D1154297

Administrative Law
Cases, Text, and Materials
SIXTH EDITION

Gus Van Harten
Osgoode Hall Law School
Faculty of Law

OCT 21 2011

PROPERTY OF
SENECA COLLEGE
LIBRARIES
@ YORK CAMPUS

Gerald Heckman
Faculty of I
University of M

David J. M
Osler, Hoskin &
Professor of Constitutional and Administrative Law
Queen's University

Founding Editors
J.M. Evans
H.N. Janisch
David J. Mulla
R.C.B. Risk

N(

2010
EMOND MONTGOMERY PUBLICATIONS
TORONTO, CANADA

Copyright © 2010 Emond Montgomery Publications Limited. All rights reserved. No part of this publication may be reproduced, stored in a retrieval system, or transmitted, in any form or by any means, photocopying, electronic, mechanical, recording, or otherwise, without the prior written permission of the copyright holder.

Emond Montgomery Publications Limited
60 Shaftesbury Avenue
Toronto ON M4T 1A3
http://www.emp.ca/lawschool

Printed in Canada.
Second printing December 2010.

We acknowledge the financial support of the Government of Canada through the Canada Book Fund for our publishing activities.

Acquisitions and development editor: Bernard Sandler
Marketing manager: Christine Davidson
Sales manager: James W. Black
Supervising editor: Jim Lyons
Copy editor: Paula Pike
Production editors: Nancy Ennis and David Handelsman
Permissions editor: Nicole Bashford

Library and Archives Canada Cataloguing in Publication

Van Harten, Gus
    Administrative law : cases, text, and materials / Gus Van Harten, Gerald Heckman, David J. Mullan. — 6th ed.

At head of title: Evans, Janisch, Mullan, and Risk.
Includes index.
Fifth ed. by David J. Mullan. Fourth ed. by J.M. Evans, H.N. Janisch, David J. Mullan.
ISBN 978-1-55239-234-8

    1. Administrative law—Canada—Cases.   I. Heckman, Gerald Paul L. R., 1967-
II. Mullan, David J., 1946-   III. Title.

KE5015.A78 2010   342.71'06   C2010-903883-5
KF5402.A4A34 2010

For John Evans, Hudson Janisch, and R.C.B. ("Dick") Risk

Preface to the Sixth Edition

In our work on this new edition of the classic textbook on Canadian administrative law, we have been guided by two principles. The first has been to maintain the overall integrity of the text and its approach to administrative law. We have sought to preserve the comprehensive treatment, coherent structure, and dialogical approach that have underlain its enduring success with students of administrative law. The second has been to "refresh" the text, not merely by updating it, but also by shifting from a historical to a step-by-step analytical approach—that is, an approach that seeks to anticipate the thought process of a lawyer or decision-maker who is tasked with analyzing a decision or decision-making process in light of the prospect of judicial review.

In pursuit of this second principle, in the area of procedural fairness, we were prompted to organize the materials so that they begin with a discussion of key sources of procedural rights and requirements and their thresholds, turn next to an analysis of the general level of fairness in a particular context, and finally discuss the specific content of various procedural rights and requirements. In the area of substantive review, the materials begin with an overview of *Dunsmuir* (rather than, for example, *CUPE* (1979)), proceed to a chapter-by-chapter examination of the various factors as framed primarily in *Dunsmuir* and, secondarily, in classic cases, provide a discussion of the specialized topics of jurisdiction and discretion, and conclude with the application of the standard of review.

In keeping with this analytical approach, we have relocated, especially in the chapters on substantive review, older cases (including some fundamental ones like *CUPE* (1979) and *Crevier*) to later stages in the discussion of the standard of review analysis. This allowed us to focus initially on the current doctrine. We recognize that this approach risks outdating the content more quickly in the face of new Supreme Court of Canada decisions on the scale of *Dunsmuir* or *Baker*, but we believe the risk is outweighed by the benefits of an up-front focus on current methods of analysis. We hope that we have struck an acceptable balance— that is, that we have introduced the main analytical frameworks of the subject in a way that, on the one hand, highlights their evolving character and the corresponding importance of basic principles, while also making clear that the principles originate in and derive much of their meaning from an understanding of the historical background.

The overall focus of the text remains on judicial review and on judge-made doctrine and statutory materials, although we afford some new space here and there for other topics and sources (such as, in chapter 4, an excerpt from the Report of the Arar Inquiry dealing with abuse of confidentiality powers and, in chapter 5, a discussion of the wider context for the dismissal of Linda Keen as president of the Canadian Nuclear Safety Commission). We appreciate that administrative law can and should be taught in a variety of ways and that a focus on doctrine alone, as it relates to judicial review, is rarely, if ever, appropriate. But we also see ongoing benefit in a text that incorporates detailed and extensive coverage of case law arising from judicial review—however rarely the courts actually intervene in the daily life of administrative decision making and its impact on Canadians—as baseline for study. We take this view on the assumption that, for students who go on to practise in administrative law, there will be valid expectations that their expertise extend precisely, though not exclusively, to matters of doctrine involving judicial review.

This edition is intended to complement the other major teaching text in this field, *Administrative Law in Context*, edited by our colleagues Colleen Flood and Lorne Sossin. We maintain in this text a detailed outline of the core elements in administrative law without delving as deeply into the rich themes and case studies that are examined in *Administrative Law in Context*. We think both approaches are vital and we have encouraged our mutual publisher to offer both these texts to instructors and students for purchase on a chapter-by-chapter basis as an electronic "mix and match," so that the materials can be tailored to the needs and demands of individual classrooms.

A criticism of past editions of this text was that it was too Ontario-centric. We have responded by taking steps to make the text more representative of the case law and statutory materials of other provinces. For example, in the material on substantive review (chapters 8 to 13), we have provided examples of appellate court decisions that apply the *Dunsmuir* framework in six provinces, one territory, and federal jurisdiction. In the chapter on the level and content of procedural fairness (chapter 4), we have incorporated a discussion of all four provincial procedural codes in the country and have reproduced in full the text of the Alberta, Ontario, and Québec codes in Appendix Three. Although in some cases other tensions, such as the importance of covering classic cases and maintaining continuity with well-known materials, have pulled against the ideal of national representation, we believe that the changes we have made will solidify this text as a widely representative work.

A further aim was to reduce the length of the textbook in this edition, while ensuring an appropriate balance between depth and manageability (and carry-ability) for students. As it turned out, we found not so much that it was impossible to trim or remove material, but that new core material, as well as new helpful examples, filled the available space nearly as quickly as we created it. So, across the text, materials have been trimmed, replaced with in-text summaries or more recent items, or simply removed outright, resulting in only a modest reduction to the length of the main text, not including the appendixes we have added. In approaching this part of the revision process, we have especially tried to balance the retention of classic cases and the addition of newer material.

There are two new authors in the list of names for the sixth edition: Gus Van Harten and Gerald Heckman. Both have welcomed the opportunity to contribute to the same text from which they learned the subject and with which they have worked over several previous editions. Both have also welcomed the opportunity to work with and continue to learn from one of the giants, if not "big beasts," of administrative law, David Mullan. David is not only delightful for his absolute mastery of the subject, but even more for his gracious, accommodating, dedicated, egalitarian, and unremittingly enthusiastic approach to a collegial project such as this. Working with David gives meaning to the phrase "it is an honour and a pleasure."

Unlike in past editions, we wish to signal to the reader the primary editors/authors of different chapters. This is less to allocate credit than to assign responsibility for possible errors, omissions, or misjudgments that may be uncovered by readers. We have placed our hands on what some might regard as a sacred text and so feel obliged to confess accordingly. Gus Van Harten was primarily responsible for chapters 7 to 17 (and made minor revisions to chapters 1 and 2), Gerald Heckman for chapters 3 to 6, and David Mullan for chapters 18 and 19. We worked in close consultation and adopted a thorough process of quality control such that all of us approved all of the chapters. It has been, as such, a team effort.

We are grateful for the support and encouragement given for this new edition by Paul Emond, Bernard Sandler, Jim Black, and Peggy Buchan at Emond Montgomery Publications. We first discussed this project in the summer of 2009, just as Bernard was joining EMP, and we found it a pleasure to work with him under the stewardship, as always, of Paul. The project proceeded more or less smoothly over the fall of 2009 and early winter of 2010, and this certainly would not have been the case without the commitment of the core EMP publication team. We are also grateful to Paula Pike, Nancy Ennis, David Handelsman, and Jim Lyons for their congenial editorial advice and expert attention to detail. Above all, we thank our families for tolerating the long days and nights that were spent by hubby or daddy with the computer instead of with them.

Acknowledgments

A book of this nature borrows heavily from other published material. We have attempted to request permission from, and to acknowledge in the text, all sources of such material. We wish to make specific references here to the authors, publishers, journals, and institutions that have generously given permission to reproduce in this text works already in print. If we have inadvertently overlooked an acknowledgment or failed to secure a permission, we offer our sincere apologies and undertake to rectify the omission in the next edition.

Canadian Bar Review	J. Willis, "Delegatus Non Protest Delegare" (1943), 21 *Can. Bar Rev.* 257.
Canadian Business Law Journal	D.S. Cohen, "The Public and Private Law Dimensions of the UFFI Problem" (1983-84), 8 *Can. Bus. LJ* 309 and 410.
Carswell	P.W. Hogg, *Constitutional Law of Canada*, 2009 Student Edition (Scarborough, ON: Carswell, 2009) 227. Reprinted by permission of Carswell, a division of Thomson Canada Limited.
	H.N. Janisch, "Case Comment: *Toshiba Corp. v. Anti-Dumping Tribunal; Trans-Quebec & Maritimes Pipeline Inc. v. National Energy Bd.*" (1984), 8 *Admin. LR* 188. Reprinted by permission of Carswell, a division of Thomson Canada Limited.
Dicey, A.V.	A.V. Dicey, "An Introduction to the Study of the Law of the Constitution" (1885), in E.C.S. Wade, *The Law of the Constitution*, 10th ed. (London: Macmillan, 1967), at 193-94.
Georgetown Law Journal	T.O. McGarity, "Substantive and Procedural Discretion in Administrative Resolution of Science Policy Questions: Regulating Carcinogens in EPA and OSHA" (1979), 67 *Georgetown LJ* 729. Reprinted with the permission of the publisher, © 1979 and Georgetown University.

Indiana University School of Law

Martin Shapiro, "Administrative Law Unbounded: Reflections on Government and Governance" (2001), 8 *Indiana Journal of Global Legal Studies* 369.

Institute of Public Administration

L. Sossin, "The Politics of Discretion: Toward a Critical Theory of Public Administration" (1993), 36 *Can. Pub. Admin.* 366. Reproduced with the permission of John Wiley and Sons, © 2008, 1993 Institute of Public Administration of Canada.

Jowell, J.

J. Jowell, *Law and Bureaucracy: Administrative Discretion and the Limits of Legal Action* (New York: Dunellen Publishing, 1975).

LexisNexis Canada Inc.

Sossin, "Developments in Administrative Law: The 1997-98 and 1998-99 Terms" (2000), 11 *Sup. Ct. LR* (2d) 37. © 2000 Butterworths Canada Ltd. Reprinted with permission.

Louisiana State University Press

K.C. Davis, *Discretionary Justice* (Baton Rouge, LA: Louisiana State University Press, 1969). Reprinted with permission. Copyright © 1969 by Louisiana State University Press.

Minister of Public Works and Government Services

Commission of Inquiry into the Actions of Canadian Officials in Relation to Maher Arar, *Report of the Events Relating to Maher Arar—Analysis and Recommendations* (2006). Reproduced with permission of the Minister of Public Works and Government Services Canada, 2010.

Economic Council of Canada, *Responsible Regulation* (1979). Reproduced with permission of the Minister of Public Works and Government Services Canada, 2010.

R.T. Franson, *Access to Information*. A Study Prepared by the Law Reform Commission of Canada. 1979. Reproduced with permission of the Minister of Public Works and Government Services Canada, 2010.

Immigration and Refugee Board of Canada, *Policy on the Use of Chairperson's Guidelines*, Policy No. 2003-07 (October 27, 2003), http://www.irb.gc.ca/eng/pages/index.aspx. Reproduced with permission of the Minister of Public Works and Government Services Canada, 2010.

The Law Reform Commission of Canada, in its working paper no. 25, "Independent Administrative Agencies" (1980). Reproduced with permission of the Minister of Public Works and Government Services Canada, 2010.

Special Committee of the House of Commons, *Third Report of the Special Committee on Statutory Instruments* (known as the MacGuigan Report), 4-6. Reproduced with permission of the Minister of Public Works and Government Services Canada, 2010.

Treasury Board of Canada, 2007 *Guidelines on International Regulatory Obligations and Cooperation*. Reproduced with permission of the Minister of Public Works and Government Services Canada, 2010.

Mullan, D.J.

D.J. Mullan, "Common and Divergent Elements of Practices of the Various Tribunals: An Overview of Present and Possible Developments" in *Special Lectures of the Law Society of Upper Canada 1992: Administrative Law—Principles, Practices, and Pluralism* (Scarborough, ON: Carswell, 1993).

Oxford University Press

D.J. Galligan, *Discretionary Powers: A Legal Study of Official Discretion* (Oxford: Oxford University Press, 1986). By permission of Oxford University Press.

Publications Ontario

Report on the Liability of the Crown, at 51-53. The Ontario Law Reform Commission, © Queen's Printer for Ontario, 1989. Reproduced with permission.

"Responsibility and Responsiveness" in *Final Report of the Ontario Task Force on Securities Regulation, 1994* (Toronto: Publications Ontario, 1994). © Queen's Printer for Ontario, 1994. Reproduced with permission.

San Diego Law Review

R.L. Rabin, "Some Thoughts on the Relationship Between Fundamental Values and Procedural Safeguards in Constitutional Right to Hearing Cases" (1979), 16 *San Diego LR* 301. Copyright 1979 *San Diego Law Review*. Reprinted with permission of the San Diego Law Review.

Vathek Publishing

G. Van Harten, "Weaknesses of Adjudication in the Face of Secret Evidence" (2009), 13 *Int'l J Evidence and Proof* 1, 20.

West Publishing Company   Davis, *Administrative Law*, 3rd ed. (St. Paul, MN:
                                 West Group, 1972). Reprinted with permission of
                                 West Publishing Company.

Yale University Press   J.L. Mashaw, *Due Process in the Administrative State*
                                 (New Haven, CT: Yale University Press, 1985). © 1985
                                 Yale University Press.

Summary Table of Contents

Detailed Table of Contents

APPENDIXES

Table of Cases

A page number in boldface type indicates that the text of the case or a portion thereof is reproduced. A page number in lightface type indicates that the case is merely quoted briefly or discussed. Cases mentioned within excerpts are not listed.

Table of Statutes

Introduction

CHAPTER ONE

The Administrative State and the Rule of Law

WHAT IS ADMINISTRATIVE LAW ABOUT?

Administrative law is a branch of public law. It applies to a wide and eclectic range of governmental activity. In particular, it applies to the exercise of public authority in ways that affect a person or group and, as such, that raise the possibility of review before a specialized tribunal or a court.

Administrative law is pervasive. It affects virtually all areas of law, even if peripherally, because in virtually all areas there is some role for government and for the legal authorization and constraint of regulatory activity. Put differently, administrative law is pervasive because of the extensive and often integral role of government in modern society.

In the law school curriculum, administrative law has the closest affinity with constitutional law in that its concerns are with the legal regulation of governmental power, both in the state's relations with individuals and in the allocation of power among various institutions. As a branch of public law, it is inevitably enmeshed in theoretical controversies about the legitimate roles of the state, the proper scope of individual autonomy, the content of democratic values, including the rule of law, and the ways in which those values can best be realized. In addition, the study of administrative law raises, particularly sharply, some fundamental questions about the nature of law: the extent to which law is discrete and autonomous from other social phenomena, on the one hand, or, on the other, is merely a vehicle for transporting to another forum debates about public policy and political power.

The subject matter of administrative law is the law governing the implementation of public programs, particularly at the point of delivery, where they are likely to have their most immediate impact on the lives and rights of individuals. Most of these programs are administered under the authority of a statute, enacted by either the Parliament of Canada or a provincial or territorial legislature, depending on the level of government with constitutional competence in the area.

Programs originate in the identification by government of a problem created by or not adequately addressed by the operation of the market or private law, often stemming from inequalities of power. Having identified a problem, often as a result of political lobbying and other forms of public pressure, government may respond in a number of ways: it may decide to do nothing; to deal with the problem through existing legal tools and institutions (the criminal law or taxation, for example); or to create a new legal framework, administered by some agency other than the courts of law, designed specifically for this purpose.

The adoption of this third option is the realm of administrative law: the fairness of administrative procedure, especially the opportunity for those immediately affected, or otherwise interested, to participate in the decision-making process; the adequacy of both the factual basis and the legal authority for administrative action, including its constitutionality; the rational exercise of discretion; and the availability of legal remedies to challenge the abuse of power by public bodies and officials.

Given its focus on the administration, a course on administrative law delves into many of the nooks and crannies of modern government. But it does not do so in a subject-specific way. Rather, administrative law aims to unpack and distil the rules and principles that apply to all public decision-makers, powers, and so on. The concerns of administrative law are general and can arise in connection with the administration of any public program. While it is necessary to acquire an understanding of the administrative, legal, and policy contexts in which questions about, for example, procedural fairness, abuse of discretion, and the interpretation of the legislation arise, the focus of administrative law is not a detailed study of the law of particular programs. Courses on labour relations, land-use planning, securities, broadcasting and communications, environmental protection, human rights, and immigration, for example, fulfill this function.

THE ADMINISTRATIVE STATE: DELIVERING PUBLIC PROGRAMS

Having indicated in abstract terms the subject matter of administrative law, we should now provide further particulars: in this section we indicate the range of contemporary public programs implemented by administrative agencies, the kinds of institutions through which the programs are delivered, and the tools typically available to enable administrators to discharge their mandates. Given the diversities within any federal system of government, this introductory description is of the broad-brush variety. Local examples and detail can be supplied by the reader.

It is important to emphasize at the outset the pervasive presence of government and its agencies in the lives of contemporary Canadians. Some of the earliest public programs concerned the regulation in the public interest of such "natural monopolies" as electricity, natural gas, railways, and telephones. Urbanization required the regulation of land use in matters such as drains and sewers, fire safety standards, the density of dwellings, and expropriation for public works. More recent administrative schemes have been created to enhance consumer protection, the protection of individuals from discrimination, and the mitigation of climate change.

Starting with the Reagan and Thatcher administrations in the United States and Britain in the 1980s, governments in many parts of the world experienced a revival of faith in market solutions. That movement finds its most clear Canadian manifestation in the policies of the current federal, Alberta, and Saskatchewan governments, but its impact over the past decade has been powerful and widespread. Deregulation, privatization, and lower taxes have been the principal rallying cries. Across the country, the issues are seldom far from the forefront of public discussion as evidenced, for instance, by ongoing debates about the role of government in managing the economy and responding to climate change.

The phenomenon of globalization, taking a rules-based form in the North American Free Trade Agreement (NAFTA) and other trade and investment agreements, also constrains the ability of governments to design and deliver programs of regulation and social benefits. Likewise, it has prompted governments to reconfigure the institutional structure of the state, including the role of domestic courts and international arbitration. Nonetheless, government appears likely to continue to be regarded in most, if not all, countries as a key player in tackling societal problems stemming from the concentration of economic power, social inequality, the threats of environmental decline or global epidemics, and other limitations of the market's capacity to regulate human behaviour for social ends.

The Subject Matter of Public Administration

The following areas of activity are the subject of diverse administrative schemes. Most of these schemes have given rise to litigation that is dealt with in this book. Needless to say, we have not attempted to compile a comprehensive list of public programs, or anything more than a thumbnail sketch of those on our list. You may be able to draw a much fuller picture of your previous study of labour relations, municipal law, or securities, for example, or from your own experience. News reports also regularly illustrate the daily working of the administrative state as well as some currently contentious issues.

Employment. The employment relationship is extensively regulated by statutory programs. The individual contract of employment and its attendant private law rights and remedies are only one component, and in many contexts they are relatively insignificant.

For example, under collective labour law, employees have a statutory right to be represented by a trade union of their choice. A union may apply to a labour relations board to be certified as the sole bargaining agent of a group of workers. If the application is granted, the board polices the relations between the union and the employer through its power to determine whether either side has committed an unfair labour practice by, for example, failing to bargain in good faith toward a collective agreement or engaging in an unlawful strike or lockout. Labour legislation commonly requires that complaints of a breach of the collective agreement (the wrongful dismissal of an employee, for example) be referred to an arbitrator appointed by the parties.

Statutes also typically prescribe basic employee entitlements that are of particular importance to those who are not covered by a collective agreement. These may include a minimum wage, holiday entitlement, and maximum hours of work, for example. Health and safety standards and the compensation of workers who are injured in the course of employment, contract a work-related illness, or suffer a disability are also the subject of legislation. Employment insurance provides some financial relief for those who lose their job, and the Canada and Quebec Pension Plans are among the most important sources of income for retired employees.

Employees and applicants for employment have a statutory right not to be discriminated against on grounds such as race, national and ethnic origin, colour, religion, sex, gender, sexual orientation, age, and mental or physical disability. Legislation ensuring equal wages for work of equal value and employment equity for underrepresented groups are among the more recent programs introduced to enhance social justice in the workplace, although the role of employment equity legislation remains contested both federally and periodically in the provinces.

Regulated industries. Since the period of rapid industrialization and urbanization of the nineteenth century, the market has proved incapable of ensuring certain public goods. As a result, the operation of some industries is subject to extensive statutory regulation. For example, as a result of their monopolistic tendencies, many utility companies require the consent of a regulator before they may increase the tariff they charge to consumers. Railway companies require regulatory consent before ceasing to provide a service on a non-economic line.

Likewise, broadcasters require a licence in order to ensure an allocation and use of the air waves that serves the public interest in the development of a national cultural identity and provide an accurate and balanced coverage of public affairs. The terms of licence may, for example, specify the kinds of programming to be carried, prescribe the amount of Canadian content and live performance, and require broadcasters to ensure that the content of their programs is balanced and impartial.

To sustain their availability, the exploitation of natural resources, both renewable and non-renewable, is heavily regulated. For example, a licence is required for the exportation of natural gas, oil, and water. The fishing and logging industries are restricted in the amount that they may cull and are required to contribute to the regeneration of the resource. To shelter both producers and consumers from the worst effects of periodic shortages and gluts, agricultural marketing schemes may regulate what and how much farmers may grow, as well as aspects of the distribution and sale of produce.

All forms of commercial transportation, both passenger and freight, are regulated in the interest of public safety. Because of their potential for causing serious and widespread illness, the production and marketing of food and the supply of drinking water are closely regulated, as is the pharmaceutical industry. Financial institutions (banks, trust companies, and the insurance and securities industries) are subject to statutory controls designed to safeguard the public interest in an orderly and honest capital market that attracts investment and in the stability and integrity of those who provide essential financial services.

Economic activities. The state regulates important aspects of economic activity, regardless of the particular industry or business in which it occurs. For example, mergers and takeovers are scrutinized for their possibly adverse impact on competition. Foreign investors who take over large Canadian companies are subject to federal approval and conditions based on a "net benefit" test. Canadian manufacturers are protected from unfair competition caused by the importation of goods for sale at less than the cost of production. The grant and regulation of rights to industrial and intellectual property are secured through legislation. Land development is regulated in the interests of community planning, including ensuring an appropriate mix of housing and other civic amenities and an adequate supply of housing for new Canadians. Public works and other major projects are subject to an assessment of their likely impact on the environment.

All economic activity is subject to taxation, imposed to raise revenue to provide public services and to redistribute wealth. "Taxes," the American jurist Oliver Wendell Holmes is thought to have said, "are the price we pay for civilization." Moreover, the imposition and level of taxation, as well as the exemption of certain activities, may be designed to achieve other policy goals: the discouragement of some businesses (the tax on tobacco products, for example) and the encouragement of others (the favourable tax treatment of the film industry and research and development, for instance).

Professions and trades. The members of most professions enjoy a statutory monopoly to render the services associated with that profession (law and health care, for example) or to use a particular professional designation (psychologist, for example). In return, applicants for membership must satisfy prescribed educational standards, and in some instances a good character requirement. Once granted a licence to practise, members of professions are subject to discipline by their governing body on grounds of incompetence or unethical conduct and, in serious cases, may lose their licence.

One of the rationales for this kind of market intervention is the lack of knowledge of consumers and their consequent inability to make an informed selection of an appropriate service provider or to assess the quality of the work performed. Power disparities between the professional and the consumer make the latter vulnerable to exploitation (overcharging or sexual impropriety, for example). Also, widespread incompetence or dishonesty in the performance of professional services may inflict more generalized public harm: a reluctance to seek medical treatment or legal advice when needed, or the collapse of poorly designed buildings, for instance.

Regulatory schemes are also in operation for trades and vocations: persons selling cars, real estate, insurance, securities, and travel typically require a licence, as do taxi drivers, street vendors, plumbers, heating engineers and others engaged in the building trades, and funeral directors.

The extension of a licensing system to those selling or providing a great variety of goods and services is explained by similar rationales of consumer protection as apply to the professions. The precise list of trades and occupations for which a licence is required varies by jurisdiction and is often determined by the scale of reported incidents of dishonesty or dangerous incompetence or by the historical experience of scandal or crisis. While the licensing and discipline of professionals is normally administered by members through the governing body of the profession as part of their professional responsibility, other forms of vocational licensing are administered by public officials.

Social control. Some public programs restrict individuals' freedom of movement. Those sentenced to imprisonment are subject to the disciplinary regime of the penal institution in which they are confined. Those guilty of infractions of the disciplinary code or believed to be engaged in unlawful activity may suffer further restrictions on their liberty by being transferred to a maximum security facility or by spending time in solitary confinement (also known as "administrative segregation"). When eligible, inmates may serve a part of their sentence on parole, a benefit that can be revoked for misconduct.

Public programs also provide for the incarceration of the mentally ill. For example, those found unfit to stand trial or not guilty by reason of insanity are detained under the warrant of the lieutenant governor and may be released only on the advice of an agency that concludes that they have recovered and are not a threat to the public. Persons who suffer from a mental illness and pose a threat to the safety of themselves or others may also be involuntarily committed to a psychiatric institution. Their detention is subject to periodic review by a specialized tribunal.

The *Immigration and Refugee Protection Act* regulates the admission to Canada of non-citizens and authorizes the detention and removal of those who enter without permission or remain in Canada in breach of the conditions imposed on their leave to remain. Even non-citizens who have lived in Canada nearly all their lives may be deported after a criminal conviction. Those charged with or convicted of criminal offences abroad, including Canadian citizens, may be extradited to the jurisdiction that has requested their surrender in order to stand trial there or to serve out their sentence.

Human rights. Public awareness and debate about the social dimensions of discrimination have made the statutory schemes for the protection of human rights of increasing importance. Typically these schemes prohibit discrimination on the grounds listed earlier in connection with the regulation of employment; protection from discrimination on these grounds also extends to housing and the provision of services offered to the public. Unlike the equality right contained in the *Canadian Charter of Rights and Freedoms*, the human rights statutory schemes apply to the activities of private individuals and corporations and government alike.

Income support. The provision of income support remains an important aspect of the Canadian state, although the legitimacy of these programs is increasingly questioned and the level of support has in some cases been reduced dramatically. We have already mentioned three types of social support: injured workers' compensation, employment-linked pensions, and employment insurance. In addition, financial benefits are available to people in need under provincially designed programs, funded in part by federal grants under the Canada Health Transfer and the Canada Social Transfer under the *Federal–Provincial Fiscal Arrangements Act*, RSC 1985, c. F-8.

Public services. Government also delivers or pays for a range of services. The most familiar are health care, education, child welfare, road construction and maintenance, public parks, fire services, police forces, garbage collection, and some public transportation and broadcasting. In nearly every case, public services are delivered under statutory authority.

Some analytical distinctions should be drawn among the array of programs described above. First, some achieve their aim by regulating a relationship between private persons: the statutory regulation of employment and the prohibition of discrimination fall into this category, although it should be remembered that, as a major employer and provider of services, the government is also subject to these programs. However, other public programs operate by requiring individuals to obtain approval from a governmental body before embarking on a course of conduct. This is the case in the regulation of immigration or of a profession or trade, for example.

Public programs may also be distinguished on the basis of whether they achieve their aims by conferring benefits on individuals or by imposing restrictions on otherwise lawful activities. This distinction can be expressed as, respectively, the welfare and regulatory roles of the state. Public education, universal health insurance, and income support are examples of the former; business licensing and land-use controls, the latter.

It should also be noted that regulatory programs are intended to confer benefits on members of the public, for example, as consumers or residents of neighbourhoods. Moreover, programs that directly regulate relationships between private individuals both create benefits and impose obligations that are legally enforceable. Thus, employees are entitled to certain statutory benefits, including wages, which employers are obliged to provide. And, while human rights and pay equity legislation regulates individuals' freedom of contract, it also provides legal redress to victims of unlawful discrimination.

The distinction between statutory restrictions on common law rights (especially physical liberty, freedom of contract, and property rights) and statutory benefits has often surfaced when administrative action has been challenged in the courts. On the whole, the courts have seemed more solicitous of existing rights that are limited by statute than eager to ensure that the intended beneficiaries of a program receive the benefits for which the statutory scheme was established. In other words, over the past two centuries, the law has more often tended to uphold the status quo than to advance the redistributive and welfare objectives of legislation.

Institutions of the Administrative State

In this section, we identify the principal institutions encountered in the study of administrative law and briefly describe the role that each plays in the design and delivery of public programs in the administrative state.

Legislatures

The legislature is the principal public forum where the most important political decisions taken in the name of the electorate are explained, debated, and (usually) approved. From a legal point of view, nearly all public programs originate with a statute enacted by either the provincial or territorial or federal legislature in order to create new legal rights and duties. In another sense, of course, the statute is the culmination of a process that may have included lobbying or other forms of pressure; a government study of the problem and possible solutions; an attempt to tackle the problem without legislation; seemingly interminable meetings among civil servants from interested departments, including government lawyers; a lengthy drafting process; and Cabinet approval in principle and the allocation of a slot in the government's legislative timetable, which is always crowded and where politics determine priorities.

In addition to debating and approving, with or without amendments, the legislation that establishes the program, the legislature will have a role to play in its subsequent administration. For example, the legislature may consider regulations made by the Cabinet or a minister under a power delegated by the statute in order to flesh out the often bare-bones terms of the legislation. The minister responsible for the program may be questioned in the legislature about its operation, possibly as a result of a report from one of the legislature's independent officers, the ombudsman, or the auditor.

Cabinet and Ministers

Typically, the Cabinet is made up of various ministers and is chaired by the Prime Minister or Premier, who assigns ministerial responsibilities. The Cabinet adopts strategic policies, sets budgets, and passes regulations and orders in council. It usually divides its tasks among a series of subject-specific policy committees. The members of Cabinet are responsible collectively to Parliament (or the legislature) for the conduct of government. Working through Cabinet, ministers must find ways to exercise their individual responsibility in a way that will be supported by all ministers. Cabinet is also known federally as the governor in council and provincially or territorially as the lieutenant governor in council, which means technically the Queen's representative as advised by the members of Cabinet.

A minister generally has responsibility for a (federal) department or (provincial) ministry that is normally established by statute. The minister is accountable for the exercise of powers assigned to her or to the officials who are subject to her direction. Officials and staff of departments or ministries comprise the core of the civil service. Ministers must also answer to the legislature for the exercise of powers assigned to agencies that are not under the minister's managerial direction and control, such as boards, commissions, tribunals, and other agencies which carry out adjudicative, regulatory, commercial, and other activities.

As already mentioned, the Cabinet, or individual ministers, may be empowered to supplement a statute with delegated legislation. The minister, through departmental officials, may also exercise discretionary powers that directly affect individuals. Under the *Immigration and Refugee Protection Act*, for example, the minister may allow a person to enter Canada who is not otherwise eligible; the minister of justice decides whether to surrender a person whose extradition has been requested by another government and upheld by a court in Canada. The minister within whose mandate an agency operates will normally be responsible for appointing the members of the agency. The minister will also report to the legislature on the operation of the program and answer questions from members of the House.

By its control of strategic policies and the allocation of funds, the Cabinet may play a decisive role in determining the shape and scope of public programs. A statute may also in rare cases provide a right of appeal to the Cabinet from decisions of administrative agencies.

Municipalities

Municipalities exercise powers that are delegated by the provincial legislature, including tax powers. Many of the programs that frequently affect people are administered at the local level of government: police and fire services, schools, child welfare, parks, roads, garbage collection, public transport, building permits, land-use planning, the taxation of property, and the licensing of many trades. The members of municipal councils and trustees of local school boards are usually elected. The elected members debate and pass the bylaws and resolutions at public meetings that elaborate the legislative framework of the programs that they administer. However, municipalities are subject to provincial guidance and control in these areas: standards may be set by the enabling legislation, ministerial policy directives or guidelines, or by the terms on which provincial funding is provided. In addition, some municipal decisions may be set aside on appeal by a provincial agency or to a provincial tribunal.

Municipal officials exercise delegated statutory power in order to deliver many of these programs. For example, an officer in the buildings department will decide whether plans to build an extension to a house comply with local fire and building codes; inspectors will ensure that construction work is carried out in accordance with approved plans; and public health inspectors will visit restaurants and can order the closure of those that do not comply with public health standards.

Crown Corporations

Some public services are provided through Crown corporations, which enjoy substantial independence in their day-to-day operations. The purpose of this independence is to enable them to make commercial decisions without government interference. However, through the power of the purse and other means, including the appointment of members of the board of directors, the government can exert considerable influence. Among the best-known federal Crown corporations are the Canadian Broadcasting Corporation, the Canada Post Corporation, the Canada Council for the Arts, the Canada Mortgage and Housing Corporation, and the National Capital Commission. Provincial Crown corporations have been responsible for, as examples, the generation, distribution, and sale of electricity and the sale of liquor.

These bodies operate on the fringes of public and private law in that they may compete with privately owned corporations, much of their decision making will be based on commercial principles, and their legal relations with suppliers and customers are governed by contract. Yet they also have governmental characteristics. For example, they were established by statute in order to perform functions that private corporations neglected, they typically occupy a powerful position in the industry (sometimes a statutory monopoly), they are in public ownership, they may be financed by government grants, their boards are appointed by government, and they report to the legislature through the minister responsible.

However, as part of a retrenchment of governmental operations, many Crown corporations have undergone important changes in recent years. These have included their outright sale (privatization) to private investors (Petro Canada, Air Canada, Alberta liquor stores, private juvenile correctional facilities, and Ontario's 407 highway); their significant reorganization and accompanying reduction in the government's financial stake (the breakup of Ontario Hydro); and their exposure to market competition, insulation from non-business concerns, and subjection to financial self-sufficiency (corporatization). Indeed, as instruments of public policy (such as the support of local industry through preferencing in the award of contracts), Crown corporations appear to have fallen from favour, whether as an imperative of international trade and investment agreements or simply as a part of a shift in ideology and policy in domestic government.

Private Bodies and Public Functions

An important array of nominally private bodies are found in the borderland between government and the private sector. Some derive their legal authority purely from contract. Yet, by virtue of the control they exercise over particular activities and the nature of the functions they perform, private bodies may resemble the administrative agencies that otherwise discharge governmental functions. Indeed, if they did not exist, such bodies would often have to be created by statute.

Perhaps the most familiar examples of this type of actor are the governing bodies of many sports. As the gatekeepers of access to the sport at the most competitive levels, they establish rules on the affiliation of clubs to the governing body and resolve disputes over the eligibility of clubs and players, for example. In other sports (for example, boxing), athletes, trainers, and managers may require a licence to participate in events under the control of the governing body.

Some regulatory functions are performed by bodies that operate under private legislation, but that rely on market power and contract, rather than a statutory monopoly, to control their industry and its members. Stock exchanges, for example, are associations of member firms that have assumed responsibility—in cooperation with the statutory regulators, the securities commissions—for protecting investors by establishing and enforcing standards in the industry.

In some provinces, private legislation has been enacted to recognize the regulatory power of real estate boards, stemming largely from their control over the multiple listing system for sale properties. Again, membership in a real estate board (as opposed to a licence from a public regulator, when one exists) is not a legal requirement for engaging in the real estate business, but it may be a practical necessity.

In Ontario, responsibility for child welfare is discharged at the local level by children's aid societies. These societies are nominally private organizations answerable to their own boards. However, provincial legislation has conferred on them coercive legal powers, including the authority to remove neglected or abused children from the custody of their parents, take them into care, and assume parental powers over them. Their operations are almost wholly funded by government, which, at both provincial and municipal levels, prescribes policies and standards.

Finally, as self-governing teaching and research institutions, universities are also located at the fringes of government. Considerations of academic freedom have contributed to placing them at arm's length from government departments with a responsibility for education and research. Universities have contractual relations with their employees and students, whose fees provide some of their university's operating budget. However, nearly all universities in Canada operate under a statutory framework, perform functions that are regarded as public in nature, and derive most of their funding from government, whether directly or indirectly in the form of research grants awarded to scholars by independent funding bodies. Also, universities are monopoly providers of academic tertiary education and degrees, and employers of those who pursue an academic career.

Independent Administrative Agencies

These are the most distinctive institutions of the administrative state. While some have a substantial history, many emerged after the Second World War with the rapid expansion of the responsibilities assumed by government. Because they are not homogeneous, they are not easily described in a few sentences. Even their names vary, often with little rhyme or reason: boards, tribunals, and commissions are the most common and, to a large extent, these labels are interchangeable. Independent administrative agencies have been created in every jurisdiction without an overall organizational plan. New programs have spawned new agencies, although in other cases existing agencies have been assigned a new but related statutory function. Despite their haphazard proliferation, they occupy a position in public law and administration in Canada of such significance as to justify an expanded introduction.

Some Family Likenesses

The independent agencies that are most frequently encountered in administrative law, and that are described here, have at least four features. First, they enjoy a measure of independence from the government department with overall responsibility for the policy area in which they operate. This means, at the very least, that the minister cannot direct what decision they must reach in a matter that is before them. In turn, the minister is not politically accountable to the legislature for the agency's individual decisions. But it would be a mistake to imagine that members of administrative agencies do or should enjoy the same level of insulation from the political process as superior court judges. For instance, members are appointed (by the minister responsible) for relatively short terms of office and their appointment may or may not be renewed. Agencies can be incapacitated by starving them of resources. A few statutes enable the Cabinet to influence the making of agency decisions, either by issuing a policy guideline that the agency must consider or, on appeal, by reversing, varying, or remitting a decision of the agency.

Civil servants in government departments are normally subject to the instructions of their superiors in the hierarchy and to departmental policy, for which the minister is ultimately responsible. In contrast, members of independent agencies are in law immune from directions from colleagues, including the agency chair, on how they should decide a case. This aspect of the legal character of agencies has received considerable attention, particularly with respect to large agencies that sit in panels to decide disputes. One example was the resignation in 1995 of the deputy chair of the Immigration and Refugee Board following allegations by members that he tried to "pressure" them over decisions that he regarded as out of line with board policy. The problem is that it is difficult to reconcile the notion that members should enjoy the same degree of autonomy as judges with the competing need to ensure that agency decisions are consistent and informed by the collective wisdom and experience of the agency as an institution.

The second feature of independent agencies is that those who are liable to be affected by a decision are given an opportunity to participate in the decision-making process by producing evidence and making submissions. Administrative hearings vary greatly: some are hardly distinguishable from those conducted in a court of law (professional discipline hearings, for example). Others are very informal and may be conducted exclusively on paper. To a large extent, procedural openness underpins the legitimacy of administrative agencies and makes good much of the "democratic deficit" that is inherent in the nature of their members' appointments and in the lack of direct political accountability for the major questions of public policy that many agencies make.

Third, independent agencies typically operate at the "sharp end" of the administrative process—that is, at the point when a program is applied to the individual. This may involve the denial of a licence, a refusal to rezone, a determination that a person is not a refugee, or the unfair dismissal of an employee. Some agencies also operate at the level of policy making and hold hearings to allow those who are interested to participate in the formulation of a policy that will guide the agency when it decides individual cases.

Fourth, all administrative agencies are specialized. They deliver a particular program or a part of one. Labour relations boards certify unions to represent groups of workers and ensure that parties do not engage in unfair labour practices that undermine the fundamental premises of collective bargaining. Assessment committees determine property taxes. Agricultural marketing boards award quotas to farmers, thus regulating the amount they can produce. International trade disputes are decided by the Canadian International Trade Tribunal. Some agencies work with one statute; others derive their jurisdiction from several. Courts of law, on the other hand, decide cases across a much broader spectrum of criminal and civil law.

Some Differences

It is more challenging to capture the generic differences among agencies. First, decisions made by agencies are found along a continuum, ranging from those that resemble courts to those that are more akin to decision making in the political process. At one end are agencies that determine individual rights based on past events or facts, a relatively precise statutory standard, and a limited degree of discretion that is exercised in the particular circumstances of the case. Examples of these agencies include human rights tribunals, labour arbitrators, the refugee protection division of the Immigration and Refugee Board, and professional discipline committees.

Other agencies have a much larger policy-making mandate and are guided more by their understanding of the broad public interest than by the conduct or impact of the decision on an individual or small group of individuals. For example, some administrative agencies approve the tariff structure for the rates to be charged to telephone subscribers or energy consumers, while others make recommendations on the siting of nuclear power stations and waste disposal facilities.

Some agencies resemble courts in their structure: there are opposing parties at the hearing; the decision is made by the members who conducted the hearing solely on the basis of the material presented to them, without the assistance of any staff, except perhaps for a lawyer to advise them on legal and procedural questions that arise during the hearing. Professional discipline committees and social assistance appeal tribunals are typically of this type. Other agencies, generally at the policy-making end of the spectrum, employ a large staff to provide expert economic, financial, policy, or legal analysis in order to assist in policy development. Counsel for the agency may participate at the hearing as a party, and outside the hearing staff will conduct research to assist the agency to reach the best decision. For these agencies the hearing represents one component of the process by which they inform themselves.

Some agencies have a massive caseload. For example, in 2009, the approximately 200 members of the Immigration and Refugee Board, the largest administrative tribunal in the country, decided 27,000 refugee claims (of 34,000 received). This is only part of the board's jurisdiction. The Canada Employment Insurance Commission and workers' compensation boards also process huge numbers of claims. On the other hand, some provincial regulatory agencies devote most of their time to one or two large rate-making utility decisions. Most agencies fall between these extremes, however. They handle a quantity of claims that is compatible with an ability to hold formal hearings before making decisions, in spite of the extensive time and resources required to conduct such hearings.

Independent agencies also vary greatly in the place that they occupy in the overall decision-making process. For instance, some only make recommendations to a body with final decision-making power. This is the role of the judge who, after an inquiry, can recommend to the attorney general or lieutenant governor that a judicial officer or a member of a tribunal be removed from office. Commissions of inquiry may be appointed to investigate and report on the object of widespread public disquiet: the collapse of the BC salmon industry, the rendition to torture of a Canadian citizen, the contamination of a municipal water supply, the safety of Canada's blood system, or the collapse of a financial institution, for example. On the strength of the commission's report, legislation may be introduced to implement its recommendations.

In contrast, other agencies make the first, and sometimes final, determination of individuals' legal rights. Provincial human rights tribunals and securities commissions are typically of this type, as is the Refugee Protection Division of the Immigration and Refugee Board. Some agencies hear appeals, which may be from another independent agency or from a decision by an officer in a mainline government department. For example, employment insurance (EI) umpires hear appeals from boards of referees, which in turn hear appeals from decisions made by an EI commission. The Immigration Appeal Division of the Immigration and Refugee Board hears appeals from the refusal of visa officers—who are civil servants in the Department of Citizenship and Immigration—to grant an entry visa to a person whose admission to Canada has been sponsored by a permanent resident.

Another important difference among independent agencies lies in the effect that their decisions have on individuals. Some can devastate the life of the person concerned. Revoking a parole may mean not only a return to prison but also the loss of remission of the sentence. Deporting a non-citizen may dispatch the person to a country where he or she has never lived as an adult, break up his family, or expose her to death or torture. Suspending a licence to practise may be a sentence of "professional death." These are some of the exceptional powers exercised by administrative agencies in Canada, to which the *Canadian Charter of Rights and Freedoms* is likely to apply.

Many agencies have a less serious impact on individuals. They may decide on the allocation of a trivial benefit: approval of a plan to build a deck on a house, for example. Or the decision may affect millions of people in a diffuse way: the approval of an increase in telephone rates, for example.

The membership of agencies varies widely. For example, discipline committees of self-governing professions typically comprise members of the same profession as the person whose conduct has been called into question. That said, in response to a public perception that complaints of professional misconduct have not always been treated seriously, lay persons are often now included on these committees.

It is common to find tribunals operating in labour relations and employment that are constituted on a tripartite basis. That is, members of the tribunal are nominated respectively by the employer and by the employee sides, with a mutually agreed independent chair. This is true of labour relations boards, labour arbitration boards (although the parties may agree to a single-member board in order to save expense), and employment insurance appeal boards.

The members of many tribunals serve on a full-time basis for the duration of their term, while others are appointed to hear a particular dispute. Labour arbitrators and human rights tribunals are typically of the latter type, although it is important to note that many of those appointed to these tribunals are often very experienced and are asked regularly to serve.

Some tribunals include lawyers among their members. Indeed, judges of the Federal Court of Canada usually act as the president of the Competition Tribunal and as umpires (the top administrative appeal body in the employment insurance system). On the other hand, members of other agencies are appointed for different kinds of experience, knowledge, or skills. Some members have a sophisticated understanding of the area in which they operate. Others have no claim to expertise, although with experience as members of the agency they are likely to acquire knowledge of the statutory framework and a "field sensitivity" to the relevant issues.

These and other variations among independent administrative agencies assume particular importance to lawyers when called on to advise an agency on the procedure that it should adopt for making its decisions, to represent a client before an agency, or to seek a legal remedy against an agency in the courts. It is a serious mistake for lawyers to stereotype agencies and to assume, for example, that because the agency in question holds hearings and is independent from the government it is functionally like a court.

The powers, membership, and procedure of many agencies are designed to perform tasks that, as we have tried to illustrate, may differ significantly from those assigned to courts. In determining the fairness of an agency's procedure or the interpretation of its enabling legislation, lawyers should familiarize themselves with the context in which the agency operates. Put differently, an agency should not be forced into a procedural mould (typically that of the courts) that unduly hampers its ability to discharge its statutory mandate effectively, with due regard to the interests of those who are affected by its decisions. Similarly, the remedial powers conferred on an agency by statute should not be presumed to be limited to those that are exercised by courts. Nor should the terms of an agency's enabling legislation be taken to have the same meaning as a rule of the common law even when expressed using the same words.

An important strand in the often conflictual history between courts and administrative agencies has been lawyers' predilection for general rules and a single model of decision making. This is usually, of course, the common law and adversarial procedure as practised in courts of law. Lawyers have too often sought to absorb administrative agencies into a vision of the legal system in which the superior courts are at the apex. The truth is that administrative agencies occupy a unique position based on their unique strengths, relative to courts. They have one foot planted firmly in the world of government and bureaucracy and the other in the world of law and the judiciary. Most, of course, lean more in one direction than the other. Agencies are part of government in that they are responsible for advancing the public interest by implementing the program that they administer. On the other hand, like courts, they may conduct hearings and must justify their decisions, which invariably affect the rights of individuals, in light of the applicable law and the evidence.

Why, then, have legislatures so regularly resorted to independent agencies, rather than mainline government departments or courts, in order to play such a major role in the delivery of public programs? Unsurprisingly, there is no single answer to this question. Here are some common answers, although we should point out that tasks seem often in practice to be allocated on the basis of chance or historical circumstances, and often according to the influence of the powerful rather than any overall plan or institutional set of principles.

Independent Agencies or Government Departments?

Independent agencies have certain advantages over government departments as makers of administrative decisions. Because they are insulated from the pressures of day-to-day partisan politics, it is easier for agencies to maintain an open process and develop longer-term consistent policies. The other side of this is that it is convenient for ministers to shed political responsibility for individual decisions, especially in sensitive areas of policy, where the chances of attracting unfavourable publicity are high.

From the perspective of the individual who is in dispute with a government department over his or her eligibility for a statutory benefit (social assistance or a pension, for example) or the imposition of a liability (deportation or the payment of taxation, perhaps), it is very important that the matter can be taken for reconsideration to a body that is perceived to be independent of the government.

The relationship between agencies and their sponsoring department may create difficulties. A recurring dilemma is the location of responsibility for policy issues, especially for federal agencies that regulate industries (such as energy, broadcasting, and telecommunications) and for provincial land-use planning agencies and securities commissions. When a legislature enacts a regulatory statute, it is impossible for the legislature to foresee or answer many of the policy questions that will arise in the delivery of the relevant programs. Hence, broad discretion is given to many administrative agencies to allow them to make additional rules or formulate policies on a case-by-case basis. Yet it has been a key principle of the Westminster system of government that major issues of public policy should be made in the name of a minister or by the Cabinet collectively, so that ministers can be held politically accountable in the legislature for their decisions.

How, then, can the virtues of agency independence in making individual decisions be reconciled with the constitutional demand for political accountability to the electorate on matters that are important to many people? One attempt to reconcile these priorities involves allocating the responsibility for formulating policy to the political branch of government (through the promulgation of regulations or less formal policy directives, for example) and leaving to the independent agencies the administrative task of applying the policy to individual cases. The basic problem is that there is no bright line to divide policy from administration; often, policy questions emerge as an agency wrestles with a particular problem. To authorize the minister at that stage to formulate a policy solution for the agency will likely leave little for the agency to do, and thus remove the benefits of independent decision making.

Another device for linking independent agencies to the traditional channels of political accountability has been to provide a right of appeal from regulatory agencies to the Cabinet. While this places responsibility for major policy decisions in the hands of the elected leadership of government, many commentators find Cabinet appeals unsatisfactory. In particular, a shroud of secrecy surrounds Cabinet decision making, which is often suspected of being more responsive to partisan political considerations than to the demands of regulatory policy. Participants in lengthy and expensive hearings who have obtained a favourable decision from the agency are liable to feel short changed if the Cabinet reverses the decision, without a hearing and without an explanation.

Perhaps it is appropriate to reconsider the extent to which we rely on traditional political institutions as the sole authentic source of democratic legitimacy for important policy decisions. Just because members of independent agencies are not elected does not make them politically unaccountable. They are after all appointed by the government and, for relatively short terms, they report to the legislature through the responsible minister or directly in parliamentary committee; their budget is allocated by the minister; they hold public hearings; consult widely on policy issues; and provide reasons for their decisions. To what extent do these characteristics satisfy your sense of democratic legitimacy?

Independent Agencies or Courts?

Who should resolve disputes that arise from the implementation of a public program? The main reasons for assigning this role to an independent agency rather than a court are as follows.

First, the nature of the decisions made by many agencies are broadly inappropriate for the courts. That is, they are far more governmental than judicial: establishing a "Canadian content" policy for broadcasters, allocating quotas to import chickens, and setting utility rates, for example. The judicial process is simply not apt for making multifaceted policy decisions of this kind. Second, it may be desirable that decisions be made by persons other than judges. Experience and expertise in areas beyond law may be required, as well as an approach to the issues that is more sympathetic to the aims of the program than that which is often displayed by judges. Trade unions, for example, had good cause historically to complain that the judiciary was quicker to understand the position of management than that of labour. Third, many of the disputes with which we are concerned involve relatively small sums (various kinds of social security benefits, for example) and, as important as these claims are to the individual, to process them through the courts would be a misallocation of public resources.

Fourth, a more informal process than that associated with the courts may enable more expeditious decisions and reduce the need for legal representation. The adversarial model of procedure assumes a rough parity of resources between the disputing parties, leaves to them the responsibility for presenting the evidence and arguments necessary for making the decision, and reduces the decision-maker to the passive roles of ensuring the proceedings are orderly and fair and deciding the case on the relative strength of the presentations of the parties. This model is unsuited to many decisions that are made in implementing public programs. For instance, a right to a full hearing, including representation by counsel, is of little practical value to most social security claimants in dispute with the government. And, when it is important that the best decision is made (on the assessment of the environmental impact of some large development project, for example), it would be inefficient to deny the decision-maker the benefit of a broad range of staff expertise in exploring the issues. Nor can the classical adversarial model readily be adapted to the mass adjudication of workers' compensation or refugee claims.

Some Current Concerns

In the last few decades, the demands on public administration have grown enormously. Pushing administrators from one direction are public demands for "transparency" and responsiveness in government decision making, the increasing role of single-issue pressure groups, and a climate of "rights consciousness" generated in part by the *Canadian Charter of Rights and Freedoms*. At the same time, the size, number, and complexity of the problems and disputes to be resolved have also grown. The administration of human rights legislation and professional discipline are examples of this.

Moreover, the budgets available for most of these purposes in many cases have shrunk. This has had a powerful impact on the operation of administrative agencies. More broadly, reform of the administrative process is a perennial topic of reports, studies, and conferences, although the talk has typically far exceeded action.

Of course, governments have taken important initiatives. Some independent agencies have been abolished (as in the case of the BC Human Rights Commission in 2002). Those that provide advice to government departments are particularly vulnerable; their advisory function can be performed less expensively by civil servants or not at all. Some agencies have been reduced in size, while others have been amalgamated, as in the instance of the Ontario Workplace Safety and Insurance Board and Appeals Tribunal, an amalgam of several employment-related agencies. The federal government is increasingly relying on those who are subject to regulation to draw up compliance plans, leaving to regulatory agencies the lesser roles of approving self-regulatory plans and monitoring adherence.

Two other examples of the impact of shrinking budgets on independent administrative agencies are as follows. First, agencies have learned what has been known in the criminal justice process for a long time: if everyone with a right to a hearing exercised it, the system would grind to a halt. Ingenuity and imagination are needed to enable agencies, without sacrificing demands for democratic accountability and individual rights, to streamline or dispense with trial-type hearings by harnessing technology, developing informal dispute resolution techniques, and using modern management theory and practice. The challenge of accommodating a "judicialized" administrative process to the need for efficient and effective decision making is also apparent in complaints that the independence of members of some agencies has been compromised by institutional pressure to ensure that their decisions comply with agency policy.

Second, attention has focused increasingly on the process by which appointments to independent agencies are made and, especially, withdrawn by the responsible minister or by Cabinet. This attention has followed heightened public suspicion of the traditional political process; a concern about political intervention in expert, independent decision making; demands by women and members of minority groups for a greater presence in public life; and a concern for value for money in times of fiscal stringency. It is also seen as unacceptable that individuals should be appointed to often well-remunerated positions of significant responsibility on the basis of their political connections.

In response to the latter concern, a number of jurisdictions, including British Columbia, Ontario, and Québec (but, notably, not the federal government) have adopted a more formalized, merit-based appointment process. The fact that very able persons have been appointed to administrative agencies (along with some substandard appointees, it is fair to say) is insufficient to meet the demand for a more open process, where job descriptions and qualifications are widely advertised and candidates are screened and ranked by an independent commission. Even so, because many independent administrative agencies make important public policy decisions, it is also appropriate for the government to retain the ultimate power to appoint members to agencies and thus to exert influence over the general policy direction to be pursued.

Administrative Tools

Public officials and institutions typically have available a wide range of tools with which to deliver the public program for which they are responsible. In contrast, courts of law discharge their mandate—the administration of justice according to law—solely through the adjudication of cases brought before them (although the courts are also attempting to lighten the load on the system by establishing an alternative dispute resolution procedure).

For many administrative agencies, adjudication is an important tool. However, an agency's adjudicative functions should always be seen in the context of its overall mandate. Take, for example, the self-governing professions. Considered in isolation, the functions of discipline committees appear to be much like those of courts of law. Their sole task is to determine, on the evidence and arguments presented to them by counsel for the member and the governing body of the profession, whether the member is guilty as charged and, if so, the appropriate penalty. But adjudication by the discipline committee is only one way in which the governing body discharges its statutory responsibility to maintain and enhance the quality of service provided to the public by the profession. Various other tools are available to carry out this task. For example, a governing body will typically ensure that, on admission to the profession, members have had a good education and training in the technical and ethical aspects of practice. It will also conduct programs of continuing professional education; provide information to the public; issue formal rules and informal explanations; define the standards of professional behaviour and competence; conduct spot checks of members' practices; and investigate complaints from the public against members.

Governing bodies of the professions usually distribute these tools to different internal committees. Other agencies, however, may not disperse their decision-making power to the same degree. For example, the Ontario Securities Commission, as a whole, makes regulations; issues policy statements and press releases advising the public and the industry of its thinking on aspects of its mandate; conducts investigations of individuals and of more widespread problems; decides whether to prosecute; and adjudicates charges brought against members of the securities industry. In other administrative schemes, testing plays an important part in decision making. Eligibility for a driver's licence, for example, is determined by a driving test, not a hearing. Testing is also used to determine whether possibly contaminated food should be removed from the shelves of a store in the interests of public health. Additionally, inspections are a familiar tool in administrative decision making, as in the case of ensuring compliance with health and safety standards in the workplace and with building codes.

Finally, public bodies may pursue governmental objectives through contract. For example, a government department may award a major construction contract to a company in an area of high unemployment as part of its regional development policy. Governments at all levels may give a preference to local industry in the award of procurement contracts.

Liquor control boards may price wines in a way that supports the provincial industry. In order to obtain the necessary land-use approvals from the planning authorities, a land developer may agree to convey land to the city for use as a park or to include affordable accommodation as part of a housing development.

POLITICAL AND ADMINISTRATIVE REDRESS OF INDIVIDUAL GRIEVANCES

Law assumes particular importance in public administration when things have gone wrong, at least in the eyes of those affected by a decision made in the course of implementing a public program. For this reason, lawyers are often involved in the design of institutional arrangements for the investigation and review of administrative action about which there is a complaint. This book is particularly concerned with forms of redress based on access to the courts. The focus is thus on the role of the courts in reviewing administrative agencies and on the remedies that a court may award where the decision-maker is found to have acted unlawfully. This focus is important because some of the most complex aspects of administrative law arise in the narrow context of judicial review. And, while a range of professional specializations may be involved in government decision making outside of the courts, it is lawyers who are expected primarily to have expertise in the litigation of disputes arising from governmental activity. To provide legal advice in many areas of practice, then, it is important to have an understanding of the underlying framework for judicial review.

Nevertheless, the focus on judicial review can also be misleading because, of course, most government decisions are never subject to litigation. An alternative approach to the subject matter of administrative law would be to examine various types of powers and responsibilities of government in general, instead of narrowing one's study to instances in which an individual or group happens to challenge administrative action in the courts (see, for example, Dussault and Borgeat, *Administrative Law: A Treatise*, 2nd ed. (1990)). Although this is not the orientation of the present text, a vital point at the outset is to emphasize the need for administrative lawyers to keep in mind that litigation may not offer a realistic or useful remedy for those affected by administrative decisions, that courts are not always (perhaps rarely) the best institutions to resolve complex policy issues, and that other forms of expertise besides legal expertise have a major role to play in developing and implementing public policy. One who works in a specialized area of law must develop an understanding of the relationships between law and government in that area.

Being a government lawyer or public official is about much more than judicial review. Likewise, in challenging or defending an administrative decision that affects one's client, it is important for a lawyer to understand how the relevant governmental apparatus works and how its decision making takes place. Moreover, it is important to put the role of the courts in context, and to be familiar with other possibilities for redress.

Legislative Oversight of the Administrative Process

As we have noted, the involvement of legislatures with public programs does not end with the enactment of the enabling statute. Delegated legislation may call for scrutiny, reports from standing committees and from the agency itself may have to be considered, and the minister with overall responsibility for the program may be questioned about its operation and desirability. Even so, legislative oversight is inadequate for investigating complaints from individuals about decisions made in the course of implementing the many public programs of the administrative state. Legislators have neither the time and resources nor the legal powers (to compel the disclosure of information, in particular) needed for the job.

Sometimes, a story about administrative injustice or apparent bungling receives extensive media coverage. Members of the legislature may be mobilized into taking up the issue, the minister responsible may intervene, and a satisfactory response developed. But these are exceptional cases. Recognizing that members of the legislature will be unable to gain redress for all of their constituents' grievances with the administration, every Canadian province has an officer of the legislature called the ombudsman, ombudsperson, citizen's representative (Newfoundland and Labrador), or protecteur des citoyens (Québec). This institutional office, originally a Scandinavian institution, was taken up with great enthusiasm in the common law world in the late 1960s and 1970s as a potential panacea for individual situations of administrative injustice.

The details of these legislative schemes for redress vary, although the essential functions and powers of the office of ombudsperson can be described succinctly. First, the ombudsperson is empowered to investigate action taken in the administration of a government organization (which may include an independent agency) that affects individuals. Second, the ombudsperson has the power to obtain information in connection with the investigation, which is conducted in private. Third, in order to set the investigative process in motion, the complainant merely has to file a complaint. Unlike those pursuing administrative appeals and redress through the courts, complainants to the ombudsperson do not bear the burden, financial and otherwise, of pursuing relief against the government. Fourth, unlike other avenues for redress, the ombudsperson can consider a wide range of possible errors that may have been committed in the delivery of a public program, including the possibility that the administrative decision or action was simply wrong. Fifth, in the event that the ombudsperson concludes that something went awry, the organization will be asked to provide a remedy, which could include a simple apology, the revision of the agency's operating procedures, or the payment of compensation. If the recommendation is not acted on, the ombudsperson may report the matter to the relevant committee of the legislature. However, because the ombudsperson's conclusions are not legally binding, any recommended remedy is ultimately enforceable only through the political pressure that can be exerted by the legislature and by public opinion.

Administrative Remedies

Administrative agencies invariably have internal mechanisms for dealing with citizens' grievances. This may be simply a matter of asking the person who made the decision to revisit it or speak with a more senior person in the agency. Sometimes there are formal levels of appeal that can be pursued within the agency. Furthermore, unlike courts of law, independent administrative agencies often have an express statutory power to reconsider their decisions.

If none of these provides a satisfactory solution, the complainant may need to consider taking the matter to an outside body that is independent of the original decision-maker. In most jurisdictions this will be the regular courts, although, since 1996, Québec has had in place the Administratif tribunal du Québec, which is the country's closest model to a general administrative appeal tribunal.

Also, statutory rights of appeal are now commonly available to an appeal tribunal from decisions made by government departments about individual entitlements. These may include, for example, appeals from the refusal or revocation of a business licence or the refusal, reduction, or termination of a social security benefit. Administrative appeal tribunals can generally reconsider the whole case after hearing from the parties and substitute the decision that, in their view, the original body should have made. On the other hand, it is relatively rare to find a right of administrative appeal from an independent agency that makes the first-level decision in a dispute. Thus, there is generally no administrative appeal from provincial human rights tribunals, labour relations boards, or labour arbitrators. Agencies that regulate industries such as communications and utilities may be subject only to a political appeal to the Cabinet.

COURTS AND ADMINISTRATIVE AGENCIES

Lawyers can be very effective in pursuing clients' grievances through the media and the various channels of political and administrative redress. Moreover, lawyers are indispensable when litigation seems appropriate. Even so, public law litigation is generally a remedy of last resort: the cost of taking the administration to court is high; the prospect of success in court is limited; and even when a favourable judicial decision is obtained, the possibility remains that, having corrected the legal error, the administration may not change the substance of the decision that generated the complaint. On the other hand, regardless of the expected result, litigation can be a tactic to delay the implementation of an agency's decision or exert pressure on the other side.

In this section, we provide an overview of the principal ways in which courts may be required to resolve disputes between the individual and an administrative official or institution. Again, we have tried to keep to a minimum the specifics of the various provincial statutory provisions, especially those relating to appeals and to the practice and procedure of the courts' supervisory jurisdiction.

Original Jurisdiction

The legislature may not have established a mechanism specifically for the purpose of challenging an administrative decision, in which case a person may take her claim against the government directly to court. Also, persons claiming that a governmental body has violated a Charter right may seek a remedy directly from a court under s. 24 of the Charter. Generally speaking, it is also possible to proceed directly to court, without recourse to administrative avenues of redress, when an administrative action has infringed an individual's private legal rights by constituting a tort, breach of contract, or some other wrong for which an award of damages may be made or specific relief (such as an injunction) granted.

Thus, in 1995 a court granted a declaration that it was a breach of contract for the Liberal government to cancel the agreement made during the Mulroney government by a consortium of developers for the renovation and privatization of Pearson International Airport:

T1T2 Limited Partnership v. Canada (1995), 23 OR (3d) 81 (Gen. Div.). One of the most famous cases dealt with in this book, *Cooper v. Board of Works for Wandsworth District,* was an action for damages for trespass dating from the 1860s. It turns on the legality of a resolution passed by the defendant, Board of Works, without prior notice to the plaintiff, authorizing its officials to demolish a house built by the plaintiff; a decision that the court found to be procedurally unfair and, therefore, invalid. (Although this is not reflected in the court's judgment in *Cooper,* the Board of Works' resolution was likely passed after the house had been built without separating its below-ground water and sewage pipes. Requirements for separate water and sewage pipes were first introduced in this era to counter the threat of cholera and other waterborne diseases in the sprawling cities of industrial England. Thus, *Cooper* points at an early stage to the tension between effective administration of public programs and judicial protection of individual property and procedural rights.)

Appeals

Since the early 1970s, statutory rights of appeal to the courts from administrative decisions have become a familiar feature of schemes established to deliver public programs. It is important to appreciate at the outset that rights of appeal are purely the creation of statute: courts have no inherent appellate jurisdiction over administrative agencies.

Rights of appeal come in different forms. The most generous provide for an appeal on questions of law, fact, and discretion and authorize the appellate court to substitute its opinion for that of the agency. Others limit the appeal to questions of fact and law, while the narrowest are confined to questions of law and jurisdiction. If the court concludes that the agency erred, it may either refer the matter back to the agency or reverse the decision and find in favour of the appellant. In recognition of the specialized expertise of the agency under appeal, an appellate court may be prepared to show deference to the agency's conclusions, even on questions of law.

It is difficult to discern any cost–benefit criteria that are used consistently by legislatures to determine when a right of appeal to a court is an appropriate form of redress or, if granted, how broad the right of appeal should be. However, there is an emerging pattern that, in the absence of a strong reason to the contrary, the legislature will include a statutory right of appeal to a court from administrative agencies where the agency exercises a power to make decisions that restrict an individual's common law rights (as in the case of human rights tribunals, land-use planning appeal tribunals, and vocational and professional licensing bodies, for example) or that refuse a significant social security benefit.

A major exception is the regulation of labour relations and employment, where the general legislative policy has been to minimize the opportunities for judicial intervention. This has been partly to avoid the damaging delays of litigation and its expense; partly because the relevant agencies are usually made up of nominees of employer and employee interests and are seen to have more understanding of labour relations than the courts; and partly because the courts and the common law were perceived historically as biased against the interests of labour, especially those based on collective rights.

Courts' Inherent Judicial Review Jurisdiction

In the absence of a statutory right of appeal to the courts, the superior courts of the provinces nevertheless retain a supervisory jurisdiction over the institutions and officials that administer our public programs. The superior courts inherited this supervisory jurisdiction from the English royal courts of justice, which exercised that jurisdiction long before the modern state and central government in order to review the activities of local justices of the peace (who had not only summary criminal jurisdiction, but also local government functions such as the repair of bridges and roads, local taxation, and liquor licensing), borough councils, commissioners of sewers, and the few other public bodies that exercised statutory powers over individual rights. Notably, since 1970, the Federal Court and the Federal Court of Appeal—which are statutory courts rather than superior courts with inherent jurisdiction under the common law—have exercised virtually exclusive jurisdiction over federal administrative agencies.

Judicial Remedies of Administrative Law

The courts exercised their supervisory jurisdiction under the common law through remedies that were available, in the main, only in respect of *public* duties or powers. They were known as the prerogative writs. Three have been particularly important in the development of administrative law. The remedy of *certiorari* is used to quash or set aside a decision. The remedy of prohibition is used to order a tribunal not to proceed in a matter. And the remedy of *mandamus* is used to order the performance of a public duty. (In Québec, where the law of judicial review is based on the common law, the remedy of *evocation* performs the functions of both *certiorari* and prohibition.)

A fourth prerogative remedy, *habeas corpus*, issues to determine the legality of a person's detention, whether by a private person or public official, with a view to ordering the release of a person who is unlawfully imprisoned. The writ of *habeas corpus* has a strong association in constitutional history with the protection of the liberty of the person and remains important today, both in criminal procedure and in areas of public administration such as immigration, prisons, extradition, and mental health. Even for federal agencies, which are otherwise subject to the jurisdiction of the Federal Court, the superior courts of the provinces retain their jurisdiction to issue *habeas corpus*. The Federal Court itself has only a limited capacity to grant this remedy. Because of its specialized nature, though, *habeas corpus* stands outside the mainstream of administrative law and thus receives less coverage in this book.

Historically, the prerogative remedies of *certiorari*, prohibition, and *mandamus* were directed as much to ensuring that bodies with limited legal powers did not exceed those powers at the potential expense of the power of central government as to vindicating the legal rights of the individual. This aspect is still apparent in that, unlike awards of damages in private law, the prerogative remedies (and their modern statutory equivalents) are granted in the discretion of the court on the basis of public interest considerations. Applicants also do not have to show that the administrative action complained of affected them in a way that infringed their private law rights; a court may instead grant relief on the basis that the applicant was an appropriate person to assert the public interest in ensuring that governmental bodies do not act unlawfully.

Since the early 1970s, courts and legislatures have vastly simplified the law relating to the remedies of judicial review (often by the creation of a single catch-all application for judicial review) and the accompanying practice and procedure. This has been a great benefit to those who study and work in administrative law. As it happened, the prerogative writs were relatively untouched by the major reforms to the law of civil procedure in the late 19th century. As a result, the forms of action and highly technical ways of thinking that these remedies encouraged in lawyers persisted into the 1960s in Canada. To an extent, the difficulty of adapting ancient remedies to the context of modern government was eased by the use in public law litigation of the (originally private but also discretionary) equitable remedies of declaration and injunction. However, with the emergence of general principles of judicial review of administrative action, the organizing ideas of administrative law shifted from the technicalities of the remedies to the grounds of review. Further, the courts have properly focused less on the anachronisms of the prerogative writs and more on ensuring, in deciding whether to grant relief, that an appropriate balance is achieved between private rights and public interest.

Grounds of Review

When the legislature has not provided a statutory right of appeal, in what circumstances may a court intervene in the administrative process at the instance of a person who has invoked its supervisory jurisdiction? There are four principal grounds of judicial review in contemporary law, although these grounds may overlap.

Procedural impropriety. Before taking action that may adversely affect the interests of individuals, administrators generally have a legal duty to act in a way that is procedurally fair. This typically requires them to give prior notice, and a reasonable opportunity to respond, to those likely to be affected. Impartiality in the decision-maker is another attribute of procedural fairness. Much of the law defining administrative action that is subject to the duty to be fair, and the precise contents of the duty in a given context, has been developed by judges as a matter of common law (sometimes disguised as statutory interpretation) and, since 1982, under the rubric of the Charter. In addition, legislation may prescribe the procedures to be followed by a particular agency, or groups of agencies, in making their decisions.

An agency that indicates that it does not intend to comply with the duty of fairness, or a statutorily required procedure, may be prohibited from proceeding to a decision or be ordered to proceed according to the proper procedure. More commonly, an applicant will ask the court to quash (or set aside) a decision that was made in breach of a procedural duty. When relief is granted, the agency will normally be free to decide again, after it has complied with its procedural duties; in substance, its second decision may be the same as the first.

Illegality. There is a strong presumption that the legal powers of governmental institutions are limited and that it is the function of the courts, as the branch of government that is independent of the executive and legislature, to determine those limits. Administrative action has no legal validity if it is not authorized by law. For the most part, the legal powers of concern to administrative law are statutory. This means that the courts must determine the scope of the legal powers and duties of the agency by interpreting the relevant legislation.

As we shall see, this is an exercise that implicates fundamental notions about law and government and about the appropriate roles of specialist agencies and the courts in the administrative state.

Unreasonableness. Administrators also have a legal duty not to exercise their powers unreasonably. This duty has emerged relatively recently as a general principle of judicial review. The principle was originally derived from a series of specific rules and principles. For example, there must be some evidence to support the material findings of fact on which an agency bases its decision. An administrative agency's interpretation of ambiguous language in its enabling legislation must be reasonable. Likewise, lack of reasonableness is a ground of review of the exercise of many discretionary powers conferred on public authorities. Similarly, when administrative action infringes a Charter right, it may be justified under s. 1 of the Charter as a reasonable limit prescribed by law.

Unconstitutionality. The constitution is an important element of the legal framework within which administrative agencies deliver public programs. Although a thorough exploration of this element is appropriately pursued in a book or course on constitutional law, it is impossible in a text on administrative law to ignore the constitutional dimensions of the subject, and its intersections with constitutional law in the formal sense: the *Constitution Acts, 1867–1982.*

Since the *Canadian Charter of Rights and Freedoms* was adopted in 1982, it has become common for lawyers to frame court challenges to administrative action in terms of both the common law and the constitution. For example, a refusal by the Immigration and Refugee Board of a claim to refugee status might be impugned both on the ground that it was made in breach of the common law duty of fairness and that it amounted to a denial of liberty or security of the person, other than in accordance with the principles of fundamental justice, contrary to s. 7 of the Charter.

It must suffice here to make two points about the relationship between administrative law and constitutional law. First, regardless of whether it is authorized by statute, administrative action may always be impugned in court on the ground that it breaches a provision of the constitution. An administrative agency cannot do what a legislature lacks the constitutional competence to authorize. Second, both constitutional law and administrative law are branches of public law and their concerns overlap. It is important, therefore, that the standards imposed by constitutional law are informed by previous experience at the level of administrative law: in balancing procedural fairness against administrative efficacy, for example. Conversely, it is important that the non-constitutional standards to which public administration is held through legislation and the common law reflect the constitutional values and principles emerging from Charter litigation.

The Reach of Administrative Law

In our overview of the institutions responsible for delivering public programs and the administrative tools that are available to them, we noted that some institutions occupy a middle ground between government and the private sector. For example, while Crown corporations are in some obvious ways public institutions, they also often provide services in competition with privately owned commercial corporations. Regulatory functions are also performed by a number of bodies that are in form private: stock exchanges and sporting associations, for instance. And governmental institutions rely on contract to regulate their relations with their employees and to purchase goods and services.

The ambivalence of these institutions and administrative tools is reflected in the law that governs them. For example, it is important to know whether, and to what extent, the remedies and grounds of review of administrative law apply to them. It may also be asked whether these institutions are "government" for the purpose of being subject to the Charter. The answer may depend very much on the particular context. For example, while universities are not, for the most part, subject to the Charter, our courts have held that, despite their institutional autonomy and the contractual nature of their relationships with students and faculty members, the decisions of university committees administering discipline to students and denying tenure to professors are subject to the prerogative remedies. Moreover, even if they are not subject to those remedies, their decisions can be challenged on the ground of procedural unfairness, by asking a court to grant a declaration of invalidity or an injunction restraining the implementation of the decision, because declaratory and injunctive remedies are not confined to breaches of public duty.

Or suppose that a government contract was awarded to a company that had financially contributed to the minister's election campaign. Could the company that entered the lowest bid, but was not awarded the contract, challenge the validity of the contract on the ground that the minister exceeded the legal limits of his powers?

THE RULE OF LAW AND THE ADMINISTRATIVE STATE

In the final section of this introduction, we identify some of the constitutional foundations of administrative law and some general themes animating the principles and doctrine examined in this book. We apply the term constitutional not only to the formal part of the law contained in the *Constitution Acts, 1867-1982*, but also to the often unarticulated ideas and understandings about democratic government, individual liberty, and the allocation of powers among the institutions of the state that have shaped public law.

The rule of law is an ideal that is regularly invoked both by proponents and by critics alike of regulatory measures and public programs. Like the concepts of liberty and democracy, the rule of law has no generally agreed meaning as applied to law and administration. In the same respect, the rule of law is rejected by few people, although specific versions of its meaning are keenly contested. It is tempting to say that an idea with no agreed content has little practical value as a critical standard by which to assess the appropriateness of the legal framework within which public programs are administered. However, the root idea— namely, that government should be subject to law—is, like democracy and liberty, an enduring one. The Preamble to the *Constitution Act, 1982* proclaims that "Canada is founded upon principles that recognize ... the rule of law." In *Re Manitoba Language Rights*, [1985] 1 SCR 721, at 747*ff.*, the court expounded on the concept in the context of constitutional interpretation. Then, in *Reference re Secession of Quebec*, [1998] 2 SCR 217, the Supreme Court of Canada recognized it as one of the four underlying principles of the Canadian constitution: federalism, democracy, constitutionalism and the rule of law, and the protection of minorities.

Most would agree, then, that an important function of administrative law, including the contribution of the courts, is the vindication of the rule of law. The challenge is to amplify this concept in a way that is compatible with the democratic claims of majoritarian government and the tasks with which it has charged the modern administrative state, including the regulation of private power, the promotion of social equality, and the redistribution of wealth. The following is an introductory sketch of some versions of the rule of law that, in our view, have significantly shaped or captured lawyers' thinking about issues of law and public administration. This seems to us part of what is needed to get started on developing an understanding of what administrative law is *really* about.

Dicey and the Liberal Idea of the Rule of Law

A.V. Dicey was a professor of English Law at the University of Oxford and then the first professor of Public Law at the London School of Economics. It was critical to Dicey, writing in the late 19th century, to establish public law as a legitimate and respected discipline alongside private law subjects, which were more established in the English common law tradition. Dicey's classic work, *An Introduction to the Study of the Law of the Constitution*, was first published in 1885. In it, Dicey defined a version of the rule of law that he thought both described English constitutional law (then found in the common law and in legislation) and explained what he saw as the success of the English constitution in protecting the liberty of the individual. For our purposes, the key elements in Dicey's definition of the rule of law were (1) that no one should be made to suffer except for a distinct breach of the law, (2) that government and citizens alike are subject to the general law of the land, and (3) that the law of government should be administered in the ordinary courts (that is, the English common law courts) and not in a specialized system of administrative courts (as in France).

Each of these notions is reflected in contemporary administrative law and in debates about the appropriate scope of government powers. The first element has been employed to attack the statutory grant of broad discretion enabling public officials to restrict individual freedom of contract and property rights. Examples are the powers of the Ontario Securities Commission to suspend the licence of a member of the industry or to issue a cease-trading order in particular securities when, in the opinion of the commission, it is in the public interest. Others have objected to the wide discretionary powers of the minister of citizenship and immigration to permit or refuse admission to Canada or to deport non-citizens. The main objections to such powers are that they may be used to discriminate improperly against or to favour particular individuals or groups, that it is difficult to hold officials democratically accountable for highly discretionary decisions, and that individuals should be able to plan their lives in accordance with known rules of general application.

A related influence on public law has come from the aspect of Dicey's definition of the rule of law that insists that, in the common law world as opposed to legal systems derived from or influenced by the Napoleonic Code, there is no distinct body of public law that applies to relations between individuals and the state and that is administered outside the "ordinary courts." Two examples, one specific and the other more general, are particularly important. First, Dicey's assertion has provided a justification for the exercise by the superior courts of their supervisory jurisdiction over administrative agencies on grounds of procedural unfairness and illegality, even when the legislature has apparently expressly excluded judicial review. Courts have regarded the powers of government as legally limited, and the judiciary as the body that is ultimately responsible for determining those limits. Indeed, in *Crevier v. Quebec (Attorney General)*, [1981] 2 SCR 220 (Que.), the Supreme Court of Canada held that it is beyond the constitutional competence of provincial legislatures to remove this jurisdiction on the basis that it is a part of the powers vested in judges who are appointed by the federal government under s. 96 of the *Constitution Act, 1867*. Subsequently, in *MacMillan Bloedel Ltd. v. Simpson*, [1995] 4 SCR 725 (BC), the court apparently extended this principle to the federal Parliament.

Second, entrenching the superior courts as the arbiters of disputes between individuals and the administrative institutions of the state has given preeminence to common law patterns of thought in shaping the legal framework for public programs. For instance, the rights most keenly protected in law are those recognized by the common law: liberty of the person, private property, and freedom of contract. On the other hand, the courts experienced difficulties in dealing with interests created by the administrative state: licences and welfare benefits, for example. Even more difficult to accommodate in a private rights model of administrative law are claims by individuals or groups based on a public right to democratic government, manifested for example in demands by members of public interest groups for an opportunity to participate before agencies that formulate important policies that are likely to affect a large number of people. Legal notions of procedural propriety in administrative decision making have been influenced more by the paradigms of litigation and the judicial process than by the bureaucratic model or the notion of participatory democracy.

The judicially enforced assimilation of administrative agencies, in their great diversity, to the "general law" administered by the "ordinary courts" is also evident in the court's common assumption that, when reviewing an agency's interpretation of its enabling statute, the court should approach the task as if it were hearing an appeal from an inferior court in the judicial hierarchy. Thus, legislation should be construed according to the general canons of statutory interpretation (however vague, malleable, or contradictory), words should be given the meaning that they have in other legal contexts, and, while the agency may have expertise in policy aspects of the program it is administering, the interpretation of legislation to determine individual rights is the province of the judiciary. It follows, therefore, that if the agency adopted an interpretation different from that preferred by the court, then it committed an error of law and its decision must be set aside.

The Functionalist Critique

Since the 1930s there have been contrary views expressed in England, the Unites States, and Canada from the dominant tradition of public law most famously associated with Dicey. In Canada, the most important proponent of a dissenting position was John Willis, whose principal writing on administrative law spanned the 1930s to the late 1960s. Functionalist criticisms of the liberal version of the rule of law, especially as propounded by Dicey and taken up in 1968 by the *Report of the Royal Commission on an Inquiry into Civil Rights in Ontario* (the McRuer Report), have taken various forms.

First, some writers challenged the historical accuracy of Dicey's assertions. They have asked whether it was ever true that the rights of English people were subject to general law, and not to official discretion, and that there was in England (fortunately, according to

Dicey) no special body of public law equivalent to the French *droit administratif* developed by *tribunaux administratifs*, headed by the *conseil d'état*, to regulate legal relations between citizens and the state. On these points, they have pointed out that at common law the Crown was immune from liability in tort, that wide discretion was exercised by local magistrates to dispense often brutal forms of criminal punishment, that Dicey misunderstood the French system of administrative law, and that Dicey overlooked the local courts and specialist agencies in England that were already hearing disputes arising from the enforcement of regulatory legislation (especially in protecting the safety of workers in factories and mines), claims for the recovery of wages, and the growth of social security.

Second, they have pointed out that Dicey's disapproval of administrative discretion and his support for affording to the "ordinary courts" (and, of necessity, the intellectual baggage of the "common law mind") a key position in the resolution of disputes between the individual and the administrative state could only thwart the implementation of legislative arrangements for regulation and redistribution in the public interest. The litigation process may have to reduce complex policy choices to crudely defined "question of law" or issue of procedural "fairness," whereas an agency that has specialized expertise and field experience, and access to a range of methods of investigation and decision making, may be better positioned to resolve multifaceted questions of policy.

Thus, far from offering a "neutral" prescription for the protection of liberty, Dicey designed his version of the rule of law to put public administration into a straitjacket. The judicial model of procedural fairness, for example, was likely to hamper an agency's capacity for effective decision making and to benefit those with the means to hire a lawyer and go to court. In addition, the courts' approach to the interpretation of legislation was driven by an ideology that generally deplored government intrusion in the market and the limitation of individual rights to pursue their economic interests without restraint.

According to functionalists, it was more likely that governments, in the face of obstruction from economic vested interests, would take the course of least resistance by curbing the effectiveness of public programs rather than risking judicial reproach in the name of private rights. Furthermore, the focus of litigation on the immediate parties to a dispute tends to downplay the interests of beneficiaries of the program, and the wider public interest, as components of judicial decision making.

Third, on a philosophical level, it was argued that the positivist legal tradition, of which Dicey's thought is a part, had failed to appreciate that law is intertwined with policy. Legislatures cannot foresee all outcomes and, by implication, statutes must often be drafted in general terms. In turn, it may be impossible to arrive at the intended meaning of the language in an agency's enabling legislation without considering the consequences that competing interpretations will have for the program that the legislation was created to deliver. The specialist agency is more able than a reviewing court to make an informed assessment of the interpretation that will enable the program to be effective. It follows, therefore, that if judicial intervention on the ground of illegality means that a reviewing court is encouraged to substitute its own interpretation of legislation for that of the agency, then the agency's ability to develop a coherent strategy to discharge its policy mandate will be undermined.

A functionalist approach to administrative law also stresses the facilitative and legitimizing roles of law. That is, as regulator and provider of benefits, the state should be regarded as a source of good. It is the function of the law to enable administrative agencies to carry out effectively and efficiently the tasks assigned to them by the legislature, the institution that, by virtue of the election of its members by universal franchise, has the greatest claim to democratic legitimacy in our system of government.

The courts have limited institutional competence on matters that are often more accurately characterized, not as questions of law or legality, but as issues of public policy and administration. Thus, the courts should have a residual role in overseeing administrative action. While insisting on procedural openness and a minimum standard of rationality in the interpretation of legislation or in the exercise of discretion, for example, a reviewing court should afford a wide measure of deference to the reasoned choices of the specialist agency made on the basis of its experience in delivering the program. That experience may place an agency in a superior position relative to the courts in matters of procedure, statutory interpretation, fact finding, and the exercise of discretion.

The functionalist approach has undoubtedly exerted a significant influence on administrative law in Canada since the early 1980s. For instance, as courts have expanded the applicability of the duty of fairness in the exercise of governmental powers, they have emphasized the importance of administrative context in deciding what procedures are legally required, including the costs and benefits to the public of affording to the litigant a particular procedural right. Context has also been considered in interpreting enabling legislation so as to give effect to legislative purpose. The courts have also been prepared to defer to an agencies' interpretations of their enabling statutes, rather than to assume that the judiciary has a monopoly on the wisdom that is needed to elaborate on the legislature's instructions.

The Rule of Law, Democratic Values, and Fundamental Rights

There is no doubt that the functionalist analysis has provided an important corrective to the view of the rule of law propounded by Dicey and other opponents of an interventionist role for the state in addressing problems unresolved or created by the operation of the market. The common law did not have satisfactory answers to these problems. However, it seems also that a functionalist approach tends to attach insufficient weight to considerations of democratic accountability and fundamental rights and to the positive contributions that courts can make to realizing these goals. Despite their well-publicized shortcomings, courts seem to enjoy more public confidence than most other institutions of government. We see no necessary inconsistency between, on the one hand, the core values of the rule of law—government that is subject to law and respectful of the claims of individual dignity and basic liberties—and, on the other hand, the public interest in an administration with the capacity to deliver public programs effectively, efficiently, and responsively.

It is possible to rework some elements of the liberal version of the rule of law in order to provide a role for the law of judicial review in advancing these values in the contemporary administrative state. This is especially so in the age of the *Canadian Charter of Rights and Freedoms*. Indeed, this is a project that has long occupied David Dyzenhaus of the University of Toronto and his position is well exemplified by "Constituting the Rule of Law: Fundamental Values in Administrative Law" (2002), 27 *Queen's LJ* 445. The following are three examples of what we have in mind.

First, with the apparent dilution of public confidence in the capacity of the traditional political process to exercise democratic control over the operations of government, it is appropriate for administrative law, both through statutory reform and judicial review, to ensure procedural openness and enhance accountability in public administration. Public participation should therefore be encouraged and not limited to those whose private rights may be adversely affected by administrative action. Direct public participation in decision making at the level of the agency that is delivering a program may go some way to compensate for the limited oversight of the legislature.

An emphasis on a democratic agency process will require the administration to disclose relevant information in its possession, ensure that public interest groups receive funding (possibly from private interests that stand to gain from a favourable decision such as an environmental assessment) to enable them to participate in a meaningful way, and provide reasons for its decision. However, because of the limitations of their institutional competence, courts should not lightly intervene if the agency has developed a procedure that represents a good faith attempt to balance the claims of democratic accountability against program effectiveness and efficiency.

Second, while reviewing courts should normally show a measure of deference to a specialist agency's interpretation of its enabling statute, it is appropriate to scrutinize more closely those decisions that seem contrary to the interests of the intended beneficiaries of the legislation or to that aspect of the public interest that the legislation was enacted to protect. Examples include: claimants under compensation and social security schemes; employees protected by labour legislation; and the protection offered by various statutory programs to members of the public in their capacities as consumer, airline passenger, or breather of air and drinker of water. In this way, the courts can provide a counterweight to the pressure that private economic interests often bring to bear on public agencies to sidestep their regulatory responsibilities.

Third, we recognize the force of the functionalist claim that it is often futile to imagine that the legislature had a "meaning" in mind when it enacted a provision in a statute that has to be applied to a set of facts that was almost certainly not foreseen at the time of enactment. We agree also with the functionalist point that the most reliable guide to the "intention of the legislature" is an interpretation that best furthers the purpose of the statute, a matter that the agency will often be better placed to determine than a reviewing court. However, the independence of the judiciary and its experience across a wide spectrum of the legal system make it appropriate for the courts to intervene when they are satisfied that—after allowance for agency expertise, linguistic ambiguity, and an approach to statutory interpretation that emphasizes legislative purpose—the agency's interpretation was nonetheless unreasonable or outright wrong. The courts have a role to play in preventing the subversion of the clear meaning of the statute by members of a specialist agency who are beholden to the government for reappointment or whose "specialization" may develop into tunnel vision. More broadly, the courts, when reviewing administrative action, have a role to play in upholding the democratic processes of the legislature.

Fourth, the rights entrenched in the *Canadian Charter of Rights and Freedoms* have been identified by the Parliament of Canada that enacted it, and the governments of the provinces that approved it, as deserving of special protection. Since the Charter applies to governments and legislatures, agencies charged with the implementation of a public program should be alert to the possibility that administrative action may violate a Charter right. However, courts have also said clearly that the Charter gives no mandate to the judiciary to roll back the statutory protections of the welfare and regulatory state. Infringements of Charter rights must therefore be weighed carefully against other competing public interests, an exercise to which administrative agencies will often be able to make an informed contribution.

The constitutional protection afforded by the Charter to certain rights may be regarded as a signal that other rights are less important and that their claim to a preferred position, even at the level of statutory interpretation, has been weakened. Thus, to the extent that freedom of contract and property rights fall outside the scope of the Charter, it should not be presumed that to remain within its legal authority an administrative agency must implement a statutory scheme for the delivery of a public program with minimum interference with their continued enjoyment.

MOVING FORWARD

The contents of this chapter suggest three directions from which administrative law should be approached. First, the details of the public program from which the particular dispute arises must be appreciated: the terms of the statute, the nature of the program, the characteristics of the officials and institutions, and the administrative and political contexts within which the statute operates. Second, a knowledge of the relevant legal principles and rules, both substantive and procedural, is essential to analyze the dispute and locate it within the elements that comprise our legal system: the rules and policies of the decision-maker, the common law, legislation, and the constitution. Third, it is important to keep in view the theoretical dimensions of a problem and to be able to consider it from the perspective of competing concepts of law and government.

Sometimes, nothing is more practical than theory. It can cut through the impenetrable and equip lawyers with an understanding of the law both as a body of principles and rules and as a political and social institution that enables them to use the law to tackle new problems. An ability to see the larger picture is particularly important for the student venturing into administrative law, where it is all too easy to get lost in the dense undergrowth of legal doctrine and program specifics. These precepts have guided our presentation of administrative law, especially as illustrated by decisions of the courts.

The next three parts of this text deal with the grounds on which individuals may challenge administrative action in court, generally by appealing (when a right of appeal exists) or invoking its supervisory jurisdiction. In the balance of this part of the text, we provide an overview and general introduction to judicial review through the vehicle of one of the most important administrative law judgments of the Supreme Court of Canada: *Baker v. Canada (Minister of Citizenship and Immigration)*, [1999] 2 SCR 817 (Can.). Part II examines administrative procedure and, in particular, the duty of decision-makers to act with procedural fairness. Part III considers the interpretation of the legislation under which public programs are administered and the role of the courts in reviewing the findings of fact and determinations of questions of law by administrative agencies. In part III, we also focus on the legal authority of administrative agencies and the power of the courts to decide the limits of that authority.

Lastly, in part IV we focus on the remedies available from the courts to those who argue that, in making a decision or taking some action, an agency has breached the duty of fairness, got the facts wrong, misinterpreted its enabling statute, or committed some other error of law or acted without legal authority by exceeding its jurisdiction or its discretionary powers. The questions considered in part IV include: who is entitled to seek relief? from what court? and what remedial orders may a court make and in what circumstances?

SOME CORE READINGS

Arthurs, H.W. "Rethinking Administrative Law: A Slightly Dicey Business" (1979), 17 *OHLJ* 1.

———. *"Without the Law": Administrative Justice and Legal Pluralism in Nineteenth Century England* (Toronto: University of Toronto Press, 1985).

Craig, P.P. *Public Law and Democracy in the United Kingdom and the United States of America* (Oxford: Clarendon Press, 1990).

Dyzenhaus, David. "Constituting the Rule of Law: Fundamental Values in Administrative Law" (2002), 27 *Queen's LJ* 445.

Loughlin, Martin. *Public Law and Political Theory* (Oxford: Clarendon Press, 1992).

———. *The Idea of Public Law* (Oxford: Oxford University Press, 2003).

Macaulay, Robert W. *Directions: Report of a Review of Ontario's Regulatory Agencies* (Toronto: Management Board of Cabinet, 1989).

Mactavish, Anne L. "Administrative Justice—Reflections on the Road Ahead" (2002), 15 *CJALP* 347.

Mullan, David J. "Administrative Tribunals: Their Evolution in Canada from 1945 to 1984" in Bernier and Lajoie, eds., *Regulations, Crown Corporations and Administrative Tribunals* (Toronto: University of Toronto Press, 1985), at 155.

Willis, John. "The McRuer Report: Lawyers' Values and Civil Servants' Values" (1968), 18 *UTLJ* 351.

———. "Three Approaches to Administrative Law: The Juridical, the Conceptual, and the Functional" (1935), 1 *UTLJ* 53.

CHAPTER TWO

The Role of Judicial Review

BAKER V. CANADA
(MINISTER OF CITIZENSHIP AND IMMIGRATION)

Introduction

Judicial review is one of the principal means of ensuring that the administrative process operates within the constraints of the principles of legality. In this chapter, we aim to provide a general overview of the system of judicial review as well as the various grounds, both substantive and procedural, on which judicial review is typically available. For these purposes, we have chosen the judgment of the Supreme Court of Canada in one of the seminal cases in Canadian administrative law—*Baker v. Canada (Minister of Citizenship and Immigration)*—a judgment in which the court not only applied existing principles of judicial review in a substantive domain that had been rife with conceptual difficulty, but also settled some long-simmering controversies in particular areas of Canadian judicial review.

In addition to being an excellent introduction to judicial review, *Baker* provides considerable insights into the way in which the legislature confers power on statutory bodies as well as the mechanics of the administrative process within government departments. In reading the case, pay attention not just to the grounds on which Mavis Baker brought her challenge to the "minister's" decision, but also to the statutory and operational framework within which that decision was taken. Also, pay attention to the way in which this case worked its way through the Federal Court system to the Supreme Court of Canada.

Baker v. Canada (Minister of Citizenship and Immigration)
[1999] 2 SCR 817 (Can.)

L'HEUREUX-DUBÉ J (Gonthier, McLachlin, Bastarache, and Binnie JJ concurring):

Regulations made pursuant to s. 114(2) of the *Immigration Act*, RSC, 1985, c. I-2 empower the respondent Minister to facilitate the admission to Canada of a person where the Minister is satisfied, owing to humanitarian and compassionate considerations, that admission should be facilitated or an exemption from the regulations made under the Act should be granted. At the centre of this appeal is the approach to be taken by a court to judicial review of such decisions, both on procedural and substantive grounds. It also raises issues of reasonable apprehension of bias, the provision of written reasons as part of the duty of fairness, and the role of children's interests in reviewing decisions made pursuant to s. 114(2).

I. Factual Background

Mavis Baker is a citizen of Jamaica who entered Canada as a visitor in August of 1981 and has remained in Canada since then. She never received permanent resident status, but supported herself illegally as a live-in domestic worker for 11 years. She has had four children (who are all Canadian citizens) while living in Canada: Paul Brown, born in 1985, twins Patricia and Peter Robinson, born in 1989, and Desmond Robinson, born in 1992. After Desmond was born, Ms. Baker suffered from post-partum psychosis and was diagnosed with paranoid schizophrenia. She applied for welfare at that time. When she was first diagnosed with mental illness, two of her children were placed in the care of their natural father, and the other two were placed in foster care. The two who were in foster care are now again under her care, since her condition has improved.

The appellant was ordered deported in December 1992, after it was determined that she had worked illegally in Canada and had overstayed her visitor's visa. In 1993, Ms. Baker applied for an exemption from the requirement to apply for permanent residence outside Canada, based upon humanitarian and compassionate considerations, pursuant to s. 114(2) of the *Immigration Act*. She had the assistance of counsel in filing this application, and included, among other documentation, submissions from her lawyer, a letter from her doctor, and a letter from a social worker with the Children's Aid Society. The documentation provided indicated that, although she was still experiencing psychiatric problems, she was making progress. It also stated that she might become ill again if she were forced to return to Jamaica, since treatment might not be available for her there. Ms. Baker's submissions also clearly indicated that she was the sole caregiver for two of her Canadian-born children, and that the other two depended on her for emotional support and were in regular contact with her. The documentation suggested that she too would suffer emotional hardship if she were separated from them.

The response to this request was contained in a letter dated April 18, 1994 and signed by Immigration Officer M. Caden, stating that a decision had been made that there were insufficient humanitarian and compassionate grounds to warrant processing Ms. Baker's application for permanent residence within Canada. This letter contained no reasons for the decision.

Upon request of the appellant's counsel, she was provided with the notes made by Immigration Officer G. Lorenz, which were used by Officer Caden when making his decision. After a summary of the history of the case, Lorenz's notes read as follows:

> PC is unemployed—on Welfare. No income shown—no assets. Has four Cdn.-born children—four other children in Jamaica—HAS A TOTAL OF EIGHT CHILDREN
>
> Says only two children are in her "direct custody." (No info on who has ghe [*sic*] other two).
>
> There is nothing for her in Jamaica—hasn't been there in a long time—no longer close to her children there—no jobs there—she has no skills other than as a domestic—children would suffer—can't take them with her and can't leave them with anyone here. Says has suffered from a mental disorder since '81—is now an outpatient and is improving. If sent back will have a relapse.
>
> Letter from Children's Aid—they say PC has been diagnosed as a paranoid schizophrenic—children would suffer if returned—

> Letter of Aug. '93 from psychiatrist from Ont. Govm't.
>
> Says PC had post-partum psychosis and had a brief episode of psychosis in Jan. when was 25 yrs. old. Is now an out-patient and is doing relatively well—deportation would be an extremely stressful experience.
>
> Lawyer says PS [*sic*] is sole caregiver and single parent of two Cdn. born children. PC's mental condition would suffer a setback if she is deported etc.
>
> This case is a catastrophy [*sic*]. It is also an indictment of our "system" that the client came as a visitor in Aug. '81, was not ordered deported until Dec. '92 and in APRIL '94 IS STILL HERE!
>
> The PC is a paranoid schizophrenic and on welfare. She has no qualifications other than as a domestic. She has FOUR CHILDREN IN JAMAICA AND ANOTHER FOUR BORN HERE. She will, of course, be a tremendous strain on our social welfare systems for (probably) the rest of her life. There are no H&C factors other than her FOUR CANADIAN-BORN CHILDREN. Do we let her stay because of that? I am of the opinion that Canada can no longer afford this type of generosity. However, because of the circumstances involved, there is a potential for adverse publicity. I recommend refusal but you may wish to clear this with someone at Region.
>
> There is also a potential for violence—see charge of "assault with a weapon." [Capitalization in original.]

Following the refusal of her application, Ms. Baker was served, on May 27, 1994, with a direction to report to Pearson Airport on June 17 for removal from Canada. Her deportation has been stayed pending the result of this appeal.

II. Relevant Statutory Provisions and Provisions of International Treaties

Immigration Act, RSC 1985, c. I-2

82.1(1) An application for judicial review under the *Federal Court Act* with respect to any decision or order made, or any matter arising, under this Act or the rules or regulations thereunder may be commenced only with leave of a judge of the Federal Court—Trial Division.

83(1) A judgment of the Federal Court—Trial Division on an application for judicial review with respect to any decision or order made, or any matter arising, under this Act or the rules or regulations thereunder may be appealed to the Federal Court of Appeal only if the Federal Court—Trial Division has at the time of rendering judgment certified that a serious question of general importance is involved and has stated that question.

· · ·

114. ...

(2) The Governor in Council may, by regulation, authorize the Minister to exempt any person from any regulation made under subsection (1) or otherwise facilitate the admission of any person where the Minister is satisfied that the person should be exempted from that regulation or that the person's admission should be facilitated owing to the existence of compassionate or humanitarian considerations.

Immigration Regulations, 1978, SOR/78-172, as amended by SOR/93-44

2.1 The Minister is hereby authorized to exempt any person from any regulation made under subsection 114(1) of the Act or otherwise facilitate the admission to Canada of any person where the Minister is satisfied that the person should be exempted from that regulation or that the person's admission should be facilitated owing to the existence of compassionate or humanitarian considerations.

Convention on the Rights of the Child, Can. TS 1992 No. 3

Article 3

1. In all actions concerning children, whether undertaken by public or private social welfare institutions, courts of law, administrative authorities or legislative bodies, the best interests of the child shall be a primary consideration.

2. States Parties undertake to ensure the child such protection and care as is necessary for his or her well-being, taking into account the rights and duties of his or her parents, legal guardians, or other individuals legally responsible for him or her, and, to this end, shall take all appropriate legislative and administrative measures.

Article 9

1. States Parties shall ensure that a child shall not be separated from his or her parents against their will, except when competent authorities subject to judicial review determine, in accordance with applicable law and procedures, that such separation is necessary for the best interests of the child. Such determination may be necessary in a particular case such as one involving abuse or neglect of the child by the parents, or one where the parents are living separately and a decision must be made as to the child's place of residence.

2. In any proceedings pursuant to paragraph 1 of the present article, all interested parties shall be given an opportunity to participate in the proceedings and make their views known.

3. States Parties shall respect the right of the child who is separated from one or both parents to maintain personal relations and direct contact with both parents on a regular basis, except if it is contrary to the child's best interests.

4. Where such separation results from any action initiated by a State Party, such as the detention, imprisonment, exile, deportation or death (including death arising from any cause while the person is in the custody of the State) of one or both parents or of the child, that State Party shall, upon request, provide the parents, the child or, if appropriate, another member of the family with the essential information concerning the whereabouts of the absent member(s) of the family unless the provision of the information would be detrimental to the well-being of the child. States Parties shall further ensure that the submission of such a request shall of itself entail no adverse consequences for the person(s) concerned.

Article 12

1. States Parties shall assure to the child who is capable of forming his or her own views the right to express those views freely in all matters affecting the child, the views of the child being given due weight in accordance with the age and maturity of the child.

2. For this purpose, the child shall in particular be provided the opportunity to be heard in any judicial and administrative proceedings affecting the child, either directly, or through a representative or an appropriate body, in a manner consistent with the procedural rules of national law.

III. Judgments

A. Federal Court—Trial Division (1995) 101 FTR 110

Simpson J delivered oral reasons dismissing the appellant's judicial review application. She held that since there were no reasons given by Officer Caden for his decision, no affidavit was provided, and no reasons were required, she would assume, in the absence of evidence to the contrary, that he acted in good faith and made a decision based on correct principles. She rejected the appellant's argument that the statement in Officer Lorenz's notes that Ms. Baker would be a strain on the welfare system was not supported by the evidence, holding that it was reasonable to conclude from the reports provided that Ms. Baker would not be able to return to work. She held that the language of Officer Lorenz did not raise a reasonable apprehension of bias, and also found that the views expressed in his notes were unimportant, because they were not those of the decision-maker, Officer Caden. She rejected the appellant's argument that the *Convention on the Rights of the Child* mandated that the appellant's interests be given priority in s. 114(2) decisions, holding that the Convention did not apply to this situation, and was not part of domestic law. She also held that the evidence showed the children were a significant factor in the decision-making process. She rejected the appellant's submission that the Convention gave rise to a legitimate expectation that the children's interests would be a primary consideration in the decision.

Simpson J certified the following as a "serious question of general importance" under s. 83(1) of the *Immigration Act*: "Given that the Immigration Act does not expressly incorporate the language of Canada's international obligations with respect to the International Convention on the Rights of the Child, must federal immigration authorities treat the best interests of the Canadian child as a primary consideration in assessing an applicant under s. 114(2) of the *Immigration Act*?"

B. Federal Court of Appeal [1997] 2 FC 127

The reasons of the Court of Appeal were delivered by Strayer JA. He held that pursuant to s. 83(1) of the *Immigration Act*, the appeal was limited to the question certified by Simpson J. He also rejected the appellant's request to challenge the constitutional validity of s. 83(1). Strayer JA noted that a treaty cannot have legal effect in Canada unless implemented through domestic legislation, and that the Convention had not been adopted in either federal or provincial legislation. He held that although legislation should be interpreted, where possible, to avoid conflicts with Canada's international obligations, interpreting s. 114(2) to require that the discretion it provides for must be exercised in accordance with the Convention would interfere with the separation of powers between the executive and legislature. He held that such a principle could also alter rights and obligations within the jurisdiction of provincial legislatures. Strayer JA also rejected the argument that any articles of the Convention could be interpreted to impose an obligation upon the government to give primacy to the interests of the children in a proceeding such as deportation. He held that the deportation of a parent was not a decision "concerning" children within the meaning of article 3. Finally, Strayer JA considered the appellant's argument based on the doctrine of legitimate expectations. He noted that because the doctrine does not create substantive rights, and because a requirement that the best interests of the children be given primacy by a decision-maker under s. 114(2) would be to create a substantive right, the doctrine did not apply.

IV. Issues

Because, in my view, the issues raised can be resolved under the principles of administrative law and statutory interpretation, I find it unnecessary to consider the various Charter issues raised by the appellant and the interveners who supported her position. The issues raised by this appeal are therefore as follows:

(1) What is the legal effect of a stated question under s. 83(1) of the *Immigration Act* on the scope of appellate review?

(2) Were the principles of procedural fairness violated in this case?

   (i) Were the participatory rights accorded consistent with the duty of procedural fairness?

   (ii) Did the failure of Officer Caden to provide his own reasons violate the principles of procedural fairness?

   (iii) Was there a reasonable apprehension of bias in the making of this decision?

(3) Was this discretion improperly exercised because of the approach taken to the interests of Ms. Baker's children?

I note that it is the third issue that raises directly the issues contained in the certified question of general importance stated by Simpson J.

V. Analysis

A. Stated Questions Under Section 83(1) of the Immigration Act

The Court of Appeal held, in accordance with its decision in *Liyanagamage v. Canada (Minister of Citizenship and Immigration)* (1994) 176 NR 4, that the requirement, in s. 83(1), that a "serious question of general importance" be certified for an appeal to be permitted restricts an appeal court to addressing the issues raised by the certified question. However, in *Pushpanathan v. Canada (Minister of Citizenship and Immigration)* [1998] 1 SCR 982 (Can.), at para. 25, this Court held that s. 83(1) does not require that the Court of Appeal address only the stated question and issues related to it:

The certification of a "question of general importance" is the trigger by which an appeal is justified. The object of the appeal is still the judgment itself, not merely the certified question.

Rothstein J noted in *Ramoutar v. Canada (Minister of Employment and Immigration)* [1993] 3 FC 370 (TD), that once a question has been certified, all aspects of the appeal may be considered by the Court of Appeal, within its jurisdiction. I agree. The wording of s. 83(1) suggests, and *Pushpanathan* confirms, that if a "question of general importance" has been certified, this allows for an appeal from the judgment of the Trial Division which would otherwise not be permitted, but does not confine the Court of Appeal or this Court to answering the stated question or issues directly related to it. All issues raised by the appeal may therefore be considered here.

B. The Statutory Scheme and the Nature of the Decision

Before examining the various grounds for judicial review, it is appropriate to discuss briefly the nature of the decision made under s. 114(2) of the *Immigration Act*, the role of this decision in the statutory scheme, and the guidelines given by the Minister to immigration officers in relation to it.

Section 114(2) itself authorizes the Governor in Council to authorize the Minister to exempt a person from a regulation made under the Act, or to facilitate the admission to Canada of any person. The Minister's power to grant an exemption based on humanitarian and compassionate (H & C) considerations arises from s. 2.1 of the *Immigration Regulations*, which I reproduce for convenience:

> The Minister is hereby authorized to exempt any person from any regulation made under subsection 114(1) of the Act or otherwise facilitate the admission to Canada of any person where the Minister is satisfied that the person should be exempted from that regulation or that the person's admission should be facilitated owing to the existence of compassionate or humanitarian considerations.

For the purpose of clarity, I will refer throughout these reasons to decisions made pursuant to the combination of s. 114(2) of the Act and s. 2.1 of the Regulations as "H & C decisions."

Applications for permanent residence must, as a general rule, be made from outside Canada, pursuant to s. 9(1) of the Act. One of the exceptions to this is when admission is facilitated owing to the existence of compassionate or humanitarian considerations. In law, pursuant to the Act and the Regulations, an H & C decision is made by the Minister, though in practice, this decision is dealt with in the name of the Minister by immigration officers: see, for example, *Minister of Employment and Immigration v. Jiminez-Perez* [1984] 2 SCR 565 (Can.), at 569. In addition, while in law, the H & C decision is one that provides for an *exemption* from regulations or from the Act, in practice, it is one that, in cases like this one, determines whether a person who has been in Canada but does not have status can stay in the country or will be required to leave a place where he or she has become established. It is an important decision that affects in a fundamental manner the future of individuals' lives. In addition, it may also have an important impact on the lives of any Canadian children of the person whose humanitarian and compassionate application is being considered, since they may be separated from one of their parents and/or uprooted from their country of citizenship, where they have settled and have connections.

Immigration officers who make H & C decisions are provided with a set of guidelines, contained in chapter 9 of the *Immigration Manual: Examination and Enforcement*. The guidelines constitute instructions to immigration officers about how to exercise the discretion delegated to them. These guidelines are also available to the public. A number of statements in the guidelines are relevant to Ms. Baker's application. Guideline 9.05 emphasizes that officers have a duty to decide which cases should be given a favourable recommendation, by carefully considering all aspects of the case, using their best judgment and asking themselves what a reasonable person would do in such a situation. It also states that although officers are not expected to "delve into areas which are not presented during examination or interviews, they should attempt to clarify possible humanitarian grounds and public policy considerations even if these are not well articulated."

The guidelines also set out the bases upon which the discretion conferred by s. 114(2) and the Regulations should be exercised. Two different types of criteria that may lead to a positive s. 114(2) decision are outlined—public policy considerations and humanitarian and compassionate grounds. Immigration officers are instructed, under guideline 9.07, to assure themselves, first, whether a public policy consideration is present, and if there is none, whether humanitarian and compassionate circumstances exist. Public policy reasons include marriage to a Canadian resident, the fact that the person has lived in Canada, has become established, and has become an "illegal de facto resident," and the fact that the person may be a long-term holder of employment authorization or has worked as a foreign domestic. Guideline 9.07 states that humanitarian and compassionate grounds will exist if "unusual, undeserved or disproportionate hardship would be caused to the person seeking consideration if he or she had to leave Canada." The guidelines also directly address situations involving family dependency, and emphasize that the requirement that a person leave Canada to apply from abroad may result in hardship for close family members of a Canadian resident, whether parents, children, or others who are close to the claimant, but not related by blood. They note that in such cases, the reasons why the person did not apply from abroad and the existence of family or other support in the person's home country should also be considered.

C. Procedural Fairness

The first ground upon which the appellant challenges the decision made by Officer Caden is the allegation that she was not accorded procedural fairness. She suggests that the following procedures are required by the duty of fairness when parents have Canadian children and they make an H & C application: an oral interview before the decision-maker, notice to her children and the other parent of that interview, a right for the children and the other parent to make submissions at that interview, and notice to the other parent of the interview and of that person's right to have counsel present. She also alleges that procedural fairness requires the provision of reasons by the decision-maker, Officer Caden, and that the notes of Officer Lorenz give rise to a reasonable apprehension of bias.

In addressing the fairness issues, I will consider first the principles relevant to the determination of the content of the duty of procedural fairness, and then address Ms. Baker's arguments that she was accorded insufficient participatory rights, that a duty to give reasons existed, and that there was a reasonable apprehension of bias.

Both parties agree that a duty of procedural fairness applies to H & C decisions. The fact that a decision is administrative and affects "the rights, privileges or interests of an individual" is sufficient to trigger the application of the duty of fairness: *Cardinal v. Director of Kent Institution* [1985] 2 SCR 643 (Can.), at 653. Clearly, the determination of whether an applicant will be exempted from the requirements of the Act falls within this category, and it has been long recognized that the duty of fairness applies to H & C decisions: *Sobrie v. Canada (Minister of Employment and Immigration)* (1987) 3 Imm. LR (2d) 81 (FCTD), at 88; *Said v. Canada (Minister of Employment and Immigration)* (1992) 6 Admin. LR (2d) 23 (FCTD); *Shah v. Minister of Employment and Immigration* (1994) 170 NR 238 (FCA).

(1) Factors Affecting the Content of the Duty of Fairness

The existence of a duty of fairness, however, does not determine what requirements will be applicable in a given set of circumstances. As I wrote in *Knight v. Indian Head School Division No. 19* [1990] 1 SCR 653 (Sask.), at 682, "the concept of procedural fairness is eminently variable and its content is to be decided in the specific context of each case." All of the circumstances must be considered in order to determine the content of the duty of procedural fairness: *Knight*, at 682-83; *Cardinal, supra*, at 654; *Old St. Boniface Residents Assn. Inc. v. Winnipeg (City)* [1990] 3 SCR 1170 (Man.), *per* Sopinka J.

Although the duty of fairness is flexible and variable, and depends on an appreciation of the context of the particular statute and the rights affected, it is helpful to review the criteria that should be used in determining what procedural rights the duty of fairness requires in a given set of circumstances. I emphasize that underlying all these factors is the notion that the purpose of the participatory rights contained within the duty of procedural fairness is to ensure that administrative decisions are made using a fair and open procedure, appropriate to the decision being made and its statutory, institutional, and social context, with an opportunity for those affected by the decision to put forward their views and evidence fully and have them considered by the decision-maker.

Several factors have been recognized in the jurisprudence as relevant to determining what is required by the common law duty of procedural fairness in a given set of circumstances. One important consideration is the nature of the decision being made and the process followed in making it. In *Knight, supra*, at 683, it was held that "the closeness of the administrative process to the judicial process should indicate how much of those governing principles should be imported into the realm of administrative decision making." The more the process provided for, the function of the tribunal, the nature of the decision-making body, and the determinations that must be made to reach a decision resemble judicial decision making, the more likely it is that procedural protections closer to the trial model will be required by the duty of fairness. See also *Old St. Boniface, supra*, at 1191; *Russell v. Duke of Norfolk* [1949] 1 All ER 109 (CA), at 118; *Syndicat des employés de production du Québec et de l'Acadie v. Canada (Canadian Human Rights Commission)* [1989] 2 SCR 879 (Qué.), at 896, *per* Sopinka J.

A second factor is the nature of the statutory scheme and the "terms of the statute pursuant to which the body operates": *Old St. Boniface, supra*, at 1191. The role of the particular decision within the statutory scheme and other surrounding indications in the statute help determine the content of the duty of fairness owed when a particular administrative decision is made. Greater procedural protections, for example, will be required when no appeal procedure is provided within the statute, or when the decision is determinative of the issue and further requests cannot be submitted: see D.J.M. Brown and J.M. Evans, *Judicial Review of Administrative Action in Canada* (loose-leaf), at 7-66 to 7-67.

A third factor in determining the nature and extent of the duty of fairness owed is the importance of the decision to the individual or individuals affected. The more important the decision is to the lives of those affected and the greater its impact on that person or those persons, the more stringent the procedural protections that will be mandated. This was expressed, for example, by Dickson J (as he then was) in *Kane v. Board of Governors of the University of British Columbia* [1980] 1 SCR 1105 (BC), at 1113:

> A high standard of justice is required when the right to continue in one's profession or employment is at stake. ... A disciplinary suspension can have grave and permanent consequences upon a professional career.

As Sedley J (now Sedley LJ) stated in *R v. Higher Education Funding Council, ex parte Institute of Dental Surgery* [1994] 1 All ER 651 (QB), at 667:

> In the modern state the decisions of administrative bodies can have a more immediate and profound impact on people's lives than the decisions of courts, and public law has since *Ridge v. Baldwin* [1964] AC 40 (HL, Eng.) been alive to that fact. While the judicial character of a function may elevate the practical requirements of fairness above what they would otherwise be, for example by requiring contentious evidence to be given and tested orally, what makes it "judicial" in this sense is principally the nature of the issue it has to determine, not the formal status of the deciding body.
>
> The importance of a decision to the individuals affected, therefore, constitutes a significant factor affecting the content of the duty of procedural fairness.

Fourth, the legitimate expectations of the person challenging the decision may also determine what procedures the duty of fairness require in given circumstances. Our Court has held that, in Canada, this doctrine is part of the doctrine of fairness or natural justice, and that it does not create substantive rights: *Old St. Boniface, supra*, at 1204; *Reference re Canada Assistance Plan (BC)* [1991] 2 SCR 525 (BC), at 557. As applied in Canada, if a legitimate expectation is found to exist, this will affect the content of the duty of fairness owed to the individual or individuals affected by the decision. If the claimant has a legitimate expectation that a certain procedure will be followed, this procedure will be required by the duty of fairness: *Qi v. Canada (Minister of Citizenship and Immigration)* (1995) 33 Imm. LR (2d) 57 (FCTD); *Mercier-Néron v. Canada (Minister of National Health and Welfare)* (1995) 98 FTR 36; *Bendahmane v. Canada (Minister of Employment and Immigration)* [1989] 3 FC 16 (CA). Similarly, if a claimant has a legitimate expectation that a certain result will be reached in his or her case, fairness may require more extensive procedural rights than would otherwise be accorded: D.J. Mullan, *Administrative Law* (3rd ed. 1996), at 214-15; D. Shapiro, "Legitimate Expectation and its

Application to Canadian Immigration Law" (1992) 8 *JL & Social Pol'y* 282, at 297; *Canada (Attorney General) v. Human Rights Tribunal Panel (Canada)* (1994) 76 FTR 1. Nevertheless, the doctrine of legitimate expectations cannot lead to substantive rights outside the procedural domain. This doctrine, as applied in Canada, is based on the principle that the "circumstances" affecting procedural fairness take into account the promises or regular practices of administrative decision-makers, and that it will generally be unfair for them to act in contravention of representations as to procedure, or to backtrack on substantive promises without according significant procedural rights.

Fifth, the analysis of what procedures the duty of fairness requires should also take into account and respect the choices of procedure made by the agency itself, particularly when the statute leaves to the decision-maker the ability to choose its own procedures, or when the agency has an expertise in determining what procedures are appropriate in the circumstances: Brown and Evans, *supra*, at 7-66 to 7-70. While this, of course, is not determinative, important weight must be given to the choice of procedures made by the agency itself and its institutional constraints: *IWA v. Consolidated-Bathurst Packaging Ltd.* [1990] 1 SCR 282 (Ont.), *per* Gonthier J.

I should note that this list of factors is not exhaustive. These principles all help a court determine whether the procedures that were followed respected the duty of fairness. Other factors may also be important, particularly when considering aspects of the duty of fairness unrelated to participatory rights. The values underlying the duty of procedural fairness relate to the principle that the individual or individuals affected should have the opportunity to present their case fully and fairly, and have decisions affecting their rights, interests, or privileges made using a fair, impartial, and open process, appropriate to the statutory, institutional, and social context of the decision.

(2) Legitimate Expectations

I turn now to an application of these principles to the circumstances of this case to determine whether the procedures followed respected the duty of procedural fairness. I will first determine whether the duty of procedural fairness that would otherwise be applicable is affected, as the appellant argues, by the existence of a legitimate expectation based upon the text of the articles of the Convention and the fact that Canada has ratified it. In my view, however, the articles of the Convention and their wording did not give rise to a legitimate expectation on the part of Ms. Baker that when the decision on her H & C application was made, specific procedural rights above what would normally be required under the duty of fairness would be accorded, a positive finding would be made, or particular criteria would be applied. This Convention is not, in my view, the equivalent of a government representation about how H & C applications will be decided, nor does it suggest that any rights beyond the participatory rights discussed below will be accorded. Therefore, in this case there is no legitimate expectation affecting the content of the duty of fairness, and the fourth factor outlined above therefore does not affect the analysis. It is unnecessary to decide whether an international instrument ratified by Canada could, in other circumstances, give rise to a legitimate expectation.

(3) Participatory Rights

The next issue is whether, taking into account the other factors related to the determination of the content of the duty of fairness, the failure to accord an oral hearing and give
notice to Ms. Baker or her children was inconsistent with the participatory rights required by the duty of fairness in these circumstances. At the heart of this analysis is
whether, considering all the circumstances, those whose interests were affected had a
meaningful opportunity to present their case fully and fairly. The procedure in this case
consisted of a written application with supporting documentation, which was summarized by the junior officer (Lorenz), with a recommendation being made by that officer.
The summary, recommendation, and material was then considered by the senior officer
(Caden), who made the decision.

Several of the factors described above enter into the determination of the type of
participatory rights the duty of procedural fairness requires in the circumstances. First,
an H & C decision is very different from a judicial decision, since it involves the exercise
of considerable discretion and requires the consideration of multiple factors. Second, its
role is also, within the statutory scheme, as an exception to the general principles of Canadian immigration law. These factors militate in favour of more relaxed requirements
under the duty of fairness. On the other hand, there is no appeal procedure, although
judicial review may be applied for with leave of the Federal Court—Trial Division. In
addition, considering the third factor, this is a decision that in practice has exceptional
importance to the lives of those with an interest in its result—the claimant and his or her
close family members—and this leads to the content of the duty of fairness being more
extensive. Finally, applying the fifth factor described above, the statute accords considerable flexibility to the Minister to decide on the proper procedure, and immigration officers, as a matter of practice, do not conduct interviews in all cases. The institutional
practices and choices made by the Minister are significant, though of course not determinative factors to be considered in the analysis. Thus, it can be seen that although some
of the factors suggest stricter requirements under the duty of fairness, others suggest
more relaxed requirements further from the judicial model.

Balancing these factors, I disagree with the holding of the Federal Court of Appeal in
Shah, supra, at 239, that the duty of fairness owed in these circumstances is simply "minimal." Rather, the circumstances require a full and fair consideration of the issues, and
the claimant and others whose important interests are affected by the decision in a fundamental way must have a meaningful opportunity to present the various types of evidence relevant to their case and have it fully and fairly considered.

However, it also cannot be said that an oral hearing is always necessary to ensure a fair
hearing and consideration of the issues involved. The flexible nature of the duty of fairness recognizes that meaningful participation can occur in different ways in different
situations. The Federal Court has held that procedural fairness does not require an oral
hearing in these circumstances: see, for example, *Said, supra,* at 30.

I agree that an oral hearing is not a general requirement for H & C decisions. An
interview is not essential for the information relevant to an H & C application to be put
before an immigration officer, so that the humanitarian and compassionate considerations presented may be considered in their entirety and in a fair manner. In this case, the

appellant had the opportunity to put forward, in written form through her lawyer, information about her situation, her children and their emotional dependence on her, and documentation in support of her application from a social worker at the Children's Aid Society and from her psychiatrist. These documents were before the decision-makers, and they contained the information relevant to making this decision. Taking all the factors relevant to determining the content of the duty of fairness into account, the lack of an oral hearing or notice of such a hearing did not, in my opinion, constitute a violation of the requirements of procedural fairness to which Ms. Baker was entitled in the circumstances, particularly given the fact that several of the factors point toward a more relaxed standard. The opportunity, which was accorded, for the appellant or her children to produce full and complete written documentation in relation to all aspects of her application satisfied the requirements of the participatory rights required by the duty of fairness in this case.

(4) The Provision of Reasons

The appellant also submits that the duty of fairness, in these circumstances, requires that reasons be given by the decision-maker. She argues either that the notes of Officer Lorenz should be considered the reasons for the decision, or that it should be held that the failure of Officer Caden to give written reasons for his decision or a subsequent affidavit explaining them should be taken to be a breach of the principles of fairness.

This issue has been addressed in several cases of judicial review of humanitarian and compassionate applications. The Federal Court of Appeal has held that reasons are unnecessary: *Shah, supra*, at 239-40. It has also been held that the case history notes prepared by a subordinate officer are not to be considered the decision-maker's reasons: see *Tylo v. Minister of Employment and Immigration* (1995) 90 FTR 157, at 159-60. In *Gheorlan v. Canada (Secretary of State)* (1995) 26 Imm. LR (2d) 170 (FCTD), and *Chan v. Canada (Minister of Citizenship and Immigration)* (1994) 87 FTR 62, it was held that the notes of the reviewing officer should not be taken to be the reasons for decision, but may help in determining whether a reviewable error exists. In *Marques v. Canada (Minister of Citizenship and Immigration) (No. 1)* (1995) 116 FTR 241, an H & C decision was set aside because the decision-making officer failed to provide reasons or an affidavit explaining the reasons for his decision.

More generally, the traditional position at common law has been that the duty of fairness does not require, as a general rule, that reasons be provided for administrative decisions: *Northwestern Utilities Ltd. v. City of Edmonton* [1979] 1 SCR 684 (Alta.); *Supermarchés Jean Labrecque Inc. v. Flamand* [1987] 2 SCR 219 (Qué.), at 233; *Public Service Board of New South Wales v. Osmond* (1986) 159 CLR 656 (HCA), at 665-66.

Courts and commentators have, however, often emphasized the usefulness of reasons in ensuring fair and transparent decision-making. Though *Northwestern Utilities* dealt with a statutory obligation to give reasons, Estey J held as follows, at 706, referring to the desirability of a common law reasons requirement:

> This obligation is a salutary one. It reduces to a considerable degree the chances of arbitrary or capricious decisions, reinforces public confidence in the judgment and fairness of administrative tribunals, and affords parties to administrative proceedings an opportunity to assess the question of appeal. ...

The importance of reasons was recently reemphasized by this Court in *Reference re Remuneration of Judges of the Provincial Court of Prince Edward Island* [1997] 3 SCR 3 (PEI), at paras. 180-81.

Reasons, it has been argued, foster better decision making by ensuring that issues and reasoning are well articulated and, therefore, more carefully thought out. The process of writing reasons for decision by itself may be a guarantee of a better decision. Reasons also allow parties to see that the applicable issues have been carefully considered, and are invaluable if a decision is to be appealed, questioned, or considered on judicial review: R.A. Macdonald and D. Lametti, "Reasons for Decision in Administrative Law" (1990) 3 *CJALP* 123, at 146; *Williams v. Canada (Minister of Citizenship and Immigration)* [1997] 2 FC 646 (CA), at para. 38. Those affected may be more likely to feel they were treated fairly and appropriately if reasons are given: de Smith, Woolf, & Jowell, *Judicial Review of Administrative Action* (5th ed. 1995), at 459-60. I agree that these are significant benefits of written reasons.

Others have expressed concerns about the desirability of a written reasons requirement at common law. In *Osmond, supra*, Gibbs CJ articulated, at 668, the concern that a reasons requirement may lead to an inappropriate burden being imposed on administrative decision-makers, that it may lead to increased cost and delay, and that it "might in some cases induce a lack of candour on the part of the administrative officers concerned." Macdonald and Lametti, *supra*, though they agree that fairness should require the provision of reasons in certain circumstances, caution against a requirement of "archival" reasons associated with court judgments, and note that the special nature of agency decision-making in different contexts should be considered in evaluating reasons requirements. In my view, however, these concerns can be accommodated by ensuring that any reasons requirement under the duty of fairness leaves sufficient flexibility to decision-makers by accepting various types of written explanations for the decision as sufficient.

In England, a common law right to reasons in certain circumstances has developed in the case law: see M.H. Morris, "Administrative Decision-makers and the Duty to Give Reasons: An Emerging Debate" (1997) 11 *CJALP* 155, at 164-68; de Smith, Woolf & Jowell, *supra*, at 462-65. In *R v. Civil Service Appeal Board, ex parte Cunningham* [1991] 4 All ER 310 (CA), reasons were required of a board deciding the appeal of the dismissal of a prison official. The House of Lords, in *R v. Secretary of State for the Home Department, ex parte Doody* [1994] 1 AC 531 (HL, Eng.), imposed a reasons requirement on the Home Secretary when exercising the statutory discretion to decide on the period of imprisonment that a prisoner who had been imposed a life sentence should serve before being entitled to a review. Lord Mustill, speaking for all the law lords on the case, held that although there was no general duty to give reasons at common law, in those circumstances, a failure to give reasons was unfair. Other English cases have held that reasons are required at common law when there is a statutory right of appeal: see *Norton Tool Co. v. Tewson* [1973] 1 WLR 45 (NIRC), at 49; *Alexander Machinery (Dudley) Ltd. v. Crabtree* [1974] ICR 120 (NIRC).

Some Canadian courts have imposed, in certain circumstances, a common law obligation on administrative decision-makers to provide reasons, while others have been more reluctant. In *Orlowski v. British Columbia (Attorney-General)* (1992) 94 DLR (4th) 541 (BC CA), at 551-52, it was held that reasons would generally be required for decisions of a review board under Part XX.1 of the *Criminal Code*, based in part on the existence of a statutory right of appeal from that decision, and also on the importance of the interests affected by the decision. In *RDR Construction Ltd. v. Rent Review Commission* (1982) 55 NSR (2d) 71 (CA), the court also held that because of the existence of a statutory right of appeal, there was an implied duty to give reasons. Smith DJ, in *Taabea v. Refugee Status Advisory Committee* [1980] 2 FC 316 (TD), imposed a reasons requirement on a ministerial decision relating to refugee status, based upon the right to apply to the Immigration Appeal Board for redetermination. Similarly, in the context of evaluating whether a statutory reasons requirement had been adequately fulfilled in *Boyle v. Workplace Health, Safety and Compensation Commission (NB)* (1996) 179 NBR (2d) 43 (CA), Bastarache JA (as he then was) emphasized, at 55, the importance of adequate reasons when appealing a decision. However, the Federal Court of Appeal recently rejected the submission that reasons were required in relation to a decision to declare a permanent resident a danger to the public under s. 70(5) of the *Immigration Act*: *Williams, supra*.

In my opinion, it is now appropriate to recognize that, in certain circumstances, the duty of procedural fairness will require the provision of a written explanation for a decision. The strong arguments demonstrating the advantages of written reasons suggest that, in cases such as this where the decision has important significance for the individual, when there is a statutory right of appeal, or in other circumstances, some form of reasons should be required. This requirement has been developing in the common law elsewhere. The circumstances of the case at bar, in my opinion, constitute one of the situations where reasons are necessary. The profound importance of an H & C decision to those affected, as with those at issue in *Orlowski, Cunningham,* and *Doody*, militates in favour of a requirement that reasons be provided. It would be unfair for a person subject to a decision such as this one which is so critical to their future not to be told why the result was reached.

In my view, however, the reasons requirement was fulfilled in this case since the appellant was provided with the notes of Officer Lorenz. The notes were given to Ms. Baker when her counsel asked for reasons. Because of this, and because there is no other record of the reasons for making the decision, the notes of the subordinate reviewing officer should be taken, by inference, to be the reasons for decision. Accepting documents such as these notes as sufficient reasons is part of the flexibility that is necessary, as emphasized by Macdonald and Lametti, *supra*, when courts evaluate the requirements of the duty of fairness with recognition of the day-to-day realities of administrative agencies and the many ways in which the values underlying the principles of procedural fairness can be assured. It upholds the principle that individuals are entitled to fair procedures and open decision-making, but recognizes that in the administrative context, this transparency may take place in various ways. I conclude that the notes of Officer Lorenz satisfy the requirement for reasons under the duty of procedural fairness in this case, and they will be taken to be the reasons for decision.

(5) Reasonable Apprehension of Bias

Procedural fairness also requires that decisions be made free from a reasonable apprehension of bias by an impartial decision-maker. The respondent argues that Simpson J was correct to find that the notes of Officer Lorenz cannot be considered to give rise to a reasonable apprehension of bias because it was Officer Caden who was the actual decision-maker, who was simply reviewing the recommendation prepared by his subordinate. In my opinion, the duty to act fairly and therefore in a manner that does not give rise to a reasonable apprehension of bias applies to all immigration officers who play a significant role in the making of decisions, whether they are subordinate reviewing officers, or those who make the final decision. The subordinate officer plays an important part in the process, and if a person with such a central role does not act impartially, the decision itself cannot be said to have been made in an impartial manner. In addition, as discussed in the previous section, the notes of Officer Lorenz constitute the reasons for the decision, and if they give rise to a reasonable apprehension of bias, this taints the decision itself.

The test for reasonable apprehension of bias was set out by de Grandpré J, writing in dissent, in *Committee for Justice and Liberty v. National Energy Board* [1978] 1 SCR 369 (Can.) at 394:

> ... [T]he apprehension of bias must be a reasonable one, held by reasonable and right minded persons, applying themselves to the question and obtaining thereon the required information. ... [T]hat test is "what would an informed person, viewing the matter realistically and practically—and having thought the matter through—conclude. Would he think that it is more likely than not that [the decision-maker], whether consciously or unconsciously, would not decide fairly."

This expression of the test has often been endorsed by this Court, most recently in *R. v. S. (R.D.)* [1997] 3 SCR 484 (NS), at para. 11, *per* Major J; at para. 31, *per* L'Heureux-Dubé and McLachlin JJ; and at para. 111, *per* Cory J.

It has been held that the standards for reasonable apprehension of bias may vary, like other aspects of procedural fairness, depending on the context and the type of function performed by the administrative decision-maker involved: *Newfoundland Telephone Co. v. Newfoundland (Board of Commissioners of Public Utilities)* [1992] 1 SCR 623 (Nfld.); *Old St. Boniface, supra,* at 1192. The context here is one where immigration officers must regularly make decisions that have great importance to the individuals affected by them, but are also often critical to the interests of Canada as a country. They are individualized, rather than decisions of a general nature. They also require special sensitivity. Canada is a nation made up largely of people whose families migrated here in recent centuries. Our history is one that shows the importance of immigration, and our society shows the benefits of having a diversity of people whose origins are in a multitude of places around the world. Because they necessarily relate to people of diverse backgrounds, from different cultures, races, and continents, immigration decisions demand sensitivity and understanding by those making them. They require a recognition of diversity, an understanding of others, and an openness to difference.

In my opinion, the well-informed member of the community would perceive bias when reading Officer Lorenz's comments. His notes, and the manner in which they are written, do not disclose the existence of an open mind or a weighing of the particular circumstances of the case free from stereotypes. Most unfortunate is the fact that they seem to make a link between Ms. Baker's mental illness, her training as a domestic worker, the fact that she has several children, and the conclusion that she would therefore be a strain on our social welfare system for the rest of her life. In addition, the conclusion drawn was contrary to the psychiatrist's letter, which stated that, with treatment, Ms. Baker could remain well and return to being a productive member of society. Whether they were intended in this manner or not, these statements give the impression that Officer Lorenz may have been drawing conclusions based not on the evidence before him, but on the fact that Ms. Baker was a single mother with several children, and had been diagnosed with a psychiatric illness. His use of capitals to highlight the number of Ms. Baker's children may also suggest to a reader that this was a reason to deny her status. Reading his comments, I do not believe that a reasonable and well-informed member of the community would conclude that he had approached this case with the impartiality appropriate to a decision made by an immigration officer. It would appear to a reasonable observer that his own frustration with the "system" interfered with his duty to consider impartially whether the appellant's admission should be facilitated owing to humanitarian or compassionate considerations. I conclude that the notes of Officer Lorenz demonstrate a reasonable apprehension of bias.

D. Review of the Exercise of the Minister's Discretion

Although the finding of reasonable apprehension of bias is sufficient to dispose of this appeal, it does not address the issues contained in the "serious question of general importance" which was certified by Simpson J relating to the approach to be taken to children's interests when reviewing the exercise of the discretion conferred by the Act and the Regulations. Since it is important to address the central questions which led to this appeal, I will also consider whether, as a substantive matter, the H & C decision was improperly made in this case.

The appellant argues that the notes provided to her show that, as a matter of law, the decision should be overturned on judicial review. She submits that the decision should be held to a standard of review of correctness, that principles of administrative law require this discretion to be exercised in accordance with the Convention, and that the Minister should apply the best interests of the child as a primary consideration in H & C decisions. The respondent submits that the Convention has not been implemented in Canadian law, and that to require that s. 114(2) and the Regulations made under it be interpreted in accordance with the Convention would be improper, since it would interfere with the broad discretion granted by Parliament, and with the division of powers between the federal and provincial governments.

(1) The Approach to Review of Discretionary Decision-Making

As stated earlier, the legislation and Regulations delegate considerable discretion to the Minister in deciding whether an exemption should be granted based upon humanitarian and compassionate considerations. The Regulations state that "[t]he Minister *is … authorized to*" grant an exemption or otherwise facilitate the admission to Canada of any person "*where the Minister is satisfied that*" this should be done "owing to the existence of compassionate or humanitarian considerations." This language signals an intention to leave considerable choice to the Minister on the question of whether to grant an H & C application.

The concept of discretion refers to decisions where the law does not dictate a specific outcome, or where the decision-maker is given a choice of options within a statutorily imposed set of boundaries. As K.C. Davis wrote in *Discretionary Justice* (1969), at 4:

> A public officer has discretion whenever the effective limits on his power leave him free to make a choice among possible courses of action or inaction.

It is necessary in this case to consider the approach to judicial review of administrative discretion, taking into account the "pragmatic and functional" approach to judicial review that was first articulated in *UES, Local 298 v. Bibeault* [1988] 2 SCR 1048 (Qué.), and has been applied in subsequent cases including *Canada (Attorney General) v. Mossop* [1993] 1 SCR 554 (Can.), at 601-7, *per* L'Heureux-Dubé J, dissenting, but not on this issue; *Pezim v. British Columbia (Superintendent of Brokers)* [1994] 2 SCR 557 (BC); *Canada (Director of Investigation and Research) v. Southam Inc.* [1997] 1 SCR 748 (Can.); and *Pushpanathan, supra.*

Administrative law has traditionally approached the review of decisions classified as discretionary separately from those seen as involving the interpretation of rules of law. The rule has been that decisions classified as discretionary may only be reviewed on limited grounds such as the bad faith of decision-makers, the exercise of discretion for an improper purpose, and the use of irrelevant considerations: see, for example, *Maple Lodge Farms Ltd. v. Government of Canada* [1982] 2 SCR 2 (Can.), at 7-8; *Shell Canada Products Ltd. v. Vancouver (City)* [1994] 1 SCR 231 (BC). A general doctrine of "unreasonableness" has also sometimes been applied to discretionary decisions: *Associated Provincial Picture Houses, Ltd. v. Wednesbury Corporation* [1948] 1 KB 223 (CA). In my opinion, these doctrines incorporate two central ideas—that discretionary decisions, like all other administrative decisions, must be made within the bounds of the jurisdiction conferred by the statute, but that considerable deference will be given to decision-makers by courts in reviewing the exercise of that discretion and determining the scope of the decision-maker's jurisdiction. These doctrines recognize that it is the intention of a legislature, when using statutory language that confers broad choices on administrative agencies, that courts should not lightly interfere with such decisions, and should give considerable respect to decision-makers when reviewing the manner in which discretion was exercised. However, discretion must still be exercised in a manner that is within a reasonable interpretation of the margin of manoeuvre contemplated by the legislature, in accordance with the principles of the rule of law (*Roncarelli v. Duplessis* [1959] SCR 121 (Qué.)), in line with general principles of administrative law governing the exercise of discretion, and consistent with the *Canadian Charter of Rights and Freedoms* (*Slaight Communications Inc. v. Davidson* [1989] 1 SCR 1038 (Can.)).

It is, however, inaccurate to speak of a rigid dichotomy of "discretionary" or "non-discretionary" decisions. Most administrative decisions involve the exercise of implicit discretion in relation to many aspects of decision making. To give just one example, decision-makers may have considerable discretion as to the remedies they order. In addition, there is no easy distinction to be made between interpretation and the exercise of discretion; interpreting legal rules involves considerable discretion to clarify, fill in legislative gaps, and make choices among various options. As stated by Brown and Evans, *supra*, at 14-47:

The degree of discretion in a grant of power can range from one where the decision-maker is constrained only by the purposes and objects of the legislation, to one where it is so specific that there is almost no discretion involved. In between, of course, there may be any number of limitations placed on the decision-maker's freedom of choice, sometimes referred to as "structured" discretion.

The "pragmatic and functional" approach recognizes that standards of review for errors of law are appropriately seen as a spectrum, with certain decisions being entitled to more deference, and others entitled to less: *Pezim, supra*, at 589-90; *Southam, supra*, at para. 30; *Pushpanathan, supra*, at para. 27. Three standards of review have been defined: patent unreasonableness, reasonableness *simpliciter*, and correctness: *Southam*, at paras. 54-56. In my opinion the standard of review of the substantive aspects of discretionary decisions is best approached within this framework, especially given the difficulty in making rigid classifications between discretionary and non-discretionary decisions. The pragmatic and functional approach takes into account considerations such as the expertise of the tribunal, the nature of the decision being made, and the language of the provision and the surrounding legislation. It includes factors such as whether a decision is "polycentric" and the intention revealed by the statutory language. The amount of choice left by Parliament to the administrative decision-maker and the nature of the decision being made are also important considerations in the analysis. The spectrum of standards of review can incorporate the principle that, in certain cases, the legislature has demonstrated its intention to leave greater choices to decision-makers than in others, but that a court must intervene where such a decision is outside the scope of the power accorded by Parliament. Finally, I would note that this Court has already applied this framework to statutory provisions that confer significant choices on administrative bodies, for example, in reviewing the exercise of the remedial powers conferred by the statute at issue in *Southam, supra*.

Incorporating judicial review of decisions that involve considerable discretion into the pragmatic and functional analysis for errors of law should not be seen as reducing the level of deference given to decisions of a highly discretionary nature. In fact, deferential standards of review may give substantial leeway to the discretionary decision-maker in determining the "proper purposes" or "relevant considerations" involved in making a given determination. The pragmatic and functional approach can take into account the fact that the more discretion that is left to a decision-maker, the more reluctant courts should be to interfere with the manner in which decision-makers have made choices among various options. However, though discretionary decisions will generally be given considerable respect, that discretion must be exercised in accordance with the boundaries imposed in the statute, the principles of the rule of law, the principles of administrative law, the fundamental values of Canadian society, and the principles of the Charter.

(2) The Standard of Review in This Case

I turn now to an application of the pragmatic and functional approach to determine the appropriate standard of review for decisions made under s. 114(2) and Regulation 2.1, and the factors affecting the determination of that standard outlined in *Pushpanathan, supra*. It was held in that case that the decision, which related to the determination of a question of law by the Immigration and Refugee Board, was subject to a standard of review of correctness. Although that decision was also one made under the *Immigration Act*, the type of decision at issue was very different, as was the decision-maker. The appropriate standard of review must, therefore, be considered separately in the present case.

The first factor to be examined is the presence or absence of a privative clause, and, in appropriate cases, the wording of that clause: *Pushpanathan*, at para. 30. There is no privative clause contained in the *Immigration Act*, although judicial review cannot be commenced without leave of the Federal Court, Trial Division under s. 82.1. As mentioned above, s. 83(1) requires the certification of a "serious question of general importance" by the Federal Court, Trial Division before that decision may be appealed to the Court of Appeal. *Pushpanathan* shows that the existence of this provision means there should be a lower level of deference on issues related to the certified question itself. However, this is only one of the factors involved in determining the standard of review, and the others must also be considered.

The second factor is the expertise of the decision-maker. The decision-maker here is the Minister of Citizenship and Immigration or his or her delegate. The fact that the formal decision-maker is the Minister is a factor militating in favour of deference. The Minister has some expertise relative to courts in immigration matters, particularly with respect to when exemptions should be given from the requirements that normally apply.

The third factor is the purpose of the provision in particular, and of the Act as a whole. This decision involves considerable choice on the part of the Minister in determining when humanitarian and compassionate considerations warrant an exemption from the requirements of the Act. The decision also involves applying relatively "open-textured" legal principles, a factor militating in favour of greater deference: *Pushpanathan, supra,* at para. 36. The purpose of the provision in question is also to *exempt* applicants, in certain circumstances, from the requirements of the Act or its Regulations. This factor, too, is a signal that greater deference should be given to the Minister. However, it should also be noted, in favour of a stricter standard, that this decision relates directly to the rights and interests of an individual in relation to the government, rather than balancing the interests of various constituencies or mediating between them. Its purpose is to decide whether the admission to Canada of a particular individual, in a given set of circumstances, should be facilitated.

The fourth factor outlined in *Pushpanathan* considers the nature of the problem in question, especially whether it relates to the determination of law or facts. The decision about whether to grant an H & C exemption involves a considerable appreciation of the facts of that person's case, and is not one which involves the application or interpretation of definitive legal rules. Given the highly discretionary and fact-based nature of this decision, this is a factor militating in favour of deference.

These factors must be balanced to arrive at the appropriate standard of review. I conclude that considerable deference should be accorded to immigration officers exercising the powers conferred by the legislation, given the fact-specific nature of the inquiry, its role within the statutory scheme as an exception, the fact that the decision-maker is the Minister, and the considerable discretion evidenced by the statutory language. Yet the absence of a privative clause, the explicit contemplation of judicial review by the Federal Court, Trial Division and the Federal Court of Appeal in certain circumstances, and the individual rather than polycentric nature of the decision, also suggest that the standard should not be as deferential as "patent unreasonableness." I conclude, weighing all these factors, that the appropriate standard of review is reasonableness *simpliciter*.

(3) Was This Decision Unreasonable?

I will next examine whether the decision in this case, and the immigration officer's interpretation of the scope of the discretion conferred upon him, were unreasonable in the sense contemplated in the judgment of Iacobucci J in *Southam, supra*, at para. 56:

> An unreasonable decision is one that, in the main, is not supported by any reasons that can stand up to a somewhat probing examination. Accordingly, a court reviewing a conclusion on the reasonableness standard must look to see whether any reasons support it. The defect, if there is one, could presumably be in the evidentiary foundation itself or in the logical process by which conclusions are sought to be drawn from it.
>
> In particular, the examination of this question should focus on the issues arising from the "serious question of general importance" stated by Simpson J: the question of the approach to be taken to the interests of children when reviewing an H & C decision.

The notes of Officer Lorenz, in relation to the consideration of "H & C factors," read as follows:

> The PC is a paranoid schizophrenic and on welfare. She has no qualifications other than as a domestic. She has FOUR CHILDREN IN JAMAICA AND ANOTHER FOUR BORN HERE. She will, of course, be a tremendous strain on our social welfare systems for (probably) the rest of her life. There are no H&C factors other than her FOUR CANADIAN-BORN CHILDREN. Do we let her stay because of that? I am of the opinion that Canada can no longer afford this type of generosity.

In my opinion, the approach taken to the children's interests shows that this decision was unreasonable in the sense contemplated in *Southam, supra*. The officer was completely dismissive of the interests of Ms. Baker's children. As I will outline in detail in the paragraphs that follow, I believe that the failure to give serious weight and consideration to the interests of the children constitutes an unreasonable exercise of the discretion conferred by the section, notwithstanding the important deference that should be given to the decision of the immigration officer. Professor Dyzenhaus has articulated the concept of "deference as respect" as follows:

> Deference as respect requires not submission but a respectful attention to the reasons offered or which could be offered in support of a decision. ...

(D. Dyzenhaus, "The Politics of Deference: Judicial Review and Democracy," in M. Taggart, ed., *The Province of Administrative Law* (1997), 279, at 286.)

The reasons of the immigration officer show that his decision was inconsistent with the values underlying the grant of discretion. They therefore cannot stand up to the somewhat probing examination required by the standard of reasonableness.

The wording of s. 114(2) and of Regulation 2.1 requires that a decision-maker exercise the power based upon "*compassionate* or *humanitarian* considerations" (emphasis added).

These words and their meaning must be central in determining whether an individual H & C decision was a reasonable exercise of the power conferred by Parliament. The legislation and regulations direct the Minister to determine whether the person's admission should be facilitated owing to the existence of such considerations. They show Parliament's intention that those exercising the discretion conferred by the statute act in a humanitarian and compassionate manner. This Court has found that it is necessary for the Minister to *consider* an H & C request when an application is made: *Jiminez-Perez, supra*. Similarly, when considering it, the request must be evaluated in a manner that is respectful of humanitarian and compassionate considerations.

Determining whether the approach taken by the immigration officer was within the boundaries set out by the words of the statute and the values of administrative law requires a contextual approach, as is taken to statutory interpretation generally: see *R v. Gladue* [1999] 1 SCR 688 (BC); *Rizzo & Rizzo Shoes Ltd. (Re)* [1998] 1 SCR 27 (Ont.), at paras. 20-23. In my opinion, a reasonable exercise of the power conferred by the section requires close attention to the interests and needs of children. Children's rights, and attention to their interests, are central humanitarian and compassionate values in Canadian society. Indications of children's interests as important considerations governing the manner in which H & C powers should be exercised may be found, for example, in the purposes of the Act, in international instruments, and in the guidelines for making H & C decisions published by the Minister herself.

(a) The Objectives of the Act

The objectives of the Act include, in s. 3(c):

> to facilitate the reunion in Canada of Canadian citizens and permanent residents with their close relatives from abroad;

Although this provision speaks of Parliament's objective of *reuniting* citizens and permanent residents with their close relatives from abroad, it is consistent, in my opinion, with a large and liberal interpretation of the values underlying this legislation and its purposes to presume that Parliament also placed a high value on keeping citizens and permanent residents together with their close relatives who are already in Canada. The obligation to take seriously and place important weight on keeping children in contact with both parents, if possible, and maintaining connections between close family members is suggested by the objective articulated in s. 3(c).

(b) International Law

Another indicator of the importance of considering the interests of children when making a compassionate and humanitarian decision is the ratification by Canada of the *Convention on the Rights of the Child*, and the recognition of the importance of children's rights and the best interests of children in other international instruments ratified by Canada. International treaties and conventions are not part of Canadian law unless they have been implemented by statute: *Francis v. The Queen* [1956] SCR 618 (Can.), at 621; *Capital Cities Communications Inc. v. Canadian Radio-Television Commission* [1978] 2 SCR 141 (Can.), at 172-73. I agree with the respondent and the Court of Appeal that the

Convention has not been implemented by Parliament. Its provisions therefore have no direct application within Canadian law.

Nevertheless, the values reflected in international human rights law may help inform the contextual approach to statutory interpretation and judicial review. As stated in R. Sullivan, *Driedger on the Construction of Statutes* (3rd ed., 1994), at 330:

> [T]he legislature is presumed to respect the values and principles enshrined in international law, both customary and conventional. These constitute a part of the legal context in which legislation is enacted and read. *In so far as possible, therefore, interpretations that reflect these values and principles are preferred.* [Emphasis added.]

The important role of international human rights law as an aid in interpreting domestic law has also been emphasized in other common law countries: see, for example, *Tavita v. Minister of Immigration* [1994] 2 NZLR 257 (CA), at 266; *Vishaka v. Rajasthan* [1997] 3 LRC 361 (SC India), at 367. It is also a critical influence on the interpretation of the scope of the rights included in the Charter: *Slaight Communications, supra*; *R v. Keegstra* [1990] 3 SCR 697 (Alta.).

The values and principles of the Convention recognize the importance of being attentive to the rights and best interests of children when decisions are made that relate to and affect their future. In addition, the preamble, recalling the *Universal Declaration of Human Rights*, recognizes that "childhood is entitled to special care and assistance." A similar emphasis on the importance of placing considerable value on the protection of children and their needs and interests is also contained in other international instruments. The United Nations *Declaration of the Rights of the Child* (1959), in its preamble, states that the child "needs special safeguards and care." The principles of the Convention and other international instruments place special importance on protections for children and childhood, and on particular consideration of their interests, needs, and rights. They help show the values that are central in determining whether this decision was a reasonable exercise of the H & C power.

(c) The Ministerial Guidelines

Third, the guidelines issued by the Minister to immigration officers recognize and reflect the values and approach discussed above and articulated in the Convention. As described above, immigration officers are expected to make the decision that a reasonable person would make, with special consideration of humanitarian values such as keeping connections between family members and avoiding hardship by sending people to places where they no longer have connections. The guidelines show what the Minister considers a humanitarian and compassionate decision, and they are of great assistance to the Court in determining whether the reasons of Officer Lorenz are supportable. They emphasize that the decision-maker should be alert to possible humanitarian grounds, should consider the hardship that a negative decision would impose upon the claimant or close family members, and should consider as an important factor the connections between family members. The guidelines are a useful indicator of what constitutes a reasonable interpretation of the power conferred by the section, and the fact that this decision was contrary to their directives is of great help in assessing whether the decision was an unreasonable exercise of the H & C power.

The above factors indicate that emphasis on the rights, interests, and needs of children and special attention to childhood are important values that should be considered in reasonably interpreting the "humanitarian" and "compassionate" considerations that guide the exercise of the discretion. I conclude that because the reasons for this decision do not indicate that it was made in a manner which was alive, attentive, or sensitive to the interests of Ms. Baker's children, and did not consider them as an important factor in making the decision, it was an unreasonable exercise of the power conferred by the legislation, and must, therefore, be overturned. In addition, the reasons for decision failed to give sufficient weight or consideration to the hardship that a return to Jamaica might cause Ms. Baker, given the fact that she had been in Canada for 12 years, was ill and might not be able to obtain treatment in Jamaica, and would necessarily be separated from at least some of her children.

It follows that I disagree with the Federal Court of Appeal's holding in *Shah, supra*, at 239, that a s. 114(2) decision is "*wholly* a matter of judgment and discretion" (emphasis added). The wording of s. 114(2) and of the Regulations shows that the discretion granted is confined within certain boundaries. While I agree with the Court of Appeal that the Act gives the applicant no right to a particular outcome or to the application of a particular legal test, and that the doctrine of legitimate expectations does not mandate a result consistent with the wording of any international instruments, the decision must be made following an approach that respects humanitarian and compassionate values. Therefore, attentiveness and sensitivity to the importance of the rights of children, to their best interests, and to the hardship that may be caused to them by a negative decision is essential for an H & C decision to be made in a reasonable manner. While deference should be given to immigration officers on s. 114(2) judicial review applications, decisions cannot stand when the manner in which the decision was made and the approach taken are in conflict with humanitarian and compassionate values. The Minister's guidelines themselves reflect this approach. However, the decision here was inconsistent with it.

The certified question asks whether the best interests of children must be *a* primary consideration when assessing an applicant under s. 114(2) and the Regulations. The principles discussed above indicate that, for the exercise of the discretion to fall within the standard of reasonableness, the decision-maker should consider children's best interests as an important factor, give them substantial weight, and be alert, alive and sensitive to them. That is not to say that children's best interests must always outweigh other considerations, or that there will not be other reasons for denying an H & C claim even when children's interests are given this consideration. However, where the interests of children are minimized, in a manner inconsistent with Canada's humanitarian and compassionate tradition and the Minister's guidelines, the decision will be unreasonable.

E. Conclusions and Disposition

Therefore, both because there was a violation of the principles of procedural fairness owing to a reasonable apprehension of bias, and because the exercise of the H & C discretion was unreasonable, I would allow this appeal.

The appellant requested that solicitor-client costs be awarded to her if she were successful in her appeal. The majority of this Court held as follows in *Young v. Young* [1993] 4 SCR 3 (BC), at 134:

> Solicitor-client costs are generally awarded only where there has been reprehensible, scandalous or outrageous conduct on the part of one of the parties.

There has been no such conduct on the part of the Minister shown during this litigation, and I do not believe that this is one of the exceptional cases where solicitor-client costs should be awarded. I would allow the appeal, and set aside the decision of Officer Caden of April 18, 1994, with party-and-party costs throughout. The matter will be returned to the Minister for redetermination by a different immigration officer.

IACOBUCCI J (Cory J concurring):

I agree with L'Heureux-Dubé J's reasons and disposition of this appeal, except to the extent that my colleague addresses the effect of international law on the exercise of ministerial discretion pursuant to s. 114(2) of the *Immigration Act*, RSC 1985, c. I-2. The certified question at issue in this appeal concerns whether federal immigration authorities must treat the best interests of the child as a primary consideration in assessing an application for humanitarian and compassionate consideration under s. 114(2) of the Act, given that the legislation does not implement the provisions contained in the *Convention on the Rights of the Child*, Can. TS 1992 No. 3, a multilateral convention to which Canada is party. In my opinion, the certified question should be answered in the negative.

It is a matter of well-settled law that an international convention ratified by the executive branch of government is of no force or effect within the Canadian legal system until such time as its provisions have been incorporated into domestic law by way of implementing legislation: *Capital Cities Communications Inc. v. Canadian Radio-Television Commission* [1978] 2 SCR 141 (Can.). I do not agree with the approach adopted by my colleague, wherein reference is made to the underlying values of an unimplemented international treaty in the course of the contextual approach to statutory interpretation and administrative law, because such an approach is not in accordance with the Court's jurisprudence concerning the status of international law within the domestic legal system.

In my view, one should proceed with caution in deciding matters of this nature, lest we adversely affect the balance maintained by our Parliamentary tradition, or inadvertently grant the executive the power to bind citizens without the necessity of involving the legislative branch. I do not share my colleague's confidence that the Court's precedent in *Capital Cities, supra*, survives intact following the adoption of a principle of law which permits reference to an unincorporated convention during the process of statutory interpretation. Instead, the result will be that the appellant is able to achieve indirectly what cannot be achieved directly, namely, to give force and effect within the domestic legal system to international obligations undertaken by the executive alone that have yet to be subject to the democratic will of Parliament.

The primacy accorded to the rights of children in the Convention, assuming for the sake of argument that the factual circumstances of this appeal are included within the scope of the relevant provisions, is irrelevant unless and until such provisions are the subject of legislation enacted by Parliament. In answering the certified question in the negative, I am mindful that the result may well have been different had my colleague concluded that the appellant's claim fell within the ambit of rights protected by the *Canadian Charter of Rights and Freedoms*. Had this been the case, the Court would have had an opportunity to consider the application of the interpretive presumption, established by the Court's decision in *Slaight Communications Inc. v. Davidson* [1989] 1 SCR 1038, and confirmed in subsequent jurisprudence, that administrative discretion involving Charter rights be exercised in accordance with similar international human rights norms.

Appeal allowed with costs.

NOTES

Legislative Structure and Decision-Making Chain

1. What was the direct legislative source of the minister's "humanitarian and compassionate" discretion? Was it the *Immigration Act*, s. 114(2) or another instrument?

2. Can you detect anything peculiar about the contents or terminology of s. 2.1 of the *Immigration Regulations*?

3. At various points in the judgment, the court refers to ministerial guidelines. What are these and what is their legal status? If they are not strictly "official" law, how do they achieve relevance in the judgment?

4. The relevant legislative instrument confers decision-making authority on the minister of citizenship and immigration. However, the facts make it clear that the minister took no personal part in the decision-making process for Baker. Officials within the department made the decision. How does this come about? In any event, why, if the statute says that the minister is to take the decision or exercise the discretion, does Baker not succeed on the simple ground that the decision was taken by the wrong official? By the way, which administrative official within the department took the decision: Lorenz or Caden? Does it matter?

The Judicial Review Process

5. The application for judicial review started in the Federal Court Trial Division. As seen in chapter 1 of this text, this is normally required in cases involving judicial review of federal statutory and prerogative decision making. However, the route by which the case reached the Federal Court Trial Division had an unusual feature, as did the subsequent appeal to the Federal Court of Appeal. What were these unusual features and what do you think might be their justification? Do you see any potential problems with these derogations from normal rights of access to judicial review?

6. Contrary to the Federal Court of Appeal, the Supreme Court of Canada held that the Federal Court of Appeal (and, as a consequence, the Supreme Court itself) was not limited in dealing with the appeal to the ground or grounds on which the Trial Division judge had certified a question for the Federal Court of Appeal's consideration. In view of your perceptions of the reasons for requiring that a question be certified, do you accept the Supreme Court's reasoning on this issue?

The Various Grounds of Judicial Review

Procedural

General

7. The court identifies several factors that bear on whether the principles of procedural fairness apply to a decision-making process even where the legislation is silent and that are used to determine the scope of the entitlement to procedural fairness once the initial threshold has been passed. What are those various factors and how were they applied to the statutory scheme and facts of this particular case?

8. There was no threshold issue in this case as to whether Baker was entitled to *any* common law procedural protection. It was a case that was about the content of the protection. Why was this so?

9. Among the factors identified by the court as relevant to the determination of procedural questions at common law is whether the decision-maker has a statutory discretion in relation to procedures or procedural rulings or can be expected to have some expertise in that domain due to its familiarity with decision making under the relevant statutory provision. How does this factor play out in the analysis? Does it mean that the court is partially abdicating its role as the guardian of the common law and as the body that is best located to make judgments on whether statutory or prerogative authorities have provided sufficient procedural protections to affected persons?

10. Baker had argued in the Supreme Court that the decision engaged her right to "life, liberty and security of the person," thus introducing a requirement for the decision-maker to comply with "the principles of fundamental justice" enshrined in s. 7 of the Charter. The court held that it did not have to decide this question. Why? What difference would or should it make, either here or more generally, if the procedural claim is being advanced within s. 7 of the Charter rather than simply a common law framework?

Oral or In-Person Hearing

11. Among the claims that Baker was making was that she and members of her family should have been given the benefit of an oral or in-person hearing by the officials within the department. Why does the court reject that argument? Do you agree with those reasons? Is the court holding that this is never a requirement of procedural fairness in cases such as this? If not, what would be needed to be able to make such a claim?

Right to Reasons

12. This was the first time that the Supreme Court of Canada recognized a common law right to reasons in the context of the administrative process. Previously, that right had been confined to situations where it existed as a result of explicit statutory direction. Why did the court "change" this area of the law? Are you convinced by the court's reasoning? What purposes does a hearing requirement seek to accomplish?

13. To the extent that the court is not accepting a universal entitlement to reasons, in what situations after *Baker* should a failure to provide reasons not attract judicial review?

14. What does the obligation to provide reasons actually involve? Even accepting that the standard is a flexible one, how could a document as flawed as that provided by the line officer in this case be seen as meeting the obligation to provide reasons? Also, by what warrant could the court conclude (contrary to Simpson J at first instance) that this was in fact the basis for the "minister's" decision given that the relevant correspondence came from other sources?

15. Why do the courts typically describe a failure to provide reasons as a procedural issue? To what extent might a failure to provide reasons compromise the procedural fairness of a hearing?

Bias

16. What was it about Officer Lorenz's notes that led the court to conclude that there was a reasonable apprehension of bias in this instance? To what extent was the official's tainted attitude attributable to Baker's particular circumstances and to what extent was it attributable to other factors? Should both aspects be relevant to the determination of a reasonable apprehension of bias?

17. Consider again, in this context, the basis on which the court associated Lorenz's attitudes with the final decision that was rendered on Baker's application.

18. To what extent does the bias portion of the judgment overlap with the subsequent substantive ground of abuse of discretion (based on taking account of irrelevant factors and failing to take account of relevant matters)? What does this say about the distinction between judicial review on procedural grounds and judicial review on substantive grounds?

Substantive

General

19. Why, having found in Baker's favour on the procedural grounds, does the court proceed to deal with the substantive arguments?

20. Before the judgment moves to the specific allegations of abuse of discretion, the court deals with the standard of review to be applied to those allegations. What is the purpose of this? How is it feasible to conceive of review for abuse of discretion within a range of various standards of review?

21. By reference to what criteria does the court say the standard of review is to be established? How within those criteria does the court establish that the appropriate standard here is "unreasonableness"? Is the court holding that this means that the decision of the official is judged by whether it is in an overall sense "unreasonable" or is the court really speaking about unreasonableness in a different sense? How does the court factor in the idea that statutory discretions "must be exercised in accordance with the boundaries imposed in the statute, the principles of the rule of law, the principles of administrative law, the fundamental values of Canadian society, and the principles of the Charter" (para. 56)? How do these concerns fit within a reasonableness standard of judicial review?

Abuse of Discretion

22. What sources does the court look to as the basis on which it will decide whether there has been reviewable unreasonableness in the exercise of discretion in this case? In what order of legal significance would you rank these sources?

23. What answer does the court provide to the question certified by Simpson J of the Federal Court Trial Division and set out in para. 9 of the judgment? More particularly, how does the majority judgment of the Supreme Court make use of the *Convention on the Rights of the Child* in determining that there has been a reviewable abuse of discretion? Why does the minority take issue with this aspect of the majority judgment? Do you agree with the minority position on this? Why does the minority concede that the position might well be different if a Charter right or freedom is at stake?

24. In the course of her judgment, L'Heureux-Dubé J insists that if immigration officers are to avoid judicial review they must be "alert, alive and sensitive" to the best interests of children affected by the exercise of humanitarian and compassionate discretion. To what extent is this a description of what constitutes reasonableness in the circumstances? How would you characterize what is required if the standard of review is one of correctness? To what extent does discerning whether a decision-maker has been "alert, alive and sensitive" involve a reweighing by the reviewing court of the way in which the officers dealt with the interests of the child in relation to other relevant considerations? If it does, how close does this come to straight reassessment of the merits of the application? (This has troubled courts subsequently: see *Suresh v. Canada (Minister of Citizenship and Immigration)*, [2002] 1 SCR 3 (Can.); *Legault v. Canada (Minister of Citizenship and Immigration)* (2002), 212 DLR (4th) 139 (FCA); rev'g. [2001] 3 FC 277 (TD)).

Remedy

25. What remedy does the court provide after holding that the appeal should be allowed? How far does this go towards Mavis Baker's ultimate goal of remaining permanently in Canada? More generally, what does this say about the capacities of judicial review?

General

26. Among the assessments of *Baker* are Sharryn Aiken and Sheena Scott, "*Baker v. Canada (Minister of Citizenship and Immigration)* and the Rights of Children" (2000), 15 *JL & Social Pol'y* 211; David Dyzenhaus and Evan Fox-Decent, "Rethinking the Process/Substance Distinction: *Baker v. Canada*" (2001), 51 *UTLJ* 193; Lorne Sossin, "Developments in Administrative Law: The 1997-98 and 1998-99 Terms" (2000), 11 *Supreme Court Law Review* (2d) 37, at 57-76; David Mullan, "*Baker v. Canada (Minister of Citizenship and Immigration)*" (1999), 7 *Reid's Administrative Law* 145; and James L.H. Sprague, "Another View of *Baker*" (1999), 7 *Reid's Administrative Law* 163. On the relevance of international law to the exercise of administrative discretion, see David Dyzenhaus, Murray Hunt, and Michael Taggart, "The Principle of Legality in Administrative Law: Internationalisation and Constitutionalisation" (2001), 1 *OUCLJ* 5. Also see, more generally, David Dyzenhaus, ed., *Baker: The Unity of Public Law?* (Oxford: Hart Publishing, 2003).

27. Over two years later, on December 21, 2001, Mavis Baker became a permanent resident of Canada. See "Mother in battle over deportation legally a resident," *National Post*, December 22, 2001.

PART II

Procedures

GENERAL INTRODUCTION

Seen from a traditional judicial review perspective, administrative law has dual concerns: the process by which a decision is reached and the merits of that decision. For the most part, the courts have claimed authority to resolve by reference to judicially developed standards procedural issues that arise or have arisen in the course of administrative decision making. In contrast, provided the decision-maker has kept within the limits of its "jurisdiction" (a weasel word, as we will come to see), the courts profess limited interest in the substantive merits of decisions.

While many question whether there is or can be a clear demarcation between issues of procedure and those of substance, and while the real profile of judicial intervention in the administrative process is somewhat at odds with (or at least more complex than) the description just provided, nonetheless, issues of procedure have played a major role in the evolution of modern judicial review law. They are worth studying in their own right.

Of course, that might not be reason in itself for placing procedural matters chronologically before those of substance in a casebook of this kind. However, there is an additional justification that has always seemed to us to be clinching. The study of procedural issues provides a more useful vehicle for revealing the nature, structure, and extent of the administrative process than would be achieved by commencing with a consideration of the scope of external review of the merits of administrative decision making. (Indeed, this is even more true in the case of the material with which many traditional administrative law courses started: a study of judicial remedies, and, most notably, the prerogative writs.) To the extent that beginning with procedures involves an outlining and evaluation of the design of a wide range of decision-making structures (the pathology of the administrative process), it serves as invaluable background to the context-sensitive inquiries that are so essential in administrative law—whether coming from a judicial review or institutional design vantage point.

Having said this, we should also confess immediately that the appropriate division of contents between part II on procedures and part III on substance was not completely self-evident. Here, we were in general influenced in our choices by a view of procedures that embraced the notion of the process and the personnel of administrative decision making; its adjectival characteristics. Thus, included within this part are chapters on bias and independence and institutional decision making, as well as a section in another chapter on the giving of reasons as an element in the administrative process. However, we also return to aspects of these issues in the part on substance and particularly in the chapters on discretion when we deal with review for bad faith, acting under dictation, and wrongful delegation as traditional categories of review for abuse of discretionary power. The links between bad faith and bias are obvious while concerns about acting under dictation and wrongful delegation are clearly ones about the personnel and process of administrative decision making. There is no need to apologize for this. At the very least, this partial overlap should reinforce the lesson that there is no complete divide between issues of procedure and substance in administrative law.

In the first two editions of this casebook, this part was labelled "Natural Justice," not "Procedures." This reflected the then prevalent terminology of the common law: judicially imposed process obligations were encapsulated as the "rules of natural justice"—the right to a decision by an impartial decision-maker after a fair hearing. This specialized meaning of an expression stolen from the arenas of philosophical and moral discourse is not only confusing, at least to neophytes, but has also diminished in currency in today's administrative law. As we will see, part of the reason for this has been an expansion of both the circumstances in which players in the administrative process are obliged to accord procedural decencies and the conceptions of the range of acceptable procedures. It is now more usual for courts and decision-makers to use the term "duty to act fairly." In common parlance, that too is just as confusing as the "rules of natural justice," in that it clearly connotes substantive as well as procedural obligations. For present purposes, "procedures" seems far more apt.

The study of procedures is the study of the procedures that agencies are required to use and should use; more particularly, it is the study of the procedural rights that individuals and groups have to participate in making decisions. These rights are not rights to vote, or rights to have some other power to make decisions. Instead, they are essentially rights to present information, analysis, and opinions to an agency that has power to make a decision (or to investigate or make a recommendation), and to test information, analysis, and opinions from other sources. The nature and extent of these rights are obviously important in any consideration of the decency and efficiency of government.

An example of these procedural rights is professional discipline. Professional associations—such as law societies, colleges of physicians and surgeons, or colleges of nurses—are usually given power to discipline members. The power to make an initial decision is usually assigned to a committee. If a committee proposes to discipline a member for misconduct, he or she is normally entitled to a set of procedural rights that are usually and expressively called a hearing. The committee must give notice of the hearing, including enough information about the alleged misconduct to enable a response to be made, and it must disclose the information it has gathered about the member. At the hearing an accuser, who is a member of the staff of the association or a lawyer retained to represent it, presents the information about the alleged misconduct, and the member may cross-examine witnesses and present witnesses, documents, and personal statements. The committee must decide on the basis of the material presented during the hearing and, now in most instances, provide reasons. The eventual effect of its decision depends on the particular structure of the association and is not important to this example.

This example is simple, or at least it will appear simple in retrospect, for three reasons. First, and most important, the hearing closely resembles the trial process so familiar to lawyers. Second, the right to these procedures is fairly well settled, although we hasten to add that much may depend on the peculiarities of context and legislation—we have presented a simple example, not a comprehensive analysis. Third, the member is usually entitled to all or almost all of the full range of the procedures that might be useful; the difficult and important problem of choosing some, but not all, of the procedures is usually not a large issue. Different sets of procedures are required for different kinds of decisions, and for many decisions no procedural rights at all are given.

The study of procedural rights can be divided into two major themes. The first is the entitlement to procedural rights, or the "threshold." What are the kinds of decisions for which some procedural rights should be given? We have already said that rights will normally be given for professional discipline. What about a decision to discipline an inmate in a prison or a student in a secondary school, a decision to expropriate land, a decision about general rules for the "Canadian content" of television programs, an investigation of the affairs of a business corporation, a decision about an application for a licence, or a decision about admission to law school? Each of these decisions presents a difficult problem at the threshold: is it a decision for which some procedural rights should be given to permit participation by the individual or groups affected? The second theme is the choice of the procedures to be required, assuming the threshold will be crossed. Consider each of the examples we have just given. What procedures are appropriate? For example, consider discipline in a secondary school. Are rights to notice and an opportunity to make a submission appropriate? And should the submission be oral or written? What about rights to disclosure of the identity of informers, to present witnesses, to cross-examine, and to be represented by a lawyer?

These two themes are interdependent. Thinking about the threshold is incomplete or meaningless without also thinking about the procedures that will be required if the threshold is crossed, and thinking about choices of procedures is incomplete without thinking about the kinds of decisions for which they will be required. The two themes are essentially different perspectives on the larger and fundamental questions of the appropriateness of procedures for making decisions. However, the distinction is justified because doctrine has tended to separate the two, and because it is convenient. Everything cannot be presented and studied at the same time.

Consider two more examples to illustrate the need to use different procedures for different kinds of decisions. The first is a decision by a workers' compensation board about compensation for an injured worker, in which the issue is whether the injury occurred in the course of the employment and, especially, the time and place it occurred. The second is a decision made by an environmental assessment board about the location of a major electrical transmission line, in which a multitude of parties participates, including landowners and public interest groups. These are disputes about the proposed location and the alternatives, including disputes about financial costs, about the effects on wildlife, farming operations, and scenery, about the reliability of the system, and disputes about the tradeoffs to be made among these interests. The range of the participants and the interests at stake in these two decisions, the nature of the issues to be considered, and the choice to be made by the agencies make different procedures appropriate for each decision.

Consideration of appropriateness requires a thorough knowledge and understanding of the structures and functions of agencies. For example, the procedures of a workers' compensation board must take account of the vast numbers of claims to be processed and the probable lack of skilled help for almost all the claimants. The procedures of an environmental assessment board must take account of the fact that some of the important issues are about values and preferences, and procedures appropriate for presenting and testing facts are not appropriate for presenting preferences. A lawyer who speculates about procedures without understanding the structure and functions of an agency takes a great risk of misunderstanding important issues and, more generally, making legalistic and monolithic prescriptions. These needs of understanding are complicated by the large number and diversity of agencies. Sheer numbers forbid treating each agency and each issue as unique. Inevitably, generalizations and groupings must be made.

The law about procedures is composed of common law, legislation and regulations, the *Canadian Bill of Rights*, the *Canadian Charter of Rights and Freedoms*, and the practices of the agencies themselves. At the very outset, when we speak of the common law, we encounter an analytical difficulty. The powers to make the decisions for which procedural rights may exist are almost always created by statutes (the exception being the limited range of surviving prerogative powers), but often the procedural rights are not mentioned at all in these statutes, and this is especially true for the cases in which the basic general principles were established. When procedural rights are established (to use a vague word) for these decisions, are they made by courts (without any authorization from the statute) or are they ultimately derived from the statute (and is the function of the courts therefore essentially interpretation)?

The common law is general, integrated, and independent and can be described in a relatively short space. The law made by legislation and regulations is very different. It differs greatly among the provinces, and in each one it is a bewildering and diverse array that defies generalized description. Some statutes and regulations govern the procedure of individual agencies, and others govern smaller or larger groups of agencies. Some specify a single procedural requirement, and others tend toward being a code of procedure. Some duplicate the common law, some expand it, and some impose requirements that are entirely different. Often, the courts must interpret these statutes, and the common law is frequently a background of standards and ideas for this interpretation. This work of the courts is important, and some cases that illustrate it are included in this part.

For much of our history and, indeed, even today in many situations, it is this common law that has been the exclusive focus of both procedural claims by affected individuals and judicial attention and elaboration. At times, however, the discourse and approach in the jurisprudence has assumed constitutional dimensions. Indeed, in this context, the use of the language of "natural justice" has had a subtle impact on judicial reasoning. To the extent that this concept in its Thomist sense is one of overarching moral imperative, it always had the potential to bring into question traditional or absolute theories of parliamentary sovereignty. While this never led to the direct assertion in Canadian law of a principle that Parliament could not expressly legislate away entitlements to a hearing, it did manifest itself in approaches to statutory interpretation and, in particular, in the assertion that the clearest possible parliamentary specification was necessary before the otherwise applicable common law entitlements to natural justice were abrogated. No purposive approach to statutory interpretation here. Indeed, to this extent, as Willis now long ago pointed out, the requirements of natural justice had a claim to be part of whatever implied bill of rights existed under the *British North America Act, 1867* (now *Constitution Act, 1867*): "Administrative Law in Canada" (1939), 53 *Harvard LR* 251. (*Quaere* whether it has any claims to be part of the current version of the implied bill of rights or the underlying principles of the Canadian constitution as recognized in *Reference re Remuneration of Judges of Provincial Court of Prince Edward Island*, [1997] 3 SCR 3 and *Reference re Secession of Quebec*, [1998] 2 SCR 217.)

With the enactment by Parliament of the *Canadian Bill of Rights* in 1960 and its self-proclaimed special or superior legislative status, the movement toward the constitutionalization of procedural entitlements seemingly made a more concrete advance. However, for two-and-a-half decades, the restrictive interpretation of its terms by Canadian courts (including the Supreme Court of Canada) made the *Bill of Rights* seem ineffective. It was reduced to being the last resort of desperate counsel. As such, it barely surfaced in the first two editions of this casebook. However, the *Bill of Rights* was rediscovered by the Supreme Court of Canada in 1985 in *Singh v. Canada (Minister of Employment and Immigration)*, [1985] 1 SCR 177 (Can.). Since then, it has assumed (as it did in *Singh* itself for three judges of the Supreme Court) an important (though still infrequently invoked) alternative source of constitutionally protected procedural rights in the federal domain to those provided by the *Canadian Charter of Rights and Freedoms*.

Far more dramatic in terms of its immediate impact was the 1982 *Canadian Charter of Rights and Freedoms*. In particular, its guarantee in s. 7 of the benefit of the "principles of fundamental justice" whenever the "right to life, liberty and security of the person" was in jeopardy not only promised much but also seemed relatively assured of an important place in the administrative law firmament after three judges of the Supreme Court in *Singh* deployed s. 7 to invalidate important features of the then *Immigration Act*'s procedures for dealing with convention refugee claims. Yet more than two decades later, while the Charter has had an impact and constitutionalized certain procedural entitlements, the precise extent to which it has marked a change or advance from the existing principles of the common law remains tantalizingly uncertain. The Charter's overall applicability is not coterminous with accepted targets of the principles of judicial review; even the general dimensions of the reach of "life, liberty and security of the person" remain uncertain at the margins; there are questions about whether "fundamental justice" involves a claim to procedures more enhanced than those afforded by traditional "natural justice" or "procedural fairness" whenever Charter rights are implicated in administrative decision making; and the extent to which s. 1 of the Charter can be advanced in an administrative setting as a justification of what are otherwise derogations from the "principles of fundamental justice" still requires further elaboration. Procedural rights have been constitutionalized by the Charter but to precisely what effect is still a significant challenge for the courts.

Agencies themselves establish many procedural requirements. Some are regulations; some are written, but are not regulations; and some are unwritten, and are either consciously made and remembered, or no more than unconsidered habit. Whether these requirements are "law" or not depends on the context and purpose of the question, but they certainly determine much of what agencies and participants do.

The appropriate allocation of responsibility among the legislatures, the courts, and the agencies for designing procedures needs to be considered throughout this part. Initially, the question may seem to be simply which institution can best design procedures, but some thought and experience demonstrates that this question is too crude. Each institution can have a distinctive role. Consider, for example, a distinction between general requirements and elaboration and detail, or a distinction between specifying procedures for agencies and giving them a prod to design procedures for themselves.

The law about procedures has changed substantially in the last 40 years and will continue to evolve particularly as conceptions about public participation in the administrative process are re-evaluated, as knowledge about the effectiveness and impact of various procedures on substantive outcomes increases, and as the courts more fully delineate the reach of the Charter. Confining ourselves for the moment to the changes of the last 30 years, we see three aspects of the evolution of the common law that have become ingrained and represent significant alterations in the traditional pattern of procedural litigation. First, the language of discourse, the words used to express the doctrine have changed. Second, the threshold below which no procedural claims will be recognized has been lowered. Third, the courts are more willing to make choices among the procedures and to require different procedures for different kinds of decision.

Associated with or part of the third phenomenon of a more context sensitive approach is a sense that, even within the traditional terrain of common law natural justice, claims to court-like procedures will not be recognized automatically. In other words, the absence of an individualized approach to procedural questions may, in some contexts, have worked a diminution in the courts' willingness to impose *any* procedural obligations. In addition, there is evidence, most dramatically manifested by the emergence of the doctrine of legitimate expectation, that procedural obligations may vary even within the context of different exercises of the same statutory power. At its most obvious, this is reflected in the recognition that representations by decision-makers to affected persons that process will be afforded may have legal effect even where that process would not normally be required in the exercise of the relevant statutory power. Here too, we anticipate further changes and refinement in the common law over the next few years.

There is another area where traditional dogma is coming under attack. As already mentioned, the courts were much more inclined to review afresh administrative rules on and decisions about procedural issues than they were to scrutinize the merits of decisions made by agencies and tribunals acting within their recognized areas of jurisdiction. In part, this willingness stemmed from a judicial sense of greater expertise than that of the challenged decision-maker over the question of what were appropriate procedures for the exercise of that decision-maker's mandate. As a consequence, the Canadian courts for the most part rejected (particularly in the domain of challenges based on the *Canadian Bill of Rights* and the Charter) arguments to the effect that administrative determinations of procedural questions are entitled to at least a measure of deference. (For a discussion of the dubiousness of these claims to expertise at least in the context of the extended reach of today's procedural fairness doctrine, see Loughlin, "Procedural Fairness: A Study of the Crisis in Administrative Law" (1978), 28 *UTLJ* 215, and for an examination of the tensions created by reason of the courts' different postures as between review of procedural and review of substantive issues, see Dyzenhaus, "Developments in Administrative Law: The 1991-92 Term" (1993), 4 *Sup. Ct. L Rev.* (2d) 177; and Dyzenhaus and Fox-Decent, "Rethinking the Process/Substance Distinction: *Baker v. Canada*" (2001), 51 *UTLJ* 193.)

To the extent that the range of administrative functions that are subject to procedural demands has increased and to the extent that the procedures deployed by those decision-makers move further and further from the paradigm of those followed by courts of law, the claim of the courts to be experts has diminished considerably. This has led to acceptance of the proposition that judges should pay respect to carefully crafted administrative processes and duly considered procedural rulings and not be so willing to intervene on a "correctness" basis from what may well be an inappropriate or uninformed view of the match between legislative mandate and procedural imperatives: *Baker v. Canada (Minister of Citizenship and Immigration)*, [1999] 2 SCR 817 (Can.). Indeed, there has been a call for some deference to procedural choices even in situations where s. 7 of the Charter applies and the applicant for relief has a constitutional entitlement to procedural protections: *Suresh v. Canada (Minister of Citizenship and Immigration)*, [2002] 1 SCR 3 (Can.).

Lawyers must consider the effects of all of this law on the procedures that agencies actually use, and the effect of procedures on agency attitudes and the decisions that agencies make. Of course in any particular dispute, especially one that involves review, procedures may be affected by a wide range of influences, but consider instead general tendencies and the vast multitude of decisions that are made without protracted dispute, without any thought for review, and perhaps without any involvement by lawyers. We believe that this law and the values it expresses tend to shape the procedures of agencies, either because the agencies share the values, or because they wish to stay comfortably far from review. We hasten to emphasize that this belief is about tendencies; failures to comply occur, both randomly and chronically, caused by ignorance, habit, arrogance, or the sheer inappropriateness of the doctrine. The effect of the procedures on attitudes and decisions is much more difficult to assess, and conclusions may in the end be no more than expressions of faith. We believe that the kind of participation that these requirements permit diminishes the effects of comfortable habit and inadequate or misguided attitudes, and permits presentation of information, analysis, and opinions that would not otherwise be considered by the agencies.

Next, we come to the justification for giving these procedural rights. Why do we give hearings? This question becomes two questions: Why do we give an opportunity for participation in governing? Why do we choose to give this form of participation—that is, a hearing—rather than others, for example, voting? Assuming we give a hearing, what shall it be? Should it be a relatively complex affair involving lawyers, or simply a conversation? The courts have understandably not undertaken comprehensive and abstract speculation about these questions, and the scholarly literature is surprisingly sparse. We return to these questions in chapter 4 of this text.

Last, a further explanation of the meanings of the terms "natural justice" and "hearing" is needed. The phrase "natural justice" has, as we said at the outset of this introduction, a rich history. It has been used in several different ways, but usually to denote a large body of common law about the procedures agencies must use (and about bias and lack of independence). The branch about procedure is often called the doctrine of *audi alteram partem* (listen to the other side), and until recently, it unambiguously included the entire range of common law procedural rights. Over 30 years ago, an expansion of rights began under the label "fairness," which caused some ambiguity and uncertainty in the meaning of "natural justice." Natural justice can, and sometimes does, include the "fairness" rights, but it can also and sometimes does exclude "fairness," and in this sense it denotes only part of the entire range of rights that we have called "procedures" and that are dealt with in this part. Neither meaning is true. The cases must occasionally be read carefully to determine which meaning is intended, but usually no more is at stake than avoiding unnecessary confusion. The word "hearing" usually, especially in older cases, has virtually the same meaning as "natural justice," and often the two terms are used together or as alternatives. However, sometimes "hearing" is used to denote a more or less formal, trial-type process. It is occasionally difficult to know which meaning is meant, in part because of a tendency, especially in older cases, to assume there is no difference.

In this part, our progression will be a consideration in chapter 3, Fairness: Sources and Thresholds, of the six principal sources of procedural entitlements: administrative decision-makers' enabling statutes, subordinate legislation, policies and guidelines, general procedural statutes, common law procedural fairness, and constitutional and quasi-constitutional enactments. Following this overview of the sources of procedures, we examine the threshold for the application of procedural entitlements under these sources. In particular, we focus on the foundations of the present threshold for the application of the rules of natural justice and duty to act fairly and evaluate whether that threshold is comprehensible and reflects an appropriate delineation of the situations where procedural claims are justified. This will involve us in an analysis of some of the key terms that are used as benchmarks in this arena: the concept of "legislative" as opposed to "administrative" and "judicial" functions; the making of "rules" and "policy" as opposed to the resolution of disputes; the "non-final" or "preliminary" as opposed to "final" nature of some decisions; the description of the interest at stake as being a "privilege" as opposed to a "right"; the pull associated with "property" claims as opposed to other types of "interest." We then move on to recent developments in procedural law associated with the doctrine of legitimate expectation. Next, we deal with the impact of the *Canadian Bill of Rights* and *Canadian Charter of Rights and Freedoms* in the domain of procedures, outlining in this context the general parameters under which both these constitutional documents operate in the domain of administrative law. Finally, we briefly review the statutory thresholds for the application of the specific protections contained in the general procedural statutes enacted by Ontario, Alberta, Québec, and British Columbia.

Once the threshold is crossed, we move in chapter 4 to outline a number of the elements associated with the detailed elaboration of the rules of procedural fairness. We begin by examining the Supreme Court's attempt, in *Baker*, to lay out a methodology to determine the appropriate content of procedural fairness and contrast this to the approach of the US Supreme Court in its seminal decisions in *Goldberg v. Kelly* and *Mathews v. Eldridge*. To provide a sense of the kinds of procedural claims that are the focus of this chapter, we examine and assess the procedural codes that have been enacted in four provinces, Ontario's *Statutory Powers Procedure Act*, RSO 1990, c. S.22; Alberta's *Administrative Procedures and Jurisdiction Act*, RSA 2000, c. A-3, as amended by SA 2005, c. 4; British Columbia's *Administrative Tribunals Act*, SBC 2004, c. 45; and Québec's *Administrative Justice Act*, SQ 1996, c. 54; and, of a somewhat less detailed variety, the relevant provisions of Québec's *Charter of Human Rights and Freedoms*, RSQ 1977, c. C-12. This leads to a discussion, principally from a common law perspective but also as a matter of appropriate decision-making structures, of some of the most frequently litigated aspects of claims to procedural protections. Here, we start with pre-hearing issues, those of notice, disclosure and discovery, and delay in the commencement and prosecution of the hearing. Then we examine matters of dispute arising in the course of the hearing itself: the right to an oral as opposed to a written hearing; whether a hearing should be open or closed; claims to representation by counsel or an agent; the extent to which each person affected is entitled to access to all relevant information; the entitlement of the decision-maker to take official notice of evidence; the applicability of the court rules of evidence; the scope of cross-examination rights; and, finally, the occasions on which the decision-maker must provide reasons, the nature of that obligation, and the consequences of failing to meet it. Of particular emphasis throughout this section will be an examination of the extent to which these claims are enhanced when rights arising under the *Canadian Charter of Rights and Freedoms* are involved. As well, there is the all-pervasive theme that we pick up again explicitly towards the end of the chapter, the influence of the concept of the traditional-type hearing.

Following our discussion of these conventional categories of procedural claim, we deal in separate chapters with some of the most contentious aspects of contemporary procedural law and debate. First, we consider what has been commonly described in the past as the second limb of the rules of natural justice—the principles of unbiased decision making. Many of the concerns here are still the predispositions and conflicts of interest of individual decision-makers. However, the dimensions of the call for impartial, detached decision making have broadened considerably in recent years to include issues of institutional autonomy and show signs of becoming subsumed under a more general category, that of decisional independence. Of considerable influence in this domain have been the provisions of the *Canadian Bill of Rights* and the Canadian and Québec Charters and their use of the dual term "impartial and independent" decision. As a consequence, this identification of the badges of structural independence serves as a convenient vehicle to return to the matter of constitutionalized procedural protections and the working out of the details of those protections in a specific context. We then proceed to the problems of institutional decision making and particularly the pressures generated by the demands of efficient, effective, and consistent decision making in accordance with the statutory mandate particularly though not exclusively in the domain of high-volume jurisdiction tribunals. These problems have manifested themselves most graphically in the case law in concerns about enforced collegiality and consultation and issues of unlawful dictation and delegation by and to fellow tribunal members (particularly the chair), staff and lawyers, both in-house and external. Finally, as we discuss in chapter 7, there is the issue whether there should be a more concerted imposition of procedures in the context of rulemaking and, if so, where this impetus should come from: the legislature or the currently diffident judiciary.

Some useful general discussions of procedures are Grey, "Procedural Fairness and Substantive Rights" (1977), XVIII *Nomos* 182; Kadish, "Methodology and Criteria in Due Process Adjudication—A Survey and Criticism" (1957), 66 *Yale LJ* 319; Macdonald, "Procedural Due Process in Canadian Constitutional Law, Natural Justice and Fundamental Justice" (1987), 39 *U of Florida LR* 217; Maher, "Natural Justice as Fairness" in MacCormick and Birks, eds., *The Legal Mind: Essays for Tony Honoré* (Oxford: Clarendon Press, 1986); Mashaw, *Due Process in the Administrative State* (New Haven, CT: Yale University Press, 1985); Michelman, "Formal and Associational Aims in Procedural Due Process" (1977), XVIII *Nomos* 126; Tucker, "The Political Economy of Administrative Fairness: A Preliminary Inquiry" (1987), 25 *Osgoode Hall LJ* 555; and Verkuil, "The Emerging Concept of Administrative Procedure" (1978), 78 *Columbia LR* 258.

CHAPTER THREE

Fairness: Sources and Thresholds

SOURCES

The *Baker* decision is the leading Canadian authority on the factors and principles considered by courts in determining the scope and content of the common law duty of procedural fairness. In other words, it addresses both the circumstances in which judges will require public authorities to observe fair procedures, affording those affected by their decisions the right to be heard by an independent and impartial decision-maker, and the specific procedures necessary to achieve this end. In many decision-making contexts, however, the common law is not the only, or even the most important, source of procedural protections. Parliament and provincial legislatures have prescribed detailed procedural requirements in statutes, or have delegated this task to Cabinet or to the administrative decision-makers themselves. This section provides a brief overview of procedural sources, approaching them in the order a tribunal would in order to determine what procedures it is required to afford parties affected by its decisions.

The Enabling Statute

To ascertain whether it is required by law to afford an affected individual procedures and, if so, what procedures, a public authority must first look to the terms of its enabling statute. Enabling statutes may set out a detailed list of procedural requirements that decision-makers must follow in making specific decisions. For example, the *Immigration Act, 1976* examined by the Supreme Court in *Singh v. Canada (MEI)* described in comprehensive terms the procedures for determination of whether an individual was a Convention refugee. These included the claimant's in-person examination by a senior immigration officer, the recommendation on status to the Minister of Employment and Immigration by a Refugee Status Advisory Committee based on its review of the claimant's examination transcript and other materials relating to country conditions, and the Immigration Appeals Board's power to reconsider the minister's denial of status through a review of the record and, if convinced there were reasonable grounds to believe the claim could be established at a hearing, through an in-person hearing of the claimant. In some circumstances, statutory procedures may constitute the clear legislative direction required by courts to limit or oust common law procedural protection.

In *Singh*, the provisions of the *Immigration Act, 1976* prescribed a complete procedural code governing refugee status determinations and thus superseded and displaced the common law duty of procedural fairness. Recognizing that it could not "import into the duty of fairness procedural constraints ... incompatible with the decision-making scheme set up by Parliament," the Supreme Court proceeded to determine whether it could override the clear statutory language based on constitutional or quasi-constitutional rights.

Subordinate Legislation: Administrative Policy and Practice

Rather than prescribing specific procedures in an administrative board's enabling statute, legislatures may choose to statutorily delegate to the executive—the (lieutenant) governor in council, an individual minister, or the board itself—the power to enact regulations or rules that establish procedural requirements. For example, Manitoba's *Regulations Act*, CCSM c. R60, s. 1 defines "regulation" as a "regulation, rule or by-law that ... governs practice or procedure in quasi-judicial proceedings and is made or approved in the execution of the power conferred by a provision of an Act of the Legislature that uses the word 'regulation' in conferring the power." Regulations and rules made pursuant to statutory authority, known as "subordinate legislation," are binding on those parties subject to them. The main reasons motivating delegation of this power include expertise and efficiency. Tribunals are more intimately familiar with the decision-making context—the impact of their decisions on affected parties and the exigencies of fair and expeditious decision making—and are best placed to craft procedures appropriate to this context. Moreover, legislatures do not have the time or information needed to tailor specific procedures for each and every tribunal or agency. This is best left to the decision-makers themselves. (See chapter 7 of this text; chapter 13 of Flood and Sossin, eds., *Administrative Law in Context* (2008).)

For example, Manitoba's *Labour Relations Act*, CCSM c. L10 confers on the Labour Relations Board of that province the power to enact rules of procedure:

> 141(1) The board may make regulations not inconsistent with this Act respecting: (a) the establishment of rules of procedure for its hearings;

In turn, Regulation 184/87R, registered pursuant to this power, sets out in great detail how board proceedings may be started and how board hearings are held, including evidentiary rules, adjournments, notices, and rules specific to certification applications.

The delegation by legislatures of rule-making powers to the executive branch, including administrative tribunals, raises a "principal–agent" problem—a risk that "those who are making the rules ... are not following the wishes and expectations of those who delegated the power (and as a consequence, at least in theory, the wishes of the electorate)" (Greene, in Flood and Sossin, eds., *Administrative Law in Context*, at 341.) To minimize this risk, delegated legislation is subjected to various mechanisms of accountability and scrutiny. Many jurisdictions in Canada have enacted laws providing for legislative scrutiny of subordinate legislation. For example, ss. 11-13 of Manitoba's *Regulations Act*, respectively, provide that regulations "stand permanently referred" to the Manitoba Legislature's Standing Committee on Statutory Regulations and Orders, require that a copy of newly registered regulations be laid before the legislature at the commencement of a legislative session, and empower the legislative assembly to direct the executive to repeal or amend the regulation. At the federal level, the minister of justice is also statutorily required to verify that statutes and regulations comply with the rights and freedoms set out in the *Canadian Bill of Rights*

(Bill, s. 3(1)) and *Charter of Rights and Freedoms* (*Department of Justice Act*, RSC 1985, c. J-2 (as amended by SC 1985, c. 26, s. 106)).

Another accountability mechanism is public consultation. The most common form of public consultation is achieved by requiring regulatory bodies or departments, by policy or statute, to provide public notice of regulatory initiatives, including draft regulations as well as an opportunity by affected parties or members of the public to comment. While some jurisdictions have applied this obligation broadly (Québec via its *Regulations Act*, SQ 1986, c. 22, ss. 8-14 and the federal government by its Federal Regulatory Plan), other jurisdictions have selectively incorporated notice and comment obligations in specific regulatory regimes. For example, in recent amendments to the Ontario *Human Rights Code* providing for direct access by individuals complaining of discrimination to the Ontario Human Rights Tribunal, the Ontario legislature required the Tribunal to "hold public consultations" before making rules to govern practice and procedure before it (OHRC, s. 43(7)). (This subject is described in greater detail in chapter 7, Rulemaking.)

Finally, a measure of accountability may be achieved through the judicial review of subordinate legislation. The validity of regulations or rules may be challenged where statutorily prescribed mandatory steps for their effective enactment were not followed. (*Immeubles Port Louis Ltée c. Lafontaine (Village)*, [1991] 1 SCR 326.) Subordinate legislation may also be challenged on substantive grounds. Just like any statute, regulations and rules must comply with the Charter and other constitutional and quasi-constitutional instruments. Moreover, they are subject to judicial review if *ultra vires*. Under the *ultra vires* doctrine, regulations and rules must fall within the scope of and respect the limits prescribed by the regulation-making or rule-making authority conferred in the delegating statute. There is a strong presumption that those statutory powers that authorized the making of rules establishing the procedures of adjudicative bodies require the subordinate legislator to comply with the principles of procedural fairness. In other words, absent express contrary language, there is an implied requirement in the delegating statute that procedural regulations and rules made under the statutory power comply with the common law, and the *vires* of non-compliant subordinate legislation is open to challenge.

Policies and Guidelines

Public authorities will frequently issue guidelines and policies, sometimes regarding the procedural aspects of decision making, which do not set down legally binding requirements. The power to make these soft law instruments may, but need not, be provided for in the authority's enabling statute. For example, the *Immigration and Refugee Protection Act*, SC 2001, c. 27 confers on the chairperson of the Immigration and Refugee Board both the power to make rules respecting "the activities, practice and procedure of each of the Divisions of the Board" (s. 161(a)) and the power to "issue guidelines in writing to members of the Board ... to assist members in carrying out their duties" (s. 159(h)). Only the rules, which are legally binding, are subject to governor in council approval and tabling in Parliament.

While not strictly law, soft law instruments like guidelines often play a dominant role in public authorities' decision making. Based on their study of social assistance decision making, Lorne Sossin and Laura Pottie have observed that front-line decision-makers will sometimes rely almost exclusively on guidelines to make decisions and refer to their enabling statute only when these guidelines are not clear. (See Pottie and Sossin, "Demystifying the Boundaries of Public Law: Policy, Discretion, and Social Welfare" (2005), 38 *UBC L Rev.* 147.) The *Baker* decision, where the Supreme Court relied on ministerial guidelines "as a useful indicator" of what constitutes a reasonable interpretation of the minister's power to grant humanitarian and compassionate exemptions to Canada's immigration law, illustrates that the rigid dichotomy between "binding" rules and "non-binding" guidelines is eroding. (See Sossin and Houle, in Jacobs and Mactavish, eds., *Dialogue Between Courts and Tribunals: Essays in Administrative Law and Justice (2001-2007)* (Montreal: Éditions Thémis, 2007).) There has been similar judicial reliance on soft law in the procedural domain. For example, in *Bezaire v. Windsor Roman Catholic Separate School Board* (1992), 9 OR (3d) 737 (Div. Ct.), an Ontario court relied on a ministerial procedural guideline on school closings and on the school board procedural policy as evidence of what procedures were required by common law procedural fairness in the context of a school closing.

General Procedural Statutes

Some Canadian jurisdictions have enacted general procedural statutes, which constitute an additional source of procedural requirements. These are the Alberta *Administrative Procedures and Jurisdiction Act*, British Columbia's *Administrative Tribunals Act*, Ontario's *Statutory Powers Procedure Act*, and Québec's *Administrative Justice Act*. The thresholds for application of these procedural codes, discussed in more detail later in this chapter, vary across jurisdictions. Once triggered, these codes prescribe common procedural standards for the decision-makers falling within their ambit. The scope of the application of these procedural codes may be modified or limited by a public authority's enabling statute and delegated legislation, and great care must be taken to read these legislative procedural sources together to determine procedural entitlements in a given case. An excellent example of this interaction is found in Ontario's recently amended *Human Rights Code*, which provides that "the provisions of the *Statutory Powers Procedure Act* apply to any proceeding before the [Human Rights] Tribunal unless they conflict with the provision of this Act, the regulations or the Tribunal rules" (s. 42(1)). These general procedural statutes, when they apply, provide for procedural standards of varying specificity, including rights to reasons for decision and the right to make representations. These issues of content or choice of procedures are discussed further in chapter 4 of this text.

Common Law Procedural Fairness

If a particular procedure is not required by a public authority's enabling statute, valid delegated legislation or a general procedural statute, or if the procedure is required only to a limited extent, the authority may nevertheless be obliged to provide an effective party with fuller procedural protection under the principles of common law procedural fairness. Under these judge-made principles, a party affected by a public authority's decision is entitled to be heard by the authority (*audi alteram partem*, the decision-maker must "hear the other side") in an impartial and independent hearing (*nemo judex in sua causa*, the decision-maker must not be "a judge in his own cause"). The concept of procedural fairness or "fairness" descends from the rules of "natural justice" which, historically, imposed on tribunals exercising judicial or quasi-judicial functions the trial-type procedures typical of courts. Today, however, it applies to a much broader spectrum of decisions, including the ministerial decision involved in *Baker* and its requirements vary accordingly, from notice of the decision and an opportunity to comment in writing to more elaborate in-person hearing requirements. The history of this evolution from natural justice to procedural fairness is briefly described later in this chapter in our discussion of thresholds for the various sources of procedure. For now, we will examine a few of the seminal cases that marked the development of the modern doctrine of procedural fairness. The first of these is an English case, *Cooper v. Board of Works for Wandsworth District*.

While *Cooper* is well over a hundred years old, it is still today as close chronologically as it was to the initial common law cases in which the courts railed against the failure of those in authority to provide a hearing before making a decision affecting the rights of a specific citizen. Indeed, in *Cooper*, reliance is placed on one of the very oldest of the known authorities, *Dr. Bentley's Case* (1723), 1 Str. 537; 93 ER 698 (KB), in which Dr. Bentley, the Master of Trinity College, Cambridge and a notorious and renegade academic, was challenging the removal of his degrees by the university and his status by the college. There, Fortescue J made his oft-quoted statement to the effect that not even God failed to provide Adam and Eve with a hearing before casting them out of the Garden of Eden. This *dictum* exemplifies the extent to which appeals were made to conceptions of morality and natural law in the foundational jurisprudence.

What is also common to *Cooper* and *Dr. Bentley's Case* is the emphasis by the respective courts on the nature of the interest that is at stake, in each instance a "property" right, and the fact that the decisions under attack involved a determination that a wrong had been committed by an individual leading to the imposition by a tribunal of a penalty. This sense that claims to implied procedural protections in the face of silent statutes were at their strongest in the case of individualized decisions involving the removal or diminution in property rights for wrongdoing was one that dominated the common law of procedural fairness until the 1960s.

When we read *Cooper* today, it seems from many perspectives thoroughly modern in its analysis of the claim to procedural fairness, particularly in so far as it adopts a functional approach to the determination whether such a duty should be imposed on the relevant statutory regime. As we have already seen in our consideration of *Baker* in chapter 2 of this text, this is very much the stuff of contemporary Canadian jurisprudence. However, it was not always thus. There are allusions in Erle CJ's judgment in *Cooper* to distinctions between functions that are judicial and those that are not. However, he expressly eschews basing his judgment on a classification of the power to order the demolition of a house as a judicial function. Regrettably, this was to change 40 to 50 years later when the English courts started restricting access to implied hearing rights. In this era (which was to last in England until well into the 1960s and beyond that in Canada), classification of the function in issue became absolutely crucial. Unless the authority being exercised was a judicial one, the courts would not impose hearing requirements. Administrative or ministerial functions did not carry with them any obligation to comply with the rules of natural justice and they were beyond the reach of the then dominant judicial review remedies of *certiorari* and prohibition, which were also seen as dependent on the presence of a judicial function.

The Traditional Common Law Doctrine

Cooper v. Board of Works for Wandsworth District
(1863), 143 ER 414 (Eng. CP)

[The *Metropolis Local Management Act 1855*, s. 76 required anyone intending to build a new house to give notice to the Board of Works seven days before beginning construction, and gave the board power "in default of such notice ... to cause such house or building to be demolished or altered ... and to recover the expenses thereof from the owner." The purpose of the notice requirement was to give the board an opportunity to give directions about drains. Cooper was a builder and was employed to build a house in Wandsworth. He claimed that he had sent notice to the board. The board denied receiving it, but Cooper admitted that he began construction within five days from the day on which he claimed to have sent the notice. He built a substantial part of the house, and the board tore it down without giving him any notice.

Cooper brought an action for damages, for trespass, and succeeded at trial. The board obtained a rule *nisi* for a non-suit.]

ERLE CJ: The contention on the part of the plaintiff has been, that, although the words of the statute, taken in their literal sense, without any qualification at all, would create a justification for the act which the district board has done, the powers granted by that statute are subject to a qualification which has been repeatedly recognised, that no man is to be deprived of his property without his having an opportunity of being heard. ... I think that the power which is granted by the 76th section is subject to the qualification suggested. It is a power carrying with it enormous consequences. The house in question was built only to a certain extent. But the power claimed would apply to a complete house. It would apply to a house of any value, and completed to any extent; and it seems to me to be a power which may be exercised most perniciously, and that the limitation which we are going to put upon it is one which ought, according to the decided cases, to be put upon it, and one which is required by a due consideration for the public interest. I think the board ought to have given notice to the plaintiff, and to have allowed him to be heard. The default in sending notice to the board of the intention to build, is a default which may be explained. There may be a great many excuses for the apparent default. The party may have intended to conform to the law. He may have actually conformed to all the regulations which they would wish to impose, though by accident his notice may have miscarried; and, under those circumstances, if he explained how it stood, the proceeding to demolish, merely because they had ill-will against the party, is a power that the legislature never intended to confer. I cannot conceive any harm that could happen to the district board from hearing the party before they subjected him to a loss so serious as the demolition of his house; but I can conceive a great many advantages which might arise in the way of public order, in the way of doing substantial justice, and in the way of fulfilling the purposes of the statute by the restriction which we put upon them, that they should hear the party before they inflict upon him such a heavy loss. I fully agree that the legislature intended to give the district board very large powers indeed: but the qualification I speak of is one which has been recognised to the full extent. It has been said that the principle that no man shall be deprived of his property without an opportunity of being heard, is limited to a judicial proceeding, and that a district board ordering a house to be pulled down cannot be said to be doing a judicial act. I do not quite agree with that; neither do I undertake to rest my judgment solely upon the ground that the district board is a court exercising judicial discretion upon the point: but the law, I think, has been applied to many exercises of power which in common understanding would not be at all more a judicial proceeding than would be the act of the district board in ordering a house to be pulled down. The case of the corporation of the University of Cambridge, who turned out Dr. Bentley, in the exercise of their assumed power of depriving a member of the University of his rights, and a number of other cases which are collected in the *Hammersmith Rent Charge Case*, 4 Exch. 96, in the judgment of Parke B, show that the principle has been very widely applied. The district board must do the thing legally; there must be a resolution; and, if there be a board, and a resolution of that board, I have not heard a word to show that it would not be salutary that they should hear the man who is to suffer from their judgment before they proceed to make the order under which they attempt to justify their act. It is said that an appeal from the district board to the metropolitan board (under s. 211) would be the mode of redress. But, if the district board have the power to do what is here stated, I am not at all clear that there would be a right of redress in that way. The metropolitan board may not have a right to give redress for that which was done under the provisions of the statute. I think the appeal clause would evidently indicate that many exercises of the power of a district board would be in the nature of judicial proceedings; because, certainly when they are appealed from, the appellant and the respondent are to be heard as parties, and the matter is to be decided at least according to judicial forms. I take that to be a principle of very wide application, and applicable to the present case; and I think this board was not justified under the statute, because they have not qualified themselves for the exercise of their power by hearing the party to be affected by their decision.

WILLES J: Then, as to the appeal section, 211, what light does that throw upon the matter? There is an appeal from the district board, not to any judicial tribunal in the sense of any tribunal more judicial in its form than the local board of works, but to the metropolitan board of works, which is just as much and just as little judicial in its acts as the board whose conduct we are now considering. What is to take place upon such appeal? "And all such appeals shall stand referred to the committee appointed by such board for hearing appeals, as herein provided; and such committee shall *hear and determine* all such appeals." Nothing can be more clear than that the legislature thought that the matters which might come before the board upon appeal, that is, the same matters which came before the local board of works in the first instance, were proper, not only to be determined, but also to be heard; and, if fit to be heard upon an appeal, *a fortiori* fit to be heard in the first instance, before a wrongful decision can make an appeal lie.

[Byles and Keating JJ gave concurring judgments. Byles J said in part, "I conceive they acted judicially, because they had to determine the offence, and they had to apportion the punishment as well as the remedy. That being so, a long course of decisions, beginning with Dr. Bentley's case, and ending with some very recent cases, establish that, although there are no positive words in a statute requiring that the party shall be heard, yet the justice of the common law will supply the omission of the legislature."]

Rule discharged.

NOTES

1. When Byles J talks about the ability of the court to "supply the omission of the legislature," there are at least three ways in which that statement might be viewed. First, it could mean that, where there is such a legislative lacuna, the role of the court is to consider what the legislature would have done had it thought about it ("the forgetful legislature" approach to statutory interpretation). Second, it could amount to an assertion that the legislature has in fact spoken indirectly. To the extent that the common law requires hearings in the face of legislative silence whenever an individualised decision is taken affecting existing property rights, the silent legislature is one that knows this common law and is impliedly assenting to or mandating judicial imposition of procedures in such cases. Third, it might not bespeak a theory of statutory interpretation at all but the assertion of a limited *common law* Bill of Rights; an autonomous power of the judges, through their control of the common law, to require a hearing unless the legislature speaks explicitly on the subject. Consider which of these theories captures most appropriately the judicial role in such cases both in relation to England of the mid-19th century and today's Canada. For these purposes, recollect our discussion in the introduction of the constitutional foundations of judicial review as well as John Willis's arguments in his article "Administrative Law in Canada" (1939), 53 *Harvard LR* 251, particularly at 274 where he makes the case for a "common law Bill of Rights." This is also a theme to which we return in our discussion of the Supreme Court of Canada's decision in *Knight*.

2. Obviously, for both Erle CJ and Willes J, the statutory language has some relevance to the applicability of the rules of natural justice. Both direct their attention to the existence of the statutory form of appeal to the metropolitan board. At one level, this consideration of the terms of the appeal provision is with a view to seeing whether Cooper could have secured a remedy there. This reflects a policy of common law judicial review that we will encounter on a number of occasions throughout this casebook and most notably in part IV, Remedies. Considerations of both economy in the use of judicial resources and expertise will frequently dictate at least the prior exhaustion and, on occasion, the exclusivity of statutory remedial regimes. Why was that principle not applied here? Second, the existence of a statutory right of appeal was seen as an indicator of the need for a hearing at first instance. Why was that so? On occasion, the reverse implication is drawn from the existence of an appeal process; it is seen as indicating that the legislature did not intend there to be a hearing at first instance. Can that ever be justified? If so, how should the decision about which is the proper implication be made?

3. *Cooper* is also a comparatively rare example of collateral attack. The remedy being sought is damages, not judicial review and the alleged illegality of the board's actions arises indirectly in an action in tort and is not the direct target of the pleadings. Construct for yourselves the logical progression of those pleadings in order to obtain a clearer sense of what collateral attack on unlawful administrative action means and involves. A somewhat

more frequent example of collateral attack is in the context of a prosecution for breach of prohibitions contained in subordinate legislation. As a defence to that prosecution, the accused puts in contention the validity of the regulation or the bylaw on which the prosecution depends. (See *R v. Sharma*, [1993] 1 SCR 650 (Ont.) and *R v. Greenbaum*, [1993] 1 SCR 674 (Ont.).) The Supreme Court of Canada, however, has condemned the use of collateral attack as a means of challenging administrative orders at the enforcement stage. The targets of administrative orders cannot wait in the weeds but rather, if concerned about the validity of such orders, must attack the decisions on which they are based directly through an application for judicial review: see *R v. Consolidated Maybrun Mines Ltd.*, [1998] 1 SCR 760 (Ont.) and *R v. Al Klippert Ltd.*, [1998] 1 SCR 737 (Alta.). We return to this issue in chapter 18, The Discretion of the Court.

The Modern Common Law Doctrine: Dimensions and Limitations of Procedural Fairness

Following *Cooper*, courts' willingness to impose hearing requirements on decision-makers became contingent on how they categorized the nature of their decision-making power. Decision-makers exercising judicial or quasi-judicial functions were required to comply with natural justice; ministers, public servants, or tribunals exercising so-called administrative functions were not. With the evolution and growth of the modern regulatory state and the multiplication of officials wielding administrative powers which significantly impacted affected parties, the all or nothing dichotomy—which denied any procedural protections to some parties based on an ill-defined distinction between judicial and administrative decisions—became increasingly untenable. In a series of decisions from 1964 to 1970, the English courts decided that they would also review administrative decisions for breach of implied procedural protections. In the first of these decisions, *Ridge v. Baldwin*, [1964] AC 40 (Eng. HL) the House of Lords determined that a watch committee could not dismiss a chief constable without first informing him of the grounds for dismissal and giving him an opportunity to respond. The House of Lords decided that the existence of the duty to comply with natural justice did not turn on finding in the enabling statute a "super-added duty to act judicially." The judicial character of the decision-maker's power could be inferred from the nature of that power and, in particular, could be implied from the mere fact that rights were being affected. The Supreme Court of Canada followed this lead in *Nicholson v. Haldimand-Norfolk (Regional) Police Commissioners*, [1979] 1 SCR 311, a case that dealt with the dismissal of a probationary police constable.

Nicholson v. Haldimand-Norfolk (Regional) Police Commissioners
[1979] 1 SCR 311 (Ont.)

[Regulations made under the *Police Act*, RSO 1970, c. 351 provided:

27. No chief of police, constable or other police officer is subject to any penalty under this Part except after a hearing and final disposition of a charge on appeal as provided by

this Part, or after the time for appeal has expired, but nothing herein affects the authority of a board or council, …

>   (b) to dispense with the services of any constable within eighteen months of his becoming a constable.

Nicholson served as a constable for 15 months and was discharged by the board without being given an opportunity to make submissions. He sought review and succeeded in the Divisional Court. An appeal by the board was allowed, and Nicholson appealed to the Supreme Court.]

LASKIN CJC: For Arnup JA, the consequence of the appellant being short of 18 months' service when he was separated from his position was that (to use his words) "the Board may act as it was entitled to act at common law, *i.e.*, without the necessity of prior notice of allegations or of a hearing, and *a fortiori*, with no right of appeal by the constable." He also relied on the *expressio unius* rule of construction by noting that "the Legislature has expressly required notice and hearing for certain purposes and has by necessary implication excluded them for other purposes." There is no recognition in his reasons, as there was in those of Hughes J, that there may be a common law duty to act fairly falling short of a requirement of a hearing or, indeed, falling short of a duty to act judicially. Counsel for the appellant asserted that there is an emerging line of authority on this distinction which this Court should approve, and that although it may be regarded as an aspect of natural justice it has a procedural content of its own. It does not, however, rise to the level of what is required to satisfy natural justice where judicial or *quasi*-judicial powers are being exercised. I shall come to this line of authority later in these reasons. …

Considerable emphasis was placed by Arnup JA on the position of a constable at common law as an office holder at pleasure who could claim no procedural protection against peremptory removal from office. We are not concerned in this case with any involvement of the Crown, with the holding of an office under the Crown, assuming that this would make any difference today. It was, however, contended in this Court, as in the Courts below, that the words in s. 27, "but nothing herein affects the authority of a board or council," point to a preservation of some pre-existing authority as contrasted with a grant of power; and hence, it was not only proper but necessary to examine the position of a constable at common law. I can see some value in this as background research, but the scheme of the *Police Act* and the involvement of statutory agencies, whether boards of commissioners of police or municipal councils, has created an entirely different frame of reference, and what is preserved of the common law is merely the fact that a constable may still be considered as the holder of an office and not simply an employee of a board or of a municipality which, for many purposes, he certainly is.

In my opinion, nothing turns on pre-existing authority but the fact is, rather, that the *Police Act* and Regulations thereunder form a code for police constables with an array of powers, some of which, as in the case of s. 27(b), are discretionary.

· · ·

The position at which I have arrived to this point is this: a constable is "the holder of a police office" (to use the description of the Privy Council in *AG New South Wales v. Perpetual Trustee Co. (Ld.)* [1955] AC 457 (PC NSW) at 489), exercising, so far as his police duties are concerned, an original authority confirmed by s. 55 of the *Police Act* and by the oath of office prescribed by s. 64 of the Act (wherein reference is made to "the duties of his office," among which are duties specified in the *Criminal Code*). He is a member of a civilian force, and I take his assimilation to a soldier, as stated by the Privy Council in the *Perpetual Trustee Co.* case, *supra*, to be an assimilation related only to whether an action *per quod* lies against a tortfeasor at common law for the loss of his services, and not to assimilation for other purposes, such as liability to peremptory discharge, if that be the case with a soldier.

The effect of the judgment below is that a constable who has served 18 months or more is afforded protection against arbitrary discipline or discharge through the requirement of notice and hearing and appellate review, but there is no protection at all, no halfway house, between the observance of natural justice aforesaid and arbitrary removal in the case of a constable who has held office for less than 18 months. In so far as the Ontario Court of Appeal based its conclusion on the *expressio unius* rule of construction, it has carried the maxim much too far. ...

Again, in so far as the judgment of the Ontario Court of Appeal is based on reading the words "at pleasure" (as importing arbitrary power) into s. 27(b), or the term "probationary" (with similar import), it results in reducing the status of the office of police constable to that involved in a master-servant relationship merely because there has been less than 18 months' service in the office, and I do not regard this as either obvious or a necessary gloss on s. 27(b). The view so taken by the Ontario Court of Appeal, and supported strongly in this Court by counsel for the respondent, relied heavily on the three-fold classification of dismissal situations formulated by Lord Reid in *Ridge v. Baldwin* [1964] AC 40 (Eng. HL). Since the present case is not one where the constable holds office at pleasure, he fits more closely into Lord Reid's third class of dismissal from an office where there must be cause for dismissing him, rather than into his second class of dismissal from an office held at pleasure.

I would observe here that the old common law rule, deriving much of its force from Crown law, that a person engaged as an office holder at pleasure may be put out without reason or prior notice ought itself to be re-examined. It has an anachronistic flavour in the light of collective agreements, which are pervasive in both public and private employment, and which offer broad protection against arbitrary dismissal in the case of employees who cannot claim the status of office holders. As S.A. de Smith pointed out in his book *Judicial Review of Administrative Action* (3rd ed. 1973), at 200, "public policy does not dictate that tenure of an office held at pleasure should be terminable without allowing its occupant any right to make prior representations on his own behalf; indeed, the unreviewability of the substantive grounds for removal indicates that procedural protection may be all the more necessary."

· · ·

In short, I am of the opinion that although the appellant clearly cannot claim the procedural protections afforded to a constable with more than 18 months' service, he cannot be denied any protection. He should be treated "fairly" not arbitrarily. I accept, therefore, for present purposes and as a common law principle what Megarry J accepted in *Bates v. Lord Hailsham of St. Marylebone* [1972] 1 WLR 1373 (Ch.) at 1378, "that in the sphere of the so-called *quasi*-judicial the rules of natural justice run, and that in the administrative or executive field there is a general duty of fairness."

The emergence of a notion of fairness involving something less than the procedural protection of traditional natural justice has been commented on in de Smith, *Judicial Review of Administrative Action, supra*, at 208-209, as follows:

> That the donee of a power must "act fairly" is a long-settled principle governing the exercise of discretion, though its meaning is inevitably imprecise. Since 1967 the concept of a duty to act fairly has often been used by judges to denote an implied procedural obligation. In general it means a duty to observe the rudiments of natural justice for a limited purpose in the exercise of functions that are not analytically judicial but administrative. Given the flexibility of natural justice, it is not strictly necessary to use the term "duty to act fairly" at all. But the term has a marginal value because of (i) the frequent reemergence of the idea that a duty to observe natural justice is not to be imported into the discharge of "administrative" functions and (ii) a tendency to assume that a duty to "act judicially" in accordance with natural justice means a duty to act like a judge in a court of law. It may therefore be less confusing to say that an immigration officer or a company inspector or a magistrate condemning food as unfit for human consumption is obliged to act fairly rather than obliged to act judicially (or to observe natural justice, which means the same thing). However, close analysis of the relevant judgments is apt to generate its own confusion, for sometimes one judge will differentiate a duty to act fairly from a duty to act judicially and another will assimilate them, both judges being in full agreement as to the scope of the procedural duty cast on the competent authority.

What rightly lies behind this emergence is the realization that the classification of statutory functions as judicial, *quasi*-judicial or administrative is often very difficult, to say the least; and to endow some with procedural protection while denying others any at all would work injustice when the results of statutory decisions raise the same serious consequences for those adversely affected, regardless of the classification of the function in question: see, generally, Mullan, "Fairness: The New Natural Justice?" (1975) 25 *UTLJ* 281.

· · ·

The present case is one where the consequences to the appellant are serious indeed in respect to his wish to continue in a public office, and yet the respondent Board has thought it fit and has asserted a legal right to dispense with his services without any indication to him of why he was deemed unsuitable to continue to hold it.

In my opinion, the appellant should have been told why his services were no longer required and given an opportunity, whether orally or in writing as the Board might determine, to respond. The Board itself, I would think, would wish to be certain that it had not made a mistake in some fact or circumstance which it deemed relevant to its determination. Once it had the appellant's response, it would be for the Board to decide on what action to take, without its decision being reviewable elsewhere, always premising good faith. Such a course provides fairness to the appellant, and it is fair as well to the Board's right, as a public authority to decide, once it had the appellant's response, whether a person in his position should be allowed to continue in office to the point where his right to procedural protection was enlarged. Status in office deserves this minimal protection, however brief the period for which the office is held.

It remains to consider whether the appellant should not be heard to complain of want of fairness because he was aware of the reason for his dismissal.

[Laskin CJC concluded that Nicholson had not been told the reason why he was dismissed. The reason is not fully apparent in any of the judgments. In the Divisional Court, Hughes J referred to an "allegation of misconduct" (1975), 61 DLR (3d) 36, at 45. Laskin CJC described an assertion by a supervisor that Nicholson had no future in the department and an incident in which Nicholson had made a phone call to headquarters, about a small administrative matter, that his immediate superior had allegedly forbidden.]

MARTLAND J (dissenting): In the present case the circumstances and the subject-matter under consideration are as follows: the respondent was not called on to make an investigation of the appellant's conduct. Its right to dispense with his services was not limited to specific causes. Its function was not to condemn or criticize him. The decision which the respondent made was that it did not wish to continue the appellant's services as a constable. His status was that of a constable on probation. The very purpose of the probationary period was to enable the respondent to decide whether it wished to continue his services beyond the probationary period. The only interest involved was that of the Board itself. Its decision was purely administrative. This being so, it was under no duty to explain to the appellant why his services were no longer required, or to give him an opportunity to be heard. It could have taken that course as a matter of courtesy, but its failure to do so was not a breach of any legal duty to the appellant.

[Ritchie, Spence, Dickson, and Estey JJ concurred with Laskin CJC; Pigeon, Beetz, and Pratte JJ concurred with Martland J.]

Appeal allowed.

NOTES

1. After the decision of the Supreme Court was given, the board told Nicholson that it would hold a hearing "to reconsider its decision" about his dismissal and, shortly afterward, it made eleven specific allegations of misconduct. Nicholson made an application for review to prevent the hearing and to recover for lost wages. The claim for prohibition was based on two arguments. First, the *Police Act* gave him a right to a full hearing, because more than 18 months had passed since he became a constable. Second, the hearing was barred by the *Public Authorities Protection Act*, RSO 1970, c. 374, s. 11, proscribing proceedings for acts done "in pursuance ... of any statutory or other public duty" that were not begun within six months. Both arguments failed, for the same reason: the hearing on December 1, 1978 would be a continuation of the original proceeding. Linden J said: "The order of the Supreme Court of Canada ... did not quash the entire proceeding of the Board; it merely quashed the decision. ... Nicholson, therefore, is to be treated, for the purposes of the continuing hearing, as a probationary constable, which he was at the time the proceeding was commenced." The claim for wages succeeded: *Re Nicholson and Haldimand-Norfolk Regional Board of Commissioners of Police* (1980), 31 OR (2d) 195 (Div. Ct.); aff'd. 31 OR (2d) 202 (CA).

Is this claim for wages really justified? What other information might you need to have to answer this question? We return to this issue in chapter 19, Money Remedies, when we consider the ability of judicial review to in effect secure financial recompense for a successful applicant. See, in particular, the decision of the Ontario Court of Appeal in an appeal from another judgment of Linden J (as he then was), *Brown v. Waterloo Regional Board of Commissioners of Police* (1983), 150 DLR (3d) 729 (Ont. CA). See also *Gerrard v. Sackville (Town)* (1992), 89 DLR (4th) 145 (NB CA) and the argument that attracted a dissenting judgment in that case—that where judicial review would lead to reinstatement in an inappropriate situation, the plaintiff should be denied public law relief and left to a damages remedy for breach of contract.

2. Nicholson's rehearing was not held until April 1981. The board allowed Nicholson to be represented by counsel, to present evidence, and to cross-examine witnesses. It concluded that he should be dismissed, and he made an application for review on several grounds, including claims that the decision was not based on the incidents of which particulars had been given, and that the conduct of the board during the hearing created a reasonable apprehension of bias. The application was dismissed: (1983), 10 OAC 65 (Div. Ct.).

3. *Nicholson* seemed likely to become a landmark when it was decided and the subsequent jurisprudence did indeed confirm its importance. Its reasoning does, though, leave questions unanswered. Here are six groups of questions that a lawyer or law student might have asked herself after reading it in 1979.

a. What is the threshold? Are all "administrative" functions to have a hearing requirement? If they are not, which functions of government will not have a hearing requirement?

b. What procedures are going to be required? Laskin CJC specified notice and "an opportunity, whether orally or in writing as the board might determine, to respond." Is this designed to be a general requirement for all administrative functions, or is it designed for this particular case? If it is designed for this case, is it appropriate, and what are the possibilities for other kinds of decisions? For example, what about permitting Nicholson to make oral submissions and have counsel? What are the criteria for appropriateness? (These questions are explored in chapter 4 of this text.)

c. What is the effect of *Nicholson* on the significance of the distinction between judicial and administrative functions? It seems no longer to mark the threshold, but does it mark a distinction between natural justice and fairness? If it does, what is the significance of this distinction? Does it mark, for example, a distinction between packages of procedures, and are natural justice and fairness two different sources of procedural requirements? Or is the old learning about judicial and administrative functions simply no longer significant for making the decisions about entitlement to hearing and the choice of procedures?

d. More generally, what is the justification for the fairness development, both for crossing the threshold and for stopping short of a trial-type hearing? (This question is also explored in chapter 4 of this text, but here, try to explain to Nicholson why he is given only limited procedural rights.)

e. Does the "fairness" development involve distinctive difficulties of administration and predictability? Will it be difficult for courts to determine whether a procedure is appropriate? Will the requirements in a particular situation depend on *ad hoc* reactions of courts that cannot be explained and justified and therefore will be difficult for administrators and lawyers to predict? How are administrators likely to react to this kind of difficulty? If it is real, to what extent is it a product of the ideals that shaped the distinction between judicial and administrative functions?

f. This "fairness" development seemed likely to impose procedural requirements on institutions that have not had these kinds of requirements imposed on them before. These institutions do not resemble courts and their procedures do not resemble trials. Are courts competent to make these decisions about procedure, especially compared to the legislature or the institutions themselves? Should this have an impact on the courts' willingness to second-guess procedural choices made by tribunals themselves, particularly in the context of a rulemaking exercise? (Recollect *Baker*'s position on judicial respect for explicit agency procedural discretion. See more generally Loughlin, "Procedural Fairness: A Study of the Crisis in Administrative Law Theory" (1978), 28 *UTLJ* 215.)

Elaborations of the Modern Doctrine

Canadian procedural fairness case law following *Nicholson* was marked by the gradual expansion of the duty of fairness to areas of administrative decision making, including the decisions of correctional authorities affecting the rights, privileges, and interests of inmates (see *Cardinal v. Director of Kent Institution*, [1985] 2 SCR 643 (BC)), that had previously escaped judicial scrutiny for compliance with the rules of natural justice. In the following seminal case, *Knight v. Indian Head School Division No. 19*, [1990] 1 SCR 653, a majority of the Supreme Court recognized that in dismissing its director, who held this office at pleasure, a school board was bound by the duty of fairness. On the one hand, by extending fairness beyond the domain of office-holders dismissible only for cause, the judgment marked a further rejection of the rigid categories that had characterized the pre-*Nicholson* and pre-*Ridge v. Baldwin* fairness case law. On the other hand, it also set down the dividing lines of a new threshold for the duty of fairness based on the distinction between decisions of a legislative and general nature and acts of an administrative and specific nature, and, as such, will be the starting point for our discussion of the common law threshold later in this chapter. Moreover, the four-judge majority in *Knight*, over the objections of three concurring colleagues, embraced the conception of procedural fairness as a free-standing common law right, thus eschewing the need to find in the decision-maker's enabling statute any provision that expressly or impliedly conferred on the office-holder a right to be heard.

Knight v. Indian Head School Division No. 19
[1990] 1 SCR 653 (Sask.)

[The appellant board of education dismissed the respondent director of education when he refused to accept a renewal of his contract for a shorter term than the original. The respondent brought an action against the appellant alleging wrongful dismissal. The Supreme Court of Canada held that the board did not need to show cause for the dismissal either under the contract of employment or under *The Education Act*. The respondent then argued that he was entitled to procedural fairness before being dismissed and that he had not been fairly treated. The court had to decide whether procedural fairness was due an office-holder at pleasure. Dickson CJ and La Forest, L'Heureux-Dubé, and Cory JJ held that procedural fairness was due but that the requirements of procedural fairness had been satisfied. Wilson, Sopinka, and McLachlin JJ held that the appellant owed no duty of fairness to the respondent. The board of education's appeal was, therefore, allowed 7:0.]

L'HEUREUX-DUBÉ J: ...

2. Procedural Fairness

The conclusion that the respondent's employment could be legally terminated without a showing of just cause does not necessarily entail that the procedure involved can be arbitrary. There may be a general right to procedural fairness, autonomous of the operation of any statute, depending on consideration of three factors which have been held by this Court to be determinative of the existence of such a right (*Cardinal v. Director of Kent Institution, supra*). If consideration of these factors in the context of the present appeal leads to the conclusion that the respondent was entitled to procedural fairness, *The Education Act* and, in this case, the terms of the contract of employment, must then be considered to determine whether this entitlement is either limited or excluded entirely. It should be noted at this point that the duty to act fairly does not depend on doctrines of employment law, but stems from the fact that the employer is a public body whose powers are derived from statute, powers that must be exercised according to the rules of administrative law. It is in that context that the employee-employer relationship between the respondent and the appellant Board must be examined, with the result that the analysis must go beyond the contract of employment to encompass arguments of public policy. ...

A. General Duty of Fairness

The existence of a general duty to act fairly will depend on the consideration of three factors: (i) the nature of the decision to be made by the administrative body; (ii) the relationship existing between that body and the individual; and (iii) the effect of that decision on the individual's rights. This Court has stated in *Cardinal v. Director of Kent Institution, supra*, that whenever those three elements are to be found, there is a general duty to act fairly on a public decision-making body (Le Dain J for the Court at 653).

(i) The Nature of the Decision

There is no longer a need, except perhaps where the statute mandates it, to distinguish between judicial, *quasi*-judicial and administrative decisions. Such a distinction may have been necessary before the decision of this Court in *Nicholson v. Haldimand-Norfolk Regional Board of Commissioners of Police* [1979] 1 SCR 311 (Ont.). Prior to this case, the "duty to act judicially" was thought to apply only to tribunals rendering decisions of a judicial or *quasi*-judicial nature, to the exclusion of those of an administrative nature. Following *Nicholson*, that distinction became less important and was found to be of little utility since both the duty to act fairly and the duty to act judicially have their roots in the same general principles of natural justice (see *Syndicat des employés de production du Quebec et de l'Acadie v. Canada (Canadian Human Rights Commission)* [1989] 2 SCR 879 (Can.) at 895-96, *per* Sopinka J for the majority).

On the other hand, not all administrative bodies are under a duty to act fairly. Over the years, legislatures have transferred to administrative bodies some of the duties they have traditionally performed. Decisions of a legislative and general nature can be distinguished in this respect from acts of a more administrative and specific nature, which do not entail such a duty (see Dussault and Borgeat, *Traité de droit administratif*, t. III, 2nd ed., 1986, at 370; *Attorney General of Canada v. Inuit Tapirisat of Canada* [1980] 2 SCR 735 (Can.) at 758, *per* Estey J for the Court). The finality of the decision will also be a factor to consider. A decision of a preliminary nature will not in general trigger the duty to act fairly, whereas a decision of a more final nature may have such an effect (Dussault and Borgeat, *op. cit.*, at 372).

In the case at bar, the decision made by the appellant Board was of a final and specific nature, directed as it was at terminating the employment of the respondent. As such, the decision to dismiss could possibly entail the existence of a duty to act fairly on the part of the appellant Board.

(ii) The Relationship Between the Employer and the Employee

The second element to be considered is the nature of the relationship between the Board and the respondent. In an oft-cited decision of the House of Lords, *Ridge v. Baldwin* [1964] AC 40 (Eng. HL), Lord Reid classified the possible employment relationship between an employer and an employee into three categories: (i) the master and servant relationship, where there is no duty to act fairly when deciding to terminate the employment; (ii) the office held at pleasure, where no duty to act fairly exists, since the employer can decide to terminate the employment for no other reason than his displeasure; and (iii) the office from which one cannot be removed except for cause, where there exists a duty to act fairly on the part of the employer. These categories are creations of the common law. They can of course be altered by the terms of an employment contract or the governing legislation, with the result that the employment relationship may fall within more than one category (see *Nova Scotia Government Employees Association v. Civil Service Commission of Nova Scotia* [1981] 1 SCR 211 (NS) at 222, *per* Laskin CJ for the majority). Lord Reid did not examine the possible implications of the non-renewal of a fixed-term employment contract, but since it was not alleged in the present appeal that the employment was terminated by non-renewal of the employee's contract, I will not address this question.

In the case at bar, the office held by the respondent was not of a "pure" master and servant type since it encompassed some elements of a public nature. The office of director of education is established by s. 106 of *The Education Act*, which requires the Board to appoint a director. His duties are at least partly set out in ss. 107 and 108 of *The Education Act*.

. . .

In a recent decision of the Saskatchewan Court of Appeal, *Barrett v. Nor. Lights Sch. Div. 113 Bd. of Educ.* [[1988] 3 WWR 500 (Sask. CA)] at 520 (*per* Sherstobitoff JA for the majority), that court found that the office of secretary treasurer under the same *Education Act* was of a statutory nature and not that of master and servant, eliminating the first of Lord Reid's category. There may be a clear contractual element to the respondent's employment, which may give the impression that his function is not "purely" statutory: I find, however, that this is not a case of a "pure master and servant" relationship but that it has on the contrary a strong "statutory flavour," so as to be categorized as an office (Wade, *Administrative Law* (5th ed. 1982) at 498-99; *Malloch v. Aberdeen Corp.* [1971] 2 All ER 1278 (HL Sc.) at 1294, *per* Lord Wilberforce).

Being an office, the respondent's situation would fall into one of the last two of Lord Reid's categories. As I have already analyzed the employment contract and *The Education Act* with regard to the question of whether the respondent could be dismissed only for cause, and concluded in the negative, the employment relation existing between the respondent and the appellant Board would fall into the second of Lord Reid's categories, *i.e.*, an office held at pleasure. I find, however, that this conclusion does not ineluctably lead to the conclusion that the appellant Board was not under a duty to act fairly, as may seem to flow from the judgment of the House of Lords in *Ridge v. Baldwin, supra.* Administrative law has evolved in recent years, particularly in the Canadian context, so as to make procedural fairness an essential requirement of an administrative decision to terminate either of the last two classes of employment described by Lord Reid. In *Nicholson, supra*, although the employee was found to be dismissable for cause, Laskin CJ, after referring to the three-class system developed by Lord Reid in *Ridge v. Baldwin, supra*, expressed some doubts about limiting the duty to act fairly to cases of dismissal for cause, to the exclusion of cases where offices are held at pleasure. He writes for the majority at 322-23:

> *I would observe here that the old common law rule, deriving much of its force from Crown law, that a person engaged as an office holder at pleasure may be put out without reason or prior notice ought itself to be re-examined.* It has an anachronistic flavour in the light of collective agreements, which are pervasive in both public and private employment, and which offer broad protection against arbitrary dismissal in the case of employees who cannot claim the status of office holders. As de Smith has pointed out in his book *Judicial Review of Administrative Action* (3rd ed. 1973), at 200, "public policy does not dictate that tenure of an office held at pleasure should be terminable without allowing its occupant any right to make prior representations on his own behalf; indeed, *the unreviewability of the substantive grounds for removal indicates that procedural protection may be all the more necessary."* [Emphasis added.]

The Chief Justice goes on to quote from a decision of the House of Lords, *Malloch v. Aberdeen Corp., supra*, in which the absence of a right to procedural fairness for those holding office at pleasure was somewhat mitigated, the court concluding that in certain circumstances procedural fairness may be necessarily implied. In that case, teachers were dismissed for refusing to register as required under a new regulation, whose validity they disputed, without being afforded either a hearing or reasons; Lord Wilberforce wrote at 1294:

> One may accept that if there are relationships in which all requirements of the observance of rules of natural justice are excluded (and I do not wish to assume that this is inevitably so), these must be confined to what have been called "pure master and servant cases," which I take to mean cases in which there is no element of public employment or service, no support by statute, nothing in the nature of an office or a status which is capable of protection. *If any of these elements exist, then, in my opinion, whatever the terminology used, and even though in some inter partes aspects the relationship may be called that of master and servant, there may be essential procedural requirements to be observed, and failure to observe them may result in a dismissal being declared to be void.* [Emphasis added.]

There is thus in England no longer an automatic exclusion of the rule of procedural fairness for employment falling into Lord Reid's second class.

The justification for granting to the holder of an office at pleasure the right to procedural fairness is that, whether or not just cause is necessary to terminate the employment, fairness dictates that the administrative body making the decision be cognizant of all relevant circumstances surrounding the employment and its termination (*Nicholson, supra*, at 328, *per* Laskin CJ). One person capable of providing the administrative body with important insights into the situation is the office holder himself. As pointed out by Lord Reid in *Malloch v. Aberdeen Corp., supra*, at 1282: "The right of a man to be heard in his own defense is the most elementary protection of all. ..." To grant such a right to the holder of an office at pleasure would not import into the termination decision the necessity to show just cause, but would only require the administrative body to give the officer holder reasons for the dismissal and an opportunity to be heard. I would adopt Wade's reasoning when he writes about offices held at pleasure (*Administrative Law* (5th ed. 1982) at 500-501):

> If the officer is subject to some accusation, justice requires that he should be allowed a fair opportunity to defend himself, whatever the terms of his tenure. *To deny it to him is to confuse the substance of the decision, which may be based on any reason at all, with the procedure which ought first to be followed for purposes of fairness.* It is then an example of the fallacy, already mentioned, that the argument for natural justice is weaker where the discretionary power is wide.
>
> [I]t would seem right therefore to protect the officer or member against wrongful deprivation of every kind and to accord him the procedural rights without which deprivation is not fair and lawful. *Whether he is removable for cause or at pleasure should in principle make no difference.* [Emphasis added.]

(See also Molot, "Employment During Good Behaviour or at Pleasure" (1989) 2 *CJALP* 238 at 250.) The argument to the effect that, since the employer can dismiss his employee for unreasonable or capricious reasons, the giving of an opportunity to participate in the decision making would be meaningless, is unconvincing. In both the situation of an office held at pleasure and an office from which one can be dismissed only for cause, one of the purposes of the imposition on the administrative body of a duty to act fairly is the same, *i.e.*, enabling the employee to try to change the employer's mind about the dismissal. The value of such an opportunity should not be dependant on the grounds triggering the dismissal.

There is also a wider public policy argument militating in favour of the imposition of a duty to act fairly on administrative bodies making decisions similar to the one impugned in the case at bar. The powers exercised by the appellant Board are delegated statutory powers which, as much as the statutory powers exercised directly by the government, should be put only to legitimate use. As opposed to the employment cases dealing with "pure master and servant" relationships, where no delegated statutory powers are involved, the public has an interest in the proper use of delegated power by administrative bodies. In the House of Lords decision of *Malloch v. Aberdeen Corp.*, *supra*, Lord Wilberforce noted this additional rationale underlying the imposition of procedural fairness (at 1293):

> The respondents are a public authority, the appellant holds a public position fortified by statute. The considerations which determine whether he has been validly removed from that position go beyond the mere contract of employment, though no doubt including it. They are, in my opinion, to be tested broadly on arguments of public policy and not to be resolved on narrow verbal distinctions.

From this perspective, the fact that an office holder could be dismissed for cause or at pleasure would not warrant a distinction with regard to the existence of a duty to act fairly, since in both cases statutory powers are exercised. As pointed out by Wade in the above-quoted passage (at 500), dismissal for displeasure should be all the more the object of scrutiny as it is a power of a wider discretionary nature.

In reaching the conclusion that both of Lord Reid's last two classes require an administrative body to act fairly, the necessity of characterizing the employment so that it fits into one or the other of those classes is rendered unnecessary. Not only does this eliminate an "anachronistic" distinction—to use the words of Laskin CJ in *Nicholson, supra*—between offices held at pleasure and offices from which one can only be dismissed with cause, but it also does away with what is in many cases a troublesome task since employment relationships are rarely easily categorized into one or the other class, being usually—as in the case at bar—of a mixed nature brought about by the terms of the employment contract or the governing legislation. In my opinion, such a simplification of these principles of administrative law is not only desirable but necessary. Of course, this does not mean that the distinction between offices from which one can be dismissed at pleasure and those from which one must be dismissed for cause becomes obsolete in all respects. In the case of an office held at pleasure, even after the giving of reasons and the granting of a hearing, the employer's mere displeasure is still justification enough to validly terminate the employment.

I conclude accordingly that the characterization of the respondent's employment as an office held at pleasure is not incompatible with the imposition of a duty to act fairly on the part of the appellant Board.

(iii) The Impact of the Decision on the Employee

This point can be dealt with summarily. There is a right to procedural fairness only if the decision is a significant one and has an important impact on the individual. Various courts have recognized that the loss of employment against the office holder's will is a significant decision that could justify imposing a duty to act fairly on the administrative decision-making body. For example, this Court in *Nicholson, supra,* found that "Status in office deserves this minimal protection, however brief the period for which the office is held" (at 328, *per* Laskin CJ). Also, in *Kane v. Board of Governors of the University of British Columbia* [1980] 1 SCR 1105 (BC), this Court noted that "A high standard of justice is required when the right to continue in one's profession or employment is at stake" (at 1113, *per* Dickson J, as he then was, for the majority). In view of this clear recognition of the importance of the right to retain one's employment, and absent any factual basis allowing us to distinguish these cases from the situation in the case at bar, there is no need to labour the point further. I conclude that the impact of the decision made by the appellant Board is compatible with the imposition of a duty to act fairly.

On the whole, the nature of the decision, the relationship existing between the respondent and the appellant Board and the impact on the respondent of the impugned decision lead to the conclusion that there was a general duty to act fairly on the part of the appellant Board in the circumstances of this case.

B. Under The Education Act

Having come to the conclusion that there exists a general right to procedural fairness, the statutory framework must be examined in order to see if it modifies this right (*Wiseman v. Borneman* [1969] 3 All ER 275 (Eng. HL) at 277, *per* Lord Reid). However, as was pointed out by Dickson J in *Kane v. Board of Governors of the University of British Columbia, supra,* at 1113: "To abrogate the rules of natural justice, express language or necessary implication must be found in the statutory instrument." Thus, the provisions of *The Education Act* must be quite clear to lead us to the conclusion that the respondent's general right to procedural fairness has been restricted.

. . .

I have thus come to the conclusion that *The Education Act* does not explicitly or implicitly excuse the appellant Board from acting fairly when terminating the employment contract of one of its administrative personnel such as the respondent. But this is not determinative of the appellant Board's obligations or the respondent's entitlement in regards to procedural fairness. Section 112 of *The Education Act* and s. 21(4) of *The Education Regulations*, enacted pursuant to that statute (Sask. Reg. 1/79), demand by necessary implication that reference be made to the contract of employment in order to determine whether the rules of natural justice have been abrogated.

[These provided as follows:

> 112. Unless otherwise provided under the contract of employment between the board and the … director, either party to that contract of employment may terminate the contract by giving, to the other party to the contract, not less than thirty days' notice in writing of his intention to terminate the contract.

21(4) A director of education shall be engaged under a written contract which shall specify:

· · ·

(d) such terms and conditions of employment, including the procedure for termination of the contract by either party, as may be mutually agreed upon.]

· · ·

We are thus led to review the employment contract in order to see if it in fact dealt fully with the termination procedure.

C. Under the Employment Contract

In interpreting the contract of employment, it will be presumed, as was the case with the statute, that the parties intended that procedural fairness would apply and it will take an explicit or clearly implicit provision to the contrary to override this presumption (*Kane v. Board of Governors of the University of British Columbia, supra*, at 1113, *per* Dickson J).

· · ·

The general duty to act fairly for an administrative decision-making body making a decision that has a significant impact on an individual would thus apply, unaltered here by either *The Education Act* or the employment contract.

3. *The Content of the Duty To Act Fairly*

Like the principles of natural justice, the concept of procedural fairness is eminently variable and its content is to be decided in the specific context of each case. In *Nicholson, supra*, at 326-27, Laskin CJ adopts the following passage from the decision of the Privy Council in *Furnell v. Whangarei High Schools Board* [1973] AC 660 (PC NZ), a New Zealand appeal where Lord Morris of Borth-y-Gest, writing for the majority, held at 679:

> *Natural justice is but fairness writ large and juridically. It has been described as "fair play in action."* Nor is it a leaven to be associated only with judicial or quasi-judicial occasions. But as was pointed out by Tucker LJ in *Russell v. Duke of Norfolk* [1949] 1 All ER 109 (CA) at 118, the requirements of natural justice must depend on the circumstances of each particular case and the subject matter under consideration. [Emphasis added.]

This was underlined again very recently by this Court in *Syndicat des employés de production du Quebec et de l'Acadie v. Canada (Canadian Human Rights Commission), supra*, where Sopinka J wrote for the majority at 895-96:

> *Both the rules of natural justice and the duty of fairness are variable standards. Their content will depend on the circumstances of the case, the statutory provision and the nature of the matter to be decided.* The distinction between them therefore becomes blurred as one approaches the lower end of the scale of judicial or quasi-judicial tribunals and the high end of the scale with respect to administrative or executive tribunals. Accordingly, the content of the rules to be followed by a tribunal is now not determined by attempting to classify them as judicial, quasi-judicial, administrative or executive. Instead, the court decides the content of these rules by reference to all the circumstances under which the tribunal operates. [Emphasis added.]

The approach to be adopted by a court in deciding if the duty to act fairly was complied with is thus close to empiric. Pépin and Ouellette, *Principes de contentieux administratif*, at 249, quote the following colourful comment of an English judge to the effect that "from time to time … lawyers and judges have tried to define what constitutes fairness. Like defining an elephant, it is not easy to do, although fairness in practice has the elephantine quality of being easy to recognize" (*Maxwell v. Department of Trade and Industry* [1974] QB 523 (CA) at 539). Of course with this flexibility comes the inherent difficulty of differing notions of fairness amongst those called upon to determine if the duty to act fairly was complied with. Therefore it is necessary to temper assertions that the concept of fairness is a purely subjective one. Like the principles of fundamental justice in s. 7 of the *Canadian Charter of Rights and Freedoms*, the concept of fairness is entrenched in the principles governing our legal system (*R v. Beare* [1988] 2 SCR 387 (Sask.) at 402-3, *per* La Forest J for the Court), and the closeness of the administrative process to the judicial process should indicate how much of those governing principles should be imported into the realm of administrative decision making.

In the case at bar the Saskatchewan Court of Appeal found that the basic requirements of the duty to act fairly are the giving of reasons for the dismissal and a hearing, adding that the content will vary according to the circumstances of each case. Since the respondent could be dismissed at pleasure, the content of the duty of fairness would be minimal and I would tend to agree that notice of the reasons for the appellant Board's dissatisfaction with the respondent's employment and affording him an opportunity to be heard would be sufficient to meet the requirement of fairness. This Court in *Nicholson, supra*, at 328, *per* Laskin CJ for the majority, found similar requirements to be sufficient in a case where the employee was dismissable from office only for cause.

4. Compliance with the Duty To Act Fairly

The trial judge and the Court of Appeal disagreed on whether the respondent was provided with reasons for his dismissal and the opportunity to be heard. In the Court of Queen's Bench, Lawton J found that through the negotiation sessions between the respondent's attorney and the appellant Board, the respondent was made fully aware of the grievances of the Board and had ample opportunity to present his side of the story. Lawton J writes at 283:

> The failure to agree on a one-year contract, which from the beginning was the major reason for the negotiations, finished them. But there had been negotiations up until that time—the lines of communication had been open and *Knight, through his solicitor, had been actively involved in presenting his case to the Board. He was being heard. By August, everything that had to be said had been said by both parties.* [Emphasis added.]

He therefore concluded that the procedure followed by the appellant Board was fair. The Saskatchewan Court of Appeal found that the respondent got neither reasons for his dismissal nor a hearing. It disagreed with the trial judge's finding that the negotiations leading to a new employment contract could be construed as equalling the giving of reasons and an opportunity to be heard. Sherstobitoff JA found for the court, at 313, that:

The trial judge seemed to proceed on the assumption that the appellant knew, or should have known, that if he did not agree to a new one-year contract that he would be fired and we must accept that finding of fact. However, *the fact remained that he was never told that he would be fired unless he accepted a one-year contract until he was actually fired. The trial judge was wrong in accepting the implied threat of termination on the part of the employer as a notice of intention to terminate and the failed negotiations as reasons for dismissal as required by the rules of procedural fairness.* It is difficult to think of anything more unfair to an employee than to tell him that he must accept a threat which he should have inferred from the employer's conduct as formal notice of intention to terminate, and must treat a purported renegotiation of an employment contract as a hearing into whether or not he should be terminated. [Emphasis added.]

The disagreement between the two courts below lies therefore not so much in the content of the communication but rather in the significance to be attached to the negotiations between the parties.

It must not be forgotten that every administrative body is the master of its own procedure and need not assume the trappings of a court. The object is not to import into administrative proceedings the rigidity of all the requirements of natural justice that must be observed by a court, but rather to allow administrative bodies to work out a system that is flexible, adapted to their needs and fair. As pointed out by de Smith (*de Smith's Judicial Review of Administrative Action* (4th ed. 1980), at 240), the aim is not to create "procedural perfection" but to achieve a certain balance between the need for fairness, efficiency and predictability of outcome. Hence, in the case at bar, if it can be found that the respondent indeed had knowledge of the reasons for his dismissal and had an opportunity to be heard by the Board, the requirements of procedural fairness will be satisfied even if there was no structured "hearing" in the judicial meaning of the word. I would agree with Wade when he writes (*Administrative Law, supra*, at 482-83):

> A "hearing" will normally be an oral hearing. But it has been held that a statutory board, acting in an administrative capacity, may decide for itself whether to deal with applications by oral hearing or merely on written evidence and argument, *provided that it does in substance "hear" them*; ... [Emphasis added; footnotes omitted.]

· · ·

In the present case, the trial judge found as a fact that the respondent knew or should have known why the appellant Board was unhappy with his employment contract and that if he did not accept a one-year contract he would be dismissed. In my view, the record amply supports this finding, which was not disputed by the Court of Appeal. I recognize the Court of Appeal's concern that the respondent was never officially notified of the reasons for his dismissal, but it is clear that he was informed of those reasons through his meetings with the appellant Board, sometimes personally, sometimes through his solicitor. In conformity with s. 2 of the contract of employment, the respondent was present at the appellant Board's meeting on May 30, 1983, where his contract was not renewed, and had the opportunity to make representations if he so wished. Further, during the summer, the respondent's attorney met twice with the appellant Board to negotiate a new contract, and all issues appeared to have been settled except as to the duration of the contract, the respondent pressing for a minimum two-year term while the Board insisted on a one-year contract. Both parties appear to have been adamant on this point and it can be presumed that it caused the negotiations to fall through. Since I accept the trial judge's finding of facts that "everything that had to be said had been said" (at 283), the requirement of the formal giving of reasons and the holding of a hearing would achieve no more, in my respectful view, than to impose upon the appellant Board a purely procedural requirement, against the above-stated principles of flexibility of administrative procedure.

In my view, the appellant Board has made itself sufficiently available for discussion through meetings with the respondent and his lawyer so that each party's concerns were made fully known to the other. This can only lead to the conclusion that the respondent knew the reasons for his dismissal and was provided with every opportunity to be heard. The requirements of the duty to act fairly in the scope of the employer–employee relationship in the case at bar have been met. I therefore conclude that the respondent was properly dismissed and that his action must fail.

Disposition

Accordingly I would allow the appeal, set aside the judgment of the Court of Appeal and restore the judgment of Lawton J in the Court of Queen's Bench, the whole with costs throughout.

The reasons of Wilson, Sopinka, and McLachlin JJ were delivered by

SOPINKA J: I have had the advantage of reading the reasons of my colleague, Justice L'Heureux-Dubé J. While I agree with her disposition of this matter, I cannot agree that in the circumstances of this case the appellant owed a duty of fairness to the respondent.

· · ·

For the reasons stated by L'Heureux-Dubé J, the appellant was entitled to dismiss the respondent without cause. Furthermore, I agree with her that the respondent's employment relationship falls into the second [*Ridge v. Baldwin*] category.

As a general rule, this category does not attract the duty of procedural fairness because the employer can terminate the employment without cause and without giving any reason. It would therefore be inconsistent with the above to require the employer to give a reason for terminating the employee's employment in order to comply with the dictates of procedural fairness. If a duty of fairness arises, it would be of a limited nature. The employer would be required to allow the employee to state his or her case. Furthermore, the employer would be bound to consider any representations made by the employee.

I am not prepared, however, to completely shut the door on the existence of a duty of fairness in relation to the termination of an office held at pleasure. An exception may be made in special cases where a sound basis for an exception is put forward. In order to bring himself or herself within the exception to the general rule, an employee in the position of the respondent must be able to identify in the statute, regulations or contractual provisions governing the relationship, provisions which expressly or by necessary implication confer upon the employee a right to be heard or to make representations.

In this regard, I accept as a correct statement of the law the following passage from the judgment of Lord Wilberforce in *Malloch v. Aberdeen Corp.* [1971] 2 All ER 1278 (HL Sc.) at 1295, which was quoted with approval by Chief Justice Laskin in *Nicholson v.*

Haldimand-Norfolk Regional Board of Commissioners of Police [1979] 1 SCR 311 (Ont.) at 323-24:

> … As a general principle, I respectfully agree; and I think it important not to weaken a principle which, for reasons of public policy, applies, at least as a starting point, to so wide a range of the public service. The difficulty arises when, as here, there are other incidents of the employment laid down by statute, or regulations, or code of employment or agreement. The rigour of the principle is often, in modern practice, mitigated for it has come to be perceived that the very possibility of dismissal without reason being given—action which may vitally affect a man's career or his pension—makes it all the more important for him, in suitable circumstances, to be able to state his case and, if denied the right to do so, to be able to have his dismissal declared void. So, while the courts will necessarily respect the right, for good reasons of public policy, to dismiss without assigned reasons, this should not, in my opinion, prevent them from examining the framework and context of the employment to see whether elementary rights are conferred on him expressly or by necessary implication, and how far these extend. The present case is, in my opinion, just such a case where there are strong indications that a right to be heard, in appropriate circumstances, should not be denied.

The strong indications in *Malloch, supra*, which led the House of Lords to find a duty of fairness were statutory requirements that enabled the employer to dismiss a teacher only after "due deliberation" at a meeting of which the teacher was required to receive notice.

In *Nicholson, supra*, the other case relied on by L'Heureux-Dubé J in finding a duty of fairness, Laskin CJ did not find it necessary to apply the above statement of Lord Wilberforce, cited by him. It was not applicable because the appellant, a probationary constable, was found not to be dismissable at pleasure. At 324, Laskin CJ stated:

> This case does not, however, fall to be determined on the ground that the appellant was dismissable at pleasure. The dropping of the phrase "at pleasure" from the statutory provision for engagement of constables, and its replacement by a regime under which regulations fix the temporal point at which full procedural protection is given to a constable, indicates to me a turning away from the old common law rule even in cases where the full period of time has not fully run. The status enjoyed by the office holder must now be taken to have more substance than to be dependent upon the whim of the Board up to the point where it has been enjoyed for eighteen months.

In her reasons, my colleague concludes, at 677, that a common law duty of fairness arises from "the nature of the decision, the relationship existing between the respondent and the appellant Board and the impact on the respondent of the impugned decision." This precedes her detailed examination of the statute, the regulations and the contract with a view to identifying therein the indicia of a duty of fairness. An examination in detail of the statute, regulations and contract is made after a common law duty is "presumed to exist" and then only to determine whether such a duty has been ruled out.

In my respectful opinion, that approach converts the exception into the rule. The correct approach requires an examination of the statute, regulations and contract to determine whether the respondent has brought himself within the exception to the general rule that an office terminable at pleasure does not attract the duty of fairness. To do so, provisions of the governing instruments must be identified which specifically or by implication point to a duty of fairness. These governing instruments are the framework and context of the employment to which Lord Wilberforce refers and which must constitute the source of the indicia of a duty of fairness.

[Sopinka J concluded that there was nothing in the contract or in *The Education Act* that would impose a requirement of fairness.]

Appeal allowed.

NOTES

1. In terms of theory, the contrasting judgments of L'Heureux-Dubé J (for the majority) and Sopinka J indicate rather different conceptions of the starting point for analysis of procedural claims. In particular, in speaking of "a general right to procedural fairness, autonomous of the operation of any statute," L'Heureux-Dubé J appears to be lending support for the implied Bill of Rights version of the basis for engrafting procedural fairness obligations onto silent statutes that we identified in the discussion of *Cooper*. What is Sopinka J's posture on this and who has the better of this debate? (See Mullan, "The Emergence of a Free Standing Right to Procedural Fairness" (1990), 43 *Admin. LR* 230.)

In this regard, contrast L'Heureux-Dubé J's approach with that of Brennan J of the High Court of Australia in *Kioa v. West* (1985), 159 CLR 551 (Aust.):

At base, the jurisdiction of a court judicially to review a decision made in the exercise of a statutory power on the ground that the decision maker has not observed the principles of natural justice depends upon the legislature's intention that observance of the principles of natural justice is a condition of the valid exercise of the power. That is clear enough when the condition is expressed; it is seen more dimly when the condition is implied, for then the condition is attributed by judicial construction of the statute. In either case, the statute determines whether the exercise of the power is conditioned on the observance of the principles of natural justice. The statute is construed, as all statutes are construed, against a background of common law notions of justice and fairness and, when the statute does not expressly require that the principles of natural justice be observed, the court construes the statute on the footing that "the justice of the common law will supply the omission of the legislature": *Cooper v. Wandsworth Board of Works*. The true intention of the legislature is thus ascertained. When the legislature creates certain powers, the courts presume that the legislature intends the principles of natural justice to be observed in their exercise in the absence of a clear contrary intention:

· · ·

Observance of the principles of natural justice is a condition attached to the power whose exercise it governs. There is no freestanding common law right to be accorded natural justice by the repository of a statutory power. There is no right to be accorded natural justice which exists independently of statute and which, in the event of a contravention, can be invoked to invalidate executive action taken in due exercise of a statutory power. There is no "right" except in the sense that a person may be entitled to apply to have a decision or action taken in purported exercise of the power set aside if the principles of natural justice have not been observed or to compel the repository of a power to observe procedures which statute obliges him to follow.

· · ·

The supremacy of Parliament, a doctrine deeply imbedded in our constitutional law and congruent with our democratic traditions, requires the courts to declare the validity or invalidity of executive action taken in purported exercise of a statutory power in accordance with criteria expressed or implied by statute. There is no jurisdiction to declare a purported exercise of statutory power invalid for failure to comply with procedural requirements other than those expressly or impliedly prescribed by statute.

2. The majority judgment clearly goes beyond *Nicholson* in its holding that procedural fairness entitlements may arise even in the case of dismissal from statutory offices held at pleasure. Is this justified? (Consider the answer to this question both in general terms and also in the precise context of this case.) What, of course, the judgment does not do is impose a duty of fairness in all cases of dismissal from employment that has a statutory basis. The applicant for relief must still establish that he or she is the holder of a position with a "sufficient statutory flavour," one that is not simply a "pure master and servant relationship." (In this regard, note also *Masters v. Ontario* (1994), 18 OR (3d) 551 (Div. Ct.), noted below, and applying the principles of *Knight* in the case of employment under the royal prerogative.) What criteria does L'Heureux-Dubé J propose for making such distinctions? Are they workable? To what extent is it relevant in considering the procedural claims of "mere statutory employees" that federally and in Nova Scotia and Québec even non-unionized workers now have a grievance process available to them after a specified number of years of service for allegedly "unfair" dismissal? For contrasting approaches to this question by first instance courts, compare the pre-*Knight* judgment of *Semchuk v. Board of Education of Regina School Division No. 4 of Saskatchewan* (1986), 26 Admin. LR 88 (Sask. QB); aff'd. (1987), 37 DLR (4th) 738 (Sask. CA) (dismissal of a graphic artist employed by a school board acting under statutory authority) with the post-*Knight* judgment of *Hill v. University College of Cape Breton* (1991), 81 DLR (4th) 302 (NS SCTD) (dismissal of president of university).

In this context, there is another very important question that arises. In such cases, is it always sufficient to establish that the employment in question had a sufficient statutory flavour? Or, are there situations where dismissal from positions with a sufficient statutory flavour will not attract procedural fairness obligations because the basis for the dismissal is legislative or general as opposed to specific to the individual affected. In thinking about this question, reflect upon what is sometimes described as the subtext of *Nicholson*: the board could not afford more permanent constables and, as a result, no one ever got beyond the probationary stage. If that had been the reason for Nicholson not becoming a fully fledged constable, would there have been a duty of procedural fairness? For these purposes, compare *Lund v. Estevan (City) Police Commissioners* (1993), 18 Admin. LR (2d) 245 (Sask. QB); var'd. (1996), 41 Admin. LR 245 (Sask. CA) (deputy chief of police held entitled to procedural fairness before dismissal even though position being eliminated for budgetary reasons) and *Bulley v. Cape Breton (Regional Municipality)* (2001), 196 NSR (2d) 1 (SC) (to the same effect), with *Vaydik v. Northwest Territories (Minister of Personnel)* (1991), 48 Admin. LR 95 (NWT SC) (layoff of civil servant because of closure of office did not attract procedural fairness obligations) and *Hickey v. Eastern Health Board*, [1991] 1 IR 208 (Eire SC).

3. In *Dunsmuir v. New Brunswick*, [2008] 1 SCR 190, the Supreme Court changed the law in relation to the application of procedural fairness to the dismissal of public office-holders as laid down in *Knight*. It held that where a public office-holder's employment is governed by an employment contract, disputes relating to his or her dismissal should be resolved according to the express or implied terms of the contract and any applicable statutes and regulations, just like any contractual employee. In other words, a public authority that dismisses an employee pursuant to an employment contract is not subject to an additional public law duty of fairness and the public employee seeking to challenge the dismissal is limited to ordinary contractual remedies.

The court justified this change on several grounds. First it noted that it was difficult to determine in practice whether a position had a sufficiently strong "statutory flavour" to be considered an office and attract the application of the duty of fairness. Second, it opined that the public law remedy for a violation of procedural fairness in this context—the quashing of the termination decision, leading to the employee's reinstatement and an entitlement to accrued salary and benefits from the time of dismissal to the court's order on judicial review—was less principled than the private law remedy of adequate notice or pay in lieu of notice because the amount of relief depended not on the employee's situation but on the length of time taken for resolution of his or her judicial review application. While *Dunsmuir* means that public office-holders can no longer be restored to their positions, a remedy not available for breach of contract, and are no longer entitled to an opportunity to meet the allegations on which their employer is dismissing them, the court was satisfied that the common law entitlements to reasonable notice or salary in lieu and the opportunity to sue for wrongful dismissal, including enhanced notice rights or damages (see *Wallace v. United Grain Growers Ltd.*, [1997] 3 SCR 701) and punitive damages, adequately protect public employees.

The court noted, at paras. 115-116, that a public law duty of fairness may still apply in the following three circumstances: (1) where a public employee is not protected by a contract of employment (judges, ministers, officials who fulfill constitutionally defined state roles); (2) where an office-holder is expressly subject to summary dismissal; and (3) where a duty of fairness "flows by necessary implication from the statutory power governing the employment relationship," including, for example, a statute that provides for notice to employees of a motion to dismiss. With regard to this last exception, do you think *Dunsmuir* has removed an office-holder's right to public law procedural fairness in the case of a statute, as in *Ridge v. Baldwin*, which allows for dismissal from statutory office but only for cause? Do you think that *Dunsmuir* means that the government, as employer, should be treated by courts no differently than any private sector employer? In other words, does the public no longer have an interest—recognized in the employment context by the majority judgment in *Knight*—in the proper use of delegated powers by administrative bodies? See generally, D. Mullan, "*Dunsmuir v. New Brunswick*, Standard of Review and Procedural Fairness for Public Servants: Let's Try Again!" (2008), 2 *CJALP* 117.

4. Finally, in terms of the questions posed at the conclusion of *Nicholson* (and here L'Heureux-Dubé and Sopinka JJ are essentially in agreement), fairness emerges as a flexible concept with quite informal opportunities to respond to allegations and to express concerns being acceptable compliance with the decision-maker's obligations in at least some contexts.

The Baker Synthesis

By the time the Supreme Court rendered its judgment in *Baker*, the leading Canadian case on procedural fairness, the basic features of the duty had been set. Whether the duty of fairness applies to a particular decision depended on a variety of contextual factors, including: the nature of the decision being made and the process followed in making it; the nature of the statutory scheme and the terms of the statute pursuant to which the decision-maker operates; the importance of the decision to the individuals affected; and the legitimate expectations of the person challenging the decision. The "degree" of fairness required for a particular decision and the specific procedural content of the duty also hinge on an assessment of these and other factors, including deference to the procedural choices made by the decision-maker. The "threshold" question will be examined later in this chapter, after our discussion of constitutional sources of procedure. The question of the degree of procedural fairness and the specific choice of procedures mandated by the duty of fairness will each be examined in chapter 4 of this text.

Constitutional and Quasi-Constitutional Sources of Procedures

Procedural rights also receive constitutional protection under the *Canadian Charter of Rights and Freedoms* and under quasi-constitutional instruments, including the *Canadian Bill of Rights* and the Québec *Charter of Human Rights and Freedoms*. From the perspective of a public authority seeking to determine the procedures it is legally obligated to provide or of a party wishing to ascertain what procedures he or she is owed in a given decision-making context, resort to constitutional and quasi-constitutional procedural sources becomes necessary in three main circumstances. First, as in the *Singh* case, legislation may expressly deny certain procedural safeguards or provide a lower level of procedural safeguards, leaving no room for common law supplementation. In such a case, only constitutional or quasi-constitutional norms may override the statute and mandate more significant procedural protections. Second, the constitutional and quasi-constitutional provisions may establish procedural claims in circumstances where none existed previously at common law. Third, these provisions may mandate a higher level of procedural protections than would the application of common law procedural fairness to the challenged species of administrative decision making. In other words, in the latter two cases, the claim is that the recognition of a protected Charter or quasi-constitutional interest serves to "boost" procedural protections beyond those recognized at common law.

The thresholds to the applicability of these constitutional and quasi-constitutional protections will be identified and explained in detail later in this section. Our primary concern at this point is to introduce the sources of these protections.

The Canadian Bill of Rights

The 1960 or "Diefenbaker" *Bill of Rights* is a federal statute. As such, despite some early suggestions to the contrary, its area of application is confined to the federal domain (ss. 5(2) and (3)). It has no relevance to provincial statutes or decision making under provincial jurisdiction. While an ordinary statute in the sense of having been enacted by the Parliament of Canada by way of simple majority in both Houses, the *Bill of Rights* nonetheless purports to be applicable to both prior and subsequent legislation in that it declares its primacy over all other legislation unless that legislation expressly provides that it overrides the *Bill of Rights* (s. 2). This "manner and form" requirement has generally been treated as effective to achieve its purposes and as giving the *Bill of Rights* its constitutional or *quasi-*constitutional status. (It is beyond the scope of our inquiry to evaluate the constitutional theory on which these assumptions are based.)

For the purposes of administrative law, the principal procedural protections of the *Bill of Rights* are found in ss. 1(a) and 2(e). They provide as follows:

> 1. It is hereby recognized and declared that in Canada there have existed and shall continue to exist without discrimination by reason of race, national origin, colour, religion or sex, the following human rights and fundamental freedoms, namely
>
> > (a) the right of the *individual* to life, liberty, security of the person and *enjoyment of property*, and the right not to be deprived thereof except by due process of law:
> >
> > · · ·
>
> 2. Every law of Canada shall, unless it is expressly declared by an Act of the Parliament of Canada that it shall operate notwithstanding the *Canadian Bill of Rights*, be so construed and applied as not to abrogate, abridge or infringe or to authorize the abrogation, abridgment or infringement of any of the rights or freedoms herein recognized and declared, and in particular, no law of Canada shall be construed and applied so as to
>
> > · · ·
>
> > (e) deprive a *person* of the right to a fair hearing in accordance with the principles of fundamental justice for the *determination of his rights and obligations*.
>
> [Emphasis added throughout.]

(Note should also be made of ss. 2(d) and (g), both of which apply to commissions, boards, and tribunals as well as to regular courts. Section 2(d) specifies that a person shall not be compelled to give evidence if denied counsel or "protection against self crimination or other constitutional safeguards" while s. 2(g) guarantees the assistance of an interpreter for those who cannot function in the language in which the proceedings are being conducted.)

While s. 1(a) could possibly be interpreted by reference to its preamble as simply an anti-discrimination provision and while s. 2(e) was thought by some to be no more than a legislated canon of statutory interpretation, those restrictive approaches are clearly no longer accepted. Each is now viewed as a vehicle for rendering inoperative federal statutes that do not provide the protections of "due process of law" and "fundamental justice," respectively.

The Canadian Charter of Rights and Freedoms

The main source of procedural protections in the Charter is s. 7, which provides:

> Everyone has the right to life, liberty and security of the person and the right not to be deprived thereof except in accordance with the principles of fundamental justice.

As opposed to s. 2(e) of the *Bill of Rights*, which has been held to be restricted to procedural claims (*Duke v. The Queen*, [1972] SCR 917 (Ont.)—"a *fair hearing* in accordance with the principles of fundamental justice"), the guarantee of the principles of fundamental justice in

s. 7 is not conditioned by any reference to a hearing. As a consequence, it was held as early as 1985 by the Supreme Court to have a substantive as well as a procedural component (*Reference re BC Motor Vehicle Act*, [1985] 2 SCR 486 (BC)). As explored later in this section, the procedural fairness rights of the party affected by a government decision is triggered only where the decision engages that party's life, liberty, or security of the person. While liberty or security of the person interests are commonly engaged in certain decision-making contexts, including refugee protection or correctional law, this is usually not the case in the sprawling domain of economic regulation, including the licensing of regulated businesses.

Initially, it was believed by some that a number of other provisions of the Charter might also be a direct source of procedural protections. However, that has proved generally not to be the case.

Any thought that s. 15 and its promise of equality "before and under the law" provided a guarantee of equality as among participants in administrative proceedings in terms of procedural rights was dashed by *Andrews v. Law Society of British Columbia*, [1989] 1 SCR 143 (BC). This case established that s. 15 was essentially an anti-discrimination provision with its protections only benefiting "discrete and insular minorities" as reflected in the categories of victim specified in the second half of the section as well as those possessing analogous characteristics. The only form of procedural discrimination that counts, therefore, is one that has the intention or effect of discriminating against persons within these groups. (See *NAPO v. Canada (Attorney General)*, below, for an example of the rejection of a s. 15 procedural inequality claim.)

As for s. 11 and its guarantees of "an independent and impartial tribunal," of no unreasonable delay in the conduct of proceedings, and of presumptions of innocence, its direct effect has been confined to criminal proceedings and those with "true penal consequences" (*R v. Wigglesworth*, [1987] 2 SCR 541 (Sask.); *R v. Shubley*, [1990] 1 SCR 3 (Ont.)). This had the effect of not only dashing the expectations of those who saw these protections as applying to professional disciplinary proceedings but also (as demonstrated by *Shubley*) of denying its effect in the context of a penitentiary superintendent imposing solitary confinement as a sanction for a prison disciplinary offence. There does, however, remain a question as to whether a fine of sufficient magnitude levied by a tribunal (such as a securities commission) would ever be a "true penal consequence," an issue that is taking on significance now that some commissions may levy fines as high as $1 million.

What remains for administrative law in ss. 8-14? As with the *Bill of Rights*, there are sections providing protection against self-incrimination (s. 13) and guaranteeing access to an interpreter (s. 14). These have obvious ramifications for administrative hearings generally (assuming that "proceedings" is not interpreted narrowly). In addition, the protections against "unreasonable search and seizure" (s. 8) and arbitrary detention or imprisonment (s. 9) have an impact on those administrative regimes with search, seizure, and detention powers. Finally, the right in s. 12 "not to be subjected to any cruel and unusual treatment or punishment" may offer protections for those who are incarcerated in penitentiaries or mental institutions.

It should also be noted that, in so far as ss. 8-14 may reflect examples in specific contexts of the principles of fundamental justice, they might also be invoked indirectly to support arguments on the content of that term in cases brought under s. 7 and where "life, liberty and security of the person" are otherwise affected. This possibility was adverted to by McLachlin J, delivering the judgment of majority of the Supreme Court of Canada in *Shubley*, above:

> Having concluded that the disciplinary proceeding to which the appellant was subject is not a proceeding for an offence within s. 11(h) on the principles set out in *Wigglesworth*, I add these comments as to the consequences of a contrary conclusion. I share the concern expressed by Wilson J in *Wigglesworth* about an overbroad application of s. 11. I agree with her conclusion (p. 558) that "it is preferable to restrict s. 11 to the most serious offences known to our law, *i.e.*, criminal and penal matters and to leave other "offences" subject to the more flexible criteria of "fundamental justice" in s. 7.
>
> The importance of this is illustrated by considering the impact of the application of s. 11 to prison discipline proceedings. Prison discipline proceedings must be expeditious and informal if the crises that inevitably occur in centres of incarceration are to be avoided. To accord to inmates facing such proceedings the constitutional rights which s. 11 confers on an accused charged with a criminal offence would be to make the task of those charged with maintaining order in our prisons immeasurably more difficult. Procedural protection for inmates affected by disciplinary measures is more properly to be found in the more flexible guarantees of s. 7 than in s. 11 of the Charter.

This statement clearly accepts that the principles found in s. 11 will not automatically apply or necessarily be as rigorous when they are contended for indirectly and by way of analogy in the context of s. 7. (See also the judgment of Iacobucci J for the Supreme Court in *Dehghani v. Canada (Minister of Employment and Immigration)*, [1993] 1 SCR 1053 (Can.).)

Québec Charter of Human Rights and Freedoms

Section 23 of the Québec Charter provides that "[e]very person has a right to a full and equal, public and fair hearing by an independent and impartial tribunal, for the determination of his rights and obligations or of the merits of any charge brought against him." It is a quasi-constitutional guarantee insofar as s. 52 of the Québec Charter specifies that no law may derogate from s. 23 unless such derogation is expressly allowed by statute.

THRESHOLDS

The previous section mapped out a veritable web of sources of procedural protections. The procedures conferred by the decision-maker's enabling legislation and related delegated legislation will protect affected parties as a matter of course. Whether general procedural codes, common law procedural fairness and constitutional and quasi-constitutional sources are available to supplement these procedures, on the other hand, will depend on whether the threshold for their application has been met. We turn now to this important question of threshold. The judge-made thresholds for the application of the duty of fairness have been to a varying extent incorporated into the thresholds for some general procedural codes, like Ontario's SPPA and for the quasi-constitutional *Canadian Bill of Rights*. Accordingly, we begin with a detailed review of the threshold for the application of common law procedural fairness.

The Common Law Threshold

Historical Overview

As noted in our discussion of the seminal English and Canadian decisions on the duty of fairness, for a large part of the 20th century, common law courts in England and the Commonwealth would not resort to the common law rules of natural justice to read in hearing requirements to otherwise silent statutes unless the decision-maker was exercising a "judicial" or "quasi-judicial" function. In *R v. Legislative Committee of the Church Assembly*, [1928] 1 KB 411, Lord Hewart, the Lord Chief Justice of England, decided that for the rules of natural justice to be imposed and for *certiorari* and prohibition to be available, a decision-maker had to have "legal authority to determine the rights of subjects" as well as the "super-added" characteristic of "a duty to act judicially."

Thus, decisions that could be characterized as preliminary and not final, bearing on "mere privileges" rather than rights, or issued from the exercise of an "administrative" or "ministerial" rather than a judicial power fell below the threshold for the application of the rules of natural justice. The situation was aggravated by the fact that the courts were unable to provide a clear and consistent definition of a "judicial" function. Following the courts' acceptance in *Ridge v. Baldwin* and *Nicholson* that, in some circumstances, administrative decision-makers owed affected parties a duty of procedural fairness, the highly formalistic judicial/administrative classification exercise lost much of its importance in administrative law. It remains relevant, as we shall see, in determining whether the procedural protections of Ontario's *Statutory Powers Procedure Act* and Québec's *Charter of Human Rights and Freedoms* are triggered.

Following *Nicholson*, it remained unclear whether there were two distinct levels of procedural protection: natural justice for decision-makers exercising judicial and quasi-judicial functions and procedural fairness for those exercising administrative functions, and whether there were any decisions to which procedural protections did not extend. In other words, was there still a threshold and, if so, how was it defined? These questions were explored by the Supreme Court of Canada very shortly after *Nicholson*. One of the first of these cases (*Martineau v. Matsqui Inmate Disciplinary Board*, [1980] 1 SCR 602 (Can.)) had two important features. First, it involved prison discipline, a domain where, prior to *Nicholson*, the courts (including the Supreme Court) had shown little or no sympathy to the procedural claims of inmates. Once incarcerated, they had ceased to be rights holders. Second, the primary concern was with a preliminary issue, the allocation of original judicial review jurisdiction between the Trial and Appeal Divisions of the Federal Court of Canada (now the Federal Court and the Federal Court of Appeal). This remained the bane of administrative lawyers' existence until the proclamation into force in early 1992 of amendments to the *Federal Court Act* by virtue of which that allocation of jurisdiction no longer depended on a virtually impenetrable statutory formula but rather on a schedule of tribunals. (See RSC 1985, c. F-7, as amended by SC 1990, c. 8; as discussed in chapter 16 of this text.)

Two inmates, Martineau and Butters, were disciplined, and alleged that they were not given a hearing. They made an application for review in the Federal Court of Appeal, which was dismissed because the court did not have jurisdiction.

Martineau and Butters also made an application for *certiorari* in the Trial Division, which has jurisdiction to grant the usual remedies for review (except for cases in which the

Court of Appeal has jurisdiction). The application was, essentially, based on the fairness requirement. They were met with the argument that *certiorari* can be used to review only judicial or *quasi*-judicial functions. (This argument was not material in *Nicholson* because of the reforms made by the *Judicial Review Procedure Act*, considered in chapter 16.)

This argument was rejected by the Supreme Court, which appeared to expand the limits of *certiorari* to include enforcement of procedural requirements generally.

The decision was limited to this remedial issue. About the substance and fairness, Pigeon J said:

> I must, however, stress that the Order issued by Mahoney J deals only with the jurisdiction of the Trial Division, not with the actual availability of the relief in the circumstances of the case. This is subject to the exercise of judicial discretion and in this respect it will be essential that the requirements of prison discipline be borne in mind. … It is specially important that the remedy be granted only in cases of serious injustice and that proper care be taken to prevent such proceedings from being used to delay deserved punishment so long that it is made ineffective, if not altogether avoided.

Dickson J said, in a set of conclusions to his judgment:

> 3. The fact that a decision maker does not have a duty to act judicially, with observance of formal procedure which that characterization entails, does not mean that there may not be a duty to act fairly which involves importing something less than the full panoply of conventional natural justice rules. In general, courts ought not to seek to distinguish between the two concepts, for the drawing of a distinction between a duty to act fairly, and a duty to act in accordance with the rules of natural justice, yields an unwieldy conceptual framework. The *Federal Court Act*, however, compels classification for review of federal decision makers.

> 4. An inmate disciplinary board is not a court. It is a tribunal which has to decide rights after hearing evidence. Even though the board is not obliged, in discharging what is essentially an administrative task, to conduct a judicial proceeding, observing the procedural and evidential rules of a court of law, it is, nonetheless, subject to a duty of fairness and a person aggrieved through breach of that duty is entitled to seek relief from the Federal Court, Trial Division, on an application for *certiorari*.

> 5. It should be emphasized that it is not every breach of prison rules of procedure which will bring intervention by the courts. The very nature of a prison institution requires officers to make "on the spot" disciplinary decisions and the power of judicial review must be exercised with restraint. Interference will not be justified in the case of trivial or merely technical incidents. The question is not whether there has been a breach of prison rules, but whether there has been a breach of the duty to act fairly in all the circumstances. The rules are of some importance in determining this latter question, as an indication of the views of prison authorities as to the degree of procedural protection to be extended to inmates.

> • • •

> 7. It is wrong, in my view, to regard natural justice and fairness as distinct and separate standards and to seek to define the procedural content of each. In *Nicholson*, the Chief Justice spoke of a "… notion of fairness involving something less than the procedural protection of the traditional natural justice." Fairness involves compliance with only some of the principles of natural justice. …

The content of the principles of natural justice and fairness in application to the individual cases will vary according to the circumstances of each case. ...

8. In the final analysis, the simple question to be answered is this: Did the tribunal on the facts of the particular case act fairly toward the person claiming to be aggrieved? It seems to me that this is the underlying question which the courts have sought to answer in all the cases dealing with natural justice and with fairness.

Martland, Ritchie, Beetz, Estey, and Pratte JJ concurred with Pigeon J; Laskin CJC and McIntyre J concurred with Dickson J.

With the 1992 proclamation of the amendments to the *Federal Court Act*, that particular need to make distinctions between judicial and administrative functions disappeared. That left as the only important domains in which such a differentiation was of continuing significance the application of the minimum procedural rules in the Ontario *Statutory Powers Procedure Act* (a matter to which we return when we discuss *Re Webb and Ontario Housing Corporation*, below); the right to a determination by an independent and impartial tribunal (s. 23) and the other procedural rights contained in chapter 3 of the Québec *Charter of Human Rights and Freedoms* (by virtue of s. 56, these attach only to judicial and *quasi*-judicial tribunals); and, finally, the application of the doctrine of *res judicata* to a statutory authority's decision.

For such purposes, Dickson J, in *MNR v. Coopers & Lybrand*, [1979] 1 SCR 495 (Can.), another *Federal Court Act* case decided in the wake of *Nicholson*, provided a restatement of the basis for that classification:

It is possible, I think, to formulate several criteria for determining whether a decision or order is one required by law to be made on a judicial or *quasi*-judicial basis. The list is not intended to be exhaustive.

(1) Is there anything in the language in which the function is conferred or in the general context in which it is exercised which suggests that a hearing is contemplated before a decision is reached?

(2) Does the decision or order directly or indirectly affect the rights and obligations of persons?

(3) Is the adversary process involved?

(4) Is there an obligation to apply substantive rules to many individual cases rather than, for example, the obligation to implement social and economic policy in a broad sense?

The cause of prisoners' procedural rights was further advanced by the judgment of Le Dain J (for the court) in *Cardinal v. Director of Kent Institution*, [1985] 2 SCR 643 (BC), where it was decided that a hearing was required for a decision by prison officials to keep a prisoner "dissociated" for security reasons. In so holding, Le Dain J stressed the "serious effect" on the prisoner and stated:

The Court has affirmed that there is, as a general common law principle, a duty of procedural fairness lying in every public authority making an administrative decision which is not of a legislative nature and which affects the rights, privileges or interests of an individual.

He went on to respond to an argument that the holding of a hearing would have been futile in this case because there was no possibility that the penitentiary authorities would have been persuaded to change their minds.

> [T]he denial of a right to a fair hearing must always render a decision invalid, whether or not it may appear to a reviewing court that the hearing would likely have resulted in a different decision. The right to a fair hearing must be regarded as an independent, unqualified right which finds its essential justification in the sense of procedural justice which any person affected by an administrative decision is entitled to have. It is not for the court to deny that right and sense of justice on the basis of speculation as to what the result might have been had there been a hearing.

Given the penitentiary discipline context and the extent of the court's support for the freestanding nature of procedural entitlements, it is difficult to see this as a judgment that is in any way restrictive of claims to procedural fairness. However, Le Dain J's formulation of the circumstances in which the duty of procedural fairness arises does contain the genesis of a new threshold, one in which the dividing lines are expressed in terms of "legislative" and all other functions and are predicated also on whether the decision is one that affects "rights, privileges or interests." These distinctions are elaborated further by L'Heureux-Dubé J in the Supreme Court's majority judgment in *Knight*. Where the decision is of "a legislative and general" as opposed to "a more administrative and specific nature," there is no duty to act fairly (at least in the procedural sense of that term). Moreover, in a statement that has echoes back to Lord Hewart and also *Guay v. Lafleur*, below, it is stated that a "decision of a preliminary nature will not in general trigger a duty to act fairly." While all this may be technically *dicta*, it does suggest the emergence of a new classification process replacing the old administrative–judicial sawoff and upon which *any* entitlement to procedural decencies will depend. We now consider this from the perspective of each of the component parts of L'Heureux-Dubé J's statement of principle.

Decisions of a Legislative and a General Nature

The notion in *Knight* that legislative functions were excluded from the ambit of any implied procedural requirements, in general, and the new, more flexible duty to act fairly, in particular, finds its genesis in the judgment of Megarry J in *Bates v. Lord Hailsham of Marylebone*, [1972] 1 WLR 1373 (Ch.), the facts of and relevant statement from which are provided in the extracts from *Canada (Attorney General) v. Inuit Tapirisat of Canada*, [1980] 2 SCR 735 (Can.) that follow. Indeed, this notion of the exclusion of legislative functions had earlier found acceptance in the judgment of Dickson J in *Martineau*, above, when he stated in his already-quoted-from doctrinal summary:

> 2. A purely ministerial decision, on broad grounds of public policy, will typically afford the individual no procedural protection, and any attack upon such a decision will have to be founded upon abuse of discretion. Similarly, public bodies exercising legislative functions may not be amenable to judicial supervision.

This statement also provides some warrant for L'Heureux-Dubé's statements in *Knight* that it is not simply legislative functions that fail to attract a duty to act fairly in a procedural sense but also decisions of a "general" nature.

What, however, these general prescriptions by and large leave undefined is the precise meaning of the crucial terminology. What counts as a "legislative" function for these purposes? What are the badges of a "purely ministerial decision, on broad grounds of public policy"? In particular, is "ministerial" being used in the limited sense of a decision taken by a minister of the Crown or in the broader sense in which it was sometimes used in pre-*Nicholson* cases as a virtual synonym for "administrative" (having to do with administering)? What are decisions of a "general" as opposed to a "specific" nature? Indeed, underlying all of this is the question whether such judicial discourse marks the re-emergence of distinctions between judicial and administrative functions under a different guise, a resurgence of the categories of decision identified and espoused by D.M. Gordon?

We begin our consideration of these questions with a judgment of the Supreme Court of Canada in which there is considerable ambiguity, in particular, about whether hearing rights are denied because of the character of the decision-maker, the nature of the decision, or both. It concerns a decision made nominally by the governor in council but on the basis of recommendations made by a Cabinet committee. Cabinets are, of course, political institutions (in every sense of that term), with many competing demands on their time, and their role in government imposes some firm procedural constraints—for example, the need for confidentiality. Yet, among the many decisions that cabinets make are those that invite demands for some form of participation—for example, decisions on appeal from agencies that have held hearings, or decisions that affect particular individuals or groups.

Cabinet and Cabinet Appeals

Canada (Attorney General) v. Inuit Tapirisat of Canada
[1980] 2 SCR 735 (Can.)

[The Canadian Radio-television and Telecommunications Commission (CRTC) had power to regulate the rates of utilities, including Bell Canada (Bell). The crucial statutory provision for these purposes was s. 64(1) of the *National Transportation Act*, RSC 1970, c. N-17, which provided:

(1) The Governor in Council may at any time, in his discretion, either upon petition of any party, person or company interested, or of his own motion, and without any petition or application, vary or rescind any order, decision, rule or regulation of the Commission, whether such order or decision is made *inter partes* or otherwise, and whether such regulation is general or limited in its scope and application;

(2) An appeal lies from the Commission to the Federal Court of Appeal upon a question of law, or a question of jurisdiction, upon leave therefor being obtained from that Court and upon notice to the parties and the Commission, and upon hearing such of them as appear and desire to be heard; and the costs of such application are in the discretion of that Court.

In 1976 Bell made an application for approval of a rate increase. The Inuit Tapirisat intervened to oppose parts of the application. More particularly, it wanted the CRTC to condition Bell Canada's rate increase on an obligation to provide better service for remote Northern communities. After an unfavourable decision, it appealed to the governor in council—the Cabinet. The CRTC made a submission to the Cabinet through the Department of Communications, and Bell also made a submission. The department made a statement that summarized the positions of the parties and gave the opinions of the department about the facts, the issues, and the proper disposition of the appeal. The Inuit Tapirisat was given none of this material except the submission by Bell. At the Cabinet meeting at which the appeal was discussed, the minister of communications made a recommendation to dismiss the appeal, which was accepted. The Inuit Tapirisat made a motion in the Federal Court for a declaration that a hearing should have been given, or that, if a hearing had been given, it did not comply with the principles of natural justice. The government applied for an order dismissing the action on the ground that the statement disclosed no reasonable cause of action. The application was granted by the Trial Division; an appeal by the Inuit Tapirisat succeeded, and the government appealed to the Supreme Court.]

ESTEY J delivered the judgment of the Court: The substance of the question before this Court in this appeal is this: is there a duty to observe natural justice in, or at least a lesser duty of fairness incumbent on, the Governor in Council in dealing with parties such as the respondents upon their submission of a petition under s. 64(1)?

Let it be said at the outset that the mere fact that a statutory power is vested in the Governor in Council does not mean that it is beyond review. If that body has failed to observe a condition precedent to the exercise of that power, the Court can declare that such purported exercise is a nullity.

However, no failure to observe a condition precedent is alleged here. Rather it is contended that, once validly seized of the respondents' petition, the Governor in Council did not fulfil the duty to be fair implicitly imposed upon him, the argument goes, by s. 64(1) of the *National Transportation Act*. While, after *Nicholson*, and *Martineau v. Matsqui Institution Disciplinary Board (No. 2)* [1980] 1 SCR 602 (Can.), the existence of such a duty no longer depends on classifying the power involved as "administrative" or "*quasi*-judicial," it is still necessary to examine closely the statutory provision in question in order to discern whether it makes the decision maker subject to any rules of procedural fairness.

It is not helpful in my view to attempt to classify the action or function by the Governor in Council (or indeed the Lieutenant-Governor in Council acting in similar circumstances) into one of the traditional categories established in the development of administrative law.

… In my view the essence of the principle of law here operating is simply that in the exercise of a statutory power the Governor in Council, like any other person or group of persons, must keep within the law as laid down by Parliament or the Legislature. Failure to do so will call into action the supervising function of the Superior Court whose responsibility is to enforce the law, that is to ensure that such actions as may be authorized by statute shall be carried out in accordance with its terms, or that a public authority shall not fail to respond to a duty assigned to it by statute.

I turn now to a consideration of s. 64(1) in light of those principles. Clearly the Governor in Council is not limited to varying orders made *inter partes* where a *lis* existed and was determined by the Commission. The Commission is empowered to approve all charges for the use of telephones of Bell Canada. In so doing the Commission determines whether the proposed tariff of tolls is just and reasonable and whether they are discriminatory.

Thus the statute delegates to the CRTC the function of approving telephone service tolls with a directive as to the standards to be applied. There is thereafter a secondary delegation of the rate-fixing function by Parliament to the Governor in Council but this function only comes into play after the Commission has approved a tariff of tolls; and on the fulfilment of that condition precedent, the power arises in the Governor in Council to establish rates for telephone service by the variation of that order, decision, rule or regulation of the CRTC. While the CRTC must operate within a certain framework when rendering its decisions, Parliament has in s. 64(1) not burdened the executive branch with any standards or guidelines in the exercise of its rate review function. Neither were procedural standards imposed or even implied. That is not to say that the Courts will not respond today … if the conditions precedent to the exercise of power so granted to the executive branch have not been observed. Such a response might also occur if, on a petition being received by the Council, no examination of its contents by the Governor in Council were undertaken. That is quite a different matter (and one with which we are not here faced) from the assertion of some principle of law that requires the Governor in Council, before discharging its duty under the section, to read either individually or *en masse* the petition itself and all supporting material, the evidence taken before the CRTC and all submissions and arguments advanced by the petitioner and responding parties. The very nature of the body must be taken into account in assessing the technique of review which has been adopted by the Governor in Council. The executive branch cannot be deprived of the right to resort to its staff, to departmental personnel concerned with the subject matter, and above all to the comments and advice of ministerial members of the Council who are by virtue of their office concerned with the policy issues arising by reason of the petition whether those policies be economic, political, commercial or of some other nature. Parliament might otherwise ordain, but in s. 64 no such limitation has been imposed on the Governor in Council in the adoption of the procedures for the hearing of petitions under s-s. (1).

This conclusion is made all the more obvious by the added right in s. 64(1) that the Governor in Council may "of his motion" vary or rescind any rule or order of the Commission. This is legislative action in its purest form where the subject matter is the fixing of rates for a public utility such as a telephone system. The practicality of giving notice to "all parties," as the respondent has put it, must have some bearing on the interpretation to be placed upon s. 64(1) in these circumstances. In these proceedings the respondent challenged the rates established by the CRTC and confirmed in effect by the Governor in Council. There are many subscribers to the Bell Canada services all of whom are and will be no doubt affected to some degree by the tariff of tolls and charges authorized by the Commission and reviewed by the Governor in Council. All subscribers should arguably receive notice before the Governor in Council proceeds with its review.

It was pointed out that in the past the Governor in Council has proceeded by way of an actual oral hearing in which the petitioner and the contending parties participated (PC 2166 dated 24/10/23; and PC 1170 dated 17/6/27). These proceedings do no more than illustrate the change in growth of our political machinery and indeed the size of the Canadian community. It was apparently possible for the national executive in those days to conduct its affairs under the *Railway Act* through meetings or hearings in which the parties appeared before some or all of the Cabinet. The population of the country was a fraction of that today. The magnitude of the government operations bears no relationship to that carried on at the federal level at present. No doubt the Governor in Council could still hold oral hearings if so disposed. Even if a Court had the power and authority to so direct (which I conclude it has not) it would be a very unwise and impractical judicial principle which would convert past practice into rigid, invariable administrative procedures. Even in cases mentioned above, while the order recites it to have been issued on the recommendation of the responsible Minister, there is nothing to indicate that the parties were informed of such a recommendation prior to the conduct of the hearing.

While it is true that a duty to observe procedural fairness, as expressed in the maxim *audi alteram partem*, need not be express … it will not be implied in every case. It is always a question of construing the statutory scheme as a whole in order to see to what degree, if any, the legislator intended the principle to apply. It is my view that the supervisory power of s. 64 … is vested in members of the Cabinet in order to enable them to respond to the political, economic and social concerns of the moment. Under s. 64 the Cabinet, as the executive branch of Government, was exercising the power delegated by Parliament to determine the appropriate tariffs for the telephone services of Bell Canada. In so doing the Cabinet, unless otherwise directed in the enabling statute, must be free to consult all sources which Parliament itself might consult had it retained this function. This is clearly so in those instances where the Council acts on its own initiative as it is authorized and required to do by the same subsection. There is no indication in s-s. (1) that a different interpretation comes into play upon the exercise of the right of a party to petition the Governor in Council to exercise this same delegated function or power. The wording adopted by Parliament in my view makes this clear. The Governor in Council may act "at any time." He may vary or rescind any order, decision, rule or regulation "in his discretion." The guidelines mandated by Parliament in the case of the CRTC are not repeated expressly or by implication in s. 64. The function applies to broad, *quasi*-legislative orders of the Commission as well as to inter-party decisions. In short, the discretion of the Governor in Council is complete provided he observes the jurisdictional boundaries of s. 64(1).

The procedure sanctioned by s. 64(1) has sometimes been criticized as an unjustifiable interference with the regulatory process: see *Independent Administrative Agencies* (Working Paper 25 of the Law Reform Commission of Canada, 1980) at 87-89. The Commission recommended that "provisions for the final disposition by the Cabinet or a minister of appeals of any agency decisions except those requesting the equivalent of the exercise of the prerogative of mercy or a decision based on humanitarian grounds, should be abolished" (at 88). Indeed it may be thought by some to be unusual and even counterproductive in an organized society that a carefully considered decision by an administrative agency, arrived at after a full public hearing in which many points of view have been advanced, should be susceptible of reversal by the Governor in Council. On the other hand, it is apparently the judgment of Parliament that this is an area inordinately sensitive to changing public policies and hence it has been reserved for the final application of such a policy by the executive branch of Government. Given the interpretation of s. 64(1) which I adopt, there is no need for the Governor in Council to give reasons for his decision, to hold any kind of a hearing, or even to acknowledge the receipt of a petition. It is not the function of this Court, however, to decide whether Cabinet appeals are desirable or not. I have only to decide whether the requirements of s. 64(1) have been satisfied.

In reaching this conclusion concerning the procedures to be followed with reference to s. 64(1), I am assisted by the reasoning of Megarry J in *Bates v. Lord Hailsham of St. Marylebone* [1972] 1 WLR 1373 (Ch.) (cited by the majority judgment of this Court in *Nicholson*). There the Court was dealing with a challenge made to the legality of an order issued under the *Solicitors Act* abolishing a tariff of fees, on the grounds that the order should have been preceded by wider consideration by the rule enacting body. In refusing to intervene, Megarry J stated (at 1378):

> Let me accept that in the sphere of the so-called *quasi*-judicial the rules of natural justice run, and that in the administrative or executive field there is a general duty of fairness. Nevertheless, these considerations do not seem to me to affect the process of legislation, whether primary or delegated. Many of those affected by delegated legislation, and affected very substantially, are never consulted in the process of enacting that legislation; and yet they have no remedy. ... I do not know of any implied right to be consulted or make objections, or any principle upon which the courts may enjoin the legislative process at the suit of those who contend that insufficient time for consultation and consideration has been given.

... It is clear that the orders in question in *Bates* and the case at bar were legislative in nature and I adopt the reasoning of Megarry J to the effect that no hearing is required in such cases. I realize, however, that the dividing line between legislative and administrative functions is not always easy to draw.

The answer is not to be found in continuing the search for words that will clearly and invariably differentiate between judicial and administrative on the one hand, or administrative and legislative on the other. It may be said that the use of the fairness principle as in *Nicholson* will obviate the need for the distinction in instances where the tribunal or agency is discharging a function with reference to something akin to a *lis* or where the agency may be described as an "investigating body" as in [*R v. Race Relations Board, ex parte Selvarajan*, [1975] 1 WLR 1686 (CA)]. Where, however, the executive branch has been assigned a function performable in the past by the Legislature itself and where the *res* or subject-matter is not an individual concern or a right unique to the petitioner or appellant, different considerations may be thought to arise. The fact that the function has been assigned as here to a tier of agencies (the CRTC in the first instance and the Governor in Council in the second) does not, in my view, alter the political science pathology of the case. In such a circumstance the Court must fall back upon the basic jurisdictional supervisory role and in so doing construe the statute to determine whether the Governor in Council has performed its functions within the boundary of the parliamentary grant and in accordance with the terms of the parliamentary mandate.

For the reasons already given I am unable, with respect, to conclude that the issue of fairness arises in these proceedings on a proper construction of s. 64(1). If there were to be a distinction between rights arising with reference to submissions from Government sources and rights arising with reference to the response from the rate applicant Bell Canada, more compelling reasons exist for disclosure of the intra-governmental communications as the respondents were, by this stage in these lengthy proceedings, very familiar with the application made by Bell Canada and the position taken by that company before the Commission by reason of the respondents' active participation in the hearings before the CRTC. In any case, I can discern nothing in s. 64(1) to justify a variable yardstick for the application to that section of the principle of fairness according to the source of the information placed before the Governor in Council for the disposition of the respondents' petition. The basic issue is the interpretation of this statutory provision in the context of the pattern of the statute in which it is found. In my view, once the proper construction of the section is determined, it applies consistently throughout the proceedings before the Governor in Council.

Appeal allowed.

NOTES

1. Does Estey J's judgment for the court preclude entirely the making of procedural demands in the context of Cabinet decision making? If the judgment leaves open some possibilities, what are they? To what extent does the judgment confine itself to arguments about the appropriateness of a hearing in front of the Cabinet itself? Are there ways of casting the applicant's procedural demands that lessen concerns about imposing procedural fairness obligations on such a political and time-constrained process? (In this regard, see Macdonald, "The Limits of Procedural Fairness: Executive Action by the Governor-in-Council" (1982), 46 *Sask. LR* 187, at 196, where, in criticizing the judgment of the majority of the court, he argues that the outcome resulted from a failure on the part of the court to conceptualize the demand for procedural fairness in other than traditional hearing terms and the unwillingness of the court to be perceived as involving itself with political matters.)

2. Subsequently, the issue of procedural rights on appeals to Cabinet under what was then s. 64(1) of the *National Telecommunications Powers and Procedures Act*, SC 1987, c. 34 was revisited in *National Anti-Poverty Organization v. Canada (Attorney-General)* (1988), 32 Admin. LR 1 (FCTD); rev'd. (1990), 60 DLR (4th) 712 (FCA). At first instance, Muldoon J held that he was not bound by *Inuit Tapirisat* because no argument had been raised in that case as to the effect of s. 2(e) of the *Canadian Bill of Rights*. However, the Federal Court of Appeal reversed on the basis that the Cabinet determination of an appeal against a CRTC order, which had an indirect impact on rates paid by subscribers, was not one that determined the "rights and obligations" of those subscribers in terms of s. 2(e). That section's mandating of the "principles of fundamental justice" was therefore not brought into operation. We return to this case and the impact of the *Canadian Bill of Rights* on procedural requirements later in this chapter.

Despite this continued judicial reticence, the *Broadcasting Act*, SC 1991, c. 1 imposed a number of procedural limits on the Cabinet. Indeed, it may be that these statutory changes altered the essential nature of Cabinet appeals. See Conklin, "The *Broadcasting Act* and the Changing Political Pathology of Cabinet Appeals" (1992), 2 *MCLR* 297.

3. In the legislative process leading up to the more recent *Telecommunications Act*, SC 1993, c. 38, an attempt was made (with mixed results) to place further restrictions on Cabinet appeals. See Janisch, "At Last! A New Canadian Telecommunications Act" (1993), 17 *Telecommunications Policy* 691:

Unlike the FCC in the USA, which is a fully fledged independent regulatory agency, the CRTC in keeping with the principles of parliamentary government is subject to having its decisions

reviewed by the elected Cabinet. Much concern as to the relationship which should exist between the CRTC and the rest of the government had been expressed before the Senate Committee, and it had made recommendations designed to protect the integrity of the Commission's
decision-making processes. These had included the elimination of the heavy-handed power to
"vary and rescind" decisions of the CRTC in favour of a more limited power to refer decisions
back for reconsideration, as contained in the 1991 *Broadcasting Act*.

In the end, the full force of the Senate Committee recommendations was not accepted and
the vary and rescind power was retained, but the Committee's recommendation for procedural
protection was adopted. There are now time limits, requirements for written petitions and responses which must be publicly filed and, most importantly, the Cabinet is now required to give
reasons for its decisions. However, unlike in the *Broadcasting Act*, there is no equivalent to the
requirement that the Cabinet only exercise its overview power where it concludes that the impugned decision "derogates from the attainment of the objectives of the broadcasting policy." A
similar provision in the *Telecommunications Act* would have met the Senate Committee's concern at suggestions that the Cabinet could legitimately take into account matters entirely extraneous to the policy objectives of the Act.

4. Notwithstanding *Inuit Tapirisat* and *NAPO*, there is authority holding that, at least in
some contexts, the Cabinet may be subject to certain implied procedural obligations. See,
for example, *Desjardins v. Bouchard*, [1983] 2 FC 641 (CA) (revocation of a criminal pardon).
In this regard, the decision of the High Court of Australia in *FAI Insurances v. Winneke*
(1982), 151 CLR 342 (Vict.) is instructive not only in terms of its different outcome but also
in its reliance on lower Canadian court authority. Legislation and regulations in the state of
Victoria required that insurers providing workers' compensation insurance have approval
from the governor in council. The approvals could be given for any period up to a year and
could be renewed. FAI had provided insurance for 20 years and its approval had been
renewed yearly. In 1979, the renewal was for only six months, and the minister of labour and
industry gave warning that some of the criteria for approval were not being met. After another six-month approval and some discussion about the criteria, the minister told FAI that
he would recommend that the current application not be approved. FAI made a request for
more information and an opportunity to make submissions. This was refused and the governor in council rejected the application. FAI sought a declaration that it was entitled to an
opportunity to be heard. At both first instance and on appeal to the Supreme Court of
Victoria, the claim was dismissed. However, on further appeal to the High Court of Australia,
FAI succeeded. Part of the reason for FAI's ultimate success was a "legitimate expectation"
of renewal based on the succession of prior approvals. We will return to this aspect of the
case when we address the scope of the doctrine of "legitimate expectation" in Canadian law.
However, the High Court also dealt with the argument that the governor in council could
not be subjected to any implied obligation of procedural fairness. Here was what Mason J
(as he then was) had to say about this argument:

> I do not accept the view that the statutory discretion given to the Governor in Council is abso-
> lute or unlimited. I concede that an exercise of the discretion may involve policy issues, *e.g.*, the
> possible need to limit the number of licences as a means of ensuring that unrestricted competi-
> tion will not result in unacceptable underwriting losses leading to inability of insurers to meet
> their commitments: see, for example, *R v. Liverpool Corporation, Ex parte Liverpool Taxi Fleet*

Operators' Association [1972] 2 QB 299 (CA). But it is not suggested that any such issue arose in the present case. At all times the central question seems to have been, as one would expect it to be in cases of application for the renewal of a licence: Was the applicant a fit and proper person to act as a workers' compensation insurer? The answer to this question seems to have turned on a view taken as to the commitments and financial position of the appellant, based on the particular matters referred to by the Minister. In these circumstances the appellant had a legitimate expectation that its approval would be renewed or at the very least that it would not be refused without its having an opportunity of meeting objections raised against it.

We are left with the argument that the Governor acting with the advice of the Executive Council is intrinsically unsuited to the making of an inquiry of the kind suggested. By reason of the nature of its proceedings, the formal nature of the business which it transacts, the nature of its membership—in Victoria it consists of all past and present Ministers of the Crown and has a quorum of two—the very heavy demands which are made on the time of many of its members in the performance of their principal duties as Ministers of the Crown and members of Parliament and the growing volume of government business, it is apparent that the Executive Council is not adapted to the conduct of proceedings similar to a judicial hearing. Rather it is adapted to the making of a formal decision based on the recommendation of the responsible Minister expressed in the papers presented to the Governor. For this reason, the court should be less inclined to hold that the Governor in Council is under an obligation to comply with the rules of natural justice than it would in the case of a statutory officer had a similar discretion been entrusted to him. It is less, perhaps much less, likely that Parliament intends the Governor in Council to be under such an obligation.

But where, as here, the function reposed in the Governor in Council, that of granting or refusing an application by an individual for the renewal of approval to act as an insurer—a matter to be decided in the circumstances of this case, not on issues of general policy, but principally, if not exclusively, by reference to the financial position and commitments of the applicant—would unquestionably attract a duty to comply with the rules of natural justice had it been reposed in a statutory officer, the difference in the nature and character of the Governor in Council is not sufficient, in my opinion, to deny the existence of some duty to accord natural justice, though the difference will be reflected in the content of the duty and what is to be expected by way of discharge of the duty, it being accepted now that the content of the duty varies with the particular circumstances of the case. It is impossible to suppose that Parliament intended that the Governor in Council would conduct a hearing similar to a judicial hearing. But it is possible, indeed proper, to attribute to Parliament the intention that the Governor in Council will act in conformity with natural justice, by giving to the applicant an adequate opportunity to present its case, as, for example, by written submissions on matters alleged to be relevant.

[A quotation from *Inuit* is omitted.]

The Governor in Council can without undue inconvenience give the appellant an adequate opportunity of presenting his case either by delegating to a committee of its members (as in *Re Gray Line of Victoria Ltd. and Chabot* (1980) 117 DLR (3d) 89 (BC SC)) or to the responsible Minister the function of considering the applicant's written submissions and reporting on them. Here the second alternative would appear to be preferable and that, after all, is what the appellant seeks. The Minister can then report on the submissions and make such recommendations as he thinks fit.

If one accepts these authorities at face value, what they reveal is that the mere fact that the designated decision-maker is the Cabinet does not automatically preclude the making of a claim to an entitlement to an opportunity to make submissions at least at some stage in the process. Where the decision is directed at a specific individual and is based on factors peculiar to that individual, the function in issue will not be classified as legislative despite the political nature of the decision-maker. Substance, not form, is crucial. This is underscored by the following judgment of the Supreme Court of Canada in which the relevant decision took the form of subsidiary legislation, the passage of a bylaw.

Bylaws and Rulemaking

Homex Realty and Development Co. Ltd. v. Wyoming (Village)
[1980] 2 SCR 1011 (Ont.)

[The municipality and Homex quarrelled about the obligation to instal services in a subdivision owned by Homex. Without giving notice to Homex, the municipality made a bylaw under the *Planning Act*, RSO 1970, c. 349, s. 29(3), designating the plan as a plan "deemed not to be a registered plan of subdivision." The effect of this designation was that lots in the subdivision could not be conveyed unless a new plan was registered or consents were obtained from the committee of adjustments of the municipality and, in either way, the municipality would have been able to impose conditions. Homex made an application for review to quash the bylaw and succeeded. An appeal by the municipality also succeeded, and Homex appealed to the Supreme Court.]

DICKSON J (dissenting): There is, of course, a long line of authority which establishes that before a public body can limit or abrogate the property rights of citizens, it must first give the individuals concerned an opportunity to be heard. This principle, of universal application, was established in the case of *Cooper v. Wandsworth Board of Works*. Nor is it necessary for the Legislature to provide explicitly for a hearing for a Court to imply such right. On the contrary, where statutory bodies seek to limit property rights, the Courts will imply a right to be heard unless there is an express declaration to the contrary.

Where the by-laws in question directly affect the land or property of specified individuals, the Courts have implied a common law right to be heard. In the present case, the Village passed two by-laws which directly and detrimentally affected the lands of Homex and, virtually, only the lands of Homex. It did so without serving any notice of its intentions. One would have thought, on the basis of the authorities, that this was a classical case in which to import rules of natural justice.

The Village advances several arguments in justification of its failure to give notice and to grant a hearing. These include: ... (ii) in passing the by-laws, the municipality was exercising a legislative function, to which no common law right to be heard applied; and (iii) even if a common law right of fairness does apply here, the municipality has satisfied the onus placed upon it.

A "Legislative" Function?

In the Court of Appeal, emphasis was placed on the "legislative" character of the acts performed by the Village of Wyoming in this case. ... The Court of Appeal held that ... the municipality is dealing with the public interest—namely who would bear the cost of servicing; the function is legislative in nature and no right to a hearing can be implied.

I find myself unable to accept the Court's exegesis.

First, the distinction sought to be made here is that there is no conflict between the competing interests of private individuals, but a question of public interest, pure and simple. That being so, the Village exercised a legislative function in passing By-laws 6 and 7. A sale of unserviced lands puts the burden of development on the municipality, which is entitled to prevent that result by enactment of a s. 29(3) by-law.

As counsel for the appellant correctly points out, this reasoning leads to anomalous results. Thus if there were two identical by-laws, each affecting only one particular piece of property, and one by-law was opposed by other private individuals or groups but the other was not, only one of the two owners would be entitled to a hearing.

The right to a hearing does not spring from the fact that there are competing groups or individuals, some of whom happen to be opposed to the by-law. It results from the fact that the by-law interferes, in particular, with the private property rights of this one owner. ...

Second, the presence of a compelling public interest does not alone abrogate or diminish a citizen's right to procedural protection. The private property interests of Homex were here at stake. The public interest, it seems to me, is best served by affording the private interest full disclosure and a fair opportunity to be heard. There is no *a priori* reason why the private interest should yield abjectly to the public interest. The Village could undoubtedly pass a by-law such as By-law 7 if it is in the public interest but, prior to deciding in favour of the public interest, the council should hear the landowner's submissions. One cannot label an act "legislative" for the purpose of dispensing with fairness. A by-law may, in the public interest, operate to the detriment of particular individuals but not without giving those individuals a right of hearing.

It was contended that if prior notice is required a sophisticated owner receiving such notice would immediately "checkerboard" and thereby defeat the intent of the section. That may be true but, if so, it is an argument which should be addressed to the Legislature accompanied by a request for an amendment which would specifically state that prior notice is not necessary.

Third, the question of the proper classification of a statutory power was, for a time, believed to be crucial in the determination of whether a right to a hearing could be implied. It was suggested that a right to a hearing only existed in circumstances where the process was judicial or *quasi*-judicial in nature. But this line of authority was rejected in England in *Ridge v. Baldwin, supra*, and, more recently, by this Court in *Re Nicholson and Haldimand-Norfolk Regional Police Com'rs*, and in *Martineau v. Matsqui Institution Disciplinary Board (No. 2)*. The latter two cases clearly establish that a right to procedural "fairness" no longer demands an *a priori* classification of a process as judicial or *quasi*-judicial.

In *Martineau*, it was said that review by *certiorari* was available whenever a public body has power to decide "any matter affecting the rights, interests, property, privileges or liberties of any person." Once it is clear that rights are being affected, it is necessary to determine the appropriate procedural standard that must be met by the statutory body. Above all, flexibility is required in this analysis. There is, as it were, a spectrum. A purely ministerial decision, on broad grounds of public policy, will typically afford the individual little or no procedural protection. On the other hand, a function that approaches the judicial end of the spectrum will entail substantial procedural safeguards, particularly when personal or property rights are targetted, directly, adversely and specifically.

It seems to me that a similar analysis should be employed in the present case. That is, it is not particularly important whether the function of the municipality be classified as "legislative" or as "*quasi*-judicial." Such an approach would only return us to the conundrums of an earlier era. One must look to the nature of the function and to the facts of each case. ...

The Court of Appeal noted that the municipality was acting out of what it conceived to be the public interest. I have no doubt this is true. Council was seeking to protect members of the public from potential injury in the purchase of unserviced land and to protect its ratepayers from paying the costs of servicing. But that is no answer to the case made by the appellant. What we have here is not a by-law of wide and general application which was to apply to all citizens of the municipality equally. Rather, it was a by-law aimed deliberately at limiting the rights of one individual, the appellant Homex. In these circumstances, I would hold that Homex was entitled to some procedural safeguards. This does not mean that the municipality was under a duty to observe the procedures appropriate to a court of law. But, at a minimum, it was under a duty to give Homex notice of the proposed by-law and the opportunity to be heard.

[Dickson J held that the hearing requirement had not been satisfied, despite the extensive exchanges, because Homex did not know that the municipality intended to pass bylaws. The majority of the court concluded that Homex was not entitled to relief because of the inconsistent and evasive conduct of its principals. Dickson J refused to consider this ground because it was not argued.]

ESTEY J: In determining the appropriate interpretation applicable to s. 29(3) of the *Planning Act*, the statutory framework, the nature of the action being undertaken by the Village Council, and the general circumstances prevailing at the time of the action by the Village Council must be taken into account.

It is clear that the passage of the by-law, if effective, has stripped Homex of its freedom to exercise the right of conveyance given by the provincial planning statute. On the other hand, it is equally clear that the balance of the township, that is to say the local ratepayers, may well be seriously affected by the action of Homex if the latter is successful in avoiding the consequences of the deregistration of Plan 567. One effect would appear to be that the other inhabitants would be obligated in theory, or in fact, or both, to service the lots of Plan 567 as and when they may be occupied by residences. It was submitted by the respondent that the argument of a notice requirement in these circumstances answers itself. The power granted the Village under s. 29(3) would be defeated by the response in fact taken by Homex in checkerboarding its lands prior to hearing of the application to quash.

Here we have the circumstance that the statute does not expressly require notice to the affected landowners. Council, of course, was aware that Homex would oppose such a by-law as By-law 7. The by-law had some characteristics of a community interest by-law, as in [*Re Hershoran and Windsor* (1973), 1 OR (2d) 291 (Div. Ct.)], but it also represented the purported culmination of an *inter partes* dispute conducted on adversarial lines between Homex and the Council. ... I would conclude that the action taken by the council was not in substance legislative but rather *quasi*-judicial in character so as to attract the principle of notice and the consequential doctrine of *audi alteram partem*, as laid down by the Courts as long ago as in *Wandsworth*. On this branch of the case all that remains is to determine whether the statutory pattern leaves this judicial principle available. The statute requires the filing of a copy of such a by-law as By-law 7 with the Minister and, in order to be effective, the by-law must be registered in the Registry Office and mailed to the registered owner of the lands affected. I draw no inference from such provisions that no prior notice may be required where the action in question is essentially *inter partes* and *quasi*-judicial in nature. Thus the statute does not displace, in my view, the very old rule of *audi alteram partem* and the resultant duty in council to hear first and decide later.

[Estey J agreed with Dickson J that the hearing requirement was not satisfied, but considered the argument about conduct and held that it succeeded. It depended on the discretion of the court in administering remedies, which is considered in chapter 18 of this text.]

[Ritchie J concurred with Dickson J; Laskin CJC and Martland, Beetz, and Chouinard JJ concurred with Estey J.]

Appeal dismissed.

NOTE

In *Homex*, the fact that a municipality had made a policy decision that had an immediate and specific target was crucial in the court's decision that Homex was entitled to procedural protections. What this does suggest clearly, however, is that where a bylaw or subordinate legislation of a more general character is being enacted or promulgated, whether by the governor in council, a minister, a municipality, a professional body, a regulatory agency, or tribunal, claims to procedural entitlements even by those affected immediately may be either diminished or eliminated. In this regard, recollect that *Bates v. Lord Hailsham*, the foundation English authority relied on by Estey J in *Inuit Tapirisat* involved a legislative-style order under the *Solicitors Act* abolishing the fees tariff. Moreover, it is this kind of analysis that has led to the Canadian courts' consistent unwillingness to impose notice and comment obligations on such bodies when they are engaged not only in the promulgation of subordinate legislation but also, to use the more expansive generic US term now in common parlance in Canada, rulemaking (see, for example, *Re Groupe des éleveurs de volailles de l'Est de l'Ontario and Chicken Marketing Agency* (1984), 14 DLR (4th) 151 (FCTD) and also *Rothmans of Pall Mall Ltd. v. Minister of National Revenue*, [1976] 2 FC 500 (CA) (decided largely by reference to principles of standing: see chapter 17 of this text)). Rulemaking is the subject of chapter 7, so we will not dwell on it further at this point.

Policy Making

Once we move away from decision making that can be classified in any formal sense as legislative, the question that still remains is where the exclusion of decisions of a "general" as well as a "legislative" nature has its bite. What seems clear is that this will have the effect of denying claims to procedural protections in relation to certain species of broadly based policy decision. Where the impact of the decision being made is diffuse, affecting a broad spectrum of the public in a generally undifferentiated manner, claims to participatory rights will be hard to justify (unless the legislation contains some indication of public participation or obligations of consultation). In this respect, two first instance BC decisions are illustrative. In *Sea Shepherd Conservation Authority v. The Queen* (1984), 11 Admin. LR 190 (BC SC), the BC Supreme Court rejected a public interest group claim to a hearing for a decision to undertake a wolf kill program, while, in *Sierra Club of Western Canada v. The Queen* (1984), 11 Admin. LR 276 (BC SC), the same result was reached in response to the grant of permits to cut timber. What, however, these two examples also suggest is that decisions about hearings are often not simply about whether there should be a hearing but also about who should be entitled to participate. In cases such as this, while public interest groups might not be seen as having an entitlement, those seeking to cut timber or hunt wolves probably do have a claim as indeed may other citizens affected directly by the decision—the neighbour whose land will erode if the timber is removed from the adjoining property. Such issues are very much part of the whole issue of standing in administrative law, a subject that we consider at length in chapter 17 of this text.

The dilemmas of identifying which decisions are so general as not to pass the threshold as well as the variations in status among those claiming participatory rights in relation to certain kinds of "policy" decisions are well illustrated by several decisions in the context of school board decisions to close schools, reallocate students and discontinue educational programs. The first case, *Vanderkloet v. Leeds & Grenville (County Board of Education)* (1985) 20 DLR (4th) 738 (Ont. CA), dealt with a school board's decision, in the face of declining enrollment, to re-organize three elementary schools by having students up to grade two attend one school and older students attend the other two schools. Acting under statutory authority, Ontario's minister of education had issued guidelines governing the closing of schools that required public consultation and participation. The board itself had prepared policies for school closings and a policy statement which required the board to make the various alternatives known to the school community before making a decision. A group of ratepayers challenged the board's decision to reallocate the students, arguing that the board had not complied with either the ministerial guidelines or the board's own policies, and that its resolutions reallocating the students were void. The Court of Appeal decided that the reallocation did not amount to a school closing and that the guidelines and policies did not apply. Turning to the claim that the school board had failed to afford the ratepayers procedural fairness, the court held:

> In my opinion, a board acting [in] good faith within its statutory authority has complete power over reallocation of students within a district and, in so doing, is not affecting the legal rights of any person.

I am not satisfied that the principles of procedural fairness are applicable to a board of education, an elected public body, who, in good faith and within the jurisdiction assigned to it by the Legislature, resolve to reallocate the student body within its school district.

In the second case, *Bezaire v. Windsor Roman Catholic Separate School Board* (1992), 9 OR (3d) 737 (Div. Ct.), the school board had decided, in the face of a financial crisis, to close nine schools. Contrary to ministerial guidelines and to the board's policy on school closings, the affected parents and students were given no opportunity for input into that decision before it was made, though there was some consultation after the decision was announced. After deciding that the ministerial guidelines were not technically subordinate legislation (and thus not strictly binding on the board), the Divisional Court considered the parents' claim that the board owed them a duty of fairness. The court distinguished *Vanderkloet* on the basis that that case had involved a reallocation of students, while the case at bar involved school closings to which the guidelines and policies applied:

> The guidelines and policies premised on public consultation attract the duty in the circumstances of this case.
>
> Unlike the decision taken by the board in *Vanderkloet* regarding the allocation of students which was held not to attract the doctrine of fairness, the guidelines, although they are ambiguous and lack the force of subordinate legislation, result in the applicability of the doctrine of fairness that was enunciated in *Nicholson* and rejected in the circumstances of *Vanderkloet*. Ambiguous though they are, the guidelines read as a whole are clearly premised on the principle that the closing of a school is the business of the community and the community, one way or another, must be consulted. The requirements of publicity, public sessions, and the importance of factors such as the social, cultural and recreational impact of a closure on the community, make it clear that real community consultation is a condition precedent to a valid decision.
>
> Although s. 149 says "require" rather than "expect," and s. 8 uses the word "require," and although s. 150 says "may," the net effect is a statutory direction that the Board will follow the public consultation expectations. Although a close parsing of these statutory provisions might suggest that public consultation is permissive or directory rather than mandatory, the overall force of the provisions supports the premise that public consultation is a condition of a valid closing decision. This is reinforced by the board's Stage II policy which requires the involvement of a committee composed of trustees, administrators, parents and board personnel.

NOTES

1. To what extent is the court's judgment in *Bezaire* contingent on the existence of the ministerial policy calling for procedures to be followed and developed? Given that this policy did not have the status of subordinate legislation, should it be even relevant? Is the court's distinguishing of *Vanderkloet* sustainable? Is the reorganization of schools involving the relocation of students all that different from a school closure? How about the decision of a school board to eliminate a program of early French immersion at the schools under its jurisdiction? Could the parents of children affected by this decision argue that they were entitled, under procedural fairness, to consultation? See *Sunshine Coast Parents for French v. Sunshine Coast (School District No. 46)* (1990), 44 Admin. LR 252, where the BC Supreme

court, while deciding the case against the parents on the basis of legitimate expectations, held that the District, in limiting the program, was exercising a legislative function.

2. Subsequently, in *Elliott v. Burin Peninsula School District No. 7* (1998), 13 Admin. LR (3d) 91, the Newfoundland Court of Appeal decided that the closing of a school was an administrative function that attracted the rules of procedural fairness. In that instance, there was no ministerial policy or internal school district policy specifying procedures to be followed.

The classification of broad regulatory functions as ministerial or policy-based has also precluded regulated industries and producers from successfully claiming an entitlement to consultation before government makes decisions with significant economic impacts. This scenario is explored in the following case.

Canadian Association of Regulated Importers v. Canada (Attorney General)
[1993] 3 FC 199 (TD); rev'd. [1994] 2 FC 247 (CA)

[At issue here was a ministerial decision changing the quota distribution system for the importation of hatching eggs and chicks, a change that significantly affected historic importers. In challenging the change, the historic importers claimed that they had not been consulted.]

REED J: ... Traditionally, a decision has been classified as being of a legislative nature if it sets out general rules which apply to a large number of persons. This is counterpoised to a decision respecting one specific individual. In the present case, the decision which is challenged sets down rules which govern a very limited segment of the populace. I am not convinced that even under the pre-*Nicholson* jurisprudence, where classification according to function was a primary consideration, that the present decision would have been characterized as being legislative in nature. I note, for example, that in *R v. Liverpool Corporation, Ex Parte Liverpool Taxi Fleet Operators' Association* [1972] 2 QB 299 (CA), a decision which was general in nature and which affected 300 taxi drivers was held to be subject to judicial review. While the main focus of that decision was the fact that representations had been made that a decision would not be taken without an opportunity to be heard being given to the taxi drivers who would be affected (the reasonable expectations doctrine), review was not refused by characterizing the decision as being as a legislative or policy one.

I think it is sufficient in this case to say that the Minister in deciding how to allocate import quota, was exercising a statutory power which had been delegated to him. While the decision made may have been general, it was general only for a small segment of the population and, in its application, it was very particular. The effect of the decision was to cause considerable economic harm to the applicants and others. There surely is an implied principle that Parliament intended that the statutory powers being exercised in this case would be exercised in accordance with the administrative law rules of fairness. These rules surely include notice to the applicants of what is being proposed and an opportunity (an effective opportunity) to comment thereon. This they did not have.

In the present case, arguments were made with respect to the nature of the applicants' "right." The applicants referred to Le Dain J's comments in *Maple Lodge Farms Ltd v.*

Government of Canada [1981] 1 FC 500 (CA) at 509, where he spoke of a "common law right to import." I have not been referred to any authority which discusses the common law right to import. At the same time, I do not think the classification of the applicants' interest as a "right" is necessary in order that they should be accorded an opportunity to make comments on and representations with respect to the particular quota system which was being adopted before it was imposed. As I read the present jurisprudence, it is not necessary to find that a "right" exists in order to bring an application for judicial review. It is sufficient if the applicant can demonstrate an "interest" which justifies the bringing by him or her of the application for judicial review. Indeed, in some cases that interest may be only a "legitimate expectation." In *Schmidt v. Home Secretary* [1969] 2 Ch 149 (CA) at 170, it was said that a person's right to be heard before an "administrative body ... depends on whether he has some right or interest, or, I would add some legitimate expectation of which it would not be fair to deprive him without hearing what he has to say."

In the present case the applicants may not have had a "right to import" but, for many years, they had in an unregulated environment been importing. They had established a position in the market and an economic viability based on this practice of importing. There is no doubt they have established an interest sufficient to found a claim for review of the decision taken by the Minister with respect to the allocation of import quotas.

With respect to the argument that it was impractical to give those affected by the allocation decision an opportunity to comment thereon before its adoption. [The evidence established that there were at the most 39 importing hatcheries and 45 chick importers affected by the decision.] ... [I]t is clear that even if all chick producers, both importing and non-importing, and all hatcheries should have had an opportunity to comment, the number of persons affected was not large. They were known. It would not have been impractical to have provided for notice and an opportunity to make recommendations.

It is trite law that the requirements of fairness differ depending upon a variety of factors including the type of decision being made. I would not want to imply that personal and individual notice to every person affected was required in the present case. But some sort of general notice, perhaps by newspaper advertisement, and an opportunity to submit representations was surely required before a decision was taken. I note that even the umbrella representative organizations, who were consulted, complained about insufficient notice being given to allow for proper consideration of the proposal. (...) I go no further than to say that the rules of fairness require that the persons affected by the decision taken, particularly those who were going to have economic rents which they enjoyed taken away and given to their competitors, should at least have had general notice of what was contemplated and an opportunity to respond thereto and comment thereon before the decision was taken.

With respect to the argument that the May 8, 1989, Notice to Importers was a policy decision only and therefore no notice was required. This characterization relies heavily on the Supreme Court decision in *Maple Lodge Farms*. ...

[After distinguishing *Maple Lodge Farms* on the basis that the decision dealt with the issuance of supplementary permits with respect to which the minister had a clearly discretionary decision-making authority, Reed J continued.]

... Secondly, however, I am not convinced that classifying a decision as being of a "policy" nature necessarily immunizes it from judicial review; see, for example, *R v. Liverpool Corporation*, (*supra*). For the same reasons that I do not think classifying the decision as "legislative" is useful in the present case, equally I do not think that classifying a decision as a policy decision is helpful either. What is important is an assessment of the effects which actually follow from the decision. In the present case, the decision was not treated as one according the Minister residual discretionary authority although it is not contested that he could have changed the decision. The decision was treated as setting down rules according to which, permits would be and were strictly issued. These were not administrative guidelines for internal administrative use. After the Notice to Importers was issued, its terms for issuing permits were followed automatically. The decision was being applied as a binding decision with respect to the issuance of permits. No discretion was left to an official acting in the name of the Minister to depart from the system of quota allocation which was detailed in the notice. The effect of the decision was to visit considerable economic loss on the applicants.

[Reed J went on to hold that the historic importers had not been accorded sufficient procedural protections before the changes were made and made an order to the effect of continuing their entitlements under the old scheme, at least until such time as the matter had been re-evaluated in the light of their submissions.]

The judgment of a Federal Court of Appeal consisting of Heald and Linden JJA and Gray DJ was delivered by

LINDEN JA: ... As for the need to comply with natural justice principles in this case, there is a fundamental disagreement. The Trial Judge held that some form of notice to the respondents was required as well as an effective opportunity to be heard. The appellants challenge this view, whereas the respondents support it.

Generally, the rules of natural justice are not applicable to legislative or policy decisions. [Linden JA here quoted from the standard Supreme Court of Canada authorities including *Inuit Tapirisat* and Dickson J in *Martineau*.]

More particularly, it has been held that the principles of natural justice are not applicable to the setting of a quota policy although they may be to individual decisions respecting grants of quotas. In *Re Bedesky and Farm Products Marketing Board of Ontario* (1975) 58 DLR (3d) 484 (Ont. Div. Ct.), aff'd. 62 DLR (3d) 266 (Ont. CA), leave to appeal refused 62 DLR (3d) 266n, Morden J stated at 507:

> No authority was cited to us for the proposition that the principles of natural justice respecting the right to notice and the right to be heard are applicable to govern a body such as the Chicken Board with respect to the devising and adopting of a quota policy. In fact, the law would appear to be to the contrary. ...

I can see no reason to differentiate the situation where, as here, it is a Minister rather than a Board that is establishing the quota. Some may be damaged while others may gain by such a quota, but the exercise is essentially a legislative or policy matter, with which Courts do not normally interfere. Any remedy that may be available would be political, not legal. It might have been a considerate thing for the Minister to give the respondents notice and an opportunity to be heard, but he was not required to do so.

In essence, what the respondents are seeking here is to impose a public consultation process on the Minister when no such thing has been contemplated by the legislation. There are statutes in which regulations or policies cannot be promulgated without notifying and consulting the public. (See, for example, *Grain Futures Act*, RSC 1985, c. G-11, s. 5(2), *Aeronautics Act*, RSC 1985, c. A-2, ss. 5 and 6; *Transportation of Dangerous Goods Act*, RSC 1985, c. T-19, s. 22(1); and *Broadcasting Act*, RSC 1985, c. B-9.01, s. 11(5).) No such legislative provision appears in the *Export and Import Permits Act*, RSC 1985, c. E-19, something that Parliament could have inserted if it wanted notice to be given and consultation with the public to be held.

. . .

Appeal allowed. Application dismissed.

NOTE

Who has the better of this argument from the perspective of both policy and precedent? Is Reed J going as far as to impose a public consultation process on all quota allocation exercises? If the procedural claim here is one that is seen as peculiar to the historic importers, does that do justice to others affected by this decision? Does Linden JA's invocation of the *expressio unius* canon of statutory interpretation carry much weight?

Individualized Decision Making Based on Exercise of Broad Discretionary Powers

In the light of *Canadian Association of Regulated Importers* and other judgments dealing with the dimensions of the term "of a legislative or general nature," how do you think a Canadian would today deal with *Calgary Power v. Copithorne*, [1959] SCR 24 (Alta.), where the Supreme Court denied the procedural claims of a farmer, a portion of whose land was being expropriated to enable the construction of power transmission lines as part of a large power delivery project, by characterizing the expropriation as a policy decision by a minister of the Crown for which he would be accountable in the legislature? (In *Favor v. Winnipeg (City)* (1988), 47 DLR (4th) 693 (Man. CA), the court applied *Calgary Power* on the basis of a statutory scheme that contemplated an inquiry into the merits of an expropriation decision after it had been taken with the lieutenant governor in council having the authority to dispense with the holding of such an inquiry.) Recollect also the cases we identified in the notes to *Knight* concerning the layoff of statutory employees for budgetary and other general policy reasons.

This whole question of the limits of procedural claims in the context of individualized decision making is also raised by the judgment of the Supreme Court of Canada in *Idziak v. Canada (Minister of Justice)*, [1992] 3 SCR 631 (Ont.). Here, the claim advanced was that the minister of justice had an obligation of procedural fairness in deciding whether to actually surrender a person to a foreign power after a deportation order had been made. In describing this function as "being at the extreme legislative end of the *continuum* of administrative decision making," Cory J made it abundantly clear that there was not a clear dichotomy in the court's mind between "legislative" decisions and decisions that have as their target a particular individual. Nonetheless, he did accept that the minister had a duty to act fairly and the majority of the court also accepted that the relevant confidential memorandum from an in-house lawyer contained no new prejudicial information. However, in a judgment concurring in the result, La Forest J placed his decision on the following basis:

> In my view, in considering the issue of surrender in the present case, the Minister was engaged in making a policy decision rather in the nature of an act of clemency. In making a decision of this kind, the Minister is entitled to consider the views of her officials who are versed in the matter. I see no reason why she should be compelled to reveal these views. She was dealing with a policy matter wholly within her discretion; see *Attorney General of Canada v. Inuit Tapirisat* [1980] 2 SCR 735 (Can.) at 753-54.

The potential implications of this line of reasoning (which now finds parallels in *Suresh v. Canada (Minister of Citizenship and Immigration)*, [2002] 1 SCR 3 (Can.)) for both the common law and *Charter of Rights and Freedoms* (which was also argued in this case) protection of procedural rights are staggering. In particular, concerns have to be raised in this context about whether the individual interest at stake in cases such as this should be subservient to broader public and political interests. Indeed, what this judgment highlights is that it presumably should not be enough for the government agency to assert broader policy considerations in defence to a procedural fairness argument. Part of the role of the courts in cases such as this is that of evaluating the legitimacy and weight of those claims against the individual interest that is at stake with a view to determining whether there are any reasons of principle or utility for allowing that interest to be trumped at the procedural fairness level.

Decisions Affecting Rights, Privileges, or Interests

When Le Dain J spoke in *Cardinal* about the existence of a duty of fairness whenever "rights, privileges or interests" were at stake, it is quite possible that he was doing so not for the purposes of setting up a test in which "rights, privileges or interests" stood in contrast to some lesser form of claim. Rather, he may have been using this term in a positive or expansive sense to indicate that the old law had ceased to be part of the terrain; that it was no longer necessary to establish that a "right" was affected but that mere privileges and interests qualified as well provided the decision in question was not a general or legislative one.

Looking at it in a slightly different way, he may have intended his expression of the basis for a claim to procedural fairness to be a compendious one and not to be disaggregated with the excluded category being those decisions that were of a general nature and that did not focus specifically on the situation of an individual or relatively discrete group of individuals. Irrespective of whether "rights, privileges or interests" were at stake, there could be no claim for procedures in relation to the exercise of such powers.

If either of these interpretations was the correct one, there would be no need to treat "rights, privileges or interests" as a possible source for the exclusion or denial of claims. Nonetheless, there are sufficient doubts as to justify some inquiry. For these purposes, we start with a judgment of the Ontario Court of Appeal that was decided almost immediately after *Nicholson* but before *Cardinal*. *Re Webb and Ontario Housing Corporation* is an important judgment for a number of reasons, including its treatment of the intersection between procedural fairness claims and the Ontario *Statutory Powers Procedure Act* and the sliding scale in procedural claims depending on the nature of the interest at stake. Even if the threshold no longer depends on a distinction between rights on the one hand and privileges and mere interests on the other, the extent of the procedures to be accorded clearly can. More particularly, however, *Webb* is included at this juncture for a point that MacKinnon JA (for the court) makes in passing about the distinctions between an applicant for accommodation in government-subsidised housing and an existing resident in such housing. This suggests a continuing relevance for threshold purposes between benefit holders and those seeking such benefits.

Re Webb and Ontario Housing Corporation
(1978), 93 DLR (3d) 187 (Ont. CA)

[Ontario Housing Corporation (OHC) owned some high-rise apartments in downtown Toronto that were managed for it by Meridian Property Management and that were leased at less than market rents to persons with low incomes. Webb and her children became tenants in August 1970. In 1973 Meridian recommended termination of the lease because of problems caused by Webb's children. OHC officials and its board of directors approved, and an application for termination of her lease was brought under the *Landlord and Tenant Act*, RSO 1970, c. 236. Webb made an application for review of the OHC decision, and the application under the *Landlord and Tenant Act* was stayed. Webb's application was dismissed and she appealed.]

MacKINNON ACJO delivered the judgment of the Court: In his able and attractive argument, Mr. Paliare made three submissions. They were:

(1) that the *Statutory Powers Procedure Act, 1971* (Ont.), c. 47, applies to a meeting of the Directors of OHC when they are considering the question of terminating a tenant's lease;

(2) if the *Statutory Powers Procedure Act, 1971* does not apply, the Court should grant an order in the nature of *certiorari* on the ground that the Board of Directors were conducting a judicial or *quasi*-judicial hearing to which the rules of natural justice applied and, in particular, the principle of *audi alteram partem*; and finally,

(3) even if the Board of Directors was performing an administrative function, on the facts of this case there was a "duty to act fairly," and the appellant had a "legitimate expectation" she would be treated fairly and this expectation was not met.

I can deal with the first two submissions very shortly. OHC is not given either the power or the obligation under the governing legislation to act judicially or *quasi*-judicially. In the instant case it did not determine the appellant's eligibility for welfare. What it did determine was whether to accept her and her family as tenants and subsequently to terminate that tenancy as part of its administration of its affairs. The lease agreement between the parties, as stated, was subject to the provisions of the *Landlord and Tenant Act* and the appellant, quite properly, took advantage of that Act in the proceedings before Judge Coo.

The OHC is given the power under the *Ontario Housing Corporation Act*, RSO 1970, c. 317, to acquire and dispose of property, to make loans and grants and to enter into agreements under the *Housing Development Act*, RSO 1970, c. 213. Under the latter Act they have the power to plan, construct and manage any housing project: s. 6(2).

. . .

Although there is a public aspect to this matter which I have noted and to which I shall refer later, the decision taken is only part of the administrative duties imposed on OHC. There is no judicial or *quasi*-judicial quality to its action in this regard. Courts must be careful not to "judicialize" every administrative act of every incorporated body (which has its powers by virtue of a statute) or life in this Province will come to a standstill.

In my view the Board of Directors was not a tribunal here exercising a statutory power of decision conferred by an Act of the Legislature where it was "required by or under such Act or otherwise by law to hold or to afford to the parties to the proceedings an opportunity for a hearing before making a decision." Accordingly, the determination to terminate the tenancy did not fall under the *Statutory Powers Procedure Act, 1971*. Equally, I do not accept the argument that there was here a *quasi*-judicial act which, at common law, required the strict application of the *audi alteram partem* principle so that the appellant was entitled to be notified of and to attend at the Board or other meeting called by OHC or its representatives to respond to the allegations made against her family prior to the final determination by the Board of Directors.

Having disposed of the first two grounds of appeal, I come to a much more difficult and, if I may say so, grayer area of the law. The submission that is made is that OHC, even if acting administratively, was required to treat this appellant "fairly." There has always seemed to me to be a rather backhanded quality to the proposition argued, as if the individual or corporate body would otherwise treat the complainant "unfairly." There surely can be actions which are neutral and which require no procedures to which the designation "fair" or "unfair" need be attached, where, in the exercise of public corporation's rights or in carrying out its obligations, the interests of others might be, quite properly, affected. The Courts are, however, increasingly applying the test of procedural "fairness" to administrative actions of donees of a power and there is, understandably and naturally, a predilection towards seeing that everyone is treated "fairly."

Is this a case where the facts warrant the application of this newly developing extension of a well-established principle?

[Discussions of *Nicholson*; *Goldberg v. Kelly*, 387 US 254 (1970); the *Family Benefits Act*, RSO 1970, c. 157; and the *General Welfare Assistance Act*, RSO 1970, c. 192 are omitted. *Goldberg v. Kelly* involved procedural requirements for termination of welfare benefits in New York. MacKinnon ACJO said that its reasoning was not useful here because the recipients had a statutory entitlement to the rights: "That, of course, is not the case here, where there is no statutory entitlement … to either secure or remain in subsidized housing."]

I recite some of the provisions of these statutes to illustrate that there is a statutory right in a person to receive assistance if he satisfies the eligibility requirements in the statutes and that, if he is not satisfied with the determination made at the first stage, he has a right to a hearing before a review tribunal. Should the respondent have the right, without notice or "hearing," to deprive the appellant of a benefit, granted by it in the carrying out of a public interest and, substantially, as an ancillary to the appellant's established welfare status? Such a proposition, submitted on behalf of the respondent, requires close examination.

It is clear in the instant case that the appellant is a welfare recipient who was accepted as a tenant because of the fact. It is common ground that the appellant would not secure a three-bedroom apartment for $95 a month rent in Toronto, other than as a tenant in publicly subsidized housing or as a matter of benevolence. As I mentioned earlier, counsel for the respondent acknowledged that there was an important public aspect to the operation of OHC and that was in providing subsidized housing, as a matter of provincial public policy, to the disadvantaged in the community. Once the appellant became a tenant she acquired a very real and substantial benefit because of her reliance on and eligibility for welfare. The determination to grant her this benefit was made when she was accepted as a tenant. That decision was one which, in my view, could be made by OHC without any intervention of a rule or principle of procedural "fairness." However, once she became a tenant and thus "qualified" for and received the very real benefit of a reduced and subsidized rent, the situation changed. As pointed out by Le Dain J, in the recent case of *Inuit Tapirisat of Canada v. Governor in Council* [[1979] 1 FC 710 (CA)], what is in issue in these cases is what is appropriate to require of a particular authority in the way of procedure, given the nature of the authority, the nature of its power and the consequences of the exercise of that power to the individuals affected, and, I would add, the nature of the relationship between the authority and the individuals affected. In my opinion, OHC, in exercising its power of termination and thereby depriving the appellant of the benefit of the lease, was required, under the circumstances, to treat the appellant fairly by telling her of the complaints(s) or case against her and giving her an opportunity, if she wished, to make an answer to those complaints.

This is not a problem area in which she can secure any relief under the *Landlord and Tenant Act*, although it is obvious that the deprivation of the benefit of subsidized housing, which she cannot secure elsewhere, would have serious adverse effects on her and on her family. She does not have the resources to substitute equivalent housing. The newly developing extension of the principle which I have recited is there equally to protect those who, because of their disadvantaged economic and social condition, are in the greatest need of protection from arbitrary and unconscionable acts of public authorities.

If no notice is given to a person who, as a result of an investigation by a public corporation in carrying out a public obligation, is in danger of losing an important benefit, and no opportunity is afforded to answer the "case" against him, such a procedure, in my view, would be unfair. Beyond that factual situation it may be that what constitutes fairness is, like beauty, to be found in the eye of the beholder. ... It is not necessary, when one is considering the question of fairness in administrative decisions that call for it, that a formal notice be given or that the trappings of formal proceedings be granted. So long as the person adversely affected is advised of the case against him and is permitted to give an answer through the servants or agents of the investigating body, that is sufficient, unless there is evidence of improper bias on the part of the servant or agent or evidence that the answer, if made, did not reach the body making the decision or determination.

. . .

On February 21, 1973 the property manager wrote to the appellant to advise her that there had been numerous complaints about the behaviour of her son and stated that if there was any repetition he would have no alternative but "to take the necessary steps to terminate her lease." On August 10, 1973, she was written to again and advised that continuance of the "anti-social behaviour" described in the letter might result in the matter being referred to the OHC "for their suitable action."

[In August 1973, OHC gave Webb a formal warning that if she did not "amend" her conduct she would be evicted.]

Although Mrs. Webb cannot read or write, her children, who lived with her, were attending school, and there is no suggestion by her that she did not receive or understand the notices sent to her. Further, Mrs. Karmanin [a "community relations worker" employed by OHC] swore that she had visited the appellant and her children on a number of occasions in her capacity as a community relations worker and discussed with her and the children the complaints and harassment of other tenants, the vandalism of the children, noise and "other related disturbances." Usually her visits to the appellant were precipitated by the receipt of a security occurrence report which cited the conduct of one of the appellant's children. Mrs. Karmainin further swore that she advised the appellant on a number of occasions prior to the notice to vacate given in October, 1973, that, if she were unable to control the behaviour of her children, management would have no alternative but to recommend that her lease be terminated. There was no denial by the appellant that these conversations took place and that this information was given to her. There is no suggestion that she had any "defence" to make to the complaints made or that, indeed, she took any interest in attempting to control her children or make an answer.

. . .

On the material which we have I am of the opinion that OHC did treat the appellant fairly. It let her know of the complaints and gave her an opportunity to remedy or answer them. There surely has to be some affirmative evidence that she did not know of the complaints or that she did answer them and the answer (or answers) was not considered by OHC. Such evidence is completely lacking in the case and indeed, as stated, the evidence is to the contrary.

. . .

The appellant has succeeded in establishing, on the facts of this case, that there was an obligation on OHC to treat her "fairly" in the conduct of its investigation and before terminating her lease. However, the evidence discloses that she was treated "fairly" as that word is now understood in its application to cases such as this. Accordingly, the appeal must fail and is dismissed without costs.

Appeal dismissed.

NOTE

At one level, *Webb* may be seen as progressive in that it at least recognizes that the holders of various forms of state assistance are entitled to some measure of procedural fairness before assistance is cut off or removed. They are no longer prevented from making such a claim on the basis that government benefits are a matter of privilege as opposed to right. Seen in this light, cases such as this expanded the reach of procedural fairness law beyond the traditional categories of property right and implicitly accorded recognition to the arguments made by Charles Reich in his seminal article, "The New Property" (1964), 73 *Yale LJ* 333.

However, aside from serious questions about whether holders of government assistance have the resources to consistently secure judicial enforcement of their procedural claims, *Webb* does not eliminate entirely the vestiges of the old hierarchy of claims or interests. Indeed, as noted already, once the initial threshold is crossed, rankings of interests still play a significant role in the assessment of what procedures are due. Why should Webb be accorded fewer procedural protections than a professional whose licence is being suspended or the owners of properties ordered "closed up" for health reasons as in *Saltfleet (Township) Board of Health v. Knapman*, [1956] SCR 877? Webb's stake in the housing unit may not be worth nearly as much money as the professional's practice or Knapman's property, but it would be a great mistake not to realize that it may be as important or much more important to her life. Can such differentiations be justified? Should it be any part of the courts' role in considering what procedures are due to take into account the extent to which the "beneficiaries" of such procedures will in fact be able to exercise them? Intuitively, one would think that a lawyer subject to professional discipline is far better located to take advantage of a trial-type hearing than welfare recipients are when their receipt of a government benefit is being threatened for cause.

To the extent that MacKinnon JA does draw a distinction between initial allocative decisions and subsequent withdrawal decisions for procedural purposes, is he justified? Obviously, there are considerations of resources and efficiency that enter into the design of processes for the distribution of "goods" for which there are a multitude of applicants: government-assisted housing; grants to cultural organizations; places in law school; membership in the judiciary. Indeed, sometimes, such goods are distributed by lottery because there seems no better way of making a decision, particularly within the limits of the granting agency's resources. On the other hand, in situations where, either as a matter of legislation or policy, qualifications and/or criteria are established for receipt of the benefit in question, distribution without regard to those qualifications and criteria would be illegal. In a sense, process is inevitable. It therefore is quite inappropriate to maintain that procedural fairness has no relevance to the allocation of benefits. Rather, the question is what level or type of process is demanded.

Often, of course, that level of process will be minimal, at least when compared to the way in which other kinds of adjudicators act. A reasonable level of fairness may be met simply by providing all applicants with the opportunity to fill in a form that seeks all the relevant information. However, for various reasons, that may not always be sufficient, and we need to ask a range of questions to decide whether more is required. Are there some interests and some types of allocative decisions where fairness demands greater procedural entitlements for applicants? Should the courts engage in a ranking of interests for these purposes? (Think again of the specific examples referred to in the previous paragraph—do some of them present claims to more extensive procedures than others?) What if the written form is not the decision-maker's only source of information? Should applicants always have access to that other information for the purposes of dealing with or countering it? Is there an obligation on the part of some allocators to hold personal interviews when the filling in of forms will exclude or prejudice some of the intended targets of a government benefit scheme? Intruding in this domain as well are two further considerations: the extent to which all applicants have to be treated alike in terms of procedures and the obligation, if any, of decision-makers to adhere to existing allocative mechanisms.

To elaborate further these concerns, we focus on the area of occupational licensing.

Hutfield v. Board of Fort Saskatchewan General Hospital District No. 98
(1986), 24 Admin. LR 250 (Alta. QB)

[In March 1984, Dr. Hutfield applied to be appointed to the medical staff of the Fort Saskatchewan General Hospital. The *Hospitals Act*, RSA 1980, c. H-11 gave the hospital board a general responsibility for its affairs and a power to make bylaws. Section 11 of the bylaws provided that applications for appointments were to be sent to the College of Physicians and Surgeons of Alberta for its recommendation and to the chief of its medical staff and to its appointments committee.

The application was sent to the college, which approved Hutfield, but in October 1984 the board rejected him. In December 1985, he applied again. The application was not sent to the college. The appointments committee considered it, without asking Hutfield to appear, and gave an oral adverse recommendation. Hutfield asked to appear before the board when it considered the application, but he was refused, and in February the board rejected him again and refused to give reasons. He sought *certiorari* to quash its decision and *mandamus* to compel a reconsideration.]

McDONALD J: ...

It is true that there are few judicial decisions evidencing the availability of *certiorari*, or the imposition of a duty to act judicially or fairly, when the exercise of the public duty has resulted not in the revocation or modification of a permission or licence, but in a refusal of a grant of permission or licence in the first place. In the latter situation, there has been a tendency to grant prerogative relief or impose such a duty only where there is some special circumstance. For example, where the permission sought is a zoning or development permit and the granting of such a permit has been refused by the body exercising statutory planning authority, the duty to act judicially is recognized, and is enforced by *certiorari* in numerous cases, because the refusal to grant the permit limits the common law right of ownership of land.

Another example is found in recent English cases which have held that judicial review will protect enhanced procedural protection when there is on the part of the applicant a "legitimate expectation" of obtaining the permission sought, as compared with a mere hope of success or benefit: See *Schmidt v. Secretary of State for Home Affairs* [1969] 2 Ch. 149 .... Another example is where the public authority is required by statute to have regard only to certain specified matters and the applicant has a legitimate expectation of obtaining the permission unless certain adverse findings are made against him in regard to those matters (*e.g.* the character and suitability of an applicant for a certificate of consent in relation to a gaming licence): See *R v. Gaming Board for Great Britain, ex p. Benaim and Khaida* [1970] 2 QB 417 (CA). ... [S]uch a case was regarded as being "different from that of applications for licences which might be granted or denied on any, or on very much wider, grounds—in such cases it would be harder to show any legitimate expectation of success." ... [A]n example of the latter ... [is] "where control of numbers may be a ground of rejection quite independent of any 'unsuitability' of the applicant." See also *McInnes v. Onslow-Fane* [1978] 1 WLR 1520 (Ch.), where Megarry V-C said that where a decision merely refuses to grant the applicant a right or position which he seeks, such as membership of an organization, or a licence to do certain acts, the applicant, particularly if he has had previous licence applications which have been unsuccessful, had no legitimate expectation of success. In that situation, Megarry V-C said, the duty of fairness applied, but required the decision-maker only to determine the application "honestly, and without bias or caprice." A final example is found where the public authority has given an undertaking as to the procedure it will follow, and fails to follow that procedure, thus defeating a legitimate expectation that there will be a hearing, for the holding of a hearing had been gratuitously promised: see *R v. Liverpool Corpn. ex p. Liverpool Taxi Fleet Operators' Association* [1972] 2 QB 299 (CA).

There are, however, cases in which the rules of natural justice were applied, and *certiorari* was held to be an appropriate remedy, where what the complainant had sought was in the nature of an initial licence or permission. One such case was *R v. Huntingdon Confirming Authority, ex p. George and Stamford Hotels Limited* [1929] 1 KB 698 (CA), although that may be regarded, one supposes, as having been a case where the refusal of a licence limited the right of a hotel proprietor to use his premises as he otherwise might do at common law. Viewed in this way, the case is of limited authority, as are all the planning cases where *certiorari* has been granted to require licensing or zoning authorities to give notice or otherwise hear the position of the applicant fairly. *Re H.K. (An infant)* [1967] 2 QB 617, one of the earliest cases recognizing a duty to act fairly, was a case in which it was held that that duty existed where what had occurred was the refusal of permission, namely permission by an immigration officer to admit a person on a specified ground. Another instance was *A-G v. Ryan* [1980] AC 718 (PC Bah.), where Lord Diplock, delivering the opinion of the Judicial Committee of the Privy Council, held that a Minister of the Bahamian government ought to have given a fair hearing to an applicant for registration as a citizen. (The remedy granted in that case was a declaration.)

In none of these cases can it be said that there was a legitimate expectation either of obtaining the permission sought, or of a particular procedure based on previous procedures or undertakings. Yet enhanced procedural standards were held to be applicable, and *certiorari* to be available.

A distinction *in kind* between the scope of judicial review and the expected standards of procedural fairness in the case of the modification or extinguishment of existing rights and interests, and the scope of judicial review and the expected standards of procedural fairness in the case of an application for a permission or consent not previously enjoyed, is a distinction that is not founded in principle. At best its source is a mixture of historical accident and of a misconception that the remedy of *certiorari* and the standards of natural justice ought to apply only where the conduct of the authority exercising the public duty determines rights in the sense of a right to which there is a corresponding obligation in law. However, that notion no longer governs, in light of:

(1) The recognition that it is not only rights but "interests" that the Courts will protect. ...

(2) The recognition that *certiorari* is available not only where there is a duty to act judicially but also where there is a duty to act fairly. ...

(3) The recognition that where there is a duty to act fairly, the content of that duty will vary from one situation to another. ...

(4) The artificiality of the distinction drawn in the recent English cases cited, that have pushed the frontiers of judicial review and procedural fairness outward but have limited them on grounds ("legitimate expectation" and "slur") that do not reflect a principle that can withstand scrutiny in the light of the object of judicial review by *certiorari*.

Three additional elements that may be present, and in this case are present, that will invite an inference that there is a duty to act judicially or fairly, and that *certiorari* will be an available remedy, are as follows:

(1) Section 11(3) of the by-laws requires the Chief of Staff and the staff committee to "investigate the credentials, training, suitability, experience and references of the applicant." As I shall later point out, these must, by implication, be the subject of reasons given in the recommendation to the Board, and must by implication be in issue before the Board itself. These specific matters involve facts or at least mixed fact and opinion. ...

(2) The nature of the specific matters that the By-laws require to be investigated by the Committee, and which as I shall point out must be the subject of reasons in the recommendations to the Board, and must by implication be in issue before the Board, gives rise to the following observation: Where a refusal of a licence casts a slur on the applicant's reputation or financial stability the duty to act fairly may well require that the body should offer an opportunity for a hearing: ...

(3) The general interests of the public may be, and in the present case, are affected by the decision of the Board to grant or not to grant hospital privileges to Dr Hutfield. A refusal of hospital privileges to him undoubtedly impairs his ability to provide that level of medical diagnosis and treatment that his licence as a member of the College of Physicians and Surgeons entitles the public to assume is within his professional reach. ...

These diverse strands of development of the principles applicable to the availability of *certiorari* as a remedy, and to the procedural standards that are expected of a body exercising a public duty pursuant to statute, may be blended into the following statements of principle: Such a body, if its decision will modify, extinguish or affect a right or interest of a person when that person's rights or interests are being considered and decided upon in a way that is in law or for practical purposes final, or final subject to appeal, must adhere to procedural standards the precise nature of which will depend upon the nature and extent of the right or interest. This will be so whether the body vested with the statutory power is effectively accountable for the exercise of its power to the executive arm of government or to an appellate body, and whether or not there is some reason, founded in principle or expedition or in a need for confidentiality or in some other factor, that dictates a particular procedural standard. A failure on the part of the adjudicating body to attain the procedural standards that are appropriate to the particular situation will attract quashing of the decision by the remedy of *certiorari* and, if thought necessary or desirable, the remedy of *mandamus* in aid. The grant of such remedies would be subject to established grounds upon which, even though the procedural standard has been breached, the court may refuse to grant a remedy in its discretion.

The Board has no duty to grant hospital privileges to an applicant such as Dr Hutfield, in the sense of a duty correlative to a right resting with Dr Hutfield to have hospital privileges. There is no such duty and no such right even if Dr Hutfield is professionally qualified. In terms of the recent English cases, it cannot even be said that he had a legitimate expectation of being granted hospital privileges by the Board; at best he had a hope of benefiting from the Board's decision on his application. Nevertheless, there is no doubt that his professional interests would be affected by the decision. Moreover, if the staff committee recommends that he be denied hospital privileges, it is a justifiable inference that there has been a finding adverse to him in regard to one or more of his "credentials, training, suitability, experience or references," and such a recommendation therefore casts a slur upon his reputation. He is a doctor practising in the district. His ability to diagnose and treat his patients is limited so long as he is refused hospital privileges by the Board of this hospital. Thus his interests are more directly affected than would be those of a doctor not practising in the district, or in Alberta at all, if such a doctor were to apply to the Board of this hospital for hospital privileges. For those reasons, in my view, Dr Hutfield's interests are affected sufficiently directly and substantially that, if the appropriate standards of procedural fairness have not been complied with by the medical staff committee in the first place, or by the Board in the second place, *certiorari* is available to quash its decision.

[McDonald J concluded that the board should have given reasons for its decision; we discuss the duty to give reasons in chapter 4 of this text. He also concluded that the board's decision was invalid because the second application had not been sent to the college and because the appointments committee had not given a written report with its reasons.]

Application allowed.

NOTES

1. *Hutfield* was affirmed on appeal ((1988), 31 Admin. LR 311 (Alta. CA)), but on somewhat narrower grounds. The Court of Appeal distinguished previous cases denying procedural protections to "privilege seekers" on the basis of the existence of strong indicia in both the statute and the bylaws of the need for a hearing.

2. In *McInnes* (discussed by McDonald J) and *Hutfield*, the judges talk of an "expectation" or "legitimate expectation" of a hearing on the part of applicants. This terminology was
shortly to find an established place in procedural fairness law and discourse and, later in this
chapter, we will examine the evolution of claims to procedural fairness based on "legitimate
expectation." However, at this juncture, it is worth asking why in *McInnes v. Onslow-Fane*, a
case involving an application for a boxing manager's licence, Megarry J was not convinced
that McInnes had such an expectation or any entitlement to a hearing even though in the
past he had held various other forms of licence from the British Boxing Board of Control, a
private organization with an effective monopoly over the conduct of the sport? In contrast,
in *Hutfield*, McDonald J was persuaded that even though Hutfield did not have an expectation in terms of the English authorities, nonetheless, he had "built up" an entitlement to a
hearing. Is such a differentiation between the two cases justified? More generally, what, if
anything, hinges on the difference between boxing and medicine as occupations or on the
fact that one involved a statutory regime and the other did not?

3. For a Canadian equivalent to *Ryan*, see the judgment of Thurlow J of the Federal
Court of Appeal in the pre-*Nicholson* case of *Lazarov v. Secretary of State of Canada*, [1973]
FC 927 (CA). *Lazarov* involved an application for Canadian citizenship. The *Citizenship Act*,
RSC 1970, c. C-19, s. 10(1) provided that an applicant must satisfy the citizenship court that
he or she met a set of specified requirements, and gave the secretary of state power, if the
court was satisfied, to grant citizenship "in his discretion." Lazarov applied and satisfied the
court about the requirements, but the secretary refused, "in the light of confidential information recently provided by the Royal Canadian Mounted Police," without giving Lazarov
any opportunity of responding to this information. Lazarov sought review and succeeded.
Thurlow J said that "it would be difficult to conceive of a broader discretion," and the government based its argument on this discretion and on the absence of any right to citizenship. Thurlow J said:

> Leaving aside any question of declining the grant of certificates to particular classes of persons
> on grounds of broad general policy, which as I see it, it is not necessary to consider, it seems to
> me that whenever the reason for contemplating refusal of an application is one that is peculiar
> to the particular applicant, the nature of citizenship and its importance to the individual are
> such that the applicant ought at least to have an opportunity of some kind and at some stage of
> the proceedings to dispute its existence.
>
> ...
>
> In my opinion, therefore, the rule *audi alteram partem* applies whenever the Minister pro-
> poses to exercise his discretion to refuse an application on the basis of facts pertaining to the
> particular applicant or his application and where he has not already had an opportunity in the
> course of the proceedings before the Citizenship Court he must be afforded a fair opportunity
> in one way or another of stating his position with respect of any matters which in the absence
> of refutation or explanation would lead to the rejection of his application. That is not to say that
> a confidential report or its contents need be disclosed to him but the pertinent allegations
> which if undenied or unresolved would lead to rejection of his application must, as I see it, be
> made known to him to an extent sufficient to enable him to respond to them and he must have
> a fair opportunity to dispute or explain them.

4. In general, as indicated by *McInnes*, when a licence is being taken away for cause, there will be an obligation of procedural fairness, more often than not requiring hearing obligations at the high end of the range. What, however, is the situation in the case of renewals? As we have seen already, the concept of "legitimate expectation" has had a role to play here: *FAI Insurances v. Winneke* (1982), 151 CLR 342 (Vict.). The longer the licence has been held, the greater the interest in renewal and the stronger the entitlement to procedural fairness. More generally, the courts have come to recognize a more general need for procedural fairness in the context of licence renewal decisions particularly to the extent that the basis for non-renewal has been cause. Thus, in *Everett v. Canada (Minister of Fisheries and Oceans)* (1994), 169 NR 100 (FCA), the Federal Court of Appeal held that a fisherman was entitled to procedural fairness notwithstanding the fact that the legislation stated that renewal of the licences in question was in the absolute discretion of the minister. To the extent that the non-renewal was based on allegations of serious infractions of conservation regulations, there was a strong claim for a hearing entitlement (though, on the facts, the court found no denial). What, however, should be the situation where such a non-renewal is the result of a ministerial decision to reduce the number of licences? Should that negate all claims to procedural fairness?

5. Another context in which a distinction has been made between the grant and removal of a benefit is to found in *Desjardins v. Bouchard*, [1983] 2 FC 641 (CA), noted already in the context of the hearing obligations of the governor in council. There, Le Dain J held that the revocation of a pardon under the *Criminal Records Act*, RSC 1970, c. 12 (1st Supp.) imposed limited procedural obligations on the governor in council whereas there was no such duty attendant upon the initial grant of a pardon. Can this differentiation be justified? One of the important distinctions between this kind of case and the benefit-seeking jurisprudence that we have been considering up to this point is that it does not involve a competition or the allocation of scarce goods. Does that consideration enhance or decrease the claims for procedural fairness?

Think about this issue in the context of other discretionary "benefits," such as the ministerial discretion under the *Immigration Act* to permit persons otherwise illegally here to remain on "humanitarian and compassionate grounds." As we have seen already in chapter 2, in *Baker*, the Supreme Court of Canada rejected *Shah v. Canada (Minister of Employment and Immigration)* (1994), 170 NR 238 (FCA), in which the court characterized the procedural obligations in such cases as minimal. Rather, it attracted a high level of procedural fairness. What does this say more generally for the whole category of application cases? Does it confirm once and for all that the court was incorrect in *Webb* in asserting no procedural protections for those applying for Ontario government subsidized housing?

Inspections and Recommendations

In the traditional doctrine, two functions were distinctive: investigating and recommending. Until the late 1970s, the doctrine was clear: no hearings were required, and this proposition was a product of the general doctrine about the threshold—the functions were not judicial. One of the leading and representative cases was *Guay v. Lafleur*, [1965] SCR 12 (Que.). Lafleur was authorized under the *Income Tax Act*, RSC 1952, s. 148 to investigate the

financial affairs of a number of taxpayers, including Guay. Lafleur began to examine witnesses, and Guay requested to be allowed to be present and to be represented by counsel
during these examinations. Lafleur refused, and Guay sought an injunction. The Supreme
Court held that Guay had no right to a hearing because the function was "purely administrative"—Lafleur was not deciding or adjudicating. Another example is *Re Training Schools
Advisory Board* (1971), 22 DLR (3d) 129 (Ont. HC). The Training Schools Advisory Board
was established by regulation to give the minister of correctional services advice about the
exercise of a power to order termination of wardships. After the board refused to recommend termination of the wardship of a girl, her mother sought disclosure of reports from
the board. Her claim failed, again because "the board does not decide anything." We also see
the lingering effects of this jurisprudence as recently as *Knight* where L'Heureux-Dubé J
stated that "[a] decision of a preliminary nature will not in general trigger the duty to act
fairly, whereas a decision of a more final nature may have that effect."

The doctrine in fact changed in England during the 1970s, and the first major case in the
course of change was *In re Pergamon Press*, [1971] Ch. 388 (CA). The Board of Trade appointed inspectors to investigate the affairs of Pergamon Press. The principals of Pergamon
demanded to see transcripts of the evidence of witnesses adverse to them, an opportunity to
cross-examine, and an opportunity to respond to proposed findings. Lord Denning MR said:

> It seems to me that this claim on their part went too far. This inquiry was not a court of law. It
> was an investigation in the public interest, in which all should surely co-operate, as they prom-
> ised to do. But if the directors went too far on their side, I am afraid that counsel for the inspec-
> tors went too far on the other. He did it very tactfully, but he did suggest that in point of law,
> the inspectors were not bound by the rules of natural justice. He said that in all the cases where
> natural justice had been applied hitherto, the tribunal was under a duty to come to a determin-
> ation or decision of some kind or other. He submitted that when there was no determination
> or decision but only an investigation or inquiry, the rules of natural justice did not apply. ... I
> cannot accept counsel for the inspectors' submission. It is true, of course, that the inspectors are
> not a court of law. Their proceedings are not judicial proceedings. ... They are not even *quasi*-
> judicial, for they decide nothing; they determine nothing. They only investigate and report.
> They sit in private and are not entitled to admit the public to their meeting. ... They do not even
> decide whether this is a *prima facie* case. ...
>
> But this should not lead us to minimise the significance of their task. They have to make a
> report which may have wide repercussions. They may, if they think fit, make findings of fact
> which are very damaging to those whom they name. They may accuse some; they may con-
> demn others; they may ruin reputations or careers. Their report may lead to judicial proceed-
> ings. It may expose persons to criminal prosecutions or to civil actions. It may bring about the
> winding-up of the company, and be used itself as material for the winding up. ... Even before
> the inspectors make their report, they may inform the Board of Trade of facts which tend to
> show that an offence has been committed—see s. 41 of the *Companies Act, 1967*. When they do
> make their report, the board are bound to send a copy of it to the company; and the board may
> in their discretion, publish it, if they think fit, to the public at large. Seeing that their work and
> their report may lead to such consequences, I am clearly of opinion that the inspectors must act
> fairly. This is a duty which rests on them, as on many other bodies, although they are not judi-
> cial, nor *quasi*-judicial, but only administrative; see *R v. Gaming Board for Great Britain, Ex*

parte Benaim [[1970] 2 QB 417 (CA)]. The inspectors can obtain information in any way which they think best, but before they condemn or criticise a man, they must give him a fair opportunity for correcting or contradicting what is said against him. They need not quote chapter and verse. An outline of the charge will usually suffice.

Very shortly after *Nicholson* and *Webb* were decided, the issue came to be re-examined in a Canadian context.

Re Abel and Advisory Review Board
(1979), 97 DLR (3d) 304 (Ont. Div. Ct.); aff'd. (1981), 119 DLR (3d) 101 (Ont. CA)

[The Advisory Review Board was created by order in council under the *Mental Health Act*, RSO 1970, c. 269. Its major function was to review annually all patients who were confined in psychiatric institutions under warrant of the lieutenant governor after being charged with criminal offences and being found not guilty by reason of insanity. It made a report about each patient to the lieutenant governor, which included any recommendations for release. The *Mental Health Act* provided:

29(1) Upon receipt of an application by the chairman, the review board shall conduct such inquiry as it considers necessary to reach a decision and may hold a hearing, which in the discretion of the review board may be held *in camera*, for the purpose of receiving oral testimony.

(2) Where a hearing is held, the patient may attend the hearing unless otherwise directed by the chairman and, where he does not attend, he may have a person appear as his representative.

(3) Where a hearing is held, the patient or his representative may call witnesses and make submissions and, with the permission of the chairman, may cross-examine witnesses.

(4) The officer in charge shall, for the purpose of an inquiry, furnish the chairman with such information and reports as the chairman requests.

(5) The review board or any member thereof may interview a patient or other person in private.

The lawyers for some patients, in preparing for this review, requested disclosure of the files kept by the institution about the patients, especially reports that were to be submitted to the board. This request was refused. At the hearing, the lawyers asked for disclosure of the reports given to the board. The chairman refused on the ground that he had no authority, and an application for review was made. The claim for access to the files of the facility failed because this disclosure was clearly prohibited by the Act. The difficult issue was disclosure from the board.]

GRANGE J: The Lieutenant-Governor is, of course, not bound to act upon the recommendations in the report, but I do not think I go too far—indeed I think I only state the obvious—when I say that a patient's only hope of release lies in a favourable recommendation by the Board.

Just as the Lieutenant-Governor need not act upon the Board's report so the Board need not act upon the information and reports of the officer in charge, but there can be no question that these will influence the Board and may in many cases be decisive. If counsel for the patient seeks, as he must, to represent his client properly, one can well understand his desire, even his imperative need, to examine such reports.

It is argued that the Board is not subject to review. The Board's report does not bind the Lieutenant-Governor and therefore the minimum rules for proceedings under the *Statutory Powers Procedure Act* do not apply, see s. 3(2)(g). ...

[Grange J discussed *certiorari* briefly and seemed to suggest that it would apply, even though the function of the board was advisory.]

One of the difficulties in determining the matter is the persistence in some judgments of the distinction between judicial and *quasi*-judicial functions on the one hand and those which are considered purely administrative on the other. In the former, it is said that the rules of natural justice apply but in the latter they do not. In England the distinction appears to have been abrogated. ...

... I find great difficulty in applying the distinction to any given situation or tribunal. I align myself with those who in this court have said that the distinction is not important, at least when the question of the duty to act fairly is concerned. ...

If then the rules of natural justice may apply notwithstanding that the proceeding will result in a recommendation only, I can think of no case where those rules should be more readily applied than the case at bar. As I said earlier, this is virtually the only chance (albeit an annual chance) that the applicants have of avoiding a lifetime of incarceration. The effect of the recommendation of the ARB is for the applicants of the most vital concern. De Smith in the 3rd edition of his work, *Judicial Review of Administrative Action* discusses the problem at 203 *et seq.*, and after concluding that the authorities are often in conflict suggests that the degree of proximity between the investigation and the decision and the exposure of the person investigated to harm are matters of paramount concern. Here the proximity is great. The second test of de Smith is easily met when one considers the effect the recommendation and its acceptance has on the freedom of the applicants.

One of the fundamental rules of natural justice is, of course, as put by de Smith (at 178), "A party must have an adequate opportunity of knowing the case he has to meet, of answering it and of putting his own case." That is not however to say that the reports must necessarily be revealed. Normally he should be given the opportunity of perusal. One can readily imagine those reports containing allegations of fact detrimental to the applicant which could readily be refuted. But there may be circumstances militating against full disclosure. ...

There is no question that the exercise of the discretion to require the production of the reports might in this instance cause grievous harm to the administration of the Centre and indeed to the patient. But the problem as I see it is that the question was never faced. The Chairman denied the request for production upon the ground that he had no jurisdiction. No doubt he meant that he had no jurisdiction to order the Medical Centre to produce the files; he needed no jurisdiction to hand over to the applicants' counsel the reports which the Board had received pursuant to s. 29(4) of the *Mental Health Act*. What was needed, in my respectful opinion, was consideration of whether or not those reports should be disclosed to the applicants. When the Chairman failed to consider that question and answer it according to proper principles there was a failure of natural justice.

It follows that in my opinion the application against the ARB must be granted, the decision of the Chairman in refusing to order production of the reports of the officer in charge quashed, and the matter remitted to the Board for reconsideration in accordance with the principles set out above. ...

For the reasons I have set forth earlier I would quash the decision of the Board notwithstanding the non-binding nature of its report. There have now been released the reasons of the Supreme Court of Canada in *Re Nicholson and Haldimand-Norfolk Regional Board of Commissioners of Police*, and those of the Court of Appeal in *Re Webb and Ontario Housing Corporation*. While neither of these cases concerned a non-binding report, they both reaffirmed and perhaps extended the duty of fairness required of all persons or bodies exercising power even though the exercise of that power might be classed as administrative rather than judicial or *quasi*-judicial. The obligation to "act fairly" perhaps lacks precision of definition and doubtless it involves something less than the strict application of the rules of natural justice but it may in some circumstances involve the application of some or all of those rules. Certainly in my opinion, it embraced in these circumstances the consideration upon proper principles of whether or not the reports should be disclosed to the applicants. In failing to give to that question that consideration, the Board, in my respectful opinion, failed to meet the legal test of fairness.

[Southey J gave a concurring judgment. O'Driscoll J dissented, in part because the board "is not subject to review because the board's report ... does not bind the Lieutenant-Governor and thus the minimum rules for proceedings under the *Statutory Powers Procedure Act, 1971* ... do not apply."]

Application granted.

[The Crown appealed. The Court of Appeal affirmed the decision of the Divisional Court about the procedures for substantially the same reasons that were given by Grange J.]

NOTES

1. For further elaboration of the procedural duties of the Advisory Review Board, see *Re Egglestone & Mousseau and Advisory Review Board* (1983), 150 DLR (3d) 86 (Ont. Div. Ct.). The process of automatic detention under s. 542(2) of the *Criminal Code* was invalidated as violating ss. 7 and 9 of the *Canadian Charter of Rights and Freedoms* (*R v. Swain*, [1991] 1 SCR 933 (Ont.)). While the review process itself was not invalidated (see (1986), 53 OR (2d) 609 (CA)), the *Criminal Code* was amended and a new review process was put in place. It provides for a review board consisting of a judge and two health-care professionals. The amendments eliminated the role of the lieutenant governors and made the review boards decisions determinative: see *Criminal Code*, RSC 1985, c. 46 (as amended by SC 1991, c. 43), part XX.1, Mental Disorder, ss. 672.1*ff.*

2. For an interesting application of *Abel* and very useful discussion of the factors involved in determining the existence and content of procedural fairness obligations in the case of non-dispositive decisions, see *Re Munro* (1993), 105 DLR (4th) 342 (Sask. CA). In a judgment delivered by Bayda CJS, the court held that the executive committee of the Saskatchewan Teachers' Federation was obliged to afford Munro procedural protections before it recommended to the minister of education that he or she not accept the recommendations of the Federation's discipline committee that Munro be suspended from teaching for five years but rather cancel his teaching certificate. Despite the fact that the executive committee was bound by the discipline committee's findings of fact, Bayda CJS, with particular reference to the importance of hearings in the context of decisions about sanctions, held that the executive committee had failed in its duty of procedural fairness by not providing Munro with a copy of the discipline committee's report and recommendations and an opportunity to address the issue of sanctions.

3. One of the questions left dangling by *Abel* (and also raised by *Munro*) is whether the affected person's entitlement to procedural fairness is exhausted at the recommendatory level or whether there might either generally or in some instances be a further claim for procedural fairness from the executive official to whom the recommendation is made. In the context of the Advisory Review Board, German J held in *Conway v. Ontario (Attorney General)* (1991), 86 DLR (4th) 655 (Ont. Div. Ct.) that there could be continuing obligations of procedural fairness even at the lieutenant governor stage, particularly in relation to reports prepared for the royal representative, which might either add new material or present an unfair picture of the prior proceedings and recommendations of the Advisory Review Board. However, this did not mean an oral or in-person hearing before the lieutenant governor, but, rather, access to the relevant material and an opportunity to make written submissions. See also *O'Shea v. Parole Board of South Australia* (1987), 163 CLR 378 (SA), rejecting any notion of a hearing by the governor in council under the South Australian equivalent but not contemplating the possibility of new material not contained in the report of the Parole Board.

4. For further elaboration of the hearing obligations of ministers of the Crown, royal representatives, and cabinets when presented with a report with recommendations, recollect *Desjardins v. Bouchard*, above, and see *Haoucher v. Minister for Immigration and Ethnic Affairs* (1990), 169 CLR 648 (Aust.) and *Thomson v. Canada (Department of Agriculture)*, [1992] 1 SCR 385 (Can.). See also *Idziak v. Canada*, above, on the procedural fairness obligations of the minister of justice in extradition proceedings.

5. Note also the disposition made in *Abel*. The outcome was not an order for production but rather a quashing and remission back for reconsideration of the procedural claims made by Abel and his counsel. This indicates at least some predisposition on the part of the court not to usurp the review board's discretion in relation to procedural matters and suggests that, at least on occasion, procedural rulings by tribunals are entitled to a measure of deference and are not to be reviewed on a simple correctness basis. This is a theme to which we return later in this chapter. However, in the context of *Abel*, consider when such a posture of judicial restraint in the review of procedural rulings might be indicated.

6. Also worth recollecting in this context is the issue we raised in the context of *Cooper*: what is the impact on procedural fairness claims of a statutory provision of a full hearing on appeal? For two cases to the effect that this does eliminate procedural fairness claims at the initial stage, see *Forsythe v. Alberta (Administrator, Private Investigators and Security Guards*

Act) (1993), 19 Admin. LR (2d) 187 (Alta. QB) (suspension of a private investigation agency's licences without a hearing on laying of charges under the *Criminal Code* against one of its principals) and *Zahab v. Salvation Army Grace Hospital—Ottawa* (1991), 3 Admin. LR (2d) 307 (Ont. Div. Ct.) (revocation of doctor's hospital privileges).

———————

What is apparent from *Abel* is that, even in the wake of *Nicholson*, not all recommendatory and investigative functions will attract an obligation of procedural fairness and this is reaffirmed by L'Heureux-Dubé J in her judgment in *Knight* when she states that a "decision of a preliminary nature will not in general trigger the duty to act fairly." While *Abel* does provide us with a useful functional test for discerning the "exceptional" cases in which that duty will be triggered, it is nonetheless not a bright line standard as the jurisprudence relating to those whose functions is primarily investigative illustrates graphically.

Dairy Producers' Co-operative Ltd. v. Saskatchewan (Human Rights Commission)
[1994] 4 WWR 90 (Sask. QB)

[Following a complaint of workplace sexual harassment, the commission had appointed an officer to investigate and provide the commission with a report on whether there was a sufficient basis for recommending the appointment of a board of inquiry to adjudicate on the complaints. This process of investigation was provided for in detail in regulations promulgated under the Act. The company was informed of the complaint and the investigation proceeded. However, throughout its progress, the company sought unsuccessfully to secure further and better particulars of the complaint. Ultimately, the investigator reported that there was probable cause to believe that there had been an infringement of the Act. As a consequence, the commission, acting under its mandate, attempted to settle the matter. In the course of these abortive efforts, the company was provided with full details of the complaints and the evidence supporting them. When settlement attempts failed, a board of inquiry was established. At this juncture, the company applied to the court for (*inter alia*) orders quashing the establishing of the board of inquiry and the investigator's report that there was "probable cause" to believe that there had been an infringement of the Act. This application was based on allegations of breach of the rules of procedural fairness during the process leading up to the striking of the board of inquiry.]

WRIGHT J: ... The test to be applied to an investigation was settled in *Syndicat des employés de production du Quebec et de l'Acadie v. Canadian Human Rights Commission* [1989] 2 SCR 879 (Can.). The following statement (at 899):

> ... It is not intended that this be a determination where the evidence is weighed as in a judicial proceeding but rather the Commission must determine whether there is a reasonable basis in the evidence for proceeding to the next stage. It was not intended that there be a formal hearing preliminary to the decision as to whether to appoint a tribunal. Rather the process moves from the investigatory stage to the judicial or quasi-judicial stage if the test

prescribed in section 36(3)(a) is met. Accordingly, I conclude from the foregoing that, in view of the nature of the Commission's function and giving effect to the statutory provisions referred to, it was not intended that the Commission comply with the formal rules of natural justice. In accordance with the principles in *Nicholson, supra*, however, I would supplement the statutory provisions by requiring the Commission to comply with the rules of procedural fairness. …

Thus the Commission is not obliged to comply with the formal rules of natural justice.

This decision repeats the conclusions reached in the earlier judgments in *Federation of Women Teachers' Association of Ontario v. Human Rights Commission (Ontario)* (1988) 30 OAC 301 and *Re Dagg and Ontario Human Rights Commission* (1979) 6 OR (2d) 100, decisions of the Ontario Divisional Court. *Dagg* contains, at 104, this statement:

> … But even assuming that the Commission and the Minister were under a duty in exercising their administrative functions to be "fair" as has been suggested in some of the cases, it is our view that duty only required the Commission and/or the Minister to receive the representations of the applicant and to give to the applicant *the substance of the information upon which the Commission* and Minister relied in arriving at their respective decisions. In this particular case, we are satisfied on the evidence that the applicant was heard fully by the Commission and was given the substance of the information which influenced the Commission in deciding not to recommend the appointment of a board of inquiry, and which no doubt equally influenced the Minister to accept that recommendation. (emphasis added)

The *Federation of Women Teachers' Association of Ontario, supra*, contains, at 310, this conclusion:

> These cases and others make it clear that the duty of fairness owed when dealing with an investigative body is to inform an interested party of *the substance of the case against it* and allow an opportunity for responding representations or submissions. There is no requirement to disclose the whole file, but a duty to provide a fair summary of the relevant evidence (emphasis added).

The Supreme Court of Canada considered the matter again in *Radulesco v. Canadian Human Rights Commission* [1984] 2 SCR 406 (Can.). The Commission made the following formal statement or acknowledgement during the course of that case:

> … It also acknowledges that procedural fairness requires that the complainant be provided with an opportunity to make submissions, at least in writing, before any action is taken on the basis of the report; however, a hearing is not necessarily required. Finally, the Commission acknowledges that in order to ensure that such submissions are made on an informed basis, it must, prior to its decision, disclose the substance of the case against the party.

The court agreed. Lamer J said (410):

> … Without pronouncing upon all aspects of the standard of conduct the Commission must meet, I agree that the standard enunciated by the respondent is one which must, in all cases, be met. …

Sopinka J made the following statement in *Syndicat des employés de production du Quebec et de l'Acadie, supra*, at 902:

> Although it is not, strictly speaking, necessary to decide this issue in view of the conclusion reached above, the matter was dealt with extensively in the Court of Appeal and was fully argued here. It is therefore appropriate to observe that had I determined that the decision of the Commission was reviewable, I would have concluded as Marceau J did that the Commission committed no reviewable error. I agree with the reasons of Marceau J that the Commission had a duty to inform the parties of the substance of the evidence obtained by the investigator and which was put before the Commission. Furthermore, it was incumbent on the Commission to give the parties the opportunity to respond to this evidence and make all relevant representations in relation thereto.

These decisions pre-suppose that the report and/or recommendation of the investigating officer will result in a decision affecting another person's rights. If it does not, no duty of procedural fairness may arise. Do the three factors outlined in *Knight, supra*, apply?

The decision in *Hawrish v. Cundall* [(1989), 39 Admin. LR 255 (Sask. QB)] is apposite. There an investigative committee of a provincial law society, after an investigation, recommended the suspension of a member. Gerein J concluded that the committee was not bound to act fairly in the broad sense of the term as its recommendations did not affect the rights of Hawrish. In a sense, he held, the committee was analogous to the prosecutor who decides if a process should be initiated which may, ultimately, affect the rights of a person.

The investigator in *Kuntz v. Saskatchewan Association of Optometrists* [(1992) 8 Admin. LR (2d) 312 (Sask. QB)], had the power not only to investigate but to determine if the member in question engaged in a conflict of interest. As such, he had a duty to act fairly.

It is necessary to review the decisions in the cases such as *Radulesco, Syndicat des employés de production du Quebec et de l'Acadie* and *Dagg, supra*, in light of the foregoing.

Analysis

I. Did the investigating officer have a duty to act fairly? The investigating officer had no power to affect the rights of the applicant. At most she could report that "probable cause" existed. That in itself did not affect the rights of the applicant. The Commission decided if the matter should proceed: s. 28, s. 27(4). It was the Commission which decided the next step.

The next step, if the complaint was not dismissed, was settlement: s. 28. The settlement negotiations were not a determination of the rights of the applicant. Quite the opposite. It was only after that process was completed, unsuccessfully, that the Commission might act to set up the Board of Inquiry. It was not bound to do so as it might have dismissed the complaint at that juncture under s. 27(4). If the Commission decided to establish a Board of Inquiry undoubtedly it had a duty to provide the applicant with the substance of the evidence against it before any hearing.

II. What is the effect of the "without prejudice" letter and addendum? Initially, the applicant took the position the letter could not be referred to as it was written "without prejudice." In other words, even though the applicant was provided with a highly detailed list of particulars prior to the negotiations that was not acceptable. That objection was not renewed in argument and counsel in the course of their arguments dealt with the addendum as constituting the particulars of the complaints against the applicant.

III. What is the effect, if any, of the settlement negotiations? If the applicant wished to impugn the conduct of the investigator in not giving the substance of the evidence to the applicant before her report and recommendation, and assuming a duty of procedural fairness then existed, which I have found did not, it could have acted. Rather, it chose to proceed with the negotiations on the basis it knew the Commission's case. With the greatest respect, that decision amounted to a waiver of its right to object if it had one. The negotiations continued for more than six months and ultimately failed. There is no suggestion the applicant did not know precisely the complaints against it.

The argument that the applicant was entitled to respond to the investigator's report before she presented it to the Commission flies in the face of *Hawrish*. It is doubly difficult to accept in light of the negotiations which undoubtedly canvassed the many allegations of harassment and abuse.

The investigator and the Commission acted appropriately throughout. There has been no breach of procedural fairness by either. If the applicant has any doubts as to the complaints it must meet before the Board of Inquiry it may confirm that the case is to meet is that set out in the addendum.

Conclusion

The application is dismissed with costs to the respondents.

NOTES

1. Where a complaint that there has been a violation of a human rights code proceeds to a board of inquiry or tribunal, there is always a full hearing. Despite this, the weight of authority is that there is, nonetheless, a duty on human rights commissions to act in a procedurally fair manner before taking that step or recommending that a board of inquiry or tribunal be struck. Why? In what sense can the commission's proceedings be more than preliminary? Should it matter for these purposes whether the complaint of a failure of procedural fairness on the part of the commission is brought to the court by the complainant or a respondent? (See Mullan, "The Procedural Obligations of Tribunals That Do Not Hold Hearings" (1991), 47 *Admin. LR* 130.)

2. In *Cashin v. Canadian Broadcasting Corporation* (1984), 8 Admin. LR 161 (FCA), the court went as far as to hold that, in the case of the dismissal of a complaint by a human rights commission without recourse to a formal hearing, there was an obligation to afford some form of oral hearing with cross-examination rights when that decision was based at least in part on an assessment of conflicting evidence. Later cases do not appear to have cast the procedural fairness rights at the commission stage in terms of any sort of oral hearing though the precise issue is still a nice one. However, in the light of her comments in *Knight* about decisions of a preliminary nature, it is worth noting that, in her dissenting judgment in *Syndicat des employés de production du Quebec et de l'Acadie*, L'Heureux-Dubé J went

even further than Sopinka J delivering the majority judgment and saw the functions of the commission as at least *quasi*-judicial and attracting a high degree of procedural fairness.

3. In the *Dairy Producers' Co-operative* case, the court, by analogy to police investigations resulting in the laying of criminal charges, was not prepared to impose any duties of procedural fairness on the official charged by the commission with investigating a complaint that a *Human Rights Code* provision had been violated. This identifies at least one domain where procedural fairness obligations do not arise in an investigative arena. However, when one considers the extent to which commissions themselves are subject to at least some level of procedural fairness obligations as well as cases such as *Abel*, does the jurisprudence really correspond to L'Heureux-Dubé J's statement in *Knight* that "generally" preliminary stages in a decision-making process do not attract procedural fairness obligations?

4. Human rights commissions are not the only context in which this issue of procedural fairness obligations attendant on decisions on whether to hold a hearing have arisen: see for example *Gerula v. Ontario (Attorney General)*, [1979] OJ no. 493 (QL) (Div. Ct.) (distinguished in *Varity Corporation v. Ontario (Director of Employment Standards Branch)* (1989), 70 OR (2d) 513 (Div. Ct.)); *Hammond v. Association of BC Professional Foresters* (1991), 47 Admin. LR 20 (BC SC). However, in other situations, the analogy with a decision to lay charges in a criminal case has prevailed with the consequence that a duty of procedural fairness was not recognized: see *MacIver v. Law Society of Alberta* (1990), 46 Admin. LR 317 (Alta. QB) (decision of chair of discipline committee to appeal the decision of an investigating committee's hearing of a complaint against a lawyer). What criteria are appropriate for deciding into which of these two categories a case fits?

5. In this context, also worth considering is the high profile case of *Masters v. Ontario* (1994), 18 OR (3d) 551 (Div. Ct.). This involved allegations of unfairness levelled at investigators appointed by the premier of Ontario to report on allegations of sexual harassment made against the agent general of the government of Ontario in New York, a prerogative appointee. Adams J (for the court) held that the investigators owed Masters a duty of procedural fairness in the conduct of the inquiry though not one that amounted to a full trial-type hearing. He then concluded that that duty had been fulfilled even though Masters (or his counsel) was not given access to the questions that were asked of those interviewed, the names of those conducting specific interviews, or any notes, transcripts, or tapes of those interviews. It was sufficient that Masters was provided with a summary of the allegations and the opportunity to interview the witnesses himself or by his lawyer (though few agreed to be interviewed). This conclusion was not affected by the fact that, on the basis of Masters' detailed response to the summary provided, some witnesses were reinterviewed and provided further details (to which Masters had no access) before a final report was submitted to the premier (to which Masters was given an opportunity to respond). It is interesting that, in holding that the rules of procedural fairness applied to the investigative process put in train here, the court relied on *Knight*, notwithstanding L'Heureux-Dubé J's reservations as to the applicability of the principles of procedural fairness to decisions of a non-final nature.

6. *Irvine v. Canada (Restrictive Trade Practices Commission)*, [1987] 1 SCR 181 involved another multi-tiered process that included both investigative and adjudicative functions. Under the *Combines Investigation Act*, RSC 1970, c. C-23, a hearing officer appointed by the commission chair conducted a fact-finding investigation into possible anti-competitive practices, produced a statement of the evidence and provided it to the commission and to

the parties under investigation. The commission considered the statement and could decide to hold a full inquiry at which everyone received full procedural protection. Though the statute provided that persons appearing before a hearing officer could be represented by counsel, it did not specify counsels' role. Irvine challenged the hearing officer's rulings that his counsel could not be present when the officer interviewed potentially adverse witnesses and could not cross-examine these witnesses, claiming that procedural fairness entitled him to such procedures. Estey J, writing for the court, noted that the director made "no decisions in the sense of a final determination of a right or interest." Rather than concluding that procedural fairness did not apply, he decided that fairness did not provide Irvine with the right to cross-examine witnesses:

> Fairness is a flexible concept and its content varies depending on the nature of the inquiry and the consequences for the individuals involved. The characteristics of the proceeding, the nature of the resulting report and its circulation to the public, and the penalties which will result when events succeeding the report are put in train will determine the extent of the right to counsel and, where counsel is authorized by statute without further directive, the role of such counsel.

The court noted that the investigation conducted by the hearing officer and director was carried out completely in private, that findings and recommendations could be made public only after a full hearing by the commission and that, while a criminal prosecution was possible, the Act prevented testimony given during the proceedings from being used against an accused individual. Estey J concluded that, in deciding whether to supplement statutory procedures through common law procedural fairness, "[c]ourts must remain alert to the danger of unduly burdening and complicating the law enforcement investigative process. Where that process is in embryonic form engaged in the gathering of the raw material for further consideration, the inclination of the courts is away from intervention. Where, on the other hand, the investigation is conducted by a body seized of powers to determine, in a final sense or in the sense that detrimental impact may be suffered by the individual, the courts are more inclined to intervene. In the present case it was sufficient that the Hearing Officer allowed all the parties to be represented by counsel who could object to improper questioning and re-examine their clients to clarify the testimony given and to ensure that the full story was communicated by the witness counsel represented."

It is, of course, interesting that the court does not rest its decision on the proposition that the rules of natural justice or procedural fairness have no application to the investigation in question. Are there aspects of those rules that the corporations and persons under investigation would or should be able to invoke successfully? For an analysis of *Irvine*, see Evans, "Developments in Administrative Law: The 1986-87 Term" (1988), 10 *Sup. Ct. L Rev.* 1, at 55-59.

7. What seems clear from the statutory context in *Irvine* is that the investigation in question was one that did involve some, albeit limited, participatory rights for those affected. In contrast, as *Dairy Producers* made clear, where the statute simply establishes an investigative capacity, there is much more of a possibility that the courts will see this capacity as being the equivalent of police investigative powers not giving rise to any "hearing" entitlements on the part of those "under suspicion."

8. In a great many contexts, the procedural entitlements of those participating or implicated in investigations or inquiries will be dealt with by specific statutory provision. The inquiry in issue may be established under the federal or provincial general inquiries legislation

in which there are specific guarantees of participatory entitlement (see, for example, *Inquiries Act*, RSC 1985, c. I-11; *Public Inquiries Act*, RSO 1990, c. P.41, s. 5 to be replaced by *Public Inquiries Act, 2009*, SO 2009, c. 33, Sched. 6, s. 15). In other statutes, inquiry and investigative functions are set up by reference to that general inquiries legislation while still others will contain their own procedural regimes (see, for example, *Coroners Act*, RSO 1990, c. C.37 and especially ss. 40-53). However, the creation of such statutory investigative regimes does not mean that there are clear answers to all procedural questions. Often, the entitlement to participate is spelled out in ambiguous terms or expressed in the form of a discretion and, not surprisingly, such provisions generate disputes (as exemplified by the amount of litigation over the entitlement to participate in coroners' inquests: see *Black Action Defence Committee v. Huxter, Coroner* (1992), 11 OR (3d) 641 (Div. Ct.) as well as Estey J's judgment in *Irvine*). The same may hold for the specific content of the participants' procedural entitlements and there is also the possibility that the procedures set out in the relevant legislation will not be exhaustive of the issues that can arise: see, for example, *Hryciuk v. Ontario (Lieutenant Governor)* (1994), 18 OR (3d) 695 (Div. Ct.) (rev'd. on other grounds (1996), 31 OR (3d) 1 (CA)). (For an in-depth consideration of the procedural issues that arise in the context of public inquiries of this kind with recommendations for reform, see Ontario Law Reform Commission, *Report on Public Inquiries* (1992), and *Report on the Law of Coroners* (1995). Incidentally, it should be noted that coroner's inquests, inquiries under the *Public Inquiries Act*, as well as investigative authorities generally are excluded from the ambit of the Ontario *Statutory Powers Procedure Act*, RSO 1990, c. S.22, ss. 3(2)(e), (f), and (g).)

9. One of the matters generally dealt with in legislation governing inquiries is the procedural entitlements of those against whom adverse conclusions are drawn in any report. Thus, s. 5(2) of the *Public Inquiries Act*, RSO 1990, c. P.41 (to be replaced by *Public Inquiries Act, 2009*, SO 2009, c. 33, Sched. 6, s. 17), provides as follows:

> (2) No finding of misconduct on the part of any person shall be made against the person in any report of a commission after an inquiry unless that person has reasonable notice of the substance of the alleged misconduct and was allowed full opportunity during the inquiry to be heard in person or by counsel.

The federal equivalent of this provision gave rise to problems about the content and timing of such notices in *Canada (Attorney General) v. Canada (Commission of Inquiry on the Blood System in Canada—Krever Commission)*, [1997] 3 SCR 440 (Can.). We consider this case in detail in the section on notice in chapter 4 of this text.

In the context of inquiries and investigations not governed by such legislation, questions can sometimes be raised by the inclusion of adverse references to those who are not the direct target of the investigation (such as witnesses) or who are named in the context of a more general inquiry under the terms of reference of which there are no named or necessary targets. In general, it has been held that those against whom adverse statements are going to be made are entitled to be confronted with the concerns about their conduct and given an opportunity to respond: see *Re Royal Commission on Thomas Case*, [1982] 1 NZLR 252 (CA); *Re Erebus Royal Commission; Air New Zealand Ltd. v. Mahon (No. 2)*, [1981] 1 NZLR 618 (CA); *Mahon v. Air New Zealand Ltd.*, [1984] 1 AC 808 (PC NZ); and *In re Pergamon*

Press, [1971] Ch. 388 (CA). However, the Ontario Court of Appeal has held by reference to the principles governing ordinary litigation that this does not apply in the case of witnesses against whom adverse conclusions are drawn in the context of administrative adjudicative proceedings (such as an arbitration over refusal to offer a tenure track position at a university): see *Hurd v. Hewitt* (1994), 20 OR (3d) 639 (CA); rev'g. (1991), 13 Admin. LR (2d) 223 (Ont. Div. Ct.). Why the differentiation between the two species of decision? There seems little basis on which it can be justified in terms of impact on the reputations of those named.

Emergencies

On occasion, despite the fact that the basis for action will be the conduct of an individual and the consequences of that action the imposition of sanctions or diminution in property rights, there will be no requirement of a prior hearing. That is in the case of emergencies.

The leading Supreme Court of Canada authority dates from 1966. In *R v. Randolph*, [1966] SCR 260 (Can.), the court held that an interim order withdrawing the provision of mail services to an individual could be made without hearing when the statutory basis for making that decision was a belief that the mails were being used for criminal purposes. What, of course, is significant here, as it is in most of the emergency cases, is that the action in question is interim only and is open to reassessment in the context of a subsequent hearing. Indeed, in *Randolph*, the court's reasoning was influenced by an explicit provision for an after-the-event hearing. In such cases, it is useful to recall the principles on which the ordinary courts grant *ex parte* injunctions—they are always interim and the affected party on receiving notice has the right to come to court and apply to have the injunction discharged.

Recall that, in *Cardinal v. Director of Kent Institution*, [1985] 2 SCR 643 (BC), Le Dain J sustained the inmates' claim to procedural protections and refused to countenance arguments that relief should be denied on the basis that no hearing could affect the outcome. However, in that case, the entitlement to procedures was in the context of a reassessment of whether the inmates should be continued in administrative segregation. No question was raised about the entitlement of the director to immediately place them in administrative segregation on their arrival from another penitentiary where they had been criminally charged with taking a guard hostage at knifepoint. Indeed, Le Dain J expressly stated (at 661):

> Because of the apparently urgent or emergency nature of the decision to impose segregation *in the particular circumstances of the case*, there could be no requirement of prior notice and an opportunity to be heard before the decision. [Emphasis added.]

Note, however, that the court is not sanctioning a general rule of after-the-event hearings in administrative segregation cases. Whether initial action without a hearing is justified depends on an assessment of whether there is genuinely a need for such action. Nevertheless, it is highly likely that the court will pay considerable deference to the relevant authority's judgment as to the urgency of the situation. (See also *Conway v. Ontario (Attorney General)* (1991), 86 DLR (4th) 655 (Ont. Div. Ct.), involving the transfer of a person to a higher security psychiatric institution.)

Of course, on occasion, the provision of a subsequent hearing after the taking of emergency action may be redundant, such as where property is destroyed. (See, for example, s. 9(4) of the *Plant Quarantine Act*, RSC 1985, c. P-15, the predecessor of which was in issue in *Bertram S. Miller Ltd. v. The Queen*, [1986] 3 FC 291 (CA), a case that establishes that emergencies may also affect constitutional procedural entitlements, in that case s. 8 of the *Canadian Charter of Rights and Freedoms* and s. 2(e) of the *Canadian Bill of Rights*, and that compensation does not necessarily flow from such actions.) There may also be occasions on which emergency action is taken on the basis of information that cannot be revealed to the affected person either before or after the event. We return to this issue in the section on notice in the next chapter.

For further elaboration of this whole issue and examples, see Dussault and Borgeat, *Administrative Law: A Treatise*, 2nd ed., trans., Breen (Toronto: Carswell, 1990), at 270-75.

Legitimate Expectation

In recent years, one of the most discussed developments in the law relating to procedural fairness has been the emergence of the doctrine of legitimate expectation. In certain circumstances, procedures will be required by reason of expectations generated in an affected person and not be entirely contingent on a detached analysis of the statutory power in question. The reasons for the emergence of this doctrine are many and complex. However, one particular reason can be located in the doctrinal position of the British courts following *Ridge v. Baldwin*.

Notwithstanding their resurrection of a *Cooper*-style functional analysis in the discernment of implied procedural protections, the British courts appeared to maintain the position that such protections attached to the statutory power in question as opposed to particular exercises of it. In other words, procedural fairness was an all or nothing proposition; either it applied every time a power was being exercised or not at all: see *Durayappah v. Fernando*, [1967] 2 AC 337 (PC Cey.). Interestingly, the Supreme Court of Canada in the post-*Nicholson* era did not espouse this theory as it recognized that procedural fairness obligations did not necessarily attach to all exercises of a particular statutory power: *T.E. Quinn Truck Lines Ltd. v. Ontario (Minister of Transport and Communications)*, [1981] 2 SCR 657 (Ont.). This may have something to do with the belated recognition of the doctrine of legitimate expectation in Canada; there was not the same doctrinal need for it.

Presumably, part of the reason for the British position stems from the theoretical bases on which judicial engrafting of procedural fairness obligations onto otherwise silent statutes are justified. Either it is obvious that the legislature would have included such protections had it thought about the matter or the legislature, in its presumed awareness of the common law, simply did not bother stating the obvious. To the extent that entitlements to procedural fairness are argued to depend on the circumstances of particular exercises of a statutory power, theories of a forgetful or an impliedly authorizing legislature become even more stretched than they are normally. In such contexts, it is rather more difficult to infer from legislative silence that there has been an implicit delegation to the courts of the task of selecting those occasions on which the decision-maker owes obligations of procedural fairness to affected persons and those where no such entitlement arises. The sometimes forgetful or impliedly authorizing legislature is one that neglects to include just a few words ("after hearing those affected"), not one that omits a whole set of criteria for the discernment of the circumstances under which a particular exercise of a statutory power attracts an obligation of procedural fairness.

It was against this background that the term "legitimate expectation" began to emerge in English caselaw. Thus, in one of the early "procedural fairness" cases, *Schmidt v. Secretary of State for Home Affairs*, [1969] 2 Ch. 149 (CA), Lord Denning MR made the following statement without any real elaboration of what he meant by the term:

> The speeches in *Ridge v. Baldwin* show that an administrative body may, in a proper case, be bound to give a person who is affected by their decision an opportunity of making representations. It all depends on whether he has some right or interest, or, I would add, some *legitimate expectation* of which it would not be fair to deprive him without hearing what he had to say. [Emphasis added.]

Initially, the concept was one that was treated as just another means of expressing the notion that the applicant's stake in the outcome was one that indicated the need for procedural fairness. Thus, in *McInnes v. Onslow-Fane*, [1978] 1 WLR 1520 (Ch.), Megarry J spoke of "legitimate expectation" cases as a category between those of someone seeking a licence or permission and those of someone from whom a licence or permission was being removed, typified most commonly by an application for renewal. Indeed, it was in this sense that the term was deployed by Gibbs CJ of the High Court of Australia in *FAI Insurances v. Winneke* (1982), 151 CLR 342 (Vict.), in the context of a claim for procedures where the applicant's licence to provide workers compensation insurance was not renewed. Of course, to the extent that such claims are seen as being of a stronger order, the longer the licensee has been in business (20 years in this case), there is a recognition that not all exercises of that authority to refuse a renewal attract the same procedural demands (compare *Durayappah*).

"Legitimate expectation" is also used to describe the nature of the substantive interest for which procedural protections were being sought in two of the Canadian cases that we encountered earlier in this chapter: *Webb* (in reference to the applicant's interest in continued occupation of government housing) and *Hutfield* (in reference to the applicant's interest in hospital admitting privileges arising from his training and entry into the general practice of medicine, though interestingly this was not seen as generating a legitimate expectation, at least in McDonald J's understanding of the term).

However, very shortly after his judgment in *Schmidt*, Lord Denning gave the concept a rather different content. This was in *R v. Liverpool Corporation, ex parte Liverpool Taxi Fleet Operators' Association*, [1972] 2 QB 299 (CA). In this case, municipal officials had given express undertakings to the association that the number of taxi licences would not be increased without a hearing, and, subsequently, following a hearing, that there would be no increases unless a private Act of Parliament was procured. Lord Denning was prepared to make these undertakings and conduct the foundation of a requirement that the association be heard or consulted if the corporation was of a mind to resile from its undertaking as to the procuring of a private Act. This was the kind of policy decision where, even after the emergence of the procedural fairness doctrine, courts were unlikely to require the affording of participatory opportunities to affected constituencies. Nevertheless, Lord Denning grounded an entitlement to such opportunities on the particular factual circumstances and thereby laid the foundations for the modern doctrine of "legitimate expectation," though without specifically using the term. Indeed, to the extent that the outcome in that case was based on the promise of a hearing and the precedent for such a hearing, it presents the archetypical kind of situation in which the doctrine applies in Canada to this day: an expectation of a hearing arising out of express representations, a practice of holding such hearings or a combination of the two. In this manifestation, the doctrine may also represent a significant evolution in the law relating to estoppel and public officials. (Note the distinguishing of *Liverpool Taxi* by the Federal Court of Appeal in *Rothmans of Pall Mall Ltd. v. Minister of National Revenue*, [1976] 2 FC 500 (CA) in which a business competitor sought review of the adoption of a new definition of the term "cigarette" for revenue purposes. In a case decided largely by reference to standing principles, the court also refused to infer any procedural fairness obligations simply on the basis of assumptions and reliance on the former definition.)

Following the *Liverpool Taxi Fleet Operators' Association* case, the development of this new branch of procedural fairness law was sporadic in the United Kingdom and, indeed, it was many years before it secured any degree of recognition in Canada. Now, however, it has been acknowledged by the Supreme Court of Canada in five cases, though in each case the court held that the grounds for successful invocation of the doctrine had not been made out. As a consequence of the lack of an example of a positive application of the doctrine, there remain many doubts as to the precise reach of the Canadian version.

In the first of the Supreme Court of Canada cases, *Old St. Boniface Residents Assn. Inc. v. Winnipeg (City)*, [1990] 3 SCR 1170 (Man.), the court was confronted with an argument that there was an expectation on the part of the residents' association that there would be no more development of the kind in issue until such time as there was a new city plan in place, a process in which the association expected to participate. As well as holding that any such expectation could not prevail against the applicant developer, the court held that such a claim could not be made in the face of all the other procedural protections provided for in the relevant legislation. In delivering the judgment of the court, Sopinka J made the following observations about the reach of the doctrine:

> The principle developed in these cases is simply an extension of the rules of natural justice and procedural fairness. It affords a party affected by the decision of a public official an opportunity to make representations in circumstances in which there otherwise would be no such opportunity. The court supplies the omission where, based on the conduct of the public official, a party has been led to believe that his or her rights would not be affected without consultation.

This statement was elaborated on by the same judge in the case that follows, one that on its face seemed to be a singularly unpromising venue for the assertion of a legitimate expectation argument (though see Dyzenhaus, "Developments in Administrative Law: The 1991-92 Term" (1993), 4 *Sup. Ct. L Rev.* 177, at 189-95).

Reference re Canada Assistance Plan
[1991] 2 SCR 525 (BC)

[The *Canada Assistance Plan*, a federal statute, authorized the government of Canada to enter into agreements with the provinces for sharing the costs of provincial social assistance and welfare programs. Section 8 of the Plan provided that these agreements would continue in force for as long as the relevant provincial law was in operation, subject to termination by consent, or unilaterally by either party on one year's notice.

As part of a deficit reduction policy, the federal government introduced a bill that limited the increase in its financial contribution to British Columbia, Alberta, and Ontario to a figure below that provided in the Plan and the agreements with the provinces. No prior notice had been given.

One of the questions referred by British Columbia to the courts was whether the government was precluded from introducing the bill by virtue of the legitimate expectation that amendments would only be made to the agreements by consent.

The judgment of the court was delivered by:]

SOPINKA J: It was held by the majority of the court below, and it was argued before us by the Attorney General of British Columbia, that the federal government acted illegally in invoking the power of Parliament to amend the *Plan* without obtaining the *consent* of British Columbia. The action was illegal because it violated a legitimate expectation of British Columbia. These submissions were adopted by the Attorney General for Alberta. This must be contrasted with a claim that there was a legitimate expectation that the federal government would not act without *consulting* British Columbia. If the doctrine of legitimate expectations required consent, and not merely consultation, then it would be the source of substantive rights; in this case, a substantive right to veto proposed federal legislation.

There is no support in Canadian or English cases for the position that the doctrine of legitimate expectations can create substantive rights. It is a part of the rules of procedural fairness which can govern administrative bodies. Where it is applicable, it can create a right to make representations or to be consulted. It does not fetter the decision following the representations or consultation.

Moreover, the rules governing procedural fairness do not apply to a body exercising purely legislative functions. Megarry J said so in *Bates v. Lord Hailsham* [1972] 3 All ER 1019 (Ch.), and this was approved by Estey J for the Court in *Attorney General of Canada v. Inuit Tapirisat of Canada, supra*. In *Martineau v. Matsqui Institution Disciplinary Board* [1980] 1 SCR 602 (Can.), Dickson J, as he then was, wrote (at 628):

> The authorities, in my view, support the following conclusions:
>
> . . .
>
> 2. A purely ministerial decision, on broad grounds of public policy, will typically afford the individual no procedural protection, and any attack upon such a decision will have to be founded upon abuse of discretion. Similarly, public bodies exercising legislative functions may not be amenable to judicial supervision.

These three cases were considered in *Penikett v. Canada* (1987) 45 DLR (4th) 108 (YTCA), leave to appeal to the Supreme Court of Canada refused [1988] 1 SCR xii, and the court concluded (at 120):

> In these circumstances, the issues sought to be raised in paras. 12 and 12(a) [right to be consulted and duty of fairness] are not justiciable because they seek to challenge the process of legislation.

The respect by the courts for the independence of the legislative power is captured by G.-A. Beaudoin, *La Constitution du Canada* (1990), in the following passage (at 92):

> [translation] The courts do not intervene, however, during the legislative process in Parliament and the legislatures. They have no interest as such in parliamentary procedure. They have made this clear in certain decisions. They respect the *lex parliamenti*.

The formulation and introduction of a bill are part of the legislative process with which the courts will not meddle. So too is the purely procedural requirement in s. 54 of the *Constitution Act, 1867*. That is not to say that this requirement is unnecessary; it must be complied with to create fiscal legislation. But it is not the place of the courts to interpose further procedural requirements in the legislative process. I leave aside the issue of review under the *Canadian Charter of Rights and Freedoms* where a guaranteed right may be affected.

The respondent seeks to avoid this proposition by pointing to the dichotomy of the executive on the one hand and Parliament on the other. He concedes that there is no legal impediment preventing Parliament from legislating but contends that the government is constrained by the doctrine of legitimate expectations from introducing the Bill to Parliament.

This submission ignores the essential role of the executive in the legislative process of which it is an integral part. The relationship was aptly described by W. Bagehot, *The English Constitution* (1872) at 14:

> A cabinet is a combining committee—a *hyphen* which joins, a buckle which fastens, the legislative part of the state to the executive part of the state. [Emphasis in original.]

Parliamentary government would be paralyzed if the doctrine of legitimate expectations could be applied to prevent the government from introducing legislation in Parliament. Such expectations might be created by statements during an election campaign. The business of government would be stalled while the application of the doctrine and its effect was argued out in the courts. Furthermore, it is fundamental to our system of government that a government is not bound by the undertakings of its predecessor. The doctrine of legitimate expectations would place a fetter on this essential feature of democracy. I adopt the words of King CJ of the Supreme Court of South Australia, *in banco*, in *West Lakes Ltd. v. South Australia* (1980) 25 SASR 389 at 390, a case strikingly similar to this one:

> Ministers of State cannot, however, by means of contractual obligations entered into on behalf of the State fetter their own freedom, or the freedom of their successors or the freedom of other members of parliament, to propose, consider and, if they think fit, vote for laws, even laws which are inconsistent with the contractual obligations.

While the statement deals with contractual obligations, it would apply, *a fortiori* to restraint imposed by other conduct which raises a legitimate expectation.

A restraint on the executive in the introduction of legislation is a fetter on the sovereignty of Parliament itself. This is particularly true when the restraint relates to the introduction of a money bill. By virtue of s. 54 of the *Constitution Act, 1867*, such a bill can only be introduced on the recommendation of the Governor General who by convention acts on the advice of the Cabinet. If the Cabinet is restrained, then so is Parliament. The legal effect of what the respondent is attempting to impugn is of no consequence to the obligations between Canada and British Columbia. The recommendation and introduction of

Bill C-69 has no effect *per se*, rather it is its impact on the legislative process that will affect those obligations. It is therefore the legislative process that is, in fact, impugned.

Appeal allowed.

NOTES

1. In delivering the judgment of the court, Sopinka J clearly rejects any notion of the doctrine of legitimate expectation being anything other than a source of procedural claims. In other words, it never generates a claim to a substantive outcome, only hearing entitlements. As seen already, L'Heureux-Dubé J reiterated this point in *Baker* and, more recently, it was reaffirmed in the concurring judgment of Binnie J (McLachlin CJ concurring) in *Mount Sinai Hospital Center v. Quebec (Minister of Health and Social Services)*, [2001] 2 SCR 281 (Que.) (though the majority expressly declined to rule on the point) (extracts follow). Is such a restriction appropriate?

2. Why did the provision that agreements would not be terminated without a year's notice not create a legitimate expectation of a *procedural* nature? Should it have limited the federal government's power to introduce the amending bill?

3. In the first case, *Old St. Boniface Residents Assn.*, Sopinka J describes the doctrine as one by virtue of which procedural claims can be made in circumstances where otherwise no procedural obligations would exist. In terms of current Canadian law, the principal domain where there is no present common law entitlement to procedural fairness is with respect to "legislative" functions. Sopinka J's statement in *Old St. Boniface Residents Assn.* would therefore seem to suggest that door may well have been opened by virtue of the legitimate expectation doctrine. However, in the *Canada Assistance Plan* case, the main reason for rejecting the applicability of the legitimate expectation argument is that it has no relevance to legislative functions. If that is so, when, if ever, will the doctrine apply? Will it be limited to situations where the applicant has an expectation of procedures in a non-final decision-making process that does not normally attract an obligation of procedural fairness or has an expectation of *more extensive* procedures in a context that normally attracts *some but limited* procedures? Does the answer to this question depend on what Sopinka J means by a "legislative" function for these purposes? If so, what does he intend when he uses that term: the process leading up to the introduction and passage of legislation by the Parliament of Canada or a provincial or territorial legislature, or some broader category of decision making (as identified earlier in this chapter)? What is to be made of his quotation of Dickson J in *Martineau* and, in particular, the statement that a "purely ministerial decision, on broad grounds of public policy, will typically afford the individual no procedural protection"? At a more practical level, what adverse consequences would have flowed from requiring the federal government to consult with the affected provinces before introducing the controversial legislative changes? Would this have placed too great a fetter on the powers of the executive? Would it have amounted to too much judicial intrusion into the executive and legislative domain? (On this latter question, see Dyzenhaus, above. See also Mullan, "*Canada Assistance Plan*: Denying Legitimate Expectation a Fair Start" (1993), 7 *Admin. LR* (2d) 269.)

4. While the cases are not ones that have been decided by reference to the doctrine of legitimate expectation, examples of the kind of situation that would presumably fit within the reach attributed to the doctrine in *Canada Assistance Plan* can be found in those cases

where the courts have held agencies to standards of procedural fairness when hearings have been held voluntarily (*Stumbilich v. Ontario (Health Disciplines Board)* (1984), 12 DLR (4th) 156 (Ont. CA); *Gaw v. Commissioner of Corrections* (1986), 19 Admin. LR 137 (FCTD); and *Dion c. Cyr* (1993), 18 Admin. LR (2d) 86 (NB QB)) or been promised (*Hammond v. Association of BC Professional Foresters* (1991), 47 Admin. LR 20 (BC SC)). In some senses, these are the Canadian equivalents of *Liverpool Taxi*. However, the entitlement has been based simply on the promise or the holding out with no associated inquiry as to whether there has been any reliance on the assurance. Public authorities break their word at their peril.

5. What is also clear in the wake of *Baker* is that in Canada substantive expectations can generate an entitlement not to substantive outcomes but procedural protections if the decision-maker is of a mind to defeat those substantive expectations. For a good example, see *Canadian Union of Public Employees and Service Employees International Union v. Ontario (Minister of Labour)* (2000), 51 OR (3d) 417 (CA), at para. 102, where the court held that the unions had an entitlement to procedural fairness arising out of their legitimate expectation that the government would not change the system for the appointment of interest arbitrators. On appeal, the Supreme Court of Canada reversed this determination on the ground that the representations and past practice claimed by the union to found their legitimate expectation could not be characterized as "clear, unambiguous and unqualified": [2003] 1 SCR 539, at para. 131.

6. A useful companion case to *Canada Assistance Plan* is the decision of the House of Lords in *Council of Civil Service Unions v. Minister for the Civil Service*, [1985] AC 374 (Eng. HL).

The Government Communications Headquarters (GCHQ) was established in 1947 to ensure the security of official and military communications and to provide the government signals intelligence. This function required handling much secret information vital to national security. From its creation, its employees were permitted to belong to national trade unions, and most of them did. There was also a well-established practice of consultation between the government and the unions about important alterations in the terms and conditions of employment. However, in the late 1970s and early 1980s, the unions initiated substantial work disruptions to support their efforts to improve the conditions of work for civil servants generally. Negotiations failed and, in late 1983, the minister for the civil service made an order forbidding the employees at GCHQ to belong to national trade unions. A council of unions and some individual employees brought an action for a declaration that the order was void because it was made without consultation. The House of Lords decided that the order could be reviewed in the same way as a statutory power, even though it was made under the prerogative, and that the employees and the unions had a legitimate expectation that they would be consulted before it was made, but their claim failed because the national security might outweigh this expectation and this choice must be made by the executive and not the courts. About the claim for a hearing, Lord Fraser of Tullybelton said:

> Mr. Blom-Cooper submitted that the Minister had a duty to consult the CCSU, on behalf of employees at GCHQ, before giving the instruction on 22 December 1983 for making an important change in their conditions of service. His main reason for so submitting was that the employees had a legitimate, or reasonable, expectation that there would be such prior consultation before any important change was made in their conditions.

It is clear that the employees did not have a legal right to prior consultation. ... But even where a person claiming some benefit or privilege has no legal right to it, as a matter of private law, he may have a legitimate expectation of receiving the benefit or privilege, and, if so, the courts will protect his expectation by judicial review as a matter of public law. ...

Legitimate, or reasonable, expectation may arise either from an express promise given on behalf of a public authority or from the existence of a regular practice which the claimant can reasonably expect to continue. ...

The submission on behalf of the appellants is that the present case is of the latter type. The test of that is whether the practice of prior consultation of the staff on significant changes in their conditions of service was so well established by 1983 that it would be unfair or inconsistent with good administration for the Government to depart from the practice in this case. Legitimate expectations such as are now under consideration will always relate to a benefit or privilege to which the claimant has no right in private law, and it may even be to one which conflicts with his private law rights. In the present case the evidence shows that, ever since GCHQ began in 1947, prior consultation has been the invariable rule when conditions of service were to be significantly altered. Accordingly in my opinion if there had been no question of national security involved, the appellants would have had a legitimate expectation that the minister would consult them before issuing the instruction of 22 December 1983. The next question, therefore, is whether it has been shown that consideration of national security supersedes the expectation. ...

Interestingly, the House of Lords was much more blunt than Sopinka J as to the reasons for denying recognition to what would otherwise have been a good claim: it was overridden by national security considerations. For these purposes, the Law Lords did not think it was necessary to carve out a more general exception to the application of the doctrine based on troubling conceptions of differences between legislative or policy and other forms of decision making.

7. See also *Hamilton-Wentworth (Regional Municipality) v. Ontario (Minister of Transportation)* (1991), 49 Admin. LR 169 (Ont. Div. Ct.) in which the claim stemmed from a decision by the minister of transportation in the new NDP government not to continue funding for a major highway construction project. The court held that it had no jurisdiction to oversee such funding decisions taken by reference to considerations of public policy, a conclusion that could not be influenced by appeals to legitimate expectation based on the previous government's fulfilment of its financial commitments and reliance by the applicants on the continuation of the funding through to the completion of the current phase of the project. The applicants' claim lay (if anywhere) in contract or restitution, not judicial review in the nature of *mandamus*.

Clearly, the future of the doctrine of legitimate expectation in Canadian law depends very much on the answers to these questions that have been raised about Sopinka J's judgment for the Supreme Court in the *Canada Assistance Plan* case. If the doctrine is to play a significant role, it will most obviously be as a surrogate for the failure of the conventional common law principles to provide for the imposition of procedural entitlements in the context of rulemaking and broadly based policy decisions. In the three subsequent Supreme Court decisions in which the doctrine is considered, *Baker, Mount Sinai*, and *CUPE v. Ontario (Minister of Labour)*, that issue does not feature and so the prospects for such a deployment of the doctrine remain very uncertain.

Once again, in this context, school closing and program modification cases are graphically illustrative. In a pre-*Canada Assistance Plan* case, Spencer J of the BC Supreme Court in an ambiguous judgment apparently rejected the application of the doctrine in the context of the elimination of a French immersion program on the basis that this was legislative action: *Sunshine Coast Parents for French v. Sunshine Coast (School District No. 46)* (1990), 44 Admin. LR 252 (BC SC). He also gave as an additional reason that only those who were aware of previous consultative practices could actually rely on those practices as generating a legitimate expectation, a reason that finds strong echoes in the Newfoundland Court of Appeal reversal of the Trial Division's judgment in the following case.

Furey v. Roman Catholic School Board for Conception Bay Centre
(1991), 2 Admin. LR (2d) 263 (Nfld. SCTD)

[The board decided to close an elementary school under its jurisdiction. Thirteen residents, most with children attending the relevant school, sought relief in the nature of *certiorari* to quash the decision of the board. They alleged that the decision was taken without an opportunity for public input and this constituted a breach of the duty of procedural fairness.

A few years earlier, when the question of the need to consolidate elementary schools within the board's jurisdiction had first arisen, parents had been involved in the discussions and these discussions had continued through the middle of 1989, at which point a decision was taken to consolidate two schools but to leave open the school that was now in jeopardy. Thereafter, in early 1991, the issue of elementary school consolidation again arose in the context of a discussion paper presented to the board by the superintendent of schools. On the basis of this paper and subsequent discussions and negotiations in which the public (parents and residents) were not involved, a motion was put at the May public meeting of the board that the school in question be closed as of the end of the 1991-92 academic year. At the meeting, that motion was amended to close the school as of the end of the current academic year and that amendment carried as did the amended motion.

In 1988, the Department of Education had issued guidelines to be followed in the case of planned consolidations and closing. These guidelines established a process of consultation and timeframes for various steps in the decision-making process. Those guidelines had not been observed by the board in this instance.]

WELLS J:

[After outlining the facts, he continued.]

I wish to make clear that a decision to close a school is a decision for a school board alone. My findings are directed to issues of procedural fairness only, and in that regard I feel it appropriate to comment on the guidelines suggested by the Department of

Education in 1988. If a board were to follow these, either to the letter or in substance, I cannot see how anyone could allege lack of procedural fairness in school closings.

A large number of cases have been provided for me by counsel. Though they provide necessary insight into judicial consideration of the concept of procedural fairness, most are not of direct application to this case, because some Canadian jurisdictions require, by statute, that the concept of procedural fairness be applied. The legislation in Newfoundland is silent on that point, and I am therefore required to consider whether or not, in the absence of specific legislation, the common law doctrines as developed by the courts with respect to procedural fairness permit this court to find that its absence is sufficient ground for setting aside a decision to close a school.

[He here quoted from the *Canada Assistance Plan* judgment on the reach of the doctrine of legitimate expectation, before continuing.]

I have no hesitation in finding that the decision of the school board in closing Assumption Elementary was an administrative decision, and not in any sense legislative. My understanding of the authorities is that legislative decisions are usually general decisions of broad application. Administrative decisions usually deal with specifics, as was the case here. That view is confirmed by a reading of recent cases such as *Blore v. Halifax (District) School Board* (1991) 105 NSR (2d) 414 (SC TD). Nunn J said at 419:

> I need not dwell on whether *certiorari* applies to this decision of the Board. There are no statutory provisions which create specific duties or obligations on the Board as to procedural fairness as there are in some provinces, and there are no specific rights of any person being affected. The only right is to an education but not a right to attend a specific school. It is suggested by the Board that the decision here and the procedures followed fall into that class of administrative decision which is outside the purview of judicial review. That may very well be the case but there seems to be a more modern concept that certain decisions, even though administrative, are subject to a duty of fairness and one would not have to strain too far to consider that a review of one whole section of the educational system, which could have profound effects not only on the children concerned but on their parents, the particular area of the community, property values and the like may very well be one where a duty of fairness exists.
>
> However, I need not make a finding on this question as I am assuming that there is such a duty and judicial review is available.

I believe that the law as enunciated by Nunn J is equally applicable under the Newfoundland legislation, and I am of the opinion that I am entitled to consider the matter on the basis that there was in this case a duty of procedural fairness, and that judicial review is available.

I am satisfied that the actions of the board in 1988 and 1989 in employing a consultative process, together with certain public communications made to parents after 1989, which referred to guidelines, did have the effect of creating the impression that the Board was operating under a system of guidelines which allowed for procedural fairness.

The 1989 procedure, and subsequent communications, could not do otherwise than raise in the minds of the parents the expectation that there would be procedural fairness in future decision making with respect to school closure. It follows that they would expect that the board would adopt and follow a requirement of procedural fairness specifically by adherence to some form of guidelines before taking a decision to close a school.

It is reasonable to contend, as did counsel for the applicants, that the parents concerned had a reasonable expectation that the board would follow a process of procedural fairness before taking a final decision to close Assumption Elementary.

Having found, as I have, that the decision was made without procedural fairness, it follows that this court has jurisdiction to grant an order in the nature of *certiorari*, setting aside the decision of May 6, 1991. I further direct that the matter be referred back to the second respondent, which is the board now having jurisdiction, for reconsideration and the making of a decision.

The applicants will have their party-and-party costs.

Application granted; decision quashed and matter remitted back for reconsideration.

NOTES

1. On appeal to the Newfoundland Court of Appeal (in which the respondent parents were unrepresented), the court reversed the judgment of Wells J: (1993), 104 DLR (4th) 455 (Nfld. CA). The court in fact accepted Wells J's conclusions for holding that this was an administrative, not a legislative, function and, in so doing, distinguished *Sunshine Coast Parents for French* on the basis that the elimination of the French immersion program in that case was a decision that affected a whole school district while this decision involved a single school. However, on perusing the affidavits of 2 of the 13 applicants for relief, the court was unable to find any evidence that those deponents had believed that the past practice would be followed in this instance. How relevant should that be? (See Mullan, "Confining the Reach of Legitimate Expectations" (1990), 44 Admin. LR 245 and Annotation to *Furey* in the Newfoundland Court of Appeal: (1993), 17 Admin. LR (2d) 46.) Also consider whether the court's distinguishing of *Sunshine Coast Parents for French* is sustainable.

2. Of course, if *Bezaire*, above, is accepted, the mere classification of the function in issue here as "administrative" rather than "legislative" should have meant that the applicants were entitled to procedural fairness irrespective of the doctrine of legitimate expectation. A differently constituted panel of the Newfoundland Court of Appeal in fact accepted this very contention in *Elliott v. Burin Peninsula School District No. 7* (1998), 13 Admin. LR (3d) 91, stating in effect that *Furey* was decided *per incuriam* on this point.

3. Following in the steps of both *Furey* and *Sunshine Coast Parents for French* is *Attaran v. University of British Columbia* (1998), 4 Admin. LR (3d) 44 (BC SC). This involved a failure by the university administration to follow its consultation policy as a prelude to an increase in student fees. Among the reasons provided for rejecting the application of the legitimate expectation doctrine were that the procedure was new and had been used only once previously; that it was in the nature of an instruction to staff, not a representation to affected constituencies; and that very few in the affected and complaining student body knew about it at the relevant time.

4. The denial of recourse to the doctrine where the applicants for relief had either no knowledge of past practices of consultation or belief that they would be followed in the par-

ticular case raises a more general question of the links between the doctrine of legitimate expectation and estoppel. Should the doctrine's application depend upon whether applicants can bring themselves within the principles normally associated with estoppel as a private law concept: with knowledge of the promise or assurance in question, the applicants acted to their detriment in such a way as to make it inequitable for the other party to now assert the strict letter of the law.

At one level, of course, as *Sunshine Coast Parents for French* and *Furey* illustrate, estoppel is a limiting concept. By focusing on the position of the particular applicants as opposed to a general theory of probity in the conduct of public affairs (which would have decision-makers acting consistently with past practice unless good reasons exist for not doing so), estoppel is concerned with the impact of the practice on the expectations of those claiming relief from the court. Of course, just as private law estoppel is now moving away from any need for proof of actual detrimental reliance, it may not be absolutely necessary, if the analogy is employed, to look for anything other than a reasonably held belief that past practice will be followed. Carried even further, however, the analogy with estoppel in private law would have the courts going against one of the apparent limitations on the doctrine of legitimate expectation: its inapplicability beyond the realm of procedures. After all, under conventional estoppel doctrine, if the person to whom the representation has been made is unable to resume her or his pre-representation position, the doctrine could affect substantive entitlements. These issues (including the expansion of the English version of the doctrine into the substantive domain) are explored in the following extracts from the judgment of Binnie J in *Mount Sinai Hospital*.

Mount Sinai Hospital v. Quebec (Minister of Health and Social Services)
[2001] 2 SCR 281 (Que.)

[For many years, the hospital had been functioning in violation of its licence. Its character had changed from a long-term care facility to a short- and medium-term care facility. Discussions took place with the minister and it was agreed that, if the hospital relocated, its licence would be regularized. The hospital engaged in extensive fund-raising efforts and relocated. When it sought to have its licence updated, a different minister in a different government refused, primarily on the basis that to issue the licence would be to commit the government to additional financial support of the hospital and that this was not one of the government's current priorities. The hospital sought *mandamus* to compel the minister to issue the revised licence. The Quebec Superior Court refused to make such an order on the basis that the doctrine of legitimate expectation could not be used to achieve substantive outcomes. The Quebec Court of Appeal accepted this but ruled that the hospital was entitled to a revised licence on the basis of the doctrine of public law estoppel: (1998), 9 Admin. LR (3d) 161 (Que. CA). The Minister appealed to the Supreme Court of Canada. Bastarache J delivered the judgment of the majority of the court and held that it was not necessary to deal with the issues of public law estoppel and legitimate expectation. The case turned on the fact that earlier ministers had already made a decision conditional on the hospital relocating and this was a decision that the current minister did not have any basis for overturning. As a consequence, the hospital had an entitlement to the formal issuance of a licence in terms of that initial decision. The concurring judgment saw it somewhat differently. The current minister had made a patently unreasonable decision and failed to act in a procedurally fair manner in refusing the licence. Since there was only one other possible outcome, *mandamus* was available to compel the issuance of the licence. Both judgments turned to a significant degree on the finding that the minister's reasons for refusing the modified licence was not supported by the facts: there was no evidence that the grant of the licence in the terms sought would involve any commitment of additional funds on the part of the government. Before reaching his conclusion, Binnie J (McLachlin CJ concurring) did deal with the public law estoppel and legitimate expectation arguments.]

BINNIE J (McLachlin CJ concurring): ...

C. The Doctrine of Legitimate Expectation

The respondents argue that the doctrine of legitimate expectations can be used to compel not only procedural protection but a substantive result provided such result is not contrary to law and is otherwise within the power of the Minister, which in this case it would be (see S.J. Schønberg, *Legitimate Expectations in Administrative Law* (2000), ch. 4). The prior jurisprudence in this Court is against such a proposition ... . However, the respondents say that this doctrine is rapidly evolving and expanding, and has been employed in Canada and elsewhere to impose a substantive rather than merely procedural result on decision makers exercising statutory or prerogative powers.

[Binnie J here listed Canadian and English authority.]

More recently in *R v. North and East Devon Health Authority, ex parte Coughlan* [2000] 3 All ER 850, the English Court of Appeal has resoundingly confirmed that in English law the doctrine of legitimate expectations *does* give rise to substantive remedies. Lord Woolf MR was unequivocal at para. 71:

> Fairness in such a situation, if it is to mean anything, must for the reasons we have considered include *fairness of outcome*. This in turn is why the doctrine of legitimate expectation has emerged as a distinct application of the concept of abuse of power in relation to *substantive* as well as procedural benefits. ... [Emphasis added.]

[Binnie J here listed further authority from Ireland, Australia, and South Africa as well as contending academic positions.]

Part of the difficulty with the contending positions in this case is that in English law, and in the law of those jurisdictions that have followed the English lead in this matter, the doctrine of legitimate expectations performs a number of functions that in Canada are kept distinct. Lord Woolf MR in *Coughlan*, *supra*, identified the unifying theme as "administrative fairness" of which procedural fairness and substantive fairness are connected parts ... . On the *substantive* side, Lord Woolf MR summarizes his position thus at para. 82:

Policy being (within the law) for the public authority alone, both it and the reasons for adopting or changing it will be accepted by the courts as part of the factual data—in other words, as not ordinarily open to judicial review. The court's task—and this is not always understood—is then limited to asking whether the application of the policy to an individual who has been led to expect something different is a just exercise of power. In many cases the authority will already have considered this and made appropriate exceptions … or resolved to pay compensation where money alone will suffice. But where no such accommodation is made, it is for the court to say whether the consequent frustration of the individual's expectation is so unfair as to be a misuse of the authority's power.

In *Coughlan* itself, a woman with severe physical disabilities was induced by the local health authority to move from a hospital to a nursing home on the promise that there she would have a "home for life" (para. 4). Five years later, after some consultation and for reasons that the court found to be perfectly rational (para. 65), the local health authority decided to close the nursing home. The decision was quashed because, though rational and reached after some consultation, the court concluded that the public authority had placed insufficient weight on its earlier promise of a "home for life."

It thus appears that the English doctrine of legitimate expectation has developed into a comprehensive code that embraces the full gamut of administrative relief from procedural fairness at the low end through "enhanced" procedural fairness based on conduct, thence onwards to estoppel (though it is not to be called that) including substantive relief at the high end, *i.e.*, the end representing the greatest intrusion by the courts into public administration. The intrusion is said to be justified by the multiplicity of conflicting decisions by a public authority on the same point directed to the same individual(s), *per* Lord Woolf MR in *Coughlan*, *supra*, at para. 66:

> In the ordinary case there is no space for intervention on grounds of abuse of power once a rational decision directed to a proper purpose has been reached by lawful process. The present class of case is visibly different. It involves not one but two lawful exercises of power (the promise and the policy change) by the same public authority, with consequences for individuals trapped between the two.

In ranging over such a vast territory under the banner of "fairness," it is inevitable that sub-classifications must be made to differentiate the situations which warrant highly intrusive relief from those which do not. Many of the English cases on legitimate expectations relied on by the respondents, at the low end, would fit comfortably within our principles of procedural fairness. At the high end they represent a level of judicial intervention in government policy that our courts, to date, have considered inappropriate in the absence of a successful challenge under the *Canadian Charter of Rights and Freedoms*.

Canadian cases tend to differentiate for analytical purposes the related concepts of procedural fairness and the doctrine of legitimate expectation. There is, on the one hand, a concern that treating procedural fairness as a subset of legitimate expectations may unnecessarily complicate and indeed inhibit rather than encourage the development of the highly flexible rules of procedural fairness: D. Wright, "Rethinking the Doctrine of Legitimate Expectations in Canadian Administrative Law" (1997) 35 *Osgoode Hall LJ* 139. On the other hand, there is a countervailing concern that using a Minister's prior conduct against him as a launching pad for substantive relief may strike the wrong balance between private and public interests, and blur the role of the court with the role of the Minister.

Under our case law the availability and content of procedural fairness are generally driven by the nature of the applicant's interest and the nature of the power exercised by the public authority in relation to that interest ... . The doctrine of legitimate expectations, on the other hand, looks to the *conduct* of the public authority in the exercise of that power (*Old St. Boniface, supra*, at p. 1204) including established practices, conduct or representations that can be characterized as clear, unambiguous and unqualified. ... The expectations must not conflict with the public authority's statutory remit.

The doctrine of legitimate expectations is sometimes treated as a form of estoppel, but the weight of authority and principle suggests that an applicant who relies on the doctrine of legitimate expectations may show, but does not necessarily have to show, that he or she was aware of such conduct, or that it was relied on with detrimental results. This is because the focus is on promoting "regularity, predictability, and certainty in government's dealing with the public": S.A. de Smith, H. Woolf and J. Jowell, *Judicial Review of Administrative Action* (5th ed. 1995), at p. 417, to which the editors add, at p. 426, that insisting on estoppel-type requirements would

> involve unfair discrimination between those who were and were not aware of the representation and would benefit the well-informed or well-advised. It would also encourage undesirable administrative practice by too readily relieving decision-makers of the normal consequences of their actions.

The High Court of Australia espouses a similar view:

> But, more importantly, the notion of legitimate expectation is not dependent upon any principle of estoppel. Whether the Minister can be estopped in the exercise of his discretion is another question; it was not a question raised by the appellant. Legitimate expectation does not depend upon the knowledge and state of mind of the individual concerned, although such an expectation may arise from the conduct of a public authority towards an individual. ...
>
> (*Haoucher v. Minister for Immigration, Local Government and Ethnic Affairs* (1990) 19 ALR 577, *per* Toohey J, at p. 590.)

See also *Minister of State for Immigration and Ethnic Affairs v. Teoh* (1995) 183 CLR 273.

It is difficult at one and the same time thus to lower the bar to the application of the doctrine of legitimate expectation (for good policy reasons) but at the same time to expand greatly its potency for overruling the Minister or other public authority on matters of substantive policy. One would normally expect *more* intrusive forms of relief to be accompanied by *more* demanding evidentiary requirements.

In *Reference re Canada Assistance Plan*, Sopinka J (citing *Old St. Boniface, supra*) regarded the doctrine of legitimate expectations as "an *extension* of the rules of natural justice and procedural fairness" which may afford "a party affected by the decision of a public official an opportunity to make representations *in circumstances in which there otherwise would be no such opportunity*" (p. 557 (emphasis added)). In referring to the making of representations, of course, Sopinka J was not limiting relief just to representations but intended to include whatever procedural remedies might be appropriate on the facts of a particular case. Procedure is a broad term. The door was shut only against substantive relief. It seems to me, notwithstanding the respondents' argument, that this conclusion should be affirmed. If the Court is to give substantive relief, more demanding conditions precedent must be fulfilled than are presently required by the doctrine of legitimate expectation.

In *Reference re Canada Assistance Plan, supra,* Sopinka J went on to note two further limitations. He quoted at p. 558 from *Martineau v. Matsqui Institution Disciplinary Board* [1980] 1 SCR 602. The first limitation was that: "A purely ministerial decision, on broad grounds of public policy, will typically afford the individual no procedural protection, and any attack upon such a decision will have to be founded upon *abuse of discretion*" (p. 558 (emphasis added)). I will return to the notion of "abuse of discretion" below.

The second limitation was that "public bodies exercising *legislative* functions may not be amenable to judicial supervision" (p. 558 (emphasis added)). *Reference re Canada Assistance Plan* dealt with the application of the doctrine of legitimate expectations to Parliament where the need for judicial restraint is obvious. There may be difficulty in other contexts in distinguishing when the legislative exception applies and where it does not, as debated in the Federal Court of Appeal in *Apotex Inc. v. Canada (Attorney General)* [2000] 4 FC 264, especially Evans JA at para. 105 *et seq.* That issue remains open for another day.

In affirming that the doctrine of legitimate expectations is limited to procedural relief, it must be acknowledged that in some cases it is difficult to distinguish the procedural from the substantive. In *Bendahmane v. Canada* [[1989] 3 FC 16], for example, a majority of the Federal Court of Appeal considered the applicant's claim to the benefit of a refugee backlog reduction program to be procedural (p. 33) whereas the dissenting judge considered the claimed relief to be substantive (p. 25). A similarly close call was made in *Canada (Attorney General) v. Canada (Commissioner of the Inquiry on the Blood System)* [1996] 3 FC 259 (TD). An undue focus on formal classification and categorization of powers at the expense of broad principles flexibly applied may do a disservice here. The inquiry is better framed in terms of the underlying principle mentioned earlier, namely that broad public policy is pre-eminently for the Minister to determine, not the courts.

The classification of relief as "substantive" however should be made in light of the principled basis for its exclusion rather than as a matter of form. Where, as in *Bendahmane v. Canada*, relief can reasonably be characterized as procedural in light of the underlying principle of deference on matters of substantive policy, then generally speaking it should be.

It follows from the foregoing that decisions of the English courts and other courts that give effect to *substantive* legitimate expectations must be read with due regard to the differences in Canadian law.

In this case, as stated earlier, the Minister's decision will be set aside through the application of the ordinary rules of procedural fairness. There is no need to expand either the availability or content of procedural fairness because of the conduct of successive Ministers which amounts, in this respect, only to an aggravating circumstance. There is, in short, no need to resort to the doctrine of legitimate expectations to achieve procedural relief and, as explained, substantive relief is not available under this doctrine.

D. Promissory Estoppel

The Quebec Court of Appeal concluded ([1998] RJQ 2707) that while the Minister was not required by the doctrine of legitimate expectations to issue the modified permit, he was estopped by his earlier representations and conduct from refusing to do so. The evidence here went well beyond what is necessary to establish legitimate expectations. ... Robert JA noted that the question whether estoppel is available against a Minister of the Crown was left open by this Court in *Comeau's Sea Foods Ltd. v. Canada (Minister of Fisheries and Oceans)* [1997] 1 SCR 12, *per* Major J, at para. 57. See also P. McDonald, "Contradictory Government Action: Estoppel of Statutory Authorities" (1979) 17 *Osgoode Hall LJ* 160, at pp. 180-81.

I agree with Robert JA that estoppel may be available against a public authority, including a Minister, in narrow circumstances. The interesting analysis of McDonald, *supra*, illustrates the variety of circumstances in which the issue has arisen, and the variegated responses given by the courts. ...

In the more recent English cases estoppel too has been swallowed up under the general heading of fairness; see *Coughlan, supra*, at para. 80:

> As Lord Donaldson MR said in *R v ITC, ex p TSW* (5 February 1992, unreported): "The test in public law is fairness, not an adaptation of the law of contract or estoppel."

It is to be emphasized that the requirements of estoppel go well beyond the requirements of the doctrine of legitimate expectations. As mentioned, the doctrine of legitimate expectations does not necessarily, though it may, involve personal knowledge by the applicant of the conduct of the public authority as well as reliance and detriment. Estoppel clearly elevates the evidentiary requirements that must be met by an applicant.

In the United States (where administrative law is heavily influenced by the due process clause in the Constitution) the courts have shown reluctance to hold government estopped. There are policy reasons for this as well as legal reasons:

> The federal government implements hundreds of extraordinarily complicated regulatory and benefit programs. Millions of civil servants give advice to citizens daily concerning their rights and duties under these programs. Erroneous advice is both inevitable and commonplace. The Internal Revenue Service (IRS) provides a good illustration. It is one of the federal agencies that is most respected for its competence. Yet, each year the General Accounting Office (GAO) conducts a study of the taxpayer advice provided by IRS, and each year that study shows that IRS gives erroneous advice in somewhere between 10 and 20 percent of all cases. Some taxpayers are injured by reliance on IRS' advice, but millions of taxpayers are benefited by its availability.
>
> (K.C. Davis and R.J. Pierce Jr., *Administrative Law Treatise* (3rd ed. 1994), vol. 2, at pp. 229-30.)

[After noting that the US Supreme Court had not ruled estoppel against government out entirely, Binnie J continued:]

Professors Davis and Pierce, *supra*, suggest at p. 231 that a successful claim for equitable estoppel in the United States would have to involve at least the following characteristics:

"(1) unequivocal advice from an unusually authoritative source; (2) reasonable reliance on that advice by an individual; (3) extreme harm resulting from that reliance; and (4) gross injustice to the individual in the absence of judicial estoppel."

In this case Robert JA adopted the private law definition of promissory estoppel provided by Sopinka J in *Maracle v. Travellers Indemnity Co. of Canada* [1991] 2 SCR 50, at p. 57:

> The principles of promissory estoppel are well settled. The party relying on the doctrine must establish that the other party has, [1] by words or conduct, made a promise or assurance [2] which was intended to affect their legal relationship and to be acted on. Furthermore, the representee must establish that, [3] in reliance on the representation, [4] he acted on it or in some way changed his position. ...
>
> [T]he promise must be unambiguous but could be inferred from circumstances.

If this were a private law case I would agree that the elements of promissory estoppel are present. The evidence goes well beyond what is necessary to trigger procedural fairness or the doctrine of legitimate expectations. Successive Ministers made clear and specific representations that were intended to be acted on, and were in fact acted upon by the respondents. Ministers encouraged the new mix of short- and long-term care beds which they knew would impact the legal relationship, *i.e.*, the respondents' compliance with the existing permit, and the resulting need for permit modifications. Assurances were given with respect to the issuance of a modified permit. If the Minister is allowed to reverse his promise of a modified permit after the respondents had made changes to their hospital operations, including the fund-raising campaign and the move to Montreal, the respondents say they would have acted on the Minister's promises to their detriment.

However this is not a private law case. Public law estoppel clearly requires an appreciation of the legislative intent embodied in the power whose exercise is sought to be estopped. The legislation is paramount. Circumstances that might otherwise create an estoppel may have to yield to an overriding public interest expressed in the legislative text. As stated in *St. Ann's Island Shooting and Fishing Club Ltd. v. The King* [1950] SCR 211, *per* Rand J, at p. 220: "there can be no estoppel in the face of an *express* provision of a statute" (emphasis added). See also *The King v. Dominion of Canada Postage Stamp Vending Co.*, [1930] SCR 500.

Here the Minister is mandated in broad terms to act in the public interest, and if the public interest as he defines it is opposed to the award of the modified permit, then I do not think a court should estop the Minister from doing what he considers to be his duty. What is at issue is not so much the Minister's ability to change policies but the fate of individuals caught in the transition between successive and inconsistent ministerial decisions on the same subject. As a matter of statutory interpretation, it seems clear from the broad test of s. 138 ("the public interest") that the legislature intended the Minister, not the courts, to determine the appropriate transitional arrangements from the old policy (which welcomed a mix of 57 long-term care beds and 50 short-term care beds) to the new policy (50 short-term care beds would only be welcome if accompanied by enhanced diagnostic and treatment services in addition to the existing operating room, laboratories and radiology facilities).

I mentioned at the outset that the wording of the particular statutory power in question and who wields it (a Minister) is important. The cases that are relied upon by the respondents generally deal with lesser powers or a narrower discretion at a lower level of officialdom. In [*Sous-ministre du Revenu du Québec v. Transport Lessard (1976) Ltée*, [1985] RDJ 502], the issue was the interpretation of a sales tax provision in relation to the bulk sale of trucking equipment (and estoppel was applied despite the caution expressed by this Court in *Granger v. Canada (Canada Employment and Immigration Commission)*, [1989] 1 SCR 141, aff'g. [1986] 3 FC 70 (CA)). The issue in *Re Multi-Malls* [*Inc. and Minister of Transportation and Communications* (1976), 14 OR (2d) 49 (CA)] was a Minister's procedural decision to decline to refer a planning document to the Ontario Municipal Board for review. In *Aurchem* [*Exploration Canada Ltd. v. Canada* (1992), 91 DLR (4th) 710] the issue was the refusal of a mining recorder to register certain mining claims because of defects of form. Strayer J emphasized that the intended effect of his order was not to impede changes in policy but to protect people caught in the transition from a relaxed regime to a more strict regime. The regulatory requirements were matters of form not substance and the statute itself contemplated the possibility of waiver. In none of these cases was the statutory power of decision framed in broad policy terms comparable to s. 138 of the legislation at issue here.

The appellant also complains that the Quebec Court of Appeal in this case used estoppel as a sword rather than a shield, but (as in *Aurchem*) this could be rationalized merely as having precluded the Minister from relying on factors that he was, in all the circumstances, estopped from taking into consideration.

There is a public law dimension to the law of estoppel which must be sensitive to the factual and legal context. Here the primary considerations are the wording of s. 138 and the status of the decision maker. Estoppel is, in my view, not available on the facts of this case in the way in which it was applied by the Quebec Court of Appeal.

Appeal dismissed.

NOTES

1. To the extent that the majority did not express any concluded opinion on the issues of legitimate expectation dealt with by Binnie J, they presumably remain open and the Supreme Court may one day have to evaluate whether it agrees with the position espoused by the chief justice and Binnie J. Seen in this light are you convinced by the arguments against expanding the doctrines of legitimate expectation and public law estoppel?

2. Before leaving the doctrine of legitimate expectation and, in particular, the question whether it can or should ever work to ensure a substantive outcome, notwithstanding the judgment of Sopinka J in *Canada Assistance Plan*, it is also worth recording that, at a more general level, there has been considerable interest in whether "fairness" itself as applied in administrative law has substantive as well as procedural dimensions. In particular, it has been suggested that fairness might involve certain guarantees of formal justice such as equality of treatment, consistency in decision making, proportionality, as well as the protection of legitimate expectations and the recognition of estoppel based on reliance. While it is now clear that this has become part of English (see Jowell and Lester, "Beyond *Wednesbury*:

Substantive Principles of Administrative Law" (1987), *Public Law* 368 as well as Binnie J's judgment in *Mount Sinai*) and also New Zealand (see *Thames Valley Electric Power Board v. NZFP Pulp & Paper Ltd.*, [1994] 2 NZLR 741 (CA) (recognizing the principle though reversing on the facts the trial judge's finding of unfairness)) judicial review law, there is little evidence of its recognition in Canadian jurisprudence.

In *Noel & Lewis Holdings Ltd. v. Canada* (1983), 1 Admin. LR 290 (FCTD), Walsh J held that it was impermissible discrimination for the fisheries authorities to deny a licence transfer to the applicant while others similarly located were being granted permission to transfer. However, that is very much a solitary beacon and, more recently, in *Domtar Inc. v. Québec (Commission d'appel en matière de lésions professionelles)*, [1993] 2 SCR 756 (Que.), the Supreme Court seemed to put beyond reach the possibility of inconsistent decision making forming an independent or freestanding basis for judicial review. In delivering the judgment of the court, L'Heureux-Dubé J expressed a preference for the arguments of MacLauchlan, "Some Problems with Judicial Review of Administrative Inconsistency" (1984), 8 *Dalhousie LJ* 435 to those of Comtois, "Le contrôle de la coherence decisionnelle au sein des tribunaux administratifs" (1990), 21 *RDUS* 77; Morrissette, "Le contrôle de la compétence d'attribution: Thèse, antithèse, et synthèse" (1986), 16 *RDUS* 591, at 631-34; and Mullan, "Natural Justice and Fairness: Substantive as Well as Procedural Standards for the Review of Administrative Decision-Making?" (1982), 27 *McGill LJ* 250. (For an analysis and criticism of *Domtar*, see Dyzenhaus, "Developments in Administrative Law: The 1992-93 Term" (1994), 5 *Sup. Ct. L Rev.* (2d) 189, at 232-40.)

Inconsistency of treatment may, however, give rise to reviewable error in the domain of procedural rights. This is well-exemplified by *Woolworth Canada Inc. v. Newfoundland (Human Rights Commission)* (1994), 114 Nfld. & PEIR 315 (Nfld. SCTD). This involved a challenge to the appointment of a board of inquiry after investigation by the commission of a complaint of discrimination. In the course of the formal investigation, the complainant was given participatory opportunities (such as access to and the right to comment on the investigator's report) that were not afforded to the respondent. This caused the appointment of the board of inquiry to be set aside though, interestingly, the inequality was not treated as an independent ground of judicial review but as the foundation for a successful allegation of a reasonable apprehension of bias.

In this context, it also should be recognized that the Supreme Court has held that the "principles of fundamental justice" as enshrined in s. 7 of the *Canadian Charter of Rights and Freedoms* have both a procedural and a substantive component: *Reference re BC Motor Vehicle Act*, [1985] 2 SCR 486 (BC). As a consequence, for those statutory authorities that affect "life, liberty and security of the person" interests, there is obviously the possibility of review by reference to substantive principles of justice. It is also worth reflecting on whether the basis on which Binnie J (and McLachlin CJ) would have decided *Mount Sinai* in favour of the hospital was a form of substantive fairness review albeit under the rubric of patent unreasonableness.

Fault as an Element in Procedural Fairness Assessments

In the vast majority of procedural fairness cases, the court will be confronting an argument to the effect that there was a denial of a proper hearing because of some conduct on the part of the decision-maker. However, on occasions, hearings do not happen or are flawed because of the intervention of external agents: notices sent do not arrive because of the negligence of couriers, postal authorities, or process servers; lawyers may fail their clients, for example, by not representing them properly at the hearing or by failing to alert them to an impending hearing date. Should this kind of situation ever give rise to a claim of breach of the rules of procedural fairness or natural justice?

In the context of solicitors misaddressing a letter to a client informing him of a deportation hearing, the House of Lords in 1990 held that there was no basis for intervention when a deportation order was made in the client's absence: *Al-Mehdawi v. Secretary of State for the Home Department*, [1990] AC 876 (CA and Eng. HL). The absence of fault on the part of the decision-maker was sufficient to settle the issue. (For a criticism of this judgment, see Herberg, "The Right to a Hearing: Breach Without Fault" (1991), *Public Law* 467.)

In Canada, there is no definitive answer to the question whether fault or responsibility on the part of the decision-maker is always a necessary ingredient in establishing a reviewable absence of procedural fairness. However, in *Shirwa v. Canada (Minister of Employment & Immigration)*, [1994] 2 FC 51 (TD), Denault J of the Federal Court Trial Division was prepared to hold that the total incompetence of the applicant's representative at an immigration hearing was, on the facts, grounds for a holding that there had been a reviewable breach of the rules of procedural fairness. In so holding, the court recognized the dangers of allowing cases to be built on allegations of incompetence on the part of representatives but felt that this was a problem that could be controlled by careful exercise of judicial discretion and a requirement of exceptional circumstances for intervention. Compare *Canada (Attorney General) v. Sorkun* (1988), 34 Admin. LR 131 (FCTD).

In a somewhat different context, Oliver J of the BC Supreme Court held that there was a failure of natural justice when the BC Human Rights Council refused to exercise a statutory discretion to reopen a matter when the applicant had prepared supplementary written representations but these had not been received: *Zutter v. British Columbia (Council on Human Rights)* (1993), 18 Admin. LR (2d) 228 (BC SC). (See also 245.) See also *Toronto Housing Co. v. Sabrie*, [2003] OJ no. 652 (Div. Ct.) (QL), in which Archie Campbell J (delivering the judgment of the court) held that the Ontario Rental Housing Tribunal had violated the principles of procedural fairness in relation to proceedings in which the person seeking a review of his eviction from rental housing did not attend because he was hospitalized at the time for a mental disorder, a fact of which the tribunal was not aware.

Which approach do you prefer: the need for a demonstration of fault on the part of the decision-maker or a consideration whether there was in fact a failure in the holding of a fair hearing and whether it is appropriate to hold the affected person responsible for that hearing? Would the latter approach be a "slippery slope" and constitute too great a threat to the need for finality in administrative decision making, or would it be sufficiently controlled by the sensitive exercise of judicial discretion? If there is no universal requirement to establish fault or responsibility on the part of the decision-maker, to what extent should the particular statutory context influence a court's assessment of such cases?

Constitutional and Quasi-Constitutional Enactments

We turn now to a consideration of the thresholds to the invocation of the procedural rights contained in the *Canadian Charter of Rights and Freedoms* and the *Canadian Bill of Rights*. There are two dimensions to the identification of these thresholds. First, there is the matter of the general reach of both these statutes; in the context of this casebook, what areas of administrative decision making do they affect? Second, there are the thresholds established in each statute by the specific provisions containing procedural guarantees. Our main attention will be directed to the second of these categories. The first raises questions generally beyond the reach of this work and is more apt for consideration in a course on constitutional law or the Charter and *Bill of Rights*. We will, nonetheless, sketch in the general parameters of each statute's application.

The Charter and the Bill of Rights: Issues of General Applicability

The *Canadian Bill of Rights* applies to the "laws of Canada," a term specified to include not only Acts of Parliament and "any order, rule or regulation thereunder" but also "any law in force in Canada" (s. 5(2)). This is presumably broad enough to encompass decisions and actions taken by those deriving their powers from federal law (including prerogative powers and action taken under them). However, it seems unlikely that it extends to the activities of bodies the functioning of which is made possible under facilitative legislation such as the *Canada Business Corporations Act*, RSC 1985, c. C-44. Putting it another way, there is an argument that, unlike the Charter, the reach of the *Bill of Rights* corresponds generally to that of judicial review under the *Federal Courts Act*.

In contrast to the *Bill of Rights*, the Charter applies throughout Canada. However, in further contrast to the *Bill of Rights*, it is clear that the ambit of the Charter is not coterminous with that of judicial review. By virtue of s. 32(1), the Charter's application is restricted to the Parliament and government of Canada (including the territories) and the legislatures and governments of the provinces. This has been held by the Supreme Court of Canada to be the controlling provision in terms of the reach of the Charter and to have the effect of restricting the Charter's application in the administrative law arena to bodies or at least activities that can be brought within the concept of "government."

Thus, in the leading authority, *McKinney v. University of Guelph*, [1990] 3 SCR 229 (Ont.), the majority held that, notwithstanding their statutory status, universities (at least as currently constituted) were not government and therefore not generally amenable to the Charter even with respect to actions and decisions that would expose them to judicial review. (See also *Harrison v. University of British Columbia*, [1990] 3 SCR 451 (BC).) The same held true for BC hospital boards (*Stoffman v. Vancouver General Hospital*, [1990] 3 SCR 483 (BC)) but not that province's community colleges (*Douglas/Kwantlen Faculty Assn. v. Douglas College*, [1990] 3 SCR 570 (BC)), a differentiation that at least on its face indicates that the dividing line between what is "government" for these purposes and what is not is certainly not a self-applying or bright-line distinction. (See also *Greater Vancouver Transportation Authority v. Canadian Federation of Students—British Columbia Component*, 2009 SCC 31 (BC).)

Thus, while it can now be asserted with some degree of confidence that, just as with the *Bill of Rights*, the Charter does not reach those bodies such as corporations the existence of which depends on and the operations of which are facilitated by statute, there are a range of other bodies, such as professional governing authorities and their disciplinary arms, where considerable controversy still remains. Nonetheless in *Harvey v. Law Society (Newfoundland)* (1992), 2 Admin. LR (2d) 306 (Nfld. SCTD), it was held that the Charter reached the disciplinary functions of the Law Society of Newfoundland. Given the self-regulating status of the legal profession, why is that so? What sorts the Law Society out from the university, given that each now operate under a statutory umbrella? Why is one a government body and the other not?

Indeed, the matter is complicated further by the suggestion in the majority judgments in *McKinney* that there may, nonetheless, be some undefined and unspecified activities of universities that partake sufficiently of the characteristics of government to be covered. This implied that the question of the general applicability of the Charter to a particular person or body will not always be determined on an all or nothing basis. Indeed, this has since been borne out in the jurisprudence. In *Eldridge v. British Columbia*, [1997] 3 SCR 624 (BC), the Supreme Court held that decisions of BC hospital boards on whether to provide translation facilities for hearing impaired patients were subject to the Charter since, in the delivery of health care services, hospitals were implementing a specific government policy. Thus, a statutory authority that is not in general government becomes subject to the Charter when charged with responsibility for the effectuation of government programs. What constitutes a governmental program for these purposes does not admit of ready answers.

Also, as exemplified by this group of cases, bodies that are not generally directly subject to the Charter may nevertheless be affected by it. To the extent that the respondent universities in *McKinney* were subject to Ontario *Human Rights Code* prohibitions against age discrimination and justified their mandatory retirement provisions on the exemptions from those prohibitions, their policies stood to be affected by a conclusion that the Ontario legislature (to which the Charter clearly applies) had transgressed s. 15(1) (the equality provision) in providing for such exemptions. (Indeed, the exemptions were held to be a violation of s. 15 but ones that could be justified by reference to s. 1.)

Finally, there may be an issue about the extent to which statutory bodies (including adjudicative tribunals), which enjoy varying degrees of independence from government or act at arm's length from government, are subject to the Charter. This issue arose in *Blencoe v. British Columbia (Human Rights Commission)*, [2000] 2 SCR 307 (BC) and we will deal with it in the context of a broader consideration of that case.

These are not the only complicated inquiries that surface with respect to the general application of the Charter. However, they are the principal ones for the purposes of administrative law and, in their complexity, provide some sense of the issues involved.

The Bill of Rights: Specific Procedural Thresholds

It is somewhat ironic that it was only after the advent of the Charter in 1982 that the *Bill of Rights* came into its own as a source of procedural protections because, in the era of the Charter, the *Bill of Rights*' real relevance is confined to those situations where it provides guarantees and the Charter does not. Seen from this perspective, there are three threshold dimensions to the *Bill of Rights* that promise a more extensive reach in terms of procedural protections than provided by the key Charter provision, s. 7. For these purposes, it is useful in this context to recall the terminology of s. 7:

> 7. *Everyone* has the right to life, liberty and security of the person and the right not to be deprived thereof except in accordance with the principles of fundamental justice. [Emphasis added.]

The three potentially significant differences between the reach of the relevant provisions in the two enactments are, first, the use of the terms "individual" and "person" in the *Bill of Rights* as opposed to "everyone" in the Charter; second, the inclusion of "enjoyment of property" in s. 1(a) of the *Bill of Rights*; and, third, the attachment in s. 2(e) of procedural guarantees to the "determination of rights and obligations." To these can also be added the fact that there is no equivalent in the *Bill of Rights* to s. 1 of the Charter, the issue of the extent that this matters being one to which we will return. As for the effect of these differences:

1. The Supreme Court of Canada has held that "life, liberty and security of the person" in s. 7 of the Charter are attributes possessed only by natural persons and, hence, "everyone" does not include corporations: for example, *Irwin Toy v. Quebec*, [1989] 1 SCR 927 (Que.). Whether the same holds for ss. 1(a) and 2(e) of the *Bill of Rights* has not been resolved definitively by the Supreme Court. While there is lower court authority to the effect that corporations are excluded from the benefit of s. 1(a) (for example, *Canada (Attorney General) v. Central Cartage Co. (No. 1)*, [1990] 2 FC 641 (CA)), there is no reason why the same should be so for s. 2(e). Under the federal *Interpretation Act*, RSC 1985, c. I-21, s. 35(1), "person" includes corporations unless the context otherwise requires and there is nothing in the nature of the concepts of "rights and obligations" that would dictate that the protections of the subsection not apply to corporations. Indeed, its application to corporations was assumed by the Federal Court of Appeal in *Central Cartage* and by the Quebec Court of Appeal in *Air Canada c. Canada (Procureure générale)*, [2003] JQ No. 21 (CA) (QL). (Note, however, that this whole question of who can invoke the Charter and the *Bill of Rights* is made more complicated by the fact that the Supreme Court in cases such as *R v. Wholesale Travel Group*, [1991] 3 SCR 154 (Ont.) held that a corporation (at least in the context of a defence to a criminal charge or in answer to a civil claim or regulatory proceedings) can argue that a legislative provision is invalid because it would violate s. 7 in its application to an individual.)

2. Quite deliberately, s. 7 of the Charter did not include protection for "property" rights. Of course, there is considerable room for debate about the extent to which property interests might achieve indirect protection in the name of "life, liberty and security of the person" and about the nature of the "property rights" that are included within s. 1(a) of the *Bill of Rights*. Nonetheless, this represents perhaps the most significant difference in terms of coverage as between the two enactments, though it must be conceded that, to this point, s. 1(a) of the *Bill of Rights* has not been frequently invoked in litigation. However, there are signs that there is life in s. 1(a). *785072 Ontario Inc. v. Canada (Minister of National Revenue)* (1994), 83 FTR 96 provides a useful example of where the *Bill of Rights* might bite in a situation

clearly not covered by s. 7 of the Charter. This case had to do with the confiscation under the *Excise Act*, RSC 1985, c. E-14, of a rental vehicle in which smuggled alcohol had been found. Under the relevant legislation, there was no guarantee that the owner of the vehicle, in this case a company that had leased the car to another company for rental purposes, would receive notice of the situation before the vehicle became forfeited to the Crown. While dealing with the issue of notice by reference to common law and statutory interpretation principles, Rothstein J also suggested that, in the event that that conclusion could not be justified on a proper reading of the statute, the legislation itself might be contrary to the *Bill of Rights*. The forfeiture of the vehicle to the Crown affected the ownership "rights" of the leasing company and the fact that this could occur without notice to it of either the seizure or the confiscation seemed to constitute a denial of the benefit of the "principles of fundamental justice." Indeed, in the case of individual (as opposed to corporate) owners of vehicles, s. 1(a) also looms as a possible basis for an attack on the legislation—the deprivation of a property right in the vehicle without "due process of law."

3. While the *Canadian Bill of Rights* does not contain an equivalent to s. 1 of the Charter, the Quebec Court of Appeal in *Air Canada c. Canada (Procureure générale)*, above, at paras. 92-99, held that, in determining the demands of the principles of fundamental justice for the purposes of s. 2(e), the court should engage in a s. 1-style balancing process akin to that set out in *R v. Oakes*, [1986] 1 SCR 103 (Ont.). *Quaere* whether such a reading in is justifiable and, if it is, does that mean that the inclusion of s. 1 in the Charter was unnecessary?

4. While initially, the term "rights and obligations" in s. 2(e) of the *Bill of Rights* was interpreted narrowly by the courts and restricted to the taking away of "strict, legal rights," all that changed with the resurrection of the *Bill of Rights* in *Singh v. Canada (Minister of Employment and Immigration)*, [1985] 1 SCR 177 (Can.), one of the seminal judgments of the Supreme Court of Canada in the early jurisprudence of the Charter and to which we turn in detail shortly. There, three members of the court held that the immigration authorities came within s. 2(e) when deciding upon a convention refugee claim. This involved "determining" whether the claimant had a statutory "right" to remain in Canada. Since then, the term has been held by the Federal Court of Appeal to embrace the investigation and hearing of a complaint of discrimination under the federal human rights legislation on the basis that those proceedings involved the determination whether the respondent had breached his legal "obligation" not to discriminate against his employees: *MacBain v. Lederman*, [1985] 1 FC 856 (CA). (For a more recent application of this, see *Bell Canada v. Canada (Human Rights Commission)*, [2001] 3 FC 481 (CA).)

The question of whether the procedural protections in ss. 1(a) and 2(e) of the *Bill of Rights* could apply to legislative proceedings, or whether they were subject to a threshold similar to that established for common law procedural fairness in *Inuit Tapirisat* and other decisions had been raised before (see *National Anti-Poverty Organization v. Canada (Attorney-General)* (1990), 60 DLR (4th) 712 (FCA)) but was only definitely answered by the Supreme Court of Canada in the following decision.

Authorson v. Canada (Attorney General)
[2003] 2 SCR 40

[Authorson was named representative plaintiff of the class of disabled veterans whose pensions and other statutory benefits received from the Crown were administered by the Department of Veterans Affairs (DVA) because the veterans were deemed incapable of managing their money. The DVA failed to invest or pay interest on these moneys until 1990 when it began to pay interest. To limit the Crown's liability for past interest, Parliament enacted s. 5.1(4) of the *Department of Veterans Affairs Act*, which provided that no claim could be made after the coming into force of the provision for or on account of interest held on moneys held or administered by the minister of veterans affairs prior to 1990. The veterans sued the Crown for breach of fiduciary duty. They argued that the statutory bar on the right to sue was inoperative because it breached their rights under ss. 1(a) and 2(e) of the *Bill of Rights*.]

MAJOR J: …

B. *Section 1(a) of the Canadian Bill of Rights*

[35] Section 1(a) of the *Bill of Rights* recognizes "… the right of the individual to life, liberty, security of the person and enjoyment of property, and the right not to be deprived thereof except by due process of law."

[36] The respondent submitted that s. 5.1(4) of the *Department of Veterans Affairs Act* took away his right to interest on his funds without due process of law. The question is what process is guaranteed by the *Bill of Rights* when property rights are extinguished? The respondent's argument encompasses three types of due process:

   (i) procedural rights before parliamentary enactment of a law;

   (ii) procedural rights before the application of a statute to his individual circumstances; and

   (iii) substantive protections against governmental expropriation of his property.

None of the claims help the respondent.

(1) *Procedural Rights in Legislative Enactment*

[37] The respondent claimed a right to notice and hearing to contest the passage of s. 5.1(4) of the *Department of Veterans Affairs Act*. However, in 1960, and today, no such right exists. Long-standing parliamentary tradition makes it clear that the only procedure due any citizen of Canada is that proposed legislation receive three readings in the Senate and House of Commons and that it receive Royal Assent. Once that process is completed, legislation within Parliament's competence is unassailable.

[A discussion of relevant authorities is omitted.]

    (i)   protections against arbitrary detention and cruel and unusual punishment;

    (ii) upon arrest, the right to information about charges laid, the right to counsel and the right to *habeas corpus*;

  (iii) evidentiary rights and rights against self-incrimination;

  (iv) the presumption of innocence;

   (v) the right to an impartial tribunal;

  (vi) the right to reasonable bail; and

 (vii) the right to an interpreter in proceedings.

All of these protections are legal rights applicable in the context of, or prior to, a hearing before a court or tribunal.

[60] The French version of s. 2(*e*) makes this distinction clearer. A fair hearing is translated as "*une audition impartiale de sa cause.*" According to *Le Grand Robert de la langue française* (2nd ed. 2001), the term "*cause*" means "*[a]ffaire, procès qui se plaide.*" This definition confirms the legalistic nature of the "fair hearing."

[61] Section 2(*e*) of the *Bill of Rights* does not impose upon Parliament the duty to provide a hearing before the enactment of legislation. Its protections are operative only in the application of law to individual circumstances in a proceeding before a court, tribunal or similar body.

V. *Conclusion*

[62] The respondent and the class of disabled veterans it represents are owed decades of interest on their pension and benefit funds. The Crown does not dispute these findings. But Parliament has chosen for undisclosed reasons to lawfully deny the veterans, to whom the Crown owed a fiduciary duty, these benefits whether legal, equitable or fiduciary. The due process protections of property in the *Bill of Rights* do not grant procedural rights in the process of legislative enactment. They do confer certain rights to notice and an opportunity to make submissions in the adjudication of individual rights and obligations, but no such rights are at issue in this appeal.

[63] While the due process guarantees may have some substantive content not apparent in this appeal, there is no due process right against duly enacted legislation unambiguously expropriating property interests.

[64] I would allow the appeal without costs. I would not disturb the order as to costs below.

NOTE

The court's decision in *Authorson* appears to mean that the quasi-constitutional norms prescribed in the *Canadian Bill of Rights* are of no assistance in decision-making contexts that fall on the legislative end of the legislative/administrative threshold for the application of common law procedural fairness. Does *Authorson* mean also that the *Bill of Rights* could not provide for procedures in other cases involving decision making that falls below the common law threshold, including investigatory processes?

Section 7 of the Charter: Specific Procedural Thresholds

The potential impact of s. 7 on administrative processes was first considered by the Supreme Court of Canada in 1984 in *Singh v. Canada (Minister of Employment and Immigration)*, [1985] 1 SCR 177 (Can.). The judgments in the Supreme Court of Canada raise issues that are still of considerable importance for the reach of s. 7 of the Charter as well as s. 2(e) of the *Bill of Rights* and we include lengthy extracts at this point for both those purposes. In reading the judgment of Wilson J (Charter) and Beetz J (*Bill of Rights*), consider the following questions:

1. On what basis does Wilson J conclude that the applicants had brought themselves within the ambit of s. 7? After all, they were not Canadian citizens, landed immigrants, or technically even residents. Moreover, the threats that they feared were based on what might happen to them were they to be returned to the country from which they came. Do you think that it was concerns about this threshold issue that led the court to reopen the hearing of the appeal so that the parties could address arguments based on s. 2(e) of the *Canadian Bill of Rights* and that led three of the judges to base their conclusions on the *Bill of Rights* rather than the Charter?

2. How does Beetz J (delivering the judgment of those three judges) justify the applicability of s. 2(e) of the *Bill of Rights*? What, if any, are the differences between these reasons and those of Wilson J?

3. What is the position of Wilson J on the applicability of s. 1 justifications in the case of violations of s. 7 of the Charter? Is she maintaining that s. 1 simply has no role to play in such cases and that breaches of the principles of fundamental justice can never be justified in a free and democratic society? If that is so, what are the practical consequences of such a position? Alternatively, is she merely saying that the Crown had not adduced adequate evidence to found a s. 1 justification? If so, what was inadequate about the evidence that was advanced? Is it a question of there being insufficient evidence of the type relied on to meet the appropriate standard of proof or is it a case where the evidence being advanced was of a species that could never provide a justification for a violation of s. 7? Does Beetz J take any position on possible justifications of breaches of s. 2(e) of the *Bill of Rights* or are such considerations and evidence totally irrelevant in that context?

Singh v. Canada (Minister of Employment and Immigration)
[1985] 1 SCR 177 (Can.)

[The appellants were all convention refugee claimants who were landed in Canada. Under the procedure then in place, the minister, acting on the advice of the Refugee Status Advisory Committee, had determined that they were not convention refugees. They all then applied to the Immigration Appeal Board for a redetermination of their status. However, their applications were not referred to an oral hearing because the board determined on the strength of the material submitted by the applicants that there were no reasonable grounds for believing that they could establish their claims at a hearing.

The appellants then applied to the Federal Court of Appeal for review of the board's decision alleging that the statutory scheme infringed s. 7 of the *Canadian Charter of Rights and Freedoms*. The applications failed and the appellants secured leave to appeal to the Supreme Court of Canada. After the conclusion of oral argument in the Supreme Court, the parties were directed to make further *written* submissions on whether the statutory scheme was consistent with s. 2(e) of the *Canadian Bill of Rights*.]

WILSON J (Dickson CJ and Lamer J concurring; Ritchie J took no part in the judgment):

· · ·

2. The Scheme of the Immigration Act, 1976

The appellants allege that the procedural mechanisms set out in the *Immigration Act, 1976* as opposed to the application of those procedures to their particular cases, have deprived them of their rights under the Charter. It is important, therefore, to understand these provisions in the context of the Act as a whole. If, as a matter of statutory interpretation, the procedural fairness sought by the appellants is not excluded by the scheme of the Act, there is, of course, no basis for resort to the Charter. The issue may be resolved on other grounds.

[Wilson J here asserted by reference to authority that the courts should in general not resort to constitutional bases for resolving cases unless it was strictly necessary.]

(a) The Rights of Convention Refugees Under the Immigration Act, 1976

The appellants make no attempt to assert a constitutional right to enter and remain in Canada analogous to the right accorded to Canadian citizens by s. 6(1) of the Charter. Equally, at common law an alien has no right to enter or remain in Canada except by leave of the Crown: *Prata v. Minister of Manpower and Immigration* [1976] 1 SCR 376 (Can.). As Martland J expressed the law in *Prata* at 380, "The right of aliens to enter and remain in Canada is governed by the *Immigration Act*" and s. 5(1) states that "No person, other than a person described in section 4, has a right to come into or remain in Canada."

However, the *Immigration Act, 1976* does provide Convention refugees with certain limited rights to enter and remain in Canada. The Act envisages the assertion of a refugee claim under s. 45 in the context of an inquiry, which presupposes that the refugee claimant is physically present in Canada and within the jurisdiction of the Canadian authorities. The Act and Regulations do envisage the resettlement in Canada of refugees who are outside the country but the following observations are not made with reference to these individuals. When a person who is in Canada has been determined to be a Convention refugee, s. 47(1) requires the adjudicator to reconvene the inquiry held pursuant to s. 23 or s. 27 in order to determine whether the individual is a person described in s. 4(2) of the Act. Section 4(2) provides that a Convention refugee "while lawfully in Canada [has] a right to remain in Canada …" except where it is established that he or she falls into the category of criminal or subversive persons set out in s. 4(2)(b). If it is determined that the person is a Convention refugee described in s. 4(2), s. 47(3) requires the adjudicator to allow the person to remain in Canada notwithstanding any other provisions of the Act or Regulations.

[After an analysis of the relevant legislative provisions and the United Nations Refugee Convention, which Canada has ratified, Wilson J concluded:]

I believe therefore that a Convention refugee who does not have a safe haven elsewhere is entitled to rely on this country's willingness to live up to the obligations it has undertaken as a signatory to the United Nations Convention Relating to the Status of Refugees. ...

(b) The Procedures for the Determination of Convention Refugee Status

The term "Convention refugee" is defined in s. 2(1) of the Act as follows:

> "Convention refugee" means any person who, by reason of a well-founded fear of persecution for reasons of race, religion, nationality, membership in a particular social group or political opinion,
>
> (a) is outside the country of his nationality and is unable or, by reason of such fear, is unwilling to avail himself of the protection of that country, or
>
> (b) not having a country of nationality, is outside the country of his former habitual residence and is unable or, by reason of such fear, is unwilling to return to that country;

As noted above, the procedures for determination of whether an individual is a Convention refugee and for redetermination of claims by the Immigration Appeal Board are set out in ss. 45 to 48 and 70 to 71 respectively. Focusing first on the initial determination, s. 45 provides as follows:

> 45.(1) Where, at any time during an inquiry, the person who is the subject of the inquiry claims that he is a Convention refugee, the inquiry shall be continued and, if it is determined that, but for the person's claim that he is a Convention refugee, a removal order or a departure notice would be made or issued with respect to that person, the inquiry shall be adjourned and that person shall be examined under oath by a senior immigration officer respecting his claim.
>
> (2) Where a person who claims that he is a Convention refugee is examined under oath pursuant to subsection (1), his claim, together with a transcript of the examination with respect thereto, shall be referred to the Minister for determination.
>
> (3) A copy of the transcript of an examination under oath referred to in subsection (1) shall be forwarded to the person who claims that he is a Convention refugee.
>
> (4) Where a person's claim is referred to the Minister pursuant to subsection (2), the Minister shall refer the claim and the transcript of the examination under oath with respect thereto to the Refugee Status Advisory Committee established pursuant to section 48 for consideration and, after having obtained the advice of that committee, shall determine whether or not the person is a Convention refugee.
>
> (5) When the Minister makes a determination with respect to a person's claim that he is a Convention refugee, the Minister shall thereupon in writing inform the senior immigration officer who conducted the examination under oath respecting the claim and the person who claimed to be a Convention refugee of his determination.
>
> (6) Every person with respect to whom an examination under oath is to be held pursuant to subsection (1) shall be informed that he has the right to obtain the services of a barrister

or solicitor or other counsel and to be represented by any such counsel at his examination and shall be given a reasonable opportunity, if he so desires and at his own expense, to obtain such counsel.

It is difficult to characterize this procedure as a "hearing" in the traditional sense. ... [T]he procedure is technically "non-adversarial" since only the claimant is entitled to be represented by counsel. ...

[After detailing the law with respect to procedural fairness and the need for the court to consider the content of the obligations of procedural fairness within the relevant statutory framework, Wilson J continued:]

Counsel for the respondent in this case submitted that the Act did not contemplate an oral hearing before the Minister or the Refugee Status Advisory Committee and that the Minister and the Committee were entitled to rely upon what he described as "the government's knowledge of world affairs" in rendering a decision. As I read s. 45, and in particular s. 45(4), these submissions appear to be correct. It is clear from s. 45(4) that the Act does not envisage an opportunity for the refugee claimant to be heard other than through his claim and the transcript of his examination under oath. Nor does the Act appear to envisage the refugee claimant's being given an opportunity to comment on the advice the Refugee Status Advisory Committee has given to the Minister. The insulation of the process is reinforced by the fact that the Minister is entitled under s. 123 of the Act to delegate his powers under s. 45 and in fact these powers are customarily delegated to the Registrar of the Refugee Status Advisory Committee ... . In substance, therefore, it would appear that the Refugee Status Advisory Committee acts as a decision-making body isolated from the persons whose status it is adjudicating and that it applies policies and makes use of information to which the refugee claimants themselves have no access. The Committee and the Minister have an obligation to act fairly in carrying out their duties in the sense that decisions cannot be made arbitrarily and they must make an effort to treat equivalent cases in equivalent fashion. I do not think, however, that the courts can import into the duty of fairness procedural constraints on the Committee's operation which are incompatible with the decision-making scheme set up by Parliament.

In any event, the Minister's exercise of his jurisdiction under s. 45 is not reviewable on these appeals. [They were only challengeable in proceedings brought before the Trial Division under s. 18 of the *Federal Courts Act*.]

The refugee claimant's status, however, need not be conclusively determined by the Minister's decision on the advice of the Refugee Status Advisory Committee made pursuant to s. 45. Under s. 70(1) of the Act a person whose refugee claim has been refused by the Minister may, within a period prescribed in Regulation 40(1) as fifteen days from the time he is so informed, apply for a redetermination of his claim by the Immigration Appeal Board. Section 70(2) requires the refugee claimant to submit with such an application a copy of the transcript of the examination under oath which was conducted pursuant to s. 45(1) and a declaration under oath setting out the basis of the application, the facts upon which the appellant relies and the information and evidence the applicant intends to offer at a redetermination hearing. The applicant is also permitted pursuant to s. 70(2)(d) to set out in his declaration such other representations as he deems relevant to his application.

The Immigration Appeal Board's duties in considering an application for redetermination of a refugee status claim are set out in s. 71 which reads as follows:

71.(1) Where the Board receives an application referred to in subsection 70(2), it shall forthwith consider the application and if, on the basis of such consideration, it is of the opinion that there are reasonable grounds to believe that a claim could, upon the hearing of the application, be established, it shall allow the application to proceed, and in any other case it shall refuse to allow the application to proceed and shall thereupon determine that the person is not a Convention refugee.

(2) Where pursuant to subsection (1) the Board allows an application to proceed, it shall notify the Minister of the time and place where the application is to be heard and afford the Minister a reasonable opportunity to be heard.

(3) Where the Board has made its determination as to whether or not a person is a Convention refugee, it shall, in writing, inform the Minister and the applicant of its decision.

(4) The Board may, and at the request of the applicant or the Minister shall, give reasons for its determination.

If the Board were to determine pursuant to s. 71(1) that the application should be allowed to proceed, the parties are all agreed that the hearing which would take place pursuant to s. 71(2) would be *quasi*-judicial one to which full natural justice would apply. The Board is not, however, empowered by the terms of the statute to allow a redetermination hearing to proceed in every case. It may only do so if "it is of the opinion that there are reasonable grounds to believe that a claim could, upon the hearing of the application, be established. ..."

. . .

The substance of the appellants' case, as I understand it, is that they did not have a fair opportunity to present their refugee status claims or to know the case they had to meet. I do not think there is any basis for suggesting that the procedures set out in the *Immigration Act, 1976* were not followed correctly in the adjudication of these individuals' claims. Nor do I believe that there is any basis for interpreting the relevant provisions of the *Immigration Act* in a way that provides a significantly greater degree of procedural fairness or natural justice than I have set out in the preceding discussion. The Act by its terms seems to preclude this. Accordingly, if the appellants are to succeed, I believe that it must be on the basis that the Charter requires the Court to override Parliament's decision to exclude the kind of procedural fairness sought by the appellant.

3. The Application of the Charter

Are the Appellants Entitled to the Protection of s. 7 of the Charter?

... Counsel for the Minister concedes that "everyone" is sufficiently broad to include the appellants in its compass and I am prepared to accept that the term includes every human being who is physically present in Canada and by virtue of such presence amenable to Canadian law.

That premise being accepted, the question then becomes whether the rights the appellants seek to assert fall within the scope of s. 7. Counsel for the Minister does not concede this. He submits that the exclusion or removal of the appellants from Canada would not infringe "the right to life, liberty and security of the person." He advances three main lines of argument in support of this submission.

The first may be described as a reliance on the "single right" theory articulated by Marceau J in *The Queen v. Operation Dismantle Inc.* [1983] 1 FC 745 (TD) at 773-74. In counsel's submission, the words "the right to life, liberty and security of the person" form a single right with closely inter-related parts and this right relates to matters of death, arrest, detention, physical liberty and physical punishment of the person. Moreover, counsel says, s. 7 only protects persons against the deprivation of that type of right if the deprivation results from a violation of the principles of fundamental justice. This argument by itself does not advance the Minister's case very far since the appellants submit that, even on this restrictive interpretation of s. 7, their rights in relation to matters of death, arrest, detention, physical liberty and physical punishment are indeed affected. Counsel for the appellants took two different approaches in their attempt to demonstrate this.

[Wilson J here set out the submissions of counsel.]

It seems to me that in attempting to decide whether the appellants have been deprived of the right to life, liberty and security of the person within the meaning of s. 7 of the Charter, we must begin by determining what rights the appellants have under the *Immigration Act, 1976.* As noted earlier, s. 5(1) of the Act excludes from persons other than those described in s. 4 the right to come into or remain in Canada. The appellants therefore do not have such a right. However, the Act does accord a Convention refugee certain rights which it does not provide to others, namely the right to a determination from the Minister based on proper principles as to whether a permit should issue entitling him to enter and remain in Canada (ss. 4(2) and 37); the right not to be returned to a country where his life or freedom would be threatened (s. 55); and the right to appeal a removal order or a deportation order made against him (ss. 72(2)(a), 72(2)(b) and 72(3)).

We must therefore ask ourselves whether the deprivation of these rights constitutes a deprivation of the right to life, liberty and security of the person within the meaning of s. 7 of the Charter. Even if we accept the "single right" theory advanced by counsel for the Minister in interpreting s. 7, I think we must recognize that the "right" which is articulated in s. 7 has three elements: life, liberty and security of the person. As I understand the "single right" theory, it is not suggested that there must be a deprivation of all three of these elements before an individual is deprived of his "right" under s. 7. In other words, I believe that it is consistent with the "single right" theory advanced by counsel to suggest that a deprivation of the appellants' "security of the person," for example, would constitute a deprivation of their "right" under s. 7, whether or not it can also be said that they have been deprived of their lives or liberty. Rather, as I understand it, the "single right" theory is advanced in support of a narrow construction of the words "life," "liberty" and "security of the person" as different aspects of a single concept rather than as separate concepts each of which must be construed independently.

· · ·

The "single right" theory advanced by counsel for the Minister would suggest that this conception of "liberty" is too broad to be employed in our interpretation of s. 7 of the

Charter. Even if this submission is sound, however, it seems to me that it is incumbent upon the Court to give meaning to each of the elements, life, liberty and security of the person, which make up the "right" contained in s. 7.

To return to the facts before the Court, it will be recalled that a Convention refugee is by definition a person who has a well-founded fear of persecution in the country from which he is fleeing. In my view, to deprive him of the avenues open to him under the Act to escape from that fear of persecution must, at the least, impair his right to life, liberty and security of the person in the narrow sense advanced by counsel for the Minister. The question, however, is whether such an impairment constitutes a "deprivation" under s. 7.

It must be acknowledged, for example, that even if a Convention refugee's fear of persecution is a well-founded one, it does not automatically follow that he will be deprived of his life or his liberty if he is returned to his homeland. Can it be said that Canadian officials have deprived a Convention refugee of his right to life, liberty and security of the person if he is wrongfully returned to a country where death, imprisonment or another form of persecution *may* await him? There may be some merit in counsel's submission that closing off the avenues of escape provided by the Act does not *per se* deprive a Convention refugee of the right to life or to liberty. It may result in his being deprived of life or liberty by others, but it is not certain that this will happen.

I cannot, however, accept the submission of counsel for the Minister that the denial of the rights possessed by a Convention refugee under the Act does not constitute a deprivation of his security of the person. Like "liberty," the phrase "security of the person" is capable of a broad range of meaning. The phrase "security of the person" is found in s. 1(a) of the *Canadian Bill of Rights* and its interpretation in that context might have assisted us in its proper interpretation under the Charter. Unfortunately no clear meaning of the words emerges from the case law ... . The Law Reform Commission, in its Working Paper No. 26, *Medical Treatment and Criminal Law* (1980), suggested at 6 that:

> The right to security of the person means not only protection of one's physical integrity, but the provision of necessaries for its support.

The Commission went on to describe the provision of necessaries in terms of Art. 25, para. 1 of the *Universal Declaration of Human Rights* (1948) which reads:

> Every one has the right to a standard of living adequate for the health and well-being of himself and of his family, including food, clothing, housing and medical care and necessary social services, and the right to security in the event of unemployment, sickness, disability, widowhood, old age, or other lack of livelihood in circumstances beyond his control.

Commentators have advocated the adoption of a similarly broad conception of "security of the person" in the interpretation of s. 7 of the Charter. ...

For purposes of the present appeal it is not necessary, in my opinion, to consider whether such an expansive approach to "security of the person" in s. 7 of the Charter should be taken. It seems to me that even if one adopts the narrow approach advocated by counsel for the Minister, "security of the person" must encompass freedom from the threat of physical punishment or suffering as well as freedom from such punishment itself. I note particularly that a Convention refugee has the right under s. 55 of the Act not to "... be removed from Canada to a country where his life or freedom would be threatened … ." In my view, the denial of such a right must amount to a deprivation of security of the person within the meaning of s. 7.

. . .

It must be recognized that the appellants are not at this stage entitled to assert rights as Convention refugees; their claim is that they are entitled to fundamental justice in the determination of whether they are Convention refugees or not. From some of the cases dealing with the application of the *Canadian Bill of Rights* to the determination of the rights of individuals under immigration legislation it might be suggested that whatever procedures the legislation itself sets out for the determination of rights constitute "due process" for purposes of s. 1(a) and "fundamental justice" for purposes of s. 2(e) of the *Canadian Bill of Rights* … As Tarnopolsky observed in his text *The Canadian Bill of Rights* (2nd ed. 1975) at 273:

> The courts have consistently held that immigration is a privilege, and not a right.

The creation of a dichotomy between privileges and rights played a significant role in narrowing the scope of the application of the *Canadian Bill of Rights*, as is apparent from the judgment of Martland J in *Mitchell v. The Queen* [1976] 2 SCR 570 (Can.). At 588 Martland J said:

> The appellant also relies upon s. 2(e) of the *Bill of Rights*, which provides that no law of Canada shall be construed or applied so as to deprive a person of the right to a fair hearing in accordance with the principles of fundamental justice for the determination of his rights and obligations. In the *McCaud* case [[1965] 1 CCC 168 (SCC)] Spence J, whose view was adopted unanimously on appeal, held that the provisions of s. 2(e) do not apply to the question of the revocation of parole under the provisions of the *Parole Act*.
>
> The appellant had no right to parole. He was granted parole as a matter of discretion by the Parole Board. He had no right to remain on parole. His parole was subject to revocation at the absolute discretion of the Board.

I do not think this kind of analysis is acceptable in relation to the Charter. It seems to me rather that the recent adoption of the Charter by Parliament and nine of the ten provinces as part of the Canadian constitutional framework has sent a clear message to the courts that the restrictive attitude which at times characterized their approach to the *Canadian Bill of Rights* ought to be re-examined. I am accordingly of the view that the approach taken by Laskin CJC dissenting in *Mitchell* is to be preferred to that of the majority as we examine the question whether the Charter has any application to the adjudication of rights granted to an individual by statute.

In *Mitchell* the issue was whether the *Canadian Bill of Rights* required s. 16(1) of the *Parole Act* to be interpreted so as to require the Parole Board to provide a parolee with a fair hearing before revoking his parole. Laskin CJC focussed on the consequences of the revocation of parole for the individual and concluded that parole could not be characterized as a "mere privilege" even although the parolee had no absolute right to be released from prison. He said at 585:

> Between them, s. 2(c)(i) and s. 2(e) [of the *Canadian Bill of Rights*] call for at least minimum procedural safeguards in parole administration where revocation is involved, despite what may be said about the confidentiality and sensitiveness of the parole system.

It seems to me that the appellants in this case have an even stronger argument to make than the appellant in Mitchell. At most Mr. Mitchell was entitled to a hearing from the Parole Board concerning the revocation of his parole and a decision from the Board based on proper considerations as to whether to continue his parole or not. He had no statutory right to the parole itself; rather he had a right to proper consideration of whether he was entitled to remain on parole. By way of contrast, if the appellants had been found to be Convention refugees as defined in s. 2(1) of the *Immigration Act, 1976* they would have been entitled as a matter of law to the incidents of that status provided for in the Act. Given the potential consequences for the appellants of a denial of that status if they are in fact persons with a "well-founded fear of persecution," it seems to me unthinkable that the Charter would not apply to entitle them to fundamental justice in the adjudication of their status.

. . .

In summary, I am of the view that the rights which the appellants are seeking to assert are ones which entitle them to the protection of s. 7 of the Charter. It is necessary therefore to consider whether the procedures for the determination of refugee status as set out in the Act accord with fundamental justice.

Is Fundamental Justice Denied by the Procedures for the Determination of Convention Refugee Status Set Out in the Act?

All counsel were agreed that at a minimum the concept of "fundamental justice" as it appears in s. 7 of the Charter includes the notion of procedural fairness articulated by Fauteux CJ in *Duke v. The Queen* [1972] SCR 917 (Ont.). At 923 he said:

> Under s. 2(e) of the *Bill of Rights* no law of Canada shall be construed or applied so as to deprive him of "a fair hearing in accordance with the principles of fundamental justice." Without attempting to formulate any final definition of those words, I would take them to mean, generally, that the tribunal which adjudicates upon his rights must act fairly, in good faith, without bias and in a judicial temper, and must give to him the opportunity adequately to state his case.

Do the procedures set out in the Act for the adjudication of refugee status claims meet this test of procedural fairness? Do they provide an adequate opportunity for a refugee claimant to state his case and know the case he has to meet? This seems to be the question we have to answer and, in approaching it, I am prepared to accept Mr. Bowie's submission that procedural fairness may demand different things in different contexts ... . Thus it is possible that an oral hearing before the decision-maker is not required in every case in which s. 7 of the Charter is called into play. However, I must confess to some difficulty in reconciling Mr. Bowie's argument that an oral hearing is not required in the context of this case with the interpretation he seeks to put on s. 7. If "the right to life, liberty and security of the person" is properly construed as relating only to matters such as death, physical liberty and physical punishment, it would seem on the surface at least that these are matters of such fundamental importance that procedural fairness would invariably require an oral hearing. I am prepared, nevertheless, to accept for present purposes that written submissions may be an adequate substitute for an oral hearing in appropriate circumstances.

I should note, however, that even if hearings based on written submissions are consistent with the principles of fundamental justice for some purposes, they will not be satisfactory for all purposes. In particular, I am of the view that where a serious issue of credibility is involved, fundamental justice requires that credibility be determined on the basis of an oral hearing. Appellate courts are well aware of the inherent weakness of written transcripts where questions of credibility are at stake and thus are extremely loath to review the findings of tribunals which have had the benefit of hearing the testimony of witnesses in person … . I find it difficult to conceive of a situation in which compliance with fundamental justice could be achieved by a tribunal making significant findings of credibility solely on the basis of written submissions.

As I have suggested, the absence of an oral hearing need not be inconsistent with fundamental justice in every case. My greatest concern about the procedural scheme envisaged by ss. 45 to 48 and 70 and 71 of the *Immigration Act, 1976* is not, therefore, with the absence of an oral hearing in and of itself, but with the inadequacy of the opportunity the scheme provides for a refugee claimant to state his case and know the case he has to meet. Mr. Bowie argued that since the procedure under s. 45 was an administrative one, it was quite proper for the Minister and the Refugee Status Advisory Committee to take into account policy considerations and information about world affairs to which the refugee claimant had no opportunity to respond. However, in my view the proceedings before the Immigration Appeal Board were *quasi*-judicial and the Board was not entitled to rely on material outside the record which the refugee claimant himself submitted on his application for redetermination … . Mr. Bowie submitted that there was no case against the refugee claimant at that stage; it was merely his responsibility to make a written submission which demonstrated on the balance of probabilities that he would be able to establish his claim at a hearing. If the applicant failed to bring forward the requisite facts his claim would not be allowed to proceed, but there was nothing fundamentally unfair in this procedure.

It seems to me that the basic flaw in Mr. Bowie's characterization of the procedure under ss. 70 and 71 is his description of the procedure as non-adversarial. It is in fact highly adversarial but the adversary, the Minister, is waiting in the wings. What the Board has before it is a determination by the Minister based in part on information and policies to which the applicant has no means of access that the applicant for redetermination is not a Convention refugee. The applicant is entitled to submit whatever relevant material he wishes to the Board but he still faces the hurdle of having to establish to the Board that on the balance of probabilities the Minister was wrong. Moreover, he must do this without any knowledge of the Minister's case beyond the rudimentary reasons which the Minister has decided to give him in rejecting his claim. It is this aspect of the procedures set out in the Act which I find impossible to reconcile with the requirements of "fundamental justice" as set out in s. 7 of the Charter.

It is perhaps worth noting that if the Immigration Appeal Board allows a redetermination hearing to proceed pursuant to s. 71(1), the Minister is entitled pursuant to s. 71(2) to notice of the time and place of the hearing and a reasonable opportunity to be heard. It seems to me that, as a matter of fundamental justice, a refugee claimant would be entitled to discovery of the Minister's case prior to such a hearing. It must be acknowledged, of course, that some of the information upon which the Minister's case would be based might be subject to Crown privilege. But the courts are well able to give the applicant relief if the Minister attempts to make an overly broad assertion of privilege: see *Canada Evidence Act*, SC 1980-81-82-83, c. 111, Schedule III, s. 36.1.

Under the Act as it presently stands, however, a refugee claimant may never have the opportunity to make an effective challenge to the information or policies which underlie the Minister's decision to reject his claim. Because s. 71(1) requires the Immigration Appeal Board to reject an application for redetermination unless it is of the view that it is more likely than not that the applicant will be able to succeed, it is apparent that an application will usually be rejected before the refugee claimant has had an opportunity to discover the Minister's case against him in the context of a hearing. Indeed, given the fact that s. 71(1) resolves any doubt as to whether or not there should be a hearing against the refugee claimant, I find it difficult to see how a successful challenge to the accuracy of the undisclosed information upon which the Minister's decision is based could ever be launched.

I am accordingly of the view that the procedures for determination of refugee status claims as set out in the *Immigration Act, 1976* do not accord refugee claimants fundamental justice in the adjudication of those claims and are thus incompatible with s. 7 of the Charter. It is therefore necessary to go forward to the third stage of the inquiry and determine whether the shortcomings of these procedures in relation to the standards set out by s. 7 constitute reasonable limits which can be demonstrably justified in a free and democratic society within the meaning of s. 1 of the Charter.

Can the Procedures Be Saved Under s. 1 of the Charter?

· · ·

The question of the standards which the Court should use in applying s. 1 is, without a doubt, a question of enormous significance for the operation of the Charter. If too low a threshold is set, the courts run the risk of emasculating the Charter. If too high a threshold is set, the courts run the risk of unjustifiably restricting government action. It is not a task to be entered upon lightly.

Unfortunately, counsel devoted relatively little time in the course of argument to the principles the Court should espouse in applying s. 1. …

Mr. Bowie's submissions on behalf of the Minister with respect to s. 1 were that Canadian procedures with respect to the adjudication of refugee claims had received the approbation of the office of the United Nations High Commissioner for Refugees and that it was not uncommon in Commonwealth and Western European countries for refugee claims to be adjudicated administratively without a right to appeal. He further argued that the Immigration Appeal Board was already subjected to a considerable strain in terms of the volume of cases which it was required to hear and that a requirement of an oral hearing in every case where an application for redetermination of a refugee claim has been made would constitute an unreasonable burden on the Board's resources.

One or two comments are in order respecting this approach to s. 1. It seems to me that it is important to bear in mind that the rights and freedoms set out in the Charter are fundamental to the political structure of Canada and are guaranteed by the Charter as part of the supreme law of our nation. I think that in determining whether a particular limitation is a reasonable limit prescribed by law which can be "demonstrably justified in a free and democratic society" it is important to remember that the courts are conducting this inquiry in light of a commitment to uphold the rights and freedoms set out in the other sections of the Charter. The issue in the present case is not simply whether the procedures set out in the *Immigration Act, 1976* for the adjudication of refugee claims are reasonable; it is whether it is reasonable to deprive the appellants of the right to life, liberty and security of the person by adopting a system for the adjudication of refugee status claims which does not accord with the principles of fundamental justice.

Seen in this light I have considerable doubt that the type of utilitarian consideration brought forward by Mr. Bowie can constitute a justification for a limitation on the rights set out in the Charter. Certainly the guarantees of the Charter would be illusory if they could be ignored because it was administratively convenient to do so. No doubt considerable time and money can be saved by adopting administrative procedures which ignore the principles of fundamental justice but such an argument, in my view, misses the point of the exercise under s. 1. The principles of natural justice and procedural fairness which have long been espoused by our courts, and the constitutional entrenchment of the principles of fundamental justice in s. 7, implicitly recognize that a balance of administrative convenience does not override the need to adhere to these principles. Whatever standard of review eventually emerges under s. 1, it seems to me that the basis of the justification for the limitation of rights under s. 7 must be more compelling than any advanced in these appeals.

Moreover, I am not convinced in light of the submissions made by the appellants that the limitations on the rights of refugee claimants which are imposed by the adjudication procedures of the *Immigration Act, 1976* are reasonable even on the respondent's own terms. It is obvious that there is a considerable degree of dissatisfaction with the present system even on the part of those who administer it.

Even if the cost of compliance with fundamental justice is a factor to which the courts would give considerable weight, I am not satisfied that the Minister has demonstrated that this cost would be so prohibitive as to constitute a justification within the meaning of s. 1. Though it is tempting to make observations about what factors might give rise to justification under s. 1, and on the standards of review which should be applied with respect to s. 1, I think it would be unwise to do so. I therefore confine my observations on the application of s. 1 to those necessary for the disposition of the appeals.

. . .

BEETZ J (Estey and McIntyre JJ concurring): Like my colleague Madame Justice Wilson, whose reasons for judgment I have had the advantage of reading, I conclude that these appeals ought to be allowed. But I do so on the basis of the *Canadian Bill of Rights*. I refrain from expressing any views on the question whether the *Canadian Charter of Rights and Freedoms* is applicable at all to the circumstances of these cases and more particularly, on the important question whether the Charter affords any protection against a deprivation or the threat of a deprivation of the right to life, liberty or security of the person by foreign governments.

Section 26 of the *Canadian Charter of Rights and Freedoms* should be kept in mind. It provides:

26. The guarantee in this Charter of certain rights and freedoms shall not be construed as denying the existence of any other rights or freedoms that exist in Canada.

Thus, the *Canadian Bill of Rights* retains all force and effect, together with the various provincial charters of rights. Because these constitutional or *quasi*-constitutional instruments are drafted differently, they are susceptible of producing cumulative effects for the better protection of rights and freedoms. But this beneficial result will be lost if the instruments fall into neglect. It is particularly so where they contain provisions not to be found in the *Canadian Charter of Rights and Freedoms* and almost tailor-made for certain factual situations such as those in the cases at bar.

. . .

The main issue, as I see it, is whether the procedures followed in these cases for the determination of Convention refugee status are in conflict with the *Canadian Bill of Rights* and more particularly with s. 2(e) thereof.

. . .

In his written submissions, Mr. Bowie, of counsel for the Attorney General of Canada, makes a concession in the following terms:

> 2. The Attorney General of Canada does not dispute that the process of determining and redetermining refugee claims involves the determination of rights and obligations of the refugee claimants. It is only in that respect that his submissions with respect to section 2(e) of the *Bill of Rights* differ from his submissions with respect to section 7 of the *Canadian Charter of Rights and Freedoms*. It was submitted upon the hearing of these appeals that a denial of a claim to refugee status by the operation of Canadian law does not deprive the claimant of "the right to life, liberty and security of the person" guaranteed by section 7 of the Charter.

In his reply, Mr. Scott refers to the Attorney General's acknowledgment that the process of adjudicating refugee claims under the *Immigration Act, 1976* involves the determination of "rights and obligations." Mr. Scott then concludes:

> The remaining issue, therefore, is whether the procedures provided by the Act conform to the dictates of "fundamental justice."

In view of the last sentence in the Attorney General's acknowledgment quoted above, I am not absolutely clear whether or not it was conceded by the Attorney General that the "rights" referred to in s. 2(e) of the *Canadian Bill of Rights* are not the same rights or rights of the same nature as those which are enumerated in s. 1, including "the right of the individual to life, liberty, security of the person ... and the right not to be deprived thereof except by due process of law."

Be that as it may, it seems clear to me that the ambit of s. 2(e) is broader than the list of rights enumerated in s. 1 which are designated as "human rights and fundamental freedoms" whereas in s. 2(e), what is protected by the right to a fair hearing is the determination of one's "rights and obligations," whatever they are and whenever the determination process is one which comes under the legislative authority of the Parliament of Canada. It is true that the first part of s. 2 refers to "the rights or freedoms herein recognized and declared," but s. 2(e) does protect a right which is fundamental, namely "the right to a fair hearing in accordance with the principles of fundamental justice" for the determination of one's rights and obligations, fundamental or not. It is my view that, as was submitted by Mr. Coveney, it is possible to apply s. 2(e) without making reference to

s. 1 and that the right guaranteed by s. 2(e) is in no way qualified by the "due process" concept mentioned in s. 1(a).

Accordingly, the process of determining and redetermining appellants' refugee claims involves the determination of rights and obligations for which the appellants have, under s. 2(e) of the *Canadian Bill of Rights*, the right to a fair hearing in accordance with the principles of fundamental justice. It follows also that this case is distinguishable from cases where a mere privilege was refused or revoked, such as *Prata v. Minister of Manpower and Immigration* [1976] 1 SCR 376 (Can.) and *Mitchell v. The Queen* [1976] 2 SCR 570 (Can.).

I therefore agree with the first branch of Mr. Scott's submission.

What remains to be decided is whether in the cases at bar, the appellants were afforded "a fair hearing in accordance with the principles of fundamental justice."

I have no doubt that they were not.

What the appellants are mainly justified of complaining about in my view is that their claims to refugee status have been finally denied without their having been afforded a full oral hearing at a single stage of the proceedings before any of the bodies or officials empowered to adjudicate upon their claim on the merits. They have actually been heard by the one official who has nothing to say in the matter, a senior immigration officer. But they have been heard neither by the Refugee Status Advisory Committee who could advise the Minister, neither by the Minister, who had the power to decide and who dismissed their claim, nor by the Immigration Appeal Board which did not allow their application to proceed and which determined, finally, that they are not Convention refugees.

I do not wish to suggest that the principles of fundamental justice will impose an oral hearing in all cases. ...

The most important factors in determining the procedural content of fundamental justice in a given case are the nature of the legal rights at issue and the severity of the consequences to the individuals concerned. ...

Again, I express no views as to the applicability of the *Canadian Charter of Rights and Freedoms*, but I otherwise agree with these submissions: threats to life or liberty by a foreign power are relevant, not with respect to the applicability of the *Canadian Bill of Rights*, but with respect to the type of hearing which is warranted in the circumstances. In my opinion, nothing will pass muster short of at least one full oral hearing before adjudication on the merits.

There are additional reasons why the appellants ought to have been given an oral hearing. They are mentioned in the following submission with which I agree:

> The appellants submit that although "fundamental justice" will not require an oral hearing in every case, where life or liberty may depend on findings of fact and credibility, and it may in these cases, the opportunity to make written submissions, even if coupled with an opportunity to reply in writing to allegations of fact and law against interest, would be insufficient.

. . .

Appeal allowed, decisions of Immigration Appeal Board set aside and applications for determination of refugee status remanded to the Board.

NOTES

1. One of the alleged consequences of *Singh* was that its apparent mandating of an oral hearing at some point in the process by someone empowered to actually render a decision made the system of refugee claim determinations immensely expensive and unworkable. Is this kind of consideration one that should at all affect courts in their judgments as to the protections afforded by s. 7 of the Charter?

Indeed, in time, this and other concerns led to legislative reform. (See SC 1988, c. 35 and c. 36, SC 1992, c. 49, and, most recently, SC 2001, c. 27.) One of these reforms was to the effect that Canada would no longer accept as refugee claimants those who arrived here by way of a "third safe country." For these purposes, a third safe country was one contained in a schedule listing countries where the refugee would have had a similar opportunity to make such a claim and through which he or she had passed in travelling to Canada. Now that this provision has been triggered as between Canada and the United States by the coming into force of an Agreement Between the Government of Canada and the Government of the United States of America for Cooperation in the Examination of Refugee Status Claims from Nationals of Third Countries (see http://www.cic.gc.ca/english/department/laws-policy/safe-third.asp), does *Singh* provide any basis for a claim that that provision is a violation of the Charter? Can Canada turn away a refugee claimant without a hearing in such circumstances? To what extent does *Singh* depend on there being a *statutory right* to make a refugee claim? If that statutory right is taken away or restricted by legislation, is there any basis for a challenge to that legislation? Is there any difference for these purposes between the ability to make a claim and the imposition of very tight limitation periods for the making of refugee determinations or the imposition of leave requirements on applications to seek judicial review in the Federal Court of claim denials (also features of the amended legislation)?

This raises very important questions about the extent to which s. 7 procedural claims are founded on the existence of statutory substantive rights as opposed to independent or freestanding constitutional rights. To take an example from US Supreme Court jurisprudence, in *Goss v. Lopez* 419 US 565 (1975), the court upheld a procedural due process, 14th amendment, deprivation of property claim by pupils expelled from school on the basis of an Ohio statute establishing school attendance as a right. Without that statutory right, the constitutional claim to due process would not have been vindicated. Should the same hold for s. 7 of the Charter or s. 2(e) of the *Bill of Rights* or do they have a different constitutional basis? If the latter, do legislative restrictions on making refugee claims necessarily fail?

2. For a detailed assessment of the potential of the Charter to have extraterritorial effect particularly in an immigration context, see Galloway, "The Extraterritorial Application of the Charter to Visa Applicants" (1991), 23 *Ottawa LR* 336.

3. While the Supreme Court of Canada has never returned directly to the issue whether the Charter does apply to convention refugee determinations, the assumption in later cases has been that the three judges who were of that view in *Singh* were correct (see, for example, the judgment of Iacobucci J in *Dehghani v. Canada (Minister of Employment and Immigration)*, [1993] 1 SCR 1053 (Can.)). Indeed, the reasoning in *Singh* has been extended to the arena of extradition proceedings, including the extradition of fugitive criminals who have arrived in Canada illegally (see, for example, *Kindler v. Canada (Minister of Justice)*, [1991]

2 SCR 779 (Que.); *Idziak v. Canada (Minister of Justice)*, [1992] 3 SCR 631 (Ont.)) to the extent of acceptance that Canada may be implicated when its actions have the effect of sub-jecting a person to the possible deprivation of his or her "life, liberty and security of the person" at the hands of a foreign government. More recently, the application of s. 7 was simply assumed by the court in a challenge to proceedings deporting a convention refugee: *Suresh v. Canada*, [2002] 1 SCR 3 (Can.).

However, in this context and others, two qualifications on *Singh* have clearly emerged: first, s. 7 does not always require an oral hearing and, second, in addition to the balancing of interests that must occur in making determinations as to the precise procedures that the "principles of fundamental justice" mandate, there is also room for s. 1 to be invoked in justification of s. 7 violations.

Thus, for example, the court held in both *Kindler* and *Idziak* that the minister had not breached the principles of fundamental justice in the procedures that had been adopted in deciding whether the applicants against whom extradition orders had been made should be surrendered to the requesting government. In that discretionary, political context, there was no need for the minister to provide the applicant with an oral hearing (*Kindler*) nor was it incumbent on the minister to reveal to the applicant a memorandum on the case from a departmental lawyer at least where that memorandum contained no new relevant informa-tion (*Idziak*). The arena for judicial type procedures was at the actual extradition hearing and there was no need for a replication of that kind of process at the surrender stage even though the issues confronting the minister were of a different order (for example, in *Kindler*'s case, whether he should be surrendered without the minister seeking an assurance from the requesting state that the death penalty not be carried out). Indeed, in setting the procedural bounds under the Charter in *Idziak*, the court relied on the spectrum analysis relied on by L'Heureux-Dubé J in *Knight* and described the ministerial surrender function as being at the extremes of the "legislative" category.

The contingent nature of claims under s. 7 is illustrated in several Supreme Court judgments regarding the constitutionality of provisions of Canada's immigration laws that allowed for proceedings leading to the deportation of permanent residents or foreign nationals on grounds of national security that could deprive these individuals of some or all of the infor-mation on which the proceedings were initiated.

In *Chiarelli v. Canada*, [1992] 1 SCR 711, Canadian authorities moved to deport Chiarelli, a permanent resident, on the grounds that he had committed a serious criminal offence rendering him inadmissible under Canada's *Immigration Act*. The solicitor general and minister of employment and immigration made a joint report to Canada's Security Intelli-gence Review Committee (SIRC) that, if allowed to remain in Canada, Chiarelli would be involved in organized crime. Under the Act, SIRC was required to investigate the ministers' report. If SIRC upheld the report, the governor in council was empowered to direct the minister of employment and immigration to issue a certificate precluding Chiarelli from appealing his deportation order. Chiarelli challenged the constitutionality of his deportation on several grounds. In particular, he claimed that the rules of procedure adopted by SIRC, which allowed the committee, in the interest of national security, to exclude him and his counsel when government witnesses were giving evidence and to limit his ability to cross-examine such witnesses, violated his s. 7 rights.

Writing for the court, Sopinka J assumed without deciding that s. 7 was engaged by the government's measures to deport Chiarelli, but found that, if there was a deprivation of Chiarelli's liberty or security of the person, it was in accordance with the principles of fundamental justice. In this respect, he noted first that, in assessing whether a procedure complied with fundamental justice, it was necessary to balance competing interests of the state and the individual:

> In the context of hearings conducted by the Review Committee pursuant to a joint report, an individual has an interest in a fair procedure, since the Committee's investigation may result in its recommending to the Governor in Council that a s. 83 certificate issue, removing an appeal on compassionate grounds. However, the state also has a considerable interest in effectively conducting national security and criminal intelligence investigations and in protecting police sources.

The court held that the review committee rules and the *Canadian Security Intelligence Service Act* under which the rules had been promulgated reasonably balanced these interests. The committee had provided Chiarelli with several documents summarizing the information it had received from the ministers as well as a summary of the *in camera* evidence presented at the hearing, which gave him "sufficient information to know the substance of the allegations against him, and to be able to respond." In addition, the committee had indicated that it would allow Chiarelli to cross-examine the RCMP witnesses who testified *in camera*. Given the information disclosed to Chiarelli, the procedural opportunities available to him, and the competing interests at play, the court found that fundamental justice had been respected.

One of the questions arising from *Chiarelli* was whether it was appropriate in s. 7 claims for courts to engage in the balancing of individual and state interests at the stage of determining the content of fundamental justice, or if such considerations should be dealt with in the justification analysis under s. 1. This issue was resolved in the next case, also involving deportation in the national security context.

Charkaoui v. Canada (Citizenship and Immigration)
[2007] 1 SCR 350

[Adil Charkaoui, a permanent resident of Canada, and Hassan Almrei and Mohamed Harkat, both foreign nationals recognized as Convention refugees, were each named in certificates of inadmissibility or "security certificates" issued by the minister of public safety and emergency preparedness and the minister of citizenship and immigration under the *Immigration and Refugee Protection Act* (IRPA). Following the issuance of the certificates, which deemed Charkaoui, Almrei, and Harkat to be threats to Canada's national security, all three individuals were detained pending the completion of proceedings for their removal. The IRPA specified that the first step of these proceedings required that, for each named individual, a federal court judge review the certificate to determine whether it was reasonable. At the ministers' request, the review was conducted *in camera* and *ex parte*, and the named individual had no right to see the material on the basis of which the certificate was issued. Non-sensitive material could be disclosed, but sensitive material could not be disclosed if the ministers objected. While the ministers and the reviewing judge could rely on undisclosed material, neither the named person nor their counsel could see it. The reviewing judge was required to disclose to the named individual a summary of the case against him or her; however, the summary could not disclose material that might compromise national security. The reviewing judge's decision that a security certificate was reasonable was final and could not be appealed. The named individuals could then be subject to additional proceedings stripping them of refugee protection and removing them from Canada, possibly to states where they faced a substantial risk of torture. The appellants challenged the constitutionality of the security certificate process on several grounds, including that the procedure established to determine the reasonableness of the certificates violated their s. 7 rights. After determining that the appellants' liberty and security of the person interests were engaged, respectively, by their detention under the Act and by their potential removal to places where their life or freedom would be threatened, the court considered whether the state's interference with the appellants' life, liberty, and security of the person conformed with the principles of fundamental justice, and most importantly, defined the content of fundamental justice in the national security context.]

McLACHLIN CJ: ...

1. *How Do Security Considerations Affect the Section 7 Analysis?*

[19] Section 7 of the *Charter* requires that laws that interfere with life, liberty and security of the person conform to the principles of fundamental justice—the basic principles that underlie our notions of justice and fair process. These principles include a guarantee of procedural fairness, having regard to the circumstances and consequences of the intrusion on life, liberty or security: *Suresh*, at para. 113.

[20] Section 7 of the *Charter* requires not a particular type of process, but a fair process having regard to the nature of the proceedings and the interests at stake: *United States of America v. Ferras*, [2006] 2 SCR 77, 2006 SCC 33, at para. 14; *R v. Rodgers*, [2006] 1 SCR 554, 2006 SCC 15, at para. 47; *Idziak v. Canada (Minister of Justice)*, [1992] 3 SCR 631 , at pp. 656-57. The procedures required to meet the demands of fundamental justice depend on the context (see *Rodgers*; *R v. Lyons*, [1987] 2 SCR 309 , at p. 361; *Chiarelli*, at pp. 743-44; *Mount Sinai Hospital Center v. Quebec (Minister of Health and Social Services)*, [2001] 2 SCR 281, 2001 SCC 41, at paras. 20-21). Societal interests may be taken into account in elucidating the applicable principles of fundamental justice: *R v. Malmo-Levine*, [2003] 3 SCR 571 , 2003 SCC 74, at para. 98.

[21] Unlike s. 1, s. 7 is not concerned with whether a limit on life, liberty or security of the person is *justified*, but with whether the limit has been imposed in a way that respects the principles of fundamental justice. Hence, it has been held that s. 7 does not permit "a free-standing inquiry ... into whether a particular legislative measure 'strikes the right balance' between individual and societal interests in general" (*Malmo-Levine*, at para. 96). Nor is "achieving the right balance ... itself an overarching principle of fundamental justice" (*ibid.*). As the majority in *Malmo-Levine* noted, to hold otherwise

"would entirely collapse the s. 1 inquiry into s. 7" (*ibid.*). This in turn would relieve the state from its burden of justifying intrusive measures, and require the *Charter* complainant to show that the measures are not justified.

[22] The question at the s. 7 stage is whether the principles of fundamental justice relevant to the case have been observed in substance, having regard to the context and the seriousness of the violation. The issue is whether the process is fundamentally unfair to the affected person. If so, the deprivation of life, liberty or security of the person simply does not conform to the requirements of s. 7. The inquiry then shifts to s. 1 of the *Charter*, at which point the government has an opportunity to establish that the flawed process is nevertheless justified having regard, notably, to the public interest.

[23] It follows that while administrative constraints associated with the context of national security may inform the analysis on whether a particular process is fundamentally unfair, security concerns cannot be used to excuse procedures that do not conform to fundamental justice at the s. 7 stage of the analysis. If the context makes it impossible to adhere to the principles of fundamental justice in their usual form, adequate substitutes may be found. But the principles must be respected to pass the hurdle of s. 7. That is the bottom line.

[24] In the instant case, the context is the detention, incidental to their removal or an attempt to remove them from the country, of permanent residents and foreign nationals who the ministers conclude pose a threat to national security. This context may impose certain administrative constraints that may be properly considered at the s. 7 stage. Full disclosure of the information relied on may not be possible. The executive branch of government may be required to act quickly, without recourse, at least in the first instance, to the judicial procedures normally required for the deprivation of liberty or security of the person.

[25] At the same time, it is a context that may have important, indeed chilling, consequences for the detainee. The seriousness of the individual interests at stake forms part of the contextual analysis. As this Court stated in *Suresh*, "[t]he greater the effect on the life of the individual by the decision, the greater the need for procedural protections to meet the common law duty of fairness and the requirements of fundamental justice under s. 7 of the *Charter*" (para. 118). Thus, "factual situations which are closer or analogous to criminal proceedings will merit greater vigilance by the courts": *Dehghani v. Canada (Minister of Employment and Immigration)*, [1993] 1 SCR 1053, at p. 1077, *per* Iacobucci J.

[26] The potential consequences of deportation combined with allegations of terrorism have been under a harsh spotlight due to the recent report of the Commission of Inquiry into the Actions of Canadian Officials in Relation to Maher Arar. Mr. Arar, a Canadian citizen born in Syria, was detained by American officials and deported to Syria. The report concludes that it is "very likely that, in making the decisions to detain and remove Mr. Arar to Syria, the U.S. authorities relied on information about Mr. Arar provided by the RCMP," including unfounded suspicions linking Mr. Arar to terrorist groups: *Report of the Events Relating to Maher Arar: Analysis and Recommendations* (2006) ("Arar Inquiry"), at p. 30. In Syria, Mr. Arar was tortured and detained under inhumane conditions for over 11 months. In his report, Commissioner O'Connor recommends enhanced review and accountability mechanisms for agencies dealing with national security, including not only the Royal Canadian Mounted Police, but also Citizenship and Immigration Canada and the Canada

Border Services Agency. He notes that these immigration-related institutions can have an important impact on individual rights but that there is a lack of transparency surrounding their activities because their activities often involve sensitive national security information that cannot be disclosed to the public: *A New Review Mechanism for the RCMP's National Security Activities* (2006), at pp. 562-65. Moreover, the sensitive nature of security information means that investigations lead to fewer prosecutions. This, in turn, restricts the ability of courts to guarantee individual rights: "Unless charges are laid, … the choice of investigative targets, methods of information collection and exchange, and means of investigation generally will not be subject to judicial scrutiny, media coverage or public debate" (p. 439).

[27] The procedures required to conform to the principles of fundamental justice must reflect the exigencies of the security context. Yet they cannot be permitted to erode the essence of s. 7. The principles of fundamental justice cannot be reduced to the point where they cease to provide the protection of due process that lies at the heart of s. 7 of the *Charter*. The protection may not be as complete as in a case where national security constraints do not operate. But to satisfy s. 7, meaningful and substantial protection there must be.

3. Relevant Principles of Fundamental Justice

[28] The overarching principle of fundamental justice that applies here is this: before the state can detain people for significant periods of time, it must accord them a fair judicial process: *New Brunswick (Minister of Health and Community Services) v. G. (J.)*, [1999] 3 SCR 46 . "It is an ancient and venerable principle that no person shall lose his or her liberty without due process according to the law, which must involve a meaningful judicial process": *Ferras*, at para. 19. This principle emerged in the era of feudal monarchy, in the form of the right to be brought before a judge on a motion of *habeas corpus*. It remains as fundamental to our modern conception of liberty as it was in the days of King John.

[29] This basic principle has a number of facets. It comprises the right to a *hearing*. It requires that the hearing be *before an independent and impartial magistrate*. It demands a *decision by the magistrate on the facts and the law*. And it entails the *right to know the case put against one*, and the *right to answer that case*. Precisely how these requirements are met will vary with the context. But for s. 7 to be satisfied, each of them must be met in substance.

[30] The *IRPA* process includes a hearing. The process consists of two phases, one executive and one judicial. There is no hearing at the executive phase that results in issuance of the certificate. However, this is followed by a review before a judge, where the named person is afforded a hearing. Thus, the first requirement, that of a hearing, is met.

[31] Questions arise, however, on the other requirements, namely: that the judge be independent and impartial; that the judge make a judicial decision based on the facts and the law; and finally, that the named person be afforded an opportunity to meet the case put against him or her by being informed of that case and being allowed to question or counter it. I conclude that the *IRPA* scheme meets the first requirement of independence and impartiality, but fails to satisfy the second and third requirements, which are interrelated here.

[Only the reasons relating to the "case to meet" principle are reproduced here. The issue of independence is addressed further in chapter 5 of this text.]

6. Is the "Case to Meet" Principle Satisfied?

[53] Last but not least, a fair hearing requires that the affected person be informed of the case against him or her, and be permitted to respond to that case. This right is well established in immigration law. The question is whether the procedures "provide an adequate opportunity for [an affected person] to state his case and know the case he has to meet" (*Singh*, at p. 213). Similarly, in *Suresh*, the Court held that a person facing deportation to torture under s. 53(1)(b) of the former *Immigration Act*, RSC 1985, c. I-2, must "[n]ot only ... be informed of the case to be met ... [but] also be given an opportunity to challenge the information of the Minister where issues as to its validity arise" (para. 123).

[54] Under the *IRPA*'s certificate scheme, the named person may be deprived of access to some or all of the information put against him or her, which would deny the person the ability to know the case to meet. Without this information, the named person may not be in a position to contradict errors, identify omissions, challenge the credibility of informants or refute false allegations. This problem is serious in itself. It also underlies the concerns, discussed above, about the independence and impartiality of the designated judge, and the ability of the judge to make a decision based on the facts and law.

[55] Confidentiality is a constant preoccupation of the certificate scheme. The judge "shall ensure" the confidentiality of the information on which the certificate is based and of any other evidence if, in the opinion of the judge, disclosure would be injurious to national security or to the safety of any person: s. 78(b). At the request of either minister "at any time during the proceedings," the judge "shall hear" information or evidence in the absence of the named person and his or her counsel if, in the opinion of the judge, its disclosure would be injurious to national security or to the safety of any person: s. 78(e). The judge "shall provide" the named person with a summary of information that enables him or her to be reasonably informed of the circumstances giving rise to the certificate, but the summary cannot include anything that would, in the opinion of the judge, be injurious to national security or to the safety of any person: s. 78(h). Ultimately, the judge may have to consider information that is not included in the summary: s. 78(g). In the result, the judge may be required to decide the case, wholly or in part, on the basis of information that the named person and his or her counsel never see. The named person may know nothing of the case to meet, and although technically afforded an opportunity to be heard, may be left in a position of having no idea as to what needs to be said.

[56] The same concerns arise with respect to the detention review process under ss. 83 and 84 of the *IRPA*. Section 78 applies to detention reviews under s. 83, and it has been found to apply to detention reviews under s. 84(2): *Almrei v. Canada (Minister of Citizenship and Immigration)*, [2005] 3 FCR 142, 2005 FCA 54, at paras. 71-72.

[57] The right to know the case to be met is not absolute. Canadian statutes sometimes provide for *ex parte* or *in camera* hearings, in which judges must decide important issues after hearing from only one side. In *Rodgers*, the majority of this Court declined to recognize notice and participation as invariable constitutional norms, emphasizing a context-sensitive approach to procedural fairness. And in *Goodis v. Ontario (Ministry of*

Correctional Services), [2006] 2 SCR 32, 2006 SCC 31, the Court, *per* Rothstein J, held that while "[h]earing from both sides of an issue is a principle to be departed from only in exceptional circumstances," in the ordinary case, a judge would be "well equipped … to determine whether a record is subject to [solicitor-client] privilege" without the assistance of counsel on both sides (para. 21).

[58] More particularly, the Court has repeatedly recognized that national security considerations can limit the extent of disclosure of information to the affected individual. In *Chiarelli*, this Court found that the Security Intelligence Review Committee could, in investigating certificates under the former *Immigration Act, 1976*, SC 1976-77, c. 52 (later RSC 1985, c. I-2), refuse to disclose details of investigation techniques and police sources. The context for elucidating the principles of fundamental justice in that case included the state's "interest in effectively conducting national security and criminal intelligence investigations and in protecting police sources" (p. 744). In *Suresh*, this Court held that a refugee facing the possibility of deportation to torture was entitled to disclosure of all the information on which the Minister was basing his or her decision, "[s]ubject to privilege or similar valid reasons for reduced disclosure, such as safeguarding confidential public security documents" (para. 122). And, in *Ruby v. Canada (Solicitor General)*, [2002] 4 SCR 3 , 2002 SCC 75, the Court upheld the section of the *Privacy Act*, RSC 1985, c. P-21, that mandates *in camera* and *ex parte* proceedings where the government claims an exemption from disclosure on grounds of national security or maintenance of foreign confidences. The Court made clear that these societal concerns formed part of the relevant context for determining the scope of the applicable principles of fundamental justice (paras. 38-44).

[59] In some contexts, substitutes for full disclosure may permit compliance with s. 7 of the *Charter*. For example, in *Rodgers*, the majority of the Court upheld the constitutionality of *ex parte* hearings for applications under s. 487.055 of the *Criminal Code* to take DNA samples from listed multiple offenders, on the ground that the protections Parliament had put in place were adequate (paras. 51-52). Similarly, in *Chiarelli*, the Court upheld the lack of disclosure on the basis that the information disclosed by way of summary and the opportunity to call witnesses and cross-examine RCMP witnesses who testified *in camera* satisfied the requirements of fundamental justice. And in *Ruby*, the Court held that the substitute measures provided by Parliament satisfied the constitutional requirements of procedural fairness (para. 42). Arbour J stated: "In such circumstances, fairness is met through other procedural safeguards such as subsequent disclosure, judicial review and rights of appeal" (para. 40).

[60] Where limited disclosure or *ex parte* hearings have been found to satisfy the principles of fundamental justice, the intrusion on liberty and security has typically been less serious than that effected by the *IRPA*: *Rodgers*, at para. 53. It is one thing to deprive a person of full information where fingerprinting is at stake, and quite another to deny him or her information where the consequences are removal from the country or indefinite detention. Moreover, even in the less intrusive situations, courts have insisted that disclosure be as specific and complete as possible.

[61] In the context of national security, non-disclosure, which may be extensive, coupled with the grave intrusions on liberty imposed on a detainee, makes it difficult, if not impossible, to find substitute procedures that will satisfy s. 7. Fundamental justice

requires substantial compliance with the venerated principle that a person whose liberty is in jeopardy must be given an opportunity to know the case to meet, and an opportunity to meet the case. Yet the imperative of the protection of society may preclude this. Information may be obtained from other countries or from informers on condition that it not be disclosed. Or it may simply be so critical that it cannot be disclosed without risking public security. This is a reality of our modern world. If s. 7 is to be satisfied, either the person must be given the necessary information, or a substantial substitute for that information must be found. Neither is the case here.

[62] The only protection the *IRPA* accords the named person is a review by a designated judge to determine whether the certificate is reasonable. The ministers argue that this is adequate in that it maintains a "delicate balance" between the right to a fair hearing and the need to protect confidential security intelligence information. The appellants, on the other hand, argue that the judge's efforts, however conscientious, cannot provide an effective substitute for informed participation.

[63] I agree with the appellants. The issue at the s. 7 stage, as discussed above, is not whether the government has struck the right balance between the need for security and individual liberties; that is the issue at the stage of s. 1 justification of an established limitation on a *Charter* right. The question at the s. 7 stage is whether the basic requirements of procedural justice have been met, either in the usual way or in an alternative fashion appropriate to the context, having regard to the government's objective and the interests of the person affected. The fairness of the *IRPA* procedure rests entirely on the shoulders of the designated judge. Those shoulders cannot by themselves bear the heavy burden of assuring, in fact and appearance, that the decision on the reasonableness of the certificate is impartial, is based on a full view of the facts and law, and reflects the named person's knowledge of the case to meet. The judge, working under the constraints imposed by the *IRPA*, simply cannot fill the vacuum left by the removal of the traditional guarantees of a fair hearing. The judge sees only what the ministers put before him or her. The judge, knowing nothing else about the case, is not in a position to identify errors, find omissions or assess the credibility and truthfulness of the information in the way the named person would be. Although the judge may ask questions of the named person when the hearing is reopened, the judge is prevented from asking questions that might disclose the protected information. Likewise, since the named person does not know what has been put against him or her, he or she does not know what the designated judge needs to hear. If the judge cannot provide the named person with a summary of the information that is sufficient to enable the person to know the case to meet, then the judge cannot be satisfied that the information before him or her is sufficient or reliable. Despite the judge's best efforts to question the government's witnesses and scrutinize the documentary evidence, he or she is placed in the situation of asking questions and ultimately deciding the issues on the basis of incomplete and potentially unreliable information.

[64] The judge is not helpless; he or she can note contradictions between documents, insist that there be at least some evidence on the critical points, and make limited inferences on the value and credibility of the information from its source. Nevertheless, the judge's activity on behalf of the named person is confined to what is presented by the ministers. The judge is therefore not in a position to compensate for the lack of informed scrutiny, challenge and counter-evidence that a person familiar with the case could

bring. Such scrutiny is the whole point of the principle that a person whose liberty is in jeopardy must know the case to meet. Here that principle has not merely been limited; it has been effectively gutted. How can one meet a case one does not know?

(b) Conclusion on Section 7

[65] In the *IRPA*, an attempt has been made to meet the requirements of fundamental justice essentially through one mechanism—the designated judge charged with reviewing the certificate of inadmissibility and the detention. To Parliament's credit, a sincere attempt has been made to give the designated judge the powers necessary to discharge the role in an independent manner, based on the facts and the law. Yet, the secrecy required by the scheme denies the named person the opportunity to know the case put against him or her, and hence to challenge the government's case. This, in turn, undermines the judge's ability to come to a decision based on all the relevant facts and law. Despite the best efforts of judges of the Federal Court to breathe judicial life into the *IRPA* procedure, it fails to assure the fair hearing that s. 7 of the *Charter* requires before the state deprives a person of life, liberty or security of the person. I therefore conclude that the *IRPA*'s procedure for determining whether a certificate is reasonable does not conform to the principles of fundamental justice as embodied in s. 7 of the *Charter*. The same conclusion necessarily applies to the detention review procedures under ss. 83 and 84 of the *IRPA*.

8. Is the Limit Justified Under Section 1 of the Charter?

[66] The *Charter* does not guarantee rights absolutely. The state is permitted to limit rights—including the s. 7 guarantee of life, liberty and security—if it can establish that the limits are demonstrably justifiable in a free and democratic society. This said, violations of s. 7 are not easily saved by s. 1. In *Re B.C. Motor Vehicle Act*, [1985] 2 SCR 486, Lamer J. (as he then was) stated, for the majority:

> (2) Section 1 may, for reasons of administrative expediency, successfully come to the rescue of an otherwise violation of s. 7, but only in cases arising out of exceptional conditions, such as natural disasters, the outbreak of war, epidemics, and the like. [p. 518]

The rights protected by s. 7—life, liberty, and security of the person—are basic to our conception of a free and democratic society, and hence are not easily overridden by competing social interests. It follows that violations of the principles of fundamental justice, specifically the right to a fair hearing, are difficult to justify under s. 1: *G. (J.)*. Nevertheless, the task may not be impossible, particularly in extraordinary circumstances where concerns are grave and the challenges complex.

[67] The test to be applied in determining whether a violation can be justified under s. 1, known as the *Oakes* test (*R v. Oakes*, [1986] 1 SCR 103), requires a pressing and substantial objective and proportional means. A finding of proportionality requires: (a) means rationally connected to the objective; (b) minimal impairment of rights; and (c) proportionality between the effects of the infringement and the importance of the objective.

[68] The protection of Canada's national security and related intelligence sources undoubtedly constitutes a pressing and substantial objective. Moreover, the *IRPA*'s provisions

regarding the non-disclosure of evidence at certificate hearings are rationally connected to this objective. The facts on this point are undisputed. Canada is a net importer of security information. This information is essential to the security and defence of Canada, and disclosure would adversely affect its flow and quality: see *Ruby*. This leaves the question whether the means Parliament has chosen, i.e. a certificate procedure leading to detention and deportation of non-citizens on the ground that they pose a threat to Canada's security, minimally impairs the rights of non-citizens.

[The court described several measures used in Canada and abroad that protected sensitive information while remaining more faithful to a traditional adversarial model. Some involved the use of security-cleared advocates who would appear at the *ex parte* hearings to make submissions and cross-examine government witnesses. It concluded that these alternatives demonstrated that the IRPA process did not minimally impair the named person's rights. The court declared the IRPA procedures unconstitutional, but suspended this declaration for one year. In *An Act to amend the Immigration and Refugee Protection Act (certificate and special advocate) and to make a consequential amendment to another Act*, SC 2008, c. 3, Parliament provided for the appointment of a special advocate who could challenge government claims to the confidentiality of evidence as well as its relevance, reliability, sufficiency and weight, make submissions, cross-examine witnesses, and, with the judge's permission, exercise any other powers required to protect the interests of a named person.]

NOTES

1.   The court observes, at para. 63, that whether the government has struck the right balance between the need for security and individual liberties is the issue at the stage of s. 1 justification, not of s. 7. When will a constraint on the "case to meet" principle provide "an adequate substitute" to this principle of fundamental justice rather than "effectively gut" it? Has the court provided sufficient guidance on this question?

2.   Hogg maintains that the absence of any equivalent to s. 1 in the *Canadian Bill of Rights* makes no difference; the courts will engage in s. 1-type balancing in the context of teasing out the content of the protections afforded by ss. 1(a) and 2(e): "A Comparison of the *Canadian Charter of Rights and Freedoms* with the *Canadian Bill of Rights*" in Beaudoin and Ratushny, eds., *The Canadian Charter of Rights and Freedoms*, 2nd ed. (Toronto: Carswell, 1989), at 7-8. See also *Air Canada c. Canada (Procureure générale)*, [2003] JQ n° 21 (QL) (CA) for support for the proposition that, in giving content to s. 2(e) and the principles of fundamental justice, it was incumbent on the court to weigh competing state interests that might justify a derogation from the normal requirements of fundamental justice. Do you agree that this should be so?

Section 7 of the Charter: "Life, Liberty and Security of the Person"

In *Singh, Suresh, Charkaoui*, and the extradition cases, there was little doubt that s. 7-type interests of the applicants for relief were at stake. In *Chiarelli*, however, the context is different and more typical: did the long-term resident have a "life, liberty and security of the person" interest in not being deported from Canada? What modes of analysis should go into determining whether such an interest does exist? The answers to these questions in this and other contexts are explored in this section, which will demonstrate that many areas of uncertainty remain.

To the extent that administrative processes have similar "liberty" dimensions to those typical of the criminal law context, of course, the modes of analysis and outcomes have been relatively predictable. We think here of cases involving prison discipline, parole granting, and revocation, as well as other custodial regimes such as compulsory detention of the insane (see, for example, *Howard v. Stony Mountain Institution*, [1984] 2 FC 642 (CA); *Gough v. Canada (National Parole Board)* (1990), 45 Admin. LR 403 (FCTD); aff'd. (1991), 47 Admin. LR 226 (FCA)). Indeed, given the history of judicial review in this arena, it is important to note that the courts have rejected arguments to resurrect a species of rights–privilege dichotomy as a basis for denying to the incarcerated procedural entitlements under s. 7. To quote from the judgment of Reed J in *Cadieux v. Director of Mountain Institution* (1984), 9 Admin. LR 50 (FCTD), in response to the argument that the revocation of an unescorted temporary absence permit was not covered by s. 7 because it was a matter of privilege, not right:

> With respect to present Canadian law, the Supreme Court decision in *Martineau v. Matsqui Institution Disciplinary Board* clearly indicates that the distinction between "rights" and "privileges" is not one which should ground a difference between allowing and not allowing judicial review. … I think it would be inconsistent with the principles underlying this decision to determine the applicability of s. 7 of the Charter on the basis of whether a right or privilege was involved, particularly when a person's liberty is at stake. It is true that s. 7 specifically applies to "*the right* to life, liberty and security of the person." But "right" is a word used in two senses: sometimes it is used in a narrow sense, as distinct from "powers," "privileges," *etc.*; at other times it is used in a more generic sense as encompassing all those concepts. I take it as being used in the latter sense in s. 7.

Far more difficult are questions about the extent to which "life, liberty and security of the person" has any application to regimes with economic consequences. While it is accepted that direct protection for traditional property rights was omitted deliberately from s. 7, are there, nonetheless, species of economic interest that transcend concepts of property and achieve protected status? To what extent is economic well-being an aspect of "life" or "security of the person" (or "physical and psychological integrity," to borrow a term from Wilson J's judgment in *R v. Morgentaler*, [1988] 1 SCR 30 (Ont.), the case in which the therapeutic abortion provisions of the *Criminal Code* were struck down on the basis of s. 7 and the threat they posed to women's security of the person interests). To what extent is the ability to carry on a chosen calling a component of "liberty"?

Moreover, the inquiries about the reach of s. 7 do not end with these questions about economic interests. The abortion judgment provides graphic evidence of this and there are still unresolved questions about the extent to which s. 7 may be invoked in relation to other administrative regimes that have an impact on the mental and physical well-being of those involved as well as their reputations. The material that follows attempts to tease out the dimensions of some of these crucial issues as to scope.

Wilson v. British Columbia (Medical Services Commission)
(1988), 53 DLR (4th) 171 (BC CA)

[In the BC medical care plan, doctors bill the government for treatment given to patients. In 1983, the commission established a scheme for limiting the numbers of practising doctors and restricting the geographic areas of their practices; the purposes of this scheme were to control the total costs of health services and to ensure the appropriate allocation of doctors throughout the province. Doctors were required to have a "practitioner number" in order to bill for their services, and there was agreement throughout that having a number was essential to practise. These numbers were assigned to current practitioners, and "newcomers" had to apply for them. The applications were made to the commission (which was one person), which was advised about need by local and regional committees.

This scheme was challenged in 1983 in *Re Mia* (1985), 17 DLR (4th) 385 (BC SC). McEachern CJSC concluded that it was not authorized by the legislation about medical services, and he also said that it violated ss. 6 and 7 of the Charter. About s. 7, he said,

> [T]here are some rights enjoyed by our people including the right to work or practise a profession that are so fundamental that they must be protected even if they include an economic element.

The government then enacted legislation under which regulations were passed implementing the previous scheme and, almost two years after *Mia*, the Charter challenge was made again and ss. 6, 7, and 15 were invoked. The plaintiffs were doctors whose personal circumstances presented different elements of the claim; for example, some sought to come from outside the province and had been denied "practitioner numbers," while others had been granted numbers subject to geographic restrictions. Their claim failed at trial (1987), 36 DLR (4th) 31 (BC SC) and they appealed. The judgment of the Court of Appeal contains extensive discussions of cases, most of which have been omitted without specific indication.]

THE COURT: The question then arises whether "liberty" in s. 7 is broad enough to encompass the opportunity of a qualified and licensed doctor to practise medicine in British Columbia without restraint as to place, time or purpose, even though there is an incidental economic component to the right being asserted.

. . .

Common sense, our history and our daily experience tell us that liberty is not unrestrained. Regulation of our activities is commonplace. Society could not survive, and chaos would result if we were all at liberty to do as we saw fit. Section 7 recognizes the validity of competing societal interests by providing that a person may be deprived of life, liberty and security in accordance with the principles of fundamental justice. Government may impose an administrative structure which limits or even deprives one of liberty to further its perception of the needs of society "unless the use of such structure is in itself so manifestly unfair, having regard to the decisions it is called upon to make, as to violate the principles of fundamental justice": *Jones v. The Queen* [1986] 2 SCR 284 (Alta.) (*per* La Forest J). ...

To summarize: "Liberty" within the meaning of s. 7 is not confined to mere freedom from bodily restraint. It does not, however, extend to protect property or pure economic rights. It may embrace individual freedom of movement, including the right to choose one's occupation and where to pursue it, subject to the right of the state to impose, in accordance with the principles of fundamental justice, legitimate and reasonable restrictions on the activities of individuals.

Is This a Case Involving Pure Economic Rights?

The trial judge appears to have concluded that the appellants, in asserting a right to pursue their profession, were asserting economic rights generally, or the right to work in particular. He said:

> The core issue can be defined more succinctly. Does the Charter's right to liberty clause guarantee a right to work? Unless it does, one does not reach second echelon issues such as whether the clause also guarantees the right to be paid for such work from public funds and the right to perform work free of statutorily mandated geographic restrictions.
>
> For purposes of classifying rights and freedoms, the right to work is commonly, if not invariably, characterized as an economic right. There is now a considerable body of case authority bearing on the question of whether the right to liberty clause confers or protects economic rights generally or the right to work in particular.

With respect, we think that puts the appellants' case on too narrow a basis. The trial judge has characterized the issue as "right to work" [a purely economic question], when he should have directed his attention to a more important aspect of liberty, the right to pursue a livelihood or profession [a matter concerning one's dignity and sense of self-worth].

The appellants' case is that the government has deprived them of the opportunity to pursue their profession, or has restricted their mobility in such a way as to deprive them of "liberty" in the broad sense in which that freedom is to be interpreted under the Charter. The government has said, in effect, that they cannot practice without a practitioner number, and that any number that is granted will restrict their movements. A geographic restriction will determine their place of residence, and a *locum tenens* number will provide only a temporary opportunity to practice and will necessitate movement from place to place, and from office to office. They assert that the scheme deprives them of choices which are fundamental to liberty in the sense in which that word should be understood in the context of Charter freedoms.

The issue then is not payment or no payment for medical services. Denial of the right to participate under the plan is not the denial of a purely economic right, but in reality is a denial of the right of the appellants to practice their chosen profession within British Columbia.

In considering the economic interests involved we must not overlook the fact that the plan does not guarantee an income to doctors. It ensures that a percentage of the bills submitted by physicians for medical services performed for insured patients will be paid. The patients who pay premiums and the governments that subsidize patient care also have an economic interest in the plan as a means by which the provincial government seeks to reduce the cost of our health care system. Cost control is admittedly a worthy purpose and a legitimate responsibility for the government. Provincial governments have considered and implemented various ways of reducing these costs including reducing the percentage paid of the medical service rendered, excluding certain services from coverage, instituting user fees for certain services, limiting the amount which will be paid for particular services and increasing premiums.

The economic component of the freedom which the doctors seek to assert is the right to be paid by or on behalf of the patient for such services as may be rendered. The problem with the impugned legislation is that the opportunity to pursue their profession, and the freedom of mobility in practice, can be denied by refusing to allow patients the right to have the doctor reimbursed under the plan. The rights being asserted in this case are personal rights affecting the freedom and quality of life of individual doctors. The effect upon them of the alleged deprivations is personal, and has far reaching implications. It is not a purely business interest which is affected.

The trial judge refused to follow *Mia* holding that:

> … Most recent decisions have declined to extend the right to liberty clause to the economic realm and indicate that the clause does not guarantee a right to engage in particular types of commercial activity, employment, or professional callings.

The decisions upon which that conclusion rests include cases of purely economic rights, cases of regulation of business, professional or occupational activity, and cases which hold that s. 7 does not guarantee a "free standing right to work." We will examine these categories in some detail as distinct from the doctors' situation.

The Economic Rights Cases

[The court discussed a group of cases in which "the 'liberty' the plaintiff was alleged to have been deprived of was a purely economic interest or freedom." A representative case in this group was *Smith Kline & French Laboratories Ltd. v. Attorney General of Canada* (1986), 24 DLR (4th) 321 (FCTD).]

At issue in *Smith, Kline & French*, was legislation which granted patentees exclusivity for 17 years (medicine patents). Strayer J was of the view that the concepts of life, liberty and security of the person have to do with the bodily well-being of a natural person. He said, at 363:

> As such, they are not apt to describe any rights of a corporation nor are they apt to describe purely economic interests of a natural person.

Strayer J in defining "liberty," accepted as correct the view expressed by Pratte J in *Operation Dismantle* that the word connoted freedom from arbitrary arrest or detention. That narrow view has not been rejected by the Supreme Court of Canada.

We do not quarrel with the conclusion reached in those cases involving corporation business interests and pure economic rights, but we do not think that they detract from the conclusion reached in *Mia*, that denying doctors the opportunity to pursue their professions falls within the rubric of "liberty" as that word is used in s. 7.

The Regulatory Cases
. . .

We have no doubt that regulation of such matters as standards of admission, mandatory insurance for the protection of the public, and standards of practice and of behaviour will not constitute an infringement of s. 7. We do not think that any of those cases detract from the conclusion reached in *Mia*.

The Right To Work Cases

To support his conclusion that s. 7 did not extend to the rights being asserted by the appellants, the trial judge equated this case with those in which it was said that there is no common law right to work.

[A long discussion of cases is omitted. The major one was *R v. Edwards Books and Art Ltd.*, [1986] 2 SCR 713 (Ont.).]

In our opinion, [these cases] ought to be regarded as cases involving the regulation of business. They established the principle that "liberty" in s. 7 is not synonymous with unconstrained freedom and that s. 7 does not extend "to an unconstrained right to transact business whenever one wishes." In our opinion they do not stand for the proposition that government may deprive an individual of the opportunity to pursue freely the practice of his profession.

In our view, the phrase "right to work" was used in [these cases] to describe the right being claimed in those cases—the right not to be regulated. It had little to do with the important personal right of otherwise qualified professional people to have an opportunity to attempt to build a practice in their province and in their chosen communities. One may be deprived of such a right in accordance with the principles of fundamental justice; however, the arbitrary nature of the deprivation effected by the *Medical Service Act* and *Regulations* as detailed later in these reasons, excludes resort by the Crown to this exception. Finally, such a right may be overriden by important societal concerns which satisfy the requirements of s. 1 of the Charter. In this case government does not assert or rely on such concerns.

We are not persuaded that the foregoing authorities relied upon by the trial judge support the conclusion that the appellants have not been deprived of the "liberty" to pursue their chosen profession.

Furthermore, we are not persuaded that the appellants are pursuing a mere economic interest in the nature of an income guaranteed by the government. The impugned enactments go beyond mere economic concerns or regulation within the profession. The appellants are all fully qualified and licensed doctors who have been excluded from pursuing the practice of their profession. It matters not whether the exclusion of the opportunity to practice is exclusion from practice everywhere in British Columbia, or exclusion from practice anywhere but specified geographic areas of the province.

Mobility: A Component of Liberty

As Chief Justice McEachern demonstrated in *Mia* (at 413), history shows that restrictions on movement for the purpose of employment were, short of imprisonment, the most severe deprivation of freedom and liberty.

Consideration of the mobility issue in the judgment appealed from is confined to the arguments under s. 6. There is no recognition in the judgment that the important freedom of mobility within a province could be embraced by the broad protection afforded by s. 7. In our view, mobility is a fundamental right, and the right to "liberty" bears directly on the right to free movement.

It may be argued that if movement within the province is a protected freedom that such right must be found in s. 6. We do not agree. The Charter is not a statute containing a number of watertight compartments. It is not a document which is to be given a narrow and legalistic interpretation.

Section 6 may or may not be restrictive to guaranteeing the right of free movement from province to province. Whatever the answer to that question may be, does not detract from the constitutional and fundamental importance of mobility as it affects the life, liberty and security of the person: "Liberty" must touch the right of free movement.

We are of the opinion, therefore, that the geographic restrictions imposed by government on the right to practice medicine in British Columbia constitute a violation of the right to liberty protected by s. 7 *unless* that right has been removed in accordance with the principles of fundamental justice, or unless the deprivation can be demonstrably justified under s. 1 of the Charter.

The Principles of Fundamental Justice
. . .

The appellants submit that the legislation, and regulatory scheme which operates under it, are unfair in both procedure and substance.

[For the procedural analysis, the court listed some objectionable omissions in the regulations—for example, the lack of any duty to make decisions about applications, the lack of a hearing, the lack of any obligation to give reasons, and the lack of any way of knowing what the current state of need for doctors was in any area or the province as a whole.]

In our opinion, the scheme offends the principles of fundamental justice. It is based on the application of vague and uncertain criteria, which combined with areas of uncontrolled discretion, leaves substantial scope for arbitrary conduct. The government does not attempt to defend the procedural deficiencies of the scheme, except to submit that the normal processes of judicial review should suffice to give a remedy to an individual applicant. We think that the scheme is so procedurally flawed that it cannot stand.

[The court also concluded that the discriminations among doctors, new and established and in and out of the province, denied fundamental justice on substantive grounds.]

Appeal allowed.

NOTES

1. The Supreme Court of Canada denied leave to appeal in this case: (1988), 92 NR 400n. Given the clear national importance of the issues, why do you think this happened?

2. Is *Wilson* about regulation of work generally or just about access to professional practice (indeed, perhaps even just the historic professions)? (For a judgment applying *Wilson* to the suspension of a private investigation agency's licences, see *Forsythe v. Alberta (Administrator, Private Investigations and Security Guards Act)* (1993), 19 Admin. LR (2d) 187 (Alta. QB).) If the latter, what are the justifications for such a restricted view of the reach of s. 7? Is the Court of Appeal ruling that the BC legislature could not restrict numbers practising medicine in the province either generally or in certain geographic areas, or is it holding that this particular way of doing it was constitutionally impermissible? If the latter, is it because of procedural or substantive defects in the legislation or both? In response to this judgment, how would you advise the government as to a constitutionally permissible manner of achieving its objectives?

3. For a critical examination of *Wilson*, see Lepofsky, "Constitutional Law—*Charter of Rights and Freedoms,* Section 7—A Problematic Judicial Foray into Legislative Policy-Making—*Wilson v. Medical Services Commission*" (1989), 68 *Can. Bar Rev.* 591. Indeed, consider whether *Wilson* can stand in the face of the following extract from the concurring judgment of Lamer J (as he then was) in *Reference re Ss. 193 and 195(1)(c) of the Criminal Code* ("the Prostitution Reference"), [1990] 1 SCR 1123 (Man.):

> In my view, it is not clear that the statement by the Chief Justice [*Reference re Public Service Employee Relations Act (Alta.),* [1987] 1 SCR 313 (Alta.)], quoted at length by the BC Court of Appeal in *Wilson,* is support for the view that s. 7 of the Charter protects a "right to pursue a livelihood or profession" as distinct from a "right to work" which is not protected. In the *Reference* case, the issue was not whether there existed an independent right to work or to pursue a profession, but rather whether the freedom of association protected by s. 2(d) of the Charter included the freedom to form and join associations and the freedom to bargain collectively and to strike. It was the view of the Chief Justice that the right to bargain collectively and to strike was essential to the capacity of individuals to ensure equitable and humane working conditions. It was in that context that the Chief Justice spoke of the importance of work to a person's sense of dignity and self-worth. There is no doubt that the non-economic or non-pecuniary aspects of work cannot be denied and are indeed important to a person's sense of identity, self-worth and emotional well-being. But it seems to me that the distinction sought to be drawn by the Court between a right to work and a right to pursue a profession is, with respect, not one that aids in an understanding of the scope of "liberty" under s. 7 of the Charter.
>
> Further, it is my view that work is not the only activity which contributes to a person's self-worth or emotional well-being. If liberty or security of the person under s. 7 of the Charter were defined in terms of attributes such as dignity, self-worth and emotional well-being, it seems that liberty under s. 7 would be all inclusive. In such a state of affairs there would be serious reason to question the independent existence in the Charter of other rights and freedoms such as freedom of religion and conscience or freedom of expression.
>
> In short then I find myself in agreement with the following statement of McIntyre J in the *Reference re Public Service Employee Relations Act (Alta.)* case, *supra,* at 412:

It is also to be observed that the Charter, with the possible exception of s. 6(2)(b) (right to earn a livelihood in any province) and s. 6(4), does not concern itself with economic rights.

I therefore reject the application of the American line of cases that suggest that liberty under the Fourteenth Amendment includes liberty of contract. As I stated earlier these cases have a specific historical context, a context that incorporated into the American jurisprudence certain *laissez-faire* principles that may not have a corresponding application to the interpretation of the Charter in the present day. There is also a significant difference in the wording of s. 7 and the Fourteenth Amendment. The American provision speaks specifically of a protection of property interests while our framers did not choose to similarly protect property rights (see *Irwin Toy Ltd. v. Quebec (Attorney General)* [1989] 1 SCR 927 (Que.) at 1033). This then, is sufficient to dispose of this ground of appeal.

· · ·

The extent to which s. 7 of the Charter can be invoked in the realm of administrative law, its implications for administrative procedures, and its relationship to the common law rules of natural justice and the duty of fairness are not before this Court, and it is preferable to develop that jurisprudence on an ongoing, case-by-case basis. What is clear, however, is that the State in certain circumstances has created bodies, such as parole boards and mental health review tribunals, that assume control over decisions affecting an individual's liberty and security of the person. Those are because they involve the restriction to an individual's physical liberty and security of the person, where the judiciary has always had a role to play as guardian of the administration of the justice system. There are also situations in which the State restricts other privileges or, broadly termed, "liberties" in the guise of regulation, but uses punitive measures in cases of non-compliance. In such situations the State is in effect punishing individuals, in the classic sense of the word, for non-compliance with a law or regulation. In all these cases, in my view, the liberty and security of the person interests protected by s. 7 would be restricted, and one would then have to determine if the restriction was in accordance with the principles of fundamental justice. By contrast, as I have stated, there is the realm of general public policy dealing with broader social, political and all issues which are much better resolved in the political or legislative forum and not in the courts.

In this respect, Professor Colvin describes the proper judicial role as follows in his article ["Section 7 of the *Canadian Charter of Rights and Freedoms*" (1989), 68 *Can. Bar Rev.* 566], at 575:

> Any claims which the judiciary can make to an "inherent domain" must be claims about means rather than ends. The judiciary should have some special expertise in matters of institutional process. The judiciary may also have certain limited powers to review governmental decisions of social policy. There is, however, no constitutional basis within the Western democratic tradition for the judiciary to claim any area of substantive policy-making as its exclusive preserve.

Put shortly, I am of the view that s. 7 is implicated when the State, by resorting to the justice system, restricts an individual's physical liberty in any circumstances. Section 7 is also implicated when the State restricts individuals' security of the person by interfering with, or removing from them, control over their physical or mental integrity. Finally, s. 7 is implicated when the State, either directly or through its agents, restricts certain privileges or liberties by using the threat of punishment in cases of non-compliance.

Although this may appear to be a limited reading of s. 7, it is my view that it is neither wise nor necessary to subsume all other rights in the Charter within s. 7. A full and generous interpretation of the Charter that extends the full benefit of its protection to individuals can be achieved without the incorporation of other rights and freedoms within s. 7.

It should be noted, however, that the other majority judges in this case did not feel it necessary for the purposes of disposing of the appeal to engage in an analysis of these issues. As a consequence, Lamer J's statements are technically no more than *dicta*, though highly influential *dicta*, as their subsequent use in more recent cases exemplifies: see, for example, the judgment of MacGuigan JA for the majority of the Federal Court of Appeal in *Canadian Association of Regulated Importers v. Canada (Attorney General)* (1991), 87 DLR (4th) 730 (FCA) and *Nisbett v. Manitoba (Human Rights Commission)* (1993), 101 DLR (4th) 744 (Man. CA). Indeed, *Walker v. PEI*, [1995] 2 SCR 407 (PEI), denying the protection of s. 7 to certified general accountants, may be read as settling the issue, although the judgment of Lamer CJC for the court is both short and cryptic. As well, in Ontario, the courts have generally taken the position that the right to practise a profession is not protected either procedurally or substantively by s. 7 of the Charter: see, for example, *Biscotti v. Ontario Securities Commission* (1990), 74 OR (2d) 119 (Div. Ct.); aff'd. (1991), 1 OR (3d) 409 (CA); leave to appeal denied 3 OR (3d) xii (SCC); *Kopyto v. Law Society of Upper Canada* (1993), 18 Admin. LR (2d) 54 (Ont. Div. Ct.). The Quebec Court of Appeal has ruled to the same effect: *Belhumeur v. Comité de discipline* (1988), 54 DLR (4th) 105 (Que. CA). However, compare *Harvey v. Law Society of Newfoundland* (1992), 2 Admin. LR (2d) 306 (Nfld. SCTD), applying s. 7 to professional discipline. Account also has to be taken of *Godbout v. Longueuil (City)*, [1997] 3 SCR 844 (Que). There, La Forest J, speaking for himself and two other members of the court, saw a municipal rule that employees of the city must live within the city as infringing on their s. 7 right to liberty. Subsequently, that concurring judgment was endorsed by a majority of the court in *Blencoe v. British Columbia (Human Rights Commission)*, [2000] 2 SCR 307 (extracted below).

4. To what extent does the position of Lamer J speak to the issue whether s. 7 can be relied on for the protection of social benefits? Is the answer to this question contingent on whether what is being asserted is a claim that s. 7 guarantees receipt of certain benefits as part of the right to life or security of the person or a claim that (as in *Webb*) certain benefits cannot be removed without the provision of adequate procedures? For discussion of these issues see Johnstone, "Section 7 of the Charter and Constitutionally Protected Welfare" (1988), 46 *UT Fac. LR* 1; Jackman, "The Protection of Welfare Rights Under the Charter" (1988), 20 *Ottawa LR* 257 and "Using the Charter to Support Social Welfare Claims" (1993), 19 *Queen's LJ* 65, both of whom argue for constitutionally guaranteed welfare rights by reference to s. 7. This issue was before the Supreme Court in *Gosselin v. Quebec (Attorney General)*, 2002 SCC 84 (Que.), a case involving (*inter alia*) a claim that s. 7 provided a right to subsistence level welfare. That claim failed on the facts, but the court left unresolved the issue of whether s. 7 could ever generate this kind of right. In dissent, Arbour J (L'Heureux-Dubé J concurring) would have sustained the claim in law and on the facts.

5. In terms of the reach of s. 7 of the Charter for the purposes of administrative law, probably the most critical question is whether involuntary subjection to the administrative process in general generates a "life, liberty and security of the person" claim. It took the Supreme Court a long time to give leave in a case that raised that question squarely. However,

in *New Brunswick (Minister of Health and Community Services) v. G. (J.) [J.G.]*, [1999] 3 SCR 46 (NB), the Supreme Court held that at least some drastic administrative proceedings may affect an individual's security of the person. Here the minister had sought to extend a judicial order granting the minister custody of the appellant's three children for an additional six months. Did fundamental justice require that she be provided with legal aid? But before that issue could be addressed, it had to be determined that the custody affected her security of the person.

Lamer CJ, speaking for a unanimous court on this issue, concluded that given the nature of the custody proceedings and their impact, she had crossed the threshold.

> Were the Minister successful in his application, the appellant would have been separated from her children for up to an additional six months. There would also be no guarantee that she would regain custody of her children at the expiry of the order. The separation of parent and child contemplated by the Minister's application would unquestionably have profound effects on both parent and child. For the purposes of this appeal, however, what must be determined is whether relieving a parent of custody of his or her child restricts a parent's right to security of the person.
>
> This Court has held on a number of occasions that the right to security of the person protects "both the physical and psychological integrity of the individual": see *R v. Morgentaler* [1988] 1 SCR 30 (Ont.), at p. 173 (*per* Wilson J); *Reference re ss. 193 and 195.1(1)(c) of the Criminal Code* [1990] 1 SCR 1123 (Man.), at p. 1177; *Rodriguez v. British Columbia (Attorney General)* [1993] 3 SCR 519 (BC), at pp. 587-88. Although these cases considered the right to security of the person in a criminal law context, I believe that the protection accorded by this right extends beyond the criminal law and can be engaged in child protection proceedings. Before addressing this issue, I will first make some general comments about the nature of the protection of "psychological integrity" included in the right to security of the person.
>
> For a restriction of security of the person to be made out, then, the impugned state action must have a serious and profound effect on a person's psychological integrity. The effects of the state interference must be assessed objectively, with a view to their impact on the psychological integrity of a person of reasonable sensibility. This need not rise to the level of nervous shock or psychiatric illness, but must be greater than ordinary stress or anxiety.
>
> I have little doubt that state removal of a child from parental custody pursuant to the state's *parens patriae* jurisdiction constitutes a serious interference with the psychological integrity of the parent. The parental interest in raising and caring for a child is, as La Forest J held in *B (R)* [*v. Children's Aid Society of Metropolitan Toronto*, [1995] 1 SCR 315 (Ont.),] at para. 83, "an individual interest of fundamental importance in our society." Besides the obvious distress arising from the loss of companionship of the child, direct state interference with the parent–child relationship, through a procedure in which the relationship is subject to state inspection and review is a gross intrusion into a private and intimate sphere. Further, the parent is often stigmatized as "unfit" when relieved of custody. As an individual's status as a parent is often fundamental to personal identity, the stigma and distress resulting from a loss of parental status is a particularly serious consequence of the state's conduct.

It should also be noted that a minority consisting of L'Heureux-Dubé, Gonthier, and McLachlin JJ, while agreeing with the chief justice with respect to the security of the person, were also of the view that the custody proceedings triggered the appellant's liberty interest.

The result of the proceedings could be that the parent is deprived of the right to make decisions on behalf of her children and guide their upbringing. Parental decision making and other attributes of custody should be considered under the liberty interest in s. 7 of the Charter. See Lorne Sossin, "Developments in Administrative Law: The 1999-2000 Term" (2000), 13 *Supreme Court LR* (2d) 45, at 50-55.

While the court as a whole had emphasized that state action must have a serious and profound effect on a person's psychological integrity in order to trigger the Charter, this judgment does suggest a potentially wider role for fundamental justice in administrative law, especially now that s. 7 is no longer associated exclusively with the criminal law. A test of how high the Charter threshold will be set was soon forthcoming in a major case involving excessive delay in a human rights context.

In reading and thinking about *Blencoe* (below) you might want to keep two ideas particularly in mind. First, here the remedial tail wagged the substantive dog in that an instinctive (and understandable) unwillingness to grant Blencoe a stay of proceedings tended to overshadow the issue whether a Charter right was at stake or whether an administrative law abuse of process right stood in need of protection. Ask yourself whether substantive legal outcomes might have been different if a remedy less likely to deprive the complainants of their rights had been sought. Or, when all is said and done, is a stay of proceedings the only way to go?

Second, note that the minority was very upset at the majority's willingness to resort to the Charter without first exploring the adequacy of an administrative law answer to delay. However, are the gloomy assessments at the close of the minority's judgment that administrative law has been frozen and sterilized, really justified? By setting the threshold as high as the majority did for access to the Charter, will this not necessitate even greater resort to administrative law remedies that will become "hot and fecund"?

Blencoe v. British Columbia (Human Rights Commission)
[2000] 2 SCR 307 (BC) (footnotes omitted)

[In March 1995, while serving as a minister in the government of British Columbia, the respondent was accused by one of his assistants of sexual harassment. A month later, the premier removed the respondent from Cabinet and dismissed him from the NDP caucus. In July and August 1995, two complaints of discriminatory conduct in the form of sexual harassment were filed with the BC Council of Human Rights (later the BC Human Rights Commission) against the respondent by two other women, W and S. The complaints centred on various incidents of sexual harassment alleged to have occurred between March 1993 and March 1995. The respondent was informed of the first complaint in July 1995 and of the second in September 1995. After the commission's investigation, hearings were scheduled before the BC Human Rights Tribunal in March 1998, over 30 months after the initial complaints were filed.

Following the allegations against the respondent, media attention was intense. The respondent suffered from severe depression. He did not stand for re-election in 1996. Considering himself "unemployable" in British Columbia due to the outstanding human rights complaints against him, the respondent commenced judicial review proceedings

in November 1997 to have the complaints stayed. He claimed that the commission had
lost jurisdiction due to unreasonable delay in processing the complaints. The respondent
alleged that the unreasonable delay caused serious prejudice to him and his family that
amounted to an abuse of process and a denial of natural justice. His petition was dismissed by the Supreme Court of British Columbia: (1998), 49 BCLR (3d) 201 (SC). A
majority of the Court of Appeal allowed the respondent's appeal and directed that the
human rights proceedings against him be stayed: (1998), 49 BCLR (3d) 216 (CA). The
majority found that the respondent had been deprived of his right under s. 7 of the *Canadian Charter of Rights and Freedoms* to security of the person in a manner that was not
in accordance with the principles of fundamental justice.]

BASTARACHE J (McLachlin CJ and L'Heureux-Dubé, Gonthier, and Major JJ concurring): ...

V. Issues

The following are the central issues to be determined for the disposition of this appeal:

A. Does the Charter apply to the actions of the British Columbia Human Rights
Commission?

B. Have the respondent's s. 7 rights to liberty and security of the person been violated by state-caused delay in the human rights proceedings?

C. If the respondent's s. 7 rights were not engaged, or if the state's actions were in
accordance with the principles of fundamental justice, was the respondent entitled to a remedy pursuant to administrative law principles where the delay did
not interfere with the right to a fair hearing?

D. If the respondent is entitled to a Charter or administrative law remedy, was the
stay of proceedings an appropriate remedy in the circumstances of this case?

VI. Analysis

A. Does the Charter Apply to the Actions of the British Columbia Human Rights Commission?

. . .

It is clear that both the federal Parliament and provincial legislatures are bound by the
Charter. However, one threshold issue which has been raised in this case is whether the
Commission and the Tribunal are agents of government pursuant to s. 32 of the Charter.
The following three factors have been put forth to support the argument that these bodies are not bound by the Charter: (i) the organizations in question are required to be
independent of government; (ii) the challenge in this case is not to any statutory provisions that might be said to be within the legislative sphere; and (iii) the organizations in
question must act judicially since their functions are analogous to those exercised by
courts of law.

For the reasons I address below, these claims are misguided with respect to their approach to the application of the Charter. Furthermore, for the purposes of this appeal, it

is only necessary to address the Charter's applicability to the actions of the Commission since the prejudice suffered by the respondent is alleged to have resulted from unreasonable delay in the actions of the Commission.

The mere fact that a body is independent of government is not determinative of the Charter's application, nor is the fact that a statutory provision is not impugned. Being autonomous or independent from government is not a conclusive basis upon which to hold that the Charter does not apply.

Bodies exercising statutory authority are bound by the Charter even though they may be independent of government. This was confirmed by La Forest J, speaking for a unanimous Court in *Eldridge v. British Columbia (Attorney General)* [1997] 3 SCR 624 (BC), at para. 21:

> There is no doubt, however, that the Charter also applies to action taken under statutory authority. The rationale for this rule flows inexorably from the logical structure of s. 32. As Professor Hogg explains in his *Constitutional Law of Canada* (3rd ed. 1992 (loose-leaf)), vol. 1, at pp. 34-8.3 and 34-9:
>
> > Action taken under statutory authority is valid only if it is within the scope of that authority. Since neither Parliament nor a Legislature can itself pass a law in breach of the Charter, neither body can authorize action which would be in breach of the Charter. Thus, the limitations on statutory authority which are imposed by the Charter will flow down the chain of statutory authority and apply to regulations, by-laws, orders, decisions and all other action (whether legislative, administrative or judicial) which depends for its validity on statutory authority.

There is no doubt that the Commission is created by statute and that all of its actions are taken pursuant to statutory authority.

One distinctive feature of actions taken under statutory authority is that they involve a power of compulsion not possessed by private individuals (P.W. Hogg, *Constitutional Law of Canada* (loose-leaf ed.), vol. 2, at p. 34-12). Clearly the Commission possesses more extensive powers than a natural person. The Commission's authority is not derived from the consent of the parties. The *Human Rights Code* grants various powers to the Commission to both investigate complaints and decide how to deal with such complaints. Section 24 of the Code specifically allows the Commissioner to compel the production of documents. ...

The Commission in this case cannot therefore escape Charter scrutiny merely because it is not part of government or controlled by government. In *Eldridge*, a unanimous Court concluded that a hospital was bound by the Charter since it was implementing a specific government policy or program. The Commission in this case is both implementing a specific government program and exercising powers of statutory compulsion.

With respect to the claim that the Commission exercises judicial functions and is thereby not subject to the Charter, the decision of this Court in *Slaight Communications Inc. v. Davidson* [1989] 1 SCR 1038, is conclusive. Lamer J (as he then was), in partial dissent but speaking for a unanimous Court on this point, held that the Charter applies to the orders of a statutorily appointed labour arbitrator. This determination was not open to challenge, as expressed by Lamer J, at pp. 1077-78:

The fact that the Charter applies to the order made by the adjudicator in the case at bar is not, in my opinion, open to question. *The adjudicator is a statutory creature: he is appointed pursuant to a legislative provision and derives all his powers from the statute.* [Emphasis added.]

The facts in *Slaight* and the case at bar share at least one salient feature: the labour arbitrator (in *Slaight*) and the Commission (in the case at bar) each exercise governmental powers conferred upon them by a legislative body. The ultimate source of authority in each of these cases is government. All of the Commission's powers are derived from the statute. The Commission is carrying out the legislative scheme of the *Human Rights Code*. It is putting into place a government program or a specific statutory scheme established by government to implement government policy (see *Eldridge, supra*, at paras. 37 and 44, and *Douglas/Kwantlen Faculty Assn. v. Douglas College* [1990] 3 SCR 570, at p. 584). The Commission must act within the limits of its enabling statute. There is clearly a "governmental quality" to the functions of a human rights commission which is created by government to promote equality in society generally.

Thus, notwithstanding that the Commission may have adjudicatory characteristics, it is a statutory creature and its actions fall under the authority of the *Human Rights Code*. The state has instituted an administrative structure, through a legislative scheme, to effectuate a governmental program to provide redress against discrimination. It is the administration of a governmental program that calls for Charter scrutiny. Once a complaint is brought before the Commission, the subsequent administrative proceedings must comply with the Charter. These entities are subject to Charter scrutiny in the performance of their functions just as government would be in like circumstances. To hold otherwise would allow the legislative branch to circumvent the Charter by establishing statutory bodies that are immune to Charter scrutiny. The above analysis leads inexorably to the conclusion that the Charter applies to the actions of the Commission.

B. Have the Respondent's Section 7 Rights to Liberty and Security of the Person Been Violated by State-Caused Delay in Human Rights Proceedings?

· · ·

(b) Applicability of Section 7 Outside the Criminal Context

Although there have been some decisions of this Court which may have supported the position that s. 7 of the Charter is restricted to the sphere of criminal law, there is no longer any doubt that s. 7 of the Charter is not confined to the penal context. This was most recently affirmed by this Court in *New Brunswick (Minister of Health and Community Services) v. G(J)* [1999] 3 SCR 46, where Lamer CJ stated that the protection of security of the person extends beyond the criminal law (at para. 58) ... . Section 7 can extend beyond the sphere of criminal law, at least where there is "state action which directly engages the justice system and its administration" (*G(J)*, at para. 66). If a case arises in the human rights context which, on its facts, meets the usual s. 7 threshold requirements, there is no specific bar against such a claim and s. 7 may be engaged. The question to be addressed, however, is not whether delays in human rights proceedings *can* engage s. 7 of the Charter but rather, whether the respondent's s. 7 rights were actually engaged by delays in the circumstances of this case. Various parties in this case seem to have conflated the delay issue with the threshold s. 7 issue. However, whether the respondent's s. 7 rights to life, liberty and security of the person are engaged is a separate issue from whether the delay itself was unreasonable. I will now examine whether the s. 7 threshold requirements have been met and whether the respondent has demonstrated a breach of his s. 7 rights.

· · ·

McEachern CJBC collapsed the s. 7 interests of "liberty" and "security of the person" into a single right protecting a person's dignity against the stigma of undue, prolonged humiliation and public degradation of the kind suffered by the respondent. In *Singh v. Minister of Employment and Immigration* [1985] 1 SCR 177, at pp. 204-5, Wilson J emphasized that "life, liberty and security of the person" are three distinct interests, and that it is incumbent on the Court to give meaning to each of these elements. This statement was endorsed by Lamer J for a majority of this Court in *Re BC Motor Vehicle Act* [1985] 2 SCR 486, at p. 500. In addressing the issue of whether the respondent's s. 7 rights have been breached in this case, I also prefer to keep the interests protected by s. 7 analytically distinct to the extent possible. For the purposes of this appeal, the outcome is dependent upon the meaning to be given to the interests of "liberty" and "security of the person."

(d) Liberty Interest

The liberty interest protected by s. 7 of the Charter is no longer restricted to mere freedom from physical restraint. Members of this Court have found that "liberty" is engaged where state compulsions or prohibitions affect important and fundamental life choices. ...

In *Godbout v. Longueuil (City)* [1997] 3 SCR 844, at para. 66, La Forest J, writing for L'Heureux-Dubé J and McLachlin J (as she then was), reiterated his position that the right to liberty in s. 7 protects the individual's right to make inherently private choices and that choosing where to establish one's home is one such inherently personal choice:

> The foregoing discussion serves simply to reiterate my general view that *the right to liberty ensh rined in s. 7 of the Charter protects within its ambit the right to an irreducible sphere of personal autonomy wherein individuals may make inherently private choices free from state interference. I must emphasize here that, as the tenor of my comments in B(R) should indicate, I do not by any means regard this sphere of autonomy as being so wide as to encompass any and all decisions that individuals might make in conducting their affairs.* Indeed, such a view would run contrary to the basic idea, expressed both at the outset of these reasons and in my reasons in *B(R)*, that individuals cannot, in any organized society, be guaranteed an unbridled freedom to do whatever they please. Moreover, I do not even consider that the sphere of autonomy includes within its scope every matter that might, however vaguely, be described as "private." *Rather, as I see it, the autonomy protected by the s. 7 right to liberty encompasses only those matters that can properly be characterized as fundamentally or inherently personal such that, by their very nature, they implicate basic choices going to the core of what it means to enjoy individual dignity and independence.* As I have already explained, I took the view in *B(R)* that parental decisions respecting the medical care provided to their children fall within this narrow class of inherently personal matters. In my view, choosing where to establish one's home is, likewise, a quintessentially private decision going to the very heart of personal or individual autonomy. [Emphasis added.]

La Forest J therefore spoke in *Godbout* of a narrow sphere of inherently personal decision-making deserving of the law's protection. Choosing where to establish one's home fell within that narrow class according to three members of this Court.

. . .

Professor Hogg, *supra*, at p. 44-9, supports a more cautious approach to the interpretation of s. 7 such that s. 7 does not become a residual right which envelopes all of the legal rights in the Charter. Professor Hogg also addresses the deliberate omission of "property" from "life, liberty and security of the person" in s. 7, and states, at p. 44-12:

> It also requires ... that those terms [liberty and security of the person] be interpreted as excluding economic liberty and economic security; otherwise, property, having been shut out of the front door, would enter by the back.

Although an individual has the right to make fundamental personal choices free from state interference, such personal autonomy is not synonymous with unconstrained freedom. In the circumstances of this case, the state has not prevented the respondent from making any "fundamental personal choices." The interests sought to be protected in this case do not in my opinion fall within the "liberty" interest protected by s. 7.

(e) Security of the Person

In the criminal context, this Court has held that state interference with bodily integrity and serious state-imposed psychological stress constitute a breach of an individual's security of the person. In this context, security of the person has been held to protect both the physical and psychological integrity of the individual ... . These decisions relate to situations where the state has taken steps to interfere, through criminal legislation, with personal autonomy and a person's ability to control his or her own physical or psychological integrity such as prohibiting assisted suicide and regulating abortion.

The principle that the right to security of the person encompasses serious state-imposed psychological stress has recently been reiterated by this Court in *G(J)*, *supra*. ... However, the former Chief Justice also set boundaries in *G(J)* for cases where one's psychological integrity is infringed upon. He referred to the attempt to delineate such boundaries as "an inexact science" (para. 59).

Not all state interference with an individual's psychological integrity will engage s. 7. Where the psychological integrity of a person is at issue, security of the person is restricted to "serious state-imposed psychological stress" (Dickson CJ in [*R v. Morgentaler*, [1988] 1 SCR 30 (Ont.),] at p. 56). I think Lamer CJ was correct in his assertion that Dickson CJ was seeking to convey something qualitative about the type of state interference that would rise to the level of infringing s. 7 (*G(J)*, at para. 59). The words "serious state-imposed psychological stress" delineate two requirements that must be met in order for security of the person to be triggered. First, the psychological harm must be *state imposed*, meaning that the harm must result from the actions of the state. Second, the psychological prejudice must be *serious*. Not all forms of psychological prejudice caused by government will lead to automatic s. 7 violations. These two requirements will be examined in turn.

(i) Was the Harm to Mr. Blencoe the Result of State-Caused Delay in the
Human Rights Process?

. . .

Stress, anxiety and stigma may arise from any criminal trial, human rights allegation, or
even a civil action, regardless of whether the trial or process occurs within a reasonable
time. We are therefore not concerned in this case with all such prejudice but only that
impairment which can be said to flow from the delay in the human rights process. It
would be inappropriate to hold government accountable for harms that are brought
about by third parties who are not in any sense acting as agents of the state.

While it is incontrovertible that the respondent has suffered serious prejudice in connection with the allegations of sexual harassment against him, there must be a sufficient
causal connection between the state-caused delay and the prejudice suffered by the respondent for s. 7 to be triggered. ...

The appellants submit that the nexus between the harm to the respondent and the alleged delay in processing the Complaints is remote. They assert that the largest measure
of prejudice to Mr. Blencoe resulted not from any delay but from the publicity surrounding the events, especially his dismissal from Cabinet and later from the NDP caucus.
They add that the respondent himself fought the allegations against him in the public
domain. For the reasons I set out below, I also have doubts whether, on the facts, the
psychological harm suffered by the respondent can be seen as the result of state-caused
delay in the human rights process.

[At this juncture, Bastarache J detailed the impact of the complaints and proceedings on
Blencoe's life and that of his family but noted that these were mostly consequences that
had occurred before there was any delay, indeed in a number of instances before the
commencement of the proceedings. He also suggested that some of the fallout during the
period of the delay was not attributable to the delay but to collateral causes. He also suggested that the delay had not exacerbated the prejudice suffered by Blencoe or at least in
a sufficiently serious manner. However, he then continued:]

At trial, Lowry J made the following finding concerning the cause of Mr. Blencoe's
suffering (at para. 13):

> The stigma attached to the outstanding complaints has certainly contributed in large meas-
> ure to the very real hardship Mr. Blencoe has experienced. His public profile as a Minister
> of the Crown rendered him particularly vulnerable to the media attention that has been
> focused on him and his family, and the hardship has, in the result, been protracted and
> severe.

Perhaps this statement supports the view that the outstanding Complaints did contribute to the stigma to some degree and that it was therefore a cause of the respondent's
suffering. Because I find in the next section that the state has not directly intruded into
a private and intimate sphere of the respondent's life, I assume without deciding that
there is a sufficient nexus between the state-caused delay and the prejudice to Mr. Blencoe. I now turn to the question of whether this interference amounts to a violation of the
respondent's security of the person.

(ii) Quality of the Interference

McEachern CJBC concluded that liberty and security of the person under s. 7 protect both the privacy and dignity of individuals against the stigma of undue, prolonged humiliation and public degradation of the kind suffered by Mr. Blencoe (at para. 101). He therefore conflated s. 7 into a general right to dignity and protection against the stigma of undue, prolonged humiliation and public degradation suffered as a result of an administrative proceeding. The question which arises is whether the rights of "liberty and security of the person" protected by s. 7 of the Charter include a generalized right to dignity, or more specifically, a right to be free from stigma associated with a human rights complaint? In my opinion, they do not.

The "right to dignity" accepted by McEachern CJBC essentially rests on several ideas. First, it is based on previous statements by this Court as to the importance and value of dignity. Second, it is based on the recognition in cases such as *Morgentaler* and *O'Connor* that state-induced psychological stress can infringe s. 7. Third, McEachern CJBC imports the notion of "stigma" as developed under s. 11(b) of the Charter in the criminal law context. Each of these bases for a generalized right to dignity under s. 7 will be addressed in turn.

1. DIGNITY

The Charter and the rights it guarantees are inextricably bound to concepts of human dignity. Indeed, notions of human dignity underlie almost every right guaranteed by the Charter (*Morgentaler, supra*, at pp. 164-66, *per* Wilson J). As professed by Dickson CJ in his discussion of s. 1 of the Charter in *R v. Oakes* [1986] 1 SCR 103, at p. 136:

> *The Court must be guided by the values and principles essential to a free and democratic society which I believe embody, to name but a few, respect for the inherent dignity of the human person,* commitment to social justice and equality, accommodation of a wide variety of beliefs, respect for cultural and group identity, and faith in social and political institutions which enhance the participation of individuals and groups in society. The underlying values and principles of a free and democratic society are the genesis of the rights and freedoms guaranteed by the Charter and the ultimate standard against which a limit on a right or freedom must be shown, despite its effect, to be reasonable and demonstrably justified. [Emphasis added.]

… Respect for the inherent dignity of persons is clearly an essential value in our free and democratic society which must guide the courts in interpreting the Charter. This does not mean, however, that dignity is elevated to a free-standing constitutional right protected by s. 7 of the Charter. Dignity has never been recognized by this Court as an independent right but has rather been viewed as finding expression in rights, such as equality, privacy or protection from state compulsion. In cases such as *Morgentaler, Rodriguez* [*v. British Columbia*, [1993] 3 SCR 519 (BC)] and *B(R)* [*v. Children's Aid Society of Metropolitan Toronto*, [1995] 1 SCR 315 (Ont.)], dignity was linked to personal autonomy over one's body or interference with fundamental personal choices. Indeed, dignity is often involved where the ability to make fundamental choices is at stake.

In my view, the notion of "dignity" in the decisions of this Court is better understood not as an autonomous Charter right, but rather, as an underlying value. …

According to the respondent, the human dignity of a person is closely tied to a person's reputation and privacy interests. Indeed, much of the harm which has been suffered by Mr. Blencoe in this case has been the damage which has been done to his reputation. Essentially, the respondent argues that his reputation has been ruined through the stigma he has suffered as a result of the publicity relating to the human rights proceedings against him. While this Court found in *Hill v. Church of Scientology of Toronto* [1995] 2 SCR 1130, that reputation was a concept underlying Charter rights, it too is not an independent Charter right in and of itself (at para. 120). ...

Respect for a person's reputation, like respect for dignity of the person, is a value that underlies the Charter. These two values do not support the respondent's proposition that protection of reputation or freedom from the stigma associated with human rights complaints are independent constitutional s. 7 rights. Moreover, the above passages from *Hill* regarding the protection of reputation were made in the context of a defamation case. Defamation laws are intended to protect reputation. Dignity and reputation are not self-standing rights. Neither is freedom from stigma. I would therefore agree with the following passage from *Reference re ss. 193 and 195.1(1)(c) of the Criminal Code* [[1990] 1 SCR 1130 (Man.)] at p.1170, wherein Lamer J cautioned:

> If liberty or security of the person under s. 7 of the Charter were defined in terms of attributes such as dignity, self-worth and emotional well-being, it seems that liberty under s. 7 would be all inclusive. In such a state of affairs there would be serious reason to question the independent existence in the Charter of other rights and freedoms such as freedom of religion and conscience or freedom of expression.

2. STATE INTERFERENCE WITH PSYCHOLOGICAL INTEGRITY

In order for security of the person to be triggered in this case, the impugned state action must have had a serious and profound effect on the respondent's psychological integrity (*G(J)*, *supra*, at para. 60). There must be state interference with an individual interest of fundamental importance (at para. 61). Lamer CJ stated in *G(J)*, at para. 59:

> It is clear that the right to security of the person does not protect the individual from the ordinary stresses and anxieties that a person of reasonable sensibility would suffer as a result of government action. If the right were interpreted with such broad sweep, countless government initiatives could be challenged on the ground that they infringe the right to security of the person, massively expanding the scope of judicial review, and, in the process, trivializing what it means for a right to be constitutionally protected.

He went on to state (at paras. 63-64):

> *Not every state action which interferes with the parent–child relationship will restrict a parent's right to security of the person.* For example, a parent's security of the person is not restricted when, without more, his or her child is sentenced to jail or conscripted into the army. Nor is it restricted when the child is negligently shot and killed by a police officer: see *Augustus v. Gosset* [1996] 3 SCR 268.
>
> *While the parent may suffer significant stress and anxiety as a result of the interference with the relationship occasioned by these actions, the quality of the "injury" to the parent is distinguishable from that in the present case.* In the aforementioned examples, the state is

making no pronouncement as to the parent's fitness or parental status, nor is it usurping the parental role or prying into the intimacies of the relationship. *In short, the state is not directly interfering with the psychological integrity of the parent qua parent.* The different effect on the psychological integrity of the parent in the above examples leads me to the conclusion that no constitutional rights of the parent are engaged. [Emphasis added.]

The quality of the injury must therefore be assessed. In my opinion, all of the cases which have come within the broad interpretation of "security of the person" outside of the penal context differ markedly from the interests that are at issue in this case. Violations of security of the person in this context include only serious psychological incursions resulting from state interference with an individual interest of fundamental importance.

It is only in exceptional cases where the state interferes in profoundly intimate and personal choices of an individual that state-caused delay in human rights proceedings could trigger the s. 7 security of the person interest. While these fundamental personal choices would include the right to make decisions concerning one's body free from state interference or the prospect of losing guardianship of one's children, they would not easily include the type of stress, anxiety and stigma that result from administrative or civil proceedings.

. . .

Few interests are as compelling as, and basic to individual autonomy than, a woman's choice to terminate her pregnancy, an individual's decision to terminate his or her life, the right to raise one's children, and the ability of sexual assault victims to seek therapy without fear of their private records being disclosed. Such interests are indeed basic to individual dignity. But the alleged right to be free from stigma associated with a human rights complaint does not fall within this narrow sphere. The state has not interfered with the respondent's right to make decisions that affect his fundamental being. The prejudice to the respondent in this case, as recognized by Lowry J, at para. 10, is essentially confined to his personal hardship. He is not "employable" as a politician, he and his family have moved residences twice, his financial resources are depleted, and he has suffered physically and psychologically. However, the state has not interfered with the respondent and his family's ability to make essential life choices. To accept that the prejudice suffered by the respondent in this case amounts to state interference with his security of the person would be to stretch the meaning of this right.

3. IMPORTING THE NOTION OF "STIGMA" FROM THE CRIMINAL LAW CONTEXT

In *Mills* [*v. The Queen*, [1986] 1 SCR 863] ... , at pp. 919-20, Lamer J, in dissent, found that the combination of loss of privacy, stigma, and disruption of family life engaged an individual's security of the person in the context of s. 11(b) of the Charter, stating that:

> ... security of the person is not restricted to physical integrity; rather, it encompasses protection against "overlong subjection to the vexations and vicissitudes of a pending criminal accusation." ... These include stigmatization of the accused, loss of privacy, stress and anxiety resulting from a multitude of factors, including possible disruption of family, social life and work, legal costs, uncertainty as to the outcome and sanction.

However, it must be emphasized that this statement was made in the context of s. 11(b) of the Charter which provides that a person charged with an offence has the right "to be tried within a reasonable time." The qualifier to this right is that it applies to individuals who have been "charged with an offence." The s. 11(b) right therefore has no application in civil or administrative proceedings. This Court has often cautioned against the direct application of criminal justice standards in the administrative law area. We should not blur concepts which under our Charter are clearly distinct. The s. 11(b) guarantee of a right to an accused person to be tried within a reasonable time cannot be imported into s. 7. There is no analogous provision to s. 11(b) which applies to administrative proceedings, nor is there a constitutional right outside the criminal context to be "tried" within a reasonable time.

. . .

In contrast to the criminal realm, the filing of a human rights complaint implies no suspicion of wrongdoing on the part of the state. The investigation by the Commission is aimed solely at determining what took place and ultimately to settle the matter in a non-adversarial manner. The purpose of human rights proceedings is not to punish but to eradicate discrimination. Tribunal orders are compensatory rather than punitive. The investigation period in the human rights process is not one where the Commission "prosecutes" the respondent. The Commission has an investigative and conciliatory role until the time comes to make a recommendation whether to refer the complaint to the Tribunal for hearing. These human rights proceedings are designed to vindicate private rights and address grievances. As stated by Dickson CJ in *Canada (Human Rights Commission) v. Taylor* [1990] 3 SCR 892, at p. 917:

> It is essential, however, to recognize that, as an instrument especially designed to prevent the spread of prejudice and to foster tolerance and equality in the community, the *Canadian Human Rights Act* is very different from the *Criminal Code*. The aim of human rights legislation, and of s. 13(1), is not to bring the full force of the state's power against a blameworthy individual for the purpose of imposing punishment. Instead, provisions found in human rights statutes generally operate in a less confrontational manner, allowing for a conciliatory settlement if possible and, where discrimination exists, gearing remedial responses more towards compensating the victim.

In criminal proceedings, the accusation alone may engage a security interest because of the grave social and personal consequences to the accused—including potential loss of physical liberty, subjection to social stigma and ostracism from the community—which are the unavoidable consequences of an open and adversarial judicial system. ...

I do not doubt that parties in human rights sex discrimination proceedings experience some level of stress and disruption of their lives as a consequence of allegations of complainants. Even accepting that the stress and anxiety experienced by the respondent in this case was linked to delays in the proceedings, I cannot conclude that the scope of his security of the person protected by s. 7 of the Charter covers such emotional effects nor that they can be equated with the kind of stigma contemplated in *Mills* (1986), *supra*, of an overlong and vexatious pending criminal trial or in *G(J)*, *supra*, where the state sought to remove a child from his or her parents. If the purpose of the impugned proceedings is to provide a vehicle or act as an arbiter for redressing private rights, some amount of stress and stigma attached to the proceedings must be accepted. This will also be the case when dealing with the regulation of a business, profession, or other activity.

A civil suit involving fraud, defamation or the tort of sexual battery will also be "stigmatizing." The Commission's investigations are not public, the respondent is asked to provide his version of events, and communication goes back and forth. While the respondent may be vilified by the press, there is no "stigmatizing" state pronouncement as to his "fitness" that would carry with it serious consequences such as those in *G(J)*. There is thus no constitutional right or freedom against such stigma protected by the s. 7 rights to "liberty" or "security of the person."

(f) Conclusion on Liberty and Security of the Person

To summarize, the stress, stigma and anxiety suffered by the respondent did not deprive him of his right to liberty or security of the person. The framers of the Charter chose to employ the words, "life, liberty and security of the person," thus limiting s. 7 rights to these three interests. While notions of dignity and reputation underlie many Charter rights, they are not stand-alone rights that trigger s. 7 in and of themselves. Freedom from the type of anxiety, stress and stigma suffered by the respondent in this case should not be elevated to the stature of a constitutionally protected s. 7 right.

My conclusion that the respondent is unable to cross the first threshold of the s. 7 Charter analysis in the circumstances of this case should not be construed as a holding that state-caused delays in human rights proceedings can *never* trigger an individual's s. 7 rights. It may well be that s. 7 rights can be engaged by a human rights process in a particular case. I leave open the possibility that in other circumstances, delays in the human rights process may violate s. 7 of the Charter.

Because of my conclusion that there was no deprivation of the respondent's right to liberty or security of the person, I need not proceed to the second stage of the analysis to determine whether the alleged deprivation was in accordance with the principles of fundamental justice. However, for the reasons that immediately follow in the administrative law section, I express the view that the delay, in the circumstances of this case, would not have violated the principles of fundamental justice.

C. Was the Respondent Entitled to a Remedy Pursuant to Administrative Law Principles?

While I have concluded that the respondent is not entitled to a remedy under the Charter, I must still address the issue of whether the respondent is entitled to a remedy under principles of administrative law. This issue was pleaded before Lowry J of the British Columbia Supreme Court. Counsel were advised by us during the hearing that, notwithstanding that pleadings were not made before this Court on administrative law *per se*, we were nevertheless prepared to deal with this issue. The question to be addressed in this section is whether the delay in this case could amount to a denial of natural justice even where the respondent's ability to have a fair hearing has not been compromised.

(a) Prejudice to the Fairness of the Hearing

In my view, there are appropriate remedies available in the administrative law context to deal with state-caused delay in human rights proceedings. However, delay, without more, will not warrant a stay of proceedings as an abuse of process at common law. Staying proceedings for the mere passage of time would be tantamount to imposing a judicially created limitation period (see: *R v. L (WK)* [1991] 1 SCR 1091, at p. 1100; *Akthar v. Canada (Minister of Employment and Immigration)* [1991] 3 FC 32 (CA). In the administrative law context, there must be proof of significant prejudice which results from an unacceptable delay.

There is no doubt that the principles of natural justice and the duty of fairness are part of every administrative proceeding. Where delay impairs a party's ability to answer the complaint against him or her, because, for example, memories have faded, essential witnesses have died or are unavailable, or evidence has been lost, then administrative delay may be invoked to impugn the validity of the administrative proceedings and provide a remedy (D.J.M. Brown and J.M. Evans, *Judicial Review of Administrative Action in Canada* (loose-leaf), at p. 9-67; W. Wade and C. Forsyth, *Administrative Law* (7th ed., 1994), at pp. 435-36). It is thus accepted that the principles of natural justice and the duty of fairness include the right to a fair hearing and that undue delay in the processing of an administrative proceeding that impairs the fairness of the hearing can be remedied. ...

The respondent argued before the British Columbia Supreme Court that the delay in the administrative process caused him prejudice that amounted to a denial of natural justice in that he could no longer receive a fair hearing. He alleged that two witnesses had died and that the memories of many witnesses might be impaired by the passage of time. Lowry J referred to these claims as "vague assertions that fall far short of establishing an inability to prove facts necessary to respond to the complaints" (para. 10). Lowry J concluded that the respondent's opportunity to make full answer and defence had not been compromised and thereby refused to terminate the proceedings.

The respondent also argued before Lowry J that he was not provided with a copy of Ms Schell's timeliness submissions for a two-month period and that he had not received proper disclosure. Lowry J did not consider the respondent prejudiced in this regard. With respect to the alleged failure to disclose information to the respondent, this is not, in my opinion, a case in which the unfairness is so obvious that there would be a denial of natural justice, or in which there was an abuse of process such that it would be inappropriate to put the respondent through hearings before the Tribunal. I would therefore adopt the finding of Lowry J that the delay in this case is not such that it would necessarily result in a hearing that lacks the essential elements of fairness. The respondent's right to a fair hearing has not been jeopardized. Proof of prejudice has not been demonstrated to be of sufficient magnitude to impact on the fairness of the hearing. This is a finding of fact made by the trial judge that has not, in my opinion, been successfully attacked on appeal. The question which must be addressed is therefore whether the delay in this case could amount to a denial of natural justice or an abuse of process even where the respondent has not been prejudiced in an evidentiary sense.

(b) Other Forms of Prejudice

· · ·

The respondent contends that the delay in the human rights proceedings constitutes a breach of procedural fairness amounting to a denial of natural justice and resulting in an abuse of process. The question is whether one can look to the psychological and

sociological harm caused by the delay rather than merely to the procedural or legal effect, namely, whether the ability to make full answer and defence has been compromised,
to determine whether there has been a denial of natural justice. This issue is a difficult
one and there is no clear authority in this area.

In cases where the Charter was held not to apply, most courts and tribunals did not
go further to decide whether the stress and stigma resulting from an unacceptable delay
were so significant as to amount to an abuse of process. On the other hand, where courts
did go further, they most often adopted a narrow approach to the principles of natural
justice. …

However, courts and tribunals have also referred to other types of prejudice than trial
fairness, holding that, where a commission or tribunal has abused its process to the detriment of an individual, a court has the discretion to grant a remedy.

[After a survey of the authorities, Bastarache J concluded:]

I would be prepared to recognize that unacceptable delay may amount to an abuse of
process in certain circumstances even where the fairness of the hearing has not been
compromised. Where inordinate delay has directly caused significant psychological
harm to a person, or attached a stigma to a person's reputation, such that the human
rights system would be brought into disrepute, such prejudice may be sufficient to constitute an abuse of process. The doctrine of abuse of process is not limited to acts giving
rise to an unfair hearing; there may be cases of abuse of process for other than evidentiary reasons brought about by delay. It must however be emphasized that few lengthy
delays will meet this threshold. I caution that in cases where there is no prejudice to
hearing fairness, the delay must be clearly unacceptable and have directly caused a significant prejudice to amount to an abuse of process. It must be a delay that would, in the
circumstances of the case, bring the human rights system into disrepute. The difficult
question before us is in deciding what is an "unacceptable delay" that amounts to an
abuse of process.

(c) Abuse of Process—Principles

The respondent's case is that there has been an unacceptable delay in the administrative
process which has caused him to be prejudiced by the stigma attached to the two Complaints to an extent that justifies the process being terminated now. Abuse of process is a
common law principle invoked principally to stay proceedings where to allow them to
continue would be oppressive. As stated by Brown and Evans, *supra*, at pp. 9-71 and 9-72:

> The stringency of the requirements for showing that delay constitutes a breach of fairness
> would seem to be due, at least in part, to the drastic nature of the only appropriate remedy.
> Unlike other instances of procedural unfairness where it is open to a court to remit the mat-
> ter for redetermination in a procedurally fair manner, *the remedy for undue delay will usu-
> ally be to prevent the tribunal from exercising its legislative authority, either by prohibiting it
> from proceeding with the hearing, or by quashing the resulting decision.* [Emphasis added.]

In the context of a breach of s. 11(b) of the Charter, a stay has been found to constitute the only possible remedy (*R v. Askov* [1990] 2 SCR 1199). The respondent asked for the same remedy in his administrative law proceedings before Lowry J. There is, however, no support for the notion that a stay is the only remedy available in administrative law proceedings. A stay accords very little importance to the interest of implementing the *Human Rights Code* and giving effect to the complainants' rights to have their cases heard. Other remedies are available for abuse of process. Where a respondent asks for a stay, he or she will have to bear a heavy burden. The discussion that follows often links abuse of process and the remedy of a stay because the stay, as I have said, is the only applicable remedy in the context of a s. 11(b) application. Nevertheless, I wish to underline that my inquiry here is directed only at the determination of the existence of an abuse of process on the facts of this case.

. . .

In order to find an abuse of process, the court must be satisfied that, "the damage to the public interest in the fairness of the administrative process should the proceeding go ahead would exceed the harm to the public interest in the enforcement of the legislation if the proceedings were halted" (Brown and Evans, *supra*, at p. 9-68). According to L'Heureux-Dubé J in [*R v. Power*, [1994] 1 SCR 601] at p. 616, "abuse of process" has been characterized in the jurisprudence as a process tainted to such a degree that it amounts to one of the clearest of cases. In my opinion, this would apply equally to abuse of process in administrative proceedings. For there to be abuse of process, the proceedings must, in the words of L'Heureux-Dubé J, be "unfair to the point that they are contrary to the interests of justice" (p. 616). "Cases of this nature will be extremely rare" (*Power, supra*, at p. 616). In the administrative context, there may be abuse of process where conduct is equally oppressive.

(d) Was the Delay Unacceptable?

To constitute a breach of the duty of fairness, the delay must have been unreasonable or inordinate (Brown and Evans, *supra*, at p. 9-68). There is no abuse of process by delay *per se*. The respondent must demonstrate that the delay was unacceptable to the point of being so oppressive as to taint the proceedings. While I am prepared to accept that the stress and stigma resulting from an inordinate delay may contribute to an abuse of process, I am not convinced that the delay in this case was "inordinate."

The determination of whether a delay has become inordinate depends on the nature of the case and its complexity, the facts and issues, the purpose and nature of the proceedings, whether the respondent contributed to the delay or waived the delay, and other circumstances of the case. As previously mentioned, the determination of whether a delay is inordinate is not based on the length of the delay alone, but on contextual factors, including the nature of the various rights at stake in the proceedings, in the attempt to determine whether the community's sense of fairness would be offended by the delay.

With respect to the actual length of the delay in this case and whether it had been "unacceptable," Lowry J noted that, unlike the cases to which he had been referred, there was no extended period without any activity in the processing of the Complaints from receipt to referral, except for an inexplicable five-month period of inaction from

April 10, 1996, when the respondent provided his substantive response to the Complaints, to September 6, 1996, when human rights officers were assigned to investigate the Complaints. The Commission's counsel provided no explanation or excuses for this five-month gap at the oral hearing. However, according to a letter to the complainant and the respondent dated March 6, 1996, the Council referred to a period of "adjustment" where investigative resources were being transferred from the Employment Standards Branch to the Council and that from then on the Council was to conduct its own investigations. This letter also stated that some investigations would be commenced prior to April 1, 1996, beginning with those complaints that had experienced the longest delays. The Council stated that it appreciated the parties' patience in waiting to be notified as to when the investigation would begin. Lowry J found that, other than during this five-month period, communication had been ongoing between the Council, solicitors and complainants, and the respondent had not been ignored. There had been a continuous dialogue between the parties (at para. 39).

With respect to calculating the delay, Lowry J found that the only time that could be considered for the delay was between the filing of the Complaint to the end of the investigation process, in July. He stated that the Tribunal could not be criticized for not setting the hearing dates earlier as the respondent did not press for earlier dates, did not question the fixed dates and cancelled the pre-hearing conference. While the respondent did at one point inquire as to whether one of the Complaints could be set for hearing without investigation, this would have required a concession that there was sufficient evidence to warrant a hearing, a concession which Mr. Blencoe was not prepared to make. Following Lowry J's reasoning, the delay would be computed until July 1997, thus reducing the delay from 32 months to 24 months.

During those 24 months, the Commission also had to deal with a challenge by the respondent as to the lateness of the Complaints and his accusation that the Complaints were in bad faith. The respondent refused to respond to the allegations until this determination was made. As a result, the process was delayed for some eight months. The respondent was perfectly entitled to bring forward allegations of bad faith and to question the timeliness of the Complaints. However, the Commission should not be held responsible for contributing to this part of the delay. In this regard, Lowry J stated (at para. 42):

> It is not suggested that Mr. Blencoe was not entitled to challenge the complaints, as he did at the outset, but having done so, and having been unsuccessful, it is not in my view open to him now to claim that the events of the eight months elapsed contributed to an unacceptable delay.

Thus, while the respondent was entitled to take the steps he did, the Court of Appeal wrongly considered the delay attributable to the aforementioned challenges in computing the delay caused by the Commission. Clearly much of this delay resulted from the respondent's actions, though there appear to be other delays caused by the Commission. As expressed by Lambert JA, at para. 29, some of the delay was attributable to the Commission, some to the respondent, but very little of it was attributable to either of the two complainants—Ms Schell or Ms Willis.

The arguments advanced by the parties before us rely heavily on criminal judgments where delay was considered in the context of s. 11(b) or s. 7 of the Charter. It must be kept in mind, as mentioned in paras. 93-95, that the human rights process of receiving complaints, investigating them, determining whether they are substantial enough to investigate and report and then to refer the matter to the Tribunal for hearing is a very different process from the criminal process. The British Columbia human rights process is designed to protect respondents by ensuring that cases are not adjudicated unless there is some basis for the claims to go forward and unless the issue cannot be disposed of prior to adjudication. Pursuant to s. 27 of the *Human Rights Code*, the Commission may dismiss a complaint if, *inter alia*, it is brought too late, the acts alleged do not contravene the Code, there is no reasonable basis for referring the complaint to a hearing, if it does not appear to be in the interest of the group bringing the complaint, the complaint was filed for improper motives or if the complaint was made in bad faith. The Commission therefore performs a gatekeeping or screening function, preventing those cases that are trivial or insubstantial from proceeding. There is also the goal of settlement through mediation which is lacking in the criminal context. The human rights process thus takes a great deal more time prior to referring a complaint to the Tribunal for hearing.

The principles of natural justice also require that both sides be given an opportunity to participate in reviewing documents at various stages in the process and to review the investigation report. The parties therefore have a chance to make submissions before a referral is made to the Tribunal. These steps in the process take time. Indeed, the Commission was under a statutory obligation to proceed as it did. The process itself was not challenged in this case. True, the Commission took longer than is desirable to process these Complaints. I am not condoning that. Nevertheless, McEachern CJBC has exaggerated in stating that "a week at the outside would have sufficed" to investigate these Complaints (para. 51). While the case may not have been an extremely complicated one, these stages are necessary for the protection of the respondents in the context of the human rights complaints system.

The Commission seems to have handled the Complaints against Mr. Blencoe in the same manner as it handles all of its human rights complaints. The respondent argues that the Commission should have been sensitive to his particular needs and to have consequently expedited his Complaints on a priority basis. However, as professed by Lowry J, there is, "little if anything in the record to suggest that Mr. Blencoe raised with the Commission any of the hardship he has suffered or that he sought to be afforded any priority on that basis" (para. 45).

In *Saskatchewan* [*(Human Rights Commission) v. Kodellas* (1989), 60 DLR (4th) 143,] the Saskatchewan Court of Appeal held that the determination of whether the delay is unreasonable is, in part, a comparative one whereby one can compare the length of delay in the case at bar with the length of time normally taken for processing in the same jurisdiction and in other jurisdictions in Canada. While this factor has limited weight, I would note that in this regard, on average, it takes the Canadian Human Rights Commission 27 months to resolve a complaint (J. Simpson, "Human Rights Commission Mill Grinds Slowly," *The Globe & Mail* (October 1, 1998), p. A18, as quoted in R.E. Hawkins, "Reputational Review III: Delay, Disrepute and Human Rights Commissions" (2000) 25 *Queen's LJ* 599, at p. 600). In Ontario, the average length of complaints, according to the *Annual Report 1997-1998 of the Ontario Human Rights Commission* (1998), at p. 24, is 19.9 months. The respondent's counsel at the oral hearing quoted a report of the British

Columbia Ministry where the average time to get to a hearing in British Columbia is three years.

The delay in the case at bar should be compared to that in analogous cases. In *Nisbett* [*v. Manitoba (Human Rights Commission)* (1993), 101 DLR (4th) 744 (Man. CA)], the sexual harassment complaint had been outstanding for approximately three years. In *Canadian Airlines* [*International Ltd. v. Canada (Human Rights Commission)*, [1996] 1 FC 638 (CA)], there was a 50-month delay between the filing of the complaint and the appointment of an investigator. In *Stefani* [*v. College of Dental Surgeons (British Columbia)* (1996), 44 Admin. LR (2d) 122 (BC SC)], there was a delay of two years and three months between the complaint and the inspection and an additional six- or seven-month delay which followed. In *Brown* [*v. Association of Professional Engineers and Geoscientists of British Columbia*, [1994] BCJ No. 2037 (QL) (BC SC)], a three-year period had elapsed prior to serving the petitioner with notice of the inquiry. In *Misra* [*v. College of Physicians & Surgeons of Saskatchewan* (1988), 52 DLR (4th) 477 (Sask. CA)], there was a five-year delay during which time Misra was suspended from the practice of medicine. Finally, in *Ratzlaff* [*v. British Columbia (Medical Services Commission)* (1996), 17 BCLR (3d) 336 (BC CA)], it had been seven years before the physician received a hearing notice.

A review of the facts in this case demonstrates that, unlike the aforementioned cases where there was complete inactivity for extremely lengthy periods, the communication between the parties in the case at bar was ongoing. While Lowry J acknowledged the five-month delay of inactivity, on balance, he found no unacceptable delay and considered the time that elapsed to be nothing more "than the time required to process complaints of this kind given the limitations imposed by the resources available" (para. 47). Lowry J concluded as follows (at para. 49):

> In my view, it cannot be said that the Commission or the Tribunal have acted unfairly toward Mr. Blencoe. They have caused neither an unacceptable delay in the process nor a prejudice to him whereby fairness of the hearings scheduled to be conducted next month have been compromised. There has been no denial of natural justice and, accordingly, Mr. Blencoe's petition for judicial review cannot succeed.

As expressed by Salmon LJ in *Allen v. Sir Alfred McAlpine & Sons Ltd.* [1968] 1 All ER 543 (CA), at p. 561, "it should not be too difficult to recognise inordinate delay when it occurs." In my opinion, the five-month inexplicable delay or even the 24-month period from the filing of the Complaints to the referral to the Tribunal was not so inordinate or inexcusable as to amount to an abuse of process. Taking into account the ongoing communication between the parties, the delay in this case does not strike me as one that would offend the community's sense of decency and fairness. While I would not presume to fix a specified period for a reasonable delay, I am satisfied that the delay in this case was not so inordinate as to amount to an abuse of process.

As noted in the discussion pertaining to the application of s. 7 of the Charter (paras. 59 to 72), I am also concerned with the causal connection in this case. There must be more than merely a lengthy delay for an abuse of process; the delay must have caused actual prejudice of such magnitude that the public's sense of decency and fairness is affected. While Mr. Blencoe and his family have suffered obvious prejudice since the various sexual harassment allegations against him were made public, as explained above, I am not convinced that such prejudice can be said to result directly from the delay in the human rights proceedings. As in the Charter analysis above, I have simply assumed without deciding, for the purpose of my analysis, that the delay caused by the Commission was a contributory cause of the respondent's prejudice.

VII. Conclusion

To summarize, it cannot be said that the respondent's s. 7 rights were violated nor that the conduct of the Commission amounted to an abuse of process. However, I emphasize that nothing in these reasons has any bearing on the merits of the case before the Tribunal.

Nevertheless, I am very concerned with the lack of efficiency of the Commission and its lack of commitment to deal more expeditiously with complaints. Lack of resources cannot explain every delay in giving information, appointing inquiry officers, filing reports, etc.; nor can it justify inordinate delay where it is found to exist. The fact that most human rights commissions experience serious delays will not justify breaches of the principles of natural justice in appropriate cases. In *R v. Morin* [1992] 1 SCR 771, at p. 795, the Court stated that in the context of s. 11(b) of the Charter, the government "has a constitutional obligation to commit sufficient resources to prevent unreasonable delay." The demands of natural justice are apposite.

I would allow the appeal. The Court of Appeal decision is set aside and the Tribunal should proceed with the hearing of the Complaints on their merits. Considering the lack of diligence displayed by the Commission, I would nevertheless exercise the Court's discretion under s. 47 of the *Supreme Court Act*, RSC, 1985, c. S-26, to award costs against the appellant Commission in favour of Robin Blencoe, Andrea Willis and Irene Schell.

LeBEL J (Iacobucci, Binnie, and Arbour JJ concurring) (dissenting in part):

I. The Issues

The parties have fought this case mainly on Charter issues. In the end, this approach turned into a constitutional problem, something that it was not. The important and determinative issue should have been the role of judicial review and administrative law principles in the control of undue delay in administrative tribunal proceedings. Given that human rights commissions are administrative law creations, the first place we should look for solutions to problems in their processes is in the realm of administrative law. If the relevant administrative law remedy had been applied, the trial judge should have found that there had been undue delay in the process of the British Columbia Human Rights Commission (formerly the British Columbia Council of Human Rights), that this delay was abusive, and that some form of remedy should have been granted to the respondent Blencoe.

Nevertheless, I agree that a stay of proceedings was not warranted in the circumstances of the case and should be lifted, as suggested by Bastarache J. Such a remedy took no consideration of the interest of the complainants Irene Schell and Andrea Willis in the proceedings of the British Columbia Human Rights Commission ("Commission"). *Nobody* benefits from delay, but the interests of innocent parties must influence our choice of remedy. The Court of Appeal seems to have dealt with this case as if it were a pure conflict between the respondent and the state, without taking into account that the complainants Schell and Willis also had an important interest in an efficient disposition of their allegations against Blencoe and in the correct and timely application of the appropriate administrative law remedies.

II. The Administrative Law Doctrine of Abuse of Process and the Control of Undue Delay

Unnecessary delay in judicial and administrative proceedings has long been an enemy of a free and fair society. At some point, it is a foe that has plagued the life of almost all courts and administrative tribunals. It's a problem that must be brought under control if we are to maintain an effective system of justice, worthy of the confidence of Canadians. The tools for this task are not to be found only in the *Canadian Charter of Rights and Freedoms*, but also in the principles of a flexible and evolving administrative law system.

The legal doctrines that have developed both under the common law and under the Charter to respond to delay are certainly not simple. But the facts of this case point to one inescapable conclusion: the respondent, Robin Blencoe, faced unreasonable delay that violated administrative law principles of fairness in the management of the process of an administrative tribunal or body. Those principles concern not only the fairness of the hearing and of the final decision, but the very conduct of the procedures leading to the disposition in the matter. In these reasons, I shall now examine those principles and the nature of the remedy that appears just and appropriate after giving due consideration to the interests of all parties concerned by this long and frustrating judicial debate.

Administrative law abuse of process doctrine is fundamentally about protecting people from unfair treatment by administrative agencies. In *Martineau v. Matsqui Institution Disciplinary Board* [1980] 1 SCR 602, at p. 631, Dickson J (as he then was) described the administrative law principle of fairness in these classic terms:

> In the final analysis, the simple question to be answered is this: Did the tribunal on the facts of the particular case act fairly toward the person claiming to be aggrieved? It seems to me that this is the underlying question which the courts have sought to answer in all the cases dealing with natural justice and fairness.

When we ask whether there has been an administrative law abuse of process, we ask the same fundamental question: has an administrative agency treated people inordinately badly?

IV. Historical Context

This question, however, does not exist outside of a legal historical context, through which we must trace the role of courts on these kinds of questions up to the present day. Two fundamental aspects of the common law's history are relevant to the rules in this area: (1) the common law system's abhorrence of delay; and (2) the common law's development as to the power of courts to monitor the processes of administrative bodies.

The notion that justice delayed is justice denied reaches back to the mists of time. In *Magna Carta* in 1215, King John promised: "To none will we sell, to none will we deny, *or delay*, right or justice" (emphasis added). As La Forest J put it, the right to a speedy trial has been "a right known to the common law ... for more than 750 years" (*R v. Rahey* [1987] 1 SCR 588, at p. 636). In criminal law cases, this Court had no difficulty determining in *R v. Askov* [1990] 2 SCR 1199, at p. 1227, that "the right to be tried within a reasonable time is an aspect of fundamental justice protected by s. 7 of the Charter." Outside the criminal law context, legislators have devised limitation periods, and courts have developed equitable doctrines such as that of laches. For centuries, those working with our legal system have recognized that unnecessary delay strikes against its core values and have done everything within their powers to combat it, albeit not always with complete success. ...

V. Modern Developments

Today, there is no doubt that *mandamus* may be used to control procedural delays. ...

The common law system has always abhorred delay. In our system's development of the courts' supervisory role over administrative processes through *mandamus*, we see a crystallizing potential to compel government officers to do their duty and, in so doing, to avoid delay in administrative processes. The historical context in which our case law is rooted is a soil of well-established principles. This ground's more modern seedlings must now be examined.

... First, courts have linked the idea of procedural fairness with a bar on abuse of process through unreasonable delay ... . Second, even on a traditional analysis, courts have expressed their preparedness to consider different kinds of adverse effects of delay, such as damage to individuals' reputations or other aspects of their lives, in conjunction with the traditionally recognized effects on the hearing ... . Third, these two evolutions have become fused along with a realization that other adverse effects can create an abusive situation *independently* of evidentiary prejudice.

Abusive administrative delay is wrong and it does not matter if it wrecks only your life and not your hearing. The cases that have been part of this evolution have sometimes expressed the point differently, but the key consideration is this: administrative delay that is determined to be unreasonable based on its length, its causes, and its effects is abusive and contrary to the administrative law principles that exist and should be applied in a fair and efficient legal system.

Unreasonable delay is not limited to situations that bring the human rights system into disrepute either by prejudicing the fairness of a hearing or by otherwise rising above a threshold of shocking abuse. Otherwise, there would not be any remedy for an individual suffering from unreasonable delay unless this same individual were unlucky enough to have suffered sufficiently to meet an additional, external test of disrepute resulting to the human rights system. Such a limitation may arise from a fear that the main remedy available would be the blunt instrument of the stay of proceedings. However, as we will see below, a remedy other than a stay may be appropriate in other cases where ongoing delay is abusive. It is true that some of the cases that have most developed the doctrine of abusive delay involved lengthier periods of time that, in conjunction with other factors, warranted stays of proceedings (see, *e.g.*, the cases cited by Bastarache J at paras. 117-18). They were cases that passed the highest threshold of abusiveness. Because of this, they did not discuss a lower threshold of unreasonable delay that might warrant some kind of judicial action and different, less radical, remedies than a stay in the administrative proceedings.

VII. Assessing Unreasonable Delay

The authorities and policy considerations that have been reviewed thus far confirm that modern administrative law is deeply averse to unreasonable delay. But nobody suggests the elimination of all delay *per se*—and with good reason. At the limit, a prohibition on delay *per se* would ban any and all delay. This would be an absurd result that would undermine rather than uphold a fair judicial system. Such an approach would, for example, deny parties on both sides the chance to prepare for the hearing (*cf. R v. Conway* [1989] 1 SCR 1659, at p. 1694). Thus, unreasonable delays must be identified within the specific circumstances of every case.

In assessing a particular delay in the process of a specific administrative body, we must keep in mind two principles: (1) not all delay is the same; and (2) not all administrative bodies are the same. First, there are different kinds of delay. There are two kinds of delay in an administrative context: general delay and individual delay. Each of these, in turn, may encompass both necessary and unnecessary delay. General delay may include certain kinds of delay due to substantive and procedural complexities inherent in the kind of matter the tribunal deals with, but it may also include delays from systemic problems. Individual delay may relate to the special complexity of a particular decision, but it may also include delays from inattention to a particular file. ...

Second, not all administrative bodies are the same. Indeed, this is an understatement. At first glance, labour boards, police commissions, and milk control boards may seem to have about as much in common as assembly lines, cops, and cows! Administrative bodies do, of course, have some common features, but the diversity of their powers, mandate and structure is such that to apply particular standards from one context to another might well be entirely inappropriate. Thus, inevitably, a court's assessment of a particular delay in a particular case before a particular administrative body has to depend on a number of contextual analytic factors.

In order to differentiate reasonable and unreasonable delay, a balancing exercise becomes necessary. Courts must, indeed, remain alive not only to the needs of administrative systems under strain, but also to their good faith efforts to provide procedural protections to alleged wrongdoers. One must approach matters with some common sense and ask whether a lengthy delay that profoundly harms an individual's life is really justified in the circumstances of a given case.

As indicated above, the central factors toward which the modern administrative law cases as a whole propel us are length, cause, and effects. Approaching these now with a more refined understanding of different kinds and contexts of delay, we see three main factors to be balanced in assessing the reasonableness of an administrative delay:

(1) *the time taken compared to the inherent time requirements* of the matter before the particular administrative body, which would encompass legal complexities (including the presence of any especially complex systemic issues) and factual complexities (including the need to gather large amounts of information or technical

data), as well as reasonable periods of time for procedural safeguards that protect parties or the public;

(2) *the causes of delay beyond the inherent time requirements of the matter*, which would include consideration of such elements as whether the affected individual contributed to or waived parts of the delay and whether the administrative body used as efficiently as possible those resources it had available; and

(3) *the impact of the delay*, considered as encompassing both prejudice in an evidentiary sense and other harms to the lives of real people impacted by the ongoing delay. This may also include a consideration of the efforts by various parties to minimize negative impacts by providing information or interim solutions.

… Obviously, considering all of these factors imposes a contextual analysis. Thus, our Court should avoid setting specific time limits in such matters. A judge should consider the specific content of the case he or she is hearing and make an assessment that takes into account the three main factors that have been identified above.

A number of parties have raised the objection that the consideration of some of those factors may extend "special treatment" to certain kinds of individuals, whether these be people who commit more stigmatizing wrongs or who are more susceptible to harms like damage to their reputations. Some interveners were afraid that the application of such factors might indeed require preferential treatment for powerful and influential people. These objections and fears are misplaced. It appears sound administrative practice for decision-making bodies to recognize the relevance of the identified factors while deciding how to process a particular case. For example, task forces analysing delay report that it is simply a good case management practice to send to different tracks cases of differing levels of complexity: see, e.g., Brookings Task Force on Civil Justice Reform, *Justice for All: Reducing Costs and Delay in Civil Litigation* (1989), at p. 3. Similarly, it only makes sense for administrative bodies seeking to minimize their negative impacts on real people to consider the ramifications of their failure to act expeditiously. In any event, every case should be processed with due dispatch.

VIII. Delays Before the British Columbia Human Rights Commission in This Case
· · ·

A. Length of Delay

The first factor to be considered is the time taken relative to the inherent time requirements of the matter. In the Court of Appeal, McEachern CJBC characterized the allegations in the case at bar as "relatively simple complaints" ((1998) 49 BCLR (3d) 216, at para. 37), stated that "[t]hese kinds of disputes are quickly resolved by courts and tribunals all the time, and there are no complex legal or factual issues" (para. 37), and concluded that "a week at the outside would have sufficed" (para. 51) for the investigation. Although McEachern CJBC perhaps puts matters a bit optimistically in suggesting that the investigation could have been wrapped up within a week, there is a good measure of truth in what he says.

At this point, a closer scrutiny of the facts is necessary in order to establish the inherent time requirements of the case. Different kinds of "allegations of sexual discrimination" may be more or less complex. A pay equity case might properly involve complex statistical analysis and innovative legal arguments and take time for those reasons. A case about other forms of well-concealed systemic discrimination might involve numerous witnesses and take time for that reason. But other cases that involve "allegations of sexual harassment" between individuals may have few complex legal or factual elements and thus appropriately should take much less time.

Considering the complexity of the allegations should not be seen to reflect in any way on their merits. This being said, the case at bar falls within a relatively less complex category. The allegations with respect to Willis, an aide to Blencoe, were that Blencoe made sexual overtures to her and inappropriately kissed her when she came to work one evening in August 1994 and that he had subsequently put his arm on her arm in a sexual manner in March 1995. The allegations with respect to Schell were that Blencoe in March 1993 had inappropriately kissed and hugged Schell, who worked for a sports organization deriving funding from Blencoe's ministry, and that he had subsequently on several occasions between July 1993 and July 1994 given her unwanted attention by inviting her for a drink. There were no other direct witnesses to any of the incidents, although there was some corroborating evidence from a small number of other witnesses. Blencoe denied some aspects of the allegations and admitted others.

Recognizing that this case is far less complex than many other sexual discrimination cases does not alleviate the seriousness of the allegations, but it is clear from the record that the allegations were not of a nature that could justify a prolonged investigation. Ultimately, the case was about a "he said/she said" scenario concerning which there should have been an adjudication. In this sense, there was little or nothing to investigate, and there was no reason for the pre-hearing investigation to take a long period of time.

Lowry J expressed serious misgivings about the delays in this case. He wrote at para. 46:

> It may well be that the structure of the Commission should be such that, given the nature of the complaints made by Ms Schell and Ms Willis, *two years would not be required to determine that they warrant a hearing.* [Emphasis added.]

While Lowry J went on to attribute the delay to a lack of resources, he questioned the effectiveness of the Commission, and his finding that two years was an inappropriately long time confirms my conclusion on this branch of the analysis. The inherent time requirements in this case were minimal.

By contrast, the time taken was anything but minimal. After five to six months spent on determining that it could hear the complaints, and once Blencoe had a chance to respond, the Commission then mysteriously took the *five months from April 1996 to September 1996 to appoint the same investigator who had been working on the file all along despite having told Blencoe that it expected to do so within two months* (appellants' record, at p. 229). The investigation took some four months. The trial judge found at para. 44 that this investigation was concluded in January 1997. Given this finding, then after this conclusion of the investigation, it apparently took the investigator *another two months to write and forward a 12-page report in early March 1997, and this only after letters from Blencoe's lawyer asking about the delay* (appellants' record, at pp. 322-35). After another four months, in July 1997, the Commission finally told Blencoe that the matter would proceed to a Tribunal hearing. It then took another two months to get a date set for the hearing, which was scheduled to be some six months later in March 1998. In all, the time for the Commission to make the determination that the complaints should go to a hearing was approximately two years. The time from the initial filing of the complaints to the scheduled hearing was approximately 32 months. While it is true that the Commission's decision to send the matter to a hearing involved a number of steps, every one of these steps involved a significant delay.

A particularly egregious example of the Commission's unacceptable lack of diligence may be found in the events during the period from October 16, 1995 to December 21, 1995. During that time, the Commission breached procedural fairness by failing to send to Blencoe Willis's October 16 response to his submissions on the timeliness of her complaint. In response to an inquiry, Blencoe received the Commission's letter dated December 21 on December 27. Although the December 21 letter denied that a decision had been made on this issue, a January 22, 1996 letter revealed that the Commission had actually already made the decision on December 18, before it even sent Blencoe the documents to which he had wished to reply and that the Commission had possessed for three months (see pp. 290-300 of the appellants' record). The Commission essentially failed even to keep those affected by its decisions up to date with what was going on.

Regardless of any arguments that parts of the time were necessary for procedural safeguards, the facts are that the Commission was slow at every step along the way. This eventually added up to a delay measured in years for a decision that was not inherently complex. Although a few letters back and forth might have been appropriate, nothing in the inherent time requirements of the case came close to requiring the delay that occurred.

B. Cause of the Delay

The second factor that we must consider is the cause of delay beyond the inherent time requirements of the matter. It is true that Blencoe sought to use those defences available to him, including an argument about whether the complaints had been correctly filed within the limitation period provided by the statute. But in so doing, he did not become responsible for the sheer inefficiency of the Commission in dealing with these and other matters.

A measure of Blencoe's determination to seek an end to the delay is that even after matters had been delayed to this point largely on account of the Commission's failures to comply with basic procedural fairness, he offered to forego the investigative stage of the complaints to bring them to a hearing. In so doing, we may infer that he made clear to the Commission that he was seeking a way past the delay and red tape in which his life had become bound. In his request, he was rebuffed, as the Commission would have required him to make major concessions on the existence of a *prima facie* case against him, if he wanted to proceed to the hearing. (Although Blencoe made the offer only on the Willis complaint, this seems to be explained by the fact that he was simultaneously trying to find out whether a decision on the timeliness issue in the Schell complaint had been made without notification as had occurred with the Willis complaint (see the appellants' record at pp. 220 and 301).) On numerous other occasions as well, Blencoe asked about when there would be a decision on the complaints. Indeed, Blencoe's inquiries of this nature comprise a significant number of the letters in the record. There can be no doubt that there was serious delay on both complaints and that Blencoe tried to find a way to end it. After being thus rebuffed, his counsel was under no obligation to beg and cry for an expedited hearing to demonstrate to the Human Rights Commission the seriousness of his requests.

A further measure of the Commission's behaviour with respect to delay is that even at the Supreme Court of Canada, the Commission admits that it cannot explain what was going on for five months of the time that it was dealing with the allegations against Blencoe. On a matter that ideally should not even have taken five months, a five-month period of *unexplained* delay remains surprising and troubling. Lowry J characterized this period as a "five-month hiatus when there appears to have been no activity in relation to the complaints" (para. 47). After the gap, the Commission sent Blencoe a letter dated September 6, 1996 to advise him that it was appointing the same person as investigator as had up to that point been dealing with the pre-investigation report. In other words, *in five months, nothing happened.* This five-month lapse is just the high mark of the Commission's ineptitude.

C. Impact of Delay on the Respondent

The third factor that we must consider is the harm accruing as a result of the delay. Although Lowry J found "that no clear case of prejudice in terms of an inability to defend has been made out" (para. 10), there is no doubt that Blencoe and his family suffered serious harm in other ways. Lowry J went so far as to write at para. 50:

> There is, however, substance to the contention that *the hardship Mr. Blencoe, his wife, and his children have suffered, and continue to suffer, is markedly disproportionate to the value there can now be in an adjudicated resolution.* [Emphasis added.]

There can be no doubt about the impact of the allegations on the respondent and his family. The respondent's career is finished. He and his family have been chased twice across the country in their attempts to make a new life. He was under medical care for clinical depression for many months. In the wake of the outstanding complaints before the Commission, even such a normal aspect of life as coaching his youngest son's soccer team has been denied to Blencoe, since he has faced stigmatization in the form of presumed guilt as a sexual harasser. As Lowry J wrote at para. 13:

> The point need not be further stressed. *The stigma attached to the outstanding complaints has certainly contributed in large measure to the very real hardship Mr. Blencoe has experienced.* His public profile as a Minister of the Crown rendered him particularly vulnerable to the media attention that has been focused on him and his family, and *the hardship has, in the result, been protracted and severe.* [Emphasis added.]

Although I do not deny that Blencoe might have taken additional steps to make the Commission more fully aware of the impact on him of continued delay, he did try to move matters along. The Commission showed next to no regard for the possible impacts of its delays, often taking long periods of time even to respond to requests for information as to the progress of the file. It certainly did nothing to minimize the impact of the delay on the respondent.

It is true that administrative delay was not the only cause of the prejudice suffered by the respondent. Nevertheless, it contributed significantly to its aggravation. It must be added, though, that this delay also frustrated the complainants in their desire for a quick disposition of their complaints. Finally, the inefficient and delay-filled process at the Commission linked with the specific blunders made in the management of those particular complaints harmed all parties involved in this sorry process. Its flaws were such that it may rightly be termed to have been abusive in respect of the respondent. In this connection, I note that my colleague, Bastarache J, despite coming to the conclusion that the conduct of the Commission did not amount to an abuse of process, nevertheless found it necessary to award costs against the Commission in light of the "lack of diligence [it] displayed" (para. 136). In my view, this further demonstrates the tension in this appeal and the fact that the conduct of the Commission in dealing with this matter was less than acceptable.

IX. *Administrative Remedy*

In the end, the specific and unexplained delay entitles Blencoe to some kind of remedy. The choice of the appropriate redress requires, though, a careful analysis of the circumstances of the case, in order to identify the causes and nature of the delay and its impact on the process, because the courts always have some discretion on orders of remedies founded on the old prerogative writs. The selection of an appropriate remedy may also impose a delicate balancing exercise between competing interests. In proceedings like those that gave rise to this appeal, we must factor in the interest of the respondent, that of the complainants themselves and finally, the public interest of the community itself which wants basic rights enforced efficiently but fairly. As we have seen above, the courts must also consider the stage of the proceedings which has been affected by the delay. A distinction must be drawn between the process leading to the hearing and the hearing itself. A different balance between conflicting interests may have to be found at different stages of the administrative process.

Several kinds of remedies are available either to prevent or remedy abusive delay within an administrative process. The main forms of redress that we need address here are a stay of proceedings, orders for an expedited hearing and costs.

Whoever asks for a stay of proceedings carries a heavy burden. In a human rights proceeding, such an order not only stops the proceedings and negates the public interest in the enforcement of human rights legislation, but it also affects, in a radical way, the interest of the complainants who lose the opportunity to have their complaints heard and dealt with. The stay of proceedings should not generally appear as the sole or even the preferred form of redress: see *R v. O'Connor* [1995] 4 SCR 411, at para. 68. A more prudent approach would limit it to those situations that compromise the very fairness of the hearing and to those cases where the delay in the conduct of the process leading to it would amount to a gross or shocking abuse of the process. In those two situations, the interest of the respondent and the protection of the integrity of the legal system become the paramount considerations. The interest of the complainants would undoubtedly be grievously affected by a stay, but the prime concern in such cases becomes the safeguard-ing of the basic rights of the respondent engaged in a human rights proceeding and the preservation of the essential fairness of the process itself: see *Ratzlaff*, *supra*, at para. 19. Whatever its consequences, a stay may thus become the sole appropriate remedy in those circumstances.

. . .

The approach of the courts should change when it appears that the hearing will re-main fair, in spite of the delay and when the delay has not risen to the level of a shocking abuse, notwithstanding its seriousness. More limited and narrowly focused remedies would then become appropriate. In the context of a judicial review procedure akin to *mandamus*, the first objective of any intervention by a court should be to make things happen, where the administrative process is not working adequately. An order for an expedited hearing within such time frame and with such conditions as the Court might set would be the most practical and effective means of judicial action. Used at the right moment, such a remedy may safeguard the interest of all parties to the process. A litigant who believes he or she is facing undue delay should probably take that route rather than letting the process decay in the hope of stopping the old process on some future date.

An order for costs is a third kind of remedy. It will not address the delay directly, but some of its consequences. If a party must resort to the courts to secure a timely hearing or to speed up the process in which he or she is engaged, some form of compensation for costs should at least be considered by the courts in their discretion.

Whenever parties are compelled to seek judicial interventions to safeguard their rights, costs must be considered to compensate at least in part the time, money and ef-forts expended in obtaining redress. Even if costs cannot indemnify the party for all the losses and prejudice arising from administrative delay, they afford at least a measure of compensation.

In the present appeal, the remedy of a pure stay of proceeding appears both excessive and unfair. First, in spite of the seriousness of the problems faced by Blencoe, the delay does not seem to compromise the fairness of the hearing. As the trial judge found at para. 10, the respondent has not established that the delay has deprived him of evidence or information important to his defence. The delay rather concerns the process leading to the hearing. It arises from a variety of causes that do not evince an intent from the Commission to harm him wilfully, but rather demonstrate grave negligence and import-ant structural problems in the processing of the complaints. Second, a stay of proceed-ings in a situation that does not compromise the fairness of the hearing and does not amount to shocking or gross abuse requires the consideration of the interest of the com-plainants in the choice of the proper remedy ([*Canada (Minister of Citizenship and Im-migration v. Tobiass*, [1997] 3 SCR 391 (Ont.)] at para. 92). In the present matter, the judgment of the Court of Appeal completely omitted any consideration of this interest (see para. 39). The lifting of the stay is thus both justified and necessary.

However, rejecting the stay as a proper remedy in the present case does not mean that Blencoe should be deprived of any redress. On the contrary, an order for an expedited hearing should have been considered as the remedy of choice. There will be some irony in granting such a remedy more than five years after the proceedings began. Such an outcome offers the respondent little solace. Nevertheless, in spite of its rather symbolic value, at the present stage of the proceedings, it appears as a critically important remedy that should have been used at an earlier stage to prod the Commission along and to control the inefficiency of its process.

In spite of the partial success of this appeal, as I agree that the stay should be lifted, Blencoe is entitled to some compensation in the form of costs in our Court and in the courts below. Section 47 of the *Supreme Court Act*, RSC, 1985, c. S-26, grants our Court broad discretion when awarding costs. In the present case, it would be both fair and appropriate to use this power as the respondent has established that the process initiated against him was deeply flawed and that its defects justified his search for a remedy, at least in administrative law. He had to fight for his rights, and it would be unfair for him to bear the costs personally. Although ultimately unsuccessful in his application for a stay, Blencoe brought to the attention of the courts the grave deficiency of the administrative processes of the Commission. He should at least not be penalized for this mixture of success and failure (*e.g.*, *Schachter v. Canada* [1992] 2 SCR 679, at p. 726).

X. Section 7 of the Charter

The application of the general principles of administrative law would have justified the intervention of the trial court without any need to demonstrate a breach of an interest protected by s. 7 of the Charter. As I think that this matter should have been resolved on the basis of administrative law principles, I do not think I have to express a definite opinion on the application of s. 7 of the Charter in the present case.

We must remember though that s. 7 expresses some of the basic values of the Charter. It is certainly true that we must avoid collapsing the contents of the Charter and perhaps of Canadian law into a flexible and complex provision like s. 7. But its importance is such for the definition of substantive and procedural guarantees in Canadian law that it would be dangerous to freeze the development of this part of the law. The full impact of s. 7 will remain difficult to foresee and assess for a long while yet. Our Court should be alive to the need to safeguard a degree of flexibility in the interpretation and evolution of s. 7 of the Charter. At the same time, the Court should remind litigants that not every case can be reduced to a Charter case.

Assuming that the Charter must solve every legal problem would be a recipe for freezing and sterilizing the natural and necessary evolution of the common law and of the civil law in this country. In the present appeal, the absence of a Charter remedy does not mean that administrative law remedies could not have been identified and applied, as we have seen above.

XI. Disposition

For these reasons, I would allow the appeal in part, lift the stay of proceedings and order an expedited hearing of the complainants Schell and Willis. I would also order the appellant British Columbia Human Rights Commission to pay costs on a party-to-party basis to the respondent Blencoe in this Court and in the British Columbia courts.

Appeal allowed with costs against the appellant Commission.

NOTES

1. Because the issue of delay was so intertwined with the whole question of the application of s. 7 of the Charter, we have not attempted to edit out the material pertaining to delay as a ground of relief at common law. However, to the extent that it is generally a content rather than a threshold issue, much of what the Supreme Court discusses on the content of and remedies for egregious delay fits more easily in chapter 4 of this text.

2. In the light of *Blencoe*, what kinds of administrative processes would you now see as subject to s. 7 of the Charter or, perhaps more accurately, what kinds of "behaviour" by statutory decision-makers would you see as implicating s. 7 and "the right to life, liberty and security of the person"? In its post-*Blencoe* decision in *Medovarski v. Canada (Minister of Citizenship and Immigration)*, [2005] 2 SCR 539, the Supreme Court re-examined the question raised in *Chiarelli* and at the start of his section: Did a permanent resident have a "life, liberty and security of the person" interest in not being deported from Canada? Medovarski, a permanent resident subject to deportation proceedings because she had been convicted of causing death while driving a car when intoxicated, argued that her deportation engaged her security of the person by subjecting her to state-imposed psychological stress and her liberty by preventing her from making the fundamental choice of remaining in Canada with her partner. Giving no reasons beyond its dicta in *Chiarelli* that "the most fundamental principle of immigration law is that non-citizens do not have an unqualified right to enter or remain in Canada," the court held that "the deportation of a non-citizen in itself cannot implicate the liberty and security interests protected by s. 7." Do you agree with the court? What more is needed to implicate s. 7?

3. For a detailed consideration of the impact of *Blencoe*, see David J. Mullan and Deirdre Harrington, "The Charter and Administrative Decision-Making: The Dampening Effects of *Blencoe*" (2002), 27 *Queen's LJ* 879.

We would be remiss if we concluded this discussion of the application of the Charter without alluding to a matter that we will examine in more detail in chapter 4 of this text. That is the issue whether there are significant differences between the "principles of fundamental justice" and those of common law "natural justice" or "procedural fairness." This has particular relevance in situations where the claim to procedures is being advanced on an implied basis as opposed to in the context of an attack on primary legislation. Is one's claim to implied procedural protections heightened in situations where you can demonstrate that a s. 7 interest is at stake? If the implication on a common law basis of additional procedural protections had not been seen in *Singh* as foreclosed by the legislation, would the common law have led the court to the same conclusion on the need for an oral hearing by an actual decision-maker as did s. 7 of the Charter?

The dilemma here is in part the resolution of the tensions between a definition of the principles of fundamental justice in terms of the "fundamental tenets of the legal system" (*Reference re BC Motor Vehicle Act*, [1985] 2 SCR 486 (BC) (*per* Lamer J)), of which presumably the rules of natural justice and procedural fairness are part, and an abiding sense that s. 7 was intended to have at least some impact on the extent of the procedural entitlements of individuals whose now constitutionalized interests are at stake. (For a discussion of this issue and a conservative view on the extent to which such appeals to Charter rights enhance procedural claims, see Evans, "The Principles of Fundamental Justice: The Constitution and the Common Law" (1991), 29 *Osgoode Hall LJ* 51.)

General Procedural Statutes

Like the other sources of procedures considered in this chapter, general procedural statutes comprise thresholds governing the application of their specific procedural protections. These thresholds are briefly reviewed here.

Ontario Statutory Powers Procedure Act

The SPPA contains a formula which provides for the Act's general application, subject to specific exceptions. Section 3(1) sets out two requirements. First, a decision-maker must exercise a statutory power of decision conferred by or under (thus catching powers conferred by subordinate legislation) an Act of the Legislature. "Statutory power of decision" is defined in s. 1 as:

> a power or right, conferred by or under a statute, to make a decision deciding or prescribing:
>
> (a) the legal rights, powers, privileges, immunities, duties or liabilities of any person or party, or
>
> (b) the eligibility of any person or party to receive, or to the continuation of, a benefit or license, whether the person is legally entitled thereto or not; …

Several important observations flow from this first requirement. First, the term "deciding or prescribing" implies that non-final decision making does not fall within the SPPA's scope, a limitation confirmed by a specific exemption in s. 3(2)(g). Second, the SPPA applies not only to decisions involving "rights" but to those involving privileges (such as licences) or benefits. Third, because the power must be conferred by a provincial statute, decisions of bodies that seem public in a way that makes administrative law doctrine and remedies appropriate—such as decisions of a union's discipline committee or a premier's appointment (or dismissal) of an official under a prerogative power (see *Masters v. Ontario*)—are not subject to the SPPA.

The second requirement for the SPPA's application is that the decision-maker be required "by or under such Act or otherwise by law to hold or to afford to the parties to the proceeding an opportunity for a hearing before making a decision." The application of the SPPA through a statutory requirement that a decision-maker hold a hearing appears straightforward, but can in fact cause considerable uncertainties and difficulties, necessitating a lengthy analysis. First, consider legislation about application: a statute may provide simply and expressly that the SPPA shall govern a particular proceeding and, if it does, it is difficult to imagine realistic difficulties. Next, a statute may provide that a "hearing" shall be held. Presumably, in most situations at least, the SPPA will apply, but what if a trial-type hearing is entirely inappropriate? Would it be reasonable to suggest that the term "hearing" does not, in that context, mean a hearing under the SPPA? Last, what if a statute uses terms that denote some procedural requirements but not the word "hearing" itself—for example, "meeting," "consultation," "an opportunity to present evidence and make representations," or "a reasonable opportunity to present his or her grievance"? Presumably, terms of this kind will often be a clear signal that a trial-type hearing is not to be required; but what if a trial-type hearing is appropriate in some particular context—would it be reasonable to suggest that a "hearing" under the SPPA is required? These questions are examples of a more general question—that is, whether and how considerations of appropriateness affect the determination of the application of the SPPA.

The application of the SPPA where a hearing is required "otherwise by law" covers situations where the common law, and presumably s. 7 of the Charter, require a hearing. However, this provision does not extend the reach of the SPPA to all statutory decision-makers now required to supply procedural fairness to the parties affected by their decisions. As demonstrated in *Re Webb and Ontario Housing Corporation*, the SPPA and its full-trial-type hearing procedures may not apply to decision-making contexts that nevertheless require decision-makers to extend more limited procedural fairness safeguards to affected parties. For purposes of the SPPA's application, a hearing will be required "otherwise" by the common law only for decision-makers exercising judicial or quasi-judicial functions. Thus, the decision-maker must exhibit characteristics identified in older Supreme Court precedents like *MNR v. Coopers & Lybrand*, [1979] 1 SCR 495 (Can.), including a focus on the determination of individuals' rights and obligations, adjudication based on the application of substantive rules to individual cases and involvement of the adversary process. Accordingly, the SPPA fits uncomfortably in the new common law world of procedural protections, where "hearings" respecting the principles of procedural fairness are required for administrative, quasi-judicial, and judicial decisions, but the precise elements of these "hearings" vary with the decision-making context.

Some useful examples are decisions to evict tenants from subsidized housing, and discipline in secondary schools. In each example, assume that some procedural requirements will be imposed, but not the requirements of the SPPA. We see four ways of approaching the analysis. (1) The function can be labelled "administrative," and the procedures labelled "fairness," not a "hearing." This approach has support in authority, especially in *Nicholson* and *Webb*, and its association of "judicial," "natural justice," and "hearings," contrasted to "administrative" and "fairness." It has the disadvantages of preserving the distinction between administrative and judicial functions, and of using different words to refer to procedural requirements, which may create confusion and inhibit developing a range of procedures from which to choose. (2) The function might be labelled "judicial." If it is, the association of "judicial" and "hearing" must be escaped; but this approach has the same disadvantages as the first. (3) The choice of procedures can be made without labelling the function, and by saying that they are not a "hearing." None of these three approaches is pleasing. (4) The appropriate procedures can be designed without mentioning the SPPA and its possible application at all. This approach has the merit of simplicity, if not thoroughness. Note that in each of these approaches—masked in the first and open in the other three—the decision that the procedures are not a "hearing" is made by considering the appropriateness of the requirements of the SPPA. In this way the effect of the SPPA may tend to be tautological: an agency will be required to give a "hearing"—that is, a hearing under the SPPA, if it is required to give a hearing—that is, the kind of hearing for which these requirements are appropriate.

Section 3(2) lists proceedings to which the SPPA does not apply. These include proceedings before the legislative assembly or its committees, the ordinary courts, arbitrators under the *Labour Relations Act* or *Arbitrations Act*, coroners' inquests, public inquiries under the *Public Inquiries Act*, and investigatory bodies whose reports are not legally binding. The section also excludes tribunals' statutory rule-making or regulation-making powers from the SPPA's reach. In exercising such functions, these bodies are subject to the procedural requirements imposed by other procedural sources, including their enabling statutes and the common law.

Even if the SPPA would otherwise apply to a decision-maker under the general application formula expressed in s. 3, the legislature is free to expressly provide in the enabling statute that the SPPA or any part of it does not apply to decision making under that statute. Accordingly, it is crucial to examine the enabling statute to determine whether a particular decision-maker is bound by any provision of the SPPA. To the extent that such a statute does not expressly exclude the SPPA and contains procedural protections of a level lower than that required by the SPPA, s. 32 of the SPPA provides that the SPPA's procedures prevail. However, an enabling statute that does expressly exclude the SPPA will not be interpreted as also ousting the application of common law procedural fairness. This was noted by Blair JA of the Ontario Court of Appeal in *Re Downing and Graydon* (1978), 92 DLR (3d) 355 (Ont. CA), a case dealing with the effects of the exclusion of the SPPA by the *Employment Standards Act* on complaining employees' common law right to be heard:

> The exclusion of the *Statutory Powers Procedure Act, 1971* does not by itself affect the employee's common law right to be heard. An express and unmistakable statement by the Legislature would be required before the exclusion of such a fundamental and deeply rooted concept as the right to be heard could be presumed. The *Statutory Powers Procedure Act, 1971* merely provides rules for the conduct of hearings which are more rigid and formal than the general and more flexible prescriptions of the common law. There is nothing in the Act which expressly or by necessary implication excludes or is repugnant to the continued operation of the *audi alteram partem* rule in cases where the *Statutory Powers Procedure Act, 1971* does not apply.

Conversely, the SPPA is not an exclusive code of procedural safeguards. Common law procedural fairness could, in respect of a particular decision-maker to which the SPPA applied, require procedural safeguards above and beyond those provided by the SPPA. This is sometimes the case for pre-hearing discovery, which is not required by the SPPA, but may be required by common law procedural fairness; see *Ontario (Human Rights Commission) v. Ontario (The Board of Inquiry into Northwestern General Hospital)* (1993) , 115 DLR (4th) 279 (Ont. Div. Ct.) (chapter 4 of this text).

Alberta Administrative Procedures and Jurisdiction Act

For a long time, the only other Canadian jurisdiction to have a statute approximating Ontario's SPPA was Alberta, whose *Administrative Procedures Act*, SA 1966, c. 1 in fact slightly pre-dated the SPPA. The Alberta *Administrative Procedures and Jurisdiction Act*, RSA 2000, c. A-3, as amended by SA 2005, c. 4 does not, like its Ontario counterpart, contain a formula to determine its general applicability. Instead, s. 2 of the Act provides that the lieutenant governor in council may designate those authorities to which the Act applies and the extent to which its provisions apply. The *Authorities Designation Regulation*, Alta. Reg. 64/2003, designates seven authorities that are subject to the *Administrative Procedures and Jurisdic-*

tion Act. In addition, the Act (or some of its provisions) are incorporated into several statutes, including, for example, the *Child, Youth and Family Enhancements Act*, RSA 2000, c. C-12, s. 119(1) and the *Widows Pension Act*, RSA 2000, c. W-7.5, s. 9(1).

British Columbia Administrative Tribunals Act

British Columbia's 2004 adoption of the *Administrative Tribunals Act*, SBC 2004, c. 45 (ATA) was the culmination of an ambitious project to reform the BC administrative justice system. The Act applies where a tribunal's enabling statute expressly makes some or all of the provisions of the ATA applicable to the tribunal. So far, ATA provisions have been "adopted" by 24 of 26 administrative tribunals in the province. The ATA, among other things, establishes common appointment provisions for tribunal members and chairs, confers rule-making powers on tribunals, strengthens their authority to enforce their orders, and sets out a detailed list of procedural powers.

Québec Act Respecting Administrative Justice

In Québec, the *Charter of Human Rights and Freedoms*, RSQ 1977, c. C-12, codifies the right to procedural fairness in a limited manner to the extent that s. 23 of the Act (which by virtue of s. 56 applies to all tribunals exercising judicial or *quasi*-judicial functions) requires a "full and equal, public and fair hearing by an independent and impartial tribunal" whenever "rights and obligations" are being determined. This is supplemented by s. 34, which enshrines "the right to be represented by an advocate or to be assisted by one before any tribunal." In 1996, Québec adopted the *Act Respecting Administrative Justice*, SQ 1996, c. 54. It applies to any organs of the provincial government and to most bodies whose membership consists of a majority of government-appointed persons and whose staff are subject to the province's public service legislation. Within this category, the Act's procedural fairness requirements apply whenever individual decisions affecting citizens are being taken on the basis of norms or standards prescribed by law. Those procedural obligations are spelled out at a greater level of generality than in the SPPA. For a general description of these developments, see D. Lemieux, "The Codification of Administrative Law in Québec" in G. Huscroft and M. Taggart, eds., *Inside and Outside Canadian Administrative Law* (Toronto: U of T Press, 2006), at 240.

CHAPTER FOUR

The Level and Choice of Procedures

THE LEVEL OF PROCEDURES

In its foundational judgment in *Nicholson*, the Supreme Court expanded the reach of the common law in the procedural realm. Whereas the rules of natural justice had previously required procedural safeguards only where decision-makers exercised judicial or quasi-judicial functions, common law procedural fairness requirements extended beyond these to administrative decisions. *Nicholson* also made clear that what constitutes sufficient procedural fairness protections—the level or content of procedural fairness required by the common law—depends on the context in which a specific decision is made. Indeed, the procedural fairness obligations of decision-makers lie on a spectrum between the trial-type procedures (for example, in-person hearing, full disclosure rights) appropriate for decision-makers exercising judicial functions and more informal procedures, such as the written notice and opportunity to comment afforded in the *Webb* case. At this latter end of the spectrum lies a new, lower threshold below which no procedural fairness is owed.

In the cases since *Nicholson*, the courts have incrementally identified factors or considerations to assist in their assessment of how full the procedural obligations of specific decision-makers must be—where they fall on this procedural fairness spectrum. Unsurprisingly, many of these factors, including the legislative or policy-driven nature of the decision and its place in the statutory decision-making framework, whether adjudicative and final or investigatory and non-dispositive, are discussed in the cases on the common law threshold in chapter 3 of this text, because both the threshold and content analyses relate to a decision-maker's position on the spectrum.

In *Baker*, the Supreme Court sought, for the first time, to lay out a methodology to determine the appropriate content of procedural fairness. It set out a non-exhaustive list of five factors or considerations to guide lower courts and decision-makers confronting this question. The first three factors are the nature of the decision, the nature of the statutory scheme and the terms of the statute pursuant to which the decision-maker operates, and the importance or significance of the decision to the affected individuals. Distilled from the procedural fairness jurisprudence, these factors mirror those identified in chapter 3 of this text as relevant to determining whether procedural fairness obligations exist at all. Two additional factors round off the list: the legitimate expectations of the person challenging the decision and the choices of procedure made by the decision-maker. We review the court's description and application of these factors in turn.

1. The nature of the decision and the process followed in making it

Relying on *Knight* and other Canadian and English authorities, Justice L'Heureux-Dubé noted, at para. 23, that "the more the process provided for, the function of the tribunal, the nature of the decision-making body, and the determinations that must be made to reach a decision resemble judicial decision-making, the more likely it is that procedural protections closer to the trial model will be required by procedural fairness." Clearly, while the "judicial" nature of the decision is no longer determinative of the existence of a duty of fairness, decisions that involve an adjudication between parties, directly or indirectly affect their rights and obligations, or require the decision-maker to apply substantive rules to individual cases (see *Canada (Minister of National Revenue—MNR) v. Coopers and Lybrand Ltd.*, [1979] 1 SCR 495) will require more extensive procedural protections than regulatory decisions bearing on the implementation of social and economic policy. In the court's view, the humanitarian and compassionate decision in *Baker*, involving a minister's exercise of considerable discretion based on the application of many "open-textured" principles and factors was very different from a judicial decision and indicated that fewer procedures were required.

2. The nature of the statutory scheme and the terms of the statute pursuant to which the decision-maker operates

As illustrated in the threshold cases, courts are very attentive to the terms of the legislation that authorizes officials to act. Where a statute provides an official with investigatory or fact-finding powers as a preliminary step to a hearing before a decision-maker with the power to make a dispositive decision, minimal procedures may be owed at the initial stage. However, as Justice L'Heureux-Dubé notes in *Baker*, at para. 24, "where no appeal procedure is provided within the statute, or when the decision is determinative of the issue and further requests may not be submitted," greater procedural protections will be owed. Conversely, in *Cooper*, the existence of a statutory administrative appeal was viewed by the court as implying the existence of a record from *some* first-instance proceeding before the Wandsworth Board of Works and thus a common law right to notice of its decision to tear down Cooper's house. The relevance of the statutory scheme is not limited to the dispositive nature of the decision or the existence of an appeal. In *Baker*, for example, the role of the minister's humanitarian and compassionate power as the source of discretionary exceptions to the normal application of the general principles of Canadian immigration law set out in the *Immigration Act* indicated that fewer procedures were warranted.

3. The importance of the decision to the affected individual(s)

The more important a decision is to the lives of those it affects, the higher the level of procedural protections mandated by common law procedural fairness. Justice L'Heureux-Dubé, by reference to English authority, emphasized that the significance of the decision's impact may elevate the requirements of fairness above what they would otherwise be, underlining the crucial importance of this factor. In *Baker*, the consequences of an unfavorable humanitarian and compassionate decision to Baker, her partner and her children, including possible separation and the interruption of Baker's psychological treatment, pointed toward a higher level of procedural fairness.

4. *The legitimate expectations of the person challenging the decision*

By including legitimate expectations in its framework for determining the level of procedural fairness, the *Baker* court confirmed the procedural focus of the doctrine. Legitimate expectations may be raised by decision-makers' representations about available procedures or substantive results. In the first scenario, where a claimant has a legitimate expectation that a certain procedure will be followed, then that procedure will be required by procedural fairness. Where a claimant legitimately expects a certain result in his or her case "fairness may require more extensive procedural rights than would otherwise be accorded"—such as notice that the decision-maker intends to renege on the substantive promise or representation and an opportunity to argue against such a course of action. In *Baker*, the court was not convinced that the Canadian government's ratification of the *Convention on the Rights of the Child* amounted to a representation on how humanitarian and compassionate applications would be decided or on the accompanying procedures, if any, and this fourth factor indicated neither a higher nor a lower level of procedures.

5. *The choices of procedure made by the agency itself*

The design of appropriate procedures is arguably situation-sensitive. An agency, with a fuller awareness of the nature of the issues that are likely to arise, of the problems of getting at the truth in the area it is regulating, and of its own personal and budgetary limitations may have a far better appreciation than the courts of what represents an appropriate compromise among the competing claims of fairness, efficiency, effectiveness, and feasibility. This is particularly compelling in the case of agencies engaged in high-volume decision making, such as refugee status determination or the processing of applications for social benefits, where a successful judicial challenge of agency procedures brought by one individual may impact thousands of other cases. In *Baker*, the Supreme Court expressly acknowledged for the first time, at para. 27, that courts should sometimes be deferential—"give important weight"—to agencies' procedural choices:

> [T]he analysis of what procedures the duty of fairness requires should also take into account and respect the choices of procedure made by the agency itself, particularly when the statute leaves to the decision-maker the ability to choose its own procedures, or when the agency has an expertise in determining what procedures are appropriate in the circumstances.

The court noted that the *Immigration Act* accorded to the minister "considerable flexibility" to decide on proper procedure. The minister's choices in this respect, including the fact that immigration officers did not conduct interviews in all cases, pointed to a lower level of procedures.

Considering each of these five factors, and noting that some factors "suggested stricter requirements under the duty of fairness" while others suggested "more relaxed requirements further from the judicial model," Justice L'Heureux-Dubé concluded, at para. 32, that, on balance, the duty of fairness was more than simply "minimal" as had previously been decided by the Federal Court of Appeal:

> [T]he circumstances require a full and fair consideration of the issues, and the claimant and others whose important interests are affected by the decision in a fundamental way must have

a meaningful opportunity to present the various types of evidence relevant to their case and have it fully and fairly considered.

This analytical framework for determining the level of procedural fairness required in a particular decision-making context, based on five non-exhaustive factors, has been widely adopted by trial and appellate courts. While it does not answer all questions regarding the details of the specific procedures required by procedural fairness in a particular case, a question explored further in this chapter, *Baker* supplies a rational framework to deal with such claims. In addition to informing the content of participatory rights, the *Baker* analysis has also been used to assess the standard of impartiality required of decision-makers by the rule against bias—the second branch of procedural fairness. That question is dealt with in greater detail in chapter 5 of this text.

The *Baker* analysis has also become an integral part of the framework for assessing the procedural content of fundamental justice in decisions that engage individuals' life, liberty, and security of the person interests. In *Suresh v. Canada (Minister of Citizenship and Immigration)*, [2002] 1 SCR 3 (Can.), a case involving the constitutionality of procedures governing a minister's power to declare Convention refugees to be a danger to Canada's security and to remove them to states where they face a substantial risk of torture (extracted and further discussed later in this chapter), a unanimous Supreme Court reasoned that, because fundamental justice demanded, at minimum, compliance with common law procedural fairness, it was appropriate to look to the factors discussed in *Baker* to "inform" its analysis of the procedural safeguards required by s. 7. The application of the *Baker* framework in the Charter context is not without problems and raises important questions. How much weight should be attributed to the fact that a Charter-protected right is allegedly infringed? Is it appropriate for courts to factor deference to the procedural choices of government officials into their assessment of the procedural requirements of fundamental justice under the Charter, an instrument whose purpose is to set out standards on which judges review the constitutionality of governmental choices? In *Suresh*, the court touches on both these questions by noting, at para. 120, that the need for deference to the minister of citizenship and immigration "must be reconciled with the elevated level of procedural protections mandated by the serious situation of refugees like Suresh, who if deported may face torture and violations of human rights in which Canada can neither constitutionally, nor under its international treaty obligations, be complicit."

A PERSPECTIVE

The framework articulated by the Supreme Court in *Baker* enables courts and tribunals to assess, in a coherent and systematic manner, where on the spectrum of procedures required by the common law duty of fairness—from notice and comment procedures to trial-type hearings—a particular decision should fall. The extent to which precise pre-hearing, hearing, and post-hearing procedures (including notice); in-person hearings; discovery; disclosure; representation; and reasons are required by the duty also depends on context and is explored in the case extracts and commentary that follow. As a bridge to understanding these materials, consider the following perspective regarding a question that was asked in the general introduction: what are the justifications for giving hearings?

Mashaw, *Due Process in the Administrative State*
(New Haven, CT: Yale University Press, 1985)

The meaning of "due process of law" can be approached from several directions. Literal interpretation, a concentration on the ordinary meaning of the words, has little to offer the scholar or the courts. The clause is obviously designed to be open textured. It is a question in the form of an answer. Of course due process is due. But what is that? The approach of courts and commentators has varied, both over time and at any one time. The variations are clustered, however, around three central themes: tradition, natural rights, and interest balancing. Each theme is complex and richly embellished in the due process jurisprudence. We will state here only the core ideas and hint at their difficulties and limitations.

Tradition

A tradition-based approach to due process analysis asks whether the procedures under consideration conform to the usual processes of law. As a historical matter, this way of putting the due process question has much to recommend it. The original understanding of the due process constraint may have been that it provided protection against oppressive governmental action enforced through special proceedings. The due process clause is thus constitutional heir to English concerns with Star Chamber proceedings and to the American revolutionary concern with an arbitrary colonial magistracy.

But tradition has serious limitations. As a jurisprudential technique, tradition's weakness lies in the difficulty of identifying a single appropriate tradition. When, for example, the Supreme Court for the first time confronted the question of an appropriate process for terminating welfare benefits, it was required to choose from among competing traditions. The long tradition of nonenforcement of gratuitous promises, including promises of continuous income support, suggested that there was no legal interest involved sufficient to activate due process concern. The tradition of commercial law remedies suggested that the welfare recipient (creditor) should have posttermination recourse to ordinary civil process to determine the legality of the government's (debtor) failure to perform. The tradition of governmental cancellation of other valuable privileges, such as common carrier certificates or professional licences, suggested that some form of pretermination proceeding was necessary. By what jurisprudential technique does a court decide which tradition should have the greatest claims of relevance?

The implicit values of a traditional approach to due process protection are also troublesome. If tradition implies adherence to the original understanding of "life, liberty, or property," then many governmental activities that encroach on modern notions of humane values (for example, privacy, beneficial social and economic relations, opportunities for education or for artistic and professional self-realization) evade the constraints of due process. And, on one original understanding of due process—meaning the processes of the ordinary courts or of the legislature—much of the regulatory apparatus of the welfare state applicable to property interests would be unconstitutional (the National Labor Relations Acts, all federal environmental quality legislation, most safety legislation, the antifraud activities of the Federal Trade Commission and the Securities and

Exchange Commission, to name a few). By modern standards the process constraints of such a traditional approach to due process (a choice limited to representative assemblies and judicial trials) are as overprotective as that traditional view's substantive values (protection only against death, incarceration, or invasion of common law property) are under-inclusive.

But a tradition-based approach need not be synonymous with a conceptually static jurisprudence. Analogical development is the principal mode of judicial law reform: thus tradition evolves. The question for contemporary scholarship is how the tradition approach actually works. What are the rules of recognition for new substantive values worthy of due process concern? What are the models and metaphors of process that have informed the comparisons that an analogical method requires? What is the continued role and relevance of traditional values and techniques in the modern administrative state? What are the normative propositions that give tradition legitimating force?

Natural Rights

A natural rights analysis takes a quite different view of the due process problem. It begins not with the historical contingencies of tradition, but with a basic moral premise concerning individual autonomy. Each citizen is an end in himself, not merely a means for the attainment of collective ends. The government cannot, therefore, pursue its purposes through processes which ignore the independent status and purposes of the individual. From the natural rights perspective this dignitary principle is what the due process clause, like other portions of the Bill of Rights, protects.

Although this secular formulation of the natural rights approach has substantial support in liberal political theory and clear connections with the individualistic ethos of ordinary political discourse, it also raises some obvious problems of application. The set of procedural rights necessary to preserve individual dignity seems infinitely expansive. Any governmentally imposed disappointment provides an occasion for invocation of the principle. And the principle implies that due process should be defined as that set of processes freely accepted by affected individuals. Because such a principle forecloses governance, limitations must be imposed. But what are the principles of limitation? Where is the objective set of truly important human values and sufficiently dignified procedures for making collective decisions about them?

The judicial dilemma is apparent. Questions of value are crucial to the application of the due process clause. The constitutional formulation requires that human interests be characterized as life, liberty, or property concerns that either have or do not have sufficient status to trigger due process protection. And, the substantive stake in decisional outcomes aside, it is surely not irrelevant to the adequacy of governmental processes that they do or do not respect individual interests in autonomy. Yet, in an increasingly secular and scientific society, confronting questions of moral value directly and in an authoritative context is embarrassing. Because they have no attachment to revealed truth and no underpinning of scientific expertise, moral pronouncements as constitutional interpretations appear radically subjective.

Interest Balancing

The functional criteria so conspicuously absent from natural rights propositions are promised by the dominant contemporary mode of due process analysis—interest balancing. Under the current Supreme Court formulation, the constitutional judgment concerning process adequacy includes consideration of (1) the magnitude of the interests of private parties, (2) the governmental interest in procedural expedition, and (3) the likely contribution of various procedural ingredients to the correct resolution of disputes. In short, the Court does a social welfare calculation to determine whether society will be better or worse off should it honor the due process claim.

The great advantages of the interest balancing approach are its adaptability to any question of procedural adequacy and its recognition that judgments about process adequacy necessarily involve trade-offs between collective and individual ends. But, as a constitutional theory, this brand of utilitarianism has the defects of its virtues. For one thing, interest balancing suggests that, given a good enough reason, the government can use any process it pleases. The Bill of Rights is, however, not meant only to facilitate adaptation of constitutional constraints to changing governmental forms. Rather, its most obvious function is to protect against encroachments on individual liberty. The interest balancing methodology seems to contradict the basic libertarian presuppositions of the text that it would implement. Moreover, the information demands of a thoroughgoing utilitarian calculus may be excessive. Can the dignitary costs of individuals and the administrative costs of government, for example, be measured in the same currency? Is it possible to predict the effect of any discrete change in the decision process on the accuracy of decision making?

The question posed by the interest balancing approach are, again, questions both of technique and of value. Can the technique deliver what it promises? Do information demands always defeat analysis, or are there acceptable strategies for dealing with uncertainties and discontinuities? Does the approach, by posing its questions in social welfare terms, misconceive the basic purposes of due process protection? Finally, does the utilitarian focus on the relationship of process to the attainment of collective ends systematically ignore or undervalue concerns that relate, not to the attainment of specific individual or collective goals, but to the place of the individual in the structure of governmental process?

NOTES

1. Does the Supreme Court's analysis of procedural fairness and fundamental justice in *Baker* and *Suresh* draw on any of these "modes of analysis"?

2. A question that is suggested by Mashaw's analysis, and which leads to the next section, is what are the general principles or ways of thinking that should govern choice of procedures at a hearing? Do these three ways of thinking help?

THE CHOICE OF PROCEDURES

We move now to a consideration of the content of procedural entitlements once the threshold to the assertion of any procedural claims has been crossed. As already suggested in the general introduction to this part, this separation of the threshold from the issue of content is to a degree artificial as reflected by the fact that you will already have discovered quite a lot about the content and strength of various claims from the previous chapter of this text. For example, *Irvine* has revealed some of the tensions that exist in determining whether someone has the right to be represented by counsel and to engage in cross-examination. *Singh* dealt in some detail with the issues of access to an oral or in-person hearing and entitlement to information in the possession of those adverse in interest or of the decision-maker. *Blencoe* provides a full account of delay as a ground for seeking relief. More generally, arguments about the threshold can scarcely avoid being influenced by the details of the procedural entitlements that the court perceives are being asserted, as exemplified most graphically by the judgment of the Supreme Court of Canada in *Inuit Tapirisat*.

Nonetheless, the nature and extent of procedural claims that are made by applicants for judicial review does not emerge fully from the discussion of sources and thresholds in chapter 3 of this text. Further elaboration is required not only in this general chapter but also in later chapters that focus on particular issues of contemporary currency—participatory rights in rulemaking and, more generally, the procedural dimensions arising out from pressures generated within certain tribunals for institutional responsibility for and influence on decisions in particular matters.

Indeed, as the threshold for the assertion of procedural claims has been lowered, the issue of procedural content has become that much more prominent and perhaps controversial. As was anticipated, the emergence of the doctrine of procedural fairness exposed certain forms of decision making to scrutiny for the first time. What rapidly became clear in a great number of these situations was that the traditional paradigm of the rules of natural justice—one based on the procedures followed by the ordinary courts of civil and criminal jurisdiction, and an adversarial model—was simply inappropriate for a wide range of administrative decisions now impressed with an obligation of procedural fairness.

The lowering of the threshold also coincided with an escalating crisis of confidence in the adversarial model as reflected in the processes of the ordinary courts of the land. The increased cost of ordinary litigation with its corresponding impact on accessibility coalesced with growing doubts about the effectiveness and efficiency of the adversarial model as a way of getting at "the truth." This led not only to the consideration of other models by law reform agencies and academics but also, at a practical level, to a constituency movement toward alternative forms of dispute resolution both within and outside the regular court structures.

Not surprisingly, of course, there have also been tugs in the other direction and, most notably, in the advocacy of greater openness or transparency in the way in which administrative agencies and tribunals do business. This has been reflected not only in the spread of access to information legislation but also in the demands through tribunal and litigation processes for fuller and more timely access to all material that has relevance or potential relevance to upcoming hearings as well as reasons for decisions. This has not, however, meant the disappearance of arguments against disclosure based on confidentiality arguments of various kinds. Just as access to information legislation is generally attended by the antidote of privacy protections, so too in the world of administrative processes are there continuing concerns for the protection of commercially sensitive material and the identity of informers and other sources of information, as well as attempts to ensure that staff advisers will still feel free to be full and frank in the provision of advice and the identification of options.

Accommodations had to be made to reflect all these realities. As a consequence, courts engaged in judicial review of administrative action on procedural grounds were expected to be much more creative and expansive in their thinking about issues of procedural design. Whether they have met that challenge is one of the underlying themes of this chapter.

The advent of the *Canadian Charter of Rights and Freedoms* added further complexity to this domain and, as anticipated in our consideration of the threshold to the assertion of constitutional procedural rights, in this chapter we examine the difficult question whether procedural entitlements are increased to the extent that rights protected by the Charter are affected. Putting it bluntly, do "the principles of fundamental justice" call for greater or different procedures than the common law rules of natural justice or procedural fairness? An examination of this question is interwoven with our exposure of the various aspects of procedural claims.

Faced with all of the uncertainties generated by the common law, the *Canadian Bill of Rights*, and the Charter as to the detail of procedural obligations, decision-makers themselves have more and more come to realize the importance of procedural design. As a consequence, one of the tasks performed frequently by contemporary administrative lawyers is the provision of advice to tribunals and other decision-makers on how to create rules of procedure that reflect the operating imperatives of that tribunal and at the same time the legal obligations of procedural fairness or fundamental justice. Indeed, even prior to the emergence of the procedural fairness doctrine, there was much debate about the desirability of legislated general procedural codes. That debate produced the Ontario *Statutory Powers Procedure Act*, SO 1971, c. 47, the Alberta *Administrative Procedures Act*, SA 1966, c. 1, the Québec *Act Respecting Administrative Justice*, SQ 1996, c. 54, and the British Columbia *Administrative Tribunals Act*, SBC 2004, c. 45. We therefore also take up in this chapter the question of the usefulness of such legislative exercises and, for these purposes, engage in a brief evaluation of the Ontario Act in particular and its judicial interpretation.

One of the themes that underlies this chapter is that exposed in the extract from Mashaw: What are the general principles or ways of thinking that should govern choice of procedures? That question is illuminated by two major judgments of the US Supreme Court with which we commence.

Goldberg v. Kelly
397 US 254 (1970)

[Welfare recipients challenged as violating the 14th amendment to the US constitution the procedures for termination of welfare payments in New York state and city. Before termination, recipients were given notice of the proposed termination and reasons (and, in New York City, the notice was preceded by a discussion with a case worker), and were entitled to make written representations. After termination, the recipients were entitled to a trial-type hearing. It was claimed that this process constituted the removal of a property right without "due process of law." The District Court held that these procedures were inadequate, and the state and the city appealed. There was no doubt that the interest of the recipients required procedural due process. The main issue was what procedures were appropriate.]

JUSTICE BRENNAN delivered the opinion of the Court: It is true, of course, that some governmental benefits may be administratively terminated without affording the recipient a pre-termination evidentiary hearing. But we agree with the District Court that when welfare is discontinued, only a pre-termination evidentiary hearing provides the recipient with procedural due process. ...

For qualified recipients, welfare provides the means to obtain essential food, clothing, housing, and medical care. ... Thus the crucial factor in this context—a factor not present in the case of the blacklisted government contractor, the discharged government employee, the taxpayer denied a tax exemption, or virtually anyone else whose governmental largesse is ended—is that termination of aid pending resolution of a controversy over eligibility may deprive an eligible recipient of the very means by which to live while he waits. Since he lacks independent resources, his situation becomes immediately desperate. His need to concentrate upon finding the means for daily subsistence, in turn, adversely affects his ability to seek redress from the welfare bureaucracy.

Moreover, important governmental interests are promoted by affording recipients a pre-termination evidentiary hearing. From its founding the Nation's basic commitment has been to foster the dignity and well-being of all persons within its borders. We have come to recognize that forces not within the control of the poor contribute to their poverty. This perception, against the background of our traditions, has significantly influenced the development of the contemporary public assistance system. Welfare, by meeting the basic demands of subsistence, can help bring within the reach of the poor the same opportunities that are available to others to participate meaningfully in the life of the community. At the same time, welfare guards against the societal malaise that may flow from a widespread sense of unjustified frustration and insecurity. Public assistance, then, is not mere charity, but a means to "promote the general Welfare, and secure the Blessings of Liberty to ourselves and our Posterity." The same governmental interests which counsel the provision of welfare, counsel as well its uninterrupted provision to those eligible to receive it; pre-termination evidentiary hearings are indispensable to that end.

Appellant does not challenge the force of these considerations but argues that they are outweighed by countervailing governmental interests in conserving fiscal and administrative resources. These interests, the argument goes, justify the delay of any evidentiary hearing until after discontinuance of the grants. Summary adjudication protects the public fisc by stopping payments promptly upon discovery of reason to believe that a recipient is no longer eligible. Since most terminations are accepted without challenge, summary adjudication also conserves both the fisc and administrative time and energy by reducing the number of evidentiary hearings actually held.

We agree with the District Court, however, that these governmental interests are not overriding in the welfare context. The requirement of a prior hearing doubtless involves some greater expense, and the benefits paid to ineligible recipients pending decision at the hearing probably cannot be recouped, since these recipients are likely to be judgment-proof. But the State is not without weapons to minimize these increased costs. Much of the drain on fiscal and administrative resources can be reduced by developing procedures for prompt pre-termination hearings and by skillful use of personnel and facilities.

· · ·

We also agree with the District Court, however, that the pre-termination hearing need not take the form of a judicial or *quasi*-judicial trial. We bear in mind that the statutory "fair hearing" will provide the recipient with a full administrative review. Accordingly, the pre-termination hearing has one function only: to produce an initial determination of the validity of the welfare department's grounds for discontinuance of payments in order to protect a recipient against an erroneous termination of his benefits. ... Thus, a complete record and a comprehensive opinion, which would serve primarily to facilitate judicial review and to guide future decisions, need not be provided at the pre-termination stage. We recognize, too, that both welfare authorities and recipients have an interest in relatively speedy resolution of questions of eligibility, that they are used to dealing with one another informally, and that some welfare departments have very burdensome caseloads.

· · ·

The city's procedures presently do not permit recipients to appear personally with or without counsel before the official who finally determines continued eligibility. Thus a recipient is not permitted to present evidence to that official orally, or to confront or cross-examine adverse witnesses. These omissions are fatal to the constitutional adequacy of the procedures.

The opportunity to be heard must be tailored to the capacities and circumstances of those who are to be heard. It is not enough that a welfare recipient may present his position to the decision maker in writing or second-hand through his caseworker. Written submissions are an unrealistic option for most recipients, who lack the educational attainment necessary to write effectively and who cannot obtain professional assistance. Moreover, written submissions do not afford the flexibility of oral presentations; they do not permit the recipient to mold his argument to the issues the decision maker appears to regard as important. Particularly where credibility and veracity are at issue, as they must be in many termination proceedings, written submissions are a wholly unsatisfactory basis for decision. The second-hand presentation to the decision maker by the caseworker has its own deficiencies; since the caseworker usually gathers the facts upon which the charge of ineligibility rests, the presentation of the recipient's side of the controversy cannot safely be left to him. Therefore a recipient must be allowed to state his position orally. Informal procedures will suffice; in this context due process does not require a particular order of proof or mode of offering evidence.

· · ·

In almost every setting where important decisions turn on questions of fact, due process requires an opportunity to confront and cross-examine adverse witnesses.

· · ·

Welfare recipients must therefore be given an opportunity to confront and cross-examine the witnesses relied on by the department.

"The right to be heard would be, in many cases, of little avail if it did not comprehend the right to be heard by counsel." *Powell v. Alabama*, 287 US 45 (1932) at 68-69. We do not say that counsel must be provided at the pre-termination hearing, but only that the recipient must be allowed to retain an attorney if he so desires. Counsel can help delineate the issues, present the factual contentions in an orderly manner, conduct cross-examination, and generally safeguard the interests of the recipient. We do not anticipate that this assistance will unduly prolong or otherwise encumber the hearing.

. . .

Finally, the decision maker's conclusion as to a recipient's eligibility must rest solely on the legal rules and evidence adduced at the hearing. ... To demonstrate compliance with this elementary requirement, the decision maker should state the reasons for his determination and indicate the evidence he relied on ... though his statement need not amount to a full opinion or even formal findings of fact and conclusions of law.

[Justice Black dissented and made two major arguments. First, the payments should not be considered property: "It somewhat strains credulity to say that a government's promise of charity to an individual is property belonging to that individual when the government denies that the individual is honestly entitled to receive such a payment." Second, the costs of the procedures required by the majority would be great and would eventually prejudice claimants by making the government reluctant to undertake payments without extensive investigation.]

Appeal dismissed.

Mathews v. Eldridge
424 US 319 (1976)

[Eldridge challenged by reference to the 5th amendment the procedures for termination of disability benefits made under the *Social Security Act*. The Act provided benefits to a worker who demonstrated that he or she was "unable to engage in any substantial gainful activity by reason of any medically determinable physical or mental impairment." The procedures established by the secretary of health, education, and welfare for making determinations about both initial and continuing eligibility required a tentative decision by a state agency based on consultation with the worker and collection of medical information and opinion. If the tentative decision was adverse, the worker was notified and given a summary of the material used and given an opportunity to respond. A final determination was made by the agency and reviewed by the social security administration. If a decision to terminate payments was approved at this stage, the payments were terminated, and the worker was entitled to reconsideration by the state agency and, ultimately, a trial-type hearing.

The District Court concluded that *Goldberg v. Kelly* governed and that the procedures were inadequate. The secretary appealed.]

JUSTICE POWELL delivered the opinion of the Court: Our prior decisions indicate that identification of the specific dictates of due process generally requires consideration of three distinct factors. First, the private interest that will be affected by the official action;

second, the risk of an erroneous deprivation of such interest through the procedures used, and the probable value, if any, of additional or substitute procedural safeguards; and finally, the Government's interest, including the function involved and the fiscal and administrative burdens that the additional or substitute procedural requirement would entail.

Since a recipient whose benefits are terminated is awarded full retroactive relief if he ultimately prevails, his sole interest is in the uninterrupted receipt of this source of income pending final administrative decision on his claim. His potential injury is thus similar in nature to that of the welfare recipient in *Goldberg*. ...

Only in *Goldberg* has the Court held that due process requires an evidentiary hearing prior to a temporary deprivation. It was emphasized there that welfare assistance is given to persons on the very margin of subsistence. ... Eligibility for disability benefits, in contrast, is not based upon financial need. Indeed, it is wholly unrelated to the worker's income or support from many other sources, such as earnings of other family members, workmen's compensation awards, tort claims awards, savings, private insurance, public or private pensions, veterans' benefits, food stamps, public assistance, or the "many other important programs, both public and private, which contain provisions for disability payments affecting a substantial portion of the work force. ..." [*Richardson v. Belcher*, 404 US 78 (1971), at 85-87 (Douglas J dissenting).]

As *Goldberg* illustrates, the degree of potential deprivation that may be created by a particular decision is a factor to be considered in assessing the validity of any administrative decision-making process. ... The potential deprivation here is generally likely to be less than in *Goldberg*, although the degree of difference can be overstated. ...

The Secretary concedes that the delay between a request for a hearing before an administrative law judge and a decision on the claim is currently between 10 and 11 months. Since a terminated recipient must first obtain a reconsideration decision as a prerequisite to invoking his right to an evidentiary hearing, the delay between the actual cutoff of benefits and final decision after a hearing exceeds one year.

In view of the torpidity of this administrative review process, and the typically modest resources of the family unit of the physically disabled worker, the hardship imposed upon the erroneously terminated disability recipient may be significant. Still, the disabled worker's need is likely to be less than that of a welfare recipient. In addition to the possibility of access to private resources, other forms of government assistance will become available where the termination of disability benefits places a worker or his family below the subsistence level. ... In view of these potential sources of temporary income, there is less reason here than in *Goldberg* to depart from the ordinary principle, established by our decisions, that something less than an evidentiary hearing is sufficient prior to adverse administrative action.

An additional factor to be considered here is the fairness and reliability of the existing pretermination procedures, and the probable value, if any, of additional procedural safeguards. Central to the evaluation of any administrative process is the nature of the relevant inquiry.

In order to remain eligible for benefits the disabled worker must demonstrate by means of "medically acceptable clinical and laboratory diagnostic techniques," that he is unable "to engage in any substantial gainful activity by reason of any *medically determinable* physical or mental impairment. ..." (Emphasis supplied.) In short, a medical assessment of the worker's physical or mental condition is required. This is a more sharply focused and easily documented decision than the typical determination of welfare entitlement. In the latter case, a wide variety of information may be deemed relevant, and issues of witness credibility and veracity often are critical to the decision-making process. *Goldberg* noted that in such circumstances "written submissions are a wholly unsatisfactory basis for decision."

By contrast, the decision whether to discontinue disability benefits will turn, in most cases, upon "routine, standard, and unbiased medical reports by physician specialists," *Richardson v. Perales* 402 US 389 (1971) at 404, concerning a subject whom they have personally examined. In *Richardson* the Court recognized the "reliability and probative worth of written medical reports," emphasizing that while there may be "professional disagreement with the medical conclusions" the "specter of questionable credibility and veracity is not present." To be sure, credibility and veracity may be a factor in the ultimate disability assessment in some cases. But procedural due process rules are shaped by the risk of error inherent in the truth-finding process as applied to the generality of cases, not the rare exceptions. The potential value of an evidentiary hearing or even oral presentation to the decision-maker, is substantially less in this context than in *Goldberg*.

The decision in *Goldberg* also was based on the Court's conclusion that written submissions were an inadequate substitute for oral presentation because they did not provide an effective means for the recipient to communicate his case to the decision-maker. Written submissions were viewed as an unrealistic option, for most recipients lacked the "educational attainment necessary to write effectively" and could not afford professional assistance. In addition, such submissions would not provide the "flexibility of oral presentations" or "permit the recipient to mold his argument to the issues the decision maker appears to regard as important." In the context of the disability-benefits-entitlement assessment the administrative procedures under review here fully answer these objections.

The detailed questionnaire which the state agency periodically sends the recipient identifies with particularity the information relevant to the entitlement decision, and the recipient is invited to obtain assistance from the local SSA office in completing the questionnaire. More important, the information critical to the entitlement decision usually is derived from medical sources, such as the treating physician. Such sources are likely to be able to communicate more effectively through written documents than are welfare recipients or the lay witnesses supporting their cause. The conclusions of physicians often are supported by X-rays and the results of clinical or laboratory tests, information typically more amenable to written than to oral presentation. ...

A further safeguard against mistake is the policy of allowing the disability recipient's representative full access to all information relied upon by the state agency. In addition, prior to the cutoff of benefits the agency informs the recipient of its tentative assessment, the reasons therefor, and provides a summary of the evidence that it considers most relevant. Opportunity is then afforded the recipient to submit additional evidence or arguments, enabling him to challenge directly the accuracy of information in his file as well as the correctness of the agency's tentative conclusions. These procedures, again as contrasted with those before the Court in *Goldberg*, enable the recipient to "mold" his argument to respond to the precise issues which the decision-maker regards as crucial.

In striking the appropriate due process balance the final factor to be assessed is the public interest. This includes the administrative burden and other societal costs that would be associated with requiring, as a matter of constitutional right an evidentiary hearing upon demand in all cases prior to the termination of disability benefits. The most visible burden would be the incremental cost resulting from the increased number of hearings and the expense of providing benefits to ineligible recipients pending decision. No one can predict the extent of the increase, but the fact that full benefits would continue until after such hearings would assure the exhaustion in most cases of this attractive option. Nor would the theoretical right of the Secretary to recover undeserved benefits result, as a practical matter, in any substantial offset to the added outlay of public funds. The parties submit widely varying estimates of the probable additional financial cost. We only need say that experience with the constitutionalizing of government procedures suggests that the ultimate additional cost in terms of money and administrative burden would not be insubstantial.

Financial cost alone is not a controlling weight in determining whether due process requires a particular procedural safeguard prior to some administrative decision. But the Government's interest, and hence that of the public, in conserving scarce fiscal and administrative resources is a factor that must be weighed. At some point the benefit of an additional safeguard to the individual affected by the administrative action and to society in terms of increased assurance that the action is just, may be outweighed by the cost. Significantly, the cost of protecting those whom the preliminary administrative process has identified as likely to be found undeserving may in the end come out of the pockets of the deserving since resources available for any particular program of social welfare are not unlimited. ...

But more is implicated in cases of this type than *ad hoc* weighing of fiscal and administrative burdens against the interests of a particular category of claimants. The ultimate balance involves a determination as to when, under our constitutional system, judicial-type procedures must be imposed upon administrative action to assure fairness. We reiterate the wise admonishment of Mr. Justice Frankfurter that differences in the origin and function of administrative agencies "preclude wholesale transplantation of the rules of procedure, trial and review which have evolved from the history and experience of courts." *FCC v. Pottsville Broadcasting Co.* 309 US 134 (1940) at 143. The judicial model of an evidentiary hearing is neither a required, nor even the most effective, method of decision-making in all circumstances. The essence of due process is the requirement that "a person in jeopardy of serious loss [be given] notice of the case against him and opportunity to meet it." *Joint Anti-Fascist Comm. v. McGrath* 341 US at 171-172 (Frankfurter J concurring). All that is necessary is that the procedures be tailored, in light of the decision to be made, to "the capacities and circumstances of those who are to be heard," *Goldberg v. Kelly* 397 US at 268-269 (footnote omitted), to insure that they are given a meaningful opportunity to present their case. In assessing what process is due in this case, substantial weight must be given to the good-faith judgments of the individuals charged by Congress with the administration of social welfare programs that the procedures they have provided assure fair consideration of the entitlement claims of individuals. See *Arnett v. Kennedy* 416 US at 202 (White J concurring in part and dissenting in part). This is especially so where, as here, the prescribed procedures not only provide the claimant with an effective process for asserting his claim prior to any administrative action, but also assure a right to an evidentiary hearing, as well as to subsequent judicial review, before the denial of his claim becomes final.

[Justices Brennan and Marshall dissented.]

Appeal allowed.

Rabin, "Some Thoughts on the Relationship Between Fundamental Values and Procedural Safeguards in Constitutional Right to Hearing Cases"
(1979), 16 *San Diego LR* 301, at 306-11

Because of their training, lawyers turn quite naturally to the adversary process as a model for articulating necessary safeguards. *Goldberg v. Kelly* reflects this inclination. After determining that a welfare recipient had an entitlement to Aid to Families with Dependent Children (AFDC) benefits, Justice Brennan went on to spell out the requisites at the pre-termination hearing: notice, an evidentiary presentation, confrontation and cross-examination of adverse witnesses, an impartial tribunal, a decision based on the evidence of record, a statement of reasons, and so on—virtually the full panoply of procedural rights that we associate with a judicial trial.

For a brief period, the Supreme Court remained faithful to the approach taken in *Goldberg*. Succeeding cases applied the trial-type adversary model to a variety of revocation situations, ranging from parole to teacher tenure cases. ...

Soon, however, the court began a gradual process of isolating *Goldberg* and treating a trial-type proceeding as an extraordinary requirement. The Court has moved in this direction for a variety of reasons that require some exploration. If *Goldberg* does set unrealistic standards, it is time to take a harder look at whether the goals of procedural due process can be implemented in other, less formal ways.

First, the *Goldberg* approach was doomed to failure because the costs of implementing trial-type procedures are almost always excessive. It is no secret, of course, that trials are expensive and time-consuming. In addition, however, the judicial model is inapposite because it understates the costs of using adjudicatory procedures in the administrative system. The fact is that the courts have developed techniques for resolving significant numbers of cases without recourse to formal adversary procedures—techniques that simply are not available to administrative agencies in contested application and revocation cases.

The courts resolve informally more than ninety percent of criminal and tort cases because there is an incentive for both parties to compromise. ... No similar incentives operate in a benefit-revocation case. Consider the AFDC recipient in a case like *Goldberg*. There is no incentive for the aggrieved claimant to stop short of exhausting every available administrative remedy, assuming benefits cannot be terminated prior to a final disposition of the case. In addition, the government has no fall-back position; either the recipient is entitled to continuing benefits or none at all—there is no room for compromise. ...

A second difficulty with the *Goldberg* approach is that it is far less universally applicable than is ordinarily thought. Apart from the cost considerations already discussed, the adversary process is simply inapposite in many cases. Consider, for example, the recent *Horowitz* case: *Board of Curators of the Univ. of Mo. v. Horowitz* 435 US 78 (1978). Horowitz, a student at a state medical school, was given an academic dismissal based on evaluation of her clinical performance. The medical school provided no "hearing." Instead it supplemented its annual review of her clinical performance by allowing her to work with seven physicians for a designated period of time. The physicians then submitted independent evaluations of her ability. The Court held that Horowitz received as much due process as was required, despite the absence of a "hearing."

Justice Rehnquist, writing for the majority, argued that there is a distinction between determining whether academic standards have been met and deciding whether rules of conduct have been broken. He suggested that trial-type procedural requirements are not well-suited to the former situations. Although there are bound to be hard cases, I think there is validity in this distinction between cases in which the issue is evaluation of performance and those involving determinations of misconduct—and I would argue that *Goldberg* has little if any relevance in the performance evaluation cases.

Consider a familiar situation: A person seeking a driver's license is told by the examiner, after taking the driving test, "Your parallel parking is terrible and you cut too sharply on left turns. You flunked the test." Does it make sense to review the examiner's decision through the use of trial-type procedures? One may even be skeptical about the utility of a more streamlined notice-and-comment hearing before an independent official. Perhaps in testing and inspection situations like *Horowitz* and the driver's license example, we ought realistically to consider the determination of competence itself as the counterpart of a "hearing." Admittedly, we then place considerable reliance on the good faith of the evaluator. But questions of competence often require subjective evaluations that simply cannot be effectively reviewed on a case-by-case basis by either adversary or inquisitorial means. The most effective safeguards in such cases may be care in the hiring and monitoring of administrative personnel, or resort to multiple evaluations. Again, the trial-type model has very little to recommend it.

A third difficulty with *Goldberg* is that it proposed, and purported to utilize, a decision-making approach that is virtually useless. The Court employed a balancing test that is supposed to determine the necessary procedural safeguards by weighing the potential loss to the recipient against the government's interest in a summary process. Yet the Court never seriously examined aggregate data on the character and quantity of claims tendered by AFDC recipients in revocation cases. Without such an analysis, focusing on the actual impact of testimonial credibility and oral advocacy in contested AFDC cases, the Court had absolutely no foundation for assessing the comparative benefits and costs of trial-type procedures.

In *Mathews v. Eldridge*, a more recent case involving the procedural safeguards constitutionally required in Social Security disability terminations, the Court essentially restated the *Goldberg* test, making explicit the need to look at the risk of error under the existing procedures. Again, the analysis is hopeless. A real effort to assign costs and benefits to various procedures would require gathering data on the number of disability termination cases and the number of appeals, and assigning quantitative values to the reasons for initial termination and the grounds for reversal. Without that data and analysis, it makes no sense to talk about costs and benefits as if some real effort at measurement has been made.

Because a court has neither the time nor the resources to undertake such an analysis, it resorts to the kind of reasoning found in *Mathews*. The Court held that a notice-and-comment type proceeding would suffice prior to termination of benefits; in other words, that a *Goldberg* trial-type proceeding was unnecessary. While I have no quarrel with the result, I find very little utility in the Court's use of its "balancing process" to distinguish between the safeguards required in AFDC and disability cases. The Court placed great weight, for example, on the fact that disability recipients are "less needy" than AFDC recipients—presumably because they need not be destitute to qualify for benefits. Yet it seems safe to say that disability recipients are not primarily drawn from the middle or upper-middle class. ...

Moreover, the Court is even less convincing when it suggests that the types of issues arising in disability cases are not as deserving of trial-type treatment as those in AFDC cases. Based admittedly on casual analysis, I have the impression that many disability cases involve questions of malingering. If I am correct, it seems arguable that these cases raise precisely the kinds of questions that seem most apt for adversary treatment—questions of testimonial credibility. Similarly, the disputes among doctors in these cases are not easily resolved on a written record.

At a minimum, the balancing test would seem to require some analysis of these issues. The *Mathews-Goldberg* approach is futile because such analysis is never undertaken. If it were, it seems unlikely that the Court would know what to make of it, in any event. How does one translate into a common currency the costs of foregoing testimonial evidence and the exigencies of financial need? The point is that the use of the balancing approach is largely futile, and has consequently undermined the authority of the *Goldberg* case for the proposition that adversary proceedings were warranted there.

If we depart from the adversary model, can we still adequately safeguard the values that are fundamental to procedural due process? In a sense, this question may be inextricably bound to the threshold issue of identifying and assigning weights to various entitlements. For one could argue that some entitlements are sufficiently important to require maximal safeguards—trial-type procedures—whatever the cost. Depriving a person of his continuing right to practice a profession, for example, could be regarded as state action of sufficient gravity to call into play every possible safeguard necessary to insure a rational decision, accountability, and an adequate explanation. Again, however, I prefer to put aside the possibility that maximal safeguards may occasionally be needed, in order to emphasize a point of at least equal importance: The fundamental values underlying procedural due process can be promoted to a very considerable degree by less stringent safeguards than those required by the adversary model.

I will demonstrate the point by brief reference to two other models. Consider, initially, a notice-and-comment type proceeding, featuring an independent hearing examiner who provides the claimant with a documented statement of reasons and an opportunity to respond through written or oral arguments—after which the examiner is required to provide a written explanation for his decision. The first point to be noted is that two of the fundamental values are safeguarded virtually as much by the notice-and-comment model as by an adversary model. Assuming adequate publication, the interplay among the notice of reasons, the claimant's response, and the examiner's subsequent justification provides the kind of record that allows for a dispassionate assessment of whether the agency is doing its job properly; in other words, it promotes accountability. The model also provides the opportunity to the claimant for participation and dialogue, and imposes the obligation on the examiner to justify—characteristics which are central to the notion of an adequate explanation.

Even with respect to the interest in a rational decision, the interplay between an impartial examiner required to make full disclosure of adverse facts—as well as to justify his subsequent determination—and a claimant bent on making the best case for maintaining his beneficial status, is likely to result in a substantial verification of factual accuracy and a good assurance of a reasonable basis for the outcome. In a teacher or student conduct inquiry, for example, if the examiner is dispassionate, surely the requirements of listening to the grievant and of writing an opinion responsive to the issues afford some safeguards against factual inaccuracy and conclusory analysis—even if not as extensive as the safeguards of confrontation, cross-examination, and other trial-type procedures. ...

Even the more limited procedural safeguard of a reasons requirement provides, in and of itself, a not insubstantial assurance that an examiner will sift through conflicting factual statements and consider whether there is a reasonable basis for his conclusions. Again, such a requirement, though modest, also provides a real measure of accountability and tangible evidence of individualized consideration—assuming it is stringently enforced.

NOTES

1. Recollect that, in *Singh v. Canada (Minister of Employment and Immigration)*, Wilson J dismissed summarily the government's attempt to justify the denial of fundamental justice by reference to s. 1 of the Charter. Not only was the evidence presented totally inadequate but she also doubted whether it was appropriate to defend derogations from s. 7 rights by means of cost–benefit analysis. Do you agree with this assessment of the situation? If cost–benefit type analysis is appropriate in considering whether a denial of procedures is justifiable either in a common law or a constitutional case, how would counsel go about making this kind of case or defence? What evidence would be relevant and how would it be taken into account as an offset against the weight of the applicant's procedural claim? Are courts really in any position to evaluate government claims that the procedures being sought are ones that, in the overall scheme of government spending, cannot be afforded? If not, can and should courts respond to arguments to the effect that the provision of an oral, as opposed to a written, hearing is likely to effect only a minimal increase in the reliability of refugee claim determinations and that such limited improvement does not justify the extra costs involved? Or, are the courts' attempts to balance the procedural claims confined, first, to evaluating, by reference to some sense of community standards, the societal worth of the interest that is at stake, and, second, to being prepared to justify the extent of the procedures that are accorded by reference to community standards and perhaps hunches or "experience" as to which kind of procedures work best in what circumstances (such as traditional beliefs that *viva voce* testimony followed by cross-examination is the best way of ascertaining the truth whenever credibility is an issue)?

2. Put differently, can or should the rules of natural justice or the principles of fundamental justice be seen as mandating the best or fullest procedures irrespective of cost? If the answer to this question is a negative, then the need to balance or weigh claims by reference

to considerations in addition to ensuring "correct" outcomes has been accepted. The obligation then rests on the courts to provide some indication of how that measurement is going to be conducted and, more particularly, the kinds of evidence that will be relevant to the performance of this function. On the other hand, even if the law is concerned only with ensuring the best or fullest procedures irrespective of cost, by what standards is "the best" to be ascertained even if it is measured simply by reference to the production of "correct" outcomes?

3. More generally, there is the issue of the extent to which the courts are or should be willing to diminish the content of fundamental justice based on countervailing considerations. This gives rise to the further question of what are legitimate countervailing considerations and where should they be considered: in the context of teasing out the content of "fundamental justice" or as the basis for a s. 1 justification of what is otherwise a violation of the principles of fundamental justice? We have already encountered these questions in *Singh* and *Charkaoui*. The following case also raises them squarely.

Suresh v. Canada (Minister of Citizenship and Immigration)
[2002] 1 SCR 3 (Can.)

[Suresh was an applicant for landed immigration status. The minister issued a certificate under s. 53(1)(b) of the *Immigration Act* to the effect that Suresh was a danger to the security of Canada. This certificate was a prelude to an order deporting Suresh from Canada. While Suresh had the opportunity to make written submissions and file material with the minister, he did not have a copy of the immigration officer's report, based on which the certificate was issued and, as a consequence, was not able to respond to it orally or in writing. That report was itself derived from material emanating from the Canadian Security Intelligence Service.]

THE COURT: ...

3. Are the Procedures for Deportation Set Out in the Immigration Act Constitutionally Valid?

This appeal requires us to determine the procedural protections to which an individual is entitled under s. 7 of the Charter. In doing so, we find it helpful to consider the common law approach to procedural fairness articulated by L'Heureux-Dubé J in *Baker* ... . In elaborating what is required by way of procedural protection under s. 7 of the Charter in cases of this kind, we wish to emphasize that our proposals should be applied in a manner sensitive to the context of specific factual situations. What is important are the basic principles underlying these procedural protections. The principles of fundamental justice of which s. 7 speaks, though not identical to the duty of fairness elucidated in *Baker*, are the same principles underlying that duty. As Professor Hogg has said, "The common law rules [of procedural fairness] are in fact basic tenets of the legal system, and they have evolved in response to the same values and objectives as s. 7": see P.W. Hogg, *Constitutional Law of Canada*, (loose-leaf) Vol. 2, at para. 44.20. In *Singh* ... at pp. 212-13, Wilson J recognized that the principles of fundamental justice demand, at a minimum, compliance with the common law requirements of procedural fairness. Section 7 protects substantive as well as procedural rights: *Re BC Motor Vehicle Act* [[1985] 2 SCR 486 (BC)]. Insofar as procedural rights are concerned, the common law doctrine summarized in *Baker* properly recognizes the ingredients of fundamental justice.

We therefore find it appropriate to look to the factors discussed in *Baker* in determining not only whether the common law duty of fairness has been met, but also in deciding whether the safeguards provided satisfy the demands of s. 7. In saying this, we emphasize that, as is the case for the substantive aspects of s. 7 in connection with deportation to torture, we look to the common law factors not as an end in themselves, but to inform the s. 7 procedural analysis. At the end of the day, the common law is not constitutionalized; it is used to inform the constitutional principles that apply to this case.

[The court here set out the five *Baker* factors.]

The nature of the decision to deport bears some resemblance to judicial proceedings. While the decision is of a serious nature and made by an individual on the basis of evaluating and weighing risks, it is also a decision to which discretion must attach. The Minister must evaluate not only the past actions of and present dangers to an individual under her consideration pursuant to s. 53, but also the future behaviour of that individual. We conclude that the nature of the decision militates neither in favour of particularly strong, nor particularly weak, procedural safeguards.

The nature of the statutory scheme suggests the need for strong procedural safeguards. While the procedures set up under s. 40.1 of the *Immigration Act* are extensive and aim to ensure that certificates under that section are issued fairly and allow for meaningful participation by the person involved, there is a disturbing lack of parity between these protections and the lack of protections under s. 53(1)(b). In the latter case, there is no provision for a hearing, no requirement of written or oral reasons, no right of appeal—no procedures at all, in fact. As L'Heureux-Dubé J stated in *Baker* "[g]reater procedural protections ... will be required when no appeal procedure is provided within the statute, or when the decision is determinative of the issue and further requests cannot be submitted" (para. 24). This is particularly so where, as here, Parliament elsewhere in the Act has constructed fair and systematic procedures for similar measures.

The third factor requires us to consider the importance of the right affected. As discussed above, the appellant's interest in remaining in Canada is highly significant, not only because of his status as a Convention refugee, but also because of the risk of torture he may face on return to Sri Lanka as a member of the LTTE. The greater the effect on the life of the individual by the decision, the greater the need for procedural protections to meet the common law duty of fairness and the requirements of fundamental justice under s. 7 of the Charter. Deportation from Canada engages serious personal, financial and emotional consequences. It follows that this factor militates in favour of heightened procedural protections under s. 53(1)(b). Where, as here, a person subject to a s. 53(1)(b) opinion may be subjected to torture, this factor requires even more substantial protections.

As discussed above, Article 3 of the CAT, which explicitly prohibits the deportation of persons to states where there are "substantial grounds" for believing that the person would be "in danger of being subjected to torture," informs s. 7 of the Charter. It is only reasonable that the same executive that bound itself to the CAT intends to act in accordance with the CAT's plain meaning. Given Canada's commitment to the CAT, we find that the appellant had the right to procedural safeguards, at the s. 53(1)(b) stage of the proceedings. More particularly, the phrase "substantial grounds" raises a duty to afford an opportunity to demonstrate and defend those grounds.

The final factor we consider is the choice of procedures made by the agency. In this case, the Minister is free under the terms of the statute to choose whatever procedures she wishes in making a s. 53(1)(b) decision. As noted above, the Minister must be allowed considerable discretion in evaluating future risk and security concerns. This factor also suggests a degree of deference to the Minister's choice of procedures since Parliament has signaled the difficulty of the decision by leaving to the Minister the choice of how best to make it. At the same time, this need for deference must be reconciled with the elevated level of procedural protections mandated by the serious situation of refugees like Suresh, who if deported may face torture and violations of human rights in which Canada can neither constitutionally, nor under its international treaty obligations, be complicit.

Weighing these factors together with all the circumstances, we are of the opinion that the procedural protections required by s. 7 in this case do not extend to the level of requiring the Minister to conduct a full oral hearing or a complete judicial process. However, they require more than the procedure required by the Act under s. 53(1)(b)—that is, none—and they require more than Suresh received.

We find that a person facing deportation to torture under s. 53(1)(b) must be informed of the case to be met. Subject to privilege or similar valid reasons for reduced disclosure, such as safeguarding confidential public security documents, this means that the material on which the Minister is basing her decision must be provided to the individual, including memoranda such as Mr. Gautier's recommendation to the Minister. Furthermore, fundamental justice requires that an opportunity be provided to respond to the case presented to the Minister. While the Minister accepted written submissions from the appellant in this case, in the absence of access to the materials she was receiving from her staff and on which she based much of her decision, Suresh and his counsel had no knowledge of which factors they specifically needed to address, nor any chance to correct any factual inaccuracies or mischaracterizations. Fundamental justice requires that written submissions be accepted from the subject of the order after the subject has been provided with an opportunity to examine the material being used against him or her. The Minister must then consider these submissions along with the submissions made by the Minister's staff.

Not only must the refugee be informed of the case to be met, the refugee must also be given an opportunity to challenge the information of the Minister where issues as to its validity arise. Thus the refugee should be permitted to present evidence pursuant to s. 19 of the Act showing that his or her continued presence in Canada will not be detrimental to Canada, notwithstanding evidence of association with a terrorist organization. The same applies to the risk of torture on return. Where the Minister is relying on written assurances from a foreign government that a person would not be tortured, the refugee must be given an opportunity to present evidence and make submissions as to the value of such assurances.

It may be useful to comment further on assurances. A distinction may be drawn between assurances given by a state that it will not apply the death penalty (through a legal process) and assurances by a state that it will not resort to torture (an illegal process). We would signal the difficulty in relying too heavily on assurances by a state that it will refrain from torture in the future when it has engaged in illegal torture or allowed others to do so on its territory in the past. This difficulty becomes acute in cases where torture is inflicted not only with the collusion but through the impotence of the state in controlling the behaviour of its officials. Hence the need to distinguish between assurances regarding the death penalty and assurances regarding torture. The former are easier to monitor and generally more reliable than the latter.

In evaluating assurances by a foreign government, the Minister may also wish to take into account the human rights record of the government giving the assurances, the government's record in complying with its assurances, and the capacity of the government to fulfill the assurances, particularly where there is doubt about the government's ability to control its security forces. In addition, it must be remembered that before becoming a Convention refugee, the individual involved must establish a well-founded fear of persecution (although not necessarily torture) if deported.

The Minister must provide written reasons for her decision. These reasons must articulate and rationally sustain a finding that there are no substantial grounds to believe that the individual who is the subject of a s. 53(1)(b) declaration will be subjected to torture, execution or other cruel or unusual treatment, so long as the person under consideration has raised those arguments. The reasons must also articulate why, subject to privilege or valid legal reasons for not disclosing detailed information, the Minister believes the individual to be a danger to the security of Canada as required by the Act. In addition, the reasons must also emanate from the person making the decision, in this case the Minister, rather than take the form of advice or suggestion, such as the memorandum of Mr. Gautier. Mr. Gautier's report, explaining to the Minister the position of Citizenship and Immigration Canada, is more like a prosecutor's brief than a statement of reasons for a decision.

These procedural protections need not be invoked in every case, as not every case of deportation of a Convention refugee under s. 53(1)(b) will involve risk to an individual's fundamental right to be protected from torture or similar abuses. It is for the refugee to establish a threshold showing that a risk of torture or similar abuse exists before the Minister is obliged to consider fully the possibility. This showing need not be proof of the risk of torture to that person, but the individual must make out a *prima facie* case that there may be a risk of torture upon deportation. If the refugee establishes that torture is a real possibility, the Minister must provide the refugee with all the relevant information and advice she intends to rely on, provide the refugee an opportunity to address that evidence in writing, and after considering all the relevant information, issue responsive written reasons. This is the minimum required to meet the duty of fairness and fulfill the requirements of fundamental justice under s. 7 of the Charter.

The Minister argues that even if the procedures used violated Suresh's s. 7 rights, that violation is justified as a reasonable limit under s. 1 of the Charter. Despite the legitimate purpose of s. 53(1)(b) of the *Immigration Act* in striking a balance between the need to fulfil Canada's commitments with respect to refugees and the maintenance of the safety and good order of Canadian society, the lack of basic procedural protections provided to Suresh cannot be justified by s. 1 in our view. Valid objectives do not, without more, suffice to justify limitations on rights. The limitations must be connected to the objective and be proportional. Here the connection is lacking. A valid purpose for excepting some Convention refugees from the protection of s. 53(1) of the Act does not justify the failure of the Minister to provide fair procedures where this exception involves a risk of torture upon deportation. Nor do the alleged fundraising activities of Suresh rise to the level of exceptional conditions contemplated by Lamer J in *Re BC Motor Vehicle Act, supra*. Consequently, the issuance of a s. 53(1)(b) opinion relating to him without the procedural protections mandated by s. 7 is not justified under s. 1.

Appeal allowed.

NOTES

1. Is it appropriate to give any deference to the procedural choices of officials when a Charter right or freedom is at stake? Why should the courts engage in anything other than correctness review in such situations?

2. Recollect our previous discussion of where balancing of interests should take place in the context of s. 7 challenges to procedures. In this case, one of the possible countervailing concerns is that of national security. Should the courts consider any claims to protect information in the name of national security as part of an evaluation of the content of the "principles of fundamental justice" or as part of a s. 1 justification for which the burden of proof or persuasion rests with the government?

GENERAL STATUTES ABOUT PROCEDURES

The idea that there was utility in the enactment of a general procedural statute applicable to a broad spectrum of administrative decision making found its most prominent early expression in the US *Administrative Procedure Act* of 1946. This statute now finds equivalents in virtually all the US states.

Relevant Statutes

In Canada, the first serious consideration of this issue occurred in the 1960s in Alberta and Ontario. In 1966, Alberta enacted its *Administrative Procedures Act* (SA 1966, c. 1). Shortly before, in 1964, the Ontario government had appointed former Chief Justice McRuer to conduct an investigation of the state of administrative justice in the province. This was the Ontario Royal Commission Inquiry into Civil Rights (more commonly known as the McRuer commission). In volume 1 of its first report, issued in 1968, the commission recommended the enactment of a general procedural statute, leading to the *Statutory Powers Procedure Act* of 1971 (SO 1971, c. 47). The provisions of the current Act, which in most respects are far more detailed than the US *Administrative Procedure Act*, are set out in Appendix Three, together with Alberta's *Administrative Procedures and Jurisdiction Act* (formerly the *Administrative Procedures Act*), Québec's *Act Respecting Administrative Justice*, and British Columbia's *Administrative Tribunals Act*.

A perusal of these statutes allows us to assess the usefulness of codification. It also provides a sense of the kinds of procedural claims that are discussed in the balance of this chapter. Indeed, the subjects of the rules in these statutory procedural codes and much of their substance are derived from the common law. Throughout this chapter, compare them to each other and to the common law. What is the continuing significance of the common law in terms of the choice of procedures? Does it govern issues that are not provided for in the rules? Is it a useful or authoritative source of experience for applying the requirements in the rules that are expressed in general terms—for example, a requirement of a "reasonable opportunity" or "reasonable information"? Should these codes be regarded as exhaustive codes of procedure for those decision-makers to which they apply? Or are there occasions where the common law might supplement them and require additional protections? Selected features of the procedural safeguards codified in these statutes are now briefly described.

Ontario's Statutory Powers Procedure Act

Among Canadian jurisdictions, Ontario has the most detailed statutory codification of procedural safeguards. Amendments to the *Statutory Powers Procedure Act*, RSO 1990, c. S.22 (SPPA) in 1994 expressly empowered tribunals to which the Act applied to make rules governing their practice and procedures (s. 25.1). Through this rule-making mechanism, the SPPA added to and refined tribunals' procedural powers and obligations. For example, while the SPPA had long required that parties to a proceeding be given reasonable notice of a hearing (s. 6(1)), the amended Act authorized tribunals to make rules providing for in-person, written, and electronic hearings (s. 5.1) and provided notice requirements specific to each type of hearing (ss. 6(3)-(5)). Similarly, while the SPPA already provided for pre-hearing disclosure of reasonable information of any allegations impugning the "good character, propriety of conduct or competence of a party" (s. 8), the amendments authorized tribunals to make rules providing for discovery and disclosure of written and oral evidence (s. 5.4).

The SPPA provides that parties (s. 10) and witnesses (s. 11) may be represented by counsel, though witness's counsel are limited to an advisory role. The Act prescribes detailed rules regarding the admissibility of evidence and the use of evidence previously admitted in another court or tribunal proceeding (ss. 15 and 15.1), and authorizes tribunals to take official notice of facts and opinions within their specialized knowledge (s. 16). It also confers on tribunals a broad discretion to order adjournments to ensure the adequacy of a hearing.

The SPPA requires tribunals to give their final decision and order in writing, and written reasons for the decision if requested by a party (s. 17). The Act specifies that these and other procedural requirements may be waived with the consent of the parties and the tribunal (s. 4).

In addition to setting out these procedural safeguards, the SPPA confers on tribunals broad powers to structure their proceedings efficiently. Tribunals are authorized to make interim decisions and orders (s. 16.1), to enact rules allowing them to classify the different kinds of proceedings and applications that come before them and apply to them different procedural rules (s. 4.7), to use alternative dispute resolution techniques (s. 4.8), to dismiss proceedings without a hearing for various reasons (s. 4.6), and to refuse to process documents relating to the commencement of a hearing that are untimely or deficient in some respect (s. 4.5).

To encourage timely decision making, tribunals are required to establish guidelines setting out the usual timeframe for completing proceedings and any interim procedural steps (s. 16.2). Like all rules made under the SPPA, these guidelines must be made available to the public (s. 17).

Alberta's Administrative Procedures and Jurisdiction Act

Alberta's *Administrative Procedures and Jurisdiction Act*, RSA 2000, c. A-3 is much less detailed than Ontario's SPPA. Where the Act applies, it provides for notice to affected parties in advance of the exercise of a statutory power (s. 3). Where an authority proposes to act in a manner that adversely affects a party's rights, the Act guarantees the party an opportunity to provide evidence and make submissions to the authority (though not necessarily at an in-person hearing) as well as a right to disclosure of facts and allegations in sufficient detail to allow the party to understand and respond to the case against it (s. 4). Finally, where an authority acts in a manner adverse to a party's rights, it must provide that party with written reasons, including its findings of fact (s. 7).

Québec's Act Respecting Administrative Justice

Québec's *Act Respecting Administrative Justice*, RSQ, c. J-3 extends the duty to act fairly to individual decisions by government departments and bodies whose members are in the majority appointed by the government or by a minister and whose personnel is appointed under the Québec *Public Service Act* (ss. 2 and 3).

The Act sets out broadly worded principles and obligations to be respected by government decision-makers, including that citizens be given an opportunity to provide information relevant to the decision, that decisions be clearly and concisely communicated, and that "directives" (policies, guidelines) relevant to the decision be publicly available (s. 4). In particular, unfavourable decisions regarding licences or permits may not be taken without prior notice to the affected citizen, disclosure of complaints or objections, and an opportunity to respond and provide relevant documentation (see s. 5 and *Sécurité 2010 (SNC) c. Ministère de la Sécurité Publique*, [2003] JQ No. 2864 (CSQ), at para. 102). Similarly, unfavourable decisions regarding benefits or indemnities may not be taken without affording the affected citizen an opportunity to provide all information useful for the making of the decision (s. 6). Decision-makers must advise citizens affected by a decision of their rights to apply for a review of the decision and to participate fairly in the review process (ss. 6-7). Finally, all decision-makers must provide reasons for any unfavourable decisions that indicate avenues for further review (including time limits) other than judicial review (s. 8).

The Act further sets out rules that govern the proceedings of tribunals empowered to adjudicate disputes between a citizen and an administrative (or decentralized) authority. These rules are also broadly framed and provide for an opportunity to be heard in (generally) public hearings. In addition to confirming that adjudicative bodies have broad, flexible powers relating to the admission of evidence, the Act requires these bodies to take measures to "where expedient," provide reconciliation between the parties and provide "if necessary" fair and impartial assistance to each party during the hearing (s. 12). All final decisions (not just unfavourable ones) must be in writing and supported by written reasons (s. 13).

British Columbia's Administrative Tribunals Act

British Columbia's *Administrative Tribunals Act*, SBC 2004, c. 45 (ATA) contains a detailed list of provisions that enable tribunals to manage the proceedings before them and ensure that parties are treated fairly. These govern, among other things: the serving of notice or documents, including the manner of service (ss. 19-21); representation (s. 32); the participatory rights of interveners (s. 33); the power to compel witness testimony or order documentary disclosure (s. 34); the form of the hearings (written, oral, or electronic); the examination of witnesses (s. 38); the adjournment of proceedings (s. 39); the admission of evidence (s. 40); and the publicity of the hearing (s. 41). These powers, authorities, and obligations may be adopted by tribunals through direct reference to the ATA within their enabling legislation. In order to reflect the unique circumstances of particular tribunals, these powers may also be adopted in modified form through appropriate amendments to the tribunals' enabling statutes. See generally D. Flood, E. Loughran, and R. Rogers, "British Columbia's New Administrative Tribunals Act" (2005), 18 *CJALP* 217.

Like Ontario's SPPA, the ATA empowers tribunals to make rules governing their practice and procedure tailored to their specific circumstances "to facilitate the just and timely resolution" of matters and requires that the tribunal make such rules accessible to the public (s. 11). The ATA sets out a non-exhaustive list of areas that may be covered by such rules, which include the receipt and disclosure of evidence before and during the hearing, notice requirements, adjournments, extension or abridgement of time limits, exclusion of witnesses, and access to tribunal documents.

In order to encourage the timely resolution of cases, the ATA requires tribunals to publish practice directives setting out the usual time period for completing the procedural steps within an application and the usual time frame to make a decision and issue reasons. Though non-binding, these directives nevertheless inform the public and parties of the timelines they may expect tribunals to meet.

Other provisions, while not linked directly to hearing procedures, allow tribunals to deal with applications before them in a more flexible, timely, and effective fashion by empowering them to dismiss applications where parties fail to comply with rules, orders, or time limits (s. 18) and to appoint tribunal members, staff, or other persons to conduct alternative dispute resolution processes (s. 28).

The Case for General Statutes: An Appraisal

Whether procedural codes are desirable is a complex and difficult issue. Its resolution ultimately depends on attitudes about allocation of responsibility for the choice and content of procedures between legislatures and courts. There are at least two kinds of reasons for adopting one. The first is a belief that the content of the common law is unsatisfactory and that the courts are not likely to make appropriate changes. The second is a desire for some distinctive attributes of the form of legislation or the legislative process. There are also two kinds of difficulties. The first is the technical or craft challenge of drafting, especially the needs to avoid inconsistencies or gaps and to integrate the statute with the common law. Throughout this chapter, consider the extent to which the Ontario, Alberta, Québec, and British Columbia statutes have met this challenge. The second difficulty is the need to accommodate diversity among the agencies, and change. That diversity has obvious implications for procedures. The change may be in the preferences about specific procedural requirements, the common law background, or the functions of agencies. One way of meeting this possibility presents again the general issue of the allocation of functions among legislatures, courts, and agencies.

Some of these difficulties can be seen in a concrete form in the SPPA, which will be the focus of our assessment of procedural codes. In proposing it, the McRuer commission made three criticisms of the work of the courts (McRuer report, no. 1, vol. 1, 146-47):

> (1) Until the courts have made a decision it cannot be said with certainty whether the rules of natural justice do or do not apply to a particular statutory power of decision. This uncertainty gives rise to two administrative difficulties:
>> (a) The tribunal itself does not know whether it is required to adhere to the rules of natural justice and to govern its procedure accordingly;
>> (b) Those who may be affected by the decisions of the tribunal do not know what their procedural rights are.
> (2) Even where it is reasonably clear that a fair procedure must be followed, the requirements of fair procedure in the exercise of a particular statutory power may be uncertain.
> (3) It is difficult for the courts to adopt rules of procedures suitable to insure the just exercise of all statutory powers of decision by the interpretative device if the rules of natural justice are to be applied. In the [*Calgary Power*] case the alternatives open to the courts were:
>> (a) To hold that the Minister before authorizing expropriation should give notice to the owner and afford him a hearing, thus permitting him to make representations;
>> (b) To hold that the rules of natural justice did not apply.
> There was no intermediate course under our law.

The commission rejected leaving development of the law to the courts, because "that development will not be systematic, and it will inevitably be a slow process attended by much uncertainty. ... The courts have not been consistent in determining the application of the rules of natural justice and there will always be areas requiring fair procedure to which the rules of natural justice do not apply." It rejected making detailed rules in each statute conferring a power to decide because the rules would be inflexible and impose too great a burden on the legislature, and it rejected making general detailed rules because of the diversity among agencies. It recommended a combination of general minimum rules and power to make detailed rules for individual agencies. The minimum general rules were to be a "procedural *Bill of Rights*" and were to govern all agencies, whether their functions were judicial or administrative. Only limited and particular exceptions were to be permitted. These rules included rights to notice, to a public hearing, to counsel, to cross-examination, to written reasons, and to an appeal. The detailed rules were to be made primarily by a statutory powers procedure rules committee (McRuer report, no. 1, vol. 1, 208-13). Obviously, these recommendations were more stringent than the Act itself. A bill based on them was introduced but withdrawn. Throughout this chapter, consider the commission's assessment of the common law—both its content and its capacity for change—and its recommendations for allocation of responsibility for specifying procedural requirements among general statutes, individual statutes, a specialized "procedures" agency, and the courts.

Contemporaneously with the enactment of the SPPA, efforts were made to tailor the procedures applicable to different agencies through the amendment of their enabling statutes to provide, among other things, for the selective application of the SPPA's provisions. The *Civil Rights Statute Law Amendment Act, 1971*, SO 1971, c. 50, for example, amended a multitude of individual statutes. Some of the recurring provisions were standards for granting licences, rights to hearings and appeals, exclusions of the SPPA, and requirements in addition to the SPPA—for example, requirements to record oral evidence. Some of the exclusions of the SPPA do not require any other procedures; for example, s. 27 amended the *Department of Correctional Services Act, 1968*, SO 1968, c. 28, by adding a provision that the SPPA "does not apply to proceedings for the discipline of inmates in correctional institutions." (Now see *Ministry of Correctional Services Act*, RSO 1990, c. M.22, s. 58.) In contrast, some of the exclusions do require different procedures. For example, s. 38 amended the *Family Benefits Act* (now RSO 1990, c. F.2) to provide that the SPPA does not apply to the determinations about entitlement made by the director (s. 13(9)), but requires the director to give notice of a proposed decision and reasons to the applicant or recipient and gives an opportunity to make written representations (s. 13(1)). The applicant or recipient may appeal to the board of review, and the SPPA applies to its proceedings—although with modifications: the hearings are to be held *in camera* and some supplementary requirements are imposed (s. 14).

During the 1970s, particular statutory provisions about the application of the SPPA continued to be made, and plans to continue this kind of individualization in a comprehensive way seemed to be in place. The *Manual of Practice*, issued by the Ontario Department of Justice and the Attorney General in 1972, stated:

> The application of the rules where a hearing is required "otherwise by law" is a transitional provision pending review and amendment of the existing statutes to provide expressly for hearings in appropriate instances. All statutes of Ontario establishing tribunals are now being reviewed for this purpose. When the amendments have been completed, the expression "otherwise by law" will cease to have significance except as a residual protection.
>
> The Minimum Rules, as their name implies, are limited to minimum procedural requirements that may be imposed generally on all tribunals to which they apply. In the course of reviewing the statutes it became apparent that additional rules for certain tribunals should be enacted and that the Minimum Rules should be varied in their application to certain tribunals to meet special circumstances. Amendments to these statutes therefore, in addition to specifying that a hearing is required, in many instances also enact provisions imposing some tribunals additional procedural requirements or overriding for some tribunals certain of the Minimum Rules.

If these plans existed, they seem to have been abandoned and, with the 1994 amendments, the heading "Minimum Rules" disappeared (though *quaere* to what effect). Since there are thousands of statutory powers, the job would have been a large one. However, the Harris Conservative government resurrected the project in 1995 to the extent that in many of its regulatory reforms, it explicitly excluded the Act's application to new or reformed decision-makers. As of the end of 2002, there were approximately 50 statutory provisions explicitly excluding the Act's operation entirely (as opposed to modifying it).

The SPPA is now almost 40 years old but its impact on Ontario administrative law has never been assessed fully. Indeed, the design of any kind of useful assessment would be a problematic exercise. Nonetheless, there are some observations that can be made with a reasonable degree of confidence.

First, the promise of the 1971 Act—that it would provide not just a model to be considered in relation to all new administrative processes in the province but also a framework for the ongoing and systematic assessment of Ontario's administrative processes—foundered. Under the original Act, as recommended by McRuer, the Statutory Powers Procedure Rules Committee was established and given responsibility for overall scrutiny of the procedural rules of virtually all administrative tribunals in the province. However, because of an absence of political and resource commitment on the part of successive Ontario governments to the committee, it never came close to achieving its goals and had effectively ceased to exist before its legal abolition in the 1994 amendments.

Second, the generality of many of the Act's provisions and, more particularly, their failure to deal with or anticipate some of the more intransigent procedural problems now being experienced by Ontario's administrative tribunals meant that the common law of judicial review remained an important forum for the development of procedural norms. Indeed, this was exacerbated with the advent of the procedural fairness doctrine and the completely understandable conclusion of the Ontario Court of Appeal in *Webb* that the Act's minimum procedural rules could not be read as applying to all bodies that after *Nicholson* had become subject to an obligation of procedural fairness.

On the positive side, the Act did establish a standard of procedural fairness that could not be ignored by those charged with the development of procedural norms. As such, the Act did have a useful educative effect and almost certainly led to a diminution in the exposure of many decision-makers to judicial review on procedural grounds.

With the 1989 release of *Directions*, a report prepared for the Ontario Liberal government by Robert W. Macaulay (a former Progressive Conservative Cabinet minister, vastly experienced administrative lawyer, and recent chair of the Ontario Energy Board), there came to be an increased interest in the revision and modernization of the Act. In May 1992, under a now NDP government, the Ministry of the Attorney General began discussions with ministries and agencies about the reforms recommended by Macaulay and possible alternatives. Then, in the fall of 1992, the Society of Ontario Adjudicators and Regulators (SOAR), which represented some 300 tribunal chairs, members, and staff, undertook a major project that involved not only responding to Macaulay but also making its own comprehensive proposals for legislative action.

This led to the formal submission of a detailed report in December 1993, *Proposal for Amendment of the SPPA*. This document ranged over a very large number of issues, including the need for additional provisions covering such matters as generic hearings, stated cases, governmental policy statements, panel consultations, complaints against members, protection from liability, mediation, costs, enforcement of undertakings, and the like. This ambitious series of recommendations did not attract Cabinet support. Instead, the government introduced more limited amendments to the Act in a *Statute Law Amendment Act*, which received Royal Assent on December 8, 1994 and was proclaimed in force on April 1, 1995 (SO 1994, c. 27). Its most notable changes were the recognition of both written and electronic hearings and the conferral of procedural rulemaking powers on bodies subject to the Act. Among its negative features was a repeal of the provisions empowering the Statutory Powers Procedure Rules Committee. Subsequently, further amendments in 1997, 1999, and 2002 added some of the other features identified in the Proposal (SO 1997, c. 23; SO 1999, c. 12, Sched. B; SO 2002, c. 17, Sched. F). These included provisions for alternative dispute resolution and the capacity to award costs. For a more detailed analysis of the impact of the 1994 amendments, see Priest and Burton, "Amendments to the *Statutory Powers Procedure Act* (Ontario); Analysis and Comments," Law Society of Upper Canada, Continuing Legal Education Program: *Recent Developments in Administrative Law* (Toronto, January 17, 1995).

Consider also Allars, "A General Tribunal Procedure Statute for New South Wales" (1993), 4 *Public Law Review* 19 (who, after an evaluation of the Ontario statute, remains sceptical about the usefulness of such an exercise for the state of New South Wales); Asimow, "Toward a New California *Administrative Procedure Act*" (1992), 39 *UCLA LR* 1067 (who is very supportive of the revision and expansion of the 1942 pioneer California Act); and the 1980 Law Reform Commission of Canada Working Paper no. 25, *Independent Administrative Agencies*, at 140-42, and 1985 *Report on Independent Administrative Agencies* (no. 26), at 51-52 and 66-72, in which the recommendation is for a compromise—a statute that sets out minimum procedural standards coupled with a conferral on all agencies of an independent authority to make procedural rules in the context of a notice and comment process. (See also Justice Canada's 1995 proposal for a federal *Administrative Hearings Powers and Procedures Act*.)

One of the arguments that Asimow makes (at 1073-79) for the revision of the California statute is that, by setting a minimum standard for all agencies and requiring formal rulemaking procedures for and publication of all additional procedural rules, it would force procedural rules out into the open and thereby facilitate more effective as well as non-lawyer representation before certain agencies. His assessment of the California situation was that there are too many agencies relying on unpublicized procedural rules that were known only to staff and those who deal regularly with that agency. That not only served to diminish the ranks of those who can represent effectively members of the public dealing with the agency but also left great leeway for inconsistent and arbitrary variation in the procedures being used. Notably, both Ontario and British Columbia require that procedural rules adopted pursuant to their statutory codes be made available to the public. Québec's *Act Respecting Administrative Justice*, while not requiring the administration to engage in a formal rulemaking process, requires that all "directives" governing decision-makers be available for consultation by citizens. In other Canadian jurisdictions, an empirical study of the extent to which agencies rely on unpublished procedural rules would be a potentially revealing exercise.

SPECIFIC CONTENT ISSUES

In this principal part of the chapter, we examine a range of specific content issues that have arisen not only in the context of common law, Charter, and *Bill of Rights* claims to procedural protections but also in the interpretation of provisions in the general statutes. We have divided our consideration of these issues into two sections. First, we look at pre-hearing content issues. These include the issues of notice, claims to pre-hearing disclosure or discovery of the evidence to be relied on, and delay in the processing of administrative proceedings. The second part involves a study of the nature of the actual hearing itself: Should it be oral or written or a mixture of both? Are the parties entitled to representation by counsel, an agent, or friend? If there is an oral hearing, is there a right to cross-examine the other witnesses? Then, and perhaps most significantly, we approach the issue of evidence in the administrative process where our main concerns will be the types of evidence that a decision-maker may rely on and the extent of the decision-maker's obligation to reveal that evidence to affected persons. In this context, we will examine confidentiality claims as advanced in a variety of situations. Indeed, these claims cut across the first and second parts of this section in that they may also be advanced at the pre-hearing stage in resistance to attempts to obtain pre-hearing discovery of the evidence that is going to be relied on. Finally, we tease out the detail of the duty to provide reasons, a topic already encountered in our consideration of *Baker* in chapter 2 of this text.

More generally, we should also concede that, particularly since the advent of the procedural fairness doctrine, a clear division between the pre-hearing and the actual hearing stage in a proceeding does not fit all forms of decision making to which procedural fairness obligations attach. This point is made cogently by Bayne ("The Content of Procedural Fairness in Administrative Decision-Making" (1994), 68 *Aust. LJ* 297, at 302) in the following extracts in which he draws a distinction between adjudicative style processes and decision making made in an administrative environment.

> The administrative process is not confined largely to the one continuous hearing which is characteristic of the adversarial process. Rather, the interchange of information and submission between the decision-maker and the person affected takes various forms, such as through letters, telephone calls, and sometimes personal interview. These interchanges occur over a lengthy period, and from the decision-maker's point of view, occur at the same time as many other matters call for attention. The decision-maker will be presented not only with new information, but sometimes with a new theory of just what are the central issues in the matter. ...
>
> The administrator is not an adjudicator supervising an adversarial proceeding within a context bounded by time and by some form of pleading which will have shaped the issues for decision.

It is within this wider decision-making context, rather than the framework that we have assumed for the general purposes of this chapter, that many procedural fairness arguments will fall for resolution. We return to this theme in the sections on oral hearings and on disclosure and official notice.

Pre-Hearing Issues

Notice

Whatever other procedural rights a person entitled to a hearing may have, notice is necessary simply because, without notice, the other rights cannot be exercised effectively or at all (assuming we may ignore alternatives such as prior knowledge from some other source, and waiver). Most of the problems about notice can be put into one or other of four groups: (1) problems about form, (2) problems about the manner of service, (3) problems about time, and (4) problems about the contents.

Two forms of notice are common—written and oral. Written notice is the more usual, and probably the norm that the courts will require unless the context permits some different form. The SPPA seems to assume the notice it requires will be written or electronic; the

Alberta Act does not. What about oral notice? The "fairness development" makes it a reasonable possibility for some situations; recall, for example, *Webb*, as discussed and extracted in chapter 3 of this text.

Personal service—that is, notice handed to or told to the party in some personal way—is another norm that the courts will probably require, unless the context permits giving notice in some other way. Some agencies—for example, an environmental assessment board—make decisions that affect large and indefinite numbers of persons in indeterminate ways. Usually, the means of giving notice is specified by legislation (see, for example, SPPA, s. 24(1)), and it is usually some form of public notice. If no legislative specification is made, presumably the courts will permit notice to be given in some public way—for example, advertisements in newspapers—although recent Canadian authority is sparse.

In *Re Hardy and Minister of Education* (1985), 22 DLR (4th) 394 (BC SC), McLachlin J (as she then was) said,

> It would be unreasonable to suggest that every resident in the school district must be personally apprised of the intention to close the school. What is required, it seems to me, is that the proposed closure be made known throughout the district generally so that it can reasonably be expected to come to the attention of interested persons, and that they be accorded sufficient time and opportunity to fairly present their side of the case before a final decision is taken.

A problem about the adequacy of notice of this kind arose in *Re Central Ontario Coalition and Ontario Hydro* (1984), 10 DLR (4th) 341 (Ont. Div. Ct.). More practically, the problem was ultimately about notice requirements for decisions about the location of electrical transmission lines, particularly large high-voltage lines. Ontario Hydro operated a large nuclear power plant on the east shore of Lake Huron. There was one large transmission line running roughly southwest from this plant to the Hydro's grid of high-voltage lines, but it was inadequate to serve the entire projected capacity of the plant. Hydro therefore wanted to build another line, and undertook an extensive study that included environmental and technical issues. It proposed that the line go south, toward London, and proposed alternatives, especially one in which the line ran east, toward a point just south of Barrie. These proposals designated broad paths, in which a precise line would be chosen later. This proposal was submitted to a "joint board," which was formed from the Ontario Municipal Board and the Environmental Assessment Board under legislation designed to enable planning and environmental considerations to be accommodated efficiently. Clearly, notice to the affected public was required and, just as clearly, service of everyone who might have been affected was not required. The board made an order for notice that included personal service on some municipalities and individuals, and for publication in newspapers. The notices were published in newspapers circulating in the location of the alternative route, but the lines were described simply as being in "southwestern Ontario," and no maps were included. A hearing was held, and very few of the participants were from the alternative route. The board rejected the proposal, and decided that the line should go east, along the alternative path. A group of people living or owning properties in this path sought review on the ground that the phrase "Southwestern Ontario" did not denote the alternative route, and succeeded.

This group submitted evidence that in a survey of 900 people living in this route, fewer than 5 percent learned of the line until after the board's decision. Reid J said:

To anyone not already familiar with Hydro's plans and what Hydro used the term "Southwest-ern Ontario" to mean, the notice published in the newspapers of the Board's first hearing would convey very little. Reference to southwestern Ontario could, and in fact did, mislead some people in areas, or with interests in an area, that could be affected in some way, into thinking that they would not be affected, believing, as they did, that they did not live in southwestern Ontario or have interests there. No idea was given, beyond that vague term, of the size or loca-tion of the six areas that were being proposed by Hydro for locating transmission lines or other installations. When it is considered that the first meeting was the first step in a process that could lead to the expropriation of private property and that people who did not appear or were not represented at that meeting would receive no further notice of plan stage hearings, the in-adequacy of the notice, judged in the light of the applicable statutes and of the common law, was, in my opinion, obvious.

· · ·

In reaching this conclusion I have not overlooked Hydro's reliance on the extensive efforts it made to acquaint the public with its plan stage proposals, efforts that did in fact generate a very considerable amount of study and discussion among an impressive number of people and considerable newspaper report and comment. Was that group so large and knowing, and that public discussion so pervasive, that any inadequacy in the notice given was a mere formality?

In other words, would a reasonable person have understood it, in all the circumstances, notwithstanding its inadequacy?

· · ·

One should take the circumstances into account in determining whether a notice was "reasonable."

There is no question that Hydro made a conscientious effort to publicize its proposed ex-pansion before the Board's hearings commenced yet there is simply no basis for concluding that, as a result, all, or even most, affected persons in the M3 route study area would, as a result, comprehend from the notice given that their property might be affected. One could thus totally disregard the testimony of individuals, to the effect that they did not so comprehend the notice, and still conclude, I think inevitably, that the notice was inherently defective.

In *Re Joint Board under the Consolidated Hearings Act and Ontario Hydro* (1985), 19 DLR (4th) 193 (Ont. CA), the notices for a similar kind of undertaking were tested. This time, Ontario Hydro sought to construct transmission lines in the eastern part of the province and used the term "Eastern Ontario" in the notices. For both the Divisional Court and the Court of Appeal, another issue was dominant, but Zuber JA referred to the *Central Ontario Coalition* case, and said, "It is not necessary to pass on the correctness of that decision. It is necessary only to say that that case is readily distinguishable from the case at hand. In the *Central Ontario* case, it was the view of the Divisional Court that the use of the term 'South-western Ontario' rendered the notice inadequate since it was far from clear that the term 'Southwestern Ontario' included the area where the undertaking was to be located. In the case at hand it cannot be said that the term 'Eastern Ontario' does not plainly include the area where the undertaking is proposed to be built. No one has argued otherwise."

The Law Reform Commission of Canada, in its working paper no. 25, "Independent Ad-ministrative Agencies" (1980), said:

5.1 Independent agencies should experiment with innovative notice techniques in connection with those types of proceedings where it is important to ensure that an agency will obtain a balanced picture of the issues at stake because there is a wide range of constituent interests affected by decisions flowing from the proceedings.

One approach might be for an agency to compile a list of persons and groups known to be interested in matters it deals with, and to provide them with comprehensive abstracts of issues coming before the agency. While the agency might be criticized as hand-picking potential intervenors, one must assume a reasonable amount of good faith on the part of the agency. As well, this is suggested as a way of augmenting more universal communication through the mass media, such as newspapers, radio and television.

One progressive approach to notice, adopted by the CRTC among other agencies, entails maintaining an extensive mailing list to which anyone can have his name added. The list includes libraries which can serve to extend notice even further. Notice is sent to everyone on the mailing list, advising of the application, where it can be inspected in Ottawa and elsewhere, and how interventions can be made. This complements another useful procedure which the CRTC requires by regulation: applicants for licence renewals are required to broadcast information regarding their applications, allowing for direct contact with the consumers of their product. New draft rules of procedure for the CRTC Telecommunications Proceedings also provide a mechanism whereby any interested subscribers may register with the CRTC and indicate specific areas of interest, for example specific carrier rates or conditions of service. They will then automatically receive copies of any applications relating thereto. The new rules would also create a subscription list of those interested in receiving copies of tariffs on a regular basis.

Giving notice by mail creates the possibility that it will not be received in time—or not be received at all. Here are two relatively simple cases that consider whether the crucial date— the date on which the notice was "given"—is the date of mailing or the date of receipt.

Re City of Winnipeg and Torchinsky (1981), 129 DLR (3d) 170 (Man. QB) involved assessment procedures specified by the *City of Winnipeg Act*, SM 1971, c. 105. Section 182(1) established procedures for making assessment rolls, and s. 182(2) provided that, if a new assessment was made, the assessor "shall send by mail or leave with the person assessed … a notice of assessment … which shall state … the reason for … the new assessment." Owners were entitled to appeal the assessments to the Board of Revision, and s. 187(1) required the board to give public notice of the dates and places for hearings of these appeals. Section 187(1)(b) required any owner who wished to appeal to give notice to the board at least ten days before the first day of the hearings. Last, s. 187(3) prohibited the board from hearing an appeal about a property if the appeal was not made "within the time limited by this section."

A new assessment was made of Torchinsky's property and on April 10, 1981 the assessor mailed her notice, which described the right of appeal and gave May 12 as the date for beginning the hearings. This notice did not arrive until May 12. Torchinsky gave notice within a few days, and the city sought to prohibit the board from hearing the appeal on the ground that the notice of appeal was late. Dewar CJQB dismissed the claim and said: "[T]he choice of messenger was an unfortunate one. … [I]f the specified date is not subject to extension or variation … the situation is as if notice has not been given. … The purpose of section 183 is to preserve the validity of an assessment affected by technical or procedural error or defect. …

[I]t does not affect or purport to affect the right to complain." Nor did s. 187(3) prohibit the board from hearing the appeal, because the 10-day period was directory and not mandatory.

Contrast *Torchinsky* to *Re Rymal and Niagara Escarpment Commission* (1981), 129 DLR (3d) 363 (Ont. CA). The *Niagara Escarpment Commission Act, 1973*, SO 1973, c. 52 gave landowners affected by decisions of the commission a right to appeal to the minister of housing. It required the commission to mail notices of decisions to owners and specified that notices of appeal must be received by the ministry within 14 days of the date of mailing by the commission. On September 8, 1980, the commission mailed notices of a decision to permit a residence to be built. One owner, Spencer, received this notice on September 17 and immediately mailed a notice of appeal that did not arrive until September 23—one day late. The owner who had sought the decision made an application to prohibit the minister from considering the appeal and failed. The Divisional Court exercised its general discretion in granting remedies, a topic considered in chapter 18 of this text, and the Court of Appeal affirmed. Cory JA (as he then was) said:

> The unreliability of the mail is a relatively new factor that has entered the lives of Canadians. This statute, among many others, clearly assumed that the mail service would be reliable and reasonably prompt. Mr Spencer obviously proceeded upon the old-fashioned but mistaken premise that the mail was still reliable and reasonably prompt when he entrusted his notice of appeal to the Post Office. The disruption of the mail at this critical time coupled with the new factor of unreliability of the mails, are aspects of this case that could properly be taken into account by the Court in refusing to exercise its discretion and grant the judicial relief sought.

The notice must be given long enough before the date of the proposed hearing to give the party enough time to decide whether to participate and to prepare. Clearly, the length of time needed will depend on the nature of the interests and the issues. The notice must also give enough information about the issues to enable the party to prepare to respond. A simple example of this requirement about the contents is *R v. Ontario Racing Commission, ex parte Taylor* (1970), 13 DLR (3d) 405 (Ont. HC); aff'd. 15 DLR (3d) 430 (Ont. CA). One of Taylor's horses had an intestinal upset and he had a veterinarian give medication that, unknown to him, contained a prohibited substance, procaine. He was questioned by the stewards, who showed him their ruling and referred it to the commission. After a hearing, he was suspended and fined. He sought *certiorari* and succeeded. There were several issues raised; about notice, Osler J said (at 411-12):

> There was undoubtedly written notice given to Mr Taylor. The notice was dated August 21st and advised that the investigation and ruling of the stewards had been referred to the Commission and that the matter had been placed on the agenda for September 2nd. It set out that the stewards had made an investigation into a positive test reported by the provincial analyst involving the horse "Simply Smashing" which was trained by Mr Taylor and that the stewards had applied rule 130(3)(a) to the case. The second paragraph of the letter addressed to Mr Taylor was in the following terms:
>
> > This matter has been placed on the agenda for the next meeting of the Commission to be held at this office on Tuesday, September 2, 1969 at 9:30 a.m., and your presence is required to provide an explanation for this positive test. You have the privilege of being

represented by counsel of your choice at this hearing, and of introducing witnesses on your behalf if you wish.

In considering the effect of this notice and whether it was adequate to advise Mr Taylor of the danger in which he stood, it is important to note that the stewards in their ruling had adopted the milder of two alternatives open to them and had ruled that Mr Taylor might carry on his business except that the horse in question was not to run again until the case had been considered by the Commission. The stewards had open to them the option provided by rule 130(3)(b) to suspend Mr Taylor pending consideration of the Commission. Had they adopted the latter alternative, it would perhaps have been obvious to Mr Taylor that it was up to him to satisfy the Commission that he had not been at fault before his suspension would be lifted. In the light of the fact that the stewards had chosen the first alternative and had not suspended Mr Taylor, there is, in my view, some ambiguity about the phrase "your presence is required to provide an explanation" and Mr Taylor could well have thought that the Commission was engaged in an investigation for the simple purpose of determining how the test made upon the horse "Simply Smashing" could have been a positive one.

In vol. 1 of Report No. 1 of the Royal Commission Inquiry Into Civil Rights, the Honourable J.C. McRuer, Commissioner, makes the forthright statement at 137 that when the rules of natural justice apply to a power of decision, "notice of the intention to make a decision should be given to the party whose rights may be affected." In this case, as was indicated by their subsequent conduct, the intention of the Commission was to make a decision as to whether or not Mr Taylor should be deprived, temporarily or permanently, of the licence given him to work at his trade as a trainer of horses under the jurisdiction of the Commission. Certainly no notice of this possible result was given to Mr Taylor and, in my view, it is not sufficient that he was advised that he was entitled to employ counsel and to summon witnesses to give evidence on his behalf. He should have been clearly advised that penalties up to and including the suspension or revocation of his licence might be imposed on him in the event of adverse findings by the Commission.

The commission appealed, and the appeal was dismissed because of a clear failure to disclose information, but Gale CJO disagreed with Osler J about the adequacy of the notice. He said (at 432-33):

I now turn to the other issue as to whether or not the respondent was denied natural justice by the action of the board. The cases establish beyond peradventure that whether a notice given in any particular case is sufficient depends entirely upon the circumstances of the case. We think that in the circumstances of this case the notice given to Mr. Taylor was adequate. When the notice itself as well as the wording of the ruling given to Mr. Taylor by the stewards before referral are taken into consideration, then we can only conclude that a man of his knowledge and experience in the racing business must have realized that he could be adversely affected by the decision of the Commission following the hearing. It would have been better, may I add, had the Commission set out in its notice that the hearing would concern Mr. Taylor's responsibility, and also set out the possible consequences of a finding against him. Had that been done, then there could have been no question about whether he had been informed as to what was going to take place at the hearing.

A similar problem arose in *R v. Chester* (1984), 5 Admin. LR 111 (Ont. HC). Chester was imprisoned in British Columbia, and the prison officials considered moving him to a special handling unit because of his general attitude and some incidents, especially one on July 6, 1982, when a visit from his fiancee was cancelled at the last minute by the authorities. The special handling units were specialized institutions designed for especially dangerous prisoners, and they imposed severe restrictions. Chester was given notice that told him that a transfer was being considered and invited submissions. It specified, "your violent and threatening behaviour and your assault on a staff member which occurred on July 6, 1982." Chester made submissions about the incident on July 6. Holland J considered the threshold, and said:

> It is my conclusion that on this issue, the protection given to a person confined as is this accused, is the right to procedural fairness whether it be considered under the common law, the *Bill of Rights* or the Charter. Each affords the same measure.

And about the notice, he said,

> The notice given to Chester was at least equivocal. A person reading that notice could fairly conclude that the reason behind the consideration was the incident of July 6, 1982. The conjunctive "and" appears just before the reference to that incident and feeds this as a rational conclusion to be drawn from the sentence. Chester's response is confirmation that this is the manner in which he interpreted the notice. His entire letter is directed to explaining his conduct on July 6, 1982. If the right of the inmate to respond in writing is to be given any weight in the sense that such response will be fairly considered in the decision to be made, then more particulars are required in the contents of the notice than was given to Chester. I find that the notice given was misleading and inadequate having in mind the severity of life in the SHU as comparable with life in the general population and failed the test of fairness.

Issues about notice are in fact not confined to pre-hearing notice but can also arise in the course of a hearing. This is no more evident than in the case of commissions of inquiry, which, as we have seen, are under a statutory duty to provide notice and an opportunity to respond to those they are of mind to name adversely in their final report. When should that notice be given and what are the limits on its contents and wording. Both issues are raised in the following extract from the judgment of the Supreme Court of Canada in the challenge to the authority of the Krever Commission of Inquiry into the operations of the blood system.

Canada (Attorney General) v. Canada (Commission of Inquiry on the Blood System in Canada—Krever Commission)
[1997] 3 SCR 440 (Can.)

The judgment of the Court was delivered by

CORY J: What limits, if any, should be imposed upon the findings of a commission of inquiry? Can a commission make findings which may indicate that there was conduct on the part of corporations or individuals which could amount to criminal culpability or civil liability? Should different limitations apply to notices warning of potential findings of misconduct? It is questions like these which must be considered on this appeal.

Factual Background

More than 1,000 Canadians became directly infected with Human Immunodeficiency Virus (HIV) from blood and blood products in the early 1980s. Approximately 12,000 Canadians became infected with Hepatitis C from blood and blood products during the same time period. This tragedy prompted the federal, provincial and territorial ministers of health to agree in September of 1993 to convene an inquiry which would examine the blood system.

On October 4, 1993, pursuant to Part I of the *Inquiries Act*, RSC 1985, c. I-11 (the Act), the Government of Canada appointed Krever JA of the Ontario Court of Appeal (the Commissioner) to review and report on the blood system in Canada. Specifically, the Order in Council directed the Commission to:

> … review and report on the mandate, organization, management, operations, financing and regulation of all activities of the blood system in Canada, including the events surrounding the contamination of the blood system in Canada in the early 1980s, by examining, without limiting the generality of the inquiry,
>
> > the organization and effectiveness of past and current systems designed to supply blood and blood products in Canada;
> >
> > the roles, views, and ideas of relevant interest groups; and
> >
> > the structures and experiences of other countries, especially those with comparable federal systems.

On November 3, 1993, an announcement of the Commissioner's appointment and a description of his mandate was published in newspapers across Canada. Subsequently, all those with an interest were provided with an opportunity to apply for standing before the Inquiry and for funding. Twenty-five interested parties were granted standing, including the appellants, The Canadian Red Cross Society and Bayer Inc., the federal government and each of the provincial governments except for Quebec. The appellant Baxter Corporation chose not to seek standing, but subsequently participated in the proceedings by supplying relevant documents and providing witnesses.

The Order in Council authorized the Commissioner to "adopt such procedures and methods as he may consider expedient for the proper conduct of the inquiry." In consultation with the parties, the Commissioner adopted rules of procedure and practice. The rules, which were agreed to by all parties, provided that in the ordinary course, Commission counsel would question witnesses first, although other counsel could apply to be the first to question any particular witness. The rules included these procedural protections:

> all parties with standing and all witnesses appearing before the Inquiry had the right to counsel, both at the Inquiry and during their pre-testimony interviews;
>
> each party had the right to have its counsel cross-examine any witness who testified and counsel for a witness who did not have standing was afforded the right to examine that witness;
>
> all parties had the right to apply to the Commissioner to have any witness called whom Commission counsel had elected not to call;

all parties had the right to receive copies of all documents entered into evidence and the right to introduce their own documentary evidence;

all hearings would be held in public unless application was made to preserve the confidentiality of information; and

although evidence could be received by the Commissioner that might not be admissible in a court of law, the Commissioner would be mindful of the dangers of such evidence and, in particular, its possible effect on reputation.

The Commission held public hearings throughout Canada between November 1993 and December 1995. In describing his mandate and intention, the Commissioner emphasized that the Inquiry "is not and it will not be a witch hunt. It is not concerned with criminal or civil liability." He said the reason the Inquiry was called was not to advance the interests of those involved with or contemplating litigation of any kind, and that he would not permit the hearings to be used for ulterior purposes. At the same time, he made it clear that he interpreted his mandate as including a fact-finding process focusing upon the events of the early 1980s and that he intended to "get to the bottom" of those events. "For those purposes it is essential to determine what caused or contributed to the contamination of the blood system in Canada in the early 1980's," he warned.

On October 26, 1995, Commission counsel delivered a memorandum to all parties inviting them to inform the Commission of the findings of misconduct they felt should be made by the Commission. The memorandum explained that under s. 13 of the Act, the Commissioner is required to give notice to any person against whom he intends to make findings of misconduct. The parties' submissions would help ensure that the notices gave warning of all the possible findings of misconduct which might be made by the Commission. These confidential submissions would be read only by Commission counsel, and would be considered for inclusion in notices issued by the Commissioner. Only those possible findings which were supported by evidence adduced in the public hearings and which were anticipated to be within the scope of the Commissioner's final report were included in the notices.

On December 21, 1995, the final day of scheduled hearings, 45 confidential notices naming 95 individuals, corporations and governments, each containing between one and 100 allegations, were delivered pursuant to s. 13 of the Act. The notices advised that the Commission might reach certain conclusions based on the evidence before it, that these conclusions may amount to misconduct within the meaning of s. 13, and that the recipients had the right to respond as to whether the Commissioner ought to reach these conclusions. The recipients were given until January 10, 1996 to announce whether and how they would respond to the notices in their final submissions.

A number of the recipients of notices brought applications for judicial review in the Federal Court. On June 27, 1996, Richard J ([1996] 3 FC 259 (TD)) declared that no findings of misconduct could be made against 47 of the applicants for judicial review, but otherwise dismissed the applications. Many recipients whose notices were not quashed appealed. The Federal Court of Appeal, [1997] 2 FC 36 (CA), quashed the notice against Dr. Craig Anhorn, but dismissed the remaining appeals.

Relevant Statutory Provisions

Inquiries Act
RSC, 1985, c. I-11

2. The Governor in Council may, whenever the Governor in Council deems it expedient, cause inquiry to be made into and concerning any matter connected with the good government of Canada or the conduct of any part of the public business thereof.

. . .

12. The commissioners may allow any person whose conduct is being investigated under this Act, and shall allow any person against whom any charge is made in the course of an investigation, to be represented by counsel.

13. No report shall be made against any person until reasonable notice has been given to the person of the charge of misconduct alleged against him and the person has been allowed full opportunity to be heard in person or by counsel.

[In order to concentrate on the procedural aspects of public inquiries, an extensive review of the history of inquiries and the scope of a commissioner's powers to make findings of misconduct has been omitted.]

What Can Be Included in a Commissioner's Report?

What then can commissioners include in their reports? The primary role, indeed the raison d'être, of an inquiry investigating a matter is to make findings of fact. In order to do so, the commissioner may have to assess and make findings as to the credibility of witnesses. From the findings of fact the commissioner may draw appropriate conclusions as to whether there has been misconduct and who appears to be responsible for it. However, the conclusions of a commissioner should not duplicate the wording of the Code defining a specific offence. If this were done it could be taken that a commissioner was finding a person guilty of a crime. This might well indicate that the commission was, in reality, a criminal investigation carried out under the guise of a commission of inquiry. Similarly, commissioners should endeavour to avoid making evaluations of their findings of fact in terms that are the same as those used by courts to express findings of civil liability. As well, efforts should be made to avoid language that is so equivocal that it appears to be a finding of civil or criminal liability. Despite these words of caution, however, commissioners should not be expected to perform linguistic contortions to avoid language that might conceivably be interpreted as importing a legal finding.

Findings of misconduct should not be the principal focus of this kind of public inquiry. Rather, they should be made only in those circumstances where they are required to carry out the mandate of the inquiry. A public inquiry was never intended to be used as a means of finding criminal or civil liability. No matter how carefully the inquiry hearings are conducted they cannot provide the evidentiary or procedural safeguards which prevail at a trial. Indeed, the very relaxation of the evidentiary rules which is so common to inquiries makes it readily apparent that findings of criminal or civil liability not only should not be made, they cannot be made.

Perhaps commissions of inquiry should preface their reports with the notice that the findings of fact and conclusions they contain cannot be taken as findings of criminal or civil liability. A commissioner could emphasize that the rules of evidence and the procedure adopted at the inquiry are very different from those of the courts. Therefore, findings of fact reached in an inquiry may not necessarily be the same as those which would be reached in a court. This may help ensure that the public understands what the findings of a commissioner are—and what they are not.

The Need for Procedural Fairness

The findings of fact and the conclusions of the commissioner may well have an adverse effect upon a witness or a party to the inquiry. Yet they must be made in order to define the nature of and responsibility for the tragedy under investigation and to make the helpful suggestions needed to rectify the problem. It is true that the findings of a commissioner cannot result in either penal or civil consequences for a witness. Further, every witness enjoys the protection of the *Canada Evidence Act* and the Charter which ensures that the evidence given cannot be used in other proceedings against the witness. Nonetheless, procedural fairness is essential for the findings of commissions may damage the reputation of a witness. For most, a good reputation is their most highly prized attribute. It follows that it is essential that procedural fairness be demonstrated in the hearings of the commission.

Fairness in Notices

That same principle of fairness must be extended to the notices pertaining to misconduct required by s. 13 of the *Inquiries Act*. A commission is required to give parties a notice warning of potential findings of misconduct which may be made against them in the final report. As long as the notices are issued in confidence to the party receiving them, they should not be subject to as strict a degree of scrutiny as the formal findings. This is because the purpose of issuing notices is to allow parties to prepare for or respond to any possible findings of misconduct which may be made against them. The more detail included in the notice, the greater the assistance it will be to the party. In addition, the only harm which could be caused by the issuing of detailed notices would be to a party's reputation. But so long as notices are released only to the party against whom the finding may be made, this cannot be an issue. The only way the public could find out about the alleged misconduct is if the party receiving the notice chose to make it public, and thus any harm to reputation would be of its own doing. Therefore, in fairness to witnesses or parties who may be the subject of findings of misconduct, the notices should be as detailed as possible. Even if the content of the notice appears to amount to a finding that would exceed the jurisdiction of the commissioner, that does not mean that the final, publicized findings will do so. It must be assumed, unless the final report demonstrates otherwise, that commissioners will not exceed their jurisdiction.

Summary

Perhaps the basic principles applicable to inquiries held pursuant to Part I of the Act may be summarized in an overly simplified manner in this way:

(a)

(i) a commission of inquiry is not a court or tribunal, and has no authority to determine legal liability;

(ii) a commission of inquiry does not necessarily follow the same laws of evidence or procedure that a court or tribunal would observe.

(iii) It follows from (i) and (ii) above that a commissioner should endeavour to avoid setting out conclusions that are couched in the specific language of criminal culpability or civil liability. Otherwise the public perception may be that specific findings of criminal or civil liability have been made.

(b) a commissioner has the power to make all relevant findings of fact necessary to explain or support the recommendations, even if these findings reflect adversely upon individuals;

(c) a commissioner may make findings of misconduct based on the factual findings, provided that they are necessary to fulfill the purpose of the inquiry as it is described in the terms of reference;

(d) a commissioner may make a finding that there has been a failure to comply with a certain standard of conduct, so long as it is clear that the standard is not a legally binding one such that the finding amounts to a conclusion of law pertaining to criminal or civil liability;

(e) a commissioner must ensure that there is procedural fairness in the conduct of the inquiry.

C. Application of the Principles to the Case at Bar

It must be remembered that in this case, the challenge brought by the appellants was triggered not by any findings of the Commission but by the s. 13 notices. Therefore, these reasons are not concerned with any challenge to the contents of the commission report or any specific findings. It will also be remembered that the Commissioner very properly stated that he would not be making findings of civil or criminal responsibility. In the interests of fairness to the parties and witnesses, the Commissioner must be bound by these statements and I am certain he will honour them. It follows that it is not appropriate in these reasons to deal with the ultimate scope of the findings that a commissioner might make in a report. The resolution of this issue will so often be governed by the nature and wording of the mandate of the commissioner and will have to be decided on that basis in each case.

The question then is whether the Commissioner exceeded his jurisdiction in the notices delivered to the appellants; I think not. The potential findings of misconduct cover areas that were within the Commissioner's responsibility to investigate. The mandate of the Inquiry was extremely broad, requiring the Commissioner to review and report on "the events surrounding the contamination of the blood system in Canada in the early 1980s, by examining ... the organization and effectiveness of past and current systems designed to supply blood and blood products in Canada." This must encompass a review of the conduct and practices of the institutions and persons responsible for the blood system. The content of the notices does not indicate that the Commissioner investigated or contemplated reporting on areas that were outside his mandate.

If the Commissioner's report had made findings worded in the same manner as the notices, then further consideration might have been warranted. However, the appellants launched this application before the Commissioner's findings had been released. Therefore, it is impossible to say what findings he will make or how they will be framed. Quite simply the appellants have launched their challenge prematurely. As a general rule, a challenge such as this should not be brought before the publication of the report, unless there are reasonable grounds to believe that the Commissioner is likely to exceed his or her jurisdiction.

Even if it could be said that the challenge was not premature, the notices are not objectionable. They indicated that there was a possibility that the Commissioner would make certain findings of fact which might amount to misconduct. While they are not all worded in the same manner, the reproduction of some of them may help illustrate the basis for this conclusion. Many of the doctors and the Red Cross received notice of a general allegation that they:

> … failed adequately to oversee, direct and provide resources for the operation of the Blood Transfusion Service (BTS) and Blood Donor Recruitment (BDR) at both the national and local level, and as a result contributed to and are responsible for the failures set out below. …

This was followed by a series of specific allegations, such as the following:

Red Cross

> 5. The CRC failed to implement in a timely manner, during January 13–March 10, 1983, any national donor-screening measures to reduce the risk of transfusion-associated AIDS, this failure causing unnecessary cases of transfusion-associated HIV infection and AIDS to occur.

The notice served on the appellant Baxter contained only one allegation:

> 1. After becoming aware in 1982 and thereafter of the possibility or likelihood that its factor concentrates transmitted the causative agent of AIDS, Baxter failed to take adequate steps to notify consumers and physicians of the risks associated with the use of its products and to advise that they consider alternative therapies.

It will be remembered that the Commissioner, from the outset of the Inquiry, wisely emphasized that he did not have the intention or the authority to make any legal determinations. Rather, his stated goal was to examine what went wrong with the blood system in the 1980s and to assess ways of resolving the problems in order to protect the blood system in the future. Thus, it was clear from the beginning that his findings would have nothing to do with criminal or civil liability.

Further, while many of the notices come close to alleging all the necessary elements of civil liability, none of them appears to exceed the Commissioner's jurisdiction. For example, if his factual findings led him to conclude that the Red Cross and its doctors failed to supervise adequately the Blood Transfusion Service and Blood Donor Recruitment, it would be appropriate and within his mandate to reach that conclusion. Some of the appellants object to the use of the word "failure" in the notices; I do not share their concern. As the Court of Appeal pointed out, there are many different types of normative standards, including moral, scientific and professional-ethical. To state that a person "failed" to do something that should have been done does not necessarily mean that the person breached a criminal or civil standard of conduct. The same is true of the word "responsible." Unless there is something more to indicate that the recipient of the notice is legally responsible, there is no reason why this should be presumed. It was noted in *Rocois Construction Inc. v. Quebec Ready Mix Inc.* [1990] 2 SCR 440 (Que.), at p. 455:

> A fact taken by itself apart from any notion of legal obligations has no meaning in itself and cannot be a cause; it only becomes a legal fact when it is characterized in accordance with some rule of law. The same body of facts may well be characterized in a number of ways and give rise to completely separate causes. ...
>
> [I]t is by the intellectual exercise of characterization, of the linking of the fact and the law, that the cause is revealed.

While the Court in *Rocois* was concerned only with facts, I believe the same principle can be applied to conclusions of fault based on standards of conduct. Unless there is something to show that the standard applied is a legal one, no conclusion of law can be said to have been reached.

There are phrases which, if used, might indicate a legal standard had been applied, such as a finding that someone "breached a duty of care," engaged in a "conspiracy," or was guilty of "criminal negligence." None of these words has been used by the Commissioner. The potential findings as set out in the notices may imply civil liability, but the Commissioner has stated that he will not make a finding of legal liability, and I am sure he will not. In my view, no error was made by the Commissioner in sending out these notices.

If the Commissioner Originally Had Such Jurisdiction, Did He Lose It by Failing To Provide Adequate Procedural Protections or by the Timing of the Release of the Notices?

a. Procedural Protections

The appellants argue that they did not have the benefit of adequate procedural protections. As a result, they contend that the Commissioner has lost the authority to make the type of findings which are referred to in the notices. They submit that they interpreted comments made by the Commissioner during the Inquiry as assurances that he had no intention of making the type of findings suggested by the notices. If these assurances had not been given the appellants say that they would have insisted upon tighter evidentiary procedures, greater ability to cross-examine, and other procedural protections.

Yet the three corporate appellants were not uninformed bystanders. Rather, they had detailed and intimate knowledge of the blood system, of the terrible tragedy resulting from its contamination with HIV, and of the public outcry and investigation which followed.

The Canadian Red Cross Society and Bayer Inc. participated in the proceedings of the Inquiry. As a result it is difficult to accept that they could have been surprised by the fact that the notices were critical. In fact, the prospect of the Commissioner's ultimately making findings adverse to a witness was specifically raised by counsel for the Red Cross during discussions among counsel in November 1993 concerning the procedural rules. In response, counsel for the Commission referred to s. 13 of the Act and indicated that a notice would have to be provided to any party who might face an adverse finding. No concern about the procedure was raised at that time. The third corporate appellant, Baxter Corporation, was not involved in the meeting and was not a party at the Inquiry. However, it knew about the Inquiry and its goals, and participated by offering witnesses and entering documentary evidence.

The position of the intervener the Canadian Hemophilia Society is both illuminating and helpful on this point. Like the appellants, the Society received a notice of a potential finding of misconduct. The Society was a party to the Inquiry, and accepted and adapted to the same procedures as the appellants. However, unlike the appellants, it continues to support the Commissioner's right to make findings of misconduct. The Society submitted and confirmed that the practices and procedures adopted at the Inquiry were, in light of its mandate, fair and appropriate. As well, it emphasized that it knew from the outset of the Inquiry that there was a risk that the Commissioner would make findings of misconduct against the group as a result of its involvement in the Canadian blood system.

Significantly, the procedural protections offered to parties to the Inquiry and to individual witnesses were extensive and exemplary. The Commission, with the full consent of the parties, offered a commendably wide range of protections. ...

These procedures were adopted on a consensual basis, after a meeting with all parties to determine which protections would be required. I am not sure what further protections the appellants could have realistically expected. The procedure adopted was eminently fair and any objections to it must be rejected. Nor can I accept that the appellants could have been misled or that they suffered prejudice as a result of any "misunderstanding" about the type of findings which would be made by the Commissioner. That submission as well must be rejected.

b. Timing of the Notices

The appellants submit that because the Commissioner waited until the last day of hearings to issue notices identifying potential findings of misconduct which might be made against them, their ability to cross-examine witnesses effectively and present evidence was compromised. They submit that there is no longer any opportunity to cure the prejudice caused by the late delivery of the notices, and that they must therefore be quashed. For the following reasons, I must disagree.

There is no statutory requirement that the commissioner give notice as soon as he or she foresees the possibility of an allegation of misconduct. While I appreciate that it might be helpful for parties to know in advance the findings of misconduct which may be made against them, the nature of an inquiry will often make this impossible. Broad inquiries are not focussed on individuals or whether they committed a crime; rather they are concerned with institutions and systems and how to improve them. It follows that in such inquiries there is no need to present individuals taking part in the inquiry with the particulars of a "case to meet" or notice of the charges against them, as there would be in criminal proceedings. Although the notices should be given as soon as it is feasible, it is unreasonable to insist that the notice of misconduct must always be given early. There will be some inquiries, such as this one, where the Commissioner cannot know what the findings may be until the end or very late in the process. So long as adequate time is given to the recipients of the notices to allow them to call the evidence and make the submissions they deem necessary, the late delivery of notices will not constitute unfair procedure.

The timing of notices will always depend upon the circumstances. Where the evidence is extensive and complex, it may be impossible to give the notices before the end of the hearings. In other situations, where the issue is more straightforward, it may be possible to give notice of potential findings of misconduct early in the process. In this case, where there was an enormous amount of information gathered over the course of the hearings, it was within the discretion of the Commissioner to issue notices when he did. As Décary JA put it at para. 79:

> ... the Commissioner enjoys considerable latitude, and is thereby permitted to use the method best suited to the needs of his inquiry. I see no objection in principle to a commissioner waiting until the end of the hearings, when he or she has all the information that is required, to give notices, rather than taking a day to day approach to it, with the uncertainty and inconvenience that this might involve.

In light of the nature and purposes of this Inquiry, it was impossible to give adequate detail in the notices before all the evidence had been heard. In the context of this Inquiry the timing of the notices was not unfair.

Further, the appellants were given an adequate opportunity to respond to the notices, and to adduce additional evidence, if they deemed it necessary. The notices were delivered on December 21, 1995, and parties were initially given until January 10, 1996 to decide whether and how they would respond. This period was then extended following requests from the parties. The time permitted for the response was adequate. It cannot be said that the timing of the delivery of the notices amounted to a violation of procedural fairness.

Appeal dismissed.

NOTES

1. For discussion, see A. Lucas, "Public Inquiries—A Green Light for the Krever Commission" (1996), 39 *Admin. LR* (2d) 291 and A. Roman, "Public Inquiries: A Brief Review of Recent Cases Involving Contaminated Blood and the Canadian Armed Forces in Somalia" (1998), 3 *Admin. LR* (3d) 319. More generally, see E. Ratushny, *The Conduct of Public Inquiries* (Toronto: Irwin Books, 2009); A. Manson and D. Mullan, eds., *Commissions of Inquiry: Praise or Reappraise?* (Toronto: Irwin Books, 2003); and G. Van Harten, "Truth Before Punishment: A Defence of Public Inquiries" (2003), 29 *Queen's LJ* 242.

2. In some instances there has been growing concern at governments "closing down" public inquiries before they have completed their work. This led to a legal challenge to the Cabinet's decision to refuse to extend the final deadline for the Somalia Report as much as

the commissioners had requested. At trial, the order in council was held to be *ultra vires* for breaching the rule of law by requiring the impossible of the commissioners and not respecting their independence. However, the Federal Court of Appeal (Marceau J with whom Isaac CJ and McDonald J concurred) reversed the trial decision and held that the impugned order was *intra vires* the governor in council (Cabinet) in *Dixon v. Commission of Inquiry into the Deployment of Canadian Forces in Somalia)*, [1997] 3 FC 169 (FCA). The commission's existence was seen as being dependent on the governor in council and it had not acquired an independent status to allow it to prevail over the will of the government. In any event, courts had no power to review the policy considerations that motivated Cabinet decisions. This was a debate that a court of law, properly confined to its adjudicative role, could not consider. Leave to appeal to the Supreme Court of Canada was denied without reasons on January 8, 1998, SCC Bulletin 1998, p. 23 (Iacobucci, Major, and Bastarache JJ).

3. Sometimes, of course, the demands that are made go beyond the identification of allegations with a sufficient degree of specificity to a claim to pre-hearing access to all relevant evidence, a form of administrative process discovery paralleling that available in the ordinary civil and now criminal litigation processes. Indeed, the evolution of such claims is contemplated in some measure by s. 8 of the Ontario SPPA, which provides for "reasonable information of any allegations" where proceedings bring into question "the good character, propriety of conduct or competence of a party." As the following materials indicate, this has been the principal terrain for the making of discovery claims at common law. Nonetheless, they have not been confined exclusively to this domain and it is to be expected that there will be further evolution in this direction in both the common law and the procedural rules governing a wide range of tribunals.

Discovery

Fuelled by the judgment of the Supreme Court of Canada in *R v. Stinchcombe*, [1991] 3 SCR 326 (Alta.) was an increasing concern with the question whether notice entitlements in the administrative process involve a claim to pre-hearing "discovery" of all relevant information in the possession of the "other side" or the "prosecution." Reid and Mulcahy suggested ("Pre-Hearing Discovery—Does *Stinchcombe* Apply to Administrative Tribunals?" (1994), 3 *Reid's Administrative Law* 97) that

> [t]he principles of *Stinchcombe* do not add anything new to administrative law. The principle of full disclosure is already part of the duty of fairness as set out in *Nicholson* … . *Stinchcombe* is important, though, because it emphasizes the required degree of disclosure. One must know the case one must meet. Disclosure must not be perfunctory; it must be complete, subject only to privilege or relevance.

However, that hides a number of questions of some considerable importance. For example, do tribunals have an inherent or an implied power to order discovery or complete disclosure where they deem it to be necessary in the interests of fairness (an issue in fact raised by Reid and Mulcahy)? Even if they do not have such a formal power, can they effectively control failures to provide such information on a voluntary basis? Even assuming that some level of advance notice of the contrary evidence is generally part of the obligations of procedural fairness, does that always encompass the levels of information-sharing that have traditionally characterized the civil litigation process and now are part of criminal procedure after *Stinchcombe*? Are there arguments against the strict application of these principles to administrative processes, at least as a general rule? If there is to be no general rule, what are the kinds of administrative decision making that might be seen as demanding a close approximation to the principles of *Stinchcombe*? Are there distinctions to be made in terms of the nature of the information in question as, for example, between material in the possession of the parties and that held by the tribunal? Indeed, in terms of the latter category, is there a still further distinction to be made between material acquired by the agency or tribunal from external sources (including the parties) and that generated within the agency or the tribunal? Another cut on this issue may be to see the entitlement as dependent on whether the proceedings are of a *lis inter partes* variety.

The answer to the initial question as to jurisdiction (and one that has important implications for other contexts in which tribunals assert the power to make procedural orders) was provided by *Canadian Pacific Airlines Ltd. v. Canadian Air Line Pilots Association*, [1993] 3 SCR 724 (Can.). This involved an order for the production of documents and other information made by the Canada Labour Relations Board at the investigative, pre-hearing stage of an application by Canadian Air Line Pilots Association (CALPA) for a "single employer" declaration. When Canadian failed to produce the information voluntarily, the board attempted to secure it relying on ss. 118(a) and 121 of the *Canada Labour Code*, RSC 1985, c. L-2. Section 118(a) provided the board with power "in relation to any proceeding before it"

> (a) to summon and enforce the attendance of witnesses and compel them to give oral or written evidence on oath and *to produce such documents and things* as the Board deems requisite to the full investigation and consideration of any matter within its jurisdiction that is before the Board in the proceeding. [Emphasis added.]

Section 121 for its part empowered the board to do such things "as may be incidental to the attainment of the objects of this Part."

According to Gonthier J, delivering the judgment of the majority, the board had no inherent or incidental powers, only those conferred on it by statute. Furthermore, the provisions relied on did not authorize compulsory discovery orders outside the context of a formal hearing. Indeed, while, at points, the court emphasized the fact that the board was still at the investigative or administrative stage in relation to the application that had been made, what is also clear in the judgment was that, even after the matter had been set down for hearing, there was no room for "pre-hearing" discovery. Section 118 was limited to orders for the production of documents in the context of witnesses being summoned to give evidence on oath. While the context of this judgment was a detailed exercise in statutory interpretation of a specific regime, what it does make clear is that any claim to exercise such a power will have to be rooted firmly in the empowering statute and that there is not likely to be any presumption drawn as to the existence of such authority in the absence of express authority to make such orders. In the judgment that follows, the court apparently found such an authority in the provisions of Ontario's *Statutory Powers Procedure Act*.

Ontario (Human Rights Commission) v. Ontario
(Board of Inquiry into Northwestern General Hospital)
(1993), 115 DLR (4th) 279 (Ont. Div. Ct.)

[A board of inquiry was set up under the Ontario *Human Rights Code* to hear a complaint of racial discrimination made by ten nurses employed by the hospital. In the context of that inquiry, the following order was made:

> I order the Commission to provide the Respondents with all statements made by the Complainants to the Commission and its investigators at the investigation stage, whether reduced to writing or copied by mechanical means. I further order the Commission to provide the Respondents with the statement and identity of any witness interviewed by the Commission or its agents who the Commission does not propose to call and whose statements might reasonably aid the Respondents in answering the Commission's case.

The commission applied for judicial review of that order.]

BY THE COURT (McMurtry ACJO, O'Driscoll and Southey JJ):

. . .

Reasons for the Decision of the Board of Inquiry

The board of inquiry considered what degree of disclosure was required to meet the duty of fairness in the circumstances of this case.

At 13 of its reasons the board of inquiry stated:

> The case before me involves the allegation that a hospital, along with certain named individuals, practices systemic discrimination based upon colour, race and associated unlawful bases. In doing so, it is alleged, they excluded those so discriminated against from positions which they were otherwise entitled to. While I have been told no more of the allegations than this, it appears to me that the allegations are very serious indeed, with the potential, if made out, to ruin reputations, and cast a pall over the future career prospects of anyone found to have so discriminated.

In rejecting the claim of privilege, the board of inquiry separated the investigation stage from the subsequent conciliation stage and the third "prosecution" stage. The board of inquiry expressed their view "that documents, including statements reduced to writing, would only very exceptionally be privileged at the investigation stage." At the same time the board held that the timing of the disclosure should be "entirely in the hands of Commission counsel."

The board concluded that the following statutory enactments are relevant to any power to order disclosure in a given case:

> 1. **Section 8 of the *Statutory Powers Procedure Act*:**
>   8. Where the good character, propriety or conduct or competence of a party is an issue in a proceeding, the party is entitled to be furnished prior to the hearing with reasonable information of any allegations with respect thereto.

2. **Section 12 of the *Statutory Powers Procedure Act*:**

> 12(1) A tribunal may require any person, including a party by summons,
>
> > (a) to give evidence on oath or affirmation at a hearing;
>
> and
>
> > (b) to produce in evidence at a hearing documents and things specified by the tribunal relevant to the subject-matter of the proceeding and admissible at a hearing.

The board expressly rejected the submission of the commission that *R v. Stinchcombe* had no applicability to human rights litigation. The board did not feel bound by *Stinchcombe*, being a case involving an indictable offence, but it did believe that *Stinchcombe* provided an important analogy between Crown counsel and commission counsel.

In the context of what is reasonably required in the way of disclosure in order to achieve the duty of fairness the board concluded:

> In a case such as this, I have decided that the *Stinchcombe* doctrine ought to be applied. The exclusion of the element of surprise in the interests of the fairness of a hearing is, I believe now required. Thus any relevant materials not otherwise privileged ought to be disclosed to counsel for the Respondents.

Decision of This Court

Section 12 of the *Statutory Powers Procedure Act* ("SPPA") clearly recognizes the authority of a board of inquiry to order the production of all the documents which are the subject of the order in this case, subject to claims of privilege.

In *R v. Stinchcombe*, Sopinka J referred to the earlier history of the adversary process of adjudication:

> Production and discovery were foreign to the adversary process of adjudication in its earlier history when the element of surprise was one of the accepted weapons in the arsenal of the adversaries. This applied to both criminal and civil proceedings. Significantly, in civil proceedings this aspect of the adversary process has long since disappeared, and full discovery of documents and oral examination of parties and even witnesses are familiar features of the practice. This change resulted from acceptance of the principle that justice was better served when the element of surprise was eliminated from the trial and the parties were prepared to address issues on the basis of complete information of the case to be met. Surprisingly, in criminal cases in which the liberty of the subject is usually at stake, this aspect of the adversary system has lingered on.

The applicant equates proceedings under the *Human Rights Code* to the civil rather than the criminal process. It is in our view significant that in civil proceedings the "full discovery of documents and oral examination of parties and even witnesses are familiar features of the practice." The important principle enunciated by Sopinka J is that "justice was better served when the element of surprise was eliminated from the trial and the parties were prepared to address issues *on the basis of complete information of the case to be met*" (emphasis added). It does not take a quantum leap to come to the conclusion that in the appropriate case, justice will be better served in proceedings under the *Human Rights Code* when there is complete information available to the respondents.

R v. Stinchcombe also recognized that the "fruits of the investigation" in the possession of the Crown "are not the property of the Crown for use in securing a conviction but the property of the public to be used to ensure that justice be done." We are of the opinion that this point applies with equal force to the proceedings before a board of inquiry and that the fruits of the investigations are not the property of the commission.

We are also of the opinion, while not necessary to our decision, that the role of commission counsel is analogous to that of the Crown in criminal proceedings (*R v. Stinchcombe*).

> It cannot be over-emphasized that the purpose of a criminal prosecution is not to obtain a conviction; it is to bring before a jury what the Crown considers to be credible evidence to what is alleged to be a crime. The tradition of Crown counsel in this country in carrying out their role as "ministers of justice" and not as adversaries has generally been very high.

[The court then went on to accept the ruling of the board of inquiry that any claim to litigation privilege for the information in question did not extend to the investigative functions of the commission. It further held that there was no class privilege for communications between complainants and officers of the commission.]

There is no dispute in these proceedings that the allegations made by the complainants are indeed extremely serious. Any racial discrimination strikes at the very heart of a democratic pluralistic society. It is, of course, of the utmost seriousness if any such racial discrimination exists or has existed in an important public institution such as a major hospital. The consequences attendant on a negative finding by a board of inquiry would be most severe for the respondents as any such finding could and should seriously damage the reputation of any such individual.

It has been submitted on behalf of the applicant that the disclosure as ordered by the board in this case could discourage victims of racial discrimination from making complaints if they knew that their original statements might be carefully scrutinized at some later stage. Obviously, the public has an important interest in the making of any legitimate complaint. However, it is of public importance as well that the complainants appreciate that allegations of racial discrimination are indeed serious and therefore should be made in a responsible and conscientious fashion. The fact that complainants are aware that their original complaint or complaints may be subsequently disclosed, might well encourage complainants to take the appropriate care in communicating their allegations. Of course, we make no comment whatsoever on the allegations in this case, as we are in no position to do so at this stage.

It is also submitted on behalf of the applicant that knowledge of such disclosure might well intimidate the potential complainant, who is often from a disadvantaged class, or place that person in an adversarial relationship with the representative of the commission whom they first encounter.

It is our opinion that any such concerns can be addressed by the procedures of the Human Rights Commission and by the provision of access to independent legal counsel. In our view this would be preferable to the denial of fundamental fairness to respondents.

The application is dismissed with costs.

NOTES

1. In the light of *Canadian Pacific*, it is significant that the court is not particularly careful about locating precisely the source of the board's authority to make the order that it did. Is it s. 8 or s. 12 of the *Statutory Powers Procedure Act* or is it derived from the presence of both these? As opposed to *Canadian Pacific*, the investigative stage has ended and the judicial phase has commenced. However, the order for production is not one that is directed to witnesses about to testify but rather to the pre-hearing stage of the inquiry. This suggests the source of the authority to make the order may be s. 8, rather than s. 12. (In terms of the precedential value of this judgment, note that it was argued on October 8, 1993 and the court released its decision on November 8. The judgment in *Canadian Pacific* was released on October 21 and is not cited in Divisional Court's judgment.) Consider also the possibilities of using s. 12 to achieve the same end and note that the 1994 amendments and new s. 5.4(1) in particular now contemplate rules incorporating a much more explicit discovery regime. The Ontario Human Rights Code Board of Inquiry (now the Human Rights Tribunal of Ontario) in fact exercised the power conferred on it by s. 25.1 of the SPPA to make such rules. In *Ontario Human Rights Commission v. Dofasco* (2001), 57 OR (3d) 693 (CA), the court held that an order made by the Board of Inquiry under rule 42 of its Rules of Practice was too broad in requiring the complainant in a physical disability discrimination case to reveal the names of all the physicians who had treated her, the nature of their expertise, and the dates and details of treatment. Such a broad order was highly intrusive on privacy and not necessarily in any way relevant to the issues raised by the case. Orders must not force production of privileged documents or extend beyond material that is relevant. Discovery and disclosure before the Ontario Human Rights Tribunal are now governed by rule 16 of its new Rules of Procedure. On the issue of privilege, see *Pritchard v. Ontario (Human Rights Commission)*, [2004] 1 SCR 809 (Ont.), holding that an opinion letter written by a commission in-house lawyer was privileged.

2. If discovery or pre-hearing disclosure is not accorded voluntarily in situations where there is no formal power to make such an order, what might be the consequences of this and what, if anything, can a tribunal do to rectify the impact of such a failure?

3. The same principles were applied (once again by way of analogy to *Stinchcombe*) by Gibson J in *Nrecaj v. Canada (Minister of Employment and Immigration)* (1993), 14 Admin. LR (2d) 161 (FCTD). At stake in this case was the failure to make pre-hearing disclosure of interview notes in the context of the adjudication of a Convention refugee claim. According to the court:

> The ability of a claimant to Convention refugee status "to make full answer and defence" to evidence adduced against his or her claim or to impeach his or her credibility is of critical importance since the claim must be based on a well-founded fear of persecution if the claim is to be recognized. And indeed, the role and duty of an RHO at a CRD hearing has many features in common with that of Crown counsel in criminal proceedings. Both the Quick Reference Book for Refugee Hearing Officers and the Refugee Hearing Officer's Manual make it clear that the RHO is required to disclose to the client and counsel all documentary evidence to be used at the hearing by the RHO and to alert the claimant and counsel to the issues and precedents he or she feels are relevant to the claim. While the "interview notes" in question may not them-

selves have been "documentary evidence," the principles enunciated with respect to documentary evidence would logically extend to them.

See also the dissenting judgment of Laskin JA in *Howe v. Institute of Chartered Accountants of Ontario* (1994), 19 OR (3d) 483 (CA), where he held that there should have been prehearing disclosure of a report prepared for the institute's disciplinary committee in relation to proceedings against Howe. The majority ruled that the application was premature since there was still a chance for any wrong to be rectified by the committee itself (the ruling having been made by the chair alone) or on subsequent appeal.

4. Subsequently, *Northwestern General Hospital* (or *House*) was distinguished by the Federal Court of Appeal in a judgment that follows. Consider whether the differentiations that the court makes between the two processes is justifiable and reflect on the circumstances where pre-hearing discovery orders are now permissible and, where permissible, a necessary component of procedural fairness when sought by one of the parties.

CIBA-Geigy Ltd. v. Canada (Patented Medicine Prices Review Board)
[1994] 3 FC 425 (CA)

[The judgment of the court (consisting otherwise of Marceau and Decary JJA) was delivered by]

MacGUIGAN JA: This appeal has to do with the extent of the disclosure required to the appellant of documents in the hands of the Patented Medicine Prices Review Board ("the Board").

Utilizing its powers under the *Patent Act* ("the Act"), the Board scheduled a hearing to determine whether the drug Habitrol marketed in Canada by the appellant is being sold at an excessive price. The consequences of such a finding under s. 83 of the Act could be an order for a price reduction in the selling price, a payment to Her Majesty in the Right of Canada of an offset amount from estimated excess corporate revenue, and, on a finding of a policy of selling the medicine at an excessive price, an offset of up to twice the amount of the estimated excess revenues. This last kind of remedial order is not in play in the instant case in its current state.

In deciding to hold a formal hearing, once a patentee has refused to make a voluntary compliance order the Chairman of the Board considers a report from the Board staff to the effect that the market price charged for the drug in Canada exceeds the Board's guidelines. The appellant seeks the disclosure to it of all documents in the Board's possession which relate to the matters in issue in the s. 83 hearing, particularly the report on which the Chairman acted in ordering the hearing. In its view such disclosure should extend to all the facets of the staff investigation and to all documents in the hands of the Board or its Chairman.

The Board refused appellant's request for such exhaustive disclosure for the following reasons (Appeal Board, I, 3):

> In the Board's view, in a hearing before it, the party to whom the hearing relates must be
> provided with a level of disclosure and production which ensures that the party is fully in-

formed of the case to be made against it. Further, the procedure followed must provide the party to whom the hearing relates a reasonable opportunity to meet that case by bringing forward its own position and by correcting or contradicting any statement or evidence related to the case which is prejudicial to its position.

It is the Board's view that, in matters of the disclosure and production of information and documents in the context of a public hearing, the Board must balance its duty to give every opportunity to a Respondent to be heard against its responsibility to ensure that its orders do not have the effect of limiting its ability to discharge its responsibilities in the public interest on an ongoing basis. In order to discharge such responsibilities, the Board must be confident that it is getting candid, complete and objective advice from its staff. This is particularly the case in respect of the preliminary views it receives as to whether there is sufficient evidence to justify calling a hearing into a matter. This balancing need not in any way affect the Board's duty in law to make its decisions on the basis of the evidence placed and tested before it during a hearing.

On a judicial review proceeding McKeown J upheld the Board's decision as follows [(1994), 77 FTR 197]:

The Board has made a decision refusing disclosure of the documents requested and I should give such a decision curial deference unless fairness or natural justice requires otherwise. Disclosure cannot be decided in the abstract. The Board is supposed to proceed efficiently and to protect the interest of the public. This requires, *inter alia*, that a hearing shall not be unduly prolonged. Certainly, the subject of an excess price hearing is entitled to know the case against it, but it should not be permitted to obtain all the evidence which has come into the possession of the Board in carrying out its regulatory functions in the public interest on the sole ground that it may be relevant to the matter at hand. The Board's function is not to obtain information solely for investigative purposes; its primary role is to monitor prices. In its decision, the Board recognized the need to balance its duty to the applicant against limiting its ability to discharge its responsibilities in the public interest on an ongoing basis. The Board has exercised its duty properly in the case at bar. ... [W]hen the statutory scheme of this Board is looked at, the Board is a regulatory board or tribunal. There is no point in the legislature creating a regulatory tribunal if the tribunal is treated as a criminal court. The obligations concerning disclosure imposed by the doctrine of fairness and natural justice are met if the subject of the inquiry is advised of the case it has to meet and is provided with all the documents that will be relied on. CIBA has been provided with much more than the minimum disclosure required to enable it to meet the case. Law and policy require that some leeway be given an administrative tribunal with economic regulatory functions, if, in pursuing its mandate, the tribunal is required by necessity to receive confidential information. It is not intended that proceedings before these tribunals be as adversarial as proceedings before a court. To require the Board to disclose all possibly relevant information gathered while fulfilling its regulatory obligations would unduly impede its work from an administrative viewpoint. Fairness is always a matter of balancing diverse interests. I find that fairness does not require the disclosure of the fruits of the investigation in this matter.

We are all agreed that the Motions Judge has correctly stated and applied the law.

Indeed, in emphasizing that its case is one of *audi alteram partem* and not of bias, counsel for the appellant expressly agreed with the law as stated by the respondent that "the concept of procedural fairness is eminently variable, and its content is to be decided in the specific context of each case" (*Knight v. Indian Head School Division No. 19 of Saskatchewan* [1990] 1 SCR 653 (Sask.) at 682 (*per* L'Heureux-Dubé J)) and the context to be thus taken into account consists of the nature and seriousness of the matters in issue, the circumstances, and of course the governing statute. This was precisely the approach of the Motions Judge.

The only real issue between the parties is as to the effect to be given in this non-criminal case to the powerful reasons for decision of Sopinka J in *R v. Stinchcombe* [1991] 3 SCR 326 (Alta.) that in a criminal case the Crown has a legal duty to make total disclosure to the defence.

[After referring to the *Northwestern General Hospital* case, MacGuigan JA continued.]

This is where any criminal analogy to the proceedings in the case at bar breaks down. There are admittedly extremely serious economic consequences for an unsuccessful patentee at a s. 83 hearing, and a possible effect on a corporation's reputation in the market place. But as McKeown J found, the administrative tribunal here has economic regulatory functions and has no power to affect human rights in a way akin to criminal proceedings.

A trustful relationship with its investigative staff and proceeding "as informally and expeditiously as the circumstances of fairness permits" are valid Board objectives.

We are all agreed with McKeown J that "law and policy require that some leeway be given an administrative tribunal with economic regulatory functions … in pursuing its mandate."

The appeal must therefore be dismissed with costs.

NOTES

1. In *May v. Ferndale Institution*, [2005] 3 SCR 809, the Supreme Court of Canada upheld the contextual approach to the scope of disclosure in administrative proceedings. May, an inmate serving a life sentence, was involuntarily transferred by Corrections Canada from a minimum-security to a medium-security institution because of a computerized reclassification of his security rating. The computer software used to reclassify May employed a "scoring matrix" that weighed an offender's risk factors, including the seriousness of the offence, criminal history, and behaviour while serving the sentence, and generated a security rating. May argued that Corrections Canada was bound by *Stinchcombe* disclosure requirements because its decision to transfer him involved a loss of liberty, and that it should have disclosed the scoring matrix. The Supreme Court agreed, at para. 91, that *Stinchcombe* was not the appropriate standard:

> It is important to bear in mind that the *Stinchcombe* principles were enunciated in the particular context of criminal proceedings where the innocence of the accused was at stake. Given the

severity of the potential consequences the appropriate level of disclosure was quite high. In these cases, the impugned decisions are purely administrative. These cases do not involve a criminal trial and innocence is not at stake. The *Stinchcombe* principles do not apply in the administrative context.

Noting that procedural fairness generally required that the decision-maker disclose the information he or she relied on and that the applicable statute—s. 27(1) of the *Corrections and Conditional Release Act*—itself required Corrections Canada to give offenders "all the information to be considered in the taking of the decision or a summary of that information," the court decided that May was entitled to disclosure of the scoring matrix. The matrix played a determinative role in reclassification decisions because it determined the weight to be attributed to different risk factors. Deprived of this information, May was unable to effectively know and respond to the case against him.

2. There may be arguments that the regulatory context in *CIBA-Geigy* was not amenable to the common law imposition of a regime of pre-hearing discovery of evidence. However, the complexity of many economic regulatory regimes indicates the almost essential nature of some form of not only pre-hearing revelation and exchange of evidence but also pre-hearing conferences for the purposes of settling and narrowing of issues as well as creating understandings for the conduct of the hearing. Without such a process, the inefficiencies of the actual hearing process are likely to be major.

In this regard, it is significant that the amendments to the Ontario SPPA also allow for rules to be made for the holding of pre-hearing conferences, orders for disclosure and discovery, as well as the examination of parties and the exchange of witness statements. Indeed, for many regulatory agencies, such provisions are no more than a reflection of their current procedural rules and practices.

3. For an affirmation of *CIBA-Geigy* in the context of a competition tribunal hearing, see *Canada (Director of Investigation and Research, Competition Act) v. D & B Companies of Canada Ltd.* (1994), 176 NR 62 (FCA). Indeed, this was in the context of a regime that has explicit discovery procedures but where there was resistance to the disclosure of particular information based on a claim to public interest privilege.

4. As indicated not only by *D & B Companies of Canada* but also by both *CIBA-Geigy*, *Northwestern General Hospital*, and *Dofasco*, the evaluation of pre-hearing discovery claims may not be based solely on considerations of administrative convenience and what is procedurally fair to those affected. As well, confidentiality and privacy claims will regularly be advanced as a justification for not providing any or full discovery: public interest privilege in *D & B Companies of Canada*, litigation privilege in *Northwestern General Hospital*, solicitor–client privilege in *Pritchard*, personal information and relevance in *Dofasco*, and protection of commercially sensitive information acquired in confidence in *CIBA-Geigy*. Indeed, as Strayer JA points out delivering the judgment of the Federal Court of Appeal in *D & B Companies of Canada*, in the civil litigation discovery process, there have always been privilege exceptions to the revelation of all relevant information. In general, however, this kind of claim transcends the arena of pre-hearing procedures and affects the whole of the administrative process. We will postpone detailed consideration of it until we reach the section on disclosure and official notice. Nonetheless, it is worth keeping in mind that, to the extent that confidentiality claims are relative or contingent, it is possible that, even where it

is denied at the pre-hearing stage, an access claim may be able to be reasserted and ultimately succeed at the actual hearing stage. At that point, it may have become clear that the ability to respond adequately depends on fuller information than was provided prior to the hearing on discovery.

Delay

In recent years, the notion that undue delay in the conduct of administrative proceedings could amount to a breach of the rules of natural justice or procedural fairness achieved a measure of acceptance. Indeed, it is one of the grounds specified in the codification of the bases of review in s. 4 of the PEI *Judicial Review Act*, SPEI 1988, c. 35 (see s. 4(1)(g)). The emergence of this species of procedural error can be attributed to a variety of causes.

At one level, it is a consequence of the exigencies of the administrative process itself. First, many administrative agencies are strapped for resources and simply cannot handle their caseload in a timely fashion. Concern over the processing of human rights complaints provides one example (see Ontario Human Rights Code Review Task Force, *Achieving Equality: A Report on Human Rights Reform* (1992)). Delay in that context was an important factor driving recent reforms to the Ontario *Human Rights Code* that stripped the Ontario Human Rights Commission of its gatekeeping function (*Human Rights Code Amendment Act, 2006*, SO 2006, c. 30) and earlier reforms to the British Columbia Code that eliminated the Human Rights Commission entirely (*Human Rights Code Amendment Act*, 2002, SBC 2002, c. 62). Second, particularly in the domain of professional discipline, hearings are often delayed pending the outcome of criminal proceedings against the member accused of professional misconduct arising out of the same circumstances. On occasion, it may be years before the criminal process is concluded. Third, there is an increasing tendency on the part of agencies that deal with complaints against individuals to accept such complaints even though they are based on conduct that occurred sometimes years previously. In all of these situations, the potential exists for the person who is the target of the proceedings to be prejudiced by the delay in the processing of the charges against him or her.

To these practical considerations can be added the impact of evolutions in the law in related areas. In the domain of criminal law, the emergence of the notion of "abuse of process" as a basis for challenges to prosecutions that were delayed unduly was seen as having a potential application to administrative proceedings. However, before the ramifications of this doctrine were explored fully in an administrative law setting, the *Canadian Charter of Rights and Freedoms* emerged with its guarantee in s. 11 of trial "within a reasonable time." While this provision's direct impact is restricted to the criminal process or situations involving true penal consequences, it has had an indirect impact on the interpretation of the "principles of fundamental justice" for the purposes of s. 7 of the Charter and on the common law in this arena.

As we have seen already, all of this surfaced in *Blencoe* where the Supreme Court accepted that both for the purposes of the Charter and the common law of procedural fairness, delay had both dimensions in the context of statutory decision making: delay that affected the ability of a person to respond adequately to proceedings in which he or she was responding to allegations and delay in its abuse of process sense. However, irrespective of category, the court also indicated that the argument was one that would be difficult to make out under either the Charter or the common law, at least where the applicant was seeking a stay of proceeding as opposed to an order for an expedited hearing. Consider the following case involving delay prejudicing the presentation of a response and consider whether it would be decided the same way in the wake of *Blencoe*. Consider also the extent to which, if at all, the court should take into account the decision-maker's institutional limitations or resources in cases such as this.

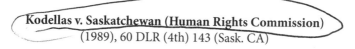

Kodellas v. Saskatchewan (Human Rights Commission)
(1989), 60 DLR (4th) 143 (Sask. CA)

BAYDA CJS: ... It is my opinion that for the purposes of determining an "unreasonable delay" in the context of s. 7 of the Charter in relation to a remedial proceeding under the Code, the factors to consider and weigh are: (1) whether the delay complained of is *prima facie* unreasonable, having regard to the time requirements inherent in such a remedial proceeding, (2) the reason or responsibility for the delay, having regard to the conduct of the complainants (at whose instance the proceedings were initiated), the conduct of the Commission (who by the provisions of the Code has carriage of the proceedings) including the inadequacy of or limitations to its institutional resources, and the conduct of the alleged discriminator, including whether he failed to object or waive any time period, and (3) the prejudice or impairment caused to the alleged discriminator by the delay. This list of factors (which I hasten to add, should not be regarded as an exclusive list) is by and large a composite of those factors outlined by the judges of the Supreme Court in *Rahey* in their respective judgments as adapted by me for use in a remedial proceeding under the Code.

[Bayda CJS determined that the 47- and 38-month delays between the filing of the two complaints and the hearing dates before a board of inquiry were much greater than the time requirements inherent in that stage of the proceedings, and that the delay was *prima facie* unreasonable having regard to those time requirements. Moreover, it appeared from the evidence that the delay was wholly ascribable to the commission. He noted that while the commission had given no explanation for the delay, there was a hint in the material before the court that inadequate institutional resources may have been a contributing factor.]

The last factor to consider and weigh is the actual prejudice which Mr. Kodellas alleges the delay has caused him. That prejudice is alleged to consist primarily, if not exclusively, of his inability to locate potential witnesses. He also complains of the fading recollection of potential witnesses. In an affidavit filed in support of his application he deposed in part:

8. That because of the time delay since I was initially notified of the complaints, it has been almost impossible to contact previous employees of the restaurant at the time of the alleged discrimination. In 1983 and early 1984 I had spoken with many people, including employees, who were prepared to testify on my behalf.

9. That it was our intention at that time to call the entire staff as witnesses to show that I have never behaved in the manner alleged by the complainants and to indicate that I

have never harassed women in general and particularly female employees. Since then, however, it has been difficult if not impossible to keep in touch with the former employees and our proposed witnesses. The witnesses that I am able to contact have difficulty recollecting things that happened three or four years ago.

10. That the restaurant industry typically attracts people who do not stay at any one particular job or residence for a long period of time and tend to be difficult to track down because of this transient nature.

11. That I am at a loss as to how I can contact former employees and witnesses to testify on my behalf so that I can defend myself properly and clear myself of these damaging allegations.

12. That these incidents happened so long ago that I myself have difficulty remembering particular things that happened during that time—in 1982 and 1983. My brothers have also informed me that they do not remember the events of that time frame very well either as it was so long ago.

In addition, there was filed an affidavit sworn by a student-at-law in the office of Mr. Kodellas' solicitors. The student deposed that he made 145 telephone calls and spent in excess of 14 hours in his endeavour to locate 50 previous employees, many of whom are potential witnesses in Mr. Kodellas' behalf. He was successful in contacting only 12 of those 50 previous employees.

There may well be some difficulty in locating many of the potential witnesses. How serious a prejudice that amounts to is not entirely clear. For example, there is nothing to suggest whether each in the group of potential witnesses has it within his or her power to disclose evidence which no other person is able to disclose or whether the evidence of many of those in the group will serve only as confirmatory evidence which Mr. Kodellas is already able to adduce. In short, there is nothing to indicate how many of the missing witnesses are essential to Mr. Kodellas' defence, how many fall into the category of "nice to have" and how many actually have nothing to add. Does it take 50 previous employees "to show that I have never behaved in the manner alleged by the complainants and to indicate that I have never harassed women in general and particularly female employees"? Would 12 not be sufficient? Moreover, even if the 50 witnesses were to affirm Mr. Kodellas's general demeanour toward women, how great an exculpatory effect would such an affirmation have respecting specific complaints by the first and second complainants? I might also add that I am also not overly impressed with the efforts that were made to locate the potential witnesses. It would seem that a little more effort by an individual experienced in locating missing persons would very quickly reveal the whereabouts of many of the remaining 38 whom the student-at-law was unable to locate. In the end I think it fair to conclude, however, that Mr. Kodellas has shown some actual prejudice caused to him by the delay.

A weighing of the factors in this series results in the conclusion that the *prima facie* unreasonable delay which I initially found, has not been explained or in any way displaced.

Appeal dismissed.

NOTES

1. Notable in this context are Ontario judgments to the effect that, in general, the issue whether there has been unreasonable delay should not be dealt with in the context of an application for relief in the nature of prohibition. Rather, the tribunal itself should be left to respond to such arguments at the hearing: *Ontario College of Art v. Ontario (Ontario Human Rights Commission)* (1992), 99 DLR (4th) 738 (Ont. Div. Ct.) and *Hughes v. Ontario College of Physician & Surgeons* (1994), 112 DLR (4th) 253 (Ont. Div. Ct.). Compare, however, *Canadian Airlines International v. Canada (Canadian Human Rights Commission)* (1992), 57 FTR 311, granting an interlocutory injunction to prevent a hearing proceeding until such time as an allegation of unreasonable delay could be dealt with on an application for prohibition. (Incidentally, this argument was also advanced in *Blencoe* at first instance but was rejected by Lowry J (at paras. 15-16), a finding that was sustained by the Court of Appeal. This issue was not argued in the Supreme Court of Canada.) Assuming that courts should generally leave tribunals to reach at least a tentative conclusion on such issues, should that be affected by whether the tribunal engages in this task as a preliminary matter or merges it with the hearing of the merits of the case before it?

2. Where the delay in question is in the processing of an application for a benefit, the only real recourse that an applicant may have will be a mandatory order that the application be dealt with. Generally, delay will not generate a claim to the benefit itself even where Charter rights are at stake. See *Akthar v. Canada (Minister of Employment and Immigration)*, [1991] 3 FC 32 (CA). Consider, however, whether that should be an unvarying rule or whether there are circumstances where a claim to the benefit could be generated.

3. You are advising a university on whether or not it should postpone disciplinary hearings against a student for alleged sexual assault when the student is also subject to criminal charges arising out of the same incident. What factors are relevant in determining what to do and, to what extent, if at all, should you be concerned about issues of delay?

The Actual Hearing

Oral Hearings

Like many terms in administrative law, the phrase "oral hearing" can have different meanings. In this section, we use it in the sense of a face to face encounter with the actual decision-maker (or someone formally and legally deputed by that decision-maker to hear and receive evidence) and, where relevant, the other party or parties. In this sense, it can be contrasted with hearings that take place purely in writing or on the basis of electronically generated data and also with decision-making processes where conclusions are based on interviews but not conducted by the actual decision-maker or in the presence of the other parties. While, in many contexts, the concept of an oral hearing also assumes the presence of other procedural entitlements, such as the formal presentation of evidence and an entitlement to counsel, we make no such assumptions in this section, seeing these as separate issues that will be taken up in the following sections of this chapter.

Traditionally, an oral hearing was usually required as an element of natural justice, although not always. In *Komo Construction Inc. v. Commission des Relations de Travail du Québec*, [1968] SCR 172 (Que.), Pigeon J said, "Turning now to the application of the *audi alteram partem* rule, it is important to note that the rule does not imply that there must always be a hearing." And in this context "hearing" clearly meant an oral hearing, contrasted to natural justice generally. Courts seemed to give agencies considerable discretion; for example, in *Hoffman-La Roche v. Delmar Chemicals*, [1965] SCR 575 (Can.), the question was about the procedures to be used by the commissioner of patents to make decisions about granting compulsory patent licences. Martland J said, "It was for him to decide whether or not the circumstances required an oral hearing, cross examination upon affidavits, or oral submissions. In my opinion, his discretion not to require any of these things cannot be considered to be a denial of natural justice to the appellant." However, cases in which these kinds of comments were made tended to be ones in which the refusal to give an oral hearing seemed sensible, and the discretion was far from being extensive. Again, the norm tended to be an oral hearing, and again it is useful to remember the allocation of responsibility for the choice between the courts and the agencies as a separate theme.

With the emergence of the procedural fairness doctrine, the presumption in favour of oral hearings as the norm disappeared in the expanded common law procedural terrain. Indeed, recollect that in the first major Canadian procedural fairness judgment, *Nicholson*, Laskin CJC, in describing the applicant's procedural entitlements at any resumed consideration of his status as a police officer, clearly left the discretion on whether to proceed by way of oral or written hearing in the hands of the Board of Commissioners of Police. This contained echoes of *Delmar Chemicals*, and the need for deference to the procedural choices of certain decision-makers (including choices about the mode of hearing) achieved even stronger affirmation in *Baker* where the Supreme Court sustained the immigration authorities' holding of a written hearing at least in that instance. The legitimacy of other forms of hearing (written and electronic) has also achieved extensive recognition in the 1994 amendments to the SPPA.

The countervailing tendency is, of course, to be found in the context of decisions affecting rights protected by the Charter and the *Bill of Rights*. In this regard, recollect Beetz J's judgment in *Singh*, condemning the statutory structure by reference to the *Bill of Rights* on the basis that the applicants' claim to Convention refugee status could be "finally denied without their having been afforded a full *oral* hearing at a single stage of the proceedings before any of the bodies or officials empowered to adjudicate on their claim on the merits" (emphasis added). It is, however, also worth recalling that Wilson J's emphasis was not so much on the absence of an oral hearing but lack of access to the ministry's case. For her, an oral hearing was not necessarily a universal component of the "principles of fundamental justice" under s. 7 of the Charter, though she did reiterate the conventional wisdom as to the need for such a procedure "where a serious issue as to credibility is involved." Subsequently, this has been confirmed in *Suresh*. Recollect also *Kindler v. Canada (Minister of Justice)*, [1991] 2 SCR 779 (Can.), in which it was held that the minister's obligation to adhere to the "principles of fundamental justice" in extradition matters did not warrant the imposition of an oral or in-person hearing prior to the making of an order surrendering a person to the requesting jurisdiction. Any submissions as to whether such an order should be made and, if so, as to its terms could be made adequately in writing. Another interesting example is *Hundal v. Superintendent of Motor Vehicles* (1985), 20 DLR (4th) 592 (BC CA), where the court accepted that the suspension of a driver's licence engaged s. 7 but went on to hold that the superintendent did not have to hold an in-person hearing when suspending a licence under a demerit points system. Such a hearing was not necessary for a proper consideration of a plea of mitigation against the operation of the normal rules. An opportunity to respond in writing would be adequate. Credibility was not a major factor.

Claims to an oral hearing are also ones that are situation sensitive in the sense that their necessity may depend on the matters that are at issue in the particular proceedings as opposed to being a feature of all exercises of the relevant statutory power. This is clear from the fact that the Supreme Court did not purport to be laying down a general rule in *Baker*. Under what circumstances should someone seeking a favourable exercise of the minister's humanitarian and compassionate jurisdiction have an entitlement to some form of oral hearing? Recollect also that the court never reached the Charter arguments in *Baker*. Should the outcome on this issue be affected by that?

As already noted, the conventional view has always been that the claim to an oral hearing is at its highest when credibility is an issue in the proceedings. Today, that view is not unchallenged and, in certain situations, is seen as being subject to competing values. Thus, arguments are made that it is preferable to gather evidence in certain kinds of cases by inquisitorial methods and to neither allow others to be present nor expose those interviewed to cross-examination. One example where such claims are made frequently is in the context of sexual harassment complaints, the justification advanced being that the trauma associated with having to confront one's harasser and to be cross-examined simply acts as too great an obstacle to formal complaints being lodged.

Of course, in this context, the issues at stake are more than simply those normally associated with debates over oral as opposed to written hearings. In addition, they also involve questions about open hearings, cross-examination rights, and access to and the opportunity to meet adverse evidence. While all the difficulties are not confronted as directly as they might have been, the following judgment provides an example of where a sexual harassment complaint was dealt with by methods of inquiry other than a regular hearing.

Masters v. Ontario
(1994), 18 OR (3d) 551 (Div. Ct.)

[Masters was the Ontario agent general in New York. He had been appointed by the premier in the exercise of prerogative power. Following complaints of sexual harassment against Masters, the premier requested a team of external investigators to ascertain the facts. Ultimately, this produced a report to the effect that Masters had sexually harassed seven women. Following a response by Masters (who had been suspended from the outset of the inquiry), the premier determined that Masters should no longer be agent general but be reassigned to another position in the civil service. Rather than accept reassignment, Masters resigned on the basis of a financial settlement.

He then applied for judicial review of the investigators' report alleging (*inter alia*) various breaches of the rules of natural justice in the conduct of the investigation. Among the concerns identified in the application for judicial review were that the 45 "witnesses" had been interviewed by the investigators without Masters or his counsel being present; that he had been refused access to the list of questions that were asked, the copies of any notes, transcripts, or tapes that were made during the interviews, and the names of the investigators who had conducted the interviews; and that, while Masters was allowed to interview the witnesses himself, few agreed to meet with him.]

ADAMS J (delivering the judgment of a court consisting otherwise of Then and Dunnet JJ): ...

Mr. Blue's central submission was that Masters was entitled to have the determination of whether he had engaged in sexual harassment placed before an impartial decision maker and to be accorded the right to cross-examine all witnesses adverse in interest.

· · ·

Also challenged in these proceedings was the refusal to provide Masters' counsel with "equal" access to the same witnesses interviewed by the investigators and that this inequality of treatment further contributed to a reasonable apprehension of bias. A related objection pertained to the investigators' "unfair" refusal to provide witness statements to MacKillop [Masters' lawyer at the investigative stage] during the investigation process. Finally, it was complained that Masters had not been given an opportunity to respond to the new allegations prior to the completion of the investigation report.

· · ·

However, the central submission of Mr. Blue was that where credibility will determine the main issue before a government decision maker, particularly where that main issue is vital to an interested party's professional career, the general duty of fairness and the rules of natural justice require that an impartial decision maker first be designated to determine credibility by way of a full trial-type hearing permitting witnesses to be subjected to cross-examination. This, of course, was not done.

· · ·

In correspondence dated September 24, 1992, over the signature of his counsel, Masters replied to the detailed allegations disclosed to him on August 25, 1992. He also met with the investigators and submitted to a lengthy interview on September 17, 1992. By letter dated October 2, 1992, he was provided with a typewritten copy of the investigators' notes of his interview to check for accuracy. With minor exceptions, Mr. Masters approved the accuracy of those notes.

[After a discussion of the authorities and particularly *Knight* as to diminished weight to be attributed to procedural fairness claims in relation to offices held at pleasure and to investigative as opposed to adjudicative functions, Adams J continued.]

In applying this framework to the facts at hand, one must not lose sight of the fact that the position held by the applicant was of high office and that he was directly accountable to the Premier. He occupied a politically sensitive position representing Ontario outside Canada. He clearly understood that his continued employment was at the discretion of the Premier and was specifically subject to the continuing confidence of the Premier. The nature of the employer and employee relationship in these circumstances, therefore, involves complete ministerial discretion ... . Masters' position was more politically accountable and more senior than those positions in *Nicholson* and *Knight*. Further, the Premier was not acting pursuant to a statute but rather was exercising a prerogative to consider revoking one of his earlier appointments. These features of the decision making distinguish this case from *Nicholson* and *Knight*, placing it even more towards the discretionary or legislative end of the spectrum referred to in *Martineau*.

On the other hand, neither the decision-making nor the investigation focused on "broad grounds of public policy." Rather, the issues became whether or not Masters could be said by his employer to have engaged in sexual harassment as alleged and, if so, what action should be taken. Both his employment and his reputation were understood to be at stake. Unfortunately, a mere allegation of sexual harassment may indelibly damage an individual ... The well-being of the women involved and the fundamental need for an harassment-free workplace, however, were also pressing concerns. Indeed, the Government of Ontario had recognized both the effect of harassment on employees and the impact of related accusations upon alleged perpetrators by promulgating [a Workplace Discrimination and Harassment Prevention Directive] through the Management Board. The Premier, on advice, decided to apply the investigatory procedures of the Directive to the accusations against Masters, as best as those procedures could be adapted to the situation. Thus, the problem was not dispatched by the exercise of a sweeping discretion on the broad policy grounds of the Premier's continuing confidence. Instead, procedures were tailored to the peculiar nature of the allegations in order to permit a more informed assessment. The duty of fairness, in these circumstances, should have its content influenced by the Directive which the government itself chose to apply.

However, the submission by Mr. Blue, that Masters was entitled to a trial-type hearing before an impartial decision maker, with a full panoply of rights including cross-examination of his accusers, is without merit. ...

[Adams J here relied principally on authorities governing investigative functions.]

No exception, as well, can be taken to MacKillop's relative lack of direct contact with witnesses. The duty of fairness did not require the government to use its coercive powers as employer and direct witnesses to subject themselves to MacKillop's questioning. Admirably, it provided the applicant's counsel with an opportunity to interview those employees who wished to be questioned. The employees could even do so on working time. No active steps were taken to hinder the preparation of Masters' case. In this respect, nothing more was required. ...

The *Statutory Powers Procedure Act*, RSO 1990, c. S.22, s. 1, has no application in the circumstances. No statutory power of decision was exercised within the meaning of that Act. No hearing was required either by statute or "otherwise by law."

. . .

MacKillop later agreed with Agnew [the Secretary of the Cabinet] that Masters would have a final right of reply to the completed report of the investigators prior to the Premier making any assessment. At the time this arrangement was made, MacKillop was well aware the investigators were following up on his client's responses to the allegations by reattending in New York and Boston to speak with the witnesses. It is clear that everyone was anxious to have the report completed as soon as possible. Indeed, MacKillop was critical of the investigators for their delay in concluding their investigation. Expedition was an important feature of the process from the outset ... . And again, this was not a hybrid dispute resolution process, combining investigatory and adjudicatory responsibilities as in *Re Downing and Graydon* (1978) 92 DLR (3d) 355 (Ont. CA). If it has any parallel, [*Inuit Tapirisat*] is more to the point and, in that case, it was held that the federal Cabinet, in entertaining a statutory appeal, had no obligation to permit a reply submission. …

I find that the witnesses' responses to Masters' denials and counter-accusations did not amount to material changes in the allegations against him. The substance of the accusations remained constant. Rather, some additional detail relating to existing allegations was recalled by some of the witnesses in response to his interview and submissions. In the circumstances, therefore, the investigators were not obliged to obtain his further response, particularly in light of the Supreme Court of Canada's explicit adoption in [*Knight*] of the excerpt from [*Selvarajan v. Race Relations Board*, [1976] 1 WLR 1686 (CA)], requiring that "the broad grounds," but not "every detail" be given. This language is to be contrasted with that found in the natural justice cases dealing with quasi-judicial functions. For example, *Re Downing and Graydon* speaks of "any information" gathered which is prejudicial, and of the opportunity to make legal argument. Similarly, *Board of Education v. Rice* [1911] AC 179 (Eng. HL) at 182, contains the phrase "any relevant statement prejudicial to their view." Furthermore, Masters was in fact given the opportunity by the Premier to make legal argument and to respond to all additional details, an opportunity he and his lawyer exercised by their very full reply of October 15, 1992. Neither the investigators nor the affected women were given the opportunity of further reply.

For similar reasons, there was no need to provide the applicant with all the witness statements. Disclosure of the substance of the accusations against him was sufficient. …

The Premier considered the applicant's October 15, 1992 submissions together with the investigators' report and concluded, in light of the number and pattern of informal complainants, that Masters could be brought back to Toronto. Nothing more was required in the circumstances. Masters was given an adequate opportunity to know the allegations against him and to state his case before the Premier considered the matter. The Directive's requirements were substantially complied with, keeping in mind MacKillop's complaints to the investigators about the delay in completing their report, the content of his meeting with Agnew on September 29, 1992, and the fact that he was given the final right of reply by the Premier. The procedures adopted were adequately tailored to the distinctive nature of harassment allegations having regard to all of the circumstances.

For the applicant's benefit, however, it must be emphasized again that the Premier was not conducting a trial. Clearly, an adversary trial is much more likely to produce "truth" and the perception of "fairness" than a mere investigation: see Fuller, "The Forms and Limits of the Adversary Process" (1978) 92 *Harv. LR* 353; and Brooks, "The Judge and the Adversary System," Linden ed., *The Canadian Judiciary* (1976) at 90-116. For example, in the criminal setting, persons are sometimes accused of criminal wrongdoing as a result of a police investigation and yet acquitted after an adversary trial. Similarly, in civil trials, we often observe employees vindicated of wrong doing despite their employers having concluded otherwise prior to dismissing them. In comparison to a trial, therefore, there is a much greater margin for error in the "findings" of any investigation. This is particularly so where findings depend on difficult determinations of credibility, motive and intent. In fact, the Premier appears to have expressed related concerns to the applicant at their meeting on either October 31 or November 7, 1992, when Masters was also told he could ultimately sue the government if need be.

It should, therefore, be understood that the allegations made against the applicant were never adjudicated. The investigatory process deployed to inquire into his alleged conduct, by its very nature, did not afford him all the safeguards of a trial and *Nicholson* and *Knight* do not require otherwise. To hold that they do would be to transform the nature of the discretion at issue. Moreover, the fact that a lawsuit for wrongful dismissal to test the allegations contained in the report may not be practically open to the applicant because of the "at pleasure" doctrine, simply recognizes the discretionary nature of his appointment: see *Re Multi-Malls Inc. and Minister of Transportation and Communications* (1976) 73 DLR (3d) 18 (Ont. CA) at 27. It is not a basis, through the fairness doctrine, for requiring the implementation of a trial or trial-like procedure prior to the discretion being exercised.

For all of these reasons, I find that Masters was aware of all the material allegations against him and was provided with an adequate opportunity to be heard. The investigation was neither unfair nor biased by reason of any of the grounds alleged. The requirements of the duty to act fairly in the scope of the employer-employee relationship in the case at bar were met.

. . .

Application dismissed.

NOTES

1. Much of Adams J's justifications for holding that Masters was not entitled to a trial-type hearing or even to confront directly either in person or through his counsel the witnesses against him stems from his analysis of the nature of the process that was being conducted as well as the nature of Masters' position. Indeed, he takes pains to point out, *inter alia*, that the Ontario *Statutory Powers Procedure Act* was not applicable to the proceedings. Should the rejection of Masters' arguments be seen as stemming solely from these considerations and, if so, are they sufficient to justify deviation from what is assumed to be the norm in dismissal from employment cases? Conversely, why should the limitations on access to one's accusers be restricted to cases such as this: see *Semchuk v. Regina Board of Education, Division No. 4* (1987), 37 DLR (4th) 738 (Sask. CA); aff'g. (1986), 26 Admin. LR 88 (Sask. QB), a judgment cited by Adams J, in which the court, as an alternative ground for its decision, held that a dismissed employee had no necessary natural justice entitlement to confront his accusers as part of the principles of procedural fairness attendant on an actual dismissal decision taken by a school board.

2. The final case in this section provides an illustration of how claims to an oral hearing (and procedural claims generally) are affected by the way the courts characterize the issue before the decision-maker and the nature of the interest that is at stake.

Khan v. University of Ottawa
(1997), 34 OR (3d) 535 (CA)

[When Khan, a second-year student, failed her evidence exam, her grade point average dipped below the faculty minimum, requiring her to complete an additional semester of courses. Khan appealed her grade to the Faculty Examinations Committee on the ground that she had submitted a fourth answer booklet that had not been graded. The committee met without providing Khan notice of the meeting or asking her to appear. After the meeting, at which the existence of the fourth booklet was the main issue, the committee dismissed Khan's appeal. After an unsuccessful appeal to a University Senate Committee, Khan sought judicial review of the decisions denying her appeal.]

LASKIN JA (Brooke JA concurring): ...

The Faculty of Law Regulations stipulate that examinations must be either two or three hours long. Ms. Khan thought that the Evidence exam was two hours long. In fact, it was set for two-and-a-half hours. During the first two hours, she answered all the exam questions in three examination booklets. Although not required to do so, she labelled her booklets "1 of 3," "2 of 3" and "3 of 3." A few minutes before what she thought was the end of the examination, she put the three booklets to the side of her table. She then looked up and saw the proctor writing on the blackboard that 35 minutes remained in the examination.

Realizing that she had been mistaken about the length of the exam, Ms. Khan began writing in a fourth examination booklet, in which she supplemented her answers to seven of the exam questions. She labelled this examination booklet "INSERT" in large red letters across the front. She said that she did not number the fourth booklet because she wanted her instructor to realize that this booklet added to answers she had already given in the first three booklets. However, she did not write anything on the first three booklets to notify the instructor of the fourth booklet.

On January 18, 1996, Ms. Khan was told that she had been given a failing grade in Evidence. On February 11, 1996, she was allowed to view her Evidence examination booklets and she realized that the fourth booklet, labelled "INSERT," was missing. She had been marked on her three examination booklets and was later told that the instructor did not recall seeing any booklet labelled "INSERT" in large red letters. A university administrator looked through the files of the other students who wrote the Evidence examination but did not find Ms. Khan's fourth booklet. On February 14, 1996 she appealed to the Faculty of Law Examinations Committee.

Ms. Khan did not fare well in her other courses during second year. Nonetheless, had she passed Evidence, she would have passed her year. But her failing grade in Evidence lowered her grade point average below the level required to pass. The university considers that she has failed her second year of law school and that she must complete an additional semester of courses before she can graduate.

. . .

The only record of the Examinations Committee's reasons is a memorandum from the chair of the Committee to the Senate Committee dated almost one month after the Examinations Committee had made its decision. That memorandum reads as follows:

> The Committee discussed Ms. Nalini [sic] application at some length, but was unable to grant her claim. In particular, the Committee took into account the following factors in coming to its decision:

— the strict procedures and extremely careful efforts made by exam invigilators and staff to ensure that all exam booklets are collected at the end of an exam and delivered to the Professor for grading;

— the fact that the alleged situation (ie: loss of an exam booklet handed in by a student in the exam hall) has not occurred in the past;

— the fact that Ms. Nalini [sic] indicated on her first exam booklet that she had completed a total of three booklets; and

— and the fact that little was written in the third of the three exam booklets which were in fact collected and graded.

The Dean of the Law School wrote a covering letter in which she said, "It is my understanding that the Committee was not convinced that a fourth booklet existed."

. . .

In my view, a university student threatened with the loss of an academic year by a failing grade is also entitled to a high standard of justice. The effect of a failed year may be very serious for a university student. It will certainly delay if not end the career for which the student was studying. It may render valueless any previous academic success. In some cases it may foreclose further university education entirely. ...

In my opinion procedural fairness before the Examinations Committee in this case required the following: first, and most important, the Committee should have given Ms. Khan an oral hearing because her credibility was a critical issue on her appeal. By an oral hearing, I mean a hearing in which she had an opportunity to appear in person before the Committee and an opportunity to make oral representations to it. Second, the Committee should have considered the procedures followed during and after the Evidence examination and made reasonable inquiries to determine whether these procedures were proper. Third, the Committee should have given Ms. Khan an opportunity to correct or contradict the three "factors" it relied on in its decision. The Examination Committee did not observe these requirements and therefore denied Ms. Khan procedural fairness.

(i) Ms. Khan Was Entitled to an Oral Hearing

Under para. 12.03(a) of the Faculty of Law Regulations, a student is entitled to have a grade reviewed "where it appears that the grade assigned to a student's work may be the result of a significant error or injustice." Under para. 12.03(b) of the Regulations, students who appeal their grades to the Examinations Committee have the onus "to identify specific facts or evidence suggesting that a significant error or injustice may have occurred." In her cross-examination the chair of the Examinations Committee acknowledged on behalf of the university that a grade given without considering the fourth booklet would amount to a significant error or injustice. The chair also acknowledged that if the fourth booklet had not been graded, Ms. Khan would be entitled to rewrite the Evidence examination.

Therefore, the question before the Examinations Committee was whether Ms. Khan had written the fourth booklet. The only direct evidence that she did a write a fourth booklet was her word. If the Committee members believed her explanation, she was entitled to relief. If they did not believe her explanation, then her appeal was properly dismissed. In short, the Committee had to decide whether Ms. Khan was telling the truth.

The Divisional Court, however, saw the matter differently. In its brief endorsement it said:

> We disagree with the applicant's position that the credibility of the applicant was the pivotal concern in the matter before the Committees. She was not accused of dishonesty by the university administration. Rather, the applicant complained about a failure on the part of the university to properly assess her effort in completing the evidence examination. ...
>
> The applicant did not discharge the burden on her of demonstrating on a balance of probabilities that the fourth examination booklet was handed in and had been mislaid.

In my view, the Divisional Court's reasoning is not persuasive. Ms. Khan's credibility was the central issue before the Committee. How else could she have demonstrated that she handed in a fourth booklet except by pledging her word that she did? If the Committee accepted her word, it was bound to allow her appeal. Certainly, the chair of the Examinations Committee recognized that the Committee's decision turned on Ms. Khan's credibility. When cross-examined on her affidavit for the judicial review application, she admitted, "I did not believe that a fourth exam booklet had been handed in. ... [I]n the end I disbelieved Ms. Khan's assertion." When the Dean said that the Committee was not convinced that a fourth booklet existed, she could only have meant that the Committee was not convinced that Ms. Khan was telling the truth. This is not an issue on which Ms. Khan could have been mistaken. She either did or did not write a fourth booklet.

Moreover, the three "factors" on which the Committee relied to justify its decision are no more than pieces of circumstantial evidence that caused the Committee members to disbelieve Ms. Khan's word. The third factor, in particular, shows that the Committee rejected Ms. Khan's statement. The Examinations Committee relied on "the fact that Ms. Khan indicated on her first exam booklet that she had completed a total of three booklets; and the fact that little was written in the third of the three exam booklets which were in fact collected and graded." Ms. Khan had an explanation for these facts. In my view, the Examinations Committee was obliged to hear her explanation before rejecting it.

In many academic appeals, procedural fairness will not demand an oral hearing. An opportunity to make a written submission may suffice. For example, I doubt that students appealing their grades because they believe they should have received a higher mark would ordinarily be entitled to an oral hearing. What distinguishes this case is that the determining issue before the Examinations Committee was Ms. Khan's credibility. In denying Ms. Khan relief the Committee judged her credibility adversely. In my view, the Committee should not have done so without affording her an in-person hearing and an opportunity to make representations orally.

[Laskin JA here dealt with the authorities, including *Singh*.]

The university submits, however, that an oral hearing was not required because Ms. Khan was not charged with any kind of misconduct. Admittedly she was not charged with dishonesty or any other wrongdoing, and the proceedings before the Examinations Committee were not strictly adversarial. But her credibility was, nonetheless, the primary issue before the Committee. The success of her appeal depended on the Committee's acceptance of her statement. If the Committee believed her assertion that she had written a fourth booklet, she would have met the onus on her to demonstrate that a significant error or injustice may have occurred. Because Ms. Khan's appeal turned on her credibility and because of the serious consequences to her of an adverse finding, fairness required an oral hearing. The Committee disbelieved Ms. Khan's explanation for the fourth booklet without hearing from her. This amounted to a denial of procedural fairness, which by itself fatally flawed the proceedings before the Committee.

. . .

Ms. Khan need not show actual prejudice to prove that she has been denied procedural fairness. She need only show that the Committee's breach of its duty of fairness may reasonably have prejudiced her: see *Kane* [*v. University of British Columbia*, [1980] 1 SCR 1105 (BC)], at p. 1116. She has met that burden.

FINLAYSON JA (dissenting): ... At the outset, as an overview to my reasons in dissent, I am compelled to comment on the appropriate standard of judicial review. In my view, this court must ensure that its judgment is not premised on a state of facts that accepts in full and without caveat every claim made by the appellant and her supporters at every stage of the proceedings in appeal, while reacting negatively to every explanation by both the Faculty and Senate Committees as to why they were not prepared to grant her appeal of a failing grade.

As a supplement to this observation, it is not up to the appellant to define the issue in appeal to her own liking. Despite the protestations of those in authority to the contrary, the appellant has consistently maintained that there is and was but one issue in these proceedings. Did the appellant lie when she said there was a fourth booklet? By insisting that this was the only matter that required a response, the appellant has co-opted the agenda of the Faculty Committee and demanded that she is entitled to a standard of justice reserved to students who face sanction because of personal misconduct. She does not acknowledge that the only issue before the Faculty Committee and later the Senate Committee was whether the grading of an examination had been subject to an error or injustice. The appellant insists upon the right to attend and assert in person that there was a fourth booklet as if establishing that fact would be conclusive, but the Committee members were aware of the quality of the work in the three booklets she did turn in, and the examining professor's assessment of the poor calibre of that work. Comments attributed to the professor regarding the examination and possibility of a fourth booklet are illuminating: "More of the same wouldn't have been beneficial."

Complementary to his argument that credibility is the issue, the appellant's counsel goes to some extremes to disparage the faculty's limited investigation of the appellant's assertion that there was a fourth booklet. This is an attempt to place the burden on the two Committees to demonstrate affirmatively that a fourth booklet did not exist, and failing that responsibility, accept the appellant's bald assertion. In my opinion, this imposes upon the respondents a standard of response that is entirely out of keeping with the issue actually before them and it unfairly ignores the investigative efforts that were made on the appellant's behalf.

. . .

As was the practice of the Committee, the appellant was given the opportunity to provide a full and detailed written account of the reasons why she deserved relief. She took full advantage of this opportunity. While she was not invited to appear before the Committee, at no time did the appellant suggest that it was important to her to appear. She did not give any indication, then or now, that the information she provided in her written brief was not complete.

. . .

Analysis

I agree with the position of the respondent Committee, also accepted by the Senate Committee and the Divisional Court, that this was not a matter which turned on credibility. There were no allegations made against the appellant and the proceedings were not adversarial in nature. The appellant had not been charged with cheating on an examination or with any other disreputable conduct as a member of the student body. The consequence to her was not expulsion from the faculty or even loss of a full academic year of study. The issue was merely, on all the evidence, including her statement, were the Faculty Committee and the Senate Committee correct in holding in the course of their review that they were not satisfied that there was a fourth booklet which made up for the gross deficiencies in the answers given by the appellant in the three booklets that they had.

The Requirements of Natural Justice

We have been referred to no authority that a student is entitled as of right to be heard in person when she or he is asking for a review of the student's marks. The suggestion that the review cannot be denied if it is implicit in the reasons of the Faculty Committee that they did not accept the self-serving statements of the student, imposes an unreasonable procedural burden on the university and its various faculties. The appellant was only entitled to a full opportunity to be heard so that her position could be fairly put and considered. The record clearly shows that the appellant was afforded the opportunity to make submissions and that she took full advantage of the opportunity to do so.

It is well established in law that an oral hearing is not required to satisfy the demands of natural justice: see *Komo Construction Inc. v. Commission des Relations de Travail du Québec* [1968] SCR 172 (Que.). ...

[Finlayson JA here dealt with the authorities.]

Courts have traditionally given administrative tribunals the discretion to determine their own procedures, including the means by which submissions are entertained: see *Hoffmann-La Roche v. Delmar Chemicals* [1965] SCR 575. The courts acknowledge that every administrative body must resolve the tension between providing procedural fairness on the one hand, and maintaining efficiency and effectiveness on the other hand. Written submissions are an accepted method of meeting these sometimes conflicting demands. The method of "hearing" submissions, whether oral or written, is less important than whether the tribunal does, in fact, receive and consider the parties' submissions. *Evans et al., Administrative Law, Cases, Text and Materials*, 4th ed. (1995), at p. 69, agree with the proposition that an administrative body may choose to proceed by way of oral or written submissions, provided that it does in substance hear the arguments.

The appellant submits that where credibility is a serious issue, there is an exception to the general proposition that written submissions will satisfy the requirements of natural justice. She relies on the judgment of Wilson J, in *Singh*. ...

The case is distinguishable from the case before us. The appellant concedes that in that case, Wilson J was dealing with an issue of fundamental justice under s. 7 of the *Canadian Charter of Rights and Freedoms*, engaging the appellants' rights to life, liberty and security of person. The reasons of Beetz J in the same case, concurring in result but differing in reasons, are instructive on this point. He agreed with Wilson J that the appellants were entitled to an oral hearing. He held that the rights at issue—life, liberty and security of person—were of such vital importance, that an oral hearing was warranted. ...

Therefore, in *Singh*, the Supreme Court's conclusion that an oral hearing to determine issues of credibility was required was inextricably linked to the serious nature of the rights at stake. Both Beetz J and Wilson J accepted that fundamental justice may not always require an oral hearing, and indeed there have been cases decided where failure to provide an oral hearing was found not to infringe the principles of fundamental justice: see *Hundal*. In the case before us, the appellant is invoking the requirements of natural justice, not the broader concepts of fundamental justice. Furthermore, the gravity of the rights in issue and the consequences of the decision significantly differ. Here, Charter rights are not in issue. The appellant, at most, will be required to prolong the completion of her education by one semester, until she has satisfied the requirements for graduation.

· · ·

The adversarial and *quasi*-criminal nature of the proceedings in [other university] cases and the gravity of consequences on the individuals must be compared with the case before us. In each of the cases cited, the applicant/appellant was responding to allegations made against them, and consequently, their credibility and that of the witnesses against them, were central issues. Here, there are no allegations made against the appellant. The proceedings were a review of the grading of her examination. The Committees did not conclude that the appellant had been dishonest. They concluded that there was insufficient evidence of the existence of a fourth booklet and could find no error or injustice in the grading of the examination. As a result, the appellant is required to complete one more semester at school to ensure that she meets the academic standards for graduation.

· · ·

Accordingly, in determining whether natural justice has been denied, it is necessary to examine the circumstances of the case before us. The legal rights involved and the consequences to the appellant do not merit the standard of justice which she would dictate. I reiterate, there were no allegations against the appellant, and certainly no accusations of dishonesty. The proceedings were not adversarial in nature. A decision affecting the right to continue in one's profession or employment may demand a higher standard of justice (see *Kane v. University of British Columbia, supra*, at p. 1113); however, that is not the case here. The appellant has not been denied an opportunity or refused entrance into the legal profession. She is merely required to prolong her schooling by one semester to allow her to demonstrate an ability to achieve the necessary academic standards. It must be noted that this outcome was brought about by the cumulative effect of the appellant's poor academic performance in her second year of school and had she produced better results in her other courses, the appellant's grade point average would have merited a pass for the year, despite a failure in the Evidence course. As it turns out, she may still graduate, achieve the qualifications to practise and enter the legal profession.

Appeal allowed.

NOTE

Some tribunals have adopted the eminently sensible practice of receiving some forms of evidence in writing and others orally. (For a sustaining of the Ontario Municipal Board's use of a process of "canned evidence," see *Morista Developments Ltd. v. Ontario Municipal Board* (1990), 2 Admin. LR (2d) 113 (Ont. Div. Ct.).)

Open Hearings

Assuming that there is to be an oral hearing, in the sense of one held at a specific place and time, the matter of whether it should be open to the public was treated traditionally as a question within the discretion of the tribunal: *Re Millward and Public Service Commission*, [1974] 2 FC 530 (TD); *Re Toronto Star and Toronto Newspaper Guild* (1976), 73 DLR (3d) 370 (Ont. Div. Ct.). However, in Ontario, for tribunals subject to the SPPA, while openness is still a matter for tribunal discretion, s. 9 of the SPPA conditions the exercise of that discretion with a presumption in favour of openness and creates specific considerations that are to form the basis of any decision to proceed *in camera* either in whole or in part.

A contrast can be found in the following provision in the *Immigration Act*, RSC 1985, c. I-2, s. 69, where the presumption was the other way. Why do you think that was so?

(2) Subject to subsection (3), proceedings before the Refugee Division shall be conducted *in camera* unless it is established to the satisfaction of the Division, on application by a member of the public, that the conduct of the proceedings in public would not impede the proceedings and that the person who is the subject of the proceedings or any member of that person's family would not be adversely affected if the proceedings were conducted in public.

Observers allowed

(3) The Refugee Division shall allow any representative or agent of the United Nations High Commissioner for Refugees to attend any proceedings before it as an observer and, at the request or with the consent of the person who is the subject of the proceedings, shall allow any other person to attend the proceedings as an observer if, in the opinion of the Division, the attendance of that other person is not likely to impede the proceedings.

In fact, the equivalent provision applicable to the conduct of inquiries by adjudicators (s. 29(3)) was found to be an infringement of s. 2(b) of the *Canadian Charter of Rights and Freedoms* and its protection of "freedom of expression" and "freedom of the press": *Pacific Press Ltd. v. Canada (Minister of Employment & Immigration)* (1991), 127 NR 325 (FCA). Proceeding on the basis that such inquiries were sufficiently judicial to qualify them as court proceedings for the purposes of s. 2(b) analysis, MacGuigan JA, delivering the judgment of the court, held that s. 29(3), as an infringement of the freedom of the press and expression, was overinclusive in terms of the objectives at which it was aimed (the protection of refugee claimants and their families) and could not be justified by reference to s. 1. It was not restricted in its application to hearings in which a refugee claim was being advanced; the onus it placed on the public seeking an open hearing was one that was impossible to discharge; it did not contemplate any intermediate possibility such as a publication ban; and it was not part of an otherwise "watertight" system, in that considerable information about refugee claims was potentially otherwise available on the public record. (The last three of these reasons seem equally applicable to s. 64(2).) The court, however, postponed the operation of its declaration of invalidity for a year to give Parliament an opportunity to amend the legislation.

As a consequence, in the controversial 1992 amendments to the *Immigration Act*, SC 1992, c. 49, s. 29 of the Act was amended to provide that all hearings before adjudicators were henceforth to be open to the public. However, an exception (subsection 2) was made in the case of situations where an adjudicator was satisfied that there was a

> serious possibility that the life, liberty and security of any person would be endangered by reason of an inquiry being conducted in public.

In such a case, the adjudicator could "take such measures and make such orders" as appeared to the adjudicator to be necessary "to ensure the confidentiality of the inquiry."

In contrast, in Convention refugee hearings before the Refugee Division of the Immigration and Refugee Board (IRB), the hearing is still conducted *in camera* unless the claimant applies to have it held in public and, even then, the panel hearing the case can make orders for maintaining the confidentiality of the proceedings (ss. 69(2) and 69(3)). It remains to be seen whether this combination of greater restrictions on access in the case of refugee hearings and more presumptive access in all other immigration matters will satisfy the courts' sense of the appropriate balance to be struck between the freedoms enshrined in s. 2(b) of the Charter and the privacy and personal security interests of those affected by proceedings under the *Immigration Act*.

One of the other domains in which this issue has surfaced most frequently is that of professional discipline. At the level of policy debate, there has been considerable public attention on the practice of many professions of keeping their disciplinary proceedings closed principally for the purpose of protecting the reputation of their members who are the subject of those proceedings. In an era of strong assertions of the need for greater public accountability of professions, this justification for secrecy has sounded increasingly hollow. When coupled with claims of press freedom based on s. 2(b) of the Charter, this argument has produced changes in the practices of many professional bodies. A prime example is provided by the change in the case of medical and related professions in the province of Ontario where s. 45 of the second schedule to the 1991 *Regulated Health Professions Act*, SO 1991, c. 18 (*Health Professions Procedural Code*) created a presumption of openness in place of the former generally closed process under the *Health Disciplines Act*, RSO 1990, c. H.4, s. 12(4). Previously, for a hearing to be open to the public, the consent of the health professional subject to discipline was required. (For the details of the previous scheme and its application in one of the most controversial cases, see *Re Yuz and Laski* (1986), 32 DLR (4th) 452 (Ont. CA).)

Indeed, similar considerations have intruded in the interpretation of s. 9 of the SPPA. In *Ottawa Police Force v. Lalande* (1986), 24 Admin. LR 145 (Ont. Dist. Ct.), a senior police officer was charged in disciplinary proceedings with having sexual relations with prostitutes while on duty. His request to have the hearing held *in camera* was opposed by newspapers, the CBC, and the police force, and rejected. Hogg DCJ said, "I believe that the press table is as much a part of any courtroom or hearing as the judge's bench, the witness box, the counsel table or the dock. Reporters bring out the exchanges between counsel and the judge and listen to the evidence and to the submissions. They should be a neutral link between the court or hearing and the vast public beyond its doors. … Unless there are compelling reasons to the contrary, a hearing, such as this, or a trial, that affects the public must be open to all citizens. … The circumstances here do not outweigh the desirability of adhering to the principle that the hearing be open to the public."

In the course of this evolution, however, it has been recognized that, on occasion, there are countervailing factors such as the protection of the privacy of victims (as opposed to that of those subject to discipline) and ensuring that witnesses are willing to testify. And, of course, in contexts other than professional discipline, there may be other concerns about the need to protect from public glare information with not only national security but also commercial competitiveness dimensions. These interests are recognized in a variety of ways from publication bans to the taking of some testimony in private. However, a full exploration of the detail of the issues raised by the competing claims in this context is beyond the scope of this work. First, it is not an issue that is peculiar to tribunals but one that tribunals share in common with regular courts. Second, as suggested by *Pacific Press*, a full appreciation of its dimensions depends on an assessment of the constitutional strength of freedom of the press claims, a subject that is more appropriately dealt with in a general constitutional law course or one on civil liberties.

The Right to Counsel

In most hearing situations, the right of the parties to representation by counsel or an agent is assumed and, indeed, in many cases will be provided for statutorily. Thus, s. 10 of the Ontario SPPA permits representation by counsel or an agent for parties to proceedings governed by that Act (though, in the case of non-lawyers, note s. 23(3)) as do s. 34 of the Québec *Charter of Human Rights and Freedoms*, s. 12(4) of the Québec *Act Respecting Administrative Justice*, and s. 32 of the British Columbia *Administrative Tribunals Act*. However, it is worth noting that s. 6 of the Alberta *Administrative Procedures and Jurisdiction Act* specifically provides that representation by counsel is not a necessary component of the procedures subject to that Act, leaving the matter to be resolved by individual statutes and regulations and the principles of the common law. Moreover, s. 11 of the SPPA places constraints on the extent to which witnesses, as opposed to parties, are entitled to be represented by counsel. What these statutory regimes clearly suggest, therefore, is that representation by counsel is not a universal right.

In this section, we therefore examine the qualifications that have been placed by the jurisprudence on representation. For these purposes, we define qualifications to include not only outright denial of such an entitlement but also limitations on the extent of counsel's participatory entitlements and on the concept of counsel "of one's choice." In evaluating the caselaw in this domain, think about why it is that representation is generally seen as an important component of natural justice and reflect on what may in some contexts be countervailing considerations. Are there circumstances where representation is unnecessary? Are there situations where representation will serve as an impediment to legislative objectives and the efficient dispatch of a statutory mandate? Putting it bluntly, are lawyers sometimes a menace to be avoided?

This general issue is faced squarely in the first case in this section.

Re Men's Clothing Manufacturers Association of Ontario and Toronto Joint Board, Amalgamated Clothing and Textile Workers' Union
(1979), 22 LAC (2d) 328; quashed 104 DLR (3d) 441 (Ont. Div. Ct.)

[Disputes in the men's clothing industry in Toronto were resolved by arbitration, and the process had been conducted for decades without lawyers. After this particular grievance was begun, the association made a general statement that it wished to change this practice and use lawyers for some disputes. This preliminary ruling was made by the arbitrator:]

ARTHURS (arbitrator): The issues that fall to be decided are:

(1) whether a party to arbitration proceedings under this collective agreement has an absolute right to legal representation, and

(2) if not, whether my discretion should be exercised in the instant proceeding so as to permit representation.

I

One must approach with some diffidence the question of whether parties to a labour arbitration do or do not enjoy an absolute right to legal representation. On the one hand, there is a widely held belief, if not in the existence of such a right, then at least in its desirability. On the other, the appearance of lawyers in labour arbitration proceedings is sufficiently common in other industries that the notion that their presence may be a matter of discretion rather than right may occasion some surprise. None the less in light of the history and special circumstances of arbitration in this industry, that question must now be decided.

It is axiomatic that a labour arbitrator must accord to parties before him all procedural rights which they have mandatorily stipulated for themselves and that, in the absence of such stipulations, he must none the less observe the basic principles of natural justice. In the instant case, the parties have obviously not addressed the question of legal representation in their collective agreement. However, if the parties have reached no agreement on the point, is a right of legal representation implied by the rules of natural justice?

[A long discussion of common law is omitted.]

While the authorities are not entirely consistent, one can fairly summarize the common law position with regard to the right to counsel this way: (1) neither in Courts nor in other forums is an absolute right to counsel regarded as an indispensable feature of natural justice; (2) generally, legal representation is desirable, and the exercise of discretion by the tribunal should favour it; and (3) there may be some circumstances where the participation of counsel is inimical to the functioning of the tribunal.

[After noting that the Ontario *Statutory Powers Procedure Act* did not apply to labour arbitrations, the arbitrator continued.]

III

I turn now to the special qualities of labour arbitration, and particularly of arbitration in the men's clothing industry, which bear upon the issues herein.

Collective bargaining in the industry is carried on between the union and the association, which comprises a number of firms, including Canadian Clothiers Corp. The collective agreement is executed only by representatives of the association and the union, although it purports throughout to bind and enure to the benefit of "the employer," obviously a manufacturing firm, rather than the association itself.

The collective agreement contains provisions for arbitration by an impartial chairman, who is to hold office for the duration of the agreement, subject to termination by the joint act of the parties.

While, of course, arbitration in the garment industry is subject to the provisions of the *Labour Relations Act*, it is important to recall that arbitration in this industry was created by the parties and not by the Legislature. (…)

For some 60 years, then, and without regard to the compulsion or assistance of law, labour and management have jointly created and administered a unique arbitration system. One feature of that system has been the apparently total absence of lawyers, at least from 1937, when my predecessor, Jacob Finkelman QC assumed the chairmanship, down to the present time, but probably from the inception of the system.

· · ·

In the absence of counsel, not unsurprisingly, various procedural arrangements developed, which in certain respects differ from those which are familiar in a Court of law and in other tribunals where counsel regularly appear.

In effect, at least during my tenure of office, all cases have been presented to the chairman in a highly informal manner. Typically, all facts are simply put before the chairman by way of assertion by the lay representatives of the parties, officials of the union, the association, or a member firm. No witnesses are called, although individuals with direct or indirect knowledge of matters in contention may be invited to contribute their knowledge for the information of the chairman. In addition, the chairman frequently questions the parties in an attempt to elicit relevant facts and arguments, if that is felt to be necessary in order to secure a full understanding of the matters at issue. On occasion, indeed, the parties have been able to agree upon the facts, and even upon the desired disposition of the grievance, and have invited the chairman to incorporate their agreement in findings or an order.

The result of these procedures has been to greatly expedite arbitration in the industry. Typically, grievances are brought to the chairman for adjudication whenever attempts to resolve them bilaterally have run their course, rather than in accordance with strict time-limits which, indeed, the agreement does not contain. Cases are scheduled for arbitration only a few days thereafter or, at most, a week or two later, unless the parties are agreeable to further delay. Hearings, which have been held after working hours in the association's boardroom, are often no more than an hour or two's duration. Awards almost always issue within a week, at most.

· · ·

It would not be accurate to say that the gains in the informality, speed, and cheapness of the arbitration process in this industry are entirely attributable to the absence of lawyers. But equally one cannot imagine that the introduction of lawyers could be accomplished without paying a substantial price in terms of the efficiency—and industrial relations effectiveness—of arbitration.

Moreover, it is not only the procedure of arbitration in the industry which has evolved in directions far removed from those of typical adversary proceedings. The scope of disputes subject to arbitration, and hence the bases of decision of disputes, differs not only from what is encountered in Courts, but also from other labour/management relationships. In effect, the association and the union have confined their formal collective agreement to a relatively limited range of issues, principally constructing a framework within which a more informal relationship might be carried on. Such an arrangement is entirely understandable in view of the nature of the industry.

· · ·

Moreover, the necessary ongoing, extensive and intimate relationships between firms in the industry and the union have given rise to many understandings which are of great concern to the parties, but which are not incorporated in the collective agreement. Sometimes these understandings are informally recorded in documents which circulate only within a particular shop or firm; sometimes they are mere shared assumptions which, though unwritten, are expected to be adhered to and are sanctified by long habits of compliance. These arrangements are, again, not surprising given substantial differences amongst the member firms of the association, and the impossibility of holding all firms, regardless of their circumstances, to identical arrangements which could be incorporated in an industry-wide collective agreement.

· · ·

It is important to understand, therefore, that what the parties meant to convey by their mutual commitment to "arbitration" in the collective agreement was their devotion to a process which differed radically not only from that of the Courts but from that of other, less venerable, labour arbitration systems. It is not too much to say that the entire viability of labour/management relations in the industry has hinged for 60 years upon the mutual presupposition of the parties that all of their conflicts should be resolved directly through negotiation without regard to the limitations of the agreement, and that if negotiation should fail, by an informal process of "arbitration" which was highly responsible to the realities and special needs and traditions of the industry.

This review of the history and practices of arbitration in the men's clothing industry leads me to the conclusion that I should, in general terms, hesitate to exercise my discretion in favour of permitting the parties to be represented by lawyers. For 60 years, the parties have been arbitrating with lay representatives only, to their apparent mutual satisfaction. Both the procedural and substantive aspects of industrial relationships throughout the industry seem to function well because they are unusually responsive to the special needs and traditions of the industry, rather than to the logic of legal analysis.

The egregious introduction of lawyers may put all of this at risk: arranging arbitration dates to convenience counsel may well delay hearings; conventional techniques of proof may well lengthen them by many hours; legal arguments based on contract analysis may shift the arbitrator's attention from issues which the parties have hitherto expected him to consider and which need to be addressed if their relationship is to remain stable; and the cost of legal representation may generate such a deterrent to arbitration—especially of minor matters such as price setting—that processes of mutual adjustment break down because the wealthier party is effectively insulated from challenge.

But general hesitancy over the introduction of lawyers does not mean that they should be excluded altogether. There may be certain kinds of issues, especially those which touch the impact of general legal rules upon the parties' special regime of understandings, which are suitable for argument by counsel.

· · ·

Finally, as a general matter, I wish to address the question of whether 60 years of history fixes the future course of this arbitration system for all time. Obviously it does not. The parties are free at any time to alter the rules of their arbitration system, as they are free to change substantive provisions of the collective agreement, or of other aspects of their understandings. But they must do so by mutual consent, or must mutually entrust the matter to me for decision.

· · ·

IV

Against the background of these general observations, I turn to the specific question of whether the parties should be entitled to representation at the hearing to consider the merits of the instant case.

[A discussion of timetabling problems, cost, and delay is omitted.]

For all of these reasons, I am not inclined to afford Mr. Stringer (or other counsel) full rights of participation in the hearing on the merits.

On the other hand, I recognize that Mr. Stringer has advanced a serious legal argument concerning the scope of the chairman's authority.

· · ·

I am therefore prepared to permit Mr. Stringer to participate in the hearing to the limited extent of making the legal argument to which I have referred, in accordance with the direction set forth below. The union and the association are likewise invited to retain counsel, who may participate on the same basis. I am not prepared to have Mr. Stringer, or other legal representatives, participate in the presentation of facts, relating to this grievance. The lay representatives of the parties have always proven fully capable of doing so in the past, with dispatch and a sense of relevance; they will obviously not be prejudiced by the absence of counsel. Other arguments, based on clothing industry practices, lie peculiarly within the knowledge of the lay representatives, and counsel can offer little assistance to them or to me on these matters.

[The Men's Clothing Manufacturers Association applied for review.]

SOUTHEY J:

[Southey J first noted that none of the parties to the arbitration—a corporate employer, an association of employers and a union—were natural persons and that each could only appear by natural persons acting as their agents.]

    … By ruling that the applicants could not be represented by legal counsel, the learned arbitrator limited the parties in their choice of agents, by denying them the right to retain as agents a particular class of persons whose members are widely retained in such matters in other industries. In my judgment, the learned arbitrator had no authority thus to limit the rights of persons who were clearly entitled to appear before him by agents, and he erred in law in so doing. As a general rule, in my judgment, a party entitled to be represented by an agent before a domestic tribunal, cannot be restricted by the tribunal in the choice of its agent, in the absence of an applicable rule or agreement containing such restriction. That is not to say that the tribunal cannot exclude persons who have misconducted themselves or are otherwise clearly inappropriate.

· · ·

    Where the arbitration arises out of an agreement, one must look at the intention of the parties as it appears from the words of the agreement and the surrounding circumstances. If it is clear from the words of the agreement, or the surrounding circumstances, that the parties intended that representation by counsel be permitted, the arbitrator has no discretion to exclude counsel.

· · ·

    In most arbitrations under collective agreements, the real adversaries are the corporate employer and the union, both of whom are entitled as of right to be represented by counsel for the reason I have given. As was recognized by the learned arbitrator, it is common in other industries for such parties to be represented by counsel. In an industry in which that is the case, I should think it would be an implied term of the collective agreement that an individual party, *i.e.* a natural person, would also be entitled as of right to representation by counsel, assuming there was no provision in the collective agreement covering the point.

    In the industry with which the learned arbitrator was concerned, however, neither side had been represented by legal counsel in arbitrations throughout a history of about 60 years. It would be impossible to find in these circumstances that the parties clearly intended to be represented by legal counsel at an arbitration hearing, if desired, and to find an implied term to that effect in the collective agreement. The result is that a natural person in the industry in question does not have an absolute right to representation by legal counsel, for the reasons given by the learned arbitrator. The point is probably entirely academic, however, because the natural person would be entitled to representation by legal counsel in any case where another party was so represented … and in any case where it would be contrary to natural justice to deny the natural person such representation. Furthermore, such representation would always be permissible by agreement, or whenever the arbitrator exercised his discretion in favour of permitting it.

On the second issue, the learned arbitrator, having found that the applicants had no absolute right to representation by legal counsel, declined to exercise his discretion to permit such representation in this case, except to a very limited extent. ...

The company established the following points in affidavit evidence that were not contradicted:

1. that the general manager of the company, who might otherwise have conducted the arbitration proceedings on behalf of the company, did not feel capable of conducting the proceedings in this case because of the complexity of the legal issues;

2. that the company would cease to be an economically viable business if the arbitrator rules that it must cease the practices under attack by the union;

3. that the compensation sought by the union could be assessed in an extremely large amount, which, if awarded by the arbitrator, would jeopardize the continued existence of the company.

The executive director of the applicant association also deposed that he would not feel competent to present properly the evidence, facts, and issues in the matter, despite his experience in the processing of arbitrations in the industry.

[Long quotations from English cases are omitted.]

Returning to the facts in the case at bar, it appears from the material that the factual issues involved in the arbitration are of considerable age and complexity, and that the arbitration will involve questions of law other than those on which the learned arbitrator gave leave to counsel to file written argument and to present further argument at the conclusion of the hearing. In view of the vital importance of the controversy to the applicant company, and the apparent complexity of the matter both in fact and in law, natural justice, in my view, requires that the applicants be represented by legal counsel at the arbitration hearing without any limitation, even if the applicants had no absolute right thereto. For this reason, the learned arbitrator, in my judgment, was in error on the second issue as well.

Application granted. Leave to appeal to the Court of Appeal refused.

Another situation in which the issue of representation by counsel has surfaced in Canadian law has been that of investigations and inquiries. In this respect, recollect that among the rulings being challenged in *Irvine v. Canada (Restrictive Trade Practices Commission)*, [1981] 1 SCR 181 (Can.), a case that we considered in chapter 3 of this text, were ones that restricted the involvement of counsel in the course of an inquiry conducted by the Restrictive Trade Practices Commission (RTPC).

As that case illustrates, there may be occasions when, in the course of hearings, counsel will be allowed to be present but not the parties counsel represent. The most common example of this is in proceedings where information of commercial significance is being adduced and it is thought inappropriate for business competitors to be present. The compromise is to allow their counsel to be present in order to safeguard their clients' interests as far as is feasible but in the context of an undertaking not to reveal commercially valuable information to those whom they represent. (Consider the potential difficulties of such a process for counsel and their relationship with their clients.) This kind of approach is also taken in cases where knowledge of information at stake may be potentially damaging to the person affected, such as medical diagnoses of the person's state of mental health: *Re Egglestone and Mousseau and Advisory Review Board* (1983), 150 DLR (3d) 86 (Ont. Div. Ct.).

Normally, of course, the situation is otherwise; counsel and client are entitled to be together and consult one another throughout the hearing. This entitlement was the basis of the holding in *Canada (Canadian Radio-television and Telecommunications Commission) v. Canada (Human Rights Tribunal)* (1990), 47 Admin. LR 302 (FCTD). There, the court held that the tribunal could not extend an order excluding witnesses from the hearing room to the person designated by the respondent Canadian Radio-television and Telecommunications Commission (CRTC) to instruct counsel in the course of the hearing. That person's presence was necessary in order to effectuate the right of the CRTC to be represented by counsel.

Irvine and its limitations on access to counsel were reassessed in the context of an accident investigation by federal transportation regulators in *Re Parrish*, [1993] 2 FC 60 (TD). Parrish, the captain of a ship that had been involved in a collision with another ship, was summoned to appear before an investigator appointed by the board to be examined in the context of an investigation being conducted under s. 14 of the *Canadian Transportation Accident Investigation and Safety Board Act*, SC 1989, c. 3. The captain appeared with two counsel, but the investigator refused to allow the captain to have counsel at the hearing. The investigator had previously allowed counsel to be present when members of the crew of the other ship were interviewed. The captain refused to testify. The board put a question to the Federal Court Trial Division under s. 18(3) of the *Federal Courts Act* as to whether it could require the captain to attend and give evidence under oath without the presence of counsel. Rouleau J held that proceedings before the Canadian Transportation Accident Investigation and Safety Board differed from those prescribed by the *Combines Investigation Act* involved in *Irvine*:

> Before this Board transcripts can, in certain circumstances, be made available. In *Re Irvine* the evidence gathered was not published but was delivered by the Director only to those against whom an allegation may have been made and that person was to be allowed full opportunity to be heard in person or by counsel. It is obvious from the evidence before me that such is not the case before this Board.
>
> . . .
>
> Undoubtedly the scope of the fairness principle depends on the consequences and nature of the inquiry as well as the repercussions on the individuals involved. In this particular case, a witness could be faced with a negative report seriously or adversely affecting his rights without being given a fair opportunity to present his case with the assistance of counsel. The fact that Parliament through this statute compels the attendance of a witness which could result in a seriously flawed published report affecting a person's reputation or livelihood, implies that the Legislature presumed that counsel would be available.

Rouleau J summarized his conclusions, addressing the board's claim that affording Parrish a right to counsel could frustrate its prompt investigation of the accident:

There has been, as I have stated before, considerable evolution in the law governing tribunals or administrative bodies in general. There is no doubt that a number of inquiries held by administrative tribunals can be conducted without the presence of counsel. My review of the jurisprudence reveals that the duty to act fairly implies the presence of counsel when a combination of some or all of the following elements are either found within the enabling legislation or implied from the practical application of the statute governing the tribunal: where an individual or a witness is subpoenaed, required to attend and testify under oath with a threat of penalty; where absolute privacy is not assured and the attendance of others is not prohibited; where reports are made public; where an individual can be deprived of his rights or his livelihood; or where some other irreparable harm can ensue. I do not intend this list to be exhaustive but I wish to highlight those factual situations in the jurisprudence giving rise to the need for adequate protection by way of counsel or some other advisor.

There is no doubt that boards or tribunals are masters of their own procedure and when witnesses appear with two or three counsel, it is certainly within the Board's domain to limit not only the number of counsel but also the scope of their participation. In this particular inquiry, Captain Parrish appeared on most occasions with lawyers representing varying interests. He had one to advise him with respect to his professional standing and others to advise him with respect to the liability interests that could be at stake. The Board may be perfectly free to prohibit the attendance of more than one counsel and it would be up to the investigator to determine if the presence of more than one would seriously impede the progress of the investigation. In most cases reviewed, the legislation provided for the presence of counsel but left the Board the power to determine its own procedure. If one finds that participation is unjustly restricted, judicial review is generally available.

The Canadian Transportation Accident Investigation and Safety Board offers to the Court but one valid argument or explanation as to why it wishes to deprive a witness of the right to counsel: that their presence would cause unwarranted delay and perhaps frustrate the immediate gathering of facts. This Court is asked to deprive an individual of his right to silence. In the event of a tragic and catastrophic incident, a witness is subpoenaed within hours and at best days to attend and give testimony under oath with the threat of penalty over his head while perhaps still in a traumatic state. He may not have the presence of mind to invoke the protection of the *Canada Evidence Act* and the British Columbia *Evidence Act*. The witness would be testifying before an investigator who is usually not legally trained, asking double barrelled questions that in some cases may even be beyond the scope of the Board's mandate; perhaps in the presence of the coroner, police authorities or some regulatory body that has the power to deprive him not only of his reputation but his professional certification and his livelihood. The witness is then faced with interim reports that are sometimes prematurely leaked to the press before having had an opportunity to comment. In such circumstances, I cannot accept the Board's argument that the need for administrative expediency in the proceedings outweighs the necessity for the protection of a witness through the presence of counsel.

After reviewing the jurisprudence and arguments submitted by the parties, I am satisfied that in these circumstances the procedural fairness requires that the witness be permitted to be accompanied by counsel when at the inquiry. ...

Obviously, the considerations that led Rouleau J to distinguish *Irvine* were his views as to the potential impact of the inquiry on Parrish's reputation and career as well as a perception that counsel might well be essential to the protection of those interests. An interesting contrast to this is provided by the judgment of the Supreme Court of Canada in *Dehghani v. Canada (Minister of Employment and Immigration)*, [1993] 1 SCR 1053 (Can.). At stake here was the procedure employed at ports of entry to Canada when the initial immigration officer has concerns about the admissibility of a person. In such cases, the person seeking entry was referred to a secondary examination at which there was no entitlement to representation by counsel. In *Dehghani*, the applicant had been referred to a secondary examination on arriving in Canada without any documents and asserting a Convention refugee claim. Later, the notes taken at that secondary examination were entered at the "credible basis" stage of the Convention refugee process, at which point Dehghani was represented by counsel. He was found not to have a "credible basis" for his claim and a removal order was made. In the ensuing judicial review proceedings, Dehghani claimed that the denial of access to counsel during the course of the secondary examination infringed both ss. 10(b) and 7 of the Charter. The Supreme Court held that s. 10(b) did not apply because the reference of a person seeking entry to Canada to a secondary examination was not a "detention." Second, while assuming that s. 7 applied to such a process and conceding that it might provide residual protection notwithstanding the rejection of the s. 10(b) claim, the court was not prepared to see access to counsel as a necessary component of the "principles of fundamental justice," at least at this stage of the process. In delivering the judgment of a unanimous court, Iacobucci J made the following statement:

> To allow counsel at port of entry interviews would, in the words of Heald JA in *Montfort v. Canada (Minister of Employment & Immigration)* [1980] 1 FC 478 (CA) at 481-482 "entail another 'mini-inquiry' or 'initial inquiry' possibly just as complex and prolonged as the inquiry provided for under the Act and Regulations." This would constitute unnecessary duplication. The purpose of the port of entry interview was, as I have already observed, to aid in the processing of the appellant's application for entry and to determine the appropriate procedures which should be invoked in order to deal with his application for Convention refugee status. The principles of fundamental justice do not include a right to counsel in these circumstances of routine information gathering.

Does this reasoning hold in the light of the use of the notes of the secondary examination in the subsequent "credible basis" hearing? In what sense is the secondary examination any less crucial to the person affected than the inquiry was to Parrish, the captain of the ship?

We turn now to an area where procedural claims generally and entitlements to counsel specifically have been affected by both the common law procedural fairness evolution and the advent of the Charter—the domain of parole and penitentiary discipline, transfer, and leave. On the matter of entitlement to counsel in prison disciplinary proceedings, the Federal Court of Canada was influenced by an English judgment, *R v. Secretary of State for the Home Department, ex p. Tarrant*, [1984] 1 All ER 799 (QB). In that case, rules made under the *Prison Act, 1952* required hearings of disciplinary charges by boards of visitors and gave each prisoner a "full opportunity of hearing what is alleged against him and of presenting his own case." Five prisoners were charged, and their requests to be represented by counsel were refused. They sought *certiorari* to quash decisions made against them and succeeded:

there was no common law right to be represented, but the boards had a discretion to allow representation that was derived from their general power to regulate their own procedures and that had not been implicitly denied by the legislation. The board had refused the requests on the ground that representation was simply not allowed, and without considering this discretion. Some of the charges raised difficult issues of interpretation and the others involved severe penalties. Therefore, representation could not reasonably have been refused. Webster J said:

> As it seems to me, the following are considerations which every board should take into account when exercising its discretion whether to allow legal representation or to allow the assistance of a friend or adviser. (This list is not, of course, intended to be comprehensive: particular cases may throw up other particular matters.)
>
> 1. The seriousness of the charge and of the potential penalty.
>
> 2. Whether any points of law are likely to arise. There is of course a duty to ensure that the prisoner understands the charge, a duty which is reflected in the guide (p. 12, para. 11): "Ask the accused whether he understands the charge(s) and explain anything to him about which he is in any doubt." But the clerks who sit with boards are not legally qualified and there may be cases where a legal point arises with which the prisoner, without legal representation cannot properly deal. A charge of mutiny, which I consider later in this judgment, is at least potentially in this category for the reasons which I will give. It was also suggested in argument that difficult questions of intent might arise; but for my part, looking at the list of disciplinary offences and the way in which those offences are described, it seems to me unlikely that such questions will arise, except very rarely, other than in charges of mutiny.
>
> 3. The capacity of a particular prisoner to present his own case. ...
>
> 4. Procedural difficulties. An affidavit has been sworn, in support of three of the applicants, by Mr. Ivan Henry, who is a member of a board of visitors, a magistrate and a legal executive. He points out that a prisoner awaiting adjudication is normally kept apart from other prisoners under r. 48(2) of the 1964 rules pending the adjudication and that this may inhibit the preparation of his defence. He points out that without the capacity to interview potential witnesses, prisoners are often unable to satisfy boards of visitors that it is reasonable to call a witness and that, where a prisoner asks questions through a chairman, there is frequently no effective presentation of a case or effective cross-examination or testing of the evidence. ... But in my view a board, when considering exercise of its discretion, should take into account any special difficulties of the kind I have mentioned and should particularly bear in mind the difficulty which some prisoners might have in cross-examining a witness, particularly a witness giving evidence of an expert nature, at short notice without previously having seen that witness's evidence.
>
> 5. The need for reasonable speed in making their adjudication, which is clearly an important consideration.
>
> 6. The need for fairness as between prisoners and as between prisoners and prison officers.

In my view, all these are matters which a board should take into account in deciding whether to allow legal representation, or the assistance of a friend or adviser, bearing in mind the overriding obligation to ensure that a prisoner "be given a full opportunity of hearing what is alleged against him and of presenting his own case."

Howard v. Stony Mountain Institution
(1985), 19 DLR (4th) 502 (FCA)

THURLOW CJ: This is an appeal from a judgment of the Trial Division which dismissed the appellant's application for an order prohibiting the respondent from continuing or concluding the hearing of certain charges against the appellant under s. 39 of the *Penitentiary Service Regulations*, CRC 1978, c. 1251, in the absence of legal counsel as requested by the appellant. The issue in the appeal is whether the request of the appellant was unlawfully refused.

As presented, it is a narrow issue.

The appellant does not claim a right to have counsel provided for him. Indeed, having had counsel available, he did not even seek a postponement to obtain counsel. On the other hand, it was not disputed by counsel for the respondent that the disciplinary court has authority and indeed a duty to permit counsel to conduct the defence of an accused inmate where to deny it would breach the obligation to deal fairly with him. This was referred to as a "discretion" vested in the presiding officer. In so far as the appellant's entitlement to representation by counsel is subject to denial by the exercise of a discretion there was no attack by the appellant either before the Trial Division or on the appeal on the exercise by the disciplinary court of such discretion by denying the appellant's request. What is in issue is thus solely whether the appellant had an undeniable right to counsel and, more particularly, whether s. 7 of the *Canadian Charter of Rights and Freedoms* guaranteed him that right.

. . .

At the material time, the appellant was an inmate of Stony Mountain Institution serving a sentence of two years and four months. On December 31, 1982, he was involved in incidents with officers of the institution as a result of which five charges were laid against him under s. 39 of the *Penitentiary Service Regulations*. These were, possessing contraband, using indecent or disrespectful language to another person, an act calculated to prejudice discipline or good order of the institution, disobeying a lawful order of a penitentiary officer and threatening to assault another person. The record does not disclose particulars of the charges other than that the first three occurred at 08.04 hours, the fourth at 09.00 hours and the fifth at 09.20 hours, all on December 31, 1982. On January 6, 1983, the appellant appeared before a presiding officer and entered pleas of guilty to the charges of possessing contraband and disobeying a lawful order and pleas of not guilty on the remaining three charges. Disposition of the charges to which he pleaded guilty was held in abeyance pending determination of the remaining three charges. Subsequently, charges of having contraband on January 4, 1983, and failing to obey a lawful order on January 20, 1983, were laid. To these the appellant pleaded not guilty. All the charges were categorized under the Commissioner's Directive No. 213 as "serious" or "flagrant" offences. On

February 3, 1983, by which time he had secured counsel, the appellant appeared before the presiding officer of the inmate disciplinary court who thereupon adjourned the hearing in order to obtain written submissions from counsel for the appellant and for the Department of Justice on the request of the appellant to have counsel represent him at the hearing. The request was denied on April 11, 1983. The presiding officer held that s. 7 of the Charter does not create "a new wave of rights" and, as he was not persuaded that there were circumstances in the particular case which precluded the possibility of a fair hearing in the absence of counsel, he exercised his discretion and denied the request.

The appellant's application for prohibition was then brought.

· · ·

On May 10, 1983, when the affidavit in support of the application for prohibition was sworn, the appellant had 267 days of earned remission standing to his credit and was due for release on mandatory supervision on June 9, 1983. The earned remission was subject to forfeiture in whole or in part as a result of the disciplinary court proceedings. Among other permissible punishments for serious or flagrant offences was solitary confinement, also referred to as punitive dissociation.

We were informed by counsel for the appellant that the hearing in the inmate disciplinary court proceeded on June 9, 1983, when the appellant was found guilty on six of the seven counts and was sentenced to forfeiture of 70 days of his earned remission. As a prohibition can no longer be effective and as the sentence which the appellant was serving has long since expired, the matter has become academic and would ordinarily not be entertained. But, as counsel for the respondent, as well as for the appellant, urged upon the court the importance, to both inmates and the penitentiary administration, of having a decision of this court as to the right of inmates to counsel in such disciplinary proceedings and in particular as to the effect of s. 7 of the Charter, the court exercised its discretion to hear the matter on its merits.

[An account of the structure for discipline is omitted.]

These statutory provisions, regulations and directives have not changed materially from what they were when the *Martineau* cases arose: *Martineau and Butters v. Matsqui Institution Inmate Disciplinary Board* [1978] 1 SCR 118 (Can.); *Martineau v. Matsqui Institution Disciplinary Board (No. 2)* [1980] 1 SCR 602 (Can.). The enactment of s. 24.1(2) of the *Penitentiary Act*, by 1976-77, c. 53, s. 41, provided for a new or additional class of persons who might preside at inmate disciplinary court proceedings but the nature of such proceedings as being essentially administrative rather than judicial or *quasi*-judicial, as held by the majority of the Supreme Court in the first *Martineau* case, remains unchanged. On the other hand, ... it appears to me to make no difference whether the appellant as an inmate was entitled to be dealt with in the disciplinary court in accordance with what are referred to as principles of natural justice or with some lesser standard referred to by the term "fairly." In neither case, apart from s. 7 of the Charter, would the appellant on the basis of existing jurisprudence have been in a position to demand as of right to be represented by counsel at the disciplinary hearing. The utmost he might have achieved was to have a discretion to permit him to be represented by counsel exercised in his favour.

[A discussion of cases, including *R v. Secretary of State for Home Department, ex p. Tarrant*, above, is omitted.]

It appears to me that the effect of this decision is that in the English system a prisoner has the right to require of the disciplinary court that it exercise on sound judicial grounds a discretion to allow representation by counsel and to require that the request be granted if, in the view of the board of visitors, the circumstances are such that legal representation is or may be required in order to comply with the prisoner's rights under the prison rules to be given a proper and full opportunity of presenting his case. This appears to me to amount in substance to a right to have counsel when the facts indicate the need for it and to a discretion to allow it in other cases as well.

I come then to s. 7 of the Charter and whether it has the effect of affording an inmate in a disciplinary proceeding a right to counsel that is not subject to denial by the presiding officer on discretionary grounds.

What was said to be at stake in the disciplinary proceedings is the liberty and security of the inmate and his right not to be deprived of them except in accordance with the principles of fundamental justice. The inmate's liberty was said to be at stake because his earned remission was in jeopardy as was also the security of his person since solitary confinement—also referred to as dissociation—was one of the punishments to which he might be subjected. I accept this analysis so far as the appellant's liberty is involved and that, as I view it, is sufficient for present purposes. At the same time it is to be noted that earned remission, which is a creation of the *Penitentiary Act*, has at all times been conditional in the sense that it has been subject to forfeiture in disciplinary proceedings of an administrative nature and thus has never had the quality of an absolute right to be set free on the completion of the unremitted portion of a sentence. To hold that an inmate's procedural rights have been increased by the enactment of s. 7 is accordingly to hold that its enactment has also enhanced the quality of the less than absolute right conferred by the *Penitentiary Act*.

In the course of their reasons both the presiding officer and the learned trial judge referred to expressions of judicial opinion in a number of reported cases supporting the view that at common law a prison inmate had no absolute right to have counsel represent him in proceedings before a disciplinary tribunal, that the legal procedures established by law before the enactment of the Charter are procedures in accordance with the principles of fundamental justice and that s. 7 of the Charter did not add to the rights of a person in the appellant's position. That may be a legitimate approach to the question. But it appears to me that in interpreting s. 7, and its meaning in the Charter, it is desirable to consider the wording of the provision in an effort to determine its ordinary meaning in its context.

The section is cast in broad terms. Its context is that of a constitutional charter. The Charter itself is part of the Constitution of Canada. These features suggest a broad interpretation. The extent of the Charter's guarantee of the rights set out in s. 7 may be limited by s. 1 but that does not, as it seems to me, bear on how s. 7 itself should be interpreted or on the breadth of what it embraces. In the present case no argument was presented on the effect of s. 1 on any right to counsel that may arise under s. 7.

Next, the subject-matter of s. 7 is the right to life, liberty and security of the person. These are matters of prime importance to everyone. Moreover, the fact that liberty and the security of the person are lumped together with life itself shows that the importance of the right to them is in the same class with that of the right to life itself. The enjoyment of property is not included in the class as it is in ss. 1(a) and 2(e) of the *Canadian Bill of Rights*.

Further, while the argument in the present case focused on the meaning and effect of the wording "in accordance with the principles of fundamental justice" as a guarantee of procedural standards, I would not rule out the possibility that the wording may also refer to or embrace substantive standards as well.

A further observation is that the standard of what is required to satisfy the section in its procedural sense, as it seems to me, is not necessarily the most sophisticated or elaborate or perfect procedure imaginable but only that of a procedure that is fundamentally just. What that may require will no doubt vary with the particular situation and the nature of the particular case. An unbiased tribunal, knowledge by the person whose life, liberty or security is in jeopardy of the case to be answered, a fair opportunity to answer and a decision reached on the basis of the material in support of the case and the answer made to it are features of such a procedure.

. . .

In this context, any right a person may have to the assistance of counsel arises from the requirement to afford the person an opportunity to adequately present his case.

Has it then become necessary, in order to afford an inmate an opportunity to be adequately heard and thus to fulfil the requirement of s. 7, to recognize his right to be represented by counsel in a disciplinary court? I hesitate to refer to pre-Charter cases on the right to counsel because to do so seems to me to beg the question whether a new right has been created. On the other hand, to hold that whenever life, liberty or security of the person is in jeopardy in administering prison discipline an absolute right to counsel arises from the requirement of s. 7 is to hold that the system before its enactment in which it was said to be within the discretion of the court to allow or deny representation by counsel was not necessarily up to that standard.

I am of the opinion that the enactment of s. 7 has not created any absolute right to counsel in all such proceedings. It is undoubtedly of the greatest importance to a person whose life, liberty or security of the person are at stake to have the opportunity to present his case as fully and adequately as possible. The advantages of having the assistance of counsel for that purpose are not in doubt. But what is required is an opportunity to present the case adequately and I do not think it can be affirmed that in no case can such an opportunity be afforded without also as part of it affording the right to representation by counsel at the hearing.

Once that position is reached it appears to me that whether or not the person has a right to representation by counsel will depend on the circumstances of the particular case, its nature, its gravity, its complexity, the capacity of the inmate himself to understand the case and present his defence. The list is not exhaustive. And from this, it seems to me, it follows that whether or not an inmate's request for representation by counsel can lawfully be refused is not properly referred to as a matter of discretion but is a matter of right where the circumstances are such that the opportunity to present the case adequately calls for representation by counsel. It may be that where the circumstances do not point to that conclusion a residual authority to permit counsel nevertheless is exercisable by the appropriate official but that area is not, I think, within the purview of s. 7.

It appears to me that the right of an inmate to counsel in a case in which under the English and United States' system it could not be denied is guaranteed in Canada by s. 7. It is guaranteed because *ex hypothesi* it is a case in which an opportunity to adequately present his case cannot be accorded without the inmate being allowed to have counsel.

. . .

This brings me to the question whether the present was a case in which the appellant's request could lawfully be refused. Its principal feature was that the whole of the appellant's 267 days of earned remission was in jeopardy. In my view, that alone suggests his need of counsel. Next, there is the lack of particulars of offences of which three are alleged to have occurred at the same instant. Conviction on the two of the charges to which he pleaded not guilty might result in consecutive losses of 30 days' remission without reference to the commissioner for what not inconceivably may have been the same act. Moreover, one of the three charges is that of an act calculated to prejudice discipline and good order, a notoriously vague and difficult charge for anyone to defend. These features, as well, suggest the need for counsel to protect the inmate.

There is not in the record anything that would indicate that the appellant suffered from physical or mental incapacity which would disable him from conducting his own defence as well as might be expected of any ordinary person without legal training. But he obviously felt the need for counsel because he obtained legal aid assistance promptly. He must also have been able to persuade those who administer the legal aid system of his need. Moreover, in a social system which recognizes the right of anyone to counsel in any of the ordinary courts of law for the defence of any charge, no matter how trivial the possible consequences may be, it seems to me to be incongruous to deny such a right to a person who, though not suffering from any physical or mental incapacity to defend himself, is faced with charges that may result in a loss of his liberty, qualified and fragile though it may have been, for some 267 days.

On the whole, I am of the opinion that the refusal of the appellant's request for counsel was a refusal of the opportunity to which he was entitled to adequately present his defence and that prohibition should have issued.

[Pratte JA concurred with Thurlow CJ; MacGuigan JA agreed, and wrote a judgment that is omitted.]

Appeal allowed.

NOTES

1. An appeal to the Supreme Court of Canada was dismissed on the grounds of mootness, [1987] 2 SCR 687.

2. In terms of Thurlow CJ's judgment, what has been the impact of the Charter on claims to representation by counsel in a prison disciplinary setting? As the person presiding over a prison disciplinary court, how, in the light of this case, would you see your role in dealing with a request to representation by counsel?

3. For the application of these principles in the context of the placing of an inmate in segregation and his transfer to a more secure form of penitentiary, see *Winters v. Canada*

(Correctional Service), [1993] 1 FC 353 (CA), in which the court held that the officials at the penitentiary had delayed unduly in providing an inmate with access to counsel. In so doing, the court rejected on the evidence justifications based on the emergency nature of the situation and other administrative exigencies.

4. An issue that has arisen in a number of cases is the extent of a person's claim to be represented by a particular lawyer. This occurs most frequently in the context of applications for adjournments because of the unavailability of a chosen lawyer at the time scheduled for the hearing. As you might expect, the right to counsel does not extend as far as an absolute right to the lawyer of one's choice irrespective of the circumstances. Indeed, the courts have generally conceded to tribunals considerable discretion on whether to grant adjournments in situations where chosen counsel are not available. For a review of the authorities in the arena where such problems seem to arise most frequently, immigration matters, see *Afrane v. Canada (Minister of Employment & Immigration)* (1994), 14 Admin. LR (2d) 201 (FCTD) and *Siloch v. Canada (Minister of Employment & Immigration)* (1993), 10 Admin. LR (2d) 285 (FCA), in both of which the courts held that there had been an abuse of discretion in the denial of an adjournment.

5. A right to counsel will, of course, mean little if a person cannot afford one. In the absence of any constitutional guarantees, the ability to exercise the right will continue to depend in large measure on the existence of provincial legal aid plans, various forms of clinics, lawyers willing to undertake *pro bono* work, and other forms of volunteer or non-fee paying legal assistance. Another way of providing assistance to those who cannot afford counsel is the creation of assistance offices within the structure of administrative tribunals. Indeed, Québec Bill 105 made express provision for this:

> 40. The members of the personnel of an administrative tribunal shall assist any person who so requests in drafting an application, a complaint, an opposition, an intervention or any other proceeding directed to the tribunal.

(This did not find its way into the *Administrative Justice Act*.) Such programs need not stop at the drafting stage—there is also the possibility of in-house advocates available for the use of "customers" of the tribunal. A prominent species of this is, of course, the responsibilities of human rights commissions in the carriage of complaints before tribunals. In Ontario, where the Ontario *Human Rights Code* now allows direct access to adjudication before the Ontario Human Rights Tribunal, a new agency—the Human Rights Legal Support Centre— is charged with providing legal assistance in the filing of tribunal applications and for representation before the tribunal: Ontario *Human Rights Code*, RSO 1990, c. H.19, s. 45.11(1). In British Columbia, privately operated legal clinics provide such assistance with funding from the Ministry of the Attorney General. In the rather different arena of economic regulation, there is also the funding in various ways of interventions by public interest groups.

The following case raises the issue whether s. 7 and/or s. 15 of the Charter will ever create an entitlement to state-provided counsel.

New Brunswick (Minister of Health and Community Services) v. G. (J.) [J.G.]
[1999] 3 SCR 46 (NB)

[At stake was whether s. 7 of the Charter required that a mother be provided with counsel for the purposes of resisting an application by the Child Welfare authorities for renewal of an order placing her three children in the custody of the state. A policy under the Legal Aid plan prohibited the granting of legal aid certificates in custody-order renewal proceedings.]

LAMER CJ (Gonthier, Cory, McLachlin, Major and Binnie JJ concurring):

· · ·

In the circumstances of this case, the appellant's right to a fair hearing required that she be represented by counsel. I have reached this conclusion through a consideration of the following factors: the seriousness of the interests at stake, the complexity of the proceedings, and the capacities of the appellant. I will consider each in turn.

The interests at stake in the custody hearing are unquestionably of the highest order. Few state actions can have a more profound effect on the lives of both parent and child. Not only is the parent's right to security of the person at stake, the child's is as well. Since the best interests of the child are presumed to lie with the parent, the child's psychological integrity and well-being may be seriously affected by the interference with the parent-child relationship.

Of particular importance is the fact that the state was seeking to extend a previous custody order by six months. A six-month separation of a parent from three young children is a significant period of time. It is even more significant when considered in light of the fact that the appellant had already been separated from her children for over a year and that generally speaking, the longer the separation of parent from child, the less likely it is that the parent will ever regain custody.

There is some debate between the parties as to whether child custody proceedings under the *Family Services Act* are more properly classified as adversarial or administrative in nature. In my view, a formalistic classification of the nature of the proceedings is not helpful in resolving the issue at hand. Child protection proceedings do not admit of easy classification. As Professor Thompson argues, the "unique amalgam of elements—criminal, civil, family, administrative—makes child protection proceedings so hard to characterize": D.A. Rollie Thompson, "Taking Children and Facts Seriously: Evidence Law in Child Protection Proceedings—Part I" (1988) 7 Can. J Fam. L 11, at p. 12.

At issue in this appeal is whether the custody hearing would have been sufficiently complex, in light of the other two factors, that the assistance of a lawyer would have been necessary to ensure the appellant her right to a fair hearing. I believe that it would have been. Although perhaps more administrative in nature than criminal proceedings, child custody proceedings are effectively adversarial proceedings which occur in a court of law. The parties are responsible for planning and presenting their cases. While the rules of evidence are somewhat relaxed, difficult evidentiary issues are frequently raised. The parent must adduce evidence, cross-examine witnesses, make objections and present legal defences in the context of what is to many a foreign environment, and under significant emotional strain. In this case, all other parties were represented by counsel. The hearing was scheduled to last three days, and counsel for the Minister planned to present 15 affidavits, including two expert reports.

In proceedings as serious and complex as these, an unrepresented parent will ordinarily need to possess superior intelligence or education, communication skills, composure, and familiarity with the legal system in order to effectively present his or her case. There is no evidence in Athey J's decision or the record to suggest that the appellant possessed such capacities.

In light of these factors, I find that the appellant needed to be represented by counsel for there to have been a fair determination of the children's best interests. Without the benefit of counsel, the appellant would not have been able to participate effectively at the hearing, creating an unacceptable risk of error in determining the children's best interests and thereby threatening to violate both the appellant's and her children's s. 7 right to security of the person.

. . .

I would like to make it clear that the right to a fair hearing will not always require an individual to be represented by counsel when a decision is made affecting that individual's right to life, liberty, or security of the person. In particular, a parent need not always be represented by counsel in order to ensure a fair custody hearing. The seriousness and complexity of a hearing and the capacities of the parent will vary from case to case. Whether it is necessary for the parent to be represented by counsel is directly proportional to the seriousness and complexity of the proceedings, and inversely proportional to the capacities of the parent.

Although all custody hearings engage serious interests, the seriousness of the interests at stake varies according to the length of the proposed separation of parent from child. For instance, permanent guardianship applications are more serious than temporary custody applications. Therefore, counsel will more likely be necessary in guardianship applications than custody applications. The difference in seriousness between these two types of applications is currently recognized by Legal Aid New Brunswick, which provides legal aid certificates to financially eligible applicants in all guardianship applications but not in all custody applications. There is also a difference in the seriousness of the interests at stake in custody hearings depending on the length of any previous separation.

The complexity of the hearing can vary dramatically from case to case. Some hearings may be very short, involve relatively simple questions of fact and credibility, and have no expert reports. Others might take days and involve complicated evidentiary questions, troublesome points of law, and multiple experts. In the former cases, the assistance of counsel will make little difference to the parent's ability to present his or her view of the child's best interests, whereas in the latter cases, the representation of counsel may be essential to ensure a fair hearing.

The parent's capacities are also variable. Some parents may be well educated, familiar with the legal system, and possess above-average communication skills and the composure to advocate effectively in an emotional setting. At the other extreme, some parents may have little education and difficulty communicating, particularly in a court of law. It is unfortunately the case that this is true of a disproportionate number of parents involved in child custody proceedings, who often are members of the least advantaged groups in society. The more serious and complex the proceedings, the more likely it will be that the parent will need to possess exceptional capacities for there to be a fair hearing if the parent is unrepresented.

. . .

I therefore conclude that the potential restriction of the appellant's right to security of the person would not have been in accordance with the principles of fundamental justice had the custody hearing proceeded with the appellant unrepresented by counsel. The potential s. 7 violation in this case would have been the result of the failure of the Government of New Brunswick to provide the appellant with state-funded counsel under its Domestic Legal Aid program after initiating proceedings under Part IV of the *Family Services Act*.

In attributing the failure to provide state-funded counsel to the government's administration of the Domestic Legal Aid program, I do not mean to suggest that the Domestic Legal Aid program as it stands is the only way the government could have fulfilled its constitutional obligation in this case. The government has wide latitude in discharging its constitutional duty to provide state-funded counsel in proceedings where that duty arises. It could have done so in any number of ways—under the *Legal Aid Act*, the *Family Services Act*, or a myriad of other legislation or programs. This Court need not and should not tell the Government of New Brunswick what specific delivery system should have been employed.

Nevertheless, notwithstanding the variety of potential delivery options, the government chose to enact a general legal aid scheme with a scope of application encompassing the proceeding at issue in this appeal. It also adopted a specific policy of not providing legal aid to respondents in custody applications. Most importantly, the Attorney General and Ministers of Justice and Health and Community Services' s. 1 arguments seeking to justify the infringement (if one were to be found) of the appellant's s. 7 rights attribute it to the administration of the legal aid scheme. Therefore, it is not unreasonable to find the Domestic Legal Aid program to be the locus of the constitutional violation in this case.

D. Section 1

Although this case involves a prospective violation of s. 7, it is still necessary to engage in a s. 1 analysis. For if the prospective s. 7 violation would otherwise have been saved by s. 1, then there would be no need to order a remedy. ...

The appellant quite rightly is not directly challenging the *Legal Aid Act*, but rather administrative decisions made pursuant to it. The *Legal Aid Act* does not expressly or by necessary implication deny state-funded counsel to respondents in custody applications. On the contrary, both Legal Aid New Brunswick, pursuant to s. 12 of the *Legal Aid Act*, and the Minister of Justice, pursuant to s. 24 may provide state-funded counsel in these circumstances.

. . .

Assuming without deciding that the policy of not providing state-funded counsel to respondents in custody applications was a limit prescribed by law, that the objective of this policy—controlling legal aid expenditures—is pressing and substantial, that the policy is rationally connected to that objective, and that it constitutes a minimal impairment of s. 7, I find that the deleterious effects of the policy far outweigh the salutary effects of any potential budgetary savings.

Section 7 violations are not easily saved by s. 1. In *Re BC Motor Vehicle Act* [[1985] 2 SCR 486 (BC),] at p. 518, I said:

> Section 1 may, for reasons of administrative expediency, successfully come to the rescue of an otherwise violation of s. 7, but only in cases arising out of exceptional conditions, such as natural disasters, the outbreak of war, epidemics, and the like.

This is so for two reasons. First, the rights protected by s. 7—life, liberty, and security of the person—are very significant and cannot ordinarily be overridden by competing social interests. Second, rarely will a violation of the principles of fundamental justice, specifically the right to a fair hearing, be upheld as a reasonable limit demonstrably justified in a free and democratic society.

In the circumstances of this case, the Government of New Brunswick argues that the objective of limiting legal aid expenditures is of sufficient importance to deny the appellant a fair hearing. The proposed budgetary savings, however, are minimal. In their factum, Legal Aid New Brunswick and the Law Society of New Brunswick report that the projected annual cost of their new policy, effective September 22, 1997, of issuing legal aid certificates to respondents in custody applications for their first hearing would be under $100,000. Although the present appeal concerns the right to state-funded counsel at a hearing to extend an original custody order, the additional cost of providing state-funded counsel in these circumstances is insufficient to constitute a justification within the meaning of s. 1. Moreover, the government is not under an obligation to provide legal aid to every parent who cannot afford a lawyer. Rather, the obligation only arises in circumstances where the representation of the parent is essential to ensure a fair hearing where the parent's life, liberty, or security is at stake. In my view, a parent's right to a fair hearing when the state seeks to suspend such parent's custody of his or her child outweighs the relatively modest sums, when considered in light of the government's entire budget, at issue in this appeal.

Appeal allowed.

NOTES

1. In crafting an appropriate remedy, Lamer CJ concluded that where a parent in a custody matter wants a lawyer, but is unable to afford one, the judge should first inquire whether the parent has applied for legal aid. If the parent has not exhausted all possible avenues for obtaining state-funded legal assistance, proceedings should be adjourned to give the parent a reasonable time to make appropriate applications provided the best interests of the child is not compromised. The court should then consider whether the parent can receive a fair hearing if unrepresented, applying the factors identified in the judgment. The judge should also bear in mind his or her ability to assist the parent within the limits of the judicial role. If, after considering these criteria, the judge is not satisfied that the parent can receive a fair hearing, and there is no other way to provide the parent with a lawyer, the judge should order the government to provide the parent with state-funded counsel under s. 24(1) of the Charter.

2. The majority appeared to believe that given their emphasis on seriousness and complexity, it would be quite exceptional to have state-provided counsel. See, for example, the passage beginning, "I would like to make it clear that the right to a fair hearing," above. However, the concurring minority (L'Heureux-Dubé, Gonthier, and McLachlin JJ) were of a more expansive view.

> Taking into account all these factors, it is likely that the situations in which counsel will be required will not necessarily be rare. Proceedings will in many cases be complex, and the consequences, when the child may be removed from the home, are generally serious. Funded counsel must be ordered whenever a fair hearing will not take place without representation. The determination of this question must take into account the important value of meaningful participation in the hearing, taking into account the rights affected, and the powerlessness that a reasonable person in the position of the claimant may legitimately feel when faced with the formal procedures and practices of the justice system. The trial judge's duty to ensure a fair trial may therefore, when necessary, involve an order that the parent be provided with legal counsel, and trial judges should not, in my view, consider the issue from the starting point that counsel will be necessary to ensure a fair hearing only in rare cases.

Disclosure and Official Notice

Imagine that an agency hears oral evidence and representations from one party in the absence of another party and does not disclose this evidence to the other party or give an opportunity to respond to it. Or imagine that the same agency receives documentary evidence or representations from one party and does not disclose it to another party or give an opportunity to respond. If the agency relies on the evidence or representations, its decisions can be challenged. There are many cases involving these kinds of situations but the general principles are clear; a party is entitled to know what evidence and representations have been given and is entitled to an adequate opportunity to respond. One example is sufficient: *Kane v. Board of Governors of the University of British Columbia*, [1980] 1 SCR 1105 (BC). Kane was a professor at UBC and was suspended by the president for improper use of computer facilities. He appealed to the board of governors, of which the president was a member. The board held a hearing, attended by Kane and the president. After the hearing, the board had dinner and met, without Kane, to discuss the case. The evidence about the role the president played at this meeting was slim and not entirely clear. A member of the board made an unchallenged and unelaborated statement that the president did not participate in the discussion or vote, but gave the board "the necessary facts." Kane made an application for review, which was dismissed, and he appealed. The appeal was dismissed, and he appealed to the Supreme Court. This appeal was allowed, and Dickson J said:

> The Board was under an obligation to postpone further consideration of the matter until such time as Doctor Kane might be present and hear the additional facts adduced; at the very least the Board should have made Doctor Kane aware of those facts and afforded him a real and effective opportunity to correct or meet any adverse statement made. In the event, the Board followed neither course. The Board heard the further facts, deliberated, and ruled against Doctor Kane. In so doing, it made a fundamental error. The danger against which the Courts must

be on guard is the possibility that further information could have been put before the Board for its consideration which affected the disposition of the appeal.

This passage is an introduction both to this section, which is about disclosure and official notice, and to the next one, which is about evidence and cross-examination.

Disclosure is the disclosure to parties of information that the agency has about the decision to be made; official notice is the extent and manner in which an agency may, in making its decisions, use material that is not introduced in evidence. The two topics overlap and are considered together because the crucial issues in official notice are the accommodation of the expertise and accumulated knowledge of the agency and the need to permit parties to know about (and respond to) material that may influence the decision. Disclosure is a basic element of the common law of natural justice and is usually required unless some competing interest prevails. The justification for the requirement is simply to enable a party to know and respond to information that the agency has and that may influence its decision.

One aspect of disclosure and official notice that we have already encountered is the matter of pre-hearing discovery. The material in that section of this chapter as well as *Chiarelli v. Canada (Minister of Justice)*, [1992] 1 SCR 711 (Can.), presage some of the difficult issues that we now take up directly in this section: limits placed on access to relevant material in the name of confidentiality claims of various kinds.

For the most part, this consideration of confidentiality is approached from a common law perspective. We make no attempt to outline and analyze all of the numerous statutory provisions that purport to deny or regulate access to information even in the course of adjudicative hearings. Before commencing on a consideration of various contexts in which confidentiality claims are asserted in response to access demands, there are, however, some legislative regimes and common law principles to which we would draw particular attention.

Access to Information Statutes

First, many jurisdictions in Canada now have "freedom of information" and privacy laws. At one level, these are potentially valuable sources of information for those involved in interrelationships with government. Indeed, at times, access to information requests may be an important aspect of preparing for a regulatory hearing, particularly as a surrogate for pre-hearing discovery. This may even include, in some situations, use of US freedom of information (FOI) laws that have been known to produce information exempted from release under Canadian FOI regimes.

However, what should also be realized is that just because information is exempted from disclosure under freedom of information legislation does not necessarily mean that its disclosure will also be denied in proceedings to which the rules of natural justice or procedural fairness apply. Thus, under the federal freedom of information legislation, it is provided that the Act is without prejudice to other laws governing access to information (*Access to Information Act*, RSC 1985, c. A-1, s. 2(2)). It "complements," not "replaces" existing entitlements to access and it is "not intended to limit in any way" existing rights of access to government information. This clearly includes the common law of natural justice and procedural fairness, and the determination of whether that common law requires disclosure is certainly not precluded by the fact that the Act provides an exemption from disclosure in the context of a freedom of information request. Reasons that dictate that not every Canadian should have access to certain kinds of information may simply lose their force in the context of proceedings that affect the particular rights or interests of a specific Canadian. (See *Gough v. Canada (National Parole Board)* (1990), 45 Admin. LR 304 (FCTD), below.) The Ontario *Freedom of Information and Protection of Privacy Act*, RSO 1990, c. F.31, deals with it slightly differently in that s. 64(2) provides that the Act does not prevail over the powers of courts and tribunals with respect to the attendance of witnesses and the production of documents.

Crown or Executive Privilege

At the federal level in Canada, the common law of Crown or executive privilege has been codified in provisions in the *Canada Evidence Act*, RSC 1985, c. C-5, ss. 37-39. As opposed to the situation with the *Access to Information Act*, these privileges are applicable to proceedings before administrative agencies. The sections provide as follows:

Canada Evidence Act
RSC 1985, c. C-5, ss. 37-39

Specified Public Interest

Objection to disclosure of information

37(1) Subject to sections 38 to 38.16, a Minister of the Crown in right of Canada or other official may object to the disclosure of information before a court, person or body with jurisdiction to compel the production of information by certifying orally or in writing to the court, person or body that the information should not be disclosed on the grounds of a specified public interest.

Obligation of court, person or body

(1.1) If an objection is made under subsection (1), the court, person or body shall ensure that the information is not disclosed other than in accordance with this Act.

Objection made to superior court

(2) If an objection to the disclosure of information is made before a superior court, that court may determine the objection.

Objection not made to superior court

(3) If an objection to the disclosure of information is made before a court, person or body other than a superior court, the objection may be determined, on application, by
   (a) the Federal Court, in the case of a person or body vested with power to compel production by or under an Act of Parliament if the person or body is not a court established under a law of a province; or
   (b) the trial division or trial court of the superior court of the province within which the court, person or body exercises its jurisdiction, in any other case.

Limitation period

(4) An application under subsection (3) shall be made within 10 days after the objection is made or within any further or lesser time that the court having jurisdiction to hear the application considers appropriate in the circumstances.

Disclosure order

(4.1) Unless the court having jurisdiction to hear the application concludes that the disclosure of the information to which the objection was made under subsection (1) would encroach upon a specified public interest, the court may authorize by order the disclosure of the information.

Disclosure order

(5) If the court having jurisdiction to hear the application concludes that the disclosure of the information to which the objection was made under subsection (1) would encroach upon a specified public interest, but that the public interest in disclosure outweighs in importance the specified public interest, the court may, by order, after considering both the public interest in disclosure and the form of and conditions to disclosure that are most likely to limit any encroachment upon the specified public interest resulting from disclosure, authorize the disclosure, subject to any conditions that the court considers appropriate, of all of the information, a part or summary of the information, or a written admission of facts relating to the information.

Prohibition order

(6) If the court does not authorize disclosure under subsection (4.1) or (5), the court shall, by order, prohibit disclosure of the information.

[Omitted are several subsections relating to the evidence that may be considered by the court hearing the application and the time at which a disclosure order becomes effective. These are followed by sections setting out appeal rights from the disclosure decision as well as the power of judges presiding at a criminal trial or other criminal proceedings to make orders to protect accused individuals' fair hearing rights following a disclosure decision. Section 38, below, sets out a comprehensive and complex code to govern the disclosure of information that, if disclosed, could injure international relations or national defence or national security.]

International Relations and National Defence and National Security

Definitions

[Duplicate titles have been removed.]

38. The following definitions apply in this section and in sections 38.01 to 38.15.

"judge" means the Chief Justice of the Federal Court or a judge of that Court designated by the Chief Justice to conduct hearings under section 38.04.

"participant" means a person who, in connection with a proceeding, is required to disclose, or expects to disclose or cause the disclosure of, information.

"potentially injurious information" means information of a type that, if it were disclosed to the public, could injure international relations or national defence or national security.

"proceeding" means a proceeding before a court, person or body with jurisdiction to compel the production of information.

"prosecutor" means an agent of the Attorney General of Canada or of the Attorney General of a province, the Director of Military Prosecutions under the *National Defence Act* or an individual who acts as a prosecutor in a proceeding.

"sensitive information" means information relating to international relations or national defence or national security that is in the possession of the Government of Canada, whether originating from inside or outside Canada, and is of a type that the Government of Canada is taking measures to safeguard.

[Section 38.01, a detailed section that requires the participants to proceedings who believe that sensitive or potentially injurious information will be disclosed to notify the attorney general of Canada, is omitted. Section 38.02, also omitted, prohibits participants from disclosing such information and from disclosing that notice has been provided, that an application for an order regarding disclosure has been made to the Federal Court, and other information relating to the disclosure proceedings except under specified conditions. Section 38.03, also omitted, provides that the attorney general may authorize disclosure or conclude a disclosure agreement regarding the information at issue (s. 38.031).]

Application to Federal Court—Attorney General of Canada

38.04(1) The Attorney General of Canada may, at any time and in any circumstances, apply to the Federal Court for an order with respect to the disclosure of information about which notice was given under any of subsections 38.01(1) to (4).

Application to Federal Court—general

(2) If, with respect to information about which notice was given under any of subsections 38.01(1) to (4), the Attorney General of Canada does not provide notice of a decision in accordance with subsection 38.03(3) or, other than by an agreement under section 38.031, authorizes the disclosure of only part of the information or disclosure subject to any conditions,

(a) the Attorney General of Canada shall apply to the Federal Court for an order with respect to disclosure of the information if a person who gave notice under subsection 38.01(1) or (2) is a witness;

(b) a person, other than a witness, who is required to disclose information in connection with a proceeding shall apply to the Federal Court for an order with respect to disclosure of the information; and

(c) a person who is not required to disclose information in connection with a proceeding but who wishes to disclose it or to cause its disclosure may apply to the Federal Court for an order with respect to disclosure of the information.

Notice to Attorney General of Canada

(3) A person who applies to the Federal Court under paragraph (2)(b) or (c) shall provide notice of the application to the Attorney General of Canada.

Court records

(4) An application under this section is confidential. Subject to section 38.12, the Chief Administrator of the Courts Administration Service may take any measure that he or she considers appropriate to protect the confidentiality of the application and the information to which it relates.

Procedure

(5) As soon as the Federal Court is seized of an application under this section, the judge

(a) shall hear the representations of the Attorney General of Canada and, in the case of a proceeding under Part III of the *National Defence Act*, the Minister of National Defence, concerning the identity of all parties or witnesses whose interests may be affected by either the prohibition of disclosure or the conditions to which disclosure is subject, and concerning the persons who should be given notice of any hearing of the matter;

(b) shall decide whether it is necessary to hold any hearing of the matter;

(c) if he or she decides that a hearing should be held, shall

(i) determine who should be given notice of the hearing,

(ii) order the Attorney General of Canada to notify those persons, and

(iii) determine the content and form of the notice; and

(d) if he or she considers it appropriate in the circumstances, may give any person the opportunity to make representations.

Disclosure agreement

(6) After the Federal Court is seized of an application made under paragraph (2)(c) or, in the case of an appeal from, or a review of, an order of the judge made under any of subsections 38.06(1) to (3) in connection with that application, before the appeal or review is disposed of,

(a) the Attorney General of Canada and the person who made the application may enter into an agreement that permits the disclosure of part of the facts referred to in paragraphs 38.02(1)(b) to (d) or part of the information or disclosure of the facts or information subject to conditions; and

(b) if an agreement is entered into, the Court's consideration of the application or any hearing, review or appeal shall be terminated.

Termination of Court consideration, hearing, review or appeal

(7) Subject to subsection (6), after the Federal Court is seized of an application made under this section or, in the case of an appeal from, or a review of, an order of the judge made under any of subsections 38.06(1) to (3), before the appeal or review is disposed

of, if the Attorney General of Canada authorizes the disclosure of all or part of the information or withdraws conditions to which the disclosure is subject, the Court's consideration of the application or any hearing, appeal or review shall be terminated in relation to that information, to the extent of the authorization or the withdrawal.

Report relating to proceedings

38.05 If he or she receives notice of a hearing under paragraph 38.04(5)(c), a person presiding or designated to preside at the proceeding to which the information relates or, if no person is designated, the person who has the authority to designate a person to preside may, within 10 days after the day on which he or she receives the notice, provide the judge with a report concerning any matter relating to the proceeding that the person considers may be of assistance to the judge.

Disclosure order

38.06(1) Unless the judge concludes that the disclosure of the information would be injurious to international relations or national defence or national security, the judge may, by order, authorize the disclosure of the information.

Disclosure order

(2) If the judge concludes that the disclosure of the information would be injurious to international relations or national defence or national security but that the public interest in disclosure outweighs in importance the public interest in non-disclosure, the judge may by order, after considering both the public interest in disclosure and the form of and conditions to disclosure that are most likely to limit any injury to international relations or national defence or national security resulting from disclosure, authorize the disclosure, subject to any conditions that the judge considers appropriate, of all of the information, a part or summary of the information, or a written admission of facts relating to the information.

Order confirming prohibition

(3) If the judge does not authorize disclosure under subsection (1) or (2), the judge shall, by order, confirm the prohibition of disclosure.

Evidence

(3.1) The judge may receive into evidence anything that, in the opinion of the judge, is reliable and appropriate, even if it would not otherwise be admissible under Canadian law, and may base his or her decision on that evidence.

Introduction into evidence

(4) A person who wishes to introduce into evidence material the disclosure of which is authorized under subsection (2) but who may not be able to do so in a proceeding by reason of the rules of admissibility that apply in the proceeding may request from a judge

an order permitting the introduction into evidence of the material in a form or subject to any conditions fixed by that judge, as long as that form and those conditions comply with the order made under subsection (2).

Relevant factors

(5) For the purpose of subsection (4), the judge shall consider all the factors that would be relevant for a determination of admissibility in the proceeding.

[Provisions relating to giving notice of the disclosure order (s. 38.07) and to reviews and appeals to the Federal Court of Appeal and Supreme Court (ss. 38.08-38.10) are omitted.]

Special rules

38.11(1) A hearing under subsection 38.04(5) or an appeal or review of an order made under any of subsections 38.06(1) to (3) shall be heard in private and, at the request of either the Attorney General of Canada or, in the case of a proceeding under Part III of the *National Defence Act*, the Minister of National Defence, shall be heard in the National Capital Region, as described in the schedule to the *National Capital Act*.

Ex parte representations

(2) The judge conducting a hearing under subsection 38.04(5) or the court hearing an appeal or review of an order made under any of subsections 38.06(1) to (3) may give any person who makes representations under paragraph 38.04(5)(d), and shall give the Attorney General of Canada and, in the case of a proceeding under Part III of the *National Defence Act*, the Minister of National Defence, the opportunity to make representations *ex parte*.

Protective order

38.12(1) The judge conducting a hearing under subsection 38.04(5) or the court hearing an appeal or review of an order made under any of subsections 38.06(1) to (3) may make any order that the judge or the court considers appropriate in the circumstances to protect the confidentiality of the information to which the hearing, appeal or review relates.

Court records

(2) The court records relating to the hearing, appeal or review are confidential. The judge or the court may order that the records be sealed and kept in a location to which the public has no access.

Certificate of Attorney General of Canada

38.13(1) The Attorney General of Canada may personally issue a certificate that prohibits the disclosure of information in connection with a proceeding for the purpose of protecting information obtained in confidence from, or in relation to, a foreign entity as defined in subsection 2(1) of the *Security of Information Act* or for the purpose of protecting national defence or national security. The certificate may only be issued after an order or decision that would result in the disclosure of the information to be subject to the certificate has been made under this or any other Act of Parliament.

[Sections 38.13(2)-38.13(4) relating to military proceedings and to service and filing of the certificate are omitted.]

Effect of certificate

(5) If the Attorney General of Canada issues a certificate, then, notwithstanding any other provision of this Act, disclosure of the information shall be prohibited in accordance with the terms of the certificate.

Statutory Instruments Act does not apply

(6) The *Statutory Instruments Act* does not apply to a certificate issued under subsection (1).

Publication

(7) The Attorney General of Canada shall, without delay after a certificate is issued, cause the certificate to be published in the *Canada Gazette*.

Restriction

(8) The certificate and any matters arising out of it are not subject to review or to be restrained, prohibited, removed, set aside or otherwise dealt with, except in accordance with section 38.131.

Expiration

(9) The certificate expires 15 years after the day on which it is issued and may be reissued.

Application for review of certificate

38.131(1) A party to the proceeding referred to in section 38.13 may apply to the Federal Court of Appeal for an order varying or cancelling a certificate issued under that section on the grounds referred to in subsection (8) or (9), as the case may be.

Notice to Attorney General of Canada

(2) The applicant shall give notice of the application to the Attorney General of Canada.

Military proceedings

(3) In the case of proceedings under Part III of the *National Defence Act*, notice under subsection (2) shall be given to both the Attorney General of Canada and the Minister of National Defence.

Single judge

(4) Notwithstanding section 16 of the *Federal Court Act*, for the purposes of the application, the Federal Court of Appeal consists of a single judge of that Court.

Admissible information

(5) In considering the application, the judge may receive into evidence anything that, in the opinion of the judge, is reliable and appropriate, even if it would not otherwise be admissible under Canadian law, and may base a determination made under any of subsections (8) to (10) on that evidence.

Special rules and protective order

(6) Sections 38.11 and 38.12 apply, with any necessary modifications, to an application made under subsection (1).

Expedited consideration

(7) The judge shall consider the application as soon as reasonably possible, but not later than 10 days after the application is made under subsection (1).

Varying the certificate

(8) If the judge determines that some of the information subject to the certificate does not relate either to information obtained in confidence from, or in relation to, a foreign entity as defined in subsection 2(1) of the *Security of Information Act*, or to national defence or national security, the judge shall make an order varying the certificate accordingly.

Cancelling the certificate

(9) If the judge determines that none of the information subject to the certificate relates to information obtained in confidence from, or in relation to, a foreign entity as defined in subsection 2(1) of the *Security of Information Act*, or to national defence or national security, the judge shall make an order cancelling the certificate.

Confirming the certificate

(10) If the judge determines that all of the information subject to the certificate relates to information obtained in confidence from, or in relation to, a foreign entity as defined in subsection 2(1) of the *Security of Information Act*, or to national defence or national security, the judge shall make an order confirming the certificate.

Determination is final

(11) Notwithstanding any other Act of Parliament, a determination of a judge under any of subsections (8) to (10) is final and is not subject to review or appeal by any court.

Publication

(12) If a certificate is varied or cancelled under this section, the Attorney General of Canada shall, as soon as possible after the decision of the judge and in a manner that mentions the original publication of the certificate, cause to be published in the *Canada Gazette*
> (a) the certificate as varied under subsection (8); or
> (b) a notice of the cancellation of the certificate under subsection (9).

[Section 38.14, which empowers judges presiding at a criminal proceeding to make orders protecting an accused person's hearing rights following the issuance and review of a certificate, is omitted.]

Fiat

38.15(1) If sensitive information or potentially injurious information may be disclosed in connection with a prosecution that is not instituted by the Attorney General of Canada or on his or her behalf, the Attorney General of Canada may issue a fiat and serve the fiat on the prosecutor.

Effect of fiat

(2) When a fiat is served on a prosecutor, the fiat establishes the exclusive authority of the Attorney General of Canada with respect to the conduct of the prosecution described in the fiat or any related process.

Fiat filed in court

(3) If a prosecution described in the fiat or any related process is conducted by or on behalf of the Attorney General of Canada, the fiat or a copy of the fiat shall be filed with the court in which the prosecution or process is conducted.

Fiat constitutes conclusive proof

(4) The fiat or a copy of the fiat
> (a) is conclusive proof that the prosecution described in the fiat or any related process may be conducted by or on behalf of the Attorney General of Canada; and
> (b) is admissible in evidence without proof of the signature or official character of the Attorney General of Canada.

Military proceedings

(5) This section does not apply to a proceeding under Part III of the *National Defence Act*.

Regulations

38.16 The Governor in Council may make any regulations that the Governor in Council considers necessary to carry into effect the purposes and provisions of sections 38 to 38.15, including regulations respecting the notices, certificates and the fiat.

Confidences of the Queen's Privy Council for Canada

Objection relating to a confidence of the Queen's Privy Council

39(1) Where a minister of the Crown or the Clerk of the Privy Council objects to the disclosure of information before a court, person or body with jurisdiction to compel the production of information by certifying in writing that the information constitutes a confidence of the Queen's Privy Council for Canada, disclosure of the information shall be refused without examination or hearing of the information by the court, person or body.

Definition

(2) For the purpose of subsection (1), "a confidence of the Queen's Privy Council for Canada" includes, without restricting the generality thereof, information contained in

(a) a memorandum the purpose of which is to present proposals or recommendations to Council;

(b) a discussion paper the purpose of which is to present background explanations, analyses of problems or policy options to Council for consideration by Council in making decisions;

(c) an agendum of Council or a record recording deliberations or decisions of Council;

(d) a record used for or reflecting communications or discussions between ministers of the Crown on matters relating to the making of government decisions or the formulation of government policy;

(e) a record the purpose of which is to brief Ministers of the Crown in relation to matters that are brought before, or are proposed to be brought before, Council or that are the subject of communications or discussions referred to in paragraph (d); and

(f) draft legislation.

Definition of "Council"

(3) For the purposes of subsection (2), "Council" means the Queen's Privy Council for Canada, committees of the Queen's Privy Council for Canada, Cabinet and committees of Cabinet.

Exception

(4) Subsection (1) does not apply in respect of

(a) a confidence of the Queen's Privy Council for Canada that has been in existence for more than twenty years; or

(b) a discussion paper described in paragraph (2)(b)

(i) if the decisions to which the discussion paper relates have been made public, or

(ii) where the decisions have not been made public, if four years have passed since the decisions were made.

Various attempts to attack the constitutionality of s. 39 and its predecessors have been unsuccessful. Most recently, in *Babcock v. Canada (Attorney General)*, 2002 SCC 57 (Can.), the court held that it infringed neither the unwritten principles of the Canadian constitution nor the guaranteed core jurisdiction of the superior courts. However, the court did seem to accept a broader jurisdiction for inquiry into the process by which the certificate was issued. Interestingly, the court did not address the issue whether s. 39 would trump rights under s. 7. For a suggestion that it would not, see *Canadian Association of Regulated Importers v. Canada (Attorney General)* (1991), 87 DLR (4th) 730 (FCA). The majority appeared to hold that such an absolute immunity was not contrary to s. 7 of the Charter. However, in a concurring judgment, Hugessen JA expressed some reservations as to whether s. 39 would always prevail over s. 7 rights, and, given that the interest at stake in this case was not one that involved a "life, liberty and security of the person" interest, there is still presumably room for doubt on this issue.

Not so in the case of a challenge based on s. 15 of the Charter. In *Canada (Attorney General) v. Central Cartage Co. (No. 1)*, [1990] 2 FC 641 (CA), the Federal Court of Appeal, in a judgment delivered by Iacobucci CJ, held that this litigation advantage possessed by the Crown was not an inequality of the kind covered by s. 15. Leave to appeal to the Supreme Court of Canada was denied on January 17, 1991.

In contrast, the constitutionality of s. 38 has been successfully challenged. In *Toronto Star Newspapers Ltd. v. Canada*, [2007] 4 FCR 434, Toronto Star Newspapers argued that ss. 38.04(4), 38.11(1), and 38.12(2), which denied the Toronto Star access to a s. 38 application and to the court records associated with it even if all parties were present at the proceedings and no secret information was disclosed, violated its s. 2(b) Charter right to freedom of expression and was not justified under s. 1. The sections were read down to apply only to the *ex parte* representations provided for in s. 38.11(2). In *Abou-Elmaati v. Attorney General*, 2010 ONSC 2055, the plaintiff and others had sued the Canadian government in tort and for breach of Charter rights for its alleged role in causing their imprisonment and torture by foreign governments. The court held that to the extent that s. 38 purported to oust, in favour of exclusive Federal Court jurisdiction, the Superior Court's jurisdiction to review a claim of federal Crown privilege on national security grounds in a matter in which individuals sought to enforce their Charter rights, it impaired the Superior Court's core jurisdiction and was unconstitutional.

Outside of the federal domain, the matter of Crown or executive privilege is still regulated by the common law. An authoritative elaboration of that common law is found in *Carey v. Ontario*, [1986] 2 SCR 637 (Ont.). Here, there is no room for absolute privilege and the last word on any claim for privilege rests with the courts, not the executive.

Other Common Law Evidential Privileges

The common law also provides for various other forms of privilege, all of which have the potential to become relevant in the context of administrative proceedings and attempts to secure information—for example, solicitor–client privilege (recollect *Idziak*, *Northwestern General Hospital*, and *Pritchard* in the section on pre-hearing discovery) and adjudicative privilege (or the presumption of deliberative secrecy). We encounter some of these incidentally both in this section and in other parts of this casebook. However, we have made no endeavour to be comprehensive in our coverage of their impact on the administrative process. As with open hearings, the issues that they raise transcend administrative law considerations for the most part and are better dealt with in a course or work on the law of evidence.

The difficulties in deciding about the existence and extent of a right to disclosure are usually the effect of competing interests. The typical difficulties and choices can be demonstrated in four groups of situations:

1. An agency may have collected information about an individual, and the individual may wish disclosure of this information;

2. An agency may have collected information about an individual from other persons, and the individual may wish to know their identity;

3. An agency may have collected information about a business, usually as a required part of an application, and other parties, often competitors, may wish disclosure; and

4. An agency may have material that it has created itself—for example, staff reports about particular corporations or about general economic conditions, or guidelines or statements of policy. Any party—for example, competitors of the particular corporations—may wish disclosure of this material.

Access to Agency Information

The problems in the first group have arisen frequently in the work of income support agencies. Claimants of benefits seek access to the files about them to prepare to present a claim or appeal, or simply to know what the agency knows about them. The best-known problem is access to the files of workers' compensation boards, especially disclosure of the medical reports in these files. These medical reports come from doctors acting in different capacities—for example, general practitioners, consultants to whom general practitioners have referred workers, company doctors, doctors on the staff of the board, and consultants to whom doctors at the board have referred workers.

Three major kinds of argument can be made for disclosure. The first is the basic and powerful belief that individuals should have the right to know what government knows about them. The second is that disclosure would increase substantially the effectiveness of the participation of workers in the decision-making process, because it would enable them to respond to information to be used by the board, and it would also increase acceptability and accountability. The third is that disclosure would tend to improve the quality of the reports, by exposing carelessness and vagueness. Some of the reasons for refusing disclosure are unimpressive—for example, a claim that the reports are confidential can hardly limit disclosure to the workers themselves. Other arguments are more substantial. Disclosure may cause suffering or harm to, for example, a worker—knowledge that terminal cancer was discovered during an examination for a sore back could cause depression or knowledge that recovery depends greatly on regaining self-confidence could prejudice recovery itself. However, even ignoring the argument that the worker—not the doctor—should have the responsibility to make the choice about disclosure, such situations are rare, and could be dealt with by giving a limited discretion to refuse disclosure. An important reason for refusing disclosure was the attitude of doctors. One specific fear was the prospect of litigation and liability. More generally, doctors suggested that disclosure would reduce the frankness and detail of the reports. The Ontario Medical Association said in a brief to the Commission on Freedom of Information and Privacy ((1977) at 4):

> Records once contained the most candid comments to enable the physician to recall, months or years later, the precise circumstances relating to a patient. The fear of such comments being read aloud in a court of law has caused many doctors to refrain from including in medical records statements which might be embarrassing under such circumstances, even though they may be extremely helpful in the care of the patient. The increasing exposure of patient records for legal and audit purposes not only dilutes the confidentiality but also can cause the quality of patient care to be jeopardized.

From a different perspective this concern can be perceived to be an unwillingness to be bothered, questioned, and challenged. However, these attitudes are powerful. The Task Force on Workmen's Compensation in Saskatchewan said ((1973), at 68):

> While the point of view of the doctors is not necessarily the correct one, the Task Force does recognize that cooperation from the medical profession is necessary if the workmen's compensation system is to function adequately.

And Terence G. Ison, who was a strong advocate of disclosure as a scholar and as a chair of the Workers' Compensation Board of British Columbia, said in 1979 in a study of the Ontario board: "[T]he traditional position of the Board has, to a large extent, been an act of deference to positions expressed by organizations of the medical profession" (*Information Access and the Workmen's Compensation Board*, a study prepared for the Commission on Freedom of Information and Individual Privacy (1979), at 89). The study from which this passage is taken contains a comprehensive survey of this problem at 74-111.

Thereafter, the practice of workers' compensation boards changed substantially, and not always simply in response to requirements of the courts. For example, in Ontario in the 1960s the practice was to give workers and their representatives summaries of the files and the medical reports. During the 1970s disclosure of this material to the workers' representatives—lawyers, law students, lay representatives, union officials, and members of parliament—was added. Discussions about further disclosure were continuing at the time the next case was decided.

Re Napoli and Workers' Compensation Board
(1981), 126 DLR (3d) 179 (BCCA)

NEMETZ CJBC: The issue before us is basically this: was the Judge right in finding that the boards of review and the commissioners of the WCB breached the rules of natural justice in failing to give the worker a full opportunity to peruse his file when he appealed from the original decision of a disability awards officer or commissioner?

In order to answer that question one must first examine the procedures provided for in such appeals. For convenience I will refer to section numbers in the 1979 Revised Statutes. Under s. 55 of the Act, an injured worker may apply for compensation. The application is heard by a disability awards officer or by a commissioner (s. 88). On such an inquiry, the officer or commissioner can compel the attendance of witnesses, examine them on oath and order production of documents. The WCB may then act on the report and award compensation.

If an officer awards compensation to the worker, the worker may appeal that ruling to a board of review within 90 days (s. 90). The boards of review are independent bodies composed of a chairman and two other persons appointed by the Lieutenant-Governor in Council, one of whom is selected after consultation with organized groups of workers and one of whom is selected after consultation with organized groups of employers (s. 89).

If the board of review does not uphold the officer's finding, its decision goes to the WCB for reconsideration (s. 90(3)). At this stage the final decision is made by a majority of the commissioners present at the WCB meeting.

If the worker is dissatisfied with the decision of the board of review, he may in some cases appeal the finding to the commissioners of the WCB (s. 91).

Following Napoli's injury he was advised, in 1977, by a disability awards officer that his compensable disability was 5% of total disability. He was awarded a disability pension of $33.56 per month, which was later increased to $50 per month. Napoli appealed this decision to a board of review. Prior to the hearing before the board of review, a WCB compensation consultant provided Napoli's counsel with a four-page summary of the information in his life.

On June 13, 1978, the board of review heard Napoli's appeal. It declined to disclose medical reports on Napoli's file. On September 5, 1978, the board of review recommended to the WCB that Napoli's appeal be denied.

Napoli applied for leave to appeal the decision of the board of review to the commissioners of the WCB, and leave was granted. An appeal to the commissioners was begun on December 1, 1978.

[A description of a companion case, one of two others forming part of the overall judgment of the Court of Appeal, *Re Bourdin and Workers' Compensation Board*, is omitted. It differed from *Napoli* in that Bourdin did not receive a summary of his file.]

Bouck J held in both cases that the rules of natural justice applied to proceedings before the boards of review and the commissioners, and that the files should be disclosed to the workers. ... He found that summaries of the file contents did not satisfy the requirements of natural justice. He went on to say that s. 10 of the British Columbia *Evidence Act* also gave a worker the right to demand disclosure, holding that the WCB was "adverse in interest" to the worker in proceedings before the board of review and the commissioners.

Did the learned Chambers Judge err? In my opinion, he did not. I do not find it necessary to examine the conclusion reached by the Judge respecting the *Evidence Act* since I agree with his finding that the rules of natural justice apply to the hearings before the boards of review and the commissioners sitting on appeal, and that therefore the file contents must be disclosed. In the hearing before us, Mr Grey frankly conceded that the rules of natural justice would be applicable on appeals to these domestic tribunals.

The issues resolve themselves into (a) do the rules of natural justice in cases of this genre require disclosure, and (b) if disclosure is required, what is its extent?

As far as the first issue is concerned, I have no difficulty in answering that question in the affirmative. …

I now turn to (b). Mr Grey, in his able submission, argued that the summaries in the Napoli case were sufficient to comply with the rules of natural justice.

We do not have a copy of the original summary produced for Napoli. We do know that a compensation consultant prepared it. This summary, as I have already indicated, was four pages in length. The second summary, signed by the Registrar to the WCB, was 16 pages in length. The 16-page document contained summaries of Napoli's previous compensation claims and disclosed a total of 30 medical and other experts' reports and opinions. None of these experts is named, and there is no way of ascertaining the extent of the original reports. However, it is instructive to read the summary when one assesses whether it constitutes a proper means of disclosing to Napoli the case made against him. I need only quote a few items from this summary to indicate its inadequacies:

> (1) It was felt that psychological and social factors were probably as critically involved in his disability as organic pathology. He expressed dismay and despair as to his plans for the future or the alternatives open to him. He seemed to have given up working at options. There was evidence of an elaboration of his medical complaints and evidence of depression suggesting development of neurotic problems.

This is a serious allegation, and counsel for Napoli would undoubtedly wish to cross-examine the writers of the original reports.

> (2) It was also requested that his tolerance for standing, bending and lifting be observed as his statement that he did not work more than 15 minutes in the garden after which he was forced to lie down was not borne out by the outstanding upkeep of his home and garden.

In a trial this observation would probably be challenged, especially since it was also known that Napoli had a family who might have assisted him in such work.

> (3) Throughout the examination, he exaggerated and simulated.

The above represents a sampling of damaging statements which counsel would undoubtedly wish to challenge in the interests of his client. To do so effectively would require production of the original reports. As this Court said in *Rammell v. Workmen's Compensation Board* (1961) 28 DLR (2d) 138 (BC CA) at 142: "If the claimant is not told the precise statement made against him, and when, where and by whom made, how can he effectively answer it?"

In these circumstances, "a high standard of justice" is required (see the remarks of Dickson J in *Kane*, particularly since Napoli's future will be largely shaped by the decision of the final domestic tribunal.

Mr Grey drew to our attention decision No. 303 of the WCB, Workers' Compensation Reporter, vol. 5, 1979, p 24 (May 24, 1979), and decision No. 119, Workers' Compensation Reporter, vol. 2, 1975-76, p 103 (June 17, 1975), and adopted the WCB's reasoning for justifying its procedure of only providing summaries in cases of this kind:

Our survey, since late 1978, of those who provide information for claim files—notably physicians, but also Adjudicators, Field Officers and Rehabilitation Consultants—has convinced us that if we were to open our files to scrutiny by claimants or their representatives, there would be a significant adverse effect on the nature and extent of evidence submitted on claims. ...

Essentially, the result is this: we have no doubt about the legitimacy of the concerns of claimants when they are unable to see for themselves all of the documentation on their Board files; but to open the files, in an effort to alleviate those concerns, would seriously damage the actual decision-making process. ...

First, there is concern about the loss of accuracy and frankness that would be likely to result. A medical report is most valuable for treatment, rehabilitation, and adjudication purposes if it is complete and frank. But a doctor may feel under considerable restraints if he felt that anything said might be disclosed to the claimant, his employer or his union. The likely result could be reports that are vague and unreliable to the point of being worthless. More examinations by Board doctors may then be needed with a consequential increase in administrative costs. ...

In my respectful opinion, this reasoning does not conform with the tenets expressed by the Courts in applying the rules of natural justice. In particular, this reasoning glosses over the valid contrary view that persons preparing reports which they know will be amenable to scrutiny will prepare them with greater care and diligence, and, more important, that fairness requires that the original reports be disclosed in order that the claimant can effectively answer the case against him.

For all of the above reasons, it is my view that the provision of summaries was not sufficient compliance with the rules of natural justice in the circumstances of the *Napoli* case. Of course, in *Bourdin* the rules of natural justice clearly were not followed since he received no summary of the file material.

Appeal dismissed.

NOTES

1. In December 1981, the Ontario Board issued a policy statement on disclosure, which provided:

The injured worker shall be provided with access to his claim file and a photocopy of the file upon request, provided there is a disputable issue. The same access shall be granted to the worker's representative upon presentation of written authorization signed by the worker.

The employer, where a disputable issue exists, shall be provided access to and a copy of the records which the Board determines to be relevant to the issue in dispute. The same access shall be granted to the employer's representative upon presentation of written authorization signed by the employer.

2. In *Re Abel and Advisory Review Board*, reproduced in chapter 3 of this text, patients confined to psychiatric institutions under warrant of the lieutenant governor sought disclosure from the Advisory Review Board. *Re Egglestone & Mousseau and Advisory Review Board* (1983), 150 DLR (3d) 86 (Ont. Div. Ct.) is an interesting sequel. Section 32 of the *Mental Health Act* provided for a hearing and in particular provided that the patient could call wit-

nesses, make submissions, and, "with the permission of the chairman, may cross-examine witnesses," and also provided that the board or any member "may interview a patient or other person in private." The practice of the board was to receive from the administrator of the institution the file for each patient, which usually included such documents as clinical records, nurse's notes, test reports, and conference reports. Egglestone requested disclosure of his hospital file, and the chairman made an order that permitted only his counsel to read it, only in the presence of a member of the board, and only on the condition that it not be disclosed to Egglestone. He sought review and failed. Griffiths J said:

> While I am sympathetic to the fact that counsel receiving the information on the limited basis here is placed in a very awkward position so far as his client is concerned, it seems to me that this is the only reasonable order that could have been made by the chairman to achieve a balance between the right of the patient to disclosure of the relevant facts, as against the right, indeed duty, of the Board to preserve confidentiality of information in sensitive areas.
>
> I would expect that faced with the order made here counsel should obtain the consent of his client to accept the documentary review on this limited basis, otherwise he may not feel at liberty to receive the information at all.

Egglestone made another claim that was not about disclosure, but that is interesting enough to include nonetheless. Two of the members of the board were psychiatrists, and the usual practice was that they would examine the patient and report their findings to the board in private, after the rest of the hearing was concluded. Egglestone sought disclosure of their notes, to be present with his counsel when they made their report, and to cross-examine. The entire Divisional Court refused cross-examination, because the statute left it to the discretion of the chair, and refused disclosure of the notes, but a majority allowed the request to be present. Griffiths J said,

> The views of the psychiatrists because of their expertise would obviously have a substantial if not dominant impact on the decision of the Board. Indeed, their analysis based on the interview and the review of the medical file may, in most cases, be a determining factor in the Board's ultimate recommendation. Here, following the reports of the psychiatrists, the Board arrived at a decision which, in effect, adopted the recommendation of the two psychiatrists.
>
> • • •
>
> The "facts" presented by the Board psychiatrists, and by facts I include their professional opinions, were obviously facts to which the Board was going to and did indeed apply its mind in arriving at its recommendations. I can see no difference in principle to the approach which should be taken to facts relied on by the Board, but contained in the reports of the Board psychiatrists and those contained in documents, which the Court of Appeal in *Abel* held were subject to disclosure, however conditional.

Trainor J dissented on this issue:

> The scheme of the legislation is investigative more than adversarial. The hearing itself cannot be conducted in an adversarial atmosphere for a number of reasons directly related to the welfare of the patient and his successful treatment. The underpinning of medical and psychiatric opinion often cannot be disclosed because of the detrimental effect disclosure would have on the patient, the staff and the public.

The Legislature has provided that members of the Board may investigate and recommend. That dual responsibility is unusual if not unique. It is foreign to an adversarial proceeding but it is the law.

Identity of Sources of Information

The second situation involves claims to disclosure of sources of information, and there is no general rule beyond "reasonableness." Consider these cases:

1. A nurse in a psychiatric hospital has been charged with abuse of patients, and a hearing will be held by the discipline committee of the College of Nurses. Clearly it must give particulars such as names of patients and dates. Must it also disclose the names of the individuals who told it about the alleged abuse? Consider the possibility that they may be personal enemies, or staff bypassed in the nurse's recent promotion.

2. A law society requires that applicants have "good character" and gives a right to "an opportunity to appear in person" before an admissions committee before refusal of admission. A would-be lawyer is told by the secretary that the society has reliable information that he was an active member of the Heritage Front. Is he entitled to know the identity of the information? Consider how the informants might confuse political organizations, or how an expression of sympathy for immigration reform might be transformed by several tellings.

3. A professor has applied for tenure, and a committee has begun to gather assessments of scholarship. Assuming this issue is not governed by valid rules, is she entitled to know the identity of the assessors? Are grant applications different?

4. Is an applicant entitled to know the identity of the persons who gave information about his citizenship application? Consider the possibilities that they may be on opposite sides of political fences in his homeland, or undercover RCMP agents.

5. A prisoner is charged in discipline proceedings with inciting a riot. Is he entitled to know the names of informers? Consider the possibilities that he may be the innocent victim of a conspiracy, or that the informers may be fellow prisoners or guards.

The dimensions of the fourth of these hypotheticals are well illustrated in the next case: *Charkaoui v. Canada (Citizenship and Immigration)* [2008] (*Charkaoui II*). The difficult issue of informants in a penitentiary setting is covered in the two cases that follow. These cases all raise again the issue of the impact of the Charter on traditional common law justifications for withholding information.

Charkaoui v. Canada (Citizenship and Immigration)
[2008] 2 SCR 326 (Can.)

[As noted in chapter 3 of this text—where portions of the earlier *Charkaoui* [2007] decision of the Supreme Court of Canada were reproduced—Mr. Charkaoui was a permanent resident who was designated by Canada's Minister of Citizenship and Immigration and Minister of Public Safety and Emergency Preparedness in a security certificate as a threat to Canada's security, and was subsequently detained. In the course of legal proceedings before a designated Federal Court judge to assess the reasonableness of the security certificate, counsel for the ministers revealed to the designated judge that they had failed, because of an oversight, to disclose to Mr. Charkaoui a summary of two interviews that he had had with CSIS officers in 2002, before his initial arrest.

When Mr. Charkaoui requested that the complete notes of these interviews be disclosed to him, the ministers informed the designated judge that these had been destroyed pursuant to an internal CSIS policy. The policy was based on CSIS's interpretation of s. 12 of the *Canadian Security Intelligence Service Act*, which required CSIS to "collect, by investigation or otherwise, to the extent that it is strictly necessary, and analyse and retain information and intelligence respecting activities that may on reasonable grounds be suspected of constituting threats to the security of Canada and, in relation thereto, shall report to and advise the Government of Canada." Under CSIS policy, all operational notes were destroyed after they had been transcribed into a report by the employee who took them.

Alleging that his right to procedural fairness had been violated by the minister's refusal to disclose the notes, Mr. Charkaoui sought an order staying the proceedings, quashing the certificate, and releasing him from custody. The Supreme Court began by reviewing the statutory framework governing CSIS's mandate and, in particular, its authority to collect and retain information in its investigations of terrorist and criminal activities. It concluded that the CSIS Act required CSIS officers investigating particular individuals or groups to retain operational notes, which may be necessary to ensure that a "complete and objective" version of the facts be available to those responsible for issuing and for reviewing the security certificates (at para. 42).

The court then turned to Mr. Charkaoui's right to disclosure of the notes. It began by addressing the Federal Court of Appeal's refusal to recognize a right to disclosure in the context of security certificate proceedings, on the basis that disclosure of this nature was required in criminal, not administrative, proceedings.]

LeBEL and FISH JJ: ...

C. Conduct of the Proceedings Relating to the Security Certificate and Duty To Disclose Information in the Possession of CSIS

[47] ... In this section, we will consider the manner in which information in CSIS's possession should be disclosed to the ministers and the designated judge in the context of the proceeding relating to the security certificate. This will require a more nuanced approach than simply importing the model developed by the courts in criminal law. All the interests at stake that relate to public safety and to certain essential functions of the state must be taken into account.

(1) Review of the Criminal Law Principles Governing Disclosure; Distinguishing the Context of the Security Certificate

(i) Review of the Criminal Law Principles Governing Disclosure

[48] We begin by reviewing the principles that apply to the disclosure of evidence in criminal law. In *R v. Stinchcombe*, [1991] 3 SCR 326, a criminal case, the Court established

the rule that a police force's investigation file must be as complete as possible, so that all evidence that might be relevant to the defence can eventually be disclosed to counsel. Otherwise, the right of the accused to make full answer and defence could be impaired. ...

[49] Later, in *R v. La*, [1997] 2 SCR 680, the Court reiterated that the duty to disclose entails a corollary duty to preserve information, exhibits, recordings, investigation notes and any other relevant evidence (see also *R v. Egger*, [1993] 2 SCR 451). There is no question that original notes and recordings are the best evidence. ...

(ii) Distinguishing the Context of the Security Certificate

[50] The principles governing the disclosure of evidence are well established in criminal law, but the proceeding in which the Federal Court determines whether a security certificate is reasonable takes place in a context different from that of a criminal trial. No charges are laid against the person named in the certificate. Instead, the ministers seek to expel the named person from Canada on grounds of prevention or public safety. However, the serious consequences of the procedure on the liberty and security of the named person bring interests protected by s. 7 of the *Charter* into play. A form of disclosure of all the information that goes beyond the mere summaries which are currently provided by CSIS to the ministers and the designated judge is required to protect the fundamental rights affected by the security certificate procedure.

[51] In the case at bar, the Federal Court of Appeal refused to impose a duty to disclose on CSIS on the basis that this duty does not apply in administrative law. It relied in particular on the following passage from *Blencoe v. British Columbia (Human Rights Commission)*, [2000] 2 SCR 307, 2000 SCC 44, a case in which this Court had held that the right to be tried within a reasonable time under s. 11(*b*) of the *Charter* applies only in criminal law matters:

> This Court has often cautioned *against the direct application of criminal justice standards in the administrative law area*. We should not blur concepts which under our *Charter* are clearly distinct. ... [para. 88]

[52] With this in mind, we pointed out in *May v. Ferndale Institution*, [2005] 3 SCR 809, 2005 SCC 82, that the consequences of a criminal prosecution are severe in comparison with those attached to a question of an administrative nature:

> It is important to bear in mind that the *Stinchcombe* principles were enunciated in the particular context of criminal proceedings where the innocence of the accused was at stake. *Given the severity of the potential consequences the appropriate level of disclosure was quite high.* In these cases, the impugned decisions are purely administrative. These cases do not involve a criminal trial and innocence is not at stake. The *Stinchcombe* principles do not apply in the administrative context. ... [para. 91]

In *May*, inmates were challenging decisions by prison authorities to transfer them.

[53] But whether or not the constitutional guarantees of s. 7 of the *Charter* apply does not turn on a formal distinction between the different areas of law. Rather, it depends on the severity of the consequences of the state's actions for the individual's fundamental

interests of liberty and security and, in some cases, the right to life. By its very nature, the security certificate procedure can place these rights in serious jeopardy, as the Court recognized in *Charkaoui*. To protect them, it becomes necessary to recognize a duty to disclose evidence based on s. 7.

[54] Investigations by CSIS play a central role in the decision on the issuance of a security certificate and the consequent removal order. The consequences of security certificates are often more severe than those of many criminal charges. For instance, the possible repercussions of the process range from detention for an indeterminate period to removal from Canada, and sometimes to a risk of persecution, infringement of the right to integrity of the person, or even death. Moreover, as Justice O'Connor observed in his report, "the security certificate process, provides for broader grounds of culpability and lower standards of proof than criminal law" (Commission of Inquiry into the Actions of Canadian Officials in Relation to Maher Arar, *A New Review Mechanism for the RCMP's National Security Activities*, at p. 436).

[55] Finally, it should be noted that the confirmation that a security certificate is reasonable is not a purely administrative measure, since a Federal Court judge must make that determination. It is therefore simplistic to characterize the proceeding to determine whether a security certificate is reasonable as a purely administrative procedure, as the respondents do.

(2) Duty To Disclose Based on Section 7 and Related to the Severity of the Consequences of the Procedure for the Named Person

[56] In *La* (at para. 20), this Court confirmed that the duty to disclose is included in the rights protected by s. 7. Similarly, in *Ruby v. Canada (Solicitor General)*, [2002] 4 SCR 3, 2002 SCC 75, at paras. 39-40, the Court stressed the importance of adopting a contextual approach in assessing the rules of natural justice and the degree of procedural fairness to which an individual is entitled. In our view, the issuance of a certificate and the consequences thereof, such as detention, demand great respect for the named person's right to procedural fairness. In this context, procedural fairness includes a procedure for verifying the evidence adduced against him or her. It also includes the disclosure of the evidence to the named person, in a manner and within limits that are consistent with legitimate public safety interests.

[57] *Suresh v. Canada (Minister of Citizenship and Immigration)*, [2002] 1 SCR 3, 2002 SCC 1, at para. 113, concerned the nature of the right to procedural fairness in a context where a person had been deprived of rights protected by s. 7 of the *Charter*. This Court emphasized the importance of being sensitive to the context of each situation:

[D]eciding what procedural protections must be provided involves consideration of the following factors: (1) the nature of the decision made and the procedures followed in making it, that is, "the closeness of the administrative process to the judicial process"; (2) the role of the particular decision within the statutory scheme; (3) the importance of the decision to the individual affected; (4) the legitimate expectations of the person challenging the decision where undertakings were made concerning the procedure to be followed; and (5) the choice of procedure made by the agency itself … . [para. 115]

[58] In the context of information provided by CSIS to the ministers and the designated judge, the factors considered in *Suresh* confirm the need for an expanded right to procedural fairness, one which requires the disclosure of information, in the procedures relating to the review of the reasonableness of a security certificate and to its implementation. As we mentioned above, these procedures may, by placing the individual in a critically vulnerable position vis-à-vis the state, have severe consequences for him or her.

[59] It is not enough to say that there is a duty to disclose. We must determine exactly how that duty is to be discharged in the context of the procedures relating to the issuance of a security certificate and the review of its reasonableness, and to the detention review.

(3) Duty Adapted to the Nature of the Procedures Designed To Ensure the Proper Performance of the Mandates of the Ministers and, in Particular, of the Designated Judge

[60] Within the statutory framework applicable to the appeal, which does not include Bill C-3 [amendments that remedied the constitutional defects outlined in the court's earlier decision in *Charkaoui*, reproduced in chapter 3 of this text], only the ministers and the designated judge have access to all the evidence. In *Charkaoui*, this Court noted the difficulties that the Act then in force caused in the review of the reasonableness of the certificate and in the detention review, particularly with respect to the assessment of the allegations of fact made against the named person:

> Despite the judge's best efforts to question the government's witnesses and scrutinize the documentary evidence, he or she is placed in the situation of asking questions and ultimately deciding the issues on the basis of incomplete and potentially unreliable information. [para. 63]

[61] The destruction of the original documents exacerbates these difficulties. If the original evidence was destroyed, the designated judge has access only to summaries prepared by the state, which means that it will be difficult, if not impossible, to verify the allegations. In criminal law matters, this Court has noted that access to original documents is useful to ensure that the probative value of certain evidence can be assessed effectively. In *R v. Oickle*, [2000] 2 SCR 3, 2000 SCC 38, at para. 46, the Court mentioned that viewing a videotape of a police interrogation can assist judges in monitoring interrogation practices, and that interview notes cannot reflect the tone of what was said and any body language that may have been employed.

[62] As things stand, the destruction by CSIS officers of their operational notes compromises the very function of judicial review. To uphold the right to procedural fairness of people in Mr. Charkaoui's position, CSIS should be required to retain all the information in its possession and to disclose it to the ministers and the designated judge. The ministers and the designated judge will in turn be responsible for verifying the information they are given. If, as we suggest, the ministers have access to all the undestroyed "original" evidence, they will be better positioned to make appropriate decisions on issuing a certificate. The designated judge, who will have access to all the evidence, will then exclude any evidence that might pose a threat to national security and summarize the remaining evidence—which he or she will have been able to check for accuracy and reliability—for the named person.

(4) Duty to the Individual Adapted to the Requirements of Confidentiality of the Information in Question That Is Being Reviewed by the Designated Judge

[63] The duty of CSIS to retain and disclose the information submitted to the ministers and the designated judge also applies with respect to the person named in the certificate. As this Court recognized in *Charkaoui*, however, confidentiality requirements related to public safety and state interests will place limits on how this duty is discharged. In short, the judge must filter the evidence he or she has verified and determine the limits of the access to which the named person will be entitled at each step of the process, both during the review of the validity of the certificate and at the detention review stage.

(5) Breach of the Duty To Retain and Disclose

[64] In conclusion, it is our view that the destruction of operational notes is a breach of CSIS's duty to retain and disclose information. CSIS is required—pursuant to s. 12 of the *CSIS Act* and based on a contextual analysis of the case law on the disclosure and retention of evidence—to retain all its operational notes and to disclose them to the ministers for the issuance of a security certificate and subsequently to the designated judge for the review of the reasonableness of the certificate and of the need to detain the named person. This conclusion flows from the serious consequences the investigation will have for the life, liberty and security of the named person. The designated judge then provides non-privileged information to the named person, as completely as the circumstances allow.

[The court determined that, by adjourning the detention review to allow Mr. Charkaoui time to prepare his testimony and defence, the designated judge had averted any prejudice that might have resulted from the delay in disclosing the interview summaries, particularly given the fact that Mr. Charkaoui had himself participated in the interviews and doubtless knew what he had said on these occasions. It refused to order a stay of proceedings, holding that the designated judge, if he ultimately upheld the certificate's reasonableness, would be in a position to determine whether the destruction of the interview notes had a prejudicial effect on Mr. Charkaoui, and the appropriate remedy.]

Appeal allowed in part.

NOTES

1. To comply with the Supreme Court's decision in *Charkaoui II*, the government asked CSIS to scrutinize its files in five security certificate cases to determine whether they contained materials which should be disclosed to the designated judge. It was determined that some original operational notes had been retained. They were provided to the designated judge, Justice Tremblay-Lamer, and to the special advocates, charged under the newly amended IRPA with the task of challenging the minister's claim that "the disclosure of information or other evidence would be injurious to national security or endanger the safety of any person." After hearing the arguments of the ministers and the special advocates, the

designated judge decided that some of the evidence could be disclosed. The ministers disagreed with the court's assessment that disclosure of the evidence would not be injurious to national security. Rather than disclosing it, the ministers withdrew the evidence, an option expressly allowed by the IRPA. Shortly after, the ministers stated that, in their opinion, the evidence remaining in the file was not sufficient to meet their burden of showing that the certificate was reasonable. Nevertheless, instead of withdrawing the security certificate, they asked the designated judge to rule on the certificate's reasonableness. Having secured a decision on the certificate's reasonableness, the Ministers intended to direct certified questions to the Court of Appeal on the proper scope of disclosure in the hope that it would cut down the scope of disclosure ordered by the designated judge, enabling the ministers to issue a new certificate based on evidence they would no longer have to disclose to Mr. Charkaoui.

The designated judge rejected the ministers' request. Tremblay-Lamer J noted that the provisions of the IRPA governing the security certificate process required the ministers to file with the court the information and evidence on which the certificate was based. She held that, in light of the ministers' withdrawal of the supporting evidence, the certificate no longer complied with the requirements for its referral to the court and declared that the certificate was void. In the alternative, she decided that the certificate was not reasonable in view of the ministers' admission that they could not meet their evidentiary burden. Finally, she refused to certify any questions for appeal, thwarting the ministers' attempt to effectively overturn the disclosure orders that had prompted the ministers to withdraw the evidence: see *Re Charkaoui*, 2009 FC 1030.

In doing so, Tremblay-Lamer J rebutted the ministers' charge that, in dismissing the disclosure orders, the court had "balanced" national security against procedural fairness, and that such balancing was inappropriate because national security must always outweigh procedural fairness. Her description of the disclosure process is reproduced below:

The Court's Methodology with Respect to Disclosure

[73] The statutory and jurisprudential framework in which the Court has operated should first be explained.

[74] First, it must be recalled that, in paragraph 85.1(2)(a) of the IRPA, Parliament has expressly given the special advocate the role of "challeng[ing]" the Minister's claim that the disclosure of information or other evidence would be injurious to national security or endanger the safety of any person." Thus, the special advocates played an active role in the disclosure process.

[75] It should also be noted that the IRPA confers an important role on the designated judge, who, under paragraph 83(1)(d), "shall ensure the confidentiality of information and other evidence provided by the Minister if, *in the judge's opinion*, its disclosure would be injurious to national security or endanger the safety of any person." Thus, each time the question arises, the designated judge must determine whether the disclosure of information would be injurious to national security or the safety of any person.

[76] Although their expertise is taken into consideration in this delicate mandate, the judge owes no deference to the assertions made by CSIS or the Ministers in this regard; nor does it owe any deference to the special advocates. The decision is the designated judge's alone. This is what Parliament decreed.

[77] Second, the Supreme Court provided several clarifications regarding the approach that designated judges must take when deciding applications for the disclosure of information and other evidence.

[78] As I have stated, the Supreme Court of Canada considered the disclosure process in the context of an examination of the reasonableness of a security certificate in *Charkaoui II*, above. At the outset of its analysis, the Supreme Court stressed, at paragraph 56, that the procedural fairness requirement, adapted to this context, includes "the *disclosure of the evidence*" on which the certificate is based "*to the named person*, in a manner and within limits that are consistent with legitimate public safety interests."

[79] The Court also specified, at paragraph 62, that in order to respect these limits, "[t]he designated judge, who will have access to all the evidence, will then exclude any evidence that might pose a threat to national security and summarize the remaining evidence—which he or she will have been able to check for accuracy and reliability—for the named person."

[80] In other words, the judge's role, as stated at paragraph 63, is to "filter the evidence he or she has verified and determine the limits of the access to which the named person will be entitled at each step of the process … ."

[81] It should be recalled that, in September 2008, the Ministers acknowledged that they have a duty to disclose the evidence on which the certificate is based. It should also be recalled that the Assistant Director of CSIS wrote to the Court that all the evidence that could be disclosed to Mr. Charkaoui without causing prejudice to national security had already been disclosed.

[82] With the statutory and case law framework discussed above in mind, the Court then ordered that a hearing *in camera* would have to be held before the disclosure of any further evidence would be permitted. In keeping with paragraph 83(1)(d) of the IRPA, ensuring the confidentiality of information that, if disclosed, would be injurious to national security or endanger the safety of any person has always been a central preoccupation of the Court, as the numerous orders, directions and communications issued by the Court in these proceedings will attest. …

[83] The purpose of the hearings *in camera* was to enable the Court, with the assistance of the special advocates and the Ministers' lawyers, to achieve this objective by means of a process of filtering and of producing neutralized summaries.

[84] To facilitate this process, the special advocates prepared disclosure proposals based on the themes developed by Justice Dawson in *Harkat* [*Re Harkat*, (2005) 2005 FC 393]: Canadian and foreign agencies, human sources, interceptions, and investigative techniques. These proposals were submitted to the Ministers, who could give or withhold their consent to the disclosure as proposed by the special advocates.

[85] Hearings *in camera* were later held with respect to the evidence that the Ministers did not agree to disclose. Applying paragraph 83(1)(d) of the IRPA, quoted above, the Court decided, item by item, whether its disclosure would injure national security or endanger the safety of any person. Whenever the Court found that it would, it refused the disclosure of the item, regardless of its potential importance to Mr. Charkaoui. In doing so, the Court rejected the special advocates' proposal that the Court weigh the interests in play and order the disclosure of information important to Mr. Charkaoui's defence despite the risk to national security.

[86] In the course of these hearings *in camera, following the Ministers' consent to the disclosure of the content of the interceptions*, the Court sought to ensure that the summaries that the Ministers had provided were in conformity with the originals.

[87] The Court issued certain oral orders intended to achieve this objective. At the same time, the Court demanded that the Ministers tell Mr. Charkaoui whether the original evidence had been retained or not, in accordance with paragraph 42 of the decision in *Charkaoui II*, above, where it was specified that "the retention and accessibility of this information is of particular

importance where the person named in the certificate and his or her counsel will often have access only to summaries or truncated versions of the intelligence … ." In the Court's opinion, this was the logical consequence of the letter of September 12, 2008, in which the Ministers acknowledged that certain notes had been retained.

[88] However, as counsel for the Ministers acknowledged at the public hearing of September 24, 2009, the Ministers responded to these orders by withdrawing all the interceptions from the evidence in support of the certificate.

[89] The withdrawal of this evidence, which was crucial to the Ministers' case, fatally obstructed the disclosure process. Given the reduced breadth of the information sources, which prevented the information from being neutralized, it became difficult to provide Mr. Charkaoui with an accurate summary of the evidence without disclosing evidence that could be injurious to national security and endanger the safety of any person.

[90] This was the breaking point that resulted in the Court's issuance of the direction dated July 9, 2009, in which the parties and the special advocates were asked for written submissions on the effect of the withdrawal of certain information tendered in support of the certificate.

Conclusion on the Certification of a Question for the Court of Appeal

[91] Thus, the true question proposed by the Ministers, which pertains to the legitimacy of a judicial balancing of national security against procedural fairness as part of the disclosure of evidence on which a security certificate is based, is not relevant to these proceedings, because the Court has never engaged in such an exercise. Thus, the question cannot be determinative of the outcome of a future appeal, and the Court cannot certify it.

[92] What the Ministers are truly seeking to do is to challenge certain disclosure orders made by this Court. In fact, they themselves assert that their ultimate goal is to "reinsert" evidence in support of the certificate, albeit without (one has to assume) having to disclose it in accordance with the Court's orders. In sum, as the special advocates point out, the Ministers' objections invite an item-by-item re-assessment of the specific summaries to the disclosure of which the Ministers object. This objection pertains to the facts of this case. It does not transcend the parties' interests and is not of general importance. It raises no question that meets the criteria of section 79 of the IRPA.

[93] Accordingly, this Court is bound by the IRPA [and] the decisions of the Federal Court of Appeal, to refuse to certify the question proposed by the Ministers.

2. In the face of Tremblay-Lamer J's disclosure orders, the ministers had to choose between disclosing the original CSIS evidence, an outcome they believed would be injurious to national security in spite of judicial conclusion to the contrary, or forgoing reliance on these materials, without which they could not meet the evidentiary burden required to uphold the security certificate. A similar dilemma is faced by the parole board in the *Gough* case, below. Note that the disclosure of confidential information can often be tailored, whether by release of summaries or by partial disclosure of sensitive information, to the demands of national security; indeed, the process of closed proceedings is often concerned with whether and how to disclose the factual details contained in sensitive information.

3. In *Re Charkaoui*, Justice Tremblay-Lamer's disclosure orders were designed to ensure that the summaries of confidential evidence that the ministers had provided to Mr. Charkaoui "were in conformity with the originals" on which the summaries were based. Both the court and the special advocates had access to these originals in the closed proceedings. Does the

fact that the ministers responded to Tremblay-Lamer J's disclosure orders by withdrawing the evidence in its entirety suggest that the concern may perhaps have been less about possible injury to national security and more about withholding embarrassing information, such as discrepancies between the originals and the summaries already disclosed, from public scrutiny? Based on past episodes, this is an important possibility to consider when national security confidentiality is invoked by the executive branch, especially in the face of a decision by a judge who has reviewed the relevant information that the disclosure in question would not injure national security.

4. See, for example, the revelations in *Re Harkat* (2009), 2009 FC 1050, also a security certificate case, in which it was found—after the matter was pursued by the special advocates appointed in that case—that CSIS had failed for a six-year period to disclose to the ministers or to the court that a confidential informant against Mr. Harkat, the named person, had failed all relevant questions on a polygraph test in 2002. Despite having knowledge of this polygraph evidence, one CSIS officer failed to disclose, when asked by the court in a 2008 closed hearing, whether there was anything unusual in the file. Another CSIS officer, after learning of the discrepancy in the file's polygraph evidence, referred the matter to CSIS's litigation department rather than to CSIS's legal counsel in the security certificate proceedings. A third CSIS officer, after undertaking to respond to questions from the court on the polygraph section of the file, gave an incomplete and inaccurate statement to the court, explaining later that he did not have time to fully prepare for his court appearance or to review his undertakings before they were filed with the court. These facts, Noël J concluded at para. 59, had "undermined the integrity of [the] Court's process," although Noël J did not find a deliberate attempt by any of the CSIS officers to hide the information from the court. Rather, at paras. 44-47, he attributed the non-disclosure to institutional failings of CSIS training and inadequate resourcing.

5. Also notable are Justice O'Connor's conclusions on the series of inaccurate and damaging leaks made by unnamed government officials against Maher Arar, both before and after Arar's release from 11 months of extra-judicial detention in Syria (where Arar was detained and tortured, the commissioner found, following his involuntary removal to Syria by US authorities). (Commission of Inquiry into the Actions of Canadian Officials in Relation to Maher Arar, *Report of the Events Relating to Maher Arar—Analysis and Recommendations* (2006).) The commissioner stated at 255-57:

> The evidence presented at the Inquiry leads me to conclude that, over time, Government of Canada officials intentionally released selected classified information about Mr. Arar or his case to the media. ...
>
> Perhaps not surprisingly, the identity of the Canadian officials responsible for the leaks remains unknown despite the fact that several administrative investigations have been conducted by the relevant government departments or agencies into the sources of the leaks. ...
>
> This case is an example of how some government officials, over an extended period of time, used the media to put a spin on an affair and unfairly damage a person's reputation. Given the content of the released information, only individuals with access to classified information could have been responsible for the leaks. The obvious inference is that this was done to paint a picture they considered favourable either to the Canadian government or to themselves.

It is worth bearing in mind that leaks of government information can have different aims. In some cases, the leakor is seeking to disclose what he or she perceived to be government wrongdoing that would not otherwise come to light.

Other leaks, however, seek to advance the interests of the Canadian government or of government officials, in some cases by disparaging the reputation of another. This was the case with some of the leaks concerning Mr. Arar, which were aimed at tarnishing Mr. Arar's reputation and undermining his credibility. Some were likely intended to persuade the Government of Canada not to call a public inquiry.

While most leaks likely involve a breach of some form of confidentiality, using confidential information to manipulate public opinion in favour of the Canadian government's interests or the interests of the leakor of the information is obviously more egregious. This is particularly so when third parties are targeted in a way that is unfairly prejudicial to them.

Because it can be so difficult to counter this type of leak, one can only hope that some of the public and the media are sophisticated enough to perceive the reality of what is occurring and to reserve judgment until there is a fair and transparent disclosure of all of the relevant facts.

6. On closed proceedings in the security context, see G. Van Harten, "Weaknesses of Adjudication in the Face of Secret Evidence" (2009), 13 *Int'l J Evidence and Proof* 1, which states at 20-25 (footnotes omitted):

Closed proceedings in the security context have a dynamic that is unlike other confidential adjudication owing to a combination of factors that may encourage the courts, sometimes in subtle ways, to favour unduly the executive's position over that of the individual. This tendency is in part the outcome of the two factors previously discussed—the absence of the individual and the public, and the courts' dependence on the executive—both of which contribute to an adjudicative environment in which the security interest obtains a privileged status as a result of its more direct and responsive representation before the court. Besides this, a judge may lean toward the executive's position for more diffuse reasons arising from the dynamic of closed proceedings and from the type of issues that arise in confidentiality review.

In the first place, closed hearings have a unique tone and atmosphere that reflects the culture of the security realm. ...

This environment need not influence the judge in an overt or conscious way, but it may contribute over time to a dynamic in which security and secrecy crowd out other priorities. One need not suspect that security officials have actively misled a judge in a particular case in order to accept that judicial review of the executive in these matters is shaped by how security officials present their activities and vet the information they collect before putting it before the court, and by their own vulnerability to errors that an open process would otherwise detect or uncover. ...

In terms of expertise, the terrain of inquiry in national security matters has an especially opaque and high-stakes quality. Threats are often not clear even to security officials and yet can easily be seen by anyone to carry potentially catastrophic consequences. This high-stakes uncertainty provides the backdrop for the "mosaic theory" of non-disclosure. The theory posits that, even where apparently innocuous information is disclosed, an informed observer may be able to piece together information or combine it with other information known to the observer in order to construct a more comprehensive picture of state secrets. The theory represents an ultra-precautionary approach to the disclosure of security intelligence. It can be used to support a claim that disclosure of virtually any evidence classified as secret by the executive will harm national security. ... The difficulty then is that the theory's breadth may cause courts to defer to the state's confidentiality claims without engaging in rigorous analysis of whether and how abstract and generalised rationales for confidentiality actually apply to specific pieces of information. ...

A judge is usually in a position to release confidential information only after a time-consuming and often testing interaction with the executive in secret. The process of confidential document review is complex and laborious. Myriad issues will arise in the assessment of the relevance of information to the underlying proceeding, the potential harm arising from disclosure, and the trade-offs between secrecy and disclosure. These issues will be multiplied by the number of distinct pieces of information that are under consideration for disclosure. The relationship between reasons for and against disclosure may be fluid, requiring ongoing review as risks evolve or other information finds its way into the public domain. The process will be cumbersome, all the more so where the executive adopts the strategy of embroiling the judge or special advocate in a contest of attrition. In such circumstances, there is a danger that the judge, facing a long and arduous struggle with the executive, will be discouraged from undertaking the meticulous scrutiny that is required to maximize disclosure. He or she may be induced to opt for secrecy as the most practical way to contend with a seemingly endless stream of objections by the executive. ...

7. The Supreme Court of Canada's decision in *Charkaoui II* was essentially an interim decision in which the court set out the scope of the ministers' disclosure obligations in security certificate proceedings. Accordingly, there was no s. 7 breach and the court was not called on to determine whether a failure to disclose, in breach of s. 7, was justified under s. 1. Each of the next two cases do consider the issue of s. 1 justification.

Gallant v. Canada (Deputy Commissioner, Correctional Service Canada)
(1989), 36 Admin. LR 261 (FCA)

[G. was a prisoner at Kent Institution, a maximum security penitentiary. He was advised that he was suspected of involvement in extortion and drugs and that the warden intended to seek his transfer to the Saskatchewan Penitentiary, a maximum-security facility. The formal notification to the prisoner explained that information had been received indicating that he was involved in the extortion of money and personal property from inmates and from members of the community, threats of violence to other persons, and the importation of drugs. More specific information was not disclosed to the prisoner on the ground that it would "jeopardize the safety of the victims" of his actions. G. applied to the Trial Division for an order quashing the ultimate decision of T., a deputy commissioner, to transfer him. *Certiorari* was granted on the ground that the notice given to the prisoner was insufficient to satisfy the requirements of procedural fairness. T. appealed.]

PRATTE JA: The requirements of procedural fairness, like those of natural justice, vary with the circumstances. Thus, the Director of a penal institution is normally obliged, before imposing administrative segregation on an inmate, to give him a fair opportunity to be heard. However, the Director is relieved of that obligation when the decision to impose administrative segregation must be made quickly in an emergency.

In the present case, notice was given to the respondent, but that notice was drafted in so general terms that it probably did not really enable the respondent, assuming his innocence, to refute the case against him. But the uncontradicted evidence given by the Warden establishes that, in his opinion, he could not give more particulars without, in effect, disclosing the identity of his six informants who would then "be in danger of death or serious bodily injury by other members of the inmate population." I do not see any reason to contest the correctness of that opinion. The question, therefore, is whether these circumstances were sufficient to relieve the appellant from the obligation to give a more detailed notice. In my view, they were. Parliament cannot have intended, when it gave the Commissioner and his delegates the power to transfer inmates from one penetentiary to another, that they should be bound by the rules of procedural fairness even when the application of those rules would endanger the lives of other inmates.

This conclusion does not conflict with the decision rendered by this Court in *Demaria v. Regional Classification Board* [1980] 1 FC 74 (CA) unless it is read as holding that an inmate is always entitled to proper notice whatever be the circumstances, a reading that could not be reconciled with that part of the decision of the Supreme Court in the *Cardinal* case to which I have already referred. In the *Demaria* case, the failure to give proper notice to the inmate was not justified by any valid reason. That is not the situation here.

I am, therefore, of opinion that the appellant's decision to transfer the respondent should not have been quashed on the ground that it had been made in disregard of the requirements of procedural fairness.

This conclusion, however, does not dispose of the case since the respondent argued that the appellant's decision violated not only the rules of procedural fairness but, also, section 7 of the *Canadian Charter of Rights and Freedoms* [being Part I of the *Constitution Act, 1982*, Schedule B, *Canada Act 1982*, 1982, c. 11 (UK)].

Since the judgments of the Supreme Court of Canada in *Martineau v. Matsqui Institution Disciplinary Board* [1980] 1 SCR 602 (Can.); *The Queen v. Miller* [1985] 2 SCR 613 (Ont.); *Cardinal v. Director of Kent Institution* [1985] 2 SCR 643 (BC); and *Morin v. National Special Handling Unit Review Committee* [1985] 2 SCR 662 (Que.), it can no longer be doubted that the decision to transfer an inmate to a penal institution where his freedom will be more severely restricted is, in effect, a committal to a "prison within a prison" which deprives the inmate of his liberty. Such a decision must therefore, according to section 7 of the Charter, be made "in accordance with the principles of fundamental justice."

It is now established that "the principles of fundamental justice are to be found in the basic tenets and principles of our legal system" and that they are not "limited solely to procedural guarantees." Here, the only attack made on the appellant's decision was that it was procedurally bad. But it can be said, without any risk of error, that the basic procedural rules that are part of the principles of fundamental justice do not differ, in substance, from the rules of natural justice and of procedural fairness. The "right to a fair opportunity to be heard" is, therefore, guaranteed by the principles of fundamental justice as well as by the principles of natural justice and procedural fairness. The question in this respect, however, is whether the rules of fundamental justice have the same flexibility as the rules of natural justice and procedural fairness.

Before answering that question, it is necessary to observe that when it is said that the rules of natural justice and of fairness are flexible and vary from case to case, two very different things may be meant. First, that assertion may merely mean that the same general rule will produce different results if it is applied to different factual contexts. In that sense, it can be said that natural justice may or may not, according to the circumstances, require an oral hearing; this is so because, in certain circumstances, it may be impossible for a person to answer adequately the case made against him, unless he is heard orally. The requirement of natural justice always remains the same: that the person concerned be given a fair opportunity to be heard. The consequences of the application of this basic requirement vary, however, with the circumstances.

The rules of natural justice and procedural fairness may also be said to be "flexible" and "variable" in a very different sense which is related to the very nature of those rules. In *Bell Canada v. Communications Workers of Canada* [1976] 1 FC 459 (CA) at 477, Jackett CJ commented as follows on the nature of the rules of natural justice:

> It is not unimportant to keep in mind in a case such as this that the so-called rules of natural justice are a means devised by the courts to interpret and apply statutory law in such a way as to avoid unjust results in particular cases. They are not rigid but flexible. They must be applied according to the exigencies of the particular case and they are not to be used as an instrumentality to defeat the achievement of the objectives of the particular statute.

In *Inuit Tapirisat of Canada v. Léger* [1979] 1 FC 710 (CA) at 717, Le Dain J said more or less the same thing with respect to the rules of procedural fairness:

> Procedural fairness, like natural justice, is a common law requirement that is applied as a matter of statutory interpretation. In the absence of express procedural provisions it must be found to be impliedly required by the statute. It is necessary to consider the legislative context of the power as a whole. What is really in issue is what it is appropriate to require of a particular authority in the way of procedure, given the nature of the authority, the nature of the power exercised by it, and the consequences of the power for the individuals affected. The requirements of fairness must be balanced by the needs of the administrative process in question.

The rules of natural justice and of fairness are common law rules which Parliament has full power to repeal or modify and which, for that reason, cannot be used "to defeat the objectives of a particular statute." They are, therefore, flexible in the sense that in each case they will have to be applied so as not to frustrate the intention of Parliament.

I have no difficulty with the proposition that the procedural rules of fundamental justice have, in the first sense that I have just explained, the same flexibility as the rules of natural justice and fairness. This is why Thurlow CJ could say in *Howard v. Stony Mountain Institution* [1984] 2 FC 642 (CA) that, whether or not the principles of fundamental justice guarantee the right to be represented by counsel depends "on the circumstances of the particular case, its nature, its gravity, its complexity."

On the other hand, it is equally clear, in my view, that the rules of substantial justice which must be applied by virtue of section 7 of the Charter are not "variable or flexible" within the second meaning of those expressions. Indeed, those rules can only be modified by Parliament in accordance with section 1 of the Charter; otherwise, Parliament would have the unfettered power to reduce to nothing the protection afforded by section 7.

The principles of fundamental justice do not have, therefore, the same flexibility as the rules of natural justice and of fairness. For that reason, I cannot escape the conclusion

that, in this case, the decision to transfer the respondent to Saskatchewan Penitentiary
was not made in accordance with the principles of fundamental justice since the respondent was not given a real opportunity to answer the allegation made against him.

There remains to be decided whether that breach of section 7 of the Charter was authorized by a law that met the requirements of section 1. The *Penitentiary Act* [RSC 1970,
c. P-6] gives the Commissioner and his delegates the discretionary power to transfer an
inmate from one institution to another, a discretion that is tempered only by the principles of procedural fairness that apply in so far as circumstances permit. It is pursuant to
that "law" that the decision to transfer the respondent was made and the question is
whether a "law" giving such a wide discretion to the authorities of the Correctional Service meets the requirements of section 1.

We have not had the benefit of any argument or of any evidence on the subject. Counsel for the appellant chose to ignore the respondent's argument based on the Charter.
However, the answer to the question appears to me to be so obvious that I do not need any
evidence or argument to conclude that, in a free and democratic society, it is reasonable,
perhaps even necessary, to confer such a wide discretion on penitentiary authorities.

I would, for these reasons, allow the appeal, set aside the order of the Trial Division
and dismiss the application for *certiorari* made by the respondent, the whole with costs
in this Court as well as in first instance.

MARCEAU JA (concurring in the result): I readily agree with Pratte JA that the judgment
appealed from here cannot be allowed to stand. I must say however, with respect, that I
have some difficulty with the reasons he gives in support of this conclusion, and I wish
to express my personal views in a few brief comments.

1. I did not understand the appellant as having at any time acknowledged that he had
somehow been compelled to breach the duty to act fairly to which he was normally
bound. What the appellant said is simply that, in fulfilling his duty to act fairly, he had
given the respondent all the information he could without, in effect, divulging the identity of his informers. So the question is not, I think, whether the rule of confidentiality
respecting informers can *relieve* a decision-maker from his duty to act fairly, it is rather
whether the rule of confidentiality can *influence*, as much as it did here, the content of
that duty. And the difference, to me, is of the utmost importance, since I have the greatest
difficulty in accepting that the *audi alteram partem* principle, which is what the duty to
act fairly is all about, can ever be completely disregarded otherwise than in a case of an
exceptional emergency and for quite a short period of time. (See: *Cardinal v. Director of
Kent Institution* [1985] 2 SCR 643 (BC).)

The rationale behind the *audi alteram partem* principle, which simply requires the
participation, in the making of a decision, of the individual whose rights or interests may
be affected, is, of course, that the individual may always be in a position to bring forth
information, in the form of facts or arguments, that could help the decision-maker reach
a fair and prudent conclusion. It has long been recognized to be only rational as well as
practical that the extent and character of such a participation should depend on the circumstances of the case and the nature of the decision to be made. This view of the manner in which the principle must be given effect in practice ought to be the same whether
it comes into play through the jurisprudential duty to act fairly, or the common law re-

quirements of natural justice, or as one of the prime constituents of the concept of fundamental justice referred to in section 7 of the Charter. The principle is obviously the same everywhere it applies.

As I see it, the problem here is whether the *audi alteram partem* principle, in the circumstances that prevailed, required that more information be given to the inmate before asking for his representations. In my judgment, having regard to the nature of the problem the appellant was facing and his responsibility toward those entrusted to his care, it did not.

2. It seems to me that, to appreciate the practical requirements of the *audi alteram partem* principle, it is wrong to put on the same level all administrative decisions involving inmates in penitentiaries, be they decisions of the National Parole Board respecting the revocation of parole, or decisions of disciplinary boards dealing with disciplinary offences for which various types of punishments, up to administrative segregation, can be imposed, or decisions, such as the one here involved, of prison authorities approving the transfer of inmates from one institution to another for administrative and good order reasons. Not only do these various decisions differ as to the individual's rights, privileges or interests they may affect, which may lead to different standards of procedural safeguards; they also differ, and even more significantly, as to their purposes and justifications, something which cannot but influence the content of the information that the individual needs to be provided with, in order to render his participation, in the making of the decision, wholly meaningful. In the case of a decision aimed at imposing a sanction or a punishment for the commission of an offence, fairness dictates that the person charged be given all available particulars of the offence. Not so in the case of a decision to transfer made for the sake of the orderly and *proper* administration of the institution and based on a belief that the inmate should, because of concerns raised as to his behaviour, not remain where he is. In such a case, there would be no basis for requiring that the inmate be given as many particulars of all the wrong doings of which he may be suspected. Indeed, in the former case, what has to be verified is the very commission of the offence and the person involved should be given the fullest opportunity to convince of his innocence; in the latter case, it is merely the reasonableness and the seriousness of the belief on which the decision would be based and the participation of the person involved has to be rendered meaningful for that but nothing more. In the situation we are dealing with here, guilt was not what had to be confirmed, it was whether the information received from six different sources was sufficient to raise a valid concern and warrant the transfer.

3. There are obvious essential differences between the situation considered by the Court in *Demaria*, on which the Trial Judge relied exclusively, and the one which is before us today:

a) In *Demaria*, the ground for transfer was the belief that the inmate had brought cyanide into the prison; it was then an act, an operation which had taken place and was not likely to be repeated. In our case, the ground is the belief that the inmate was involved in a system of extortion, which could very well be still going on or reactivated.

b) In *Demaria*, there was no direct reason to believe that the safety of fellow prisoners was involved; there were no obvious victims of the alleged misconduct. Here, on the contrary, extortion through threat of violence, by its very nature, implicates victims and spells danger for the safety of others.

c) In *Demaria*, there was independent evidence obtained by the police. Here, the entire body of evidence was obtained from informants who had obvious objective and realistic fears of reprisals at the hands of the alleged extortionists.

d) In *Demaria*, the withholding of information was almost complete and merely justified by a blanket claim, as characterized by Hugessen JA [at 78], that " 'all preventive security information' is confidential and (cannot) be released." Here, on the one hand, the information given is definitely more substantial—including the inmate's Progress Summary Report in its entirety, the extent of the concern of the Warden, and cogent reasons for non-disclosure of further particulars. On the other hand, we have the unequivocal sworn statement of the prison authorities that no further information could be safely released, notably the statement of the Warden who, as the Trial Judge so rightly proclaims, "is more familiar with prison conditions than the court and is in a position to give a more realistic appraisal of what the inmate population is able to deduce from any given information."

I would dispose of the appeal as suggested by Pratte JA.

. . .

DESJARDINS JA (dissenting): … In the case at bar, the prison authorities are claiming, through their affidavits, much more than the simple confidentiality of the identity of their informers under the rule of *Bisaillon v. Keable* [[1979] 1 SCR 218 (Que.)]. They are claiming that they cannot give more details to the respondent than those given to him because to do so would, in all likelihood, endanger the lives or safety of the informers. Although not in those words, they are in fact claiming the right of other inmates and of a member of the community to the security of the person, a right also entrusted in section 7 of the *Canadian Charter of Rights and Freedoms*.

The transfer of a prisoner from one institution to another is a disciplinary measure. The test to be applied is one of administrative law, not criminal law. At this stage, the prisoner is not deprived of the absolute liberty to which every citizen is entitled. He has already lost it by virtue of a lawful incarceration. The full panoply of rights due an accused in a criminal proceeding does not apply to him. A transfer involves changes in the conditions of his detention. This type of loss of liberty is of consequence and attracts the protection of procedural fairness both at common law and under section 7 of the Charter.

Procedural fairness varies according to the circumstances. The American courts have been careful while elaborating the standards of due process to examine the nature of the Government decision involved and the degree of the loss to the prisoner. I would think our law on this matter would be no different from what was said in *Wolff v. McDonnell*, 418 US 539 (1974) at 560 by the United States Supreme Court:

… "The very nature of due process *negates any concept of inflexible procedures universally applicable to every imaginable situation.*" *Cafeteria Workers v. McElroy*, 367 US, at 895. "[C]onsideration of what procedures due process may require under any given set of circumstances must begin with a determination of the precise nature of the government function involved as well as of the private interest that has been affected by government action." *Ibid.: Morrissey*, 408 US, at 481. Viewed in this light it is immediately apparent that *one cannot automatically apply procedural rules designed for free citizens in an open society, or for parolees or probationers under only limited restraints, to the very different situation presented by a disciplinary proceeding in a state prison.* [Emphasis added.]

That same Court in *Bell v. Wolfish*, 441 US 520 at 547 said:

> Prison administrators ... should be accorded wide-ranging deference in the adoption and executions of policies and practices that in their judgment are needed to preserve internal order and discipline and to maintain institutional security.

I am reminded that in *Solosky v. The Queen* [1980] 1 SCR 821 (Can.) at 839-840, Dickson J [as he then was] said for the Court:

> As a general rule, I do not think it is open to the courts to question the judgment of the institutional head as to what may, or may not, be necessary in order to maintain security within a penitentiary.

Indeed, in *Wolff v. McDonnell, supra*, at 566, the United States Supreme Court recognized that "[t]he operation of a correctional institution is at best an extraordinarily difficult undertaking." The substantial risks that informers in prisons run when they cooperate with prison officials should not be underestimated and it is possible that in such situation, prison authorities might lean on the prudent side rather than the risky side. But at the same time, the burden is on these authorities, when a disciplinary measure is taken, to demonstrate that the circumstances are such that they cannot inform the respondent of the facts on which the charge is based. This burden is not a light one since the protection of the law and of the Constitution does not stop at the prison gate.

The respondent probably did not have enough information to adequately defend himself. He claims that while the notice given to him was undeniably more voluminous than the one given in the case of *Demaria*, it provided no greater detail of the allegations than the notice that was found wanting in *Demaria*. For instance, he says the notice in the case at bar fails to state what types of drugs were allegedly involved and in what quantity, with what frequency they were brought into the institution over the year period in which it is alleged that they were brought into the institution, how much money and what kind of property was extorted and which community outside the prison was targeted by this scheme. In addition, no information is given as to whether the police have conducted an investigation and if so, what are the results of their enquiries.

Before a claim, such as the one made here by the prison authorities, can succeed, measures ought to be taken so as to minimize errors. And I am not satisfied that they have all been taken in the present case.

I have noted that in the case of *Cadieux v. Director of Mountain Institution* [1985] 1 FC 378 (TD) at 402, Reed J, who was dealing with an application for a writ of *certiorari* to quash a decision of the National Parole Board which had cancelled the applicant's unescorted temporary absence programme, considered (at 402) the possibility that courts of law might require in certain circumstances the production of affidavits in a sealed envelope together with a specific explanation as to why non-disclosure would be justified, a procedure she noted is similar to that developed at common law in privilege cases and to that existing under section 36.1 [as enacted by SC 1980-81-82-83, c. 111, s. 4, Sched. III] of the *Canada Evidence Act*, RSC 1970, c. E-10. Measures of such a nature might however not be practical with regards to prison authorities and I agree with Marceau JA (at 342 paragraph 2 of his reasons for judgment) that "it is wrong to put on the same level all administrative decisions involving inmates in penitentiaries, be they decisions of the National Parole Board … or decisions of disciplinary boards … or decisions, … of prison authorities." This point was also made in *Wolff v. McDonnell*.

I do not understand this case as being one where emergency was claimed by the prison authorities to justify the transfer of the respondent, although there might have been one when the respondent was segregated pending the outcome of the investigation. No complaint was however made by him about the first phase of the disciplinary measure.

Confidential information was used and the notification given to the respondent claims that "Information has been received that *reliably* indicates" (emphasis added). The affidavits however do not explain why the prison authorities thought the information obtained was reliable.

I retain from the American decisions [a list follows], which all have some similarities with the present case, that when confidential information is relied on by prison authorities so as to justify a disciplinary measure, the record must contain some underlying factual information from which the authorities can reasonably conclude that the informer was credible or the information reliable. Where cross-examination, confrontation or adequate information are not available to sift out the truth, some measures must exist so as to ensure that the investigation is a genuine fact-finding procedure verifying the truth of wrongdoing and that the informers are not engaged in a private vendetta. None of the courts in the cases cited have examined *in camera* the confidential information except [in one case] where it was done pursuant to an agreement by the parties and not *proprio motu* by the Court. In many of these cases, there are indications that administrative rules had been designed to assist and guide prison authorities in accommodating the need for fairness in disciplinary proceedings with prison security. None are present in this case.

Reliability may be demonstrated in a number of ways, as for instance, by an independent investigation or by corroborating information from independent sources. The affidavits produced by the appellant indicate that no independent investigation was carried on. Why then did the prison authorities feel they had the assurance of the reliability of the information received? Were the statements made under oath? Were there elements in the information gathered from the six informers that corroborated essential facts? Why was the respondent not put under a tight surveillance so as to allow the possible gathering of evidence against him? Was there anything that prevented the taking of this measure? Were the police informed particularly with regard to the activity outside the prison?

I would have dismissed the appeal for lack of satisfying affidavits.

Appeal allowed.

NOTES

1. The judgment of Pratte JA in this case raises important questions as to the timing in s. 7 cases of any consideration of administrative imperatives. Is it part of any delineation of the content of the "principles of fundamental justice" in particular cases or should any assessment of these asserted justifications be performed in the context of s. 1 or do these arguments have relevance in both contexts? If the latter, how precisely should this occur? (For some discussion of this issue, see Evans, "The Principles of Fundamental Justice: The Constitution and the Common Law" (1991), 29 *Osgoode Hall LJ* 51).

2. The dissenting judgment of Desjardins JA raises somewhat different issues and possibilities that have relevance to the determination of confidentiality arguments against disclosure in both Charter and common law procedural fairness cases: the development of surrogate checks on the reliability of information that, it is argued, cannot be revealed to the affected person. Is the regime that she suggests impractical? Aside from that question, does it involve the court inappropriately in the design of institutional procedures? This issue surfaces again in the next case, also drawn from the correctional law arena.

Gough v. Canada (National Parole Board)
(1990), 45 Admin. LR 304 (FCTD)

[G. had been on parole for five-and-a-half years and was subject to the least restrictive form of parole. As a result of complaints made to the Correctional Service Office involving allegations of sexual assault and other forms of coercion as well as drug use, his parole was suspended and ultimately revoked. The National Parole Board ("the board"), relying on s. 17(5) of the *Parole Regulations* and the authority it created to refuse disclosure of information, never revealed at G.'s post-suspension hearing or at any other time the details of the dates and places of the alleged incidents or the names of the victims.

G. applied to have the revocation quashed on the basis that it violated his rights under s. 7 of the *Canadian Charter of Rights and Freedoms*. The application was allowed to the extent that the board was given the option of an order either quashing the decision or requiring the submission of the relevant information to the court for an *in camera* hearing at which counsel for G. would be given the opportunity of arguing that the non-disclosure was not justified. The board chose the latter option and appealed the order to the Federal Court of Appeal. The Court of Appeal allowed the appeal on the basis that s. 24(1) of the Charter did not extend to authorizing the court to compel the production of information for the purposes of such an *in camera* hearing. The matter was referred back to Reed J for a resumption of the hearing.]

REED J:

. . .

He Already Knows?

The Board's first argument is that the applicant has been given enough information to enable him to answer the allegations against him because he knows of the incidents in question. This first contention can be easily answered. If the applicant has knowledge of the alleged incidents which underlie his parole suspension, then, there can be no reason not to disclose to him the Board's information concerning those incidents. If he knows about the incidents he will know the alleged victims. He may not know the informants but this is not, in any event, a relevant fact. To repeat, it is no answer to say that the applicant need not be given the information because he already knows it.

Compliance with Regulation 17(5)

Even if the applicant does not know exactly which precise incidents were referred to in the information upon which the Board relied, it is argued that the non-disclosure is justified by virtue of subs. 17(5) of the *Parole Regulations*. Subsection 17(5) authorizes the Parole Board not to disclose (to an inmate or paroled inmate) information on which it is basing its decision when, in the Board's opinion, disclosure of the information:

> (a) could reasonably be expected to threaten the safety of individuals;
>
>   . . .
>
> (e) could reasonably be expected to be injurious to the conduct of lawful investigations or the conduct of reviews pursuant to the Act or these Regulations, including any such information that would reveal the source of information obtained in confidence.

[Justice Reed noted that whether or not the board had complied with regulation 17(5) in refusing did not matter. The relevant question was whether and in what circumstances the board could revoke the parole of a person in the applicant's position without giving him enough information to answer the case against him, and in so doing not offend s. 7 of the Charter.]

Section 7 of the Charter

Section 7 of the *Canadian Charter of Rights and Freedoms* provides:

> Everyone has the right to life, liberty and security of the person and the right not to be deprived thereof except in accordance with the principles of fundamental justice.

It is trite law that both at common law and under s. 7 of the Charter the rules of fundamental justice require that an individual is entitled to know the case against him in a decision-making process which leads to a diminution of his liberty. The Board concedes that if the applicant were not a paroled inmate it would be a flagrant breach of his Charter rights for him to be deprived of his liberty without being given details of the allegations which underlie that deprivation. Concomitantly, counsel for the applicant points out that his client would be much better off if he had been charged with criminal offences in relation to the incidents which are alleged. If charges had been laid, there would be an obligation to reveal the names of the victims and to disclose some degree of specificity regarding dates, times and places of the events.

The requirement that an individual is entitled to know and be given an opportunity to respond to the case against him is essential not only to prevent abuses by people making false accusations but also to give the person who has been accused the assurance that he or she is not being dealt with arbitrarily or capriciously. ...

Guarantees Provided by Section 7 Will Vary with the Circumstances

It is clear that the requirements of fundamental justice operate on a spectrum. The content of such requirements vary with the circumstances of the case.

. . .

Paroled Inmate—Conditional Liberty Only

The respondent argues that the applicant, as a paroled inmate, enjoys only a conditional liberty and that this reduced right to liberty justifies the refusal by the Board to make the information in question available. It is argued that the public interest in non-disclosure (as expressed in regulation 17(5)) must be weighed against the individual's interest in having sufficient information to answer the case against him. It is argued that the parole system will break down and become unworkable if individuals are not able to supply information to Correctional Service officers without fear of reprisal. It is argued that people must be able to supply information concerning the activities of paroled inmates on the understanding that that information will be kept confidential and that the Parole Board must be allowed to rely on this information in making decisions respecting the continuation of an inmate's parole.

There is no doubt that the applicant's liberty is conditional. It can be revoked without the requirement to prove criminal offences beyond a reasonable doubt and without all the procedural guarantees which pertain in a court of law. At the same time, there can be little doubt that the applicant's conditional liberty interest, in this case, is at the high end of the spectrum. The applicant's position is close to that of an individual who has unconditional liberty. It is as close to that position as it can be within the correctional system. The applicant is on full parole and has been for many years. He has a "parole reduced" status. The incidents which allegedly took place, took place outside the prison situation. Institutional considerations with respect to the identification of informants within the prison walls do not exist. An individual's liberty (even the conditional liberty which a parolee enjoys) weighs very heavily in the scales when compared to competing interests.

I would note in passing that while it is usual to characterize the applicant's rights as "individual" rights, which are counterpoised to the public interest (in ensuring that paroled inmates do not commit acts harmful to members of the public) there is also a public interest in employing procedures which are fair, for dealing with all members of society including paroled inmates. Procedures which have the appearance of being arbitrary and capricious are by their very nature not in the public interest.

Section 7 Requirements in the Parole/Penitentiary Context

[After reviewing several cases involving disclosure in the parole revocation context, including *Cadieux v. Director of Mountain Institution*, [1985] 1 FC 378 (TD), *Latham v. Solicitor General (Canada)*, [1984] 2 FC 734 (TD), and *Demaria v. Regional Classification Board (Canada)*, [1980] 1 FC 74 (CA), which held that s. 7 entitled inmates to "the gist" or "an outline" of the allegations against them, Reed J continued.]

The *Latham*, *Cadieux* and *Demaria* cases all dealt with situations in which the inmate had a much more limited liberty interest than does the applicant in the present case.

Those cases dealt with day parole, the unescorted temporary absence program and a transfer between penitentiaries. There is no doubt that the applicant, in the present case, is entitled to sufficient detail respecting the allegations being made against him to enable him to respond intelligently thereto unless the respondent can demonstrate otherwise.

Limitation "Prescribed by Law"—Section 1

. . .

In the case of s. 7, since the rights guaranteed thereunder constitute a spectrum of guarantees, [s. 1 justification] involves first determining the content of the principles of fundamental justice flowing from s. 7 applicable to the particular decision-making process being challenged (by reference to the particular circumstances of the case, the nature of the interests involved, and the reasons and evidence which have been put forward to justify the limitations which have been placed in what are claimed as s. 7 guarantees). When the limitations are not "prescribed by law" the enquiry stops at that stage. When the limitations are prescribed by law, however, the enquiry moves on to consider whether a s. 1 justification might exist.

Regulation 17(5) is a limitation prescribed by law. The burden, then, is on the respondent to demonstrate that it is a "reasonable limit … demonstrably justified in a free and democratic society."

National Parole Board's Justification

Three affidavits were filed, two by a Mr. Stienburg and one by a Mr. Harvey. The justifications set out therein can, in a general sense, be characterized as asserting that non-disclosure is necessary for the operation and effective working of the parole system. Indeed, counsel for the respondent went so far as to assert that an order which did not protect the type of confidential information which is in question in this case would undermine the whole parole system and the Board would simply have to cease granting paroles. (This was counsel's argument, it is not a consequence asserted in the affidavits filed.) Another ground upon which non-disclosure of the information is claimed to be justified is that the accuracy of that information is carefully checked before it is relied upon by the Board. I will quote from the affidavits.

[Reed J here quoted at length from the affidavits.]

Assessment of the Affidavits

In assessing the affidavits filed on behalf of the National Parole Board, it is important, first, to keep clearly in mind that the issue in this case does not challenge the right of Correctional Service officers to receive information in confidence and keep it confidential. The issue in this case does not affect the process of information gathering by the Correctional Service of Canada (para. 16 of Mr. Stienburg's affidavit of November 20, 1990). The issue is not whether the Parole Board should be required to disclose the *complete* Correctional Services' file to the paroled inmate (para. 16 of Mr. Stienburg's affidavit of November 20, 1990). The issue is not whether the Board has to disclose the identity of informants. It clearly does not. There is never a requirement to disclose the names of informants since that fact is never relevant to the decision which must be made. An issue only arises when the disclosure of information will necessarily disclose the identity of the informant. The issue is whether the National Parole Board is required to either release information to the applicant (when disclosure will necessarily reveal the source of that information) or forego reliance on that information in making a decision on the applicant's parole.

With respect to the particular points made in the affidavits, there is no evidence that there is an on-going police investigation, in this case, which investigation would be prejudiced by the disclosure of the information in question (para. 12 of Mr. Harvey's affidavit). The only investigation about which there is any evidence is the one pursuant to the *Parole Act* and *Regulations* which led to the revocation of the applicant's parole (paras. 14 and 17 of the Stienburg affidavit of November 20, 1990). It was established in *Singh v. Minister of Employment & Immigration* [1985] 1 SCR 177 (Can.) that administrative convenience does not justify a denial of fundamental justice. As I understand the respondent's argument, in this case, it is more than just administrative convenience which is alleged to require the limitations which have been imposed. Nevertheless, to the extent that any part of the respondent's argument might be based on administrative convenience, that argument has been answered by the decision in the *Singh* case.

The reliance on provisions of the *Access to Information Act*, RSC 1985, c. A-1 and the *Privacy Act*, RSC 1985, c. P-21, is misplaced. As has been said before those legislative provisions prescribe circumstances under which individuals will not be given certain information which they seek from the government. Those exemptions, however, are not designed to operate in the context of a situation where the individual seeking the information is faced with serious consequences respecting his liberty as a result of decisions being made on the basis of that information. Those statutes prescribe limits to an individual's access to information when the information being sought may be required for no more serious reason than idle curiosity. Also, in that context, this Court has a reviewing function which ensures that the exemptions claimed are properly so claimed—a role which the respondent categorically denies is appropriate in the more serious circumstances in which the applicant finds himself.

The respondent claims that the accuracy of the information in question has been carefully vetted. That may be true but I do not think it justifies refusing to provide the applicant with the information he seeks. The assertion, that the information is accurate, is self-serving and it is no answer to the applicant's perception that he is being dealt with arbitrarily and capriciously. The process of restricting an individual's liberty without being required to give details of the accusations against him is not rescued from invalidity by the decision-maker's assertion that the information is true.

This leaves for consideration the main focus of the respondent's argument: the information was provided in confidence; the individuals who provided the information expressed concern that if their identities were known they would suffer reprisals at the hands of the applicant; the information cannot be disclosed without disclosing, at the same time, the identity of the informers. And, if the Parole Board cannot rely on such information, the ability of the Board to assess risk is seriously impaired and the functioning of the parole system undermined.

The affidavits address two questions: the particular facts of the applicant's case, and the rationale for the procedure established by, and content of Reg. 17(5). Evidence with respect to the particular circumstances of the applicant's case might more properly be seen as relevant in determining whether or not a breach of fundamental justice has occurred than to determining whether a s. 1 justification exists. In any event, insofar as the particular circumstances of the applicant's case is concerned, Mr. Stienburg's assertion that on the basis of statements set out in the various confidential reports, the Parole Board panel is persuaded that disclosure of additional information to the applicant would disclose the identity of the source, is not compelling evidence as to whether disclosure would in fact have that consequence. Similarly, Mr. Stienburg's assertion that, on the basis of the descriptions contained in the confidential reports (of the alleged assaults and the expressions of fear by the informants) the panel concluded that a threat to the safety of the informants would exist if disclosure took place, is not convincing evidence that in fact disclosure would have that result.

One wonders, for example, why the difficulties of protecting the informants in the present circumstances is any more severe than is the case with many situations of domestic violence. One wonders why the difficulty is any greater than that of protecting many witnesses who testify at criminal trials. These types of problems are not unique to the situation of a paroled inmate.

Insofar as the evidence concerning the procedure of refusing disclosure, in accordance with Reg. 17(5), is concerned, again there is a lack of persuasive evidence. The assertion that the operation of the parole system will be undermined if information of the kind in question is disclosed to the applicant (and by analogy to other applicants in similar situations) is an expression of opinion unsupported by any factual underpinnings. In addition, I note that there is a complete lack of evidence of the usual comparative nature, which is often adduced in these kinds of cases, to demonstrate that other democratic jurisdictions have found it necessary to establish procedures of a similar kind.

The respondent was given the opportunity to bring specific evidence forward to demonstrate that either the particular circumstances of the claimant's case justified the limitation which had been imposed, or that the operation of a parole system which authorizes the Parole Board to refuse disclosure of information in accordance with the terms of Reg. 17(5) is justifiable pursuant to s. 1 of the Charter. The Board did not adduce any such specific evidence.

Review by the Courts

The respondent was offered an *in camera* hearing for the purpose of establishing a factual basis for its assertions, accompanied by an undertaking from counsel for the applicant that any confidential information to which he became privy would not be disclosed to his client, nor indeed to any other person. The respondent alleges that even this would have a serious and adverse effect on the working of the parole system (para. 16 of Mr. Stienburg's affidavit). This is simply not credible.

This Court deals with many situations in which confidential information is brought before it and used or not used in litigation, as the case may be. Often restrictions are imposed with respect to the use of that information in order to protect its confidentiality. Under some procedures, only the court and the party tendering the information has access to it. Under other procedures, while counsel and the court have access to the information, the relevant opposing party does not. (In this case, the respondent had no objection to applicant's counsel seeing the information; what was objected to was the setting of a precedent.)

As has already been noted, this Court performs a reviewing function under the *Access to Information Act*. This Court has jurisdiction under the *Canada Evidence Act*, RSC 1985, c. C-5, to decide issues such as whether national defence or security might be injuriously affected by the public disclosure of certain information in a court. It may also be asked to decide whether international relations might be injuriously affected by the disclosure of information. Under s. 37 of the *Canada Evidence Act*, the Court is authorized to determine whether information which a Minister considers should not be disclosed "in the public interest" is rightly so characterized. It is hard to conclude that a disclosure to this Court of specific information regarding the applicant's particular situation or to support a justification for a non-disclosure rule as set out in Reg. 17(5) would have the adverse consequences which are alleged.

The respondent asserts that it is not within this Court's jurisdiction to compel production of the confidential information reports concerning the applicant or other types of information relevant to the present case. Whether or not the information respecting the applicant is part of the record and could be compelled to be brought before the Court, on that basis, is an argument which has been eclipsed by the arguments respecting the applicant's Charter rights. An argument that such could be compelled, as part of the record, was initially asserted, but it has not been pursued as a vigorous argument in the more recent phase of these proceedings. Regardless of whether or not the Court has any compulsory authority, in this regard, the consequence of not adducing further evidence is that the respondent, in this case, has not established an evidentiary base to support the arguments it seeks to make.

Limitation by Regulation 17(5)

I turn to the text of Reg. 17(5) itself. The policy considerations underlying that regulation and the particular facts relating to the applicant's case, as attested to in the affidavits of Mr. Stienburg and Mr. Harvey, have been considered. But what of the provisions of the regulation itself?

I note, first of all, that Reg. 17(5) is very broadly framed. No distinction is made between the non-disclosure of information essential to allow an individual to know the case against him or her and the non-disclosure of information which is more peripheral in nature. In addition, para. 17(5)(e) is so broad that it seems to authorize non-disclosure merely because the information was received in confidence. This can never be a justification for limiting the guarantees of fundamental justice as was clearly set out in the *Demaria* case, at 78. What is more, para. 17(5)(a) seems to require only the possibility of a threat and not a probability that harm would likely occur to an individual. These are disturbingly broad provisions. While I do not find it necessary to decide whether Reg. 17(5) is *ultra vires* (perhaps it can operate in certain circumstances), it suffices to say that when that regulation is used to deny a paroled inmate the kind of information which was denied in this case, it is inapplicable for that purpose.

In addition, I am not convinced that a system which puts in the hands of the same body both the decision on the merits (the applicant's parole revocation) and the decision as to how much of the information which is before it will be disclosed to the applicant, is one which can meet the requirements of s. 1 of the Charter. I certainly doubt that such a procedure can be justified when dealing with a person in the applicant's position. (A person who has been paroled for many years and whose record is exemplary.) A parallel can be drawn to the decision in *Hunter v. Southam Inc.* [1984] 2 SCR 145 (Alta.) where it was held that a search warrant was invalid if not issued by a judicial body independent of the investigating agency.

Conclusion

In conclusion, the applicant's s. 7 Charter rights have been infringed by the refusal to provide him with the confidential information upon which the Board is relying. The respondent has not established an evidentiary basis justifying non-disclosure neither with respect to the specific circumstances of this applicant's case nor by justifying Reg. 17(5) as establishing a reasonable limitation on the applicant's rights pursuant to s. 1 of the Charter. Accordingly, an order will issue quashing the Board's decision and an order of mandamus will issue requiring a new hearing by a differently constituted panel of the National Parole Board.

Application allowed.

[An appeal to the Federal Court of Appeal was dismissed (1991), 47 Admin. LR 226 (FCA).]

NOTE

Consider the following dilemma. Mary is a sexual harassment officer at a university. Over the years, she has on five occasions had female students complain informally to her about serious sexually harassing conduct by a senior male faculty member. In each instance, however, the students have been unwilling to make a formal complaint. On all these occasions, Mary has made a private note of the nature and the details of the complaint. She is now about to retire from her position and seeks advice from you about what, if anything, she should do about this information. Should she pass it on to her successor? Should she be able to create an official university file in which this and similar information may be placed? In that event, should the faculty member be informed about it? Are there ways in which the official collection of such information could be sanctioned without having to provide the named faculty member with knowledge of what is going on and an opportunity to object? If such information can be retained either formally or informally, to what uses may it be put if there is another complaint against the same professor?

Commercially Sensitive Information

The third situation presents the possibility of disclosure of information about a business that may generally be regarded as confidential and that may give competitors an advantage because, for example, it may reveal its pricing practices or contract terms it has been willing to accept.

The *Anti-Dumping Act*, RSC 1970, c. A-15 established arrangements for determining whether dumping of goods into Canada caused "material injury to the production in Canada of like goods." One of the stages was an inquiry under s. 16 by the Anti-Dumping Tribunal (now replaced by the Canadian International Trade Tribunal). Section 29 provided:

> 3) Where evidence or information that is in its nature confidential, relating to the business or affairs of any person, firm or corporation, is given or elicited in the course of any inquiry under section 16, the evidence or information shall not be made public in such a manner as to be available for the use of any business competitor or rival of the person, firm or corporation.

In *Magnasonic Canada v. Anti-Dumping Tribunal*, [1972] FC 1239 (CA), Jackett CJ said:

> We do not think that s. 29(3) requires a departure from the pattern of hearings dictated by the other provisions of the statute. What it does require, on that view as to its meaning, is that, when information of a confidential character is tendered at a hearing, a decision must be made as to what steps are required to comply with s. 29(3). The obvious first step in the ordinary case would seem to be that the evidence be taken *in camera*. What further steps require to be taken would depend on the circumstances. The most extreme step that might be required would be, we should have thought, to exclude all competitors or rivals while the evidence is being taken and to provide such parties afterwards with the sort of report of the evidence taken in their absence that is contemplated for the parties with reference to confidential evidence taken under s. 28.

Slayton, *The Anti-Dumping Tribunal*
A Study Prepared for the Law Reform Commission of Canada (1979), at 47

Another nettle grasped by the Tribunal hearings is the problem of confidentiality. Business adversaries face each other across the floor. To support their positions, these combatants must describe themselves and their business in great detail. Such intelligence is of commercial value, and must be kept out of the hands of competitors. Procedures to do so must be in place, all the while ensuring adherence to the strictures of *Magnasonic*. Confidential briefs, documents and exhibits are made available by the Tribunal only to counsel who are appearing for parties represented at the hearings, and those counsel are required to give an undertaking not to reveal confidential information to their clients. Confidential material made available must be returned by counsel at the conclusion of the hearings. Expert advisers to counsel—accountants, for example—may be given access to confidential information at the Tribunal's discretion and with the consent of other parties. In-house counsel and those on the boards of directors of their clients are not given access to such material. When confidential information will be given in evidence, the Tribunal goes behind closed doors, excluding everyone except the various counsel (and any expert advisers who have given the undertaking and are permitted to remain).

NOTES

1. The *Canadian International Trade Tribunal Act*, RSC 1985, c. 47 (4th Supp.) now contains a much more detailed provision on disclosure reflecting in part the practice described by Slayton:

45(1) Where a person designates information as confidential pursuant to paragraph 46(1)(a) and that designation is not withdrawn by that person, no member and no person employed in the federal public administration who comes into possession of that information while holding that office or being so employed shall, either before or after ceasing to hold that office or being so employed, knowingly disclose that information, or knowingly allow it to be disclosed, to any other person in any manner that is calculated or likely to make it available for the use of any business competitor or rival of any person to whose business or affairs the information relates.

Disclosure of summary or statement

(2) Subsection (1) does not apply in respect of any non-confidential edited version or non-confidential summary of information or statement referred to in paragraph 46(1)(b).

Disclosure to counsel and experts

(3) Notwithstanding subsection (1), information to which that subsection applies that has been provided to the Tribunal in any proceedings before the Tribunal may be disclosed by the Tribunal to counsel for any party to those proceedings or to other proceedings arising out of those proceedings or to an expert, acting under the control or direction of that counsel, for use, notwithstanding any other Act or law, by that counsel or expert only in those proceedings, subject to any conditions that the Tribunal considers reasonably necessary or desirable to ensure that the information will not, without the written consent of the person who provided the information to the Tribunal, be disclosed by counsel or the expert to any person in any manner that is calculated or likely to make it available to

(a) any party to the proceedings or other proceedings, including a party who is represented by that counsel or on whose behalf the expert is acting; or

(b) any business competitor or rival of any person to whose business or affairs the information relates.

Disclosure to Tribunal's experts

(3.1) Notwithstanding subsection (1), the Tribunal may disclose information to which that subsection applies to an expert retained by the Tribunal for use, notwithstanding any other Act or law, by the expert only in proceedings before the Tribunal under the *Special Import Measures Act* or this Act, subject to any conditions that the Tribunal considers reasonably necessary or desirable to ensure that the information will not, without the written consent of the person who provided the information to the Tribunal, be disclosed by the expert to any person in any manner that is calculated or likely to make it available to

(a) any party to the proceedings; or

(b) any business competitor or rival of any person to whose business or affairs the information relates.

Disclosure to persons described in subsection (5)

(3.2) For greater certainty, disclosure of information under subsection (3) or (3.1) to a person described in subsection (5) who is an employee of an institution of the Government of Canada that is a party to the proceedings or, in the case of subsection (3), other proceedings is not disclosure to a party to those proceedings for the purposes of subsection (3) or (3.1).

Definition of "counsel"

(4) In subsection (3), "counsel," in relation to a party to proceedings, includes any person, other than a director, servant or employee of the party, who acts in the proceedings on behalf of the party.

Persons who may be recognized as experts

(5) In subsections (3) and (3.1), "expert" includes any of the following persons whom the Tribunal recognizes as an expert:

> (a) persons whose duties involve the carrying out of the *Competition Act* and who are referred to in section 25 of that Act, other than persons authorized by the Governor in Council to exercise the powers and perform the duties of the Director of Investigation and Research;

> (b) in respect of the determination of damages and costs in procurement review proceedings, persons employed in the government institution involved in the procurement under review; and

> (c) any prescribed person.

[Provisions on sanctions follow.]

2. Another example of agency rules about disclosure is regulations made by the CRTC (SOR/79-554) for practice in its telecommunications proceedings. Any document submitted to the commission is public, unless a claim for confidentiality is made and the commission rules that disclosure be restricted or denied. The claim for confidentiality must describe "specific direct harm" that would be caused by disclosure, and if claim is made, any party (or the commission itself) may request disclosure. The commission may decide on the basis of the written submission, or it may order a conference, disposition, or an oral hearing. It must consider the "public interest" in disclosure and the "specific direct harm" that would be caused, and it may order: (1) disclosure, (2) non-disclosure, (3) disclosure at an *in camera* hearing, or (4) disclosure "of an abridged version of the document."

Staff Studies

The fourth group is composed of claims to disclosure of materials created by an agency itself—for example, reports prepared by its staff, or guidelines and statements of policy—an issue that we encountered earlier in the discovery case of *CIBA-Geigy Ltd. v. Canada (Patented Medicine Prices Review Board)*, above.

> **Franson, *Access to Information: Independent Administrative Agencies***
> A Study Prepared for the Law Reform Commission of Canada (1979), at 28-34

> Unlike the courts, administrative agencies usually have large staffs assigned to them. The staff of an agency is intended to conduct investigations and studies necessary to assure that the agency has all the information it needs to make fully informed decisions. The reports prepared by the staff are, or should be, a valuable source of information about subjects within the agency's jurisdiction. Because of this, members of the public and participants in the administrative process often request disclosure of staff reports.

Reports prepared by an agency's staff can cover a wide variety of subjects. Some reports deal with inspection of firms that are subject to regulatory control. These might cover such subjects of public interest as safety, pricing, and profitability. Other reports might describe general studies of particular industries, perhaps seeking to identify important trends and problems that might emerge in the future. Some reports will simply summarize the evidence and submissions made at public hearings for the convenience of the members of the agency. The CRTC, for example, follows the practice of having its staff submit a report following each hearing summarizing the material put forward at the hearing. In other cases, the staff may actually prepare a draft decision following a hearing, which the agency may ultimately accept as its own.

Such information may clearly be of great interest to both participants in administrative matters and to the general public. For example, a firm that is subject to disciplinary action is very likely to want to see any inspection reports that may have been filed about its operations. Similarly, the consuming public, and particularly consumer interest organizations, will be very anxious to see any inspection reports relating to the safety or quality of products or services they buy.

Participants in the administrative process argue that they should be entitled to see any staff documents bearing on the matter under consideration. Their arguments are well taken for two reasons. First, information that might assist them in preparing their submissions may be effectively denied if they do not have access to staff reports. The result is to diminish the value of their participation and, therefore, to diminish the usefulness of the hearing to the agency itself. Second, the confidence that the participants have in the fairness and impartiality of an agency is undermined when participants become aware that staff submissions have been received in confidence. They have no opportunity to correct what may be erroneous information and can easily fear that staff biases have entered into the decision-making process.

. . .

Most agencies take the position that staff reports are confidential, and will not disclose them. They do, however, recognize exceptions to the general rule. I was told, for example, that information would not be used against someone in a proceeding that would affect his rights in a substantial way, unless it could be disclosed to him. However, there is no guarantee of this, except in those cases where the rules of natural justice apply. … Moreover, situations have clearly arisen where staff reports have been used against people even though they were not disclosed. Sometimes, in such situations, the reports are not officially disclosed, but the participants get to see them anyway through some informal leak, often too late to use effectively. Needless to say, such abuses are very difficult to document. There may be many cases where secret reports have been used but the participants never became aware of the fact. What is important to note, in this context, is that staff reports are not disclosed as a matter of general practice, and participants believe that they are influential and feel that the proceedings are unfair. This fact adversely affects the acceptability of agency decisions.

Public interest representatives also argue that staff reports and documents should be made available to the public. They assert two interests. First, they say that it is not possible to assess the performance of the agency and its staff unless it is possible to see what information the staff has access to and also its analysis of that information. One can be much more critical, for example, of an agency that failed to take action against a known peril, or of an agency that was caught by surprise because it did not enter into sufficient investigations, than one can be of an agency that conscientiously tried to obtain all the information necessary for its tasks but has been caught by a surprising turn of events.

The second reason disclosure of staff reports has been urged by public interest representatives is simply that the public is entitled to have much of the information contained in staff reports because it affects the public. The best example again involves inspection reports. These often deal with matters of health and safety, for example the cleanliness of eating establishments and food processing plants. It is argued that the public is entitled to this information simply to enable individuals to protect themselves and bring pressure to bear on the proper authorities to cure the existing deficiencies.

. . .

A number of concerns have been voiced by administrators concerning disclosure of staff documents. First, there are two general concerns that have been expressed in the hearings conducted by the Standing Joint Committee on Regulations and Other Statutory Instruments. These include the arguments that ministerial responsibility would be undermined by disclosure of staff documents and that disclosure would serve to politicize the public service. Neither of these arguments is persuasive, at least as they apply to agencies. In the first place, agencies have, and should continue to have, some measure of independence from the government of the day and from the ministers responsible for their area. For this reason, the arguments that have been offered concerning ministerial responsibility have less force when applied to agencies than they have when applied to the departments of government. The ministers are not supposed to run the agencies and their staffs. Second, while we probably shouldn't politicize the Public Service unduly, or subject individual public servants to political embarrassment, we should try to assure that the agencies are publicly accountable for their action and for their inaction. To this extent politicization, if that's the proper word for it, is desirable.

More particular concerns were voiced when research for this paper was being conducted. First, fear was expressed that disclosure requirements would force the agencies to make public each and every draft of their decisions. Obviously this would lengthen every decision-making process unduly. Fear was also expressed that every scrap of paper in every file would have to be made public, including the handwritten analysis that a staff member might work up concerning a particular proposal. These are legitimate concerns, but it should be possible to include, in any disclosure legislation, exemptions that would adequately protect draft decisions, day-to-day operating notes, and so on. . . .

A final concern relates to the candour of advice that is offered to the agency by its staff. It is argued that disclosure requirements would result in the staff being less candid in its advice. There is probably some truth to this although it can be argued that advice that has to be disclosed is likely to be more well thought out and more carefully based on accurate information. On its face, the candour argument seems to have some merit, but it has to be weighed against the legitimate interests in disclosure mentioned above.

. . .

The approach that seems to offer the best balance between the competing interests is to distinguish between the factual portions of staff documents and the actual advice given. The factual portions should be available to any requester, regardless of the context of the request, unless the particular context of the document must be withheld on some other ground (*e.g.*, protection of privacy, *etc.*). The advice should be regarded as confidential, in order to protect the agency's interest in obtaining candid staff advice, unless, in the particular context of the request, the interest of the requester or the public interest in disclosure becomes paramount. There may be situations, for example licence revocations, where the parties affected should have the right to challenge the construction placed on facts and conclusions drawn from those facts by the staff, as well as the right to challenge the facts themselves, and therefore where the whole document should be released. Such a policy would recognize the agency's need for candid advice by protecting the actual advice that is given; it would recognize the public's need for information about agencies by requiring the release of the factual portions of reports; and it would recognize the overriding interest in fairness by allowing the release of the staff advice if the interest of the requester and the context made this essential.

NOTES

1. Disclosure of staff studies was considered subsequently in two Federal Court of Appeal judgments. In *Toshiba Corporation v. Anti-Dumping Tribunal* (1984), 8 Admin. LR 173 (CA), Toshiba sought review of a decision of the then Anti-Dumping Tribunal on the ground that it had relied on two reports prepared by its staff and not disclosed to the parties. The Court of Appeal dismissed the application and Hugessen J said:

> The issue upon which some comment is required relates to the use made by the Tribunal of reports prepared for it by its staff. In the present case, the Tribunal's staff prepared two reports, the first prior to the commencement of the public hearings and the second after the hearings were over. These reports raise different questions and it is appropriate to deal with them separately.
>
> The preliminary report is, in effect, an introduction to the subject-matter of the inquiry prepared with the obvious intention of allowing the Tribunal members to approach their difficult task (which the statute requires them to complete within a very limited time-frame (s. 16)) in an intelligent and rational manner. Inevitably it contains a number of statements of fact which bear directly upon the ultimate issue which the Tribunal was called upon to decide. It was not revealed to the parties or their counsel. This is a dangerous practice:
>
> • • •
>
> Upon analysis, however, I am satisfied that everything contained in the preliminary staff report is either a matter of general or public knowledge or is based upon facts and sources which were, in due course, properly brought out at the hearing in such a manner that all the parties to that hearing had a full opportunity to test them. Thus, while, in my view, there might have been a technical breach of the rules of natural justice, it can be said with confidence at the end of the day that such breach was minor and inconsequential and that the result of the inquiry would not have been different had such breach not occurred.
>
> • • •
>
> Quite different considerations apply to the final staff report. It consists of summary and commentary on the evidence and submissions made at the inquiry. There is nothing whatever improper in this and it is not dissimilar to the kind of work that law clerks sometimes do for Judges. It is a proper part of the functions of the Tribunal's staff. Nothing requires that such

reports be revealed to the parties. They are simply part of the Tribunal's own internal decision-making process for which, of course, the Tribunal alone is responsible. In my view, they should not even form part of the record in this Court.

2. In *Trans-Quebec & Maritimes Pipeline Inc. v. National Energy Board* (1984), 8 Admin. LR 177 (FCA), Trans-Quebec sought leave to appeal two decisions of the National Energy Board, and applied for disclosure of any staff papers prepared for the board. Again the Federal Court of Appeal dismissed the application, and Thurlow CJ said:

> On the whole, I do not think the order so made should be regarded as authority for a general proposition that staff reports prepared for the assistance of members of a tribunal either in the course of a proceeding or in the judgment making process are papers that must be included in the material on which the tribunal's decision is to be reviewed. As it appears to me, where the decision of a tribunal can be shown to have been based on staff reports to which the parties have not had access containing evidentiary material to which the parties have not had an opportunity to respond, it may well be possible to make out a case for requiring that they be included in the case for review. Further, in such a situation the fact that the reports were prepared and submitted on a confidential basis, in my view, would not afford them protection. But no such case has been made out here.
>
> The applicant's memorandum indicates that the principal reason for seeking the inclusion of staff memoranda in the case is to attempt to establish the Board's reasons for decision. The analysis and opinion in staff memoranda are irrelevant to the ascertainment of the Board's reasons for decision because they cannot be assumed to have been adopted by it as its reasons. The Board's reasons for decision are those which it chooses to express or which can otherwise be clearly shown from its own words or actions to have been its reasons.

These two cases prompted an annotation by Janisch, (1984), 8 *Admin. LR* 188 (footnotes omitted):

> Close consultation between decision makers and their advisers is likely to produce better decisions. Such "institutional" decisions allow for collaborative effort, a broadening of the range of specialist skills and a higher level of sophistication in analysis than that attainable by the ablest of administrators who are cut off from their advisers.
>
> There are, however, drawbacks associated with institutional decision making in that arguments may not be made directly to the real decision makers and outcomes may be greatly influenced by staff whose views and assessments are not made part of the public record. ...
>
> American experience suggests that there are no easy answers which will preserve the undoubted strengths of group work and at the same time ensure procedural fairness. However, it should be noted that the view of Hugessen J that an analogy may be drawn between the role of a staff specialist and that of a law clerk has been decisively rejected. As K.C. Davis has noted:
>
> > The contrast with a typical federal district judge is instructive. The judge's decision is almost entirely personal, for he hears the evidence and the argument and makes the decision. He may have law clerks, who may sometimes play a significant role, but the decision is almost always entirely his, almost never even partially theirs. An agency head may sometimes defer to what he deems to be the superior judgment of a staff specialist, but such deference of a judge to the judgment of a law clerk is relatively rare. Judges' law

clerks are typically neophytes, not specialists. Even when a law clerk's view prevails, the decision is likely to be mainly or entirely that of the judge. But an agency head may often be the intellectual inferior of an agency specialist with respect to particular subject matter, so that the decision may be mainly or entirely that of the specialist.

Moreover, Hugessen J's reassuring analogy to the law clerk is particularly inappropriate in view of his characterization of the final staff report as consisting of "... summary and *commentary* on the evidence and submissions made at the inquiry." (emphasis added) Once it is conceded that staff do more than summarize, there must be concern as to how any evaluative role may be reconciled with procedural fairness. Consider, for example, *Denton v. Auckland City* [[1969] NZLR 256 (SC)] where the concern was with a report from municipal planning officials in a zoning application matter to be decided by the city council. The report included factual matters and matters of opinion. The latter were of great concern to Speight J, especially as they commented directly on the merits of objectors' case.

> [I]t will be observed that the comments and criticisms of the objectors' arguments were received by the Committee unbeknown to the objectors from a person whose expert knowledge and experience as a professional adviser would be likely to be most impressive and compelling to a committee comprised of laymen, albeit experienced laymen, and such opinions in so far as they may be adverse (as some of these were) would be devastating to the objectors who had been deprived of the opportunity to answering.

> Speight J added that it was, of course, highly desirable that a decision maker draw on its general knowledge and a distillation of a mass of experience "... but to do so is far removed from receiving and acting on confidential information in relation to the matter in issue given by a person whose face is not seen and whose voice is not heard by the parties whose rights are being affected."

> Speight J concluded by drawing a distinction between a "factual summary" and "comment." He was persuaded that any comment on the merits and demerits of particular points of objection had to be disclosed. As for purely factual summaries, he expressed the view that it might be better that there be disclosure in the interests of accuracy in a complex area where it is only natural that errors may creep in.

> This is surely the type of analysis needed. It goes somewhat further than the test suggested by Thurlow CJ in *Trans Quebec and Maritimes Pipeline*. ...

> Both these decisions are greatly disappointing not only because they fail to come to grips with the difficult issues involved, and indicate no awareness of a rich body of American experience which should have been of considerable assistance, but because they make no reference whatsoever to Canadian thinking on this very subject.

> For instance, the issue of staff studies are addressed at length in a 1979 study for the Law Reform Commission of Canada and in its 1980 working paper Independent Administrative Agencies. It has also been dealt with in agency studies such as that on the CTC and the CRTC.

> As well, Canadian agencies themselves have struggled with the procedural aspects of institutional decision making in general and staff studies in particular. Consider, for example, the following extract from the CRTC's 1978 proposals for new procedures with respect to broadcasting matters[:]

It is a fundamental principle that an applicant before a tribunal is entitled to know and to have the opportunity to reply to relevant evidence prejudicial to its interests which is in the tribunal's possession and which may have an influence on the tribunal's decision. This principle does not and cannot extend, however, to all documentation possessed or prepared by the tribunal or to its expertise and acquired knowledge.

Staff documents can be divided generally into two categories:

(i) Documents which add evidence: *e.g.*, information gathered by staff from physical inspection visits, monitoring and analyzing programs, *etc.*

(ii) Documents prepared by staff summarizing applications, summarizing evidence, discussing Commission regulations and policies and discussing their applicability to a particular application; in sum, documents which do not add evidence.

The Commission proposes that in the case of staff documents containing evidence which is not on the public file but which relates directly to an application to be heard, such evidence will be made public by the Commission in advance of the hearing if it is to be considered by the Commission in the course of its decision-making. The other category of staff documents may continue to be held confidential, in the Commission's discretion.

It is striking that none of this body of relevant thinking and experience is reflected in these cases. Indeed, they do little more than indicate some of the potential problems involved in institutional decision making. However disappointing this initial judicial response may have been, the fact remains that conscientious administrators, even in the absence of guidance from the Courts, are going to have to struggle with the four objections to any major role for staff in decision making namely, the dilution of the influence of the advocate; the introduction of extra-record facts or factual impressions; the introduction of new ideas that may be decisive even though parties have no chance to respond to them, and the separation of deciding from the discipline of decision making. As K.C. Davis has suggested, while each of these objections has some validity, even in combination they are not enough to prohibit group work. But that is not to say that there cannot be improvements.

The agencies should do what they reasonably can do to diminish the four objections. They should adopt formal rules and informal policies that will strive to assure (1) that the influence of the advocate is not lost from the case, (2) that parties have opportunity to meet in the appropriate fashion whatever extrarecord facts are introduced through consultation, (3) that parties have a chance to respond to new ideas that may be decisive, and (4) that opinion writers' reactions to their systematic examination of specifics of a case play as large a role as they deserve in the decision-making. An enterprising agency can and should put real meaning into these somewhat platitudinous suggestions.

While this leaves much to conscientious administrators, it is to be hoped that more encouragement and guidance will be forthcoming from Canadian Courts than we have seen up to this point. The objective should not be to impose judicial standards, but to reinforce the strength of institutional decision making by reconciling effectiveness with fairness.

Somewhat surprisingly, the question of access to material prepared by staff still remains a comparatively untilled terrain. However, as we have already seen, the recent cases in which applicants attempted to extend *Stinchcombe* to the arena of economic regulation were singularly unsympathetic to the existence of any general obligation that documents prepared by staff and provided to decision-makers about upcoming hearings had to be revealed at least in advance of the hearing. On the other hand, at least two judgments of the Supreme Court of Canada, which we will discuss in chapter 6, Institutional Decisions, clearly prevent decision-makers from listening to, let alone taking account of, new material and arguments fed to them by fellow non-sitting tribunal members. In such situations, the parties must be put on notice. To the extent that this restriction operates among tribunal members, it must perforce apply to new arguments and information provided by staff. See *Tremblay v. Québec (Commission des affaires sociales)*, [1992] 1 SCR 952 (Que.) and the earlier judgment in *IWA, Local 2-69 v. Consolidated-Bathurst Packaging Ltd.*, [1990] 1 SCR 282 (Ont.). Indeed, these judgments would seem to speak to both pre- and post-hearing material prepared by staff save to the extent that, in the case of pre-hearing reports, the contents come out in other ways at the hearing. But see *Armstrong v. Canada (Royal Canadian Mounted Police)*, [1998] 2 FC 666 (CA), where the Federal Court of Appeal upheld the non-disclosure of a staff report in a disciplinary context. The commissioner of the RCMP relied on a staff summary of evidence, including psychological assessments, to dismiss an appeal from a discharge and demotion board and order Armstrong's discharge from the RCMP. The staff member had noted in her report that "one psychologist was unaware of [Armstrong's] history of problems with paperwork, a fact which may have influenced his opinion had it been known during his evaluation of her." McDonald JA was of the view that the staff member was not qualified to assert this opinion, characterized the comment as "exceptionally close to the line" and suggested that it should have been disclosed to allow Armstrong to respond. However, Stone JA held that the comment was appropriate because it did not "suggest that the result was forgone" or "recommend how the appeal should be disposed of by the Commissioner." Desjardins JA, relying on *Toshiba Corporation*, concluded that it was the staff member's role to "sift and summarize the evidence" and that it was not improper for her "to flag possible weaknesses in the evidence for the commissioner's consideration and reflexion." See also *Devon Canada Corporation v. Alberta (Energy and Utilities Board)*, 2003 ABCA 167, 3 Admin. LR (4th) 154, at para. 24, which raises, but does not decide, whether it is appropriate for board members to examine and discuss geological core samples relevant to a licence application with members of the board's expert staff in the absence of the parties.

The Law Reform Commission of Canada, in its working paper no. 25, "Independent Administrative Agencies" (1980), recommended that

> agencies should, in appropriate cases, release and distribute information at their disposal, including research papers prepared by individual staff members which outline issues and disclose relevant information not elsewhere disclosed in documentation available to participants; but agency documents should not attribute to the staff as a whole any official position taken with respect to any issues raised.

The commission recognized the problem of confidentiality, but said only: "Agencies must ... reconcile as best they can the competing values of confidentiality and fairness to fulfil their responsibilities."

Berger, "The MacKenzie Valley Pipeline Inquiry"
(1976), 3 *Queen's LJ* 3, at 14

Then there is the problem of assuring that the Inquiry's own staff do not wind up writing the report of the Inquiry. To put it another way, there is the problem of ensuring that the Inquiry staff are not allowed to put their arguments privately to the Commissioner or to the Inquiry. I have sought to overcome this by laying down a ruling that the recommendations that the Inquiry staff wish to develop should be presented to the Inquiry by Commission Counsel at the formal hearings. In this way the Inquiry staff will be developing what they conceive to be the appropriate terms and conditions to be applied, but they will not be enabled to do so privately. It will be necessary for them to place them before the Inquiry, where they can be challenged, adopted or ignored by the other participants in the Inquiry.

Official Notice

Davis, *Administrative Law*
3rd ed. (St. Paul, MN: West Publishing Company, 1972), at 291-314

Section 556(e) of the [United States] *Administrative Procedure Act* deals with the problem in a single sentence: "Where an agency decision rests on official notice of a material fact not appearing in the evidence in the record, a party is entitled, on timely request, to an opportunity to show the contrary." This provision is clearly sound and satisfactory as far as it goes, but it does not answer the principal question of whether or when an agency may properly go beyond the record for a material fact. For an answer to that question and other principal questions about official notice, we must turn to the case law, to the practices of the agencies, to an analysis of the combined needs of fair hearing and of enlightened administrative action, and to the law of judicial notice, including the proposed Federal Rules of Evidence.

The nub of the central problem is to reconcile the needs of procedural fairness with the need for full and free use of whatever expertness the agency may have, including the kind of understanding that is based upon an inseparable mixture of experience and information.

In many circumstances the only orderly and fair method for resolving some issues of fact is to put all the evidence in the record so that each party will have an unabridged opportunity to cross-examine, to explain, to present rebuttal evidence, and to offer written and oral argument. Indeed, cutting off such an opportunity may often be a denial of due process of law.

Yet in some circumstances an agency must be free to go beyond the record for some of its facts. Even the courts may and do commonly rely upon extra-record facts, and such leading evidence scholars as Thayer, Wigmore and McCormick have asserted that the scope of judicial notice should be expanded, not restricted.

When an agency is confronted with a problem of policy or of discretion, we want it to come forth with something we call wisdom. But how much of wisdom in practical contexts is factual? It is made up of multifarious ingredients all stirred up together—knowledge of specific facts, understanding of general facts, prior experience in trying to solve similar problems, scientific information, mental processes such as logic or reasoning, mental processes such as appraising or estimating or guessing, formulation and application of notions about policy, imagination or inventiveness, intuition, controlled emotional reactions.

When an assessment board's appraisal of property was challenged because members of the board necessarily relied to some extent upon their own knowledge, Mr. Justice Holmes observed that many honest and sensible judgments "express an intuition of experience which outruns analysis and sums up many unnamed and tangled impressions. ... The Board was created for the purpose of using its judgment and its knowledge."

The mental equipment that men bring to the task of exercising judgment—whether about questions of fact or law or policy or discretion—includes understanding and experience and perhaps specialization or expertness, and these qualities in turn depend to a considerable extent upon knowledge of facts. But what are the boundaries of such mental equipment? What of the books and files that an administrator may have at his fingertips? If the administrator may rely upon his own past experience, may he rely upon that of his colleague, that of his subordinate, that of the author of the treatise on law or the treatise on medicine, or that of the witness who testified in a case recently decided? Does the mental equipment of one who has become accustomed to directing a staff in a specialized field encompass whatever may be conveniently at the fingertips of assistants—many portions of the agency's files and whole segments of the agency's library?

But even if we say yes to such questions as these, what of it? Should we not still require all facts the agency uses in making a decision to be made part of the record? The answer is that they should be to the extent that that is practicable. But as soon as we take account of some of the realities of the workaday handling of ordinary cases, we begin to see the central problem. One of the realities is that neither the parties nor their counsel nor the examiner nor other officers can anticipate all the facts that may be needed for making an enlightened decision. Theoretically, to be sure, the examiner could be instructed to make a full investigation and to do all the necessary research in advance of the hearing, and to spread the results on the record at the hearing. Such a system would satisfy the requirements of both informed decisions and fair procedure. But reasons of economy usually require that staff research should merely supplement rather than duplicate the work of counsel for private parties.

The crucial problem of official notice normally arises for the first time when the examiner is studying the record to prepare his proposed report and discovers points on which additional information or advice is needed. It is then that he discovers the need of help from an agency specialist, or begins to remember that another case or a record of an investigation or reports to the agency by the parties or previous staff studies may illuminate what he now realizes to be one of the dark corners of the case. The same basic problem of official notice may arise a second time when the case comes to the heads of the agency for final decision. By then the issues of law and policy and discretion may have crystallized and the agency heads, with a broader perspective of such issues than that of the examiner, may feel the need for use of specialized understanding which may include materials in the files or in the library.

What should they do? Reopen the hearing? Send the examiner back from Washington to Los Angeles? Ignore the information of which they are fully aware? Use the information but conceal its use? Use the information and notify the parties of its use? These are the main alternatives. The choice among the alternatives depends upon many variables that we are going to explore in this chapter. Sometimes nothing short of reopening the hearing will suffice. Sometimes the information may be used without mentioning it. Usually the proper course is to use it and to set it forth, together with its source, in the report.

· · ·

The cardinal distinction which more than any other governs the use of extra-record facts by courts and agencies is the distinction between legislative facts and adjudicative facts. When a court or an agency finds facts concerning the immediate parties—who did what, where, when, how, and with what motive or intent—the court or agency is performing an adjudicative function, and the facts are conveniently called adjudicative facts. When a court or an agency develops law or policy, it is acting legislatively; the courts have created the common law through judicial legislation, and the facts which inform the tribunal's legislative judgments are called legislative facts.

Stated in other terms, the adjudicative facts are those to which the law is applied in the process of adjudication. They are the facts that normally go to the jury in a jury case. They relate to the parties, their activities, their properties, their businesses. Legislative facts are the facts which help the tribunal determine the content of law and of policy and help the tribunal to exercise its judgment or discretion in determining what course of action to take. Legislative facts are ordinarily general and do not concern the immediate parties. In the great mass of cases decided by courts and by agencies, the legislative element is either absent or unimportant or interstitial, because in most cases the applicable law and policy have been previously established. But whenever a tribunal engages in the creation of law or of policy, it may need to resort to legislative facts, whether or not these facts have been developed on the record.

The exceedingly practical difference between legislative and adjudicative facts is that, apart from facts properly noticed, the tribunal's findings of adjudicative facts must be supported by evidence, but findings or assumptions of legislative facts need not be, frequently are not, and sometimes cannot be supported by evidence.

· · ·

In our search for principle we should reorient ourselves in fundamentals which are easily overlooked or forgotten. Why do we use trial-type procedure in our courts and in our agencies? Why do we want adjudicative facts to be determined on the record? Why do we decide that findings must be made on the record—and then carve out an exception for facts that may be judicially noticed? The law of judicial and official notice should emerge from the answers to such basic questions as these.

The reason we use trial-type procedure is that we make the practical judgment, on the basis of much experience, that taking evidence, subject to cross-examination and rebuttal, is the best way to resolve controversies involving disputes of adjudicative facts. The reason we require a determination on the record is that we think fair procedure in resolving disputes of adjudicative facts calls for giving each party a chance to meet in the appropriate fashion the facts that come to the tribunal's attention, and the appropriate fashion for meeting disputed adjudicative facts includes rebuttal evidence, cross-examination, usually confrontation, and argument (written or oral or both). The key to a fair trial is opportunity to use the appropriate weapons (rebuttal evidence, cross-examination, and argument) to meet adverse materials that come to the tribunal's attention.

The reason we allow judicial or official notice to be taken of extra-record facts is not to promote fairness but to promote convenience. Tribunals make factual assumptions because it is convenient to do so. Indeed, to fail to make factual assumptions would mean extreme inconvenience, even to such an extent that probably both courts and agencies would find the adjudication of cases impracticable.

The two major considerations in developing a system of judicial notice are fairness and convenience, and the essential problem is to accommodate the one to the other in such a way that neither will be unduly sacrificed.

The accommodation of fairness to convenience cannot be made by limiting judicial notice of adjudicative facts to those "not subject to reasonable dispute" because such a limitation sacrifices convenience much more than is necessary for protecting procedural fairness. The convenient system is to assume all facts that are unlikely to be challenged, taking care to state those that might possibly be erroneously assumed, while keeping the door open to challenge.

The basic principle is that extra-record facts should be assumed whenever it is convenient to assume them, except that convenience should always yield to the requirement of procedural fairness that parties should have opportunity to meet in the appropriate fashion all facts that influence the disposition of the case. What is the appropriate fashion depends upon three main variables—the extent to which the facts are adjudicative about the parties or legislative facts of a general character, the degree to which the facts are critical or peripheral, and the extent of uncertainty or apparent certainty of the facts.

NOTES

1. The Ontario SPPA deals with official notice in s. 16, but does it respond to Davis's "central problem"?

2. For a rare instance in which the court considered the issue of official notice (in that case, by the Ontario Municipal Board), see *Township of Innisfil v. Township of Vespra*, [1981] 2 SCR 145 (Ont.); rev'g. (1978), 95 DLR (3d) 298 (Ont. CA); aff'g. (1978), 7 OMBR 233 (Ont. Div. Ct.). See also *Sivaguru v. Canada (Minister of Employment and Immigration)* (1992), 16 Imm. R (2d) 85 (FCA), in which the court held that a member of the Refugee Board acted outside his authority under s. 68(4) of the *Immigration Act*, RSC 1985, c. I-2 "to take notice of any facts that may be judicially noticed and ... of any other generally recognized facts and any information or opinion that is within its specialized knowledge that authorized the taking of notice of facts." The board member had been suspicious of evidence given by the claimant and sought material from the board's documentation centre, which the board member then used to lay a trap for the claimant in the course of questioning. The court held that this was not sanctioned by the legislation and that it created a reasonable apprehension of bias. For a discussion of this historical provision for official notice in the immigration context, see Houle, "The Use of Official Notice in a Refugee Determination Process" (1993), 34 *Cahiers de Droit* 573; and Houle, "The Credibility and the Authoritativeness of the Documents of the Documentation, Information and Research Branch of the Immigration and Refugee Board" (1994), 6 *Int. J Ref. Law* 6.

3. The independent, extra-judicial gathering of evidence also surfaced in the Federal Court of Canada in a different context in *Canadian Cable Television Association v. American College Sports Collective of Canada Inc.* (1991), 81 DLR (4th) 376 (FCA). Here, in proceedings before the Copyright Board, one of the members of the board had secured data and other information outside the hearing that he used in questioning witnesses and in writing his decision. While the court, after a discussion of the authorities, condemned this conduct, it declined to grant a remedy. The member, whose activities were in question, was in dissent and there was no proof that his conduct had a prejudicial effect on the outcome as reflected in the majority decision.

4. The issues raised by these cases also involve more general questions about evidence in the administrative process and, indirectly, entitlement to cross-examine. As such, they serve as a useful link to that section of this chapter. For a general elaboration of the whole topic, see Lemieux and Clocchiatti, "Official Notice and Specialized Knowledge" (1990), 46 *Admin. LR* 126.

Admissibility of Evidence

The first materials in this section are about the admissibility of evidence. This topic is closely related to others, especially control of jurisdiction and the accuracy and adequacy of fact finding. Admissibility is included in this chapter because it is part of an important general procedural issue: what procedures should agencies use for fact finding, especially for facts that are different from the kinds of facts that usually concern courts.

It is well settled that agencies are not governed by the rules of evidence used by courts unless some statutory provision requires them, and such provisions are rare. For example, in *Miller (T.A.) v. Minister of Housing and Local Government*, [1968] 1 WLR 992 (CA), the major factual issue was whether a piece of land had been used by a business for retail sale of garden supplies during a particular period. Evidence that the property was used for this purpose was given by four witnesses. A contradictory letter from the managing director of the business was introduced, and the witnesses were given an opportunity to comment. They disagreed with it, but the decision relied on it. Leave to appeal was refused. Lord Denning said:

> A tribunal of this kind is master of its own procedure, provided that the rules of natural justice are applied. Most of the evidence here was on oath, but that is no reason why hearsay should not be admitted where it can fairly be regarded as reliable. Tribunals are entitled to act on any material which is logically probative, even though it is not evidence in a court of law. ...
>
> During this very week in Parliament we have had the second reading of the *Civil Evidence Bill*. It abolishes the rule against hearsay, even in the ordinary courts of the land. It allows first-hand hearsay to be admitted in civil proceedings, subject to safeguards. Hearsay is clearly admissible before a tribunal. No doubt in admitting it, the tribunal must observe the rules of natural justice, but this does not mean that it must be tested by cross-examination. It only means that the tribunal must give the other side a fair opportunity of commenting on it and of contradicting it. ...
>
> The inspector here did that. Mr. Fogwill's letter of November 19, 1964, was put to the witnesses and they contradicted it. No application was made for an adjournment to deal further with it. In these circumstances I do not see there was anything contrary to natural justice in admitting it.

Indeed, in many statutes establishing administrative tribunals and in both the SPPA (s. 15(1)) and Alberta *Administrative Procedures and Jurisdiction Act* (s. 9), the disregarding of the normal rules of evidence is sanctioned. Nonetheless, as the quotation from Lord Denning makes clear, this does not necessarily make the common law rules of evidence irrelevant or generally inapplicable. To the extent that the rules of natural justice or procedural fairness condition decisions about evidence, the discretionary authority of boards and tribunals over questions of admissibility and requirements of proof is subject to limits and those limits may, on occasion at least, be influenced by normal common law evidential principles. Two examples will suffice to illustrate this point.

In *Université du Québec à Trois-Rivières v. Larocque*, [1993] 1 SCR 471 (Que.), the Supreme Court of Canada sustained the quashing of an arbitration award by reason of wrongful refusal to admit evidence. While the arbitrator had a broad statutory discretion over questions of procedure and evidence, the inadmissibility ruling in this instance had led to a denial of natural justice. The evidence in question was held to be both relevant and crucial to the defence that the university was advancing in the context of a grievance against a dismissal. While this decision is not without its difficulties in that it also reflects upon the tribunal's legal characterization of the issues at stake (see Reid, "Not All Evidentiary Errors Are Reviewable—Only Violations of Natural Justice" (1993), 2 *Reid's Administrative Law* 144 and Dyzenhaus, "Developments in Administrative Law: The 1992-93 Term" (1994), 5 *Sup. Ct. L Rev.* (2d) 189, at 213-15), it does reflect a fairly obvious truism—discretionary decisions over the admissibility of evidence must not remove the entitlement of affected persons to have a reasonable opportunity to make their case. Indeed, in the SPPA, this is reflected in s. 10.1(a) and the entitlement that it creates in parties to "call and examine witnesses and present arguments and submissions."

Conversely, of course, natural justice considerations can also arise by reason of the admission of and weight attributed to certain kinds of evidence. Given not only evolutions in the common law relating to the use of hearsay evidence in regular court proceedings (*R v. Khan*, [1990] 2 SCR 531 (Ont.)) and the historically more relaxed attitude of the court to the use of hearsay evidence in administrative proceedings, it is unlikely that the mere admission of hearsay evidence will lead to a breach of the rules of natural justice. (Indeed, to deny admission of hearsay evidence may itself be a problem in some contexts.) Thus, in the subsequent professional disciplinary proceedings arising out of *Khan v. College of Physicians and Surgeons of Ontario* (1992), 94 DLR (4th) 193 (Ont. CA), the Ontario Court of Appeal sustained the admission of hearsay evidence. This was in the context of an allegation of professional misconduct by way of sexual assault on a three-and-a-half-year-old girl. The hearsay evidence was not only reasonably necessary but there were sufficient indicia of its reliability.

However, exclusive reliance on hearsay and opinion evidence may have the consequence of leading to a denial of natural justice. Thus, in *Bond v. New Brunswick (Management Board)* (1992), 95 DLR (4th) 733 (NB CA), the NB Court of Appeal set aside an arbitrator's sustaining of a dismissal for sexual assault. The victim did not testify; rather the arbitrator relied simply on hearsay evidence of what the victim had told others as well as opinion evidence. Given the sanction and the seriousness of the allegations, this was not sufficient to meet the requirements of natural justice. Once again, there are obvious links here between evidential questions and both cross-examination rights and the standard of proof to be met in such cases by the employer in justifying the discharge.

A variation on this theme emerges from *Re Clarke and Superintendent of Brokers, Insurance, and Real Estate* (1985), 23 DLR (4th) 315 (BC CA). Clarke surrendered her licence as a real estate salesperson when she was charged with theft and fraud in connection with a sale of a home owned by Jakobsen. She was acquitted and applied for the reissue of her licence. This application was made to the superintendent, who held a hearing. Counsel for the superintendent sought to introduce the transcripts of the evidence Jakobsen had given at the criminal trial, with the explanation that her health did not permit her to attend. The transcripts were admitted, and the superintendent decided not to reissue the licence, although he said that he did not give much weight to Jakobsen's evidence. Clarke appealed to the Commercial Appeals Commission, which was governed by a statutory provision virtually identical to s. 15(1) of the SPPA. Her appeal was dismissed and leave to appeal to the Court of Appeal was refused. The Court of Appeal asserted that by implication the superintendent was governed by the same provision, and Hutcheon JA said:

> The consequence is that the transcript evidence of Mrs. Jakobsen was admissible and the superintendent in admitting the evidence and giving it little weight made no error in law or in fact. In turn, the Commercial Appeals Commission would have been in error if it had reversed the superintendent's decision on the ground that the transcript evidence was not admissible in a court of law.

Subsequently, *Clarke* was cited with approval in *Re OEX Electromagnetic Inc. and British Columbia Securities Commission* (1990), 43 Admin. LR 274 (BC CA), where the court sustained the admissibility of depositions of evidence before the United States Securities and Exchange Commission in a BC Securities Commission hearing. Though only one of the deponents was available for cross-examination, there was other relevant oral and documentary evidence before the commission and the depositions were used with caution by the commission.

The extent to which these holdings can be generalized will, however, not be fully apparent until after our consideration of cross-examination and fact finding.

Problems about admissibility are often a product of problems about statutory interpretation. *Timpauer v. Air Canada* (1986), 18 Admin. LR 192 (FCA) is a good example, which also includes an interesting comment about review generally. Timpauer complained that excessive tobacco smoke at his workplace presented an "imminent danger" to his health. Eventually his complaint reached the Canada Labour Relations Board, and he sought to call experts to testify generally about the dangers of tobacco smoke and about the inadequacies of ventilation as a means of controlling these dangers, as well as doctors to testify about the effects of the smoke on him personally. The board ruled that the issue was the effect of the smoke on Timpauer and not the dangers of smoking generally, and it interpreted "imminent danger" to mean an immediate crisis and not a continuing condition. It refused to hear Timpauer's witnesses, and dismissed the complaint. He sought review and succeeded. Stone JA concluded that the board's interpretation of "imminent danger" was "not unreasonable," and continued,

> In my view, the board could not properly decide the impact of the smoke upon the health of the applicant by relying simply on the description he gave of his reaction to tobacco smoke. That evidence might not have had told the full story. The physician and the allergist, with their special

skills and knowledge, might have added a dimension of critical importance. By refusing to hear their evidence the board denied the applicant natural justice. The fact that such evidence might not have assisted the applicant was not a valid reason for refusing to hear it. The remaining witnesses, it seems to me, would have testified on matters of a more general nature not specifically directed toward the impact of the smoke upon the health of the applicant at the relevant time. I do not see that the board's refusal to receive that evidence involved reviewable error.

(The legislation that created the Labour Board included a broad privative clause.)

Before leaving the matter I wish also to deal with a point addressed to us by counsel for the board. It is to the effect that this aspect of it does not involve a denial of natural justice as such but, rather, that it involves solely a question of statutory interpretation. In essence, counsel submits that even if natural justice had been denied, that denial arose out of the board's interpretation of the term "imminent danger" and as that interpretation is not patently unreasonable this Court cannot interfere. As authority for that proposition the decision of the Supreme Court of Canada in the *Bibeault* case, supra, is relied upon. In my view, that was an altogether different case.

. . .

The Supreme Court of Canada held that the decisions of the commissioners and of the Labour Court, not being patently unreasonable, should not be interfered with. There was therefore no room for an argument that natural justice had been denied.

. . .

In the present case, on the other hand, even though in my view the board's interpretation cannot be successfully challenged, it had yet to decide whether or not the circumstances disclosed the existence of an "imminent danger" to the health of the applicant. To do that, it had first to hear all relevant evidence either party wished to adduce and then to determine the facts. Only after doing so could it decide the merits of the matter on the basis of its interpretation of the Code.

Cross-Examination

One of the major founding cases on cross-examination is *Re Toronto Newspaper Guild and Globe Printing*, [1951] 3 DLR 162 (Ont. HC); aff'd. [1952] 2 DLR 302 (Ont. CA); aff'd. [1953] 2 SCR 18 (Ont.). The guild applied to the Labour Relations Board to be certified as bargaining agent for employees of Globe Printing Company. In support of its contention that it represented a majority of employees, an official of the guild submitted membership cards. The company, suspecting that some employees had left the union after the application was made, sought to cross-examine. The board refused and refused to undertake cross-examination itself or to order a secret vote. It certified the union, and Globe's application for *certiorari* succeeded. Gale J said, "The most effective way in which the Company could have tested the merits of the application was to cross-examine the person who was presenting it to the Board. Unfortunately, in this case the right to cross-examination was not granted and in that fact alone I think the Company was improperly excluded from a cardinal privilege which it enjoys under our jurisprudence; that exclusion, of itself, was tantamount to a denial of basic justice."

This principle is now enshrined in s. 10.1(b) of the SPPA though conditioned on the cross-examination being "reasonably required for a full and fair disclosure of all matters relevant to the issues in the proceeding." What kinds of considerations are permitted or required by the phrase "reasonably required"?

Innisfil (Township) v. Vespra (Township)
[1981] 2 SCR 145 (Ont.)

[This case was mentioned earlier in this chapter in the material on official notice. In the course of an application by the city of Barrie to the Ontario Municipal Board for permission to annex land in adjacent townships, Barrie claimed that it needed the land to accommodate a projected population of 125,000. This figure had been recommended by a government-appointed task force on the region's future and had been approved by the government. A letter from the minister of treasury, economics, an intergovernmental affairs stating this government policy was introduced at the Municipal Board hearing. When it reached the Supreme Court of Canada, the issue whether the board was obliged to accept the letter had been settled: the letter was admissible, and the policy was relevant evidence, but the board had a duty to make up its own mind. The major issue at the Supreme Court was whether the opposing municipalities were entitled to cross-examine the official of the ministry who had presented the letter.]

ESTEY J delivered the judgment of the Court: I turn first to the question of the right of the appellant to cross-examine the department representative on the letter transmitted to the Board by the Minister, the provincial Treasurer. It will afford a better appreciation of the issue to set out the relevant parts of this letter:

> I refer to my previous letter regarding the matter of the City of Barrie's application to annex part of the neighbouring townships. At that time, I indicated that the report of the Simcoe-Georgian Task Force had been accepted in principle by the Government.
>
> I understand from my staff, who are attending the hearings, that the Board is uncertain about the degree to which the Government has accepted the report as Government policy, in view of the statement that it has been accepted "in principle." I confirm that, in particular, the population allocations contained in the report have been approved by the Government. In the case of the Barrie Urban Area, this is 125 000.
>
> • • •
>
> I understand that my previous letters have not been placed in the record and that the Board would prefer that a witness be available to present such letters and to testify.
>
> In this regard, I have instructed Mr E.M. Fleming to deliver this letter.

The *Statutory Powers Procedure Act, 1971* does not assist the respondent or the intervenant, the Attorney General of Ontario, in their opposition to the cross-examination of Mr Fleming on the letter. Section 3 of that Act clearly makes that statute applicable to the hearing under s. 14 of the *Municipal Act*. Section 10(c) [now s. 10.1(b)] is directly applicable to the issue at hand. Here the Ministry volunteered a witness and at one stage or another the Board and all the parties before it assumed cross-examination of that witness should and would take place. Clause (c) makes no exception in favour of a member of the executive, nor does it leave any discretion in any agency or tribunal, subject to its provisions, to escape from them. By s. 12 the Board is authorized to compel a person without limitation to give evidence. Here the difficulty of an unwilling witness does not arise, except in the case of the Minister, but no issue has been made of his election not to testify because all parties appeared to accept the reasonableness of having a departmental official attend the hearing as a witness. Counsel for an objector questioned Mr Fleming's competency for the task without some further description of his qualifications to testify on the population policy on behalf of the Minister.

It is within the context of a statutory process that it must be noted that cross-examination is a vital element of the adversarial system applied and followed in our legal system, including, in many instances, before administrative tribunals since the earliest times. Indeed the adversarial system, founded on cross-examination and the right to meet the case being made against the litigant, civil or criminal, is the procedural substructure upon which the common law itself has been built. That is not to say that because our Court system is founded upon these institutions and procedures that administrative tribunals must apply the same techniques. Indeed, there are many tribunals in the modern community which do not follow the traditional adversarial road. On the other hand, where the rights of the citizen are involved and the statute affords him the right to a full hearing, including a hearing of his demonstration of his rights, one would expect to find the clearest statutory curtailment of the citizen's right to meet the case made against him by cross-examination. ...

The procedural format adopted by the administrative tribunal must adhere to the provisions of the parent statute of the Board. The process of interpreting and applying statutory policy will be the dominant influence in the workings of such an administrative tribunal. Where the Board proceeds in the discharge of its mandate to determine the rights of the contending parties before it on the traditional basis wherein the onus falls upon the contender to introduce the facts and submissions upon which he will rely, the Board technique will take on something of the appearance of a traditional Court. Where, on the other hand, the Board, by its legislative mandate or the nature of the subject-matter assigned to its administration, is more concerned with community interests at large, and with technical policy aspects of a specialized subject, one cannot expect the tribunal to function in the manner of the traditional Court. This is particularly so where Board membership is drawn partly or entirely from persons experienced or trained in the sector of activity consigned to the administrative supervision of the Board. Again where the Board in its statutory role takes on the complexion of a department of the executive branch of Government concerned with the execution of a policy laid down in broad concept by the Legislature, and where the Board has the delegated authority to issue regulations or has a broad discretionary power to license persons or activities, the trappings and habits of the traditional Courts have long ago been discarded.

We are here concerned with that sector of the common law sometimes referred to as the principles of natural justice, fairness and *audi alteram partem*. These principles, of course, are of diminished impact in instances such as we have here where the constituting statutes themselves outline the necessity for a hearing and, by direction and indirection, establish the procedure to be followed in the conduct of such hearing. In proceeding to examine some of the authorities, new and old, one must constantly be cautious that the overriding consideration is the statutes themselves. ...

It must be emphasized that if the appellant has here the right to cross-examine the representative of the Ministry, as I believe he does, it is not for the appellate Court to withhold such right because in its judgment it is doubtful, or even impossible, in the view of the Court for the appellant to advance its case by such cross-examination. The decision to exercise the right is solely that of the holder of the right. He, of course, must exercise it at his peril as is the case in any other administrative or judicial proceeding where such a right arises.

The relationship of "independent" agencies to the executive branch of Government, in so far as that relationship affects the procedural rights of parties before the tribunal, can only be determined by reference to the agency's parent statute, and other relevant statute or common law prescribing procedural norms. It is not for a Court to go behind these ground rules or modify them because of perceived far-reaching effects. If on its face an agency is held out in the constituting legislation as "independent" of the executive, that is with functions independent of the executive branch, it remains that way for all purposes until the Legislature exercises its undoubted right to alter, by providing for policy directions for example, the position and procedure of the agency. ...

A court will require the clearest statutory direction along the lines, for example, of the *Broadcasting Act* to enable the executive branch of Government to give binding policy directions of an administrative tribunal and to make such directions immune from challenge by cross-examination or otherwise by the objectors. It is, of course, open to the Legislature at any time to make provision for the issuance of binding directions by the executive branch to the Board whereby the Board would be required to conform strictly to the announced policies of the executive branch or its agent, a Minister; and thereby to withdraw the subject of the policies so announced from the hearing procedure. ...

This is not a case of the right to cross-examination being used to challenge the policies of the executive branch of Government in such a way as to bring the administrative tribunal into the political arena. It is merely the exercise by a party properly before the Board on an annexation application of a right accorded to that party by the Legislature. The Legislature has, of course, granted by s. 14 of the *Municipal Act* an identical right to all other parties who wish to object to applications for annexation. The role assigned to the Board by the Legislature in the legislation as now drafted may entail some conflict between the administrative result and certain Government policies or actions. The remedy does not lie in the Board and the Court denying the citizen has statutory right to oppose annexation, but in achieving by legislative adjustment some better integration of Board and executive branch actions.

Appeal allowed.

NOTE

The Supreme Court highlighted once again the importance of cross-examination to procedural fairness and fundamental justice in the national security context in its first *Charkaoui* decision: *Charkaoui v. Canada (Citizenship and Immigration)*, [2007] 1 SCR 350 (reproduced in chapter 3 of this text). The court held that the statutory regimes to ascertain the reasonableness of security certificates, which provided for the *ex parte* and *in camera* presentation and assessment of secret government evidence, did not minimally impair Mr. Charkaoui's right not to be deprived of life, liberty, and security of the person except in accordance with fundamental justice. In doing so, it pointed to various mechanisms, in Canada and abroad, that made use of special advocates whose "vigorous" cross-examination of government evidence assisted decision-makers' assessment of the government's evidence and of government claims that disclosure of the evidence to the affected party threatened national security.

Re County of Strathcona No. 20 and MacLab Enterprises
(1971), 20 DLR (3d) 200 (Alta. SCAD)

[The Provincial Planning Board directed that lands owned by a developer be rezoned from "agricultural general reserve" to "general urban." This decision was appealed to a judge in chambers by a group that felt that the area was unsuitable for residential housing because of odours emitted by nearby industries. They succeeded on the ground that they had not been given an opportunity to test all the evidence by cross-examination. The developer appealed to the Alberta Supreme Court, Appeal Division. The appeal raised several issues about cross-examination, and only one is discussed in this excerpt.]

JOHNSON JA: A person appearing before *quasi*-judicial bodies is entitled to be heard and to present his case, and when this is not permitted there is a denial of natural justice. In the process of presenting his own case he is entitled to weaken and destroy the case that is made against him. In trials in Court this is often effectively done by cross-examination. A party is often able to advance his own case from the mouths of his opponent's witnesses. It does not follow that the refusal of or the placing of limitations upon the right of cross-examination will always require that the Court quash an order made in proceedings in which these restrictions are enforced. If he is afforded an equally effective method of answering the case made against him, in other words is given "a fair opportunity to correct or controvert any relevant statement brought forward to his prejudice" (to quote the words used above), the requirements of natural justice will be met. The importance of cross-examination will vary with the nature of the case being heard.

· · ·

The Bernhart report remains to be considered. While Mr MacTaggart was making submissions on behalf of the appellant, he asked the Board to accept a report from a Dr Bernhart who, he said, had made a study of pollution in this area. He explained that Dr Bernhart could not be present because he was then in Germany. It was vigorously argued by the respondents that the report should not be accepted unless Dr Bernhart was produced for cross-examination as to his qualifications as an expert in this field. The Board ruled, however, that the report be admitted, and directed that copies be given to all the parties and that the respondents could file answers to any points raised in that report. With the appellant's submission was filed, as an addendum, a document setting forth the doctor's degrees, his previous experience, his membership in various professional associations and a list of papers published by him. Two documents, one by Dr Turk and the other by Dr Kleppinger, answered the Bernhart report and the arguments advanced by it.

Section 8 of the *Planning Act, 1963* (Alta.) c. 43 [now RSA 1970, c. 276, proclaimed in force March 1, 1971], contains the following subsections:

8.(3) The Board may make and adopt rules of practice, not inconsistent with this Act, regulating its procedure and the times of its sittings.

(4) In the conduct of inquiries and hearings before it, the Board is not bound by the technical rules of evidence.

• • •

There is thus no question of Dr Bernhart's report being admissible once the Board decided to accept it. The absence of its author with the consequent inability to cross-examine him goes to the weight to be given to it, not its admissibility.

• • •

Have the respondents been afforded "a fair opportunity" to "correct or contradict" the contents of the report to Dr Bernhart? They have been deprived of doing so by cross-examination because its author was not present, but cross-examination is but one method by which this can be done. In the present case, the Board invited written answers to the matters contained in the report. To one who reads the critique of Dr Turk and the shorter one by Dr Kleppinger, it is impossible to say the respondents have not taken full advantage of the opportunity afforded to them to "correct or contradict" any "statement prejudicial to their view" in the Bernhart report.

[Kane and McDermid JJA concurred.]

Appeal allowed.

Re B and Catholic Children's Aid Society of Metropolitan Toronto
(1987), 38 DLR (4th) 106 (Ont. Div. Ct.)

[The *Child Welfare Act*, RSO 1980, c. 66 included terms that established a "child abuse register." It was a list of individuals who had been reported by children's aid societies as having abused children. If an individual was included on the list, he or she was entitled to notice and to make an application to be removed from the list to the director of the Ontario Centre for the Prevention of Child Abuse, or his or her delegate. A hearing was required for this application, and an appeal could be made to the Divisional Court.]

CRAIG J: The appellant appeals to this court from the decision of Hearing Officer Barry Lowes dated May 17, 1985, as affirmed on May 28, 1985, by the Director, Ontario Centre for the Prevention of Child Abuse, Ministry of Community and Social Services, denying the appellant's application to have his name expunged from the Child Abuse Register pursuant to s. 51 of the *Child Welfare Act*, RSO 1980, c. 66 (the Act).

As a result of an investigation conducted on and subsequent to September 7, 1983, the Catholic Children's Aid Society of Metropolitan Toronto (the Society) alleged that the appellant J.B. sexually molested Haley B, the 12-year-old daughter of J.B.'s girlfriend, Margaret B.

On September 16, 1983, the social worker from the Society, June De Maat, met with officers of the Metropolitan Toronto Police. The police felt there was not enough evidence to charge J.B. As a result no charges were laid.

· · ·

At the hearing the Society called only one witness, June De Maat, the social worker. Miss De Maat related her investigation to the hearing frequently relating out-of-court conversations she had with the alleged victim, Haley B. Haley B. was not called as a witness and as a result counsel for the appellant did not have the opportunity to test the veracity of her evidence by cross-examination. The appellant testified and flatly denied that he inflicted any sexual abuse upon the alleged victim.

Counsel for the appellant appeals upon three grounds:

(1) The hearing officer found against the appellant on the hearsay evidence of June De Maat (some of it hearsay upon hearsay) who repeated the complaints and later denials made to her by Haley B; and that in so doing there was a denial of natural justice. This hearsay evidence was admissible because s. 15(1) of the *Statutory Powers Procedure Act*, RSO 1980, c. 484, is made applicable to the hearing by s. 52(14) of the Act.

· · ·

In argument before us counsel for the respondent quite candidly admitted that the alleged victim was not called to testify because she had changed her "story" and would not say that she had been abused or molested by the appellant. The alleged victim was aged 12 at the time of the alleged abuse and aged 14 at the time of the hearing. There was no indication of any kind that she could not have testified at the hearing or that there were any impediments to having her sworn as a witness. As I understand the submission of counsel for the respondent, he conceded that he could not have succeeded had she been called as a witness because she would deny any molestation by the appellant. Had she been called to testify and made that denial, leave might well have been given to counsel for the respondent to cross-examine her as to her alleged previous inconsistent statements. (There is no indication that she made any statements in writing.) If the alleged victim then admitted that she made the previous inconsistent statements but did not adopt them as being true, those statements would be of limited evidential value, that is, they would only go to her credibility and not to the truth of the facts referred to in the statements: Sopinka and Lederman, *Evidence in Civil Cases* at 505-8. Therefore, had she been called as a witness, it seems to me that it would be almost impossible for the hearing officer to make a finding against the appellant upon hearsay evidence in the face of a denial of sexual abuse by the alleged victim and the appellant. Because of s. 15(1) of the *Statutory Powers Procedure Act* the hearing officer was able to rely upon hearsay evidence. In so doing he stated in part: "I believe the child's first account of what happened." He did not give any reasons why he rejected the denial evidence of the appellant J.B.

It is our view that in the circumstances mentioned, where the appellant was denied the right to cross-examine the alleged victim, the admission of the hearsay evidence did amount to a denial of natural justice; the hearing in this case fell below the minimum requirement of fairness. The appellant was not convicted of sexual molestation but nevertheless it is a grievous stigma to have one's name in the Child Abuse Register where it may remain for 25 years.

Appeal allowed.

NOTE

See to the same effect *S(I) v. Child and Family Services of Western Manitoba* (1993), 99 DLR (4th) 760 (Man. CA). Access to the alleged victim for the purposes of cross-examination in contexts such as this remains controversial. See, in the context of sexual harassment complaints, the contrasting judgments of *Masters*, above; *Semchuk v. Regina School Division No. 4* (1987), 37 DLR (4th) 738 (Sask. CA); aff'g. (1986), 26 Admin. LR 88 (Sask. QB); and *YB v. RW* (1985), 16 Admin. LR 99 (Ont. Div. Ct.), all denying an entitlement to cross-examine; and *Healey v. Memorial University of Newfoundland* (1993), 14 Admin. LR (2d) 259 (Nfld. SC), sustaining such a claim.

THE LIMITS OF THE TRIAL-TYPE HEARING

An important and general problem for lawyers is the appropriate uses and limits of the trial-type hearing. This problem can most usefully be examined at this point, after a study of its characteristic element, cross-examination.

Consider a proposal by an electric utility to construct and operate a large generating plant. A proposal of this kind involves at least three general questions:

1. Is the power needed? This question involves projections about population and economic growth for decades, estimates of the availability of alternative sources of energy, and values about the kind of society "we" desire and the price to be paid for it.

2. What shall be the technology? This question involves knowledge and choices about the scale of technology to be used (shall we continue to use large generating plants or shift to smaller more decentralized plants?) and fuels.

3. What shall be the environmental tradeoffs? The environmental impact of any large generating plant is large, and therefore this question is part of the first two. How can the impacts be minimized, to the extent that they are inescapable, and are we willing to bear them and, if so, on whom shall they be imposed?

Consider in particular one apparently small issue of environmental tailoring. Assume that decisions have been made to have a large plant on the shore of a lake and to use water from the lake for cooling. The plant will take immense amounts of water from the lake and will return it at a higher temperature than it was taken. The effect on aquatic life of an increase in water temperature of this kind is uncertain and debated. Assume that there is a spawning ground close to the shore and close to the proposed location. If the outlet pipe for the water is near the shore, the warm water may destroy or seriously damage this spawning ground. The total effect will depend not only on the uncertain effect of the warm water, but on its size and on the number of other spawning grounds—in this lake or in the country or in the world. Should the pipe be extended far out into the lake, at a cost of millions of dollars? Or will the lake currents simply push the warm water back to shore?

Assume that the decisions about the proposal generally and about the length of the outlet pipe will be made by an environmental assessment board. (The decisions may ultimately be made by the government, for example, through a requirement of approval or a right of appeal.) What kind of hearing is appropriate, and what kind of hearing is required?

We suggest that the decision has two characteristics that can usefully be separated: fact findings and choice. The fact finding is a determination of the current knowledge about the nature and extent of the harm, if any, to aquatic life that will be caused by the warm water, and the cost and effectiveness of longer and shorter outlet pipes. We do not mean to suggest that the board can hope to determine what the effect will be (even apart from difficulties about the word "fact" and the difficulties implicit in a determination that a plaintiff was not telling the truth, or exceeding the speed limit). One of the elements of the determination will be the extent and risks of uncertainty. This determination involves an understanding and assessment of complex technology, and it may be facilitated by the distinction between legislative and adjudicative facts introduced in the reading from Davis about official notice. What do the readings from Robinson and McGarity (below) suggest about the uses and limits of cross-examination?

Given the determination about "facts," the board must make a choice that is ultimately between money and an (uncertain) harm to the fish. In other contexts, the choice might be more complex and might not involve any element that could be easily expressed in money. For example, the location of a transmission line from the plant might involve a choice among blighting an attractive landscape, using prime agricultural land, and endangering rare animal life in a swamp. A trial is an awkward process for making a choice of this kind. "The decision to go forward with nuclear plants is ... a value judgment that the risk is worth assuming. One can argue whether a risk should be taken, but it is not useful to try that question in the traditional adjudicatory setting" (Murphy, "The *National Environmental Policy Act* and the Licencing Process" (1972), 72 *Columbia LR* 963 at 991). A trial process may often disguise choice as fact finding or the application of general standards. But what hearing procedures are appropriate for making a choice?

McGarity, "Substantive and Procedural Discretion in Administrative Resolution of Science Policy Questions: Regulating Carcinogens in EPA and OSHA" (1979), 67 *Georgetown LJ* 729, at 776-78

The purpose of trial-type procedures is to increase the accuracy of agency factual determinations. A court should not insist that the agency utilize wasteful formal factfinding procedures for issues in which such procedures cannot increase the accuracy of the agency's decision. Even the old paradigm, which provides informal summary judgment procedures for policy issues, recognizes that trial-type procedures will not increase the "accuracy" of a policy decision. Similarly, no amount of confrontation and cross-examination will increase the accuracy with which an agency determines trans-scientific questions that cannot be resolved by experimentation. Furthermore, trial-type procedures will not aid in resolving questions plagued by insufficient data, although they might be useful in identifying and quantifying the costs and benefits of delay pending further experimentation.

When the experts disagree in their interpretations of scientific data, trial-type procedure at first glance might seem appropriate. Extensive cross-examination could probe the real differences in interpretation and might provide the decision-maker with some basis for choosing between the experts. Unfortunately, cross-examination usually reveals only the depth of the disagreement among the experts; it rarely reveals any basis for choosing one expert's interpretation of the data over another's.

Cross-examination, however, can be of great value in probing inferences. Direct oral testimony and cross-examination provide an opportunity to examine the assumptions upon which an expert bases his interpretation. The assumptions an expert uses can be result-oriented and highly policy-dominated. The validity of the scientist's assumptions will obviously affect the accuracy of his inferences. The decision-maker should be aware of those assumptions to be able to draw his own conclusions.

Agencies should engage in formal factfinding to enhance factual accuracy. But countervailing considerations exist in the form of reduced administrative efficiency and increased expense to all parties to the proceedings. Thus, even when formal factfinding enhances accuracy, these "transaction costs" may outweigh any benefits derived from increased accuracy.

A more detailed breakdown of transaction costs would include the resources lost to the agency, the resources lost to all other parties participating in the hearing, and the harm resulting from *status quo* during the additional time it takes to conduct the formal proceedings. On the benefit side, the need for formal proceedings would depend on the value of the affected interests, the degree to which inaccurate decisions would affect those interests, and the likelihood that formal factfinding will reduce uncertainty on the particular issue in question.

Robinson, "The Making of Administrative Policy: Another Look at Rulemaking and Adjudication and Administrative Procedure Reform"
(1970), 118 *U Pa. L Rev.* 485, at 521-23

Challenges to the suitability of adjudicative methods (particularly the reliance on testimonial evidence and cross-examination) where the issues involve policy planning, appear to rest in large part on the notion that "policy," or, to use Professor Davis' phrase, "legislative fact," is something pure, uncontaminated by particular data and questions, assumptions, opinions and biases which have been regarded as properly the subject of such methods in other contexts. But a judgment on policy or "legislative fact" invariably involves an admixture of particular facts, opinions, and biases, some of which may and some of which may not be appropriate for exploration by testimony and cross-examination. To say categorically that general policy questions or "legislative facts" cannot fruitfully be explored by testimonial procedures and cross-examination is to generalize to an extent which can only obscure analysis. Noteworthy in this respect is the *Blocked Space* court's statement that the principal issue in that case called for "expert opinions and forecasts" which "cannot be decisively resolved by testimony" and is therefore the "kind of issue where a month of experience will be worth a year of hearings": *American Airlines Inc. v. CAB*, 359 F (2d) 624 (DC Cir. 1966). The theory, apparently, is that predictive judgments or forecasts are a class apart from "historical facts," and techniques of testimonial proof and cross-examination are inappropriate in determining the former even though appropriate for the latter. Such a distinction seems untenable.

First, it is doubtful that predictive judgment is radically different from determinations of historical fact. In both cases the determination must almost invariably rest on general conclusions that are inferred from particular factual data and an evaluation of probabilities that may be as appropriate for testimonial proof and cross-examination in one case as in the other.

Second, in some cases testimonial proof and cross-examination can serve a more valuable function in testing forecasts and generalized conclusions underlying future policy planning than in making findings concerning specific past events. For example, assume that a witness testifies before the CAB that in 1960 there were X tons of air freight carried by combination carriers. American Airlines disputes this by showing that it was only Y tons of freight. Cross-examination of the witness would generally be of little utility in situations like this where the fact in question can be readily and effectively disputed simply by offering contradictory data. Suppose, however, there is no dispute over the number of tons involved, but the witness takes the position that most of the X tons of freight should be carried not by combination carriers but by all-cargo carriers because this will strengthen these specialized service carriers, which in turn will promote air freight and also serve the public interest. If the witness's testimony is disputed, the fact in controversy is what the *Blocked Space* opinion evidently regards as "legislative fact," not appropriate for testimonial proof and cross-examination. But is this sound? Even if there is no dispute about specific identifiable "facts," such as number of freight tons involved, and even if the Board's judgment cannot be proved or disproved as easily as its finding as to the number of tons, it may still be desirable to force the Board, through cross-examination of its experts, to disclose the particular premises, including facts, opinions, and reasoning, which underlie its "policy" conclusions. Notwithstanding the absence of any contest over the one readily identifiable "fact," cross-examination of Board witnesses could play an important role in exposing possible error, bias, or lack of solid foundation which cannot be effectively brought to light simply by introducing rebuttal argument against the generalized policy statements. At the very least it puts some burden on the agency to explain and articulate the assumptions and the foundations on which its policy rests. It has been observed that cross-examination may not only expose many errors of judgment, but the very prospect of cross-examination can impose a discipline on the presentation. Thus, the knowledge that a written exhibit containing economic data and judgments cannot simply slide surreptitiously into a giant record, but is subject to publicity by cross-examination, can have a healthy disciplinary effect on the presentation of the evidence and the ultimate decision-making process.

The Law Reform Commission of Canada, in its working paper no. 25, "Independent Administrative Agencies" (1980), said:

> Generally the courts have determined that the closer administrative proceedings come to deciding questions involving initial restraints on liberty, confiscation of property rights, or the

imposition of other significant sanctions, the stricter should be the procedural guarantees of fairness. We are in accord with this position, and recommend that:

> 6.2 Hearings with the full panoply of traditional legal procedural safeguards, including the right of parties to call and examine witnesses and present their arguments and submissions, the conducting of cross-examination of witnesses, and the making of decisions based on the hearings record, should be used by agencies when dealing with issues of this kind.

After emphasizing the costs of hearings and the need to develop modification and alternatives, the commission continued:

> There are many types of cases where a court-like hearing is not warranted, but some kind of hearing is required for the sake of fairness or accuracy. To cover these situations, we recommend that:

> 6.3 Minimum procedural safeguards should be adopted requiring that appropriate notice of hearings be given, written comment from interested persons be solicited and considered, and the supplementary use be made of written interrogatories, oral comment and cross-examination in certain cases or on specific issues, at the discretion of the agency. This kind of hearing would include rule-making proceedings.

There has been concern in some quarters with the length and expense of hearings into major government projects and an emerging sense of the need to re-evaluate the process under which such public inquiries take place. As the title of the following article indicates, many critics place the blame for the situation on lawyers and the imposition of court-like processes: Shier and Speigal, "Environmental Approvals: Are Lawyers to Blame for Interminable Hearings?" (1990), 6 *Admin. LJ* 18. See also D. Mullan, "Tribunals Imitating Courts—Foolish Flattery or Sound Policy?" (2005), 28 *Dal. LJ* 1. We examine some of these problems in greater detail in chapter 7, Rulemaking.

POST-HEARING ISSUES

Reasons

As we have seen, both the SPPA (s. 17(1)) and the Alberta *Administrative Procedures and Jurisdiction Act* (s. 7) require decision-makers coming within their purview to give reasons for their decisions (though, in the case of the SPPA only on request). Section 8 of the Québec *Act Respecting Administrative Justice* and s. 51 of the British Columbia *Administrative Tribunals Act* each have a similar provision. We have also seen that, until recently, the common law was reluctant to impose on statutory and prerogative decision-makers an obligation to give reasons for their decisions. All of that changed in 1999 with the judgment of the Supreme Court of Canada in *Baker v. Canada (Minister of Citizenship and Immigration)*, [1999] 2 SCR 817 (Can.) (see chapter 2 of this text).

Clearly, the Supreme Court did not hold that all exercises of statutory or prerogative power now involve the giving of reasons. In *Baker* itself, it was obviously the importance of the interest at stake that triggered the obligation. As in other parts of judicial review law, that begs the question where the threshold of sufficient importance lies. The judgment, echoing earlier authority, also seems to accept that the existence of a statutory right of appeal from the decision will normally generate an entitlement to reasons. It is, however, interesting that the court does not cite two judgments in which reasons were held to be a requirement where necessary to facilitate the constitutionally guaranteed right to judicial review for jurisdictional error: *Société des services Ozanam Inc. v. Commission municipale du Québec*, [1994] RJQ 364 (Que. SC) and *Future Inns Canada Inc. v. Nova Scotia (Labour Relations Board)* (1997), 4 Admin. LR (3d) 248 (NS CA). Nonetheless, in another context, the court did refer to the need to ensure that an affected person's entitlement to judicial review is not frustrated. This was in *CUPE, Local No. 301 v. Montreal (City)*, [1997] 1 SCR 793 (Que.) where L'Heureux-Dubé J, delivering the judgment of the court, held that the absence of a transcript of a tribunal's proceedings could be a fatal error if that led to an inability to make out a case for judicial review on the grounds alleged. It is, therefore, puzzling why there is no explicit reference in *Baker* to the facilitation of judicial review. Of course, that does not preclude such a consideration coming within the tantalizingly vague residual category: "other circumstances."

More generally, as we will see below, the tendency of the courts since *Baker* has been to require the provision of reasons. However, that has not universally been the case, as in *Service Corp. International (Canada) Inc. v. Burnaby (City)* (1999), 9 MPLR (3d) 242 (BC SC), where it was held that municipal corporations were not obliged even after *Baker* to provide reasons for decisions in planning matters. See also *Gigliotti v. Conseil d'administration du Collège des Grands Lacs* (2005), 76 OR (3d) 581, where the Ontario Divisional Court held, at para. 54, that a minister's decision to close a college was a "policy decision" and that "[n]o reasons are required to establish or close a college."

The Content of the Duty To Give Reasons

When an administrative body is legally required to give reasons for its decisions, what are the contents of this duty? Obviously, giving no explanation at all for its decision will not satisfy the common law or statutory standard. A duty to give reasons means that adequate reasons must be given; but how do we measure the "adequacy" of a tribunal's reasons? Do they have to deal with every possible question of law, fact, or discretion that may bear on the decision?

Do they have to explain how the tribunal dealt with each and every point made in oral or written representations submitted to it? How specific do they have to be? If a tribunal's duty to give reasons includes a statement of its findings of material fact, must the tribunal set out the supporting evidence? Do they even have to be in the form of the reasons given by judges? Might it sometimes be appropriate simply to refer to existing agency policy statements? As so often in administrative law, when rules that are stated in general language have to be applied to very different contexts, it is difficult to give a simple answer that will hold true in all cases.

Any attempt to formulate a standard of adequacy that must be met before a tribunal can be said to have discharged its duty to give reasons must ultimately reflect the purposes served by a duty to give reasons. For example, in order to assure the parties that the hearing has given them a meaningful opportunity to influence the decision-maker, and to limit the risk of error by the tribunal, the reasons should show that the tribunal addressed itself to the parties' arguments on any significant question of law relevant to the case, and should indicate the basis on which it resolved the dispute.

If the decision is challenged on an appeal or an application for judicial review, the court will test the adequacy of the reasons by asking whether, in the light of the issues in dispute and the arguments and evidence advanced by the parties at the hearing before the tribunal, the tribunal's reasons are sufficient to enable the court effectively to scrutinize the decision. To be balanced against these is the consideration that to require unduly elaborate and punctilious reasons and findings may put unjustifiable burdens on the tribunal. A requirement to give reasons should be interpreted in such a way that the extra costs, such as delayed decision making and the waste involved in encouraging administrative decisions to be challenged on formalistic grounds, do not exceed any perceptible improvements in the quality of either the overall standard of administrative justice in the agency's work or the substantive merits of the individual decision. These ideas are well illustrated in *Lake v. Canada (Minister of Justice)*, 2008 SCC 23, where the Supreme Court, at para. 46, dismissed Lake's claim that the reasons delivered by the minister of justice in support of his decision to extradite Lake to face drug trafficking charges in the United States were inadequate because they did not fully canvass the close to a dozen relevant factors outlined in *United States of America v. Cotroni*, [1989] 1 SCR 564—the leading extradition case:

> [The minister's] reasons need not be comprehensive. The purpose of providing reasons is two-fold: to allow the individual to understand why the decision was made; and to allow the reviewing court to assess the validity of the decision. The Minister's reasons must make it clear that he considered the individual's submissions against extradition and must provide some basis for understanding why those submissions were rejected. Though the Minister's Cotroni analysis was brief in the instant case, it was in my view sufficient. The Minister is not required to provide a detailed analysis for every factor. An explanation based on what the Minister considers the most persuasive factors will be sufficient for a reviewing court to determine whether his conclusion was reasonable.

If the decision involved an exercise of discretion, the reasons should demonstrate that the tribunal recognized that it had a power to choose and the factors that it considered in exercising it. When the tribunal's application of a statutory standard depends on the existence of certain facts, the reasons should include the findings of fact made by the tribunal and indicate the evidence on which the tribunal based its findings. See, for example, *Canadian Association of Broadcasters v. Society of Composers, Authors and Music Publishers of Canada*, 2006 FCA 337, where the Federal Court of Appeal quashed a decision of the Copyright Board certifying tariffs of the royalties payable by commercial radio broadcasters to composers, authors, and music publishers. The board had determined that the previous tariff had underestimated by 10 to 15 percent the value of music to commercial broadcasters, warranting a 10 percent increase in the SOCAN tariff. However, it based its quantification of the undervaluation on "the evidence taken as a whole" without referring to any specific evidence, as none of the parties had adduced evidence bearing on this point. In setting aside the board's decision, Evans JA stated, at para. 17:

> In my view, it was not sufficient in the circumstances of this case for the Board to justify its quantification ... by merely referring to the evidence taken as a whole. It is not enough to say

in effect: "We are the experts. This is the figure: trust us." The Board's reasons on this issue served neither to facilitate a meaningful judicial review, nor to provide future guidance for regulatees.

As noted by the Ontario Court of Appeal in *Clifford v. Ontario Municipal Employees Retirement System*, 2009 ONCA 670 (CanLII), at para. 40, a tribunal is not required by the duty to give reasons to refer to evidence that could have led it to decide differently: "[R]easons need not refer to every piece of evidence to be sufficient, but must simply provide an adequate explanation of the basis upon which the decision was reached."

When a tribunal's findings depend on the assessment of the credibility of witnesses who gave conflicting accounts of the relevant facts, it may often be unrealistic to require a tribunal to elaborate its conclusion. However, courts are liable to require more specificity when the tribunal rejected the only *viva voce* evidence in favour of either hearsay or the tribunal's general impression of the witness. Consider, for example, *Hilo v. Minister of Employment and Immigration* (1991), 130 NR 236 (FCA), an appeal from a rejection by the Immigration and Refugee Board of the appellant's claim to refugee status. The board had stated that

> [t]he claimant's testimony lacked detail and was sometimes inconsistent. He was often unable to answer questions and sometimes appeared uninterested in doing so. While this may be partly due to the claimant's young age, the panel was not fully satisfied of his credibility as a witness.

In allowing the appeal Heald J said (at 238):

> The appellant was the only witness who gave oral testimony before the Board. His evidence was uncontradicted. The only comments as to his credibility are contained in the short passage quoted *supra*. That passage is troublesome because of its ambiguity. It does not amount to an outright rejection of the appellant's evidence but it appears to cast a nebulous cloud over its reliability. In my view, the Board was under a duty to give its reasons for casting doubt. ... Surely particulars of the lack of detail and of the inconsistencies should have been provided. Likewise, particulars of his inability to answer questions should have been made available.

And for the factors that a tribunal should consider when making a finding about the credibility of a witness, see *Pitts v. Ontario (Ministry of Community and Social Services, Director of Family Benefits Branch)* (1985), 51 OR (2d) 302 (Div. Ct.) and *College of Nurses of Ontario v. Quiogue* (1993), 13 OR (3d) 325 (Div. Ct.).

In the wake of *Baker*, Lorne Sossin expressed a concern that the seemingly broad reach of the duty to give reasons might lead to that requirement having only symbolic value. He saw in some of the first decisions applying a reasons requirement ominous support for this concern. See Sossin, "Developments in Administrative Law: The 1997-98 and 1998-99 Terms" (2000), 11 *Sup. Ct. LR* (2d) 37, at 74-75:

> The danger in the Court's approach is that it may be perceived as casting the net too broadly in terms of what will constitute reasons. The Court clearly is mindful of the administrative burden that requiring written reasons may occasion. Indeed, this was often cited as a principal justification for why no duty to provide reasons was appropriate in the administrative sphere. However, it is possible to read this aspect of *Baker* as an indication that the reasons requirement may be satisfied in an informal and even ad hoc fashion. This would be an unfortunate result.
>
> Regrettably, the lower courts applying *Baker* do appear to be interpreting the written reasons requirement as more of a symbolic than a substantive burden on the government. For example, in *Xu v. Canada (Minister of Citizenship and Immigration)* [(1999), 172 FTR 294],

Gibson J considered a judicial review of a decision of a visa officer rejecting the applicant's application for an authorization to study in Canada on a visitor's visa. A letter setting out the reasons denying the application was prepared and dated several days prior to the visa officer interviewing the applicant. This letter was handed to the applicant at the conclusion of the interview. While Gibson J had little trouble concluding that pre-written reasons constituted bias, as well as a fettering of discretion, he went on to acknowledge, in obiter, that a form letter prepared prior to an interview, but modified subsequently to fit the facts of the application, would likely meet the reasons requirement. In *Liang v. Canada (Minister of Citizenship and Immigration)* [1999] FCJ No. 1301 (QL) (TD), Evans J considered a judicial review arising from a consular program manager's decision to reject an application for humanitarian and compassionate considerations from a citizen of China who wished to join his father in Canada. No reasons were provided beyond the ticking of a box marked "denied" on a form. Applying *Baker*, Evans J first held that the requirement to provide reasons only applies where an applicant has requested and been denied reasons (in the case before him, no such request had been made). If it were necessary, however, Evans J indicated that he would be prepared to infer reasons from the ticking of the "denied" box on the form based on the facts before the immigration official.

If the requirement to provide written reasons is to be a meaningful component of the duty of fairness, those reasons must, at a minimum, shed some light on the actual reasoning of the decision-maker. Elevating form letters and tick boxes to the status of reasons, even if appropriate in some specific institutional and factual contexts, may seriously erode the fairness of the administrative process. Further, on this standard, the notes of the first-level immigration officer in *Baker* appear to shed little, if any, light on the thinking of the decision-making officer, on whom the duty to provide reasons rests.

Sossin's fear of symbolic interpretation may have been justified during the immediate aftermath of *Baker* (*Xu v. Canada*, above, was decided just three weeks after the *Baker* judgment, and *Liang v. Canada*, above, in the following month). However, the subsequent case law now suggests that the lower courts are giving *Baker* a substantive reading. A case survey conducted in June 2001 by Bruce Ettis and Evan Smith of the University of Toronto Faculty of Law revealed that, in a majority of the 50 lower-court decisions sampled, the remaining courts required more or less formal reasons and did not subscribe to a symbolic notion of the reasons requirement. In *Suresh v. Canada (Minister of Citizenship and Immigration)*, [2002] 1 SCR 3 (Can.), at para. 126, the Supreme Court required that substantial reasons be provided to individuals targeted for deportation based on the claim that they are a "danger to the public or the security of Canada":

The Minister must provide reasons for her decision. These reasons must articulate and sustain a finding that there are no substantial grounds to believe that the individual who is subject to the [ministerial] declaration will be subjected to torture, execution or other cruel or unusual treatment, so long as the person under consideration has raised those arguments. The reasons must also articulate why, subject to privilege or valid legal reasons for not disclosing detailed information, the Minister believes the individual to be a danger to the security of Canada as required by the Act. In addition, the reasons must emanate from the person making the decision, in this case the Minister, rather than take the form of advice or suggestion, such as the memorandum of Mr. Gautier. Mr. Gautier's report, explaining the position of Citizenship and Immigration Canada is more like a prosecutor's brief than a statement of reasons for a decision.

The following judgment of the Federal Court of Appeal is further evidence that courts are giving the *Baker* reasons requirement a substantive reading, although in a setting far removed from *Baker* and *Suresh*.

VIA Rail Canada Inc. v. National Transportation Agency
[2001] 2 FC 25 (CA) (footnotes omitted)

SEXTON JA (Linden and Evans JJA concurring):
This is an appeal from a decision of the National Transportation Agency (the "Agency") dated November 28, 1995 that held that a portion of VIA Rail's Special and Joint Passenger Tariff (the "tariff") constitutes an undue obstacle to the mobility of persons with disabilities.

Facts

In December, 1993, a team of wheelchair basketball athletes travelled from Saint-Hyacinthe to Toronto using VIA Rail. Eight members of the group were physically disabled persons travelling in wheelchairs. Each was accompanied by an attendant to assist them with their basic needs during the trip. In accordance with the provisions of the tariff, the attendants travelled for free. The group encountered a number of difficulties related to the accessibility of VIA's services to the disabled passengers.

Upon application by M. Jean Lemonde, the party's leader for the trip, the Agency conducted an investigation into a number of specific complaints. The Agency concluded that certain actions and practices of VIA constituted obstacles to the mobility of the persons with disabilities in the party and that those obstacles "were undue because they could have easily been avoided by the carrier." In a decision communicated by letter dated November 4, 1994, it ordered VIA to take a number of corrective measures. VIA subsequently complied with those orders to the satisfaction of the Agency.

In the same November, 1994 decision, the Agency called attention to Section 13-D of VIA's Special and Joint Passenger Tariff 1, NTA 1, the relevant portions of which are reproduced below:

Section 13-D DISABLED PERSON AND ATTENDANT

1. CONDITIONS
A ticket may be sold for the transportation of a disabled person and one adult attendant (at the fare authorized in 3 upon ... [a list of conditions follows].
. . .
The attendant must be capable of assisting the disabled person to get on and off trains and of attending to his/her personal needs throughout the trip.
. . .

3. FARE BASIS
One fare (any fare which the disabled person would pay if travelling alone) will apply for the transportation of both passengers.

Thus, the tariff provides that an attendant who is capable of providing assistance to a disabled person who is unable to travel alone is entitled to travel for free.

With respect to the provisions of the tariff, the Agency made the following statements:

> The Agency specifies that the presence of an attendant is no excuse not to provide assistance to a person during boarding and deboarding.
>
> The Agency supports the principle pursuant to which the attendant must be capable of meeting the basic needs of the person s/he is accompanying and of offering the services which are not usually offered by a carrier. However, providing assistance during boarding and deboarding is the carrier's responsibility. Consequently, this assistance should not be imposed on the attendant. The obligation imposed on the latter to board and deboard a disabled person constitutes an obstacle to the mobility of the person and the Agency believes that disabled persons are entitled to receive the same level of service whether they are travelling alone or with an escort.

As a result of this finding, the Agency required VIA to show cause that the Agency should not find the obstacle "undue" and order VIA to remove the requirement from its tariff.

Decision Appealed From

Following the receipt of VIA's submissions, the Agency issued a further order and decision on November 28, 1995. It ordered that the words "[t]he attendant must be capable of assisting the disabled person to get on and off trains" be struck from the tariff and that a provision be added to clearly indicate VIA's responsibility to board and deboard all of its passengers. It indicated that VIA could add to the amended tariff a proviso allowing it to inquire, at the time of booking, whether the passenger's attendant would be able to assist VIA personnel, if necessary. It also ordered VIA to issue a bulletin to its employees informing them of the changes and to make consequential amendments to various printed materials.

The Agency's main finding with respect to the tariff was reported as follows:

> The Agency remains of the opinion that it is the responsibility of VIA to board and deboard its passengers. Under normal conditions and with sufficient advance notice, the carrier should be in a position to control the quality and level of services—both personnel and equipment—to accommodate the boarding and deboarding needs of passengers with disabilities. As a general principle, attendants are there to provide assistance of a personal nature to the person during the trip. To put the onus on the attendant that "the attendant must be capable of assisting the disabled person to get on or off trains ..." as found in VIA's Special Local and Joint Passenger tariff, is an undue obstacle to the mobility of persons with disabilities.

[After setting out the relevant legislation and describing the proceedings, Sexton JA continued:]

It is necessary, therefore, to deal with the questions of whether or not the Agency erred in law by failing to articulate adequate reasons for:

1. Its finding that s. 13-D of the tariff constituted an obstacle to the mobility of disabled persons; and

2. Its finding that such obstacle is "undue."

For the reasons which appear below, I believe that the reasons given by the Agency were inadequate.

Analysis

The Duty To Give Reasons

Although the Act itself imposes no duty on the Agency to give reasons, s. 39 of the *National Transportation Agency General Rules* does impose such a duty. In this case, the Agency chose to provide its reasons in writing.

The duty to provide reasons is a salutary one. Reasons serve a number of beneficial purposes including that of focusing the decision-maker on the relevant factors and evidence. In the words of the Supreme Court of Canada:

> Reasons, it has been argued, foster better decision making by ensuring that issues and reasoning are well articulated and, therefore, more carefully thought out. The process of writing reasons for decision by itself may be a guarantee of a better decision. [*Baker*, at 845.]

Reasons also provide the parties with the assurance that their representations have been considered.

In addition, reasons allow the parties to effectuate any right of appeal or judicial review that they might have. They provide a basis for an assessment of possible grounds for appeal or review. They allow the appellate or reviewing body to determine whether the decision-maker erred and thereby render him or her accountable to that body. This is particularly important when the decision is subject to a deferential standard of review.

Finally, in the case of a regulated industry, the regulator's reasons for making a particular decision provide guidance to others who are subject to the regulator's jurisdiction. They provide a standard by which future activities of those affected by the decision can be measured.

The duty to give reasons is only fulfilled if the reasons provided are adequate. What constitutes adequate reasons is a matter to be determined in light of the particular circumstances of each case. However, as a general rule, adequate reasons are those that serve the functions for which the duty to provide them was imposed. In the words of my learned colleague Evans JA, "Any attempt to formulate a standard of adequacy that must be met before a tribunal can be said to have discharged its duty to give reasons must ultimately reflect the purposes served by a duty to give reasons." [J.M. Evans et al., *Administrative Law*, 4th ed. (Toronto: Emond Montgomery, 1995), at 507.]

The obligation to provide adequate reasons is not satisfied by merely reciting the submissions and evidence of the parties and stating a conclusion. Rather, the decision-maker must set out its findings of fact and the principal evidence upon which those findings were based. The reasons must address the major points in issue. The reasoning process followed by the decision-maker must be set out and must reflect consideration of the main relevant factors.

In my view, the general propositions stated above are all applicable in the circumstances of the case at bar. However, in this case, I believe that the adequacy of the Agency's reasons must be measured with particular reference to the extent to which they provide VIA with sufficient guidance to formulate their tariff without running afoul of the Agency and to the extent to which they give effect to VIA's right of appeal by providing this Court with sufficient insight into the Agency's reasoning process and the factors that it considered.

Therefore, I believe that for this Court to hold that the Agency's reasons are adequate, we must find that those reasons set out the basis upon which the Agency found that the existence of the tariff constituted an obstacle, that they reflect the reasoning process by which the Agency determined that the obstacle was undue and include a consideration of the main factors relevant to such a determination.

I now turn to the questions posed above.

Issue 1: Did the Agency provide adequate reasons for its finding that Section 13-D of the tariff constitutes an obstacle to the mobility of passengers with disabilities?

In the words of the tariff, did the Agency's reasons provide sufficient indication of the reasoning process by which it determined that it is an obstacle to the mobility of a disabled passenger to require that an attendant, travelling on the same ticket as the passenger, be capable of assisting the passenger in getting on and off the train?

The Agency determined that the tariff was an obstacle in its November, 1994 decision. The decision under appeal treats this earlier finding as a given. The only portion of the 1994 decision dealing with the reasons for the Agency's determination is reproduced in paragraph 6 above. It is worth noting that the tariff was not a subject of the original complaint filed by M. Lemonde. Its provisions seem to have come before the Agency only as a result of VIA's reference to it in its submission responding to the complaint.

In my view, the conclusion that the tariff was an obstacle is not supported by sufficient indication of the reasoning process engaged in by the Agency. The reasons provide no intimation of what constitutes an obstacle to the mobility of a disabled passenger nor are they sufficiently clear.

The Concise Oxford Dictionary defines "obstacle" as a "thing that obstructs progress." Not only has the Agency failed to articulate any definition but it also does not appear to have engaged in any reasoned consideration of the tariff provisions. How does the requirement that an attendant be capable of assisting the disabled person with whom they are travelling to board and deboard a train constitute an obstacle to the mobility of the disabled person? This is a question which the Agency did not answer and hence it erred in law.

There are a number of other inconsistencies on the face of the reasons that provide support for my view that the reasons with respect to the finding that the tariff was an obstacle were inadequate. In both its 1994 and 1995 decisions, the Agency accepted that an attendant must be capable of meeting the basic needs of the person he or she is accompanying and of offering services which are not usually offered by the carrier. One example of this would be in assisting the disabled passenger to travel to and from the washroom. Presumably, therefore, the attendant would be required to be capable of providing such assistance. This activity, like boarding or deboarding a train, involves physically assisting the disabled person in moving from one place to another and potentially into and out of a wheelchair. The Agency does not explain why the obligation of the attendant in respect of personal needs on board the train does not constitute an obstacle while any obligation in respect of being capable of providing help in boarding or deboarding does.

Another inconsistency is apparent in relation to an error made by the Agency in describing the condition imposed by the tariff. In the 1994 decision, it said: "The obligation imposed on the [attendant] to board and deboard a disabled person constitutes an obstacle to the mobility of the person. ..." This is not the obligation imposed by the tariff. The tariff merely provides that the attendant be capable of providing such assistance. While it implies the possibility that an attendant might be requested by VIA to provide physical assistance in boarding and deboarding disabled passengers, the condition does not impose a general obligation that the attendant do so in all circumstances. Indeed, the Agency accepted in its 1995 decision that, in general, VIA did provide such assistance to disabled passengers.

The Agency did use the proper wording when requiring VIA to show cause why the condition should not be removed and again in its 1995 decision. However, both of these references were made in contexts that arose after the Agency had reached the conclusion that the tariff was an obstacle.

I conclude, therefore, that the Agency erred in law by failing to provide adequate reasons for its decision that the tariff was an obstacle. Its reasons did not provide sufficient insight into the reasoning process followed. Moreover, they were not sufficiently clear with respect to the conclusion that is in issue.

Issue 2: Did the Agency err in law by failing to provide adequate reasons for its conclusion that any obstacle posed by the tariff was "undue"?

While there seems to be no jurisprudence dealing with what constitutes an undue obstacle to the mobility of disabled persons, the Courts have had ample opportunity to consider the use and interpretation of the term "undue" in other legislative contexts.

These include undue prevention or lessening of competition (*Combines Investigation Act*, now the *Competition Act*, RSC 1985, c. C-34), undue exploitation of sex (the *Criminal Code*, RSC 1985, c. C-46), undue delay in movement of freight (*Lord's Day Act*, RSC 1970, c. L-13) and undue hardship (human rights legislation).

While "undue" is a word of common usage which does not have a precise technical meaning the Supreme Court has variously defined "undue" to mean "improper, inordinate, excessive or oppressive" or to express "a notion of seriousness or significance." To this list of synonyms, the *Concise Oxford Dictionary* adds "disproportionate."

What is clear from all of these terms is that "undueness" is a relative concept. I agree with the position expressed by Cartwright J, as he then was:

> "Undue" and "unduly" are not absolute terms whose meaning is self-evident. Their use presupposes the existence of a rule or standard defining what is "due." Their interpretation does not appear to me to be assisted by substituting the adjectives "improper," "inordinate," "excessive," "oppressive" or "wrong," or the corresponding adverbs, in the absence of a statement as to what, in this connection, is proper, ordinate, permissible or right [*R v. Howard Smith Paper Mills Ltd.*, [1957] SCR 403, at 425].

The proper approach to determining if something is "undue," then, is a contextual one. "Undueness" must be defined in light of the aim of the relevant enactment. It can be useful to assess the consequences or effect if the undue thing is allowed to remain in place.

· · ·

In the case at bar, the Agency's reasons do not reveal sufficient indicators of the reasoning process it followed in interpreting the term "undue." They include no definition of the term "undue" or any indication of a "rule or standard defining what is 'due.'" In its submissions to this Court, the Agency argued that the definition that it had applied was that articulated in its November 1994 reasons: "... the obstacles ... were undue because they could have easily been avoided by the carrier." Even if this could be said to be true, the statement can only lead me to conclude that the Agency undertook no contextual analysis of the issue. It looked only to its perception of VIA's ability to avoid the obstacle. In my opinion, this was not sufficient.

In determining whether the obstacle was undue, the Agency should have first considered the aim of the *National Transportation Act, 1987*. This is found in s. 3(1), which provides that the nation's transportation network should be, *inter alia*, economic, efficient, viable and effective. The network must serve the needs of all travellers, including those with disabilities. In my opinion, the possibility that the economic and commercial objectives of the Act, the needs of non-disabled passengers and those of disabled passengers might be inconsistent in some circumstances was contemplated by Parliament and addressed by s-s. 3(1)(g). This provision provides that each carrier, so far as practicable, should conduct its business under conditions which do not constitute an undue obstacle to the mobility of disabled persons. The use of the words "so far as practicable," in addition to the use of the term "undue" provides further support for my view that the Agency was required to undertake a balancing of interests such that the satisfaction of one interest does not create disproportionate hardship affecting the other interest.

In its decision the Agency made no mention of s. 3 of the Act. I am forced to conclude that it did not have regard to it. Nor do the reasons indicate that the Agency engaged in any consideration of the impact upon VIA and all of its passengers of leaving the tariff in place as compared to removing it.

The Agency was required to consider all of the relevant factors and to balance them against each other. With respect to the interests of the disabled passengers the following factors might be relevant:

1. The difficulty of providing an escort who is capable of assisting the disabled person in boarding the train;

2. The difficulty of providing an escort who is willing to assist the disabled person in boarding the train;

3. The importance to the dignity of the individual that they be able to travel with as much independence as possible and their right to accessible travel.

With respect to VIA, the relevant factors may be collectively termed operational factors and commercial or economic factors. They might include the following:

1. The reasonable availability of personnel and equipment to assist in the boarding and disembarkation from trains;

2. The time required for providing assistance in boarding and deboarding;

3. The effect on scheduling of trains which are required to spend time boarding disabled persons in excess of that scheduled;

4. The impact of delays incurred as a result of boarding disabled persons on all passengers;

5. The impact of unscheduled delays on passenger confidence and the continued viability of VIA's passenger rail service;

6. VIA's ability to contract occasional workers to assist in boarding and deboarding, having regard to any collective bargaining agreements to which VIA is a party;

7. The requirement that such occasional workers be properly trained and insured to carry out their duties; and

8. The expense of providing additional personnel for boarding disabled persons, especially at small stations where only a modest complement of staff is available.

I note that the Agency did refer to some of the factors impacting upon VIA's operational requirements and its commercial viability. It did so mainly in the context of simply reciting VIA's submissions. The Agency agreed with VIA's position that it had an obligation to provide a timely and effective service to all of its passengers and accepted that, in general, VIA does provide assistance in boarding and deboarding to all of its passengers, whether disabled or not. It also recognized that scheduling constraints, large numbers of disabled passengers and insufficient personnel at some stations might impact upon VIA's ability to provide services to disabled passengers. Unfortunately, rather than dealing with those submissions in a reasoned manner, it simply expressed the belief that with sufficient advance notice and consultation between VIA and disabled passengers, problems of accessibility could be avoided.

In summary, the Agency failed to provide sufficient insight into the reasoning process that it followed or the factors that it considered in determining that any obstacle provided by the tariff was undue. In so doing, it erred in law.

Appeal allowed; matter remitted to National Transportation Agency.

NOTES

1. Consider the extent to which the court, under the guise of reviewing whether the reasons were adequate, in fact has conducted appellate reassessment of the agency's conclusions. This blurring of the divide between substantive and procedural review was specifically addressed by the Newfoundland and Labrador Court of Appeal in *Newfoundland and Labrador (Treasury Board) v. Newfoundland and Labrador Nurses' Union*, 2010 NLCA 13, at para. 12:

[A] comment may be of assistance regarding the interplay between adequacy of reasons in the context of procedural fairness and the first prong of the *Dunsmuir* analysis, that is, the aspect of reasonableness directed to the process of articulating the reasons, requiring justification, transparency and intelligibility in the decision-making process. Clearly, the *Dunsmuir* analysis requires a consideration of the reasons provided by the tribunal. A failure to give reasons, or inadequate reasons, would be decisive in the reasonableness assessment. A complete lack of or inadequate reasons could not be said to provide the justification, transparency and intelligibility in the decision-making process required to satisfy reasonableness under the *Dunsmuir* analysis. Unless legislation eliminates the necessity for reasons, reasonableness is the standard required to be met by a tribunal. Since reasons, including adequacy thereof, constitute a component of reasonableness, a separate examination of procedural fairness is an unnecessary and unhelpful complication.

For a contrary view, see *Clifford v. Ontario Municipal Employees Retirement System*, 2009 ONCA 670 (CanLII), at paras. 31-32.

2. For an application of *VIA Rail*, see *Gray v. Ontario (Director, Disability Support Program)* (2002), 59 OR 364 (CA).

Effect of Breach of the Duty To Give Reasons

Whenever an administrative authority fails to comply with some formal or procedural requirement, whether imposed by the common law, statute, or the Charter, a question may arise about the legal consequences of the breach. Here we deal with this question in the context of a failure to discharge a legal duty to give reasons.

If it is apparent from the reasons for a decision, whether given voluntarily or under legal obligation, that the decision-maker misinterpreted the legislation or committed some other error of law, then the decision may be set aside. In addition, if a tribunal's reasons deal with some of the arguments and evidence adduced by the individual, a reviewing court may conclude that the tribunal failed to consider other relevant issues and set the decision aside on this ground: *MacDonald v. The Queen*, [1977] 2 SCR 665 (Can.); *R v. Burns*, [1994] 1 SCR 656 (BC). However, if the tribunal's reasons, read in a realistic manner, indicate that it applied its mind to the most important issues, a court will not necessarily infer from its silence about others that it ignored them altogether: *Kindler v. Attorney General of Canada*, [1987] 2 FC 145 (CA).

When the reasons given do contain some legal error, public authorities are not normally permitted to justify their decision, when challenged, on grounds not included in or contradictory to their stated reasons. When there is a legal duty to give reasons a court will generally regard the duty as mandatory, in the sense that if a tribunal refuses or fails to give reasons for a decision, it may be required by an order of *mandamus* to do so.

Two other questions are, however, somewhat less straightforward. First, if a tribunal gives reasons that do not reveal some legal error in its approach to the legislation but are unduly vague or ambiguous, can a court nonetheless, on an appeal or an application for judicial review, allow the appeal or set the decision aside as being wrong in law, even though in a substantive sense the decision was one that the tribunal could properly reach? Second, is a decision of a tribunal that is supported by bad reasons liable to be set aside, even though the tribunal has also included reasons that in law justify its conclusion?

The traditional judicial reluctance to require tribunals to give reasons for their decisions has reappeared in some jurisdictions as a refusal by the courts to hold that a failure to discharge a *statutory* duty to give adequate reasons does not necessarily render the decision erroneous in law and liable to be set aside on appeal or an application for judicial review. This is especially true in England, where the law seems to be that a tribunal's failure to give adequate reasons will only vitiate the decision if it can be inferred from the reasons given that the tribunal failed to take into account a matter that it was legally obliged to consider or took into consideration some irrelevant factor. If the court is left in doubt about the legal propriety of the tribunal's decision, then it should remit the case for further consideration by the tribunal. See especially, *Crake v. Supplementary Benefits Commission*, [1982] All ER 498 (Eng. QBD). In *Save Britain's Heritage v. Number 1 Poultry Ltd.*, [1991] 1 WLR 153 (Eng. HL), Lord Bridge, at 167, formulated the following test in the context of a statutory appeal in a land use planning matter, where it was argued that the decision of the tribunal should be set aside because its reasons were inadequate.

> The alleged deficiency will only afford a ground for quashing the decision if the court is satis-fied that the interests of the applicant have been substantially prejudiced by it.

It is not clear whether Lord Bridge intended this *dictum* to be of general application or to apply to decisions of the kind under consideration in that case, land-use planning appeals. However, in *R v. Higher Education Funding Council, ex parte Institute of Dental Surgery*, [1994] 1 WLR 242 (Eng. QBD), Sedley J said that a failure to give adequate reasons rendered the decision a nullity, although the court had discretion over the grant of relief.

On the whole, courts in Canada have taken the more robust view suggested by Sedley J. The trend in the more recent case law is that a decision that is not accompanied by adequate reasons may be set aside as erroneous in law. There are also suggestions that, if no reasons are given at all, the decision is null and void. See, for example, *Proulx v. Public Service Staff Relations Board*, [1978] 2 FC 133 (CA); *Northwestern Utilities Ltd. v. City of Edmonton*, [1979] 1 SCR 684, 706 (Alta.); *Blanchard v. Control Data Canada Ltd.*, [1984] 2 SCR 476, 500-1 (Que.); *Re Minister of Employment and Immigration and Singh* (1987), 35 DLR (4th) 680, 683-84 (FCA).

For a helpful summary of the relevant law, see Kushner, "The Right to Reasons in Administrative Law" (1976), 24 *Alta. LR* 305, 328-32; and for the theoretical implications of the diversity of judicial opinions on this issue, see Richardson, "The Duty To Give Reasons: Potential and Practice" (1986), *Public Law* 437, 450-57.

One explanation for the courts' surprisingly ambivalent attitude to the legal effect of a tribunal's breach of a statutory duty to provide adequate reasons is that it can be difficult to fashion the appropriate relief. If the absence of reasons is a legal flaw in the decision, the court will generally remit it to the tribunal, although there are cases where, on an appeal from the tribunal, the court has reversed the decision, and ended the dispute altogether: see, for example, *Wrights' Canadian Ropes Ltd. v. Minister of National Revenue*, [1947] AC 109 (Can. PC); *Re Alkali Lake Indian Band and Westcoast Transmission Co.* (1984), 8 DLR (4th) 610 (BC CA).

If the case is to be remitted, for what purpose? If all that is required is that the tribunal must give better reasons, is this not an invitation to provide an *ex post facto* rationalization, and no more than a mere formality? There may also be a practical difficulty in attempting to schedule a meeting of the members of the tribunal who heard the case. Alternatively, the case could be remitted for a complete rehearing before different members of the tribunal. But may this not be unduly onerous on the parties and on the agency, especially since there may be nothing substantively wrong with the decision? A less drastic option is to remit the case for a rehearing on those aspects not adequately dealt with in the tribunal's reasons; see, for example, *Orlowski v. British Columbia (Att. Gen.)* (1992), 94 DLR (4th) 541, 553 (BC CA).

A more limited hearing of this nature should be conducted by the original members of the tribunal, although their possible unavailability may make this solution unattractive as a practical matter.

The principal common law remedies available when the courts exercise a supervisory jurisdiction over administrative tribunals, *certiorari*, prohibition, *mandamus*, injunctions, and declarations are discretionary. One ground upon which a remedy may be refused that may be relevant here is contained in the Ontario *Judicial Review Procedure Act*, RSO 1980, c. 224, s. 3:

> On an application for judicial review in relation to a statutory power of decision, where the sole ground for relief established is a defect in form or a technical irregularity, if the court finds that no substantial wrong or miscarriage of justice has occurred, the court may refuse relief and, where the decision has already been made, may make an order validating the decision, notwithstanding such defect, to have effect from such time and on such terms as the court considers proper.

Should this provision or the courts' discretion at common law over granting the remedies be used to refuse relief or to validate a decision for which adequate reasons have not been given, but which in other respects seems correct?

In *Re Howatson and Assiniboine Park Community Committee* (1973), 37 DLR (3d) 584 (Man. QB), the court rejected an argument that the failure of a community committee, an advisory body on planning matters, to support its recommendations with reasons, as required by statute, could be cured by a provision in the legislation relating to "formal defects or omissions." Wilson J stated (at 596) that the purpose of the planning machinery was "to ensure that in each of the communities established, the residents shall enjoy in the fullest measure possible the right to watch their councillors at work upon the business of the community. And, where there is a zoning variation, to hear the reasons which the community committee accept as persuading them to recommend the change." And in *Re Don Howson Chevrolet Oldsmobile Ltd. and Registrar of Motor Vehicle Dealers and Salesmen* (1974), 51 DLR (3d) 683 (Ont. Div. Ct.), it was said that a statement of reasons by the registrar for proposing to suspend or revoke a licence was essential to the valid exercise of his power and that the Commercial Registration Appeal Tribunal, to which a licensee dissatisfied with the registrar's proposal may appeal, had no jurisdiction to hear an appeal against a proposal that was unsupported by reasons. This decision implicitly supports the view that a failure to give reasons when legally required will not normally be viewed as a mere formal error that can be excused by a higher administrative body or a reviewing court.

The effect on a decision of the presence of bad reasons as well as good would appear to be that, if a court is satisfied that the reasons given are independent or alternative, then the decision may be upheld on the basis of the valid reasons. Where the reasons appear cumulative, the decision will generally be set aside. However, it is sometimes possible to sever an invalid reason, particularly where it is clearly subsidiary. It is more usual, though, for a court to decline to speculate whether the tribunal would have decided the dispute in the same way if it had realized that it could not in law rely upon all the reasons given.

For example, in *Malloch v. Aberdeen Corporation (No. 2)*, [1974] SLT 253 (Scot. First Div.), the defendants dismissed a school teacher in Scotland on the grounds that, by virtue of certain regulations, he was ineligible for employment and that "in any event" the defendants chose as a matter of their own policy not to employ a person who did not have the qualifications set out in the regulations. The regulations were subsequently held to be *ultra vires*; the decision to dismiss was upheld because the second reason for the decision was independent of the first and did not fall with it. Similarly, in *International Longshoremen's and Warehousemen's Union, Local 502 v. Matus*, [1982] 2 FC 549 (CA), it was held that the principal reason given by the Canada Labour Relations Board for its decision was based on a patently unreasonable interpretation of a provision of the *Canada Labour Code*. However, the decision was not set aside because the board had given as an alternative reason one that was plainly correct.

On the other hand, in *Re DiNardo and the Liquor Licence Board of Ontario* (1974), 49 DLR (3d) 537 (Ont. HC), the board had given three reasons for suspending a tavern-owner's licence: non-compliance with fire safety regulations, the "deplorable" condition of the premises, and a lack of "co-operation" on the part of the licensee with the police department. The court found that the last two reasons were defective. In the course of his judgment Morden J said:

> I have found that one of the reasons was based on an extraneous consideration, one either reflects an extraneous consideration or alternatively lacks any evidence in support of it and the third is relevant and there is some evidence on which it could be found. Can the decision stand? In my view it cannot. In coming to the decision that it did, the Board appears to rely upon the cumulative effect of the three findings. It has not based its decision on each of these findings considered alternatively. In the face of this, it is not for me to speculate on what the Board would have done if it had considered whether or not to base its decision on the one finding which I have held cannot be successfully challenged. In these circumstances, the decision itself must be set aside.

Finally, it should be remembered that it is the decision that can be set aside, and not simply the reasons, so that a party cannot ask a court to review the legality of the reasons if the decision ultimately was not adverse to the applicant: see *Re Libby, McNeill and Libby of Canada Ltd. and United Automobile etc. Workers of America* (1978), 91 DLR (3d) 281 (Ont. CA).

CHAPTER FIVE

Bias and Lack of Independence

INTRODUCTION

In this chapter, we consider in detail the second limb of the rules of natural justice or procedural fairness: the principle that decision-makers should be unbiased. Of course, if applied absolutely, this principle would result in the disqualification of all decision-makers. After all, everyone has biases in the sense of preferences, preconceptions, or predispositions. It is also the case that, whatever the issue for decision, adjudicators, by virtue of their backgrounds, personality, and training (everything that we think of as part of a person's "makeup"), are always going to possess tendencies (often deeply hidden and not part of their self-perception) to lean in one direction rather than another. Indeed, frequently, in the appointment of adjudicators, the possession of such attributes is regarded as a virtue. Thus, for example, the fact that a judge has demonstrated a particular commitment to the values seemingly inherent in the *Canadian Charter of Rights and Freedoms* may be one of a number of considerations that will influence the minister of justice in deciding whether to recommend the appointment of that person to the Supreme Court of Canada. This reflects not only a bias on the part of the appointing authority but also an appointment *for* or by reason of an apparently discernible bias. Few question the legitimacy of such practices (though many would argue that they should become more transparent in the sense, for example, of required parliamentary confirmation hearings).

What, therefore, is at stake is not disqualification for any form of bias but the identification of what constitute impermissible biases. In at least one sense, the Latin phrasing of the principle captures the essence of the range of inquiry: *nemo judex in causa propria sua debet esse*. Literally translated, this has it that no one ought to be a judge in his or her own cause. What this maxim most obviously envisages is a situation where an adjudicator is called upon to decide a matter where he or she will benefit directly from one of the possible outcomes. In fact, as we will see shortly, it is here that the common law takes its firmest stance against participation. However, in everyday speech, "cause" is far more commonly understood as connoting a position that is adhered to or advocated actively than in the sense of a "legal cause of action." In this context, the inquiry then becomes what levels of advocacy or adherence to particular causes or points of view should be seen as disqualifying.

However, bias as deployed as a disqualifying concept by the courts is about more than cause or causes in either of the senses identified already. It is also concerned with associations that are likely to produce predispositions—professional, familial, and other forms of personal link with the persons (or groups) (including their advocates) who are parties to the proceedings or who stand to benefit or suffer as a result of the decision to be taken. Here, the connection with the concept of "cause," even in its most generous colloquial sense, becomes tenuous though not necessarily overextended. The association in question means that the "causes" of others are attributed to the adjudicator in either a positive (one favours one's friends) or negative (one does not confer advantages on one's enemies) sense.

In appreciating the courts' general approach to challenges to participation based on bias, it is also useful to ask: How does one know whether a person against whom an allegation of bias is made is in fact too predisposed for whatever reason to a particular outcome? Even to pose that question is to suggest its problematic nature. Despite a direct interest in the outcome, despite prior advocacy of a particular position, despite kinship, despite enmity, certain altruistic individuals may be able to divorce themselves from those considerations and decide a matter as "objectively" as the mythical truly disinterested or dispassionate person. However, how a court could discern whether that will in fact happen or has in fact happened defies description or elaboration. Moreover, even if this could be done, there is also the just as problematic possibility that, in striving for impartiality, such an altruistic but suspect decision-maker will stray too far in the direction of the opposite or another outcome or point of view.

Indeed, there is yet another reason for not trying to establish by evidence and other inquiry the actual state of an adjudicator's mind. To endeavour to do so would almost invariably involve the adjudicator testifying either in-person or by way of affidavit subject to cross-examination. Such a process could not only involve a compromise of the principle of confidentiality in decision making by tribunals but also subject adjudicators to a species of in-person scrutiny from which they are generally immune (see *R v. Gough (RB)* (1993), 155 NR 81 (Eng. HL), at 97 (*per* Lord Woolf)).

As a consequence, courts almost invariably eschew any inquiry into the actual state of an adjudicator's mind but rather generally ask whether the particular situation of the decision-maker is such as to give rise to a sufficient risk that an impermissible degree of bias will in fact exist. In fact, in the case of a direct stake in the outcome of proceedings, the mere existence of that pecuniary or financial interest has always (absent statutory authorization) been held to be in itself sufficient to disqualify a decision-maker. The courts' refusal to investigate the decision-maker's actual state of mind also reflects another strong policy underlying the principle of unbiased adjudication: the public is entitled to have confidence in the impartial resolution of disputes and that confidence is undermined when the facts are such as to create an impression in the public mind that a decision-maker is too predisposed toward a particular outcome. This notion is well-captured in the oft-quoted statement of Lord Hewart CJ in the bias case of *R v. Sussex Justices, ex parte McCarthy*, [1924] 1 KB 256, at 259:

> It is of fundamental importance that justice should not only be done, but should manifestly and undoubtedly be seen to be done.

Another factor or consideration that intrudes frequently in the cases, particularly since the rules of natural justice or procedural fairness have been applied to a broader range of decision making, is that the courts' tolerance for attitudes, prior involvements, and relationships on the part of decision-makers will vary with the statutory context in which the allegation of disqualifying bias is raised. Where the principle of unbiased decision making has its genesis in what is appropriate for judges of the regular courts, such deviations should be neither surprising nor unwelcome. What may seem dictated in the case of a generalist superior court judge operating within a system of a strict separation of functions and presiding over and deciding cases in solitary splendour in the context of the adversary system may not be appropriate for all of the great variety of administrative agencies that are subject to the dictates of procedural fairness. After all, agencies may have a range of functions of which adjudication is only a part, their members may be appointed from and continue to operate in a small community of experts or peers and may be expected to engage in collegial or collective decision making, their processes may be far less adversarial than those of the regular courts and involve inquisitorial and generally activist approaches, and they may be engaged in decision making with an explicit and high policy content.

Thus, the courts have been willing to concede to municipal politicians considerably more latitude in terms of their prior involvement with and attitude toward a particular outcome in a policy matter that is subject to a public hearing than they would be to human rights adjudicators having a prior involvement with and position on a particular case now before them for decision. In a somewhat different vein, prior associations are less likely to disqualify someone from sitting at a disciplinary hearing of one of the historically self-governing professions or being involved in peer consideration of a candidate for tenure or promotion at a university. In short, there is something of a sliding scale in effect here with greater leniency or toleration in evidence in the domain of discretionary decision making having a high policy content than in the case of more highly judicialized proceedings determining objective facts and questions of law and focussed on an individual or a narrow range of individuals. Moreover, even in the latter situation, as illustrated by the professional discipline and university preferment examples, context may also be highly relevant in determining the appropriate standards of judicial scrutiny.

In the Anglo-Canadian tradition, the issue of bias has been determined for the most part by reference to common law standards, the only exception being those situations where the empowering statute has spoken to the question of bias generally by way of authorizing the participation of those who by reference to regular common law standards would be seen as disqualified. Now, however, the common law has been supplemented by constitutional and quasi-constitutional norms and these may not only result in the disqualification of individual adjudicators but also the disregarding of statutory authorizations for otherwise disqualifying biases and, indeed, the striking down of regimes. Most important for administrative law purposes are s. 7 of the *Canadian Charter of Rights and Freedoms* with its guarantee of the benefit of the "principles of fundamental justice" when someone's "life, liberty and security of the person" are at stake and ss. 1(a) and 2(e) of the *Canadian Bill of Rights*, which respectively require "due process" when "life, liberty, security of the person and enjoyment of property" are involved and "fundamental justice" in the context of the determination of a person's "rights and obligations." In the provincial domain, Alberta and Quebec also have bills of rights. Section 1(a) of the *Alberta Bill of Rights* is virtually identical to s. 1(a) of the *Canadian Bill of Rights*, while s. 23 of the Québec *Charter of Human Rights and Freedoms* contains an assurance of

> a full and equal, public and fair hearing by *an independent and impartial tribunal*, for the determination of [a person's] rights and obligations or of the merits of any charge brought against him. [Emphasis added.]

This chapter begins with a consideration of the general test applied by Canadian courts to determine whether a decision-maker should be disqualified for breaching the *nemo judex* principle: that of reasonable apprehension of bias. It then identifies the kinds of interests and involvements that are generally disqualifying, including a decision-maker's antagonism toward or association with the parties and prior involvement in the proceedings. In this context, we evaluate the various tests that the courts have proposed for isolating those circumstances. We then review the issue of statutory authorization of otherwise disqualifying bias and the limits that this places on the courts' application of general common law tests for bias and principles of disqualification. We then introduce the concept of institutional as opposed to personal or individual bias. Following that, we take up the very difficult questions of attitudinal bias (that is, predisposition toward an outcome based on a view about or prior involvement with the matter in issue) and bias by reason of pecuniary or other direct stake in the outcome of the proceedings and link these with an examination of the factors or contexts that lead a court to exercise greater restraint in intervention on the basis of allegations of bias.

Finally, we deal with what is becoming an increasingly common aspect of challenges to tribunal members and structures particularly in the wake of the Charter: the concept of "independence." What the emergent jurisprudence clearly establishes is that, in both its individual and structural senses, the notion of independent decision making provides a more extensive basis for challenging adjudicators and statutory regimes than has been envisaged under traditional common law conceptions of bias.

Before proceeding with a detailed examination of bias, impartiality and independence, it is necessary to briefly explain the relationship between these concepts. A decision is tainted by bias if it is driven or based on illegitimate interests or irrelevant considerations, such as the decision-maker's pecuniary interests, relationships with parties, and preconceived attitudes toward the issues at stake in the proceedings. Even the perception, by a reasonable observer, that the decision-maker is predisposed toward a particular outcome undermines public confidence in the administration of justice. Without this confidence, the justice system, including the administrative justice system, cannot command the respect and acceptance that are essential to its effective operation. Accordingly, impartiality, as the Supreme Court noted in the context of judicial proceedings, refers to "a state of mind or attitude of the tribunal in relation to the issues and the parties in a particular case": *R v. Valente*, [1985] 2 SCR 673, at para. 15. An impartial decision-maker, in other words, approaches a decision with an open mind, without bias, actual or perceived. Judicial independence, in contrast, has as its core "the complete liberty of individual judges to hear and decide the cases that come before them: no outsider—the government, pressure group, individual or even another judge—should interfere in fact, or attempt to interfere, with the way in which a judge conducts his or her case or makes his or her decision": *Beauregard v. Canada*, [1986] 2 SCR 56, at para. 21. Independence, then, connotes "a status or relationship to others, particularly to the executive branch of government, that rests on objective conditions or guarantees," including financial security, security of tenure, and administrative control. The objective of judicial independence is to ensure the public's perception of impartiality; if the government of the day can arbitrarily change a judge's remuneration, dismiss a judge, or interfere with the administration of the courts, a reasonable observer would apprehend that judges may be predisposed toward outcomes that do not displease the government. Accordingly, independence has been described as a "component," a "cornerstone," and a "necessary prerequisite" for impartiality: *R v. Lippé*, [1990] 2 SCR 114, at paras. 48-49 (*per* Lamer CJ). Having laid the groundwork for our discussion of these important concepts, we focus now on the common law definition of bias.

BIAS: THE GENERAL TEST

The general test applied by the Canadian courts for the determination of whether an adjudicator or other decision-maker should be disqualified is that of a reasonable apprehension of bias. That test was elaborated by de Grandpré J of the Supreme Court of Canada in *Committee for Justice and Liberty v. National Energy Board*, [1978] 1 SCR 369 (Can.), at 394-95 and, while contained in a dissenting judgment, this formulation has since achieved acceptance (see, for example, *Canadian Pacific Ltd. v. Matsqui Indian Band*, [1995] 1 SCR 3 (Can.)) as establishing the appropriate reference points by which the existence of a reasonable apprehension is to be discerned:

> [T]he apprehension of bias must be a reasonable one, held by reasonable and rightminded people, applying themselves to the question and obtaining thereon the required information. In the words of the Court of Appeal, that test is "what would an informed person, viewing the matter realistically and practically—and having thought the matter through—conclude."

Lord Denning MR also captured the essence of the inquiry in his judgment in *Metropolitan Properties v. Lannon*, [1969] 1 QB 577 (CA), at 579:

> In considering whether there was a real likelihood of bias, the court does not look at the mind of the justice himself or at the mind of the chairman of the tribunal, or whoever it may be, who sits in a judicial capacity. It does not look to see if there was a real likelihood that he would, or did, in fact favour one side at the expense of the other. The court looks at the impression which would be given to other people. Even if he was as impartial as could be, nevertheless if a right-minded person would think that, in the circumstances, there was a real likelihood of bias on his part, then he should not sit. And if he does sit, his decision cannot stand. ... Nevertheless there must appear to be a real likelihood of bias. Surmise or conjecture is not enough. ... There must be circumstances from which a reasonable man would think it likely or probable that the justice or chairman, as the case may be, would, or did, favour one side unfairly at the expense of the other. The court will not inquire whether he did, in fact, favour one side unfairly. Suffice it that reasonable people might think he did. The reason is plain enough. Justice must be rooted in confidence: and confidence is destroyed when right-minded people go away thinking: "The judge was biased."

While the Master of the Rolls speaks in terms of a "real likelihood" rather than a "reasonable apprehension," de Grandpré J took pains to state in *Committee for Justice and Liberty* that such variations in the expressions used should not generally be treated as involving any substantive difference in the approach to be taken. "Reasonable apprehension," "real likelihood," "reasonable likelihood," and "reasonable suspicion" amount to the same standard. Nonetheless, in other common law jurisdictions, there continue to be concerns about the links between the language of the test adopted by the courts and the substance of the inquiry to be conducted. In particular, this manifests itself in discussions as to which expression captures correctly the proper balance to be struck between maintaining public confidence in the due delivery of even-handed justice and ensuring that adjudicators can get on with their work and not be disqualified because of fears on the part of the oversensitive or unduly suspicious.

Of somewhat more practical importance, however, is the question what knowledge is to be attributed to the observer of events. While this obviously involves a fictional construct, it may have a considerable impact on the evidence adduced by the parties and the admissibility of and relevance attached to that evidence by the court. Should, for example, a respondent be able to adduce evidence to demonstrate that, despite newspaper reports to the contrary, there is not any sort of business link between an adjudicator and one of the parties? Should it matter for these purposes that the evidence to support this position is evidence that would not be available readily to those challenging the adjudicator's position or to the general public? Should relief be available to an applicant (anxious to disqualify a particular adjudicator or simply to delay proceedings) on the basis of the likely impressions of a reasonably informed observer of the proceedings when that party's own more particular knowledge of the situation would suggest that there is no real likelihood of bias?

The Canadian courts have not been all that consistent in the knowledge that is to be attributed to the reasonable bystander. On occasion, it has been expressed in terms of the "readily ascertainable and easily verifiable facts." On other occasions, such as *Committee for Justice and Liberty* itself, the expression used is the tantalizingly vague "informed." In the constitutional case of *R v. Lippé*, [1991] 2 SCR 114 (Que.), Lamer CJC stated the test for institutional (as opposed to personal or individual) bias in terms of the apprehensions of a "fully informed" reasonable person (at 144); yet, in *Old St. Boniface Residents Assn. Inc. v. Winnipeg (City)*, [1990] 3 SCR 1170 (Man.), a policy bias case, Sopinka J used the expression "reasonably well-informed person" to describe the appropriate vantage point. Ironically, the positions of Lamer CJC and Sopinka J were in a sense reversed in the later judgment of *Canadian Pacific Ltd. v. Matsqui Indian Band*, above, to which we return in detail in the section on institutional independence. However, suffice it to say for present purposes that Sopinka J accused Lamer CJC of taking too narrow a focus in terms of the knowledge that he attributed to the reasonable person in that case by failing to require knowledge of how an allegedly impaired tribunal structure operated in practice.

These and other issues are canvassed by Kelly in "Reviewing the Observer of Bias" (1993), 67 *Aust. LJ* 340 and have given rise to a restatement by the House of Lords in *R v. Gough (R.B.)*, [1993] AC 646 (Eng. HL) of the test to be applied. Lord Goff of Chieveley, after stating that the standard of scrutiny should be the same whether the target be justices, tribunal members, arbitrators, or jurors, continued (at 670):

> Furthermore, I think it unnecessary, in formulating the appropriate test, to require that the court should look at the matter through the eyes of a reasonable man, because the court in cases such as these personifies the reasonable man; and in any event the court has first to ascertain the relevant circumstances from the available evidence, knowledge of which would not necessarily be available to an observer [present] at the relevant time. Finally, for the avoidance of doubt, I prefer to state the test in terms of *real danger* rather than real likelihood, to ensure that the court is thinking in terms of possibility rather than probability of bias. Accordingly, having ascertained the relevant circumstances, the court should ask itself whether, having regard to those circumstances, there was a real danger of bias on the part of the relevant member of the tribunal in question, in the sense that he might unfairly regard (or have unfairly regarded) with favour, or disfavour, the case of a party to the issue under consideration by him. [Emphasis added.]

In a concurring judgment, Lord Woolf (at 673) responds to the possible criticism that such a test pays too little heed to the concern that in the public mind there must be an appearance of unbiased appraisal:

> It is because the court in the majority of cases does not inquire whether actual bias exists that the maxim that justice must not only be done but be seen to be done applies. When considering whether there is a real danger of injustice, the court gives effect to the maxim, but does so by examining all the material available and giving its conclusion on that material. If the court having done so is satisfied that there is no danger of the alleged bias having created injustice, then the application to quash the decision should be dismissed.

To the extent that the fictional observer of events remains relevant under this formulation, what the House of Lords appears to be saying is that the initial impressions of that fictional observer may well be modified once the complete evidence is adduced in the judicial review proceedings. If that evidence now establishes that there is no real danger of biased appraisal, the fictional observer of events will be satisfied and the public's interest in the appearance of justice will be maintained as a result of the court's inquiries. Indeed, to disqualify an adjudicator where the evidence before the court establishes that previous apprehensions were unfounded would be a disservice to both the challenged adjudicator and the administrative process.

This interpretation of *Gough* has the apparent support of Simon Brown LJ of the English Court of Appeal in *R v. Inner West London Coroner, ex parte Dallaglio*, [1994] 4 All ER 139 (CA), at 151-52, when he summarizes *Gough* as standing for the following propositions:

(1) Any court seised of a challenge on the ground of apparent bias must ascertain the relevant circumstances and consider all the evidence for itself so as to reach its own conclusion on the facts.

(2) It necessarily follows that the factual position may appear quite differently as between the time when the challenge is launched and the time when it comes to be decided by the court. What may appear at the leave stage to be a strong case of "justice [not] manifestly and undoubtedly be[ing] seen to be done," may, following the court's investigation, nevertheless fail. Or, of course, although perhaps less probably, the case may have become stronger.

(3) In reaching its conclusion the court "personifies the reasonable man."

(4) The question upon which the court must reach its own factual conclusion is this: is there a real danger of injustice having occurred as a result of bias? By "real" is meant not without substance. A real danger clearly involves more than a minimal risk, less than a probability. One could, I think, as well speak of a real risk or a real possibility.

(5) Injustice will have occurred as a result of bias if "the decision maker unfairly regarded with disfavour the case of a party to the issue under consideration by him." I take "unfairly regarded with disfavour" to mean "was pre-disposed or prejudiced against one party's case for reasons unconnected with the merits of the issue."

(6) A decision maker may have unfairly regarded with disfavour one party's case either consciously or unconsciously. Where, as here, the applicants expressly disavow any suggestion of actual bias, it seems to me that the court must necessarily be asking itself whether there is a real danger that the decision maker was unconsciously biased.

(7) It will be seen, therefore, that by the time the legal challenge comes to be resolved, the court is no longer concerned strictly with the appearance of bias but rather with establishing the possibility that there was actual though unconscious bias. ...

(9) It is not necessary for the applicants to demonstrate a real possibility that the coroner's decision would have been different but for bias; what must be established is the real danger of bias having affected the decision in the sense of having caused the decision maker, albeit unconsciously, to weigh the competing considerations, and so decide the merits, unfairly.

Consider whether the House of Lords (as interpreted by Simon Brown LJ) has adopted a more realistic test for bias and also whether the use of the language "real danger" rather than "real" or "reasonable likelihood" involves a more appropriate standard of scrutiny.

Whatever test is used to establish whether disqualifying bias is present, there are certain interests that traditionally have been seen as giving rise to disqualification. Marceau J provides a useful general list in *Energy Probe v. Canada (Atomic Energy Control Board)* (1984), 15 DLR (4th) 48 (FCA), discussed below in the section on pecuniary bias:

kinship, friendship, partisanship, particular professional or business relationship with one of the parties, animosity towards someone interested, predetermined mind as to the issue involved, *etc.*

In each of these instances, however, questions of degree may arise (for example, how close a familial connection should be seen as disqualifying?) and the regulatory context may be highly relevant.

For purposes of elaboration, it is useful to break this list of disqualifying conditions down into four categories: (1) antagonism during a hearing by a decision-maker toward a party or his or her counsel or witnesses; (2) an association between one of the parties and a decision-maker; (3) an involvement by a decision-maker in a preliminary stage of the decision; and (4) an attitude of a decision-maker toward the outcome. While these categories are by no means mutually exclusive (as the cases that follow will demonstrate), they each present their own problems in terms of establishing a reasonable apprehension of bias. (We deal with the first three categories in the balance of this part of the chapter and return later to the issue of attitudinal bias.)

Antagonism During the Hearing

To the extent that this ground of attack is based on the way in which the hearing is being or has been conducted, it is sometimes categorized as a denial of fair procedures—the victim has been denied the opportunity to present his or her case. However, the jurisprudence also classifies such behaviour by a decision-maker as giving rise to a reasonable apprehension of bias.

Its most common manifestations are unreasonably aggressive questioning or comments about testimony (see, for example, *Gooliah v. Canada (Minister of Citizenship and Immigration)* (1967), 63 DLR (2d) 224 (Man. CA) and *Golomb v. Ontario (College of Physicians and Surgeons)* (1976), 68 DLR (3d) 25 (Ont. Div. Ct.). Such conduct may also manifest an attitude toward the issue to be decided. Thus, in *Yusuf v. Canada (Minister of Employment & Immigration)* (1991), 7 Admin. LR (2d) 86 (FCA), members of a panel of the Immigration and Refugee Board had engaged in injudicious cross-examination (involving harassing and unfair comments) of a Convention refugee claimant as well as directed gratuitous and irrelevant sexist comments at her. This behaviour could be seen as coming just as much from an attitude to the claim being advanced as personal dislike of the claimant. As the Federal Court of Appeal noted, such actions achieved particularly significant dimensions where the panel's role was confined to determining whether there was a "credible basis" for the claim being advanced and where the claimant was the only witness. Similarly, in *Sparvier v. Cowessess Indian Band No. 73* (1993), 63 FTR 242, the antagonism demonstrated by a member of an Indian Band election appeal tribunal toward the person whose election was being challenged stemmed clearly from prior dealings between the member and the winner of the election and indicated a predisposition toward the outcome of the appeal. Indeed, had it been necessary, Rothstein J would have found that the challenged member was biased in fact.

As we saw in chapter 2 in *Baker v. Canada (Minister of Citizenship and Immigration)*, antagonism may also be a problem in written or paper hearings—that is, the court may disqualify a decision-maker who reveals in the course of a paper hearing an antagonism toward a party or a lack of sympathy with legislative objectives and the way the legislation is being enforced. In *Baker*, the evidence of that antagonism was found in the memorandum on which the decision was based.

This requirement of balanced and proper behaviour during the hearing is not confined to the designated decision-makers but also reaches lawyers who are employed to assist a tribunal at the hearing. Thus, in *Brett v. Ontario (Board of Directors of Physiotherapy)*, 77 DLR (4th) 144 (Ont. Div. Ct.); aff'd. (1993), 104 DLR (4th) 421 (Ont. CA), the conduct of the lawyer for the profession's discipline committee led to the quashing of its decision. In the course of the hearing, counsel had told the lawyer presenting the case against the member subject to discipline when to object to questions, when to put forward arguments favourable to the "prosecution," and suggested to the prosecution's witnesses answers to questions that assisted the prosecution's case. Here too, of course, there are links not only with other aspects of bias (prejudgment of the issues) but also with the rules against delegation of decision-making functions. Indeed, the principal concern in many of these cases is the creation of an impression that the decision-making function of the tribunal has been taken over by counsel and the language frequently used is the broader concept of an "appearance of unfairness" rather than simply of bias. (See *Adair v. Ontario (Health Disciplines Board)* (1993), 15 OR (3d) 705 (Div. Ct.).)

In such cases, the balance to be struck is that the courts should not inhibit tribunals from controlling their proceedings to ensure that they do not become too protracted and that parties, witnesses, and their counsel keep to the point and generally conduct themselves appropriately. That will frequently require firmness on the part of the tribunal and/or its counsel and, indeed, on occasion, measured expressions of disapproval and even anger. (For an example of where an allegation of bias was resisted successfully on this basis, see *Chromex Nickel Mines v. British Columbia (Securities Commission)* (1992), 6 Admin. LR (2d) 268 (BC SC). Here, the unsuccessful challenge was based on the chair of the hearing panel admonishing counsel for making deprecating remarks about both the commission and the superintendent of brokers.)

Association Between Party and Decision-Maker

A simple example of this group of cases is *Convent of the Sacred Heart v. Armstrong's Point Association and Bulgin*, which has already been used as an example of material interest. The other co-owner of the residence was the member's wife, who was a member of the executive of a ratepayers group that opposed the modification. This relationship was an alternative ground for quashing the decision.

Another simple example is *Marques v. Dylex Ltd.* (1977), 81 DLR (4th) 554 (Ont. Div. Ct.). An employer challenged a decision of the Ontario Labour Relations Board to certify a union because one of the members of the board, who had been a lawyer before his appointment, had been a member of a firm that acted for a union that became part of the union that was certified. The challenge failed; Morden J said:

> In looking at the cumulative effect of the factors relied upon by counsel for the employer there are certain other factors which have to be weighed in the balance. They are as follows. The vice-chairman had nothing to do with any aspect of the present proceedings, as part of his association with the law firm or otherwise, and neither did the law firm itself during the currency of his association with it. Over a year had elapsed since he had anything to do with the union, or more correctly, one of its predecessors. Almost a year had elapsed since his connection with the law firm terminated.
>
> Further, on a more general plane, the nature and functions of the Board itself have to be regarded. The fact that a Judge in similar circumstances would not, I would think, have heard the case is not determinative. (In saying this I am not expressing an opinion on minimum *legal* standards.) We can take judicial notice, if it is not apparent from the *Labour Relations Act*, RSO 1970, c. 232, itself, that members of the Labour Relations Board and in particular the chairmen of panels will have had experience and expertise in the law and labour relations. The Government of Ontario looks to people with such a background in making appointments. Most, if not all of those appointed, are bound to have some prior association with parties coming before the Board.

An interesting contrast is provided by *Ontario Hydro v. Ontario (Ontario Energy Board)* (1994), 114 DLR (4th) 341 (Ont. Div. Ct.), in which the court held that the Energy Board could not employ as its counsel at an Ontario Hydro rate hearing a lawyer who had acted for Hydro in the annual rate hearings between 1976 and 1986 with the exception of 1980. Here, however, the application for disqualification was made by Ontario Hydro itself and the formal basis was not that this would create a reasonable apprehension of biased appraisal but that serving the board could involve a situation of conflict of interest to the potential detriment of the lawyer's former client.

A further variation is provided by *CNG Transmission Corporation v. Canada (National Energy Board)*, [1992] 1 FC 346 (TD), in which a meeting took place between representatives of one of the parties to a proceeding and representatives of the National Energy Board (the chair, a member and counsel to the board). This encounter, in which matters relevant to the ongoing proceeding were discussed, was held by Cullen J to have produced a reasonable apprehension of bias, a finding that was reinforced by the fact that, among the representatives of the party was a former chair of the board. In seeking the meeting, the former chair had not gone through the board's secretary as required by the relevant protocol but had contacted the present chair personally. If it had been anyone else, Cullen J opined, the chair would have refused the approach in that form.

Later, we return to a further variation on this type of situation when we consider *MacBain v. Canada (Human Rights Commission)* (1985), 22 DLR (4th) 119 (FCA), where one of the elements of a successful challenge was that the Canadian Human Rights Tribunal members were appointed by the commission, which then carried the case for the complainant at the hearing.

Involvement of Decision-Maker in Earlier Stage of Process

The leading Canadian case on the test for bias, *Committee for Justice and Liberty v. National Energy Board*, [1978] 1 SCR 369 (Can.), is one which spans bias by reason of association with a party and involvement in an earlier stage of the process. An application was made under s. 44 of the *National Energy Board Act*, RSC 1970, c. N-6, to the National Energy Board by Canadian Arctic Gas Pipeline for construction of a natural gas pipeline from Prudhoe Bay and the MacKenzie Delta down the MacKenzie Valley. The chairman of the board at the time of the application was Marshall Crowe, who had been president of Canada Development Corporation before his appointment. The applicant, the Arctic Gas Pipeline Company, was formed in November 1972 by a "study group" of companies interested in constructing a pipeline from the north. This study group was formed in June 1972, and Development Corporation became a member in the following November. Crowe had been involved in its discussions and planning from the time the Development Corporation became a member until he left to join the Energy Board. For example, he was a member of the management committee and joined in its decisions about ownership and routing of the proposed pipeline.

Some of the participants in the hearing claimed that this apparent commitment to a pipeline created a reasonable apprehension of bias, and a majority of the Supreme Court agreed. Laskin CJ said,

> To say, that the issues before the Board are different from those to which the Study Group directed itself is not entirely correct, save as it reflects the different roles of the Board and of the Study Group. Moreover, it does not meet the central issue in this case, namely, whether the presiding member of a panel hearing an application under s. 44 can be said to be free from any reasonable apprehension of bias on his part when he had a hand in developing and approving important underpinnings of the very application which eventually was brought before the panel.

> There was some inconsistency in the approaches taken by counsel for the Attorney General of Canada and counsel for the Canadian Arctic Gas Pipeline Limited, who made the main submissions in support of the position of all the respondents. The former asserted at one point in his submissions that the decision to seek a pipeline had already been made by the Study Group before Canada Development Corporation became a participant. It was his further contention that Mr Crowe participated only in the decisions as to routing and as to single ownership of the proposed pipeline and as to the appointment of auditors and bankers. In his view, these decisions fell short of an involvement in the crucial considerations of economic and financial feasibility which, presumably, were either determined before Mr Crowe became a representative member of the Study Group or were redetermined after he ceased to be such a member. This is an untenable position. Economic and financial feasibility were involved in the very decision to pursue the pipeline project by an application to the Board, and the fact that the proposed application was later refined or revised did not make it one to which Mr Crowe was a stranger before it came to the Board.

Counsel for Canadian Arctic Gas Pipeline Limited appeared to say that there was no concluded decision to apply for a certificate while Mr Crowe was a representative member of the Study Group. He did agree that economic and financial feasibility were involved in decisions made by the Study Group in which Mr Crowe participated, but he contended that, in so far as this affected a decision to apply for a certificate, it was not conclusive on the question whether public convenience and necessity existed or would exist two years hence. This submission either begs the question of reasonable apprehension of bias or makes it depend on whether the Study Group can be said to have made the very decision which the Board is called upon to make. There can be no such dependence. Any application under s. 44 would, of course, be pitched to securing a favourable decision, but the Board's powers are wide enough to entitle it to insist on changes in a proposal as a condition of the grant of a certificate. The vice of reasonable apprehension of bias lies not in finding correspondence between the decisions in which Mr Crowe participated and all the statutory prescriptions under s. 44, especially when that provision gives the Board broad discretion "to take into account all such matters as to it appear to be relevant," but rather in the fact that he participated in working out some at least of the terms on which the application was later made and supported the decision to make it. The Federal Court of Appeal had no doubt that Mr Crowe (to use its words) "took part in [the] meetings and in the decisions taken which ... dealt with fairly advanced plans for the implementation of the pipeline project."

The more usual situations of prior involvement are ones in which a decision-maker has in the same or another capacity already heard the matter before the tribunal (rehearing after successful judicial review or appeal or sitting in appeal from a decision in which one has participated) or been involved in the investigation and decision to proceed with the matter being heard.

A simple example of the former is *Township of Vespra v. Ontario (Municipal Board)* (1983), 2 DLR (4th) 303 (Ont. Div. Ct.), which was a sequel to the *Innisfil* case. The result of the decision of the Supreme Court was that the application was still pending. Barrie came to an agreement with Innisfil and decided not to proceed with the application to annex the land in Oro. Therefore only the application to annex the land in Vespra remained. The hearing began again early in 1983, and the members of the board were the members who had made the original decision. Vespra objected that their presence created an apprehension of bias, but the hearing continued despite this objection. However, the board refused to receive any new evidence because of a deadline imposed by the *Municipal Boundary Negotiations Act, 1981*, SO 1981, c. 70, s. 24(1), which provided that the application would lapse unless a decision was made before February 1984. The board made a decision on the merits, and Vespra made an application for review and succeeded, because the refusal to hear evidence was considered to be a denial of the obligation to give a hearing. Smith J said:

> The question that remains is solely one of deciding whether there should be either a renewal of the hearing or a new hearing before a different panel. It is inevitable, of course, that if a different panel is constituted a complete hearing *de novo* will be required.
>
> In the course of giving their reasons for the 1977 decision the Arrell/Charron panel stated, *inter alia*, and I quote from 229 of that decision:
>
> > We are of the opinion that this development, outside the city's boundaries, should never have been allowed and was and is poor planning. ... It is essential that the city have the

control and management of this area for the benefit of its existing commercial areas and
as a support for the urbanization provided in the new city.

· · ·

It would be the absolute height of folly to allow this question of Vespra's financial
viability to determine where the boundaries of a city of the magnitude of 125 000 people
should be drawn.

These statements must, of course, be kept in perspective. The members of the board were in
the process of making their decision. The statements are nevertheless emphatic and perhaps
rightly so, in the circumstances, but they could lead a reasonable person to the conclusion that
human nature might conceivably come into play and make it difficult for the panel to draw back
from the positions expressed in that fashion and to bring an impartial mind to bear on the issue
to be determined. Standing alone, these emphatic expressions of opinion on the part of the
panel would not lead this court to a conclusion that there was a reasonable apprehension of
bias. But, when there is added to those strong statements the actual decision of 1983, … made
without jurisdiction and contrary to natural justice, based upon the evidence of 1976 without
regard for any change in circumstances in the intervening seven-year period and, in particular,
without evidence of population projections, the government policy having lost its relevancy, the
reasonable apprehension of bias by Vespra is inevitable in our view.

The board may well have unwittingly placed itself in a position from which it felt with sin-
cerity and honesty of purpose, we allow readily, it could not extricate itself except by finalizing
the matter at once. It is the unanimous view of this court that in doing so, it embarked upon a
course which cannot be countenanced and which leads to the inevitable conclusion, as just
stated, of a reasonable apprehension of bias.

Problems about prior involvement can arise in situations where an appeal from a decision is permitted. In the realm of appeals, the most obvious possibility is that a person
makes the initial decision and then hears the appeal, either alone or as part of an appeal
tribunal. This arrangement is generally accepted as creating a reasonable apprehension of
bias. A more difficult problem arose in *Law Society of Upper Canada v. French*, [1975] 2 SCR
767 (Ont.), which was created by the complex structure for professional discipline created
by the *Law Society Act, 1970*, SO 1970, c. 19. The governing body of the Law Society of
Upper Canada was the benchers, and allegations of misconduct were heard by the discipline
committee. Section 33(12) provided that if the committee found a member guilty of misconduct, it was to give a copy of its decision to the member, together with notice "of his right
of appeal." Section 37 gave the committee power to reprimand the lawyer, and s. 34 gave
Convocation (the assembly of benchers) power to order disbarment or suspension. Section
39 provided that a member reprimanded under s. 37 could appeal to Convocation, and
members of the discipline committee could not participate in considering the appeal.

The discipline committee heard allegations of professional misconduct against French,
found him guilty of seven of them, and recommended suspension. Convocation met to
consider this recommendation and two members of the committee were present. French
objected to their participation; he was granted an adjournment and made a motion for review. He succeeded and an appeal to the Supreme Court was allowed.

French's claim was that the proceeding in Convocation was essentially consideration of
an appeal from the discipline committee, and therefore the participation of the two members

created an apprehension of bias. One argument for the Society was even if the proceedings were an appeal, the maxim *expressio unius est exclusio alterius* permitted the members to participate. Section 39 prohibited committee members from participating in one kind of appeal, therefore implicitly permitting them to participate in others. Spence J, writing for the majority of the court, accepted this argument; Laskin J, dissenting, said, "It seems to me a curious, if not inverted view of *expressio unius, exclusio alterius* to urge that where a graver penalty than a mere reprimand is recommended there is no disqualification. I should have thought it *a fortiori*, without the need of express reference; at the worst, I would consider it a *casus omissus* which cries for judicial intervention in accordance with accepted principles of administrative law."

Considering the question of the nature of the proceeding, Spence J concluded that Convocation was not considering an appeal. Quoting from *Merchant v. Law Society of Saskatchewan* (1972), 32 DLR (3d) 178 (Sask. CA), he said that the discipline process was "a single proceeding in which there are two stages: First, the inquiry and investigation into the complaint by the discipline committee, the results of which are embodied in a report to the Benchers; and secondly, the consideration and disposition of the report by the Benchers in Convocation. That being so, I can see no basis for the submission that the Benchers who were members of the discipline committee would be precluded from participating in the deliberations of the Benchers in Convocation." Laskin J said:

> I do not think that the issue herein falls to be decided according to whether the proceedings in Convocation are or amount to an appeal or are or amount to a review under a two-stage scheme of inquiry into allegations of professional misconduct. No doubt, characterization of the proceedings as an appeal may lend weight to the contention of the appellant solicitor, but the principle underlying his position rises above any such formalistic approach. The principle is immanent in the ancient *nemo judex in causa sua*, expressed by Coke in *Dr Bonham's Case* (1610) 8 Co. Rep. 113b, 77 ER 646, and in its evolutionary application to statutory tribunals, has been examined in depth by de Smith, *Judicial Review of Administrative Action* (3rd ed. 1973), c. 5, especially at 227ff. and 237ff.
>
> · · ·
>
> Again, the hearing before Convocation was not a hearing *de novo*, nor one in which Convocation was presented with merely factual findings for its consideration. It was a hearing based on findings of guilt which the adversely affected solicitor was seeking to reverse and which he was invited to challenge by the notice served upon him by the Law Society that the Discipline Committee's report and findings would be considered by Convocation at a stated time and place.
>
> The likelihood that members of the Discipline Committee would stand above their findings and conclusions could be best ensured if they abstained from participating in the ensuing Convocation proceedings. That they should do so as a matter of law seems to me to be the more obvious when it is the organized legal profession whose conduct is under scrutiny. It is a reasonable expectation that lawyers, in their organized capacity as the governing body of their profession, should be most sensitive to the application of the rationale underlying the principle of impartiality. Indeed, whether or not the law was on their side—and I think it is not—it would have been a simple matter to have acceded to the request of the solicitor that members of the Discipline Committee abstain from participation in proceedings consequent upon their report and findings of guilt. One such member did abstain on his own. That way this protracted litigation might have been avoided without sacrifice by the Law Society of either principle or authority.

I do not think that I stretch the conception of bias beyond reasonable limits in supporting the disqualification of members of an adjudicative body when they come to its proceedings with their names attached to previous findings of guilt upon which those proceedings are based.

The nature of these proceedings was considered again in *Emerson v. Law Society of Upper Canada* (1984), 5 DLR (4th) 294 (Ont. HC). The discipline committee found Emerson guilty of misconduct and recommended disbarment, which Convocation imposed. Emerson sought review on the ground that the committee had not proceeded properly, especially because its report was drafted by the secretary of the Law Society and signed by an assistant secretary on behalf of the chairman. (We considered this ground in chapter 4 of this text, dealing with reasons.) The Law Society argued that, because the function of the committee was to investigate and report, the court should not review, and it pointed especially to s. 3(2)(g) of the *Statutory Powers Procedure Act* (which provides that the minimum rules do not apply to a tribunal "required to make an investigation and to make a report"). Henry J dismissed this argument, and said:

> The two-stage disciplinary proceeding under the *Law Society Act*, which the Supreme Court of Canada views as a single proceeding, results in a decision reflecting upon the solicitor's conduct which may include suspension from practice or disbarment. There can be no question that the proceedings as authorized by the *Law Society Act* must be conducted judicially, not only before convocation, which takes the final step in the process, but at all stages.
>
> · · ·
>
> I have concluded that the exclusion in s. 3(2)(g) does not apply to the discipline committee because, first, the proceedings before the discipline committee are the first stage of a single disciplinary proceeding culminating with final decision by convocation as to penalty without a hearing *de novo* on the findings and decision of the discipline committee. Secondly, the discipline committee, in addition to finding the facts on the evidence, makes a decision that the solicitor is guilty of professional misconduct or otherwise which, as I interpret s. 34 of the *Law Society Act*, is not a matter that convocation is *by the Act*, empowered to determine;

(As a result of 1998 amendments to the *Law Society Act* (RSO 1990, c. L.8, as am. by SO 1998, c. 21), the adjudicative role of Convocation disappeared. The amendments created three separate bodies: the Proceeding Authorization Committee, the Hearing Panel, and the Appeal Panel with a further appeal from the Appeal Panel to the Divisional Court. Section 49.21(2)1 of the Act now provides that there can be no overlap of membership between the Proceeding Authorization Committee and the Hearing Panel. While there is no similar provision in relation to the Appeal Panel, it would seem to be necessarily implicit in the new structure.)

The concern that members of agencies have no prior involvement in disputes that they adjudicate is, in Ontario, often enshrined in legislation See, for example, s. 23 of the *Health Insurance Act*, RSO 1990, c. H.6 with respect to the Appeal Board under the Ontario Health Insurance Plan:

> (2) Members of the Appeal Board holding a hearing shall not have taken part, before the hearing, in any investigation or consideration of the subject-matter of the hearing and shall not communicate directly or indirectly in relation to the subject-matter of the hearing with any person or with any party or representative of the party except upon notice to and with opportunity for all parties to participate, but the Appeal Board may seek legal advice from an adviser

independent from the parties and in such case the nature of the advice should be made known to the parties so that they may make submissions as to the law.

The general rules about bias and provisions of this kind are often a problem for agencies that make decisions about entitlement to income support payments—for example, workers' compensation boards. Most of the claimants, like most people, cannot present their claims effectively, and most do not have advisors or counsel. Should the agency respond by investigating, counselling, and organizing facts and issues? For example, should such an agency tell a claimant: "We have just taken a preliminary look at your file. We understand you want to establish X, but so far you don't seem to have enough evidence. Can you get more? For example, can you get A, or B, or C? If you want help, call our claims adviser." If the agency could usefully undertake these functions, can it, given the common law rules about this kind of conduct? Should it, given lawyers' fears about "inquisitorial" procedures?

STATUTORY AUTHORIZATION

One of the most common responses to an allegation of bias by reason of prior involvement is that of statutory authorization. Before moving to deal with the problem of attitudinal bias, we therefore pause to consider the limits of the statutory authorization defence. Part of the context in which we do this are two decisions involving securities commissions and, in fact, these judgments not only will serve as a link to the issue of attitudinal bias but also will introduce the possibility of constitutional challenges to statutorily authorized bias.

Brosseau v. Alberta (Securities Commission)
[1989] 1 SCR 301 (Alta.)

[Brosseau alleged that the chair of the commission was disqualified from sitting in an adjudicative capacity because, at the request of a senior civil servant, he had instructed commission staff to review their files and information in the possession of the police about a company of which Brosseau was the solicitor. The chair had also received a copy of the resulting report of the commission staff. A notice of hearing was issued against Brosseau alleging that false or misleading statements were contained in the company prospectus filed with the commission. The judgment of the court was delivered by]

L'HEUREUX-DUBÉ J:

. . .

Reasonable Apprehension of Bias

The appellant contends that a reasonable apprehension of bias arose from the fact that the Chairman, who had received the investigative report, was also designated to sit on the panel at the hearing of the matter. He objects to the Chairman's participation at both the investigatory and adjudicatory levels.

The maxim *nemo judex in causa sua debet esse* underlies the doctrine of "reasonable apprehension of bias." It translates into the principle that no one ought to be a judge in his own cause. In this case, it is contended that the Chairman, in acting as both investigator and adjudicator in the same case, created a reasonable apprehension of bias. As a general principle, this is not permitted in law because the taint of bias would destroy the integrity of proceedings conducted in such a manner.

As with most principles, there are exceptions. One exception to the "*nemo judex*" principle is where the overlap of functions which occurs has been authorized by statute, assuming the constitutionality of the statute is not in issue. A case in point relied on by the respondents, *Re W.D. Latimer Co. and Attorney-General for Ontario* (1973) 2 OR (2d) 391 (Div. Ct.), aff'd. *sub nom. Re W. D. Latimer Co. and Bray* (1974) 6 OR (2d) 129 (CA), addresses this particular issue with respect to the activities of a securities commission. In that case, as in this one, members of the panel assigned to hear proceedings had also been involved in the investigatory process. Dubin JA for the Court of Appeal found that the structure of the Act itself, whereby commissioners could be involved in both the investigatory and adjudicatory functions did not, by itself, give rise to a reasonable apprehension of bias.

. . .

In order to disqualify the Commission from hearing the matter in the present case, some act of the Commission going beyond its statutory duties must be found.

Administrative tribunals are created for a variety of reasons and to respond to a variety of needs. In establishing such tribunals, the legislator is free to choose the structure of the administrative body. The legislator will determine, among other things, its composition and the particular degrees of formality required in its operation. In some cases, the legislator will determine that it is desirable, in achieving the ends of the statute, to allow for an overlap of functions which in normal judicial proceedings would be kept separate. In assessing the activities of administrative tribunals, the courts must be sensitive to the nature of the body created by the legislator. If a certain degree of overlapping of functions is authorized by statute, then, to the extent that it is authorized, it will not generally be subject to the doctrine of "reasonable apprehension of bias" *per se*. In this case, the appellant complains that the Chairman was both the investigator and adjudicator and that therefore, the hearing should be prevented from continuing on the grounds of reasonable apprehension of bias.

In the course of deciding this case, it became clear to this Court that the arguments presented by the parties in their factums and in oral argument before this Court were insufficient to properly address these questions. As a result, the parties were requested to provide written submissions in answer to the following questions:

(1) pursuant to what statutory authority was the investigation directed?

(2) was the investigation directed solely at the initiative of the Chairman?

(3) was the investigation confined to documents on file with the Commission, *i.e.* was it a purely internal investigation or was it broader in scope?

In his written submissions, the appellant claimed that there was no authority for the investigation. He maintained that it was directed solely at the initiative of the Chairman, and was not confined to documents on file. Not surprisingly, the respondents disagreed.

They argued that while not specifically authorized by statute, implicit authority for the investigation could be found in the general scheme of the *Securities Act.*

If the investigation was without statutory authority, and if it was also directed at the initiative of the Chairman, then it is clear that the Chairman was attempting to act in the role of both investigator and adjudicator in circumstances which would not permit an abrogation of the general rules against bias. The appellant claims that the investigation was initiated by the Chairman. The respondent contends that it was, in fact, the Director who ordered the investigation. In my view, the available evidence does not favour one position over the other. While it appears that the Chairman may have had some role in "initiating" the investigation, it is far from clear that he initiated it in the sense of directing what should be done, how, and by whom. However, I do not feel it necessary to decide this point since I believe that the Act contemplates the involvement of the Chairman at several stages of proceedings.

Section 28 of the *Securities Act* provides authority for the Commission to carry out a full scale investigation which includes a wide range of powers. The person appointed to make the investigation under s. 28 has, by virtue of s. 29, "the same power as is vested in the Court of Queen's Bench for the trial of civil actions." Because of the extensive nature of the powers granted to an investigator under s. 28, such an investigation must be ordered by the Commission, and not by the Chairman alone.

There is no evidence in the present case that a s. 28 investigation was ordered by the Commission. In fact, the record and submissions suggest that this was not the route chosen by the Commission. The appellant contends that the only permissible route for an investigation is s. 28, and that therefore there was no statutory authorization for the action taken by the Chairman.

The respondent argues that the Act implies powers on a different level from the s. 28 formal investigative procedures. It contends that an informal "enforcement review" is the mechanism used by the Commission to bring to its attention those matters which warrant a more in depth investigation. Because of the formalities surrounding the s. 28 investigation, and because of the broad powers conferred, I am inclined to agree that the Commission must have the implied authority to conduct a more informal internal review. It would be unreasonable to say that a securities commission requires express statutory authority to review the documents it has on file, or to keep itself informed of the course of an RCMP investigation. To do so would be to make mandatory a resort to a s. 28 investigation for what are often simple administrative purposes. Such an approach might have the effect of paralysing the operations of the Commission. It would seem logical that before ordering a s. 28 investigation, the Commission would have first investigated the facts. If no wrongdoing is found, that would end the matter. If irregularities are uncovered, then the Commission could proceed either to a more thorough s. 28 investigation or to order a hearing, as in this case, to probe more deeply into the matter.

Section 11 of the *Securities Act* provides that the Chairman of the Commission is its Chief Executive Officer. As such, it appears to me that he would necessarily have the authority to receive information from the Assistant Deputy Minister or from the RCMP, pass this material along to the Director of the Commission, require that the Director verify the allegations and complaints, and receive a report of any review made by the

Director. There is no evidence that his participation went beyond these bounds. It is also to be noted that the report in question was made available to the appellant.

Certain other factors should be taken into consideration along with the question of statutory authorization. For example, in a specialized body such as the Commission, it is more than likely that the same decision-makers will have repeated dealings with a given party on a number of occasions and for a variety of reasons. It is hardly surprising, given the fact that there is only one Alberta Securities Commission, that the Commission in this case was required to deal with many aspects of the failure of Dial over a period of years.

Securities commissions, by their nature, undertake several different functions. They are involved in overseeing the filing of prospectuses, regulating the trade in securities, registering persons and companies who trade in securities, carrying out investigations and enforcing the provisions of the Act. By their nature, they will have repeated dealings with the same parties. The dealings could be in an administrative or adjudicative capacity. When a party is subjected to the enforcement proceedings contemplated by ss. 165 or 166 of the Act, that party is given an opportunity to present its case in a hearing before the Commission, as was done in this case. The Commission both orders the hearing and decides the matter. Given the circumstances, it is not enough for the appellant to merely claim bias because the Commission, in undertaking this preliminary internal review, did not act like a court. It is clear from its empowering legislation that, in such circumstances, the Commission is not meant to act like a court, and that certain activities which might otherwise be considered "biased" form an integral part of its operations. A section 28 investigation is of a different nature from this type of proceeding.

Securities Acts in general can be said to be aimed at regulating the market and protecting the general public.

. . .

This protective role, common to all securities commissions, gives a special character to such bodies which must be recognized when assessing the way in which their functions are carried out under their Acts.

The special circumstances of the tribunal in this case are substantially the same as those in the case of *Re W.D. Latimer Co. and Attorney-General for Ontario, supra*. In the Supreme Court of Ontario, Wright J made the following observation at 404:

> What fair play is in particular circumstances, and whether and how the power of the Courts to enforce it should be exercised are what the Court must decide. It must on the one hand see that the citizen is not unfairly dealt with or put in a position of potential unjustified peril at the hands of some person or body exercising jurisdiction. It must on the other hand see that such persons or bodies seeking to perform their public duty are not unduly hampered in their work and that the purpose of the Legislature, if it be the source of their jurisdiction, is respected and realized as it has been expressed.

The particular structure and responsibilities of the Commission must be considered in assessing allegations of bias. Upon the appeal of *Latimer* to the Ontario Court of Appeal, Dubin JA, for a unanimous Court, dismissed the complaint of bias. He acknowledged that the Commission had a responsibility both to the public and to its registrants.

. . .

Dubin JA found that the structure of the Act whereby commissioners could be involved in both the investigatory and adjudicatory functions did not, by itself, give rise to a reasonable apprehension of bias.

I am in agreement with this proposition. So long as the Chairman did not act outside of his statutory authority, and so long as there is no evidence to show involvement above and beyond the mere fact of the Chairman's fulfilling his statutory duties, a "reasonable apprehension of bias" affecting the Commission as a whole cannot be said to exist.

Appeal dismissed.

NOTES

1. In the Alberta Court of Appeal ((1986), 25 DLR (4th) 730), but not in the Supreme Court of Canada, arguments were made that the conduct of the proceedings violated s. 11(d) (presumption of innocence and right to an "independent and impartial tribunal") and s. 11(h) (double jeopardy) of the *Canadian Charter of Rights and Freedoms*. They were not successful and presumably were not re-advanced in the Supreme Court of Canada because of the intervening judgment of that court in *Wigglesworth v. The Queen*, [1987] 2 SCR 541 (Can.), in which it was held that s. 11 applied only to criminal matters or proceedings with the potential for truly penal consequences. That question may, however, be resurfacing given recent extensions in the capacities of some securities commissions to levy fines. Thus, under amendments to s. 127 of the *Securities Act*, RSO 1990, c. S.5, as am. by SO 2002, c. 22, s. 183, the commission now has authority to levy "administrative" fines up to $1 million as well as to make disgorgement orders. There is a serious question whether this passes into the domain of the truly penal, though the BC Court of Appeal has indicated that a $100,000 fine authority did not do so: *Johnson v. British Columbia (Securities Commission)* (2001), 206 DLR (4th) 711 (BC CA). For a more detailed analysis of this question, see Hon. C.A. Osborne, Q.C., D. Mullan and B. Finlay, Q.C., *Report of the Fairness Committee to the Ontario Securities Commission*, March 5, 2004, at 54. There also appears little likelihood, however, that s. 7 of the Charter could be invoked in relation to the activities of securities commissions, save perhaps (and even this is dubious) to the extent that they exercise regulatory authority over participation in certain occupations (securities dealers): *Malarctic Hygrade Gold Mines (Canada) Ltd. v. Ontario (Securities Commission)* (1986), 27 DLR (4th) 112 (Ont. Div. Ct.). There is also a question whether the "principles of fundamental justice" involve necessarily a complete separation of functions in situations such as this. In this regard, consider the extent to which the arguments advanced by L'Heureux-Dubé J in the course of her judgment would be equally relevant in the context of an argument that the statutory scheme was not contrary to the "principles of fundamental justice" or could be justified by reference to s. 1 of the Charter. (For a discussion of *Brosseau* in general and this issue in particular, see Evans, "Developments in Administrative Law; The 1988-89 Term" (1990), 1 *Sup. Ct. L Rev.* (2d) 1, at 64-72 (generally) and 69-72 (Charter). We also return to this theme when we deal more fully with the constitutional dimensions of bias.)

2. While *Brosseau* was under appeal to the Supreme Court of Canada, legislation was enacted splitting the commission into two separate bodies for enforcement and adjudicative purposes: a board and an agency. See *Alberta Securities Commission Reorganization Act*, SA

1998, c. 7. However, that experiment was abandoned and the previous structure reinstated. See *Securities Act*, RSA 2000, c. S.4.

3. In many senses, the type of attack in *Brosseau* has more to do with the structure of the decision-making process at issue than the state of mind of particular members of tribunals. In recent times, this has spawned a classification of bias cases on the basis of whether they involve an allegation of bias against an individual or the decision-making process itself. A similar distinction is made in the cases involving an allegation of independence.

4. As suggested by Evans in his commentary (at 68) and L'Heureux-Dubé J in her judgment, the defence of statutory authorization will not be an answer in every case where allegations of bias by reason of prior involvement are raised against the members of a securities commission or similarly structured body. The following judgment exemplifies this and also provides a further example of a reasonable apprehension of bias of the fourth category, that involving an attitude toward the outcome of the matter.

E.A. Manning Ltd. v. Ontario Securities Commission
(1994), 18 OR (3d) 97 (Div. Ct.); aff'd. (1995), 125 DLR (4th) 305 (Ont. CA)

[In a policy statement, the Ontario Securities Commission ("the OSC") indicated that it considered the actions of some ten securities dealers and salespersons, who were not members of the stock exchange, to be improper and to amount to unfair sales practices. Subsequently, the OSC issued two notices of hearing against the applicant, one of those dealers implicated in the practices denounced in the policy statement, and its principals and various employees. In the interim, the Ontario Court of Justice had declared the policy statement to be without statutory authority and, in so doing, had also stated that the OSC had determined by that policy statement that certain dealers (including the applicant) had been guilty of various abuses (*Ainsley Financial Corporation v. Ontario Securities Commission* (1993), 106 DLR (4th) 507 (Ont. Gen. Div.)). The commission appealed that decision and, in that context, issued a press release reiterating the concerns addressed in the policy statement. The chair of the OSC also gave a press interview to the same effect.

The applicant applied for an order in the nature of prohibition to prevent the OSC from proceeding with the two hearings.]

MONTGOMERY J (Dunnet and Howden JJ concurring): … The conclusions stated by the OSC in Policy 1.10 reflected the findings made in a staff report of July 8, 1992 which the Commissioners had before them and relied upon in formulating and approving Policy 1.10. The staff report sets out in detail the same allegations of ongoing improper conduct which are now the subject matter of the second notice of hearing. The sort of conclusions made in the staff report, which was in turn adopted by the OSC, can be observed in the following passage:

> Based upon our examination of the penny stock industry, we believe that as a result of the unfair sales practices engaged in by broker/dealers in the marketing of penny stocks;
>> (a) Investors purchase penny stocks unaware of risks that:
>>> (i) there may be no market to sell their penny stocks after the broker/dealer has sold its inventory position; and

(ii) they are likely to lose a significant portion of their investment.

(b) Investors are unaware of the commission and/or mark-up charged by salespersons and broker-dealers;

(c) Investors are pressured into purchasing penny stocks over the phone; and

(d) Broker/dealers do not comply with their know-your-client obligations.

As can be seen, the unfair conduct alleged in the second notice of hearing has already been found to exist by the Commissioners. The *conclusions* stated in Policy 1.10 and the *conclusions* stated in the staff report, which the OSC expressly adopted in approving Policy 1.10, demonstrate that the subject matter of the hearing has already been decided by the Commissioners.

The affidavit of Mr. Gordon, a staff lawyer for the OSC, sufficiently creates the link between the unfair conduct alleged and the applicants. Mr. Gordon's affidavit was just part of the evidence relied upon by the OSC in the *Ainsley* case to support Policy 1.10. The conduct of Manning Limited which Mr. Gordon calls "unfair sales practices" is the same conduct alleged in the second notice of hearing.

Having considered all of the evidence filed by the OSC in the *Ainsley* case, R.A. Blair J made a finding that the OSC had *concluded* that the plaintiff securities dealers (including Manning Limited) were guilty of various abuses. He said at 515:

> With the completion of this review, the Commission was satisfied that it had found cogent evidence of abusive and unfair sales practices in the marketing of penny stocks, and in addition, I think it is fair to say, *had concluded that these abuses were centred in the practices of the plaintiff securities dealers*. It set out to remedy the situation for the reasons and in the manner outlined above [*i.e.*, by implementing Policy 1.10]. (Emphasis added.)

On the material filed before me, it appears that the OSC has already decided that Manning Limited and related parties are guilty of these unfair practices.

The first notice of hearing merely goes through substantially the same allegations of improper conduct repeated in the second notice but relates them to the securities of two named companies, BelTeco and Torvalon, after certain dates in 1992 and 1994. These allegations are based on complaints of particular conduct about Manning Limited and other securities dealers which were before the Commissioners when they concluded such conduct was in fact occurring widely and approved Policy 1.10. In addition, on December 22, 1992, copies of the pleadings against the OSC in the *Ainsley* action were distributed to the Commissioners "to assist them in their review of the Draft Policy." In that action, substantial material was filed by the OSC specifically pertaining to complaints and practices now alleged against Manning Limited, its officers and employees and to be dealt with at the upcoming hearings.

Even if OSC staff tried to separate their investigative role from the Commissioners' role as adjudicators, the creation and adoption of Policy 1.10 and the additional evidence, including the mass of complaints specifically regarding Manning Limited and others in the staff report and the material led by the OSC in *Ainsley*, lead me to the irresistible conclusion that the roles have become so interwoven that there is a reasonable apprehension of bias against all Commissioners who took office prior to November 1993.

In a press interview, the Chair of the OSC, Mr. Waitzer, stated that dealing with penny stock dealers is a "perennial priority." "There will always be marginal players in the securities industry. Our task is to get these players into the self-regulatory system or get them out of the jurisdiction."

I conclude that Mr. Waitzer cannot sit on either hearing because of a reasonable apprehension of bias.

[After referring to *Newfoundland Telephone Co. v. Newfoundland (Board of Commissioners of Public Utilities)*, [1992] 1 SCR 623 (Nfld.) (below); *W.D Latimer Co. v. Bray* (1974), 52 DLR (3d) 161 (Ont. CA); and *Brosseau*, Montgomery J continued:]

In finding that there was no reasonable apprehension of bias on these facts, L'Heureux-Dubé J, delivering the judgment of the court, relied heavily on the Court of Appeal's decision in *Latimer*. She said at 315:

> Dubin JA found that the structure of the Act whereby commissioners could be involved in both the investigatory and adjudicatory functions did not, by itself, give rise to a reasonable apprehension of bias.
>
> I am in agreement with this proposition. So long as the Chairman did not act outside of his statutory authority, and so long as there is no evidence to show involvement above and beyond the mere fact of the Chairman's fulfilling his statutory duties, a "reasonable apprehension of bias" affecting the Commission as a whole cannot be said to exist.

In the case at hand, the OSC did act outside its statutory authority in adopting Policy 1.10. The Commissioners, in effect, sought to legislate. This, as found by *Ainsley*, was *ultra vires*. In the process of formulating and deciding to issue the mandatory regulation presented by Policy 1.10, the Commissioners in March 1993 closed their minds to the issue of whether securities dealers, including Manning Limited, are guilty of unfair sales practices. This constitutes prejudgment.

In the context of the litigation brought by the securities dealers, including the motion for judgment in the *Ainsley* case and the pending appeal, the OSC went beyond merely defending itself and its jurisdiction and adopted the role of advocate against them and strenuously sought to demonstrate that Manning Limited and others are guilty of the very conduct which is now the subject of the current notices of hearing.

The affidavits filed on behalf of the OSC speak loudly in what they fail to address. The affidavit of Mr. Gordon does not say that there was no discussion between the staff and Commissioners about Manning Limited when Policy 1.10 was being prepared. There is no affidavit evidence to say the Commissioners have been canvassed and individually could make an unbiased decision. Further, there is no evidence to show that the 55 complaints about Manning, which were made to OSC staff and made known to the Commissioners in the 1992 report accepted by them, have not tainted them. It is reasonable to assume that the complaints played a part in the desire to establish Policy 1.10. Given these gaps in the respondent's material, it seems to me that "the informed bystander," to use the words of Cory J in *Newfoundland Telephone*, "could reasonably perceive bias on the part of an adjudicator."

The OSC (both staff and Commissioners) were acting within the ambit of their statutory duties in assembling and considering information in respect of a certain segment of the securities market. But in using that information to conclude that the securities dealers (including Manning Limited) were in fact engaging in the practices alleged in Policy 1.10, and now in the notices of hearing, the Commissioners prejudged the case. They pursued a course in excess of their policy and regulatory functions due to a too narrow focus on a small number of parties and very particular allegations of practices and that, in turn, has produced an overly specific regulation beyond the OSC's jurisdiction. It has also produced an obvious apprehension of bias, quite distinct from the situation in *Latimer*.

The OSC has repeatedly recorded its conclusion that the targeted dealers engaged in unfair sales practices. The OSC issued Policy 1.10 in an effort to protect the public from unfair sales practices it "had found to exist." In my view, this prejudgment coupled with the continued effort of the OSC to vindicate its position through the ongoing litigation with the security dealers, including the appeal in *Ainsley*, created a reasonable apprehension of bias that precludes all members of the OSC who were Commissioners prior to the fall of 1993 from sitting at the hearings involving the applicants. In addition, the new Chair, Mr. Waitzer, is precluded from sitting for reasons stated earlier.

[The Divisional Court then went on to deal with the argument that there was such a degree of corporate tainting that even those members of the Securities Commission appointed subsequently were disqualified from sitting on this matter. This argument was rejected by the Divisional Court, which held that the hearing could proceed in front of two identified subsequent appointees as well as any later appointees. In so doing, the court doubted the existence of a doctrine of corporate taint; held that, in any event, it could not be invoked on the present facts; and stated further that, even if made out on the facts, it was subject to the overriding doctrine of necessity.

The applicants secured leave to appeal against this ruling, which in effect amounted to a rejection of their application for an order prohibiting the hearing from taking place in front of anyone. The commission itself did not cross-appeal the ruling that the other members of the commission (including the chair) were disqualified by reason of a reasonable apprehension of bias and the Court of Appeal dealt with the appeal on the assumption that that holding was correct. In the meantime, the Ontario Court of Appeal had sustained the judgment of the Divisional Court in *Ainsley*: (1994), 21 OR (3d) 104 (CA). The judgment of the Court of Appeal was delivered by:]

DUBIN CJO (Labrosse and Doherty JJA concurring):

The appellants submitted that the Divisional Court erred in failing to give effect to their submissions that the conduct of the Commission in its formulation and adoption of the Policy Statement, its defence to the *Ainsley* action, and the comments of its Chair, Mr. Waitzer, had so tainted the entire Commission that even newly-appointed Commissioners should be excluded from sitting on the hearings to consider the allegations in the first and second notices of hearing. They also submitted that the Divisional Court erred in holding that even if the concept of corporate taint could be invoked to otherwise disqualify the new Commissioners, the doctrine of necessity would apply.

· · ·

Disqualification by Reason of Corporate Taint

· · ·

It should be noted that the Policy Statement was held to be beyond the jurisdiction of the Commission because it had crossed the line between a non-mandatory guideline, and a mandatory pronouncement having the same effect as a statutory instrument, without the appropriate statutory authority (Doherty JA in *Ainsley, supra*). However, there is no suggestion of bad faith.

· · ·

Assuming that the Divisional Court was correct in finding [that the members of the commission who participated in the formulation and support of the *ultra vires* policy were disqualified], I agree with its conclusion that such a finding did not disqualify the new Commissioners. Montgomery J, at 116, stated, in part, as follows:

> It is argued by the applicant that there is a corporate taint affecting all those Commissioners subsequently appointed to the OSC. There is no judicial authority for this proposition. Bias is a lack of neutrality.
>
> Blake in *Administrative Law in Canada* (1992) states at 92:
>
>> Many tribunals are part of a larger administrative body. The fact that one branch of that administrative body is biased does not mean that another branch that has carriage of the matter is biased. Bias on the part of an employee of the tribunal or a member who is not on the panel hearing the matter usually does not give rise to a reasonable apprehension of bias on the part of the tribunal. Even bias on the part of the Minister in charge of the department does not necessarily make the adjudicator employed by the Ministry biased.

There was no evidence of prejudgment on the part of the new Commissioners. They were not involved in the consideration and adoption of the Policy Statement. Furthermore, none of the evidence which the staff of the Enforcement Branch proposed to adduce at the hearings was provided to them.

It should also be noted that the evidence to be adduced in connection with the second notice of hearing only came to the attention of Commission staff after final approval of the Policy Statement by the Commissioners. Furthermore, none of the details of the evidence proposed to be presented to the Commissioners in connection with the first notice of hearing formed part of the staff report presented to those Commissioners who were present when the Policy Statement was adopted.

It is assumed, of course, that the new Commissioners would be familiar with the Policy Statement and the concerns of the Commission with respect to the trading in penny stocks.

Securities Commissions, by their very nature, are expert tribunals, the members of which are expected to have special knowledge of matters within their jurisdiction. They may have repeated dealings with the same parties in carrying out their statutory duties and obligations. It must be presumed, in the absence of any evidence to the contrary, that the Commissioners will act fairly and impartially in discharging their adjudicative responsibilities and will consider the particular facts and circumstances of each case.

As noted earlier, even advance information as to the nature of a complaint and the grounds for it, which are not present here, are not a basis for disqualification.

In *Brosseau, supra*, the fact that the Chairman of the Commission had received the investigative report and sat on the panel hearing the matter did not give rise to a finding of a reasonable apprehension of bias.

In *Bennett v. British Columbia (Securities Commission)* (1992) 69 BCLR (2d) 171 (CA), an allegation of bias against the Commission was made because the staff of the Commission had cooperated with Crown counsel in *quasi*-criminal proceedings against those who were subsequently to appear before the British Columbia Securities Commission.

[The BC Court of Appeal had rejected a motion to stay the proceedings before the commission by reason of the participation of staff in swearing information used by the Crown in quasi-criminal proceedings, finding that such activities could not found a reasonable apprehension of bias. Dubin CJO quoted from the *Bennett* judgment, at 180-81:]

> We wish to add one further observation and that is as to the target of a bias allegation. Bias is an attitude of mind unique to an individual. An allegation of bias must be directed against a particular individual alleged, because of the circumstances, to be unable to bring an impartial mind to bear. No individual is identified here. Rather, the effect of the submissions is that all of the members of the commission appointed pursuant to s. 4 of the *Securities Act*, regardless of who they may be, are so tainted by staff conduct that none will be able to be an impartial judge. Counsel were unable to refer us to a single reported case where an entire tribunal of unidentified members had been disqualified from carrying out statutory responsibilities by reason of real or apprehended bias. We think that not to be surprising. The very proposition is so unlikely that it does not warrant serious consideration.

A case very much in point is *Laws v. Australian Broadcasting Tribunal* (1990) 93 ALR 435 (HCA). In that case, three members of the Australian Broadcasting Tribunal, during the course of what was intended to be a preliminary investigation, concluded that the appellant (Laws) had breached broadcasting standards. Subsequently, the tribunal, as a whole, decided to hold a formal inquiry to consider whether it should exercise any of its regulatory powers against the appellant including the withdrawal of its licence. The appellant sought an order prohibiting the broadcasting tribunal from conducting such a hearing on the ground that the entire tribunal was tainted by reason of the prejudgment of three of its members. An employee of the tribunal, Ms Paramore, the Director of its Programs Division, later gave an interview on behalf of the tribunal in which she repeated the conclusions made earlier by the three tribunal members. Mr. Laws submitted that this was a further ground for disqualification.

An action for defamation was commenced by Mr. Laws against the tribunal and Ms Paramore arising from the radio interview. In defence, the tribunal pleaded justification. That also formed the basis of the appellant's application to prohibit the tribunal from proceeding with its formal inquiry. I find it convenient to deal with the impact of the lawsuit later.

At first instance, Morling J concluded that the three members of the tribunal who had undertaken the preliminary investigation had gone much further and had made a positive finding that the appellant had violated broadcasting standards. He held that they were precluded from participating in the formal inquiry, but the appellant was not entitled to an order prohibiting the formal inquiry from continuing so long as it was conducted by other members of the tribunal who had not participated in the preliminary investigation. That conclusion was upheld by the full court and by the High Court of Australia.

With respect to the statements made by Ms Paramore, the appellant contended that those statements reflected the corporate view of the members of the tribunal and thus formed the basis for an order of prohibition against the tribunal itself.

Morling J held that there was no justification for attributing Ms Paramore's views to the members of the tribunal who were to conduct a formal inquiry. That conclusion was upheld in the High Court of Australia. On that issue, Mason CJ and Brennan J stated at 444-45:

> In order to examine this submission it is necessary to consider the interview given by Ms Paramore. Although the Act did not authorise [*sic*] the publication of the findings of non-compliance by the appellant with RPS 3 [broadcasting standards], it was not disputed that Ms Paramore spoke for the tribunal when she gave an account of the vitiated decision of 24 November. The tribunal is constituted by the Act as a body corporate (s. 7(1), (2)(a)) and it consists of a chairman, a vice-chairman and at least one other member but not more than six other members: s. 8(1). There is nothing to identify the source of Ms. Paramore's authority to make the statements which she made in the interview on behalf of the tribunal. It is very likely that her authority arose from her responsibility as Director of the Programs Division; in other words, it was part of her general responsibility to publish and explain, by way of broadcast, interview and otherwise, decisions made by the tribunal. The fact that the decision which she sought to report and explain was vitiated, at least so far as it related to the appellant, did not deny to the interview the character of a corporate act performed in purported pursuance of s. 17(1). However, though it might be correct to regard the interview as a corporate act, it was not necessarily an act done on behalf of each of the individual members of the corporation. The circumstances are not such as to justify the drawing of an inference that each of the individual members of the tribunal authorised the interview or approved of its content. At best, from the appellant's viewpoint, it might be inferred that the three members of the tribunal who made the decision of 24 November so authorised or approved the interview. Accordingly, the interview does not entitle the appellant to wider relief than that granted at first instance by Morling J.

Although there may be circumstances where the conduct of a tribunal, or its members, could constitute institutional bias and preclude a tribunal from proceeding further, this is not such a case. This is not a case where the Commission has already passed judgment upon the very matters which are to be considered in the pending hearings by the new Commissioners. ...

Disqualification by Reason of the Comments of the Chair, Mr. Waitzer

· · ·

The appellants submitted that the statements of the Chair exhibited a bias against them which was reflective of the Commission as a whole, and, therefore, they could not get a fair hearing from any members of the Commission. They submitted that, having found Mr. Waitzer was disqualified by reason of a reasonable apprehension of bias, the Divisional Court erred in not prohibiting the hearings from proceeding.

[Dubin CJO examined Mr. Waitzer's comments to the media, published in a series of four articles in the Dow Jones News, and found that, properly contextualized, his statements about getting penny stock dealers in the self-regulating system was a solution he advocated for all market players, not just the appellants and other penny stock dealers.]

With respect, I fail to see how what was said by Mr. Waitzer could form any basis for concluding that there was a reasonable apprehension of bias if he were to sit on either of the pending hearings, let alone disqualify the other Commissioners from conducting the hearings. In making the comments complained of here, Mr. Waitzer was fulfilling his mandate as Chair of the Commission.

[The court then quoted a passage from the court's judgment in *Ainsley Financial Corporation v. Ontario Securities Commission*, above, at 108-109, which confirmed the commission's authority, as a regulator, to issue non-binding statements, guidelines, speeches, and communiqués to inform and guide those subject to regulation.]

Mr. Waitzer's comments did not in any way relate to the subject matter of the complaints made against the appellants in the pending proceedings, nor should they be viewed as a veiled threat against the appellants, as was contended.

However, even if statements by a regulator relate to the very matters which he or she is considering, that, in itself, is not a basis for concluding that the regulator has prejudged the matter.

[Dubin CJO here quoted from the judgment of Cory J in *Newfoundland Telephone Co. v. Newfoundland (Board of Commissioners of Public Utilities)*, [1992] 1 SCR 623 (Nfld.), at 639, reproduced below.]

Even if it could be said that the statements of the Chair exhibited some bias against the appellants that, in itself, would not disqualify the other Commissioners from conducting the hearings.

In *Van Rassel v. Canada (Superintendent of the RCMP)* [1987] 1 FC 473 (TD) it was alleged that the commissioner of the RCMP made a public comment strongly critical of the RCMP officer who faced a trial before the RCMP service tribunal. Joyal J held that even if such a statement were made, it could not lead to a reasonable apprehension of bias against the whole tribunal, at 487:

> Assuming for the moment that the document is authentic and that the words were directed to the applicant, it would not on that basis constitute the kind of ground to justify my intervention at this time. The Commissioner of the RCM Police is not the tribunal. It is true that he has appointed the tribunal but once appointed, the tribunal is as independent and as seemingly impartial as any tribunal dealing with a service-related offence. One cannot reasonably conclude that the bias of the Commissioner, if bias there is, is the bias of the tribunal and that as a result the applicant would not get a fair trial.

As I indicated earlier, in my opinion, there was no merit in the contention that the new Commissioners were disqualified by reason of the comments made by the Chair.

Bias Resulting from Commission's Defence in the Ainsley Action

• • •

In the action, the plaintiffs claimed, in part, that the Commission staff could neither establish the public interest basis for the Policy Statement, nor the truth of the conclusions reached in the staff report upon which it was based. The plaintiffs also alleged bad faith, harassment, intimidation, and intentional interference with their business interests and claimed damages in the amount of $1 million.

These were very serious allegations and certainly called for a vigorous defence. The Divisional Court did not detail the manner in which they felt that the Commission in its defence to the *Ainsley* action went beyond defending itself and its jurisdiction. It would be a strange result if a securities dealer, whose conduct is under investigation, could, by the institution of an action calling for a defence, prevent the Commission from taking proceedings against it.

However, it is unnecessary to determine whether the Divisional Court was correct in holding that the defence of the *Ainsley* action was a basis for disqualification of certain of the Commissioners.

It was the Commission staff, along with counsel, who were responsible for assembling the materials that formed the basis of the Commission's response to the plaintiffs' allegations in the *Ainsley* action. None of the Commissioners, with the exception of the former Chair, Robert Wright, participated in any way in assembling those materials, or preparing the Commission's response to the action.

In my opinion, it cannot be said that the defence of the action was a basis to conclude that the new Commissioners had prejudged the complaints which were the subject matter of the notices of hearing, and, in this respect, I agree with the Divisional Court.

I agree with the way that this issue was dealt with in *Laws v. Australian Broadcasting Tribunal, supra*.

As noted above, in that case, an action for defamation had been commenced against the tribunal and one of its employees. The tribunal, in its defence, relied upon justification which, in effect, alleged that what the employee of the tribunal had stated was true, *ie*, that Laws had violated the broadcasting standards. The High Court of Australia did not accede to the submission of the appellant in that case that the defence in the civil action demonstrated bias, or a reasonable apprehension of bias, on the part of all the members of the Commission, including those who had not participated in the preliminary investigation.

The court concluded that the defence in the defamation action did not preclude members of the tribunal who had not participated in the preliminary investigation from conducting the pending inquiry.

• • •

Gaudron and McHugh JJ, concurring, added the following at 457-58:

In the present case, the most that can be said against those members of the tribunal who were parties to the filing of the defamation defences is that they believed that, upon the evidence then known to them, the assertions in the defences were true and that on that evidence they would probably have decided the s. 17c issues adversely to the appellant. But to attribute that belief and that decision to them does not give rise to a reasonable fear that they would not fairly consider any evidence or arguments presented by the appellant at the s. 17c inquiry or that they would not be prepared to change their views about the issues. When the defamation proceedings against the tribunal were commenced, the members of the tribunal were required to file the tribunal's defence on the evidence that they then had in their possession and without the benefit of evidence or argument from the appellant. When all the evidence is heard and the case argued, it may become apparent to them that the defences which the tribunal filed cannot succeed. However, there is no suggestion that the filing of the defences was itself an abuse of process or the product of prejudice. *To the contrary, the hypothesis is that the members of the tribunal believed that the assertions in the defences were true. But neither logic nor the evidence makes it reasonable to fear that, because of that belief, the members of the tribunal will not decide the case impartially when they hear the evidence and arguments for the appellant at the s. 17c inquiry.* [Emphasis added.]

As indicated earlier, I would reject the submission that the defence in the *Ainsley* action precluded the new Commissioners from presiding over the pending hearings.

Doctrine of Necessity

As noted earlier, the Divisional Court held that even if this were a case of "corporate taint," the doctrine of necessity could be invoked, which would all allow those Commissioners against whom no specific reasonable apprehension of bias was found to form a quorum for the hearings.

In the view that I take of the matter, it is not necessary to consider the doctrine of necessity.

. . .

Appeal dismissed.

NOTES

1. While the Divisional Court's disqualification of the members who had participated in the formulation of the *ultra vires* policy and of the chair of the commission was not in issue on the appeal, does the judgment of Dubin CJO speak indirectly to either of these conclusions? If so, to what effect?

2. On the scope and application of the doctrine of necessity, the Divisional Court had had the following to say:

If it is felt elsewhere that there is some corporate taint, I would allow the above two or three persons, as the case may be, to sit on the basis of the doctrine of necessity. Natural justice must give way to necessity. The doctrine of necessity was enunciated by Jackett CJ in *Caccamo v. Canada (Minister of Manpower & Immigration)* [1978] 1 FC 366 (CA) at 373:

As I understand the law concerning judicial bias, however, even where actual bias in the sense of a monetary interest in the subject of the litigation is involved, if all eligible adjudicating officers are subject to the same potential disqualification, the law must be carried out notwithstanding that potential disqualification. ... If this is the rule to be applied where actual bias is involved, as it seems to me, it must also be the rule where there is no actual case of bias but only a "probability" or reasonable suspicion arising from the impact of unfortunate statements on the public mind.

This case does not require the doctrine of necessity to be applied to the extent of the example referred to in *Caccamo v. Canada (Minister of Manpower & Immigration)*. The doctrine of necessity is properly used to prevent a failure of justice and not as an affront to justice: de Smith's *Judicial Review of Administrative Action*, (4th ed. 1980) at 276-77. Neither new member has acted in any way or even participated in any process which could give rise to a reasonable apprehension of bias on their part. Therefore the doctrine of necessity is rightly applied in these facts to allow a panel to be constituted, in case any general corporate disqualification beyond those members' control were found: Tracey, "Disqualified Adjudicators: The Doctrine of Necessity in Public Law" [1982] *Public Law* 628 at 632.

See also *Milne v. Joint Chiropractic Review Committee*, [1992] 3 WWR 354 (Sask. CA), where the application of the doctrine of necessity was rendered unnecessary by the presence of a regulation authorizing the appointment of temporary members. However, in Ontario, it is possible to finesse this problem. Section 16 of the *Public Officers Act*, RSO 1990, c. P.45 provides for the judicial appointment of *ad hoc* replacements whenever a public officer is "disqualified by interest" from performance of his or her duties. For an example of the use of this section in the instance of the province's Labour Relations Board, see *Service Employees International Union v. Johnson* (1997), 35 OR (3d) 345 (OC GD).

3. The British Columbia Securities Commission's investigations of the affairs of former Premier Bennett and business person Harb Doman gave rise to a mass of litigation, including the case referred to by Dubin CJO. In subsequent proceedings, a member of the hearing panel of the commission was held to be disqualified because he was a business competitor of those being proceeded against: *Bennett v. British Columbia (Superintendent of Brokers)* (1993), 17 Admin. LR (2d) 222 (BC CA). Nevertheless, despite the fact that the hearing had been proceeding for some time (mainly dealing with preliminary motions but also hearing one witness) and that the panel itself (minus the challenged member) had ruled against the objection based on its member's bias, the court refused to disqualify the whole of the panel. It was simply stated (at 232) that the other members had not been "tainted" by the participation up until that point of the disqualified member. This conclusion is unusual since the normal position is that the bias of one member is sufficient to disqualify the whole of a panel: *Sparvier v. Cowessess Indian Band* (1993), 63 FTR 242. Given that, the Court of Appeal's judgment should perhaps be seen as reflecting a view that the proceedings were not sufficiently far along to justify the usual inference of possible influence by the disqualified member.

4. The aftermath of this litigation challenging the structures of securities commissions brought both statutory and in-house changes. Section 3.5(4) of the Ontario *Securities Act*, RSO 1990, c. S.5, as am. SO 1997, c. 10, s. 37 and SO 1999, c. 9, s. 197 now provides generally that members of the commission who perform any of the commission's duties with respect to investigations and examinations may not, save with the written consent of the parties, sit on any subsequent hearing involving those matters. Internally, the OSC has also created various barriers to ensure greater separation of the various enforcement and adjudicative roles of the commission and its staff. See also the cautions issued in *Applebaum v. Ontario (Securities Commission)*, [1993] OJ No. 649 (Div. Ct.) (QL).

5. Legislative authorization may also justify the participation of those with a firm attitude or point of view or having a relationship with one of the parties or stake in the outcome. Labour relations boards and arbitration boards are typically composed of a representative of each of employers and labour, and an independent chairperson. The general purposes of this arrangement are described by Arthurs, in "The Three Faces of Justice" (1963), 28 *Sask. B Rev.* 147-48:

> The appeal of tripartitism is threefold. First, the parties may commit their dispute to an impartial arbiter, yet seek assurance that his decision will be influenced by knowledge of their special customs and relationship. Here the representative member provides a form of "judicial notice." Secondly, in both labour relations and international relations, adjudication is increasingly sought as a substitute for battle. Where the tribunal is created to adjust interests rather than merely to decide disputes over pre-existing rights, the representative member serves as a negotiator *vis-à-vis* the tribunal, while exerting moral suasion upon the party that nominated him. Thirdly, even where the tribunal functions in a more purely adjudicative fashion, parties who are committed to an ongoing relationship may wish to be assured of an "acceptable," if not a favourable, decision. The representative member provides the neutral arbiter with a sounding board upon which proposed rulings may be tested for this quality of acceptability. Of course, each of these virtues contains the seeds of its own negation. "Judicial notice" may extend to improper *ex parte* reception of evidence. Negotiation in the deliberations of the tribunal may degenerate to bluster or bullying. "Acceptability" may be incompatible with justice.

Note, however, *Refrigeration Workers Union, Local 516 v. Labour Relations Board of British Columbia* (1986), 27 DLR (4th) 676 (BC CA); aff'g. (1985), 19 Admin. LR 65 (BC SC); rev'g. (1985), 19 Admin. LR 43 (LRB BC), where the Court of Appeal held that a union member of the board was disqualified in the context of what the court saw as an inter-union dispute. See, however, the criticism of this case in Kuttner, "Is the Doctrine of Bias Compatible with the Tri-Partite Labour Tribunal?" (1986), 19 *Admin. LR* 81 and "Bias and the Labour Boards Redux" (1989), 31 *Admin. LR* 216.

6. In both *Brosseau* and *E.A. Manning*, much of the concern was with the way in which the respective Securities Commissions operated in an institutional sense. In the aftermath of these cases, and conscious of case law that dealt with problems of an institutional lack of independence (to which we turn later in this chapter), the Supreme Court finally recognized that bias too could be both individual or personal and institutional. This meant that, on occasion, when a tribunal was set up in such a way as to create a reasonable apprehension of bias, the court could set aside a decision on the basis of institutional bias. Where the institutional problems were the result of internal choices about modes of operation, this intervention was on the basis of the common law. Where the structures were statutorily provided for, as in *Brosseau*, the court needed a constitutional or *quasi*-constitutional basis on which to intervene. To conclude this section, we present examples of each.

2747-3174 Québec Inc. v. Quebec (Régie des permis d'alcool)
[1996] 3 SCR 919

[The régie revoked the company's liquor permits for violations of the statute. The company sought a declaration that various provisions of the Quebec liquor licensing statute were invalid in terms of s. 23 of the Québec *Charter of Human Rights and Freedoms*. As noted earlier, this section requires that where a tribunal is acting in a judicial or a *quasi*-judicial fashion, it be both "independent and impartial." In both the Quebec Superior Court and Court of Appeal ((1994), 122 DLR (4th) 553 (Que. CA)), the company was successful and the government obtained leave to appeal to the Supreme Court of Canada.]

GONTHIER J (Lamer CJ, La Forest, Sopinka, Cory, McLachlin, Iacobucci, and Major JJ concurring):

[After concluding that the régie did exercise judicial or *quasi*-judicial powers for the purposes of s. 23 of the Québec Charter, Gonthier J proceeded to deal with the claim that the operational structure of the régie gave rise to a reasonable apprehension of bias.]

Since [*R v. Lippé*, [1991] 2 SCR 114 (Que.)] there is no longer any doubt that impartiality, like independence, has an institutional aspect. Lamer CJ, speaking for the Court on this point, stated the following at 140:

> Notwithstanding judicial independence, there may also exist a reasonable apprehension of bias on an institutional or structural level. Although the concept of institutional impartiality has never before been recognized by this Court, the constitutional guarantee of an "independent and impartial tribunal" has to be broad enough to encompass this. Just as the requirement of judicial independence has both an individual and institutional aspect ([*R v. Valente*, [1985] 2 SCR 673 (Ont.)], at 687), so too must the requirement of judicial impartiality. I cannot interpret the Canadian *Charter* as guaranteeing one on an institutional level and the other only on a case-by-case basis.
>
> · · ·
>
> The objective *status* of the tribunal can be as relevant for the "impartiality" requirement as it is for "independence." Therefore, whether or not any particular judge harboured preconceived ideas or biases, if the system is structured in such a way as to create a reasonable apprehension of bias on an institutional level, the requirement of impartiality is not met. [Emphasis in original.]

In the case at bar, the respondent's concerns are related first to the Régie's multiple functions and to the impact of that multiplicity of functions on the duties of its various employees. The respondent thus concentrated on the context in which the decision makers operate and noted certain institutional characteristics capable in its view of affecting their state of mind, and accordingly raising an apprehension of bias. These submissions therefore concerned impartiality.

· · ·

(1) Institutional Bias

As a result of *Lippé, supra*, and *Ruffo v. Conseil de la magistrature*, [1995] 4 SCR 267 (Que.), *inter alia*, the test for institutional impartiality is well established. It is clear that the governing factors are those put forward by de Grandpré J in *Committee for Justice and Liberty v. National Energy Board*, [1978] 1 SCR 369 (Can.), at 394. The determination of institutional bias presupposes that a well-informed person, viewing the matter realistically and practically—and having thought the matter through—would have a reasonable apprehension of bias *in a substantial number of cases*. In this regard, all factors must be considered, but the guarantees provided for in the legislation to counter the prejudicial effects of certain institutional characteristics must be given special attention.

This test is perfectly suited, under s. 23 of the [Québec] *Charter*, to a review of the structure of administrative agencies exercising quasi-judicial functions. Whether appearing before an administrative tribunal or a court of law, a litigant has a right to expect that an impartial adjudicator will deal with his or her claims. As is the case with the courts, an informed observer analysing the structure of an administrative tribunal will reach one of two conclusions: he or she either will or will not have a reasonable apprehension of bias. That having been said, the informed person's assessment will always depend on the circumstances. The nature of the dispute to be decided, the other duties of the administrative agency and the operational context as a whole will of course affect the assessment. In a criminal trial, the smallest detail capable of casting doubt on the judge's impartiality will be cause for alarm, whereas greater flexibility must be shown toward administrative tribunals. As Lamer CJ noted in *Lippé, supra*, at 142, constitutional and quasi-constitutional provisions do not always guarantee an ideal system. Rather, their purpose is to ensure that, considering all of their characteristics, the structures of judicial and quasi-judicial bodies do not raise a reasonable apprehension of bias. This is analogous to the application of the principles of natural justice, which reconcile the requirements of the decision-making process of specialized tribunals with the parties' rights. ...

I note, however, that this necessary flexibility, and the difficulty involved in isolating the essential elements of institutional impartiality, must not be used to justify ignoring serious deficiencies in a quasi-judicial process. The perception of impartiality remains essential to maintaining public confidence in the justice system.

(i) The Liquor Permit Cancellation Process

The arguments against the Régie des permis d'alcool relate primarily to its role at various stages in the liquor permit cancellation process. The Act authorizes employees of the Régie to participate in the investigation, the filing of complaints, the presentation of the case to the directors and the decision.

I note at the outset that a plurality of functions in a single administrative agency is not necessarily problematic. This Court has already suggested that such a multifunctional structure does not in itself always raise an apprehension of bias. [Gonthier J here quoted from other Supreme Court authorities, principally *Brosseau*.]

Although an overlapping of functions is not always a ground for concern, it must nevertheless not result in excessively close relations among employees involved in different stages of the process. The lack of separation of roles within the Régie des permis d'alcool was the principal basis for the Court of Appeal's decision in the present case, which means that a thorough review of its institutional structure will be necessary.

The Régie is composed of at least six directors, including a chairman and a vice-chairman (s. 4). The directors are appointed by the government for a term of not over five years. Their remuneration, social benefits and conditions of employment are also determined by the government. Once fixed, however, their remuneration cannot be reduced (s. 5). The directors are prohibited from holding offices incompatible with the functions assigned to them by the Act (s. 9). They are also prohibited, under pain of forfeiture of office, from having any direct or indirect interest in an undertaking likely to make their personal interest in conflict with the duties of their office (s. 10). The directors have the powers and immunity of commissioners appointed under the *Act respecting public inquiry commissions*, RSQ, c. C-37 (s. 11). In addition, neither the Régie nor the directors can be prosecuted for official acts done in good faith in the exercise of their functions (s. 12).

The chairman, in addition to his or her role as a director, is responsible for the administration and the general direction of the affairs of the Régie (s. 8). The chairman's duties include presiding over the plenary sessions of the Régie, informing the directors on any questions of general policy, signing the documents and instruments within the Régie's jurisdiction either alone or with any other designated person, and preparing the roll (s. 15 of the *Règles de régie interne de la Régie des permis d'alcool du Québec*, RRQ 1981, c. P-9.1, r. 9). Moreover, the parties admitted that the chairman conducts an annual evaluation, on the basis of a rating guide, of the performance of the Régie's members and employees. The chairman is in turn evaluated by the Minister of Public Security. These assessments appear to be used to calculate bonuses. The vice-chairman replaces the chairman in his or her absence (s. 8). The Régie's 1991-92 annual report, which was filed in evidence, describes the vice-chairman's duties as follows, (at p. 21):

> [translation] The incumbent of this position co-ordinates and supervises the legal advice and support functions of the Régie's directors and legal advisers. She ensures that the Régie's decisions are consistent and that files for submission to the courts are in order.

The other employees of the Régie work in various administrative units. Only the secretariat is of interest in this appeal, as it is responsible, *inter alia*, for the legal services unit, which includes lawyers appointed and remunerated in accordance with the *Public Service Act*, RSQ, c. F-3.1.1. Their role is described as follows in the annual report (at p. 22):

> [translation] Members of legal services review any files that may result in notices to appear before the Régie to ensure that they comply with the law.
>
> These advisers also meet with the solicitors of record to clarify certain aspects of the cases, see that notices of summons are drafted and sent, and present arguments to the Régie sitting in public hearings. Legal services also give legal opinions to the managers and directors, perform legal research and draft opinions, prepare draft regulations on matters within the Régie's jurisdiction and provide the public with information on statutes and regulations.

In practice, employees of the Régie are involved at every stage of the process leading up to the cancellation of a liquor permit, from investigation to adjudication. Thus, the Act authorizes the Régie to require permit holders to provide information (s. 110). Members of the Régie's staff designated by the chairman, or members of police forces, may also inspect establishments during business hours (s. 111). The Régie has signed memorandums of understanding with certain police forces to establish a framework for their role of inspection and seizure. The Régie can thus initiate the investigation process. However, a formal investigation is not an absolute prerequisite for cancellation of a permit. The Régie may summon a permit holder of its own initiative or on the application of any interested person, including the Minister of Public Security (s. 85). As the annual report indicates, legal services lawyers participate in the preliminary review of files before the decision to summon a permit holder is made. Where the application for cancellation is made by a third party, s. 26 of the *Regulation respecting the procedure applicable before the Régie des permis d'alcool du Québec*, requires that the Régie summon the permit holder if the facts mentioned call *prima facie* for the enforcement of ss. 86 to 90 of the Act. The Act and regulations do not, however, specify the circumstances in which the Régie may proceed *proprio motu*.

If the Régie decides to hold a hearing, a notice of summons drafted by a legal services lawyer is sent to the permit holder. In the case at bar, the notice was signed by the chairman of the Régie. Where a ground related to public tranquility is involved, a hearing is then held before at least two directors designated by the chairman (ss. 15 and 16). One of the legal services lawyers acts as counsel for the Régie at that hearing. The directors must decide the matter and, in the case of a tied vote, the matter is referred to the Régie sitting in plenary session. The proceedings are completed with the publication of written reasons.

(ii) Role of the Régie's Lawyers

This detailed description of the Régie's structure and operations shows that the issue of the role of the lawyers employed by legal services is at the heart of this appeal. In my view, an informed person having thought the matter through would in this regard have a reasonable apprehension of bias in a substantial number of cases. The Act and regulations do not define the duties of these jurists. The Régie's annual report, however, and the description of their jobs at the Régie, show that they are called upon to review files in order to advise the Régie on the action to be taken, prepare files, draft notices of summons, present arguments to the directors and draft opinions. The annual report and the silence of the Act and regulations leave open the possibility of the same jurist performing these various functions in the same matter. The annual report mentions no measures taken to separate the lawyers involved at different stages of the process. Yet it seems to me that such measures, the precise limits of which I will deliberately refrain from outlining, are essential in the circumstances. Evidence as to the role of the lawyers and the allocation of tasks among them is incomplete, but the possibility that a jurist who has made submissions to the directors might then advise them in respect of the same matter is disturbing, especially since some of the directors have no legal training. In this regard, I agree with Brossard JA (at 581):

> [translation] The appellants invite us to presume that their opinions are general or related to the administrative functions of the directors and point out that the Régie's annual report does not establish the existence of any practice by which the prosecuting lawyers would also be called on to give legal opinions in the context of the exercise of the directors' adjudicative function. However, the report does not rule out this possibility. Yet in matters of institu-

tional bias, it is the reasonable apprehension of the informed person that we must consider and not the proven or presumed existence of an actual conflict of interest.

Furthermore, the courts have not hesitated to declare on the basis of the rules of natural justice that such a lack of separation of functions in a lawyer raises a reasonable apprehension of bias. In *Re Sawyer and Ontario Racing Commission* (1979) 24 OR (2d) 673 (CA), for example, the lawyer who presented the administrative agency's point of view subsequently took part in the review of the reasons for the decision. Brooke JA described the role of that lawyer as follows, at 676:

> But there is no doubt that his role was to prosecute the case against the appellant and he was not present in a role comparable to that of a legal assessor to the Commission. ... He was counsel for the appellant's adversary in proceedings to determine the appellant's guilt or innocence on the charge against him. It is basic that persons entrusted to judge or determine the rights of others must, for reasons arrived at independently, make that decision whether it or the reasons be right or wrong. It was wrong for the Commission, who were the judges, to privately involve either party in the Commission's function once the case began and certainly after the case was left to them for ultimate disposition. To do so must amount to a denial of natural justice because it would not unreasonably raise a suspicion of bias in others, including the appellant, who were not present and later learned what transpired.

See also *Després v. Association des arpenteurs-géomètres du Nouveau-Brunswick* (1992) 130 NBR (2d) 210 (CA); *Khan v. College of Physicians and Surgeons of Ontario* (1992) 76 CCC (3d) 10 (Ont. CA), at 41.

Similarly, in the case at bar, the Régie's lawyers could not advise the directors and make submissions to them without there being a reasonable apprehension of bias. This is not to say that jurists in the employ of an administrative tribunal can never play any role in the preparation of reasons. An examination of the consequences of such a practice would exceed the limits of this appeal, however, as I need only note, to dispose of it, that prosecuting counsel must in no circumstances be in a position to participate in the adjudication process. The functions of prosecutor and adjudicator cannot be exercised together in this manner.

(iii) Role of the Directors

The Court of Appeal's decision was also based on the fact that the directors could intervene at various stages in the permit cancellation process. The Régie, which is composed of the incumbent directors, may require permit holders to provide information (s. 110) and may assign one of its employees or a member of a police force to inspect an establishment (s. 111). The directors, including the chairman first and foremost, may thus initiate the review of a specific case. Similarly, the decision to hold a hearing presupposes a certain participation by the directors. It is the Régie that is responsible for sending notices of summons. Where a complaint is submitted to it by a third party, the Régie must hold a hearing if the allegations of fact call *prima facie* for the enforcement of the relevant provisions (s. 26 of the *Regulation respecting the procedure applicable before the Régie des permis d'alcool du Québec*). The circumstances in which the Régie may decide to summon a permit holder of its own initiative are not specified, but it may be concluded by analogy that similar criteria would be applied. Although the Act and the various regulations are silent on this subject, the Court of Appeal held in *Jacob et Bar Le Morency* [(1988), 16 QAC 308] that the decision to summon was an administrative decision within the chairman's authority that did not have to be made in plenary session. Gendreau JA described this power of the chairman as follows, at 311:

> [translation] The chairman determines only one simple question that boils down to deciding whether it is appropriate, in light of the information obtained and placed in the record kept under s. 20(1) of the Act, to constitute a panel of the Régie to determine whether the permit holder's use complies with the Act. The purpose of the chairman's power is therefore limited to setting the quasi-judicial investigation process in motion, and this power is included among those conferred by the Act.
>
> Furthermore, neither the purpose nor the effect of the chairman's decision is to affect the permit holder's rights; the operation of his or her establishment is not prevented, suspended or restricted. Nor does the notice include a decision or a statement of a presumption of unlawful exercise of trade that the appellants would have to rebut to retain their permit. In short, the chairman, in assigning the case to a panel of the Régie, in no way hinders the appellants either in putting their arguments to the directors in timely fashion or in acting as the authorized managers of their bar until the adjudication, the result of which is not prejudged.

Although the evidence was silent as to the Régie's practice, that judgment indicates that the decision to summon may be made by the chairman acting alone. In the case at bar, at the very least, the notice of summons bears the chairman's signature. The annual report, however, describes the duties of the directors as follows (at 23):

> [translation] In addition, they must take turns in assuming internal responsibility for verifying and, where appropriate, authorizing the draft decisions submitted by the retailers' and manufacturers' permit directorates, *reviewing administrative files submitted by legal services or the above-mentioned directorates in order to decide whether a summons is necessary*, having a draft decision prepared or taking any other appropriate action. [Emphasis added.]

Furthermore, once a notice of summons has been sent, the chairman has the power to designate the directors responsible for deciding the case in question (s. 15 of the *Règles de régie interne de la Régie des permis d'alcool du Québec*).

A lack of evidence makes it difficult to assess the Régie's operations. It must be noted, however, that the Act and regulations authorize the chairman to initiate an investigation, decide to hold a hearing, constitute the panel that is to hear the case and include himself or herself thereon if he or she so desires. Furthermore, the annual report suggests that other directors sometimes make the decision to hold a hearing, and it does not rule out the possibility that those directors might then decide the case on its merits. In the case at bar, these factors can only reinforce the reasonable apprehension of bias an informed person would have in respect of the Régie owing to the role of counsel.

Having said this, I agree with the opinion expressed by Gendreau JA in *Jacob et Bar Le Morency* that the decision to hold a hearing does not amount to a prior determination of the validity of the allegations against the permit holder. The fact that the Régie, as an institution, participates in the process of investigation, summoning and adjudication is not in itself problematic. However, the possibility that a particular director could, following the investigation, decide to hold a hearing and could then participate in the decision-making process would cause an informed person to have a reasonable apprehension of bias in a substantial number of cases. It seems to me that, as with the Régie's jurists, a form of separation among the directors involved in the various stages of the process is necessary to counter that apprehension of bias.

[The court subsequently rejected the company's other challenge based on a lack of institutional independence: below. In terms of relief, the court was also of the view that the problem of institutional bias was not a statutory one but could be dealt with internally by changing the way in which the régie operated. As a result, the appeal was technically allowed and the claim for a declaration dismissed. Instead, the court awarded the company a writ of evocation quashing the revocation of its licence.]

Appeal allowed.

NOTES

1. Contrast this judgment with that in *Brosseau*. Acting within its operational sphere, could not the Alberta Securities Commission have avoided the overlapping roles that were the subject of the challenge in that case? If so, why did the court allow the defence of statutory authorization to work there rather than here? Of course, if in this case, the court had held that the problem was with the statute, s. 23 of the Québec Charter would have prevailed over the statute.

2. Note how in this context the court took account of the way in which the régie in fact operated. In other words, the mere fact that the relevant act might leave open the possibility of a tribunal operating in a way that gives rise to a reasonable apprehension of institutional bias does not mean that the statute is flawed. Provided the tribunal operates in such a way as not to create an apprehension of bias, it will be secure from such an allegation. This issue of how the tribunal actually operates in practice also arises in the lack of independence cases that we consider below.

3. How might the régie have gone about restructuring its operations to meet the court's concerns?

4. In the case that follows, the Federal Court of Appeal was unable to deal with the problem of structural bias by telling the tribunal to restructure the way in which it operated. The institutional bias arose in this case out of provisions of the relevant statute. The court therefore required a constitutional or *quasi*-constitutional basis for overriding the statute. This is found in s. 2(e) of the *Canadian Bill of Rights*. The challenger had also advanced s. 7 of the Charter but the court did not feel it necessary to address that.

MacBain v. Canada (Human Rights Commission)
(1985), 22 DLR (4th) 119 (FCA)

[The *Canadian Human Rights Act*, SC 1976-77, c. 33 prohibited discrimination of various kinds and established the Canadian Human Rights Commission to administer its requirements. If a complaint was made to the commission, it could appoint an official to investigate and report. Section 36(3) provided that the commission could "adopt the report if it is satisfied that the complaint to which the report relates has been substantiated." Section 39 provided that it could at any time after a complaint was filed appoint a human rights tribunal from a panel of prospective members "established and maintained by the Governor in Council." The tribunal was to hold a hearing into the complaint, and "if it finds the complaint … is substantiated," it had power to make various remedial orders.

The complainant, Potapczyk, filed a complaint that MacBain had discriminated against her on the basis of her sex during the course of her employment. The commission appointed a staff member to investigate and, after she made her report, the commission decided that the complaint was substantiated and appointed a tribunal from the list established under s. 39.

MacBain sought a declaration that the legislation violated the Charter and the *Bill of Rights* because the arrangements specified by the Act for appointment of the tribunal created an apprehension of bias. The hearing proceeded, with the commission prosecuting the complaint, and the tribunal concluded that the complaint was justified. MacBain's action was dismissed by the Trial Division of the Federal Court, and MacBain appealed and succeeded. One major issue, which appeared in chapter 3 of this text, was whether the *Bill of Rights* applied.]

HEALD J delivered the judgment of the court: In essence [MacBain's] submission was to the following effect: in the instant case, and pursuant to the scheme envisaged in the Act, the Commission investigated, made findings of substantiation and then prosecuted this complaint; the very same Commission also appointed the Tribunal members who heard and decided the case adversely to the appellant/applicant. Such a scheme violates the principle that no one will judge his own cause since it cannot be said that there is any meaningful distinction between being your own judge and selecting the judges in your own cause. Accordingly, the scheme is inherently offensive and gives rise to a reasonable apprehension of bias thereby violating the principles of natural justice.

Collier J, after reviewing the facts, the scheme of the Act and the test set out in the *Crowe* case, concluded that

> … the reaction of a reasonable and right-minded person, viewing the whole procedure as set out in the statute and as adopted in respect of this particular complaint, would be to say: "There is something wrong here; the complaint against me has been ruled proved; now that complaint is going to be heard by a tribunal appointed by the body who said the complaint has been proved; that same body is going to appear against me in that hearing and urge the complaint to be found to be proved."

It is clear from a perusal of the reasons of the learned trial judge in their entirety that, in his view, the most serious problem with the scheme of the Act is the requirement initially for the Commission to determine whether the complaint has been "substantiated" (s-s. 36(3)) whereas the Tribunal is obligated in its deliberations to make the same determination—namely substantiation of the complaint (s-ss. 41(1) and (2)). He observed that the same word "substantiate" was used in both subsections and it was his opinion that the same meaning should be ascribed to that word in both subsections. He defined "substantiate" to mean "prove" and applied that definition to both subsections. In his view, it was the fact that the Commission had already found that the case against MacBain had been "proved" prior to the appointment of the Tribunal that gave rise to a reasonable apprehension of bias. The trial judge made it clear that his finding of apprehension of bias rested on the provisions requiring substantiation and that if the statute had simply required the Commission to be satisfied that there was enough evidence to warrant a hearing, no apprehension of bias would exist.

. . .

With respect, I differ from the view of the learned trial judge that the issue of substantiation is the only factor when considering apprehension of bias. In my view, the apprehension of bias also exists in this case because there is a direct connection between the prosecutor of the complaint (the Commission) and the decision maker (the Tribunal). That connection easily gives rise, in my view, to a suspicion of influence or dependency. After considering a case and deciding that the complaint has been substantiated, the "prosecutor" picks the Tribunal which will hear the case. It is my opinion that even if the statute only required the Commission to decide whether there was sufficient evidence to warrant the appointment of a Tribunal, reasonable apprehension of bias would still exist.

[Discussion of an argument about the appropriate standard is omitted.]

Counsel for the Attorney-General opened his oral submissions with a frank concession that "What we have here is an appearance of unfairness" which "may deserve relief." He then went on to urge that any relief granted should not "demolish the statute." He proceeded to emphasize that in this case we are dealing with an administrative tribunal and not a court in the traditional sense. He submitted that, in these circumstances, the procedure set out in the Act should be seen "… through the eyes of an informed person examining this tribunal and its functions realistically and practically." He then proceeded to detail numerous features of the scheme of the Act. With respect, it seems to me that this analysis begs the question because it fails to consider whether the respondent was afforded fundamental justice under that scheme. Some of the features mentioned by counsel relate to "utilitarian considerations" such as volume, expense, efficiency and expediency. In this connection, I think the observations made by Wilson J in *Re Singh and Minister of Employment & Immigration* are relevant.

Appeal allowed.

NOTES

1. Contrast the court's concern in *MacBain* over the overlapping functions of the commission with the judgment of the Supreme Court of Canada in *Idziak v. Canada (Minister of Justice)*, [1992] 3 SCR 631 (Can.). Here, the dual functions of the minister of justice in extradition proceedings were at issue. Under the *Extradition Act*, it was the responsibility of the minister to decide whether to respond favourably to a "requesting" nation and appoint an agent to "prosecute" a matter at an extradition hearing. Thereafter, if the extradition judge issued a warrant of committal, it was also for the minister to decide whether to surrender

the person to the requesting nation. Cory J, for the court, following *USA v. Cotroni*, [1989] 1 SCR 1 (Que.), held that this overlapping of functions was not contrary to s. 7 of the Charter and the "principles of fundamental justice." In so doing, he emphasized the flexible content of those principles and, against this background, referred to the buffer provided by the extradition hearing conducted by a judge and at which the affected individual had full procedural protections as well as the highly political nature of the minister's discretionary power not to issue a warrant of surrender despite the existence of a warrant of committal. This latter function, he described as being very much at the legislative end of the continuum between highly judicialized and legislative functions. As a consequence, there was no basis for a claim that the conferring of dual roles was unconstitutional.

2. The Supreme Court had also earlier visited the constitutional dimensions of overlapping functions in *R v. Jones*, [1986] 2 SCR 284 (Alta.). Here, it rejected the argument that s. 7 was infringed by a process in which a departmental official decided whether there was sufficient proof of effective instruction to warrant allowing a child to be taught outside the regular school system. It was not persuaded by the contention that a reasonable apprehension of bias existed on the basis that such an official would have a strong commitment to enrolment in the regular school system.

3. In *R v. Lippé*, above (referred to with approval in *Idziak*), Lamer CJ (at 144) stated that the appropriate standpoint from which to consider such allegations of institutional bias or impartiality was that of "a fully informed person" and whether that person would have a reasonable apprehension of bias in "a substantial number of cases." If the answer to that question was in the negative, to succeed, the applicant would then have to establish a reasonable apprehension of bias in the context of his or her particular case. In this context, recollect the earlier discussion of whether the vantage point is or should now be that of a *fully informed* reasonable person in all bias cases. (We return to this theme below in considering *Alex Couture Inc. v. Canada (Attorney-General)*.)

4. *MacBain* was an important case in the resurrection of the *Canadian Bill of Rights* as a vehicle for challenging the validity of statutory schemes on the basis that they did not conform to the "principles of fundamental justice." As we saw in chapter 3 of this text, the basis on which the Court of Appeal was prepared to do this was that the commission and its tribunal were engaged in a "determination" of whether MacBain had breached his legal "obligation" under the federal *Human Rights Act* not to discriminate on the basis of sex, thus bringing the proceedings within s. 2(e). This, of course, is not a basis for attacks on provincial human rights bodies. For s. 7 of the Charter to be invoked, a "life, liberty and security of the person" interest has to be identified and, as we have seen already and especially in the wake of *Blencoe v. British Columbia (Human Rights Commission)*, [2000] 2 SCR 307, that may in fact be a comparatively rare occurrence.

5. While *MacBain* was still being litigated, amendments to the federal *Human Rights Act* were in train. First, the standard to be applied by the commission in requiring the striking of a panel was changed. Now, the judgment to be made was whether "having regard to all the circumstances of the complaint, an inquiry thereinto is warranted." In addition, the panel to hear the matter was no longer appointed by the commission itself but by a new official, the president of the Canadian Human Rights Tribunal panel, though, as before, the selection was made from a list designated by the governor in council. (See SC 1985, c. 26, ss. 69-71.) However, that did not end the problems with the Act. In *Bell Canada v. Canadian*

Telephone Employees Association, [1998] 3 FC 244 (TD), in the context of a pay equity hearing before the tribunal, the Federal Court Trial Division sustained a further challenge to the Act. There were two bases for the holding that the tribunal was insufficiently independent: first, because the minister was responsible for deciding whether to extend the term of office of a member whose term expired during a hearing and, second, because the commission prescribed the rate of remuneration (and expenses policies) for members of the tribunal. The appeal in this case was adjourned *sine die* to allow the government time to change the Act yet again: (1999), 246 NR 368 (FCA). This indeed happened: SC 1998, c. 9. Under the revisions to the Act, the discretion on whether to allow a member whose term of office was expiring to continue to hear a case was conferred on the president of the tribunal and issues of remuneration and expenses were subjected to a process that was at arm's length from the commission. The Act was challenged once more in *Canadian Telephone Employees Association v. Bell Canada*, [2001] 3 FC 481 (CA), where the Court of Appeal, reversing the Trial Division ([2001] 2 FC 392 (TD)), held, in the context of the same pay equity hearing, that the independence of the tribunal was not compromised by virtue of the fact that the commission had exercised its statutory authority and issued general directives to the tribunal in the domain of pay equity. The court also rejected an additional challenge to the legislative amendments prompted by the previous litigation. Giving the president of the tribunal a discretion as to whether a member would be allowed to complete a hearing notwithstanding the expiry of his or her term of office did not threaten that member's independence. This judgment was upheld by the Supreme Court of Canada: [2003] 1 SCR 884.

6. The issue of the links between adjudicators and those appointing them is one that we have also encountered earlier in the domain of tripartite arbitrations. There, as in the field of human rights adjudications, the fear sometimes expressed is not so much one based on a perception of the appointee's known attitudes toward the specific issue but rather on a concern that the appointee will tend to favour the position of the appointing agency for other reasons and, most notably, to ensure continuing access to this and other types of appointment or benefit. In the case of tripartite arbitrations, such a situation can be described readily as one involving association with one of the parties but, in the case of human rights adjudications, that analysis does not necessarily hold to the extent that the appointing authority is not really a party to the proceedings. As a consequence, this type of problem now tends to be classified as one of insufficient independence, a somewhat broader category than that of bias. To that problem, we turn in a separate section.

ATTITUDINAL BIAS

The first case that we consider in this section is one that spans the issues of prior involvement and attitudinal bias. It is about the mechanisms for awarding tenure at a university. To the extent that that process is one which involves ongoing peer evaluation, colleagues, who are responsible for the actual collection and assessment of data and opinion and for making recommendations based on that and their own views, will have had a prior involvement in the matter. In so far as this is an inevitable part of the whole process, what also becomes relevant in this context is the issue of implied statutory authorization or, putting it another way, a consideration of the extent to which the exigencies of statutory context dictate a movement away from normal standards and tests for bias.

Paine v. University of Toronto
(1980), 115 DLR (3d) 461 (Ont. Div. Ct.); rev'd. (1981), 131 DLR (3d) 325 (Ont. CA)

BY THE COURT: This is an application for judicial review brought by Anthony Paine, an assistant professor in the Department of Fine Arts at the University of Toronto, following the denial of his application for tenure in April, 1975. Hereafter, the applicant will be described as the Candidate, the Governing Council as the Council, the Tenure Committee as the Committee and the Tenure Appeal Committee as the Appeal Committee.

In 1972, the "Haist Rules" were adopted by the Council's predecessors and became part of the terms of employment of all professorial members of the staff of the university following their adoption. These rules, which are not specifically authorized by any statutory provisions, deal with the subject of academic tenure and their most important features, so far as this appeal is concerned, are to be found in the following excerpts:

The Nature of Academic Tenure
Tenure, as understood, herein, is the holding by a member of the professorial staff of the University of a continuing full-time appointment which the University has relinquished the freedom to terminate before the normal age of retirement except for cause and under the conditions specified in (14) to (30) below:

. . .

Tenure shall be granted only by a definite act, under stipulated conditions on the basis of merit.

The Granting of Tenure
(1) To qualify for tenure the individual should have demonstrated academic excellence in his field and should have shown his willingness to accept reasonable university responsibilities.

. . .

(5) Assistant Professors shall be considered for tenure after a probationary period of six years.

(6) In the spring term of the year preceding the last year of the probationary period, a Tenure Committee shall meet to decide whether or not the member of the professorial staff shall be recommended for tenure. The Tenure Committee shall be appointed by the Dean of the Faculty, Director of the School or Principal of the College in consultation with the Chairman of the Department concerned. The Chairman of the Department shall be the Chairman of the Committee. The Committee shall, in addition to its Chairman, the Dean, Director or Principal, and the Dean of the School of Graduate Studies or his representative, consist of four members of the professorial staff having tenure, at least two of whom should be from the Department involved. … A recommendation to grant tenure must be approved by at least five of the seven members of the Committee.

An assessment was requested from all tenured members of the Department of Fine Arts as internal referees. One such internal assessment was negative, the referee stating that it was clear in his mind for some time that the Candidate was not acceptable for tenure.

The Candidate was advised by letter dated March 5, 1975, that the membership of the Committee would probably include three tenured department members and at least one tenured person from outside the department but within the university in a cognate discipline. He was advised "it is up to you to let me know, with substantive reasons, whether there are any potential members in those categories to whom you wish to object. If you enter no objections, I must assume you have none … ."

The Committee was set up consisting of four tenured members of the Department of Fine Arts, including the chairman, Professor Winter; a tenured member of the Department of Architecture, a "cognate" department; a representative of the School of Graduate Studies and the Dean of the Faculty of Arts and Science, the latter two sitting as *ex officio* members. One of the tenured members of the department who was asked to serve on the Committee declined and it is said that it was at that time that the tenured member who had made the negative assessment previously was invited to serve.

On April 11 and 15, 1975, the Committee met and decided to recommend denial of tenure and termination of the Candidate's appointment as of June 30, 1976, by a vote of five to zero with two abstentions. …

In our view, the one overwhelming consideration which points to procedural unfairness is the fact that, with prior knowledge of the views that he had previously expressed, the chairman of the Tenure Committee appointed to it a tenured senior member of the Department of Fine Arts who had submitted a thoroughly negative assessment of Mr Paine's merits as an instructor and artist concluding with a statement to the effect that the writer had concluded some time before that Mr Paine was "not acceptable for tenure."

The presence of that member constituted unfairness and certainly made the likelihood of unfairness apparent to any who knew or became aware of the member's previous statement. While the decision is, of course, ultimately within the jurisdiction of a reviewing Court, we think the matter was well expressed at 201 of the report made on this matter by the university ombudsman where he has this to say:

> Irrespective of whatever qualifications such a member might have for sitting on a tenure committee, I cannot see how a suspicion that he might be, either consciously or unconsciously, incapable of making an objective decision could ever be dispelled. Even if justice were done, it most certainly would not be seen to be done in such circumstances. In my opinion, then, the presence of Referee A on Mr Paine's Tenure Committee did indeed constitute an irregularity and unfairness.

Regardless of the fact that there was an appeal to the Appeals Committee and indeed a second appeal directed by the president after receiving the report of the ombudsman, there was really no *de novo* hearing on fresh material and we do not think that any of the subsequent appeals or hearings had or could have had the effect of validating the decision of the Tenure Committee so constituted.

It is argued that such a body is not in fact acting in a judicial or *quasi*-judicial capacity but rather as a jury of the applicant's peers. Certain American authorities are cited in support of this proposition and it is argued that anything like judicial fairness is not required of such a body.

In our view, there is nothing inconsistent with the concept of judgment by one's peers in a requirement that proceedings must be fair. Our criminal justice system is based fundamentally upon the procedure of trial by jury which is historically founded upon the concept of judgment by one's peers. Nevertheless, bias or apprehended bias has long been recognized by statute and by common law as a valid ground upon which to challenge a potential juryman. A trial is no less a trial by one's peers if those among them who are obviously biased have been previously eliminated.

Application granted.

[The university appealed.]

WEATHERSTON JA: I turn then to the question of whether the Court ought to intervene in the present case. The Divisional Court found that there was unfairness in the presence on the tenure committee of a member who, as a referee, had submitted a thoroughly negative assessment of Mr Paine's merits as an instructor and artist, concluding with a statement to the effect that the writer had concluded some time before that Mr Paine was "not acceptable for tenure." Mr Genest, for the university, argues that there was no unfairness at all, given the nature of the process by which tenure is granted or withheld. Members of the tenure committee are tenured members of the professorial staff of the candidate's department, or a cognate department. As a matter of course they must all, in the course of their association with the candidate, have formed general opinions as to his suitability for tenure, and it makes little difference whether that opinion was expressed before or at the meetings of the committee. There is much force in that argument. The tenure committee does not sit as a tribunal, acting only on the evidence placed before it. The members act on their own knowledge of the candidate, as well as the assessments and references that are provided to them. A recommendation to grant tenure need be approved by only five of the seven members of the committee, and it is worth noting that not one of the members approved Mr Paine's application.

Of course it is possible that a member of the tenure committee, with a preconceived opinion as to a candidate's suitability for tenure, could dominate the proceedings and persuade the others to accept his opinion. That seems unlikely, in view of the composition of this committee, and there is no suggestion that it happened in this case.

There is a procedure for review by a tenure appeal committee. This is not a new hearing that would cure any defects in the first proceedings, but a person who has been denied tenure has the right to appeal on one or more of the following grounds:

(a) a significant irregularity or unfairness in the procedure followed by the tenure committee or in the selection of its members;

(b) improper bias or motive on the part of any member of the tenure committee;

(c) improper bias or motive on the part of any person whose opinion may have materially influenced the decision of the committee; or

(d) the decision is one which, in the light of the evidence before the committee and the standards that should have been applied, was unreasonable.

Mr Paine appealed on all those grounds, specifically complaining of the presence on the tenure committee of the member who had written the unfavourable assessment. The tenure appeal committee, and a second tenure appeal committee appointed by the president of the university, rejected all grounds of appeal.

The question is whether, at the end of the day (to use an English expression), Mr Paine has shown that he was treated with such manifest unfairness as to call for intervention by the Court. It may be that a Judge would think it wrong and unfair for the chairman to have selected, as a member of the tenure committee, a man who had written an adverse assessment of the candidate; but the members of the university community to which Mr Paine belonged, and to whose judgment he submitted, thought otherwise. I think this is not a case where the Court should intervene to substitute its own views for those of the review committee's.

I would allow the appeal with costs, and dismiss the application with costs.

MacKINNON ACJO: I agree with the conclusion to which my brother Weatherston has come and the reasons for that conclusion and I have only a brief comment to add. *Calvin v. Carr* [[1984] AC 574 (PC NSW)] is cogent authority for the view that, generally speaking, Courts should leave domestic disputes to be settled by methods agreed on by the parties. In that case Lord Wilberforce, speaking for the Judicial Committee, said this (at 593):

> ... it is for the court, *in the light of the agreements made*, and in addition having regard to the course of proceedings, to decide whether, at the end of the day, there has been a fair result, reached by fair methods, such as the parties should fairly be taken to have accepted when they joined the association.

In the instant case the respondent had two university tenure appeal committee hearings, the second one with a different chairman from the first and in which the respondent had the assistance of counsel. There is no complaint about the conduct or procedures of those hearings, only with the results. The very complaints (without detailing them) which were made by the respondent to the Courts, were the complaints that were thoroughly thrashed out before the tenure appeal committees and rejected by them.

The parties to the instant appeal had contractually agreed to have their domestic disputes resolved in a certain way, and as I have noted, there is no suggestion that there were "flagrant violations" of procedural fairness or otherwise, in the proceedings before the tenure appeal committees. The validity of the rejection of tenure rested, in the last resort, on the decision of the tenure appeal committee which the parties by their agreement and actions had determined to be the knowledgeable arbiter of the issues raised. This is not, in my view, the exceptional case in which there is manifest error on the part of the appeal tribunals nor is it a flagrant case of injustice at any level of the proceedings which demands that the Court interfere.

[Brooke JA concurred with Weatherston JA.]

Appeal allowed.

NOTE

In requiring that the applicant in such cases demonstrate "manifest unfairness" or "flagrant violations of procedural fairness," the Ontario Court of Appeal appears to be adopting a higher threshold for judicial intervention than is normally applied in procedural fairness cases. In part, this is contingent on the court's deference to the internal processes of the university, once again a posture that before *Baker* was not adopted customarily in procedural fairness litigation. Is there anything in the particular context that justifies this "exception" to the normal principles of scrutiny?

One domain where the issue of attitudinal bias has a high profile is that of *Human Rights Code* adjudications. To what extent should attitudes toward the enforcement of anti-discrimination protections in general and the evolution of specific areas of human rights law in particular lead to exposure to a challenge based on a reasonable apprehension of bias? In the first case that we consider, that issue was avoided by the court focusing its attention on a link between the adjudicator and the prosecuting commission. However, the more general issue was clearly present as well.

Great Atlantic & Pacific Co. of Canada v. Ontario (Human Rights Commission)
(1993), 12 Admin. LR (2d) 267 (Ont. Div. Ct.)

PER CURIAM [Montgomery, Carruthers, and Campbell JJ]: ... It is the position of both A&P, and the Union, that there exists a real and reasonable apprehension of bias, and perhaps acts of bias, on the part of Constance Backhouse as the Board appointed [in 1991] to hear and decide the complaints in issue.

This position is based upon both the background of Miss Backhouse as an "advocate" in matters and issues involving sex discrimination, and the fact of her being a party in proceedings outstanding before the Commission in which that issue is raised. At the time of her appointment, Miss Backhouse was an associate professor at the Faculty of Law, University of Western Ontario. She had been a member of that faculty for several years and during that time she had written extensively on the subject of "sex discrimination." In this respect, all counsel referred to her as an advocate.

In September of 1987, Miss Backhouse was one of 120 people who filed a complaint with the Commission. That complaint alleges, generally speaking, that Osgoode Hall Law School, York University, had violated the provisions of the Code by reason of systemic sex discrimination ("the Osgoode Hall Complaint"). Miss Backhouse was elected by the complainants to serve as one of a 12 member steering committee.

The material indicates that some question remains as to whether the memorandum of settlement of the issues raised in the Osgoode Hall Complaint, entered into in September, 1989, has been completely fulfilled. Since that time the matter has been designated as "inactive" by the Commission. However, there is no question that, because there has been no formal settlement of the issues and the complaint has not been withdrawn, it remains at this time classified as being "outstanding."

On April 20, 1992, Miss Backhouse wrote to the Commission requesting that her name be withdrawn from the list of complainants in the Osgoode Hall Complaint. At the same time she caused her membership in the steering committee to end. By letter dated the 29th of March, 1993, the Commission acknowledged that it had acceded to Miss Backhouse's request withdrawing her name as a complainant.

Counsel appears for the Board to defend its decision on the issue of reasonable apprehension of bias. Generally speaking, we consider it wrong for individual adjudicators to so retain counsel. In the unusual circumstances of this case, however, we exercised our discretion so as to permit counsel for Miss Backhouse to argue this issue of bias in order to expedite the hearing before us and to avoid unnecessary argument.

During the course of argument, we advised counsel that we did not think it necessary to decide whether Miss Backhouse's public advocacy in favour of the same position advanced before her by the Commission in relation to systemic sex discrimination went so far as to create a reasonable apprehension of bias in relation to this case. Rather, we told counsel that for the purposes of determining this issue, our attention was focused only upon the fact of Miss Backhouse's involvement in the proceedings outstanding before the Commission in which she was, at the relevant times, one of the complainants.

All counsel agree that the appropriate test to employ when determining if there is a reasonable apprehension of bias is derived from de Grandpré J's dissenting opinion in *Committee for Justice and Liberty v. Canada (National Energy Board)* [1978] 1 SCR 369 (Can.) at 394-95. The test put forward in that case would require an analysis of the relevant facts by a reasonable and right-minded person who was well informed as to the issues.

In our view, the unique aspect of this case is that Miss Backhouse went beyond the position of an advocate and descended personally, as a party, into the very arena over which she has been appointed to preside in relation to the very same issues she has to decide.

By becoming a personal complainant before the very commission that was prosecuting the similar case before her, she personally selected one of the parties before her as her own advocate to pursue her personal complaint about the same issue.

Counsel are in agreement that there has been no decided case in this province which deals with an allegation of systemic discrimination on the grounds of sex. Miss Backhouse is therefore in a position, in this case, should she continue as the Board, to vindicate the position she had taken as a personal complainant in a similar case. It is trite to state that simple justice requires a high degree of neutrality. We do not think that would be attained if Miss Backhouse was to continue as the Board. In our opinion, the appropriate test has not been met.

Therefore, because there is, in our opinion, a reasonable apprehension of bias, the application of the Union in this respect is allowed and the proceedings before the Board are quashed. The Minister is at liberty to appoint another board to adjudicate the remaining complaints against the Union if so requested to do so.

With respect to the matter of costs, counsel are in agreement that the amount of $10,000 is due to both the Union and A&P on account of the appearances before this Court last December and now. We are of the opinion that both the Commission and the Board are liable to pay these amounts on a joint and several basis.

Order accordingly.

NOTE

The case raises starkly the issue of the appointment of human rights activists to adjudicate on complaints of discrimination under human rights codes. Should involvement as one of a large number of complainants in another case in which the limits of the Act are being tested prevent service as an adjudicator in subsequent hearings? Should a record as an advocate of an expansion or expansive interpretation of the *Human Rights Code* disqualify a person from service? If such activities limit those who have taken a pro-human-rights stance, should there be corresponding restrictions on those who advocate retrenchment or narrow interpretations of human rights codes? Should the answer to these questions depend on whether the tribunal is a three-person or single-member one and on whether the issue in the proceedings is one with respect to which the challenged member has taken a prior position or been active? To what extent should the approach to these questions be conditioned by the desirability of having experts with a sympathy toward the purposes of the Code adjudicate on complaints?

In fact, in an earlier *Human Rights Code* judgment, the Ontario Divisional Court dealt with such a challenge in a way that suggested at least some room for prior expression of views on and involvement with human rights causes though note how the court draws a distinction between the matter on which the single member tribunal had expressed an opinion and the issue for decision.

Large v. Stratford (City)
(1992), 9 OR (3d) 104 (Div. Ct.)

ARCHIE CAMPBELL J (Callaghan CJOC and Zuber SJ concurring on this issue):

Alleged Bias

The appellant [employer] argues that board chair Professor Robert W. Kerr was biased, as evidenced by his public statements as president of the Canadian Association of University Teachers, after he released his decision in this case and before he dealt with the question of compensation. His remarks included statements that flexible rather than mandatory retirement is a sensible way to deal with older men and women, that it should be negotiated at the bargaining table, and that governments should be lobbied to abolish mandatory retirement. During the course of the impugned comments he said:

> Human rights laws which recognize *bona fide* occupational requirements are the appropriate way to deal with those few situations where it [is] impractical to deal with each man or woman individually.

The professor took a public position on a public issue—the general desirability of mandatory retirement. That question was never in issue before him in this case and he was not called upon to decide it. The parties avoided that question by agreeing that mandatory retirement at age 60 was *prima facie* discriminatory. Professor Kerr was called upon to decide a quite different issue, whether the evidence established that retirement at age 60 was a *bona fide* occupational requirement of the Stratford police force.

Professor Kerr took the public position that the best way to deal with retirement was on the basis of *bona fide* occupational requirement, the very issue remitted to him in this case.

These comments do not violate the well-established standards of administrative neutrality. Human rights inquiry boards are drawn from those who have some experience and understanding of human rights issues. To exclude everyone who ever expressed a view on human rights issues would exclude those best qualified to adjudicate fairly and knowledgeably in a sensitive area of public policy.

This is not a case like *Committee for Justice and Liberty v. Canada (National Energy Board)* [1978] 1 SCR 369 (Can.), where the adjudicator had been involved in a corporate pipeline study whose conclusions were in issue before his tribunal. This is not a case like *Newfoundland Telephone Co. v. Newfoundland (Board of Commissioners of Public Utilities)* [1992] 1 SCR 623 (Nfld.), where the adjudicator demonstrated that he had a closed mind on the subject in issue.

Whatever his views on questions which were not in issue in this case, there is no evidence of any reasonable apprehension of bias on the questions to be decided by the chair of the board of inquiry.

Appeal dismissed.

NOTES

1. Linked with this issue of attitudinal bias in *Human Rights Code* and other adjudications is the whole question of how the members of human rights tribunals and boards of inquiry are appointed. Consider, for example, the following advertisement for a chair of the now defunct Ontario Employment Equity Tribunal, which appeared some years ago in the Ontario Reports ((1994), 17 OR (3d) (pt. 7), xliii):

> The Government of Ontario is committed to fairness and equity in employment throughout the province. The *Employment Equity Act*, which will be proclaimed in 1994, will help to remove barriers to employment for Aboriginal people, people with disabilities, members of racial minorities and women.
>
> The Act provides for the establishment of the Employment Equity Tribunal. This independent adjudicative body will hear and decide matters under this new legislation.
>
> We seek an exceptional leader to establish and chair the Tribunal. The immediate priorities are to adjudicate first cases and to develop and implement policies, procedures and hearing practices to ensure the fair and consistent application of rights to all parties.
>
> Candidates must have experience in adjudication and administrative law as well as knowledge of mediation practices and principles. A sound knowledge of equality issues is essential. Knowledge of the *Employment Equity Act* and related legislation such as the *Human Rights Code*, the *Advocacy Act*, the *Pay Equity Act*, labor law and employment standards is necessary.
>
> Sound judgment is critical as early decisions will set the jurisprudence in this new and complex area of administrative law. Excellent communication, interpersonal, decision-making and administrative skills are required.
>
> This important opportunity will appeal to those who have demonstrated a commitment to social justice, equity and access issues. Appointment is by Order-in-Council for an initial three-year term.
>
> In accordance with our employment equity goals, applications are particularly encouraged from aboriginal peoples, francophones, persons with disabilities, racial minorities and women. Reply in confidence to 102 Bloor Street West, Ste. 900, Toronto, Ontario M5S 1M8.

Should the contents of this advertisement give any cause for concern? Or, is it directed at no more than emphasizing that the successful applicant will be someone who shares the policy objectives of the relevant legislation? Issues of appointment and reappointment of members of tribunals also raise issues of structural or institutional bias to which we return when we consider the possibility of constitutional challenges based on bias and lack of independence.

2. Of course, as *Baker* establishes clearly, a *lack* of sympathy with legislative objectives is a basis for disqualification.

3. For an interesting example of a similar argument being made in the context of a challenge to the adjudication of a matter by a s. 96 court judge, see *Ellis-Don Ltd. v. Ontario (Labour Relations Board)* (1992), 98 DLR (4th) 762 (Ont. Div. Ct.). The substantive issue was whether members of the Ontario Labour Relations Board had an immunity against testifying about the processes by which they reached their decision in a particular case. The challenged judge was Adams J, who, some ten years previously as chair of the same board, had rendered the decision justifying the board's practice of meeting collectively to discuss cases heard by various panels of the board, a justification approved subsequently though subject to limits (that were being tested in *Ellis-Don*) by the Supreme Court of Canada in *Consolidated-Bathurst Packaging Ltd. v. International Woodworkers of America, Local 2-69*, [1990] 1 SCR 282 (Ont.). The Ontario Divisional Court held that the issue before the court of which Adams J was a member and the issue before the board that he had chaired earlier were not the same and that, in any event, judges of the superior courts were not to be subject to disqualification merely because they "once took a position in days of yore before being appointed a judge" (at 765). The court's robust defence of its own judges and their ability to dissociate themselves from prior involvements and prior points of view contrasts with the attitude sometimes exhibited by courts toward members of administrative tribunals and their past involvement with issues and causes. On the other hand, the fact that the court was prepared to be so forgiving in the context of regular court proceedings provides a very useful precedent for situations where similar issues arise in relation to tribunals and agencies and where one would normally expect the extent of tolerance to be even greater. However, this does not mean that judges are immune from such challenges. In *Locabail (UK) Ltd. v. Bayfield Properties Ltd.*, above, the English Court of Appeal upheld an allegation of a reasonable apprehension of bias claim made by an insurance company litigant on the basis of articles he had written for professional journals in which he was critical of the way in which insurance companies conducted litigation. Also, in a case reminiscent of *Gale*, above, in *Benedict v. Ontario* (2000), 51 OR (3d) 147 (CA), the court held that a judge was disqualified from hearing a wrongful dismissal case against the Crown, when she herself was still engaged in a similar claim against the Crown in which similar issues were likely to arise. More generally, on the principles governing allegations of bias against judges, see *R v. RDS*, [1997] 3 SCR 484.

PECUNIARY AND OTHER MATERIAL INTERESTS

The common law has always treated a direct pecuniary or other material interest in the outcome of a matter as disqualifying an adjudicator or decision-maker automatically. The classic case is one involving a member of the regular judiciary, indeed the Lord Chancellor of England.

In *Dimes v. Proprietors of the Grand Junction Canal* (1852), 10 ER 301 (Eng. HL), Lord Chancellor Cottenham confirmed orders (made by the vice-chancellor) in favour of the canal company. Later, the party against whom the orders had been made discovered that the Lord Chancellor owned shares in the company and appealed. The House of Lords held that the orders should be reversed, and Lord Campbell said: "No one can suppose that Lord Cottenham could be, in the remotest degree, influenced by the interest that he had in this concern; but, my Lords, it is of the last importance that the maxim that no man is to be a judge in his own cause should be held sacred. And that is not to be confined to a cause in which he is a party, but applies to a cause in which he has an interest."

In a more modern Canadian example, *Convent of the Sacred Heart v. Armstrong's Point Association and Bulgin* (1961), 29 DLR (2d) 373 (Man. CA), a decision of the Municipal Board of Manitoba about zoning was quashed because a member of the board was co-owner of a residence in an area that was, arguably, enhanced or protected by the decision.

For the longest time, it was accepted that even the slightest whiff of a financial interest was sufficient to disqualify. However, the English Court of Appeal sensibly recognized a *de minimis* exception: *Locabail (UK) Ltd. v. Bayfield Properties Ltd.*, [2000] 1 All ER 65 (CA). Presumably, this would deal, for example, with situations of adjudicators holding mutual funds or being members of a pension plan with a diverse portfolio and allow them to sit on cases involving companies within that portfolio.

Our illustrative modern case is *Energy Probe v. Canada (Atomic Energy Control Board)*. The various judgments revisit the question whether directness is indeed the appropriate standard to apply in deciding whether a material interest is disqualifying and, if so, what constitutes a "direct" interest. What is also suggested is that, to the extent that an interest is not direct, it may nevertheless still be relevant and have to be dealt with by reference to the normal tests for identifying disqualifying bias. The case, therefore, also revisits the general standards by which courts consider challenges to adjudicators on the basis of a perceived bias. Finally, to the extent that the licensing function of the AECB had previously been held to be administrative (rather than judicial in the traditional sense), *Energy Probe* deals with the issue whether the threshold for the application of the principle of unbiased decision making has been lowered as a consequence of *Nicholson* to the same extent as it was lowered for claims to other procedural entitlements.

Energy Probe v. Canada (Atomic Energy Control Board)
(1984), 8 DLR (4th) 735 (FCTD); aff'd. (1984), 15 DLR (4th) 48 (FCA)

[The AECB proposed to renew the operating licence for a nuclear generating station operated by Ontario Hydro, and Energy Probe made some objections, including an objection to participation by one board member, Olsen. Energy Probe alleged that Olsen was president of a company that supplied cables to nuclear power plants and was an official or member of several organizations that supported use of nuclear power. AECB rejected this objection and renewed the licence. Energy Probe challenged this decision, and it limited its challenge to an allegation of material interest.]

REED J: The issues raised by this application are: (1) does the doctrine of fairness as enunciated by the Supreme Court in *Nicholson v. Haldimand-Norfolk Regional Board of Com'rs of Police* apply to the licensing function of the Atomic Energy Control Board and, particularly, does that doctrine of fairness include a requirement of a lack of bias on the part of the board members?; (2) did Mr Olsen have a pecuniary interest in the outcome

of that decision sufficient to constitute pecuniary bias as that term has been defined?; and
(3) in any event, does the applicant Energy Probe have standing to challenge the board's
decision?

Fairness Doctrine

All parties agree that the licensing function of the AECB is an administrative one and not
quasi-judicial or judicial.

It seems clear, therefore, that the doctrine of fairness, as enunciated by the Supreme
Court in *Nicholson v. Haldimand-Norfolk Regional Board of Com'rs of Police*, applies to
AECB licensing decisions.

· · ·

[T]he requirements of fairness may be different from and less than those required by
the rules of natural justice. They may very well vary depending upon the exact nature of
the administrative function to which they are being applied. In addition, Canadian cases,
so far, have all dealt only with the procedural aspects of fairness: a right to notice and to
know the case against you. I was not referred to any Canadian authority which had discussed whether or not a requirement of lack of bias also applied.

· · ·

I have no doubt that the duty to act fairly as enunciated by the Supreme Court in the
Nicholson case must include a requirement for an unbiased decision maker. Any other
conclusion would undercut the whole concept of the requirement of a duty of fairness.

It would indeed be anomalous that there exist a requirement that rules of procedural
fairness be followed in making an administrative decision but not a requirement for an
unbiased decision maker. A biased tribunal would be a much more serious lack of fairness than non-compliance with procedural requirements.

Direct Pecuniary Bias?

It is necessary, therefore, to examine the facts in this case to see whether a sufficient degree of bias exists to offend the fairness principle. Only pecuniary bias has been alleged;
there has been no allegation of reasonable apprehension of bias.

The rule relating to pecuniary bias, as it has been articulated, is that a *direct* pecuniary
interest, no matter how trivial, will constitute bias: refer to Mullan, "Administrative Law,"
1 CED (Ont. 3rd) at 3-128, s. 50; and de Smith, *Judicial Review of Administrative Action*,
(4th ed. 1980) at 258.

In this case the pecuniary interest of Mr Olsen was alleged to arise because of his
course of business dealings with Ontario Hydro. He had in the past sold radioactive-re-
sistant cables to Ontario Hydro. It is clear he could expect to do so again in the future.
But, I can find no *direct* pecuniary interest, as that concept has been defined in the jurisprudence, held by Mr Olsen *at the date of the hearings* in question: June 27, 1983 and
September 12, 1983. There was no contract conditionally in effect pending the outcome
of the new licences to Ontario Hydro. There was no certainty that Mr Olsen would sell
additional cables to Ontario Hydro for the Pickering units, during the life of the new licence. Also, it was admitted by counsel for the applicant that the purchase of such cables
by Ontario Hydro was through a tendering process. The most that could be said of

Mr Olsen as of the date of the hearing was that he could entertain a reasonable expectation of pecuniary gain as a result of approval of the licences.

I was not referred to any case, nor was I able to find any, which has held that this kind of contingent expectation constitutes *direct* pecuniary bias. All of the jurisprudence respecting pecuniary bias that I have seen involves individuals who at the date of the hearing held some sort of direct relationship with the beneficiary of the decision such that pecuniary benefit might with certainty arise even though that benefit might be minuscule, *e.g.*: as a ratepayer, as an estate agent for the transaction in question, as a shareholder.

. . .

Mr Olsen, however, did not stand in a direct and certain relationship with Ontario Hydro at the date of the licensing decisions.

[Discussion of the standing issue is omitted. It will appear later, in chapter 17 of this text. The challenge failed, and Probe appealed.

The Federal Court of Appeal unanimously dismissed the appeal, and the majority (Heald and Stone JJ) essentially agreed with Reed J. Heald J said, "Olsen's interest was indirect and uncertain and too remote to constitute either direct pecuniary interest, or bias." Marceau J concurred, but asserted that his reasons differed.]

MARCEAU J: In dealing with the basic features of the common law rules against bias so as to apply them to the facts of the case, the learned motions judge, in her reasons, seems to be drawing a straight opposition between "pecuniary bias" and "reasonable apprehension of bias" and stands firm to the idea that only a "direct" and "certain"—as strictly opposed to an indirect or uncertain—pecuniary interest may constitute "pecuniary bias." In fact, her whole reasoning is supported by these two distinctions. It is indeed on the basis of the second one that Reed J could form the opinion that even if "Mr Olsen as of the date of the hearing ... could entertain a reasonable expectation of pecuniary gain as a result of approval of the licences," such a gain would be coming to him indirectly, not directly, and therefore could not legally constitute "pecuniary bias"; and it is on the basis of the first opposition that she could decide that while the case made against Mr Olsen could well be one of reasonable apprehension of bias ... the court could not examine the situation in that perspective, counsel having limited his allegation to "pecuniary bias." These legal propositions upon which the learned motions judge built her reasoning and founded her findings do not appear to me in complete harmony with the teachings of the jurisprudence, as I read it, and I must, with respect, express my disagreement with them.

The principle of natural justice involved in all matters of bias is, of course, that a tribunal called upon to settle disputes between individuals ought to be independent, disinterested and impartial and it is trite to say that the most obvious and most easily perceived practical application of that principle is that no one should be permitted to be judge in his own cause. It was soon "discovered"—it is taught in all the textbooks—that the common law, like the Roman law and the Canon law long before it, did not permit a judge to determine a matter in which he had a pecuniary or proprietary interest: see *de Smith's Judicial Review of Administrative Action*, (4th ed. 1980) at 248. From that early moment on, the law in that respect has evolved, as I understand it, on the strength of two ideas. One is that there are many interests other than pecuniary which may affect the impartiality of a decision maker, emotional type interests one might say (see Pépin and Ouellette, *Principes de contentieux administratif*, (2nd ed. 1977) at 253), such as kinship, friendship, partisanship, particular professional or business relationship with one of the parties, animosity towards someone interested, predetermined mind as to the issue involved, *etc.* The other, which has since become a sort of legal axiom, is that it "is of fundamental importance that justice should not only be done but should manifestly and undoubtedly be seen to be done." The result of the evolution of the law on the basis of these two ideas is that a distinction is today well recognized and acknowledged between situations where the decision maker has a pecuniary interest in the outcome of the decision, and situations where his interest is of another type.

· · ·

It is clear that this view I take of the law of bias as it is now applied by the common law courts does not permit me to subscribe to the learned trial judge's reasoning, and if on the two essential points I have just referred to I agree with her conclusions, it is for completely different reasons.

(a) I do not think that the word "direct," when used by the judges and the textbooks to qualify the interest required to constitute the peremptorily disqualifying pecuniary bias, should be given such a strict and narrow interpretation that any indirect or uncertain advantage would not have to be considered; the word, in my view, is used in the sense of not too remote or too contingent or too speculative. Having regard to the purpose of the rule, *i.e.*, that no one charged with the power and the duty to adjudicate upon the rights of opposing parties should be allowed to exercise his jurisdiction for his own profit and material interest, there is no reason to draw a strict distinction between direct and indirect or certain and uncertain as regards the monetary benefit the adjudicator could expect from his determination. The only rational requirements are that the benefit come from the decision itself and that it be a likely enough effect to "colour" the case in his eyes. It would appear to me that the presence of an immediate possibility, not to say probability, of gain to be coming to him directly or indirectly as a result of his decision would be enough to render someone unfit to make it.

If I were to accept literally the statement of the learned judge referred to above, to the effect that "Mr Olsen … could entertain a reasonable expectation of pecuniary gain as a result of approval of the licences," I would definitely be inclined to conclude that pecuniary bias was here present. I do not think, however, that the statement was meant to express a clear finding of fact and, in any event, it is not supported by the evidence. As recalled above, the licences were only operating licences and Mr Olsen's company could expect no extra business and obviously no gain as a result of their approval. The mere possibility that a profit could be realized in the future out of other contracts awarded in the course of construction of other units was no doubt too alien, contingent and remote to constitute pecuniary bias with respect to the decision to be made at that time.

(b) I do not see "pecuniary bias" and "reasonable apprehension of bias" as being two subcategories of bias. Such a distinction would appear to me somewhat difficult to defend logically since it would present no basis for comparison, one group being identified by the nature of the interest, the other by the possible reaction the presence thereof may inspire in the mind of the public. The distinction to me, as I said earlier, is between pecuniary and non-pecuniary interests, and if I agree with the learned judge that reasonable apprehension of bias was not an issue here, it is not because of the presentation of counsel, but simply because no interest other than a pecuniary one was alleged and even alluded to. If the evidence had revealed a non-pecuniary interest capable of being influential and sufficient to raise a real likelihood of bias, I would have thought that even if counsel had improperly presented his case, the learned judge would not have been precluded from dealing with it.

· · ·

If I have chosen to approach the matter and set forth my view thereof on the assumed basis that the common law rules against bias, as they have evolved in the jurisprudence, were fully applicable to an administrative body like the respondent, it is because of the position to that effect adopted by my brother judges in their reasons for judgment. But, in fact, I think that a difficult problem lies behind such an assumption and the learned judge of first instance was, in my opinion, perfectly right in considering that the first issue she had to determine was whether or not it was justified. The law of bias was developed with regard to the exercise of all sorts of judicial or *quasi*-judicial functions, so that, in the process, it was easily extended from courts to tribunals and to all other bodies called upon to determine questions affecting the civil rights of individuals. But there seems to be so far no authority for the proposition that it has to be applied to a purely administrative forum like the board which does not deal with private rights, has no adjudicative powers in the proper sense and has no resemblance whatever with a court of justice.

· · ·

It is obvious that there is indeed "a requirement for an unbiased decision-maker." It cannot be doubted that the law imposes a duty on anyone called upon to decide anything under a statute to act in good faith and with an open mind.

· · ·

But the rules referred to in the so-called law of bias go much further since, having been developed with a view to preventing all possibilities of bias and making sure that even reasonable apprehension thereof will be eliminated, they never require that actual bias be established. The issue is, therefore, not resolved by remarks to the effect that fairness would be incompatible with bias.

In a preceding paragraph of her reasons, after having quoted long passages of the reasons for judgment given by Laskin CJC in the *Nicholson* case, Reed J had observed that it was clear from the remarks of the Chief Justice that "the requirements of fairness may be different from and less than those required by the rules of natural justice." There, I think, lies the solution. It seems to me quite normal that the rules of fairness cover the two aspects of those of natural justice from which they derive so as to establish safeguards not only against arbitrariness and despotism but also against bias. I am even quite prepared to concede that, in order to assure the complete confidence of the public in the decisions of those advisory and regulatory bodies, it is necessary that there be rules aimed at protecting their objectivity. But I would be of the view that the standard to be achieved does not have to be as high as that required of an adjudicative tribunal and the rules applicable should therefore be less strict. As I see it in practice, to operate disqualification, the pecuniary interest ought to be more immediate and certain and the non-pecuniary interest must give rise to very substantial grounds for apprehending lack of objectivity. All this may give rise to difficult problems of application in real life but the idea is of course valid. …

This view that the rules of the law of bias cannot be applied with all their rigidity to a board like the respondent reinforces (if need be) my conviction in this case that the pecuniary interest Mr Olsen is said to have had in the decision was far too remote and uncertain to have been a cause for his disqualification.

Appeal dismissed.

NOTES

1. Subsequently, the Supreme Court of Canada sustained the position that classification of the function as judicial or *quasi*-judicial was no longer a prerequisite to a challenge on the basis of bias. The court also accepted, however, that just as with the *audi alteram partem* component of the rules of natural justice, the standards of detachment expected of decision-makers varied according to the nature of the role being performed: *Old St. Boniface Residents Assn. Inc. v. Winnipeg (City)*, [1990] 3 SCR 1170 (Man.). We return to this case and this issue below.

2. As with other forms of bias, a pecuniary or other material interest may be statutorily authorized. Indeed, some of the most interesting cases in this domain involve that possibility.

For example, many of the agencies that regulate the marketing of agricultural products are composed, in part, of producers whose interests may conflict with the interests of other participants in the market. In *Burnbrae Farms v. Canadian Egg Marketing Agency*, [1976] 2 FC 217 (CA), a disgruntled egg producer in Ontario withheld a levy imposed by the Canadian Egg Marketing Agency (CEMA). The agency held a hearing and withdrew its licence. The producer sought review on several grounds, including bias, and particularly because some of the members who participated in the hearing were producers in other provinces and their interests under the marketing scheme therefore conflicted with the producer's. However, the legislation and regulations required at least 7 of the 12 members to be producers in other provinces (and the *Interpretation Act*, RSC 1970, c. I-23 made at least half the members a quorum). Jackett CJ said:

> In such a statutory scheme, it does not appear to me that an apprehension of bias that is based only on the fact that some of the members have, by virtue of the part of the country from which they come, a business background with economic interests that conflict with those of a particular licensee whose licence is in jeopardy can be regarded as a disqualification.

Contrast *Moskalyk-Walter v. Ontario (College of Pharmacy)* (1975), 58 DLR (3d) 665 (Ont. Div. Ct.), which involved discipline by the College of Pharmacy. The Discipline Committee imposed a suspension on a pharmacist in Fort Erie, a town of about 7,500 persons. He successfully appealed, because one of the members who participated in the hearing owned one store in Fort Erie and operated another.

In this regard, see also *Pearlman v. Manitoba Law Society Disciplinary Committee*, [1991] 2 SCR 869 (Man.), where the Supreme Court rejected summarily the argument that a professional discipline committee composed of fellow members was structurally biased because of the self-interest of the committee members in the reduction of competition by way of suspending or expelling others. Similarly, the Supreme Court of Canada in *Canadian Pacific Ltd. v. Matsqui Indian Band*, [1995] 1 SCR 3 (Can.), rejected an assertion of disqualifying pecuniary bias against members of Indian bands being called upon to adjudicate on appeals by non-Indians against tax assessments levied against them in relation to their use of land on Indian reserves. To quote from the judgment of Lamer CJC:

> There is clearly an important interest in having band members sit on appeal tribunals. The concern that these members might be inclined to increase taxes in order to maximize the income flowing to the band is simply too remote to constitute a reasonable apprehension of bias at a structural level. More to the point, the income raised through the tax assessment scheme does not accrue to any individual, but rather to the community as a whole. There is, as Iacobucci J stated at 892 [in *Pearlman*], "no personal and distinct interest on the part of" tribunal members. In my view, the potential for conflict between the interests of members of the tribunal and those of parties appearing before them is, at this stage, speculative. Therefore, it cannot be said that a reasonable apprehension of bias would exist in the mind of a fully informed person in a substantial number of cases. Any allegations of bias which might arise must be dealt with on a case-by-case basis. …

3. On the basis of the judgments in *Energy Probe*, should directness be the test in determining if a pecuniary or other material interest is disqualifying? For those judges who accepted this as the appropriate criterion, why was Olsen's pecuniary interest not direct? If the interest is not direct but merely contingent, should that be decisive on the question of disqualification? If not, what arguments are available to support the proposition that Olsen should be removed from the hearing by reference to the general test for bias? Do these arguments pay sufficient regard to the desirability of having at least some industry members on the Atomic Energy Control Board? Is there any role for the courts in policing appointments to regulatory bodies such as this to ensure that there is an overall balance among those appointed in terms of the competing interests that are at stake in the agency's proceedings? (We return to this issue in *Newfoundland Telephone Co. v. Newfoundland (Board of Commissioners of Public Utilities)*, [1992] 1 SCR 623 (Nfld.) and also in considering the scope for constitution-based challenges.)

4. For an interesting example of a case where the court treated the pecuniary interest as "indirect" and therefore appropriately dealt with by reference to the test of a "reasonable apprehension of bias," see again *Pearlman v. Manitoba Law Society Judicial Committee*, above. Another issue in that case involved whether the authority of the disciplinary committee to award costs against a member found guilty of professional misconduct gave rise to disqualifying bias rendering the relevant provision in the legislation invalid by reference to s. 7 of the *Canadian Charter of Rights and Freedoms*. The Supreme Court, assuming but not deciding that a "life, liberty and security of the person" interest was at stake, held that any financial interest in the outcome of the proceedings on the part of the members of the committee was indirect rather than direct. It then found that that indirect interest was sufficiently attenuated and small as to not give rise to a reasonable apprehension that the members would be biased against those subject to discipline because of an incentive to find guilt and award costs, thereby potentially reducing their membership fees. The court also emphasized that the costs that could be legitimately awarded were restricted to the recovery of actual Law

Society expenditures and could not involve a profit component. (See also *McAllister v. New Brunswick (Veterinary Medical Association)* (1986), 71 NBR (2d) 109 (QB), approved by the Supreme Court in *Pearlman*.)

VARIATIONS IN STANDARDS

As indicated by the judgment of Marceau JA in *Energy Probe*, with the extension of the rules against bias to decision-makers not previously subject to the rules of natural justice has come a heightened realization that, just as with the *audi alteram partem* principle, the standard of what constitutes disqualifying bias may vary dramatically with context. This is particularly so in the arena of prior involvement with and attitudes toward the matter to be decided. The following Supreme Court of Canada judgments are graphically illustrative.

Old St. Boniface Residents Assn. Inc. v. Winnipeg (City)
[1990] 3 SCR 1170 (Man.)

[S, a Winnipeg municipal councillor, was involved from the start in the movement through the municipal approval process for a residential development that, *inter alia*, required a change of zoning. S had been one of the city's representatives who initially discussed the project with the developer. Subsequently, he had attended and spoken in favour of the project at *in camera* meetings of the finance committee, a committee of which he was not a member. This meeting was for the purpose of considering whether the development would be given an option to buy city lands that were an integral part of the development. Subsequently, after the option had been given and after the developer had been authorized to proceed with a rezoning application in respect of the city-owned lands, S was a member of the community committee of the ward in which the lands were located, which after public hearings had recommended that the developer's application be approved subject to the city's usual requirements as well as the necessary street closing bylaws.

During these meetings, the association, having learned of S's appearances before the finance committee, had asked him to withdraw from further participation but S had declined. Ultimately, the matter came before a plenary session of city council and, after full debate, the council gave its approval to the rezoning and asked that a rezoning bylaw be prepared. It also gave approval to the necessary street closing bylaw.

At this juncture, however, before the rezoning bylaw had been passed, the association moved for orders quashing the decision of the community committee, an order prohibiting the council from proceeding with third reading of the bylaw and an order quashing the street closing bylaw.

The Court of Queen's Bench quashed the committee's decision, prohibited the third reading of the zoning bylaw, and adjourned the motion to quash the street closing bylaw, but prohibited the city from implementing this bylaw until further order. The Manitoba Court of Appeal allowed an appeal from this judgment and dismissed the association's cross-appeal in respect of the street closing bylaw. The association obtained leave to appeal to the Supreme Court of Canada.]

SOPINKA J (Dickson CJC, Wilson, Gonthier, and McLachlin JJ concurring):

1. Bias

Natural Justice: Application to Local Government Bodies

The rules which require a tribunal to maintain an open mind and to be free of bias, actual or perceived, are part of the *audi alteram partem* principle which applies to decision makers. The appellant contends that it applies in its full vigour to members of a municipal council when deciding whether to vote in favour of a by-law which in this case involves zoning. It relies, principally, on *Wiswell v. Metropolitan Corp. of Greater Winnipeg* [1965] SCR 512 (Man.) in support of this proposition.

· · ·

Wiswell [in which the court held that the council was acting in a *quasi*-judicial capacity and obliged to give a hearing in considering a zoning bylaw] must be read in light of comparatively recent changes that have occurred in applying the rules of natural justice. The content of the rules of natural justice and procedural fairness were formerly determined according to the classification of the functions of the tribunal or other public body or official. This is no longer the case and the content of these rules is based on a number of factors including the terms of the statute pursuant to which the body operates, the nature of the particular function of which it is seized and the type of decision it is called upon to make. This change in approach was summarized in *Syndicat des employées de production du Québec et de l'Acadie v. Canada (Canadian Human Rights Commission)* [1989] 2 SCR 879 (Can.). I stated at 895-96:

> Both the rules of natural justice and the duty of fairness are variable standards. Their content will depend on the circumstances of the case, the statutory provisions and the nature of the matter to be decided. The distinction between them therefore becomes blurred as one approaches the lower end of the scale of judicial or *quasi*-judicial tribunals and the high end of the scale with respect to administrative or executive tribunals. Accordingly, the content of the rules to be followed by a tribunal is now not determined by attempting to classify them as judicial, *quasi*-judicial, administrative or executive. Instead, *the court decides the content of these rules by reference to all the circumstances under which the tribunal operates.* [Emphasis added.]

It is therefore necessary to examine all the factors under which a committee of Council operates. I start with the most significant fact that the statute provides for a hearing before a committee of members of Council. There is nothing in the legislation to indicate that they are to act in a capacity other than municipal councillors. In this regard I must assume that the Legislature was aware that in this capacity the members of Council will have fought an election in which the matter upon which they are called upon to decide may have been debated and on which the would-be councillors may have taken a stand some pro and some con. Indeed, the election of a particular councillor may have depended on the position taken. Furthermore, with respect to the enactment of zoning by-laws and amendments to zoning by-laws, it is well known that numerous committees are involved at which members of Council are expected to vote before being called upon to hear representations and decide the question. Moreover, in the preparation and processing of a development, a municipal councillor is often involved in assisting parties supporting and opposing the development with respect to their presentations. In the course of this process, a councillor can and often does take a stand either for or against the development. This degree of prejudgment would run afoul of the ordinary rule which disqualifies a decision maker on the basis of a reasonable apprehension of bias. Accordingly, it could not have been intended by the Legislature that this rule apply to members of Council with the same force as in the case of other tribunals whose character and functions more closely resemble those of a court.

The nature and functions of a municipal body and their influence on the rules of natural justice have been examined in a number of cases which I have found of assistance.

In *Re Cadillac Development Corp. Ltd. and Toronto (City)* (1973) 39 DLR (3d) 188 (Ont. HC), the Council was called upon to consider the repeal of a land-use by-law. A majority of Council had already made up their minds and had said so. In dismissing an application to quash the by-law on this ground, Henry J stated:

> In respect of a *quasi*-judicial tribunal in the fullest sense of that concept required to adhere to principles of natural justice this would amount to an allegation of bias such as might be ground for quashing the decision. But regard must be had to the nature of the body reviewing the matter. A municipal council is an elected body having a legislative function within a limited and delegated jurisdiction. Under the democratic process the elected representatives are expected to form views as to matters of public policy affecting the municipality. Indeed, they will have been elected in order to give effect to public views as to important policies to be effected in the community.
>
> . . .
>
> They are not Judges, but legislators from whom the ultimate recourse is to the electorate. Once having given notice and fairly heard the objections, the Council is of course free to decide as it sees fit in the public interest.

Henry J had further occasion to elaborate on the subject in *Re McGill and Brantford (City)* [(1980), 111 DLR (3d) 405 (Ont. Div. Ct.)]. It involved a motion to quash a by-law to close certain city streets on the grounds of bias. At the hearing, objectors took the position that the Council had already committed itself to the street closing and that it was therefore unlikely that it could act impartially and in a judicial manner.

After describing the legislative and political nature of a municipal council's function, Henry J stated:

> On this process, which is simply our concept of democracy in action, is imposed the requirement to hold a hearing before roads are closed. What then is the character of such a hearing? Its purpose is to ensure that the Council, before exercising its power to enact a law closing specific roads, must provide a forum in which those whose private rights are adversely affected may assert their objections. It fortifies by law the right every ratepayer has to write to his alderman, organize and address a meeting or conduct a peaceable demonstration. By statute, he is to be *heard*, and that by the whole Council, who must provide the opportunity to do so.

In his view it was only when Council had made an irrevocable decision on the matter that a disqualifying bias was made out. He continued:

So if it could be shown, the onus being on the objectors to do so, that the Council before the hearing had irrevocably decided to pass the by-law to close the roads, that would reflect disabling bias. No hearing in the true sense of that concept was or could be held. As such a hearing is a condition precedent, its absence would be fatal to the exercise of the legislative power.

. . .

The role of a municipal councillor is quite different from that of the Chairman of the National Energy Board which was considered in *Committee for Justice v. National Energy Board*. In that case, a majority of our Court concluded that the Chairman of the Board was disqualified from presiding over an application for a certificate of public convenience and necessity in connection with the MacKenzie Valley Pipeline pursuant to s. 44 of the *National Energy Board Act*, RSC 1970, c. N-6, by reason of his participation in the work of a Study Group made up of parties interested in the project. Chief Justice Laskin on behalf of the majority stressed that the Chairman had participated in discussions material to the s. 44 application with members of the group which included the applicant for the licence. In this capacity he had assisted in the preparation of the s. 44 application. Moreover, the Crown Corporation of which he was the president contributed funds to the Study Group. In short, his relationship with parties to the application had been such that he virtually had a personal interest in the s. 44 application and its outcome which created a reasonable apprehension of bias.

The members of the National Energy Board do not have political or legislative duties. Prejudgment of issues is not inherent in the nature of their extra-adjudicative functions. While it was argued that the Chairman was required to deal, in the course of his duties, with matters of supply and the requirements for natural gas and that these matters would have some relevance to the s. 44 application, Chief Justice Laskin discounted them as merely preparing the Chairman for the main hearing.

I would distinguish between a case of partiality by reason of pre-judgment on the one hand and by reason of personal interest on the other. It is apparent from the facts of this case, for example, that some degree of prejudgment is inherent in the role of a councillor. That is not the case in respect of interest. There is nothing inherent in the hybrid functions, political, legislative or otherwise, of municipal councillors that would make it mandatory or desirable to excuse them from the requirement that they refrain from dealing with matters in respect of which they have a personal or other interest. It is not part of the job description that municipal councillors be personally interested in matters that come before them beyond the interest that they have in common with the other citizens in the municipality. Where such an interest is found, both at common law and by statute, a member of Council is disqualified if the interest is so related to the exercise of public duty that a reasonably well-informed person would conclude that the interest might influence the exercise of that duty. This is commonly referred to as a conflict of interest. [A list of cases is omitted.]

Statutory provisions in various provincial Municipal Acts tend to parallel the common law but typically provide a definition of the kind of interest which will give rise to a conflict of interest. ... In Manitoba, the relevant provisions are found in the *Municipal Council Conflict of Interest Act*, RSM 1987, c. M-255, ss. 4, 5 and 8. No reference is made to these sections in this appeal nor is there any suggestion that they have been contravened.

In my opinion, the test that is consistent with the functions of a municipal councillor and enables him or her to carry out the political and legislative duties entrusted to the councillor is one which requires that the objectors or supporters be heard by members of Council who are capable of being persuaded. The Legislature could not have intended to have a hearing before a body who has already made a decision which is irreversible. The party alleging disqualifying bias must establish that there is a prejudgment of the matter, in fact, to the extent that any representations at variance with the view, which has been adopted, would be futile. Statements by individual members of Council while they may very well give rise to an appearance of bias will not satisfy the test unless the court concludes that they are the expression of a final opinion on the matter, which cannot be dislodged. In this regard it is important to keep in mind that support in favour of a measure before a committee and a vote in favour will not constitute disqualifying bias in the absence of some indication that the position taken is incapable of change. The contrary conclusion would result in the disqualification of a majority of Council in respect of all matters that are decided at public meetings at which objectors are entitled to be heard.

Application to This Appeal

The disqualifying conduct relied on in this case consists of Councillor Savoie appearing before the Finance Committee and speaking on behalf of the developer. This in itself would not necessarily lead to the conclusion that his mind could not be changed. It is, however, suggested that this places him in the role of advocate for the developer thus giving him an interest in the issue which goes beyond the public interest. This submission would have substance if there was something to suggest that the Councillor's support was motivated by some relationship with or interest in the developer rather than in the development. The evidence shows, however, that he had previously supported the development on its merits and there is no evidence that suggests any relationship with the developer. Furthermore, the Judge of first instance found as a fact that the Councillor had no such interest. In his reasons Schwartz J stated [54 Man. R (2d) 252, at 260]:

> There is no suggestion that Councillor Savoie did what he did for any reason other than what he believed to be the best interests of his community.
>
> There is no suggestion that he had any personal interest in the success of Tyrone's application other than what he thought was his duty.

Schwartz J did refer to the fact that Councillor Savoie acted as an advocate for the development but in light of the above finding this reference must be taken to mean nothing more than that he argued in favour of it. It was error, therefore, for the learned Judge to apply the reasonable apprehension of bias test. This test would have been appropriate if it had been found that the Councillor had a personal interest in the development, either pecuniary or by reason of a relationship with the developer. In such circumstances, the test is that which applies to all public officials: Would a reasonably well-informed person consider that the interest might have an influence on the exercise of the official's public duty? If that duty is to hear and decide, the test is expressed in terms of a reasonable apprehension of bias. As I have stated above, there is nothing arising from the political and legislative nature of a councillor's duties that requires a relaxation of this test. The situation is quite distinct from a prejudgment case. In this case no personal interest exists or was found and it is purely a prejudgment case. Councillor Savoie had not prejudged the case to the extent that he was disqualified on the basis of the principles outlined above. The Court of Appeal was right, therefore, in reversing the Judge of first instance on this point. The appeal on this ground must therefore fail.

[Lamer J concurred on the basis of La Forest J's articulation of the appropriate test for bias in *Save Richmond Farmland Society v. Richmond (Township)*, [1990] 3 SCR 1213 (BC), below.

La Forest J (L'Heureux-Dubé and Cory JJ concurring) dissented on an issue other than bias.]

Appeal dismissed.

Save Richmond Farmland Society v. Richmond (Township)
[1990] 3 SCR 1213 (BC)

[An area of agricultural land reserve in Richmond known as the Terra Nova lands had been the subject of municipal controversy for some years. M was an alderman who had campaigned for office in part as being in favour of rezoning these lands for some form of development. He had then voted in favour of two bylaws that would have rezoned the lands to being predominantly residential. However, these bylaws were declared void by the Supreme Court. While these bylaws were subject to judicial review, a comprehensive zoning bylaw that designated the Terra Nova lands as available for development was introduced for the entire municipality of Richmond. After first reading and prior to the public hearing on that bylaw, M gave an interview to the press in which he allegedly said that, while he would listen attentively at the public hearing, he would not change his mind. Subsequently, while the public hearings were proceeding, he appeared on a television show and advocated residential zoning for the Terra Nova lands, stating that it would take something significant for him to change his mind though he would be interested to see what emerged in the balance of the hearings.

After the public hearings, both the second and third readings of the bylaw passed by five-to-four margins, reflecting the known division of opinion on council as revealed in the earlier campaign positions of the aldermen in question. After the second reading, Save Richmond Farmland Society (SRFS) petitioned for judicial review for an order preventing M from voting and further participation because of a disqualifying reasonable apprehension of bias. The petition was dismissed and SRFS appealed to the British Columbia Court of Appeal. Fourth reading of the bylaw was stayed by judicial order pending the disposition of the appeal.

The BC Court of Appeal dismissed the appeal and the petitioners obtained leave to appeal to the Supreme Court of Canada. In the meantime, the bylaw was read a fourth time and was formally adopted.]

[Sopinka J (Dickson CJC, Wilson, Gonthier, Cory, and McLachlin JJ concurring) dismissed the appeal on the basis of the test elaborated in the *Old St. Boniface Residents Assn.* case, above.]

La FOREST J (Lamer and L'Heureux-Dubé JJ concurring): ... Though I have reached the same conclusion as my colleague, I approach the issue differently and I have, therefore, prepared my own reasons. My colleague has set forth the facts, judicial history and applicable legislation and I can, therefore, proceed directly to an analysis of the issue.

Analysis

I underscore the fact that in this appeal it is clear that the municipality made a policy choice to emphasize the provision of housing rather than the preservation of agricultural land in that portion of the municipality called the Terra Nova lands. This necessitated a zoning change for the lands in question, and, as is clear from s. 956 of British Columbia's *Municipal Act*, a statutory duty is placed on municipal councils to hold a public hearing prior to the adoption of a zoning by-law. The issue raised by this appeal is that of defining what standard of fairness is owed to the participants in this hearing process.

This poses the problem of defining in what capacity the council acts when conducting a zoning by-law hearing such as that mandated by the above-noted section. The appellant association, relying on *Karamanian v. Richmond* (1982) 38 BCLR 106 (SC), submitted that the council acts in a *quasi*-judicial capacity. The respondent municipality, stressing the high policy content of the decision to change the zoning of the lands in question, counters by suggesting that the council acts in its legislative capacity. I consider the implications of both alternatives.

[La Forest J here detailed the competing arguments and principles including the split within the BC Court of Appeal. There, the majority had accepted that it mattered not in such situations whether the councillors went into the public hearings with closed minds. Lambert JA, however, accepted there must be a degree of openmindedness, which he was prepared to find on the basis of the councillor's statements during the television show. La Forest J also accepted that, if Lambert JA's test were the appropriate one, he was also correct in finding that the councillor had indeed retained a sufficiently open mind. However, he then continued:]

"Amenable to Persuasion"—A Valid Test?

Both judgments of the Court of Appeal are premised on the notion that it is an error, in the context of a rezoning application, to imply bias from the fact that a municipal councillor holds very firm and strongly stated views on the matter. The difference between the two approaches lies in the fact that Lambert JA would hold to the notion that having taken a firm position on a given proposal is not a licence to close one's mind entirely to being persuaded otherwise.

This sounds good in theory, but breaks down in practice. Southin JA's approach might seem drastic, but is the more realistic of the two. There is no way of gauging the "openness" of a person's mind, and indeed it would be pointless to attempt to do so. In the result, it seems to me that if this Court is to adopt the "amenable to persuasion" test, this is bound to lead to a lot of posturing. Politicians who have campaigned on a given issue, and owe their election to it, can be expected to make solemn pronouncements to the effect that they remain "amenable to persuasion" if a truly convincing argument is presented to them. There would seem to be little to be gained by enforcing a campaign of "lip-service" to this ideal.

In conclusion, I think that Southin JA is correct when she holds that a "closed mind" (provided it is not a corrupt mind) should not disentitle an alderman from participating in the electoral process.

Woolf LJ puts the matter well in *R v. Amber Valley District Council, Ex parte Jackson* [1985] 1 WLR 298 (CA) at 307:

> But does this have the effect of disqualifying the Labour majority from considering the planning application? It would be a surprising result if it did since in the case of a development of this sort, I would have thought that it was almost inevitable, now that party politics play so large a part in local government, that the majority group on a council would decide on the party line in respect of the proposal. If this was to be regarded as disqualifying the district council from dealing with the planning application, then if that disqualification is to be avoided, the members of the planning committee at any rate will have to adopt standards of conduct which I suspect will be almost impossible to achieve in practice.

It might be objected that this approach makes the public meeting called for by s. 956 a mere charade. By way of answer, it must be assumed that the Legislature will have been well aware of the fact that the very aldermen who are called on by statute to make the final decision on zoning by-laws initiated by municipalities themselves will often have run for office on the strength of their support or opposition to these measures. If this seemingly guarantees that zoning applications of this nature are decided before ever reaching the hearing stage, this inconsistency should be for the Legislature to iron out, and not the courts.

Secondly, I think that Lambert JA is correct in his submission that s. 956 should not be interpreted as meant to apply in exactly the same way to all matters it covers [at 162]:

> If the by-law affects a specific solution to a specific problem of a narrow scope that only touches the people it immediately concerns, different obligations of fairness may arise than if the by-law affects a comprehensive solution to an overall policy problem confronting the whole municipality. *The section is sufficiently flexible to allow the appropriate standards of fairness to be applied to the particular circumstances.* [Emphasis added.]

In the particular circumstances of this appeal, I think that the respondent municipality is correct in its submission that in respect of a rezoning initiated by Council itself and driven by policy:

> The emphasis is on the legislative nature of the process and thus on compelling "the elected" to listen to the views of "the electors." It is not, as in an adjudicative process, on compelling the hearing tribunal to find the facts by means of a hearing or inquiry and then to determine the issue on the facts as found.

If this is indeed the correct characterization of the purpose served by the meeting in the context of a "policy driven" zoning initiative, it follows that the standard of fairness mandated by s. 956 places on the council members little more than the obligation of ensuring that due notice is given to those who do stand to be affected, and of affording them a reasonable opportunity to express their views.

In the final analysis, I think that the association's position is an unrealistic one in the case of a hearing that is mandated in order to consider a rezoning "initiated by Council itself and driven by policy." A community plan, or a comprehensive zoning by-law represents a general statement of the broad objectives and policies of the local government respecting the form and character of existing and proposed land use (see s. 945(1) *Municipal Act*), and the adoption of such a measure is less a judicial process than a legislative one. The aldermen who participate in such a process should be viewed accordingly not as Judges, but as elected representatives who are answerable to the concerns of their constituents.

. . .

Clearly, in this instance, the decision-making process is to be located at the legislative end of the spectrum. Accordingly, the threshold test for establishing bias should be a very high one. In my view, Southin JA is correct in her view that a decision maker is entitled to bring a closed mind to this decision-making process, provided that the "closed mind is the result not of corruption, but of honest opinions strongly held."

Appeal dismissed.

NOTE

These two judgments reveal a Supreme Court divided on the standard to apply when dealing with allegations of bias made against municipal councillors holding public hearings on broad matters of zoning on which they have already taken strong public positions, often in the setting of an election. Do the majority, in a practical sense and short of actual conflict of interest, leave any room for court policing of the behaviour of councillors? Or, is La Forest J correct, both in terms of theory and reality, when he says that the process is one in which closed minds should be tolerated and where to demand that councillors maintain a willingness to be convinced or still "amenable to persuasion" is simply an invitation to hypocritical political posturing? Keep that question in mind as well when reading the following judgment.

Newfoundland Telephone Co. v. Newfoundland (Board of Commissioners of Public Utilities)
[1992] 1 SCR 623 (Nfld.)

CORY J: Two issues are raised on this appeal. The first requires a consideration of the extent to which an administrative board member may be permitted to comment upon matters before the board. The second, raises the question as to what the result should be if a decision of a board is made in circumstances where there is found to be a reasonable apprehension of bias.

The Factual Background

Pursuant to the provisions of *The Public Utilities Act*, RSN 1970, c. 322, the Board of Commissioners of Public Utilities ("the Board") is responsible for the regulation of the Newfoundland Telephone Company Limited. Commissioners of the Board are appointed by the Lieutenant-Governor in Council. The statute simply provides that commissioners cannot be employed by, or have any interest, in a public utility (s. 6). In 1985, Andy Wells was appointed as a Commissioner to the Board. Earlier, while a municipal councillor, Wells had acted as an advocate for consumers' rights. When he was appointed, Wells publicly stated that he intended to play an adversarial role on the Board as a champion of consumers' rights. *The Public Utilities Act* neither provides for the appointment of commissioners as representatives of any specific group nor does it prohibit such appointments. The appointment of Wells has not been challenged.

Acting in accordance with *The Public Utilities Act*, the Board commissioned an independent accounting firm to provide an analysis of the costs and of the accounts of Newfoundland Telephone for the period between 1981 and 1987. The Board received the report from the accountants on November 3, 1988. In light of the report the Board, on November 10, decided to hold a public hearing. The hearing was to be before five commissioners including Wells and was to commence on December 19.

On November 13, 1988, *The Sunday Express*, a weekly newspaper published in St. John's, reported that Wells had described the pay and benefits package of appellant's executives as "ludicrous" and "unconscionable." Wells was quoted as saying:

If they want to give Brait [the chief executive officer of the appellant] and the boys extra fancy pensions, then the shareholders should pay it, not the rate payers.

. . .

So I want the company hauled in here—all them fat cats with their big pensions—to justify (these expenses) under the public glare ... I think the rate payers have a right to be assured that we are not permitting this company to be too extravagant.

On November 26, *The Evening Telegram*, a daily newspaper, published in St. John's, quoted Wells:

"Who the hell do they think they are?" Mr. Wells asked. "The guys doing the real work, climbing the poles never got any 21 per cent increase."

"Why should we, the rate payers, pay for an extra pension plan," he continued, adding that if the executive employees want more money put in their pensions they should take it out of shareholders' profits.

. . .

Mr. Wells said he senses an attitude of contempt by the telephone company towards the Public Utilities Board. The company seems to expect to always get its own way, he said, adding that the auditors had problems getting information from the company to do the audit requested by PUB. "But, I'm not having anything to do with the salary increases and big fat pensions," said Mr. Wells.

. . .

The telephone company wants the report kept confidential, "but, who do they think they are," said Mr. Wells. This document should be public.

When the hearing commenced on December 19, the appellant objected to Wells' participation on the panel on the grounds that his statements had created an apprehension of bias. The Board found that there was no provision in the Act which would allow it to rule on its own members and it decided that it did not have jurisdiction to do so. The Board rejected the appellant's submission and ruled that the panel would continue as constituted.

On December 20, *The Evening Telegram* reported the previous day's events at the hearing. The article read in part:

> Following Monday's proceedings, Mr. Wells said he was not surprised by the request to remove him from the PUB panel for the Newfoundland Telephone hearing.
>
> "I don't think those expenses can be justified," said Mr. Wells. "I'm concerned about bias the other way."

On January 24, 1989, the "NTV Evening News" (a television news program originating in St. John's) reported on the continuation of the hearing. That report contained the following statements made by a reporter, Jim Thoms, and by Mr. Wells. They were as follows:

> Jim Thoms: Before the hearing began last night board member Andy Wells went public with what he thought of the phone company. He nailed in particular increases in salary and pension benefits for top executives including president Anthony Brait and let it be known even before the board heard any evidence what his judgment would be.
>
> . . .
>
> Andy Wells: I was absolutely astounded to find out for 1988 that, that Brait is now about up to two hundred and thirty-five thousand dollars and I think that's an incredible sum of money to be paid for to manage a small telephone company.
>
> Jim Thoms: Now Mr. Wells is trying to find out what happened for this year. He was going after '89 salary figures at a meeting today.
>
> Andy Wells: And I just think that it is unfair to expect ratepayers, the consumers, you and I to pay for this kind of extravagance.
>
> Jim Thoms: Okay now. … Mr. Wells has left no doubt how his vote will come down in this matter. He wants the board to disallow the salary and pension increases as unreasonable for rate making purpose and to tell the stockholders to pick up the tab.
>
> Andy Wells: And I think that's, that's a reasonable way of proceeding, it's too easy, it's too easy for, for the Company to pass off all these expenses as, onto the ratepayers. …

On January 30, 1989 *The Evening Telegram* reported further comments of Mr. Wells pertaining to the salaries of the executives. The article read in part:

> Mr. Wells complained in December that the salaries paid to the company executives, in particular to president Anthony Brait, were so high they were driving up the cost of telephone service to consumers.
>
> . . .
>
> Mr. Wells said Sunday that additional company documents subpoenaed by the board indicate Mr. Brait's salary for 1988 was close to $235,000, a figure Mr. Wells described as "ludicrous."
>
> . . .

"I can't see what circumstances would justify that kind of money," Mr. Wells said.

"I don't think the ratepayers of this province should be expected to pay that kind of salary. The company can bloody well take it out of the shareholders' profits."

. . .

Mr. Wells said he doesn't know when the case will be before the court, but said if he is biased, it is on the side of the consumers who pay too much for their phone bills.

On April 4, Mr. Wells discussed the issue that was before the Board on the CBC morning radio program. His comments in part are as follows:

What's wrong is that it's not necessary to provide telephone services to the people of this Province for chief executive officer of a company operating in a protected enclave in the economy like that where revenues are down too where there's no real business pressure. To be paid at that level, I think the company is asking the board, I suppose, or asking the rate payers to approve a level of compensation which is excessive and I just don't know, there's absolutely no justification for it at all. The company, obviously, is out of touch with reality and insensitive to the cold hard facts of life that many Newfoundlanders face in earning living from day to day.

During the same program Commissioner Wells also commented:

There's no question about that, the question is whether or not this is excessive and very clearly, in my mind, it's certainly is and when you're as I say, you're not talking about a free enterprise situation where you have the competitive pressures in the market place, you're talking about a monopoly that's got a guaranteed situation and if something goes wrong then they can come crying to the board and get rate relief.

. . .

Well that's the point, that's the point, I mean I don't particularly care what the company decides to pay its top executives. I care about how much of that compensation is to be paid for by rate payers, by you, as consumers of telephone services and very clearly that issue has to be addressed and I hope when we have an order out on this issue later on the month, they, they will in fact, be addressed. No justification whatsoever to expect the consumers of telephone services in this Province to be paying the full cost of salary levels for these people, no justification whatsoever.

. . .

Very clearly, very clearly there is a significant level of executive over compensation and very clearly the board has to deal with that. To what degree the board does in fact deal with it, by that I mean, to what level we're, we're prepared to allow for rate making purposes, of course, awaits determination and the result of the hearing.

. . .

Well I, no you're right, it's not the amount of money, I mean the amount of money relative to the overall revenues of the company is in fact incidental, it's peanuts but what's important here is the issue of equity, the issue of fairness. ... what's important is that pay levels be set with in tune with what's paid generally in the community and that they be fair and be perceived to be fair, very clearly in the minds of I suppose, 99 percent of Newfoundlanders, paying Mr. Brait over $200,000.00 a year along with what's being paid to the rest of the executives is not fair in the minds of ordinary Newfoundlanders and I think they're perfectly right and indeed, I think it's incumbent on this board to address that inequity even though as you say, it's not going to result in lower telephone bills. But as somebody once said if you watch the pennies the dollars look after themselves you know.

It is to be noted that all these comments were made before the Board released its decision on the matter. The decision was contained in Order No. P.U. 20 (1989) dated August 3, 1989. In that order, the Board (i) disallowed the "cost of the enhanced pension plan" for certain senior executive officers of the appellant as an expense for rate-making purposes, and (ii) directed the appellant to refund to its customers in the former operating territory of the Newfoundland Telephone Company Limited the sums of $472,300 and $490,300 which were the amounts charged as expenses to the appellant's operating account for 1987 and 1988 to cover the costs of the enhanced pension plan; (iii) made no order respecting the individual salaries of the senior executive officers of the appellant.

Mr. Wells and two others constituted the majority of the Board which disallowed the costs of the enhanced pension plan for executive officers of the appellant. A minority of the Board would have allowed this item as a reasonable and prudent expense. Although the Board made no order respecting the salaries of senior executive officers, Mr. Wells added a concurring opinion and comment in which he stated:

> Because the Board failed to properly address those issues and on the basis of the evidence presented, I have to agree with the rest of the Board.
>
>   . . .
>
> In conclusion I am in complete agreement with the Majority on the issue of the special executive retirement plan and given the evidence as presented at the hearing, I have to concur with the rest of the Board on the issue of executive salaries. However, the latter issue requires a more thorough examination by the Board in the future. It is not an issue that has been finally resolved.
>
>   . . .

Analysis

The Composition and Function of Administrative Boards

Administrative boards play an increasingly important role in our society. They regulate many aspects of our life, from beginning to end. Hospital and medical boards regulate the methods and practice of the doctors that bring us into this world. Boards regulate the licensing and the operation of morticians who are concerned with our mortal remains. Marketing boards regulate the farm products we eat; transport boards regulate the means and flow of our travel; energy boards control the price and distribution of the forms of energy we use; planning boards and city councils regulate the location and types of buildings in which we live and work. In Canada, boards are a way of life. Boards and the functions they fulfil are legion.

Some boards will have a function that is investigative, prosecutorial and adjudicative. It is only boards with these three powers that can be expected to regulate adequately complex or monopolistic industries that supply essential services.

The composition of boards can, and often should, reflect all aspects of society. Members may include the experts who give advice on the technical nature of the operations to be considered by the board, as well as representatives of government and of the community. There is no reason why advocates for the consumer or ultimate user of the regulated product should not, in appropriate circumstances, be members of boards. No doubt many boards will operate more effectively with representation from all segments of society who are interested in the operations of the Board.

Nor should there be undue concern that a board which draws its membership from a wide spectrum will act unfairly. It might be expected that a board member who holds directorships in leading corporations will espouse their viewpoint. Yet I am certain that although the corporate perspective will be put forward, such a member will strive to act fairly. Similarly, a consumer advocate who has spoken out on numerous occasions about practices which he, or she, considers unfair to the consumer will be expected to put forward the consumer point of view. Yet that same person will also strive for fairness and a just result. Boards need not be limited solely to experts or to bureaucrats.

· · ·

It can be seen that there is a great diversity of administrative boards. Those that are primarily adjudicative in their functions will be expected to comply with the standard applicable to courts. That is to say that the conduct of the members of the board should be such that there could be no reasonable apprehension of bias with regard to their decision. At the other end of the scale are boards with popularly elected members such as those dealing with planning and development whose members are municipal councillors. With those boards, the standard will be much more lenient. In order to disqualify the members a challenging party must establish that there has been a pre-judgment of the matter to such an extent that any representations to the contrary would be futile. Administrative boards that deal with matters of policy will be closely comparable to the boards composed of municipal councillors. For those boards, a strict application of a reasonable apprehension of bias as a test might undermine the very role which has been entrusted to them by the legislature.

Janisch published a very apt and useful Case Comment on *Nfld. Light & Power Co. v. P.U.C. (Bd.)* (1987) 25 Admin. LR 196. He observed that Public Utilities Commissioners, unlike judges, do not have to apply abstract legal principles to resolve disputes. As a result, no useful purpose would be served by holding them to a standard of judicial neutrality. In fact to do so might undermine the legislature's goal of regulating utilities since it would encourage the appointment of those who had never been actively involved in the field. This would, Janisch wrote at 198, result in the appointment of "the main line party faithful and bland civil servants." Certainly there appears to be great merit in appointing to boards representatives of interested sectors of society including those who are dedicated to forwarding the interest of consumers.

Further, a member of a board which performs a policy formation function should not be susceptible to a charge of bias simply because of the expression of strong opinions prior to the hearing. This does not of course mean that there are no limits to the conduct of board members. It is simply a confirmation of the principle that the courts must take a flexible approach to the problem so that the standard which is applied varies with the role and function of the Board which is being considered. In the end, however, commissioners must base their decision on the evidence which is before them. Although they may draw upon their relevant expertise and their background of knowledge and understanding, this must be applied to the evidence which has been adduced before the board.

. . .

It can be seen that the Board has been given the general supervision of provincial public utilities. In that role it must supervise the operation of Newfoundland Telephone which has a monopoly on the provision of telephone services in the Province of Newfoundland. The Board, when it believes any charges or expenses of a utility are unreasonable, may of its own volition summarily investigate the charges or expenses. As a result of the investigation it may order a public hearing regarding the expenses. In turn, at the hearing the utility must be accorded the fundamental rights of procedural fairness. That is to say, the utility must be given notice of the complaint, the right to enforce the attendance of witnesses and to make submissions in support of its position.

When determining whether any rate or charge is "unreasonable" or "unjustly discriminatory" the Board will assess the charges and rates in economic terms. In those circumstances the Board will not be dealing with legal questions but rather policy issues. The decision-making process of this Board will come closer to the legislative end of the spectrum of administrative boards than to the adjudicative end.

It can be seen that the Board, pursuant to s. 79, has a duty to act as an investigator with regard to rates or charges and may have a duty to act as prosecutor and adjudicator with regard to these same expenses pursuant to ss. 83, 85 and 86.

What then of the statements made by Mr. Wells? Certainly it would be open to a commissioner during the investigative process to make public statements pertaining to the investigation. Although it might be more appropriate to say nothing, there would be no irreparable damage caused by a commissioner saying that he, or she, was concerned with the size of executive salaries and the executive pension package. Nor would it be inappropriate to emphasize on behalf of all consumers that the investigation would "leave no stone unturned" to ascertain whether the expenses or rates were appropriate and reasonable. During the investigative stage, a wide licence must be given to board members to make public comment. As long as those statements do not indicate a mind so closed that any submissions would be futile, they should not be subject to attack on the basis of bias.

The statements made by Mr. Wells before the hearing began on December 19 did not indicate that he had a closed mind. For example, his statement: "[s]o I want the company hauled in here—all them fat cats with their big pensions—to justify (these expenses) under the public glare ... I think the rate payers have a right to be assured that we are not permitting this company to be too extravagant" is not objectionable. That comment is no more than a colourful expression of an opinion that the salaries and pension benefits seemed to be unreasonably high. It does not indicate a closed mind. Even Wells' statement that he did not think that the expenses could be justified, did not indicate a closed mind. However, should a commissioner state that, no matter what evidence might be disclosed as a result of the investigation, his or her position would not change, this would indicate a closed mind. Even at the investigatory stage statements manifesting a mind so closed as to make submissions futile would constitute a basis for raising an issue of apprehended bias. However the quoted statement of Mr. Wells was made on November 13, three days after the hearing was ordered. Once the hearing date had been set, the parties were entitled to expect that the conduct of the commissioners would be such that it would not raise a reasonable apprehension of bias. The comment of Mr. Wells did just that.

Once the matter reaches the hearing stage a greater degree of discretion is required of a member. Although the standard for a commissioner sitting in a hearing of the Board of Commissioners of Public Utilities need not be as strict and rigid as that expected of a judge presiding at a trial, nonetheless procedural fairness must be maintained. The statements of Commissioner Wells made during and subsequent to the hearing, viewed cumulatively, lead inexorably to the conclusion that a reasonable person appraised of the situation would have an apprehension of bias.

On January 24, while the hearing was already in progress, Wells was making statements that might readily be understood by a reasonable observer, as they were by the telecast reporter Jim Thoms, that Wells had made up his mind what his judgment would be even before the Board had heard all the evidence. Evidence sufficient to create a reasonable apprehension of bias can be found in some of the statements made by Wells during the course of a January 24th telecast, and in the subsequent comments to the press and to the radio. …

These statements, taken together, give a clear indication that not only was there a reasonable apprehension of bias but that Mr. Wells had demonstrated that he had a closed mind on the subject.

Once the order directing the holding of the hearing was given the Utility was entitled to procedural fairness. At that stage something more could and should be expected of the conduct of board members. At the investigative stage, the "closed mind" test was applicable. Once matters proceeded to a hearing, a higher standard had to be applied. Procedural fairness then required the board members to conduct themselves so that there could be no reasonable apprehension of bias. The application of that test must be flexible. It need not be as strict for this Board dealing with policy matters as it would be for a board acting solely in an adjudicative capacity. This standard of conduct will not of course inhibit the most vigorous questioning of witnesses and counsel by board members. Wells' statements, however, were such that so long as he remained a member of the Board hearing the matter, a reasonable apprehension of bias existed. It follows that the hearing proceeded unfairly and was invalid.

The Consequences of a Finding of Bias

Everyone appearing before administrative boards is entitled to be treated fairly. It is an independent and unqualified right. As I have stated, it is impossible to have a fair hearing or to have procedural fairness if a reasonable apprehension of bias has been established. If there has been a denial of a right to a fair hearing it cannot be cured by the tribunal's subsequent decision. A decision of a tribunal which denied the parties a fair hearing cannot be simply voidable and rendered valid as a result of the subsequent decision of the tribunal. Procedural fairness is an essential aspect of any hearing before a tribunal. The damage created by apprehension of bias cannot be remedied. The hearing, and any subsequent order resulting from it, is void. In *Cardinal v. Director of Kent Institution* [1985] 2 SCR 643 (BC) at 661, Le Dain J speaking for the Court put his position in this way:

… I find it necessary to affirm that the denial of a right to a fair hearing must always render a decision invalid, whether or not it may appear to a reviewing court that the hearing would likely have resulted in a different decision. The right to a fair hearing must be regarded as an independent, unqualified right which finds its essential justification in the sense of procedural justice which any person affected by an administrative decision is entitled to have. It is not for a court to deny that right and sense of justice on the basis of speculation as to what the result might have been had there been a hearing.

In my view, this principle is also applicable to this case. In the circumstances, there is no alternative but to declare that the Order of the Board of Commissioners of Public Utilities is void.

Appeal allowed.

NOTES

1. Consider the following criticism of Cory J's judgment advanced in Dyzenhaus, "Developments in Administrative Law: The 1991-92 Term" (1993), 4 *Sup. Ct. L Rev.* (2d) 177, at 207-8:

Suppose that Wells had in fact conducted himself as Cory J suggested. That is, suppose that he had made his opposition very clear and public until the stage of hearing the matter had been reached and had then shut up. Would a reasonably informed bystander have any less reason to suspect that Wells' views were continuing to operate on his judgment? Suppose further that Wells had followed Cory J's advice even more carefully and had remained silent from the start of the process, although his views were still well known. Here the bystander might surely find silence more suspicious than golden.

My reasonable bystander is different from the figure that the Court has in mind, but she is, I suggest, at least no less reasonable and in my view much more so. My reasonable bystander thinks that where decision makers have strong views it is better to have those views out in the open where they can be challenged at every stage of the decision process. She thinks that it is on a challenge-allowing openness that any hope of eliminating a biased decision rests.

2. For a rather different context in which the standard of an open mind rather than that of a reasonable apprehension of bias has been applied, see *Reimer v. Saskatchewan (Human Rights Commission)* (1992), 8 Admin. LR (2d) 1 (Sask. CA), the context being the investigative function of the commission and the decision whether to establish a board of inquiry to adjudicate on an allegation of discrimination.

3. The *Newfoundland Telephone* case illustrates the tension between the desire of members of agencies with a public interest mandate to be accessible and transparent to the media, and through the media, to the public, and the right of parties to agency proceedings to a hearing free of actual or apparent bias. In reading the following judgment, which involved a claim of apprehended bias by a former prime minister and his chief of staff against the retired Superior Court judge heading a commission of inquiry into the alleged mismanagement of government funds, ask yourself whether transparency and fairness in such a context are irreconcilable. Significantly, the extensive media coverage of the commission of inquiry and the commission's findings played no small part in the minority Liberal government's electoral defeat in January 2006.

Pelletier v. Canada (Attorney General)
(2008), 84 Admin. LR (4th) 1, 333 FTR 190

[In 1996, on the heels of the narrow defeat of the sovereigntist option in the 1995 referendum on Québec sovereignty, the government of Canada, led by Prime Minister Jean Chrétien, decided to take measures to counteract the Québec sovereignty movement. Mr. Chrétien placed Jean Pelletier, his chief of staff, in charge of Canada's national unity strategy, which sought to enhance federal visibility and presence in Canada, but particularly in Québec. One way to achieve this was through federal sponsorship of cultural, community, and sporting events, where promotional material and Canadian symbols would be displayed. Through the sponsorship program, administered by the Department of Public Works and Government Services Canada, the federal government spent $250 million between 1997 and 2003, of which $100 million was awarded to advertising and communication agencies in the form of production fees and commissions. Following the auditor general's publication of a report detailing irregularities in the operation of the sponsorship program, a commission of inquiry, headed by retired Québec Superior Court Justice John Howard Gomery was established with a mandate to investigate and report on the program and advertising activities of the government and to make recommendations to prevent mismanagement of such programs in the future.

In an effort to permit the media to have a better understanding of the commission's proceedings, Commissioner Gomery granted several media interviews in the course of the inquiry. In view of certain comments made by the commissioner at these interviews, Mr. Chrétien's counsel asked Mr. Gomery to recuse himself. He dismissed the motion for recusal and eventually issued a report setting out the commission's findings. In a section of his first report (Commission of Inquiry into the Sponsorship Program and Advertising Activities, *Who Is Responsible? Fact Finding Report* (2005)), Commissioner Gomery expressly addressed the responsibility of Mr. Chrétien and Mr. Pelletier. After noting that there was no evidence that they were involved in kickback schemes, he stated, at 428-29:

> But they are to be blamed for omissions. Since Mr. Chrétien chose to run the Program from his own office, and to have his own exempt staff take charge of its direction, he is accountable for the defective manner in which the Sponsorship Program and initiatives were implemented. Mr. Pelletier, for whom Mr. Chrétien was responsible, failed to take the most elementary precautions against mismanagement. ...
>
> They should also have done precisely what [clerk of the Privy Council] Ms. [Jocelyne] Bourgon counselled the Prime Minister to do, which was to postpone making decisions about sponsorship initiatives until a formal process had been adopted for evaluating them. It would have been more prudent for Mr. Chrétien to have accepted her suggestion that responsibility for the administration of the Program be transferred to the PCO or to a Minister, instead of being retained within the PMO. He chose to disregard this advice and, since he is directly responsible for errors committed by Mr. Pelletier, he must share the blame for the mismanagement that ensued. ...

Mr. Chrétien and Mr. Pelletier sought judicial review of the commissioner's report and an order that the commissioner's findings relating to them be set aside on the grounds that there was a reasonable apprehension of bias on the part of Commissioner Gomery toward them.]

TEITELBAUM DJ:

[Teitelbaum DJ, applying the *Baker* factors, determined that the applicant Jean Pelletier, and former Prime Minister Jean Chrétien, were entitled to a high degree of fairness due to the serious potential damage that the commission's findings could have on their reputations. He then considered the issue of reasonable apprehension of bias.]

Issue 3: Did the Commissioner breach the duty of procedural fairness?

A. Was there a reasonable apprehension of bias on the Commissioner's part toward the Applicant?

[65] Procedural fairness requires that decisions be made free from a reasonable apprehension of bias by an impartial decision-maker (*Baker, supra*, at para. 45). The standard of impartiality expected of a decision-maker is variable depending on the role and function of the decision-maker involved (*Newfoundland Telephone Co. v. Newfoundland (Board of Commissioners of Public Utilities)*, [1992] 1 SCR 623, *per* Cory J [hereinafter *Newfoundland Telephone*]). In *Newfoundland Telephone*, the Supreme Court established a spectrum for assessing allegations of bias against members of commissions or administrative boards: [An extract from *Newfoundland Telephone* is omitted.]

[66] Justice Cory stressed in that case "that the courts must take a flexible approach to the problem so that the standard which is applied varies with the role and function of the Board which is being considered" (*Newfoundland Telephone, supra*, at p. 639). Applying this flexible approach, he then concluded that the applicable standard for assessing the Board's impartiality during the investigative stage was the closed-mind standard. He also found that when the matter reached the hearing stage, the Board's role had changed and, as a result, the standard used to assess the Board's conduct at that stage was the reasonable apprehension of bias standard.

[67] In *Beno (FCA), supra*, the Federal Court of Appeal considered the nature, mandate and function of the Commission of Inquiry into the Deployment of Canadian Forces to Somalia and determined that the Commission was situated somewhere between the legislative and adjudicative extremes on the spectrum, stating the following at paragraphs 26-27:

> It is not necessary, for the purposes of this appeal, to determine with precision the test of impartiality that is applicable to members of commissions of inquiry. Depending on its nature, mandate and function, the Somalia Inquiry must be situated along the Newfoundland Telephone spectrum somewhere between its legislative and adjudicative extremes. Because of the significant differences between this Inquiry and a civil or criminal proceeding, the adjudicative extreme would be inappropriate in this case. On the other hand, in view of the serious consequences that the report of a commission may have for those who have been served with a section 13 notice, the permissive "closed mind" standard at the legislative extreme would also be inappropriate. We are of the opinion that the Commissioners of the Somalia Inquiry must perform their duties in a way which, having regard to the special nature of their functions, does not give rise to a reasonable apprehension of bias. As in Newfoundland Telephone, the reasonable apprehension of bias standard must be applied flexibly. Cory J held (supra, at pages 644-645):

Once matters proceeded to a hearing, a higher standard had to be applied. Procedural fairness then required the board members to conduct themselves so that there could be no reasonable apprehension of bias. The application of that test must be flexible. It need not be as strict for this Board dealing with policy matters as it would be for a board acting solely in an adjudicative capacity. This standard of conduct will not of course inhibit the most vigorous questioning of witnesses and counsel by board members.

Applying that test, we cannot but disagree with the findings of the Judge of first instance. A commissioner should be disqualified for bias only if the challenger establishes a reasonable apprehension that the commissioner would reach a conclusion on a basis other than the evidence. In this case, a flexible application of the reasonable apprehension of bias test requires that the reviewing court take into consideration the fact that the commissioners were acting as investigators in the context of a long, arduous and complex inquiry. The Judge failed to appreciate this context in applying the test.

[68] Relying on the Federal Court of Appeal's decision in *Beno*, the Attorney General submits that the Commission falls between the middle and the closed-mind end of the *Newfoundland Telephone* spectrum and argues that the applicable test is whether there is a reasonable apprehension that the Commissioner would reach a conclusion on a basis other than the evidence. In the alternative, the Attorney General submits that the applicable test is the reasonable apprehension of bias test as enunciated in the dissenting judgment of Justice de Grandpré in *Committee for Justice and Liberty v. National Energy Board*, [1978] 1 SCR 369 [hereinafter *Committee for Justice and Liberty*] and adopted subsequently by the Supreme Court of Canada.

[69] The Applicant submits that the test for assessing Commissioner Gomery's impartiality is the reasonable apprehension of bias test or reasonable person test established in *Committee for Justice and Liberty*. The Applicant argues that since the Commissioner is a judge and was appointed as Commissioner because of his judicial skills, the applicable test for determining whether or not there is a reasonable apprehension of bias on the part of the Commissioner is the same as that which is applied when assessing the impartiality of a judge presiding over a trial. Put simply, the Applicant argues that because the Commissioner in this case was selected because of his skills as a judge, although he was sitting as a Commissioner in the hearings, he should be held to the same standard of judicial neutrality expected of a judge presiding over a trial.

[70] Although the Commissioner's experience as a judge may have assisted him in his role as Commissioner, he was not sitting as a judge while performing his duties as a Commissioner. Thus, it does not necessarily follow that his impartiality is to be assessed using a strict application of the reasonable apprehension of bias test.

[71] After considering the jurisprudence cited by the parties, I conclude that the Commission falls somewhere between the middle and high end of the *Newfoundland Telephone* spectrum. Thus, using a flexible application of the reasonable apprehension of bias test, I adopt the test enunciated by Justice de Grandpré in *Committee for Justice and Liberty* ... .

[After discussing the test for bias, including the evidentiary onus and the legal effect of a finding of reasonable apprehension of bias, Teitelbaum DJ continued.]

Application of Reasonable Apprehension of Bias Test in the Present Case

[75] The Applicant alleges that the following indicate a reasonable apprehension of bias: (1) the public statements made in the course of the interviews granted by Commissioner Gomery in December 2004, before all the evidence had been submitted and all the witnesses had testified; (2) the August 2007 interview in which the Commissioner confirmed that some of the December 2004 comments were a mistake; (3) the August 2007 newspaper articles in which the Commissioner was quoted as stating that the Commission was "an amazing spectacle" and that he "had the best seat in the house for the best show in town"; (4) the public statements made by Mr. François Perreault, the Commission's spokesperson, and more generally, the role played by Mr. Perreault in ensuring media attention on the Commission; (5) Commissioner Gomery's declaration to Mr. Alex Himelfarb, then Clerk of the Privy Council, revealing his preoccupation with media coverage; and (6) that the Commission's lead counsel, Me Roy, was the Secretary to the Prime Minister of Canada, the Right Honourable Brian Mulroney, from 1984 to 1988 and is now a partner of Mr. Mulroney and Me Sally Gomery, the Commissioner's daughter, at the law firm of Ogilvy Renault LLP. I have already determined that the documents evidencing the relationship between the Commissioner's lead counsel and Mr. Mulroney and Me Gomery are not relevant. Thus, I need not consider this ground in my analysis on this part.

[76] The Applicant submits that the Commissioner's comments, on the record, to the media, and after the Inquiry had concluded establish a reasonable apprehension of bias. He further argues that Commissioner Gomery was seduced by the media and the limelight to such an extent that the judicial instinct for fairness, objectivity and restraint which the Applicant was entitled to expect of him gave way to a preoccupation on his part with focusing media (and public) attention upon himself, a course of conduct which preordained unfavourable findings about the Applicant in the Report.

[77] The Attorney General argues that the Court, in assessing the allegations of a reasonable apprehension of bias, must be cautious not to confound the Commissioner's personality with his state of mind. He suggests that the Commissioner was outspoken and transparent, and even though the Commissioner himself acknowledged that some of his comments were a mistake, the Attorney General maintains that these comments do not establish that the Commissioner would decide on something other than the evidence or, in the alternative, that there is a reasonable apprehension of bias toward the Applicant.

[78] I also add that counsel for the Attorney General admitted that some of the Commissioner's remarks to the journalists were inappropriate.

[79] After reviewing the evidence placed before me on this issue, I am convinced that there is more than sufficient evidence to find that an informed person, viewing the matter realistically and practically and having thought the matter through would find a reasonable apprehension of bias on the part of the Commissioner. The comments made by the Commissioner, viewed cumulatively, not only indicate that he prejudged issues but also that he was not impartial toward the Applicant.

[80] Statements made by the Commissioner indicate that while conducting the hearings, the Commissioner formed conclusions about issues he was to investigate and report before having heard all the evidence. In December 2004, when the Commission's Phase I hearings had recessed for the holidays, the Commissioner granted interviews to jour-

nalists, which resulted in the publication of a number of newspaper articles. As noted above, the Commissioner does not contest the accuracy of the statements *in quotations* in the articles.

[81] In an article in the *Ottawa Citizen*, dated December 16, 2004, the Commissioner is quoted as having stated: "I'm coming to the same conclusion as (Auditor General) Sheila Fraser that this was a government program which was run in a catastrophically bad way. I haven't been astonished with what I'm hearing, but it's dismaying." In an article published the following day in the *National Post*, Commissioner Gomery, speaking of his previous comment that the Sponsorship Program "was run in a catastrophically bad way," stated: "Does anyone have a different opinion on that subject?" "I simply *confirmed* the findings that Sheila Fraser had made, which I think I am in a position to do after three months of hearings" [my emphasis].

[82] The Attorney General submits that the Commissioner was indeed in a position to determine at the time he made these statements that the Sponsorship Program was "run in a catastrophically bad way," since this was, in essence, one of the conclusions of the Auditor General's Report on which the Commissioner's mandate was based. In other words, the Commissioner's mandate had the premise that there had been very bad mismanagement of the Program. Further, the Attorney General states that none of the Auditor General's conclusions were ever challenged by the parties, despite Commissioner Gomery's invitation to do so. The Attorney General submits that in fact, "everybody admitted" the problems noted in the Auditor General's Report.

[83] I cannot agree with the Attorney General that the Commissioner, after conducting only three of nine months of hearings, was in a position to confirm the findings of the Auditor General or to conclude that the Sponsorship Program was "run in a catastrophically bad way." First, unlike the Auditor General's investigation, the Commissioner's mandate, as set out in the Terms of Reference, was not limited to investigating and reporting only the way in which the Program was managed by public servants. I stress that section (iii) of Part I of the Commissioner's mandate provided that the Commissioner was to investigate and report on "the management of the sponsorship program and advertising activities by government officials at *all* levels" [my emphasis]. Thus, the Commissioner was not in a position to conclude that the program was mismanaged before having heard from government officials of *all* levels who were set to testify. This is especially so given that the Commissioner ultimately concluded that the Sponsorship Program was run out of the Prime Minister's Office under the direct supervision of the Applicant (who had yet to testify), who "for all practical purposes, assumed the role, the functions and the responsibilities of a Minister of a department charged with the implementation of a program." Without having heard the testimony of all witnesses who were to appear before the Commission, especially those whom he found to be in charge of the program, the Commissioner was not and could not be in a position to conclude that the Program was "run in a catastrophically bad way."

[84] Second, to conclude that the mismanagement was "catastrophic" before hearing all the evidence undermined the very purpose of the commission of inquiry, creating a sense that the proceedings were perfunctory in nature. The Commissioner's remarks indicate that he had reached conclusions or drawn inferences of fact before the evidence was complete and submissions had been received from all participants. The Commissioner

had a duty not to reach conclusions about the management of the sponsorship program until having heard all the evidence, and he was not in a position to do so until then. The objective of the Inquiry was to get to the truth of the matters that were the subject of chapters 3 and 4 of the Auditor General's Report. By stating that he "was coming to the same conclusion" and that he "simply confirmed the findings that Sheila Fraser had made" after only three months of hearings would, in my view, leave the reasonable person with the view that the Commissioner had prejudged some of the very matters he was tasked to investigate before hearing all the evidence.

[85] There is other evidence to lead a reasonable observer to conclude that the Commissioner prejudged the outcome of the investigation. In Mr. Perreault's book entitled *Inside Gomery* (which the Commissioner in the foreword to the book described as "accurate" ["exacte" in the original, French version]) and in an article in the *Toronto Star*, dated March 1, 2006, Commissioner Gomery is cited as having stated the following with respect to the answer given by Mr. Chrétien when asked who was responsible for managing the Sponsorship Program: "And the very answer he gave me was the only answer that counted as far as I was concerned." "So, with this answer, I had everything that I needed." Mr. Chrétien's answer referred to by Commissioner Gomery was given in the course of the following exchange between Me Roy, Commissioner Gomery, and Mr. Chrétien at the February 8, 2005 hearing of the Commission:

> Mr. Roy: And you, did you have in your office, the PMO, had you directed certain people to get involved in the post-referendum strategy file?
>
> Mr. Chrétien: Mr. Pelletier, who had been mayor of Quebec City, he knew Quebec well and he was my chief of staff and he had the same commitment as I did to ensure that Quebec was going to stay in confederation, took up those responsibilities afterwards.
>
> Mr. Roy: So, my question, more precisely, is as follows: who, inside the PMO, from your cabinet, had the responsibility for ensuring that the game plan would be followed and that the government would be ready to face a future referendum campaign? …
>
> The Commissioner: But Mr. Chrétien, I would really like to have an answer to this question. Did you designate someone to take charge—
>
> Mr. Chrétien: I already said that Mr. Pelletier was responsible for the unity file in my office.
>
> The Commissioner: Thank you.

Commissioner Gomery's intervention at the hearing, combined with his subsequent comment that Mr. Chrétien's answer "was the only answer that counted" and that it gave him "everything that [he] needed," raises doubt as to whether Commissioner Gomery was indeed impartial in his fact-finding mission, or if he was in search of specific answers that supported pre-determined conclusions.

[86] Again, this comment was made before all the evidence had been heard from the witnesses who were called to testify or were to be called to testify. A reasonable, well-informed person, viewing this statement, would conclude that, instead of sitting as a dispassionate decision-maker presiding over the hearings with no pre-established ideas regarding the conclusions he would eventually reach after hearing all the evidence, the

Commissioner had a plan or checklist of the evidence that was expected and which was required in order to support pre-determined conclusions.

[87] Also, in an article in the *Ottawa Citizen*, dated December 16, 2004, the Commissioner is quoted as having stated, in reference to upcoming evidence that was to be heard by the Commission, that the "juicy stuff" was yet to come. The term "juicy" is defined by the Canadian Oxford Dictionary as meaning "racy or scandalous."

[88] This comment trivialized the proceedings, which had enormous stakes for the witnesses involved in the proceedings, especially those who had yet to testify. It telegraphed to the public a prediction that evidence of wrongdoing was forthcoming, and, because in terms of public interest the most important witnesses were yet to come (including the Applicant, other senior officials, the Prime Minister and cabinet ministers), the comment was clearly directed at what might be expected from or about them. Whatever interpretation is given to this comment, the comment bears a pejorative connotation to which no witness ought to have been subjected.

[89] I note that on a number of occasions, the Commissioner gave assurances that he had not prejudged any issues and that his impartiality remained intact. First, in an article in the *National Post* on December 17, 2004, the Commissioner was quoted as stating: "I don't think I am in danger of having prejudged an issue that I shouldn't have prejudged," and "I haven't made any judgments or prejudged any issue. I just made a comment on the personality of one of the witnesses." This second statement was made with respect to a comment the Commissioner had made in an interview the previous day about Mr. Guité: "It's impossible not to like Chuck Guité." "Let's face it, he's a charming scamp and he had his department mesmerized. He got himself promoted just before his retirement and thereby built up his pension. I'm going to hear more about Mr. Guité. He will probably have to testify again."

[90] When the hearings resumed in January 2005, counsel for the Applicant expressed concern about the statements the Commissioner had made to the media. The Commissioner expressed regret if his comments had caused anxiety or concern and reassured the parties that he had not reached any conclusions and would not do so until having heard all the evidence. However, the Commissioner went on to justify his conduct by stating that there had been a change in what was considered proper judicial conduct and stated:

> We have also seen over the last decades an increasing pressure for judges to come out of their ivory towers to establish some sort of a relationship with the media and to permit the media to have a better understanding of what it is that is taking place in the courtrooms or before commissions of inquiry of this kind.
>
> It was on the understanding of this evolution that led me to make—to grant certain interviews at the end of the year. I was told by representatives of the media that there was a desire to know a little bit better what was going on and what could be expected. It was in that context that these press interviews were granted.

In the Commissioner's dismissal of the Motion for Recusal brought against him by Mr. Chrétien, the Commissioner provided further reassurances that he had not prejudged any issues and that he remained impartial, stating:

In the representations made before me on January 11th, Mr. Scott declared and I quote: "You have closed your mind." That statement was factually incorrect. I am the only person in the world who could know if I had closed my mind, and I said then, to reassure Mr. Scott and others, that my mind remained open. It is still open today and I repeat that I have not yet reached any final conclusion on any of the questions which the Inquiry calls upon me to decide. ...

When I referred to the report of the Auditor General, I am quoted as saying that I "was coming" to the same conclusions as she did, not that I had so concluded. In other words, I indicated that my mental processes were ongoing; I have not closed my mind to contrary evidence, should such evidence be adduced.

When I made reference to autographed golf balls, I said that it was disappointing to have heard evidence that a Prime Minister *would* allow (note the use of the conditional tense) his name to be used in this way. My mind remains open to any reasonable explanation, and it is a small point in any event. I am looking forward to hearing Mr. Chrétien's testimony.

I have heard contradictory evidence, from various witnesses. I must conclude that some witnesses have not been truthful, but I did not say which witness or witnesses I was talking about, or indicate which of the conflicting versions I may be inclined to prefer. As to the relative truthfulness of various witnesses, these are conclusions I will draw only in light of all the evidence thus far and yet to come.

Finally, my description of Mr. Guité and the characterization of him as a "charming scamp," which is admittedly the kind of colourful language that judges should avoid using, does not in any way betray how I feel about his credibility. Sometimes charming people are credible and sometimes not. It is too soon to decide what weight I will give to Mr. Guité's testimony. That remains to be decided when the hearings are completed ... .

[91] The Attorney General relies heavily on these assurances by the Commissioner in support of the argument that the Commissioner had not formed premature conclusions. That the Commissioner made assurances that he had not prejudged any issue is irrelevant, as one may be unaware of their own biases. In *R v. Gough*, [1993] AC 646 (HL) at p. 655 (quoted by the Supreme Court of Canada in *Wewaykum Indian Band v. Canada*, [2003] 2 SCR 259), Lord Goff, quoting Devlin LJ in *The Queen v. Barnsley Licensing Justices*, [1960] 2 QB 167 (C.A.), stated:

Bias is or may be an unconscious thing and a man may honestly say that he was not actually biased and did not allow his interest to affect his mind, although nevertheless, he may have allowed it unconsciously to do so. The matter must be determined upon the probabilities to be inferred from the circumstances in which the justices sit.

[92] The determinative test, as stated above, is whether a reasonably well-informed person, viewing the matter realistically and practically, would conclude that there is a reasonable apprehension of bias. As I have already stated, I am satisfied that the test for a reasonable apprehension of bias has been met in this case.

[93] Lastly, I note that the Commissioner made other inappropriate comments that seemingly tainted the purpose and focus of the Inquiry. On a number of occasions, the Commissioner referred to the proceedings as a "show" or "spectacle" and even declared: "I have the best seat in the house for the best show in town." Upon his retirement, the

Commissioner further commented: "I was criticized for saying it but I stand by what I said—I had the best seat in the house for the best show in town." "It was an amazing spectacle. It was a drama with surprise discoveries almost every day, with eminently competent lawyers. It was an ideal situation for the person running the show." "It wasn't a rehearsed spectacle, but to see witnesses, one after the other, making startling revelations after being confronted with documents they couldn't explain was exciting and engrossing." Although these statements do not indicate a reasonable apprehension of bias toward the Applicant *per se*, they had the effect of transforming the nature of the inquiry from one that was a fact-finding mission with the hallmarks of fairness into an "exhibition" of misconduct on the part of senior government officials.

[94] The Applicant has also raised concerns about the Commissioner's preoccupation with the media. He argues that Commissioner Gomery was seduced by the media and the limelight to such an extent that the judicial instinct for fairness, objectivity and restraint which the Applicant was entitled to expect of him gave way to a preoccupation on his part with focusing media (and public) attention upon himself, a course of conduct which preordained unfavourable findings about the Applicant in the Report.

[95] I agree with the Applicant that the Commissioner became preoccupied with ensuring that the spotlight of the media remained on the Commission's inquiry, and he went to great lengths to ensure that the public's interest in the Commission did not wane. An example of the Commissioner's obvious preoccupation with the media is the following statement he made during Mr. Himelfarb's testimony:

> You know that both the opposition parties and the public would not be satisfied by saying "Well, we know that there was money lost but we have corrected that for the future." That is not going to satisfy the public, I don't think. *Certainly it isn't going to satisfy the media, which represents the public to some degree.* [my emphasis]
>
> This preoccupation with the media outside the hearing room had a detrimental impact on the fairness of the proceedings as it applies to the Applicant and, as I have said in my decision, as it applies to Mr. Chrétien.

[96] I note that although the Commissioner, in his ruling on the Motion for Recusal brought against him by Mr. Chrétien, acknowledged that some of the statements he had made during the interviews were, in his words, "ill-advised" and "inappropriate." He further acknowledged that his statements detracted attention from "the real objective of the Inquiry, which [was] to get at the truth of the matters which were subject of Chapters 3 and 4 of the Report of the Auditor General" and expressed his regret for this distraction. However, this acknowledgement and expression of regret, in my view, were incapable of repairing the harm that the Commissioner caused to the Applicant's reputation and the irreparable harm caused to the fairness or apparent fairness of the proceedings.

[97] Considering again the basic principles applicable to commissions of inquiries so succinctly set down by Justice Cory in *Krever*, above, I do not read that it is a function of a Commissioner to grant press interviews nor to express, during such an interview or interviews, an opinion as to what the evidence showed, and more particularly, to express that opinion before *all* of the evidence had been heard from the witnesses who were called to testify or were to be called to testify. I find that the Commissioner's conduct outside the hearing room had a detrimental effect on the fairness of the proceedings in

that the Applicant was put in a position in which he was caused to appear before a Commission that had publicly questioned the conduct and integrity of witnesses, including Mr. Chrétien, to which the Applicant was, in many respects, the *alter ego*, before they had even appeared before the Commission. This is sufficient to instill doubt in the mind of the reasonable person as to the fairness of the inquiry process.

[98] The media is not an appropriate forum in which a decision-maker is to become engaged while presiding over a commission of inquiry, a trial, or any other type of hearing or proceeding. Indeed, the only appropriate forum in which a decision-maker is to become engaged is within the hearing room of the very proceeding over which he or she is presiding. Comments revealing impressions and conclusions related to the proceedings should not be made extraneous to the proceedings either prior, concurrently *or even after* the proceedings have concluded.

[99] I stress that even in public inquiries where the purpose of the proceedings is to educate and inform the public, it is not the role of decision-makers to become active participants in the media. First and foremost, a decision-maker's primary duty is to remain impartial, with an open mind that is amenable to persuasion. It is only when all the evidence is heard and after deliberating on that evidence that a decision-maker is to form conclusions and, finally, to issue a judgment or report on the basis of these conclusions. It follows that a decision-maker speaks by way of his or her decision. This is the only appropriate forum in which a decision-maker should state his or her conclusions. As my colleague, mentor and friend, the late Justice Frank Collier once said to me when I was first appointed as a judge, "Let the decision speak for itself."

[100] I am convinced that an informed person, viewing the matter realistically and practically and having thought the matter through would find that the Commissioner's statements to the media during the Phase I hearings, after the release of the Report and upon his retirement, viewed cumulatively, indicate that the Commissioner prejudged issues under investigation and that he was not impartial toward the Applicant. The nature of the comments made to the media are such that no reasonable person, looking realistically and practically at the issue, and thinking the matter through, could possibly conclude that the Commissioner would decide the issues fairly.

[101] Given that I have already found a reasonable apprehension of bias on the part of the Commissioner toward the Applicant, I need not address the remaining issues in this application. At the hearing, the parties made submissions regarding the effect of a finding of a reasonable apprehension of bias on the Commissioner's Report if one were to be found. I conclude that, as a result of my finding that there existed a reasonable apprehension of bias on the part of the Commissioner toward the Applicant, the findings in the Report, as they relate to the Applicant, must be set aside. This is consistent with the decision of the Supreme Court of Canada in *Newfoundland Telephone, supra*, wherein Justice Cory, writing for the Court, held that where a reasonable apprehension of bias is found to exist on the part of a tribunal, its decision must be treated as void.

NOTES

1. Teitelbaum DJ simultaneously released a companion decision in *Chrétien v. Canada (Commission of Inquiry into the Sponsorship Program and Advertising Activities, Gomery Commission)* (2008), 2008 FC 802 finding a reasonable apprehension of bias on the part of Commissioner Gomery toward Mr. Chrétien.

2. The applicants Chrétien and Pelletier also pointed to the fact that Mr. Bernard Roy, lead commission counsel, had been principal secretary to former Conservative Prime Minister Brian Mulroney and was a partner in the same law firm as Mr. Mulroney and Ms. Sally Gomery, the commissioner's daughter. They claimed that these relationships supported their allegation that Commissioner Gomery had shown a reasonable apprehension of bias toward them. Teitelbaum DJ decided, in an interlocutory motion, that the paragraphs in the affidavits filed by the applicants were not relevant to their claims and ordered them struck.

3. Do you agree with Teitelbaum DJ that it is not the role of decision-makers to become active participants in the media? Is this true only in the context of a commission of inquiry or in all circumstances?

4. Should the fact that Commissioner Gomery was formerly a Superior Court judge affect the choice of the appropriate standard for assessing the claim of reasonable apprehension of bias?

5. Teitelbaum DJ determines the standard of disqualifying bias applicable to the commissioner's findings by reference to the spectrum established by the Supreme Court in *Newfoundland Telephone*. Accordingly, the utility of the very detailed analysis of the *Baker* factors preceding this part of his judgment is somewhat unclear. The Federal Court of Appeal has also linked the *Baker* "spectrum" to the standard of disqualifying bias—this time expressly—in *Kozak v. Canada (Minister of Citizenship and Immigration)*, 2006 FCA 124, at paras. 53-54. There, Evans JA states:

> [53] ... [T]he standard of impartiality expected of a particular administrative decision maker depends on context and is to be measured by reference to the factors identified by L'Heureux-Dubé J in *Baker* ... . The independence of the [Immigration and Refugee] Board, its adjudicative procedure and functions, and the fact that its decisions affect the Charter rights of claimants, indicate that the content of the duty of fairness owed by the Board, including the duty of impartiality, falls at the high end of the continuum of procedural fairness.
>
> [54] ... [T]he high standard of impartiality and independence applicable to the Board will be reflected in the determination of whether the appellants have established a reasonable apprehension of bias.

The Court of Appeal's reliance on the *Baker* analysis can be linked back to the Supreme Court's analysis in *Newfoundland Telephone*. Where the reasonable apprehension of bias standard is appropriate (for example, once a matter has proceeded to a hearing), the Supreme Court noted that its application must be "flexible"—less strict for a board dealing with policy matters than an adjudicative board. In *Kozak*, the court appears to have linked the strictness of its application of the standard to the proceeding's position on the *Baker* spectrum.

INDEPENDENCE

Over the years, the notion of independent decision making by tribunals and agencies has provided the fuel for continuing controversy about the wisdom of Cabinet directives and appeals (a subject we will return to later). Does the subjection of the decisions of allegedly independent regulatory agencies to the possibility of dictation or reversal by Cabinet on "political" grounds amount to an inappropriate compromise of the independence of those agencies? The use of independence in this context is, of course, a reflection of concerns about the integrity of agencies as collectivities or, as it is frequently described, "institutional independence." More recently, however, discussions of independence have come to focus more on the adjudicative freedom of individual members. In particular, this finds expression in debate about the extent to which their relative lack of security of tenure has an impact on their capacity for independent judgment.

One important aspect of this concern arises in the context of the relationship between panels of multimember tribunals and the collectivity in the context of pending adjudications. In chapter 6 of this text, we consider the whole issue of the extent to which it is appropriate for panels to discuss specific matters over which they are presiding with their colleagues. However, it merits noting in this context that at least part of the reason for this issue arising and the resulting jurisprudence placing restrictions on such contacts was based on the extent to which "toeing the line" might be seen by some adjudicators as important in terms of pleasing the other members of the tribunal. This consideration is, of course, a particular concern in the case of the chair who might be expected to play some role not only in the assignment of cases and making life within the tribunal tolerable but also in having an influence when reappointment is pending. Obviously, difficult questions are raised by such considerations and the need to determine where the line between impermissible pressures ends and essential performance evaluation and effective management of the collective enterprise begins.

Of course, in most instances, reappointment and preferment depend much more on the minister and the Cabinet than on pleasing one's colleagues, including the chair (for example, in the case of appointment to provincial human rights tribunals) and, in this context, there has been some litigation. Ministers of the Crown are unlikely to be as blunt as Premier Duplessis was in ordering the chair of the Liquor Commission to withdraw Roncarelli's licence (*Roncarelli v. Duplessis*, [1959] SCR 121 (Que.)). However, the high profile of many tribunals (for example, National Parole Board and Immigration and Refugee Board) and the criticisms directed at their responsible ministers by members of the public and Her Majesty's Loyal Opposition when those tribunals are perceived to have performed badly, ensures a level of interest on the part of the executive branch with the personnel who make up their membership. In such an environment, it would not be surprising if on occasion this produced a willingness to please in some contexts, particularly around renewal time.

Sethi v. Canada (Minister of Employment and Immigration), [1988] 2 FC 537 (TD); rev'd. [1988] 2 FC 552 (CA) provides an example.

Sethi claimed to be a Convention refugee. The minister disagreed, and Sethi made an application to the Immigration Appeal Board for a redetermination. He then claimed an apprehension of bias because of the apparent effects of proposed legislation about the board. Bill C-55 abolished the board and discharged the members without any compensation for the loss of their jobs. There were 49 members who would be discharged; 3 held appointments for life (during good behaviour) and the others had been appointed for terms ranging from 2 (the majority) to 10 years. The Bill created a replacement, the Immigration and Refugee Board, to which the members of the abolished board would be eligible for appointment. Sethi's argument was that the board could not appear to be indifferent between him and the government, because hopes of appointment to the new board by the government created a reasonable likelihood that members of the board would be sympathetic to the government's arguments against him. At the time of Sethi's application hearing, the Bill had passed third reading in Commons, and at the time of the appeal it had been reported back to the Senate by its committee. At first instance, Reed J said:

> In this case, the Board members were appointed for varying terms … . They would have undertaken the appointment on that basis and arranged or planned their financial affairs accordingly. What *Bill C-55* does is to undercut that financial planning, that financial security. By threatening to "throw" all the members of the Board out of office, it threatens the financial security of the members, while at the same time, holding out the possibility that some of them will be reappointed full time. In my view, given the fact that it is the government which will select from the existing Board members those that will be reappointed full time, and it is the government which is opposing the applicant's claim before the Board, I accept the applicant's contention that a reasonable apprehension of bias exists.

The Federal Court of Appeal allowed the government's appeal, and Mahoney JA said:

> In the first place, an affirmative answer would require the informed, right minded person to conclude the Board will tend, consciously or unconsciously, to perceive the government's interest lying in denial to applicants and appellants of rights accorded them by the law.
>
> · · ·
>
> In my opinion, no informed, right minded person would conclude that members of the Board would, in fact, please the government if they decided that disagreement unfairly. Members of the Board, taken collectively, are well informed as to the administration and policy of the Act, and, I trust, right minded. They would not think that such conduct would, in fact, please the government.
>
> · · ·
>
> In the second place, the mere expression of a government's intentions toward an administrative tribunal cannot, in my opinion, give rise to a probability that the tribunal will react to those intentions in a particular way relative to the decisions it is required to make.
>
> · · ·
>
> A more profound reason for rejecting an announcement of the government's intentions as to a tribunal as a basis for holding that it cannot continue to function, at least insofar as those who choose to object are concerned, is found in the chilling effect that would have on the democratic process as it has developed in Canada. Public debate, consultation and input have become important elements in the government's decision-making process. Much of it is now out of the backroom. Unless the government can make public its intentions without risk to the ability of the tribunal concerned to continue to function, it seems to me inevitable that it will be the opportunity for and benefit of public input that will be lost. On the dubious assumption that a Court could find, in a statement of government intention, sufficient certainty upon which to base a conclusion having legal effect, it should be slow to do so.

For a trenchant criticism of the judgment of the Federal Court of Appeal in this case, see the Canadian Bar Association Report, *The Independence of Federal Administrative Tribunals and Agencies in Canada* (1990) ("the Ratushny Report"), at 96-102. Also, for a rather different perspective on the issue in the context of the right of the Minister of Defence to reappoint military trial judges, see *R v. Lauzon* (1998), 8 Admin. LR (2d) 33 (CMAC).

Another reason for the emergence of "lack of independence" as a basis for challenge to participation, particularly in the constitutional domain, can be found in the employment of the expression "independent and impartial tribunal" in both s. 2(f) of the *Canadian Bill of Rights* and s. 11(d) of the *Canadian Charter of Rights and Freedoms*. While both these provisions have marginal relevance to the administrative process—they are each concerned primarily with the hearing and determination of criminal charges—some of the definitions of "independence" provided by the courts in applying these provisions clearly have resonances beyond their precise context and are suggestive of attacks on administrative decision making either on a common law basis or by reference to ss. 1(a) and 2(e) of the *Bill of Rights* and s. 7 of the Charter in situations where the more expansive thresholds for the applicability of those provisions can be crossed.

> Historically, the generally accepted core of the principle of judicial independence has been the complete liberty of individual judges to hear and decide cases that come before them: no outsider—be it government, pressure group or even another judge—should interfere in fact, or attempt to interfere, with the way in which a judge conducts his or her case and makes his or her decision. (Dickson CJ in *R v. Beauregard*, [1986] 2 SCR 56 (Que.) at 69.)

This theme as well as that of the difference between guarantees of impartiality and independence are developed in the following case where s. 11(d) and s. 7 of the Charter were held applicable to the federal competition tribunal because of its contempt powers.

Alex Couture Inc. v. Canada (Attorney-General)
(1991), 83 DLR (4th) 577 (Que. CA)

ROUSSEAU-HOULE JA (Bisson CJQ and Dussault JA concurring) [Translation]:

· · ·

1. The Interpretation of the Guarantees of Independence and Impartiality for the Purposes of s. 11(d) of the Charter

Judicial independence as a constitutional guarantee for the purposes of s. 11(d) of the Charter has been interpreted by Le Dain J in *R v. Valente* [[1985] 2 SCR 673 (Ont.)] as "referring to the status or relationship of judicial independence as well as to the state of mind or attitude of the tribunal in the actual exercise of its judicial function."

The test or criterion for assessing the independence of the judge or tribunal must, according to Le Dain J, be the one of reasonable apprehension of bias proposed by de Grandpré J in *Committee for Justice and Liberty v. National Energy Board* [1978] 1 SCR 369 (Can.):

> ... the apprehension of bias must be a reasonable one, held by reasonable and right-minded persons, applying themselves to the question and obtaining thereon the required informa-

tion. In the words of the Court of Appeal, that test is "what would an informed person, viewing the matter realistically and practically—and having thought the matter through—conclude."

Le Dain J added that this perception of a reasonable and informed person must be one "of whether the tribunal enjoys the essential objective conditions or guarantees of judicial independence, and not a perception of how it will in fact act, regardless of whether it enjoys such conditions or guarantees."

In order to decide whether the guarantee of judicial independence has been respected, three essential conditions must, according to Le Dain J, be analyzed. They are: (1) security of tenure, (2) financial security and (3) the institutional independence of the tribunal with respect to administrative decisions bearing directly on the exercise of its judicial functions.

These essential conditions for independence for the purposes of s. 11(d) must have a reasonable connection with the diversity of institutions to which s. 11(d) applies. The essence of the guarantee of independence was not expressed, however, by Le Dain J in the form of a principle giving rise to standards of varying content, but rather in the form of minimal conditions with respect to security of tenure, financial security and institutional independence: *cf.* Blache, "L'impartialité et l'indépendance selon les articles 7 et 11(d) de la *Charte canadienne*" in 2 *Développements recents en droit administratif* (1989) at 62. See also Pépin, "Indépendance judiciaire, L'article 11(d) de la *Charte canadienne*" (1986) 64 *Can. Bar Rev.* 550.

These minimal conditions which arise from the status or collective independence of the judge are in addition to the individual aspect of judicial independence which is reflected in the state of mind or attitude of the court in the exercise of its judicial functions in a particular case.

Judicial independence in its individual aspect is closely related to the guarantee of impartiality. Although it was not necessary to deal with the application of the guarantee of impartiality in *Valente*, Le Dain J distinguished the concept of independence from that of impartiality:

> Although there is obviously a close relationship between independence and impartiality, they are nevertheless separate and distinct values or requirements. Impartiality refers to a state of mind or attitude of the tribunal in relation to issues and the parties in a particular case. The word "impartial," as Howland CJO noted, connotes absence of bias, actual or perceived. The word "independent" in s. 11(d) reflects or embodies the traditional constitutional value of judicial independence. As such, it connotes not merely a state of mind or attitude in the actual exercise of judicial functions, but a status or relationship to others, particularly to the Executive Branch of government, that rest on objective conditions or guarantees.

For Le Dain J, the notion of attitude or state of mind which characterizes impartiality is not foreign to the notion of independence but it is the relationship which in his view is the primary meaning of independence. A tribunal which lacks the objective status or relationship of independence cannot be considered independent within the meaning of s. 11(d), regardless of how it may appear to have acted in the particular adjudication.

Le Dain J seems to have tried to situate impartiality within the concept of independence so that it would appear to be a dimension of independence in its broad sense (*cf.*

Blache, *id.* at 57) or as a minimal condition of the status of independence (Pépin, "L'indépendance des tribunaux administratifs et l'article 23 de *la Charte des droits et libertés de la personne*" (1990) 50 R du B 766 at 781).

In *R v. Lippé* [[1991] 2 SCR 114 (Que.)] Lamer CJC, writing for the court on this issue, noted that while the significance of the distinction between impartiality and independence is not always apparent, in a case involving allegations of partiality on an institutional level, it becomes particularly important. While reaffirming that judicial independence is a fundamental condition which contributes to the guarantee of a trial in which there is no partiality and which is critical to the public perception of impartiality, he held that judicial independence may not be sufficient. Notwithstanding judicial independence, there may also exist a reasonable apprehension of bias on an institutional or structural level.

Like the requirement of judicial independence, the requirement of institutional impartiality must, for the purposes of s. 11(d), form part of the constitutional guarantee because the constitutional guarantee of an independent and impartial tribunal has to be broad enough to encompass this.

As the respondents advance in the present case that the appointment of part-time lay members puts the impartiality of the Competition Tribunal in issue, it would be appropriate to examine, in addition to the three conditions of security of tenure, financial security and institutional independence, the condition of institutional impartiality.

2. *The Guarantees of Independence and Impartiality for the Purposes of s. 11(d)*

Security of Tenure

Security of tenure is the most important essential condition of judicial independence for the purposes of s. 11(d) of the Charter because of the importance which has traditionally been attached to it. In *Valente*, Le Dain J defined the essence of security of tenure as follows:

> The essence of security of tenure for purposes of s. 11(d) is a tenure, whether until an age of retirement, for a fixed term, or for a specific adjudicative task, that is secure against interference by the executive or other appointing authority in a discretionary or arbitrary manner.
>
> . . .

The Act establishing the Competition Tribunal [*Competition Tribunal Act*, RSC 1985, c. 19 (2nd Supp.)] provides, as we have seen, that each judicial member is appointed for a term not exceeding seven years and holds office so long as he remains a judge of the Federal Court (s. 5(1)). Pursuant to the statutes which govern them, Federal Court of Canada judges hold office during good behaviour until the age specified for retirement and may only be removed by the Governor-General on address of the Senate and House of Commons. They enjoy what is generally considered to be the highest degree of security of tenure.

Each lay member shall be appointed for a term not exceeding seven years and holds office during good behaviour, but may be removed by the Governor in Council for cause (s. 5(2)). Security of tenure is therefore expressly provided for the lay members and it is for a fixed period.

. . .

Since Mr. Roseman is at the present time a member of the tribunal during good behaviour for a term of seven years, it would not be appropriate to examine the effect of the very short previous appointments in relation to the requirements of independence and impartiality. It has not been proven that this practice of short appointments constituted an ongoing practice and that it had in fact been used in cases other than Mr. Roseman's at the time the tribunal was set up.

· · ·

The documentary evidence in the record shows that the lay members who sit on the tribunal were appointed for terms of five to seven years. However, it would be appropriate to examine whether the method and procedure for removing the lay members has the effect of destroying the security of tenure afforded by s. 5(2) of the Act.

The lay members may be removed before the end of their appointment by the Governor in Council. Such removal must be for cause (s. 5(2)). The Act does not specify the specific cause for removal but this is not required as an essential condition for judicial independence for the purposes of s. 11(d) of the Charter. As the lay members are appointed to hold office during good behaviour, the Governor in Council can only remove them for some cause related to the exercise of their function. In this regard, the method of removal would appear to be sufficient. As Le Dain J wrote in *Valente* at 179:

> It may be that the requirement of an address of the legislature makes removal of a judge more difficult in practice because of the solemn, cumbersome and publicly visible nature of the process, but the requirement of cause, as defined by statute, together with a provision for judicial inquiry at which the judge affected is given a full opportunity to be heard, is in my opinion a sufficient restraint upon the power of removal for purposes of s. 11(d).

The *Competition Tribunal Act* does not specifically provide for the holding of a prior hearing in a proceeding in which the person in question is given an opportunity to be heard. The rules of natural justice and s. 69 of the *Judges Act*, RSC 1985, c. J-1, supplement the absence of a specific legislative provision in a satisfactory fashion. Should the Governor in Council be called upon to exercise his power to remove a lay member, he would be obliged to adopt a fair process which would provide the opportunity for the person in question to be heard: *AG Can. v. Inuit Tapirisat of Canada* [1980] 2 SCR 735 (Can.). Moreover, s. 69 of the *Judges Act* provides that, at the request of the Minister of Justice for Canada, the Canadian Judicial Council shall hold an inquiry to establish whether a person appointed pursuant to an enactment of Parliament to hold office during good behaviour other than the holders of certain offices mentioned in paras. (a) and (b) of s. 69, should be removed from office for any of the reasons set out in s. 65(2) of the *Judges Act*. The causes are age or infirmity, misconduct, failure in the due execution of one's office, and having been placed, by his conduct or otherwise, in a position incompatible with the due execution of that office.

If it were called upon to hold such inquiry concerning a lay member of the Competition Tribunal, the council would be required, pursuant to s. 64 of the *Judges Act*, to afford the member an opportunity to be heard and to adduce evidence that he considers relevant. The report of the inquiry is submitted to the Minister of Justice who may remove the person in question on the basis of this report. The fact that the commencement of this inquiry process is left to the discretion of the Minister of Justice does not permit, in my view, the conclusion that the minimum standard required by *Valente* has not been met.

The whole of these provisions and the rules of natural justice concerning security of tenure sufficiently demonstrate, in my view, that the office of the lay members of the tribunal is secure against interference in a discretionary or arbitrary manner by the Governor in Council, who is responsible for appointments.

Financial Security

The second condition of judicial independence for the purposes of s. 11(d) of the Charter is financial security. The essence of this security, according to Le Dain J in *Valente*, "is that the right to salary and pension should be established by law and not be subject to arbitrary interference by the executive in a manner that could affect judicial independence."

Le Dain J added that although it may be theoretically preferable that judicial salaries should be fixed by the legislature rather than by the executive government and should be made a charge on the Consolidated Revenue Fund rather than requiring annual appropriation, he did not think that either of these features should be regarded as essential to the financial security that may be reasonably perceived as sufficient for independence under s. 11(d) of the Charter.

The *Competition Tribunal Act* provides that the lay members shall be paid such remuneration as may be fixed by the Governor in Council. They are entitled to be paid the travel allowances that a judge is entitled to be paid under the *Judges Act* and are deemed to be employed in the federal public service for the purposes of the *Government Employees Compensation Act* [RSC 1985, c. G-5] and regulations made under s. 9 of the *Aeronautics Act* [RSC 1985, c. 33 (1st Supp.)] (s. 6).

Under the public service system of remuneration, Mr. Roseman received in October, 1989, a salary of between $82,000 to $96,500. At the same date, Ms. Sarrazin received, when she sat on the tribunal, an allowance based on a *per diem* rate of between $355 and $415.

The respondents submit that the salary of the lay members remains subject to arbitrary interference by the executive, because there is no guarantee in the Act that the initial salary, once set, will not be decreased. The chairperson of the tribunal would be able to influence the members' salary through her appraisal of their performance. In addition, the present appraisal system described in the administrative documents concerning "Benefits and Employment Conditions, Governor in Council Appointees, Public Service of Canada" only constitutes a policy or a practice which may change over time in the discretion of the executive so that the financial security of a judge considered individually is not ensured in an objective manner.

The document, which relates the administrative policy with respect to benefits and employment conditions of the lay members, mentions at Title III, Compensation Policy:

> The Governor in Council establishes the salary rates for all Governor in Council appointees. The Treasury Board establishes salary ranges and other terms and conditions applicable to the GIC 1-11 and DM 1-3 groups.
>
> The policy currently applicable to senior executive compensation is based on the principle of aggregate compensation comparability with the average of other sectors of the economy up to the EX-1 level of the Public Service Management Category (GIC 4 equivalent). Beyond this level, appropriate salary differentials are set for the more senior executive and DM levels.

At Title IV: GIC and DM Levels and Salary Ranges:

> Salary ranges are set by the Treasury Board following submission of the Advisory Group's recommendations to the Prime Minister. The Advisory Group makes its recommendations by examining the relationship of the SM and EX-1 levels of compensation with their external counterparts, the appropriateness of the differentials for successively higher level positions and other factors which the Advisory Group believes warrant consideration.

At Title V: Performance Appraisal:

> The performance of individual members of boards, commission, *etc.*, is evaluated with respect to policy formulation and advice, management and administration, adjudication and regulation, interface and coordination, analysis and interpretation, and length of time in the position.
>
> The final decision on personal salary rates in all cases resides with the Governor in Council.
>
> Performance appraisals of members of *quasi*-judicial boards and agencies are completed by the head of the organization. Reports are submitted to the Privy Council Office for *human resource planning purposes only*. The personal salaries of the members of each of these boards and agencies are set at the same rate. (Emphasis added.)

This document only constitutes an administrative policy, but it none the less indicates the present government practice in setting salary ranges and remuneration rates for the lay members. In light of this policy, one cannot conclude that the determination of the lay members' salary is subject to arbitrary interference by the executive.

With respect to the effect of their appraisal on their salary, the document distinguishes between the appraisal of persons who hold an office reporting to a department or to the government and who are eligible for performance pay, and members of quasi-judicial agencies. In respect of the latter, their appraisals are completed by the head of the organization they report to and are submitted to the Privy Council Office for human resource planning purposes only.

Unlike the trial judge who found that the fact that the setting of the lay members' remuneration by the Governor in Council and the appraisal mechanism for the lay members constituted obstacles to the perception of independence and impartiality of the tribunal, it appears to me that a reasonably well-informed person could not seriously fear that the lay members of the tribunal did not enjoy, during their appointment, the guarantee of financial security required for the purposes of s. 11(d) of the Charter.

Institutional Independence

The third condition for judicial independence for the purposes of s. 11(d) of the Charter is the institutional independence of the tribunal with respect to matters of administration bearing directly on the exercise of its judicial functions. In *R v. Lippé, supra*, Lamer CJC for the majority, held that the content of the principle of judicial independence, analyzed in a context of the relationship existing between the judicial branch and the executive branch of government, must be limited to independence from the government. He added that the fact of giving judicial independence narrowed content does not result in a narrowed constitutional guarantee. Section 11(d) of the *Canadian Charter* and s. 23 of the *Quebec Charter* guarantee impartiality.

In the present case, the Superior Court judge held that the Competition Tribunal did not meet this condition of institutional independence because of the close connection existing between one lay member, Mr. Roseman, and the executive branch of the government.

It is admitted that Mr. Roseman in 1987 held, and continues to hold, the office of a member of the former Restrictive Trade Practices Commission in accordance with the transitory provisions of the *Competition Act* [RSC 1985, c. C-34].

[Rousseau-Houle JA, after a close examination of the transitory arrangements, came to the conclusion that the continuing exercise of both roles by Roseman, until such time as the outstanding work of the Restrictive Trade Practices Commission, an investigative arm of government, was concluded, did not jeopardize the institutional independence of the tribunal.]

With respect to the possibility that Mr. Roseman will hear, as a member of the tribunal, a matter with which he has already been seized as a member of the commission and in respect of which he had made an inquiry, this is a purely hypothetical situation. It would presuppose that Mr. Roseman would be called upon to form part of the panel designated by the chairperson of the tribunal to hear the case. Should that happen, the appropriate recourse could be an application for his disqualification (recusation) or an application for prohibition to prevent him from hearing the matter. As the facts at the origin of the present dispute all arose subsequent to the coming into force of the Act on June 19, 1986, the possibility of conflicts between his functions does not exist because no matter or inquiry could have been commenced under the transitory provisions of the Act.

The respondents argued before the Court of Appeal that institutional independence may still be jeopardized by the fact that no provision of the Act provides that the office of the chairperson of the tribunal is to be held during good behaviour and, as a result, the chairperson may be dismissed without cause. The institutional independence of the tribunal is, in my view, sufficiently safeguarded by the provisions of ss. 4 and 5(1) of the Act.

Given the legislation applicable to this tribunal, the situation which prevails in its relationship with the government, the individual independence which its members enjoy because of their personal objective status guaranteeing their security of tenure and their financial security, one can conclude that a realistic and well-informed person would be of the view that there is no reason to apprehend that the tribunal would not feel totally free to render its decisions and that it therefore has the guarantees of independence required for the purposes of s. 11(d) of the Charter.

The Guarantee of Impartiality

Individual partiality or bias on the part of one member of the tribunal is not alleged in the present case. The partiality or bias mentioned by the trial judge concerns the very institution of the tribunal. In my view, the possibility that lay members may hold double functions or offices as both members of the commission and of the tribunal, and the appointment of lay persons who sit part-time, may constitute an infringement of impartiality.

The question of double functions does not raise, as we have seen, serious fears with respect to judicial independence. However, the question of part-time judges merits examination. The Act does not provide that the lay members of the tribunal must have any particular qualifications in order to be appointed members of the tribunal. Section 3(3) only permits the Governor in Council to establish an advisory council to advise him with respect to appointments. Given the applications with which the tribunal is seized and its vocation, one can presume that the lay members will have an education and active professional experience in the fields of commerce, finance or economics. The lay member who at present sits part-time continues to have other functions in the area of economics and finance. A conflict of interests may therefore result which could give rise to doubts as to the impartiality of the tribunal.

Lamer CJC in *R v. Lippé* sketched out the contours of the concept of institutional impartiality found in the constitutional guarantee of an "independent and impartial tribunal." He recognized that:

> The objective status of the tribunal can be as relevant for the "impartiality" requirement as it is for "independence." Therefore, whether or not any particular judge harboured preconceived ideas or biases, if the system is structured in such a way as to create a reasonable apprehension of bias on an institutional level, the requirement of impartiality is not met.

The test for institutional impartiality is the same as the test adopted in the *Valente* case with respect to the issue of judicial independence, that is the apprehension of an informed person, viewing the matter realistically and practically, and having thought the matter through. According to Lamer CJC, for such person, the fact that a judge is part-time does not in or of itself raise a reasonable apprehension of bias. However, the activities in which a judge engages when he is not sitting may give rise to such an apprehension.

In order to determine which occupations will raise a reasonable apprehension of bias on an institutional level, Lamer CJC proposed a two-step test:

> Step One: Having regard for a number of factors including, but not limited to, the nature of the occupation and the parties who appear before this type of judge, will there be a reasonable apprehension of bias in the mind of a fully informed person in a substantial number of cases?

> Step Two: If the answer to that question is no, allegations of an apprehension of bias cannot be brought on an institutional level, but must be dealt with on a case-by-case basis.

> However, if the answer to that question is yes, this occupation is *per se* incompatible with the functions of a judge. At this point in the analysis, one must consider what safeguards are in place to minimize the prejudicial effects and whether they are sufficient to meet the guarantee of institutional impartiality under s. 11(d) of the *Canadian Charter*.

If we apply this test to the facts of the present case, it may happen, as the respondents submit, that a consultant in the area of business acquisitions, who works for a firm of accountants or business consultants and who, as such, dedicates his time to the pursuit of the interests of clients whose identity is not always known, may be appointed to the Competition Tribunal. This consultant, as a member of the tribunal, may be called upon to decide disputes which may involve persons whose interests are opposed to those of his clients.

The high degree of improbability of this example demonstrates quite clearly, in my view, that this situation is not likely to arise in a large number of cases. If one considers, in addition, the limited number of matters brought before the Competition Tribunal, one cannot reasonably think that in the matters in which he sits, numerous conflicts of interests would slip the mind of the part-time member, as well as the litigants.

The *Competition Tribunal Act* also contains sufficient safeguards to ensure, in principle, the impartiality of the tribunal. These are s. 7 concerning the oath of office which every member of the tribunal must take, s. 5(3) which limits the number of times a member can be reappointed and s. 10(3) which prohibits a member from sitting in a matter in which he has a direct or indirect financial interest. Protection against conflicts of interests is also ensured by the *Code of Conflict of Interests and Post Employment for Public Office Holders* to which the lay members are subject.

In these circumstances, one cannot successfully argue that there is an apprehension of bias on an institutional level.

The Competition Tribunal therefore meets all the requirements of the constitutional guarantee of an independent and impartial tribunal under s. 11(d). The mechanism adopted in the Act therefore ensures the right to a fair hearing in accordance with the principles of fundamental justice so that the tribunal definitely possesses all the essential attributes of an independent and impartial tribunal.

· · ·

Appeal allowed. Action dismissed.

NOTES

1. For another judicial elaboration of this issue, see *Mohammad v. Canada (Minister of Employment and Immigration)*, [1989] 2 FC 363 (CA), a case rejecting a challenge to the independence of adjudicators presiding at deportation hearings under the *Immigration Act*. Despite their status as civil servants, the Federal Court of Appeal found sufficient guarantees of independence in the terms and conditions under which they functioned to meet the requirements of s. 7 of the Charter. And, for discussion of the issue, see Evans, "The Principles of Fundamental Justice: The Constitution and the Common Law" (1991), 29 *Osgoode Hall LJ* 52, at 61-66.

2. There is a sense in which independence and impartiality can be a two-edged sword. This is exemplified by another episode in the saga involving former BC Premier Bennett, businessman Harb Doman, and the BC Securities Commission. One of Bennett's and Doman's many attacks on the processes of the commission was based on the fact that the BC Securities Commission is required by statute to be self-financing. To the extent that this empowers the commission to raise money to support its activities, such a requirement ensures a certain level of financial independence from government. On the other hand, to the extent that the commission obtains its funds from fines and awards of costs, there is at least an argument that it has a financial stake in the outcome of all of its proceedings. Consider the likelihood of a successful challenge based on this element of the regulatory scheme in the light of *Pearlman v. Manitoba Law Society Judicial Committee*, [1991] 2 SCR 869 (Man.), outlined above. In fact, the BC Court of Appeal rejected the argument on the basis that the

regime was statutorily authorized: *Doman v. British Columbia (Superintendent of Brokers)* (1996), 31 BCLR (3d) 357 (CA).

3. The case that follows provides another context in which to raise challenges based on a lack of structural independence—tribunals established by subordinate legislation. It also graphically makes the point that the principle of independence is a contingent one. What is demanded may vary considerably depending on the nature of the issues with which the tribunal deals. Finally, the case also bears on the question of the timing and context of the consideration of such challenges, a matter on which the Supreme Court was divided and that raises some concerns about the evidential base or record on which issues involving structural independence should be adjudicated.

<h3 style="text-align:center">Canadian Pacific Ltd. v. Matsqui Indian Band</h3>
[1995] 1 SCR 3 (Can.)

[Acting under authority conferred by the *Indian Act*, RSC 1985, c. I-5, Indian bands across Canada passed bylaws creating a tax regime for real property on reserve land. Each of the regimes also included a means of challenging an initial assessment. The Matsqui Band bylaw created a two tier internal appeal structure (a Court of Revision then an Assessment Review Committee) and then a further appeal on questions of law to the Federal Court of Canada. With the other bands involved in these proceedings, there was only one level of internal appeal before an appeal to the Federal Court. Members of the appeal tribunals could but need not be paid and they had no tenure of office. Band members were eligible appointees.

CP and Unitel were each assessed in respect of land they were using that ran through reserve lands and each applied to the Federal Court Trial Division for judicial review of the assessment. They claimed that the bands lacked jurisdiction to impose a tax since the land in question was not, in terms of the legislation, "in the reserve." The assessing bands then moved for an order striking out this application and Joyal J allowed the application on the basis that the companies had an adequate alternative remedy—the relevant appeal regime: [1993] 1 FC 74 (TD). The companies appealed and their appeal was allowed ([1993] 2 FC 641 (CA)). The Court of Appeal justified its interference with the motions judge's exercise of discretion on the basis, *inter alia*, that direct access to the Federal Court by way of judicial review was a more appropriate vehicle for contesting the validity of the assessment than by using the internal appeal routes. The bands obtained leave to appeal to the Supreme Court of Canada.

The appeal was dismissed by a nine-judge court (5:4). Two members of the majority held that the only reason for interference with the exercise of discretion by the trial judge was the lack of institutional independence enjoyed by the appeal tribunals. The other three members of the majority held that the companies should be allowed direct access to the Federal Court because they were raising a jurisdictional challenge to the imposition of the taxes (a ground rejected by the other two members of the majority) and expressly declined to rule on any other issue including that of institutional independence. The minority of four agreed with the first two members of the majority on every issue except that of institutional independence. As a consequence, the breakdown of the court on the institutional independence issue was four (no basis for challenge at this time), two (independence impaired), and three abstentions.]

LAMER CJC (Cory J concurring):

· · ·

[Lamer CJC rejected as too "speculative" the argument that there was a reasonable apprehension of bias in a structural sense because band members serving on the appeal tribunals would have a financial stake in the outcome of the proceedings. He then moved on to consider the argument of lack of structural independence.]

Thus, I am left with the allegation that a reasonable apprehension of bias exists because tribunal members may not be paid, lack security of tenure, and are appointed by the Band Chiefs and Councils. It is here that I part company with my colleague Sopinka J In my opinion, the respondents' submissions concerning institutional independence raise serious questions about the structure of the appeal tribunals established by the appellant bands. These questions cannot be avoided by simply deferring to Joyal J's exercise of discretion. The issue of bias was raised before Joyal J, and was argued before both the Federal Court of Appeal and this Court. If the bands' tribunals lack sufficient institutional independence, then this is a relevant factor which must be taken into account in determining whether the respondents should be required to pursue their jurisdictional challenge before those tribunals.

Moreover, while I agree that the larger context of Aboriginal self-government informs the determination of whether the statutory appeal procedures established by the appellants constitute an adequate alternative remedy for the respondents, I cannot agree with Sopinka J's conclusion that this context is relevant to the question of whether the bands' tribunals give rise to a reasonable apprehension of bias at an institutional level. In my view, principles of natural justice apply to the bands' tribunals as they would apply to any tribunal performing similar functions. The fact that the tribunals have been constituted within the context of a federal policy promoting Aboriginal self-government does not, in itself, dilute natural justice. The Indian Taxation Advisory Board, which intervened before this Court on behalf of the appellant bands, has itself determined that appeal tribunals constituted under s. 83(3) of the *Indian Act* must comply with the principles of natural justice. I would cite the following excerpt from the Board's *Introduction to Property Taxation on Reserves* (1990), a manual designed to assist Aboriginal Bands in establishing their taxation tribunals:

> Subsection 83(3) of the *Indian Act* requires taxation by-laws to provide "an appeal procedure in respect of assessments made for the purposes of taxation." A statutory right of appeal is fundamental to any tax assessment process for two reasons. First the nature of the assessment process is such that an assessment decision is made only on the strength of an assessor's judgment, without any prior hearing providing input from the party assessed. Second, a fundamental rule of the common law relating to administrative procedures, like assessments, is that everyone has a right to a hearing where matters are involved affecting that person's liberty or property rights. This rule is derived from the principles of administrative

law that basically ensure (i) a person's right to a hearing and (ii) that the person is heard by an impartial tribunal.

* * *

The *Indian Act* does not detail the types of appeal processes that councils should establish in their taxation by-laws. *However, whatever appeal mechanisms are put in place, they will have to adhere to the principles of natural justice, since, as mentioned above, the appeal is in effect a subsequent hearing* (emphasis added, p. 23).

With respect, I do not believe that either *Nowegijick v. The Queen* [1983] 1 SCR 29 (Can.), or *Mitchell v. Peguis Indian Band* [1990] 2 SCR 85 (Man.), the cases cited by Sopinka J, support the view that the policy of Aboriginal self-government is relevant to a determination of whether the appellant Band's taxation tribunals comply with the principles of natural justice.

[After setting out relevant extracts from *Valente v. The Queen*, [1985] 2 SCR 673 (Ont.) and citing cases that accepted the relevance of the *Valente* principles to administrative tribunals, Lamer CJC continued:]

I agree and conclude that it is a principle of natural justice that a party should receive a hearing before a tribunal which is not only independent, but also appears independent. Where a party has a reasonable apprehension of bias, it should not be required to submit to the tribunal giving rise to this apprehension. Moreover, the principles for judicial independence outlined in *Valente* are applicable in the case of an administrative tribunal, where the tribunal is functioning as an adjudicative body settling disputes and determining the rights of parties. However, I recognize that a strict application of these principles is not always warranted. In *Valente*, supra, Le Dain J wrote at 692-93,

It would not be feasible, however, to apply the most rigorous and elaborate conditions of judicial independence to the constitutional requirement of independence in s. 11(d) of the Charter, which may have to be applied to a variety of tribunals ... The essential conditions of judicial independence for purposes of s. 11(d) must bear some relationship to that variety.

* * *

Therefore, while administrative tribunals are subject to the *Valente* principles, the test for institutional independence must be applied in light of the functions being performed by the particular tribunal at issue. The requisite level of institutional independence (*i.e.*, security of tenure, financial security and administrative control) will depend on the nature of the tribunal, the interests at stake, and other indices of independence such as oaths of office.

In some cases, a high level of independence will be required. For example, where the decisions of a tribunal affect the security of the person of a party (such as the Immigration Adjudicators in *Mohammad* [*v. Canada (Minister of Employment and Immigration)*, [1989] 2 FC 363 (CA)], a more strict application of the *Valente* principles may be warranted. In this case, we are dealing with an administrative tribunal adjudicating disputes relating to the assessment of property taxes. In my view, this is a case where a more flexible approach is clearly warranted.

I would therefore apply this approach to the question of whether the members of the appellants' appeal tribunals are sufficiently independent. The *Valente* principles must be considered in light of the nature of the appeal tribunals themselves, the interests at stake, and other indices of independence, in order to determine whether a reasonable and right-minded person, viewing the whole procedure as set out in the assessment by-laws, would have a reasonable apprehension of bias on the basis that the members of the appeal tribunals are not independent.

It is first necessary to examine the provisions of the assessment by-laws dealing with the powers of appeal tribunals and the appointment and remuneration of their members. For this purpose, the by-laws of the Matsqui and Siska bands will be considered. It should be noted that the Siska By-law is identical to those of the other five appellant bands.

[Lamer CJC here set out the details of the two appeal regimes.]

I have quoted these excerpts from the bands' by-laws to demonstrate that members of the appeal tribunals perform adjudicative functions not unlike those of courts. However, members of the Siska Board of Review and the Matsqui Court of Revision have no guarantee of salary. Under the Matsqui By-law, members of the Court of Revision "may" receive remuneration, while the Siska By-law also uses permissive language.

On the subject of security of tenure, the Matsqui tribunals are to be appointed each year, although the terms of appointment are to be left to the Chief and Band Council. One might presume that the members of the tribunals are appointed for one-year terms; however, there is nothing in the Matsqui By-law protecting members from arbitrary dismissal mid-term. The Siska By-law is silent on all aspects of the appointment of tribunal members.

This raises some serious concerns. For example, under the By-laws, there is nothing to prevent the Band Chiefs and Councils from paying tribunal members only after they have reached a decision in a particular case, or not paying the members at all. The Siska Band could, if it wished, appoint tribunals members on an *ad hoc* basis, since there is no requirement that members be appointed for a specific term. Siska could then refuse to re-appoint members who reached decisions contrary to the interests of the band. In all cases, it would appear that tribunal members may be removed from their positions at any time by the bands, which leaves open the possibility of considerable abuse.

A further factor contributing to an apprehension of insufficient institutional independence arises when one considers that the Chiefs and Band Councils select the members of their tribunals, in addition to controlling their remuneration and tenure. This fact contributes to the appearance of a dependency relationship between the tribunal and the band, particularly in the case at bar where the interests of the band are clearly at odds with the interests of the respondents. In fact, both the Matsqui and Siska by-laws allow the bands themselves to be parties before their respective tribunals (s. 49(A) of the Matsqui By-law and s. 41(4) of the Siska By-law). The respondents are thus faced with presenting their case before a tribunal whose members were appointed by the very Band Chiefs and Councils who oppose their claim. This raises a problem similar to that addressed in *MacBain* [*v. Lederman*, [1985] 1 FC 856 (CA)]. In that case, the Federal Court of Appeal found a reasonable apprehension of bias where the prosecutor of the human rights infringement (*i.e.*, the Human Rights Commission) also selected the members of the panel which would adjudicate the matter. This case, though not identical, raises the similar concern that a party should not be required to present its case before a tribunal whose members have been appointed by an opposing party.

The appellants rely heavily on the fact that members of the appeal tribunals are required to take an oath of office that they will be impartial. This is one factor to take into account in assessing the independence of an administrative tribunal. However, the fact that an oath is taken cannot act as a substitute for financial security or security of tenure. The *Valente* principles are flexible in their application to administrative tribunals, but they cannot be ignored.

Similarly, the fact that the interest at stake in the case, tax assessment, is of a lesser form than interests like the one identified in *Sethi* [*v. Canada (Minister of Employment and Immigration)*, [1988] 2 FC 552 (CA)] (*i.e.*, security of the person) is a consideration in applying the *Valente* principles. Again, however, I am not prepared to discard the *Valente* principles on the basis that the property interests implicated in this case are not as important as other interests.

In my view, even a flexible application of the *Valente* principles leads to the inevitable conclusion that a reasonable and right-minded person, viewing the whole procedure in the assessment by-laws, would have a reasonable apprehension that members of the appeal tribunals are not sufficiently independent. Three factors lead me to this conclusion:

(1) There is a complete absence of financial security for members of the tribunals;

(2) Security of tenure is either completely absent (in the case of Siska), or ambiguous and therefore inadequate (in the case of Matsqui);

(3) The tribunals, whose members are appointed by the Band Chiefs and Councils, are being asked to adjudicate a dispute pitting the interests of the bands against outside interests (*i.e.*, those of the respondents). Effectively, the tribunal members must determine the interests of the very people, the bands, to whom they owe their appointments.

In reaching this conclusion, I wish to emphasize that it is these three factors in combination which lead me to the conclusion that the appeal tribunals lack sufficient independence in this case. I am not saying that any one of these factors, considered in isolation, would have led me to the same conclusion. For example, most of the provincial tax assessment appeal tribunals are appointed by the provincial government, rather than by the municipalities. ...

These provincial regimes effectively address the third problem with the band tribunals noted above, since a different level of government is making the tribunal appointments than the level whose interests are directly at stake in proceedings before that tribunal. I am satisfied that such tribunals have sufficient independence, even where other indices of independence such as security of tenure or security of remuneration are not guaranteed in the statute authorizing the creation of the tribunal.

Of course, Indian bands may be reluctant to cede the power to appoint tribunal members to the federal government, given that one of the purposes of the new tax assessment regime is to facilitate the development of Aboriginal self-government. Thus, to conform to the requirements of institutional independence, the appellant bands' by-laws will have to guarantee remuneration and stipulate periods of tenure for tribunal members. The by-laws will also have to ensure that members may only be dismissed during their tenure "with cause."

One final matter concerning the bias issue should be addressed. The appellants argued before this Court that all the allegations of bias raised here were speculative. Sopinka J adopts this position. While I agree that the allegations concerning an absence of institutional impartiality are premature, I disagree that this necessarily results in the allegations surrounding institutional independence being premature as well. The two concepts are quite distinct. It is mere speculation to suggest that members of the tribunals will lack impartiality, since we cannot possibly know in advance of an actual hearing what these members think. The mere fact that the structure of the tribunals allows band members to sit on appeals tells us nothing (unless we assume that all band members are biased, which is clearly not correct). However, in assessing the institutional independence of the appeal tribunals, the inquiry focuses on an objective assessment of the actual structure of the tribunals. We can examine the by-laws, apply the *Valente* principles, and reach a conclusion. This kind of analysis is hardly speculative, since the by-laws are conclusive evidence that the tribunals are not sufficiently independent from the Band Chiefs and Councils.

My colleague Sopinka J does not dispute that institutional independence is a principle of natural justice which applies to the band tribunals. He argues, however, that institutional independence should be assessed in the context of an actual tribunal hearing, thereby taking the position that institutional independence could arise in the circumstances of the appointment of the tribunal members, or in the manner in which the tribunals conduct their hearings.

With respect, I cannot agree. The function of institutional independence is to ensure that a tribunal is legally structured such that its members are reasonably independent of those who appoint them. My colleague Sopinka J appears to be of the view that it is possible for the appellant bands to exercise their discretion under the by-laws with respect to financial and tenure matters in such a way that the fundamental inadequacies of the by-laws will be cured. With respect, it is always possible for discretion to be exercised consistent with natural justice. The problem is the discretion itself, since the point of the institutional independence doctrine is to ensure that tribunal independence is not left to the discretion of those who appoint the tribunals. It is, in my opinion, inconsistent to concede that institutional independence applies in this case, yet go on to conclude that the lack of institutional independence in the by-laws may be addressed through the exercise of the discretionary powers granted to the Band Chiefs and Councils under the by-laws. Institutional independence and the discretion to provide for institutional independence (or not to so provide) are very different things. Independence premised on discretion is illusory.

V. Conclusion

Joyal J, in the Federal Court, Trial Division, did not consider irrelevant factors, nor did he reach an unreasonable conclusion on the basis of the factors which he did consider. However, he erred in exercising his discretion by failing to take into account the fact that the appeal tribunals established under s. 83(3) of the Indian Act lack sufficient independence from the Band Chiefs and Councils. Had Joyal J considered this factor, he would have concluded that the appeal tribunals are not an adequate alternative remedy, and would therefore have exercised his discretion in favour of undertaking judicial review as sought by the respondents. ...

SOPINKA J (L'Heureux-Dubé, Gonthier and Iacobucci JJ concurring):

· · ·

[Sopinka J first expressed agreement with Joyal J's treatment of the lack of institutional independence argument as premature because it was raised only in oral argument and lacked a sufficient factual basis for determination. He then went on to say that the standards for appellate intervention in the exercise of discretion by a first instance judge (as articulated by La Forest J in *Friends of the Oldman River Society v. Canada (Minister of Transport)*, [1992] 1 SCR 3, at 76 (Can.)) had not been met in terms of a justification for interfering with Joyal J's discretionary determination that the matter of structural independence was premature.]

In this appeal, a very significant contextual factor is that the band taxation scheme, under the *Indian Act*, RSC 1985, c. I-5, as amended, is part of a nascent attempt to foster Aboriginal self-government. This was considered by Joyal J, at first instance, as follows:

> Although there is no direct evidence on the point, there is another aspect to this case which deserves mention. It is obvious, from an examination of all the material before me, that the whole legislative scheme found in the Indian band by-laws reflects extremely important policy issues. One need not be a participant in the scheme to observe the departure from long-established norms respecting the taxing of lands and improvements on Indian reserves. One can also presume that intensive discussions took place between public authorities in British Columbia, the federal authorities at Ottawa and, for that matter, the Indian bands concerned, in setting up an elaborate system of assessment and taxation. I conclude that effectively, the provincial authorities, as a policy matter, have relinquished their historical field of taxation over reserve lands, with the collaboration of the federal authorities in giving the force of law to the by-laws pursuant to section 83 of the *Indian Act*, have clothed the respective Indian band councils with the mantle of legitimacy in running their own system of taxation. It leads me to conclude that for purposes of settling the issue before me, it would not be in the public interest and it would not favour public policy at this time to bypass the appeal provisions in the by-laws.

The Chief Justice has stated that this context was reasonably taken into account by Joyal J respecting the band taxation appeal procedures. In my view, this same contextual consideration also applies to assessing Joyal J's conclusion that the bias issue was premature. The self-government policy context is relevant to the entire exercise of judicial discretion. In this regard, it is pertinent to refer to the principle of statutory interpretation set forth by Dickson CJ in *Nowegijick v. The Queen*, [1983] 1 SCR 29 (Can.) at 36, a case involving interpretation of the *Indian Act* tax exemption rights:

It is legal lore that, to be valid, exemptions to tax laws should be clearly expressed. It seems to me, however, that treaties and statutes relating to Indians should be liberally construed and doubtful expressions resolved in favour of Indians.

This principle was affirmed by La Forest J in *Mitchell v. Peguis Indian Band*, [1990] 2 SCR 85 (Man.) at 143, also in the tax exemption rights context:

> ... it is clear that in the interpretation of any statutory enactment dealing with Indians, and particularly the *Indian Act*, it is appropriate to interpret in a broad manner provisions that are aimed at maintaining Indian rights, and to interpret narrowly provisions aimed at limiting or abrogating them.

These are broad, general interpretive principles and they apply equally to assessing institutional bias on the face of band taxation tribunal by-laws established under s. 83 of the *Indian Act* as they do to directly interpreting the *Indian Act*. Accordingly, before concluding that the by-laws in question do not establish band taxation tribunals with sufficient institutional independence, they should be interpreted in the context of the fullest knowledge of how they are applied in practice.

4. Relevance of the Practice of a Tribunal as Depicted in the Context of an Actual Hearing in Order to Assess Institutional Independence

I agree with the Chief Justice that the *Valente, supra*, principles are to be applied in the context of the test that applies in determining impartiality, that is, whether a reasonable and right-minded person would have a reasonable apprehension of bias. I also agree that the hypothetical reasonable, right-minded person must view the matter on the basis of being provided with the relevant information. In this regard, the judgment of de Grandpré J in *Committee for Justice and Liberty v. National Energy Board* [1978] 1 SCR 369 (Can.) at 394-5, which was approved in *Valente, supra*, referred to "reasonable and right-minded persons, applying themselves to the question and obtaining thereon the required information."

The difference between us in this regard is that, while the Chief Justice would limit the information to the procedure set out in the by-laws, I would defer application of the test so that the reasonable person will have the benefit of knowing how the tribunal operates in actual practice. That the principles of natural justice are flexible and must be viewed in their contextual setting has become almost a trite observation. As de Grandpré J stated in *Committee for Justice and Liberty, supra*, at 395:

> The basic principle is of course the same, namely that natural justice be rendered. But its application must take into consideration the special circumstances of the tribunal. As stated by Reid, *Administrative Law and Practice* (1971) at 220:
>
> > ... "tribunals" is a basket word embracing many kinds and sorts. It is quickly obvious that a standard appropriate to one may be inappropriate to another. Hence, facts which may constitute bias in one, may not amount to bias in another.

. . .

I do not disagree with the Chief Justice that the band taxation tribunals must comply with the principles of natural justice, but without a clear understanding of the relevant, operational context, these principles cannot be applied.

[Sopinka J here referred to a range of institutional independence cases (*Lippé*, *Alex Couture*, *MacBain*, and *Mohammad*) as examples of the court making an assessment of that issue in the context of the actual operations of the relevant tribunal.]

Case law has thus tended to consider the institutional bias question after the tribunal has been appointed and/or actually rendered judgment. That institutional independence must be considered "objectively" does not preclude considering the operation of a legislative scheme which creates an administrative tribunal, but only vaguely or partly sets out the three *Valente* elements, as in this appeal, where the taxation by-laws in issue are silent with regard to details relating to tenure and remuneration. It is not safe to form final conclusions as to the workings of this institution on the wording of the by-laws alone. Knowledge of the operational reality of these missing elements may very well provide a significantly richer context for objective consideration of the institution and its relationships. Otherwise, the administrative law hypothetical "right minded person" is right-minded, but uninformed. Although in this appeal, information regarding the appointment of a tribunal was not provided and it is unclear whether the tribunal members who are to hear the taxation assessment appeal have even been designated, tenure and remuneration may be established by the bands on appointment of the taxation tribunals.

Appeal dismissed.

NOTES

1. We return to this judgment and the whole question of the timeliness (or prematurity) of seeking judicial review in chapter 18, The Discretion of the Court, where we also consider the standard to be applied in appellate review of first instance judges' exercise of remedial discretions in judicial review cases.

2. In terms of the split between Lamer CJ and Sopinka J on the timeliness of the challenge in this case, Lamer CJ seems to accept that the structures created by the regulations simply cannot operate without compromising the independence of the appeal structures. Sopinka J is of the opinion that these concerns might be laid to rest by the way in which the tribunals operate in practice. Given that the tribunals are new institutions, they should be given a chance to prove themselves. How might they do that in an operational sense?

3. More generally, the court has accepted that if the possibility exists under the relevant legislation that the challenged tribunal could act in an institutionally independent manner, it is appropriate to consider the way the tribunal in fact operates in practice. See *2747-3174 Québec Inc. v. Quebec (Régie des permis d'alcool)*, [1996] 3 SCR 919 (Que.) and *Katz v. Vancouver Stock Exchange*, [1996] 3 SCR 405 (BC); aff'g. (1995), 128 DLR (4th) 424 (BC CA).

4. As is the case with bias or impartiality, if the relevant statute clearly authorizes the existence of a statutory scheme that does not meet appropriate standards of independence for the tribunal in question, there will be no remedy available unless those affected can rely

on a constitutional or *quasi*-constitutional argument: *Ocean Port Hotel Ltd. v. British Columbia (Liquor Control and Licensing Branch, General Manager)*, [2001] 2 SCR 781 (BC). There, the court rejected an argument to the effect that the province's liquor licensing regime, which provided for the at-pleasure appointment of decision-makers, was required to be independent by reference to the Preamble to the *Constitution Act, 1867*. While this might require that provincial court judges be independent (*Reference re Remuneration of Provincial Court Judges of Prince Edward Island*, [1997] 3 SCR 3), it did not provide a basis for independence for administrative tribunals (or at least for those which performed an executive licensing function).

5. In *Bell Canada v. Canadian Telephone Employees Assn.*, [2003] 1 SCR 884, a quasi-constitutional guarantee of independence—s. 2(e) of the *Canadian Bill of Rights*—was invoked to challenge several aspects of the *Canadian Human Rights Act*. Notably, the Act empowered the Canadian Human Rights Commission to issue guidelines that were binding on the Canadian Human Rights Tribunal regarding interpretations of the Act in "a class of cases." Also, the Act authorized the tribunal's chair to extend the terms of tribunal members in ongoing inquiries. The Supreme Court observed that, while a high degree of independence was required by the Bill and the common law due to the tribunal's adjudicative functions, the tribunal's role in implementing government policy as part of a legislative scheme for rectifying discrimination meant that the applicable standard of independence was lower than that of a court. The Supreme Court determined that neither the guideline power nor the power to extend appointments undermined the independence of the tribunal or its members.

6. McEwan J of the BC Supreme Court distinguished *Ocean Port* in *McKenzie v. Minister of Public Safety and Solicitor General et al.* (2006), 61 BCLR (4th) 57, a case involving a residential tendency adjudicator whose appointment was rescinded mid-term. The court decided that the unwritten constitutional guarantees of judicial independence, as a reflection of the rule of law, extended to residential tendency adjudicators. It noted that the Supreme Court of Canada, in *Ell v. Alberta*, [2003] 1 SCR 857, extended the constitutional principle of judicial independence to justices of the peace on the basis that they exercised judicial functions directly related to the enforcement of law and the court system. By analogy, the court held that residential tenancy adjudicators, whose functions were highly adjudicative and whose jurisdiction had been taken directly from courts of civil jurisdiction, should also enjoy unwritten guarantees of independence. The BC Court of Appeal dismissed an appeal from the trial judgment as moot because the provincial legislature had since amended the statute on which the government relied to rescind McKenzie's appointment: (2007), 71 BCLR (4th) 1, 287 DLR (4th) 313 (CA). In doing so, the Court of Appeal did not rule on the constitutional issues arising from the decision of the BC Supreme Court. The Supreme Court of Canada denied leave to appeal: [2007] SCCA No. 601 (QL), 2008 CanLII 18936. See Bryden, "*McKenzie v. British Columbia (Minister of Public Safety and Solicitor General)*: A Constitutional Guarantee of Tribunal Independence?" (2007), 40 *UBC LR* 679. See also Jacobs, "Independence, Impartiality, and Bias" in Flood and Sossin, eds., *Administrative Law in Context* (2008).

See also *Saskatchewan Federation of Labour v. Saskatchewan (Attorney General, Department of Advanced Education, Employment and Labour)*, 2010 SKCA 27 for an extraordinary example of statutorily authorized interference with the tenure of tribunal members. Following the 2007 defeat of Saskatchewan's NDP government and the election of a new govern-

ment led by the Saskatchewan Party, the new government issued an order-in-council terminating the terms of office of the chair and two vice-chairs of the Labour Relations Board.
According to the new premier of Saskatchewan, this decision was necessary because his
government lacked confidence in the willingness or ability of the current chair and vice-
chairs to give effect to the policy choices embodied in proposed amendments to Saskatchewan's labour legislation. Several unions sought an order quashing the order-in-council. The
Saskatchewan Court of Appeal decided that it was clearly authorized by s. 20 of Saskatchewan's *Interpretation Act, 1995*, SS 1995, c. I-11.2, which provides that:

> 20(1) Subject to subsection (2), notwithstanding any other enactment or any agreement, if
> a person is a member of a board, commission or other appointed body of the Government of
> Saskatchewan or any of its agencies or Crown Corporations on the day on which the Executive
> Council is first installed following a general election as defined in The Election Act, the term of
> office for which that person was appointed is deemed to end on the earlier of:
>
>> (a) the last day of the term for which that person was appointed; or
>>
>> (b) a day designated by the Lieutenant Governor in Council or the person who made
>> the appointment.
>
> (2) Subsection (1) does not apply to a person whose appointment is expressly stated in an
> Act to be subject to termination by the Legislative Assembly.

The purpose of the provision was explained by the attorney general responsible for passage of the bill on its second reading in a statement quoted by the court, at para. 55:

> Mr. Speaker, the purpose of the amendment is quite clear. When any new government is
> elected, it cannot have its hands tied by the previous government's actions. This amendment
> will assist any new government … to move to implement its policies through its various boards,
> commissions, and agencies, by changing memberships on those bodies as is necessary.

The court dismissed the possibility that the legislature had intended to exclude quasi-
judicial tribunals, like the Labour Relations Board, from the application of s. 20, since an
amendment to that effect had been proposed and overwhelmingly defeated. Significantly,
the court noted that the unions had not challenged the order-in-council's validity or the
validity of s. 20 on the basis that they violated the unwritten constitutional principle of
independence.

7. At a policy level, there have been a number of studies and papers on the question of
independence (including, for example, the appointments process, the issue of security of
tenure, and the role of chairs). For a discussion of the various suggestions and initiatives, see
Priest, "Structure and Accountability of Administrative Agencies," in Law Society of Upper
Canada Special Lectures, *Administrative Law—Principles, Practice and Pluralism* (1992), at
11. See also Bryden and Hatch, "British Columbia Council of Administrative Tribunals
Research and Policy Committee: Report on Independence, Accountability and Appointment Processes in British Columbia Tribunals" (1999), 12 *CJALP* 235; Bryden, "Structural
Independence in the Wake of *Ocean Port*" (2003), 16 *CJALP* 125; Wyman, "The Independence of Administrative Tribunals in an Era of Ever Expansive Judicialization" (2001), 14
CJALP 61; and Des Rosiers, "Toward an Administrative Model of Independence and Accountability for Administrative Tribunals," in *Justice to Order—Adjustment to Changing*

Demands and Coordination Issues in the Justice System in Canada (Montréal: Éditions Thémis, 1999), at 53.

8. We now return to a case in which the issues of security of tenure and institutional independence from government were considered.

2747-3174 Québec Inc. v. Quebec (Régie des permis d'alcool)
[1996] 3 SCR 919

[After finding that the way the régie operated in practice led to a reasonable apprehension of bias in an institutional sense, the court went on to deal with the further argument of lack of independence.]

GONTHIER J: ...

(i) Security of Tenure

The respondent relied primarily on the term of office of the directors and the method of dismissal. They are appointed by the government for a term of not more than five years (s. 4). Supplementary directors may also be appointed for as long as the government determines. The orders of appointment adduced in evidence refer to terms of two, three and five years. Once appointed, at least judging by the orders of appointment adduced in evidence, the directors can be dismissed only for specific reasons. All the contracts contain the following clause, which is taken from the agreement between the government and the chairman of the Régie:

[TRANSLATION]

5.2 Dismissal

Mr. Laflamme also agrees that the government may revoke this appointment at any time, without notice or compensation, on grounds of defalcation, mismanagement, gross fault or any ground of equal seriousness, proof of which lies upon the government.

Some of the employment contracts also contain the following clause:

[TRANSLATION]

7. Renewal

As provided for in article 2, Mr. Laflamme's term shall end on May 31, 1995. If the minister responsible intends to recommend to the government that his term as director and chairman of the Régie be renewed, the said minister shall notify him at least six months prior to the expiry of the present term.

If this appointment is not renewed or if the government does not appoint Mr. Laflamme to another position, Mr. Laflamme shall rejoin the staff of the Ministère de la Sécurité publique on the terms and conditions set out in article 6.

In my view, the directors' conditions of employment meet the minimum requirements of independence. These do not require that all administrative adjudicators, like judges of courts of law, hold office for life. Fixed-term appointments, which are common, are acceptable. However, the removal of adjudicators must not simply be at the pleasure of the executive. Le Dain J summarized the requirements of security of tenure as follows in *Valente*, at 698:

> ... that the judge be removable only for cause, and that cause be subject to independent review and determination by a process at which the judge affected is afforded a full opportunity to be heard. The essence of security of tenure for purposes of s. 11(d) is a tenure, whether until an age of retirement, for a fixed term, or for a specific adjudicative task, that is secure against interference by the Executive or other appointing authority in a discretionary or arbitrary manner.

In the case at bar, the orders of appointment provide expressly that the directors can be dismissed only for certain specific reasons. In addition, it is possible for the directors to apply to the ordinary courts to contest an unlawful dismissal. In these circumstances, I am of the view that the directors have sufficient security of tenure within the meaning of *Valente*, since sanctions are available for any arbitrary interference by the executive during a director's term of office.

(ii) Institutional Independence

It was suggested that the large number of points of contact between the Régie and the Minister of Public Security was problematic. The Minister is responsible for the application of the Act (s. 175). The Régie is required to submit a report to the Minister each year (s. 21) and the Minister may require information from the chairman on the agency's activities (s. 22). In addition, the Minister of Public Security must approve any rules the Régie might adopt in plenary session for its internal management (s. 4), and the Government must approve the various regulations made by the Régie (s. 16). Each year, the Minister also conducts the evaluation of the chairman of the Régie. Furthermore, the Minister is responsible for the various police forces that may, at the Régie's request, conduct investigations. Finally, the Minister may initiate the permit cancellation process by submitting an application to the Régie under s. 85.

In light of the evidence as a whole, I do not consider these various factors sufficient to raise a reasonable apprehension with respect to the institutional independence of the Régie. It is not unusual for an administrative agency to be subject to the general supervision of a member of the executive with respect to its management. As Le Dain J stated in *Valente*, at 712, the essential elements of institutional independence may be summed up as judicial control over the administrative decisions that bear directly and immediately on the exercise of the judicial function. It has not been shown how the Minister might influence the decision-making process. The chairman is responsible for monitoring the Régie's day-to-day activities and its various employees, and for preparing the rolls. The fact that the Minister of Public Security is ultimately responsible for both the Régie and the various police forces conducting investigations would not in my view cause an informed person to have a reasonable apprehension with respect to the independence of the directors. The directors swear an oath requiring them to perform the duties of their office honestly and fairly. The Minister's links with the various parties involved are accordingly not sufficient to raise concerns.

Appeal allowed.

NOTES

1. The court seems to accept that, in the case of administrative tribunals, as long as the members do not serve purely at pleasure, there will be sufficient security of tenure. In other words, terms of office as short as two years will do. What about the situation in *Ocean Port*, above, where the members of the liquor licensing appeal authority were part-time, held their offices at pleasure, and were on year-to-year appointments? If this scheme had not been set up legislatively, would it have passed muster?

2. One of the best illustrations of the extent to which the issue of lack of independence is context-sensitive is provided by *Katz*, above. There, the members of the Disciplinary Committee of the Vancouver Stock Exchange were not appointed for any particular term of office and, aside from the external legal member, were not paid for their work. Indeed, there were no set rules governing the emoluments for the legal member. Nonetheless, the Supreme Court, sustaining the BC Court of Appeal, held that these institutional aspects did not pose a problem. In the circumstances, the fact that the members did not depend financially on their work at the disciplinary committee for their livelihood contributed to, rather than detracted from, their independence. Also, in the practice of the tribunal, members seemed to continue to serve until voluntary resignation or death. More generally, the Exchange was a self-governing body, which called for different standards from those applying to such tribunals as the taxation appeal tribunals in *Matsqui Indian Band*, above.

3. The degree of independence required of a tribunal under s. 23 of the Québec *Charter of Human Rights and Freedoms* depends on where the tribunal falls on a spectrum ranging from regulatory to purely adjudicative tribunals. A tribunal's place on that spectrum is determined by reference to several factors, including the tribunal's function, its attributes and procedures, its powers, the parties to its proceedings and their interests, and the attributes of its members. In *Barreau de Montréal v. Québec (Procureure générale)*, [2001] JQ No. 3882 (CA), the Québec Court of Appeal concluded that members of the Tribunal administratif du Québec, a super-tribunal with appellate jurisdiction in various decision-making contexts including social assistance, municipal property assessments, and economic regulation, required a high level of independence. The court scrutinized regulations governing the reappointment of tribunal members and found that an informed observer would have a reasonable apprehension that tribunal members may not be sufficiently independent to adjudicate cases objectively, because the committee struck to decide their reappointment included a Justice Ministry official and the tribunal chair. It ruled that an independent committee be struck to make reappointment recommendations and that tribunal members be afforded an opportunity to be heard by the committee. The court was equally concerned with provisions linking members' salary increases with the outcome of periodic performance evaluations conducted by the tribunal chair. It found that such a regime imperiled the tribunal members' independence and recommended that the members' salaries be automatically stepped up throughout their tenure. Québec's National Assembly ultimately re-

sponded to the judgment by amending the tribunal's enabling statute to provide for the appointment of tribunal members during good behaviour: *An Act to amend the Act respecting administrative justice and other legislative provisions*, SQ 2005, c. 17, s. 2. For a critical perspective on this change, see Ellis, "Misconceiving Tribunal Members: Memorandum to Québec" (2005), 18 *CJALP* 189. Ellis observes, at 206:

> A life-time appointments regime is not consistent with a tribunal's legitimate need to insist that its members co-operate fully in its institutional strategies and accept and meet its institutional standards. In a term appointment regime, provided the re-appointments process is objective and independent, one can make co-operation with a tribunal's corporate strategies and compliance with its performance standards a principled condition of re-appointment. Moreover, the mere existence of such conditions for re-appointment will promote an institutional culture of collegiality in which such co-operation and performance becomes an integral and natural feature of the tribunal's environment.
>
> However, if tribunal members are protected by tenured appointments, the tribunal culture will be dramatically different. The autonomy of individual members will become the dominant theme, and the tribunals' corporate role will be correspondingly diminished, if not emasculated.

Do you agree?

A Summary of Linda Keen's Dismissal

What kinds of relationships between a tribunal and the minister to which it reports would or should give rise to lack of independence problems? Consider the following case, which offers an illuminating case study of both agency independence and the role of judicial review.

Linda Keen was appointed president of the Canadian Nuclear Safety Commission—Canada's nuclear safety watchdog—in 2001 and reappointed as president in 2006 after the conclusion of her first five-year term. In January 2008, she was removed as president of the commission by federal Natural Resources Minister Gary Lunn. In November 2007, during a planned shutdown of the Chalk River nuclear facility owned by Atomic Energy Canada Ltd. (AECL), a Crown corporation, commission inspectors discovered that the facility was in breach of the conditions of its operating licence. In particular, two reactor coolant pumps, which were required for the reactor's safe operation, were not connected to an emergency power supply. AECL decided to extend the shutdown of the reactor to allow time for AECL to complete mandatory safety upgrades. However, the prolonged closure of the facility, which normally produced a substantial proportion of the world's radio-isotopes used in medical procedures and tests, was contributing to a shortage in the world supply of this essential material.

In a December 5 teleconference call with AECL and the commission, Minister Lunn requested the parties to work together to resolve the matter. The commission advised AECL that it was willing to hold an expedited hearing into amending the terms of AECL's licence if this was needed to restart the reactor. Shortly after, in another teleconference call, Minister Lunn requested that a hearing be convened immediately to approve a restart of the reactor. Ms. Keen, as president of the commission, responded that, once the commission received an application from AECL to amend its licence including a complete safety case, it would hold an expedited hearing. AECL stated that it could do so within a few days. On the morning of December 11, however, the governor in council delivered a directive to the commission, as authorized under s. 19 of the *Nuclear Safety and Control Act*, SC 1997, c. 9, that had been prepared the previous day and that directed the commission to take into account in its decision making the health of Canadians who, for medical purposes, depend on nuclear isotopes. On the afternoon of the same day, a bill to authorize the reopening of the Chalk River facility for 120 days, despite any conditions in its licence, was introduced in Parliament and assented to the following day. The facility reopened and resumed production of isotopes on December 16.

A few weeks later, Minister Lunn, in a letter to Ms. Keen, expressed "deep concern" with respect to the commission's failure "to initiate the process to permit the return to operation of the NRU reactor." He also expressed doubt on whether Ms. Keen possessed "the fundamental good judgment" required by her office and advised Ms. Keen that he was considering making a recommendation to the governor in council that her designation as president be terminated (while maintaining her as a full-time member of the commission). The letter invited Ms. Keen to provide submissions to the minister before a decision was made on her role as president.

In her written response to the minister, Ms. Keen claimed that the minister's actions jeopardized the commission's institutional independence:

> As the head of an independent quasi-judicial administrative tribunal, I was and remain deeply troubled by both the tone and content of your letter. The nature of the allegations which have been made, coupled with your threat to have me removed as President, seriously undermine the independence of the CNSC. The manner in which you have sought to approach these issues, absent or in advance of any formal inquiry, highlights a significant misunderstanding of the relationship between yourself, as Minister of Natural Resources, and the CNSC. ...
>
> While the CNSC reports through you to Parliament, neither the CNSC nor its President are obliged to report to you on the status of particular licensing matters before the CNSC. ...
>
> In our view, your comments concerning the NRU reactor which were made during the December 8, 2007 telephone call with me and one of my officials—a matter with which the CNSC was and continues to be seized—and the demand noted in your letter... requiring that we, an independent quasi-judicial administrative tribunal, answer to you about this case, are examples of improper interference with both the institutional independence of the CNSC and with the administration of justice.

Ms. Keen also noted that the threat to remove her as president of the commission interfered with her security of tenure, another "fundamental element of independence of quasi-judicial bodies like the CNSC." A week after Ms. Keen's response and on the eve of her scheduled appearance before a House of Commons committee, the governor in council on Minister Lunn's recommendation removed her as president of the commission.

Do you think that Minister Lunn's interventions on the Chalk River file cross the line and inappropriately undermine the commission's institutional independence, or was the minister entitled to ask the commission to account for actions relating to a matter falling within his responsibility as natural resources minister? Would the fact that one of the responsibilities of the minister of natural resources is to promote the use of nuclear energy be relevant to your answer? Was Parliament's enactment of *An Act to permit the resumption and con-*

tinuation of the operation of the National Research Universal Reactor at Chalk River, SC 2007, c. 31 inconsistent with the commission's institutional independence?

Why would the government go so far as to introduce an Act of Parliament authorizing the reopening of the Chalk River nuclear facility, and to dismiss Ms. Keen, when the minister had the power simply to issue a directive that was binding on the commission under s. 19 of the *Nuclear Safety and Control Act*?

Following Ms. Keen's removal as president of the commission, Minister Lunn appointed as interim president and subsequently confirmed as president an assistant deputy minister from within the Ministry of Industry. What implications, if any, does the appointment of a former civil servant to this position in the wake of the Chalk River saga have for the commission's institutional independence?

In September 2008, Ms. Keen resigned her position as a member of the commission, claiming that she had been constructively dismissed from that position by the government, and filed an application for an order quashing the order in council that terminated her designation as commission president. This application was denied by the Federal Court on the grounds that, while her statutory appointment to the commission provided that she would be a member during her good behaviour, she held the president's office only at pleasure. By providing her with notice and the opportunity to make submissions before its final decision on her status with the commission, the government complied with the post-*Dunsmuir* requirements of procedural fairness governing the dismissal of public officers: *Keen v. Canada (Attorney General)* (2009), 2009 FC 353. Ms. Keen is reported to have said after the decision: "One would have thought that a regulatory agency of a serious thing like nuclear energy—you would have thought that would have been something that would have been independent." (S. Chase, "Ottawa's ouster of nuclear watchdog lawful, court rules," *The Globe and Mail* (April 11, 2009).)

Continuing the story, in May 2008, after these projects had gone hundreds of millions of dollars over budget, the federal government cancelled two AECL projects for new MAPLE nuclear reactors to produce medical isotopes and to replace Chalk River. In May 2009, AECL discovered a heavy water leak from the Chalk River reactor and announced that the facility would be taken out of service for several months. A week later, the federal government announced that it would put AECL up for sale and exit the supply of medical isotopes by 2016. During summer 2009, the closure of the Chalk River facility was reportedly described by the president of the Canadian Association of Nuclear Medicine as "a catastrophe for the patients, for the health-care system in general, and for the profession," and by the International Society of Nuclear Medicine as one of the biggest crises in the history of the nuclear medicine profession. A worldwide survey of 1,000 members of the International Society indicated that 90 percent had had to cancel or delay half their scanning procedures or switch to less effective methods (G. Galloway, "Reactor shutdown called a catastrophe as isotopes dry up," *The Globe and Mail* (May 21, 2009); J. Hall and J. Smith, "Isotope shortage endangers patients, say experts," *Toronto Star* (June 16, 2009)). In August 2009, the Ontario minister of health called on the federal government to compensate the province for hundreds of millions of dollars in additional health-care costs due to the Chalk River shutdown (G. Galloway, "Maples reactors no solution to isotope shortage," *The Globe and Mail* (August 21, 2009)).

At the time of writing (June 2010), the Chalk River facility is scheduled to reopen in late July 2010, after a shutdown of 14 months. In comparison, the shutdown of the facility in late

2007, as required by the commission while Ms. Keen was its president and concerning which she was dismissed by the minister, lasted about one month.

CHAPTER SIX

Institutional Decisions

INTRODUCTION

In this chapter we consider a number of situations where lawyers' traditional notions of procedural fairness seem to be at odds with the ability of some administrative agencies to efficiently deliver consistent and high quality decisions. The difficulties of adhering to an essentially judicial model of procedure are particularly acute for agencies that decide thousands or even hundreds of thousands of claims each year: workers' compensation boards, employment insurance tribunals, and the Immigration and Refugee Board, for example. These and other administrative agencies have a large number of members who typically sit in panels to hear and decide individual cases, and a staff, including legal advisers, to assist them to discharge their functions.

The paradigm of the legal concept of procedural fairness was developed in the context of the judicial decision-making process, in which judges decide cases personally. They hear evidence and argument, read whatever other material they believe to be necessary, make decisions, and write reasons personally and essentially alone, without help from other judges or a staff. Clerks and discussion with other judges, especially among the members of a court of appeal, doubtless have some role that varies among different times and jurisdictions but is generally not large.

Some decisions of administrative agencies are made in the same personal way: an identified individual official (or a small group of officials) makes a decision and takes responsibility for it. However, other decisions are the product of institutions and institutional processes, and they can usefully be described as "institutional decisions." There are many different degrees, processes, and reasons for these decisions, but two themes are dominant: (1) The sheer volume of the decisions to be made may demand a large staff and some arrangement for dispersal of authority, specialization, and control. For example, in Canada some agencies that provide income support benefits make hundreds of thousands of decisions each year and, in the United States, some make millions of decisions. (2) The range and complexity of the issues may make it impossible for any individual or small group of individuals to have the time, expertise, and perspective to make an intelligent decision. For example, consider the range and complexity of issues involved in a decision by an energy board about the export of natural gas, or a decision about the location and safety of a nuclear power plant.

The strengths of institutional decisions are the ability to make large volumes of decisions and the opportunities to establish internal checks and balances; specialization among staff members; and a sharing of expertise, opinions, and perspective. The weaknesses are the general weaknesses of bureaucracies, especially the large possibilities for anonymity, loss of authority by the senior levels, inconsistency, and impersonal treatment of those who are affected by their decisions.

The objective is to design procedures that combine the strengths of both individual and institutional decision making. When considering an application for judicial review of a decision for procedural unfairness, the reviewing court is not equipped to prescribe the optimal procedure for the agency. Its role is the more modest but nonetheless challenging one of understanding the administrative context of the decision and fashioning the content of the duty of fairness so as to retain its essential values and insights without depriving the agency of the institutional means available to enable it to discharge its statutory mandate effectively and efficiently.

There is no discrete legal doctrine about institutional decision making, although some aspects of the duty of fairness have proved particularly relevant: the rule restricting the delegation of legal powers and duties, the principle that only those who heard the evidence and argument may participate in making the decision, the duty of disclosure, and the impartiality and independence of the decision-maker. The materials presented here illustrate the operation of several concepts already encountered in previous chapters, and may assist reflection on some of the pervasive themes of this part of the book.

Before—and during and after—reading the material that follows, consider these four scenarios:

1. An agency decides appeals from decisions about entitlement to income support benefits—for example, family benefits. It is composed of 30 members of whom 2 are a quorum. Because the volume of decisions to be made is large—from 2,000 to 3,000 appeals each year—and much of the work is done at different places, usually only 2 members hear a case. Except for the chair and vice-chair, the members all serve part-time, and for short terms. The chair proposes to have weekly meetings of the entire board to discuss appeals, especially the proposed decisions. The objective of these meetings is to avoid glaring mistakes, to enable members to pool their experience, and to eliminate unnecessary inconsistencies. Is the proposal permitted? Are there any other ways to achieve the chair's objectives?

2. The governing body of a university is composed of 60 members of whom 30 are a quorum. It has power to expel individual staff and student members for cause, but it has no express authority to delegate this power. Assuming that a hearing must be given, is there any way to avoid tying up 30 or more busy people for days? For example, can the power to expel be delegated to a committee? If not, can the job of gathering the facts be done by a committee?

3. An agency regulates a major economic field such as transport or communications. It is composed of 12 members, usually 3 of whom sit at a hearing. It is concerned about consistency, although its smaller size and the continuous experience and personal contacts of the members make the problem smaller than it is for the agency in the second scenario. It has four different concerns:

   a. Hearings may take months. Can parts of them be assigned to an individual member or a member of the staff?

b. It wishes to have hearings "from coast to coast" to collect public opinion, as well as a central and more technical hearing in Ottawa. Can the job of travelling about the country be assigned to an individual member or a member of the staff?

c. It believes strongly in collegiality—that is, in having all the members participate in making the decisions and taking responsibility. Is this possible?

d. Expertise in a wide range of disciplines is useful or necessary to understand and make decisions about many of the issues. None of the members has or can be expected to have this expertise, but the staff does. May the members consult the staff?

4. An agency is responsible for administering a rather complex statute around which a body of case law is rapidly developing. The agency has a large membership; to enable it to handle its high volume of cases, it sits across the country in panels of two. Inconsistencies among the panels in the way that statutory discretion is exercised and provisions in the statute are interpreted have become a serious problem. The chair has instituted a policy that no decision of the agency will be released until it has first been reviewed by the agency's legal services department so that the deciding members' attention can be drawn to apparent errors, inconsistencies with the decisions of other panels, and oversights. Is this policy open to legal challenge? After careful consultations with members and other interested individuals and groups, the chair of the agency has issued guidelines to members setting out the agency's preferred interpretation of provisions in the statute on which there is as yet little jurisprudence. Is this permissible?

DELEGATION

Willis, "Delegatus Non Potest Delegare"
(1943), 21 *Can. Bar Rev.* 257-61

The administrative law which has grown up around the Latin maxim *delegatus non potest delegare*, a delegate may not re-delegate, deals with the extent to which an authority may permit another to exercise a discretion entrusted by a statute to itself. The maxim is derived from and is most frequently applied in matters relating to principal and agent but it is not confined thereto; it is basic in administrative law, the law relating to discretions conferred by statute. The maxim does not state a rule of law; it is "at most a rule of construction" and in applying it to a statute "there, of course, must be a consideration of the language of the whole enactment and of its purposes and objects." As a rule of construction for a section in the statute which confers a discretion on an authority named therein, the maxim applies: to an authority empowered to lay down general rules (legislative power); to an authority empowered to decide a particular issue affecting the rights of an individual, be it a magistrate, a municipal authority, a wartime controller or a minister of the Crown (judicial and *quasi*-judicial power); to an authority empowered to determine whether legal proceedings shall or shall not be initiated against an individual; and even to an authority empowered to do an act involving the exercise of practically no discretion, such as a utility company operating under a charter, and a person serving a distress warrant. It applies, in short, to all persons who are empowered by statute to do anything. Its most important application, however, is to authorities which are by statute empowered to exercise discretions affecting the rights and interests of the public; and it is this aspect of it that will be dealt with here.

The maxim deals with "delegation" by an authority of its statutory discretion. What is "delegation"? "Delegation, as the word is generally used, does not imply a parting with powers by the person who grants the delegation, but points rather to the conferring of an authority to do things which otherwise that person would have to do himself … it is never used by legal writers, so far as I am aware, as implying that the delegating person parts with this power in such a way as to denude himself of his rights." The fact that the authority named in the statute has and retains a general control over the activities of the person to whom it has entrusted the exercise of its statutory discretion does not, therefore, save its act of so entrusting to him the discretion from being "delegation" and so falling within the ambit of the maxim. If, however, the authority exercises such a substantial degree of control over the actual exercises of the discretion so entrusted and it can be said to direct its own mind to it, there is in law no "delegation" and the maxim does not apply.

. . .

A wartime controller who appoints someone to assist him in carrying out his duties but does not authorize him to exercise any of his powers, and a Minister of Justice who signs an order suppressing a newspaper but acts, in accordance with ordinary departmental practice, not of his own knowledge but on the recommendation of his subordinates are not delegating their powers and no further question arises. A county council which is empowered to grant movie licences "on such terms and conditions … as the Council may by the respective licences determine" delegates its powers if it inserts a condition "that no film be shown which has not been certified for public exhibition by the British Board of Film Censors," but does not delegate them if it adds thereto a rider reserving to itself the right to dispense with that condition. A local authority which is required by statute to "approve" the acts of one of its committees or officers delegates its powers and so does not "approve" if it passes a resolution allowing them to decide any matter independently of the authority and requiring them only to report quarterly the number of cases decided; it does not delegate its powers and so does "approve" if in a particular case the committee or officer has decided a matter independently of the authority and the authority later ratifies the decision but without inquiring into it.

When is delegation permissible? The answer to this question depends entirely on the interpretation of the statute which confers the discretion. A discretion conferred by statute is *prima facie* intended to be exercised by the authority on which the statute has conferred it and by no other authority, but this intention may be negatived by any contrary indications found in the language, scope or object of the statute; to put the matter in another way, the word "personally" is to be read into the statute after the name of the authority on which the discretion is conferred unless the language, scope or object of the statute shows that the words "or any person authorized by it" are to be read thereinto in its place. This *prima facie* rule of construction dealing with delegation is derived in part from the "literal" rule of construction, in part from the political theory known as "the rule of law," and in part from the presumption that the naming of a person to exercise some discretion indicates that he was deliberately selected because of some aptitude peculiar to himself. The literal rule of construction prescribes that nothing is to be added to a statute unless there are adequate grounds to justify the inference that the legislature intended something which it omitted to express; to read in the word "personally" adds nothing to the statute, to read in the words "or any person authorized by it" does. The "rule of law" says that, since the common law recognizes no distinction between government officials and private citizens, all being equal before the law, no official can justify interference with the common law rights of the citizen unless he can point to some statutory provision which expressly or impliedly permits him to do so; to point to a provision justifying interference by A does not, of course, justify interference by B. The presumption that the person named was selected because of some aptitude peculiar to himself requires the authority named in the statute to use its own peculiar aptitude and forbids it to entrust its statutory discretion to another who may be less apt than it, unless it is clear from the circumstances that some reason other than its aptitude dictated the naming of it to exercise the discretion. Because, however, the courts will readily mould the literal words of a statute to such a construction as will best achieve its object; because they will, recognizing the facts of modern government, readily imply in an authority such powers as it would normally be expected to possess; because the presumption of deliberate selection, strong when applied to the case of a principal who appoints an agent or a testator who selects a trustee, wears thin when applied to a statute which authorizes some governmental authority, sometimes with a fictitious name such as "Governor-in-Council" or "Minister of Justice," to exercise a discretion which everyone, even the legislature, knows will in fact be exercised by an unknown underling in the employ of the authority, the *prima facie* rule of *delegatus non potest delegare* will readily give way, like the principles on which it rests, to slight indications of a contrary intent.

What are these indications? The *prima facie* rule is displaced, of course, by a section in the statute which expressly permits the authority entrusted with a discretion to delegate it to another. In the absence of such a provision, how does the court decide whether the rule is or is not intended to apply; how does it decide whether to read in the word "personally" or the words "or any person authorized by it"? The language of the statute does not, *ex hypothesi*, help it: it is driven therefore to the scope and object of the statute. Is there anything in the nature of the authority to which the discretion is entrusted, in the situation in which the discretion is to be exercised, in the object which its exercise is expected to achieve to suggest that the legislature did not intend to confine the authority to the personal exercise of its discretion? This question is answered in practice by comparing the *prima facie* rule with the known practices or the apprehended needs of the authority in doing its work; the court inquires whether the policy-scheme of the statute is such as could not easily be realized unless the policy which requires that a discretion be exercised by the authority named thereto be displaced; it weighs the presumed desire of the legislature for the judgment of the authority it has named against the presumed desire of the legislature that the process of government shall go on in its accustomed and most effective manner and where there is a conflict between the two policies it determines which, under all the circumstances, is the most important.

Vine v. National Dock Labour Board
[1957] AC 488 (Eng. HL)

[The National Dock Labour Board was responsible for allocating dock labourers to steve-doring companies, and had express power to delegate its functions to local dock labour boards. Vine was assigned work but did not report; the company complained, and a discipline committee of the local dock labour board ordered Vine discharged. Vine brought an action for damages for wrongful dismissal and for a declaration that the action of the discipline committee was void because the local board had no power to delegate its disciplinary powers. He succeeded at trial and before the Court of Appeal on the delegation issue, and the board appealed to the House of Lords.]

LORD SOMERVELL: In deciding whether a "person" has power to delegate one has to consider the nature of the duty and the character of the person. Judicial authority nor-mally cannot, of course, be delegated, though no one doubted in *Arlidge's Case* [1915] AC 120 (HL), that the Local Government Board, which consisted of the President, the Lord President of the Council, the Secretaries of State, the Lord Privy Seal and the Chancellor of the Exchequer (*Local Government Board Act, 1871*), could act by officials duly deputed for the purpose, whether or not the act to be done had judicial ingredients. There are, on the other hand, many administrative duties which cannot be delegated. Appointment to an office or position is plainly an administrative act. If under a statute a duty to appoint is placed on the holder of an office, whether under the Crown or not, he would, normally, have no authority to delegate. He could take advice, of course, but he could not by a min-ute authorize someone else to make the appointment without further reference to him. ...
I am, however, clear that the disciplinary powers, whether "judicial" or not, cannot be delegated. The non-entitlement to pay, the suspension, the notice or the dismissal must be a step taken by the board and not by a delegate. The penalties, in some cases, may be slight but, in some cases, very great. A man who has worked all his life in the docks may find himself precluded altogether from doing so. Today it may be easy for him to get other work, but that has not always been so. The constitution of the board also supports the conclusion. It is clearly constituted so as to inspire confidence and weigh fairly the interests of employers and employed. The purported delegation in the present case was to a representative of each side, but it is impossible to imply a limited right of delegation. *Osgoode v. Nelson* [(1872), LR 5 HL 636] decides that in somewhat similar circumstances the appointment of a committee to take evidence and report is not in itself a delegation of authority. If there are administrative difficulties, this may be an answer to them.

VISCOUNT KILMUIR LC: I now turn to the contention that the local board could delegate its functions to the disciplinary committee. I have had the advantage of seeing in print the opinion which my noble and learned friend, Lord Somervell of Harrow, is about to express and, on this part of the case, I find myself in complete agreement with it. It was urged that the very idea was negatived by the fact that this was a *quasi*-judicial act. I am not prepared to lay down that no *quasi*-judicial function can be delegated, because the presence of the qualifying word "*quasi*" means that the functions so described can vary from those which are almost entirely judicial to those in which the judicial constituent is small indeed. ...

Nevertheless, that is not the end of the matter. It is necessary to consider the import-ance of the duty which is delegated and the people who delegate. In this case the duty is to consider whether a man will be outlawed from the occupation of a lifetime. The scheme will not work unless discipline is maintained by the wise use of that power. I do not make any reflection on the ability or sense of justice of the pairs of gentlemen who from time to time form the committee. I notice that the pair would always consist of one representative of the employers and one of the workers, but my view is that this duty in this scheme is too important to delegate unless there is an express power.

I reach the same conclusion when I consider this from the aspect of who may dele-gate. The duty is placed on the local board. It is obviously possible that cases may occur in which not only the man but his trade union and employers may want a decision of the whole board. Again, I think that they are entitled to have it unless the scheme says other-wise. Further, as was mentioned in the argument, if one allows the principle of delega-tion, it would then be possible, although neither probable nor practicable, for the board to delegate its functions to a committee which was not a microcosm of itself but a body on which employers and employed were no longer equally represented.

Appeal dismissed.

NOTES

1. *Morgan v. Acadia University* (1985), 15 Admin. LR 61 (NS SC) involved review of a disciplinary decision. The *Acadia University Act*, SNS 1891, c. 134, s. 8 provided that the board of governors had "power to adopt and carry into effect by-laws, resolutions, and regulations touching and concerning the instruction, care, government, and discipline of the students." The board delegated its responsibility for discipline to the dean of students. The structure for making and hearing charges against individual students was composed of several levels, formal and informal, and the last stage was an appeal to the Judicial Appeals Committee composed of students and faculty. Charges were made against Morgan and were considered throughout the various stages. After he was found guilty, he sought review and failed. One of the grounds was delegation, and Grant J quoted from the article by Willis and continued:

> I find the very nature of the duty required by the scope and objects of the legislation is such that a delegation be envisioned in interpreting the section. It would, I find, be impractical and inap-propriate to consider otherwise. With several residences, with female and male students living in the contemporary university setting, such delegation is only fair and practical. The delega-tion to the Dean and by him to students and faculty seems to me to be also fair and practical. To hold otherwise I find would be unrealistic today.

2. In *King v. Institute of Chartered Accountants (Nova Scotia)* (1993), 99 DLR (4th) 425 (NS SCTD), counsel for the institute argued that, in determining whether in the absence of express statutory authority the institute could validly delegate to a committee the function of disciplining members, the court should ask, "What meaning provides the most practical interpretation consistent with language used, the purpose of the legislation, and the prin-ciples of natural justice?" Macdonald J responded to this approach as follows (at 432):

This rhetorical question, as a proposed principle of law, appears to be contrary to the present rule that quasi-judicial functions can only be delegated by express authority.

The court quashed the discipline committee's decision finding King guilty of professional misconduct.

3. The principle of non-delegation also requires that all members of the tribunal hearing a dispute participate in a substantive sense in the making of the decision. In *IBM Canada Ltd. v. Deputy Minister of National Revenue, Customs and Excise*, [1992] 1 FC 663 (FCA), a decision of the tariff board was challenged on the ground that it was signed by only two of the members; reasons of the dissenting member were released later. The court concluded that the applicant had failed to prove that the third member of the quorum had not in fact participated in the deliberations. However, Décary JA said (at 673-75):

> In setting a quorum and requiring that a minimum number of persons participate in a decision, Parliament reposes its faith in collective wisdom, does so for the benefit of the public as well as for the benefit of those who might be affected by the decision, and expects those who participate in the decision either as members of the majority or as dissenting members to act together up to the very last moment which is the making of one united, though not necessarily unanimous, decision. Having the proper quorum at all relevant times, from the beginning up to the very last moment is a question of principle, of public policy and of sound and fair administration of justice.
>
> The nature, degree and form of this "acting together" need not, cannot and should not be defined. Tribunals have their own ways and their own rules. Members of a panel have their own personality and habits and cannot be expected to hold hands from the time a case is heard until the time it is decided. What must be done, however, is that at some point in time, the panel must reach a decision collectively and each member must "participate" individually in that collective decision in agreeing with it or dissenting from it. There has to be a meeting of the minds, each member being informed at least in a general way of the point of view of each of his colleagues.

4. Finally, questions have arisen about the powers exercisable by the chair of an administrative agency, either by virtue of her office (statutes sometimes designate the chair as chief executive officer of the agency) or as a result of the delegation of authority by other members. In the absence of clear statutory language to the contrary, the chair probably cannot be authorized to exercise alone any of the agency's quasi-judicial functions "in the sense they entail the exercise of significant discretionary and judgmental powers in relation to the vital interests of other persons" (*Volk v. Saskatchewan (Public Service Commission)* (1993), 12 Admin. LR (2d) 293, 298 (Sask. CA). However, if at the hearing the chair assumes responsibility for ruling on questions of law, and the other members are present and do not object when the rulings are made, they may be held to have adopted by acquiescence the chair's rulings as their own (*Re Schabas and Caput of the University of Toronto* (1974), 52 DLR (3d) 495 (Ont. Div. Ct.)).

DECIDING WITHOUT HEARING

An aspect of the duty of fairness that we have not so far encountered is the general principle that only those members of an agency who hear a particular case may decide it. However, like other incidents of fairness, this one should be applied with sensitivity to the administrative and legal contexts in which the impugned decision was made.

The rationale of the requirement is that a person is denied an adequate opportunity to influence the decision if unable to address directly those who make or participate in making it. A simple illustration is that it will normally be a breach of the duty of fairness for a member of a hearing panel who is unable to attend for part of the hearing subsequently to resume sitting and to participate in making the decision. The decision must be made by the members who heard all the evidence and argument, provided of course that they constitute a quorum. If they do not, the proceeding must be abandoned and started afresh.

For two illustrative cases, see *Re Ramm* (1957), 7 DLR (2d) 378 (Ont. CA) and *Western Realty Projects Ltd. v. City of Edmonton and Triple Five Corporation Ltd.*, [1974] 5 WWR 131 (Alta. DC). And see *Gratton v. Canadian Judicial Council*, [1994] 2 FC 769 (TD), where the implications of the delegation doctrine and the rule that only those who hear may decide are considered in the context of proceedings for the dismissal from office of a superior court judge.

Delegating the Duty To Hear

Local Government Board v. Arlidge
[1915] AC 120 (Eng. HL)

[The *Housing and Town Planning Act, 1909* gave borough councils authority to make orders closing dwelling houses that they were satisfied were unfit for human habitation. It also gave authority to terminate such orders if the council was satisfied that adequate corrective measures have been taken. The owner of the dwelling house was given a right of appeal to the Local Government Board, a government department, against both a closing order and a refusal to terminate. The board was given power to determine its own procedure for these appeals, provided that it did not dismiss any appeal without holding a public local inquiry.

The Hampstead Borough Council made a closing order against a house owned by Arlidge, and Arlidge appealed to the board. The board appointed an inspector who held a public inquiry and made a report. Arlidge made an application to present his case before the actual decision-maker in the board, but this was refused and the board confirmed the order. Arlidge then undertook repairs and applied to the council to have the closing order terminated. This application was refused and Arlidge appealed again to the board. Another public inquiry was held and the board again confirmed the decision of the council.

Arlidge sought *certiorari* on three grounds: (1) The order of the board did not disclose the officer who had made the decision, and therefore the appeal could not be shown to have been decided by the board or by someone authorized to act for it. (2) Arlidge was entitled to be heard orally by the board. (3) He was entitled to disclosure of the inspector's report. The application was dismissed, and Arlidge appealed. The appeal succeeded, but the board appealed to the House of Lords, which allowed the appeal. Only the passages about delegation are reproduced here.]

VISCOUNT HALDANE LC: The Minister at the head of the Board is directly responsible to Parliament like other Ministers. He is responsible not only for what he himself does but for all that is done in his department. The volume of work entrusted to him is very great and he cannot do the great bulk of it himself. He is expected to obtain his materials vicariously through his officials, and he has discharged his duty if he sees that they obtain these materials for him properly. To try to extend his duty beyond this and to insist that he and other members of the Board should do everything personally would be to impair his efficiency. Unlike a judge in a Court he is not only at liberty but is compelled to rely on the assistance of his staff. When, therefore, the Board is directed to dispose of an appeal, that does not mean that any particular official of the Board is to dispose of it.

LORD SHAW: [I]t is said that the respondent is entitled to know his particular judge or judges, to individualize the Board, and to demand that that person or those persons so discovered shall give him, the respondent, an audience on the whole material available, including the result of the public local inquiry and the report made thereupon by the Board's inspector. In the first place, of the demand to know the individual judge or judges. My Lords, how can the judiciary be blind to the well-known facts applicable not only to the constitution but to the working of such branches of the Executive? The department is represented in Parliament by its responsible head. On the one hand he manages its affairs with such assistance as the Treasury sanctions, and on the other he becomes answerable in Parliament for every departmental act. His Board—that is, all the members of it together—may never meet, or they may only be convened on some question of policy; but a determination, signed and sealed and issued in correct form, stands as the deliverance of the Board as such, for which determination the President becomes answerable to Parliament. This is the general rule, acknowledged and familiar, of departmental action and responsibility.

NOTE

The reasoning in *Arlidge* about the propriety of the procedural arrangements made by the minister for hearing appeals must be considered within its wider doctrinal context: the reluctance of courts to apply the non-delegation principle to the exercise by civil servants of statutory powers conferred on their minister. The argument from practicality is bolstered by the fact that ministers remain legally and politically accountable for decisions made in their name by departmental officials. English courts have come close to saying that, when statutory powers conferred on a minister are exercised in the name of the minister within the department in accordance with normal practice, no delegation is involved at all: see Molot, "The *Carltona* Doctrine and Recent Amendments to the *Interpretation Act*" (1994), 26 Ottawa LR 259.

In Canada, however, while our courts do not require powers to be delegated expressly by the minister to the civil servants in the department, they continue to find that some decisions exceptionally require the minister's personal decision—for example, *Quebec (Attorney General) v. Carrières Ste-Thérèse Ltée*, [1985] 1 SCR 831 (Que.), involving an order closing down a hazardous factory, and *Suresh v. Canada (Minister of Citizenship and Immigration)*, [2002] 1 SCR 3 (Can.), at para. 126, especially where the court seems to demand that the minister personally provide reasons when making a deportation order of a person likely to suffer torture on return to his or her country of origin. On the other hand, the principle that powers exercised by departmental officials in the name of the minister is not a delegation of authority has been extended to the exercise at the local level of a power to make an assessment of tax liability conferred by statute on a senior civil servant, the deputy minister of the Department of National Revenue: *Canada v. BM Enterprises*, [1992] 3 FC 409 (TD).

The procedural latitude shown in *Arlidge* may therefore not be afforded to attempts by other decision-makers to delegate their hearing responsibilities.

Jeffs v. New Zealand Dairy Production and Marketing Board
[1967] 1 AC 551 (NZ PC)

[The board had general powers to govern the production and marketing of milk, including the power to establish zones for exclusive supply arrangements. When an informal agreement between the Northern Wairoa Co-operative Dairy Co. and the Ruawai Co-operative Dairy Co. regarding the allocation of the supply of whole milk from local producers between the two dairies was due to expire, the board resolved that a zoning committee consisting of three members of the board should be set up to investigate the question of supply and report back to the board. The committee decided to proceed with a public hearing of zoning applications that had previously been made to the board. Following a two-day hearing, at which the committee heard witnesses and received written evidence, the committee prepared a written report to the board setting out its recommendations on zoning of whole milk supply as between Northern Wairoa company and Ruawai company. The board accepted the recommendations without alteration and passed resolutions to give effect to them.]

VISCOUNT DILHORNE: … Mr. Green, the secretary of the board, in the course of his evidence at the trial of this case stated that the members of the board who were not on the committee received the report of the committee when they received the agenda for the meeting on the 30th or sat down for that meeting. As the report is dated May 30 it is unlikely that any members of the board who were not on the committee saw it before the morning of the day on which the board decided to give effect to the committee's recommendations. The minutes and draft minutes record that Mr. Green read the report to the board.

That report does not record, even in summary form, the evidence given at the public hearing. It does contain a statement of the submissions made by those who represented interested parties at the hearing. Mr. Green testified that at the public hearing the chairman had said that the committee were prepared to receive written submissions after the conclusion of the hearing. Mr. Dyson, who appeared on behalf of the appellant Mr. Jeffs, and Mr. Spring, who appeared for the Ruawai company, sent in written submissions. Mr. Green also testified that he had drafted the committee's report according to discussions that had taken place in the car as the members of the committee were returning from the public hearing to Auckland. Although the members of the committee saw after May 17 the written submissions that were sent in, they were not seen by the other members of the board.

[Farmers in the Ruawai district made an application for *certiorari*. The application and an appeal were dismissed and they appealed to the Privy Council. Discussion of an unsuccessful argument that an appearance of bias was created by a debt owed by the Ruawai company to the board is omitted.]

The appellants further contended that the board had improperly delegated its judicial task of hearing evidence and submissions to the committee; that its duty was to consider all the evidence, notes and submissions relative to the zoning applications and it should not have relied on the report of the committee; and so it had failed to comply with the requirements of natural justice.

It is clear from the board's resolutions appointing the committee, from the letter sent to the shareholders in the Ruawai company on March 28, 1963, by Mr. Green and from the minutes of the meeting of May 30 that the board did not delegate to the committee the duty of deciding on zoning applications. The committee was appointed by the board to "investigate the question of supply between the two companies and to report back to the board." It was not expressly authorized to hold a public hearing. It appears to have done so on its own initiative when there was lack of sufficient support for amalgamation. The committee was appointed to investigate and report and was not charged with the duty of collecting evidence for consideration by the board.

The only material the board had before it when reaching its decision was the report of the committee. In the discharge of its duty to act judicially, it was the board's duty to "hear" interested parties. In *R v. Local Government Board, ex p. Arlidge* [1914] 1 KB 160 (CA), at 191 Hamilton LJ said:

> In my opinion, the question whether the deciding officer "hears" the appellant audibly addressing him or "hears" him only through the medium of his written statement is, in a matter of this kind, one of pure procedure.

In this case the board did not hear the persons interested orally nor did it see their written statements. It did not see the written statements produced by witnesses at the hearing. Its members, other than the members of the committee, were not informed of the evidence given. The report stated what submissions were made at the hearing but did not state what evidence was given nor did it contain a summary of the evidence. The members of the board other than the members of the committee did not see the written submissions sent in response to the chairman of the committee's statement at the hearing.

On the facts of this case it does not appear that the board asked the committee to hold the public hearing or delegated to the committee any part of its duties. Subject to the provisions of the Act and of any regulations thereunder, the board can regulate its procedure in such manner as it thinks fit (1961 Act, s. 12(10)). Whether the board heard the interested parties orally or by receiving written statements from them, is, as Hamilton LJ said in *R v. Local Government Board, ex p. Arlidge*, a matter of procedure. Equally it would have been a matter of procedure if the board had appointed a person or persons to hear and receive evidence and submissions from interested parties for the purpose of informing the board of the evidence and submissions. ... This procedure may be convenient when the credibility of witnesses is not involved, and if it had been followed in this case and as a result the board, before it reached a decision, was fully informed of the evidence given and the submissions made and had considered them, then it could not have been said that the board had not heard the interested parties and had acted contrary to the principles of natural justice. In some circumstances it may suffice for the board to have before it and to consider an accurate summary of the relevant evidence and submissions if the summary adequately discloses the evidence and submissions to the board.

Unfortunately no such procedure was followed in this case. The committee was not appointed by the board, nor was it asked by the board to receive evidence for transmission to it. The committee's report did not state what the evidence was and the board reached its decision without consideration of and in ignorance of the evidence.

The board thus failed to hear the interested parties as it was under an obligation to do in order to discharge its duty to act judicially in the determination of zoning applications.

Appeal allowed.

Consultations Among Agency Members

The following materials present an issue that is of great practical importance to the work of many administrative agencies and goes to the heart of some critical differences between courts and agencies in function, process, and structure. It represents one of the most significant points of tension between the process values typically ascribed respectively to lawyers and administrators. The question is whether, and if so to what extent, the duty of fairness precludes the members of an agency panel who heard a case from discussing it with other members of the agency after the hearing has ended, but before they have rendered their decision.

International Woodworkers of America, Local 2-69 v. Consolidated-Bathurst Packaging Ltd.
(1983), 5 CLRBR (NS) 79 (OLRB), [1990] 1 SCR 282 (Ont.)

[The union made an application to the Ontario Labour Relations Board (OLRB) for a determination that the employer had failed to bargain in good faith, and raised a difficult and important issue about the extent of the employer's duty to disclose its business affairs during negotiations for a collective agreement—in particular, a decision to close one of its plants. In its previous jurisprudence, the board had developed a test that imposed a duty of disclosure on the employer when it had taken a hard or firm decision to close a plant prior to or during the bargaining process. Three members of the board held a hearing. In the course of that hearing both the employer and the union argued that the current test should be changed. After the hearing was concluded these members discussed the case with other members of the board at a "full-board" meeting and then gave a decision upholding the existing test but in favour of the union's application on the facts. The employer requested the board to reconsider this decision and argued that, if any evidence given at the hearing was discussed with other members or if any opinions of other members were considered, the decision had been improperly made.]

DECISION OF THE BOARD: It must be kept in mind that the Ontario Labour Relations Board is a relatively large tripartite administrative agency first established in 1944. ... At the end of fiscal year 1982-83, the Board employed a total of 94 persons on a full-time basis. ... In the same fiscal year the Board received a total of 2,762 applications and complaints. In addition to these cases, 427 were carried over from the previous year, making a total caseload of 3,189 cases in 1982-83. Of the total, 2,445 were disposed of during the year producing an average workload of 266 cases for the Board's full-time chairmen and vice-chairmen. Currently, the Board employs 12 full-time chairmen and vice-chairmen and 4 part-time vice-chairmen. There are 10 full-time Board members representing labour and management and another 22 part-time Board members representing the parties. ... The unique tripartite nature of the Ontario Labour Relations Board and the difficulty of strictly applying common law concepts such as bias to this agency are highlighted in Arthurs, "The Three Faces of Justice: Bias in the Tripartite Tribunal" (1963) 28 *Sask. Bar Rev.* 147. ...

Sections 102 and 103 [of Ontario's *Labour Relations Act*] establish the Board and set out many of its general procedural powers. Section 102(9) provides that the Chairman or a vice-chairman, one member representative of employers and one member representative of employees constitute a quorum. ... Today, the constitution of the Board, sitting in three person panels, lends itself to hundreds of different combinations of Board members and vice-chairmen who may sit on any given case. What are the implications of these diverse panel configurations to the administration of the Act and to the attainment of the statute's objectives?

In considering this question, it is to be noted that the Act confers many areas of broad discretion on the Board in determining how the statute should be interpreted or applied to an infinite variety of factual situations. Within these areas of discretion, decision-making has to turn on policy considerations. At this level of "administrative law," law and policy are to a large degree inseparable. In effect, law and policy come to be promulgated through the form of case by case decisions rendered by panels. It is in this context that the Board is sometimes criticized for not creating enough certainty in "Board law" to facilitate the planning of the parties regulated by the statute. This criticism, however, ignores the fact that there is a huge corpus of Board law much of which is almost as old as the legislation itself and as settled and stable as law can be. Board decision-making has recognized the need for uniformity and stability in the application of the statute and the discretions contained therein. Indeed, it is because there is so much settled law and policy that upwards to 80% of unfair labour practice charges are withdrawn, dismissed, settled or adjusted without the issuance of a decision and that a high percentage of other matters are either settled or withdrawn without the need for a hearing. ... Thus, there is a great incentive for the Board to articulate its policies clearly and, once articulated, to maintain, and apply them. Nevertheless, there remains, even in applying an established policy, an inevitable area of discretion in applying the statute to each fact situation. Moreover, the Board reserves the right to change its policies as required and new amendments to the Act create additional requirements for ongoing policy analysis. To perform its job effectively, the Board needs all the insight it can muster to evaluate the practical consequences of its decisions, for it lacks the capacity to ascertain by research and investigation just what impact its decisions have on labour relations and the economy generally.

In this context therefore, and accepting that no one panel of the Board can bind another panel by any decision rendered, what institutional procedures has the Board developed to foster greater insightfulness in the exercise of the Board's powers by particular panels? What internal mechanisms has the Board developed to establish a level of thoughtfulness in the creation of policies which will meet the labour relations community's needs and stand the test of time? What internal procedures has the Board developed to ensure the greatest possible understanding of these policies by all Board members in order to facilitate a more or less uniform application of such policies? The meeting impugned by the respondent must be seen as only part of the internal administrative arrangements of the Board which have evolved to achieve a maximum regulatory effectiveness in a labour relations setting.

Since the inception of the Board, it has been understood that a division or panel which hears a case, ultimately, is alone responsible for deciding it. Panels deliberate on their own in executive sessions following the conclusion of hearings. At this session the vice-chairman is invariably charged with the responsibility of preparing a draft decision for the consideration of his or her two colleagues. ... A second executive session will usually be convened by the panel to consider the draft decision. ...

After deliberating over a draft decision, any panel of the Board contemplating a major policy issue may, through the Chairman, cause a meeting of all Board members and vice-chairmen to be held to acquaint them with this issue and the decision the panel is inclined to make. These "Full Board" meetings have been institutionalized to facilitate a maximum understanding and appreciation throughout the Board of policy developments and to evaluate fully the practical consequences of proposed policy initiatives on labour relations and the economy in the Province. But this institutional purpose is subject to the clear understanding that it is for the panel hearing the case to make the ultimate decision and that discussion at a "Full Board" meeting is limited to the policy implications of a draft decision. The draft decision of a panel is placed before those attending the meeting by the panel and is explained by the panel members. The facts set out in the draft are taken as given and do not become the subject of discussion. No vote is taken at these meetings nor is any other procedure employed to identify a consensus. The meetings invariably conclude with the Chairman thanking the members of the panel for outlining their problem to the entire Board and indicating that all Board members look forward to that panel's final decision whatever it might be. ...

"Full Board" meetings are as important to fashioning informed and practical decisions which will withstand the scrutiny of subsequent panels as is the research and reflection undertaken by the vice-chairmen, in preparing their draft decisions. As learned articles, labour relations texts, memoranda prepared by Board lawyers and law students, and previous decisions of the Board can provide insightful guidance on difficult policy issues, so can general discussion with the experienced full and part-time management and labour Board members who make up the tripartite Board and who have to live with the decisions rendered by individual panels hearing cases. Indeed, in the absence of a formalized Full Board meeting, Board members and vice-chairmen would be driven to discuss their cases with each other informally in order to better appreciate the issues involved and to develop a level of understanding and insight consistent with the large measure of deference the labour relations system needs to be paid to rendered decisions.

The "Full Board" meeting merely institutionalizes these discussions and better emphasizes the broad ranging policy implications of individual decisions. The decisions therefore remain the individual decisions of particular panels and vice-chairmen. The "Full
Board" meetings are merely reflective of the institutional setting in which these individual decisions are made.

The respondent's submission is really attempting to probe the mental processes of the
panel which rendered the decision in question and in so doing ignores the inherent nature of judicial decision-making and administrative law making. See K.C. Davis, *Administrative Law Treatise* (2d ed. 1980) §17. In general, the deliberations of this panel were not
unlike those engaged in by a judge sitting in court. The "Full Board" meeting, to the extent
there is no judicial analogy, distinguishes an administrative agency from somewhat more
individual common law judging. But, as an extra-record event, "Full Board" meetings are
in substance no different from the post-hearing consultation of a judge with his law clerks
or the informal discussions that inevitably occur between brother judges. Such meetings,
we also suggest, have no greater or lesser effect than a judge's post-hearing reading of
reports and periodicals which may not have been cited or relied on by the advocates. Is
it seriously open for a litigant to question Supreme Court justices or other judges about
their post-hearing reading, their thinking, and the contribution of their law clerks or
brother judges to the ideas expressed in an opinion published under a justice's name? For
example, could it be asked of a judge "Did you make a false start that your law clerk or
brother judge in consultation corrected?" If such questions are improper for a judge, as
we think they are, why are they not equally improper to be put to an administrator of an
important public statute embracing a complex of socio-economic objectives. ...

[Consolidated-Bathurst made an application for judicial review, which succeeded before
the Divisional Court: (1985), 20 DLR (4th) 84. The Court of Appeal reversed: (1988), 31
DLR (4th) 444. The company appealed to the Supreme Court of Canada.]

SOPINKA J (dissenting): The issue in this case is the propriety of a practice of the Ontario
Labour Relations Board pursuant to which a full Board session is held to discuss a draft
decision of a three-person panel.

· · ·

Although we are told that the full Board consists of 48 members, it does not appear
from the record how many attended the meeting in question and whether labour and
management were equally represented as contemplated by s. 102(9) of the Act. The affidavit of Mr. Michael Gordon, filed on behalf of the appellant, identifies thirteen of the
people present, among them an alternate chairman, several vice-chairmen, a number of
Board members, solicitors and senior employees of the Board. Of those specifically identified, only Board member Wightman was a member of the panel which heard the case.
Nevertheless it appears from the Board's reasons on reconsideration that the other members of the panel of three were also present.

While it is not contested that no evidence was introduced at this full board meeting,
it is not clear from the record what was discussed. The meeting took several hours but no
minutes were kept. The reasons of the Board on reconsideration describe the practice of
the Board in relation to full board hearings but provide no details as to what was dis-

cussed. It may be assumed that the matters discussed were in accordance with the Board's practice in this regard. ...

There is no evidence that the procedure at the meeting in question departed from the Board's usual practice, whereby discussion is limited to the policy implications of a draft decision, the facts contained in the decision are taken as given, no vote or consensus is taken, no minutes are kept, and no attendance is recorded. The practice is not a recent innovation. It goes back at least as far as 1971 when it was referred to, disapprovingly, in Chief Justice McRuer's report in the *Royal Commission Inquiry into Civil Rights*, February 22, 1971, pp. 2004-6. ...

Issues

The issue in this appeal is whether the following rules of natural justice have been violated:

   (a) he who decides must hear;
   (b) the right to know the case to be met.

The Effect of the Full Board Procedure

The first step in deciding whether the rules of natural justice have been breached is to assess what role, if any, the full board procedure played in the decision-making process. The appellant submits that the outcome of its case may have been influenced by a formalized meeting of the full Board. The respondent Union counters by submitting that the appellant must establish a breach of the rules of natural justice but can point to no new evidence or arguments in the decision of the Board that were obtained as a result of the full board procedure. The purport of the Board's reasons on the application for reconsideration is that the ultimate decision was left to the panel and therefore presumably that the discussion of policy implications did not influence the final decision.

. . .

[Sopinka J examined the reasons for full-board meetings generally and in the context of this case.]

Given the number of Board members present and the fact that included were an alternate Chairman, Vice-chairmen and solicitors, the views expressed were potentially very influential.

   In view of the above I adopt the following from the reasons of the majority of the Divisional Court, at pp. 94-5, as a correct statement as to the effect of the full board meeting:

Chairman Shaw [*sic*] states in his reasons that the final decision was made by the three members who heard evidence and argument. He cannot be heard to state that he and his fellow members were not influenced by the discussion at the full board meeting. The format of the full board meeting made it clear that it was important to have input from other members of the board who had not heard the evidence or argument before the final decision was made. The tabling of the draft decision to all of the members of the board plus all of the support staff involved a substantial risk that opinions would be advanced by others and arguments presented. It is probable that some of the people involved in the meeting would express points of view. The full board meeting was only called when important questions of policy were being considered. Surely, the discussion would involve policy reasons why s. 15 should be given either a broad or narrow interpretation. Members or support staff might relate matters from their own practical experience which might be tantamount to giving evidence. The parties to the dispute would have no way of knowing what was being said in these discussions and no opportunity to respond.

I would conclude from the foregoing that the full Board meeting might very well have affected the outcome. The Board in its reasons on reconsideration does not directly seek to refute this inference. It does affirm that the final decision was that of the panel. There are two difficulties which confront the Board in seeking to negate the inference. First, I find it difficult to understand how the full board practice can achieve its purpose of bringing about uniformity without affecting the decision of individual panels. Uniformity can only be achieved if some decisions are brought into line with others by the uniform application of policy. The second difficulty is that in matters affecting the integrity of the decision-making process, it is sufficient if there is an appearance of injustice. The tribunal will not be heard to deny what appears as a plausible objective conclusion. The principle was expressed by Mackay J in *Re Ramm* (1957) 7 DLR (2d) 378 (Ont. CA). Mackay J wrote, at p. 382:

> With respect to the difference in the constitution of members of the Public Accountants Council on the first and second hearings, it may very well be that the two members of the Public Accountants Council who were not present at the earlier hearing, abstained from argument on the issues which fell for determination. It appears, however, that they did vote inasmuch as the decision to revoke the licence of the appellant Ramm was unanimous. It is well established that it is not merely of some importance but of fundamental importance, that "justice should not only be done but should manifestly and undoubtedly be seen to be done." In a word, it is not irrelevant to inquire whether two members of the Council who were not present at the earlier meeting took part in the proceeding in the Council's deliberation on the subsequent hearing. *What is objectionable is their presence during the consultation when they were in a position which made it impossible for them to discuss in a judicial way, the evidence that had been given on oath days before and in their absence and on which a finding must be based.* [Emphasis added.]

> . . .

I turn next to consider whether a discussion of policy matters at the full board meeting which may have affected the outcome constituted a breach of the rules of natural justice.

The Principles of Natural Justice

Section 102(13) of the Act provides that the Board shall give full opportunity to the parties to present their evidence and make their submissions. The Board is empowered to determine its own practice and procedure but rules governing its practice and procedure are subject to the approval of the Lieutenant Governor in Council. While not every practice of the Board would necessarily be subject to the approval of the Lieutenant Governor, the full board practice is one which might require such approval. No such approval has been given and indeed the practice does not appear to have been adopted formally as a rule of the Board. In view of the fact, however, that this point was not argued I do not propose to deal with it further.

The full board hearing in this case is said to violate the principles of natural justice in two respects: first, that members of the Board who did not preside at the hearing participated in the decision; and second, that the case is decided at least in part on the basis of materials which were not disclosed at the hearing and in respect of which there was no opportunity to make submissions.

Although these are distinct principles of natural justice, they have evolved out of the same concern: a party to an administrative proceeding entitled to a hearing is entitled to a meaningful hearing in the sense that the party must be given an opportunity to deal with the material that will influence the tribunal in coming to its decision, and to deal with it in the presence of those who make the decision. As stated by Crane in his case comment on the *Consolidated-Bathurst* decision (1988) 1 *CJALP* 215, at p. 217: "The two rules have the same purpose: to preserve the integrity and fairness of the process." In the first case the party has had no opportunity to persuade some of the members at all, while in the second the party has not been afforded an opportunity to persuade the tribunal as to the impact of material obtained outside the hearing.

The concern for justice is aptly put by the pithy statement in the McRuer Report criticizing the full board procedure. At pages 2005-6, the former Chief Justice of the High Court of Ontario states:

> To take a matter before the full Board for a discussion and obtain the views of others who have not participated in the hearing and without the parties affected having an opportunity to present their views is a violation of the principle that he who decides must hear.
>
> • • •
>
> Notwithstanding that the ultimate decision is made by those who were present at the hearing, where a division of the Board considers that a matter should be discussed before the full Board or a larger division, the parties should be notified and given an opportunity to be heard.

Although I am satisfied that, at least formally, the decision here was made by the three-member panel, that does not determine the matter. The question, rather, is whether the introduction of policy considerations in the decision-making process by members of the Board who were not present at the hearing and their application by members who were present but who heard no submissions from the parties in respect thereto, violates the rationale underlying the above principles.

In answering this question, it is necessary to consider the role of policy in the decision-making processes of administrative tribunals. There is no question that the Labour Board is entitled to consider policy in arriving at its decisions. See Dickson J (as he then was) in *Canadian Union of Public Employees, Local 963 v. New Brunswick Liquor Corp.* [1979] 2 SCR 227, at pp. 235-36:

> The labour board is a specialized tribunal which administers a comprehensive statute regulating labour relations. In the administration of that regime, a board is called upon not only

to find facts and decide questions of law, but also to exercise its understanding of the body of jurisprudence that has developed around the collective bargaining system, as understood in Canada, and its labour relations sense acquired from accumulated experience in the area.

The Board, then, is obliged by statute to hold a hearing and to give the parties a full opportunity to present evidence and submissions. It is also entitled to apply policy. At a time when the content of the rules of natural justice was determined by classifying tribunals as quasi-judicial or administrative, the Board would have been classified as exercising hybrid functions. A tribunal exercising hybrid functions did so in two stages. As a quasi-judicial tribunal it was required to comply with the rules of natural justice. In making its decision, however, it assumed its administrative phase and could overrule the conclusion which was indicated at the hearing by the application of administrative policy. Examples of this type of tribunal and the jurisprudence relating to its functions can be found in cases such as *B. Johnson & Co. (Builders), Ltd. v. Minister of Health* [1947] 2 All ER 395, and *Re Cloverdale Shopping Centre and Township of Etobicoke* (1966) 2 OR 439 (Ont. CA). In this state of the law there was no obligation on a tribunal during its administrative phase to comply with the rules of natural justice and hence to disclose policy which was being applied. Although tribunals exercising so-called administrative functions were subject to a general duty of fairness, disclosure of the policy to be applied by the tribunal was generally not a requirement. In the case of hybrid tribunals, therefore, such non-disclosure at the quasi-judicial stage would not have been considered a breach of the rules of natural justice. In this respect policy was treated on the same footing as the law. Both law and policy might be dealt with at the hearing but the tribunal was entitled to supplement it by its own researches without disclosure to the parties.

This view of the role of policy must be reappraised in light of the evolution of the law relating to the classification of tribunals and the application to them of the rules of natural justice and fairness. The content of these rules is no longer dictated by classification as judicial, quasi-judicial or executive, but by reference to the circumstances of the case, the governing statutory provisions and the nature of the matters to be determined. ...

It is no longer appropriate, therefore, to conclude that failure to disclose policy to be applied by a tribunal is not a denial of natural justice without examining all the circumstances under which the tribunal operates.

The proceedings which are the subject of this appeal involve the exercise of extraordinary powers by the Board. In this case the Board was asked to order reopening of the Hamilton plant although it had operated at a loss. Although the Board declined to make that order, it apparently considered that it had jurisdiction to do so. In lieu thereof the employer was ordered to pay damages. These are civil consequences that affect the rights of employers to a greater degree than many civil actions in the courts in which a litigant enjoys the whole panoply of protection afforded by the rules of practice, procedure and the rules of evidence. The Act, here, provides for a full opportunity to the parties to present evidence and to make submissions. Is this opportunity denied when the tribunal considers and applies policy without giving the parties an opportunity to deal with it at the hearing? Is it a breach of the standard of fairness which underlies the rules of natural justice?

The answers to these questions lie in the nature of policy and whether it is correct to treat it on the same footing as the law. In *Innisfil (Corporation of the Township) v. Corporation of Township of Vespra* [1981] 2 SCR 145, this Court was called upon to deal with the question whether a party to a proceeding before the Ontario Municipal Board was entitled to challenge policy by leading evidence and by cross-examination—the traditional methods for contesting fact. The Court of Appeal of Ontario had held that government policy introduced at the hearing was not binding but could be met by other evidence. Cross-examination was, however, denied. In this Court, the right to challenge policy by evidence was affirmed. In addition, the appellants were accorded the right to cross-examine and the Court of Appeal was reversed in this respect. Estey J, who delivered the judgment of the Court, stated, at p. 167:

> On the other hand, where the rights of the citizen are involved and the statute affords him the right to a full hearing, including a hearing of his demonstration of his rights, one would expect to find the clearest statutory curtailment of the citizen's right to meet the case made against him by cross-examination.

If a party has the right to attack policy in the same fashion as fact, it follows that to deprive the party of that right is a denial of a full opportunity to present evidence and is unfair. Policy in this respect is not like the law which cannot be the subject of evidence or cross-examination. Policy often has a factual component which the law does not. Furthermore, under our system of justice it is crucial that the law be correctly applied. The court or tribunal is not bound to rely solely on the law as presented by the parties. Accordingly, a tribunal can rely on its own research and if that differs from what has been presented at the hearing, it is bound to apply the law as found. Ordinarily there is no obligation to disclose to the parties the fruits of the tribunal's research as to the law, although it is a salutary practice to obtain their views in respect of an authority which has come to the tribunal's attention and which may have an important influence on the case. For an example of the application of this practice in this Court, see *City of Kamloops v. Nielsen* [1984] 2 SCR 2, at p. 36. We do not have the same attitude to policy. There is not necessarily one policy that is the right policy. Often there are competing policies, selection of the better policy being dependent on being subjected to the type of scrutiny which was ordered in *Innisfil, supra*.

Ample support can be found in the cases and writings for the proposition that generally policy is to be treated more like fact than law. In *Capital Cities Communications Inc. v. Canadian Radio-Television Commission* [1978] 2 SCR 141, Laskin CJ, in holding that the Commission was entitled to rely on policy, stated at p. 171:

> … it was eminently proper that it lay down guidelines from time to time as it did in respect of cable television. The guidelines on this matter were arrived at after extensive hearings at which interested parties were present and made submissions. An overall policy is demanded in the interests of prospective licensees and of the public under such a regulatory regime as is set up by the *Broadcasting Act*. Although one could mature as a result of a succession of applications, there is merit in having it known in advance.

In *de Smith's Judicial Review of Administrative Action* (4th ed. 1980), at p. 223, the learned author states:

> … an opportunity to be heard, both on the application and the merits of the policy, may be required in order to prevent a fettering of discretion.

In support, the learned author cites *R v. Criminal Injuries Compensation Board, ex p. Ince* [1973] 1 WLR 1334, at p. 1345, *per* Megaw LJ:

> As to the question of the board's minutes, I think that justice and paragraph 22 of the Scheme alike require that if the board in any particular case are minded to be guided by any principle laid down in any pre-existing minute of the board, the applicant must be informed of the existence and terms of that minute, so that he can, if he wishes, make his submissions with regard thereto: that is, submissions on the questions whether the principle is right or wrong in relation to the terms of the Scheme and whether the principle, if right, is applicable or inapplicable to the facts of the particular case.

Another comment from de Smith is found in the section on the right to a hearing, at p. 182, note 92:

> Whilst it would be going too far to assert that in all circumstances there is an implied right to be apprised of and to argue against policy proposals, there are some indications pointing in this direction: see for example, *British Oxygen Co. Ltd. v. Board of Trade* [1971] AC 610, 625, 631 (desirable that notice be given to applicants for industrial grants of any rule or policy generally followed by the Department, and an opportunity for the applicants to make representations on the soundness or applicability of the policy or rule: this would make applications more effective and prevent the Department from fettering its statutory discretion).

. . .

In the discussion of "The Duty of Disclosure" Aronson and Franklin in *Review of Administrative Action* write, at p. 183:

> The extent to which policy, expertise and independent inquiry are integral to the decision-making process will inevitably vary according to the subject matter for decision or investigation. But even in a trial-type hearing, the adjudicator is not bound exclusively by the parties' proofs and arguments, and will need to accommodate public and institutional interests. The more "polycentric," policy-oriented or technical a problem, the greater is the pressure on decision-makers to seek out solutions, to confer separately with interested persons, and to use their experience to find a settlement. The ability of administrators to inform themselves, and to apply their expertise and accumulated experience, and the expectation that they will do so, makes the duty of disclosure sometimes difficult to define, and to observe. *At the same time, however, it enhances the importance of the duty. Disclosure can act as an important safeguard against the use of inaccurate material or untested theories.* It can also contribute to the efficiency of the hearing by directing argument and information to the relevant issues and materials. [Emphasis added.]

Wade, *Administrative Law* (4th ed. 1977) states, at p. 470:

> Policy is of course the basis of administrative discretion in a great many cases, but this is no reason why the discretion should not be exercised fairly *vis-a-vis* any person who will be adversely affected. The decision will require the weighing of any such person's interests against the claims of policy; and this cannot fairly be done without giving that person an opportunity to be heard.

In my opinion, therefore, the full Board hearing deprived the appellant of a full opportunity to present evidence and submissions and constituted a denial of natural justice.

While it cannot be determined with certainty from the record that a policy developed at the full Board hearing and not disclosed to the parties was a factor in the decision, it is fatal to the decision of the Board that this is what might very well have happened.

While achieving uniformity in the decisions of individual boards is a laudable purpose, it cannot be done at the expense of the rules of natural justice. If it is the desire of the legislature that this purpose be pursued it is free to authorize the full board procedure. It is worthy of note that Parliament has given first reading to Bill C-40, a revised *Broadcasting Act* which authorizes individual panels to consult with the Commission and officers of the Commission in order to achieve uniformity in the application of policy (s. 19(4)). Provision is made, however, for the timely issue of guidelines and statements with respect to matters within the jurisdiction of the Commission.

Section 114

The respondents do not contend that if a breach of natural justice has occurred, the privative clause in s. 108 of the Act would apply. They have, however, submitted that if there was a breach of natural justice, it was technical only and hence no remedy should be available. The respondents cite s. 114 of the Act as well as *Toshiba Corp. v. Anti-Dumping Tribunal* (1984), 8 Admin. LR 173 (FCA). Section 114 reads:

> 114. No proceedings under this Act are invalid by reason of any defect of form or any technical irregularity and no such proceedings shall be quashed or set aside if no substantial wrong or miscarriage of justice has occurred.

Toshiba concerned a preliminary staff report prepared for the Anti-Dumping Tribunal which was not revealed to the parties and which the Court described as "a dangerous practice." Nonetheless, the Court of Appeal was satisfied that the report contained only matters of general knowledge or was based upon facts and sources which were brought out at the hearing in such a manner that the parties had the opportunity to test them. Thus any breach of natural justice was minor and inconsequential and the application for judicial review was dismissed.

The submission that there is no prejudice as a result of a technical breach of rules of natural justice requires that the party making the allegation establish this fact. To do so in this case it would be necessary for the respondents to satisfy the court that the matters discussed were all matters that had been brought out at the hearing. This has not occurred; unlike *Toshiba* there is no report or minutes of the full board meeting against which the hearing proceedings can be compared. The appellant can hardly be expected to establish prejudice when it was not privy to the discussion before the full Board and there is no evidence as to what in fact was discussed. In the absence of such evidence the gravity of the breach of natural justice cannot be assessed, and I cannot conclude that no substantial wrong has occurred.

Section 102(13)

Nor can I conclude that the full Board procedure is saved by virtue of s. 102(13) of the *Labour Relations Act*. Section 102(13) reads:

102. ...

(13) The Board shall determine its own practice and procedure *but shall give full opportunity to the parties to any proceedings to present their evidence and to make their submissions,* and the Board may, subject to the approval of the Lieutenant Governor in Council, make rules governing its practice and procedure and the exercise of its powers and prescribing such forms as are considered advisable. [Emphasis added.]

I recognize the importance of deference to a Board's choice of procedures expressed by this Court in *Komo Construction Inc. v. Commission des Relations de Travail du Québec* [1968] SCR 172 at 176, *per* Pigeon J:

While upholding the rule that the fundamental principles of justice must be respected, it is important to refrain from imposing a code of procedure upon an entity which the law has sought to make master of its own procedure.

However, in this case the appellant was not given a full opportunity to present evidence and make submissions, which is an explicit limit placed by statute on the Board's control of its procedure. Furthermore, when the rules of natural justice collide with a practice of the Board, the latter must give way.

[Lamer CJC concurred with Sopinka J. The judgment of Wilson, La Forest, L'Heureux-Dubé, Gonthier, and McLachlin JJ was delivered by]

GONTHIER J:

. . .

It will be noted that Chairman Adams does not claim that the purpose of full Board meetings is to achieve absolute uniformity in decisions made by different panels in factually similar situations. Chairman Adams accepts that "no one panel of the Board can bind another panel by any decision rendered" (at p. 2001). The methods used at those meetings to discuss policy issues reflect the need to maintain an atmosphere wherein each attending Board member retains the freedom to make up his mind on any given issue and to preserve the panel members' ultimate responsibility for the outcome of the final decision. Thus, Chairman Adams states that discussions at full Board meetings are limited to policy issues, that the facts of each case must be taken as presented and that no votes are taken nor any attendance recorded, at p. 2002. ... At page 2004 of his reasons, Chairman Adams confirmed that the impugned meeting was held in accordance with the above-mentioned rules.

Finally, Chairman Adams rejected the idea that full Board meetings could have an overbearing effect on the panel members' capacity to decide the issues at hand in accordance with their opinion, at p. 2003. ... It follows that the full board meetings held by the Board are designed to promote discussion on important policy issues and to provide an opportunity for members to share their personal experiences in the regulation of labour relations. There is no evidence that the particular meeting impugned in this case was used to impose any given opinion upon the members of the panel or that the spirit of discussion and exchange sought through those meetings was not present during those deliberations. Moreover, three sets of reasons were issued by the members of the panel, one member dissenting in part while another dissented on the principal substantive issue at stake in this case. If this meeting had been held for the purpose of imposing policy directives on the members of the panel, it certainly did not meet its objective.

. . .

III—Analysis

(a) Introduction

It is useful to begin with a summary of the arguments submitted by the parties. The appellant argues that the practice of holding full board meetings on policy issues constitutes a breach of a rule of natural justice appropriately referred to as "he who decides must hear." According to the appellant's version of this rule, a decision-maker must not be placed in a situation where he can be "influenced" by persons who have not heard the evidence or the arguments. Thus, the appellant's position is that panel members must be totally shielded from any discussion which may cause them to change their minds even if this change of opinion is honest, because the possibility of undue pressure by other Board members is too ominous to be compatible with principles of natural justice. The appellant also claims that full board meetings do not provide the parties with an adequate opportunity to answer arguments which may be voiced by Board members who have not heard the case.

It is important to note at the outset that the appellant's arguments raise issues with respect to two important and distinct rules of natural justice. It has often been said that these rules can be separated in two categories, namely "that an adjudicator be disinterested and unbiased (*nemo judex in causa sua*) and that the parties be given adequate notice and opportunity to be heard (*audi alteram partem*)": Evans, *de Smith's Judicial Review of Administrative Action* (4th ed. 1980), at p. 156; see also Pépin and Ouellette, *Principes de contentieux administratif* (2nd ed. 1982), at pp. 148-49. While the appellant does not claim that the panel was biased, it does claim that full board meetings may prevent a panel member from deciding the topic of discussion freely and independently from the opinions voiced at the meeting. Independence is an essential ingredient of the capacity to act fairly and judicially and any procedure or practice which unduly reduces this capacity must surely be contrary to the rules of natural justice.

The respondent union argues that the practice of holding full board meetings on important policy issues is one which is justified for the reasons set forth by Chairman Adams in the reconsideration decision quoted previously.

Before embarking on an analysis of these arguments, one should keep in mind the difference between a full board meeting and a full board hearing: a full board hearing is simply a normal hearing where representations are made by both parties in front of an enlarged panel comprised of all the members of the Board in the manner prescribed by s. 102 of the *Labour Relations Act*; on the other hand, a full board meeting does not entail representations by the parties since they are not invited to or even notified of the meeting. The procedure recommended by the McRuer Report is somewhat different in that it entails the presence of the parties at an informal meeting where they would have the right to answer the arguments raised by members of the Board. In this case, the parties have not made any arguments on the relative virtues of these procedures and have restricted their arguments to the legality of the full board meeting procedure in relation to the rules of natural justice.

I agree with the respondent union that the rules of natural justice must take into account the institutional constraints faced by an administrative tribunal. These tribunals are created to increase the efficiency of the administration of justice and are often called upon to handle heavy caseloads. It is unrealistic to expect an administrative tribunal such as the Board to abide strictly by the rules applicable to courts of law. In fact, it has long been recognized that the rules of natural justice do not have a fixed content irrespective of the nature of the tribunal and of the institutional constraints it faces. This principle was reiterated by Dickson J (as he then was) in *Kane v. Board of Governors of the University of British Columbia* [1980] 1 SCR 1105 at 1113:

> As a constituent of the autonomy it enjoys, the tribunal must observe natural justice which, as Harman LJ said, [*Ridge v. Baldwin*, [1963] 1 QB 539, 578] is only "fair play in action." *In any particular case, the requirements of natural justice will depend on "the circumstances of the case, the nature of the inquiry, the rules under which the tribunal is acting, the subject-matter which is being dealt with, and so forth": per* Tucker LJ in *Russell v. Duke of Norfolk* [1949] 1 All ER 109, 118. To abrogate the rules of natural justice, express language or necessary implication must be found in the statutory instrument. [Emphasis added.]

The main issue is whether, given the importance of the policy issue at stake in this case and the necessity of maintaining a high degree of quality and coherence in Board decisions, the rules of natural justice allow a full board meeting to take place subject to the conditions outlined by the Court of Appeal and, if not, whether a procedure which allows the parties to be present, such as a full board hearing, is the only acceptable alternative. The advantages of the practice of holding full board meetings must be weighed against the disadvantages involved in holding discussions in the absence of the parties.

(b) The Consequences of the Institutional Constraints Faced by the Board

The *Labour Relations Act* has entrusted the Board with the responsibility of fostering harmonious labour relations through collective bargaining, as appears clearly in the preamble of the Act:

> WHEREAS it is in the public interest of the Province of Ontario to further harmonious relations between employers and employees by encouraging the practice and procedure of collective bargaining between employers and trade unions as the freely designated representatives of employees.

The Board has been granted the powers thought necessary to achieve this task, not the least of which is the power to decide in a final and conclusive manner all matters which fall within its jurisdiction: s. 106(1) of the *Labour Relations Act*. As was stated by Chairman Adams in his reconsideration decision, the Board has also been given very broad discretionary powers as is the case with the power to determine what constitutes "bargaining in good faith" (s. 15).

The immensity of the task entrusted to the Board should not be underestimated. As Chairman Adams wrote in the reconsideration decision, the Board had a caseload of

3,189 cases to handle in 1982-83 and employed 12 full-time chairman and vice-chairmen, 4 part-time vice-chairmen, 10 full-time Board members representing labour and management as well as another 22 part-time Board members to hear and decide those cases. The Board's full-time chairman and vice-chairmen have an average caseload of 266 cases per year. Moreover, the tripartite nature of the Board makes it necessary to have an equal representation from management and labour unions on each panel as appears clearly from s. 102 of the *Labour Relations Act*:

> 102(1) The Ontario Labour Relations Board is continued.
>
> (2) The Board shall be composed of a chairman, one or more vice-chairmen and as many members equal in number representative of employers and employees respectively as the Lieutenant Governor in Council considers proper, all of whom shall be appointed by the Lieutenant Governor in Council.
>
> . . .
>
> (9) The chairman or a vice-chairman, one member representative of employers and one member representative of employees constitute a quorum and are sufficient for the exercise of all the jurisdiction and powers of the Board.
>
> . . .
>
> (11) The decision of the majority of the members of the Board present and constituting a quorum is the decision of the Board, but, if there is no majority, the decision of the chairman or vice-chairman governs.

The rules governing the quorum of any panel of the Board are especially suited for panels of three although they do not appear to prevent the formation of a larger panel. However, even if the *Labour Relations Act* allows full board hearings, such a procedure would not necessarily be practical every time an important policy issue is at stake.

Indeed, it is apparent from the size of the Board's caseload and from the number of persons which would sit on such an enlarged panel that holding full board hearings is a highly impractical way of solving important policy issues. Furthermore, the difficulties involved in setting up a panel comprised of an equal number of management and labour representatives and in scheduling such a meeting are also obvious when one takes into consideration the large number of Board members who would have to be present. In fact, one wonders whether it is really possible to call a full board hearing every time an important policy issue arises. The solution proposed in the McRuer Report, i.e., allowing the parties to be present and to answer the arguments made at the meeting, would entail similar difficulties since their presence would necessitate some formal procedure and involve organizational difficulties as well.

The first rationale behind the need to hold full board meetings on important policy issues is the importance of benefiting from the acquired experience of all the members, chairman and vice-chairmen of the Board. Moreover, the tripartite nature of the Board makes it even more imperative to promote exchanges of opinions between management and union representatives. As was pointed out clearly by Dickson J (as he then was) in *Canadian Union of Public Employees, Local 963 v. New Brunswick Liquor Corp.* [1979] 2 SCR 227, the primary purpose of the creation of administrative bodies such as the Ontario Labour Relations Board is to confer a wide jurisdiction to solve labour disputes on those who are best able, in light of their experience, to provide satisfactory solutions to these disputes, at pp. 235-36:

> Section 101 constitutes a clear statutory direction on the part of the Legislature that public sector labour matters be promptly and finally decided by the Board. Privative clauses of this type are typically found in labour relations legislation. The rationale for protection of a labour board's decisions within jurisdiction is straightforward and compelling. The labour board is a specialized tribunal which administers a comprehensive statute regulating labour relations. In the administration of that regime, a board is called upon not only to find facts and decide questions of law, but also to exercise its understanding of the body of jurisprudence that has developed around the collective bargaining system, as understood in Canada, and its labour relations sense acquired from accumulated experience in the area.

The rules of natural justice should not discourage administrative bodies from taking advantage of the accumulated experience of its members. On the contrary, the rules of natural justice should in their application reconcile the characteristics and exigencies of decision-making by specialized tribunals with the procedural rights of the parties.

The second rationale for the practice of holding full board meetings is the fact that the large number of persons who participate in Board decisions creates the possibility that different panels will decide similar issues in a different manner. It is obvious that coherence in administrative decision-making must be fostered. The outcome of disputes should not depend on the identity of the persons sitting on the panel for this result would be [Translation] "difficult to reconcile with the notion of equality before the law, which is one of the main corollaries of the rule of law, and perhaps also the most intelligible one," Morissette, "Le contrôle de la competence d'attribution: thèse, antithèse et synthèse" (1986) 16 *RDUS* 591, at p. 632. Given the large number of decisions rendered in the field of labour law, the Board is justified in taking appropriate measures to ensure that conflicting results are not inadvertently reached in similar cases. The fact that the Board's decisions are protected by a privative clause (s. 108) makes it even more imperative to take measures such as full board meetings in order to avoid such conflicting results. At the same time, the decision of one panel cannot bind another panel and the measures taken by the Board to foster coherence in its decision-making must not compromise any panel member's capacity to decide in accordance with his conscience and opinions.

A full board meeting is a forum for discussion which, in Cory JA's words (as he then was) is "no more than an amplification of the research of the hearing panel carried out before they delivered their decision" (at p. 517). Like many other judicial practices, however, full board meetings entail some imperfections, especially with respect to the opportunity to be heard and the judicial independence of the decision-maker, as is correctly pointed out by Professors Blache and Comtois in "La décision institutionnelle" (1986) 16 *RDUS* 645, at pp. 707-8:

> [TRANSLATION] There are advantages and disadvantages to institutionalizing the decision-making process. The main advantages with which it is credited are increasing the efficiency of the organization as well as the quality and consistency of decisions. It is felt that institutional decisions tend to promote the equal treatment of individuals in similar circumstances, increase the likelihood of better quality decisions and lead to a better allocation of

resources. Against this it is feared that institutionalization creates a danger of the introduction, without the parties' knowledge, of evidence and ideas obtained extraneously and reduces the decision-maker's personal responsibility for the decision to be made.

The question before this Court is whether the disadvantages involved in this practice are sufficiently important to warrant a holding that it constitutes a breach of the rules of natural justice or whether full board meetings are consistent with these rules provided that certain safeguards be observed.

(c) The Judicial Independence of Panel Members in the Context of a Full Board Meeting

The appellant argues that persons who did not hear the evidence or the submissions of the parties should not be in a position to "influence" those who will ultimately participate in the decision, i.e., vote for one side or the other. The appellant cites the following authorities in support of its argument [a list of cases is omitted].

. . .

In all those decisions with the exception of *Re Rogers* [(1978), 20 Nfld. & PEIR 484], some of the members of the panel which rendered the impugned decision had not heard all the evidence or all the representations of the parties: their vote was cast even though some of the members of these panels did not have the benefit of assessing the credibility of the witnesses or the validity of the factual and legal arguments. I agree that, as a general rule, the members of a panel who actually participate in the decision must have heard all the evidence as well as all the arguments presented by the parties and in this respect I adopt Pratte J's words in *Doyle v. Restrictive Trade Practices Commission* [[1985] 1 FC 362] at 368-69:

> The important issue is whether the maxim "he who decides must hear" invoked by the applicant should be applied here.
>
> This maxim expresses a well-known rule according to which, where a tribunal is responsible for hearing and deciding a case, only those members of the tribunal who heard the case may take part in the decision. It has sometimes been said that this rule is a corollary of the *audi alteram partem* rule. This is true to the extent a litigant is not truly "heard" unless he is heard by the person who will be deciding his case. ... This having been said, it must be realized that the rule "he who decides must hear," important though it may be, is based on the legislator's supposed intentions. It therefore does not apply where this is expressly stated to be the case; nor does it apply where a review of all the provisions governing the activities of a tribunal leads to the conclusion that the legislator could not have intended them to apply. Where the rule does apply to a tribunal, finally, it requires that all members of the tribunal who take part in a decision must have heard the evidence and the representations of the parties in the manner in which the law requires that they be heard.

In that case, one of the issues was whether it was sufficient for the members of the panel who had not heard the evidence to read the transcripts and this question was answered in the negative in light of the relevant statutory provisions. In this case, however, the members of the panel who participated in the impugned decision, i.e., Chairman Adams and Messrs. Wightman and Lee, heard all the evidence and all the arguments. It follows that the cases cited by the appellant cannot support its argument, nor can the presence of other Board members at the full board meeting amount to "participation" in the final decision even though their contribution to the discussions which took place at that meeting can be seen as a "participation" in the decision-making process in the widest sense of that expression.

However, the appellant claims that the following extract from the reasons of Romer J in *R v. Huntingdon Confirming Authority* [1929] 1 KB 698 constitutes the basis of a rule whereby decision-makers who have heard all the evidence and representations should not be influenced by persons who have not, at p. 717:

> Further, I would merely like to point this out: that at that meeting of May 16 there were present three justices who had never heard the evidence that had been given on oath on April 25. There was a division of opinion. The resolution in favour of confirmation was carried by eight to two, and *it is at least possible that that majority was induced to vote in the way it did by the eloquence of those members who had not been present on April 25, to whom the facts were entirely unknown.* [Emphasis added.]

Thus, Romer J was of the opinion that the influence of those who did not hear the evidence could go beyond their vote and that this influence constituted a denial of natural justice. Following that reasoning, it was held in *Re Rogers* that the presence of a person who heard neither the evidence nor the representations at one of the meetings where a quorum of the Prince Edward Island Land Use Commission was deliberating invalidated the decision of the Commission even though that person did not vote on the matter. The opposite result was reached in *Underwater Gas Developers Ltd. v. Ontario Labour Relations Board* (1960) 24 DLR (2d) 673 (Ont. CA), where it was held that the presence of Board members who neither heard the evidence nor voted on the matter did not invalidate the Board's decision, at p. 675.

I am unable to agree with the proposition that any discussion with a person who has not heard the evidence necessarily vitiates the resulting decision because this discussion might "influence" the decision-maker. In this respect, I adopt Meredith CJCP's words in *Re Toronto and Hamilton Highway Commission and Crabb* (1916) 37 OLR 656 (CA), at p. 659:

> The Board is composed of persons occupying positions analogous to those of judges rather than of arbitrators merely; and it is not suggested that they heard any evidence behind the back of either party; the most that can be said is that they—that is, those members of the Board who heard the evidence and made the award—allowed another member of the Board, who had not heard the evidence, or taken part in the inquiry before, to read the evidence and to express some of his views regarding the case to them. ... *[B]ut it is only fair to add that if every Judge's judgment were vitiated because he discussed the case with some other Judge a good many judgments existing as valid and unimpeachable ought to fall; and that if such discussions were prohibited many more judgments might fall in an appellate Court because of a defect which must have been detected if the subject had been so discussed.* [Emphasis added.]

The appellant's main argument against the practice of holding full board meetings is that these meetings can be used to fetter the independence of the panel members. Judicial independence is a long standing principle of our constitutional law which is also part of the rules of natural justice even in the absence of constitutional protection. It is useful to define this concept before discussing the effect of full board meetings on panel members. In *Beauregard v. Canada* [1986] 2 SCR 56, Dickson CJ described the "accepted core of the principle of judicial independence" as a complete liberty to decide a given case in accordance with one's conscience and opinions without interference from other persons, including judges, at p. 69:

> Historically, the generally accepted core of the principle of judicial independence has been the complete liberty of individual judges to hear and decide the cases that come before them: no outsider—be it government, pressure group, individual or even another judge— should interfere in fact, or attempt to interfere, with the way in which a judge conducts his or her case and makes his or her decision. This core continues to be central to the principle of judicial independence.

See also *Valente v. The Queen* [1985] 2 SCR 673, at pp. 686-87, and Benyekhlef, *Les garanties constitutionnelles relatives à l'indépendance du pouvoir judiciaire au Canada* (1988), at p. 48.

It is obvious that no outside interference may be used to compel or pressure a decision-maker to participate in discussions on policy issues raised by a case on which he must render a decision. It also goes without saying that a formalized consultation process could not be used to force or induce decision-makers to adopt positions with which they do not agree. Nevertheless, discussions with colleagues do not constitute, in and of themselves, infringements on the panel members' capacity to decide the issues at stake independently. A discussion does not prevent a decision-maker from adjudicating in accordance with his own conscience and opinions nor does it constitute an obstacle to this freedom. Whatever discussion may take place, the ultimate decision will be that of the decision-maker for which he assumes full responsibility.

The essential difference between full board meetings and informal discussions with colleagues is the possibility that moral suasion may be felt by the members of the panel if their opinions are not shared by other Board members, the chairman or vice-chairmen. However, decision-makers are entitled to change their minds whether this change of mind is the result of discussions with colleagues or the result of their own reflection on the matter. A decision-maker may also be swayed by the opinion of the majority of his colleagues in the interest of adjudicative coherence since this is a relevant criterion to be taken into consideration even when the decision-maker is not bound by any *stare decisis* rule.

It follows that the relevant issue in this case is not whether the practice of holding full board meetings can cause panel members to change their minds but whether this practice impinges on the ability of panel members to decide according to their opinions. There is nothing in the *Labour Relations Act* which gives either the chairman, the vice-chairmen or other Board members the power to impose his opinion on any other Board member. However, this *de jure* situation must not be thwarted by procedures which may effectively compel or induce panel members to decide against their own conscience and opinions.

It is pointed out that "justice should not only be done, but should manifestly and undoubtedly be seen to be done": see *Rex v. Sussex Justices*, [1924] 1 KB 256, at p. 259. This maxim applies whenever the circumstances create the danger of an injustice, for example when there is a reasonable apprehension of bias, even if the decision-maker has completely disregarded these circumstances. However, in my opinion and for the reasons which follow, the danger that full board meetings may fetter the judicial independence of panel members is not sufficiently present to give rise to a reasonable apprehension of bias or lack of independence within the meaning of the test stated by this Court in *Committee for Justice and Liberty v. National Energy Board*, [1978] 1 SCR 369, at p. 394, reaffirmed and applied as the criteria for judicial independence in *Valente v. The Queen*, *supra*, at p. 684:

> … the apprehension of bias must be a reasonable one, held by reasonable and right minded persons, applying themselves to the question and obtaining thereon the required information. In the words of the Court of Appeal, that test is "what would an informed person, viewing the matter realistically and practically—and having thought the matter through—conclude. …"

A full board meeting set up in accordance with the procedure described by Chairman Adams is not imposed: it is called at the request of the hearing panel or any of its members. It is carefully designed to foster discussion without trying to verify whether a consensus has been reached: no minutes are kept, no votes are taken, attendance is voluntary and presence at the full board meeting is not recorded. The decision is left entirely to the hearing panel. It cannot be said that this practice is meant to convey to panel members the message that the opinion of the majority of the Board members present has to be followed. On the other hand, it is true that a consensus can be measured without a vote and that this institutionalization of the consultation process carries with it a potential for greater influence on the panel members. However, the criteria for independence is not absence of influence but rather the freedom to decide according to one's own conscience and opinions. In fact, the record shows that each panel member held to his own opinion since Mr. Wightman dissented and Mr. Lee only concurred in part with Chairman Adams. It is my opinion, in agreement with the Court of Appeal, that the full board meeting was an important element of a legitimate consultation process and not a participation in the decision of persons who had not heard the parties. The Board's practice of holding full board meetings or the full board meeting held on September 23, 1983 would not be perceived by an informed person viewing the matter realistically and practically—and having thought the matter through—as having breached his right to a decision reached by an independent tribunal thereby infringing this principle of natural justice.

(d) Full Board Meetings and the Audi Alteram Partem Rule

Full board meetings held on an *ex parte* basis do entail some disadvantages from the point of view of the *audi alteram partem* rule because the parties are not aware of what is said at those meetings and do not have an opportunity to reply to new arguments made by the persons present at the meeting. In addition, there is always the danger that the persons present at the meeting may discuss the evidence.

For the purpose of the application of the *audi alteram partem* rule, a distinction must be drawn between discussions on factual matters and discussions on legal or policy issues. In every decision, panel members must determine what the facts are, what legal standards apply to those facts and, finally, they must assess the evidence in accordance with these legal standards. In this case, for example, the Board had to determine which events led to the decision to close the Hamilton plant and, in turn, decide whether the appellant had failed to bargain in good faith by not informing of an impending plant closing either on the basis that a *"de facto* decision" had been taken or on some other basis. The determination and assessment of facts are delicate tasks which turn on the credibility of the witnesses and an overall evaluation of the relevancy of all the information presented as evidence. As a general rule, these tasks cannot be properly performed by persons who have not heard all the evidence and the rules of natural justice do not allow such persons to vote on the result. Their participation in discussions dealing with such factual issues is less problematic when there is no participation in the final decision. However, I am of the view that generally such discussions constitute a breach of the rules of natural justice because they allow persons other than the parties to make representations on factual issues when they have not heard the evidence.

It is already recognized that no new evidence may be presented to panel members in the absence of the parties: *Kane v. Board of Governors of the University of British Columbia, supra,* at pp. 1113-14. The appellant does not claim that new evidence was adduced at the meeting and the record does not disclose any such breach of the *audi alteram partem* rule. The defined practice of the Board at full board meetings is to discuss policy issues on the basis of the facts as they were determined by the panel. The benefits to be derived from the proper use of this consultation process must not be denied because of the mere concern that this established practice might be disregarded, in the absence of any evidence that this has occurred. In this case, the record contains no evidence that factual issues were discussed by the Board at the September 23, 1983 meeting.

In his reasons for judgment, Rosenberg J [delivering the judgment of the majority in the Divisional Court] has raised the issue of whether discussions on policy issues can be completely divorced from the factual findings, at p. 95:

> In this case there was a minority report. Although the chairman states that the facts in the draft decision were taken as given there is no evidence before us to indicate whether the facts referred to those in the majority report or the minority report or both. Also, without in any way doubting the sincerity and integrity of the chairman in making such a statement, it is not practical to have all of the facts decided except against a background of determination of the principles of law involved. For example, a finding that Consolidated-Bathurst was seriously considering closing the Hamilton plant is of no significance if the requirement is that the failure to bargain in good faith must be a *de facto* decision to close. Accordingly, until the board decides what the test is the findings of fact cannot be finalized.

With respect, I must disagree with Rosenberg J if he suggests that it is not practical to discuss policy issues against the factual background provided by the panel.

It is true that the evidence cannot always be assessed in a final manner until the appropriate legal test has been chosen by the panel and until all the members of the panel have evaluated the credibility of each witness. However, it is possible to discuss the policy issues arising from the body of evidence filed before the panel even though this evidence may give rise to a wide variety of factual conclusions. In this case, Mr. Wightman seemed to disagree with Chairman Adams with respect to the credibility of the testimonies of some of the appellant's witnesses. While this might be relevant to Mr. Wightman's conclusions, it was nevertheless possible to outline the policy issues at stake in this case from the summary of the facts prepared by Chairman Adams. In turn, it was possible to outline the various tests which could be adopted by the panel and to discuss their appropriateness from a policy point of view. These discussions can be segregated from the factual decisions which will determine the outcome of the case once a test is adopted by the panel. The purpose of the policy discussions is not to determine which of the parties will eventually win the case but rather to outline the various legal standards which may be adopted by the Board and discuss their relative value.

Policy issues must be approached in a different manner because they have, by definition, an impact which goes beyond the resolution of the dispute between the parties. While they are adopted in a factual context, they are an expression of principle or standards akin to law. Since these issues involve the consideration of statutes, past decisions and perceived social needs, the impact of a policy decision by the Board is, to a certain extent, independent from the immediate interests of the parties even though it has an effect on the outcome of the complaint.

I have already outlined the reasons which justify discussions between panel members and other members of the Board. It is now necessary to consider the conditions under which full board meetings must be held in order to abide by the *audi alteram partem* rule. In this respect, the only possible breach of this rule arises where a new policy or a new argument is proposed at a full board meeting and a decision is rendered on the basis of this policy or argument without giving the parties an opportunity to respond.

I agree with Cory JA (as he then was) that the parties must be informed of any new ground on which they have not made any representations. In such a case, the parties must be given a reasonable opportunity to respond and the calling of a supplementary hearing may be appropriate. The decision to call such a hearing is left to the Board as master of its own procedure: s. 102(13) of the *Labour Relations Act*. However, this is not a case where a new policy undisclosed or unknown to the parties was introduced or applied. The extent of the obligation of an employer engaged in collective bargaining to disclose information regarding the possibility of a plant closing was at the very heart of the debate from the outset and had been the subject of a policy decision previously in the *Westinghouse* case. The parties had every opportunity to deal with the matter at the hearing and indeed presented diverging proposals for modifying the policy. There is no evidence that any new grounds were put forward at the meeting and each of the reasons rendered by Chairman Adams and Messrs. Wightman and Lee simply adopts one of the arguments presented by the parties and summarized at pp. 1427-30 of the Chairman Adams' decision. Though the reasons are expressed in great detail, the appellant does not identify any of them as being new nor does it contend that it did not have an opportunity to be heard or to deal with them.

Since its earliest development, the essence of the *audi alteram partem* rule has been to give the parties a "fair opportunity of answering the case against [them]": Evans, *de Smith's Judicial Review of Administrative Action, supra*, at p. 158. It is true that on factual matters the parties must be given a "fair opportunity … for correcting or contradicting any relevant statement prejudicial to their view": *Board of Education v. Rice* [1911] AC 179, at p. 182, see also *Local Government Board v. Arlidge* [1915] AC 120, at pp. 133 and 141, and *Kane v. Board of Governors of the University of British Columbia, supra*, at p. 1113. However, the rule with respect to legal or policy arguments not raising issues of fact is somewhat more lenient because the parties only have the right to state their case adequately and to answer contrary arguments. This right does not encompass the right to repeat arguments every time the panel convenes to discuss the case. For obvious practical reasons, superior courts, in particular courts of appeal, do not have to call back the parties every time an argument is discredited by a member of the panel and it would be anomalous to require more of administrative tribunals through the rules of natural justice. Indeed, a reason for their very existence is the specialized knowledge and expertise which they are expected to apply.

I therefore conclude that the consultation process described by Chairman Adams in his reconsideration decision does not violate the *audi alteram partem* rule provided that factual issues are not discussed at a full board meeting and that the parties are given a reasonable opportunity to respond to any new ground arising from such a meeting. In this case, an important policy issue, namely the validity of the test adopted in the *Westinghouse* case, was at stake and the Board was entitled to call a full board meeting to discuss it. There is no evidence that any other issues were discussed or indeed that any other arguments were raised at that meeting and it follows that the appellant has failed to prove that it has been the victim of any violation of the *audi alteram partem* rule. Indeed, the decision itself indicates that it rests on considerations known to the parties upon which they had full opportunity to be heard.

IV—Conclusion

The institutionalization of the consultation process adopted by the Board provides a framework within which the experience of the chairman, vice-chairmen and members of the Board can be shared to improve the overall quality of its decisions. Although respect for the judicial independence of Board members will impede total coherence in decision-making, the Board through this consultation process seeks to avoid inadvertent contradictory results and to achieve the highest degree of coherence possible under these circumstances. An institutionalized consultation process will not necessarily lead Board members to reach a consensus but it provides a forum where such a consensus can be reached freely as a result of thoughtful discussion on the issues at hand.

The advantages of an institutionalized consultation process are obvious and I cannot agree with the proposition that this practice necessarily conflicts with the rules of natural justice. The rules of natural justice must have the flexibility required to take into account the institutional pressures faced by modern administrative tribunals as well as the risks inherent in such a practice. In this respect, I adopt the words of Professors Blache and Comtois in "La décision institutionnelle," *supra*, at p. 708:

> [Translation] The institutionalizing of decisions exists in our law and appears to be there to stay. The problem is thus not whether institutional decisions should be sanctioned, but to organize the process in such a way as to limit its dangers. There is nothing revolutionary in this approach: it falls naturally into the tradition of English and Canadian jurisprudence that the rules of natural justice should be flexibly interpreted.

The consultation process adopted by the Board formally recognizes the disadvantages inherent in full board meetings, namely that the judicial independence of the panel members may be fettered by such a practice and that the parties do not have the opportunity to respond to all the arguments raised at the meeting. The safeguards attached to this consultation process are, in my opinion, sufficient to allay any fear of violations of the rules of natural justice provided as well that the parties be advised of any new evidence or grounds and given an opportunity to respond. The balance so achieved between the rights of the parties and the institutional pressures the Board faces are consistent with the nature and purpose of the rules of natural justice.

Appeal dismissed.

NOTES

1. *Law, fact, and policy.* To what extent do the minority and majority judgments proceed from different premises about the nature of law and, in particular, its relationship to policy? How would you locate them within the broad categories of public law thought?

If Sopinka J was right to draw a sharp distinction between law and policy, describe how the board could think sensibly about the scope of the statutory duty to bargain in good faith without also considering matters such as the appropriate balance between employer interests in not revealing prematurely its corporate plans and union interests in obtaining complete information, and the public policy implications of how these interests are balanced, especially for the province's ability to retain existing industry and attract new investment.

Are you persuaded by Sopinka J's reliance on the *Innisfil Township* case (chapter 4 of this text) as authority for the proposition that "policy" is to be characterized as a question of fact? Incidentally, counsel for the winning appellants in that case was John Sopinka QC.

Nor is the distinction between fact and policy that Gonthier J relies on always clearcut. The collective experience and expertise of the agency may assist individual members to draw the appropriate inference from the evidence when deciding regularly recurring questions of fact on which direct evidence may be lacking, incomplete, or unreliable. For example, labour boards often have to decide whether a person has a genuine religious objection to belonging to a union, or whether an employer's conduct is intended to hinder attempts to unionize employees. The Immigration and Refugee Board is regularly required to decide whether a couple's marriage is genuine, and not an "immigration marriage of convenience," or whether an applicant for a Canadian visa is, as he alleges, the 18-year-old unmarried son of his sponsor, a Canadian permanent resident, when the country of origin does not maintain a comprehensive register of births and marriages.

2. *Tribunal chairs and members' independence.* One factor not mentioned by the majority is the power (actual or perceived) possessed by the chairs of the Ontario Labour Relations Board and many other administrative agencies. It is reasonable to expect that members are liable to give particular weight to the opinions expressed at full-board meetings and informally by the chair and perhaps other senior members as well. This may be because their views are well-informed and persuasive. But it may also be because members believe that if their decisions do not conform to the position taken by the chair, their prospects of reappointment at the end of their term are liable to be diminished. Ministers often rely heavily on the recommendations of the chair when deciding whether to reappoint a member. (See, for example, Ontario's *Adjudicative Tribunals Accountability, Governance and Appointments Act, 2009*, SO 2009, c. 33, Sched. 5, s. 14(4), which specifies that tribunal member reappointments will only be made upon the chair's recommendation.)

Unlike judges, members of administrative agencies are typically appointed for relatively short terms (three years is not uncommon), with the possibility of reappointment. This contributes to the hierarchical structure of many administrative agencies.

In November 1994, the deputy chair of the Immigration and Refugee Board was suspended by the chair, following complaints from some members that he had "pressured" them to increase the percentage of refugee claims that they accepted and had "called them to account" for some of the negative decisions that they had rendered in the past.

3. *Adjudication or rulemaking?* It has been suggested that, in order to retain the effectiveness of the right to be heard, it would be preferable for an agency panel when encountering a major policy issue that has arisen in the course of a proceeding to adjourn the hearing so that, emergency situations apart, the agency can initiate a notice and comment procedure and make a generic rule or policy. This would broaden the range of participation beyond the parties to the adjudicative proceeding in which the issue first arose. It would also enable the panel simply to apply the rule or policy to the facts of the particular dispute, without the need to consult other members of the agency; this would avoid jeopardizing the parties' procedural right to address the decision-makers directly.

What do you think about this suggestion? See further, on this and other aspects of the case, Roman (1990), 42 *Admin. LR* 109 and Janisch, "Consistency, Rulemaking and *Consolidated-Bathurst*" (1991), 16 *Queen's LJ* 95.

For a legislative endorsement of intra-agency consultation, see the *Broadcasting Act*, SC 1991, c. 11, s. 20(4), which provides that the members of a panel established to hear a matter *shall* consult with the Canadian Radio-television and Telecommunications Commission (CRTC), and *may* consult with any officer of the commission for the purpose of ensuring a consistent interpretation of broadcasting and regulatory policy set out in the Act, and of the regulations made by the commission.

Tremblay v. Québec (Commission des affaires sociales)
[1992] 1 SCR 952 (Que.)

GONTHIER J: The case at bar provides an opportunity for the Court to apply the rules already stated by it in *IWA v. Consolidated-Bathurst Packaging Ltd.* [1990] 1 SCR 282, on so-called "institutional" decisions. The Court must accordingly decide whether the decision of the appellant, the Commission des affaires sociales ("the Commission"), which refused to reimburse the respondent Noémie Tremblay for certain dressings and bandages was made contrary to the rules of natural justice. This decision of the Commission was the end result of an internal consultation process established by the Commission to ensure consistency in its decisions.

At the hearing, the Court dismissed the principal and incidental appeals from the bench with costs. The reasons that follow are in support of that disposition.

Statement of Facts

At the relevant time, the respondent Noémie Tremblay was receiving social aid. The Ministère de la Main-d'oeuvre et de la Sécurité du revenu denied her claim to be reimbursed for the cost of certain dressings and bandages. The respondent appealed this decision to the Commission in accordance with the *Social Aid Act*, RSQ 1977, c. A-16. This appeal is governed by the *Act respecting the Commission des affaires sociales*, RSQ, c. C-34.

On January 20, 1983 the appeal was heard in the social aid and allowances division by a "quorum" consisting of a member of the Commission, Mr. Claude Pothier, and an assessor, Mrs. Dolorès Landry. The point at issue was whether the dressings and bandages came within the definition of "medical equipment" within the meaning of s. 10.04 of the *Regulation on Social Aid* then in effect. As this point was purely one of law, the parties proceeded by admissions and argued in writing. No witnesses were heard.

At the close of the hearing, Mr. Pothier undertook to draft a decision which he then sent to Mrs. Landry for comments and approval. This draft decision was favourable to the respondent. Mrs. Landry signed the draft, which was then sent to the Commission's legal counsel for verification and consultation in accordance with established practice at the Commission. As the legal counsel was on vacation, it was the president of the Commission, Hon. Gilles Poirier, who reviewed the draft. He then sent the decision-makers a memorandum dated March 8, 1983 in which he explained his position, which was contrary to their own. On receiving this memorandum, Mr. Pothier asked that the point of law raised by the case be submitted to the "consensus table" machinery of the Commission. The respondent's case was accordingly placed on the agenda for the next plenary meeting of the Commission.

At that meeting, a majority of members present supported the viewpoint opposed to that originally taken by Mr. Pothier and Mrs. Landry. Shortly after this meeting, Mrs. Landry changed her mind and decided to write an opinion unfavourable to the respondent. As the quorum was thereby in disagreement, the matter was submitted to the president of the Commission, Judge Poirier, as required by the *Act respecting the Commission des affaires sociales*. Judge Poirier then decided the matter in the way he had already indicated to the decision-makers in his memorandum of March 8, 1983. The Commission accordingly dismissed the respondent's appeal: [1983] CAS 713 (*sub nom. Aide social—86*).

The respondent then challenged the Commission's decision by an action in nullity: she alleged a breach of the rules of natural justice. The respondent further asked that the first draft decision written by the members of the Commission who heard her appeal be declared the Commission's true decision. In the Superior Court, Dugas J concluded that the Commission's decision contravened the rules of natural justice, but he refused to regard the first draft of the decision as the Commission's true decision: [1985] CS 490. The Court of Appeal upheld the trial judgment: [1989] RJQ 2053.

On the principal appeal, Jacques and Mailhot JJA concluded that the Commission's decision was made in breach of the rules of natural justice, Monet JA dissenting; on the incidental appeal, Monet and Mailhot JJA refused to regard the first version of the Commission's decision as the true one. Jacques JA differed on this point.

Relevant Legislation

An Act respecting the Commission des affaires sociales, RSQ, c. C-34

> 10. A matter shall be decided by the majority of the members and assessors having heard it.
>
> When opinions are equally divided on a question, it shall be decided by the president or the vice-president he designates.
>
> . . .

Points at Issue

Principal Appeal

1. Should the Superior Court have allowed the objection to the evidence made by counsel for the Commission and based on deliberative secrecy?

2. Does the machinery established by the Commission to ensure adjudicative coherence give rise to a reasonable apprehension of bias?

3. Is the part played by the president in the case at bar a breach of the rules of natural justice?

Incidental Appeal

4. Should document P-10 (the first "decision") be regarded as the Commission's true decision?

Analysis

I will deal with these four questions in order.

1. Confidentiality of Deliberations

At the trial, counsel for the Commission made several objections to the evidence based on the principle of deliberative secrecy. The Commission objected in particular to the Commission secretary answering the questions of counsel for the respondent on the process for dealing with draft decisions within the Commission (approval by legal counsel, discussion at plenary meeting, and so on). In his judgment, Dugas J did not expressly deal with these objections; however, he dismissed them implicitly by ruling on the internal consultation procedure followed by the Commission.

In my opinion, the objections made by the Commission should be dismissed. The questions raised by the respondent did not touch on matters of substance or the decision-makers' thinking on such matters. These questions were directed instead at the *formal process* established by the Commission to ensure consistency in its decisions. They were concerned first with the institutional setting in which the decision was made and how it functioned, and second with its actual or apparent influence on the intellectual freedom of the decision-makers. This discussion was noted by Dugas J during the interrogatories themselves.

In the case of administrative tribunals, the difficulty of distinguishing between facts relating to an aspect of the deliberations which can be entered in evidence and those which cannot is quite understandable. The institutionalization of the decisions of administrative tribunals creates a tension between on one hand the traditional concept of deliberative secrecy and on the other the fundamental right of a party to know that the decision was made in accordance with the rules of natural justice. The institutionalized consultation process involving deliberation is the subject of rules of procedure designed to regulate the "consensus tables" process. Paradoxically, it is the public nature of these rules which, while highly desirable, may open the door to an action in nullity or an evocation. It may be questioned whether justice is seen to be done. Accordingly, the very special way in which the practice of administrative tribunals has developed requires the Court to become involved in areas into which, if a judicial tribunal were in question, it would probably refuse to venture:

> The judge's right to refuse to answer to the executive or legislative branches of government or their appointees as to *how* and why the judge arrived at a particular judicial conclusion is essential to the personal independence of the judge, one of the two main aspects of judicial independence: *Valente v. The Queen, supra; Beauregard v. Canada.* ... To entertain the demand that a judge testify before a civil body, an emanation of the legislature or executive, on how or why he or she made his or her decision would be to strike at the most sacrosanct core of judicial independence. [Emphasis added.]

(*MacKeigan v. Hickman* [1989] 2 SCR 796, at 830-31.)

Additionally, when there is no appeal from the decision of an administrative tribunal, as is the case with the Commission, that decision can only be reviewed in one way: as to legality by judicial review. It is of the very nature of judicial review to examine *inter alia* the decision-maker's decision-making process. Some of the grounds on which a decision may be challenged even concern the internal aspect of that process: for example, was the decision made at the dictate of a third party? Is it the result of the blind application of a previously established directive or policy? All these events accompany the deliberations or are part of them.

Accordingly, it seems to me that by the very nature of the control exercised over their decisions administrative tribunals cannot rely on deliberative secrecy to the same extent as judicial tribunals. Of course, secrecy remains the rule, but it may nonetheless be lifted when the litigant can present valid reasons for believing that the process followed did not comply with the rules of natural justice. This is indeed the conclusion at which the majority of the Court of Appeal arrived, at pp. 2074-75:

> [TRANSLATION] However, this confidentiality yields to application of the rules of natural justice, as observance of these rules is the bedrock of any legal system.
>
> In exceptional cases, therefore, the confidentiality requirement may be lifted when good grounds for doing so are first submitted to the tribunal.

I would therefore dismiss this first ground of appeal.

2. Legality of the "Institutionalized" Decision-Making Process Established by the Commission

Of the four questions raised by this appeal, the second is clearly the central one. The Commission is arguing that the consultation machinery which it has created is consistent with the rules of natural justice. It describes this consultation machinery not as a compulsory process of consultation but rather as an "automated" process, the purpose of which is not to impose any particular viewpoint but to assist the decision-maker by informing him of the existence of precedents.

The following internal directives are significant. They are taken from the "Directives on the holding of general meetings and creation of a reading committee" adopted by the Commission in September 1984:

> 4. A unanimous quorum may also suggest that a given problem be discussed at a general meeting, whether the decision has already been issued or not.

> 5. The president may suggest discussion at a general meeting of a unanimous decision, in cases where:
>
>   (a) the principles stated in that decision or its application contravene or depart from a consensus or precedent decided on by the Commission;
>   (b) the decision is a ruling in principle on a new point, or develops a new interpretation which sets an important precedent for the Commission.
>
>   . . .

> 34. Discussions will generally develop as follows:
>
>   • presentation by the persons concerned (members of the quorum or, if applicable, the legal counsel, a member of the reading committee, the president and so on) of the problem and arguments on either side, and this presentation shall be made without becoming involved in arguments on either side of the issue;
>   • questions by the meeting to the authors;
>   • additional comments by members and assessors on the point;
>   • (possible roundtable of views);
>   • brief final comments by the persons concerned;
>   • ensuring that the meeting fully understands the question;
>   • re-reading of the question by the president;
>   • vote by the meeting (show of hands).

> 35. A vote is not regarded as the necessary outcome of a discussion: it is only required if the points for consideration have validly emerged from the discussion and a sufficient number of those present feel well enough informed to make a decision. ...

> 39. A formal voting process or vote by show of hands is used in place of the "roundtable" process. ...

> 41. The president may decide, when he considers that the matter discussed is of great importance, to extend the consultation to members and assessors absent from the general meeting. ...

44. Any vote taken at a general meeting must be compiled and its result announced at the meeting and entered in the minutes.

45. Consensus is intended to ensure greater consistency in Commission decisions. It will be obtained following thorough discussion and by means of an unambiguous vote; but in the last analysis the quorum retains control of its decision.

46. The consensus is entered in the minutes of the general meeting, with reference to the decision it will be reflected in and the breakdown of the number of votes.

It is true that the system for verifying decisions established in the case at bar was created at the request of the decision-makers themselves. In view of the large number of decisions made by the Commission (on the evidence, 2,871 decisions for 1983), members and assessors very soon felt the need to consult their colleagues to ensure consistent and carefully reasoned decisions. As the Commission noted, the objective of consistency responds to litigants' need for stability but also to the dictates of justice. As the Commission's decisions are not subject to appeal, it is the Commission itself which has the duty of preventing inconsistent decision-making.

However, that does not mean that the actual structure of the machinery created to promote collegiality is unimportant. Clearly, by its very nature administrative law encompasses a wide variety of types of decision-making. Nonetheless, these must be in keeping with natural justice: accordingly, they should not impede the ability of the members of an administrative tribunal to decide as they see fit nor should they create an appearance of bias in the minds of litigants.

[Gonthier J here quoted at length from *Consolidated-Bathurst*.]

The institutionalized decision-making process in the case at bar is rather different from that considered by the Court in *IWA*. Although the "consensus tables" held by the Commission are optional in theory, it appeared from the testimony of the member Claude Pothier that these collegiate discussions are in practice compulsory when the legal counsel determines that the proposed decision is contrary to previous decisions:

A. ... So this time, literally *in order not to hold up the case, we sent—it was the only way—sent the Noémie Tremblay file to the discussion table.*

Q. When you say—in order not to hold up the case?

A. Well, listen, it is difficult because we were—at least I for one was in a difficult situation in which the quorum had disposed of a matter which was not contrary to principle or the previous decisions of the Commission, because there were none, I think there was one and it was more favourable to the decision being taken than the other possibility. There was Judge Poirier's memo, which was in the file, so we could hardly not take it into account. *The only way was to have a general discussion around the table to get the file moving, to move it forward.*

Q. Could you have sent the original of document P-10 to the Commission's secretary?

A. Listen, the administrative procedure did not authorize us to do that. I think I would have been squarely blamed if I had gone over their heads, especially the administrative office, and rendered a decision directly from my office; the discussion took place in my office at the time, and we decided to make this decision for a very good reason.

Q. I did not ask you whether you could have sent it directly to the parties; my question was whether you could have sent the decision to the Commission's secretary for it to be issued?

A. *I could not do that either, because the procedure set up was compulsory, all files of whatever kind had to go through the legal counsel.* So the only route was to send my file to my secretary who sent it on to the legal counsel's office, and then it went from there to be issued. If anything held it up, such as the legal counsel finding an inadvertent error in the citation of a regulation … the file was sent back to us. …

Additionally, in other cases where the decision was contrary to earlier decisions of the Commission … or contrary to the consensus established around the table by my colleagues together, the legal counsel still held up the file, to my personal knowledge of the matter, and if the quorum did not change its opinion, the file to my personal knowledge—in which I was involved in any case—the files went either to the office of the president or the vice-president and eventually came back to the general discussion table. That is the procedure in the Commission as I have known it for nine (9) years. [Emphasis added.]

Dugas J, who heard the parties and was therefore in a better position to assess the specific concrete aspects of the case, concluded from the testimony that there was undeniable "compulsory consultation" and "systemic pressure." In such circumstances, the fact that at the end of his testimony Mr. Pothier admitted that the vote taken at the plenary meeting had not prevented him from abiding by his decision in no way shows absence of constraint.

The Commission argued that under directive 45, the quorum still retains full control of its decision. As the Court observed in *IWA*, mere "influence" is to be distinguished from "constraint"; but what is crucial is to determine the *actual situation* prevailing in the body in question. In the case at bar on the facts do

[t]he methods used at those meetings to discuss policy issues reflect the need to maintain an atmosphere wherein each attending Board member retains the freedom to make up his mind on any given issue and to preserve the panel members' ultimate responsibility for the outcome of the final decision?

(*IWA, supra*, at p. 316.)

I do not think so. The testimony of the member Claude Pothier depicts a system in which in actual fact constraint seems to have outweighed influence, regardless of any internal directive to the contrary.

Additionally, reading the rules for holding plenary meetings of the Commission discloses a number of points which taken together could create an appearance of bias. In my opinion, the key indicator in this regard is to be found in directive 5, which provides that a plenary meeting may be requested not only by the quorum responsible for making the decision but also by the president of the Commission.

The fact that under directive 5 the president of the Commission can raise a question at a plenary meeting without the approval of the quorum responsible for deciding the matter presents a particular problem in light of the following passage from the judgment in *IWA, supra*, at p. 332:

It is obvious that no outside interference may be used to compel or pressure a decision-maker to participate in discussions on policy issues raised by a case on which he must render a decision.

In my view, the mere fact that the president can of his own motion refer a matter for plenary discussion may in itself be a constraint on decision-makers. In such circumstances, they may not feel free to refuse to submit a question to the "consensus table" when the president suggests this. Further, the statute clearly provides that it is the decision-makers who must decide a matter. Accordingly, it is those decision-makers who must retain the right to initiate consultation; imposing it on them amounts to an act of compulsion towards them and a denial of the choice expressly made by the legislature.

The Commission apparently wishes by this machinery to make the expertise of the Commission as a whole available to its members and to inform them of existing precedents. This is a praiseworthy motive. If the quorum has the advantage of the experience and opinions of its colleagues it may be in a position to render a more thoughtful decision. However, it is the quorum, and *only the quorum*, which has the responsibility of rendering the decision. If it does not wish to consult, it must be truly free not to do so. This constraint, which is subjective for the decision-makers, may also cause litigants to have an impression of objective bias. Compulsory consultation creates at the very least an appearance of a lack of independence, if not actual constraint.

The referral process mentioned in directive 5 in cases of new subject-matter also circumvents the will of the legislature by seeking to establish a prior consensus by persons not responsible for deciding the case. Ordinarily, precedent is developed by the actual decision-makers over a series of decisions. The tribunal hearing a new question may thus render a number of contradictory judgments before a consensus naturally emerges. This of course is a longer process; but there is no indication that the legislature intended it to be otherwise. Bearing this in mind, I consider it is particularly important for the persons responsible for hearing a case to be the ones to decide it.

There are other facts which support this conclusion of an apparent lack of independence. For example, plenary meetings of the Commission are held so as to arrive at a consensus: a vote by a show of hands is generally taken, as well as attendance; minutes are kept (directives 34, 35, 39, 44 and 46). The process created by the Commission thus contains very few of the protective devices which led this Court to conclude that the practice of the OLRB was in keeping with natural justice. Such protective devices are important when, as here, what is at issue is also to determine whether there was an *appearance of bias or lack of independence*. Certain aspects of the system established by the Commission create at the very least an appearance of "systemic pressure," to use the words of Dugas J.

Accordingly the Commission's decision, as a product of this system of internal consultation, seems to me to have been made in breach of the rules of natural justice. The present practice of the Commission of holding plenary meetings without members of a quorum having requested them, as well as the voting procedure and the keeping of minutes, may exert undue pressure on decision-makers. Such pressure may be an infringement of a litigant's right to a decision by an independent tribunal. I consider that the institutionalized consultation process currently being used by the Commission may also give rise to a reasonable apprehension of bias in an informed litigant.

I would accordingly dismiss the principal appeal for this reason.

It should not be concluded from all this that the Court does not regard the objective sought by the Commission, of ensuring adjudicative coherence, as important. On the contrary, it has already recognized the manifest benefits which may be obtained from an institutionalized consultation process. The Court is also aware of the breadth of the task which has been entrusted to the Commission by the legislature and of the difficulties which the Commission may face in performing these quasi-judicial duties.

As it said earlier in *IWA, supra*, plenary meetings may be a consultation tool which is entirely in keeping with the rules of natural justice. However, they should not be imposed on decision-makers and should be held in such a way as to leave decision-makers free to decide according to their own consciences and opinions. Voting, the taking of attendance and the keeping of minutes are therefore not to be recommended. There are in any case a number of other methods which can be used to inform members of the Commission of applicable adjudicative trends or to prompt discussion on points of importance; the task of devising these may be left to the Commission.

3. Part Played by the President in the Case at Bar and Appearance of Bias

Though this question does not have to be decided in order to dispose of the principal appeal, I will still make certain observations on the part played by Judge Poirier in the case at bar.

The *Act respecting the Commission des affaires sociales* gives the president of the Commission the power to settle disputes that may arise within a quorum:

> 10. A matter shall be decided by the majority of the members and assessors having heard it.
>
> When opinions are equally divided on a question, it shall be decided by the president or the vice-president he designates.

What part did the president of the Commission play here? In the case at bar, it is the president who raised the question by sending the quorum a memorandum in which he indicated the interpretation he would have given to the regulation at issue. This led to engaging the consultation process which eventually led to the disagreement between the two previously unanimous decision-makers. Once the disagreement emerged, it was the president again who resolved the matter in the way he had indicated in his first intervention.

[Justice Gonthier held that the fact that the president had expressed his opinion to the panel, invited them to reconsider their decision, and then become the decision-maker raised a reasonable apprehension of bias; the president had committed himself to a particular outcome. After referring to the principle that the overlapping duties of tribunal members may be statutorily authorized, he continued:]

… The demands of natural justice must therefore be reconciled with the deliberate intent of the legislature to give an administrative tribunal several overlapping duties. In the case at bar, the internal consultation procedure used by the Commission was not created by the legislature; and even if it had been, it does not contemplate the president taking control of cases in place of the legal counsel. There is accordingly less reason to tolerate the president playing several parts within the decision-making process.

Moreover, s. 10 of the *Act respecting the Commission des affaires sociales* expressly authorizes the president to designate a vice-president to resolve disputes between the members of a quorum. In view of the active part he took in the discussion, the president should have delegated the decision to one of his vice-presidents. He did not do so. The active part played by Mr. Poirier in this matter thus seems to me likely to create a reasonable apprehension of bias in an informed observer.

The respondent further argued that the procedure used infringes the *audi alteram partem* rule in that the president did not hear the parties when he finally decided the matter. The Court has already considered this point in *IWA*. ...

[The passage from *Consolidated-Bathurst* distinguishing between discussions bearing on questions of fact and those relating to questions of law, reproduced earlier in this chapter, is omitted.]

The question on which the Commission had to rule was clearly a point of law, namely whether "dressings and bandages were included in the definition of medical equipment" within the meaning of s. 10.04 of the *Regulation on Social Aid* then in effect. Furthermore, the parties chose to plead in writing and so far as one can tell made no representations at the hearing.

In the case at bar, there is no evidence that new arguments of law were raised at the "consensus table." The consultation process therefore did not infringe the *audi alteram partem* rule. Turning to the next stage, it also seems that no new points were considered by the president at the decision-making stage. He in fact decided on the basis of the written file as prepared by the quorum. As the Court observed in *IWA*, *supra*, at p. 339:

> ... the rule with respect to legal or policy arguments not raising issues of fact is somewhat more lenient because the parties only have the right to state their case adequately and to answer contrary arguments. This right does not encompass the right to repeat arguments every time the panel convenes to discuss the case.

I therefore do not feel the facts of the instant case established a breach of the *audi alteram partem* rule. The Court moreover notes that the Commission has subsequently altered its practice and has taken the sensible step of giving parties an opportunity to be heard by the president or vice-president responsible for resolving a disagreement. In the case at bar, the only blame which can attach to the president is thus of having resolved the disagreement between the decision-makers when he had already spoken on the matter.

4. Nature of First "Decision"

I concur on this point with the disposition chosen by Dugas J, namely that the only decision in the case at bar is that contained in document P-9 (the "second" decision, [1983] CAS 713). Like Dugas J, I consider that the first "decision" rendered by the members of the quorum was in their minds only a draft, a provisional opinion.

In this regard, the intent of the decision-makers must be analysed in terms of the institutionalized consultation process that existed at the time the decision was made, even though that process now proves to have contravened the rules of natural justice. The Court cannot disregard the setting in which the decision was made in deciding whether it was conclusive.

Finally, I would note that the procedure of early signature of draft decisions by members and assessors followed in the case at bar seems to me unadvisable. Although this procedure may be practical, it only adds to the appearance of bias when a decision-maker decides to alter his opinion after free consultation with his colleagues. A litigant who sees a "decision" favourable to him changed to an unfavourable one will not think that there has been a normal consultation process; rather, he will have the impression that external pressure has definitely led persons who were initially favourable to his case to change their minds.

Appeal dismissed.

NOTES

1. Subsequently, the Ontario Divisional Court approved a practice of the Pay Equity Hearings Tribunal under which members hearing a case that raised issues of general importance could meet and engage in discussions with various caucuses of members of the entire tribunal: *Glengarry Memorial Hospital v. Ontario (Pay Equity Hearings Tribunal)* (1993), 110 DLR (4th) 260 (Ont. Div. Ct.).

2. For a recent decision considering *Tremblay*, see *Cherubini Metal Works Ltd. v. Nova Scotia (Attorney General)* (2007), 253 NSR (2d) 134, 282 DLR (4th) 538. In that case, the Nova Scotia Court of Appeal concluded, at paras. 19-22, that the administrative law principle of deliberative secrecy operated to preclude an attempt in a tort case to compel former board of examiners members under the *Stationary Engineers Act*, RSNS 1989, c. 440, to testify on discovery.

Mullan, "Common and Divergent Elements of Practices of the Various Tribunals: An Overview of Present and Possible Developments"
in *Administrative Law: Principles, Practice and Pluralism*
(Special Lectures of the Law Society of Upper Canada 1992)
(Toronto: Carswell, 1993), 461, at 469-74 (footnotes omitted)

[After describing the reasons given by Gonthier J in *Tremblay* for distinguishing *Consolidated-Bathurst*, the author continues:]

To me, there are a significant number of problems with all of this. First, the determination of whether there has been illegitimate compulsion, as opposed to permissible pressure, seems to be related solely to form as opposed to substance. In reality, of course, the process of the Labour Relations Board could, as a matter of fact, be just as conducive to compliance with the wishes of the other members of the tribunal as the formal structure of the Commission des affaires sociales. It is all a matter of power relationships within the tribunal. Of course, perhaps the Supreme Court was able to discern such a distinction in fact as between the two cases and was simply using the formal indicators as a surrogate for other more concrete evidence and in justification of its hunch. However, that is scarcely an adequate basis on which to build a rule applicable to other contexts. To the extent that compulsion is illegitimate, it should be founded on hard evidence, not simply a structure of consultation that gives some cause for suspicion.

More importantly, however, the designation as decisive in all such cases of the answer to the question whether the process amounted to compulsion as to opposed to merely influence without regard to statutory context is to my mind most unfortunate. Simply put, it is very restrictive of the opportunities for mass adjudication tribunals to choose the kind of process that will best forward the objectives of the statutory programme on which they are called to adjudicate.

If we look at this in the particular context of *Tremblay*, what is ironic is that the nature of what was at stake was the grant of a form of government benefit or "largesse" which, at least, until recently would not have attracted the application of the common law rules of natural justice. However, once the benefit in question was put in the statutory context of "right" or "entitlement" and its disallowance made subject to a right of appeal, the court seemed impelled to apply to the regime in question traditional judicial values. Whether this is a fair reflection of either statutory intention or functional or operating imperatives is, however, a matter of some doubt.

At the September 1988 Conference, *Law and Leviathan* staged jointly by the Law Reform Commission of Canada and the University of Toronto, John Evans expressed considerable sanguinity at the extent to which Canadian mass adjudication tribunals were able to engage in devices and techniques that enabled them to handle their caseload despite resource problems and to ensure some measure of consistency in their decision-making processes (Evans, "Problems in Mass Adjudication: The Courts' Contribution" (1990) 40 *UTLJ* 606).

However, he noted that this issue was one that had not by and large spilled over into the courts, the one major exception being *Singh v. Canada (Minister of Employment & Immigration)*. Before the published version of his paper appeared, *Consolidated-Bathurst* had been decided by the Supreme Court of Canada and Evans saw this as confirming the idea that the courts would not be interventionist in the arena of process developed by high volume administrative agencies (at p. 609).

> When Charter rights are not at stake, courts are now much less prepared to second-guess administrators by tampering with well-established schemes of administrative procedures, even if they deviate significantly from the judicial model.

That is a judgment that after *Tremblay* would have to be reconsidered. As the Supreme Court itself pointed out, the Commission des affaires sociales had a caseload of 2,871 decisions in 1983. There were no appeals from its decisions to the courts, only judicial review, and that presumably subject to the principle of deference so that the courts would not really be in a position to resolve problems of internal conflict on matters of law and principle. In those circumstances, some mediating processes were needed if different rules were not to prevail depending on which panel of the Commission a claimant encountered in an appeal, if surgical bandages were to be consistently paid for or not. Given that context, there have to be serious doubts about whether notions of adjudicative independence and the principle that the person who hears must decide should prevail to produce a result which favours the autonomy of individual members over collective consistency. Indeed, to ask whether the process of consultation amounted to effective compulsion amounts to answering without discussion the question that really needs to be asked in such cases: Why not compulsion on issues of law and policy?

Such concerns become even more palpable if one considers a body such as the [Immigration and] Refugee Board consisting of over two hundred members sitting all across the country and dealing with a five digit caseload. It is simply unacceptable for the possibility to exist that there can be significant deviations in the acceptance figures for claimants from certain countries depending upon the region of Canada in which the claim is heard. In such contexts, there has to be some way of ensuring uniform policies and a large measure of consistent treatment, and, to a certain extent, that may have to involve the heavy hand of executive or corporate dictation if the system is going to work.

As it is, the impact of the Supreme Court of Canada's decision may well be not only to forbid this kind of activity but also to discourage generally such collective discussions of common problems. In this regard, one aspect of the judgment may well have a major impact. This is the court's ruling that, in the face of an allegation, of a breach of the rules of natural justice where "the litigant can present valid reasons for believing" that allegation, the principle of deliberative secrecy gave way and the Commission secretary could be obliged to answer questions about the process of how draft decisions were dealt with within the Commission. Now, that has been extended by Steele J of the Ontario Court of Justice in *Ellis-Don Ltd. v. Ontario (Labour Relations Board)* (1992) 95 DLR (4th) 56 (Ont. Gen. Div.) to permit the Chair and Vice-Chair of the Board to be ordered to attend before an official examiner to answer questions not simply about the general practice of the Board in relation to its method of dealing with draft decisions but about how there was an apparent change in a finding of "fact" after the consideration by the whole Board of a draft decision in a particular matter. If this judgment is sustained on appeal and the practice of calling tribunal members to account in this way becomes a regular practice, it is easy to see how such consultation practices will wither and die as such and move underground! Indeed, it is also ironic that it was the level of formality and the fact that the practice had been laid down in rules that doomed the process in *Tremblay*, a process that had in fact resulted from a request by the members of the Commission.

Some would not, however, lament the passing of such consultations. Andrew Roman, for example, views the whole process and the constraints placed on discussion by *Consolidated-Bathurst* as matters that cannot be policed, and, therefore, one that should be dispensed with: Roman, (1990) 42 Admin. LR 109 at 115. To him, *Ellis-Don* is presumably just confirmation of this in the sense that the demands that it places on tribunal members are simply inappropriate. While I concede that policing is going to be difficult and that there are problems with *Ellis-Don*, this certainly becomes less of a difficulty if one accepts the legitimacy of a greater level of compulsion in relation to disputed matters of law and policy. Moreover, with respect to new arguments of law and policy not raised at the hearing itself, there is always the discipline of the requirement to give reasons as a check on the intrusion of such arguments without the benefit of a reopening of the hearing to hear the parties' views.

Hudson Janisch's paper, "The Choice of Decisionmaking Method: Adjudication, Policies and Rulemaking," *supra*, at 259, however, suggests that this kind of process is but a poor surrogate for open rule-making and I certainly concede that that is so in many situations and that to deal with such issues simply in the context of collegial discussion is to deny to the tribunal the benefit of broader constituency views on matters of significance. Nonetheless, in an era of severe resource constraints (adverted to by Margot Priest, "Structure and Accountability of Administrative Agencies," *supra*, at 11) and the sheer difficulty of setting up a policy or rule-making hearing, there are problems for administrative tribunals wishing to move in this direction though some, such as the Ontario Securities Commission, manage to do so regularly. More importantly, however, some of the issues that seem appropriate for collective consultation (Should the cost of surgical bandages be reimbursed (as arose in *Tremblay*)?) are matters that are not terribly well-suited to a rule-making hearing. To the extent that they involve the resolution of a disputed but narrow issue of law, rather than a proposed change in tribunal policy, a rule-making hearing or process may amount to overkill.

That brings me finally in this specific context to what may be another objection emerging from Margot Priest's presentation. As an obvious supporter of independence for the members of administrative tribunals and agencies, she condemns those criticisms of the Ratushny Report that its proposals for greater independence for tribunal members are too much based on a judicial model. While generally supportive of the entitlement of tribunals to move away from the judicial model, she views independence as a special issue, not subject to such variations. And, of course, many, with some justification, see the *Consolidated-Bathurst* and *Tremblay* cases as essentially being about independence. The ultimate compromise of independence is to allow those who hear cases to be subject to virtual dictation in how they decide them.

In this context, it seems to me that there is a case for reconceiving what is meant by adjudicative independence. In general terms, there will be situations in which it is more appropriate to conceive of independence in the sense of the corporate independence of the tribunal, the entitlement of the collectivity to go about its business of dispensing justice, of making decisions without being subject to extra-judicial pressures. Within that cocoon of corporate independence, judgments will have to be made in some instances about the scope of the individual autonomy of particular members. Clearly, on matters of fact and judgment arising in individual cases, the tribunal member is generally in the best position to make the call and should be able to do so without fear of reprisal or being subject to collective check. Nonetheless, in relation to issues of law and policy that have ramifications beyond the particular case, the demand for complete independence in their decision-making role by individual members sounds somewhat hollow and, under at least some statutory configurations such as in *Tremblay*, should give way to the collective interests of the whole tribunal.

According to some, to allow this to happen places too much power in the hands of a strong chair and leads to compliance through fear of non-renewal or marginalization, and I have heard it suggested that this is in fact the non-articulated sub-text of *Tremblay*. However, that is something that can occur completely irrespective of the existence of a process of consultation or collective consideration of individual cases. Indeed, the more formal the consultative processes are made and the more one accepts the legitimacy of the collective will prevailing in such matters, the more the chances of this occurring are diminished. In sum, I therefore see *Tremblay* as far too much of a brake upon the devising of appropriate techniques for the handling of mass adjudication situations and as placing far too much emphasis on traditional judicial values at the expense of other more important considerations.

NOTE

An obvious problem with the *Consolidated-Bathurst* rules is the challenge of policing their observance. Tribunals are not obliged to disclose whether they engage in such practices let alone whether a particular case has been the subject of a consultation. As a consequence, it will often be a matter of happenstance whether the holding of such a consultation has taken place. In *Consolidated-Bathurst* itself, the employer's lawyer was at the board offices, eavesdropping, on the day the case was discussed. In *Glengarry Memorial Hospital*, the consultations came to light as a consequence of some elliptical comments in the reasons for decision penned by a dissenting member of the panel. In *Ellis-Don Ltd.*, the company received a copy of the original draft decision in the proverbial anonymous brown paper envelope. Indeed, even when the parties are aware that such a meeting has taken place, as *Tremblay* suggests, there may be serious impediments to obtaining evidence as to how the consultation actually proceeded. This dilemma is illustrated by the second round of litigation involving the *Ellis-Don* case.

Ellis-Don Ltd. v. Ontario (Labour Relations Board)
[2001] 1 SCR 221 (Ont.)

[In 1962, the appellant entered into a collective bargaining agreement to contract or subcontract only to individuals or companies whose employees were members of the affiliated unions of the Toronto Building and Construction Trades Council. In 1971, the Electrical Contractors Association of Toronto applied to the respondent board to be certified as a bargaining agent for the electrical contractors of Toronto. In that accreditation process, the IBEW, Local 353 filed a required document listing all employers for which it claimed bargaining rights but it did not include the appellant's name. In 1978, when province-wide bargaining was introduced, the bargaining rights of Local 353 were extended to Local 894. In 1990, Local 894 filed a grievance with the board alleging that the appellant had subcontracted electrical construction work to non-union subcontractors contrary to the provincial collective agreement. A three-member panel of the board heard the grievance. The appellant argued that Local 353 had abandoned its bargaining rights in part because it omitted the appellant's name from the document filed in the 1971 accreditation proceedings and Local 894 offered no explanation for the omission. A first draft of the panel's decision would have dismissed the grievance based on the abandonment of bargaining rights. However, after a full board meeting discussed the draft, a majority of the panel found that there had been no abandonment of bargaining rights and upheld the grievance. The appellant applied for judicial review. It alleged that the change between the draft and the final decision was of a factual nature as opposed to a legal or policy change, and claimed that there was a breach of natural justice and a violation of the rules governing institutional consultations. Prior to the hearing of the application for judicial review, the appellant obtained an order compelling the chair of the board, the vice-chair who presided over the panel, and the registrar of the board to give evidence with respect to the procedures implemented by the board in arriving at its final decision. This order was reversed on appeal based on a finding of statutory testimonial immunity. The Divisional Court later dismissed the application for judicial review and the Court of Appeal affirmed the decision.]

LeBEL J (McLachlin CJ, L'Heureux-Dubé, Gonthier, Iacobucci, Bastarache, and Arbour JJ concurring):

The appellant faced difficult evidentiary problems when it launched its application for judicial review. The only facts it knew were that a draft decision dismissing the grievance had been circulated, that a full meeting of the OLRB had been called at the request of Vice-Chair Susan Tacon, that such a meeting had indeed been held and that the final arbitration award upheld the grievance.

The final decision was silent as to what had happened during the full Board meeting. As stated above, there has been no request for reconsideration, and thus, perhaps, an opportunity was lost to obtain information on the consultation process within the OLRB. From these facts, there is no direct evidence of improper tampering with the decision of the panel. Ellis-Don sought to strengthen its case by obtaining evidence of what had happened during the consultation process. The appellant tried to get this evidence through an interlocutory motion to examine certain members and officers of the OLRB. After the dismissal of its motion by the Divisional Court, Ellis-Don found itself in an impasse, as it could not obtain evidence of the process followed in the particular case from the OLRB through the interrogation of its members or officers.

The appellant then tried a new tack during the hearing of its application for judicial review. The purpose of its argument remained the same: to establish an improper interference by the full Board in the decision of the panel. Thus, it sought to convince the courts that the change in the decision was of a factual nature and that it could properly be implied that a discussion of the facts had occurred at the full Board meeting. It also suggested that the threshold for judicial review in such a case was an apprehension of breach of natural justice and that there was no need to establish an actual breach of the audi alteram partem rule. It argued that such an apprehended breach of natural justice had been established through a displacement of the presumption of regularity of the administrative proceedings of the Board. According to the appellant, it fell to the respondents to establish that the proceedings had not been tainted by any breach of natural justice. Absent evidence to this effect, the Court should find that there was a breach of natural justice, that the Board had been biased and that the audi alteram partem rule had been violated. This unrebutted presumption would justify granting the application for judicial review and quashing the decision of the Board.

[In response to the appellant's argument that there had been a reassessment of particular facts, not simply a discussion of law and policy, LeBel J concluded: "On the record before us, this amounts to little more than speculation."]

The case reveals a tension between the fairness of the process and the principle of deliberative secrecy. The existence of this tension was conceded by Gonthier J in *Tremblay*. Undoubtedly, the principle of deliberative secrecy creates serious difficulties for parties who fear that they may have been the victims of inappropriate tampering with the decision of the adjudicators who actually heard them. Even if this Court has refused to grant the same level of protection to the deliberations of administrative tribunals as to those of the civil and criminal courts, and would allow interrogation and discovery as to the process followed, Gonthier J recognized that this principle of deliberative secrecy played an important role in safeguarding the independence of administrative adjudicators.

Deliberative secrecy also favours administrative consistency by granting protection to a consultative process that involves interaction between the adjudicators who have heard the case and the members who have not, within the rules set down in *Consolidated-Bathurst, supra*. Without such protection, there could be a chilling effect on institutional consultations, thereby depriving administrative tribunals of a critically important means of achieving consistency.

Satisfying those requirements of consistency and independence comes undoubtedly at a price, this price being that the process becomes less open and that litigants face tough hurdles when attempting to build the evidentiary foundation for a successful challenge based on alleged breaches of natural justice (see, *e.g.*, H.N. Janisch, "Consistency, Rule-Making and *Consolidated-Bathurst*" (1991), 16 *Queen's LJ* 95; D. Lemieux, "L'équilibre nécessaire entre la cohérence institutionnelle et l'indépendance des membres d'un tribunal administratif: *Tremblay c. Québec (Commission des affaires sociales)*" (1992), 71 *Can. Bar Rev.* 734). The present case provides an excellent example of those difficulties.

After the dismissal of its interlocutory motion, the appellant could not examine the officers of the Board on the process that had been followed. In the absence of any further evidence, this Court cannot reverse the presumption of regularity of the administrative process simply because of a change in the reasons for the decision, especially when the change is limited on its face to questions of law and policy, as discussed above. A contrary approach to the presumption would deprive administrative tribunals of the independence that the principle of deliberative secrecy assures them in their decision-making process. It could also jeopardize institutionalized consultation proceedings that have become more necessary than ever to ensure the consistency and predictability of the decisions of administrative tribunals.

BINNIE J (dissenting) (Major J concurring): When this Court decided in *IWA v. Consolidated-Bathurst Packaging Ltd.*, that panel members could consult with the full Board on matters of policy as opposed to issues of fact, it was feared in some quarters that the integrity of administrative decision-making could appear to be compromised without effective redress. This appeal tests the limits of the *Consolidated-Bathurst* rule. It also tests the availability of effective redress for non-observance of those limits.

[Contrary to LeBel J, he concluded on a close review of both the draft and final decision that what had happened before the board indicated that "the evidence was reweighed or reassessed, apparently as a result of the full-board meeting. This was contrary to *Consolidated-Bathurst.*"]

In my view, the Board cannot have it both ways. It cannot, with the assistance of the legislature, deny a person in the position of the appellant all legitimate access to relevant information, then rely on the absence of this same information as a conclusive answer to the appellant's complaint. We are not in the business of playing Catch 22. The record discloses a change of position by the panel on an issue of fact. This runs counter to *Consolidated-Bathurst* and has to be dealt with properly if confidence in the integrity of the Board's decision making is to be maintained.

Where, as here, a serious question is raised on material emanating from the Board itself as to whether the *Consolidated-Bathurst* limits were respected, I do not think it is for the Board to claim that the failure of the party to obtain the additional evidence that the Board itself has fought to withhold is a complete answer to the claim. The strength of the evidence necessary to displace the presumption of regularity depends on the nature of the case: W. Wade and C. Forsyth, *Administrative Law* (7th ed. 1994), at p. 334. Having regard to the difficulties put in the way of the appellant to obtain evidence to which at common law it would have been entitled (*Tremblay*, at 965-66), I think the appellant discharged its evidentiary onus to displace the "presumption" of regularity.

The Board relies on the public interest in the effective operation of its docket, but that is not the only public interest at stake here. Public confidence in the integrity of decision-making by courts and adjudicative tribunals is of the highest importance. Parties coming before the Board should not come away with a reasonable apprehension that they were subject to a rogue process. Once it was determined here that the change between the initial decision and the final decision related to an issue that was almost entirely factual, and was nevertheless put up for discussion at a full Board meeting, I think the appellant has made out a prima facie basis for judicial review which in this case the Board chose not to rebut. To hold otherwise would suggest that the Court in *Consolidated-Bathurst* affirmed procedural limitations on full board meetings for breach of which there is no effective remedy.

Appeal dismissed.

NOTES

1. Can the majority judgment in this case be reconciled with the judgment of Gonthier J in *Tremblay*?

2. For an example of the significant burden faced by parties seeking to establish a breach of the *audi alteram partem* principle in deliberations between members of a hearing panel of Alberta's Energy and Utilities Board and its expert staff, see *Devon Canada Corporation v. Alberta (Energy and Utilities Board)*, 2003 ABCA 167, 3 Admin. LR (4th) 154, at para. 21.

3. It is important to note that in *Ellis-Don* the majority did not rely on s. 114(1) of the *Labour Relations Act*, SO 1995, c. 1. It provides:

Except with the consent of the Board, no member of the Board, nor its registrar, nor any of its other officers, nor any of its clerks or servants shall be required to give testimony in any civil proceeding before the Board or in any proceeding before any other tribunal respecting information obtained in discharge of their duties or while acting within the scope of their employment under this Act.

Rather, they grounded their commitment to deliberative secrecy on broad common law concerns about the need to protect institutional decisions from attack. This makes the following earlier Ontario Court of Appeal judgment particularly interesting.

Payne v. Ontario (Human Rights Commission)
(2000), 192 DLR (4th) 315 (Ont. CA)

SHARPE JA (O'Connor JA concurring): The appellant made a complaint to the respondent Ontario Human Rights Commission (the "Commission") alleging that she had been the victim of discrimination at the hands of her employer. The Commission staff investigated her complaint. A report of the investigation recommended that the Commission refer the appellant's complaint to a board of inquiry. The matter was considered at three meetings of the Commission. In the end, the Commission decided not to request the minister to appoint a board of inquiry and, in effect, dismissed the appellant's complaint.

The appellant brought an application for judicial review, challenging the decision dismissing her complaint on the grounds, inter alia, that it was made on inappropriate grounds and that she had been denied procedural fairness. The appellant filed the affidavit of a former member of the Commission who had been present at the first of the three meetings at which the appellant's complaint had been considered. The former member swore that when the complaint was considered, Commission staff members made recommendations to the Commissioners that the complaint not be referred to a board of inquiry based on facts or considerations that ought not to have been taken into account by the Commission. The statements or recommendations of the Commission staff were not revealed in the record filed by the Commission for the judicial review application.

The principal issue on this appeal is whether the appellant is entitled to full disclosure and production of all facts, arguments and considerations that were presented to the Commission when it considered her complaints.

[The short answer is that the appellant was not entitled to any right of discovery to rummage through the commission's files in hope of uncovering something helpful to her case, but this did not mean that she was not entitled to a "more focussed examination." This conclusion was arrived at first by identifying what had to be disclosed in order to ensure that the procedures were fair, and then by considering whether concerns for deliberative secrecy should limit this disclosure. The need for disclosure was identified in the following terms:]

... As I see it, the only legitimate factor to be considered by the Commission in the exercise of its discretion is whether there is any merit in the complaint. If the Commission were to base its decision on some extraneous factor, the court would intervene on judicial review. I did not understand counsel appearing on behalf of the Commission to dispute this basic point which flows from the nature of the Commission's statutory mandate. The decision not to refer a complaint puts an end to an allegation that a fundamental human right has been violated. In my opinion, it would be entirely inconsistent with the nature of a fundamental human right if the Commission were, as is alleged in the Wharton affidavit, to dismiss a complaint for reasons of cost or because of "strategic concerns." ...

In any event, procedural fairness dictates that the complainant and other parties who may be affected by a decision of the Commission be given notice of the facts, arguments and considerations upon which the decision is to be based and an opportunity to make submissions. Under the procedures adopted by the Commission, the complainant and others who may be affected by the decision are not entitled to attend the meeting at which the complaint is considered by the Commissioners. In advance of that meeting, they are provided with a copy of the Case Analysis Report that will be put before the Commissioners and are given an opportunity to make written submissions. If the Commission were to proceed on a different recommendation or to base its decision on factors or considerations undisclosed to the complainant and the others there would be no opportunity to respond and the right to fairness would be infringed.

Finally, the complainant has a statutory right to be given the Commission's reasons for refusing to proceed with the complaint or for refusing to refer it to a board of inquiry. It would make a mockery of that statutory right if the complainant were told that the complaint was dismissed for want of merit while the Commissioners' real reason was want of resources or some other unexplained strategic concern.

[Sharpe JA then turned to consider whether concerns for deliberative secrecy should prevent even a focused examination. He noted that three purposes had been put forward in favour of deliberative secrecy: first, a practical concern that if no limits were imposed, tribunal members would be exposed to unduly burdensome examinations; second, the need for finality and the need for decisions to rest on reasons given; and, third, the need to protect the process of debate, discussion, and compromise inherent in collegial decision making.]

However, it has also been held on the highest authority that limitations on the right to conduct examinations designed to protect the interests of tribunal members must be balanced with the right of the citizen who has been affected by the tribunal's decision to effective judicial review. When applying the principle of deliberative secrecy to protect the integrity of the decision-making process, the courts must take into account the fact that administrative decisions are subject to the inherent power of judicial review. In this regard, a distinction has been drawn between the deliberations of administrative and judicial officers. The deliberative secrecy of administrative decision-makers is not absolute and must yield, where necessary, to the certain overarching principles. As was pointed out by Gonthier J in *Tremblay v. Quebec (Commission des Affaires Sociales)*, [1992] 1 SCR 952 at 965-6, an allegation that the right to natural justice has been infringed may require scrutiny of the decision-making process. Tribunal members do not have an unqualified right to shelter their decision-making process from scrutiny. ...

In the present case, the doctrine of deliberative secrecy must be taken into account. The appellant does not seek to examine a member of the Commission as to confidential discussions with other Commissioners. She does, however, seek to examine a senior official, privy to the deliberations of the Commission, and to obtain disclosure of facts and arguments that were put before the Commissioners by senior staff members and considered by the Commissioners in determining the fate of her complaint. I note, however, that the application of deliberative secrecy to these proceedings is not without difficulty. The Commissioners apparently conduct their discussions at the same time they entertain submissions and input from staff members and it would seem difficult to identify a discrete, deliberative phase of the process. In view of that practice, it seems to me that the claim of protection for deliberative secrecy has considerably less force than in cases where tribunal members actually retire to consider the case in private. This factor must be added to what was said in *Tremblay* regarding the qualified protection accorded deliberative secrecy in the administrative law setting in determining the extent to which the Commission can shelter its process from disclosure. ...

I would summarize the effect of these authorities and considerations in the following manner. There is a prima facie right to resort to a Rule 39.03 examination in relation to an application for judicial review and there is no onus on the party seeking the examination to prove any facts as a precondition. However, as there is no general right to discovery on a judicial review application, the party serving a notice of examination may be required to specify the scope of the proposed examination. The matters intended to be covered in the examination must be relevant to a ground that would justify judicial review. The evidence must not be excluded by statute. The proposed examination will not be allowed where it is being used for some improper purpose or where the examination or the application for judicial review would constitute an abuse of the process of the court. Where it is proposed to examine a tribunal member or senior tribunal official privy to the decision-making process, the right to conduct the examination must be balanced with the principle of deliberative secrecy. The examination will not be permitted unless the party proposing it can present some basis for a clearly articulated and objectively reasonable concern that a relevant legal right may have been infringed. Examinations based on conjecture or mere speculation will not be allowed.

ABELLA JA (dissenting):

[Unlike Sharpe JA, in her dissent Abella JA sets out in detail events leading up to the appeal, especially the extraordinary breadth of the examination sought in the application for judicial review. (She certainly was not prepared to salvage the application by identifying some more focused examination). As well, again unlike Sharpe JA, she was highly critical of the affidavit of a former member of the Human Rights Commission.]

It is, with respect, difficult to understand why or how Mr. Wharton felt entitled to engage in such an astonishing breach of his duty to protect the confidentiality of the Commission's deliberations, and to so sweepingly assault the Commissioners' integrity and their capacity for independent decision-making. He smears by innuendo the bona fides of the Commission's staff and process and, inferentially, the legitimacy of every Commission decision made during his six year tenure. It is not at all surprising that the

Commission refused to exacerbate or appear to condone the impropriety by cross-examining Mr. Wharton.

There is nothing in the record to indicate whether at any time in his six years as a Commissioner Mr. Wharton ever raised these concerns either with fellow Commissioners, the Chief Commissioners, or Commission staff, or, if he did not, why he chose to raise them so publicly when he did.

There is no doubt that Mr. Wharton disagrees with and is upset by the Commissioners' decision not to refer Ms. Payne's complaint to a Board of Inquiry. This may explain his swearing the affidavit, but it in no way justifies this extraordinary, selective breach of his duty to protect the confidentiality of the Commission's deliberative process. The Commission, by its nature, is frequently called upon to deal with highly sensitive matters of intense public interest. Not unlike judicial deliberations, it would totally undermine the required frank exchange of competing views to render the deliberations routinely subject to public disclosure by disaffected Commission members or staff or, for that matter, through Rule 39.03 examinations.

[Abella JA went on to dismiss the Wharton affidavit as a mere repetition of conjecture and argument bereft of facts relevant to the arguments advanced in the judicial review proceeding. "Conjecture does not, by virtue of its repetition, thereby transform itself from theory into evidence." As such it could not form the basis for an examination of commission staff as it did not amount to evidence of wrongdoing. Referring specifically to rule 39.03, which provides that a person may be examined as a witness before the hearing of a pending motion or application, Abella JA brought together her concern that if deliberative secrecy was not observed, the role of staff would be significantly undermined and the integrity of the administrative process unjustifiably compromised.]

The statutory duty to decide whether to refer a complaint to a Board of Inquiry is assigned by s. 36 of the Code to the Commission. The fact that a staff member—either in person or through a report—recommends one course of action and the Commissioners decide on another, is, by itself, arguably more reflective of the proper interplay between discrete and independent institutional functions within the Commission than of a tainted decision-making process.

The staff, who are responsible for investigating complaints, are not discouraged from offering their opinions at Commission meetings. This, it seems to me, is a salutary part of informed decision-making. So is the Commission's ultimate duty to make a decision regardless of these opinions. It may be that a consensus regularly emerges between staff opinions and the Commissioners' decisions, but this should be no more surprising among people who share the same statutory and policy expertise than is the occasional difference of opinion.

Nor can it be said that there is anything inappropriate in having the staff participate in discussions about cases. In *Consolidated-Bathurst Packaging Ltd. v. International Woodworkers of America, Local 2-69*, the Supreme Court of Canada held that discussions with persons who do not have decision-making responsibility in a particular case, do not automatically pollute the final decision. As Gonthier J stated, at 561:

Discussions with colleagues do not constitute, in and of themselves, infringements on the panel members' capacity to decide the issues at stake independently. A discussion does not prevent a decision-maker from adjudicating in accordance with his own conscience and opinions nor does it constitute an obstacle to this freedom. Whatever discussion may take place, the ultimate decision will be that of the decision-maker for which he assumes full responsibility.

The spectre of impropriety is not raised by the presence and participation of staff members. There is no evidence that any member of the staff made inappropriate comments at the relevant meetings, made comments that were not based on information contained in the Reports, or made any comments that unduly influenced or interfered with the Commission's ability to make up its own mind based on relevant and appropriate factors.

I cannot accept the submission that the Commissioners should be presumed collectively to be so completely weak and vulnerable to the importunings of staff that the presence of staff impairs their capacity for independent decision-making, or that any decision diverging from a staff recommendation reflects the application of inappropriate considerations. Yet this is in essence what the appellant is arguing: by looking at the result in this case, we are invited, in the absence of evidence, to conclude that something sufficiently improper has taken place to invoke the otherwise uninvocable Rule 39.03.

In my view, the appellant's proposed Rule 39.03 examination is essentially ... an attempt through examinations of the Commission Registrar and staff to ascertain how the deliberative process worked in this case. It is, with respect, difficult to see this as anything other than a fishing expedition.

Appeal dismissed.

NOTES

1. Can this judgment stand in the wake of *Ellis-Don*?

2. In *Milner Power Inc. v. Alberta (Energy and Utilities Board)* (2007), 417 AR 115, 65 Admin. LR (4th) 296, [2007] 12 WWR 389 (CA), the appellant Milner Power brought a motion for disclosure of additional documents and for leave to examine tribunal members and staff of the Energy and Utilities Board. A majority of the Alberta Court of Appeal directed that additional documents be disclosed but declined to order the requested examinations. Slatter J, in his separate opinion, would have dismissed entirely the application for further disclosure on the basis that Milner Power did not satisfy the legal threshold for a court to direct that an administrative tribunal make further disclosure. He stated, at paras. 54-59:

[54] As mentioned ... Milner Power asserts a right to examine Board members and Board staff if it is not satisfied with the document production it gets. In *Payne v. Ontario Human Rights Commission*, *supra*, the court discussed the threshold that would have to be met before an applicant could examine the tribunal or its staff. While the majority thought that resort could generally be had as of course to the Ontario equivalent of R. 266 [of the Alberta Rules of Court, Alta. Reg. 390/1968], even they placed restrictions when an attempt was made to examine the members of the tribunal. At para. 172 the majority held:

... In view of these authorities and in keeping with what was said in *Canada Metal* and *Tremblay*, it seems to me that an applicant for judicial review who seeks to conduct an examination that will touch upon the deliberative secrecy of the decision-maker must present some basis for a clearly articulated and objectively reasonable concern that a relevant legal right may have been infringed. I would emphasize that in view of the importance of the principle of deliberative secrecy in the administrative decision-making process, examinations based on conjecture or mere speculation will not be allowed.

Abella JA, dissenting at para. 100, felt that there was a need for "reasonable, reliable, relevant evidence" to justify any use of the rule, and an even higher standard when adjudicative secrecy was to be breached. While I prefer the approach of Abella JA, the evidence tendered by Milner Power does not meet even the lower standard set by the majority: it does not rise above speculation.

[55] In *Cherubini Metal Works Ltd. v. Nova Scotia (Attorney General)*, 2007 NSCA 37, 253 NSR (2d) 134, the applicant wanted to examine members of an administrative tribunal in a tort action. The court held that a threshold must be met before the general rule of adjudicative secrecy can be displaced:

> [36] What is the threshold for lifting deliberative secrecy in the context of a tort action? By analogy to the judicial review cases, it would seem that there must be evidence of a clearly articulated and objectively reasonable concern that a relevant legal right may have been infringed and that the proposed discovery will afford evidence of it. This is a slightly modified version of the approach taken by the Ontario Court of Appeal in a judicial review case in *Payne v. Ontario Human Rights Commission* (2000), 192 DLR (4th) 315; OJ No. 2987 (QL) (CA) at para. 172 and which is adopted in Brown and Evans, *Judicial Review of Administrative Action in Canada*, vol. 2 (looseleaf, updated to July 2, 2006) (Toronto: Canvasback Publishing, 1998), section 6:5620. It serves at least as a useful starting point for defining the threshold in civil litigation as opposed to judicial review and related proceedings.

While the applicant argued there had been improper influence on the decision making process, the court concluded it had "not provided any clearly articulated basis to displace deliberative secrecy, let alone provide evidence to support it."

[56] This Court has on previous occasions confirmed that a threshold must be met before an administrative tribunal will be directed to make further disclosure. ... [discussion of earlier decisions omitted.]

[57] Where the applicant for leave to appeal could show some clear evidence of an error of law or jurisdiction, but it appeared that the error was not fully disclosed on the record, further production or examination might be ordered. The applicant is not however entitled to embark on a fishing expedition. There is no entitlement to a general examination for discovery prior to the application for leave to appeal. ... There is simply not anything on this record suggesting that there is "missing evidence" that would show that the Department of Energy influenced the A.E.U.B. improperly or at all, or that the A.E.U.B. fettered its discretion, such as would entitle Milner Power to further disclosure.

[58] Milner Power argues (factum, para. 65) that the A.E.U.B. refuses "otherwise to admit its consideration of materials outside of the official record." The panel of the A.E.U.B. stated (in its

reasons) what it relied on. There is nothing on the record, apart from conjecture, to suggest it relied on anything else, or that there is anything for the panel to "admit." There is not a scintilla of evidence of any "government directives" on how the Milner complaint should be decided.

[59] Milner Power argues that if applicants are not able to supplement the record, some tribunal misconduct may go undetected. If that is so, it is the price that must be paid for deliberative confidentiality, which is vital to the efficient and effective functioning of tribunals. As the Court noted in *Ellis-Don Ltd. v. Ontario (Labour Relations Board)*, *supra*, at para. 54:

> Satisfying those requirements of consistency and independence comes undoubtedly at a price, this price being that the process becomes less open and that litigants face tough hurdles when attempting to build the evidentiary foundation for a successful challenge based on alleged breaches of natural justice.
>
> Deliberative confidentiality is a core value, not to be lightly set aside: *R v. Pan*, 2001 SCC 42, [2001] 2 SCR 344, at para. 45. It is also a type of shield that prevents the interruption of tribunal business by unfounded suspicions, or by a desire applicants may have to satisfy themselves that they have been fairly treated when there is no objective evidence to the contrary: *Potter v. Nova Scotia (Securities Commission)*, 2006 NSCA 45, 266 DLR (4th) 147, at paras. 20-23; *Cherubini Metals*, *supra*, at para. 14. In any event such undiscovered misconduct must be rare, as it assumes a lack of candor by tribunals in their reasons or the records they file with the courts. The theoretical benefits that might result from placing every tribunal under a microscope do not outweigh the very real costs of such a procedure. Where there is some reasonable evidence of misconduct, further inquiry is justified. Where there is no evidence of misconduct, it is not.

3. For academic discussion, see Ellis and Alterman, "Deliberative Secrecy and Adjudicative Independence: The *Glengarry* Principle" (1994), 7 *CJALP* 171; Hawkins, "Behind Closed Doors I: The Substantive Problem—Full Boards, Consensus Tables and Caucus Cabals" (1995), 9 *CJALP* 39 and "Behind Closed Doors II: The Operational Problem—Deliberative Secrecy, Statutory Immunity and Testimonial Privilege" (1996), 10 *CJALP* 39; and Chambers, "Behind Closed Doors: Publicity, Secrecy, and the Quality of Deliberation" (2004), 12 *J Political Philosophy* 389.

AGENCY COUNSEL

Nearly all administrative agencies have some professional staff, including a secretary. They also have access to legal counsel, who may be employed full-time in a variety of roles, or may be lawyers in private practice engaged on a retainer to give legal advice as and when required. As we saw in chapter 5, Bias and Lack of Independence, where an agency is responsible not just for hearing cases but also for investigating and making decisions to proceed against someone, it is now seen as imperative that those involved do not generally have overlapping functions. Lawyers or staff involved in investigations and prosecutions should not also be engaged in assisting those who adjudicate, particularly in the instance of files with which they have had some prior involvement: *2747-3174 Québec Inc. v. Quebec (Régie des permis d'alcool)*, [1999] 3 SCR 919.

In this section we consider some of the other limitations that the duty of fairness may impose on agencies' ability to seek the assistance of counsel in the discharge of their adjudicative functions. For a useful overview, see Rankin and Greathead, "Advising the Board: The Scope of Counsel's Role in Advising Administrative Tribunals" (1993), 7 *CJALP* 29 and Mullan, "The Role of Lawyers to Professional Disciplinary Bodies" (Dec. 1994), 13 *Advoc. Soc. J* 10.

At the Hearing

It is common for tribunals, especially when sitting without a member who is legally trained, to have counsel available to advise on the admissibility of evidence, procedure, or other questions of law that arise during the hearing. Sometimes the lawyer actually sits in the hearing room and gives advice when asked. However, since this can be very expensive, the tribunal may be content to have the lawyer available by telephone. In either case, the parties should be apprised of counsel's advice, and given an opportunity to make submissions to the tribunal before it decides the issue. Legal opinions given to an agency by the staff counsel are the subject of lawyer–client privilege: *Pritchard v. Ontario (Human Rights Commission)*, [2004] 1 SCR 809 (Ont.).

The problem most likely to arise from these arrangements is that counsel may overstep the role of adviser to assume functions more appropriate for the chair or other members of the tribunal—for example, making rulings, intervening to raise issues or question witnesses, or deciding on adjournments. The impression may be created that counsel, not the panel, is in fact running the hearing. This could give rise to a challenge for bias on the ground that a reasonable observer might conclude that someone other than one statutorily authorized to decide was in reality the decision-maker. See, for example, *Venczel v. Association of Architects (Ontario)* (1990), 74 OR (2d) 755 (Ont. Div. Ct.). The degree of intervention permitted may also depend on the nature of the proceeding—in an adversarial proceeding, less active intervention on the part of tribunal counsel is likely to be allowed by the duty of fairness than in a proceeding that is more inquisitorial, such as a Convention refugee determination hearing, where the refugee hearing officer questions the claimant in an attempt to ensure that the panel has the full story before it.

It is an additional ground for impugning the proceeding that counsel's interventions seemed to favour one party to the dispute: *Brett v. Ontario (Board of Directors of Physiotherapy)* (1991), 77 DLR (4th) 144 (Ont. Div. Ct.); aff'd. (1993), 104 DLR (4th) 421 (Ont. CA). However, if an objection to the conduct of counsel at the hearing is not made at the time, an application for judicial review made after the tribunal releases its decision may be dismissed for acquiescence. Of course, the person to whom the panel looks for legal advice should be in fact and appearance independent of the parties: *Hutterian Brethren Church of Starland v. Starland No. 47 (Municipal District)* (1993), 14 Admin. LR (2d) 186 (Alta. CA). Compare *Omineca Enterprises Ltd. v. British Columbia (Minister of Forests)* (1993), 18 Admin. LR (2d) 210 (BC CA) (not bias for board to engage as its counsel a lawyer paid by the attorney general's department, even in a proceeding to which another government department was a party).

The Preparation of Reasons

Writing reasons for decision can be an onerous and daunting task for the members of many administrative tribunals. Members of self-governing professions serve on the discipline committee of the governing body of their profession on a part-time basis as a matter of professional duty, and with no or very modest remuneration. In recent years, the volume and complexity of disciplinary proceedings in many professions have grown alarmingly. Governments have also started to appoint members of tribunals from a wider cross-section of the population in an attempt to ensure that the problems of more claimants are fully understood. For example, the Social Assistance Review Board in Ontario has included people with personal experience of living on welfare, and the membership of the Immigration and Refugee Board is intended to reflect Canada's ethnic diversity.

Consequently, members of tribunals may find that they do not have the time needed to write reasons for a decision that may be based on a hearing that lasted several days. Or, they may have little experience with writing reports or anything analogous to reasons for decision, which require them to make and explain findings of fact on the basis of the evidence produced at the hearing and to draw legal conclusions from the parties' submissions.

The practical problem is this: how far may tribunals take advantage of the expertise of their staff, including their counsel, in the preparation of the reasons for decision, without breaching some aspect of the duty of fairness—the delegation doctrine and apprehended bias, in particular? To put the question on a more theoretical level, to what extent is the giving of reasons a function that must be performed *personally* by the statutorily designated decision-makers, rather than *bureaucratically* (or institutionally) through the use of the full range of agency resources?

The relevant black-letter law can be stated simply. First, the decision made must be that of the tribunal members themselves. For this reason, counsel who, without the consent of the parties, retire with the tribunal while it deliberates may thereby create a reasonable apprehension of bias: the participation of a non-member in making the tribunal's decision. Second, the reasons for decision must be in substance those of the tribunal members, not their clerk's or their counsel's.

The courts have recognized in two ways the difficulties that may be caused by insisting that agency members write their own reasons for decision. First, in *Re Del Core and Ontario College of Pharmacists* (1985), 19 DLR (4th) 68 (Ont. CA), Finlayson JA said that "courts should not be overly critical of the language employed by [discipline committees of self-governing] bodies and seize on a few words as being destructive of the entire disciplinary process" (at 74). Other judges have also recognized that, when interpreting administrative decisions and other documents, they should remember that their author may not be a lawyer and be prepared to overlook infelicities in expression or possible ambiguities, if the document otherwise gives a reasonably clear account of the reasons for decision: see, for example, *International Woodworkers of America, Local 217 v. Weldwood of Canada, Ltd.*, [1977] 1 SCR 703, at 710 (BC) and *Brown v. Public Service Commission*, [1975] FC 345, at 374-75. Nonetheless, courts are still liable to scrutinize reasons for decisions, especially from professional discipline committees, for example, with considerable care.

Second, the courts have also permitted tribunals to seek the assistance of counsel (or some other staff member: *Armstrong v. Canada (Commissioner of the RCMP)*, [1994] 2 FC

356 (TD)) in the preparation of the statement of their reasons for decision. In *Spring v. Law Society of Upper Canada* (1988), 60 OR (2d) 719, 50 DLR (4th) 523 (Div. Ct.), the Law Society discipline committee's decision to disbar one of its members was upheld despite the fact that the committee's reasons were prepared by the clerk of the committee who was not a member of it. However, a committee member had received the draft decision, made changes, and drafted the conclusion on penalty; furthermore, the final draft was concurred in by all panel members.

On the other hand, it is impermissible for the tribunal to ask for help from counsel for one of the parties: this would give rise to a reasonable apprehension of bias. See *Re Sawyer and Ontario Racing Commission* (1979), 99 DLR (3d) 561 (Ont. CA) and *Després v. New Brunswick Lands Surveyors Association* (1992), 8 Admin. LR (2d) 136 (NB CA).

Khan v. College of Physicians and Surgeons of Ontario
(1992), 94 DLR (4th) 193 (Ont. CA)

[Khan was found guilty of professional misconduct by the discipline committee of the college and his licence was revoked. He appealed to the Divisional Court, which allowed the appeal: (1990), 76 DLR (4th) 179. The Court of Appeal allowed the college's appeal, holding that, despite the evidential errors that the committee had made, the case against Khan was so strong that the committee would necessarily have reached the same result on the basis of the admissible evidence that it heard.

Khan had also appealed on the ground that the committee breached the duty of procedural fairness by permitting its counsel to play so significant a role in the preparation of its reasons for decision as to create a reasonable apprehension of bias. The Divisional Court allowed the appeal on this ground as well. The following extract from the Court of Appeal's judgment deals only with this issue.]

DOHERTY JA: ...

E. Did counsel's involvement in the preparation of the Committee's reasons contravene the Health Disciplines Act or the principles of natural justice?

(i) Background

The Committee is entitled to the legal assistance of its own counsel during the hearing. It received such assistance in this case and there is no suggestion that counsel's conduct during the actual hearing was improper. It is also not suggested that counsel played any role in the Committee's deliberation or its decisions to find Dr. Khan guilty of professional misconduct and revoke his licence.

The Committee did not give any reasons for its decision at the time it was announced to the parties. Reasons were released about three months later. It is counsel's involvement in the preparation of those reasons which is in issue.

After the Committee had released the reasons, counsel for Dr. Khan inquired of counsel for the Committee as to his involvement in the preparation of the reasons. Counsel replied, in part:

[W]e provide no legal advice to the Committee in their preparation of written reasons for their decision. The Committee understands that they are obligated to provide the reasons for their decision. The written Decision and Reasons for Decision is in every case drafted in the first instance by the Chairman of the panel or a member of the panel designated by the Chairman for that purpose. In the ordinary course we are provided with a copy of the draft, review it with the Chairman and assist the Chairman to express the reasons of the Committee. The draft Decision and Reasons for Decision in this case went through this process, and through subsequent review and revision by members of the Committee in conference, and was ultimately approved and signed by each Committee member.

In the *Khan* case, as in all others, the Decision and Reasons for Decision are those of the Committee. We are satisfied that the journalistic and administrative assistance that we provide in the above respect is not "legal advice" within the meaning of Section 12(3) of the Act. Our role here is to assist the Committee to express their decision and their reasons for that decision.

Counsel for Dr. Khan subsequently requested access to the drafts referred to in the above-quoted letter. The Committee declined to produce them.

In the Divisional Court, counsel for Dr. Khan did not challenge the description provided in counsel's letter to him. Nor did he seek production of any drafts of the reasons of the Committee. This appeal must proceed on the basis that the counsel's letter provides an accurate and complete description of the reason-writing process. That process had three distinct phases. First, a member of the Committee prepared a draft. That draft was then reviewed and revised by counsel for the Committee, in consultation with the chairman. This second draft then went back to the entire Committee for review, revision and eventual release. Counsel for the Committee was not involved in this final revision of the reasons. The final draft was approved and signed by each member of the Committee.

(ii) Section 12(3) of the Health Disciplines Act

The majority in the Divisional Court held that s. 12(3) of the *Health Disciplines Act* precluded the kind of assistance given by counsel during the drafting process. [This part of s. 12(3) is now contained in the *Regulated Health Professions Act*, SO 1991, c. 18, Sched. 2 *(Health Professions Procedural Code)*, s. 44.]

Section 12(3) provides:

12(3) Members of a discipline committee holding a hearing shall not have taken part before the hearing in any investigation of the subject-matter of the hearing other than as a member of the Council considering the referral of the matter to the discipline committee or at a previous hearing of the committee, and shall not communicate directly or indirectly in relation to the subject-matter of the hearing with any person or with any party or his representative except upon notice to and opportunity for all parties to participate, but the committee may seek legal advice from an adviser independent from the parties and in such case the nature of the advice should be made known to the parties in order that they may make submissions as to the law.

Rosenberg J, for the majority, held that counsel's advice to the Committee must have amounted to legal advice. He wrote at p. 200:

Without suggesting that the letter is not a straightforward attempt to give the court the facts, it is difficult to see how a lawyer trained as he is and whose role is counsel for the committee can distinguish between changes that are made for journalistic and administrative reasons and those that are made for legal reasons. If a sentence is left out, does it change the meaning of what is being said and might it not affect the court's view of the reasons? Lawyers are not retained for their journalistic or administrative abilities and it is unlikely that a lawyer with the best of intentions can confine his advice to be only of journalistic and administrative assistance.

Before turning to the nature of the advice supplied by counsel, the scope of s. 12(3) of the *Health Disciplines Act* must be addressed. Mr. Scott argued that the section had no application beyond the hearing stage of the discipline process. I agree. This is apparent from a consideration of s. 12 as a whole, and the language of s. 12(3).

Section 12(1) designates the parties to the hearing; s. 12(2) refers to the disclosure of material to be relied on at the hearing; s. 12(4) is concerned with public access to the hearing; s. 12(5) and (6) deal with the rules of evidence and the recording of proceedings during the hearing; s. 12(7) sets out the nature of the participation in the hearing required before a committee member can take part in the decision-making process; and s. 12(8) deals with the return of materials used during the hearing. The context provided by the other parts of s. 12 strongly suggests that the hearing is the focal point of s. 12 and that the section is directed only to that part of the discipline process.

The language of s. 12(3) confirms this assessment by its opening reference to "members of a discipline committee holding a hearing." The terms of s. 12(3) address the requirements of a fair hearing. They speak to bias, the right to know the case made by the other party, and the right to present one's own case. Section 12(3), like the rest of s. 12, refers to the hearing stage of the proceedings. The legal advice refers to advice given during the hearing by counsel for the Committee.

In my view, the hearing phase of the discipline process encompasses the taking of evidence, the hearing of argument and the rendering of the decision required by s. 61(2) of the *Health Disciplines Act*. It does not include the preparation of reasons for that decision. The *Health Disciplines Act* distinguishes between decisions and reasons for those decisions (*e.g.*, ss. 58(3) and 8). It does not require that the Committee provide reasons for its findings of professional misconduct. The hearing stage of the discipline process was over when the Committee announced its decision and imposed a penalty. Nothing done by counsel for the Committee after that point could contravene s. 12(3).

Even if s. 12(3) of the *Health Disciplines Act* reached beyond the hearing stage to the writing of the reasons for the decision, the section was not contravened in this case. Counsel for the Committee specifically disavowed providing any legal advice to the Committee during the writing of the reasons. His assertion was not challenged.

I cannot accept the view that any advice given by counsel for the Committee which affects the substance of the Committee's reasons amounts to legal advice. It is the nature of the advice, not its effect on the final product, which must be considered. The phrase "legal advice" in s. 12(3) must refer to advice on matters of law. Advice intended to improve the quality of the Committee's reasons by, for example, deleting erroneous references to the evidence or adding additional relevant references to the evidence, is not advice on a matter of law but is rather advice as to how the Committee should frame its reasons in support of its decision. If the Committee accepts such advice, it may improve the quality of the reasons ultimately provided by the Committee and render the decision of the Committee less susceptible to reversal on appeal. This does not, however, transform advice as to the content and formulation of reasons into advice on a matter of law.

Even if s. 12(3) of the *Health Disciplines Act* applied after the hearing was completed, Dr. Khan had the burden of showing that counsel for the Committee provided "legal advice" to the Committee during the drafting process. On this record, there is no evidence to support that contention.

(iii) The Propriety of Counsel's Involvement in the Drafting Process Apart from s. 12(3) of the Health Disciplines Act

Apart from any specific statutory requirement, the involvement of counsel in the preparation of the reasons for the Committee's decision may raise questions as to the fairness and integrity of the proceedings before the Committee. Mr. Thomson, for the Committee, and Mr. Scott as *amicus curiae*, addressed these broader concerns. Both argued that the Committee was entitled to the assistance of counsel in the preparation of their reasons. At the same time, both recognized that there were limitations on the extent and nature of the assistance which counsel could provide. They submitted that the involvement of counsel for the Committee in the drafting process fell well within the bounds of permissible assistance and did not impair either the fairness or integrity of the discipline process.

I accept both of the underlying principles put forward by Mr. Thomson and Mr. Scott. The reasons for a decision made by the Committee must be those of the Committee: *Del Core v. Ontario College of Pharmacists* (1985) 19 DLR (4th) 68 at 74 (Ont. CA); leave to appeal to the Supreme Court of Canada refused, [1986] 1 SCR viii. The rationale underlying this principle is self-evident. In discipline proceedings the parties are entitled to know, and if so inclined challenge on appeal, the Committee's decision. Someone else's explanation for or rationalization of that decision is no substitute for the Committee's reasons. Without the reasons of the Committee, a party cannot know why the decision was made, or who made the decision. The right of appeal also becomes illusory.

The Committee's ultimate responsibility for the authorship of the reasons is not inconsistent with the Committee availing itself of counsel's assistance during the drafting process. It is well-established that a tribunal such as the Committee may look to outside sources for assistance in the preparation of its reasons: *Spring v. Law Society of Upper Canada* (1988) 50 DLR (4th) 523 (Ont. Div. Ct.); Macaulay, *Practice and Procedure Before Administrative Tribunals* (1988), at pp. 22-10 to 22-10.21. That assistance should not be discouraged or deprecated. In *Consolidated-Bathurst Packaging Ltd. v. I.W.A. Local 2-69* [1990] 1 SCR 282, at 327 Gonthier J, for the majority observed that tribunals must marry their use of "outside" assistance with procedural fairness:

> The rules of natural justice should not discourage administrative bodies from taking advantage of the accumulated experience of its members. On the contrary, the rules of natural justice should in their application reconcile the characteristics and exigencies of decision-making by specialized tribunals with the procedural rights of the parties.

That same reconciliation must be achieved during the drafting of reasons. The ultimate aim of the drafting process is a set of reasons which accurately and fully reflects the thought processes of the Committee. To the extent that consultation with counsel promotes that aim, it is to be encouraged. The debate must fix, not on the Committee's entitlement to assistance in the drafting of reasons, but on the acceptable limits of that assistance.

The line between permissible assistance and that which is forbidden must be drawn by regard to the effect of counsel's involvement in the drafting process, on the fairness of the proceedings and the integrity of the overall discipline process. Without attempting an exhaustive description of these concepts, fairness includes considerations of bias, real or apprehended, independence, and each party's right to know the case made against them and to present their own case. Integrity concerns encompass those fairness concerns but include the broader need to ensure that the body charged with the responsibility of making the particular decision in fact makes that decision after a proper consideration of the merits. If the reasons presented for the decision are not those of the decision-maker, or do not appear to be so, it raises real concerns about the validity of the decision and the genuineness of the entire inquiry.

There is no single formula or procedure referable to the drafting process that can be uniformly applied across the very broad spectrum of decision-making, when determining whether the involvement of the non-decision-maker in the drafting process compromised the fairness of the proceedings or the integrity of the process. The nature of the proceedings, the issues raised in those proceedings, the composition of the tribunal, the terms of the enabling legislation, the support structure available to the tribunal, the tribunal's workload, and other factors will impact on the assessment of the propriety of procedures used in the preparation of reasons. Certainly, the judicial paradigm of reason-writing cannot be imposed on all boards and tribunals: *Consolidated-Bathurst Packaging Ltd. v. I.W.A., supra*, at pp. 554-5.

It must also be recognized that the volume and complexity of modern decision-making all but necessitates resort to "outside" sources during the drafting process. Contemporary reason-writing is very much a consultive process during which the writer of the reasons resorts to many sources, including persons not charged with the responsibility of deciding the matter, in formulating his or her reasons. It is inevitable that the author of the reasons will be influenced by some of these sources. To hold that any "outside" influence vitiates the validity of the proceedings or the decision reached is to insist on a degree of isolation which is not only totally unrealistic but also destructive of effective reason-writing.

In deciding whether the involvement of counsel in the drafting of the reasons operated unfairly against Dr. Khan or appeared to do so, I take the words of Gonthier J in *Tremblay v. Québec (Commission des affaires sociales)*, a decision of the Supreme Court of Canada released April 16, 1992 [since reported, [1992] 1 SCR 952, 971], as an appropriate starting place:

> A consultation process by plenary meeting designed to promote adjudicative coherence may thus prove acceptable and even desirable for a body like the Commission, *provided this process does not involve an interference with the freedom of decision-makers to decide according to their consciences and opinions. The process must also, even if it does not interfere with*

the actual freedom of the decision-makers, not be designed so as to create an appearance of bias or lack of independence.

(Emphasis added.) Where counsel is connected with one of the parties to the hearing an appearance of bias will result if that counsel participates in the drafting process: *Re Sawyer and Ontario Racing Com'n* (1979) 99 DLR (3d) 561 at 564-5 (Ont. CA); *Re Emerson and Law Society of Upper Canada* (1983) 5 DLR (4th) 294 at 324 (Ont. Div. Ct.). Also where the decision-maker is compelled to consult with others, who are not charged with the responsibility of deciding the case, the appearance of independence may be lost: *Tremblay v. Quebec (Commission des affaires sociales), supra,* at 971-3. No doubt other factors could affect the independence or impartiality of the tribunal or the appearance of independence and impartiality.

Nothing in this record suggests that counsel's involvement in the writing of the reasons compromised the independence or impartiality of the Committee. Counsel for the Committee was the servant of the Committee and was totally independent from the College or Dr. Khan. His involvement in the writing of the reasons was not mandatory, and was entirely under the control of the Committee. Counsel's assistance could not have had any coercive effect on the Committee.

I am also satisfied that counsel's involvement in the drafting process did not undermine Dr. Khan's ability to know the case made against him or to present his own case. There is no evidence that counsel assumed the role of an advocate, advancing one position over another during the drafting process, or that he presented any new facts, arguments or legal issues for the Committee's consideration during the drafting process. He merely assisted in the preparation of an intermediate draft. The reasons released by the Committee reflect the evidence heard, the arguments made, and the legal advice given at the hearing. On this record, it would be sheer speculation to hold that during the drafting stage, counsel led the Committee outside of the confines of the evidence heard, the arguments made and the legal advice given at the hearing, so as to deny Dr. Khan a fair hearing and a proper adjudication.

In my opinion, no legitimate concerns as to the fairness of the proceedings arise from counsel's very limited involvement in the reason-writing process.

I am also persuaded that counsel's involvement in the drafting process did not impair the integrity of the discipline proceedings. The drafting process followed by the Committee maintained the responsibility of authorship with the Committee and avoided any inference that counsel had co-opted or had delegated to him the reason-writing function. In that regard, the following features of the process are significant, although none are determinative:

(i) A Committee member prepared the first draft of the reasons.

(ii) Counsel, with the chairman of the Committee, revised and clarified the first draft but did not write independently of that draft.

(iii) The Committee met to consider and revise the draft as amended by counsel and the chairman; counsel played no role in this review and revision.

(iv) The final product which emerged from the drafting process was signed by each member of the Committee.

In referring to these factors, I do not suggest that the presence or absence of any one of these features will be determinative when addressing the effect of the drafting process on the integrity of the discipline process. The entire process must be considered. Nor do I suggest that the procedure followed here sets either a maximum standard for the involvement of counsel in the drafting of reasons, or that it is the only appropriate procedure. I am, however, satisfied that this procedure, considered as a whole, effectively counteracts any legitimate concerns as to the authorship of the reasons.

Appeal allowed.

Reasons Review

In the cases considered above, assistance was given by a person assigned to assist the hearing panel with a particular case. Some agencies also employ lawyers, either on staff or on retainer from private practice, to assist the agency in its corporate capacity to develop policy and oversee its implementation by panels of the agency.

The chairs of many agencies take the view that there is a corporate responsibility for the quality of the agency's work, including the decisions made by its members after a hearing. The argument is that, when sitting on a hearing panel, members exercise their powers, not with total independence, like judges, but as members of an agency with a statutory mandate to discharge, which accordingly gives to the agency a legitimate interest in the substance and technical quality of members' decisions.

Bovbel v. Canada (Minister of Employment and Immigration)
[1994] 2 FC 563 (CA)

PRATTE JA: This is an appeal from an order of the Trial Division allowing the respondent's application for judicial review of a decision of the Immigration and Refugee Board determining that the respondent was not a Convention refugee.

In the court below, the respondent attacked the decision of the board on two grounds, namely, that the board had erred in failing to find that he was a Convention refugee and, second, that "contrary to the principles of natural justice and the provisions of the *Immigration Act*," the board had "referred a draft of its written decision to legal counsel who [was] not a member of the Board and who [had] not participate[d] in or attend[ed] at the applicant's hearing."

The motion judge rejected the respondent's first ground of attack but allowed the application for judicial review on the second ground. He found that the members of the board were governed by a Policy—the Reasons Review policy—according to which they were expected to submit a draft of their reasons for decision to legal advisors before issuing them to the parties. The mere existence of that policy, according to the judge, was sufficient to taint all the decisions rendered by the board while the policy was in force since it created a reasonable apprehension of lack of independence on the part of its members.

The only evidence on the record of the board's Reasons Review Policy is found in documents that, following a request made by the appellant pursuant to Rule 1612, were forwarded to the registry by the board. There is no evidence of the manner in which that policy was understood and applied by the members of the board. More importantly, the record does not show whether the two members of the board who disposed of the respondent's claim to Convention refugee status actually followed that policy in this case. Their reasons may or may not have been submitted to the board's legal advisors; we do not know. This lack of evidence, according to the judge of first instance, was of no consequence ([1994] 1 FC 340). The issue before him, as he saw it, was simply whether the board's Reasons Review Policy breached the rules of natural justice. We have difficulty understanding the judge's position on this point. If, as he found, the Reasons Review Policy prescribed a procedure that offended the principles of natural justice, certainly that defect could only affect the validity of decisions rendered in accordance with that procedure. For that reason alone, the order appealed from should be set aside. The application for judicial review was not directed against the policy of the board but against the decision determining that the respondent was not a Convention refugee; if it was not established that this decision had been illegally made, the application could not succeed.

But there is more. Even if, contrary to our view, the motion judge correctly defined the issue before him and correctly assumed that a Reasons Review Policy endangering the independence of the members of the board could create a reasonable apprehension of bias on their part, sufficient to vitiate all their decisions, the appeal should still be allowed for the very simple reason that there was nothing wrong with the policy followed by the board.

The board's policy, in so far as it can be understood from the documents on the record, encourages the members of the board, the great majority of whom have no legal training, to submit their reasons for decision to the Legal Services Branch (which is composed of lawyers who do not participate in the hearings of the board) prior to putting their reasons in final form. The goals pursued by that policy are expressed in the following terms in a document filed by the board:

The goals of the reasons review process prior to January 1992 were:

1. To ensure that the reasons are written in an appropriate style and form.

2. To ensure that the reasons address the issues which need to be dealt with.

3. To ensure that decisions of the IRB, IAB or the courts are not overlooked by the panel.

4. To ensure that the decisions which depart from precedent are made knowingly and after full consideration of the existing jurisprudence.

5. To ensure that the reasons are consistently of as superior a quality as possible by drawing upon the legal unit's knowledge and expertise.

6. To ensure that the legal unit is aware of the decisions being made so that the bank of jurisprudence is updated and complete.

Chapter 15 of the Convention Refugee Determination Division Member's Handbook of October 16, 1990, is entitled "Decisions and Reasons." It refers in many places to the role played by the members of the Legal Services Branch. The following passages of that handbook are of interest:

1. INTRODUCTION

This chapter deals with decisions and reasons following a Refugee Division hearing into a claim. ...

A "decision" is a panel's final determination on a claim or application, while "reasons" are the panel's explanation for the decision.

This chapter explains when Refugee Division members must give written reasons. ...

The chapter also discusses the role of the Board's legal advisers in reviewing reasons for decision.

• • •

4. CONSULTATION AND COLLEGIALITY IN DECISION-MAKING

Between Panel Members and Other CRDD Members

It is suggested that Refugee Division members may consult with one another, subject to the following limitations:

(i) No new evidence should be considered in reaching a decision, unless the participants at the hearing are given an opportunity to respond. ...

(ii) A panel should not decide a case on a new ground, one not raised at the hearing, unless the participants are given an opportunity to respond. ...

(iii) While a panel may receive the advice of the other members, only the panel members should participate in the final decision. This simply means that panel members should not abdicate in any way their responsibility to decide the case themselves.

Between Panel Members and Board's Lawyers

The considerations set out above apply equally well to discussions between panel members and the Board's legal advisers. While the Board's lawyers may give advice, it is the panel members themselves who must decide the case. Members, of course, are free to accept or reject the advice of legal advisers, as the members see fit.

The Board's lawyers may suggest that a case would be better decided on different grounds than what the panel has proposed, but the panel should not decide the case on those different grounds if the grounds were not raised at the hearing or unless the parties were given an additional opportunity to comment.

14. ROLE OF THE LEGAL SERVICES BRANCH

The Board's legal advisers provide opinions on request to the members and staff of the Board on a variety of legal matters. ...

Legal advisers try to provide whatever legal assistance a Refugee Division panel may require. ...

Legal advisers provide written opinions on legal issues that have been raised at hearings, if a panel member so requests. ... In this context, the role of the legal adviser is an extension of the research function of the individual member.

• • •

Written reasons for Refugee Division members may be submitted in preliminary draft form to legal advisers in advance of the release of the reasons to the parties affected. A legal adviser peruses the draft reasons with certain objectives in mind. These are mainly:

(a) to ensure that the reasons address the issues which need to be dealt with, and

(b) to ensure that decisions which depart from precedent are made knowingly and after full consideration of the jurisprudence.

The review procedure does not result in restricting or imposing in any way upon the authority and responsibility of a panel to decide a case or to express the reasons in any manner it may choose. Once the legal adviser has made comments or suggestions, the panel or any member of it is free to adopt or reject them. This practice has the further purpose of ensuring that the legal branch is aware of the decisions being made so that the bank of jurisprudence is updated and complete.

. . .

16. ADMINISTRATIVE ROUTING OF WRITTEN REASONS

When a member has completed a draft set of reasons, the following steps are followed at the present time:

1. The completed draft and the case file are sent to the regional legal advisers. Some files may be sent on to be reviewed by legal advisers in Ottawa.

2. A legal adviser will review the draft reasons and comment, if necessary, directly on the draft. …

3. The legal adviser who reviewed the reasons will return the draft reasons, with comments, and the file to the author of the reasons. The author will decide whether or not to make changes to the reasons based on the comments. If major changes are made, the reasons may be returned to Legal Services for a review of only those aspects of the decision that are new. …

4. When the review process has been completed and the author is satisfied with the reasons, the reasons and the file in the case will be sent to any other panel members. The author of the reasons should not remove the draft reasons with the legal adviser's comments from the file. It may be that those comments trigger a concern in other panel members prompting them to dissent or to write separate, concurring reasons, or even to convince the author of the reasons to make further changes.

5. The co-panel member in the case will either sign the reasons to show that he or she concurs, or write dissenting or concurring reasons. In the latter two cases, the reasons may be sent to Legal Services for review (usually the same lawyer will be assigned to review majority and minority reasons in a case) and the steps outlined above are applicable to these reasons.

It appears that on December 8, 1989, the Director of Legal Services sent a memo to the senior legal advisors of the board notifying them that a new "Reasons Review Policy," designed "to streamline the reasons review process and to decrease the turn around time for files in Legal Services," was to be implemented immediately. A document entitled "Reasons Review—Temporary Measures CRDD Reasons" was attached to that memo. After stating the goals of the new policy, that document described the reasons review process in the following terms:

The Interim Reasons Review Process

1. Grammatical Indiscretions and Matters of Style

Corrections of grammatical errors will be made only where the change is necessary or obvious. ...

Stylistic changes should be kept to a minimum. ... It may be necessary to suggest stylistic changes where the style affects the substance of the reasons. For example, where because of the style the reasons do not convey the message in a clear and concise manner it may be necessary to suggest style changes.

. . .

4. Legal Issues

Our primary focus in reasons review will continue to be the identification of errors of law, areas where the member should be made aware of the existing jurisprudence and advising the member generally on the legal issues arising from the case. Our comments will be made within the following general guidelines:

(a) comments should be made in a brief and concise manner;

. . .

(f) do not spend a great deal of time verifying facts and names; it is important to look for inconsistencies that signal a problem with the facts before embarking on a time consuming review of the transcript.

The IRB Case Processing Manual, a manual intended to serve as an operational guide to all employees of the Immigration and Refugee Board who are involved in the processing of cases that come before the board, also makes reference to the review of draft reasons by the Legal Services in a chapter entitled "Decisions and Reasons," where it describes the procedure followed when reasons are given in support of a decision:

Decision and Reasons prepared—Reserved decisions finalized, and Bench Decisions with reasons to follow:

1. The presiding member records the disposition on the *CRDD Hearing Disposition Record* and ensures that it is dated and signed by him/herself and the other panel member. ...

2. The presiding member has reasons drafted and provides to his/her secretary for typing.

3. The member's secretary types the draft reasons, returns them to the member for verification and forwards them with the file to Legal Services for review.

4. Legal Services returns the reasons with the file to the member's secretary.

5. The presiding member reviews the reasons returned from Legal, has final reasons typed (the members proofread the final reasons), signs them and forwards the files to the other panel member for signature or to write concurring reasons.

. . .

8. Where concurring reasons are written, the member forwards them to Legal Services for review and the reasons review process repeats itself.

This is all that we know of the board's Reasons Review Policy.

There is no doubt that the participation of "outsiders" in the decision-making process of an administrative tribunal may sometimes cause problems. The decisions of the tribunal must, indeed, be rendered by those on whom Parliament has conferred power to decide and their decisions must, unless the relevant legislation impliedly or expressly provides otherwise, meet the requirements of natural justice. However, when the practice followed by members of an administrative tribunal does not violate natural justice and does not infringe on their ability to decide according to their opinion even though it may influence that opinion, it cannot be criticized.

[The judge cited *Consolidated-Bathurst*, *Tremblay*, and *Khan*.]

This is why this court, in *Weerasinge v. Canada (Minister of Employment and Immigration)* [1994] 1 FC 330 (CA), approved the practice of the Immigration and Refugee Board to have the reasons of its members reviewed by legal advisors before their release. Mahoney JA, speaking for the majority of the court, expressed himself as follows (at 337-38):

> The Refugee Division consists of such number of full and part-time members as the Governor in Council may decide. They are appointed for terms of up to seven years. A minimum of one-tenth are required to be barristers or advocates of at least five years standing. It would be pure coincidence if either member of a panel hearing a particular claim were legally qualified.
>
> The Refugee Division is a lay tribunal required to decide claims which, as I have observed, involve the life, liberty and security of the person. It must do so within the framework of extensive, confusing, and sometimes confused, jurisprudence. It is required to give written reasons for decisions not favourable to claimants. The desirability of legal review of those reasons is manifest. Having come to a decision on what is essentially a question of fact: whether the claimant has a well-founded fear of persecution for a reason that engages the Convention refugee definition, a tribunal does not, in my opinion, offend any tenet of natural justice by taking advice as to legal matters contained in its reasons.
>
> While the reasons review process, both in the more limited format described in the memorandum and the full review format suggested, could be abused and result in the reviewing lawyers influencing the decisions to which the reasons relate, there is, in my opinion, simply no foundation for a conclusion that it has been, in fact, abused, either in the case before us or generally. Any consultation by a decision-maker before publishing a decision, including consultation by a judge with a law clerk, could be abused. As to whether there is an appearance offensive to our notions of natural justice, it seems to me that the question to be asked is, as in dealing with an assertion of a reasonable apprehension of bias, namely, whether an informed person, viewing the matter realistically and practically and having thought it through, would think it more likely than not that the tribunal's decision that a claimant was, or was not, a Convention refugee had been influenced by the review of its reasons by its staff lawyers. In my opinion, that person would not think it likely.

The motion judge gave these reasons for not following that decision.

His first reason was that the board's Reasons Review Policy, although not mandatory, was formulated so as to give the impression that draft reasons were to be reviewed as a general rule. Assuming the correctness of that finding, we fail to understand how, if the board's policy was otherwise unobjectionable, the fact that it was generally applied could make it bad.

Another reason given by the motion judge in support of his decision was founded on the passage of the member's handbook directing the authors of draft reasons which had been submitted to a legal advisor to leave those draft reasons in the file with the comments of the legal advisor so that they could be seen by the other member participating in the decision. This provision, according to the judge, was "a blatant attempt to influence." Again, we do not understand. Surely, if there is nothing wrong in the author of the reasons receiving the comments of a legal advisor, there cannot be any wrong in making those comments known to the other member of the board who is asked to concur in the reasons.

The main ground for the judge's decision, however, was based on the fact that the legal advisor reviewing the draft reasons had access to the entire file and on the recommendation made to legal advisors in December, 1989, that they should "not spend a great deal of time verifying facts and names" and should "before embarking on a time consuming review of the transcript" look for "inconsistencies that signal a problem with the facts." From this, the judge inferred that the legal advisors had, according to the policy, the authority to discuss the findings of facts made by the member. This, he considered to be objectionable in view of the assertion made by Gonthier J in *Consolidated-Bathurst*, *supra*, that discussions between members of a tribunal having to determine questions of facts and other persons generally constitute a breach of natural justice if those discussions relate to the determination and assessment that the tribunal must make of the facts.

We are all of opinion that this last reason is also without merit. A fair reading of the documents on the record shows, in our view, that the legal advisors were not expected to discuss the findings of facts made by the members but merely, if there was a factual inconsistency in the reasons, to look at the file in order to determine, if possible, how the inconsistency could be resolved. True, there was always the possibility that the legal advisors might, since they were in possession of the file, exceed their mandate and try to influence the factual findings of the board. However, as mentioned by Mahoney JA in *Weerasinge*, any policy is susceptible to abuse.

Appeal allowed.

[On September 8, 1994, the Supreme Court of Canada dismissed a motion for leave to appeal.]

AGENCY GUIDELINES

Some administrative agencies make extensive use of guidelines on the interpretation of their enabling legislation and the exercise of their statutory discretion. Guidelines can provide valuable assistance to agency members sitting on a panel that will hear and decide a particular case. They can be an effective way of maximizing the coherence of agency decisions and of transmitting to individual members the benefit of the agency's collective experience with and thought about the subject matter of the guidelines. Unlike the devices of institutional decision making considered previously, guidelines are proactive and can be used to formulate a general and comprehensive approach to a problem without being confined by the facts of a particular dispute. They should, of course, always be published and made available to those appearing before the agency.

In chapter 15 of this text we consider the strengths and weaknesses of general rules and individualized discretion as tools of administrative decision making and the extent to which the law encourages, discourages, or takes into account non-statutory rulemaking by agencies. Here, however, we are concerned only with the extent to which the duty of fairness limits the effective use of guidelines—in particular, the tension between the "due process" value represented by the principle that judicial decision-makers should be independent and the "bureaucratic" value that, as governmental institutions responsible for the delivery of public programs, administrative agencies should adopt measures to ensure that their decisions are coherent, thoughtful, and consistent.

The Immigration and Refugee Board, Canada's largest administrative tribunal, has been very active in drafting guidelines to assist board members to deal with both the procedural and substantive aspects of the exercise of their powers under the *Immigration and Refugee Protection Act*. In 2003, Chairperson Jean-Guy Fleury issued the following policy (footnotes have been omitted from the text below; emphasis from the original) governing the chairperson's exercise of the statutory authority to issue guidelines.

Immigration and Refugee Board of Canada,
Policy on the Use of Chairperson's Guidelines
Policy No. 2003-07 (October 27, 2003),
http://www.irb.gc.ca/eng/pages/index.aspx

1. Background

This policy governs the exercise of the Chairperson's authority to issue written guidelines in the Immigration Division (ID), the Immigration Appeal Division (IAD) and the Refugee Protection Division (RPD) of the Immigration and Refugee Board (IRB, or the Board). This policy establishes:

- a framework that guides in which circumstances the exercise of that authority may be carried out, and
- the process for deciding to issue guidelines.

1.1 Statutory Authority

The Chairperson has the statutory authority [pursuant to s. 159(1)(h) of the *Immigration and Refugee Protection Act*, SC 2001, c. 27] to issue guidelines and to identify decisions as jurisprudential guides to assist members in carrying out their duties:

> 159(1) The Chairperson is, by virtue of holding that office, a member of each Division of the Board and is the chief executive officer of the Board. In that capacity, the Chairperson …
>
> (h) may issue guidelines in writing to members of the Board and identify decisions of the Board as jurisprudential guides, after consulting with the Deputy Chairpersons and the Director General of the Immigration Division, to assist members in carrying out their duties;

A similar authority to issue guidelines existed under the former *Immigration Act*. Four sets of guidelines were issued: *Women Refugee Claimants Fearing Gender-Related Persecution*; *Child Refugee Claimants: Procedural and Evidentiary Issues*; *Civilian Non-Combatants Fearing Persecution in Civil War Situations*; and *Guidelines on Detention*.

In *Fouchong* [*Fouchong v. Canada (Secretary of State)*, [1994] FCJ No. 1727 (MacKay J)], the Federal Court—Trial Division upheld the legality of the *Guidelines on Women Refugee Claimants Fearing Gender-Related Persecution*:

> The Guidelines are not law, but they are authorized under s. 65(3) of the Act. They are not binding but they are intended to be considered by members of the tribunal in appropriate cases.

The Court then referred to the part of the Chairperson's memorandum that accompanied the release of the guidelines regarding their effect.

More recently, the decision of the Supreme Court of Canada in *Bell Canada* [*Bell Canada v. Canadian Telephone Employees Association*, [2003] 1 SCR 884] strengthened the legitimacy of a tribunal's use of statutory tools, such as guidelines, to support its adjudication strategy.

1.2 Adjudication Strategy

The IRB's ability to establish a consistent and coherent body of jurisprudence depends, in part, on the establishment of a coordinated and rational approach to its adjudicative function, including its procedure.

To be most effective, each division must establish a selective and strategic approach to the adjudication of issues. One aspect of this adjudication strategy involves identifying the recurring issues that have the potential to shape the Board's jurisprudence or practice. As Chairperson's guidelines may possibly affect a great number of cases before the Board, they constitute a major part of any strategic approach to the adjudication of issues.

Another aspect of a division's adjudication strategy revolves around procedure. Each division must continually work towards having in place the most efficient national and regional procedures, in order to improve the quality, consistency and efficiency of decision-making, which is part of the Board's key strategic priorities. The Board must respond to these operational challenges on an institutional level, given the Board's position as the country's largest administrative tribunal, spread out across Canada in five regions, with many decision-makers who render tens of thousands of decisions every year.

A number of different options are available that, taken together, constitute the tools that the Board has at its disposal to support its adjudication strategy. These are not mutually exclusive options, and any or all of them could be exercised at any particular time. These tools include the following:

- Chairperson's guidelines
- Identification of decisions as jurisprudential guides
- Identification of decisions as persuasive decisions
- Use of three-member panels (RPD and IAD)
- Conduct of a lead case

- Consultation amongst members on draft decisions in accordance with the principles in *Consolidated-Bathurst* [reproduced earlier in this chapter of the text]
- The Board seeking leave to intervene in a Higher Court proceeding

Guidelines and jurisprudential guides are complementary tools, the purpose of which is to promote consistency, coherence and fairness in the treatment of cases at the Board. The inclusion of such a statutory provision on guidelines and jurisprudential guides indicates Parliament's intent that the Chairperson should be involved in the adjudication strategy of the IRB as a whole, in order to assist decision-makers on matters of substantive and procedural importance.

Accordingly, the IRB has developed this policy, which governs the exercise of the Chairperson's authority to issue guidelines.

2. Process for Proposing Guidelines

The relevant Division Head may, after consultation with the Executive Director on any operational impact, make a written submission to the Chairperson's Executive Committee (CEC), regarding any issue or matter that he or she believes is suitable for the issuance of a set of guidelines, using the criteria set out in section 3 below.

The Executive Director may, after consultation with the relevant Division Head, make a written submission to the CEC, regarding any operational issue or matter that he or she believes is suitable for the issuance of a set of guidelines, in accordance with the criterion set out in subsection 3.4 below.

Any such submission shall be accompanied by a memorandum from staff, countersigned by the General Counsel, evaluating the legal considerations that could flow from guidelines on that issue or matter. The CEC will recommend to the Chairperson if the issue or matter should be pursued as a set of guidelines. However, it is only the Chairperson who has the authority to decide to proceed with a set of guidelines.

3. Circumstances for Exercise of Chairperson's Authority

Section 159(1)(h) of the *Act* gives the Chairperson two separate powers—1) to issue guidelines and 2) to identify decisions as jurisprudential guides. The stated purpose for the exercise of both of these powers is the same—*to assist members in carrying out their duties*. Where appropriate, guidelines may be issued to apply to more than one division of the Board.

There are four circumstances in which the Chairperson may consider exercising his or her authority to issue a set of guidelines. These four circumstances are as follows:

3.1 To Address Specific Legal Issues

The need to address specific legal issues has various components. For example, a division may identify one of the following needs:

- To address an emerging issue,
- To resolve an ambiguity in the law,
- To resolve inconsistency in decision-making, or
- To establish legal interpretations as preferred positions.

3.2 To Provide Guidance on Questions of Mixed Fact and Law

In addition to addressing issues that are strictly legal in nature as set out in section 3.1 above, guidelines may also provide guidance on questions of mixed fact and law.

Questions of mixed fact and law are found in between questions of law, which apply to all cases, and questions of fact, which apply only to the specific case. The Supreme Court of Canada distinguished them as follows in *Southam* [*Canada (Director of Investigation and Research, Competition Act) v. Southam Inc.*, [1997] 1 SCR 748]:

Briefly stated, questions of law are questions about what the correct legal test is; questions of fact are questions about what actually took place between the parties; and questions of mixed law and fact are questions about whether the facts satisfy the legal tests.

Guidelines could address, for example, certain aspects of country conditions in a refugee source country.

3.3 To Codify the Exercise of Discretion

There are many instances where the exercise of a decision-maker's discretion is not codified in the *Act* or the *IRB Rules*, nor set out in Higher Court jurisprudence. Absent any statutory or other direction, such guidelines may be issued. Guidelines may also be issued where such statutory or other direction has been provided, in order to give additional guidance to decision-makers.

For example, guidelines could set out the preferred approach to dealing with the exercise of discretion in a procedural matter.

3.4 To Provide Guidance on Procedural Issues

Guidelines may be used to provide guidance on procedural issues. These guidelines would be different from the *IRB Rules* in that they would provide the Board with flexibility in managing procedural issues. They could be revised more easily than the *IRB Rules*, if necessary. Guidelines could be issued for specific procedural issues, such as the scheduling of proceedings, or they could be quite general in nature, such as providing broad guidance on how hearings are to be conducted.

4. Consultation

Where the Chairperson has decided to exercise his or her authority to issue a set of guidelines, the Chairperson shall consult with the Deputy Chairpersons and the Director General of the ID, as applicable, as required by s. 159(1)(h) of the Act. Other consultation shall also take place, that is appropriate for the nature of the issue or matter being addressed in the guidelines, including consultation with the Executive Director.

External consultation shall also take place, the extent of which shall be determined at the discretion of the Chairperson.

5. *Whether Guidelines Expire?*

Guidelines remain in effect unless and until the Chairperson expressly revokes them.

The Board will continue to monitor the review of IRB decisions by Higher Courts. In the event that a set of guidelines becomes inconsistent with a subsequent Higher Court decision, the guidelines will either be revised in order to be consistent with the Higher Court decision, or revoked. The decision whether to revise or revoke the guidelines shall be determined at the discretion of the Chairperson, after consulting with the Deputy Chairpersons, the Director General of the ID, and the Executive Director, as applicable.

In any other case, the decision whether or not to revoke a set of guidelines is left to the Chairperson's discretion, after consulting with the Deputy Chairpersons, the Director General of the ID, and the Executive Director, as applicable.

6. *Effect of Issuance of Guidelines*

The issuance of a set of guidelines will be communicated to the public. Parties and their counsel will therefore be expected to know that a set of guidelines have been issued on a particular subject.

Although not binding, members are *expected to follow guidelines*, unless compelling or exceptional reasons exist to depart from them.

A member must *explain in his or her reasoning* why he or she is not following a set of guidelines when, based on the facts or circumstances of the case, they would otherwise be expected to follow them.

In December 2003, the IRB chair released Guideline 7, "Concerning Preparation and Conduct of a Hearing in the Refugee Protection Division." The guideline set out in detail how the Refugee Protection Division (RPD) member, refugee protection officer (RPO), refugee claimant, and counsel (for the claimant and for the minister) were expected to act in order to ensure fair and efficient refugee status determination proceedings.

The most controversial aspect of the guideline was its directions regarding the proper order of questioning at the hearing. RPD members in several Canadian localities had traditionally allowed claimants to be examined in chief by their counsel before being questioned by the member or RPO (an IRB employee who assists the RPD member to ensure that all relevant evidence is presented). Guideline 7 reversed this order of questioning by providing that the standard practice would be for the RPO or member to start questioning the claimant, though the member could vary this order in exceptional circumstances. It was expected that allowing members or RPOs to focus on those aspects of the claim of concern to them and dispensing with the often unfocused examinations in chief would make the hearing more efficient.

Refugee claimants and advocates challenged the validity of the guideline, arguing that the "reverse order questioning" violated claimants' rights to a fair hearing and that the guideline unlawfully fettered RPO members' discretion. The following case deals with the fettering claim.

Thamotharem v. Canada (Minister of Citizenship and Immigration)
[2008] 1 FCR 385, 60 Admin. LR (4th) 247

EVANS JA: ...

Issue 3: Is Guideline 7 unauthorized by paragraph 159(1)(h) because it is a fetter
on RPD members' exercise of discretion in the conduct of hearings?

. . .

(i) Rules, Discretion and Fettering

[55] Effective decision-making by administrative agencies often involves striking a balance between general rules and the exercise of *ad hoc* discretion or, to put it another way, between the benefits of certainty and consistency on the one hand, and of flexibility and fact-specific solutions on the other. Legislative instruments (including such non-legally binding "soft law" documents as policy statements, guidelines, manuals, and handbooks) can assist members of the public to predict how an agency is likely to exercise its statutory discretion and to arrange their affairs accordingly, and enable an agency to deal with a problem comprehensively and proactively, rather than incrementally and reactively on a case by case basis.

[56] Through the use of "soft law" an agency can communicate prospectively its thinking on an issue to agency members and staff, as well as to the public at large and to the agency's "stakeholders" in particular. Because "soft law" instruments may be put in place relatively easily and adjusted in the light of day-to-day experience, they may be preferable to formal rules requiring external approval and, possibly, drafting appropriate for legislation. Indeed, an administrative agency does not require an express grant of statutory authority in order to issue guidelines and policies to structure the exercise of its discretion or the interpretation of its enabling legislation: *Ainsley Financial Corp. v. Ontario (Securities Commission)* (1994), 121 DLR (4th) 79 (Ont. CA) at 83 ("*Ainsley*").

[57] Both academic commentators and the courts have emphasized the importance of these tools for good public administration, and have explored their legal significance. See, for example, Hudson N. Janisch, "The Choice of Decision-Making Method: Adjudication, Policies and Rule-Making" in Special Lectures of the Law Society of Upper Canada 1992, *Administrative Law: Principles, Practice and Pluralism*; David J. Mullan, *Administrative Law* (Toronto: Irwin Law, 2001) at 374-79; P.P. Craig, *Administrative Law*, 5th edn. (London: Thomson, 2003) at 398-405, 536-40; *Capital Cities Communications Inc. v. CRTC*, [1978] 2 SCR 141 at 171; *Vidal v. Canada (Minister of Employment and Immigration)* (1991), 49 Admin. LR 118 (FCTD) at 131; *Ainsley* at 82-83.

[58] Legal rules and discretion do not inhabit different universes, but are arrayed along a continuum. In our system of law and government, the exercise of even the broadest grant of statutory discretion which may adversely affect individuals is never absolute and beyond legal control: *Roncarelli v. Duplessis*, [1959] SCR 121 at 140 (*per* Rand J). Conversely, few, if any, legal rules admit of no element of discretion in their interpretation and application: *Baker* at para. 54.

[59] Although not legally binding on a decision-maker in the sense that it may be an error of law to misinterpret or misapply them, guidelines may validly influence a deci-

sion-maker's conduct. Indeed, in *Maple Lodge Farms Ltd. v. Canada*, [1982] 2 SCR 2, McIntyre J, writing for the Court, said (at 6):

> The fact that the Minister in his policy guidelines issued in the Notice to Importers employed the words: "If Canadian product is not offered at the market price, a permit will *normally* be issued; …" does not fetter the exercise of that discretion. [Emphasis added]

The line between law and guideline was further blurred by *Baker* at para. 72, where, writing for a majority of the Court, L'Heureux-Dubé J said that the fact that administrative action is contrary to a guideline "is of great help" in assessing whether it is unreasonable.

[60] The use of guidelines, and other "soft law" techniques, to achieve an acceptable level of consistency in administrative decisions is particularly important for tribunals exercising discretion, whether on procedural, evidential or substantive issues, in the performance of adjudicative functions. This is especially true for large tribunals, such as the Board, which sit in panels; in the case of the RPD, as already noted, a panel typically comprises a single member.

[61] It is fundamental to the idea of justice that adjudicators, whether in administrative tribunals or courts, strive to ensure that similar cases receive the same treatment. This point was made eloquently by Gonthier J. when writing for the majority in *Consolidated-Bathurst Packaging Ltd. v. International Woodworkers of America, Local 2-69*, [1990] 1 SCR 282 at 327 ("*Consolidated-Bathurst*"):

> It is obvious that coherence in administrative decision-making must be fostered. The outcome of disputes should not depend on the identity of the persons sitting on the panel for this result would be "difficult to reconcile with the notion of equality before the law, which is one of the main corollaries of the rule of law, and perhaps also the most intelligible one." [Citation omitted]

[62] Nonetheless, while agencies may issue guidelines or policy statements to structure the exercise of statutory discretion in order to enhance consistency, administrative decision-makers may not apply them as if they were law. Thus, a decision made solely by reference to the mandatory prescription of a guideline, despite a request to deviate from it in the light of the particular facts, may be set aside, on the ground that the decision-maker's exercise of discretion was unlawfully fettered: see, for example, *Maple Lodge Farms* at 7. This level of compliance may only be achieved through the exercise of a statutory power to make "hard" law, through, for example, regulations or statutory rules made in accordance with statutorily prescribed procedure.

[63] In addition, the validity of a rule or policy itself has sometimes been impugned independently of its application in the making of a particular decision. *Ainsley* is the best known example. That case concerned a challenge to the validity of a non-statutory policy statement issued by the Ontario Securities Commission setting out business practices which would satisfy the public interest in the marketing of penny stocks by certain securities dealers. The policy also stated that the Commission would not necessarily impose a sanction for non-compliance on a dealer under its "public interest" jurisdiction, but would consider the particular circumstances of each case.

[64] Writing for the Court in *Ainsley*, Doherty JA adopted the criteria formulated by the trial judge for determining if the policy statement was "a mere guideline" or was

"mandatory," namely, its language, the practical effect of non-compliance, and the expectations of the agency and its staff regarding its implementation. On the basis of these criteria, Doherty JA concluded that the policy statement was invalid. He emphasized, in particular, its minute detail, which "reads like a statute or regulation" (at 85), and the threat of sanctions for non-compliance. He found this threat to be implicit in the Commission's pronouncement that the business practices it described complied with the public interest, and was evident in the attitude of enforcement staff, who treated the policy as if it were a statute or regulation, breach of which was liable to trigger enforcement proceedings.

(ii) Guideline 7 and the Fettering of Discretion

(a) Is Guideline 7 delegated legislation?

[Based on an analysis of the statutory provisions authorizing the issuance of the Chairperson's guidelines and, in particular, their inclusion of a potentially overlapping rule-making power and the absence of a provision that the guidelines were binding, Evans JA determined that the guidelines did not have the same legally binding effect as statutory rules.]

(b) Is Guideline 7 an unlawful fetter on members' discretion?

[73] Since guidelines issued by the Chairperson of the Board do not have the full force of law, the next question is whether, in its language and effect, Guideline 7 unduly fetters RPD members' discretion to determine for themselves, case-by-case, the order of questioning at refugee protection hearings. In my opinion, language is likely to be a more important factor than effect in determining whether Guideline 7 constitutes an unlawful fetter. It is inherently difficult to predict how decision-makers will apply a guideline, especially in an agency, like the Board, with a large membership sitting in panels.

[74] Consequently, since the language of Guideline 7 expressly permits members to depart from the standard order of questioning in exceptional circumstances, the Court should be slow to conclude that members will regard themselves as bound to follow the standard order, in the absence of clear evidence to the contrary, such as that members have routinely refused to consider whether the facts of particular cases require an exception to be made.

[75] I turn first to language. The Board's *Policy on the Use of Chairperson's Guidelines*, issued in 2003, states that guidelines are not legally binding on members: section 6. The introduction to Guideline 7 states: "The guidelines apply to most cases heard by the RPD. However, in compelling or exceptional circumstances, the members will use their discretion not to apply some guidelines or to apply them less strictly."

[76] The text of the provisions of Guideline 7 of most immediate relevance to this appeal. Paragraph 19 states that it "will be" standard practice for the RPO to question the claimant first; this is less obligatory than "must" or some similarly mandatory language. The discretionary element of Guideline 7 is emphasized in paragraph 19, which provides that, while "the *standard practice* will be for the RPO to start questioning the claimant" (emphasis added), a member may vary the order "in exceptional circumstances."

[77] Claimants who believe that exceptional circumstances exist in their case must apply to the RPD, before the start of the hearing, for a change in the order of questioning. The examples, and they are only examples, of exceptional circumstances given in paragraph 23 suggest that only the most unusual cases will warrant a variation. However, the parameters of "exceptional circumstances" will no doubt be made more precise, and likely expanded incrementally, on a case-by-case basis.

[78] I agree with Justice Blanchard's [the motions judge] conclusion (at para. 119) that the language of Guideline 7 is more than "a recommended but optional process." However, as *Maple Lodge Farms* makes clear, the fact that a guideline is intended to establish how discretion will *normally* be exercised is not enough to make it an unlawful fetter, as long as it does not preclude the possibility that the decision-maker may deviate from normal practice in the light of particular facts: see *Ha v. Canada (Minister of Citizenship and Immigration)*, 2004 FCA 49, [2004] 3 FCR 195.

[79] To turn to the effect of Guideline 7, there was evidence that, when requested by counsel, members of the RPD had exercised their discretion and varied the standard order of questioning in cases which they regarded as exceptional. No such request was made on behalf of Mr Thamotharem. In any event, members must permit a claimant to be questioned first by her or his counsel when the duty of fairness so requires.

[80] In at least one case, however, a member wrongly regarded himself as having no discretion to vary the standard order of questioning prescribed in Guideline 7. On July 3, 2005, this decision was set aside on consent on an application for judicial review, on the ground that the member had fettered the exercise of his discretion, and the matter remitted for re-determination by a different member of the RPD: *Baskaran v. Canada (Minister of Citizenship and Immigration)* (Court File No. IMM-7189-04). Nonetheless, the fact that some members may erroneously believe that Guideline 7 removes their discretion to depart from the standard practice in exceptional circumstances does not warrant invalidating the Guideline. In such cases, the appropriate remedy for an unsuccessful claimant is to seek judicial review to have the RPD's decision set aside.

[81] There was also evidence from Professor Donald Galloway, an immigration and refugee law scholar, a consultant to the Board and a former Board member, that RPD members would feel constrained from departing from the standard order of questioning. However, he did not base his opinion on the actual conduct of members with respect to Guideline 7.

[82] In short, those challenging the validity of Guideline 7 did not produce evidence establishing on a balance of probabilities that members rigidly apply the standard order of questioning without regard to its appropriateness in particular circumstances.

[83] I recognize that members of the RPD must perform their adjudicative functions without improper influence from others, including the Chairperson and other members of the Board. However, the jurisprudence also recognizes that administrative agencies must be free to devise processes for ensuring an acceptable level of consistency and quality in their decisions, a particular challenge for large tribunals which, like the Board, sit in panels.

[84] Most notably, the Supreme Court of Canada in *Consolidated-Bathurst* upheld the Ontario Labour Relations Board's practice of inviting members of panels who had heard but not yet decided cases to bring them to "full Board meetings," where the legal

or policy issues that they raised could be discussed in the absence of the parties. This practice was held not to impinge improperly on members' adjudicative independence, or to breach the principle of procedural fairness that those who hear must also decide. Writing for the majority of the Court, Gonthier J said (at 340):

> The institutionalization of the consultation process adopted by the Board provides a framework within which the experience of the chairman, vice-chairmen and members of the Board can be shared to improve the overall quality of its decisions. Although respect for the judicial independence of Board members will impede total coherence in decision making, the Board through this consultation process seeks to avoid inadvertent contradictory results and to achieve the highest degree of coherence possible under these circumstances. ... The advantages of an institutionalized consultation process are obvious and I cannot agree with the proposition that this practice necessarily conflicts with the rules of natural justice. The rules of natural justice must have the flexibility required to take into account the institutional pressures faced by modern administrative tribunals as well as the risks inherent in such a practice. ...

[85] However, the arrangements made for discussions within an agency with members who have heard a case must not be so coercive as to raise a reasonable apprehension that members' ability to decide cases free from improper constraints has been undermined: *Tremblay v. Québec (Commission des affaires sociales)*, [1992] 1 SCR 952.

[86] Evidence that the Immigration and Refugee Board "monitors" members' deviations from the standard order of questioning does not, in my opinion, create the kind of coercive environment which would make Guideline 7 an improper fetter on members' exercise of their decision-making powers. On a voluntary basis, members complete, infrequently and inconsistently, a hearing information sheet asking them, among other things, to explain when and why they had not followed "standard practice" on the order of questioning. There was no evidence that any member had been threatened with a sanction for non-compliance. Given the Board's legitimate interest in promoting consistency, I do not find it at all sinister that the Board does not attempt to monitor the frequency of members' compliance with the "standard practice."

[87] Nor is it an infringement of members' independence that they are expected to explain in their reasons why a case is exceptional and warrants a departure from the standard order of questioning. Such an expectation serves the interests of coherence and consistency in the Board's decision-making in at least two ways. First, it helps to ensure that members do not arbitrarily ignore Guideline 7. Second, it is a way of developing criteria for determining if circumstances are "exceptional" for the purpose of paragraph 23 and of providing guidance to other members, and to the Bar, on the exercise of discretion to depart from the standard order of questioning in future cases.

[88] In my opinion, therefore, the evidence in the present case does not establish that a reasonable person would think that RPD members' independence was unduly constrained by Guideline 7, particularly in view of: the terms of the Guideline; the evidence of members' deviation from "standard practice"; and the need for the Board, the largest administrative agency in Canada, to attain an acceptable level of consistency at hearings, conducted mostly be single members.

[89] Adjudicative "independence" is not an all or nothing thing, but is a question of degree. The independence of judges, for example, is balanced against public accountability, through the Canadian Judicial Council, for misconduct. The independence of members of administrative agencies must be balanced against the institutional interest of the agency in the quality and consistency of the decisions, from which there are normally only limited rights of access to the courts, rendered by individual members in the agency's name.

[The Court of Appeal also dismissed the appellant's claim that reverse-order questioning violated refugee claimants' right to procedural fairness. It agreed with the trial judge that in the context of the inquisitorial and relatively informal nature of refugee status determination hearings established by Parliament in the IRPA, the duty of fairness did not invariably require that claimants be given the opportunity to be questioned first by their counsel.]

NOTES

1. Evans JA observes that Guideline 7 is aimed at ensuring an acceptable level of consistency and quality in IRB decisions, and, drawing an analogy to a full board hearing, applies the *Consolidated-Bathurst* framework to determine the guideline's validity. Is his characterization of Guideline 7 accurate? Would the analysis change if Guideline 7 were characterized as a procedural guideline (as opposed to the substantive policies at play in *Consolidated-Bathurst*) aimed at maximizing expediency in decision making rather than consistency? See, on this point, F. Houle, "*Thamotharem* and Guideline 7 of the IRB: Rethinking the Scope of the Fettering of Discretion Doctrine" (2009), *Refuge* (forthcoming).

2. Do you agree with Evans JA that "language is likely to be a more important factor than effect" in determining whether a guideline constitutes an unlawful fetter, especially for a large, multi-member board like the IRB? Can boards avoid a finding of fettering simply through clever drafting of guidelines and by avoiding the use of mandatory language?

CHAPTER SEVEN

Rulemaking

Rulemaking is a branch of administrative law that in the Anglo-Canadian tradition has received relatively little attention. While there has been considerable concern to develop procedures appropriate for adjudication, much less has been done with respect to formal opportunities for participation in rulemaking. However, for some time there have been signs that this historic position is being revisited.

CONCEPTUAL ASPECTS

A Quiet Revolution

In 1976, K.C. Davis proclaimed: "The United States is entering the age of rulemaking, and the rest of the world, in governments of all kinds, is likely to follow. The main tool of getting governmental jobs done will be rulemaking, authorized by legislative bodies and checked by courts" (*Administrative Law of the Seventies* (Rochester, NY: The Lawyers Co-operative Publishing Co., 1976), at 168). It is now evident that Canada has entered the age of rule-making, bringing with it internal processes of regulatory impact assessment, although there has been little fanfare announcing this important development. Only one province, Québec, has adopted a general statute allowing for public participation in rulemaking. However, there have been significant changes in administrative practice at the federal level and, in Ontario, legislation governing environmentally significant decision making and securities regulation has introduced sophisticated systems of participation in rulemaking. In the other provinces a practice of widespread consultation has grown, and it appears that either the Québec example will be followed or the practice of consultation will become sufficiently entrenched to attract more legal and judicial attention than has been given to rulemaking in the past.

What Is Meant by Rulemaking?

To the extent that there has been legal and judicial interest in rules, the focus has been on formal regulations made directly under authority of statutes with the concern being whether the regulation is *intra vires* the statutory grant of subordinate legislative power. From a more functional perspective, it has to be recognized that rules are employed far more widely than regulations in the form of policies, manuals, guidelines, standards and the like. This is a matter dealt with more fully in chapter 15, The Use and Misuse of Discretion.

The essence of a rule, as opposed to an adjudication, is that the former lays down a norm of conduct of general application while the latter deals only with the immediate parties to a particular dispute. Of course, some rules may only affect a very limited class of persons, and, in a regime of precedent, an adjudication may affect many persons. As we have seen in *Homex v. Village of Wyoming*, [1980] 2 SCR 1011 (Ont.), chapter 3 of this text, it is sometimes necessary to discard nomenclature in favour of functional assessment. Nevertheless, it is generally true that a rule is of general application, and an adjudication of particular application.

When considering the appropriate procedure in rulemaking, the courts have not been able to analogize to their own judicial process. This has made it very difficult for them to envisage, on their own, a procedural design appropriate to multi-party rulemaking. Typically, the courts become more actively involved once the general outline of a participatory requirement is settled, whether in a statute or in clearly established administrative practice.

The Importance of Rules

It is totally unrealistic today to expect legislatures to deal with the minute details of implementation in their legislation. Typically, modern legislation takes the form of a skeleton of principles onto which a mass of formal regulations (and less formal policies and guidelines) are then added to give life to the statutory scheme. It is routine for ministers and agencies to be given broad powers by legislatures to enact what is known as "subordinate" or "delegated" legislation.

Thus, it may seem that the child has outgrown the parent. Even when a statute lays out a narrow definition of a rule, it usually contains a provision for formal regulations to allow for further elaboration and evolution of the rule. Subordinate legislation is not limited to unimportant and trivial matters of detail. Rules constitute a little-known "cutting edge" of law. This was recognized 60 years ago by Lord Hewart in *The New Despotism* (London: Benn, 1929), at 98, when he pointed out the paradox that, while statutes that set out general legislative principles are readily available, that is not necessarily so for rules laying down the particulars that are of real concern to the citizen.

> The paradox is that it is precisely in the labyrinth of departmental legislation that the citizen, if time permitted, might find the particular order or prohibition which should direct his conduct and which, if it is to be ignored, is ignored at his peril. As a rule he is not interested in what may be termed the immensities and eternities of legislation or of jurisprudence. But he is, or may be, profoundly interested in the rules or orders subsidiary to a statute for the very reason that they deal with particulars, and the particular is the thing to be done.

A major review of subordinate legislation at the federal level was undertaken in 1968 by a special committee of the House of Commons. Its report, *Third Report of the Special Committee on Statutory Instruments* (known as the *MacGuigan Report* after the committee's chairman, Mark MacGuigan MP) summarized the reasons for and criticisms of the ever-expanding use of delegated legislation (at 4-6):

> The reasons usually given to justify the delegation by Parliament of the power to make laws are: lack of parliamentary time; lack of parliamentary knowledge on technical matters; the necessity of rapid decisions in cases of emergency; the need to experiment with legislation, especially in

a new field; the need for flexibility in the application of laws; and unforeseen contingencies which may arise during the introduction of new and complex pieces of legislation. It also seems that the force of precedent has some bearing on it; sections conferring powers of delegated legislation now tend to be considered as standard clauses by the draftsmen of statutes.

Uneasiness respecting the extent of delegated legislation began to be evident in England toward the end of the nineteenth century, just at the time it began to be a frequently used device. The concern multiplied in proportion with the growth of delegated legislation. Hence, delegated legislation formed one of the matters referred to the United Kingdom Committee on Ministers' Powers, whose report was published in 1932 (Cmd. 4060); it was also of some concern to the American Committee on Administrative Procedure, whose report was published in 1941. Since that time, although it has continued to grow in bulk and importance, in Britain, in Canada, in the United States and elsewhere, delegated legislation has not been a subject of such controversy. In the United States, the practice has been accepted by the courts, although the U.S. Constitution prescribes explicitly that "All legislative powers herein granted shall be vested in a Congress" (Article 1). The contemporary consensus was probably put by Mr. A. Beuvan, before the British Select Committee on Delegated Legislation, in 1953:

> There is now general agreement about the necessity for delegated legislation; the real problem is how this legislation can be reconciled with the processes of democratic consultation, scrutiny and control.

. . .

> Today, therefore, critics of regulation-making do not seek to deny its necessity in some form; their complaints have been aimed rather against the volume and character of delegated legislation than against the practice itself. (*Report of the Committee on Ministers' Powers*, 1932, p. 53). The more fundamental of the criticisms can be summarized as follows: the parliamentary tendency to enact statutes in skeleton form, leaving the "details" to be filled in by regulations—such regulations being often the very matters that are of most importance to the citizen; uncertainty in enabling statutes as to the extent of the area regulations are intended to cover; sweeping or subjective terms used in enabling acts which exclude the judicial control of the regulations made under their authority; lack of public debate, and inadequate consultation of all interested parties before the making of the regulations; lack of precision in the form and content of the regulations; inadequate publicity given to the regulations after they are made; inadequate parliamentary control over the regulations; and the danger that civil servants may be transformed into our masters.

. . .

> Your Committee does not accept an abstract analysis of the principle of the separation of powers which would regard regulation-making as a proper function of the legislative branch of government, grudgingly bestowed on the executive because of the human deficiencies of legislators. We believe rather that there is, properly as well as practically, an executive function of subordinate law-making. But we also believe that, because it is a delegated power, the delegator, Parliament, has a continuing responsibility to ensure its well-functioning in the public interest.

CASE STUDIES

Rulemaking and Common Law Procedural Fairness

As we saw in chapter 3, Fairness: Sources and Thresholds, the courts have not been prepared to spread the requirement of procedural fairness to include legislative functions. In *Canada (Attorney General) v. Inuit Tapirisat of Canada*, [1980] 2 SCR 735 (Can.), chapter 3 of this text, Estey J started out by acknowledging that, in the post-*Nicholson* era, a duty of fairness no longer depended on classifying the function involved as being "administrative" or "*quasi*-judicial." Indeed, he went on to say that it was not helpful to classify an action or function into one of the "traditional" categories established in the development of administrative law. However, he was not prepared to abandon a labelling approach. To the traditional categories he added "legislative" and announced that the dictates of procedural fairness did not apply to legislative functions.

In so doing, Estey J adopted Megarry J's stance in *Bates v. Lord Hailsham*, [1972] 1 WLR 1373 (Ch.), chapter 3 of this text. "Many of those affected by delegated legislation, and affected very substantially, are never consulted in the process of enacting that legislation; and yet they have no remedy." The courts have clearly balked at the prospect of having to design procedures appropriate to multi-party rulemaking. Unable to analogize to its own judicial process, the courts essentially gave up. As Craig has observed, "The courts have been dormant, anaesthetized by the mention of the word legislative." (*Public Law and Democracy in the United Kingdom and the United States of America* (Oxford: Clarendon Press, 1990), at 174. We also saw in *Canadian Association of Regulated Importers v. Canada (Attorney General)*, [1993] 3 FC 199 (TD); rev'd. [1994] 2 FC 247 (CA), chapter 3 of this text, how the Federal Court of Appeal used the fact that there were rulemaking procedures in some federal statutes to reject an argument that a duty to consult could be engrafted onto a quota-setting exercise in the context of a statute that was silent on process.

The courts may be willing to impose procedural requirements, such as a hearing, where the judicial analogy seems compelling, as where a bylaw has a specific impact on specific individuals. See *Homex v. Wyoming (Village)*, [1980] 2 SCR 1011 (Ont.). In approving the practice of certain tribunals, when meeting as a whole, to discuss issues that have come before particular panels of the tribunal (*Re Consolidated-Bathurst Packaging Ltd. and International Woodworkers of America, Local 2-69* (1985), 20 DLR (4th) 84 (Ont. Div. Ct.)), the Supreme Court has also recognized the importance of providing support for internal mechanisms that seek to ensure coherence in decision making. Nevertheless, the courts have often shown indifference to rulemaking even though it provides a more effective mechanism for increasing consistency.

Initial Attitudes Toward Consultation

Outside of the courts, various steps have been pursued to develop procedural rights in rulemaking. In the 1960s, the prevailing attitude toward consultation was that it was a "good thing" best left informal and unstructured. The McRuer commission stated that "extensive consultations usually take place" and that a notice and comment requirement "would cause unnecessary delay and merely duplicate the time already spent in informal consultation" (Report no. 1, vol. 1, at 362). In 1969, the MacGuigan committee concluded:

The advantages of prior consultation before the making of regulations is obvious, and your Committee therefore recommends that, before making regulations, regulation-making authorities should engage in the widest feasible consultation, not only with the most directly affected persons, but also with the public at large where this would be relevant. Where a large body of new regulations is contemplated, the Government should consider submitting a White Paper … stating its views as to the substance of the regulations, to the appropriate Standing Committee, which might conduct hearings with respect thereto. It is essential that all relevant facts and viewpoints should be taken into account before regulations are finally made.

Having said this, we should state that we are of the opinion that no useful purpose would be served by laying down in legislation of general application minimum procedures respecting prior consultation or hearings which would apply to the making of all regulations. However, your Committee recommends that, when enabling provisions and statutes are being drawn, consideration should be given to providing for some type of formalized hearing or consultation procedure where appropriate, e.g. where all affected parties may be easily identifiable and the matters to be covered by the regulations lend themselves to a hearing or consultation type of procedure. It should be left to the individual enabling sections, where feasible and practical, to provide for the appropriate type of consultation procedure.

The experience in the United States has been substantially different. The federal government and many of the states have legislation that imposes rights to participate in rulemaking. The federal statute is the *Administrative Procedure Act* (APA). It establishes two different procedures: "on-the-record" rulemaking and "notice-and-comment" rulemaking. On-the-record rulemaking is essentially a trial-type process, is relatively uncommon, and has been generally unsuccessful. Notice-and-comment rulemaking is more simple. The agency must publish notice of the proposed rules in the *Federal Register* and must give "interested persons an opportunity to participate in the rulemaking through submission of written data, views, or arguments with or without opportunity for oral presentation." It must consider the submissions and "incorporate in the rules adopted a concise general statement of their basis and purpose." One or the other of these procedures is required for all rulemaking that is not excluded by the exceptions in the Act. Two of the exceptions are paramount; the entire scheme does not apply to rules about "a military or foreign affairs function of the United States" or to rules about "agency management or personnel, or … public property, loans, grants, benefits or contracts." Notice-and-comment rulemaking is required for all other rulemaking, except for rules that are specifically required "by statute" to be made on the record and for "interpretive rules; general statements of policy; or rules of agency, organization, procedure, or practice," unless the agency decides that the process is "impracticable, unnecessary, or contrary to the public interest."

Overall, it is widely agreed that as long as the trial-type process is avoided, the APA's s. 553 notice-and-comment procedure has worked well. As Davis once put it: "The system is simple and overwhelmingly successful" (*Administrative Law of the Seventies*, at 170).

Changing Attitudes

In the late 1970s, a decade after the McRuer and MacGuigan reports, three major reports appeared that included extensive discussions of rulemaking. The first was an interim report from the Economic Council of Canada requested by Prime Minister Trudeau as part of an extensive review of economic regulation. Rather than await the completion of numerous studies spanning many areas of regulation, the council, in *Responsible Regulation* (1979), set out its proposals with respect to procedural matters and urged that there be the earliest possible informal consultation about rulemaking:

> Consultation is the process of exchanging information and advice between government departments and agencies and private sector groups and individuals. While it is not part of the process of making a final decision about regulatory intervention, it serves important functions, particularly at the problem identification and problem definition stages. Both government and the private sector should benefit from consultation. Governments are better able to assess whether intervention is necessary, gain a better understanding of the implications of their proposals, and may be able to identify alternatives to the proposed form of intervention. Private sector groups will have an opportunity early in the process to influence the regulations with which they must live and may provide valuable information that a regulatory authority will use in deciding an appropriate form or standard of regulation. The net result should be more rational development of proposals for regulatory intervention and a better understanding of the problems and attitudes on both sides. In the long run, success in achieving regulatory objectives may be facilitated and time spent in consultation may ensure easier and more immediate compliance. … A number of problems need to be resolved in consulting with the private sector. First, there is the question of timing. On one hand, if consultation is undertaken "too early," governments may be accused of not providing enough information to which the private sector can respond. Governments, like other decision makers, consider many courses of action in varying detail and intent. Consultation at a very early "idea-floating" stage may raise false hopes or fears. Frequent consultation on inadequate proposals may overload private sector groups, particularly "public interest groups." On the other hand, if consultation is "too late," governments may be seen as being committed to a given fully developed proposal. Indeed, the greater the investment that has been made in refining a proposal, the less likely it is to be changed. The full benefits of consultation would then be lost.
>
> The second problem is answering the question of how much consultation is appropriate. While enough input to give a full range of information is desired, the private sector may complain of excessive government demands for information. Furthermore, there is a danger of confusing inadequate consultation with failure of governments to agree with the positions of those consulted. Sharing of information does not necessarily imply a sharing of decision-making authority.
>
> The question of whom to consult raises the third problem. While there will undoubtedly be a set of obvious candidates in most instances, governments should avoid the convenient habit of consulting only with "established" groups. …
>
> In view of these problems, we conclude that it would be difficult, if not impossible, to institutionalize, particularly in the form of legislation, any meaningful requirement for a consultative process. The Council, however, urges government departments and agencies to continue and, when appropriate, expand their informal procedures for consultation with individuals and groups that might be affected by regulatory intervention.

In addition to informal consultation, the council proposed the establishment of a formal opportunity to comment, including a requirement of publication of notice of intent to create a new regulation and an opportunity to comment on draft regulations. Major draft regulations would have to be accompanied by a regulatory impact analysis statement that estimated the costs and benefits involved.

While not as ambitious as the Economic Council of Canada's proposals, the recommendations of the other two reports of the late 1970s were unanimous in their criticism of the status quo and in their insistence on substantial improvements in procedures for rulemaking.

The federal Standing Joint Committee on Regulations and Other Statutory Instruments in its *Fourth Report* (1980) concluded that: "Despite the reluctance of the MacGuigan Committee to recommend a mandatory notice-and-comment procedure, your Committee believes that it should now be introduced in Canada" (at 7:21). The Standing Joint Committee had been impressed by what it had learned of the workings of s. 553 of the APA and emphasized that an "opportunity to participate" need seldom involve a "true hearing." Indeed, it was the very "modesty of the aims" of s. 553 that led to its success.

The third report was made by the House of Commons Special Committee on Regulatory Reform (known as the Peterson Committee, after its chairman, Jim Peterson MP). It did not support a general requirement, but it did encourage the creation of better voluntary and informal opportunities for participation. However, it felt that this type of notice-and-comment procedure should complement and not substitute for even earlier, informal consultation: "It is difficult to persuade regulators to make major changes after a final draft has been published. Too much has been invested in the form of the regulation by that time. Only early notice and consultation will result in the exchange of views and consideration of alternatives that will yield more efficient and effective regulation. Publication of draft regulations, however, does provide an excellent opportunity for 'fine tuning' and last minute adjustments" (*Report of the House of Commons Special Committee on Regulatory Reform* (First Session, Thirty-Second Parliament, December 1980), at 9). Also, both the Standing Joint Committee and the Peterson Committee noted that participation was voluntarily encouraged by some departments and agencies.

Québec's Approach to Public Consultation

Despite this work at the federal level, the first general statutory reform came in Québec. As Michel Leclerc, Director, Quebec Regulations Office, explained to the Fleet Committee in Ontario (see below), there were already 79 provisions in the *Revised Statutes of Quebec* prescribing publication in the *Gazette officielle du Québec* before regulations could be made (*Reply to Questions Concerning the Regulations Act*, Exhibit 1/01/001, filed March 21, 1988, at 2). The *Regulations Act*, RSQ c. R-18.1, provides:

Publication of Proposed Regulations
8. Every proposed regulation shall be published in the *Gazette officielle du Québec*.

9. Section 8 does not require the publication in the *Gazette officielle du Québec* of any text referred to in a proposed regulation.

10. Every proposed regulation published in the *Gazette officielle du Québec* shall be accompanied with a notice stating, in particular, the period within which no proposed regulation may be made or submitted for approval but within which interested persons may transmit their comments to a person designated in the notice.

11. No proposed regulation may be made or submitted for approval before the expiry of 45 days from its publication in the *Gazette officielle du Québec*, or before the expiry of the period indicated in the notice accompanying it or in the Act under which the proposed regulation may be made or approved, where the notice or the Act provides for a longer period.

12. A proposed regulation may be made or approved at the expiry of a shorter period than the period applicable to it, or without having been published, if the authority making or approving it is of the opinion that a reason provided for in the Act under which the proposed regulation may be made or approved, or one of the following circumstances, warrants it:

    (1) the urgency of the situation requires it;

    (2) the proposed regulation is designed to establish, amend or repeal norms of a fiscal nature.

13. The reason justifying a shorter publication period shall be published with the proposed regulation, and the reason justifying the absence of such publication shall be published with the regulation.

14. A proposed regulation may be amended after its publication without being published a second time.

It should be noted that the 45-day comment period is a minimum that may be extended where the empowering Act provides for a longer period. It is not entirely clear what is meant in s. 12 by an exemption from publication "if the authority making or approving it is of the opinion that a reason provided for in the Act under which the proposed regulation may be made ... warrants it." It should also be noted that exemption from notice and comment is not left entirely to the determination of the regulation-making authority because objective "circumstances" must exist as a prerequisite to the subjective "opinion."

Public Participation and Regulatory Impact Assessment at the Federal Level

Unlike Québec with its general statute, the federal government took the approach of increasing the number of statutes that require consultation and of reforming administrative practice. In 1969, the MacGuigan Committee noted that only two Canadian statutes provided for formalized consultation. Of the two, the best known was the *Broadcasting Act*, RSC 1970, c. B-11, s. 16(2) (now SC 1991, c. 11, s. 10(3)), which provides: "A copy of each regulation that the Commission proposes to make under this section shall be published in the *Canada Gazette* and a reasonable opportunity shall be given to licensees and other interested persons to make representations with respect thereto." By the early 1980s, most new federal statutes that gave major regulation-making powers contained a similar clause. Typical is s. 17 of the *Canada Post Corporation Act*, SC 1980-81-82-83, c. 54, which provided that the corporation may, with the approval of the governor in council, make regulations for the efficient operation of its business and for carrying the Act into effect; s. 17(3) required that a copy of each regulation shall be published in the *Canada Gazette* and "a reasonable opportunity shall be afforded to interested persons to make representations ... with respect thereto" (now RSC 1985, c. C-10, s. 20). This approach has continued. See, for example, the *Transportation of Dangerous Goods Act*, SC 1992, c. 34, s. 30(1).

As important as these statutory provisions (which are now almost standard legislative "boilerplate") is the actual policy and practice of government. Growing out of a series of administrative initiatives in the mid-1980s designed to allow for greater public participation in regulation, a fully fledged system of notice and comment in federal rulemaking was established.

The process has evolved significantly since that time. The current 2007 policy (derived from the *Cabinet Directive on Streamlining Regulation* and various supporting documents) applies to all "regulatory organizations," including all federal departments and agencies, Crown corporations, commissions, and other bodies that are authorized by a parliamentary statute to develop and propose regulations in specified areas of public policy. Every regulation put forward must be accompanied by a Regulatory Impact Analysis Statement (RIAS). This is designed to identify the purpose of the proposed regulation, provide an analysis of its costs and benefits, and explain why a regulatory proposal is considered necessary. The RIAS is then published, along with proposed regulations, in the *Canada Gazette Part I* and with final regulations in the *Canada Gazette Part II*. The RIAS describes the regulation and its anticipated impact, alternatives considered, compliance with international obligations, and the extent of consultation that took place in the design of the regulation. Draft regulations are "prepublished" in the *Canada Gazette Part I* and an opportunity is provided for public comment. There are several exceptions to prepublication; the two main ones in the 2007 policy are cases where the regulation responds to an emergency that poses "major risks to health, safety, the environment, or security" and cases where prepublication "would cause demonstrable adverse effects or undermine the intent of the regulations, such as those affecting subsidy changes and interest rate changes."

The RIAS process may have an important impact on rulemaking. In the 2007 policy, for instance, proposed regulations are subject to the following set of questions regarding Canada's international obligations (Treasury Board of Canada, 2007 *Guidelines on International Regulatory Obligations and Cooperation*) (footnotes omitted):

- Do relevant international standards exist or is their completion imminent? If so, would such international standards be an effective and appropriate means for achieving Canada's stated policy objectives? If this is the case, then such international standards should be used as a basis for domestic regulation. If not, has the rationale been fully and transparently documented?

- Is the proposed regulation compatible with existing regulations of Canada's NAFTA partners? If not, are there practical ways to promote greater compatibility without compromising the achievement of Canada's policy objective? Would the different approach used by our NAFTA partners be equally effective and appropriate in the Canadian context?

- Does the proposed regulation create an unnecessary obstacle to trade? Is the policy objective underlying the proposed regulation legitimate in the context of trade obligations? Is the proposed regulation rationally connected to the achievement of a legitimate policy objective in the context of trade obligations? Are there less trade-restrictive alternatives that would equally achieve the legitimate policy objective? Is there sufficient documentation to support the conclusions and analysis of each of these steps?

- Does the proposed regulation discriminate against imported products or services either on its face or in its effect? If so, is this discrimination justified under applicable exemptions from trade obligations?

- Is the proposed regulation a legitimate exercise of governmental regulatory power? Could it constitute expropriation?

- Does the regulation comply with other international obligations, such as those found in environmental treaties?

- If the proposed regulatory approach differs from international standards or the approaches of key international counterparts, how is it different and why are the specific Canadian requirements necessary? How does this approach provide greater overall benefits to Canadians?

- Where proposed regulations may have a significant effect on trade, have the appropriate international bodies been notified in accordance with the notification obligations set out in Canada's trade agreements?

- Are resources and a strategy in place to reduce the impact of regulatory differences on regulated parties in the implementation of the regulation?

These questions reflect a wide range of considerations and raise questions about, for example, the degree to which Canada should defer to regulatory standards developed elsewhere and, if so, whether the external standard-setting process reflects Canadian values of participation and accountability. They also create in-built hurdles for new regulations, such as the concern that a regulation not be more trade restrictive than necessary to achieve its end. Consider also whether there are areas of international obligation, highlighted in *Baker*, for example, that are absent from the list of questions here and whether, as a result, some considerations have been given undue weight. Finally, how might this process for screening regulations affect the allocation of power among federal departments and agencies, and how might it affect the responsiveness of the federal government as a whole to emerging regulatory concerns?

In a footnote to the question that is reproduced above on whether a proposed regulation constitutes "expropriation," the Guidelines state:

Canada's international trade and investment treaties typically contain a provision prohibiting the nationalization or expropriation of an investment of an investor from another party to that agreement, except where certain conditions have been met, including the payment of compensation at fair market value. Expropriation can be either direct or indirect. Indirect expropriation typically involves such a substantial interference with the investment as to support a conclusion that the investment has been taken from the investor. It is Canada's position, accepted by numerous international tribunals, that non-discriminatory regulations designed and applied to protect legitimate public welfare obligations, such as health, safety, and the environment, do not constitute indirect expropriation but are legitimate exercises of governmental "police powers." However, given that expropriation can be very fact-specific, in situations where a proposed regulation has the potential to substantially interfere with the operations of an investment in

Canada, the regulatory body proposing such a regulation should seek legal advice from the Trade Law Bureau to ensure compliance with Canada's international obligations.

The screening of regulations for "indirect expropriations" stems mainly from provisions under Chapter 11 of the North American Free Trade Agreement, which allow foreign investors to sue Canada under a special investor–state arbitration mechanism. Legislative, judicial, and executive measures adopted by any level of government can be challenged in this way where they affect the value of the investor's assets. Foreign investors need not resort to a Canadian court or tribunal before bringing a claim and can obtain an internationally enforceable damages award against Canada if successful. The investor–state arbitration mechanism and its substantive provisions of investor protection prompted an extensive debate in Canada, Mexico, and the United States about their impact on government policy space and about their lack of provision for institutional safeguards of judicial independence. Specifically on expropriation, however, the NAFTA mechanism is controversial because in Canadian law there is no general concept of "indirect expropriation" requiring payment of compensation for regulatory measures (see R.E. Young, "A Canadian Commentary on Constructive Expropriation Law Under NAFTA Article 1110" (2006), 43 *Alberta L Rev.* 1001). Furthermore, some arbitration tribunals have interpreted the notion of indirect expropriation to require payment of compensation even for non-discriminatory measures adopted in good faith for a legitimate public purpose. To date, measures challenged by investors under the NAFTA mechanism have included a federal order in council banning exports of polychlorinated biphenyls (PCBs) from Canada, an Act of Parliament prohibiting the interprovincial trade of a gasoline additive, limits on pesticide use in the Québec *Pesticides Management Code*, and the enforcement of the *Canada Health Act* with respect to a proposed private health clinic in British Columbia. Information on NAFTA claims is published by the Department of Foreign Affairs and International Trade: http://www.international.gc.ca/trade-agreements-accords-commerciaux/disp-diff/NAFTA.aspx?lang=en. For general commentary on this area of interaction between international obligations and domestic rulemaking, see, for example, Van Harten, *Investment Treaty Arbitration and Public Law* (2007), Schneiderman, *Constitutionalizing Economic Globalization* (2008), and Clarkson and Wood, *A Perilous Imbalance—The Globalization of Canadian Law and Governance* (2009).

Developments in Ontario

Until the 1990s, McRuer's reassurance of extensive informal consultation tended to mute proposals for public notice and comment provisions in Ontario. In 1983, the Standing Committee on Regulations and Private Bills (popularly known as the Fleet committee after the chair of the committee, David Fleet MPP) did recommend that a notice-and-comment procedure should be incorporated into appropriate legislation on a statute-by-statute basis. However, as the standing committee noted in its *Second Report 1988*, "Unfortunately, we can find few signs of its implementation. In theory, this option may be well suited to meeting Ontario's needs; but in practice, as the past five years have shown, it just does not work. What can best be described as 'inertia' appears to have set in" (at 10).

The Fleet committee, after carefully reviewing the federal comprehensive but non-statutory option, the Québec general statute option, and its own earlier statute-by-statute option, unanimously concluded that a general notice-and-comment procedure along the lines of the 1986 Québec statute was most appropriate in that it could improve public participation "without impeding the efficient operation of government" (at 14). While this recommendation was not acted on, a perceived crisis in securities regulation led to an important legislative reform that seems likely to have a broad impact on rulemaking in Ontario, particularly by administrative agencies.

The Ontario Securities Commission (OSC) long employed "policies" as a major instrument in its regulatory arsenal. While lacking formal statutory authorization, these policies were routinely treated as having the force of law. Despite warnings from some as to their legality, a complex policy edifice was put in place to serve as the primary day-to-day means of regulating the securities industry. However, in 1993, in *Ainsley Financial Corporation v. Ontario Securities Commission* (1993), 14 OR (3d) 280 (Gen. Div.); aff'd. (1995), 21 OR (3d) 104 (CA), this practice of using policies as mandatory rules was struck down. This led to the setting up of the Ontario Task Force on Securities Regulation and its Final Report, *Responsibility and Responsiveness* (Toronto: Queen's Printer for Ontario, 1994). The task force recommended that the OSC be given statutory authority to issue mandatory rules subject, however, to Cabinet disapproval.

The following extracts from the task force's Final Report highlight first, the importance of rules in regulation; second, the need for formal notice-and-comment procedures; and third, based on what it had learned through its own extensive consultation, the nature of the dynamics of public participation and the type of linkages necessary to assure participants that their input will be treated seriously.

Responsibility and Responsiveness: Final Report of the Ontario Task Force on Securities Regulation
(Toronto: Queen's Printer for Ontario, 1994), at 2-3, 35-40

The Role of Subordinate Regulatory Instruments in the Modern System of Securities Regulation

It is essential that the importance of so-called subordinate instruments to the modern system of securities regulation be recognized. The subordinate instruments occupy 63% of the total number of pages in the standard 1994 industry consolidation of securities materials in Ontario, with legislation and regulations comprising the remainder (37%). Review of the subjects covered by these subordinate instruments underscores their scope and importance. For instance, rules (or "requirements") governing the structure and operation of the mutual fund industry (a $114 billion industry in Canada in 1993); the nature, form and timing of information that senior issuers must disclose pursuant to the prompt offering qualification system for prospectuses; and the manner in which a related party transaction can be effected (including disclosure, valuation, review, and approval requirements) are entirely or primarily lodged in these instruments.

Moreover, subordinate instruments play an important role in facilitating interprovincial and international cooperation. There are currently 37 National Policy Statements and 12 Uniform Act Policy Statements in force. Further, the OSC has entered into memoranda of understanding ("MOU") with other regulatory agencies and governments, such as the enforcement and information sharing memoranda concluded among the OSC and various other Canadian securities commissions and with the United States' Securities and Exchange Commission ("SEC").

To the extent that uncertainty exists as to the status of some of these instruments, public confidence in the soundness and integrity of the securities regulatory regime in Ontario may be undermined.

. . .

Notice and Comment

(i) Codification of Notice and Comment Obligation

It has been said that the regulatory agency is a "government in miniature." If so, the nature of the processes used to facilitate active and informed participation in policy development is critical to the legitimacy of the product. The vast majority of submissions we received endorsed the statutory entrenchment of a structured notice and comment procedure for the making of rules by the Commission.

The magnitude of the rulemaking power recommended for the Commission requires considerable attention to the checks and balances that will accompany its exercise. We regard an effective notice and comment procedure as the central mechanism for ensuring the accountability and transparency of Commission rulemaking. While the substantive standards we enumerate … will impart critical guidance to the Commission and the public regarding the scope of Commission rulemaking, ultimately, informed involvement by stakeholders in the rulemaking process will be necessary to ensure the production of responsive and responsible rules.

Notice and comment consultation is by no means novel to the Commission. In the past, it has been used regularly and effectively in the development and adoption of policy statements.

. . .

The Task Force recommends that the Commission be required to submit all proposed rules to a notice and comment procedure prior to their adoption. Under the notice and comment procedure, the Commission would be obliged to publish a proposed instrument along with a request for comments in the OSC Bulletin. The public would be allowed at least 90 days to consider the proposed rule and furnish any submission to the Commission. If material amendments to a rule were made by the Commission after the conclusion of the initial notice and comment period, the Commission would be obliged to remit the amended instrument to a subsequent round of notice and comment. However, given public familiarity with the general content and design of the amended instrument, we believe that the public would not be adversely affected by a more circumscribed period of consultation on subsequent rounds, and we would remit to the Commission the discretion to determine the appropriate length of time for successive rounds of consultation.

. . .

Finally, we recommend that the Commission not be bound to follow the prescribed notice and comment procedure when:

(a) *the effects of the rule are restricted to certain named individuals who are provided an opportunity for a hearing on the proposed rule;*

(b) the rule relates only to organizational or procedural matters internal to the Commission, and is not likely to have a substantial impact on the interests of persons or companies, other than members of the Commission or employees of the Commission, who are affected by it;

(c) the rule grants an exemption or removes a restriction and is not likely to have a substantial impact on the interests of persons or companies other than those who benefit under it; or

(d) the rule makes no material change to an existing rule.

(ii) Request for Comments and Supporting Statement

Some of the submissions we received expressed concern with the amount of supporting material distributed by the Commission at the time of publication of a proposed policy statement. Without sufficient background information, it is difficult for the public to assess meaningfully the factual basis for or merits of a proposed rule or policy statement. This impairs the goals of transparency, accountability and participation in public decision-making.

To address the need for increased information, we recommend that the Commission be required as part of its notice and comment process to publish a Supporting Statement that would, in general, include the following materials: a description of the objective of the proposed rule, the statutory power relied upon, and the alternatives, if any, that were considered and why those alternatives were rejected, a reference to any significant unpublished study, and, finally, a qualitative description of the anticipated costs and benefits of the proposed rule. The general content of this statement could be informed by the purposes and principles of the Act.

By and large, as demonstrated by past practice, the Staff have been successful in furnishing the public with well articulated and coherent statements in support of policy statements. *To ensure the efficacy of the Supporting Statement, we recommend periodic public review of the content and use of the statement with the Commission. In this way, the Commission could experiment with different forms of the statement, and could adopt those forms which had proven most useful to the public.*

We emphasize that the preparation and circulation of a Supporting Statement constitutes only a minimum standard of disclosure. We encourage the Commission to adopt a presumption in favour of disclosure of any and all materials that would assist the public in evaluating the case for a given policy initiative, subject to the obvious proviso that the Commission not compromise its enforcement or investigative activities through such disclosure.

. . .

(iii) Staff Summary of Public Comments and the Commission's Reply

Several First Round public submissions [to the Task Force] focused on the need for the Commission to demonstrate a clearer link between the comments it receives from the notice and comment process and the final form of the proposed policy statement or rule. In the view of the Task Force, the rulemaking process would be enhanced if the public were advised in summary fashion of the range of views reflected in comments received with respect to a proposed rule and provided with an analysis of the reasoning behind the Commission's conclusions, as reflected in the ultimate policy.

To increase public confidence in the integrity of the notice and comment process, we recommend that the Commission be required to publish a summary of comments received from the public during each round of consultations. The Summary of Public Comments would permit the public to discern the essence of each of the submissions filed, as well as the thrust of the submissions taken as a whole. For purposes of economy and accuracy, we recommend that the Commission consider encouraging commentators to furnish the OSC with a summary of materials submitted in response to a request for comments.

One particularly difficult issue concerns the role, if any, for confidential comments tendered during the notice and comment process. It is around this issue that two of our foundational principles, namely transparency and broad participation, directly collided. In its Second Round brief to us, the OSC stated that

> While we appreciate the benefits of public disclosure of comments in order to ensure a full and thorough canvassing of issues, we note that confidentiality may be warranted in a variety of circumstances (e.g., proprietary trade information and information that would, if disclosed, adversely affect relationships with clients). It has been our experience that information which is sensitive may be invaluable for purposes of appreciating the relevant issues. (at 9-10)

We concur with the OSC, and recommend that the Commission have authority to determine on a case-by-case basis whether or not it can grant confidentiality at the request of a commentator, subject to the Freedom of Information Act. We would expect that the weight of confidential submissions would be appropriately discounted by the Commission to the extent that public testing of the substance of the submission is lacking.

We further recommend that the Commission be required to respond to the material issues and concerns raised in the notice and comment process in a statement ("Commission's Reply") published with the adopted rule. Particularly where there has been concentrated public opposition to or concern expressed with certain aspects of a proposed rule, the Commission's Reply would afford the public the opportunity to understand clearly the reasons for the final form of the policy instrument. The preparation of the Commission's Reply reinforces the Commissioners' central responsibility for the integrity of the Province's securities regime.

(iv) Public Hearings

Several submissions identified the contribution that public hearings could make, in some circumstances, to the notice and comment process. Through face-to-face meetings, the public would be able to clarify their written comments and respond to specific questions and concerns raised by the Commission. In this way, the Commission would be able to test the factual premises upon which submissions were made and appreciate more fully their implications.

While the greater use of public hearings in the notice and comment process was endorsed in some of the submissions, most parties also recognized the time and resource constraints inherent in the process, and did not advocate that the hearing be a mandatory component of the notice and comment procedure. We share this view.

We endorse the use of public hearings to the extent they may enhance the development of certain policy instruments in appropriate circumstances.

(v) Waiver for Exceptional Circumstances

We considered the desirability of delegating to the Commission the authority to make rules in exceptional circumstances without submitting the proposed rule to the notice and comment process. The submissions were divided on this issue. Several expressed scepticism of the need to create exemptions from the notice and comment procedure. Some conceded the possibility that exceptions to the notice and comment procedure may be necessary to enable the Commission to respond to particularly abusive situations, but were not fully persuaded of the necessity for what they termed to be "extraordinary power."

Other commentators were in favour of conferring a power on the Commission to waive the application of the notice and comment process in exceptional circumstances. They noted that this power was vested in the SEC and endorsed it for circumstances of a pressing or immediate nature where consultations would be impracticable or would defeat the purpose of the rule. In such cases, the waiver would permit the enactment of a rule on an interim basis only. The interim rule would have an expiry date and would be subject to notice and comment scrutiny before being enacted on a permanent basis.

. . .

We recommend that the Commission be permitted to waive or abridge the notice and comment process in the event of matters of urgency as evidenced by the risk of material harm to investors or the integrity of capital markets. Such an interim rule would only be permitted to remain in force for a period of 9 months. We further recommend that the adoption of an interim rule be made only with the express approval of the Minister. Finally, we recommend that the Commission be bound to publish in the OSC Bulletin its reasons for waiver or abridgement for the notice and comment process at the time of enactment of the interim rule.

The recommendations of the task force were largely implemented in Bill 190, *An Act to Amend the Securities Act* (SO 1994, c. 33). The general requirement for public participation in rulemaking is now found in s. 143.2(1) of the *Securities Act*, RSO 1990, c. S.5, which obliges the OSC to publish a notice of any proposed rule in its bulletin. In s. 143.2(2) notice must include:

1. The proposed rule.

2. A statement of the substance and purpose of the proposed rule.

3. A summary of the proposed rule.

4. A reference to the authority under which the rule is proposed or a statement that the Commission is seeking legislative amendments to provide the requisite rule-making authority.

5. A discussion of all alternatives to the proposed rule that were considered by the Commission and the reasons for not proposing the adoption of the alternatives considered.

6. A reference to any significant unpublished study, report or other written materials on which the Commission relies in proposing the rule.

7. A description of the anticipated costs and benefits of the proposed rule.

Requirements for an analysis of alternatives, along with the release of any written materials relied on and an estimate of anticipated costs and benefits, are expected to enhance the effectiveness of public comment. Comment is limited to written representations in s. 143.2(4):

Upon publication of a notice under subsection (1), the Commission shall invite, and shall give a reasonable opportunity to, interested persons and companies to make written representations with respect to the proposed rule within a period of at least 90 days after the publication.

It is further provided in s. 143.2(10):

In cases where a notice and comment process is required, the Commission may make the rule only at the end of the notice and comment process and after considering all representations made as a result of that process.

While this is clearly a call for meaningful participation, one might also ask what assurance there will be (aside from the good faith of the rulemaker) that public participation will be taken seriously.

Several of the *Securities Act* provisions introduced in Bill 190 appear designed to put the OSC on the spot if it simply ignores notice-and-comment submissions or if it give credence to only one viewpoint. Thus, should the commission propose to make material changes to a proposed rule after considering representations, it must give notice of such changes including a concise statement of the purposes of the changes and reasons for the changes. Thereafter, a reasonable opportunity has to be provided for written representations with respect to such changes (ss. 143.2(7)-(9)). As well, in publishing the final version of a rule, the commission is obliged to explain how it responded to representations made to it. Consider s. 143.3(2):

The Commission shall publish in its Bulletin every rule made by it as soon after the rule is made as practicable together with the following:

· · ·

4. A summary of the written comments received during the comment periods if notice and comment were required.

5. A statement of the Commission setting out its response to the significant issues and concerns brought to the attention of the Commission during the comment periods.

Requirements of reasons for changes, summaries of written comments, and responses to significant issues and concerns go further than what is required by the bare bones of s. 553 of the APA, federal practice, or the Québec legislation. Are reasons, or even responses to significant issues and concerns, appropriate in a legislative task that does not involve a principled choice between competing arguments in a focused adversary process? Are reasons appropriate where the decision-making exercise involves a largely intuitive estimate of what is in the public interest based on a mix of fact, experience, and instinct?

In seeking to devise procedures appropriate to rulemaking, care must be taken to ensure that the pendulum does not swing too far and that we do not end up seeking to transpose methods that are suitable for adjudication into the legislative arena. It seems appropriate to bear this in mind as we look briefly at some further procedural issues.

First let us consider claims to confidentiality. The Ontario Task Force on Securities Regulation noted, "One particularly difficult issue concerns the role, if any, for confidential comments tendered during the notice and comment process. It is around this issue that two of our foundational principles, namely transparency and broad participation, directly collide" (38). The OSC itself asserted that sensitive information (such as proprietary trade information and information that would, if disclosed, adversely affect relationships with clients) could often be invaluable for an appreciation of relevant issues. The task force recommended that the commission be given authority to grant confidentiality on a case-by-case basis and added, "We would expect that the weight of confidential submissions would be appropriately discounted by the Commission to the extent that public testing of the substance of the submission is lacking" (*ibid.*).

Section 143.2(3) of the *Securities Act*, RSO 1990, c. S.5 provides:

> The Commission does not have to make reference to written material that, in the opinion of the Commission, should be held in confidence because it discloses intimate financial, personal or other information and the desirability of avoiding disclosure of the substance of it or its existence in the interests of any person or company affected outweighs the desirability of making it or knowledge of its existence available to the public.

Philip Anisman, in a submission to the Standing Committee on Financial and Economic Affairs of the Ontario legislature concerning Bill 190 (November 16, 1994), which introduced this provision, was trenchantly critical of this approach (at 35-36).

> In view of the importance of public participation in the rulemaking process and its central role in the Commission's accountability, confidential treatment of significant information and of submissions is counterproductive. It would deprive persons who may be affected by a rule of an opportunity to address issues that may influence its adoption or the terms on which it is adopted. This potential undercuts both meaningful participation in rulemaking and the role of the rulemaking procedure as a check on the Commission. It is contrary to the openness that should accompany rulemaking.

Do you agree? Or would this be to apply an essentially adjudicative standard of disclosure to the legislative process? Would it be possible to devise a unique standard for rulemaking that could reassure participants that their submissions would not be undermined by reliance on undisclosed information, but that would not, as the OSC emphasized, cut rulemakers off from invaluable information? How much confidence do you place in the task force's expectation that less weight be given to confidential information? Isn't the opposite more likely?

Another issue is that of exceptions to public notice and comment. As we saw above, the task force indicated that provision should be made for waiver in exceptional circumstances. Following Bill 190, s. 143.2(5) of the *Securities Act* provides:

> (5) Publication of a notice is not required if,
>
>   (a) all persons and companies who would be subject to the proposed rule are named, the information set out in subsection (2) is sent to each of them and they and any other

person or company whose interests are likely to be substantially affected by the proposed rule are given an opportunity to make written representations with respect to it;

(b) the proposed rule grants an exemption or removes a restriction and is not likely to have a substantial effect on the interests of persons or companies other than those who benefit under it;

(c) what is proposed is only an amendment that does not materially change an existing rule;

(d) the Commission,

(i) believes that there is an urgent need for the proposed rule and that, without it, there is a substantial risk of material harm to investors or to the integrity of the capital markets, and

(ii) has the approval of the Minister to make the rule without publication of notice;

. . .

(6) When a rule to which clause (5)(d) applies comes into force, the Commission shall publish in its Bulletin a statement setting out the substance and purpose of the rule and the nature of the urgency and the risk.

Do you think that the task force was on the right track when it recommended that, should the OSC be permitted to waive or abridge the notice and comment process in the extent of matters of urgency, it should only be authorized to enact "interim rules" that could remain in force for a period of nine months? Note that s. 143.4(6) provides: "Every rule to which clause 143.2(5)(d) applies is revoked on the 275th day after it comes into force."

Next, consider the issue of oral hearings. As we have seen, the task force, Bill 190, and now the *Securities Act* favoured written submissions as the means of implementing a notice-and-comment regime. However, the task force did acknowledge that several of the submissions it received favoured oral hearings as a means of testing factual premises and providing a forum at which the public would be able to clarify its written submissions and respond to specific questions and concerns raised by the commission. Nevertheless, the task force was not prepared to advocate that the hearing be a mandatory component of the notice-and-comment procedure, although it endorsed the use of public hearings "to the extent that they may enhance the development of certain policy instruments in appropriate circumstances" (at 39).

Is this all that can be done? Might it be possible to nudge rulemakers to make limited use of oral procedures where facts are in dispute? What do you think of the following provisions in the *Draft Act* of Anisman's *Proposals for a Securities Market Law for Canada* (1979)?

15.15(2) After a proposed regulation is published … the Commission shall afford a reasonable opportunity to interested persons to make representations in writing with respect to the proposed regulation and all such representations shall be available to the public.

(3) The Commission may convene a hearing for the presentation of oral argument or the submission of evidence orally and may permit cross-examination by interested persons in order to determine an issue of specific fact that is material to its consideration of a proposed regulation.

Finally, who should be entitled to initiate a rulemaking proceeding? The Ontario Task Force on Securities Regulations' "Proposed Amendments and Commentary" provide in s. 143(a)7 that "[a]ny person may petition the Commission to make, amend or repeal a rule."

This provision was not included in Bill 190's reforms to the *Securities Act*. According to Anisman in his submission to the Standing Committee on Finance and Economic Affairs:

> Although it is open to any member of the public to request the Commission to consider making, amending or repealing a rule, such a request will be taken more seriously if it is authorized expressly in the Act. Indeed, the inclusion of such a provision will further the participatory process contemplated by the Task Force in that it will, in effect, require the Commission to consider such a request. Similar provisions in the United States not only authorize such a request but prescribe the contents for a request and require that the Commission notify the petitioner of its decision with respect to the request within a specified period of time.
>
> The recommendation of the Task Force should be included in the Bill. It would emphasize the fact that the Commission should be responsive to public investors and others who are affected by rules under the Securities Act.

Do you believe that the power to initiate a rulemaking proceeding should rest solely with the rulemaking authority? What role should private actors play in initiating policy making? In 1979, Anisman proposed a similar provision to that favoured by the task force. In his *Commentary* he observed that it was included "to make it clear that any person may petition the Commission in relation to rulemaking and to ensure that the Commission must consider such requests." Is this an idea whose time has come? What reasons might weigh against it?

Notice and comment provisions are still relatively uncommon in provincial legislation. Two Ontario statutes that contain obligations in this respect are the *Ontario Energy Board Act, 1998*, SO 1998, c. 15, Sch. B, s. 45 and the *Ontarians with Disabilities Act*, SO 2001, c. 32, s. 23(2). Further examples include the *Clean Air Act*, SNB 1997, c. C-5.2, s. 8(2); and the *Electric Utilities Act*, RSA 2000, c. E-5, ss. 20.2 and 20.4. Advocacy for such procedures also continues: Berzins, "Policy Development by Labour Relations Boards in Canada: Is There a Case for Rulemaking?" (2000), 25 *Queen's LJ* 479.

The following example is a broadly framed statutory regime designed to facilitate public participation and accountability in environmentally significant decision making.

Environmental Bill of Rights, 1993
SO 1993, c. 28

Preamble

The people of Ontario recognize the inherent value of the natural environment.

The people of Ontario have a right to a healthful environment.

The people of Ontario have as a common goal the protection, conservation and restoration of the natural environment for the benefit of present and future generations.

While the government has the primary responsibility for achieving this goal, the people should have means to ensure that it is achieved in an effective, timely, open and fair manner.

Therefore, Her Majesty, by and with the advice and consent of the Legislative Assembly of the Province of Ontario, enacts as follows:

PART I

DEFINITIONS AND PURPOSES

. . .

2(1) The purposes of this Act are,

(a) to protect, conserve and, where reasonable, restore the integrity of the environment by the means provided in this Act;

(b) to provide sustainability of the environment by the means provided in this Act; and

(c) to protect the right to a healthful environment by the means provided in this Act.

(2) The purposes set out in subsection (1) include the following:

1. The prevention, reduction and elimination of the use, generation and release of pollutants that are an unreasonable threat to the integrity of the environment.

2. The protection and conservation of biological, ecological and genetic diversity.

3. The protection and conservation of natural resources, including plant life, animal life and ecological systems.

4. The encouragement of the wise management of our natural resources, including plant life, animal life and ecological systems.

5. The identification, protection and conservation of ecologically sensitive areas or processes.

(3) In order to fulfil the purposes set out in subsections (1) and (2), this Act provides,

(a) means by which residents of Ontario may participate in the making of environmentally significant decisions by the Government of Ontario;

(b) increased accountability of the Government of Ontario for its environmental decision-making;

(c) increased access to the courts by residents of Ontario for the protection of the environment; and

(d) enhanced protection for employees who take action in respect of environmental harm.

PART II

PUBLIC PARTICIPATION IN GOVERNMENT DECISION-MAKING

3(1) This Part sets out minimum levels of public participation that must be met before the Government of Ontario makes decisions on certain kinds of environmentally significant proposals for policies, Acts, regulations and instruments.

. . .

5(1) An environmental registry shall be established as prescribed.

. . .

6(1) The purpose of the registry is to provide a means of giving information about the environment to the public.

. . .

7. Within three months after the date on which this section begins to apply to a ministry, the minister shall prepare a draft ministry statement of environmental values that,

(a) explains how the purposes of this Act are to be applied when decisions that might significantly affect the environment are made in the ministry; and

(b) explains how consideration of the purposes of this Act should be integrated with other considerations, including social, economic and scientific considerations, that are part of decision-making in the ministry.

8(1) After the draft ministry statement of environmental values is prepared and not later than three months after the day on which this section begins to apply to a ministry, the minister shall give notice to the public that he or she is developing the ministry statement of environmental values.

(2) Notice under this section shall be given in the registry and by any other means the minister considers appropriate.

. . .

(4) The minister shall not finalize the ministry statement of environmental values until at least thirty days after giving the notice under this section.

(5) The minister shall consider allowing more than thirty days between giving the notice under this section and finalizing the statement in order to permit more informed public consultation on the statement.

(6) In considering how much time ought to be allowed under subsection (5), the minister shall consider the following factors:

1. The complexity of the matters on which comments are invited.

2. The level of public interest in the matters on which comments are invited.

3. The period of time the public may require to make informed comment.

4. Any private or public interest, including any governmental interest, in resolving the matters on which comments are invited in a timely manner.

5. Any other factor that the minister considers relevant.

9(1) Within nine months after the day on which this section begins to apply to a ministry, the minister shall finalize the ministry statement of environmental values and give notice of it to the public.

(2) Notice under this section shall be given in the registry and by any other means the minister considers appropriate.

(3) The notice shall include a brief explanation of the effect, if any, of comments from members of the public on the development of the statement and any other information that the minister considers appropriate.

. . .

11. The minister shall take every reasonable step to ensure that the ministry statement of environmental values is considered whenever decisions that might significantly affect the environment are made in the ministry.

. . .

14. In determining, under section 15 or 16, whether a proposal for a policy, Act or regulation could, if implemented, have a significant effect on the environment, a minister shall consider the following factors:

1. The extent and nature of the measures that might be required to mitigate or prevent any harm to the environment that could result from a decision whether or not to implement the proposal.

2. The geographic extent, whether local, regional or provincial, of any harm to the environment that could result from a decision whether or not to implement the proposal.

3. The nature of the private and public interests, including governmental interests, involved in the decision whether or not to implement the proposal.

4. Any other matter that the minister considers relevant.

15(1) If a minister considers that a proposal under consideration in his or her ministry for a policy or Act could, if implemented, have a significant effect on the environment, and the minister considers that the public should have an opportunity to comment on the proposal before implementation, the minister shall do everything in his or her power to give notice of the proposal to the public at least thirty days before the proposal is implemented.

(2) Subsection (1) does not apply to a policy or Act that is predominantly financial or administrative in nature.

16(1) If a minister considers that a proposal under consideration in his or her ministry for a regulation under a prescribed Act could, if implemented, have a significant effect on the environment, the minister shall do everything in his or her power to give notice of the proposal to the public at least thirty days before the proposal is implemented.

(2) Subsection (1) does not apply to a regulation that is predominantly financial or administrative in nature.

17(1) The minister shall consider allowing more than thirty days between giving notice of a proposal under section 15 or 16 and implementation of the proposal in order to permit more informed public consultation on the proposal.

(2) In considering how much time ought to be allowed under subsection (1), the minister shall consider the factors set out in subsection 8(6).

18. Notice under section 15 or 16 shall be given in accordance with section 27.

19. Within a reasonable time after this section begins to apply to a ministry, the minister for the ministry shall prepare a proposal for a regulation to classify proposals for instruments as Class I, II or III proposals for the purposes of this Act and the regulations under it.

· · ·

22(1) The minister shall do everything in his or her power to give notice to the public of a Class I, II or III proposal for an instrument under consideration in his or her ministry at least thirty days before a decision is made whether or not to implement the proposal.

· · ·

(3) Despite subsection (1), the minister need not give notice of a proposal to amend or revoke an instrument if the minister considers that the potential effect of the amendment or revocation on the environment is insignificant.

(4) Notice under this section shall be given in accordance with section 27.

. . .

24(1) A minister required to give notice under section 22 of a Class II proposal for an instrument shall also consider enhancing the right of members of the public to participate in decision-making on the proposal by providing for one or more of the following:

1. Opportunities for oral representations by members of the public to the minister or a person or body designated by the minister.

2. Public meetings.

3. Mediation among persons with different views on issues arising out of the proposal.

4. Any other process that would facilitate more informed public participation in decision-making on the proposal.

(2) In exercising his or her discretion under subsection (1), the minister shall consider the factors set out in section 14.

. . .

27(1) Notice of a proposal under section 15, 16 or 22 shall be given in the registry and by any other means the minister giving the notice considers appropriate.

(2) Notice of a proposal given under section 15, 16 or 22 in the registry shall include the following:

1. A brief description of the proposal.

2. A statement of the manner by which and time within which members of the public may participate in decision-making on the proposal.

3. A statement of where and when members of the public may review written information about the proposal.

. . .

6. Any other information that the minister giving the notice considers appropriate.

. . .

(4) The minister shall include a regulatory impact statement in a notice of a proposal given under section 16 in the registry if the minister considers that it is necessary to do so in order to permit more informed public consultation on the proposal.

(5) A regulatory impact statement shall include the following:

1. A brief statement of the objectives of the proposal.

2. A preliminary assessment of the environmental, social and economic consequences of implementing the proposal.

3. An explanation of why the environmental objectives, if any, of the proposal would be appropriately achieved by making, amending or revoking a regulation.

. . .

29(1) Sections 15, 16 and 22 do not apply where, in the minister's opinion, the delay involved in giving notice to the public, in allowing time for public response to the notice or in considering the response to the notice would result in,

(a) danger to the health or safety of any person;

(b) harm or serious risk of harm to the environment; or

(c) injury or damage or serious risk of injury or damage to any property.

(2) If a minister decides under subsection (1) not to give notice of a proposal under section 15, 16 or 22, the minister shall give notice of the decision to the public and to the Environmental Commissioner.

(3) Notice under subsection (2) shall be given as soon as reasonably possible after the decision is made and shall include a brief statement of the minister's reasons for the decision and any other information about the decision that the minister considers appropriate.

30(1) Sections 15, 16 and 22 do not apply where, in the minister's opinion, the environmentally significant aspects of a proposal for a policy, Act, regulation or instrument,

(a) have already been considered in a process of public participation, under this Act, under another Act or otherwise, that was substantially equivalent to the process required in relation to the proposal under this Act; or

(b) are required to be considered in a process of public participation under another Act that is substantially equivalent to the process required in relation to the proposal under this Act.

. . .

32(1) Section 22 does not apply where, in the minister's opinion, the issuance, amendment or revocation of an instrument would be a step towards implementing an undertaking or other project approved by,

(a) a decision made by a tribunal under an Act after affording an opportunity for public participation; or

(b) a decision made under the *Environmental Assessment Act*.

. . .

33(1) A minister need not give notice under section 15, 16 or 22 of a proposal that would, if implemented, form part of or give effect to a budget or economic statement presented to the Assembly.

. . .

35(1) A minister who gives notice of a proposal under section 15, 16 or 22 shall take every reasonable step to ensure that all comments relevant to the proposal that are received as part of the public participation process described in the notice of the proposal are considered when decisions about the proposal are made in the ministry.

. . .

36(1) As soon as reasonably possible after a proposal for a policy, Act or regulation in respect of which notice was given under section 15 or 16 is implemented, the minister shall give notice to the public of the implementation.

(2) As soon as reasonably possible after a decision is made whether or not to implement a proposal for an instrument in respect of which notice was given under section 22, the minister shall give notice to the public of the decision.

. . .

Contents of notice

(4) The notice shall include a brief explanation of the effect, if any, of public participation on decision-making on the proposal and any other information that the minister considers appropriate.

To summarize these provisions, the purposes of the *Environmental Bill of Rights* (EBR)—all relating to the protection and conservation of the environment—are to be furthered by providing a means, in the case of environmentally significant decisions, for public participation and public accountability (along with increased access to the courts and enhanced protections for environmental whistleblowers) (s. 2(3)). Part II of the EBR requires Ontario ministries to prepare a statement of environmental values, subject to public notice and comment, that explains how the ministry will apply the purposes of the EBR when making potentially environmentally significant decisions and how those purposes should be integrated with other considerations including social, economic, and scientific considerations (s. 7). In turn, the minister must take "every reasonable step" to ensure that the statement of environmental values is considered in ministry decision making (s. 11). Furthermore, any ministerial proposal for a policy, Act, regulation, or instrument (other than an Act, policy, or regulation that is not "predominantly financial or administrative in nature") that could have a significant effect on the environment is subject to a 30-day notice period (s. 15) including posting on an environmental registry. Detailed provisions are included on the requirements for public notice of proposals (s. 27(2)) and, in the case of proposals for regulations, on the need to include a regulatory impact statement "if the minister considers that it is necessary to do so in order to permit more informed public consultation on the proposal" (s. 27(4)). Where a regulatory impact assessment is included, it must contain a statement of the objectives of the proposed regulation, a preliminary assessment of its expected environmental, social, and economic consequences, and an explanation of why its environmental objectives, if any, would be appropriately achieved by making, amending, or revoking a regulation (s. 27(5)).

How does this approach to public participation and regulatory impact assessment compare with that in the federal *Cabinet Directive on Streamlining Regulation* and the *Guidelines on International Regulatory Obligations and Cooperation*? Is it fair to say that the EBR focuses more on public participation whereas the federal process emphasizes vetting of the substantive content of proposed regulations prior to their submission for approval? If so, what does this say about the purposes of the two regimes and to what extent do you think each will be effective in achieving its purpose?

Notably, it is provided in ss. 37-38 of the EBR that failure to comply with the EBR requirements for public participation does not affect the validity of a policy, Act, regulation, or instrument. However, any Ontario resident may seek leave to appeal a decision on an instrument where the person has an interest in the decision (including where the person commented on the proposal) and where implementation of the decision could be appealed by a person under another Act. Implementation of the EBR is also supervised by the environmental commissioner of Ontario, whose office, function, and powers are established under Part III of the EBR.

EMERGING PROCEDURAL ISSUES

The examples of securities reform and the EBR present wider questions about the appropriate scope and about the utility of public consultation. Without careful analysis, "consultation" may quickly become platitudinous rhetoric. Who could be against consultation? The hard questions are more specific and more difficult.

With whom should there be consultation—with those most immediately affected or some wider group? Where a proposed rule has a great impact on a particular industry and only a very minor one on individuals, what steps should be taken, if any, to provide financial support for the involvement of non-industry public-interest groups?

At what stage should there be consultation? Should the concern be with the identifying of problems and possible alternatives to rulemaking or should the focus be on types and terms of rules? Should there be consultation prior to draft rules and how will this consultation dovetail with subsequent more formal participation? How different should procedures be for early consultation and for consultation about draft rules?

What right of access should there be to explore the factual basis on which rules are developed? Are written comments always enough? If not, when should oral proceedings be employed, and what would be included: cross-examination; interrogatories? Would this involve the agency staff who drafted the rules? Would it involve an opportunity to adduce evidence? What *ex parte* contact should there be between the rulemaking agency and interested participants? Should the rule against bias apply in rulemaking?

A somewhat skeptical perspective on public consultation and participation in decision making, and its implications for the democratic process, is offered by political scientist Martin Shapiro, "Administrative Law Unbounded: Reflections on Government and Governance" (2001), 8 *Ind. J Global Legal Stud.* 369. Reflecting on what Shapiro calls a wider trend in public decision making from government to "governance"—in which "everyone, or at least potentially everyone is also seen as a participant in the collective decision-making process" (at 369)—Shapiro says at 372-73:

> The erosion of the boundary between government and nongovernment decisionmaking generates several new problems for those who seek to make an administrative law that focuses on governance rather than government. From the perspective of pluralist democracy, an administrative law that maximizes transparency and participation is democratic—it maximizes the access of "outside" interest groups to the government decision-making process. But from the standpoint of individual, popular, or majoritarian democracy, an administrative law that promotes transparency and participation to such a degree that government becomes governance may actually undermine democracy.
>
> As public policy decisionmaking is diffused among various government and nongovernment actors in an amorphous, non-rule-defined manner, democratic accountability is destroyed. Reference to some standard observations on the operation of parliamentary government may make this point clearer and less abstract. Where a parliamentary government coincides with a two-party system with strong party discipline, decisionmaking is concentrated in a cabinet that bears collective responsibility. This approach to government epitomizes democratic accountability. Voters know exactly whom to hold electorally accountable for everything that the government does or fails to do … . "Governance" by "network" and "epistemic community" has the

opposite effect. While every interested group may participate in the decisionmaking process, the voters have no idea whom to reward or blame for results they like or dislike.

In light of Shapiro's comment, how might provisions for public participation be designed to maintain easily identifiable lines of accountability for government decisions?

PART III

Substantive Review

GENERAL INTRODUCTION

For over 60 years, there have been serious issues about the scope of judicial review on substantive grounds. These issues emerged during the early part of the era of more activist government. Among the features of these new government initiatives were the development of social programs of various kinds, the arrival of new regulatory agencies, and an increasing use of tribunals in place of the courts to settle disputes arising out of the new social programs and regulatory regimes. All of these features, once innovations, are now integral aspects of modern government.

Historically, judicial review of the substance of statutory decision making was very confined. The courts essentially policed the outer limits of the jurisdiction of statutory authorities. When operating within their jurisdiction or home territory, statutory authorities were left pretty much alone provided they did not act in bad faith or for purposes not contemplated by the empowering Act. For a while, there was a claim of an entitlement to review for all errors of law at least in the case of truly adjudicative bodies that kept a formal record of their proceedings. However, this lapsed for a considerable time in the face of various legislative devices aimed at squelching this nascent threat to the autonomy of these specialist bodies. Privative clauses—that is, provisions intended to limit the scope of judicial review of tribunals—were one such device. Beyond that, judicial review of a tribunal's findings of fact (save in the instance of facts on which the tribunal's jurisdiction was said to depend) was extremely rare. It was confined to situations where there was absolutely no evidence to support the conclusion reached by the tribunal. There were also serious doubts as to whether this basis for review survived the presence of a privative clause in the empowering legislation.

With greater government intervention in the private sector, increased social programs, and legislative derogation from the traditional jurisdiction of the courts came a rather different attitude on the part of the Canadian courts. While they still paid obeisance to the prerogatives of Cabinet and ministerial decision making, they were far less hospitable to the advent of many administrative tribunals and, more generally, the new social order. This was particularly so in the courts' response to those who were charged with administering a new regime of labour relations, one based on collective bargaining instead of traditional employment law and on administrative substitutes for the restrictive tort law that had applied to the lot of employees injured at work. Indeed, in a number of judgments of this era, over several decades during the mid-20th century, the attitude of the courts was one of downright hostility to legislative objectives and the removal of the courts' traditional jurisdiction.

The Supreme Court of Canada was often at the forefront of this rearguard action (to mix metaphors). Privative clauses were interpreted in a very restrictive fashion. The concept of

674 Part III Substantive Review

jurisdictional error was distorted and expanded to such an extent as to potentially subject any determination of law that a tribunal or other form of statutory authority might make to full correctness review. In short, there were aspects of the courts' practice of judicial review that were the equivalent of a war between the courts and the legislature, a war in which the casual victims were often the intended beneficiaries of new programs: those injured at work; those seeking the benefits of collective bargaining and especially the right to take collective action; and, with the advent of human rights commissions and tribunals, those alleging discrimination. The technical requirements for access to the common law remedies of judicial review were also frequently a trap for the unwary, a group that included often otherwise competent lawyers who were ensnared by the arcane rules surrounding the availability of the ancient prerogative writs that continued to provide the principal route by which administrative wrongs could be redressed.

This is to a certain extent a caricature of judicial review as it was practised in Canada in the second and third quarters of the 20th century, though one that in general has considerable support in the history of the case law: see David Mullan, "The Supreme Court of Canada and Tribunals—Deference to the Administrative Process: A Recent Phenomenon or a Return to Basics?" (2001), 80 *Can. Bar Rev.* 399. What should be added to the picture, though, is that frequently the courts had "right" on their side in that the legislature in many instances actually conferred a right of appeal to the courts from a tribunal or other statutory authority. The presence of such a statutory right invited intrusive curial scrutiny of not just the legal determinations of the decision-maker subject to appeal but also, where the terms of the appeal right were sufficiently broad, of the very substantive merits of the determination by the relevant statutory authority. It was also the case that many administrative tribunals were little deserving of respect from the superior courts in that their members frequently owed their appointments to even more crass political considerations than was the case with the superior courts themselves. In short, appointees to many administrative tribunals tended to have both less political clout and less ability than those appointed to s. 96 courts.

We enter this story at a recent point where the "modern" approach of the Supreme Court of Canada to administrative decision-makers—an approach that is more respectful of the comparative strengths of tribunals and other non-judicial actors and of legislative intentions regarding their expanded role—was affirmed, but also clarified and refined. At this point, we begin also with a case involving judicial review in the labour relations context, this being the same context in which the modern turn in substantive review was signalled in 1979 with the seminal decision in *CUPE* (see chapter 12 of this text). In labour law especially, competence or indeed excellence had become the characteristic of many of those who were members of labour boards or who acted as arbitrators of disputes arising from collective agreements. The same was often true of workers' compensation regimes. As well, service on those agencies charged with economic regulation was beginning to attract some of the best and brightest talents in the country at a time when public service was regarded as a significant virtue or, at the very least, a path to lucrative employment in the private sector. The late 1960s and early 1970s was also an era in which the evils of racist and sexist discrimination achieved a high profile and many eminently qualified people with a commitment to social justice were anxious to lend their skills to effecting the aims of human rights codes. In short, across a broad range of tribunals (though admittedly not all and in varying degrees) the profile of the administrative process improved dramatically. It was also the case that many of these legislative initiatives previously perceived as radical, socialist, or as taking away a God-given right to adjudication by a "real judge" were now seen not just as the accepted way of doing things but also as an improvement on the institutions and substantive entitlements that they replaced. Finally, many lawyers—both practising and academic—educated under and participating in the world of the "new administrative law" and generally sympathetic to its objectives were receiving judicial appointment. Of these, the most notable was Bora Laskin, who as judge on both the Ontario Court of Appeal and the Supreme Court of Canada was to play an important role in the transformation of conceptions of the proper role and methodology of judicial review of statutory and prerogative decision making.

The new era that persists to today was one in which reviewing courts were instructed by the Supreme Court of Canada to assess the extent of their engagement with the administrative process from a "pragmatic and functional" perspective. This dictated respect for the legislature's choice as to the decision-maker that was designated as the primary vehicle for carrying out the statutory mandate. It called also for greater attention to legislative signposts indicating restraint on the part of the reviewing courts, awareness of the expertise of many statutory regimes and the courts' own lack of working familiarity with the detailed working of those regimes, and, in the actual assessment of the decision taken in the particular case, a far more purposive or contextual approach to statutory interpretation. In many instances this has produced a cautious approach to the scope of the courts' judicial review authority or powers of intervention. The outcome of this pragmatic and functional approach is the courts' selection of a "standard of review" that determines the intensity with which they review an administrative decision.

This approach to substantive review was reaffirmed, but renovated, in *Dunsmuir v. New Brunswick*, [2008] 1 SCR 190, 2008 SCC 9 (CanLII). The "pragmatic and functional approach" that was applied in past by the courts to determine the appropriate level of deference to an administrative actor is now called the "standard of review analysis." All of the factors in the analysis remain, although the role that each plays has been clarified and recalibrated. The possible standards of review have been narrowed to two: an intrusive correctness standard and a deferential reasonableness standard. Moreover, the Supreme Court of Canada has conveyed that lower-court judges, counsel, and the parties involved in a judicial review should be encouraged to simplify the process of determining the appropriate standard of review. According to the concurring reasons of Binnie J in *Dunsmuir*, at para. 154:

> The problem is that courts have lately felt obliged to devote too much time to multi-part threshold tests instead of focusing on the who, what, why and where for of the litigant's complaint on its merits.

Seeking to address this problem, *Dunsmuir* clarifies that, where there is existing jurisprudence that determines "in a satisfactory manner" the applicable standard of review, then it should be applied without further consideration of the various factors in the standard of review analysis. In the absence of such guidance from past decisions, *Dunsmuir* clarifies further that it is sometimes unnecessary for a court to review all of these factors, such that the standard of review may be assumed to apply automatically based, for example, on the nature of the question at stake. This streamlining of the methodology is helpful, one might say even pragmatic, in its response to what had become an abstract and at times confounding effort to decide the question of curial deference. On the other hand, in a field as wide-ranging and diverse as administrative law—encompassing hundreds of decision-makers and probably tens of thousands of regulatory and statutory habitats for decision making—it remains to be seen whether *Dunsmuir* has revealed further challenges in how best to reconcile the principles of legislative supremacy, judicial independence, and administrative expertise.

There are eight chapters in this part of the book. In the first, chapter 8, we outline the analytical framework in *Dunsmuir*. We then turn in the following three chapters to the factors that apply to a court's determination of the standard of review in the absence of a past decision that governs the question. In chapter 9, we discuss the role and significance of a statutory privative clause or right of appeal, if any, applying to the administrative decision that is under review. In chapter 10, we examine the role of the specialized expertise and field sensitivity of administrative decision-makers in assessing what deference is owed by courts to their decisions. Also in that chapter, we discuss the factor of statutory purpose, one that gives context for and thus may inform other factors in the analysis. Chapter 11 focuses on how the court's characterization of the nature of the question that is under review may affect the standard of review analysis. The discussion turns also to the challenges of distinguishing between different types of questions, accounting for discretionary or mixed law and fact decision making, and ensuring that the concept of jurisdiction does not envelope the wider decision-making process, especially on questions of law and discretion. Then, in chapter 12, we expand on the concept of jurisdiction and jurisdictional error as a particularly complex subcategory of questions of law. Generally in our review of the *Dunsmuir* framework, we review Supreme Court decisions that contributed to the evolution of the standard of review analysis, that elaborate on the role of the various factors within it, and that suggest how the framework may change in future.

The next chapter in this part of the book, chapter 13, moves beyond the standard of review analysis in general to examine how the courts have used *Dunsmuir* to decide the standard of review and, in turn, how they have applied the resulting standard—whether correctness or reasonableness—to the administrative decision before them. This is the "nitty gritty" of judicial review: the day-to-day task of reading and interpreting the relevant statutory regime and evaluating the evidence against the backdrop of the applicable standard of review and by reference to the statutory authority's own assessment of questions of law, fact, mixed law and fact, or discretion. It also highlights lingering questions about the standard of review analysis. By reducing the available standards of review from the three which applied from 1997 until *Dunsmuir* (correctness, reasonableness *simpliciter*, and patent unreasonableness; from 1979 to 1997 there were two standards: correctness and patent unreasonableness) to two standards (correctness and "reasonableness"), the Supreme Court of Canada appears implicitly to have adopted a highly contextualized approach to what deference entails in individual cases under the new "reasonableness" standard. We ask whether this shift of approach will have the desired outcome of clarifying the overall analysis or whether it might instead lead us to another body of murky water.

The part concludes with two discrete areas in substantive review, each with both a unique history and a current doctrine. Chapter 14 examines a narrow set of issues that has arisen more frequently since the advent of the *Canadian Charter of Rights and Freedoms*: the extent to which statutory authorities have the capacity and perhaps even the duty, not only to take constitutional instruments into account in performing their interpretative and discretionary tasks, but also to resolve constitutional questions in ways that might go so far as to treat the statutory regime under which the decision-maker is acting as invalid. We treat this as a case study in jurisdiction, considering that it reveals an area in which the courts may be called on to decide, based on what may be complex and ambiguous statutory language, whether a decision-maker has been given the authority to resolve constitutional questions.

Finally, in chapter 15, we enter a domain that until recently was largely treated as a stand-alone category: judicial review of the exercise of discretion by administrative actors. This involves the grounds of judicial review of statutory and prerogative powers that leave the decision-maker considerable room for the exercise of judgment or choice in what course of action to take, as opposed to the exercise of deciding on the meaning of more precise statutory provisions or determining questions of law or jurisdiction. Now, the Supreme Court has integrated the extent to which the courts should be prepared to become involved in these kinds of decision-making powers within the ambit of the standard of review analysis. We consider how this phenomenon, arising out of *Baker v. Canada (Minister of Citizenship and Immigration)* (chapter 2 of this text), has evolved in the subsequent jurisprudence. In chapter 15, we also consider other ways of checking and constraining the exercise of statutory discretion.

CHAPTER EIGHT

The Standard of Review

INTRODUCTION

As mentioned in the introduction to part III, our preoccupation in this chapter is with the standard of review that the courts should apply in exercising their review powers over various forms of statutory authorities (and in many cases tribunals) charged with implementing the mandate of the administrative scheme created by their empowering statute. More concretely, when the courts are asked to review determinations of questions of law, fact, mixed law and fact, and discretion made by these decision-makers, what approach should they bring to that task and what tests should they apply? The *Dunsmuir* decision lays out the current framework. It calls this the standard of review analysis, although the analysis encompasses the factors that previously applied under the pragmatic and functional approach. These are: (1) the presence and terms of a privative clause or right of appeal in the statute, (2) the nature of the question that is under review, (3) the expertise of the decision-maker, and (4) the statutory purpose and context in which the decision making took place. In reviewing *Dunsmuir*, pay particular attention to how these factors are to be applied and how they interact. In later chapters, each of the factors is examined in greater detail, both conceptually and historically.

THE STANDARD OF REVIEW ANALYSIS

The Supreme Court of Canada's judgment in *Baker v. Canada (Minister of Citizenship and Immigration)*, discussed in chapter 2, had a profound effect on many critical issues in Canadian judicial review of administrative action on both substantive and procedural grounds. The majority reasons of the court in *Dunsmuir* proclaim similar ambitions to provide a comprehensive review of the system of judicial review and a "holistic approach" to fundamental principles of substantive review. And, even if *Dunsmuir* did not radically alter the court's commitment to judicial deference for administrative decision making, it made significant changes to the method of implementation of that commitment. The first was to reduce the number of standards of review in Canadian judicial review from three to two. The highly deferential "patent unreasonableness" standard does not entirely disappear from the lexicon, but rather seems to live on only where its usage is dictated by a past decision or by an express statutory provision. Likewise, the new standard of reasonableness is not necessarily the same as the old reasonableness *simpliciter* and appears to convey an adaptable approach to deference in different circumstances, thus shifting many questions in the standard of review analysis to the stage at which the standard of reasonableness, once arrived at, is applied. The standard of correctness, on the other hand, retains more or less the same meaning.

The first stage of substantive review is to determine the appropriate standard of review. In other words, must an administrative decision be unreasonable or simply incorrect, in the court's view, for the court to set it aside? The second stage is to apply that standard on the merits of the case at hand in order to decide the outcome of judicial review. Our concern in this chapter is with the first stage, governed by what is now called the standard of review analysis, at which a court decides whether to defer to the administrative decision-maker—by adopting a reasonableness standard—or whether to decline to defer based on the correctness standard. As we see in *Dunsmuir*, this first stage is built on a series of factors that courts use to guide themselves in asking the right sort of questions, so as to decide the appropriate standard of review.

Dunsmuir v. New Brunswick
[2008] 1 SCR 190 (NB)

[Dunsmuir was a court official with the New Brunswick Department of Justice. As such, he was both a provincial public servant and legally a statutory office holder at pleasure. He was dismissed, after having been reprimanded on three occasions, and given four and a half months' salary in lieu of notice. In dismissing him by way of an order of the Lieutenant Governor of the province, the government relied on s. 20 of the *Civil Service Act*, SNB 1984, c. C-5.1. It provided that "[s]ubject to the provisions of this Act and any other Act" termination of any employees "shall be governed by the ordinary rules of contract." According to the government, this meant that it could dismiss Dunsmuir simply by providing him with reasonable notice or salary in lieu of notice. It did not have to establish cause or give him a hearing before dismissing him.

However, s. 100.1 of the *Public Service Labour Relations Act*, RSNB 1973, c. P-25 (as amended) extended grievance rights to non-unionized employees such as Dunsmuir, and incorporated s. 97(2.1) of the PSLRA, which provided that "[w]here an adjudicator determines that [the] employee has been discharged or otherwise disciplined *for cause* ... the adjudicator may substitute such other penalty for the discharge or the discipline as to the adjudicator seems just and reasonable in all the circumstances." Apparently to avoid the effect of this provision, the official reason provided by the government for Dunsmuir's dismissal was that he was not suitable for the position he was occupying, not that there was cause for the dismissal. Dunsmuir argued that the government had in reality dismissed him for cause and that, if he established that this was the case and also that the government did not have cause, he was entitled to seek reinstatement based on the common law of dismissal of public officers.

A mutually agreed PSLRA adjudicator heard the case. Acting under s. 97(2.1), the adjudicator concluded that an employer could not avoid an inquiry into its real reasons for dismissing an employee by stating that cause was not alleged. Rather, an employee was entitled to an adjudication on whether a discharge purportedly with notice or pay in lieu thereof was in fact for cause. He then held that, on his view of the evidence, the termination was not disciplinary but rather was based on the employer's concerns about the appellant's performance and suitability for the positions he held. Based on the law on dismissal of public officers, pursuant to the decision in *Knight v. Indian Head School Div-*

ision, the adjudicator held that Dunsmuir should have been informed of the reasons for this dissatisfaction and given an opportunity to respond. He declared that the termination was void and ordered the appellant reinstated as of the date of dismissal. The adjudicator added that, in the event that his reinstatement order was quashed on judicial review, he would find the appropriate notice period to be eight months.

On judicial review, Rideout J of the New Brunswick Court of Queen's Bench applied the pragmatic and functional approach and concluded that the appropriate standard of review was correctness and that the court need not show deference to the adjudicator's interpretation of the *Civil Service Act* and the PSLRA (in spite of the presence of a full privative clause in the PSLRA and the relative expertise of adjudicators appointed under the PSLRA). On this basis, Rideout J concluded that the adjudicator wrongly interpreted the relevant statutes and that he lacked jurisdiction to review the circumstances of Dunsmuir's dismissal under the PSLRA. At the Court of Appeal for New Brunswick, in contrast, it was held that the appropriate standard of review was that of reasonableness *simpliciter* but that it was unreasonable, based on the relevant statutes, for the adjudicator not to accept the employer's portrayal of the dismissal as not for cause. The only right of the employee in the circumstances was to challenge the length of the notice period.]

The judgment of McLachlin CJ and Bastarache, LeBel, Fish, and Abella JJ was delivered by BASTARACHE and LeBEL JJ.

I. Introduction

[1] This appeal calls on the Court to consider, once again, the troubling question of the approach to be taken in judicial review of decisions of administrative tribunals. The recent history of judicial review in Canada has been marked by ebbs and flows of deference, confounding tests and new words for old problems, but no solutions that provide real guidance for litigants, counsel, administrative decision makers or judicial review judges. The time has arrived for a reassessment of the question.

[Summary of facts and decisions below omitted.]

II. Issues

[24] At issue, firstly is the approach to be taken in the judicial review of a decision of a particular adjudicative tribunal which was seized of a grievance filed by the appellant after his employment was terminated. This appeal gives us the opportunity to re-examine the foundations of judicial review and the standards of review applicable in various situations.

[25] The second issue involves examining whether the appellant who held an office "at pleasure" in the civil service of New Brunswick, had the right to procedural fairness in the employer's decision to terminate him. On this occasion, we will reassess the rule that has found formal expression in *Knight*.

[26] The two types of judicial review, on the merits and on the process, are therefore engaged in this case. Our review of the system will therefore be comprehensive, which is preferable since a holistic approach is needed when considering fundamental principles.

III. Issue 1: Review of the Adjudicator's Statutory Interpretation Determination

A. Judicial Review

[27] As a matter of constitutional law, judicial review is intimately connected with the preservation of the rule of law. It is essentially that constitutional foundation which explains the purpose of judicial review and guides its function and operation. Judicial review seeks to address an underlying tension between the rule of law and the foundational democratic principle, which finds an expression in the initiatives of Parliament and legislatures to create various administrative bodies and endow them with broad powers. Courts, while exercising their constitutional functions of judicial review, must be sensitive not only to the need to uphold the rule of law, but also to the necessity of avoiding undue interference with the discharge of administrative functions in respect of the matters delegated to administrative bodies by Parliament and legislatures.

[28] By virtue of the rule of law principle, all exercises of public authority must find their source in law. All decision-making powers have legal limits, derived from the enabling statute itself, the common or civil law or the Constitution. Judicial review is the means by which the courts supervise those who exercise statutory powers, to ensure that they do not overstep their legal authority. The function of judicial review is therefore to ensure the legality, the reasonableness and the fairness of the administrative process and its outcomes.

[28] Administrative powers are exercised by decision makers according to statutory regimes that are themselves confined. A decision maker may not exercise authority not specifically assigned to him or her. By acting in the absence of legal authority, the decision maker transgresses the principle of the rule of law. Thus, when a reviewing court considers the scope of a decision-making power or the jurisdiction conferred by a statute, the standard of review analysis strives to determine what authority was intended to be given to the body in relation to the subject matter. This is done within the context of the courts' constitutional duty to ensure that public authorities do not overreach their lawful powers: *Crevier v. Attorney General of Quebec*, [1981] 2 SCR 220, at p. 234; also *Dr. Q v. College of Physicians and Surgeons of British Columbia*, [2003] 1 SCR 226, 2003 SCC 19 at para. 21.

[30] In addition to the role judicial review plays in upholding the rule of law, it also performs an important constitutional function in maintaining legislative supremacy. As noted by Justice Thomas Cromwell, "the rule of law is affirmed by assuring that the courts have the final say on the jurisdictional limits of a tribunal's authority; second, legislative supremacy is affirmed by adopting the principle that the concept of jurisdiction should be narrowly circumscribed and defined according to the intent of the legislature in a contextual and purposeful way; third, legislative supremacy is affirmed and the court-centric conception of the rule of law is reined in by acknowledging that the courts do not have a monopoly on deciding all questions of law" ("Appellate Review: Policy and Pragmatism," in *2006 Isaac Pitblado Lectures, Appellate Courts: Policy, Law and Practice*, V-1, at p. V-12). In essence, the rule of law is maintained because the courts have the last word on jurisdiction, and legislative supremacy is assured because determining the applicable standard of review is accomplished by establishing legislative intent.

[31] The legislative branch of government cannot remove the judiciary's power to review actions and decisions of administrative bodies for compliance with the constitutional capacities of the government. Even a privative clause, which provides a strong indication of legislative intent, cannot be determinative in this respect (*Executors of the Woodward Estate v. Minister of Finance*, [1973] SCR 120, at p. 127). The inherent power of superior courts to review administrative action and ensure that it does not exceed its jurisdiction stems from the judicature provisions in ss. 96 to 101 of the *Constitution Act, 1867*: *Crevier*. As noted by Beetz J in *U.E.S., Local 298 v. Bibeault*, [1988] 2 SCR 1048, at p. 1090, "[t]he role of the superior courts in maintaining the rule of law is so important that it is given constitutional protection." In short, judicial review is constitutionally guaranteed in Canada, particularly with regard to the definition and enforcement of jurisdictional limits. As Laskin CJ explained in *Crevier*:

> Where ... questions of law have been specifically covered in a privative enactment, this Court, as in *Farrah*, has not hesitated to recognize this limitation on judicial review as serving the interests of an express legislative policy to protect decisions of adjudicative agencies from external correction. Thus, it has, in my opinion, balanced the competing interests of a provincial Legislature in its enactment of substantively valid legislation and of the courts as ultimate interpreters of the *British North America Act* and s. 96 thereof. The same considerations do not, however, apply to issues of jurisdiction which are not far removed from issues of constitutionality. It cannot be left to a provincial statutory tribunal, in the face of s. 96, to determine the limits of its own jurisdiction without appeal or review. [pp. 237-38]

See also D.J. Mullan, *Administrative Law* (2001), at p. 50.

[32] Despite the clear, stable constitutional foundations of the system of judicial review, the operation of judicial review in Canada has been in a constant state of evolution over the years, as courts have attempted to devise approaches to judicial review that are both theoretically sound and effective in practice. Despite efforts to refine and clarify it, the present system has proven to be difficult to implement. The time has arrived to re-examine the Canadian approach to judicial review of administrative decisions and develop a principled framework that is more coherent and workable.

[33] Although the instant appeal deals with the particular problem of judicial review of the decisions of an adjudicative tribunal, these reasons will address first and foremost the structure and characteristics of the system of judicial review as a whole. ...

B. Reconsidering the Standards of Judicial Review

[34] The current approach to judicial review involves three standards of review, which range from correctness, where no deference is shown, to patent unreasonableness, which is most deferential to the decision maker, the standard of reasonableness *simpliciter* lying, theoretically, in the middle. In our view, it is necessary to reconsider both the number and definitions of the various standards of review, and the analytical process employed to determine which standard applies in a given situation. We conclude that there ought to be two standards of review—correctness and reasonableness.

[Here Bastarache and LeBel JJ discuss the evolution of the three standards of review in Canadian administrative law, some criticisms of those standards, and their rationale for the new standards of correctness and reasonableness; see chapter 13 of this text.]

C. Two Standards of Review

[43] The Court has moved from a highly formalistic, artificial "jurisdiction" test that could easily be manipulated, to a highly contextual "functional" test that provides great flexibility but little real on-the-ground guidance, and offers too many standards of review. What is needed is a test that offers guidance, is not formalistic or artificial, and permits review where justice requires it, but not otherwise. A simpler test is needed.

(1) Defining the Concepts of Reasonableness and Correctness

[Here the two standards of review, reasonableness and correctness, are discussed; see chapter 13 of this text.]

(2) Determining the Appropriate Standard of Review

[51] Having dealt with the nature of the standards of review, we now turn our attention to the method for selecting the appropriate standard in individual cases. As we will now demonstrate, questions of fact, discretion and policy as well as questions where the legal issues cannot be easily separated from the factual issues generally attract a standard of reasonableness while many legal issues attract a standard of correctness. Some legal issues, however, attract the more deferential standard of reasonableness.

[52] The existence of a privative or preclusive clause gives rise to a strong indication of review pursuant to the reasonableness standard. This conclusion is appropriate because a privative clause is evidence of Parliament or a legislature's intent that an administrative decision maker be given greater deference and that interference by reviewing courts be minimized. This does not mean, however, that the presence of a privative clause is determinative. The rule of law requires that the constitutional role of superior courts be preserved and, as indicated above, neither Parliament nor any legislature can completely remove the courts' power to review the actions and decisions of administrative bodies. This power is constitutionally protected. Judicial review is necessary to ensure that the privative clause is read in its appropriate statutory context and that administrative bodies do not exceed their jurisdiction.

[53] Where the question is one of fact, discretion or policy, deference will usually apply automatically (*Mossop*, at pp. 599-600; *Dr. Q*, at para. 29; *Suresh*, at paras. 29-30). We believe that the same standard must apply to the review of questions where the legal and factual issues are intertwined with and cannot be readily separated.

[54] Guidance with regard to the questions that will be reviewed on a reasonableness standard can be found in the existing case law. Deference will usually result where a tribunal is interpreting its own statute or statutes closely connected to its function, with which it will have particular familiarity: *Canadian Broadcasting Corp. v. Canada (Labour Relations Board)*, [1995] 1 SCR 157, at para. 48; *Toronto (City) Board of Education v. OSSTF, District 15*, [1997] 1 SCR 487, at para. 39. Deference may also be warranted where an

administrative tribunal has developed particular expertise in the application of a general common law or civil law rule in relation to a specific statutory context: *Toronto (City) v. CUPE*, at para. 72. Adjudication in labour law remains a good example of the relevance of this approach. The case law has moved away considerably from the strict position evidenced in *McLeod v. Egan*, [1975] 1 SCR 517, where it was held that an administrative decision maker will always risk having its interpretation of an external statute set aside upon judicial review.

[55] A consideration of the following factors will lead to the conclusion that the decision maker should be given deference and a reasonableness test applied:

- A privative clause: this is a statutory direction from Parliament or a legislature indicating the need for deference.

- A discrete and special administrative regime in which the decision maker has special expertise (labour relations for instance).

- The nature of the question of law. A question of law that is of "central importance to the legal system … and outside the … specialized area of expertise" of the administrative decision maker will always attract a correctness standard (*Toronto (City) v. CUPE*, at para. 62). On the other hand, a question of law that does not rise to this level may be compatible with a reasonableness standard where the two above factors so indicate.

[56] If these factors, considered together, point to a standard of reasonableness, the decision maker's decision must be approached with deference in the sense of respect discussed earlier in these reasons. There is nothing unprincipled in the fact that some questions of law will be decided on the basis of reasonableness. It simply means giving the adjudicator's decision appropriate deference in deciding whether a decision should be upheld, bearing in mind the factors indicated.

[57] An exhaustive review is not required in every case to determine the proper standard of review. Here again, existing jurisprudence may be helpful in identifying some of the questions that generally fall to be determined according to the correctness standard (*Cartaway Resources Corp. (Re)*, [2004] 1 SCR 672, 2004 SCC 26). This simply means that the analysis required is already deemed to have been performed and need not be repeated.

[58] For example, correctness review has been found to apply to constitutional questions regarding the division of powers between Parliament and the provinces in the *Constitution Act, 1867*: *Westcoast Energy Inc. v. Canada (National Energy Board)*, [1998] 1 SCR 322. Such questions, as well as other constitutional issues, are necessarily subject to correctness review because of the unique role of s. 96 courts as interpreters of the Constitution: *Nova Scotia (Workers' Compensation Board) v. Martin*, [2003] 2 SCR 504, 2003 SCC 54; Mullan, *Administrative Law*, at p. 60.

[59] Administrative bodies must also be correct in their determinations of true questions of jurisdiction or *vires*. We mention true questions of *vires* to distance ourselves from the extended definitions adopted before *CUPE*. It is important here to take a robust view of jurisdiction. We neither wish nor intend to return to the jurisdiction/preliminary question doctrine that plagued the jurisprudence in this area for many years. "Jurisdiction" is intended in the narrow sense of whether or not the tribunal had the authority to make

the inquiry. In other words, true jurisdiction questions arise where the tribunal must explicitly determine whether its statutory grant of power gives it the authority to decide a particular matter. The tribunal must interpret the grant of authority correctly or its action will be found to be *ultra vires* or to constitute a wrongful decline of jurisdiction: D.J.M. Brown and J.M. Evans, *Judicial Review of Administrative Action in Canada* (looseleaf), at pp. 14-3 to 14-6. An example may be found in *United Taxi Drivers' Fellowship of Southern Alberta v. Calgary (City)*, [2004] 1 SCR 485, 2004 SCC 19. In that case, the issue was whether the City of Calgary was authorized under the relevant municipal acts to enact bylaws limiting the number of taxi plate licences (para. 5, *per* Bastarache J). That case involved the decision-making powers of a municipality and exemplifies a true question of jurisdiction or *vires*. These questions will be narrow. We reiterate the caution of Dickson J in *CUPE* that reviewing judges must not brand as jurisdictional issues that are doubtfully so.

[60] As mentioned earlier, courts must also continue to substitute their own view of the correct answer where the question at issue is one of general law "that is both of central importance to the legal system as a whole and outside the adjudicator's specialized area of expertise" (*Toronto (City) v. CUPE*, at para. 62, *per* LeBel J). Because of their impact on the administration of justice as a whole, such questions require uniform and consistent answers. Such was the case in *Toronto (City) v. CUPE*, which dealt with complex common law rules and conflicting jurisprudence on the doctrines of *res judicata* and abuse of process—issues that are at the heart of the administration of justice (see para. 15, *per* Arbour J).

[61] Questions regarding the jurisdictional lines between two or more competing specialized tribunals have also been subject to review on a correctness basis: *Regina Police Assn. Inc. v. Regina (City) Board of Police Commissioners*, [2000] 1 SCR 360, 2000 SCC 14; *Quebec (Commission des droits de la personne et des droits de la jeunesse) v. Quebec (Attorney General)*, [2004] 2 SCR 185, 2004 SCC 39.

[62] In summary, the process of judicial review involves two steps. First, courts ascertain whether the jurisprudence has already determined in a satisfactory manner the degree of deference to be accorded with regard to a particular category of question. Second, where the first inquiry proves unfruitful, courts must proceed to an analysis of the factors making it possible to identify the proper standard of review.

[63] The existing approach to determining the appropriate standard of review has commonly been referred to as "pragmatic and functional." That name is unimportant. Reviewing courts must not get fixated on the label at the expense of a proper understanding of what the inquiry actually entails. Because the phrase "pragmatic and functional approach" may have misguided courts in the past, we prefer to refer simply to the "standard of review analysis" in the future.

[64] The analysis must be contextual. As mentioned above, it is dependent on the application of a number of relevant factors, including: (1) the presence or absence of a privative clause; (2) the purpose of the tribunal as determined by interpretation of enabling legislation; (3) the nature of the question at issue, and; (4) the expertise of the tribunal. In many cases, it will not be necessary to consider all of the factors, as some of them may be determinative in the application of the reasonableness standard in a specific case.

D. *Application*

[65] Returning to the instant appeal and bearing in mind the foregoing discussion, we must determine the standard of review applicable to the adjudicator's interpretation of the *PSLRA*, in particular ss. 97(2.1) and 100.1, and s. 20 of the *Civil Service Act*. That standard of review must then be applied to the adjudicator's decision. In order to determine the applicable standard, we will now examine the factors relevant to the standard of review analysis.

(1) *Proper Standard of Review on the Statutory Interpretation Issue*

[66] The specific question on this front is whether the combined effect of s. 97(2.1) and s. 100.1 of the *PSLRA* permits the adjudicator to inquire into the employer's reason for dismissing an employee with notice or pay in lieu of notice. This is a question of law. The question to be answered is therefore whether in light of the privative clause, the regime under which the adjudicator acted, and the nature of the question of law involved, a standard of correctness should apply.

[67] The adjudicator was appointed and empowered under the *PSLRA*; s. 101(1) of that statute contains a full privative clause, stating in no uncertain terms that "every order, award, direction, decision, declaration or ruling of ... an adjudicator is final and shall not be questioned or reviewed in any court." Section 101(2) adds that "[n]o order shall be made or process entered, and no proceedings shall be taken in any court, whether by way of injunction, judicial review, or otherwise, to question, review, prohibit or restrain ... an adjudicator in any of its or his proceedings." The inclusion of a full privative clause in the *PSLRA* gives rise to a strong indication that the reasonableness standard of review will apply.

[68] The nature of the regime also favours the standard of reasonableness. This Court has often recognized the relative expertise of labour arbitrators in the interpretation of collective agreements, and counselled that the review of their decisions should be approached with deference: *CUPE*, at pp. 235-36; *Canada Safeway Ltd. v. RWDSU, Local 454*, [1998] 1 SCR 1079, at para. 58; *Voice Construction*, at para. 22. The adjudicator in this case was, in fact, interpreting his enabling statute. Although the adjudicator was appointed on an *ad hoc* basis, he was selected by the mutual agreement of the parties and, at an institutional level, adjudicators acting under the *PSLRA* can be presumed to hold relative expertise in the interpretation of the legislation that gives them their mandate, as well as related legislation that they might often encounter in the course of their functions. See *Alberta Union of Provincial Employees v. Lethbridge Community College*. This factor also suggests a reasonableness standard of review.

[69] The legislative purpose confirms this view of the regime. The *PSLRA* establishes a time- and cost-effective method of resolving employment disputes. It provides an alternative to judicial determination. Section 100.1 of the *PSLRA* defines the adjudicator's powers in deciding a dispute, but it also provides remedial protection for employees who are not unionized. The remedial nature of s. 100.1 and its provision for timely and binding settlements of disputes also imply that a reasonableness review is appropriate.

[70] Finally, the nature of the legal question at issue is not one that is of central importance to the legal system and outside the specialized expertise of the adjudicator. This also suggests that the standard of reasonableness should apply.

[71] Considering the privative clause, the nature of the regime, and the nature of the question of law here at issue, we conclude that the appropriate standard is reasonableness. ...

[The majority's application of the reasonableness standard is omitted as is its reasoning on the issue of procedural fairness in the dismissal of public officers.]

The majority decision in *Dunsmuir* reinforces the principle of judicial deference in administrative law, while varying the methodology that is used to apply that principle in specific cases. A very different methodology emerges, on the other hand, from the concurring reasons of Deschamps J in *Dunsmuir* and from the reasons of Rothstein J in *Canada (Citizenship and Immigration) v. Khosa*, 2009 SCC 12 (CanLII). This alternative approach aims in part to recharacterize the issue of judicial deference in the review of administrative actors based on the method that is used by appellate courts to scrutinize lower court decisions. Focusing on the nature of the question, to a greater degree even than the *Dunsmuir* majority, the alternative approach says that courts—absent a statutory direction to the contrary—should defer to administrative tribunals on questions of fact, and usually on questions of mixed fact and law or of discretion, but presumptively not on questions of law. On questions of law, deference is warranted only where there is a privative clause and specifically not where there is a statutory right of appeal on such questions. Deference is also precluded where the issue falls outside the regular activities of the decision-maker and its expertise.

Thus, according to Deschamps J's reasons in *Dunsmuir*:

[161] ... when the issue is limited to questions of fact, there is no need to enquire into any other factor in order to determine that deference is owed to an administrative decision maker.

[162] Questions of law, by contrast, require more thorough scrutiny when deference is evaluated, and the particular context of administrative decision making can make judicial review different than appellate review. Although superior courts have a core expertise to interpret questions of law, Parliament or a legislature may have provided that the decision of an administrative body is protected from judicial review by a privative clause. ...

[163] However, privative clauses cannot totally shield an administrative body from review. Parliament, or a legislature, cannot have intended that the body would be protected were it to overstep its delegated powers. Moreover, if such a body is asked to interpret laws in respect of which it does not have expertise, the constitutional responsibility of the superior courts as guardians of the rule of law compels them to insure that laws falling outside an administrative body's core expertise are interpreted correctly. ... Finally, deference is not owed on questions of law where Parliament or a legislature has provided for a statutory right of review on such questions.

• • •

[172] ... The judicial review of administrative action need not be a complex area of law in itself. Every day, reviewing courts decide cases raising multiple questions, some of fact, some of mixed fact and law and some purely of law; in various contexts, the first two of these types of

questions tend to require deference, while the third often does not. Reviewing courts are already amply equipped to resolve such questions and do not need a specialized analytical toolbox in order to review administrative decisions.

Does this alternative approach help to simplify the standard of review, even beyond the steps taken by the majority in *Dunsmuir*? If so, does it do so at the expense (or with the aim) of establishing a system of administrative law in which administrative decision-makers are regarded simply as a lower tier in a hierarchical structure, with courts at the top? At least in effect, the alternative approach appears to revisit the court's well-established commitment to deference to administrative actors and acceptance that, on this issue, legislative intent is often unclear. In *Dunsmuir*, Deschamps J came to adopt a correctness standard and to overturn the decision, despite the presence of a strong privative clause and the longstanding role of labour adjudicators in resolving workplace dismissal grievances. She did so on the following basis (at para. 168):

> In the case at bar, the adjudicator was asked to adjudicate the grievance of a non-unionized employee. This meant that he had to identify the rules governing the contract. Identifying those rules is a question of law. ... The common law rules relating to the dismissal of an employee differ completely from the ones provided for in the *PSLRA* that the adjudicator is regularly required to interpret. Since the common law, not the adjudicator's enabling statute, is the starting point of the analysis, and since the adjudicator does not have specific expertise in interpreting the common law, the reviewing court does not have to defer to his decision on the basis of expertise. This leads me to conclude that the reviewing court can proceed to its own interpretation of the rules applicable to the non-unionized employee's contract of employment and determine whether the adjudicator could enquire into the cause of the dismissal. The applicable standard of review is correctness.

In contrast, consider this statement of Binnie J in *Dunsmuir* (at para. 130):

> ... When the applicant for judicial review challenges the substantive *outcome* of an administrative action, the judge is invited to cross the line into second-guessing matters that lie within the function of the administrator. This is controversial because it is not immediately obvious why a judge's view of the reasonableness of an administrative policy or the exercise of an administrative discretion should be preferred to that of the administrator to whom Parliament or a legislature has allocated the decision, unless there is a full statutory right of appeal to the courts, or it is otherwise indicated in the conferring legislation that a "correctness" standard is intended.

The alternative approach thus diverges sharply from the majority in *Dunsmuir* in its ambition to revisit earlier decisions of the Supreme Court of Canada that prioritize deference where an administrative actor is found to have greater expertise than the courts. Deschamps and Rothstein JJ reject this prioritization for reasons of legislative intent, although the presumptions they then adopt in order to read intention into privative clauses and rights of appeal are themselves debatable. Rothstein J elaborates in his separate (concurring) reasons in *Khosa*, at para. 95:

> Far from subscribing to the view that courts should be reviewing the actual expertise of administrative decision makers, it is my position that this is the function of the legislature. In my view, the discordance between imputed versus actual expertise is simply one manifestation of the

larger conceptual unhinging of tribunal expertise from the privative clause. The legislatures that create administrative decision makers are better able to consider the relative qualifications, specialization and day-to-day workings of tribunals, boards and other decision makers which they themselves have constituted. Where the legislature believes that an administrative decision maker possesses superior expertise on questions that are normally within the traditional baili-wick of courts (law, jurisdiction, fraud, natural justice, etc.), it can express this by enacting a privative clause.

For Rothstein J the presence of a privative clause should be treated as determinative of whether the legislature believed a statutory decision-maker to have greater expertise than the courts. Is that a credible presumption? Or might one also assume—even in the absence of a privative clause or indeed in the face of a broad right of appeal—that the legislature intended a decision-maker to develop its own expertise and field sensitivity over time and that this was part of the rationale for creating the tribunal or agency in the first place? More generally, is it realistic to think that legislatures assess the expertise of administrative tribu-nals or agencies, relative to the courts, when they draft statutes, and is it even desirable for them to attempt to do so without knowledge of the future circumstances that will lead to judicial review? Perhaps legislatures may just as well intend for the reviewing court, in an individual case, to assess expertise and, in turn, to incorporate this assessment into the wider analysis of deference?

The conflict here between the majority view and what we have described as the alterna-tive approach of Deschamps and Rothstein JJ can thus be distilled to a difference of view over what to presume in the face of silence or ambiguity in a statute on the specific issue of the appropriate standard of review. This root difference is revealed by Binnie J's response, for the majority, in *Khosa*, at paras. 21-26:

> [21] My colleague Justice Rothstein adopts the perspective that in the absence of a privative clause or statutory direction to the contrary, express or implied, judicial review under s. 18.1 [of the *Federal Courts Act*, RSC 1985, c. F-7] is to proceed "as it does in the regular appellate context" (para. 117). Rothstein J writes:
>
> > On my reading, where Parliament intended a deferential standard of review in s. 18.1(4), it used clear and unambiguous language. The necessary implication is that where Parlia-ment did not provide for deferential review, *it intended the reviewing court to apply a cor-rectness standard as it does in the regular appellate context*. [Emphasis added by Binnie J.]
>
> I do not agree that such an implication is either necessary or desirable. My colleague states that "where a legal question can be extricated from a factual or policy inquiry, it is inappropriate to presume deference where Parliament has not indicated this via a privative clause" (para. 90), citing *Housen v. Nikolaisen*, 2002 SCC 33, [2002] 2 SCR 235, at paras. 8 and 13. *Housen*, of course, was a regular appeal in a civil negligence case.
>
> [22] On this view, the reviewing court applies a standard of review of correctness unless otherwise directed to proceed (expressly or by necessary implication) by the legislature.
>
> [23] Rothstein J writes, at para. 87, that the Court "depart[ed] from the conceptual origin of standard of review" in *Pezim v. British Columbia (Superintendent of Brokers)*, [1994] 2 SCR 557. *Pezim* was a unanimous decision of the Court which deferred to the expertise of a special-ized tribunal in the interpretation of provisions of the *Securities Act*, SBC 1985, c. 83, despite the presence of a right of appeal and the absence of a privative clause.

[24] The conceptual underpinning of the law of judicial review was "further blurred," my colleague writes, by *Pushpanathan v. Canada (Minister of Citizenship and Immigration)*, [1998] 1 SCR 982, which treated the privative clause "simply as one of several factors in the calibration of deference (standard of review)" (para. 92). In my colleague's view, "[i]t is not for the court to impute tribunal expertise on legal questions, absent a privative clause and, in doing so, assume the role of the legislature to determine when deference is or is not owed" (para. 91).

[25] I do not share Rothstein J's view that absent statutory direction, explicit or by necessary implication, no deference is owed to administrative decision-makers in matters that relate to their special role, function and expertise. ...

[26] *Dunsmuir* stands against the idea that in the absence of express statutory language or necessary implication, a reviewing court is "to apply a correctness standard as it does in the regular appellate context" (Rothstein J, at para. 117). *Pezim* has been cited and applied in numerous cases over the last 15 years. Its teaching is reflected in *Dunsmuir*. With respect, I would reject my colleague's effort to roll back the *Dunsmuir* clock to an era where some courts asserted a level of skill and knowledge in administrative matters which further experience showed they did not possess.

We see, then, that a court may look to the implicit as well as explicit signals in a statute that support or refute the case for deference. Yet rarely if ever will a statute settle unquestionably, without some discretionary role for the judge, just what the appropriate standard should be and, of course, how it should be applied. As we discuss below, the BC *Administrative Tribunals Act*, SBC 2004, c. 45, dictates the adoption of a correctness standard for various decision-makers and decisions, and a patent unreasonableness standard for others. This has raised questions about how such a statutory direction should be integrated into the post-*Dunsmuir* analysis.

LINGERING QUESTIONS AFTER DUNSMUIR

Dunsmuir aspires to a coherent and workable method for deciding the question of judicial deference. It offers guidance on how to address uncertainties in the standard of review analysis that could otherwise frustrate the resolution of administrative disputes. In his concurring reasons in *Dunsmuir*, at para. 133, Binnie J captured a widespread sentiment when he described the then-operating pragmatic and functional approach as "unduly subtle, unproductive [and] esoteric," as contributing to "lengthy and arcane" discussions in both factums and on the hearing of applications and appeals, and as creating "undue cost and delay." But will the adjustments in *Dunsmuir* solve this dilemma? According to Alice Woolley, "The Metaphysical Court: *Dunsmuir v. New Brunswick* and the Standard of Review" (2008), 21 *CJALP* 259, at 269:

[I]t may be that any radical change in direction in this area is impossible, that the major flaw in *Dunsmuir* is the judgment's illusion that it can fix the problem, not that it does not do so. Why? Because the questions posed by substantive judicial review are impossible to answer. No generic formula can decide when a specific question is better answered by an administrative decision maker and when it is better answered by the court. No test can tell one how to be deferential; since deference is neither capitulation or substitution of judgment it necessarily requires the drawing of fine lines in particular cases.

At the very least, and for the time being, several questions linger about how the reno-vated approach in *Dunsmuir* will unfold. As Woolley suggests, this may be an inevitable consequence of the challenges of implementing the principle of judicial deference in admin-istrative law in a way that balances predictability with flexibility. We highlight some of the tensions below.

First is the role of precedent. According to *Dunsmuir*, at paras. 57 and 62, the standard of review should follow "existing jurisprudence" where it "has already determined in a satis-factory manner the degree of deference to be accorded." Yet, in all cases where a past deci-sion is said to resolve an issue, it must be decided whether the past decision is sufficiently like the case at hand. From *Dunsmuir* one may deduce that a past decision should govern where it involves the same decision-maker, the same "category" of question (and it is an open question just how broadly this should extend), and sufficiently comparable statutory terms including any privative clause or right of appeal. But what if some but not all of these conditions apply? And, what if all of the relevant characteristics are very similar but the purpose of the statutory regime has evolved since the previous decision, or the decision-maker itself has undergone some crisis of its legitimacy? More technically, where the past decision is by a court that is not superior in the judicial hierarchy to the court that is exercis-ing judicial review, should the latter court take the opportunity to contribute to the develop-ment of a sound approach to the standard of review in the particular context? Should it go so far as to revisit decisions that appear to contradict the balance that is struck in *Dunsmuir*, especially regarding a decision-maker's interpretations of its home statute?

Perhaps these questions are best answered by examining how courts since *Dunsmuir* have used existing jurisprudence to decide the standard of review. In subsequent chapters we examine examples of such responses. In the meantime, it is clear that judges, lawyers, and the parties should avoid allowing the standard of review to occupy a central role in liti-gation where there is a sufficiently clear record of past decisions that govern the issue. But, where the existing jurisprudence amounts to one or two decisions by a lower court—even an appellate court—there is a residual case to be made for applying the standard of review analysis in full, so as to confirm that any movement toward precedent is otherwise harmoni-ous with the factor-based messages in *Dunsmuir*. Paying attention to precedent may con-tribute to a more coherent as well as a more streamlined approach to deference. On the other hand, the drawing of parallels and distinctions between cases is one of the great chal-lenges of the common law and there will undoubtedly be differences among judges, let alone among disputing parties, about what qualifies as satisfactory guidance. Particular difficulties may emerge if decisions on the standard of review come to be entrenched following a soli-tary court decision, without further consideration by other courts.

A second tension after *Dunsmuir* was what to do about cases where a statute or the exist-ing jurisprudence dictates a standard of review that is no longer available in the common law after *Dunsmuir*. This was especially pertinent to the BC *Administrative Tribunals Act*, SBC 2004, c. 45, ss. 57-58, which explicitly requires the adoption of particular standards in certain circumstances:

> 58(1) If the tribunal's enabling Act contains a privative clause, relative to the courts the tri-bunal must be considered to be an expert tribunal in relation to all matters over which it has exclusive jurisdiction.

(2) In a judicial review proceeding relating to expert tribunals under subsection (1)

(a) a finding of fact or law or an exercise of discretion by the tribunal in respect of a matter over which it has exclusive jurisdiction under a privative clause must not be interfered with unless it is patently unreasonable,

(b) questions about the application of common law rules of natural justice and procedural fairness must be decided having regard to whether, in all of the circumstances, the tribunal acted fairly, and

(c) for all matters other than those identified in paragraphs (a) and (b), the standard of review to be applied to the tribunal's decision is correctness.

(3) For the purposes of subsection (2) (a), a discretionary decision is patently unreasonable if the discretion

(a) is exercised arbitrarily or in bad faith,

(b) is exercised for an improper purpose,

(c) is based entirely or predominantly on irrelevant factors, or

(d) fails to take statutory requirements into account.

59(1) In a judicial review proceeding, the standard of review to be applied to a decision of the tribunal is correctness for all questions except those respecting the exercise of discretion, findings of fact and the application of the common law rules of natural justice and procedural fairness.

(2) A court must not set aside a finding of fact by the tribunal unless there is no evidence to support it or if, in light of all the evidence, the finding is otherwise unreasonable.

(3) A court must not set aside a discretionary decision of the tribunal unless it is patently unreasonable.

(4) For the purposes of subsection (3), a discretionary decision is patently unreasonable if the discretion

(a) is exercised arbitrarily or in bad faith,

(b) is exercised for an improper purpose,

(c) is based entirely or predominantly on irrelevant factors, or

(d) fails to take statutory requirements into account.

(5) Questions about the application of common law rules of natural justice and procedural fairness must be decided having regard to whether, in all of the circumstances, the tribunal acted fairly.

Various considerations follow from these provisions. For example, do the provisions simply displace the standard of review analysis in all respects or do they feed into aspects of that analysis? Also, do they have the effect of freezing the meaning of a particular standard under the common law? More discretely, an obvious question after *Dunsmuir* was whether the standard of patent unreasonableness—or indeed reasonableness *simpliciter*—could live on under a statute despite the shift in *Dunsmuir* to the single, deferential standard of reasonableness. This was addressed in *Canada (Citizenship and Immigration) v. Khosa*, 2009 SCC 12 (CanLII), at para. 19, where Binnie J said for the majority:

Generally speaking, most if not all judicial review statutes are drafted against the background of the common law of judicial review. Even the more comprehensive among them, such as the British Columbia *Administrative Tribunals Act*, SBC 2004, c. 45, can only sensibly be interpreted in the common law context because, for example, it provides in s. 58(2)(a) that "a finding of fact or law or an exercise of discretion by the tribunal in respect of a matter over which it has exclusive jurisdiction under a privative clause must not be interfered with *unless it is patently unreasonable*." The expression "patently unreasonable" did not spring unassisted from the mind of the legislator. It was obviously intended to be understood in the context of the common law jurisprudence, although a number of *indicia* of patent unreasonableness are given in s. 58(3). Despite *Dunsmuir*, "patent unreasonableness" will live on in British Columbia, but the *content* of the expression, and the precise degree of deference it commands in the diverse circumstances of a large provincial administration, will necessarily continue to be calibrated according to general principles of administrative law. That said, of course, the legislature in s. 58 was and is directing the BC courts to afford administrators a high degree of deference on issues of fact, and effect must be given to this clearly expressed legislative intention.

Thus, a pre-*Dunsmuir* standard of review may live on where it is preserved by express statutory language, although its meaning both originates in and will continue to evolve with the common law. But what about where it is the existing jurisprudence, rather than a statute, that calls for a pre-*Dunsmuir* standard such as patent unreasonableness? It is unlikely that *Dunsmuir* leaves it open for a lower court to adopt patent unreasonableness as a continuing standard based on past decisions. On the other hand, it is open for a court to adopt reasonableness as the standard but then apply that standard in a manner that is like the "old" patent unreasonableness. In either case, a highly deferential approach would be maintained.

A third tension is that *Dunsmuir* introduces new questions about the proper scope of judicial review on questions of law. According to *Dunsmuir*, at para. 54, deference will usually be shown where "a tribunal is interpreting its own statute or statutes closely connected to its function, with which it will have particular familiarity" or where "an administrative tribunal has developed particular expertise in the application of a general common law or civil law rule in relation to a specific statutory context." On the other hand, the court left room in *Dunsmuir*, at para. 60, for intervention where a question of law is one of general law "that is both of central importance to the legal system as a whole and outside the adjudicator's specialized area of expertise." Also, "a question of law that does not rise to this level *may* be compatible with a reasonableness standard where the two above factors so indicate" [emphasis added]. Binnie J laments in *Dunsmuir*, at para. 128, that the majority's reference to a new category of questions of law will cause unnecessary confusion:

> It is, with respect, a distraction to unleash a debate in the reviewing judge's courtroom about whether or not a particular question of law is "of central importance to the legal system as a whole." It should be sufficient to frame a rule exempting from the correctness standard the provisions of the home statute and closely related statutes which require the expertise of the administrative decision maker (as in the labour board example). Apart from that exception, we should prefer clarity to needless complexity and hold that the last word on questions of general law should be left to judges.

Clearly, the category of questions of law that are of central importance to the legal system as a whole includes constitutional questions, issues involving an overlap between the jurisdictions of different tribunals, and apparent conflicts between statutes that fall outside the decision-maker's expertise. But does it justify intervention on questions of law relating to the decision-maker's core mandate, as apparently did the interpretations of the *Civil Service*

Act and the PSLRA by the adjudicator in *Dunsmuir*? And to what extent does it call for deference to a decision-maker's resolution of a narrow question of law that is nonetheless outside its expertise?

A fourth area of uncertainty after *Dunsmuir* concerns the role of the factors in general in the standard of review analysis. To what extent is it necessary for a court (or a disputing party) to refer explicitly to several or all of the factors when explaining its reasoning in support of a correctness or reasonableness standard?

On the one hand, it may be that the presumptive role of the nature of the question and of existing jurisprudence in the standard of review analysis will make reference to other factors increasingly redundant in many instances of judicial review. On the other hand, the responses of many provincial appellate courts to the post-*Dunsmuir* framework suggest that a discussion of the factors, even if fairly brief, provides a useful means to support and solidify a court's conclusions on the appropriate standard by demonstrating the court's awareness of the wider factors in play. Indeed, it is difficult to understand the standard of review analysis without appreciating the role that is played by privative clauses and rights of appeal, by one's characterization of agency expertise, and by one's framing of the motivations of the statutory scheme, in the construction of the analytical framework itself. Even where a court does not refer explicitly to the underlying factors in the standard of review analysis, therefore, one should appreciate that those factors should always play some role in a court's decision on whether to defer.

For this reason, we consider it appropriate at this early stage in the post-*Dunsmuir* jurisprudence to organize our elaboration of the standard of review analysis, in the next four chapters of this text, in terms of the factors that emerged from the Supreme Court of Canada jurisprudence in this area over the past 30 years, while acknowledging also that, with *Dunsmuir*, the factors may come to play a less explicit role over time in the standard of review analysis.

A fifth tension follows from Binnie J's query in *Dunsmuir*, at para. 120, whether the majority's approach will provide, as it aspires to do, a coherent and workable framework for the system of judicial review *as a whole*. Is this really possible, Binnie J asks, where the majority focuses so clearly on the review of administrative tribunals? Binnie J offered an answer (at para. 123) by suggesting that the *Dunsmuir* framework is applicable to all administrative actors:

> Parliament or a provincial legislature is often well advised to allocate an administrative decision to someone other than a judge. The judge is on the outside of the administration looking in. The legislators are entitled to put their trust in the viewpoint of the designated decision maker (particularly as to what constitutes a reasonable outcome), not only in the case of the administrative tribunals of principal concern to my colleagues but ... also in the case of a minister, a board, a public servant, a commission, an elected council or other administrative bodies and statutory decision makers. In the absence of a full statutory right of appeal, the court ought generally to respect the exercise of the administrative discretion, particularly in the face of a privative clause.

Moreover, since *Dunsmuir*, the Supreme Court of Canada has referred to the standard of review analysis to administrative actors other than tribunals. See *Lake v. Canada (Minister of Justice)*, [2008] 1 SCR 761, 2008 SCC 23 (CanLII), where the court referred to *Dunsmuir* in relation to a highly discretionary decision of the federal minister of justice to surrender a fugitive to US authorities rather than prosecute him in Canada.

Last, there is a tension in *Dunsmuir* involving the interaction between the different factors in the standard of review analysis, in particular the role of privative clauses. We discuss this tension in the next chapter. In this respect, however, it is notably ironic that in *Dunsmuir* the court affirmed its longstanding commitment to judicial deference, only to overturn unanimously the adjudicator's decision. Even Binnie J agreed with this outcome despite his observation that "[l]abour arbitrators, as in this case, command deference on legal matters within their enabling statute or on legal matters intimately connected thereto" and that "[i]n this case, the adjudicator was dealing with his 'home statute' plus other statutes intimately linked to public sector relations in New Brunswick." We revisit just how the reasonableness standard was applied in *Dunsmuir* in chapter 13 of this text. Suffice it to say that *Dunsmuir* may not instill quite the confidence in the ability of judges to resist the temptation to intervene, even under the guise of deference, in the face of a strong privative clause and accumulated administrative expertise.

CHAPTER NINE

Privative Clauses and Statutory Rights of Appeal

INTRODUCTION

This chapter deals with an important consideration in the standard of review analysis: privative clauses and statutory rights of appeal. We are concerned here with the statute (or statutes) under which a decision-maker acts and, in particular, with statutory provisions that speak to the relationship between the courts and the relevant decision-maker or decision. An examination of privative clauses and rights of appeal thus involves statutory interpretation in that the court must formulate an understanding of legislative intent on the issue of judicial deference. (Recall also that, in the absence of an express right of appeal in a statute, a person may still be able to seek judicial review before the superior courts of the relevant province based on the common law.)

Only rarely does Parliament or a provincial legislature indicate precisely in a statute what standard of review a court should apply. And, even where a legislature does just this—so as to provide clarity in judicial review—the meaning of the words used to describe the relevant standard may evolve over time. Thus, the BC *Administrative Tribunals Act* has stated since its enactment in 2004 that the courts should apply a patent unreasonableness standard to the review of certain tribunal decisions. But, as we saw in the previous chapter of this text, the Supreme Court of Canada in *Canada (Citizenship and Immigration) v. Khosa*, 2009 SCC 12 (CanLII), at para. 19, concluded that the meaning of this statutory provision, and particularly its reference to "patent unreasonableness," will continue to evolve over time according to the common law.

On the other hand, legislatures have for decades included provisions in statutes that direct the courts not to review the decisions taken under the statute. These provisions are referred to as privative (or preclusive) clauses. Although the meaning and impact of privative clauses varies, depending on their wording, the inclusion of such a clause is always taken to signal deference by the courts. Alternatively, where the legislature indicates a role for judges by including a statutory right of appeal to a particular court, this will generally weigh against deference for the issues that are subject to the right of appeal. Even so, where a privative clause or a right of appeal (or both) are present in a statute, they will influence, but not determine outright, the standard of review. Moreover, even where a court decides to show deference based on a reasonableness standard, it may of course go on to overturn the decision in question despite the presence of a privative clause (and vice versa in the case of a broad right of appeal).

The courts' treatment of privative clauses, in particular, has provoked impassioned debate within the judiciary and the wider legal community. It is not hard to understand why. A statutory direction that the decisions of a particular tribunal are not to be questioned or reviewed in any legal proceeding whatsoever challenges the pervasive assumption that it is ultimately the constitutional function of an independent judiciary to determine the rights of individuals according to law. In particular, it is ultimately for the courts, not administrative agencies, whose members may not be lawyers or who may be appointed for a relatively short term, to interpret statutes and apply them to the facts of the individual case and to ensure that administrative decisions are made on the basis of a procedure that meets minimum standards of reasoning and fairness.

In addition, a principal area in which privative clauses are common is the regulation of the employment relationship. Thus, statutory privative clauses of various kinds regularly shelter from judicial review the proceedings and decisions of labour relations boards, labour arbitrators, workers' compensation boards, and the tribunals charged with implementing the principles of equal pay for work of equal value and employment equity.

In this chapter, we begin with sections on the general role of privative clauses and rights of appeal in light of the *Dunsmuir* decision. We then examine the historical debate about privative clauses, focusing especially on the position of the courts—based on the judicature provisions (ss. 96-101) of the *Constitution Act, 1867*—that a legislature cannot completely remove the authority of superior courts to review administrative decision making.

PRIVATIVE (OR PRECLUSIVE) CLAUSES AND RIGHTS OF APPEAL

Privative clauses are statutory provisions by which a legislature purports to limit the scope or intensity of judicial review of a statutory decision-maker. The language used in privative clauses varies and, as such, so too do their effects and their interpretations by courts. Generally, courts distinguish between "full" or "strong" privative clauses and "weak" privative clauses.

The former typically use broad language to preclude any form of review by a court, while also establishing that the decisions of the relevant actor are "final and conclusive." Thus, the clearest form of a full privative clause, according to *Pasiechnyk v. Saskatchewan (Workers' Compensation Board)*, [1997] 2 SCR 890, at para. 17, is "one that declares that decisions of the tribunal are final and conclusive from which no appeal lies and all forms of judicial review are excluded," although "[w]here the legislation employs words that purport to limit review but fall short of the traditional wording of a full privative clause, it is necessary to determine whether the words were intended to have full privative effect or a lesser standard of deference." As such, a privative clause can be full in its effect even where it does not satisfy the clearest definition of a full privative clause as laid out in *Pasiechnyk*.

On the other hand, weak privative clauses (sometimes called finality clauses or exclusive jurisdiction clauses) fall short of this broad language. Typically they state simply that the decisions of a decision-maker are "final and conclusive" or that a decision-maker has the "sole" or "exclusive" jurisdiction in certain matters, without expressly precluding the role of the courts from any "review" of the decision-maker.

Interpretation of a privative clause may depend also on whether other provisions of the statute provide for an appeal to a court from the decision-maker on questions of fact, law, mixed fact and law, or another category of decisions (or combination of categories). In such cases, the legislature may be said both to have authorized and to have circumscribed the court's role, leaving the disputing parties and the court to sort out any tensions or ambiguities arising from the statute. Notably, a privative clause cannot oust the authority of the superior courts to carry out judicial review on constitutional issues or its authority to ensure that an administrative actor has the statutory authority that it claims and that it is acting within the bounds of (or *intra vires*, as opposed to *ultra vires*) this authority.

Some examples of privative clauses and rights of appeal are reproduced below.

A STRONG PRIVATIVE CLAUSE:

No decision, order, direction, declaration or ruling of the Board shall be questioned or reviewed in any court, and no order shall be made or process entered, or proceedings taken in any court, whether by way of injunction, declaratory judgment, certiorari, mandamus, prohibition, quo warranto, or otherwise, to question, review, prohibit or restrain the Board or any of its proceedings.

Labour Relations Act, 1995, SO 1995, c. 1, Sched. A, s. 116

A FINALITY CLAUSE:

The decision and finding of the board under this Act upon all questions of fact and law are final and conclusive ... .

Workers' Compensation Act, 1979, SS 1979, c. W-17.1, s. 22(2)

A FINALITY CLAUSE COMBINED WITH A REQUIREMENT TO PROVIDE WRITTEN REASONS:

All orders and decisions of a Board of Inquiry are final and shall be made in writing, together with a written statement of the reasons therefor ... .

Human Rights Act, RSNB 1973, c. H-11, s. 21(1)

A BROAD RIGHT OF APPEAL:

(1) Any party to the proceedings before the [Health Services Appeal and Review Board] under this Act may appeal from its decision or order to the Divisional Court in accordance with the rules of court.

(5) An appeal under this section may be made on questions of law or fact or both and the court may confirm, alter or rescind the decision of the Board and may exercise all powers of the Board to confirm, alter or rescind the order as the court considers proper, or the court may refer the matter back to the Board for rehearing, in whole or in part, in accordance with such directions as the court considers proper.

Health Protection and Promotion Act, RSO 1990, c. H.7, s. 46

A RIGHT OF APPEAL REQUIRING LEAVE TO APPEAL FROM A JUDGE OF THE FEDERAL COURT, ALLOWING A LIMITED FURTHER APPEAL TO THE FEDERAL COURT OF APPEAL, AND INCORPORATING AN EXCLUSIVE JURISDICTION CLAUSE:

72(1) Judicial review by the Federal Court with respect to any matter—a decision, determination or order made, a measure taken or a question raised—under this Act is commenced by making an application for leave to the Court. ...

74. Judicial review is subject to the following provisions: ... (d) an appeal to the Federal Court of Appeal may be made only if, in rendering judgment, the judge certifies that a serious question of general importance is involved and states the question ... .

162(1) Each Division of the Board has, in respect of proceedings brought before it under this Act, sole and exclusive jurisdiction to hear and determine all questions of law and fact, including questions of jurisdiction.

Immigration and Refugee Protection Act, SC 2001, c. 27, ss. 72(1), 74, and 162(1)

In light of the variation in the terms of privative clauses and rights of appeal, it is important to examine closely the statute under which a decision has been taken so as to determine the appropriate route for any statutory appeal and to assess the likelihood that a court will show deference to the decision-maker. Likewise, based on *Dunsmuir*, one must review past cases in which comparable decisions have been reviewed by a court in order to locate existing jurisprudence on the standard of review.

PRIVATIVE CLAUSES IN THE STANDARD OF REVIEW ANALYSIS

Generally, in determining whether judicial deference should be shown to an administrative decision-maker, a court will accept that the presence of a privative clause in a statute calls for the court to show deference, although this may be influenced also by other factors. That said, there is an unfortunate history of judicial resistance to privative clauses, especially in the labour relations context, and one should therefore be prepared to scrutinize whether a court in a specific judgment has indeed respected any clear directions of the legislature. At times, cases arise where a court appears to have contorted its reasoning on the standard of review so as to justify an interventionist stance in the face of a strong privative clause.

In *Dunsmuir*, the majority described a privative clause rather modestly as "a statutory direction from Parliament or a legislature indicating the need for deference." This statement gives meaning to the privative clause, but arguably does not ring as loudly as one might expect in favour of deference where the clause in question is strongly worded. Recall also this statement by the majority in *Dunsmuir* (at para. 52):

The existence of a privative or preclusive clause gives rise to a strong indication of review pursuant to the reasonableness standard. This conclusion is appropriate because a privative clause is evidence of Parliament or a legislature's intent that an administrative decision maker be given greater deference and that interference by reviewing courts be minimized. This does not mean, however, that the presence of a privative clause is determinative. The rule of law requires that the constitutional role of superior courts be preserved and, as indicated above, neither Parliament nor any legislature can completely remove the courts' power to review the actions and decisions of administrative bodies. This power is constitutionally protected. Judicial review is necessary to ensure that the privative clause is read in its appropriate statutory context and that administrative bodies do not exceed their jurisdiction.

Despite the presence of a full privative clause, therefore, the superior courts retain a fundamental constitutional authority to review administrative action in order to ensure that a statutory decision-maker has not exceeded its delegated authority. On the other hand, judges should also not twist the concept of jurisdiction in artificial ways so as to justify overturning a decision where it appears clearly to warrant deference. As stated in *Dunsmuir*, at para. 35 (citing *CUPE, Local 963 v. New Brunswick Liquor Corporation*, [1979] 2 SCR 227, at 233), courts "should not be alert to brand as jurisdictional, and therefore subject to broader curial review, that which may be doubtfully so." Why would the majority in *Dunsmuir* find it important to give this caution? Even today, there remain instances in which courts appear to downplay the presence of a privative clause by expanding the concept of jurisdictional error. In *Dunsmuir*, Binnie J invoked Bora Laskin to criticize this tactic:

> Chief Justice Laskin during argument once memorably condemned the quashing of a labour board decision protected by a strong privative clause, by saying "what's wrong with these people [the judges], can't they read?"

Furthermore, Binnie J stated, more in criticism of the majority reasons in *Dunsmuir*, that

> [a] system of judicial review based on the rule of law ought not to treat a privative clause as conclusive, but it is more than just another "factor" in the hopper of pragmatism and functionality. Its existence should presumptively foreclose judicial review on the basis of *outcome* on substantive grounds unless the applicant can show that the clause, properly interpreted, permits it or there is some legal reason why it cannot be given effect.

Differences of view over privative clauses are about more than technical questions of statutory interpretation. They arise within a wider debate about the role of the courts in the regulation of property and contract rights where the legislature has assigned the responsibilities of economic regulation and social affairs to non-judicial bodies. Take for example the following reasons for why legislatures in Canada inserted privative clauses in legislation to protect the decisions of administrative agencies charged with regulating labour relations.

First, legislatures were aware that the protracted delays that accompany applications for judicial review to seek a second opinion on an arbitrator's interpretation of the collective agreement have the effect of postponing the resolution of a grievance, to the potential detriment of the parties' labour relations as well as the aim of expeditious dispute resolution. Time is generally of the essence, for instance, when a union is seeking certification from a labour relations board; delay often works in favour of the employer who is resisting certification by allowing the employer more time to try to persuade the employees that unionization will not serve their interests.

Second, the conduct of litigation through the courts is expensive. Employers generally have more resources at their disposal for this purpose than employees or their trade union. To allow unrestricted access to the courts would, therefore, confer an advantage on the employer and might well discourage the employee side from resorting to the tribunal in the first place on the ground that a favourable decision was likely to be challenged and defending the decision in court would prove too expensive.

Third, administrative tribunals sometimes have been created for the very purpose of keeping the dispute out of the courts; to allow the courts to scrutinize decisions made by these bodies for error of law would frustrate this purpose. For example, a specialist tribunal is generally preferred to a court as the forum for resolving disputes because its members have an understanding of the subject matter and an approach to the issues that is informed by an understanding of workplace realities and labour relations policy. A full right of judicial review would tend to force on the tribunal the distinctively "legal" approach of the generalist courts to issues of process and interpretation.

Some of these ideas were well captured by Iacobucci J in *Canadian Broadcasting Corporation v. Canada (Labour Relations Board)*, [1995] 1 SCR 157 (Can.), at para. 31:

> The CLRB must develop a coherent and workable structure for the application of the numerous provisions which govern the labour relations of the employers and employees whose operations fall within federal jurisdiction. In order for these workers and their employers to receive rapid resolution of their disputes in a manner which can be rationalized with their other rights and duties under the *Canada Labour Code*, the decisions of the Board cannot be routinely overturned by the courts whenever they disagree with the Board's treatment of an isolated issue.

Moreover, most tribunals in the labour area are tripartite in their composition—that is, they comprise representatives of labour and management, with a chair appointed by agreement or by an outside authority. There has been a widespread view, on the other hand, that the courts and the common law have historically been unsympathetic to the aspirations of labour: individual rights of freedom of contract and property have too often taken precedence over the statutory scheme of regulation and the notion of collective rights. In short, the regulation of labour relations readily gives rise to heated debate about the legitimacy of legislative intervention in the operation of the market and to clashes between collective and individual rights. This has been one of the principal arenas in which Canadian lawyers have struggled to reconcile traditional understandings of the concept of the rule of law with the mission of the modern administrative state to address the shortcomings of *laissez-faire* capitalism and its legal supports—namely, the common law and the courts of general jurisdiction.

Where then do we stand on the role of privative clauses in current doctrine? On the one hand, privative clauses retain their importance in the standard of review analysis as a signal of deference. On the other hand, other aspects of the *Dunsmuir* framework—the positioning of privative clauses as but one factor alongside others and the withdrawal of the highly deferential standard of patent unreasonableness—suggest a turn away from the view that privative clauses convey a clear message about legislative intent. Thus, *Dunsmuir* could in time dilute the impact of full privative clauses, especially, in spite of the majority's admonition against an expansive approach to jurisdictional review. That said, *Dunsmuir* also leaves room to maintain the effect of a privative clause in areas such as labour relations, based on the role of existing jurisprudence and on the context-driven nature of the reasonableness standard. It seems to remain important, at least, to examine closely the reasons given by a court to justify overturning a decision where the decision was protected by a full privative clause.

In its post-*Dunsmuir* decision in *Hibernia Management and Development Company Ltd. v. Canada-Newfoundland and Labrador Offshore Petroleum Board*, 2008 NLCA 46 (CanLII), the Newfoundland and Labrador Court of Appeal analyzed a complex set of privative provisions in the *Canada-Newfoundland Atlantic Accord Implementation Act*, SC 1987, c. 3. The purpose of this legislation was to implement the 1985 Atlantic Accord between Canada and Newfoundland and Labrador by which the Canada-Newfoundland and Labrador Offshore Petroleum Board had been established. The board had the authority to issue licences and approve development plans for offshore oil development projects, and had issued guidelines in 2004 on the required research and development expenditures by companies operating such projects. The board's authority to issue and apply these guidelines was challenged by the Hibernia Management and Development Company and by Petro-Canada, the respective operators of the Hibernia and Terra Nova offshore projects. In its standard of review analysis, the court examined closely the privative provisions under the Act:

[47] In submitting that correctness is the appropriate standard of review, Hibernia Management and Petro-Canada argued that there is no privative clause in the legislation protecting the Board's decisions from review by the courts. In response, the Board submitted that section 30 constitutes a privative clause because it provides that "the exercise of a power or the performance of a duty by the Board pursuant to this Act is final and not subject to the review or approval of either government or either Minister."

[48] The language of section 30, particularly compared with other provisions in the Act, is ambiguous. There are at least three other provisions in the legislation that use language consistent with a privative clause. Two of these are confined in their application to decisions, and the particular operations, of the Oil and Gas Committee [a separate entity from the board], and are, therefore, not directly relevant to this appeal. However, it is useful to review the language used:

145(3) The finding or determination of the [Oil and Gas] Committee on any question of fact within its jurisdiction is binding and conclusive.

184(1) Except as provided in this Division, every decision or order of the [Oil and Gas] Committee is final and conclusive.

[49] By contrast, again in the context of the Oil and Gas Committee, section 124(10) specifically provides for review by the courts:

Any order, decision or action in respect of which a hearing is held under this section is subject to review and to be set aside by the Trial Division of the Supreme Court of Newfoundland.

[50] The third provision of the legislation containing language that may be characterized as a form of privative clause is found in the same Part as section 30. Section 38 states:

Where a determination referred to in section 36 or 37 [regarding self-sufficiency and unreasonable delay] is made by a panel pursuant to that section, that determination is not subject to be reviewed or set aside by any government, court or other body.

[51] Of particular interest is the specific reference to "court." Section 30, by contrast, omits that reference. It may be argued, therefore, that, in light of the reference to governments and ministers in section 30, if the intention had been to restrict review by the courts, then the courts would have been specifically mentioned. Applying this interpretation, section 30 would not be characterized as a privative clause.

[52] On the other hand, the argument can be made that the essence of section 30 is that the exercise of a power by the Board, including the making of a decision, is final, and that the remaining language simply emphasizes that governments and ministers may not interfere. This

interpretation flows from the language of section 30 which specifies that the exercise of a power by the Board under the Act "is final" and "not subject to the review or approval of either government or either Minister" ... . This interpretation would result in characterization of section 30 as at least a partial privative clause.

[53] Ambiguity in the language of section 30 must be considered in the context of the legislation as a whole. As noted above, under the statute, the Board has an extensive mandate. The Board falls within the description of a "discrete and special administrative regime in which the decision maker has special expertise," and, therefore, a regime where the reasonableness standard would generally apply (*Dunsmuir*, at paragraph 55).

[54] In the circumstances, on balance, I would characterize section 30 as a partial privative clause which would support a review by the courts on a standard of reasonableness.

[55] Even if this section did not constitute a partial privative clause, the absence of such a clause is not determinative. In the circumstances of this case, other factors, particularly the mandate and expertise of the Board, lead to the conclusion that the courts should show deference to the Board's decisions by applying a reasonableness standard.

[56] Finally, it is important to note that the question of whether the Board has authority to apply the 2004 Guidelines to the Hibernia and Terra Nova projects does not involve any questions of law of central importance to the legal system (*Dunsmuir*, at paragraph 55). Accordingly, the standard of correctness is not, for that reason, necessarily engaged.

[57] Further, the question of whether the Board has authority to issue the 2004 Guidelines and to apply them to the Hibernia and Terra Nova Projects is not a true question of *vires* as discussed in *Dunsmuir*. As noted above, the Board has broad authority with respect to approving benefits plans, including the research and development component. Section 151.1 of the Act specifically authorizes the Board to issue "guidelines and interpretation notes with respect to the application and administration" of the sections of the Act dealing with benefits plans, operating licences and production authorizations. As discussed below, the question of whether the 2004 Guidelines can properly be applied to companies already in the production phase depends primarily on the interpretation of the language of the benefits plans as approved in the Board's decisions. In the circumstances, it cannot be said that, in issuing and applying the Guidelines, the Board acted beyond its authority in the sense of a true question of *vires*.

[58] In the result, I conclude that reasonableness is the appropriate standard of review in assessing whether the Board has authority to apply the 2004 Guidelines to the Hibernia and Terra Nova projects.

We discuss, in chapter 12 of this text, the concept of jurisdiction and, in particular, the direction in *Dunsmuir* that the courts exercise caution in characterizing questions as jurisdictional. The decision in *Hibernia Management* is an example of such caution. What is important to review for present purposes, however, is the careful approach that was taken by the court in *Hibernia Management* to identifying the ambiguity in s. 30 and to reaching the conclusion that, "on balance," s. 30 should be read as a partial privative clause.

RIGHTS OF APPEAL IN THE STANDARD OF REVIEW ANALYSIS

Many statutes provide a right of appeal to a specific court—in Ontario, for instance, this is typically to the Divisional Court, whereas at the federal level it is the Federal Court or the Federal Court of Appeal—on questions of fact or law (or both; or some other combination) that have been determined by the statutory decision-maker. Some examples of rights of appeal were provided above.

A right of appeal is broadest when it encompasses all of the possible questions that a decision-maker might make, and its inclusion in a statute tends to weigh against deference by a court. Nevertheless, a separate purpose of a right of appeal is to clarify the route that the legislature intends a judicial review application to follow. Where no right of appeal is included in a statute, then, by default, the common law reserves judicial review for the superior courts of the respective province (which may carry other common law requirements of standing and the exhaustion of internal remedies, for example). Often legislatures provide in statutes for a right of appeal to a court that is itself established by statute—as in the case of the Federal Court, the various federal and provincial Courts of Appeal, and numerous courts in the provinces—in connection with a particular realm of decision making. For this reason, the judicial deference signals given by a right of appeal are not as singular as in the case of a privative clause: they are one, but not the only, function of a right of appeal in assigning and delineating the task of judicial review.

In *Dunsmuir*, the majority did not mention rights of appeal and their impact on the standard of review analysis. In one way this is not surprising given that the PSLRA did not contain a right of appeal, but rather a strong privative clause, with respect to the decision of the adjudicator in that case. On the other hand, *Dunsmuir* aspires to give wide-ranging guidance, and so one might expect rights of appeal to appear in the reasoning of the majority. Differences of view among those justices who made up the majority in *Dunsmuir* may explain this lack of clarification about just how rights of appeal fit in.

The clearest view on rights of appeal in *Dunsmuir* was expressed by Binnie J in his separate reasons. He emphasized the role that a broad right of appeal plays in signalling legislative intent that the courts not defer to the substantive decisions of an administration actor. According to Binnie J, at para. 146, "[the] fact that the legislature designated someone other than the court as the decision-maker calls for deference to (or judicial respect for) the outcome, absent a broad statutory right of appeal."

One might assume that the majority in *Dunsmuir* does not seek to alter the position on statutory rights of appeal. Before *Dunsmuir*, the general position was that, where questions of *fact* fell within the scope of the right of appeal, there was a tendency nonetheless to defer to the findings of the trier of fact. Where the issue was one of *law*, on the other hand, the assumption was that the right of appeal indicated a legislative intent for the court to feel free to intervene on the basis of its own conclusions on the relevant legal issues. In contrast to the red or amber lights of privative-clause protected decisions, a right of appeal on questions of law was taken as a green light for judicial intervention.

However, that this was not a totally safe assumption was revealed as far back as in *Bell Canada v. Canada (CRTC)*, [1989] 1 SCR 1722 (Can.). Here, at 1744-45, Gonthier J, delivering the judgment of the court, said that, even within statutory appeals, "the principle of specialization of duties justifies curial deference … on issues which fall squarely within its area of expertise." In other words, the nature of the question and the degree of the tribunal's expected expertise were beginning to emerge as relevant concerns even when there was a statutory right of appeal. As we discuss in chapter 10 of this text, this concern was incorporated into the pragmatic and functional approach when, in both *Pezim* and *Southam*, the deferential standard of reasonableness *simpliciter* was adopted in the face of a statutory right of appeal and in the absence of a privative clause.

Other pre-*Dunsmuir* decisions of the Supreme Court of Canada affirmed this position. For example, in *Law Society of New Brunswick v. Ryan*, [2003] 1 SCR 247, at para. 29, Iacobucci J stated for a unanimous court:

> The existence of a broad statutory right of appeal indicates that less deference may be due to decisions of the Discipline Committee [of the Law Society of New Brunswick]. However, as Bastarache J noted in *Pushpanathan*, *supra*, at para. 30: "The absence of a privative clause does not imply a high standard of scrutiny, where other factors bespeak a lower standard." The specialization of duties intended by the legislature may warrant deference notwithstanding the absence of a privative clause.

In terms of a right of appeal that encompasses questions of law, then, *Dunsmuir* suggests implicitly that the conventional position may be altered, or at least clarified. The majority says that the decisions of a tribunal or agency on the interpretation of its own statute, or closely related statutes, are "usually" entitled to deference and that questions of law—where not both of central importance to the legal system and outside the decision-maker's expertise—"may" be compatible with the standard of reasonableness. Furthermore, in *Khosa*, at para. 55, Binnie J stated for the majority that "[w]hile privative clauses deter judicial intervention, a statutory right of appeal may be at ease with it, depending on its terms." These carefully framed statements seem to allow for the application of a correctness standard on questions of law where there is a full statutory right of appeal. But they suggest also that deference may be appropriate where the question of law arises from the decision-maker's home statute or from closely related statutes. Thus, the more important issue appears to be, not the presence of a right of appeal on questions of law, but rather the context in which a question of law has arisen and the degree to which it engages the mandate and expertise of the decision-maker.

THE CONSTITUTIONAL LIMITS OF PRIVATIVE CLAUSES

In this section, we consider the doctrine, led in particular by the decision in *Crevier v. Quebec (Attorney General)*, [1981] 2 SCR 220 (Que.), that the constitution implicitly guarantees the authority of the courts to review the decisions of administrative agencies for errors of law or jurisdiction and for procedural unfairness. The issue is of special significance to privative clauses because it restrains the ability of Parliament or a provincial legislature to limit the scope of judicial review. Indeed, the discussion and jurisprudence on the constitutional basis for judicial review arose from litigation over the effect of privative clauses.

It is important to emphasize that, at this point, we are not concerned with judicial review of the entire universe of administrative decision making. When speaking of the constitutional basis for judicial review, the focus is on challenges to administrative action on grounds that a tribunal or agency made an error of jurisdiction (although this may be defined in a range of ways) or of constitutional interpretation or that it denied procedural fairness to an individual. These are the ultimate questions that the courts are most concerned to protect, invoking the constitution itself if necessary to do so.

As we have seen, it is a foundational principle that public statutory authorities have only those powers conferred on them by legislation. Their powers are legally limited and it is ultimately the role of the courts to determine what those limits are, especially when they affect the rights of individuals. Put differently, statutory interpretation is informed by the judiciary's ideas about the appropriate distribution of decision-making power between courts and administrative agencies in a system of government subject to the law. As the majority said in *Dunsmuir* (at para. 31):

> The legislative branch of government cannot remove the judiciary's power to review actions and decisions of administrative bodies for compliance with the constitutional capacities of the government. Even a privative clause, which provides a strong indication of legislative intent, cannot be determinative in this respect. ... The inherent power of superior courts to review administrative action and ensure that it does not exceed its jurisdiction stems from the judicature provisions in ss. 96 to 101 of the *Constitution Act, 1867*: *Crevier*. As noted by Beetz J in *U.E.S., Local 298 v. Bibeault*, [1988] 2 SCR 1048, at p. 1090, "[t]he role of the superior courts in maintaining the rule of law is so important that it is given constitutional protection." In short, judicial review is constitutionally guaranteed in Canada, particularly with regard to the definition and enforcement of jurisdictional limits.

Moving from the level of what is, in a formal sense at least, a question of statutory interpretation, our inquiry here is whether Parliament or a provincial legislature has the constitutional capacity to exclude all judicial review of an administrative agency that it has created. The proposition that a legislature has such authority is an assertion of parliamentary supremacy in the allocation of responsibilities between legislature and judiciary. It is thus not without its own powerful normative force, counter to that of the rule of law.

It is now generally agreed that a legislature cannot oust the courts' power to review a decision of an administrative agency, or its enabling statute, on the ground that either is beyond the constitutional capacity of that legislature. Thus, legislation that confers power on public authorities—and those public authorities in the exercise of that power—are always subject to challenge on the basis that there has been a disregard of the division of powers between Parliament and the provincial legislatures provided for primarily in ss. 91 and 92 of the *Constitution Act, 1867*. Legislation cannot take this right away. Nor can it remove the right to launch a constitutional challenge on other grounds such as violation of the *Canadian Charter of Rights and Freedoms* and failures to observe other limits on legislative capacity in the *Constitution Acts, 1867-1982*, in other constitutional instruments, and also in unwritten principles of the Canadian constitution as recognized in *Reference re Secession of Quebec*, [1998] 2 SCR 217 (Can.).

However, the *Constitution Acts, 1867-1982* contain no provision that explicitly deals with the power of the courts to review decisions of administrative agencies. This reflects the (British) Westminster style of parliamentary democracy. Thus, unlike the constitutions of some other federalist states, such as the United States and Australia, our constitution does not outline a general separation of powers doctrine in that it does not confer on Parliament and the provincial legislatures exclusive authority to exercise the legislative power of the

Canadian state; nor on the Crown, its executive powers; nor on the judiciary, its judicial powers. The absence of an express guarantee of judicial review of government contrasts to the South African constitution, for example, which declares not only a "right to administrative action that is lawful, reasonable and procedurally fair" (s. 33(1)), but also a right to review of administrative action by either a court or "an independent and impartial tribunal" (s. 33(3)(a)).

Of course, it is always possible to argue that what is not expressly provided for in the constitution is nonetheless implicit within it. In Canada, in the absence of any express separation of powers provision, it was claimed that a right to the judicial review of administrative action should be implied in the constitution based on the judicature provisions of the *Constitution Act, 1867*, ss. 96-101. These sections provide for the appointment, by Canada's governor general, of judges of the superior, district, and county courts in each province (s. 96) from among members of the bars of their respective provinces (ss. 97 and 98), for the security of tenure of judges of superior courts (s. 99), and for the salary and pension of judges of the superior, district, and county courts to be fixed and provided by the Parliament of Canada (s. 100). Also, when considering the prospect of constitutional limits on the power of Parliament to exclude federal tribunals from judicial review, it is necessary to consider s. 101, which says: "The Parliament of Canada may, notwithstanding anything in this Act ... provide for ... the establishment of any additional courts for the better administration of the laws of Canada."

COURTS AND TRIBUNALS: CONSTITUTIONAL BACKGROUND

In the first place, one should be familiar with the original context in which questions about the legislative capacity to create administrative agencies arose. This context involved the creation by provincial legislatures of tribunals whose members did not and do not have all of the attributes of ss. 96-100 judges. Despite this, the tribunals in question were given authority over matters that came within the historical jurisdiction of the courts as presided over by such judges. Could a provincial legislature validly confer such authority on an administrative tribunal, for what are no doubt very defensible reasons, thus effectively displacing the role of the courts? If not, then what aspects of the courts' historical role are protected and how are they to be defined? The following summary by Peter Hogg outlines the doctrine of the Supreme Court of Canada on these questions.

Hogg, *Constitutional Law of Canada*
(Toronto: Carswell, 2009 Student Edition), at 227-34
(footnotes omitted; emphasis in original)

The last 100 years have seen a great increase in the number of administrative tribunals in Canada (and elsewhere), to the point that administrative tribunals undoubtedly decide more cases and probably dispose of more dollars than do the ordinary courts. The cause of this development is the vast increase in social and economic regulation which has occurred in the last 100 years. The novel tasks of adjudication which are entailed by new schemes of regulation have commonly been entrusted to administrative tribunals rather than to the courts. Some of the reasons for this preference can be identified. First is the desire for a specialist body: specially qualified personnel can be appointed to a tribunal, and those who do not start off specially qualified can acquire experience and expertise in the field of regulation (whether it be labour relations, marketing of agricultural products, transportation, broadcasting, liquor licensing, or whatever). Second is the desire for innovation: a tribunal can be given broad discretion to develop the policies and remedies required to implement a new scheme of regulation (such as foreign investment review, control of pay television). Third is the desire for initiative: a tribunal (such as a human rights commission or a securities commission) can be given power to initiate proceedings, to undertake investigations, to do research, and to play an educative and policy-formulating role as well as an adjudicative one. Fourth is the problem of volume: if adjudication is required with great frequency (as in workers' compensation, unemployment insurance, immigration, income tax objections, for example), the tribunal can develop procedures to handle a case-load that would choke the ordinary court system. Fifth is economy: a tribunal can be structured and mandated to be less formal, speedier and less expensive than the ordinary courts (although in many fields the complexity of the issues and the sums at stake preclude this kind of advantage).

When the advantages of administrative adjudication are reviewed, it is easy to see why legislative bodies have chosen to confer many adjudicative functions on administrative tribunals rather than the ordinary courts. But the ordinary courts, through their exegesis of s. 96 and the other judicature sections of the *Constitution Act, 1867*, have assumed the power to review legislation investing a provincially-established administrative tribunal with adjudicative functions: if those functions ought properly to belong to a superior, district or county court, then the legislation will be unconstitutional. By this means, the courts have erected constitutional barriers to legislative encroachments on their own traditional functions.

The leading case on the impact of s. 96 on the creation of provincial administrative tribunals is the decision of the Supreme Court of Canada in *Re Residential Tenancies Act* [[1981] 1 SCR 714 (Ont.)]. In that case, Dickson J for the Court suggested a three-step approach to the resolution of a s. 96 challenge to an administrative tribunal's powers. The first step is an historical inquiry into whether the impugned power broadly conforms to a power exercised by a superior, district or county court at confederation. The second step, reached only if the answer to the historical inquiry is yes, is an inquiry into whether the impugned power is a "judicial" power. The third step, reached only if the answer to both the historical inquiry and the judicial inquiry is yes, is an inquiry into whether the power in its institutional setting has changed its character sufficiently to negate the broad conformity with superior, district or county court jurisdiction.

The first step—the historical inquiry—involves an investigation of whether the impugned power was one that was within the powers of a superior, district or county court at confederation. A negative answer to this inquiry will resolve the s. 96 issue in favour of the validity of the power without the necessity to proceed to steps (2) and (3).

For a tribunal's power to be held to be a s. 96 power at confederation, it is clear that the impugned power must have been within the *exclusive* jurisdiction of s. 96 courts at confederation. If there was even concurrent jurisdiction in inferior courts or tribunals at confederation, then this will lead to a negative answer to the historical inquiry. This rule

places great weight on the way in which the impugned power is characterized. For example, a tribunal's remedial powers may have been within the exclusive jurisdiction of
s. 96 courts at confederation, while its subject-matter jurisdiction was only concurrent.
And with respect to subject-matter, jurisdiction can be expressed broadly (e.g., labour
relations), which may give rise to concurrent jurisdiction, or narrowly (e.g., unjust dismissal), which may not. In *Sobeys Stores v. Yeomans* [[1989] 1 SCR 238 (NS)], which was
a challenge to a reinstatement order made by a labour standards tribunal, Wilson J for
the majority of the Supreme Court of Canada recognized the existence of these choices.
She suggested that the Court should lean in the direction of an affirmative answer to the
historical test, that is, a finding that the tribunal's power was within the exclusive powers
of a superior, district or county court at confederation, so as to protect the traditional
jurisdiction of the s. 96 courts. In that way, the historical inquiry would become a rather
low threshold, easily crossed, and the issue of validity would be resolved in steps (2) and
(3) of the s. 96 reasoning.

. . .

The second step in the s. 96 reasoning—the "judicial" inquiry—involves the notoriously elusive task of characterizing the impugned power as "judicial" (in which case the
s. 96 inquiry must proceed) or as "administrative" or "legislative" (in which case the s. 96
inquiry can stop). In *Re Residential Tenancies Act*, Dickson J suggested that a power was
"judicial" if it involved (1) "a private dispute between parties," (2) that must be adjudicated "through the application of a recognized body of rules," and (3) that must be adjudicated "in a manner consistent with fairness and impartiality." He concluded that these
characteristics were all present in the powers of the rent tribunal in that case. Of course,
in the case of an inferior court (as opposed to an administrative tribunal), the power in
question is almost certainly to be classified as judicial, and this step of the inquiry is not
significant. Even in the case of an administrative tribunal, where the historical inquiry
(the first step) has yielded the answer that the power in question was one that was exercised by a superior court at the time of confederation, in most cases the power will be
classified as judicial. But in some cases a power, challenged for breach of s. 96, has been
upheld as insufficiently judicial, either for absence of a private dispute between parties,
or for absence of a controlling body of rules, or for both reasons.

The third step in the s. 96 reasoning—the "institutional setting" inquiry—involves an
examination of the power in its institutional setting to see whether it still broadly conforms to a s. 96 power. This step of the process had been emphasized before *Residential
Tenancies* in *Tomko v. Labour Relations Board (Nova Scotia)* [[1977] 1 SCR 112 (NS)]
where, in upholding a labour relations board's power to issue a cease and desist order,
Laskin CJ for the majority of the Supreme Court of Canada said that the superficially
close analogy with superior-court injunctions was not decisive, because it was necessary
to consider not the "detached jurisdiction or power alone," but rather "its setting in the
institutional arrangements in which it appears." The Privy Council in the *John East* case
[(*Labour Relations Board (Sask.) v. John East Ironworks Ltd.*, [1949] AC 134 (Sask. PC)]
had also decided that the institutional setting of a labour relations regime transformed a
power to enforce contracts into a non-s. 96 function. In both *Tomko* and *John East*, the
court-like adjudicative function of the labour relations board was ancillary to a broader
administrative and policy-making role as administrator of the labour relations legisla-

tion. A similar argument carried the day in *Sobeys Stores*, where a labour standards tribunal's power to reinstate employees was upheld as "a necessarily incidental aspect of the broader social policy goal of providing minimum standards of protection for non-unionized employees." In settings other than labour relations, the institutional setting has sustained many other adjudicative functions vested in administrative tribunals.

The institutional setting will not save an adjudicative function which, having been held to be a s. 96 function at confederation (step (1)), and having been characterized as judicial (step (2)), is the "sole or central function" of the tribunal. That was the case in *Re Residential Tenancies Act*, where the Supreme Court of Canada held that, although the rent tribunal did perform other functions in the administration of Ontario's residential tenancy legislation, the other functions were ancillary to the central function of adjudicating disputes between landlords and tenants.

The institutional setting was also unavailing to save the impugned power in *A.-G. Que. v. Farrah* [[1978] 2 SCR 638 (Que.)] where the sole function of the Quebec Transport Tribunal was to sit on appeal from a tribunal of first instance and decide "any question of law"; this was held to be an unconstitutional s. 96 function. That was also the holding in *Crevier v. A.-G. Que.* [[1981] 2 SCR 220 (Que.)] where the sole function of the Quebec Professions Tribunal was to sit on appeal from several tribunals of first instance; the Professions Tribunal also had the power to decide questions of law. In both *Farrah* and *Crevier*, a privative clause purported to exclude superior-court review of the appellate tribunal's decisions; that aspect of the cases is discussed in the next section of this chapter. The three concurring opinions in *Farrah* emphasized the exclusion of superior-court review as if it was the unreviewable character of the authority of the Quebec Transport Tribunal that was important. But, in *Crevier*, Laskin CJ for the Court, as well as holding the privative clause unconstitutional, seemed to hold that the fact that the sole function of the Quebec Professions Tribunal was that of "a general tribunal of appeal" was a fatal flaw by itself.

The three-step approach now favoured by the Supreme Court of Canada is no doubt a sound synthesis of the prior case-law. But it is not satisfactory as constitutional-law doctrine. Each of the three steps is vague and disputable in many situations, and small differences between the provinces in their history or institutional arrangements can spell the difference between the validity and invalidity of apparently similar administrative tribunals. The Supreme Court of Canada's holdings of invalidity in the *Residential Tenancies*, *Farrah* and *Crevier* cases (as well as in the *B.C. Family Relations Act*, *McEvoy* and *MacMillan Bloedel* cases, discussed in the earlier section of this chapter on inferior courts) have cast doubt on the constitutionality of many provincial administrative tribunals (and some inferior courts), have encouraged a spate of litigation on this issue, and have led to pressure from the provinces for an amendment to s. 96. I think an amendment is the only solution. The courts are unlikely to abandon doctrine which has been built up over a long time; nor are they likely to abandon their concern (which I regard as extravagant) to prevent the erosion of superior-court jurisdiction. To me, the allocation of jurisdiction between different levels of courts and administrative tribunals is primarily a political question, upon which the inevitably self-interested views of the courts should not be unduly influential. An amendment proposal which has been circulated for discussion by the federal Department of Justice would specifically grant to the provinces the power to confer on an administrative tribunal (but not an inferior court) any function within provincial legislative competence (including a s. 96 function), so long as the tribunal's decisions remained subject to superior-court review. This proposal would remove a swamp of uncertainty from our constitutional law, and give to the provinces more security in assigning functions to administrative tribunals.

STATUTORY REMOVAL OF JUDICIAL REVIEW

Crevier v. Quebec (Attorney General)
[1981] 2 SCR 220 (Que.)

[This case addresses the limits of a provincial legislature's power to create an administrative tribunal with authority over matters conventionally dealt with by ss. 96-101 courts. The case concerns the validity of aspects of the *Professional Code*, RSQ 1977, c. C-26. This statute was novel in that it created a Professions Tribunal that had exclusive appellate jurisdiction, protected by a full privative clause, over the disciplinary committees of most of the statutory professional bodies in Quebec. The Professions Tribunal was composed of six judges of the Provincial Court, where judges are appointed pursuant to provincial statute rather than by the federal Cabinet (as in the case of ss. 96-101 courts). The statute provided that the decisions of the tribunal were final.]

LASKIN CJC delivered the judgment of the Court: ... Two other sections of the *Professional Code* are relevant, s. 193 providing for certain immunity for acts done in good faith in the performance by, *inter alia*, a discipline committee or an appeal tribunal of their duties; and s. 194, a privative provision, excluding recourse to the supervisory authority of the Superior Court under certain aspects of the *Code of Civil Procedure*, RSQ 1977, c. C-25. These sections read:

> 193. The syndics, assistant syndics, corresponding syndics, the investigators and experts of a professional inspection committee, the members of the Office, of a Bureau, of a committee on discipline, of a professional inspection committee or of a committee of inquiry established by a Bureau, and the members of a tribunal hearing an appeal from a decision by a committee on discipline, shall not be prosecuted for acts done in good faith in the performance of their duties.
>
> 194. No extraordinary recourse contemplated in articles 834 to 850 of the *Code of Civil Procedure* shall be exercised and no injunction granted against the persons mentioned in section 193 acting in their official capacities.
>
> ...

Section 195 should also be mentioned, reading as follows:

> 195. Article 33 of the *Code of Civil Procedure* does not apply to the persons mentioned in section 193 acting in their official capacities.

It is sufficient in the present case, in adverting to the reference in s. 194 to arts. 834 to 850 of the *Code of Civil Procedure*, to reproduce only art. 846 which is in these terms:

846. The Superior Court may, at the demand of one of the parties, evoke before judgment a case pending before a court subject to its superintending and reforming power, or revise a judgment already rendered by such court, in the following cases:

(1) when there is want or excess of jurisdiction;

(2) when the enactment upon which the proceedings have been based or the judgment rendered is null or of no effect;

(3) when the proceedings are affected by some gross irregularity, and there is reason to believe that justice has not been, or will not be done;

(4) when there has been a violation of the law or an abuse of authority amounting to fraud and of such a nature as to cause a flagrant injustice.

However, in the cases provided in paragraphs 2, 3 and 4 above, the remedy lies only if, in the particular case, the judgments of the court seized with the proceeding are not susceptible of appeal.

Article 33 of the *Code of Civil Procedure*, excluded by s. 195 is as follows:

33. Excepting the Court of Appeal, the courts within the jurisdiction of the legislature of Quebec, and bodies politic and corporate within Quebec are subject to the superintending and reforming power of the Superior Court in such manner and forms as by law provided, save in matters declared by law to be of the exclusive competency of such courts or of any one of the latter, and save in cases where the jurisdiction resulting from this article is excluded by some provision of a general or special law.

The Court of Appeal majority viewed the preclusive words of s. 194 as not touching the power and right of the Superior Court to issue a writ of evocation where there has been a want or excess of jurisdiction. Section 194 itself, however, does not recognize this supervisory authority of the Superior Court. If it did, it would be arguable that so long as the Professions Tribunal was subject to the superintendence of the Superior Court on questions of jurisdiction, it would not be tainted as exercising a power belonging to a s. 96 court by an initial but reviewable conclusion that a Discipline Committee had exceeded its jurisdiction. That is not this case, having regard to the embracive terms of s. 194 of the *Professional Code*. Even if it were otherwise and the supervisory authority of the Superior Court on questions of jurisdiction was expressly preserved, it would still not be a complete answer to a contention that the Professions Tribunal is exercising powers more conformable to those belonging to a s. 96 court than those properly exercisable by a provincial administrative or *quasi*-judicial tribunal or even a provincial judicial tribunal.

· · ·

Three issues arise from the reasons in the Court of Appeal. The first, which I think may be quickly disposed of, concerns the intimation by Jacques J of a *Tomko v. Labour Relations Board (NS)* [1977] 1 SCR 112 (NS) situation. The Professions Tribunal is given no function other than that of a general tribunal of appeal in respect of all professions covered by the *Professional Code* and it is, therefore, impossible to see its final appellate jurisdiction as part of an institutional arrangement by way of a regulatory scheme for the governance of the various professions. The Professions Tribunal is not so much integrated into any scheme as it is sitting on top of the various schemes and with an authority de-tached from them, although, of course, exercising that authority in relation to each scheme as the occasion requires. There is no valid comparison with the cease and desist orders which the Labour Relations Board in the *Tomko* case was authorized to issue in its administration of a collective bargaining statute.

[Here Laskin CJC distinguished *Tomko* by relying on *Reference re Residential Tenancies Act*, [1981] 1 SCR 714 (Ont.).]

The second issue arising from the reasons of the Quebec Court of Appeal concerns the effect upon s. 96 of a privative clause of a statute which purports to insulate a prov-incial adjudicative tribunal from any review of its decisions. Is it enough to deflect s. 96 if the privative clause is construed to preserve Superior Court supervision over questions of jurisdiction, and if (as in this case) such a construction is not open because of the wording of the privative clause, is the clause constitutionally valid? In my opinion, where a provincial Legislature purports to insulate one of its statutory tribunals from any curial review of its adjudicative functions, the insulation encompassing jurisdiction, such prov-incial legislation must be struck down as unconstitutional by reason of having the effect of constituting the tribunal a s. 96 Court.

• • •

In *Executors of Woodward Estate v. Minister of Finance* [1973] SCR 120 (BC), this court was concerned, *inter alia*, with a provincial statutory provision which purported to make certain determinations by the Minister final and conclusive and not open to appeal or review in any Court. Martland J, speaking for this Court, dealt with this provision as fol-lows (at 127):

> The effect which has been given to a provision of this kind is that, while it precludes a su-perior Court from reviewing, by way of *certiorari*, a decision of an inferior tribunal on the basis of error of law on the face of the record, if such error occurs in the proper exercise of its jurisdiction, it does not preclude such review if the inferior tribunal has acted outside its defined jurisdiction. The basis of such decisions is that if such a tribunal has acted beyond its jurisdiction in making a decision, it is not a decision at all within the meaning of the statute which defines its powers because Parliament could not have intended to clothe such tribunal with the power to expand its statutory jurisdiction by an erroneous decision as to the scope of its own powers.

Although this was not a direct pronouncement on constitutional power (jurisdiction as such was not expressly involved as it is in the case at bar), it was a clear indication that the constitutional issue was in the background. It is necessary to bring it forward, how-ever, when it is raised as squarely as it has been under the *Professional Code*.

It is true that this is the first time that this Court has declared unequivocally that a provincially constituted statutory tribunal cannot constitutionally be immunized from review of decisions on questions of jurisdiction. In my opinion, this limitation, arising by virtue of s. 96, stands on the same footing as the well-accepted limitation on the power of provincial statutory tribunals to make unreviewable determinations of constitutional-ity. There may be differences of opinion as to what are questions of jurisdiction but, in my lexicon, they rise above and are different from errors of law, whether involving statutory construction or evidentiary matters or other matters. It is now unquestioned that privative clauses may, when properly framed, effectively oust judicial review on questions of law and, indeed, on other issues not touching jurisdiction. However, given that s. 96 is in the *British North America Act, 1867* and that it would make a mockery of it to treat it in non-functional formal terms as a mere appointing power, I can think of nothing that is more the hallmark of a Superior Court than the vesting of power in a provincial statutory tribunal to determine the limits of its jurisdiction without appeal or other review.

There has been academic concern with the permitted scope of privative clauses referable to determinations of provincial adjudicative agencies. Opinion has varied from a position that even errors of law cannot validly be immunized from review (see Lyon, "Comment" (1971) 49 *Can. Bar Rev.* 365), to a position that at least jurisdictional review is constitutionally guaranteed (see Lederman, "The Independence of the Judiciary" (1956) 34 *Can. Bar Rev.* 1139, 1174) to a position that jurisdictional determinations may, constitutionally, also be denied judicial review (see Hogg, "Is Judicial Review of Administrative Action Guaranteed by the *British North America Act?*" (1976) 54 *Can. Bar Rev.* 716, and see also Dussault, *Le Contrôle Judiciaire de l'Administration au Québec* (1969), especially at pp. 110-113).

This Court has hitherto been content to look at privative clauses in terms of proper construction and, no doubt, with a disposition to read them narrowly against the long history of judicial review on questions of law and questions of jurisdiction. Where, however, questions of law have been specifically covered in a privative enactment, this Court, as in *Farrah* [[1978] 2 SCR 638 (Que.)], has not hesitated to recognize this limitation on judicial review as serving the interests of an express legislative policy to protect decisions of adjudicative agencies from external correction. Thus, it has, in my opinion, balanced the competing interests of a provincial Legislature in its enactment of substantively valid legislation and of the Courts as ultimate interpreters of the *British North America Act, 1867*, and s. 96 thereof. The same considerations do not, however, apply to issues of jurisdiction which are not far removed from issues of constitutionality. It cannot be left to a provincial statutory tribunal, in the face of s. 96, to determine the limits of its own jurisdiction without appeal or review.

The third issue that emerges from the reasons of the Court of Appeal relates to the impact of the *Farrah* case. There, as here, the provincial Legislature established a statutory tribunal of appeal. The relevant statute, the Quebec *Transport Act, 1972* (Qué.), c. 55 [now RSQ 1977, c. T-12] confided to the Transport Tribunal, under s. 58(a) of the *Transport Act*, "jurisdiction to the exclusion of any other court, to hear and dispose of in appeal, on any question of law, any decision of the [Quebec Transport] Commission which terminates a matter." This authority was reinforced by the privative provisions of ss. 24 and 72 which, respectively, precluded recourse under arts. 834 to 850 of the *Code of Civil Procedure* as against the Commission and as against the Transport Tribunal. The effect of the foregoing provisions, taken together, was to transfer the supervisory jurisdiction of the Quebec Superior Court, as it existed at Confederation and afterwards, to the Transport Tribunal, and this was beyond provincial competence. It was a supporting consideration that s. 58(a) put the Transport Tribunal in place of the Quebec Court of Appeal to which there was previously a right of appeal on questions of law and of jurisdiction.

In short, what the *Farrah* case decided was that to give a provincially constituted statutory tribunal a jurisdiction in appeal on questions of law without limitation, and to reinforce this appellate authority by excluding any supervisory recourse to the Quebec Superior Court, was to create a s. 96 court. The present case is no different in principle, even though in ss. 162 and 175 of the *Professional Code*, dealing with the appellate authority of the Professions Tribunal, there is no mention of the word "law" or the word "jurisdiction." When regard is had to the privative terms of ss. 194 and 195, added to the fact that by s. 175 the Professions Tribunal's decisions are final, I see no significant distinction between the present case and the *Farrah* case in the fact that in the latter the authority granted to the appeal tribunal was "to the exclusion of any other court." In both cases there was a purported exclusion of the reviewing authority of any other court, whether by appeal or by evocation.

Appeal allowed.

Crevier: Context and Criticism

As the judgment of Laskin CJC indicates, prior to *Crevier* there had been considerable controversy among commentators about whether the right to judicial review of administrative agencies was constitutionally guaranteed. One school of thought—skeptical of the view that ss. 96-101 of the *Constitution Act, 1867* constrain the creation of administrative tribunals by provincial legislatures—was represented, rather ironically, by (then-Professor) Bora Laskin in "*Certiorari* to Labour Boards: The Apparent Futility of Privative Clauses" (1952), 30 *Can. Bar Rev.* 986, at 989-90:

> At the threshold of this inquiry it may be well to make the assertion that there is no constitutional principle on which courts can rest any claim to review administrative board decisions. In so far as such review is based on the historic supervisory authority of superior courts through the use of the prerogative writs of *certiorari* or their modern equivalents, it must bow to the higher authority of a legislature to withdraw this function from them. The question would then become whether the legislature has used apt words to effect this result. ...
>
> We may well feel that judicial supremacy is the highest of all values under a democratic regime of law, and a value to which even the legislature should pay tribute. But we have not enshrined it in any fundamental constitutional law or in our political system. On the contrary, the cardinal principle of our system of representative government, inherited from Great Britain, has been the supremacy of the legislature. ... We must not then delude ourselves that judicial review rests on any higher ground than that of being implicit in statutory interpretation.

An alternative perspective, this time expressed by Chief Justice Bora Laskin, appeared in (1977), 51 *Aust. LJ* 450. Here, Laskin CJC discussed the separation of powers under the Canadian constitution as follows (at 457):

> On the administrative agency side of the problem under discussion, it is obvious that such agencies cannot escape making determinations of law in the course of their regulatory or *quasi-judicial* operations, and to deny them such leeway would weaken considerably their utility. The reasonable compromise here is to deny them unreviewable authority to make such determina-

tions, and equally to deny them power to determine finally the limits of their jurisdiction. These are matters with which Canada is quite familiar without being bound by a strict separation of powers doctrine. They arise under accepted conceptions of administrative law and, as is well known, privative clauses have not proved very effective to oust all judicial review. ...

What might explain this evolution of Bora Laskin's perspective over the course of his legal career? The narrow point that was settled by *Crevier*, authored by Laskin CJC, is that a provincial legislature cannot insulate from review *on jurisdictional grounds* the decisions of a provincial appellate tribunal. Moreover, the Supreme Court of Canada seemed to indicate that the appellate jurisdiction of the Professions Tribunal in Quebec, even without a full privative clause, could only be conferred constitutionally on a s. 96 court. Indeed, there were lingering doubts after *Crevier* about the validity of provincial legislation that created administrative agencies with appellate powers: see, for example, *Reference Re Residential Tenancies Act (NS)* (1994), 115 DLR (4th) 129 (NS CA).

Commentators who had criticized the courts' previous interventions in the administrative process were dismayed that the Supreme Court of Canada entrenched in *Crevier* a constitutional right to judicial review on jurisdictional grounds. This was seen to reinforce the notion that administrative agencies and the courts are part of a single decision-making system of which the courts sit at the apex with "inferior tribunals" at the bottom. A stultifying implication of Dicey's version of the rule of law was thus incorporated, by an implied reading, into the constitution. See in particular, Arthurs, "Protection Against Judicial Review" (1983), 47 *La Revue du Barreau* 277. For other analyses of *Crevier*, see Mullan, "The Uncertain Constitutional Position of Canada's Administrative Appeal Tribunals" (1982), 14 *Ottawa L Rev.* 239, and Macdonald, "Comment" (1983), 17 *UBC L Rev.* 111. For an in-depth treatment of the constitutional justifications for judicial review in the United Kingdom context, see Elliott, *The Constitutional Foundations of Judicial Review* (Oxford: Hart Publishing, 2001).

An assessment of the significance of *Crevier* depends partly on one's sense of how courts will handle their authority to review for "jurisdictional" error. Even before *Crevier*, privative clauses were presumed, in spite of their clear wording to the contrary, not to oust the courts' right to determine whether an agency's decision was within its jurisdiction. Further, the courts interpreted statutory provisions—which on their face precluded judicial review of the proceedings or of decisions of a particular agency—as applicable only to those questions that were remitted expressly to the agency to decide. Thus, the courts assigned themselves as a backstop by scrutinizing any language in a statute that could be said to raise "preliminary" questions, deemed in turn to be outside the agency's jurisdiction.

If this constitutional power of judicial review were confined to guarding against procedural unfairness or bad faith decision making, and to ensuring that an exercise of authority was at least traceable to a granting power in a statute, then *Crevier* might be uncontroversial. Hogg (above, at 7-42, note 193) has criticized *Crevier*, however, on the grounds that the definition of jurisdictional error has been notoriously elusive and prone to judicial manipulation: "It is alarming that this concept should now be enshrined in our constitutional law, immune from legislative change." We discuss this history of jurisdictional review in chapter 12 of this text.

Crevier: Federalism or Separation of Powers?

The normative basis of the rule in *Crevier* is not clear. Was the court's concern that, by immunizing the Professions Tribunal from judicial review, the Québec legislature had conferred on the tribunal an essential characteristic of a superior court—namely, that its decisions were immune from judicial review and could only be challenged if there was a statutory right of appeal? Or was it that the power to review tribunals for jurisdictional error is part of the constitutionally guaranteed core of the authority of superior courts? In other words, is *Crevier* ultimately about preventing the provinces from encroaching on the federal government's power to appoint judges to the superior courts by the creation of tribunals that have an essential characteristic of superior courts? Or is it about protecting the individual's right to seek a determination from an independent judiciary—constituted under s. 96, with the attributes laid out in ss. 97-100—of the legality of administrative action?

Since *Crevier*, the case law has generally supported the view that the courts' power to subject tribunals to jurisdictional review has a constitutional foundation. That is, what was objectionable about the legislation considered in *Crevier* was that it purported to remove part of the courts' core jurisdiction, rather than that it made the Professions Tribunal the sole arbiter of the limits of its own statutory powers. While the original purpose of the judicature sections of the *Constitution Act, 1867* was probably to ensure a large measure of control by the federal government over the justice system, those sections are now understood primarily as entrenching the right of individuals to seek legal protection from an independent judiciary. See, for example, *UES, Local 298 v. Bibeault*, [1988] 2 SCR 1048, 1080 (Que.).

On this, note the statements in *Dunsmuir*, at para. 29 citing *Crevier* at 234, that the standard of review analysis "strives to determine what authority was intended to be given to the body in relation to the subject matter" and that "[t]his is done within the context of *the courts' constitutional duty to ensure that public authorities do not overreach their lawful powers*"; and, further, that "[t]he *inherent power of superior courts to review administrative action* and ensure that it does not exceed its jurisdiction stems from the judicature provisions in ss. 96 to 101 of the *Constitution Act, 1867*" (emphasis added). Recall also the statement of Binnie J in *Dunsmuir* (at para. 127):

> [T]he Constitution restricts the legislator's ability to allocate issues to administrative bodies which s. 96 of the *Constitution Act, 1867* has allocated to the courts. The logic of the constitutional limitation is obvious. If the limitation did not exist, the government could transfer the work of the courts to administrative bodies that are not independent of the executive and by statute immunize the decisions of these bodies from effective judicial review. The country would still possess an independent judiciary, but the courts would not be available to citizens whose rights or interests are trapped in the administration.

If the Supreme Court of Canada has endorsed the view that, implicit in ss. 96-100, there is a constitutionally guaranteed right of an individual to seek judicial review of administrative action on the grounds of jurisdictional error or illegality, then two practical consequences follow. The first is that *Crevier* extends to all administrative decision-makers, including tribunals with original decision-making authority (that is, not just appellate tribunals) as well as public bodies that are vested with wide statutory discretion (such as ministers and municipalities), whether or not they are required to hold a hearing before exercising their powers.

The second consequence is that it also applies to judicial review of federal administrative agencies. That is, if the concepts of the rule of law and a notion of the separation of powers are the normative basis for *Crevier*, then a constitutional right to judicial review for jurisdictional error should apply to federal tribunals and agencies, as well as those established by provincial legislation. On the other hand, if review for jurisdictional error were based only on the view that s. 96 implicitly prohibits the conferral of a superior court power on another body, a federal tribunal would probably not fall within the words "a superior, district or county court *in each province*." Moreover, s. 101 of the *Constitution Act, 1867* expressly enables Parliament, "notwithstanding anything in this Act," to create "additional courts for the better administration of the laws of Canada."

CHAPTER TEN

Expertise and Statutory Purpose

INTRODUCTION

In this chapter we examine two of the factors in the standard of review analysis. The first is the expertise of the administrative decision-maker as measured by the court in light of relevant statutory provisions and relative to the court's understanding of its own expertise. Indicators of expertise may be present in the statute itself, but may also emerge from the court's understanding of the legislature's aim when it created a statutory regime and the relevant decision-makers within it. In the words of McLachlin CJC in *Dr. Q v. College of Physicians and Surgeons of British Columbia*, [2003] 1 SCR 226, at para. 29:

> Relative expertise can arise from a number of sources .... The composition of an administrative body might endow it with knowledge uniquely suited to the questions put before it and deference might, therefore, be called for .... For example, a statute may call for decision-makers to have expert qualifications, to have accumulated experience in a particular area, or to play a particular role in policy development .... Similarly, an administrative body might be so habitually called upon to make findings of fact in a distinctive legislative context that it can be said to have gained a measure of relative institutional expertise .... Simply put, "whether because of the specialized knowledge of its decision-makers, special procedure, or non-judicial means of implementing the Act," an administrative body called upon to answer a question that falls within its area of relative expertise will generally be entitled to greater curial deference.

Closely connected to the consideration of expertise is consideration of the purpose of a decision-maker as determined by its enabling legislation. This factor was not examined in great detail in *Dunsmuir* but has long history in the pragmatic and functional approach. An assessment of statutory purpose does not itself determine the standard of review without resort to other factors. However, it can provide important support for the assessment of other aspects of the decision-making process and, more generally, for the court's characterization of the role of a decision-maker in its regulatory field.

We present these two factors by reviewing their origins in Supreme Court of Canada decisions on deference in substantive review. While the factor of statutory purpose has been integral to the court's approach to deference since the *CUPE* decision of 1979, expertise came to the fore more recently, in the mid-1990s, with the decisions in *Pezim* and *Southam*. Recall that these latter decisions were the focal point of disagreement on the court in *Dunsmuir* between, on the one hand, the view of Deschamps and Rothstein JJ—who reject the role of a broader inquiry into expertise by courts in favour of a more strict set of presumptions about legislative intent—and the majority view, which retained expertise as an important component and justification for deference.

EXPERTISE AS A FACTOR IN THE STANDARD OF REVIEW ANALYSIS

The expertise of an administrative decision-maker may arise in various ways. It may be traced to the personal and professional background of an individual member of a tribunal or member. More commonly, it is recognized in the collective history and institutional memory of a decision-maker and its membership as a whole. Expertise may relate to a superior technical capacity or understanding in a particular subject matter, but may also follow from the "field sensitivity" that a decision-maker acquires from years of operation in its assigned area of specialization. These markers of expertise are not always clearly present in a case, nor do they necessarily offer a compelling rationale for deference where other characteristics—such as a lack of independence or electoral accountability—call for final decisions to be taken elsewhere. But they can weigh in favour of the courts accepting that the legislature has assigned certain tasks to a tribunal or agency, in part because the legislature itself has recognized the superior expertise and thus capability of that entity.

In this respect, the consideration of expertise requires a court to put itself into the mind of the legislature at the time that it created or subsequently endorsed a statutory regime. It looks to explicit markers in the statute to guide itself in this manner, such as a provision that states expressly the type of expertise that members of tribunal possess, or at least should possess, as a condition of their appointments. Also, a court may find indirect indicators of the legislature's intentions, such as a requirement that a tribunal include members who are lawyers or judges (thus indicating a degree of preference for legal expertise) or in more general statements about the aims and purpose of the statute. In turn, statutory markers of expertise also contribute to an understanding of the intentions of the legislature when it established the statutory regime. Expertise and statutory purpose are thus closely related.

By its silence on statutory rights of appeal, combined with its endorsement of judicial respect for the expertise of tribunals, *Dunsmuir* retains expertise as an important factor in the standard of review analysis. According to the majority reasons of Bastarache and LeBel JJ in *Dunsmuir*, at para. 55, the existence of a "discrete and special administrative regime in which the decision-maker has special expertise (labour relations for instance)" is a consideration that may lead to deference based on a reasonableness standard. The rationale for this is stated at para. 49:

> Deference in the context of the reasonableness standard therefore implies that courts will give due consideration to the determinations of decision makers. As Mullan explains, a policy of deference "recognizes the reality that, in many instances, those working day to day in the implementation of frequently complex administrative schemes have or will develop a considerable degree of expertise or field sensitivity to the imperatives and nuances of the legislative regime": D.J. Mullan, "Establishing the Standard of Review: The Struggle for Complexity?" (2004), 17 *CJALP* 59, at p. 93. In short, deference requires respect for the legislative choices to leave some matters in the hands of administrative decision makers, for the processes and determinations that draw on particular expertise and experiences, and for the different roles of the courts and administrative bodies within the Canadian constitutional system.

Additionally, the majority in *Dunsmuir*, at para. 54, concluded that deference will usually extend to the resolution of questions of law "where a tribunal is interpreting its own statute or statutes closely connected to its function, with which it will have particular familiarity" or "where an administrative tribunal has developed particular expertise in the application of a general common law or civil law rule in relation to a specific statutory context." The role of adjudicators in labour law was highlighted as an example.

These references draw on past Supreme Court decisions that established the pragmatic and functional approach to judicial review. Two decisions, in particular, were important markers of the court's endorsement of deference on questions of law, as well as questions of fact or mixed questions, even in the absence of a privative clause and in the face of a broad right of appeal. This more flexible approach to deference arose from the court's acknowledgment that some administrative actors develop highly specialized expertise going beyond that of a generalist court. More fundamentally, the court accepted implicitly that the court-based model is not always the most effective or appropriate means of decision making and that administrative arrangements deserve respect in their own right where they have been created by legislatures to govern economic and social affairs.

THE DECISIONS IN PEZIM AND SOUTHAM

Pezim v. British Columbia (Superintendent of Brokers)
[1994] 2 SCR 557 (BC)

[The BC Securities Commission had found that the respondents (Pezim and others) had failed to make timely disclosure in respect of certain transactions as required by the *Securities Act*, SBC 1985, c. 83. As a result, it suspended them from trading in shares for a year and ordered them to pay costs. The respondents exercised their right under s. 149 of the *Securities Act* to appeal this decision on questions of law to the Court of Appeal, with leave of that court. They argued that the commission had erred in law in its interpretation of the phrase "material change" in the affairs of a reporting issuer of shares. The Court of Appeal allowed the appeal (1992), 96 DLR (4th) 137 (BC CA), and the superintendent and the commission appealed to the Supreme Court of Canada.]

IACOBUCCI J:

. . .

1. *What is the appropriate standard of review for an appellate court reviewing a decision of a securities commission not protected by a privative clause when there exists a statutory right of appeal and where the case turns on a question of interpretation?*

In order to answer this first question, I should like to discuss a number of factors and principles which come into play.

A. The Nature of the Statute

It is important to note from the outset that the *Securities Act* is regulatory in nature. In fact, it is part of a much larger framework which regulates the securities industry throughout Canada. Its primary goal is the protection of the investor but other goals include capital market efficiency and ensuring public confidence in the system.

Within this large framework of securities regulation, there are various government administrative agencies which are responsible for the securities legislation within their respective jurisdictions. The British Columbia Securities Commission is one such agency. Also within this large framework are self-regulatory organizations which possess the power to admit and discipline members and issuers. The VSE falls under this head. Having regard to this rather elaborate framework, it is not surprising that securities regulation is a highly specialized activity which requires specific knowledge and expertise in what have become complex and essential capital and financial markets.

B. Principles of Judicial Review

From the outset, it is important to set forth certain principles of judicial review. There exist various standards of review with respect to the myriad of administrative agencies that exist in our country. The central question in ascertaining the standard of review is to determine the legislative intent in conferring jurisdiction on the administrative tribunal. In answering this question, the courts have looked at various factors. Included in the analysis is an examination of the tribunal's role or function. Also crucial is whether or not the agency's decisions are protected by a privative clause. Finally, of fundamental importance, is whether or not the question goes to the jurisdiction of the tribunal involved.

Having regard to the large number of factors relevant in determining the applicable standard of review, the courts have developed a spectrum that ranges from the standard of reasonableness to that of correctness. Courts have also enunciated a principle of deference that applies not just to the facts as found by the tribunal, but also to the legal questions before the tribunal in the light of its role and expertise. At the reasonableness end of the spectrum, where deference is at its highest, are those cases where a tribunal protected by a true privative clause, is deciding a matter within its jurisdiction and where there is no statutory right of appeal. [The cases cited for this proposition are omitted.]

At the correctness end of the spectrum, where deference in terms of legal questions is at its lowest, are those cases where the issues concern the interpretation of a provision limiting the tribunal's jurisdiction (jurisdictional error) or where there is a statutory right of appeal which allows the reviewing court to substitute its opinion for that of the tribunal and where the tribunal has no greater expertise than the court on the issue in question, as for example in the area of human rights. See for example *Zurich Insurance Co. v. Ontario (Human Rights Commission)* [1992] 2 SCR 321, *Canada (Attorney General) v. Mossop* [1993] 1 SCR 554 and *University of British Columbia v. Berg* [1993] 2 SCR 353.

The case at bar falls between these two extremes. On one hand, we are dealing with a statutory right of appeal pursuant to s. 149 of the *Securities Act*. On the other hand, we are dealing with an appeal from a highly specialized tribunal on an issue which arguably goes to the core of its regulatory mandate and expertise.

[Iacobucci J here quoted from Gonthier J's judgment in *Bell Canada*.]

Consequently, even where there is no privative clause and where there is a statutory right of appeal, the concept of the specialization of duties requires that deference be shown to decisions of specialized tribunals on matters which fall squarely within the tribunal's expertise.

. . .

In my view, the pragmatic or functional approach articulated in *UES, Local 963 v. Bibeault* [1988] 2 SCR 1048 is also helpful in determining the standard of review applicable in this case. At p. 1088 of that decision, Beetz J, writing for the Court, stated the following:

> … the Court examines not only the wording of the enactment conferring jurisdiction on the administrative tribunal, but the purpose of the statute creating the tribunal, the reason for its existence, the area of expertise of its members and the nature of the problem before the tribunal.

As already mentioned, the primary goal of securities legislation is the protection of the investing public. The importance of that goal in assessing the decisions of securities commissions has been recognized by this Court in *Brosseau v. Alberta Securities Commission* [1989] 1 SCR 301 … , where L'Heureux-Dubé J, writing for the Court, stated the following at p. 314:

> Securities acts in general can be said to be aimed at regulating the market and protecting the general public. This role was recognized by this Court in *Gregory & Co. v. Quebec Securities Commission* [1961] SCR 584, where Fauteux J observed at p. 588:
>
> > The paramount object of the Act is to ensure that persons who, in the province, carry on the business of trading in securities or acting as investment counsel, shall be honest and of good repute and, in this way, to protect the public, in the province or elsewhere, from being defrauded as a result of certain activities initiated in the province by persons therein carrying on such a business.
>
> This protective role, common to all securities commissions, gives a special character to such bodies which must be recognized when assessing the way in which their functions are carried out under their Acts.

In *National Corn Growers Assn. v. Canada (Import Tribunal)* [1990] 2 SCR 1324 at pp. 1369-70, L'Heureux-Dubé J, in a concurring judgment, referred at p. 1336 to financial markets as a field where specialized tribunals have an important role to play:

> Canadian courts have struggled over time to move away from the picture that Dicey painted toward a more sophisticated understanding of the role of administrative tribunals in the modern Canadian state. Part of this process has involved a growing recognition on the part of courts that they may simply not be as well equipped as administrative tribunals or agencies to deal with issues which Parliament has chosen to regulate through bodies exercising delegated power, e.g., labour relations, telecommunications, *financial markets* and international economic relations. Careful management of these sectors often requires the use of experts who have accumulated years of experience and a specialized understanding of the activities they supervise.
>
> Courts have also come to accept that they may not be as well qualified as a given agency to provide interpretations of that agency's constitutive statute that make sense given the broad policy context within which that agency must work. [Emphasis added.]

The breadth of the Commission's expertise and specialisation is reflected in the provisions of the *Securities Act*. Section 4 of the Act identifies the Commission as being responsible for the administration of the Act. The Commission also has broad powers with respect to investigations, audits, hearings and orders. Section 144.2 provides that any decision of the Commission filed in the Registry of the Supreme Court of British Columbia has the force and effect of a decision of that court. Finally, pursuant to s. 153 of the Act, the Commission has the power to revoke or vary any of its decisions. Sections 14 and 144 are of particular importance as they reveal the breadth of the Commission's public interest mandate:

14(1) The commission may, where it considers it to be in the public interest, make any decision respecting

(a) a bylaw, rule or other regulatory instrument or policy, or a direction, decision, order or ruling made under a bylaw, rule or other regulatory instrument or policy, of a self regulatory body or stock exchange,

(b) the procedures or practices of a self regulatory body or stock exchange,

(c) the manner in which a stock exchange carries on business,

(d) the trading of securities on or through the facilities of a stock exchange,

(e) a security listed and posted for trading on a stock exchange, and

(f) issuers, whose securities are listed and posted for trading on a stock exchange, to ensure that they comply with this Act and the regulations.

(2) A person affected by a decision made by the commission under subsection (1) shall act in accordance with it.

144(1) Where the commission or the superintendent considers it to be in the public interest, the commission or the superintendent, after a hearing, may order

(a) that a person comply with or cease contravening, and that the directors and senior officers of the person cause the person to comply with or cease contravening,

(i) a provision of this Act or the regulations,

(ii) a decision, whether or not the decision has been filed under section 144.2, or

(iii) a bylaw, rule, or other regulatory instrument or policy or a direction, decision, order or ruling made under a bylaw, rule or other regulatory instrument or policy of a self regulatory body or stock exchange, as the case may be, which has been recognized by the commission under section 11,

(b) that

(i) all persons

(ii) the person or persons named in the order, or

(iii) one or more classes of persons cease trading in a specified security or in a class of security,

(c) that any or all of the exemptions described in any of sections 30 to 21, 55, 58, 80 or 81 do not apply to a person,

(d) that a person

(i) resign any position that the person holds as a director or officer of an issuer, and

(ii) is prohibited from becoming or acting as a director or officer of any issuer, …

. . .

In reading these powerful provisions, it is clear that it was the legislature's intention to give the Commission a very broad discretion to determine what is in the public's interest. To me, this is an additional basis for judicial deference.

It must also be noted that the definitions in the *Securities Act* exist in a factual or regulatory context. They are part of the larger regulatory framework discussed above. They are not to be analyzed in isolation but rather in their regulatory context. This is something that requires expertise and thus falls within the jurisdiction of the Commission. This is yet another basis for curial deference.

[Iacobucci J cited a list of cases, which has been omitted.]

C. The Role of the Commission

Where a tribunal plays a role in policy development, a higher degree of judicial deference is warranted with respect to its interpretation of the law. This was stated by the majority of this Court in *United Brotherhood of Carpenters and Joiners of America, Local 579 v. Bradco Construction Ltd.* [1993] 2 SCR 316 at pp. 336-37:

> ... a distinction can be drawn between arbitrators, appointed on an *ad hoc* basis to decide a particular dispute arising under a collective agreement, and labour relations boards responsible for overseeing the ongoing interpretation of legislation and development of labour relations policy and precedent within a given labour jurisdiction. *To the latter, and other similar specialized tribunals responsible for the regulation of a specific industrial or technological sphere, a greater degree of deference is due their interpretation of the law notwithstanding the absence of a privative clause.* [Emphasis added.]

In the case at bar, the Commission's primary role is to administer and apply the *Securities Act*. It also plays a policy development role. Thus, this is an additional basis for deference. However, it is important to note that the Commission's policy-making role is limited. By that I mean that their policies cannot be elevated to the status of law; they are not to be treated as legal pronouncements absent legal authority mandating such treatment.

Thus on precedent, principle and policy, I conclude as a general proposition that the decisions of the Commission, falling within its expertise, warrant judicial deference.

D. The Questions of Law at Issue

As mentioned above, it is also necessary to focus on the specific question of law at issue to determine whether it falls within the tribunal's expertise and whether deference is warranted. The specific sections at issue in this case are ss. 67, 144 and 154.2 of the *Securities Act*.

The decision to make an order and the precise nature of that order, under s. 144, as well as any decision obliging a person to pay the costs of a hearing necessitated by his or her conduct, pursuant to s. 154.2, are clearly within the jurisdiction and expertise of the Commission. The other provision at issue is s. 67 which involves an interpretation of the words "material change" and "as soon as practicable."

Both "material change" and "material fact" are defined in s. 1 of the Act. They are defined in terms of the significance of their impact on the market price or value of the securities of an issuer. The definition of "material fact" is broader than that of "material change"; it encompasses any fact that can "reasonably be expected to significantly affect" the market price or value of the securities of an issuer, and not only changes "in the business, operations, assets or ownership of the issuer" that would reasonably be expected to have such an effect.

· · ·

As already mentioned, the present case turns partly on the definition of "material change." Three elements emerge from that definition: the change must be (a) "in relation to the affairs of an issuer," (b) "in the business, operations, assets or ownership of the issuer" and (c) material, i.e., would reasonably be expected to have a significant effect on the market price or value of the securities of the issuer. Thus, not all changes are material changes; the latter are set in the context of making sure that issuers keep investors up to date. Consequently, it would seem wholly uncontroversial that the determination of what information should be disclosed is an issue which goes to the heart of the regulatory expertise and mandate of the Commission, i.e., regulating the securities markets in the public's interest.

This case also turns on the meaning of the words "as soon as practicable" in s. 67 of the Act which reveal when a material change should be disclosed to the public. In my view, the timeliness of disclosure also falls within the Commission's regulatory jurisdiction.

In summary, having regard to the nature of the securities industry, the Commission's specialization of duties and policy development role as well as the nature of the problem before the court, considerable deference is warranted in the present case notwithstanding the fact that there is a statutory right of appeal and there is no privative clause.

[Iacobucci J then turned to the second question, whether the Court of Appeal had applied the appropriate standard of review to the commission's determinations. He concluded that, in rejecting the commission's view and substituting its own, "[t]he majority of the Court of Appeal erred in failing to appreciate the commission's role in an area requiring special knowledge and sophistication" (at 609). Iacobucci J clearly intimated that, on the principal points in dispute, he thought that the commission's interpretation was right and the Court of Appeal's wrong.]

Appeal allowed.

NOTES

1. Do you agree with this extension of the principle of deference or does it perhaps flout the legislative intention that aggrieved parties are entitled to have the merits of disputed determinations resolved by a court? Is it a case of the court allowing its conceptions of expertise to override a clear legislative signpost, as Rothstein J suggested in *Khosa* (see chapter 8 of this text)?

2. We see in *Pezim* a discussion of the expertise of securities commissions but also of the link between that expertise and the purpose of a specialized regime for securities regulation.

According to Iacobucci J, the primary goal of securities regulation is "the protection of the investing public" and the importance of that goal calls for respect to the decision-makers charged by the legislature with achieving it. Thus, Iacobucci J says, the "protective role, common to all securities commissions, gives a special character to such bodies which must be recognized when assessing the way in which their functions are carried out under their Acts." In this respect, a wider reading of the purpose of the BC *Securities Act* was a major factor in the decision to elevate the significance of expertise as a factor in the court's doctrine of judicial deference.

3. As mentioned, *Pezim* was groundbreaking because it established that courts should defer to an agency's resolution of an issue of statutory interpretation even in the face of a right of appeal on such issues. Since that time, the principle of deference to agency determinations even on questions of law has been consolidated, culminating in the statements in *Dunsmuir* and *Khosa* that administrative decision-makers enjoy a margin of appreciation when interpreting their home statutes or other statutes closely related to their functions. The significance of the decision in *Southam*, which closely followed *Pezim*, was to discuss further the basis for deference based on expertise.

Incidentally, *Southam* is also significant because it introduced the third "middle" standard, reasonableness *simpliciter*, in Canadian judicial review (*Pezim* did not articulate a standard of review, referring instead to a need for "considerable deference"). As such, *Southam* provides an interesting supplement to our discussion of the nature of the question in chapter 11 of this text. Recall however that this middle standard—along with the highly deferential standard of patent unreasonableness—have been replaced in *Dunsmuir* with the single standard of reasonableness. Likewise, one's approach to the application of the standard of reasonableness should now look first to *Dunsmuir* and to the post-*Dunsmuir* jurisprudence, and only secondarily, if at all, to *Southam*.

Canada (Director of Investigation and Research) v. Southam Inc.
[1997] 1 SCR 748 (Can.)

[Vancouver's two daily newspapers (owned by Southam Inc.) were less successful, when compared with daily newspapers in other regions of Canada, relative to smaller community newspapers circulating in their distribution area. The community newspapers differed from the dailies in that they served a smaller area, were distributed free of charge, and were printed from one to three times a week. In 1989, Southam Inc. began to acquire community and specialized newspapers in the area, and one year later had obtained a controlling interest in 13 community newspapers (including the two strongest ones, the *North Shore News* and the *Vancouver Courier*), a real estate advertising publication, three distribution services, and two printing concerns. Southam Inc. also established a local supplement to one of its dailies but eventually discontinued it.

The respondent applied for an order requiring Southam to divest itself of the *North Shore News*, the *Vancouver Courier*, and the *Real Estate Weekly*, alleging that the concentration of these properties in the hands of one publisher was likely to lessen competition substantially in the retail print advertising and real estate print advertising markets in the Lower Mainland. The Competition Tribunal found a substantial lessening in competition in the real estate print advertising market in the North Shore. It ordered Southam to divest itself, at its option, of either the *North Shore News* or the *Real Estate Weekly*. It rejected Southam's proposal that it sell the real estate section of the *North Shore News*. The director of investigation and research appealed the tribunal's decision on the merits and Southam appealed the tribunal's decision on the remedy. The Federal Court of Appeal allowed the first appeal and dismissed the second.

The appeal to the Supreme Court of Canada raised two issues. The first was whether the Federal Court of Appeal erred in concluding that it owed no deference to the tribunal's finding about the dimensions of the relevant market and in subsequently substituting for that finding one of its own. The second was whether the Federal Court of Appeal erred in refusing to set aside the tribunal's remedial order. (Taken from the headnote.)]

IACOBUCCI J: ...

5. *Analysis*

The principal question in this appeal concerns the limits that an appellate court should observe in deciding a statutory appeal from a decision like the one that the Tribunal reached in this case. Ultimately, this comes down to a question about the standard of review that an appellate court should apply in a case such as this one. In the reasons that follow, the answer given is that the Tribunal should be held to the standard of reasonableness *simpliciter*. In other words, a court, in reviewing the Tribunal's decision, must inquire whether that decision was reasonable. If it was, then the decision should stand. Otherwise, it must fall.

The secondary question is whether the Tribunal chose an appropriate remedy. My conclusion is that, even though the Tribunal imposed too strict a test, its chosen remedy is appropriate.

A. *Statutory Right of Appeal*

In *Pezim v. British Columbia (Superintendent of Brokers)* [1994] 2 SCR 557 (BC), a decision which, like this one, concerned a decision of an expert tribunal that was subject to a statutory right of appeal, the Court declared that the standard of review is a function of many factors. Depending on how the factors play out in a particular instance, the standard may fall somewhere between correctness, at the more exacting end of the spectrum, and patently unreasonable, at the more deferential end. ...

An appellate court must consider the factors with a view to determining the approach that it should take as a court sitting in appeal of the decision of the tribunal. There is no privative clause, and so jurisdiction is not at issue. The tribunal enjoys jurisdiction by virtue of its constating statute and the appellate court enjoys jurisdiction by virtue of a statutory right of appeal. The legislative intent is clear. The question is what limits an appellate court should observe in the exercise of its statutorily mandated appellate function.

I wish to emphasize that in cases like the instant appeal no question arises about the extent of the tribunal's jurisdiction. Where the statute confers a right of appeal, an appellate court need not look to see whether the tribunal has exceeded its jurisdiction by breaching the rules of natural justice or by rendering a decision that is patently unreasonable. The manner and standard of review will be determined in the way that appellate courts generally determine the posture they will take with respect to the decisions of courts below. In particular, appellate courts must have regard to the nature of the problem, to the applicable law properly interpreted in the light of its purpose, and to the expertise of the tribunal.

I propose to consider each of the relevant factors in turn.

B. The Nature of the Problem Before the Tribunal

The parties vigorously dispute the nature of the problem before the Tribunal. The appellants say that the problem is one of fact. The respondent insists that the problem is one of law. In my view, the problem is one of mixed law and fact.

Section 12(1) of the *Competition Tribunal Act* contemplates a tripartite classification of questions before the Tribunal into questions of law, questions of fact, and questions of mixed law and fact. Briefly stated, questions of law are questions about what the correct legal test is; questions of fact are questions about what actually took place between the parties; and questions of mixed law and fact are questions about whether the facts satisfy the legal tests. A simple example will illustrate these concepts. In the law of tort, the question what "negligence" means is a question of law. The question whether the defendant did this or that is a question of fact. And, once it has been decided that the applicable standard is one of negligence, the question whether the defendant satisfied the appropriate standard of care is a question of mixed law and fact. I recognize, however, that the distinction between law on the one hand and mixed law and fact on the other is difficult. On occasion, what appears to be mixed law and fact turns out to be law, or vice versa.

For example, the majority of the British Columbia Court of Appeal in *Pezim, supra*, concluded that it was an error of law to regard newly acquired information on the value of assets as a "material change" in the affairs of a company. It was common ground in that case that the proper test was whether the information constituted a material change; the argument was about whether the acquisition of information of a certain kind qualified as such a change. To some extent, then, the question resembled one of mixed law and fact. But the question was one of law, in part because the words in question were present in a statutory provision and questions of statutory interpretation are generally questions of law, but also because the point in controversy was one that might potentially arise in many cases in the future: the argument was about kinds of information and not merely about the particular information that was at issue in that case. The rule on which the British Columbia Securities Commission seemed to rely—that newly acquired information about the value of assets can constitute a material change—was a matter of law, because it had the potential to apply widely to many cases.

By contrast, the matrices of facts at issue in some cases are so particular, indeed so unique, that decisions about whether they satisfy legal tests do not have any great precedential value. If a court were to decide that driving at a certain speed on a certain road under certain conditions was negligent, its decision would not have any great value as a precedent. In short, as the level of generality of the challenged proposition approaches utter particularity, the matter approaches pure application, and hence draws nigh to being an unqualified question of mixed law and fact. See R.P. Kerans, *Standards of Review Employed by Appellate Courts* (1994) at 103-108. Of course, it is not easy to say precisely where the line should be drawn; though in most cases it should be sufficiently clear whether the dispute is over a general proposition that might qualify as a principle of law or over a very particular set of circumstances that is not apt to be of much interest to judges and lawyers in the future.

Part of the confusion in this case arises from the fact that the parties are arguing about two different questions. On the surface, it appears that the parties agree about the law: both say that, in determining the dimensions of the relevant market, the Tribunal must consider indirect evidence of cross-elasticity of demand. No one quarrels with the Tribunal's understanding of the kinds of indirect evidence it should consider.

However, the respondent says that, having informed itself correctly on the law, the Tribunal proceeded nevertheless to ignore certain kinds of indirect evidence. Because the Tribunal must be judged according to what it does and not according to what it says, the import of the respondent's submission is that the Tribunal erred in law. After all, if a decision-maker says that the correct test requires him or her to consider A, B, C, and D, but in fact the decision-maker considers only A, B, and C, then the outcome is as if he or she had applied a law that required consideration of only A, B, and C. If the correct test requires him or her to consider D as well, then the decision-maker has in effect applied the wrong law, and so has made an error of law.

The appellants, for their part, maintain that the Tribunal considered all the relevant kinds of indirect evidence, including the kinds that the respondent says it ignored. Accordingly, the appellants argue that if the Tribunal erred, it can only have been in applying the correct legal test to the facts. Such an error, say the appellants, is an error of fact. As authority for their position, they cite a passage from the decision of this Court in *R v. Nova Scotia Pharmaceutical Society* [1992] 2 SCR 606 (NS) at 647:

> In the context of s. 32(1)(c), the process followed and the criteria used to arrive at a determination of "undueness" are questions of law and as such are reviewable by an appellate court. The application of this process and these criteria, that is the full inquiry, often involving complicated economic issues, into whether the impugned agreement was an undue restriction on competition, remains a question of fact. The general rule that appellate courts should be reluctant to venture into a re-examination of the factual conclusions of the trial judge applies with special force in a complex matter such as here.

Both positions, so far as they go, are correct. If the Tribunal did ignore items of evidence that the law requires it to consider, then the Tribunal erred in law. Similarly, if the Tribunal considered all the mandatory kinds of evidence but still reached the wrong conclusion, then its error was one of mixed law and fact. The question, then, becomes whether the Tribunal erred in the way that the respondent says it erred.

Even a cursory reading of the Tribunal's reasons discloses that the Tribunal did not fail to consider relevant items of evidence. The respondent charges—and the Federal Court of Appeal agreed with him on this point—that the Tribunal ignored evidence of functional interchangeability and of inter-industry competition. But this overlooks the 14 pages that the Tribunal devoted to functional interchangeability, and the 28 pages that the Tribunal devoted to inter-industry competition. See 191-218 and 225-38. A great part, if not actually the bulk of the Tribunal's decision is taken up with an examination of the very factors that the respondent says it ignored. Therefore, the Tribunal did not err in law by failing to consider relevant factors.

The suggestion remains, however, that the Tribunal might have erred in law by failing to accord adequate weight to certain factors. The problem with this suggestion is that it is inimical to the very notion of a balancing test. A balancing test is a legal rule whose application should be subtle and flexible, but not mechanical. It would be dangerous in the extreme to accord certain kinds of evidence decisive weight as, for example, by saying that evidence of inter-industry competition should always be sufficient to prove that two companies are operating in the same market. A test would be stilted and impossible of application if it purported to assign fixed weights to certain factors as, for example, by saying that evidence of inter-industry competition should weigh 10 times as heavily in the Tribunal's deliberations as does evidence of physical similarities between the products in question. These sorts of things are not readily quantifiable. They should not be considered as matters of law but should be left initially at least to determination by the Tribunal. The most that can be said, as a matter of law, is that the Tribunal should consider each factor; but the according of weight to the factors should be left to the Tribunal.

It seems, then, that if the Tribunal erred, it was in applying the law to the facts; and that is a matter of mixed law and fact. This is especially so if, as here, the legal principle being applied involves a balancing test, because with a typical multi-factored balancing test so many factors weigh in the balance that a duplication of any one set of relevant circumstances in the future is unlikely. At the outside, the decision of the Tribunal in this case stands for the proposition that a large daily newspaper does not compete for retail advertising business with small community newspapers though probably it does not stand even for so general a proposition as that, because the Tribunal's decision rested in part on its assessment of the behaviour of these parties. Depending as it does so fully on the facts and circumstances of the case, the decision is too particular to have any great value as a general precedent.

In short, the Tribunal forged no new legal principle, and so its error, if there was an error, can only have been of mixed law and fact. It should be noted that no one has suggested that the Tribunal erred in its findings of fact. All of this tends to suggest that some measure of deference is owed to the decision of the Tribunal because, to paraphrase what Gonthier J stated in *Nova Scotia Pharmaceutical Society, supra*, appellate courts should be reluctant to venture into a re-examination of the conclusions of the Tribunal on questions of mixed law and fact.

C. The Words of the Tribunal's Constating Statute

Section 13 of the *Competition Tribunal Act* confers a right of appeal from orders and decisions of the Tribunal:

> 13(1) Subject to subsection (2), an appeal lies to the Federal Court of Appeal from any decision or order, whether final, interlocutory or interim, of the Tribunal as if it were a judgment of the Federal Court—Trial Division.
>
> (2) An appeal on a question of fact lies under subsection (1) only with the leave of the Federal Court of Appeal.

That Parliament granted such a broad, even unfettered right of appeal, as if from a judgment of a trial court, perhaps counsels a less-than-deferential posture for appellate courts than would be appropriate if a privative clause were present. However, as this Court has noted several times recently, the absence of a privative clause does not settle the question. See *Pezim, supra*, at 591; *Bell Canada v. Canada (Canadian Radio-television and Telecommunications Commission)* [1989] 1 SCR 1722 (Can) at 1746.

D. The Purpose of the Statute That the Tribunal Administers

Parliament has described the purpose of the *Competition Act* in the following terms:

> 1.1 The purpose of this Act is to maintain and encourage competition in Canada in order to promote the efficiency and adaptability of the Canadian economy, in order to expand opportunities for Canadian participation in world markets while at the same time recognizing the role of foreign competition in Canada, in order to ensure that small and medium-sized enterprises have an equitable opportunity to participate in the Canadian economy and in order to provide consumers with competitive prices and product choices.

Competition Act, s. 1.1, as am. by RSC 1985, c. 19, s. 19 (2nd Supp.).

The aims of the Act are more "economic" than they are strictly "legal." The "efficiency and adaptability of the Canadian economy" and the relationships among Canadian companies and their foreign competitors are matters that business women and men and economists are better able to understand than is a typical judge. Perhaps recognizing this, Parliament created a specialized Competition Tribunal and invested it with responsibility for the administration of the civil part of the *Competition Act*. See *Competition Tribunal Act*, s. 8(1).

This Court has said in the past that the Tribunal is especially well-suited to the task of overseeing a complex statutory scheme whose objectives are peculiarly economic:

> Section 8(1) [of the *Competition Tribunal Act*] confirms the jurisdiction of the Tribunal over Part VIII. The civil part of the [*Competition Act*] therefore falls entirely under the Tribunal's jurisdiction. It is readily apparent from the [*Competition Act*] and the [*Competition Tribunal Act*] that Parliament created the Tribunal as a specialized body to deal solely and exclusively with Part VIII [of the *Competition Act*], since it involves complex issues of competition law, such as abuses of dominant position and mergers.

Chrysler Canada Ltd. v. Canada (Competition Tribunal) [1992] 2 SCR 394 (Can.) at 406.

Because an appellate court is likely to encounter difficulties in understanding the economic and commercial ramifications of the Tribunal's decisions and consequently to be less able to secure the fulfilment of the purpose of the *Competition Act* than is the Tribunal, the natural inference is that the purpose of the Act is better served by appellate deference to the Tribunal's decisions.

E. The Area of the Tribunal's Expertise

Expertise, which in this case overlaps with the purpose of the statute that the tribunal administers, is the most important of the factors that a court must consider in settling on a standard of review. This Court has said as much several times before, though perhaps never so clearly as in the following passage, from *United Brotherhood of Carpenters and Joiners of America, Local 579 v. Bradco Construction Ltd.* [1993] 2 SCR 316 (Nfld.) at 335:

> ... the expertise of the tribunal is of the utmost importance in determining the intention of the legislator with respect to the degree of deference to be shown to a tribunal's decision in the absence of a full privative clause. Even where the tribunal's enabling statute provides explicitly for appellate review, as was the case in *Bell Canada* ..., it has been stressed that deference should be shown by the appellate tribunal to the opinions of the specialized lower tribunal on matters squarely within its jurisdiction.

As I have already said, the Tribunal's expertise lies in economics and in commerce. The Tribunal comprises not more than four judicial members, all of whom are judges of the Federal Court—Trial Division, and not more than eight lay members, who are appointed on the advice of a council of persons learned in "economics, industry, commerce or public affairs." See *Competition Tribunal Act*, s. 3. The preponderance of lay members reflects the judgment of Parliament that, for purposes of administering the *Competition Act*, economic or commercial expertise is more desirable and important than legal acumen.

The particular dispute in this case concerns the definition of the relevant product market—a matter that falls squarely within the area of the Tribunal's economic or commercial expertise. Undeniably, the determination of cross-elasticity of demand, which is in theory the truest *indicium* of the dimensions of a product market, requires some economic or statistical skill. But even an assessment of indirect evidence of substitutability, such as evidence that two kinds of products are functionally interchangeable, needs a variety of discernment that has more to do with business experience than with legal training. Someone with experience in business will be better able to predict likely consumer behaviour than a judge will be. What is more, indirect evidence is useful only as a surrogate for cross-elasticity of demand, so that what is required in the end is an assessment of the *economic* significance of the evidence; and to this task an economist is almost by definition better suited than is a judge.

All of this is not to say that judges are somehow incompetent in matters of competition law. Significantly, Parliament mandated that the Tribunal should include judicial members, and that the Chairman should always be a judge. See *Competition Tribunal Act*, s. 4. Clearly it was Parliament's view that questions of competition law are not altogether beyond the ken of judges. However, one of the principal roles of the judicial members is to decide such questions of pure law as may arise before the Tribunal. Over those questions they have exclusive jurisdiction. See *supra* at s. 12(1)(a). But over questions of fact and of mixed law and fact, the judicial members share their jurisdiction with the lay members. See, *supra*, at s. 12(1)(b). Thus, while judges are able to pronounce on questions of the latter kind, they may do so only together with the lay members; and, in a typically constituted panel, such as the one that sat in this case, the lay members outnumber the judicial ones, so that in the event of a disagreement between the two camps, the lay members as a group will prevail. This makes sense because, as I have observed, the expertise of the lay members is invaluable in the application of the principles of competition law.

[Iacobucci J then proceeded to deal with the appeal and the cross-appeal by reference to what was then (pre-*Dunsmuir*) a new "middle" standard of reasonableness *simpliciter*.]

Appeal on the merits allowed with costs; appeal on the remedy dismissed with costs.

NOTES

1. It is interesting in this case that Iacobucci J recognized expertise as the single most important factor in divining the standard of review. Consider the extent to which this relegates legislative *indicia* to a subsidiary category, especially as indicated by the inclusion of a statutory right of appeal. After *Dunsmuir*, it appears that the nature of the question has become the primary factor in the standard of review analysis, at least by its pointing presumptively to a correctness or reasonableness standard in many cases.

2. In the wake of *Southam*, there were suggestions from some judges that available standards of review were not confined to the three possibilities accepted to that point. Further nuances and variations might well be appropriate. Thus, Lambert JA of the BC Court of Appeal, delivering the judgment of the majority, expressed the view that at least on occasion there was room for some degree of deference within the correctness standard: *Northwood Inc. v. British Columbia (Forest Products Board)* (2001), 86 BCLR (3d) 215 (CA), at para. 21. For a critical appraisal of *Southam* on this point, which bears also on the reduction to two standards in *Dunsmuir*, see David P. Jones, "The Concept of a Spectrum of Standards of Review: Is There a Different Standard of Review for Appeals? The *Southam* Case and 'Reasonableness *Simpliciter*'" (1997), 50 *Admin. LR* (2d) 260.

The issue of the standard of review when there is a statutory right of appeal did not in fact arise for the first time in *Pezim* and *Southam*. Earlier, there was a lively debate as to whether the courts should afford any deference to professional disciplinary committees interpreting legislative provisions creating disciplinary offence. For example, in *Re Shulman and College of Physicians & Surgeons of Ontario* (1980), 111 DLR (3d) 689 (Ont. Div. Ct.), Montgomery J held that the court should not intervene unless the disciplinary committee's decision was unreasonable. Reid J explicitly rejected this in *Re Feingold and Discipline Committee of College of Optometrists of Ontario* (1981), 123 DLR (3d) 667 (Ont. Div. Ct.), holding that, in the face of a broad right of appeal, the court should not be deferential but is obliged to deal with the determination under appeal on a correctness basis. This issue came before the Supreme Court of Canada in *Law Society of New Brunswick v. Ryan*, [2003] 1 SCR 247, in which the court determined that deference was due to the determination by a law society of the appropriate penalty for a lawyer who was found guilty of serious professional misconduct.

This deferential position toward professional disciplinary committees was reiterated lately by the Alberta Court of Appeal in *Bishop v. Alberta College of Optometrists*, 2009 ABCA 175, based on the *Dunsmuir* framework:

> [1] Optometrists have two methods of testing visual fields: a screening test and a threshold test. Both may be conducted with the assistance of a computer. A threshold test is more complex and time consuming than a screening test. The Council of the Alberta College of Optometrists (the "Council") found that the appellant, Dr. Bishop, and his associates, were conducting screening tests but billing for threshold tests. The Council concluded that Dr. Bishop was guilty of unprofessional conduct and imposed a reprimand, fines of $8,750 and costs of over $73,000. Dr. Bishop appeals.

> [The court's discussion of the background of the case and the decisions below, including that of the council, have been omitted.]

[15] Dr. Bishop argues that his first ground of appeal [that the council misinterpreted an agreement between Alberta Health and Wellness and the Alberta Association of Optometrists, based on which Alberta optometrists can bill for insured services] raises a question of law reviewable on the correctness standard because it challenges the Council's interpretation of the Agreement and its regulatory regime. ...

[16] In *Dunsmuir* ... , the Supreme Court set out a two-step process for determining the applicable standard of review for administrative decisions. The first step is to ascertain whether the jurisprudence has already determined the degree of deference attributable to the type of question in issue. If not, the next step involves performing a contextual analysis of the relevant factors to determine whether correctness or reasonableness is the appropriate standard of review: *Dunsmuir*, at paras. 62-64.

[17] The jurisprudence has not determined the degree of deference attributable to the questions at issue in this appeal. Therefore, it is necessary to conduct a contextual standard of review analysis.

[18] The [*Health Professions Act*, RSA 2000, c. H-7 (the "HPA")] provides a full right of appeal without a leave requirement. Although this factor suggests less deference to the Council, it is not decisive. It is also necessary to consider the purpose of the Council, the nature of the questions at issue and the expertise of the Council: ... *Dunsmuir* at para. 64.

[19] The purpose of the College is to regulate the practice of optometry in Alberta in a manner that protects and serves the public interest: *HPA*, s. 3(1). A review of the *HPA* suggests that the Council plays an important role in setting standards for the optometry profession and ensuring that those standards are upheld. This factor suggests that deference is owed to the Council's decisions. See *Zenner v. Prince Edward Island College of Optometrists*, 2005 SCC 77, [2005] 3 SCR 645 at para. 23.

[20] Dr. Bishop's first ground of appeal raises questions central to the Council's oversight jurisdiction, within its relative expertise and containing large factual components. The Council was required to interpret documents that establish professional billing practices. This function is central to the Council's duty to set standards and regulate professional conduct. In arriving at its interpretation of the documents, the Council assessed and weighed expert evidence of professional practice. It also applied the knowledge and expertise of the panel members on appropriate billing practices and professional conduct. These factors suggest that the Council's decision on the first ground is entitled to deference: *Litchfield v. College of Physicians and Surgeons of Alberta*, 2008 ABCA 164, 432 A.R. 131 at para. 11.

[21] Based on the foregoing analysis, the standard of review applicable to the first ground of appeal is reasonableness. We agree with Dr. Bishop that the reasonableness standard also applies to his second and third grounds of appeal. A decision is reasonable if it is justifiable, transparent and intelligible and "falls within a range of possible, acceptable outcomes which are defensible in respect of the facts and law": *Dunsmuir* at para. 47.

[The court then applied the reasonableness standard in its review of the council's interpretation of the agreement, its conclusion that Dr. Bishop was guilty of unprofessional conduct, and its imposition of penalties, and concluded that each was reasonable.]

[34] The appeal is dismissed.

THE ROLE OF STATUTORY PURPOSE

This factor has a long pedigree. In *Roncarelli v. Duplessis*, [1959] SCR 122, at 140, Rand J famously said, "there is always a [legislative] perspective within which a statute is intended to operate." Yet who is to formulate that perspective if not the courts, expressly or implicitly, in the course of judicial review? A component of the functionalist approach to substantive review and to deference was a call for courts to inquire into the purposes of a regulatory regime in order to avoid legal interpretations that contradicted or frustrated that purpose. As Binnie J put it in *Dunsmuir*, at para. 151, a reviewing judge must consider "the precise nature and function of the decision-maker including its expertise [and] the terms and objectives of the governing statute (or common law) conferring the power of decision." He continued (at para. 151):

> In some cases, the court will have to recognize that the decision maker was required to strike a proper balance (or achieve proportionality) between the adverse impact of a decision on the rights and interests of the applicant or others directly affected weighed against the public purpose which is sought to be advanced.

While the courts may refer to the factor of a decision-maker's (or a statute's) purpose in order to obtain an overall sense of the decision-making context, the role of this factor is perhaps most important to steer the courts away from judicial decisions that run counter to the overall rationale for which a specialized administrative regime was established. Respect for purpose may be just another way of saying that the courts should respect the substantive choices of legislatures but also of those to whom a legislature has delegated public powers.

The framing of a decision-maker's purpose thus interacts with all of the other factors in the standard of review analysis. It informs, and is informed by the terms of the statute, by the nature of the question addressed by the decision-maker, and by an assessment of the decision-maker's relative expertise. In this respect, purpose and regulatory context pervade many aspects of the evaluation of deference. On the other hand, it is also difficult to imagine a court relying on purpose alone to decide whether to defer, especially where the other factors point in an opposite direction.

Placing too much emphasis on purpose might also defeat the aim of *Dunsmuir* to clarify the standard of review analysis. Even so, it must be kept in mind that the interpretation of statutory provisions, where they are open to a range of reasonable interpretations, must not be at the expense of the statute as a whole and its regulatory aims, and that the inclinations arising from other factors in the analysis should support, and not contradict, that framing of purpose. All are examined in order to reveal legislative intent. For a court to intervene where a decision-maker has made choices that go to the core of its regulatory mandate—by making policy choices based on broad statement of principle in its statute, for example— runs contrary to the purpose of the decision-maker, as well as to assumptions of deference based on expertise and the nature of the question. Likewise, for a court to defer where a decision-maker has contradicted the purpose of its regime or significantly limited its decision-making role—perhaps by declining to exercise jurisdiction over an entire class of claims in a regime for human rights protection—raises concerns in relation to various factors in the standard of review analysis, including statutory purpose.

The reasoning in *Pezim* and *Southam* point to the role of the purpose of a decision-maker. Likewise, the following extract from a recent decision of the Supreme Court links statutory purpose more closely to the nature of the question. In this case, observe how the specific terms of the statute cause the court to defer to a discretionary and policy-based decision of a major regulatory agency, the Canadian Radio-television and Telecommunications Commission (CRTC), in its rate-setting role.

Bell Canada v. Bell Aliant Regional Communications
2009 SCC 40 (CanLII)

ABELLA J: [1] The *Telecommunications Act*, SC 1993, c. 38, sets out certain broad telecommunications policy objectives. It directs the Canadian Radio-television and Telecommunications Commission to implement them in the exercise of its statutory authority, balancing the interests of consumers, carriers and competitors in the context of the Canadian telecommunications industry. The issue in these appeals is whether this authority was properly exercised.

[2] While distinct questions arise in each of the appeals before us, the common problem is whether the CRTC, in the exercise of its rate-setting authority, appropriately directed the allocation of funds to various purposes. In the Bell Canada and TELUS Communications Inc. appeal, the challenged purpose is the distribution of funds to customers, while in the Consumers' Association of Canada and National Anti-Poverty Organization appeal, the impugned allocation was directed at the expansion of broadband infrastructure. For the reasons that follow, in my view the CRTC's allocations were reasonable based on the Canadian telecommunications policy objectives that it is obliged to consider in the exercise of all of its powers, including its authority to approve just and reasonable rates.

Background

[3] The CRTC issued its landmark "Price Caps Decision" in May 2002. Exercising its rate-setting authority, the CRTC established a formula to regulate the maximum prices charged for certain services offered by incumbent local exchange carriers ("ILECs"), who are primarily well-established telecommunications carriers.

[4] As part of its decision, the CRTC ordered the affected carriers to create separate accounting entries in their ledgers. These were called "deferral accounts." The funds contained in these deferral accounts were derived from residential telephone service revenues in non-high cost serving areas ("non-HCSAs"), which are mainly urban. Under the formula established by the Price Caps Decision, any increase in the price charged for these services in a given year was limited to an inflationary cap, less a productivity offset to reflect the low degree of competition in that particular market.

[5] More specifically, the effect of the inflationary cap was to bar carriers from increasing their prices at a rate greater than inflation. The productivity offset, on the other hand, put downward pressure on the rates to be charged. While market forces would normally serve to encourage carriers to reduce both their costs and their prices, the low

level of competition in the non-HCSA market led the CRTC to conclude that an offsetting factor was necessary as a proxy for the effect of competition.

[6] Given the countervailing factors at work in the Price Caps Decision formula, there was the potential for a decrease in the price of residential services in these areas if inflation fell below a certain level. Rather than mandating such a decrease, however, the CRTC concluded that lower prices, and therefore the prospect of lower revenues, would constitute a barrier to the entry of new carriers into this particular telecommunications market. It therefore ordered that amounts representing the difference between the rates *actually* charged, not including the decrease mandated by the Price Caps Decision formula, and the rates as *otherwise determined* through the formula, were to be collected from subscribers and recorded in deferral accounts held by each carrier. These accounts were to be reviewed annually by the CRTC. The intent of the Price Caps Decision was, therefore, that prices for these services would remain at a level sufficient to encourage market entry, while at the same time maintaining the pressure on the incumbent carriers to reduce their costs.

[7] The principal objectives the CRTC intended the Price Caps Decision to achieve were the following:

a) to render reliable and affordable services of high quality, accessible to both urban and rural area customers;

b) to balance the interests of the three main stakeholders in telecommunications markets, i.e., customers, competitors and incumbent telephone companies;

c) to foster facilities-based competition in Canadian telecommunications markets;

d) to provide incumbents with incentives to increase efficiencies and to be more innovative; and

e) to adopt regulatory approaches that impose the minimum regulatory burden compatible with the achievement of the previous four objectives. [para. 99]

[8] The CRTC discussed the future use of the deferral account funds as follows:

> The Commission anticipates that an adjustment to the deferral account would be made whenever the Commission approves rate reductions for residential local services that are proposed by the ILECs as a result of competitive pressures. The Commission also anticipates that the deferral account would be drawn down to mitigate rate increases for residential service that could result from the approval of exogenous factors or when inflation exceeds productivity. *Other draw downs could occur, for example, through subscriber rebates or the funding of initiatives that would benefit residential customers in other ways.* [Emphasis added; para. 412.]

At the time, it did not specifically direct how the deferral account funds were to be used, leaving the issue subject to further submissions. While some participants objected to the creation of the deferral accounts, no one appealed the Price Caps Decision (*Bell Canada v. Canadian Radio-television and Telecommunications Commission*, 2008 FCA 91, 375 NR 124, at para. 14).

[9] The Price Caps Decision was to apply to services offered by Bell Canada, TELUS, and other affected carriers for the four-year period from June 1, 2002 to May 31, 2006. In a decision in 2005, the CRTC extended this price regulation regime for another year to May 31, 2007. The CRTC allowed some draw-downs of the deferral accounts following the Price Caps Decision that are not at issue in these appeals.

[10] In March 2003, in two separate decisions, the CRTC approved the rates for Bell Canada and TELUS. In the Bell Canada decision, the CRTC appeared to contemplate the continued operation of the deferral accounts established in the Price Caps Decision. It ordered, for example, that certain tax savings be allocated to the deferral accounts:

> The Commission, in Decision 2002-34, established a deferral account in conjunction with the application of a basket constraint equal to the rate of inflation less a productivity offset to all revenues from residential services in non-HCSAs. The Commission considers that AT&T Canada's proposal to allocate the Ontario GRT and the Quebec TGE tax savings associated with all capped services to the price cap deferral account is inconsistent with that determination. *The Commission finds that Bell Canada's proposal to include the Ontario GRT and Quebec TGE tax savings associated with the residential local services in non-HCSAs basket in the price cap deferral account is consistent with that determination.* [Emphasis added; para. 32.]

[11] On December 2, 2003, Bell Canada sought the approval of the CRTC to use the balance in its deferral account to expand high-speed broadband internet service to remote and rural communities. In response, on March 24, 2004, the CRTC issued a public notice requesting submissions on the appropriate disposition of the deferral accounts. Pursuant to this notice, the CRTC conducted a public process whereby proposals were invited for the disposition of the affected carriers' deferral accounts. The review was extensive and proposals were received from numerous parties.

[12] This led to the release of the "Deferral Accounts Decision" on February 16, 2006. In this decision, the CRTC directed how the funds in the deferral accounts were to be used. These directions form the foundation of these appeals.

[13] After considering the various policy objectives outlined in the applicable statute, the *Telecommunications Act*, and the purposes set out in the Price Caps Decision, the CRTC concluded that all funds in the deferral accounts should be targeted for disposal by a designated date in 2006:

> The attachment to this Decision provides preliminary estimates of the deferral account balances as of the end of the fourth year of the current price cap period in 2006. *The Commission notes that the deferral account balances are expected to be very large for some ILECs. It also notes the concern that allowing funds to continue to accumulate in the accounts would create inefficiencies and uncertainties.*
>
> . . .
>
> *Accordingly, the Commission considers it appropriate not only to provide directions on the disposition of all the funds that will have accumulated in the ILECs' deferral accounts by the end of the fourth year of the price cap period in 2006, but also to provide directions to address amounts recurring beyond this period in order to prevent further accumulation of funds in the deferral accounts.* The Commission will provide directions and guidelines for disposing of these amounts later in this Decision. [Emphasis added; paras. 58 and 60.]

[14] The CRTC further decided that the deferral accounts should be disbursed primarily for two purposes. As a priority, at least 5 percent of the accounts was to be used for improving accessibility to telecommunications services for individuals with disabilities. The other 95 percent was to be used for broadband expansion in rural and remote communities. Proposals were invited on how the deferral account funds should be applied. If the proposal as approved was for less than the balance of its deferral account, an affected carrier was to distribute the remaining amount to consumers.

[15] In summary, therefore, the CRTC decided that the affected carriers should focus on broadband expansion and accessibility improvement. It also decided that if these two objectives could be fulfilled for an amount less than the full deferral account balances, credits to subscribers would be ordered out of the remainder. It should be noted that customers were not to be compensated in proportion to what they had paid through these credits because of the potential administrative complexity of identifying these individuals and quantifying their respective shares. Instead, the credits were to be provided to certain current subscribers. Prospective rate reductions could also be used to eliminate recurring amounts in the accounts.

[16] At the time, the balance in the deferral accounts established under the Price Caps Decision was considerable. Bell Canada's account was estimated to contain approximately $480.5 million, while the TELUS account was estimated at about $170 million.

[17] It is helpful to set out how the CRTC explained its decision on the allocation of the deferral account funds. Referencing the importance of telecommunications in connecting Canada's "vast geography and relatively dispersed population," it stressed that Canada had fallen behind in the adoption of broadband services (at paras. 73-74). It contrasted the wide availability of broadband service in urban areas with the less developed network in rural and remote communities. Further, it noted that the objectives outlined in the Price Caps Decision and in the *Telecommunications Act* at s. 7(b) provided for improving the quality of telecommunications services in those communities, and that their social and economic development would be favoured by an expansion of the national broadband network. In its view, this initiative would also provide a helpful complement to the efforts of both levels of government to expand broadband coverage. It therefore concluded that broadband expansion was an appropriate use of a part of the deferral account funds (at paras. 73-80).

[18] The CRTC also explained that while customer credits would be consistent with the objectives set out in s. 7 of the *Telecommunications Act* and with the Price Caps Decision, these disbursements should not be given priority because broadband expansion and accessibility services provided greater long-term benefits. Nevertheless, credits effectively balanced the interests of the "three main stakeholders in the telecommunications markets" (at para. 115), namely customers, competitors and carriers. It concluded that credits did not contradict the purpose of the deferral accounts, and contrasted one-time credits with a reduction of rates. In its view, credits, unlike rate reductions, did not have a sustained negative impact on competition in these markets, which was the concern the deferral accounts were set up to address (at paras. 112-16).

[19] A dissenting Commissioner expressed concerns over the disposition of the deferral account funds. In her view, the CRTC had no mandate to direct the expansion of broadband networks across the country. The CRTC's policy had generally been to ensure

the provision of a basic level of service, not services like broadband, and she therefore considered the CRTC's reliance on the objectives of the *Telecommunications Act* to be inappropriate.

[20] On January 17, 2008, the CRTC issued another decision dealing with the carriers' proposals to use their deferral account balances for the purposes set out in the Deferral Accounts Decision. Some carriers' plans were approved in part, with the result that only a portion of their deferral account balances was allocated to those projects. Consequently, the CRTC required them to submit, by March 25, 2008, a plan for crediting the balance in their deferral accounts to residential subscribers in non-HCSAs.

[21] Bell Canada, as well as the Consumers' Association of Canada and the National Anti-Poverty Organization, appealed the CRTC's Deferral Accounts Decision to the Federal Court of Appeal. The Deferral Accounts Decision was stayed by Richard CJ in the Federal Court of Appeal on January 25, 2008. The decision requiring further submissions on plans to distribute the deferral account balances was also stayed by Sharlow JA pending the filing of an application for leave to appeal to this Court on April 23, 2008. Both stay orders were extended by this Court on September 25, 2008. The stay orders do not apply to the funds allocated for the improvement of accessibility for individuals with disabilities.

[22] In a careful judgment by Sharlow JA, the court unanimously dismissed the appeals, concluding that the Price Caps Decision regime always contemplated the future disposition of the deferral account funds as the CRTC would direct, and that the CRTC acted within its broad mandate to pursue its regulatory objectives. For the reasons that follow, I agree with the conclusions reached by Sharlow JA.

Analysis

[23] The parties have staked out diametrically opposite positions on how the balance of the deferral account funds should be allocated.

[24] Bell Canada argued that the CRTC had no statutory authority to order what it claimed amounted to retrospective "rebates" to consumers. In its view, the distributions ordered by the CRTC were in substance a variation of rates that had been declared final. TELUS joined Bell Canada in this Court, and argued that the CRTC's order for "rebates" constituted an unjust confiscation of property.

[25] In response, the CRTC contended that its broad mandate to set rates under the *Telecommunications Act* includes establishing and ordering the disposal of funds from deferral accounts. Because the deferral account funds had always been subject to the possibility of disbursement to customers, there was therefore no variation of a final rate or any impermissible confiscation.

[26] The Consumers' Association of Canada was the only party to oppose the allocation of 5 percent of the deferral account balances to improving accessibility, but abandoned this argument during the hearing before the Federal Court of Appeal. Together with the National Anti-Poverty Organization, it argued before this Court that the rest of the deferral account balances should be distributed to customers in full, and that the CRTC had no authority to allow the use of the funds for broadband expansion.

[27] These arguments bring us directly to the statutory scheme at issue.

[28] The *Telecommunications Act* lays out the basic legislative framework of the Canadian telecommunications industry. In addition to setting out numerous specific powers, the statute's guiding objectives are set out in s. 7. Pursuant to s. 47(a), the CRTC must consider these objectives in the exercise of *all* of its powers. These provisions state:

> 7. It is hereby affirmed that telecommunications performs an essential role in the maintenance of Canada's identity and sovereignty and that the Canadian telecommunications policy has as its objectives
>
> (a) *to facilitate the orderly development throughout Canada of a telecommunications system that serves to safeguard, enrich and strengthen the social and economic fabric of Canada and its regions;*
>
> (b) *to render reliable and affordable telecommunications services of high quality accessible to Canadians in both urban and rural areas in all regions of Canada;*
>
> (c) *to enhance the efficiency and competitiveness, at the national and international levels, of Canadian telecommunications;*
>
> (d) to promote the ownership and control of Canadian carriers by Canadians;
>
> (e) to promote the use of Canadian transmission facilities for telecommunications within Canada and between Canada and points outside Canada;
>
> (f) *to foster increased reliance on market forces for the provision of telecommunications services and to ensure that regulation, where required, is efficient and effective;*
>
> (g) *to stimulate research and development in Canada in the field of telecommunications and to encourage innovation in the provision of telecommunications services;*
>
> (h) *to respond to the economic and social requirements of users of telecommunications services;* and
>
> (i) to contribute to the protection of the privacy of persons.
>
> . . .
>
> 47. The Commission *shall exercise its powers and perform its duties* under this Act and any special Act
>
> (a) *with a view to implementing the Canadian telecommunications policy objectives and ensuring that Canadian carriers provide telecommunications services and charge rates in accordance with section 27;*

The CRTC relied on these two provisions in arguing that it was required to take into account a broad spectrum of considerations in the exercise of its rate-setting powers, and that the Deferral Accounts Decision was simply an extension of this approach.

[29] The *Telecommunications Act* grants the CRTC the general power to set and regulate rates for telecommunications services in Canada. All tariffs imposed by carriers, including rates for services, must be submitted to it for approval, and it may decide any matter with respect to rates in the telecommunications services industry, as the following provisions show:

> 24. *The offering and provision of any telecommunications service by a Canadian carrier are subject to any conditions imposed by the Commission* or included in a tariff approved by the Commission.

25(1) No Canadian carrier shall provide a telecommunications service except in accordance with a tariff filed with and approved by the Commission that specifies the rate or the maximum or minimum rate, or both, to be charged for the service.

. . .

32. The Commission may, for the purposes of this Part,

. . .

(g) in the absence of any applicable provision in this Part, *determine any matter and make any order relating to the rates, tariffs or telecommunications services of Canadian carriers.*

[30] The guiding rule of rate-setting under the *Telecommunications Act* is that the rates be "just and reasonable," a longstanding regulatory principle. To determine whether rates meet this standard, the CRTC has a wide discretion which is protected by a privative clause:

27(1) Every rate charged by a Canadian carrier for a telecommunications service shall be just and reasonable.

. . .

(3) The Commission may determine in any case, as a question of fact, whether a Canadian carrier has complied with section 25, this section or section 29, or with any decision made under section 24, 25, 29, 34 or 40.

. . .

(5) In determining whether a rate is just and reasonable, the Commission may adopt any method or technique that it considers appropriate, whether based on a carrier's return on its rate base or otherwise.

. . .

52(1) The Commission may, in exercising its powers and performing its duties under this Act or any special Act, determine any question of law or of fact, and its determination on a question of fact is binding and conclusive.

[31] In addition to the power under s. 27(5) to adopt "any method or technique that it considers appropriate" for determining whether a rate is just and reasonable, the CRTC also has the authority under s. 37(1) to order a carrier to adopt "any accounting method or system of accounts" in view of the proper administration of the *Telecommunications Act*. Section 37(1) states:

37(1) The Commission may require a Canadian carrier
(a) *to adopt any method of identifying the costs of providing telecommunications services and to adopt any accounting method or system of accounts* for the purposes of the administration of this Act;

[32] The CRTC has other broad powers which, while not at issue in this case, nevertheless further demonstrate the comprehensive regulatory powers Parliament intended to grant. These include the ability to order a Canadian carrier to provide any service in certain circumstances (s. 35(1)); to require communications facilities to be provided or constructed (s. 42(1)); and to establish any sort of fund for the purpose of supporting access to basic telecommunications services (s. 46.5(1)).

[33] This statutory overview assists in dealing with the preliminary issue of the applicable standard of review. Although the Federal Court of Appeal accepted the parties' position that the applicable standard of review was correctness, Sharlow JA acknowledged that the standard of review could be more deferential in light of this Court's decision in *Council of Canadians with Disabilities v. VIA Rail Canada Inc.*, 2007 SCC 15, [2007] 1 SCR 650, at paras. 98-100. This was an invitation, it seems to me, to clarify what the appropriate standard is.

[34] Bell Canada and TELUS concede that the CRTC had the authority to approve disbursements from the deferral accounts for initiatives to improve broadband expansion and accessibility to telecommunications services for persons with disabilities, and that they actually sought such approval. In their view, however, this authority did not extend to what they characterized as retrospective "rebates." Similarly, in the Consumers' appeal the crux of the complaint is with whether the CRTC could direct that the funds be disbursed in certain ways, not with whether it had the authority to direct how the funds ought to be spent generally.

[35] This means that for Bell Canada and TELUS appeal, the dispute is over the CRTC's authority and discretion under the *Telecommunications Act* in connection with ordering credits to customers from the deferral accounts. In the Consumers' appeal, it is over its authority and discretion in ordering that funds from the deferral accounts be used for the expansion of broadband services.

[36] A central responsibility of the CRTC is to determine and approve just and reasonable rates to be charged for telecommunications services. Together with its rate-setting power, the CRTC has the ability to impose *any* condition on the provision of a service, adopt *any* method to determine whether a rate is just and reasonable and require a carrier to adopt *any* accounting method. It is obliged to exercise all of its powers and duties with a view to implementing the Canadian telecommunications policy objectives set out in s. 7.

[37] The CRTC's authority to establish the deferral accounts is found through a combined reading of ss. 27 and 37(1). The authority to establish these accounts necessarily includes the disposition of the funds they contain, a disposition which represents the final step in a process set in motion by the Price Caps Decision. It is self-evident that the CRTC has considerable expertise with respect to this type of question. This observation is reflected in its extensive statutory powers in this regard and in the strong privative clause in s. 52(1) protecting its determinations on questions of fact from appeal, including whether a carrier has adopted a just and reasonable rate.

[38] In my view, therefore, the issues raised in these appeals go to the very heart of the CRTC's specialized expertise. In the appeals before us, the core of the quarrel in effect is with the methodology for setting rates and the allocation of certain proceeds derived from those rates, a polycentric exercise with which the CRTC is statutorily charged and which it is uniquely qualified to undertake. This argues for a more deferential standard of review, which leads us to consider whether the CRTC was reasonable in directing how the funds from the deferral accounts were to be used. (See *Dunsmuir v. New Brunswick*, 2008 SCC 9, [2008] 1 SCR 190, at para. 54; *Canada (Citizenship and Immigration) v. Khosa*, 2009 SCC 12, [2009] 1 SCR 339, at para. 25; and *VIA Rail Canada Inc.*, at paras. 88-100.)

[39] This brings us to the nature of the CRTC's rate-setting power in the context of this case. The predecessor statute for telecommunications rate-setting, the *Railway Act*,

RSC 1985, c. R-3, also stipulated that rates be "just and reasonable" (s. 340(1)). Traditionally, those rates were based on a balancing between a fair rate for the consumer and a fair return on the carrier's investment. (See, e.g., *Northwestern Utilities Ltd. v. City of Edmonton*, [1929] SCR 186, at pp. 192-93 and *ATCO Gas and Pipelines Ltd. v. Alberta (Energy and Utilities Board)*, 2006 SCC 4, [2006] 1 SCR 140, at para. 65.)

[40] Even before the expansive language now found in the *Telecommunications Act*, regulatory agencies had enjoyed considerable discretion in determining the factors to be considered and the methodology that could be adopted for assessing whether rates were just and reasonable. For instance, in dismissing a leave application in *Re General Increase in Freight Rates* (1954), 76 CRTC 12 (SCC), Taschereau J wrote:

> [I]f the Board is bound to grant a relief which is just to the public and secures to the railways a fair return, it is not bound to accept for the determination of the rates to be charged, the sole method proposed by the applicant. *The obligation to act is a question of law, but the choice of the method to be adopted is a question of discretion with which, under the statute, no Court of law may interfere.* [Emphasis added; p. 13.]

In making this determination, he relied on Duff CJ's judgment in *Canadian National Railways Co. v. Bell Telephone Co. of Canada*, [1939] SCR 308, for the following proposition in the particular statutory context of that case:

> The law dictates neither the order to be made in a given case nor the considerations by which the Board is to be guided in arriving at the conclusion that an order, or what order, is necessary or proper in a given case. True, it is the duty of all public bodies and others invested with statutory powers to act reasonably in the execution of them, but the policy of the statue [*sic*] is that, subject to the appeal to the Governor in Council under s. 52, in exercising an administrative discretion entrusted to it, the Board itself is to be the final arbiter as to the order to be made. [p. 315]

(See also Michael H. Ryan, *Canadian Telecommunications Law and Regulation* (loose-leaf ed.), at §612.)

[41] The CRTC's already broad discretion in determining whether rates are just and reasonable has been further enhanced by the inclusion of s. 27(5) in the *Telecommunications Act* permitting the CRTC to adopt "any method," language which was absent from the *Railway Act*.

[42] Even more significantly, the *Railway Act* contained nothing analogous to the statutory direction under s. 47 that the CRTC must exercise its rate-setting powers with a view to implementing the Canadian telecommunications objectives set out in s. 7. These statutory additions are significant. Coupled with its rate-setting power, and its ability to use any method for arriving at a just and reasonable rate, these provisions contradict the restrictive interpretation of the CRTC's authority proposed by various parties in these appeals.

[43] This was highlighted by Sharlow JA when she stated:

> Because of the combined operation of section 47 and section 7 of the *Telecommunications Act* ... , the CRTC's rating jurisdiction is not limited to considerations that have traditionally been considered relevant to ensuring a fair price for consumers and a fair rate of return

to the provider of telecommunication services. Section 47 of the *Telecommunications Act* expressly requires the CRTC to consider, as well, the policy objectives listed in section 7 of the *Telecommunications Act*. What that means, in my view, is that in rating decisions under the *Telecommunications Act*, the CRTC is entitled to consider any or all of the policy objectives listed in section 7. [para. 35]

[44] It is true that the CRTC had previously used a "rate base rate of return" method, based on a combination of a rate of return for investors in telecommunications carriers and a rate base calculated using the carriers' assets. This resulted in rates charged for the carrier's services that would, on the one hand, provide a fair return for the capital invested in the carrier, and, on the other, be fair to the customers of the carrier.

[45] However, these expansive provisions mean that the rate base rate of return approach is not necessarily the only basis for setting a just and reasonable rate. Furthermore, based on ss. 7, 27(5) and 47, the CRTC is not required to confine itself to balancing only the interests of subscribers and carriers with respect to a particular service. In the Price Caps Decision, for example, the CRTC chose to focus on maximum prices for services, rather than on the rate base rate of return approach. It did so, in part, to foster competition in certain markets, a goal untethered to the direct relationship between the carrier and subscriber in the traditional rate base rate of return approach. A similar pricing approach was adopted by the CRTC in a decision preceding the Price Caps Decision.

[46] The CRTC has interpreted these provisions broadly and identified them as responsive to the evolved industry context in which it operates. In its "Review of Regulatory Framework" decision, it wrote:

> *The Act ... provides the tools necessary to allow the Commission to alter the traditional manner in which it regulates* (i.e., to depart from rate base rate of return regulation).
>
> · · ·
>
> *In brief, telecommunications today transcends traditional boundaries and simple definition.* It is an industry, a market and a means of doing business that encompasses a constantly evolving range of voice, data and video products and services.
>
> · · ·
>
> *In this context, the Commission notes that the Act contemplates the evolution of basic service by setting out as an objective the provision of reliable and affordable telecommunications,* rather than merely affordable telephone service. [Emphasis added; pp. 6 and 10.]

[47] In *Edmonton (City) v. 360Networks Canada Ltd.*, 2007 FCA 106, [2007] 4 FCR 747, leave to appeal refused, [2007], 3 SCR vii, the Federal Court of Appeal drew similar conclusions, observing that the *Telecommunications Act* should be interpreted by reference to the policy objectives, and that s. 7 justified in part the view that the "Act should be interpreted as creating a comprehensive regulatory scheme" (at para. 46). A duty to take a more comprehensive approach was also noted by Ryan, who observed:

> Because of the importance of the telecommunications industry to the country as a whole, rate-making issues may sometimes assume a dimension that gives them a significance that extends beyond the immediate interests of the carrier, its shareholders and its customers, and engages the interests of the public at large. It is also part of the duty of the regulator to take these more far-reaching interests into account. [§604]

[48] This leads inevitably, it seems to me, to the conclusion that the CRTC may set rates that are just and reasonable for the purposes of the *Telecommunications Act* through a diverse range of methods, taking into account a variety of different constituencies and interests referred to in s. 7, not simply those it had previously considered when it was operating under the more restrictive provisions of the *Railway Act*. This observation will also be apposite later in these reasons when the question of "final rates" is discussed in connection with the Bell Canada appeal.

[49] I see nothing in this conclusion which contradicts the ratio in *Barrie Public Utilities v. Canadian Cable Television Assn.*, 2003 SCC 28, [2003] 1 SCR 476. In that case, the issue was whether the CRTC could make an order granting cable companies access to certain utilities' power poles. In that decision, the CRTC had relied on the Canadian telecommunications policy objectives to inform its interpretation of the relevant provisions. In deciding that the language of the *Telecommunications Act* did not give the CRTC the power to grant access to the power poles, Gonthier J for the majority concluded that the CRTC had inappropriately interpreted the Canadian telecommunications policy objectives in s. 7 as power-conferring (at para. 42).

[50] The circumstances of *Barrie Public Utilities* are entirely distinct from those at issue before us. Here, we are dealing with the CRTC setting rates that were required to be just and reasonable, an authority fully supported by unambiguous statutory language. In so doing, the CRTC was exercising a broad authority, which, according to s. 47, it was required to do "with a view to implementing the Canadian telecommunications policy objectives ... ." The policy considerations in s. 7 were factors that the CRTC was required to, and did, take into account.

[51] Nor does this Court's decision in *ATCO* preclude the pursuit of public interest objectives through rate-setting. In that case, Bastarache J for the majority, took a strict approach to the Alberta Energy and Utilities Board's powers under the applicable statute. The issue was whether the Board had the authority to order the distribution of proceeds by a regulated company to its subscribers from an asset sale it had approved. It was argued that because the Board had the authority to make "further orders" and impose conditions "in the public interest" on any order, it therefore had the ability to order the disposition of the sale proceeds.

[52] In holding that the Board had no such authority, Bastarache J relied in part on the conclusion that the Board's statutory power to make orders or impose conditions in the public interest was insufficiently precise to grant the ability to distribute sale proceeds to ratepayers (at para. 46). The ability of the Board to approve an asset sale, and its authority to make any order it wished in the public interest, were necessarily limited by the context of the relevant provisions (at paras. 46-48 and 50). It was obliged too to adopt a rate base rate of return method to determine rates, pursuant to its governing statute (at paras. 65-66).

[53] Unlike *ATCO*, in the case before us the CRTC's rate-setting authority, and its ability to establish deferral accounts for this purpose, are at the very core of its competence. The CRTC is statutorily authorized to adopt any method of determining just and reasonable rates. Furthermore, it is required to consider the statutory objectives in the exercise of its authority, in contrast to the permissive, free-floating direction to consider

the public interest that existed in *ATCO*. The *Telecommunications Act* displaces many of the traditional restrictions on rate-setting described in *ATCO*, thereby granting the CRTC the ability to balance the interests of carriers, consumers and competitors in the broader context of the Canadian telecommunications industry (Review of Regulatory Framework Decision, at pp. 6 and 10).

[54] The fact that deferral accounts are at issue does nothing to change this framework. No party objected to the CRTC's authority to establish the deferral accounts themselves. These accounts are accepted regulatory tools, available as a part of the Commission's rate-setting powers. As the CRTC has noted, deferral accounts "enabl[e] a regulator to defer consideration of a particular item of expense or revenue that is incapable of being forecast with certainty for the test year." They have traditionally protected against future eventualities, particularly the difference between forecasted and actual costs and revenues, allowing a regulator to shift costs and expenses from one regulatory period to another. While the CRTC's creation and use of the deferral accounts for broadband expansion and consumer credits may have been innovative, it was fully supported by the provisions of the *Telecommunications Act*.

[55] In my view, it follows from the CRTC's broad discretion to determine just and reasonable rates under s. 27, its power to order a carrier to adopt any accounting method under s. 37, and its statutory mandate under s. 47 to implement the wide-ranging Canadian telecommunications policy objectives set out in s. 7, that the *Telecommunications Act* provides the CRTC with considerable scope in establishing and approving the use to be made of deferral accounts. They were created in accordance both with the CRTC's rate-setting authority and with the goal that all rates charged by carriers were and would remain just and reasonable.

[56] A deferral account would not serve its purpose if the CRTC did not also have the power to order the disposition of the funds contained in it. In my view, the CRTC had the authority to order the disposition of the accounts in the exercise of its rate-setting power, provided that this exercise was reasonable.

[57] I therefore agree with the following observation by Sharlow JA:

> The Price Caps Decision required Bell Canada to credit a portion of its final rates to a deferral account, which the CRTC had clearly indicated would be disposed of in due course as the CRTC would direct. There is no dispute that the CRTC is entitled to use the device of a mandatory deferral account to impose a contingent obligation on a telecommunication service provider to make expenditures that the CRTC may direct in the future. *It necessarily follows that the CRTC is entitled to make an order crystallizing that obligation and directing a particular expenditure, provided the expenditure can reasonably be justified by one or more of the policy objectives listed in section 7 of the Telecommunications Act.* [Emphasis added; para. 52.]

[58] This general analytical framework brings us to the more specific questions in these appeals. In the first appeal, Bell Canada relied on Gonthier J's decision *Bell Canada v. Canada (Canadian Radio-Television and Telecommunications Commission)*, [1989] 1 SCR 1722 ("*Bell Canada (1989)*"), to argue that "final" rates cannot be changed and that the funds in the deferral accounts could not, therefore, be distributed as "rebates" to customers.

[59] In *Bell Canada (1989)*, the CRTC approved a series of interim rates. It subsequently reviewed them in light of Bell Canada's changed financial situation, and ordered

the carrier to credit what it considered to be excess revenues to its current subscribers. Arguing against the CRTC's authority to do so, Bell Canada contended that the CRTC could not order a one-time credit with respect to revenues earned from rates approved by the CRTC, whether the rate order was an interim one or not. Gonthier J observed that while the *Railway Act* contemplated a positive approval scheme that only allowed for prospective, not retroactive or retrospective rate-setting, the one-time credit at issue was nevertheless permissible because the original rates were interim and therefore inherently subject to change.

[60] In the current case, Bell Canada argued that the rates had been made final, and that the disposition of the deferral accounts for one-time credits was therefore impermissible. More specifically, it argued that the CRTC's order of one-time credits from the deferral accounts amounted to retrospective rate-setting as the term was used in *Bell Canada (1989)*, at p. 1749, namely, that their "purpose is to remedy the imposition of rates approved in the past and found in the final analysis to be excessive" (at p. 1749).

[61] In my view, because this case concerns encumbered revenues in deferral accounts (referred to by Sharlow JA as contingent obligations or liabilities), we are not dealing with the variation of final rates. As Sharlow JA pointed out, *Bell Canada (1989)* is inapplicable because it was known from the outset in the case before us that Bell Canada would be obliged to use the balance of its deferral account in accordance with the CRTC's subsequent direction (at para. 53).

[62] It would, with respect, be an oversimplification to consider that *Bell Canada (1989)* applies to bar the provision of credits to consumers in this case. *Bell Canada (1989)* was decided under the *Railway Act*, a statutory scheme that, significantly, did not include any of the considerations or mandates set out in ss. 7, 27(5) and 47 of the *Telecommunications Act*. Nor did it involve the disposition of funds contained in deferral accounts.

[63] In my view, the credits ordered out of the deferral accounts in the case before us are neither retroactive nor retrospective. They do not vary the original rate as approved, which included the deferral accounts, nor do they seek to remedy a deficiency in the rate order through later measures, since these credits or reductions were contemplated as a possible disposition of the deferral account balances from the beginning. These funds can properly be characterized as encumbered revenues, because the rates *always* remained subject to the deferral accounts mechanism established in the Price Caps Decision. The use of deferral accounts therefore precludes a finding of retroactivity or retrospectivity. Furthermore, using deferral accounts to account for the difference between forecast and actual costs and revenues has traditionally been held not to constitute retroactive rate-setting (*EPCOR Generation Inc. v. Energy and Utilities Board*, 2003 ABCA 374, 346 AR 281, at para. 12, and *Reference Re Section 101 of the Public Utilities Act* (1998), 164 Nfld. & PEIR 60 (Nfld. CA), at paras. 97-98 and 175).

[64] The Deferral Accounts Decision was the culmination of a process undertaken in the Price Caps Decision. In the Price Caps Decision, the CRTC indicated that the amounts in the deferral accounts were to be used in a manner contributing to achieving the CRTC's objectives (at paras. 409 and 412). In the Deferral Accounts Decision, the CRTC summarized its earlier findings that draw-downs could occur for various purposes, including through subscriber credits (at para. 6). When the CRTC approved the rates derived from the Price Caps Decision, the portion of the revenues that went into

the deferral accounts remained encumbered. The deferral accounts, and the encumbrance to which the funds recorded in them were subject, were therefore an integral part of the rate-setting exercise ensuring that the rates approved were just and reasonable. It follows that nothing in the Deferral Accounts Decision changed either the Price Caps Decision or any other prior CRTC decision on this point. The CRTC's later allocation of deferral account balances for various purposes, therefore, including customer credits, was not a variation of a final rate order.

[65] The allocation of deferral account funds to consumers was not, strictly speaking, a "rebate" in any event. Instead, as in *Bell Canada (1989)*, these allocations were one-time disbursements or rate reductions the carriers were required to make out of the deferral accounts to their *current* subscribers. The possibility of one-time credits was present from the inception of the rate-setting exercise. From the Price Caps Decision onwards, it was understood that the disposition of the deferral account funds might include an eventual credit to subscribers once the CRTC determined the appropriate allocation. It was precisely because the rate-setting mechanism approved by the CRTC included accumulation in and disposition from the deferral accounts pursuant to further CRTC orders, that the rates were and continued to be just and reasonable.

[66] Therefore, rather than viewing *Bell Canada (1989)* as setting a strict rule that subscriber credits can never be ordered out of revenues derived from final rates, it is important to remember Gonthier J's concern that the financial stability of regulated utilities could be undermined if rates were open to indiscriminate variation (at p. 1760). Nothing in the Deferral Accounts Decision undermined the financial stability of the affected carriers. The amounts at issue were always treated differently for accounting purposes, and the regulated carriers were aware of the fact that the portion of their revenues going into the deferral accounts remained encumbered. In fact, the Price Caps Decision formula would have allowed for *lower* rates than the ones ultimately set, were it not for the creation of the deferral accounts. Those lower rates could conceivably have been considered sufficient to maintain the financial stability of the carriers and were increased only in an effort to encourage market entry by new competitors.

[67] TELUS argued additionally that the Deferral Accounts Decision constituted a confiscation of its property. This is an argument I have difficulty accepting. The funds in the accounts never belonged unequivocally to the carriers, and always consisted of encumbered revenues. Had the CRTC intended that these revenues be used for any purposes the affected carriers wanted, it could simply have approved the rates as just and reasonable and ordered the balance of the deferral accounts turned over to them. It chose not to do so.

[68] It is also worth noting that in approving Bell Canada's rates, the CRTC ordered it to allocate certain tax savings to the deferral accounts. Neither the CRTC, nor Bell Canada, could possibly have expected that the company would be able to keep that portion of its rate revenue representing a past liability for taxes that it was in fact not currently liable to pay or defer.

[69] For the above reasons, I would dismiss the Bell Canada and TELUS appeal.

[70] The premise underlying the Consumers' Association of Canada appeal is that the disposition of some deferral account funds for broadband expansion highlighted the fact

that the rates charged by carriers were, in a certain sense, not just and reasonable. Consumers can only succeed if it can demonstrate that the CRTC's decision was unreasonable.

[71] At its core, Consumers' primary argument was that the Deferral Accounts Decision effectively forced users of a certain service (residential subscribers in certain areas) to subsidize users of another service (the future users of broadband services) once the expansion of broadband infrastructure was completed. In its view, this was an indication that the rates charged to residential users were not in fact just and reasonable, and that therefore the balance in the deferral accounts, excluding the disbursements for accessibility services, should be distributed to customers.

[72] As previously noted, the deferral accounts were created and disbursed pursuant to the CRTC's power to approve just and reasonable rates, and were an integral part of such rates. Far from rendering these rates inappropriate, the deferral accounts ensured that the rates were just and reasonable. And the policy objectives in s. 7, which the CRTC is always obliged to consider, demonstrate that the CRTC need not limit itself to considering solely the service at issue in determining whether rates are just and reasonable. The statute contemplates a comprehensive national telecommunications framework. It does not require the CRTC to atomize individual services. It is for the CRTC to determine a tolerable level of cross-subsidization.

[73] Nor does the traditional approach to telecommunications regulation support Consumers' argument. Long-distance telephone users have long subsidized local telephone users (Price Caps Decision, at para. 2). Therefore, while rates for individual services covered by the *Telecommunications Act* may be evaluated on a just and reasonable basis, rates are not necessarily rendered unreasonable or unjust simply because there is some cross-subsidization between services. (See Ryan, at §604, for the proposition that the CRTC can determine the appropriate extent of cross-subsidization for a given telecommunications carrier.)

[74] In my view, the CRTC properly considered the objectives set out in s. 7 when it ordered expenditures for the expansion of broadband infrastructure and consumer credits. In doing so, it treated the statutory objectives as guiding principles in the exercise of its rate-setting authority. Pursuing policy objectives through the exercise of its rate-setting power is precisely what s. 47 requires the CRTC to do in setting just and reasonable rates.

[75] In deciding to allocate the deferral account funds to improving accessibility services and broadband expansion in rural and remote areas, the CRTC had in mind its statutorily mandated objectives of facilitating "the orderly development throughout Canada of a telecommunications system that serves to … strengthen the social and economic fabric of Canada" under s. 7(a); rendering "reliable and affordable telecommunications services … to Canadians in both urban and rural areas" under s. 7(b); and responding "to the economic and social requirements of users of telecommunications services" pursuant to s. 7(h).

[76] The CRTC heard from several parties, considered its statutorily mandated objectives in exercising its powers, and decided on an appropriate course of action. Under the circumstances, I have no hesitation in holding that the CRTC made a reasonable decision in ordering broadband expansion.

[77] I would therefore conclude that the CRTC did exactly what it was mandated to do under the *Telecommunications Act*. It had the statutory authority to set just and reasonable

rates, to establish the deferral accounts, and to direct the disposition of the funds in those accounts. It was obliged to do so in accordance with the telecommunications policy objectives set out in the legislation and, as a result, to balance and consider a wide variety of objectives and interests. It did so in these appeals in a reasonable way, both in ordering subscriber credits and in approving the use of the funds for broadband expansion.

[78] I would dismiss the appeals. At the request of all parties, there will be no order for costs.

Appeals dismissed.

NOTES

1. To which instruments does Abella J refer in determining the statutory purpose underlying the CRTC's rate-setting power? How does this factor interact with others relating to the CRTC's decision? In particular, on what basis does Abella J conclude, at para. 37, that it is "self-evident that the CRTC has considerable expertise" on rate-setting?

2. Abella J finds, at para. 48, that the CRTC has the power to set "just and reasonable" rates for the purposes of the *Telecommunications Act* and "through a diverse range of methods, taking into account a variety of different constituencies and interests." This invokes the category of policy—or polycentric—questions, described in the court's decision in *Pushpanathan*, at para. 36 (excerpted in chapter 11 of this text) in these terms:

> Where the purposes of the statute and of the decision-maker are conceived not primarily in terms of establishing rights as between parties, or as entitlements, but rather as a delicate balancing between different constituencies, then the appropriateness of court supervision diminishes. ... That legal principles are vague, open-textured, or involve a "multi-factored balancing test" may also militate in favour of a lower standard of review ... . These considerations are all specific articulations of the broad principles of "polycentricity" well known to academic commentators who suggest that it provides the best rationale for judicial deference to non-judicial agencies ... . [S]ome problems require the consideration of numerous interests simultaneously, and the promulgation of solutions which concurrently balance benefits and costs for many different parties.

Such a situation of polycentricity was classically described by the American legal scholar Lon L. Fuller in these evocative terms (Lon L. Fuller, "The Forms and Limits of Adjudication" (1978), 92 *Harv. L Rev.* 353, at 395):

> We may visualize this kind of situation by thinking of a spider web. A pull on one strand will distribute tensions after a complicated pattern throughout the web as a whole. Doubling the original pull will, in all likelihood, not simply double each of the resulting tensions but will rather create a different complicated pattern of tensions. This would certainly occur, for example, if the doubled pull caused one or more of the weaker strands to snap. This is a "polycentric" situation because it is "many centered"—each crossing of strands is a distinct centre for distributing tensions.

3. In its earlier decision in *ATCO Gas & Pipelines Ltd. v. Alberta (Energy & Utilities Board)*, 2006 SCC 4, [2006] 1 SCR 140, the Supreme Court held by a 4:3 majority that the

Alberta Energy and Utilities Board lacked the jurisdiction to order a disbursement to a utility's subscribers of a portion of the proceeds of an asset sale by the utility (the dissenting judges would have upheld the decision, after concluding that it was highly discretionary and protected by a full privative clause and thus entitled to deference). This decision was heavily criticized for its de-emphasis of the broad statutory language used to describe the board's authority to make orders and impose conditions "in the public interest." How does Abella J distinguish the CRTC's rate-setting power in the *Telecommunications Act* from those of the Alberta Energy and Utilities Board? Is this a credible basis for distinction or does it simply reflect a more permissive approach by the court, relative to its earlier decision in *ATCO*, to discretionary or policy decisions by economic regulators?

4. Abella J notes the elaborate process of public consultation that was conducted by the CRTC prior to its decisions on the Price Caps Decision and on the deferral accounts. Might this feature of the case have had some bearing on the court's dismissal of the objections by Bell Canada and TELUS? Should it?

5. For another recent decision of the Supreme Court of Canada on statutory purpose, see *Montréal (City) v. Montreal Port Authority*, 2010 SCC 14 (CanLII), in which the court concluded that the discretionary decisions of the two federal Crown corporations on how to calculate payments they owed in lieu of property tax to the City of Montreal were unreasonable.

CHAPTER ELEVEN

The Nature of the Question

INTRODUCTION

Before *Dunsmuir*, the most important factor in the pragmatic and functional approach appeared to be that of expertise. Iacobucci J said as much in *Canada (Director of Investigation and Research) v. Southam Inc.*, [1997] 1 SCR 748 (Can.), as we saw in the previous chapter of this text. However, *Dunsmuir* shifted the focus to the nature of the question by emphasizing that a determination of the nature of the question may create a strong presumption in favour of deference, such that it may be unnecessary to examine other factors in detail. What then do we mean by the nature of the question and is it feasible to categorize administrative decisions as reflecting—or turning on—one particular type of question rather than another?

Conventionally, the courts have distinguished the decisions of administrative actors based on whether they engaged questions of law, questions of fact, or questions of mixed law and fact. These categories were discussed by Iacobucci J in *Southam*, at para. 35:

> Briefly stated, questions of law are questions about what the correct legal test is; questions of fact are questions about what actually took place between the parties; and questions of mixed law and fact are questions about whether the facts satisfy the legal tests. A simple example will illustrate these concepts. In the law of tort, the question what "negligence" means is a question of law. The question whether the defendant did this or that is a question of fact. And, once it has been decided that the applicable standard is one of negligence, the question whether the defendant satisfied the appropriate standard of care is a question of mixed law and fact. I recognize, however, that the distinction between law on the one hand and mixed law and fact on the other is difficult. On occasion, what appears to be mixed law and fact turns out to be law, or *vice versa*.

As helpful as this guidance is, it is as we shall see not always straightforward to classify a decision of a tribunal or agency, or one single question arising from that decision, as one of law, fact, or mixed fact and law. Likewise, it may be challenging to distinguish these categories from the further category of "discretionary" questions given that the resolution of issues of law and fact always involve some element of discretion, although to widely varying degrees. As we shall see, the further category of discretionary questions (and the closely connected "policy" questions), as identified in *Dunsmuir*, refers not so much to the use of discretion in general in decision making, but rather to a category of questions that are *sufficiently* discretionary based primarily on the language of the relevant statute.

Dunsmuir instructs that in some cases an assessment of the nature of the question will presumptively determine the standard of review. This will be especially clear where the question is of constitutional importance or where it involves general issues of law such as a resolution of apparent conflicts of jurisdiction between different tribunals, leading to a correctness standard. Other types of questions, including many questions of law, will "usually" result in a reasonableness standard, according to *Dunsmuir*. Despite this guidance, however, it is not straightforward to characterize the nature of the question before a court. Heckman writes that "the nature of the question is the most amenable to manipulation by the parties and, possibly, by reviewing courts" (G. Heckman, "Dunsmuir and Substantive Review— Implications and Impact: A Preliminary Assessment," presentation to the Canadian Institute for the Administration of Justice National Roundtable on Administrative Law, Halifax, Nova Scotia (May 2009), at 26-29).

Generally speaking, the analytical process of issue selection in litigation entails a host of subtle choices by the disputing parties about how to frame a case before the court. And, facing the record before it, the court will itself have to make choices about how to orient its analysis and resolution of the issues in dispute. At various stages, it may be difficult to distinguish between different types of questions, giving counsel and judges alike the opportunity to shape the construction of the case in the manner that either favours or eschews deference to the administrative decision-maker. Likewise, it may be difficult to decide whether to divide—or "disaggregate"—the overall decision of a decision-maker into a series of more precise questions of law, fact, and so on. Taken to an extreme, the tool of disaggregation could be used to divide an administrative decision into numerous separate components; more typically, a court will disaggregate in order to isolate a particular question of law from the wider decision under review in order to subject it to correctness review. However, any choice by a court to disaggregate implies that one component of the decision calls for an exceptional level of judicial scrutiny (or deference), creating opportunities for short-cuts around (or to) judicial deference. See M.G. Underhill, "*Dunsmuir v. New Brunswick*: A Rose by Any Other Name?" (2008), 21 *CJALP* 247, at 257-58.

There is a long and controversial history on a further category: jurisdictional questions. The meaning of this category is especially tortuous to pin down because of the many ways in which courts have sought to identify jurisdictional issues in the context of what might otherwise be treated as simply questions of law or mixed fact and law. For much of the 20th century, the doctrines of "preliminary question" and "collateral fact" were used in order to "find" jurisdictional errors, in turn enabling the court to assert its authority to correct the interpretations of administrative actors even in the face of a strong privative clause. This led to a great deal of criticism and, in its classic decision in *CUPE, Local 963 v. New Brunswick Liquor Corporation*, [1979] 2 SCR 227, the Supreme Court emphasized that judges should not substitute their views about how to interpret a statute (or make policy decisions) by artificially classifying some aspect of an administrative decision as "going to" jurisdiction. This point of caution on the concept of jurisdictional error was reinforced in subsequent decisions, including *Dunsmuir*.

In this chapter, we elaborate on the nature of the question as a factor in the standard of review analysis. To do so, we examine various challenges arising from the attempt to distinguish between different types of questions and decisions. We focus first on the role of the nature of the question after *Dunsmuir*, providing examples of cases in which the court has focused on this factor in relation both to fact-laden questions and to general questions of law. Next we introduce the subcategory of discretionary questions, which were brought within the general analytical framework of substantive review by the *Baker* decision (discretionary decisions are discussed further in chapter 15 of this text). This leads to a discussion of the vexing issue of whether and how a court should disaggregate (or "segment") a decision into multiple questions, each potentially subject to a different standard of review. We reserve for chapter 12 our discussion of jurisdictional questions and the historical evolution of the pragmatic and functional approach to substantive review, dating from the *CUPE* decision of 1979.

FACTUAL QUESTIONS

According to *Dunsmuir* (at para. 53):

> Where the question is one of fact, discretion or policy, deference will usually apply automatically. … We believe that the same standard must apply to the review of questions where the legal and factual issues are intertwined with and cannot be readily separated.

The excerpt from *Southam* that was reproduced in the introduction to this chapter offers a sense of what the court means when it refers to questions of fact and to mixed questions in which the legal and factual issues are intertwined. Why in turn should such questions call presumptively for deference? There are various reasons in the case of the factual determinations of administrative actors. Most importantly, it is the primary decision-maker that has had first-hand access to the information on which a factual assessment was based, and also to the regulatory context in which the decision was made. The primary decision-maker is thus better positioned to evaluate and weigh the evidence in relation to the factual issues in dispute, particularly where the evidence flows from *viva voce* testimony. In addition, the courts often appear to be swayed by the reality that the factual findings made in a specific case are of less concern for the courts where they are unlikely to affect future cases or the legal system in general. So long as a decision-maker arrived at its factual conclusions reasonably, by ensuring that there was evidence to support them and by considering all of the relevant evidence, the courts will not interfere. (On the other hand, this might arguably present opportunities for a decision-maker to insulate a decision from review by structuring it so that it turns on "reasonable" determinations of fact.)

The same justification for deference extends to questions in which the factual issues cannot readily be separated from the questions of law. The great majority of administrative decisions involve factual as well as legal issues. Typically, a court will treat a decision as a single act, subject to a single standard of review. The category of mixed fact and law allows for decisions to be characterized in this way by recognizing that the core of many decisions is the activity of applying a rule or standard to the facts of a particular case. This was emphasized by the Supreme Court of Canada in *Law Society of New Brunswick v. Ryan*, [2003] 1 SCR 247, at para. 41, where the court deferred to and reinstated the decision of a disciplinary committee of a law society to disbar one of its members:

> The question of what sanction Mr. Ryan should face as a result of his misconduct is a question of mixed fact and law since it involves the application of general principles of the Act to specific circumstances. The Court of Appeal impugned the weight that the Committee assigned to particular mitigating evidence and also disapproved of the Committee's selection of factually similar cases. These are fact-intensive elements within the question of mixed fact and law. They do

not involve easily extracted and discretely framed questions of law. The Committee's decision on sanction is not one that will determine future cases except insofar as it is a useful case for comparison. The decision is intricately bound to many factual findings and inferences about the misconduct of Mr. Ryan and the interests of the public and the profession. The Committee clearly benefited from the opportunity to hear the testimony and cross-examination of Mr. Ryan and of the expert witnesses. All this suggests that a higher degree of deference should be afforded to the Disciplinary Committee.

In the following decision, which like *Ryan* pre-dates *Dunsmuir*, the Supreme Court of Canada emphasized the factual aspects of the decision of another professional disciplinary committee (here, for doctors)—especially its basis in the assessment of the credibility of witnesses—to justify a reasonableness standard, even in the face of a broad statutory right of appeal and relatively limited expertise of the decision-maker. Observe also, as a prelude to *Dunsmuir*, how McLachlin CJC summarized the factors at stake in the pragmatic and functional approach.

Dr. Q v. College of Physicians and Surgeons of British Columbia
[2003] 1 SCR 226

[In 1998, an inquiry committee of the appellant college found that the respondent physician had taken physical and emotional advantage of one of his female patients and was guilty of infamous conduct. The Council of the College suspended the respondent from the practice of medicine for 18 months, with stringent conditions for his return to the profession. On an appeal under the *Medical Practitioners Act*, RSBC 1996, c. 285, the reviewing judge set aside the inquiry committee's decision, disagreeing with its findings as to credibility. The Court of Appeal dismissed the college's appeal. (Taken from the headnote.)]

McLACHLIN CJ:

I. Introduction

[Factual introduction omitted.]

[3] This appeal raises a number of questions about the legal relationships between administrative bodies, reviewing courts, and courts of appeal. The result in this case, therefore, depends upon a clear understanding, and calls for a clear articulation, of the legal principles that guide review at each of these levels.

[4] I conclude that the reviewing judge of the British Columbia Supreme Court exceeded the limits of judicial review authorized by the Act by engaging in a reconsideration of the Committee's findings of fact and that the Court of Appeal erred in failing to set aside the order of the reviewing judge. In the result, I would allow the appeal and reinstate the order of the College of Physicians and Surgeons against Dr. Q.

II. *The Facts and Decisions*

[5] The relationship between Dr. Q and Ms. T began in early 1994 as a therapeutic one. Ms. T sought Dr. Q's help in treating her depression. Ms. T alleged that, at some point in the spring of 1995, the relationship became sexual and that this sexual relationship lasted for approximately 16 months. The case ultimately turned on an assessment of credibility. Dr. Q flatly denied Ms. T's allegations that they had been involved sexually. The Committee heard the oral evidence of both parties and considered corroborative evidence. In reaching its conclusion that sexual acts had occurred, the Committee stated that it accepted Ms. T's evidence and disbelieved that of Dr. Q (Report of the Inquiry Committee, January 5, 1998, p. 20).

[6] Section 73 of the Act affords an appeal to the courts "on the merits" of the case. Dr. Q appealed to the British Columbia Supreme Court. On appeal, Koenigsberg J, in chambers, accepted that "[t]he task of the Committee was to determine the guilt or innocence of Dr. Q. based almost completely on the credibility of the witnesses" (para. 2). Koenigsberg J posed the question before her as follows (at para. 4):

> The issue is whether the evidence before the Committee objectively assessed meets the standard of clear and cogent evidence to support the finding that Dr. Q. was guilty.

She reviewed the evidence and disagreed with the Committee's findings as to credibility. As a result, Koenigsberg J held that the evidence was not "sufficiently cogent" (para. 39) to make it safe to uphold the findings of the panel. She allowed the appeal and set aside the finding of infamous conduct.

[7] The College appealed to the British Columbia Court of Appeal. The Court of Appeal reviewed Koenigsberg J's decision, felt that it could not reach the conclusion that she was "clearly wrong" (para. 30) and, therefore, dismissed the appeal.

III. *Analysis*

[8] Since this case turns on the respective roles of an administrative tribunal and the courts, it is necessary to consider in turn the legal principles that guide the Committee, the reviewing judge, and the Court of Appeal.

A. *The Role of the Committee*

[9] The Province of British Columbia has ultimate authority and responsibility for the governance of the medical profession in that province. It has delegated part of this responsibility to the College of Physicians and Surgeons through the mechanism of an Inquiry Committee whose task it is to investigate complaints against members of the profession. The Committee gives its opinion to the College, which imposes a sanction if the complaint is found to have merit.

[10] The Inquiry Committee in this case consisted of two physicians, a public representative, and a member of the Bar of British Columbia. Sections 53 and 60 of the Act empowered it to decide the issues raised by the complaint. The merits of the complaint are to be determined by the Committee on the basis of the evidence and its findings on credibility.

[11] The Committee had three tasks before it in dealing with the allegations levelled against Dr. Q: first, it had to make findings of fact, including assessments of credibility; second, it had to select the appropriate standard of proof; and, third, it had to apply the standard of proof to the facts as found to determine whether the alleged impropriety had been proven. The Committee applied the standard of "clear and cogent evidence," enunciated in *Jory v. College of Physicians and Surgeons of British Columbia*, [1985] BCJ No. 320 (QL) (SC), and all parties accepted that this was appropriate. This standard was not challenged in the courts below nor in this Court, and the case law demonstrates that it is routinely used in professional conduct inquiries in the Province of British Columbia. The determination of whether the allegations had been proven to this standard followed irresistibly from the Committee's assessment of the witnesses' evidence, leaving credibility as the main issue before the Committee.

[12] The Committee heard the oral evidence of both Dr. Q and Ms. T and made assessments of the manner in which each had delivered their evidence. The Committee found Ms. T to be "forthright and direct" and stated that, even on questions of a very personal nature, she "answered questions directly and responsively" (p. 20). In contrast, the Committee felt that Dr. Q was "initially nervous in giving his evidence" and, even after he settled down, "he was nonetheless somewhat hesitant and evasive when dealing with difficult questions" (p. 20). But the Committee also looked to the internal consistency of both parties' evidence. In a letter written to the College, Dr. Q had stated that he "did see Ms. [T] for lunch *on at least one occasion* after she stopped seeing [him] as a patient" (p. 20 (emphasis added)). Yet on cross-examination, Dr. Q admitted to having lunch with Ms. T on between 10 and 15 occasions. The Committee viewed this discrepancy as diminishing Dr. Q's credibility.

[13] The Committee also assessed the substance of both stories in light of potentially corroborative evidence. On a number of important details, the Committee found that the external evidence was corroborative of Ms. T's testimony. For example, Ms. T was able to describe particular physical features of Dr. Q in a way that the Committee found was more "consistent with her visual observation" (p. 26) of Dr. Q's body than having heard about them from Dr. Q, as he had suggested. The Committee concluded that Ms. T's ability to provide a vivid description of Dr. Q's new office, which he had moved into after they had ceased their therapeutic relationship, was inconsistent with Dr. Q's assertion that Ms. T had only been in the new office on one occasion, and even then only briefly. Furthermore, contrary to Ms. T's version of events, Dr. Q denied that he had ever dined at a particular restaurant with Ms. T. Yet the owner of the restaurant confirmed that a reservation in Dr. Q's name was made and used at a time consistent with the evidence given by Ms. T. The Committee examined a letter written by Dr. Q to Ms. T and concluded that its contents were "likewise more consistent with a relationship which has gone beyond the platonic" (p. 28). Finally, the Committee considered Ms. T's evidence that, subsequent to the termination of their therapeutic relationship, she and Dr. Q would meet at his office at the end of the day, at which point they would engage in sexual activity. The Committee heard evidence from a witness, Ms. K, which confirmed that Ms. T had, indeed, been in Dr. Q's office at the end of the day, well after their therapeutic relationship had ended. Dr. Q offered no explanation (p. 29).

[14] On the basis of the manner and internal consistency of their testimony, as well as all of the corroborative evidence, the Committee stated that it "accepts the evidence of Ms. [T] as to the occurrence of the sexual acts described in her evidence and disbelieves Dr. [Q] in his evidence where he denies that the sexual encounters occurred" (p. 20). As noted, the conclusion that a sexual relationship had existed and that this constituted infamous and unprofessional conduct flowed inexorably once these findings of credibility had been made. As such, the key question in this case is whether the reviewing judge should have interfered with the findings of credibility made by the Committee.

[15] Having set out the responsibility and tasks of the Committee in this case, and summarized its conclusions, I turn to the duties of the reviewing judge in the Supreme Court of British Columbia.

B. The Role of the Reviewing Judge

[16] The Act permits an appeal to the Supreme Court of British Columbia. As Koenigsberg J noted, the reviewing judge's task is not to substitute his or her views of the evidence for those of the tribunal, but to review the decision with the appropriate degree of curial deference. However, having said this, Koenigsberg J engaged in a wide-ranging review of the evidence and in effect substituted her views on the credibility of the witnesses for those of the Committee.

[17] This approach appears to have been connected to two assumptions. The first was the apparent assumption that since the standard of proof was the intermediate standard of clear and cogent evidence, the reviewing judge was required to review the evidence and make her own evaluation of whether it reached this standard. The second was the assumption that because the Act expressly confers a right of appeal, the review was not to be treated like the usual review of the decision of an administrative tribunal, which requires the reviewing judge to first determine the appropriate standard of review and then apply that standard to the decision. In my view, both of these assumptions are mistaken. As a result of their application, the reviewing judge applied the wrong standard of review and interfered unduly in the Committee's findings of credibility and fact.

(1) The Distinction Between Standard of Proof at First Instance and Standard of Judicial Review

[18] The first erroneous assumption was that because the standard was that of clear and cogent evidence, the reviewing judge was required to revisit the Committee's findings of credibility and fact. The reviewing judge took the requirement for clear and cogent evidence as an entree into a reconsideration of the facts. She stated at para. 4:

> Thus guided it remains to consider the findings of the Committee in this case in relation to credibility. The issue is whether the evidence before the Committee objectively assessed meets the standard of clear and cogent evidence to support the finding that Dr. Q. was guilty.

[19] The standard of clear and cogent evidence does not permit the reviewing judge to enter into a re-evaluation of the evidence. Indeed, *Jory, supra*, upon which the reviewing judge relied, emphasized that findings of fact or credibility are generally due considerable deference (paras. 12-13). The requirement for "clear and cogent evidence" is a

matter relating to the standard of proof employed at the Committee level, ensuring that the Committee is alive to the gravity of the consequences of their decision. It is a legal standard that the administrative decision-maker must apply to the evidence in order to determine the outcome of the case. It does not instruct a reviewing court on how to scrutinize the decision of the administrative decision-maker. This is solely a question of standard of review, to be resolved by applying the pragmatic and functional approach.

(2) The Primacy of the Pragmatic and Functional Approach

[Here the chief justice discussed the need for a court to apply the usual administrative law principles pertaining to the standard of review.]

(3) A Review of the Pragmatic and Functional Factors

[26] In the pragmatic and functional approach, the standard of review is determined by considering four contextual factors—the presence or absence of a privative clause or statutory right of appeal; the expertise of the tribunal relative to that of the reviewing court on the issue in question; the purposes of the legislation and the provision in particular; and, the nature of the question—law, fact, or mixed law and fact. The factors may overlap. The overall aim is to discern legislative intent, keeping in mind the constitutional role of the courts in maintaining the rule of law. I find the approach taken in the courts below problematic. As a result, I believe it will be helpful to re-articulate the focus of the factors involved and update the considerations relevant to each. Before doing this, I must emphasize that consideration of the four factors should enable the reviewing judge to address the core issues in determining the degree of deference. It should not be viewed as an empty ritual, or applied mechanically. The virtue of the pragmatic and functional approach lies in its capacity to draw out the information that may be relevant to the issue of curial deference.

[27] The first factor focuses generally on the statutory mechanism of review. A statute may afford a broad right of appeal to a superior court or provide for a certified question to be posed to the reviewing court, suggesting a more searching standard of review: see *Southam, supra,* at para. 46; *Baker, supra,* at para. 58. A statute may be silent on the question of review; silence is neutral, and "does not imply a high standard of scrutiny": *Push-panathan, supra,* at para. 30. Finally, a statute may contain a privative clause, militating in favour of a more deferential posture. The stronger a privative clause, the more deference is generally due.

[28] The second factor, relative expertise, recognizes that legislatures will sometimes remit an issue to a decision-making body that has particular topical expertise or is adept in the determination of particular issues. Where this is so, courts will seek to respect this legislative choice when conducting judicial review. Yet expertise is a relative concept, not an absolute one. Greater deference will be called for only where the decision-making body is, in some way, *more expert than the courts* and the question under consideration is one that *falls within the scope of this greater expertise*: see *Moreau-Bérubé v. New Brunswick (Judicial Council),* [2002] 1 SCR 249, 2002 SCC 11, at para. 50. Thus, the analysis under this heading "has three dimensions: the court must characterize the expertise of the tribunal in question; it must consider its own expertise relative to that of the tribunal;

and it must identify the nature of the specific issue before the administrative decision-maker relative to this expertise": *Pushpanathan, supra*, at para. 33.

[29] Relative expertise can arise from a number of sources and can relate to questions of pure law, mixed fact and law, or fact alone. The composition of an administrative body might endow it with knowledge uniquely suited to the questions put before it and deference might, therefore, be called for under this factor: *Pezim v. British Columbia (Superintendent of Brokers)*, [1994] 2 SCR 557, at pp. 591-92. For example, a statute may call for decision-makers to have expert qualifications, to have accumulated experience in a particular area, or to play a particular role in policy development: *Mattel, supra*, at paras. 28-31. Similarly, an administrative body might be so habitually called upon to make findings of fact in a distinctive legislative context that it can be said to have gained a measure of relative institutional expertise: e.g., *Canada (Attorney General) v. Mossop*, [1993] 1 SCR 554. Simply put, "whether because of the specialized knowledge of its decision-makers, special procedure, or non-judicial means of implementing the Act," an administrative body called upon to answer a question that falls within its area of relative expertise will generally be entitled to greater curial deference: *Pushpanathan, supra*, at para. 32.

[30] The third factor is the purpose of the statute. Since the conceptual focus of the pragmatic and functional approach is upon discerning the intent of the legislature, it is fitting that reviewing courts are called upon to consider the general purpose of the statutory scheme within which the administrative decision is taking place. If the question before the administrative body is one of law or engages a particular aspect of the legislation, the analysis under this factor must also consider the specific legislative purpose of the provision(s) implicated in the review. As a general principle, increased deference is called for where legislation is intended to resolve and balance competing policy objectives or the interests of various constituencies: see *Pushpanathan, supra*, at para. 36, where Bastarache J used the term "polycentric" to describe these legislative characteristics.

[31] A statutory purpose that requires a tribunal to select from a range of remedial choices or administrative responses, is concerned with the protection of the public, engages policy issues, or involves the balancing of multiple sets of interests or considerations will demand greater deference from a reviewing court: see *Pezim, supra*, and *Southam, supra*. In *Mount Sinai, supra*, at para. 57, Binnie J recognized that the express language of a statute may help to identify such a purpose. For example, provisions that require the decision-maker to "have regard to all such circumstances as it considers relevant" or confer a broad discretionary power upon a decision-maker will generally suggest policy-laden purposes and, consequently, a less searching standard of review (see also *Baker, supra*, at para. 56). Reviewing courts should also consider the breadth, specialization, and technical or scientific nature of the issues that the legislation asks the administrative tribunal to consider. In this respect, the principles animating the factors of relative expertise and legislative purpose tend to overlap. A legislative purpose that deviates substantially from the normal role of the courts suggests that the legislature intended to leave the issue to the discretion of the administrative decision-maker and, therefore, militates in favour of greater deference.

[32] In contrast, a piece of legislation or a statutory provision that essentially seeks to resolve disputes or determine rights between two parties will demand less deference. The more the legislation approximates a conventional judicial paradigm involving a pure *lis*

inter partes determined largely by the facts before the tribunal, the less deference the reviewing court will tend to show.

[33] The final factor is the nature of the problem. In appellate review of judicial decisions, the nature of the question is almost entirely determinative of standard of review: *Housen v. Nikolaisen*, [2002] 2 SCR 235, 2002 SCC 33. For example, as the *Stein v. The Ship "Kathy K,"* [1976] 2 SCR 802, and *Toneguzzo-Norvell (Guardian ad litem of) v. Burnaby Hospital*, [1994] 1 SCR 114, line of cases has made clear, judicial decisions of first instance on factual issues will only be interfered with where the appellate court can identify a "palpable and overriding error" or where the finding was "clearly wrong": *Kathy K*, at pp. 806 and 808. But the conceptual foundation of review of administrative decisions is fundamentally different than that of appeals from judicial decisions. Consequently, in the context of judicial review of administrative action, the nature of the question is just one of four factors to consider when determining standard of review.

[34] When the finding being reviewed is one of pure fact, this factor will militate in favour of showing more deference towards the tribunal's decision. Conversely, an issue of pure law counsels in favour of a more searching review. This is particularly so where the decision will be one of general importance or great precedential value: *Chieu v. Canada (Minister of Citizenship and Immigration)*, [2002] 1 SCR 84, 2002 SCC 3, at para. 23. Finally, with respect to questions of mixed fact and law, this factor will call for more deference if the question is fact-intensive, and less deference if it is law-intensive.

[35] Having considered each of these factors, a reviewing court must settle upon one of three currently recognized standards of review: see *Law Society of New Brunswick v. Ryan*, [2003] 1 SCR 247, 2003 SCC 20, released concurrently. Where the balancing of the four factors above suggests considerable deference, the patent unreasonableness standard will be appropriate. Where little or no deference is called for, a correctness standard will suffice. If the balancing of factors suggests a standard of deference somewhere in the middle, the reasonableness *simpliciter* standard will apply.

(4) Application to the Case at Bar

[36] Applying the pragmatic and functional approach in this case, the four factors lead to a standard of reasonableness *simpliciter*. The fact that the statute provides a broad right of appeal and that the Committee is no more expert than the courts on the issue in question suggests a low degree of deference.

[37] An assessment of the purpose of the statute and the provision in particular yields an ambivalent result. On one hand, the legislature's intent for the legislation as a whole was to assign to the College the role of balancing competing interests and multiple policy objectives, like the protection of the public, education and qualification of members, the setting of standards of ethics and practice, and the administration of privacy regimes: the Act, s. 3. This purpose suggests considerable deference. However, the discrete issue of adjudicating a claim of professional misconduct—the particular issue that the statute puts before the Committee—is quasi-judicial in nature, and therefore militates against deference. In the result, the purpose analysis counsels neither for great deference, nor for exacting scrutiny.

[38] Finally, however, the need for deference is greatly heightened by the nature of the problem—a finding of credibility. Assessments of credibility are quintessentially

questions of fact. The relative advantage enjoyed by the Committee, who heard the *viva voce* evidence, must be respected.

[39] Balancing these factors, I am satisfied that the appropriate standard of review is reasonableness *simpliciter*. ...

[Here the chief justice discussed the application of the standard; see chapter 13 of this text.]

[42] I conclude that the reviewing judge erred by applying too exacting a standard of review and substituting her own view of the evidence for that of the Committee.

C. The Role of the Court of Appeal

[43] The Court of Appeal stated that "[t]he standard that we must apply in assessing the judgment of Madam Justice Koenigsberg is whether in her re-weighing of the evidence she was clearly wrong" (para. 25). This is not the appropriate test at the secondary appellate level. The role of the Court of Appeal was to determine whether the reviewing judge had chosen and applied the correct standard of review, and in the event she had not, to assess the administrative body's decision in light of the correct standard of review, reasonableness. At this stage in the analysis, the Court of Appeal is dealing with appellate review of a subordinate court, not judicial review of an administrative decision. As such, the normal rules of appellate review of lower courts as articulated in *Housen, supra*, apply. The question of the right standard to select and apply is one of law and, therefore, must be answered correctly by a reviewing judge. The Court of Appeal erred by affording deference where none was due.

[44] The Court of Appeal should have corrected the reviewing judge's error, substituted the appropriate standard of administrative review, and assessed the Committee's decision on this basis. Judged on the proper standard of reasonableness, there was ample evidence to support the Committee's conclusions on credibility, burden of proof and application of the burden of proof to the factual findings. It follows that the decisions of the reviewing judge and the Court of Appeal should be set aside and the order of the College restored.

· · ·

Appeal allowed with costs.

QUESTIONS OF LAW

In *Dunsmuir*, the majority stated that a court should also adopt a correctness standard in the case of certain questions of law. A correctness standard is said to be required for "constitutional questions regarding the division of powers between Parliament and the provinces in the *Constitution Act, 1867* ... as well as other constitutional issues" and of "[q]uestions regarding the jurisdictional lines between two or more competing specialized tribunals." More generally, correctness is required for questions of "general law" that are both "of central importance to the legal system as a whole" and "outside the adjudicator's specialized area of expertise," and that "impact on the administration of justice as a whole." The reason for judicial intervention on such questions is to ensure "uniform and consistent answers" from the courts. As an example, the majority referred to the "complex common law rules and conflicting jurisprudence on the doctrines of *res judicata* and abuse of process" (as in

Toronto (City) v. CUPE, Local 79, [2003] 3 SCR 77, 2003 SCC 63). Finally, the majority in *Dunsmuir* reserved a correctness standard for the well-established, but widely debated, category of jurisdictional questions.

This outline of categories of questions of law implies that such questions can be readily isolated from the factual or contextual aspects of a tribunal or agency decision. In the case of constitutional questions, this may indeed be straightforward given the obvious need for a party to invoke the constitution in order to make a constitutional argument. On the other hand, non-constitutional "general" questions of law may be difficult to identify and disaggregate for the purpose of subjecting them to a distinct standard of review. *Dunsmuir* instructs that such questions are identified by their central importance to the legal system but also in light of the expertise of the decision-maker. But is such expertise to be approached in terms of the wider decision taken by a tribunal or agency, or in terms of the act of legal interpretation upon which a court has chosen to focus? The extract below dates from well before *Dunsmuir*, but offers nonetheless a good example of a question of law that appears to fall within the *Dunsmuir* subcategory of "general" questions of law. Observe how the court emphasizes both the importance of the issue of legal interpretation for future cases and the relative lack of expertise of the Immigration and Refugee Board in the definition of human rights guarantees.

Pushpanathan v. Canada (Minister of Citizenship and Immigration)
[1998] 1 SCR 982 (Can.)

[In 1985, the appellant claimed refugee status under the United Nations *Convention Relating to the Status of Refugees* ("Convention"), but his claim was never adjudicated because he was granted permanent residence status in Canada. The appellant was later arrested in Canada and charged with conspiracy to traffic in a narcotic. At the time of his arrest, he was a member of a group in possession of heroin with a street value of some $10 million. He pleaded guilty and was sentenced to eight years in prison. In 1991, the appellant renewed his claim for Convention refugee status. Employment and Immigration Canada subsequently issued a conditional deportation order against him under ss. 27(1)(d) and 32.1(2) of the *Immigration Act*. The deportation pursuant to those sections was conditional on a determination that the claimant was not a Convention refugee. To determine this, the appellant's claim was referred to the Convention Refugee Determination Division of the Immigration and Refugee Board. The board decided that the appellant was not a refugee based on an exclusion clause in article 1F(c) of the Convention, which provided that the provisions of the Convention did not apply to a person who "has been guilty of acts contrary to the purposes and principles of the United Nations." The Federal Court Trial Division dismissed the appellant's application for judicial review and certified the following as a serious question of general importance for consideration: Is it an error of law for the Refugee Division to interpret article 1F(c) of the Convention to exclude from refugee status an individual guilty of a serious narcotics offence committed in Canada? The Federal Court of Appeal answered "no" to this question and upheld the Trial Division's judgment.]

BASTARACHE J (L'Heureux-Dubé, Gonthier, McLachlin JJ concurring): This appeal raises two important questions relating to who may be admitted to Canada as a refugee: first, the proper standard of judicial review over decisions of the Immigration and Refugee Board; second, the meaning of the exclusion from refugee status of those who are "guilty of acts contrary to the purposes and principles of the United Nations." That exclusion, in Article 1F(c) of the United Nations *Convention Relating to the Status of Refugees*, Can. TS 1969 No. 6, is incorporated into Canadian law by s. 2(1) of the *Immigration Act*, RSC 1985, c. I-2, requiring a definition of that phrase with respect to the domestic law of Canada.

. . .

V. Analysis

A. Standard of Review

[23] Neither in the decisions below, nor in the written submissions before this Court, was the issue of the proper standard of review of the decision of the Convention Refugee Determination Division of the Immigration and Refugee Board addressed. McKeown J, at the Trial Division level, did find that the Board had "reasonably concluded" and that there were "serious reasons for considering" that the appellant was excluded by Article 1F(c) of the Convention, implying a standard of reasonableness. However, in certifying the question to be posed to the Court of Appeal, he asked whether the Board's determination was an "error of law," suggesting a standard of correctness. The Court of Appeal confined itself to answering the certified question. The court did not consider what standard of review had been applied below, nor whether that was the correct standard.

[24] Nevertheless, s. 83(1) requires such an inquiry. It states:

> 83(1) A *judgment* of the Federal Court—Trial Division on an application for judicial review … *may be appealed* to the Federal Court of Appeal only if the Federal Court—Trial Division has at the time of rendering judgment certified that a serious question of general importance *is involved* and has stated that question. [Emphasis added.]

[25] The certification of a "question of general importance" is the trigger by which an appeal is justified. The object of the appeal is still the judgment itself, not merely the certified question. One of the elements necessary for the disposition of an application for judicial review is the standard of review of the decision of the administrative tribunal whose decision is being reviewed, and that question is clearly in issue in this case. Reluctant as this Court is to decide issues not fully argued before it, determining the standard of review is a prerequisite to the disposition of this case.

[26] The central inquiry in determining the standard of review exercisable by a court of law is the legislative intent of the statute creating the tribunal whose decision is being reviewed. More specifically, the reviewing court must ask: "[W]as the question which the provision raises one that was intended by the legislators to be left to the exclusive decision of the Board?" (*Pasiechnyk v. Saskatchewan (Workers' Compensation Board)* [1997] 2 SCR 890 (Sask.) at para. 18, *per* Sopinka J).

[Bastarache J here summarized *Bibeault* and *Southam*.]

[28] Although the language and approach of the "preliminary," "collateral" or "jurisdictional" question has been replaced by this pragmatic and functional approach, the focus of the inquiry is still on the particular, individual provision being invoked and interpreted by the tribunal. Some provisions within the same Act may require greater curial deference than others, depending on the factors which will be described in more detail below. To this extent, it is still appropriate and helpful to speak of "jurisdictional questions" which must be answered correctly by the tribunal in order to be acting *intra vires*. But it should be understood that a question which "goes to jurisdiction" is simply descriptive of a provision for which the proper standard of review is correctness, based upon the outcome of the pragmatic and functional analysis. In other words, "jurisdictional error" is simply an error on an issue with respect to which, according to the outcome of the pragmatic and functional analysis, the tribunal must make a correct interpretation and to which no deference will be shown.

(1) Factors To Be Taken into Account

[29] The factors to be taken into account in determining the standard of review have been canvassed in a number of recent decisions of this Court, and may be divided into four categories.

[Here Bastarache J discussed in general the factors of privative clauses and expertise.]

(iii) Purpose of the Act as a Whole, and the Provision in Particular

[36] As Iacobucci J noted in *Southam* ... , at para. 50, purpose and expertise often overlap. The purpose of a statute is often indicated by the specialized nature of the legislative structure and dispute-settlement mechanism, and the need for expertise is often manifested as much by the requirements of the statute as by the specific qualifications of its members. Where the purposes of the statute and of the decision-maker are conceived not primarily in terms of establishing rights as between parties, or as entitlements, but rather as a delicate balancing between different constituencies, then the appropriateness of court supervision diminishes. Thus, in *National Corn Growers*, *supra*, at 1336, Wilson J characterized the function of the board in question as one of "management," partially because of the specialized knowledge of the members of the board, but also because of the range of remedies available upon a determination, including the imposition of countervailing duties by the Minister (at 1346). In *Southam*, the Court found (at para. 48) that the "aims of the Act are more 'economic' than they are strictly 'legal'" because the broad goals of the Act "are matters that business women and men and economists are better able to understand than is a typical judge." This conclusion was reinforced by the creation in the statute of a tribunal with members having a special expertise in those domains. Also of significance are the range of administrative responses, the fact that an administrative commission plays a "protective role" *vis-à-vis* the investing public, and that it plays a role in policy development; *Pezim*, *supra*, at 596. That legal principles are vague, open-textured, or involve a "multi-factored balancing test" may also militate in favour of a lower standard of review (*Southam*, at para. 44). These considerations are all specific articulations of the broad principle of "polycentricity" well known to academic com-

mentators who suggest that it provides the best rationale for judicial deference to non-judicial agencies. A "polycentric issue is one which involves a large number of interlocking and interacting interests and considerations" (P. Cane, *An Introduction to Administrative Law* (3rd ed. 1996) at 35). While judicial procedure is premised on a bipolar opposition of parties, interests, and factual discovery, some problems require the consideration of numerous interests simultaneously, and the promulgation of solutions which concurrently balance benefits and costs for many different parties. Where an administrative structure more closely resembles this model, courts will exercise restraint. The polycentricity principle is a helpful way of understanding the variety of criteria developed under the rubric of the "statutory purpose."

(iv) The "Nature of the Problem": A Question of Law or Fact?

[37] As mentioned above, even pure questions of law may be granted a wide degree of deference where other factors of the pragmatic and functional analysis suggest that such deference is the legislative intention, as this Court found to be the case in *Pasiechnyk, supra*. Where, however, other factors leave that intention ambiguous, courts should be less deferential of decisions which are pure determinations of law. The justification for this position relates to the question of relative expertise mentioned previously. There is no clear line to be drawn between questions of law and questions of fact, and, in any event, many determinations involve questions of mixed law and fact. An appropriate litmus test was set out in *Southam* ... , at para. 37, by Iacobucci J, who stated:

> Of course, it is not easy to say precisely where the line should be drawn; though in most cases it should be sufficiently clear whether the dispute is over a general proposition that might qualify as a principle of law or over a very particular set of circumstances that is not apt to be of much interest to judges and lawyers in the future.

This principle was also articulated by L'Heureux-Dubé J in *Canada (Attorney General) v. Mossop* [1993] 1 SCR 554 (Can.) at 599-600, who sought to clarify the limitations of distinctions based on this criterion:

> In general, deference is given on questions of fact because of the "signal advantage" enjoyed by the primary finder of fact. Less deference is warranted on questions of law, in part because the finder of fact may not have developed any particular familiarity with issues of law. While there is merit in the distinction between fact and law, the distinction is not always so clear. Specialized boards are often called upon to make difficult findings of both fact and law. In some circumstances, the two are inextricably linked. Further, the "correct" interpretation of a term may be dictated by the mandate of the board and by the coherent body of jurisprudence it has developed. In some cases, even where courts might not agree with a given interpretation, the integrity of certain administrative processes may demand that deference be shown to that interpretation of law.

Her dissent in that case was founded essentially on her disapproval of the views of the majority on the characterization of the human rights tribunal as enjoying no expertise relative to courts in the understanding and interpretation of human rights Acts. Nevertheless, the principles discussed in the above quotation correctly state the law. This was confirmed in *Pasiechnyk*, at paras. 36 to 42, where the broad expertise of the Workers'

Compensation Board to determine all aspects of "eligibility" under that system was considered sufficiently broad to include the determination that the term "employer" included claims against the government for its alleged negligence in regulating the works of two companies which had led to workers' injuries. Claims against the government as regulator were thus barred by virtue of the determination in issue. To allow such a claim "would undermine the purposes of the scheme" which was to "solve ... the problem of employers becoming insolvent as a result of high damage awards" (para. 42). Such a finding falls squarely within Iacobucci J's description of a question of law: a finding which will be of great, even determinative import for future decisions of lawyers and judges. The creation of a legislative "scheme" combined with the creation of a highly specialized administrative decision-maker, as well as the presence of a strong privative clause was sufficient to grant an expansive deference even over extremely general questions of law.

[38] Keeping in mind that all the factors discussed here must be taken together to come to a view of the proper standard of review, the generality of the proposition decided will be a factor in favour of the imposition of a correctness standard. This factor necessarily intersects with the criteria described above, which may contradict such a presumption, as the majority of this Court found to be the case in *Pasiechnyk, supra*. In the usual case, however, the broader the propositions asserted, and the further the implications of such decisions stray from the core expertise of the tribunal, the less likelihood that deference will be shown. Without an implied or express legislative intent to the contrary as manifested in the criteria above, legislatures should be assumed to have left highly generalized propositions of law to courts.

(2) The Immigration Act

[39] Jurisdiction is granted to the Convention Refugee Determination Division of the Immigration and Refugee Board in the following terms:

> 67(1) The Refugee Division has, in respect of proceedings under sections 69.1 and 69.2, sole and exclusive jurisdiction to hear and determine all questions of law and fact, including questions of jurisdiction.

> 82.1(1) An application for judicial review under the *Federal Court Act* with respect to any decision or order made, or any matter arising, under this Act or the rules or regulations thereunder may be commenced only with leave of a judge of the Federal Court—Trial Division.

> 83(1) A judgment of the Federal Court—Trial Division on an application for judicial review with respect to any decision or order made, or any matter arising, under this Act or the rules or regulations thereunder may be appealed to the Federal Court of Appeal only if the Federal Court—Trial Division has at the time of rendering judgment certified that a serious question of general importance is involved and has stated that question.

(3) Previous Jurisprudence on the Standard of Review

[40] This is the first time this Court has had the opportunity of considering the standard of review over decisions of the Immigration and Refugee Board. There is surprisingly scant discussion of the issue in previous Federal Court decisions. In most cases, a

patent unreasonableness or "perverse or capricious" standard is applied. Those cases involved reviews of findings of credibility of witnesses by the Board. ...

[41] In the thorough decision of Richard J in *Sivasamboo v. Canada (Minister of Citizenship and Immigration)* [1995] 1 FC 741 (TD), however, the question before this Court is directly addressed. The case involved a Board determination that the applicants were not refugees because they had an "internal flight alternative." Richard J examines s. 82.1 of the *Immigration Act* and s. 18.1 of the *Federal Court Act*, which set out the possibility of an application for judicial review of a Board decision, and the grounds upon which such a decision may be reversed. He considers many of the controlling authorities of the day, including *Pezim* and *Bradco*. Although conceding that s. 67(1) of the *Immigration Act* is not a strong privative clause, he points out that many cases rely more on the specialized nature of the tribunal in question than on the presence or absence of a privative clause and notes: (a) that there is a limited structure for applying for judicial review; (b) that appeals from the Trial Division may only be taken when certified as a "serious question of general importance" under s. 83(1) of the *Immigration Act*; (c) that the structure of refugee determination is not typically adversarial in nature, and that members of the Board have wide powers as to production of evidence and fact-finding; (d) that there is no adverse party; (e) that the international law context, and the implementation of the Refugee Convention in Canadian law is highly complex and therefore requires specialized knowledge; (f) that the members of the Board are experts in their field and draw upon detailed, expert reports from the Documentation Centre of Employment and Immigration Canada. He relies extensively on a commentary by Professor James Hathaway on the Refugee Division, including, at 758, the following excerpt:

> These evidentiary and contextual concerns make departure from traditional modes of adjudication imperative. We need expert, engaged, activist decision-makers who will pursue substantive fairness rather than technocratic justice. We must not view refugee claimants as opponents or threats, but rather as persons seeking to invoke a right derived from international law. It is the commitment to this kind of flexibility and sensitivity which led Parliament to abolish the previous court of record charged with refugee status determination, and to replace it with an expert tribunal with inquisitorial, non-adversarial jurisdiction.

Finally, he distinguishes this Court's decision in *Mossop, supra*, contending that the position of a human rights tribunal is different because its "determination is unrelated to issues of expertise or specialized knowledge and does not require a high degree of deference." He goes on to say: "The questions at issue here are not broad questions involving general principles of statutory interpretation and legal reasoning, but the interpretation of a statutory definition within a specific international law and regulatory framework." He concludes from all these considerations that the standard is patent unreasonableness, and that standard ought to apply even to "legal questions before it" (at 761). On this basis, Richard J rejected the application for judicial review, finding that the determination of "internal flight alternative" was not patently unreasonable.

(4) The Proper Standard: Correctness

[42] Richard J's judgment in *Sivasamboo*, described above in some detail, presents admirably the case for a high level of deference to the decision of the Board. In my judgment, however, applying the pragmatic and functional analysis to the Act indicates that the decision of the Board in this case should be subjected to a standard of correctness.

[43] First, s. 83(1) would be incoherent if the standard of review were anything other than correctness. The key to the legislative intention as to the standard of review is the use of the words "a serious question of *general* importance" (emphasis added). The general importance of the question, that is, its applicability to numerous future cases, warrants the review by a court of justice. Would that review serve any purpose if the Court of Appeal were obliged to defer to incorrect decisions of the Board? Is it possible that the legislator would have provided for an exceptional appeal to the Court of Appeal on questions of "general importance," but then required that despite the "general importance" of the question, the court accept decisions of the Board which are wrong in law, even clearly wrong in law, but not patently unreasonable? The only way in which s. 83(1) can be given its explicitly articulated scope is if the Court of Appeal—and inferentially, the Federal Court, Trial Division—is permitted to substitute its own opinion for that of the Board in respect of questions of general importance. This view accords with the observations of Iacobucci J in *Southam* ... , at para. 36, that a determination which has "the potential to apply widely to many cases" should be a factor in determining whether deference should be shown. While previous Federal Court decisions, including, arguably, the dispute in *Sivasamboo*, involve significant determinations of facts, or at the highest, questions of mixed fact and law, with little or no precedential value, this case involves a determination which could disqualify numerous future refugee applicants as a matter of law. Indeed, the decision of the Board in this case would significantly narrow its own role as an evaluator of fact in numerous cases.

[44] In short, s. 83(1) of the Act grants a statutory right of appeal based upon the criterion of "generality." The principle described in *Southam* and applied in many other cases, which is really no more than an assumption as to legislative intent, is reinforced by explicit statutory inclusion.

[45] Moreover, the Board appears to enjoy no relative expertise in the matter of law which is the object of judicial review here. A clear majority of this Court has found in a number of cases that deference should not be shown by courts to human rights tribunals with respect to "general questions of law" (*Mossop, supra*, at 585), even legal rules indisputably at the core of human rights adjudication. The categorical nature of this rule has been mitigated by observations in other cases, however. As La Forest J stated for the entire Court in *Ross v. New Brunswick School District No. 15* [1996] 1 SCR 825 (NB) at para. 29:

> That having been said, I do not think the fact-finding expertise of human rights tribunals should be restrictively interpreted, and it must be assessed against the backdrop of *the particular decision the tribunal is called upon to make*. ... A finding of discrimination is impregnated with facts, facts which the Board of Inquiry is in the best position to evaluate. ... Given the complexity of the evidentiary inferences made on the basis of the facts before the Board, it is appropriate to exercise a relative degree of deference to the finding of discrimination, in light of the Board's superior expertise in fact-finding, a conclusion supported by

the existence of words importing a limited privative effect into the constituent legislation. [Emphasis added.]

A similar approach is adopted by the majority in *University of British Columbia v. Berg* [1993] 2 SCR 353 (BC) at 370.

[46] Although the precise degree of deference which should be accorded to a human rights tribunal may still be open to question, the factors militating against deference in those cases apply with much greater force to the issues here. In those cases, the relationship relevant for considering the proper standard of review was that between a tribunal with specific expertise and experience in human rights adjudication, and provisions whose purpose is to protect human rights. The provision in question here shares that purpose. In *Canada (Attorney General) v. Ward* [1993] 2 SCR 689 (Can.) at 733, La Forest J found the purpose underlying the Convention to be "the international community's commitment to the assurance of basic human rights without discrimination." As I will explain in the course of the next section, Article 1F(c) is at the core of this human rights purpose.

[47] But the Board's expertise in matters relating to human rights is far less developed than that of human rights tribunals. The expertise of the Board is in accurately evaluating whether the criteria for refugee status have been met and, in particular, assessing the nature of the risk of persecution faced by the applicant if returned to his or her country of origin. Unlike the situation of a human rights tribunal, the relationship between the expertise and the provision in question here is remote. Only 10 percent of the members of the Board are required to be lawyers (s. 61(2)) and there is no requirement that there be a lawyer on every panel. While this may not be a liability for the purposes of assessing the risk of persecution of an applicant if returned to his or her country of nationality, it renders unthinkable reposing the broad definition of a basic human rights guarantee exclusively in the hands of the Board. Nor is there any indication that the Board's experience with previous factual determinations of risk of persecution gives it any added insight into the meaning or desirable future development of the provision in question here. Unlike many cases involving determinations by human rights tribunals, this case does not involve any significant "impregnation" of legal principle with fact, as demonstrated by the ease with which the reviewing court was able to extract a question of general importance for the purposes of s. 83(1). Here, the legal principle is easily separable from the undisputed facts of the case and would undoubtedly have a wide precedential value. It bears repeating that with this determination, the tribunal is in fact seeking to stifle the application of its own expertise, rather than exercise it. The factual expertise enjoyed by this administrative decision-maker does not aid it in the interpretation of this general legal principle.

[48] Nor can the Board be characterized as performing a "managing" or "supervisory" function, as was found in *Southam* and *National Corn Growers*. The Board itself is not responsible for policy evolution. The purpose of the Convention—and particularly that of the exclusions contained in Article 1F—is clearly not the management of flows of people, but rather the conferral of minimum human rights' protection. The context in which the adjudicative function takes place is not a "polycentric" one of give-and-take between different groups, but rather the vindication of a set of relatively static human rights, and ensuring that those who fall within the prescribed categories are protected.

[49] Added to these indications of the intent of the legislator with regard to the development of general legal principles is the absence of a strong privative clause. Indeed, read in the light of s. 83(1), it appears quite clear that the privative clause, such as it is, is superseded with respect to questions of "general importance." As has been emphasized above, the "pragmatic and functional" approach allows differing standards of deference even within different sections of the same Act, and with regard to different types of decisions taken by the tribunal in question. Here, the wording of the privative clause goes hand in hand with the fourth factor of the functional and pragmatic analysis, namely, that determinations of abstract principles with wide application is a factor militating against deference.

[50] I conclude that a correctness standard applies to determinations of law by the Board. *Sivasamboo* dealt with review of a question of a significantly different nature and I wish to emphasize that I make no comment about the correctness of that decision, specific as it is to the facts presented there.

[Bastarache J went on to hold that the board had erred. His application of the correctness standard is excerpted in chapter 13 of this text.]

[Cory and Major JJ dissented on the merits but agreed that the appropriate standard of review was that of correctness.]

Appeal allowed.

NOTES

1. As noted above, one of the critical factors in *Pushpanathan* was the court's conception of the question as one of general international law, thus putting it beyond the expertise of the board. In light of this, would an application of the *Dunsmuir* framework in this case also have led to a correctness standard? In particular, would Bastarache J's definition of questions of general importance rise to the level of *Dunsmuir*'s questions "of central importance to the legal system as a whole"? Given the link to expertise in the definition of this subcategory, it appears—especially after *Dunsmuir*—that an expert decision-maker is entitled to deference even when resolving a question of central importance to the legal system that falls within its expertise, and that non-expert decision-makers may be shown deference when resolving legal issues of more discrete significance. Why would either be desirable?

2. How does the court in *Pushpanathan* treat the provision governing leave to appeal to the Federal Court of Appeal as a deference indicator? Based on its reasoning, should the standard not always be correctness? Recall *Baker*, however, which went to the Federal Court of Appeal under the same provision.

3. Bastarache J refers approvingly to the judgment of Sopinka J in *Pasiechnyk v. Saskatchewan (Workers' Compensation Board)*, [1997] 2 SCR 890. That judgment is in one sense the high watermark of deference in that the court held that an administrative tribunal's determination of whether there was a surviving right of action in the regular courts was not a jurisdictional question but one that engaged the patent unreasonableness standard. This ceding to administrative tribunals' final word on whether the statute has effectively excluded

common law actions in the regular courts went a long way in adopting deference doctrine. For an evaluation of *Pasiechynk* and *Pushpanathan*, see David Mullan, "Recent Developments in Administrative Law: The Apparent Triumph of Deference" (1999), 12 *CJALP* 191.

4. The question in *Pushpanathan* was reviewed on a correctness standard not simply because of the generality of the issue at stake but also because of the limited expertise of the decision-maker in treaty interpretation. In terms of the relationship between treaty interpretation and expertise, was it appropriate for the court's evaluation in *Pushpanathan* to focus on the board's relative lack of expertise in the definition of human rights guarantees, rather than its expertise in the resolution of refugee claims? Or did the court underestimate the capacities of the Immigration and Refugee Board?

A recent decision in which the question under review was treated, perhaps somewhat questionably, as one of law is *Elgie v. Alberta (Workers' Compensation, Appeals Commission)*, 2009 ABCA 277 (CanLII), where the Alberta Court of Appeal set aside a decision of the appeals commission and remitted the matter to the commission for a disposition according to the court's reasons. The commission's decision had upheld the denial of a claim for compensation by the legal spouse of a worker who was killed in a workplace accident on the basis that the claimant and her child were not receiving compensation from the worker at the time of his fatal accident and thus did not qualify as "dependents" under the *Workers' Compensation Act*, RSA 2000, c. W-15. The court treated the commission's decision as a question of law although, unlike in *Pushpanathan*, the issues of interpretation arose solely from the commission's home statute. As framed by the court, these issues arose from the definition of "dependent" in s. 1(1)(h) of the Act:

> "dependent" means a member of the family of a worker who was wholly or partially dependent on the worker's earnings at the time of the worker's death or who, but for the death or disability due to accident, would have been so dependent, but a person is not a partial dependent of a worker unless the person was partially dependent on contribution from the worker for the provision of the ordinary necessaries of life;

In the following excerpt, at paras. 30-32 of *Elgie*, the court characterized the question before the commission, in its decision to uphold the denial of the claim, as one of law that fell outside the expertise of the commission:

> [30] In my view, to determine whether the appellant and her son fell within the statutory definition it was necessary for the Commission to interpret two key phrases within the definition: "but for the death or disability due to the accident" and "the ordinary necessaries of life." The interpretation of statutory provisions such as these is a matter of law which brings this task under the appeal provisions of the Act. It also means, as noted above, that the privative clause found in section 13(1) does not apply, signalling the need for less deference.
>
> [31] Moreover, as the Supreme Court noted in *Dunsmuir* at para. 55 … : "A question of law that is of 'central importance to the legal system … and outside the … specialized area of expertise' of the administrative decision maker will always attract a correctness standard." While the Commission is a specialized tribunal that has been given the task of adjudicating disputes between workers and the [Workers' Compensation Board], resolving the question of law here

falls outside of that scope. It involves applying the principles of statutory interpretation to terms that are not specific to the workers' compensation context, and deciding questions of family law, including legal entitlement to spousal support. In addition, in interpreting the intended scope of subsection 1(1)(h), it is necessary to review the Legislature's overall scheme of accident victim compensation, including the *Fatal Accidents Act*, RSA 2000, c. F-8.

[32] For all these reasons, this question of law does not engage the Commission's specialized expertise. This fact is borne out by the Commission's reliance on *Black's Law Dictionary* to supply the definition of "necessaries" when interpreting the phrase "ordinary necessaries of life," and by the Commission's own admission that questions of family law fell outside its jurisdiction. It was open to the Legislature to provide its own statutory definition to these terms, such as to remove them from the body of general law and into the specific area of the Commission's jurisdiction. Had it done so, the argument would be stronger that a reasonableness standard should apply in reviewing the Commission's reading of its internal legislative language. However, the Legislature here chose to import significant legal concepts from outside the workers' compensation context with those external meanings intact. Therefore, the Commission should apply the same legal meanings to those concepts as tribunals and courts do in other legal contexts. Based on the foregoing and the lack of a privative clause, I conclude that the appropriate standard of review … is correctness.

See also the decision of the Manitoba Court of Appeal in *Gardentree Village Inc. v. Winnipeg (City) Assessor*, 2009 MBCA 79 (CanLII), where decisions of the Municipal Board of Manitoba on the allocation of the onus in an appeal from a property assessment and on the available remedy were both reviewed on a correctness standard.

A major fault line in judicial review has been whether deference should be given to a tribunal's interpretation of its own statute. Some who have little problem with increased judicial interventionism hold the view that it would be an abdication by the courts of their constitutional responsibility to uphold the rule of law if they were to defer to an agency's interpretation of its legislation whenever it could be read plausibly in more than one way. A critique of this perspective was provided by Allars, "On Deference to Tribunals, with Deference to Dworkin" (1994), 20 *Queen's LJ* 208-9 (footnotes omitted):

The legal norms and the non-legal norms comprising the tribunal member's working conception are clearly very different from those comprising a judge's working conception of law as integrity. The judge's working conception is comprised of legal principles fanning across all departments of the law, although one or a limited number of departments loom large in the context of each hard case. By contrast a member of a labour tribunal is likely to perceive herself as having a more limited and more complex task of trying to make labour laws, including the informal norms governing their implementation in particular labour contexts, the best they can be. The moral and political norms which Dworkin says judges take into account in justifying one interpretation as better than another are those of fairness, justice and procedural due process. These factors have closely structured and limited roles, and operate to exclude some moral and political norms. Policies, and the organizational and informal norms which structure specialized areas of administrative decision-making, are not part of the picture of law as integrity, except insofar as policies underlying legislative history enter into the interpretation of the statute.

The strong discretion exercised by an administrator within a statutory framework has yet to be explained by integrity. The tribunal member and the judge are engaged in different enterprises and are situated in different interpretive communities. Rationality for the tribunal member does not match the rationality of law as integrity. The tribunal member and the judge march to the beat of different traditions.

In *Dunsmuir* and *Khosa* (which is excerpted below), the Supreme Court answered this question clearly by stating that an administrative tribunal is to be shown deference in the interpretation of its home statute or of statutes closely related to its function. In doing so, the court reinforced a position originating in the decision in *CUPE, Local 963 v. New Brunswick Liquor Corporation*, [1979] 2 SCR 227, in which Dickson J acknowledged that statutory language may be open to a range of interpretations and that it is not up to a court to substitute its preferred reading for that of an expert decision-maker operating on its specialized terrain. We examine the *CUPE* decision in the next chapter of this text.

The decision in *Investment Dealer's Association of Canada v. Dass*, 2008 BCCA 413 (CanLII), offers a recent example of judicial deference to a tribunal's interpretation of its home statute. The case involved a self-regulatory association's interpretation of its authorizing statute and its bylaws to conclude that a former member of the association, Dass, was subject to its requirements for a period of five years after leaving the association. Dass exercised his statutory right to appeal to the BC Securities Commission, which upheld the relevant interpretation and outcome in the case. According to the Court of Appeal:

[1] The appellant, a former member of the Investment Dealers Association of Canada (the "IDA"), appeals from a decision of the British Columbia Securities Commission (the "Commission") of May 11, 2007, holding that a panel of the Pacific District of the IDA did not err in law when it concluded that he remains subject to the IDA's investigatory and disciplinary by-laws.

[2] The questions before the Commission were whether the IDA's disciplinary jurisdiction is located in its by-laws, which represent terms of a contract between the appellant and the IDA, or whether the jurisdiction is statutory and if so, whether the statute limits the IDA's jurisdiction to current members. The Commission held the source of jurisdiction is the by-laws and that the jurisdiction is not limited by statute. The appellant says the Commission erred in law and asks us to declare that the IDA does not have jurisdiction over him.

[3] The threshold question in this Court is what is the applicable standard of review of the Commission's decision. For the following reasons I find that the Commission's decision must be reviewed on a standard of reasonableness. Applying that standard, I find the Commission's decision was reasonable. I would therefore dismiss the appeal.

[Discussion of the background of the case, the IDA's investigation and decision, a review by the BC Securities Commission, and the *Dunsmuir* decision has been omitted.]

[25] The appellant says the question is whether the IDA retains jurisdiction over former members. In his submission this is a jurisdictional question and the jurisprudence has determined that jurisdictional questions attract a correctness standard of review.

[26] The respondents submit that the question is one of statutory interpretation and that judicial precedents establish that the decision of the Commission should be reviewed on a standard of reasonableness.

Analysis

[27] The appellant submits that the issue is the correct interpretation of s. 26(1) of the *Act* [which read "Subject to this Act, the regulations and any decision made by the commission, a self regulatory body … must regulate the operations, standards of practice and business conduct of its members or participants, and the representatives of its members or participants, in accordance with its bylaws, rules or other regulatory instruments."] as it relates to the jurisdiction of the IDA. He argues that this is purely a question of law and jurisdiction and that a correctness standard therefore applies.

[28] The appellant relies on *ATCO Gas & Pipelines Ltd. v. Alberta (Energy & Utilities Board)*, 2006 SCC 4, [2006] 1 SCR 140, and *Barrie Public Utilities v. Canadian Television Assn.*, [2003] 1 SCR 476, in support of his submission. These cases hold that decisions of administrative tribunals as to the extent of their own jurisdiction are reviewable on a correctness standard. However, they are of no assistance here since the Commission's jurisdiction under s. 28 of the *Act* to review the decision of the IDA hearing panel and, in doing so, to interpret s. 26(1) of the *Act* is undisputed. We are not asked to review the Commission's jurisdiction to make its decision and I would accordingly reject the appellant's submission that the question is jurisdictional and that the standard of review is therefore correctness.

[29] That is not to say that correctness is necessarily ruled out as the appropriate standard of review. Decisions of administrative tribunals on some questions of law will be subject to review on a correctness standard. As was said in *Dunsmuir* at para. 60,

> … courts must also continue to substitute their own view of the correct answer where the question at issue is one of general law "that is both of central importance to the legal system as a whole and outside the adjudicator's specialized area of expertise" (*Toronto (City) v. CUPE*, at para. 62, *per* LeBel J). Because of their impact on the administration of justice as a whole, such questions require uniform and consistent answers.

However, the question at issue in this case is not such a question. Whether s. 26(1) of the *Act* limits the jurisdiction of the IDA as contended by the appellant is not a question of general law that is of central importance to the legal system as a whole nor is it one that is outside the Commission's specialized area of expertise. Rather, I agree with the respondents that the question is one of statutory interpretation by a specialized tribunal of its own statute and that judicial precedents indicate such questions should be reviewed on a standard of reasonableness … .

[Discussion of *Dunsmuir* and earlier cases, including *Pezim* (see chapter 10 of this text), has been omitted.]

[34] Returning to the case at hand, s. 26(1) is contained in Part 4 of the *Act*, which provides for a self-regulatory scheme supervised by the Commission. The goals of the *Act* were identified in *Pezim* as primarily the protection of investors and, in addition, the ensuring of capital market efficiency and public confidence in the system (at 589). It is self-evident that an integral part of these goals is the regulation of the conduct of persons employed in the securities industry. Thus, the question in issue here, whether s. 26(1) limits the disciplinary jurisdiction of the IDA to current members despite their contractual submission to jurisdiction for five years after termination of membership, is at the core of the Commission's function and expertise. In my view, this question is within a category for which *Pezim* and *Re Cartaway* have established a standard of review of reasonableness.

[35] I add that I would reach the same conclusion on a second-stage analysis of the standard of review. The four factors mentioned in para. 64 of *Dunsmuir* were considered in *Pezim* and in *Re Cartaway*. The reasons given in those cases move me to conclude that these factors point to a standard of reasonableness in this case as well.

DISCRETIONARY AND POLICY QUESTIONS IN THE STANDARD OF REVIEW ANALYSIS

The category of discretionary decisions was brought within the pragmatic and functional approach in the *Baker* decision (see chapter 2). Prior to *Baker*, such decisions were subject to review based on a complex series of discrete grounds of review, involving assessments of whether the decision-maker used its power for an improper purpose, took into account an irrelevant consideration or failed to consider some relevant factor, acted in bad faith, wrongly delegated its powers, improperly fettered its exercise of discretion, or acted under the dictation of another actor. As we discuss in chapter 15 of this text, these conventional approaches to discretion and to abuse of discretion may survive in various ways, such that it may yet be premature to claim that discretionary decisions will no longer be dealt with distinctly from the standard of review analysis. Yet in the post-*Dunsmuir* era (let alone the post-*Baker* era) it is also clear that questions of discretion (and policy) are to be identified as such and dealt with using the standard of review analysis. We therefore introduce discretionary questions here in light of the *Dunsmuir* framework.

What is a discretionary question? We should first dispel the notion that this category is entirely exclusive of the categories of law, fact, or mixed fact and law. All of the latter types of questions may involve discretion, understood simply as a choice between different options. Legal issues arising from silence or ambiguity in a statute allow for different interpretations, each of which may be reasonably supported by the terms used, their context, and the purpose of the statutory scheme. Resolving a question of fact likewise involves discretionary choices in the evaluation of factual assertions by the parties or in the judgment of whether an evidentiary threshold has been met so as to satisfy the burden of proof. Questions of mixed fact and law raise complex questions arising from the need to evaluate factual findings in light of the tests laid out in law. Even the choice to make a decision, or to enter into an inquiry in the first place, involves the exercise of discretion. So we should not approach discretion as something that is present only in the case of certain kinds of decisions, and never in others. It is, on the contrary, inherent to all forms of decision making.

It is thus more accurate to approach this topic—the identification of discretionary questions in the standard of review analysis—as an inquiry into the foremost or pre-eminent nature of a question, based on the terms of the statute that bestows authority on the decision-maker. To identify discretionary questions, then, the key is to look to the relevant statute in order to determine whether the statute frames the decision-maker's authority in broad and general terms, such that it requires choices to be made from a wide range of options, usually involving broadly framed policy considerations. Where such language is present in the statutory provision that grants the authority, then the question may be framed as discretionary based on *Dunsmuir*. Often, such questions will also mix general principles or aims with the assessment of complex factual information arising from a specific case or group of cases.

Various indicators in a statute may point to the discretionary nature of a particular authority. To bestow wide discretion, the legislature may use phrases such as "in the public interest," "in the circumstances," or "in the opinion of." Each conveys that the legislature intends the decision-maker to use its judgment, often guided by a list of purposes or guidelines laid out in the statute. Although the use of such phrases may suggest that there are no limits to the discretionary activities of a decision-maker, it is always the case that a decision-maker must use its powers in good faith and for the purposes that the legislature connected to the statute in question. Rand J put it this way in *Roncarelli v. Duplessis*, [1959] SCR 121 (Que.), at 140, so as to condemn an abuse of discretion by then-Premier Maurice Duplessis in his direction that Roncarelli's liquor licence be removed to punish him for his support of the Jehovah's Witnesses:

> In public regulation of this sort there is no such thing as absolute and untrammelled "discretion," that is that action can be taken on any ground or for any reason that can be suggested to the mind of the administrator; no legislative Act can, without express language, be taken to contemplate an unlimited arbitrary power exercisable for any purpose, however capricious or irrelevant, regardless of the nature or purpose of the statute.

Thus, the exercise of discretion always has implicit boundaries, even if the courts typically defer to a decision-maker's discretionary choices. See also *Montréal (City) v. Montreal Port Authority*, 2010 SCC 14 (CanLII), in which the Supreme Court found the discretionary decisions of two Crown corporations to be unreasonable on the basis that they were inconsistent with the principles governing the application of the relevant statute and regulations and with Parliament's intention.

There is a longstanding debate about discretionary decision making in public law. At its crux is the issue of whether and how a legislature should delegate discretion to other decision-makers. On the one hand, the delegation of any authority to administrative actors inherently involves the delegation of discretion. In turn, this presents a risk that public power may be used in ways not intended or approved of by the legislature. But to what extent should a legislature attempt to include specific statutory language that indicates clearly how it expects decisions to be taken? Can a legislature realistically do this when it cannot predict the varied situations in which subsequent administrative decisions will need to be taken? Is it even appropriate for the legislature to allow its anticipation of future cases to affect the drafting of general laws? Or is it sometimes more appropriate to bound discretion by using broadly framed standards, or lists of factors, rather than binary rules? These questions, involving how best to reconcile clarity with flexibility, engage aspects of both substantive review and procedural fairness, and are discussed in more detail in chapter 15 of this text.

The decision of the Supreme Court in *Khosa* provides an example of how the standard of review analysis may apply to a discretionary decision. It thus also elaborates a context in which courts will show deference based on the nature of the question before an administrative actor. Thus, *Khosa* reiterates the important role of the nature of the question, post-*Dunsmuir*. The court's characterization of the question as discretionary, based on the applicable statutory language, did not determine outright the standard of review. But it clearly played an important role in supporting the court's decision to apply a reasonableness standard.

Canada (Citizenship and Immigration) v. Khosa
2009 SCC 12 (CanLII)

[Khosa was a citizen of India and a landed immigrant to Canada. It was concluded at his criminal trial that he took part in "street racing" in Vancouver. Khosa was prepared to plead guilty to a charge of dangerous driving, but not to the more serious charge of criminal negligence causing death of which he was eventually convicted. Khosa applied unsuccessfully to the Immigration Appeal Division (IAD) of the Immigration and Refugee Board to remain in Canada, notwithstanding this conviction. A valid removal order was issued to return him to India. The majority of the IAD did not accept that there were "sufficient humanitarian and compassionate considerations [to] warrant special relief [against the removal order] in light of all the circumstances of the case" within the meaning of s. 67(1)(c) of the *Immigration and Refugee Protection Act* (IRPA), SC 2001, c. 27. Applying the patent unreasonableness standard of review, the reviewing judge at first instance dismissed Khosa's challenge to the IAD decision. However, applying a reasonableness *simpliciter* standard, a majority of the Federal Court of Appeal set aside the IAD decision. Both court decisions were decided prior to *Dunsmuir*, which did away with the distinction between patent unreasonableness and reasonableness *simpliciter*.]

BINNIE J (McLachlin CJ and Binnie, LeBel, Abella, and Charron JJ concurring):

[Introductory discussion of the *Federal Courts Act*, RSC 1985, c. F-7, omitted.]

[4] *Dunsmuir* teaches that judicial review should be less concerned with the formulation of different standards of review and more focussed on substance, particularly on the nature of the issue that was before the administrative tribunal under review. Here, the decision of the IAD required the application of broad policy considerations to the facts as found to be relevant, and weighed for importance, by the IAD itself. The question whether Khosa had shown "sufficient humanitarian and compassionate considerations" to warrant relief from his removal order, which all parties acknowledged to be valid, was a decision which Parliament confided to the IAD, not to the courts. I conclude that on general principles of administrative law, including our Court's recent decision in *Dunsmuir*, the applications judge was right to give a higher degree of deference to the IAD decision than seemed appropriate to the Federal Court of Appeal majority. In my view, the majority decision of the IAD was within a range of reasonable outcomes and the majority of the Federal Court of Appeal erred in intervening in this case to quash it. The appeal is therefore allowed and the decision of the Immigration Appeal Division is restored.

[Discussion of the facts, judicial history, and relevant statutory provisions omitted.]

IV. Analysis

[17] This appeal provides a good illustration of why the adjustment made by *Dunsmuir* was timely. By switching the standard of review from patent unreasonableness to reasonableness *simpliciter*, the Federal Court of Appeal majority felt empowered to retry the

case in important respects, even though the issues to be resolved had to do with immigration policy, not law. Clearly, the majority felt that the IAD disposition was unjust to Khosa. However, Parliament saw fit to confide that particular decision to the IAD, not to the judges.

[18] In cases where the legislature has enacted judicial review legislation, an analysis of that legislation is the first order of business. Our Court had earlier affirmed that, within constitutional limits, Parliament may by legislation specify a particular standard of review: see *R v. Owen*, 2003 SCC 33, [2003] 1 SCR 779. Nevertheless, the intended scope of judicial review legislation is to be interpreted in accordance with the usual rule that the terms of a statute are to be read purposefully in light of its text, context and objectives.

[19] Generally speaking, most if not all judicial review statutes are drafted against the background of the common law of judicial review. Even the more comprehensive among them, such as the British Columbia *Administrative Tribunals Act*, SBC 2004, c. 45, can only sensibly be interpreted in the common law context because, for example, it provides in s. 58(2)(a) that "a finding of fact or law or an exercise of discretion by the tribunal in respect of a matter over which it has exclusive jurisdiction under a privative clause must not be interfered with *unless it is patently unreasonable.*" The expression "patently unreasonable" did not spring unassisted from the mind of the legislator. It was obviously intended to be understood in the context of the common law jurisprudence, although a number of *indicia* of patent unreasonableness are given in s. 58(3). Despite *Dunsmuir*, "patent unreasonableness" will live on in British Columbia, but the *content* of the expression, and the precise degree of deference it commands in the diverse circumstances of a large provincial administration, will necessarily continue to be calibrated according to general principles of administrative law. That said, of course, the legislature in s. 58 was and is directing the BC courts to afford administrators a high degree of deference on issues of fact, and effect must be given to this clearly expressed legislative intention.

[Binnie J's discussion of the different perspective of Rothstein J and of s. 18.1 of the *Federal Courts Act* omitted.]

D. Standard of Review Analysis

[52] *Dunsmuir* states that "courts, while exercising their constitutional functions of judicial review, must be sensitive not only to the need to uphold the rule of law, but also to the necessity of avoiding undue interference with the discharge of administrative functions in respect of the matters delegated to administrative bodies by Parliament and legislatures" (para. 27).

[53] The process of judicial review involves two steps. First, *Dunsmuir* says that "[a]n exhaustive review is not required in every case to determine the proper standard of review" (para. 57). As between correctness and reasonableness, the "existing jurisprudence may be helpful" (para. 57). And so it is in this case. *Dunsmuir* renders moot the dispute in the lower courts between patent unreasonableness and reasonableness. No authority was cited to us that suggests a "correctness" standard of review is appropriate for IAD decisions under s. 67(1)(*c*) of the *IRPA*. Accordingly, "existing jurisprudence" points to adoption of a "reasonableness" standard.

[54] This conclusion is reinforced by the second step of the analysis when jurispru-dential categories are not conclusive. Factors then to be considered include: (1) the pres-ence or absence of a privative clause; (2) the purpose of the IAD as determined by its enabling legislation; (3) the nature of the question at issue before the IAD; and (4) the expertise of the IAD in dealing with immigration policy (*Dunsmuir*, at para. 64). Those factors have to be considered as a whole, bearing in mind that not all factors will neces-sarily be relevant for every single case. A contextualized approach is required. Factors should not be taken as items on a check list of criteria that need to be individually anal-ysed, categorized and balanced in each case to determine whether deference is appropri-ate or not. What is required is an overall evaluation. Nevertheless, having regard to the argument made before us, I propose to comment on the different factors identified in *Dunsmuir*, all of which in my view point to a reasonableness standard.

[55] As to the presence of a privative clause, s. 162(1) of the *IRPA* provides that "[e]ach Division of the Board has, in respect of proceedings brought before it under this Act, sole and exclusive jurisdiction to hear and determine all questions of law and fact, including questions of jurisdiction." A privative clause is an important indicator of legislative in-tent. While privative clauses deter judicial intervention, a statutory right of appeal may be at ease with it, depending on its terms. Here, there is no statutory right of appeal.

[56] As to the purpose of the IAD as determined by its enabling legislation, the IAD determines a wide range of appeals under the *IRPA*, including appeals from permanent residents or protected persons of their deportation orders, appeals from persons seeking to sponsor members of the family class, and appeals by permanent residents against deci-sions made outside of Canada on their residency obligations, as well as appeals by the Minister against decisions of the Immigration Division taken at admissibility hearings (s. 63). A decision of the IAD is reviewable only if the Federal Court grants leave to com-mence judicial review (s. 72).

[57] In recognition that hardship may come from removal, Parliament has provided in s. 67(1)(c) a power to grant exceptional relief. The nature of the question posed by s. 67(1)(c) requires the IAD to be "satisfied that, at the time that the appeal is disposed of … sufficient humanitarian and compassionate considerations warrant special relief." Not only is it left to the IAD to determine what constitute "humanitarian and compas-sionate considerations," but the "sufficiency" of such considerations in a particular case as well. Section 67(1)(c) calls for a fact-dependent and policy-driven assessment by the IAD itself. As noted in *Prata v. Minister of Manpower and Immigration*, [1976] 1 SCR 376, at p. 380, a removal order

> establishes that, in the absence of some special privilege existing, [an individual subject to a lawful removal order] has no right whatever to remain in Canada. *[An individual appealing a lawful removal order] does not, therefore, attempt to assert a right, but, rather, attempts to obtain a discretionary privilege.* [Emphasis added.]

[58] The respondent raised no issue of practice or procedure. He accepted that the removal order had been validly made against him pursuant to s. 36(1) of the *IRPA*. His attack was simply a frontal challenge to the IAD's refusal to grant him a "discretionary privilege." The IAD decision to withhold relief was based on an assessment of the facts of the file. The IAD had the advantage of conducting the hearings and assessing the evidence

presented, including the evidence of the respondent himself. IAD members have considerable expertise in determining appeals under the *IRPA*. Those factors, considered altogether, clearly point to the application of a reasonableness standard of review. There are no considerations that might lead to a different result. Nor is there anything in s. 18.1(4) that would conflict with the adoption of a "reasonableness" standard of review in s. 67(1)(*c*) cases. I conclude, accordingly, that "reasonableness" is the appropriate standard of review.

[Binnie J's application of the reasonableness standard omitted.]

V. Disposition

[68] The appeal is allowed and the decision of the IAD is restored.

NOTES

1. As in *Baker*, *Khosa* involved a decision to refuse to allow a non-citizen to remain in Canada following an administrative decision to reject the individual's petition for relief on humanitarian and compassionate grounds. Unlike in *Baker*, where the decision was made by an immigration officer, the decision in *Khosa* was taken after a hearing by a tribunal of the Immigration Appeal Division. Also, in *Baker*, the decision to refuse Ms. Baker's application was overturned by the Supreme Court on the basis that the immigration officer failed to consider the best interests of Ms. Baker's children, making the decision unreasonable. This outcome was groundbreaking at the time because the court established that even discretionary choices of administrative agencies were not entitled automatically to the highest level of deference (the court applied the pre-*Dunsmuir* standard of reasonableness rather than patent unreasonableness) simply because they were discretionary.

2. In *Khosa*, the question was classified as discretionary because of the breadth of the statutory language granting the Immigration Appeal Division its authority to review Mr. Khosa's application. The IAD was authorized to give special relief from removal on the basis of "humanitarian and compassionate considerations ... in all the circumstances." By rejecting Mr. Khosa's application for judicial review and upholding the IAD's decision, the court in *Khosa* clearly signalled a reluctance to interfere with the discretionary choices of an administrative tribunal. On what basis would you reconcile this outcome with that in *Baker*, given that in both cases the court was applying a deferential standard? We discuss the application of the reasonableness standard, post-*Dunsmuir*, in chapter 13 of this text.

3. Closely connected to the category of discretionary questions is that of policy questions. Indeed, in *Dunsmuir*, the court refers to both in tandem as "questions of discretion or policy." Are these the same categories and, if not, how do they interact? To what extent is the characterization of a question as one of policy driven by a court's characterization of the purpose of a statute? Note the discussion in *Pushpanathan*, excerpted above, of the polycentricity principle.

THE DISAGGREGATION DILEMMA: LÉVIS AND VIA RAIL

In most cases, a court will review the decision of an administrative actor without discussing whether and how the decision has been narrowed to focus on one or a few questions and subjected to a particular standard of review on this basis. Rather, it will be implicit within a judgment that the court has opted to focus the decision in one or another way as part of the analytical process of refining the issues at stake in the case. On the other hand, in some cases, a court may explicitly disaggregate an aspect of the overall decision that is under review, typically but not always a question of law, in order to subject that discrete question to a standard of review that is different from that applied to the decision as a whole. In either circumstance, questions may arise about just when and how a court should isolate one question from others incumbent in a decision in the course of the standard of review analysis.

This issue of disaggregation (or "segmentation" or "segregation") has been a thorny one for the Supreme Court in recent years. It may in the first place be difficult to distinguish a question of fact or law from the convenient catch-all of questions of mixed fact and law. More fundamentally, the choice to isolate a question of law (whether also constitutional or jurisdictional) often leads to a correctness standard and to the court's substitution of its answer for the tribunal's. As such, the decision to extract an issue of legal principle from a tribunal's ruling (or to downplay factual elements) and then review it on a correctness basis may be seen as a sleight of hand by which the court can avoid the basic purpose of deference doctrine. This perception will be especially acute where disaggregation takes place in the face of an expert, specialized decision that is protected by a full privative clause.

The challenges of outlining when and how to segregate one question from various other questions at play in a decision is a lurking issue after *Dunsmuir*, in which the issue of disaggregation was not discussed overtly by the majority. Rather, in *Dunsmuir*, the adjudicator's interpretation of provisions in the *Public Service Labour Relations Act* and the *Civil Service Act* was treated as a question of law that fell within the adjudicator's expertise in a highly specialized context, justifying deference. The court then applied a reasonableness standard to the legal (and other) aspects of the adjudicator's decision.

Despite its silence on the issue, however, *Dunsmuir* implies that disaggregation is appropriate in cases where the nature of the question calls presumptively for a correctness standard. This implication follows from the majority's discussion of types of questions of law that will not attract deference in contrast to the general categories of fact, mixed fact and law, and discretion or policy. The following statement of Binnie J in *Dunsmuir*, at para. 142, also indicates that disaggregation remains an important part of the standard of review analysis:

> Mention should be made of a further feature that also reflects the complexity of the subject matter of judicial review. An applicant may advance several grounds for quashing an administrative decision. He or she may contend that the decision maker has misinterpreted the general law. He or she may argue, in the alternative, that even if the decision maker got the general law straight (an issue on which the court's view of what is correct will prevail), the decision maker did not properly apply it to the facts (an issue on which the decision maker is entitled to deference). In a challenge under the *Canadian Charter of Rights and Freedoms* to a surrender for extradition, for example, the minister will have to comply with the Court's view of *Charter* principles (the "correctness" standard), but if he or she correctly appreciates the applicable law,

the court will properly recognize a wide discretion in the application of those principles to the particular facts. The same approach is taken to less exalted decision makers (*Moreau-Bérubé v. New Brunswick (Judicial Council)*, [2002] 1 SCR 249, 2002 SCC 11). In the jargon of the judicial review bar, this is known as "segmentation."

Two prominent cases on segmentation, both preceding *Dunsmuir*, are *Lévis (City) v. Fraternité des policiers de Lévis Inc.*, [2007] 1 SCR 591, and *Council of Canadians with Disabilities v. VIA Rail Canada Inc.*, [2007] 1 SCR 650. In these two cases, the Supreme Court sought to clarify when and why it was appropriate to isolate a question of law from a tribunal's ruling so as to subject it to a higher level of judicial scrutiny. Unfortunately, in both cases the court split dramatically on whether disaggregation was necessary and, in turn, on the appropriate standard of review. In *Lévis*, the majority found that the decision of a Québec labour arbitrator should be disaggregated because it involved an apparent conflict between two statutes, the *Police Act* and the *Cities and Towns Act*; the arbitrator's resolution of the apparent conflict was reviewed on a correctness standard while the rest of the decision attracted a reasonableness standard. Bastarache J wrote as follows for the majority in *Lévis* on the issue of disaggregation:

> [19] It is clear that the pragmatic and functional approach may lead to different standards of review for separate findings made by an arbitrator in the course of his or her decision. ... This will most frequently be the case when an arbitrator is called upon to construe legislation. The arbitrator's interpretation of the legislation—a question of law—*may* be reviewable on a different standard than the rest of the decision. ... While interpretations of general public statutes or statutes external to an administrative decision maker's constituting legislation will often be reviewed on a standard of correctness, this will not always be so. ... The answer in each case will depend on the proper application of the pragmatic and functional approach, which requires various factors be taken into account such as the presence or absence of a privative clause, the expertise of the decision maker, the purpose of the governing legislation and the nature of the question under review. ... Since the presence or absence of a privative clause will likely be the same for all aspects of an administrative decision, whether there is a possibility of more than a single standard of review under the pragmatic and functional approach will largely depend on whether there exist questions of different natures and whether those questions engage the decision maker's expertise and the legislative objective in different ways. Of course it may not always be easy or necessary to separate individual questions from the decision taken as a whole. The possibility of multiple standards should not be taken as a licence to parse an administrative decision into myriad parts in order to subject it to heightened scrutiny. However, reviewing courts must be careful not to subsume distinct questions into one broad standard of review. Multiple standards of review should be adopted when there are clearly defined questions that engage different concerns under the pragmatic and functional approach.

> [20] The question whether s. 119, para. 2 *P.A.* [*Police Act*] and s. 116(6) *C.T.A.* [*Cities and Towns Act*] are in conflict and, if so, which one should prevail, clearly raises separate concerns from the question of whether the arbitrator properly interpreted and applied s. 119, para. 2 *P.A.* The one factor that is common to both questions is the presence of a privative clause. By virtue of s. 101 *L.C.* [Québec *Labour Code*], the arbitrator's decision is not subject to appeal. Combined with ss. 139, 139.1 and 140 *L.C.*, s. 101 forms a relatively strong privative clause. However, a privative clause is not determinative and regard must be had to the other factors under the pragmatic

and functional approach. … In this case, the privative clause suggests greater deference in general but does not shed light on whether the level of scrutiny should be different for each question.

In her dissent in *Lévis*, Abella J concluded that the arbitrator's decision as a whole should be subjected to the highly deferential standard of patent unreasonableness. As follows, she disagreed in particular on the majority's approach to segmentation in the face of a strong privative clause:

[107] The primary concern I have relates to [Justice Bastarache's] determination that the arbitrator's decision *whether* to apply s. 119, para. 2 should be subjected to a different standard than his decision on *how* to apply it. It seems to me that applying the factors in *Pushpanathan v. Canada (Minister of Citizenship and Immigration)*, [1998] 1 SCR 982, the clear legislative directive here is that the arbitrator's decision as a whole is entitled to deference.

[108] First, there is an unequivocal privative clause in s. 101 of the Quebec *Labour Code*, RSQ, c. C-27, stating that the arbitrator's award is "without appeal" and "binds the parties." Second, s. 100.12(a) of the *Labour Code* authorizes the arbitrator to "interpret and apply any Act or regulation to the extent necessary to settle a grievance."

[109] The privative clause is the legislature's way of protecting the arbitrator's exclusive responsibility for deciding the grievance, and s. 100.12(a) clothes him with the authority to determine how *any* relevant statutory provision ought to apply to it. Any assessment of the degree of deference owed to the arbitrator must be respectful of these unambiguous legislative instructions. Combined with the expertise of the arbitrator in labour disputes and the legislative objective of having them resolved expeditiously and conclusively, there seems to me to be a strong argument in favour of an integrated standard for assessing the arbitrator's interpretation both of his jurisdictional mandate and its application.

[110] As this Court held in *Toronto (City) Board of Education v. OSSTF, District 15*, [1997] 1 SCR 487, at para. 39, the interpretation of legislation, external or otherwise, that is "intimately connected with the mandate of the tribunal and is encountered frequently as a result" is entitled to deference. … In interpreting the applicability of s. 119, para. 2 of the *Police Act* and s. 116(6) of the *Cities and Towns Act*, the arbitrator was interpreting and applying legislation relating to issues of the discipline and sanctioning of police officers. Both issues are central to his mandate to decide the grievance under the collective agreement and the *Labour Code*.

[111] There is a danger that the routine segmentation of such mandates leads to an unduly interventionist approach more reminiscent of "the wrong question" or "preliminary or collateral matter" doctrines … [see chapter 12 of this text], than of the more deferential approach applied by Dickson J in *Canadian Union of Public Employees, Local 963 v. New Brunswick Liquor Corp.*, [1979] 2 SCR 227, at p. 233. Dickson J's admonition in *CUPE* remains instructive:

The question of what is and is not jurisdictional is often very difficult to determine. The courts, in my view, should not be alert to brand as jurisdictional, and therefore subject to broader curial review, that which may be doubtfully so.

[112] Similarly, legal issues ought not to be declared readily extricable when they are legitimately and necessarily intertwined with the adjudicator's mandate and expertise. In such circumstances, the decision ought to be reviewed as a whole, not as a segmented compilation subject to an increased degree of scrutiny and intervention. As LeBel J observed in *Toronto (City) v. C.U.P.E., Local 79*, [2003] 3 SCR 77, 2003 SCC 63, at para. 76:

[T]he various strands that go into a decision are more likely to be inextricably inter-twined, particularly in a complex field such as labour relations, such that the reviewing court should view the adjudicator's decision as an integrated whole.

• • •

[115] If, on the other hand, the legal issue is genuinely external to the adjudicator's mandate or expertise and easily differentiated from other issues in the case, such heightened scrutiny is entirely warranted: *Canadian Broadcasting Corp. v. Canada (Labour Relations Board)*, [1995] 1 SCR 157.

[116] In this case, the labour arbitrator's mandate and expertise merge to entitle him to a single deferential standard of review both for his decision as to the scope of the relevant legis-lation and its application to this case.

Abella J's more circumspect approach to disaggregation won the day in *VIA Rail*, re-leased a day after the decision in *Lévis*, where a five-judge majority of the Supreme Court reviewed and upheld a decision of the Canadian Transportation Tribunal on a single defer-ential standard. The tribunal had ordered, pursuant to the *Canada Transportation Act*, SC 1996, c. 10, that VIA Rail implement a series of remedial measures—estimated by VIA to cost $48 million—aimed at addressing undue obstacles to the mobility of persons with dis-abilities in 30 of VIA's train cars. For the majority, at paras. 93-100, Abella J explained why the tribunal's decision as a whole was entitled to deference on a single standard:

[93] The Agency's enabling legislation clearly shows that its interpretation of its authority to proceed with CCD's [Council of Canadians with Disabilities'] application is a question Par-liament intended to fall squarely within its jurisdiction and expert assessment. Under s. 172(1) [of the *Canada Transportation Act*], "[t]he Agency may, on application, inquire into a matter in relation to which a regulation could be made under subsection 170(1)." Section 170(1) gives the Agency discretionary authority to "make regulations for the purpose of eliminating undue obstacles in the transportation network under the legislative authority of Parliament." A list of four particular areas in which the Agency may make regulations is provided, but this list is not exhaustive. Instead, Parliament gave the Agency discretionary authority to determine whether regulations directed toward eliminating undue obstacles in the federal transportation system *could* be made, without circumscribing the Agency's discretion to identify the specific matters these regulations might address.

[94] In accepting CCD's application, the Agency relied on its express authority to make regulations respecting "the design, construction or modification of ... means of transportation" and the "conditions of carriage applicable in respect of the transportation of persons with dis-abilities" under s. 170(1)(a) and (c) to find that it had jurisdiction to entertain CCD's complaint. Since CCD's application clearly concerned the "design, construction or modification" of the Renaissance cars and the "conditions of carriage" confronting persons with disabilities, no ju-risdictional question legitimately arises from this ground of appeal on these facts. If an experi-ence-based complaint were required to operationalize the Agency's adjudicative authority, we would not expect to find authority to make regulations respecting the "design" or "construc-tion" of rail cars in s. 170(1)(c).

[95] The Agency's authority to entertain CCD's complaint, in any event, depended on its own discretionary determination of whether CCD's complaint raised an issue for which a regu-lation directed toward eliminating undue obstacles *could* be made. This falls squarely within the

Agency's jurisdiction. Given that the Agency's jurisdiction to entertain CCD's complaint under s. 172(1) turns almost exclusively on its own discretionary decision-making, s. 172(1) is a jurisdiction-granting, not jurisdiction-limiting, provision.

[96] It seems to me counterproductive for courts to parse and recharacterize aspects of a tribunal's core jurisdiction, like the Agency's discretionary authority to make regulations and adjudicate complaints, in a way that undermines the deference that jurisdiction was conferred to protect. By attributing a jurisdiction-limiting label, such as "statutory interpretation" or "human rights," to what is in reality a function assigned and properly exercised under the enabling legislation, a tribunal's expertise is made to defer to a court's generalism rather than the other way around.

[97] I do not share the view that the issue before the Agency was, as a human rights matter, subject to review on a standard of correctness. This unduly narrows the characterization of what the Agency was called upon to decide and disregards how inextricably interwoven the human rights and transportation issues are. Parliament gave the Agency a specific mandate to determine how to render transportation systems more accessible for persons with disabilities. This undoubtedly has a human rights aspect. But that does not take the questions of how and when the Agency exercises its human rights expertise outside the mandate conferred on it by Parliament.

[98] The human rights issues the Agency is called upon to address arise in a particular—and particularly complex—context: the federal transportation system. The *Canada Transportation Act* is highly specialized regulatory legislation with a strong policy focus. The scheme and object of the Act are the oxygen the Agency breathes. When interpreting the Act, including its human rights components, the Agency is expected to bring its transportation policy knowledge and experience to bear on its interpretations of its assigned statutory mandate: *Pushpanathan*, at para. 26.

[99] The allegedly jurisdictional determination the Agency was being asked to make, like the "undueness" inquiry, falls squarely within its statutory mandate. It did not involve answering a legal question beyond its expertise, but rather requires the Agency to apply its expertise to the legal issue assigned to it by statute. The Agency, and not a reviewing court, is best placed to determine whether the Agency may exercise its discretion to make a regulation for the purpose of eliminating an undue obstacle to the mobility of persons with disabilities—a determination on which the Agency's jurisdiction to entertain applications depends.

[100] The Agency is responsible for interpreting its own legislation, including what that statutory responsibility includes. The Agency made a decision with many component parts, each of which fell squarely and inextricably within its expertise and mandate. It was therefore entitled to a single, deferential standard of review.

In contrast, the four dissenting judges in *VIA Rail* focused on two discrete questions of law that formed part of the decision—one of which was characterized as a jurisdictional issue and the other as an issue of human rights principle—and applied a correctness standard to both, and found that the tribunal's interpretation of the human rights principles of "undue obstacle" and "reasonable accommodation" was incorrect. For the dissenting justices, Deschamps and Rothstein JJ concluded as follows on disaggregation:

[278] The standard of review jurisprudence recognizes that segmentation of a decision is appropriate in order to ascertain the nature of the questions before the tribunal and the degree of deference to be accorded to the tribunal's decisions on those questions.

[References to authorities omitted.]

Subjecting all aspects of a decision to a single standard of review does not account for the diversity of questions under review and either insulates the decision from a more exacting review where the pragmatic and functional considerations call for greater intensity in the review of specific legal questions, or subjects questions of fact to a standard that is too exacting. A tribunal's decision must therefore be subject to segmentation to enable a reviewing court to apply the appropriate degree of scrutiny to the various aspects of the decision which call for greater or lesser deference.

. . .

[282] The Agency's jurisdiction and the determination of the applicable human rights law principles in the federal transportation context are pure questions of law. ...

[283] Furthermore, the Agency is not protected by a privative clause in respect of questions of law or jurisdiction. Rather, there is a statutory appeal procedure on such questions under s. 41(1) of the Act. This contrasts with the Agency's factual determinations which are "binding and conclusive," under s. 31 of the Act.

[284] On questions of jurisdiction and the determination of the applicable human rights law principles, the Agency does not have greater relative expertise than a court. The Agency is required to resort to human rights principles which are not comprehensively set out in its home statute and in respect of which the Agency, whose prime function is economic regulation of transportation in a largely deregulated environment, does not have specific expertise. This factor points to a standard of review that will be less deferential.

[285] Finally, the purpose of s. 172 of the Act is to grant the Agency an adjudicative role to consider applications from persons with disabilities who allege the existence of undue obstacles to their mobility in respect of a federal transportation carrier. The issues generally involve a dispute between an aggrieved party and the transportation carrier. While the Agency's ultimate analysis, in those cases, involves a balancing of interests, the questions of the Agency's jurisdiction and the determination of the applicable human rights law, do not.

[286] Considering all of these factors, the questions of the Agency's jurisdiction and the determination of the applicable human rights law principles in the federal transportation context are both to be reviewed on the standard of correctness.

As indicated by these contrasting reasons from both *Lévis* and *VIA Rail*, disaggregation is a vexing issue and it has caused major differences of view on the court. There are several reasons why this is so. For one, in many cases, segmentation occurs inherently without the court explaining why it has focused on one question or issue among the others that arise in a judicial review. It may be that the analytical process leading to disaggregation—involving an assessment of the relationship between legal and factual considerations, and shaped by how the case was framed by the parties and other decision-makers—is simply not reducible to a pithy statement of rules or guidelines that will apply satisfactorily in all cases. On the other hand, technical discussions of disaggregation may also mask controversial choices by a court that effectively downplay other features of the standard of review analysis, such as the presence of a privative clause (where the court disaggregates in order to intervene) or the possible infringement of Charter rights (where the court disaggregates in order to defer; see the discussion in *Suresh* as reproduced in chapter 15 of this text). Thus, a court's reasons on disaggregation may speak indirectly to more fundamental differences. Partly for this reason, judges of the Supreme Court may feel compelled to elaborate on why they have chosen or refused to disaggregate only in cases where they are split on the appropriate outcome of the standard of review analysis. In *Lévis*, the disagreement turned on the impact of a full privative clause; in *VIA Rail*, it involved the role of tribunal expertise and the degree to which legal issues fell within a specialized area.

In its post-*Dunsmuir* decision in *Workers' Compensation Act (Re) and O'Donnell*, 2008 YKCA 9 (CanLII), the Yukon Court of Appeal considered and rejected the option of disaggregating a question of law from the decision as a whole. The case involved an appeal from a Yukon Supreme Court decision that had quashed a decision of the Yukon Workers' Compensation Appeal Tribunal. The Supreme Court chambers judge based his decision to quash on the conclusion that the tribunal—in rejecting a claim for compensation by O'Donnell—decided incorrectly a number of "pure legal questions" arising from the *Workers' Compensation Act*, RSY 2002, c. 231, and a Yukon Workers' Compensation Health and Safety Board Policy, and, in turn, that the tribunal's findings and reasoning were flawed and unreasonable. This decision was appealed by O'Donnell's employer, the government of the Yukon. Focus on how the Court of Appeal rejects the chambers judge's disaggregation of the matters before the tribunal:

> [28] The essential basis of the employer's appeal is that the chambers judge failed to properly apply the reasonableness standard of review. The employer contends that the chambers judge re-weighed the evidence, doubted the factual findings of the Tribunal, unfairly criticized the Tribunal's reasoning, and generally accorded the Tribunal no deference.

[A summary of *Dunsmuir* has been omitted.]

> [33] The Tribunal's jurisdiction is defined in s. 25 of the *Act*, the relevant subsections of which read:

> 25(1) The appeal tribunal has exclusive jurisdiction to examine, inquire into, hear, and determine all matters arising in respect of an appeal from a decision of the board under subsection 8(1), from a decision of a hearing officer under subsection 20(1), or from a decision of the president under subsection 27(4) and it may confirm, reverse, or vary the decision.

> (2) Without restricting the generality of subsection (1), the exclusive jurisdiction includes the power to determine, on an appeal pursuant to subsection 8(2) or 21(1)

> (a) whether a worker's disability was work-related;

> (b) the duration and degree of a disability;

> (c) the weekly loss of earnings of a worker resulting from a work-related disability;

> (d) the average weekly earnings of a worker;

> (e) whether a person is a member of the family of a worker;

> (f) whether a person is a dependant;

> (g) whether a person is a worker, and to deem a person to be a worker; and

(h) whether a worker or a dependant is entitled to compensation.

(3) Subject to subsections 24(8) and (13), the acts or decisions of the appeal tribunal on any matter within its jurisdiction are final and conclusive and not open to question or review in any court.

(4) No proceedings by or before the appeal tribunal shall be restrained by injunction, declaration, prohibition, or other process or proceedings in any court or be removed by *certiorari*, judicial review, or otherwise in any court, in respect of any act or decision of the appeal tribunal within its jurisdiction.

. . .

(8) The appeal tribunal has the same powers as the Supreme Court for compelling the attendance of witnesses, examining witnesses under oath, and compelling the production and inspection of books, papers, documents, and objects relevant to the hearing.

(9) The appeal tribunal may cause depositions of witnesses residing in or outside of the Yukon to be taken before any person appointed by it in the same way as the Supreme Court can in civil actions.

. . .

(11) Despite subsections (3) and (4), a worker, a dependant of a deceased worker, or an employer may make an application for judicial review of a decision of the appeal tribunal if there has been an error in law or in jurisdiction.

[34] One of the objects of the *Act* is "to provide an appeal procedure that is simple, fair, and accessible, with minimal delays" (s. 1(e)).

[35] A committee of the Tribunal consists of the chair or alternate chair and a representative each of employers and workers (s-s. 24(1)).

[36] The Tribunal had, under s-s. 25(2), exclusive jurisdiction to determine whether Ms. O'Donnell's disability was work-related. The Tribunal asked itself two questions: first, did Ms. O'Donnell suffer a work-related disability?; and second, was there an "adjustment disorder" which constitutes a work-related disability?

[37] Subsection 25(3) protects the Tribunal's decisions on any matter within its jurisdiction from review in any court, *except in circumstances where the Tribunal errs in law or in jurisdiction* (s-s. 25(11)).

[38] Thus, the privative clause in respect of the Tribunal, while not "full," is nevertheless robust in that it reserves for review only errors of law or jurisdiction.

[39] As the Supreme Court stated in *Dunsmuir* at para. 59, "'[j]urisdiction' is intended in the narrow sense of whether or not the tribunal had the authority to make the inquiry." There can be no doubt that the Tribunal in this case was acting within its jurisdiction.

[40] The nature of the legislative regime is identified in the preamble to the *Act* as "recognizing that the historic principles of workers' compensation, namely the collective liability of employers for workplace disabilities, guaranteed, no fault compensation for disabled workers, immunity of employers and workers from civil suits, should be maintained." The objects of the *Act* and the powers of the Tribunal suggest a speedy, efficient and final process that is fair to both employers and workers. From this, it can be taken that the legislature intended that the Tribunal hold relative expertise in the interpretation of the *Act* that creates its mandate and in the application of the policies of the Board, which the Tribunal is bound to consider.

[41] Finally, the question at issue, whether Ms. O'Donnell's disability was work-related, is a question of mixed fact and law. In this case, in my view, the legal and factual issues were intertwined and not readily separated (*Dunsmuir* at para. 53). This case warranted one standard of review, not multiple standards. As a majority of the Supreme Court of Canada stated in *Lévis (City) v. Fraternité des policiers de Lévis Inc.*, [2007] 1 SCR 591, 2007 SCC 14 at para. 19:

> … Since the presence or absence of a privative clause will likely be the same for all aspects of an administrative decision, whether there is a possibility of more than a single standard of review under the pragmatic and functional approach will largely depend on whether there exist questions of different natures and whether those questions engage the decision maker's expertise and the legislative objective in different ways. Of course it may not always be easy or necessary to separate individual questions from the decision taken as a whole. The possibility of multiple standards should not be taken as a licence to parse an administrative decision into myriad parts in order to subject it to heightened scrutiny. However, reviewing courts must be careful not to subsume distinct questions into one broad standard of review. Multiple standards of review should be adopted when there are clearly defined questions that engage different concerns under the pragmatic and functional approach.

[42] In my view, it is questionable whether the "pure legal questions" identified by the chambers judge in this case were in fact all questions of law. What is certain is that they were not readily separated from the general question in issue and were not "of central importance to the legal system and outside the specialized expertise" of the Tribunal (*Dunsmuir* at para. 55).

[43] Considering all of the relevant factors, there can be no doubt that the appropriate standard of review in this case was one of reasonableness. Indeed, as I have noted, that was the standard chosen by the chambers judge, preferring that standard over the standard of patent unreasonableness urged by the employer. The issue on this appeal really concerns whether the reasonableness standard was properly applied by the chambers judge.

[A discussion of how the chambers judge failed to show any deference to the tribunal's decision has been omitted.]

[62] In summary, I would allow the appeal, restore the Tribunal's decision, and order that each party bear its own costs.

SOME CONCLUDING THOUGHTS

The complexity of characterizing the nature of a question reflects wider challenges in the implementation of deference doctrine. It is extraordinarily difficult for the Supreme Court—tasked with resolving disputes that emerge from widely varying administrative, statutory, and factual contexts—to fashion a broad consensus and steer a straight course in the face of competing positions on curial deference. Often the question boils down to an exercise in statutory interpretation. In that respect there is little doubt that the court now addresses more directly and with more sophistication than ever before the underlying tensions in the exercise of statutory interpretation. In doing so, the court has become more open about its approaches to the institutional competence of generalist courts and specialist agencies, to weighing regulatory goals and individual rights, and to administrative expertise and democratic accountability.

It may also be that there is simply no viable alternative to the course that the court has charted in *Dunsmuir* and, more fully, in its jurisprudence on the standard of review analysis. This is not to say that one will always agree with the way in which the court weighs the competing considerations or evaluates its institutional ability to come to grips with the complexities of regulatory schemes and the dynamics of administration. One may still find too much formalism in the court's approach to statutory interpretation and too little concern for attaining the goals of a statutory scheme. Perhaps the most that can be asked of the law on the standard of review is that it should push judges to address the relevant questions. The law cannot constrain those who are predisposed toward doing "the wrong thing," but it should help others to consider thoughtfully what "the right thing" is and not hamper them from doing it.

CHAPTER TWELVE

Jurisdictional Questions and the Origins of the Standard of Review Analysis

INTRODUCTION

A subcategory of the question of law is the jurisdictional question. However, the concept of jurisdiction lends itself to a wide range of meanings, some of which have drifted far from the root meaning of the term as simply a statutory authority to enter into an inquiry.

The concept of jurisdiction is at once central to judicial review—it provides the foundation for the constitutional role of the courts to ensure that administrative decision-makers do not exceed the scope of their delegated powers—and to many of the deep-set controversies in administrative law. At the heart of these controversies is a difference of views over the circumstances in which an administrative decision-maker can have jurisdiction to decide on the scope of its own jurisdiction (in the civil law tradition, this is referred to as *kompetenz kompetenz*). At one extreme is the restrictive view that an administrative decision-maker cannot act unless a court has determined that it has the jurisdiction to act, or at least that its actions are always subject to the court's review of its ability to decide its own authority to act. At the other extreme is the permissive view that a court has no greater right to interpret the terms of a statutory grant of power than does the grant-holder, and so the courts should not question the conclusions reached by administrative decision-makers. Between these two extremes is a wide landscape on which those who favour judicial intervention have historically done battle with those who are suspicious of ever-expanding notions of jurisdiction in the name of judicial review, especially in the face of privative clauses that appeared to preclude any review by the court including on matters of jurisdiction.

In *Dunsmuir*, the majority reiterated the position that the courts, through judicial review, play a constitutional role in ensuring that administrative tribunals exercise only authority that they have been granted by statute. The court invoked both the rule of law and legislative supremacy in support of this, stressing that the courts serve as a check against administrative excess—ensuring tribunals act *intra vires* and not *ultra vires* their statutory authority—and as the guarantor that legislative intentions are met. However, the court also made clear that the concept of "jurisdictional error" must not be stretched by courts beyond the narrow domain of a decision-maker's authority to enter into an inquiry. According to the majority reasons in *Dunsmuir* (at para. 59):

> Administrative bodies must also be correct in their determinations of true questions of jurisdiction or *vires*. We mention true questions of *vires* to distance ourselves from the extended

definitions adopted before *CUPE*. It is important here to take a robust view of jurisdiction. We neither wish nor intend to return to the jurisdiction/preliminary question doctrine that plagued the jurisprudence in this area for many years. "Jurisdiction" is intended in the narrow sense of whether or not the tribunal had the authority to make the inquiry. In other words, true jurisdiction questions arise where the tribunal must explicitly determine whether its statutory grant of power gives it the authority to decide a particular matter. The tribunal must interpret the grant of authority correctly or its action will be found to be *ultra vires* or to constitute a wrongful decline of jurisdiction. ... We reiterate the caution of Dickson J in *CUPE* that reviewing judges must not brand as jurisdictional issues that are doubtfully so.

This reference to the *CUPE* decision—*CUPE, Local 963 v. New Brunswick Liquor Corporation*, [1979] 2 SCR 227—is important because that decision marked a turning point in the jurisprudence of the Supreme Court of Canada away from earlier expansive approaches to the notion of jurisdiction. In *Dunsmuir*, at para. 59, the court took care to preserve the spirit of *CUPE* by characterizing jurisdiction in the "narrow sense" of the "authority to make the inquiry." Put differently, the position from *CUPE* to *Dunsmuir* reflects an approach by which a reviewing court must confirm that a statute implies that the legislature intended for the decision-maker to decide whether it should answer a question or engage in an activity connected to its statutory authority. So long as the statute implies that the decision-maker has this authority to decide on the scope of its own authority, a court should be satisfied that the decision-maker's interpretation of its parent statute has not engaged a question of jurisdiction but rather (at most) a question of law.

This point was emphasized in *Nolan v. Kerry (Canada) Inc.*, 2009 SCC 39 (CanLII), where Rothstein J pointed to *Dunsmuir* in order to emphasize the need for caution in determining whether a decision by the Ontario Financial Services Tribunal to award costs should be characterized as jurisdictional and thus subjected to a less deferential standard. Rothstein J concluded as follows for the majority:

[32] ... para. 59 of *Dunsmuir* states that "administrative bodies must also be correct in their determinations of true questions of jurisdiction or vires." However, para. 59 goes on to note that it is important "to take a robust view of jurisdiction" and that true questions of jurisdiction "will be narrow."

[33] Administrative tribunals are creatures of statute and questions that arise over a tribunal's authority that engage the interpretation of a tribunal's constating statute might in one sense be characterized as jurisdictional. However, the admonition of para. 59 of *Dunsmuir* is that courts should be cautious in doing so for fear of returning "to the jurisdiction/preliminary question doctrine that plagued the jurisprudence in this area for many years."

[34] The inference to be drawn from paras. 54 and 59 of *Dunsmuir* is that courts should usually defer when the tribunal is interpreting its own statute and will only exceptionally apply a correctness of standard when interpretation of that statute raises a broad question of the tribunal's authority.

[35] Here there is no question that the Tribunal has the statutory authority to enquire into the matter of costs; the issue involves the Tribunal interpreting its constating statute to determine the parameters of the costs order it may make. The question of costs is one that is incidental to the broad power of the Tribunal to review decisions of the Superintendent in the context

of the regulation of pensions. It is one over which the Court should adopt a deferential standard of review to the Tribunal's decision.

In spite of these clarifications, there remains uncertainty today about just how far the concept of "true" questions of jurisdiction now extends. This is particularly so in light of the pervasiveness of broad approaches to jurisdictional error in the history of Canadian judicial review, as *Dunsmuir* warns against. Indeed, for the longest time, the theory and practice of substantive review were dominated by the concept of jurisdiction. Courts deemed statutory authorities to have only as much jurisdiction or authority as the legislature conferred on them, and the primary task of the courts was to ensure that the tribunal or agency stayed within those boundaries. This meant reviewing on a correctness basis all determinations of law and fact that affected or "went to" the statutory authority's jurisdiction (as opposed to the exercise of the jurisdiction that was actually conferred, where the opportunities for review were limited or non-existent). But, in the face of statutory provisions that clearly sought to restrict the review powers of the courts, what were the badges of questions that transcended the language of privative clauses and on which correctness review by the courts was assured? What is it that amounts in *Dunsmuir* to a "true" question of *vires*?

THE CONCEPT OF JURISDICTIONAL ERROR

One of the technical explanations given for the courts' restrictive interpretation of privative clauses that preclude any legal challenge to the decision of an administrative agency is that the statutory reference to "decision" means a *valid* decision. Outside its jurisdiction, the agency had no legal power to make any decision at all, and any attempt to do so is null and void and merely something that *purports* to be a decision. Thus, Dickson J offered this justification for not interpreting blanket preclusive clauses literally in *Jacmain v. Attorney General (Canada) et al.*, [1978] 2 SCR 15, at 29 (Can.):

> The intractable difficulty is this. It is hard to believe that a legislature would create a tribunal with a limited jurisdiction and yet bestow on such tribunal an unlimited power to determine the extent of its jurisdiction.

An underlying assumption of this rationale for judicial surveillance is that, left to its own devices, an administrative agency will tend to implement its enabling legislation in a way that expands its regulatory reach. Further, this may be at the expense of the existing legal rights of those engaged in the regulated activity and without adequate regard to the limits imposed by the legislature on the scope of the agency's mandate. Foxes, it is often observed, do not make ideal guards for chicken houses. A response to this line of argument has been that the courts and the common law are no more neutral than administrative agencies, and that their approach to statutory interpretation has often exhibited an anti-regulation and pro *status quo* bias. Moreover, as interpreters of public policy statutes, courts are at a serious disadvantage when compared with the specialist agency to which the legislature has entrusted the administration of the legislation. They are removed from the realities of administering a public program and are unable to formulate comprehensive solutions to what are often complex choices of public policy and its effective delivery and not legal questions suitable for determination by courts.

At one level, it is perhaps illusory to distinguish the question of whether an agency has the power to decide from the question of whether it has exercised its power properly. In many instances throughout the decision-making process, a decision-maker may need to work out, sometimes in very subtle or passing ways, just whether it can continue on a particular path of inquiry without offending the aims of its empowering statute and the scope of its statutory grant of authority. The search, then, is as much about finding a framework that will enable courts to distinguish questions of law that should be left to an agency from those that, despite the presence of a privative clause, must be decided by the court. The concept of jurisdiction may aid this search, but only in limited ways and at the risk of obfuscation and confusion.

The following excerpt from the decision of Evans JA offers further assistance in understanding how the concept of jurisdiction can be understood. The case involved an appeal to the Federal Court of Canada under the *Federal Courts Act*. The appeal was from a decision of the Public Service Labour Relations Board to allocate three positions in the federal public service to an occupational group other than that which would accord with the definitions of the occupational group and its bargaining unit in the relevant job descriptions. Both the Public Service Alliance of Canada and the Attorney General of Canada appealed the PSLRB's decision. They argued, among other things, that the PSLRB had made a jurisdictional error and that its decision should therefore be set aside pursuant to s. 18.1(4)(a) of the *Federal Courts Act*, which allowed the Federal Court to provide relief where a federal board, commission or tribunal "acted without jurisdiction, acted beyond its jurisdiction or refused to exercise its jurisdiction." In response, Evans JA inquired into the concept of jurisdictional error after *Dunsmuir*.

Public Service Alliance of Canada v. Canadian Federal Pilots Association
2009 FCA 223

Issue 2: Did the Board exceed its jurisdiction by allocating the positions to the AO bargaining unit?

[27] The applicants argue that the Board exceeded its jurisdiction when, on a section 58 application [pursuant to the *Public Service Labour Relations Act*, SC 2003, c. 22 (PSLRA)], it allocated an employee to a bargaining unit comprising an occupational group from which the position held by the employee was specifically excluded. They say that this amounts to a change to the certified bargaining units, something which the Board only has the legal authority to do in accordance with section 70.

[28] They submit that whether section 58 enables the Board to, in effect, amend the definition of a bargaining unit is a jurisdictional question and therefore must be decided correctly: *Dunsmuir v. New Brunswick* ... at paras. 30, 31 and 59 ("*Dunsmuir*").

. . .

[30] Jurisdictional error (*Federal Courts Act*, paragraph 18.1(4)(*a*)) is the only *ground* of review available to the applicants on the facts of this case. The preclusive clause in section 51 [of the PSLRA] ousts the Court's power to review the decisions of federal tribunals for "mere" error of law under paragraph 18.1(4)(c). In the absence of any indication to the contrary, the references in paragraph 18.1(4)(a) to the wrongful assumption or

declining of jurisdiction should be understood to connote the concept of jurisdictional error in the common law of judicial review of administrative action: *Canada (Minister of Immigration and Citizenship) v. Khosa*, 2009 SCC 12 (CanLII), 2009 SCC 12, especially at para. 19 ("*Khosa*").

[31] Paragraph 18.1(4)(a) does not prescribe a *standard* of review for determining whether a federal tribunal has exceeded its jurisdiction. As Justice Binnie said in *Khosa* (at para. 42) of paragraph 18.1(4)(a):

> No standard of review is specified. *Dunsmuir* says that jurisdictional issues command a correctness standard (majority at para. 59).

However, it is important to emphasize that a tribunal may exceed its jurisdiction in one of two ways.

[32] First, a tribunal will have "acted beyond its jurisdiction" if it had decided incorrectly a legal question for which correctness is the applicable standard of review. Such questions have been labelled "jurisdictional questions" or, to adopt the terminology of Justice Binnie referred to above, "jurisdictional issues." They may include provisions of a tribunal's enabling statute.

[33] Second, even if the question decided by a tribunal is not "jurisdictional" in this sense, but is a "mere" question of law, the Court may nonetheless intervene on an application for judicial review if the tribunal's decision is unreasonable.

[34] Thus, the Board will have "acted beyond its jurisdiction" if the Court concludes that the Board had to be correct in deciding whether the discretion conferred by section 58 authorized it to include a position in a bargaining unit when the definition of the unit specifically excluded it, and the Court disagrees with the Board's conclusion.

[35] Even if its interpretation of section 58 is not subject to review for correctness, the Board will nonetheless have "acted beyond its jurisdiction" if its interpretation is unreasonable. Like other administrative tribunals, the Board is not authorized by Parliament to make a decision that is based on an unreasonable interpretation of its enabling legislation. Fidelity to the rule of law requires that individuals be afforded this minimum protection from the arbitrary exercise of public power by administrative decision-makers, whether or not they are protected by a preclusive clause: *Khosa* at para. 42.

(i) Correctness Review and "Jurisdictional Questions"

[36] Recent decisions of the Supreme Court of Canada have clarified many aspects of the standard of review applicable to the decisions of adjudicative administrative tribunals, like the Board. Of particular importance in the context of the present case is the Court's enunciation of a presumption that tribunals' interpretation of their enabling legislation is normally reviewable on a standard of unreasonableness: *Dunsmuir* at paras. 54-55; *Association des courtiers et agents immobiliers du Québec v. Proprio Direct Inc.*, [2008] 2 SCR 195, at para. 21; *Khosa* at para. 25.

[37] However, the Court's retention in *Dunsmuir* (at para. 59) of a category of "questions of pure jurisdiction or *vires*" reviewable on a standard of correctness is apt to cause confusion if such questions are to be identified independently of a standard of review analysis.

[38] It would be difficult, in my view, to reconcile the Court's well-established pragmatic and functional approach to the standard of review (as now streamlined and renamed by *Dunsmuir*) with the abstract approach inherent in the concept of a jurisdictional question. In particular, if a standard of review analysis indicates that a tribunal's interpretation of a particular provision in its enabling statute is reviewable for unreasonableness, on what basis could it be characterized as a "jurisdictional issue" and thus reviewable for correctness?

[39] I well appreciate why correctness is the appropriate standard of review for the interpretation of a statutory provision which demarcates the authority of competing different administrative regimes: *Dunsmuir* at para. 61. However, I can see no justification in contemporary approaches to the roles of specialist tribunals and generalist courts in administrative law for characterizing as a "jurisdictional issue," and thus reviewable on a standard of correctness, the interpretation of other provisions in a tribunal's enabling statute that do not raise a "question of law that is of 'central importance to the legal system ... and outside the ... specialized area of expertise' of the administrative decision maker" (*Dunsmuir* at para. 55).

[40] In my view, the analytical emptiness of the concept of a "jurisdictional issue" was deftly exposed by Justice Bastarache in *Pushpanathan v. Canada (Minister of Citizenship and Immigration)*, 1998 CanLII 778 (SCC), [1998] 1 SCR 982 at para. 28 when he said:

> ... "jurisdictional error" is simply an error on an issue with respect to which, according to the outcome of the pragmatic and functional analysis, the tribunal must make a correct interpretation and to which no deference will be shown.

Indeed, the Court in *Dunsmuir* seems to have been thinking along the same lines when Justices Bastarache and LeBel, writing for the majority, said (at para. 29):

> Thus, when a reviewing court considers the scope of a decision-making power or the jurisdiction conferred by a statute, the standard of review analysis strives to determine what authority was intended to be given to the body in relation to the subject matter.

[41] To the extent that the Court in *Dunsmuir* has retained the concept of a jurisdictional question to identify the provisions of an enabling statute which the administrative decision maker must decide correctly, it has done so in a very limited way. I say this for the following three reasons.

[42] First, it is clear from the reasons in *Dunsmuir* (at para. 59) that the Supreme Court did not intend to turn back the clock to the days before 1979 when virtually any question of law decided by a tribunal could be, and routinely was, characterized as a jurisdictional issue, and thus subject to *de novo* judicial review, notwithstanding the presence of a strong preclusive clause. Thus, the Court repeated with approval (at para. 35) the warning of Justice Dickson (as he then was) that "courts ... should not be alert to brand as jurisdictional, and therefore subject to broader curial review, that which may be doubtfully so": *CUPE, Local 963 v. New Brunswick Liquor Corporation*, [1979] 2 SCR 227 at 233.

[43] In a similar vein, Justice Abella had noted in *Council of Canadians With Disabilities v. VIA Rail Canada Inc.*, [2007] 1 SCR 650, at para. 88, that invoking "preliminary jurisdictional questions" as a basis for subjecting a tribunal's interpretation of its enabling legislation to review for correctness:

... has the capacity to unravel the essence of the decision and undermine the very characteristic of the Agency which entitles it to the highest level of deference from a court—its specialized expertise.

[44] Second, the Court indicated the limited range of issues that it had in mind when it stated (at para. 59) that jurisdictional questions are to be limited to "*true* questions of jurisdiction or *vires*" (my emphasis):

"Jurisdiction" is intended in the narrow sense of whether or not the tribunal had the authority to make the inquiry. In other words, true jurisdiction questions arise where the tribunal must explicitly determine whether its statutory grant of power gives it the authority to decide a particular matter.

[45] Despite the vagueness of the phrases "the authority to make the inquiry" and "the authority to decide a particular matter," and the similar phrases used in the pre-*New Brunswick Liquor* jurisprudence, I am satisfied that the Court in *Dunsmuir* did not intend to return the law to that era. This is apparent, not only from the passages quoted earlier where the Court expressly disavowed such an intention, but also from the manner in which the Court disposed of the question before it.

[46] The issue in contention in *Dunsmuir* was whether a labour adjudicator had exceeded his jurisdiction by going behind the terms of the letter terminating Mr Dunsmuir's employment and considering whether he was in fact being dismissed for disciplinary reasons. On the basis of the four-factor standard of review analysis (at paras. 66-71), the Court concluded that the standard of review was unreasonableness. It went on to find that the adjudicator's interpretation of the relevant provisions of the enabling statute was unreasonable and that, despite the privative clause, he had thereby exceeded his jurisdiction.

[47] Significantly, in my view, the Court did *not* say that, since the adjudicator had no authority to inquire into the "real reason" for the employee's dismissal, he had exceeded his jurisdiction because he had no authority to make that inquiry or to decide that question. Indeed, having found that the standard of review analysis indicated that unreasonableness was the applicable standard of review, the Court did not canvass the possibility that the interpretation of the statutory provision in question might raise a "jurisdictional issue." Similarly, there is no consideration in the Court's important post-*Dunsmuir* standard of review decisions, *Proprio Direct* and *Khosa*, of the possibility that the interpretation of the statutory provisions in question in those cases involved a "jurisdictional issue."

[48] Third, the only example given by the Court in *Dunsmuir* of a "true question of jurisdiction or *vires*" is its decision in *United Taxi Drivers' Fellowship of Southern Alberta v. Calgary (City)*, 2004 SCC, 2004 SCC 19 (CanLII), [2004] 1 SCR 485. The issue in that case was whether a resolution by the City of Calgary was within the legal authority delegated to it by the *Municipal Act*. Writing for the Court, Justice Bastarache said (at para. 5):

Municipalities do not possess any greater institutional competence or expertise than the courts in delineating their jurisdiction. Such a question will always be reviewed on a standard of correctness: *Nanaimo (City) v. Rascal Trucking Ltd.*, 2000 1 SCR 342, at para. 29. There is no need to engage in the pragmatic and functional approach in a review for *vires*; such an inquiry is only required where a municipality's adjudicative or policy-making function is being exercised.

[49] In my view, this suggests that a standard of review analysis *is* required when an adjudicative administrative tribunal is said to have exceeded its jurisdiction because it has misinterpreted a provision of its enabling statute. This is because Justice Bastarache only excluded the need for "a pragmatic and functional approach" (now, a standard of review analysis) on "a review for *vires*" when a municipality's delegated legislation is being challenged, but not when the exercise of its "adjudicative or policy-making function" is in issue.

[50] To conclude, in order to establish that the Board has exceeded its jurisdiction by misinterpreting a provision in its enabling statute, which neither raises a question of law of central importance to the legal system nor demarcates its authority *vis-à-vis* another tribunal, an applicant must demonstrate that the Board's interpretation was unreasonable.

[51] The only qualification that I would add is that the tribunal must have the legal authority to interpret and apply the disputed provision of its enabling legislation. However, administrative tribunals performing adjudicative functions, such as the Board, normally have explicit or implied authority to decide all questions of law, including the interpretation of its enabling statute, necessary for disposing of the matter before it: *Nova Scotia (Workers' Compensation Board) v. Martin*, [2003] 2 SCR 504, at paras. 40-41.

[52] In my view, it is too late in the development of administrative law in Canada for an applicant to invoke the ghost of jurisdiction past to inveigle the Court into reviewing for correctness a tribunal's interpretation of a provision in its enabling statute, without subjecting it to a standard of review analysis. It would, in my view, make no sense to apply a correctness standard when the tribunal has the authority to interpret and apply the provision to the facts, and a standard of review analysis indicates that the legislature intended the tribunal's interpretation to be reviewed only for unreasonableness.

NOTE

To what extent does this interpretation of *Dunsmuir* address loose ends about what amounts to a "true" error of jurisdiction? Is Evans JA's reasoning limited to the specific references to jurisdictional error that are contained in s. 18.1(4)(d) of the *Federal Courts Act* or does it extend to the wider issue of jurisdiction as an aspect of the nature of the question in the standard of review analysis? Most notable about the decision, perhaps, is its emphasis that *Dunsmuir* does not "turn back the clock to the days before 1979" when questions of law were routinely characterized as questions of jurisdiction. We examine below that history and, in particular, the significance of the *CUPE* decision of 1979 as a turning point.

The "Preliminary Question" Doctrine

The *Dunsmuir* decision warns against a return to the preliminary questions of doctrine that preceded the *CUPE* decision of 1979. For a long time, the courts allocated decision-making power between courts and administrative agencies (that were protected by a privative clause) by attempting to distinguish between those questions of law that were within the area of decision-making authority, or jurisdiction, of the agency, on the one hand, and those that were either "preliminary" to the exercise of the agency's jurisdiction, or "collateral" to the merits of the decision, on the other. Despite the privative clause, a court was entitled on this theory to intervene in the administrative process if it found that some condition precedent to the agency's exercise of its jurisdiction was not satisfied. The agency's determinations of preliminary questions were subject to review by the courts on the basis of their correctness. In contrast, any question of law within the agency's jurisdiction was entirely immune from judicial review (no matter, it seemed, how serious the error) because of the privative clause.

The preliminary question doctrine was unsatisfactory in both theory and practice. First, no test was ever devised to identify which questions of law that an administrative tribunal might decide in the course of resolving a dispute were preliminary and which were part of the merits. Indeed, virtually any question of statutory interpretation could logically be styled as preliminary to the agency's ultimate decision. To say that the preliminary nature of a question depended on the interpretation of the particular statute offered no real guidance. Second, the search for preliminary questions distracted attention from the substantive issues at stake: to match the institutional strengths of the reviewing court and the specialist agency to the particular question in dispute and to account for the public interest in both effective administration and the protection of constitutional values. Third, because the preliminary question doctrine lacked logical and policy coherence, courts were able to set aside administrative decisions whenever they disagreed with its determination of a question of law. Only a modest level of judicial craft was needed to present an issue of statutory interpretation as preliminary to the merits of the decision and therefore subject to judicial review for correctness.

It seems clear after *Dunsmuir* that the preliminary (or collateral) question approach is no longer part of Canadian administrative law. The most important judicial repudiations of this doctrine, historically, were the unanimous judgments of the Supreme Court of Canada in *CUPE, Local 963 v. New Brunswick Liquor Corporation*, [1979] 2 SCR 227, at 233 (Dickson J) and in *UES, Local 298 v. Bibeault*, [1988] 2 SCR 1048, at 1083-84 and 1087 (Beetz J). That said, a basic idea at the core of the doctrine has not been abandoned. This is that the decision-making power of administrative agencies is legally limited and that it is the function of the courts to ensure that agencies do not exceed the limits imposed by the legislature on their authority to decide. Thus, despite the presence of a privative clause, the courts must determine whether the agency correctly interpreted any provision in its enabling statute that confers, limits, or describes its jurisdiction. However, jurisdiction-limiting clauses are to be identified by the standard of review analysis as a whole, and not by the formalistic approach to statutory language that followed from the preliminary question doctrine.

Wrong Questions and Irrelevant Considerations

As part of the expansion of judicial review of administrative action that occurred in England in the late 1960s, the House of Lords abandoned the preliminary question approach to defining those questions of law that remained subject to judicial review. It was held in *Anisminic Ltd. v. Foreign Compensation Commission*, [1969] 2 AC 147 (Eng. HL) that the decision of an administrative tribunal could be set aside as being outside its jurisdiction if, in the course of making the decision, the tribunal had asked itself the "wrong question," taken into consideration legally irrelevant factors, or ignored factors that it was legally required to consider. The House of Lords reversed the Court of Appeal, which, applying the more traditional "preliminary question" doctrine, had held that the interpretation of the disputed provision in the tribunal's enabling legislation was part of the "merits" of the decision, and thus within its jurisdiction.

It was widely recognized that *Anisminic* expanded the scope of judicial review for jurisdictional error. It was not entirely clear, however, whether it eliminated entirely the distinction between questions of law and questions of jurisdiction. Courts in Canada did not embrace *Anisminic* wholeheartedly, although, shortly after it was decided, the Supreme Court of Canada in *Metropolitan Life Insurance Co. v. International Union of Operating Engineers, Local 796*, [1970] SCR 425 (Ont.) expressly adopted its doctrinal language and supporting philosophy. This reflected an assumption that the interpretation of an agency's enabling statute was a matter for the courts and, despite a strong privative clause, the agency's decision could be set aside if the court thought it was based on an error of law, including a misinterpretation of the agency's enabling statute.

There are two major problems with this *Anisminic*-based approach to the definition of jurisdictional review. First, denying that administrative agencies have the authority to decide questions of law conclusively in effect nullifies clearly worded privative clauses. This is difficult to reconcile with the constitutional principle of legislative supremacy, subject to the limits imposed by the *Constitution Acts, 1867-1982*. Second, the reasoning in *Metropolitan Life* is based on widely discredited views about statutory interpretation. In particular, it assumes that statutory language always has a determinate meaning and that the courts are uniquely qualified to divine the "correct" interpretation. On this view, since statutory interpretation is a legalistic exercise, the specialist expertise of the agency is irrelevant.

A related assumption is that the meaning of statutory language does not vary according to the context in which it is used. But might the terms found in regulatory legislation deviate from their conventional meaning in the common law? In *Metropolitan Life* itself the question was whether a person could be a "member" of a trade union, within the meaning of that term as used in a labour relations statute, even if he or she was not eligible for membership under the union's constitution. The labour board gave a persuasive explanation of why it made little sense from an industrial relations perspective to approach the union constitution as dispositive of the issue given that such a constitution may have not been updated to follow changing patterns of work. Nonetheless, the Supreme Court quashed the decision on the assumption that the word "member" had the same meaning in the statute as in the common law relating, for instance, to clubs and associations.

The Supreme Court of Canada has clearly rendered of historical interest only the approach to jurisdictional review contained in *Metropolitan Life*. It has also sought to limit an expansive approach to jurisdiction along the lines of the preliminary question doctrine, while preserving a role for "true" questions of jurisdiction, understood in the narrow sense of the authority to enter into an inquiry. To shed further light on what the narrow concept of jurisdiction is meant to capture, it is essential to examine one of the seminal decisions in Canadian substantive review.

THE ORIGINS OF THE STANDARD OF REVIEW ANALYSIS: CUPE (1979)

Dunsmuir adopted a cautious approach to the concept of jurisdiction. It did so, in part, by referring to Dickson J's decision in *CUPE* (1979). The *CUPE* decision marked a major turning point in Canadian administrative law. Past approaches to substantive review had permitted virtually any question of law to be approached as a question of jurisdiction and thus reviewed on a correctness standard. On the other hand, where a question was not treated as jurisdictional and was protected by a full privative clause, it would be entirely insulated from review. *CUPE* initiated a move away from the existing approaches to review for jurisdictional error. The decision called in particular for restraint by courts when reviewing administrative decision-makers, even in matters of statutory interpretation. In reading *CUPE*, one should look for the indicators of just how and why the courts are expected to limit their role. One should also reflect on the degree to which *Dunsmuir* maintains the spirit of deference evinced by *CUPE*.

Canadian Union of Public Employees, Local 963 v. New Brunswick Liquor Corporation
[1979] 2 SCR 227 (NB)

DICKSON J (for the Court): On August 22, 1977, during the course of a lawful strike, the Canadian Union of Public Employees, Local 963, laid a complaint with the Public Service Labour Relations Board of New Brunswick, pursuant to the *Public Service Labour Relations Act*, RSNB 1973, c. P-25, s. 19. The Union complained that the New Brunswick Liquor Corporation, the employer of their members, was replacing striking employees with management personnel contrary to s. 102(3)(a) of the Act. The Liquor Corporation denied the complaint and countered with a complaint against the Union, alleging picketing in violation of s. 102(3)(b) of the Act.

The two complaints were heard at the same time. The Board found the employer's complaint to be well-founded, and an appropriate order was made requiring the Union to cease and desist its then current picketing practices. The employer's complaint against the Union is, therefore, no longer of concern. The Union's complaint against the employer is another matter. It has given rise to some considerable difficulty and is the subject of the appeal now before the Court.

The facts of the case are brief and simply stated, by agreement of the parties before the Board:

Agreements as to the Complaint by the Union against Management

(1) Management personnel are and have been doing the work of bargaining unit personnel at the Fredericton warehouse since August 19, 1977.

(2) The Manager of Store No. 60 in Fredericton, N.B. opened that store and filled an order for a licensee at some unspecified date since August 19, 1977.

(3) All liquor received and sold in the Province by the New Brunswick Liquor Corporation is processed through bargaining unit personnel in normal circumstances. Managers do sometimes participate in sales.

The centre of the controversy is the interpretation of s. 102(3) of the *Public Service Labour Relations Act*:

102(3) Where subsection (1) and subsection (2) are complied with employees may strike and during the continuance of the strike

(a) the employer shall not replace the striking employees or fill their position with any other employee, and

(b) no employee shall picket, parade or in any manner demonstrate in or near any place of business of the employer.

On one point there can be little doubt—section 102(3)(a) is very badly drafted. It bristles with ambiguities. Mr Justice Limerick of the New Brunswick Appeal Division, in the course of his reasons in the present litigation, said: "Four possible interpretations immediately come to mind."

In argument before the Public Service Labour Relations Board, counsel for the employer contended that the words "with any other employee" referred to the word "replace" as well as the words "fill their positions." He went on to argue that the activities of the employer were not a violation of the Act, because management personnel are not "employees" as defined in the *Public Service Labour Relations Act*. Seven different classes of people are excluded from the definition of "employee" in s. 1 of the Act, including "(g) a person employed in a managerial or confidential capacity."

. . .

The major argument of the employer before the Board was that to which I have alluded, quite simply that the phrase "with any other employee" in s. 102(3)(a) covered *both* earlier branches of that paragraph, i.e. "replace the striking employees" or "fill their position." The only intent of the section, on this view, was to ensure that the jobs remained open for the employees after the strike was over.

This interpretation was rejected by the Board. It was the opinion of the Board that when the Legislature saw fit to grant the right to strike to public employees, it intended through the enactment of s. 102(3) to restrict the possibility of picket-line violence by prohibiting strikebreaking, on the one hand, and picketing, on the other. This apparent intention, the Board held, would be frustrated if the words "with any other employee" were to be interpreted as modifying "replace" as well as "fill their position," "for in that case there would be nothing to stop the Employer from replacing the strikers with anyone not coming within the definition of 'employee' in the *Public Service Labour Relations Act* ... . The result of such an interpretation would be that the strikers would have been deprived of their right to picket, but the employer would not have been deprived of the right to employ strike-breakers." The Board recognized the reach of their decision: "In coming to this conclusion we have been mindful of the fact that the result of our decision will force the Employer to close down some of the operations which are now being carried on and that this may have far reaching effects." The Board ordered the employer to refrain from the use of management personnel to do work normally done by the members of the bargaining unit in any of the employer's places of business.

Before entering upon a discussion of the conflicting interpretations of s. 102(3)(a) found in the judgments in the Court of Appeal, there is the critical characterization of the interpretation of s. 102(3) as a "preliminary or collateral matter" by that court, in the reasons of Mr Justice Limerick ((1978) 21 NBR (2d) 441, 448 (SC AD)):

> The Board is empowered to inquire into a complaint that the employer *has failed to observe a prohibition* in the Act and not to determine what is prohibited by the Act or to interpret it except as necessary to determine its jurisdiction.
>
> Two questions are therefore raised by the complaint:
>
> 1. Does the Act prohibit management personnel replacing striking employees? and if so
>
> 2. did management personnel replace employees?
>
> It is the latter question which is the subject-matter of the complaint and the primary matter for enquiry by the Board. The first question is a condition precedent to and collateral to determining the second.
>
> It is true the Board must determine the first question to vest itself with the jurisdiction to enquire into the second, but it is equally true the Board cannot by wrongly deciding the first question confer a jurisdiction on itself it cannot otherwise acquire. See judgment of Pigeon J in *Jacmain v. Att. Gen. of Canada* [1978] 2 SCR 15 (Can.). See also *Jarvis v. Associated Medical Services Inc. et al.* [1964] SCR 497 (Ont.), and *Parkhill Bedding & Furniture Ltd. v. International Molders & Foundry Workers Union of North America, Local 174 and Manitoba Labour Board* (1961) 26 DLR (2d) 589, 593 (Man. CA).

With respect, I do not think that the language of "preliminary or collateral matter" assists in the inquiry into the Board's jurisdiction. One can, I suppose, in most circumstances subdivide the matter before an administrative tribunal into a series of tasks or questions and, without too much difficulty, characterize one of those questions as a "preliminary or collateral matter." As Wade suggests in his *Administrative Law* (4th ed. 1977), p. 245, questions of fact will naturally be regarded as "the primary and central questions for decision," whereas the "prescribed statutory ingredients will be more readily found to be collateral." This is precisely what has occurred in this case, the existence of the prohibition described in the statute becoming the "collateral matter," and the facts possibly constituting breach of the prohibition, however interpreted, the "primary matter for enquiry." Underlying this sort of language is, however, another and, in my opinion, a preferable approach to jurisdictional problems, namely, that jurisdiction is typically to be determined at the outset of the inquiry.

The question of what is and is not jurisdictional is often very difficult to determine. The courts, in my view, should not be alert to brand as jurisdictional, and therefore subject to broader curial review, that which may be doubtfully so.

Broadly speaking, the Public Service Labour Relations Board acquires its jurisdiction to consider a complaint of violation of the Act under s. 19(1)(a):

> 19(1) The Board shall examine and inquire into any complaint made to it that the employer, or any person acting on its behalf, or that an employee organization, or any person acting on its behalf, or any other person, has failed
>
> (a) to observe any prohibition or to give effect to any provision contained in this Act or the regulations under this Act.

The parties before the Board, a separate employer identified in the Act, and a bargaining agent duly certified under the Act, were certainly those entitled to initiate the inquiry according to s. 19(1), and to be parties to that inquiry. The general subject-matter of the dispute between the parties unquestionably fell within the confines of the Act, that is, the situation of a strike by employees which is considered lawful by the very provisions of the Act. The Board was asked by the parties to determine whether certain activities of the Union and of the employer during that lawful strike were in violation of a prohibition in the Act, *i.e.*, section 102(3). The Union took no jurisdictional objection to the ban on picketing contrary to s. 102(3)(b), nor did the employer. The employer, in its reply to the Union complaint of violation of s. 102(3)(a), only contended that the Liquor Corporation "has not in any way violated" that provision. One cannot therefore suggest that the Board did not have "jurisdiction in the narrow sense of authority to enter upon an inquiry": *Service Employees' International Union v. Nipawin Union Hospital* [1975] 1 SCR 382, 389 (Sask.).

On this view of the matters before the Board, it is difficult to conceive how the existence of the prohibition can be a question "preliminary" to the Board's jurisdiction, in the sense of determining the scope of the Board's capacity to hear and decide the issues before them. Thus, the cases cited by the Court of Appeal in support of their view do not have any application in the case at bar. In *Jacmain v. Attorney General of Canada* [1978] 2 SCR 15 (Can.), the adjudicator's characterization of the employer's action as a disciplinary dismissal, or a rejection for unsuitability, could be seen as crucial to his ability even to enter upon a consideration of the grievance. In *Parkhill Bedding and Furniture, supra*, the issue was whether the Board could hear the Union's application under the successor rights provision of the Manitoba *Labour Relations Act* and, therefore, rule the purchaser of the defunct company's assets bound by the existing agreement. Had the Board not found the purchaser to be a "successor" employer, then the Union would have had to apply anew for certification under the normal certification procedures. In the *Jarvis* case, the interpretation given to the Ontario *Labour Relations Act* by this court was that the unfair practice provisions of that Act were only intended to benefit persons who were "employees" as defined by the Act. In this context, the Board's finding that Mrs. Jarvis was not an "employee" left the Board without jurisdiction to inquire into whether she was dismissed contrary to the Act, or to exercise its remedial powers of reinstatement. In each of these cases, at the threshold of the inquiry, the Board or the adjudicator had to determine whether the case before them was one of the kind upon which the empowering statute permitted entering an inquiry.

At this stage, it is important to have in mind the privative clause found in s. 101 of the Act, which protects the decisions of the Board made within jurisdiction. Section 101 reads:

> 101(1) Except as provided in this Act, every order, award, direction, decision, declaration, or ruling of the Board, the Arbitration Tribunal or an adjudicator is final and shall not be questioned or reviewed in any court.
>
> 101(2) No order shall be made or process entered, and no proceedings shall be taken in any court, whether by way of injunction, *certiorari*, prohibition, *quo warranto*, or otherwise, to question, review, prohibit or restrain the Board, the Arbitration Tribunal or an adjudicator in any of its or his proceedings.

Section 101 constitutes a clear statutory direction on the part of the Legislature that public sector labour matters be promptly and finally decided by the Board. Privative clauses of this type are typically found in labour relations legislation. The rationale for protection of a labour board's decisions within jurisdiction is straightforward and compelling. The labour board is a specialized tribunal which administers a comprehensive statute regulating labour relations. In the administration of that regime, a board is called upon not only to find facts and decide questions of law, but also to exercise its understanding of the body of jurisprudence that has developed around the collective bargaining system, as understood in Canada, and its labour relations sense acquired from accumulated experience in the area.

The usual reasons for judicial restraint upon review of labour board decisions are only reinforced in a case such as the one at bar. Not only has the Legislature confided certain decisions to an administrative board, but to a separate and distinct Public Service Labour Relations Board. That Board is given broad powers—broader than those typically vested in a labour board—to supervise and administer the novel system of collective bargaining created by the *Public Service Labour Relations Act*. The Act calls for a delicate balance between the need to maintain public services, and the need to maintain collective bargaining. Considerable sensitivity and unique expertise on the part of Board members is all the more required if the twin purposes of the legislation are to be met. Nowhere is the application of those skills more evident than in the supervision of a lawful strike by public service employees under the Act. Although the New Brunswick Act is patterned closely upon the federal *Public Service Staff Relations Act*, 1966-67 (Can.), c. 72, section 102(3) is not found in the federal legislation nor, in fact, in any other public sector labour legislation in Canada. The interpretation of s. 102(3) would seem to lie logically at the heart of the specialized jurisdiction confided to the Board. In that case, not only would the Board not be required to be "correct" in its interpretations, but one would think that the Board was entitled to err and any such error would be protected from review by the privative clause in s. 101. ...

I would take the position that the Board decided a matter which was plainly confided to it, for it alone to decide within its jurisdiction. It is contended, however, that the interpretation placed upon s. 102(3)(a) was so patently unreasonable that the Board, although possessing "jurisdiction in the narrow sense of authority to enter upon an inquiry," in the course of that inquiry did "something which takes the exercise of its powers outside the protection of the privative or preclusive clause." In the *Nipawin* case, in a unanimous judgment of this Court, it was held that examples of such error would include (at 389):

> ... acting in bad faith, basing the decision on extraneous matters, failing to take relevant factors into account, breaching the provisions of natural justice or misinterpreting the provisions of the Act so as to embark on an inquiry or answer a question not remitted to it.

Did the Board here so misinterpret the provisions of the Act as to embark on an inquiry or answer a question not remitted to it? Put another way, was the Board's interpretation so patently unreasonable that its construction cannot be rationally supported by the relevant legislation and demands intervention by the court upon review?

I do not see how one can properly so characterize the interpretation of the Board. The ambiguity of s. 102(3)(a) is acknowledged and undoubted. There is no one interpretation which can be said to be "right." The judgments of the Court of Appeal are in irreconcilable conflict. Mr Justice Limerick took the view that "replace" dealt with permanent effects, and "fill their position" with temporary actions by the employer. Chief Justice Hughes found the converse, that "replace" meant "replace temporarily," while "fill their position" meant "fill their position on a permanent basis." Mr Justice Bugold agreed in the result, but did not indicate which of the two versions he would adopt.

[After examining the reasoning of Limerick JA, Dickson J stated:]

This appears to be a reasonable interpretation on first reading but, with all due respect, no more or less reasonable than the interpretation which found favour with the Board.

· · ·

At this point, it might be useful to review the purpose of s. 102(3)(a) within the general context of the New Brunswick *Public Service Labour Relations Act*. Clearly s. 102(3) is an attempt to maintain the balance of power with a *quid pro quo*. Its intent, no doubt, is to avoid picket lines outside government buildings, for two reasons: as the Board indicates, to avoid picket line violence, but also to avoid the impact of picket lines for one bargaining group upon the remainder of government operations in a given building. Collective bargaining in the New Brunswick public service takes place in bargaining units formed out of "occupational groups" and thus, there are a large number of bargaining units in any one government operation. In one department, there may be employees in units of "scientific and professional," "technical," "administrative," "administrative support," "operational," or other employees. Also, in any one government building, there will typically be more than one department as well as one bargaining unit of employees. As a consequence, if one of the bargaining agents chooses the conciliation-strike route under the Act, some employees may go on strike while their fellow employees in the department and other departments stay on the job.

By reference to the private sector strike, one can see the importance of s. 102(3). The traditional view of the picket line is that it is simply informative. But its real purpose, as recognized by Mr Justice Limerick, goes beyond that. Generally, the purpose is to shut down the employer's operation, or at least to make it difficult to maintain the operation. This is done by dissuading various groups and individuals from having anything to do with the employer. In a heated confrontation, this attempt to discourage extends also to managerial personnel. The employer, by contrast, tries to maintain his operations by using managerial personnel to do the work of the strikers, by hiring strike-breakers, and by maintaining lines of communication for incoming supplies and services, and outgoing products. In private sector labour relations, these efforts on both sides are typically legal and an integral part of the economic conflict.

Hence, the enactment of s. 102(3). On the one hand, the striking employees are barred from picketing "in or near any place of business of the employer." On the other hand, the employer is barred either from "replacing" the striking employees, or from "filling their positions with any other employee." Both branches are purely temporary in nature, i.e. "during the continuance of the strike." The latter branch of the clause can be seen as cutting two ways: for the benefit of the striking employees, it bars the employer from temporarily filling the positions of the striking employees, and at the same time protects the "employees" in other bargaining units, who are still at work in the same government department or some other government department, from being required to fill the positions of their striking fellow employees during the period of the strike. The first branch ensures similar protection to the striking employees in a more general manner, in that they cannot be "replaced" by any person and not simply "with any other employee."

If one were to read "with any other employee" as applicable to "replace," then there is the obvious problem that any individual not an employee under the Act in s. 1 could work in maintaining the employer's operation. Aside from individuals completely outside the ambit of the Act, the definition of "employee" in s. 1 excludes a number of categories within the potential application of the Act—not just clause (g) managerial and confidential employees, but also (a) Order in Council appointments, (d) part-time employees, and (e) casual or temporary employees employed for less than six months. The result would be that the striking employees would be deprived of their right to picket, while the employer could maintain a high level of services, in the absence of the picket line, with suppliers and customers coming and going at will and the work being performed by anyone other than "employees" under the Act. The right to strike would be sterilized and the supposed choice of settlement techniques, spelled out in ss. 70 to 75, would become illusory.

. . .

I have discussed the possible interpretations of s. 102(3)(a) at some length only because, to some, the Board's interpretation may, at first glance, seem unreasonable if one draws too heavily upon private sector experience. Upon a careful reading of the Act, the Board's decision, and the judgments in the Court of Appeal, however, I find it difficult to brand as "patently unreasonable" the interpretation given to s. 102(3)(a) by the Board in this case. At a minimum, the Board's interpretation would seem at least as reasonable as the alternative interpretations suggested in the Court of Appeal. Certainly the Board cannot be said to have so misinterpreted the provision in question as to "embark on an inquiry or answer a question not remitted to it."

Appeal allowed.

NOTES

1. This excerpt from *CUPE* includes not only the standard of review discussion but also the court's application of the patent unreasonableness standard that it established to the matters in issue. Thus, the decision provides a further glimpse of how the courts integrate the theory and the practice of judicial review of substantive decisions. The question of how courts will apply the post-*Dunsmuir* standards of reasonableness and correctness is addressed in more detail in chapter 13 of this text.

2. An important feature of the *CUPE* decision is its emphasis on statutory context and legislative purpose, rather than common law concepts or presumptions, as key to interpreting the administrative statutes in question. However, it also illustrates two further insights that follow from a functionalist approach to statutory interpretation. The first involves the recognition that the meaning of statutory language may be ambiguous: Dickson J acknowledged not only that the statutory terminology that was in dispute "bristles with ambiguities" but also that "there is no one interpretation which can be said to be right."

Related to this is the insight that a court's determination of the meaning of an ambiguous word or phrase in a statute involves an institutional choice about who is best positioned to make that determination. But should the responsibility for interpreting an administrative statute lie with the specialist agency that makes decisions in the course of implementing the statute in question? Or should it lie with the court before which the agency's interpretation is challenged? Dickson J in *CUPE* concluded that it was not the responsibility of the court to resolve the statutory ambiguity in that case. This, he said, was a matter for the board, using its understanding of the collective bargaining system and "its labour relations sense acquired from accumulated experience in the area." It was for a reviewing court to ensure only that the board's interpretation of the relevant section was not "patently unreasonable," especially in light of the privative clause protecting the board's decisions from review.

On the standard of review, Dickson J's judgment was a landmark in the development of Canadian administrative law. Its historical significance is perhaps matched only by the judgment given for the majority by Laskin CJC in *Nicholson*, the harbinger of the "fairness revolution" that was discussed in chapter 3 of this text. In these cases the court exposed the shortcomings of abstract and formalistic doctrines by which judges had previously sought answers to two fundamental issues of administrative law: in *Nicholson*, the role of the courts in setting minimum standards of procedural fairness in public administration; in *CUPE*, the allocation of responsibility between courts and agencies for interpreting the legislation administered by specialist agencies.

In these two cases the court dismissed legal doctrine that purported to regulate the imposition of procedural duties using the elusive conceptual distinction between an "administrative" and a "judicial" power, and to define the limits of a tribunal's decision-making authority by slicing the non-factual issues decided by an agency into a series of "preliminary questions." In each case, the court indicated that procedural unfairness and jurisdictional error, as grounds of review, should be shaped by an examination of the legal and administrative contexts from which the dispute arose and by an understanding of the functional considerations and constitutional values that should inform any understanding of the role of the courts in the modern administrative state.

Notably, in *Nicholson* the court increased the role of the courts as arbiters of the adequacy of administrative procedure, while in *CUPE* it clearly sought to restrict judicial scrutiny of administrative interpretations of enabling statutes. Considered in this light, do you think that the impulses underlying these decisions are compatible?

Although the reasons for judgment given by Dickson J in *CUPE* broke new ground for the court, the judgment can also be located within some familiar contours of Canadian public law. The influence of the functionalist tradition (represented in Canada by the writings of, for example, Willis, Laskin (both as professor and as judge), and Arthurs) is apparent in the frank recognition of the ambiguities and silences in statutory texts, of the relevance of the expertise of the specialist agency to their satisfactory resolution, and of the importance of a policy of judicial restraint so as to avoid conjuring "jurisdictional" issues out of labour relations policy.

CUPE's principal doctrinal importance is that it shifted the focus of jurisdictional review by directing attention to the rationality of the agency's interpretation of its enabling statute rather than to an *a priori* classification of the statutory provision in dispute. *CUPE* was not the first case in which Dickson J adopted a policy of restraint by limiting jurisdictional review, in matters other than procedural fairness, to ensuring that the agency's interpretation of its enabling legislation was not patently unreasonable. See, for example, *Service Employees International Union, Local 333 v. Nipawin District Staff Nurses' Association*, [1975] 1 SCR 382 (Sask.), at 388-89; and *Jacmain v. Att. Gen. of Canada*, [1978] 2 SCR 15 (Can.), at 29 (dissenting). His judgment in *CUPE*, however, was a more explicit formulation of a policy of judicial restraint that clearly marked a new start.

On the other hand, despite the *CUPE* decision's message of judicial restraint (to be implemented by a refusal to overturn agencies' interpretations of their enabling legislation except when "patently unreasonable"), Dickson J's judgment did not unequivocally wrench the law from its old moorings. What examples of the "old" reasoning can you find in the judgment? Perhaps leaving these ambiguities in the law was the price paid for obtaining a unanimous decision from the court. Or perhaps it is simply the nature of the judicial process to gloss over the extent to which a judgment, even at the level of the Supreme Court of Canada, represents a radical departure from what has gone before.

AFTER CUPE: EVOLUTION OF THE PRAGMATIC AND FUNCTIONAL APPROACH

Naturally, many issues raised in *CUPE* have been revisited and elaborated in numerous decisions, most recently in *Dunsmuir*. For example, as we saw in *Dunsmuir*, not all questions of law arising from the interpretation of a decision-maker's enabling statute are said to warrant deference. This is so, according to *Dunsmuir*, where the question of law is considered to be of central importance to the legal system as a whole and outside of the specialized expertise of the decision-maker. One might indeed treat this description as a definition of the very concept of jurisdiction, such that a question of jurisdiction is understood simply to be a question of law which, based on the pragmatic and functional approach, attracts a correctness standard (see *Pushpanathan*, at para. 28). In elaborating this point, *Dunsmuir* echoes the reaction to *CUPE* that emanated from later decisions such as *Syndicat des employés de production du Québec et de l'Acadie v. Canada Labour Relations Board*, [1984] 2 SCR 412 (Can.) (the *CBC* case), where the board's decision was challenged as beyond its jurisdiction on the ground that the remedy awarded by the board was not authorized by the *Canada Labour Code*. Writing for a unanimous court, Beetz J said (at 440) that, even though the remedial issue arose at the end of the case and not "at the outset of the inquiry," as Dickson J in *CUPE* suggested jurisdictional questions normally should, "it is not doubtful but manifest that the interpretation of these provisions raises a question of jurisdiction about which the Board cannot err without committing an excess of jurisdiction."

Another marker of the origins of the standard review analysis is the decision of the Supreme Court of Canada in *Union des employés de service, Local 298 v. Bibeault*, [1988] 2 SCR 1048 (Que.). This was the case that first named the modern approach to the standard of review as the "pragmatic and functional approach," while also explicitly rejecting the preliminary question doctrine:

The formalistic analysis of the preliminary or collateral question theory is giving way to a pragmatic and functional analysis, hitherto associated with the concept of the patently unreasonable
error. At first sight it may appear that the functional analysis applied to cases of patently unreasonable error is not suitable for cases in which an error is alleged in respect of a legislative
provision limiting a tribunal's jurisdiction. The difference between these two types of error is
clear: only a patently unreasonable error results in an excess of jurisdiction when the question
at issue is within the tribunal's jurisdiction, whereas in the case of a legislative provision limiting the tribunal's jurisdiction, a simple error will result in a loss of jurisdiction. It is nevertheless
true that the first step in the analysis necessary in the concept of a "patently unreasonable" error
involves determining the jurisdiction of the administrative tribunal. At this stage, the Court
examines not only the wording of the enactment conferring jurisdiction on the administrative
tribunal, but the purpose of the statute creating the tribunal, the reason for its existence, the
area of expertise of its members and the nature of the problem before the tribunal. At this initial
stage a pragmatic or functional analysis is just as suited to a case in which an error is alleged in
the interpretation of a provision limiting the administrative tribunal's jurisdiction: in a case
where a patently unreasonable error is alleged on a question within the jurisdiction of the tribunal, as in a case where simple error is alleged regarding a provision limiting that jurisdiction,
the first step involves determining the tribunal's jurisdiction.

This development seems to me to offer three advantages. First, it focuses the Court's inquiry
directly on the intent of the legislator rather than on interpretation of an isolated provision.
Determining the legislator's intent is especially desirable when the Court has to intervene in the
decisions of administrative tribunals such as the labour commissioner or Labour Court. ...

Second, a pragmatic or functional analysis is better suited to the concept of jurisdiction and
the consequences that flow from a grant of powers. In *Judicial Review of Administrative Action*,
op. cit., at p. 110, S.A. de Smith writes:

> Jurisdiction means authority to decide. Whenever a judicial tribunal is empowered or
> required to inquire into a question of law or fact for the purpose of giving a decision on
> it, its findings thereon cannot be impeached collaterally or on an application for certiorari
> but are binding until reversed on appeal.

Under the preliminary or collateral question theory, the mere fact that an administrative
tribunal must answer a preliminary or collateral question before it may exercise its powers suffices to transform the question into a jurisdictional question. Thus, the order in which the tribunal deals with the questions presented to it may determine the nature of those questions.
Such a theory tends to empty the concept of jurisdiction of its content. Jurisdiction *stricto sensu*
is defined as the power to decide. The importance of a grant of jurisdiction relates not to the
tribunal's capacity or duty to decide a question but to the determining effect of its decision. As
S.A. de Smith points out, the tribunal's decision on a question within its jurisdiction is binding
on the parties to the dispute. In the exercise of its superintending and reforming power, a superior court must not limit its inquiry to identifying the questions to be dealt with by the tribunal. The true problem of judicial review is to discover whether the legislator intended the
tribunal's decision on these matters to be binding on the parties to the dispute, subject to the
right of appeal if any.

The third and perhaps the most important of the reasons why a pragmatic or functional
analysis seems more advantageous is that it puts renewed emphasis on the superintending and

reforming function of the superior courts. When an administrative tribunal exceeds its juris-diction, the illegality of its act is as serious as if it had acted in bad faith or ignored the rules of natural justice. The role of the superior courts in maintaining the rule of law is so important that it is given constitutional protection: *Crevier v. Attorney General of Quebec* [1981] 2 SCR 220. Yet, the importance of judicial review implies that it should not be exercised unnecessarily, lest this extraordinary remedy lose its meaning.

The motivation underlying the pragmatic and functional approach was also captured, in somewhat idealized terms, by the decision in *IAM, Lodge 692 v. BC (Industrial Relations Council)* (1993), 110 DLR (4th) 418, at 424-25 (BCCA), where Lambert JA offered this description of the phrase (at 425):

The *pragmatic and functional* approach requires the courts to rise above technicalities of all kinds, particularly legal and drafting technicalities, and to respond to the fundamental issues of democratic government, in particular, the paramount authority of Parliament and legisla-tures to confer ample jurisdiction on experienced people in statutory tribunals to regulate particularly difficult social interactions, and the obligation of the courts to check arbitrary acts against the individual or group beyond what Parliament and legislatures must be taken to have conceived.

The introduction of a factor-based approach to the standard of review analysis raised the prospect that a factor other than the presence of a strong privative clause could lead a court to defer, even on questions of law, to an administrative decision-maker. It might allow a tri-bunal to claim deference based on its specialized expertise alone, for example, as in *Pezim* and *Southam* (see chapter 10 of this text). To this day, the role of expertise as a counter to a statutory right of appeal on a question of law has led to differences of view. As we saw in *Dunsmuir*, the majority left open the possibility of deference to a tribunal on this basis, while Deschamps and Rothstein JJ rejected it.

We conclude this chapter with the following excerpt from the decision of the Alberta Court of Appeal in *Border Paving Ltd. v. Alberta (Occupational Health and Safety Council)*, 2009 ABCA 37. The reasons of the Alberta Court of Appeal here provide a useful example of a cautious approach—as dictated by *CUPE* (1979) and by *Dunsmuir*—to an attempt by a party to classify an issue of statutory interpretation as a jurisdictional question:

[1] This appeal concerns an order ("Order") by the respondent occupational health and safety officer ("Officer") that directs the appellant employer, Border Paving Ltd., to take certain steps following a workplace injury accident. The appellant has twice unsuccessfully appealed the Order. The appeal is dismissed.

Background

[2] A paving machine's rollover which resulted in serious injury to its operator caused the Officer, among other things, to order the appellant to equip all RayGo 304A road roller paving machines ("RayGo") with rollover protection, and provide documentation for review and lift-ing of the associated stop work order.

[3] The appellant's appeal to the Occupational Health and Safety Council ("Council") pur-suant to section 16(1) of the *Occupational Health and Safety Act*, RSA 2000, c. O-2 ("*OHSA*") was rejected. Appeals from Council decisions on questions of law or jurisdiction may be made

to the Court of Queen's Bench: s. 16(5). The employer's appeal from the Council's decision to the Court of Queen's Bench was dismissed: *Border Paving Ltd. v. Alberta (Occupational Health and Safety Council)*, 2006 ABQB 893, 408 AR 312.

[4]   The appeal judge concluded that reasonableness was the appropriate standard of review to apply to the Council's decision. Among other things, he relied on the employer's "sorry record" (it was the appellant's third injury accident involving RayGo rollovers) to conclude that the "health and safety of Alberta workers employed by Border" justified the Order, and the Council's decision to uphold it was reasonable: paras. 19-21.

[Discussion of preliminary matters and of the legislation has been omitted.]

Standard of Review and Grounds of Appeal

[Discussion of past cases, including *Dunsmuir*, has been omitted.]

[11]   The appellant's factum outlines three main grounds of appeal: the Officer lacked jurisdiction to make the Order, and there was no or insufficient evidence to support the Order or the finding that the Officer acted reasonably in making it. All three, the appellant suggests, are reviewable by this Court on the correctness standard.

[12]   Statutory appeals from Council decisions are permitted only on "questions of law and questions of jurisdiction": *OHSA*, s. 16(5).

[13]   "[W]hen the governing legislation grants a right of appeal on questions of law or jurisdiction, questions of mixed fact and law are not appealable unless there is an extricable legal question. ... Even then, only the pure legal question will be considered. ... [W]hen the issue on appeal involves a trial judge's interpretation of the evidence as a whole, or the application of the correct legal test to the evidence, there is no extricable error of law": *Alberta (Workers' Compensation Board) v. Appeals Commission*, 2005 ABCA 276 at paras. 27-29, 371 AR 318.

[14]   Accordingly, the two grounds of appeal that concern the adequacy of evidence or the reasonableness of the Order are not reviewable in this statutory appeal. Although the appellant asserts otherwise, in our view these points raise questions of mixed fact and law from which there is no extricable legal issue.

[15]   The remaining issue is whether the Officer had jurisdiction to make the Order and what standard of review applies. In its factum at para. 1, the appellant framed the question as whether the Officer could "issue an Order requiring the Appellant to adhere to a more stringent standard than that specified in the [Code]." At para. 17, it phrased the question as whether the appellant could be required to install rollover protection "when the Legislation does not require it, [the Officer] effectively amending the Legislation." In our view, both descriptions of the issue, as well as the appellant's arguments, are captured by considering whether the Officer had jurisdiction to make the Order.

[16]   As recently summarized in *Macdonald v. Mineral Springs Hospital*, 2008 ABCA 273 at paras. 27-30, 437 AR 7, true jurisdictional questions do not require a standard of review analysis since they are reviewable on the correctness standard: *United Taxi Drivers' Fellowship of Southern Alberta v. Calgary (City)*, [2004] 1 SCR 485 at para. 5. True jurisdictional questions "arise where the tribunal must explicitly determine whether its statutory grant of power gives it the authority to decide a particular matter": *Dunsmuir* at para. 59. Such questions will be narrow. An overly broad approach to characterizing issues as jurisdictional is misplaced: *VIA Rail* at para. 89.

[17] Whether the Officer had the jurisdiction to make the Order is not, in our view, a true question of jurisdiction as described in *Dunsmuir*. To explain why requires a brief detour into the authority under which the Officer was acting when he made the Order. The Order itself does not refer to its underlying authority, that is, what section of the *OHSA* was engaged.

[18] Before the Council, the appellant referred both to subsections 9(1) and (2) of the *OHSA*: AB E270 and E276. At the latter place, the appellant's counsel said they inferred that the Officer was using section 9(2), but did not explain why. The respondent's counsel referred to section 10(1)(c) as the basis for the Order: AB E264 and E303. Neither the Council nor the appeal judge opined about what section the Officer employed, although the appeal judge cited section 9. Nor does it appear to have been an issue of significance raised by the appellant.

[19] We return to this issue at para. 33. For present purposes it is sufficient to note that all three subsections permit the Officer to make certain orders when, *in his opinion*, work is being conducted unsafely or contrary to the legislated scheme for worker safety. This makes it apparent that the legal issue raised in this case is not a matter of true jurisdiction in the sense that the term is employed in *Dunsmuir*. Since the Officer was entitled to make orders if he thought that certain facts existed, a review of his order by the courts cannot question whether the legislation gave him that power, but only whether he exercised it appropriately in all the circumstances. Consequently, a standard of review analysis is necessary.

[20] The four factors to consider in the contextual standard of review analysis are whether there is a privative clause in the legislation, the purpose of the tribunal as determined by the interpretation of enabling legislation, the nature of the question at issue and the expertise of the tribunal: *Dunsmuir* at para. 64.

[21] Existing standard of review analyses concerning the tribunal may be used: *Dunsmuir* at paras. 57 and 62. This Court previously concluded that the Council is a specialized tribunal that commands curial deference and has developed an institutionalized expertise in the interpretation of the *OHSA*'s provisions and their application: *Navrot v. Alberta Occupational Health and Safety Council*, 2005 ABCA 398 at para. 11, 376 AR 161. We adopt this conclusion and it points to deference. By contrast, the statutory right of appeal in section 16(5) suggests less deference. This leaves consideration of the nature of the question at issue.

[22] As emphasized in the reproduction of subsections 9(1) and (2), and 10(1) above, the enabling provisions grant an officer considerable latitude in determining whether work is being conducted safely or in accordance with the legislation, as well as in selecting the appropriate measures to remedy safety concerns. And, as noted in *Dunsmuir* at para. 53, "deference will usually apply automatically" to questions of discretion decided by a tribunal interpreting its own statute. Accordingly, this factor also indicates deference to the Council.

[23] In summary, although the *OHSA* grants a statutory right of appeal, the Council is a specialized tribunal interpreting a provision of its enabling statute which grants a health and safety officer broad discretion to direct remedial measures in response to safety concerns. Therefore, a reasonableness standard applies to the Council's decision.

[The court's analysis of the application of the reasonableness standard has been omitted.]

[34] The appeal is dismissed.

CHAPTER THIRTEEN

Applying the Standard of Review

INTRODUCTION

In the preceding chapters on substantive review, we dealt with the extensive case law in which the Supreme Court has forged the principles by which the appropriate standard of review is selected. We saw how in the first of the modern cases, *Canadian Union of Public Employees, Local 963 v. New Brunswick Liquor Corporation*, [1979] 2 SCR 227 (NB), the Supreme Court applied the most deferential standard of "patent unreasonableness" to the issues in that case, how the then-middle standard of "reasonableness *simpliciter*" was introduced in *Canada (Director of Investigation and Research) v. Southam Inc.*, [1997] 1 SCR 748 (Can.), and in turn how these standards were reshaped in *Dunsmuir* by its adoption of the new, unified standard of reasonableness. In this chapter, we sample a range of cases that illustrate how the two post-*Dunsmuir* standards of review—correctness and reasonableness—are applied in order to decide whether the administrative decision under review should be upheld, varied, overturned, or otherwise interfered with by a court. We pay particular attention to the reasonableness standard, which is not the same as either reasonableness *simpliciter* or patent unreasonableness, but which also takes its meaning from past experiences with those standards. Before turning to the application of the reasonableness standard, however, we examine the standard of correctness.

CORRECTNESS REVIEW

When applying the correctness standard, according to the majority in *Dunsmuir*, at para. 50:

> [A] reviewing court will not show deference to the decision maker's reasoning process; it will rather undertake its own analysis of the question. The analysis will bring the court to decide whether it agrees with the determination of the decision maker; if not, the court will substitute its own view and provide the correct answer. From the outset, the court must ask whether the tribunal's decision was correct.

The brevity of this definition reflects that correctness review is well-established. For example, appellate courts have traditionally applied a correctness standard to the review of decisions of lower courts on questions of law (although in *Housen v. Nikolaisen*, [2002] 2 SCR 235, the Supreme Court established that appellate courts should defer to lower courts in civil proceedings on questions of mixed fact and law, as well as questions of law). Likewise, it is generally a more straightforward exercise of analysis for a court to revisit a decision in its entirety—by reviewing the record before the decision-maker alongside its decision(s) and any reasons given—in order to formulate and substitute its own position

821

than to exercise deference in some way. As we see in the excerpt below from *Pushpanathan*, when reviewing a legal question on a correctness standard, a court will carry out its own analysis of the statute or other legal instrument in order to arrive at an autonomous understanding of how silence or ambiguity should be resolved and of how the legal standard should be applied.

Pushpanathan v. Canada (Minister of Citizenship and Immigration)
[1998] 1 SCR 982 (Can.)

[Other portions of this decision are reproduced in chapter 11 of this text. In the following excerpt, the Supreme Court applied a correctness standard in its review of the interpretation given by a panel of the Immigration and Refugee Board to article 1F(c) of the United Nations *Convention Relating to the Status of Refugees* ("Convention"), which provided that the refugee protection provisions of the Convention did not apply to a person who "has been guilty of acts contrary to the purposes and principles of the United Nations." On the basis of its interpretation of this clause, the board interpreted article 1F(c) to exclude from refugee status an individual who had been found guilty of a serious narcotics offence committed in Canada. The board's decision was upheld by the Federal Court Trial Division and by the Federal Court of Appeal.]

B. *Principles of Treaty Interpretation: Determining the Purpose of Article 1F(c)*

[51] Although some non-governmental organizations advocated the determination of exclusion under Article 1F(c) of the Convention by the United Nations High Commissioner for Refugees, it was ultimately decided that each contracting state would decide for itself when a refugee claimant is within the scope of the exclusion clause (J.C. Hathaway, *The Law of Refugee Status* (1991), at pp. 214-15). Since the purpose of the Act incorporating Article 1F(c) is to implement the underlying Convention, the Court must adopt an interpretation consistent with Canada's obligations under the Convention. The wording of the Convention and the rules of treaty interpretation will therefore be applied to determine the meaning of Article 1F(c) in domestic law (*Ward* [*Canada (Attorney General) v.*, [1993] 2 SCR 689], at pp. 713-16).

[52] Those rules are succinctly articulated in the *Vienna Convention on the Law of Treaties*, Can. TS 1980 No. 37 ("Vienna Convention"), which states:

Article 31
General rule of interpretation
   1. A treaty shall be interpreted in good faith in accordance with the ordinary meaning to be given to the terms of the treaty in their context and in light of its object and purpose.
   2. The context for the purpose of the interpretation of a treaty shall comprise, in addition to the text, including its preamble and annexes:
        (a) any agreement relating to the treaty which was made between all the parties in connexion with the conclusion of the treaty;
        (b) any instrument which was made by one or more parties in connexion with the conclusion of the treaty and accepted by the other parties as an instrument related to the treaty.

3. There shall be taken into account, together with the context:

(a) any subsequent agreement between the parties regarding the interpretation of the treaty or the application of its provisions;

(b) any subsequent practice in the application of the treaty which establishes the agreement of the parties regarding its interpretation;

(c) any relevant rules of international law applicable in the relations between the parties.

4. A special meaning shall be given to a term if it is established that the parties so intended.

Article 32

Supplementary means of interpretation

Recourse may be had to supplementary means of interpretation, including the preparatory work of the treaty and the circumstances of its conclusion, in order to confirm the meaning resulting from the application of article 31, or to determine the meaning when the interpretation according to article 31:

(a) leaves the meaning ambiguous or obscure; or

(b) leads to a result which is manifestly absurd or unreasonable.

[53] These rules have been applied by this Court in two recent cases, one involving direct incorporation of treaty provisions (*Thomson v. Thomson*, [1994] 3 SCR 551, 1994 CanLII 26 (SCC), and another involving a section of the *Immigration Act* intended to implement Canada's obligations under the Convention (*Ward, supra*). In the latter case, La Forest J makes use of several interpretative devices: the drafting history of, and preparatory work on the provision in question; the United Nations High Commissioner for Refugees' *Handbook on Procedures and Criteria for Determining Refugee Status* ("UNHCR Handbook"), and previous judicial comment on the purpose and object of the treaty. Indeed, at p. 713, La Forest J was willing to consider submissions of individual delegations in the *travaux préparatoires*, although he recognized that, depending on their content and on the context, such statements "may not go far" in supporting one interpretation over another.

[54] Although these rules of interpretation were accepted in general terms in the courts below and by the parties, there is substantial disagreement as to precisely what those rules mean in the context of Article 1F(c) of the Convention as incorporated by s. 2(1) of the Act. In deciding on the relative weight to be accorded the various interpretative sources made available under the Vienna Convention, Strayer JA found that the terms "purposes and principles of the United Nations" were relatively clear. He was also of the opinion that the *travaux préparatoires* were confused, ambiguous, or unrepresentative, and therefore, "completely unhelpful." The UNHCR Handbook, which was accepted as a valid source under Article 31(3)(b) of the Vienna Convention, was considered "far from emphatic" as to the meaning of Article 1F(c). Finally, the categorization of the purpose of the Convention as a "'human rights' instrument" did not favour the applicant. Indeed, Strayer JA tacitly rejected this purpose as an interpretative guide by adopting the words of Robertson JA in *Moreno v. Canada (Minister of Employment and Immigration)*, [1994] 1 FC 298 (CA), at p. 307:

As persuasive as the commentaries may be, I am bound to approach the application of the exclusion clause, first, by reference to the existing jurisprudence of this Court and, second, by reference to the clear intent of the signatories to the Convention. Where, however, there is an unresolved ambiguity or issue, the construction most agreeable to justice and reason must prevail.

[55] In my view, the Federal Court of Appeal erred in dismissing the objects and purposes of the treaty, and in according virtually no weight to the indications provided in the *travaux préparatoires*. As will be seen later, the legislative history of Article 1F indicates that the signatories to the Convention wished to ascribe a special meaning to the words "purposes and principles of the United Nations" in the context of the Convention. In *Ward*, La Forest J carefully used each of these interpretative tools as a means of understanding the objects and purposes of the Convention as a whole, and the particular provisions being interpreted. The extremely general words in Article 1F(c) are not so unambiguous as to foreclose examination of other indications of the proper scope of the provision. An examination of the purpose and context of the treaty as a whole, as well as the purpose of the individual provision in question as suggested by the *travaux préparatoires*, provide helpful interpretative guidelines.

[56] The starting point of the interpretative exercise is, first, to define the purpose of the Convention as a whole, and, second, the purpose and place of Article 1F(c) within that scheme. In *Ward*, La Forest J, speaking for the entire Court at p. 709, stated that:

> International refugee law was formulated to serve as a back-up to the protection one expects from the state of which an individual is a national. It was meant to come into play only in situations when that protection is unavailable, and then only in certain situations. The international community intended that persecuted individuals be required to approach their home state for protection before the responsibility of other states becomes engaged. For this reason, James Hathaway refers to the refugee scheme as "surrogate or substitute protection," activated only upon failure of national protection; see *The Law of Refugee Status* (1991), at p. 135.

Using a textual analysis of the Convention itself, and taking account of the views of commentators, La Forest J, at p. 733, defines the purpose of the Convention with reference to the specific issue of the definition of refugee, which is precisely the issue in this case as well:

> Underlying the Convention is the international community's commitment to the assurance of basic human rights without discrimination. This is indicated in the preamble to the treaty as follows:
>
> > CONSIDERING that the Charter of the United Nations and the Universal Declaration of Human Rights approved on 10 December 1948 by the General Assembly have affirmed the principle that human beings shall enjoy fundamental rights and freedoms without discrimination.

This theme outlines the boundaries of the objectives sought to be achieved and consented to by the delegates. It sets out, in a general fashion, the intention of the drafters and thereby provides an inherent limit to the cases embraced by the Convention. Hathaway, *supra*, at p. 108, thus explains the impact of this general tone of the treaty on refugee law:

The dominant view however, is that refugee law ought to concern itself with actions which deny human dignity in any key way, and that the sustained or systemic denial of core human rights is the appropriate standard.

This theme sets the boundaries for many of the elements of the definition of "Convention refugee."

[57] The human rights character of the Convention is further confirmed by the "Objectives" section of the Act:

> 3. It is hereby declared that Canadian immigration policy and the rules and regulations made under this Act shall be designed and administered in such a manner as to promote the domestic and international interests of Canada recognizing the need
>
> . . .
>
> (g) to fulfil Canada's international legal obligations with respect to refugees *and to uphold its humanitarian tradition with respect to the displaced and the persecuted*; [Emphasis added.]

This overarching and clear human rights object and purpose is the background against which interpretation of individual provisions must take place.

[58] The purpose of Article 1 is to define who is a refugee. Article 1F then establishes categories of persons who are specifically excluded from that definition. The purpose of Article 33 of the Convention, by contrast, is not to define who is and who is not a refugee, but rather to allow for the *refoulement* of a *bona fide* refugee to his or her native country where he or she poses a danger to the security of the country of refuge, or to the safety of the community. This functional distinction is reflected in the Act, which adopts Article 1F as part of s. 2, the definitional section, and provides for the Minister's power to deport an admitted refugee under s. 53, which generally incorporates Article 33. Thus, the general purpose of Article 1F is not the protection of the society of refuge from dangerous refugees, whether because of acts committed before or after the presentation of a refugee claim; that purpose is served by Article 33 of the Convention. Rather, it is to exclude *ab initio* those who are not *bona fide* refugees at the time of their claim for refugee status. Although all of the acts described in Article 1F could presumably fall within the grounds for *refoulement* described in Article 33, the two are distinct. This reasoning must also be applied when considering whether the acts falling under Article 1F(c) must be acts performed outside the country of refuge, as argued by the appellant. In my opinion, the *refoulement* provisions cannot be invoked to read into Article 1F(c) any such limitation. Where geographical limitations were required, the Convention specifically provided for them, as evidenced by the terms of Article 1F(b). The relevant criterion here is the time at which refugee status is obtained. In other words, Article 1F(c) being referable to the recognition of refugee status, any act performed before a person has obtained that status must be considered relevant pursuant to Article 1F(c).

[59] Some light may be shed on the purpose of Article 1F(c) as distinct from Article 1F(a) and F(b) from the *travaux préparatoires* and from the contemporaneous meaning of the terms used. The precursor of Article 1F stated:

Article I: Definition of the term "refugee"

   D. No contracting State shall apply the benefits of this Convention to any person who in its opinion has committed a crime specified in article VI of the London Charter of the International Military Tribunal *or any other act contrary to the purposes and principles of the Charter of the United Nations.* [Emphasis added.] (UN Doc. E/L. 82)

The inclusion of the underlined words, which eventually were incorporated as Article 1F(c), generated considerable discussion in the Social Committee of the Economic and Social Council where the Convention was being negotiated. The Canadian, Chilean, and Pakistani delegates all expressed concern that the vague and potentially overbroad exclusionary clause would undermine the primary purpose of the Convention, and give states a means to easily reject individuals who deserved protection. The French delegate responded that the provision was aimed at "certain individuals who, though not guilty of war crimes, might have committed acts of similar gravity against the principles of the United Nations, in other words, crimes against humanity" (UN Doc. E/AC.7/SR.166, 22 August 1950, at p. 4). He was concerned that acts criminalized by the London *Charter of the International Military Tribunal*, 82 UNTS 280, would only be found to exist where a war had actually taken place. This would allow all manner of atrocities to be committed without the London Charter being violated simply because of the absence of military, interstate conflict. The reference to the London Charter alone, therefore, would fail to include

> tyrants ... guilty of acts contrary to the purposes and principles of the Charter, who had by such acts helped to create the fear from which the refugees had fled. The fact that they had themselves become suspect to their superiors and were in their turn a prey to the fear which they had themselves created, would ... certainly not [entitle them] to the automatic benefit of the international protection granted to refugees. (E/AC.7/SR.166, at p. 6)

[60] While a statement such as this one is far from authoritative in determining the purpose of what emerged as Article 1F(c), two points may be taken from these statements. The first is that the London Charter, in addition to describing crimes against the peace and war crimes, also described "crimes against humanity" such as "murder, extermination, enslavement, deportation, and other inhumane acts committed against any civilian population, *before or during the war*, or persecutions on political, racial or religious grounds *in execution of or in connection with any crime within the jurisdiction of the Tribunal*" (as quoted in H.M. Kindred et al., *International Law Chiefly as Interpreted and Applied in Canada* (1993)), at p. 448 (emphasis added). As articulated in the London Charter, then, a crime against humanity was tied to the punishment of crimes of war and crimes in times of peace. Although as it finally emerged, Article 1F(a) actually spelled out the individual offences contained in the London Charter, including "a crime against humanity, as defined in the international instruments drawn up to make provision in respect of such crimes," there is a clearly articulated concern by the French delegate, of which he persuaded the other delegations, that the crimes against humanity described in the London Charter were confined to those related to the occurrence of a war. Though initially one of the objectors who considered the provision dangerously vague, the Canadian delegate eventually agreed that the individuals caught by Article 1F(c) and not otherwise identified by the London Charter were those "persons who had abused positions of

authority by committing crimes against humanity, *other than war crimes*" (E/AC.7/SR.166, at p. 10 (emphasis added)). In short, the delegates whose minds were changed by the statement of the French delegate believed that they were identifying non-war-related crimes against humanity and that this was a distinct concept worthy of a separate provision, even if the acts falling into that category could not be clearly enumerated at that time.

[61] It must also be noted that the principle of exclusion by reason of acts contrary to the purposes and principles of the United Nations was found in embryonic form in the International Refugee Organization Constitution which also sought to exclude "those who, since the end of the Second World War, had participated in any organization seeking the overthrow by armed force of a government of a UN member State, or in any terrorist organization; or who were leaders of movements hostile to their government or sponsors of movements encouraging refugees not to return to their country of origin" (G.S. Goodwin-Gill, *The Refugee in International Law* (2nd ed. 1996), at p. 108). This is consistent with the position of the British representative who stated that acts contrary to the purposes and principles of the UN comprised the subversion and overthrow of democratic regimes. Other participants were opposed to this interpretation, however, because it was seen to conflict with the right to self-determination (Hathaway, *supra*, at p. 228). The confusion probably explains why the UNHCR Handbook, at paras. 162-63, does not consider that Article 1F(c) introduces "any specific new element."

[62] Of course, the purposes and principles of the United Nations are set out in the Preamble and Articles 1 and 2 of the *Charter of the United Nations*, Can. TS 1945 No. 7. But the statement found there is principally organizational; its general wording also allows for a dynamic interpretation of state obligations, which must be adapted to the changing international context. The principles set out in the UN Charter are in fact often developed in other international instruments and in decisions of the International Court of Justice, as well as in the jurisprudence of signatory states. Hathaway, *supra*, at p. 227, concludes that the multiple interpretations of Article 1F(c) "mirror its confused drafting history." The article is a residual clause which the UNHCR Handbook suggests, "due to its very general character, should be applied with caution" (para. 163). In reading the *travaux préparatoires*, one is easily convinced that the delegates participating in the Social Committee meetings intended to give the words "purposes and principles of the United Nations" a narrower and more focused meaning than that which would naturally be inferred by reading the UN Charter. The work of the drafting subcommittee and the resolutions of various bodies that followed are evidence of an effort to create a consensus on the special meaning to be given to the terms used in Article 1F(c).

[63] What is crucial, in my opinion, is the manner in which the logic of the exclusion in Article 1F generally, and Article 1F(c) in particular, is related to the purpose of the Convention as a whole. The rationale is that those who are responsible for the persecution which creates refugees should not enjoy the benefits of a Convention designed to protect those refugees. As La Forest J observes in *Ward*, *supra*, at p. 733, "actions which deny human dignity in any key way" and "the sustained or systemic denial of core human rights ... se[t] the boundaries for many of the elements of the definition of 'Convention refugee.'" This purpose has been explicitly recognized by the Federal Court of Appeal in the context of the grounds specifically enumerated in Article 1F(a) in *Sivakumar v. Canada (Minister of Employment and Immigration)*, [1994] 1 FC 433, where Linden JA stated

(at p. 445): "When the tables are turned on persecutors, who suddenly become the persecuted, they cannot claim refugee status. International criminals, on all sides of the conflicts, are rightly unable to claim refugee status."

[64] This brings me back to the second point to be taken from the declarations of the French delegate referred to earlier. In the light of the general purposes of the Convention, as described in *Ward*, and elsewhere, and the indications in the *travaux préparatoires* as to the relative ambit of Article 1F(a) and F(c), the purpose of Article 1F(c) can be characterized in the following terms: to exclude those individuals responsible for serious, sustained or systemic violations of fundamental human rights which amount to persecution in a non-war setting.

C. What Acts Are "Contrary to the Purposes and Principles of the United Nations"?

[65] Determining the precise content of this phrase is significantly easier having defined a discrete purpose which Article 1F(c) was intended to play within the structure and purposes of the Convention. The parties before us presented various alternatives as to what should be included within the section and sought to do so with a high degree of particularity. In my view, attempting to enumerate a precise or exhaustive list stands in opposition to the purpose of the section and the intentions of the parties to the Convention. There are, however, several types of acts which clearly fall within the section. The guiding principle is that where there is consensus in international law that particular acts constitute sufficiently serious and sustained violations of fundamental human rights as to amount to persecution, or are explicitly recognized as contrary to the purposes and principles of the United Nations, then Article 1F(c) will be applicable.

[66] Several categories of acts fall within this principle. First, where a widely accepted international agreement or United Nations resolution explicitly declares that the commission of certain acts is contrary to the purposes and principles of the United Nations, then there is a strong indication that those acts will fall within Article 1F(c). The *Declaration on the Protection of All Persons from Enforced Disappearance* (GA Res. 47/133, 18 December 1992, Article 1(1)), the *Declaration on the Protection of All Persons from Being Subjected to Torture and Other Cruel, Inhuman or Degrading Treatment or Punishment* (GA Res. 3452 (XXX), 9 December 1975, Article 2), and the *Declaration to Supplement the 1994 Declaration on Measures to Eliminate International Terrorism* (GA Res. 51/210, 16 January 1997, Annex, Article 2), all designate acts which are contrary to the purposes and principles of the United Nations. Where such declarations or resolutions represent a reasonable consensus of the international community, then that designation should be considered determinative.

[67] Similarly, other sources of international law may be relevant in a court's determination of whether an act falls within Article 1F(c). For example, determinations by the International Court of Justice may be compelling. In the case *United States Diplomatic and Consular Staff in Tehran*, ICJ Reports 1980, p. 3, at para. 91, the court found:

> Wrongfully to deprive human beings of their freedom and to subject them to physical constraint in conditions of hardship is in itself manifestly incompatible with the principles of the Charter of the United Nations, as well as with the fundamental principles enunciated in the Universal Declaration of Human Rights.

The International Court of Justice used even stronger language in the advisory opinion concerning the Legal Consequences for States of the Continued Presence of South Africa in Namibia (South West Africa) notwithstanding Security Council Resolution 276 (1970), ICJ Reports 1971, p. 16, at para. 131, finding that the policy of apartheid "constitute[s] a denial of fundamental human rights [and] is a flagrant violation of the purposes and principles of the Charter."

[68] Another important aspect of the exclusion under Article 1F(c) is the inference that violators of the principles and purposes of the UN must be persons in positions of power. This inference is drawn by the UNHCR Handbook at paras. 162-63 and in particular by the Canadian delegate to the Social Committee meetings of 1950 and 1951. While many commentators share this view (Hathaway, *supra*, at p. 229; A. Grahl-Madsen, *The Status of Refugees in International Law* (1966), vol. 1, at p. 286; and Kälin, Köfner and Nicolaus, in Goodwin-Gill, *supra*, at p. 110, note 162), the jurisprudence of signatory states is evolving along a different stream. Goodwin-Gill reports in his treatise, at p. 113, that the *Tehran* decision was the basis of the exclusion of a refugee under Article 1F(c) by Australian immigration authorities, indicating that it may be possible for non-state actors to be excluded by the provision. He contrasts this approach with that in France and Germany which appear to require that the acts be clothed in the authority of the state. Although it may be more difficult for a non-state actor to perpetrate human rights violations on a scale amounting to persecution without the state thereby implicitly adopting those acts, the possibility should not be excluded *a priori*. As mentioned earlier, the Court must also take into consideration that some crimes that have specifically been declared to contravene the purposes and principles of the United Nations are not restricted to state actors.

[69] In this case, we are concerned with drug trafficking. There is no indication in international law that drug trafficking on any scale is to be considered contrary to the purposes and principles of the United Nations. The respondent submitted evidence that the international community had developed a co-ordinated effort to stop trafficking in illicit substances through numerous UN treaties, declarations, and institutions. It has not, however, been able to point to any explicit declaration that drug trafficking is contrary to the purposes and principles of the United Nations, nor that such acts should be taken into consideration in deciding whether to grant a refugee claimant asylum. Such an explicit declaration would be an expression of the international community's judgment that such acts should qualify as tantamount to serious, sustained and systemic violations of fundamental human rights constituting persecution.

[70] The second category of acts which fall within the scope of Article 1F(c) are those which a court is able, for itself, to characterize as serious, sustained and systemic violations of fundamental human rights constituting persecution. This analysis involves a factual and a legal component. The court must assess the status of the rule which has been violated. Where the rule which has been violated is very near the core of the most valued principles of human rights and is recognized as immediately subject to international condemnation and punishment, then even an isolated violation could lead to an exclusion under Article 1F(c). The status of a violated rule as a universal jurisdiction offence would be a compelling indication that even an isolated violation constitutes persecution. To that end, if the international community were ever to adopt the *Draft Statute*

of the International Criminal Court, UN Doc. A/CN.4/L.491/Rev.2, which currently includes trafficking in narcotics within its jurisdiction, along with war crimes, torture and genocide, then there would be a much greater likelihood of a court being able to find a serious violation of human rights by virtue of those activities.

[71] A serious and sustained violation of human rights amounting to persecution may also arise from a particularly egregious factual situation, including the extent of the complicity of the applicant. Assessing the factual circumstances of a human rights violation as well as the nature of the right violated would allow a domestic court, for example, to determine on its own that the events in the Tehran hostage-taking warrant exclusion under Article 1F(c).

[72] In this case there is simply no indication that the drug trafficking comes close to the core, or even forms a part of the corpus of fundamental human rights. The respondent sought to bring the Court's attention to a novel category of international offence devised by M.C. Bassiouni called "crimes of international concern" (*International Criminal Law*, vol. 1, *Crimes* (1986), at pp. 135-63). Those "crimes" evince certain characteristics indicating that the international community does view their violation as particularly serious and worthy of immediate sanction; however, the bar appears to be set too low, including such categories of offence as "interference with submarine cables" and "environmental protection," as well as drug trafficking and eight other categories.

[73] It is also necessary to take account of the possible overlap of Article 1F(c) and F(b) with regard to drug trafficking. It is quite clear that Article 1F(b) is generally meant to prevent ordinary criminals extraditable by treaty from seeking refugee status, but that this exclusion is limited to serious crimes committed before entry in the state of asylum. Goodwin-Gill, *supra*, at p. 107, says:

> With a view to promoting consistent decisions, UNHCR proposed that, in the absence of any political factors, a presumption of serious crime might be considered as raised by evidence of commission of any of the following offences: homicide, rape, child molesting, wounding, arson, drugs trafficking, and armed robbery.

The parties sought to ensure that common criminals should not be able to avoid extradition and prosecution by claiming refugee status. Given the precisely drawn scope of Article 1F(b), limited as it is to "serious" "non-political crimes" committed outside the country of refuge, the unavoidable inference is that serious non-political crimes are not included in the general, unqualified language of Article 1F(c). Article 1F(b) identifies non-political crimes committed outside the country of refuge, while Article 33(2) addresses non-political crimes committed within the country of refuge. Article 1F(b) contains a balancing mechanism in so far as the specific adjectives "serious" and "non-political" must be satisfied, while Article 33(2) as implemented in the Act by ss. 53 and 19 provides for weighing of the seriousness of the danger posed to Canadian society against the danger of persecution upon *refoulement*. This approach reflects the intention of the signatory states to create a humanitarian balance between the individual in fear of persecution on the one hand, and the legitimate concern of states to sanction criminal activity on the other. The presence of Article 1F(b) suggests that even a serious non-political crime such as drug trafficking should not be included in Article 1F(c). This is consistent with the expression of opinion of the delegates in the *Collected Travaux Préparatoires of the 1951 Geneva Convention Relating to the Status of Refugees* (1989), vol. III, at p. 89.

[74] There is no rational connection between the objectives of the Convention and the objectives of the limitation on Article 1F(c) as stated by the respondent. Until the international community makes clear its view that drug trafficking, in one form or another, is a serious violation of fundamental human rights amounting to persecution, then there can be no rationale for counting it among the grounds of exclusion. The connection between persecution and the international refugee problem is what justifies the definitional exclusions in Article 1F(a) and F(c). Acts which fall short of persecution may well warrant *refoulement* under Article 33, and the Act has provided a procedure for determination of the merits of that issue. The *a priori* denial of the fundamental protections of a treaty whose purpose is the protection of human rights is a drastic exception to the purposes of the Convention as articulated in *Ward, supra*, and can only be justified where the protection of those rights is furthered by the exclusion.

VI. Disposition

[75] Even though international trafficking in drugs is an extremely serious problem that the United Nations has taken extraordinary measures to eradicate, in the absence of clear indications that the international community recognizes drug trafficking as a sufficiently serious and sustained violation of fundamental human rights as to amount to persecution, either through a specific designation as an act contrary to the purposes and principles of the United Nations (the first category), or through international instruments which otherwise indicate that trafficking is a serious violation of fundamental human rights (the second category), individuals should not be deprived of the essential protections contained in the Convention for having committed those acts. Article 33 and its counterparts in the Act are designed to deal with the expulsion of individuals who present a threat to Canadian society, and the grounds for such a determination are wider and more clearly articulated. It is therefore clear that my determination of the scope of Article 1F(c) of the Convention, as incorporated in domestic law by s. 2(1) of the Act, does not preclude the Minister from taking appropriate measures to ensure the safety of Canadians.

[76] In my view, the appellant's conspiring to traffic in a narcotic is not a violation of Article 1F(c).

[77] I would allow the appeal and return the matter to the Convention Refugee Determination Division for consideration under Article 33 of the Convention, and ss. 19 and 53 of the Act, if the respondent chooses to proceed.

[The dissenting reasons of Cory and Major JJ, who would have upheld the board's interpretation of article 1F(c) of the Convention on a correctness standard, have been omitted.]

NOTES

1. Bastarache J applied the rules of treaty interpretation derived from articles 31 and 32 of the *Vienna Convention on the Law of Treaties*. These direct the interpreter of a treaty, in article 31(1), to examine "the ordinary meaning to be given to the terms of the treaty in

their context and in light of its object and purpose" before turning, in certain cases, to the "supplementary means of interpretation" that are laid out in article 32. To what extent did these rules of treaty interpretation provide a clear path in *Pushpanathan* for the court to interpret article 1F(c) of the *Convention Relating to the Status of Refugees*? What means of interpretation did the Supreme Court majority rely on most clearly in reaching its view of the correct interpretation?

2. Might the earlier decisions of the Federal Court Trial Division and the Federal Court of Appeal in *Pushpanathan*, as well as the view of the dissenting Supreme Court judges, that the board's interpretation of article 1F(c) was correct pose a challenge to the enterprise of correctness review? Or is it simply a natural outcome of the structure of appellate review? In considering this question, reflect on the decision in *CUPE, Local 963 v. New Brunswick Liquor Corporation*, [1979] 2 SCR 227 (reproduced in chapter 12 of this text).

3. In a recent decision, the Supreme Court of Canada applied a correctness standard to a decision of the Canadian International Trade Tribunal (CITT) on a jurisdictional issue: see *Northrup Grumman Overseas Services Corporation v. Canada (Attorney General)*, 2009 SCC 50. In its decision, the court revisited the CITT's interpretation of Canada's inter-governmental *Agreement on Internal Trade* (AIT), the *Canadian International Trade Tribunal Act*, RSC 1985, c. 47 (4th Supp.) and the CITT Regulations, and concluded that the CITT had incorrectly allowed a non-Canadian supplier to bring a complaint under the AIT. After analyzing and interpreting these instruments, the court made this further comment on the wider rationales that had been offered to support the CITT's decision to allow a non-Canadian supplier to bring a claim under the AIT. The comment points to the sorts of issues, including policy implications, that a court will be inclined to decide for itself when applying a correctness standard.

Problems with the AIT Applying to Non-Canadian Suppliers

[41] Northrop Overseas' argument that non-Canadian suppliers have standing to bring complaints based on the AIT to the CITT leads to problematic results. If the argument of Northrop Overseas were correct, it would gain rights under the AIT despite its government (here, the U.S.) not being a party to the AIT. This poses difficulties. First, the goods that were the subject of this procurement were excluded from the [*North American Free Trade Agreement*] and the [World Trade Organization *Agreement on Government Procurement*]. Allowing non-Canadian suppliers to gain rights under the AIT where those rights were specifically excluded from agreements signed with their country's government would undercut the exclusion. Canada has negotiated similar exclusions for the military goods at issue in this case in trade agreements with Chile, Colombia and Peru ... .

[42] Second, Northrop Overseas's interpretation undermines the Canadian government's approach to negotiating trade agreements. Access to an accelerated alternative dispute resolution body for procurement disputes, such as the CITT, is a concession that Canada can offer other countries in negotiating trade agreements with the intent of obtaining reciprocal concessions in the other country. If access to the CITT were freely available to suppliers of all countries, access to it would have no value as a concession and Canada would have greater difficulty securing the equivalent access for its own suppliers in foreign countries ... .

• • •

The Jurisdictions of the CITT and the Federal Court

[44] It is suggested that the CITT provides an efficient dispute resolution mechanism to which there should be ready access. While the CITT may be an efficient dispute resolution vehicle, it is a statutory tribunal and access to it must be found in the relevant statutory instrument. The statutory provisions provide that access to the CITT is pursuant to specific trade agreements negotiated by governments. If the government of a supplier did not negotiate access to the CITT for its suppliers, there is no access for them.

[45] Northrop Overseas says that such an interpretation produces anomalous results. A Canadian supplier would have standing to challenge a contract awarded to a non-Canadian supplier but the reverse would not be true. Again, this is the result of the agreements negotiated by the governments who are parties to the various agreements under which the terms of access to the CITT are determined.

[46] It should be noted that a non-Canadian supplier of goods is not without recourse. Decisions of governments and government entities are subject to judicial review. In the case of the Government of Canada and its entities and, in particular, PW, there is recourse to the Federal Court by way of judicial review. It is argued that such recourse is limited and duplicative by comparison to that available through the CITT. While that may be so, again, access to the CITT is the product of the trade agreements entered into between the governments who are parties to such agreements and the legislation adopted to implement those agreements. The rights of suppliers are subject to the rights negotiated for them by their governments.

[47] Northrop Canada apparently has a place of business in Canada and if it, instead of Northrop Overseas, had bid on the procurement in this case, then, as the potential supplier in this case, it may well have had standing to complain about the award to Lockheed before the CITT. The majority of the Federal Court of Appeal suggested that income tax considerations may have been the reason Northrop Overseas was the potential supplier ... . Whatever the reason, standing before the CITT is determined by the agreements entered into by the governments of suppliers. As Northrop Overseas is within the jurisdiction of a government that did not negotiate access to the CITT for this type of military procurement by the Government of Canada, its recourse is judicial review in the Federal Court.

In the following decision, the New Brunswick Court of Appeal applied a correctness standard to an interpretation by the Appeals Tribunal of the provincial Workplace Health, Safety and Compensation Commission of the term "accident" in a federal statute. The Appeals Tribunal had resolved the issue of interpretation by looking to the meaning given to the term "accident" in a comparable provincial statute. In examining the Court of Appeal's reasoning below, consider first whether its rationale for applying a correctness standard was compelling in light of *Dunsmuir*. Then observe how the court applied the correctness standard in a manner that (properly) eschewed any deference to the Appeals Tribunal's interpretation.

Stewart v. Workplace Health, Safety and Compensation Commission
2008 NBCA 45

BELL JA:

I. Introduction

[1] This appeal addresses the extent, if any, to which the definition of "accident" in the provincial *Workers' Compensation Act*, RSNB 1973, c. W-13 (*WCA*) determines the interpretation of "accident" as that word is defined in the federal *Government Employees Compensation Act*, RSC 1985, c. G-5 (*GECA*). In a decision dated February 19, 2007, the Appeals Tribunal concluded the term "accident" under *GECA* does not include the gradual onset of stress as a compensable injury because, pursuant to s. 4(2) of *GECA*, a claimant can "only expect to be eligible for the same benefits as provided for under the *Act* [*Workers' Compensation Act*]." For the reasons set out below, I respectfully disagree. I would allow the appeal, set aside the Appeals Tribunal's decision, and remit the matter back to the Appeals Tribunal to determine whether, in light of these reasons, the gradual onset of stress in the present case is compensable under *GECA*.

II. Background

[2] Sheila Stewart is presently 60 years of age. In September of 2003, she was placed on stress leave because of stress-related symptoms including insomnia, crying spells, feelings of uselessness, fatigue, and lack of concentration. At that time, she had been employed by Public Works and Government Services Canada for approximately 23 years. As a result of the symptoms she experienced, Ms. Stewart ceased work in September 2003 and has been unable to return to work since that time.

[3] On February 26, 2004, Sharon Dea, a licensed psychologist, reported that Ms. Stewart suffered from depression and anxiety due to the ill effects of her job. She concluded the "stress overload" at Ms. Stewart's job had affected her physical and emotional well-being. Dr. Preston Smith, Ms. Stewart's family physician, made similar observations. By April 5, 2004, Dr. Dinesh Bhalla, psychiatrist, diagnosed Ms. Stewart with Major Depressive Disorder precipitated by "the distress caused by her work situation."

[4] On March 10, 2004, Ms. Stewart filed a claim with the Workplace Health, Safety and Compensation Commission (the "Commission") for compensation benefits because of her inability to attend work due to work-related stress. The Commission denied Ms. Stewart's claim on the basis that the incidents about which she complained did not "constitute an 'accident' within the meaning of [*GECA*]." Following requests for reconsideration, as permitted by s. 22(1) of the *Workplace Health, Safety and Compensation Commission Act*, SNB 1994, c. W-14 (*WHSCCA*), the Commission maintained its position and denied the claim. Ms. Stewart appealed to the Appeals Tribunal. In dismissing Ms. Stewart's appeal the Appeals Tribunal concluded she could only be eligible for the same benefits as were available pursuant to the provincial compensation scheme. It reached this conclusion because s. 4(2) of *GECA* provides, in part, that federal employees are "entitled to receive compensation at the same rate and under the same conditions as are provided under the law of the province where the employee is usually employed."

[5] Ms. Stewart now challenges the Appeals Tribunal's decision on the basis that, unlike the definition of "accident" in the provincial *WCA*, the definition in *GECA* does not exclude gradual onset of stress. Furthermore, she submits that the only purpose of s. 4(2) of *GECA* is to ensure parity for compensation purposes once a claimant has established eligibility for benefits independent of that section.

III. Analysis

A. The Applicable Standard of Review

[6] Since this Court is reviewing the decision of an administrative tribunal, the analysis must begin by applying the standard of review analysis set out in *Dunsmuir v. New Brunswick*, [2008] SCJ No. 9 (QL), 2008 SCC 9. This analysis replaces the pragmatic and functional approach previously applied in order to determine the appropriate standard of review: *Dr. Q. v. College of Physicians and Surgeons of British Columbia*, [2003] 1 SCR 226, [2003] S.C.J. No. 18 (QL), 2003 SCC 19, at para. 21 and *D.W. v. New Brunswick (Workplace Health, Safety and Compensation Commission)* (2005), 288 NBR (2d) 26, [2005] NBJ No. 282 (QL), 2005 NBCA 70, at para. 12. The objective of the standard of review analysis is to determine the degree of curial deference the legislator intended for the decision under review.

[7] The present appeal is heard by virtue of a statutory right of appeal as set out in s. 21(12) of the *WHSCCA*. That section specifically grants a right of appeal on questions of jurisdiction and law. It is my opinion the Appeals Tribunal's interpretation of the word "accident" raises a question of law. In the absence of a privative clause in relation to such questions, and, given the presence of a statutory right of appeal, it is my view the Appeals Tribunal must be correct in order for its decision to stand: *Gallant v. New Brunswick (Health, Safety and Compensation Commission)* (2000), 228 NBR (2d) 98 (CA), [2000] NBJ No. 320 (QL), at para. 12; *Keddy v. New Brunswick (Workplace Health, Safety and Compensation Commission)* (2002), 247 NBR (2d) 284 (CA), [2002] NBJ No. 91 (QL), 2002 NBCA 24, and *T.S. Simms & Co. v. New Brunswick (Workplace Health, Safety and Compensation Commission)* (2004), 279 NBR (2d) 56, [2004] NBJ No. 469 (QL), 2004 NBCA 92, at para. 15, all of which, in my view, continue to be valid law in the post *Dunsmuir* era. I leave to another time a consideration of whether the interpretation of the word "accident" also raises a jurisdictional issue within the relatively narrow approach advocated by the Supreme Court in paragraph 59 of *Dunsmuir*.

B. Interpretation of "Accident" as Defined in GECA

[8] "Accident" is defined in section 2 of *GECA* as follows:

> 2. In this Act,

> "accident" includes a wilful and an intentional act, not being the act of the employee, and a fortuitous event occasioned by a physical or natural cause;

Section 4(2) of *GECA* states that certain employees and dependents "are, notwithstanding the nature or class of the employment, entitled to receive compensation at the same rate and under the same conditions as are provided under the law of the province where the employee is usually employed respecting [workplace] compensation" when those employees are "caused personal injuries in that province by accidents arising out of and in the course of their employment." The definition of "accident" in the provincial *WCA* excludes disablement caused by mental stress, "other than as an acute reaction to a traumatic event."

[9] In *D.W.*, at para. 38, this Court set out the relevant factors to be considered in order to determine whether a stress-related claim is compensable under the *WCA*. This Court opined that "cases of chronic or gradual onset stress, being cumulative in nature, do not qualify as a traumatic event." In the present case, because of the language of s. 4(2) of *GECA*, the Appeals Tribunal concluded at p. 5 that the *D.W.* factors applied equally to the determination of whether an "accident" had occurred for purposes of *GECA*:

> It follows, therefore, in the Appeals Tribunal's view, that the term "accident" under *GECA* would not include the gradual onset of stress as being compensable because a claimant under *GECA* could only expect to be eligible for the same benefits as provided for under the *Act* [the provincial *Workers' Compensation Act*]. Those benefits for stress-related claims in New Brunswick are as outlined in *D.W.*

[10] It is my view the only purpose of s. 4(2) of *GECA* is to ensure the rates and conditions of compensation payable to injured federal employees mirror the rates and conditions for other injured workers in New Brunswick once the threshold of entitlement has been determined. Parliament has not, in my view, delegated to the legislature of each province the right to amend federal legislation by redefining "accident" in *GECA* in the province's own image; nor did Parliament intend to create a patchwork across Canada whereby federal employees in different provinces are faced with different thresholds for proving a compensable injury.

[11] I find support for this view in *Canada Post Corp. v. Nova Scotia (Workers' Compensation Appeals Tribunal)* (2004), 224 NSR (2d) 276, [2004] NSJ No. 242 (QL), 2004 NSCA 83 and *Rees v. Canada (Royal Canadian Mounted Police)* (2005), 246 Nfld. & PEIR 79, [2005] NJ No. 103 (QL), 2005 NLCA 15, leave to appeal to the Supreme Court denied [2005] SCCA No. 246 (QL). In *Canada Post Corporation* the Court was called upon to apply *GECA* to a claim of gradual onset of stress. As is currently the case in New Brunswick, the provincial *Workers' Compensation Act*, SNS 1994-95, c. 10 specifically excluded such claims. Relying upon the earlier Nova Scotia case of *Cape Breton Development Corp. v. Morrison (Estate) et al.* (2003), 218 NSR (2d) 53, [2003] NSJ No. 353 (QL), 2003 NSCA 103, leave to appeal to the Supreme Court dismissed [2003] SCCA 525 (QL), the Workers' Compensation Board of Nova Scotia argued that, given the language employed in that province's *Workers' Compensation Act*, such claims were excluded by operation of s. 4(2) of *GECA*. Cromwell JA rejected that hypothesis at para. 13:

> In my respectful view, *Morrison* does not support this position at all. As Freeman JA for the Court said at para. 55 of *Morrison*, in evaluating a claim, the Board must first of all determine whether the federal worker has suffered an accident pursuant to s. 4(1) of *GECA*. Further, at para. 54, he said that workers "… made eligible by the GECA definitions in s. 2, …" are entitled to file claims. Thus, the Court made it clear that the fundamental question of whether the worker has suffered an accident is to be determined having regard to the inclusions in that term found in *GECA*.

[12] The Newfoundland and Labrador Court of Appeal reached the same conclusion in *Rees*. After quoting extensively from Cromwell JA's judgment in *Canada Post Corp.*, Wells CJNL concluded as follows at para. 28:

> Before section 4(2) of the Act is engaged, thereby triggering compensation "at the same rate and under the same conditions as are provided under the law of the province," the provincial workers' compensation authority must first determine whether Mr. Rees is eligible, by virtue of section 4(1), to make a claim under the Act. This requires an interpretation of the word "accident" to ascertain whether it includes gradual onset stress.

[13] As noted by Wells CJNL in *Rees*, s. 4(2) of *GECA* is not engaged until it has been determined that s. 4(1) includes the gradual onset of stress.

IV. Conclusion

[14] Based upon all of the above it is my view the Appeals Tribunal erred in concluding the definition of "accident" in the *Workers' Compensation Act* is imported into the definition of "accident" set out in *GECA*. I would therefore allow the appeal and remit the matter back to the Appeals Tribunal for determination of whether, in light of these reasons, the gradual onset of stress in the present case is compensable under *GECA*.

NOTES

1. The New Brunswick Court of Appeal's substitution of its own interpretation of the term "accident" in the federal *Government Employees Compensation Act* was motivated by its view that the Appeals Tribunal had wrongly concluded that the interpretation of that term should track the meaning given to the same term (by the Court of Appeal in another decision) in the provincial *Workers' Compensation Act*. Imagine if the Court of Appeal had instead applied a reasonableness standard: would this have led it to defer to the Appeals Tribunal's interpretation such that the decision to apply a correctness standard decided the outcome of the case? Would it be reasonable for the Appeals Tribunal to assume that the interpretation of a term in a federal statute should track the meaning given to the same term in a provincial statute serving a similar purpose? Or is this very question—the relevance of an interpretation of one statute to the interpretation of another—one on which the courts should always have the final word, without the prospect of deference to administrative actors in the field?

2. What role did s. 4(2) of the *Government Employees Compensation Act* play in the Appeals Tribunal's decision and on what basis did the Court of Appeal reach a different conclusion?

3. The court's rationale for applying a correctness standard, based on the *Dunsmuir* framework, emphasized the presence of a statutory right of appeal on questions of jurisdiction and law, as well as past court decisions involving the same decision-maker on questions of law. Is this consistent with the majority reasons in *Dunsmuir* or with the dissenting approach to rights of appeal that was adopted in *Dunsmuir* by Deschamps and Rothstein JJ? And, if a series of pre-*Dunsmuir* court decisions in New Brunswick tended toward the approach of Deschamps and Rothstein JJ, is it appropriate to use the reference to "existing

jurisprudence" by the majority in *Dunsmuir* in order to elevate the importance of a statutory right of appeal as a factor in the standard of review analysis?

Rights of Appeal on Questions of Fact

Based on *Dunsmuir*, one might expect that correctness review would never apply in the case of a question of fact (or of mixed fact and law). Where there is a statutory right of appeal on questions of fact, however, a reviewing court may approach the task of review differently depending on the precise nature of the appeal. Thus, if the legislation specifies a very broad appeal, by way of hearing *de novo*, it is likely that the court will rehear the evidence and be prepared to reach a totally different conclusion from that of the tribunal. However, where the appeal is on the record of the proceedings below, the court will more likely pay some regard to the findings made by the initial decision-maker. Consider the extent to which a degree of deference in correctness review itself was applied in the following historical example.

Re Reddall and College of Nurses of Ontario
(1981), 123 DLR (3d) 678 (Ont. Div. Ct.)

[The appellant's employment as a nurse at a hospital was terminated for incompetence after she had had obvious difficulties in discharging nursing responsibilities in an intensive care unit (ICU). An investigation was conducted by the college, as a result of which she was found guilty of incompetence by the discipline committee of the college and her certificate was revoked.

The appellant appealed under s. 13(2) of the *Health Disciplines Act*, which provides a broad right of appeal:

An appeal under this section may be made on questions of law or fact or both and the court may affirm or rescind the decision of the committee appealed from and may exercise all the powers of the committee and may direct the committee or the College to take any action which the court considers proper, and for such purposes the court may substitute its opinion for that of the committee, or the court may refer the matter back to the committee for rehearing, in whole or in part, in accordance with such directions as the court considers proper.]

REID J: Appellant was charged with 21 different errors or omissions in three different categories: (1) patient care and treatment, (2) administration and recording of medication, and (3) reporting and recording. She admitted all allegations except two. Those two the Committee did not consider serious enough to constitute incompetence.

In its decision the Committee made the following findings:

Miss Reddall has demonstrated and admitted to a difficulty in organizing her work load and setting priorities, and showed a lack of insight in dealing with her own problems. Miss Reddall committed serious errors which endangered the life of the patients assigned to her care. (Reference Standards of Nursing Practice: Sections I, II, III B, and IV.) The Committee finds Miss Linda Reddall guilty of incompetence as per Section 84(4) of the *Health Disciplines Act, 1974*, Part IV Nursing, in that she has displayed, in her professional care of her patients, a lack of knowledge, skill and judgment and disregard for the welfare of the patient of a nature and to an extent that demonstrates she is unfit to continue in practice.

Section 13 of the Act confers extremely wide powers on this Court. ... We may consider questions of law and questions of fact. We may affirm or rescind the Committee's decision. We may exercise all of the Committee's powers. We may direct the Committee to take any action open to it that we consider proper. We may substitute our opinion for the Committee's or require the Committee to hold a rehearing, in whole or in part, in accordance with our directions.

The mandate so conferred is not an easy one to execute. For instance, we are told by counsel for the College that certain things should be left to the Committee's expertise. We should not expect to see evidence in the record to support certain of the findings. That submission arose in connection with the Committee's finding that "Miss Reddall committed serious errors which endangered the life of the patients assigned to her care." The gravity of that finding is obvious. When we asked to see the evidence supporting that finding we were told we would not find it in the record. The conclusion was not grounded in any expert opinion given in evidence before the Committee: it was grounded in the Committee's "expertise."

The consequence is that the Committee's conclusion is unreviewable. We are not experts in medicine or nursing. We cannot, or speaking for myself, I cannot, read the 19 admitted errors and omissions and decide whether any one or all of them endangered life. I do not say it was not so; I say merely that I am without the capacity to decide it on my own.

The difficulty we face is this. We are asked to review the Committee's decision that Miss Reddall was incompetent. We are asked, as well, to review the penalty imposed; revocation of her certificate, and therefore her right to practise nursing. Both of these issues raise the question: how serious were her 19 errors? If all were serious enough to endanger life could a finding of incompetence or the revocation of the right to practise seriously be questioned? Even if some were that serious would the decision not remain difficult to challenge? The Committee's decision does not make clear whether it was "some" or "all." It refers merely to "errors which endangered" lives.

The seriousness of Miss Reddall's errors is thus central to the issue of the appropriateness of the Committee's decision both on incompetence and on penalty. Yet, if there is no framework of expert evidence against which the Committee's decision can be measured in this Court, how can this Court perform its function? We are asked, in effect, to accept the most fundamental conclusion reached by the Committee without proof. We are asked to review the unreviewable.

I find this the most intractable problem in this case. I can illustrate it further by setting out the errors Miss Reddall admitted. They are taken from the Committee's decision. Some appear to me to be trivial. But what may appear trivial to a layman may be serious to a medical doctor or nurse. Without evidence, I cannot judge.

[The court then set out the specific errors and omissions allegedly committed by the appellant in her care of patients and treatments, including such allegations as "failure to administer KC1 elixir q 4h" and "infusing Normal Saline with 20 mEq KC1 instead of ⅔ and ⅓ with 20 mEq KC1" as ordered for named patients on specified days.]

Should we "for practical purposes," as we are invited, simply leave it to the Committee? Courts have been known to defer to the expertise of tribunals; indeed, the whole of the law of judicial review accepts the expertise of tribunals in their own fields. The law, however, does not lie in those fields; it lies within the domain of the Court's own expertise. The extent of a tribunal's powers under its legislation; the manner in which it shall proceed with its task: these, and like questions, are all, ultimately, for the Courts to decide.

The question is: may the Committee rely at all on its own expertise? By that I mean, in the confines of this case, is the Committee authorized to express an opinion without having heard expert opinion evidence directed to the point? Is the Committee not obliged, in order to create a record that this Court can review, to have heard opinions sufficient to support the opinion it adopts?

There is much to suggest it must. The implication of the breadth of the powers granted to this Court, and the Court's concomitant obligations I have already mentioned. Linden J, speaking for this Court in *Re Matheson and College of Nurses of Ontario* [(1979), 107 DLR (3d) 430, at 431] said:

> It is clear that, under this section, extremely wide powers are granted to this Court, far in excess of the authority it normally possesses in cases of judicial review. In essence, the Court appears to have *carte blanche* to rectify any errors of fact or law and to do what it thinks is appropriate in the circumstances of the case.

How can we perform that task properly unless we are able to assess the Committee's opinion against the evidence?

There are other indications in the legislation that suggest that we were not expected to. The Act, as I read it, suggests strongly that a case against a member must be laid out fully on the record. Section 83(2) provides:

> 83(2) In the case of hearings into allegations of professional misconduct or incompetence, the Discipline Committee shall,
>
>   (a) consider the allegations, hear the evidence and ascertain the facts of the case;
>
>   (b) determine whether upon the evidence and the facts so ascertained the allegations have been proved;
>
>   (c) determine whether in respect of the allegations so proved the member is guilty of professional misconduct or incompetence;
>
>   (d) determine the penalty to be imposed as hereinafter provided in cases in which it finds the member guilty of professional misconduct or of incompetence.

It might, as well, be asked whether the Discipline Committee was "expert" in the sense that the term has been applied to other tribunals. The members were not all registered nurses; indeed, we are told that only one was an RN. One member was a clergyman. Others were another lay person and two registered nursing assistants. There was nothing improper about the constitution of the Committee; it was appointed in accordance with s. 82 of the Act which requires the inclusion of lay persons. Should we not be reluctant to accept the term "expert" as appropriate to a Committee that could not even be described as a registered nurse's professional peers? Does the Committee, in the light of this, justify the kind of deference allowed to the Labour Relations Board in *Canadian Union of Public Employees, Local 963 v. New Brunswick Liquor Corp.* [1979] 2 SCR 227?

The question whether the Committee was justified in its conclusion that Miss Reddall's errors endangered lives is not only a serious but a pervasive one. It relates both to the finding of incompetence and to penalty. It is submitted that Miss Reddall's failures occurred only in the ICU, and that any incompetence proven was not across the broad field of nursing. Thus, it is submitted, the Committee's decision to prohibit her from nursing, from all or any nursing, was unjustified and harsh.

There were indeed areas of nursing in which her competence was not only unchallenged; it was endorsed. According to Dr Newhouse she was an effective respiratory care unit nurse. The doctors who employed her after her termination said she was a diligent and capable office nurse. All of this was before the Committee. None of it was contradicted.

It was open to the Committee, if it found incompetence, to revoke the nurse's certificate. But it was open to it instead to: "(c) impose such restrictions on the certificate of the member for such a period and subject to such conditions as the Committee designates." The submission is that the Committee should have done no more than restrict Miss Reddall's certificate in a way that would prevent her from nursing in an ICU: see s. 84(5)(c) [now s. 83(5)(c)].

So goes the argument. Again, in order to weigh it, we must return to the nature of Miss Reddall's failures. Certainly they were confined to the ICU. Yet, if they were so serious as to endanger life, does that matter? If they were that serious, is her general competence not in question? Should she be permitted the care of patients at all?

In my opinion, it does not follow necessarily that an error, or errors, committed in one area of nursing imply incompetence in others. They may, or they may not. It depends upon the nature and gravity of the errors. The seriousness of the errors is, again, the test of the appropriateness of the Committee's decision; this time in reference to the penalty imposed. If the Committee found that the error, although committed in only one area, was so serious as to show incompetence beyond that, the Committee would be justified in imposing a penalty reaching beyond that one area. (These considerations again reflect views expressed in *Re Matheson*.)

In the case before us, if the Committee has properly found that the errors endangered the lives of patients and was justifiably of the view that the nature of the errors demonstrated a general propensity for incompetence that would, in my opinion, make the penalty unassailable. But, again, whether they have properly made those findings, notwithstanding that the first was expressed and the second only implied, is not something that on the record before us I have the means to judge.

These are weighty considerations. I set them out because they have troubled me greatly. If they were to be given literal effect the result would be to deny almost completely any expertise in the Committee. There are countervailing factors. The Committee might not all be the peers of an RN but the majority are trained nurses or nursing assistants. They are in a far better position to judge the seriousness of a nursing error than we are. In pondering the implication of individual parts of the legislation one should not lose sight of its general thrust. The Legislature committed the responsibility for disciplinary matters in the nursing profession in clear terms to the members of that profession. Had the Legislature not wished to take advantage of the Committee's expertise why would it have done this? By denying to the Committee any expertise would one not be denying the implication of the entire Act as it relates to nursing? I fear one would.

It seems to me that, on balance, we should be reluctant to deny the Committee's expertise. Thus, on a point where the Committee, taken as a whole, may be accepted as expert the obligation on this Court to measure its findings against the record is, at the least, lessened. I do not suggest that we are bound to accept without question the opinion of the Committee on such a matter as the seriousness of error. There may be circumstances where it may properly be challenged in this Court.

I am willing to accept the Committee's conclusion in this case because (1) it was not directly challenged—the point arose only during argument—and (2) we were not shown anything in the record that would support a challenge. I thus accept that Miss Reddall "committed serious errors which endangered the life of the patients assigned to her care."

[The appellant appealed to the Court of Appeal: (1983), 149 DLR (3d) 60 (Ont. CA):]

MacKINNON ACJO delivered the judgment of the Court: By virtue of [s. 13(2) of the *Health Disciplines Act*] the Divisional Court clearly has all the powers of the discipline committee to assess and weigh the evidence and determine whether incompetence or professional misconduct has been established by that evidence and, if so established, the seriousness of the offences alleged in determining the penalty to be imposed.

[MacKinnon ACJO quoted from the judgment of Reid J, including the passages explaining the difficulty facing the court in reviewing the discipline committee's findings.]

His first reason for accepting the committee's conclusion that the appellant's errors had been life-threatening was that this position has not been directly challenged before the committee. However, we are advised by counsel for the appellant, and an affidavit which we accepted today, sworn by the appellant's counsel at trial, supports this, that it had been argued on behalf of the appellant that none of the errors or omissions caused any harm or was likely to cause harm to any patient.

Mr Justice Reid's second ground for accepting the conclusion that the appellant "committed errors which endangered the life of the patients assigned to her care" was that the court "was not shown anything in the record that would support a challenge." It should be noted that the notice of hearing served on the appellant setting out the counts or allegations of incompetence does not allege that her errors or omissions were such as to endanger the lives of patients. It is difficult to accept the proposition that an onus is placed on an individual charged to challenge an allegation that is not made in the charge and upon which no evidence is led which can be challenged by cross-examination or otherwise. The onus is surely on the college to establish its case on the admissible evidence.

We do not think that the Divisional Court was being asked "to review the unreviewable." It is only so if the mere *ipse dixit* of the discipline committee, without more, is enough in all cases to establish the seriousness of the incompetence. Such an approach, with deference, emasculates the broad right of appeal given by s. 13(2) quoted above. There were two laymen on the committee and it cannot be that they are to act outside the evidence given at the hearing. Indeed they are directed, as are all members of the committee, to base their finding on the evidence before them (s. 12(6) and s. 83(2)(b)—this in sharp contrast to ss. 15 and 16 of the *Statutory Powers Procedure Act*, RSO 1980,

c. 484). Are the laymen on the committee to take evidence and expert opinion from their professional colleagues on the committee in executive session without the person charged having an opportunity to challenge the evidence or opinion by cross-examination and rebuttal? It would appear to be a denial of the right to a fair hearing and of natural justice as well as a breach of the sections referred to, to allow this to be so. Further, the members of the Divisional Court are in the same position as the lay members of the discipline committee. Yet they are given the same powers as that committee to weigh and assess the evidence and indeed to exercise all of its powers. They, like the committee, can only act on the evidence which is in the record.

There was clearly evidence to support a finding of incompetence against the appellant but the seriousness of the errors and omissions leading to that finding has not been established on the record. It is obvious, we think, that the finding that she is unfit to continue in practice and the revocation of her certificate was based on the finding that her errors had endangered the lives of patients assigned to her care. The necessary evidence to support this conclusion is missing and the penalty cannot stand. This view of the record does not mean that the members of the committee cannot use their expertise in assessing all the evidence which is before them. But the evidence has to be before them before they can assess it. On any appeal one would expect the Divisional Court to give considerable weight to the decisions of the tribunal which has weighed the admissible evidence in light of its expertise and we do not deny the value of that expertise.

In the result, the appeal against the finding of incompetence is dismissed and the appeal against the penalty imposed is allowed, and to that extent the order of the Divisional Court is set aside and the penalty imposed by the discipline committee is quashed. The matter of penalty is remitted to the discipline committee for a rehearing on evidence as the parties may be advised.

Appeal allowed in part.

NOTE

The *Health Disciplines Act* was repealed by the *Regulated Health Professions Act 1991*, SO 1991, c. 18. The appeal provisions are contained in Schedule 2 of the *Health Professions Procedural Code*, s. 70, which specifies that appeals from a panel of a discipline committee may be made "on questions of law or fact or both" and that on an appeal "the Court has all the powers of the panel that dealt with the matter" (s. 70(3)). How does s. 70 differ from the repealed s. 13(2)? Why do you think the changes were made and what difference, if any, do you think they will make to the court's exercise of its appellate jurisdiction?

THE ESTABLISHMENT OF A SINGLE DEFERENTIAL STANDARD

In the following excerpt from *Dunsmuir* ([2008] 1 SCR 190 (NB)) the majority of the Supreme Court explained its decision to replace the standards of reasonableness *simpliciter* and patent unreasonableness with a single deferential standard of reasonableness. The discussion also provides useful background on the evolution of deferential standards of review in Canada since *CUPE, Local 963 v. New Brunswick Liquor Corporation*, [1979] 2 SCR 227:

Reconsidering the Standards of Judicial Review

[34] The current approach to judicial review involves three standards of review, which range from correctness, where no deference is shown, to patent unreasonableness, which is most deferential to the decision maker, the standard of reasonableness *simpliciter* lying, theoretically, in the middle. In our view, it is necessary to reconsider both the number and definitions of the various standards of review, and the analytical process employed to determine which standard applies in a given situation. We conclude that there ought to be two standards of review—correctness and reasonableness.

[35] The existing system of judicial review has its roots in several landmark decisions beginning in the late 1970s in which this Court developed the theory of substantive review to be applied to determinations of law, and determinations of fact and of mixed law and fact made by administrative tribunals. In *Canadian Union of Public Employees, Local 963 v. New Brunswick Liquor Corp.*, [1979] 2 SCR 227 ("*CUPE*"), Dickson J introduced the idea that, depending on the legal and administrative contexts, a specialized administrative tribunal with particular expertise, which has been given the protection of a privative clause, if acting within its jurisdiction, could provide an interpretation of its enabling legislation that would be allowed to stand unless "so patently unreasonable that its construction cannot be rationally supported by the relevant legislation and demands intervention by the court upon review" (p. 237). Prior to *CUPE*, judicial review followed the "preliminary question doctrine," which inquired into whether a tribunal had erred in determining the scope of its jurisdiction. By simply branding an issue as "jurisdictional," courts could replace a decision of the tribunal with one they preferred, often at the expense of a legislative intention that the matter lie in the hands of the administrative tribunal. *CUPE* marked a significant turning point in the approach of courts to judicial review, most notably in Dickson J's warning that courts "should not be alert to brand as jurisdictional, and therefore subject to broader curial review, that which may be doubtfully so" (p. 233). Dickson J's policy of judicial respect for administrative decision making marked the beginning of the modern era of Canadian administrative law.

[36] *CUPE* did not do away with correctness review altogether and in *Bibeault*, the Court affirmed that there are still questions on which a tribunal must be correct. As Beetz J explained, "the jurisdiction conferred on administrative tribunals and other bodies created by statute is limited, and ... such a tribunal cannot by a misinterpretation of an enactment assume a power not given to it by the legislator" (p. 1086). *Bibeault* introduced the concept of a "pragmatic and functional analysis" to determine the jurisdiction of a tribunal, abandoning the "preliminary question" theory. In arriving at the appropriate standard of review, courts were to consider a number of factors including the wording of the provision conferring jurisdiction on the tribunal, the purpose of the enabling statute, the reason for the existence of the tribunal, the expertise of its members, and the nature of the problem (p. 1088). The new approach would put "renewed emphasis on the superintending and reforming function of the superior courts" (p. 1090). The "pragmatic and functional analysis," as it came to be known, was later expanded to determine the appropriate degree of deference in respect of various forms of administrative decision making.

[37] In *Canada (Director of Investigation and Research) v. Southam Inc.*, [1997] 1 SCR 748, a third standard of review was introduced into Canadian administrative law. The legislative context of that case, which provided a statutory right of appeal from the decision of a specialized tribunal, suggested that none of the existing standards was entirely satisfactory. As a result, the reasonableness *simpliciter* standard was introduced. It asks whether the tribunal's decision

was reasonable. If so, the decision should stand; if not, it must fall. In *Southam*, Iacobucci J described an unreasonable decision as one that "is not supported by any reasons that can stand up to a somewhat probing examination" (para. 56) and explained that the difference between patent unreasonableness and reasonableness *simpliciter* is the "immediacy" or "obviousness" of the defect in the tribunal's decision (para. 57). The defect will appear on the face of a patently unreasonable decision, but where the decision is merely unreasonable, it will take a searching review to find the defect.

[38] The three standards of review have since remained in Canadian administrative law, the approach to determining the appropriate standard of review having been refined in *Pushpana-than v. Canada (Minister of Citizenship and Immigration)*, [1998] 1 SCR 982.

[39] The operation of three standards of review has not been without practical and theoretical difficulties, neither has it been free of criticism. One major problem lies in distinguishing between the patent unreasonableness standard and the reasonableness *simpliciter* standard. The difficulty in distinguishing between those standards contributes to the problem of choosing the right standard of review. An even greater problem lies in the application of the patent unreasonableness standard, which at times seems to require parties to accept an unreasonable decision.

[40] The definitions of the patent unreasonableness standard that arise from the case law tend to focus on the magnitude of the defect and on the immediacy of the defect (see *Toronto (City) v. CUPE, Local 79*, [2003] 3 SCR 77, 2003 SCC 63, at para. 78, *per* LeBel J). Those two hallmarks of review under the patent unreasonableness standard have been used consistently in the jurisprudence to distinguish it from review under the standard of reasonableness *simpliciter*. As it had become clear that, after *Southam*, lower courts were struggling with the conceptual distinction between patent unreasonableness and reasonableness *simpliciter*, Iacobucci J, writing for the Court in *Law Society of New Brunswick v. Ryan*, [2003] 1 SCR 247, 2003 SCC 20, attempted to bring some clarity to the issue. He explained the different operations of the two deferential standards as follows, at paras. 52-53:

> [A] patently unreasonable defect, once identified, can be explained simply and easily, leaving no real possibility of doubting that the decision is defective. A patently unreasonable decision has been described as "clearly irrational" or "evidently not in accordance with reason." ... A decision that is patently unreasonable is so flawed that no amount of curial deference can justify letting it stand.
>
> A decision may be unreasonable without being patently unreasonable when the defect in the decision is less obvious and might only be discovered after "significant searching or testing" (*Southam*, *supra*, at para. 57). Explaining the defect may require a detailed exposition to show that there are no lines of reasoning supporting the decision which could reasonably lead that tribunal to reach the decision it did.

[41] As discussed by LeBel J at length in *Toronto (City) v. CUPE*, notwithstanding the increased clarity that *Ryan* brought to the issue and the theoretical differences between the standards of patent unreasonableness and reasonableness *simpliciter*, a review of the cases reveals that any actual difference between them in terms of their operation appears to be illusory (see also the comments of Abella J in *Council of Canadians with Disabilities v. Via Rail Canada Inc.*, [2007] 1 SCR 650, 2007 SCC 15, at paras. 101-3). Indeed, even this Court divided when attempting to determine whether a particular decision was "patently unreasonable," although this should have been self-evident under the existing test (see *CUPE v. Ontario (Minister of*

Labour)). This result is explained by the fact that both standards are based on the idea that there might be multiple valid interpretations of a statutory provision or answers to a legal dispute and that courts ought not to interfere where the tribunal's decision is rationally supported. Looking to either the magnitude or the immediacy of the defect in the tribunal's decision provides no meaningful way in practice of distinguishing between a patently unreasonable and an unreasonable decision. As Mullan has explained:

> [T]o maintain a position that it is only the "clearly irrational" that will cross the threshold of patent unreasonableness while irrationality *simpliciter* will not is to make a nonsense of the law. Attaching the adjective "clearly" to irrational is surely a tautology. Like "uniqueness," irrationality either exists or it does not. There cannot be shades of irrationality.

See D.J. Mullan, "Recent Developments in Standard of Review," in Canadian Bar Association (Ontario), *Taking the Tribunal to Court: A Practical Guide for Administrative Law Practitioners* (2000), at p. 25.

[42] Moreover, even if one could conceive of a situation in which a clearly or highly irrational decision were distinguishable from a merely irrational decision, it would be unpalatable to require parties to accept an irrational decision simply because, on a deferential standard, the irrationality of the decision is not clear *enough*. It is also inconsistent with the rule of law to retain an irrational decision. As LeBel J. explained in his concurring reasons in *Toronto (City) v. CUPE*, at para. 108:

> In the end, the essential question remains the same under both standards: was the decision of the adjudicator taken in accordance with reason? Where the answer is no, for instance because the legislation in question cannot rationally support the adjudicator's interpretation, the error will invalidate the decision, regardless of whether the standard applied is reasonableness *simpliciter* or patent unreasonableness. ...

See also *Voice Construction Ltd. v. Construction & General Workers' Union, Local 92*, [2004] 1 SCR 609, 2004 SCC 23, at paras. 40-41, *per* LeBel J.

An obvious benefit of a single deferential standard is that it avoids any need to devise a clear and workable methodology to differentiate review based on reasonableness *simpliciter* from that based on patent unreasonableness. As emphasized by the majority in *Dunsmuir*, any drawing of distinctions between concepts that are themselves abstract and highly flexible is very difficult and will always leave cases at the boundaries that are difficult to classify.

On the other hand, in defence of the pre-*Dunsmuir* approach (which originated in *Southam*; see chapter 10 of this text), it was arguably helpful to know that there were two—and only two—choices in terms of the degree of deference to be shown to a decision-maker, and that further inquiry into the precise degree of deference that should be applied was unnecessary once a court arrived at the reasonableness *simpliciter* or patent unreasonableness standard. The former, according to *Dr. Q. v. College of Physicians and Surgeons of British Columbia*, [2003] 1 SCR 226, at para. 35, called for "considerable deference," whereas the latter called for "something in the middle" between patent unreasonableness and the correctness standard of "little or no deference." *Dunsmuir*'s replacement of these two standards with a single deferential standard could, thus, ironically make applying the standard more complex where it leads a court and the litigating parties to examine at length the precise degree of deference that is called for in a case. This concern was highlighted by Binnie J in his separate reasons in *Dunsmuir*, at paras. 139 and 152:

> [139] The judicial sensitivity to different levels of respect (or deference) required in different situations is quite legitimate. "Contextualizing" a single standard of review will shift the debate (slightly) from choosing *between* two standards of reasonableness that each represent a different level of deference to a debate *within* a single standard of reasonableness to determine the appropriate level of deference. In practice, the result of today's decision may be like the bold innovations of a traffic engineer that in the end do no more than shift rush hour congestion from one road intersection to another without any overall saving to motorists in time or expense.
>
> . . .
>
> [152] … In *Law Society of New Brunswick v. Ryan*, for example, the Court *rejected* the argument that "it is sometimes appropriate to apply the reasonableness standard more deferentially and sometimes less deferentially depending on the circumstances" (para. 43). It seems to me that collapsing everything beyond "correctness" into a single "reasonableness" standard will require a reviewing court to do exactly that.

As we shall see, in decisions after *Dunsmuir*, provincial appellate courts and then the Supreme Court itself sought to address the issue of whether the single reasonableness standard entailed a "spectrum" of deference rather than a singular approach to deference. They clarified, in particular, that reasonableness was not a spectrum; rather, as Binnie J put it in *Khosa*, 2009 SCC 12 (CanLII), reasonableness "is a single standard that takes its colour from the context." Consider in the next section how the need to "contextualize" the act of deference affects or clarifies the process of reasonableness review.

REASONABLENESS REVIEW

After laying out its rationale for moving to a single deferential standard in *Dunsmuir*, the majority turned to explaining the reasonableness standard:

> [46] What does this revised reasonableness standard mean? Reasonableness is one of the most widely used and yet most complex legal concepts. In any area of the law we turn our attention to, we find ourselves dealing with the reasonable, reasonableness or rationality. But what is a reasonable decision? How are reviewing courts to identify an unreasonable decision in the context of administrative law and, especially, of judicial review?
>
> [47] Reasonableness is a deferential standard animated by the principle that underlies the development of the two previous standards of reasonableness: certain questions that come before administrative tribunals do not lend themselves to one specific, particular result. Instead, they may give rise to a number of possible, reasonable conclusions. Tribunals have a margin of appreciation within the range of acceptable and rational solutions. A court conducting a review for reasonableness inquires into the qualities that make a decision reasonable, referring both to the process of articulating the reasons and to outcomes. In judicial review, reasonableness is concerned mostly with the existence of justification, transparency and intelligibility within the decision-making process. But it is also concerned with whether the decision falls within a range of possible, acceptable outcomes which are defensible in respect of the facts and law.

[48] The move towards a single reasonableness standard does not pave the way for a more intrusive review by courts and does not represent a return to pre-*Southam* formalism. In this respect, the concept of deference, so central to judicial review in administrative law, has perhaps been insufficiently explored in the case law. What does deference mean in this context? Deference is both an attitude of the court and a requirement of the law of judicial review. It does not mean that courts are subservient to the determinations of decision makers, or that courts must show blind reverence to their interpretations, or that they may be content to pay lip service to the concept of reasonableness review while in fact imposing their own view. Rather, deference imports respect for the decision-making process of adjudicative bodies with regard to both the facts and the law. The notion of deference "is rooted in part in a respect for governmental decisions to create administrative bodies with delegated powers" (*Canada (Attorney General) v. Mossop*, [1993] 1 SCR 554, at p. 596, *per* L'Heureux-Dubé J, dissenting). We agree with David Dyzenhaus where he states that the concept of "deference as respect" requires of the courts "not submission but a respectful attention to the reasons offered or which could be offered in support of a decision": "The Politics of Deference: Judicial Review and Democracy," in M. Taggart, ed., *The Province of Administrative Law* (1997), 279, at p. 286 (quoted with approval in *Baker*, at para. 65, *per* L'Heureux-Dubé J; *Ryan*, at para. 49).

[49] Deference in the context of the reasonableness standard therefore implies that courts will give due consideration to the determinations of decision makers. As Mullan explains, a policy of deference "recognizes the reality that, in many instances, those working day to day in the implementation of frequently complex administrative schemes have or will develop a considerable degree of expertise or field sensitivity to the imperatives and nuances of the legislative regime": D.J. Mullan, "Establishing the Standard of Review: The Struggle for Complexity?" (2004), 17 *CJALP* 59, at p. 93. In short, deference requires respect for the legislative choices to leave some matters in the hands of administrative decision makers, for the processes and determinations that draw on particular expertise and experiences, and for the different roles of the courts and administrative bodies within the Canadian constitutional system.

[50] As important as it is that courts have a proper understanding of reasonableness review as a deferential standard, it is also without question that the standard of correctness must be maintained in respect of jurisdictional and some other questions of law. This promotes just decisions and avoids inconsistent and unauthorized application of law. When applying the correctness standard, a reviewing court will not show deference to the decision maker's reasoning process; it will rather undertake its own analysis of the question. The analysis will bring the court to decide whether it agrees with the determination of the decision maker; if not, the court will substitute its own view and provide the correct answer. From the outset, the court must ask whether the tribunal's decision was correct.

This is more a broad description than a definition of reasonableness. It reiterates the principle, dating at least from *CUPE, Local 963 v. New Brunswick Liquor Corporation*, [1979] 2 SCR 227 (see chapter 12 of this text), that "certain questions that come before administrative tribunals do not lend themselves to one specific, particular result" (*Dunsmuir*, para. 47). It explains also that administrative decision-makers should be afforded a margin of appreciation such that a decision will be held reasonable where it "falls within a range of possible, acceptable outcomes which are defensible in respect of the facts and law" (*Dunsmuir*, para. 47). Further, the Supreme Court indicates—acknowledging, perhaps, the potential overlaps between substantive review and procedural fairness—that a court's inquiry into "the qualities that make a decision reasonable" refers "both to the process of articulating the reasons and to outcomes" and mentions that the main concern of reasonableness review is "with the existence of justification, transparency and intelligibility within the decision-making process" (*Dunsmuir*, para. 47). However, the court in *Dunsmuir* clearly did not seek to provide more than general guidance on reasonableness review, eschewing the more precise prescriptions of pre-*Dunsmuir* decisions like *Southam*. The latter decision, at paras. 56-57, had instructed lower courts (when applying the reasonableness *simpliciter* standard) to look for a "defect"—such as "an assumption that had no basis in the evidence, or that was contrary to the overwhelming weight of the evidence"—whether or not the defect was apparent on the face of the tribunal's reasons or otherwise obvious to the reviewing court.

One of the references in *Dunsmuir*, at para. 48, is to an article by Professor David Dyzenhaus ("The Politics of Deference: Judicial Review and Democracy," in M. Taggart, ed., *The Province of Administrative Law* (1997), 279, at p. 286) in which he stated that "deference as respect" requires of the courts "not submission but a respectful attention to the reasons offered or which could be offered in support of a decision." Dyzenhaus further described and contextualized this notion as follows:

> The task ... is no less than providing a theory of democratic legal order, one which justifies a workable account of the role for judicial review in the new political context.
>
> In this paper, I hope to show that a close examination of some leading Canadian decisions, mainly on the topic of judicial deference to administrative decisions, can assist us in this task. I will argue that [Albert Venn] Dicey's model requires judges to adopt a principle of deference which has to be rejected. This is the principle I will call submissive deference, since what it requires of judges is that they submit to the intention of the legislature, on a positivist understanding of intention.
>
> The alternative principle is the principle of deference as respect. Deference as respect requires not submission but a respectful attention to the reasons offered or which could be offered in support of a decision, whether that decision be the statutory decision of the legislature, a judgment of another court, or the decision of an administrative agency. I will argue that only this principle can rearticulate the proper relationship between the legislature, administrative agencies and the courts. I will argue further that the sense it makes requires the courts to reject the Diceyan model of law in which the idea of submissive deference is an essential component. I also suggest that the model of the rule of law to which the principle of deference as respect is committed might well prove fruitful in the new political context of administrative law, in particular because of its explicit commitment to the value of equality.

Here, then, Dyzenhaus introduces "deference as respect" by contrasting it with the Diceyan model of law. What do you think motivates Dyzenhaus to do this and can it be said that the same concerns influenced the Supreme Court in its delineation of substantive review in *Dunsmuir*? If so, how do we explain the *Dunsmuir* majority's invocation of classical (Diceyan) notions of the rule of law (para. 52) alongside Dyzenhaus' concept of deference as respect (para. 48)?

The flexible approach in *Dunsmuir* to the actual process of deference is based, we may assume, on the Supreme Court's confidence that lower courts will know how best to show deference in the circumstances of individual cases and that they will be faithful to the spirit of deference that is evident in the Supreme Court's jurisprudence from the *CUPE* decision of 1979 to *Dunsmuir* itself. Yet *Dunsmuir* does not provide specific guidance on just how a court should go about applying the reasonableness standard. To a large extent, this is an outcome of the need for the court to characterize reasonableness in a way that can be adapted to an extraordinary range of circumstances. But it also invites further questions about whether courts can and should achieve greater clarity for those affected by substantive review and for those who make administrative decisions. This reflects, of course, a fundamental conflict underlying judicial review, which Philip Bryden described in these terms ("Standards of Review and Sufficiency of Reasons: Some Practical Considerations" (2006), 19 *Can. J Admin. Law & P* 191, at 192):

> [A] tension between the desire of judges to develop a jurisprudence that is both principled and sufficiently flexible to address a broad range of administrative decision making and the desire of administrative law practitioners (whether they be parties to administrative proceedings, lawyers or administrative decision-makers) to operate in a legal environment that enables them to achieve practical solutions to their problems.

In the following post-*Dunsmuir* decision, the Alberta Court of Appeal applied a reasonableness standard in its review of a narrow question of statutory interpretation that arose from a municipal tax assessment of commercial property. The case is of interest here primarily for its concise discussion of the standard of review analysis and for its reasoning on why the provincial Municipal Government Board's interpretation of its home statute should be upheld as reasonable.

Calgary (City) v. Alberta (Municipal Government Board)
2008 ABCA 187

McFADYEN JA (Ritter and Rowbotham JJA concurring): [1] The main issue in this appeal is whether the Hudson's Bay Company ("the Bay") is entitled, under s. 460(3) of the *Municipal Government Act*, RSA 2000, c. M-26 [*MGA*], to make a complaint to an assessment of property that it occupies as a tenant.

Facts

[2] The City of Calgary ("the City") issued its 2004 property assessments to the owners of four Calgary shopping centres (Southcentre Mall, Sunridge Mall, Chinook Centre, and Deer Valley Shopping Centre) as the assessed persons. In each case, the Bay, or its wholly owned subsidiary, Zellers Inc., are anchor tenants in the shopping centres, and their leases required payment by them of the proportionate share of property taxes based on the space occupied by them as anchor tenants.

[3] The Bay also owns the downtown Bay store, and is the "assessed person" in respect of that property. There is no evidence that Zellers owns property in Calgary.

[4] The owners of each shopping centre filed a complaint with the Assessment Review Board ("ARB"). The owners subsequently reached settlements with the City, and the ARB accepted the agreed revised property assessments, and issued the necessary orders.

[5] The Bay, on its own behalf and on behalf of Zellers, also filed separate complaints in regard to these assessments, disputing the assessments in respect of the space occupied by the Bay or Zellers, as the case may be. These complaints were dismissed by the ARB on the basis that it had no jurisdiction to hear the complaints because it had already decided the assessments by accepting the settlements of the City and the owners. Although the Bay filed separate complaints, it had not been invited to participate in the settlement negotiations, which resulted in the settlement and reassessment.

[6] The Bay appealed to the Municipal Government Board ("MGB").

Decisions Below

A. Municipal Government Board

[7] The MGB decided that the Bay was entitled to file a complaint against the assessments on the basis that ss. 460(3) and (4) provide that "an assessed person" may make a complaint respecting "any assessed property or tax." Although it recognized that the Bay was not the "assessed person" for the assessed properties that were the subject matter of the complaints, the MGB concluded that the Bay was an "assessed person" entitled to file the complaint because it owned other property that was the subject of an assessment. The MGB considered the wording of s. 460(3) to be broad enough to permit that interpretation, and that no policy reason existed to justify restricting the right of complaint only to owners of the assessed property. The MGB determined that multiple complainants would not overburden the complaint process.

B. Court of Queen's Bench

[8] The City of Calgary applied for judicial review of the MGB's decision: *Calgary (City) v. Alberta (Municipal Government Board)*, 2007 ABQB 47, 70 Alta. LR (4th) 98. The chambers judge conducted the pragmatic and functional analysis anticipated by *Pushpanathan v. Canada (Minister of Citizenship and Immigration)*, [1998] 1 SCR 982, 160 DLR (4th) 193 [*Pushpanathan*] and concluded that the standard of correctness applied. She further concluded that the MGB erred in its interpretation of s. 460(3), as the term "an assessed person" refers only to the assessed person for the property that is subject to the complaint. Therefore, the *MGA* only permitted the shopping centre owners to file complaints to the assessments. She came to this conclusion by considering s. 460(3), together with ss. 284(1)(a) and 304, and found that the *MGA* requires a connection between an assessed person and the particular property in question, so "an assessed person" in s. 460(3) should be read as "*the* owner of *the* assessed property": at para. 81 [emphasis in original]. She also determined that "a taxpayer" refers to a payer of property tax and that it must be the person liable for tax on the property in question, which meant essentially that "an assessed person" and "a taxpayer" are the same person—the owner of the property. As the Bay and Zellers were not owners of the properties subject to the complaints, they could not complain about the assessments.

Legislation

[9] Section 460 of the *MGA* sets out the procedure for complaints against property assessments, and defines who may make a complaint:

460(1) A person wishing to make a complaint about any assessment or tax must do so in accordance with this section. ...

(3) A complaint may be made only by an assessed person or a taxpayer.

(4) A complaint may relate to any assessed property or business.

[10] The definitions for "tax," "taxpayer," "assessed person" and "assessed property" are also relevant, and are defined as follows:

1(1)(aa) "tax" means

(i) a property tax,

(ii) a business tax,

(iii) a business revitalization zone tax,

(iii.1) a community revitalization levy,

(iv) a special tax,

(v) a well drilling equipment tax,

(vi) a local improvement tax, and

(vii) a community aggregate payment levy;

1(1)(bb) "taxpayer" means a person liable to pay a tax; ...

284(1) In this Part and Parts 10, 11 and 12,

(a) "assessed person" means a person who is named on an assessment roll in accordance with section 304;

(b) "assessed property" means property in respect of which an assessment has been prepared or adopted;

[11] Section 304, which is referred to in the definition of assessed person, provides, in part:

304(1) The name of the person described in column 2 must be recorded on the assessment roll as the assessed person in respect of the assessed property described in column 1.

Column 1 Assessed Property	Column 2 Assessed Person
...	...
(b) a parcel of land and the improvements to it, unless otherwise dealt with in this subsection;	(b) the owner of the parcel of land;

[12] Other provisions of the *MGA* use the phrase "an assessed person," and are also relevant to its interpretation. In particular, ss. 299(1) and 300(1) provide:

299(1) An assessed person may ask the municipality, in the manner required by the municipality, to let the assessed person see or receive sufficient information to show how the assessor prepared the assessment of that person's property.

300(1) An assessed person may ask the municipality, in the manner required by the municipality, to let the assessed person see or receive a summary of the assessment of any assessed property in the municipality.

Issues

A. Did the chambers judge select the appropriate standard of review?

B. Does s. 460(3) limit the right of complaint about a property assessment to "*the owner of the* assessed property"?

Standard of Review

[13] This Court reviews the chambers judge's selection of the standard of review on the standard of correctness. ... If the court decides that the chambers judge adopted the appropriate standard of review, the court must also decide whether that standard was correctly applied ... . [case citations omitted].

[14] After conducting a pragmatic and functional analysis, the chambers judge concluded that the correctness standard of review applied. The parties' submissions before us on this issue were similarly premised on the pragmatic and functional approach. However, the Supreme Court has since reconsidered the analytical process employed by a court to ascertain the appropriate standard of review in the judicial review of administrative tribunal decisions: *Dunsmuir v. New Brunswick*, 2008 SCC 9.

[Summary of *Dunsmuir* omitted.]

[20] The nature of the question in this appeal, whether a party is entitled to file a complaint, is a question of law involving the interpretation of s. 460(3) of the *MGA*. This question involves the MGB interpreting its own statute, and typically will be subject to deference: *Dunsmuir*, at para. 54. Morever, while the appeal involves an issue of law, it also requires consideration of policy issues, since a proper interpretation of the *MGA* in this instance requires an understanding as to the effective functioning of the complaint process and considers the extent to which an assessed person or taxpayer has an interest in making a complaint of another person's property assessment. The MGB is particularly familiar with such issues, and is well-suited to address these considerations. This question of law does not fall within the scope of one of the examples cited in *Dunsmuir*; it is not a jurisdictional question in the narrow sense (see *United Taxi Drivers' Fellowship of Southern Alberta v. Calgary (City)*, 2004 SCC 19, [2004] 1 SCR 485), and it does not constitute a question of importance to the legal system as a whole. These comments apply to the standard of review applicable to the interpretation of s. 460(3) of the *MGA*, and do not necessarily govern the standard of review applicable to other MGB decisions.

[21] The Supreme Court in *Dunsmuir* also pointed out that the existence of a privative clause is a "strong indication" of the legislative intent to give deference to the decision of the administrative tribunal: para. 52. While the *MGA*'s privative clause has been characterized as "weak," it nonetheless signals that some deference should be given to the MGB's decisions: *Telus* at para. 31.

[22] Taking these factors into account leads to the conclusion that the standard of reasonableness applies to a review of the MGB's decision. Reasonableness, according to the majority of the Supreme Court in *Dunsmuir*, requires that deference be accorded to the underlying decision, which "imports respect for the decision-making process of adjudicative bodies with regard to both the facts and the law," (para. 48) and "implies that courts will give due consideration to the determinations of decision makers" (para. 49).

[23] The appropriate standard of review is reasonableness. The question on this appeal is the reasonableness of the decision of the MGB that "any assessed person" has the right to file a complaint about an assessment, and that the right is not limited to the assessed person named in the assessment rolls for the property that is the subject of the complaint.

Position of the Parties

[24] The chambers judge determined that the MGB erred in its interpretation of s. 460(1), and concluded that the only person who can make a complaint is the person whose name appears on the assessment role as the "assessed person" with respect to the assessed property referred to in the complaint. On appeal, the appellant submits that the chambers judge erred in this conclusion. The appellant says that the ordinary meaning of the words used in s. 460(1), as read in the context of the *MGA* as a whole, permits an appeal by any assessed person in respect of any assessed property. The appellant submits that the chambers judge erred in deciding that "*an* assessed person" in s. 460(3) has the same meaning as the phrase "*the* assessed person" in s. 304(1)(b).

[25] The respondent adopts the reasons of the chambers judge's and submits that the phrase "assessed person" used in s. 460(1) is determined by s. 304(1).

Analysis

[26] The modern, preferred approach to statutory interpretation mandates that the Court interpret the words of the legislative provision in their entire context and in their grammatical and ordinary sense, harmoniously with the scheme of the Act, the object of the Act and the intention of the Legislature: *Rizzo & Rizzo Shoes Ltd.*, [1998] 1 SCR 27 at para. 21; *Bell ExpressVu Ltd. Partnership v. Rex*, 2002 SCC 42, [2002] 2 SCR 559 at para. 26.

Ordinary Meaning

[27] The MGB appropriately noted that s. 460 addresses the question of who may file an assessment complaint, and considered the ordinary meaning of ss. 460(3) and (4) to be clear. Read together, they provide that "an assessed person" may make a complaint relating to "any assessed property." The MGB considered that this wording provided broad appeal rights to assessed persons to make a complaint about property assessment, including persons other than those whose name appears on the assessment roll as the assessed person of the subject property.

[28] This approach is certainly reasonable, as the ordinary meaning of "*an* assessed person" and "*a* taxpayer" is not restrictive. "A" and "an" are indefinite articles, defined as "one, some, any": *Canadian Oxford Dictionary*, 2d ed., *s.v.* "a." The ordinary meaning

implies that any assessed person or taxpayer may make a complaint in respect of any assessed property.

[29] The ordinary meaning is confirmed by the definitions for "assessed person" and "assessed property," which provide that an assessed person is any person whose name appears on an assessment roll. That language indicates a broad unrestricted interpretation.

[30] The respondent submits that s. 304(1) defines the term "assessed person." However, s. 304(1) does not purport to define the terminology used in the *MGA*, but merely sets out what information is to be included in the assessment rolls, and identifies and links the assessed person and the specified classes of property. Nothing in this language requires a linkage between the person who may make a complaint and the property in respect of which the complaint is made. Had the Legislature intended to restrict the right of complaint to the person who owned or was the assessed person in respect of the assessed property that is the subject matter of the complaint, it could easily have said so.

Consistency of Meaning

[31] Legislation must be read in context and other parts of the statute inform the ordinary meaning of the provision in question: Pierre-André Côté, *The Interpretation of Legislation in Canada*, 3d ed. (Scarborough: Thomson Canada Limited, 2000) at 309. Similarities and differences in choice of words are significant. "It is presumed that the legislature uses language carefully and consistently so that within a statute or other legislative instrument the same words have the same meaning and different words have different meanings": Ruth Sullivan, *Driedger on the Construction of Statutes*, 4th ed. (Markham: Butterworths Canada Ltd., 2002) at 162.

[32] Generally, when ss. 460(3) and (4) are read with other parts of the statute, the ordinary meaning is reinforced. For instance, the MGB considered s. 462(1)(b) to be instructive. It requires the designated officer to, at least fourteen days prior to the hearing, notify "the municipality, the complainant, and *any assessed person other than the complainant who is affected by the complaint*, of the date time and location of the hearing." [Emphasis added.] This provision recognizes that the complainant and the assessed person for the property that is the subject of the complaint may be two distinct entities, and ensures that notice of a hearing is given to the owner of the assessed property where the complaint is made by someone other than the owner.

[33] The chambers judge reasoned that this provision did not refer to the owner but to the assessed owners of other similarly situated assessed properties. However, the complaint process under the *MGA* deals with individual complaints relating to individual properties, and nothing in the *MGA* suggests that an ARB decision relating to the assessment of one property will bind or affect owners of unrelated similarly situated properties. If the *MGA* intended to refer only to owners of similarly situated properties, some guidance would have been provided as to the manner in which the officer would decide what constituted a similarly situated property.

[34] Certainly, other sections of the *MGA* clearly identify when the assessed person of the subject property is specified and when the more general term is used. In particular, s. 304(1) provides that the name of "the person" described in column 2 must be recorded

on the assessment role as "the assessed person" in respect of "the assessed property" described in column 1.

[35] Where the Legislature intended to link an assessed person to that assessed person's assessed property, it has expressly done so. Specifically, s. 299(1) permits "an assessed person" to request sufficient information to show how the assessor prepared the assessment "of that person's property." If "an assessed person" meant "*the* owner of *the* assessed property," or "the assessed person in respect of the assessed property," it would be unnecessary to use the words "of that person's property." To cite another example, s. 300(1) permits "an assessed person" to request a summary of the assessment for any assessed property in the municipality. The wording in ss. 300(1) and 460(4), both of which use the term "an assessed person," can only be consistent if "an assessed person" means any person who is named on an assessment roll, whether or not she is the owner of the subject property. If "any assessed property" is limited to only the property owned by that person, s. 300(1) would be meaningless. Section 460(4) would still have meaning, as allowing any assessed person to make a complaint about her own property, but it would be inconsistent with s. 300(1) despite containing the same words.

[36] The City submits that the broad interpretation suggested by the Bay will render the complaints process unworkable. The MGB decided otherwise, and noted in its reasons that multiple complaints have not caused significant problems to date. Section 460(3) limits the right to make a complaint to assessed persons or taxpayers, both of whom have an interest in the fairness of the tax regime. Owners of assessed property and other taxpayers have an interest in ensuring that other assessments reflect full value, and could have reason to make a complaint. This issue deals largely with policy and the efficient functioning of the appeals process provided by the *MGA*, and deference must be accorded to the MGB decision.

[37] For these reasons, the MGB's decision is reasonable.

. . .

Conclusion

[40] The Bay is an assessed person, by virtue of its ownership of the downtown Bay store. It therefore has the right to make a complaint about the assessment of the shopping centres in question. Zellers is not a party to this appeal. The appeal is allowed and returned to the MGB for decision.

As indicated above, there was some debate after *Dunsmuir* about whether the reasonableness standard reflected a spectrum, such that a court, having decided to defer, would then need to determine more precisely how much deference was required in the case before it. Indeed, prior to the decision in *Law Society of New Brunswick v. Ryan*, [2003] 1 SCR 247, some lower courts in Canada approached the standards of correctness, reasonableness *simpliciter*, and patent unreasonableness as if they reflected merely points on a wider spectrum. Moreover, in *Dunsmuir* itself, at para. 153, Binnie J appeared to read the majority's reasons in that case as indicating that reasonableness was a spectrum-based concept "that covers ... the reviewing court's evaluation, *in light of the appropriate degree of deference*, of whether the decision falls within a range of reasonable administrative choices" (emphasis added).

This view of reasonableness as a spectrum was canvassed and rejected by the Ontario Court of Appeal in *Mills v. Ontario (Workplace Safety and Insurance Appeals Tribunal)*, 2008 ONCA 436, where Rouleau JA stated:

[14] As noted, both parties agree that, in accordance with the Supreme Court of Canada's recent decision in *Dunsmuir*, the standard of reasonableness applies to the review of the Tribunal's decision. … Where the parties diverge is on the level of deference to be accorded to the decision within the "reasonableness" standard. In essence, the appellant submits that, within the reasonableness standard, there are varying degrees of deference that apply. The level of deference to be accorded will be determined by reference to existing jurisprudence. In this case, the jurisprudence has established that the highest level of deference applies to Tribunal decisions.

[15] In contrast, the respondent submits that the "reasonableness standard" does not contain varying degrees of deference. He relies on the decision in *Law Society of New Brunswick v. Ryan* 2003 SCC 20 (CanLII), (2003), 223 DLR (4th) 577 (SCC), which rejected the argument that "it is sometimes appropriate to apply the reasonableness standard more deferentially and sometimes less deferentially depending on the circumstances" (para. 43).

[16] The appellant argues that *Law Society of New Brunswick v. Ryan* predates the decision in *Dunsmuir* and therefore has not considered the approach to deference when the standards of reasonableness and patent unreasonableness have been collapsed into a single standard. Although the majority in *Dunsmuir* did not offer specific comment on whether there are varying degrees of deference within the reasonableness standard, the appellant relies on the views expressed by Binnie J in his concurring opinion. At para. 139, Binnie J notes that the decision to collapse reasonableness *simpliciter* and patent unreasonableness served to "shift the debate (slightly) from choosing *between* two standards of reasonableness that each represent a different level of deference to a debate *within* a single standard of reasonableness to determine the appropriate level of deference." [Emphasis in original.]

[17] The appellant argues that the reference in paragraph 62 of the majority reasons to the "degree of deference" lends further support to its submission. …

[18] I understand the majority in *Dunsmuir* to be referring now to only two degrees of deference, correctness, where no deference is accorded, and reasonableness, where deference is accorded. It is not necessary or appropriate to then assess the degree of deference within the reasonableness standard.

[19] In my view, by collapsing the patently unreasonable standard and the reasonable standard, the majority has not set aside the court's earlier decision in *Law Society of New Brunswick v. Ryan*, nor has it signalled that courts must now puzzle over the degree of deference to give to a tribunal within the reasonableness standard. The existence of varying degrees of deference within the single reasonableness standard suggests that a decision made by a tribunal will be found to be unreasonable if the court accords the tribunal a low degree of deference but that same decision will be found to be reasonable if the court decides to accord the tribunal a high degree of deference. I do not read the decision of the majority in *Dunsmuir* as encompassing any such approach.

· · ·

[21] The "revised system" established in *Dunsmuir* was designed in part to make the approach to judicial review of administrative decisions "simpler and more workable" (para. 45).

An analysis of the varying degrees of deference to be accorded to the tribunal within the reasonableness standard, as submitted by the appellant, fails to comply with this objective.

[22] My conclusion does not signal that factors such as the nature and mandate of the decision-maker and the nature of the question being decided are to be ignored. Applying the reasonableness standard will now require a contextual approach to deference where factors such as the decision-making process, the type and expertise of the decision-maker, as well as the nature and complexity of the decision will be taken into account. Where, for example, the decision-maker is a minister of the Crown and the decision is one of public policy, the range of decisions that will fall within the ambit of reasonableness is very broad. In contrast, where there is no real dispute on the facts and the tribunal need only determine whether an individual breached a provision of its constituent statute, the range of reasonable outcomes is, perforce, much narrower.

[23] My interpretation on this issue is strengthened by the majority description of "reasonableness." The description provided by the majority did not articulate varying degrees of deference, but instead referred simply to a deferential standard that mandates respect for the "decision-making process of adjudicative bodies with regard to both the facts and the law." *Dunsmuir* at para. 48. The concept of reasonableness does not turn on a detailed analysis of whether the tribunal's decision is subject to a high or low degree of deference. In defining the concept of reasonableness, the majority in *Dunsmuir* instead emphasized the following at para. 47:

> A court conducting a review for reasonableness inquires into the qualities that make a decision reasonable, referring both to the process of articulating the reasons and to outcomes. In judicial review, reasonableness is concerned mostly with the existence of justification, transparency and intelligibility within the decision-making process. But it is also concerned with whether the decision falls within a range of possible, acceptable outcomes which are defensible in respect of the facts and law.

[24] In the present case, the issues raised on appeal relate to findings of fact made by the Tribunal. These findings fall squarely within the Tribunal's area of experience and expertise and the basis for the findings is articulated in the Tribunal's reasons. It is in this context that the guiding principles from *Dunsmuir* are to be applied to review the reasonableness of the Tribunal's decision.

Subsequently, the Supreme Court also confirmed in *Canada (Citizenship and Immigration) v. Khosa*, 2009 SCC 12 (CanLII), excerpted below, that reasonableness was not a spectrum, by referring to reasonableness as "a single standard that takes its colour from the context." Observe in the reasons of Binnie J how the Supreme Court defers to the fact-driven conclusions of the majority of the Immigration Appeals Division based on its weighing of the evidence before it. (The facts of this case were summarized in chapter 11 of this text.)

Applying the "Reasonableness" Standard

[59] Reasonableness is a single standard that takes its colour from the context. One of the objectives of *Dunsmuir* was to liberate judicial review courts from what came to be seen as undue complexity and formalism. Where the reasonableness standard applies, it requires deference. Reviewing courts cannot substitute their own appreciation of the appropriate solution, but must rather determine if the outcome falls within "a range of possible, acceptable outcomes which are defensible in respect of the facts and law" (*Dunsmuir*, at para. 47). There might be

more than one reasonable outcome. However, as long as the process and the outcome fit comfortably with the principles of justification, transparency and intelligibility, it is not open to a reviewing court to substitute its own view of a preferable outcome.

[60] In my view, having in mind the considerable deference owed to the IAD [the Immigration Appeal Division of the Immigration and Refugee Board] and the broad scope of discretion conferred by the *IRPA*, there was no basis for the Federal Court of Appeal to interfere with the IAD decision to refuse special relief in this case.

[61] My colleague Fish J agrees that the standard of review is reasonableness, but he would allow the appeal. He writes:

> While Mr. Khosa's denial of street racing may well evidence some "lack of insight" into his own conduct, it cannot reasonably be said to contradict—still less to outweigh, on a balance of probabilities—all of the evidence in his favour on the issues of remorse, rehabilitation and likelihood of reoffence. [para. 149]

I do not believe that it is the function of the reviewing court to reweigh the evidence.

[62] It is apparent that Fish J takes a different view than I do of the range of outcomes reasonably open to the IAD in the circumstances of this case. My view is predicated on what I have already said about the role and function of the IAD as well as the fact that Khosa does not contest the validity of the removal order made against him. He seeks exceptional and discretionary relief that is available only if the IAD itself is satisfied that "sufficient humanitarian and compassionate considerations warrant special relief." The IAD majority was not so satisfied. Whether we agree with a particular IAD decision or not is beside the point. The decision was entrusted by Parliament to the IAD, not to the judges.

[63] The *Dunsmuir* majority held:

> A court conducting a review for reasonableness inquires into the qualities that make a decision reasonable, referring both to the process of articulating the reasons and to outcomes. In judicial review, reasonableness is concerned mostly with the existence of justification, transparency and intelligibility within the decision-making process. But it is also concerned with whether the decision falls within a range of possible, acceptable outcomes which are defensible in respect of the facts and law. [para. 47]

Dunsmuir thus reinforces in the context of adjudicative tribunals the importance of reasons, which constitute the primary form of accountability of the decision maker to the applicant, to the public and to a reviewing court. Although the *Dunsmuir* majority refers with approval to the proposition that an appropriate degree of deference "requires of the courts 'not submission but a respectful attention to the reasons offered *or which could be offered* in support of a decision'" (para. 48 (emphasis added)), I do not think the reference to reasons which "could be offered" (but were not) should be taken as diluting the importance of giving proper reasons for an administrative decision, as stated in *Baker v. Canada (Minister of Citizenship and Immigration)*, [1999] 2 SCR 817, at para. 43. *Baker* itself was concerned with an application on "humanitarian and compassionate grounds" for relief from a removal order.

[64] In this case, both the majority and dissenting reasons of the IAD disclose with clarity the considerations in support of both points of view, and the reasons for the disagreement as to outcome. At the factual level, the IAD divided in large part over differing interpretations of Khosa's expression of remorse, as was pointed out by Lutfy CJ. According to the IAD majority:

It is troublesome to the panel that [Khosa] continues to deny that his participation in a "street-race" led to the disastrous consequences. ... At the same time, I am mindful of [Khosa's] show of *relative remorse* at this hearing for his excessive speed in a public road-way and note the trial judge's finding of this remorse. ... This show of remorse is a posi-tive factor going to the exercise of special relief. However, I do not see it as a compelling feature of the case in light of the *limited nature of [Khosa's] admissions* at this hearing. [Emphasis added; para. 15.]

According to the IAD dissent on the other hand:

... from early on he [Khosa] has accepted responsibility for his actions. He was prepared to plead guilty to dangerous driving causing death ...

I find that [Khosa] is contrite and remorseful. [Khosa] at hearing was regretful, his voice tremulous and filled with emotion. ...

The majority of this panel have placed great significance on [Khosa's] dispute that he was racing, when the criminal court found he was. And while they concluded this was "not fatal" to his appeal, they also determined that his continued denial that he was rac-ing "reflects a lack of insight." The panel concluded that this "is not to his credit." The panel found that [Khosa] was remorseful, but concluded it was not a "compelling feature in light of the limited nature of [Khosa's] admissions."

However I find [Khosa's] remorse, even in light of his denial he was racing, is genuine and is evidence that [Khosa] will in future be more thoughtful and will avoid such reck-lessness. [paras. 50-51 and 53-54]

It seems evident that this is the sort of factual dispute which should be resolved by the IAD in the application of immigration policy, and not reweighed in the courts.

[65] In terms of transparent and intelligible reasons, the majority considered each of the *Ribic* factors. It rightly observed that the factors are not exhaustive and that the weight to be attributed to them will vary from case to case (para. 12). The majority reviewed the evidence and decided that, in the circumstances of this case, most of the factors did not militate strongly for or against relief. Acknowledging the findings of the criminal courts on the seriousness of the offence and possibility of rehabilitation (the first and second of the *Ribic* factors), it found that the offence of which the respondent was convicted was serious and that the prospects of rehabilitation were difficult to assess (para. 23).

[66] The weight to be given to the respondent's evidence of remorse and his prospects for rehabilitation depended on an assessment of his evidence in light of all the circumstances of the case. The IAD has a mandate different from that of the criminal courts. Khosa did not testify at his criminal trial, but he did before the IAD. The issue before the IAD was not the potential for rehabilitation for purposes of sentencing, but rather whether the prospects for rehabilitation were such that, alone or in combination with other factors, they warranted special relief from a valid removal order. The IAD was required to reach its own conclusions based on its own appreciation of the evidence. It did so.

[67] As mentioned, the courts below recognized some merit in Khosa's complaint. Lutfy CJ recognized that the majority "chose to place greater weight on his denial that he participated in a 'race' than others might have" (para. 36). Décary JA described the majority's preoccupation with street racing as "some kind of fixation" (para. 18). My colleague Fish J also decries the

weight put on this factor by the majority (para. 141). However, as emphasized in *Dunsmuir*, "certain questions that come before administrative tribunals do not lend themselves to one specific, particular result. Instead, they may give rise to a number of possible, reasonable conclusions. Tribunals have a margin of appreciation within the range of acceptable and rational solutions" (para. 47). In light of the deference properly owed to the IAD under s. 67(1)(c) of the *IRPA*, I cannot, with respect, agree with my colleague Fish J that the decision reached by the majority in this case to deny special discretionary relief against a valid removal order fell outside the range of reasonable outcomes.

V. Disposition

[68] The appeal is allowed and the decision of the IAD is restored.

What, one may ask, is the difference between reasonableness as a spectrum and reasonableness as a single standard that is contextual in its application? The answer may simply be the practical one that a spectrum-based approach to reasonableness would invite a distracting discussion in all cases regarding where on the spectrum a particular case should be positioned. A contextual approach, on the other hand, directs a court more to the specific circumstances, and as such to the merits, of the case, without requiring any particular outcome to the application of the standard beyond the outcome of the substantive review itself. It seems it is not so much that a spectrum is an inappropriate metaphor to convey the varying ways in which deference may be shown, but rather that the invitation to engage in a forensic inquiry regarding where on a spectrum a case is located itself creates unnecessary complexity and diversion from the main purpose of the review exercise. Thus, it may be said as an introductory statement that a court, applying the reasonableness standard, has determined that it should show deference, although the manner in which it defers will depend on the circumstances.

The Relevance of the Factors in the Standard of Review Analysis

Based on *Khosa*, then, the application of the reasonableness standards will vary with the context. This "context" could include various components, such as the identity and institutional make-up of the decision-maker, the type of decision, the nature of the evidence before the decision-maker and the degree to which the decision-maker's weighing of the evidence drove its decision, the relevant terms of the statute, the purpose of the statutory scheme, and past practice in the judicial review of that decision-maker in comparable circumstances. Moreover, these components may interact with each other in ways that guide the court's approach to deference. The nature of the expertise applied by a tribunal to resolve a legal issue, for instance, may itself be informed by the terms of the statute or by the design of the decision-making apparatus. As such, in applying reasonableness, a court may find it useful to refer in its analysis to factors that informed its initial determination of the standard of review. Likewise, where the court relied on past decisions to determine the standard of review, it may look to those decisions in order to highlight just how the courts have shown deference previously in the relevant context.

The pre-*Dunsmuir* decision of the Supreme Court in the following case revealed that a court, while deferring, may also need to review carefully the key evidence before a decision-maker in order to work out whether the decision-maker's conclusions were reasonable. Note also how the court's definition of reasonableness, in the first paragraph below, has changed with *Dunsmuir*.

Dr. Q v. College of Physicians and Surgeons of British Columbia
[2003] 1 SCR 226, 2003 SCC 19

[The facts of this case were summarized in chapter 11 of this text.]

McLACHLIN CJ (for the Court):

. . .

[39] ... The reviewing judge should have asked herself whether the Committee's assessment of credibility and application of the standard of proof to the evidence was unreasonable, in the sense of not being supported by any reasons that can bear somewhat probing examination (see *Ryan, supra*, at para. 46).

[40] The reviewing judge did not adopt this analysis. Indeed, she made no reference at all to the pragmatic and functional approach. The effect of the reviewing judge's failure to conduct the usual administrative law analysis was essentially to proceed on what amounted to a correctness standard. One of the factors under the pragmatic and functional approach is whether the statute grants a right of appeal. But it is only one. The reviewing judge considered only this factor and, as a result, she applied too strict a standard. Specifically, she failed to address the need for deference in view of the purpose of the Act and the nature of the problem, credibility. A proper consideration of all the factors required by the pragmatic and functional approach would have yielded a standard of reasonableness *simpliciter*, not correctness. In effect, the reviewing judge erroneously instructed herself to review the Committee's findings of fact on a correctness basis.

[41] The reviewing judge's analysis of the corroborative evidence confirms that she assessed the Committee's findings of credibility from the perspective of correctness, rather than reasonableness. For example, when addressing the Committee's reliance upon the discrepancy between Dr. Q's letter to the College and the number of times he had actually had lunch with Ms. T, the reviewing judge argued that "one explanation for Dr. Q's less than forthright description of his lunch relationship with Ms. T is that the letter was written without dealing with specific allegations pursuant to legal advice" (para. 13). Yet when the standard of review is reasonableness, the reviewing judge's role is not to posit alternate interpretations of the evidence; rather, it is to determine whether *the Committee's* interpretation is unreasonable. When considering the Committee's conclusion that Ms. T's ability to describe distinct bodily markings suggested an intimate relationship between Ms. T and Dr. Q, the reviewing judge noted that Ms. T had some experience as a surgical nurse and asserted that, "[i]n my view, her description is no more vivid than one might expect from someone who has experience with surgical scars if such a scar had been described to her as Dr. Q testified he had done" (para. 20). With respect, when applying a standard of reasonableness *simpliciter*, the reviewing judge's view of the evidence is beside the point; rather, the reviewing judge should have asked whether the Committee's conclusion on this point had some basis in the evidence (see *Ryan, supra*). Finally, when assessing the Committee's finding that a letter sent by Dr. Q

to Ms. T supported the conclusion that a sexual relationship existed, the reviewing judge stated the following (at para. 25):

> While there is no doubt that for many the wording of the letter is such as to raise a suspicion or question as to the nature of the relationship; nevertheless it is, in my view, not clear and cogent evidence corroborative of a sexual relationship as testified to by Ms. T.

If there is "no doubt" that the letter could be interpreted as evidence of a sexual relationship, such an interpretation cannot be unreasonable and, therefore, the reviewing judge's preferred view is irrelevant.

In both *Dr. Q* and *Khosa* we see how deferential review of fact-laden decisions may paradoxically require a court to examine closely how the decision-maker dealt with and weighed the evidence before it. The court may need to do this in order to isolate a factual issue that was central to the decision as a whole. It may also need to examine how the tribunal's apprehended the evidence in answering the relevant issue. However, the purpose of a court's close examination either of the tribunal's reasoning on factual issues or of the evidence itself should be to determine whether the decision fell within the range of acceptable options. It is not an opportunity for the court to form and substitute its own conclusions. Thus, in *Khosa*, so long as the decision of the IAD majority reached "its own conclusions based on its own appreciation of the evidence" and so long as its decision fell within "the range of reasonable outcomes," the decision would stand.

In the following case, the Saskatchewan Court of Appeal applied the reasonableness standard to an arbitration board's interpretation of a collective agreement in a highly specific negotiating context. Observe how the court's review of the board's interpretation was affected by its appreciation of that context. Notice also how the court's assessment of various factors in the standard of review analysis was invoked by the court in its application of the reasonableness standard.

Art Hauser Centre Board Inc. (City of Prince Albert) v. CUPE Local No. 882
2008 SKCA 121

JACKSON JA [Lane and Hunter JJA concurring]:

1. Introduction

[1] The sports complex in Prince Albert, known as the Art Hauser Centre, was formerly operated by the City of Prince Albert (the "City"). The Canadian Union of Public Employees, Local No. 882 ("CUPE") is the Union that represents City employees pursuant to the terms of a collective agreement between the City and CUPE. The City created a separate body to operate the sports complex, with its own board of directors, called the Art Hauser Centre Board Inc. (the "Centre"). The Centre, however, continued to be bound by the City's collective agreement with CUPE.

[2] The Centre decided to contract out the concession services of the sports complex. CUPE grieved this decision on the basis that the collective agreement prohibits contract-

ing out except in certain circumstances, and where contracting out is possible, consultation must take place before the decision to contract out is made. The majority of an arbitral board, which for ease of reference I will call "the Board," agreed.

[3] On judicial review in the Queen's Bench, the learned Chambers judge found the standard of review to be reasonableness, but she found the Board's interpretation of the contracting out clause to be unreasonable [*Art Hauser Centre Board Inc. (City of Prince Albert) v. Canadian Union of Public Employees Local No. 882 and Bob Pelton, Q.C. sitting as arbitration chair*, 2007 SKQB 306, (2007), 300 Sask. R 217]. While I agree that the standard of review is reasonableness, I respectfully find that the Chambers judge erred in concluding that the Board's interpretation of the contracting out clause is unreasonable. I also find that the Board's opinion that a prior letter of understanding can be considered in interpreting the collective agreement is reasonable, and that the letter lends force to the Board's interpretation. I would allow the appeal and restore the Board's decision.

2. Legal and Factual Context

2.1 Factual Context

[4] The pertinent circumstances are taken from the Chambers judge's decision [paras. 2-3]:

> The Employer operates a multi-use facility in Prince Albert (the "Centre") which is used primarily as a hockey rink for the local junior hockey club. Prior to September, 2005, the City of Prince Albert operated the Centre, including its concession services. The City employed non-permanent, part-time recreation employees, represented by the Union, to operate the concession. Because of the Centre's fluctuating use, the demand for employees at the concession also fluctuated. In September, 2005, the City created a new model to operate the Centre, with its own non-profit board of directors. The Centre is a related business to the City of Prince Albert within the meaning of s. 37.3 of *The Trade Union Act*, RSS 1978, c. T-17, and is bound by the Collective Agreement between the City and the Union.
>
> The new board of directors was responsible for the operation of the concession at the Centre effective August 1, 2005. In July, 2005, the board of directors placed a call for bids for the operation of the concession at the Centre. On September 7, 2005, the Optimist Club of Prince Albert was awarded the contract to operate the concession. The Employer notified the Union on September 9, 2005, that the concession's operation was contracted out to the Optimist Club. On September 21, 2005, the Union filed a grievance alleging that the Employer was limited by Article 12.07 of the Collective Agreement from contracting out the concession on a permanent basis.

2.2 Clause To Be Interpreted

[5] Article 12.07 is the Article of the collective agreement that the Board was called upon to interpret. It reads:

ARTICLE 12: LAYOFFS AND RECALLS

. . .

12.07 Contracting Out Work

Having regard to the desirability of maintaining a stable work force and having regard to periodic peaks in work load dictating the necessity of contracting work out, the City agrees to notify and consult with the Union prior to making any final decision to contract work out presently being performed by City employees. The Union will be a participant in studying any contracting out plans and will be supplied with all information and research done prior to the final decision being made. ...

The Board was required to construe the underlined phrase. Thus, the issue facing the Board was this: what did the parties to the collective agreement intend when they added the words "[h]aving regard to the desirability of maintaining a stable work force and having regard to periodic peaks in work load dictating the necessity of contracting work out"?

2.3 The Board's Decision

[6] While the issue before the Board can be simply stated, the Board was not asked to interpret Article 12.07 devoid of context. The Board heard testimony for three days from two representatives of CUPE and a member of the Centre's board of directors, who is also a member of City Council. The testimony canvassed how it came to be that the Centre was created, the involvement of CUPE in the decision to contract out services, the role of the Centre board of directors, and so on. The Board summarized this evidence over some 100 paragraphs of text. It was against this factual and legal backdrop that the Board considered the meaning of the specific phrase: "having regard to periodic peaks in work load dictating the necessity of contracting work out."

[Summary and excerpts of the board's decision, and discussion of the chambers judge's decision, have been omitted. Discussion of *Dunsmuir* and of past decisions on the standard of review has also been omitted.]

4. Analysis

[21] Applying the standard of review to the task at hand, I observe that there are two alternative interpretations of Article 12.07 before the Court:

1. The Board's interpretation: The employer is prohibited from contracting out work unless "periodic peaks in work load dictating the necessity of contracting work out" exist. Where such circumstances exist, the City will notify and consult with the Union before making its final decision.

2. The Chambers judge's interpretation: The only restriction on the City's right to contract out is that it must notify and consult.

[22] In my respectful view, the Chambers judge substituted her interpretation of Article 12.07 for that of the Board without according the Board's interpretation sufficient deference and, in so doing, incorrectly applied the reasonableness standard. The Supreme Court of Canada's reasons in *Dunsmuir* demonstrate the need for greater deference to a consensual labour board's decision than was demonstrated in this case.

[23] When reviewing the decision of an administrative tribunal, the context in which the decision arises and the nature of the question to be decided must be considered. The context in which this decision arises is that of labour relations. The decision to be reviewed is that of a labour arbitrator, chosen by the parties pursuant to a process established in a collective agreement. There is a long list of cases that could be cited in support of the proposition that consensual labour arbitrators are to be accorded a high degree of deference. In addition to the authorities cited earlier in these reasons, in the section pertaining to the standard of review, I need only quote the words of LeBel J in *Toronto (City) v. CUPE, Local 79*, [2003] 3 SCR 77 [at para. 68]:

> *This Court has repeatedly stressed the importance of judicial deference in the context of labour law.* Labour relations statutes typically bestow broad powers on arbitrators and labour boards to resolve the wide range of problems that may arise in this field and protect the decisions of these adjudicators by privative clauses. Such legislative choices reflect the fact that, as Cory J noted in *Toronto (City) Board of Education v. OSSTF District 15*, [1997] 1 SCR 487, at para. 35, *the field of labour relations is "sensitive and volatile" and "[i]t is essential that there be a means of providing speedy decisions by experts in the field who are sensitive to the situation, and which can be considered by both sides to be final and binding"* (see also *Canada (Attorney General) v. Public Service Alliance of Canada*, [1993] 1 SCR 941 ("PSAC"), at pp. 960-61; and *Ivanhoe inc. v. UFCW, Local 500*, [2001] 2 SCR 565, 2001 SCC 47, at para. 32). The application of a standard of review of correctness in the context of judicial review of labour adjudication is thus rare. ...

[24] An important aspect of this context is the extent to which the legislature has isolated the decision from judicial review. The Board's decision in this case is protected by a privative clause—a section added relatively recently by the Saskatchewan legislature to *The Trade Union Act*, RSS 1978, c. T-17:

> 25(1) All differences between the parties to a collective bargaining agreement or persons bound by the collective bargaining agreement or on whose behalf the collective bargaining agreement was entered into respecting its meaning, application or alleged violation, including a question as to whether a matter is arbitrable, are to be settled by arbitration after exhausting any grievance procedure established by the collective bargaining agreement. ...
>
> (1.2) The finding of an arbitrator or an arbitration board is:
>
> (a) final and conclusive;
>
> (b) binding on the parties with respect to all matters within the legislative jurisdiction of the Government of Saskatchewan; and
>
> (c) enforceable in the same manner as an order of the board made pursuant to this Act. ...

That is not to say that a privative clause or a near privative clause completely insulates a decision from review and intervention, but its presence is a factor in considering the context of the decision under review. The Chambers judge makes no mention of s. 25(1.2), or its effect, on her reasoning process.

[25] The nature of the question also plays a role in determining the need for deference in this case. The Board was not considering a principle of general law, or one of significant impact on labour relations as a whole, for which one might expect there to be

one answer only. Instead, the Board was called upon to interpret a clause in a collective agreement—a contracting out clause negotiated by a public sector employer with its union—and the interpretation of this clause was the very issue referred to the Board. I agree with CUPE's counsel that this is a classic case of rights arbitration. The rights accorded to CUPE by Article 12.07 are real rights that must be interpreted according to the process outlined in s. 25(1) of *The Trade Union Act* and the collective agreement.

[26] The clause that the Board was required to interpret admits of more than one interpretation. That is why the matter was referred for arbitration. The parties agree that the wording is not clear. Article 12.07 does not say explicitly that the employer cannot contract out except where periodic peaks in work load exist, but the Board recognized this, and recognized alternative interpretations also existed [citing the board's decision, *Canadian Union of Public Employees Local No. 882 v. Art Hauser Centre Board Inc. (City of Prince Albert)* [Contracting Out Grievance], [2006] SLAA No. 18 (QL), at para. 150]:

> Counsel for the Employer argued that this case is distinguishable, from those relied upon by the Union, in that Article 12.07 does not open with a general prohibition against contracting out, followed by defined exceptions in which contracting out will be allowed. Certainly Article 12.07 does not read:
>
> > Having regard to the desirability of maintaining a stable work force, the City agrees to not contract out work presently being performed by City employees, unless periodic peaks in work load dictate the necessity of contracting work out. ...

[27] The Board considered and rejected the very interpretation of the Article that the Chambers judge accepted. On this point, the Board wrote [paras. 147 and 151]:

> The Collective Bargaining Agreement in the present case falls between the two ends of what Counsel for the Union described as a continuum. On the one hand the Collective Bargaining Agreement does not contain an absolute prohibition against contracting out bargaining unit work; indeed Article 12.07 contemplates that there may be contracting out. By the same token, the Collective Bargaining Agreement is not silent on the issue, such that the Employer, acting reasonably and in good faith, is free to contract out bargaining unit work as it sees fit.
>
> ... By the same token Article 12.07 does more than simply provide that the City will notify and consult with the Union and provide that the Union will be a participant, which would be the case if Article 12.07 read:
>
> > The City agrees to notify and consult with the Union prior to making any final decision to contract out work presently being performed by City employees. The Union will be a participant in studying any contracting out plans and will be supplied with all information and research done prior to the final decision being made. ...

And yet, it is this last interpretation that the Chambers judge accepted.

[28] Moreover, the Chambers judge's decision does not take into account the Board's interpretation and reliance upon the specific body of jurisprudence pertaining to contracting out clauses. ... [Excerpts from the board's discussion of past arbitration awards have been omitted.] Based on this, the Board went on to say that the City, which was the original signatory to the Collective Agreement, and CUPE are *"presumed to know the Employer is free to contract out bargaining unit work in the absence of contractual language*

to the contrary." By agreeing to the words contained within the first two lines of the Article, the City agreed to a limitation on its management rights.

[29] If we consider the two alternative interpretations of Article 12.07 against the backdrop of the jurisprudence and the evidence, it is not unreasonable to assume, as the Board did, that the parties contemplated consultations would be required in the only circumstance where the employer had the authority to contract out: when periodic peaks in work load exist. By virtue of the fact that the parties turned their minds to the question of contracting out by agreeing to Article 12.07, it is not unreasonable to conclude that restrictions above and beyond the duty to consult would be placed upon the City's right to contract out. At the very least, it must be said, using the language of *Dunsmuir* [at para. 72], that the Board's decision falls within the range of acceptable contractual interpretations.

[30] The Chambers judge's decision does not give any meaning to the phrase "periodic peaks in work load dictating the necessity of contracting work out." The Board interpreted the words as being a restriction, i.e., the employer can only negotiate contracting out if there are "periodic peaks in work load dictating the necessity of contracting work out." Thus, for the Board, if there are no periodic peaks in work load, there can be no contracting out. The Chambers judge interpreted the phrase in issue as not adding anything to the analysis, but without these words, the Centre could have done exactly what was done in this case. Contractual interpretation, like statutory interpretation, must consider and give meaning to all the words to be construed.

[31] The Board's primary decision is that the employer cannot contract out. The secondary aspect of the Board's decision is that the employer can contract out if the precondition of periodic peaks in work load exists. The Chambers judge used this second aspect of the interpretation to conclude that the first aspect is not reasonable, i.e, by concluding that the only circumstance where the employer can contract out is when periodic peaks in work load exist, consultation becomes meaningless because the existence of periodic peaks in work load would mean that the employer would have little choice but to contract out. But the meaningfulness of that type of negotiations was not before the Court. If anything, the narrowness of the circumstance where consultation was required does as much to support the Union's interpretation of Article 12.07 as to detract from it.

[32] The narrowness of the clause is consistent with an interpretation that the employer has chosen, as a result of the negotiation process, to restrict its rights to contract out. Moreover, as the Board pointed out, the closing words of Article 12.07, to the effect that the "Union will be a participant in studying any contracting out plans and will be supplied with all information and research done prior to the final decision being made" does "speak to a greater role for the Union than would be the case if that sentence was not present." These words are consistent with an interpretation of Article 12.07 that contemplates a larger role for the Union generally in the employer's right to contract out.

[33] In summary, the task is to determine whether the Board's decision fell within a range of reasonable outcomes. As soon as it is determined that the Board's interpretation is one of the possible reasonable interpretations, that ends the matter. The Chambers judge's interpretation is also reasonable, and arguably even more reasonable, but that opinion is irrelevant for the purposes of answering the question before the Court. As soon as a reviewing court begins to consider degrees of reasonableness, and passes judg-

ment based on a perceived improved reasonableness, it falls within the trap identified by Binnie J., in his minority reasons in *Dunsmuir* [at para. 125]:

> Thus the law (or, more grandly, the "rule of law") sets the boundaries of potential administrative action. It is sometimes said by judges that an administrator acting within his or her discretion "has the right to be wrong." This reflects an unduly court-centred view of the universe. *A disagreement between the court and an administrator does not necessarily mean that the administrator is wrong. ...*

[34]   Finally, the Board found that its interpretation of Article 12.07 was supported by Letter of Understanding #6, which forms part of the collective agreement between the City and CUPE. ... [Excerpts of the board's and the chambers judge's interpretations of this letter have been omitted.]

[35]   ... The first part of [the chambers judge's] determination contradicts the Board's express finding that the Letter of Understanding forms part of the Collective Agreement, which is supported by the documentary evidence. Given this, and as counsel for CUPE points out, the Board did no more than follow an accepted principle of interpretation in arbitral jurisprudence that words under consideration should be read in the context of the sentence, section and agreement as a whole [Donald J.M. Brown and David M. Beatty, *Canadian Labour Arbitration*, 4th ed., vol. 1 (Aurora, ON: Canada Law Book, 2008), at 4:1250 (looseleaf)].

· · ·

5. *Conclusion*

[37]   While I agree with the Chambers judge that the appropriate standard of review is reasonableness, the application of that standard requires the reviewing judge to determine whether the decision under review falls within a range of acceptable outcomes. After having considered the nature of the Board, the question it was required to decide and the evidence before it, the Board's reasons, the law pertaining to contracting out in the labour relations setting, the possible alternative interpretations of Article 12.07 and the language of the clause, I conclude that the Board's decision represents one of the acceptable reasonable interpretations of Article 12.07.

[38]   For these reasons, the appeal is allowed and the decision of the Board is restored with costs on Column 2 in this Court and on the appropriate tariff in the Queen's Bench.

Correctness Review in the Guise of Reasonableness?

Occasionally, there are cases, usually involving issues of legal interpretation, where a court applies the reasonableness standard in a way that appears to show little if any deference to the decision-maker. In such cases, it is pertinent to ask whether the court carried through on its commitment to defer or whether, instead, the court engaged in correctness review "in disguise." As good a case as any to test this proposition of interventionist review in the name of deference is the decision in *Dunsmuir* itself.

Recall that in *Dunsmuir* the majority (with Binnie J concurring on a reasonableness standard, and Rothstein and Deschamp JJ concurring on a correctness standard) overturned the labour adjudicator's interpretation of (especially) s. 97(2.1) of the *Public Service*

Labour Relations Act, RSNB 1973, c. P-25 (as amended) (the "PSLRA"), in light of the *Civil Service Act*, SNB 1984, c. C-5.1. Dunsmuir's employer had relied on the *Civil Service Act* to assert a right to dismiss Dunsmuir, without alleging cause, according to the ordinary rules of contract, and claimed that there was no requirement to afford Dunsmuir a hearing even though a hearing was required at the time as a matter of common law procedural fairness in the dismissal of public officers. Of particular relevance was s. 20 of the *Civil Service Act*, which provided: "Subject to the provisions of this Act and any other Act ... [termination] shall be governed by the ordinary rules of contract." Given that the *Civil Service Act* was, based on this provision, subject to the provisions of other statutes, the adjudicator had considered Dunsmuir's grievance of his dismissal under the PSLRA, which itself stated in s. 97(2.1):

> Where an adjudicator determines that an employee has been discharged or otherwise disciplined for cause and the collective agreement or arbitral award does not contain a specific penalty for the infraction that resulted in the employee being discharged or otherwise disciplined, the adjudicator may substitute such other penalty for the discharge or the discipline as to the adjudicator seems just and reasonable in all the circumstances.

Interpreting this provision, the adjudicator concluded that it was open to him to reach his own conclusion on whether Dunsmuir had been "discharged or otherwise disciplined *for cause*" as provided in s. 97(2.1). In adopting this interpretation of s. 97(2.1), the adjudicator rejected the employer's argument that the adjudicator did not have the authority to look behind the employer's characterization of the dismissal as being not for cause. The adjudicator found further, on the facts, that Dunsmuir's dismissal had been a disguised dismissal for cause and ordered that Dunsmuir be reinstated on the basis that he was denied a hearing.

The key question of statutory interpretation in *Dunsmuir*, then, was whether the adjudicator had the authority, pursuant to s. 97(2.1) of the PSLRA, to look behind the employer's characterization of Dunsmuir's dismissal as being not for cause. Consider, then, the following extract from *Dunsmuir*, in which the majority reviewed the adjudicator's interpretation of the PSLRA, and ask whether the majority really deferred to the adjudicator in its application of the reasonableness standard. Keep in mind also that the PSLRA and the *Civil Service Act* were both connected to the adjudicator's usual task of resolving grievances in the public service and that the adjudicator's interpretation of the PSLRA was protected by a full privative clause.

> [71] ... We must now apply that standard [reasonableness] to the issue considered by the adjudicator in his preliminary ruling.
>
> **Was the Adjudicator's Interpretation Unreasonable?**
>
> [72] While we are required to give deference to the determination of the adjudicator, considering the decision in the preliminary ruling as a whole, we are unable to accept that it reaches the standard of reasonableness. The reasoning process of the adjudicator was deeply flawed. It relied on and led to a construction of the statute that fell outside the range of admissible statutory interpretations.
>
> [73] The adjudicator considered the New Brunswick Court of Appeal decision in *Chalmers (Dr. Everett) Hospital v. Mills* as well as amendments made to the *PSLRA* in 1990 (SNB 1990, c. 30). Under the former version of the Act, an employee could grieve "with respect to ... dis-

ciplinary action resulting in discharge, suspension or a financial penalty" (s. 92(1)). The amended legislation grants the right to grieve "with respect to discharge, suspension or a financial penalty" (*PSLRA*, s. 100.1(2)). The adjudicator reasoned that the referential incorporation of s. 97(2.1) in s. 100.1(5) "necessarily means that an adjudicator has jurisdiction to make the determination described in subsection 97(2.1), i.e. that an employee has been discharged or otherwise disciplined for cause" (p. 5). He further stated that an employer "cannot avoid an inquiry into its real reasons for a discharge, or exclude resort to subsection 97(2.1), *by simply stating that cause is not alleged*" (*ibid.* (emphasis added)). The adjudicator concluded that he could determine whether a discharge purportedly with notice or pay in lieu of notice was in reality for cause.

[74] The interpretation of the law is always contextual. The law does not operate in a vacuum. The adjudicator was required to take into account the legal context in which he was to apply the law. The employment relationship between the parties in this case was governed by private law. The contractual terms of employment could not reasonably be ignored. That is made clear by s. 20 of the *Civil Service Act*. Under the ordinary rules of contract, the employer is entitled to discharge an employee for cause, with notice or with pay in lieu of notice. Where the employer chooses to exercise its right to discharge with reasonable notice or pay in lieu thereof, the employer is not required to assert cause for discharge. The grievance process cannot have the effect of changing the terms of the contract of employment. The respondent chose to exercise its right to terminate without alleging cause in this case. By giving the *PSLRA* an interpretation that allowed him to inquire into the reasons for discharge where the employer had the right not to provide—or even have—such reasons, the adjudicator adopted a reasoning process that was fundamentally inconsistent with the employment contract and, thus, fatally flawed. For this reason, the decision does not fall within the range of acceptable outcomes that are defensible in respect of the facts and the law.

[75] The decision of the adjudicator treated the appellant, a non-unionized employee, as a unionized employee. His interpretation of the *PSLRA*, which permits an adjudicator to inquire into the reasons for discharge where notice is given and, under s. 97(2.1), substitute a penalty that he or she determines just and reasonable in the circumstances, creates a requirement that the employer show cause before dismissal. There can be no justification for this; no reasonable interpretation can lead to that result. Section 100.1(5) incorporates s. 97(2.1) by reference into the determination of grievances brought by non-unionized employees. The employees subject to the *PSLRA* are usually unionized and the terms of their employment are determined by collective agreement; s. 97(2.1) explicitly refers to the collective agreement context. Section 100.1(5) referentially incorporates s. 97(2.1) *mutatis mutandis* into the non-collective agreement context so that non-unionized employees who are discharged *for cause and without notice* have the right to grieve the discharge and have the adjudicator substitute another penalty as seems just and reasonable in the circumstances. Therefore, the combined effect of s. 97(2.1) and s. 100.1 cannot, on any reasonable interpretation, remove the employer's right under contract law to discharge an employee with reasonable notice or pay in lieu of notice.

[76] The interpretation of the adjudicator was simply unreasonable in the context of the legislative wording and the larger labour context in which it is embedded. It must be set aside. Nevertheless, it must be acknowledged that his interpretation of the *PSLRA* was ultimately inconsequential to the overall determination of the grievance, since the adjudicator made no finding as to whether the discharge was or was not, in fact, for cause. The decision on the

merits, which resulted in an order that the appellant be reinstated, instead turned on the adjudicator's decision on a separate issue—whether the appellant was entitled to and, if so, received procedural fairness with regard to the employer's decision to terminate his employment. This issue is discrete and isolated from the statutory interpretation issue, and it raises very different considerations.

NOTE

Does the majority's invocation of the wider context for the adjudicator's decision provide a compelling basis for the court's substitution of a different interpretation of the PSLRA? In this respect, the majority's reasoning must support its interpretation of the PSLRA but must also establish that the labour adjudicator's interpretation was unreasonable—that is, that it did not fall within the range of acceptable outcomes that are defensible in respect of the facts and the law. It is not a matter of choosing whether the court's interpretation of the PSLRA was the correct one, so much as assessing whether there were sufficient flaws in the adjudicator's interpretation to justify it being overturned. Thus, was it unreasonable—or, as the majority says, "deeply flawed" reasoning (para. 72)—for the adjudicator to decide that s. 97(2.1) (and especially the first four words of that section) allowed him to form his own conclusion on whether an employee had been dismissed for cause?

In the following decision, the BC Court of Appeal applied a reasonableness standard to an issue of legal interpretation that was decided by a commercial arbitrator. The court concluded that the arbitrator's interpretation of the term "unfairly" in a provincial regulation dealing with the allocation of logging subcontracts by timber companies was unreasonable. As in the case of *Dunsmuir*, one may ask whether the Court of Appeal effectively engaged in correctness review, in the guise of deference.

Western Forest Products Inc. v. Hayes Forest Services Limited
2009 BCCA 316

Reasons for Judgment of the Honourable Madam Justice HUDDART (Lowry and Bauman JJA concurring):

[1] This appeal focuses on the meaning of the word "fairly" in s. 33.22(h) of the *Timber Harvesting Contract and Subcontract Regulation*, BC Reg. 22/96 (the "*Regulation*"), made under the *Forest Act*, RSBC 1996, c. 157. That provision requires a timber licence holder to apply four prescribed criteria "fairly, impartially and without regard to any past disagreements between the parties" in making a proposal in response to a ministerial order allocating its allowable annual cut ("AAC") reduction under the *Forestry Revitalization Act*, SBC 2003, c. 17, s. 3(2).

[2] That Act was a legislative response to public pressure for access to forest resources to meet needs of small community loggers and First Nations. It provides for damages to be paid from a revitalization trust if operating efficiency criteria are not applied properly, and for damages from the licence holder if they are not applied fairly.

[3] The *Forestry Revitalization Act* required the respondent, Western Forest Products Inc. ("Western"), to reduce its AAC by 20% or approximately 685,000 cubic metres of

timber across the province, and a ministerial order allocated a reduction of about 76,000 cubic metres to its Plumper Harbour operation in the Nootka Region of Vancouver Island. To this end, Western made a forestry revitalization proposal to its logging contractors operating at Plumper Harbour.

[4] Section 33.2(1) of the *Regulation* permits a licence holder in those circumstances to:

(a) vary the amount of work specified in, or to terminate, one or more of those replaceable contracts, or

(b) change a contract such that it pertains to a different licence.

[5] Western's proposal included the termination of a replaceable logging contract held by the appellant, Hayes Forest Services Ltd. ("Hayes"), while continuing those of its other contractors. Pursuant to s. 33.4(1) of the *Regulation*, Hayes gave notice of its belief that the proposal did not comply with the AAC reduction criteria, and included a fairness objection under s. 33.4(5). Because no other impacted contractor objected, by ss. 33.41(3) and 33.42(1)(a) of the *Regulation*, the proposal was deemed accepted and the contracts amended accordingly, thereby extinguishing Hayes' right to advance an objection on the general ground that the proposal does not comply with the AAC reduction criteria.

[6] However, because Hayes had made a fairness objection, s. 33.42(1)(b) deemed a dispute to exist between the parties to this appeal as well as with a subcontractor of Hayes. The parties appointed Paul Pearlman, QC, to arbitrate the dispute under. s. 33.1(8) of the *Regulation*. Although not a requirement of his appointment, Mr. Pearlman was a designated and registered mediator and arbitrator under s. 7 of the *Regulation*. The *Commercial Arbitration Act*, RSBC 1996, c. 55, applied to the dispute by reason of s. 6(2) of the *Regulation*.

[7] On the fairness objection, under s. 33.42(2)(a), the sole issue was whether the respondent's proposal met the requirements of s. 33.22(h) with respect to the appellant contractor. As I noted above, that meant applying the AAC reduction criteria "fairly, impartially and without regard to past disputes." Those criteria are defined in s. 1(1) of the *Regulation* to mean:

... each of the following factors:

(a) achieving a contractor configuration that optimizes the effective utilization of capital within all timber harvesting operations carried out under all licences included by a licence holder in an AAC reduction proposal or a forestry revitalization proposal;

(b) achieving a contractor configuration that optimizes the efficiency of all timber harvesting operations carried out under all licences included in an AAC reduction proposal or a forestry revitalization proposal by a licence holder;

(c) the demonstrated historical operational effectiveness, ability to carry out timber harvesting operations and compliance with safety, environmental and other applicable laws of each contractor with a replaceable contract pertaining to any licences held by a licence holder;

(d) minimizing the overall need for geographic relocation by contractors and company operations to operating areas different than those they have traditionally operated in;

[8] In arriving at his decision, the arbitrator could also "have regard to other forestry revitalization proposals made by the licence holder" (s. 33.42(2)(b)). If he concluded the fairness requirements were not met, he could assess damages to be paid by the licence holder, Western, to the contractor, Hayes (s. 33.42(2)(c)). By agreement with the parties, the assessment of damages was deferred to await the decision on liability.

[9] Counsel agree s. 33.22(h) had not been judicially interpreted prior to the chambers judge's decision and that Mr. Pearlman was the first arbitrator to consider it. He came to this provision with an extensive background in arbitrating disputes under the *Forest Act*, including objections to AAC reductions pursuant to that Act. Division 5 of Part 5 of the *Regulation*, which governs the resolution of such disputes, does not provide for a "fairness objection" or include any provision comparable to s. 33.22(h).

[10] The chambers judge characterized the point of law on which she granted leave to appeal as whether "the arbitrator erred in law by interpreting s. 33.22(h) and the definition of AAC reduction criteria to require Western to consider or propose potential alternatives to the termination of Hayes' contract, including the provision of replaceable heli-logging rights to Hayes": 2007 BCSC 1469 at para. 35.

The Arbitral Decision

[11] Mr. Pearlman concluded that Hayes' fairness objection "succeeds." He explained at paragraph 25 of his reasons:

> … Although I have rejected many of the grounds advanced by Hayes in support of its fairness objection, *I have found that Western unfairly and unreasonably failed to consider alternatives which had the potential to mitigate the impact of the take back in the Nootka region on Hayes.* Those alternatives included the provision of a dedicated phase heli-logging contract to Hayes for all contractor logging operations in the Nootka region in exchange for Hayes' loss of its Bill 13 conventional logging rights at Plumper Harbour. [emphasis added]

[12] Before resolving the parties' dispute about the test for application of the fairness criteria, he had regard to other forestry revitalization proposals Western had made, writing [at paras. 45-46]:

> In assessing Hayes' complaints of unfairness, I do so having regard to the fact that this Proposal is only one of the forestry revitalization proposals which Western made, and that the licence holder's overall response to the Bill 28 take back of 685,000 m^3 of AAC resulted in the termination of 15 contracts, reductions in the amount of work for a number of additional contractors, as well as impacts on Western's own company operations. There is no question that Western, confronted by the need to respond to a twenty percent reduction in its AAC, had to make difficult business decisions while attempting to ensure its own continuing viability during a period when the Doman Group of Companies were either under protection from their creditors under the CCAA, or were just emerging from that protection.
>
> However, ultimately, I must determine whether Hayes, who bears the onus of proof in this case, has made out its fairness objection to this particular Proposal, which is confined to the fibre basket in the Nootka region.

[13] To craft a test for the application of the fairness criteria in the *Regulation*, the arbitrator found some assistance in *Francisco Gold Corp (Re)*, 2002 BCSC 1054, where H. Holmes J cited an observation made in *Maple Leaf Foods v. Schneider Corp.*, (1998), 42 OR (3d) 177 (CA), at 192. He then stated the test this way [at paras. 49-50]:

> I agree that the test here is not perfection, but rather whether Western, in making the Proposal, has applied the AAC reduction criteria in a manner that a reasonable person would regard as fair, impartial, and made without regard to any past disagreements between the parties.
>
> It is therefore necessary to review Western's proposal, and the specific complaints advanced by Hayes with respect to the alleged unfairness of the proposal, on a standard of reasonableness.

[14] Importantly, in view of his final conclusion and the parties' grounds for appeal, he added [at para. 51]:

> I find additional support for this approach in the Minister of Forests' letter of April 19, 2005 to licensees affected by the *Forestry Revitalization Act* … :
>
>> The overall spirit and intent of the proposal process provides for replaceable contractors to be dealt with fairly, impartially and without regard to past disagreements between the parties. In addition, Bill 13 requires each proposal to include sufficient information so that compliance with the cap can be readily confirmed by any impacted contractors.
>>
>> Bill 13 establishes the cap for an ungrouped licence or group of licences (as defined under the *Forestry Revitalization Act*) and allows me to waive that cap.
>>
>> I will waive the cap in situations where a minister's order or set of orders affecting a single licensee under the *Forestry Revitalization Act* applies a company's AAC reduction to its licences *such that all options that would result in compliance with the cap are unreasonable.* The licensee will be required to demonstrate that the proposal is consistent with the AAC reduction criteria *and that every reasonable effort has been made to mitigate the impact on replaceable contractors.* [emphasis added]

[15] The arbitrator read the language of s. 33.22(h) disjunctively (as the parties now agree it should be read), considered Hayes' specific complaints in support of its fairness objection, and rejected all but the alleged failure to consider alternatives to termination of its logging contract. Implicit in his conclusions was a determination that the termination was reasonably required by Western, particularly when the impact of the required AAC reduction on other locally-based contractors was taken into account.

[16] In the course of his discussion of these complaints, the arbitrator commented at some length on Western's application to the Minister of Forests for a cap variance, finding in it no support for Hayes' fairness objection. He noted [at para. 120]:

> In its application for the cap variance, Western made the point that in both regions, existing contract volumes were at marginal levels for efficiency and capital utilization, that in both regions it intended to terminate one full phase contractor while retaining the remaining contractors at their pre-Bill 28 harvesting levels, and that this approach would provide for effective capital utilization, efficiency of timber harvesting operations for the non-impacted contractors, and would also minimize disruptions to local communities.

[17] At para. 123 of his reasons, the arbitrator observed the Minister, in granting the application, was satisfied "the request for the cap variance was consistent with the situations in which he would grant relief, as stated in his letter of April 19, 2005."

[18] He also considered Western's view that its options were constricted by commitments it had made to three First Nations and concluded [at para. 149]:

> Although I accept that Mr. Boniface and Western had a *bona fide* belief that the written agreements with the First Nations produced in this arbitration all imposed some constraints on Western's ability to utilize timber volumes within the traditional territories of each of the three First Nations, *I am not satisfied that when Western made its Proposal, it gave any meaningful consideration to the extent to which these agreements did or did not limit its options to mitigate the impact of the 75,760 m³ take back AAC reduction in the Nootka region.* [emphasis added]

[19] Included in those agreements with First Nations was one with the Ehattesaht First Nation about heli-logging. The arbitrator had earlier noted (at para. 60) that Hayes had made a proposal to Western in 1999 "to give up its conventional logging cut for redistribution among the remaining contractors, in exchange for a phase heli-logging contract for all of the helicopter logging in the Nootka fibre basket." The arbitrator was not persuaded the Ehattesaht agreement was an impediment to such a proposal. He concluded [at paras. 158-159 and 161-162]:

> I am concerned about the fact that Western made no effort at all to pursue this as an alternative, particularly when Hayes had twice before proposed a similar exchange of conventional for heli-logging volumes. While there is no question that Western was required to make hard decisions regarding the rationalization of all its operations affected by the Bill 28 take backs, the fact is that it gave no consideration at all to the exchange of Hayes' conventional logging rights for heli-logging volume, an alternative to the complete loss of Hayes' replaceable contract which had the potential to mitigate that loss.
>
> In my view, it is no answer to say that it might be difficult to determine a particular replaceable volume for a dedicated phase heli-logging contract on an annual basis, in order to meet the requirements of section 17 of the *Regulation*. Western made absolutely no effort to do so. Given Hayes' capability to perform heli-logging, and the potential to mitigate the complete loss of Hayes' replaceable logging contract at Plumper Harbour, Western's failure to even consider this alternative was, in my view, both unreasonable, and unfair to Hayes. *To say that Western ought to have pursued this alternative is not to demand a standard of perfection. Rather, in all of the circumstances of this case, Western's failure to do so meant that it did not meet the objective standard of fairness mandated by section 33.22(h) of the Regulation.*
>
>   . . .
>
> Hayes also suggested that Western could have made inquiries to determine whether Hayes' replaceable contract at Plumper Harbour might be replaced with a dedicated phase heli-logging contract for the provision of heli-logging services in a joint venture arrangement with one or more First Nations. Mr. Boniface characterized this as "theoretical and speculative" but acknowledged that Western had made no inquiries of Hayes or any First Nation about whether this was a possibility.

Of the various mitigation measures suggested by Hayes, the exchange of Hayes' replaceable logging contract for a dedicated phase heli-logging contract in the Nootka region is the one which, in my view, had the greatest potential for success in providing a reasonable means of mitigating Hayes' loss of conventional logging volume while still minimizing the need for any relocation of contractors or company operations into operating areas different from those where they had traditionally operated. [emphasis added]

[20] Thus, the arbitrator determined the liability issue in favour of the contractor, Hayes. In effect, he decided that a fair application of the AAC reduction criteria required Western to consider all reasonable operational alternatives to mitigate a reasonably necessary termination decision.

[21] As permitted by s. 33(1) of the *Commercial Arbitration Act*, Western sought leave to appeal the arbitrator's decision on the ground that the arbitrator had committed an error of law which it stated this way:

[I]n concluding that Western had acted unfairly under section 33.22(h) of the Regulation, the Arbitrator erred in concluding that the AAC reduction criteria required Western to consider or propose alternatives to the termination of Hayes' replaceable logging contract at Plumper Harbour.

[22] Although Hayes disagreed with that statement of the arbitrator's conclusion, it did not resist the application and leave was granted. It pointed out that the arbitrator had decided Western's proposal was unfair because it had failed to consider potential alternatives to the contract termination and therefore did not comply with s. 33.22(h) of the *Regulation*.

[Summary of the decisions of the chambers judge, who applied a correctness standard and set aside the portion of the arbitrator's award finding Western's proposal to be unfair, has been omitted.]

Grounds of Appeal

[30] In its factum, Hayes states the chambers judge erred:

(a) By giving the term "fairly" an unduly restrictive meaning and effectively equating the licence holder's obligation to act "fairly" under subsection 33.22(h) with the obligation to take into account the AAC reduction criteria;

· · ·

[Discussion of *Dunsmuir* and *Khosa* and the standard of review analysis for questions of law decided by an arbitrator under the *Commercial Arbitrations Act* has been omitted.]

[58] When I consider these factors [of the standard of review analysis] together, they point to a standard of reasonableness. This means that the arbitrator's interpretation of s. 33.22(h) of the *Regulation* must be given the "respectful attention" discussed at paras. 48 and 49 in *Dunsmuir*. The final question is whether his interpretation is unreasonable.

Was the arbitrator's decision unreasonable?

[59] I am persuaded the arbitrator's reasoning process was so flawed as to take his interpretation of s. 33.22(h) of the *Regulation* beyond the range of reasonableness. Although he stated the test for fairness correctly at para. 49 of his reasons for the award, he then followed a path of reasoning that led him to import a criterion not included in the provision he was applying, thereby unreasonably taking it upon himself to depart from the legislated factors to be considered when resolving a fairness objection under the *Regulation*.

[60] The appellant would have this Court find the term "fairly" to be "deliberately ambiguous," thereby permitting the arbitrator to use his expertise in the forest industry to resolve the "polycentric" question, whose nature is revealed by the purpose of the *Regulation*. The parties agree a healthy and vibrant forest industry is the broad policy objective of the *Regulation*. However, that objective does not permit an arbitrator to import a criterion said by the Minister to be relevant to Western's cap variance application into the resolution of the distinct question, whether Western applied four operational efficiency criteria "fairly" in making a forestry revitalization proposal to its logging contractors. The arbitrator is in no different position from that of a judge whose exercise of discretion is limited to a consideration of a closed list of factors.

[61] I agree with the chambers judge that the language of s. 33.22(h) is not ambiguous and cannot and need not be read to justify an expansion of the criteria applied in resolving a fairness objection in order to better balance the competing interests in the forestry industry.

[62] A fairness objection is defined in s. 33.1 of the *Regulation* to mean:

> ... the inclusion in an objection to a forestry revitalization proposal under section 33.4 by an impacted contractor of notice that the contractor believes the requirements of section 33.22(h) have not been met in respect of that contractor and the reasons why the requirements have not been met.

[63] Leaving aside the fact that Hayes did not include the failure to consider mitigation alternatives in its objection and the fact that the Minister was sufficiently satisfied with Western's efforts to mitigate to permit the cap variance, s. 33.22(h) cannot reasonably bear the interpretation Hayes puts forward. As it was permitted to do by its authorizing statute, the executive chose to require the four listed reduction criteria be applied "fairly." If the executive had intended that a licence holder consider additional fairness criteria, it could have expressed that obligation in the definition of "fairness objection" or by expanding the "AAC reduction criteria" it required be applied "fairly."

[64] The *Regulation* sets down the criteria to control the resolution of a fairness objection. It does not provide an arbitrator with uncontrolled discretion to import criteria beyond those listed. Section 33.42(2)(a) of the *Regulation* is clear: the sole issue on a fairness objection is that the proposal meet the requirements of s. 33.22(h). The restricted scope of a fairness objection is understandable in its context: s. 33.22(h) is part of a remedial scheme.

[65] If a licence holder does not apply the four AAC reduction criteria "fairly," it must pay compensation for the consequences of its failure. Consistency and predictability are

vital to the scheme's effectiveness. A licence holder who reads the *Regulation* would reasonably understand it to mean that it would be required to pay compensation only if it applied the four AAC reduction criteria unfairly, with partiality, or with regard to past disagreements between it and a logging contractor. It could not be expected to consider all reasonable potential mitigation alternatives to termination or proportionate reduction of the cut demanded of it.

[66]   Nowhere in his reasons, does the arbitrator tie the obligation to consider mitigation alternatives to any of the four AAC reduction criteria such that it could be said he concluded Western applied one or more of them unfairly. Nor does Hayes suggest he did so.

[67]   For these reasons, I would dismiss the appeal.

[Separate reasons were issued by Mackenzie JA (Smith JA concurring), who would have also dismissed the appeal, but on grounds of procedural fairness rather than unreasonableness.]

NOTES

1.   In concluding that the arbitrator's reasoning went "beyond the range of reasonableness," Huddart JA focused closely on the choice of criteria applied by the arbitrator. Would this have been the appropriate focus if the arbitrator's decision had been classified as discretionary and polycentric, as Hayes argued, rather than strictly an issue of legal interpretation? If so, the court's characterization of the nature of the question appears also to have driven the application of the reasonableness standard.

2.   To address whether the Court of Appeal in this case engaged in correctness review in the guise of reasonableness, on a question of law, one must examine whether the language in the regulation lent itself to multiple answers and whether the answer given by the arbitrator fell within the acceptable range, or—to use the famous words of Dickson J in *CUPE, Local 963 v. New Brunswick Liquor Corporation*, [1979] 2 SCR 227, at 237—whether the arbitrator's interpretation was "so patently unreasonable that its construction cannot be rationally supported by the relevant legislation and demands intervention by the court upon review." What do you think?

Reasonableness and the Giving of Reasons

As discussed in chapter 4 of this text, the giving of reasons is a requirement of procedural fairness, based on *Baker* (para. 43), "where the decision has important significance for the individual, where there is a statutory right of appeal, or in other circumstances." That said, the giving of reasons is also important for the reasonableness review of substantive decisions. Thus, in *Dunsmuir*, the majority stated that an examination of "the qualities that make a decision reasonable" entails reference "both to the process of articulating the reasons and to outcomes." Also, the main concern of reasonableness review is said in *Dunsmuir* to be "with the existence of justification, transparency and intelligibility within the decision-making process." These statements indicate that the giving of reasons may be an important prerequisite for a court to conclude that a substantive decision of an administrative actor was reasonable. On the other hand, the majority in *Dunsmuir* (at para. 48, citing Dyzenhaus) referred also to the proposition that an administrative decision may be found to be reasonable based on "the reasons ... *which could be offered* in support of a decision" (emphasis added), suggesting that a court might invite from the parties, or indeed develop for itself, reasons to support a decision that are not present explicitly in the reasons of the decision-maker, or indeed where the decision-maker's reasons do not capture (or perhaps even where they contradict) a court's rationale for the decision.

These references in *Dunsmuir* raise challenging questions about the extent to which a court should revisit the reasons of a decision-maker in the course of substantive review. They indicate that a court may require a decision-maker to give express reasons, beyond the content of the record that was before the decision-maker. They suggest that there is also room for a court to supplement or even substitute the reasons of the decision-maker and that this is consistent with the principles of justification, transparency, and intelligibility in administrative decision making. However, where a tribunal has offered elaborate reasons for a decision, the court should presumably look first—or even exclusively—to those reasons in order to frame and understand the decision. In other words, the courts should not jump to elaborate or spice up the decision-maker's expression of its own deliberations. Further, a court will presumably only rarely disregard the rationale offered by a decision-maker, in favour of the court's own rationale, on the basis that the core purpose of reasonableness review is to defer to the decision-maker's own choices. As we see in the next case, the absence of reasons that are adequate to allow the evaluation of a substantive decision may prompt a court to refer the case back to the administrative decision-maker for a proper explanation. This is not as a matter of procedural fairness, we should be clear, but on the basis that the reasons given were inadequate for the court to determine whether the decision was reasonable.

Macdonald v. Mineral Springs Hotel
2008 ABCA 273

The Honourable Madam Justice HUNT [O'Brien JA concurring]:

[1] This is an appeal from a chambers decision that held that the Hospital Privileges Appeal Board ("HPAB") incorrectly concluded it had no jurisdiction to hear Macdonald's appeal from a refusal by the Operating Room Committee ("OR Committee") of the Mineral Springs Hospital ("Hospital") to increase his operating room ("OR") time.

[2] I would allow the appeal but remit the matter to the HPAB.

Facts

[3] The respondent, Macdonald, is a physician with medical staff privileges at the Hospital. In mid-2002 he asked the OR Committee for more OR time, which request it considered. In February 2003 he wrote the Hospital's Chief of Staff asking him to increase his allocation of OR time from one day every three weeks to one day every two weeks. The matter was referred to the OR Committee, which formed a sub-committee to re-evaluate the OR allocation process. Both the sub-committee (of which Macdonald was a member) and the OR Committee refused his request.

[4] He appealed to the HPAB, a majority of which concluded it had no jurisdiction to hear his appeal because it did not involve the matter of his "privileges." The HPAB's decision is elaborated below beginning at para. 14.

[Review of the legislative framework omitted.]

HPAB Decision

[14] The HPAB set out the three grounds for the Hospital's objection to the Board's jurisdiction:

> (1) The decision was not appealable under section 21(1) of the *Act*;
>
> (2) If appealable, it did not relate to "privileges" under section 21(1) of the *Act*; and
>
> (3) If a question of "privileges" under section 21(1) of the *Act*, it did not concern the termination, suspension or variation of a Physician's privileges.

[15] The HPAB referred to certain documents in addressing the first ground, including letters and minutes of meetings. It concluded at A.B. F9 that "there is an appealable decision ... there has been a delegation, express or implied, of the Hospital Board's authority to make a decision to the OR Committee." This part of the HPAB's decision seems to conclude that the OR Committee's decision was, in effect, a decision by "the board of the approved hospital," as required by section 21(1). This point was not pursued before the courts by either party.

[16] On the second ground, the HPAB decision simply said that its majority found that "the decision made not to vary Dr. Macdonald's OR time is not a question of privileges within the meaning of section 21(1) of the Hospitals Act or the medical staff bylaws ...": at A.B. F9. In coming to this bare conclusion, the Board neither found facts nor referred to any facts. It added that it did not need to rule on the Hospital's third ground.

[17] It then outlined the minority decision as follows:

Operating room time is a matter of allocation of hospital privileges. Reference is made to tab C of Exhibit 1 at page 8, which defines privileges as follows, (AS READ):

Privileges are defined as the ability to access specific resources of the hospital in order to provide specified health care services as determined for each physician by the Board to patients in the hospital.

The minority is of the opinion that because OR time is a matter of allocation of resources, it comes within the hospital's definition of privileges, as I've described from the medical staff bylaws. The definition of privileges is not ambiguous so as to necessitate the application of the doctorate [*sic*] of contra proferentum.

There then remains the question of whether, within the meaning of section 21(1) of the *Hospitals Act*, the appealable decision made by the OR committee was a termination, suspension, or variation of Dr. Macdonald's privileges.

Dr. Macdonald applied to have his existing privileges of one day of OR time every three weeks varied to one day of OR time every two weeks.

The word "varying" in section 21(1)(c) of the *Hospitals Act* is broad enough to include a decision not to vary, and it is not necessary that there be an expressed variation before section 21(1)(c) becomes applicable.

The minority stresses that its opinion that this Board has jurisdiction does not presuppose a finding that the appeal should be dismissed or allowed, only that this Board has jurisdiction to hear the appeal.

It is manifest that, unlike the majority decision, the minority considered both the *Act* and bylaws in explaining its conclusion.

Chambers Decision

[18] The chambers judge focused on the definition of "privileges" in the Hospital's bylaws, concluding that the "denial of the respondent to return Dr. MacDonald to his original OR time clearly in my view affects his privileges": A.B. F17/15-17. He also held that this decision fell under the definition of varying the member's hospital privileges in section 21(1)(c) of the *Act*. He then considered what standard of review applied to the HPAB's decision, concluding that it was correctness because it was an issue of statutory interpretation. This led him to hold that the HPAB erred in law in concluding it had no jurisdiction over the OR Committee's decision. He set aside the HPAB decision and directed the HPAB to hear the merits of Macdonald's appeal.

[Discussion of the standard of review analysis, by which the Court of Appeal concluded that the appropriate standard based on *Dunsmuir* was reasonableness, has been omitted.]

Ground 3—Was the HPAB decision reasonable?

[38] Reasonableness applies not only to the outcome of a tribunal's decision but also to its "process of articulating reasons" and the "existence of justification, transparency and intelligibility within the decision-making process": *Dunsmuir* at para. 47. The notion of deference requires "a respectful attention *to the reasons offered*": *Dunsmuir* at para. 48 (emphasis added).

[39] The HPAB gave no reasons for its conclusion that the matter before it was not a question of privilege. Nor are any reasons for this conclusion apparent from the totality of its decision.

[40] The *Act* does not require the HPAB to give reasons and the *Administrative Procedures and Jurisdiction Act*, RSA 2000, c. A-3, s. 7(b) (which requires certain statutory delegates to give reasons) does not apply to the HPAB. Neither does an administrative tribunal have a common law duty to give reasons: *Northwestern Utilities Ltd. v. City of Edmonton*, [1979] 1 SCR 684, (1978) 12 AR 449; *Supermarchés Jean Labrecque Inc. v. Flamand*, [1987] 2 SCR 219 at 233, 43 DLR (4th) 1. However, in *Baker v. Canada (Minister of Citizenship and Immigration)*, [1999] 2 SCR 817, 174 DLR (4th) 193, the Court concluded that there were some circumstances which required the provision of a written explanation for a decision: at para. 43. To similar effect see *Cook v. Alberta (Minister of Environmental Protection)*, 2001 ABCA 276, 293 AR 237; *Fenske v. Alberta (Minister of Environment)*, 2002 ABCA 135, 303 AR 356 at para. 36.

[41] The Supreme Court has applied to civil cases the "functional test" for whether reasons are required first established in *R v. Sheppard*, 2002 SCC 26, [2002] 1 SCR 869 at para. 55: *Hill v. Hamilton-Wentworth Regional Police Services Board*, 2007 SCC 41, 285 DLR (4th) 620. At para. 100 the Court explained that the "question is whether the reasons are sufficient to allow for meaningful appellate review and whether the parties' 'functional need to know' why the trial judge's decision has been made has been met." This assessment takes into consideration the "context of the record before the court. Where the record discloses all that is required to be known to permit appellate review, less detailed reasons may be acceptable": para. 101. There does not appear to be any principled reason why, when there exists a statutory right of appeal and the context makes it impossible to apply a reasonableness test to the tribunal's decision, the tribunal ought not to be required to give reasons.

[42] Each party offered arguments in support of or against the HPAB's conclusion based in part on an analysis of the *Act* and the bylaws. It is perhaps the case that such *ex post facto* reasoning could support the view that the decision was reasonable. Doing so, however, would undermine one of the fundamental reasons why courts must defer to tribunals in cases such as this: because they have expertise about how hospitals function. Accepting the reasonableness of their decisions absent so much as a hint as to how they reached them would also encourage tribunals not to explain themselves. Moreover, it would engage courts in doing the very work that legislatures intended tribunals to do. This outcome would also work against the basic purpose of judicial review, which is "to ensure the legality, the reasonableness and the fairness of the administrative process and its outcomes." *Dunsmuir* at para. 28.

[43] There may be cases where the reasons for a tribunal's decision are apparent from the totality of the record. That is unlikely to be the case, when, as here, the decision has to be grounded on analysis of complicated statutory-type provisions that can only be understood in the context in which they operate.

[44] Nothing can be gleaned here by examining the reasonableness of the outcome, because only two are possible: either HPAB had jurisdiction or it did not. Therefore, in applying the reasonableness standard it is necessary to focus on matters such as justification, transparency and intelligibility. Without the benefit of the HPAB's reasoning about how it employed its expertise to interpret its home statute, it is impossible to determine whether its decision was reasonable.

Conclusion

[45] As a result, under section 21(3) of the *Act* the issue must be remitted to the HPAB with a direction that it explain why it concluded that the decision not to vary Macdonald's OR time is not a question of privilege. The reasons must be sufficient to allow for meaningful appellate review (given that there is a statutory right of appeal on questions of law) and answer Macdonald's 'functional need to know' why the decision has been made.

[46] Given this conclusion, it would not be appropriate to opine on whether this involved a variation of Macdonald's privileges, a point on which the majority of the HPAB itself declined to rule.

. . .

[Berger JA dissented, concluding that the HPAB's decision was reasonable. His conclusions on the question of whether the HPAB majority's reasons were sufficient to find its decision reasonable are elaborated in the following paragraphs.]

[94] The majority opinion contends that the failure of the HPAB to give reasons warrants returning the matter to the Board with a direction that the refusal to entertain Dr. Macdonald's appeal be explained. My colleagues' analysis and reasoning is tantamount to an invocation of *R v. Sheppard*, [2002] 1 SCR 869 in an administrative law context absent a statutory command that the tribunal must provide reasons (see, for example, s. 687(2) of the *Municipal Government Act*, RSA 2000, c. M-26).

[95] In my opinion, the relevant inquiry is whether meaningful appellate review is possible on this record. In the Court of Queen's Bench and on appeal to this Court from the disposition below, neither party argued that the failure of the HPAB to give reasons amounted to a breach of natural justice or a denial of procedural fairness. No one contended that meaningful appellate review was frustrated by the absence of reasons.

[96] As I have already pointed out, the HPAB heard and considered *viva voce* evidence and competing argument was advanced for the Board's consideration. The appeal to the Court of Queen's Bench and to this Court is with respect to the conclusion reached premised upon precisely the same record that was available to the HPAB. To the extent that interpretation of the language of the enactment or of the Bylaws is in issue, the absence of reasons does not preclude meaningful appellate review on the question of law that is arguably engaged. The majority concedes that the question that came before the Tribunal does not lend itself to one specific, particular result. That said, the conclusion reached by the HPAB is certainly one of a number of possible reasonable conclusions. The Board is entitled to a margin of appreciation within the range of acceptable and rational solutions (*Dunsmuir, supra*, at para. 47).

· · ·

[101] It follows, in my opinion, that on this basis also, the decision of the HPAB was not unreasonable. Appellate interference by the Court of Queen's Bench was not warranted.

[Berger JA would have allowed the appeal and restored the decision of the HPAB.]

NOTES

1. The majority reasons of Hunt JA refer to the statement in *Dunsmuir*, at para. 48, that a reviewing court should show "a respectful attention to the reasons offered." However, they do not mention the possibility of respect for the reasons that "could be offered" for the decision, as referenced in the same paragraph of *Dunsmuir*. Rather, Hunt JA, at para. 43 of her reasons, discounted the prospect that reasons might be derived from the record in circumstances, such as this case, where the decision was "grounded on analysis of complicated statutory-type provisions that can only be understood in the context in which they operate." Do you think that this offers a viable basis for distinguishing cases in which a court may seek to construct its own understanding of the reasons for a decision from cases in which it should not do so?

2. In dissent, Berger JA allowed for greater flexibility in the review of the HPAB decision and the degree to which it fell within the range of acceptable and rational outcomes. What aspects of the HPAB's decision making did he emphasize, in contrast to Hunt JA, to conclude that meaningful appellate review was possible? Do you agree that the fact that neither of the parties argued that the failure of HPAB to give reasons was a breach of procedural justice, as Berger JA mentioned at para. 95, was relevant to the issue of whether the absence of reasons frustrated appellate review? For a close examination of this issue, which led the court to distinguish issues of procedural fairness from substantive review based on a reasonableness standard, see *Clifford v. Ontario Municipal Employees Retirement System* (2009), 2009 ONCA 670.

A Historical Example of Reasonableness Review

Southam was the first case in which the Supreme Court expressly identified reasonableness *simpliciter* as a third (or middle) category of review. It thus provides an interesting example of how to show deference based on the pre-*Dunsmuir* distinction between reasonableness *simpliciter* and patent unreasonableness. Also evident in the excerpt below, and of ongoing relevance today, is the court's choice to defer to a decision of a federal tribunal in spite of its own doubts about the appropriateness of the tribunal's decision. As such, *Southam* offers an example of deference doctrine in its most genuine form: an instance in which the court, out of respect for legislative choices about administrative decision making, disciplines itself by declining to interfere with a decision about which it holds significant reservations.

Canada (Director of Investigation and Research) v. Southam Inc.
[1997] 1 SCR 748 (BC)

[The facts of this case were summarized in chapter 10 of this text.]

IACOBUCCI J (delivering the judgment of the Court):

. . .

G. *Application of the Standard*

The question, then, is whether the Tribunal acted unreasonably when it decided that Southam's daily newspapers and community newspapers are in different product markets. I conclude that it did not.

The Federal Court of Appeal identified what it thought were two defects in the Tribunal's decision. The first is that the Tribunal failed to consider evidence that daily newspapers and community newspapers are functionally interchangeable. The second is that the Tribunal failed to consider evidence that Southam considered the community newspapers to be its principal rivals in the Lower Mainland.

By "functional interchangeability," the Federal Court of Appeal apparently meant "end use" or "purpose." See [[1995] 3 FC 557 (CA),] at 636-37. The Tribunal, for its part, elaborated (at 225-38) at great length on the use to which advertisers put daily and community newspapers. At the end of 14 pages, it came to the conclusion with which the Federal

Court of Appeal would later take issue: that advertisers use daily newspapers to reach consumers throughout the entire Lower Mainland and use community newspapers to reach smaller, "local" audiences.

The Federal Court of Appeal quarreled with this conclusion on several grounds. Its first, and most general objection, was to the weight that the Tribunal assigned to the criterion of functional interchangeability. In the court's view, at 635, the Tribunal gave this important criterion short shrift: "the Tribunal clearly failed to consider the importance of functional interchangeability, which is not simply one of many criteria to be considered but a central part of the framework." However, as I have already noted, the weighing of criteria in a balancing test must be largely a matter of discretion. The very purpose of a multi-factored test, such as the one that the Tribunal used to determine the dimensions of the relevant product market, is to permit triers of fact to do justice in diverse particular cases.

As a general matter, in cases like this one, the aims and objectives of the statute may not be served by assigning principal or overriding importance to any one factor. It cannot be said as a matter of law that evidence of functional interchangeability should weigh more heavily in the balance than other kinds of evidence. The question therefore must be whether the Tribunal's attention to functional interchangeability was reasonable on the facts of this case.

For my part, I cannot say that the Tribunal acted unreasonably to discount the evidence of functional interchangeability. It had its reasons for doing so, and those reasons cannot be said to be without foundation or logical coherence. In particular, the Tribunal seems to have thought that daily newspapers and community newspapers serve different purposes. The former appeal to large advertisers who wish to convey their message throughout a metropolitan region. The latter appeal to smaller advertisers, who wish to reach all or many of the consumers living in a particular neighbourhood or district of a city. See the Tribunal's decision at 238. While I might not agree, as a matter of empirical "fact," that this description of the purposes of the respective kinds of newspaper is exhaustive, I think that it is not without its reasons. It is reasonable, if only reasonable, to suppose that advertisers are sufficiently discerning about the media they employ that they are unlikely to respond to changes in the relative prices of the two kinds of newspaper by taking their business from the one to the other. Fortunately for the Tribunal, its decision need only be reasonable and not necessarily correct.

However, that does not finish the matter. The Federal Court of Appeal had two other difficulties with the Tribunal's approach, and they appear to go to the reasoning that underlies the Tribunal's conclusion. The first is that it is inconsistent to lump together daily newspapers and community newspapers for purposes of distinguishing them from broadcast media but then to separate the two kinds of newspapers for purposes of distinguishing them from one another. The second is that the Tribunal's conclusion confuses geographical scope with purpose. Both alleged difficulties turn out on closer inspection not to be troubling.

The Federal Court of Appeal, at 636, described the first alleged difficulty in these terms: "If 'multiple price/product' advertising is a relevant purpose for distinguishing between print and electronic media then it must also be relevant as between advertising in daily and community newspapers." But, with respect, this conclusion does not follow. It is perfectly consistent to distinguish between the broadcast media and the print media on one ground and to distinguish further between two kinds of print media on another ground. Broadcasters attract advertisers who want to convey an "image." See the Tribunal's decision at 221. Newspapers attract advertisers who want to convey a great deal of specific information about a variety of products all at once. Accordingly, the two kinds of media serve different markets. However, from the fact that newspapers in general serve a certain broad class of advertiser, it does not follow that all newspapers serve precisely the same particular advertisers, or the same relevant advertising markets. Further division of the market is possible. Thus, daily newspapers serve advertisers who wish to reach even a relatively small proportion of people throughout a large region. Community newspapers serve advertisers who wish to reach a large proportion of people in a small region. See, *supra*, at 238. These markets are at least possibly, and therefore reasonably, different.

If the identification of an overarching, broad purpose that two kinds of products serve were sufficient to place those products in the same market, then all products could be placed in the same market, because all products serve the general purpose of satisfying consumers' needs. Certainly, following the Federal Court of Appeal's reasoning it would be possible to argue that broadcast media and print media are in the same market because both kinds of media serve advertisers. But it is not so, and the Federal Court of Appeal admitted at 636 that it is not so. The trick is to settle on the correct level of generality. Canadian courts have recognized as much in the past:

> … speaking generally, it is of importance to bear in mind that the term "market" is a relative concept. In one sense, there is only one market in an economy since, to some extent, all products and services are substitutes for each other in competing for the customer's dollar.
>
> In another sense, almost every firm has its own market since, in most industries, each firm's product is differentiated, to some extent, from that of all other firms.
>
> Defining the relevant market in any particular case, therefore, requires a balanced consideration of a number of characteristics or dimensions to meet the analytical needs of the specific matter under consideration.

The Queen v. J.W. Mills & Son Ltd., [1968] 2 Ex. CR 275, at 305.

What has to be kept in mind is that purposes are as various as markets, and both come in different sizes. Consequently it is unhelpful to suggest that once a purpose has been identified, all those products that serve that purpose should be considered to fall within a single market. It is the *correct* or *relevant* purpose that must be found, which is to say the broadest purpose that is consistent with a high cross-elasticity of demand. For example, cars and tanks both serve the general purpose of conveying people from place to place. But no one would suggest that cars and tanks are in the same market. The reason is that consumers do not modify their car-purchasing behaviour in response to slight changes in the price of tanks, and governments do not modify their tank-purchasing behaviour in response to slight changes in the price of cars. A person who is in the market for a station wagon does not shop with an eye on the price of armaments. Again, the Minister of National Defence does not check prices at local car dealerships before announcing an acquisition of new military hardware.

The relevant purpose is a function of the psychology of consumption or preference. Consequently, in order to choose the relevant purpose, the adjudicator must possess in advance some idea about the behaviour of consumers. In this way, the purpose inquiry is a little circular. Tribunals inquire into purpose in order to get a grip on the tendency of consumers to substitute one product for another, but they will not hit on the right purpose unless they already have a notion of what consumers will substitute for what. This circularity does not, however, alter the fact that more is needed to establish functional interchangeability than citation of a common purpose. That daily newspapers and community newspapers both seek the trade of "multiple price/product" advertisers does not show, without more, that they are competing in the same market. It was open to the Tribunal to conclude, after consulting evidence of the behaviour of advertisers, that purchasing decisions in the real world are taken on the basis of some more particular purpose than to convey information about several products at once.

The Federal Court of Appeal at 636-37 also took issue, at a theoretical level, with the Tribunal's attention to the geographic scope of the different kinds of newspapers:

> But the fact that the community newspapers are more local in nature does not go to the question of functional interchangeability, but to the behaviour of buyers as to preference for geographical scope. This latter subjective factor should not be mingled with the purely objective factor of functional interchangeability which focuses on use or purpose.

Immediately, any argument that depends on a classification of purpose as "objective" is suspect. Purpose is at least, in part, a matter of intention and so is at least, in part, "subjective." Presumably, almost any object can be put to a multitude of uses. An axe handle, for example, can serve as a bludgeon or as an axe handle. The purpose it serves depends on the intention of the person in whose hand it is. In like manner, the purposes daily newspapers and community newspapers serve depend on the intentions of their users.

In the right hands, both could function as birdcage liners or as wrapping for fish and chips. At times, both probably do. However, those functions are uninteresting because they are atypical, and the Tribunal was right not to mention them. But in order to exclude those purposes and settle on the relevant ones, the Tribunal had to consider, at least implicitly, the intentions of the users of the two kinds of newspaper. Therefore, it was not illegitimate for the Tribunal to look to what the Federal Court of Appeal at 636 called "preference for geographical scope." Reaching consumers throughout a large region is one purpose. Reaching consumers in a neighbourhood is another purpose. It does not matter that the difference between them is in the intention of the advertiser. Intention is a component of purpose. Of course, "objective" considerations also play a part. A newspaper cannot be an aircraft, however much someone might wish that it could be. And this is reflected in the Tribunal's distinction. A community newspaper cannot reach a large audience, however much an advertiser might wish that it could, and a daily newspaper cannot reach only the consumers in a small locality.

It appears, then, that the Tribunal considered at length, at much greater length than did the Federal Court of Appeal, whether daily newspapers and community newspapers serve the same purpose. It concluded that they do not, and gave reasons for its conclusion. The reasons that the Federal Court of Appeal offered for questioning that conclusion are, with respect, unconvincing. Accordingly, failing the appearance of some other basic objection to the Tribunal's conclusion about functional interchangeability, that conclusion should stand.

The Federal Court of Appeal also found fault with the Tribunal's treatment of evidence that Southam regarded the community newspapers as its chief competitors. In particular, it objected to the Tribunal's preference for a "more focused analysis" of the evidence of inter-industry competition. In the court's view at 638, "[t]he evidence of broad competitiveness is sufficient to show that there is competition in fact between the Pacific Dailies and the community newspapers." It was error, said the Federal Court of Appeal, for the Tribunal to ignore that evidence.

In fact, the Tribunal devoted 28 pages of its reasons (at 191-218) to the question of inter-industry competition. The Tribunal did not "ignore" evidence of broad inter-industry competition. It simply did not regard that evidence as decisive (at 191-92):

> … determining that Pacific Press regarded the community newspapers as "competitors" is not by itself enough to place them in the same market. Competition means many things to many people. What the tribunal must establish is whether dailies and the community newspapers are in the same product market for the purposes of assessing the implications of the acquisitions in question in this case. As discussed above in general terms, that exercise involves resolving whether dailies and community newspapers are effective substitutes for newspaper retail advertising services. The actions taken and the views expressed by participants in the alleged market are recognized by both parties and by expert witnesses as an important source of information in trying to answer this question. [Emphasis added.]

In short, the Tribunal found that although evidence of inter-industry competition suggests a certain conclusion, it is not sufficient by itself to establish that conclusion. In this it relied on the elementary principle that thinking something is so does not make it so. A company can believe that it is competing with another company without it actually (or legally) being so.

It is possible that if I were deciding this case *de novo*, I might not dismiss so readily as the Tribunal did what is admittedly weighty evidence of inter-industry competition. In my view, it is very revealing that Southam's own expert, an American newspaper consultant, identified the community newspapers as the source of Southam's difficulties in the Lower Mainland. To find, in the face of such evidence, that the daily newspapers and the community newspapers are not competitors is perhaps unusual. In that sense, the Tribunal's finding is difficult to accept. However, it is not unreasonable. The Tribunal explained that, in its view, Southam was mistaken about who its competitors were; and though I may not consider that reason compelling, I cannot say that it is not a reason for which there is a logical and evidentiary underpinning. More generally, I notice that the Tribunal seems to have been preoccupied with the definition of the relevant market. It is possible that the members may occasionally have lost sight of the ultimate inquiry, which is whether the acquisition of the community newspapers by Southam substantially lessened competition. But again, I cannot say that the Tribunal's approach was unreasonable. Definition of the relevant market is indeed a necessary step in the inquiry; and the fact that the Tribunal dwelled on it is perhaps understandable if, as seems to have been the case, the bounds of the relevant market were not clear.

I wish to observe, by way of concluding my discussion of this issue, that a reviewer, and even one who has embarked upon review on a standard of reasonableness *simpliciter*, will often be tempted to find some way to intervene when the reviewer him- or herself would have come to a conclusion opposite to the tribunal's. Appellate courts must resist such temptations. My statement that I might not have come to the same conclusion as the Tribunal should not be taken as an invitation to appellate courts to intervene in cases such as this one but rather as a caution against such intervention and a call for restraint. Judicial restraint is needed if a cohesive, rational, and, I believe, sensible system of judicial review is to be fashioned.

Accordingly, the Tribunal's conclusion must stand.

H. Remedy

Having found that Southam's acquisitions had produced a substantial lessening of competition in the market for real estate print advertising on the North Shore, the Tribunal ordered Southam to divest itself, at its own option, of either the *Real Estate Weekly* or the *North Shore News*. The Federal Court of Appeal declined to disturb this remedy. I agree with the Federal Court of Appeal that the remedy settled upon by the Tribunal should be allowed to stand.

The appellants submit that the correct test for a remedy under the *Competition Act* is whether it eliminates any substantial lessening of competition that the merger may have caused. The appellants observe that this is the standard that has been applied in cases under s. 92(1)(e)(iii) of the *Competition Act*, in which the parties have consented to the remedy. See *e.g. Canada (Director of Investigation & Research) v. Air Canada* (1989) 27 CPR (3d) 476 (Comp. Trib.) at 513-14. They observe also that substantial lessening of competition is the evil that Parliament has sought to address in the Act. Mergers themselves are not considered to be objectionable except in so far as they produce a substantial lessening of competition. Therefore, restoration to the pre-merger situation is not what is wanted. Indeed, presumably *some* lessening of competition following a merger is tolerated, because the Act proscribes only a *substantial* lessening of competition. The appellants object further to what they see as the punitive quality of the remedy that the Tribunal imposed, and to what they regard as the illicit shifting to them of the burden of showing that the proposed remedy would be effective.

The respondent, for his part, says that the test of a remedy is whether it restores the parties to the pre-merger competitive situation. I believe that the appellants' test is the better one.

The evil to which the drafters of the *Competition Act* addressed themselves is substantial lessening of competition. See *Competition Act*, s. 92(1). It hardly needs arguing that the appropriate remedy for a substantial lessening of competition is to restore competition to the point at which it can no longer be said to be substantially less than it was before the merger. This is the test that the Tribunal has applied in consent cases. The Tribunal attempted to distinguish this case from those cases on precisely the ground that here the Director did not consent to the appellants' proposed remedy. But the distinction is not a sensible one. I can think of only two reasons why the test should be more forgiving where the parties have consented to a remedy. The first is that parties who have not consented should be punished for their obduracy. The second, which is related to the first, is that the law should provide parties with an incentive to come to a consensual arrangement. Neither reason is valid on closer analysis. The burden of a harsh standard falls entirely on one of the parties: the company. No punishment falls on the Director when he or she is obdurate, and the harsh standard gives him or her no incentive to consent to a remedy. Therefore, even if there is a policy of encouraging consent and punishing obduracy, it is not well served by the imposition of a more stringent standard in cases in which the parties have not consented. The better approach is to apply the same standard in contested proceedings as in consent proceedings.

However, the appellants do not benefit by their proposed standard. The reason is that the Tribunal expressly found that, even accepting that the appropriate standard is the one used in consent proceedings, Southam's proposed remedy fails because it would not likely be effective in eliminating the substantial lessening of competition. Robertson JA accepted this finding, saying that it was entitled to deference. I agree.

The Tribunal's choice of remedy is a matter of mixed law and fact. The question whether a particular remedy eliminates the substantial lessening of competition is a matter of the application of a legal standard to a particular set of facts. Therefore, for reasons I have already given, the Tribunal's decision must be reviewed according to a standard of reasonableness.

Because the Tribunal did not decide unreasonably when it decided that Southam's proposed remedy would not be effective, its decision should be allowed to stand. What Southam proposed was that it should sell the real estate supplement that appears weekly in the *North Shore News*. But, as the Tribunal very properly pointed out, it is not clear that the supplement would prosper or even survive on its own. Even if the supplement continued to enjoy the advantages of a close association with the *North Shore News*, the closeness of the association would not tend to foster competition. See the Tribunal's decision, *supra*, at 252.

The appellants' other objections to the remedy are unconvincing. The remedy is not punitive, because the Tribunal found that it was the only effective remedy. If the choice is between a remedy that goes farther than is strictly necessary to restore competition to an acceptable level and a remedy that does not go far enough even to reach the acceptable level, then surely the former option must be preferred. At the very least, a remedy must be effective. If the least intrusive of the possible effective remedies overshoots the mark, that is perhaps unfortunate but, from a legal point of view, such a remedy is not defective. As for the claim that the Tribunal wrongly required the appellants to demonstrate the effectiveness of their proposed remedy, no more need be said than that he who asserts should prove, as Robertson JA so aptly put it [(1995), 127 DLR (4th) 329,] at 337.

Therefore, I would dismiss the appeal of the remedy.

Appeal on the merits allowed with costs; appeal on the remedy dismissed with costs.

NOTES

1. If the standard of review had been correctness, how would this part of the judgment in *Southam* have been written?

2. Return to *Baker* (chapter 2 of this text) and reassess how the Supreme Court conducted reasonableness review in that case. To what extent does reasonableness review involve an assessment of the weight attributed to various factors or considerations or to items

of evidence? Recollect Iacobucci J's statement in *Law Society of New Brunswick v. Ryan*, [2003] 1 SCR 247 (see chapter 10 of this text), at para. 41, that reasonableness review does not involve the court reweighing or reassessing the evidence. Should that always be the case? To what extent is that consistent with the judgment of L'Heureux-Dubé J in *Baker*?

PATENT UNREASONABLENESS REVIEW

For a fascinating decision in which the Supreme Court diverged on its approach to the pre-*Dunsmuir* standard of patent unreasonableness (which was the sole deferential standard at the time), framed against an extensive discussion of the reasons for deference, see *National Corn Growers Assn. v. Canada (Import Tribunal)*, [1990] 2 SCR 3124 (Can.). Notably, the difference of view of the court in that case did not involve what patent unreasonableness actually meant but rather what material the court should look at and, more specifically, how deeply it should probe.

In its decision in *Manz v. Sundher*, 2009 BCCA 92, the BC Court of Appeal concluded that the patent unreasonableness standard lived on after *Dunsmuir* and that it retained its old meaning, based on the direction in ss. 58-59 of the BC *Administrative Tribunals Act* that the courts apply patent unreasonableness in certain circumstances (ss. 58-59 are reproduced in chapter 8 of this text). The Court of Appeal also addressed an argument that the concerns raised in *Crevier* (chapter 9 of this text) called into question the constitutionality of ss. 58-59 of the *Administrative Tribunals Act*. This argument was rejected by Saunders JA on the basis that the constitutional foundations of judicial review, especially on jurisdictional questions, are distinct from the issue of how a court decides whether and how to defer to a decision-maker. Saunders JA stated for the court:

Constitutional Question

[21] Mr. Manz's thesis is that in legislating on the standard of review of the superior courts through the device of ss. 58 and 59 of the *Administrative Tribunals Act*, the legislature has impermissibly sought to control the supervisory function of a superior court, which cannot be done without trenching upon s. 96 of the *Constitution Act, 1867*.

· · ·

[24] The Attorney General responds that the exercise of a superior court on a judicial review petition is the supervision of the inferior tribunal to ensure it keeps to its statutory mandate, a question that is fundamentally a question of statutory interpretation to determine legislative intent. The only limitation on a legislature's ability to legislate in respect to an administrative tribunal within its general legislative competence is that expressed in *Crevier v. The Queen*, where, in considering a privative clause, the Supreme Court of Canada held that a legislature may not exclude judicial review on issues touching jurisdiction because to do so is to impinge upon the jurisdiction of courts established under s. 96 of the *Constitution Act, 1867*.

[25] In my view, the British Columbia legislature has not, by enacting ss. 58 and 59 of the *Administrative Tribunals Act*, stepped outside its legislative competence.

[26] Mr. Ishkanian frames the issue as encroaching on the inherent jurisdiction of the superior courts. I am not at all persuaded that judicial review is properly characterized as part of inherent jurisdiction of superior courts. Rather, modern judicial review (in British Columbia under the *Judicial Review Procedure Act*, RSBC 1996, c. 241) is a restatement of the law of pre-

rogative writs whereby the Sovereign called on the tribunal to ensure compliance with its mandate, using the court as the medium. ...

[27] Judicial review however, does hold a constitutionally protected place in the jurisdiction of superior courts. In *Crevier* Chief Justice Laskin said at p. 236 and 237:

> It is true that this is the first time that this Court has declared unequivocally that a provincially-constituted statutory tribunal cannot constitutionally be immunized from review of decisions on questions of jurisdiction. In my opinion, this limitation, arising by virtue of s. 96, stands on the same footing as the well-accepted limitation on the power of provincial statutory tribunals to make unreviewable determinations of constitutionality.

> ...

[30] The question posed on behalf of Mr. Manz is whether this constitutional guarantee of judicial review requires that the standard applied by a court in determining the legislative intent must be determined by the courts. In my view the answer is no. The constitutionally protected role of the superior courts, confirmed in *Crevier*, is supervision of the administrative tribunal's conformity with the jurisdiction assigned to it by the enabling legislation. This is, as said in *Dunsmuir*, a duty "to ensure public authorities do not overreach their lawful powers." Nothing in ss. 58 or 59, in my view, detracts from that constitutional role held by the superior court, the Supreme Court of British Columbia.

[31] This discussion is an example of the difference between "what is done" and "how that what is done." In this case the "what" is supervision of tribunals to ensure they do not overstep their legislated mandate. The standard of review analysis is a question of "how." The common law of standard of review has been developed as an interpretive guide for use in determining the Legislature's intent as to the jurisdiction accorded by it to the Tribunal.

[32] There is, in my view, no constitutional imperative to the method employed by the courts in the supervision of administrative tribunals *so long as the core requirement of ensuring the tribunal keeps to its mandate is preserved*. I do not consider that the *Administrative Tribunals Act* generally derogates from the constitutional demand described in *Crevier*.

[33] In particular, to the extent that either ss. 58 or 59 refers to a standard of correctness, there can be no complaint a superintending role of the Courts has been removed. Nor, to the extent that s. 59 refers to reasonableness, can there be any complaint by Mr. Manz as he seeks to apply that standard to all matters for which correctness is not required. His challenge is simply to application of the standard of patent unreasonableness. But that standard is a standard that demands a tribunal's compliance with its jurisdiction, comporting with the language of Chief Justice Laskin in *Crevier*.

[34] It is my opinion the impugned provisions do not remove a s. 96 court function, there is no impairment of the key, constitutional, superintending role of the courts over administrative tribunals to which the *Administrative Tribunals Act* applies, and no basis for constitutional complaint as to the standard that the statute directs a court to consider upon a judicial review application.

Also of interest is the decision of the Supreme Court, and especially the dissenting reasons of L'Heureux-Dubé J, in *Canada (Attorney General) v. Mossop*, [1993] 1 SCR 554 (Can.), where the court divided on the extent to which Charter values (in this case, freedom from discrimination) should oust the more traditional concerns and techniques of statutory interpretation. For the majority, which concluded that the term "family status" did not extend to a relationship that was dependent on a same-sex living arrangement, the plain meaning of the statutory language and the clear intention of Parliament not to include sexual orientation as a proscribed ground of discrimination under the *Canadian Human Rights Act* prevailed over the broad, anti-discriminatory purpose of the Act. In contrast, the judgment of L'Heureux-Dubé J emphasized the ambiguity of the statutory text, elaborated its meaning by reference to evolving notions of human rights and to changes in society, and accepted that legislation acquires a life of its own that is to an extent independent of the intention of those who originally enacted it. Can you spot any decision(s) in this chapter where the same sort of difference was played out in the majority as opposed to the dissenting reasons of the court?

CHAPTER FOURTEEN

The Jurisdiction of Tribunals and the Constitution

In this chapter, we consider five questions about the allocation of functions between courts and administrative tribunals when a constitutional issue arises from a dispute that is within the jurisdiction of a statutory court or tribunal.

First, do administrative agencies have jurisdiction to decide Charter or other constitutional challenges to the validity of the legislation that they administer, or are these issues that only superior courts may decide? The second and third questions arise if a positive answer is given to the first. Must a litigant resort exclusively to, or at least exhaust, the statutory remedies specifically provided before going to the superior courts? Third, may administrative agencies grant constitutional remedies and can an administrative tribunal ever be a court of competent jurisdiction for the purposes of s. 24(1), the remedies provision of the Charter? Fourth, what standard of review applies when an administrative agency makes a pronouncement on a constitutional question or provides a constitutional remedy? Finally, to what extent does the court's analysis of jurisdiction and constitutional questions extend also to a tribunal's application of "quasi-constitutional" statutes, such as a human rights code?

THE JURISDICTION OF TRIBUNALS TO DECIDE CONSTITUTIONAL CHALLENGES

It is clear that, in exercising their statutory powers, administrative tribunals should take the constitution including the Charter into account. For instance, they should whenever possible interpret their legislation in a way that is consistent with the constitution. A statutory power that may seem wide enough to authorize the infringement of a Charter-protected right should be "read down": it is a principle of statutory interpretation that legislatures are presumed not to authorize, or to require, unconstitutional conduct. In these cases, the tribunal engages the Charter as part of its general responsibilities for interpreting and applying its enabling statute.

But what if a party to a proceeding over which the tribunal has jurisdiction argues that the tribunal's enabling legislation is invalid, in whole or in part, because it is contrary to the division of powers in ss. 91 and 92 of the *Constitution Act, 1867* or violates a Charter-protected right? Does the administrative tribunal have the legal authority to decide a challenge to the validity of its own legislation? If not, it presumably must either adjourn the proceeding to enable the party to obtain a ruling from the courts, or proceed with the hearing on the assumption that its legislation is valid.

Many tribunals have been faced with these questions; an indication of their practical importance is that the Supreme Court of Canada visited this question on five separate occasions until the issue was resolved with relative clarity in the Supreme Court's decision in *Martin*, excerpted below. This decision is now the starting point for an analysis of whether a tribunal, based on the terms of its empowering statute, has the authority to decide a constitutional question and, in turn, to decline to apply a provision of a statute in a dispute before the tribunal on grounds that the provision is unconstitutional.

Briefly, according to *Martin*, an administrative decision-maker has the authority to decide constitutional questions where, based on its statute, it has the explicit or implicit authority to decide questions of law, unless the authority to decide constitutional questions has been removed, explicitly or implicitly, by the statute. Notably, the *Martin* decision adopted a position of openness to administrative actors interpreting and applying the Charter. This position was reflected originally in the dissent by McLachlin J (as she then was) in *Cooper*, portions of which are also excerpted at the end of this section because of the extent to which they demonstrate the historical differences of view over whether constitutional questions should be decided outside of the courts.

Nova Scotia (Workers' Compensation Board) v. Martin;
Nova Scotia (Workers' Compensation Board) v. Laseur
[2003] 2 SCR 504

GONTHIER J:

I. Introduction

[1] Chronic pain syndrome and related medical conditions have emerged in recent years as one of the most difficult problems facing workers' compensation schemes in Canada and around the world. There is no authoritative definition of chronic pain. It is, however, generally considered to be pain that persists beyond the normal healing time for the underlying injury or is disproportionate to such injury, and whose existence is not supported by objective findings at the site of the injury under current medical techniques. Despite this lack of objective findings, there is no doubt that chronic pain patients are suffering and in distress, and that the disability they experience is real. While there is at this time no clear explanation for chronic pain, recent work on the nervous system suggests that it may result from pathological changes in the nervous mechanisms that result in pain continuing and non-painful stimuli being perceived as painful. These changes, it is believed, may be precipitated by peripheral events, such as an accident, but may persist well beyond the normal recovery time for the precipitating event. Despite this reality, since chronic pain sufferers are impaired by a condition that cannot be supported by objective findings, they have been subjected to persistent suspicions of malingering on the part of employers, compensation officials and even physicians. Ruth Laseur and Donald Martin are the appellants in this case. Both suffer from the disability of chronic pain.

[2] Courts are not the appropriate forum for an evaluation of the available medical evidence concerning chronic pain for general scientific purposes. Nevertheless, because disability is an enumerated ground in s. 15(1) of the *Canadian Charter of Rights and*

Freedoms, the question whether the way in which a government handles chronic pain in providing services amounts to discrimination is a proper subject of judicial review. More specifically, these appeals concern the constitutional validity of s. 10B of the Nova Scotia *Workers' Compensation Act*, SNS 1994-95, c. 10, as amended by SNS 1999, c. 1 (the "Act"), and of the *Functional Restoration (Multi-Faceted Pain Services) Program Regulations*, NS Reg. 57/96 (the "FRP Regulations"), adopted under that Act. These provisions exclude chronic pain from the purview of the regular workers' compensation system and provide, in lieu of the benefits normally available to injured workers, a four-week Functional Restoration (Multi-Faceted Pain Services) Program (the "Functional Restoration Program") beyond which no further benefits are available. A preliminary issue is whether the Nova Scotia Workers' Compensation Appeals Tribunal (the "Appeals Tribunal"), an administrative tribunal set up to hear appeals from decisions of the Workers' Compensation Board of Nova Scotia (the "Board"), had jurisdiction to decline to apply the challenged provisions to the appellants on the ground that these provisions violate the *Charter*.

[3] In my view, the Nova Scotia Court of Appeal erred in concluding that the Appeals Tribunal did not have jurisdiction to consider the constitutionality of the challenged provisions of the Act and the FRP Regulations. I am of the view that the rules concerning the jurisdiction of administrative tribunals to apply the *Charter* established by this Court in *Douglas/Kwantlen Faculty Assn. v. Douglas College*, [1990] 3 SCR 570, *Cuddy Chicks Ltd. v. Ontario (Labour Relations Board)*, [1991] 2 SCR 5, and *Tétreault-Gadoury v. Canada (Employment and Immigration Commission)*, [1991] 2 SCR 22, ought to be reappraised and restated as a clear set of guidelines. Administrative tribunals which have jurisdiction—whether explicit or implied—to decide questions of law arising under a legislative provision are presumed to have concomitant jurisdiction to decide the constitutional validity of that provision. This presumption may only be rebutted by showing that the legislature clearly intended to exclude *Charter* issues from the tribunal's authority over questions of law. To the extent that the majority reasons in *Cooper v. Canada (Human Rights Commission)*, [1996] 3 SCR 854, are inconsistent with this approach, I am of the view that they should no longer be relied upon.

[4] Here, the Nova Scotia legislature expressly conferred on the Appeals Tribunal the authority to decide questions of law by providing, in s. 252(1) of the Act, that it "may confirm, vary or reverse the decision of a hearing officer" exercising the authority conferred upon the Board by s. 185(1) of the Act to "determine all questions of fact and law arising pursuant to this Part." Other provisions of the Act also confirm the legislature's intention that the Appeals Tribunal decide questions of law, for instance by allowing the Chair, under certain circumstances, to direct cases involving "important or novel questions or issues of general significance" or issues of "law and general policy" to the Appeals Tribunal for consideration (s. 199(1) and (2)), and by providing for a further appeal to the Nova Scotia Court of Appeal "on any question of law" (s. 256(1)). The Appeals Tribunal thus has explicit jurisdiction to decide questions of law arising under the challenged provisions, a jurisdiction which is presumed to include the authority to consider their constitutional validity. This presumption is not rebutted in this case, as there is no clear implication arising from the Act that the legislature intended to exclude the *Charter* from the scope of the Appeals Tribunal's authority.

[Gonthier J here summarized his conclusion that the challenged provisions of the Act and its Regulations violated s. 15(1) of the Charter and that the violation was not saved by s. 1 of the Charter. His review of the facts and the decisions below has also been omitted.]

V. Analysis

A. Jurisdiction of the Appeals Tribunal To Apply the Charter

1. The Policy Adopted by This Court in the Trilogy

[27] This Court has examined the jurisdiction of administrative tribunals to consider the constitutional validity of a provision of their enabling statute in *Douglas College, supra*, *Cuddy Chicks, supra*, and *Tétreault-Gadoury, supra* (together, the "trilogy"). On each occasion, the Court emphasized the strong reasons, of principle as well as policy, for allowing administrative tribunals to make such determinations and to refuse to apply a challenged provision found to violate the Constitution.

[28] First, and most importantly, the Constitution is, under s. 52(1) of the *Constitution Act, 1982*, "the supreme law of Canada, and any law that is inconsistent with the provisions of the Constitution is, to the extent of the inconsistency, of no force or effect." The invalidity of a legislative provision inconsistent with the *Charter* does not arise from the fact of its being declared unconstitutional by a court, but from the operation of s. 52(1). Thus, in principle, such a provision is invalid from the moment it is enacted, and a judicial declaration to this effect is but one remedy amongst others to protect those whom it adversely affects. In that sense, by virtue of s. 52(1), the question of constitutional validity inheres in every legislative enactment. Courts may not apply invalid laws, and the same obligation applies to every level and branch of government, including the administrative organs of the state. Obviously, it cannot be the case that every government official has to consider and decide for herself the constitutional validity of every provision she is called upon to apply. If, however, she is endowed with the power to consider questions of law relating to a provision, that power will normally extend to assessing the constitutional validity of that provision. This is because the consistency of a provision with the Constitution is a question of law arising under that provision. It is, indeed, the most fundamental question of law one could conceive, as it will determine whether the enactment is in fact valid law, and thus whether it ought to be interpreted and applied as such or disregarded.

[29] From this principle of constitutional supremacy also flows, as a practical corollary, the idea that Canadians should be entitled to assert the rights and freedoms that the Constitution guarantees them in the most accessible forum available, without the need for parallel proceedings before the courts: see *Douglas College, supra*, at pp. 603-4. In La Forest J's words, "there cannot be a Constitution for arbitrators and another for the courts" (*Douglas College, supra*, at p. 597). This accessibility concern is particularly pressing given that many administrative tribunals have exclusive initial jurisdiction over disputes relating to their enabling legislation, so that forcing litigants to refer *Charter* issues to the courts would result in costly and time-consuming bifurcation of proceedings. As McLachlin J (as she then was) stated in her dissent in *Cooper, supra*, at para. 70:

> The *Charter* is not some holy grail which only judicial initiates of the superior courts may touch. The *Charter* belongs to the people. All law and law-makers that touch the people

must conform to it. Tribunals and commissions charged with deciding legal issues are no exception. Many more citizens have their rights determined by these tribunals than by the courts. If the *Charter* is to be meaningful to ordinary people, then it must find its expression in the decisions of these tribunals.

Similar views had been expressed by the majority in *Weber v. Ontario Hydro*, [1995] 2 SCR 929.

[30] Second, *Charter* disputes do not take place in a vacuum. They require a thorough understanding of the objectives of the legislative scheme being challenged, as well as of the practical constraints it faces and the consequences of proposed constitutional remedies. This need is heightened when, as is often the case, it becomes necessary to determine whether a *prima facie* violation of a *Charter* right is justified under s. 1. In this respect, the factual findings and record compiled by an administrative tribunal, as well as its informed and expert view of the various issues raised by a constitutional challenge, will often be invaluable to a reviewing court: see *Douglas College, supra*, at pp. 604-5. As La Forest J correctly observed in *Cuddy Chicks, supra*, at pp. 16-17:

> It must be emphasized that the process of *Charter* decision making is not confined to abstract ruminations on constitutional theory. In the case of *Charter* matters which arise in a particular regulatory context, the ability of the decision maker to analyze competing policy concerns is critical. ... The informed view of the Board, as manifested in a sensitivity to relevant facts and an ability to compile a cogent record, is also of invaluable assistance.

[31] Third, administrative tribunal decisions based on the *Charter* are subject to judicial review on a correctness standard: see *Cuddy Chicks, supra*, at p. 17. An error of law by an administrative tribunal interpreting the Constitution can always be reviewed fully by a superior court. In addition, the constitutional remedies available to administrative tribunals are limited and do not include general declarations of invalidity. A determination by a tribunal that a provision of its enabling statute is invalid pursuant to the *Charter* is not binding on future decision makers, within or outside the tribunal's administrative scheme. Only by obtaining a formal declaration of invalidity by a court can a litigant establish the general invalidity of a legislative provision for all future cases. Therefore, allowing administrative tribunals to decide *Charter* issues does not undermine the role of the courts as final arbiters of constitutionality in Canada.

[32] In *Douglas College, supra*, La Forest J expressly considered and rejected several general arguments made against recognizing that administrative tribunals that have jurisdiction to decide questions of law possess a concomitant jurisdiction to apply the *Charter*. He noted that some authors had pointed to practical concerns with respect to the desirability of such adjudication, such as the lack of legal expertise of some administrative tribunals, the differences between their rules of procedure and evidence and those followed by courts, and the need to maintain the accessibility and timeliness of their procedures. Nevertheless, La Forest J concluded, at p. 603, that these considerations, "though not without weight, should [not] dissuade this Court from adopting what has now become the clearly dominant view in the courts of this country." Nor, in my view, should such practical considerations surreptitiously find their way back into the courts' analysis of a particular tribunal's jurisdiction despite a clear expression of legislative intent to

endow it with authority to decide questions of law, including constitutional issues. I now turn to the rules governing this analysis.

2. *The Applicable Law*

[33] In view of the policy considerations outlined above, this Court has adopted a general approach for the determination of whether a particular administrative tribunal or agency can decline to apply a provision of its enabling statute on the ground that the provision violates the *Charter*. This approach rests on the principle that, since administrative tribunals are creatures of Parliament and the legislatures, their jurisdiction must in every case "be found in a statute and must extend not only to the subject matter of the application and the parties, but also to the remedy sought": *Douglas College, supra*, at p. 595; see also *Cuddy Chicks, supra*, at pp. 14-15. When a case brought before an administrative tribunal involves a challenge to the constitutionality of a provision of its enabling statute, the tribunal is asked to interpret the relevant *Charter* right, apply it to the impugned provision, and if it finds a breach and concludes that the provision is not saved under s. 1, to disregard the provision on constitutional grounds and rule on the applicant's claim as if the impugned provision were not in force.

[34] Since the subject matter and the remedy in such a case are premised on the application of the *Charter*, the question becomes whether the tribunal's mandate includes jurisdiction to rule on the constitutionality of the challenged provision: see *Douglas College, supra*, at p. 596; *Cuddy Chicks, supra*, at p. 15. This question is answered by applying a presumption, based on the principle of constitutional supremacy outlined above, that all legal decisions will take into account the supreme law of the land. Thus, as a rule, "an administrative tribunal which has been conferred the power to interpret law holds a concomitant power to determine whether that law is constitutionally valid": *Cuddy Chicks, supra*, at p. 13; or, as stated in *Cooper, supra*, at para. 46:

> If a tribunal does have the power to consider questions of law, then it follows by the operation of s. 52(1) that it must be able to address constitutional issues, including the constitutional validity of its enabling statute.

While the general principles outlined above have been consistently reaffirmed by this Court and remain sound, their application has been fraught with difficulties, as evidenced by the disagreements that arose in *Cooper, supra*. I am of the view that it is now time to reappraise the case law and to provide a single set of rules concerning the jurisdiction of administrative tribunals to consider *Charter* challenges to a legislative provision.

[35] In each case, the first question to be addressed is whether the administrative tribunal at issue has jurisdiction, explicit or implied, to decide questions of law arising under the challenged provision. While, as stated in the trilogy and *Cooper, supra*, this question is one of legislative intent, it is crucial that the relevant intent be clearly defined. The question is not whether Parliament or the legislature intended the tribunal to apply the *Charter*. As has often been pointed out, such an attribution of intent would be artificial, given that many of the relevant enabling provisions pre-date the *Charter*. ... That attribution of intent would also be incompatible with the principle stated above that the question of constitutional validity inheres in every legislative enactment by virtue of

s. 52(1) of the *Constitution Act, 1982*. Therefore, in my view, to the extent that passages in the trilogy and *Cooper, supra*, suggest that the relevant legislative intention to be sought is one that the tribunal apply the *Charter* itself, those passages should be disregarded.

[36] Rather, one must ask whether the empowering legislation implicitly or explicitly grants to the tribunal the jurisdiction to interpret or decide *any* question of law. If it does, then the tribunal will be presumed to have the concomitant jurisdiction to interpret or decide that question in light of the *Charter*, unless the legislator has removed that power from the tribunal. Thus, an administrative tribunal that has the power to decide questions of law arising under a particular legislative provision will be presumed to have the power to determine the constitutional validity of that provision. In other words, the power to decide a question of law is the power to decide by applying only valid laws.

[37] Often the statute will expressly confer on the tribunal jurisdiction to decide certain questions of law. Thus, in *Cuddy Chicks, supra*, the Ontario *Labour Relations Act* granted the Labour Relations Board jurisdiction "to determine all questions of fact or law that arise in any matter before it." This provision was held to provide a clear jurisdictional basis for the Labour Relations Board to consider the constitutional validity of a provision of the *Labour Relations Act* excluding agricultural employees from its purview. Yet, while obviously adequate, such a broad grant of jurisdiction is not necessary to confer on an administrative tribunal the power to apply the *Charter*. It suffices that the legislator endow the tribunal with power to decide questions of law arising under the challenged provision, and that the constitutional question relate to that provision.

[38] This nuance was sometimes overlooked in the trilogy. Thus, in *Douglas College, supra*, La Forest J held that an arbitration board had jurisdiction to apply the *Charter* to a provision in the collective agreement that the board was empowered to interpret and apply. While that conclusion was certainly correct, courts should use some care in relying on the reasoning used to support it. The British Columbia *Labour Code* provided that the arbitration board had authority to "interpret and apply any Act intended to regulate the employment relationship of the persons bound by a collective agreement." La Forest J found that the *Charter* was intended to be included within the meaning of the term "Act" in that section. With respect, I believe the better view is that, since the board had undisputed jurisdiction to decide questions of law arising under the collective agreement, and the agreement constituted "law" within the meaning of s. 52(1) of the *Constitution Act, 1982*, the board could consider the constitutional validity of the agreement's provisions. This conclusion would have been true regardless of whether the *Charter* is truly an "Act intended to regulate the employment relationship of the persons bound by a collective agreement."

[39] In other words, the relevant question in each case is not whether the terms of the express grant of jurisdiction are sufficiently broad to encompass the *Charter* itself, but rather whether the express grant of jurisdiction confers upon the tribunal the power to decide questions of law arising under the challenged provision, in which case the tribunal will be presumed to have jurisdiction to decide the constitutional validity of that provision. The *Charter* is not invoked as a separate subject matter; rather, it is a controlling norm in decisions over matters within the tribunal's jurisdiction.

[40] In cases where the empowering legislation contains an express grant of jurisdiction to decide questions of law, there is no need to go beyond the language of the statute. An express grant of authority to consider or decide questions of law arising under

a legislative provision is presumed to extend to determining the constitutional validity of that provision.

[41] Absent an explicit grant, it becomes necessary to consider whether the legislator intended to confer upon the tribunal implied jurisdiction to decide questions of law arising under the challenged provision. Implied jurisdiction must be discerned by looking at the statute as a whole. Relevant factors will include the statutory mandate of the tribunal in issue and whether deciding questions of law is necessary to fulfilling this mandate effectively; the interaction of the tribunal in question with other elements of the administrative system; whether the tribunal is adjudicative in nature; and practical considerations, including the tribunal's capacity to consider questions of law. Practical considerations, however, cannot override a clear implication from the statute itself, particularly when depriving the tribunal of the power to decide questions of law would impair its capacity to fulfill its intended mandate. As is the case for explicit jurisdiction, if the tribunal is found to have implied jurisdiction to decide questions of law arising under a legislative provision, this power will be presumed to include jurisdiction to determine the constitutional validity of that provision.

[42] Once this presumption has been raised, either by an explicit or implicit grant of authority to decide questions of law, the second question that arises is whether it has been rebutted. The burden of establishing this lies on the party who alleges that the administrative body at issue lacks jurisdiction to apply the *Charter*. In general terms, the presumption may only be rebutted by an explicit withdrawal of authority to decide constitutional questions or by a clear implication to the same effect, arising from the statute itself rather than from external considerations. The question to be asked is whether an examination of the statutory provisions clearly leads to the conclusion that the legislature intended to exclude the *Charter*, or more broadly, a category of questions of law encompassing the *Charter*, from the scope of the questions of law to be addressed by the tribunal. For instance, an express conferral of jurisdiction to another administrative body to consider *Charter* issues or certain complex questions of law deemed too difficult or time-consuming for the initial decision maker, along with a procedure allowing such issues to be efficiently redirected to such body, could give rise to a clear implication that the initial decision maker was not intended to decide constitutional questions.

[43] As La Forest J stated in *Tétreault-Gadoury, supra*, at p. 33, "the power to interpret law is not one which the legislature has conferred lightly upon administrative tribunals." When a legislature chooses to do so, whether explicitly or by implication, the courts must assume that the administrative body at issue was intended to be an appropriate forum for the resolution of complex legal issues, including the interpretation and application of the *Charter*. Thus, while, as noted above, considerations concerning an administrative body's practical capacity to address such issues may be relevant in determining the scope of a tribunal's implicit authority to decide questions of law, they generally will not suffice on their own to rebut the presumption that arises from such authority, whether explicit or implied, once that presumption has been found to apply. In my view, lower court cases which suggest otherwise, such as *Bell Canada v. Canada (Human Rights Commission)*, [2001] 2 FC 392 (TD), rev'd on other grounds, [2001] 3 FC 481 (CA), and *Canada (Minister of Citizenship and Immigration) v. Reynolds* (1997), 139 FTR 315, as well as the Court of Appeal's decision in the present case, are erroneous in this respect.

[44] I refrain, however, from expressing any opinion as to the constitutionality of a provision that would place procedural barriers in the way of claimants seeking to assert their rights in a timely and effective manner, for instance by removing *Charter* jurisdiction from a tribunal without providing an effective alternative administrative route for *Charter* claims.

[45] In applying the approach set out above, there is in my view no need to draw any distinction between "general" and "limited" questions of law, as was admittedly done in *Cooper, supra*. An administrative body will normally either have or not have the power to decide questions of law. As stated above, administrative bodies that do have that power may presumptively go beyond the bounds of their enabling statute and decide issues of common law or statutory interpretation that arise in the course of a case properly before them, subject to judicial review on the appropriate standard: see, e.g., *McLeod v. Egan*, [1975] 1 SCR 517; *David Taylor & Son, Ltd. v. Barnett*, [1953] 1 All ER 843 (CA); *Canadian Broadcasting Corp. v. Canada (Labour Relations Board)*, [1995] 1 SCR 157. Absent a clear expression or implication of contrary intent, such administrative bodies will also have jurisdiction to subject the statutory provisions over which they have jurisdiction to *Charter* scrutiny, while those tribunals without power to decide questions of law will not.

[46] In *Cooper, supra*, this Court considered the jurisdiction of the Canadian Human Rights Commission or a tribunal appointed by it to consider the validity of s. 15(c) of the *Canadian Human Rights Act* under s. 15(1) of the *Charter*. The challenged section provided that no discrimination occurred when persons were forced to retire at the normal age for employees working in similar positions in the same industry. La Forest J first noted the absence of any explicit grant of jurisdiction to consider questions of law, which raised the need to determine whether such jurisdiction was implied. Turning to an examination of the statutory scheme under the *Canadian Human Rights Act*, he concluded that Parliament did not intend the Commission to decide questions of law arising under s. 15(c), but rather to serve as a screening mechanism for a tribunal endowed with broader jurisdiction to decide such questions as well as with greater capacity to do so. In those specific circumstances, he concluded that a series of well-circumscribed provisions allowing the Commission to consider other questions of law necessary to the exercise of its limited statutory functions as a screening body could not endow it with such power.

[47] In my view, the result reached in *Cooper* could have been reached under the current restated rules, given La Forest J's finding that the Commission had no authority, either explicit or implicit, to decide questions of law arising under s. 15(c) of the *Canadian Human Rights Act*. It is thus unnecessary at this time to revisit the holding in that case. To the extent that it is incompatible with the present reasons, however, I am of the view that the *ratio* of the majority judgment in *Cooper* is no longer good law. This is particularly true insofar as it implies that the distinction between general and limited questions of law is generally relevant to the analysis of an administrative tribunal's jurisdiction to apply the *Charter*, or that the adjudicative nature of the administrative body is a necessary (or even preponderant) factor in the search for implicit jurisdiction. Likewise, the views expressed by Lamer CJ in his concurrence are at odds with the current approach and should not be relied on.

[48] The current, restated approach to the jurisdiction of administrative tribunals to subject legislative provisions to *Charter* scrutiny can be summarized as follows: (1) The first

question is whether the administrative tribunal has jurisdiction, explicit *or* implied, to decide questions of law arising under the challenged provision. (2)(a) Explicit jurisdiction must be found in the terms of the statutory grant of authority. (b) Implied jurisdiction must be discerned by looking at the statute as a whole. Relevant factors will include the statutory mandate of the tribunal in issue and whether deciding questions of law is necessary to fulfilling this mandate effectively; the interaction of the tribunal in question with other elements of the administrative system; whether the tribunal is adjudicative in nature; and practical considerations, including the tribunal's capacity to consider questions of law. Practical considerations, however, cannot override a clear implication from the statute itself. (3) If the tribunal is found to have jurisdiction to decide questions of law arising under a legislative provision, this power will be presumed to include jurisdiction to determine the constitutional validity of that provision under the *Charter*. (4) The party alleging that the tribunal lacks jurisdiction to apply the *Charter* may rebut the presumption by (a) pointing to an explicit withdrawal of authority to consider the *Charter*; or (b) convincing the court that an examination of the statutory scheme clearly leads to the conclusion that the legislature intended to exclude the *Charter* (or a category of questions that would include the *Charter*, such as constitutional questions generally) from the scope of the questions of law to be addressed by the tribunal. Such an implication should generally arise from the statute itself, rather than from external considerations.

3. Application to the Facts

[49] In the case at bar, the jurisdiction of the Board is primarily determined by s. 185(1) of the Act. That provision states that "[s]ubject to the rights of appeal provided in this Act, the Board has exclusive jurisdiction to inquire into, hear and determine all questions of fact and law arising pursuant to this Part." The right of appeal contemplated by this section is to the Appeals Tribunal, which under s. 243 and s. 252(1) "may confirm, vary or reverse the decision of a hearing officer." It follows, then, that s. 185(1) also confers upon the Appeals Tribunal jurisdiction to "determine all questions of fact and law arising pursuant to this Part." This provision is, of course, almost identical to the one considered by this Court in *Cuddy Chicks*. In addition, s. 256(1) allows for an appeal from the Appeals Tribunal to the Nova Scotia Court of Appeal "on any question of law," which suggests that the Appeals Tribunal may deal initially with such questions.

[50] Section 10B is found in Part I of the Act, and the FRP Regulations were adopted under that Part. Thus, it is clear that the Act confers upon the Appeals Tribunal explicit jurisdiction to decide questions of law arising under the challenged provisions.

[51] Given this conclusion, it is not strictly necessary to consider other aspects of the statutory scheme or the practical considerations raised by the respondents. Nevertheless, since much of the parties' submissions relate to considerations of this nature, and since I believe that an examination of the statutory scheme as a whole supports the conclusion that the legislature intended the Appeals Tribunal to decide questions of law, I will discuss this question briefly. I repeat, however, that the explicit jurisdiction to determine questions of law would alone have been determinative.

[52] First, and most importantly, there can be no doubt that the power to decide questions of law arising under the Act is necessary in order for the Appeals Tribunal ef-

fectively to fulfill its mandate. Any conclusion to the contrary would contradict the legislature's clear intent to create a comprehensive scheme for resolving workers' compensation disputes, notably by barring access to the courts in cases covered by the Act: see *Pasiechnyk v. Saskatchewan (Workers' Compensation Board)*, [1997] 2 SCR 890, at paras. 23-29. Moreover, the Appeals Tribunal's implied jurisdiction clearly extends even beyond the Act itself, to other questions of statutory interpretation or common law raised in the course of a dispute arising from the operation of the workers' compensation scheme. This conclusion is supported by the common law presumption, alluded to above, that administrative tribunals can interpret laws other than their enabling statute when necessary to resolve a case over which they otherwise have jurisdiction, subject to judicial review. It is also consistent with the practice of the Appeals Tribunal, which regularly decides questions of law involving the interpretation of common law principles and statutes other than the Act. These questions include the law of contracts, evidence, causation, employment, corporate relationships, conflicts of law, administration of foreign workers' compensation schemes, and motor vehicles, to name but a few. Denying the Appeals Tribunal the authority to decide such questions would seriously impede its work and threaten the access by injured workers to a forum capable of deciding all aspects of their case.

[53] Second, the Appeals Tribunal is fully adjudicative in nature. It is independent of the Board and is placed under the supervision of the Minister of Justice, whereas the Board is supervised by the Minister of Labour. The Appeals Tribunal establishes its own rules of procedure (s. 240(1)), can consider all relevant evidence (s. 246(1)), and records any oral evidence for future reference (s. 253(1)). Its members have the powers, privileges and immunities of a commissioner appointed under the *Public Inquiries Act*, RSNS 1989, c. 372 (s. 178(1)), including the power to summon witnesses, compel testimony, require production of documents, and punish persons guilty of contempt; they also have certain powers of entry (s. 180). Although the Appeals Tribunal is normally required to render its decision within 60 days of the hearing, or if there is no hearing, of the day on which all submissions have been received (s. 246(3)), it may "at any time, extend any time limit prescribed by this Part or the regulations where, in the opinion of the Appeals Tribunal, an injustice would otherwise result" (s. 240(2)). This extension power allows it to give proper consideration to the more intricate issues raised by a *Charter* appeal, as was done in this case. While only the Chief Appeal Commissioner is required to be a practising lawyer (s. 238(5)), in reality all appeal commissioners have been admitted to the bar. Moreover, this Court has recognized that non-lawyers sitting on specialized tribunals can make important contributions to *Charter* adjudication: *Cuddy Chicks, supra*, at pp. 16-17. In my view, there is no reason to doubt that the Appeals Tribunal is an adjudicative body fully capable of deciding *Charter* issues, as demonstrated by its competent reasons on the s. 15(1) issue in the case at bar.

[54] I hasten to add, however, that while the presence of an adjudicative process is an important factor in finding an implied power to decide questions of law, its absence would not by itself be determinative. An examination of the statutory scheme as a whole may lead to the conclusion that the legislature intended a non-adjudicative body to consider and decide questions of law.

[55] Third, under the *Constitutional Questions Act*, RSNS 1989, c. 89, and under s. 245(1)(d) of the Act, the Attorney General may be provided with an opportunity to

intervene in any proceedings involving a constitutional question, as was done in this case. Such interventions diminish the relative disadvantage of administrative tribunals as compared to courts by relieving private parties or administrative agencies from the burden of defending the validity of legislation: see *Cuddy Chicks, supra*, at pp. 17-18.

[56] Finally, the Court of Appeal was wrong to take into consideration the backlog of cases that had accumulated at the Appeals Tribunal prior to the 1999 amendments. Practical considerations of this nature, while they may in certain circumstances be helpful to confirm the legislature's intent, are of little weight when faced with clear legislative intent, arising from the statutory scheme as a whole, to confer upon an administrative body the power to consider and decide questions of law. Such considerations "can never supplant the intention of the legislature" (*Cooper, supra*, at para. 47). Moreover, as the Appeals Tribunal itself argues in its submissions, the backlog has since been completely eliminated. Counsel for the Appeals Tribunal informed us at the hearing that *Charter* challenges were not the cause of the backlog and would not significantly increase its workload or cause undue delay. Since the Appeals Tribunal itself does not believe that deciding *Charter* cases would aggravate matters, and in the absence of other evidence, I fail to see on what basis the Court of Appeal could have reached such a conclusion. In contrast, allowing the Appeals Tribunal to apply the *Charter* clearly furthers the policy objectives outlined in the trilogy. It allows courts to benefit from a full record established by a specialized tribunal fully apprised of the policy and practical issues relevant to the *Charter* claim, and permits workers to have their *Charter* rights recognized within the relatively fast and inexpensive adjudicative scheme created by the Act, rather than having to take separate proceedings in the courts in addition to their compensation claim before the administrative tribunal.

[57] These aspects of the legislative scheme all militate in favour of allowing the Appeals Tribunal to apply the *Charter*, in conformity with the legislature's intent to create a comprehensive scheme for the treatment of workers' compensation claims and related disputes. Thus, even if there had been no express provision endowing the Appeals Tribunal to consider and decide questions of law arising under the Act, I would have found that it had implied jurisdiction to do so. I have already noted that, in assessing implied jurisdiction, the adjudicative or non-adjudicative character of a tribunal is not dispositive. Given the rich variety of administrative schemes and enabling statutes, I would not wish to suggest either that the other factors present in this case are individually or collectively essential to finding implied jurisdiction to decide questions of law. The question is, in each case, to be decided by looking at the relevant statutory scheme as a whole.

[58] The Appeals Tribunal's jurisdiction to decide questions of law arising under the challenged provisions is presumed to include the authority to consider their constitutional validity. Is this presumption rebutted by other provisions of the Act?

[59] The respondents argue that the authority conferred upon the Chair of the Board to direct certain issues from the Appeals Tribunal to the Board of Directors is incompatible with the idea that the Appeals Tribunal was itself intended by the legislature to decide *Charter* questions. Surely, it is said, the legislature cannot have intended that *Charter* issues be postponed to a policy-making executive body with no special expertise or powers of ultimate disposition of the issue. I disagree with this description of the procedure allowed by the Act. Section 248(1) provides that the Chair may postpone or adjourn an

appeal before the Appeals Tribunal when he or she is of the opinion that the appeal raises "an issue of law and general policy that should be reviewed by the Board of Directors pursuant to Section 183." It is s. 183 that grants the Board of Directors authority to adopt policies. Pursuant to s. 202(a), an adjournment to the Board of Directors lasts no longer than three months or, "where the Board determines that exceptional circumstances exist," twelve months. If the Board of Directors issues a policy with respect to the issue raised in the appeal or notifies the hearing officer that it will not issue a policy, the postponement also comes to an end. Section 248(3) provides that "where the Chair postpones or adjourns a hearing pursuant to subsection (1), the Chief Appeal Commissioner shall ensure that the final disposition of the appeal is left solely to the independent judgment of the Appeals Tribunal."

[60] In my view, these provisions do no more than allow the Board of Directors to respond to the issues of law and general policy raised by an appeal by adopting a policy on the matter, enabling the Workers' Compensation Board to deal consistently with future similar cases on a principled basis. As s. 248(3) attests, this does not mean that the Board of Directors is entitled to take over an appeal raising a *Charter* issue and decide the issue itself. Rather, at most, the Board of Directors can suspend the appeal for up to twelve months in order to adopt a policy that properly responds to the general issues raised. For instance, the Board of Directors may recognize that one of its policies is inconsistent with the *Charter* or the Act and reformulate that policy, rather than litigating the *Charter* issue further. If the Board of Directors declines to do so, or if the policy as reformulated remains inconsistent with the *Charter* or the Act, the Appeals Tribunal will have the authority to refuse to apply that policy when the appeal is resumed. This is the effect of s. 183(5A), which provides that "a policy adopted by the Board is only binding on the Appeals Tribunal where the policy is consistent with this Part or the regulations." In addition, as the Appeals Tribunal correctly pointed out, even taking into consideration the additional delay that may be imposed by the Chair, the cost and length of an appeal before the Appeals Tribunal would still compare favourably to those of a *Charter* challenge before the courts.

[61] Consequently, nothing in the Act produces the kind of clear implication capable of rebutting the presumption that the Appeals Tribunal may consider the constitutionality of the Act that it is called upon to interpret and apply. The Appeals Tribunal could properly consider and decide the *Charter* issue raised in this case because it could properly consider and decide questions of law.

4. *The Relationship Between the Charter Jurisdictions of the Board and the Appeals Tribunal*

[62] The reasons outlined in the previous section establish that, even if s. 185(1) of the Act had not provided the Appeals Tribunal with explicit authority to decide questions of law, an examination of the statutory scheme set out by the Act would lead to the conclusion that it has implied authority to do so. The determinative explicit conferral of jurisdiction in this case raises one last question. Section 185(1) of the Act defines the jurisdiction of both the Board and the Appeals Tribunal. Therefore, our holding that this section confers explicit jurisdiction upon the Appeals Tribunal to decide questions of

law, including *Charter* issues, appears to lead to the conclusion that such jurisdiction is also vested in the Board, despite the considerably different characteristics of its claims adjudication process. In particular, I note a distinction between the Appeals Tribunal and the Board. In its submissions, the Appeals Tribunal argued confidently for its ability to apply the *Charter*. In contrast, the Board itself argues that it does not possess the resources or expertise to deal with numerous *Charter* cases, and that doing so would compromise its efficiency and timeliness in handling vast numbers of compensation cases.

[63] Of course, as a matter of statutory interpretation, the Board's own view is not determinative of its jurisdiction. As La Forest J noted in *Cuddy Chicks*, referring to the Ontario Labour Relations Board (at p. 18):

> At the end of the day, the legal process will be better served where the Board makes an initial determination of the jurisdictional issue arising from a constitutional challenge. *In such circumstances, the Board not only has the authority but a duty to ascertain the constitutional validity of s. 2(b) of the Labour Relations Act.* [Emphasis added.]

Likewise, in the present appeals, the Act clearly contemplates that the Board will decide questions of law. Practical considerations cannot override the clear expression of legislative intent in s. 185(1). The legislature also seems to have contemplated, however, that it may be preferable, as a matter of administrative convenience, to refer *Charter* questions raised before the Board to the Appeals Tribunal or to the courts. Thus, s. 199(1)(b) provides that when a hearing officer "is of the opinion ... that an appeal raises important or novel questions or issues of general significance that should be decided by the Appeals Tribunal pursuant to Part II, ... the hearing officer shall postpone or adjourn the appeal and refer the appeal to the Chair." The Chair may then, under s. 199(2)(b) and (c), refer the appeal to the Appeals Tribunal or return it to the hearing officer. Likewise, under s. 200(1)(b), when an appeal before a hearing officer raises such questions, the Chair "may postpone or adjourn the appeal and direct that the appeal be ... heard and decided by the Appeals Tribunal."

[64] Under these provisions, it seems to be entirely within the Board's discretion to refer complex *Charter* cases to the Appeals Tribunal, either on a case-by-case basis or as a matter of policy. As noted above, since an administrative process which avoids parallel proceedings in the courts is preserved, I believe that the Board would not infringe its duty to consider the constitutionality of the Act by referring such cases to the Appeals Tribunal: see generally *Tétreault-Gadoury, supra*, at pp. 35-36. Therefore, I believe that the practical concerns raised by the respondents concerning the Board's capacity to handle complex *Charter* cases do not require a conclusion that either the Board or the Appeals Tribunal lacks jurisdiction to apply the *Charter*. On the contrary, they explain the choice made by the legislature in providing a procedural mechanism to allow such complex issues to be redirected from the Board to the Appeals Tribunal when the Chair of the Board of Directors deems it appropriate.

5. Conclusion

[65] I conclude that the Appeals Tribunal has explicit jurisdiction to decide questions of law arising under the challenged provisions of the Act. It is thus presumed to have

jurisdiction to consider the validity of these provisions under s. 15(1) of the *Charter*, and to disregard these provisions if it finds them to be unconstitutional. This presumption is not rebutted by the statute, either explicitly or by necessary implication. Since the remedy requested arises from s. 52(1) of the *Constitution Act, 1982*, it is not necessary to determine whether the Appeals Tribunal is a "court of competent jurisdiction" within the meaning of s. 24(1) of the *Charter*: see *Douglas College, supra*, at pp. 594-95 and 605. However, as the Appeals Tribunal's decision on the constitutionality of the challenged provisions is to be reviewed on a correctness standard, I now turn to the substantive *Charter* questions.

[Gonthier J's analysis of ss. 15 and 1 of the Charter has been omitted.]

The test that was applied by the Supreme Court in *Martin* had been developed in earlier cases, including *Cooper* below. However, *Martin* refined the application of that test in important ways. For one, the court adopted a liberal approach to its interpretation of whether an administrative decision-maker was implicitly granted the authority to decide questions of law, alongside a restrictive approach to the issue of whether the decision-maker's authority to decide constitutional questions was implicitly removed. This effectively expanded the likelihood that administrative actors would be deemed to have the authority to decide constitutional questions. In addition, the court clarified in *Martin* that policy considerations could not be used to rebut a presumption, based on an explicit or implicit statutory granting of the authority to decide questions of law, that a decision-maker was authorized to decide constitutional questions. In reviewing the following excerpts from *Cooper*, consider the underlying debate over whether administrative actors should be permitted to decide constitutional questions as well as those aspects of the reasons of La Forest J and (more obviously) of Lamer CJ that were overturned in *Martin*.

The decision in *Martin* reaffirmed a flexible approach of the Supreme Court—originally laid out in the trilogy of *Douglas College*, *Cuddy Chicks*, and *Tétreault-Gadoury*—to the power of administrative tribunals to decline to apply a provision on the basis that it failed to comply with (often broadly framed) Charter rights. This remedial power is unlike that of a court acting under s. 24(1) of the Charter or s. 52(1) of the *Constitution Act, 1982* in that an administrative decision-maker's determination of constitutionality, as a matter of law, is limited to the particular case before it and does not extend to the validity of the provision as a whole. This reflects the fact that the authority of a tribunal to find a provision unconstitutional derives not from the constitution but from the tribunal's authorizing statute.

However, before *Martin*, the Supreme Court had for a time adopted a much more restrictive position based on its assessment of institutional and policy consequences of allowing particular decision-makers to decide constitutional questions. In *Cooper*, reservations were expressed by a majority of the Supreme Court on the prospect of the Canadian Human Rights Commission deciding constitutional questions, most fundamentally by Lamer CJ but also in the "pragmatic and functional policy concerns" of La Forest J, writing for the majority. As we saw in *Martin*, the role of these policy concerns has now been discounted in favour of an emphasis on interpretive presumptions arising from the language of the decision-maker's authorizing Act. But they are still worth considering as an illustration of deeper questions of the separation of powers and parliamentary sovereignty, for example, which inescapably arise when a legislature or a court is allocating the power to decide whether a law is unconstitutional.

Cooper v. Canada (Human Rights Commission)
[1996] 3 SCR 854 (Can.)

LAMER CJ:

Introduction

These appeals are the latest in a series of decisions from this Court which have examined the ability of administrative tribunals to determine the constitutionality of their enabling legislation. Although my colleagues disagree on the outcome of these appeals, they nevertheless agree on the governing legal proposition: that tribunals which have jurisdiction over the general law, have jurisdiction to refuse to apply—and hence effectively to render inoperative—laws that they find to be unconstitutional, since through the operation of s. 52 of the *Constitution Act, 1982*, the Constitution is the supreme law of Canada. I agree with them that this proposition emerges from previous decisions of this Court and that it binds us today. However, I hope that a full bench of this Court will eventually be afforded the opportunity to revisit this proposition.

Although there are pragmatic reasons for reconsidering that proposition, my concerns mainly emerge from a consideration of some of the fundamental features of the Canadian constitutional order. Canada is a Parliamentary democracy, and is hence based on the belief that those who exercise public power should be held accountable to the electorate. Legislation is the ultimate embodiment of that public power, because it reflects the measured and considered judgment of the legislature itself on a matter of public policy. In Canada, the decisions of our democratic institutions are subject to judicial review, which allows courts to strike down the enactments of those legislatures when those enactments contradict constitutional norms. Although judicial review is necessary to preserve important constitutional values, in a democracy like Canada it is inherently controversial, because it confers on unelected officials the power to question decisions which are arrived at through the democratic process. For this reason, in my view, *as a matter of constitutional principle* that power must be reserved to the courts and should not be given over to bodies that are mere creatures of the legislature, whose members are usually vulnerable to removal with every change of government, and whose decisions in some circumstances are made within the parameters of guidelines established by the executive branch of government.

I fear that in seeking to give the fullest possible effect to the Charter's promise of rights-protection, the previous judgments of this Court may have misunderstood and distorted the web of institutional relationships between the legislature, the executive and the judiciary which continue to form the backbone of our constitutional system, even in the post-Charter era. This distortion has been achieved by giving administrative tribunals access to s. 52. But in my opinion, s. 52 can only be used by the courts of this country, because the task of declaring invalid legislation enacted by a democratically elected legislature is within the exclusive domain of the judiciary. I should make it very clear at the outset of my reasons that I *am not* addressing the role of administrative tribunals in relation to s. 24(1) of the *Canadian Charter of Rights and Freedoms*.

. . .

The Issue in This Case

I approach this *conceptual* problem by reference to the *practical* question which my colleagues address in this case—did Parliament intend to confer on the Canadian Human Rights Commission, and on tribunals which adjudicate upon the *Canadian Human Rights Act*, RSC 1985, c. H-6, the power to decide general questions of law? Justices La Forest and McLachlin agree that the bodies in question have not been expressly granted this power. Where they disagree is whether those bodies have the implied jurisdiction to consider the general law. ...

[I]n my respectful opinion, this exercise is deeply flawed because the premise upon which my colleagues rely—that the intent to confer on tribunals a power to interpret general law in turn implies an intent to confer on tribunals a power to refuse systematically to apply laws which violate the Charter—is suspect. I say that for two reasons. One is that such an inference is artificial. Many, if not most of the tribunals which have been set up by Parliament and the provincial legislatures were created *before* the enactment of the Charter in 1982. Granting the power to tribunals to refuse systemically to apply laws which violate the Charter could not have possibly been within the contemplation of Canada's legislatures. ...

Moreover, inferring the power to refuse systematically to apply laws which violate the Charter from the power to interpret and apply the general law strikes me as profoundly illogical. A legislature could only intend to confer on a tribunal the power to judge the constitutionality of that tribunal's enabling legislation if the legislature had knowingly passed a constitutionally suspect law; otherwise, the conferral of the power would be unnecessary. But it is very hard to imagine a situation in which a legislature would know that it was passing constitutionally suspect legislation. If anything, the presumption of constitutionality seems to suggest that legislatures assume the constitutionality of their enactments. In any event, if the legislature did know that a piece of legislation was constitutionally suspect, and nonetheless enacted it into law, it is not readily apparent why the legislature would also confer on the tribunal to which the legislature assigns the responsibility of giving effect to that legislation the power to hold various provisions of the legislation inoperative. Surely, a legislature intent on passing a constitutionally suspect law would not plant within that law the seeds of its own demise.

The suspect nature of the inference that jurisdiction over the general law in turn leads to jurisdiction over the Charter requires us to return to the first principles of the Constitution, in order to comprehend properly the relationship between s. 52 and administrative tribunals. I will discuss two of these principles here. These are the separation of powers and Parliamentary democracy.

The Separation of Powers

. . .

The centrality of courts to determinations of constitutional validity suggests that no other bodies should exercise this function. Indeed, this Court openly acknowledged in *Cuddy Chicks* that a tribunal *could not* make a declaration of invalidity, because it was not a court: *Cuddy Chicks, supra*, at p. 17. Thus, even in that decision, there was a recognition of the fundamental constitutional difference between courts and tribunals. However, despite the Court's awareness of this difference, the Court in that case rejected the view that when a tribunal refuses to apply its enabling legislation for the purposes of the proceeding before it, it effectively makes a declaration of invalidity: *Cuddy Chicks*, at p. 17; also see *Douglas College, supra*, at p. 599. However, the distinction between declarations of invalidity and refusals to apply is hard to sustain. The distinction relies on the assumption that decisions of one tribunal do not bind another tribunal operating under the same statutory regime.

. . .

The *de facto* equivalence between refusals to apply and declarations of invalidity decisively demonstrates that tribunals, when they refuse to apply their enabling legislation under s. 52 of the *Constitution Act, 1982*, are improperly exercising the role of the courts. As a result, the decisions of this Court which authorize tribunals to overstep their constitutional role, in my opinion, are in serious need of revision. Furthermore, although the case at bar concerns the implied power to decide Charter questions, I would even go so far as to say that tribunals cannot be *expressly* given the power to consider the constitutionality of their enabling legislation, for the same reasons. ...

Parliamentary Democracy

The assumption by administrative tribunals of jurisdiction over the Charter does no less than to invert this hierarchical relationship. Instead of putting the intent of the legislature into effect, the case law of this Court enables tribunals to challenge the decisions of the democratically elected legislature "by the assertion of overriding constitutional norm." ... Instead of being subject to the laws of the legislature, the executive can defeat the laws of the legislature. On each occasion that this occurs, a tribunal has disrupted the proper constitutional relationship between it and the legislature. Indeed, I would go so far as to say that a tribunal has, in these circumstances, unconstitutionally usurped power which it did not have.

The unconstitutional usurpation of power by tribunals can be illustrated by the decision of this Court in *Cuddy Chicks*. In that case, the Ontario Labour Relations Board (OLRB) held that a provision of its enabling legislation which barred agricultural workers from access to collective bargaining violated the equality rights guaranteed by s. 15 of the Charter. That decision was upheld by this Court. The effect of the decision, of course, was to expand the jurisdiction of the OLRB to cover a class of persons whom the legislature had decided should not have the right to collectively bargain. Instead of the legislature's determining the jurisdiction of the OLRB, the OLRB determined its own jurisdiction.

I cannot imagine that the intent of the framers of the Charter was to alter so fundamentally the nature of the relationship between the executive and the legislature.

La FOREST J (Sopinka, Gonthier and Iacobucci JJ concurring): At issue in these appeals is whether the Canadian Human Rights Commission or a tribunal appointed by it to investigate a complaint has power to determine the constitutionality of a provision of their enabling statute, the *Canadian Human Rights Act*, RSC 1985, c. H-6. In particular, is it open to the Commission to ignore s. 15(c) of the Act, which provides that it is not a discriminatory practice for an individual to be terminated from employment because that individual has reached the normal age of retirement for employees in similar positions?

· · ·

Analysis
· · ·

In three previous cases, *Douglas College, supra*, *Cuddy Chicks, supra*, and *Tétreault-Gadoury, supra*, this Court has had the opportunity to address the principles underlying an administrative tribunal's jurisdiction to consider the constitutionality of its enabling statute. These authorities make it clear that no administrative tribunal has an independent source of jurisdiction pursuant to s. 52(1) of the *Constitution Act, 1982*. Rather, the essential question facing a court is one of statutory interpretation—has the legislature, in this case Parliament, granted the administrative tribunal through its enabling statute the power to determine questions of law? ...

The power of an administrative tribunal to consider Charter issues was addressed recently by this Court in *Douglas/Kwantlen Faculty Assn. v. Douglas College*. ... That case concerned the jurisdiction of an arbitration board, appointed by the parties under a collective agreement in conjunction with the British Columbia *Labour Code*, to determine the constitutionality of a mandatory retirement provision in the collective agreement. In ruling that the arbitrator did have such jurisdiction, this Court articulated the basic principle that an administrative tribunal which has been conferred the power to interpret law holds a concomitant power to determine whether that law is constitutionally valid. This conclusion ensues from the principle of supremacy of the Constitution, which is confirmed by s. 52(1) of the *Constitution Act, 1982*:

> 52(1) The Constitution of Canada is the supreme law of Canada, and any law that is inconsistent with the provisions of the Constitution is, to the extent of the inconsistency, of no force or effect.

Distilled to its basics, the rationale for recognizing jurisdiction in the arbitrator in the *Douglas College* case is that the Constitution, as the supreme law, must be respected by an administrative tribunal called upon to interpret law.

It should be emphasized that there is no need to determine if either the Commission or a tribunal under the Act is a court of competent jurisdiction under s. 24(1) of the Charter. That is not the inquiry before us. Rather, what must be scrutinized is the mandate given under the Act to the Commission and the tribunals. There is no doubt that the power to consider questions of law can be bestowed on an administrative tribunal either explicitly or implicitly by the legislature. All the parties agree that there is no provision in the Act that expressly confers on the Commission a general power to consider questions of law. There being no such express authority, it becomes necessary to determine whether Parliament has granted it implicit jurisdiction to consider such questions. ...

In considering whether a tribunal has jurisdiction over the parties, the subject matter before it, and the remedy sought by the parties, it is appropriate to take into account various practical matters such as the composition and structure of the tribunal, the procedure before the tribunal, the appeal route from the tribunal, and the expertise of the tribunal. These practical considerations, in so far as they reflect the scheme of the enabling statute, provide an insight into the mandate given to the administrative tribunal by the legislature. At the same time there may be pragmatic and functional policy concerns that argue for or against the tribunal having constitutional competence, though such concerns can never supplant the intention of the legislature.

The Scheme of the Act

[La Forest J here described the way in which the federal human rights legislation operated.]

The Jurisdiction of the Commission

With the exception to be noted later, there is no explicit provision in the Act giving to the Commission power to determine questions of law. Nor is there anything in the scheme of the Act to imply that the Commission has this power. Looking at the Act as a whole it is evident that the role of the Commission is to deal with the intake of complaints and to screen them for proper disposition. ...

The Commission is not an adjudicative body; that is the role of a tribunal appointed under the Act. When deciding whether a complaint should proceed to be inquired into by a tribunal, the Commission fulfills a screening analysis somewhat analogous to that of a judge at a preliminary inquiry. It is not the job of the Commission to determine if the complaint is made out. Rather its duty is to decide if, under the provisions of the Act, an inquiry is warranted having regard to all the facts. The central component of the Commission's role, then, is that of assessing the sufficiency of the evidence before it. ...

The striking down of s. 15(c) by the Commission, which is what a referral to a tribunal in the present case would amount to, would be an assumption by the Commission of an adjudicative role for which it has no mandate. When Parliament has failed to vest an administrative body with such a jurisdiction (which is the case here), then it is not the role of a court to create such jurisdiction. Administrative bodies and tribunals are creatures of statute; the will of the legislature as it appears therein must be respected.

Notwithstanding the general scheme of the Act, there are specific provisions, notably ss. 27, 40 and 41, that both the appellants and the Commission fastened upon as indicating an intent by Parliament to have the Commission determine questions of law. However, these sections amount to no more than that the Commission has power to interpret and apply its enabling statute. It does not follow that it then has a jurisdiction to address general questions of law. Every administrative body, to one degree or another, must have the power to interpret and apply its own enabling statute. If this were not the case, it would be at the mercy of the parties before it and would never be the master of its own proceedings. The power to refuse to accept a complaint, or to turn down an application, or to refuse to do one of the countless duties that administrative bodies are charged with, does not amount to a power to determine questions of law as envisaged in *Douglas/*

Kwantlen, *Cuddy Chicks* and *Tétreault-Gadoury*. To decide otherwise would be to accept that all administrative bodies and tribunals are competent to question the constitutional validity of their enabling statutes, a position this Court has consistently rejected. ...

The role of the Commission as an administrative and screening body, with no appreciable and adjudicative role, is a clear indication that Parliament did not intend the Commission to have the power to consider questions of law. There is simply nothing in the Act indicating that the Commission has the mandate which the appellants and the Commission would wish it to have. ...

Practical Considerations

It must be recognized at the outset that practical considerations cannot dictate the outcome of the issue presently before this Court. As I have already emphasized, the focus of the Court's inquiry must be the mandate given to the Commission by Parliament. In such an endeavour practical considerations may be of assistance in determining the intention of Parliament, but they are not determinative. ...

In the present case the practical advantages in having the Commission consider the constitutionality of its own statute are limited. First, since the Commission is not an adjudicative body it cannot be considered a proper forum in which to address fundamental constitutional issues. As this Court has previously found, there is no requirement for anything more than a "paper hearing" for the parties before the Commission. Although I readily acknowledge that the informal and accessible process of administrative bodies may well be a considerable advantage to a party, as compared to the regular court system, there comes a point where a body such as the Commission simply does not have the mechanism in place to adequately deal with multifaceted constitutional issues. For example, the Commission is not bound by the traditional rules of evidence. This means that it is open to the Commission to receive unsworn evidence, hearsay evidence, and simple opinion evidence. Such an unrestricted flow of information may be well suited to deciding the threshold question facing the Commission, but it is inappropriate when determining the constitutional validity of a legislative provision. In the latter case, suitable evidentiary safeguards are desirable. Related to this problem is the concern that one of the aims of the Commission, to deal with human right complaints in an accessible, efficient and timely manner, would be disrupted and interfered with by allowing the parties to raise constitutional issues before the Commission. Such issues would of necessity require a more involved and lengthy process than is presently the case. In my view, it was not the intention of Parliament that the Commission's screening function become entangled in this manner.

A second and more telling problem in the case of the Commission is its lack of expertise. ... [T]his Court has made clear in *Mossop* [*Canada (Attorney General) v.*, [1993] 1 SCR 554 (Can.)], at pp. 584-85, and reiterated in *Gould v. Yukon Order of Pioneers* [1996] 1 SCR 571, at pp. 599-600, that a human rights tribunal, unlike a labour arbitrator or labour board, has no special expertise with respect to questions of law. What is true of a tribunal is even more true of the Commission which, as was noted in *Mossop*, is lacking the adjudicative role of a tribunal.

To my mind the relevant practical considerations do not argue in favour of having the Commission consider Charter issues. Without question there is on the surface an attraction and efficiency, at least for the complainant, in having the constitutional matter first heard by the Commission. That will always be so, however, and in the present situation I am of the view that the reality would in fact be different. It is likely that in a case such as the one presently before us the decision of the Commission on the validity of a provision of the Act under the Charter would be the subject of judicial review proceedings in the Federal Court. It would be more efficient, both to the parties and to the system in general, to have a complainant seek a declaration of constitutional invalidity in either the Federal Court or a provincial superior court. In such a setting the question can be debated in the fullness it requires and the proper expertise can be brought to bear on its resolution.

The Jurisdiction of a Tribunal Under the Act

Given my finding that the Commission does not have the jurisdiction to question the constitutional validity of its enabling statute, it logically follows that a tribunal appointed under the Act, and indeed a review tribunal appointed pursuant to s. 56, must also lack the jurisdiction to declare unconstitutional a limiting provision of the Act. Take for example the case presently before us: if the Commission must apply the Act as it is written, then the appellants cannot get their complaint before a tribunal, depending as it does on s. 15(c) being found to be inoperative. The same is true of any complaint that requires the Commission to arrive at a decision on a constitutional matter before being able to find that the complaint warrants further inquiry by a tribunal. It would be something of a paradox for Parliament to grant tribunals under the Act a jurisdiction that could never be exercised.

As with the Commission there is no explicit power given to a tribunal to consider questions of law. Taken together, ss. 50(1) and 53(2) of the Act state that a tribunal shall inquire into the complaint referred to it by the Commission to determine if it is substantiated. This is primarily and essentially a fact-finding inquiry with the aim of establishing whether or not a discriminatory practice occurred. In the course of such an inquiry a tribunal may indeed consider questions of law. As with the Commission, these questions will often centre around the interpretation of the enabling legislation. However, unlike the Commission, it is implicit in the scheme of the Act that a tribunal possess a more general power to deal with questions of law. Thus tribunals have been recognized as having jurisdiction to interpret statutes other than the Act (see *Canada (Attorney General) v. Druken* [1989] 2 FC 24 (CA)) and as having jurisdiction to consider constitutional questions other than those noted above. In particular, it is well accepted that a tribunal has the power to address questions on the constitutional division of powers (*Public Service Alliance of Canada v. Qu'Appelle Indian Residential Council* (1986) 7 CHRR D/3600 (CHRT)), on the validity of a ground of discrimination under the Act (*Nealy v. Johnston* (1989) 10 CHRR D/6450 (CHRT)), and it is foreseeable that a tribunal could entertain Charter arguments on the constitutionality of available remedies in a particular case (see *Canada (Human Rights Commission) v. Taylor* [1990] 3 SCR 892). Even in such instances, however, the legal findings of a tribunal receive no deference from the courts. This position was firmly established by this Court in *Mossop, supra,* at p. 585:

The superior expertise of a human rights tribunal relates to fact-finding and adjudication in a human rights context. It does not extend to general questions of law such as the one at issue in this case. These are ultimately matters within the province of the judiciary, and involve concepts of statutory interpretation and general legal reasoning which the courts must be supposed competent to perform.

I would add a practical note of caution with respect to a tribunal's jurisdiction to consider Charter arguments. First, as already noted, a tribunal does not have any special expertise except in the area of factual determinations in the human rights context. Second, any efficiencies that are *prima facie* gained by avoiding the court system will be lost when the inevitable judicial review proceeding is brought in the Federal Court. Third, the unfettered ability of a tribunal to accept any evidence it sees fit is well suited to a human rights complaint determination but is inappropriate when addressing the constitutionality of a legislative provision. Finally, and perhaps most decisively, the added complexity, cost, and time that would be involved when a tribunal is to hear a constitutional question would erode to a large degree the primary goal sought in creating the tribunals, i.e., the efficient and timely adjudication of human rights complaints.

Taking all these factors into consideration, I am of the view that while a tribunal may have jurisdiction to consider general legal and constitutional questions, logic demands that it has no ability to question the constitutional validity of a limiting provision of the Act.

Conclusion

To conclude, the Canadian Human Rights Commission has no jurisdiction under the *Canadian Human Rights Act* to subject provisions of that statute to constitutional scrutiny. The Commission is limited in its jurisdiction by the dictates of the Act. Similarly, a tribunal appointed at the request of the Commission is also without jurisdiction to determine the constitutional validity of limiting provisions of the Act.

McLACHLIN J (L'Heureux-Dubé J concurring) (dissenting): …

I. Introduction

In my respectful view, the majority approach depreciates the language of s. 52 of the *Constitution Act, 1982*, makes it more difficult for the Human Rights Commission to fulfil its mandate, and places burdens on the victims of discrimination in their fight for equality that Parliament cannot have intended. If this is the clear effect of the Act and the law, then these results, however illogical, unjust and inconvenient they may be, must be accepted. But, unlike the majority, I do not find this to be the clear effect of the law. In my view, every tribunal charged with the duty of deciding issues of law has the concomitant power to do so. The fact that the question of law concerns the effect of the Charter does not change the matter. The Charter is not some holy grail which only judicial initiates of the superior courts may touch. The Charter belongs to the people. All law and law-makers that touch the people must conform to it. Tribunals and commissions charged with deciding legal issues are no exception. Many more citizens have their rights determined by these tribunals than by the courts. If the Charter is to be meaningful to ordinary people, then it must find its expression in the decisions of these tribunals. If Parliament makes it clear that a particular tribunal can decide facts and facts alone, so be it. But if Parliament confers on the tribunal the power to decide questions of law, that power must, in the absence of counter-indications, be taken to extend to the Charter, and to the question of whether the Charter renders portions of its enabling statute unconstitutional.

What is at stake may be judged by the case before us. The appellants contend that they are the victims of discrimination on the basis of age. Like many people who bring complaints before human rights tribunals, they have no lawyer. As is usual, they asked the Commission to consider their claim and refer it to a tribunal for investigation and hearing. Consistent with its goal of helping the disadvantaged, the Act establishes procedures for all this to be done at little or no cost to the complainant.

Everyone who appeared before this Court, with the exception of *amicus curiae* appointed at the direction of this Court, agreed that the Commission should be able to initiate proceedings to determine the constitutional validity of the "normal retirement age" exemption of the Act. The appellants, having fought their way all the way to this Court without counsel, submit that the Commission should refer their complaint to a tribunal for consideration of both the facts and the legal issues. The respondent employer, Canadian Airlines, suggests that the Commission should be permitted to refer the legal question to the Federal Court, which will permit it, upon obtaining the answer, to decide whether the complaint has sufficient merit to justify appointing a tribunal. The Canadian Human Rights Commission, for its part, submits that the Commission has the power as a screening body to consider the constitutional issue in a preliminary way and either appoint a tribunal if it finds a meritorious case to be made out considering the law and the facts, or decline to do so if it finds no such case. In the event a tribunal were appointed, the Commission submits that the tribunal would have the power to consider and decide the entire matter, including arguments that the "normal age of retirement" exemption is rendered void by s. 52 of the *Constitution Act, 1982*. Aggrieved parties could take appeals to the courts as permitted by the *Canadian Human Rights Act*.

It behooves this Court to ask why every party with a stake in the matter urges this Court to find that the Human Rights Commission may deal with the issue of the constitutionality of the "normal age of retirement" exemption in one way or another. The answer, I venture to suggest, is that this is the result which best achieves the economical and effective resolution of human rights disputes and best serves the values entrenched in the *Canadian Human Rights Act* and the Charter.

Applicants like the appellants suffer the greatest prejudice from a ruling that the Commission has no choice but to ignore the Charter challenge and to proceed on the basis that the law is valid. They must first launch their complaint with the Human Rights Commission, knowing that this is a useless *pro forma* step. When the complaint is refused, as it inevitably must be, they must then bring an action in Federal Court for a declaration that the section of the *Canadian Human Rights Act* at issue offends the Charter and is invalid. The requirement of this *pro forma* step can only serve to discourage complainants from challenging the constitutionality of a provision of the *Canadian Human Rights Act*. Moreover, the Commission itself may be unable to refer the constitutionality of a provision of the *Canadian Human Rights Act* to the court: see *Re Rosen* [1987] 3 FC 238, where the Federal Court of Appeal held that it lacked jurisdiction to hear a reference from the Human Rights Commission on a question arguably similar to that raised by this appeal.

Nor does the process the majority envisions serve the employer; while the employer may be better able to bear the legal expense of a litigation detour than the appellants, the process may never provide an answer to the question of whether its policy violates the *Canadian Human Rights Act*. Unless the private complainants muster courage and enough money to pursue a collateral court challenge to the *Canadian Human Rights Act*, the employer will not know what policy is required to conform to the law and the Charter.

Finally, the Canadian public is ill-served by the process proposed by the majority on this appeal. Unless and until private individuals mount a successful court challenge under the Charter, administrative agencies like the Canadian Human Rights Commission must proceed to deal with people's rights as though the Charter had never been enacted. If and when the Charter issue is brought before the courts, it will be decided in a vacuum. Under the majority's suggested process of a declaratory action in Federal Court, there will be no factual record or tribunal findings to assist the courts in deciding whether or not to declare that the impugned section of *Canadian Human Rights Act* offends the Charter.

Why, one must ask, is it necessary to conclude, against the submissions of all the parties, that the Canadian Human Rights Commission has no jurisdiction to consider, even in its limited capacity as a screening body, the question of whether the "normal age of retirement" defence may have been invalidated by the Charter? In my view, it is not necessary. The authorities, in my opinion, point to a more efficient process, a process which will not place unnecessary roadblocks in the way of complainants like the appellants. The Canadian Human Rights Commission seeks to do only what its statute obliges it to do— to carry out preliminary investigations of complaints and, if warranted, appoint tribunals to investigate and hear them.

Appeals dismissed.

NOTES

1. The majority position (as opposed to that of Lamer CJ) places primacy on the intention of the legislature, at least to the extent that if the legislature explicitly confers the power on a statutory authority to determine Charter questions (including those as to the validity of the empowering legislation) then that legislative statement is conclusive. Lamer CJ would seemingly see it as constitutionally invalid. Why? Are you convinced?

2. In the trilogy that led to *Cooper*, the court in two of the cases found express authority in the relevant statute for the tribunal to consider the relevant constitutional challenge. Thus, in *Cuddy Chicks*, the court pointed to the provision in the Act that gave the Labour Relations Board exclusive jurisdiction "to determine all questions of fact and law that arise in any matter before it." Then, in *Douglas College*, La Forest J's judgment seemed to rely on his view that the phrase in s. 98(g) of the *Labour Code* authorizing arbitrators to interpret and apply "any Act intended to regulate employment" was broad enough to include the Charter. In reality, how explicit are these provisions? Consider, for instance, that in *Douglas College*, while the *Labour Code* itself contained no definition of the word "Act," the *Interpretation*

Act, RSBC 1979, c. 206, ss. 1 and 29 provide that "Act" means an enactment of the legislature of British Columbia. This point is made by Irvine, "*Douglas College*: Administrative Tribunals, Charter Jurisdiction and Statutory Interpretation" (1992), 5 *Admin. LR* (2d) 225. More generally, note Lamer CJ's pointed remarks in *Cooper* about the fiction of legislative intention in this domain.

3. Where a statutory authority has jurisdiction to consider the relevant Charter question, the statutory authority "not only has the authority but a duty to ascertain the answer to the constitutional challenge": La Forest J in *Cuddy Chicks*, at 18. Thus, in *Douglas College*, the constitutional question was remitted to the arbitrator who had declined to deal with the question. See also *Falkiner v. Ontario (Minister of Community and Social Services)* (1996), 140 DLR (4th) 114 (Div. Ct.). Why is this so? Should a tribunal have discretion not to exercise its jurisdiction if, in the circumstances of the case and in the light of the nature of the constitutional issue raised, it concludes that the costs of prolonging the proceedings to hear and determine the constitutional question would likely outweigh the benefits of the tribunal's deciding it?

4. In *Cooper*, La Forest J not only holds that the commission but also the Human Rights Tribunal cannot entertain the question. However, the judgment hinged not on this logic but on a pragmatic and functional analysis of the Human Rights Tribunal's capacities. Why is the Human Rights Tribunal unsuited to consider issues of constitutional validity that the Ontario Labour Relations Board (*Cuddy Chicks*) and a labour arbitrator under a collective agreement (*Douglas College*) can consider? This was a question that posed problems for the lower courts in the wake of *Cooper* and that was responded to in *Martin* by the Supreme Court's emphasis on presumptions arising from the language of the statute rather than policy considerations arising from the allocation of authority.

5. For discussion of *Martin*, see Fox-Decent, "The Charter and Administrative Law: Cross-Fertilization in Public Law" in Flood and Sossin, eds., *Administrative Law in Context* (2008), at 189-94; B. Bilson, "The Voice from the Trenches: Administrative Tribunals and The Interpretation of the Charter" (2006), 69 *Sask. LR* 3; and L. Smith, "Administrative Tribunals as Constitutional Decision-Makers" (2004), 17 *CJALP* 113. For earlier commentary on *Cooper*, see M.C. Crane, "Administrative Tribunals, Charter Challenges, and the Web of 'Institutional Relationships'" (1998), 61 *Sask. LR* 495; G.-A. Beaudoin, "Les tribunaux administratifs et la *Charte canadienne de droits and libertés*" (1998), 61 *Sask. LR* 277; J. McMillan, "Tribunals and the Charter: The Search for Implied Jurisdiction—A Case Comment on *Cooper v. Canada (Human Rights Commission)*" (1998), 32 *UBCLR* 365; A.J. Roman, "Case Comment: *Cooper v. Canada (Human Rights Commission*" (1997), 43 *Admin. LR* (2d) 243; and K. Schucher, "A Further Diminishing of the Role of Human Rights Tribunals: *Cooper v. Canadian Human Rights Commission, Bell v. Canadian Human Rights Commission*" (1997), 5 *CLELJ* 173.

CONSTITUTIONAL CHALLENGES AND REMEDIES: THE APPROPRIATE FORUM

One of the premises of the cases considered above is that, at least on occasion, the knowledge, perspective, and experience of members of specialized administrative tribunals is sufficiently relevant to deciding the constitutional validity of their enabling legislation that the quality of decisions will often be enhanced if they are authorized to make the first determination of the issue. Taking the matter a step further, we now ask (1) whether these considerations may also support the view that a person who alleges a violation of a constitutional right ought to be able to litigate it in court before it has been decided by a specialized administrative tribunal, and (2) whether such a tribunal will be "a court of competent jurisdiction" for the purposes of providing relief under s. 24(1) of the Charter. Both these issues were dealt with comprehensively in the following decision of the Supreme Court of Canada. Specifically before the court was the issue whether the Ontario Review Board, in reviewing a mentally ill offender's continued detention in a mental health facility, had the jurisdiction to award him an absolute discharge as a s. 24(1) remedy.

R v. Conway
2010 SCC 22

ABELLA J (for the Court): [1] The specific issue in this appeal is the remedial jurisdiction of the Ontario Review Board under s. 24(1) of the *Canadian Charter of Rights and Freedoms*. The wider issue is the relationship between the *Charter*, its remedial provisions and administrative tribunals generally.

[2] There are two provisions in the *Charter* dealing with remedies: s. 24(1) and s. 24(2). Section 24(1) states that anyone whose *Charter* rights or freedoms have been infringed or denied may apply to a "court of competent jurisdiction" to obtain a remedy that is "appropriate and just in the circumstances." Section 24(2) states that in those proceedings, a court can exclude evidence obtained in violation of the *Charter* if its admission would bring the administration of justice into disrepute. A constitutional remedy is also available under s. 52(1) of the *Constitution Act, 1982*, which states that the Constitution is the supreme law of Canada, and that any law inconsistent with its provisions is, to the extent of the inconsistency, of no force or effect.

[3] When the *Charter* was proclaimed in 1982, its relationship with administrative tribunals was a *tabula rasa*. It was not long, however, before various dimensions of the relationship found their way to this Court.

[4] The first relevant wave of cases started in 1986 with *Mills v. The Queen*, [1986] 1 SCR 863. The philosophical legacy of *Mills* was in its conclusion that for the purposes of s. 24(1) of the *Charter*, a "court of competent jurisdiction" was a "court" with jurisdiction over the person, the subject matter, and the remedy sought. For the next 25 years, this three-part test served as the grid for determining whether a court or administrative tribunal was a "court of competent jurisdiction" under s. 24(1) of the *Charter* (*Carter v. The Queen*, [1986] 1 SCR 981; *Argentina v. Mellino*, [1987] 1 SCR 536; *United States v. Allard*, [1987] 1 SCR 564; ... *R v. Gamble*, [1988] 2 SCR 595; ... *Weber v. Ontario Hydro*, [1995] 2 SCR 929; *Mooring v. Canada (National Parole Board)*, [1996] 1 SCR 75; *R v. 974649 Ontario Inc.*, 2001 SCC 81, [2001] 3 SCR 575 ("*Dunedin*") [some case citations omitted].

[5] The second wave started in 1989 with *Slaight Communications Inc. v. Davidson*, [1989] 1 SCR 1038. Although *Slaight* did not—and does not—offer any direct guidance on what constitutes a "court of competent jurisdiction," its legacy was in its conclusion

that any exercise of statutory discretion is subject to the *Charter* and its values [case citations omitted].

[6] The third and final wave started in 1990 with *Douglas/Kwantlen Faculty Assn. v. Douglas College*, [1990] 3 SCR 570, followed in 1991 by *Cuddy Chicks Ltd. v. Ontario (Labour Relations Board)*, [1991] 2 SCR 5, and *Tétreault-Gadoury v. Canada (Employment and Immigration Commission)*, [1991] 2 SCR 22. The legacy of these cases—the *Cuddy Chicks* trilogy—is in their conclusion that specialized tribunals with both the expertise and authority to decide questions of law are in the best position to hear and decide constitutional questions related to their statutory mandates (*Nova Scotia (Workers' Compensation Board) v. Martin*, 2003 SCC 54, [2003] 2 SCR 504; *Paul v. British Columbia (Forest Appeals Commission)*, 2003 SCC 55, [2003] 2 SCR 585; *Quebec (Attorney General) v. Quebec (Human Rights Tribunal)*, 2004 SCC 40, [2004] 2 SCR 223; *Okwuobi v. Lester B. Pearson School Board*, 2005 SCC 16, [2005] 1 SCR 257).

[7] The impact of these three jurisprudential waves has been to confine constitutional issues for administrative tribunals to three discrete universes. It seems to me that after 25 years of parallel evolution, it is time to consider whether the universes can appropriately be merged.

Background

[Discussion of the factual background has been omitted. Summary of the decisions of the Ontario Review Board and the Ontario Court of Appeal, both of which concluded that the board lacked jurisdiction under s. 24(1) of the *Charter*, has also been omitted.]

[18] This Court, in order to decide whether Mr. Conway is entitled to the *Charter* remedies he is seeking, must first determine whether the Ontario Review Board is a court of competent jurisdiction which can grant *Charter* remedies under s. 24(1). In accordance with the new approach developed in these reasons, I am of the view that it is. On the other hand, I am not persuaded that Mr. Conway is entitled to the particular *Charter* remedies he seeks and would therefore dismiss the appeal.

Analysis

[19] Section 24(1) states:

Anyone whose rights or freedoms, as guaranteed by this Charter, have been infringed or denied may apply to a court of competent jurisdiction to obtain such remedy as the court considers appropriate and just in the circumstances.

[20] We do not have one *Charter* for the courts and another for administrative tribunals (*Cooper v. Canada (Human Rights Commission)*, [1996] 3 SCR 854, *per* McLachlin J (in dissent), at para. 70; *Dunedin*; *Douglas College*; *Martin*). This truism is reflected in this Court's recognition that the principles governing remedial jurisdiction under the *Charter* apply to both courts *and* administrative tribunals. It is also reflected in the jurisprudence flowing from *Mills* and the *Cuddy Chicks* trilogy according to which, with rare exceptions, administrative tribunals with the authority to apply the law have the jurisdiction to apply the *Charter* to the issues that arise in the proper exercise of their statutory functions.

[21] The jurisprudential evolution has resulted in this Court's acceptance not only of the proposition that expert tribunals should play a primary role in the determination of *Charter* issues falling within their specialized jurisdiction, but also that in exercising their statutory discretion, they must comply with the *Charter*.

[22] All of these developments serve to cement the direct relationship between the *Charter*, its remedial provisions and administrative tribunals. In light of this evolution, it seems to me to be no longer helpful to limit the inquiry to whether a court or tribunal is a court of competent jurisdiction only for the purposes of a particular remedy. The question instead should be institutional: does this particular tribunal have the jurisdiction to grant *Charter* remedies generally? The result of this question will flow from whether the tribunal has the power to decide questions of law. If it does, and if *Charter* jurisdiction has not been excluded by statute, the tribunal will have the jurisdiction to grant *Charter* remedies in relation to *Charter* issues arising in the course of carrying out its statutory mandate (*Cuddy Chicks* trilogy; *Martin*). A tribunal which has the jurisdiction to grant *Charter* remedies is a court of competent jurisdiction. The tribunal must then decide, given this jurisdiction, whether it can grant the particular remedy sought based on its statutory mandate. The answer to this question will depend on legislative intent, as discerned from the tribunal's statutory mandate (the *Mills* cases).

[23] This approach has the benefit of attributing *Charter* jurisdiction to the tribunal as an institution, rather than requiring litigants to test, remedy by remedy, whether it is a court of competent jurisdiction. It is also an approach which emerges from a review of the three distinct constitutional streams flowing from this Court's jurisprudence. As the following review shows, this Court has gradually expanded the approach to the scope of the *Charter* and its relationship with administrative tribunals. These reasons are an attempt to consolidate the results of that expansion.

The Mills Cases

[24] In *Mills*, it was decided that relief is available under s. 24(1) of the *Charter* if the "court" from which relief is sought has jurisdiction over the parties, the subject matter and the remedy sought. Since 1986, the *Mills* test has been consistently applied to determine whether courts and tribunals acting under specific statutory schemes are courts of competent jurisdiction to grant particular remedies under s. 24(1).

[25] The early cases considered the remedial jurisdiction of statutory and superior courts. In *Mills* and *Carter*, this Court held that a provincial court judge sitting as a preliminary inquiry court was not a court of competent jurisdiction for the purpose of ordering a stay of proceedings for an alleged s. 11(b) violation. The following year, this Court concluded that extradition judges had the same institutional features as preliminary inquiry judges, and could therefore not order a stay in the event of a *Charter* breach (*Mellino*; *Allard*). Further, in *Mellino*, the Court observed that since extradition proceedings were reviewable by superior courts by way of *habeas corpus*, those superior courts were the courts of competent jurisdiction to grant a stay under s. 24(1), not the extradition judge.

[26] In 1988, in *Gamble*, the Court held that a superior court in the province where an individual is in custody is a court of competent jurisdiction to hear an application for *habeas corpus*, stating:

Where the courts of Ontario have jurisdiction over the subject matter and the person, it seems to me that they may, under the broad provisions of s. 24(1) of the *Charter*, grant such relief as it is within their jurisdiction to grant and as they consider appropriate and just in the circumstances. [p. 631]

[27] In 1995, in *Weber*, the Court expanded the scope of the *Mills* inquiry to cover administrative tribunals. The issue was whether a labour arbitrator appointed under the *Labour Relations Act*, RSO 1990, c. L.2, was a court of competent jurisdiction for the purpose of granting damages and a declaration under s. 24(1) in relation to disputes which in their essential character arose out of the collective agreement between the parties. Weber had sought relief for what he alleged were breaches of ss. 7 and 8 of the *Charter* committed by his employer, Ontario Hydro, who had gathered surveillance evidence about him during his extended sick leave. The Court had to determine whether Weber was required to raise his *Charter* claims before a labour arbitrator or before the superior court.

[28] For the majority, McLachlin J rejected an approach that would bifurcate the proceedings between the arbitrator and the courts. In her view, the "essential character" of Weber's claim was unfair treatment by the employer. The collective agreement expressly stated that the grievance procedure applied to "[a]ny allegation that an employee has been subjected to unfair treatment." Weber's *Charter* claims were therefore found to be within the arbitrator's exclusive jurisdiction:

> [W]hile the informal processes of such tribunals might not be entirely suited to dealing with constitutional issues, clear advantages to the practice exist. Citizens are permitted to assert their *Charter* rights in a prompt, inexpensive, informal way. The parties are not required to duplicate submissions on the case in two different fora, for determination of two different legal issues. A specialized tribunal can quickly sift the facts and compile a record for the reviewing court. And the specialized competence of the tribunal may provide assistance to the reviewing court.
>
> . . .
>
> [I]t is not the name of the tribunal that determines the matter, but its powers ... . The practical import of fitting *Charter* remedies into the existing system of tribunals, as McIntyre J notes, [in *Mills*] is that litigants have "direct" access to *Charter* remedies in the tribunal charged with deciding their case. [paras. 60 and 65]

[29] Foreshadowing the debate that is before us in this case, Iacobucci J in dissent, expressed the view that the arbitrator was neither a "court" nor of "competent jurisdiction" for the purpose of granting *Charter* remedies under s. 24(1). In his view, Weber was entitled to seek labour remedies from the arbitrator, but not those under the *Charter*.

[30] The *Weber* "exclusive jurisdiction model" enunciated by McLachlin J, which directed that an administrative tribunal should decide *all* matters whose essential character falls within the tribunal's specialized statutory jurisdiction, is now a well-established principle of administrative law (*Regina Police Assn. Inc. v. Regina (City) Board of Police Commissioners*, 2000 SCC 14, [2000] 1 SCR 360; *Québec (Commission des droits de la personne et des droits de la jeunesse) v. Québec (Attorney General)*, 2004 SCC 39, [2004] 2 SCR 185; *Québec (Human Rights Tribunal)*; *Vaughan v. Canada*, 2005 SCC 11, [2005] 1 SCR 146; *Okwuobi*; Andrew K. Lokan and Christopher M. Dassios, *Constitutional Litigation in Canada* (2006), at p. 4-15).

[Discussion of the court's decision in *Mooring* and subsequent cases has been omitted.]

[40] This review of *Mills*' progeny gives rise to three observations. First, this Court has accepted that the *Mills* test applies to courts as well as to administrative tribunals. Second, although *Mills* set out a three-pronged definition of "court of competent jurisdiction," the first two steps have almost never been relied on. Twenty-five years later, "jurisdiction over the parties" and "jurisdiction over the subject matter" remain undefined for the purposes of the test. The inquiry has almost always turned on whether the court or tribunal had jurisdiction to award the *particular* remedy sought under s. 24(1). In other words, the inquiry is less into whether the adjudicative body is institutionally a court of competent jurisdiction, and more into whether it is a court of competent jurisdiction *for the purposes of granting a particular remedy*. Third, while there appears to be agreement that s. 24(1) jurisdiction is a function of legislative intent, the authoritative comments of the majorities in *Weber* and *Dunedin* eschewing bifurcated proceedings and heralding early and accessible adjudication of *Charter* applications, may have been slightly unmoored by the majority in *Mooring*.

The Slaight Cases

[41] The cases flowing from *Slaight*, while of no direct assistance on what constitutes a court of competent jurisdiction, are of interest as they too show how the Court increasingly came to expand the application of the *Charter* in the administrative sphere. In 1989, *Slaight* established that any exercise of statutory discretion must comply with the *Charter* and its values ... .

[Discussion of *Slaight* and subsequent case law has been omitted.]

The Cuddy Chicks Trilogy

[49] While the courts and tribunals were preoccupied with the proper application of the principles in *Mills* and *Slaight*, another line of authority regarding the constitutional jurisdiction of statutory tribunals was emerging. These cases dealt with whether administrative tribunals could decide the constitutionality of the provisions of their own statutory schemes and decline to apply them because they are "of no force or effect" under s. 52(1) of the *Constitution Act, 1982*.

[Discussion of *Cuddy Chicks*, *Douglas College*, and *Tétreault-Gadoury* as well as *Cooper*, *Martin*, and *Okwuobi* has been omitted. On these cases, see the preceding section of this chapter of the text.]

[77] These cases confirm that administrative tribunals with the authority to decide questions of law and whose *Charter* jurisdiction has not been clearly withdrawn have the corresponding authority—and duty—to consider and apply the Constitution, including the *Charter*, when answering those legal questions. As McLachlin J observed in *Cooper*:

> [E]very tribunal charged with the duty of deciding issues of law has the concomitant power to do so. The fact that the question of law concerns the effect of the *Charter* does not change

the matter. The *Charter* is not some holy grail which only judicial initiates of the superior courts may touch. The *Charter* belongs to the people. All law and law-makers that touch the people must conform to it. Tribunals and commissions charged with deciding legal issues are no exception. Many more citizens have their rights determined by these tribunals than by the courts. If the *Charter* is to be meaningful to ordinary people, then it must find its expression in the decisions of these tribunals. [para. 70]

The Merger

[78] The jurisprudential evolution leads to the following two observations: first, that administrative tribunals with the power to decide questions of law, and from whom constitutional jurisdiction has not been clearly withdrawn, have the authority to resolve constitutional questions that are linked to matters properly before them. And secondly, they must act consistently with the *Charter* and its values when exercising their statutory functions. It strikes me as somewhat unhelpful, therefore, to subject every such tribunal from which a *Charter* remedy is sought to an inquiry asking whether it is "competent" to grant a particular remedy within the meaning of s. 24(1).

[79] Over two decades of jurisprudence has confirmed the practical advantages and constitutional basis for allowing Canadians to assert their *Charter* rights in the most accessible forum available, without the need for bifurcated proceedings between superior courts and administrative tribunals (*Douglas College*, at pp. 603-604; *Weber*, at para. 60; *Cooper*, at para. 70; *Martin*, at para. 29). The denial of early access to remedies is a denial of an appropriate and just remedy, as Lamer J pointed out in *Mills*, at p. 891. And a scheme that favours bifurcating claims is inconsistent with the well-established principle that an administrative tribunal is to decide all matters, including constitutional questions, whose essential factual character falls within the tribunal's specialized statutory jurisdiction (*Weber*; *Regina Police Assn.*; *Québec (Commission des droits de la personne et des droits de la jeunesse)*; *Québec (Human Rights Tribunal)*; *Vaughan*; *Okwuobi*. See also *Dunsmuir v. New Brunswick*, 2008 SCC 9, [2008] 1 SCR 190, at para. 49).

[80] If, as in the *Cuddy Chicks* trilogy, expert and specialized tribunals with the authority to decide questions of law are in the best position to decide constitutional questions when a remedy is sought under s. 52 of the *Constitution Act, 1982*, there is no reason why such tribunals are not also in the best position to assess constitutional questions when a remedy is sought under s. 24(1) of the *Charter*. As McLachlin J said in *Weber*, "[i]f an arbitrator can find a law violative of the *Charter*, it would seem he or she can determine whether conduct in the administration of the collective agreement violates the *Charter* and likewise grant remedies" (para. 61). I agree with the submission of both the Ontario Review Board and the British Columbia Review Board that in both types of cases, the analysis is the same.

[81] Building on the jurisprudence, therefore, when a remedy is sought from an administrative tribunal under s. 24(1), the proper initial inquiry is whether the tribunal can grant *Charter* remedies generally. To make this determination, the first question is whether the administrative tribunal has jurisdiction, explicit or implied, to decide questions of law. If it does, and unless it is clearly demonstrated that the legislature intended to exclude the *Charter* from the tribunal's jurisdiction, the tribunal is a court of compe-

tent jurisdiction and can consider and apply the *Charter*—and *Charter* remedies—when resolving the matters properly before it.

[82] Once the threshold question has been resolved in favour of *Charter* jurisdiction, the remaining question is whether the tribunal can grant the particular remedy sought, given the relevant statutory scheme. Answering this question is necessarily an exercise in discerning legislative intent. On this approach, what will always be at issue is whether the remedy sought is the kind of remedy that the legislature intended would fit within the statutory framework of the particular tribunal. Relevant considerations in discerning legislative intent will include those that have guided the courts in past cases, such as the tribunal's statutory mandate, structure and function (*Dunedin*).

Application to This Case

[83] The question before the Court is whether the Ontario Review Board is authorized to provide certain remedies to Mr. Conway under s. 24(1) of the *Charter*. Before the Board, Mr. Conway sought an absolute discharge. At the hearing before this Court, and for the first time, he requested additional remedies dealing with his conditions of detention: an order directing CAMH to provide him with access to psychotherapy, and an order prohibiting CAMH from housing him near a construction site.

[84] The first inquiry is whether the Board is a court of competent jurisdiction. In my view, it is. The Board is a quasi-judicial body with significant authority over a vulnerable population. It is unquestionably authorized to decide questions of law. It was established by, and operates under, Part XX.1 of the *Criminal Code* as a specialized statutory tribunal with ongoing supervisory jurisdiction over the treatment, assessment, detention and discharge of those accused who have been found not criminally responsible by reason of mental disorder ("NCR patient"). Section 672.72(1) provides that any party may appeal a board's disposition on any ground of appeal that raises a question of law, fact or mixed fact and law. Further, s. 672.78(1) authorizes an appellate court to allow an appeal against a review board's disposition where the court is of the opinion that the board's disposition was based on a wrong decision on a question of law. I agree with the conclusion of Lang JA. and the submission of the British Columbia Review Board that, as in *Martin* and *Paul*, this language is indicative of the Board's power to decide legal questions. And there is nothing in Part XX.1 of the *Criminal Code*—the Board's statutory scheme—which permits us to conclude that Parliament intended to withdraw *Charter* jurisdiction from the scope of the Board's mandate. It follows that the Board is entitled to decide constitutional questions, including *Charter* questions, that arise in the course of its proceedings.

[85] The question for the Court to decide therefore is whether the particular remedies sought by Mr. Conway are the kinds of remedies that Parliament appeared to have anticipated would fit within the statutory scheme governing the Ontario Review Board. This requires us to consider the scope and nature of the Board's statutory mandate and functions.

[86] Part XX.1 of the *Criminal Code* was enacted after this Court struck down the traditional regime for dealing with mentally ill offenders as contrary to s. 7 of the *Charter* in *R v. Swain*, [1991] 1 SCR 933. The traditional system subjected offenders with mental illness to automatic and indefinite detention at the pleasure of the Lieutenant Governor

in Council (*Criminal Code*, s. 614(2) (formerly s. 542.2(2)) (repealed SC 1991, c. 43, s. 3); *Winko v. British Columbia (Forensic Psychiatric Institute)*, [1999] 2 SCR 625). Part XX.1 was designed to address the concerns raised in *Swain* and was intended to highlight that offenders with a mental illness must be "treated with the utmost dignity and afforded the utmost liberty compatible with [their] situation" (*Winko*, at para. 42; *Penetanguishene Mental Health Centre v. Ontario (Attorney General)*, 2004 SCC 20, [2004] 1 SCR 498, at para. 22).

[87] Part XX.1 introduced a new verdict—"not criminally responsible on account of mental disorder"—into the traditional guilt/innocence dichotomy. This verdict is neither an acquittal nor a conviction; rather, it diverts offenders to a special stream that provides individualized assessment and treatment for those found to be a significant danger to the public (*Winko*, at para. 21; *R v. Owen*, 2003 SCC 33, [2003] 1 SCR 779, at para. 90; *Penetanguishene*, at para. 21). Those NCR patients who are not a significant danger to the public must be unconditionally released.

[88] The Ontario Board manages and supervises the assessment and treatment of each NCR patient in Ontario by holding annual hearings and making dispositions for each patient (ss. 672.38(1), 672.54, 672.81(1) and 672.83(1); *Mazzei v. British Columbia (Director of Adult Forensic Psychiatric Services)*, 2006 SCC 7, [2006] 1 SCR 326, at para. 29). It is well established that the review board regime is intended to reconcile the "twin goals" of protecting the public from dangerous offenders, and treating NCR patients fairly and appropriately (*Winko*, at para. 20; House of Commons, *Minutes of Proceedings and Evidence of the Standing Committee on Justice and the Solicitor General*, No. 7, 3rd Sess., 34th Parl., October 9, 1991, at p. 6). While public safety is the paramount concern, an NCR patient's liberty interest has been held to be the Board's "major preoccupation" within the fence posts staked by public safety (*Pinet v. St. Thomas Psychiatric Hospital*, 2004 SCC 21, [2004] 1 SCR 528, at para. 19). The Board fulfills its "primary purpose" therefore by protecting the public while minimizing incursions on patients' liberty and treating patients fairly (*Mazzei*, at para. 32; *Winko*, at paras. 64-71; *Penetanguishene*, at para. 51).

[89] Section 672.54 of the *Criminal Code* sets out the remedial jurisdiction of review boards, stating:

> Where a court or Review Board makes a disposition under subsection 672.45(2) or section 672.47 or 672.83, it shall, taking into consideration the need to protect the public from dangerous persons, the mental condition of the accused, the reintegration of the accused into society and the other needs of the accused, make one of the following dispositions that is the least onerous and least restrictive to the accused:
>
> (a) where a verdict of not criminally responsible on account of mental disorder has been rendered in respect of the accused and, in the opinion of the court or Review Board, the accused is not a significant threat to the safety of the public, by order, direct that the accused be discharged absolutely;
>
> (b) by order, direct that the accused be discharged subject to such conditions as the court or Review Board considers appropriate; or
>
> (c) by order, direct that the accused be detained in custody in a hospital, subject to such conditions as the court or Review Board considers appropriate.

Accordingly, at a disposition hearing regarding an NCR patient, the Ontario Review Board is authorized to make one of three dispositions: an absolute discharge, a conditional discharge or a detention order. When making its disposition, the Board must consider the four statutory criteria: the need to protect the public from dangerous persons, the patient's mental condition, the reintegration of the patient into society and the patient's other needs.

[90] The Board has a "necessarily broad" discretion to consider a large range of evidence in order to fulfill this mandate (*Winko*, at para. 61). The Board's assessment of the evidence must "take place in an environment respectful of the NCR accused's constitutional rights, free from the negative stereotypes that have too often in the past prejudiced the mentally ill who come into contact with the justice system" (*Winko*, at para. 61). Upon considering the evidence, if the Board is not of the opinion that the patient is a significant threat to public safety, it must direct that the patient be discharged absolutely (s. 672.54(a); *Winko*, at para. 62). On the other hand, if the Board finds that the patient is, as in Mr. Conway's case, a significant threat to public safety, an absolute discharge is not statutorily available as a disposition (s. 672.54; *Winko*, at para. 62).

[91] A patient is not a significant threat to public safety unless he or she is a "real risk of physical or psychological harm to members of the public that is serious in the sense of going beyond the merely trivial or annoying" (*Winko*, at para. 62). The conduct giving rise to the harm must be criminal in nature (*Winko*, at paras. 57 and 62).

[92] Once a patient is absolutely discharged, he or she is no longer subject to the criminal justice system or to the Board's jurisdiction (*Mazzei*, at para. 34). However, pending an absolute discharge, NCR patients are subject to a detention or conditional discharge order. The Board is entitled to include appropriate conditions in its orders (s. 672.54(b) and (c)). The appropriateness of conditions is tied, at least in part, to the framework for making the least onerous and least restrictive disposition consistent with public safety, the patient's mental condition and other needs, and the patient's reintegration into the community (s. 672.54(b), (c); *Penetanguishene*, at paras. 51 and 56).

[93] The Board is not entitled to include any conditions that prescribe or impose treatment on an NCR patient (s. 672.55; *Mazzei*) and any conditions must withstand *Charter* scrutiny (*Slaight*). In addition, disposition orders, including any conditions, are subject to appeal. The Court of Appeal is entitled to allow an appeal against a disposition if it is unreasonable, cannot be supported by the evidence, is based on a wrong decision on a question of law, or gives rise to a miscarriage of justice (s. 672.78(1); *Owen*).

[94] Subject to these limits, the content of the conditions included in a disposition is at the Board's discretion. In this way, the Board has the statutory tools to supervise the treatment and detention of dangerous NCR patients in a responsive, *Charter*-compliant fashion and has a broad power to attach flexible, individualized, creative conditions to the discharge and detention orders it devises for dangerous NCR patients.

[95] The Board's task calls for "significant expertise" (*Owen*, at paras. 29-30) and the Board's membership, which sits in five-member panels comprised of the chairperson (a judge or a person qualified for or retired from appointment to the bench), a second legal member, a psychiatrist, a second psychiatrist or psychologist and one public member (ss. 672.39 and 672.4(1)), guarantees that the requisite experts perform the Board's challenging task (*Owen*, at para. 29; s. 672.39). Further, as almost one-quarter of NCR

patients and accused found unfit to stand trial spend at least 10 years in the review board system, with some, like Mr. Conway, spending significantly longer (Jeff Latimer and Austin Lawrence, *Research Report—The Review Board Systems in Canada: Overview of Results from the Mentally Disordered Accused Data Collection Study* (Department of Justice Canada, January 2006, at p. v), review boards become intimately familiar with the patients under their supervision. In light of this expertise, the appellate courts are "not to be too quick to overturn" a review board's "expert opinion" on how best to manage a patient's risk to the public (*Owen*, at para. 69; *Winko*, at para. 61).

[96] Mr. Conway submits that, pursuant to s. 24(1) of the *Charter*, and notwithstanding the Board's finding that he is a significant threat to public safety, he is entitled to an absolute discharge or, in the absence of a discharge, an order directing CAMH to provide him with alternative treatment and/or an order directing CAMH to ensure that he can access psychotherapy. Mr. Conway admits that these remedies are outside the Board's statutory jurisdiction, but asserts that s. 24(1) of the *Charter* frees the Board from statutory limits on its jurisdiction.

[97] I disagree. Part XX.1 of the *Code* provides the Board with "wide latitude" in the exercise of its powers (*Winko*, at para. 27; *Mazzei*, at para. 43). However, Parliament did not imbue the Board with free remedial rein, and in fact withdrew certain remedies from the Board's statutory arsenal. As noted above, Part XX.1 of the *Code* precludes the Board from granting either an absolute discharge to an NCR patient found to be dangerous or an order directing that a hospital authority provide an NCR patient with particular treatment (ss. 672.54(a) and 672.55; *Winko*; *Mazzei*). Parliament was entitled to withdraw these powers from the Board and, barring a constitutional challenge to the legislation, no judicial fiat can overrule Parliament's clear expression of intent.

[98] Granting the Board the jurisdiction to unconditionally release a dangerous patient without the requisite treatment to resolve the dangerousness would frustrate the Board's mandate to supervise the special needs of those who are found to require the treatment/assessment regime (*Winko*, at paras. 39-42). It would also undermine the balance required by s. 672.54: it not only threatens public safety, it jeopardizes the interests of the NCR patient by failing to adequately prepare him or her for reintegration and, as a result, creating a substantial risk of re-offending and re-entry into the Part XX.1 regime (*Winko*, at paras. 39-41). As McLachlin J wrote in *Winko*, at paras. 39-41:

> Treatment ... is necessary to stabilize the mental condition of a dangerous NCR accused and reduce the threat to public safety created by that condition ... .
>
> Part XX.1 protects society. If society is to be protected on a long-term basis, it must address the cause of the offending behaviour—the mental illness. ...
>
> Part XX.1 also protects the NCR offender. The assessment-treatment model introduced by Part XX.1 of the *Criminal Code* is fairer to the NCR offender than the traditional common law model. The NCR offender is not criminally responsible, but ill. Providing opportunities to receive treatment, not imposing punishment, is the just and appropriate response.

[99] The Board's duty to protect public safety, its statutory authority to grant absolute discharges only to non-dangerous NCR patients, and its mandate to assess and treat NCR patients with a view to reintegration rather than recidivism, all point to Parliament's intent not to permit NCR patients who are dangerous to have access to absolute

discharges as a remedy. These factors are determinative in this case and lead to the conclusion that it would not be appropriate and just in Mr. Conway's current circumstances for the Board to grant him an absolute discharge.

[100] The same is true of Mr. Conway's request for a treatment order. Allowing the Board to prescribe or impose treatment is not only expressly prohibited by the *Criminal Code* (s. 672.55); it is also inconsistent with the constitutional division of powers (*Mazzei*). The authority to make treatment decisions lies exclusively within the mandate of provincial health authorities in charge of the hospital where an NCR patient is detained, pursuant to various provincial laws governing the provision of medical services. "It would be an inappropriate interference with provincial legislative authority (and with hospitals' treatment plans and practices) for Review Boards to require hospital authorities to administer particular courses of medical treatment for the benefit of an NCR accused" (*Mazzei*, at para. 31).

[101] A finding that the Board is entitled to grant Mr. Conway an absolute discharge despite its conclusion that he is a significant threat to public safety, or to direct CAMH to provide him with a particular treatment, would be a clear contradiction of Parliament's intent. Given the statutory scheme and the constitutional considerations, the Board cannot grant these remedies to Mr. Conway.

[102] Finally, Mr. Conway complains about where his room is located and seeks an order under s. 24(1) prohibiting CAMH from housing him near a construction site. Neither the validity of this complaint, nor, obviously, the propriety of any redress, has yet been determined by the Board.

[103] Remedies granted to redress *Charter* wrongs are intended to meaningfully vindicate a claimant's rights and freedoms (*Doucet-Boudreau v. Nova Scotia (Minister of Education)*, 2003 SCC 62, [2003] 3 SCR 3, at para. 55; *Canada (Prime Minister) v. Khadr*, 2010 SCC 3, [2010] 1 SCR 44, at para. 30). Yet, it is not the case that effective, vindicatory remedies for harm flowing from unconstitutional conduct are available only through separate and distinct *Charter* applications (*R v. Nasogaluak*, 2010 SCC 6, [2010] 1 SCR 206, at para. 2). *Charter* rights can be effectively vindicated through the exercise of statutory powers and processes (*Nasogaluak; Dagenais; Okwuobi*). In this case, it may well be that the substance of Mr. Conway's complaint about where his room is located can be fully addressed within the framework of the Board's statutory mandate and the exercise of its discretion in accordance with *Charter* values. If that is what the Board ultimately concludes to be the case, resort to s. 24(1) of the *Charter* may not add either to the Board's capacity to address the substance of the complaint or to provide appropriate redress.

[104] I would dismiss the appeal … .

NOTES

1. *Conway* harmonizes the framework for analyzing tribunal jurisdiction over the Charter. It employs the test in *Cooper* and *Martin*—that is, where a tribunal has statutory authority to decide questions of law, it is assumed to have jurisdiction over Charter questions unless that jurisdiction is specifically removed by statute—to resolve the particular issue of a tribunal's remedial jurisdiction under s. 24(1). However, the court makes clear that s. 24(1) does not expand the range of remedies that a tribunal may award pursuant to statute (para. 82)

and that "*Charter* rights can be effectively vindicated through the exercise of statutory pow-ers and processes" (para. 103). In what circumstances might a tribunal decline to award a remedy under its statute, but be prepared to do so under s. 24(1)? If those circumstances will be limited, is there much significance for the tribunal to possess jurisdiction under s. 24(1) only to the extent that the remedy in question is otherwise authorized by a statute?

2. *Conway* demonstrates the strong preference of the Supreme Court against the bifurca-tion of administrative proceedings that involve Charter issues. What are the rationales against such bifurcation? What arguments could be made in favour of it?

3. If administrative tribunals that decide questions of law are "courts of competent juris-diction" under s. 24(1) of the Charter, should they not also be treated as "courts" for the purpose of constitutional principles of judicial independence? Put differently, might *Con-way* undermine the court's decision in *Ocean Port*, as discussed in chapter 5 of this text?

THE STANDARD OF REVIEW

Whether an administrative tribunal has authority to deal with constitutional questions or is a court of competent jurisdiction is a jurisdictional question on which the tribunal must be correct (*Martin*; *Dunsmuir*). The tribunal's position on this issue is ostensibly not entitled to any deference. Indeed, the cases all proceed without any standard of review analysis on this point. It is simply assumed.

Also, once the courts have acknowledged that an administrative tribunal has jurisdiction to determine a constitutional challenge to its enabling legislation, either on its face or as applied to the particular dispute, they have often added that the tribunal's decision on the constitutional question is subject to judicial review for correctness. Thus, in *Cuddy Chicks*, La Forest J stated at 17 that, while the board had jurisdiction to entertain the constitutional challenge to the validity of the relevant provision, "it can expect no curial deference with respect to constitutional decisions." An administrative tribunal should not be able to extend the constitutional reach of the legislature that created it by some erroneous conclusion of law. This proposition has also on occasion been applied to findings of fact made by the agency that have constitutional significance.

For example, in *Northern Telecom Ltd. v. Communications Workers of Canada*, [1980] 1 SCR 115 (Can.), Dickson J said that, on an application for judicial review of the decision of the Canada Labour Relations Board to certify a union as the sole bargaining agent for a group of employees, the reviewing court should be prepared to determine for itself any fact that was relevant to whether the employees were engaged in a federal or interprovincial work or undertaking, and thus constitutionally subject to the jurisdiction of the board. However, the board's procedure, as well as its industrial relations experience, may make its findings worthy of some measure of deference on questions such as the extent of the inter-provincial aspect of the employer's business, and the role within it of the department where the employees worked.

For a more deferential view of the role of a reviewing court toward the findings of fact made by an administrative agency to establish that a matter was within the jurisdiction that could constitutionally be given to it, see, for example, *Re Windsor Airline Limousine Services Ltd.* (1980), 117 DLR (3rd) 400, at 403-4 (Ont. Div. Ct.) and *Re 50478 Ontario Ltd. and Great Lakes Fishermen etc. Union* (1986), 31 DLR (4th) 765 (Ont. HC).

Suppose that, as in *Cuddy Chicks*, a union brought a s. 15 Charter challenge to the exclusion from the benefits of collective bargaining of workers employed in a particular industry. The board rejected the employer's s. 1 defence, finding that, contrary to the evidence produced by the employer, the extension of collective bargaining would not undermine the economic viability of the industry. Should the court on review make its own independent findings of fact on this question, or may it properly give some weight to the board's? And what about a finding by a prison discipline tribunal that to disclose any more details to the inmate about information given in confidence would deter future informants, and thus was not required by the principles of fundamental justice under s. 7 of the Charter?

In fact, in another context, the Supreme Court has recognized the need for judicial deference to agency findings of constitutional or Charter facts. This was in *Suresh v. Canada (Minister of Citizenship and Immigration)*, [2002] 1 SCR 3 (Can.), at para. 39. It involved the exercise of a ministerial discretion to order deportation in a situation where s. 7 was engaged by the possibility that the deportee would face a substantial risk of torture if returned to the country from which he came. Not only did the court accept the need for deference to the minister's factual determinations on which the existence of the constitutional claim depended but it also seemed to suggest that the weight to be given to the Charter right in question in the principles of fundamental justice assessment was also not a matter for the courts. Provided it was taken into account and the decision was not patently unreasonable, the court "should not reweigh" the correct factors. We return to this issue in the next chapter, The Use and Misuse of Discretion. In the meantime, consider whether, in the light of this judgment, it would now be appropriate to defer to a tribunal's assessment of the various facts that go into determining whether it has an implicit jurisdiction to consider the validity of its empowering legislation.

JURISDICTION TO CONSIDER QUASI-CONSTITUTIONAL STATUTES

The question of a tribunal's jurisdiction to decide a specified category of legal questions is not confined to Charter and *Constitution Act* questions. In *Paul v. British Columbia (Forest Appeals Commission)*, [2003] 2 SCR 585 (released concurrently with *Martin*), for example, the Supreme Court held unanimously that the BC Forest Appeals Commission had jurisdiction to deal with questions of aboriginal rights and title in the context of an appeal from a seizure of logs from the member of a First Nations band. According to the Bastarache J:

[36] As a preliminary issue, I note that there is no basis for requiring an express empowerment that an administrative tribunal be able to apply s. 35 of the *Constitution Act, 1982*. There is no persuasive basis for distinguishing the power to determine s. 35 questions from the power to determine other constitutional questions, such as the division of powers under the *Constitution Act, 1867* or a right under the *Charter*. Section 35 is not, any more than the *Charter*, "some holy grail which only judicial initiates of the superior courts may touch" (*Cooper, supra*, at para. 70, *per* McLachlin J (as she then was), dissenting). ... The arguments that s. 35 rights are qualitatively different—that they are more complex, and require greater expertise in relation to the evidence adduced—have little merit. ... To the extent that aboriginal rights are unwritten, communal or subject to extinguishment, and thus a factual inquiry is required, it is worth noting

that administrative tribunals, like courts, have fact-finding functions. Boards are not necessarily in an inferior position to undertake such tasks. Indeed, the more relaxed evidentiary rules of administrative tribunals may in fact be more conducive than a superior court to the airing of an aboriginal rights claim.

        . . .

[38] I conclude, therefore, that there is no principled basis for distinguishing s. 35 rights from other constitutional questions.

        . . .

[39] The facts and arguments in this appeal and those in *Martin, supra*, have presented this Court with an opportunity to review its jurisprudence on the power of administrative tribunals to determine questions of constitutional law. As Gonthier J notes in *Martin*, at para. 34, the principle of constitutional supremacy in s. 52 of the *Constitution Act, 1982* leads to a presumption that all legal decisions will take into account the supreme law of the land. "In other words," as he writes, "the power to decide a question of law is the power to decide by applying only valid laws" (para. 36). One could modify that statement for the present appeal by saying that the power of an administrative board to apply valid laws is the power to apply valid laws only to those factual situations to which they are constitutionally applicable, or to the extent that they do not run afoul of s. 35 rights. This Court's decision in *Cooper, supra*, has too easily been taken as suggesting that practical considerations relating to a tribunal may readily overcome this presumption. I am of the view that the approach set out in *Martin*, in the context of determining a tribunal's power to apply the *Charter*, is also the approach to be taken in determining a tribunal's power to apply s. 35 of the *Constitution Act, 1982*. ...

Beyond the constitution itself, some statutes are said to be "quasi-constitutional" where Parliament or a legislature has provided that the statute takes precedence over all other statutes (enacted by the same legislative body) unless the other statute provides expressly to the contrary. An example of a primacy clause is the language in s. 2 of the *Canadian Bill of Rights*, SC 1960, c. 44, which states:

> Every law of Canada shall, unless it is expressly declared by an Act of the Parliament of Canada that it shall operate notwithstanding the *Canadian Bill of Rights*, be so construed and applied as not to abrogate, abridge or infringe or to authorize the abrogation, abridgment or infringement of any of the rights or freedoms herein recognized and declared. ...

Provincial human rights statutes also typically contain a primacy clause, as we see in the next case, which deals with the Ontario *Human Rights Code*.

In the following case, the Supreme Court split 4:3 on whether the Ontario Social Benefits Tribunal could decline to apply a provision of its authorizing legislation on the basis that the provision violated the Ontario *Human Rights Code*. The tribunal's authorizing legislation, the *Ontario Works Act, 1997*, s. 67(2), expressly removed the tribunal's authority to decide "the constitutional validity of a provision of an Act or a regulation" but did not refer expressly to the Ontario *Human Rights Code*. Did the inclusion of s. 67(2) nevertheless convey an intention by the legislature to remove the tribunal's authority to apply the *Human Rights Code* so as to "trump" a provision of the *Ontario Works Act, 1997*? Review the reasons of the majority and dissent in this case with the analytical framework in *Martin* in mind.

Tranchemontagne v. Ontario (Director, Disability Support Program)
[2006] 1 SCR 513

The judgment of McLachlin CJ and Bastarache, Binnie, and Fish JJ was delivered by
BASTARACHE J:

1. Introduction

[1] Is the Social Benefits Tribunal ("SBT"), a provincially created statutory tribunal, obligated to follow provincial human rights legislation in rendering its decisions? That is the question raised by this appeal.

[2] The roots of this dispute can be traced back to November 1998 and July 1999, when the appellants Robert Tranchemontagne and Norman Werbeski respectively applied to the Director of the Ontario Disability Support Program ("Director") for support pursuant to the *Ontario Disability Support Program Act, 1997*, SO 1997, c. 25, Sch. B ("ODSPA"). If successful, the appellants would have received financial assistance in order to help them cope with their substantial impairments. If unsuccessful, the appellants would be left to apply for the appreciably lower levels of assistance offered pursuant to the *Ontario Works Act, 1997*, SO 1997, c. 25, Sch. A ("OWA").

[3] It is clear that the ODSPA and the OWA are meant to serve very different goals. The former statute is meant to ensure support for disabled applicants, recognizing that the government shares in the responsibility of providing such support (ODSPA, s. 1). The latter statute, on the other hand, seeks to provide only temporary assistance premised on the concept of individual responsibility (OWA, s. 1). ...

[4] The Director determined that the appellants were not entitled to benefits under the ODSPA regime. Following the procedure set out in the ODSPA, the appellants requested an internal review of the Director's decision. Rejected at this stage as well, the appellants then appealed to the intervener SBT.

[5] The rulings of the SBT in the appellants' individual appeals were rendered on February 7, 2001, for the appellant Werbeski, and September 18, 2001, for the appellant Tranchemontagne. In both decisions, the SBT found that the appellants suffered from alcoholism. The SBT held alcoholism to be a "disabling condition," in the case of the appellant Tranchemontagne, and a "substantial impairment" that "substantially restricts" working ability, in the case of the appellant Werbeski. The SBT dismissed both appellants' appeals.

[6] The SBT based its decisions on s. 5(2) of the ODSPA. That section provides:

5. ...

(2) A person is not eligible for income support if,

(a) the person is dependent on or addicted to alcohol, a drug or some other chemically active substance;

(b) the alcohol, drug or other substance has not been authorized by prescription as provided for in the regulations; and

(c) the only substantial restriction in activities of daily living is attributable to the use or cessation of use of the alcohol, drug or other substance at the time of determining or reviewing eligibility.

[7] The appellants do not dispute that, if applicable, s. 5(2) functions to deny them support on the basis of their alcoholism. In front of the SBT, they each argued that they had impairments other than alcoholism; these arguments were rejected and the SBT's findings have not been appealed to this Court. But the appellants also argued that s. 5(2) was inapplicable by virtue of the Ontario *Human Rights Code*, RSO 1990, c. H.19 ("Code"). By purporting to refuse them support on the basis of their alcoholism, which the appellants assert is a disability within the meaning of the Code, the appellants argued that s. 5(2) of the ODSPA constituted discrimination and was therefore inapplicable because of the primacy of the Code over other legislation.

[8] Instead of analyzing this argument, the SBT held that it did not have the jurisdiction to consider the applicability of s. 5(2) pursuant to the Code. The appellants' appeals were therefore dismissed without the benefit of a ruling that their treatment was not discriminatory.

[9] Their cases now joined, the appellants appealed to the Divisional Court. In brief oral reasons, the bench of Then, Cameron and Desotti JJ agreed with the SBT that the authority to consider the Code could not be found in its enabling statutes ([2003] OJ No. 1409 (QL), at para. 3). The appellants then appealed to the Ontario Court of Appeal.

[10] On behalf of a unanimous bench, Weiler JA examined the ODSPA and OWA in detail. She concluded that the legislature did not remove jurisdiction to consider the Code from the SBT, and that accordingly the SBT possessed the power to declare a provision of the ODSPA inapplicable by virtue of its discriminatory nature ((2004), 72 OR (3d) 457, at paras. 58-59 and 62). However, Weiler JA then went on to consider whether the SBT should have declined to exercise its Code jurisdiction in the present appeal. She held that the SBT was not the most appropriate forum in which the Code issue could be decided, leading her to ultimately dismiss the appeal (para. 70).

[11] The substance of the appellants' argument before the SBT is not at issue before this Court. Since the appeal is allowed, this issue will be remitted to the SBT. In the event the appeal would have been dismissed, the appellants would have pursued a judicial review application, which is presently being held in abeyance before the Divisional Court. It is thus not for this Court to consider whether s. 5(2) of the ODSPA conflicts with the Code. Rather, this Court is only concerned with the SBT's decision that it could not decide these issues for itself.

[12] It has been almost five years since the appellants' applications were denied by the Director. During this time, the appellants have not received any disability support pursuant to the ODSPA. If the appellants are ultimately successful in their substantive claims, no amount of interest could negate the fact that they have lived the past five years without the assistance they were owed. Accordingly, much argument before this Court centred on concerns as to the vulnerability of the appellants and their need to have their appeals settled fully by the SBT. Nevertheless, these concerns must be tempered by the importance of the efficient operation of the SBT more generally, lest other applicants suffer needlessly while waiting for the results of their appeals. Ultimately, however, this appeal is not decided by matters of practicality for applicants or matters of expediency for administrative tribunals. It is decided by following the statutory scheme enacted by the legislature.

[13] The Code is fundamental law. The Ontario legislature affirmed the primacy of the Code in the law itself, as applicable both to private citizens and public bodies. Further, the adjudication of Code issues is no longer confined to the exclusive domain of the intervener the Ontario Human Rights Commission ("OHRC"): s. 34 of the Code. The legislature has thus contemplated that this fundamental law could be applied by other administrative bodies and has amended the Code accordingly.

[14] The laudatory goals of the Code are not well served by reading in limitations to its application. It is settled law that statutory tribunals empowered to decide questions of law are presumed to have the power to look beyond their enabling statutes in order to apply the whole law to a matter properly in front of them. By applying this principle to the present appeal, it becomes clear that the SBT had the jurisdiction to consider the Code in determining whether the appellants were eligible for support pursuant to the ODSPA. At that point, the SBT had the responsibility of applying the Code in order to render a decision that reflected the whole law of the province.

2. Issues

[15] This appeal raises two issues:

(1) Does the SBT have the jurisdiction to consider the Code in rendering its decisions?

(2) If the answer to the first question is "yes," should the SBT have declined to exercise its jurisdiction in the present cases?

3. Analysis

Does the SBT Have the Jurisdiction To Consider the Code?

[16] Statutory tribunals like the SBT do not enjoy any inherent jurisdiction. It is therefore necessary to examine the enabling statutes of the SBT in order to determine what powers it possesses: *Nova Scotia (Workers' Compensation Board) v. Martin*, [2003] 2 SCR 504, 2003 SCC 54, at para. 33; *Cuddy Chicks Ltd. v. Ontario (Labour Relations Board)*, [1991] 2 SCR 5, at p. 14; *Douglas/Kwantlen Faculty Assn. v. Douglas College*, [1990] 3 SCR 570, at p. 595. For the SBT, the relevant statutes are the ODSPA and the OWA. In the context of the present appeal, however, the legislative scheme surrounding the Code cannot be ignored. The enabling statutes and the Code will all be considered in turn.

The ODSPA and the OWA

[17] The ODSPA and the OWA are twin components of the Ontario government's scheme for delivering social assistance to deserving applicants. The ODSPA deals with disabled applicants, while the OWA provides assistance for eligible applicants who are not disabled. Reference can be made to the opening sections of each statute in order to discern the policy differences between the two. Section 1 of the ODPSA reads:

1. [Purpose of Act] The purpose of this Act is to establish a program that,

(a) *provides income and employment supports to eligible persons with disabilities;*

(b) *recognizes that government, communities, families and individuals share responsibility for providing such supports;*

(c) effectively serves persons with disabilities who need assistance; and

(d) is accountable to the taxpayers of Ontario.

Section 1 of the OWA reads:

1. [Purpose of Act] The purpose of this Act is to establish a program that,

(a) *recognizes individual responsibility and promotes self reliance through employment;*

(b) *provides temporary financial assistance to those most in need while they satisfy obligations to become and stay employed;*

(c) effectively serves people needing assistance; and

(d) is accountable to the taxpayers of Ontario.

[18] As mentioned above, the levels of support also vary greatly between the two regimes. For instance, the amount payable for basic needs for a single recipient with no dependents, pursuant to the OWA, is $201 per month (O Reg. 134/98, s. 41(1)). The comparable figure for the ODSPA regime is $532 per month (O Reg. 222/98, s. 30(1)1). The single shelter allowance under the OWA is $335 (O Reg. 134/98, s. 42(2)2), while the comparable ODSPA figure is $427 (O Reg. 222/98, s. 31(2)2). The provision of assistance under the OWA may also be subject to conditions, like participating in employment measures: s. 7(4)(b).

[19] The ODSPA provides a detailed framework for the handling of a disability benefits application. The Director receives applications for income support: s. 38(a). Whether a person is disabled is decided through reference to ss. 4 and 5 of the ODSPA: ... [omitting reproduction of these sections of the Act].

[20] As s. 4(2) makes clear, it is not the Director who personally decides whether a person is disabled within the meaning of s. 4(1). The Director may also allow any of his or her duties to be performed by another under his or her supervision and direction: s. 37(3). However the ultimate determination of eligibility, including the application of s. 5(2), falls within the responsibilities of the Director: s. 38(b).

Once an applicant is found to be eligible for support, it is also the Director who determines the amount and directs its provision: s. 38(c).

[21] An appeal to the SBT is generally permitted, with the legislature specifying certain exceptional cases where an appeal will not lie: s. 21. But an applicant must request an internal review before appealing to the SBT: s. 22. The internal review need not conform to the *Statutory Powers Procedure Act*, RSO 1990, c. S.22: s. 22(4). After the internal review, an applicant can appeal the Director's decision to the SBT: s. 23(1). The onus is on the applicant to satisfy the SBT that the Director is wrong: s. 23(10).

[22] I should emphasize at this point that, for an applicant whose application for income support is still denied after the internal review, the SBT is a forum that cannot easily be avoided. It is the SBT that is empowered by the legislature to decide income support appeals binding on the Director: s. 26(3). Given the existence of an appeal to the SBT, it is not at all clear that an applicant could seek judicial review of the Director's decision without first arguing before the SBT: see *Canadian Pacific Ltd. v. Matsqui Indian*

Band, [1995] 1 SCR 3, at paras. 32-38, 112 and 140-53. And while an applicant who is denied benefits for discriminatory reasons may indeed seek recourse through the OHRC, applicants will not always realize that they are victims of discrimination. For instance, in the present appeal, the letters from the Director to the appellants concerning the initial application and the internal review never mention that the appellants' alcoholism was being ignored as a potential basis for disability. The appellants were simply told that they were not found to be persons with a disability. The adjudication summaries of the cases raise the issue of alcoholism, but there is no evidence that these documents were appended to the Director's letters; it would seem they were obtained by the appellants on discovery.

[23] The ODSPA also provides for an appeal, on questions of law, from the SBT to the Divisional Court: s. 31(1). Such questions of law can routinely arise during the course of the SBT's normal operations: for example, it may need to determine the legal meaning of "substantial physical or mental impairment" under s. 4(1)(a), or even "chemically active substance" under s. 5(2)(a). There is little doubt, therefore, that the SBT is empowered to decide questions of law: see *Paul v. British Columbia (Forest Appeals Commission)*, [2003] 2 SCR 585, 2003 SCC 55, at para. 41. Important implications flow from this power.

[24] In *Martin*, this Court repeated the principle that administrative bodies empowered to decide questions of law "may presumptively go beyond the bounds of their enabling statute and decide issues of common law or statutory interpretation that arise in the course of a case properly before them, subject to judicial review on the appropriate standard": see para. 45. I must emphasize that the presumptive power to look beyond a tribunal's enabling statute is triggered simply where a tribunal (with the authority to decide questions of law) is confronted with "issues ... that arise in the course of a case properly before" it. This can be contrasted with the power to subject a statutory provision to *Charter* scrutiny, which will only be found where the tribunal has jurisdiction to decide questions of law *relating to that specific provision*: see *Martin*, at para. 3.

[25] I must conclude that the contrast in the wording of *Martin* is deliberate. Where a specific provision is being declared invalid, it is necessary to ensure that the tribunal is empowered to scrutinize it. Power to scrutinize other provisions is not sufficient, because the constitutional analysis is targeting one specific provision. But the same does not hold true when a tribunal is merely being asked to consider external sources of law. In such a situation, a specific statutory provision is not necessarily placed at the heart of the analysis; for instance, the tribunal may be asked to look beyond its enabling statute because its enabling statute is silent on an issue. Although consideration of the external source in the present appeal might lead to the inapplicability of a specific provision, this does not imply that the process is analogous to that of constitutional invalidation. ...

[26] The presumption that a tribunal can go beyond its enabling statute—unlike the presumption that a tribunal can pronounce on constitutional validity—exists because it is undesirable for a tribunal to limit itself to some of the law while shutting its eyes to the rest of the law. The law is not so easily compartmentalized that all relevant sources on a given issue can be found in the provisions of a tribunal's enabling statute. Accordingly, to limit the tribunal's ability to consider the whole law is to increase the probability that a tribunal will come to a misinformed conclusion. In turn, misinformed conclusions lead to inefficient appeals or, more unfortunately, the denial of justice.

[27] Yet the power to decide questions of law will not always imply the power to apply legal principles beyond the tribunal's enabling legislation. As noted above, statutory creatures are necessarily limited by the boundaries placed upon them by the legislature. Subject to its own constitutional constraints, a legislature may restrict the jurisdiction of its tribunals however it sees fit. The respondent points to two provisions in the ODSPA and OWA to argue that this is precisely what the legislature sought to do with respect to the SBT.

[28] Section 29(3) of the ODSPA provides that the "Tribunal shall not make a decision in an appeal under this Act that the Director would not have authority to make." The respondent suggests that the Director, and the Director's delegates, cannot possibly have the power to use the Code to deny application of the ODSPA, and it therefore follows that the SBT does not have this power either. I believe this argument can be dealt with easily.

[29] Section 29(3) is not as extreme as the respondent suggests. The section merely states that the SBT cannot make a decision that the Director would not have the authority to make. Thus the SBT could not decide to award an applicant income support in an amount inconsistent with the regulations, because the Director does not have the authority to award income support in an amount inconsistent with the regulations: see s. 11. Yet allowing the Code to inform an eligibility determination can hardly be characterized as a "decision" itself; it is simply a power that the SBT may possess. And the ODSPA does not limit the SBT's *powers* to those possessed by the Director. In fact, the ODSPA itself contemplates powers that the SBT has and the Director does not. For instance, pursuant to s. 38(b), the Director must determine each applicant's eligibility for income support, but s. 28 obliges the SBT to refuse to hear frivolous or vexatious appeals. I conclude that s. 29(3) does not preclude the possibility of the SBT considering the Code.

[30] The second provision to which the respondent points in suggesting that the SBT does not have the jurisdiction to consider the Code is s. 67(2) of the OWA. That section provides that the SBT cannot determine the constitutional validity of a provision or regulation and cannot determine the legislative authority for making a regulation. The respondent's argument is thus premised on the notion that scrutiny pursuant to the Code is analogous to the kind of scrutiny explicitly prohibited by s. 67(2). Once again, I cannot agree.

[31] The Code emanates from the Ontario legislature. As I will elaborate below, it is one thing to preclude a statutory tribunal from *invalidating* legislation enacted by the legislature that created it. It is completely different to preclude that body from *applying* legislation enacted by that legislature in order to resolve apparent conflicts between statutes. The former power—an act of defying legislative intent—is one that is clearly more offensive to the legislature; it should not be surprising, therefore, when the legislature eliminates it. Yet the latter power represents nothing more than an instantiation of legislative intent—a legislative intent, I should note, that includes the primacy of the Code and the concurrent jurisdiction of administrative bodies to apply it.

[32] Thus the argument based on s. 67(2) is defeated because the legislature could not possibly have intended that the Code be denied application by analogy to the Constitution. While it clearly prohibited the SBT from considering the constitutional validity of laws and regulations, it equally clearly chose not to invoke the same prohibition with respect to the Code. In the context of this distinction, I must conclude that the legislature

envisioned constitutional and Code issues as being in different "categor[ies] of questions of law," to use the language of *Martin*, at para. 42. Consistent with the human rights regime it crafted, the legislature has afforded the Code the possibility of broad application even while denying the SBT the authority to determine constitutional issues.

The Code

[33] The most important characteristic of the Code for the purposes of this appeal is that it is fundamental, quasi-constitutional law. ... Accordingly, it is to be interpreted in a liberal and purposive manner, with a view towards broadly protecting the human rights of those to whom it applies. ... And not only must the content of the Code be understood in the context of its purpose, but like the *Canadian Charter of Rights and Freedoms*, it must be recognized as being the law of the people: see *Cooper v. Canada (Human Rights Commission)*, [1996] 3 SCR 854, at para. 70, aff'd in *Martin*, at para. 29, and *Quebec (Attorney General) v. Quebec (Human Rights Tribunal)*, [2004] 2 SCR 223, 2004 SCC 40 ("*Charette*"), at para. 28. Accordingly, it must not only be given expansive meaning, but also offered accessible application.

[34] The importance of the Code is not merely an assertion of this Court. The Ontario legislature has seen fit to bind itself and all its agents through the Code: s. 47(1). Further, it has given the Code primacy over all other legislative enactments: s. 47(2). As a result of this primacy clause, where provisions of the Code conflict with provisions in another provincial law, it is the provisions of the Code that are to apply.

[35] This primacy provision has both similarities and differences with s. 52 of the *Constitution Act, 1982*, which announces the supremacy of the Constitution. In terms of similarities, both provisions function to eliminate the effects of inconsistent legislation. At the end of the day, whether there is a conflict with the Code or the Constitution, the ultimate effect is that the other provision is not followed and, for the purposes of that particular application, it is as if the legislation was never enacted. But in my view, the differences between the two provisions are far more important. A provision declared invalid pursuant to s. 52 of the *Constitution Act, 1982* was never validly enacted to begin with. It never existed as valid law because the legislature enacting it never had the authority to pass it. But when a provision is inapplicable pursuant to s. 47 of the Code, there is no statement being made as to its validity. The legislature had the power to enact the conflicting provision; it just so happens that the legislature also enacted another law that takes precedence. ...

[Bastarache J's analysis and rejection of the related argument that there was a substantive similarity between s. 1 of the Code and s. 15 of the Charter have been omitted.]

[38] Rather, it is most consistent with the legislative scheme surrounding the Code to differentiate the Code from the Constitution and allow the SBT to consider the former. Two elements of the Code regime, in addition to those discussed under the ODSPA and OWA, confirm this legislative intention. The first is found at s. 47(2). This section provides not simply that the Code takes primacy over other legislative enactments, but that this primacy applies "unless the [other] Act or regulation *specifically* provides that it is to

apply *despite this Act* [the Code]." Thus the legislature put its mind to conflicts between the Code and other enactments, declared that the Code will prevail as a general rule and also developed instructions for how it is to avoid application of Code primacy. Given that the legislature did not follow the procedure it declared mandatory for overruling the primacy of the Code, this Court is in no position to deduce that it meant to do so or that it came close enough. This is especially so given that the consequence of this deduction would be that the application of human rights law is curtailed.

[39] The second element in the statutory scheme that confirms the jurisdiction of the SBT to apply the Code is the non-exclusive jurisdiction of the OHRC concerning the interpretation and application of the Code. While s. 14b(6) of *The Ontario Human Rights Code*, RSO 1970, c. 318, as amended by SO 1971, c. 50 (Supp.), s. 63, previously gave a board of inquiry exclusive jurisdiction to determine contraventions of the Code, the legislature has since altered its regime. In its present form, the Code can be interpreted and applied by a myriad of administrative actors. Nothing in the current legislative scheme suggests that the OHRC is the guardian or the gatekeeper for human rights law in Ontario. …

Conclusion on Jurisdiction

[40] I therefore conclude that the SBT has jurisdiction to consider the Code. The ODSPA and OWA confirm that the SBT can decide questions of law. It follows that the SBT is presumed to have the jurisdiction to consider the whole law. More specifically, when it decides whether an applicant is eligible for income support, the SBT is presumed able to consider any legal source that might influence its decision on eligibility. In the present appeal, the Code is one such source.

[41] There is no indication that the legislature has sought to rebut this presumption. To the contrary, the legislature has announced the primacy of the Code and has given itself clear directions for how this primacy can be eliminated in particular circumstances. The legislature has indeed prohibited the SBT from considering the constitutional valid-ity of enactments, or the *vires* of regulations, but it did nothing to suggest that the SBT could not consider the Code. I cannot impute to the legislature the intention that the SBT ignore the Code when the legislature did not even follow its own instructions for yielding this result.

[42] The ODSPA and OWA do evince a legislative intent to prevent the SBT from looking behind the statutory and regulatory scheme enacted by the legislature and its delegated actors. However, consideration of the Code is not analogous. Far from being used to look behind the legislative scheme, the Code forms part of the legislative scheme. It would be contrary to legislative intention to demand that the SBT ignore it.

Should the SBT Have Declined To Exercise Its Jurisdiction in the Present Cases?

[43] Although I have established that the SBT has the jurisdiction to apply the Code in rendering its income support decisions, the respondent argues that a further analysis remains. It suggests that, in cases where two administrative bodies—the SBT and the OHRC, in the present appeal—have jurisdiction over an issue, there should be a deter-mination of which one is the better forum before an applicant is allowed to proceed in

either one. Following the Court of Appeal's reasoning, this approach would use the framework developed in the context of disputes over exclusive jurisdiction ... to determine the most appropriate forum in cases of concurrent jurisdiction.

[44] The analysis that the respondent invites is premised on the assumption that the SBT could decline jurisdiction if it determines that the OHRC is a more appropriate forum in which the applicants could advance their claim. This premise is unnecessary when a tribunal is determining whether another decision maker has exclusive jurisdiction; in that context, the tribunal is not deciding which of two forums is preferable, but rather which of two forums has jurisdiction in the first place. But this premise is vital in the present appeal because the jurisdiction of the SBT has already been triggered. In order for the SBT to be able to decline to hear the issue properly in front of it, the legislature must have granted it this power.

[45] An investigation of the ODSPA and the OWA reveals that the legislature did not grant the SBT such a power. While the SBT must refuse to hear an appeal that is frivolous or vexatious pursuant to s. 28 of the ODSPA, at no point does the legislature offer the SBT the discretion to decline to hear an issue of which it is properly seized. This approach can be contrasted with the Ontario legislature's regime surrounding the OHRC (which possesses a discretion to decline to hear complaints better considered under another Act pursuant to s. 34 of the Code) and its courts (which may stay proceedings "on such terms as are considered just" pursuant to s. 106 of the *Courts of Justice Act*, RSO 1990, c. C.43).

[46] Since the SBT has not been granted the authority to decline jurisdiction, it cannot avoid considering the Code issues in the appellants' appeals. This is sufficient to decide the appeal.

[47] Having the SBT apply the Code in rendering its decisions also has many salutary effects and is consistent with this Court's jurisprudence affirming the importance of accessible human rights legislation. Before reviewing these effects, however, I should stress that they were not determinative in deciding the outcome of this appeal. While the SBT happens to be the best forum to decide Code issues in this particular case, even if it was not, its lack of authority to decline jurisdiction would be conclusive. The legislature defines the jurisdiction of the tribunals that it creates and, so long as it defines their jurisdiction in a way that does not infringe the Constitution, it is not for those tribunals (or the courts) to decide that the jurisdiction granted is in some way deficient. Accordingly, important as they may be to applicants and administrative bodies, factors like expertise and practical constraints are insufficient to bestow a power that the legislature did not see fit to grant a tribunal.

[48] In this case, the applicability of s. 5(2) of the ODSPA is best decided by the SBT because the SBT is practically unavoidable for the vulnerable applicants who have been denied financial assistance under the ODSPA. Appellants to the SBT, like applicants in front of many administrative tribunals, are not individuals who have time on their side, nor will they necessarily be willing to start afresh with an application to the OHRC if their appeal to the SBT is dismissed. And if they try this alternate route, there is no guarantee that they would even have the chance to argue their case before the Human Rights Tribunal of Ontario. ... These applicants merit prompt, final and binding resolutions for their disputes. ... It is truly exceptional that the appellants in the present appeal have

been able to ride the waves of this legal battle for almost five years, without ever collecting benefits under the ODSPA and without even having their substantive argument adjudicated yet.

[49] The intersection of the ODSPA regime with human rights law in the present dispute only accentuates the importance of the SBT deciding the entire dispute in front of it. In *Zurich Insurance Co. v. Ontario (Human Rights Commission)*, [1992] 2 SCR 321, at p. 339, Sopinka J described human rights legislation as often being the "final refuge of the disadvantaged and the disenfranchised" and the "last protection of the most vulnerable members of society." But this refuge can be rendered meaningless by placing barriers in front of it. Human rights remedies must be accessible in order to be effective.

[50] Where a tribunal is properly seized of an issue pursuant to a statutory appeal, and especially where a vulnerable appellant is advancing arguments in defence of his or her human rights, I would think it extremely rare for this tribunal to not be the one most appropriate to hear the entirety of the dispute. I am unable to think of any situation where such a tribunal would be justified in ignoring the human rights argument, applying a potentially discriminatory provision, referring the legislative challenge to another forum, and leaving the appellant without benefits in the meantime.

[51] The practical constraints that burden the SBT are of an entirely different character than those facing applicants. It is true that the efficient functioning of tribunals is important. And the presence of another tribunal with greater institutional capacity may indeed signal that this other forum is more appropriate to deal with the case at hand: see *Paul*, at para. 39. But tribunals should be loath to avoid cases on the assumption that the legislature gave them insufficient tools to handle matters within their jurisdiction. In those instances where the legislature does grant a tribunal the power to decline jurisdiction, the scope of this power should be carefully observed in order to ensure that the tribunal does not improperly ignore issues that the legislature intended it to consider.

[52] I conclude that the SBT is a highly appropriate forum in which to argue the applicability of s. 5(2) of the ODSPA under the Code. In general, encouraging administrative tribunals to exercise their jurisdiction to decide human rights issues fulfills the laudable goal of bringing justice closer to the people. But more crucial for the purposes of the present appeal is the fact that the legislature did not grant the SBT the power to defer to another forum when it is properly seized of an issue. Absent such authority, the SBT could not decline to deal with the Code issue on the basis that a more appropriate forum existed.

4. Disposition

[53] The appeal is allowed. The case will be remitted to the SBT so that it can rule on the applicability of s. 5(2) of the ODSPA.

5. Costs

[54] The appellants' request for reimbursement of their disbursements before this Court will be granted. The parties did not seek costs and therefore none will be awarded.

[ABELLA J (LeBel, Deschamps, and Abella JJ concurring) (dissenting)]:

[55] The government of Ontario created a special program for the efficient and effective delivery of income support benefits to persons with disabilities. Though not excluded from general social assistance benefits, those whose sole impairment is alcohol or drug addiction are excluded from this particular program.

[56] This case is not about access, about the applicability of human rights legislation, or about whether the government is entitled to refuse to provide disability benefits to individuals whose only substantial impairment is an alcohol or drug dependency. It is about statutory interpretation. Specifically, it is about the scope of the legislature's intention when it enacted a statutory provision depriving an administrative tribunal of jurisdiction to decide whether any of its enabling provisions were *ultra vires* or violated the *Canadian Charter of Rights and Freedoms*. With respect, I do not share the view of my colleague Bastarache J that this legislative direction has no effect on a tribunal's ability to apply the Ontario *Human Rights Code*, RSO 1990, c. H.19 ("Code"), so as to render legislation inapplicable.

[57] The Social Benefits Tribunal ("SBT") was created to hear appeals dealing with Ontario's general social assistance regime under the *Ontario Works Act, 1997*, SO 1997, c. 25, Sch. A ("OWA"), and Ontario's special income support program for persons with disabilities under the *Ontario Disability Support Program Act, 1997*, SO 1997, c. 25, Sch. B ("ODSPA"). The OWA prescribes the general structure, composition, procedures and jurisdiction of the SBT.

[58] Section 5(2) of the ODSPA provides that an individual whose only disabling condition is an alcohol or non-prescription drug dependency is not eligible for income support under the ODSPA. The question in this appeal is whether the SBT has jurisdiction to refuse to apply this provision, based on its purported inconsistency with the Code, or whether it is precluded from doing so by s. 67(2) of the OWA, which states:

> 67. …
>
> (2) The Tribunal shall not inquire into or make a decision concerning,
>> (a) the constitutional validity of a provision of an Act or a regulation; or
>> (b) the legislative authority for a regulation made under an Act.

[59] In *Nova Scotia (Workers' Compensation Board) v. Martin*, [2003] 2 SCR 504, 2003 SCC 54, at para. 42, this Court said: "The question to be asked is whether an examination of the statutory provisions clearly leads to the conclusion that the legislature intended to exclude the *Charter*, or more broadly, a *category of questions of law* encompassing the *Charter*, from the scope of the questions of law to be addressed by the tribunal" (emphasis added).

[60] In my view, s. 67(2) creates a "category of questions of law" that have been explicitly removed from the SBT's jurisdiction, namely any legal question the answer to which might result in the SBT finding a provision of its own legislation inoperative.

[Abella J's review of the factual background and decisions below has been omitted.]

Analysis

[69] The issue is not *whether* a party can challenge a provision of the ODSPA as being inconsistent with the Code; it is *where* the challenge can be made and, specifically, whether it can be made before the Director or SBT.

[70] Through s. 5 of the ODSPA, the legislature has imposed some restrictions on eligibility for income support. Under s. 5(2), the Director is required to determine whether "the only substantial restriction in activities of daily living" the applicant experiences is attributable to the use of drugs, alcohol or some other substance. If so, the applicant is ineligible for income support.

[71] This provision, it is argued, is discriminatory and must defer to the paramountcy of the Code. Section 47(2) of the Code provides that where a provision in an Act or regulation purports to require or authorize conduct in contravention of the Code, the Code prevails in the absence of specific legislative language to the contrary:

> Where a provision in an Act or regulation purports to require or authorize conduct that is a contravention of Part I, this Act applies and prevails unless the Act or regulation specifically provides that it is to apply despite this Act.

[72] Clearly, the values and rights expressed in the Code are fundamental. This, however, is different from a derivative conclusion that as a result of s. 47(2), all administrative bodies in Ontario are *ad hoc* Human Rights Commissions capable of applying the Code. Section 47(2) of the Code does not confer jurisdiction; it announces the primacy of the Code. It represents a legislative direction that when a body *with the authority to do so* is asked to apply the Code, the provisions of the Code will prevail over an inconsistent statutory provision.

[73] The question in this case, then, is whether the Director or the SBT have the jurisdiction to apply the Code in a way that renders a provision inoperable. If they do not, the Code's primacy is of no interpretive assistance in this regard.

[74] In *Martin*, this Court decided that the authority to assess the constitutional validity of a legislative provision flows from the powers to decide questions of law the legislature conferred on the administrative body:

> Administrative tribunals which have jurisdiction—whether explicit or implied—to decide questions of law *arising under a legislative provision* are presumed to have concomitant jurisdiction to decide the constitutional validity of *that provision*. [Emphasis added; para. 3.]

This recognizes the truism that the jurisdictional range of administrative tribunals is determined by their enabling legislation. It also recognizes that the legislature may have intended that an administrative decision maker be authorized to resolve some legal issues, but not others.

[75] The following powers and duties of the Director are prescribed in s. 38 of the ODSPA:

> 38. The Director shall,
>   (a) receive applications for income support;
>   (b) determine the eligibility of each applicant for income support;

(c) if an applicant is found eligible for income support, determine the amount of the income support and direct its provision;

(d) administer the provisions of this Act and the regulations;

(e) determine how the payment of the costs of administering this Act and providing income support is to be allocated;

(f) ensure that the appropriate payments are made or withheld, as the case may be; and

(g) exercise the prescribed powers and duties.

[76] Following an internal review, an appeal lies from the Director to the SBT. Section 26(1) of the ODSPA provides that on appeal, the SBT is limited to denying the appeal, granting the appeal, granting the appeal in part or referring "the matter back to the Director for reconsideration in accordance with any directions the Tribunal considers proper."

[77] The SBT's authority is limited by s. 29(3) of the ODSPA. Section 29(3) states that the "Tribunal shall not make a decision in an appeal under this Act that the Director would not have authority to make," confining the SBT to exercising the limited jurisdiction of the Director. While the ODSPA provides the SBT with greater procedural powers than the Director, it is clear from s. 29(3) that the SBT has no broader decision-making powers or jurisdiction than the Director.

[78] Section 67(2) of the OWA was enacted in 1997 in response to a decision of the prior SBT interpreting its legislation to give itself *Charter* jurisdiction. As previously noted, s. 67(2) provides that the SBT "shall not inquire into or make a decision concerning" either "the constitutional validity of a provision of an Act or a regulation" or "the legislative authority for a regulation made under an Act." The potential effect of either inquiry may be to render a regulation or provision inapplicable.

[79] The reasons of my colleague Bastarache J suggest that the s. 67(2) revocation of *Charter* jurisdiction does not extend to Code jurisdiction because the consequence of a *Charter* breach is legislative invalidity while non-compliance with the Code gives rise only to inoperability. The difference between invalidity and inoperability explains why, in his view, the legislature revoked *Charter* jurisdiction but not Code jurisdiction. This, with respect, overlooks the fact that administrative tribunals lack the power to make formal declarations of invalidity. A tribunal only has jurisdiction to decline to apply the offending provision. The legislature revoked the SBT's *Charter* jurisdiction because it did not want the SBT to declare any part of the legislation inapplicable. That is precisely what the effect could be of applying the Code.

[80] An obvious deduction from the specific withdrawal of *Charter* and *ultra vires* determinations, it seems to me, is that the legislature did not want the SBT to be able to refuse to apply any of its enabling provisions by finding these to be inoperable, period. In the face of such a clear legislative direction, one wonders why it can be assumed that the intent was, nonetheless, to permit such a finding under the Code.

[81] In enacting s. 67(2), the legislature did everything it could reasonably have been expected to do to signal its intention that the SBT not decide the validity of any aspect of the ODSPA. What the legislature specifically excluded from the SBT's determinations was that "category of questions of law," to use the language of *Martin*, which engaged the validity, and thus the applicability, of any of the statutory provisions or regulations the SBT was created to administer.

[82] The fact that the Code is not mentioned specifically in the taxonomy of prohibited determinations in s. 67(2) is not determinative. The overlapping nature of the rights and remedies guaranteed under the *Charter* and the Code, including disability rights, is such that it would be anomalous if the SBT were empowered to assess whether an ODSPA provision was discriminatory on grounds of disability under the Code but not under the *Charter*.

[A discussion of authorities has been omitted.]

[84] The Code and the *Charter* are both legal instruments capable of remedying discrimination based on disability. The result of a challenge under either may very well be the same. From the perspective of a claimant before the SBT, the result of a Code or a *Charter* violation would be the same—s. 5(2) would be rendered inapplicable to them.

[85] By revoking jurisdiction over *Charter* questions, the legislature unequivocally expressed its intent that the SBT not hear and decide legal issues that may result in the inoperability of a provision. Even though s. 67(2) refers to constitutional validity, but not to compliance with the Code, the remedial and conceptual similarities between the *Charter* and the Code are such that the legislature has, by clear implication, withdrawn authority to grant the remedy of inoperability under *either* mandate.

[86] In addition to the wording of the operative legislation, *Martin* also holds that practical considerations, including its institutional capacity, may indicate the legislature's intention that a tribunal not consider legal questions that go to the applicability of its enabling statute. Assessing the applicability of the legislature's decision to make those whose sole incapacitating impairment is drug or alcohol addiction ineligible for income support under the ODSPA, requires an inquiry into the legislature's justification, which is a complicated evidentiary and legal determination. On second reading of the OWA, the Parliamentary Assistant to the Minister of Community and Social Services said, about s. 67(2), "… we are proposing to remove jurisdiction from the tribunal to consider constitutional issues. The reason for this proposed change is simple: Constitutional questions involve complex legal issues and can have far-reaching consequences that are better addressed, in our opinion, by the courts": Legislative Assembly of Ontario, *Official Report of Debates*, No. 222B, September 2, 1997, at p. 11708 (Mr. F. Klees).

[87] Clearly, a legal inquiry into the operability of a provision by either the Director or the SBT was deemed inappropriate. A brief review of their institutional characteristics confirms why neither the Director nor the SBT was deemed to have the capacity to decide such complex, time-consuming legal issues.

[88] The Director does not hold hearings or receive evidence beyond that filed by an applicant. An appeal to the SBT from the Director's decision is commenced by filing with the SBT a notice of appeal form on which an applicant is simply asked to explain what he or she disagrees with in the Director's original decision and why. The Director has the option of making only written submissions before the SBT. Following receipt of an applicant's notice of appeal form, the Director has 30 days to file any written submissions in response.

[89] The SBT's decisions are not publicly available. The hearings are informal and private. Most hearings last no longer than one and a half hours.

[90] The SBT is meant to be an efficient, effective, and quick process. Yet it seems to be having difficulty meeting this mandate. In 2004-2005, the SBT had a backlog of 9,042 cases and received 11,127 new appeals under the OWA and the ODSPA. ...

[91] Imposing Code compliance hearings on the SBT will similarly and inevitably impact its ability to assist the disabled community it was established to benefit in a timely way. It will be difficult to explain to the thousands of disabled individuals waiting for their appeals to be heard—many without any interim support—that there is any public benefit in the SBT hearing a complex, lengthy, and inevitably delaying jurisprudential issue with no precedential value. That is the real access issue in this case.

[92] The SBT's institutional capacity and procedural practices differ markedly from those of a tribunal appointed under the Code ("Human Rights Tribunal"). The Human Rights Tribunal's Rules of Practice foster full adversarial debate and provide for full disclosure and production obligations. I acknowledge that the Human Rights Tribunal's greater institutional powers and capacity do not mean that only a Human Rights Tribunal can apply the Code.

[93] Formerly, the Ontario Human Rights Commission had exclusive jurisdiction to decide human rights complaints. ... In 1981, the legislature enacted what is now s. 34(1)(a) of the Code, giving the Commission a discretion to refer a human rights complaint to another body. ...

[94] While s. 34(1)(a) of the Code may signal that the Commission no longer has exclusive jurisdiction to decide complaints under the Code, the legislature does not seem to have replaced that exclusivity with a scheme whereby all provincial tribunals have concurrent, free-standing jurisdiction with the Commission to enforce the Code. Such jurisdiction would have to be found in the enabling legislation of the tribunal. Under s. 48(12)(j) of the *Labour Relations Act, 1995*, SO 1995, c. 1, Sch. A, for example, labour arbitrators are authorized "to interpret and apply human rights and other employment-related statutes." ...

[95] The existence of a dedicated human rights body like the Commission reflects how complex and nuanced human rights determinations necessarily are, as manifested in the many checks and balances in the Code itself, and protects the integrity of the Code, of human rights adjudication, and of the interests of the parties and the public.

[96] The inability to declare a provision inoperative under the Code does not mean that in making their determinations, the Director and the SBT are precluded from applying the human rights values and principles found in it. It does mean, however, that those principles cannot be used to "invalidate" a provision which defines their mandate.

[97] Nor does it mean that a litigant cannot challenge a provision of the OPSDA for incompatibility with the Code, or even with the *Charter*. It means that the challenge must be made in the proper forum. That is exactly what the parties in this case have done by bringing a joint *Charter* and Code challenge before the Divisional Court.

[98] I would accordingly dismiss the appeal without costs and restore the SBT's decision that it lacked jurisdiction to find s. 5(2) inoperable under the Code.

Appeal allowed.

NOTES

1. At which step in the *Martin* analytical framework would you position the disagreement between the majority and the dissent in this case? As a matter of statutory interpretation, whose reasons are more compelling? Can the court's decision to allow the Social Benefits Tribunal to consider a *Human Rights Code* complaint be understood simply as a matter of statutory interpretation, as *Martin* appears to suggest? Or is it also valid and important for a court, when reading statutory language, to account for the policy consequences of the allocation of authority to decide *Human Rights Code* questions?

2. Most applicants for social benefits will not appeal a decision to deny them social benefits, let alone seek judicial review: see Pottie and Sossin, "Demystifying the Boundaries of Public Law: Policy, Discretion, and Social Welfare" (2005), 38 *UBC Law Rev.* 147. In light of this, is the majority decision in *Tranchemontagne* more likely than the dissenting approach to enhance access to social support by those who are wrongly denied benefits by administrative staff? In turn, which is more likely to enhance access to the *Human Rights Code* by those whose human rights have been denied?

3. To differentiate Charter jurisdiction from *Human Rights Code* jurisdiction, Bastarache J, at para. 31, differentiates the concept of constitutional invalidity from that of inapplicability in the face of a conflicting statute. Is this a compelling distinction? Or is Abella J right, at para. 79, that the distinction overlooks that administrative tribunals cannot make formal declarations of invalidity in any case because their authority is limited to disregarding the offending provision?

4. As Bastarache J observed, by the time of the Supreme Court's decision in *Tranchemontagne*, it had been nearly five years since the appellants' applications were denied by the Director; during that time, the appellants had not received any disability support. Why then did the Supreme Court remit the question of the applicability of s. 5(2) of the *Ontario Disability Support Program Act, 1997* to the Social Benefits Tribunal rather than decide the question once and for all?

CHAPTER FIFTEEN

The Use and Misuse of Discretion

INTRODUCTION

No aspect of administrative law has attracted worse press from opponents of an activist state than the discretionary powers regularly conferred on and exercised by agencies and officials in the course of carrying out statutory schemes. Writing at the end of the 19th century, Dicey seemed to regard the presence of discretion as inimical to a system of government that was subject to the rule of law. Explaining the meaning of the rule of law, he said in *An Introduction to the Study of the Constitution*:

> We mean, in the first place, that no man is punishable or can be lawfully made to suffer in body or goods except for a distinct breach of law established in the ordinary manner before the ordinary courts of the land. In this sense the rule of law is contrasted with every system of government based on the exercise by persons in authority of wide, arbitrary, or discretionary powers of constraint.

Dicey's subsequent discussion indicates that here he was primarily concerned with discretionary powers exercisable over freedom of speech, public meetings, and personal liberty. In his later writings (for example, "The Development of Administrative Law in England" (1915), 31 *LQR* 148), he also observed that the delivery of social programs (such as pensions, education, and insurance) required the grant of broad discretion to officials. He sought to elevate his political opposition to collectivist social policies to the level of constitutional principle by warning that the implementation of these policies required extensive discretion and that officials were always likely to abuse powers that were not strictly confined by law.

Dicey's concerns about the growth of discretion in the administrative state were echoed in the 1920s in *The New Despotism* (London: Benn, 1929), a series of lectures given by Lord Hewart, then lord chief justice of England. Lord Hewart inveighed particularly against the broad discretionary powers delegated by Parliament to ministers to make regulations to implement the administrative schemes established by an enabling statute.

More recently, the 1968 Report of the Royal Commission, *An Inquiry into Civil Rights*, chaired by J.C. McRuer, then chief justice of the High Court of Justice of Ontario, grudgingly accepted the need for discretion in the modern state. However, the report warned (vol. 1, no. 1, at 95) that discretion should be strictly limited to what is

> necessary and unavoidable in order to achieve the social objective or policy of the statute. It ought not to be conferred where rules or standards for judicial application can be stated. Where an administrative power is necessary and unavoidable, the power should be no wider in scope than is demanded to meet the necessity.

A strong aversion to discretion is also an important ingredient of the writings of F.A. Hayek, one of the most influential modern political philosophers of the neo-conservative, free market school. In *Discretionary Powers* (Oxford: Clarendon Press, 1986), Galligan has said (at 202-3):

> [D]iscretion is anathema to the liberal state when it means that officials have powers which affect the private domain of the individual, and that the criteria for their exercise are left to the officials themselves. The danger of discretion in this sense is that its exercise depends upon the preferences of officials, which may in turn be determined by variable values and purposes. This means, according to Hayek, that the individual is subject to coercion by state officials, in that they have control over his affairs in such a way as to prevent him from planning his life, secure in the knowledge of the nature and limits of official powers.
>
> Coercion of this kind is a deprivation of liberty in a special and negative sense; that is, the liberty that results from having a sphere of activity protected by rules, and with which officials may not interfere except in accordance with the rules. Now, any state control involves coercion or the threat of coercion, but not all coercion, on Hayek's view, constitutes a deprivation of liberty. Where power is exercised according to known general rules, the individual is able to live within those rules, and will be coerced only if by his own choice he puts himself in violation. In such a situation he is free in so far as there are parameters within which he must live, and within those parameters he may make his choices, and he is free from official interference in doing so. Conversely, where officials are given powers which may be exercised in ways which interfere with the individual and his private interests, and where it is left to officials to decide in their discretion under what circumstances and in what ways interference may occur, then the individual is threatened with a form of coercion that infringes his liberty.
>
> This argument forms part of a wider theory of constitutional government. According to Hayek there is a particular conception of law to be found in the classical, liberal tradition which has been lost in modern democracies. Within that tradition, law is the principal guardian of freedom, but not every act or decree of government constitutes law in its special sense. Government by law requires the formulation of general rules, and the even-handed application of those rules to all who fall within their terms in an unknown number of future instances. But not merely any rules will do; Hayek argues for a conception of justice according to which rules are just only if they are both general in nature and would receive universal consent.

This is a powerful denouncement of official discretion. Nonetheless, no commentator on contemporary government who wishes to be taken seriously can now contend that broad statutory grants of discretion to public officials are in themselves inconsistent with either democratic ideals or an appropriate concern for the rights of individuals. It has become obvious to all that discretion is the very life blood of the administrative state. It would be inconsistent with achieving the legislative aim of protecting the public interest identified by particular programs if the enabling statute was expected to define with precision all the situations in which, for example, non-citizens who have committed criminal offences should be excluded from Canada or deported; those engaged in regulated businesses and professions (such as the sale of used cars and securities, law, and medicine) should either be refused a licence to practise or have their licence revoked; or land may be expropriated for public purposes.

This is not to say that the grant and exercise of discretionary powers by administrative agencies, especially when they curtail common law rights of freedom of contract and private property, are now uncontroversial. Nothing could be further from the truth. In the area of the regulation of economic activities, proponents of market capitalism still argue against the broad grant of discretion and in favour of subjecting its exercise to tight legal constraints. On the other hand, those who favour a more activist role for the state in the regulation of the market in order to protect members of the public in their capacities of consumer, resident of a neighbourhood, or employee, for example, are more likely to observe that administrative agencies need ample discretion to discharge their mandate and that the scope of their powers should therefore not be unduly constrained by legal limitations.

When it comes to discretionary powers that may infringe on human rights, including those protected by the *Canadian Charter of Rights and Freedoms*, the supporters of broad grants and bold exercises of discretion to regulate private market power are likely to be much less enthusiastic about, for example, the discretion exercisable by customs officers to exclude pornographic material from entering Canada or by immigration officials to refuse entry to or remove from Canada persons perceived to endanger national security. Conversely, those who see threats to liberty and the rule of law in the grant of broad discretionary powers in the area of economic regulation have often been much more understanding of the need for discretion in the state's dealings with dissenters and others on the margins of society and have generally not objected to the discretionary nature of the positive benefits that legislation may authorize an agency to confer, such as compensation for the victims of crime or social assistance.

Recently, another dimension has emerged (or perhaps re-emerged) in the criticism of broad grants of statutory discretion. In an era in which it is fashionable to talk about the democratic deficit in the sense of a weakening of parliamentary institutions, increasingly broad grants of discretion to executive officials (especially by governments with a deregulatory, privatization, and corporatization agenda) are treated as one of the major contributing factors to this phenomenon. Skeletal legislation, sometimes accompanied by the conferral of power to promulgate regulations or make orders dispensing with or even amending provisions in the empowering Act (so-called King Henry VIII clauses), creates a sense of the further marginalization of the legislative branch. In turn, this has apparently concentrated political power in the hands of Cabinet and, indeed, in increasingly small groups of ministers and unelected officials.

A philosophical analysis of discretion is beyond the scope of this book; Galligan, *Discretionary Powers* (Oxford: Clarendon Press, 1986) is a good introduction; additional contributions include Hawkins, ed., *The Uses of Discretion* (Oxford: Clarendon Press, 1992) and Pottie and Sossin, "Demystifying the Boundaries of Public Law: Policy, Discretion, and Social Welfare" (2005), 38 *UBC Law Rev.* 147. It must suffice here to say that by discretion we mean an express legal power to choose a course of action from a range of permissible options, including the option of inaction. The discretion may authorize administrative action, a decision that is aimed at an individual or a small group, or the making of a rule that will affect a large number of people. Lawyers and others have often contrasted decisions taken by an official in the exercise of discretion with those prescribed by law. However, the simplistic distinction between a "government of laws" and a "government of men" obscures the fact that, while in their ideal types discretion and law may lie at opposite ends of a spectrum, most of the legal rules and discretionary powers that are encountered in real life administrative law fall somewhere in between.

The following four observations indicate that it is misleading to attempt to draw too sharp a distinction between law and discretion as administrative tools, a point that was clearly accepted by the Supreme Court of Canada in *Baker*. First, as we have seen in earlier chapters of this text, the terms of an agency's enabling statute frequently do not yield a clear meaning that identifies the "correct" answer to a specific problem. Because many situations are not foreseen at the time of enactment, statutory provisions require interpretation by officials. The process of filling the silences and resolving the ambiguities in statutory language that interpretation so often involves can be described as the exercise of an *implicit* discretion to elaborate unclear or incomplete legislative instructions. Second, even the most detailed and precise regulatory codes are not self-enforcing; typically, officials are left with ample and unstated discretion about the circumstances in which they will actually be enforced against individuals.

Third, just as rules contain grants of implicit discretion (both of interpretation and enforcement), so all express grants of discretion to public officials are subject to some legal limits, at least when their exercise affects the rights and interests of individuals. The courts have normally asserted that in our system of constitutional government there are no legally unlimited public powers, regardless of whether they are claimed by an independent administrative agency, a municipality, a minister of the Crown or the governor (or lieutenant governor) in council. Moreover, it is an essential function of the courts to determine what those limits are by reference to the terms of the enabling statute, common law principles, the *Constitution Acts, 1867-1982* (including the Charter), and now, on occasion, the underlying principles of the constitution.

Fourth, it is sometimes assumed, especially by lawyers, that, while a rule-bound solution to a dispute requires the decision-maker to base it on precedent and general legal principles, those exercising discretion need to consult only their own preferences. However, this is a caricature of the exercise of discretion. Discretionary decisions must be made by reference not only to the statutory purposes and other legal limits of the power, but they should also be informed by any policy objectives formulated by the agency, guidelines that it has issued, and its past practice. Arbitrariness is as much the antithesis of the effective exercise of discretion as the mechanical application of rules is the antithesis of the just administration of the law. The differences between discretionary and rule-based decisions are a matter of degree, not of kind.

In this chapter we are concerned primarily with some of the doctrinal devices developed by the courts to review the legality of the exercise of discretion by an administrative agency. We also raise the question of the roles that should be played in administration by rule and discretion, respectively, and the extent to which the law of judicial review is alert to, encourages, or discourages the structuring of administrative discretion through measures such as, for example, the formulation of statutory rules, informal guidelines, and policy statements.

ABUSE OF DISCRETION AS A GROUND OF JUDICIAL REVIEW

At common law, there have always been a number of discrete grounds of judicial review for abuse of discretion. The decision-maker may have acted in bad faith, wrongfully delegated its powers, fettered its exercise of discretion by laying down a general rule and not responding to individual situations, or acted under the dictation of another. However, in the overall lexicon of judicial review, these grounds of review feature relatively infrequently.

Another and far more common ground of judicial review of discretion is that the agency to which discretionary power has been given has exercised it in order to achieve some purpose not contemplated by its grant. A closely related, and often overlapping ground is that, in exercising its discretion, the agency has taken into consideration some factor that is irrelevant to achieving the ends for which the power was granted or, conversely, that the agency neglected to take into consideration some factor that was relevant. Statutes often do not set out either the purposes for which the discretionary powers that they grant may be exercised or the factors that are relevant to their exercise. And even when legislation contains an objects clause, such clauses are often stated at such a level of generality or are so mutually incompatible as to be of limited assistance in deciding whether any given exercise of discretion was within the scope of the power conferred by the statute.

Issues of relevancy and purpose thus normally boil down to questions of statutory interpretation. And since, as we have seen in previous chapters of this text, the interpretation of statutes is far from being value-free or scientific, there is plenty of scope for differences of view about how narrowly or broadly the interpreter should draw the legal boundaries of the discretion. As you read the materials in this chapter, note the reappearance of the various interpretative "backgrounds" used by the courts when fixing the legal limits of a discretion: backgrounds such as the protection of common law rights of contract and property, functional considerations of governmental effectiveness, democratic values, and human rights.

It is also helpful to identify some points of reference that courts use when sizing up the breadth of a discretionary power and assessing the intensity with which the courts should review its exercise or the degree of latitude that they should be prepared to accede to the body or official to which or to whom the legislature has granted the power.

First and most obvious is the statutory language in which the discretion is granted. Is it couched in objective or subjective terms? Is it related to a specific purpose or is it granted for more general purposes? Second is the nature of the interest affected by the discretionary power. Is it one to which our legal system normally gives a high degree of protection? How seriously is it affected by the decision? Third is the character of the decision. Are there effective alternative checks, such as political accountability, that will prevent the abuse of discretion? Fourth is the character of the decision-maker. In the previous chapters on substantive review, as well as in those dealing with procedure, it has been suggested that courts should show some deference to the expertise of well-established administrative agencies, at least when the expertise is relevant to the interpretation of the statutory term in dispute. However, not all discretionary powers are exercised after a hearing, nor are reasons necessarily given. Moreover, discretionary powers are vested in a wide range of officials and bodies whose claim to relevant expertise may be much less compelling than those of, for example, labour relations boards. On the other hand, when the power is exercised by the governor in council or a minister of the Crown, another dimension is present: respect for the judgment of those with direct lines of electoral political accountability.

In the absence of a right of appeal from the exercise of discretion, the legal basis of the courts' intervention was traditionally subsumed under the doctrine of *ultra vires*. The theory is that the agency to which the legislature has granted discretion may decide how or whether to exercise it. However, it is a requirement of the concept of government under law that discretionary powers are presumptively limited in scope and the agency's discretion does not extend to defining the limits of its own powers. It is for the courts to ensure that the agency does not use its power for some purpose not authorized by the legislature or base its decision on a range of factors that are either narrower or broader than those intended by the legislature to inform the exercise of the discretion. It is appropriate for the courts to perform this function because of their independence from the administration and their expertise in the interpretation of statutes.

This principle was most famously formulated in Canada in *Roncarelli v. Duplessis*, [1959] SCR 121 (Que.), a case concerning an order by Premier Duplessis to the liquor licensing commission to revoke the restaurant licence held by Roncarelli because he had posted bail bonds for Jehovah's Witnesses who had been charged with distributing their literature in violation of municipal bylaws. The liquor licensing statute simply stated that licences could be revoked in the discretion of the commission and did not specify the circumstances in which, or the purposes for which, the power was exercisable. In his memorable reasons in *Roncarelli*, Rand J said (at 140):

> The field of licensed occupations and businesses of this nature is steadily becoming of greater concern to citizens generally. It is a matter of vital importance that a public administration that can refuse to allow a person to enter or continue a calling which, in the absence of regulation, would be free and legitimate, should be conducted with complete impartiality and integrity; and that the grounds for refusing or cancelling a permit should unquestionably be such and such only as are incompatible with the purposes envisaged by the statute: the duty of a Commission is to serve those purposes and those only. A decision to deny or cancel such a privilege lies within the "discretion" of the Commission; but that means that decision is to be based upon a weighing of considerations pertinent to the object of the administration.
>
> In public regulation of this sort there is no such thing as absolute and untrammelled "discretion," that is that action can be taken on any ground or for any reason that can be suggested to the mind of the administrator; no legislative Act can, without express language, be taken to contemplate an unlimited arbitrary power exercisable for any purpose, however capricious or irrelevant, regardless of the nature or purpose of the statute. Fraud and corruption in the Commission may not be mentioned in such statutes but they are always implied as exceptions. "Discretion" necessarily implies good faith in discharging public duty; there is always a perspective within which a statute is intended to operate; and any clear departure from its lines or objects is just as objectionable as fraud or corruption. Could an applicant be refused a permit because he had been born in another province, or because of the colour of his hair? The ordinary language of the legislature cannot be so distorted.

The theoretical basis for the judicial review of the exercise of statutory discretion is essentially the same as that advanced for the courts' power to set aside as null and void agency decisions that are based on a misinterpretation by the agency of a provision in its statute that limits or confers its jurisdiction. Administrative action that is not authorized by law is of no legal force or effect. When interpreting a statute to determine either the purposes for which the discretion was conferred or the matters that are relevant to its exercise, the courts traditionally showed no more deference to the agency's views on these questions than they do when reviewing the agency's interpretation of the "jurisdictional" provisions in that agency's enabling legislation.

Thus, courts typically assumed that it was their function on an application for review to determine independently the scope of the agency's statutory discretion: whether a factor considered by the agency was relevant or a purpose pursued was authorized is reviewable by a standard of correctness, not reasonableness. Even in *CUPE*, Dickson J cited with approval a statement that he had made in *Service Employees' International Union, Local No. 333 v. Nipawin District Staff Nurses Association*, [1975] 1 SCR 382, 389 (Sask.), to the effect that "basing the decision on extraneous matters" and "failing to take relevant factors into account" were examples of an exercise of an agency's power that would take it outside its jurisdiction and the protection of a privative clause.

Indeed, for many years following the judgment in *U.E.S., Local 298 v. Bibeault*, [1988] 2 SCR 1048, the Supreme Court of Canada did not consider whether a pragmatic and functional approach to the standard of review applicable to the decisions of an independent administrative agency inevitably required that questions of relevancy and propriety of purpose should be characterized as jurisdictional, and thus reviewable for correctness, when the agency's decisions are protected by a privative clause. Rather, the court simply substituted its view for that of labour relations boards (for example) as to whether the remedy granted under a broad statutory power does, as the statute provides, further the objectives of the legislation or counter the consequences of the unfair labour practice that has been committed: see *National Bank of Canada v. Retail Clerks' International Union*, [1984] 1 SCR 269 (Can.).

However, as we saw in chapter 2 of this text, the traditional approach to judicial review of discretionary decisions changed dramatically in *Baker*. In that case, the Supreme Court emphasized the lack of a bright-line distinction at the margins between questions of law and exercises of discretion. This led to the court recognizing for the first time explicitly that the "pragmatic and functional approach" was also of use in determining the intensity with which reviewing courts should be approaching decisions in the discretionary section of the spectrum between pure questions of law, at one end, and completely unfettered discretion (to be exercised on the basis of the subjective judgment of the repository of power), at the other end. Standard of review discourse was introduced to the world of abuse of discretion.

This means little or nothing in the case of traditional common law doctrines of bad faith, acting under dictation, unlawful subdelegation, and wrongful fettering, given that these are largely fact-based grounds of abuse of discretion review. However, in the realm of failing to take account of relevant factors, taking account of irrelevant factors, and even acting for an improper purpose, it is now necessary to ask whether the standard of review is that of correctness or reasonableness. Indeed, when one also takes into account the *Baker* and *Dunsmuir* courts' recognition of at least the occasional need for deference to discretionary procedural choices, it is evident that the "pragmatic and functional" approach to judicial review—now the standard of review analysis—has become an overarching concept applicable across almost the entire gamut of the grounds of judicial review.

In the world of review for abuse of discretion, this is even more obvious in the extension (in the following case) of the standard of review analysis to a challenge based on an alleged failure to observe or have regard to Charter rights and freedoms in the exercise of discretion.

Suresh v. Canada (Minister of Citizenship and Immigration)
[2002] 1 SCR 3 (Can.)

[One of the issues at stake in this case was a ministerial discretion to deport someone who was a danger to the security of Canada, even when there was a possibility that that person's "life, liberty and security of the person" would be in serious jeopardy in his or her country of origin by reason of a serious prospect of torture. Note that the reasons for judgment in the case were issued four months after the attacks of September 11, 2001 against the United States.]

THE COURT:

[At the outset, the court identified the principles that affected its judgment on all the issues raised by the case.]

[3] The issues engage concerns and values fundamental to Canada and indeed the world. On the one hand stands the manifest evil of terrorism and the random and arbitrary taking of innocent lives, rippling out in an ever-widening spiral of loss and fear. Governments, expressing the will of the governed, need the legal tools to effectively meet this challenge.

[4] On the other hand stands the need to ensure that those legal tools do not undermine values that are fundamental to our democratic society—liberty, the rule of law, and the principles of fundamental justice—values that lie at the heart of the Canadian constitutional order and the international instruments that Canada has signed. In the end, it would be a Pyrrhic victory if terrorism were defeated at the cost of sacrificing our commitment to those values. Parliament's challenge is to draft laws that effectively combat terrorism and conform to the requirements of our Constitution and our international commitments.

[5] We conclude that to deport a refugee to face a substantial risk of torture would generally violate s. 7 of the Charter. The Minister must exercise her discretion to deport under the *Immigration Act* accordingly. ...

[The court then recited the applicable legislative provisions including the section conferring the ministerial discretion.]

[24] ...

Immigration Act, RSC 1985, c. I-2

19(1) No person shall be granted admission who is a member of any of the following classes:

· · ·

(e) persons who there are reasonable grounds to believe ...

(iv) are members of an organization that there are reasonable grounds to believe will ...

(C) engage in terrorism;

(f) persons who there are reasonable grounds to believe ...

(ii) have engaged in terrorism, or

(iii) are or were members of an organization that there are reasonable grounds to believe is or was engaged in ...

(B) terrorism,

except persons who have satisfied the Minister that their admission would not be detrimental to the national interest;

53(1) Notwithstanding subsections 52(2) and (3), no person who is determined under this Act or the regulations to be a Convention refugee, nor any person who has been determined to be not eligible to have a claim to be a Convention refugee determined by the Refugee Division on the basis that the person is a person described in paragraph 46.01(1)(a), shall be removed from Canada to a country where the person's life or freedom would be threatened for reasons of race, religion, nationality, membership in a particular social group or political opinion unless ...

(b) the person is a member of an inadmissible class described in paragraph 19(1)(e), (f), (g), (j), (k) or (l) and the Minister is of the opinion that the person constitutes a danger to the security of Canada;

· · ·

1. Standard of Review

[26] This appeal involves a consideration of four types of issues: (1) constitutional review of the provisions of the *Immigration Act*; (2) whether Suresh's presence in Canada constitutes a danger to national security; (3) whether Suresh faces a substantial risk of torture upon return to Sri Lanka; and (4) whether the procedures used by the Minister under the Act were adequate to protect Suresh's constitutional rights.

[27] The issues of the constitutionality of the deportation provisions of the *Immigration Act* do not involve review of ministerial decision-making. The fourth issue of the adequacy of the procedures under the Act will be considered separately later in these reasons. At this point, our inquiry is into the standard of review to be applied to the second and third issues—the Minister's decisions on whether Suresh poses a risk to the security of Canada and whether he faces a substantial risk of torture on deportation. The latter was characterized by Robertson JA [[2000] 2 FC 592 (CA)] as a constitutional decision and hence requires separate treatment. It is our view that the threshold question is factual, that is whether there is a substantial risk of torture if the appellant is sent back, although this inquiry is mandated by s. 7 of the Charter. The constitutional issue is whether it would shock the Canadian conscience to deport Suresh once a substantial risk of torture has been established. This is when s. 7 is engaged. Since we are ordering a new hearing on procedural grounds, we are not required in this appeal to review the Minister's decisions on whether Suresh's presence constitutes a danger to the security of Canada and whether he faces a substantial risk of torture on deportation. However, we offer the following comments to assist courts in future ministerial review.

[28] The trial judge and the Court of Appeal rejected Suresh's submission that the highest standard of review should apply to the determination of the rights of refugees. Robertson JA, while inclined to apply a deferential standard of review to whether Suresh constituted a danger to the security of Canada, concluded that the decision could be

maintained on any standard. Robertson JA went on to state (at paras. 131-36) that while the Act and the Constitution place constraints on the Minister's exercise of her discretion, these do not extend to a judicially-imposed obligation to give particular weight to particular factors. On the question of whether he would face a substantial risk of torture on return, a question that he viewed as constitutional rather than merely one of judicial review, Robertson JA did not determine the applicable standard of review, concluding that even on the stringent standard of correctness the Minister's decision should be upheld.

[29] The first question is what standard should be adopted with respect to the Minister's decision that a refugee constitutes a danger to the security of Canada. We agree with Robertson JA that the reviewing court should adopt a deferential approach to this question and should set aside the Minister's discretionary decision if it is patently unreasonable in the sense that it was made arbitrarily or in bad faith, it cannot be supported on the evidence, or the Minister failed to consider the appropriate factors. The court should not reweigh the factors or interfere merely because it would have come to a different conclusion.

[30] This conclusion is mandated by *Pushpanathan v. Canada (Minister of Citizenship and Immigration)* [1998] 1 SCR 982 (Can.), which reviewed the principles for determining the standard of review according to the functional and pragmatic approach. In *Pushpanathan*, the Court emphasized that the ultimate question is always what the legislature intended. One looks to the language of the statute as well as a number of factors to determine that intention. Here the language of the Act (the Minister must be "of the *opinion*" that the person constitutes a danger to the security of Canada) suggests a standard of deference. So, on the whole, do the factors to be considered: (1) the presence or absence of a clause negating the right of appeal; (2) the relative expertise of the decision-maker; (3) the purpose of the provision and the legislation generally; and (4) the nature of the question. (*Pushpanathan, supra*, at paras. 29-38).

[31] The first factor suggests that Parliament intended only a limited right of appeal. Although the Minister's s. 53(1)(b) opinion is not protected by a privative clause, it may only be appealed by leave of the Federal Court—Trial Division (s. 82.1(1)), and that leave decision may not itself be appealed (s. 82.2)). The second factor, the relative expertise of the decision-maker, again favours deference. As stated in *Baker v. Canada (Minister of Citizenship and Immigration)* [1999] 2 SCR 817 (Can.), "[t]he fact that the formal decision-maker is the Minister is a factor militating in favour of deference" (para. 59). The Minister, as noted by Lord Hoffmann in *Secretary of State for the Home Department v. Rehman* [2001] 3 WLR 877 (HL Eng.) at para. 62, "has access to special information and expertise in ... matters [of national security]." The third factor—the purpose of the legislation—again favours deference. This purpose, as discussed in *Pushpanathan, supra*, at para. 73, is to permit a "humanitarian balance" of various interests—"the seriousness of the danger posed to Canadian society" on the one hand, and "the danger of persecution upon *refoulement*" on the other. Again, the Minister is in a superior position to a court in making this assessment. Finally, the nature of the case points to deference. The inquiry is highly fact-based and contextual. As in *Baker, supra*, at para. 61, the s. 53(1)(b) danger opinion "involves a considerable appreciation of the facts of that person's case, and is not one which involves the application or interpretation of definitive legal rules," suggesting it merits a wide degree of deference.

[32] These factors suggest that Parliament intended to grant the Minister a broad discretion in issuing a s. 53(1)(b) opinion, reviewable only where the Minister makes a patently unreasonable decision. It is true that the question of whether a refugee constitutes a danger to the security of Canada relates to human rights and engages fundamental human interests. However, it is our view that a deferential standard of ministerial review will not prevent human rights issues from being fully addressed, provided proper procedural safeguards are in place and provided that any decision to deport meets the constitutional requirements of the Charter.

[33] The House of Lords has taken the same view in *Rehman, supra*. Lord Hoffmann, following the events of September 11, 2001, added the following postscript to his speech (at para. 62):

> I wrote this speech some three months before the recent events in New York and Washington. They are a reminder that in matters of national security, the cost of failure can be high. *This seems to me to underline the need for the judicial arm of government to respect the decisions of ministers of the Crown on the question of whether support for terrorist activities in a foreign country constitutes a threat to national security.* It is not only that the executive has access to special information and expertise in these matters. It is also that such decisions, with serious potential results for the community, require a legitimacy which can be conferred only by entrusting them to persons responsible to the community through the democratic process. If the people are to accept the consequences of such decisions, they must be made by persons whom the people have elected and whom they can remove. [Emphasis added.]

[34] It follows that the weighing of relevant factors is not the function of a court reviewing the exercise of ministerial discretion (see, for instance, *Pezim v. British Columbia (Superintendant of Brokers)* [1994] 2 SCR 577 (BC) at 607, where Iacobucci J explained that a reviewing court should not disturb a decision based on a "broad discretion" unless the tribunal has "made some error in principle in exercising its discretion or has exercised its discretion in a capricious or vexatious manner").

[35] The Court's recent decision in *Baker, supra*, did not depart from this view. Rather, it confirmed that the pragmatic and functional approach should be applied to all types of administrative decisions in recognition of the fact that a uniform approach to the determination of the proper standard of review is preferable, and that there may be special situations where even traditionally discretionary decisions will best be reviewed according to a standard other than the deferential standard which was universally applied in the past to ministerial decisions (see *Dagg v. Canada (Minister of Finance)* [1997] 2 SCR 403 (Can.)).

[36] The Court specified in *Baker, supra*, that a nuanced approach to determining the appropriate standard of review was necessary given the difficulty in rigidly classifying discretionary and non-discretionary decisions (paras. 54 and 55). The Court also made it clear in *Baker* that its approach "should not be seen as reducing the level of deference given to decisions of a highly discretionary nature" (para. 56) and, moreover, that any ministerial obligation to consider certain factors "gives the applicant no right to a particular outcome or to the application of a particular legal test" (para. 74). To the extent this Court reviewed the Minister's discretion in that case, its decision was based on the ministerial delegate's failure to comply with *self-imposed* ministerial guidelines, as reflected

in the objectives of the Act, international treaty obligations and, most importantly, a set of published instructions to immigration officers.

[37] The passages in *Baker* referring to the "weight" of particular factors (see paras. 68 and 73-75) must be read in this context. It is the Minister who was obliged to give proper weight to the relevant factors and none other. *Baker* does not authorize courts reviewing decisions on the discretionary end of the spectrum to engage in a new weighing process, but draws on an established line of cases concerning the failure of ministerial delegates to consider and weigh implied limitations and/or patently relevant factors: see *Anisminic Ltd. v. Foreign Compensation Commission* [1969] 2 AC 147 (HL Eng.); *Sheehan v. Ontario (Criminal Injuries Compensation Board)* (1974) 52 DLR (3d) 728 (Ont. CA); *Maple Lodge Farms Ltd. v. Canada* [1982] 2 SCR 2 (Can.); *Dagg, supra,* at paras. 111-12, *per* La Forest J (dissenting on other grounds).

[38] This standard appropriately reflects the different obligations of Parliament, the Minister and the reviewing court. Parliament's task is to establish the criteria and procedures governing deportation, within the limits of the Constitution. The Minister's task is to make a decision that conforms to Parliament's criteria and procedures as well as the Constitution. The court's task, if called upon to review the Minister's decision, is to determine whether the Minister has exercised her decision-making power within the constraints imposed by Parliament's legislation and the Constitution. If the Minister has considered the appropriate factors in conformity with these constraints, the court must uphold her decision. It cannot set it aside even if it would have weighed the factors differently and arrived at a different conclusion.

[39] This brings us to the question of the standard of review of the Minister's decision on whether the refugee faces a substantial risk of torture upon deportation. This question is characterized as constitutional by Robertson JA, to the extent that the Minister's decision to deport to torture must ultimately conform to s. 7 of the Charter: see *Kindler v. Canada (Minister of Justice)* [1991] 2 SCR 779 (Can.), *per* La Forest J; and *United States v. Burns* [2001] 1 SCR 283 (Can.) at para. 32. As mentioned earlier, whether there is a substantial risk of torture if Suresh is deported is a threshold question. The threshold question here is in large part a fact-driven inquiry. It requires consideration of the human rights record of the home state, the personal risk faced by the claimant, any assurances that the claimant will not be tortured and their worth and, in that respect, the ability of the home state to control its own security forces, and more. It may also involve a reassessment of the refugee's initial claim and a determination of whether a third country is willing to accept the refugee. Such issues are largely outside the realm of expertise of reviewing courts and possess a negligible legal dimension. We are accordingly of the view that the threshold finding of whether Suresh faces a substantial risk of torture, as an aspect of the larger s. 53(1)(b) opinion, attracts deference by the reviewing court to the Minister's decision. The court may not reweigh the factors considered by the Minister, but may intervene if the decision is not supported by the evidence or fails to consider the appropriate factors. It must be recognized that the nature of the evidence required may be limited by the nature of the inquiry. This is consistent with the reasoning of this Court in *Kindler, supra,* at 836-37, where considerable deference was shown to ministerial decisions involving similar considerations in the context of a constitutional revision, that is in the context of a decision where the s. 7 interest was engaged.

[40] Before leaving the issue of standard of review, it is useful to underline the distinction between standard of review and the evidence required to establish particular facts in issue. For example, some authors suggest a lower evidentiary standard may govern decisions at entry (under ss. 2 and 19 of the Act) than applies to decisions to deport a landed Convention refugee under s. 53(1)(b): see J.C. Hathaway and C.J. Harvey "Framing Refugee Protection in the New World Disorder" (2001) 34 *Cornell Int'l LJ* 257 at 288. This does not imply different standards of review. Different administrative decisions involve different factors, stemming from the statutory scheme and the particular issues raised. Yet the same standard of review may apply.

[41] We conclude that in reviewing ministerial decisions to deport under the Act, courts must accord deference to those decisions. If the Minister has considered the correct factors, the courts should not reweigh them. Provided the s. 53(1)(b) decision is not patently unreasonable—unreasonable on its face, unsupported by evidence, or vitiated by failure to consider the proper factors or apply the appropriate procedures—it should be upheld. At the same time, the courts have an important role to play in ensuring that the Minister has considered the relevant factors and complied with the requirements of the Act and the Constitution.

[The court went on to hold that the authority of the minister to order deportation despite the serious possibility of torture did not violate the principles of fundamental justice. It was justifiable as an exceptional measure. However, because Suresh had raised a *prima facie* case of a substantial risk of torture, he was entitled to a level of procedural fairness. As he had not received it, the decision was quashed and the matter remitted.]

Appeal allowed with costs.

NOTES

1. For the purposes of its standard of review analysis, the court segments the minister's decision-making process into two stages: the determination of whether Suresh was a danger to national security (which did not engage the Charter) and the determination of whether there was a substantial risk of torture and, if so, whether the minister should nonetheless order deportation (subject to s. 7 of the Charter). Is there anything problematic about that segmentation?

2. Why in reviewing the first question (the danger assessment) does the court depart from the earlier decision in *Baker* and apply a patent unreasonableness standard?

3. In reviewing the second question (substantial risk and whether to deport despite that risk), the court held that at least aspects of the process attracted deference by the court. What are those aspects? Should deference ever enter the picture when the exercise of a discretion engages Charter rights? What is to be made of the court's subsequent holding that deportation to torture can be justified under s. 7 of the Charter only in the most exceptional circumstances? Does that suggest that, where there is found to be a substantial risk of torture, the courts should at that point be much more intrusive in exercising their review powers?

4. We return shortly to the constitutional dimensions of review for abuse of discretion, but before doing that we consider two pre-*Baker* judgments on review for taking account of

irrelevant factors (*Sheehan*) and wrongful purpose (*Shell Canada*). Note that *Sheehan* is cited by the court in *Suresh* and consider also the extent to which the Ontario Court of Appeal judgment presages *Baker*.

Re Sheehan and Criminal Injuries Compensation Board
(1973), 37 DLR (3d) 336 (Ont. Div. Ct.); rev'd. (1975), 52 DLR (3d) 728 (Ont. CA)

HOLLAND J: This is an application for judicial review of a decision made by the Criminal Injuries Compensation Board, dated January 12, 1973, whereby two applications on behalf of Robert James Sheehan, hereinafter called Sheehan, were refused, A. Roy Wilmott QC dissenting.

The first application arises out of an incident which occurred on January 2, 1970, while Sheehan was an inmate of Kingston Penitentiary, a federal penitentiary. He was assaulted and injured by a fellow prisoner.

The second application arises out of an incident which occurred on April 18, 1971, while Sheehan was an inmate of Kingston Penitentiary and occurred during the Kingston riot. Sheehan had been housed in protective custody and shortly after midnight on April 18, 1971, during the riot, he was forcibly removed, with other inmates, from a cell block, bound to a chair and assaulted over a considerable period of time by fellow inmates. As a result of this latter series of assaults Sheehan was most seriously injured.

In addition to the application of Sheehan, arising out of the Kingston riot, five other applications were brought before the Board arising out of this riot, four on behalf of inmates and one on behalf of a prison guard. The decision of the Board dealt with all of the applications above referred to.

In refusing the applications for compensation the Board considered three circumstances:

(1) The fact that Sheehan before the commission of the criminal assault above referred to, by which he suffered injury, had himself been guilty of criminal behaviour for which he had been convicted;

(2) The fact that the criminal assaults took place within the walls of Kingston Penitentiary, and at all relevant times Sheehan and his assailants were in the official and exclusive custody of another Government, under conditions which were totally outside the power and jurisdiction of Ontario to deal with; and

(3) The fact that there was no evidence adduced before the Board to indicate that any application had been made to or proceedings taken on behalf of Sheehan against any other Government department, ministry or agency, to obtain compensation for damages.

The relevant legislation applicable to both of Sheehan's applications is the *Law Enforcement Compensation Act*, RSO 1970, c. 237.

The relevant sections of the *Law Enforcement Compensation Act* are as follows:

3(1) Where any person is injured or killed by any act or omission of any other person occurring in or resulting directly from,

(a) the commission of an offence against any statute of Canada or Ontario ... the Board may, on application therefor and after a hearing, make an order in its discretion in accordance with this Act for the payment of compensation and the decision of the Board is final and conclusive for all purposes.

. . .

5. In determining whether to make an order for compensation and the amount thereof, the Board may have regard to all such circumstances as it considers relevant, including any behaviour of the victim that directly or indirectly contributed to his injury or death.

. . .

7(2) An order for compensation does not affect the right of any person to recover from any other person by civil proceedings lawful damages in respect of the injury or death, but, where the Board has granted an order, the Board is subrogated to all the rights of the person in whose favour the order is granted in respect of the injury or death to the extent of the amount awarded in the order.

If the three circumstances set out above, upon which the Board based its decision, are relevant then any attack on such decision must fail. I will consider the relevance of each of the above circumstances in order.

It appears to me to be completely irrelevant that the victim before the commission of the criminal assault, giving rise to the claim, had himself been guilty of criminal behaviour for which he had been convicted. Counsel for the Board suggested that such was a proper consideration in view of the wording of s. 5 which includes as a proper consideration "any behaviour of the victim that directly or indirectly contributed to his injury. ..." This surely must be restricted to relevant behaviour. If the victim is, for example, guilty of insulting behaviour that results in an assault such would be a relevant consideration but the fact that the victim was guilty of criminal behaviour unconnected with the incident in question to my mind cannot be considered to be relevant.

It is to be noted that the prison guard, on whose behalf an application for compensation had also been made, was not incarcerated by reason of his previous criminal behaviour and yet his application was also refused.

I turn now to the second matter considered by the Board, that is that the assaults took place within the walls of Kingston Penitentiary and that at all relevant times both the victim and assailant or assailants were in official and exclusive custody of another Government under conditions which were totally outside the power and jurisdiction of the Government of Ontario to deal with. Without going into the matter I have some doubts that the area within the walls of Kingston Penitentiary is totally outside the power and jurisdiction of the Government of Ontario to deal with. Be that as it may, from a practical point of view the maintenance of order and the protection of persons and property within the walls of a federal penitentiary are dealt with by federal authorities without the intervention of provincial authorities. In considering this circumstance the Board, in its majority reasons, stated:

The Board considers the foregoing circumstances to be not only relevant but persuasive in determining whether an Order should be made for payment of compensation—compensation moreover, which is to be paid out of moneys appropriated by the Legislature of Ontario—in this case.

. . .

The Board is at pains to point out that there has been no arbitrary or discriminatory exclusion. To be specific, the fact that the applicants were or are inmates of a penitentiary does not, of itself, in any way disentitle the applicants to compensation. In general the Board is ready to order payment of compensation to any member of any class of persons, so long as the circumstances in the individual case appear to the Board to justify such an order.

In this case in the assaults to Sheehan arising out of the riot, I think it can hardly be said that Sheehan contributed in any way to such assaults. He was forcibly removed from the cell block by other inmates and severely beaten, after having been tied to a chair. If compensation is to be refused in this case I can hardly think of any circumstances that would warrant the Board in the future, if it follows its own decisions, allowing compensation to an inmate of a federal penitentiary. As such, the Board, notwithstanding its expression to the contrary, has disentitled inmates of federal penitentiaries, as a class, to compensation under the Act.

In my view, the fact that Sheehan was an inmate of a federal institution or "an enclave situate within the Province of Ontario," as referred to by the Board, is not a proper consideration. If the Legislature intended to exclude under the Act inmates of federal penitentiaries it should have said so.

I now turn to the third circumstance considered by the Board and that is that there was no evidence to indicate that any application had been made by or on behalf of Sheehan to any other Government department, ministry or agency to obtain compensation for damages. Section 7(2) of the *Law Enforcement Compensation Act* provides that an order for compensation does not affect the right of any person to recover from any other person by civil proceedings lawful damages in respect of the injury and further provides that where the Board has granted an order, the Board is subrogated to the rights of the person in whose favour the order is granted to the extent of the amount awarded in the order. No section imposes an obligation on an applicant to make an application or take any other proceedings against any other individual or authority. I suppose that technically an action would lie against the federal authorities in connection with the injuries sustained by Sheehan: see the *Crown Liability Act*, RSC 1970, c. C-38; *MacLean v. The Queen* (1972) 27 DLR (3d) 365.

I can hardly conceive, however, of any such action being successful. I consider that the third circumstance considered by the Board was not a relevant circumstance to be considered by the Board.

For the above reasons I have come to the conclusion that none of the three circumstances considered by the Board were relevant. The question remains whether this Court can, in view of the wording of s. 3(1) and (5) of the Act, set aside the dismissal of the application and direct that the matter be remitted to the Board for further consideration.

There is no obligation on the Board to award compensation. It could be argued that the payment is an *ex gratia* payment. Even so the general intent of the Act is clear and that is to provide compensation to victims of crime. Claimants to *ex gratia* payments are entitled to have their claims considered on a proper basis: *Joy Oil Co. Ltd. v. The King* [1951] SCR 624.

In the case of *CNR v. Canada Steamship Lines Ltd. et al.* [1945] 3 DLR 417, the Privy Council considered the effect of s. 35(13) of the *Transport Act, 1938* (Can.), c. 53, which stated that in considering an application for the approval of agreed charges, the Board of Transport Commissioners "shall have regard to all considerations which appear to it to be relevant." In that case the Board refused to approve the charges because it would have had the effect of depriving the respondent steamship companies of most, if not all, of their business in that sector. Speaking for the Privy Council, Lord Macmillan referred to s. 35(13) and said (at 420):

> It would be difficult to conceive a wider discretion than is conferred on the Board as to the considerations to which it is to have regard in disposing of an application for the approval of an agreed charge. It is to have regard to "all considerations which appear to it to be relevant." Not only is it not precluded negatively from having regard to any considerations but it is enjoined positively to have regard to every consideration which in its opinion is relevant. So long as that discretion is exercised in good faith the decision of the Board as to what considerations are relevant would appear to be unchallengeable.

It should be noted that under the terms of the *Transport Act, 1938* the Board was charged with the regulation of rail, air and water transport. Surely it would be a highly relevant consideration to a Board which was charged by s. 3(2) of the Act with "co-ordinating and harmonizing the operations of all carriers engaged in transport by railways, ships and aircraft" that the approval of a rate request by one class of carrier would seriously affect another class of carrier.

But what if a tribunal acts on irrelevant considerations, i.e., ones which have no rational bearing given the terms of the enabling statute or ones which are based on an erroneous view of the law? It seems clear that the Courts will interfere in such circumstances, even if the tribunal is vested with broad discretion. In *The Queen v. Vestry of St. Pancras* (1890) 24 QBD 371, 375-376 (Eng. CA), Lord Esher MR said:

> But they must fairly consider the application and exercise their discretion on it fairly, and not take into account any reason for their decision which is not a legal one. If people who have to exercise a public duty by exercising their discretion take into account matters which the Courts consider not to be proper for the guidance of their discretion, then in the eye of the law they have not exercised their discretion.

The above quotation was approved by the Supreme Court of Canada in *CPR v. Province of Alberta et al.* [1950] SCR 25, 34 (*per* Kellock J).

[Holland J then cited Lord Reid's statement in *Anisminic Ltd. v. Foreign Compensation Commission*, [1969] 2 AC 147 (Eng. HL) that a tribunal may lose its jurisdiction should it, *inter alia*, decide a question not remitted to it, refuse to take into account something that it was required to take into account, or base its decision on a matter it had no right to take into account. He added that *Anisminic* had been approved and followed by the Supreme Court of Canada in *Metropolitan Life Insurance Company v. International Union of Operating Engineers, Local 796*, [1970] SCR 425 (Ont.).]

I conclude that the Court may properly review the decision of the Board in this case and that the matters considered by the Board were not relevant. In the circumstances the decision of the Board will be quashed and the matter remitted to the Board for consideration.

Application granted.

[This decision was appealed to the Ontario Court of Appeal.]

KELLY JA: In proceedings in the nature of judicial review, either under the *Judicial Review Procedure Act, 1971* (Ont.), SO 1971, Vol. 2, c. 48, or upon an application for one of the prerogative writs, the primary consideration is the nature of the jurisdiction of the body whose decision is sought to be brought under review. In this matter the heart of the issue is this—has the Board in refusing the application done so within the proper limits of its discretionary function established by its parent statute, or has the Board, in ascribing its refusal to one or more of the circumstances above referred to, exceeded its statutory jurisdiction so as to bring its decision within the proper reach of judicial review?

The principal argument proffered in support of the contention that the Board had exceeded its jurisdiction and was accordingly subject to judicial review, was that the Board had escalated one or more of the circumstances above set out to the status of statutory conditions of eligibility and had thereby purported to vary the statute under which its authority was to be found. If the Board had said that the presence of any one or more of the factors would disentitle any applicant from receiving compensation it might be arguable that it had exceeded its authority under the Act. But a clear-cut distinction must be drawn between the Board giving consideration to certain circumstances and the Board holding that a particular circumstance *ipso facto* disqualified an applicant from benefits under the Act.

In appraising what the Board did it is essential to observe the very wide discretion given to the Board as set out in s. 3:

> 3(1) … make an order in its discretion exercised in accordance with this Act for the payment of compensation. …

Further direction is given to the Board in s. 5 where the Legislature authorizes the Board to:

> 5. … have regard to all such circumstances as it considers relevant, including any behaviour of the victim that directly or indirectly contributed to his injury or death.

It should be emphasized that this is not an instance where the Board has a precise jurisdiction within which it may, by its decisions, hold that an applicant is one entitled to the *rights* granted under statute, regulation or contract. The applicant has, under this legislation, no right to compensation, his right being limited to making an application therefor to the Board.

Apart from the obligation not to act arbitrarily or capriciously and to observe the principles of natural justice (and there is no allegation that the Board offended in any of these regards) the jurisdiction of the Board to determine in each case what were the relevant circumstances and to decide having regard to these circumstances is untrammelled.

The Board did not hold that as a matter of statutory interpretation any of the recited circumstances would render an applicant ineligible for payment of compensation. The Board, in holding that the applicant was a victim as defined by s. 1(f) and a person in whose favour its discretion could have been exercised, made it clear that these factors were merely circumstances which in the Board's opinion were relevant to determine whether compensation should be awarded to the applicant who was unquestionably eligible for such an award.

In the reasons for judgment of the Divisional Court the Divisional Court purported to "consider the relevance of each of the above circumstances" [at 339], and concluded that "the Court may properly review the decision of the Board in this case, and that the matters considered by the Board were not relevant" [at 342-343].

While the foregoing might have been a proper expression of the powers of the Board had it been directed to regard all relevant circumstances, by s. 5 the Board was given the right and duty to make compensation when, in its discretion, it deemed fit to do so and in reaching its decision the Act states that the Board is to be the judge of that which is relevant.

The Board having considered that, in the light of the discretion given by the statute to the Board, the circumstances outlined above are relevant and that the payments provided by the statute are gratuitous, and not having held out that any of the factors considered by it were prerequisites to eligibility, no misconstruction of ss. 3(1), 5 or 7(2) has been made and accordingly no error in law appears on the face of the record.

To this situation the words of Judson J, in *Labour Relations Board and A.G. BC et al. v. Traders' Service Ltd.* [1958] SCR 672, 678, are peculiarly appropriate:

> The matter, therefore, was solely within the Board's jurisdiction and it is not open to judicial review. In making its finding of fact, the Board proceeded exactly as it was authorized to do by statute. There was no refusal of jurisdiction or lack of jurisdiction or conduct outside or in excess of its jurisdiction.

While even such a broad conferring of the power to act on what the Board considers relevant would not extend to authorize the Board to make relevant a consideration which is patently irrelevant, simply by the act of the Board expressing that it considers it to be relevant, there is nothing in the record before this Court to indicate that the Board has so acted—to the contrary, the reasons advanced by the Board in its disposition of the application indicate a careful and thoughtful review of the circumstances and a considered decision as to their relevancy.

. . .

With respect I do not construe the Act as authorizing the Court to review the correctness of the Board's decision made within the scope of its authority. The Legislature has expressly assigned to the Board and not to the Courts the discretionary authority to grant or deny compensation.

Within the confines of its convening statute the Board may, indeed must, perform this function and may do so free from judicial intervention however a Court may view any particular exercise of its proper discretion.

In my opinion the Divisional Court erred when it considered that its task was to determine if the said circumstances were relevant. In the light of the discretion vested in the Board to have regard to all circumstances which it considered relevant so long as it acted in good faith, the decision of the Board as to what considerations are relevant are unchallengeable: see *CNR et al. v. Canada Steamship Lines Ltd. et al.* [1945] 3 DLR 417, 420.

I would therefore allow the appeal with costs if demanded, set aside the order of the Divisional Court and in its place substitute an order directing that the application for judicial review be dismissed, also with costs if demanded.

Appeal allowed.

NOTES

1. On what issues do the Divisional Court and the Court of Appeal disagree? Is it on the interpretation of the legislation and, if so, is this because they are using different interpretative backgrounds? Do they disagree about the standard of review that should apply to the board's exercise of discretion? Are the factors described in the introduction to abuse of discretion as a ground of judicial review helpful in considering the problem?

2. Suppose that the claimant had been a prison guard or a person injured on a Canadian Forces base or at a federal airport. Could the board have lawfully included these factors in its reasons for refusing compensation? The Court of Appeal stated that the board had not decided that all prison inmates were ineligible for compensation. What evidence is there that the board regarded Sheehan as different from others? Would it ever be unlawful for the board to state in its reasons for refusing compensation that the claimant was an inmate?

3. The essential difficulty, of course, is that the legislation neither gave a right to compensation to all who suffered personal injuries as a result of another's criminal conduct nor indicated the factors to be considered in deciding in what circumstances compensation should be paid or refused. This was left largely to the discretion of the board as it administered the scheme.

4. The current legislation, *Compensation for Victims of Crime Act*, RSO 1990, c. C.24, s. 17 provides that, in determining whether to make an order for compensation and the amount thereof, "the board *shall have regard to all relevant circumstances*"; these are now expressly stated to include the refusal of the claimant to cooperate with, or the failure to report the offence promptly to, a law enforcement agency and the amount of any benefit or other compensation received, other than social assistance. There is also a right of appeal from the board to the Divisional Court on any question of law: s. 23.

It is apparent from recent cases that, despite the protection given to the accused in the criminal process, people may be wrongly convicted of serious criminal offences and required to serve long prison sentences. For understandable reasons, governments have not enacted statutes establishing permanent administrative agencies to award compensation to such victims of the criminal justice system. Compensation is paid *ex gratia* and is generally awarded through the Ministry of the Attorney General on a case-by-case basis. Could a wrongly convicted person who was refused compensation ever make a successful legal challenge to the exercise of discretion? Suppose, for example, that the minister refused to compensate family and friends who had contributed to the individual's legal expenses? Or that the minister refused a claim for compensation made on behalf of a wrongly convicted person by his parents because the person had died?

In *Shell Canada Products Ltd. v. Vancouver (City)*, below, the applicant attacked the validity of resolutions passed by the Vancouver city council. The resolutions, passed in 1989, were to refrain from doing business with Shell as long as it continued to do business in apartheid South Africa. These resolutions were overturned by a 5:4 majority of the Supreme Court of Canada on the basis that the council had exercised its statutory discretion for an improper purpose. The excerpts below deal with this issue.

Shell Canada Products Ltd. v. Vancouver (City)
[1994] 1 SCR 231 (BC)

McLACHLIN J (Lamer CJ and L'Heureux-Dubé and Gonthier JJ concurring) (dissenting): This appeal raises the issue of whether the elected representatives of a municipality may vote to refuse to give the municipality's business to a firm because of the conduct of the firm outside the municipality.

The facts are simple. In 1989 the Council of the City of Vancouver passed two resolutions (the "Resolutions"): first, not to do business with Shell Canada and Royal Dutch/ Shell as long as Shell continues to do business in South Africa; and second, to declare the City a "Shell Free" zone until such time as Shell should disinvest from South Africa. At the time, apartheid was the legal regime in South Africa. The legalized discrimination which that regime sustained was abhorrent to many Canadians. Nations throughout the world had imposed trade embargoes against South Africa in protest against the regime. Canada was among those nations. Shell, however, continued to do business with South Africa, supplying it with fuel and other products vital to its economy. In particular, Shell was exporting sulphur to South Africa through the port of Vancouver. Many Vancouverites found this conduct to be offensive.

A delegation of citizens made representations to City Council seeking support for a boycott against Shell. On September 12, 1989, Council considered the matter. The councillors heard representations from people supporting the boycott. It also heard representations and received a brief from Shell Canada's representative, arguing against the boycott. Council was told that approximately 30 cities had adopted a preferential purchasing policy boycotting Shell products. After hearing both sides of the issue, the elected representatives of the government of the City of Vancouver passed the Resolutions impugned on this appeal.

The City's refusal to do business with Shell, standing alone, is not attacked, nor could it be. The City undoubtedly possesses a general power to buy its fuel from whomever it chooses. It is the reasons or motives for choosing not to deal with Shell which are attacked. They are attacked on the ground that they relate to the conduct of Shell *outside* the City, and hence to matters that are *irrelevant* to municipal concerns. The decision not to deal with Shell, valid in itself, is said to become invalid because it was made for purposes which are beyond the power of the City.

As will become apparent, I take the view that this case requires us to consider the appropriate approach to judicial review of municipal decisions. Broadly speaking, two approaches may be drawn from the cases: a narrow confining approach, and a broader more deferential approach. My colleague Justice Sopinka, as I understand his reasons, takes a narrow view of municipal powers and a strict approach to judicial review of municipal decisions. I advocate a more generous view of municipal powers and a more deferential approach to judicial review. In my view, the latter approach is the better of the two, having regard both to the authorities and to the modern conception of cities and municipalities.

. . .

A. The Availability and Standard of Judicial Review

1. Are the Resolutions Subject to Judicial Review?

[McLachlin J reviewed the law of government procurement and the traditional assumption that governmental contractual powers were not subject to judicial review. She concluded that such powers should be subject to judicial review where a municipality has exercised them for improper purposes or in an improper manner.]

2. The Proper Scope of Judicial Review

Judicial review of municipal decisions is necessary. It is important that municipalities not assume powers which have not been conferred on them, that they not violate civil liberties, that disputes between them and other statutory bodies be resolved, and that abuses of power are checked. On the other hand, it is important that the courts not unduly confine municipalities in the responsible exercise of the powers which the legislature has conferred on them.

The two different approaches to construction of municipal powers alluded to earlier confronts us at this point: see A. McDonald, "In the Public Interest: Judicial Review of Local Government" (1983) 9 *Queen's LJ* 62, at p. 64. The first approach is the narrow construction—pro-interventionist approach, expressed by the Ontario Court of Appeal in *Merritt v. City of Toronto* (1895) 22 OAR 205, at p. 207:

> Municipal corporations, in the exercise of the statutory powers conferred upon them to make by-laws, should be confined strictly within the limits of their authority, and all attempts on their part to exceed it should be firmly repelled by the Courts.

The second approach is typified by the oft-cited decision *City of Hamilton v. Hamilton Distillery Co.* (1907) 38 SCR 239, at p. 249. It was there held:

> In interpreting this legislation I would not desire to apply the technical or strict canons of construction sometimes applied to legislation authorizing taxation. I think the sections are, considering the subject matter and the intention obviously in view, entitled to a broad and reasonable if not, as Lord Chief Justice Russell said in *Kruse v. Johnson* [[1898] 2 QB 91], at p. 99, a "benevolent construction," and if the language used fell short of expressly conferring the powers claimed, but did confer them by a fair and reasonable implication I would not hesitate to adopt the construction sanctioned by the implication. ...

The weight of current commentary tends to be critical of the narrow, pro-interventionist approach to the review of municipal powers, supporting instead a more generous, deferential approach: S.M. Makuch, *Canadian Municipal and Planning Law* (1983), at pp. 5-6; McDonald, *supra*; Arrowsmith, *supra*, at p. 219. Such criticism is not unfounded. Rather than confining themselves to rectification of clear excesses of authority, courts under the guise of vague doctrinal terms such as "irrelevant considerations," "improper purpose," "reasonableness," or "bad faith," have not infrequently arrogated to themselves a wide and sweeping power to substitute their views for those of the elected representatives of municipalities. To the same effect, they have "read in" principles of statutory construction such as the one which states that a by-law cannot affect "common law rights" unless the statute confers authority to do so "in plain language or by necessary implication"; *City of Prince George v. Payne* [1978] 1 SCR 458, at p. 463. The result is that, to quote McDonald (at p. 79), "despite the court's protestations to the contrary, they do, in fact, interfere with the wisdom which municipal councils exercise."

Recent commentary suggests an emerging consensus that courts must respect the responsibility of elected municipal bodies to serve the people who elected them and exercise caution to avoid substituting their views of what is best for the citizens for those of municipal councils. Barring clear demonstration that a municipal decision was beyond its powers, courts should not so hold. In cases where powers are not expressly conferred but may be implied, courts must be prepared to adopt the "benevolent construction" which this Court referred to in *Greenbaum*, and confer the powers by reasonable implication. Whatever rules of construction are applied, they must not be used to usurp the legitimate role of municipal bodies as community representatives.

Such an approach serves a number of purposes which the narrow interventionist approach does not. First, it adheres to the fundamental axiom that courts must accord proper respect to the democratic responsibilities of elected municipal officials and the rights of those who elect them. This is important to the continued healthy functioning of democracy at the municipal level. If municipalities are to be able to respond to the needs and wishes of their citizens, they must be given broad jurisdiction to make local decisions reflecting local values.

Second, a generous approach to municipal powers will aid the efficient functioning of municipal bodies and avoid the costs and uncertainty attendant on excessive litigation. Excessive judicial interference in municipal decision-making can have the unintended and unfortunate result of large amounts of public funds being expended by municipal councils in the attempt to defend the validity of their exercise of statutory powers. The object of judicial review of municipal powers should be to accord municipalities the autonomy to undertake their activities without judicial interference unless clearly warranted.

Thirdly, a generous approach to municipal powers is arguably more in keeping with the true nature of modern municipalities. As McDonald asserts (*supra*, at p. 100), the municipal corporation "has come a long way from its origins in a rural age of simple government demands." She and other commentators (see Makuch and Arrowsmith) advocate that municipal councils should be free to define for themselves, as much as possible, the scope of their statutory authority. Excessive judicial interference in the decisions of elected municipal councils may, as this case illustrates, have the effect of confining modern municipalities in the straitjackets of tradition. ...

Finally, the broader, more deferential approach to judicial intervention in the decisions of municipalities is more in keeping with the flexible, more deferential approach this Court has adopted in recent cases to the judicial review of administrative agencies. ...

The Court has repeatedly stressed the need for sensitivity to context and to the special expertise of tribunals. Where such expertise is established, deference may be warranted even to a tribunal's interpretation of its statutory powers: *Teamsters Union, Local 938 v. Massicotte* [1982] 1 SCR 710. There can be little justification for holding decisions on the welfare of the citizens by municipal councillors to a higher standard of review than the decisions of non-elected statutory boards and agencies.

These considerations lead me to conclude that courts should adopt a generous, deferential standard of review toward the decisions of municipalities. To say this is not new.

[McLachlin J mentioned here the continuing tendency of many courts to take a narrow, interventionist approach to municipal decisions and the recommendation by commentators that the courts develop a "threshold" test for judicial interference.]

It may be that, as jurisprudence accumulates, a threshold test for judicial intervention in municipal decisions will develop. For the purposes of the present case, however, I find it sufficient to suggest that judicial review of municipal decisions should be confined to clear cases. The elected members of council are discharging a statutory duty. The right to exercise that duty freely and in accordance with the perceived wishes of the people they represent is vital to local democracy. Consequently, courts should be reluctant to interfere with the decisions of municipal councils. Judicial intervention is warranted only where a municipality's exercise of its powers is clearly *ultra vires*, or where council has run afoul of one of the other accepted limits on municipal power.

This must be the theme. Against this background, I turn to the grounds of review advanced on this appeal: (1) that the Resolutions were beyond the City's powers; and (2) that the Resolutions violate the rule against discrimination.

B. Were the Resolutions Beyond the City's Powers?

The City's powers are determined by the *Vancouver Charter*, enacted by the Legislature of British Columbia. Generally, the Council may provide for "the good rule and government of the city": s. 189. This is in accordance with the purpose generally ascribed to municipal legislation—to promote the health, welfare, safety or good government of the municipality.

...

Specifically, "the City has full power to engage in any commercial, industrial or business undertaking": s. 137(1). This power extends to doing anything which is related to the commercial or business undertaking: "The Council, in addition to the powers specifically allotted to it, shall have power to do all such things as are incidental or conducive to the exercise of the allotted powers": s. 199. The City also has the power to acquire personal property required for the purposes of the City: s. 190.

Having conferred these broad powers on City Council, the *Vancouver Charter* goes on to specifically state areas in which Council can differentiate or discriminate between groups or classes—the areas of licensing and taxation: s. 203. Similarly, the grant of a special franchise, privilege, immunity or exception must be authorized by a by-law requiring the assent of the electors: s. 153.

The first Resolution in issue on this appeal, the Resolution not to do business with Shell until it stops trading with South Africa, clearly can be defended under the power of the City to engage in commercial and business activities. The City needs fuel. Fuel may be purchased from a variety of firms. This means that the City must of necessity discriminate between suppliers of fuel, as Sopinka J concedes (at p. 282). The City and its agents doubtless make thousands of similar decisions each month, without any suggestion that the City must justify the reason why it chooses one firm over another.

The attack on this Resolution as well as on the second Resolution is based solely on the motives that led to its adoption. It is said the motives for choosing other companies over Shell are unrelated to the business of the City and that these improper purposes render the otherwise legitimate decision invalid.

At this point, we must inquire into the legal principles relevant to review of municipal decisions on the basis of motive. The actions of a statutory body or municipality can be said to be beyond its powers in one of two ways. First, it may be alleged that the *action* itself is beyond the authority's powers. Second, it may be alleged that while the action is within the municipality's powers, the *purpose* for which the action was taken was outside the municipality's powers, thereby rendering the action itself invalid. This case falls into the second category.

The law governing review under this head is sometimes referred to as the "doctrine of improper purposes."

. . .

This doctrine has been applied to municipalities as well as to administrative agencies.

Recently, in England, it was used to invalidate a by-law similar to the resolutions at issue on this appeal: *R v. Lewisham Borough Council, ex parte Shell UK Ltd.* [1988] 1 All ER 938 (QBD).

Nevertheless, application of the doctrine of improper purposes to municipal authorities remains problematic. Municipal legislation is governmental legislation, effected by duly elected representatives. It is often difficult to determine precisely what considerations may have led to the passage of legislation. Even where the preamble or text purports to give reasons, votes may have been cast for quite different reasons. While administrative boards give reasons expressly explaining the basis of their decision, this is not the case for governmental bodies. Thus Dickson J noted in *Thorne's Hardware Ltd. v. The Queen* [1983] 1 SCR 106, at pp. 112-13: "governments may be moved by any number of political, economic, social or partisan considerations." He went on to state that as a general rule the motives of governments enacting subordinate legislation should not be inquired into.

A number of Canadian courts have rejected the notion that municipal legislation, short of evidence of bad faith, should be invalidated on the ground that it was passed for improper purposes, particularly in cases where the municipality can be seen as expressing the moral view of its citizens. ... [A discussion of Canadian authorities has been omitted.]

On the basis of these Canadian authorities, a case might be made that the court on this appeal should not inquire into the motives of the City of Vancouver in deciding not to deal with Shell. That question, however, need not be decided on this appeal, since I am satisfied that in any event, the motives of the City of Vancouver cannot be said to have exceeded the powers which the Legislature has conferred on it.

The question is whether City Council's motives in this case fall outside the area of the City's legitimate concern. The *Vancouver Charter* empowers Council to "provide for the good rule and government of the city": s. 189. My colleague and I agree that this clause permits Vancouver City Council to enact measures for the benefit or welfare of the inhabitants of the City. We part company on what this phrase includes.

My colleague adopts a narrow view of the welfare of the inhabitants of the City. He asserts that the City's Resolutions effect a purpose "without any identifiable benefit to its inhabitants" (p. 280) and speaks of "matters external to the interests of the citizens" (p. 279). He appears to define "municipal purposes" essentially in terms of provision of basic services to the inhabitants of the City.

I would cast the proper functions of a municipality in a larger mould. The term "welfare of the citizens," it seems to me, is capable of embracing not only their immediate needs, but also the psychological welfare of the citizens as members of a community who have an interest in expressing their identity as a community. Our language recognizes this: we speak of civic spirit, of city pride. This suggests that City Council may properly take measures related to fostering and maintaining this sense of community identity and pride. Among such measures may be found community expression of disapproval or approval of different types of conduct, wherever it is found. The right of free expression, one of the most fundamental values of our society, may be exercised individually or collectively. Are the citizens of a city to be prevented from expressing through their elected representatives their disapproval of conduct which they feel to be improper? Are they to be forced to do business with a firm whose conduct they see as objectionable, simply because the conduct occurs outside the territorial boundaries of the city? Can the desire of the citizens' elected representatives to express their views on such matters and to withdraw support for the conduct to which they object by refusing to do business with its perpetrators be said to be totally unrelated to the welfare and interests of the citizens of the city? To all these questions I would answer no.

A number of considerations support this view. The first is the need, referred to earlier, to adopt a generous approach toward municipal legislation. Courts should not be quick to substitute their views for those of elected council members on what will best serve the welfare of the city's citizens. That is the responsibility of the elected councillors. Unless they have clearly gone beyond the city's powers, the courts should not interfere.

The second consideration supporting this view is the wording of the *Vancouver Charter*. As I read it, it amply supports a broad view of the City's proper concerns. The Council is to "provide for the good rule and government of the city": s. 189. These words are not restricted to the provision of services. They are broad enough to encompass expression of community concerns about what is happening outside the community's boundaries. Collective expression through elected representatives may be seen as a proper function of "government." As such, it falls within s. 189 of the *Vancouver Charter*. A broad approach to the powers of the City finds further support in s. 199, which allows Council "to do all such things as are incidental or conducive to the exercise of the allotted powers."

My colleague Sopinka J dismisses these provisions as "general sections found in most if not all municipal Acts" which "must be construed subject to the limitations imposed by the purpose of the statute as a whole" (p. 278). He concludes that "[a]ny powers implied from their general language must be restricted to municipal purposes and cannot extend to include the imposition of a boycott based on matters external to the interests of the citizens of the municipality" (pp. 278-79). It seems to me that this reasoning begs the essential question: what are proper "municipal purposes"? What matters are truly "external to the interests of the citizens"? In determining the answers to these questions, it is important to recognize the changing nature and role of municipal government in Canada. As noted earlier, municipalities have evolved significantly over the last century, in both size and purpose. As Rogers states, *supra*, § 63.31, at p. 357: "Functions generally accepted as being within the purview of legitimate municipal endeavour today were not always so regarded. ..." Thus, even if the expression of collective values was not traditionally seen as a function of municipal authorities, the growing sophistication and stature of a contemporary city such as Vancouver requires that the scope of "municipal purposes" be determined with reference to this current reality.

Nor can I agree that the fact that the *Vancouver Charter* authorizes the City to participate in public works projects with other municipalities and to acquire property for City purposes indicates the intent that in no other cases may the Council consider matters or events outside the boundaries of the City. These provisions seem to me not to be directed at the issue of territorial boundaries, so much as to defining the sorts of activities the municipality can engage in, wherever they may take place.

Finally, I cannot agree with my colleague that the phrase "good rule and government of the city" (p. 278) places a territorial limit on the factors which Council may consider in making decisions which are within its express power to make. The phrase is capable of encompassing matters outside the City's boundaries, provided they relate to the welfare of its citizens.

The truth of the matter is that provisions in municipal Acts for the "good government" or general welfare of the citizens, far from being mere surplusage as my colleague suggests, found their origin in the desire of legislatures to prevent the decisions of municipal councillors being struck down by the courts. If the courts interpret them narrowly, they will defeat the very purpose for which these provisions were enacted. Rogers states, [*The Law of Canadian Municipal Corporations* (2nd ed. 1971)], § 63.35, at p. 364:

> Undoubtedly the inclusion of "general welfare" provisions was intended to circumvent, to some extent, the effect of the doctrine of *ultra vires* which puts the municipalities in the position of having to point to an express grant of authority to justify each corporate act.

Even accepting that lower courts have held that these phrases must be read "subject to the general intent and purport of legislation respecting municipal institutions" (Rogers, *supra*, § 63.35, at p. 366), the fact remains that legislatures introduce clauses such as these for the very purpose of permitting municipalities themselves to decide what is in the best interests of their citizenry.

A third consideration supporting a broader view of the City's powers is the fact that many other municipalities interpret their mandate in similar terms. The City of Vancouver does not stand alone in its view that the welfare of its citizens extends to action based on the community's moral views about what may be happening outside the municipality. Council was advised, before adopting the Resolutions, that approximately 30 cities had adopted a preferential purchasing policy boycotting Shell products. The brief which Shell filed before City Council contains a copy of a publication which informs us that "[a] number of local governments in the US are relentlessly pursuing pledges they made a few years ago to stop doing business with companies that continue to sell to South Africa. ... One such local government is Dade County, Florida, which includes the city of Miami." Clearly many municipalities share the view that the welfare of the citizens of a city extends to declining to do business with companies whose conduct the citizenry finds to be morally unacceptable.

[McLachlin J then discussed, and distinguished, an English case in which a municipal bylaw similar to Vancouver's resolution was held to be invalid.]

As discussed earlier, scholars are critical of the frequency with which courts disguise an assessment for reasonableness in the cloak of a review for *vires*. On one view of my colleague's reasons, they do this very thing. Sopinka J correctly states that the reasonableness of the Resolutions is not in issue, only the power of the City to pass them (p. 274). Yet he goes on to hold that the Resolutions must fall because they are "based on matters external to the interests of the citizens of the municipality" (p. 279). But that is the very question at stake. What *is* external to the interests of the citizens? What, conversely, is in their interests? The City councillors, after hearing both sides, took one view—a view which many other municipal councils have taken. My colleague takes another. In my view, it is the Council's judgment which should prevail. ...

In summary on the first issue, I am satisfied that the purposes of City Council in resolving not to do business with Shell was proper and fell within the powers of the City under the *Vancouver Charter*.

[The judgment of La Forest, Sopinka, Cory, Iacobucci, and Major JJ was delivered by:]

SOPINKA J:

· · ·

Reviewability

The respondent submits that the Resolutions are not law enacted by it pursuant to its legislative powers but rather an exercise of its corporate power and hence not reviewable by the court. A variant of this argument is that if the Resolutions are a legal emanation of Council, since the same result could have been achieved by simply refusing to deal with Shell in awarding contracts, the court should not interfere. This latter argument applies only to the first Resolution.

The powers of a municipality are classified for some purposes. The classifications include legislative functions, quasi-judicial functions and business functions. The nature of the function may affect the duties and liabilities of the municipality. Accordingly, it may be liable in contract or tort in respect of its business function but civil liability in respect of its legislative or quasi-judicial function is problematic. In its quasi-judicial function, Council may have a duty of fairness which does not apply in respect of the exercise of its legislative powers. ... See *Welbridge Holdings Ltd. v. Metropolitan Corporation of Greater*

Winnipeg [1971] SCR 957, and *Wiswell v. Metropolitan Corporation of Greater Winnipeg* [1965] SCR 512. As creatures of statute, however, municipalities must stay within the powers conferred on them by the provincial legislature. In *R v. Greenbaum* [1993] 1 SCR 674, Iacobucci J, speaking for the Court, stated, at p. 687:

> Municipalities are entirely the creatures of provincial statutes. Accordingly, they can exercise only those powers which are explicitly conferred upon them by a provincial statute.

It follows that the exercise of a municipality's statutory powers, whatever the classification, is reviewable to the extent of determining whether the actions are *intra vires*. Normally this is done by a motion to quash or a declaration of invalidity with respect to the act of Council which is impugned. The authorities referred to in argument do not support the contention that the exercise of business or corporate powers is immune from review.

Moreover, there does not appear to be any valid policy ground for providing such immunity. There is good reason to encourage municipalities to act within their statutory powers. An absence of judicial review would leave some ratepayers without an effective remedy. The suggestion that the only remedy is at the polls is of no value to the minority who would be left with no remedy and Council could continue to enlarge its statutory powers as long as it was able to retain its majority support. The public policy in favour of restricting a municipality to its statutory powers exists as much for the minority as for the majority.

The City of Vancouver took action herein by passing resolutions. Clearly this was a purported exercise of its statutory powers. Section 223 of the *Municipal Act*, RSBC 1979, c. 290, indicates that all powers of a council may be exercised by by-law or by resolution. Section 151 of the *Vancouver Charter* repeats this proviso, adding that the powers of Council may be exercised by resolution only where a by-law is not specifically required. A resolution is an act which binds Council and municipal officers and officials until repealed. See I.M. Rogers, *The Law of Canadian Municipal Corporations* (2nd ed. 1971), at pp. 406.8 and 406.9. In these circumstances, I do not appreciate the force of the argument that the respondent could have accomplished its purpose in some other fashion which would have been immune from judicial review. The respondent argues that it could simply have refused to deal with the appellant. I have difficulty envisaging how this would have been possible without direction from Council. An individual who wishes to engage in conduct and avoid scrutiny of his or her reasons or motives can simply decide to act in a certain fashion. A municipality cannot do this. Any policy or plan not to deal with the appellant would require a decision of Council. Any such decision must be grounded in a statutory power and, whatever its form, would be reviewable. In the absence of such a decision, any attempt to have the staff refuse to deal with the appellant on the basis of a "wink and a nod" would be vulnerable to attack on the basis of absence of authority from Council and would expose the staff to civil liability.

Impermissible Purpose

Generally, a municipal authority is authorized to act only for municipal purposes. In *R v. Sharma* [1993] 1 SCR 650, at p. 668, Iacobucci J, speaking for the Court, adopted the principle from S.M. Makuch, *Canadian Municipal and Planning Law* (1983), at p. 115, that as statutory bodies, municipalities

> ... may exercise only those powers expressly conferred by statute, those powers necessarily or fairly implied by the expressed power in the statute, and those indispensable powers essential and not merely convenient to the effectuation of the purposes of the corporation.

The "purposes of the corporation" or "municipal purposes" are determined by reference to not only those that are expressly stated but those that are compatible with the purpose and objects of the enabling statute.

· · ·

In most cases, as here, the problem arises with respect to the exercise of a power that is not expressly conferred but is sought to be implied on the basis of a general grant of power. It is in these cases that the purposes of the enabling statute assume great importance. The approach in such circumstances is set out in the following excerpt in Rogers, *The Law of Canadian Municipal Corporations, supra,* § 64.1, at p. 387, with which I agree:

> In approaching a problem of construing a municipal enactment a court should endeavour firstly to interpret it so that the powers sought to be exercised are in consonance with the purposes of the corporation. The provision at hand should be construed with reference to the object of the municipality: to render services to a group of persons in a locality with a view to advancing their health, welfare, safety and good government.

Any ambiguity or doubt is to be resolved in favour of the citizen especially when the grant of power contended for is out of the "usual range."

I must, therefore, determine whether the Resolutions were passed for a municipal purpose. Their purpose is amply defined in the preambles and the operative parts of the Resolutions. The explicit purpose is to influence Shell to divest in South Africa by expressing moral outrage against the apartheid regime and to join the alleged international boycott of its subsidiaries and products until Shell "completely withdraws from South Africa." There is no mention as to how the good government, health or welfare of the City or its citizens is affected or promoted thereby. Specifically, there is no mention of any objective of improving relations among its citizens. In view of the detailed recital of the purposes of the Resolutions, no such implicit purpose can be read in. The fourth recital hints at the existence of a broader program to control with whom the City does business. It refers to doing business with South Africa as one of the criteria to be employed. There is, however, no evidence that such a program exists and, indeed, its existence is contradicted by the fact that the City continued to purchase from Chevron. I therefore agree with the trial judge that the respondent was seeking to use its powers to do business "to affect matters in another part of the world" (pp. 348-49), a purpose which is directed at matters outside the territorial limits of the City.

Is this in relation to a municipal purpose? Clearly there is no express power in the *Vancouver Charter* authorizing the Resolutions and if they are valid the respondent must rely on such powers being implied. This requires a consideration of the relevant provisions of the *Vancouver Charter* on the basis of the principles outlined above. So far as the purpose of the *Vancouver Charter* is concerned it is perhaps best expressed in s. 189, which provides that "Council may provide for the good rule and government of the city."

In this regard its purpose does not differ from the purpose generally of municipal legislation which, as stated above, is to promote the health, welfare, safety or good government of the municipality. This places a territorial limit on Council's jurisdiction. No doubt Council can have regard for matters beyond its boundaries in exercising its powers but in so doing any action taken must have as its purpose benefit to the citizens of the City. The *Vancouver Charter* is careful to expressly provide for activities in which Council is permitted to engage outside of its limits even when such activities clearly redound to the benefit of the inhabitants of the City. Such activities include participation in public works projects with other municipalities (s. 188) and acquiring property required for the purposes of the City (s. 190).

The respondent relied on several other sections of the *Vancouver Charter* to support the Resolutions. Section 137 gives the City power to engage in commercial, industrial or business undertakings; s. 190 empowers Council to acquire such personal property as may be required for the purposes of the City; and s. 199 allows Council "to do all such things as are incidental or conducive to the exercise of the allotted powers." These sections are general sections found in most if not all municipal Acts and must be construed subject to the limitations imposed by the purpose of the statute as a whole. Any powers implied from their general language must be restricted to municipal purposes and cannot extend to include the imposition of a boycott based on matters external to the interests of the citizens of the municipality.

[Sopinka J found the reasoning of the analogous English case "highly persuasive" and followed it.]

Appeal allowed.

NOTES

1. To what extent can differences between the majority and minority judgments in *Shell Canada* be attributed to the interpretative "backgrounds" used for determining the scope of the city's legal powers? How in a post-*Baker* world do you think this case would be decided? Does McLachlin J's plea for deference to the judgment of elected officials in the exercise of broad discretion now take on a much stronger dimension even for wrongful purpose review?

2. All members of the court agree that resolution on procurement is subject to the principles of public law judicial review. Should the same hold for individual procurement decisions such as the award of the city's advertising contract on the basis of a tendering process? See *Gestion Complexe Cousineau (1989) Inc. v. Canada*, [1995] 2 FC 694 (CA) and below.

3. *Shell Canada* can be compared in one respect with a line of English cases in which municipalities were held to have acted *ultra vires* when they exercised commercial or contractual powers to advance a social policy objective. The policy was often characterized by the courts as legally irrelevant, and the expenditure of public funds for redistributive purposes exposed the municipalities to the charge of failing to have regard to the "fiduciary" duties that they owed to the local property taxpayers.

For example, having decided that it should act as a responsible employer, a municipality used its statutory power to pay to its employees such wages as it thought fit to remunerate them at above the prevailing labour market rate, especially for women: *Roberts v. Hopwood*, [1925] AC 579 (Eng. HL). In *Prescott v. Birmingham Corporation*, [1995] Ch. 210, the municipality permitted senior citizens to ride on its buses free of charge, pursuant to a discretion to charge such fares as it thought fit. More recently, the Greater London Council honoured an election pledge to reduce fares on public transport in London, even though it thereby forfeited a large operating grant from central government: *Bromley London Borough Council v. Greater London Council*, [1983] 1 AC 768 (Eng. HL). In each case the court held that the municipality had acted *ultra vires* and overturned its decision.

Failure To Consider Relevant Factors

The previous two cases involved challenges to an agency's exercise of discretion on the ground that it took into consideration a factor that was not legally relevant or that it was pursuing some improper purpose.

Failing to take into consideration a relevant factor is also a basis for impugning the *vires* of an agency's exercise of discretion, although there is some doubt about the scope of this doctrine. On one view, the doctrine requires decision-makers to assemble for consideration all the factors that they may lawfully take into account when exercising their discretion. However, this would be an extraordinarily onerous and sometimes impossible standard to meet. The costs of trying to comply would generally not be offset by any increase in the quality of the decision made.

A more limited and plausible version is that, while an agency *may* consider a large number of factors in the exercise of a discretionary power (permissive relevant considerations), it is *required* to consider only some of them (mandatory relevant considerations). An exercise of discretion will therefore be *ultra vires* only if the agency has overlooked a factor that its enabling statute (whether expressly or impliedly) *obliged* it to consider. Whether a particular factor was one that the agency had to take into account in exercising its discretion should be determined by reference to the importance of that factor to the discharge of its statutory mandate. (The origin of this distinction is the judgment of Cooke P in *Tavita v. Minister of Immigration*, [1993] 2 NZLR 257 (CA).)

In the aftermath of *Baker*, it is now clear that international law (including unincorporated ratified treaties) will have to be taken into account in the exercise of statutory and prerogative powers. Similarly, *Reference re Secession of Quebec*, [1998] 2 SCR 217 (Can.) will on occasion require the taking into account of one or more of the four underlying principles of Canadian constitutional law. In these cases, there is little doubt that these will be mandatory relevant considerations. What is, however, problematic, as we saw in *Baker*, is the extent to which these constitutional principles have to be taken into account or the weight that must be given to them. Does *Suresh* settle this question and hold that the question of weight is no concern of the courts?

If an agency is found to have taken into consideration a factor that is irrelevant to the exercise of its discretion, or has acted for some improper purpose, this is normally because the reviewing court has rejected the agency's interpretation of its statutory power. However, an allegation that an agency has failed to consider something that it ought to have considered sometimes means not that it has misinterpreted its statute, but that it has overlooked evidence that would establish whether a legally relevant fact existed.

For example, in *Oakwood Developments Ltd. v. Rural Municipality of St. François Xavier*, [1985] 2 SCR 164 (Man.), a municipality refused a developer permission to subdivide land for residential development because of the danger of flooding. However, the council had declined to read an engineer's report that described measures that could be taken to avoid the problem. Delivering the judgment of the court, Wilson J said that, because the process of regulating the division of land into smaller lots curtailed the common law rights of landowners, it must be specifically authorized by statute. She concluded that, while flood control and soil erosion were relevant to the exercise of the power to refuse permission, the refusal of permission in this case was *ultra vires* because the municipality failed to consider evidence that was highly material to its legitimate concerns. Although not mentioned in the judgment, the municipality's error presumably could also have been described as a breach of the duty of procedural fairness because it denied the developer an opportunity to tender evidence in support of its claim.

Multiple Purposes and Considerations

What if an agency exercised a statutory discretion to achieve several purposes, only one of which is improper? Or, what if the irrelevant factor that was taken into account is only one of several relevant considerations that shaped the decision? While judicial support can be found for a range of tests, the prevailing view appears to be that the court will only hold such decisions to be *ultra vires* if the unlawful purpose or consideration played a dominant or material role in the exercise of discretion. See, for example, *Canadian Assn. of Regulated Importers v. Canada (Attorney General)*, [1994] 2 FC 247, 260 (CA) (concluding that a decision based entirely or predominantly on irrelevant factors is liable to be set aside).

Professional Licensing and the Relevancy Principle

Legislative schemes that create statutory monopolies for, and regulate entry to, the professions often provide that, in addition to satisfying standards of competence, applicants for registration must be of "good character." After admission, a member may be subject to disciplinary proceedings for engaging in "conduct unbecoming" a member of the profession. Responsibility for elaborating these open-ended standards is normally left to the governing body of the profession, often subject to a right of appeal to the courts.

A recognition that these powers are conferred in order to protect the public, rather than, for example, to boost the image of the profession, by no means eliminates all the potential difficulties in deciding whether a particular factor is legally relevant to the power to exclude from registration or to discipline. Consider these hypotheticals.

1. After graduating from an accredited law school, a student-at-law has successfully completed his articles and the bar admission examinations and has accepted a position in the corporate department of the law firm where he was an articling student. It has come to the attention of the law society that the student was convicted six

years earlier of sexually assaulting his wife's daughter. Is this a "relevant consideration" in determining whether to admit him to membership of the law society?

2. A lawyer has been reported to the law society for regularly picking up prostitutes in his car. He is also in default in his child support payments. Is either, or both, "conduct unbecoming" for which he could be disciplined?

For further reading on the good character requirement in the legal profession in the United States, see Rhode, "Moral Character as a Professional Credential" (1985), 94 *Yale LJ* 491.

DISCRETION AND THE CHARTER, UNDERLYING PRINCIPLES OF THE CONSTITUTION, AND INTERNATIONAL LAW

Before the Charter, the courts used presumptions of statutory construction to protect fundamental rights from being infringed by the exercise of administrative discretion. In other words, in the absence of express words or necessary implication in a statute, it was presumed that the legislature did not intend a discretion to be exercised so as to curtail basic liberties. Rights protected in this way included freedom of speech and association, the right not to have one's property expropriated without compensation, and the right to earn a living.

In this regard, mention should be made of two important administrative law decisions of the Supreme Court of Canada in the 1950s, a time when the civil liberties of dissenters from majority opinion were not well protected. In both decisions, the judgments delivered by Rand J are especially powerful. The first case, *Roncarelli v. Duplessis*, was referred to earlier in this chapter. It is a ringing vindication of freedom of religion from attack by the state through a statutory liquor licensing power. The second, *Smith and Rhuland v. The Queen*, [1953] 2 SCR 95 (NS), arose from a labour board's refusal in its discretion to certify a union as the sole bargaining agent for a group of employees because a senior union official was a member of the Communist Party. Despite the significant backwash experienced in Canada from the witch hunt for communists in the United States by Senator Eugene McCarthy, the Supreme Court held that the fact that the board found a union official's political views to be dangerous was insufficient to deny to employees the right to be represented by a union of their choosing. However, Rand J qualified his judgment (at 100) by indicating that the board's decision would have been upheld if there had been some evidence that "with the acquiescence of the members, [the influence of the official] has been directed to ends destructive of the legitimate purposes of the union."

The Charter improved in at least three ways on the protection of individual rights previously provided by the common law. First, while there is no authoritative list of rights regarded by the common law as fundamental, the Charter identifies those that are to receive particular protection by their entrenchment in the constitution. This does not mean that the scope of these rights is precisely defined: the phrase "life, liberty and security of the person" in s. 7 conveys a very broad concept. On the other hand, rights of property (though *cf.* s. 1(a) of the *Canadian Bill of Rights*) and freedom of contract are not as such protected. Second, the inclusion of s. 1 makes it clear that Charter rights are not absolute and may have to be accommodated to other claims. While it is far from clear how these provisions should be applied, the analytical framework developed by the courts for balancing competing claims (principally the *Oakes* test) provides a more overt and structured methodology than anything that the courts evolved at common law. Third, the Charter operates independently of statute. This means that it normally prevails over even express statutory language authorizing the curtailment of Charter-protected rights, and emphasizes that "reading down" grants of discretion so as not to authorize the violation of fundamental rights involves more than the interpretation of the enabling statute.

A substantive analysis of the use of the Charter to invalidate the grant or exercise of statutory discretion is more appropriate for books about constitutional law. Early examples included the invalidation of powers of search and seizure without warrants for the purpose of anti-combines investigation (*Hunter v. Southam Inc.*, [1984] 2 SCR 145 (Alta.)); regulations restricting advertising by members of a profession (*Rocket v. Royal College of Dental Surgeons of Ontario*, [1990] 2 SCR 232 (Ont.)); a policy prohibiting "leafletting" at an airport owned by the federal government (*Committee for the Commonwealth of Canada v. Canada*, [1991] 1 SCR 139 (Can.)); and municipal bylaws prohibiting "postering" on public property (*Ramsden v. Peterborough (City)*, [1993] 2 SCR 1084 (Ont.)). Note also on the scope of "life, liberty and security of the person": *R v. Morgentaler*, [1988] 1 SCR 30 (Ont.) and *Wilson v. Medical Services Commission of British Columbia* (1988), 53 DLR (4th) 171 (BC CA).

However, the mere fact that a statutory discretionary has the potential to be exercised in a way that infringes Charter rights and freedoms does not give rise automatically to invalidation: *R v. Jones*, [1986] 2 SCR 284 (Alta.). In such cases, the attack will have to be on the individual exercise of discretion, not the authorizing provision: *Eldridge v. British Columbia*, [1997] 3 SCR 624 (BC). See also *Little Sisters Book and Art Emporium v. Canada (Minister of Justice)*, [2000] 2 SCR 1120 (BC) and, for useful academic discussion, see June Ross, "Applying the Charter to Discretionary Authority" (1991), 29 *Alta. LR* 382. Note also the very limited use of the Charter to strike down legislation as void for vagueness under the principles of *R v. Nova Scotia Pharmaceutical Society*, [1992] 2 SCR 606 (NS); and *Canadian Foundation for Children, Youth and the Law v. Canada (Attorney General)*, [2004] 1 SCR 76; see, for example, *Trang v. Alberta (Edmonton Remand Centre)* (2010), 2010 ABQB 6 (CanLII), paras. 1131-42, in which Marceau J concluded that the power of a disciplinary board to punish an inmate at a provincial correctional institution for doing anything that is "prejudicial to the good order and discipline of the institution" was not unconstitutionally vague in a context where "a statement of the particulars" that contains "meaningful details" of the charge "is given to the accused at the same time as his notice to attend a disciplinary hearing."

For a discussion of the relationship between administrative law and constitutional law with respect to the control of discretionary power and the restrictions of fundamental rights, see *Slaight Communications Inc. v. Davidson*, [1989] 1 SCR 1038. See also Fox-Decent, "The Charter and Administrative Law: Cross-Fertilization in Public Law" in Flood and Sossin, eds., *Administrative Law in Context* (2008), at 181-89; and Gratton, "Standing at the Divide: The Relationship Between Administrative Law and the Charter Post-*Multani*" (2008), 53 *McGill LJ* 477.

Besides the Charter, other underlying constitutional principles as well as international law may be relevant to the exercise of discretionary power. This is made clear in the *Secession Reference* ([1998] 2 SCR 217) and in *Baker*. See, for example, *Lalonde v. Ontario (Commission de restructuration des services de santé)* (2001), 56 OR (3d) 505 (CA), where the Ontario Court of Appeal upheld a decision of the Divisional Court that overturned a discretionary order of the commission to downsize the Montfort Hospital in Ottawa as part of a restructuring of health-care services in the province. The Court of Appeal concluded that, in exercising its discretion, the commission failed to give serious weight and consideration to the linguistic and cultural significance of Montfort to the survival of the Franco-Ontarian minority, contrary to the constitutional principle of respect for and protection of minorities.

On the relevance of international law, see *114957 Canada Ltée (Spraytech, Société d'arrosage) v. Hudson (Town)*, [2001] 2 SCR 241 (Que.), where emerging international law on the precautionary principle of sustainable development was deployed as part of the justification for a bylaw banning the recreational use of pesticides. In contrast, recall that the Supreme Court in *Suresh* was not willing to hold that the absolute prohibition in the *Convention Against Torture*, which Canada has ratified, signalled the invalidity of a provision that allowed deportation for national security reasons even where that might jeopardize s. 7 Charter rights. Domestic law and the Charter permitted such deportations in exceptional circumstances, according to the court.

DELEGATED LEGISLATION

We have so far focused on the individual exercise of discretion. Equally important as an administrative tool is the power, frequently delegated by statute, to make rules of more general application. This is often called delegated legislation. It is a large topic that can only be touched on here.

While rules made within the bounds of statutory authority have the same legal effect as if they had been contained in the statute itself, delegated legislation, like other exercises of discretion, is subject to judicial review. Of course, the legislature itself may also establish a special process or dedicated committee to review delegated legislation introduced by administrative actors pursuant to statute; see Marleau and Montpetit, *House of Commons Procedures and Practice* (2000 edition), c. 17, online: Parliament of Canada.

Because the theoretical bases for judicial review of the exercise of discretion is of general application, one would expect the grounds for challenging delegated legislation to be the same as those for challenging individualized discretionary decisions. And, indeed, delegated legislation is subject to judicial review on the ground of *ultra vires*. Further, the following presumptions seem to be of particular importance when the courts determine the scope of authority delegated by the legislature: statutes are presumed not to authorize the exercise of rule-making power to impose taxation, to operate retroactively, or to contradict a provision in the enabling statute. Despite the general relevance of common law principles of judicial review, a discrete body of doctrine has evolved around the judicial review of the exercise of delegated legislative powers. A book-length treatment of this topic is provided by Holland and McGowan, *Delegated Legislation in Canada* (Scarborough, ON: Carswell, 1989). See also the discussion of delegation in chapter 6 of this text.

Notably, the courts have been especially prepared to review delegated legislation passed by municipalities, generally in the form of bylaws. A judicial attitude of suspicion toward municipal bylaws has a long history; in England it stretches back to a time when local government was not elected and when local centres of power represented a threat to the central government, of which the royal courts were an emanation. As we have noted elsewhere in this text, these conflicts continued throughout the 20th century, typically when collectivist policies of municipal councils, with a Labour Party majority, incurred the displeasure of a Conservative central government or local taxpayers.

In particular, with respect to municipal bylaws, the courts historically employed the concept of abuse of power to develop various categories where bylaws would be subjected to closer scrutiny than delegated legislation passed by Cabinet or individual ministers, for example. See *Kruse v. Johnson*, [1898] 2 QB 91 (Eng. QBD). In the Canadian context, see, for example, *R v. Bell*, [1979] 2 SCR 212 (Ont.) (where the court struck down a zoning bylaw that restricted the use of dwelling units to single-family occupation) and *Montreal (City of) v. Arcade Amusements Inc.*, [1985] 1 SCR 368 (Que.) (where Beetz J concluded that a bylaw that prohibited persons under the age of 18 from using amusement machines and frequenting arcades was discriminatory and therefore invalid, although the city had acted in good faith pursuant to its power to enact bylaws to regulate the use of slot machines and, more generally, to ensure the peace, order, and good government of the city).

UNREVIEWABLE DISCRETIONARY POWERS?

Prerogative Powers and Non-Justiciability

Until the mid-1980s, it was normally assumed that the principles of judicial review applicable to the exercise of statutory discretion did not extend to non-statutory powers of government. While the vast majority of administrative programs are delivered under statutory authority, there are some areas in which government relies on the common law powers of the Crown, including the royal prerogative. For example, prerogative powers provide the legal foundation for the issue and refusal of passports to citizens, the award of honours (including the title of Queen's Counsel (QC)), the signing of treaties and the conduct of foreign affairs, and the disposition of the armed forces.

It was established conclusively in England in the 17th century that the ordinary courts could determine the existence and scope of a prerogative power claimed by the Crown. Prerogative powers are also subject to statute, and may be limited or abolished expressly or by implication. Again, it is the role of the courts to determine whether and to what extent a prerogative power has been superseded by statute. However, it was assumed until quite recently that the courts could not impose on the exercise of an existing prerogative power the kinds of limitations to which statutory powers are subject: the duty of fairness and requirements of relevancy, propriety of purpose, and reasonableness, for example.

Two primary factors have contributed to the view that the exercise of prerogative powers is not subject to the normal range of judicial review. First, the role of the courts in administrative law has traditionally been said to ensure that government agencies comply with the duly expressed instructions of the legislature and that the principles of administrative law are essentially rules of statutory interpretation. Based on these assumptions, which, as we have tried to show in this text, represent only a part of the truth, it is easy to understand why the courts did not focus on the exercise of non-statutory government powers.

Second, the exercise of most of the prerogative powers that have survived until today does not impinge directly on the legal rights of individuals. Typically, they concern the grant of privileges (passports and QCs) that are not legally required for any activity, or action that affects the public in much the same way (the signing of treaties, and measures taken under them, for instance). And if the role of the courts in administrative law is limited to the protection of individuals' legal rights (that is, those recognized by the common law or conferred by statute) from unauthorized governmental action, then it is difficult to justify judicial intervention in decisions that do not have this effect. Given also the large issues of public policy that influence the exercise of many prerogative powers, it is legitimate to wonder whether grievances about the propriety of their exercise are more appropriately addressed in the political forum rather than the courts.

It is now clear that the courts, in determining whether a discretionary power is exempt from review, will be influenced more by the nature of the power in question and less by its legal source. A prominent example of this functional approach to the scope of judicial review of discretionary power is the House of Lords' decision in *Council of Civil Service Unions v. Minister for the Civil Service*, [1985] AC 374 (Eng. HL). In this case, the Lords denied relief to the applicants in their application for judicial review of the minister's decision to disallow them from continuing to belong to a national trade union. The minister stated that her decision to bar civil servants employed at an intelligence gathering facility, Government Communications Headquarters (GCHQ), from continuing to belong to a national trade union was based on considerations of national security. If she had consulted, the minister's affidavit said, there might have been a work stoppage which would have endangered security. The House of Lords accepted this argument and denied relief on this basis.

More significantly, the Lords held that, because the minister had consulted the council in the past about changes to the terms and conditions of employment of civil servants, the council had a legitimate expectation of being consulted in future. Thus it would normally be a breach of the duty of fairness for the minister to effect a change without prior consultation with the council. Here, the source of the minister's authority to issue instructions on civil servants' terms and conditions of employment came from an order in council that was issued pursuant to the Crown prerogative. Thus, on the general issue of justiciability and the Crown prerogative, the Lords concluded that the minister's exercise of discretion was reviewable in the courts. According to Lord Diplock:

> For a decision to be susceptible to judicial review the decision-maker must be empowered by public law (and not merely, as in arbitration, by agreement between private parties) to make decisions that, if validly made, will lead to administrative action or abstention from action by an authority endowed by law with executive powers, which have one or other of the consequences mentioned in the preceding paragraph. The ultimate source of the decision-making power is nearly always nowadays a statute or subordinate legislation made under the statute; but in the absence of any statute regulating the subject matter of the decision the source of the decision-making power may still be the common law itself, i.e., that part of the common law that is given by lawyers the label of "the prerogative." Where this is the source of decision-making power, the power is confined to executive officers of central as distinct from local government and in constitutional practice is generally exercised by those holding ministerial rank.
>
> It was the prerogative that was relied on as the source of the power of the Minister for the Civil Service in reaching her decision of 22 December 1983 that membership of national trade unions should in future be barred to all members of the home civil service employed at GCHQ.

My Lords, I intend no discourtesy to counsel when I say that, intellectual interest apart, in answering the question of law raised in this appeal, I have derived little practical assistance from learned and esoteric analyses of the precise legal nature, boundaries and historical origin of "the prerogative," or of what powers exercisable by executive officers acting on behalf of central government that are not shared by private citizens qualify for inclusion under this particular label. It does not, for instance, seem to me to matter whether today the right of the executive government that happens to be in power to dismiss without notice any member of the home civil service upon which perforce it must rely for the administration of its policies, and the correlative disability of the executive government that is in power to agree with a civil servant that his service should be on terms that did not make him subject to instant dismissal, should be ascribed to "the prerogative" or merely to a consequence of the survival, for entirely different reasons, of a rule of constitutional law whose origin is to be found in the theory that those by whom the administration of the realm is carried on do so as personal servants of the monarch who can dismiss them at will, because the King can do no wrong.

Nevertheless, whatever label may be attached to them there have unquestionably survived into the present day a residue of miscellaneous fields of law in which the executive government retains decision-making powers that are not dependent upon any statutory authority but nevertheless have consequences on the private rights or legitimate expectations of other persons which would render the decision subject to judicial review if the power of the decision-maker to make them were statutory in origin. From matters so relatively minor as the grant of pardons to condemned criminals, of honours to the good and great, of corporate personality to deserving bodies of persons, and of bounty from moneys made available to the executive government by Parliament, they extend to matters so vital to the survival and welfare of the nation as the conduct of relations with foreign states and—what lies at the heart of the present case—the defence of the realm against potential enemies. Adopting the phraseology used in the European Convention on Human Rights 1953 (Convention for the Protection of Human Rights and Fundamental Freedoms (1953) (Cmd. 8969)) to which the United Kingdom is a party it has now become usual in statutes to refer to the latter as "national security."

My Lords, I see no reason why simply because a decision-making power is derived from a common law and not a statutory source, it should *for that reason only* be immune from judicial review. ...

Lord Diplock stated that a decision made under a prerogative power was, in most cases, subject to review for procedural propriety.

Compare, however, Lord Roskill's reasoning in *Council of Civil Service Unions* as follows on the boundaries of judicial review of prerogative powers (after he agreed in principle that a decision was not immune from judicial review simply because its source was the prerogative rather than a statute):

But I do not think that that right of challenge can be unqualified. It must, I think, depend upon the subject matter of the prerogative power which is exercised. Many examples were given during the argument of prerogative powers which as at present advised I do not think could properly be made the subject of judicial review. Prerogative powers such as those relating to the making of treaties, the defence of the realm, the prerogative of mercy, the grant of honours, the dissolution of Parliament and the appointment of ministers as well as others are not, I think, susceptible to judicial review because their nature and subject matter are such as not to be amenable to the judicial process. The courts are not the place wherein to determine whether a treaty should be concluded or the armed forces disposed in a particular manner or Parliament dissolved on one date rather than another.

Do you agree with Lord Roskill's list of prerogative powers that are excluded from judicial review? Suppose, for example, a Canadian citizen was, because she had not repaid a loan, refused a passport by the Canadian consulate in London, thus preventing her from flying home to Canada at short notice where her father was dying? Or what if the Order of Canada was revoked from a distinguished poet when he was convicted of fraud?

Black v. Canada (Prime Minister)
(2001), 54 OR (3d) 215 (CA)

[The main question in this appeal was whether the prerogative power exercised by Prime Minister Chrétien to advise the Queen on the conferral of honours was reviewable in the courts. In concluding that it was reviewable, Laskin JA (Goudge and Feldman JJA concurring) stated: "I agree with Mr. Black that the source of the power—statute or prerogative—should not determine whether the action complained of is reviewable" (at para. 44). He went on to endorse the comprehensive approach adopted by the House of Lords in *Council of Civil Service Unions v. Minister for the Civil Service*.]

LASKIN JA:

. . .

Apart from the Charter, the expanding scope of judicial review and of Crown liability make it no longer tenable to hold that the exercise of a prerogative power is insulated from judicial review merely because it is a prerogative and not a statutory power. The preferable approach is that adopted by the House of Lords in the *Civil Service Unions* case, *supra*. There, the House of Lords emphasized that the controlling consideration in determining whether the exercise of a prerogative power is judicially reviewable is its subject matter, not its source. If, in the words of Lord Roskill, the subject matter of the prerogative power is "amenable to the judicial process," it is reviewable; if not, it is not reviewable. Lord Roskill provided content to this subject matter test of reviewability by explaining that the exercise of the prerogative will be amenable to the judicial process if it affects the rights of individuals. Again, in his words at 417:

... If the executive in pursuance of the statutory power does an act affecting the rights of the citizen, it is beyond question that in principle the manner of the exercise of that power may today be challenged on one or more of the three grounds which I have mentioned earlier in this speech. If the executive instead of acting under a statutory power acts under a prerogative power and in particular a prerogative power delegated to the respondent under article 4 of the Order in Council of 1982, so as to affect the rights of the citizen, I am unable to see, subject to what I shall say later, that there is any logical reason why the fact that the source of the power is the prerogative and not statute should today deprive the citizen of that right of challenge to the manner of its exercise which he would possess were the source of the power statutory. In either case the act in question is the act of the executive. ...

[Laskin JA thus concluded that the proper test for review of the prerogative was a "subject matter" test and that justiciability was at the core of the subject matter test. Subject matters of the prerogative ranged from the signing of treaties and declaring war (powers that were not judicially reviewable apart from Charter claims) to, at the other end of the spectrum, the refusal of a passport or exercise of mercy (powers that were clearly reviewable). In between lay matters such as the "honours prerogative." How then were the prime minister's actions to be characterized?]

… Mr. Black characterizes the subject matter of the Prime Minister's actions in one of two ways: first, as giving unsolicited and wrong legal advice to the Queen, which detrimentally affected Mr. Black; or second, as an administrative decision involving the improper interpretation and application of Canadian policy, the Nickle Resolution, to the granting of an honour.

In my opinion, these are not accurate characterizations of Prime Minister Chrétien's actions as pleaded in the amended statement of claim. Prime Minister Chrétien was not giving legal advice or making an administrative decision. Focusing on wrong legal advice or the improper interpretation of a policy misses what this case is about. As I see it the action of Prime Minister Chrétien complained of by Mr. Black is his giving advice to the Queen about the conferral of an honour on a Canadian citizen. The Prime Minister communicated Canada's policy on honours to the Queen and advised her against conferring an honour on Mr. Black.

So characterized, it is plain and obvious that the Prime Minister's exercise of the honours prerogative is not judicially reviewable.

* * *

The refusal to grant an honour is far removed from the refusal to grant a passport or a pardon, where important individual interests are at stake. Unlike the refusal of a peerage, the refusal of a passport or a pardon has real adverse consequences for the person affected. Here, no important individual interests are at stake. Mr. Black's rights were not affected, however broadly "rights" are construed. No Canadian citizen has a right to an honour.

And no Canadian citizen can have a legitimate expectation of receiving an honour. In Canada the doctrine of legitimate expectations informs the duty of procedural fairness; it gives no substantive rights. … Here Mr. Black does not assert that he was denied procedural fairness. Indeed, he had no procedural rights.

But even if the doctrine of legitimate expectations could give substantive rights, neither Mr. Black nor any other Canadian citizen can claim a legitimate expectation of receiving an honour. The receipt of an honour lies entirely within the discretion of the conferring body. The conferral of the honour at issue in this case, a British peerage, is a discretionary favour bestowed by the Queen. It engages no liberty, no property, no economic interests. It enjoys no procedural protection. It does not have a sufficient legal component to warrant the court's intervention. Instead, it involves "moral and political considerations which it is not within the province of the courts to assess." See *Operation Dismantle, supra.*

Appeal dismissed.

NOTE

Were the prime minister's actions in this case confined to giving advice on the conferral of an honour on a Canadian citizen? Laskin JA conceded that his actions also involved communicating Canada's "policy" on honours (para. 56). Was there any basis to conclude that they involved more than that?

The Supreme Court of Canada has considered in the context of constitutional law the central issues in the *Council of Civil Service Unions* case. These issues include the reviewability of Cabinet decisions made in the exercise of a prerogative power and whether the courts are precluded from reviewing decisions said to be based on national security. See *Operation Dismantle v. The Queen*, [1985] 1 SCR 441 (Can.).

The "Private" Powers of Public Authorities

In addition to the more obvious government powers, generally conferred by statute, that public bodies exercise, public bodies also usually have the capacity to enter into contracts and to own and manage property. Sometimes, these powers are expressly granted, or their exercise is regulated, by statute, and the public authority must observe the statutory limits imposed. Often, though, the powers are implied in the body's constitutive statute. As a common law corporation sole, the Crown has the full capacity and powers of a natural person, subject to any modification by statute.

In the exercise of the powers of contract and property ownership, the liability of public bodies for breach of contract and for tort is determined for the most part by the general law, without regard to the public or governmental character of the power. See chapter 19 of this text, dealing with Money Remedies. An important question that has not yet been fully explored by the courts is the extent to which the exercise of these "private" powers is also subject to review on public law grounds and, in particular, for abuse of discretion.

The principal theoretical objection to the extension of the principles of administrative law to decisions taken by public authorities in their "private" capacity as contracting party or property owner has been the strong belief that public bodies should be subject to the same law as private individuals. In the common law tradition, there is no separate body of public law that comprehensively regulates all the legal relationships of governmental bodies with individuals. At a more pragmatic level, it may be appropriate to introduce into a legal relationship governed by a contract, for example, another layer of legal regulation—namely, administrative law grounds of review and public law remedies. This could have an unsettling effect on the parties' understandings and expectations.

On the other hand, it can be said that since public bodies enjoy powers of contract and property, not to advance their own interests but for the benefit of the public, it is mistaken to assume that the exercise of these powers should be subject only to the law that was developed to regulate the conduct of private individuals acting on their own behalf. For instance, because government exercises all its powers in the name of the community, it should be held to standards of decency and accountability beyond those required of private persons by the law of contract. There is also a public interest in ensuring that any procedures prescribed by the legislature are observed and that the contracting process is calculated to result in the making of the "best" decision. To draw a bright line between administrative action and contract overlooks the fact that contract can be an important tool for implementing public policy, as the *Shell* case illustrates. Should an agency be able to escape judicial surveillance by choosing to proceed by contract rather than by unilateral order?

We have already encountered instances when the courts have injected public law principles that also had private law elements into a relationship between a public body and an individual. For example, the courts have in the past imposed a duty to hear before "office holders," who also are normally in a contractual relationship with the employer, are dismissed (*Nicholson, Knight*; now modified by *Dunsmuir*). The right to be heard has not been extended, however, to employees of a public body who are in a purely contractual master-and-servant relationship although, if unionized, they will normally have procedural protections under the collective agreement. As their operating budgets shrink, public authorities often rely increasingly on "independent contractors" who are not unionized, receive minimal benefits, and can be hired and fired as needed. Should they be protected by public law? How far should the exercise of government contracting power (including the tendering process, the selection of the contractor, the terms of the contract, and performance) be brought within the scope of judicial review on normal administrative law grounds?

See, generally, Arrowsmith, *Government Procurement and Judicial Review* (Scarborough, ON: Carswell, 1988); see also Taggart, "Corporatisation, Contracting and the Courts" (1994), *Public Law* 351; and Mullan and Ceddia, "The Impact on Public Law of Privatization, Deregulation, Outsourcing, and Downsizing: A Canadian Perspective" (2003), 10 *Indiana Journal of Global Legal Studies* 199. For two cases holding that the government contracting process is not subject to administrative law principles, see *Associated Respiratory Services Inc. v. British Columbia* (1992), 7 Admin. LR (2d) 104 (BC SC) and *Peter Kiewit & Sons Co. v. Richmond (City)* (1992), 7 Admin. LR (2d) 124 (BC CA); but see *Gestion Complexe Cousineau (1989) Inc. v. Canada*, [1995] 2 FC 694 (CA) and for municipalities, at least in the setting of procurement policies by formal resolution, see *Shell Canada* (above). For a recent decision cautioning against the application of public law values—as opposed to general contract law—to procurement contracting by government, see *Irving Shipbuilding Inc. v. Canada (Attorney General)* (2009), 2009 FCA 116 (CanLII), paras. 44-62.

CONFINING AND STRUCTURING DISCRETION

Introduction

All too often the discretion granted by legislatures to administrative agencies is overly broad. Sometimes, ironically, this is precisely because of concern for individualization in decision making. Rigid rules may lead to great hardship and this can be alleviated only by the use of discretion. Yet if carried too far wide discretion can, in turn, lead to hardship of its own in that it allows for arbitrariness and unequal treatment. In theory, the legislature itself should be able to strike a balance between rules and discretion for the particular situation in which it has chosen to legislate. In reality, the task is left largely to the administrative agencies, with the legislature usually erring on the side of more rather than less discretion.

The other major cause of overly broad discretionary power is that the legislature can seldom identify the exact nature of the problem it wishes to deal with or its precise cure. This leads to the granting of power in vague terms such as the "public interest." K.C. Davis has pointed out that "[s]ometimes telling the agency to do what is in the public interest is the practical equivalent of instructing it 'Here is the problem. Deal with it.'"

As noted at the start of this chapter, the current challenge to lawyers and the courts is whether they can shift away from a negative response to the spread of discretionary power toward a more accepting position that, while recognizing that discretionary power is here to stay, seeks nevertheless to humanize its use rather than simply set legal limits on its existence. In the past, lawyers have largely contented themselves with denouncing the growth of discretionary power and have offered few concrete suggestions about how it could be tamed and channeled to a positive end. This Canute-like response has resulted, ironically, in a massive growth of largely unchecked discretionary power with virtually no empirical investigation of the role for open-ended power or for the development of imaginative techniques to restrain such power without destroying the flexibility, adaptability, and human responsiveness that discretion makes possible.

Philip Anisman, in his pioneering study of statutory grants of discretionary power, *A Catalogue of Discretionary Powers in the Revised Statutes of Canada* (Law Reform Commission of Canada, 1975), determined that there were 14,885 such powers, of which 5,938 were "judicial"; 2,933 "administrative"; 1,298 "investigative"; and 3,467 "rulemaking." He went on to conclude that "the number of powers discovered should neither be a surprise nor a ground of either praise or criticism. The fact is that they exist and that they will continue to do so. What is important is to discover how they are exercised; and for that empirical study is required" (at 24). Indeed, as John Willis reminded us, it was time for lawyers long ago to stop declaiming and to focus instead on the actual use to which discretion is put and to propose specific improvements grounded on observable experience rather than visceral ideological responses to "big government." See, for example, "The McRuer Report: Lawyers' Values and Civil Servants' Values" (1968), 18 *UTLJ* 351.

It is perhaps difficult for lawyers to be balanced in their views on discretion in the administrative process because all too often they only become involved on behalf of individual clients who complain of being caught in the thraldom of the bureaucratic state. Their focus is at times too much on individual complaints rather than the administrative process as a whole. A lawyer should be able to understand the workings of an administrative scheme and to propose constructive improvements that do not compromise the social goals of that scheme.

CONFINING AND STRUCTURING DISCRETION: RULES, PRECEDENTS, AND POLICY STATEMENTS

One of the most distinctive aspects of the administrative process is the flexibility that it affords in the selection of methods of decision making. A legislature must normally confine itself to the declaration of generally applicable standards of conduct, whereas a court must deal with a problem as defined by the particular controversy before it. An administrative agency, on the other hand, may often choose between these approaches, or even reject them both in favour of more informal means of decision making.

In the 1960s and 1970s, K.C. Davis made a major contribution to the debate about how lawyers and administrators should respond to the wide grants of discretionary power that are so characteristic of modern government. He urged lawyers to break away from a simplistic notion of a rule of law that denies the legitimacy of broad discretionary power, a position which Davis dismissed as unrealistic and counterproductive. For Davis, the answer was not to deny discretion but to seek imaginative means to control it. The following excerpts from Davis's 1969 study of discretion offer an introduction to his attempt to locate the optimum degree of structuring in respect of each discretionary power.

Davis, *Discretionary Justice*
(Baton Rouge, LA: Louisiana State University Press, 1969),
at 55-57, 65-67, 97-99, 102-103, and 106-107

The principal ways of controlling are structuring and checking. Structuring includes plans, policy statements, and rules, as well as open findings, open rules, and open precedents. ... Checking includes both administrative and judicial supervision and review. Our present concern is with eliminating and limiting discretionary power, that is, confining discretion. By confining is meant fixing the boundaries and keeping discretion within them. The ideal, of course, is to put all necessary discretionary power within the boundaries, to put all unnecessary such power outside the boundaries, and to draw clean lines. The ideal is seldom realized, and many of the failures are rather miserable ones, for they frequently result in avoidable injustice.

Statutes which delegate discretionary power often fix some of the boundaries but leave others largely open. By and large, although some opinions differ, I think that legislative bodies usually do about as much as they reasonably can do in specifying the limits on delegated power, but they are often deficient in failing to provide further clarification after experience provides a foundation for it, and they are almost flagrantly deficient in failing to correct the administrative assumption of discretionary power which is illegal or of doubtful legality. Perhaps the greatest single area of discretionary power which legislative bodies should cut back is the power of the police to nullify legislation through non-enforcement or partial enforcement.

Altogether, the chief hope for confining discretionary power does not lie in statutory enactments but in much more extensive administrative rulemaking, and legislative bodies need to do more than they have been doing to prod the administrators.

Administrative rulemaking to confine discretion. When legislative bodies delegate discretionary power without meaningful standards, administrators should develop standards at the earliest feasible time, and then, as circumstances permit, should further confine their own discretion through principles and rules. The movement from vague standards to definite standards to broad principles to rules may be accomplished by policy statements in any form, by adjudicatory opinions, or by exercise of the rulemaking power. When rulemaking procedure is used, even a statement which changes a vague statutory standard into an administrative standard which is as vague or only slightly less vague is called, in our somewhat confusing language, a "rule."

Earlier and more diligent use of agencies' rulemaking power is a far more promising means of confining excessive discretionary power than urging legislative bodies to enact more meaningful standards. This is not because administrative clarification of law is preferable to legislative clarification; the opposite is often true. The reason administrative clarification is more promising is that legislative bodies may not be *expected* to provide the needed clarification. Legislators and their staffs know their own limitations, they know they are ill-equipped to plan detailed programs, and they know that administrators and their staffs are better equipped because they can work continuously for long periods in limited areas. On the basis of careful examination of what happens when legislative bodies undertake to determine detailed policies, as distinguished from broad outlines of policy accompanied by largely unguided delegation, one may conclude that legislators are usually wise in refraining from trying to legislate detailed policies. But anyone who doubts that conclusion is immediately confronted with the undeniable fact that legislators at all levels—federal, state, and local—make the choice with increasing frequency in favor of delegation of broad discretionary power without meaningful guides, and, even if opinions may differ about the wisdom of that choice, perhaps the people's representatives should be allowed to govern on the question of how far they should refrain from governing detail.

The hope lies in administrative clarification of vague statutory standards. *The typical failure in our system that is correctible is not legislative delegation of broad discretionary power with vague standards; it is the procrastination of administrators in resorting to the rulemaking power to replace vagueness with clarity.* All concerned should push administrators toward earlier and more diligent use of the rulemaking power: Affected parties should push, legislators and legislative committees should push, appropriations committees should push, bar groups should push, and reviewing courts should push.

The typical tendency of agencies to hold back from resort to the rulemaking power is understandable and often it is justifiable. Waiting for a case to arise, then clarifying only to the extent necessary to decide the case, and then waiting for the next case is one way to build cautiously. In some circumstances, the slow process of making law only through adjudication is a necessity, for administrators may be truly unable to do more than to decide one case at a time. And sometimes, even when they can do more, they properly refrain from early rulemaking. Building law through adjudication is a sound and necessary process; the great bulk of American law is the product of that process.

Even so, I think that American administrators, by and large, have fallen into habits of unnecessarily delaying the use of their rulemaking power. They too often hold back even when their understanding suffices for useful clarification through rulemaking. This is the point at which significant reform is needed, and this is the point at which significant reform can be accomplished.

. . .

Rulemaking procedure is one of the greatest inventions of modern government. When more than a handful of parties are affected, creation of new law through either statutory enactment or administrative rulemaking is much more desirable than creation of new law through either judicial decision or administrative adjudication. True, the Supreme Court of the United States decides great policy issues affecting millions of people, but its procedure is geared to a few parties, not to many, even though occasionally it may receive a dozen or even two dozen briefs from *amici curiae*. By contrast, the legislative committee system at its best is a superb procedure for the development of understanding and for the reflection of democratic desires.

The procedure of administrative rulemaking is in my opinion one of the greatest inventions of modern government. It can be, when the agency so desires, a virtual duplicate of legislative committee procedure. More often it is quicker and less expensive. The usual procedure is that prescribed by the *Administrative Procedure Act*, the central feature of which is publishing proposed rules and inviting interested parties to make written comments. Anyone and everyone is allowed to express himself and to call attention to the impact of various possible policies on his business, activity, or interest. The agency's staff sifts and summarizes the presentations and prepares its own studies. The procedure is both fair and efficient. Much experience proves that it usually works beautifully.

For making policy affecting large numbers, rulemaking procedure is superior to adjudicative procedure in many ways, including the following six: (1) All who may be interested are systematically notified; for instance, the *Administrative Procedure Act* requires that notice of rulemaking be published in the Federal Register. Notice to non-parties of contemplated policy-making through adjudication is unusual. (2) Tentative rules are usually published and written comments received before final rules are adopted. In an adjudication a tribunal may adopt a policy without knowing and without having means of discovering what its impact may be on unrepresented parties. (3) Rulemaking procedure which allows all interested parties to participate is democratic procedure. Adjudication procedure is undemocratic to the extent that it allows creation of policy affecting many unrepresented parties. (4) An administrator who is formulating a set of rules is free to consult informally anyone in a position to help, such as the business executive, the trade association representative, the labor leader. An administrator who determines policy in an adjudication is usually inhibited from going outside the record for informal consultation with people who have interests that may be affected. In policy-making through adjudication, either the quest for understanding is likely to be impaired or the tribunal's judicial image is likely to be damaged. (5) Even when retroactive law-making through adjudication is not so unfair as to be a denial of due process, the retroactive feature may still be sufficiently unfair that good administrators ought to try to avoid it. Much law-making that is now retroactive can and should be avoided. For this reason alone, prospective rules often should be preferred to retroactive law-making through adjudication. (6) Congressional committees often provide useful supervision of administration, even though it is usually unsystematic and spotty. Such supervision can be quite effective in reaching contemplated rulemaking, but is almost always ineffective in influencing administrative law-making and policy-making through adjudication.

· · ·

Recognition of the superiority of rulemaking procedure over adjudicative procedure for making law or policy affecting more than a few parties means that agencies should strive to use rulemaking procedure to the greatest extent they find feasible, but it does not mean that agencies should avoid making law or policy through adjudication. For complex subject matter, rules can never provide all the answers in advance. When facts about parties are in dispute, the methods of adjudication are indispensable, and whole problems must be disposed of, including whatever law-making or policy-making may be necessary. The vastly increased rulemaking that I think desirable can never be carried so far as to eliminate all development of law and policy through case-to-case adjudication.

· · ·

The meaning of structuring. The principal question in this chapter is: How can administrators structure the exercise of their discretionary power, that is, how can they regularize it, organize it, produce order in it, so that their decisions affecting individual parties will achieve a higher quality of justice? One who thinks about this question is likely to discover that the answer has to grow out of particular subject matter, and I agree. But the question I am raising is more difficult: What can we do about structuring administrative discretion in general, irrespective of subject matter? The question leads into pioneer territory where the literature of jurisprudence, of public administration, and of administrative law is of little or no assistance.

Structuring discretionary power is different from confining it, although the two may overlap. The purpose of confining is to keep discretionary power within designated boundaries, and this can be accomplished through statutory enactments, through administrative rules, or by avoiding the development of discretionary power beyond the boundaries. The purpose of structuring is to control the manner of the exercise of discretionary power within the boundaries, and this, too, can be accomplished through statutory enactments, through administrative rules, and by other means. Administrative rulemaking is an especially important tool both for confining discretionary power and for structuring it; rules which establish limits on discretionary power confine it, and rules which specify what the administrator is to do within the limits structure the discretionary power.

The seven instruments that are most useful in the structuring of discretionary powers are open plans, open policy statements, open rules, open findings, open reasons, open precedents, and fair informal procedure. The reason for repeating the word "open" is a powerful one: Openness is the natural enemy of arbitrariness and a natural ally in the fight against injustice. We should enlist it much more than we do. When plans and policies and rules are kept secret, as through confidential instruction to staffs, private parties are prevented from checking arbitrary or unintended departures from them. Findings are a better protection against arbitrariness if affected parties can point to needed corrections. Reasoned opinions pull toward evenhanded justice but the pull is stronger if the opinions are out in the open. The difference between a system of precedents and a system of open precedents is enormous; for instance, because the Visa Office of the State Department uses a system of precedents but keeps them secret, parties often cannot ascertain whether discretion has been abused.

Plans, policy statements, and rules are three facets of essentially the same thing; all are designed to clarify and to regularize the purpose of the governmental activity. Similarly, findings and reasons are two facets of somewhat the same thing; findings summarize the facts, and reasons explain why the discretionary choices are made as they are. We have long realized the value of findings and reasons when cases go to hearing; we need to learn their value when discretionary determinations are made without hearings. The use of precedents—striving for consistency—has to be a central feature of any system which adequately structures discretionary power. Reasoned opinions and the use of precedents work together as a strong team, constantly structuring discretion as well as changing the exercise of discretion into the making of law. In addition to the procedural requirement of findings, reasons, and precedents, fair informal procedure includes opportunity for the affected party to know what is considered and to respond to it before a decision is made; requirements of fair procedure are not limited to hearing procedure.

Some discretionary power is beyond the reach of all seven methods of structuring, some can be reached by some of the seven, and some is subject to all seven. New discretionary functions may for long periods defy application of any of the seven methods of structuring and then may gradually yield to some or all of them. An exceedingly important fact is that when many or most apply, they help each other, producing an aggregate effect that may be profound, changing a disorderly system of ad hoc decisions that frequently result in avoidable injustice into an orderly system that may do reasonably well in minimizing injustice. Of course, even when the seven methods are possible, they are not always desirable for particular governmental tasks; *the purpose is not to maximize the use of the seven methods of structuring but to locate the optimum degree of structuring in each respect for each discretionary power.*

. . .

Open plans. The structuring of a particular discretionary power begins when the administrator first has some thought about his long-term objectives in the exercise of the power. Structuring occurs as the objectives take shape and as discretionary choices are made in the light of the objectives. In some circumstances executives are forced at an early time to do significant overall planning in order to instruct their staffs, who are immediately confronted with day-to-day choices. But regulatory agencies characteristically sit back and wait for questions to arise in particular cases, and the members of the agencies typically do little policy thinking except in the process of adjudicating single cases. Because the resulting case law is often spotty and even self-contradictory, the regulatory law remains uncertain over long periods. Indeed, regulatory agencies are notoriously deficient not only in doing the needed overall planning but also in announcing the results of such little planning as is done.

Policy statements and rules. When an agency knows what it is doing, it should say in some form what it is. The goal should be to close the gap between what the agency and its staff know about the agency's law and policy and what an outsider can know. The gap can probably never be completely closed, but the effort should always continue.

The means by which an agency can make known its law and policy range from the least formal to the most formal—an informal remark of a staff member, a whispered statement by an agency member, a public speech by a representative of the agency, a press release by the agency, a policy statement issued as such, a formal statement in an adjudicatory opinion, an interpretative rule, a legislative rule. All these means of communication are useful and all are used. Often the legal effect of what is said is difficult to ascertain. Sometimes a policy statement or rule is judicially reviewable and a less formal statement is not, but the lines are not clearly drawn.

Policy statements are usually looser than rules and are not necessarily binding on the agency, as legislative rules may be. Policy statements may still be very helpful. Such a statement may be appropriate when the agency feels that it is not quite prepared to issue rules; the agency may say, in effect: We are feeling our way in this direction, and this is where we want to go if we can get there. A policy statement may be essentially an announcement of a plan for an area of the agency's activities and therefore may be very helpful in structuring discretion. In general, policy statements should be used much more freely. Whatever understanding an agency may have about any subject that affects private parties should usually be made known to them except when the agency has a sufficient reason for not doing so.

At some point policy statements shade into interpretative rules which in turn shade into legislative rules. Interpretative rules are considered slightly more formal than policy statements, and they usually have a slightly greater degree of binding effect on the agency—a degree that is seldom clear. Legislative rules are the product of grants of power to make law and when valid have substantially the same legal effect as a statute.

. . .

Open precedents. The main difference between what we call case law and what we call discretion lies in the presence or absence of an expectation that the tribunal will strive for consistency. As soon as a tribunal shows that it is in a sufficient degree striving for consistency, it is making law and not merely exercising discretion. Striving for consistency normally pulls along with it the writing of reasoned opinions, and opinion-writing tends to yield principles and then rules. The key element is the degree of attention given to consistency.

Law and discretion are not separated by a sharp line but by a zone, much as night and day are separated by dawn. Instead of the two categories of law and discretion, we could recognize five or fifty, as may be convenient. For present purposes, five seem convenient—those in which the tribunal's prevailing attitude is that precedents are (1) almost always binding, (2) always considered and usually binding, (3) usually considered but seldom binding, (4) occasionally considered but never binding, and (5) almost never considered. The first two categories fit what we usually call case law, the last two fit what we usually call discretion, and the third is the zone between law and discretion.

One's first impulse is to prefer law to discretion and therefore to suppose that the greater the role of precedents the better. After all, consistency is clearly desirable for two main reasons: Equality is a major ingredient of justice, and striving for consistency reduces arbitrariness. But other factors also must be considered. Turning all discretion into law would destroy the individualizing element of equity and of discretion. Binding precedents may make for undue rigidity. For instance, we do not want precedents to be as strongly binding on some of the looser problems of public law as they are and ought to be in some areas of real property law. Precedents have greater force in English courts than in American courts, and my opinion is that we would lose much if our courts were to imitate the English courts; we benefit by the flexibility which helps keep our law abreast of changing conditions and new understanding. Near the other end of the scale, we do not want the President and the State Department to be bound by precedents in making foreign policy, and the same is true of any agency's broad policy positions. We must remember that although the inequality caused by inconsistency can mean injustice, excessive rigidity can mean not only injustice but also a failure to make use of better understanding.

Our sound objective, therefore, is not to maximize law and to minimize discretion, and it is not to maximize consistency and to minimize inconsistency. Our sound objective is to locate the optimum degree of binding effect of precedents for each particular subject matter, so that the role of precedents will be in each instance neither too strong nor too weak.

NOTE

The Davis approach to discretion places heavy emphasis on a shift to rules at an early stage. However, as others such as Jowell later pointed out, there may be a price to pay for an unthinking or premature shift from discretion to rules.

Jowell, *Law and Bureaucracy*
(New York: Dunellen Publishing, 1975), at 21-31

The Defects of Rules

Rules possess merits and demerits—in the abstract. A major thesis of this study is that the argument for or against legalization should not be pursued in the abstract, but in the light of the particular task to be performed, and in the knowledge that the perspective of the actor (official or public) often determines the perception of rules as a merit or defect.

Rigidity and Legalism

When bureaucracy is charged with the application of rules, organizational routines are set in motion whenever a set of categorized facts occur. We have seen that some problems must be solved by a minimum of routine handling through the categorization of data. The effect of this is to reduce the personality both of the official and of the affected client who is seen as a "carrier of data" relevant to the task at hand. He is thus a "complainant of discrimination," a "welfare applicant," a "speeder." Weber's "objective" discharge of business "without regard to persons" thus occurs.

On the other hand, all persons who come into contact with rules will have noted that, as categorizing general directions, rules may easily catch within their ambit technical violators whose actions have not contravened the objectives of the enforcing bureaucracy. For example, a parking meter will not show understanding or mercy to the person who was one minute over the limit because he was helping a blind man cross the street. Rules thus permit legalism, which, because of its close affinity to arbitrariness (i.e., lack of rational relation to official ends), may cause dissatisfaction on the part of technical violators.

However understandable his breach of a parking by-law may have been, the rule categorizes the person who helped the blind man as a violator of the law. Nor is the rule able to justify this. Unlike a reasoned adjudicative decision, rules do not carry with them any explanations (apart from the occasional vague preamble of a statute and insofar as they may receive judicial elaboration). For example, nothing in the rule itself explains to a welfare recipient why she may be permitted, as a "special need," a washing machine, but not a television set or dishwasher.

Furthermore, the content of rules varies. The advocates of rules *qua* rules tend to assume that all rules are good rules. Commentators have proposed, for example, that rules should specify criteria for eviction from public housing, thus giving tenants certain specified "rights." If the rules are intended to prohibit improper and arbitrary conduct, then the case for rules is sound. However, rules may impose hardships—for example, insisting that a welfare recipient bring a support action against her husband, or prohibiting public housing tenants from keeping pets. As Lawrence Friedman has pointed out:

It is so easy to forbid pets—a stroke of the pen will do it. It is not quite so easy to calculate the costs and the benefits of cats and dogs and to try to devise some method of letting tenants have their pets without harming the project.

Rules, therefore, permit official behavior that may show no apparent relation between fidelity to the rule and organizational ends. However, techniques to temper strict rule-enforcement do exist. One judicial technique is the imposition of a nominal penalty (where a rule imposing a minimum penalty does not exist) or nominal damages. An administrative technique is selective enforcement or non-enforcement allowing, for example, a police officer to refrain from fining a doctor speeding to the scene of an accident, or a driver narrowly exceeding a speed limit in the early hours of the morning. But, as we have seen, selective enforcement creates as many problems as it solves and is only possible where the administrator has the opportunity to refrain from setting legal enforcement in motion.

We shall see the apparent legalism of rules relating to welfare need, where, in a manner that appears nonrational, a caseworker has no power to grant a recipient a nonallowable dishwasher in place of the allowed clothes washer. It would be a bold public housing administrator who exempted from a prohibition against dogs the Seeing-Eye dog of a blind tenant.

Organization theorists have pointed out certain legalistic tendencies within organizations that arise from ritualistic attachment to routines and procedures. Victor Thompson refers to these patterns as "bureaupathic," because they do not advance organizational goals but rather reflect the status needs of individuals in the organization. Rules are used by superordinates to control subordinates, who in turn go strictly "by the book," follow precedent, and avoid innovations or chances of error by developing an exaggerated dependence upon regulations and quantitative standards: "Everybody, including the supervisor, is simply carrying out instructions imposed from above. If they are unpleasant instructions, it is not the supervisor's fault. …"

These remarks, from the intraorganizational perspective, reflect a propensity among officials to hide behind a rule. The need on their part for routinization and protection from the continuing obligation of discretionary decision is understandable. "Bureaupathic" behavior, however, within an organization or between an organization and its clientele, bears no relation to organizational ends.

To the client, therefore, the official refuge behind rules might be seen as an excuse to ignore valid claims. The obligation of a reasoned decision *de novo*, while not guaranteeing the absence of official ignorance or prejudice, constitutes at least some protection against the mechanical application of rules in situations that do not further rational objectives; at best it provides an assurance of personal attention, and "individualized justice." The administrator might also prefer to look at each case anew, and to preserve the flexibility that a rule may preclude.

Adjudication

The second technique proposed by advocates of the legal control of the administrative process is the use of adjudicatory procedures. Charles Reich wants welfare rights to be determined by means of the usual protections and participation of affected interests that surround this method of institutional decision making.

The concept of adjudication adopted here will closely follow Lon Fuller's. Fuller has defined adjudication as "a social process of decision which assures to the affected party a particular form of participation, that of presenting proofs and arguments for a decision in his favor." Adjudication is thus a means of institutionally guaranteed participation because each party to the dispute may present proofs and arguments. Other institutionally guaranteed means of participation are, for example, elections, where the means of participation is the vote and contracts, where the means of participation is negotiation.

The main consequence of Fuller's concept of adjudication is the restraint associated with the judicial role. The proofs and arguments of the litigants ought to be presented to an impartial and unbiased decision maker. The decision maker should not hold private conferences with either party, otherwise the excluded party may not know to what issue he should direct his proofs and arguments. Each party should have the opportunity to cross-examine the other.

In addition, adjudication implies what might be called functional prerequisites. For a decision to be amenable to resolution by adjudication, the decision maker must be able to reach a decision on the basis of some rule, standard, or principle that is generalizable and applicable to all future "like" cases. This prerequisite flows from the method of institutional participation because, for a participant to present proofs and arguments for a decision in his favor, he must appeal to some decision-making guide, which ideally is sufficiently specific to qualify as a rule, principle, or standard. If there were no such narrowly drawn guides, the participation of the litigants would not be meaningful because they would be joining issue in an "intellectual void."

It should be stressed that the adjudicative model we are discussing is an ideal-typical characterization. Reality will frequently fall short of the ideal. Some decisions within an adjudicative framework are no more than *ex post facto* rationalizations of positions formulated in advance. In addition, the symbols surrounding the judicial format may be manipulated to reassure people that the "rules of the game" have been followed, thereby obtaining their "quiescence" in the face of decisions that would otherwise be unacceptable.

Adjudication will thus refer here to the technique of decision making that guarantees participation to parties affected, through a number of procedural devices. The more procedural devices used, the more "judicialized" the process will be. The technique may be the sole forum for the elaboration of policies (as for example in many licence-applications) or it may be a forum where previous administrative determinations are challenged (as for example in welfare appeals). We shall be comparing adjudication as case-by-case elaboration of legislative policy both with administrative decision making by rules determined in advance of specific dispute-situations and with case-by-case discretionary determination that is not controlled by predetermined rules, nor by the adjudicative format.

The Merits of Adjudication

Perhaps the most obvious merits of adjudication for the litigant arise from the fact that it guarantees participation to affected parties. Although they do not make the final decision, the litigants are involved in the decision making process, and are permitted to plead for a decision in their favor and to challenge each other's proofs and arguments. Being immediately involved, they are well placed to advance the strongest case for their proposition.

Rules, as we have seen, are in a sense nonrational. Whatever the reasoning behind the enactment of a rule, the rule itself appears as an injunction—for example, not to exceed 55 miles per hour or park 15 feet from a fire hydrant. The adjudicator's obligation to reason will provide a check against the use of criteria that are improper, arbitrary, or legalistic, or fail to achieve congruence between the effect of the decision and official objectives. Adjudication contains a desire to give "formal and institutional expression to the influence of reasoned argument in human affairs." The requirement that a decision be justified, and the justification be published, implies that the justification is open to public criticism. Thus adjudication normally provides an opportunity for scrutiny and thus for the accountability of the decision makers to their clientele and to the public.

What strengthens this point is the *nature* of the justifications embodied in judicial decisions. Such decisions must be justified by a rule, standard, or principle. Ascriptive or particularistic criteria are illegitimate. Litigants will make their claims as members of a generalized category. In consequence, an appeal to power, private interests, or political expediency will be inappropriate. The adjudicator will in turn be bound to evaluate the claims by means of accepted techniques and by reference to authoritative guides, rather than his personal interest in the result or his personal predisposition towards the claimants.

A rule might provide administrators with a welcome refuge from the obligation of reasoned decision and from political and personal pressures. Adjudication, on the other hand, might require a reasoned decision. However, the claimant's appeal to a rule, principle, or standard reduces the possibility of litigants' appealing to political or private interests. In this sense, therefore, the decision maker will be somewhat insulated from such pressures.

Administrators might also derive benefits from the fact that a reasoned decision was made and openly arrived at with equal participation. The process of adjudication, whatever the decision, might therefore provide administrative action with the gloss of legitimacy.

A final merit of adjudication is the fact that it involves incremental elaboration of laws on a case-by-case basis. Although an organization might feel itself bound by its own decisions, adjudication deals with a specific fact situation, and later cases can be "distinguished" from earlier ones on the basis of the facts. Thus, despite pressures for consistency, which might lead to a rule's ossification, and for the gradual reduction of discretion (features that students of the common law know too well), the case-by-case approach of adjudication allows an administrative body to deal with cases as they arise and to build its commitments gradually, and even to change its mind.

The Defects of Adjudication

The opportunity to challenge an administrative decision through adjudication does not speak to the nature of the substantive right in question. A welfare recipient, for example, who has the procedural right to appeal the decision of a caseworker, might be told by the appeals referee that what she is asserting does not exist. In other words, she may be told through the exercise of her procedural right that in fact she has no substantive right.

We should also repeat what was stated in connection with rules: The existence of rule-determined (or, in this case, adjudication-determined) rights or obligations does not reflect upon the content of the right or obligation. For example, a welfare "right" to a given amount per month does not imply that the right will be generous or fair, or even that it will be more generous or more fair than a "privilege" given through an official's discretion. The existence of a right *qua* right simply informs us of two factors: that the official's discretion to act is limited and that all persons equally situated ought to receive equal treatment in connection with the right.

Moreover, the adversary structure of adjudication might contain costs. In welfare cases, we shall see that the continuing relationship between the caseworker and recipient might make a recipient reluctant to risk antagonizing her caseworker through challenge in an adversary situation. Tenants might fear that a legal challenge to their landlord would provoke retaliation. Adversary challenge in a university setting might prove threatening to the pursuit of learning.

The adversary-adjudicative situation also places the participants in what game theorists call a "zero-sum" situation. One side must win; the other must lose. The defendant is liable or not liable, guilty or not guilty. Except for the possibility of a flexible settlement out of court, the matter is placed in a clear yes-no, either-or, more-or-less setting. Matters that are suited to compromise, mediation, and accommodation are not best pursued in the structured adversary setting of adjudication.

Rules, as we have seen, may be of benefit to officials as a means of announcing policies to affected parties. Individual application of laws is thus possible without the necessity of administrative intervention. Adjudicative decisions, however, are less possible of communication because they arise in the context of specific dispute-situations. In addition, the adjudicative decision is less available to the lay public. Even lawyers may have difficulty in extrapolating the *ratio* from a decision and in knowing the precise content of a rule.

The specific dispute orientation of adjudication highlights another defect from the administrative perspective: it concerns individual rights and may thus bear little relation to the primary administration function, which involves the performance of a particular task. A particular case, for example, may raise questions wider than the question at issue. The adjudicator may deal with the wider questions but is not required to do so, and remarks made on the wider issue are considered strictly *obiter dicta* and thus not binding on future cases. Furthermore, although the specific decision may affect outside parties, the decision maker is not required to consult or to notify these wider interests. For example, a welfare recipient may complain to a referee that she was refused a winter coat by her caseworker. The grant of the coat is of interest to other recipients and to welfare rights organizations. The referee, however, would not normally consult or notify the other recipients or organization and would confine his decision to the particular recipient at hand.

These defects of adjudication point up its limitations as a planning device. In fact, decision makers in the adjudicative context may lay their own complaints, announce their rules clearly, deal with issues wider than the question at issue, and consult interests wider than those directly represented by the litigants. Normally, however, adjudication is deficient in wide-range planning because it is geared to the resolution of individual disputes rather than to the managerial tasks required to "get the work of society done."

Summary of Merits and Defects

What conclusions can we draw from the checklist of merits and defects of rules and adjudication? The answer is surely none, other than that as methods of controlling administrative discretion each possesses both costs and benefits to the bureaucrat, affected persons, and public. What is gained in uniformity may be lost in flexibility; rules to prevent the arbitrary may encourage the legalistic; case-by-case adjudication may prevent comprehensive planning; rules that may shield the bureaucracy from pressures and allow the efficient and speedy dispatch of cases, may offend the client who desires individually tailored justice.

It is thus clearly futile to propose legal control of administrative discretion in the abstract, for in the abstract the relative merits of devices of legal control may seem evenly balanced by their defects. In assessing whether any given administrative task ought to be subjected to legal control, it is necessary first to recognize that costs and benefits exist and then to weigh one against the other.

As Jowell points out, in thinking about the relative role for rules, adjudication, and policies, it is particularly important for lawyers to keep in mind the institutional context within which decisions have to be made. Decision making within an organization is not immune from diverse influences that are internal to the organization, let alone external influences. These may include the beliefs and interests of individuals in the organization, their surrounding culture and managerial structure, and the ideology and sense of purpose that is instilled by the organizational leadership. In a complex institutional context, the dichotomy between rules and discretion is only a starting point for capturing the dynamics of decision making.

It has to be recognized that the Davis approach to discretion was developed in a specifically American context. Are Canadian administrative processes and constitutional arrangements sufficiently similar to allow for the importation of US notions of confining and structuring discretion? In their comparative study of American and British administrative law, *Legal Control of Government* (Oxford: Clarendon Press, 1972), Schwartz and Wade suggested that different political and constitutional traditions may have led to different approaches to discretion (at 106):

> The American conception is that discretion, whether judicial or administrative, should in all possible cases be exercised in accordance with rules ascertainable in advance, and that the policy to be applied should somehow be fixed or standardized. The British conception is that within its legal limits administrative discretion must be free, and that the object of policy should be to produce the best solution as it appears at any particular time. ... The main cause of the difference, such as it may be, is probably the constitutional background in each country. Abuse of political discretion may be a more imminent danger in the United States where the executive is not directly responsible to the elected legislature and where so much vital power is in the hands of independent agencies which are responsible to no-one. The American yearning for the crystallization of policy by rules may be prompted by the desire to fill this void.

It cannot realistically be said in Canada—if, indeed, it can be said in Britain—that executive responsibility to the legislature effectively reduces the dangers of untrammelled discretionary power. Discretionary power is commonly granted in Canada to bodies similar in many ways to American independent agencies. Moreover, the widespread delegation of discretionary power well down the hierarchy of decision making makes it unlikely that political accountability will be an effective alternative to confining and structuring discretion. Nevertheless, as Schwartz and Wade caution, it is always important to bear in mind the total context within which discretion is exercised.

For a particularly useful assessment of the Davis approach and its applicability to Canada, see Anisman, "Book Review of *Discretionary Justice: A Preliminary Inquiry*" (1969), 47 *Can. Bar Rev.* 670.

There remains room in Canada for the adoption of rulemaking to confine discretion. On the other hand, some critics assert that the focus should be on the potential of discretionary decision making to foster a dialogue about the important judgments that administrators make. This, it is argued, would make is possible to see the value of a critical approach to administrative structures and to allow analysis to shift away from sterile concerns about simply confining discretion. Consider this extract.

Sossin, "The Politics of Discretion: Toward a Critical Theory of Public Administration"
(1993), 36 *Can. Pub. Admin.* 366

The key to revitalizing the welfare state, and transforming its citizenry from the object to the subject of government, lies, I would argue, within the ambit of administrative discretion. The purpose of this paper is to explore new ways of understanding and legitimating the important discretionary judgments public officials make. In my view, just as laws and government policies make claims to validity that must be justified publicly before they will be accepted politically, so do the administration of those laws and policies. More importantly, the welfare state embodies important social values that cannot be realized in a value-free, instrumentally rational form of public administration. The analysis must, therefore, shift from the question of whether an official has the right to exercise discretion to focus on whether it can be democratically established that such discretion is right. Therefore, rather than seek new ways to confine and control bureaucracy, I argue that it is necessary to seek new ways of legitimating bureaucracy as an independent political institution.

I seek to undertake such an analysis into public administration from within the framework of critical theory. Such a framework takes as its goal the establishment, through reason, of forms of life free from unnecessary domination. Applying critical theory in this fashion is thus two-pronged: it entails both an inquiry into "reason" as well as an examination of "domination" in order to determine what forms of life contain or promote the highest degree of "freedom." This approach, I believe, finally allows the loss of meaning and subjectivity in the administrative relations of advanced capitalist societies to assume the primary focus of social inquiry. It provides a basis for establishing a bureaucratic discourse that is participatory and free of the "scientization" that has tended to render the machinery of administration accessible only to so-called experts.

Through integrating various strands of critical theory into a coherent research program, Jurgen Habermas's theory of communicative action provides a starting point for a critical analysis of public administration. ...

The crisis of meaning which characterizes administrative action under the welfare state has resulted in what Habermas terms the "cleansing of political participation from any participatory content." This critique amounts to a rallying cry for the establishment of new democratic forms of public administration. ...

See Sossin, "Redistributing Democracy: An Inquiry into Authority, Discretion and the Possibility of Engagement in the Welfare State" (1994), 26 *Ottawa L Rev.* 1; Janisch, "Further Developments with Respect to Rulemaking by Administrative Agencies" (1995), 9 *CJALP* 1; Berzins, "Policy Development by Labour Boards: Is There a Case for Rulemaking?" (2000), 25 *Queen's LJ* 479; and Zaring, "Rulemaking and Adjudication in International Law" (2008), 46 *Col. J Transnat'l L* 563.

PART IV

Remedies

GENERAL INTRODUCTION

By this point in the text, the names and purposes of the remedies, both statutory and common law, that are available in Canada for challenging administrative action will have become familiar. Some of this part of the text may therefore be repetitive. Nevertheless, the material on remedies to this point has been fragmentary and for the most part focused on the relationship between remedies and substantive review. Because of the significance of remedial choices in adjudication, it is important before leaving a course on administrative law to take an overview of the remedial package in order to see the points of distinction as well as those of overlap among remedies, and to be able to discern the bases on which counsel may choose to pursue one avenue of relief rather than another.

It is at the outset important to consider the relationship between review in the courts and other methods of challenging the decision of a statutory body. These other methods may be internal to the statutory process itself (see Ford, "Dogs and Tails: Remedies in Administrative Law" in Flood and Sossin, eds., *Administrative Law in Context* (2008), at 47-56) or external in that they involve non-judicial appeal bodies or officials like the ombudsperson. For counsel, the crucial questions are those of determining when as a matter of law and when as a matter of expedience they should use a route other than the regular courts to challenge a decision.

The picture presented in this part of the text is, however, somewhat incomplete in three respects. First, the procedure for obtaining a particular remedy in administrative law may differ from one province to another, and there are minor variations across jurisdictions—sometimes resulting from the differing procedures—in the scope of review that is available under the various remedies. No attempt is made here to be comprehensive in such matters nor does this part purport to be otherwise comprehensive. That would require a separate book and course.

Instead, particular attention is paid to the statutory regimes for judicial review that are in place at the federal level and in British Columbia and Ontario. Along with Québec, these are the three most frequently invoked judicial review regimes in the country and they provide useful vehicles for a study of the process of transformation that has taken place in different ways across Canada, from the old prerogative writ procedures for challenging governmental action to simpler statutory-based regimes.

The second caution is a practical one. Litigation costs money and, although some judicial review proceedings are relatively simple, significant outlays cannot be avoided. In some jurisdictions, legal aid may not be available or readily available for the commencement of judicial review proceedings. Moreover, costs may not necessarily follow a successful application

for review as they do in other forms of civil litigation, while there always remains the possibility that an unsuccessful applicant may have to pay costs, particularly if the court considers that groundless allegations of impropriety have been made against a tribunal or public
official (see *Sierra Club of Western Canada v. British Columbia (Chief Forester)* (1994), 117
DLR (4th) 395 (BC SC)).

There is another important factor that enters the picture here. Unlike most situations,
success in court does not necessarily mean wider success for the judicial review applicant.
The clearest illustration of this is where the basis of judicial review is a procedural deficiency. The quashing of a decision on this basis generally gives the decision-maker the option of proceeding again and possibly reaching the same result. Even review for abuse of
discretion does not guarantee a favourable result on any subsequent reconsideration. Tacti-
cal considerations such as these should be foremost in the mind of counsel advising clients
on the utility of judicial review. Counsel should also be constantly aware of the opportunities
that exist for non-judicial resolution of many administrative law disputes—for example,
negotiating for a reconsideration by the statutory authority, resorting to alternative dispute
resolution mechanisms, lobbying for legislative change or authorized political intervention
or reversal, or, at a more formal level but at far less cost to the client, approaching the provincial ombudsman. Finally, notwithstanding an apparently strong case for judicial review,
restraint may be the best advice because of a need to maintain an amicable relationship with
a particular statutory authority. On the other hand, there are those who advocate that counsel who are involved frequently with a particular statutory authority should periodically
confront it with a judicial review application in order to keep the authority on its toes.

The final matter to note is the overlap between remedies and substance. What at first may
appear to be a technical limitation associated with a particular remedy is often in fact the
product of decisions about the substance of judicial review. Thus, in reading cases in which
remedies have been denied, one should always ask whether the reason for the denial of relief
was indeed related to the remedy itself, or whether the judge was really rejecting the arguments on substantive grounds, notwithstanding the use of language on remedies. Conversely,
one should be alert to situations in which judges, under the guise of dispensing with or ignoring a rule on remedies, are in fact creating a cause of action where none existed previously.

These considerations are part of a more general problem with any section on remedies in
an administrative law casebook—namely, the difficulty of discerning how frequently remedies
really matter in judicial review. Simply presenting a series of cases in which there has been a
remedies difficulty may give little idea of the extent to which remedial choices are an issue in
practice. In the first 75 years of the 20th century of administrative law in Canada, it seemed
as if technical rules on the availability of remedies too often blocked the courts from dealing
with the substantive issues at stake in applications for judicial review. This has been the
subject of scathing criticism, none more damning than that of the US academic, K.C. Davis,
who wrote in 1961 about English remedial law ("The Future of Judge-Made Public Law in
England: A Problem of Practical Jurisprudence" (1961), 61 *Columbia LR* 201, at 204):

> My own view is that either Parliament or the Law Lords should throw the entire set of preroga-
> tive writs into the Thames River, heavily weighted with sinkers to prevent them from rising
> again.

Fortunately, the present reality in Canada is far removed from this state of affairs. Reform of statutory and procedural rules have dealt with many anomalies from the law of remedies in judicial review. Judges are also less inclined to allow technical issues on remedy to drive the outcome in a case. Even so, there are significant pockets in which remedial difficulties continue to exist. Thus, while amendments in 1992 to the *Federal Courts Act* removed many of the bizarre remedial difficulties under that Act, problems involving how to allocate jurisdiction between the provincial superior courts and the Federal Court still arise and still make it to the Supreme Court, as evidenced by *Reza v. Canada*, [1994] 2 SCR 394 (Ont.). As well, there continue to be cases in which courts are confronted with issues about whether the pursuit of judicial review, rather than another form of action, is the appropriate way to proceed. With the advent of the *Canadian Charter of Rights and Freedoms*, questions were raised about the appropriate vehicles for the vindication of the rights that it conferred and, in particular, the extent to which the remedial discretion in s. 24(1) of the Charter opened possibilities for innovative remedies. Many such questions remain unresolved. (Note that, from 1970 to 2003, the *Federal Courts Act* was called the *Federal Court Act*; in this chapter it is referred to generally by its current name.)

In addition to threshold issues, there are three areas where first instance courts are frequently faced with difficult remedial issues. The first is in the context of applications for interim or interlocutory relief to prevent governmental action (including the holding of hearings) pending the determination of an application for judicial review. Second, there are arguments to the effect that the court, as a matter of discretion and irrespective of the merits of the claim being advanced, should deny relief; for example, in cases where another potentially effective avenue of redress is available. Third, there are the continuing problems of standing or *locus standi* to seek judicial review.

The scheme of this part follows the path of these difficulties. In the initial general chapter, we commence with a consideration of two of the threshold issues identified above. Is the matter in question something that can be dealt with in a judicial review application? That is, what is the reach of the public law remedies available on judicial review, beyond the core rubric of statutory authority exercised in a public capacity by a governmental body or official? Further, if the matter is properly the subject of judicial review, under what regime should it be brought, the *Federal Courts Act* or the relevant provincial rules or statute on judicial review? At this juncture, we identify the forms of relief that are generally available regardless of the judicial review regime under which the application is made. In so doing, we also canvass the "modern" remedial reforms that have taken place in Canadian jurisdictions as well as some of the limitations that apply to the various modes of relief. This includes a separate section on the availability of interlocutory or interim remedies. Throughout, we consider periodically the impact of the *Canadian Charter of Rights and Freedoms* on the remedies of judicial review. Thereafter, separate chapters are devoted to the perennial issues of standing and discretion to deny relief. We conclude with a chapter on the availability of money remedies in an administrative law setting.

For practical purposes, it is helpful to keep in mind a set of questions that may alert you to potential remedial problems once you have identified an apparent reason for redress. In some respects, these questions have been framed from the perspective of the person who is seeking relief. However, they are easily modified to reflect the position of government and agency lawyers and other potential respondents or defendants who wish to resist an application for judicial review.

1. Are there alternatives other than recourse to the courts for resolving the matter in dispute? Are there potential choices that have to be made as between tribunals other than the courts? If so, what legal and practical considerations are important in the making of those choices? Is there statutory or informal access to reconsideration of the decision by the initial decision-maker? Is there an internal right of appeal or recourse to arbitration or other form of alternative dispute resolution? Does the authority come within the jurisdiction of the ombudsman or some other external complaint mechanism (such as a human rights commission, a privacy and freedom of information commission, or, in the case of some universities, the visitor) capable of dealing with the matter?

2. If recourse to the courts appears to be the appropriate course of action, what is the nature of that recourse: judicial review or some other form of remedy under the common law, equity, or a statute (such as a right of appeal)? Is the situation one where it might be safe to ignore the decision of the agency in question and postpone any challenge to the decision until a later stage, where one can initiate a collateral attack on the decision or order in the context of an enforcement proceeding? What is the nature of the body against which relief is sought? Is it public or private, statutory or non-statutory in nature? What kind of claim is being considered? Is it more in the nature of a contractual or tortious claim rather than a matter of public law? Is the aim a damages award or specific relief (such as the mandating or prevention of governmental action)?

3. If judicial review is the appropriate course of action, does the matter in dispute involve federal or provincial agencies? If the former, does the application for judicial review have to be made to the Federal Court under the *Federal Courts Act* or does it come within the residual jurisdiction of the provincial superior courts over a federal statutory authority? If there is concurrent or overlapping jurisdiction between the Federal Court and the provincial superior courts, in which of those venues is the matter more appropriately litigated?

4. Among the options provided by the public law of judicial review, what is the nature of the relief that is required? What are the grounds on which relief is being sought? What modes of relief provide potential vindication on those grounds? Has a decision been taken or an order made, or is it a situation where the aim is to prevent or compel a decision? Would interim or interlocutory relief, pending final disposition of a judicial review, be useful?

5. Are there limitations on the availability and scope of judicial review, as manifested in leave to apply requirements, privative clauses, limitation periods, or immunities from suit and testifying? What are the notice requirements? Who has to be served, with what, and within which time period?

6. From the perspectives of procedure and evidence, is the matter one that is capable of satisfactory resolution based on affidavit evidence in the context of summary proceedings? Or is a trial-like process with *viva voce* evidence more desirable? If the latter, is this even an option and, if so, how is it best pursued?

7. Is there any potential problem with the standing of the person who is seeking judicial review? Is there any empirical data or other evidence that needs to be assembled to deal with those difficulties? Is this a matter in which the decision-maker itself will also have standing or be accorded intervenor status? Who else might seek intervenor status and on what basis might this be resisted?

8. Are there any discretionary reasons that may cause a court to refuse or limit the relief that is available? Is this affected by the ground on which judicial review is sought and the form of relief that is pursued?

As this framework suggests, the issue of remedies is a highly technical aspect of judicial review. Knowledge of and an ability to work with the details count. However, this should not distract one from scrutinizing the efficacy of the remedial scheme that Canadian courts, legislatures, and other decision-makers have fashioned. Do the remedies that have been developed achieve the aims of judicial review? What is the purpose of a technical rule on remedies and does the rule serve that purpose? The remedial issues before a judge increasingly involve these broad questions as the courts have been liberated (whether by statutory or procedural reform or by judicial common sense) from old forms of action that were beset with technicalities and as remedial issues have been reduced to exercises of judicial discretion. The key question now is usually: as a matter of judicial review policy, which remedy should be available to this successful applicant? Counsel must therefore develop a reasoned response to this question. As in our consideration of the grounds of judicial review, the most effective arguments will depend in part on an appreciation of the balance that needs to be struck between the often competing interests of effective government action, on the one hand, and the interests of particular individuals, corporations, and groups on the other.

In many respects, this part of the text is about the interplay between the substantive principles of judicial review and the rules on remedies and procedure. In studying the material, however, one should not simply look for more detailed knowledge of this interplay but also inquire about it in a more fundamental way. What is the significance of a legal right if the law presents barriers, perhaps impenetrable, to its vindication? If a decision is a nullity under the substantive rules of judicial review, what is the effect of allowing a residual discretion by which the court can deny relief? Some of these problems are among the most difficult in law.

CHAPTER SIXTEEN

Remedies for Unlawful Administrative Action

JUDICIAL REVIEW AT COMMON LAW

Introduction

Judicial review of administrative action originates in the various prerogative writs by which the monarch, through the Court of King's or Queen's Bench, controlled the exercise of authority by officials who acted or purported to act under royal or parliamentary warrant. Thus, the most common of these writs, *certiorari*, was associated in its early history with the proceedings of inferior courts of record, as personified in magistrates and justices of the peace, and with the very early administrative tribunals such as the commissioners of sewers. It was a process by which the formal record of a proceeding before such a body was delivered to the Court of King's or Queen's Bench for inspection so that the court was able "to be informed." If the formal record revealed that the body was acting without jurisdiction or, somewhat later in the development of the remedy of *certiorari*, that it had committed an error of law on the face of the record, its process would be quashed.

In essence, *certiorari* and the other prerogative writs (principally *mandamus*, prohibition, and *habeas corpus*) were vehicles for ensuring that the administrative arms of government were kept under control. In other words, it was a system of review aimed at the control of *public* as opposed to *private* bodies. This sense of judicial review as a public law remedy remains a crucial element even today in determining the appropriate reach of the remedies that have succeeded the prerogative writs. Thus: is this body sufficiently public in its origins, purposes, or powers to make it subject to the supervisory authority of the superior courts as exercised through judicial review?

The Reach of Public Law Remedies

Unfortunately, this basic question—whether an entity is public, such that it is subject to judicial review—can be difficult to answer. It has been affected in recent times by a more expansive approach to what counts as "public." It has also been complicated by the fact that there are private law analogues to some of the old prerogative writs. Likewise, certain private law remedies—the declaration and the injunction, in particular—expanded over time such that they became available for both private and public law purposes. Finally, some of the substantive grounds of judicial review are not peculiar to the public domain. The private law of associations (including corporations) is founded at least in part on concepts of jurisdiction, while the notion of procedural fairness has played a prominent role in the judicial policing of "private" clubs and organizations.

As a result, there are some contexts in which it matters little whether the litigation is technically public or private. The remedy sought will be the same and the allegations may be appropriately located in either the public or the private domain. Thus, in the case of a challenge to the procedurally unfair expulsion of a member from an association that had its own constitutive statute (such as many Canadian universities), there may be doubts about whether this is a question of private or public law. Even so, subject to reservations, this question may be made irrelevant by a decision to initiate proceedings for declaratory and/or injunctive relief.

On the other hand, there are occasions when public–private distinctions among remedial options is crucial. For example, there is some common law (still potentially relevant in certain Canadian jurisdictions) that declaratory relief is not available against public authorities where *certiorari* and its late 20th-century successors provide adequate relief. If that rule is potentially applicable, then it is vital to make the correct assessment of the nature of the body and decision that is under attack. More importantly, the principal statutes and amalgamations of the judicial review remedies, as found in the *Federal Courts Act* and the *Judicial Review Procedure Act* of both British Columbia and Ontario, contain formulas that force the issue of whether the matter in dispute falls within the statute's conception of the reach of public law remedies.

Of even greater significance are situations where the issue of whether the body is sufficiently public to qualify for review via public law remedies is in reality an issue on the extent to which the courts can interfere with the decision in question. Thus, as the Supreme Court of Canada decided in *Dunsmuir*, not all employees under statute are entitled to a fair hearing before they are dismissed. Those who are excluded are said to have no access to public law remedies—only contractual ones—such that they may have no entitlement to a hearing before dismissal and no possibility of reinstatement as a remedy.

What these types of cases reveal most clearly are the policy choices behind technical issues. In some instances, the need to choose between public and private law remedies is predicated on the principle that governments are sometimes subject to higher obligations than actors in the private sector. While, at common law, private sector employers are not obliged to provide hearings before dismissing an employee and are not subject to specific performance where there has been a wrongful dismissal, more is often expected of governments in both respects. Likewise, when they act as commercial operators, governments may be held to higher standards of probity and good faith dealing than private businesses. While this distinction between government and the private sector is not maintained rigidly in the jurisprudence, and while there are signs of the law governing the two sectors tending to merge in these matters, the different conceptions of their roles and obligations often lead to disputes about the availability of judicial review.

For a recent case in which these tensions were manifest, see *Société de l'assurance automobile du Québec v. Cyr*, [2008] 1 SCR 338, a 6:3 decision of the court in which the majority concluded that public law remedies were available to allow an automobile mechanic to challenge the SAAQ's decision to revoke his accreditation, despite the SAAQ having contracted out the duty to inspect autobiles to the mechanic's employer. Public law remedies were available pursuant to the *Act Respecting Administrative Justice*, RSQ, c. J-3, s. 5, which placed procedural requirements on an administrative authority prior to its making "an unfavour-able decision concerning a permit or licence or other authorization of like nature." Although the case can be understood simply as an interpretation of this provision, Bastarache J char-acterized the case more broadly at paras. 1 and 25 of his majority reasons:

[1] This appeal raises the issue of distinguishing between the private and public actions of a public authority. ... More generally, the Court has to decide whether the SAAQ has insulated itself from the requirements of administrative law by implementing a contract-based scheme to meet its statutory duties.

. . .

[25] In an era of increased privatization of public services and the rise of public-private partnerships, this case provides an opportunity to consider whether a government body will avoid public law duties when delegating its functions by way of contract or other form of agreement.

Notably, in its application of remedies in public law to this area of contractual relation-ships between government and private actors, the *Cyr* decision contrasts sharply with the court's contemporaneous decision in *Dunsmuir* on procedural fairness in the dismissal of public officers.

Historically, the law on the availability of public law remedies has been bedevilled by the so-called Atkin *dictum* in *R v. Electricity Commissioners, ex parte London Electricity Joint Committee Co.*, [1924] 1 KB 171 (CA) (as glossed by Lord Hewart CJ in *R v. Church Assem-bly Legislative Committee, ex parte Haynes-Smith*, [1928] 1 KB 411). Atkin LJ (as he then was) said in that case that the remedies of *certiorari* and prohibition were available "[w]herever any body of persons having legal authority to determine questions." This was interpreted subsequently as confining the reach of public law remedies to bodies that were genuinely *statutory*. As a result, the inquiry on whether a body was sufficiently public in its origins, its purposes, or its powers was often determined by an examination of whether it exercised a "statutory power." For a time, this excluded judicial review of powers exercised under the royal prerogative and, even today, it sometimes causes judicial review applications to be rejected when brought against governmental bodies on the basis that they do not have a clear warrant for existence in statute. Indeed, this was an important component of the first instance judgment in the following case, which is an example of the debate about public law and private law remedies in a modern context.

Government in the Conduct of Business

Volker Stevin NWT (1992) Ltd. v. Northwest Territories (Commissioner)
(1994), 113 DLR (4th) 639 (NWT CA)

[An advisory committee of civil servants and business representatives was established under a directive attached to a policy document of the government of the Northwest Territories. Its purpose was to designate businesses as "northern businesses" that were eligible for various government incentives, including preference in the award of govern-ment procurement contracts. The directive also set out the criteria for qualifying as a northern business and provided for appeals from decisions of the advisory committee to a committee of deputy ministers, the Senior Management Preference Committee.

The advisory committee revoked the applicant's designation and the applicant applied for an order in *certiorari* to quash the decision. Richard J of the Northwest Territories Supreme Court dismissed the application ((1993), 15 Admin. LR (2d) 211 (NWT SC)), holding that decisions under the policy document were not amenable to judicial review. The company appealed.]

BY THE COURT (consisting of de Weerdt, McFadyen, and Hudson JJA): … The learned chambers judge found that the revocation of the designation of a business as a Northern Business is not subject to judicial review. He found that, in the context of this case, judicial review is available only to review the exercise of statutory authority. The adoption of the policy and its administration were not an exercise of statutory authority but government's procurement of goods and services. Being commercial decisions, these were not subject to review.

I disagree with this decision in two respects:

1. Judicial review is available to review decisions, not only of public bodies exercising statutory duties but also of those administrative bodies which obtain authority from prerogative powers; their decisions affect rights of others who come under their direction.

2. The committees, the business incentive policy and authority exercised by virtue of the policy go beyond mere decisions by civil servants regarding procurement of goods and services. The Advisory Committee is a public body exercising a power which affects the status of business enterprises, and their ability to compete effectively in the Northwest Territories. The decisions affect the right of a business to contract not only with the Government of the Northwest Territories but also with organizations funded by it and others who have adopted the policy.

. . .

The argument for reviewing not just the source of the power but also its nature flows from the line of English authorities which began with *R v. Criminal Injuries Compensation Board, Ex parte Lain* [1967] 2 QB 864 (CA), in which the English Court of Appeal held that the power of review goes beyond statutory powers of decision to include powers of a board constituted under the prerogative: see also *Council of Civil Service Unions v. Minister for the Civil Service* [1985] AC 374 (Eng. HL).

While the court must be careful not to assume jurisdiction where none exists, the availability of judicial review has expanded over the years. In *Martineau* [*v. Matsqui Inmate Disciplinary Board No. 2*, [1980] 1 SCR 602 (Can.)], Dickson J also quotes from the judgment of Lord Parker CJ in *Lain*, at 882:

The position as I see it is that the exact limits of the ancient remedy by way of *certiorari* have never been and ought not to be specifically defined. They have varied from time to time being extended to meet changing conditions. At one time the writ only went to an inferior court. Later its ambit was extended to statutory tribunals determining a *lis inter partes*. Later again it extended to cases where there was no *lis* in the strict sense of the word but where

immediate or subsequent rights of a citizen were affected. The only constant limits throughout were that it was performing a public duty.

[Further discussion of the case law on the scope of judicial review has been omitted.]

The *Vander Zalm* [*v. British Columbia (Commissioner of Conflict of Interest)* (1991), 80
DLR (4th) 291 (BC SC)] and the *Datafin* [*R v. Panel on Take-overs and Mergers, Ex parte
Datafin PLC*, [1987] QB 815 (Eng. CA)] cases were applied by Saunders J of the Ontario
Court of Justice (General Division), in *Masters v. Ontario* (1993) 110 DLR (4th) 407.
Saunders J had before him an application of a senior civil servant to quash on grounds of
lack of procedural fairness, investigative reports made into his conduct following a complaint of sexual harassment. The investigation was conducted pursuant to a policy directive dealing with workplace discrimination and harassment prevention. The directive
had no statutory basis. Saunders J found that the applicant was entitled to procedural
fairness in the investigation of allegations against him and refused to quash the application for *certiorari*. While not bound by any statutory duty, the investigators making the
report were part of the machinery of government decision-making. The senior officials
who initiated the investigation were under a duty of fairness, as were the investigators
who were carrying out a public duty of investigating his conduct.

Decisions of administrative bodies are reviewable on *certiorari* if an analysis of their
functions discloses a duty of procedural fairness. ...

The business incentive policy monitoring office, its officers, and the committees created by the policy are part of the machinery of government decision-making. While the
source of the power of the business incentive policy office and committees is not statutory,
the policy is recognized in the government contract regulations and must be applied by
all government departments in assessing tenders submitted to the government.

· · ·

While I agree with the learned chambers judge that purely commercial decisions relating to the procurement by government of goods and services generally do not fall
within the class of cases which will be subjected to judicial review, the decisions here go
beyond this category. This is not a simple procurement decision which deals with the
acceptance or rejection of a specific tender or a bid. ... The decision of the Advisory
Committee to reject an application or to revoke a designation affects, not the individual
contract, but the ability of the business to compete with others in contracting with the
government generally and with organizations funded by the government. The decision
also affects the availability of financial assistance through government departments. The
business incentive policy creates a central registry for businesses designated as Northern
Businesses. Government departments and organizations funded by government must
apply the policy in determining, who the successful bidder will be. The decisions deal
with and affect the status of the business and its right and ability to compete with other
business in contracting generally with the government, and with organizations funded
by the government, with others who have adopted the policy. It affects its ability to effectively carry on business in the Northwest Territories. It is this aspect that brings in the
public duty and fairness component referred to in the authorities cited above.

[After finding that the decision was amenable to review for procedural unfairness in an application for *certiorari*, the court remitted the matter to the chambers judge for consideration of whether there was a denial of procedural fairness in the revocation of the applicant's designation.]

Appeal allowed.

NOTES

1. In holding that the decision in issue was amenable to judicial review in public law, the Northwest Territories Court of Appeal was more influenced by the nature of the power than its origins. The same is true of the judgment of Saunders J in *Masters*, which was approved on this point by a full panel of the Divisional Court in *Masters v. Ontario* (1994), 18 OR (3d) 551 (Div. Ct.), at 593-94. The threshold for the availability of the remedy is determined on the basis of the need for procedural fairness rather than procedural fairness entitlements being contingent on the technical rules governing the remedy that is sought. Is this approach satisfactory?

2. The Court of Appeal seems to accept that the actual procurement decisions of government are not appropriate for judicial review because they represent government acting in a purely commercial capacity. Is this an appropriate stance for the court to take? Does it mean that there are some exercises of power under statutory authorization that are not sufficiently public to attract judicial review? If so, on what bases should this distinction be drawn? Note the judgment of Strayer J, then of the Federal Court Trial Division, in *Assaly (Thomas C.) Corporation v. Canada* (1990), 44 Admin. LR 89, in which he held that unfairness in a government tendering process was subject to judicial review. For an affirmation of *Assaly*, see *Gestion Complexe Cousineau (1989) Inc. v. Canada (Minister of Public Works and Government Services)*, [1995] 2 FC 694 (CA); *Cougar Aviation Ltd. v. Canada (Minister of Public Works and Government Services)* (2009), 26 Admin. LR (3d) 30. In contrast, see the post-*Dunsmuir* decision in *Irving Shipbuilding Inc. v. Canada (Attorney General)* (2009), 2009 FCA 116 (CanLII), leave to appeal refused (2009), 2009 CanLII 575521 (SCC), where Evans JA concluded that the subcontractor of an unsuccessful bidder for a government procurement contract (to supply in-service support to Canada's Victoria Class submarines) could not apply for judicial review in order to challenge the fairness of the process for awarding the contract when the unsuccessful bidder had decided not to litigate. After discussing various reasons for this holding, all related to Irving Shipbuilding's status as a subcontractor rather than a contracting party to the tendering process, Evans JA then offered this last rationale, at para. 54, which would apply more generally to limit the availability of judicial review to challenge government procurement where it is subject to contract:

> [O]nce a contract has been awarded, the public has an interest in the avoidance of undue delays in its performance, and in ensuring that government is able promptly to acquire the goods and services that it needs for the discharge of its responsibilities. The normal remedy for breach of contract is a simple award of damages, which does not delay the performance of the contract by the winning bidder. In contrast, the more intrusive public law remedy sought by the appellants is that the contract awarded to CSMG [the successful bidder] be set aside, so that the

tendering process can start again. Governments' recent resort to funding "shovel-ready" infra-structure projects as part of a strategy for promoting economic recovery vividly illustrates that delays in getting publicly financed work underway may be detrimental to the public interest.

3. *Volker Stevin* and *Masters* (and the English authorities relied on) called into question a range of earlier jurisprudence in which judicial review of the decisions of various "inter-nal" committees was denied because the committee lacked a clear statutory basis. Among these earlier authorities is a group of decisions involving challenges to decision making within universities in which the availability of judicial review was either denied or doubted: *R v. Royal Institution for the Advancement of Learning, ex parte Fekete* (1969), 2 DLR (3d) 129 (Que. QB, appeal side); *Diamond v. Hickling* (1987), 24 Admin. LR 30 (BC SC); aff'd. (1988), 36 Admin. LR 129 (BC CA); *MacLean v. University of British Columbia Appeal Board* (1993), 109 DLR (4th) 569 (BC CA); *Wade v. University of British Columbia* (1994), 94 BCLR (2d) 354 (BC SC); and *Vinogradov v. University of Calgary* (1987), 25 Admin. LR 203 (Alta. CA). Should it make any difference for these purposes that universities are not gener-ally seen as part of the apparatus of government? (See Mullan, "The Universities and the Principles and Remedies of Public Law" (1987), 25 *Admin. LR* 212.)

4. Recall also in this context the judgment of McLachlin J in *Shell Canada Products Ltd. v. Vancouver (City)*, [1994] 1 SCR 231 (BC) (see chapter 15 of this text). There, she held (in a part of her judgment in which all of the court concurred) that resolutions passed by Van-couver city council to boycott trade with apartheid South Africa were subject to judicial review under the BC *Judicial Review Procedure Act*.

"Voluntary" Associations

Another area where there have been doubts about the availability of judicial review in public law is that of so-called voluntary associations, which, by law or *de facto*, control access to or opportunities in a particular occupation. The next two cases (both from Nova Scotia) pro-vide contrasting approaches to this issue. In reading them, consider whether the judgment of the court in *Ripley* can still be sustained in the light of *Volker Stevin* and *Masters*.

R v. Halifax-Dartmouth Real Estate Board, ex parte Seaside Real Estate Ltd.
(1963), 42 DLR (2d) 442 (NS SC); rev'd. (1964), 44 DLR (2d) 248 (NS SC *en banc*)

[The Halifax-Dartmouth Real Estate Board expelled Seaside from membership for vari-ous alleged breaches of the association's rules and regulations with respect to the listing and sale of properties. Seaside sought *certiorari* on the basis of failure to give adequate notice of the charges against it. The decision was quashed for this reason: (1963), 40 DLR (2d) 1010 (NS SC). However, subsequently, the matter was reconsidered by the court.]

COFFIN J: Some time after this decision, counsel for the Halifax-Dartmouth Real Estate Board raised a point, which had not been put forward, or argued, on the original hearing, namely, that *certiorari* did not lie at all in this particular case, because there was no duty imposed by statute in the interests of the community and in the nature of public jurisdic-tion to act judicially.

The specific case on which this submission was based was *Re McComb and Vancouver Real Estate Board* (1960) 32 WWR 385 (BC SC). The real estate board in question was a society incorporated under the *Societies Act*, RSBC 1948, c. 311. As Lord J, by whom the case was heard, pointed out, the objects were set out in the constitution and by-laws of the Board, generally to "establish good public relations, to advance and promote the interests of those engaged in the real estate business in the Vancouver area, and to adopt and enforce sound rules of business conduct among all its members. The by-laws provide a complete code for admission of members, and procedure for inquiring into the conduct of its members and giving power to suspend or dismiss from membership."

Lord J continued (at 386): "I can see no distinction between the organization and set-up of this body and the association described in *Re Ness and Incorporated Canadian Racing Ass'ns.*"

The learned judge quoted de Smith's *Judicial Review of Administrative Action* (1959) at 275: "it now seems to be clearly established that neither prohibition nor *certiorari* will issue to a body exercising a jurisdiction that is other than statutory." ...

On these authorities counsel for Halifax-Dartmouth Real Estate Board contends that there is nothing in the statute incorporating the Board which empowers it to act judicially and certainly nothing that makes its deliberations such that they involve the public interest.

[After citing the Atkin *dictum*, Coffin J continued:]

The Halifax-Dartmouth Real Estate Board was not incorporated under the *Societies Act* but by special Act, SNS 1958, c. 110. The aims, objects and purposes of the Board are set forth in s. 2:

> 2(a) to establish and standardize the real estate business so that it shall enjoy and retain the confidence of the general public and serve the interests of owners and purchasers of real estate; ...
>
> (c) to foster and maintain the general development and economic growth of Halifax, Dartmouth, the County of Halifax and Province of Nova Scotia; ...
>
> (e) to promote individual ownership of homes in the cities, towns, villages and rural areas of the Province of Nova Scotia; ...
>
> (h) to raise and maintain the ethical standards of the real estate profession in Halifax, Dartmouth, the County of Halifax and throughout the Province of Nova Scotia;
>
> (i) to establish, promote, manage and administer a co-operative listing system with the object of rendering improved service to the public by providing sellers of real estate and personal property with a wider potential market; ...
>
> (k) to adopt and enforce the code of ethics of the Canadian Association of Real Estate Boards.

Section 4 provides for by-laws and regulations:

> 4. The Board may make, alter, amend or repeal by-laws, rules and regulations as are deemed necessary or convenient to the carrying out of its objects and for the conduct and management of its affairs and for any purpose incidental thereto and to provide for distribution of any surplus funds of the Board whether upon winding up, dissolution or otherwise

to such Nova Scotia universities as the Board may designate for the purpose of extension courses and adult education.

The by-laws themselves provide for fines and expulsions in the following words:

> Members may be fined, suspended or expelled by the majority action of the Board of Directors for violations of the regulations of the Board or for any other conduct which discredits this organization or the real estate business, providing the member shall be given reasonable opportunity to defend himself before such final action is taken. Such decisions of the Board of Directors shall be final.

Thus the general provisions for making by-laws are in the statute, the specific procedure for expulsion is found in the by-laws.

I have examined the statute under which the Vancouver Real Estate Board, the subject-matter of the *McComb* case, was incorporated, namely c. 311 of the Revised Statutes of British Columbia, 1948. It was entitled, "An Act to facilitate the Incorporation of Societies for Provident and other Useful Purposes, and to provide for their Regulation." Section 24(1) provides: "The by-laws of a society incorporated under this Act shall contain provisions in respect of the several matters mentioned in Schedule B."

Schedule B set forth ten matters pursuant to s. 24(1), the relevant clause being: "(2) Conditions under which membership ceases and manner (if any) in which a member may be expelled."

It, therefore, appears that the Vancouver statute is, if anything, stronger than the Nova Scotia statute incorporating the real estate board. The Nova Scotia statute gives the right to make by-laws but does not specifically mention the matter of membership or expulsions in the statute itself, although there is a section in the by-laws dealing with that subject-matter. On the other hand, the Vancouver Act provides in the statute itself that the by-laws shall contain provisions in respect of several matters mentioned in Schedule B, and Schedule B itself includes as one of those matters conditions under which membership ceases and the manner, if any, in which a member may be expelled. Yet despite this, the British Columbia Court held that *certiorari* did not lie.

Counsel for the applicant, in referring to *Re Ness* and the *McComb* cases, accepts the position that if these two cases were strictly applied in Nova Scotia, they would preclude the issuance of *certiorari* against the real estate board in the present case. He also very fairly points out that the extract from Mr de Smith (at 275) extends the English rigidity on *certiorari*.

[After discussing Nova Scotia authority that it was not necessary for a body to be acting judicially or *quasi*-judicially to be amenable to *certiorari*, Coffin J held that this was a requirement and then held that the board had in fact acted judicially. He then continued:]

The Act of Incorporation of the Board gives it power to make rules and regulations for the conduct and management of its affairs and for any purpose incidental thereto. The procedure for fines and expulsions is set forth in the by-laws which were made pursuant to the statute.

The main point urged by the Board is that there must be imposed by statute not only a duty to act judicially but that this duty must be in the interests of the community within the meaning of *Re Ness*, and *Re McComb and Vancouver Real Estate Board*.

It appears to me that the restrictions set forth in these two cases are greater than the Courts in this Province have required, but in any event I cannot agree with the reasoning in the *McComb* case that matters affecting membership in a real estate board are not in the interests of the community. They affect the community just as do the disciplinary regulations of other professional societies.

The Board was established, among other things, to standardize the real estate business, to foster and maintain the general development and economic growth of Halifax, Dartmouth, the County of Halifax and Province of Nova Scotia, and to maintain ethical standards of the real estate profession.

With the greatest deference, in my opinion, these are matters of interest to the community.

I, therefore, confirm my original decision of August 21, 1963.

Order accordingly.

NOTES

1. On appeal, Ilsley J (with whom MacQuarrie J concurred) allowed the appeal on the basis that the board of directors, not the real estate board itself, should have been sued. The majority were prepared to allow the proceedings to be amended. They also held that the board, being statutory in origin, was amenable to *certiorari*. However, they allowed the appeal on other substantive grounds.

2. To what extent was this case affected by the fact that it was possible to carry on the business of selling realty in Halifax and Dartmouth without being a member of the real estate board? Is there any difference between a case like this and the case of a lawyer expelled from a law society (for example, *Barristers and Solicitors Act*, RSNS 1989, c. 30 and *Law Society Act*, RSO 1990, c. L.8)? If *certiorari* is not the appropriate remedy in the case of an expulsion or suspension from a society, what remedies are appropriate? What would be the legal basis of the cause of action in such a case?

Ripley v. Investment Dealers Association of Canada (No. 2)
(1990), 99 NSR (2d) 338 (TD); aff'd. (1991), 108 NSR (2d) 38 (AD)

[Ripley was fined and suspended from membership in the Investment Dealers Association (IDA) for professional misconduct following a hearing by the IDA's discipline committee. He sought various forms of relief against the association, including *certiorari*, prohibition, and a declaration. He alleged that the proceedings were invalid on the basis of, among other things, jurisdictional error and breach of the rules of natural justice.]

ROSCOE J: ... The IDA is one of a number of self-regulatory organizations ([SRO]'s) which operate within the securities industry in Canada. The other [SRO]'s are the

Toronto, Montreal, Vancouver, Alberta and Winnipeg Stock Exchanges, the Winnipeg Commodity Exchange and the Toronto Futures Exchange. All of the stock brokerage firms in Canada are members of one or more of the [SRO]'s, depending on their location and type of business. The [SRO]'s have protocol agreements with each other, providing for procedures and responsibilities for conducting investigations into the activities of firms and employees of firms who are members of more than one [SRO], in order to avoid duplication and confusion. Firms who have membership in more than one [SRO] are called joint members.

. . .

b) Certiorari

The applicant argues that, although the IDA is a non-statutory domestic tribunal, it performs a public function and, therefore, it is an inferior tribunal over which the court has some control by way of the prerogative remedy of *certiorari*, and in particular, *certiorari* may be used to review the decision of the disciplinary tribunal to determine if it exceeded its jurisdiction or made an error of law on the face of the record.

The respondent submits that the IDA does not derive any authority from statute and it is not exercising any government function by either implied or explicit delegation of the legislature, and, therefore, its Disciplinary Committee is not subject to *certiorari* for error of law on the face of the record.

The applicant, in his argument, reviews the *Securities Act*, SNS 1984, c. 11, which regulates trading in securities and in particular, those sections dealing with registration of investment dealers, the bonding of dealers and procedures for segregation of funds. The Act, in s. 150(f), authorizes the Governor in Council to make Regulations authorizing the delegation by the Minister to a stock exchange or the Investment Dealers Association of Canada of any powers or duties of the registrar respecting the registration or renewal of registration of a dealer. However, it does not appear that any such Regulations delegating powers to the IDA have yet been proclaimed. Under s. 150(g) the Act provides that regulations may be made classifying registrants into different categories but indicates that no registrant shall be included in a category designated as an "investment dealer" unless he is a member of the Atlantic District of the Investment Dealers Association of Canada. The applicant also points out that, under certain Regulations that have been made under the Act, members of the Investment Dealers Association are exempt from certain requirements regarding bonding and participation in a compensation fund. In addition, another regulation regarding business procedures indicates that compliance may be effected by following the guidelines established by the IDA. The applicant submits that, by these references to the IDA, in the Statute and the Regulations, the legislation "adopts the IDA as an arm of its regulatory scheme."

Since no regulation has been passed which delegates any authority to the IDA, under the *Securities Act*, and since it is not the registrar, under the *Securities Act*, who is empowered to discipline registrants, I am in agreement with the argument by the respondent that mere reference to the IDA in the Statute and recognition of its registration requirements, does not transform the IDA into a statutory tribunal or an agent of the government. It is the Securities Commission, established by the *Securities Act*, that has the power to enforce compliance with the Act, and there is no suggestion that the IDA acts as a delegate or agent of the Securities Commission. I agree with the respondent's submission that the Regulations simply recognize that the Association has procedures and rules that are acceptable to the registrar. It should be noted that, if the IDA disciplinary panel were to revoke the approval of Mr. Ripley, it would not result in automatic revocation of his registration under the *Securities Act.*

In coming to the conclusion that the IDA is not performing a public function or acting as an agent of the government, I have specifically reviewed the following cases cited by the applicant:

1. *R v. Panel on Take-overs and Mergers, Ex parte Datafin plc* [1987] QB 815 (CA);
2. *Martineau v. Matsqui Institution Disciplinary Board, No. 2* [1980] 1 SCR 602 (Can.);

and the following cases referred to by the respondents:

1. *Re Peg-Win Real Estate Ltd. and Winnipeg Real Estate Board* (1985) 19 DLR (4th) 438 (Man. QB);
2. *Chyz v. Appraisal Institute of Canada* (1984) 36 Sask. R 266 (QB).

I have compared the functions of the IDA with the respondents in the cases noted and have come to the conclusion that the IDA is much more similar to the organizations involved in the two cases referred to by the respondent, in which the courts found that *certiorari* for error on the face of the record was not an available remedy. In *Chyz v. Appraisal Institute of Canada*, Wright J (at 273) described the respondent as:

> ... a voluntary, private organization incorporated without share capital under the *Companies Act* of Canada. While membership in the institute is certainly and obviously important to any person practising as an appraiser in Canada, membership is voluntary as is the case with the local real estate boards referred to in the decisions first cited. There is no evidence before me that lack of membership in the institute would preclude an appraiser from carrying on his or her practice in this province however prestigious and helpful membership in the institute might be in the way of qualifications. The authority exercised by the Committee as a creation of the institute is not statutory. *Certiorari* and prohibition, generally speaking, will not lie against a private body which derives its jurisdiction from the consent of its members banded together in a voluntary association. The institute is such an association.

I should note that *Chyz* was reversed on appeal in a decision reported in (1985) 44 Sask. R 165 (CA) on the grounds that the trial judge had erred in not finding a breach of the rules of natural justice.

In the *Peg-Win Real Estate* case the court, after pointing out that the board, in that case, was voluntary and that its objects were to regulate its members, followed *Re Ness and Incorporated Canadian Racing Ass'ns* [1946] 3 DLR 91 (Ont. CA) where it was decided that *certiorari* will not lie to a person or body of persons, where there is no duty to decide, cast upon it by law. Although it may be adjudicating upon the rights of individuals, in order for *certiorari* to lie, the duty to decide must be one such as is imposed by statute in the interest of the community and must be of the nature of a public jurisdiction.

In summary, then, I find that the IDA and its Disciplinary Committee are not subject to *certiorari* for error on the face of the record since its authority over its members and employees of members is derived solely from contract, and although the organization is recognized by Statute, it does not derive any authority to discipline its members from the Statute nor is it acting as an agent or delegate of the Crown in the exercise of its functions.

. . .

Applications dismissed.

NOTES

1. On appeal, the Appeal Division of the NS Supreme Court upheld Roscoe J's holding that *certiorari* was not available to challenge the jurisdiction and procedure of the IDA and its discipline committee. However, the court (as had Roscoe J) accepted that such a challenge could properly be brought in Nova Scotia by way of an application for declaratory relief, which Ripley had also sought. Even so, his claim for declaratory relief failed on the merits.

2. In its judgment, 1991 CanLII 2445, the Appeal Division provided more details of the nature of the regulatory role played by the IDA:

The Investment Dealers Association (IDA), as explained at some length in the appellant's factum, is an unincorporated association which oversees the investment and brokerage business in Canada, serving as the professional organization of, and regulating, member brokerage houses and their employees. It is not specifically empowered under any statute, although its existence is recognized in some securities legislation. It has its own constitution, by-laws and regulations to which its members bind themselves by contract to comply. The IDA establishes requirements for capitalization, procedures for purchase, sale and registration of securities for clients, audit procedures and other matters that govern the internal and external operations of national and local investment firms. The IDA also sets standards of qualifications for, and for the discipline of, persons engaged in the industry. Its authority does not extend to regulating the actual issuance of securities: that is vested in provincial securities commissions and the various stock exchanges sold. The sale of securities is regulated by statute in all Provinces. It is the persons and the firms who sell the securities that are regulated by the IDA.

. . .

It was acknowledged that the appellant had agreed to bind himself to the by-laws, rules and regulations of the IDA and made himself responsible for knowing their contents. IDA approval is required at various career stages beginning with securities salesman, or registered representative, and Mr. Ripley had in fact signed similar undertakings several times occasioned by his promotions.

Does this affect your views as to the degree of control that the IDA had over Ripley's occupational opportunities and, as a consequence, the holding that the IDA and its disciplinary committee were not exercising authority that was amenable to public law review?

3. More generally, *Ripley* raises questions about the extent to which "private" bodies exercising "public" powers conferred on or delegated to them by statute should be subject to public law remedies. Given the extent of privatization, deregulation, and outsourcing over the past two decades, it is inevitable that this issue will continue to arise. For example, should private correctional facilities be amenable to public law remedies in exercising their disciplinary powers? To what extent should stock exchanges be subject to judicial review in

public law when exercising authority conferred directly on them by statute or delegated to them under the statutory mandate of a securities commission?

4. An example of a recent decision involving a voluntary association is *Wang v. British Columbia Medical Association* (2008), 2008 BCSC 1559 (CanLII), where Ballance J concluded that the relationship between the BC Medical Association and Dr. Wang, one of its members, was contractual in nature. As a result, Dr. Wang's challenge to the Association based on jurisdictional and procedural fairness grounds was subject to the contractual documents of the association, supplemented by the common law of voluntary associations, rather than public law principles.

The Impact of Statutory Remedial Regimes

The language of statutes such as Ontario's *Judicial Review Procedure Act*, in which the remedies of public law are not only replaced but consolidated and codified in a single application for judicial review, can have an impact on the extent of relief.

The Federal Courts Act

Under the *Federal Courts Act*, RSC 1985, c. F-7, the Federal Court's original judicial review jurisdiction is expressed in s. 18 in terms of the review of a "federal board, commission or other tribunal." Section 2 of the *Federal Courts Act*, RSC 1985, c. F-7, defines that term as follows:

> [A]ny body, person or persons having, exercising or purporting to exercise jurisdiction or powers conferred by or under an Act of Parliament *or by or under an order made pursuant to a prerogative of the Crown*, other than the Tax Court of Canada or any of its judges, any such body constituted or established by or under a law of a province or any such person or persons appointed under or in accordance with a law of a province or under section 96 of the *Constitution Act, 1867*. [Emphasis added.]

Notable in this definition is the inclusion in 1990 of specific reference to prerogative powers, a puzzling omission from the original 1970 version. However, the relevant wording is problematic. Does it apply to direct exercises of the prerogative as opposed to decisions made or actions taken under formal instruments that were issued in the exercise of the royal prerogative? In *Black v. Canada* (2001), 54 OR (3d) 215 (CA), it was held that when the prime minister was advising the British government on whether Conrad Black should be made a peer, he was exercising a prerogative power rather than acting under an order made by virtue of the prerogative. On the court's interpretation, this did not come within the definition and, as a result, the Ontario courts were properly seized of the matter; it was not within the jurisdiction of the Federal Court.

The term "by or under an Act of Parliament" obviously extends to powers conferred by subordinate as well as primary legislation. However, the same questions that surfaced in *Volker Stevin* could arise under the *Federal Courts Act*. To what extent does the Act justify the review of decision-making bodies that do not have a clear warrant in either an Act or a regulation? Can intervention be justified either on a theory of implied legislative mandate or, now, by reference to the residual royal prerogative?

What was clear, even before the 1990 amendments, was that the term "by or under an Act of Parliament" was not broad enough to embrace all corporate bodies established under federal legislation. Thus, Laskin CJC suggested in *Attorney General of Canada v. Lavell*, [1974] SCR 1349 (Can. and Ont.), at 1379, that Crown corporations, boards of directors of corporations incorporated under the general federal statute, and band councils having certain powers by virtue of the *Indian Act*, RSC 1970, c. I-6, s. 81, did not come within the definition of "federal board, commission or other tribunal." They were thus excluded from the reach of the judicial review provisions of that Act. See also *Canada Metal Co. Ltd. v. CBC (No. 2)* (1972), 27 DLR (3d) 385 (Ont. CA) and *Wilcox v. CBC*, [1980] 1 FC 326 (TD), which held the CBC to be excluded. Here too, however, difficulties of the kind identified in the *Halifax-Dartmouth Real Estate Board* case and *Ripley* may arise. Take, for example, the Canadian Medical Council, incorporated by Special Act of Parliament (see *Canada Medical Act*, RSC 1952, c. 26) and possessing certain authority with respect to the establishing of criteria for the national registration of medical practitioners and the certification of doctors as specialists. Would the exercise of all or any of the council's powers be subject to review under the *Federal Courts Act*?

In this context, it is interesting that in New Zealand, there was considerable judicial and academic debate on whether the new species of state-owned enterprise created as part of a 1980s government corporatization of many of its trading activities immunized such bodies from judicial review under that country's judicial review procedure legislation, the *Judicature Amendment Act, 1972*. Eventually, the Judicial Committee of the Privy Council—anachronistically still New Zealand's highest court—ruled in favour of the Act's application but on a very restricted substantive basis: *Mercury Energy Ltd. v. Electricity Corporation of New Zealand*, [1994] 1 WLR 521 (PC NZ). See Taggart, "Corporatisation, Contracting and the Courts" (1994), *Public Law* 351 for a discussion of the issue and the judgment.

The Judicial Review Procedure Acts of British Columbia and Ontario

The key sections in each of these Acts are worded similarly. Section 2 of the BC *Judicial Review Procedure Act* (RSBC 1996, c. 241) provides as follows:

2(1) An application for judicial review is an originating application and must be brought by petition.

(2) On an application for judicial review, the court may grant any relief that the applicant would be entitled to in any one or more of the proceedings for

(a) relief *in the nature of* mandamus, prohibition or certiorari;

(b) a declaration or injunction, or both, in relation to the exercise, refusal to exercise, or proposed or purported exercise, of a *statutory power*. [Emphasis added.]

The term "statutory power" is then defined in s. 1 as

a power or right conferred by an enactment

(a) to make a regulation, rule, bylaw or order,

(b) to exercise a *statutory power of decision*,

(c) to require a person to do or to refrain from doing an act or thing that, but for that requirement, the person would not be required by law to do or to refrain from doing,

(d) to do an act or thing that would, but for that power or right, be a breach of a legal right of any person, or

(e) to make an investigation or inquiry into a person's legal right, power, privilege, immunity, duty or liability. ... [Emphasis added.]

Finally, "statutory power of decision" is also defined as

a power or right conferred by an enactment to make a decision deciding or prescribing

(a) the legal rights, powers, privileges, immunities, duties or liabilities of a person, or

(b) the eligibility of a person to receive, or to continue to receive, a benefit or licence, whether or not the person is legally entitled to it,

and includes the powers of the Provincial Court.

(The only substantial difference between the provisions of the BC Act and those of the Ontario *Judicial Review Procedure Act*, RSO 1990, c. J.1, is the omission from the Ontario Act of paragraph (e) of the definition of statutory power.)

Three points should be made here about these two regimes.

The Scope of the New Remedy: Frozen or Evolutionary

First, there was some question whether the public law remedies that provide the reference point—the common law prerogative writs—for the new application for judicial review established in the two Acts were to be given the content that they had at the time of the creation of the new remedy or whether their content should be delineated on the basis of the scope that they came to possess in other jurisdictions over the course of time. It is now clear that their content is not frozen as of the time of the enactment of the two statutes. However, that does not mean that the courts of British Columbia and Ontario have to maintain a "shadow" law relating to the old remedies as the yardstick against which to measure the scope of the new remedy. According to Lambert JA of the BC Court of Appeal in *Culhane v. Attorney General of British Columbia* (1980), 108 DLR (3d) 648 (BC CA), at paras. 39-51, the Act's objective was simply to deal with the procedure of judicial review. It did not have substantive objectives, leaving the courts free, within the framework of the new remedy, to attribute a scope for judicial review that seemed appropriate in an evolutionary common law framework. While the other judges in that case did not consider it necessary to go this far, it seems a sensible and suitably purposive approach.

"In the Nature of"

Second, there is an issue about the meaning and impact of the words "in the nature of." Before these statutes were enacted, the courts did not issue the prerogative writs. Rather, as a result of earlier procedural reforms, they issued orders "in the nature of" the prerogative writs. This suggested that the use of this language in the Acts had no aim other than a reference to the existing terminology of public law relief.

However, at least some Ontario judges attributed a more far-reaching intention to the drafters of the legislation. These words were held to have the effect of bringing within the ambit of the *Judicial Review Procedure Act* not only the successors of the old prerogative writs but also other remedial regimes that were similar to the prerogative writs in their effects (such as an application to set aside the award of a consensual arbitrator): *Re Ontario Provincial Police Association and the Queen* (1974), 46 DLR (3d) 518 (Ont. Div. Ct.). This reasoning—which is criticized in Evans, "Comment" (1977), 55 *Can. Bar Rev.* 148, at 159-69—has not been repudiated by a higher Ontario court and therefore must still be taken as a possible interpretation of the impact of that province's Act.

Indeed, the reasoning in that case was taken up by Henry J (sitting as a single Divisional Court judge) in *Re Rees and United Association of Journeymen & Apprentices of the Plumbing & Pipefitting Industry of the United States and Canada, Local 527* (1983), 150 DLR (3d) 493 (Ont. Div. Ct.) and applied to the suspension from membership and fining of the member of a trade union. Henry J justified this by a combination of the language of "in the nature of," a sense that there was room for evolution in the remedies of public law, and the fact that the relationship between trade unions and their members had come, as a result of public and legislative policy, to have a public rather than a purely private dimension.

In British Columbia, the courts have not been so expansive in interpreting the reach of the *Judicial Review Procedure Act* and the meaning of "in the nature of." In the same context, an application for judicial review of the expulsion of a member from a trade union, the BC Court of Appeal held that relief was unavailable. While the court was not confined to the review of statutory powers under the Act, nonetheless the target of the application had to be affecting public rights. It did not reach domestic, non-statutory tribunals, and "in the nature of" did not have the effect accepted in the Ontario cases. See *Mohr v. Vancouver, New Westminster and Fraser Valley District Council of Carpenters* (1988), 33 Admin. LR 154 (BC CA). A similar conclusion was reached by the Alberta Court of Appeal in an application to review an expulsion from a trade union by way of an application for an order in the nature of *certiorari: Skoreyko v. Belleville* (1991), 47 Admin. LR 228 (Alta. CA) (but see *Kaplan v. Canadian Institute of Actuaries* (1994), 161 AR 321 (QB); aff'd. (1997), 206 AR 268 (CA); leave to appeal refused [1997] SCCA No. 563 (SCC); *IABSOI v. Boilermakers' Union* (2001), 272 AR 1, 85 Alta. LR (3d) 147).

The Relevance of Statutory Power

Finally, these two statutes framed the new remedy differently in relation to prerogative-style relief, on the one hand, and injunctive and declaratory relief on the other. The purpose of linking relief by way of injunction and declaration to the exercise of a "statutory power" always seemed fairly clear: the object of the Act was to capture only the public law (and not the private law) uses of those remedies. However, this limitation was unnecessary for relief in the nature of the prerogative writs because, by their nature, the prerogative writs were exclusively public law remedies.

However, in Ontario, early interpretations of the Act linked the availability of relief in the nature of the prerogative writs to the "statutory power" requirement. Such an interpretation is in fact not sustainable and has now been rejected decisively by later Ontario authority: *Bezaire v. Windsor Roman Catholic Separate School Board* (1992), 9 OR (3d) 737 (Div. Ct.). The same conclusion was reached by the BC Court of Appeal in *Mohr v. Vancouver, New Westminster and Fraser Valley District Council of Carpenters* (1988), 33 Admin. LR 154

(BC CA): relief in the nature of *certiorari* under that province's *Judicial Review Procedure Act* was not contingent on the presence of a statutory power.

In the Prince Edward Island *Judicial Review Act*, SPEI 1988, c. 35, the equivalent statutory provision is s. 1(b), which defines "application for judicial review":

> (b) "application for judicial review" means an application to determine whether or not authority conferred on a tribunal by an enactment has been exercised in accordance with the enactment in respect to a decision of the tribunal in relation to the legal rights, powers, privileges, immunities, duties or liabilities of a person or the eligibility of a person to receive, or to continue to receive, a benefit or license.

"Tribunal" is then defined in s. 1(h) to mean

> a person or group of persons upon whom an enactment confers authority to make a decision, whether styled a board or a commission or by any other title.

In contrast, the *Alberta Rules of Court*, Part 56.1 simply creates an application for judicial review in the domain of the remedies of public law and provides in rule 753.01 that

> "person" *includes* a board, commission, tribunal or other body whose decision, act or omission is subject to judicial review.

Consider how the courts of these two provinces might handle the cases we have identified where the application of the BC and Ontario *Judicial Review Procedure Acts* was contentious.

It is clear that the availability of declaratory and injunctive relief under the BC and Ontario *Judicial Review Procedure Acts* depends on there being an exercise of a statutory power and that this requirement may remove from the ambit of the Act some aspects of the modern uses of declaratory and injunctive relief as public law remedies. A related question is whether the fact that a body has been created by statute is itself sufficient to bring the body within the ambit of the Act. In Ontario, for example, the statutory origins of the United Church of Canada have led the courts to hold that the disciplining of United Church clergy comes within the ambit of the Act: *Lindenberger v. United Church of Canada* (1985), 17 CCEL 143 (Ont. Div. Ct.) and *Davis v. United Church of Canada* (1991), 8 OR (3d) 75 (Div. Ct.). (See also *Bruker v. Marcovitz*, [2007] 3 SCR 607, in which Abella J for the majority, at para. 44, cited *Lindberger* as an example of a case in which a case involving a religious dispute was justiciable in the courts.)

Interestingly, the United Church was incorporated by federal legislation (SC 1926, c. 100) and this raises questions as to whether judicial review (if available) should be sought in the Federal Court. More fundamentally, the award of relief in the nature of *certiorari* in *Davis* in the context of church discipline directly raised the issue of the extent to which review under the *Judicial Review Procedure Act* is confined to the domain of public law. After all, in terms of any distinction between the domain of the public and the private, at least under traditional notions of that distinction, religious bodies are private bodies. Moreover, if the United Church is subject to judicial review on the basis that it was incorporated by statute, does that open up the possibility of all corporate decision making being subject to judicial review?

Excluded Public Bodies

Superior Courts

The prerogative writs developed as a means for the monarch and his or her courts to call on officials, including inferior courts such as magistrates and justices of the peace, to account for their actions. As such, there was always a logic in their non-application to superior court judges. More generally, there is the further justification that decisions of first instance judges are usually subject to a right of appeal to a higher court and, to the extent they are not, this reflects a deliberate legislative choice.

Even so, there may be exceptions to a general rule. This is demonstrated by the judgment of the Supreme Court of Canada in *Dagenais v. Canadian Broadcasting Corp.*, [1994] 3 SCR 835 (Ont.), which sustained the applicability of the general rule but, on its facts, raising questions about the court should have created an exception to accommodate what appeared to be an obvious legislative lacuna. At issue in the case were bans on the telecasting of a fictional drama and media reporting of that drama and the judicial proceedings surrounding it. The basis for the initial ban issued by a superior court judge was that the telecast might prejudice criminal trials that were ongoing or upcoming. One of the issues was the extent to which such interlocutory orders could be challenged by the affected media in an application for relief in the nature of *certiorari*. The Supreme Court sustained the availability of *certiorari* as a means to challenge such orders when made by a provincial court or non-s. 96 court judge. However, when such a ban was issued by a superior court judge, the court reaffirmed the general immunity of such judges from prerogative relief, even though this meant that the only way in which an order could be challenged was by proceeding immediately to the Supreme Court of Canada and seeking leave to appeal under s. 40(1) of the *Supreme Court Act*. The only solution to this situation, according to the court, was legislative action.

The Crown

As a matter of the common law, the Crown is also excluded from the ambit of the prerogative writs. This is based on a similar historical explanation as that which applies to the superior courts. To the extent that the royal courts in their prerogative writ jurisdiction were exercising authority derived from the monarch that was based on the monarch's officials being called on to account for themselves, it was illogical and unseemly for the Crown to be called to account in its own courts. At another level was the question of enforcement. It was not seen as appropriate or even possible for the Crown to be cited for contempt of its own courts. Crown immunity from the processes of the superior courts was removed, however, by legislation on Crown proceedings and Crown liability in the second half of the 20th century.

In the domain of the prerogative writs, Crown immunity now has little practical significance. While the prerogative writs and their modern statutory equivalents may still not technically be available against the Crown in the sense of the Queen in right of Canada or the provinces, to the extent that the modern day powers of the Crown (or the governments of Canada and the provinces) are in large measure exercised by officials or agencies named in statutes, the restriction is avoided by naming the designated official as the respondent or defendant. Indeed, this can hold even where the designated decision-maker is the governor or lieutenant governor in council, as confirmed in the context of the *Federal Courts Act* by the interpretation of the term "federal board, commission or other tribunal" to include the governor in council. The definition of "federal board, commission or other tribunal" in s. 2(1) of that Act also now makes clear that the Act's judicial review provisions apply to persons "exercising or purporting to exercise jurisdiction or powers conferred ... by or under an order made pursuant to a prerogative of the Crown."

Moreover, at the federal level and then in all the provinces, legislation on Crown proceedings or Crown liability legislation has expressly subjected the Crown to the declaratory judgment or order jurisdiction of the superior courts. This exposed the Crown to a declaration even in the limited situations where the exercise of a power was still considered a function of the Crown itself rather than a named or designated official.

Even so, the old Crown immunity may still have a bite in contexts where the courts are asked to make mandatory or injunctive orders against the government. On occasion, whether in the context of an application for *mandamus* or, more commonly, an action for an injunction, the defence will be raised by government lawyers that such relief is not available against the Crown and that the action or inaction complained of is really that of the Crown. Warrant for this position is found in Crown proceedings and Crown liability legislation in the form of the provisions that authorize the courts to award declaratory relief against the Crown. Thus, for example, s. 18(1) of the Ontario *Proceedings Against the Crown Act*, RSO 1990, c. P.27, provides as follows:

> 18(1) Where in proceedings against the Crown any relief is sought that might, in proceedings between persons, be granted by way of injunction or specific performance, the court shall not, as against the Crown, grant an injunction or make an order for specific performance, but in lieu thereof may make an order declaratory of the rights of the parties.
>
> (2) The court shall not in any proceedings grant an injunction or make an order against a servant of the Crown if the effect of granting the injunction or making the order would be to give any relief against the Crown that could not have been obtained in proceedings against the Crown, but in lieu thereof may make an order declaratory of the rights of the parties.

For the remedy of *mandamus*, the tradition of Crown immunity from the prerogative writs lived on for many years in the jurisprudence on whether a minister of the Crown, when acting under legislation, is exercising statutory power as a servant of the Crown or a designated official (*persona designata*). Put differently, was the duty in question one that was owed to the Crown or to those affected by its exercise? (*In re M*, [1994] 1 AC 377 (Eng. HL).) Today, it is rare to find instances of the former. The courts regularly assert jurisdiction to award *mandamus* against the Crown on the basis that the duty in question was owed to the applicant. See, for example, *Apotex Inc. v. Canada (Attorney General)*, [1994] 1 FC 742 (CA); aff'd. [1994] 3 SCR 1100 (Can.). There is also authority to the effect that the Crown is subject to *mandamus* where constitutional rights are at stake. Thus, in *Levesque v. Canada (Attorney General)* (1986), 25 DLR (4th) 184 (FCTD), Rouleau J issued an order in the nature of *mandamus* against the Crown, ordering it to facilitate the exercise by a penitentiary inmate of his Charter right to vote in a provincial election (see also *Auton v. A.G.B.C.* (2001), 84 BCLR (3d) 259, 197 DLR (4th) 165, at paras. 16-18 and 48).

Injunctive Relief Against the Crown

The availability of injunctive relief against ministers of the Crown (as opposed to the Crown itself) appears to be undergoing a similar re-evaluation as in the case of *mandamus*. While Crown proceedings legislation generally still acts as an impediment (save for unconstitutional action) to the award of injunctive relief against the Crown—or against servants or agents of the Crown where the effect is to grant relief against the Crown itself—nonetheless some judges appear to have attributed in this context a broader expanse to the domain in which ministers, Crown agents, and their servants are amenable to injunctions (both permanent and interlocutory).

Many of the cases in this domain do not really involve judicial review in the sense in which we have been using it in this chapter. Often the issue arises in the context of a plaintiff or applicant seeking to enjoin a statutory body from acting in breach of contract or in disregard of its incorporating statute in the same manner as such an action would be brought against a private body, and the defence raised is that such relief is not available because the body in question is the Crown, or the effect of granting the relief would be the same as granting relief against the Crown. See, for example, *Smith v. Attorney General (N.S.)* (2004), 226 NSR (2d) 344, 244 DLR (4th) 649 (CA); *Mil Systems v. Canada (International Trade Tribunal)* (1999), 1999 CanLII 9244 (FCA); and *Canada (Attorney General) v. Saskatchewan Water Corporation* (1993), 18 Admin. LR (2d) 91 (Sask. CA).

Nonetheless, the jurisprudence on the scope of the prohibition on the award of injunctions against the Crown does include a significant body of cases in which the objective is to prevent the exercise of what is clearly public law, statutory, or prerogative power. Notwithstanding the theoretical growth in the reach of the prerogative remedy of prohibition, it still tends to be confined to situations in which the objective is the prevention of a process being engaged in, while injunctions remain the remedy of choice where the aim is the halting of the exercise of a substantive statutory power. (In some jurisdictions, this assumes an added dimension to the extent that preliminary relief is still not available in aid of an application for relief in the nature of the prerogative writs. Where such interim relief is vital if any ultimate remedy at trial is to be efficacious, the only alternative in the public law domain remains the commencement of an action for an injunction coupled with an application for an interim or interlocutory injunction.)

Government of PEI v. Summerside Seafood
(2006), 256 Nfld. & PEIR 277, 271 DLR (4th) 530, 48 Admin. LR (2d) 91 (CA)

[A motions judge declared that Summerside Seafood Supreme (SSS) had a right to have its 2004 fishing licence issued and to have the licence renewed until the final determination of SSS's judicial review in the matter. SSS had sought judicial review against the government of PEI in relation to alleged government decisions declaring SSS to be in default of its financial obligations to the government, listing SSS on a registry of defaulted loans, and revoking or refusing SSS's fish processing licence. The motions judge concluded that SSS was not entitled to an interim injunction because an injunction could not issue against the Crown and so, instead, the motions judge granted SSS an interim declaration against the government. The government appealed.]

WEBBER JA: ... [35] [W]ith respect I would disagree with the premise upon which the motions judge based his decision to proceed with an interim declaratory remedy. That premise was that an injunction was not available against the Government/Crown in the instant case.

[Webber JA reviewed s. 13 of the *Crown Proceedings Act*, RSPEI 1988, c. C-32, which prohibited the granting of an injunction against the Crown or against "an officer of the Crown if the effect of granting the injunction ... would be to give any relief against the Crown that could not have been obtained in proceedings against the Crown." Webber JA also examined academic materials indicating that an injunction could be granted against Crown agents and servants, although not against the Crown itself, where they were acting contrary to their statutory grant of authority.]

[40] Overall, the position of the appellant is that no interlocutory injunction should issue in this case because there is no wrong in this case, i.e. the Crown servants were acting lawfully. However, that is the very issue to be decided at trial or on judicial review. Essentially, the argument of SSS is that the appellant acted in bad faith or in a biased manner when it acted to deprive SSS of a licence. ... SSS's alternative argument is that the Government acted without authority because SSS does not owe the money alleged; the government should not have paid out what it did on the guarantee and so SSS was wrongly placed on the Loans in Default Central Registry; such debt has not been proven. If either proposition is supported at trial, the Crown servant will be found to have acted without authority. So an injunction could issue. The only question is whether or not the same, albeit temporary, injunction should be issued prior to the full hearing of the merits.

[41] Neither the cases nor the texts dealing with the subject of injunctive relief against Crown servants or agents suggest that where such relief is available, it is for some reason available only on a permanent basis. I can find no reason in logic or law to make such a distinction.

[42] Therefore, as the sought-after injunctive relief is available against Crown servants or agents, there is no need to consider the issue of interim declaratory relief.

NOTES

1. The approach adopted by Webber JA is similar to that of Lord Woolf, delivering the judgment of the House of Lords in *In re M*, mentioned above. In that case, the House of Lords sustained the Court of Appeal's holding that the acting Secretary of State for Home Affairs was guilty of contempt of court for failing to comply with an interim injunction. The injunction had prevented the removal of a foreign national from the United Kingdom pending the determination of a challenge by way of judicial review to the validity of a Home Office decision that he was not entitled to asylum in the United Kingdom. According to Lord Woolf, this was the first time a minister of the Crown had been found in contempt of court. (See, in a Canadian context, *Bhatnager v. Canada (Minister of Employment & Immigration)*, [1990] 2 SCR 217 (Can.), where the Supreme Court accepted the possibility of ministerial contempt but rejected the Federal Court of Appeal's conclusion that it had been established in law.) In the course of his judgment, in referring to s. 21 of the *Crown Proceedings Act,*

1947 [the equivalent of s. 18 of the Ontario legislation], Lord Woolf made the following observations:

> The position so far as civil wrongs are concerned, prior to the *Crown Proceedings Act*, can be summarised, therefore, by saying that as long as the plaintiffs sued the actual wrongdoer or the person who ordered the wrongdoing he could bring an action against officials personally, in particular as to torts committed by them and they were not able to hide behind the immunity of the Crown. This was the position even though at the time they committed the alleged tort they were acting in their official capacity. In those proceedings an injunction, including, if appropriate, an interlocutory injunction, could be granted. The problem which existed in seeking a remedy against the Crown was not confined to injunctions. It applied to any form of proceedings and where proceedings were possible by suing the wrongdoer personally then an injunction would be available in the same circumstances as other remedies. If such a position required reconciling with the historic maxim as to the Crown doing no wrong, then this could be achieved by an approach, which Mr. Richards endorsed in the course of argument, by saying that, as the Crown could do no wrong, the Crown could not be considered to have authorised the doing of wrong, so the tortfeasor was not acting with the authority of the Crown.
>
> • • •
>
> Returning to section 21, what is clear is that in relation to proceedings to which section 21(1) provisos (a) and (b) apply, no injunction can be granted against the Crown. In addition there is the further restriction on granting an injunction against an officer of the Crown under section 21(2). That subsection is restricted in its application to situations where the effect of the grant of an injunction or an order against an officer of the Crown will be to give any relief against the Crown which could not have been obtained in proceedings against the Crown prior to the Act. Applying those words literally, their effect is reasonably obvious. Where, prior to 1947, an injunction could be obtained against an officer of the Crown, because he had personally committed or authorised a tort, an injunction could still be granted on precisely the same basis as previously since, as already explained, to grant an injunction could not affect the Crown because of the assumption that the Crown could do no wrong. The proceedings would, however, have to be brought against the tortfeasor personally in the same manner as they would have been brought prior to the 1947 Act. If, on the other hand, the officer was being sued in a representative capacity, whether as an authorised government department, for example, one of the named Director-Generals or as Attorney-General, no injunction could be granted because in such a situation the effect would be to give relief against the Crown. The position would be the same in those situations where proceedings would previously have been brought by petition of right or for a declaration but could now be brought against the authorised department.
>
> There appears to be no reason in principle why, if a statute places a duty on a specified Minister or other official which creates a cause of action, an action cannot not be brought for breach of statutory duty claiming damages or for an injunction, in the limited circumstances where injunctive relief would be appropriate, against the specified Minister personally by any person entitled to the benefit of the cause of action. If, on the other hand, the duty is placed on the Crown in general, then section 21(2) would appear to prevent injunctive relief being granted, but as Professor Sir William Wade QC has pointed out ("Injunctive Relief against the Crown and Ministers" (1991) 107 *LQR* 4 at 4-5) there are likely to be few situations when there will be statutory duties which place a duty on the Crown in general instead of on a named Minister. In

broad terms therefore the effect of the Act can be summarised by saying that it is only in those situations where prior to the Act no injunctive relief could be obtained that section 21 prevents an injunction being granted. In other words it restricts the effect of the procedural reforms that it implemented so that they did not extend the power of the courts to grant injunctions. This is the least that can be expected from legislation intended to make it easier for proceedings to be brought against the Crown.

2. The Ontario Law Reform Commission in its *Report on the Liability of the Crown* recommended the repeal of s. 18 of Ontario's *Proceedings Against the Crown Act*, at 51-53. It justified the recommendation as follows (footnotes omitted):

(b) Case for Reform and Recommendation

As we have indicated, the principal reason why the coercive remedies, including injunction, specific performance, and *mandamus*, are not available against the Crown has been the refusal of the courts to attempt to coerce the Crown. This refusal was based on two related concerns. ...

The first concern is the alleged incongruity of one branch of government, the courts, commanding another branch, the executive. In our view, this concern is largely anachronistic and no longer constitutes a problem. There appears to be no reason in principle why the Crown should not be subject to the same remedies as other legal persons. As we have indicated, the Crown in right of Ontario is for most purposes treated by the courts as a legal person, capable of suing and being sued. The Crown has, from the earliest times, been obliged to pay damages ordered by the courts. Discovery, a "coercive" procedure that is discussed below, has been available against the Crown for some time in Ontario.

The second concern is the difficulty of enforcing such a command. The coercive remedies are enforced by bringing an application for civil contempt of court against the contemnor. The penalties for such a breach, in the discretion of the court, are fine or imprisonment. It is said that the possibility that the Crown may be held in contempt raises the potential of damaging or even irreconcilable constitutional confrontation.

The Commission does not find this argument persuasive. For the reasons given in chapter 6, we will recommend that orders against the Crown should be subject to enforcement by way of contempt proceedings. Moreover, we believe that, even if the Crown remained immune from civil contempt, such orders would be worth making. As a matter of principle, the full range of remedies ought be available against the Crown, as it is against any other person, so that the court is in a position to make whatever order is appropriate in the situation. We feel confident that, as with declarations, the Crown would nearly always obey the order, and therefore the issue of enforcement would rarely arise. To be sure, in the exceptional case where the Crown refused to obey and remained immune from contempt proceedings, the plaintiff would have no further legal recourse. However, that rare case would not be a sufficient reason for denying the court the power to grant an injunction against the Crown in all appropriate cases.

It may be argued that, because the remedy of a declaration is available against the Crown, there is no need to alter the law with respect to the Crown's immunity from injunction or specific performance. Our response to this suggestion is twofold. First, as a matter of principle, it is undesirable to have a special regime of remedial law applicable to the Crown, which is the effect of substituting the declaration for the injunction in proceedings against the Crown. Secondly, as we have indicated, the declaration is an inadequate substitute for the injunction, since interlocutory relief is not available in the form of a declaration. Interlocutory relief is sought in private litigation in Canadian courts almost every day. It is clear to us that this relief would also be useful against the Crown, and, in our view, should be available.

It has also been suggested that Crown immunity from the coercive remedies generally is justifiable on the ground that the Crown ought to be free to act unlawfully, without risk of judicial intervention, where compelling interests of state require, as, for example, in an emergency. However, we agree with the observation that such an exception to the rule of law is too sweeping. These are discretionary remedies. Even given the possibility that some unforeseen crisis might compel illegal action by the Crown, we believe that the courts can be relied upon to take account of any compelling state interests that would be injured by any order sought. Moreover, the ultimate safeguard of such interests is the power of the Legislature to reverse the decision of a court granting an injunction against the Crown.

Accordingly, we recommend that section 18 of the *Proceedings Against the Crown Act* should be repealed. A new *Crown Liability Act* should provide that the remedies of injunction and specific performance are available against the Crown.

3. Even assuming a more liberal stance by the courts to the availability of injunctive relief against Crown servants and ministers particularly does not necessarily guarantee that such relief will always be available. The following cautionary statement by Lord Woolf in *In re M* makes this point:

> The fact that, in my view, the court should be regarded as having jurisdiction to grant interim and final injunctions against Officers of the Crown does not mean that that jurisdiction should be exercised except in the most limited circumstances. In the majority of situations so far as final relief is concerned, a declaration will continue to be the appropriate remedy on an application for judicial review involving officers of the Crown. As has been the position in the past, the Crown can be relied upon to co-operate fully with such declarations. To avoid having to grant interim injunctions against officers of the Crown, I can see advantages in the courts being able to grant interim declarations. However, it is obviously not desirable to deal with this topic, if it is not necessary to do so, until the view of the Law Commission are known.

ALLOCATION OF REVIEW AUTHORITY: FEDERAL COURT AND PROVINCIAL SUPERIOR COURTS

Introduction

As we have seen, judicial review jurisdiction in Canada is divided between the superior courts of the provinces and the Federal Court. In most instances, the choice whether to proceed in one of the Federal Court or in a provincial superior court depends on whether the source of the power or authority in question is federal or provincial in nature. However, as we will see in this section, this may not be entirely determinative because the provincial superior courts continue to have jurisdiction over aspects of federal statutory regimes. Despite the Federal Court's generally exclusive jurisdiction over the review of federal statutory authorities, the superior courts, by virtue of the *Constitution Act, 1867* and the *Federal Courts Act* itself, still have concurrent and, in some situations, exclusive jurisdiction over a range of challenges to the exercise of federal statutory power. This means that, on occasion, counsel first will have to evaluate whether a matter is one of concurrent or overlapping jurisdiction and, if so, which court is the appropriate venue for the commencement of proceedings.

As well as examining these aspects of the allocation of review authority between the superior courts and the Federal Court, we will examine the way in which judicial review occurs in the Federal Court. This is pertinent because, despite statutory reforms, there remain aspects of the Federal Court's judicial review powers that distinguish it from the provincial superior courts. In this section it is important to consider the justifications for this bifurcation of judicial review authority in Canada and to ask whether it might be better (as has been asserted from time to time by some provincial attorneys general and bars) to restore a unitary system of judicial review. What are the advantages and disadvantages of a system of review that, by and large, compels litigants to have recourse to the Federal Court when review is sought of the exercise of federal statutory power?

Relevant Provisions of the Federal Courts Act

Unlike the provincial superior courts, the Federal Court and Federal Court of Appeal are statutory courts in that their judicial review jurisdiction derives from an Act of Parliament, as reproduced below.

Federal Courts Act
RSC 1985, c. F-7

2(1) … "[F]ederal board, commission or other tribunal" means any body, person or persons having, exercising or purporting to exercise jurisdiction or powers conferred by or under an Act of Parliament or by or under an order made pursuant to a prerogative of the Crown, other than the Tax Court of Canada or any of its judges, any such body constituted or established by or under a law of a province or any such person or persons appointed under or in accordance with a law of a province or under section 96 of the *Constitution Act, 1867*;

(2) For greater certainty, the expression "federal board, commission or other tribunal," as defined in subsection (1), does not include the Senate, the House of Commons, any committee or member of either House, the Senate Ethics Officer or the Conflict of Interest and Ethics Commissioner with respect to the exercise of the jurisdiction or powers referred to in sections 41.1 to 41.5 and 86 of the *Parliament of Canada Act*.

. . .

16(1) Except as otherwise provided in this Act or any other Act of Parliament, every appeal and every application for leave to appeal to the Federal Court of Appeal, and every application for judicial review or reference to that court, shall be heard in that court before not fewer than three judges sitting together and always before an uneven number of judges. Otherwise, the business of the Federal Court of Appeal shall be dealt with by such judge or judges as the Chief Justice of that court may arrange.

17(1) Except as otherwise provided in this Act or any other Act of Parliament, the Federal Court has concurrent original jurisdiction in all cases in which relief is claimed against the Crown.

(2) Without restricting the generality of subsection (1), the Federal Court has concurrent original jurisdiction, except as otherwise provided, in all cases in which

(a) the land, goods or money of any person is in the possession of the Crown;

(b) the claim arises out of a contract entered into by or on behalf of the Crown;

(c) there is a claim against the Crown for injurious affection; or

(d) the claim is for damages under the *Crown Liability and Proceedings Act.*

. . .

(5) The Federal Court has concurrent original jurisdiction

(a) in proceedings of a civil nature in which the Crown or the Attorney General of Canada claims relief; and

(b) in proceedings in which relief is sought against any person for anything done or omitted to be done in the performance of the duties of that person as an officer, servant or agent of the Crown.

(6) If an Act of Parliament confers jurisdiction in respect of a matter on a court constituted or established by or under a law of a province, the Federal Court has no jurisdiction to entertain any proceeding in respect of the same matter unless the Act expressly confers that jurisdiction on that court.

18(1) Subject to section 28, the Federal Court has exclusive original jurisdiction

(a) to issue an injunction, writ of *certiorari*, writ of prohibition, writ of *mandamus* or writ of *quo warranto*, or grant declaratory relief, against any federal board, commission or other tribunal; and

(b) to hear and determine any application or other proceeding for relief in the nature of relief contemplated by paragraph (a), including any proceeding brought against the Attorney General of Canada, to obtain relief against a federal board, commission or other tribunal.

(2) The Federal Court has exclusive original jurisdiction to hear and determine every application for a writ of *habeas corpus ad subjiciendum*, writ of *certiorari*, writ of prohibition or writ of *mandamus* in relation to any member of the Canadian Forces serving outside Canada.

(3) The remedies provided for in subsections (1) and (2) may be obtained only on an application for judicial review made under section 18.1.

18.1(1) An application for judicial review may be made by the Attorney General of Canada or by anyone directly affected by the matter in respect of which relief is sought.

(2) An application for judicial review in respect of a decision or order of a federal board, commission or other tribunal shall be made within 30 days after the time the decision or order was first communicated by the federal board, commission or other tribunal to the office of the Deputy Attorney General of Canada or to the party directly affected by it, or within any further time that a judge of the Federal Court may fix or allow before or after the end of those 30 days.

(3) On an application for judicial review, the Federal Court may

(a) order a federal board, commission or other tribunal to do any act or thing it has unlawfully failed or refused to do or has unreasonably delayed in doing; or

(b) declare invalid or unlawful, or quash, set aside or set aside and refer back for determination in accordance with such directions as it considers to be appropriate, prohibit or restrain, a decision, order, act or proceeding of a federal board, commission or other tribunal.

(4) The Federal Court may grant relief under subsection (3) if it is satisfied that the federal board, commission or other tribunal

(a) acted without jurisdiction, acted beyond its jurisdiction or refused to exercise its jurisdiction;

(b) failed to observe a principle of natural justice, procedural fairness or other procedure that it was required by law to observe;

(c) erred in law in making a decision or an order, whether or not the error appears on the face of the record;

(d) based its decision or order on an erroneous finding of fact that it made in a perverse or capricious manner or without regard for the material before it;

(e) acted, or failed to act, by reason of fraud or perjured evidence; or

(f) acted in any other way that was contrary to law.

(5) If the sole ground for relief established on an application for judicial review is a defect in form or a technical irregularity, the Federal Court may

(a) refuse the relief if it finds that no substantial wrong or miscarriage of justice has occurred; and

(b) in the case of a defect in form or a technical irregularity in a decision or an order, make an order validating the decision or order, to have effect from any time and on any terms that it considers appropriate.

18.2 On an application for judicial review, the Federal Court may make any interim orders that it considers appropriate pending the final disposition of the application.

18.3(1) A federal board, commission or other tribunal may at any stage of its proceedings refer any question or issue of law, of jurisdiction or of practice and procedure to the Federal Court for hearing and determination.

(2) The Attorney General of Canada may, at any stage of the proceedings of a federal board, commission or other tribunal, other than a service tribunal within the meaning of the *National Defence Act*, refer any question or issue of the constitutional validity, applicability or operability of an Act of Parliament or of regulations made under an Act of Parliament to the Federal Court for hearing and determination.

18.4(1) Subject to subsection (2), an application or reference to the Federal Court under any of sections 18.1 to 18.3 shall be heard and determined without delay and in a summary way.

(2) The Federal Court may, if it considers it appropriate, direct that an application for judicial review be treated and proceeded with as an action.

18.5 Despite sections 18 and 18.1, if an Act of Parliament expressly provides for an appeal to the Federal Court, the Federal Court of Appeal, the Supreme Court of Canada, the Court Martial Appeal Court, the Tax Court of Canada, the Governor in Council or the Treasury Board from a decision or an order of a federal board, commission or other tribunal made by or in the course of proceedings before that board, commission or tribunal, that decision or order is not, to the extent that it may be so appealed, subject to review or to be restrained, prohibited, removed, set aside or otherwise dealt with, except in accordance with that Act.

. . .

28(1) The Federal Court of Appeal has jurisdiction to hear and determine applications for judicial review made in respect of any of the following federal boards, commissions or other tribunals:

(a) the Board of Arbitration established by the *Canada Agricultural Products Act*;

(b) the Review Tribunal established by the *Canada Agricultural Products Act*;

(b.1) the Conflict of Interest and Ethics Commissioner appointed under section 18.1 of the *Parliament of Canada Act*;

(c) the Canadian Radio-television and Telecommunications Commission established by the *Canadian Radio-television and Telecommunications Commission Act*;

(d) the Pension Appeals Board established by the *Canada Pension Plan*;

(e) the Canadian International Trade Tribunal established by the *Canadian International Trade Tribunal Act*;

(f) the National Energy Board established by the *National Energy Board Act*;

. . .

(h) the Canada Industrial Relations Board established by the *Canada Labour Code*;

(i) the Public Service Labour Relations Board established by the *Public Service Labour Relations Act*;

(j) the Copyright Board established by the *Copyright Act*;

(k) the Canadian Transportation Agency established by the *Canada Transportation Act*;

. . .

(m) umpires appointed under the *Employment Insurance Act*;

(n) the Competition Tribunal established by the *Competition Tribunal Act*;

(o) assessors appointed under the *Canada Deposit Insurance Corporation Act*;

(p) the Canadian Artists and Producers Professional Relations Tribunal established by subsection 10(1) of the *Status of the Artist Act*;

(q) the Public Servants Disclosure Protection Tribunal established by the *Public Servants Disclosure Protection Act*; and

(r) the Specific Claims Tribunal established by the *Specific Claims Tribunal Act*.

(2) Sections 18 to 18.5, except subsection 18.4(2), apply, with any modifications that the circumstances require, in respect of any matter within the jurisdiction of the Federal Court of Appeal under subsection (1) and, where they apply, a reference to the Federal Court shall be read as a reference to the Federal Court of Appeal.

(3) If the Federal Court of Appeal has jurisdiction to hear and determine a matter, the Federal Court has no jurisdiction to entertain any proceeding in respect of that matter.

History and Constitutional Considerations

The Federal Court of Canada (as it was then called) was established in 1971. Before then, the Exchequer Court of Canada—a federal court created by virtue of s. 101 of the *Constitution Act, 1867*—had jurisdiction in several areas of federal law, such as admiralty matters, income tax appeals, and tortious liability of the federal Crown. The Exchequer Court also served as an appellate court from the decisions of certain federal statutory authorities. However, other than a relatively unexplored jurisdiction to grant declaratory relief (*Jones v.*

Gamache, [1969] SCR 119 (Can.)), the Exchequer Court did not possess any general judicial review jurisdiction.

The jurisdiction of the Exchequer Court was restructured considerably by the *Federal Court Act*, RSC 1970, c. 10 (2nd Supp.). The name of the court was changed from the Exchequer Court to the Federal Court of Canada and it thereafter consisted of two divisions, a Trial Division and a Court of Appeal, until those divisions were reconstituted in 2003 as the Federal Court and the Federal Court of Appeal. As part of the creation of the Federal Court of Canada in 1971, a significant component was added to the jurisdiction of the new court as compared with the Exchequer Court: it was assigned a virtually exclusive review authority over the affairs of federal statutory bodies. Previously, general jurisdiction over judicial review of such authorities was exercised by the provincial superior courts. However, those responsible for the legislation felt that the quantity and nature of judicial review involving federal statutory authorities called for a judicial review jurisdiction in the new court. There was also a sense that, with ten superior courts across the country adjudicating in judicial review proceedings involving federal authorities, conflicts would arise in the jurisprudence on particular exercises of power.

At the time of the original *Federal Court Act* in 1970, concerns were expressed that the creation of a Federal Court of Canada with largely exclusive review power over federal statutory authorities was unconstitutional. To the extent that it diminished the judicial review jurisdiction of the provincial superior courts and replaced the historically important prerogative writs as the means of reviewing the decisions of federal administrative tribunals and agencies, it was said by some that the Act infringed ss. 96-100—the judicature provisions of the *Constitution Act, 1867*.

In 1972, the Supreme Court of Canada in *Pringle v. Fraser*, [1972] SCR 821 (Ont.) determined, not only that the prerogative writs themselves had no constitutionally guaranteed existence, but also that judicial review jurisdiction over federal statutory authorities could be constitutionally taken from the provincial superior courts and conferred on a federal court such as the Federal Court of Canada. The source of this authority was s. 101 of the *Constitution Act*, which entitled Parliament, notwithstanding anything else in the Act, to create courts in addition to the Supreme Court of Canada for the "better administration of the laws of Canada." Further support for this proposition was provided by *Canada Labour Relations Board v. Paul L'Anglais Inc.*, [1983] 1 SCR 147 (Que.).

Even so, this determination by the Supreme Court did not exhaust the constitutional questions that arose from the Federal Court's exclusive judicial review jurisdiction. As we saw in chapter 9 of this text, the Supreme Court of Canada in *Crevier v. Attorney General of Quebec*, [1981] 2 SCR 220 (Que.) held that a provincial legislature could immunize an administrative regime from judicial review for jurisdictional error, prompting the question of whether this limitation extended to the Parliament of Canada. That question appears to have been resolved in favour of the application of *Crevier* in the federal domain: *MacMillan Bloedel Ltd. v. Simpson*, [1995] 4 SCR 725 (BC); *Dunsmuir*, at para. 29 (see also the discussion in chapter 9 of this text).

Specific to the Federal Court was the further issue of whether the provincial superior courts maintained any authority over a constitutional challenge involving a federal statutory regime. Did the Federal Court's exclusive review authority under the *Federal Court Act* apply to such matters? Here, the Supreme Court of Canada held that s. 96 of the *Constitu-*

tion Act was triggered and that the *Federal Court Act* could not constitutionally remove the superior courts' jurisdiction over constitutional challenges to the jurisdiction of federal statutory regimes (*Attorney General of Canada v. Law Society of British Columbia*, [1982] 2 SCR 307 (BC) ("the *Jabour* case")) or to action taken or proposed under a federal statute (*Paul L'Anglais*, above).

Yet these rulings still did not exhaust the constitutional questions. In particular, there was the problem of what amounted to a constitutional challenge for these purposes. This issue first arose in challenges to the validity of subordinate legislation promulgated under federal legislation. Here, it was argued that the *ultra vires* promulgation of a regulation was a constitutional matter because it involved the unconstitutional arrogation of legislative power by the executive branch. The issue surfaced in another context with the advent of the *Charter of Rights and Freedoms*. To the extent that a federal statutory regime or exercise of power was challenged under the Charter, was this a constitutional challenge within the *Jabour* and *Paul L'Anglais* rules, cases that involved constitutional challenges based on the division of powers under ss. 91 and 92 of the *Constitution Act, 1867*? There was also the question of whether, in cases where a constitutional challenge to the exercise of federal statutory power was brought in a provincial superior court, it was permissible to join associated administrative law grounds in the same proceedings? Or did the *Federal Court Act* require that the administrative law attacks had to be made separately in the Federal Court? Other litigation raised the question of whether, in cases where there was concurrent jurisdiction between the provincial superior courts and the Federal Court, the provincial superior courts were obliged to accept jurisdiction or, alternatively, whether they could defer to the Federal Court's jurisdiction under the *Federal Courts Act*.

On the question of whether challenges to federal subordinate legislation raised an issue of constitutional law that justified the assertion of jurisdiction by a provincial superior court, there was, surprisingly, no significant conflict between some provincial superior courts (*Waddell v. Shreyer* (1981), 126 DLR (3d) 431 (BC SC) and *Re Williams and the Attorney General for Canada* (1983), 6 DLR (4th) 329 (Ont. Div. Ct)) and the Federal Court. In particular, in *Re Groupe des Éleveurs de Volailles de l'Est de l'Ontario and Canadian Chicken Marketing Board* (1984), 14 DLR (4th) 151 (FCTD), Strayer J held (at 165-66) that the only authority of provincial superior courts to rule on the validity of federal subordinate legislation, other than on *Constitution Act* grounds, was where that issue arose collaterally in proceedings otherwise within the jurisdiction of a provincial superior court.

Subsequently, there was provincial Court of Appeal support for this position: *Saskatchewan Wheat Pool v. Canada (Attorney General)* (1993), 17 Admin. LR (2d) 236 (Sask. CA). The Wheat Pool had commenced an action in the Saskatchewan Court of Queen's Bench for a declaration that a 1993 order in council promulgated under the *Canadian Wheat Board Act*, RSC 1985, c. C-24, was beyond the authority conferred on the governor in council by the Act. The attorney general moved to strike out the action on the basis that such a challenge was within the exclusive jurisdiction of the Federal Court. Wakeling JA delivered the judgment of the Saskatchewan Court of Appeal allowing the motion, stating:

> In this action we are not asked to rule on the constitutional validity of the *Canadian Wheat Board Act*, RSC 1985, c. C-24, nor has any Charter issue been raised. The issue here is purely and simply a request for a declaration that the Governor in Council has acted in excess of the authority

it was granted by a federal statute when it issued the Order in Council in question. In our view, this case comes as close as it can come to being a situation which was intended to be within the exclusive jurisdiction of the Federal Court. All of the attributes of what might be termed a federal case are firmly in place and the exception identified by Strayer J has no application.

There are some sound reasons for this position. If an *ultra vires* regulation is said to raise a constitutional issue on the theory that such an instrument involves an unconstitutional bypassing of Parliament, the logical extension of this argument is that any federal statutory authority that exceeds its statutory mandate is attempting to bypass Parliament by ignoring the constraints placed on it by its empowering legislation. On this theory, one could characterize any jurisdictional-error case as raising a constitutional issue, a determination that would render largely meaningless the Federal Court exclusivity provisions in the *Federal Courts Act*.

The issue of whether a Charter challenge involves constitutional issues for these purposes was mentioned but not resolved in the *Saskatchewan Wheat Pool* case. However, in *Reza*, the Supreme Court of Canada judgment that follows, it is assumed by the Supreme Court that, where Charter issues are raised in an attack on a federal legislative regime, there is concurrent jurisdiction between the Federal Court and the provincial superior courts. This position was also endorsed (albeit in *obiter dicta*) by three judges of the Supreme Court of Canada, at least where the challenge is to legislation. According to Sopinka J, delivering one of two three-judge judgments in *Kourtessis v. Canada (Minister of National Revenue)*, [1993] 2 SCR 53 (BC), at 113-14:

> The jurisdiction of the provincial superior courts to issue declaratory judgments on the constitutional validity of provincial and federal legislation (whether as to *vires* or consistency with the Charter) is fundamental to Canada's federal system ... . This plenary jurisdiction is necessary to enable provincial courts to discriminate between valid and invalid federal laws so as to refuse to apply the invalid ones ... and to ensure that the subject always has access to a remedy for violation of his or her Charter rights and freedoms.

Is this position justified? Do the provincial superior courts have the same claim to concurrent jurisdiction that they do in cases involving the ss. 91-92 allocation of legislative authority between the Parliament of Canada and the provincial legislatures? Should it be relevant for such purposes whether the challenge is to legislation as opposed to a decision or order of a federal authority? (For an articulation of the argument that the provincial superior courts lack this jurisdiction when the challenge is to the actions of a federal statutory body, see *Canada (Attorney General) v. Mousseau* (1993), 126 NSR (2d) 33, 107 DLR (4th) 727 (NS CA).)

Assuming that concurrent jurisdiction in both of these situations is justified, should the exercise of that jurisdiction be a matter of discretion for the provincial superior court (as ruled by the Supreme Court of Canada in *Reza*) or should the court be obliged to hear the case? What if the challenge involves Charter and non-Charter grounds of attack (such as an allegation of a violation of both the principles of fundamental justice as guaranteed by s. 7 and those of common law procedural fairness as well as a claim of patent unreasonableness)? What does the Supreme Court tell first instance judges about the principles on which they should exercise their discretion should these issues arise?

Reza v. Canada
[1994] 2 SCR 394 (Ont.)

[Reza had made a Convention refugee claim under the *Immigration Act* (Can.). A two-member tribunal decided that he did not have a "credible basis" for his claim. As a consequence, it was not considered by the Immigration and Refugee Board and a deportation order was issued. The Federal Court of Appeal denied Reza leave to apply to have the deportation order set aside. Reza was also unsuccessful in having his case reviewed by the immigration authorities on humanitarian and compassionate grounds. The Federal Court Trial Division then refused him leave to seek judicial review of this denial.

At this juncture, Reza applied to the Ontario Court (General Division) for declaratory and associated interlocutory relief. He asserted that various provisions of the *Immigration Act* pertinent to his situation were contrary to the *Canadian Charter of Rights and Freedoms* and the *Canadian Bill of Rights*. Among the provisions challenged was the requirement that leave be obtained to seek judicial review of a deportation order by the Federal Court, a decision from which there was no appeal.

Ferrier J allowed a motion by Canada to stay Reza's application, but this decision was reversed by the Ontario Court of Appeal ((1992), 11 OR (3d) 65) (Abella JA dissenting). Canada obtained leave to appeal this decision to the Supreme Court of Canada.]

BY THE COURT (La Forest, L'Heureux-Dubé, Sopinka, Gonthier, Cory, McLachlin, and Major JJ): ...

III. *Judgments Below*

... Ferrier J stated, "[t]his Court clearly has jurisdiction to grant the relief sought by the Applicant. The issue is whether the Court may decline to exercise its jurisdiction and if so, whether the Court ought to so decline in this case." He then went on to state:

> In the absence of any showing that the available review process and appeal process is inappropriate or less advantageous than the *habeas corpus* jurisdiction of this Court, this Court should, in the exercise of its discretion, decline to grant relief on a *habeas corpus* application. Both jurisprudence and logic would support that this Court should leave the review of immigration matters with the Federal Court: *Re Peiroo* (1989) 69 OR (2d) 253 (CA). To the same effect is the Court of Appeal decision in [*Shepherd v. Canada (Minister of Employment & Immigration)* (1989), 63 DLR (4th) 687 (Ont. CA)]. I am of course bound by these decisions.
>
> The case at bar does not involve an application for *habeas corpus* relief, but the relief sought, by way of declaration and injunctive relief, is also discretionary in this Court. The Federal Court has jurisdiction to grant the relief sought in this application and in my view the principles set out by the Court of Appeal in *Peiroo* and in *Shepherd* are applicable to the case at bar. The circumstances described by Campbell J in [*Bembenek v. Canada (Minister of Employment & Immigration)* (1991), 69 CCC (3d) 34 (OC (Gen. Div.))], which influenced the Court to take jurisdiction, are not present here.
>
> As to whether the process is less advantageous in the Federal Court, as indicated, the relief is available in that Court and in my view the requirement of leave in that Court to make a claim for a declaratory judgment does not make the process less advantageous. ...
>
> Accordingly, it is my view that this proceeding should be stayed and I so order.

Ontario Court of Appeal (1992) 11 OR (3d) 65

Arbour JA (Carthy JA concurring)

Arbour JA held that the sole issue before the Court was: assuming that the Federal Court would have jurisdiction to hear the respondent's application, upon what principles should a provincial superior court decline to hear an application for a remedy under the Charter in deference to a prospective litigation of the issue in the Federal Court?

Dealing first with the argument that the issue falls to be decided by the *habeas corpus* jurisprudence, Arbour JA found that the cases relied upon by the motions court judge merely affirm that a provincial superior court may decline to entertain an application for *habeas corpus* when the applicant is attempting to bypass a statutory scheme. She held that those cases offered little guidance in the present case where the comprehensive statutory scheme has been exhausted.

Arbour JA expressed the view that, assuming that both the Federal Court and the Ontario Court had jurisdiction, the *prima facie* choice of jurisdiction should have been that of the respondent. She saw no reason why the Ontario Court should defer to the expertise of the Federal Court since this was not an immigration case, but a constitutional one. She held that no principle of curial deference in constitutional adjudication could be relied upon by a provincial superior court to defer to the expertise of the Federal Court merely because the constitutional violation is said to have occurred in the context of an immigration matter.

Although the issue of convenience was not raised as such, Arbour JA felt that the trial judge's reference to advantage and inconvenience seemed to originate in the doctrine of *forum non conveniens*. Referring to the opinion of Lamer J (as he then was) in *Mills v. The Queen* [1986] 1 SCR 863 (Ont.), she stated that the test articulated under that doctrine should not be determinative of the jurisdictional conflict in this case, but agreed that the principles offer useful guidance for the proper exercise of discretion.

After stating the *forum conveniens* test to be applied where the appropriate forum is at issue, Arbour JA said that she disagreed with Ferrier J's conclusion that the leave requirement to proceed before the Federal Court did not make the process less advantageous. She was of the view that the leave threshold would operate as a juridical disadvantage to the respondent who could commence the identical procedure as of right in the Ontario Court. Arbour JA also noted that the Federal Court of Appeal had already decided against the contentions of the respondent and thus his application was likely to fail in that forum. She held that the respondent was entitled to avail himself of the juridical advantage he would enjoy in the Ontario courts and to choose, between two equally competent forums, the one in which the law was not already settled against his contention. Arbour JA concluded by acknowledging the limited usefulness of the *forum non conveniens* test in constitutional cases, but held that if applied to the present case it could not support the granting of a stay.

Finally, Arbour JA stated at 72:

> In my opinion, the factors relied upon by the motions court judge in this case did not justify his decision to decline to exercise his jurisdiction and I see no other relevant factor that would. There is no principle which justifies a provincial superior court declining jurisdic-

tion simply because the identical remedy could be pursued in the Federal Court, when a constitutional remedy is sought in good faith before a court fully competent to grant it.

Abella JA (dissenting)

Abella JA emphasized the breadth of a motions court judge's discretion to grant a stay but held that the discretion should not be exercised in a patently unreasonable manner. She described the respondent's application as follows at 76:

> The [respondent] could have raised virtually all of his Charter arguments in his numerous immigration and judicial review proceedings. This action is, at heart, an attempt to have the credible basis decision and the deportation order reviewed and relitigated by a different forum by recharacterizing and reformulating as constitutional the outcomes and procedures the [respondent] had previously (and unsuccessfully) invoked. Every opportunity existed for the raising of all of these Charter challenges. But the [respondent] chose instead first to exhaust the forums available in the pursuit of his statutory rights in immigration matters, then to re-explore them in other forums available in the pursuit of his Charter ones.
>
> This application is essentially an application to declare the [respondent's] deportation order and the Federal Court's process unconstitutional. The entire background presented in this appeal through extensive documents and submissions to this court, is based on the particular facts which arose in the [respondent's] own immigration proceedings, proceedings which have been declared by Parliament to be within the jurisdiction of the Federal Court. The [respondent's] application is, while now designated to be constitutional in nature, a constitutional challenge to the results in his own case.

Abella JA referred to *Maynard v. Maynard* [1951] SCR 346 (Ont.), in support of the proposition that parties are not permitted to begin fresh litigation because of new views they may entertain of the law of the case. That case also suggested that the plea of *res judicata* applies when parties seek to bring forward points which could have been raised in earlier litigation. Abella JA found both these propositions germane to the case at bar.

Abella JA went on to state that, even if she was wrong to suggest that the new proceedings before the Ontario Court could and should have been raised in any of the immigration and Federal Court procedures, Ferrier J did not err by deferring this new application to another court of concurrent jurisdiction. In her view there was no obligation on the part of the Ontario Court (General Division) to hear every case presented for adjudication in which there is a constitutional issue raised. She held that the discretion to decline to hear such a case surely exists when not only does the Federal Court have concurrent jurisdiction to deal with the matter, it also has expertise and experience in immigration law, administrative law and Federal Court procedure, the core issues of the respondent's application. She also found it significant that the Federal Court has an exclusive mandate over immigration matters and found the principles from *Peiroo v. Canada (Minister of Employment and Immigration)* (1989) 69 OR (2d) 253 (CA) (dealing with *habeas corpus*), were applicable. Abella JA noted that the failure to decline to exercise jurisdiction would raise concerns over forum-shopping, inconsistency and multiplicity of proceedings.

In conclusion, Abella JA held that a categorical denial of a superior court judge's discretion to decline to exercise jurisdiction in favour of a tribunal of concurrent jurisdiction was not warranted. She held that the discretion not only existed, but should not have been interfered with when, as in the present case, it was reasonably exercised.

III. Analysis

We are all of the view that this appeal should be allowed. We are generally in agreement with the dissenting reasons delivered by Abella JA in the Court of Appeal. We are unable to agree, however, with two aspects of Abella JA's reasons.

First, citing cases which deal with the doctrine of *res judicata*, Abella JA concluded that all of the issues raised in the respondent's application to the Ontario Court (General Division) could and should have been raised in the proceedings in the Federal Court. We interpret this as a finding that the issues were either *res judicata* or subject to issue estoppel. In view of the fact that leave to commence judicial review was required in both the Federal Court of Appeal and the Federal Court, Trial Division and one of the issues was the constitutional validity of the leave procedure itself we have serious doubts about the application of either *res judicata* or issue estoppel. Moreover, in view of the conclusion reached by Abella JA and which we share, it was and is unnecessary to address this issue.

Second, Abella JA stated that the standard of review for an appellate court reviewing a lower court's exercise of discretion is whether the exercise of discretion is patently unreasonable. While the latter is appropriate in review of decisions of administrative tribunals, the test for appellate review of the exercise of judicial discretion is whether the judge at first instance has given sufficient weight to all relevant considerations: *Friends of the Oldman River Society v. Canada (Minister of Transport)* [1992] 1 SCR 3 (Can.) at 76-77, *per* La Forest J. See also *Manitoba (Attorney General) v. Metropolitan Stores Ltd.* [1987] 1 SCR 110 (Man.) at 154-55.

These two points aside, we agree with Abella JA's conclusion that there is no basis for interfering with Ferrier J's decision to stay the proceedings commenced by the respondent. The Ontario Court (General Division) and the Federal Court had concurrent jurisdiction to hear the respondent's application but, under s. 106 of the *Courts of Justice Act*, any judge of the General Division had a discretion to stay the proceedings. Ferrier J properly exercised his discretion on the basis that Parliament had created a comprehensive scheme of review of immigration matters and the Federal Court was an effective and appropriate forum. In view of our decision in *Kourtessis v. MNR* [1993] 2 SCR 53 (BC), this was the correct approach.

Since Ferrier J took into account all relevant considerations in exercising his discretion to grant a stay, there is no basis for an appellate court to interfere with his decision. The majority in the Ontario Court of Appeal erred in doing so. Accordingly, the appeal is allowed.

Appeal allowed.

NOTES

1. Would it have been appropriate in this case for the court to consider that the Charter challenges were in part predicated on the fact that the success of an application for leave to seek review from a Federal Court judge in an immigration matter apparently depended very

much on the specific judge that was hearing the application? See Green and Schaffer, "Leave to Appeal and Leave to Commence Judicial Review in Canada's Refugee Determination System: Is the Process Fair?" (1992), 4 *Int. J of Refugee Law* 71. Does this consideration and the fact that the challenge was to the way in which jurisdiction had been created in the Federal Court in immigration matters speak in any way to the exercise of discretion in allowing the matter to proceed in the provincial superior court?

2. Where did the judgment of the Supreme Court of Canada leave Reza and the Federal Court? Should Reza have been able to recommence proceedings in the Federal Court for declarations based on his allegations that various provisions of the *Immigration Act* were unconstitutional or did the Supreme Court of Canada not determine that issue?

The Federal Courts Act's Allocation of Jurisdiction as Between the Federal Court and Provincial Courts

The mere fact that the Federal Court was established with the objective of providing a special forum for the judicial review of federal statutory authorities does not mean that the court always has jurisdiction over all such bodies. The Federal Court, as a statutorily created court, is not regarded as having any inherent jurisdiction, at least in the fullest sense in which that is characteristic of the provincial superior courts. As a result, whether the Federal Court has jurisdiction over any particular federal statutory power depends on whether there has been a specific conferral of that jurisdiction either in the *Federal Courts Act* or the legislation establishing that statutory authority.

As we have seen, the principal threshold issue in the *Federal Courts Act* is the definition in s. 2 of "federal board, commission or other tribunal." That term is defined expansively to include not only tribunals and agencies but also those exercising executive power (such as the governor in council). Even so, it does not reach all bodies that owe their existence to federal statutes or regulations. Recall in this context the exclusion of companies incorporated under the *Canada Business Corporations Act* and the likely exclusions of other bodies incorporated under federal statute to conduct business on behalf of the government or to fulfill a specific policy mandate (for example, the Canadian Broadcasting Corporation; see *Montréal (Ville) v. Canadian Broadcasting Corporation* (2006), 292 FTR 16 (FC), at paras. 14-16). Where the precise line is to be drawn in this respect remains somewhat unclear.

On its face, the definition contains explicit exclusions (bodies or persons exercising powers under federal statute but appointed by or under the law of a province as well as persons appointed under s. 96 of the *Constitution Act, 1867*—that is, superior court judges). The precise extent of these exclusions has been subject to extensive litigation.

First, there is an exclusion for bodies or persons appointed under the law of a province. This exclusion seems to apply most clearly where the powers created by a federal statute are conferred on or delegated to a provincially appointed decision-maker. This may include, for example, the powers exercised by provincial highway transport boards over interprovincial trucking operations and the exercise of jurisdiction by provincial or non-s. 96 court judges under the *Criminal Code* (see, for example, *Dagenais*, above).

A complicated issue under this definition arose from the authority of s. 96 judges who exercised special (federal) statutory powers. It was asked in the case law, were they acting as s. 96 judges or were they acting under the authority of the statute (as so-called *personae designatae*) and thus subject to judicial review in the Federal Court? In *Re Herman and Deputy Attorney General for Canada*, [1979] 1 SCR 729 (Can.) and *Minister of Indian Affairs and Northern Development v. Ranville*, [1982] 2 SCR 518 (Can.), the Supreme Court held that, unless the statute expressly provided otherwise, s. 96 court judges exercised all powers conferred on them by statute in their capacity as superior court judges. Thus, their decisions in such matters were not reviewable under the *Federal Courts Act*. See Macdonald, "Federal Judicial Review Jurisdiction Under Section 2(g) of the Federal Court Act: The Position of Section 96 Judges" (1979), 11 *Ottawa L Rev*. 9.

Beyond exclusions in the definition of "federal board, commission or other tribunal" under the *Federal Courts Act*, there is the possibility that an empowering statute will exclude the jurisdiction of the Federal Court. Thus, the *Canada Labour Code*, RSC 1985, c. L-2, s. 58(3), provides: "For the purposes of the Federal Courts Act, an arbitrator appointed pursuant to a collective agreement or an arbitration board is not a federal board, commission or other tribunal within the meaning of that Act." In effect, this returns the judicial review of that process to the provincial superior courts.

The judicial review jurisdiction of the Federal Court and the provincial superior courts was affected by the provisions of the Canada–US Free Trade Agreement (FTA) and the North American Free Trade Agreement (NAFTA) and their creation of a supranational process for the review of decisions of panels that have adjudicated trade disputes under those agreements as an alternative to review in the Federal Court. The review provisions of the treaties are given effect by the *Special Import Measures Act*, RSC 1985, c. S-15 (as amended), Part I.1 (NAFTA) and Part II (FTA); see Lemieux and Stuhec, *Review of Administrative Action Under NAFTA* (1999). More broadly, the investment provisions of Canada's trade agreements (for example, Chapter 11 of NAFTA) and bilateral investment treaties authorize a novel process of supranational review by international arbitrators of Canada's federal and provincial governments (including legislative and judicial acts as well as administrative action); see Van Harten, *Investment Treaty Arbitration and Public Law* (2007), especially chapters 3 and 5.

In some domains, the provincial superior courts continue to possess judicial review jurisdiction over federal decision making. Section 18 of the *Federal Courts Act* has never provided for the issue by the Federal Court of the prerogative writ of *habeas corpus* in relation to detentions by federal statutory authorities (other than in the case of members of the Canadian Armed Forces serving abroad). Thus, in such cases, the potential existed for challenges in both the Federal Court (by way of the *Federal Courts Act* remedies) and the provincial superior courts by way of an application for relief in the nature of *habeas corpus* under provincial legislation and court rules governing that relief.

In that respect, in *R v. Miller*, [1985] 2 SCR 613 (Ont.), the Supreme Court held that *certiorari* in aid of *habeas corpus* was not the same remedy as *certiorari* alone, over which the Federal Court had exclusive jurisdiction in matters involving federal statutory bodies. As a result, *habeas corpus* could be used to challenge any discrete form of confinement (such as segregation in a prison facility) and did not have to lead to complete release from imprisonment. Notably, the ability to link an application for *habeas corpus* in the superior courts with *certiorari*-type relief in the Federal Court meant that affidavits or transcripts (if available) detailing the process and the nature of the detention could be filed, allowing an applicant a much stronger evidential base on which to make her or his case.

The holding in *Miller* was reaffirmed by the Supreme Court in *May v. Ferndale Institution*, [2005] 3 SCR 809, at para. 32:

> First and foremost, provincial superior courts have jurisdiction to issue certiorari in aid of habeas corpus in respect of detention in federal penitentiaries in order to protect residual liberty interests. This principle is crucial in these cases. In the prison context, the applicant is thus entitled to choose the forum in which to challenge an allegedly unlawful restriction of liberty. Under Miller, if the applicant chooses habeas corpus, his or her claim should be dealt with on the merits, without regard to other potential remedies in the Federal Court. The second proposition ... is that habeas corpus will lie to determine the validity of the confinement of an inmate in administrative segregation, and if such confinement is found unlawful, to order his or her release into the general inmate population of the institution.

The court also clarified, at para. 44, that a provincial superior court should decline to exercise its *habeas corpus* jurisdiction only "in limited circumstances" and "not ... merely because another alternative remedy exists and would appear as or more convenient in the eyes of the court." The Supreme Court referred to two established examples of these limited circumstances: where "a statute confers jurisdiction on a court of appeal to correct the errors of a lower court and release the applicant if need be" and where "there is in place a complete, comprehensive and expert procedure for review of an administrative decision" (as in the field of immigration law but not in the prison context).

Within their inherent jurisdiction of judicial review, the provincial superior courts can issue interlocutory injunctions in aid of administrative processes created by federal legislation: *Brotherhood of Maintenance Way Employees, Canadian Pacific System Federation v. Canadian Pacific Ltd.*, [1996] 2 SCR 495 (BC). Later in this chapter we examine the availability of interlocutory relief from a superior court where there is no underlying proceeding in the court that is asked to provide that relief.

A final context in which the superior courts may be involved (albeit indirectly or collaterally) in the review of federal administrative action is that of claims in damages against the federal Crown. To the extent that the 1990 amendments to the *Federal Courts Act* designate the Federal Court and the provincial courts as having concurrent jurisdiction over such claims, the provincial courts could conceivably have to rule on the validity of federal administrative action in a situation where a damages claim against the federal Crown is an element in the litigation. See, for example, *TeleZone Inc. v. Attorney General (Canada)* (2008), 94 OR (3d) 19, 2008 ONCA 892 (CanLII).

As Between the Federal Court and the Federal Court of Appeal

Under the original *Federal Courts Act*, the original jurisdiction of the Federal Court to review federal statutory decision-makers was split between the court's Trial Division and its Appeal Division (which in 2003 were reconstituted as the Federal Court and the Federal Court of Appeal). However, in 1990, a major change was made to the way in which the statute allocated jurisdiction between the Trial Division and the Appeal Division. Previously, the issue of which division of the court had jurisdiction depended on the interpretation of complex language in the statute (a matter that caused a mass of litigation). After 1990, jurisdiction was allocated simply by listing in s. 28(1) the tribunals that were subject to the initial jurisdiction of the Appeal Division, leaving all other decision-makers covered by the Act to the Trial Division (s. 28(3)). This method of allocating jurisdiction continues to apply in the case of the Federal Court and the Federal Court of Appeal.

The major practical impact of the reform in 1990 was to exclude first-level decision-makers in immigration and refugee matters, and subsequently the Immigration and Refugee Board, from the list of decision-makers that were allocated to the Appeal Division. Previously, the Appeal Division was, by virtue of a complex statutory formula, the principal court of original jurisdiction in such cases. The heavy caseload in immigration and refugee matters is now carried by the Federal Court.

While there may be debate about aspects of the list of authorities in s. 28(1) (such as the exclusion of human rights tribunals under the *Canadian Human Rights Act*) and generally about a bifurcated system of judicial review, the list approach at least eliminates the vexing problem of wasteful litigation on whether a proceeding should be as commenced in the Federal Court or the Federal Court of Appeal.

Incidentally, the arguments for the split in original judicial review jurisdiction are essentially that the tribunals on the list are among the more important federal agencies, making them more appropriately reviewed at first instance by the Federal Court of Appeal, and that the exercise of their mandate should not be delayed by the prospect of two levels of court before an application for judicial review reaches the Supreme Court of Canada. Is this a compelling justification?

There is a further reservation about this allocation of jurisdiction: it affects only the judicial review jurisdiction of the Federal Court and the Federal Court of Appeal. This has two consequences. First, to the extent that a claim for damages is made on the basis of the conduct of any of the bodies listed in s. 28(1) of the *Federal Courts Act*, the proceedings come within the original jurisdiction of either the Federal Court or the appropriate provincial court, not the Federal Court of Appeal (s. 17). Second, by virtue of ss. 18(5) and 28(2), the judicial review jurisdiction of the Federal Court and the Federal Court of Appeal is conditioned on the extent to which the decision under review is subject to a statutory appeal. In federal statutes, an express right of appeal is often authorized to the Federal Court or Federal Court of Appeal, the Supreme Court of Canada, the Court Martial Appeal Court, the Tax Court of Canada, the governor in council, or the Treasury Board. Where a statutory appeal right exists, it must be exercised, thus excluding the possibility of judicial review under the *Federal Courts Act*. Notably, statutory appeals may be created by subordinate as well as primary legislation, so long as the authorization in the subordinate legislation falls within a regulation or bylaw-making power conferred by an Act of Parliament: *Canadian Pacific Ltd. v. Matsqui Indian Band*, [1995] 1 SCR 3 (Can.). In the case of a statutory appeal, one must also account for restrictions on the availability of judicial review in the statute, such as a requirement that the court grant leave to appeal.

Claims for Damages in the Federal Court

Applications for judicial review in the Federal Court are commenced by way of application (s. 18.1). However, claims for damages against the Crown and federal statutory authorities are commenced by way of an action under s. 17 of the *Federal Courts Act*. This raises some difficulties. In particular, it seems to preclude the joining of proceedings for judicial review and damages in relation to an exercise of federal statutory powers. However, pursuant to s. 18.4(2), with respect to bodies that are subject to the original judicial review jurisdiction of the Federal Court (although strangely not the Federal Court of Appeal: s. 28(2)), the Federal Court "may, if it considers it appropriate, direct that an application for judicial review be treated and proceeded with as an action."

A logical candidate for such a direction by the Federal Court is the case where the applicant/ plaintiff is pursuing both judicial review and damages against the Crown. However, the Federal Court has declined to use s. 18.4(2) for this purpose: *Zubi v. Canada* (1991), 71 FTR 168 (FCTD). This appears to leave the person affected in the position of having to commence two separate proceedings. However, see *Hinton v. Canada (Minister of Citizenship and Immigration)* (2009), [2009] 1 FCR 476 (FCA), at para. 49, in which Sexton JA took a liberal approach to the conversion of an application into an action in order to permit a damages claim:

> I am not convinced that subsection 18.4(2) should be read narrowly so as to only apply to the procedural aspects of an action, such as discoveries, the admission of *viva voce* evidence, and the like. It is well recognized that the right to treat an application as if it were an action is to compensate for certain procedural inadequacies with the process underlying applications. In my mind, however, I think it may sometimes also be appropriate to consider the *remedial* inadequacies of an application for judicial review, as well. One problem with applications for judicial review is that a remedy for damages cannot be sought. In most applications for judicial review, this is not a major concern as the desired remedy will usually lie in the form of *mandamus*, *certiorari*, or a declaration. Where it is of concern, however, is when a totally separate action afterwards may be necessary in either Federal Court or a provincial court to advance a claim of damages: this is a potentially undesirable situation. [Emphasis in original.]

Notably, before the 1990 amendments to the *Federal Courts Act*, declarations had to be sought by way of action, thus allowing a combined action for both review and damages. (For a discussion of the general principles that govern s. 18.4(2), see *MacInnis v. Canada*, [1994] 2 FC 464 (CA).)

FORMS OF PERMANENT RELIEF

Statutory Appeals

The present chapter is primarily about remedies of judicial review. However, it should be recognized that the most common way to challenge administrative action is by the huge variety of statutory appeals that exist in individual statutes creating specific tribunals, agencies, and statutory powers. The scope of those appellate provisions varies greatly but, at their broadest, they authorize judicial reversal of the decision under attack on both questions of law and fact, sometimes after a complete rehearing of the matter in issue. As we have seen, such an intrusive review of an administrative decision is not a characteristic of common law judicial review or indeed of modern forms of statutory review.

To the extent that the empowering statute creates a right of appeal, these are viewed by the courts as the legislatively preferred mode of challenging a decision. In chapter 18 of this text, we cover in some detail the principles on which the courts evaluate the effectiveness of and necessity to resort to statutory rights of appeal rather than judicial review.

What should be emphasized in this context, however, is the importance of consulting the statute that created the statutory power the exercise of which has become a matter of concern. For one, the statute may provide for a more extensive mode of relief than allowed for under the principles of judicial review. Moreover, you may be expected to use that avenue of recourse even where its reach is the same as, or in some cases narrower than, that of judicial review; if the statutory appeal route will address the grounds on which you are seeking to challenge a decision, it should generally be used.

Judicial Review

Collateral Attack

The bulk of judicial review of administrative action takes place within the framework of direct attack—that is, in proceedings where the challenged administrative action or inaction is the direct focus of the pleadings and of the remedy sought. However, this is not always the case. As we saw in *Cooper v. Board of Works for Wandsworth District*, in chapter 3 of this text, collateral attack retains a limited role in judicial review. Recall that the validity of the Board of Works' proceedings in *Cooper* was relevant only in the context of a pleading by the board that its demolition of the structure was justified by a valid order and therefore was not an actionable trespass. The plaintiff countered that this justification could not be advanced because the board's order was tainted by a breach of the rules of natural justice. Put simply, the validity of the board's order was not the direct target of the proceedings. The validity of the order was raised indirectly as part of the board's defence to a tort action in trespass.

A similar analysis can be applied to cases where, in the context of a prosecution for violation of a bylaw or regulation, the defendant challenges the validity of the relevant statutory instrument: see, for example, *R v. Sharma*, [1993] 1 SCR 650 (Ont.) and *R v. Greenbaum*, [1993] 1 SCR 674 (Ont.). The Supreme Court has made it clear that collateral attack is not a matter of right but should be circumscribed by judicial discretion. See *R v. Consolidated Maybrun Mines Ltd.*, [1998] 1 SCR 706 (Ont.) and *R v. Al Klippert Ltd.*, [1998] 1 SCR 737 (Alta.).

Direct Attack

Until recently, the substantive scope of judicial review of administrative action was largely dictated by the rules on the availability of the various public law remedies. To the extent that many of those rules were arcane, complex, and, most significantly, had long ceased to have any justifiable policy basis, this situation did not serve the overall interests of governments or the public. In some contexts, the rules imported limitations into the law that could be used (mainly by government) to prevent courts ever reaching the substantive merits of a claim. In contrast, the "chilling" effect of making an application for one of the various forms of judicial review remedy meant that, in many contexts, those who were threatened by the prospect of administrative proceedings could delay or avoid submission to that process by launching an application for judicial review regardless of its likelihood of success.

Not surprisingly, this state of affairs created pressures for legislative and judicial reform of the law governing the scope and availability of the judicial review remedies. In particular, it created pressures to remove unnecessary technicalities and to expand the various forms of relief to enable courts to have more flexibility in fashioning relief that was appropriate to the circumstances of particular cases. Such was the variety of governmental decision making coming before courts that, for example, the inability of a judge on an application for relief in the nature of *certiorari* to do anything other than quash a decision or refuse the application for relief was a real impediment to administrative justice. The remedial instrument was simply too blunt.

Fortunately, steps were taken to eliminate impediments to an effective system of administrative law remedies. Indeed, while there is still work to be done—not all jurisdictions have undergone comprehensive reforms and there are still minor glitches in the remedial regimes of those where there has been comprehensive reform—we no longer cover all details of the traditional remedies or, for that matter, all of the various statutory reforms that took place in Canada over the past few decades. For the most part, the key remedial issues are now raised appropriately as part of the general law of standing and in the wide terrain of judicial discretion.

At the legislative level, the provisions of the Prince Edward Island *Judicial Review Act*, SPEI 1988, c. 35, typify the remedial reform initiatives taken to simplify judicial review and the availability of public law remedies. As with the BC and Ontario *Judicial Review Procedure Acts*, the *Alberta Rules of Court* (Parts 56 and 56.1), and the *Federal Courts Act*, s. 2 of the PEI *Judicial Review Act* creates a single application for judicial review, encompassing the existing remedies of judicial review and apparently replacing those remedies (although see, in the PEI context, the judgments in *National Farmers Union v. Prince Edward Island (Prince Edward Island Potato Marketing Council)* (1989), 56 DLR (4th) 753 (PEI SC); *CJA, Local 1388 v. Prince Edward Island (Labour Relations Board)* (1990), 81 Nfld. & PEIR 40 (PEI SC); and *Big John Holdings Ltd. v. Island Regulatory and Appeals Commission* (1993), 111 Nfld & PEIR 297, 18 Admin. LR (2d) 307 (PEI SC), asserting the continued existence of the prerogative writs).

Besides consolidating the process of applying for judicial review, the PEI Act provides in s. 3(1) that, while the applicant must set out the grounds on which relief is being sought, the application does not have to link specifically the relief in question to one or another of the former remedies. Section 4 (in the manner of the *Federal Courts Act*) in turn lays out a non-exclusive list of grounds on which relief may be sought. The Act also specifies the kinds of relief that the court may grant. According to s. 3(3):

> (3) Subject to this Act, a judge, on an application for judicial review, may by order
>
> (a) nullify an act of a tribunal not done pursuant to authority conferred by an enactment;
>
> (b) prohibit an act of a tribunal that would not be an act done pursuant to authority conferred by an enactment:
>
> (c) direct an act by a tribunal in accordance with authority conferred by an enactment if a duty to act is not performed;
>
> (d) declare a right of a person in respect to the exercise of authority conferred by an enactment on a tribunal;
>
> (e) refer a matter back to a tribunal for further consideration either generally or in accordance with specific findings of the judge.

(Notably, in the Alberta, BC, and Ontario procedures, perhaps out of an abundance of caution, the court's ability to make a declaration is reinforced by a provision to the effect that, in any case where a declaration is available, the court may instead set aside the decision under attack.)

In addition, s. 3(4) of the PEI Act provides for interim orders (including a stay of proceedings or an interim declaration) pending judicial review. On the other hand, s. 8(3) clarifies—probably codifying the common law position—that an application for judicial review does not automatically stay the proceedings or any act that is the subject of the application for judicial review.

These provisions of the Act are supported by a requirement that, on being served with an application for judicial review, the decision-maker must file with the court the record of the matter that is under challenge (s. 8(1)). For these purposes, the record is defined expansively in s. 1(g) to include:

> (i) a document by which the proceeding is commenced,
>
> (ii) a notice of a hearing in the proceeding,
>
> (iii) an intermediate order made by the tribunal,
>
> (iv) a document produced in evidence at a hearing before the tribunal, subject to any limitation expressly imposed by any other enactment on the extent to or the purpose for which a document may by used in evidence in a proceeding,
>
> (v) a transcript, if any, of the oral evidence given at a hearing, and
>
> (vi) the decision of the tribunal and any reasons given by it.

This provision, which has equivalents in the *Judicial Review Procedure Acts* of British Columbia and Ontario and the *Alberta Rules of Court*, arguably increased the scope of the record that had to be produced by a decision-maker at common law (in order to allow judicial review for errors of law on the face of the record review). At the very least, it resolved any doubts in that domain.

In large measure, the species of relief specified in this modern legislation do no more than codify the remedial outcomes of a successful application for the former remedies: *certiorari* would quash or nullify a decision; prohibition and the injunction would prohibit or enjoin action; *mandamus* would direct the performance of duties; and the declarations would declare rights as between the parties. Nonetheless, putting all of these modes of relief under one judicial review remedy meant that the difficulties in choosing the correct remedy were removed or minimized, provided that the Act's initial thresholds were crossed.

Second, the ability of the court to refer a matter back for reconsideration in accordance with specific findings of the court or "with directions" (as in the *Judicial Review Procedure Acts* of British Columbia and Ontario, the *Alberta Rules of Court*, and the *Federal Courts Act*) is a significant remedial addition to the judicial review powers of the court. Previously, an order in the nature of *mandamus* to compel the retaking of a decision, this time in accordance with law, was the only approximation to such a power and a more limited one at that.

Finally, the general availability of interim relief is a major improvement over the situation where interim relief was thought to be unavailable in support of an application for a prerogative remedy or by way of declaration, and where the only mode of interim relief was by an application for an interim injunction or stay of proceedings generally restricted to situations where the applicant was proceeding by way of action (rather than simplified application) and subject to all the restrictions and limitations of injunctive relief generally. Without doubt, the modern statutory reform of judicial review proceedings addressed many of these tortuous complexities.

Of course, such statutory reforms have not dealt with all remedial problems and uncertainties. For example, can the court engage in partial quashing or setting aside of a decision? Does the court have authority to vary a decision or an order rather than quash it? May the court postpone the operation of its remedial orders to avoid consequences that undermine the interests of one or more of the parties or the public generally?

Despite this, the courts have worked to find creative and sensible solutions to remedial dilemmas. In some measure, this sense of liberation was enhanced by the spur to remedial innovation and flexibility that was provided by the Charter. See, for example, *Dagenais v. Canadian Broadcasting Corp.*, [1994] 3 SCR 835 (Ont.), where the court held that *certiorari* was available not only to quash but also to vary a publication ban issued by a county court judge. The court found justification for this extension of the reach of *certiorari* in s. 24(1), the remedial provision of the Charter that confers the right on those with a Charter claim "to obtain such remedy as the court considers appropriate and just in the circumstances."

The notion of a court varying an order rather than setting it aside makes sense in the context of orders that infringe the Charter and that have been made by provincial court judges. After all, the Supreme Court of Canada has made it clear that statutory authorities have no claim to deference in relation to aspects of their decisions that involve the Charter. Also, provincial court judges who exercise authority in criminal law matters are part of the court-based system of which the Supreme Court of Canada is the apex. But to what extent, if at all, would the exercise of a power to vary rather than to quash a decision be appropriate in the context of a non-Charter challenge to the exercise of jurisdiction by a regulatory agency or tribunal?

Dagenais is significant to the extent that it affirms the principle that Charter challenges not only can be raised in regular judicial review proceedings but also should be raised within that framework, where feasible, rather than by reference to an independent species of relief created by s. 24(1). While this solves most problems in terms of the relationship between judicial review and s. 24(1), there is an issue in jurisdictions such as Alberta, British Columbia, Ontario, and Prince Edward Island, as well as federally, as to whether their statutory regimes of judicial review allow a person to seek a bare declaration that an administrative regime violates the Charter. In fact, this problem may arise beyond the Charter itself in all situations where a bare declaration of rights or of invalidity is sought, divorced from any decision.

For example, the right of the PEI Supreme Court under its *Judicial Review Act* to issue a declaration is tied in s. 2(3)(d) to the "exercise of authority conferred by an enactment on a tribunal." In Ontario, the Court of Appeal held in *Re Service Employees International Union, Local 204 and Broadway Manor Nursing Home* (1984), 13 DLR (4th) 220 (Ont. CA) that there was no room for a bare declaration, under the Ontario *Judicial Review Procedure Act*, that provisions in a regulatory statute infringed the *Canadian Charter of Rights and Freedoms*. Applied generally, this means that bare declarations of this kind must still be sought under those statutory provisions or rules of court that establish the general jurisdiction of the court to grant declaratory relief. In some jurisdictions, this may involve having to proceed by way of action rather than by a simplified application for judicial review. However, to the extent that the relevant rules of civil procedure permit the commencement of proceedings for a bare declaration by way of application, and allow the joinder of such an application with an application for judicial review of a related decision, there may not be a serious problem in practice where the applicant seeks both a declaration of unconstitutionality of a statute and review of a decision in the same proceeding: *Halpern v. Toronto (City Clerk)*, [2000] OJ No. 3213 (QL) (SCJ).

For other examples of judicial flexibility and creativity in fashioning appropriate remedies within the framework of the traditional remedies and their modern statutory equivalents, see *Sparvier v. Cowessess Indian Band No. 73* (1993), 13 Admin. LR (2d) 266 (FCTD) (postponing the quashing of a decision until the conduct of a statutory appeal was concluded) (for further elaboration, see chapter 18 of this text, The Discretion of the Court) and *Re Milstein and Ontario College of Pharmacy* (1978), 87 DLR (3d) 392 (Ont. CA) (severing and quashing the invalid part of a penalty imposed in professional disciplinary proceedings).

Two specific remedial problems should also be addressed before we conclude this section on permanent relief. The first concerns the impact on the continuing jurisdiction of a statutory authority over a matter when a quashing order has been made against it. Second, although it relates as much to the nature of the statutory power in issue and to questions of standing (both of which are dealt with elsewhere in this text), we identify some limitations on the availability of relief in the nature of *mandamus*.

Effects of Certiorari Relief

In some instances the award of relief in the nature of *certiorari* or prohibition (or a declaration or an injunction for that matter) will have the effect of leaving the authority under attack with no residual jurisdiction in the matter. For example, if a provincial labour relations board is prohibited from proceeding in a matter because the employment relationship in question comes within federal jurisdiction, the board has been excluded completely from that matter.

However, judicial review does not always undermine the whole authority of the decision-maker whose action is under challenge. Thus, the quashing of a certification on the basis of the impropriety of a pre-hearing vote in *Re Little Narrows Gypsum Co. Ltd. and Labour Relations Board (Nova Scotia)* (1977), 73 DLR (3d) 161 (NS SCAD) did not call into question the general jurisdiction of the board to consider the application of the bargaining unit for certification. Even so, when the board in that case purported to resume its consideration of the application, it was prohibited from doing so by the Supreme Court, which held (in an unreported decision in 1976 of the Trial Division of the Supreme Court of Nova Scotia) that the tribunal had exhausted its jurisdiction and could not resume it without an affirmative order in the nature of *mandamus* from the trial judge. On appeal, this was reversed by the Appeal Division: *Re Labour Relations Board (Nova Scotia) and Little Narrows Gypsum Co. Ltd.* (1977), 82 DLR (3d) 693, which held that the effect of the award of *certiorari* was to wipe out the certification order and the pre-hearing vote on which it was based, leaving the application for certification still not dealt with. The board then had a duty to proceed and *mandamus*-type relief was necessary only if the board refused to act, not when it wanted to proceed.

Indeed, the court held that, in such cases, the board did not have to start over but rather could resume at the point where the error was made. This was a sensible approach.

In *Gill v. Canada (Minister of Employment & Immigration)* (1987), 27 Admin. LR 257 (FCA), an Immigration Appeal Board decision was set aside and the matter was referred back to the board. The board then decided that it did not have authority to reopen a Convention refugee redetermination hearing that was tainted by breaches of the rules of natural justice, of s. 2(e) of the *Canadian Bill of Rights*, and of s. 7 of the *Canadian Charter of Rights and Freedoms*. The Federal Court of Appeal held that, even absent a specific statutory authority to reopen or rehear a case, a tribunal in such circumstances had the implied authority to do so and rectify such wrongs. In contrast, de Weerdt J of the Northwest Territories Supreme Court in *841638 NWT Ltd. v. Labour Standards Officer*, [1998] NWTR 239 (SC), relied on the absence of a power to rehear in refusing to order the rehearing of a labour standards board decision that was tainted by a breach of the rules of natural justice. The unfortunate effect, considering the purpose of the statutory scheme, was to preclude the adjudication of the employees' claims for wages where the initial failure to afford natural justice to their alleged employer was no fault of theirs.

Limits of Mandamus Relief

In *Karavos v. City of Toronto*, [1948] 3 DLR 294 (Ont. CA), at 297, Laidlaw JA cited High's *Extra-Ordinary Legal Remedies*, 3rd ed. (1896) on the remedy of *mandamus*:

> [*Mandamus*] is appropriate to overcome the inaction or misconduct of persons charged with the performance of duties of a public nature.
>
> Before the remedy can be given, the applicant for it must show:
>
> (1) "a clear, legal right to have the thing sought by it done, and done in the manner and by the person sought to be coerced."
>
> (2) "The duty whose performance it is sought to coerce by *mandamus* must be actually due and incumbent upon the officer at the time of seeking the relief, and the writ will not lie to compel the doing of an act which he is not yet under obligation to perform."
>
> (3) That duty must be purely ministerial in nature, "plainly incumbent upon an officer by operation of law or by virtue of his office, and concerning which he possesses no discretionary powers."
>
> (4) There must be a demand and refusal to perform the act which it is sought to coerce by legal remedy.

Laidlaw JA indicated that he was not providing a comprehensive list of the jurisdictional prerequisites for the issue of *mandamus*. Even so, the statement above reflects the principal points that must be demonstrated before the remedy of *mandamus* will be granted. (See also the discussion of *mandamus* in *Apotex Inc. v. Canada (Attorney General)*, [1994] 1 FC 742 (CA), *per* Robertson JA; aff'd. [1994] 3 SCR 1100 (Can.).) Some of the language, however, calls for further explanation, particularly the terms "ministerial," "public," and "clear, legal right."

If by "ministerial" Laidlaw JA intended to state that *mandamus* was only available with respect to administrative, as opposed to judicial or *quasi*-judicial functions, then his view is out of line with present authority. For example, it is common for a court to use *mandamus* in order to compel the observance of the rules of natural justice.

The use of the word "public" raises an issue canvassed above in relation to *certiorari* and prohibition, especially in our consideration of the *Halifax-Dartmouth Real Estate Board* case. As seen there, not all power created by statute is "public." However, it may be that, for the purposes of *mandamus*, there are "public" duties that exist other than by virtue of statute or an exercise of the royal prerogative. To illustrate, in *Re Morris and Morris* (1973), 36 DLR (3d) 447 (Man. QB), Wilson J issued *mandamus* to compel the defendant to commence proceedings before a Jewish religious court for the recognition of his civil divorce. While this judgment was reversed (1973), 42 DLR (3d) 550 (Man. CA), the grounds for reversal did not disavow the use of *mandamus* to compel non-statutory public duties.

Laidlaw JA described the prerequisites for *mandamus* in terms of the existence of "a clear, legal right" to performance of the duty on the part of the applicant. This was an overstatement in current practice so far as it emphasizes that the duty must be owed to the applicant personally rather than as a member of a wider class. The liberalization of standing requirements discussed in chapter 17 of this text has also liberalized this aspect of the remedy of *mandamus*.

That said, not all statutory provisions that are described in terms of "duties" give rise to a claim for enforcement by members of the public. Sometimes the duties will be stated at a level of generality that makes clear that the provision is for the guidance of the statutory authority in question and not intended to confer rights on members of the public. Consider, for example, this section from the former Ontario *Labour-Management Arbitration Commission Act*, RSO 1970, c. 320. Which, if any, of the duties specified in this section might be the subject of *mandamus* proceedings?

> 5. The duties and functions of the Commission are to,
>
> (a) maintain for the use of parties to an arbitration a register of approved arbitrators;
>
> (b) assist arbitrators by making the administrative arrangements required for the conduct of arbitrations;
>
> (c) sponsor training programs for arbitrators;
>
> (d) sponsor the publication and distribution of information in respect of arbitration process and awards; and
>
> (e) sponsor research in respect of arbitration processes and awards.

An interesting example is *Victoria University of Wellington Students' Association Inc. v. Shearer (Government Printer)*, [1973] 2 NZLR 21 (SC). Here the association, representing law students, attempted through *mandamus* to compel the respondent to print a consolidated version of the New Zealand Code of Civil Procedure. The basis for this claim was a statutory provision requiring all Acts to "be procurable by purchase at the offices of the Government Printer." Wild CJ concluded that this was a duty of the Crown and thus was not compellable by *mandamus*. This certainly makes sense if viewed from the perspective of a general organizational duty of the Government Printing Office that is not intended to confer rights on the public in general or law students in particular.

In contrast to the New Zealand case is the judgment of de Weerdt J of the Northwest Territories Supreme Court in *Union of Northern Workers v. Jewell* (1991), 49 Admin. LR 280 (NWT SC). This case involved an application for an order in the nature of *mandamus* compelling the appointment by a minister of the members of an occupational health and safety board, a body that was assigned the statutory responsibility to advise the minister on safety in mines. The court held that the applicant, a union representative, had standing to seek such relief and that the appointment of the members was statutorily mandated, notwithstanding the fact that the Act called for a process to be devised for the appointment of certain members of the board. Although such a process had not been set up (in part because of an ongoing standoff between the union and the government), the court held that relief in the nature of *mandamus* was available. De Weerdt J also distinguished *Karavos* by holding that a valid formal demand was not a necessary prelude to the granting of relief in a situation that was apparent for a number of years and where it was clear to the minister that the appointment of the board was sought.

Mandamus is sometimes sought together with *certiorari*. The remedy of *certiorari* is sought to quash a decision already taken; *mandamus* is sought to compel that the decision be retaken in accordance with the law. However, unless the case involves non-jurisdictional error of law or perhaps breach of procedural fairness, the use of *certiorari* is probably redundant in such cases. *Mandamus* is theoretically available alone because the person who brings the complaint alleges that the administrative body has a duty to take a decision according to the law and that this duty remains unfulfilled, notwithstanding an (unlawful) attempt by the body to take the decision. Therefore, the decision already taken is a nullity and does not need to be quashed by way of *certiorari*.

INTERIM AND INTERLOCUTORY RELIEF AND STAYS OF PROCEEDINGS

Introduction

This section would not be necessary if the filing and service of an application for judicial review acted as a stay on further proceedings (including execution of a decision already taken by an administrative actor) in the matter in contention. Indeed, there is authority that the service of an application for *certiorari* automatically stays a tribunal's proceedings until the application has been determined: *UFCW, Local 1252 v. Prince Edward Island (Labour Relations Board)* (1987), 67 Nfld. & PEIR 148 (PEI SC).

However, in judicial review proceedings, an application for judicial review generally does not have the effect of staying proceedings in the underlying decision-making process. In *Re Cedarvale Tree Services Ltd. and Labourers' International Union* (1972), 22 DLR (3d) 40 (Ont. CA) (see also *Prassad v. Canada (Minister of Employment and Immigration)*, [1989] 1 SCR 560, at 568-69), the Ontario Court of Appeal had held that a tribunal was not obliged to halt its proceedings after being served with an application for *certiorari* and prohibition. According to Arnup JA in *Cedarvale Trade Services* (at 49-50), halting the proceedings was a matter of courtesy and common sense for the statutory authority rather than a legal obligation. Thus, in *Communications, Energy and Paperworkers Union of Canada v. Native Child and Family Support Services of Toronto* (2009), 2009 CanLII 9047 (ON LRB), the Ontario Labour Relations Board determined for itself whether to suspend its proceedings while a judicial review was pending:

[10] The employer asserts it is improper for the Board to determine this application while the trade union is pursuing its Federal application through the appeals process. In its view, it is apparent that the union does not agree that the Board has jurisdiction over the matter and ought not to be permitted to essentially be certified as a fall back position if its appeal to Supreme Court fails.

[11] I am satisfied that the Board has the authority to defer the determination of this application pending the resolution of the appeal of the Federal Court's decision. As the Court of Appeal stated in *Cedarvale Tree Services Ltd. and Labourers' International Union of North America*, [1971] 3 OR 832 [para. 25]:

> It is clear to me that under the Labour Relations Act the Board is master of its own house not only as to all questions of fact and law falling within the ambit of the jurisdiction conferred upon it by the Act, but with respect to all questions of procedure when acting within that jurisdiction. In my view, the only rule which should be stated by the Court (if it be a rule at all) is that the Board should, when its jurisdiction is questioned, adopt such procedure as appears to it to be just and convenient in the particular circumstances of the case before it. While it may be convenient, if a motion for certiorari is later brought, to have a record from the Board in which the factual background to the issue of jurisdiction is fully explored this is not a necessary prerequisite to the exercise of the jurisdiction of the Court. An applicant is entitled to put before the Court in any way he chooses the facts necessary to determine the question of jurisdiction.

[12] The question therefore in this case is: should the Board exercise its discretion to hold this application in abeyance? This is the kind of issue the Board frequently considers when its own decisions are under review. These decisions disclose that it is the Board's general practice not to stay its own proceedings until judicial proceedings are complete, although there may be exceptions (for example, perhaps if the judicial process is to commence immediately). However, it is notable that in most of the circumstances where the Board has determined this issue it is the responding party which has commenced the judicial proceedings. It is unusual for an applicant to make an application for certification while at the same time challenging, in effect, the jurisdiction of the Board to entertain the application.

[13] That being said, the Board is mindful that during the lengthy time that the squabbling between the parties about which Board will certify this employer has been going on (there being no doubt that it will be certified), the employees, who clearly wish to be represented, have been left in limbo. To require them to wait an additional and indefinite period of time, which may substantial, is not desirable.

[14] The Board is also mindful of the fact that as it stands, it has the jurisdiction to deal with this application. The Federal Court of Appeal has made that clear. There also appears to be no policy or practical reason not to certify. The CIRB [Canada Industrial Relations Board] have already issued a certificate. That has been overturned by the Federal Court of Appeal. That decision will either be confirmed by the Supreme Court or be overturned. In either case, any bargaining done by the parties will not have gone to waste.

[15] Accordingly, we find it appropriate to certify the applicant pursuant to section 9(2) of the Act.

Section 8(3) of the PEI *Judicial Review Act*, SPEI 1988, c. 35, provides explicitly that the launching of an application for judicial review under that Act does not automatically stay further proceedings or acts whose validity depends on the decision that is being challenged. While there is no equivalent provision in the BC and Ontario *Judicial Review Procedure Acts*, the Alberta Rules, or the *Federal Courts Act*, the provisions that authorize interim relief in those instruments could be interpreted as an implicit recognition of the same position. Also, in the Ontario *Statutory Powers Procedure Act*, s. 25(1) provides that the launching of an appeal stays the implementation of the decision under appeal, absent a statutory provision to the contrary or an order from the appellate body. However, s. 25(2) of the SPPA clarifies that an application for judicial review does not qualify as an appeal for these purposes.

Yet, the absence of any capacity on the part of the courts to provide interim relief in support of an application for judicial review would appear to be inappropriate in some situations. Think of the consequences of a court being unable to make an order to prevent the deportation of a Convention refugee claimant pending determination of a claim that the rejection of her claim violated procedural fairness or the *Charter of Rights and Freedoms*.

As we saw above, in the modern judicial review regimes, express provision is made for the award of interim relief pending the disposition of an application for judicial review. These provisions overcome an apparent limitation of the prerogative remedies: interim relief was not available as an adjunct to such relief (obliging those who needed interim relief to proceed by way of an action for an injunction).

In general, the availability of interim relief to halt the administrative process—whether the relief takes the form of a stay of proceedings, an interlocutory injunction, or an order under the relevant legislation or rules on judicial review procedure—is subject to the same principles that govern the availability of interim injunctions in the private domain. A key consideration in the balancing of the various interests involved is the public interest, however, in the efficient and timely exercise of a statutory power. The importance of this consideration distinguishes these judicial review cases from most situations in which interlocutory relief is sought in private litigation. Moreover, in many cases, Charter interests are at stake, adding a countervailing consideration in the exercise of the courts' discretion over the availability of such relief. In the following material, we examine these elements of interlocutory relief in public law litigation.

There is another potential use of interlocutory relief in the administrative process. While the bulk of the litigation is about attempts to prevent the administrative process from proceeding pending the disposition of an application for judicial review, it is possible to seek interlocutory relief *in aid of* the administrative process—that is, to prevent actions being taken by those who are subject to the administrative process pending the conclusion of a hearing or an investigation. This raises the controversial issue of the availability of interlocutory relief in aid of the proceedings of bodies other than a court. We examine this question in the second part of this section.

Stays of the Administrative Process

Manitoba (Attorney General) v. Metropolitan Stores (MTS) Ltd.
[1987] 1 SCR 110 (Man.)

[A union applied to the Manitoba Labour Relations Board for the imposition of a first contract. In reply, the employer sought a declaration that the provisions of the Manitoba *Labour Relations Act* authorizing such applications violated the *Canadian Charter of Rights and Freedoms*. In the proceedings, the employer sought a stay of further action by the board until the court disposed of the Charter challenge. After Krindle J refused the stay ((1985), 36 Man. R (2d) 152), the board indicated its intention to impose a first contract if one was not negotiated by a designated date. The Manitoba Court of Appeal allowed an appeal from Krindle J's judgment ((1985), 37 Man. R (2d) 181). The attorney general then appealed to the Supreme Court of Canada.]

The judgment of a court consisting of Beetz, McIntyre, Lamer, Le Dain, and La Forest JJ was delivered by BEETZ J:

[Beetz J summarized the facts and the judgments below before dealing with an argument that there should be a presumption of validity, for the purposes of interlocutory relief, where a statutory regime is challenged for non-compliance with the *Canadian Charter of Rights and Freedoms*. This argument was rejected. If it were accepted, then it would be open to rebuttal, which would be inappropriate in interlocutory proceedings because, contrary to the intent of such proceedings, it would lead to lengthier hearings. The court noted also that the recognition of such a presumption was undesirable given the "innovative and evolutive character of" the Charter. Beetz J then continued.]

IV The Principles Which Govern the Exercise of the Discretionary Power To Order a Stay of Proceedings Pending the Constitutional Challenge of a Legislative Provision

The second question in issue involves a study of the principles which govern the granting of a stay of proceedings while the constitutionality of a legislative provision is challenged in court by the plaintiff.

It should be observed that none of the parties has disputed the existence of the discretionary power to order a stay in such a case and, in my view, the parties were right in conceding that the trial judge had jurisdiction to order a stay: see *Attorney General of Canada v. Law Society of British Columbia* [1982] 2 SCR 307 (BC) at 330.

(1) The Usual Conditions for the Granting of a Stay

Prior to the *Supreme Court of Judicature Act, 1873*, 36 & 37 Vict., c. 66, no distinction between injunctions restraining proceedings and other sorts of injunctions was drawn in English law (*Halsbury's Laws of England*, vol. 24, 4th ed., at 577). The Parliament of Westminster then enacted the Act referred to above, which in the main has been adopted by all of the provinces of Canada except Quebec where the distinction between equity and law is unknown. The distinction the English *Judicature Act* created between a stay of proceedings and an injunction was, however, essentially procedural. ...

A stay of proceedings and an interlocutory injunction are remedies of the same nature. In the absence of a different test prescribed by statute, they have sufficient characteristics in common to be governed by the same rules and the courts have rightly tended to apply to the granting of interlocutory stays the principles which they follow with respect to interlocutory injunctions: ... .

The case law is abundant as well as relatively fluid with regard to the tests developed by the courts in order to help better delineate the situations in which it is just and equitable to grant an interlocutory injunction. Reviewing it is the function of doctrinal analysis rather than that of judicial decision-making and I simply propose to give a bare outline of the three main tests currently applied.

The first test is a preliminary and tentative assessment of the merits of the case, but there is more than one way to describe this first test. The traditional way consists in asking whether the litigant who seeks the interlocutory injunction can make out a *prima facie* case. The injunction will be refused unless he can: *Chesapeake and Ohio Railway Co. v. Ball*, [1953] OR 843 (HC), *per* McRuer CJHC at 854-55. The House of Lords has somewhat relaxed this first test in *American Cyanamid Co. v. Ethicon Ltd.*, [1975] 1 All ER 504 (Eng. HL), where it held that all that was necessary to meet this test was to satisfy the Court that there was a serious question to be tried as opposed to a frivolous or vexatious claim. ...

In the case at bar, it is neither necessary nor advisable to choose, for all purposes, between the traditional formulation and the *American Cyanamid* description of the first test: the British case law illustrates that the formulation of a rigid test for all types of cases, without considering their nature, is not to be favoured. ... In my view, however, the *American Cyanamid* "serious question" formulation is sufficient in a constitutional case where, as indicated below in these reasons, the public interest is taken into consideration in the balance of convenience. But I refrain from expressing any view with respect to the sufficiency or adequacy of this formulation in any other type of case.

The second test consists in deciding whether the litigant who seeks the interlocutory injunction would, unless the injunction is granted, suffer irreparable harm, that is harm not susceptible or difficult to be compensated in damages. Some judges consider at the same time the situation of the other party to the litigation and ask themselves whether the granting of the interlocutory injunction would cause irreparable harm to this other party if the main action fails. Other judges take the view that this last aspect forms part of the balance of convenience.

The third test, called the balance of convenience and which ought perhaps to be called more appropriately the balance of inconvenience, is a determination of which of the two parties will suffer the greater harm from the granting or refusal of an interlocutory injunction, pending a decision on the merits.

I now propose to consider the particular application of the test of the balance of convenience in a case where the constitutional validity of a legislative provision is challenged. As Lord Diplock said in *American Cyanamid, supra*, at 511:

> ... [T]here may be many other special factors to be taken into consideration in the particular circumstances of individual cases.

It will be seen in what follows that the consequences for the public as well as for the parties, of granting a stay in a constitutional case, do constitute "special factors" to be taken into consideration.

(2) The Balance of Convenience and the Public Interest

A review of the case law indicates that, when the constitutional validity of a legislative provision is challenged, the courts consider that they ought not to be restricted to the application of traditional criteria which govern the granting or refusal of interlocutory injunctive relief in ordinary private or civil law cases. Unless the public interest is also taken into consideration in evaluating the balance of convenience, they very often express their disinclination to grant injunctive relief before constitutional invalidity has been finally decided on the merits.

The reasons for this disinclination become readily understandable when one contrasts the uncertainty in which a court finds itself with respect to the merits at the interlocutory stage, with the sometimes far-reaching albeit temporary practical consequences of a stay of proceedings, not only for the parties to the litigation but also for the public at large.

(i) Difficulty or Impossibility To Decide the Merits at the Interlocutory Stage

The limited role of a court at the interlocutory stage was well described by Lord Diplock in the *American Cyanamid* case, *supra*, at 510:

> It is no part of the court's function at this stage of the litigation to try to resolve conflicts of evidence on affidavit as to facts on which the claims of either party may ultimately depend nor to decide difficult questions of law which call for detailed argument and mature considerations. These are matters to be dealt with at the trial.

The *American Cyanamid* case was a complicated civil case but Lord Diplock's *dictum*, just quoted, should *a fortiori* be followed for several reasons in a Charter case and in other constitutional cases when the validity of a law is challenged.

First, the extent and exact meaning of the rights guaranteed by the Charter are often far from clear and the interlocutory procedure rarely enables a motion judge to ascertain these crucial questions. Constitutional adjudication is particularly unsuited to the expeditious and informal proceedings of a weekly court where there are little or no pleadings and submissions in writing, and where the Attorney General of Canada or of the Province may not yet have been notified as is usually required by law. ...

Still, in Charter cases such as those which may arise under s. 23 relating to Minority Language Educational Rights, the factual situation as well as the law may be so uncertain at the interlocutory stage as to prevent the court from forming even a tentative opinion on the case of the plaintiff; *Marchand v. Simcoe County Board of Education* (1984) 10 CRR 169 (Ont. HC) at 174.

Furthermore, in many Charter cases such as the case at bar, some party may find it necessary or prudent to adduce evidence tending to establish that the impugned provision, although *prima facie* in violation of a guaranteed right or freedom, can be saved under s. 1 of the Charter. But evidence adduced pursuant to s. 1 of the Charter essentially addresses the merits of the case. ... [Beetz J's discussion of the earlier decision in *Gould v. Attorney General of Canada*, [1984] 2 SCR 124 (Can.); aff'g. [1984] 1 FC 1133 (CA), which set aside [1984] 1 FC 1119 (TD), has been omitted.]

[At the interlocutory stage of a proceeding, a judicial approach based on] cautious restraint respects the right of both parties to a full trial. … Also, it is consistent with the fact that, in some cases, the impugned provision will not be found to violate a right or freedom protected by the Charter after all and thus will not need to be saved under s. 1. …

In addition, to think that the question of constitutional validity can be determined at the interlocutory stage is to ignore the many hazards of litigation, constitutional or otherwise. A plaintiff may fail for lack of standing, lack of adequate proof, procedural or other defect. …

However, the principle I am discussing is not absolute. There may be rare cases where the question of constitutionality will present itself as a simple question of law alone which can be finally settled by a motion judge. A theoretical example which comes to mind is one where Parliament or a legislature would purport to pass a law imposing the beliefs of a state religion. Such a law would violate s. 2(a) of the Canadian *Charter of Rights and Freedoms*, could not possibly be saved under s. 1 of the Charter and might perhaps be struck down right away; see *Attorney General of Quebec v. Quebec Association of Protestant School Boards* [1984] 2 SCR 66 (Que.) at 88. It is trite to say that these cases are exceptional.

Most of the difficulties encountered by a trial judge at the interlocutory stage, which are raised above, apply not only in Charter cases but also in other constitutional challenges of a law. I therefore fully agree with what Professor R.J. Sharpe wrote in *Injunctions and Specific Performance*, at 177, in particular with respect to constitutional cases that "the courts have sensibly paid heed to the fact that at the interlocutory stage they cannot fully explore the merits of the plaintiff's case." At this stage, even in cases where the plaintiff has a serious question to be tried or even a *prima facie* case, the court is generally much too uncertain as to the facts and the law to be in a position to decide the merits.

(ii) The Consequences of Granting a Stay in Constitutional Cases

Keeping in mind the state of uncertainty above referred to, I turn to the consequences that will certainly or probably follow the granting of a stay of proceedings. As previously said, I will not restrict myself to Charter instances.

· · ·

Although constitutional cases are often the result of a *lis* between private litigants, they sometimes involve some public authority interposed between the litigants, such as the Board in the case at bar. In other constitutional cases, the controversy or the *lis*, if it can be called a *lis*, will arise directly between a private litigant and the State represented by some public authority. …

In both sorts of cases, the granting of a stay requested by the private litigants or by one of them is usually aimed at the public authority, law enforcement agency, administrative board, public official or minister responsible for the implementation or administration of the impugned legislation and generally works in one of two ways. Either the law enforcement agency is enjoined from enforcing the impugned provisions in all respects until the question of their validity has been finally determined, or the law enforcement agency is enjoined from enforcing the impugned provisions with respect to the specific litigant or litigants who request the granting of a stay. In the first branch of the alternative, the operation of the impugned provisions is temporarily suspended for all practical purposes. Instances of this type can perhaps be referred to as suspension cases. In the second branch of the alternative, the litigant who is granted a stay is in fact exempted from the impugned legislation which, in the meanwhile, continues to operate with respect to others. Instances of this other type, I will call exemption cases.

Whether or not they are ultimately held to be constitutional, the laws which litigants seek to suspend or from which they seek to be exempted by way of interlocutory injunctive relief have been enacted by democratically-elected legislatures and are generally passed for the common good, for instance: the providing and financing of public services such as educational services, or of public utilities such as electricity, the protection of public health, natural resources and the environment, the repression of what is considered to be criminal activity, the controlling of economic activity such as the containing of inflation, the regulation of labour relations, *etc.* It seems axiomatic that the granting of interlocutory injunctive relief in most suspension cases and, up to a point, as will be seen later, in quite a few exemption cases, is susceptible temporarily to frustrate the pursuit of the common good.

While respect for the Constitution must remain paramount, the question then arises whether it is equitable and just to deprive the public, or important sectors thereof, from the protection and advantages of impugned legislation, the invalidity of which is merely uncertain, unless the public interest is taken into consideration in the balance of convenience and is given the weight it deserves. As could be expected, the courts have generally answered this question in the negative. In looking at the balance of convenience, they have found it necessary to rise above the interests of private litigants up to the level of the public interest, and, in cases involving interlocutory injunctions directed at statutory authorities, they have correctly held it is erroneous to deal with these authorities as if they have any interest distinct from that of the public to which they owe the duties imposed upon them by statute.

[Beetz J here discussed a number of earlier decisions.]

(iii) Conclusion

It has been seen from what precedes that suspension cases and exemption cases are governed by the same basic rule according to which, in constitutional litigation, an interlocutory stay of proceedings ought not be granted unless the public interest is taken into consideration in the balance of convenience and weighted together with the interest of private litigants.

The reason why exemption cases are assimilated to suspension cases is the precedential value and exemplary effect of exemption cases. Depending on the nature of the cases, to grant an exemption in the form of a stay to one litigant is often to make it difficult to refuse the same remedy to other litigants who find themselves in essentially the same situation, and to risk provoking a cascade of stays and exemptions, the sum of which make them tantamount to a suspension case. ...

In short, I conclude that in a case where the authority of a law enforcement agency is constitutionally challenged, no interlocutory injunction or stay should issue to restrain that authority from performing its duties to the public unless, in the balance of convenience, the public interest is taken into consideration and given the weight it should carry. Such is the rule where the case against the authority of the law enforcement agency is serious, for if it were not, the question of granting interlocutory relief should not even arise. But that is the rule also even where there is a *prima facie* case against the enforcement agency, such as one which would require the coming into play of s. 1 of the Canadian *Charter of Rights and Freedoms.*

I should point out that I would have reached the same conclusion had s. 24 of the Charter been relied upon by counsel. Assuming for the purpose of the discussion that this provision applies to interlocutory relief in the nature of the one sought in this case, I would still hold that the public interest must be weighed as part of the balance of convenience: s. 24 of the Charter clearly indicates that the remedy sought can be refused if it is not considered by the court to be "appropriate and just in the circumstances."

On the whole, I thus find myself in agreement with the following excerpt from Sharpe, *op. cit.,* at 176-77:

> Indeed, in many situations, problems will arise if no account is taken of the general public interest where interlocutory relief is sought. In assessing the risk of harm to the defendant from an interlocutory injunction which might later be dissolved at trial, the courts may be expected to be conscious of the public interest. Too ready availability of interlocutory relief against government and its agencies could disrupt the orderly functioning of government.

I would finally add that in cases where an interlocutory injunction issues in accordance with the above-stated principles, the parties should generally be required to abide by the dates of a preferential calendar so as to avoid undue delay and reduce to the minimum the period during which a possibly valid law is deprived of its effect in whole or in part … .

V Review of the Judgments of the Courts Below

Finally, it is now appropriate to review the judgments of the courts below in light of the principles set out above.

The main legislative provision under attack is s. 75.1 of the *Labour Relations Act* of Manitoba, enacted in SM 1984-85, c. 21, s. 37, which enables the Board to settle the provisions of a first collective agreement. It is alleged by the employer that these provisions in question violate ss. 2(b), (d) and 7 of the *Canadian Charter of Rights and Freedoms* relating respectively to freedom of expression, freedom of association, liberty and security of the person. The Manitoba Court of Appeal has taken the view that the employer raises "a serious challenge" to the constitutional validity of the impugned provision and all the parties have conceded that the constitutional challenge is indeed a serious one. The test of a "serious question" applicable in a constitutional challenge of a law has therefore been met.

The "irreparable harm" test also clearly appears to have been satisfied.

As I read her reasons, Krindle J, at 153, implicitly accepted the employer's argument that the imposition of a first contract was susceptible to prejudice its position:

It may give to the union a semblance of bargaining strength which the union does not in fact possess. It may permit the union to benefit from a contract which, left to its own devices, it could not have successfully negotiated. That, however, was the object of the legislation.

It is difficult to imagine how the employer can be compensated satisfactorily in damages, for instance for the imposition of possibly higher wages or of better conditions of work, if it is later to be held that the imposed collective agreement is a constitutional nullity.

The same observation should be made with respect to the position of the union; as I understand the findings of Krindle J, the very existence of the unit was compromised without the imposition of a first collective agreement.

Krindle J's findings of facts have not been questioned by the Court of Appeal and it is not for this Court to review these findings.

Krindle J then considered the balance of convenience and I refer in this respect to the above-quoted parts of her reasons for judgment. I am of the view that she applied the correct principles. More particularly, at 154, she looked at the public interest and at the inhibitory impact of a stay of proceedings upon the Board, in addition to its effect upon the employer and the union:

> It would seem to me that the granting of a stay in this case would invite the granting of stays in most other cases of applications for first agreements or applications involving the mandatory inclusion of sections within negotiated agreements. In effect, for a two or three year period, prior to any finding of invalidity of those sections, their operation would be suspended, suspended in circumstances where the *status quo* cannot, practically speaking, be maintained.
>
> In my opinion, in both the circumstances of this particular case and more generally, the balance of convenience favours proceeding as though the sections were valid unless and until the contrary is found.

While this is an exemption case, not a suspension case, and each case, including *a fortiori* an exemption case, turns on its own particular facts, yet, the inconvenience suffered by the parties is likely to be quite similar in most cases involving the imposition of a first collective agreement. Accordingly, the motion judge was not only entitled to but required to weigh the precedential value and exemplary effect of granting a stay of proceedings before the Board. I have not been persuaded that she committed reversible error in concluding that "the granting of a stay in this case would invite the granting of stays in most other cases of applications for first agreements."

[Beetz J then held that the Manitoba Court of Appeal erred in the principles that it adopted with respect to an appeal from a trial judge's exercise of judicial discretion. The Court of Appeal overreached in its perception of the scope for intervention in such cases. It also erred in the substantive principles that were applicable to the grant of stays in constitutional litigation. On this point, Beetz J summarized the court's conclusions as follows:]

The Court of Appeal did not exercise its fresh discretion in accordance with the above-stated principles. It did not itself proceed to consider the balance of convenience nor did it consider the public interest as well as the interest of the parties. It only urged the parties to be expeditious. But urging or even ordering the parties to be expeditious does not dispense from weighing the public interest in the balance of convenience. It simply attenuates the unfavourable consequences of a stay for the public where those consequences are limited.

The judgment of the Court of Appeal could be construed as meaning that an interlocutory stay of proceedings may be granted as a matter of course whenever a serious argument is invoked against the validity of legislation or, at least, whenever a *prima facie* case of violation of the *Canadian Charter of Rights and Freedoms* will normally trigger a recourse to the saving effect of s. 1 of the Charter. If this is what the Court of Appeal meant, it was clearly in error ... .

VI Conclusions

I would allow the appeal and set aside the stay of proceedings ordered by the Manitoba Court of Appeal.

Appeal allowed.

In *RJR-MacDonald Ltd. v. Canada (Attorney General)*, [1994] 1 SCR 311 (Que.), the Supreme Court of Canada, in a judgment by Cory and Sopinka JJ, affirmed the approach adopted by Beetz J in *Metropolitan Stores*. In doing so, the court elaborated on a number of points in that judgment.

First, the court made it clear that *American Cyanamid*, [1975] AC 396 (Eng. HL), provided the general test for the availability of interlocutory relief in Canada, be it in the private or the public law domain:

B. The Strength of the Plaintiff's Case

Prior to the decision of the House of Lords in *American Cyanamid Co. v. Ethicon Ltd.* [1975] AC 396 (Eng. HL), an applicant for interlocutory relief was required to demonstrate a "strong *prima facie* case" on the merits in order to satisfy the first test. In *American Cyanamid*, however, Lord Diplock stated that an applicant need no longer demonstrate a strong *prima facie* case. Rather it would suffice if he or she could satisfy the court that "the claim is not frivolous or vexatious; in other words, that there is a serious question to be tried." The *American Cyanamid* standard is now generally accepted by the Canadian courts, subject to the occasional reversion to a stricter standard. ...

In *Metropolitan Stores*, Beetz J advanced several reasons why the *American Cyanamid* test rather than any more stringent review of the merits is appropriate in Charter cases. These included the difficulties involved in deciding complex factual and legal issues based upon the limited evidence available in an interlocutory proceeding, the impracticality of undertaking a s. 1 analysis at that stage, and the risk that a tentative determination on the merits would be made in the absence of complete pleadings or prior to the notification of any Attorneys General.

The court also refined what "irreparable harm" meant in a public law setting:

The assessment of irreparable harm in interlocutory applications involving Charter rights is a task which will often be more difficult than a comparable assessment in a private law application. One reason for this is that the notion of irreparable harm is closely tied to the remedy of damages, but damages are not the primary remedy in Charter cases.

This Court has on several occasions accepted the principle that damages may be awarded for a breach of Charter rights. ... However, no body of jurisprudence has yet developed in respect of the principles which might govern the award of damages under s. 24(1) of the Charter. In light of the uncertain state of the law regarding the award of damages for a Charter breach, it will in most cases be impossible for a judge on an interlocutory application to determine whether adequate compensation could ever be obtained at trial. Therefore, until the law in this area has developed further, it is appropriate to assume that the financial damage which will be suffered by an applicant following a refusal of relief, even though capable of quantification, constitutes irreparable harm.

The court also identified how this was relevant to the facts of the case before it—an attempt to enjoin the enforcement of tobacco advertising restriction legislation and regulations pending the final determination of their constitutional status:

The applicants allege that if they are not granted interlocutory relief they will be forced to spend very large sums of money immediately in order to comply with the regulations. In the event that their appeals are allowed by this Court, the applicants contend that they will not be able either to recover their costs from the government or to revert to their current packaging practices without again incurring the same expense.

Monetary loss of this nature will not usually amount to irreparable harm in private law cases. Where the government is the unsuccessful party in a constitutional claim, however, a plaintiff will face a much more difficult task in establishing constitutional liability and obtaining monetary redress. The expenditures which the new regulations require will therefore impose irreparable harm on the applicants if these motions are denied but the main actions are successful on appeal.

Then the court built on Beetz J's identification of how the public interest should be dealt with in this kind of Charter litigation:

1. The Public Interest

Some general guidelines as to the methods to be used in assessing the balance of inconvenience were elaborated by Beetz J in *Metropolitan Stores*. A few additional points may be made. It is the "polycentric" nature of the Charter which requires a consideration of the public interest in determining the balance of convenience: see Cassels, "An Inconvenient Balance: The Injunction as a Charter Remedy" in Berryman, ed., *Remedies: Issues and Perspectives* (1991) 271 at 301-5. However, the government does not have a monopoly on the public interest. ...

It is, we think, appropriate that it be open to both parties in an interlocutory Charter proceeding to rely upon considerations of the public interest. Each party is entitled to make the court aware of the damage it might suffer prior to a decision on the merits. In addition, either the applicant or the respondent may tip the scales of convenience in its favour by demonstrating to the court a compelling public interest in the granting or refusal of the relief sought. "Public interest" includes both the concerns of society generally and the particular interests of identifiable groups.

We would therefore reject an approach which excludes consideration of any harm not directly suffered by a party to the application. ...

When a private applicant alleges that the public interest is at risk that harm must be demonstrated. This is since private applicants are normally presumed to be pursuing their own interests rather than those of the public at large. In considering the balance of convenience and the public interest, it does not assist an applicant to claim that a given government authority does not represent the public interest. Rather, the applicant must convince the court of the public interest benefits which will flow from the granting of the relief sought.

Courts have addressed the issue of the harm to the public interest which can be relied upon by a public authority in different ways. [Discussion of earlier cases is omitted.]

In our view, the concept of inconvenience should be widely construed in Charter cases. In the case of a public authority, the onus of demonstrating irreparable harm to the public interest is less than that of a private applicant. This is partly a function of the nature of the public authority and partly a function of the action sought to be enjoined. The test will nearly always be satisfied simply upon proof that the authority is charged with the duty of promoting or protecting the public interest and upon some indication that the impugned legislation, regulation, or activity was undertaken pursuant to that responsibility. Once these minimal requirements have been met, the court should in most cases assume that irreparable harm to the public interest would result from the restraint of that action.

A court should not, as a general rule, attempt to ascertain whether actual harm would result from the restraint sought. To do so would in effect require judicial inquiry into whether the government is governing well, since it implies the possibility that the government action does not have the effect of promoting the public interest and that the restraint of the action would therefore not harm the public interest. The Charter does not give the courts a licence to evaluate the effectiveness of government action, but only to restrain it where it encroaches upon fundamental rights.

Consideration of the public interest may also be influenced by other factors. In *Metropolitan Stores*, it was observed that public interest considerations will weigh more heavily in a "suspension" case than in an "exemption" case. The reason for this is that the public interest is much less likely to be detrimentally affected when a discrete and limited number of applicants are exempted from the application of certain provisions of a law than when the application of certain provisions of a law than when the application of the law is suspended entirely. ...

Similarly, even in suspension cases, a court may be able to provide some relief if it can sufficiently limit the scope of the applicant's request for relief so that the general public interest in the continued application of the law is not affected. Thus in *Ontario Jockey Club v. Smith* (1922) 22 OWN 373 (HC), the court restrained the enforcement of an impugned taxation statute against the applicant but ordered him to pay an amount equivalent to the tax into court pending the disposition of the main action.

2. The Status Quo

In the course of discussing the balance of convenience in *American Cyanamid*, Lord Diplock stated at 408 that when everything else is equal, "it is a counsel of prudence to ... preserve the *status quo*." This approach would seem to be of limited value in private law cases, and, although there may be exceptions, as a general rule it has no merit as such in the face of the alleged violation of fundamental rights. One of the functions of the Charter is to provide individuals with a tool to challenge the existing order of things or *status quo*. The issues have to be balanced in the manner described in these reasons.

Earlier, the court had identified its general sense of the competing interests in litigation of this kind:

> On one hand, courts must be sensitive to and cautious of making rulings which deprive legislation enacted by elected officials of its effect.
>
> On the other hand, the Charter charges the courts with the responsibility of safeguarding fundamental rights. For the courts to insist rigidly that all legislation be enforced to the letter until the moment that it is struck down as unconstitutional might in some instances be to condone the most blatant violation of Charter rights. Such a practice would undermine the spirit and the purpose of the Charter and might encourage a government to prolong unduly final resolution of a dispute.

NOTES

1. One question after the Supreme Court of Canada's judgments in these two cases was the extent to which they were relevant outside of the Charter in judicial review applications for interlocutory relief. For example, would the approach of the court have been exactly the same had the applicants in *Metropolitan Stores* been challenging the labour board imposition of a first contract on the basis that the board had made a patently unreasonable decision, or if in *RJR-MacDonald* the regulations had been attacked as *ultra vires* the empowering statute? In *Sobeys Inc. v. UFCW, Local 1000A* (1993), 12 OR (3d) 157 (Div. Ct.), it was held that, as opposed to the situation in Charter cases (where the standard of review is correctness), the applicant for a stay of proceedings in relation to decisions that were protected by a privative clause, and where the resulting standard of judicial review was that of patent unreasonableness, had to establish that it had a strong *prima facie* case on the merits, not just a serious issue to be tried. However, other courts have not adopted this position: *International Brotherhood of Locomotive Engineers v. Cairns* (2000), 252 NR 160 (FCA); *Windsor Airline Limousine Services Ltd. v. Ontario Taxi Union, CAW Local 1688*, [2001] OJ No. 5633 (QL) (SCJ).

2. What do you make of the court's assertion in *RJR-MacDonald* that, because of uncertainty in the law on the availability of damages against government for losses arising from compliance with legislation that is later found to violate the Charter, the applicants in such cases should always be considered as suffering potentially irreparable harm if the interlocutory relief is denied? Given that the occasions on which financial compensation is available for unlawful administrative action are few, should the opposite apply in that realm or does the proposition hold with even greater certainty in the administrative law realm?

Injunctions in Aid of the Administrative Process

Administrative tribunals are sometimes given the authority to make interim rulings pending the disposition of a matter before them. What happens, however, if there is no such explicit power? One area in which this question arose was human rights adjudication, where the inquiry is complicated first by doubts about the capacity of the courts to award interlocutory injunctions in support of proceedings other than their own (so-called freestanding interlocutory injunctions). Second, the question is complicated by the holding of the Supreme Court of Canada in *Board of Governors of Seneca College of Applied Arts & Technology v. Bhadauria*, [1981] 2 SCR 181 (Ont.) that, in general, human rights codes are comprehensive codes leaving no room for the independent seeking of court remedies in aid of alleged human rights violations (in *Bhadauria*, an action for damages for the tort of discrimination or breach of statutory duty). The following cases provide a resolution of this problem.

Brotherhood of Maintenance of Way Employees, Canadian Pacific System Federation v. Canadian Pacific Ltd.
[1996] 2 SCR 495 (BC)

[At issue was whether the BC Supreme Court had jurisdiction to award an interlocutory injunction to restrain an employer from implementing a change to work schedules pending the outcome of the arbitration of a union grievance brought under the collective agreement.]

McLACHLIN J (delivering the judgment of the Court): ...

III. Legislation

Canada Labour Code, RSC, 1985, c. L-2

> 57(1) Every collective agreement shall contain a provision for final settlement without stoppage of work, by arbitration or otherwise, of all differences between the parties to or employees bound by the collective agreement, concerning its interpretation, application, administration or alleged contravention.

Law and Equity Act, RSBC 1979, c. 224

> 36. A mandamus or an injunction may be granted or a receiver or receiver manager appointed by an interlocutory order of the court in all cases in which it appears to the court to be just or convenient that the order should be made, and the order may be made either unconditionally or on terms and conditions the court thinks just. ...

IV. Points in Issue

1. Do the superior courts in British Columbia have jurisdiction to issue injunctions in connection with disputes between federally regulated employers and employees concerning the interpretation, application, administration or alleged contravention of collective agreements?

2. Can the superior courts in British Columbia issue interlocutory injunctions in circumstances where there is no cause of action to which the injunction is ancillary?

V. Analysis

A) Jurisdiction of the Superior Courts in British Columbia To Grant an Injunction

The governing principle on this issue is that notwithstanding the existence of a comprehensive code for settling labour disputes, where "no adequate alternative remedy exists" the courts retain a residual discretionary power to grant interlocutory relief such as injunctions, a power which flows from the inherent jurisdiction of the courts over interlocutory matters: *St. Anne Nackawic Pulp & Paper Co. v. Canadian Paper Workers Union, Local 219* [1986] 1 SCR 704 (NB) at 727 ... . The "residual discretionary jurisdiction in courts of inherent jurisdiction to grant relief not available under the statutory arbitration scheme" was most recently affirmed by this Court in *Weber v. Ontario Hydro* [1995] 2 SCR 929 (Ont.) at paras. 41, 54, 57 and 67, and *New Brunswick v. O'Leary* [1995] 2 SCR 967 (NB), at para. 3.

Applying this principle to the facts in the case at bar, the first question is whether the *Canada Labour Code* provides an adequate remedy for the claim raised before the British Columbia Supreme Court. That claim, as stated above, was for a postponement of the employer's disputed decision to reschedule the work in such a way that the employees would lose their Sunday rest days, pending a decision on the legality of the new schedule by an arbitrator appointed under the *Canada Labour Code*. It is not disputed that the collective agreement and the machinery provided under the *Canada Labour Code* provided no means to secure the postponement of implementation of the new schedule. I can put it no better than Hutcheon JA in the Court of Appeal ((1994) 93 BCLR (2d) 176 at 182-3):

> The important circumstances in the present case are that there is no forum for interlocutory injunctions available through the *Canada Labour Code*; the work of the track crews is seasonal and from approximately March to the end of October; the arbitration proceeding was not finished until March 1994, several months after the 1993 work season; and without a restraining order there would be no way to remedy the loss of Sunday rest days.

There was, in the words of this Court in *St. Anne Nackawic*, "no adequate alternative remedy." The British Columbia Supreme Court, by contrast, was empowered to grant interlocutory injunctions such as that which the union sought in the exercise of its inherent jurisdiction: *Law and Equity Act*, s. 36. It would appear to follow that the court had the power to grant an injunction against imposition of the new schedule for the interim period pending a decision from the arbitrator appointed under the Code. ...

[McLachlin J proceeded to review and reject various arguments by the employer, concluding that allowing the court to grant an interim objection would not undermine the collective agreement and the *Canada Labour Code*; that the dispute mechanism under the *Canada Labour Code* was not exclusive because it did not cover all aspects of labour disputes, thus leaving a role for the common law and the courts' inherent jurisdiction; and that there was no evidence in the case at hand that granting an interim injunction would interfere with the employer's management of its enterprise. McLachlin J then continued:]

B) Need for an Underlying Cause of Action

The appellant employer submits that a court has power to grant an interim injunction only as an adjunct to a cause of action properly instituted in the court. It contends that the jurisdiction to grant interim injunctions under s. 36 of the *Law and Equity Act* is ancillary to and dependant upon a claim for final relief to the court from which the interim relief is sought. It is not disputed that at the time the injunction was granted, there was no claim for final relief before the Supreme Court of British Columbia.

The notion that a court could not entertain an application for an interim injunction unless the court had before it an action claiming final relief finds expression in *Lamont v. Air Canada* (1981) 126 DLR (3d) 266 (Ont. HC), where Griffiths J wrote (at 272):

> I know of no authority, nor has counsel been able to cite one in which the Court may issue an injunction to preserve the *status quo* while the plaintiff pursues his remedy before a statutory body over which the Court has no control.

Other cases relied on by the employer are readily distinguishable. In *Burkart v. Dairy Producers Co-operative Ltd.* (1990) 74 DLR (4th) 694, the Saskatchewan Court of Appeal acknowledged that the court did retain limited jurisdiction over labour matters. In *Iron Ore Co. of Canada v. United Steelworkers of America, Local 5795* (1984) 5 DLR (4th) 24 (Nfld. CA), the governing statute requires that there be a "civil cause or matter commenced in the Supreme Court," as contrasted with the more general language of the British Columbia *Law and Equity Act*.

Put at their highest, these cases may be seen as reflections of the doubt that existed in this area following the decision of the House of Lords in *Siskina (Cargo Owners) v. Distos Compania Naviera SA* [1979] AC 210 (Eng. HL). The House of Lords removed that doubt in its decision in *Channel Tunnel Group Ltd. v. Balfour Beatty Construction Ltd.* [1993] 2 WLR 262 (Eng. HL), categorically rejecting the submission that to grant interim relief, the courts must have jurisdiction over the cause of action. The concurring judgment of Lord Browne-Wilkinson held at 267 that:

> In my judgment that submission is not well founded. I can see nothing in the language employed by Lord Diplock (or in later cases in this House commenting on the *Siskina*) which suggest that a court has to be satisfied, at the time it grants interlocutory relief, that the final order, if any, will be made by an English court.
>
> • • •
>
> ... Even applying the test laid down by the *Siskina* the court has power to grant interlocutory relief based on a cause of action recognised by English law against a defendant duly served where such relief is ancillary to a final order whether to be granted by the English court or some other court *or arbitral body*. [Emphasis added.]

Canadian courts since *Channel Tunnel* have applied it for the proposition that the courts have jurisdiction to grant an injunction where there is a justiciable right, wherever that right may fall to be determined. ... This accords with the more general recognition throughout Canada that the court may grant interim relief where final relief will be granted in another forum. ...

I conclude that the absence of a cause of action claiming final relief in the Supreme Court of British Columbia did not deprive the court of jurisdiction to grant an interim injunction.

The Supreme Court of Canada reached the same conclusion in *Canada (Human Rights Commission) v. Canadian Liberty Net*, [1998] 1 SCR 626 (Can.). In that case, the Federal Court Trial Division had issued an interlocutory injunction at the suit of the Canadian Human Rights Commission. The injunction enjoined Canadian Liberty Net from operating a phone message service until a human rights tribunal determined whether the Net's activities infringed the *Canadian Human Rights Act*. Unlike the situation of the Supreme Court of British Columbia, however, the Federal Court was a statutory court with no inherent jurisdiction. Even so, the Supreme Court was prepared to find a statutory grant of jurisdiction to make such orders in s. 44 of the *Federal Courts Act*. This jurisdiction was concurrent to the inherent jurisdiction exercised in such matters by the provincial superior courts. In other words, in relation to federal statutory regimes, an applicant may have a choice of forum for seeking interlocutory relief.

The next case offers an example in which, based on *Brotherhood*, a court issued an interlocutory injunction in support of a statutory decision-making process. The injunction was issued to delay the construction of a business park on land in Guelph, Ontario for 30 days in order to allow the minister of natural resources to decide whether to make a stop-work order pursuant to s. 28(1) of the *Endangered Species Act, 2007*, SO 2007, c. 6. The minister might wish to make a stop-work order, the court concluded, due to tentative evidence that the land provided habitat for an endangered species.

Guelph (City) v. Soltys
(2009), 2009 CanLII 42449 (Ont. Sup. Ct.)

GRAY J:

[1] It is likely that most citizens will not have heard of the Jefferson Salamander. As it happens, the Jefferson Salamander is a "threatened species," within the meaning of the *Endangered Species Act, 2007*. The issue before me is what effect, if any, this has on the right of the City of Guelph to proceed with the development of a project known as the Hanlon Creek Business Park.

Background

[2] The City of Guelph and Belmont Equity (HCBP) Holdings Ltd. are the owners of about 271 hectares of land, bordered, in part, by Downey Road, Forestell Road and Hanlon Parkway, in the City of Guelph. ... The plaintiffs intend to develop these lands as a corporate and industrial business park. ... All necessary assessments, approvals, certificates and permits to develop Phase 1 of the park have been obtained. An environment impact study was completed in August, 2000. Further environmental impact studies have been done. An appeal to the Ontario Municipal Board was resolved, as a result of which the OMB ordered that a draft plan of subdivision be approved, subject to certain condi-

tions arrived at during the settlement process. Approximately $20 million has been spent on the project so far.

[3] In the past, the lands had been used for agricultural purposes. There are areas of uncleared forest and wetlands, and a tributary of Hanlon Creek runs through the property. As part of the approved draft plan of subdivision, a roadway will be built that crosses the creek. The creek crossing will be by way of a culvert that crosses the creek in an east-west direction. Due to time constraints, the culvert must be built first, with the rest of the infrastructure for Phase 1 of the project to follow. The culvert is likely to take six weeks to build, and the plaintiffs suggest that it must be completed on or before September 15, 2009. It is said that if this date is missed the entire project must be delayed at least one year.

[4] In early 2009, the City was contacted by individuals who expressed concern about environmental issues regarding development of the park. Some of these people belonged to a group called Land Is More Important Than Sprawl (LIMITS). One of the main supporters of LIMITS is the defendant Matthew Soltys. ...

[5] On April 20, 2009, a dead hybrid salamander was discovered along Laird Road, within the park. This specimen was collected and provided to Dr. James Bogart at the University of Guelph.

[6] Dr. Bogart has provided an affidavit in these proceedings. There is no doubt that he is eminently qualified to discuss issues surrounding the Jefferson Salamander; indeed, from 2002 to the present, he has been Chair of the Jefferson Salamander Recovery Team (Canadian Species at Risk).

[7] In the spring of 2009, the City retained Natural Resource Solutions Inc. (NRSI) to provide an opinion on the existence of the Jefferson Salamander on the property. NRSI performed various tests, and, in substance, has concluded that it is likely that the habitat of the Jefferson Salamander does not exist within the vicinity of the location where it is proposed that the culvert be installed.

[8] The information regarding the finding of the dead salamander, and other information in the City's possession, has been shared with the Ministry of Natural Resources. The Ministry's recommendation has been that development of the road that will cross the creek, and the building of the culvert, be postponed due to the unknown location of Jefferson Salamander breeding points on the property.

[9] Dr. Bogart identified the dead salamander as an LJJ unisexual salamander, that exists with Jefferson Salamander and uses that species for reproduction. Dr. Bogart has expressed the view that it is very difficult to document the absence of breeding in particular ponds, especially when the individual salamanders are few in number. Because the majority of LJJ females remain within 800 metres of a breeding pond, the particular breeding pond is expected to be within an 800 metre circumference of the collected specimen. Also, there is the possibility that successful breeding does not occur every year. Dr. Bogart has expressed the view that additional survey work should be performed at the site prior to environmental disturbance in order to find the breeding pond or ponds that are being used. Additional survey work could take up to three years.

[10] With leave, Dan Hagman was called to give *viva voce* evidence. He is the Guelph District Manager of the Ministry of Natural Resources. He is familiar with the project, has visited the site, and is familiar with the issue involving the Jefferson Salamander. He

testified that no formal approval of the MNR is required to proceed with the work, and that the MNR has taken no formal steps to prevent the work being done. He testified that the City has been working with the MNR in an attempt to address the Jefferson Salamander issue. The MNR's preference is that work on the culvert, and the road leading up to it, be suspended until further study has been done regarding the habitat of the Jefferson Salamander in the area. However, he recently attended a meeting in which it apparently was acknowledged that the City would proceed with the culvert work. When asked how this is consistent with the MNR's view that the work should be suspended, he said the MNR did not have the power to issue a stop work order under s. 27 of the [*Endangered Species Act, 2007*] because a regulation had not been promulgated defining the area of habitat of the Jefferson Salamander.

[11] Commencing on or about July 27, 2009, a number of individuals, including the defendants, entered the property and shut down construction of the culvert. Some of these people wore bandanas and sunglasses that hid their facial features. Demands that they leave the property have been ignored. Since that date, the blockading has continued, so that the contractor retained by the City has been unable to do any work on the culvert and the roadway leading to it.

[12] The plaintiffs bring this motion for an injunction, effectively to restrain the defendants from trespassing on the lands and impeding the construction activities.

[Gray J's discussion of the arguments of the plaintiffs and defendants on whether an injunction should be issued to restrain the defendants from trespass has been omitted.]

[17] Counsel for the defendants asserts that the defendants do not intend to continue their occupation of the property. However, counsel submits that if I determine that an injunction in favour of the plaintiffs is appropriate, I should only issue such an injunction, prohibiting the defendants from trespassing or blocking construction, on condition that the plaintiffs are themselves enjoined from engaging in any construction activities, for a reasonable period, that may interfere with the habitat of the Jefferson Salamander, and specifically suspend construction of the culvert over the creek. A reasonable period, in counsel's submission, would be for the duration of the anticipated breeding season, which would run until mid to late fall, 2009. Mr. Gillespie submits, in the alternative, that if I am not persuaded that I should enjoin the plaintiffs in the context of their injunction motion, I should grant the defendants an injunction in the same terms, based on the motion for an injunction that they have brought themselves.

[18] Counsel for the defendants submits that I should have regard for the "precautionary principle," which, simply put, contemplates that where there is a threat of a significant reduction or loss of biological diversity, lack of full scientific certainty should not be used as a reason for postponing measures to avoid or minimize such a threat. Reliance in this respect is placed on *114957 Canada Ltée (Spraytech, Société d'arrosage) v. Hudson (Town)*, [2001] 2 SCR 241, at paras. 31 and 32. In this case, the Jefferson Salamander is clearly recognized as a threatened species, as contemplated in the *Endangered Species Act, 2007*. Since a dead salamander was discovered within the lands slated for development, and close to the location of the creek crossing, it is a virtual certainty that breeding grounds for the salamander are somewhere within the park. Just because it is presently unknown

where those breeding grounds are is not sufficient reason to decline to take steps to avoid the potential destruction or interference with the habitat of the Jefferson Salamander. To fail to do so would be directly contrary to the precautionary principle. Mr. Gillespie notes that Dr. Bogart is of the view that up to three years may be required in order to adequately investigate the matter, and he asserts that an injunction lasting until the end of the breeding season in 2009 would be entirely reasonable in the circumstances.

[19] Mr. Gillespie submits that if construction is allowed to continue, and it develops that breeding grounds have been destroyed as a result, that consequence is irreversible. Any delay in pursuing the construction of the works is, in the circumstances, a small price to pay.

[Gray J noted that the defendants would require standing as public interest litigants in order to seek an injunction against the plaintiffs, before continuing:]

[21] In reply, counsel for the plaintiff submits that, whether it is done as a condition to the plaintiffs' injunction, or as a separate injunction granted to the defendants, the plaintiffs should not be restrained in continuing their construction activities, specifically the construction of the culvert at the creek crossing. Mr. Bordin submits that the defendants do not qualify as public interest litigants. Further, it is submitted that the Minister of Natural Resources, and her Ministry, are charged with the responsibility of enforcing the *Endangered Species Act, 2007*. The plaintiffs have cooperated with the Ministry, and are continuing to work with the Ministry to proceed carefully with the construction activities, so that any habitat of the salamander can be discovered at the earliest opportunity, and means can be taken to ameliorate any potential damage. While it is the Ministry's preference that construction of the culvert be postponed until further study can be done, most recently the Ministry has signalled its acceptance of the construction of the culvert, provided it is done carefully and in consultation with the Ministry.

[22] Mr. Bordin submits that the enforcement mechanisms conferred on the Ministry and the Minister under the *Act* are exclusive, and accordingly the Court is deprived of jurisdiction to grant an injunction to the defendants, even if they are granted standing as public interest litigants. Since the Minister and/or the Ministry have not issued orders under the *Act*, the Court should not do so.

Analysis

[23] I will consider the matter in two stages. First, I will consider whether the plaintiffs should be granted the injunction they seek, to prevent trespassing and interference with the construction activities in the park. Second, I will consider the defendants' request for an injunction to restrain the plaintiffs from continuing construction activities, at least for some period.

[Gray J's reasons for granting an injunction in favour of the plaintiffs, to restrain trespassing and interference with construction activities, have been omitted.]

[29] That brings me to the defendants' motion for an injunction.

[30] I do not intend to entertain the defendants' request for injunctive relief within the context of the plaintiffs' motion. I doubt that, as a condition of granting an injunction to the plaintiffs, I could grant a corresponding injunction to the defendants. However, even if I could, I am not prepared to allow the defendants to do so as a convenient way of allowing them to sidestep the requirement that they establish their right to pursue an injunction as public interest litigants. If the defendants are entitled to injunctive relief, they must persuade me that they are entitled to such relief in the context of their own motion. As part of the analysis, I must consider whether they should be granted standing as public interest litigants.

[31] In order to succeed in obtaining an interlocutory injunction, the defendants must satisfy the three-part test discussed in *R.J.R. MacDonald, supra* ... .

[32] Fundamentally, the defendants argue that it is necessary to grant an injunction in order to preserve the ability to determine whether the construction activities will adversely impact on the habitat of the Jefferson Salamander. In order to appreciate the defendants' submissions, it is necessary to have regard for certain of the provisions of the *Endangered Species Act, 2007.* ...

[34] First, it is apparent from the Preamble to the *Act*, and from the purposes of the *Act* described in s. 1, that the policy reflected in the *Act* is considered, by the legislators, to be of importance. ...

[35] Second, the term "habitat" has both a geographical and non-geographical component. Where a regulation has been made defining a specific area, that area is deemed to be the habitat of the species in question. However, where no such regulation is made, the area is undefined, and is simply defined as "an area on which the species depends, directly or indirectly, to carry on its life processes, including life processes such as reproduction, rearing, hibernation, migration or feeding."

[36] Third, the Jefferson Salamander is specifically defined, by statute, as a threatened species.

[37] Fourth, it is clear that, while the destruction or damage of habitat of an endangered or threatened species is prohibited, wherever it may occur, the treatment of habitat for enforcement purposes before the making of a regulation defining the habitat's area is different. The combined effect of s. 10(1) and (3) of the *Act* is to create a prohibition on the damaging or destruction of habitat, but to suspend that prohibition until a regulation defining the area is made, subject only to the power of the Minister of Natural Resources to make a stop work order in some circumstances. ...

[38] Under s. 27 an "enforcement officer" of the Ministry can make an order requiring a person to stop engaging in an activity if a person is contravening s. 10 of the *Act*. However, pursuant to s. 10(3), there is no contravention if a regulation defining the area of habitat is not in force. In that circumstance, s. 28 applies. ... To paraphrase, these provisions [of s. 28] authorize the Minister to make an order requiring a person to stop engaging in an activity if that person is about to engage in an activity that is destroying or is about to destroy or seriously damage an important feature of an area used as habitat, even if s. 10(3) would otherwise neutralize the prohibition in s. 10(1).

[39] Thus, the statutory scheme of enforcement is complete: an enforcement officer can make a stop work order if a regulation defining the area of habitat is in force, and if there is no such regulation, the Minister can make an order pursuant to the terms of s. 28. ...

[40] Where the Legislature has specified a tribunal having jurisdiction to adjudicate matters of a specified nature, it is generally understood that the jurisdiction of such a tribunal is exclusive, and the jurisdiction of the ordinary courts is ousted. This is particularly so where the jurisdiction of the tribunal is defined under the specific statute under which the rights being adjudicated are created or governed: see *Seneca College v. Bhadauria*, [1981] 2 SCR 181; and *Weber v. Ontario Hydro*, [1995] 2 SCR 929.

[41] In this case, as part of the public policy considerations reflected in the substantive provisions of the *Act* itself, the Legislature has chosen to confer enforcement powers on the Ministry of Natural Resources and, in some respects, on the Minister. Specifically, the Minister has power to determine the very matter in issue in the defendants' motion for an injunction: namely, whether work on the project should be stopped, and if so, to what degree and for how long, because of some anticipated negative impact on the habitat of the Jefferson Salamander. The Minister can make that assessment on an ongoing basis, and is in a much better position to assess the competing policy considerations, as well as legal considerations, than is the Court. Thus, in my view, the Court is deprived of jurisdiction to grant an injunction.

[42] An exception to the general principle exists where it is sought to enjoin an activity until the statutory tribunal can exercise the statutory decision-making power: see *Brotherhood of Maintenance of Way Employees Canadian Pacific System Federation v. Canadian Pacific Ltd.*, [1996] 2 SCR 495.

[43] In this case, Mr. Hagman testified that the Ministry's preference is that work on the culvert, and the road leading up to it, be suspended until further investigation can be done as to the habitat of the Jefferson Salamander. When asked why a stop work order has not been made, he testified that one could not be issued because a regulation defining the area of habitat has not yet been made. To this extent, Mr. Hagman's evidence is consistent with s. 27(1), which limits the power of an enforcement officer to make an order to those circumstances where a regulation defining the area of habitat has been made.

[44] There is no evidence before me, however, that the Minister has even considered making an order under s. 28 of the *Act*. If the construction activity commences immediately, it may prevent, or at least seriously limit, any opportunity for the Minister to consider making such an order.

[45] In this context, the defendants have satisfied the three-part test for an injunction, at least to allow the Minister to make a decision one way or the other. If necessary, I will grant standing to the defendants as public interest litigants for this purpose: see *Finlay v. Canada (Minister of Finance)*, [1986] 2 SCR 607. There is obviously a serious question to be tried, at least by the Minister, as to whether a stop work order should be issued. If the injunction is not granted, the work is commenced, and habitat is destroyed, the harm will be irreparable. I am persuaded that the balance of convenience favours an injunction of short duration.

[46] It is for the Minister to decide whether the circumstances are such that an order under s. 28(1) of the *Act* is justified, and if so, whether her discretion should be exercised to grant one. She may decide that the informal monitoring by the MNR is sufficient. These considerations are for the Minister, and it is not for the Court to usurp the Minister's authority. The residual jurisdiction of the Court to grant injunctive relief

should be sparingly exercised, and should be exercised in aid of, rather than in substitution for, the jurisdiction of the Minister.

[47] I will grant an injunction to prevent any further work on the culvert and the road leading up to it for a period of up to 30 days. That will give the Minister enough time to decide whether she will make an order pursuant to s. 28 of the *Act*. If the Minister issues an order under s. 28, or if she signifies, in writing, that she does not intend to issue such an order, my order will terminate. If the Minister does nothing, my order will expire 30 days from today.

[48] I am not persuaded that the deadline for finishing the culvert work, said to be September 15, 2009, is immutable. I expect that, if necessary, the work can be speeded up, or the City can live with an extension of the deadline, or both. If that is not the case, and it turns out that the project must be delayed for a year, so be it. The policies enshrined in the *Endangered Species Act, 2007* must prevail in these circumstances.

[49] I request that counsel for both parties apprise the proper officials within the Ministry of Natural Resources of this decision.

CHAPTER SEVENTEEN

Standing

INTRODUCTION

This chapter is principally concerned with standing to seek judicial review of administrative action. What are the limitations on the bringing of judicial review applications by individuals and groups concerned with apparently unlawful administrative action?

Despite the important role of judicial review in public law, historically, the common law did not treat judicial review as a means of rooting out or getting at illegality in governmental action no matter where it was occurring or in whose name the challenge was brought. Rather, judicial review was much more individually focused. It represented a way for citizens to complain about unlawful exercises of government power that affected them personally. It was perceived by the courts as a bulwark between the individual and a coercive state, particularly to the extent that the state impinged on traditional property rights. Where unlawful administrative action affected a broader public interest, the launching of a challenge in the courts was largely left to the unreviewable discretion of the attorney general. Individual citizens were not seen as appropriate vindicators of the public interest nor as the carriers of rights of groups in which they were members. The common law was extremely conservative in its recognition of collective or group rights. (See, in particular, Vining, *Legal Identity: The Coming of Age of Public Law* (New Haven, CT: Yale University Press, 1978).)

As modern regulatory regimes became more complex, however, there came a realization that the issue of government illegality could not always be reduced to a contest between a target individual and the state. Often, illegal government action affected large numbers of people in indistinguishable ways; no one person could be said to be more specially affected than another. As well, many statutory regimes have layered or disparate impacts. They affect more than one group in society and they do so in varying ways. In a standing regime that emphasized individual interests, this situation raised questions about where to draw the line. At what point in the layers of effects on individuals and groups should the law decide that the impact was too remote to allow for standing in judicial review? What should be done if those primarily or most directly affected do not have the inclination or the resources to mount an effective challenge?

More fundamental changes also began to occur. The position of the attorney general as the sole vindicator of that public interest came to be seen as anomalous. This was particularly so in situations where the attorney general was a member of the Cabinet containing the minister whose own or whose department's conduct was the subject of scrutiny. It also reflected a growing awareness of the diversity of the public interest and the impracticability of the attorney general being sufficiently attentive in reviewing all forms of governmental action.

Recognition of the diffuse nature of the public interest manifested itself initially in the political process with the growth of lobby and public interest groups. It soon was felt in the proceedings of regulatory agencies as the same or sometimes different groups clamoured for participatory rights. This led in turn, perhaps inevitably, to claims for an entitlement to mount challenges in the courts as well. From this perspective, judicial review can be analyzed not only as a process by which to police the legality of governmental conduct but also as a path to another form of democratic accountability. As Cane argued in "Statutes, Standing and Representation" (1990), *Public Law* 307, at 312:

> It is now a truism that representative interest and pressure groups play a very important part in the governmental system of modern democracies. But it is also well known that the influence of particular groups on the governmental policy-making process varies widely, and that governments are free to choose their own counsellors with no obligation to ensure balance. To the extent that judicial review operates as a check on the exercise of governmental power, the courts must be willing to give serious consideration to the claims of representative groups to forward their causes through the judicial process. ... It is only when the role of individuals and groups in activating the judicial process is considered in the light of a clear understanding of the function of standing rules that the "new law of standing" will begin to develop in a reasoned and rational way.

Within the Canadian constitutional framework there has been further impetus for this evolution in the enactment of the *Canadian Bill of Rights* and the adoption of the *Charter of Rights and Freedoms*. The promise of these constitutional documents was clearly one of the subjection of parliamentary will and executive power to the scrutiny of the regular courts. The terms of the Charter also created expectations of greater judicial recognition of group rights. Moreover, once the Supreme Court of Canada recognized a more liberal law of standing in the context of constitutional challenges generally, it seemed inevitable that those policies would impact the law of standing in relation to non-constitutional challenges to governmental action, the arena of judicial review of administrative action.

Despite this historical trajectory by which access to the courts has expanded, largely due to decisions by the courts themselves, the adoption of an expansive or liberal law of standing is not a matter of universal agreement. At one level, it is said to draw too much on the resources of an already overtaxed court system. Sometimes linked to this are concerns about the conditions under which the litigation process works best. This has at least two dimensions: first, only those with a real stake in the outcome of litigation have the incentive to provide the court with the best arguments and, second, courts generally see the real issues in disputes most clearly when they are confronted with them in the context of a claim by someone who is affected directly. On the other hand, the courts may be at a disadvantage in having to deal with questions in a more abstract setting against the background of arguments made by those claiming to represent a general public interest and not having a concrete stake in the outcome.

More fundamentally, there remain significant pockets of concern, even in the age of the Charter, about the "politicization" of the courts. To the extent that an expanded law of public interest standing contributes to this phenomenon, it may be thought to be undesirable. In one sense, this is an argument about institutional competence and legitimacy. Not only does it reflect a worry about the judiciary trespassing in the domain of party politics and legislative choice; it is also based on a belief that there are certain questions that are not for the courts in the sense that they are not considered justiciable. At another level, it casts doubt on the arguments of Cane. There is no guarantee that liberalizing access to the courts for public interest groups will enhance democratic and participatory values. In the face of the high costs of litigation and of unequal access to legal services and to the courts, a "liberal" standing law may simply confer further advantages on those who are already privileged in the political process or sustain the attacks by vested interests on "socially progressive" government policies and programs. In that sense, the promise of a liberal standing law for those who are disadvantaged in society and in politics is a snare and a delusion.

The foregoing is intended to explain the often ambivalent attitude of courts, lawyers, and commentators to an expanded law of standing. Further, one must also take into account the fact that judicial review remains rooted in the concept of individual claims of public law wrongs. Despite the public interest in the legality of governmental action, most applications for judicial review are brought by the persons most directly affected or, more specifically, the sole target of the action under challenge. In most cases, we still conceive of the cause of action as theirs and theirs alone. In this sense, the law of standing raises yet another dimension of the interplay between public and private and the difficult problem of the circumstances in which, no matter how liberal our law of standing, we should still be willing to concede that the private interest behind the commencement of a judicial review should be determinative. Put differently, there may be occasions where a purely private interest dictates that a public wrong should go unchallenged.

To complicate the matter even further, it will frequently be impossible or imprudent to disentangle the issue of standing from the merits of the claim that is advanced. A person's or a group's claim to be an appropriate plaintiff or applicant will often only be appreciated based on an awareness of the claim itself and its factual and legal underpinnings. For courts and litigants, then, there is always the dilemma of whether to treat an issue of standing as a threshold matter or as integrally related to the merits of the claim. Moreover, that decision cannot be made without a consideration of the practical litigation concerns arising from a dissociation of the merits of a case from other considerations. This choice is manifested in the context of an application by the body under attack to strike out the judicial review application on the basis of the applicant's lack of standing. As you move through this chapter, keep these competing considerations in mind when you evaluate the state of Canadian law as well as the individual judgments.

The chapter commences with an examination of the leading Canadian judgment in the area, *Minister of Finance of Canada v. Finlay*, [1986] 2 SCR 607 (Can.). We then consider the extent to which this judgment has expanded access to the courts to challenge administrative action beyond those whose rights or interested are affected directly by the administrative action. When will public interest standing be granted? To what extent do current principles of standing allow for private law enforcement by way of an administrative law remedy? We then turn to the role of the attorney general in a legal environment in which that office is no longer the exclusive vindicator of the public interest in judicial review. We examine also the question of whether and to what extent tribunals and agencies should have standing to participate in legal proceedings in which their decisions are under scrutiny. In some cases, for instance, a tribunal may be granted limited standing to participate in a judicial review of its decision only a narrow range of issues; alternatively, the decision-maker may be granted the status of an intervenor rather than a party. Intervenor status (and *amicus curiae* status) is also an alternative way for individuals and public interest groups to play a role in judicial review proceedings at the discretion of the court. We consider the notion of intervention as a separate category of participation, in both court and tribunal proceedings, from that of standing as a party.

Related to status to commence or participate in a judicial review is the issue of standing to participate in the hearings of an administrative tribunal as either a party or an intervenor. In one sense, this request to participate is another way of advancing a claim of procedural fairness: Who is entitled to notice of a proceeding and who is entitled to participatory rights? Where an administrative tribunal or agency has discretion about how to conduct its proceedings or, in some cases, about those who it allows to participate, the issue can be framed in terms of the controls that the courts impose on the exercise of discretionary powers. In both respects, we have touched on the issue in other chapters of this text.

To the extent that a tribunal or agency's decision to grant standing will in turn determine a person's entitlement to review the administrative decision, such decisions on standing are central to judicial review in the courts. Moreover, many of the same considerations that are relevant to a court's consideration of whether to grant standing or intervenor status in a judicial review are relevant to a tribunal or agency's determination of the same issue (see, for example, *Imperial Tobacco Ltd. v. Canada (PG)* (1988), 38 Admin. LR 74 (Que. SC)). Accordingly, we return to this matter at the end of the chapter and, in particular, consider whether there should be an exact parallel between the principles of standing and intervention applied by the courts in judicial review proceedings and those relevant to tribunal and agency hearings.

STANDING IN JUDICIAL REVIEW PROCEEDINGS

General

Who is entitled to bring judicial review proceedings? Historically, the context and the remedy sought would prompt one of a wide variety of answers. Here are a few of them. Mere strangers could seek *certiorari* and prohibition but the court possessed an overriding discretion to refuse relief at the suit of such a person. On the other hand, when a person was directly affected or "aggrieved" and the error was patent rather than latent in the case of prohibition, the remedy was available as of right (or, to use the old Latin term, *ex debito justitiae*). For *mandamus*, the person seeking the remedy had to be a person to whom performance of the duty was owed or, in terms of more recent authority, someone sufficiently interested in its performance. When declaratory and injunctive relief were sought, the plaintiffs were required to show interference with a private right of theirs or, when the interference was with public rights, to show that they would be affected or suffer loss over and above other members of the community. Otherwise, the only appropriate plaintiff was the attorney general. Indeed, the status of the attorney general to seek any remedy seemed beyond question by the courts. Private individuals, not otherwise having status, who could convince the attorney general to lend support to proceedings brought by them (so-called relator proceedings) seemed assured of being able to shelter behind the attorney general's title. This stemmed from the attorney general's recognized position as the guardian of the public interest. One exception was that ratepayers, perhaps even inhabitants, of a municipality were recognized by the courts as having status to challenge the validity of municipal bylaws involving the expenditure of public funds.

Superficially, these principles of standing may appear to be relatively clear, although not perhaps consistent or logical. Yet, behind the buzzwords used were a host of difficulties. What exactly did being "aggrieved," "specially affected," or "suffering loss over and above the rest of the community" mean? If an administrative duty was owed to the public at large, who could ever seek *mandamus*? What were the obligations of attorneys general if they were requested to lend their names in relator proceedings? What if they refused? Could class actions be employed to aggregate individually insufficient interests into a recognizable standing? It was also clear that different people were affected in different ways by the operation of statutes and regulatory schemes created by statutes. In such instances, distinctions based on the categorization of some as "directly" or "specially affected" were highly problematic.

From a policy perspective, it is possible to discern two extremes in positions on the issue of standing. On the one hand, one can assert that there is a general public interest in the legality of administrative action and that anyone should be able to bring illegality to the attention of the courts. On the other hand, one may argue that the benefits of litigation should be available only to those who are the direct targets of individualized, administrative decision making and whose financial or property interests are affected in a substantial way. On this view, public interest in legality, and any other public interest considerations, should be for the attorney general alone.

Canadian law has never adopted either of these extremes although, until recently, it seemed closer to the latter rather than the former. Unfortunately, however, in the struggle over the intermediate territory, there was little careful policy analysis and too much appeal to past judicial decisions which themselves did not stand scrutiny and were often in conflict. The result was a body of law that was difficult to describe and by and large unprincipled in its approach. (For an account of the traditional Canadian law, see Cromwell, *Locus Standi— A Commentary on the Law of Standing in Canada* (Scarborough, ON: Carswell, 1986), at chapter 3 particularly.)

That said, there is of course no problem, in most cases, with the standing of an applicant to seek relief. The bulk of proceedings for judicial review are brought by a person who is the direct object of the decision-maker's attention—a licence is refused, property is expropriated, money is not paid, and the person affected goes to court. Once we move out of that class of cases, however, difficulties arise. For example, what about the interests of neighbouring property owners when property is rezoned? What types of interest will be sufficient to give them standing?

In *Lord Nelson Hotel Ltd. v. City of Halifax* (1972), 33 DLR (3d) 98 (NS SCAD), the court held that the hotel company had standing to challenge such a decision. It operated a hotel on one corner and owned a residential property on another; the rezoning would have permitted the erection of another hotel on a third corner. The company had exercised a right of appeal to the Planning Appeal Board, because of which its interests were held to be affected materially. But how much less would have sufficed? If it had been an insurance company that owned a building two blocks away, would that have been enough of an interest? Which, if any, of the factors identified by the court were crucial, or was it the combination of all of the factors?

A quite different case is presented by *Young v. Attorney General of Manitoba* (1961), 25 DLR (2d) 352 (Man. CA). In a coroner's verdict, a child was held to have died because of "an excessive dosage of morphine and lack of any actual treatment." The "treating" doctor sought to have the inquest quashed on various procedural grounds. According to one majority judge, only people named as responsible criminally for the death or the personal representative of the deceased have standing to challenge a coroner's verdict. Why is their claim better than that of the doctor here? Should the damage to his reputation not generate a claim to standing? What if, as was the case, the verdict gave rise to professional disciplinary proceedings?

To these complications with the traditional law of standing, new factors emerged. The proliferation of public interest groups led to demand that they be recognized as not only having the right to participate in regulatory processes but also to challenge the outcome of those processes in the courts, whether by statutory appeal or judicial review. This was prompted in part by the success of such groups to obtain access to regulatory processes and to the courts in the United States. Generally, the attempts to secure recognition in judicial review proceedings took one of two forms. Either the group itself commenced the proceedings and asserted itself as a representative of the collective interest (for example, a ratepayers' or residents' association) or the group sponsored an individual, presumably with a recognized interest, to bring the proceedings. Initially, the first method proved risky and the second much safer, save for possible problems with the tort of maintenance.

Over time, however, the courts' attitude began to change. The most significant developments were the decisions of the Supreme Court of Canada in *Thorson v. Attorney General of Canada*, [1975] 1 SCR 138 (Ont.); *Nova Scotia Board of Censors v. McNeil*, [1976] 2 SCR 265 (NS); and *Minister of Justice of Canada v. Borowski*, [1981] 2 SCR 575 (Sask.). Each of these cases involved attempts to challenge the constitutionality of legislation by private individuals with no particular stake beyond that of being citizens and taxpayers. Thorson challenged the validity of the *Official Languages Act*, RSC 1970, c. O-2, while McNeil targetted Nova Scotia's movie censor, the Amusement Regulation Board. Borowski challenged the validity of the therapeutic abortion committee provisions of the *Criminal Code*, RSC 1970, c. C-34, s. 251, though not on the basis that they contravened the *Constitution Act, 1867*; his allegations were that they were contrary to the "right to life" provisions of the *Canadian Bill of Rights*, RSC 1970, App. III, s. 1(a). In each case, the Supreme Court upheld the applicant's status to commence a declaratory proceeding and, more generally, the court held that judges had broad discretion, at least in constitutional matters, to allow proceedings by private individuals with no direct stake in the dispute.

Once the Supreme Court of Canada liberalized the law of standing in the constitutional arena, litigants urged the acceptance of the same principles in the judicial review of administrative action. This question reached the Supreme Court of Canada in following case.

Finlay v. Canada (Minister of Finance)
[1986] 2 SCR 607 (Can.)

[Finlay was a resident of Manitoba who relied on social assistance. He sought declaratory and injunctive relief from the Trial Division of the Federal Court to the effect that the transfer payments made by the federal government to Manitoba under the *Canada*

Assistance Plan, RSC 1970, c. C-1 were illegal. The basis for this claim was that the relevant Manitoba social welfare legislation did not comply with the plan's requirements for transfer payments to the provinces. Compliance allegedly would have produced a higher level of assistance for Finlay. Nitikman DJ struck out Finlay's statement of claim on the basis of his lack of standing and because it did not disclose a reasonable cause of action. This order was reversed by the Federal Court of Appeal ([1984] 1 FC 516 (CA)) and the Crown appealed to the Supreme Court of Canada.

Le DAIN J delivered the judgment of the Supreme Court of Canada, consisting of Dickson CJ, Beetz, McIntyre, Chouinard, Wilson, La Forest JJ, and himself:]

· · ·

The issue of standing in this appeal, as I conceived it, may be approached by asking the following questions:

1. Does the respondent have a sufficient personal interest in the legality of the federal cost-sharing payments to bring him within the general requirement for standing to challenge an exercise of statutory authority by an action for a declaration or an injunction?

2. If not, does the Court have a discretion to recognize public interest standing in the circumstances of the present case?

3. If the Court does have such a discretion should it be exercised in favour of the respondent?

These questions involve a consideration of the discretionary control over standing to assert a purely public right or interest by an action for a declaration or an injunction that has traditionally vested in the Attorney General and the extent to which that control has been displaced or qualified by the judgments of this Court in [the trilogy of constitutional standing cases]. More specifically, they involve a consideration of whether the approach to public interest standing reflected in those cases, in which there was a challenge to the constitutionality or operative effect of legislation, applies to a non-constitutional challenge to the statutory authority for administrative action.

In the course of his submissions on the issue of standing counsel for the appellants also raised an issue of justiciability. He contended that the question of provincial compliance with the conditions of federal cost-sharing was not an issue appropriate for determination by a court, but was rather one that should be left to government review and inter-governmental resolution. The respondent contended that the particular questions of provincial non-compliance raised by the statement of claim were questions of law appropriate for judicial determination. Justiciability was held by this Court in *Thorson* to be a central consideration in the exercise of the judicial discretion to recognize public interest standing in certain cases. I propose to consider it in that context.

[Le Dain J initially considered whether this was a case in which it was appropriate to deal with an allegation of lack of standing in the context of a motion to strike out a statement of claim. He concluded that it was for the following reasons:]

It depends on the nature of the issues raised and whether the court has sufficient material before it, in the way of allegations of fact, considerations of law, and argument, for a proper understanding at a preliminary stage of the nature of the interest asserted. In my opinion the present case is one in which the question of standing can be properly determined on a motion to strike. The nature of the respondent's interest in the substantive issues raised by his action is sufficiently clearly established by the allegations and contentions in the statement of claim and the statutory and contractual provisions relied on without the need of evidence or full argument on the merits.

III

I turn to the question whether the respondent has a sufficient personal interest in the legality of the federal cost-sharing payments to bring him within the general requirement for standing to challenge an exercise of statutory authority by an action for a declaration or an injunction. The nature of the interest required by a private individual for standing to sue for declaratory or injunctive relief where, as in the present case, a question of public right or interest is raised, has been defined with reference to the role of the Attorney General as the guardian of public rights. Only the Attorney General has traditionally been regarded as having standing to assert a purely public right or interest by the institution of proceedings for declaratory or injunctive relief of his own motion or on the relation of another person. His exercise of discretion as to whether or not to give his consent to relator proceedings is not reviewable by the courts. See *London County Council v. Attorney-General* [1902] AC 165 (Eng. HL), and *Gouriet v. Union of Post Office Workers* [1978] AC 435 (Eng. HL). In such a case a private individual may not sue for a declaratory or injunctive relief without the consent of the Attorney General unless he can show what amounts to a sufficient private or personal interest in the subject matter of the proceedings. It is in this sense that I have referred to the discretionary control of the Attorney General over public interest standing. *Thorson, McNeil* and *Borowski* represent a departure from or exception to that general rule, but before considering their application in the present case it is necessary to consider whether the respondent has a sufficient interest in the legality of the federal cost-sharing payments to bring him within the general rule.

The general rule was laid down in cases involving the private action for public nuisance but it has been applied in a variety of public law contexts where an issue of public right or interest has been raised. The statement of the rule that has been most often cited is that of Buckley J in *Boyce v. Paddington Borough Council* [1903] 1 Ch. 109, in which the issue was whether the plaintiff, a private individual, could bring an action, without the consent of the Attorney General, for an injunction to restrain a public authority from erecting an obstruction in an open space that interfered with the access of light to the windows of the plaintiff's property. The case involved the public right to the open space and the private right to access of light to private property. It was held that the plaintiff could sue without joining the Attorney General because, although the right to the open space was a public right, the plaintiff sought to restrain an interference with his private right to access of light to his property, and he also suffered special damage peculiar to himself from the interference with the public right. Buckley J stated the rule as follows at 114:

A plaintiff can sue without joining the Attorney-General in two cases: first, where the interference with the public right is such that some private right of his is at the same time interfered with (*eg*, where an obstruction is so placed in a highway that the owner of the premises abutting upon the highway is specially affected by reason that the obstruction interferes with his private right to access from and to his premises to and from the highway); and, secondly, where no private right is interfered with, but the plaintiff, in respect of his public right, suffers special damage peculiar to himself from the interference with the public right.

· · ·

While the authority of the rule is well established the precise nature of the two exceptions stated by Buckley J—interference with a private right and special damage peculiar to oneself—has been the subject of a variety of commentary and expression. The "private right" referred to by Buckley J has been said to be "a right the invasion of which gives rise to an actionable wrong within the categories of private law, for example, a breach of contract or trust or the commission of a tort": Thio, *Locus Standi and Judicial Review* (1971), at 161. It has also been observed that the exception for private rights applies not only to common law rights but to a right created by statute for the benefit of a plaintiff: Zamir, *The Declaratory Judgment* (1962), at 269. The nature of the interest reflected by the words "special damage peculiar to himself" in the second exception in *Boyce* has been variously characterized in the cases. For a convenient reference to the conflicting meanings given to these words in the private action for public nuisance see Cromwell, *Locus Standi: A Commentary on the Law of Standing in Canada* (1986), at 24-27. In *Smith v. Attorney General of Ontario* [1924] SCR 331 (Ont.), which was considered by this Court in *Thorson*, Duff J referred to the general rule as follows at 337: "An individual, for example, has no status to maintain an action restraining a wrongful violation of a public right unless he is exceptionally prejudiced by the wrongful act." In *Cowan* [*v. Canadian Broadcasting Corporation* (1966), 56 DLR (2d) 578 (Ont. CA)] in which the standing requirement laid down in *Boyce* was applied by the Ontario Court of Appeal to an action for declaratory and injunctive relief alleging that the Canadian Broadcasting Corporation had exceeded its statutory authority by operating a French language broadcasting station, Schroeder JA said at 311:

> A plaintiff, in attempting to restrain, control or confine within proper limits, the act of a public or *quasi*-public body which affects the public generally, is an outsider unless he has sustained special damage or can show that he has some "special interest, private interest, or sufficient interest." These are terms which are found in the law of nuisance but they have been introduced into cases which also involve an alleged lack of authority. Therefore, in an action where it is alleged that a public or *quasi*-public body has exceeded or abused its authority in such a manner as to affect the public, whether a nuisance be involved or not, the right of the individual to bring the action will accrue as it accrues in cases of nuisance on proof that he is more particularly affected than other people.

In *Australian Conservation Foundation* [*v. Commonwealth of Australia* (1980), 28 ALR 257 (HCA)] in which the High Court of Australia applied the rule in *Boyce* to deny public interest standing to challenge the validity of administrative procedures respecting a requirement for an environmental impact statement, Gibbs J at 268, made the following observations concerning the meaning to be given to the words "special damage peculiar to himself" in *Boyce*:

Although the general rule is clear, the formulation of the exceptions to it which Buckley J made in *Boyce v. Paddington Borough Council* is not altogether satisfactory. Indeed the words which he used are apt to be misleading. His reference to "special damage" cannot be limited to actual pecuniary loss, and the words "peculiar to himself" do not mean that the plaintiff, and no one else, must have suffered damage. However, the expression "special damage peculiar to himself," in my opinion should be regarded as equivalent in meaning to "have a special interest in the subject matter of the action."

In *Borowski, supra*, Laskin CJ, dissenting, referred to the general rule as follows at 578: "Unless the legislation itself provides for a challenge to its meaning or application or validity by any citizen or taxpayer, the prevailing policy is that a challenger must show some special interest in the operation of the legislation beyond the general interest that is common to all members of the relevant society."

The precise nature of the respondent's interest in the legality of the federal cost-sharing payments is not easy to characterize in terms of the general rule. The respondent sues as a person in need within the meaning of the Plan who claims to have been prejudiced by the alleged provincial non-compliance with the conditions and undertakings to which the federal cost-sharing payments are made subject by the Plan. He alleges the prejudice caused by the deduction from his monthly social allowance payment of an amount to repay an overpayment of allowance, which he contends was caused by administrative error. Counsel for the appellants conceded that the deduction reduced the amount of the respondent's monthly social allowance payment below that required to meet the cost of basic requirements or necessities. The respondent alleges the further prejudice arising from the fact that he remains indebted for the municipal assistance which he received prior to qualifying for social allowance. Although the Plan was enacted for the benefit of persons in need it does not confer any rights on such persons; their entitlement to assistance arises under the provincial legislation. Nor can the federal cost-sharing payments be said to affect such entitlement directly. The respondent contends, however, that the continued payment of the federal contributions, despite the alleged provincial non-compliance with the conditions and undertakings imposed by the Plan, is in effect a cause of such non-compliance and the resulting prejudice to the respondent. He argues that it is the federal failure to insist on provincial compliance with the conditions and undertakings imposed by the Plan that permits or encourages such continued non-compliance by the province. What the respondent seeks by a declaration that the federal payments are illegal and an injunction to stop them is to compel the province to comply with the conditions and undertakings imposed by the Plan.

Counsel for the appellants contended that there was an insufficient "nexus" between the alleged provincial non-compliance with the conditions and undertakings imposed by the Plan and the alleged illegality of the federal payments to satisfy the general requirement for standing to bring an action for a declaration. The term "nexus" was apparently borrowed from American cases on standing to which we were referred in the course of argument. As formulated in *Flast v. Cohen* 392 US 83 (1968), a case of taxpayer's standing to challenge the constitutionality of federal public expenditure, the nexus requirement has a two-fold aspect of a special nature based on particular features of the American Constitution. The term "nexus" is used in a more general sense in other cases, such as *Linda R.S. v. Richard D.* 410 US 614 (1973), to refer to the causative relationship that must exist between the injury or prejudice complained of and the action attacked. The action attacked must have been a cause of the injury or prejudice complained of, and the plaintiff must have a personal stake in the outcome of the litigation—that is, stand to benefit in his personal interests from the relief sought. It is in this general sense that I understood counsel for the appellants to use the word "nexus." The American requirement of "nexus" or "directness," as it is sometimes referred to (*cf. Joint Anti-Fascist Refugee Committee v. McGrath* 341 US 123 (1951), *per* Frankfurter J at 152-53), stems from the special constitutional requirement of case or controversy for federal jurisdiction under Article III of the Constitution, and for this reason the American cases on standing must be treated with some caution. I am of the opinion, however, that a similar requirement of directness or causal relationship between the alleged prejudice or grievance and the challenged action is implicit in the notions of interference with private right and special damage. I note that Thio, *op. cit.*, at 5-6, refers to the general requirement for standing in administrative law as being that of a "direct, personal interest." In *Australian Conservation Foundation, supra*, Gibbs J, referring to the general rule, stated the requirement of a personal stake in the outcome of the litigation as follows at 270:

> A person is not interested within the meaning of the rule, unless he is likely to gain some advantage, other than the satisfaction of righting a wrong, upholding a principle or winning a contest, if his action succeeds or to suffer some disadvantage, other than a sense of grievance or a debt for costs, if his action fails.

There is no doubt that the respondent has a direct, personal interest in the alleged provincial non-compliance with the conditions and undertakings imposed by the Plan. A declaration that the federal cost-sharing payments are illegal would necessarily involve a finding that the province had failed to comply with the conditions and undertakings imposed by the Plan, but this would not affect the validity of the provincial legislative provisions about which complaint is made. Cf. *Re Lofstrom and Murphy* (1971) 22 DLR (3d) 120 (Sask. CA). See also *LeBlanc v. City of Transcona* [1974] SCR 1261 (Man.), *per* Spence J at 1268. It cannot be asserted for a certainty that the province would feel compelled by such a finding to change the offending legislative provisions. The effect on provincial action of a declaration that the federal payments are illegal and even an injunction to stop them is also necessarily a matter of speculation. For a somewhat analogous relationship between the prejudice suffered and the action attacked that was held to be too speculative for standing see *Simon v. Eastern Kentucky Welfare Rights Organization* 426 US 26 (1979). Although I have experienced some difficulty on this question, I am on balance of the view that the relationship between the prejudice allegedly caused to the respondent by the provincial non-compliance with the conditions and undertakings imposed by the Plan and the alleged illegality of the federal payments is too indirect, remote or speculative to be a sufficient causative relationship for standing under the general rule. The respondent must therefore in my opinion rely for standing on what is essentially a public interest in the legality of the federal cost-sharing payments, albeit that of a particular class of the public defined by the Plan as persons in need. It is accordingly necessary to consider whether the respondent should be recognized as having standing, as a matter of judicial discretion, by application of the principle or approach reflected in the decisions of this Court in *Thorson, McNeil* and *Borowski.*

[Le Dain J here considered whether, as a matter of precedent, the three earlier constitutional cases had resolved the issue of public interest standing in administrative law contexts. He decided that they were not decisive one way or the other, before continuing:]

... The issue, then, as I see it, is whether the principle reflected in *Thorson*, *McNeil* and *Borowski* should be extended by this Court to such cases. This question raises again the policy considerations underlying judicial attitudes to public interest standing, and in particular, whether the same value is to be assigned to the public interest in the maintenance of respect for the limits of administrative authority as was assigned by this Court in *Thorson*, *McNeil* and *Borowski* to the public interest in the maintenance of respect for the limits of legislative authority.

In my view an affirmative answer should be given to this question. The recognized standing of the Attorney General to assert a purely public interest in the limits of statutory authority by an action of his own motion or on the relation of another person is a recognition of the public interest in the maintenance of respect for such limits. For the reasons indicated in *Thorson*, I do not think that his refusal to act in such a case should bar a court from the recognition, as a matter of discretion in accordance with the criteria affirmed in *Borowski*, of public interest standing in a private individual to institute proceedings. The traditional judicial concerns about the expansion of public interest standing may be summarized as follows: the concern about the allocation of scarce judicial resources and the need to screen out the mere busybody; the concern that in the determination of issues the courts should have the benefit of the contending points of view of those most directly affected by them; and the concern about the proper role of the courts and their constitutional relationship to the other branches of government. These concerns are addressed by the criteria for the exercise of the judicial discretion to recognize public interest standing to bring an action for a declaration that were laid down in *Thorson*, *McNeil* and *Borowski*. I shall deal with each of them in relation to the question of the respondent's standing in the present case.

The concern about the proper role of the courts and their constitutional relationship to the other branches of government is addressed by the requirement of justiciability, which Laskin J held in *Thorson* to be central to the exercise of the judicial discretion whether or not to recognize public interest standing. Of course, justiciability is always a matter of concern for the courts, but the implication of what was said by Laskin J in *Thorson* is that it is a matter of particular concern in the recognition of public interest standing. As I indicated earlier in these reasons, counsel for the appellants raised the issue of justiciability with reference to judicial review of a question of provincial compliance with the conditions of federal cost-sharing. The requirement of justiciability was considered by this Court in *Operation Dismantle Inc. v. The Queen* [1985] 1 SCR 441 (Can.), where reference was made to both the institutional and constitutional aspects of justiciability. The question of justiciability in that case was considered in the context of a challenge, based on the *Canadian Charter of Rights and Freedoms*, to the constitutionality of a decision of the executive government of Canada in the realms of foreign policy and national defence. As I read the reasons of Wilson J, with whom Dickson J (now CJ) concurred on the question of justiciability, they affirm that where there is an issue which is appropriate for judicial determination the courts should not decline to determine it on the ground that because of its policy context or implications it is better left for review and determination by the legislative or executive branches of government. That was, of course, said in the context of the judicial duty to rule on issues of constitutionality under the Charter, but I take it to be equally applicable to a non-constitutional issue of the limits of statutory authority. There will no doubt be cases in which the question of provincial compliance with the conditions of federal cost-sharing will raise issues that are not appropriate for judicial determination, but the particular issues of provincial non-compliance raised by the respondent's statement of claim are questions of law and as such clearly justiciable. The same is, of course, true of the issue of statutory authority under s. 7 of the Plan. I am, therefore, of the opinion that the recognition of public interest standing in this case should not be refused on the ground of justiciability.

The judicial concern about the allocation of scarce judicial resources and the need to screen out the mere busybody is addressed by the requirements affirmed in *Borowski* that there be a serious issue raised and that a citizen have a genuine interest in the issue. I think the respondent meets both of these requirements. The issues of law raised with respect to the alleged provincial non-compliance with the conditions and undertakings to which the federal cost-sharing payments are made subject by the Plan and with respect to the statutory authority for such payments are in my opinion far from frivolous. They merit the consideration of a court. The status of the respondent as a person in need within the contemplation of the Plan who complains of having been prejudiced by the alleged provincial non-compliance shows that he is a person with a genuine interest in these issues and not a mere busybody.

The judicial concern that in the determination of an issue a court should have the benefit of the contending views of the persons most directly affected by the issue—a consideration that was particularly emphasized by Laskin CJ in *Borowski*—is addressed by the requirement affirmed in *Borowski* that there be no other reasonable and effective manner in which the issue may be brought before a court. In *Thorson*, *McNeil* and *Borowski* that requirement was held to be satisfied by the nature of the legislation challenged and the fact that the Attorney General had refused to institute proceedings although requested to do so. In *Borowski*, the majority and the minority differed essentially, as I read their reasons, on the question whether there was anyone with a more direct interest than the plaintiff who would be likely to challenge the legislation. Here it is quite clear from the nature of the legislation in issue that there could be no one with a more direct interest than the plaintiff in a position to challenge the statutory authority to make the federal cost-sharing payments. In so far as a prior request to the Attorney General to intervene might be considered to be necessary in certain cases to show that there is no other way in which the issue may be brought before a court, I do not think it should be regarded as necessary in a case such as this one, where it is clear from the position adopted by the Attorney General in the case that he would not have consented to the institution of proceedings. I am accordingly of the view that the respondent meets the requirement that there should be no other reasonable and effective manner in which the issue of statutory authority raised by the respondent's statement of claim may be brought before a court.

For all of these reasons I am of the opinion that the respondent should be recognized as having standing to bring his action for a declaration to challenge the legality of the federal cost-sharing payments under s. 7 of the Plan.

As I indicated above, the Federal Court of Appeal did not, at least explicitly, address the question of standing to seek the injunctive relief prayed for by the respondent, as distinct from standing to seek the declaratory relief. The Court dismissed the appeals from the orders in the Trial Division refusing an injunction by way of originating notice of motion and an interim injunction in the action on the ground, as I read the reasons of Thurlow CJ, of lack of urgency and not lack of standing. In his reasons for judgment Thurlow CJ referred throughout to standing to seek a declaration. After giving his reasons for dismissing the appeals from the orders refusing an injunction, he said at 522: "That leaves for consideration the questions whether the appellant has standing to bring the action and whether the statement of claim disclosed a reasonable cause of action for declaratory relief." In this Court counsel for the appellants did not contend that there was a significant distinction to be drawn, for purposes of the issue in the appeal, between standing for a declaration and standing for an injunction. Indeed, that question was simply not addressed in argument. The Federal Court of Appeal and counsel in this Court may well have proceeded on the assumption that there is no significant difference between these remedies, in so far as standing is concerned, as distinct from the conditions of entitlement to them in a particular case. If so, that is in my opinion a sound assumption. It is essential to distinguish, I think, between standing, or the right to seek particular relief, and the entitlement to such relief. The general rule respecting standing to seek a declaration or an injunction, to which I have referred above, has generally been regarded as essentially the same for the two forms of relief. *Cf.* Cromwell, *op. cit.*, at 157-58. I can see no sound reason why the exceptional recognition to public interest standing, as a matter of judicial discretion, which is being affirmed in these reasons should not apply to injunctive as well as declaratory relief. If the respondent is recognized as having standing to seek the declaratory relief then I cannot see why he should not be recognized as also having standing to seek the ancillary injunctive relief. Whether a plaintiff should be granted either declaratory relief or injunctive relief in a particular case is a matter of judicial discretion to be exercised according to criteria and considerations which are somewhat different for the two forms of relief. In the exercise of that discretion in the present case consideration would have to be given to the role of injunction as a public law remedy, including the question whether it will lie against Ministers of the Crown. Those are questions to be left to the trial court. The respondent should in my opinion be recognized as having standing to seek the injunctive relief prayed for in his statement of claim.

[After brief consideration, Le Dain J then rejected the contention that the statement of claim should be struck out because there was not an arguable case.]

Appeal dismissed.

NOTES

1. Why does the court reject the argument that Finlay had standing as of right to challenge the legality of the federal transfer payments? Do you agree with Le Dain J's conclusions on this point? Is Finlay's status as a welfare recipient in any way relevant to the court's

ultimate decision to accord him standing? What reasons does Le Dain J then advance for extending the principle of the constitutional standing cases to "administrative law" cases?

2. What criteria does the Supreme Court lay down as determinative of whether public interest litigants should be afforded standing? In what ways does the Supreme Court believe that these criteria will eliminate inappropriate litigants? Do you agree? Must the applicant establish an entitlement under each of these criteria or are they more in the nature of a list of individually non-definitive factors that are to be considered and weighed by the court? For what reasons does the Supreme Court reject the exclusive status of the attorney general as the initiator of litigation to protect the public interest? Are these convincing? Is the traditional role of the attorney general in any way relevant to the discretion of the court to recognize private individuals or groups as vindicators of the public interest or aspects of it? (We return to the role of the attorney general later.)

3. One consideration that Le Dain J identifies as relevant to the determination whether to accord public interest standing is "justiciability." While accepting that justiciability "is always a matter of concern to the courts," he then states that this is especially so in the case of a claim by a public interest litigant to standing. What does he mean by "justiciability"? Can there be gradations in the justiciability of a dispute? If not, then should this not be treated as an independent criterion for being able to seek relief beyond the issue of standing? (See Allars, "Standing: The Role and Evolution of the Test" (1991), 20 *Fed. LR* 83, at 96-97.)

4. Do the court's concerns about the role of "busybodies" in public interest standing speak more to individual litigants or to the court's understanding of its role and the resources available to support that role? For a detailed examination of the busybody rationale for limited standing and an argument for a more interdependent approach to personal autonomy in the choice to litigate, see Binch, "The Mere Busybody: Autonomy, Equality and Standing" (2002), 40 *Alta. L Rev.* 367.

5. One of the implications of *Finlay* seems to be that the discretion of the court only comes into play when the applicant or plaintiff fails to establish standing by reference to the traditional common law rules or any relevant statutory provisions with respect to standing. Where those standards are met, the plaintiff is entitled to bring the case as of right. As a result, it is to be expected that in many instances where standing is an issue, the argument will proceed in the same way that it did in *Finlay*, with the plaintiff first trying to establish an entitlement to litigate by reference to accepted principles and then, if unsuccessful, seeking to invoke the discretion of the court as recognized by *Finlay*. Given this, consider the following examples and ask yourself whether those seeking relief are sufficiently affected to be entitled to standing as of right and, if not, whether the discretionary considerations established by *Finlay* indicate that they should be recognized by the court.

a) A husband seeks judicial review on administrative law grounds of the decision of a therapeutic abortion committee giving permission for his wife to have an abortion. (See *Medhurst v. Medhurst* (1984), 9 DLR (4th) 252 (Ont. HC).)

b) Parents of children attending a school seek judicial review of the school board's decision to dismiss a popular teacher. The basis of the application is that the teacher was denied natural justice. (See *Re Ratepayers of the New Ross Consolidated School* (1979), 102 DLR (3d) 486 (NS SCTD).)

c) A postmaster challenges the decision of Canada Post to close his post office on the grounds that it is not paying its way. He claims that the decision is patently unreasonable and without any support in fact. His claim to standing is based on the fact that if the closure proceeds, he will be transferred to another branch and will lose the subsidized accommodation that comes with the present position. What if the postmaster fails? Should any member or group of members of the community served by the post office in question be allowed to mount a challenge? (See *Stammers v. Broadbridge* (1987), 73 ALR 523 (FCA GD), and see also *Rural Dignity of Canada v. Canada Post Corp.* (1991-92), 7 Admin. LR (2d) 242 (FCTD and CA).)

d) An organization representing grocers in border towns challenges the enforcement policies with respect to customs duties on groceries bought in the United States. (See *Distribution Canada Inc. v. Canada (Minister of National Revenue)* (1993), 149 NR 152 (FCA).)

e) A trade union challenges the approval of a pesticide by the Minister of Agriculture. It does so on behalf of its members working in a plant where the pesticide will be used. (See *Pulp & Paper Workers of Canada, Local 8 v. Canada (Minister of Agriculture)*, [1992] 1 FC 372 (TD).)

f) A person appointed to the Order of Canada by the governor general objects to the appointment of another person to the Order of Canada and seeks to review judicially the process by which the person was appointed. (See *Chauvin v. Canada* (2009), 2009 FC 1202 (CanLII).)

PUBLIC INTEREST STANDING

In the context of Charter challenges, the Supreme Court revisited the issue of public interest standing and the discretionary considerations that were identified by Le Dain J in *Finlay*. The focus has tended to be on the question whether there is a more appropriate litigant of the issues than the individual or public interest group bringing the cause of action. The first of these judgments involved a challenge by a public interest group to various provisions in an Act that amended Canada's Convention refugee laws.

Canadian Council of Churches v. Canada
(Minister of Employment and Immigration)
[1992] 1 SCR 236 (Can.)

CORY J delivered the judgment of a Court otherwise consisting of La Forest, L'Heureux-Dubé, Sopinka, and Gonthier JJ:

At issue on this appeal is whether the Canadian Council of Churches should be granted status to proceed with an action challenging, almost in its entirety, the validity of the amended *Immigration Act, 1976*, which came into effect January 1, 1989.

Factual Background

The Canadian Council of Churches (the Council), a federal corporation, represents the interests of a broad group of member churches. Through an Inter-Church Committee for

Refugees it co-ordinates the work of the churches aimed at the protection and resettlement of refugees. The Council together with other interested organizations has created an organization known as the Concerned Delegation of Church, Legal, Medical and Humanitarian Organizations. Through this body the Council has commented on the development of refugee policy and procedures both in this country and in others.

In 1988 the Parliament of Canada passed amendments to the *Immigration Act, 1976,* SC 1976-77, c. 52, by SC 1988, c. 35 and c. 36. The amended act came into force on January 1, 1989. It completely changed the procedures for determining whether applicants come within the definition of a Convention Refugee. While the amendments were still under consideration the Council expressed its concerns about the proposed new refugee determination process to members of the government and to the parliamentary committees which considered the legislation. On the first business day after the amended act came into force, the Council commenced this action, seeking a declaration that many if not most of the amended provisions violated the *Canadian Charter of Rights and Freedoms* and the *Canadian Bill of Rights,* RSC 1985, App. III. The Attorney General of Canada brought a motion to strike out the claim on the basis that the Council did not have standing to bring the action and had not demonstrated a cause of action.

[Rouleau J of the Federal Court Trial Division dismissed this application ([1989] 3 FC 3 (TD)) stating in part:

> Finally, I am satisfied that there exists no reasonable, effective or practical manner for the class of persons more directly affected by the legislation, that is refugees, to bring before the court the constitutional issues raised in the plaintiff's statement of claim. There is little question that this new legislation has accelerated the procedure for those persons making application for refugee status in this country. Such applicants are subject to a 72 hour removal order. In that short period of time, an applicant must consult with counsel; a procedure which in itself may take a fair amount of time due to language barriers and the difficulty of a solicitor establishing a proper solicitor-client relationship with an individual who, in some instances, may be from a country where human rights have been disregarded and who is understandably slow to trust anyone in authority.
>
> Even accepting the defendants' argument that a refugee who has had a removal order made against him may seek a stay or injunction from the Federal Court in order to challenge the removal order, such an injunction cannot be considered by the Court before a minimum of 10 days has elapsed from the time of filing the applicant's materials. Consequently, the harm to the refugee will have already occurred, and any remedy granted by the Court may be illusory given that the refugee will be under the jurisdiction of another state.

The Federal Court of Appeal, in a judgment delivered by MacGuigan JA ([1990] 2 FC 534), allowed an appeal save for the challenge to four provisions in the legislation that he said might not be able to be challenged effectively by Convention refugee claimants because of the time limits referred to by Rouleau J at first instance. These provisions, which were the subject of a cross-appeal, were detailed by Cory J.]

1. The claim in paragraph 3(c) of the statement of claim which alleges that the requirement that detainees obtain counsel within 24 hours from the making of a removal order violates s. 7 of the Charter (at 558);

2. The claim in paragraph 6(a) which alleges that provisions temporarily excluding claimants from having claims considered violate s. 7 of the Charter (at 554);

3. The claim in paragraph 10(a) which alleges that provisions allowing the removal of a claimant within 72 hours leave too short a time to consult counsel and violate s. 7 of the Charter (at 561);

4. The claim in paragraph 14(c) which alleges that the provisions permitting the removal of a claimant with a right to appeal within 24 hours if a notice of appeal is not filed in that time violate the Constitution (at 562).

The appellant seeks to have the order of the Federal Court of Appeal set aside. The respondent has cross-appealed to have the remaining positions of the statement of claim struck out.

Issues

The principal question to be resolved is whether the Federal Court of Appeal erred in holding that the Canadian Council of Churches should be denied standing to challenge many of the provisions of the *Immigration Act, 1976*.

The Approaches Taken in Other Common Law Jurisdictions To Granting Parties' Status To Bring Action

It may be illuminating to consider by way of comparison the position taken in other common law jurisdictions on this issue of standing. The highest Courts of the United Kingdom, Australia and the United States have struggled with the problem. They have all recognized the need to balance the access of public interest groups to the Courts against the need to conserve scarce judicial resources. It will be seen that each of these jurisdictions has taken a more restrictive approach to granting status to parties than have the courts in Canada.

[Cory J reviewed the leading cases in these jurisdictions.]

The Question of Standing in Canada

Courts in Canada like those in other common law jurisdictions traditionally dealt with individuals. For example, courts determine whether an individual is guilty of a crime; they determine rights as between individuals; they determine the rights of individuals in their relationships with the state in all its various manifestations. One great advantage of operating in the traditional mode is that the courts can reach their decisions based on facts that have been clearly established. It was by acting in this manner that the courts established the rule of law and provided a peaceful means of resolving disputes. Operating primarily, if not almost exclusively, in the traditional manner courts in most regions operate to capacity. Courts play an important role in our society. If they are to continue to do so care must be taken to ensure that judicial resources are not over-extended. This is a factor that will always have to be placed in the balance when consideration is given to extending standing.

On the other hand there can be no doubt that the complexity of society has spawned ever more complex issues for resolution by the courts. Modern society requires regulation to survive. Transportation by motor vehicle and aircraft requires greater regulation for public safety than did travel by covered wagon. Light and power provided by nuclear energy requires greater control than did the kerosene lamp.

The state has been required to intervene in an ever more extensive manner in the affairs of its citizens. The increase of state activism has led to the growth of the concept of public rights. The validity of government intervention must be reviewed by courts. Even before the passage of the Charter this Court had considered and weighed the merits of broadening access to the courts against the need to conserve scarce judicial resources. It expanded the rules of standing in a trilogy of cases; *Thorson v. Attorney General of Canada*, *Nova Scotia Board of Censors v. McNeil* and *Minister of Justice of Canada v. Borowski*. Writing for the majority in *Borowski, supra*, Martland J set forth the conditions which a plaintiff must satisfy in order to be granted standing, at 598:

> … to establish status as a plaintiff in a suit seeking a declaration that legislation is invalid, if there is a serious issue as to its invalidity, a person need only to show that he is affected by it directly or that he has a genuine interest as a citizen in the validity of the legislation and that there is no other reasonable and effective manner in which the issue may be brought before the Court.

Those then were the conditions which had to be met in 1981.

In 1982 with the passage of the Charter there was for the first time a restraint placed on the sovereignty of Parliament to pass legislation that fell within its jurisdiction. The Charter enshrines the rights and freedoms of Canadians. It is the courts which have the jurisdiction to preserve and to enforce those Charter rights. This is achieved, in part, by ensuring that legislation does not infringe the provisions of the Charter. By its terms the Charter indicates that a generous and liberal approach should be taken to the issue of standing. If that were not done, Charter rights might be unenforced and Charter freedoms shackled. The *Constitution Act, 1982* does not of course affect the discretion courts possess to grant standing to public litigants. What it does is entrench the fundamental right of the public to government in accordance with the law.

The rule of law is recognized in the preamble of the Charter which reads:

> Whereas Canada is founded upon principles that recognize the supremacy of God and the rule of law:

The rule of law is thus recognized as a corner stone of our democratic form of government. It is the rule of law which guarantees the rights of citizens to protection against arbitrary and unconstitutional government action. This same right is affirmed in s. 52(1) which states:

> 52(1) The Constitution of Canada is the supreme law of Canada, and any law that is inconsistent with the provisions of the Constitution is, to the extent of the inconsistency, of no force or effect.

Parliament and the legislatures are thus required to act within the bounds of the constitution and in accordance with the Charter. Courts are the final arbiters as to when that duty has been breached. As a result, courts will undoubtedly seek to ensure that their discretion is exercised so that standing is granted in those situations where it is necessary to ensure that legislation conforms to the Constitution and the Charter.

[Cory J here summarized *Finlay*.]

Should the Current Test for Public Interest Standing Be Extended?

The increasing recognition of the importance of public rights in our society confirms the need to extend the right to standing from the private law tradition which limited party status to those who possessed a private interest. In addition, some extension of standing beyond the traditional parties accords with the provisions of the *Constitution Act, 1982*. However, I would stress that the recognition of the need to grant public interest standing in some circumstances does not amount to a blanket approval to grant standing to all who wish to litigate an issue. It is essential that a balance be struck between ensuring access to the courts and preserving judicial resources. It would be disastrous if the courts were allowed to become hopelessly overburdened as a result of the unnecessary proliferation of marginal or redundant suits brought by well-meaning organizations pursuing their own particular cases certain in the knowledge that their cause is all-important. It would be detrimental, if not devastating, to our system of justice and unfair to private litigants.

The whole purpose of granting status is to prevent the immunization of legislation or public acts from any challenge. The granting of public interest standing is not required when, on a balance of probabilities, it can be shown that the measure will be subject to attack by a private litigant. The principles for granting public standing set forth by this court need not and should not be expanded. The decision whether to grant status is a discretionary one with all which that designation implies. Thus, undeserving applications may be refused. Nonetheless, when exercising the discretion the applicable principles should be interpreted in a liberal and generous manner.

The Application of the Principles for Public Interest Standing to This Case

It has been seen that when public interest standing is sought, consideration must be given to three aspects. First, is there a serious issue raised as to the invalidity of legislation in question? Second, has it been established that the plaintiff is directly affected by the legislation or if not does the plaintiff have a genuine interest in its invalidity? Third, is there another reasonable and effective way to bring the issue before the court?

(1) Serious Issue of Invalidity

It was noted in *Finlay, supra,* that the issues of standing and of whether there is a reasonable cause of action are closely related and indeed tend to merge. In the case at bar the

Federal Court of Appeal in its careful reasons turned its attention to the question of whether the amended statement of claim raised a reasonable cause of action. The claim makes a wide-sweeping and somewhat disjointed attack upon most of the multitudinous amendments to the *Immigration Act, 1976*. Some of the allegations are so hypothetical in nature that it would be impossible for any court to make a determination with regard to them. In many ways the statement of claim more closely resembles submissions that might be made to a parliamentary committee considering the legislation than it does an attack on the validity of the provisions of the legislation. No doubt the similarity can be explained by the fact that the action was brought on the first working day following the passage of the legislation. It is perhaps unfortunate that this court is asked to fulfill the function of a motions court judge reviewing the provisions of a statement of claim. However, I am prepared to accept that some aspects of the statement of claim could be said to raise a serious issue as to the validity of the legislation.

(2) Has the Plaintiff Demonstrated a Genuine Interest?

There can be no doubt that the applicant has satisfied this part of the test. The council enjoys the highest possible reputation and has demonstrated a real and continuing interest in the problems of the refugees and immigrants.

(3) Whether There Is Another Reasonable and Effective Way To Bring the Issue Before the Court

It is this third issue that gives rise to the real difficulty in this case. The challenged legislation is regulatory in nature and directly affects all refugee claimants in this country. Each one of them has standing to initiate a constitutional challenge to secure his or her own rights under the Charter. The applicant council recognizes the possibility that such actions could be brought but argues that the disadvantages which refugees face as a group preclude their effective use of access to the court. I cannot accept that submission. Since the institution of this action by the council, a great many refugee claimants have, pursuant to the provisions of the statute, appealed administrative decisions which affected them. The respondents have advised that nearly 33,000 claims for refugee status were submitted in the first 15 months following the enactment of the legislation. In 1990, some 3,000 individuals initiated claims every month. The Federal Court of Appeal has a wide experience in this field. MacGuigan JA, writing for the court, took judicial notice of the fact that refugee claimants were bringing forward claims akin to those brought by the council on a daily basis. I accept without hesitation this observation. It is clear therefore that many refugee claimants can and have appealed administrative decisions under the statute. These actions have frequently been before the courts. Each case presented a clear concrete factual background upon which the decision of the court could be based.

The appellant also argued that the possibility of the imposition of a 72-hour removal order against refugee claimants undermines their ability to challenge the legislative scheme. I cannot accept that contention. It is clear that the Federal Court has jurisdiction to grant injunctive relief against a removal order: see *Toth v. Canada (Minister of Employment & Immigration)* (1988) 6 Imm. LR (2d) 123 (FCA). Further, from the information submitted by the respondents it is evident that persons submitting claims to refugee status in Canada are in no danger of early or speedy removal. As of March 31, 1990, it required an average of five months for a claim to be considered at the initial "credible basis" hearing. It is therefore clear that in the ordinary case there is more than adequate time for a claimant to prepare to litigate the possible rejection of the claim. However, even where the claims have not been accepted "the majority of removal orders affecting refugee claimants have not been carried out." (See *Report of the Auditor General of Canada to the House of Commons, Fiscal Year Ended 31 March 1990*, pp. 352-353, at para. 14.43.) Even though the Federal Court has been prepared in appropriate cases to exercise its jurisdiction to prevent removal of refugee claimants there is apparently very little need for it to do so. The means exist to ensure that the issues which are sought to be litigated on behalf of individual applicants may readily be brought before the court without any fear that a 72-hour removal order will deprive them of their rights.

From the material presented, it is clear that individual claimants for refugee status, who have every right to challenge the legislation, have in fact done so. There are, therefore, other reasonable methods of bringing the matter before the court. On this ground the applicant council must fail. I would hasten to add that this should not be interpreted as a mechanistic application of a technical requirement. Rather it must be remembered that the basic purpose for allowing public interest standing is to ensure that legislation is not immunized from challenge. Here there is no such immunization as plaintiff refugee claimants are challenging the legislation. Thus the very rationale for the public interest litigation party disappears. The council must, therefore, be denied standing on each of the counts of the statement of claims. This is sufficient to dispose of the appeal. The respondents must also succeed on their cross-appeal to strike out what remained of the claim as the plaintiff council does not satisfy the test for standing on any part of the statement of claim. I would simply mention two other matters.

Intervenor Status

It has been seen that a public interest litigant is more likely to be granted standing in Canada than in other common law jurisdictions. Indeed, if the basis for granting status were significantly broadened, these public interest litigants would displace the private litigant. Yet the views of the public litigant who cannot obtain standing need not be lost. Public interest organizations are, as they should be, frequently granted intervenor status. The views and submissions of intervenors on issues of public importance frequently provide great assistance to the courts. Yet that assistance is given against a background of established facts and in a time-frame and context that is controlled by the courts. A proper balance between providing for the submissions of public interest groups and preserving judicial resources is maintained.

Appeal dismissed; cross-appeal allowed.

NOTES

1. In his judgment, one of Cory J's primary concerns is that of conserving judicial resources. How does exclusion of the Canadian Council of Churches assist in that policy?

Would it not be more efficient for the court to resolve these issues of constitutionality once and for all in proceedings brought by a public interest group that was well-equipped to advance all the relevant arguments rather than have them dealt with in numerous proceedings brought by unevenly represented Convention refugees over years? What countervailing considerations are referred to by Cory J? Where the attack is against a range of provisions in a new statutory regime, is it not more appropriate to deal with such claims of unconstitutionality as a whole rather than piecemeal and case by case? Aside from considerations of judicial resources, is it not likely that some of the dimensions of the legislative regime under attack will be missed if the challenges proceed on such a case-by-case, uncoordinated manner?

2. There seems to be some considerable disagreement among the three courts that dealt with this matter about the ability of Convention refugees to call into question the impugned provisions. What evidence does Cory J rely on for his conclusion that there is scope for all of the provisions to be challenged effectively by refugee claimants? Is this acceptable proof that there is another reasonable and effective way to bring the issue before the courts? Should the relative capacity of the Canadian Council of Churches and Convention refugee claimants have been considered at this point?

3. Cory J recognized that the Council of Churches had a genuine interest in the matters in question and also seemed willing to concede it status as an intervenor when these issues arise in the context of challenges by individual refugee claimants. To what extent should such matters depend on the enjoyment of the "highest possible reputation" and demonstration of "a real and continuing interest in the problems" of the group or individual litigant in question?

4. In addition to the formal legal obstacles to public interest group litigation of public law issues, one must also account for the economic realities of litigation. To the extent that the courts become more willing to make orders for costs against unsuccessful applicants for judicial review, the dimensions of that problem are exacerbated. See, for example, *Sierra Club of Western Canada v. British Columbia (Chief Forester)* (1994), 117 DLR (4th) 395 (BC SC).

5. The court seemingly has also changed its position on the capacity of groups to represent the interests of their members in public law litigation. In 1974, in *L'Association des propriétaires des Jardins Tâché v. Les entreprises Dasken Inc.*, [1974] SCR 2 (Que.), the court denied standing to a non-profit corporation with the object of preserving the residential character of a neighbourhood in the context of a challenge to the allegedly illegal issuance of building permits with respect to the area of the association's concern. Notwithstanding the fact that its members were all property owners in the affected area, Pigeon J, delivering the judgment of the majority, held (at 10) that the "organization was not entitled to exercise the rights of its members." However, as opposed to the minority judges, Pigeon J was prepared to accord standing to seek review to an individual property owner and ratepayer in terms that suggested that she could do so at least in part in a representative capacity. However, in 1991, the court, endorsing a dissenting judgment in the Québec Court of Appeal, held that an employers' organization could bring an action as a representative of its members challenging the validity of anti-scab labour legislation: *Conseil du Patronat du Québec c. Québec (PG)*, [1991] 3 SCR 685. This indicates that in many situations suitably representative bodies may seek judicial review under normal standing principles on behalf of those who are affected directly. Subject to possible concerns about the representative nature and capacities of the organization, it does not have to rely on public interest standing principles.

6. For an application of *Canadian Council of Churches*, see *Lexogest Inc. v. Manitoba (Attorney General)* (1993), 16 Admin. LR (2d) 144 (Man. CA). This case involved a challenge to the validity of a Manitoba regulation that restricted health insurance coverage for abortions to those performed in public hospitals. A corporation that owned and operated an abortion clinic in Winnipeg and two of the physicians employed at that clinic challenged the regulation on administrative and constitutional law grounds. The Court of Appeal had no difficulty in according them standing to raise the administrative *ultra vires* issue ("it directly impacts on their entitlement to payment for a required medical service"). However, it rejected their standing to raise *Constitution Act* and *Charter of Rights and Freedoms* issues; these could be brought more effectively to the court's attention "on the initiative of the patients directly affected by it." How can this differentiation between the administrative and constitutional law aspects of the case be justified?

In contrast, in *Unishare Investments Ltd. v. The Queen* (1994), 18 OR (3d) 603 (Gen. Div.), MacPherson J allowed a corporation that sold flowers to street vendors to proceed with a challenge on Charter grounds to a bylaw that allowed the police to confiscate flowers being sold in violation of the bylaw. Not only did he hold that the corporation was directly affected by the bylaw but also that, given their limited means, it was highly unlikely that individual vendors would ever have the resources to mount such a challenge. This distinguished the case from *Canadian Council of Churches*.

7. Cory J himself revisited the issue of standing in another high-profile Charter case, *Vriend v. Alberta*.

Vriend v. Alberta
[1998] 1 SCR 493 (Alta.)

[Vriend lost his position as a teacher at a private religious school in Alberta when he admitted that he was a homosexual. The Alberta Human Rights Commission rejected his complaint of discrimination on the basis that the Alberta *Individual Rights Protection Act* (IRPA) did not prohibit discrimination on the basis of sexual orientation. Vriend and three lesbian and gay organizations sought a declaration that the omission of sexual orientation from the list of proscribed species of discrimination was contrary to s. 15 of the Charter. They did not confine their challenge to the employment provisions of the IRPA but rather sought to raise the issue generally in relation to all provisions in the Act spelling out the proscribed species of discrimination. The respondent challenged their standing to make such a broad challenge. The majority judgment of the Supreme Court was delivered by Cory and Iacobucci JJ, with the former identified as being responsible for the section on standing. There was no dissent on this aspect of the case.]

CORY J: ...

A. Standing

The appellants seek to challenge the preamble and ss. 2(1), 3, 4, 7(1), 8(1), 10 and 16(1) of the IRPA. The respondents on this appeal submitted that the appellants should have standing to challenge only the sections of the IRPA relating to employment, namely ss. 7(1), 8(1) and 10, since the factual background of the case involves discrimination in employment. The Attorney General of Canada goes even further by arguing that the only provision at issue in this case is s. 7(1), which specifically addresses discrimination in employment practices. ...

In *Canadian Council of Churches* (at p. 253), it was stated that three aspects should be considered:

First, is there a serious issue raised as to the invalidity of legislation in question? Second, has it been established that the plaintiff is directly affected by the legislation or if not does the plaintiff have a genuine interest in its validity? Third, is there another reasonable and effective way to bring the issue before the court?

It is my opinion that these criteria are met with respect to all of the provisions named by the appellants (the preamble and ss. 2(1), 3, 4, 7(1), 8(1), 10 and 16(1)).

A serious issue as to constitutional validity is raised with respect to all of these provisions. The issue is substantially the same for all of the provisions from which sexual orientation is excluded as a prohibited ground of discrimination. There is nothing in particular about s. 7(1) or ss. 7(1), 8(1) and 10 that makes their validity any more questionable than the other provisions dealing with discrimination. The respondents argue that there is no serious issue as to the constitutional validity of the preamble and s. 16 (which sets out the functions of the Human Rights Commission), because those provisions do not confer any specific benefit or protection. Although neither of these two provisions directly confers a benefit or protection, arguably they do so indirectly. An omission from those provisions could well have at least some of the same effects as the omission of these rights from the other sections and therefore raises a serious issue of constitutional validity.

Further Vriend and the other appellants have a genuine and valid interest in all of the provisions they seek to challenge. Both Vriend as an individual and the appellant organizations have a direct interest in the exclusion of sexual orientation from all forms of discrimination. What is at issue here is the exclusion of sexual orientation as a protected ground from the IRPA and its procedures for the protection of human rights. This is not a case about employment discrimination as distinct from any other form of discrimination that occurs within the private sphere and is covered by provincial human rights legislation. Insofar as the particular situation and factual background of the appellant Vriend is relevant to establishing the issues on appeal, it is the denial of access to the complaint procedures of the Alberta Human Rights Commission that is the essential element of this case and not his dismissal from King's College. The particular issues relating to his loss of employment would be for the Human Rights Commission to resolve and do not form part of this appeal. It must also be remembered that Vriend is only one of four appellants. The other three are organizations which are generally concerned with the rights of gays and lesbians and their protection from discrimination in all areas of their lives. There is nothing to restrict their involvement in this appeal to matters of employment.

With respect to the third criterion, the only other way the issue could be brought before the Court with respect to the other sections would be to wait until someone is discriminated against on the ground of sexual orientation in housing, goods and services, etc. and challenge the validity of the provision in each appropriate case. This would not only be wasteful of judicial resources, but also unfair in that it would impose burdens of delay, cost and personal vulnerability to discrimination for the individuals involved in those eventual cases. This cannot be a satisfactory result.

As well it is important to recall that all of the provisions are very similar and do not depend on any particular factual context in order to resolve their constitutional status. The fact that homosexuals have suffered discrimination in all aspects of their lives was accepted in *Egan* [*v. Canada*, [1995] 2 SCR 513 (CA)]. It follows that there is really no need to adduce additional evidence regarding the provisions concerned with discrimination in areas other than employment.

Therefore, the appellants have standing to challenge the validity of all of the provisions named in the constitutional questions, namely the preamble and ss. 2(1), 3, 4, 7(1), 8(1), 10 and 16(1) of the IRPA.

[The court (Major J dissenting in part) went on to find that the omission of sexual orientation from the Act infringed s. 15 of the Charter and was not saved by s. 1. The appeal was therefore allowed and a declaration made reading "sexual orientation" into the relevant provisions.]

Appeal dismissed.

NOTES

1. What distinguishes this case and *Canadian Council of Churches* so as to justify the court giving standing to allow challenges to provisions in the IRPA that were not in issue on the facts of Vriend's own case? Why did the court not hold that allowing Vriend to challenge those other provisions should await cases in which their validity was raised directly? To what extent does the court's decision in this case depend on a greater emphasis on judicial economy than in *Canadian Council of Churches*?

2. The court later added a further dimension to the standing doctrine by recognizing an overriding discretion to hear a case even where the normal rules of standing and public interest standing might not indicate the according of status to the plaintiff or applicant. (See *Canadian Egg Marketing Agency v. Richardson*, [1998] 3 SCR 157 (NWT).)

A critical aspect of *Finlay* was the fact that the case involved a situation where Finlay, a private citizen, was alleging that the federal government was not enforcing the law in that it was allowing Manitoba not to live up to the terms on which it was eligible to receive transfer payments from the federal government under the *Canada Assistance Plan*. Traditionally, the courts were unwilling to allow private citizens to take over the law enforcement role, in effect, in such situations. Compare, however, the decision in the following case involving the entitlement of an individual taxpayer to challenge the government's favourable treatment of another taxpayer.

Harris v. Canada
[2000] 4 FC 37 (CA)

[Harris, a taxpayer, sought a declaration that the minister of national revenue had acted illegally in providing another taxpayer with a favourable private advance ruling while maintaining a different position publicly on the taxability of the funds in question. He alleged that the minister had ulterior motives for providing this preferential treatment. The minister sought to have the proceedings struck out as not disclosing a reasonable cause of action and also for Harris' lack of standing. A prothonotary granted the motion to strike out. The Federal Court Trial Division reversed that decision and the minister appealed to the Federal Court of Appeal.]

SEXTON JA (Létourneau and Robertston JJA concurring): ...

[After rejecting the argument that the proceedings did not reveal a reasonable cause of action, the court dealt with the issue whether Harris should be accorded public interest standing.]

This Court has recognized that where strong public interest issues arise, a court may exercise its discretion to recognize public interest standing. In *Distribution Canada Inc. v. MNR* [[1993] 2 FC 26 (CA)], a case in which a plaintiff sought to require the Minister to comply with certain provisions of the Customs Tariff [RSC 1985 (3d Supp.), c. 41], Desjardins JA held that public interest standing may exist where "the matter raised ... is one of strong public interest and there may be no other way such an issue could be brought to the attention of the Court, were it not for the efforts of the [public interest litigant]" [*Distribution Canada Inc. v. MNR*, above, at 39. Discussion of the House of Lords decision in *National Federation of Self-Employed* omitted.]

I now turn to the four criteria established in *Finlay* to determine whether this Court should exercise its discretion to recognize Mr. Harris' public interest standing.

In *Finlay*, Le Dain J held that courts should be concerned about their proper role and their constitutional relationship to other branches of governments. He held that where an issue may be appropriately decided by a court, a court "should not decline to determine it on the ground that because of its policy context or implications it is better left for review and determination by the legislative or executive branches of government."

In my view, Mr. Harris' statement of claim raises a justiciable issue. His claim that the Minister of National Revenue acted illegally or improperly or for ulterior motives, namely favouritism and preferential treatment by way of a covert deal when he interpreted the provisions of the Act in favour of a specific trust, raises a question of a potential violation of the Act that a court may assess by reference to the Minister's duty to follow the Act "absolutely," as this Court held in *Ludmer* [*v. Canada*, [1995] 2 FC3 (CA), at 17].

The second criterion established by Le Dain J in *Finlay* was that a public interest litigant must raise a serious issue. As Le Dain J concluded in *Finlay*, the issues raised by Mr. Harris are "far from frivolous." Mr. Harris does not merely bring an action to obtain a declaration for an interpretation of particular sections of the Act. Rather, as stated above, he alleges that the Minister of National Revenue acted for ulterior motives with a view to favouring particular taxpayers, in circumstances where there was a "lack of documentation and analysis of key decisions made by Crown officials in this regard." [Statement of claim, at para. 13.] The issues are serious.

The third criterion is that the public interest litigant must have a genuine interest in the issue. On appeal, the Attorney General did not seriously contest that Mr. Harris did have a genuine interest in the issues he raises. Mr. Harris is a taxpayer. He is a member of an organization that seeks to ensure the fair administration of the taxation system. Accordingly, I conclude that Mr. Harris has a genuine interest in the issues he raises.

Finally, in exercising its discretion to recognize public interest standing, a court must be satisfied that there is no other reasonable and effective manner in which the issue may be brought before a court. Here too, the Attorney General did not seriously contend that there was another reasonable or effective manner in which the issue could be brought before a court. Mr. Harris requested the Attorney General to do so twice, but to this date, the Attorney General has not yet complied. It cannot be seriously contended that the taxpayers who were provided with the 1991 ruling favourable to them would raise the issues brought by Mr. Harris. Therefore, I conclude that there is no other reasonable and effective manner in which the issue could be brought before a court.

Conclusion on Standing

Public interest standing has been granted in analogous cases. For example, in *Greater Victoria Concerned Citizens Assn. v. Provincial Capital Commission* [(1990), 46 Admin. LR 74 (BC SC)], a citizens group successfully obtained standing to seek to obtain a declaration that an agreement to lease certain heritage property as a tourist attraction was beyond the Provincial Capital Commission's jurisdiction. In *Union of Nor. Wkrs. v. NWT (Min. of Safety & Pub. Services)* [[1991] NWTR 103 (SC)], a union was granted public interest standing to seek to compel a government minister to hold occupational health and safety board meetings. In *Sierra Club of Canada v. Canada (Minister of Finance)* [[1999] 2 FC 211 (TD)], an organization promoting protection of the environment was granted standing to seek to compel several government ministers to subject the sale of nuclear reactors to a full environmental assessment under the *Canadian Environmental Assessment Act* [SC 1992, c. 37], the absence of which was said to be unlawful.

I do not think that there is a principled basis for concluding that the Minister of National Revenue is somehow protected from a similar action by a public interest litigant to compel the Minister to perform his or her statutory duties. Accordingly, I conclude that Muldoon J properly ruled that Mr. Harris could be granted public interest standing and therefore correctly set aside the Prothonotary's granting of the Crown's motion to strike.

I wish to emphasize the narrow cause of action for which public interest standing has been granted. Mr. Harris does not merely seek to obtain the interpretation of a particular provision of the Act, akin to requesting a court to provide a legal opinion. A mere *bona fide* change of position on interpretation of a statute, without more, would be insufficient to constitute a cause of action and would have been insufficient to persuade this Court to exercise its discretion to recognize public interest standing.

Nevertheless, in considering Mr. Harris' cause of action for which public interest standing has been granted, the Trial Judge may incidentally find it necessary to consider whether, on a proper construction of the Act, "taxable Canadian property" may be held by a resident of Canada. …

I would therefore dismiss the appeal, with costs.

Appeal dismissed.

NOTE

In his judgment, Sexton JA emphasized that the court gave Harris standing because he alleged that the minister acted for ulterior motives in taking the position he did. He indicated also that the situation would have been different had the allegation been merely that the minister erred in law in his interpretation of the Act. In terms of the second *Finlay* criterion, the allegation of ulterior motives or the equivalent of bad faith made this a "serious" issue. This indicates that, in at least some circumstances, the courts will look to the basis on which judicial review is sought and that a mere error of law may not count for as much as an assertion of abuse of discretion. There is no whiff of this in *Finlay*. Can it be justified by reference to the particular context, the administration of the tax scheme? If so, what other contexts might demand this higher standard on the second criterion?

THE ROLE OF THE ATTORNEY GENERAL

As noted above, the attorney general was traditionally the only appropriate person to commence litigation in the name of the public interest. That position must now be re-evaluated in administrative law after the decision in *Finlay*. Are there in fact circumstances in which, in the absence of anyone with standing as of right, the only appropriate plaintiff or applicant is the attorney general either on his or her own initiative or by allowing the use of his or her name in relator proceedings? As we have seen, there may be situations where the courts will accept that law enforcement lies in the hands of the attorney general or other designated authorities and will not allow claims by private citizens or groups as surrogates. However, *Harris* suggests that there are a range of situations where citizens will have status to assume a law enforcement role. The other side of the coin is the question whether the attorney general has standing as of right or automatically to seek judicial review.

Until the emergence of public interest standing, the assumption was that the status of the attorney general to seek judicial review was beyond question. This proposition arose in the following case. Reed J's judgment on this point is useful both in establishing the legal status of the attorney general in such matters and in introducing the problem of the right of a statutory authority to defend in its own name challenges to its decisions and to appeal against adverse judgments.

Energy Probe v. Canada (Atomic Energy Control Board)
[1984] 2 FC 138 (TD)

[As we saw earlier, in chapter 5 of this text, Bias and Lack of Independence, Energy Probe challenged the renewal of a nuclear reactor's licence on the basis of the bias of a member of the licensing authority. The board challenged Energy Probe's standing, but the court accorded the group standing in the public interest. Energy Probe also contested the attorney general of Canada's right to be a party to the proceedings.]

REED J: … The applicant, Energy Probe, does not object to the Attorney General making arguments to the Court on the issues but contends that he should do so only as an *amicus curiae*. The Attorney General on the other hand wants full party status. The immediate cause of this difference is that the Attorney General wishes to ensure himself of a right to appeal any decision I might take on the *certiorari* motion while the applicant wishes to preclude that possibility. It is not likely that either Ontario Hydro or the Atomic Energy Control Board would appeal a decision not in their favour. Rather, they would proceed immediately to cure the defect, as soon as possible by a rehearing.

It should be noted that the Attorney General could not be precluded, in any event, from having the legal issues raised by this case finally determined since authority exists under section 55 of the *Supreme Court Act* for the Governor-in-Council to refer questions to the Supreme Court.

The Attorney General argues that he should be allowed standing because: (1) a decision in the main action will affect Crown interests or the public interest generally; (2) an analogy should be drawn to the status given to the Attorney General in constitutional cases; (3) this Court has discretion pursuant to section 18 of the *Federal Court Act* and Rules 1101 and 1716(2)(b) which it should exercise because of the important issues of public concern (policy) raised; and (4) since the Atomic Energy Control Board itself cannot appear except for restricted purposes (see *Northwestern Utilities Ltd. v. City of Edmonton*, [1979] 1 SCR 684 (Alta.)), the Attorney General of Canada should be allowed standing in order to ensure that all relevant arguments are made to the Court.

Counsel for Ontario Hydro supported the arguments of the Attorney General noting particularly that his client's interests did not coincide with those of the Attorney General. In addition he relied heavily on the decision of the Supreme Court in *PPG Industries Canada Ltd. v. Attorney General of Canada* [1976] SCR 739 (Can.). In that case the Attorney General was given standing to seek an order to quash a decision of the Anti-Dumping Tribunal on the basis of bias two years after the decision in question had been made.

Counsel for the applicant, Energy Probe, as would be expected, took the opposing view on almost all the above arguments. He argued that the issue was not one affecting Crown interests or the public interest generally but was very restricted and specific in nature, concerning the alleged pecuniary bias of only one member of the Atomic Energy Control Board. He argued that an analogy could not be drawn to the status given to the Attorney General in constitutional cases. He contended that the Attorney General's right of standing in those cases was based on a doctrine of "legislative trespass": a doctrine, I might say, borrowed from the Australian jurisprudence and which does not in any event fit well into the Canadian context. In any event, it must be noted that counsel for the applicant was rather on the horns of a dilemma in making these arguments since it was obvious that it would become important to him in making argument for his own client's claim of standing on the *certiorari* application to argue that an issue of significant public importance was involved; the issue of the right of the citizenry to have AECB decisions made by a tribunal untainted by pecuniary interest.

I have no doubt that this is an appropriate case in which the Attorney General should be given permission to be added as a party. The Attorney General has a direct interest in the outcome of this case. It is alleged that one of the members of the AECB has a pecuniary bias in the decisions of the Board because he is president and director of a company which sells significant quantities of radiation-resistant cables for nuclear reactors to Ontario Hydro. It is not a case of bias being alleged with respect to one isolated transaction but because of a continuing business activity. If bias exists in this case then the Board member will be an ineffective member for many decisions which the Board makes. Thus the issue raised challenges the practice of the Governor-in-Council in appointing as part-time AECB members persons having interests in the industry of the nature described above. The issue relates to the *choosing* of persons for appointment to the Board and to the requirements that would have to be placed upon them (*eg*, divestiture of interests) to make them effective members of the Board.

In addition I think the Attorney General should be added on the ground that a "question of general importance is raised" in these proceedings on which the Court should have his arguments. (Refer: Rule 1101 of the *Federal Court Rules*.)

I cannot accept Energy Probe's argument that the issue here is merely confined to Mr Olsen's alleged bias and is a "one-shot affair." The ramifications are much broader. They do involve as noted above questions relating to the composition of the Board, and perhaps other Boards similarly constituted; they do involve, as counsel for Energy Probe was bound to argue on the main motion, questions relating to the general public confidence in boards of this nature.

Counsel for Energy Probe argued that the Attorney General was entitled to no higher standing than the AECB. In *Northwestern Utilities Ltd. v. City of Edmonton*, [1979] 1 SCR 684 (Alta.) at 708-709, the Supreme Court held:

> Section 65 no doubt confers upon the Board the right to participate on appeals from its decisions, but in the absence of a clear expression of intention on the part of the Legislature, this right is a limited one. The Board is given *locus standi* as a participant in the nature of an *amicus curiae* but not as a party. That this is so is made evident by s. 63(2) of the *Public Utilities Board Act* which reads as follows:
>
> > 63(2) The party appealing shall, within ten days after the appeal has been set down, give to the parties affected by the appeal or the respective solicitors by whom the parties were represented before the Board, and to the secretary of the Board, notice in writing that the case has been set down to be heard in appeal, and the appeal shall be heard by the court of appeal as speedily as practicable.
>
> Under s. 63(2) a distinction is drawn between "parties" who seek to appeal a decision of the Board or were represented before the Board, and the Board itself. The Board has a limited status before the Court, and may not be considered as a party, in the full sense of that

term, to an appeal from its own decisions. In my view, this limitation is entirely proper. This limitation was no doubt consciously imposed by the Legislature in order to avoid placing an unfair burden on an appellant who, in the nature of things, must on another day and in another cause again submit itself to the rate-fixing activities of the Board. It also recognizes the universal human frailties which are revealed when persons or organizations are placed in such adversarial positions.

This appeal involves an adjudication of the Board's decision on two grounds both of which involve the legality of administrative action. One of the two appellants is the Board itself, which through counsel presented detailed and elaborate arguments in support of its decision in favour of the Company. Such active and even aggressive participation can have no other effect than to discredit the impartiality of an administrative tribunal either in the case where the matter is referred back to it, or in future proceedings involving similar interests and issues or the same parties. The Board is given a clear opportunity to make its point in its reasons for its decision, and it abuses one's notion of propriety to countenance its participation as a full-fledged litigant in this Court, in complete adversarial confrontation with one of the principals in the contest before the Board itself in the first instance.

It has been the policy in this Court to limit the role of an administrative tribunal whose decision is at issue before the Court, even where the right to appear is given by statute, to an explanatory role with reference to the record before the Board and to the making of representations relating to jurisdiction: *vide Labour Relations Board of New Brunswick v. Eastern Bakeries Ltd.* [1961] SCR 72 (NB) and *Labour Relations Board of Saskatchewan v. Dominion Fire Brick & Clay Products Ltd.* [1947] SCR 336 (Sask.).

Accordingly, counsel for Energy Probe argued that since the Board's role could only be that of *amicus curiae* or defender of the Board's jurisdiction (in the narrow sense of that word) the Attorney General, equally, could only play that role.

I do not agree. It is not the Attorney General who is being attacked for bias. None of the reasons for which the Board is excluded apply to the Attorney General. It is not the Attorney General who will hear any rehearing of a licence application should an order for *certiorari* be given. It is not a decision by the Attorney General which is under review. Accordingly, I find no reason in the *Northwestern Utilities* case or the other cases to which it refers which create an implied or express limitation on the propriety of the Attorney General obtaining standing in this case. This is so even considering the fact that under section 3 of the *Atomic Energy Control Act* the Board is an agent of Her Majesty. While the position of a principal may be similar to that of his agent for many purposes, they are not identical and their interests are not necessarily identical. Having come to this conclusion it is unnecessary for me to deal with much of the argument made by counsel to the effect that the Attorney General can only be heard as an *amicus curiae*.

Counsel's second argument was that the Attorney General had neither a statutory right nor a common law right to intervene. With respect to the first half of this argument he referred to section 4 of the *Department of Justice Act*:

The Minister of Justice shall ...
    (b) see that the administration of public affairs is in accordance with law;
    (c) have the superintendence of all matters connected with the administration of justice in Canada, not within the jurisdiction of the governments of the provinces.

He proceeded then to argue that, while the Attorney General might have authority to intervene to quash a tribunal decision for bias, he could not intervene to try to defend one from a charge of bias. I must admit I do not see this argument. If the duty imposed by section 4 is to see that the administration of public affairs is in accordance with law or to superintend "matters connected with the administration of justice in Canada" this would include seeing that decisions were made in accordance with law, and this should involve the right to argue either side of a case depending upon which in the Attorney General's opinion was more consonant with the law as he viewed it.

I note however that Chief Justice Laskin in the PPG case (*supra*) seems to cast doubt on whether section 4(b) had any relevance at all to the role of the Attorney General in this type of situation because subsection (b) refers to "public affairs." I wondered too whether section 4 was relevant at all to the role of the Attorney General. That section addresses itself to the role of the Minister of Justice and while the two may be embodied in one person in our system, the offices are different. In my view it is section 5 of the *Department of Justice Act* which is relevant:

> 5. The Attorney General of Canada shall
> (a) be entrusted with the powers and charged with the duties that belong to the office of the Attorney General of England by law or usage, so far as those powers and duties are *applicable to Canada*. ... [Italics added.]

Counsel argued that the roles of the Attorney General in England and in Canada are different and that in order to rely on the common law rules respecting that role as developed in England the Attorney General of Canada must demonstrate a relevant similarity between his role and that of his United Kingdom counterpart. Reference was made to *Re Bisaillon and Keable* (1981) 127 DLR (3d) 368 (Que. CA) at 374-76 and 397; overruled on other grounds by the Supreme Court (1983) 2 DLR (4th) 193 (SCC Que.).

It is trite law that the role of the Attorney General in Canada differs from that of his counterpart in England but none of the differences referred to either in the *Basaillon* case or by counsel for Energy Probe were relevant to drawing a difference between the roles that both might seek in this case.

The two grounds on which the Attorney General seeks and should be given standing to appear in this case are equally applicable in both countries.

He is appearing to protect a Crown interest which at one level is not qualitatively different from the right given to any person to appear before a court to make representations when his interest will be affected by a decision of the Court. Secondly the issue before the Court is one of general public importance and of such a nature that the Court deems it beneficial to hear argument of the Attorney General on the issue in order to ensure that all arguments are adequately canvassed. Reference might be made in this regard to *Adams v. Adams* [1971] P 188.

Accordingly the application to add the Attorney General as an intervenor is granted.

NOTES

1. Why is it ironic that Energy Probe resisted the attempt of the attorney general to be recognized as a party-intervenor in these proceedings? What, if anything, does this case say

about the role of the attorney general as representative of the public interest and the nature of the public interest? Does this have any bearing on Energy Probe's own claim to standing to seek judicial review?

2. On appeal, the Federal Court of Appeal upheld Reed J's holding in favour of the attorney general, but in general terms: [1985] FC 563 (CA), at 575-79 and 585.

3. Subsequently, the Canadian courts have been consistent in their recognition of the attorney general's status in other contexts. Thus, in *Canada (Attorney General) v. Gaboreault*, [1992] 3 FC 566 (CA), the Federal Court of Appeal sustained the right of the federal attorney general to pursue a judicial review application under then s. 28 of the *Federal Court Act* even after the union, the members of which were the targets of the Canada Labour Relations Board order under challenge, discontinued its application. The court doubted whether it had any discretion over the matter of the attorney general's status given the language of s. 28 of the *Federal Court Act*, which provided that the attorney general could bring such an application; but, in any event, it was prepared to recognize the attorney general's interest in continuing the litigation. That interest was one of preventing the perpetuation of a ruling that would be a precedent in future matters before the board and that would leave a void in the law.

4. Similarly, the Ontario Divisional Court, in *Latif v. Ontario (Human Rights Commission)* (1992), 4 Admin. LR (2d) 227 (Ont. Div. Ct.), recognized the entitlement of the attorney general to intervene in a judicial review application and apply for an order striking out that application as premature, in the sense that the designated human rights board of inquiry should have an opportunity to itself deal with an issue of allegedly unreasonable and prejudicial delay before it was subject to judicial review. This entitlement was said to arise out of the provisions of s. 9(4) of the *Judicial Review Procedure Act*, RSO 1990, c. J.1, providing not only that the attorney general was to be given notice of any judicial review application under the Act but also that he was "entitled as of right to be heard in person or by counsel on the application."

5. More recently, in *Sutcliffe v. Ontario (Environment)* (2004), 69 OR (3d) 257, 242 DLR (4th) 709, 14 Admin. LR (4th) 294 (CA), Rosenberg JA refused a motion to strike a notice of intervention by the attorney general of Ontario. The attorney general gave notice of her intent to intervene in the proceeding only at the stage of an appeal from a judicial review decision by the Divisional Court, in which the Divisional Court quashed the terms of reference issued by the minister of the environment in connection with an environmental assessment (the minister of the environment did not seek to appeal the Divisional Court's decision). Rosenberg JA found that the attorney general had a right to be heard in any judicial review proceeding, apart from s. 9(4) of the *Judicial Review Procedure Act*, as a modern embodiment of the common law prerogative writs. On the other hand, the attorney general's right to intervene on a statute-based appeal came only from the statute and had no independent basis in common law. In the proceeding at hand, however, the appeal from the Divisional Court decision derived from a judicial review application, such that the attorney general could seek an appeal based on the broad terms of s. 9(4) of the *Judicial Review Procedure Act*.

6. For a discussion of the history and statutory authority of the attorney general's powers to represent the public in relator and other proceedings, see McAllister, "The Attorney General's Role as Guardian of the Public Interest in Charter Litigation" (2002), 21 *Windsor YB Access to Justice* 47.

THE STATUS OF THE AUTHORITY UNDER ATTACK

Aside from any general public interest and constitutional reasons for according recognition as a party to the attorney general, the lengthy excerpt from Estey J's judgment in *Northwestern Utilities Ltd. v. City of Edmonton*, [1979] 1 SCR 684 (Alta.) provides Reed J with a specific reason for allowing the attorney general's application in *Energy Board*—namely, the inability of the board to appeal a judgment quashing its decision for breach of procedural fairness. In this judgment, Estey J goes on to elaborate the appropriate role of a statutory authority under challenge and the reasons for this position (at 709-11):

> Where the right to appear and present arguments is granted, an administrative tribunal would be well advised to adhere to the principles enunciated by Aylesworth JA in *Int'l Ass'n. of Machinists v. Genaire Ltd.* (1958) 18 DLR (2d) 588 (CA) at 589-590:
>
>> Clearly upon an appeal from the Board, counsel may appear on behalf of the Board and may present argument to the appellant tribunal. We think in all propriety, however, such argument should be addressed not to the merits of the case as between the parties appearing before the Board, but rather to the jurisdiction or lack of jurisdiction of the Board. If argument by counsel for the Board is directed to such matters as we have indicated, the impartiality of the Board will be the better emphasized and its dignity and authority the better preserved, while at the same time the appellate tribunal will have the advantage of any submissions as to jurisdiction which counsel for the Board may see fit to advance.
>
> Where the parent or authorizing statute is silent as to the role or status of the tribunal in appeal or review proceedings, this Court has confined the tribunal strictly to the issue of its jurisdiction to make the order in question (*vide Central Broadcasting Co. Ltd. v. Canada Labour Relations Board* [1977] 2 SCR 112 (Can.)).
>
> In the sense the term has been employed by me here, "jurisdiction" does not include the transgression of the authority of a tribunal by its failure to adhere to the rules of natural justice. In such an issue, when it is joined by a party to proceedings before that tribunal in a review process, it is the tribunal which finds itself under examination. To allow an administrative board the opportunity to justify its action and indeed to vindicate itself would produce a spectacle not ordinarily contemplated in our judicial traditions. In *Re Canada Labour Relations Board and Transair Ltd.* [1977] 1 SCR 722 (Can.) at 746-747, Spence J, speaking on this point, stated:
>
>> It is true that the finding that an administrative tribunal has not acted in accord with the principles of natural justice has been used frequently to determine that the Board has declined to exercise its jurisdiction and therefore has had no jurisdiction to make the decision which it has purported to make. I am of the opinion, however, that this is a mere matter of technique in determining the jurisdiction of the Court to exercise the remedy of *certiorari* and is not a matter of the tribunal's defence of its jurisdiction. The issue of whether or not a board has acted in accordance with the principles of natural justice is surely not a matter upon which the board, whose exercise of its functions is under attack, should debate, in appeal, as a protagonist and that issue should be fought out before the appellate or reviewing Court by the parties and not by the tribunal whose actions are under review.

Do you agree with the justifications advanced by the court for a limited view of the right of the board to participate in court proceedings? Are there countervailing considerations? After all, if the courts are moving in the direction of according greater deference to tribunal expertise, should not the tribunal be able to justify its procedures and decisions? Recall also that many administrative decisions are the product of an unopposed application. There will be no "winner" to defend the tribunal's position on judicial review. In such cases, indeed generally, is it appropriate to allow the attorney general to represent the position of the tribunal that is under attack? Is the impartiality of the statutory authority less discredited when its case is being put by the attorney general? See Falzon, "Tribunal Standing on Judicial Review" (2008), 21 *CJALP* 21; Semple, "The Case for Tribunal Standing in Canada" (2007), 20 *CJALP* 305; Jacobs and Kuttner, "Discovering What Tribunals Do: Tribunal Standing Before the Courts" (2002), 81 *Can. Bar Rev.* 616; Campbell, "Appearances of Courts and Tribunals as Respondents to Applications for Judicial Review" (1982), 56 *Aust. LJ* 293; and Picher, "Adjudicator, Administrator or Advocate? The Role of the Labour Board in Judicial Review Proceedings" (1984), 62 *Can. Bar Rev.* 22.

Ten years after the Supreme Court of Canada's restrictive approach to tribunal standing in *Northwestern Utilities*, in *CAIMAW Local 14 v. Paccar of Canada Ltd.*, [1989] 2 SCR 983 (BC), La Forest J revisited the wider issue in the context of a decision on whether a tribunal should be able to be a party and defend itself in proceedings where the allegation was one of patent unreasonableness:

Standing of the Industrial Relations Council

The union argued that the Industrial Relations Council, having had the opportunity in two lengthy sets of reasons to offer a rational basis for its conclusion, has no standing to make submissions before this court in support of the reasonableness of its decision. It takes the position that while the board could legitimately show that it had jurisdiction to embark upon the inquiry it did, a point the union concedes in any event, it cannot argue that it has not subsequently lost that jurisdiction through a patently unreasonable decision. With respect, I cannot accept this argument. In my view, the Industrial Relations Council has standing before this court to make submissions not only explaining the record before the court, but also to show that it had jurisdiction to embark upon the inquiry and that it has not lost that jurisdiction through a patently unreasonable interpretation of its powers. ...

In *BCGEU v. Industrial Relations Council* (unreported, BC CA, May 24, 1988), the British Columbia Court of Appeal held that the Industrial Relations Council had the right to make the submissions that the court below had erred in substituting its judgment for that of the Industrial Relations Council, and that the court erred in finding the council's interpretation of the Act to be patently unreasonable. In the course of his judgment, Taggart JA for the court made the following statement with which I am in complete agreement, at 13:

> The traditional basis for holding that a tribunal should not appear to defend the correctness of its decision has been the feeling that it is unseemly and inappropriate for it to put itself in that position. But when the issue becomes, as it does in relation to the patently unreasonable test, whether the decision was reasonable, there is a powerful policy reason in favour of permitting the tribunal to make submissions. That is, the tribunal is in the best position to draw the attention of the court to those considerations, rooted in the specialized jurisdiction or expertise of the tribunal, which may render reasonable what

would otherwise appear unreasonable to someone not versed in the intricacies of the specialized area. In some cases, the parties to the dispute may not adequately place those considerations before the court, either because the parties do not perceive them or do not regard it as being in their interest to stress them.

Before this court, the Industrial Relations Council confined its submissions to two points. It first argued that the Court of Appeal erred in applying the wrong standard of review to the decision of the Board. It submitted that the Court of Appeal reviewed for correctness instead of for reasonableness. As I have already indicated, I agree that the Court of Appeal erred in adopting such an approach. The second branch of the council's submissions was to show that the Board had considered each of the union's submissions before it, and had given reasoned, rational rejections to each of the arguments. The argument before us emphasized that the council had made a careful review of the relevant authorities and had made a decision that was within its exclusive jurisdiction. At no point did it argue that the decision of the Board was correct. Rather it argued that it was a reasonable approach for the Board to adopt. The council had standing to make all these arguments, and in doing so it did not exceed the limited role the court allows an administrative tribunal in judicial review proceedings.

Falzon ("Tribunal Standing on Judicial Review" (2008), 21 *CJALP* 21, at 34) discussed *Paccar's* permissive approach to tribunal standing as follows:

Paccar recognizes what experience shows—that private parties argue what it is in their interest to argue, and that two adversarial private parties will not necessarily provide the court with a full and proper context for deciding public law cases, particularly when a decision will have implications beyond the case itself. …

Many examples of this could be given. In some cases, private parties will find it to be in their interests to "defend" a tribunal's decision on the narrowest basis possible. They will not regard it as being in their interest to advance arguments taking a broad view of a tribunal's powers, or advancing a broad view of deference, as such a position might make it more difficult for them in a future case as a petitioner or appellant. In other cases, a private party respondent, who may have only a single foray before the tribunal, may have very limited resources and ability to advance a full and proper administrative law defence of the tribunal's decision which reflects an informed understanding of the tribunal's legislative history, operational reality and jurisprudence.

In the aftermath of *Paccar* and *Northwestern Utilities*, the law of tribunal standing in Canada has not been clear. However, the general law may be clarified somewhat by statutory provisions on the status of an administrative decision-maker to participate in judicial review proceedings. This is the case in Ontario, for example, by virtue of s. 9(2) of the *Judicial Review Procedure Act*, RSO 1990, c. J.1. The following decision indicates the role of the Act in informing judicial discretion on the question of tribunal standing, against the backdrop of the permissive and restrictive approaches in *Paccar* and *Northwestern Utilities*, which may themselves be difficult to reconcile

Children's Lawyer for Ontario v. Goodis
(2005), 75 OR (3d) 309, 253 DLR (4th) 489, 29 Admin. LR (4th) 86 (CA)

[At issue in this case was the entitlement to standing of the information and privacy commissioner of Ontario in a judicial review proceeding against it. The application for judicial review was brought by the Children's Lawyer after the commissioner ordered disclosure of records held by the Children's Lawyer to a person who, when she was a child, was represented by the Children's Lawyer in legal proceedings. In the judicial review proceeding, the Children's Lawyer requested that the commissioner be denied standing, or at least be prohibited from arguing that the commissioner's decision was correct on a basis that was not given in her original decision. The Divisional Court refused the Children's Lawyer's request as well as the application for judicial review, leading the Children's Lawyer to appeal to the Court of Appeal. The person who requested the records did not respond to the judicial review application or participate in the court proceedings.]

GOUDGE JA: ...

[Discussion of the facts and the case law from *Northwestern Utilities* to *Paccar* has been omitted.]

[24] Since *Paccar* [*CAIMAW Local 14 v. Paccar of Canada Ltd.*, [1989] 2 SCR 983] the fundamental values of maintaining tribunal impartiality and facilitating a fully informed adjudication have been employed in a number of cases—separately or together—to underpin decisions on this issue. Some have followed *Northwestern Utilities* [*Northwestern Utilities Ltd. v. City of Edmonton*, [1979] 1 SCR 684]. Some have followed *Paccar*. In other cases, the courts have simply given full standing as a matter of course to tribunals to defend their decisions without even broaching, let alone discussing, the limits of their standing. In a thoughtful article on the subject, Laverne Jacobs and Thomas Kuttner cite as two examples of this method *Quebec (Commission des affaires sociales) v. Daigle*, [1992] 1 SCR 952 and *Ellis-Don Ltd. v. Ontario (Labour Relations Board)*, [2001] 1 SCR 221. See Laverne A. Jacobs and Thomas S. Kuttner, "Discovering What Tribunals Do: Tribunal Standing before the Courts" (2002) 8 Can. Bar. Rev. 616.

[25] Against this rather clouded jurisprudential backdrop, I think the analysis of the scope of standing to be accorded to the Commissioner in this case must begin with the relevant legislation. Section 9(2) of the *Judicial Review Procedure Act* reads:

> For the purposes of an application for judicial review in relation to the exercise, refusal to exercise or proposed or purported exercise of a statutory power, the person who is authorized to exercise the power may be a party to the application.

[26] The ordinary meaning of this provision gives the administrative tribunal the right to be a party to the proceeding if it chooses to do so. It leaves to the tribunal rather than the court the decision of whether to become a party to the application for judicial review.

[27] However, once a party, the scope of a tribunal's standing is a subject not addressed by the legislation. Although the legislature could have pre-empted the debate by

spelling out precise limits to a tribunal's participation, it has chosen not to do so. The legislation's silence necessarily leaves this issue to the court's discretion, as part of its task of ensuring that its procedures serve the interests of justice. Where the issue arises, the court must exercise this discretion to determine the scope of standing to be accorded to a tribunal that is a party to a judicial review proceeding.

[28] This approach to s. 9(2) was well described by the Divisional Court in *Re Consolidated-Bathurst Packaging Ltd. and International Woodworkers of America Local 2-69 et al.* (1985), 51 OR (2d) 481. In that case, judicial review was sought of a decision of the Ontario Labour Relations Board on the basis that the draft decision by the hearing panel was presented to the full Board for discussion of policy, thereby violating the principle of natural justice.

[29] The applicant objected to counsel for the Board making submissions about its own procedure. However, the Divisional Court unanimously rejected this argument. It found that s. 9(2) entitled the Board to be a party to the proceedings and it then exercised its discretion to permit Board counsel full latitude to answer the submissions of the applicant.

[30] When the case was appealed to the Court of Appeal for Ontario and then to the Supreme Court of Canada, Board counsel was again permitted to argue fully. In neither court was the scope of standing raised, let alone commented upon.

[31] In the decision under appeal here, the Divisional Court adopted the approach used in *Consolidated Bathurst, supra*. It held that the scope of standing accorded to the Commissioner is best left to judicial discretion. In exercising that discretion to permit the Commissioner to respond fully to the applicant, the court appeared to be most moved by the desire to avoid denying itself legitimate, helpful submissions. On this basis, the Children's Lawyer's motion to deny or limit the Commissioner's standing was dismissed.

[32] In this court, all parties took similar positions, at least at the broadest level of generality. They all argued that the court should approach the scope of standing issue contextually and should avoid the formalism of fixed rules that turn on whether the question before the court is one of jurisdiction, natural justice, or the applicable standard of review. They all urged the same "pragmatic and functional" label for this approach but disagreed on the considerations that should inform the court's decision.

[33] As I have said, s. 9(2) of the *Judicial Review Procedure Act* entitles the administrative tribunal to be a party to the proceedings but leaves to the court's discretion the scope of its standing. Given the wide variety of administrative tribunals and types of decisions that are today subjected to judicial review, I agree that the court should exercise this discretion paying attention to the context presented in the particular application. However, I think it is both unnecessary and confusing to use the "pragmatic and functional" label. This phrase has developed a strong association with the quite different task of determining the proper standard of review and with the well-known factors embodied in that approach, which will not automatically be useful in determining the scope of standing.

[34] However, I agree with the parties that a context-specific solution to the scope of tribunal standing is preferable to precise *a priori* rules that depend either on the grounds being pursued in the application or on the applicable standard of review. For example, a categorical rule denying standing if the attack asserts a denial of natural justice could deprive the court of vital submissions if the attack is based on alleged deficiencies in the structure or operation of the tribunal, since these are submissions that the tribunal is

uniquely placed to make. Similarly, a rule that would permit a tribunal standing to defend its decision against the standard of reasonableness but not against one of correctness, would allow unnecessary and prevent useful argument. Because the best argument that a decision is reasonable may be that it is correct, a rule based on this distinction seems tenuously founded at best as Robertson JA said in *United Brotherhood of Carpenters and Joiners of America Local 1368 v. Bransen Construction Ltd. et al.* (2002), 249 NBR (2d) 93, at para. 32.

[35] Nor do I think cases like *Northwestern Utilities* and *Paccar, supra*, dictate the use of precise rules of this sort. Particularly in light of the recent evolution of administrative law away from formalism and towards the more flexible practical approach exemplified by *Pushpanathan v. Canada (Minister of Citizenship and Immigration)*, [1998] 1 SCR 982, I think these cases are best viewed as sources of the fundamental considerations that should inform the court's discretion in the context of a particular case. Resolving the scope of standing on this basis rather than by means of a set of fixed rules is likely to produce the most effective interplay between the array of different administrative decision makers and the courts.

[36] If this is so, what are the important considerations that should guide the court in the exercise of its discretion? In my view, the two most important considerations are those reflected in the two seminal cases on this issue: *Paccar* and *Northwestern Utilities, supra*.

[37] In *Paccar*, La Forest J articulated the importance of having a fully informed adjudication of the issues before the court. Because of its specialized expertise, or for want of an alternative knowledgeable advocate, submissions from the tribunal may be essential to achieve this objective. In these circumstances, a broader standing adds value to the court proceedings. Because sound decision making is most likely to come from a fully informed court, this consideration will frequently be of most importance. Professor Mullan [*Essentials of Canadian Law: Administrative Law* (Toronto: Irwin, 2001)] put it this way, at 459:

> Under a discretionary approach, the principal question should probably be whether the participation of the tribunal is needed to enable a proper defence or justification of the decision under attack. If that decision will almost certainly be presented adequately by the losing party at first instance or by some other party or intervenor such as the attorney general, there may be no need for tribunal representation irrespective of the ground of judicial review or appeal. On the other hand, where no one is appearing to defend the tribunal's decision, where the matter in issue involves factors or considerations peculiarly within the decision maker's knowledge or expertise, or where the tribunal wishes to provide dimensions or explanations that are not necessarily going to be put by a party respondent, then there should clearly be room for that kind of representation to be allowed within the discretion of the reviewing or appellate court. Indeed, in at least some instances, a true commitment to deference and restraint in intervention would seem to necessitate it.

[38] In *Northwestern Utilities, supra*, Estey J articulated the other significant consideration, namely the importance of maintaining tribunal impartiality. This obviously matters to the parties to the decision, particularly if the application results in the matter being referred back to the tribunal. More broadly however, in future cases before the tribunal where similar interests arise, or where the tribunal serves a defined and specialized

community, there may be a risk that full-fledged participation by a tribunal as an adversary in a judicial review proceeding will undermine future confidence in its objectivity.

[39] This risk may be enhanced where the tribunal's role is not to evaluate the interests of an applicant against a legislative standard but is to resolve private disputes between two litigants where the perception of favouring one side over the other may be felt more acutely.

[40] I also agree with Jacobs and Kuttner, *supra*, that the nature of the issue under review may affect the apprehension of partiality arising from the unconstrained participation of the tribunal before the court. For example, if the question is whether the tribunal has treated a particular litigant fairly, impartiality may suggest a more limited standing than if the allegation is that the structure of the tribunal itself compromises natural justice.

[41] Although these two considerations are primary and will have to be weighed and balanced in almost every case where the scope of a tribunal's standing is in issue, there will undoubtedly be other considerations that will be relevant in particular cases.

[42] In this case the Children's Lawyer raises such a consideration. She says that the tribunal's standing should not extend to defending its decision on a ground that it did not rely on in the decision under review. The argument is that this "bootstrapping" undermines the integrity of the tribunal's decision-making process. It is akin to the impartiality concern in that a tribunal seeking to justify its decision in court on an entirely different basis than that offered in its reasons may well cause those adversely affected to feel unfairly dealt with. However, it goes beyond impartiality. The importance of reasoned decision making may be undermined if, when attacked in court, a tribunal can simply offer different, better, or even contrary reasons to support its decision. Where a tribunal takes such a course, this will become an important consideration in determining the extent of the tribunal's standing.

[43] Ultimately, if the legislation does not clearly articulate the tribunal's role, the scope of standing accorded to a tribunal whose decision is under review must be a matter for the court's discretion. The court must have regard in each case, to the importance of a fully informed adjudication of the issues before it and to the importance of maintaining tribunal impartiality. The nature of the problem, the purpose of the legislation, the extent of the tribunal's expertise, and the availability of another party able to knowledgeably respond to the attack on the tribunal's decision, may all be relevant in assessing the seriousness of the impartiality concern and the need for full argument.

[44] The last of these factors will undoubtedly loom largest where the judicial review application would otherwise be completely unopposed. In such a case, the concern to ensure fully informed adjudication is at its highest, the more so where the case arises in a specialized and complex legislative or administrative context. If the standing of the tribunal is significantly curtailed, the court may properly be concerned that something of importance will not be brought to its attention, given the unfamiliarity of the particular context, something that would not be so in hearing an appeal from a lower court. In such circumstances the desirability of fully informed adjudication may well be the governing consideration.

[45] In addition to fully informed adjudication and tribunal impartiality, there may be other considerations that arise in particular cases, as the appellant argues here. In the

end however, the court must balance the various considerations in determining the scope of standing that best serves the interests of justice.

[46] It remains to apply these considerations to this case to assess whether the Divisional Court erred in exercising its discretion to dismiss the appellant's attempt to deny or limit the standing of the Commissioner in these judicial review proceedings.

[47] Several aspects of this case clearly demonstrate the importance of full tribunal participation in the judicial review to ensure a fully informed adjudication of the issues.

[48] From the beginning, the requester has played no part in the proceedings. As the Divisional Court noted, it would be left with only one party, the Children's Lawyer, if the tribunal were denied standing. There would be nobody charged with defending the decision under review, a problem not solved by the appointment of the *amicus*, whose appointment was for the purpose of making the submissions it deemed appropriate. Traditionally, an *amicus* does not act on behalf of any party nor is it meant to defend the position of the tribunal.

[49] As well, the specialized nature of the statutory scheme administered by the Commissioner has long been recognized by this court. See *Ontario (Workers' Compensation Board) v. Ontario (Assistant Information and Privacy Commissioner)*, (1998), 41 OR (3d) 464 (CA) at 472-73. The issues raised in the judicial review require the court to understand two specific provisions in that scheme (s. 13 relating to the advice of a public servant and s. 19 relating to Crown litigation privilege). With full standing, the Commissioner's expert familiarity with the statute provides an important assurance of a fully informed adjudication. This is not a role that an *amicus* could be expected to fill.

[50] On the other hand, both the nature of the tribunal here and the nature of the issues suggest that the impartiality consideration is not a significant brake on full standing for the Commissioner.

[51] Under *FIPPA* [*Freedom of Information and Protection of Privacy Act*, RSO 1990, c. F.31], the Commissioner sits on the appeal from a decision of the head of a government institution about whether the legislation requires disclosure of records to the public at the behest of a requester. On appeal, the head is not defending his or her private interest, or that of the institution, but his or her decision interpreting the legislation and applying it to the circumstances. Nor is the requester seeking private access but access for the public. *FIPPA* provides that the process used by the Commissioner to decide the appeal is inquisitorial not simply adversarial. All of this shifts the nature of the tribunal somewhat away from a court-like model and mutes the impartiality concern.

[52] Similarly the issues raised by this judicial review application are fundamentally ones of statutory interpretation. Although they arise in a particular factual context, they are not applicable only to the Children's Lawyer and the requester. If the Commissioner were to address the court on these issues, its ability to act impartially in future cases, even ones involving this government head and this requester, would not be adversely affected any more than its original decision on the same issues could be said to carry that consequence.

[53] The final consideration in this case is the importance of preserving the integrity of the administrative tribunal's decision making. The appellant argues that this is undermined if the Commissioner is given standing to defend her decision in court on an entirely different basis than that offered in her reasons for decision. There is no doubt that

this is a valid consideration. The only question is whether in this case it warrants curtailing the scope of the Commissioner's standing.

[54] In my view it does not. There is no doubt that the Commissioner's original decision that the second branch of s. 19 of *FIPPA* did not provide the Children's Lawyer with a basis to refuse to disclosure rested on her conclusion that this provision offered the Children's Lawyer no protection from the individual she represents. It did not rest on an express finding that the Children's Lawyer was not "Crown counsel" in the circumstances. In the Divisional Court that is the argument the Commissioner sought to put in defence of its decision.

[55] Clearly an administrative tribunal must strive to provide fully reasoned decisions. However I do not think the absence of the "Crown counsel" argument in the decision should prevent the Commissioner from advancing it to the court on judicial review. It is not inconsistent with the reason offered in the decision. Indeed it could be said to be implicit in it. If the Children's Lawyer was the legal representative of the requester in the proceedings for which records are sought (the reason relied upon by the Commissioner in her original decision) it could not have been Crown counsel in those proceedings.

[56] Moreover, the Children's Lawyer was required by this section of *FIPPA* to positively establish that it was Crown counsel in order to take advantage of the protection offered by the second branch of s. 19. It appears that the Children's Lawyer did not seek to do so before the Commissioner either by evidence or argument. The result was that the decision under review was simply silent on the question.

[57] Finally, if the Commissioner's standing were to preclude her from making this argument there would be no guarantee that the Divisional Court would hear it from anyone else with a resulting risk to a fully informed adjudication.

[58] It was therefore proper for the Commissioner to be permitted to raise this argument before the Divisional Court and equally proper for the court to decide on that basis.

[59] In summary, I conclude that allowing the Commissioner full standing in the judicial review proceedings assures a fully informed adjudication of the issues without significantly compromising her impartiality or undermining the integrity of her decision-making process. The Divisional Court did not err in exercising its discretion to refuse the appellant's attempt to preclude or limit the Commissioner's standing.

[60] Before leaving this appeal, I would add a word about procedure. Where a party to a judicial review application seeks to limit the standing of the administrative tribunal, it should do as the appellant did here. It should serve a notice of motion saying why, so that the issue can be properly joined. Although this may require additional factums and perhaps additional material, it ought not normally require a separate preliminary hearing. Submissions on this issue can be made at the hearing on the merits of the application. If the decision on the scope of standing is reserved, the written and oral submissions of the tribunal on the merits that go beyond the scope of standing ultimately permitted will, of course, be disregarded. With this approach, the scope of standing issue ought not to unduly complicate judicial review proceedings.

[61] Finally, I think it important that if an administrative tribunal seeks to make submissions on a judicial review of its decision, it pay careful attention to the tone with which it does so. Although this is not a discrete basis upon which its standing might be limited, there is no doubt that the tone of the proposed submissions provides the background for

the determination of that issue. A tribunal that seeks to resist a judicial review application will be of assistance to the court to the degree its submissions are characterized by the helpful elucidation of the issues, informed by its specialized position, rather than by the aggressive partisanship of an adversary.

[62] I hasten to add that before us all counsel were exemplary. We are grateful for their able submissions.

[63] The appeal is dismissed. No party sought costs, and none are ordered.

NOTES

1. To what extent is this "context-specific" approach to tribunal standing of assistance beyond Ontario, given the role of s. 9 of the *Judicial Review Procedure Act* in Goudge JA's decision? See *BC Teachers' Federation, Nanaimo District Teachers' Association et al. v. Information and Privacy Commissioner (B.C.) et al.* (2005), 50 BCLR (4th) 151, 34 Admin. LR (4th) 151, at paras. 34-46, where Garson J also adopted a flexible approach to the commissioner standing to defend his decision and to inform the court in the judicial review proceedings, so long as the commissioner did not take an overly adversarial role. See also *Rowel v. The Union Centre Inc. et al.* (2008), 227 Man. R (2d) 315, [2008] 7 WWR 341, 75 Admin. LR (4th) 67 (MB QB), at paras. 18-25, where the Manitoba Human Rights Commission was granted standing to play "a significant role" in the judicial review of its decision to dismiss a human rights complaint in the face of an allegation that the commission breached the rules of natural justice in its investigation of the complaint.

2. Under the BC *Judicial Review Procedure Act*, RSBC 1996, c. 241, the status of the statutory authority whose decision is under attack seems even clearer than in the Ontario Act, in that s. 15 of the BC Act (the equivalent of s. 9(2)) is couched in terms of the respondent becoming a party at its "option." For a discussion, see Falzon, "Tribunal Standing on Judicial Review" (2008), 21 *CJALP* 21, at 22-24.

3. Compare *Children's Lawyer* with the recent decision in *Pacific Newspapers Group Inc. v. Communications, Energy and Paperworkers Union of Canada, Local 2000* (2009), 2009 BCSC 962 (CanLII), at paras. 40-42, where the BC Labour Relations Board was granted limited standing only in a judicial review of its decision, such that its role was restricted to making submissions and argument on the jurisdiction of the board and to explaining the record. Adair J concluded that the factors favouring broad standing for the board were outweighed by the need to maintain the board's impartiality in its role to resolve adversarial disputes between the relevant parties. She referred, at para. 29, to a "rejuvenation" of the *Northwestern Utilities* principle of limited standing, although stressing that the principle could be understood only in the relevant decision-making context, and referring in turn to the factors discussed in *Children's Lawyer*.

4. For an argument in favour of a liberal approach to tribunal standing, see N. Semple, "The Case for Tribunal Standing in Canada" (2007), 20 *CJALP* 305; see also Jacobs and Kuttner, "Discovering What Tribunals Do: Tribunal Standing Before the Courts" (2002), 81 *Can. Bar Rev.* 616.

5. In the federal domain, the Federal Court of Appeal held in *Canada (Human Rights Commission) v. Canada (Attorney General)* (1994), 17 Admin. LR (2d) 2, that, under the 1992 *Federal Court Rules*, the decision-maker under challenge was not entitled to be a party

to judicial review proceedings. Rather, the appropriate step for the Canadian Human Rights Commission (which was being challenged for allowing a complaint to be processed outside the normal limitation period) was to apply under rule 1611 to be an intervenor in the proceedings. The court then had a discretion to recognize that status as an intervenor to the extent that it was appropriate for the tribunal to defend its jurisdiction without compromising its independence. In rendering one of the two majority judgments in this case, Décary JA stated (at 10):

> The [Canadian Human Rights Commission] ... has been granted by its enabling statute a very special status in some circumstances, none of which are present here. Provisions granting tribunals status to participate in proceedings where their decisions are attacked are exceptional and should be interpreted restrictively. Courts should go no further than Parliament has. Parliament, had it intended to grant full party status to the Commission in a case where it had not initiated the complaint itself or in a case where the decision attacked was its own rather than one of a Human Rights Tribunal would have been expected to do so in express terms.

The other majority judge, Desjardins JA, essentially agreed with this proposition (at 15). This continues to be the situation under the current *Federal Courts Rules*, SOR/98-106, rule 109. See *Gardner v. Canada (Attorney General)* (2004), 2004 FCA 322 (CanLII); *Hoechst Marion Roussel Canada v. Canada (Attorney General)* (2001), 208 FTR 223, 13 CPR (4th) 446, 42 Admin. LR (3d) 193. In the wake of the Federal Court of Appeal's decision in *Canada (Human Rights Commission)*, and somewhat ironically, Reed J (in *Canada (Attorney General) v. Canada (Human Rights Tribunal)* (1994), 19 Admin. LR (2d) 69 (FCTD)) concluded that the Canadian Human Rights Commission in its capacity as an intervenor under rule 1611 of the *Federal Court Rules* was entitled to respond in the manner of a party to allegations of procedural unfairness based on the creation of legitimate expectations.

6. In *United Brotherhood of Carpenters and Joiners of America, Local 1386 v. Bransen Construction Ltd.* (2002), 249 NBR (2d) 93, 39 Admin. LR (3d) 1, at paras. 32-37, Robertson JA for the New Brunswick Court of Appeal developed a flexible approach to the issue of intervenor status for a tribunal whose decision was under attack:

> It seems to me that the true issue is whether the tribunal seeking intervener status has something to contribute, beyond that expected of the parties. If that can be established, the tribunal should be permitted to address the merits in its written submission. I say this for two reasons. First, the distinction between a tribunal that seeks to defend its jurisdiction in the narrow as opposed to broad sense is, with respect, tenuous. If a tribunal is entitled to defend its interpretation of jurisdictional provisions then why shouldn't it be permitted to defend its interpretation of non-jurisdictional provisions? In both instances the purpose underscoring the value of tribunal participation is the same: to enable the reviewing court to make an informed decision as to why one interpretation was or should be preferred to another. My second reason for permitting tribunals to address the merits of their decisions is that in *Northwestern Utilities* Justice Estey was driven to articulating a broad rule when a narrow one would have sufficed. Provided the tribunal is not seeking to bootstrap its decision, the tribunal cannot be accused of breaching the principle of impartiality. This leads me to the problem of bootstrapping.
>
> No tribunal should be permitted to bootstrap its decisions. If the tribunal fails to provide a rational explanation for its interpretative decision, why should it be given a second opportunity

to do so? Those that fail to provide sufficient reasons to support their interpretative decisions run the risk of having the matter remitted to them for reconsideration, as was ordered in *Northwestern Utilities*. Another possibility is that the tribunal will have to live with the interpretative arguments presented by the parties. If the issue is decided against the tribunal, in future it must be content to direct its submissions to the legislature. ...

Frankly, the only tribunals that fail to clothe their reasons with juristic respectability are those lacking legal expertise. These are the tribunals whose principal mandate is to make findings of fact. At the same time, I do not wish to leave the impression that all tribunal decisions must be fortified by extensive reasons. If the issue is one that had been adduced in an earlier decision, there is no need to reproduce legal reasoning found elsewhere.

When it comes to the application of the principle of impartiality it is helpful to distinguish between a tribunal's written and oral submissions. In my experience, tribunals accept that the principle of impartiality limits their ability to engage fully in the adversarial process. Typically, a written submission is filed without objection from opposing counsel. Costs are neither sought by, nor awarded against, the intervener who qualifies as a friend of the court. Tribunal counsel rarely walk to the podium to argue in support of the tribunal's decision. If they do, it is to respond only to questions posed by the court. On occasion it may be necessary for the intervener to address briefly matters raised in argument. There is a reason why this is so. All counsel are acutely aware of the reality that a carefully crafted written submission virtually displaces the need for oral argument. In this way the appearance of impartiality is retained. The Board in this case so conducted itself.

In summary, a tribunal seeking intervener status must persuade the court that: the case is of precedential significance; the tribunal can contribute to the proceedings in a way not reasonably expected of the parties; and the principle of impartiality can and will be respected. Written submissions that address the merits of the decision do not offend this principle, except those intended to bootstrap tribunal reasons that are materially deficient. Oral submissions that respond only to questions posed by the reviewing court, or are of brief duration, qualify as non-aggressive participation that respect the principle of impartiality.

In the present case, it is understandable that the Board would seek intervener status. The central issue involves the interpretation of ss. 13 and 40 of the *Industrial Relations Act*. The interpretative issue involves a fundamental question: May the Board look only to the date of the application for certification to determine if there is a unit of employees that is appropriate for collective bargaining? The Board's written submissions on this issue were helpful and simply amplified that contained within its reasons for decision. This is not a case of bootstrapping. The Board's oral argument was succinct and did not qualify as "aggressive participation" of the kind contemplated by Justice Estey in *Northwestern Utilities*. Hindsight reveals that without coaching from this Court, the Board in both its written and oral argument maintained an air of impartiality. In short, the Board had something to contribute, beyond that expected of the parties. That something was tied to the Board's specialized jurisdiction and expertise.

INTERVENORS

Issues of standing can also arise in applications for status to participate in litigation to which the applicant has not been named as a party. In general, such applications take one of two forms: an application to be added as an intervenor party or an application to be added as a friend of the court (*amicus curiae*). The difference between the two categories is that the first confers on a successful applicant all the rights of the original parties to the litigation, including the right to appeal, while the second is restricted to the level of participation that is specified by the court and does not extend to conferring appeal rights.

In general, intervention is covered by the appropriate rules of court and the interpretations and common law principles developed under those rules. While the form of these rules differ across the country, the Prince Edward Island *Rules of Civil Procedure* provide an example:

> 13.01(1) Where a person who is not a party to a proceeding claims,
>
> (a) an interest in the subject matter of the proceeding;
>
> (b) that he or she may be adversely affected by a judgment in the proceeding; or
>
> (c) that there exists between him or her and one or more of the parties to the proceeding a question of law or fact in common with one or more of the questions in issue in the proceeding,
>
> the person may move for leave to intervene as an added party.
>
> (2) On the motion, the court shall consider whether the intervention will unduly delay or prejudice the determination of the rights of the parties to the proceeding and the court may add the person as a party to the proceeding and may make such order for pleadings and discovery as is just. …
>
> 13.02 Any person may, with leave of a judge or at the invitation of the presiding judge, and without becoming a party to the proceeding, intervene as a friend of the court for the purpose of rendering assistance to the court by way of argument. …
>
> 13.03(2) Leave to intervene as an added party or as a friend of the court in the Appeal Division may be granted by a panel of the court or the Chief Justice of Prince Edward Island.

It seems likely that this codifies the principles of intervention in Prince Edward Island. However, in the context of the Québec *Code of Civil Procedure*, the Québec Superior Court has recognized the existence of a residual judicial discretion to afford intervenor status to those who do not qualify under the relevant articles if necessary to ensure justice: *Imperial Tobacco Ltd. v. Canada (PG)* (1988), 38 Admin. LR 74 (Que. SC). It should also be noted that under the BC and Ontario *Judicial Review Procedure Acts* the ability of the attorney general to intervene in judicial review applications is specifically recognized (see RSBC 1996, c. 241, s. 16(2) and RSO 1990, c. J.1, s. 9(4)) and, as indicated by Rosenberg JA's reasons in *Sutcliffe* and by Reed J's judgment in *Energy Probe*, this constitutes generally one of the prerogatives of that office irrespective of the relevant rules of court (see also *Salutin v. Prince* (1997), 1997 CanLII 5803 (FCA)).

With the possible exception of interventions by the attorney general, the recognition of such status and the extent of participatory rights accorded is a matter within the discretion of the court, subject to limitations imposed by the language of the relevant rules. In so far as those rules use terms such as "interest" or "sufficient interest" as the basis for the exercise of discretion, questions arise about the extent that such language imports the normal standing principles into this realm of public law litigation and, if they are imported, whether those principles include the *Finlay* concept of public interest standing.

In *Finlay*, one of the major concerns of the Supreme Court of Canada was whether there were others better placed and likely to initiate the challenge for which the public interest litigant was seeking standing. In intervention applications, another person has already taken action and so the public interest litigant will generally have to show is that there are yet other interests that are not represented by the parties already before the court or, alternatively, that it has something to add in support of the interests represented by the current parties, but which they cannot be relied on to bring forward adequately. In addition, the court must consider other factors that are relevant to intervenor applications in both the public and the private sphere: concerns about broadening the issues, taking the litigation out of the hands of the original parties, and increasing the costs of the litigation both to the existing parties and in terms of the court's resources. These further concerns are discussed in *Attorney General of Canada v. Aluminum Co. of Canada Ltd.* (1987), 35 DLR (4th) 495 (BC CA), where the court noted that the position in Canada was more in accord with the liberal United States principles for according intervenor status than with the more restrictive English principles on *amicus curiae* status. Even so, intervention was not allowed under the BC rule where to do so involved raising new issues not raised by the parties and not relevant to the determination of the litigation. The court also applied the principle that intervention should not be allowed if the effect would be for the intervenors to take the litigation away from those directly affected by it. (For a discussion of this case, see Roman and Hemingway, "Standing to Intervene" (1987), 26 *Admin. LR* 49).

In the *Canadian Council of Churches* case, above, Cory J suggested that the council might be able to intervene in challenges to the legislation brought by individual Convention refugee claimants. In light of the rules governing interventions by public interest litigants, in what kind of scenario would the Canadian Council of Churches be an appropriate intervenor?

RECOMMENDATIONS FOR STATUTORY REFORM

Over the years, there have been numerous reports by law reform bodies and other agencies on the subject of standing and intervention. Among the notable Commonwealth papers are: Law Reform Commission of British Columbia, *Report on Civil Litigation in the Public Interest*, LRC 46 (1980); Australian Law Reform Commission, *Access to Courts—1 Standing: Public Interest Suits*, Working Paper No. 7 (1977); English Law Commission, *Report on Remedies in Administrative Law*, Law Com. No. 73 (Cmnd. 6407, 1976) (and now see The Law Commission, Consultation Paper No. 126, *Administrative Law: Judicial Review and Statutory Appeals* (1992)); New Zealand Public and Administrative Law Reform Committee, *Standing in Administrative Law*, Report No. 11 (1978); and Ontario Law Reform Commission, *Report on the Law of Standing* (1989). Among the themes explored in these reports was whether existing common law principles were too restrictive and whether there needed to be statutory reform of the common law rules. The Ontario report answered both of these questions in the affirmative and recommended statutory reform to widen access to the courts based on a liberal approach to standing.

STANDING AND INTERVENTION BEFORE TRIBUNALS

The question of standing to participate in the proceedings of tribunals is one that is surfacing more and more frequently. In part, this may be attributed to the expansion in the reach of the principles of procedural fairness as a result of *Nicholson v. Haldimand Norfolk (Regional) Police Commissioners*, [1979] 1 SCR 311 (Ont.) and *Cardinal v. Director of Kent Institution*, [1985] 2 SCR 643 (BC), at 653, and, in particular, Le Dain J's assertion in the latter that a duty of procedural fairness is owed to anyone whose "rights, privileges or interests" are affected by statutory decision making. It is also promoted by the evolution of powerful, well-funded and skilled public interest groups with a participatory agenda and the recognition by tribunals and agencies of the claims of such groups to participate in proceedings affecting the relevant constituencies. Finally, it finds expression in legislative provision for hearings on a range of issues with public dimensions and the clear message of many such enactments that broad-based representation of opinion at such hearings should be encouraged. At times, this commitment has been backed by extensive government support of such groups to enable effective participation.

Not surprisingly, disputes about participatory entitlements often reach the courts in the context of a common law claim that the rules of natural justice have been breached either in a failure to give notice to an affected person or group or in the direct denial of requested participatory opportunities. On occasion, the claim will be complicated by the fact that the dispute arises in the context of an explicit legislative grant of power to the tribunal to make decisions on participatory entitlements or, more generally, in relation to the procedures it follows. As we have seen, the conferral of this power raises issues about the appropriate standard of review. Should the court, as in an ordinary common law natural justice or procedural fairness case, decide the procedural issue afresh on the basis of its conception of the demands of procedural fairness as elaborated in Supreme Court of Canada jurisprudence, or is the judgment of the tribunal entitled to deference? (In this context, recall *Baker*, in chapter 2 of this text, and its recognition of the need for deference to a decision-maker's choices where the decision-maker has an explicit statutory discretion in matters of procedure.) Indeed, in the converse situation, the courts have generally tended to treat as conclusive, or as a very strong factor regarding standing to seek judicial review, tribunal recognition of an entitlement to participate in the proceedings before it: *Energy Probe v. Canada (Atomic Energy Control Board)*, above, and *Canadian Broadcasting League v. Canadian Radio-television and Telecommunications Commission (No. 2)*, [1980] 1 FC 396 (CA).

More commonly, questions as to standing to participate in tribunal proceedings have arisen in the context of legislative language defining participatory entitlements, but with no express conferral of discretion on the tribunal with respect to the meaning of the relevant language. In this context, tribunals and the courts most frequently make reference to the common law of standing and intervention in relation to court proceedings as a guide to the meaning of the statutory terms. Common law principles of standing were decisive in the judgment of Puddester J of the Newfoundland Supreme Court in *Re Bambrick* (1992), 101 Nfld & PEIR 181 (Nfld. SCTD). This involved a challenge to a ruling by the Workers' Compensation Appeal Tribunal that the Workers' Compensation Commission was entitled to participate as a party in an appeal from one of its decisions. In holding that the commission was not, in terms of the relevant legislative provision, "a person with an interest," the court relied on the

Northwestern Utilities line of cases on the participation of tribunals in judicial review and appeal proceedings.

Notwithstanding this tendency to apply traditional principles to such issues, it has been argued that, as a general proposition, the relevant considerations on standing or intervention before tribunals are quite different from applying in court proceedings. Consider this comment by Larry Fox (17 *Admin. LR* 317, at 317-18), criticizing the Ontario Securities Commission decision in *Re Torstar and Southam* (1985), 17 Admin. LR 303 (Ont. Sec. Comm.). Here, the commission denied an application by investors and the Toronto Stock Exchange for full intervention rights in a disciplinary hearing against directors of two corporations. Instead, the intervenors were restricted to the making of argument.

> In a Court setting, intervenor status is for a party without sufficient interest to be either a plaintiff or defendant, in a dispute over whether the plaintiff has the right to the remedy sought against the defendant. The Court's traditional reluctance to allow intervention, at least at the trial level, is to avoid burdening the plaintiff's case for the sake of those with only peripheral interests. In this OSC hearing, the issues were by no means so bipolar, and the interests of the would-be intervenors were certainly not peripheral. In other words, the "intervenor" label before a board means something quite different from that same label in a Court of law. Normally, the roles before a board are not like those of plaintiffs and defendants seeking or opposing judicial remedies; hence, "intervenor" will mean only "another party," since board hearings usually have one applicant or principal party, with all other parties being called "intervenors," whether they support or oppose the principal party. For this reason, boards do not, *stricto sensu*, determine "standing to sue" or "standing to intervene" as does a Court of law. Rather, they determine the right to participate, in accordance with whether the prospective participant has any interests which may be affected (without construing "interests" in any narrow, technical legal sense), assessed in the context of the purpose and scheme of the applicable statutes empowering the board.

Fox goes on to criticize the notion of restricted intervention. Consider whether such a restrictive approach is ever justified. Compare, for example, the more flexible approach leading to the BC Court of Appeal's decision in *Global Securities Corp. v. British Columbia (Executive Director, Securities Commission)* (2006), 56 BCLR (4th) 79, 274 DLR (4th) 523, 47 Admin. LR (4th) 260 (CA). Here, the court upheld a decision of the BC Securities Commission that granted standing to the TSX Venture Exchange, a regulatory body in the securities industry, to make submissions on the merits before the commission in defence of a disciplinary decision by the Exchange finding misconduct by Global Securities Inc. Applying a reasonableness standard, the Court of Appeal upheld the commission's decision, concluding:

> [54] There can be no doubt that the Commission Panel was well aware of the rationale for not permitting a tribunal to argue before a reviewing court the merits of a decision it has made. After quoting the salient paragraphs of Estey J's reasons in *Northwestern Utilities*, the Commission Panel carefully distinguished that case from the one before it by drawing out the differences in function between the Exchange and the Hearing Panel [of the Exchange].
>
> [55] Global's argument is predicated on the assumption that the Hearing Panel's decision is a decision made by the Exchange itself. The assumption does not withstand scrutiny. The Exchange is responsible for conducting the investigation of infractions and prosecuting them

whereas the Hearing Panel is entirely limited in function to its adjudicative role. It is the Exchange, not the Hearing Panel, which sought a review and hearing under s. 28(1) of the Act [*Securities Act*, RSBC 1996, c. 418] and it is the Exchange, not the Hearing Panel, that wishes to make submissions on the merits of the decision of the Hearing Panel.

. . .

[57] While the Hearing Panel was constituted under the rules and by-laws of the Exchange, its sole task in the regulatory scheme was to act as an independent tribunal in relation to the particular disciplinary hearing for which it was selected. There is no evidence to show that the Hearing Panel stepped beyond its role as an adjudicative body independent of the Exchange. The analogy suggested by the Executive Director is apt: the role of the Exchange was that of a prosecutor; the role of the Commission Panel was that of the judge.

In a different context, a restrictive approach to intervention before a tribunal was taken in Grange J's ruling, as commissioner of a public inquiry, that the parents of deceased children were not entitled to participate in the police conduct phase of his inquiry into the deaths of children at the Toronto Hospital for Sick Children. Grange J ruled:

The parents' position is very difficult and evokes the greatest sympathy. They are, of course, immensely interested in the investigation and prosecution of the killer or killers (if there be any) of their children, but I cannot find that their interest (in a legal sense) is any greater than that of the public at large who are represented by Commission Counsel. It may be a delicate distinction but I held in effect that there was a direct and substantial interest for the parents in Phase I. One might say that the interest was largely emotional but it was nevertheless direct and substantial. They are the only representatives of the babies themselves. The interests of the parents in the investigation and prosecution is also natural and understandable but it is not in my view either a direct or substantial interest within the meaning of the statute. The legal interests of the parents cannot conceivably be affected either by the Inquiry or the Report.

This ruling was sustained by the Divisional Court in *Parents of Babies Gosselin v. Grange* (1984), 8 Admin. LR 250 (Ont. Div. Ct.).

A related area of controversy regarding public participation is coroner inquests. The history and the jurisprudence is reviewed in *Black Action Defence Committee v. Huxter, Coroner* (1992), 11 OR (3d) 641 (Div. Ct.) in the context of a provision giving status to those "substantially and directly interested." In this situation, the court was prepared to concede considerable autonomy to the presiding coroner and to intervene in a coroner's decision only in the case of "manifest error."

However liberal a tribunal is in according standing to public interest litigants to participate in its proceedings, the reality is that such groups need funding to exercise effectively any rights they are given. In an era when direct government financial support of such groups has declined dramatically, they have had to depend on the resources of their members, external private funding, legal aid, and the power of the tribunal to award costs (both after the event and in advance). Legal aid budgets are also under considerable pressure and are not open to tribunal proceedings in all provinces. Moreover, not all tribunals have the jurisdiction to award costs. For a consideration of the bases on which costs are awarded by a tribunal with authority to do so, see *Re Durham (Regional Municipality)* (1991), 50 Admin. LR 163 (Ont. Joint Bd.—OMB and OEAB). See also Sossin, "Access to Administrative Justice and Other Worries" in Flood and Sossin, eds., *Administrative Law in Context* (2008), at 403-6.

For an example of an ambitious public litigant funding plan, see the *Intervenor Funding Project Act*, RSO 1990, c. I.13, which provided for funding of public interest intervenors before the Ontario Energy Board, the Environmental Appeal Board, and Joint Boards established under the *Consolidated Hearings Act*, RSO 1990, c. C.19. Section 7 of the IFPA made intervenor funding (payable by the proponents) contingent on a consideration by the relevant tribunal of the following factors:

7(1) Intervenor funding may be awarded only in relation to issues,

(a) which, in the opinion of the funding panel, affect a significant segment of the public; and

(b) which, in the opinion of the funding panel, affect the public interest and not just private interests.

(2) In deciding whether to award intervenor funding to an intervenor, the funding panel shall consider whether,

(a) the intervenor represents a clearly ascertainable interest that should be represented at the hearing;

(b) separate and adequate representation of the interest would assist the board and contribute substantially to the hearing;

(c) the intervenor does not have sufficient financial resources to enable it to adequately represent the interest;

(d) the intervenor has made reasonable efforts to raise funding from other sources;

(e) the intervenor has an established record of concern for and commitment to the interest;

(f) the intervenor has attempted to bring related interests of which it was aware into an umbrella group to represent the related interests at the hearing;

(g) the intervenor has a clear proposal for its use of any funds which might be awarded; and

(h) the intervenor has appropriate financial controls to ensure that the funds, if awarded, are spent for the purposes of the award.

(3) In determining the amount of an award of intervenor funding, the funding panel shall,

(a) if the proposal includes the use of lawyers in private practice, assess legal fees at the legal aid rate under the legal aid plan in effect on the day of the award for work necessarily and reasonably performed;

(b) set a ceiling in respect of disbursements that may be paid as part of the award and such disbursements shall be restricted to eligible disbursements;

(c) deduct from the award funds that are reasonably available to the applicant from other sources.

(4) A funding panel may award intervenor funding subject to such conditions as it sets out in its order.

(5) In clause (3)(b), "eligible disbursements" means disbursements for consultants, expert witnesses, typing, printing, copying and transcripts necessary for the representation of the interest and such other expenditures as may be named in the regulations made under this Act as eligible disbursements.

For an assessment of the operation of the *Intervenor Funding Project Act*, see Bogart and Valiante, *Access and Intent* (1992), a study prepared for the Ontario ministries of the Attorney General, Energy, and Environment. On the basis of that assessment, the Ontario government extended the Act's life by an additional four years from 1992 to 1996: "*Intervenor Funding Act* will be extended 4 years, Ont. gov't. says," *The Lawyers Weekly*, April 18, 1992. However, the legislation was ultimately allowed to lapse on April 1, 1996.

CHAPTER EIGHTEEN

The Discretion of the Court

INTRODUCTION

We have already seen a variety of devices that the courts have used in the control of access to a determination on the merits of a judicial review application: the matter is one of private, not public, law; the issue is not justiciable or otherwise unreviewable; there has been no final decision by a statutory authority; and the applicant lacks standing.

In addition to these grounds for denying access to a merits determination or a remedy, the courts also assert an overriding discretion to deny relief. The common grounds for such refusals to intervene are the existence of alternative avenues of recourse, such as a statutory right of appeal or a more convenient court remedy; prematurity and its opposites, delay and mootness; lack of practical utility; the misconduct of the applicant; waiver; and, occasionally, the balance of convenience or the public interest. In 2009, in *Canada (Citizenship and Immigration) v. Khosa*, [2009] 1 SCR 339 (Can.), Rothstein J summarized as follows:

> The traditional common law discretion to refuse relief on judicial review concerns the parties' conduct, any undue delay and the existence of alternative remedies. ... [C]ourts may exercise their discretion to refuse relief to applicants "if they have been guilty of unreasonable delay or misconduct or if an alternative remedy exists, notwithstanding that they have proved a usurpation of jurisdiction by the inferior tribunal or an omission to perform a public duty." As in the case of interlocutory injunctions, courts exercising discretion to grant relief on judicial review will take into account the public interest, any disproportionate impact on the parties and the interests of third parties. This is [a] type of "balance of convenience" analysis.

To the extent that most of these bases for the denial of relief are rooted in concerns for the integrity and the functioning of the administrative process, the appropriateness of the discretionary denial of relief raises issues that have recurred throughout this casebook and, in particular, the extent of the claim that the administrative process has over the courts for deference and institutional respect.

However, in so far as some of the discretionary grounds for refusing relief (misconduct, waiver, and delay) also involve as a crucial element judicial assessment of the actions of the applicant for relief, different questions surface. In the face of unlawful administrative action, should the court be at all concerned with the motives or behaviour of the person bringing the matter to the attention of the court?

Here, the links are with the law of standing rather than with the theme of institutional imperatives. As we saw in the previous chapter of this text, the law traditionally required that, in general, only those who had suffered specific harm or damage could seek judicial review and, even now that Canadian law recognizes categories of public interest standing, the nature or status of the public interest applicant or plaintiff is one of the relevant concerns in the exercise of the court's discretion over standing. The spectre of the "meddler" or the "busybody" is always present in such considerations. Does the conduct or actions of someone with incontrovertible standing also merit the court's attention and for the same or different reasons?

As with the other control mechanisms, the discretionary grounds for the refusal of relief have the potential to legitimate unlawful administrative action and part of our objective in this chapter is to raise questions as to when it is appropriate for the courts to take that risk of allowing an unlawful decision or course of action to achieve *de facto* legal status. Indeed, much of the concern that has been expressed about the very existence of judicial discretion in this area has its roots in the notion that the courts should have no part in the effective validating of *ultra vires* decisions.

Nonetheless, the concepts of "voidness" and "nullity" are generally relative rather than absolute. Even if one accepts that breach of the rules of natural justice renders a decision "void" or a "nullity" for the purposes of evading the effects of a privative clause, that does not mean that decisions tainted by such errors can never achieve legally impregnable status. Where, for example, there is a statutory limitation period for the bringing of challenges on such grounds, it is almost certainly the case that the limitation period will be effective and the decision in question will be immune from attack.

A recognition that there are necessarily varying degrees of "nullity" or "voidness" or that "null" or "void" decisions can have partial or complete legal effect should at least clear away some of the seemingly principled objections to the existence of judicial discretion in the granting of remedies for unlawful administrative action. In fact, as has been suggested by some authors and carried forward in some authorities (see, for example, *R v. Consolidated Maybrun Mines Ltd.*, [1998] 1 SCR 706 (Ont.) (extracted below)), there may be some merit in dispensing entirely in this context with expressions such as "nullity," "voidness," and "*ultra vires*" and, in particular, in ceasing to try to resolve difficult policy issues by pretending that everything depends on whether a decision is "void" as opposed to merely "voidable," as though these were self-evident, objective, neutral, organizing principles. Rather than engagement in that charade, what may be more appropriate is a balancing of the relative seriousness of the wrong against the various considerations that detract from the award of a remedy to the applicant.

Indeed, as Sedley writing in an English context suggested, there are lessons in this area to be derived from the development of flexibility in the awarding of relief in the context of Charter litigation. In "Judicial Review II: The Good, the Bad and the Voidable," [1989] *Public Law* 32, at 37, he refers to the *Manitoba Language Rights Case*, [1985] 1 SCR 721 (Man.) and comments:

> The Canadian Supreme Court faced the fact that there can be no degrees of nullity and asked itself the frank question: what does the rule of law call for to fill the subsequent void? With scholarly help from the Bar, the court deployed an impressive range of authority for its ultimate proposition that the law, abhorring a vacuum, would give recognition to acts done under colour of authority in Manitoba but would deny any recognition to the authority claimed for them. It made an order which continued this application of the *de facto* doctrine of constitutional law for just long enough to let Manitoba carry out its obligation to re-legislate bilingually, explicitly

giving temporary validity meanwhile to the effects, though not the sources, of existing Manitoba law—with liberty, of course, to apply.

What, of course, this example also suggests is that discretion with respect to the remedies of judicial review should not be seen as simply raising two alternatives—either the immediate setting aside of the decision or the outright refusal of any relief.

An example of this in the administrative law context is provided by *Sparvier v. Cowessess Indian Band No. 73* (1993), 13 Admin. LR (2d) 266 (FCTD). This case concerned the election of the chief of a band. An appeal tribunal had ordered a new election on the basis of irregularities in the original election process and, at that new election, a different chief was elected. Thereafter, however, there was a successful challenge to the decision of the appeal tribunal necessitating a rehearing by a differently constituted panel. This placed the court in a dilemma because the effect of a quashing order would be to restore the results of the initial election but still subject to the appeal. In order to minimize the potential for further disruption of the band's chieftaincy, Rothstein J in effect left the second election result undisturbed until the appeal had been reheard. He did this by postponing the quashing order until either the new appeal tribunal had upheld the original election or the day after the election should that appeal tribunal allow the appeal and order yet another election.

Such remedial flexibility is obviously very useful in terms of diminishing the disruptive effects of judicial review and adds another dimension to the concept of judicial discretion as to remedies. What it also suggests is that the assertion of greater choice as to the appropriate remedy may enable the courts to resolve some of the technically difficult problems of judicial review. Recollect how the Supreme Court in *Dunsmuir v. New Brunswick*, [2008] 1 SCR 190 (NB) dealt with what it saw as the problem of judicial review in effect amounting to an order for reinstatement when a court quashed a decision dismissing a public office holder. Henceforth, in such cases, the affected office holder will generally have to rest content with an action for damages in private law and only rarely be able to assert a right to a public law application for judicial review. Subsequently, in *Irving Shipbuilding Inc v. Canada (Attorney General)*, 2009 FCA 116, 389 NR 72 (Can.), Evans JA (delivering the judgment of the majority of the court) asserted the general primacy of a contractual action for damages over public law relief in the case of government procurement processes tainted by procedural unfairness.

In contrast, we have already encountered situations where the courts have eschewed the use of discretion at the remedial stage. Recollect how in *Cardinal v. Director of Kent Institution* (chapter 3 of this text), Le Dain J for the Supreme Court of Canada rejected the arguments for refusing relief for breach of the rules of natural justice based on the proposition that the outcome would have been the same even if the rules of natural justice had been complied with. While the denial of discretion to refuse relief on this basis is controversial and arguably not consistent with English authority (see also *Mobil Oil Canada Ltd. v. Canada-Newfoundland Offshore Petroleum Board*, [1994] 1 SCR 202 (Nfld.) (discussed below)), the court's position can be justified on purely pragmatic grounds; it need not be seen as an inevitable consequence of the principle that breach of the rules of natural justice or procedural fairness renders a decision void or as part of a general desire on the part of the Supreme Court to reduce the ambit of judicial discretion over remedies.

Those pragmatic grounds are, of course, that the evidence before the courts in such cases has as its primary focus the alleged procedural defects, not the merits. Anything that the court learns about the merits occurs incidentally and possibly very incompletely. It may therefore be very dangerous for the court to speculate about what the outcome would have been had the procedural decencies been observed. Moreover, the acceptance of such a discretion in cases of this kind would act as a spur to the parties to try to present the court with as much evidence on the merits as they could. Not only would this increase the costs of judicial review but it also entails the arrogation to itself by the court of a function that properly belongs to the decision-maker whose procedures have been brought into question. Thus, respect for legislative allocation of functions as well as limits on judicial competence may be seen as dictating this self-denial of remedial discretion.

Of course, the converse may also be true in other situations. As we have seen already in the chapters in part III, Substantive Review, considerations of respect for legislative choice and tribunal expertise will frequently dictate that the courts dismiss an application for judicial review as premature. Where one of the parties engages in a pre-emptive strike on the proceedings of an administrative tribunal, it is only sensible to ask questions such as whether there is any possibility that the problems raised will be dealt with by the tribunal itself in such a way as to avoid the necessity for judicial review. Also relevant is whether the court's exercise of its judicial review functions would be better informed by the building by the tribunal of a more complete evidential record than is available in the context of the application for prohibitory or injunctive relief and by the tribunal's considered views on the matter that is the subject of the judicial review challenge. Indeed, as we saw in *Nova Scotia (Workers' Compensation Board) v. Martin*, [2003] 2 SCR 504 (NS) (discussed in chapter 14), these considerations are ones that can come into play even in relation to questions on which a tribunal is seen as having no entitlement to judicial deference, such as Charter issues.

What is also important in relation to the exercise of discretion against the grant of a remedy on the basis of prematurity as well as some of the other related institutional respect grounds, such as the existence of appeal rights and the availability of a more convenient remedy, is that in these situations the court is not really in the position of having to condone the *de facto* legal effects of invalid decisions. They all proceed on the supposition that there are other ways in which any unlawful action can be dealt with more effectively or appropriately.

Perhaps implicit in all of this is the proposition that remedial discretion can be justified by explanations as to the contingent nature of concepts such as "voidness," "nullity," and "*ultra vires*," by the identification of situations where the exercise of that power does not in fact amount to judicial approbation of unlawful administrative action, and by the arguments for recognition of institutional imperatives. However, it is incorrect to think that this exhausts all of the concerns with the existence of discretionary power over the remedies of judicial review.

As with the canons of equity, on which many of the discretionary considerations are based, it is possible to identify a number of discrete situations where the raising of such a challenge is likely. Nevertheless, it is frequently problematic to predict how a court is going to react to such an appeal to its discretion. In common with much of judicial review law, the particular factual configuration will be crucial. Second, the various grounds for refusing to intervene are stated at a high level of generality. These two factors tend to a situation where appeal courts are unlikely to intervene and set aside such a denial of relief. Indeed, the bulk of the "law" in this area is found in a variegated collection of first instance judgments. Moreover, as we will see in the course of this chapter, on the comparatively rare occasions on which such issues have been confronted by the Supreme Court of Canada, the members of the court were prone to divide and there has on occasion been an uncharacteristic willingness to disregard precedent. All of this contributes to a very fluid set of principles and applications of those principles.

In an English context, this has led to some arguments for the narrowing of the limits of judicial discretion over remedies either by way of judicial self-restraint or by legislation. For example, Cane asserted in *Administrative Law*, 4th ed. (Oxford: Clarendon Press, 2004), at 94, that remedial discretion has been used too frequently as a substitute for careful definition and articulation of the substantive grounds of review. He went on to assert:

> It is certainly essential that the grounds on which the discretion to refuse relief can be exercised should be spelled out as clearly as possible, and that those grounds should be supportable by rational argument. The courts will always wish to retain a residual and undefined discretion to deal with unexpected cases, but the scope for its operation must be kept as narrow as possible.

Similarly, Lewis proposed in *Judicial Remedies in Public Law*, 4th ed. (London: Sweet & Maxwell, 2009), at 427, that remedial discretion,

> like all discretions, should be exercised on the basis of clear, consistent and defensible principles, otherwise there is a risk that this judicial discretion may become arbitrary making it impossible to predict the attitude of the courts.

Perhaps, in contrast, Sedley (above, at 37) would lament not only the undue confusion of substantive principles and remedial alternatives but also the lack of remedial flexibility:

> There is no need for the law of remedies to fossilise in this way, but the English lawyer's habit of pretending that there is nothing new under the sun dies hard. Because of it, we may need primary or delegated legislation to unblock the channel. If it is not done we may end up in a situation where it is possible to advise with near certainty on the legal strength of a claim without being able to offer any worthwhile advice as to what relief the court will give.

While concerns and suggestions such as those expressed by Cane, Lewis, and Sedley largely have to be seen as the product of a context in which there have been some notable examples of allegedly undue manipulation of remedies as a surrogate for dealing more directly with issues of substance, Canadian jurisprudence (as suggested already) has its analogues. What Cane, Lewis, and Sedley also highlight is a more general concern. That is the problem of how to rein in judicial remedial discretion and subject it to appropriate ordering principles, while at the same time ensuring that the judges have sufficient remedial flexibility and room for creativity in dealing with the complexities of regulatory structures and specific fact situations. Obviously, these are considerations that should be borne in mind when assessing the various exercises of remedial discretion that are featured in the cases in this chapter of the text.

Also, evaluate whether the law is well-served by the current principles governing appeal court intervention in the exercise of remedial discretions by first instance judges. That approach was well-encapsulated by Lamer CJC in *Canadian Pacific Ltd. v. Matsqui Indian Band*, [1995] 1 SCR 3 (Can.), at para. 39:

This discretionary determination should not be taken lightly by reviewing courts. It was [the judge's] discretion to exercise, and unless he considered irrelevant factors, failed to consider relevant factors, or reached an unreasonable conclusion, then his decision should be respected. To quote Lord Diplock in *Hadmor Productions Ltd. v. Hamilton* [1982] 1 All ER 1042 (Eng. HL) at 1046, an appellate court "must defer to the judge's exercise of his discretion and must not interfere with it merely on the ground that the members of the appellate court would have exercised the discretion differently."

For other Supreme Court of Canada expressions of the standard of intervention in such matters, see La Forest J in *Friends of the Oldman River Society v. Canada (Minister of Transport)*, [1992] 1 SCR 3 (Can.), at 76 (below); *Reza v. Canada*, [1994] 2 SCR 394 (Ont.), at 404 (chapter 16 of this text), rejecting the use of the term "*patently* unreasonable" in this context; and Rothstein J in *MiningWatch Canada v. Canada (Fisheries and Oceans)*, 2010 SCC 2 (Can.), at para. 43 (below) ("whether the judge at first instance has given weight to all relevant considerations").

Finally, note that, as with questions of standing, the issue of discretion may sometimes be raised before there has been any consideration of the merits of the claim. In some jurisdictions, this will occur in the context of an application for leave to seek review. However, such requirements are uncommon in Canada save where leave is needed to appeal to the courts from the decisions of certain tribunals (though see *Immigration and Refugee Protection Act*, SC 2001, c. 27, s. 72(1) of which creates a leave requirement in the case of judicial review of Immigration and Refugee Board determinations of Convention refugee claims). Rather, these challenges are made most frequently by way of a motion to have the application for judicial review struck out. As with claims of a lack of standing, are there arguments that in general such discretionary matters should not be dissociated from a consideration of the merits of the case for judicial review? In other words, should the courts deal with such challenges only after hearing and perhaps even deciding the merits of the case for judicial review (as in *Sparvier* and *Cardinal*)?

This chapter of the text commences with a consideration of those factors that are essentially concerned with the timeliness of judicial review (the availability of appeals and other avenues of recourse, prematurity in a more general sense, and mootness) before focusing on the discretionary grounds for denial of relief based essentially on the conduct of the applicant (delay, misconduct, and waiver). It then concludes with the most controversial aspect of remedial discretion, that which focuses on the impact of successful judicial review on the administrative process, third parties, and the public generally. In this context, these concerns have been subsumed under the general title of "balance of convenience."

For a useful discussion in a British context, see Bingham, "Should Public Law Remedies Be Discretionary?" [1991] *Public Law* 64.

ALTERNATIVE REMEDIES

As we have seen already, the courts will sometimes regard the existence of a specific remedy in the empowering statute as excluding the availability of common law judicial review as a matter of jurisdiction. More frequently, however, the question of alternative remedies is dealt with by reference to the courts' overriding discretion to refuse relief even where the substance of the applicant's or plaintiff's case may have been made out. In such instances, the questions asked tend to be about the relative or comparative convenience of judicial review as opposed to the alternative forms of relief that are also available. It is not simply enough to assert that there are alternative avenues of relief available and that, given the historically "extraordinary" nature of prerogative relief in particular, those other avenues are, therefore, the more appropriate ones to pursue.

Indeed, as the following materials demonstrate, the issue whether a particular remedy is the more appropriate is not always easy to resolve. In reading these cases, try to develop a list of the considerations that might be relevant to the resolution of such questions.

For a consideration of this issue from a British perspective, see Lewis, "The Exhaustion of Alternative Remedies in Administrative Law" (1992), 51 *Camb. LJ* 58; for a survey of Canadian authorities on this and the often related ground of prematurity, see Reid and Leafloor, "Prematurity, Alternative Remedies and Special Circumstances" (1994), 3 *Reid's Administrative Law* 73.

Statutory Appeals

Harelkin v. University of Regina
[1979] 2 SCR 561 (Sask.)

[This case involved a student who was required to withdraw from the university's faculty of social work. His appeal to a university committee was dismissed without his being given a hearing. He then applied for *certiorari* and *mandamus*, rather than pursuing the available right of appeal to a committee of the university senate. His application was allowed by the Saskatchewan Queen's Bench, but this decision was reversed by the Court of Appeal. The case proceeded to the Supreme Court of Canada. There was no doubt that there had been a breach of the rules of natural justice.]

BEETZ J: The contentions made against the judgment of the Court of Appeal can be summarized in four main propositions: first, failure by the council committee to respect the principle *audi alteram partem* was akin to a jurisdictional error and the writs should issue *ex debito justitiae*; second, the decision of the council committee was an absolute nullity from which there could be no appeal to the senate committee; third, even if there could be an appeal to the senate committee, appellant's right of appeal was not an adequate alternative remedy; fourth, the principle *audi alteram partem* had in this case been given statutory force and the Courts should exercise their discretion with a view to enforcing the statute.

I propose to deal in turn with each of these propositions.

. . .

III Failure To Respect the Principle audi alteram partem and Issuance of the Writs ex debito justitiae

The principle that *certiorari* and *mandamus* are discretionary remedies by nature cannot be disputed. The principle was recently reaffirmed with respect to *certiorari* in a unanimous decision of this Court, *PPG Industries Canada Ltd. v. A.G. Can.* [1976] 2 SCR 739 (Can.) at 749. And *mandamus* is certainly not less discretionary than *certiorari*:

> The award of the writs usually lies within the discretion of the court.
>
> The court is entitled to refuse *certiorari* and *mandamus* to applicants if they have been guilty of unreasonable delay or misconduct or if an adequate alternative remedy exists, notwithstanding that they have proved a usurpation of jurisdiction by the inferior tribunal or an omission to perform a public duty. On applications by subjects for *certiorari* to remove indictments the courts have always exercised a very wide discretion.
>
> The fact that some of the prerogative writs were discretionary came to be directly linked with their designation as prerogative writs. Thus, in one case, it was said: "An application for *mandamus* is an application to the discretion of the court; a *mandamus* is a prerogative writ and is not a writ of right" (*R v. Excise Commissioners* (1788) 2 TR 381 at 385). But although none of the prerogative writs is a writ of course, not all are discretionary. Prohibition, for example, issues as of right in certain cases, and *habeas corpus ad subjiciendum*, the most famous of them all, is a writ of right which issues *ex debito justitiae* when the applicant has satisfied the court that his detention was unlawful. These two writs, therefore, are not in the fullest sense writs of grace.

See de Smith, *Judicial Review of Administrative Action* (3rd ed 1973) at 510, App. 1.

Over the years, the Courts have elaborated various criteria which provide guidance as to how the discretion should be exercised. In the process, the area of discretion has been more or less reduced depending on the circumstances of each case. In some cases, particularly those involving lack of jurisdiction, Courts have gone as far to say that *certiorari* should issue *ex debito justitiae*. And, on the more than dubious assumption that cases involving a denial of natural justice could be equated with those involving a lack of jurisdiction, it has also been said that *certiorari* should issue *ex debito justitiae* where there was a denial of natural justice.

The use of the expression *ex debito justitiae* in conjunction with the discretionary remedies of *certiorari* and *mandamus* is unfortunate. It is based on a contradiction and imports a great deal of confusion into the law.

Ex debito justitiae literally means "as of right," in opposition to "as of grace" (Osborne, *A Concise Law Dictionary* (5th ed.); *Black's Law Dictionary* (4th ed.)). A writ cannot at once be a writ of grace and a writ of right. To say in a case that the writ should issue *ex debito justitiae* simply means that the circumstances militate strongly in favour of the issuance of the writ rather than for refusal. But the expression, *albeit* Latin, has no magic virtue and cannot change a writ of grace into a writ of right nor destroy the discretion even in cases involving lack of jurisdiction.

A fortiori does the discretion remain in cases not of lack of jurisdiction, but of excess or abuse of jurisdiction such as those involving a breach of natural justice.

[Beetz J then discussed a number of Canadian and English cases, including *Halifax-Dartmouth Real Estate Board* (1964), 44 DLR (2d) 248 (NSSC), to support his arguments about the discretionary nature of the relief being sought. He then proceeded to deal with the issue whether the decision of the council was a nullity from which there could be no appeal (see 580-87). On this point, he held that breach of the rules of natural justice did not nullify a decision and he contrasted such breaches with "want" of jurisdiction. In the alternative, he held that, even if the effect of the breach was to nullify the council's decision, a fair reading of the relevant appeal provision led him to the conclusion that such "nullities" were subject to it (that is, could be appealed). See further on this point, *Calvin v. Carr*, [1980] AC 574 (PC NSW), which also held that there was no general rule that breach of the rules of natural justice could not be cured on appeal.]

V Whether Appellant's Right of Appeal to the Senate Committee Was an Adequate Alternative Remedy: The Balance of Convenience

. . .

In order to evaluate whether appellant's right of appeal to the senate committee constituted an adequate alternative remedy and even a better remedy than a recourse to the Courts by way of prerogative writs, several factors should have been taken into consideration among which the procedure on the appeal, the composition of the senate committee, its powers and the manner in which they were probably to be exercised by a body which was not a professional Court of Appeal and was not bound to act exactly as one nor likely to do so. Other relevant factors include the burden of a previous finding, expeditiousness and costs.

[After noting that, at the time, there was nothing in the university's statute or bylaws with respect to procedures to be followed by the senate appeals committee, Beetz J continued:]

In my view, appellant was not entitled to assume that, because of the lack of such bylaws at the relevant time, the senate committee would have denied him a hearing within the meaning of s. 33(1)(e) of the Act. Nor should he have assumed that, since one of the governing bodies of the university had erroneously failed to comply with the principles of natural justice, another governing body of superior jurisdiction would do the same. He should on the contrary have assumed that the body of superior jurisdiction would give him justice, as was held by the Judicial Committee in *White v. Kuzych* [[1951] 3 DLR 641 (PC BC) at 651]:

> Their Lordships are therefore constrained to hold that the conclusion reached by the general committee was subject to appeal. And they must respectfully repudiate both the correctness and the relevance of the view that it would have been useless for the respondent to appeal, because the federation would be sure to decide against him. They see no reason why the federation, if called on to deal with the appeal, should be assumed to be incapable of giving its honest attention to a complaint of unfairness or of undue severity, and of endeavouring to arrive at the right final decision.

Section 33(1)(e) of the Act does not spell out the detailed powers of the senate appeals committee but there is no reason to doubt that such powers comprise the ordinary powers of an appellate jurisdiction including, if the appeal be allowed, the power to set aside the decision of the council committee and render on the merits the decision that the council committee should have rendered or send it back before the council committee for a proper hearing. There is thus no jurisdictional lacuna in the senate committee which could have prevented it from giving full justice to appellant.

On the other hand, in the context of a statute providing for the constitution of a body such as a university, there is every reason to construe the word "appeal" in the most flexible manner with respect to the mode of appeal, and as capable of meaning "review," "retrial" or "new trial." One should also expect that, in this context, an appeal is more likely to take a form resembling that of a trial *de novo* than that of a "pure" appeal. There are three main reasons for this. First, nothing in the Act nor in the new by-laws indicates that the council committee's record shall be transferred to the senate committee on an appeal from a council committee decision. Second, university bodies like the Faculty of Social Work and the council are not courts of records. Such records as they keep are not kept for the sole purpose of facilitating *quasi*-judicial proceedings, appeals or review. They ordinarily consist of terse minutes, bare resolutions and concise documents. Given these circumstances, the senate committee should in practice have to try a case anew in a great number of situations. Sub-section 4.2.6 of the new senate by-laws, quoted above, illustrates this point: it does not merely empower the senate committee to hear additional or new evidence as pure appellate jurisdictions sometimes do; it is broad enough to enable the senate committee to try the case afresh. The third reason why an "appeal" within a university should not be given a restricted or technical meaning flows from the fact that the members of a university appeal committee are not usually trained in the law. Even in cases where they would not be called upon to hear any evidence, they would be almost irresistibly inclined to "re-try" the case, apart from any finding in the impeached decision. This inclination is so strong that professional appellate Courts sometimes find it difficult to resist. It would be more realistic to expect that a body of laymen would abide by technically less strict standards than a professional Court of Appeal.

In the case at bar, in so far as an appeal to the senate committee would have taken the form of a trial *de novo*, appellant would not have been confronted with the adverse finding of the council committee. But even if this appeal to the senate committee had not taken the form of a pure trial *de novo*, appellant would still not have been confronted with such an adverse finding, since the senate committee would have been bound, as a matter of law, to set aside the decision of the council committee which was vitiated by the failure to hear appellant. Again it should not be presumed that the senate committee would have erred in law and decided that appellant was not entitled to be heard by the council committee. It must be assumed that the senate committee would have reached the correct decision and, if it did not, a Superior Court could quash its decision.

In the result, appellant's position before the senate committee, unencumbered by any valid finding of the council committee, would have been similar to his initial position before the council committee. The only finding against him, if it can be called a finding, would have been that of the Faculty of Social Work. But this finding was already before the council committee. Appellant, being the grievor, would have had the burden of establishing that his examination papers had been improperly marked; again this burden would have been upon him before the council committee.

As to the contention that difference in membership between the senate committee and the council committee should result in a difference in approach to the issue, it does not in my view carry great weight. Appellant could not expect the members of either committee themselves to read and re-mark his examination papers. This could not be part of their function and they would be unable to do so, the members of the council committee because they would in the main be academics of different disciplines, and the members of the senate committee, because they would be students and lay members. Assuming also that academic expertise was useful or necessary to decide the case, there would have been no lack of such expertise in a university and it would have been equally available to the senate committee and to the council committee, in the form of expert testimony. Furthermore, the Legislature, in its wisdom, has decided that the lay body of the senate committee should occupy a position superior to that of the academic or expert body of the council committee. I fail to see how appellant could complain that his case be decided by the body whom the Legislature has placed in the superior position.

For the same reasons, I do not see much substance in the assertion that appellant was in effect deprived of his right of appeal to the council committee. This may be so, but it is of little importance where the superior appellate jurisdiction is equipped with the means to remedy all injustices.

I have reached the conclusion that appellant's right of appeal to the senate committee provided him with an adequate alternative remedy. In addition, this remedy was in my opinion a more convenient remedy for appellant as well as for the university in terms of costs and expeditiousness.

If appellant had followed throughout the wise counsel given to him at the beginning by his advocate Ms Lemire to settle his difficulties with the mechanisms which existed within before going to an outside body, he would have saved a great deal of time and money. But he has from the start shown a preference for external forums, beginning with the Ombudsman and hindering the initial review of his academic situation. He has now gone before three Courts. Three years after the event, the merits of his case remain undetermined from an academic point of view. Furthermore, and as was conceded by his counsel, there remains some uncertainty as to the modalities of a hearing before the council committee, more particularly with respect to his right to counsel. His counsel did not foreclose the right to challenge any decision of the council committee on this point. It is therefore possible that, if appellant were successful in this Court and the council committee refused him permission to be represented by counsel, appellant would, instead of going before the senate committee, again apply for *certiorari* and *mandamus* with consequential appeal and that a few more years and considerably more money would be lost before a final determination of his case could even be considered. If this is the law, then the law has reached a dangerous stage of complication, for all of appellant's difficulties could have been resolved fairly, within a reasonable time and at little cost to himself and to the university, had he simply wanted to use all the remedies put at his disposal by the Act.

The courts should not use their discretion to promote delay and expenditure unless there is no other way to protect a right. I believe the correct view was expressed by O'Halloran JA, in *The King, ex rel. Lee v. Workmen's Compensation Board* [1942] 2 DLR 665 (BC CA) at 677-678, dealing with *mandamus* but equally applicable to *certiorari*:

> Once it appears a public body has neglected or refused to perform a statutory duty to a person entitled to call for its exercise, then *mandamus* issues *ex debito justitiae*, if there is no other convenient remedy. ... If however, there is a convenient alternative remedy, the granting of *mandamus* is discretionary, *but to be governed by considerations which tend to the speedy and inexpensive as well as efficacious administration of justice.* ... (The italics are mine.)

This passage was quoted with approval by the British Columbia Court of Appeal in *R v. Spalding* [1955] 5 DLR 374 (BC CA) at 382, in which it was held that the failure to respect the principle of natural justice in first instance could not be cured by the exercise of a right of appeal where the latter, apart from the risk of being futile, could not be exercised except at considerable expense and inconvenience. It is not the case here. (O'Halloran JA also said in *Lee* that *mandamus* was not to be regarded as a secondary or unusual remedy but as a speedy, inexpensive and efficacious remedy; times have changed and certainly in this case, an appeal to the senate committee would be speedier than *mandamus* and *certiorari*, less expensive and as efficacious.)

One last point should be mentioned in relation to appellant's right to alternative remedies, namely, appellant's right to a rehearing before the council committee. It will be recalled that appellant's counsel had unsuccessfully asked for a rehearing, and this is a factor which must be weighed together with all the others. Thus, in *Glynn v. Keele University* [[1971] 1 WLR 487 (Ch.)], Pennycuick V-C said (at 495) that the result might have been different had the applicant applied for a fresh hearing to the appeal council. Lord Denning was of the same view in the *Baldwin & Francis* case [[1959] AC 663 (Eng. HL)]. But in both cases, the applicant had already reached the ultimate appellate level and had nowhere else to go, whereas in this case, the senate committee exercised the ultimate appeal jurisdiction and the mode of redress prescribed by the Act is not a rehearing by the council committee but an appeal to the senate committee. It is also arguable that fresh consideration of the issues involved by another body of superior jurisdiction may be preferable to a hearing by the tribunal which had previously ruled against appellant. Accordingly the council committee's refusal to grant a rehearing to appellant is not a sufficient reason, in my view, for issuing *certiorari* and *mandamus*.

[In then rejecting the argument that the appellant's case was strengthened by the fact that the hearing was statutorily mandated, rather than judicially implied, Beetz J stated:]

The Act incorporates a university and does not alter the traditional nature of such an institution as a community of scholars and students enjoying a substantial internal autonomy. While a university incorporated by statute and subsidized by public funds may in a sense be regarded as a public service entrusted with the responsibility of insuring the higher education of a large number of citizens, as was held in *Polten* [*Re Polten and Governing Council of The University of Toronto* (1975), 59 DLR (3d) 197 (Ont. Div. Ct.)], its immediate and direct responsibility extends primarily to its present members and, in practice, its governing bodies function as domestic tribunals when they act in a *quasi-judicial* capacity. The Act countenances the domestic autonomy of the university by making provision for the solution of conflicts within the university. Thus, s. 55 provides:

> 55. The senate may make provision for the hearing and final determination of all appeals and complaints respecting the election of its members and the election of the chancellor.

Section 66 has a similar purpose:

> 66. Where any question arises respecting the powers and duties of convocation, the senate, board, council or any officer or servant of the university, the question shall be settled by a committee composed of the chancellor, the president and the board chairman.

Furthermore, s. 78(1)(c) contains within itself the qualification that the power of the council committee to hear and decide upon all applications and memorials by students is "subject to an appeal to the senate." These words give weight to the proposition that the legislator attached importance on the student proceeding through the stages established by the Act for the protection of student interests.

Sections 78(1)(c) and 33(1)(e) are, in my view, inspired by the general intent of the Legislature that intestine grievances preferably be resolved internally by the means provided in the Act, the university thus being given the chance to correct its own errors, consonantly with the traditional autonomy of universities, as well as with expeditiousness and low cost for the public and the members of the university. While, of course, not amounting to privative clauses, provisions like ss. 55, 66, 33(1)(e) and 78(1)(c) are a clear signal to the Courts that they should use restraint and be slow to intervene in university affairs by means of discretionary writs whenever it is still possible for the university to correct its errors with its own institutional means. In using restraint, the Courts do not refuse to enforce statutory duties imposed upon the governing bodies of the university. They simply exercise their discretion in such a way as to implement the general intent of the Legislature. I believe this intent to be a most important element to take into consideration in resolving the case and, indeed, to be a conclusive one when taken in conjunction with the others.

[Martland, Pigeon, and Pratte JJ concurred with Beetz J's judgment. Dickson J (with whom Spence and Estey JJ concurred) dissented. After holding that there had been a breach of the natural justice rules, referring to *Smith*, *inter alia*, and arguing that breach of the rules of natural justice amounted to jurisdictional error, he continued:]

DICKSON J:

(3) Where there has been a denial of natural justice (and hence a lack of jurisdiction) *certiorari* will issue, notwithstanding a right of appeal to an administrative or domestic body, where that body exercises purely appellate functions.

This point raises the general issue of the discretionary nature of *certiorari*. In this context the authorities, as I have earlier indicated, draw a distinction between jurisdictional and non-jurisdictional error and between a right of appeal to an administrative or domestic tribunal and a right of appeal to the Courts. Generally speaking, the rule is that, if the error is jurisdictional, *certiorari* will issue *ex debito justitiae*, but if the error is error in law, then in the absence of a privative clause, *certiorari* may issue. The discretion is broad when the error is non-jurisdictional and there is an appeal to the Courts, but virtually disappears when the error is jurisdictional and the right of appeal, if any, is to an administrative or domestic tribunal sitting in a purely appellate role.

Counsel has not cited a single case—and I know of none—in which *certiorari* has been denied when the ground of complaint has been failure to accord a statutory right resulting in a denial of natural justice and the appeal is to a domestic tribunal exercising purely appellate functions.

. . .

There are several broad principles operative in this general area of want of jurisdiction, and alternative remedies. Generally speaking, *certiorari* is a matter of discretion. The discretion must, of course, be exercised judicially and, in the absence of something in the circumstances of the case which makes it proper to refuse the relief, the writ will issue *ex debito justitiae* in an excess of jurisdiction situation. The phrase *ex debito justitiae* is merely a shorthand for referring to those cases where "the Court, although nominally it has a discretion, if it is to act according to the ordinary principles upon which judicial discretion is exercised, must exercise that discretion in a particular way": *per* Sir Wilfrid Greene MR in *The King v. Stafford Justices, Ex parte Stafford Corp.* [1940] 2 KB 33 (CA) at 43. This does not rule out inquiry into the conduct of the applicant and the circumstances of the case. Inordinate delay may be ground for refusing relief. Where an alternative remedy exists, in the case of want of jurisdiction, *certiorari* remains available but, in each case, the Court in exercising its discretion must consider the convenience and adequacy of the alternative remedy. An example will be found in *R v. Brighton Justices, Ex parte Robinson* [1973] 1 WLR 69 (QB), in which a traffic summons against Mrs Robinson was heard in her absence. The *Criminal Justice Act, 1967* (UK) provided a procedure whereby in that situation a statutory declaration could be filed with the clerk to the Justices, the result of which was to render the summons and all subsequent proceedings void. An application for an order of *certiorari* was granted quashing the conviction notwithstanding the alternative remedy. It should be added that the Court made it clear that an order of *certiorari* would not go as a matter of course and that, in future, regard would be had as to why the applicant had not used the alternative procedure.

The nature of the error will also be a circumstance for consideration. If the loss of jurisdiction derives from a misinterpretation of a statute, a statutory right of appeal may well be adequate. On the other hand, a breach of natural justice in all but the rarest of cases will render inadequate the remedy. A possible exception is the availability of a hearing *de novo* on appeal to a body exercising original jurisdiction.

The nature of the appellate body may also be of concern. Where a statutory right of appeal is provided directly to the Courts, the reviewing Court is more likely to refuse *certiorari*, especially on questions of statutory interpretation. ...

On the other hand, as one moves away from a right of appeal to the Courts to a right of appeal to a statutory tribunal (see *R v. Paddington Valuation Officer, Ex parte Peachey Property Corp. Ltd.* [1966] 1 QB 380 (CA)), or an appeal to administrative officials, even ministers (see *R v. Spalding* [1955] 5 DLR 374 (BC CA)) and, ultimately, domestic bodies (see *O'Laughlin v. Halifax Longshoremen's Ass'n.* (1972) 28 DLR (3d) 315 (NS SCAD)), the alternative remedies are more frequently found to be inadequate. ...

The capacity of the remedial body may be of importance. Where the body which may grant the remedy exercises original jurisdiction (*King v. University of Saskatchewan* [1969] SCR 678 (Sask.); *Re Chromex Nickel Mines Ltd.* (1970) 16 DLR (3d) 273 (BC CA) [appeal quashed [1972] SCR 119 (BC)]), perhaps even hearing the matter *de novo*, the remedy will be more often perceived as adequate, even conceivably in cases of denial of natural justice. On the other hand, the normal sort of purely appellate function will rarely be seen as capable of curing a breach of natural justice. ...

[Dickson J then held that, save in exceptional circumstances not present here, breach of the rules of natural justice cannot be cured on appeal.]

It is the convenience and adequacy of the alternative remedy, that is, an appeal to the senate appeals committee, which should be the focus of attention. The case at bar, in my opinion, is a classic example of the situation where the discretion of the reviewing Court is "nominal" and, upon the facts, ought to be exercised in favour of Mr Harelkin. The fundamental reason underlying all of this is that an appeal is simply not a sufficient remedy for the failure to do justice in the first place. Take the present case. Assume an appeal to the senate appeals committee. The ground of appeal would be that the council committee had erred in failing to afford the student an opportunity to be heard. The appeals committee would be placed immediately in the invidious position of having to decide, as a question of law, an issue already decided in favour of the student in the Saskatchewan Courts. What then would be the proper course for the appeals committee—send the matter back to council for rehearing? Hear the case anew despite its appellate role? Does the senate appeals committee have the power to do either?

A person appealing a decision made against him without a hearing is at a grave disadvantage. At the first level, the burden of persuasion lies with the other side to show some reason why a decision adverse to this individual should be made. At the appeal level the burden changes. The present case is a good example. Should Mr Harelkin be expected to go to the senate not knowing what has been placed against him at council or the real reason for his expulsion—bad marks or neurosis?

There are no minutes of the committee of council available. There is nothing to show whether the real core of Mr Harelkin's complaint—that he was being rejected because of mental instability rather than low marks—was ever placed before the committee. If the appeal body were specifically charged with determining whether the lower decision was properly made, and if not, that it should remit the matter to the lower level for rehearing, the matter might be different: see Mullan, "Comment" (1971) 49 *Can. Bar Rev.* 624. Appeal might conceivably be equally as effective as review. But that is not this case.

The dynamic of ascending rigidity is readily apparent in structures such as a university. Who could possibly pretend that a student starts the day with as fair a chance in a hearing before the university senate, or its committee, faced with adverse decisions from the faculty studies committee and a council committee, both made with no hearing, as he would have before the first body to have considered the matter? Furthermore, there is a world of difference between these bodies, as the faculty committee and the council committee are composed of academics, with expertise in judging the quality of a student's work and whether it warrants expulsion, while the senate is composed in the main of administrators, lay people and students. The key decision is by the academic committee. Thus, it is before this committee that the person should be heard above all: see *Leary v. National Union of Vehicle Builders* [[1971] Ch. 34 (Ch.)].

Professor de Smith sums up the position in the following words (210-211) which I would like to adopt:

[T]he present weight of authority appears to support the view that a breach of natural justice in the first instance can be rectified only by a full and fair *de novo* hearing given either (i) by the body perpetrating the original breach, or (if possible) a differently constituted body with the same powers and status, or (ii) (exceptionally) an appellate body, if that body also has original jurisdiction and exercises that jurisdiction in the particular case.

Mr Harelkin should be able to look to the Courts for relief if he is treated unfairly by the council, regardless of what might have occurred before the senate, had he pursued that route. At the time he was faced with the choice of senate appeal or *certiorari* he had no assurance that he would be heard by the senate appeals committee. The council committee, whose statutory duty to "hear and decide" was framed in the same terms as senate, had preferred an *in camera* session from which he was excluded. There was nothing, at the time, to say that senate would not adopt the same attitude. The fact that the senate has adopted procedural safeguards since these proceedings were initiated clarifies that issue for the future, but it does not in any way, in my view, affect the outcome of this appeal.

The university says that to require the full hearing of the type which the applicant seeks could be interpreted as a requirement to have at least two full-scale confrontations between student and university in the process of having a student discontinue his studies. That may be so. But the fault, if fault it is, lies in the legislation, and not in the expectations of the student. The *University of Regina Act, 1974,* for reasons best known to the legislators, gives a student believing himself aggrieved two hearings, *ie,* one original hearing and one on appeal. The student in the case at bar has not waived his right to either hearing, and it would be wrong, in my view, to deny him that which the statute expressly accords him.

On the footing (i) that the council of the University of Regina had no jurisdiction to deny the appellant a hearing, and (ii) that the appeal given the appellant is administrative and not to the Courts, there is simply no authority for the decision of the Court below.

Counsel for the university referred the Court to two other sections of the *University of Regina Act, 1974,* ss. 9 and 66, which read:

> 9. The Lieutenant Governor shall be the visitor of the university with authority to do all those acts that pertain to visitors as to him seem proper.
>
> . . .
>
> 66. Where any question arises respecting the powers and duties of convocation, the senate, board, council or any officer or servant of the university, the question shall be settled by a committee composed of the chancellor, the president and the board chairman.

Neither of these sections was relied upon as offering an alternative remedy on its own. Both were referred to in support of the broader contention that the Legislature intended that disputes be resolved within the university community. Section 66 clearly has no application in this case, as we are not concerned with uncertainty respecting the powers or duties of either senate or council. As for s. 9, it might be noted that the "visitor" has experienced somewhat of a renaissance of late in English university cases, notably in the recent decision in *Patel v. University of Bradford Senate* [1978] 3 All ER 841 (Ch.). Academic writers have suggested that the rehabilitation of the role of the "visitor" may be the cure to the internal ills of the university: see Bridge, "Keeping Peace in the Universities" (1970) 86 *LQR* 531 and Ricquier, "The University Visitor" (1978) 4 *Dal. LJ* 647. Be that as it may, the university did not argue that exclusive jurisdiction here lay in the "visitor," and one might well question the practical relevance of this English institution to the modern Canadian university.

Appeal dismissed.

NOTES

1. Do the majority and the minority have different views as to the nature of judicial discretion over the grant of relief for unlawful administrative action or is their disagreement merely factual? How do they differ in their assessment of the facts? Which criteria would you identify as relevant in advising a client to seek judicial review as opposed to pursuing a statutory appeal?

2. The status of *Harelkin* was for a long time subject to considerable doubt. First, it attracted academic criticism that derived support from the strong dissent of Dickson J. Second, the Supreme Court itself did not seem wholly committed to the principles espoused by the majority. Despite these and other doubts as to its authority and reach, *Harelkin* was ultimately reconfirmed by the Supreme Court in *Canadian Pacific Ltd. v. Matsqui Indian Band*, set out in part in chapter 5, Bias and Lack of Independence. At stake was whether the applicants, who were contesting a real property tax assessment, could proceed directly to the Federal Court by way of application for judicial review and bypass the appeal tribunals established by the taxing Indian bands by way of bylaw. Among the substantive issues raised by the applicants was a claim that the lands in question were not subject to assessment, a matter that all members of the court seemed to regard as a question going to jurisdiction in a preliminary or jurisdiction-limiting sense. Nonetheless, by a majority of six to three (on this issue), the court held that that challenge should have been made initially before the appeal tribunals rather than by way of a preemptive application for judicial review. Extracts from the judgment of Lamer CJC follow.

Canadian Pacific Ltd. v. Matsqui Indian Band
[1995] 1 SCR 3 (Can.)

LAMER CJC (Cory, L'Heureux-Dubé, Sopinka, Gonthier, and Iacobucci JJ concurring on this point): …

IV. Analysis

A. Introduction

The respondents argue that their land is not "in the reserve" as required by s. 83(1)(a) of the *Indian Act*, and therefore the land may not be taxed by the appellant bands under their new tax assessment powers. This Court is not being asked to determine whether the land is, or is not, "in the reserve." Instead, we must decide whether Joyal J properly exercised his discretion in refusing to entertain the respondents' application for judicial review, thereby requiring the respondents to pursue their jurisdictional challenge through the appeal procedures established by the appellant bands under s. 83(3) of the *Indian Act*.

In considering whether Joyal J exercised his discretion reasonably, it is important that we not lose sight of Parliament's objective in creating the new Indian taxation powers. The regime which came into force in 1988 is intended to facilitate the development of Aboriginal self-government by allowing bands to exercise the inherently governmental power of taxation on their reserves. Though this Court is not faced with the issue of Aboriginal self-government directly, the underlying purpose and functions of the Indian tax assessment scheme provide considerable guidance in applying the principles of administrative law to the statutory provisions at issue here. I will therefore employ a purposive and functional approach where appropriate in this ruling.

[Lamer CJC here considered whether the tribunals had authority to even entertain the question whether the land in question was "in the reserve." After accepting that the issue was indeed a jurisdictional one, he nonetheless concluded that the appeal bodies could consider this question, albeit that their conclusions on it would attract little deference on subsequent judicial review. He concluded on this point:]

A purposive analysis also leads me to favour the "process approach." Parliament clearly intended bands to assume control over the assessment process on the reserves, since the entire scheme would be pointless if assessors were unable to engage in the preliminary determination of whether land should be classified as taxable and thereby placed on the taxation rolls. Given this, I see no reason to interpret s. 83(3) of the *Indian Act* as authorizing appeal procedures relating only to the valuation step of the assessment process. Such narrow supervisory control would be inconsistent with Parliament's purpose in authorizing Bands to value and classify property for taxation.

[He then embarked on a consideration whether the appeals constituted an adequate alternative remedy, citing *Harelkin* with approval.]

On the basis of the above, I conclude that a variety of factors should be considered by courts in determining whether they should enter into judicial review, or alternatively should require an applicant to proceed through a statutory appeal procedure. These factors include: the convenience of the alternative remedy, the nature of the error, and the nature of the appellate body (*ie*, its investigatory, decision-making and remedial capacities). I do not believe that the category of factors should be closed, as it is for courts in particular circumstances to isolate and balance the factors which are relevant.

In this case, when applying the adequate alternative remedy principle, we must consider the adequacy of the statutory appeal procedures created by the bands, and not simply the adequacy of the appeal tribunals. This is because the bands have provided for appeals from the tribunals to the Federal Court, Trial Division. I recognize that certain factors will be relevant only to the appeal tribunals (*ie*, the expertise of members, or allegations of bias) or to the appeal to the Federal Court, Trial Division (*ie*, whether this appeal is *intra vires* the bands). In applying the adequate alternative remedy principle, all these factors must be considered in order to assess the overall statutory scheme.

[Lamer CJC then held that Joyal J had not erred in taking into account the policy considerations behind the assessment bylaws. As well, he held that the creation in the bylaws of a right of appeal from the appeal tribunal to the Federal Court Trial Division had implicit statutory authorization. He then moved to consider the adequacy of the alternative remedies.]

Joyal J and Pratte JA engaged in a debate within their respective rulings as to whether the statutory appeal tribunals or the Federal Court, Trial Division, is the preferable forum in which to consider at first instance the issue of whether the respondents' lands are "in the reserve." Joyal J ... reasoned as follows:

> ... I observe that section 18 motions, as for all prerogative writ applications, are heard summarily. It seems to me that a board or court of revision is a better forum to receive and consider all the evidence material to the issue. It is not presumptuous of me to imagine that the respondents have built up some armour to respond to the main thrust of the applicant's case and that the enquiry might be extensive and far-reaching. Whatever the decision below, it is probable that the Federal Court would be called upon to deal with an appeal from it. In that respect, it may be generally stated that the field of enquiry of an appeal court and the remedies available to it are far more extensive than those available in *certiorari* proceedings.

Pratte JA disagreed: ...

> ... [W]hile the Judge realized that it would be necessary, in order to answer the questions raised by the appellants, to introduce evidence on complex factual issues, he expressed the view ... that since "section 18 motions ... are heard summarily" the tribunals created under the Assessment By-law were "a better forum to receive and consider all the evidence material to the issue." That opinion does not take into account the fact that those who are appointed to the tribunals created by the Assessment By-law are not likely to have any experience in the difficult task of presiding over a trial and will not be governed by any rules of procedure enabling them to perform that function. That opinion also ignores that, under subsection 18.4(2) (as enacted by SC 1990, c. 8, s. 5) of the *Federal Court Act*, the Trial Division may, if an application for judicial review raises complex factual issues, order that it be treated and proceeded with as an action.

With respect to both Joyal J and Pratte JA, I believe that they may have asked themselves the wrong question. In the case of the adequate alternative remedy principle, the question which should be posed is: Is an appeal tribunal established under s. 83(3) of the *Indian Act* an adequate forum for resolving, at first instance, the respondents' jurisdictional challenge? This does not necessarily require a finding that the tribunals are a better forum than the courts.

Having considered the factors raised by both Joyal J and Pratte JA, I find that it was not unreasonable for Joyal J to conclude that the appeal tribunals are an adequate forum. Whether or not Joyal J was wrong to conclude that the tribunals are a better forum is irrelevant. As Joyal J noted, a hearing before the appeal tribunal will allow for a wide-ranging inquiry into all of the evidence. Moreover, although the issues may be complex, to suggest (as Pratte JA does) that the appeal tribunals are ill-equipped to consider such issues is contrary to the intention of Parliament, as evidenced by s. 83(3) of the *Indian*

Act. When Parliament required bands to establish appeal procedures on both the classification and valuation aspects of the assessment process, Parliament must have believed that the appeal tribunals would be capable of resolving the issues on which they had authority to adjudicate. Otherwise, the existence of a requirement that appeal procedures be established makes no sense.

It is interesting to note s. 18.3(1) of the *Federal Court Act*, which states:

> 18.3(1) A federal board, commission or other tribunal may at any stage of its proceedings refer any question or issue of law, of jurisdiction or of practice and procedure to the Trial Division for hearing and determination.

Section 18.3(1) allows an appeal tribunal to seek the guidance of the courts if it encounters legal, procedural or other issues which it cannot resolve.

On the basis of my analysis above, I would conclude that it was not unreasonable for Joyal J to consider the following factors in exercising his discretion:

(1) The appeal tribunals are an adequate forum for considering at first instance the issue raised by the respondents. In particular, it was not unreasonable to conclude that the appeal tribunals would be an adequate forum on the basis that a far-reaching and extensive inquiry could be conducted in which both sides could fully present their evidence and arguments.

(2) The statutory appeal procedure provides to the respondents an appeal from the appeal tribunals to the Federal Court, Trial Division. Effectively, the respondents will be able to bring their case before the Federal Court, Trial Division, which may fully review the findings of the appeal tribunals. Any decision of that Court will have the force of *res judicata*. To deny the respondents judicial review in no way prevents them from obtaining a full judicial examination of the issue of whether their lands are "in the reserve."

(3) The purpose of Parliament in enacting the Indian tax assessment scheme was to promote the development of Aboriginal governmental institutions. It is therefore preferable for issues concerning Indian tax assessment to be resolved within the statutory appeal procedures developed by Aboriginal peoples. In particular, it is preferable that assessment errors be corrected within the institutions of the bands.

[As we have already seen, however, Lamer CJC went on to hold that Joyal J had erred in failing to take into account the appeal tribunal's lack of independence. While only one other judge agreed with him on this point, the combination of those two and the three judges who held that the applicants should have direct access to the Federal Court on their jurisdictional challenge meant that the appeal was dismissed and the application for judicial review allowed to proceed.]

NOTES

1. For strong reaffirmation of this aspect of *Matsqui*, see *President of the Canada Border Services Agency v. C.B. Powell Ltd.*, 2010 FCA 61, where the Federal Court of Appeal held

that, even where the agency declined to deal with a matter because it was outside of its jurisdiction, this did not excuse the affected company from appealing that ruling to the Canadian International Trade Tribunal. As a consequence, an application for judicial review of that ruling was premature whether or not the issue was truly jurisdictional.

2. To what extent does *Matsqui* stand for the proposition that, if an appeal on the issues raised does exist, it should always be used in preference to judicial review? If the judgment does not go this far, under what circumstances will a court be justified in assuming judicial review jurisdiction over a matter that could have been appealed? Has the Supreme Court put out of contention the argument that, while the appeal tribunal could jurisdictionally deal with the issues that are raised, judicial review is a better route for resolving such matters? Would it be appropriate to argue that the result of an appeal would be a foregone conclusion because of the appeal body's precedents? In the light of the Supreme Court's judgment consider the case digests of earlier judgments that follow:

a. In *Spence v. Prince Albert (City) Police Commissioners* (1987), 25 Admin. LR 90 (Sask. CA), the court excused a failure to exercise a statutory right of appeal from a first instance police disciplinary process. Notwithstanding the breadth of the appeal provisions, the court (in distinguishing *Harelkin*) ruled that exhaustion of appeal rights was not required in situations where, as here, it was likely that the appeal authority would deal with the matter on the merits rather than considering the applicant's principal basis for seeking judicial review: an allegation of bias against the first instance body.

b. In *Banks v. Workers' Compensation Board of British Columbia* (1988), 25 BCLR (2d) 282 (SC), a defence based on a failure to exhaust appeal rights was defeated, the court giving as one of its reasons that the first instance decision depended on a longstanding policy of the board. Because it was highly unlikely, given the commitment of the board to this policy, that there would be a reversal of the decision at either of two levels of appeal, an appeal was said to be futile and the petition for judicial review entertained. However, in such cases, there are competing considerations. What are they? Indeed, even where the application for review raises constitutional, or preliminary or collateral jurisdictional questions, there may still be arguments for compelling resort to a statutory appeal body before a judicial review application is considered.

c. In *Richmond Cabs Ltd. v. British Columbia (Motor Carrier Commission)* (1992), 69 BCLR (2d) 149 (SC), Shaw J rejected an argument that rival companies seeking judicial review on natural justice grounds to an extension of a cab company's licences should have exercised a statutory right of appeal to the lieutenant governor in council rather than seeking judicial review. The court simply did not see the Cabinet appeal as an adequate surrogate for judicial review in such a case given the limited procedural obligations of Cabinet and the potential for lengthy delays in having the matter determined at that level. Shaw J also intimated (echoing *Spencer v. Spencer*) that Cabinet appeals are more concerned with the merits than technical procedural fairness claims and that, in this instance, any such engagement with the merits would be hampered by the deficiencies of the record coming from the commission, deficiencies resulting from the failure of the commission to hear the objectors properly.

3. Concern about whether the appeal tribunal can afford appropriate relief is also a relevant factor in cases such as this. Thus, in *Misra v. College of Physicians and Surgeons* (1988),

52 DLR (4th) 477 (Sask. CA), in which a doctor was trying to have a disciplinary committee suspension of his licence to practise medicine quashed as well as an order prohibiting the committee proceeding to hear the charges against him, the court (relying on *Harelkin*) rejected the argument that he should have appealed to an appeal tribunal as provided for under the relevant legislation. In doing so, the court not only referred to the possibility of requiring recourse to the appeal tribunal (which was to proceed by way of *de novo* hearing) compounding the unreasonable delay that Misra was alleging but also doubted the capacity of the tribunal to give the relief that he was seeking—the dismissal of the proceedings against him for natural justice reasons. (See also *Aylward v. McMaster University* (1991), 79 DLR (4th) 119 (Ont. Div. Ct.).)

4. The converse may also be true in that, in terms of the range of solutions that is available, it is more appropriate to have the matter dealt with by an administrative tribunal than the courts. A good example of this is provided by *Canadian National Railway Co. v. Toronto (City)* (1992), 91 DLR (4th) 255 (Ont. Div. Ct.). Here, Canadian National had appealed to the Ontario Municipal Board against amendments to Toronto's official plan and zoning bylaws, which, *inter alia*, provided that developers of the Toronto "Railway Lands" would have to provide a certain proportion of social housing. Canadian National also sought judicial review of that portion of the zoning bylaw pertaining to social housing. In refusing judicial review as a matter of discretion, the Divisional Court stated as follows:

> The Board has all the powers of a court of record and has the authority to hear and determine all questions of law or fact concerning matters within its jurisdiction. It also has exclusive jurisdiction in all cases and in respect of all matters in which jurisdiction is conferred upon by it by any Act: the *Ontario Municipal Board Act*, RSO 1990, c. O.28, ss. 34, 35 and 36. Also an appeal lies from the Board to the Divisional Court with leave of the Divisional Court on a question of law. In addition the Board may, of its motion or on the application of a party, state a case to the Divisional Court upon a question that in the opinion of the Board is a question of law: the *Ontario Municipal Board Act*, ss. 96(1) and 94(1). In our opinion it is quite clear that the Board is empowered to consider questions of law relating to the validity of the by-law in question provided that in so doing it is ancillary to or necessarily incidental to determining its own jurisdiction in dealing with a by-law enacted pursuant to the various statutes giving the Board jurisdiction. In this case jurisdiction is given to the Board by the *Planning Act* and the *City of Toronto Act, 1988 (No. 2)*, SO 1988, c. Pr1. In the instant case in exercising its planning jurisdiction the Board will be required to determine whether the provisions for social housing are good planning. If it decides that question in the affirmative it will be required to decide whether the method adopted by the respondent is proper.
>
> In determining whether legislative provisions which confer judicial powers on an administrative body are valid the court must be concerned, not simply with a particular power or authority detached from the legislative scheme in which it is included but with its intimate relations to the working of the scheme. A legislative provision conferring judicial power on the Board in the context of the restructuring and reorganization of a municipal institution was upheld by the Supreme Court of Canada in *Mississauga (City) v. Peel (Regional Municipality)* [1979] 2 SCR 244 (Ont.). We refer also to the case of *Reference Re Residential Tenancies Act (Ont.)* [1981] 1 SCR 714 (Ont.). It should be remembered that the Board is a specialized tribunal having an intimate knowledge and expertise in relation to all aspects of planning and planning legislation.

The applicant has chosen the remedy of appealing the zoning by-law together with the underlying official plan by-law to the Board. In our opinion this court ought not to exercise its discretion in considering only one aspect of the much larger issue which will be considered by the Board.

If this court were to grant the applicant's request and strike down s. 6(4)(8) of By-law 637-91 the result would be that the subject lands could then be used for all of the wide range of residential and non-residential uses permitted under By-law 637-91. A decision with such significant planning and land use results should properly be considered by the Board in the context of the hearings set to commence on June 22nd next rather than by this court. The Board will then determine whether or not social housing should be provided on the blocks the city has specified. If the Board determines that the specified blocks should not be secured for social housing the Board has jurisdiction to: (a) address the relevant provisions of the official plan amendment; (b) refuse to approve the social housing designation of the specific lands contained in the zoning by-law; and (c) to designate other specified lands for social housing pursuant to the provisions of the *Planning Act*. If required the city can regulate the use of land for social housing purposes in a manner which would otherwise be considered unreasonable, oppressive and contrary to the decision of the Supreme Court of Canada in *Bell v. The Queen* [1979] 2 SCR 212 (Ont.). For example the *City of Toronto Act, 1988 (No. 2)* enables the city to restrict occupancy of social housing to persons or classes of persons such as senior citizens or persons under a disability.

Finally, where a statutory right of appeal exists as in this case the weight of authority favours a denial of an application for judicial review. For example: see *Re Woodglen and Co. and City of North York* (1983) 149 DLR (3d) 186 (Ont. Div. Ct.) and *Taylor v. Metropolitan Toronto (Municipality) Metropolitan Licensing Commission* (1989), 63 DLR (4th) 599 (Ont. Div. Ct.). The reasons for adopting that practice in this case are particularly compelling.

Therefore in the exercise of our discretion we dismiss this application for all of the above reasons.

5. Among the remedial capacities that are relevant is the power of tribunals and agencies to award Charter remedies as clarified and expanded in *R v. Conway*, 2010 SCC 22.

Statutory Appeals to the Courts

In addition to cases where the argument is based on the exhaustion of the administrative process through recourse to statutory appeals to higher tribunals or, sometimes, applications for reconsideration, claims of a sufficient statutory right of appeal also surface when someone has commenced an application for judicial review rather than using a statutory right of appeal to the courts provided for in the empowering statute. Generally, Canadian courts take the position that, if the grounds on which the applicant for judicial review is relying could have been raised in the context of a statutory appeal, the application will be dismissed: *Milner Power Inc. v. Alberta Energy and Utilities Board* (2007), 80 Alta. LR (4th) 35 (CA). In this regard, consider the appropriateness of the court allowing an application for judicial review to proceed in the following circumstances.

Under the Newfoundland *Public Utilities Act*, provision was made for an appeal from decisions of the Public Utilities Board on questions of law and jurisdiction to the Newfoundland Court of Appeal. Such appeals had to be brought within 15 days of the decision being rendered. In the context of an application to the Newfoundland Supreme Court (Trial Division) for judicial review of a rate ruling that imposed a municipal tax surcharge, an argument was made that the application should be denied because of the existence of a statutory right of appeal. The principal allegation was one of breach of the rules of natural justice. Is this not an allegation that the Court of Appeal would have been perfectly at ease with handling in the context of an appeal on questions of law and jurisdiction? Does it make any difference to your thinking that the allegation was one of lack of notice and that the applicants did not come to learn of the relevant part of the rate ruling until after the 15-day period for appealing had expired? (See *Conception Bay South (Town) v. Public Utilities Board (Nfld.)* (1991), 85 Nfld. & PEIR 33 (Nfld. SC).)

Another dimension of the issue of the more appropriate way of seeking court intervention is provided by *Reza* (chapter 16 of this text), in which, in the case of concurrent jurisdiction between the Federal Court and a provincial superior court, the Ontario Court of Appeal evaluated which was the more appropriate court for the determination of the particular issues.

The matter of appeals to both the courts and other statutory bodies is also dealt with in the Ontario *Judicial Review Procedure Act* and the *Federal Courts Act*. The Ontario *Judicial Review Procedure Act*, RSO 1990, c. J.1, s. 2 provides that, on application for judicial review under that Act, the court "may" grant relief "despite any right of appeal." However, in *City of Mississauga v. Director, Environmental Protection Act* (1978), 8 CPC 292 (Ont. HC), this was held not to affect the principle that such relief should not be awarded when a right of appeal exists, save in very special circumstances. Support for this was gleaned from s. 2(5) of the Act, which preserves the courts' former discretions in the reformed remedial arrangements in Ontario. In the BC *Judicial Review Procedure Act*, RSBC 1979, c. 209, s. 2, the words "despite any right of appeal" or similar language was omitted. Also relevant is the *Federal Courts Act*, RSC 1985, c. F-10, s. 18.5 (as amended by SC 1990, c. 8), which provides that the original judicial review authority of the court is subordinate to statutory rights of appeal to the court and other assorted authorities covering the same grounds.

Alternative Methods of Establishing Rights or Enforcing Observance of Statutes and Orders

A somewhat different aspect of the issue of alternative remedies is raised when an attempt is made to use the courts to vindicate rights created by or arising under a statute or to enforce statutory or administrative prohibitions. There may well be other methods established for the resolution of such matters—administrative rather than judicial determination or enforcement, prosecution rather than declaratory or injunctive relief. Also, questions of entitlement to seek a determination or enforcement may also arise, as discussed in chapter 17 of this text. The following case brings together a number of these considerations.

Shore Disposal Ltd. v. Ed de Wolfe Trucking Ltd.
(1976), 72 DLR (3d) 219 (NS SCAD)

MacKEIGAN CJNS: By the order allowing the appeal the Court set aside the decision of the learned trial Judge, MacIntosh J, whereby he granted the respondents a declaratory judgment that the appellant "is presently operating in the business of collection and disposal of refuse in the County of Halifax, contrary to the provisions of the *Motor Carrier Act*, RSNS 1967, Chapter 190."

The alleged contravention of that Act was that the appellant was operating a "freight vehicle" upon a provincial highway "without holding a licence issued by the Board [of Commissioners of Public Utilities] allowing the vehicle to be so operated" contrary to s. 6(1)(a) of the Act. Section 1(b) defines a "freight vehicle" as a "vehicle operated by or on behalf of any person carrying on upon any highway the business of a carrier of freight for gain." Section (1)(f) defines a "motor carrier" as "a person operating ... a motor vehicle ... as a freight vehicle." Finally, s. 33 makes it an offence liable to a penalty, of not more than $100 for a first offence, not more than $200 for a second offence, and not more than $500 for a third or subsequent offence, for a motor carrier to violate or fail to observe "any provision of this Act." An alleged offender may be prosecuted on summary conviction proceedings in a Provincial Magistrate's Court under the *Summary Proceedings Act, 1972*, SNS 1972, c. 18.

The learned trial Judge held that the appellant was a carrier of freight for gain, that it had no licence from the Public Utilities Board and that it was therefore violating the *Motor Carrier Act*, RSNS 1967, c. 190. He then granted the declaratory judgment sought, but without costs.

He declined to grant an injunction to restrain the appellant from engaging in the business of collecting and disposing of garbage until such time as it was licensed under the Act. He based his refusal on the fact that the Act "contains sufficient remedies to ensure due compliance with its provisions, without the necessity in this instance of a Court injunction." This issue is not under appeal.

· · ·

The principle that a declaration should not be granted merely to enforce a criminal or penal offence is in my view a branch of a wider principle, that the Supreme Court should not usually interfere by declaration where the matter in issue is placed within the exclusive jurisdiction of another tribunal: ... . In *Cassidy v. Stuart* [1928] 3 DLR 879 (Ont. CA) at 883, Masten JA said: the "... jurisdiction will not, as a rule, be exercised where the declaration would be useless or embarrassing or where some other statutory mode of proceeding is provided." Orde JA (at 887) stated it would be "grossly impertinent" for the Court to express an opinion on a matter within the jurisdiction of another tribunal, there the Exchequer Court: see also Spence J, in *Hollinger Bus Lines Ltd. v. Ontario Labour Relations Board* [1951] 4 DLR 47 (Ont. HC) at 54-55, refusing to grant a declaration as to the status of a collective agreement in issue before the Board.

Here, the question of licensing motor carriers is placed within the exclusive jurisdiction of the Public Utilities Board, and, so far as enforcement by prosecution is concerned, within the exclusive jurisdiction of the Provincial Magistrate's Court.

Not only did those tribunals have exclusive jurisdiction but had actually begun to exercise their jurisdiction. An information had been laid on April 8, 1976, charging the appellant with unlawfully operating a freight vehicle upon a highway without licence issued by the Board contrary to s. 6(1) of the *Motor Carrier Act*. Following appearance and plea of "not guilty," trial in Provincial Magistrate's Court was set for June 22, 1976; I do not know whether trial then occurred.

Proceedings were also pending before the Public Utilities Board. The appellant, although it has contended vigorously at all stages, including this appeal, that the licensing provisions do not apply to its operations, applied to the Board on March 2, 1976, for a licence, to protect its position in case it was convicted despite its protestations. The application to the Board was set down for hearing on June 29, 1976.

The learned trial Judge held that the appellant's vehicle was a "freight vehicle" requiring licensing. The appellant contended then, and before this Court, that it did not carry "freight," *ie*, its customer's goods, at all, because it acquired title to these goods, *viz.*, the garbage, when it picked it up from the customer. The garbage was then its property when it processed it in its truck and transported it to the disposal point. It thus, it claimed, carried no freight for gain within the meaning of the *Motor Carrier Act*, but merely supplied a service in which it at its customer's premises, acquired the garbage as its own goods and then disposed of it. We express no view on that issue.

This matter might be approached, as we have seen, on the basis that the respondents have no standing to take the action or on the closely related basis that they have no rights which would be protected, defined or declared by the declaration sought. It is better, however, to base our judgment on the principle that the Court, in proceedings where the plaintiffs are virtually private prosecutors, should not grant a declaration that the defendant has committed an offence. Such a declaration is gratuitous and almost impertinent advice to the summary conviction Court and to the Public Utilities Board, and may also be in effect an injunction disregard of which may visit upon the defendant penalties harsher far than the Legislature ordained.

Basic freedoms may be grossly infringed by a person thus being convicted in civil proceedings without the protection of the criminal laws of burden of proof and evidence, including the ban against self-incrimination. On this appeal the respondents are merely special prosecutors seeking condemnation of past crimes by declaration alone without due process of criminal law; they have no special rights which might have warranted granting them an injunction to ensure their future protection.

[Macdonald JA concurred with MacKeigan CJNS; Cooper JA delivered a separate judgment to much the same effect.]

Appeal allowed.

NOTE

There is other Canadian authority on the same issue raised by *Shore Disposal*. In *St. Andrews Airways Ltd. v. Anishenineo Piminagan Inc.* (1977), 80 DLR (3d) 645 (Man. QB), an unlicensed airline was successfully sued by a licensed airline for an injunction and damages. See also *Lambair Ltd. v. Aero Trades (Western) Ltd.* (1978), 87 DLR (3d) 500 (Man. CA), in which an action for damages brought by a competitor against another airline for failure to assess proper charges for its services as required by a CTC order was allowed to proceed to trial. Does it make any difference that in these two cases monetary relief was being sought as opposed to a mere declaration? Would that have given *Shore Disposal* a stronger case? Subsequently, in *Rogers Cable TV Ltd. v. 373041 Ontario Ltd.*, [1998] OJ No. 5125 (CA), the court granted a competitor declaratory and injunctive relief against an activity that did not come within the defendant's licence. There was no claim for monetary relief.

PREMATURITY

Prematurity, or an absence of "ripeness" (as it is described in US public law), involves an assertion by the court that, while the applicant may potentially have a good cause of action, the matter is inappropriate for judicial intervention at present. There are a number of reasons why this might be so. First, there is the possibility that the matter may be resolved internally or without the need for court intervention. As seen already, this is one of the reasons for the court requiring recourse to internal appeal regimes rather than seeking judicial review. It also surfaces in the context of applications to prohibit a tribunal from dealing with an issue in favour of its resolution by a court. Here too there is always the possibility in such cases that the tribunal itself will resolve the matter to the parties' satisfaction or, alternatively, will render it moot because of its decision on some other aspect of the proceeding.

In such instances, the reviewing court will generally take into account the legal question whether the statutory regime itself obliges the tribunal to have "first crack" at resolving the issue in question (a much more frequent obligation since *Nova Scotia (Workers' Compensation Board) v. Martin*, [2003] 2 SCR 504 (NS) (chapter 14 of this text)) and, from a practical perspective, the advantages and disadvantages of a pre-emptive ruling by the court. In this latter regard, the relevant questions are the ones we have in general identified already in considering the issue of statutory appeals: Is the tribunal likely to deal with the issue that is being raised by the applicant? If so, is the tribunal's conclusion on that issue highly predictable, making judicial review an inevitability anyway? Does the court have an advantage over the tribunal in terms of its expertise in relation to the issue at stake? Will any party be disadvantaged in a participatory sense by allowing the matter to be resolved by the court rather than leaving it to the tribunal? How will the encouragement of recourse to the courts in a case such as this ultimately tax judicial resources?

Prematurity or lack of ripeness also has another dimension. Aside from questions of comparative expertise with respect to the issue in question, one of the frequent advantages of allowing the tribunal to proceed to a conclusion on the issue in question is that it will thereby be building an evidential record that will facilitate subsequent judicial review. In this context, recollect not only the evidential limitations of most judicial review proceedings but also the various advantages of allowing the evidence to be collected, sifted and analyzed by the tribunal. Indeed, even with respect to mixed questions of law and fact and pure questions of law (including questions of jurisdiction), ultimate judicial review will often be better informed if the tribunal is given the opportunity to make an initial determination of such questions.

The case that follows brings together the issues of prematurity and availability of an adequate right of appeal in that the applicant for relief was confronted by the dual argument that the tribunal itself had not finally ruled on the issue and that there was a right of appeal from the ultimate decision of the tribunal anyway. While this was sufficient for a majority of the Ontario Court of Appeal, there was a spirited dissent that deserves serious consideration in any assessment of the appropriateness of the majority's position.

Howe v. Institute of Chartered Accountants of Ontario
(1994), 19 OR (3d) 483 (CA)

[Following an investigation into Howe's conduct, charges of professional misconduct were laid against him. Prior to the convening of the discipline committee, the Institute provided Howe with disclosure of various materials pertaining to the case. However, the investigating committee refused to release the report of its investigator, claiming that it contained confidential and privileged information. That decision was confirmed by the chair of the discipline committee and Howe then applied for judicial review claiming that he was entitled to discovery of this material under the principles in *R v. Stinchcombe*, [1991] 3 SCR 326 (Alta.). (For a consideration of the merits of such a claim, see chapter 4 of this text.) The Divisional Court dismissed the application and Howe appealed to the Ontario Court of Appeal.]

FINLAYSON JA (Brooke JA concurring):

[Finlayson JA detailed how Howe would have a right of appeal to the appeal committee from an adverse decision of the discipline committee. It was specifically provided that allegations of breach of the rules of natural justice could be raised in such an appeal and there was also room for the appeal to proceed by way of *de novo* hearing. He then went on to assert that the panel discipline committee to hear the case had still not been struck and that it was perfectly in order for Howe to challenge the chair's ruling before the panel. Moreover, if the panel ruled that the report should be disclosed, it could then adjourn the hearing to give Howe an opportunity to consider the contents of that report for the purposes of preparing his defence. Finlayson JA then continued:]

It seems to me that we are being asked to rule on the adequacy of the disclosure made to date by the prosecution when we do not have the means of gauging the significance of what has been disclosed against what is contained in the Johnston report. We do not have the Johnston report before us. We do not even have the 26-page "will say" statement. We do not know what ruling the panel of the Discipline Committee might make on this issue if it is raised again at any time during the hearing. We certainly do not know what final disposition will be forthcoming from the panel of the Discipline Committee that finally hears this matter, or what will happen if and when the appeal procedure is exhausted. In consequence, we are not in a position to identify and weigh the non-disclosure against the evidence actually given against the appellant.

In short, I agree with the Divisional Court that this application is premature. I think it is trite law that the court will only interfere with a preliminary ruling made by an administrative tribunal where the tribunal never had jurisdiction or has irretrievably lost it: see *Gage v. Ontario (Attorney General)* (1992) 90 DLR (4th) 537 (Ont. Div. Ct.), and *Roosma v. Ford Motor Co. of Canada Ltd.* (1988) 53 DLR (4th) 90 (Ont. Div. Ct.). In *Gage, supra,* the court found that the failure of the board of inquiry to provide a policeman with timely written notice of its decision to order a hearing into a complaint regarding his behaviour, pursuant to its statutory obligation, was a denial of natural justice which resulted in a loss of jurisdiction. In *Roosma, supra,* the court held that judicial review was open to challenge proceedings tainted with a fatal jurisdictional defect at the outset even where an appeal was provided.

It is not at all clear that a refusal to order production of documents goes to jurisdiction: see *Patterson v. [The Queen]* [1970] SCR 409 (Alta.), much less that it is a denial of natural justice or a fatal flaw to the exercise by the tribunal of that jurisdiction. Additionally, on the pivotal question of whether the claim of privilege was valid, I am not persuaded on this record that the conclusion reached by the chair of the Discipline Committee is not reasonable. It seems to be conceded that the applicable legal principles are Wigmore's four tests and, that being so, normally we are obliged to defer to the unchallenged findings of fact and policy made by the chair: see *Zurich Insurance Co. v. Ontario (Human Rights Commission)* [1992] 2 SCR 321 (Ont.).

I do not think that we should encourage applications such as these which have the effect of fragmenting and protracting the proceedings except in the clearest of cases. In my opinion, the Divisional Court was correct in exercising its discretion not to grant prerogative relief in this case.

Accordingly, I would dismiss the appeal.

LASKIN JA (dissenting): ...

2. Is the Application for Judicial Review Premature?

There are two branches to the argument that this application is premature. The first is that the court should not encourage applications for judicial review of preliminary rulings or interlocutory orders of an administrative tribunal, especially where the aggrieved party has an adequate right of appeal. The second is that the appellant is entitled to renew his motion for disclosure before the panel that will hear the charges of professional misconduct and that that panel should be given the opportunity to rule on the motion.

(i) The court's unwillingness to review evidentiary or disclosure rulings made by an administrative tribunal in the midst of a hearing, or even before the hearing starts, is understandable where the ruling, even if wrong, is an error within the tribunal's jurisdiction. Although an application for judicial review does not require an administrative tribunal to bring its proceedings to a halt, an aggrieved party should not be encouraged to rush off to the Divisional Court every time it is dissatisfied with a ruling made by the tribunal. ...

But where the ruling amounts to a breach of the tribunal's duty of fairness, or a breach of natural justice, then different considerations apply. A breach of natural justice

amounts to or is akin to jurisdictional error; and in administrative law language, a tribunal which begins with jurisdiction to decide will lose jurisdiction or act in excess of its
jurisdiction if, in the course of deciding, it breaches natural justice: see *SEIU, Local 333
v. Nipawin District Staff Nurses' Assn.* [1975] 1 SCR 382 (Sask.) at 389.

Where there is jurisdictional error arising from a breach of natural justice during the
course of the proceedings, a court is entitled to intervene to correct the error though the
party affected has a right of appeal. This was the central point of Dickson J's strong dissent in *Harelkin v. University of Regina, supra.*

· · ·

This court recently granted judicial review of an interlocutory order of a tribunal refusing disclosure because the erroneous ruling was so fundamental to a fair hearing that
it amounted to a breach of natural justice and thus jurisdictional error. In *People First of
Ontario v. Porter, Regional Coroner Niagara* (1991) 85 DLR (4th) 174 (Ont. Div. Ct.),
rev'd. (1992) 87 DLR (4th) 765 (Ont. CA), a coroner refused to order production of
medical reports to a public interest group that had been granted standing at an inquest,
although the other parties had copies of the reports. The Divisional Court dismissed an
application for judicial review brought after the inquest had started, emphasizing that the
application was premature. This court reversed and ordered production, stating at 768:

> In our view, in the particular circumstances of this inquest, it was unfair to withhold that
> information from the appellants, particularly when, as noted earlier, the records were re-
> leased by the coroner to the other parties. The failure of the coroner to give the medical
> records to the applicants prevented them from participating as they were entitled to in the
> inquest and the coroner lost jurisdiction in so doing.

Admittedly, the aggrieved party in *People First* did not have a right of appeal. The
existence of an adequate, alternative remedy by appeal prompted Beetz J writing for a
narrow majority of the court in *Harelkin, supra,* to refuse *certiorari,* and was a ground on
which the Divisional Court dismissed the appellant's application. It seems to me, respectfully, that the majority judgment in *Harelkin* has to be applied with caution. The basis of
the judgment is the proposition that a denial of natural justice renders a decision voidable not void and therefore can be "cured" on appeal: *Harelkin, supra,* at 581-82. That
proposition was implicitly rejected, albeit without reference to *Harelkin,* in the subsequent case of *Cardinal v. Director of Kent Institution* [1985] 2 SCR 643 (BC). Le Dain J,
writing for the court, said at 661:

> ... I find it necessary to affirm that the denial of a right to a fair hearing must always render
> a decision invalid, whether or not it may appear to a reviewing court that the hearing would
> likely have resulted in a different decision. The right to a fair hearing must be regarded as an
> independent, unqualified right which finds its essential justification in the sense of proced-
> ural justice which any person affected by an administrative decision is entitled to have. It is
> not for a court to deny that right and sense of justice on the basis of speculation as to what
> the result might have been had there been a hearing.

This passage was in turn cited with approval by Lamer CJC in *Université du Québec à
Trois-Rivières v. Larocque* [[1993] 1 SCR 471 (Que.)].

Assuming, however, that the existence of an adequate alternative remedy by appeal affords a sound basis to refuse judicial review, the question remains whether the appellant's right of appeal is an "adequate alternative remedy" for the breach complained of. In my view it is not. In this case it would be more efficient and less costly to determine the disclosure issue now. There would be no fragmenting or protracting of the proceedings since the hearing has not started. The appellant's appeal is not to a court but to another internal tribunal and therefore the court would be in no better position to ensure the fairness of the appeal. Refusing judicial review would have the further effect of denying the appellant's right to two procedurally fair hearings, one at first instance (where the prosecution bears the burden of proof), and the other, if required, on appeal. In short, I see no valid reason why the appellant should have to go through a lengthy and costly public hearing that is flawed at the outset when this court can correct the flaw now: *Harelkin, supra, per* Beetz J at 587-88, and see Jones, "Discretionary Refusal of Judicial Review in Administrative Law" (1981) 19 *Alta. LR* 483. ...

(ii) While in my view the decision of the chair of the Discipline Committee is reviewable, I recognize there is some merit to the position that the panel hearing the case against the appellant should decide the issue before the court considers it. There are, however, at least four considerations against this position. First, the prospect that the panel will take a view different from the chair of the Discipline Committee is, I think, slight. This is not the first time an accountant facing discipline charges has sought disclosure of the investigation report which formed the basis of the charges. The record before us indicates that each time disclosure was denied, and in one case by the Appeal Committee. Indeed, the reasons of the chair in the present case reflect what seems to me to amount to a policy on the part of the respondents against disclosure of these reports. Second, disclosure issues should be determined sooner rather than later. The goals of fairness, efficiency and the early resolution of charges, all argue against waiting until the hearing commences to determine whether Mr. Johnston's report ought to be produced. Disclosure of experts' reports prior to trial is required in civil cases by the *Rules of Civil Procedure. The Report of the Attorney General's Advisory Committee on Charge Screening, Disclosure and Resolution Discussions, 1993* ("the Martin Report"), made the important point (at 195-97) that full and timely disclosure not only benefits an accused person but enhances the administration of justice as a whole. Third, there is a sufficient factual record to decide the issue, and the arguments for and against judicial review were fully canvassed by counsel. Fourth, since this court granted leave, the issue is before us, and in my view we ought to decide it if we can. Although Mr. Binnie opposed the application, he did fairly acknowledge in his factum, "this court having granted leave to hear this appeal, it is in the interest of the parties to have the issue determined on the merits."

For all of these reasons, in my opinion it is no answer to the appellant's position to say that the application is premature.

Appeal dismissed.

NOTES

1. While *Howe* involved an allegation of procedural unfairness, it is also clear that prematurity may be invoked in situations where the ground of attack is of a jurisdictional and even a constitutional variety. As we saw in relation to the jurisdictional issue in *Matsqui Indian Band*, the majority of the court held that the appeal tribunals should be given an opportunity to deal with that question in advance of the courts. Similar examples can also be found in the domain of Charter challenges, at least in relation to tribunals that have the capacity to deal with Charter issues: see, for example, *Falkiner v. Ontario (Ministry of Community and Social Services* (1996), 140 DLR (4th) 115 (Div. Ct.) and *Douglas/Kwantlen Faculty Association v. Douglas College*, [1990] 3 SCR 570 (BC). Frequently, the principal basis for denying relief in these cases will be the court's sense that the tribunal setting will provide a better forum for the creation of a factual record on the basis of which judicial review will then take place. (A further consideration after *R v. Conway*, 2010 SCC 22 is the capacity of the tribunal or agency to grant Charter remedies.) Given this line of jurisprudence, evaluate what Finlayson JA means in *Howe* when he refers to prematurity not being an issue "where the tribunal never had jurisdiction or has irretrievably lost it." What situations might he be referring to?

2. Is *Howe* the kind of situation where the members of the panel hearing the case should be given an opportunity to review the chair's preliminary determination denying pre-hearing disclosure of the report? Given that once the hearing has started one of the purposes of seeking discovery has disappeared (preparation and developing responses), is not a panel reversal of the initial decision too late and should not the court have been willing to intervene before that point? The majority was not unconscious of this argument and they suggested a way of overcoming it; is their solution a practicable one?

3. Should the conclusion in this case have been any different if the matter of disclosure had reached the panel itself and the chair's preliminary ruling been confirmed? Consider Laskin JA's dissent on this point in the light of the Supreme Court's reassertion of the principles of *Harelkin* in *Canadian Pacific Ltd. v. Matsqui Indian Band*, above, and the disagreement among the judges in that case as to whether the motions judge should have considered the challenge based on the tribunals' lack of structural independence in the context of a motion to strike out the applicant's application for judicial review, an application brought instead of an appeal to the tribunals against an initial real property tax assessment. More generally, in what circumstances should a challenge based on a reasonable apprehension of bias or a lack of independence be held to be premature? Should the court at least wait until the tribunal itself has had an opportunity to deal with the challenge? Are there situations where the affected party should postpone any judicial review application on the basis of bias or lack of independence until the end of the hearing? These issues are raised by the following case.

Air Canada v. Lorenz
[2000] 1 FC 494 (TD)

[Lorenz made an unjust dismissal complaint against Air Canada. After five days of hearing, Air Canada learned that the adjudicator's law practice included labour and employment law and, more particularly, that he was acting for a client in an unjust dismissal complaint against an employer other than Air Canada under equivalent Québec legislation. When confronted with this, the adjudicator refused to provide the parties with any further details of the Québec case or of other unjust dismissal cases in which he was acting. Air Canada requested that the adjudicator recuse himself on the basis of a reasonable apprehension of bias. He declined to do so. Air Canada applied for judicial review of that ruling. Pending the disposition of the application for judicial review, the hearing did not proceed. Nearly two years elapsed before the application was heard. It was contended that the application for judicial review on the basis of a reasonable apprehension of bias was premature and should not proceed until such time as the adjudicator determined the complaint on its merits.]

EVANS J:

Having heard full argument on this interesting question I have nonetheless decided that it would be inappropriate for the Court to make a ruling before the adjudicator has rendered a final decision on the unjust dismissal complaint. Air Canada has put the bias objection on the record and, if the adjudicator finds in favour of the employee, Air Canada will be able to apply for judicial review on the ground of bias and, at the same time, raise any other reviewable error that it believes that the adjudicator's award contains. Of course, if the adjudicator dismisses the complaint then the bias issue becomes moot. ...

C. Analysis

I invited counsel to make their submissions on whether this application for judicial review should be dismissed for prematurity as part of their argument on the merits, and not as a preliminary objection. Hearing the case in its entirety has provided a valuable context within which to consider the exercise of my discretion over the grant of relief.

However, this does not necessarily mean that the allegation of bias should be decided before the Court considers the exercise of its remedial discretion. As Vertes J in *Woloshyn v. Yukon Teachers Assn.* [1999] YJ No. 69 (SC) (QL) pointed out, it would seem quite inappropriate to compel an applicant to complete an administrative hearing before a tribunal which a reviewing court has found to be disqualified by bias.

But it does not follow, either, that an applicant is entitled to have a bias question determined at any time of its choosing, simply for the asking. The time and resources put into preparing the written submissions and making the oral argument are not necessarily wasted if it is not. Should the matter be brought back to the Court on the issue of bias after the tribunal has rendered its final decision, counsel will already have done most of the necessary work.

It was agreed by counsel that it is within the jurisdiction of the Court on an application for judicial review alleging bias to refuse relief on the ground of prematurity. Counsel for the Attorney General submitted that it was only in the most unusual and exceptional cases that the Court will intervene in an administrative proceeding before the final decision has been rendered. Counsel for Air Canada, on the other hand, maintained that allegations of bias stand apart from most other grounds of review, and that the courts are less reluctant to intervene on this ground than on others before the administrative process is complete.

As a general rule it is much more difficult nowadays for a litigant to persuade a court to intervene before the applicant has exhausted the available administrative remedies than it was when *Bell v. Ontario Human Rights Commission* [1971] SCR 756 (Ont.) was decided. Thus, relief may be refused on the ground that a litigant has not taken advantage of a right of appeal to an administrative tribunal when this is an adequate alternative remedy to an application for judicial review, even when the ground of review is the wrongful denial of a participatory right in breach of the duty of fairness (*Harelkin v. University of Regina* [1979] 2 SCR 561 (Sask.), or even a substantive jurisdictional error (*Canadian Pacific Ltd. v. Matsqui Indian Band* [1995] 1 SCR 3 (Can.)).

Courts are similarly reluctant to intervene to review an interim or interlocutory decision prior to the conclusion of the proceeding before the administrative tribunal. There are a number of cases in which relief has been refused when the applicant has challenged the proceeding of a human rights tribunal prior to its rendering a final decision, including some involving allegations of bias: see, for example, *Ontario College of Art v. Ontario (Human Rights Commission)* (1993), 11 OR (3d) 798 (Div. Ct.).

In other cases, however, the Court has found that an allegation of bias against a tribunal should be determined without requiring the applicant to complete the administrative hearing and await a decision: *Great Atlantic & Pacific Co. of Canada Ltd. v. Ontario (Minister of Citizenship)* (1993) 62 OAC 1 (Div. Ct.). More recently, there was found to be a reasonable apprehension of bias with respect to one of the members of a Canadian Human Rights Tribunal. The Tribunal was prohibited from proceeding with the hearing as it was then constituted, even though the hearing had lasted for approximately 40 days and was expected to take more than a few days to complete: *Zündel v. Citron* [1999] 3 FC 409 (TD). However, the question of the prematurity of granting relief seems not to have been addressed by the Court, perhaps because the Court permitted the Tribunal to continue without the disqualified member.

I should make it clear that, unlike the cases cited above (with the exception of *Zündel*), there is in this case no broad statutory right of appeal from the adjudicator to another administrative tribunal or to this Court. Nor is this a case where non-intervention can be justified by the policy of curial deference to the expertise of administrative tribunals. Despite *dicta* to the contrary in *Re Refrigeration Workers Union, Local 516 and Labour Relations Board of British Columbia* (1986) 27 DLR (4th) 676 (BCCA), at 681-682, whether Mr. Marchessault is disqualified for bias must be decided independently by a reviewing court on a standard of correctness. Nor is this a case where a better record will be compiled for the conduct of the judicial review on the ground of bias if it is postponed until after the adjudicator has rendered his final decision.

Rather, the exercise of the Court's discretion here turns principally on a weighing of two competing considerations. On the one hand are the possible hardships caused to Air Canada, and the time and resources that will have been wasted, if the bias question is not determined prior to the completion of the proceeding before the adjudicator. On the other hand, there are the adverse consequences of delaying the administrative process and of countenancing a multiplicity of litigation.

(i) The Factors To Be Considered

(a) Hardship to the Applicant

Counsel submitted that an allegation of bias casts a cloud over the legitimacy of the entire proceeding before the adjudicator, and to require Air Canada to push through to the end without having this question resolved would impose serious hardships. A party should not be subject to the exercise of legal powers by a tribunal whose very authority to hear the dispute the party has called into question.

This factor cannot be determinative, however, because otherwise a reviewing court would always have to decide allegations of bias and to award relief when they are upheld, even though raised before the completion of the administrative process. This would mean, in effect, that a court would have no discretion to dismiss an application for judicial review for prematurity when bias is alleged or, putting it another way, an allegation of bias always constitutes "exceptional circumstances" justifying judicial intervention before the administrative process is complete. In my opinion this is not the law. Further, counsel argued, even if the adjudicator ultimately decides in favour of Air Canada he may make rulings in his reasons that are adverse to it, which it has no means of challenging, whether by an application for judicial review or otherwise. This does not seem to me to be a particularly pressing concern.

(b) Waste

Air Canada raised the bias allegation on what would have been the sixth day of a hearing that is predicted to last for a total of 23 days. If Air Canada is required to postpone its challenge to the proceeding on the ground of the adjudicator's apprehended bias until the end of that hearing, and its application is then successful, the resources devoted to the last 18 days of the hearing will have been wasted. This concern is only relevant, however, if Air Canada is found to have dismissed Mr. Lorenz unjustly, something that is still in the realm of the unknown.

(c) Delay

There is no doubt that the completion of the hearing before the adjudicator has been delayed by Air Canada's application for judicial review: the last day on which the merits of Mr. Lorenz's complaint was heard was in October 1997, nearly two years ago. Thus, if Air Canada's application is unsuccessful on the merits, it will nonetheless have delayed the determination of the substantive issues in Mr. Lorenz's complaint.

Delay should be considered as a factor as it may affect not only the parties in this particular case, but also the conduct of other administrative proceedings. If the Court were to decide Air Canada's allegation of bias prior to the completion of the administrative process it is all too likely that participants in other administrative proceedings may resort to judicial review on this ground for the purpose of delaying the proceedings, or forcing the more vulnerable party to surrender or settle.

(d) Fragmentation

A determination of Air Canada's bias allegation at this time may also proliferate litigation. If the allegation were found to be misconceived then, when the ultimate decision is made by another adjudicator, an aggrieved party could make a second application for judicial review on other issues. Fragmentation of the issues raised by an administrative proceeding is wasteful of court resources and unduly burdens the administration of public programs.

(e) Strength of the Case

The potential harmful consequences of deciding or not deciding the merits of this application for judicial review prior to the determination of the administrative process are largely premised on the eventual success or failure of the allegation of bias. It is therefore appropriate to consider the strength of the case made by the applicant.

Counsel for Air Canada conceded that the question on which he has asked the Court to rule is largely one of first impression. While there is no authority directly on point, he argued that in *R v. Lippé* [1991] 2 SCR 114 (Que.), the Supreme Court of Canada expressed the view that, in the absence of adequate safeguards, the appointment of part-time judges who continued their legal practice breached the constitutional requirement of institutional impartiality and independence.

It is an open question whether similar concerns are applicable to specialized administrative tribunals. For example, a consequence of a finding that Mr. Marchessault was disqualified by bias from acting as an adjudicator in this case would be that lawyers practising labour and employment law would be generally ineligible for an appointment under section 240 [as amended by RSC 1985 (1st Supp.), c. 9, s. 15] of the *Canada Labour Code*. This might result in the loss of a valuable source of relevant expertise. However, in the absence of any evidence about the frequency with which adjudicators are appointed from the ranks of practising labour and employment lawyers I can make no finding on this point. Of course, a claim is not doomed to failure by virtue of its legal novelty or the practical fall out from its success. Nonetheless, the fact is that no court appears to have been called upon before to rule on the question raised by Air Canada in this proceeding. This may be some evidence that at least labour and employment law practitioners do not regard combining the duties of an adjudicator and a lawyer practising in the area as giving rise to a reasonable apprehension of bias, especially when, as here, the adjudicator in his legal practice represents both management and employees.

However, I should state again that there was no evidence before me about the prevalence of the appointment of adjudicators who actively practise labour and employment law. Hence, I do not know how often this occurs. Indeed, the only evidence in the record on the issue is the expression of surprise by a partner in the law firm representing Air Canada in this matter that an adjudicator was also actively practising labour and employment law. This suggests that it may be unusual for adjudicators also to represent clients in this area of the law.

Air Canada did not satisfy me that this is a clear and obvious case of bias. On the other hand, it clearly cannot be characterized as frivolous either. The concerns expressed in *Lippé, supra*, and, to a lesser extent, codes of ethics from other jurisdictions put into evidence by counsel, suggest that Air Canada's allegation of bias is by no means fanciful.

(f) Statutory Context

The factors outlined above must be evaluated, not only on the basis of the facts of the particular case, but also in the context of the statutory scheme from which the application for judicial review arises. Parliament conferred on adjudicators, appointed *ad hoc*, jurisdiction to determine unjust dismissal complaints in order to minimize the expense and delays that dismissed employees, often still out of work and typically far from being among the highest income earners, could have expected to encounter in the courts. The absence of a right of appeal and the inclusion of a strong preclusive provision in the Code (section 243) evidence a legislative intention to keep to a minimum judicial oversight of the proceedings before adjudicators.

While timing may not have quite the same significance in unjust dismissal cases as it does in industrial disputes and contested union certifications, it would seem quite inconsistent with the unjust dismissal provisions in the Code for the Court to exercise its discretion in a way that potentially increases delays and the costs of adjudication. Accordingly, in my opinion the avoidance of delay and fragmentation of the issues are factors that should be regarded in the context of this statutory scheme as carrying considerable weight. Thus, even when an adjudicator is impugned for bias, it will be the rare case indeed when the Court should determine the merits of the claim prior to the release of the adjudicator's ultimate decision, such as when the allegation reveals a very clear case of bias and the issue arises at the outset of a hearing that is scheduled to last for a significant length of time.

(ii) The Jurisprudence

Previous jurisprudence involving judicial discretion can provide valuable guidance on the test to be applied and the general approach to be taken to the exercise of that discretion. It can also identify the factors that a judge should take into account when making a decision. However, an examination of the actual disposition of particular cases is apt to yield only limited and indirect assistance on the way in which the discretion ought to be exercised in a given case. The factual and legal matrices of each case makes generalization difficult.

There is judicial authority on the test to be applied on an application for judicial review when the applicant has alleged that an administrative tribunal was biased, and there is no right of appeal from that tribunal to another administrative body. Thus, it has been said that a court should only intervene before the tribunal has rendered its final decision in "exceptional circumstances" (*University of Toronto v. Canadian Union of Education Workers, Local 2* (1988) 28 OAC 295 (Div. Ct.), at 306), in "exceptional or extraordinary circumstances" (*Ontario College of Art v. Ontario (Human Rights Commission), supra*, at 799), or where the attack is on the "very existence of the tribunal" (*Pfeiffer v. Canada (Superintendent of Bankruptcy)* [1996] 3 FC 584 (TD) 596).

In other words, the test applied when other grounds of review are asserted is equally applicable to allegations of bias. However, judicial review for bias does not engage the policy either of curial deference to the expertise of the tribunal, or of postponing review until a complete factual record is compiled. Accordingly, I accept that the burden of demonstrating the existence of "exceptional circumstances" may be somewhat easier to discharge when the impartiality of the tribunal is impeached in judicial review proceedings before the administrative process has run its course than it is when the applicant alleges other reviewable errors.

Nonetheless, I find no authority for the proposition that an allegation of bias *ipso facto* constitutes "exceptional circumstances" justifying judicial review before the tribunal has rendered its final decision ... . Although a case in which the applicant had a right of appeal to another tribunal, *Canadian Pacific, supra*, would appear clearly to indicate that the "jurisdictional" nature of a ground of review does not in itself deprive a reviewing court of its discretion in the exercise of its supervisory jurisdiction.

Counsel for Air Canada also relied on the statement by Cory J in *Newfoundland Telephone Co. v. Newfoundland (Board of Commissioners of Public Utilities)* [1992] 1 SCR 623 (Nfld.) at 645 that when "a reasonable apprehension of bias has been established," the ensuing decision of the tribunal "cannot be simply voidable and rendered valid as a result of the subsequent decision of the tribunal." However, these comments are not relevant to the issue in this case where no finding of bias has been made; they do not speak to the discretion of the Court to dismiss an application for prematurity without determining whether a reasonable apprehension of bias existed.

Counsel for Air Canada sought to distinguish the cases in which the Court had declined to intervene on grounds of prematurity where bias was alleged and where there was no right to an administrative appeal. For example, in the *Ontario College of Art* case, *supra*, the bias alleged was that of the officer appointed by the Ontario Human Rights Commission to investigate the complaint, not of the board of inquiry appointed to adjudicate it. The board was presumably capable of taking into account in its determination any possible bias by Commission staff.

In *Coopers & Lybrand Ltd. v. Wacyk* (1996) 23 CCEL (2d) 165 (Ont. Div. Ct.), counsel pointed out, the application for judicial review had been filed 13 months after the impugned decision had been made. However, the Court did not mention in its discussion of the prematurity issue the late filing of the application as a reason for refusing relief. Instead, it simply relied on the case law establishing that only in exceptional circumstances will relief be granted before the tribunal has made its final decision. Obviously, the allegation of bias and the absence of any right of appeal from the tribunal were regarded as insufficient in *Coopers & Lybrand* to constitute "exceptional circumstances." A reviewing court may also be more willing to intervene when the applicant alleges that the tribunal's enabling statute is constitutionally flawed: *Pfeiffer v. Canada (Superintendent of Bankruptcy), supra*; *Cannon v. Canada (Assistant Commissioner, RCMP)* [1998] 2 FC 104 (TD).

However, even in these circumstances a challenge may be dismissed for prematurity if more factual material is required in order properly to address the question of the tribunal's independence: *Bissett v. Canada (Minister of Labour)* [1995] 3 FC 762 (TD). Counsel for Air Canada also relied heavily on the dissenting judgment in *Howe v. Institute of Chartered Accountants of Ontario* (1994) 19 OR (3d) 483 (CA), at 502-507, where Laskin JA held that a failure to disclose the report of an investigation of a complaint to a professional regulatory body constituted a breach of the duty of fairness and that the application for judicial review was not premature. However, in that case it was also said (at 506) that:

> There would be no fragmenting or protracting of the proceedings since the hearing has not started.

This is not, of course, the situation in our case where five days of hearings have already been held. Moreover, to the extent that Laskin JA's judgment rested on an assumption that courts should generally be ready to intervene whenever a jurisdictional error is alleged, including a denial of procedural fairness, it has been weakened by the subsequent decision of the Supreme Court of Canada in the *Canadian Pacific* case, *supra*.

D. Conclusion

It is not, of course, disputed that Air Canada has a right to a fair hearing before an adjudicator that is free from any reasonable apprehension of bias. The question, here, however, is the point in the administrative process at which the applicant is entitled to a determination of its allegation and the grant of relief if it is upheld. In my opinion the substantial delay that has arisen from this application for judicial review is a vivid illustration of the dangers of a practice that, in all but truly exceptional circumstances, does not seek firmly to discourage applications for judicial review before an administrative tribunal has rendered its decision. Delay of this kind is antithetical to the legislative purpose underlying the creation of a specialized tribunal to adjudicate the claims of dismissed employees that their dismissal was unjust. Fragmentation of the issues in multiple litigation remains a real possibility.

The fact that the proceeding before the adjudicator was already well under way mitigates the waste factor in the exercise of discretion, even though the hearing had only gone for about a quarter of its projected length. The possibility of waste is also reduced by the fact that it cannot be said that it is plain and obvious in law that the adjudicator's activities disqualified him on the ground of bias. A non-frivolous allegation of bias that falls short of a cast-iron case does not *per se* constitute "exceptional circumstances," even when the hearing before the tribunal is still some way from completion, and there is no broad right of appeal from the tribunal. Nor is it to be equated with a constitutional attack on the "very existence of a tribunal" considered in *Pfeiffer v. Canada (Superintendent of Bankruptcy)*, *supra*.

For these reasons the application for judicial review is dismissed.

Application dismissed.

NOTES

1. While Evans J refers to *Matsqui*, he does so solely with reference to the issue of prematurity that attracted a majority of the court—whether the appeal tribunal should be allowed to deal with the substantive jurisdictional issue of whether the land in question was in the reserve. On the issue of lack of independence, as noted already, the court split. For Sopinka J and the three judges who supported him, such allegations could not be determined simply on an examination of the relevant legislative provisions but rather depended on knowledge of the way in which the Indian band property tax appeal tribunals functioned in practice. Of course, this may be not so much an argument for the tribunals themselves considering the issue and building up a review record before the matter reaches the court as it is a criticism of the material placed before the court by the applicants. Indeed, Lamer CJ

(with whom Cory J concurred and who, for other reasons, was part of the 5:4 majority) held that the judge had erred in failing to deal with this issue on the strength of the provisions of the relevant bylaw and there is no suggestion here that the tribunals be given first crack at assessing the validity of the regime under which they were operating. Subsequently, the court has clearly accepted that, at least on occasion, how the tribunal operates in practice will be a very important consideration in determining whether there is a lack of independence: *Katz v. Vancouver Stock Exchange*, [1996] 3 SCR 405 (BC). However, that may not necessarily mean that Lamer CJ was incorrect on the facts of *Matsqui*. If the legislation is structurally flawed to an extent that cannot be cured by the way the tribunal operates in practice, is there any point in allowing the tribunal to continue with the hearing? Are there other considerations that might outweigh immediate intervention even in that situation?

2. Related to the issue of prematurity is the unwillingness of the courts to consider purely hypothetical questions. The problem most commonly arises in situations in which declaratory relief is being sought.

Consider in this context *Jamieson v. Attorney General of British Columbia* (1971), 21 DLR (3d) 313 (BC SC). The plaintiff teachers sought a declaration as to the validity of a regulation prohibiting the continued employment of teachers who advocated the policies of the FLQ or the overthrow of the government by force. The court refused relief on the bases that the plaintiffs were not breaching the regulation and were not in jeopardy because of the regulation. Their concern was purely hypothetical. What interests are the courts protecting in refusing to deal with an issue because it is hypothetical? Consider also whether *Operation Dismantle v. The Queen*, [1985] 1 SCR 441 (Can.) is a case about prematurity and the hypothetical nature of the issues raised.

MOOTNESS

On occasion, by the time an application for judicial review comes on for a hearing or, more commonly, by the time it reaches the appropriate Court of Appeal or the Supreme Court of Canada, the dispute will have ceased to have practical significance for the applicant. As, for example, in *Cardinal*, the inmate applicants will have been released from penitentiary or the particular form of incarceration before their challenge to the way in which they have been treated has been resolved finally by the courts. Such cases always raise questions as to whether the court should, nonetheless, proceed to deal with the matter.

The general principles governing mootness have been laid down by the Supreme Court of Canada in *Borowski v. Attorney General*, [1989] 1 SCR 342 (Sask.), at 353, as follows:

The doctrine of mootness is an aspect of a general policy or practice that a court may decline to decide a case which raises merely a hypothetical or an abstract question. The general principle applies when the decision of the court will not have the effect of resolving some controversy which affects or may affect the rights of the parties. If the decision of the court will have no practical effect on such rights, the court will decline to decide the case. This essential ingredient must be present not only when the action or proceeding is commenced but at the time when the court is called upon to reach a decision. Accordingly, if, subsequent to the initiation of the action or the proceeding, events occur which affect the relationship of the parties so that no present live controversy exists which affects the rights of the parties, the case is said to be moot. The general policy is enforced in moot cases unless the court exercises its discretion to depart from its policy or practice.

Among the reasons that Sopinka J (delivering the judgment of the court) identified for departing from the general policy or practice were situations where there were still collateral consequences to the proceedings (such as in *Vic Restaurant v. City of Montreal*, [1959] SCR 58 (Que.)); where the restaurant that was the subject of proceedings seeking *mandamus* to compel the issue of permits to sell liquor and operate a restaurant had been sold, but there were still outstanding prosecutions for alleged violation of the impugned bylaw; where the issue at stake was one of a recurring nature, particularly in cases where the substratum of any particular challenge will have disappeared before the matter can be resolved; and where, in a case of public importance, there remained a public interest in the resolution of the issue raised by the litigation. However, in all these situations, it was necessary to weigh the countervailing considerations of the need for issues to be dealt with in a truly adversarial context, concern for the scarce resources of the court, and the importance of the courts not departing from their appropriate role under Canadian law as essentially the resolvers of live disputes.

Borowski was applied in *Pulp, Paper & Woodworkers, Local 8 v. Canada (Minister of Agriculture)*, [1992] 1 FC 372 (TD), a case involving a challenge by a trade union on behalf of its members to the licensing of a pesticide. The application was challenged on the basis that the pesticide in question was no longer being used in the workplace where the members of the union were employed. Did the dispute become moot as a result of this? Even if it did, should the court have exercised its discretion to enable the application for relief to proceed nonetheless?

A useful pre-*Borowski* example is afforded by *Landreville v. The Queen*, [1973] FC 1223 (TD). Landreville, a judge of the Ontario High Court, had resigned following an unfavourable report by a commissioner appointed to investigate his conduct under the federal inquiries legislation. Six years later he commenced an action seeking, among other relief, declarations with respect to the validity of the commission of inquiry. In response to an argument that at this stage a declaration of invalidity would be purely academic, the court held that, though the award of a declaration would be devoid of legal effect, it might serve such purposes as restoring Landreville's reputation and persuading the government to compensate him as well as being in the general interest that any invalidity of the commission be known publicly. (Subsequently Landreville was vindicated to the extent that he obtained a declaration of entitlement to a pension: [1981] FC 15 (TD).)

DELAY

Delay in commencing proceedings may go either to the jurisdiction or the discretion of the reviewing court. Failure to adhere to mandatory limitation statutes or provisions will prevent the court from even considering the case. However, if there is no limitation period, or even within a limitation period, the courts will on occasion deny relief to the applicant on the ground of undue delay, the doctrine of *lâches*.

In fact, limitation periods surprisingly do not often intrude in judicial review proceedings. However, the *Federal Courts Act*, RSC 1985, c. F-7, s. 18.1(2) contains a very short limitation period: 30 days from the communication of the order, though a judge may extend that period. In other jurisdictions, there are variations on this. For example, under Rule 7.05(1), *Nova Scotia Civil Procedure Rules, 2008,* there is a limitation period of either 25 days from the date the decision was communicated or 6 months from the date of the decision, whichever is the shorter. Also, some statutory forms of review are subject to a limitation period; for example, the *Municipal Act,* SO 2001, c. 25, s. 273 imposes a 12-month limitation on the availability of the statutory motion to quash a municipal bylaw. (This limitation is preserved in the legislation reforming the Ontario law of limitations: *Limitations Act, 2002,* being Sched. B to the *Justice Statute Law Amendment Act, 2002,* SO 2002, c. 24. See s. 19(a) and the Schedule to the Act.) In all such cases, questions are raised about the availability of alternate modes of relief once the limitation period has expired (for example, a declaratory action instead of *certiorari*; an application for judicial review under the Ontario *JRPA* instead of the statutory motion to quash).

There is also an issue as to whether the imposition of limitation periods can be accomplished by subordinate legislation or rules of court. In this regard, see *Ostrowski v. Saskatchewan (Beef Stabilization Board)* (1993), 101 DLR (4th) 311 (Sask. CA), in which a six-month limitation period on seeking *certiorari* contained in rules of court was found to be *ultra vires.* However, that proved to be a Pyrrhic victory, since the application was subsequently dismissed on the basis of prejudicial delay by reference to common law principles: see (1993), 109 DLR (4th) 385 (Sask. QB).

Other significant limitation periods are those relating to particular types of decision-makers—for example, the *Public Officers Act,* RSM 1987, c. P230, s. 21(1) imposed a two-year limitation period on certain actions:

> 7. No action, prosecution or other proceedings lies or shall be instituted against a person for an act done in pursuance or execution or intended execution of a statute or of a rule or regulation made thereunder, or of a public duty or authority, or in respect of an alleged neglect or default in the execution of the statute, rule, regulation, duty or authority, unless it is commenced within two years next after the act, neglect or default complained of, or in case of continuance of injury or damage, within two years next after the ceasing thereof.

For an interpretation of such a provision, see *Roncarelli v. Duplessis,* [1959] SCR 121 (Que.), where the claim was for damages, and *Berardinelli v. Ontario Housing Corporation,* [1979] 1 SCR 275 (Ont.). See also Hogg, "The Supreme Court of Canada and Administrative Law, 1949-71" (1973), 11 *Osgoode Hall LJ* 187, at 199-202.

As far as delay as a discretionary consideration is concerned, read the following cases in the context of these questions: Is it better, at least as far as judicial review is concerned, to leave it all to the court as in effect is done in Ontario? Or should there be legislatively prescribed limitation periods? Should delay on its own ever be a ground for the denial of relief?

Friends of the Oldman River Society v. Canada (Minister of Transport)
[1992] 1 SCR 3

[This complex case arose from the failure of the federal minister of transport to conduct an environmental assessment review, pursuant to federal guidelines, of a proposal by the province of Alberta for the construction of a dam on the Oldman River. Attempts made in the Alberta courts by environmental groups and native peoples' organizations to halt the approval of the dam failed. The minister approved the proposal in September 1986, and the construction contract was awarded by the province of Alberta in 1988. By the time that this proceeding was instituted in the Federal Court in April 1989 the project was 40 percent complete.

The society won on the principal issues, but the minister argued that the Federal Court of Appeal had erred in exercising its discretion to grant an order of *certiorari* to quash the minister's decision to approve construction of the dam. The judgment of the majority was delivered by:]

La FOREST J: The protection of the environment has become one of the major challenges of our time. To respond to this challenge, governments and international organizations have been engaged in the creation of a wide variety of legislative schemes and administrative structures. In Canada, both the federal and provincial governments have established Departments of the Environment, which have been in place for about twenty years. More recently, however, it was realized that a department of the environment was one among many other departments, many of which pursued policies that came into conflict with its goals. Accordingly at the federal level steps were taken to give a central role to that department, and to expand the role of other government departments and agencies so as to ensure that they took account of environmental concerns in taking decisions that could have an environmental impact.

. . .

The last substantive issue raised in this appeal is whether the Federal Court of Appeal erred in interfering with the motions judge's discretion not to grant the remedies sought, namely orders in the nature of *certiorari* and mandamus, on the grounds of unreasonable delay and futility. Stone JA found that the motions judge had erred in a way that warranted interference with the exercise of his discretion on both grounds.

The principles governing appellate review of a lower court's exercise of discretion were not extensively considered, only their application to this case. Stone JA cited *Polylok Corp. v. Montreal Fast Print (1975) Ltd.* [1984] 1 FC 713 (CA), which in turn approved of the following statement of Viscount Simon LC in *Charles Osenton & Co. v. Johnston* [1942] AC 130 (Eng. HL), at 138:

> The law as to the reversal by a court of appeal of an order made by the judge below in the exercise of his discretion is well-established, and any difficulty that arises is due only to the application of well-settled principles in an individual case. The appellate tribunal is not at liberty merely to substitute its own exercise of discretion for the discretion already exercised by the judge. In other words, appellate authorities ought not to reverse the order merely because they would themselves have exercised the original discretion, had it attached to them, in a different way. But if the appellate tribunal reaches the clear conclusion that there has been a wrongful exercise of discretion in that no weight, or no sufficient weight, has been given to relevant considerations such as those urged before us by the appellant, then the reversal of the order on appeal may be justified.

That was essentially the standard adopted by this Court in *Harelkin v. University of Regina* [1979] 2 SCR 561 (Sask.), where Beetz J said, at 588:

Second, in declining to evaluate, difficult as it may have been, whether or not the failure to render natural justice could be cured in the appeal, *the learned trial judge refused to take into consideration a major element for the determination of the case*, thereby failing to exercise his discretion on relevant grounds and giving no choice to the Court of Appeal but to intervene. [Emphasis added.]

What, then, are the relevant considerations that should have been weighed by the motions judge in exercising his discretion? The first ground on which the motions judge exercised his discretion to refuse prerogative relief was delay. There is no question that unreasonable delay may bar an applicant from obtaining a discretionary remedy, particularly where that delay would result in prejudice to other parties who have relied on the challenged decision to their detriment, and the question of unreasonableness will turn on the facts of each case; see de Smith, *Judicial Review of Administrative Action* (4th ed. 1980) at 423, and Jones and de Villars, *Principles of Administrative Law* (1985) at 373-74. The motions judge took cognizance of the period of time that elapsed between approval being granted by the Minister of Transport on September 18, 1987 and the filing of the notice of motion in this action on April 21, 1989, and the fact that the project was approximately 40 percent complete by that time. With respect, however, he ignored a considerable amount of activity undertaken by the respondent Society before taking this action, some of which was referred to by Stone JA. I should note at this point that Stone JA was mistaken when he stated that this action was taken only two months after the Society became aware that approval had been granted. During cross-examination on her affidavit in support of the application, Ms. Kostuch, the vice-president of the Society, admitted that the Society became aware of the approval on February 16, 1988, some 14 months before the present action was launched.

This was not the only action taken by the Society in opposition to the dam, however. The Society first brought an action in October 1987 seeking *certiorari* with prohibition in aid to quash an interim licence issued by the Minister of the Environment of Alberta pursuant to the *Water Resources Act*. On December 8, 1987 Moore CJQB quashed all licences and permits issued by the Minister on the grounds that the department had not filed the requisite approvals with its application, that it had not referred the matter to the Energy Resources Conservation Board as required by s. 17 of the Act, and that the Minister's delegate had wrongfully exercised his discretion in waiving the public notice requirements set out in the Act: *Friends of the Oldman River Society v. Alberta (Minister of the Environment)* (1987) 85 AR 321 (QB). Another interim licence was issued on February 5, 1988 and again the respondent brought an application to quash that licence, principally on the ground that the requirement for giving public notice had been improperly waived. The application was dismissed by Picard J who held that the appropriate material had been filed with the application for the licence and that the Minister's delegate had acted within his jurisdiction in waiving public notice: *Friends of Oldman River Society v. Alberta (Minister of the Environment)* (1988) 89 AR 339 (QB).

In the meantime, the respondent Society had been petitioning the Alberta Energy Resources Conservation Board to conduct a public hearing into the hydro-electric aspects of the dam pursuant to the *Hydro and Electric Energy Act*. The Board replied on December 18, 1987 refusing the Society's request for the reason that the dam did not constitute a "hydro development" within the meaning of the Act. An application was taken for leave to appeal that decision to the Alberta Court of Appeal which refused leave, agreeing with the Board that the project was not a hydro development, even though it was designed to allow for the future installation of a power generating facility: *Friends of the Old Man River Society v. Energy Resources Conservation Board (Alta.)* (1988) 89 AR 280 (CA). Finally, Ms. Kostuch swore an information before a justice of the peace alleging that an offence had been committed under s. 35 of the *Fisheries Act*. After summonses were issued, the Attorney General for Alberta intervened and stayed the proceedings on August 19, 1988. I have already documented the correspondence directed to the federal Minister of the Environment and Minister of Fisheries and Oceans through 1987 and 1988 in which members of the Society sought to have the *Guidelines Order* invoked, all to no avail. This action was taken shortly after the Trial Division of the Federal Court in *Canadian Wildlife* held that the *Guidelines Order* was binding on the Minister of the Environment.

In my view, this chronology of events represents a concerted and sustained effort on the part of the Society to challenge the legality of the process followed by Alberta to build this dam and the acquiescence of the appellant Ministers. While these events were taking place, construction of the dam continued, despite ongoing legal proceedings, and as at the date of the hearing before this Court, counsel for Alberta advised that the dam had been substantially completed. I can find no evidence that Alberta has suffered any prejudice from any delay in taking this action; there is no indication whatever that the province was prepared to accede to an environmental impact assessment under the *Guidelines Order* until it had exhausted all legal avenues, including an appeal to this Court. The motions judge did not weigh these considerations adequately or at all. Accordingly, the Court of Appeal was justified in interfering with the exercise of his discretion on this point.

The remaining ground for refusing to grant prerogative relief was on the basis of futility, namely that environmental impact assessment under the *Guidelines Order* would be needlessly repetitive in view of the studies that were conducted in the past. In my view this was not a proper ground to refuse a remedy in these circumstances. Prerogative relief should only be refused on the ground of futility in those few instances where the issuance of a prerogative writ would be effectively nugatory. For example, a case where the order could not possibly be implemented, such as an order of prohibition to a tribunal if nothing is left for it to do that can be prohibited: see de Smith, *supra*, at 427-28. It is a different matter, though, where it cannot be determined *a priori* that an order in the nature of prerogative relief will have no practical effect. In the present case, aside from what Stone JA has already said concerning the qualitative differences between the process mandated by the *Guidelines Order* and what has gone before, it is not at all obvious that the implementation of the *Guidelines Order* even at this late stage will not have some influence over the mitigative measures that may be taken to ameliorate any deleterious environmental impact from the dam on an area of federal jurisdiction. I have therefore concluded that the Court of Appeal did not err in interfering with the motions judge's exercise of discretion to deny the relief sought.

STEVENSON J (dissenting): ... The Federal Court of Appeal was clearly wrong in dismissing the motions judge's conclusion on the question of delay, which it was "not persuaded" was well-founded in principle. The Court of Appeal says the respondent Society did not become aware of the grant of the approval under the *NWPA* until some two months before the proceedings were actually launched. In fact, it knew of the approval some 14 months beforehand and the principal promoters of the Society knew even before then.

The common law has always imposed a duty on an applicant to act promptly in seeking extraordinary remedies:

> Owing to their discretionary nature, extraordinary and ordinary review remedies must be exercised promptly. Donaldson LJ of the Court of Appeal of England aptly explained the principle in *R v. Aston University Senate* [[1969] 2 QB 538 (CA) at 555]: "The prerogative remedies are exceptional in their nature and should not be made available to those who sleep upon their rights."

(Dussault and Borgeat, *Administrative Law* (2nd ed. 1990), vol. 4, at 468-69.)

That duty was recognized by Laskin CJ on behalf of this Court in *PPG Industries Canada Ltd. v. Attorney General of Canada* [1976] 2 SCR 739 (Can.) at 749:

> In my opinion, discretionary bars are as applicable to the Attorney General on motions to quash as they admittedly are on motions by him for prohibition or in actions for declaratory orders. The present case is an eminently proper one for the exercise of discretion to refuse the relief sought by the Attorney General. *Foremost among the factors which persuade me to this view is the unexplained two year delay in moving against the Anti-dumping Tribunal's decision.* [Emphasis added.]

The importance of acting promptly when seeking prerogative relief has also been recognized in much of the legislation now governing judicial review. For example, Ontario's *Judicial Review Procedure Act*, RSO 1990, c. J.1, empowers a court to extend the prescribed time for initiating an application for judicial review, but only where it is satisfied that there are *prima facie* grounds for relief and no substantial prejudice or hardship will result to those who would be affected by the delay (s. 5). Under British Columbia's *Judicial Review Procedure Act*, RSBC 1979, c. 209, an application for judicial review may be barred by the affluxion of time if a court considers that substantial prejudice or hardship will result by reason of the delay (s. 11). The *Federal Court Act*, RSC 1985, c. F-7, s. 28(2) stipulates that an application for judicial review before the Federal Court of Appeal must be made within ten days from the time the impugned decision or order is first communicated. That time limit can only be extended with leave of the court. In Alberta, Rule 753.11(1) of the *Alberta Rules of Court* (Alta. Reg. 390/68) stipulates that where the relief sought is the setting aside of a decision or act, the application for judicial review must be filed and served within six months after that decision or act. Finally, in art. 835.1 of Quebec's *Code of Civil Procedure*, RSQ, c. C-25, which applies to all extraordinary remedies, it is stipulated that motions must be served "within a reasonable time." The Court of Appeal of Quebec held in *Syndicat des employés du commerce de Rivière-du-Loup (section Émilio Boucher, CSN) v. Turcotte* [1984] CA 316, at 318, that: [Translation] "This article [835.1] merely codified the common law rule that the remedy must be exercised within a reasonable time."

By the time this application was brought, the dam was 40 percent complete. A significant amount of public money had already been spent. It is a matter of public record that individual members of the respondent Society were aware of the approval issued under the *NWPA* prior to February, 1988. Even if such were not the case, the respondent Society still could have launched its action in early 1988. At that time, major construction had not yet taken place. Had the respondent Society initiated proceedings then as compared to April of 1989, the appellant Alberta would have been in a much better position objectively to assess any potential legal risk associated with continuing. Faced with the possibility of invalid federal approval, it may well have chosen at that point not to put out the public funds that it did.

After years of extensive planning, innumerable public hearings, environmental studies and reports, and after the establishment of various councils and committees for the purpose of reviewing proposals that were put forward, the appellant Alberta embarked upon an enormous undertaking to meet the needs of its constituents. It did so at the expense of the public. And it did so after having been advised by the federal government that it could legitimately proceed. The Oldman River dam no doubt necessitates comprehensive administration. Its construction also involves a significant number of contracts with third parties. Given the enormity of the project and the interests at stake, it was unreasonable for the respondent Society to wait 14 months before challenging the decision of the Minister of Transport. In the context of this case, it was imperative that the respondent Society respect the common law duty to act promptly.

Had the respondent Society acted more promptly, the appellant Alberta would have been able to assess its position without regard to the economic and administrative commitment that was a reality by the time these proceedings were launched. It is impossible to conclude that the appellant Alberta was not prejudiced by the delay. Moreover, the motions judge made a finding on prejudice, and found that there was no justification for waiting to launch the attack until the dam was nearly 40 percent completed.

The rationale for requiring applicants for prerogative relief to act promptly is to enable their erstwhile respondents to act upon the authority given to them. The applicant cannot invoke the fact that the respondent did what he or she was legally entitled to do as an answer to its own delay. Such a view would put a premium on delay and deliver the wrong message to those who plan prerogative challenges.

My colleague, La Forest J, would also give some weight to the fact that the appellant Alberta was aware of the opposition of the respondent Society and others because of the other unsuccessful challenges by the Society and others. In my view, those challenges are completely irrelevant to this question. Those attacks were all ill-founded, and the appellant Alberta was not bound to expect that these peripheral and collateral proceedings presaged a fundamental attack on the original permit. The fact that detractors are harassing a travelling train does not put one on guard against the proposition that they are going to attack the authority to depart in the first instance. In my opinion, those activities need not have been taken into consideration by the motions judge. None of the activities undertaken by the Society or its members precluded the respondent Society from undertaking this challenge.

The activities referred to by my colleague were qualitatively different from that which is sought in this action, and irrelevant to the issue at hand. The applications for *certiorari* brought by the respondent Society in October 1987 and early 1988 respectively, were directed at interim licences issued by Alberta's Minister of Environment pursuant to that province's *Water Resources Act*, RSA 1980, c. W-5. The petitioning of the Alberta Energy Resources Conservation Board focused on the hydro-electric aspects of the dam. The information sworn before a justice of the peace alleged an offence pursuant to the federal *Fisheries Act*, RSC 1985, c. F-14.

This action centres on the constitutionality and applicability of the *Environmental Assessment and Review Process Guidelines Order*. It raises new and different issues. The previous efforts of the respondent Society were not necessary preliminaries; they were separate and distinct from the relief sought here. It is my view that in determining whether he should exercise his discretion against the respondent Society, Jerome ACJ was obliged to look only at those factors which he considered were directly connected to the application before him. He was clearly in the best position to assess the relevancy of that put forward by the parties. Interference with his exercise of discretion is not warranted unless it can be said with certainty that he was wrong in doing what he did. For the reasons stated above, I am of the opinion that the test has not been met in this case.

Appeal dismissed.

NOTES

1. If the application for judicial review had been made earlier, could the applicants have been met with a prematurity argument or the contention that the Federal Court should not deal with the case while proceedings were still pending in the Alberta courts? To what extent, if at all, do these considerations have relevance to a claim that the applicants delayed unduly in asserting their rights?

2. Consider the futility argument in the context of the previous section on mootness as well as that which follows on balance of convenience.

3. Take particular note of the portion of Stevenson J's dissent in which he refers to the fact that delay and other discretionary bars can be invoked even in situations where the applicant for relief or the appellant is the attorney general. There is no doubt that this is still good law.

4. An interesting contrast with *Friends of the Oldman River Society* is provided by *R v. Board of Broadcast Governors, ex parte Swift Current Telecasting Co. Ltd.* (1962), 33 DLR (2d) 449 (Ont. CA), in which the court refused to entertain a procedural unfairness attack on the grant of a broadcasting licence. There, with full knowledge of the grant of a licence, the applicant had waited until the construction of the new station was well under way before launching its challenge.

5. Should it matter whether the basis for attack is breach of the rules of natural justice or procedural fairness as opposed to a challenge founded on a complete lack of jurisdiction or substantive *ultra vires*? See *R v. Consolidated Maybrun Ltd.*, below.

6. Frequently, as with other matters going to the courts' discretion to deny relief, the issue of delay will be affected by the merits of the applicant's case for judicial review. In other words, it will not be appropriate to deal with the delay issue in isolation. See, in this regard, the judgment of the BC Court of Appeal in *MacLean v. University of British Columbia* (1993), 109 DLR (4th) 569 (BC CA), declining to deal with an allegation of undue delay in the context of an application to dismiss a petition for judicial review. In that case, the peti-

tioner had delayed a year in commencing his challenge to a decision denying him a renewal of his university position, allegedly because of a lack of funds. In the meantime, the university had hired another professor. The judgment of the court was delivered by Lambert JA:

> When the petition came on for hearing, counsel for the university took the position on a preliminary motion that the merits of the petition for judicial review should not be considered but that instead the petition should be dismissed because of delay in bringing it. Reference was made to s. 11 of the *Judicial Review Procedure Act*, RSBC 1979, c. 209, which reads in this way:
>
> > 11. Unless an enactment otherwise provides, and unless the court considers that substantial prejudice or hardship will result to any other person affected by reason of delay, an application for judicial review is not barred by effluxion of time.
>
> It was argued that substantial prejudice or hardship, to both the university and Professor Kay [the alleged replacement for MacLean], would result if the petition were granted and that the substantial prejudice and hardship flowed from the delay in launching the petition and not from the passage of time itself. That is, it was said on behalf of the university that it was the failure to launch the petition that caused the prejudice, not the simple passage of time.
>
> . . .
>
> In my opinion, a decision on a question of delay should not be made as a preliminary matter based on assumptions such as those which have been conceded in this case. In my opinion, the question of whether delays should affect the outcome of a judicial review application must be made in conjunction with the merits of the judicial review application itself. It is only when those merits are weighed and the prejudice to both sides has been weighed that it is possible for the chambers judge to exercise the principled and guided discretion that is conferred on a chambers judge in relation to granting a remedy under the *Judicial Review Procedure Act*.

7. Delay is also a major consideration in the position that the Supreme Court has taken on collateral attack. Particularly where there is a right of appeal, those affected by the decisions of administrative tribunals should not postpone their challenge to the validity of such orders until such time as they are confronted with enforcement proceedings. The following case exemplifies this well.

R v. Consolidated Maybrun Mines Ltd.
[1998] 1 SCR 706 (Ont.)

[The appellant company operated a gold and copper mine. Officials of the Ontario Ministry of the Environment concluded that the mine had been abandoned and that transformers containing PCBs presented a risk of environmental contamination. Despite numerous efforts to have the company take corrective action, the condition of the site did not change. The company was ordered to clean up, but it ignored the order. When charged by the ministry with failing to comply with the order, the appellant sought to go behind the order and have it declared invalid by the provincial court judge before whom the order had been charged. The Court of Appeal for Ontario affirmed the judgment of the Ontario Court (General Division) that by reviewing the validity of the order, the trial provincial court judge had exceeded his jurisdiction.]

L'HEUREUX-DUBÉ J (delivering the judgment of the Court): ... Before trying to answer the question raised by this appeal, it may be helpful to define its parameters somewhat and review the context in which this question arises.

It must be mentioned at the outset that the issues involved in the question of "collateral attacks" on administrative orders are different from those traditionally encountered in the judicial review context. Cases involving the superintending and reforming power of the superior courts are generally concerned with determining whether courts must show deference in reviewing a decision by an administrative tribunal. Although administrative orders like the one in the case at bar can be subject to judicial review by the superior courts, the problem before us presupposes, inter alia, that the affected party did not apply for review. Thus, the question that arises is, instead, whether a penal court, which is not necessarily a superior court, can determine the validity of an administrative order when the case before it concerns primarily a charge of a penal nature.

Admittedly, the issue before this Court involves considerations that are not entirely foreign to those which inform the superintending and reforming power of the superior courts. In both cases, the lawfulness of government actions is at issue. In the United States, the question of collateral attacks in penal proceedings has been resolved by means of the "exhaustion doctrine," which is intended primarily to protect the integrity of administrative mechanisms set up by law. See, in particular, *McGee v. United States*, 402 US 479 (1971). Our own administrative law recognizes a similar doctrine relating to the discretion enjoyed by the superior courts in exercising their superintending and reforming power. *See: Harelkin v. University of Regina* [1979] 2 SCR 561 (Sask.); *Commission des accidents du travail du Québec v. Valade* [1982] 1 SCR 1103 (Que.); *Abel Skiver Farm Corp. v. Town of Sainte-Foy* [1983] 1 SCR 403 (Que.); *Canadian Pacific Ltd. v. Matsqui Indian Band* [1995] 1 SCR 3 (Can.). Although I will be discussing the American case law on collateral attacks below, I simply point out here that it would be wrong to think that the considerations underlying the exhaustion doctrine in the judicial review context are irrelevant to the issue before this Court. However, this is insufficient to deprive the problem submitted to the Court of its inherent originality and permit it to be resolved by directly transposing principles developed in another context, *i.e.* the superintending and reviewing power of superior courts.

On the other hand, while it is true that the instant case does not arise in a judicial review context, it does not involve a court sitting on appeal from an administrative decision either. Indeed, the question of collateral attacks clearly arises precisely when the relevant statute provides for no right of appeal to the court responsible for trying the charge. As will be seen below, this does not necessarily mean that no appeal otherwise lies to another forum or that the existence of such a right of appeal is not a relevant factor. However, the problem raised by collateral attacks requires us, at the outset, to take into account the legislature's decision not to confer the power to hear an appeal from the administrative order on the court responsible for hearing the charge. From this perspective, the question is, accordingly, the extent to which, where no right of appeal confers express jurisdiction on the trial judge, the rule of law enables a penal court, here a provincial court, to consider the validity of an administrative order where a person is charged with failing to comply with such order.

The rule of law viewed, in particular, as the submission of the executive branch to the authority of the law, is clearly an essential component of our constitutional structure. This principle requires that it be open to concerned citizens to bring the excesses of government to the attention of the courts, especially where penal sanctions are involved. It explains *inter alia* why a party against whom a regulatory provision is raised may collaterally attack the validity of the provision, as is generally the case, for example, with municipal by-laws—see *R v. Greenbaum* [1993] 1 SCR 674 (Ont.); *R v. Sharma* [1993] 1 SCR 650 (Ont.); *Khanna v. Procureur général du Québec* (1984) 10 Admin. LR 210 (Que. CA); as well as *R v. Rice* [1980] CA 310, concerning a regulation enacted by a band council. However, the rule of law does not imply that the procedures for achieving it can be disregarded, nor does it necessarily empower an individual to apply to whatever forum he or she wishes in order to enforce compliance with it.

Finally, in resolving the problem of collateral attacks on administrative orders, it is necessary to bear in mind the role and importance of administrative structures in the organization of the various sectors of activity characteristic of contemporary society. The growing number of regulatory mechanisms and the corresponding administrative structures are a reflection of the state's will to intervene in spheres of activity, such as economics, communications media, health technology or the environment, whose growing complexity requires constantly evolving expertise and normative instruments permitting a pointed and rapid intervention consistent with the specific circumstances of the situation. The effectiveness of these instruments depends to a large extent on the penal sanctions that ensure their authority. As Cory J wrote in *R v. Wholesale Travel Group Inc.* [1991] 3 SCR 154 (Ont.) at 233:

> The realities and complexities of a modern industrial society coupled with the very real need to protect all of society and particularly its vulnerable members, emphasize the critical importance of regulatory offences in Canada today. Our country simply could not function without extensive regulatory legislation.

In order to ensure the integrity of these administrative structures, while at the same time seeking to protect the rights of individuals affected by government actions, the legislature is free to set up internal mechanisms and establish appropriate forums to enable such individuals to assert their rights. In considering the requirements resulting from the rule of law and the rights of a person accused of non-compliance with an administrative order, it is important not to isolate the penal proceedings from the whole of the process established by the legislature.

Laskin JA, writing for the Court of Appeal, proposed five factors to be considered in determining whether a court can rule on the validity of an administrative order collaterally attacked in penal proceedings: (1) the wording of the statute from which the power to issue the order derives; (2) the purpose of the legislation; (3) the availability of an appeal; (4) the nature of collateral attack; and (5) the penalty on a conviction for failing to comply with the order.

Subject to the comments below on the fourth factor, this approach seems to me to be satisfactory, provided, however, that it reflects a general approach aimed at determining the legislature's intention as to the appropriate forum. From this perspective, the factors set out above are not independent and absolute criteria, but important clues, among others, for determining the legislature's intention. In doing this, it must, *inter alia*, be presumed that the legislature did not intend to deprive citizens affected by government actions of an adequate opportunity to raise the validity of the order. The interpretation process must, therefore, determine not whether a person can challenge the validity of an order that affects his or her rights, but whether the law prescribes a specific forum for doing so.

The basis for my reservation concerning the fourth factor is that the Court of Appeal, in answering the question as to the nature of the collateral attack, suggests that a distinction be drawn between invalidity for lack of jurisdiction *ab initio* and invalidity resulting from loss of jurisdiction, which is not open to a collateral attack. However, it is not clear that this distinction can always be drawn in practice, nor is it clear how it really makes it possible to determine the legislature's intention as to the appropriate forum.

As regards the problems raised by the dichotomy between lack of jurisdiction and loss of jurisdiction, it must be recognized that the distinction between an order in respect of which an agent of the state lacks jurisdiction from the outset and an order that is so unreasonable as to result in a loss of jurisdiction, is not the easiest one to draw. Since *UES, Local 298 v. Bibeault* [1988] 2 SCR 1048 (Que.), the judgments of this Court have shown the clearest possible determination to avoid the problems connected with this type of distinction.

However, Laskin JA's approach to the nature of the collateral attack has an even more fundamental flaw. The distinction he proposes implies an approach that focuses exclusively on the jurisdiction of the authority that issued the order and disregards any relationship between the kind of collateral attack and the jurisdiction or *raison d'être* of the appeal tribunal. The jurisdiction of the authority that issued the order is, of course, relevant to the case, since it is the subject of the attack. However, what this Court must do is determine the forum in which the attack should be made, assuming for discussion purposes that the order does in fact contain a jurisdictional defect. Where the legislature has established an administrative appeal tribunal, it must be asked whether it intended that tribunal to have jurisdiction, to the exclusion of a penal court, to determine the validity of the impugned order. For this purpose, the nature of the collateral attack is, of course, relevant to determine not whether it raises an excess or lack of jurisdiction on the part of the agent or official who issued the administrative order, but rather to determine whether the attack involves considerations that fall within the jurisdiction conferred by statute on the appeal tribunal. Where the appropriate forum must be determined, it is, indeed, the jurisdiction of the appeal tribunal that is at issue rather than that of the Director, even though it is the Director's jurisdiction that is attacked.

Thus, where an attack on an order requires the consideration of factors that fall within the specific expertise of an administrative appeal tribunal, this is a strong indication that the legislature wanted that tribunal to decide the question rather than a court of penal jurisdiction. Conversely, where an attack on an order is based on considerations which are foreign to an administrative appeal tribunal's expertise or *raison d'être*, this suggests, although it is not conclusive in itself, that the legislature did not intend to reserve the exclusive authority to rule on the validity of the order to that tribunal. This analysis must be conducted in light of the specific characteristics of each administrative scheme. An approach, such as the one suggested by the Court of Appeal, aimed at establishing a general rule relating to the nature of the attack does not recognize the importance that must be given to the legislature's intention.

I would, accordingly, reformulate the fourth factor suggested by the Court of Appeal to take into account the nature of the collateral attack in light of the appeal tribunal's expertise and *raison d'être*.

(c) Conclusion

In summary, the question whether a penal court may determine the validity of an administrative order on a collateral basis depends on the statute under which the order was made and must be answered in light of the legislature's intention as to the appropriate forum. In doing this, it must be presumed that the legislature did not intend to deprive a person to whom an order is directed of an opportunity to assert his or her rights. For this purpose, the five factors suggested by the Court of Appeal, as reformulated here, constitute important clues for determining the legislature's intention as to the appropriate forum for raising the validity of an administrative order.

3. Application of the Principles to the Case at Bar

The purpose of the *Environmental Protection Act* is "to provide for the protection and conservation of the natural environment" (s. 2). It accordingly confers on the directors appointed by the Minister under the Act a certain number of powers of a considerable scope which are essentially preventive in nature. Thus, under s. 7, the Director is authorized to issue a stop order requiring the cessation of any activity resulting in the discharge of contaminants that constitute, or the level of which constitutes, a danger to human life or health. Furthermore, the construction or alteration of any plant, structure or apparatus that may discharge a contaminant into the environment, or any alteration of a process or rate of production entailing the discharge of contaminants into the environment, is subject to prior approval by the Director by means of a certificate (s. 8). Finally, s. 17 authorizes the Director to order the owner of, or person who controls, an undertaking or property to take steps to prevent or reduce the risk of environmental contamination. These are clearly broad powers that are, where ss. 7 and 17 are concerned, subject only to the condition that the Director base such a decision on reasonable and probable grounds that there is a risk of contamination based on the definition of the word "contaminant" in s. 1 of the Act.

The very fact that the Act gives the Director a certain number of powers of a preventive nature, including those set out in s. 17, which are at issue here, is a clear indication that the purpose of the Act is not just to remedy environmental contamination, but also to prevent it. This purpose must, therefore, be borne in mind in interpreting the scheme and procedures established by the Act.

It is true that the Act also has a remedial dimension. Thus, it confers on the Minister a power, now exercised by the Director under the present s. 17 (RSO 1990, c. E.19), to order repairs where a contaminant is emitted or discharged into the environment (s. 16). This power to order repairs, like the fact that s. 143 authorizes the government, as it did in the case at bar, to take any necessary action to protect the environment and bring proceedings to recover any amounts disbursed, cannot be read as reducing the importance of the Act's preventive purpose. On the contrary, it is my view that s. 143 shows the concern of the legislature with giving the government the tools needed to guarantee prompt compliance with orders issued under the Act, since a person to whom an order is directed could be required to bear the cost of any steps he or she neglects or refuses to take.

[A] person affected by a decision of the Director is not without recourse under the Act. On the contrary, ss. 120 *et seq.* of the Act provide for the creation of an Environmental Appeal Board, whose sole function is to hear appeals from decisions of the Director. In particular, s. 122 authorizes a person to whom an order is directed to appeal to the Board within 15 days after service of the order. Sitting as a panel of three, the Board has full power to review the Director's decision and take any action it deems necessary and may substitute its own opinion for that of the Director (s. 123). It is, therefore, a *de novo* process whose purpose is to permit the Director's decision to be reviewed in light of submissions by the affected party. Furthermore, should this party not be satisfied with the outcome, he or she has a right of appeal to the Divisional Court on a question of law, and a right of appeal to the Minister on any other matter.

In establishing this process, the legislature clearly intended to set up a complete procedure, independent of any right to apply to a superior court for review, in order to ensure that there would be a rapid and effective means to resolve any disputes that might arise between the Director and the persons to whom an order is directed. The decision to establish a specialized tribunal reflects the complex and technical nature of questions that might be raised regarding the nature and extent of contamination, and the appropriate action to take. In this respect, the Board plays a role that is essential if the system is to be effective, while at the same time ensuring a balance between the conflicting interests involved in environmental protection. ...

In the case at bar, the appellants elected to disregard not only the order, but also the appeal mechanism, preferring to wait until charges had been laid before asserting their position. Eleven years later, these proceedings are still in progress, and the appellants are still arguing that the order ought never to have been issued. It seems clear to me that the Board could have dealt with this entire matter more rapidly and more sensibly. The appellants' attitude forced the government to undertake the necessary measures to prevent a PCB spill. While the Act does contemplate such course of action, it cannot be said to encourage it. I agree with Laskin JA of the Ontario Court of Appeal that to permit the appellants to collaterally attack the order at the stage of penal proceedings would encourage conduct contrary to the Act's objectives and would tend to undermine its effectiveness. ...

In concluding, I cannot refrain from pointing out that the appellants, by systematically refusing to co-operate with the Ministry of the Environment and to participate in any dialogue, have shown an inflexible attitude for which they must now bear the consequences. Such an attitude serves neither the interests of society in environmental protection nor the interests of those who are subject to administrative orders. While penal sanctions will, perhaps, always be a necessary component of any regulatory scheme, they must not become the principal or a customary instrument for relations between the government and its citizens.

VI. Disposition

Considering the purpose of the Environmental Protection Act and the procedural mechanisms established to guarantee that a person to whom an order is directed can assert his or her rights, I conclude that persons charged with failing to comply with an order issued under the Act cannot attack the validity of the order by way of defence after failing to avail themselves of the appeal mechanisms available under the Act. The trial judge accordingly lacked jurisdiction to rule on the validity of the order.

Appeal dismissed.

NOTES

1. In this instance, the company was attempting to attack the order collaterally on the basis that it was completely unsupported by the evidence, the "no evidence" ground of judicial review. In the companion judgment of *R v. Al Klippert Ltd.*, [1998] 1 SCR 737 (Alta.), the company was charged with disobeying an order to cease operating a sand and gravel pit on the basis that it was a non-conforming use. The company's basis for attacking this order was that it was made without jurisdiction in the sense that the operation was indeed a permitted use. Despite the fact that this was much nearer the classic species of jurisdictional error allegation, the court came to the same result.

2. In each of *Consolidated Maybrun* and *Al Klippert*, there was a right of appeal to a court from the orders in question. The Supreme Court seemed to treat this as a highly relevant, if not decisive, factor in its rejection of the availability of collateral attack. What if the decision in question is not subject to appeal and protected by a privative clause? Should this make a difference?

3. In the course of its judgment, the court refers to its own precedents where persons charged with breaching bylaws have been allowed to impugn the validity of those bylaws collaterally. What differentiates those situations?

4. See also *Canada (Canadian Human Rights Commission) v. Taylor*, [1990] 3 SCR 892 (Can.), where it was held that it was too late to attack a tribunal order in the course of contempt proceedings. The affected person should have commenced a timely application for judicial review.

5. See Bilson, "Lying in Wait for Justice: Collateral Attacks on Administrative and Regulatory Orders" (1999), 12 *CJALP* 289.

MISCONDUCT OF APPLICANT

On occasion, the courts will deny a remedy because of the way in which the person seeking relief has behaved. This, of course, is a well-known ground for the refusal of equitable relief, the courts invoking the hoary old maxim that whoever comes to equity must come with clean hands. The courts have also imported the same type of consideration into the law relating to public law judicial review.

Homex Realty and Development Co. Ltd. v. Wyoming (Village)
[1980] 2 SCR 1011 (Ont.)

ESTEY J delivered the judgment of the majority of the Court: We come then to the last substantive test. Having thus determined that Homex had the right to an opportunity to be heard and that Homex did not receive such an opportunity before the passage by the Village of By-law 7, is Homex in all these circumstances entitled to the remedy sought, that is the quashing of the by-law on judicial review? These proceedings are brought under the *Judicial Review Procedure Act, 1971*. The procedure on this application is that formerly available under the Rules of Court where an application was made for an order in lieu of *certiorari*. The statute in s. 2(5) preserves the discretion of the Court under the former procedure:

> 2(5) Where, in any of the proceedings enumerated in subsection 1, the court had before the coming into force of this Act a discretion to refuse to grant relief on any grounds, the court has a like discretion on like grounds to refuse to grant any relief on an application for judicial review.

The discretionary nature of the remedy is undoubted: *vide* Laskin CJC in *PPG Industries Canada Ltd. v. A.G. Canada* [1976] 2 SCR 739 (Can.) at 749, where the Court exercised its discretion to deny *certiorari* to an applicant otherwise in law entitled. …

[Estey J then cited *Harelkin*.]

… The principles governing the exercise of discretion to decline the grant of the extraordinary remedy of *certiorari* are gathered in 1 Hals. (4th ed.), at 157 at para. 162: including, from the point of view of this appeal, "… if the conduct of the party applying has not been such as to disentitle him to relief." Examples of such conduct are found (in addition to those already enumerated above) in *F. Hoffmann-La Roche & Co. a.g. v. Secretary of State for Trade and Industry* [1975] AC 295 (Eng. HL); *Watson v. Northern School Board* [1976] 5 WWR 703 (Sask. QB), where the applicant had breached a contract and then sought to quash an award by a board established to determine the financial entitlements of the applicant as a result of such breach; *Re Falconbridge Nickel Mines Ltd. and United Steelworkers of America* (1972) 26 DLR (3d) 513 (Ont. HC), where the Judge of first instance refused *certiorari* because the applicant had acted unconscionably during the proceedings before the administrative tribunal. The Court of Appeal, adopting the same general principles of law, found that on the facts the applicant was not guilty of disentitling conduct ((1973) 30 DLR (3d) 412 (Ont. CA)).

I recognize that there has been some criticism of this exercise of judicial discretion to deny the remedy, which criticism has generally viewed the discretion as an attempt by a Court to apply or impose its own code of morality. This observation, however, denies or overlooks the very history of *certiorari*, an extraordinary and discretionary remedy coming down to present-day Courts from ancient times. To say that the writ is universally available where the rights of an individual are adversely affected by action of some public authorities taken in excess of jurisdiction or in some circumstances where an error of law has been committed in the course of the exercise of its jurisdiction, is not to say that the reviewing tribunal must slavishly apply the rules surrounding the issuance of *certiorari* and automatically respond to the application of the person affected without any further scrutiny. The principles upon which *certiorari*, and now the modern order in judicial review, have been issued have long included the principle of disentitlement where a Court, because of the conduct of the applicant, will decline the grant of the discretionary remedy.

... There are many examples to which one can turn. The British Columbia Court of Appeal in *Cock v. Labour Relations Board* (1960) 26 DLR (2d) 127 (BC CA) reversed an order of the Court below quashing, by *certiorari*, an award by a labour relations board, and in so doing stated through Davey JA (at 129):

> While the point was not taken below, in my respectful opinion, these writs should not be granted, even upon grounds otherwise legally sufficient, to applicants who in the matters before the Board have committed the fraud, trickery, and apparently perjury, found against the respondent here.

It is to be noted that the Court there regarded the discretion to be one springing not from the adversarial position of the parties but from the responsibility of the Court in the administration of Superior Court review to match the application of the extraordinary remedy to the circumstances of each case. Other authorities to the same point are *Ex parte Fry* [1954] 1 WLR 730 (CA) at 737; *R v. Kensington Income Tax Commissioners, Ex parte Princess Edmond de Polignac* [1917] 1 KB 486 (KB) at 519; *R v. Williams, Ex parte Phillips* [1914] KB 608 (KB) at 614, as to the exercise of discretion in the first instance. Thus it will be seen that the governing principles surrounding the issuance or withholding of the extraordinary remedy of *certiorari* in old or modern form operate up through the levels of the Superior Courts. Indeed, it is incumbent upon all Courts to apply those principles where the circumstances so require whether or not the parties address themselves to the latter.

Turning now to the application of this principle to the circumstances of this appeal, I do not propose to repeat but merely refer back to the history of the dealings by Homex with its predecessor in title Atkinson, and with the Village. Homex has sought throughout all these proceedings to avoid the burden associated with the subdivision of the lands comprised in Plan 567. In the preliminary stages of this application for judicial review, Homex has taken inconsistent and even contradictory positions. Examinations on affidavits were protracted because of a lack of simple frankness on the part of its president. Homex has sought, after its application to this Court to set aside the by-law, to put its lands beyond the reach of municipal regulations by means of checkerboarding. This it apparently is entitled to do at law but it does not follow that the exercise of such a legal right may not be a factor for assessment by a court which Homex invites to exercise a discretion in its favour in connection with *certiorari* or now judicial review concerning By-law 7. Of primary concern in my view is the attempt by Homex to avoid the burden of the "Atkinson" agreement to service these lands by shifting that burden to the ratepayers in the Village by the undoing of the municipal action taken in the form of By-law 7. There is nothing in the Council's conduct of negotiations to indicate the presence of any motive in Council other than its desire to protect its constituents from an expense which had been undertaken by the owners of Plan 567 when seeking the right to subdivide their land. This objective the Village had facilitated first by entering into a subdivision agreement with the then owner Atkinson, and thereafter by consenting to a conveyance of the subdivided lands to the applicant Homex. Furthermore, Homex appears to be secure against other forms of action for the recovery of the cost of services by the Village. It is not a party to the Atkinson-Village agreement and the agreement could not be registered and did not therefore run with the land at the time of the Homex acquisition. It might be that the Village could prove prior notice and somehow overcome want of privity in an action on the agreement. But Homex erected another obstacle in the path of the Village by resorting to checkerboarding in December, 1976. Such litigation by the Village would be difficult, no doubt protracted as were these proceedings, expensive, and of doubtful outcome. In any case, Homex and its "nominees" on title might, in the meantime, have disposed of the land and the Village would be left submerged in litigation with the new owners over the cost of services. Indeed, there is presently at least one outstanding action brought against Homex by a purchaser in which the Village is a third party.

I would, by reason of these special circumstances, deny the issuance of the order of judicial review with reference to By-law 7.

DICKSON J (dissenting): ... Two points in closing. First, the question of whether Mr Redick knew of the terms of the Atkinson agreement at the time of purchase was not the subject of argument in this Court. Neither factum saw this question as being relevant to the issues at bar. In the Divisional Court only passing reference was made to the agreement. Anderson J, for the Court, said:

> There appears to be some dispute as to whether the applicant did or did not have notice as to the existence and terms of the subdivision agreement at the time of purchase. There is reference to it in the offer to purchase. In my view nothing turns on this in any event.

Second, the respondent did not in this Court, nor, apparently, in the Court of Appeal, take the technical point that the conduct of the appellant was such as to disentitle the appellant to relief by way of *certiorari*. The appellant was not called upon to face this issue in either Court. I would not deny relief on a ground not raised nor argued.

[Ritchie J concurred with Dickson J.]

Appeal dismissed.

NOTE

Sometimes the issue of misconduct arises in the context of persons who have defied administrative rulings later established to have been made improperly. Should defiance ever be treated as misconduct justifying the denial of relief? Consider the following two decisions.

In *Re Tomaro and City of Vanier* (1978), 89 DLR (3d) 265 (Ont. CA), Tomaro was seeking *mandamus* to compel the municipality to issue him with a licence for a body-rub parlour. The Divisional Court, after holding that the municipality's refusal of a licence was wrongful, denied him relief on the basis that he had operated a body-rub parlour anyway and this had not emerged until he had been cross-examined on his affidavit. The Ontario Court of Appeal reversed the Divisional Court, Lacourcière JA dissenting and stating that the operation of the parlour revealed "a serious flaw in his character and integrity." This case is also interesting because the court awarded *mandamus* to compel the issue of the licence and not simply to compel consideration of the applicant's application for a licence according to law. Is the operation of the parlour without a permit more relevant if the entitlement to *mandamus* is of the latter rather than the former variety? Earlier, in *Re Slau Ltd. and City of Ottawa* (1976), 74 DLR (3d) 181 (Ont. Div. Ct.), *mandamus* was granted to compel issue of a building permit that had been refused wrongfully, notwithstanding the fact that the applicant had erected the building without a permit after the initial refusal.

WAIVER

On occasion, relief may be denied to an applicant on the basis of waiver or acquiescence. Most commonly, this occurs where the defect complained of is breach of the rules of natural justice or bias. Thus, in the *Halifax-Dartmouth Real Estate Board* case (chapter 16 of this text), one of the alternate grounds for the denial of relief given by MacDonald J was the failure of the applicants to object at the hearing to the lack of notice on one of the charges, this being the basis of the application for *certiorari*. What this seems to indicate is that it is dangerous to participate in a hearing without at least objecting when you believe that the decision-maker is transgressing the rules of natural justice in some way. Of course, if you do not know or have cause to know, then it is difficult to see any rationale for a failure to object being held against you: *Radio Iberville Ltée v. Board of Broadcast Governors*, [1965] 2 Ex CR 43; *UNA, Local 1 v. Calgary General Hospital* (1989), 63 DLR (4th) 440 (Alta. QB); aff'd. (1990), 77 DLR (4th) 732 (Alta. CA); *McGuire v. Royal College of Dental Surgeons (Ontario)* (1991), 49 Admin. LR 293 (Ont. Div. Ct.).

A more difficult question is whether in such cases you should not only object but also withdraw from further participation if your objections are overruled. How do you think a court should deal with this question? Note also *Millward v. Public Service Commission*, [1974] 2 FC 530 (TD), in which the applicants lost the opportunity of full participation in a hearing by withdrawing from the proceedings when their ill-founded request that the tribunal proceed in private was rejected, and *Pierre v. Minister of Manpower and Immigration*, [1978] 2 FC 849 (CA), in which the same result occurred after the applicant's counsel withdrew when an adjournment, in view of the court, was rightfully refused.

There are, however, limits to the extent that waiver will be operative. For example, an Ontario Racing Commission agreement to reinstate a racing licence, without holding the public hearing required by the rules, was not binding on the commission on the basis that it could not waive a requirement that had been enacted in the public interest: *Wassilyn v. Ontario (Racing Commission)* (1993), 10 Admin. LR (2d) 157 (Ont. Div. Ct.).

At times, as seen earlier, breach of the rules of natural justice is regarded as a category of jurisdictional error and this raises some theoretical problems with using waiver or acquiescence as a basis for the denial of relief in such cases. As with the ordinary courts, jurisdiction cannot be conferred on statutory authorities by consent or acquiescence (for example, *Re Rosenfeld and College of Physicians and Surgeons* (1970), 11 DLR (3d) 148 (Ont. HC)). Accepting this proposition of law, how then is it possible to justify ever allowing waiver or acquiescence to defeat an allegation of breach of the rules of natural justice? Does the same consideration raise any difficulties for other discretionary grounds for refusing relief, for

example delay? Should breach of the rules of natural justice be differentiated for these purposes from other types of reviewable error? What if the breach of the rules of natural justice
in question is also a violation of s. 7 of the *Canadian Charter of Rights and Freedoms*?

BALANCE OF CONVENIENCE

Much of this chapter has involved a consideration of the balance of convenience. In a very
direct sense, the refusal of relief because the applicant had other avenues of recourse available, or on the basis that there was a chance that the completion of the proceedings by the
tribunal would eliminate the applicant's concerns, is based on the premise that it is more
convenient to use alternative means of solving the problem before or as a substitute for seeking judicial review. Moreover, those discretionary grounds that focus on the conduct of the
applicant generally involve balance of convenience considerations. In delay cases, the question is asked whether the administrative process and third parties have been prejudiced by
the applicant's tardiness in commencing or pursuing an application for judicial review.
Where disqualifying misconduct is alleged, the applicant's behaviour frequently is balanced
against the administrative convenience of the process that is being challenged. Also, the
extent to which there has been reliance by either the administrative structure or third parties is relevant to arguments as to whether there has been an effective waiver of rights. Earlier, we also saw the centrality of a consideration of the balance of convenience where the
applicant is seeking interlocutory relief to prevent further processing of or action on a matter until such time as the merits of an application for judicial review can be dealt with.

However, considerations of balance of convenience sometimes surface as an independent
basis on which judicial review is denied and other avenues of relief effectively foreclosed,
notwithstanding the fact that the applicant has made out the merits of the case for judicial
review.

In the introduction to this chapter, we referred to the prospect of a court refusing relief, in
the face of a denial of procedural fairness, on the basis that the outcome would have been
the same even if the applicant had been treated in a procedurally fair manner. The justifications for such a stance are usually identified as the general consideration that the courts
should not be awarding remedies that are practically futile and, more specifically, the inappropriateness of forcing the decision-maker to engage in a reconsideration, the outcome of
which is inevitable.

Lewis, in *Judicial Remedies in Public Law* (above), at 437-39, identifies this as an accepted
factor in the exercise of remedial discretion in English law and favourable references may be
found in *Swift Current Telecasting*, above. However, the Supreme Court of Canada in *Cardinal* rejected such a ground for refusing relief on the basis that the denial of the benefit of the
rules of natural justice is a "free standing" ground of judicial review As noted earlier, the
practical justification for such a stance can be found in the dangers of the court speculating
as to inevitability of outcomes on the basis of incomplete material in relation to a matter
where it is not the statutorily designated decision-maker. There is also a sense, conveyed by
the reference to "free standing," that it is important that there always be sanctions for such
wrongs and that the inconvenience of reconsidering the matter counts for less than the imposition of some cost or penalty for the decision-maker's wrongful behaviour.

In *Mobil Oil Canada Ltd. v. Canada–Newfoundland Offshore Petroleum Board*, [1994] 1 SCR 202 (Nfld.), the Supreme Court of Canada revisited this issue in the context of the denial of a fair hearing by the board to companies that had requested "a significant discovery declaration" in respect of an offshore gas well. In fact, the chair of the board had refused to put the matter before the board. The court held that the board had not delegated authority to the chair to make such decisions and that this had amounted to a failure on the part of the board to afford the companies procedural fairness. However, relief was refused (at 228-29) because the court had, on a cross-appeal by the board, held that the board would *as a matter of law* have had to refuse the application anyway.

In so doing, the court acknowledged (at 228) the authority of *Cardinal*, but held that this was one of those exceptional cases where the refusal of a remedy in the face of a denial of natural justice was justified on the basis of futility. For these purposes, the court relied on the following statement by Wade in *Administrative Law*, 6th ed. (Oxford: Clarendon Press, 1988), at 535:

> A distinction might perhaps be made according to the nature of the decision. In the case of a tribunal which must decide according to law, it may be justifiable to disregard a breach of natural justice where the demerits of the claim are such that it would in any case be hopeless.

How far this exception goes, however, is problematic in that, in many situations, the tribunal under attack will have at least initial and often, because of privative clauses, virtually unreviewable authority over questions of law that arise before it. Thus, for a reviewing court to speculate on the outcome of such questions of law can be seen as just as much an arrogation of authority as the determination of questions of fact. Thus, it may be that the only occasion where it is appropriate for the court to enter into such an inquiry is where the merits of the legal issue have also been put before it by the tribunal itself and argued fully in the same judicial review proceedings, and where that issue is one that is in relation to a jurisdiction-conferring provision. This certainly seems to have been the situation in *Mobil Oil*. Moreover, the court was very careful to emphasize the exceptional nature of what it was doing, with Iacobucci J concluding (for the court) that he "would not wish to apply it broadly" (at 229). In general, the freestanding nature of breach of the rules of natural justice still leads to the virtually automatic grant of relief in such cases.

How should a court respond when a decision-maker asserts in the context of the judicial review proceedings that, even if the initial decision was tainted, he or she would have reached the same conclusion irrespective of the defect? This unusual situation arose in the New Zealand case of *Chieu v. Minister of Immigration*, [1994] 2 NZLR 541 (CA), where an alien was refused a residence permit on the basis of a ministerial misinterpretation of the Act and an operative guideline. In response to a judicial review application, the minister's successor swore an affidavit to the effect that, operating within the Act and guideline as interpreted properly, he would still have exercised his residual discretion to refuse the permit. The Court of Appeal (at 552-53) refused to use this as a basis for a discretionary denial of relief. It was not prepared to see such an affidavit as conclusive as to what would happen once the matter was referred back and reconsidered, particularly given that the affidavit was sworn at a time when the precise grounds on which the court might intervene were unknown and where, on the reconsideration, there might be new arguments and evidence, and perhaps even a new decision-maker. Fisher J, delivering the judgment of the court, was also impressed by the fact that, in such a case, an appearance of fairness would never be achieved in the absence of a formal reconsideration. He then concluded:

> Finally, the availability of judicial review could at times have a deterrent function. In at least some cases, decision-makers may be encouraged to avoid error if they appreciate that their efforts can attract judicial scrutiny and intervention. It would be unfortunate if the idea gained currency that in the event of challenge, flawed procedures and decisions could be protected by the simple expedient of giving evidence which predicted the same result.

It is worth contrasting this position with that adopted in another New Zealand decision, *Fitzgerald v. Muldoon*, [1976] 2 NZLR 615 (SC), involving futility or lack of utility in a different sense. There, the prime minister of New Zealand, lacking any statutory authority, had ordered the responsible government agency not to abide by its statutory obligation to collect and enforce government superannuation deductions by employers from employees' wages. The reason for this direction was the prime minister's anticipation of the introduction and passage of legislation abolishing the national superannuation scheme. The court was willing to recognize the inevitability of this legislation and dismissed the applications for mandatory and injunctive relief. However, it did declare the prime minister's actions to be illegal. Is this an adequate compromise in such cases? (Compare *Re McKay and Minister of Municipal Affairs* (1973), 35 DLR (3d) 627 (BC SC), rejecting an "imminent" legislation argument, but note that Cane, above, at 93, sees this as an acceptable alternative in natural justice cases, though noting the lack of incentive for applicants to commence proceedings if that is going to be the only likely remedy.)

One of the difficulties with *Fitzgerald v. Muldoon* is that the actions in question were clearly *ultra vires* in a substantive sense. This raises the problem of whether the court's toleration of illegalities because of considerations of futility should at the most be recognized in cases that are essentially procedural. In this context, it is worth considering how this discussion relates to the issue (considered in chapter 15, The Use and Misuse of Discretion) of the courts' response to an exercise of statutory discretion, one of the reasons for which was legally irrelevant. If we concede the entitlement of the courts to speculate in that class of case as to what the outcome would have been had the irrelevant factor not been taken into account, have we not both undercut *Cardinal* and rejected any distinction for these purposes between procedural and substantive error? In any event, how should we view a case such as *R v. Monopolies and Mergers Commission, ex parte Argyll Group*, [1986] 1 WLR 763 (CA) (highlighted by both Lewis (*Judicial Remedies in Public Law*, at 298-301) and Cane (at 92) in which a takeover was approved by the wrong person (the chair of the commission rather than the commission itself) but where the required statutory approval had been given by the secretary of state?

While it is possible to analyze the *Argyll Group* judgment in terms of procedural rather than substantive error in a situation where the outcome would have been the same if the correct body had taken the decision, Donaldson MR (in delivering the judgment of the court) ranged more broadly than that in references to the reliance on the decision by third parties and, in particular, the economic consequences of too readily allowing decisions of this kind to be quashed by judicial review. This parallels *Re Central Canada Potash Co. Ltd. and Minister of Mineral Resources of Saskatchewan* (1972), 32 DLR (3d) 107 (Sask. CA) and an alternative ground for denial of relief in that case—namely, that to grant *mandamus* compelling the minister to issue licences on the basis of the previously applicable criteria "would lead to confusion and disorder in the potash industry."

To the extent that these factors are taken into account, they depend on an overriding sense that the public interest in certain instances dictates that illegalities be ignored by the courts. Irrespective of whether the outcome would have been the same had the statutory body acted legally, the court should recognize the disruptive effects of granting judicial review and allow the impugned decision or action to stand. The courts clearly condone such an approach in their acceptance of the often blurred distinction between mandatory and directory procedural requirements. However, even there, there is a considerable nod to the impact of the error on the applicant's procedural rights: if the applicant has been substantially prejudiced by the non-observance of a directory procedural provision, then relief will be granted.

In the *Argyll Group* case, the motivations of the applicant in seeking judicial review could be seen as stemming from a desire to achieve a competitive advantage over a rival. This was a further reason why the applicant's position did not deserve much recognition from the court. It is somewhat more difficult to make this claim about the applicant's interest in *Central Canada Potash*. However, in some other Canadian cases where the public interest in this form has intruded, that kind of consideration has seemingly been present—the particular nature of the applicant's interest when balanced against other aspects of the public interest.

MiningWatch Canada v. Canada (Fisheries and Oceans)
2010 SCC 2

[Following a favourable environmental assessment of an open pit mining and milling operation by British Columbia authorities, the federal Department of Fisheries and Oceans determined that a comprehensive federal environmental assessment was not necessary. Rather, all that it required was assessment by way of screening. MiningWatch, a public interest group, applied for judicial review of the decision to proceed in this manner. After concluding that the department had acted without statutory authority, the Supreme Court went on to assess what relief, if any, it should award.]

ROTHSTEIN J: In my respectful view, in exercising his discretion to grant the broad relief he did, the learned trial judge did not take account of a number of relevant and significant considerations. Because of this, he granted broader relief than was appropriate.

Martineau J set aside the RAs' decision to proceed by way of screening and prohibited the issuing of permits and approvals under s. 5(1)(d) and s. 5(2) until the completion of a comprehensive study pursuant to s. 21 and, based thereon, a decision whether to permit the project to be carried out in whole or in part pursuant to s. 37. In simple terms, the parties have been ordered to substantially re-do the environmental assessment. I do not think such relief is warranted.

First, at para. 292, the trial judge states that "[i]t is not entirely clear to the Court why, once it had been determined the Project, as described by the RCDC, was included in the CSL, the decision was subsequently made to downgrade the extent of the assessment required to that of a screening." While he says that he does not define the scoping decision to be "capricious and arbitrary" (para. 294), his reasons indicate a suspicion of the motive of the RAs. However, it is apparent that the environmental assessment was converted to a screening assessment on or about December 9, 2004, because of new information and because of the issuance of the *TrueNorth* decision by the Federal Court on September 16, 2004 (2004 FC 1265. 257 FTR 212), after the initial scoping decision had been made. Indeed, the trial judge, in his reasons, quoted a letter of DFO dated December 9, 2004 to the Canadian Environmental Assessment Agency explaining that the RAs were influenced by new information and by the *TrueNorth* decision (para. 108). Yet, he still questioned the motives of the RAs in scoping. It is difficult to fault the RAs for following a decision of the Federal Court on the very matter with which they were dealing.

Second, the trial judge does not appear to have considered that, although it is Red Chris that will be prejudiced by incurring further delay and costs as a result of his order, Red Chris did nothing wrong. The approach to the environmental assessment was determined by the government.

Third, according to the evidence, Red Chris cooperated fully with the environmental assessment conducted by the BCEAO. It proposed terms of reference for a working group which included federal and provincial agencies and local First Nation groups. Red Chris sought public comment on the project through several open house meetings. Once Red Chris submitted its application for a provincial environmental assessment certificate, the BCEAO posted the application online for public comment, and members of the public submitted several comments in response to the Red Chris application. These facts do not appear to have been considered by the trial judge in exercising his discretion to grant relief.

Further, in a letter to the Deputy Minister of Natural Resources Canada dated August 24, 2006, MiningWatch stated that it "brought this application as a test case of the federal government's obligations under section 21." It would be incorrect to say that the parties in test cases may not still be interested in preserving their claims that gave rise to the litigation in the first place. However, this is not such a case.

MiningWatch says it has no proprietary or pecuniary interest in the outcome of the proceedings (affidavit of Joan Kuyek, AR vol. 2, p. 1, at para. 32). MiningWatch did not participate in the environmental assessment conducted by the BCEAO. Its first involvement was in commencing judicial review in the Federal Court. It has not brought forward any evidence of dissatisfaction with the environmental assessments conducted by the BCEAO or the RAs; nor is there evidence of dissatisfaction with the assessment process from anyone else. MiningWatch says it has brought this judicial review as a test case of the federal government's obligations under s. 21. Indeed, they made a strategic decision not to challenge the substantive scoping decision. This is an appropriate case in which to take the position expressed by MiningWatch at face value. A declaration as to the proper interpretation of s. 21 and the obligations of the federal government achieves MiningWatch's stated objective and grants a substantial portion of the relief it requested.

In my opinion, the appropriate relief in this case would be to allow the application for judicial review and declare that the RAs erred in failing to conduct a comprehensive study. Pursuant to s. 18.1(3) of the *Federal Courts Act*, I would decline to grant any further relief.

I acknowledge that in exercising discretion to grant declaratory relief without requiring the parties to substantially redo the environmental assessment, the result is to allow a process found not to comply with the requirements of the *CEAA* to stand in this case. But the fact that an appellant would otherwise be entitled to a remedy does not alter the fact that the court has the power to exercise its discretion not to grant such a remedy, or at least not the entire remedy sought. However, because such discretionary power may make inroads upon the rule of law, it must be exercised with the greatest care. See Wade, *Administrative Law* (10th ed. 2009), at 599 and *Immeubles Port Louis Ltée v. Lafontaine (Village)*, [1991] 1 SCR 326 (Que.), at 361. In the exercise of that discretion to deny a portion of the relief sought, balance of convenience considerations are involved. See D.J.M. Brown and J.M. Evans, *Judicial Review of Administrative Action in Canada* (looseleaf), at pp. 3-88 and 3-89, referred to by Binnie J in *Canada (Citizenship and Immigration) v. Khosa*, 2009 SCC 12, [2009] 1 SCR 339 (Can.), at para. 36. Such considerations will include any disproportionate impact on the parties or the interests of third parties (Brown and Evans, at p. 3-88, footnote 454). In my respectful opinion, that is the situation here. The focus of MiningWatch's interest as a public interest litigant is the legal point to which the declaration will respond. On the other hand, I can see no justification in requiring Red Chris to repeat the environmental assessment process when there was no challenge to the substantive decisions made by the RAs.

NOTE

Given that MiningWatch was before the Supreme Court as a public interest litigant (and presumably had standing as such), is the court justified in focusing on the positions taken by and litigation strategy of MiningWatch? Or should the court, in weighing the balance of convenience, have paid more attention to the broader public interest considerations in allowing a project to proceed when there had not been a proper federal environmental assessment?

CHAPTER NINETEEN

Money Remedies

INTRODUCTION

Frequently, the wrongful action or inaction of statutory authorities will cause damage to those affected by it. Money may have been paid under a regulation or order subsequently found to be *ultra vires*. A licence may have been cancelled or a statutory position taken away wrongfully, leaving the victim with a loss of business or personal income. Those charged with administering a statutory scheme may have performed their functions carelessly or negligently causing physical and/or economic harm to private citizens as, for example, in the case of the negligent inspection of a building under construction (the defects in which lead to personal injury, diminished property value, or both). In this chapter, our aim is to explore the extent to which such losses may be recovered from public authorities and their officials.

In terms of causes of action, these scenarios will lead us to consider the application of the principles of restitution or unjust enrichment to public authorities. We will also look briefly at how the granting of judicial review may in itself create a direct claim on the public purse for moneys due and owing. We then turn to the availability of damages in tort against public authorities and their officials. Here, we will concentrate principally on claims in negligence but, in addition, will evaluate the extent to which the courts recognize a separate tort of misfeasance in public office or bad faith in the exercise of statutory powers. We will also raise the question of the extent to which Canadian law recognizes separate principles of liability when wrongful administrative action involves a violation of rights and freedoms protected by the *Canadian Charter of Rights and Freedoms* and other constitutional principles, the domain of "constitutional tort."

Underlying all these various possibilities for financial recompense from the government and its officials is the crucial question of the extent to which the relevant liability rules and principles for the availability of money remedies should be the same as in the case of private sector defendants.

The traditional starting point for considerations of this topic is the assertion by Dicey in *The Law of the Constitution*, 10th ed. (London: Macmillan, 1967), at 193-94 (and first written in 1885) that no person is above the law and that officials are as liable as ordinary citizens for harmful acts done without justification.

> We mean in the second place, when we speak of the "rule of law" as a characteristic of our country, not only that with us no man is above the law, but (what is a different thing) that here every man, whatever be his rank or condition, is subject to the ordinary law of the realm and amenable to the jurisdiction of the ordinary tribunals.
>
> In England the idea of legal equality, or of the universal subjection of all classes to one law administered by the ordinary courts, has been pushed to its utmost limit. With us every official,

from the Prime Minister down to a constable or a collector of taxes, is under the same responsibility for every act done without legal justification as any other citizen. The Reports abound with cases in which officials have been brought before the courts, and made, in their personal capacity, liable to punishment, or to the payment of damages, for acts done in their official character but in excess of their lawful authority. A colonial governor, a secretary of state, a military officer, and all subordinates, though carrying out the commands of their official superiors, are as responsible for any act which the law does not authorise as is any private and unofficial person. Officials, such for example as soldiers or clergyman of the Established Church, are, it is true, in England as elsewhere, subject to laws which do not affect the rest of the nation, and are in some instances amenable to tribunals which have no jurisdiction over their fellow-countrymen; officials, that is to say, are to a certain extent governed under what may be termed official law. But this fact is in no way inconsistent with the principle that all men are in England subject to the law of the realm; for though a soldier or a clergyman incurs from his position legal liabilities from which other men are exempt, he does not (speaking generally) escape thereby from the duties of an ordinary citizen.

Given the extent to which both the Crown and public officials personally enjoyed an immunity from suit when this was first written, there is considerable room for questioning the accuracy or at least completeness of Dicey's description of the law of his day. Nonetheless, as a prescriptive statement, it still has considerable attraction as reflected in the following statement in the introduction to Hogg's and Monahan's *Liability of the Crown*, 3rd ed. (Toronto: Carswell, 2000), at iii:

> However, the general thesis of the book remains the same as that of the first edition and the second edition: in our view, the government ought usually be subject to the same rules of legal liability as the subject. We continue to reject the European-derived alternative of a distinctive public law of government liability and we also reject the French model of special courts to administer the public law. This approach leads us to criticize most of the immunities and privileges that still apply to the Crown although we acknowledge that some adaptation of the general law is needed to accommodate the special needs of government.

While it may well be that, as a matter of prescription, both Hogg and Dicey are correct and that the occasions for special treatment of the government in litigation should be few, it is also clear that this is not an easy issue in many contexts and particularly those which are the principal concern of this book: the exercise of explicit statutory powers by government officials. Of course, it may be difficult to sustain an argument for the immunity of either the Crown (vicariously as employer) or its servant in a situation where the minister of finance's chauffeur negligently injures a private citizen while on official business. However, in many other situations, the proper governing principles are neither self-evident nor do they necessarily involve the choice of either immunity or liability on the same basis as that pertaining to private citizens. There are at least arguments that, in some contexts, the government should be under a greater obligation than that which applies normally.

While it is still seldom explicitly articulated in the cases, one of the issues that arises in fixing liability in general tort law is that of resource allocation and ability to pay. However, it did, for example, surface in an action brought against the British Railways Board for injuries suffered by a trespasser. In *British Railways Board v. Herrington*, [1972] AC 877 (Eng. HL), at 899, Lord Reid asserted that the board had a greater ability than private individuals to avoid dangers to trespassers. What that may be seen as suggesting is that governments and their agencies, because of their deep pockets, their unenviable capacity as loss spreaders or reallocators, and their ability to exercise control through the creation and exercise of statutory powers, should be more readily liable than private citizens for certain kinds of harm.

There is also an argument stemming from the fact that at least some of the activities of government either have no private sector analogues or are of an ultra-hazardous variety (such as the production and storage of nuclear materials). To the extent that the general populace benefits from these activities, those who happen to be the chance victims of mishaps involved in their operation should perhaps be compensated irrespective of fault.

Finally, there is the commonly held view that there are contexts where governments wielding power by virtue of public trust should be held to high moral and legal responsibilities for the lawful and prudent exercise of that authority. This argument has greatest weight in the domain of intentional torts and government's coercive powers, such as those of arrest, imprisonment, and the confiscation of property. It reflects itself, for example, in the English position that the commission of torts in such contexts represents one of the extremely limited number of situations in which exemplary damages should be available: *Rookes v. Barnard*, [1964] AC 1129 (Eng. HL) ("oppressive, arbitrary or unconstitutional action by the servants of government"). It is also a consideration that surfaces in some of the debate as to the existence of a constitutional tort in cases of violations of the Charter.

However, these arguments may be controversial as a matter of principle and difficult to sustain as an empirical matter. The arguments based on the deep pocket of the government have little or no relevance when it comes to the personal liability of officials, save to the extent that governments are under a legal obligation (as, for example, under a collective agreement) or prepared voluntarily to indemnify officials when they are subjected to such a cause of action. Moreover, even in terms of government itself, such arguments are not always convincing. For example, municipalities are not nearly as well-placed to act as loss spreaders as are central governments, and the cost of insurance against many of their potential liabilities may be such as to cause them to become self-insurers against claims of that kind. Indeed, in the present context of massive central government deficits and cutbacks in services, there is a certain hollowness to appeals to the deep pocket of governments as a justification for even the same, let alone greater, liability on their part as applies to the private sector. Finally, not all find convincing the moral claim that all citizens, through their taxes, should pay for harms suffered by the chance victims of government programs and activities that are carried on for the general public benefit. At least as far as tort claims (as opposed to participation in various forms of government benefits) are concerned, many would argue that such harms are part of the risk of living in a society and beyond the bounds of that for which the state should be responsible. In recognition of the possibility of such risks, private citizens should protect themselves by private insurance and not expect the state to answer a claim for tort-level damages.

Integrally linked with this series of arguments is also the contention that care must be taken in devising principles of governmental and public official liability to ensure that they do not act as a disincentive to the creation of programs that are generally in the public interest or an undue influence in the performance of official duties. This point is made graphically by Aman and Mayton, *Administrative Law*, 2d ed. (St. Paul, MN: West Group, 2001), at 552-53, writing in the context of public official liability under American law:

> It may be unfair to hold an official liable in damages as she in good faith tries to perform the hard task that the public demands of her. These tasks demand difficult judgments, and these judgments often bear down on people in such a way as to offend them and to make them likely plaintiffs. The teacher who disciplines, the policeman who searches and arrests, these officials and many others like them have to make difficult judgments that are painful to those subject to them ... [A]long with possibility of injustice to the individual official, official liability may also diminish the general public welfare ... . The deterrence to vigorous official action is not just the amount of damages that officials may have to pay. It also includes litigation costs such as legal fees, time, embarrassment, and so forth. ...
>
> Consequently, the potential of official liability is that of a range of public action that is not as vigorous as it ought to be: police may not be enthusiastic law enforcers, parole boards may refuse to parole, public employers may overlook malingerers, teachers may not make hard disciplinary choices. The diminishment of public action may not be just a reluctance to take action, it may as well be an increased formality and awkwardness in that action as the official shields herself with layers of documentation and decisional processes [footnotes omitted].

To these concerns can be added the disincentives that liability rules may create for the acceptance of appointments to agencies and tribunals such as the National Parole Board.

In terms of the liability of government itself and the creation of programs, the following example is instructive. It is a decision of the Supreme Court of Canada in a case from Québec in which it was argued that there should be government liability in delict, irrespective of fault, for the harm suffered by the chance victim of a government program.

Lapierre v. Attorney-General of Quebec, [1985] 1 SCR 241 (Que.) involved an attempt to make the government of Québec liable for the illness of a child who was allergic to a measles vaccine that was urged on parents by health authorities. In the Supreme Court, the case was fought on the assumption that the government had not been guilty of negligence and the issue was whether the situation called for the imposition of "no fault" liability. In a remarkable judgment, Chouinard J, writing for the Supreme Court, decided the case almost solely by reference to whether a private individual could be held liable for such losses under the *Quebec Civil Code*, with barely an acknowledgment of the possibility of the case not being governed solely by considerations of private law.

Of course, it might be said that there is nothing problematic about this. If the normal rule is that statutory authorities are less readily to be found liable than private individuals or groups, the matter is clinched if there is no private liability. However, the plaintiff's lawyers, under the rubric of the "theory of risk," advanced an opposing argument that deserved far more attention than the cursory statement that it represented neither the law of Québec nor that of France. The thrust of the argument is put forward in the following extract from a text cited by Chouinard J, though ultimately dismissed in one sentence:

> [Translation] Perhaps in terms of equity the theory of risk raises fewer objections in public law. When it is the State or a public body which has caused damage through its representatives, there is no moral objection to requiring it to make compensation, though it may be clear that no one was at fault. This is no longer a question of causing pecuniary loss to an individual,

against which equity rebels when the latter's conduct is free of fault; the question is whether a single individual, the victim, should bear the burden caused by operation of the service which injured him, or whether all individuals, represented by the State, should share that burden. The question arises in completely new circumstances: there is a problem of "distributing public burdens," "individual equality with respect to public burdens." However, no contemporary publicist accepts the theory of risk outright.

What we have here is a competing theory of state liability or, at least, a theory of state liability that posits the possibility of different approaches to the liability of the state depending on the context in which the issue is being raised. Unfortunately, that argument was simply not addressed in *Lapierre*. Instead, the ultimate in positivistic responses is given: "This is not the law." (Subsequently, in 1985, the Québec National Assembly passed a law establishing a fund against which victims of the vaccination program, including Lapierre, could claim: SQ 1985, c. 23, s. 18, inserting ss. 16.1-16.9 in the *Public Health Protection Act*, RSQ, c. P-35, and see also s. 26 making the regime applicable to Lapierre and two others. This remains the only example of such legislation in Canada: "Only Quebec pays out for vaccine injuries," *Globe and Mail*, November 18, 2002.)

It is worthwhile to contrast *Lapierre* with the judgment of La Forest J in *Tock v. St. John's Metropolitan Area Board*, [1989] 2 SCR 1181 (Nfld.), in which he advocated deciding on questions pertaining to the nuisance liability of public authorities by reference to a form of risk allocation and enterprise liability analysis. While admittedly this approach was not adopted by a majority of the court, there are real problems in conceding the utility of such an approach in the domain of nuisance and rejecting outright its application as a basis for imposing limited no fault liability on public authorities in relation to certain of their activities. (For a discussion of this issue, see Mullan, "The Law of Canada" in Bell and Bradley, eds., *Governmental Liability: A Comparative Study* (London: United Kingdom National Committee of Comparative Law, 1991), at 59.)

Despite many opportunities, our courts have seldom discussed directly the difficult issues raised by various attempts to make the state liable for the losses caused by it and its numerous organs. As a result, our law is still far removed from a developed, coherent theory of state liability. Not surprisingly, there have been many academic attempts to fill that void. Among those dealing with the cases extracted in this chapter, see Craig, "Negligence in the Exercise of Statutory Power" (1978), 94 *LQR* 428; Seddon, "The Negligence Liability of Statutory Authorities: *Dutton* Reinterpreted" (1978), 9 *Fed. LR* 326; Harlow, *Compensation and Government Torts* (1982); and Makuch, *Canadian Municipal and Planning Law* (1983), at 140-72. In the following extract, David Cohen identified the complexity of the issues involved and, at the same time, attempted to provide a direction for thinking about this area.

Cohen, "The Public and Private Law Dimensions of the UFFI Problem"
(1983-1984), 8 *Can. Bus. LJ* 309 and 410, at 419-434

[The impetus for and focal point of this article was the commencement of actions against various arms of the federal government for their part in the endorsement and subsidization of the use in housing of a type of foam insulation that was alleged to be toxic to some people.]

The issue of judicial review of bureaucratic incompetence in the performance of mandatory statutory duties or in the exercise of statutory discretion will, it seems, be considered in the context of a negligence action. At one time it was thought that breach of a statutory duty would develop as a conceptually distinct private law action. Recent cases suggest however, that traditional negligence concepts will be applied both to activities rendered pursuant to mandatory statutory duties and to discretionary statutory directives. In the former case, which may arise under the *Department of Supply and Services Act*, the action may be framed as a "breach of statutory duty," while in the latter case it will be framed in common law negligence terms. In both cases, the court must determine whether a bureaucrat (or a group of bureaucrats) in carrying out statutory responsibilities, owed a legal duty of care to the person who alleges that he was injured as a result of the negligent performance of those statutory responsibilities.

The decision to impose a private legal duty on bureaucratic activity has been said to depend on the nature of the activity under review. Where the bureaucratic decision takes place within the *operational* sphere of government, the court will hold that the bureaucrat owes the individual a private, legal duty of care. Conversely, policy or planning decisions of bureaucrats are beyond judicial review. This categorical distinction has been adverted to with increasing frequency since the House of Lords' decision in *Anns v. Merton London Borough Council* [[1978] AC 728 (Eng. HL) (extracted below)].

The categorization of governmental functions into policy and operational spheres, even if we could agree on the criteria to use in determining into which camp one should put a particular decision, is entirely artificial. The description of the foam insulation approval process which took place in the context of a financial incentive grant programme, which itself was an element in a multi-sector conservation policy, which itself was an aspect of a national energy programme designed to achieve energy self-sufficiency in Canada suggests that each bureaucratic decision is both an operational and a policy or planning decision. Each decision, in most cases, will be made in the context of implementing a superior policy decision; and will itself constitute a superior policy decision which will be implemented by inferior operational (policy) decisions. It is not that a decision has both operational and policy *aspects*, and that as the former predominates the court is more likely to review it. Rather, the decision is both a planning and an operational decision, and the court must decide whether it will review the policy/operational decision.

The categorization demanded by *Anns* will certainly breed apparently inconsistent decisions, and produce simplistic definitions of policy decisions contrasted with operational decisions. What we must keep in mind is that we do not have policy and operational decisions in government. We have decisions, some of which are appropriate for judicial review, and some of which are not. What we need are the tools to assist us in making the distinction. For the time being we are working within a conceptual framework which, at the very least, should require the courts to formulate their reasons for deciding that a particular act is appropriate for review. I have identified several interdependent variables which I consider to be relevant to this determination. No doubt there are many others.

I have chosen to describe the first variable as "standards of conduct." To a very large degree, the reticence of the courts to review bureaucratic behaviour is due to their inability to identify an independent, external, pre-existing objective standard against which to assess the executive decision. Where the court is able to identify a superior bureaucratic standard pursuant to which the decision under review ought to have been exercised, it is able to assert that the fault of the latter consists of a departure from a standard. The court can thus avoid evaluating "fault" in terms of the abstract propriety of the conduct according to the personal view of the judge as to the correctness of the decision. The existence of a standard is important for several reasons. First, it reduces the risk that the legitimacy of judicial discretion will be questioned. Second, the court need not spend inordinate amounts of time and resources developing the standard against which to assess the bureaucratic conduct. Finally, the court, where it applies a superior bureaucratic standard, is in fact reinforcing the position of the superior bureaucrat, by adding a legal sanction to whatever internal disciplinary measures exist. Thus Lord Diplock in *Dorset Yacht* [*Co. Ltd. v. Home Office*, [1970] AC 1004 (Eng. HL)] could state that the role of the court was to deter the government employees from completely disregarding the interests of the escaped prisoners; and in *Anns*, the standard against which the inspector's conduct was assessed was to take reasonable care to observe that the government's *own* bylaws were observed.

The identification of an independent standard of conduct developed within the bureaucracy may be facilitated where the alleged negligence takes place in the context of "programmed decisions." This second variable acknowledges that the bureaucratic process may be described as a series of discretionary decisions with varying degrees of uniqueness. As decisions become routine, and must be made more frequently, it is less likely that discretion can be exercised, and the "correctness" of a particular programmed decision can be evaluated through a comparison with other decisions of the same class. The bureaucrat's own decision becomes the standard. In the foam insulation case, one might examine the governmental standard-setting process, including evaluative techniques, variables under inquiry, the identity of the participants and the independence of the research data, which was applied in the case of the several insulation products for which standards were set. These programmed decisions may provide an objective basis upon which to determine the "reasonableness" of the state conduct in the particular case of establishing a foam insulation standard.

The third variable which the courts have recognized as an element in the establishment of a legal duty of care is the degree of discretion exercised by the bureaucrat whose conduct is under inquiry. Even where a superior standard of conduct can be identified, it may be that the inferior bureaucratic conduct is characterized by substantial discretionary elements which point away from judicial review. While it is true that the mere presence of discretion will not preclude review, the court must be aware of the political risks which it runs were it to identify conflicting interests of the classes of persons likely to be affected by the decision, place a value or weight on those interests, and perhaps identify a general public interest in the pursuit of the activity in question. The court, even in this case, has standards which it can apply—the difficulty is that the criteria involve elements of social wisdom, political practicability, and economic expediency, whose application might expose the court to political retaliation and social criticism. As well, the self-defined role of the courts has been to deny the exercise of judicial discretion and, as the bureaucratic decision is characterized by increasing discretionary authority, it becomes difficult to disguise what the court is doing.

The fourth variable which should be considered focuses on the nature of the private interest affected by the bureaucratic activity. It is possible that the long history of judicial review of nuisance cases involving interference with use of land, and a similar willing-ness to review police enforcement practices, reflects judicial values which demand a greater degree of bureaucratic circumspection where land ownership or occupation, or individual freedom, are at stake. This consideration may have been influencing Linden J in *Johnston v. A.G. Can.* [(1981), 128 DLR (3d) 459 (Ont. HC)], who refused to follow an earlier decision denying the existence of a duty of care in similar circumstances. One explanation offered by Linden J was that in the former case the plaintiff suffered personal injuries, while in the latter the alleged loss was purely economic. It may be that the nature of the injuries in the foam insulation case, where they can be identified as the loss of the family home and serious risks of personal injury, will point towards judicial review.

A fifth variable which may be relevant in deciding if judicial review ought to take place looks to the *unintentional* nature of the government activity. Where a bureaucrat makes a deliberate choice to injure a particular class of individuals, or to expose that class to the risk of injury, the question as to whether the losers should be compensated has not been perceived as a question for the judiciary. In such cases, the decision will most likely have been authorized, and where the injury is deliberate, the combination of lawfulness and intentional infliction of injury suggests that political review will be the appropriate mechanism for redress. It is difficult to picture deliberate, lawful activity as wrongful in the context of the corrective justice model of law-making. As well, judicial sanctions imposed on deliberate governmental activity may result in retaliation, which may not take place where judicial review is restricted to unintentional conduct. It is always open to the bureaucracy to argue that it decided to expose a large class of homeowners to the risk of personal injury in order to expedite the establishment of a home insulation pro-gramme, and that this decision was authorized under the relevant statutory mandate.

The sixth variable involving judicial review looks to the nature of the government activity which is alleged to have been negligent. It seems that the courts will be much more willing to exercise a supervisory jurisdiction where the state is engaged in an activ-ity which can be identified as "commercial" in nature, as opposed to activities which are characterized as "governmental." The distinction, which admittedly is not an easy one, is based on a number of factors. First, the court, in assessing a commercial activity carried out by government will be able to turn to the behaviour and practice of private enter-prises as an independent, objective standard against which to gauge the reasonableness of the government behaviour. Secondly, where the state is engaged in commercial activ-ities in competition with private enterprise, the court may be concerned that the state not be given competitive advantages, and thus will subject the public enterprise to the same constraints as its private counterparts. Where, on the other hand, the state is engaged in providing a service which would not, for a variety of reasons, be produced through the market, the court may consider it inappropriate to impose market constraints. In the latter case, the traditional test of negligence which looks to the cost of injury prevention in light of the probability, nature and extent of the injury, gives rise to serious inconsis-tencies. The public, non-commercial enterprise does not necessarily operate subject to the pricing and budgetary constraints imposed by the costs of labour, capital and other inputs, and by market competition. Where the activity is commercial in nature, however, it may be subject to constraints analogous to those operating in private enterprises.

In addition, the state, where it is engaged in a commercial activity, may be able to pass on the costs of the negligence liability to the users of the government service or product. This loss allocation mechanism may not be as easy to implement in the case of non-commercial, governmental activities, where access to the service cannot be controlled to the same degree. In the case of commercial activities the loss will be borne, to some degree, by the users of the service or good. The beneficiaries of the government programme and policy decisions will, in the commercial context, be compensating the losers. This transfer from winners to losers may take place in "governmental" activities as well, but the redistribution is more likely to take place through pricing decisions in the provision of commercial services. In governmental activities the bureaucratic and political embarrassment accompanied by public, forced compensation may point away from a decision to allocate the costs of regulation to the beneficiaries of government decisions. Finally, the willingness of the court to review commercial governmental activities may be justified on the basis of protecting expectations of individuals who may find it difficult to distinguish between private and public enterprises when the latter are carrying on commercial activities.

The activity of the government in the foam insulation case runs from the creation of an energy conservation programme, to standard setting of product quality, to the encouragement of product purchases through information dissemination. The standard-setting process has been classified as a policy decision in several American cases, even though political scientists might describe this activity as administrative rather than policy-making in nature. Cases of government information transfer to encourage or facilitate private transactions have, however, been the subject of judicial review on several occasions. The explanation for the willingness of the court to review the government's role as an information broker is that to require the government to disseminate accurate information is a relatively non-intrusive judicial role. In many cases the transaction costs of the information transfer will be relatively insignificant, especially where, as in the foam insulation case, the state has decided to establish an information transfer system in the pursuit of its policy objectives. As well, the courts are quite familiar with the regulation of information transfer in the private sector. Thus, while the provision of information by the state in the case of insulation may not have been a "pure" commercial activity, the nature of the enterprise was such that the courts may be able to invoke private standards which they can apply to the governmental behaviour.

A court may, however, hesitate to impose liability on the state where the issue is not the duty to transfer information which the state possesses, but to investigate certain matters and acquire information which must then be transferred. In the latter case, the costs of information acquisition may suggest to the court that a private duty of care should not be established. The issue is a relative one, and in two recent cases the Federal Court has suggested that the information-gathering activities of Treasury Board officials and officials of the Food and Drug Directorate will be subject to judicial review.

A seventh variable which may influence a decision to impose civil liability on the state relates to the status or identity of the government actor. At the ultimate level of governmental decision-making, the court will be asked to assess the negligence of legislative acts—a responsibility which they deny absolutely. In most cases, however, the determination of bureaucratic status will require an assessment of the bureaucratic infra-structure

in which the decision was made, in an effort to determine the responsibility and authority of this bureaucrat and his relationship with other political actors. The requirement
that the court investigate the *actual* bureaucratic decision-making process and the *actual*
nature and extent of scrutiny of the decision by specific bureaucratic and political actors
is important for a number of reasons. As the behaviour of more senior bureaucrats is
scrutinized, it becomes increasingly likely that political and broad discretionary
decision-making will be involved. Further, where the court attempts to review the activities of more senior bureaucrats it may risk political retaliation, and thus it is not at all
surprising to discover that the majority of cases involving judicial review of governmental activity have involved municipal governments—the one tier of government which
cannot retaliate directly by withdrawing its operations from judicial review. Finally, by
demanding that the government identify the bureaucrat or group of bureaucrats who
participated in the decision under review, the court will encourage political accountability where appropriate. The government can identify a lower level bureaucrat where it
wants to minimize direct political responsibility, but when it does so, it risks legal liability. At the same time, where the state points to bureaucratic seniority to avoid legal responsibility, it increases the likelihood of political responsibility.

The question as to the status and identity of the bureaucrat who made the decision
under review is complemented by judicial concern that courts not interfere officiously in
broadly based social disputes which may be resolved through non-legal processes. The
availability of limited judicial resources is only one aspect of this attitude. The courts are
also aware of the risk of conflicting judicial/political solutions to the dispute. The availability of alternative sources of accountability—whether through political action or
through the doctrines of ministerial and bureaucratic responsibility—has been noted by
the courts as a relevant factor in deciding whether to create a private right of action.

Possibly the most significant factor which the courts recognize in determining whether a private legal duty of care should be imposed on the bureaucracy is the requirement
of an individualized wrong. The nature of corrective justice is that it is designed to redress a perceived wrong which one party has committed against another. This suggests
that the alleged wrong must be individualized in nature—there must be an "individualization of responsibility" for the alleged negligence founded on a direct relation between
the state employee and an individual member of the public. In fact, in almost all cases in
which the state has been found liable for the acts of its employees the alleged negligent
behaviour occurred in this "one-on-one" bilateral relationship.

This requirement of individualization of harm can be justified on a number of
grounds. First, the courts ameliorate the interjurisdictional tension between the judiciary
and executive when they restrict themselves to compensating individual wrongs. Second,
the requirement of an individual nexus reduces the potential impact of the decision on
the exercise of broadly described bureaucratic discretion. Third, by requiring an individualistic aspect, the courts avoid the substantial administrative costs of determining
the identity of numerous claimants, and the nature and extent of their alleged losses. As
well, the existing procedural rules and administrative structure of the court system are
singularly ill-suited to the resolution of group wrongs. Fourth, the courts recognize the
potential instrumental effect of damage awards which, where they involve increasing
numbers of plaintiffs, may have a significant prospective, instrumental influence on

bureaucratic behaviour. In addition, the courts are aware that as the number of losers increases, the prospect of political or parliamentary accountability increases. Finally, where a large number of potential losers exists, the ability of the court to entertain a range of interests in its decision-making process may be limited. The "losers" are not a homogeneous group, and the technical and quite artificial rules of evidence and procedure may distort the adequate representation of these disparate interests.

The tenth variable is probably the judicial favourite. The decision of the state to engage in certain activities will often involve an allocation of public resources, and the decision will be made in the context of competing claims for government largesse and programmes, both from within and from without the bureaucracy. If the alleged negligent decision involved the allocation of resources among competing claims for social resources, or if the impact of the decision will influence future resource allocation decisions, the decision is less likely to be reviewed. Once the resource allocation decision has taken place, then the inferior decision as to how the activity should be carried out may be reviewed.

I have no difficulty accepting the general proposition that resource allocation is a function which almost by definition will require that particular interests be sacrificed. It is also difficult to see how the reasonableness of a particular resource allocation decision could be objectively assessed by a court. At the same time, the court should appreciate that resource allocation is a question of degree; and that the state can obtain insurance to spread the costs of its activities.

The courts have also turned to the misfeasance/nonfeasance distinction as a relevant variable in determining whether to impose a private duty of care on bureaucratic actors, although it is unclear whether the distinction is still doctrinally correct after the decision of the House of Lords in *Anns v. Merton London Borough Council*. At best it may have been a categorical relative of the policy/operational distinction. The distinction between nonfeasance and misfeasance is a difficult one to draw at best, and adds little to the analysis of the propriety of judicial review of state behaviour. None the less, judicial deference to bureaucratic "nonfeasance" may be understood as a reflection of several concerns. First, where a bureaucrat has acted, it may be possible to use his own intended behaviour as an objective standard against which to assess the reasonableness of his actual behaviour. Second, where an alleged loss is incurred as a result of governmental *inactivity*, the injury may be a foregone opportunity which may be viewed as a less substantial injury than an actual incurred loss. Finally, a concern with "pure" inaction will often result in an inquiry as to whether the defendant's conduct created or increased the risk of injury. This risk creation concept brings us to the final variable which I have identified in the judicial decision to impose a legal duty of care on a state employee—the concept of reliance.

The courts appear to react to two categories of reliance. The first is direct reliance, common in the "individualized wrong" discussed earlier, where a member of the public relies upon acts or representations of a particular bureaucrat. The second is what may be called institutional reliance—the creation of an environment by the state in which members of the public assume that the state will be taking adequate precautions to ensure that their interests will be safeguarded. Thus in cases of pure omission the court may be willing to impose liability where the state has established an institutional framework upon which the public relies and where an individual refrains from adopting alternate measures to reduce the risk of injury, or from insuring against the risk.

The reliance issue is, I think, a central concept in the decision to impose a legal duty on the bureaucrat. It reflects the overriding corrective justice philosophy which operates in this area, in that it demands a bilateral relationship. The bureaucrat or bureaucracy assumes responsibility for a certain activity which creates a reciprocal sense of trust and dependence. More generally, we may be able to see a more general interest in compensating disappointed individuals whose expectations were created by a governmental, institutional arrangement, and who relied on that arrangement to protect their interests.

NOTE

Cohen continued to develop these themes in later articles. See Cohen and Smith, "Entitlement and the Body Politic: Rethinking Negligence in Public Law" (1986), 64 *Can. Bar Rev.* 1; Cohen, "Suing the State" (1990), 40 *UTLJ* 630; and Cohen, "Government Liability for Economic Losses: The Case of Regulatory Failure" (1992), 20 *Can. Bus. LJ* 215. As far as the urea formaldehyde litigation was concerned, the most prominent of numerous lawsuits was unsuccessful after the longest civil trial in Québec history. The Québec Superior Court judge who heard the case (lasting over 8 years and costing an estimated $20 million in legal fees) delivered a 1,200-page judgment on December 12, 1991, holding that the 6 families who were suing in a test case on behalf of 7,200 other Québec residents had not proved a connection between urea formaldehyde and the physical harm alleged. The Québec government paid the plaintiff's costs. The Court of Appeal affirmed this judgment. See *Berthiaume v. Val Royal Lasalle Ltée* (1991), [1992] RJQ 76 (SC); aff'd. [1996] RJQ 46 (CA). In reading the materials that follow, keep Cohen's concerns and the lessons of this litigation in mind.

MONEYS MISTAKENLY PAID TO AND BENEFITS MISTAKENLY CONFERRED ON STATUTORY AUTHORITIES

As far as any claims against the government are concerned, there is intuitive appeal in the notion that monetary relief should be most readily available in situations where payments were made mistakenly. However, traditionally, the Supreme Court of Canada accepted that, subject to very limited exceptions (such as compulsion), moneys paid under a mistake of law (as opposed to a mistake of fact) were not recoverable, irrespective of whether the context was private or public: *Hydro Electric Commission of Nepean v. Ontario Hydro*, [1982] 1 SCR 347 (Ont.). As a consequence, there was considerable confusion as to when (if at all) there was a claim for moneys paid under an unconstitutional statute, an *ultra vires* bylaw or regulation, an unlawful agency decision or order, or by reason of a mistaken interpretation or misapplication of a statutory provision.

Fortunately, given the difficulties at the margin of distinguishing for these purposes between a mistake of law and a mistake of fact and the general lack of a sound policy foundation for any such differentiation, the Supreme Court has now repudiated this position for both private and public law purposes, and adopted the position that the recovery of moneys paid mistakenly should no longer depend on whether the error is one of fact as opposed to law.

On the other hand, in *Air Canada v. British Columbia*, [1989] 1 SCR 1161 (BC), the court split on whether there were special reasons that such recovery should be more limited in public than in private law. Some members of the court in that case accepted that, whether the payments in issue were made mistakenly or not, there were distinctions to be drawn for the purposes of recovery among the various categories of payments to state authorities. Specifically, it was suggested that recovery of payments made under unconstitutional statutes was more restricted than where the payment resulted from an *ultra vires* (in its administrative law sense) regulation, bylaw, or order. In substantial part, that position depends on a perception that, especially in the case of unconstitutionally required payments, there are policy reasons for restricting recovery based on considerations of disruption to the public treasury.

In reading the materials that follow, keep this now discredited position in mind and consider whether and, if so, to what extent such differentiations are justifiable in this domain. For example, should recovery be more readily available for payments made under an *ultra vires* municipal bylaw (see, for example, *Air Canada v. Dorval (City)*, [1985] 1 SCR 861 (Que.)) than for those made under an unconstitutional statute?

Kingstreet Investments Ltd. v. New Brunswick (Department of Finance)
[2007] 1 SCR 3 (NB)

[At issue here was a claim for the recovery of all money paid under an unconstitutional user charge applied to New Brunswick nightclubs when purchasing alcohol. At first instance, the New Brunswick Court of Queen's Bench, applying restitutionary principles, denied recovery on the basis that the nightclubs had passed the tax on to their patrons. The Court of Appeal allowed the appeal in part, denying recovery for moneys paid prior to the commencement of legal proceedings, holding that those payments had not been paid under protest and also relying on the passing-on defence. The case came before the Supreme Court of Canada on an appeal from the nightclubs and a cross-appeal by the Crown.]

BASTARACHE J delivered the judgment of the Court: ...

Restitution for Ultra Vires Taxes

Constitutional Remedy

[13] This case is about the consequences of the injustice created where a government attempts to retain unconstitutionally collected taxes. Because of the constitutional rule at play, the claim can be dealt with more simply than one for unjust enrichment in the private domain. Taxes were illegally collected. Taxes must be returned subject to limitation periods and remedial legislation, when such a measure is deemed appropriate. As will later be discussed, no passing-on defence should be entertained.

[14] The Court's central concern must be to guarantee respect for constitutional principles. One such principle is that the Crown may not levy a tax except with authority of the Parliament or the legislature: *Constitution Act, 1867*, ss. 53 and 90. This principle of "no taxation without representation" is central to our conception of democracy and

the rule of law. As Hogg and Monahan explain, this principle "ensures not merely that the executive branch is subject to the rule of law, but also that the executive branch must call the legislative branch into session to raise taxes" (P.W. Hogg and P.J. Monahan, *Liability of the Crown* (3rd ed. 2000), at 246. See also P.W. Hogg, *Constitutional Law of Canada* (loose-leaf ed.), vol. 2, at 55-16 and 55-17; *Eurig [Estate (Re),* [1998] 2 SCR 565 (Ont.)] at para. 31, *per* Major J).

[15] When the government collects and retains taxes pursuant to *ultra vires* legislation, it undermines the rule of law. To permit the Crown to retain an *ultra vires* tax would condone a breach of this most fundamental constitutional principle. As a result, a citizen who has made a payment pursuant to *ultra vires* legislation has a right to restitution: P. Birks, "Restitution from the Executive: A Tercentenary Footnote to the Bill of Rights," in P.D. Finn, ed., *Essays on Restitution* (1990), c. 6, at 168.

[16] This Court has previously recognized this right. In *Amax Potash Ltd. v. Government of Saskatchewan,* [1977] 2 SCR 576 (Sask.), the Court struck down a provision that purported to bar recovery of *ultra vires* taxes. At 590, Dickson J (as he then was) based his holding on constitutional principles:

> Section 5(7) of *The Proceedings against the Crown Act,* in my opinion, has much broader implications than mere Crown immunity. In the present context, it directly concerns the right to tax. It affects, therefore, the division of powers under *The British North America Act, 1867.* It also brings into question the right of a Province, or the federal Parliament for that matter, to act in violation of the Canadian Constitution. Since it is manifest that if either the federal Parliament or a provincial Legislature can tax beyond the limit of its powers, and by prior or *ex post facto* legislation give itself immunity from such illegal act, it could readily place itself in the same position as if the act had been done within proper constitutional limits. To allow moneys collected under compulsion, pursuant to an *ultra vires* statute, to be retained would be tantamount to allowing the provincial Legislature to do indirectly what it could not do directly, and by covert means to impose illegal burdens.

[17] In *Woolwich Equitable Building Society v. Inland Revenue Commissioners,* [1993] AC 70 (HL, Eng.), the House of Lords has also recognized a right to restitution for payments made pursuant to *ultra vires* taxes. Without even referring to unjust enrichment, Lord Goff held, at 172, that restitution was available as a matter of "common justice":

> ... the retention by the state of taxes unlawfully exacted is particularly obnoxious, because it is one of the most fundamental principles of our law—enshrined in a famous constitutional document, the Bill of Rights 1688—that taxes should not be levied without the authority of Parliament; and full effect can only be given to that principle if the return of taxes exacted under an unlawful demand can be enforced as a matter of right.

[18] However, the general availability of restitution for *ultra vires* taxes has to date not been clearly established. In *Air Canada [v. British Columbia,* [1989] 1 SCR 1161 (BC)], La Forest J was of the opinion that policy considerations operated to take claims for taxes paid pursuant to unlawful legislation outside of the restitutionary context. He proposed a general rule that the Crown should be immune to claims for recovery of unconstitutional and *ultra vires* levies. But La Forest J did not command a majority in that case and so the status of his proposed immunity rule was never clear. It is necessary,

therefore, to consider why such an immunity rule should be rejected before discussing the proper basis for restitution in this case.

Rejecting the Immunity Rule

[19] In *obiter* statements pronounced in *Air Canada*, La Forest J explained on behalf of three members of a six-judge panel that, while

> [i]t is clear that the principles of unjust enrichment can operate against a government to ground restitutionary recovery … *in this kind of case, where the effect of an unconstitutional or ultra vires statute is in issue, I am of the opinion that special considerations operate to take this case out of the normal restitutionary framework, and require a rule responding to the specific underlying policy concerns in this area.* [Emphasis added; at 1203.]

[20] Like Robertson JA, I accept Wilson J's rationale for rejecting a rule which would immunize public authorities from restitutionary claims with respect to monies paid under invalid legislation. Wilson J was of the view that "[w]here the payments were made pursuant to an unconstitutional statute there is no legitimate basis on which they can be retained" (*Air Canada*, at 1216). As Professor Hogg explained at 55-13:

> Where a tax has been paid to government under a statute subsequently held to be unconstitutional, can the tax be recovered by the taxpayer? In principle, the answer should be yes. The government's right to the tax was destroyed by the holding of unconstitutionality, and the tax should be refunded to the taxpayer. [Footnote omitted.]

This very principle was recognized by a unanimous Court in *Reference re Goods and Services Tax*, [1992] 2 SCR 445 (Alta.), where it was held that an *ultra vires* law cannot constitute a juristic reason for the state's enrichment.

[21] As Wilson J explained in dissent in *Air Canada*, the immunity rule proposed by La Forest J amounts to saying that "the principle should be reversed *for policy reasons* in the case of payments made to governmental bodies" (1215 (emphasis in original)). Those policy reasons, according to La Forest J, included the fact that the unconstitutional tax at issue in *Air Canada* came close to raising a merely technical issue. Relying on this passage, the trial judge in the present case held that the impugned regulation was deficient only in form, insofar as it resulted from the Province's failure to tailor the charge to the cost of regulating the licensees. In my view, privileging policy considerations in the case of *ultra vires* taxes threatens to undermine the rule of law.

[22] Professor Hogg has explained that

> the constitutional principle that ought to dominate all others in this context is the principle that the Crown may not levy a tax except by the authority of the Parliament or Legislature. This principle, enshrined in the Bill of Rights of 1688, ensures not merely that the executive branch is subject to the rule of law, but also that the executive branch must call the legislative branch into session to raise taxes (and vote supply). To permit the Crown to retain a tax that has been levied without legislative authority is to condone a breach of one of the most fundamental constitutional principles. [Footnote omitted; 55-16 and 55-17.]

[23] Professors Hogg and Monahan argue, at 246-47, that permitting taxpayers to recover taxes paid pursuant to unconstitutional statutes is more consistent with the well-settled rule that the Crown may recover monies paid out of the consolidated revenue fund without legislative authority, where the expenditure was not authorized. Such has always been the case,

> even if it was made under a mistake of law, and even if the recipient could have raised the defences of estoppel or change of position to an action by a private plaintiff. In this situation, the governing rule is the fundamental constitutional principle that prohibits the Crown from spending public funds except under the authority of the Parliament or Legislature. To apply the ordinary rules of restitution so as to render an unauthorized expenditure irrecoverable would in effect permit an important constitutional safeguard to be evaded. *The same reasoning ought to apply when it is the subject suing the Crown to recover a payment made to the Crown, since the same constitutional principle is in issue.* [Emphasis added; footnotes omitted; 247.]

[24] If the constitutional rule requiring the Crown to only spend public funds under legislative authority has sufficient weight to compel recovery of an unauthorized expenditure by the Crown, notwithstanding the principles of unjust enrichment, then it is difficult to understand a common law bar to the recovery of unconstitutionally imposed taxes. Presumably, the constitutional limitations on the Crown's power to spend are of equal importance as the constitutional limitations on the Crown's power to raise revenue. In my view, these principles are really two sides of the same coin.

[25] Another policy reason given by La Forest J for the immunity rule was a concern for fiscal inefficiency and fiscal chaos (1207). My view is that concerns regarding potential fiscal chaos are best left to Parliament and the legislatures to address, should they choose to do so. Where the state leads evidence before the court establishing a real concern about fiscal chaos, it is open to the court to suspend the declaration of invalidity to enable government to address the issue. In *Eurig*, Major J suspended a declaration of invalidity for six months. Because, in that case, unconstitutionally levied probate fees were used to defray the costs of court administration in the Province, he expressed concern that an immediate deprivation of this source of revenue might have harmful consequences for the administration of justice. Moreover, this Court's decision in *Air Canada* demonstrates that it will be open to Parliament and to the legislatures to enact valid taxes and apply them retroactively, so as to limit or deny recovery of *ultra vires* taxes. Obviously, such legislation must also be constitutionally sound.

                                          . . .

[28] Turning to La Forest J's concern about potential fiscal inefficiency, I agree with Wilson J in *Air Canada*, where she queries:

> Why should the individual taxpayer, as opposed to taxpayers as a whole, bear the burden of government's mistake? I would respectfully suggest that it is grossly unfair that X, who may not be (as in this case) a large corporate enterprise, should absorb the cost of government's unconstitutional act. If it is appropriate for the courts to adopt some kind of policy in order to protect government against itself (and I cannot say that the idea particularly appeals to me) it should be one which distributes the loss fairly across the public. The loss should not fall on the totally innocent taxpayer whose only fault is that it paid what the legislature improperly said was due. [1215]

[29] Concerns about fiscal chaos and inefficiency should not be incorporated into the applicable rule. I agree with Professor Birks that

> [s]o far as concerns the fear of wholesale reopening of past transactions and the danger of fiscal disruption, the principle of legality [including that government must tax with legislative authorization and within its constitutional limitations] outweighs those dangers and requires that judges leave it to legislatures to impose what restrictions on the right of restitution they think necessary, wise and proper. At all events, a merely hypothetical danger of disruption certainly does not warrant an undiscriminating denial of restitution. [204]

[30] For these reasons, I would not adopt the general immunity rule proposed by La Forest J. It is important to note, however, that La Forest J had envisioned the rule against recovery of *ultra vires* taxes as operating outside of the private law context. In his view, the special policy concerns meant that the issue of recovery of *ultra vires* taxes was outside of the normal unjust enrichment and restitution framework … .

[31] Having rejected the immunity rule, this raises the question of whether claims for the recovery of unconstitutional taxes should be analysed on the basis of the private law rules of unjust enrichment or constitutional principles. As explained above, the recovery of unconstitutional taxes is warranted on the basis of limitations to the state's constitutional authority to tax, and in particular on the fundamental constitutional principle that there shall be no taxation without representation (see Birks, at c. 6; Hogg, at 55-16; and Hogg and Monahan, at 246-47). This would place the restitutionary right clearly within a public law context. However, there is no question that the law of unjust enrichment, although developed in the private law context, can apply to public bodies. Indeed, the present case was argued at the lower courts and before this Court on the grounds of unjust enrichment. I must therefore discuss why, in my view, an unjust enrichment analysis is inappropriate in this case before setting out the proper restitutionary basis for the repayment of *ultra vires* taxes.

Basis for the Constitutional Remedy: Why an Unjust Enrichment Framework Is Inappropriate

[32] Restitution is a tool of corrective justice. When a transfer of value between two parties is normatively defective, restitution functions to correct that transfer by restoring parties to their pre-transfer positions. In *Peel (Regional Municipality) v. Canada*, [1992] 3 SCR 762 (Ont.), McLachlin J (as she then was) neatly encapsulated this normative framework: "The concept of 'injustice' in the context of the law of restitution harkens back to the Aristotelian notion of correcting a balance or equilibrium that had been disrupted" (804).

[33] There are at least two distinct categories of restitution: (1) restitution for wrongdoing; and (2) restitution for unjust enrichment: P.D. Maddaugh and J.D. McCamus, *The Law of Restitution* (loose-leaf ed.), at 3-7. This case raises the separate notion of restitution based on the constitutional principle that taxes should not be levied without proper legal authority. The first category is not readily applicable here since, in the case of *ultra vires* taxes enacted in good faith, it cannot be said that the government was acting as a "wrong-doer." The choice, then, is between restitution for unjust enrichment or restitution based on constitutional grounds.

[34] The Province submits that, from a moral and public policy perspective, it cannot be said to have unjustly benefited from an enrichment as a result of the *ultra vires* charges. I would not decide this appeal as a matter of unjust enrichment. The taxpayers in this case has [*sic*] recourse to a remedy as a matter of constitutional right. This remedy is in fact the only appropriate remedy because it raises important constitutional principles which would be ignored by treating the claim under another category of restitution. Claims of unjust enrichment against the government may still be appropriate in certain circumstances (see *Pacific National Investments Ltd. v. Victoria (City)*, [2004] 3 SCR 575, 2004 SCC 75 (BC)). Nevertheless, it is my view that the analytical framework of the modern doctrine of unjust enrichment is inappropriate in this case.

[35] In a colloquial sense, it might be said that the retention of improperly collected taxes unjustly enriches governments. However, a technical interpretation of "benefit" and "loss" is hard to apply in tax recovery cases. Furthermore, in the context of this case, the unjust enrichment framework adds an unnecessary layer of complexity to the real legal issues. Some of the components of the modern doctrine are of little use to a principled disposition of the matter, but are rather liable to confuse the proper application of the key principles of constitutional law at issue.

[36] The application of private law principles in the realm of public and constitutional law is not without its difficulties. These difficulties have in the past been resolved by a flexible application of the unjust enrichment principle. McLachlin J had explained in *Peel* that the three-part formulation of the unjust enrichment principle was capable of going beyond the traditional categories of recovery and of allowing the law to develop in a flexible way as required to meet changing perceptions of justice. This restitutionary framework was recently restated and refined in *Garland v. Consumers' Gas Co.*, [2004] 1 SCR 629, 2004 SCC 25 (Ont.). *Garland* established a two-part analysis for determining whether there was a juristic reason for the enrichment that should operate to deny recovery. First, the plaintiff is required to show that no established category of juristic reason for the enrichment exists. If no reason exists, the burden shifts to the defendant to show that there is some other reason why recovery should be denied. At this point of the analysis, the Court explicitly recognized that the juristic reasons for the enrichment had to be considered in light of the reasonable expectation of the parties and certain public policy considerations (para. 46). It is at this second stage of the test that courts would weigh the equities in the particular circumstances of each case.

[37] McLachlin J had previously explained in *Peel* that

> [t]he courts' concern to strike an appropriate balance between predictability in the law and justice in the individual case has led them in this area, as in others, to choose a middle course between the extremes of inflexible rules and case by case "palm tree" justice. The middle course consists in adhering to legal principles, but recognizing that those principles must be sufficiently flexible to permit recovery where justice so requires having regard to the reasonable expectations of the parties in all the circumstances of the case as well as to public policy. [802]

[38] The *Garland* approach is, as one can see, very complex; it requires that courts look only to *proper* policy considerations. By proper policy considerations, I mean those that have traditionally informed the development of restitutionary law. Otherwise, they

risk turning the test into a subjective analysis that has less to do with legal reasoning than with the dispensing of "palm tree" justice. As previously explained, La Forest J was prepared to immunize public bodies in *Air Canada* where monies were paid pursuant to an unconstitutional statute for reasons of public policy. He explained that "[c]hief among these are the protection of the treasury, and a recognition of the reality that if the tax were refunded, modern government would be driven to the inefficient course of reimposing it either on the same, or on a new generation of taxpayers, to finance the operations of government" (1207). The question in the present case became, ultimately, whether such concerns are properly considered within the *Garland* test. In my view, they are not. Considerations related to preserving the public purse do not properly fall within the second branch of the juristic reason analysis, which is more concerned with broad principles of fairness. In *Garland*, for example, the overriding public policy concern was ensuring that criminals do not profit from their crime (para. 57). This is not to say that any and all fairness considerations are appropriate. As I said above, they must be rooted in the policy considerations that are traditionally found in unjust enrichment cases.

[39] For the above reasons, I would conclude that the ordinary principles of unjust enrichment should not be applied to claims for the recovery of monies paid pursuant to a statute held to be unconstitutional. I do not therefore need to address in any length the distinction between mistake of law and mistake of fact, which used to be of significance in unjust enrichment cases for mistaken payments. Traditionally, although monies paid under mutual mistake of fact were recoverable, monies paid under mutual mistake of law were not. However, this Court has abandoned the distinction between mistake of fact and mistake of law as it applies to the law of unjust enrichment: see *Air Canada; Canadian Pacific Air Lines Ltd. v. British Columbia*, [1989] 1 SCR 1133 (BC); and *Pacific National Investments*. There can be no doubt that the ordinary principles of unjust enrichment now apply in cases of payments made pursuant to mutual mistake of law. While this point perhaps needed to be clarified, it is of little moment in this case given that unjust enrichment is an inappropriate framework for restitution.

[40] Restitution for *ultra vires* taxes does not fit squarely within either of the established categories of restitution. The better view is that it comprises a third category distinct from unjust enrichment. Actions for recovery of taxes collected without legal authority and actions of unjust enrichment both address concerns of restitutionary justice, but these remedies developed in our legal system along separate paths for distinct purposes. The action for recovery of taxes is firmly grounded, as a public law remedy in a constitutional principle stemming from democracy's earliest attempts to circumscribe government's power within the rule of law. Unjust enrichment, on the other hand, originally evolved from the common law action of *indebitatus assumpsit* as a means of granting plaintiffs relief for quasi-contractual damages (Maddaugh and McCamus, at 1-4; Goff and Jones, *The Law of Restitution* (4th ed. 1993), at 7; Peel, at 784 and 788, *per* McLachlin J).

[41] From a comparative perspective, it is interesting to note that in Quebec our Court has expressed the view that actions for recovery of illegally collected taxes could be brought by the more simple route that I suggest. In its opinion, such claims could be brought under art. 1491 of the *Civil Code of Québec*, SQ 1991, c. 64, or under the predecessor provisions, arts. 1047 and 1048 of the *Civil Code of Lower Canada*, as actions for "undue payment" (*Ross v. The King* (1902), 32 SCR 532 (Que.); *Abel Skiver Farm Corp. v.*

Town of Sainte-Foy, [1983] 1 SCR 403 (Que.), at 423, *per* Beetz J; *Willmor Discount Corp. v. Vaudreuil (City)*, [1994] 2 SCR 210 (Que.), at 218, *per* Gonthier J; see also J-L. Baudouin and P.-G. Jobin, *Les obligations* (6th ed. 2005), at 556-58; *Ville de Sept-Îles v. Lussier*, [1993] RJQ 2717 (CA)).

Passing-On Defence

[42] Robertson JA found that the only possible defence the Province could raise in the present case was that the appellants had passed on the cost of the charge (paras. 46-48). The basic premise of the passing-on defence is that if the taxpayer has passed on the burden of the tax payments to others, usually via price increases charged to its customers, the taxpayer has not suffered a deprivation, the taxing authority's enrichment was not at its expense, and it would receive a windfall if it were awarded recovery. However, unlike Robertson JA, I would reject the passing-on defence in the context of the recovery of taxes paid pursuant to *ultra vires* legislation.

[43] La Forest J would have applied the defence, if necessary, so as to deny recovery in *Air Canada*. He found that

> the evidence supports that the airlines had passed on to their customers the burden of the tax imposed upon them. The law of restitution is not intended to provide windfalls to plaintiffs who have suffered no loss. Its function is to ensure that where a plaintiff has been deprived of wealth that is either in his possession or would have accrued for his benefit, it is restored to him. The measure of restitutionary recovery is the gain the province made at the airlines' expense. If the airlines have not shown that they bore the burden of the tax, then they have not made out their claim. What the province received is relevant only in so far as it was received at the airlines' expense. [1202-3]

[44] There are three major criticisms of the passing-on defence: first, that it is inconsistent with the basic premise of restitution law; second, that it is economically misconceived; and third, that the task of determining the ultimate location of the burden of a tax is exceedingly difficult and constitutes an inappropriate basis for denying relief.

[45] The defence of passing on has developed almost exclusively in the context of recovery of taxes and other charges paid under a mistake of law. If, as La Forest J suggests in *Air Canada*, "[t]he law of restitution is not intended to provide windfalls to plaintiffs who have suffered no loss" (1202), then the defence ought to have arisen in other contexts as well. At the very least, the defence of passing on should also apply to mistaken payments, whether of fact or law, but such has generally not been the case in Canada (see Maddaugh and McCamus, at 11-46). Professors Maddaugh and McCamus suggest that the reason the defence has not been applied outside the context of *ultra vires* taxes is because it is inconsistent with the basic principles of restitutionary law. They argue that "the mere fact that the taxpayer has mistakenly paid, with its own money, the revenue authority is sufficient to establish an unjust enrichment at the plaintiff's expense. As between the taxpayer and the Crown, the question of whether the taxpayer has been able to recoup its loss from some other source is simply irrelevant" (11-45).

[Bastarache J then found support for this position in *Commissioner of State Revenue (Victoria) v. Royal Insurance Australia Ltd.* (1994), 182 CLR 51, a High Court of Australia decision involving the overpayment of taxes, not the levying of an unconstitutional tax.]

[47] … As mentioned earlier, restitutionary principles provide for restoration of "what has been taken or received from the plaintiff without justification" (*Royal Insurance*, at 71). Restitution law is not concerned by the possibility of the plaintiff obtaining a windfall precisely because it is not founded on the concept of compensation for loss.

[48] In addition to being contrary to the basic principles of restitution law, the defence of passing on has also been criticized for being economically misconceived and for creating serious difficulties of proof. In *British Columbia v. Canadian Forest Products Ltd.*, [2004] 2 SCR 74, 2004 SCC 38 (BC), LeBel J, writing in dissent but not on this point, commented on the inherent difficulties in a commercial marketplace of proving that the loss was not passed on to consumers. LeBel J noted that every commercial entity could be accused of passing on all or part of any damages suffered by it, by its own rates or charges to its customer. This is because it is difficult to determine what effect a change in a company's prices will have on its total sales. Unless the elasticity of demand is very low, the plaintiff is bound to suffer a loss, either because of reduced sales or because of reduced profit per sale. Where elasticity is low, and it can be demonstrated that the tax was passed on through higher prices that did not affect profits per sale or the volume of sales, it would be impossible to demonstrate that the plaintiff could not or would not have raised its prices had the tax not been imposed, thereby increasing its profits even further. LeBel J referred to these various figures as "virtually unascertainable" (para. 205, citing White J in *Hanover Shoe, Inc. v. United Shoe Machinery Corp.*, 392 US 481 (1968), at 493). LeBel J ultimately concluded that "[t]he passing on defence would, in effect, result in an argument that no damages are ever recoverable in commercial litigation because anyone who claimed to have suffered damages but was still solvent had obviously found a way to pass the loss on" (para. 206, citing Ground J in *Law Society of Upper Canada v. Ernst & Young* (2002), 59 OR (3d) 214 (SCJ), at para. 40).

[49] Although LeBel J was criticizing the application of the passing-on defence in tort law, his criticisms are equally appropriate, if perhaps not more so, in the context of restitution law. This is because, unlike restitution law, tort law is premised on the concept of compensation for loss, such that concerns about potential windfalls are appropriate.

[50] Recognition of the defence in *Air Canada* has also led to uncertainty in its application. In *Canadian Pacific Air Lines*, released contemporaneously with *Air Canada*, the defence was applied to the claim for recovery of a beverage tax, which the Court noted was imposed on passengers, not on the airline. The airline was simply a collector of the tax. This holding is uncontentious insofar as the airline was merely collecting the tax as an agent of the Crown. In my view, the defence of passing on was not necessary to arrive at that conclusion. In the same case, the airline was allowed to recover the social services tax paid on the value of the aircraft and aircraft parts with no discussion of the defence. However, La Forest J in *Air Canada* found the defence to be applicable to the tax on fuel so as to deny recovery. The holdings in these cases with respect to the application of the passing-on defence are difficult to reconcile.

[51] For the above reasons, I would reject the passing-on defence in its entirety.

Application of the Doctrine of Protest and Compulsion

[52] Robertson JA granted recovery of the illegal user charge on the basis that it was paid under protest. This is another issue that had posed problems in the context of recovery of money paid under an *ultra vires* tax. The doctrine of protest and compulsion functions as an exception to the passing-on defence. As Professors Maddaugh and McCamus explain, "the defence [of passing on] would no longer be available once the taxpayer signaled, through protest, that the unlawfulness of the taxation measure was being challenged" (11-44 and 11-45). Thus, even though Robertson JA accepted the Province's argument that the appellants had passed on the cost of the tax, he found that the payments made under protest and compulsion were recoverable. Because I have rejected the passing-on defence as generally inapplicable in the context of *ultra vires* taxes, it is not necessary to deal with the doctrine of protest and compulsion. I think some general comments will, however, be useful.

[53] In my view, the doctrine of protest and compulsion is simply not applicable to cases such as the present. This flows from the constitutional basis for the right of restitution in this case: that the Crown should not be able to retain taxes that lack legal authority. It therefore matters little whether the taxpayer paid under protest and compulsion. If the law proves to be invalid, then there should be no burden on the taxpayer to prove that they were paying under protest. Such a finding would be inconsistent with the nature of the cause of action in this case. As Lord Goff said in *Woolwich*, at 172, "full effect can only be given to that principle [that taxes should not be levied without proper authority] if the return of taxes exacted under an unlawful demand can be enforced as a matter of right." The right of the party to obtain restitution for taxes paid under *ultra vires* legislation does not depend on the behaviour of each party but on the objective consideration of whether the tax was exacted without proper legal authority.

[54] I also have concerns about the applicability of the doctrine of protest and compulsion to cases where the tax, although collected pursuant to valid legislation, was misapplied in relation to the taxpayer. The tax is valid, but the taxpayer should never have had to pay it. The problem, in my view, stems from the notion of compulsion in the context of payments made pursuant to law. Duress first found recognition as a limited ground for the recovery of damages against an intimidating party in tort. A contract entered into under duress was held to be voidable at the instance of the coerced party (see Maddaugh and McCamus, at 26-2 and 26-3). The recovery of benefits conferred under duress is achieved via an action in restitution (*ibid.*, at 26-6.1). Duress vitiates the voluntary nature of the payment.

[55] Professors Maddaugh and McCamus explain, at 11-20, that "if one is mistaken about the law, one pays because one believes one is obliged to do so by law. If one is responding to duress, it must be that the individual believes or strongly suspects that there is no legal requirement to pay." However, in my opinion, the absence of duress on the part of the taxpayer should not be an important factor. It is not up to the taxpayer but rather to the party that makes and administers the law to bear the responsibility of ensuring the validity and applicability of the law (see also *Ontario (Liquor Control Board)*). I agree with Wilson J in *Air Canada* that

payments made under unconstitutional legislation are not "voluntary" in a sense which should prejudice the taxpayer. The taxpayer, assuming the validity of the statute as I believe it is entitled to do, considers itself obligated to pay. Citizens are expected to be law-abiding. They are expected to pay their taxes. Pay first and object later is the general rule. The payments are made pursuant to a perceived obligation to pay which results from the combined presumption of constitutional validity of duly enacted legislation and the holding out of such validity by the legislature. In such circumstances I consider it quite unrealistic to expect the taxpayer to make its payments "under protest." Any taxpayer paying taxes exigible under a statute which it has no reason to believe or suspect is other than valid should be viewed as having paid pursuant to the statutory obligation to do so. [1214-15]

Although made in the context of *ultra vires* legislation, Wilson J's comments are equally applicable to the situation where a taxpayer is required to pay a levy because of an incorrect application of the law. In either case, the protest requirement is inappropriate.

[56] There is a second concern which arises in cases where monies have been paid to public authorities pursuant to unconstitutional legislation or as a result of the misapplication of an otherwise valid law. In *Eurig*, for example, payment under protest and the commencement of legal proceedings was held to be sufficient to trigger the exception allowing recovery. The end result is that whenever a tax is declared *ultra vires*, only the successful litigants will be granted recovery of the unconstitutional charges. All other similarly situated persons will not benefit from the Court's holding. This raises concerns about horizontal equity that are similar to those raised by the doctrine of constitutional exemption. This Court has alluded to such concerns in *Mackin v. New Brunswick (Minister of Finance)*, [2002] 1 SCR 405, 2002 SCC 13 (NB), and in *Miron v. Trudel*, [1995] 2 SCR 418 (Ont.). In my view, constitutional law should apply fairly and evenly, so that all similarly situated persons are treated the same.

[57] I would therefore discard the doctrine of protest and compulsion insofar as it applies to payments made to public authorities, whether pursuant to unconstitutional legislation or as the result of a misapplication of otherwise valid legislation. Once the immunity rule is rejected, there is no need to distinguish between cases involving unconstitutional legislation and cases where delegated legislation is merely *ultra vires* in the administrative law sense. In all such cases, the payment of the charge should not be viewed as voluntary in a sense that would prejudice the taxpayer. Rather, the plaintiff is entitled to rely on the presumption of validity of the legislation, and on the representation as to its applicability by the public authority in charge of administering it.

[58] In cases not involving payments made to public authorities pursuant to unconstitutional legislation or the misapplication of an otherwise valid law, my view is that courts should insist on proof of compulsion in fact. The mere fact that the payment was made in protest should be neither necessary nor sufficient to establish compulsion. Protest may accompany a voluntary payment (in order to protect a hypothetical restitutionary entitlement), and compulsion may occur without any evidence of formal protest. Insisting on compulsion in fact is more principled and ensures that all similarly situated persons will be treated equally, regardless of protest.

[Bastarache J then went on to hold that a properly enacted limitations statute in this case limited the taxpayers' claims.]

Conclusion

[62] For the above reasons, I would allow the appeal in part and dismiss the cross-appeal. The appellants are entitled to recover all user charges paid on or after May 25, 1995, with interest. However, I conclude that this is not an appropriate case for the awarding of compound interest as the appellants did not allege any wrongful conduct on behalf of the Province that might warrant moral sanction (see *Bank of America Canada v. Mutual Trust Co.*, [2002] 2 SCR 601, 2002 SCC 43 (Ont.)). The appellants are entitled to their costs in this Court and in the courts below.

Appeal allowed in part and cross-appeal dismissed, with costs.

NOTES

1. Obviously, this judgment is about the repayment of moneys paid under an unconstitutional law. However, in the course of his judgment, Bastarache J accepted that at least some of the principles will also apply in the case of moneys paid under invalid subordinate legislation as well as invalid orders and demands by government for money. To what extent might or should there be a difference among these various categories of mistaken payment?

2. In *Peel (Regional Municipality) v. Canada*, [1992] 3 SCR 672 (Ont.), cited by Bastarache J, the court, on the basis of restitutionary principles, held that the municipality had no claim against the federal and provincial governments for the cost of housing juvenile offenders imposed by an unconstitutional statute. The municipality had not established "an incontrovertible benefit" to either of the levels of government. Would the analysis propounded in *Kingstreet Investments Ltd.* have produced a different result or is this one of those public law cases in which relief would or should only be available by reference to the principles of restitution? In this regard, consider also *Pacific National Investments Ltd. v. Victoria (City)*, [2004] 3 SCR 575 (BC). Bastarache J gave this as an example where recovery was properly dealt with under restitutionary principles. It involved a successful claim against the municipality for benefits received as a result of an *ultra vires* commitment with respect to rezoning—a commitment that both parties had assumed the city was entitled to make.

3. If symmetry or reciprocity in terms of the respective rights and obligations of individual and state should count for anything in this area, it is probably useful to consider the judgment of the Supreme Court of Canada in *Kenora (Town) Hydro Electric Commission v. Vacationland Dairy Co-operative Ltd.*, [1994] 1 SCR 80 (Ont.). Here, by a 5:4 majority, the court rejected the claim of the commission to recover the amount by which it had undercharged the dairy for electricity over a seven-year period. As a consequence of a clerical error, the dairy had been charged only half the amount that it actually owed. The majority decided that the commission was estopped from making a claim and, in so doing, referred not only to the dairy's reliance in terms of its own business operations and the hardship that a judgment for the commission would impose, but also to the fact that, over the years, the financial consequences of the mistake had been spread among the commission's other customers.

MONEY REMEDIES THROUGH JUDICIAL REVIEW

Monetary compensation or relief can, on occasion, be achieved through the medium of judicial review. Most directly, if a public official is in breach of a legal duty to remit a specific sum of money from an already allocated budget, this may be enforced by way of relief in the nature of *mandamus*. (See, for example, *R ex. rel. Lee v. WCB*, [1942] 2 DLR 665 (BC CA) (*mandamus* issued to compel payment of pension).) However, this mode of relief does not go as far as enabling the courts to force governments to appropriate funds for particular projects. This is exemplified by *Hamilton-Wentworth (Regional Municipality) v. Ontario (Minister of Transportation)* (1991), 49 Admin. LR 169 (Ont. Div. Ct.), where the court held that it had no authority to require the Ontario government to appropriate money for a highway project that it was alleged had been halted unlawfully. This was seen as too great an interference with a Crown or government prerogative. According to the court:

> The evidence leads to the conclusion that the decision was one announced by the Minister after approval of the Cabinet and in substance constitutes an expression of the intention of the government not to provide any further funding for construction of the Project. The government has the right to order its priorities and direct its fiscal resources towards those initiatives or programmes which are most compatible with the policy conclusions guiding that particular government's action. This was simply a statement of funding policy and priorities and not the exercise of a statutory power of decision attracting judicial review.
>
> While it would appear that in basing its decision on environmental concerns the government is ignoring the statutory framework established to deal with environmental matters, that does not affect its jurisdiction to make the decision in question. Such a decision is not subject to judicial review. It is in substance a decision for the disbursement of public funds. It has been a constitutional principle of our parliamentary system for at least three centuries that such disbursement is within the authority of the Legislature alone. The appropriation, allocation or disbursement of such funds by a court is offensive to principle.
>
> As was said by Lush J in *The Queen v. Lords Com'rs of the Treasury* (1872) LR 7 QB 387 at 402:

> > I think that the applicants have failed to make out that which is essential to entitle them to a writ of *mandamus*, namely, that there is a legal duty imposed upon the Lords of the Treasury—a duty as between them and the applicants—to pay over this sum of money. The only statute which can be brought to aid at all is the *Appropriation Act*, and that, as it seems to me, clearly shews that the money is voted to the Crown upon trust that the Crown will dispense it for certain specified purposes. When the money gets to the hands of the Lords dispensing it, it is in their hands as servants and agents of the Crown, and they are accountable theoretically to the Crown, but practically to the House of Commons, and in no sense are they accountable to this or any other court of justice. There is not a word, to my mind, in this Act or any other Act shewing an intention on the part of the legislature to impose any such obligation on the officers of the Crown, so as to subject them to the jurisdiction of this Court in reference to the disbursement of moneys voted by the Crown for specific purposes.

See also Wade, *Administrative Law* (6th ed., 1988) at 662. It follows that a Minister of the Crown cannot be required to make a particular expenditure of public funds.

In the instant case the Minister responsible on behalf of the Cabinet has clearly indicated Cabinet's priorities for spending. While the matter has not been put before the Legislative Assembly, I am prepared to accept as inevitable that the result of such a decision will be the non-allocation of funds. Were this court to use its authority to direct the government to appropriate funds for the completion of this Project by way of declaration or any other order, it would be trenching on the exclusive control of the revenue of a sovereign Legislative Assembly in relation to fiscal matters. In these circumstances, there is no decision which is subject to judicial review.

The nature of the action under review here is, in my view, observably and significantly different from those situations where the court requires government, be they municipal or provincial, to carry out mandates according to law and which require the expenditure of money. The decision in issue represents an exercise of the government's right to allocate its funds as it sees proper. Such a conclusion is essential to the parliamentary system of democracy. That, however, does not foreclose the applicant or the intervenants from pursuing by way of action any claim for damages or other remedy they may be advised exists in these circumstances.

The court then went on to conclude that this basic position could not be affected by arguments of estoppel, reliance, or legitimate expectation.

However, prior to *Dunsmuir v. New Brunswick*, [2009] 1 SCR 339 (NB), the domain in which the possibility of financial recompense through judicial review arose most frequently was that of the loss of statutory office or position.

If a decision dismissing the holder of a paid statutory office is quashed or held to be invalid (a phenomenon that presumably will be relatively infrequent after *Dunsmuir*), what are the financial consequences of such a judgment? Does the holder of the statutory office then become entitled automatically to all of the emoluments of that office that have been withheld in the period between the illegal dismissal and the decision of the court? If it is accepted that the original decision is void *ab initio*, then it might be argued that the right to financial relief flows automatically from the quashing of the decision. However, even in *Ridge v. Baldwin*, [1964] AC 40 (Eng. HL), where the dismissal decision was expressly declared to be void, there was not a declaration that Ridge was entitled to his salary in the six-year interim. Rather, the case was remitted to the Queen's Bench Division for "further procedure" (at 91, *per* Lord Reid). In contrast, in the equivalent Canadian police constable case, *Re Nicholson and Haldimand-Norfolk Regional Board of Commissioners of Police*, the Ontario Divisional Court and Court of Appeal followed the "logic" of the *Ridge v. Baldwin* decision, quashing Nicholson's dismissal and holding him entitled to arrears of salary: (1980), 117 DLR (3d) 604 (Ont. Div. Ct. and CA). According to Linden J, delivering the judgment of the Divisional Court: "there has been no valid discharge of Nicholson. Consequently, he has not lost his status as a police constable. He remains a police constable to this day and will remain so until his status is legally ended. As a logical consequence of this, Nicholson is entitled to be paid any wages that he would have earned were it not for the aborted dismissal. ... This is so even though the Board has not permitted Nicholson to remain on active duty, because a police constable's salary is due to him as the holder of a police office, and not in consideration of his services." However, there was a deduction for salary earned elsewhere and his entitlement was held to cease as of the date when the board wished to rehear the allegations against him, a rehearing that was frustrated by Nicholson's ultimately unsuccessful attempt to seek a court order prohibiting the board from proceeding again. (Subsequently, this approach was affirmed in *Re Hallyburton and Town of Markham* (1988), 47 DLR (4th) 640 (Ont. CA).)

The notion of a deduction for moneys earned elsewhere in the meantime is in accord with this excerpt from the judgment of Pigeon J in *Emms v. The Queen*, [1979] 2 SCR 1148, at 1164-65 (Can.), a case concerned, *inter alia*, with a claim for arrears of salary by a civil servant dismissed in breach of statute:

> The situation in the present case is not identical with that in *Ouimet*. There were allegations and there was evidence given of what occurred after Emms' employment by the Department of Indian Affairs and Northern Development was *de facto* terminated. He promptly obtained employment with the Government of Saskatchewan, at first on a temporary basis, later on a permanent basis. The trial Judge allowed damages only for the few days during which Emms was unemployed, saying:

> > The relief sought in paragraph (c) [damages] is mutually inconsistent with the relief sought in paragraphs (a) and (b) which I have granted. Since I have found that the plaintiff's employment was not terminated, it follows that the plaintiff is entitled to continue in his employment and to receive his salary therefor. But to be entitled to receive his salary the plaintiff must perform the duties of his office or indicate his willingness to do so.

> As against this, counsel for the Crown referred us to the judgment of the Privy Council in *Francis v. Municipal Councillors of Kuala Lumpur* [1962] 1 WLR 1411 (PC Mal.), where Lord Morris of Borth-y-Gest said (at 1417-1418):

> > Accepting, however, the decision of the Court of Appeal, which, as has been pointed out, has not been the subject of any cross-appeal, the position on Oct. 1 was that the removal of the appellant was a removal by the council and not by the president. The council were his employers, but having regard to the provisions of the ordinance their termination of his service constituted wrongful dismissal. Their Lordships consider that it is beyond doubt that on Oct. 1, 1957, there was *de facto* a dismissal of the appellant by his employers, the respondents. On that date, he was excluded from the council's premises. Since then he has not done any work for the council. In all these circumstances, it seems to their Lordships that the appellant must be treated as having been wrongly dismissed on Oct. 1, 1957, and that his remedy lies in a claim for damages. It would be wholly unreal to accede to the contention that since Oct. 1, 1957, he had continued to be and that he still continues to be in the employment of the respondents.

> > In their Lordships' view, when there has been a purported termination of a contract of service a declaration to the effect that the contract of service still subsists will rarely be made. This is a consequence of the general principle of law that the courts will not grant specific performance of contracts of service. Special circumstances will be required before such a declaration is made and its making will normally be in the discretion of the court. In their Lordships' view there are no circumstances in the present case which would make it either just or proper to make such a declaration.

> In my view, the circumstances in the present case do not justify the making of a declaration of continued employment. It would imply that Emms is entitled to his salary for the whole period since the date of his *de facto* termination of employment, although he made himself unavailable

by taking other employment which became of a permanent character. Also it seems this would mean that Emms would be entitled to receive back pay irrespective of what he has received from other employment. This last consequence might be avoided by amending the declaration. However, bearing in mind that the making of such a declaration is an equitable remedy seldom allowed, it appears to me that the circumstances are not such as to justify it here and the proper remedy is in damages.

At the hearing in this Court, counsel for Emms referred to an admission by the parties at trial that the difference in salary and benefits that Emms would have received had he been allowed to continue his employment with the Department amounted to $6,899.40. This sum was claimed as damages which this Court was requested to assess. No objection to this request having been made, it appears proper to render judgment accordingly.

Indeed, what this judgment suggested is that, at least in relation to certain kinds of "statutory employment," private law employment principles should be relevant. Now, following *Dunsmuir*, not only will private law employment principles be applicable in almost all of these situations but also the affected employee or office holder will be confined to a private law cause of action.

TORT LIABILITY FOR UNLAWFUL ADMINISTRATIVE ACTION OR INACTION

Introduction

The scope of the availability of damages for unlawful administrative action or inaction tends to be much more commonly considered in the context of actions in tort than those for breach of contract. By and large, with the occasional exception of judicial review of procurement processes, in the domain of contract, ordinary private law doctrine governs principles of both liability and monetary relief (though, as we have seen already, some Crown proceedings or liability legislation prevents the award of injunctions and specific performance against the Crown).

Indeed, notwithstanding the historically special position in law of the Crown as contracting party (a stance based at least in part on the proposition that government should have a much greater capacity to both breach its contracts and not be held liable for the financial consequences than that possessed by the private sector), such "special treatment" is today the stuff of high political controversy. If evidence of this is needed, one only has to look to the furore generated by the cancellation in 1994 by the new Liberal federal government of the contract for the privatization of Pearson International Airport and the introduction of legislation to both nullify the deal and deny access to judicial review of the amounts of compensation determined by the minister of transport. Not only did this allegedly unjustifiable infringement of property rights engender fierce partisan debates in Parliament but it also generated academic disagreement in the pages of *The Globe and Mail*: contrast Bakan and Schneiderman, "The Pearson Bill would pass legal muster," January 2, 1995, with Norman, "The Pearson Act offends the rule of law," December 8, 1994. As well, the members of the disappointed consortium obtained a declaration that the government had acted in breach of contract: *T1T2 Limited Partnership v. Canada* (1995), 23 OR (3d) 81 (Gen. Div.); aff'd. (1995), 24 OR (3d) 546 (CA).

In the domain of tort liability, on which this section of the chapter concentrates, there is far more judicial acceptance of the need to apply different or at least modified standards to the liability of governments. For many of the reasons identified in the introduction to the chapter, the determination of tortious or delictual responsibility on the part of government responds to what is perceived to be the special status or position of government and its servants and agents in the exercise of at least some statutory powers and responsibilities. The identification of these special considerations and resulting legal treatment, as well as an assessment of their appropriateness, provide the primary focus of the material that follows.

It is important at the outset to make one thing clear: for there to be tort liability on the part of a statutory authority, plaintiffs must be able to fit their case within a known head of tort liability. Thus, in *Cooper v. Board of Works for Wandsworth District* (1863), 143 ER 414 (CP) (chapter 3 of this text), the plaintiff recovered damages in tort because he was able to show that the unlawful administrative action gave rise to the tort of trespass. Similarly, in this section of the materials, we see attempts made to show that administrative action or inaction involved a negligent misrepresentation giving rise to a claim for damages under the principles of *Hedley Byrne v. Heller*, [1964] AC 415 (Eng. HL).

Of more pervading significance, however, are the following problems:

1. the extent to which *ultra vires* action or abuse of statutory authority *per se* constitutes an independent tort; and

2. the application of general principles of tort law, and particularly liability for negligence, to the exercise of statutory functions.

In considering these problems, we will again be entering the familiar but confusing territory of classification of functions, and the meaning of the terms "bad faith" and "malice" as well as that of "duty," "right," "power," and "discretion." Relevant also will be distinctions between "misfeasance" and "non-feasance" and the "policy making" and "operational" aspects of the functioning of statutory authorities. One thing to be alert to is the extent to which courts in this area are or might be using this language in a different manner from that encountered in other areas of law.

Do not allow the terminology to distract you from the basic concern here: the extent to which, as a matter of policy, statutory authorities should be accountable in tort for their actions, and the extent to which in answering that question traditional private law concerns and thinking are relevant. In fixing liability in general tort law, the courts seldom refer explicitly to the issues of resource allocation and the ability of litigants to act as loss bearers. However, as noted already, in *British Railways Board v. Herrington*, [1972] AC 877 (Eng. HL), at 899, Lord Reid asserted that the board had greater abilities than private individuals to avoid dangers to trespassers. Does this consideration have a greater claim to recognition where the defendant is a public body with all the resources of the state theoretically behind it? Should we be entitled to expect higher standards of risk avoidance from public bodies as opposed to individuals and corporations (however large)? How relevant is it to this issue that public authorities operate or regulate enterprises with the potential for horrendous or unmanageable disaster such as nuclear power plants, defence facilities, and the use of dangerous commodities? Is the public purse really as bottomless as is sometimes asserted? Clearly not, as exemplified by the case of municipalities and the difficulties that they have had in obtaining liability insurance for various social programs in which they are engaged. Do such considerations of fiscal constraint and a desire not to hamper or discourage public bodies in the undertaking of initiatives of various sorts point, in fact, in the other direction—namely, less strict liability than that of the private sector? (See Harlow, *State Liability: Tort Law and Beyond* (2004); and Harlow, "Fault Liability in French and English Public Law" (1976), 39 *Mod. LR* 516.) To what extent, if at all, do distinctions now made in the jurisprudence between "duties" and "discretions," "policy making" and "operations," and "misfeasance" and "non-feasance" bear upon these concerns and what position, if any, do they indicate that the courts have taken with respect to these competing tensions?

Abuse of Power by Statutory Authorities

While it is accepted that the *ultra vires* exercise of power generally does not in itself attract civil liability (as exemplified by the Canadian rejection of the tort of breach of statutory duty: *Canada v. Saskatchewan Wheat Pool*, [1983] 1 SCR 205 (Sask.)), there are nonetheless occasions where the circumstances in which *ultra vires* conduct occurs will give rise to a claim by those suffering harm or damage. This is the territory of tort or extra-contractuelle liability arising out of misconduct on the part of public officials and variously described as misfeasance in public office or bad faith in the exercise of public power

The cases in this section commence with the consideration of a particular problem: the potential tort or extra-contractuelle liability of licensing authorities for misuse or abuse of power. As well as setting the scene for a more general evaluation of the existence of a special public law tort, these judgments also serve to underscore one of the subtexts of this whole section. That subtext is the extent to which, irrespective of the nature of the harm caused, certain government functionaries enjoy immunity from suit as a result of the position that they occupy or the functions that they exercise.

McGillivray v. Kimber
(1915), 52 SCR 146 (NS)

[The appellant's pilot's licence was suspended by a resolution of the pilotage authority for "neglect and incapacity." The statutory requirements for such an action were not observed; there was no formal complaint, notice, or investigation. The appellant sought damages for the wrongful revocation of his licence. He was successful at trial, recovering $1,800 for his likely earnings during 1912 and 1913, but the Supreme Court of Nova Scotia reversed on the basis that damages were not available against an authority acting in a *quasi*-judicial capacity without proof of malice. He then appealed to the Supreme Court of Canada.]

SIR CHARLES FITZPATRICK CJ (dissenting): In my opinion the judgment appealed from is right. There can, I think, be no doubt that in discharging the pilot the respondents were acting in a *quasi*-judicial capacity, and it is settled law that those acting in a judicial or *quasi*-judicial capacity incur no liability for acts performed within their jurisdiction unless actuated by malice. Many American cases indeed go so far as to hold that even malice will not affect the immunity of those performing such functions. It is unnecessary to consider this in the present instance as malice has not been charged.

This freedom from liability of those discharging *quasi*-judicial functions does not, of course, in any way prevent the courts interfering to review the proceedings. The courts do so in every variety of cases, quashing convictions, setting aside awards, granting *mandamus* such as would undoubtedly have been done on application in the present case. The proceedings by the Pilotage Authority were clearly irregular and the *mandamus* would have directed them to hear and determine the matter in a proper manner. Freedom from liability for the consequences of such acts is, however, precisely the protection which the law gives to those discharging such duties. Were it otherwise no one could venture to undertake the discharge of the duties of many public positions.

The appeal should be dismissed with costs.

DUFF J: As to the law, assuming there had been an intention to exercise authority under by-law 9 since there was no hearing, no evidence on oath, no judicial determination, it follows that no "forfeiture" to use the language of the by-law, took place and consequently there is nothing amounting to a justification of the so called dismissal; which is, therefore, an actionable wrong under the principle of [*Mogul Steam Ship Co. v. McGregor* (1889), 23 QBD 598 (CA)]. Moreover, the rule is sufficiently established that persons in the position of the respondents exercising *quasi*-judicial powers are only protected from civil liability if they observe the statutory rules conditioning their powers as well as the rules of natural justice.

. . .

I have not, of course, overlooked the argument of Mr. Rogers founded upon authorities relating to the responsibility of the judicial officers strictly so called, judges of the inferior courts and magistrates. Generally, no doubt, in the absence of bad faith such judicial officers are not responsible for harm caused by acts otherwise wrongful when such acts are judicial acts done in the course of some judicial proceedings in which the officer has jurisdiction as regards the persons affected, and the matter before him is some matter with which he has authority judicially to deal. No authority has been cited, however, for the extension of this principle to protect administrative officers such as the respondents from the consequences of injurious acts for which authority is wanting owing to the omission of the essential statutory prerequisites. Even as regards the acts of judicial officers strictly so called in respect of matters in which there is jurisdiction over the person affected as well as over the subject matter where the jurisdiction is purely statutory, the statutory conditions must be observed at the peril of the officer, assuming, at all events, that he is under no mistake as to the facts. Thus, a magistrate being empowered by a statute to issue a warrant on complaint in writing before him on oath, the issue of a warrant in the absence of evidence on oath is an act for the consequences of which he is civilly responsible. ...

There remains the question of damages.

[After considering the statutory provisions, Duff J held that licences were to be for a minimum of two years. He then continued:]

It must be assumed that the Pilotage Authority intended to grant a valid licence, and if the proper assumption is that the intention was to grant a licence only for the minimum period permitted by the law, then, on that assumption, each of the licences must be treated as a licence valid for a period of two years.

On these assumptions the appellant's licence held by him in June, 1912, did not expire until August, 1913, and the position taken by the respondents in their statement of defence and sustained by the full court that the appellant ceased in law to be a licensed pilot after June, 1912, necessarily fails.

Assuming that the proper course is to treat the appellant's licence as a licence limited as to duration under section 454, and that the discretion to renew, conferred upon the Pilotage Authority by sub-section (b) of that section, is an absolute and not a judicial discretion; it would still, I think, be wrong to deal with the question of damages on the footing of the consequences of the proceedings in 1912 having ceased to operate with the expiry of the licence in August, 1913. The proceedings in evidence in August, October and November of 1913, shew that the majority of the Board insisted at that time on treating the appellant as compulsorily retired from the service and disqualified from holding a licence. This loss of status and the prejudice thereby occasioned him in his character of applicant for a licence in August, 1913, is one of the consequences natural and intended of the respondents' conduct in respect of which the appellant is entitled to reparation.

On this footing the appellant would not be entitled to recover compensation *nominatim* for the loss of prospective earnings in the season of 1913-1914. But without deciding whether or not the appellant's position was that of a licensee with a licence limited as to time under section 454, I still think the damages found by the learned trial judge are not excessive. Apart altogether from the right to reparation just mentioned this is emphatically not a case for measuring damages with nicety.

There was some suggestion, although I do not think it was seriously pressed, that substantial damages ought not to be awarded on the ground that the evidence shews the appellant's habits to have been so notorious that, if there had been an investigation conducted as the law required, the respondents must have reached the conclusion judicially that the appellant was incapacitated as an inebriate. But the findings of the learned trial judge dispose of this contention effectually. Not only does the finding as to damages tacitly involve a rejection of any such contention, but the learned judge explicitly holds that the appellant had successfully repelled the attack upon his character. The statements of some of the respondents must be evaluated in light of the fact that they were seeking some refuge from legal responsibility and of the strong suspicion, not to say probability, that the respondents as a whole whatever may have been their beliefs as to the appellant's conduct, were not free in the impeached proceedings from the influence of other motives than a desire to elevate the character of the pilotage service. In this aspect of the case, it is eminently one in which the view of the trial judge ought to guide a court of appeal.

[Idington and Anglin JJ were also in favour of restoring the judgment at first instance. Davis J concurred with Sir Charles Fitzpatrick CJ's dissent.]

Appeal allowed with costs.

NOTE

What tort has been committed here? Should there be any difference for the purposes of liability between a licensing authority (such as in issue here) and regular judicial officers (for example, superior court judges or statutory authorities designated as courts of record or otherwise obliged to act by way of formal hearings)? See, for example, the later judgment of the Supreme Court of Canada in *Harris v. The Law Society of Alberta*, [1936] SCR 88 (Alta.), also delivered by Duff, then CJC. Here, the court, absent proof of malice, dismissed a claim for damages against the Law Society for striking Harris from the rolls without (technically) according him a hearing. Applying *Partridge v. General Council of Medical Education* (1890), 25 QBD 90 (CA), the court held that the Law Society's Disciplinary Committee had been acting in a judicial rather than ministerial capacity.

On what basis, in *McGillivray*, does Duff J allow damages for the period beyond the regular expiry date of the licence? See also on this same point *Roncarelli v. Duplessis*, below. In the course of his judgment, Idington J referred to the evidence at trial:

> Q. Why was John McGillivray dismissed?
>
> A. Well, I can give you my own reasons. I had two. One was political and I considered him a disgrace to the service.
>
> Q. What was the political reason?
>
> A. I got it in the neck myself once and I thought I would return the compliment when I got the chance.
>
> Q. You had been dismissed when the Liberals were in office and you thought you would return the compliment to him?
>
> A. That was one reason and one was just as strong as the other.

What is the possible relevance of such evidence?

Roncarelli v. Duplessis
[1959] SCR 121 (Que.)

[The essential facts are set out in chapter 15, The Use and Misuse of Discretion.]

RAND J: To deny or revoke a permit because a citizen exercises an unchallengeable right totally irrelevant to the sale of liquor in a restaurant is equally beyond the scope of the discretion conferred. There was here not only revocation of the existing permit but a declaration of a future, definitive disqualification of the appellant to obtain one: it was to be "forever." This purports to divest his citizenship status of its incident of membership in the class of those of the public to whom such a privilege could be extended. Under the statutory language here, that is not competent to the Commission and *a fortiori* to the Government or the respondent: *McGillivray v. Kimber* (1915) 52 SCR 146 (NS). There is here an administrative tribunal which, in certain respects, is to act in a judicial manner; and even on the view of the dissenting Justices in *McGillivray*, there is liability: what could be more malicious than to punish this licensee for having done what he had an absolute right to do in a matter utterly irrelevant to the *Alcoholic Liquor Act*? Malice in the proper sense is simply acting for a reason and purpose knowingly foreign to the administration, to which was added here the element of intentional punishment by what was virtually vocation outlawry.

It may be difficult if not impossible in cases generally to demonstrate a breach of this public duty in the illegal purpose served; there may be no means, even if proceedings against the Commission were permitted by the Attorney General, as here they were refused, of compelling the Commission to justify a refusal or revocation or to give reasons for its action; on these questions I make no observation; but in the case before us that difficulty is not present: the reasons are openly avowed.

The act of the respondent through the instrumentality of the Commission brought about a breach of an implied public statutory duty toward the appellant; it was a gross abuse of legal power expressly intended to punish him for an act wholly irrelevant to the statute, a punishment which inflicted on him, as it was intended to do, the destruction of his economic life as a restaurant keeper within the Province. Whatever may be the immunity of the Commission or its member from an action for damages, there is none in the respondent. He was under no duty in relation to the appellant and his act was an intrusion upon the functions of a statutory body. The injury done by him was a fault engaging liability within the principles of the underlying public law of Quebec: *Mostyn v. Fabrigas* (1774) 98 ER 1021, and under art. 1053 of the Civil Code. That, in the presence of expanding administrative regulation of economic activities, such a step and its consequences are to be suffered by the victim without recourse or remedy, that an administration according to law is to be superseded by action dictated by and according to the arbitrary likes, dislikes and irrelevant purposes of public officers acting beyond their duty, would signalize the beginning of disintegration of the rule of law as a fundamental postulate of our constitutional structure. An administration of licences on the highest level of fair and impartial treatment to all may be forced to follow the practice of "first come first served," which makes the strictest observance of equal responsibility to all of even greater importance; at this stage of developing government it would be a danger of high consequence to tolerate such a departure from good faith in executing the legislative purpose. It should be added, however, that that principle is not, by this language, intended to be extended to ordinary governmental employment: with that we are not here concerned.

It was urged by Mr. Beaulieu that the respondent, as the incumbent of an office of state, so long as he was proceeding in "good faith," was free to act in a matter of this kind virtually as he pleased. The office of Attorney General traditionally and by statute carries duties that relate to advising the Executive, including here, administrative bodies, enforcing the public law and directing the administration of justice. In any decision of the statutory body in this case, he had no part to play beyond giving advice on legal questions arising. In that role his action should have been limited to advice on the validity of a revocation for such a reason or purpose and what that advice should have been does not seem to me to admit of any doubt. To pass from this limited scope of action to that of bringing about a step by the Commission beyond the bounds prescribed by the Legislature for its exclusive action converted what was done into his personal act.

"Good faith" in this context, applicable both to the respondent and the General Manager, means carrying out the statute according to its intent and for its purpose; it means good faith in acting with a rational appreciation of that intent and purpose and not with an improper intent and for an alien purpose; it does not mean for the purposes of punishing a person for exercising an unchallengeable right; it does not mean arbitrarily and illegally attempting to divest a citizen of an incident of his civil status.

I mention, in order to make clear that it has not been overlooked, the decision of the House of Lords in *Allen v. Flood* [1898] AC 1 (Eng. HL), in which the principle was laid down that an act of an individual otherwise not actionable does not become so because of the motive or reason for doing it, even maliciously to injure, as distinguished from an act done by two or more persons. No contention was made in the present case based on agreed action by the respondent and Mr. Archambault. In *Allen v. Flood* the actor was a labour leader and the victims non-union workmen who were lawfully dismissed by their employer to avoid a strike involving no breach of contract or law. Here the act done was in relation to a public administration affecting the rights of a citizen to enjoy a public privilege, and a duty implied by the statute toward the victim was violated. The existing permit was an interest for which the appellant was entitled to protection against any unauthorized interference, and the illegal destruction of which gave rise to a remedy for the damages suffered. In *Allen v. Flood* there were no such elements.

Nor is it necessary to examine the question whether on the basis of an improper revocation the appellant could have compelled the issue of a new permit or whether the purported revocation was a void act. The revocation was *de facto*, it was intended to end the privilege and to bring about the consequences that followed. As against the respondent, the appellant was entitled to treat the breach of duty as effecting a revocation and to elect for damages.

Mr. Scott argued further that even if the revocation were within the scope of discretion and not a breach of duty, the intervention of the respondent in so using the Commission was equally at fault. The proposition generalized is this: where, by a statute restricting the ordinary activities of citizens, a privilege is conferred by an administrative body, the continuance of that enjoyment is to be free from the influence of third persons on that body for the purpose only of injuring the privilege holder. It is the application to such a privilege of the proposition urged but rejected in *Allen v. Flood* in the case of a private employment. The grounds of distinction between the two cases have been pointed out; but for the reasons given consideration of this ground is unnecessary and I express no opinion for or against it.

MARTLAND J: On the issue of liability, I have, for the foregoing reasons, reached the conclusion that the respondent, by acts not justifiable in law, wrongfully caused the cancellation of the appellant's permit and thus caused damage to the appellant. The respondent intentionally inflicted damage upon the appellant and, therefore, in the absence of lawful justification, which I do not find, he is liable to the appellant for the commission of a fault under art. 1053 of the *Civil Code*.

I now turn to the matter of damages.

The learned trial Judge awarded damages to the appellant in the sum of $8,123.53, made up of $1,123.53 for loss of value of liquor seized by the Commission, $6,000 for loss of profits from the restaurant from December 4, 1946, the date of the cancellation of the permit, to May 1, 1947, the date when the permit would normally have expired, and $1,000 for damages to his personal reputation. No objection is taken by the appellant in respect of these awards, but he contends that he is also entitled to compensation under certain other heads of damage in respect of which no award was made by the learned trial judge. These are in respect of damage to the goodwill and reputation of his business, loss of property rights in his permit and loss of future profits for a period of at least one year from May 1, 1947. Damages in respect of these items, were not allowed by the learned trial Judge because of the fact that the appellant's permit was "only a temporary asset."

The appellant contends that, although his permit was not permanent, yet, in the light of the long history of his restaurant and the continuous renewals of the permit previously, he had a reasonable expectation of renewal in the future, had not the cancellation been effected in December 1946. He contends that the value of the goodwill of his business was substantially damaged by that cancellation.

His position on this point is supported by the reasoning of Duff J (as he then was) in *McGillivray v. Kimber* (1915) 52 SCR 146 (NS). That was an action claiming damages for the wrongful cancellation of the appellant's pilot's licence by the Sydney Pilotage Authority. At 163-164 he says: "The statement of defence seems to proceed upon the theory that for the purpose of measuring legal responsibility, the consequences of this dismissal came to an end with the expiry of the term, and that I shall discuss; but for the present it is sufficient to repeat that the dismissal was an act which being not only calculated but intended to prevent the appellant continuing the exercise of his calling had in fact this intended effect; and the respondents are consequently answerable in damages unless there was in law justification or excuse for what they did. *Per* Bowen LJ: *Mogul S.S. Co. v. McGregor* (1889) 23 QBD 598 (CA)."

The statement by Bowen LJ to which he refers appears at 613 of the report and is also of significance in relation to the appellant's right of action in this case. It is as follows: "Now, intentionally to do that which is calculated in the ordinary course of events to damage, and which does, in fact, damage another in that other person's property or trade, is actionable if done without just cause or excuse."

The evidence establishes that there was a substantial reduction in the value of the goodwill of the appellant's restaurant business as a result of what occurred, apart from the matter of any loss which might have resulted on the sale of the physical assets. It is difficult to assess this loss and there is not a great deal of evidence to assist in so doing. The appellant did file, as exhibits, income tax returns for the three years prior to 1946, which showed in those years a total net income from the business of $23,578.88. The profit-making possibilities of the business are certainly an item to be considered in determining the value of the goodwill.

However, in all the circumstances, the amount of these damages must be determined in a somewhat arbitrary fashion. I consider that $25,000 should be allowed as damages for the diminution of the value of the goodwill and for the loss of future profits.

I would allow both appeals, with costs here and below, and order the respondent to pay to the appellant damages in the total amount of $33,123.53, with interest from the date of the judgment in the Superior Court, and costs.

[Abbott J's judgment on this point is to much the same effect as that of Martland J. Taschereau, Cartwright, and Fauteux JJ delivered dissenting judgments, although not on the basis of this issue. However, Cartwright J did express doubt as to the availability of a cause of action in damages. Locke J and for the most part Kerwin CJC concurred with Martland J; Judson J concurred with Rand J.]

Appeal allowed with costs.

NOTES

1. Article 1053 (now reworked as article 1457) of the *Quebec Civil Code* provided for delictual or extra-contractuelle liability in the following terms:

Every person capable of discerning right from wrong is responsible for the damage caused by his fault to another, whether by positive act, imprudence, neglect or want of skill.

To what extent does this affect the applicability of *Roncarelli v. Duplessis* in common law jurisdictions? How precisely would you characterize the wrong that Rand J finds in this case? Is it the same as the tort in *McGillivray v. Kimber*? (For the first authoritative application of *Roncarelli v. Duplessis* in a common law province, see the judgment of the Manitoba Court of Appeal in *Gershman v. Manitoba Vegetable Producers' Marketing Board* (1976), 69 DLR (3d) 114 (Man. CA), a case involving the board taking retaliatory action against Gershman for challenging the constitutionality of legislation establishing the board. In so doing, the court upheld the first instance court's award of both compensatory and punitive damages.) How does the court in *Roncarelli* go about calculating the damages to be awarded? Is this appropriate?

2. A related context in which questions of immunity have arisen is that of the exercise of prosecutorial discretion. In this instance, however, the debate about immunity and its extent takes place within the rubric of another tort or delict, albeit one very close in concept to that of abuse of power—namely, malicious prosecution. In *Nelles v. Ontario*, [1989] 2 SCR 170 (Ont.), the issue was whether the province, its attorney general, and involved Crown attorneys had an immunity from liability for malicious prosecution and, for that matter, for claims based on alleged Charter violations. While the court determined that, though the province itself could not be sued by reason of a specific immunity provided for in s. 5(6) of the Ontario *Proceedings Against the Crown Act*, RSO 1980, c. 393 (now RSO 1990, c. P.27), the action could proceed against the attorney general and the Crown attorneys. Lamer J (as he then was) summarized the court's conclusions as follows:

III. CONCLUSION

A review of the authorities on the issue of prosecutorial immunity reveals that the matter ultimately boils down to a question of policy. For the reasons I have stated above I am of the view that absolute immunity for the Attorney-General and his agents, the Crown Attorneys, is not justified in the interests of public policy. We must be mindful that an absolute immunity has the effect of negating a private right of action and in some cases may bar a remedy under the Charter. As such, the existence of absolute immunity is a threat to the individual rights of citizens who have been wrongly and maliciously prosecuted. Further, it is important to note that what we are dealing with here is an immunity from suit for malicious prosecution; we are not dealing with errors in judgment or discretion or even professional negligence. By contrast the tort of malicious prosecution requires proof of an improper purpose or motive, a motive that involves an abuse or perversion of the system of criminal justice for ends it was not designed to serve and as such incorporates an abuse of the office of the Attorney-General and his agents the Crown Attorneys.

There is no doubt that the policy considerations in favour of absolute immunity have some merit. But in my view those considerations must give way to the right of a private citizen to seek a remedy when the prosecutor acts maliciously in fraud of his duties with the result that he causes damage to the victim. In my view the inherent difficulty in proving a case of malicious prosecution combined with the mechanisms available within the system of civil procedure to weed out meritless claims is sufficient to ensure that the Attorney-General and Crown Attorneys will not be hindered in the proper execution of their important public duties. Attempts to qualify prosecutorial immunity in the United States by the so-called functional approach and its many variations have proven to be unsuccessful and unprincipled as I have previously noted. As a result I conclude that the Attorney-General and Crown Attorneys do not enjoy an absolute immunity in respect of suits for malicious prosecution.

See also *Proulx v. Quebec (Attorney General)*, [2001] 3 SCR 9 (Que.), reaffirming *Nelles* in a Québec context. However, more recently, see *Miazga v. Kvello Estate*, [2009] 3 SCR 339, 2009 SCC 51, emphasizing that malice in this context required proof not only of a lack of subjective belief in the existence of reasonable and probable grounds to prosecute but also of an improper purpose. Consider as well *Prete v. Ontario (Attorney General)* (1993), 110 DLR (4th) 94 (Ont. CA), holding that s. 5(6) did not apply where the action against the Crown in right of Ontario was for violation of a Charter right. The province could not constitutionally immunize itself from liability for violations of the Charter. Also consider *Milgaard v. Kujawa* (1993), 112 Sask. R 241 (QB); aff'd. [1994] 9 WWR 305 (Sask. CA), leave to appeal to the Supreme Court of Canada refused, February 2, 1995.

3. Another of the major issues in *Roncarelli* was whether the action could be maintained at all because of failure to comply with a notice provision imposed by the Québec *Code of Civil Procedure* when suing public officers who are acting in the exercise of their functions. The majority were able to avoid this provision by holding that the conduct in question was not engaged in as part of Duplessis's public functions. This device is used frequently by the courts to defeat not only notice provisions but also limitation periods and even immunities from liability when statutory authorities are being sued for damages.

See also in this regard the decision of the Supreme Court of Canada in *Berardinelli v. Ontario Housing Corporation*, [1979] 1 SCR 275 (Ont.), in which the court held that the then six months' limitation period of the Ontario *Public Authorities Protection Act*, RSO 1980, c. 406 (now repealed by *Limitations Act, 2002*, being Sched. B to the *Justice Statute Law Amendment Act, 2002*, SO 2002, c. 24, see s. 25.20) did not apply to the activities of the corporation, which were of an internal or operational nature with a predominantly private aspect, as opposed to those with a public aspect or of an inherently public nature. As a result, a claim for damages arising out of injuries suffered when the plaintiff slipped on snow at one of the corporation's housing units was allowed to proceed. (See also *Berendsen v. Ontario*, 2001 SCC 55 (Ont.) and *Des Champs v. Conseil des écoles séparées catholiques de langue française de Prescott-Russell*, [1999] 3 SCR 281 (Ont.) to the same effect.)

4. In terms of the liability of public officers and especially members of tribunals, limiting statutory provisions take a variety of forms. For example, in some instances, there will be

immunity provided functions are performed in good faith (for example, s. 34A(5) of the *Motor Carrier Act*, RSN 1970, c. 242 (now RSNL 1990, c. M-19), as interpreted in *King v. Newfoundland (Commissioners of Public Utilities)* (1991), 78 DLR (4th) 719 (Nfld. CA)). On other occasions, there will no liability save where the tribunal or authority acts without or in excess of jurisdiction (for example, s. 15 of the *Magistrates' Courts Act (Northern Ireland), 1964*, as interpreted in *McC v. Mullan*, [1984] 3 All ER 908 (HL NI)). Sometimes, these two concepts are combined to create an immunity for tribunals acting within jurisdiction provided they do so in good faith and without malice (for example, *Coroners Act*, RSBC 1996, c. 72).

A 1985 Supreme Court of Canada examination of this question involved another variation, one in which the immunities of superior court judges were extended to a tribunal. This was in *Morier v. Rivard*, [1985] 2 SCR 716 (Que.), an attempt to sue the Quebec Police Commission for damages for conducting an inquiry contrary to its statutory mandate. Among the allegations were a failure to comply with a statutory provision conferring procedural protections on those against whom adverse findings were made, breach of the rules of natural justice and the provisions of the Québec *Charter of Human Rights and Freedoms*, RSQ, c. C-12, discriminatory treatment, and improper purposes and motivations. In restoring a Quebec Superior Court judgment allowing a motion to strike out the proceedings, Chouinard J, delivering the judgment of the majority, considered the common law governing the immunities of superior court judges before stating:

> Indeed, there is no question in the case at bar that appellants, members of the Commission de police, had the necessary jurisdiction to conduct an inquiry and to submit a report. It is possible that they exceeded their jurisdiction by doing or failing to do the acts mentioned in the statement of claim. It is possible that they contravened the rules of natural justice, that they did not inform respondent of the facts alleged against him or that they did not give him an opportunity to be heard. It is possible that they contravened the *Charter of Human Rights and Freedoms* [Québec]. All of these are allegations which may be used to support the respondent's other action to quash the report of the Commission de police and the evidence obtained. This action continues to be before the Superior Court, and of course I shall make no ruling upon it; but in my opinion these are not allegations which may be used as the basis for an action in damages.

In *dicta*, the court also seemed to accept that, even in situations where judicial bodies either by statute or by common law were subject to liability for acting without or in excess of jurisdiction, the scope of jurisdiction for these purposes was not as extensive as the reach of that term in the domain of judicial review. No question was apparently raised in this case as to whether the relevant provision could prevail in the face of the guarantees in the Québec *Charter of Human Rights and Freedoms*, RSQ, c. C-12, which is not only a source of procedural rights (s. 23) but which also provides for a damages remedy for those whose rights have been interfered with (s. 49). In s. 52, ss. 1-38 (though not s. 49) of the Québec Charter are also expressed to apply notwithstanding the provisions of any other Act.

5. While there now is no doubt that the principles enunciated in *Roncarelli* are also part of the common law, there is a paucity of cases in which a plaintiff has successfully sued for the tort of abuse of power or misfeasance in public office. The evidential burdens are considerable, and it may also be the case that the standards of probity among Canadian public officials are for the most part exemplary. There has also been an active judicial debate as to whether the bases for this kind of liability should be expanded. A prominent example was

Alberta (Minister of Public Works, Supply and Services) v. Nilsson (1999), 246 AR 201 (QB); aff'd. (2002), 220 DLR (4th) 474 (CA). Here, the court held that the minister was liable for abuse of office in a case involving a land freeze and subsequent acquisition. After a survey of the relevant authorities, Marceau J (at first instance) concluded that the tort should not be restricted to instances of targeted malice as in *Roncarelli*. Rather, it should extend to the following situations:

1. an intentional illegal act, which is either [*sic*]:
   (a) an intentional use of statutory authority for an improper purpose; or
   (b) actual knowledge that the act (or omission) is beyond statutory authority; or
   (c) reckless indifference, or willful blindness to the lack of statutory authority for the act;
2. intent to harm an individual or class of individual, which is satisfied by either [*sic*]:
   (d) an actual intention to harm; or
   (e) actual knowledge that harm will result; or
   (f) reckless indifference or willful blindness to the harm that can be foreseen to result.

This analysis built on a judgment of the English Court of Appeal that subsequently went on appeal to the House of Lords: *Three Rivers District Council v. Bank of England (No. 3)*, [2000] 2 WLR 1220 (Eng. HL). The judgments in this case accept that there are two categories of conduct that come within the reach of the tort: targeted malice, as in *Roncarelli*, and acting in the knowledge that there was no power and that those actions would probably cause injury. As part of the second (or perhaps as a separate third category), there is acting with wilful indifference in the subjective sense as to presence of power and the outcome. Consider the extent to which the Supreme Court of Canada has endorsed this version of the test for liability in the following judgment.

Odhavji Estate v. Woodhouse
[2003] 3 SCR 263, 2003 SCC 69 (Ont.)

[Members of the Toronto Police shot and killed Odhavji, who was fleeing following a bank robbery. As required by legislation, the Special Investigations Unit (SIU) commenced an investigation into the death. The police officers involved refused to cooperate with the SIU, although they were under a statutory obligation to do so. The chief of police was also under a statutory obligation to ensure that the police officers cooperated with the SIU. Ultimately, the SIU cleared the police officers of any wrongdoing. Odhavji's estate and family then commenced a variety of actions against the police officers, the chief of police, the Toronto Police Services Board, and the province of Ontario. These included claims of misfeasance in public office against the officers and the chief of police and negligence against the chief of police, the Police Services Board, and the province. The defendants moved to strike out the plaintiffs' statement of claim as not disclosing any reasonable causes of action. Some of these motions ultimately reached the Supreme Court of Canada. More specifically, the plaintiffs obtained leave to appeal the Court of Appeal's striking out the misfeasance in public office claims and the claims in negligence against the

Police Services Board and the province. The chief of police cross-appealed the Court of Appeal's decision to allow the claim in negligence against him to proceed.]

IACOBUCCI J: ...

[After setting out the "stringent" test for the striking out of a statement of claim as disclosing no reasonable cause of action, a test that required the court to assume the truth of the facts as pleaded, Iacobucci J proceeded to outline and apply the components of the test for an action in misfeasance in public office.]

The Actions for Misfeasance in a Public Office

[16] The essence of the Court of Appeal's decision is that the "radical defect" from which the actions for misfeasance in a public office suffer is their failure to plead the constituent elements of the tort. In particular, the Court of Appeal held that the defining element of the tort is the unlawful exercise of the statutory or prerogative powers that adhere to the defendant's office. Because the alleged misconduct involved the breach of a statutory duty rather than the improper or unlawful exercise of a statutory or prerogative power, it is "plain and obvious," on this view, that the actions for misfeasance in a public office cannot succeed.

[17] Consequently, I begin by considering the Court of Appeal's conclusion that the unlawful exercise of a statutory or prerogative power is a constituent element of the tort. With respect, a review of the leading cases clearly reveals that the tort is not limited to circumstances in which the defendant officer is engaged in the unlawful exercise of a particular statutory or prerogative power. As I will discuss, the class of conduct at which the tort is targeted is not as narrow as the unlawful exercise of a particular statutory or prerogative power, but more broadly based on unlawful conduct in the exercise of public functions generally.

(1) The Defining Elements of the Tort

[18] The origins of the tort of misfeasance in a public office can be traced to *Ashby v. White* (1703) 2 Ld Raym 938, 92 ER 126 [KB], in which Holt CJ found that a cause of action lay against an elections officer who maliciously and fraudulently deprived Mr. White of the right to vote. Although the defendant possessed the power to deprive certain persons from participating in the election, he did not have the power to do so for an improper purpose. Although the original judgment suggests that he was simply applying the principle *ubi jus ibi remedium*, Holt CJ produced a revised form of the judgment in which he stated that it was because fraud and malice were proven that the action lay: J.W. Smith, *A Selection of Leading Cases on Various Branches of the Law* (13th ed. 1929) at 282. Thus, in its earliest form it is arguable that misfeasance in a public office was limited to circumstances in which a public officer abused a power actually possessed.

[19] Subsequent cases, however, have made clear that the ambit of the tort is not restricted in this manner. In *Roncarelli v. Duplessis*, [1959] SCR 121 [Que.], this Court found the defendant Premier of Quebec liable for directing the manager of the Quebec Liquor Commission to revoke the plaintiff's liquor licence. Although *Roncarelli* was decided at

least in part on the basis of the Quebec civil law of delictual responsibility, it is widely regarded as having established that misfeasance in a public office is a recognized tort in Canada. See for example *Powder Mountain Resorts Ltd. v. British Columbia* (2001) 94 BCLR (3d) 14, 2001 BCCA 619; and *Alberta (Minister of Public Works, Supply and Services) v. Nilsson* (2002) 220 DLR (4th) 474, 2002 ABCA 283. In *Roncarelli*, the Premier was authorized to give advice to the Commission in respect of any legal questions that might arise, but had no authority to involve himself in a decision to revoke a particular licence. As Abbott J observed, at 184, Mr. Duplessis "was given no statutory power to interfere in the administration or direction of the Quebec Liquor Commission." Martland J made a similar observation, at 158, stating that Mr. Duplessis' conduct involved "the exercise of powers which, in law, he did not possess at all." From this, it is clear that the tort is not restricted to the abuse of a statutory or prerogative power actually held. If that were the case, there would have been no grounds on which to find Mr. Duplessis liable.

[20] This understanding of the tort is consistent with the widespread consensus in other common law jurisdictions that there is a broad range of misconduct that can found an action for misfeasance in a public office. For example, in *Northern Territory of Australia v. Mengel* (1995) 129 ALR 1 (HCA), Brennan J wrote as follows, at 25:

> The tort is not limited to an abuse of office by exercise of a statutory power. *Henly v. Mayor of Lyme* [(1828) 5 Bing. 91, 130 ER 995] was not a case arising from an impugned exercise of a statutory power. It arose from an alleged failure to maintain a sea wall or bank, the maintenance of which was a condition of the grant to the corporation of Lyme of the sea wall or bank and the appurtenant right to tolls. *Any act or omission done or made by a public official in the purported performance of the functions of the office can found an action for misfeasance in public office.* [Emphasis added.]

In *Garrett v. Attorney-General*, [1997] 2 NZLR 332 [CA], the Court of Appeal for New Zealand considered an allegation that a sergeant failed to investigate properly the plaintiff's claim that she had been sexually assaulted by a police constable. Blanchard J concluded, at 344, that the tort can be committed "by an official who acts or omits to act in breach of duty knowing about the breach and also knowing harm or loss is thereby likely to be occasioned to the plaintiff."

[21] The House of Lords reached the same conclusion in *Three Rivers District Council v. Bank of England (No. 3)*, [2000] 2 WLR 1220 (HL, Eng.). In *Three Rivers*, the plaintiffs alleged that officers with the Bank of England improperly issued a licence to the Bank of Credit and Commerce International and then failed to close the bank once it became evident that such action was necessary. Forced to consider whether the tort could apply in the case of omissions, the House of Lords concluded that "the tort can be constituted by an omission by a public officer as well as by acts on his part" (*per* Lord Hutton, at 1267). In Australia, New Zealand and the United Kingdom, it is equally clear that the tort of misfeasance is not limited to the unlawful exercise of a statutory or prerogative power actually held.

[22] What then are the essential ingredients of the tort, at least insofar as it is necessary to determine the issues that arise on the pleadings in this case? In *Three Rivers*, the House of Lords held that the tort of misfeasance in a public office can arise in one of two ways, what I shall call Category A and Category B. Category A involves conduct that is

specifically intended to injure a person or class of persons. Category B involves a public officer who acts with knowledge both that she or he has no power to do the act complained of and that the act is likely to injure the plaintiff. This understanding of the tort has been endorsed by a number of Canadian courts: see for example *Powder Mountain Resorts, supra; Alberta (Minister of Public Works, Supply and Services)* (CA), *supra*; and *Granite Power Corp. v. Ontario*, [2002] OJ No. 2188 (QL) (SCJ). It is important, however, to recall that the two categories merely represent two different ways in which a public officer can commit the tort; in each instance, the plaintiff must prove each of the tort's constituent elements. It is thus necessary to consider the elements that are common to each form of the tort.

[23] In my view, there are two such elements. First, the public officer must have engaged in deliberate and unlawful conduct in his or her capacity as a public officer. Second, the public officer must have been aware both that his or her conduct was unlawful and that it was likely to harm the plaintiff. What distinguishes one form of misfeasance in a public office from the other is the manner in which the plaintiff proves each ingredient of the tort. In Category B, the plaintiff must prove the two ingredients of the tort independently of one another. In Category A, the fact that the public officer has acted for the express purpose of harming the plaintiff is sufficient to satisfy each ingredient of the tort, owing to the fact that a public officer does not have the authority to exercise his or her powers for an improper purpose, such as deliberately harming a member of the public. In each instance, the tort involves deliberate disregard of official duty coupled with knowledge that the misconduct is likely to injure the plaintiff.

[24] Insofar as the nature of the misconduct is concerned, the essential question to be determined is not whether the officer has unlawfully exercised a power actually possessed, but whether the alleged misconduct is deliberate and unlawful. As Lord Hobhouse wrote in *Three Rivers, supra*, at 1269:

> The relevant act (or omission, in the sense described) must be unlawful. This may arise from a straightforward breach of the relevant statutory provisions or from acting in excess of the powers granted or for an improper purpose.

Lord Millett reached a similar conclusion, namely, that a failure to act can amount to misfeasance in a public office, but only in those circumstances in which the public officer is under a legal obligation to act. Lord Hobhouse stated the principle in the following terms, at 1269: "If there is a legal duty to act and the decision not to act amounts to an unlawful breach of that legal duty, the omission can amount to misfeasance [in a public office]." See also *R v. Dytham*, [1979] QB 722 (CA). So, in the United Kingdom, a failure to act can constitute misfeasance in a public office, but only if the failure to act constitutes a deliberate breach of official duty.

[25] Canadian courts also have made a deliberate unlawful act a focal point of the inquiry. In *Alberta (Minister of Public Works, Supply and Services) v. Nilsson* (1999) 70 Alta. LR (3d) 267, 1999 ABQB 440, at para. 108, the Court of Queen's Bench stated that the essential question to be determined is whether there has been deliberate misconduct on the part of a public official. Deliberate misconduct, on this view, consists of: (i) an intentional illegal act; and (ii) an intent to harm an individual or class of individuals. See also *Uni-Jet Industrial Pipe Ltd. v. Canada (Attorney General)* (2001) 156 Man. R (2d) 14,

2001 MBCA 40, in which Kroft JA adopted the same test. In *Powder Mountain Resorts*, *supra*, Newbury JA described the tort in similar terms, at para. 7:

> [I]t may, I think, now be accepted that the tort of abuse of public office will be made out in Canada where a public official is shown either to have exercised power for the specific purpose of injuring the plaintiff (i.e., to have acted in "bad faith in the sense of the exercise of public power for an improper or ulterior motive") or to have acted "unlawfully with a mind of reckless indifference to the illegality of his act" and to the probability of injury to the plaintiff. (See Lord Steyn in *Three Rivers*, at [1231].) Thus there remains what in theory at least is a clear line between this tort on the one hand, and what on the other hand may be called negligent excess of power—i.e., an act committed without knowledge of (or *subjective* recklessness as to) its unlawfulness and the probable consequences for the plaintiff. [Emphasis in original.]

Under this view, the ambit of the tort is limited not by the requirement that the defendant must have been engaged in a particular type of unlawful conduct, but by the requirement that the unlawful conduct must have been deliberate and the defendant must have been aware that the unlawful conduct was likely to harm the plaintiff.

[26] As is often the case, there are a number of phrases that might be used to describe the essence of the tort. In *Garrett*, *supra*, Blanchard J stated, at 350, that "[t]he purpose behind the imposition of this form of tortious liability is to prevent the deliberate injuring of members of the public by deliberate disregard of official duty." In *Three Rivers*, *supra*, Lord Steyn stated, at 1230, that "[t]he rationale of the tort is that in a legal system based on the rule of law executive or administrative power 'may be exercised only for the public good' and not for ulterior and improper purposes." As each passage makes clear, misfeasance in a public office is not directed at a public officer who inadvertently or negligently fails adequately to discharge the obligations of his or her office: see *Three Rivers*, at 1273, *per* Lord Millett. Nor is the tort directed at a public officer who fails adequately to discharge the obligations of the office as a consequence of budgetary constraints or other factors beyond his or her control. A public officer who cannot adequately discharge his or her duties because of budgetary constraints has not deliberately disregarded his or her official duties. The tort is not directed at a public officer who is *unable* to discharge his or her obligations because of factors beyond his or her control but, rather, at a public officer who *could* have discharged his or her public obligations, yet wilfully chose to do otherwise.

[27] Another factor that may remove an official's conduct from the scope of the tort of misfeasance in a public office is a conflict with the officer's statutory obligations and his or her constitutionally protected rights, such as the right against self-incrimination. Should such circumstances arise, a public officer's decision not to comply with his or her statutory obligation may not amount to misfeasance in a public office. I need not decide that question here except that it could be argued. A public officer who properly insists on asserting his or her constitutional rights cannot accurately be said to have deliberately disregarded the legal obligations of his or her office. Under this argument, an obligation inconsistent with the officer's constitutional rights is not itself lawful.

[28] As a matter of policy, I do not believe that it is necessary to place any further restrictions on the ambit of the tort. The requirement that the defendant must have been aware that his or her conduct was unlawful reflects the well-established principle that misfeasance in a public office requires an element of "bad faith" or "dishonesty." In a

democracy, public officers must retain the authority to make decisions that, where appropriate, are adverse to the interests of certain citizens. Knowledge of harm is thus an insufficient basis on which to conclude that the defendant has acted in bad faith or dishonestly. A public officer may in good faith make a decision that she or he knows to be adverse to interests of certain members of the public. In order for the conduct to fall within the scope of the tort, the officer must deliberately engage in conduct that he or she knows to be inconsistent with the obligations of the office.

[29] The requirement that the defendant must have been aware that his or her unlawful conduct would harm the plaintiff further restricts the ambit of the tort. Liability does not attach to each officer who blatantly disregards his or her official duty, but only to a public officer who, in addition, demonstrates a conscious disregard for the interests of those who will be affected by the misconduct in question. This requirement establishes the required nexus between the parties. Unlawful conduct in the exercise of public functions is a public wrong, but absent some awareness of harm there is no basis on which to conclude that the defendant has breached an obligation that she or he owes to the plaintiff, *as an individual*. And absent the breach of an obligation that the defendant owes to the plaintiff, there can be no liability in tort.

[30] In sum, I believe that the underlying purpose of the tort is to protect each citizen's reasonable expectation that a public officer will not intentionally injure a member of the public through deliberate and unlawful conduct in the exercise of public functions. Once these requirements have been satisfied, it is unclear why the tort would be restricted to a public officer who engaged in the unlawful exercise of a statutory power that she or he actually possesses. If the tort were restricted in this manner, the tort would not extend to a public officer, such as Mr. Duplessis, who intentionally *exceeded* his powers for the express purpose of interfering with a citizen's economic interests. Nor would it extend to a public officer who breached a statutory obligation for the same purpose. But there is no principled reason, in my view, why a public officer who wilfully injures a member of the public through intentional *abuse* of a statutory power would be liable, but not a public officer who wilfully injures a member of the public through an intentional *excess* of power or a deliberate failure to discharge a statutory duty. In each instance, the alleged misconduct is equally inconsistent with the obligation of a public officer not to intentionally injure a member of the public through deliberate and unlawful conduct in the exercise of public functions.

[31] I wish to stress that this conclusion is not inconsistent with *R v. Saskatchewan Wheat Pool*, [1983] 1 SCR 205 [Sask.], in which the Court established that the nominate tort of statutory breach does not exist. *Saskatchewan Wheat Pool* states only that it is *insufficient* that the defendant has breached the statute. It does not, however, establish that the breach of a statute cannot give rise to liability if the constituent elements of tortious responsibility have been satisfied. Put a different way, the mere fact that the alleged misconduct also constitutes a breach of statute is insufficient to exempt the officer from civil liability. Just as a public officer who breaches a statute might be liable for negligence, so too might a public officer who breaches a statute be liable for misfeasance in a public office. *Saskatchewan Wheat Pool* would only be relevant to this motion if the appellants had pleaded no more than a failure to discharge a statutory obligation. This, however, is not

the case. The principle established in *Saskatchewan Wheat Pool* has no bearing on the outcome of the motion on this appeal.

[32] To summarize, I am of the opinion that the tort of misfeasance in a public office is an intentional tort whose distinguishing elements are twofold: (i) deliberate unlawful conduct in the exercise of public functions; and (ii) awareness that the conduct is unlawful and likely to injure the plaintiff. Alongside deliberate unlawful conduct and the requisite knowledge, a plaintiff must also prove the other requirements common to all torts. More specifically, the plaintiff must prove that the tortious conduct was the legal cause of his or her injuries, and that the injuries suffered are compensable in tort law.

(2) Application to the Case at Hand

[33] As outlined earlier, on a motion to strike on the basis that the statement of claim discloses no reasonable cause of action, the facts are taken as pleaded. Consequently, the primary question that arises on this appeal is whether the statement of claim pleads each of the constituent elements of the tort.

[34] In respect of the first constituent element, namely, unlawful conduct in the exercise of public functions, the statement of claim alleges that the defendant officers did not cooperate with the SIU investigation, but, rather, took positive steps to frustrate the investigation. As described above, police officers are under a statutory obligation to cooperate fully with members of the SIU in the conduct of investigations, pursuant to s. 113(9) of the *Police Services Act*. On the face of it, the decision not to cooperate with an investigation constitutes an unlawful breach of statutory duty. Similarly, the alleged failure of the Chief to ensure that the defendant officers cooperated with the investigation also would seem to constitute an unlawful breach of duty. Under s. 41(1)(b) of the *Police Services Act*, the duties of a chief of police include ensuring that members of the police force carry out their duties in accordance with the Act. A decision not to ensure that police officers cooperate with the SIU is inconsistent with the statutory obligations of the office.

[35] As discussed above, an obligation inconsistent with a public officer's constitutional rights cannot give rise to misfeasance in a public office. It is arguable that the statutory obligation to cooperate fully with the members of the SIU cannot trump a police officer's constitutional right against self-incrimination. I do not need to answer this question because it has not been argued that the SIU's requests were inconsistent with the officers' constitutional rights. Nor has it been argued that the alleged misconduct, which includes submitting inaccurate and misleading shift notes and disobeying an order to remain segregated, is privileged by the right against self-incrimination. As a consequence, it is not "plain and obvious" that the officers were faced with a stark choice between complying with the SIU's requests and abandoning their right against self-incrimination, either as a matter of fact or law. The potential conflict between the duty to cooperate with the SIU and the right against self-incrimination cannot be relied on to dismiss the action at this stage of the proceedings.

[36] Insofar as the second requirement is concerned, the statement of claim alleges that the acts and omissions of the defendant officers "represented intentional breaches of their legal duties as police officers." This plainly satisfies the requirement that the officers were aware that the alleged failure to cooperate with the investigation was unlawful. The

allegation is not simply that the officers failed to comply with s. 113(9) of the *Police Services Act*, but that the failure to comply was intentional and deliberate. Insofar as the Chief is concerned, the statement of claim alleges as follows:

(i)   Chief Boothby, through his legal counsel, was directed by SIU officers to segregate the defendant officers and he deliberately failed to do so;

(ii) Chief Boothby failed to ensure that defendant police officers produced timely and complete notes;

(iii) Chief Boothby failed to ensure that the defendant police officers attended for requested interviews by SIU in a timely manner; and

(iv) Chief Boothby failed to ensure that the defendant police officers gave accurate and complete accounts of the specifics of the shooting incident.

[37] Although the allegation that the Chief *deliberately* failed to segregate the officers satisfies the requirement that the Chief *intentionally* breached his legal obligation to ensure compliance with the *Police Services Act*, the same cannot be said of his alleged failure to ensure that the defendant officers produced timely and complete notes, attended for interviews in a timely manner, and provided accurate and complete accounts of the incident. As above, inadvertence or negligence will not suffice; a mere failure to discharge the obligations of the office cannot constitute misfeasance in a public office. In light of the allegation that the Chief's failure to segregate the officers was deliberate, this is not a sufficient basis on which to strike the pleading. Suffice it to say, the failure to issue orders for the purpose of ensuring that the defendant officers cooperated with the investigation will only constitute misfeasance in a public office if the plaintiffs prove that the Chief deliberately failed to comply with the standard established by s. 41(1)(b) of the *Police Services Act*.

[38] The statement of claim also alleges that the defendant officers and the Chief "knew or ought to have known" that the alleged misconduct would cause the plaintiffs to suffer physically, psychologically and emotionally. Although the allegation that the defendants *knew* that a failure to cooperate with the investigation would injure the plaintiffs satisfies the requirement that the alleged misconduct was likely to injure the plaintiffs, misfeasance in a public office is an intentional tort that requires subjective awareness that harm to the plaintiff is a likely consequence of the alleged misconduct. At the very least, according to a number of cases, the defendant must have been subjectively reckless or wilfully blind as to the possibility that harm was a likely consequence of the alleged misconduct: see for example *Three Rivers, supra; Powder Mountain Resorts, supra;* and *Alberta (Minister of Public Works, Supply and Services)* (CA), *supra*. This, again, is not a sufficient basis on which to strike the pleading. It is clear, however, that the phrase "or ought to have known" must be struck from the statement of claim.

[39] The final factor to be considered is whether the damages that the plaintiffs claim to have suffered as a consequence of the aforementioned misconduct are compensable. In the defendant officers' submission, the alleged damages are non-compensable. Consequently, it is their submission that even if the plaintiffs could prove the other elements of the tort, it still would be plain and obvious that the actions for misfeasance in a public office must fail.

[40] In the defendant officers' submission, the essence of the plaintiffs' claim is that they were deprived of a thorough, competent and credible investigation. And owing to the fact that no individual has a private right to a thorough, competent and credible criminal investigation, the plaintiffs have suffered no compensable damages. If this were an accurate assessment of the plaintiffs' claim, I would agree. Individual citizens might desire a thorough investigation, or even that the investigation result in a certain outcome, but they are not entitled to compensation in the absence of a thorough investigation or if the desired outcome fails to materialize. This, however, is not an accurate assessment of the plaintiffs' submission. In their statement of claim, the plaintiffs also allege that they have suffered physically, psychologically and emotionally, in the form of mental distress, anger, depression and anxiety as a direct result of the defendant officers' failure to co-operate with the SIU.

[41] Although courts have been cautious in protecting an individual's right to psychiatric well-being, compensation for damages of this kind is not foreign to tort law. As the law currently stands, that the appellant has suffered grief or emotional distress is insufficient. Nevertheless, it is well established that compensation for psychiatric damages is available in instances in which the plaintiff suffers from a "visible and provable illness" or "recognizable physical or psychopathological harm": see for example *Guay v. Sun Publishing Co.*, [1953] 2 SCR 216 (BC), and *Frame v. Smith*, [1987] 2 SCR 99 (Ont.). Consequently, even if the plaintiffs could prove that they had suffered psychiatric damage, in the form of anxiety or depression, they still would have to prove both that it was caused by the alleged misconduct and that it was of sufficient magnitude to warrant compensation. But the causation and magnitude of psychiatric damage are matters to be determined at trial. At the pleadings stage, it is sufficient that the statement of claim alleges that the plaintiffs have suffered mental distress, anger, depression and anxiety as a consequence of the alleged misconduct.

[42] In the final analysis, I would allow the appeal in respect of the actions for misfeasance in a public office. If the facts are taken as pleaded, it is not plain and obvious that the actions for misfeasance in a public office against the defendant officers and the Chief must fail. The plaintiffs may well face an uphill battle, but they should not be deprived of the opportunity to prove each of the constituent elements of the tort.

. . .

Appeal against Court of Appeal's decision to strike the action for misfeasance in public office allowed.

NOTE

For decisions of the Supreme Court of Canada dealing with liability for the bad faith exercise of power under article 1457 of the *Quebec Civil Code*, see *Finney v. Barreau du Québec*, [2004] 2 SCR 17, 2004 SCC 36 (Que.) and *Les Enterprises Sibeca Inc. v. Frelighsburg (Municipality)*, [2004] 3 SCR 304, 2004 SCC 61 (Que.). See also Mrozinski, "Monetary Remedies for Administrative Law Errors" (2009), *CJALP* 133, at 135-52, for a discussion of the post-*Odhavji* common law cases.

Negligence in the Exercise of Statutory Powers

In certain circumstances, plaintiffs do not have to go as far as establishing malice, misfeasance in public office, or abuse of power to succeed in a tort or extra-contractuelle claim against a public authority. Sometimes, negligence or the civil law equivalent will be enough. As in the consideration of the existence and scope of the tort of misfeasance in the exercise of statutory powers or abuse of power, we commence this section with a case involving an attempt to fix a statutory "licensing" authority with liability—in this instance, a municipality acting in the exercise of its zoning powers to permit the development of a property. Here, too, principles of immunity from suit in the performance of certain kinds of function were crucial in the Supreme Court of Canada's determination that the municipality was not liable.

Welbridge Holdings Ltd. v. Winnipeg (Greater)
[1971] SCR 957 (Man.)

[This case arose out of the decision of the Supreme Court of Canada in *Wiswell v. Winnipeg (Greater)*, [1965] SCR 512 (Man.) in which the court struck down a zoning bylaw because of a lack of notice to a homeowners' association.

The plaintiff, a lessee of the relevant land, incurred expense in reliance on that bylaw, which would have allowed its proposed development. When the Supreme Court struck down the bylaw, the plaintiff brought an action for damages in tort alleging negligence against the municipality. This was dismissed in both Manitoba courts (1969), 4 DLR (3d) 509 (Man. QB) and (1970), 12 DLR (3d) 124 (Man. CA) and an appeal was taken to the Supreme Court of Canada.]

LASKIN CJC delivered the judgment of the Court:

[After detailing the facts, including the judgment of the Supreme Court in the earlier *Wiswell* decision, he continued:]

The liability in negligence sought to be imposed upon the defendant is not a vicarious one, resting upon the fault of a servant or agent of the defendant, but rather an original, independent liability. As I took the argument, it was said to proceed from a duty of the defendant, in enacting a rezoning by-law enlarging the development possibilities of designated land, to exercise reasonable care to see that the procedures upon which valid enactment depended were followed; and this duty was owed specially to those persons having or obtaining an interest in the affected land which enabled them to exploit those possibilities. There was, in the circumstances, more than merely a duty at large to the residents of the municipality or to the smaller number residing in the affected area. If a duty such as is urged exists, I would not exclude the appellant from the class of those to whom it was owing, merely because the appellant did not come into existence until after the invalid by-law was passed and did not acquire any interest in the affected land until about 16 months after its passage.

It is important to emphasize in this case that a duty of care of the defendant to the plaintiff cannot be based merely on the fact that economic loss would foreseeably result to the latter if By-law 177 should prove to be invalid. Indeed, it has long been recognized, as Lord Wright said in *"Liesbosch," Dredger v. SS. "Edison"* [1933] AC 449 (Eng. HL), at 460, that "the law cannot take account of everything that follows a wrongful act," a proposition that was recently applied in *SCM (United Kingdom) Ltd. v. W.J. Whittal & Son Ltd.* [1970] 3 All ER 245 (CA). However, the concern here is not with the consequences for which reparation should be made, but with whether there is liability for any consequences, however direct they be. On this issue, the *Hedley Byrne* case does not assist the plaintiff-appellant, even apart from the fact that it dealt with negligent words and not with negligent acts of omission as in the present case.

Accepting that *Hedley Byrne* has expanded the concept of duty of care, whether in amplification or extension of *M'Alister (or Donoghue) v. Stevenson* [1932] AC 562 (HL Sc.), it does not, nor, in my view, would any underlying principle which animates it, reach the case of a legislative body, or other statutory tribunal with *quasi*-judicial functions, which in the good faith exercise of its powers promulgates an enactment or makes a decision which turns out to be invalid because of anterior procedural defects. *McGillivray v. Kimber* (1915) 52 SCR 146 (NS), so far as it has a majority *rationale*, rests either on a complete want of jurisdiction or on intentional wrongdoing which might, in any event, be said to be reflected in the want of jurisdiction. It was not concerned with negligence. I refer also to what Rand J said about that case in *Roncarelli v. Duplessis* [1959] SCR 121 (Que.), at 141.

Under the considerations on which the *Hedley Byrne* enunciation of principle rests, it cannot be said in the present case either that a special relationship arose between the plaintiff and the defendant or that the defendant assumed any responsibility to the plaintiff with respect to procedural regularity. This would equally be my view if the plaintiff had been the applicant for the rezoning by-law. A rezoning application merely invokes the defendant's legislative authority and does not bring the applicant in respect of his particular interest into any private nexus with the defendant, whose concern is a public one in respect of the matter brought before it. The applicant in such case can reasonably expect honesty from the defendant but not a wider duty. Beyond this, I would adapt to the present case what the late Jackson J said in dissent in *Dalehite v. US*, 346 US 15 (1953) at 59 (a case concerned with the *Federal Tort Claims Act, 1946*, of the United States), as follows:

> When a [municipality] exerts governmental authority in a manner which legally binds one or many, [it] is acting in a way in which no private person could. Such activities do and are designed to affect, often deleteriously, the affairs of individuals, but courts have long recognized the public policy that such [municipality] shall be controlled solely by the statutory or administrative mandate and not by the added threat of private damage suits. [The words in brackets are mine.]

The defendant is a municipal corporation with a variety of functions, some legislative, some with also a *quasi*-judicial component (as the *Wiswell* case determined) and some administrative or ministerial, or perhaps better categorized as business powers. In exercising the latter, the defendant may undoubtedly (subject to statutory qualification) incur liabilities in contract and in tort, including liability in negligence. There may, therefore, be an individualization of responsibility for negligence in the exercise of business powers which does not exist when the defendant acts in a legislative capacity or performs a *quasi*-judicial duty.

Its public character, involving its political and social responsibility to all those who live and work within its territorial limits, distinguishes it, even as respects its exercise of any *quasi*-judicial function, from the position of a voluntary or statutory body such as a trade union or trade association which may have *quasi*-judicial and contractual obligations in dealing with its members: *cf. Abbott v. Sullivan* [1952] 1 All ER 226 (CA), and *Orchard v. Tunney* [1957] SCR 436 (Man.). A municipality at what may be called the operating level is different in kind from the same municipality at the legislative or *quasi*-judicial level where it is exercising discretionary statutory authority. In exercising such authority, a municipality (no less than a provincial Legislature or the Parliament of Canada) may act beyond its powers in the ultimate view of a Court, albeit it acted on the advice of counsel. It would be incredible to say in such circumstances that it owed a duty of care giving rise to liability in damages for its breach. "Invalidity is not the test of fault and it should not be the test of liability": see Davis, 3 *Administrative Law Treatise* (1958), at 487.

A narrower basis of liability is, however, proposed in the present case, one founded only on the failure to carry out the anterior procedural requirements for the enactment of By-law 177. Although those requirements were held in the *Wiswell* case to be expressions of a *quasi*-judicial function, this did not mean that the hearing to which they were relevant was a step unrelated to the legislative exercise in which the defendant was engaged. In approving what Freedman JA said in the *Wiswell* case in the Manitoba Court of Appeal, Hall J agreed that the enactment of the by-law was "[not] simply a legislative act": see 51 DLR (2d) 754 (SCC Man.), at 763. But that did not import that there was no legislative function involved in the enactment. There clearly was.

Moreover, even if the *quasi*-judicial function be taken in isolation, I cannot agree that the defendant in holding a public hearing as required by statute comes under a private tort duty, in bringing it on and in carrying it to a conclusion, to use due care to see that the dictates of natural justice are observed. Its failure in this respect may make its ultimate decision vulnerable, but no right to damages for negligence flows to any adversely affected person, albeit private property values are diminished or expense is incurred without recoverable benefit. If, instead of rezoning the land involved herein to enhance its development value, the defendant had rezoned so as to reduce its value and the owners had sold it thereafter, could it be successfully contended, when the rezoning by-law was declared invalid on the same ground as By-law 177, that the owners were entitled to recoup their losses from the municipality? I think not, because the risk of loss from the exercise of legislative or adjudicative authority is a general public risk and not one for which compensation can be supported on the basis of a private duty of care. The situation is different where a claim for damages for negligence is based on acts done in pursuance or in implementation of legislation or of adjudicative decrees.

Windsor Motors Ltd. v. District of Powell River (1969) 4 DLR (3d) 155 (BC CA), a judgment of the British Columbia Court of Appeal, is a useful illustration in this connection. The *Hedley Byrne* case was applied against a municipality by reason of advice negligently given by its licence inspector to the plaintiff that he could lawfully open a used car business in a certain location. The inspector went further and issued a licence to the plaintiff who had gone into business in reliance on the advice and licence. In fact, the zoning regulations forbade a used car business at the particular location, and the plaintiff had to move at considerable loss. The municipality's liability, moreover, was vicarious, arising upon a conclusion that it had to answer for its employee who knew of the plaintiff's reliance on his special knowledge when the plaintiff sought the employee's advice.

Finally, I refer to what appears to me to be the main ground upon which Freedman JA, dissenting in the present case in the Manitoba Court of Appeal, would have imposed liability upon the defendant, relying on the *Hedley Byrne* doctrine. He said this (see 12 DLR (3d) 124 (Man. CA) at 138-39):

> Metro's negligence was not spent with [the] omissions [as to notice]. ... It extended to its continuing representation that an apartment block could lawfully be erected on the site by reason of By-law 177 rezoning the land. With respect to that continuing representation Metro most assuredly owed a duty to the plaintiff. Indeed, it is clear from the evidence that the plaintiff received specific assurances from Metro that the land in question had been rezoned and that a high-rise apartment block could be erected there. It was on the faith of that continuing representation that the plaintiff proceeded with its plans, with resultant loss and damage.

I do not see how actionable negligence flows from the representation. Although I do not read the evidence as strongly against the defendant as did Freedman JA, the fact was that the land had been rezoned. There was, therefore, nothing false or misleading or careless in the representations or statements made to the plaintiff. I cannot accept what must be implicit in the learned Judge's reasoning that the representations involved an assumption of responsibility to the plaintiff for the procedural regularity of the rezoning proceedings. If the passage quoted is intended to suggest a vicarious liability, as in the *Windsor Motors Ltd.* case, there is no factual basis on which it can be put. I have already noted that the argument before this Court charged the defendant itself with actionable negligence. What has gone before in these reasons covers this issue, and I need not repeat it.

Since the action fails on the main substantive point it is unnecessary to deal with a number of preliminary issues raised in the case touching statutory and other bars to the plaintiff's action. Accordingly, the appeal is dismissed with costs.

Appeal dismissed.

NOTES

1. Why was the plaintiff relying principally on a negligence claim in this case? Would it have mattered here if the municipality had been acting in bad faith or maliciously in enacting the relevant rezoning bylaw? Does it matter for the purposes of this action that the plaintiff was suing for reliance expenses incurred for the purposes of enabling him to take advantage of the subsequently impugned bylaw, as opposed to suing for losses incurred by reason of disadvantages suffered as a result of the seeming effects of the bylaw—for example, a neighbour who had sold his house at what was ultimately undervalue because of the bylaw? Does the latter situation involve a higher claim for relief?

2. Laskin J, in the course of his judgment, suggests that, for the purposes of liability in negligence, there is a difference between the legislative and adjudicative functions of statutory authorities and those that can be classified as ministerial, administrative, or business

functions. This is similar to the distinction outlined by Estey J in *Berardinelli*, above. Is it a sensible distinction? Why does Laskin CJC emphasize the legislative aspect of the bylaw when, in *Wiswell*, the court took pains to classify the function as *quasi*-judicial? Does this make his arguments stronger than if it were a purely judicial function?

3. More recently, the Supreme Court of Canada has relied on Laskin J's distinction between the exercise of legislative or adjudicative authority and "acts done in pursuance or in implementation of legislation or of adjudicative decrees" to hold that government officials could be liable for negligent failure to implement a judicial decree: see *Holland v. Saskatchewan*, [2008] 2 SCR 551, 2008 SCC 42 (Sask.), at para. 14. In so holding, the court also linked its reasoning to the subsequent case law drawing a distinction between policy and operational decisions (see *infra*). For these purposes, decisions about the implementation of judicial decrees were operational, not policy decisions.

Anns v. Merton London Borough Council
[1978] AC 728 (Eng. HL)

[The *Public Health Act* created a wide range of duties and powers for local authorities to enable the safeguarding and promoting of the health of the public at large. Through building bylaws, local authorities were enabled to supervise and control the construction of buildings in their area and, in particular, the foundations of buildings.]

LORD WILBERFORCE: Building byelaws were duly made, under these powers, by the borough of Mitcham in 1953 and confirmed by the Minister in 1957. Byelaw 2 imposes an obligation on a person who erects any building to comply with the requirements of the byelaws. It imposes an obligation to submit plans. Byelaw 6 requires the builder to give to the council not less than 24 hours notice in writing: (a) of the date and time at which an operation will be commenced, and (b) before the covering up of any drain, private sewer, concrete or other material laid over a site, foundation or damp-proof course. Byelaws 18 and 19 contain requirements as to foundations. The relevant provision (18(1)(b)) is that the foundations of every building shall be taken down to such a depth, or be so designed and constructed as to safeguard the building against damage by swelling or shrinking of the subsoil.

Acting under these byelaws, the first defendants on 30th January 1962 gave notice to the Mitcham borough council of their intention to erect a new building (*viz.*, the block of maisonettes) in accordance with accompanying plans. The plans showed the base walls and concrete strip foundations of the block and stated, in relation to the depth from ground level to the underside of the concrete foundations, (3 feet or deeper to the approval of local authority). These plans were approved on 8th February 1962. The written notice of approval dated 9th February 1962 drew attention to the requirement of the byelaws that notice should be given to the surveyor at each of the following stages: before the commencement of the work and when the foundations were ready to be covered up.

The builders in fact constructed the foundations to a depth of only two feet six inches below ground level. It is not, at this stage, established when or whether any inspection was made.

[In 1970, after the builder-owner leased the block of maisonettes, there were structural movements and, among other defects, cracks appeared in the walls and the floors started sloping. The plaintiffs, who were lessees (two original, the rest by assignment), sued the builder and the council for damages, claiming that the damage was attributable to inadequate foundations. As against the council, they pleaded negligence by its servants or agents in approving the foundation and failing to inspect.

After stating the facts and reciting the history of the proceedings, Lord Wilberforce elaborated on the general development of the law in relation to the duty of care before commencing a consideration of the specifics of this case.]

One of the particular matters within the area of local authority supervision is the foundations of buildings—clearly a matter of vital importance, particularly because this part of the building comes to be covered up as building proceeds. Thus any weakness or inadequacy will create a hidden defect which whoever acquires the building has no means of discovering: in legal parlance there is no opportunity for intermediate inspection. So, by the byelaws, a definite standard is set for foundation work (see byelaw 18(1)(b) referred to above); the builder is under a statutory (*sc.* byelaw) duty to notify the local authority before covering up the foundations: the local authority has at this stage the right to inspect and to insist on any correction necessary to bring the work into conformity with the byelaws. It must be in the reasonable contemplation not only of the builder but also of the local authority that failure to comply with the byelaws' requirement as to foundations may give rise to a hidden defect which in the future may cause damage to the building affecting the safety and health of owners and occupiers. And as the building is intended to last, the class of owners and occupiers likely to be affected cannot be limited to those who go in immediately after construction.

What then is the extent of the local authority's duty towards these persons? Although, as I have suggested, a situation of "proximity" existed between the council and owners and occupiers of the houses, I do not think that a description of the council's duty can be based upon the "neighbourhood" principle alone or upon merely any such factual relationship as "control" as suggested by the Court of Appeal. So to base it would be to neglect an essential factor which is that the local authority is a public body, discharging functions under statute: its powers and duties are definable in terms of public not private law. The problem which this type of action creates, is to define the circumstances in which the law should impose, over and above, or perhaps alongside, these public law powers and duties, a duty in private law towards individuals such that they may sue for damages in a civil court. It is in this context that the distinction sought to be drawn between duties and mere powers has to be examined.

Most, indeed probably all, statutes relating to public authorities or public bodies, contain in them a large area of policy. The courts call this "discretion" meaning that the decision is one for the authority or body to make, and not for the courts. Many statutes also prescribe or at least presuppose the practical execution of policy decisions: a convenient description of this is to say that in addition to the area of policy or discretion, there is an operational area. Although this distinction between the policy area and the operational area is convenient, and illuminating, it is probably a distinction of degree; many "operational" powers or duties have in them some element of "discretion." It can safely be said that the more "operational" a power or duty may be, the easier it is to superimpose upon it a common law duty of care.

I do not think that it is right to limit this to a duty to avoid causing extra or additional damage beyond what must be expected to arise from the exercise of the power or duty. That may be correct when the act done under the statute *inherently* must adversely *affect* the interest of individuals. But many other acts can be done without causing any harm to anyone—indeed may be directed to preventing harm from occurring. In these cases the duty is the normal one of taking care to avoid harm to those likely to be affected.

Let us examine the *Public Health Act, 1936* in the light of this. Undoubtedly it lays out a wide area of policy. It is for the local authority, a public and elected body, to decide upon the scale of resources which it can make available in order to carry out its functions under Part II of the Act—how many inspectors, with what expert qualifications, it should recruit, how often inspections are to be made, what tests are to be carried out, must be for its decision. It is no accident that the Act is drafted in terms of functions and powers rather than in terms of positive duty. As was well said, public authorities have to strike a balance between the claims of efficiency and thrift (du Parcq LJ in *Kent v. East Suffolk Rivers Catchment Board* [1940] 1 KB 319 (CA), at 338): whether they get the balance right can only be decided through the ballot box, not in the courts. It is said—there are reflections of this in the judgments in *Dutton v. Bognor Regis Urban District Council* [1972] 1 QB 373 (CA)—that the local authority is under no duty to inspect, and this is used as the foundation for an argument, also found in some of the cases, that if it need not inspect all, it cannot be liable for negligent inspection: if it were to be held so liable, so it is said, councils would simply decide against inspection. I think that this is too crude an argument. It overlooks the fact that local authorities are public bodies operating under statute with a clear responsibility for public health in their area. They must, and in fact do, make their discretionary decisions responsibly and for reasons which accord with the statutory purpose; see *Ayr Harbour Trustees v. Oswald* (1883) 8 App. Cas. 623 (HL Sc.), at 639, *per* Lord Watson:

> the powers which [s. 10] confers are discretionary. ... But it is the plain import of the clause that the harbour trustees ... shall be vested with, and shall avail themselves of, these discretionary powers, whenever and as often as they may be of opinion that the public interest will be promoted by their exercise.

If they do not exercise their discretion in this way they can be challenged in the courts. Thus, to say that councils are under no duty to inspect, is not a sufficient statement of the position. They are under a duty to give proper consideration to the question whether they should inspect or not. Their immunity from attack, in the event of failure to inspect, in other words, though great is not absolute. And because it is not absolute, the necessary premise for the proposition "if no duty to inspect, then no duty to take care in inspection" vanishes.

Passing then to the duty as regards inspection, if made. On principle there must surely be a duty to exercise reasonable care. The standard of care must be related to the duty to be performed—namely to ensure compliance with the byelaws. It must be related to the fact that the person responsible for construction in accordance with the byelaws is the builder, and that the inspector's function is supervisory. It must be related to the fact that once the inspector has passed the foundations they will be covered up, with no subsequent opportunity for inspection. But his duty, heavily operational though it may be, is still a duty arising under the statute. There may be a discretionary element in its exercise— discretionary as to the time and manner of inspection, and the techniques to be used. A plaintiff complaining of negligence must prove, the burden being on him, that action taken was not within the limits of a discretion *bona fide* exercised, before he can begin to rely upon a common law duty of care. But if he can do this, he should, in principle, be able to sue.

Is there then, authority against the existence of any such duty or any reason to restrict it? It is said that there is an absolute distinction in the law between statutory duty and statutory power—the former giving rise to possible liability, the latter not, or at least not doing so unless the exercise of the power involves some positive act creating some fresh or additional damage.

My Lords, I do not believe that any such absolute rule exists: or perhaps, more accurately, that such rules as exist in relation to powers and duties existing under particular statutes, provide sufficient definition of the rights of individuals affected by their exercise, or indeed their non-exercise, unless they take account of the possibility that, parallel with public law duties there may coexist those duties which persons—private or public— are under at common law to avoid causing damage to others in sufficient proximity to them. This is, I think, the key to understanding of the main authority relied upon by the appellants—*East Suffolk Rivers Catchment Board v. Kent* [1941] AC 74 (Eng. HL).

The statutory provisions in that case were contained in the *Land Drainage Act, 1930* and were in the form of a power to repair drainage works including walls or banks. The facts are well known: there was a very high tide which burst the banks protecting the respondent's land. The Catchment Board, requested to take action, did so with an allocation of manpower and resources (graphically described by MacKinnon LJ [1940] 1 KB 319 (CA), at 330) which was hopelessly inadequate and which resulted in the respondent's land being flooded for much longer than it need have been. There was a considerable difference of judicial opinion. Hilbery J [1939] 2 All ER 207 (QB), who tried the case, held the board liable for the damage caused by the extended flooding and his decision was upheld by a majority of the Court of Appeal [1940] 1 KB 319. This House, by majority of four to one, reached the opposite conclusion [1941] AC 74. The speeches of their Lordships contain discussion of earlier authorities, which well illustrate the different types of statutory enactment under which these cases may arise. There are private Acts conferring powers—necessarily—to interfere with the rights of individuals: in such cases, an action in respect of damage caused by the exercise of the powers generally does not lie, but it may do so "for doing that which the legislature has authorised, if it be done negligently": see *Geddis v. Bann Reservoir Proprietors* (1878) 3 App. Cas. 430 (HL Ire.), at 456, *per* Lord Blackburn. Then there are cases where a statutory power is conferred, but the scale on which it is exercised is left to a local authority: *Sheppard v. Glossop Corporation* [1921] 3 KB 132 (CA). That concerned a power to light streets and the corporation decided, for economy reasons, to extinguish the lighting on Christmas night. Clearly this was within the discretion of the authority but Scrutton LJ in the Court of Appeal, at 146, contrasted this situation with one where "an option is given by statute to an authority to do or not to do a thing and it elects to do the thing and does it negligently." (Compare

Indian Towing Co. Inc. v. United States, 350 US 61 (1955), which makes just this distinction between a discretion to provide a lighthouse, and at operational level, a duty, if one is provided, to use due care to keep the light in working order.) Other illustrations are given.

My Lords, a number of reasons were suggested for distinguishing the *East Suffolk Case*—apart from the relevant fact that it was concerned with a different Act, indeed type of Act. It was said to be a decision on causation: I think that this is true of at least two of their Lordships (Viscount Simon LC and Lord Thankerton). It was said that the damage was already there before the board came on the scene: so it was but the board's action or inaction undoubtedly prolonged it, and the action was in respect of the prolongation. I should not think it right to put the case aside on such arguments. To me the two significant points about the case are, first, that it is an example, and a good one, where operational activity—at the breach in the wall—was still well within a discretionary area, so that the plaintiff's task in contending for a duty of care was a difficult one. This is clearly the basis on which Lord Romer, whose speech is often quoted as a proposition of law, proceeded. Secondly, although the case was decided in 1940, only one of their Lordships considered it in relation to a duty of care at common law. It need cause no surprise that this was Lord Atkin. His speech starts with this passage (at 88):

> On the first point [sc. whether there was a duty owed to the plaintiff and what was its nature] I cannot help thinking that the argument did not sufficiently distinguish between two kinds of duties: (1) A statutory duty to do or abstain from doing something. (2) A common law duty to conduct yourself with reasonable care so as not to injure persons liable to be affected by your conduct.

And later he refers to *Donoghue v. Stevenson* [1932] AC 562 (HL Sc.)—the only one of their Lordships to do so—though I think it fair to say that Lord Thankerton (who decided the case on causation) in his formulation of the duty must have been thinking in terms of that case. My Lords, I believe that the conception of a general duty of care, not limited to particular accepted situations, but extending generally over all relations of sufficient proximity, and even pervading the sphere of statutory functions of public bodies, had not at that time become fully recognised. Indeed it may well be that full recognition of the impact of *Donoghue v. Stevenson* in the latter sphere only came with the decision of this House in *Dorset Yacht Co. Ltd. v. Home Office* [1970] AC 1004 (Eng. HL).

· · ·

It is for this reason that the law, as stated in some of the speeches in *East Suffolk Rivers Catchment Board v. Kent* [1941] AC 74 (Eng. HL), but not in those of Lord Atkin or Lord Thankerton, requires at the present time to be understood and applied with the recognition that, quite apart from such consequences as may flow from an examination of the duties laid down by the particular statute, there may be room, once one is outside the area of legitimate discretion or policy, for a duty of care at common law. It is irrelevant to the existence of this duty of care whether what is created by the statute is a duty or a power: the duty of care may exist in either case. The difference between the two lies in this, that, in the case of a power, liability cannot exist unless the act complained of lies outside the ambit of the power. In *Dorset Yacht Co. Ltd. v. Home Office* [1970] AC 1004 (Eng. HL) the officers may (on the assumed facts) have acted outside any discretion delegated to them and having disregarded their instructions as to the precautions which they should take to prevent the trainees from escaping: see *per* Lord Diplock, at 1069. So in the present case, the allegations made are consistent with the council or its inspector having acted outside any delegated discretion either as to the making of an inspection, or as to the manner in which an inspection was made. Whether they did so must be determined at the trial. In the event of a positive determination, and only so, can a duty of care arise. I respectfully think that Lord Denning MR in *Dutton v. Bognor Regis Urban District Council* [1972] 1 QB 373 (CA), at 392 puts the duty too high.

[Lord Wilberforce concluded that a duty was owed to an owner or occupier of the building, that duty being to take reasonable care to see that a builder does not cover in foundations that do not comply with the bylaw. He then went on to state that, while it would be unreasonable to hold the council liable if the builder himself were immune, he agreed that the builder was also liable if not for common law negligence then at least for breach of a statutory duty. Damages recoverable would include all those that foreseeably arose from the breach of the duty including personal injury, damage to property, and damage to the dwelling place itself.

Lords Diplock, Simon of Glaisdale, and Russell of Killowen concurred with Lord Wilberforce. Lord Salmon delivered a separate judgment in which he reached the same result.]

Appeal dismissed.

Kamloops (City) v. Nielsen
[1984] 2 SCR 2 (BC)

[Nielsen had purchased a house from Hughes senior in December 1977. The house had defective foundations, a fact that was not ascertained by Nielsen until he was in occupation and it was drawn to his attention by a plumber when a pipe burst in November 1978. The house had been built by Hughes junior for his father. It had not been constructed in accordance with the requirements laid down by the city's building inspector. Indeed, the city had put a stop-work order on the further construction of the house until its requirements were satisfied. The requirements were not met, but Hughes junior, despite inspections and warnings, proceeded with the construction anyway, during which time he sold the property to his father in April 1974. Hughes senior was also advised of the city's concerns. He was an alderman and at that point made a plea for tolerance in the council chamber. There was then a strike of city employees and no further inspections were carried out by the city, though a plumbing permit was issued before Hughes senior occupied the house in February 1975.

The *Municipal Act* gave municipalities a discretion to promulgate bylaws regulating the construction of buildings. The city here had in fact promulgated such bylaws requiring buildings and occupancy permits, providing for a system of inspection, requiring builders to notify at various stages of construction, and requiring building inspectors to enforce the bylaws.

Nielsen sued both the city and Hughes senior for damages. As against Hughes senior, he alleged fraudulent misrepresentation, breach of contract, and negligence in the construction of the house. As against the city, he alleged negligence in failing to enforce the stop-work order or, alternatively, in failing to condemn the building as unfit for habitation.

At trial, the judge found both defendants liable and apportioned the liability on the basis of 75 percent attributable to Hughes senior and 25 percent to the city. The damages were held to be the cost of putting the house in the condition it should have been in had it been constructed properly. Only the city appealed, but its appeal was dismissed by the BC Court of Appeal. The city then appealed to the Supreme Court of Canada.]

WILSON J (Dickson and Ritchie JJ concurring): …

[After outlining the facts, then discussing *Anns*, she continued:]

It seems to me that, applying the principle in *Anns*, it is fair to say that the City of Kamloops had a statutory power to regulate construction by by-law. It did not have to do so. It was in its discretion whether to do so or not. It was, in other words, a "policy" decision. However, not only did it make the policy decision in favour of regulating construction by by-law, it also imposed on the city's building inspector a duty to enforce the provisions of the by-law. This would be Lord Wilberforce's "operational" duty. Is the city not then in the position where in discharging its operational duty it must take care not to injure persons such as the plaintiff whose relationship to the city was sufficiently close that the city ought reasonably to have had him in contemplation?

[Wilson J then rejected the argument that there was not a causal link between the actions of the city and the harm suffered by Nielsen before continuing:]

4. Non-feasance and Misfeasance

The second proposition put forward on behalf of the city goes directly to the central issue in the case, namely what, if any, duty was owed by the city to the plaintiff. Counsel submits that even if this Court were to adopt the principle in *Anns*, it should not be applied in this case because at most the city was guilty of nonfeasance rather than misfeasance. He submits that this distinction between nonfeasance and misfeasance is well established in Canadian law and that nonfeasance does not give rise to a liability in negligence. Accordingly, he submits, the principle in *Anns*, if adopted, should be confined in Canada to misfeasance cases. It is necessary to consider this submission in some detail.

A good starting point is the case most strongly relied upon by counsel, namely *McCrea v. White Rock* (1975) 56 DLR (3d) 525 (BC CA). The circumstances giving rise to that litigation are not dissimilar to those arising here. An owner of a building sued the municipality for negligent inspection of the structure after it collapsed. Alterations had been made to the building to substitute a beam supported by two columns for a bearing wall. Three inspections were made at the call of the contractor, one at the time of the pouring of the cement floor, another in relation to a laminated fire wall and the third in connection with the floor repair. Maclean JA summarizes the crucial facts as follows (at 528-29):

There was evidence that the practice in White Rock was for the contractor to call for inspections on behalf of the owner. No further calls for inspections were made and the inspector did not inspect the beam. In fact, the contractor did not follow the plan which he had submitted in support of the application for the building permit. However, the inspector had no reason to believe that an inspection other than one called for by the owner or his agent was required.

Berger J found that the city had been negligent, applying the reasoning in *Dutton v. Bognor Regis Urban Dist. Council* [1972] 1 QB 373 (CA). The Court of Appeal of British Columbia reversed the trial Judge. Maclean JA distinguished the *Dutton* case on the basis of the distinction between nonfeasance and misfeasance. Quoting from his judgment at 529-30:

> *In my view, if it could be said that the building inspector was at fault at all, his fault was one of non-feasance at the worst, rather than misfeasance.* The respondents relied on the case of *Dutton v. Bognor Regis Urban District Council* [1972] 1 QB 373 (CA). In that case the builder erected the building on a rubbish tip, and upon discovering the nature of the ground, he enlarged the foundations and made other provisions in an attempt to ensure the safety of the building. These attempts were futile, however, and the building became an almost total loss because of settling of the foundations. The building inspector had passed the foundations following an inadequate inspection. There is no doubt that his inspection was inadequate and careless in the extreme. The negligent inspection by the building inspector was clearly an act of misfeasance as Lord Denning MR, said at 475 of the report of the *Dutton* case:
>
>> It was his job to examine the foundations to see if they would take the load of the house. He failed to do it properly. In the third place, the council should answer for his failure. They were entrusted by Parliament with the task of seeing that houses were properly built. They received public funds for the purpose. ... Yet, they failed to protect them. *Their shoulders are broad enough to bear the loss.* [Emphasis added.]
>
> It should be noted that the building inspector was also held liable for the loss, but, as previously noted, the *Dutton* case was clearly a case of misfeasance on the part of the servant, the building inspector. Liability was imposed upon him by the law of England, but in my view, the same result does not necessarily follow here. *In any event, the Dutton case is distinguishable because that was a case of misfeasance whereas in my view this is a case of non-feasance if it is anything* (my emphasis).

Robertson JA agreed with Mclean JA that the *Dutton* case was distinguishable on this basis. In the course of his reasons for judgment he made reference to the judgment of Schroeder JA in *Schacht v. R* (1973) 30 DLR (3d) 641 (Ont. CA) [varied, *sub nom. O'Rourke v. Schacht*, [1976] 1 SCR 53 (Ont.)] in which certain police officers failed to warn the plaintiff of an excavation on the highway and as a result he suffered personal injuries. Action was brought against the Crown. After reviewing a number of cases and statutory provisions Schroeder JA, delivering the judgment of the Court, said

> Looked upon superficially the passivity of these two officers in the face of the manifest dangers inherent in the inadequately guarded depression across the highway may appear to be nothing more than non-feasance, but in the case of public servants subject not to a mere

social obligation, but to what I feel bound to regard as a legal obligation, it was *non-feasance amounting to misfeasance* (my emphasis).

Seaton JA commented on *Schacht* at pp 548-49 as follows:

In *Schacht* there is reference to non-feasance amounting to misfeasance. I do not understand that statement. In *Dutton* Sachs LJ, dealt with the borderline between non-feasance and misfeasance so as to much reduce the area termed non-feasance. The judgment under appeal adopts that reasoning and carried it further. I think that the result is not consistent with the decisions in England (for example, *East Suffolk, supra*), this jurisdiction (for example, *Stevens & Willson v. Chatham*, [[1934] SCR 353 (Ont.)], *Mainwaring v. Nanaimo* [1951] 4 DLR 519 (BC CA), and *Miller & Brown Ltd. v. City of Vancouver* (1966) 59 DLR (2d) 640 (BC CA), or elsewhere (for example, *Gorringe v. Transport Com'n (Tas.)* (1950) 80 CLR 357 (Tas), and *Oamaru Borough v. McLeod* [1967] NZLR 940 (SC)). *I think that this case must turn upon the presence or absence of a duty to inspect. If a duty is discovered the non-feasance/misfeasance dichotomy is not necessary* (my emphasis).

Seaton JA concluded that there was no duty on the appellant in the *McCrea* case to inspect and that was sufficient to dispose of the appeal. He was able to reach this conclusion because there was no obligation on the inspector to inspect until the owner had given notice and no notice had been given in respect of the beam.

The *McCrea* case, of course, predates *Anns*. Counsel relies also therefore on a number of Canadian decisions since *Anns* including a decision of this Court. In *Barratt v. North Vancouver* [1980] 2 SCR 418 (BC), a plaintiff was thrown from his bicycle and injured when he rode into a deep pothole in the road surface. The evidence indicated that the municipality had a once-every-2-weeks inspection system, that the road was properly inspected 1 week before the accident and that the pothole developed between the time of that inspection and the date of the accident. It was held that the plaintiff could not recover in negligence from the municipality on the ground that it should have provided for more frequent inspections. It should be noted that s. 513(2) of the *British Columbia Municipal Act* gave the municipality authority to lay out, construct, maintain and improve highways but it imposed no duty on the municipality to maintain its highways. Martland J said at 428:

In my opinion, no such duty existed. The Municipality, a public authority, exercised its power to maintain Marine Drive. It was under no statutory duty to do so. Its method of exercising its power was a matter of policy to be determined by the Municipality itself. If, in the implementation of its policy its servants acted negligently, causing damage, liability could arise, but the Municipality cannot be held to be negligent because it formulated one policy of operation rather than another.

The position of the Municipality is well stated in the judgment of du Parcq LJ in the Court of Appeal in *Kent v. East Suffolk Rivers Catchment Board* [1940] 1 KB 319 (CA) at 338:

The law would perhaps be more satisfactory, or at any rate seem more satisfactory in some hard cases, if a body which chose to exercise its powers were regarded as being in exactly the same position as one upon which an Act of Parliament imposed a duty. On the other hand, it must be remembered that when Parliament has left it to a public authority to decide which of its powers it shall exercise, and when and to what extent it shall exercise them, there would be some inconvenience in submitting to the subsequent decision of a jury, or judge of fact, the question whether the authority had acted reasonably, a question involving the consideration of matters of policy and sometimes the striking of a just balance between the rival claims of efficiency and thrift.

Martland J then stated his conclusion as follows (428):

> My conclusion is that the trial judge sought to impose upon the Municipality too heavy a duty, that the determination of the method by which the Municipality decided to exercise its power to maintain the highway, including its inspection system, was a matter of policy or planning, and that, absent negligence in the actual operational performance of that plan, the appellant's claim fails.

Two things are of interest about Martland J's reasons for judgment in *Barratt*. The first is that he makes no reference to any distinction between non-feasance and misfeasance although presumably, if the distinction was significant, this would be categorized as a non-feasance case. The second is that it seems to be central to his judgment that no duty was imposed upon the municipality. It was in the discretion of the municipality whether or to what extent it exercised its maintenance power. The Courts could not therefore interfere in the absence of negligence in the implementation of the policy it adopted with respect to inspection. This, it appears to me, is the *ratio* of the decision in *Barratt*.

This Court did, however, indicate some support for the non-feasance/misfeasance distinction in its earlier decision in *Stevens-Wilson v. Chatham* [1934] SCR 353 (Ont.). Indeed, that case may be viewed as the primary source of the distinction. The facts in brief were that the plaintiff's building burned while firemen stood by helplessly because they did not know how to turn off the electricity which was the source of the fire. The fireman telephoned the Public Utilities Commission to get them to turn off the electricity but by the time this was done the fire was out of control and the building could not be saved. Duff CJ and Smith J agreed with the trial Judge and the majority of the Ontario Court of Appeal that the firemen were not in these circumstances negligent. Rinfret J concurred but added (at 363):

> The City is not legally responsible in damages, in this case, for mere inactivity on the part of its firemen.

Crocket J dissented, expressing no opinion on whether the firemen were negligent in their "non-feasance or misfeasance" in waiting for the commission to shut off the power. He found that the commission had been negligent in being slow to shut off the power. Only Lamont J based his judgment primarily on the ground that the city was not liable "for mere inactivity on the part of its servants" (at 364). The "mere inactivity" approach would appear to have formed the basis of the non-feasance/misfeasance distinction adopted and applied in cases such as *Wing v. Moncton* [1940] 2 DLR 740 (NB CA); *Neabel v. Ingersoll* 63 DLR (2d) 484 (Ont. HC); and *McCrea v. White Rock, supra*.

5. *The Nature of the Alleged Breach*

Two important questions that must be answered in the present case are: (1) What was it that the building inspector failed to do in this case that is alleged to have contributed to the plaintiff's damage? and (2) Was he under a duty to do that thing? If the building inspector was under a duty to do the thing he failed to do, then it seems to me that Seaton JA was right in *McCrea* when he stated that the non-feasance/misfeasance dichotomy becomes irrelevant. He is in breach of a duty and, if his breach caused the plaintiff's damage, liability must ensue. If, however, he is under no duty to do the thing he failed to do, there can be no liability. Again, the non-feasance/misfeasance dichotomy is irrelevant.

Lambert JA, speaking for the Court of Appeal, found that the building inspector was under a public law duty to prevent the continuation of the construction of the building on structurally unsound foundations once he became aware that the foundations were structurally unsound. He was also under a public law duty to prevent the occupancy of the building by the Hughes or the plaintiff. He failed to discharge either of those public law duties. Lambert JA then went on to discuss the nature of the private law duty he was under. He said ((1981) 31 BCLR 311 (CA) at 319):

> I turn now to the private law duty. The conduct of the building inspector in response to the public law duties involved decisions on alternative courses of conduct which were, in my opinion, operational in character. The building was a danger to the occupant of the house and to adjoining property owners. It may have been a danger to anyone in the house. *Policy decisions could have confronted the city as to whether to prosecute or to seek an injunction. There may have been other policy choices. But a decision not to act at all, or a failure to decide to act, cannot be supported by any reasonable policy choice. That decision or failure was not "within the limits of a discretion bona fide exercised," using again the words of Lord Wilberforce.* It was certainly open to the trial judge to reach that conclusion. Indeed, having regard to the evidence of Mr Backmeyer, it was open to the trial judge to conclude that the decision not to act or the failure to decide to act, was influenced by the pressure exerted by Mr Hughes Sr in his capacity as alderman.
>
> I would follow the reasons of Lord Wilberforce in *Anns* in concluding that a private law duty was owed to Mr Nielsen as the owner and occupier of the house at the time when the defective foundations first became apparent by causing actual subsidence and damage. (my emphasis)

It seems to me that Lambert JA was correct in concluding that the courses of conduct open to the building inspector called for "operational" decisions. The essential question was what steps to take to enforce the provisions of the by-law in the circumstances that had arisen. He had a duty to enforce its provisions. He did not have a discretion whether to enforce them or not. He did, however, have a discretion as to how to go about it. This may, therefore, be the kind of situation envisaged by Lord Wilberforce when, after discussing the distinction between decisions and operational decisions, he added the rider:

> Although this distinction between the policy area and the operational area is convenient, and illuminating, it is probably a distinction of degree; many "operational" powers or duties have in them some element of "discretion." It can safely be said that the more "operational"

a power or duty may be, the easier it is to superimpose upon it a common law duty of care
([1978] AC at 754).

It may be, for example, that although the building inspector had a duty to enforce the
by-law, the lengths to which he should go in doing so involved policy considerations. The
making of inspections, the issuance of stop orders and the withholding of occupancy permits may be one thing; resort to litigation, if this became necessary, may be quite another.
Must the city enforce infractions by legal proceedings or does there come a point at which
economic considerations, for example, enter in? And if so, how do you measure the "operational" against the "policy" content of the decision in order to decide whether it is more
"operational" than "policy" or *vice versa*? Clearly this is a matter of very fine distinctions.

Lambert JA resolves this problem, as I apprehend the passage already quoted from his
reasons, by concluding that the city could have made a policy decision either to prosecute or to seek an injunction. If it had taken either of those steps, it could not be faulted.
Moreover, if it had considered taking either of those steps and decided against them, it
could likewise not be faulted. But not to consider taking them at all was not open to it.
In other words, as I read his reasons, his view was that the city at the very least had to
give serious consideration to taking the steps toward enforcement that were open to it. If
it decided against taking them, say on economic grounds, then that would be a legitimate
policy decision within the operational context and the Courts should not interfere with
it. It would be a decision made, as Lord Wilberforce put it, within the limits of a discretion *bona fide* exercised.

There is no evidence to support the proposition that the city gave serious consideration to legal proceedings and decided against them on policy grounds. Rather the evidence gives rise to a strong inference that the city, with full knowledge that the work was
progressing in violation of the by-law and that the house was being occupied without a
permit, dropped the matter because one of its aldermen was involved. Having regard to
the fact that we are here concerned with a statutory duty and that the plaintiff was clearly
a person who should have been in the contemplation of the city as someone who might
be injured by any breach of that duty, I think this is an appropriate case for the application of the principle in *Anns*. I do not think the appellant can take any comfort from the
distinction between non-feasance and misfeasance where there is a duty to act or, at the
very least, to make a conscious decision not to act on policy grounds. In my view, inaction for no reason or inaction for an improper reason cannot be a policy decision taken
in the *bona fide* exercise of discretion. Where the question whether the requisite action
should be taken has not been considered by the public authority, or at least has not been
considered in good faith, it seems clear that for that very reason the authority has not
acted with reasonable care. I conclude therefore that the conditions for liability of the city
to the plaintiff have been met.

It is of interest to note in this connection that other courses were open to the city. It
could have posted warning notices on the building and it could have condemned it. In
fact, it did neither even although it knew that work was continuing despite the stop work
order and that the house was being occupied without an occupancy permit. Indeed, it
issued a plumbing permit in August 1974 before the Hughes moved in.

6. The "Floodgates" Argument

Before leaving the issue of the liability of public officials and moving on to the equally vexatious issue of recovery for pure economic loss, I should like to say a word or two about what has come to be known as the "floodgates" argument. The floodgates argument would discourage a finding of private law duties owed by public officials on the ground that such a finding would open the floodgates and create an open season on municipalities. No doubt a similar type of concern was expressed about the vulnerability of manufacturers following the decision in *Donoghue v. Stevenson*. While I think this is an argument which cannot be dismissed lightly, I believe that the decision in *Anns* contains its own built-in barriers against the flood. For example, the applicable legislation or the subordinate legislation enacted pursuant to it must impose a private law duty on the municipality or public official before the principle in *Anns* applies. Further, the principle will not apply to purely policy decisions made in the *bona fide* exercise of discretion. This is, in my view, an extremely important feature of the *Anns* principle because it prevents the Courts from usurping the proper authority of elected representatives and their officials. At the same time, however, the principle ensures that in the operational area, *i.e.*, in implementing their policy decisions, public officials will be exposed to the same liability as other people if they fail in discharging their duty to take reasonable care to avoid injury to their neighbours. The only area, in my view, which leaves scope for honest concern is that difficult area identified by Lord Wilberforce where the operational subsumes what might be called secondary policy considerations, *i.e.*, policy considerations at the secondary level. This, I believe, is the area into which this case falls. This case, however, is more easily disposed of by virtue of the complete failure of the municipality to deal with the policy considerations. On the assumption that by and large municipalities and their officials discharge their responsibilities in a conscientious fashion, I believe that such a failure will be the exception rather than the rule and that the scope for application of the principle in *Anns* will be relatively narrow. I do not see it, as do some commentators, as potentially ruinous financially to municipalities. I do see it as a useful protection to the citizen whose ever-increasing reliance on public officials seem to be a feature of our age: see Linden, "Tort Law's Role in the Regulation and Control of the Abuse of Power," Law Society of Upper Canada, Special Lectures (1979), at 67.

[Wilson J then ruled that recovery for economic loss was not precluded in this case by *Rivtow Marine Ltd. v. Washington Iron Works*, [1974] SCR 1189 (BC).]

I said earlier in commenting upon the floodgates argument in relation to the imposition of a private law duty of care that I was not troubled by the thought that public officials in discharging their duties should incur the same liability as ordinary citizens. It may be that in exposing public authorities to liability for economic loss when under our law as it presently stands a private litigant may not be so exposed, the Court would be extending the liability of public authorities beyond that of private litigants. I am not, however, persuaded that this is so. Like Lambert JA I tend to think that the problem of concurrent liability in contract and tort played a major role in the restrictive approach taken by the majority in *Rivtow* and that, as in the case of *Hedley Byrne*, we will have to await the outcome of a developing jurisprudence around that decision also ... .

I do not believe that to permit recovery in this case is to expose public authorities to the indeterminate liability referred to in *Ultramares* [*v. Touche*, 255 NY 170 (1931)]. In order to obtain recovery for economic loss the statute has to create a private law duty to the plaintiff alongside the public law duty. The plaintiff has to belong to the limited class of owners or occupiers of the property at the time the damage manifests itself. Loss caused as a result of policy decisions made by the public authority in the *bona fide* exercise of discretion will not be compensable. Loss caused in the implementation of policy decisions will not be compensable if the operational decision includes a policy element. Loss caused in the implementation of policy decisions, *i.e.*, operational negligence will be compensable. Loss will also be compensable if the implementation involves policy considerations and the discretion exercised by the public authority is not exercised in good faith. Finally, and perhaps this merits some emphasis, economic loss will only be recoverable if as a matter of statutory interpretation it is a type of loss the statute intended to guard against.

It seems to me that recovery for economic loss on the foregoing basis accomplishes a number of worthy objectives. It avoids undue interference by the courts in the affairs of public authorities. It gives a remedy where the Legislature has impliedly sanctioned it and justice clearly requires it. It imposes enough of a burden on public authorities to act as a check on the arbitrary and negligent discharge of statutory duties. For these reasons I would permit recovery of the economic loss in this case.

McINTYRE J (Estey J concurring) dissenting: Liability for negligence of a public authority, as dealt with in *Anns* and the other cases considered with it, would arise out of the activities of the public authority in the conduct of its business. Public authorities, in addition to their administrative and regulatory functions, must perform many tasks. They enter into a wide variety of contracts covering business, commercial and industrial enterprises, and public works. They enter the market place and operate as do private corporations and private individuals. In these circumstances there would seem to be no reason why a public authority should not be liable for its own acts of negligence and vicariously liable for the negligence of its servants in the performance of their duties of employment. The public authority, as has been noted in *Anns*, differs from the private citizen in that, while it must undertake much in accordance with its mandate, it has as a rule limited resources and frequently limited credit and relatively fixed revenues. The employment of those resources, frequently not sufficient to cover completely all responsibilities, will involve policy choices as to their application. The policy choice protective provision developed in *Anns* meets this problem. It will be observed, however, that in *Anns* and in the various other cases which preceded it (*Dutton v. Bognor Regis* and *Dorset Yacht Co. v. Home Office*) and in many later cases which have applied it, the policy choice required of the public authority was one which would protect it against negligence in carrying out the corporate functions and such negligence is ordinarily found in the conduct of its employees for which the authority may be vicariously liable.

No such negligence occurred in the case at bar. The building inspectors, as has been pointed out, fully and adequately carried out their duties and I am unable to agree with Lambert JA when he said [at 319]:

> The conduct of the building inspector in response to the public law duties involved decisions on alternative courses of conduct which were, in my opinion, operational in character.

The building inspector in his response to the problems he discovered faced no alternative course of action. His duty was to report, and he did so, and any alternative courses of conduct in response to public duties were for the council, the city itself, and I am wholly unable to characterize them as operational in character.

The exercise of the discretion by the city regarding enforcement proceedings in Court differs fundamentally from the "policy choice" contemplated by *Anns*. In my opinion, it does not involve considerations of negligence because it is not properly subject to restriction by a private law duty of care. It involves, in my view, such considerations as those discussed by Laskin J (as he then was) in *Welbridge Hldgs. Ltd. v. Winnipeg* [1971] SCR 957 (Man.).

> ⋯

The facts in *Welbridge* differ widely from the facts at Bar, but the case emphasizes the different consequences that may flow from the exercise or non-exercise of *quasi*-judicial powers by a public authority. Laskin J also pointed out the difference between a public body vicariously liable in negligence for the conduct of its employees and a public body charged with "an original independent liability." This factor is of fundamental importance and goes far to distinguish the case at Bar from the trilogy of cases culminating in *Anns*. Here we have a public body against whom it is said, you are negligent in that you failed to exercise what is essentially a *quasi*-judicial function, that is, you failed to enforce your by-law by proceeding in Court. It is my view that a public body, vested with the discretion of by-law enforcement, may not be required by a Court to exercise that power in a certain way and is not under a private law duty to do so. I draw support in reaching this conclusion from *Welbridge*.

Finding that the City is not under a private law duty to enforce its building by-law by Court proceedings or demolition does not mean that its discretion is completely unfettered. This becomes clear from a reference to *Roncarelli v. Duplessis* [1959] SCR 121 (Que.) at 140, where Rand J said:

> In public regulation of this sort there is no such thing as absolute and untrammelled "discretion," that is that action can be taken on any ground or for any reason that can be suggested to the mind of the administrator; no legislative Act can, without express language, be taken to contemplate an unlimited arbitrary power exercisable for any purpose, however capricious or irrelevant, regardless of the nature or purpose of the statute. Fraud and corruption in the Commission may not be mentioned in such statutes but they are always implied as exceptions. "Discretion" necessarily implies good faith in discharging public duty; there is always a perspective within which a statute is intended to operate; and any clear departure from its lines or objects is just as objectionable as fraud or corruption.

These words have the support of Martland J in his reasons in the same case, at 155-57, which was concurred in by Kerwin CJ and Locke J. The plaintiff might have succeeded in this case on a showing of corruption upon the part of the city officials and council, or upon showing that the failure to prosecute resulted from consideration of extraneous or improper matters or from bad faith. But the scanty evidence in the perhaps inadequate record before this Court would allow no such conclusion to be drawn.

In the case at Bar the record discloses little as to what, if any, steps were taken by the Council towards the enforcement of its by-law. It is clear that the defective foundations rendered the house unsafe. It is equally clear that the building inspectors, having found the defective work, reported the matter to the council and took such steps as were open to them to correct matters including the refusal to lift the "stop work" order or give an occupancy permit. It is also evident that the council was aware of the infraction of the by-law and that the respondents Hughes were living in the house. There is no evidence of any positive step taken in the matter by the council, save that at one time it consulted its city solicitor who shortly after returned the file with a covering letter which is not before us. From all this, the only conclusion that can be reached is that the council took no further step towards enforcement and there is no evidence which would justify any inference of bad faith or impropriety.

Appeal dismissed.

NOTES

1. Is the difference between the majority and minority judgments in this case one with respect to the interpretation of the facts or is it based on a variation of views with respect to the applicable principles? In dissent, McIntyre J seems to place much reliance on the presence of a *quasi*-judicial function. What is that function and do you agree with McIntyre J's classification and use of it as an excluder of liability? In the course of her judgment, Wilson J confronts the arguments with respect to unlimited and indeterminate liability on the part of municipalities and concludes that the effect of a judgment in favour of Nielsen will not be such as to open the floodgates of liability as had been claimed by counsel for the municipality. Do you agree with this conclusion? To what extent does the majority position act as an incentive for municipalities to curtail their regulation of construction activities within their jurisdiction? If a municipality has a choice under its empowering legislation as to whether to regulate a particular area of activity, a choice that in no way attracts the possibility of liability in negligence, why should the making of a positive decision to regulate open up that possibility? Does this not simply create an incentive for inaction? Counsel for the City of Kamloops argued that the *Anns* principles did not apply here because what was involved was non-feasance rather than misfeasance. How was this argument treated by the majority? Where does Wilson J's judgment leave the non-feasance–misfeasance distinction in this branch of Canadian law?

2. Clearly, Wilson J accepts the *Anns* principle that for the purposes of the negligence liability of public authorities, a distinction is to be drawn between policy and operational decisions and, indeed, that liability should not exist for the policy elements in the exercise of operational functions. Wilson J herself admits that the drawing of such distinctions will not be easy but obviously she also believes that they have a legitimate policy foundation. Do you agree with this conclusion? What are or will be the criteria for distinguishing between purely

operational activities and operational activities involving policy choices? Recollect the extract from Cohen and his concerns about the utility of the policy-operational distinction.

Just v. British Columbia
[1989] 2 SCR 1228 (BC)

[Just was injured and his daughter killed when a rock fell on their car while they were stopped on a highway in British Columbia. At the time of the tragedy, the Department of Highways had in place a system of inspection aimed at preventing the fall of boulders onto highways. At trial, McLachlin J (as she then was) held that this matter came within the policy domain and was therefore incapable of supporting a duty of care to Just and his daughter ((1985), 64 BCLR 349 (SC)) and this conclusion was sustained on appeal ((1986), 10 BCLR (2d) 223 (CA)). Just obtained leave to appeal to the Supreme Court of Canada.]

CORY J (concurred in by Dickson CJ, Wilson, La Forest, L'Heureux-Dubé, and Gonthier JJ with Sopinka J dissenting): ... In the case at bar the accident occurred on a well used major highway in the Province of British Columbia. All the provinces across Canada extol their attributes and attractions in the fierce competition for tourist business. The skiing facilities at Whistler are undoubtedly just such a magnificent attraction. It would be hard to imagine a more open and welcoming invitation to use those facilities than that extended by the provincial highway leading to them. In light of that invitation to use both the facilities and the highway leading to them, it would appear that apart from some specific exemption, arising from a statutory provision or established common law principle, a duty of care was owed by the province to those that use its highways. That duty of care would extend ordinarily to reasonable maintenance of those roads. The appellant as a user of the highway was certainly in sufficient proximity to the respondent to come within the purview of that duty of care. In this case it can be said that it would be eminently reasonable for the appellant as a user of the highway to expect that it would be reasonably maintained. For the Department of Highways it would be a readily foreseeable risk that harm might befall users of a highway if it were not reasonably maintained. That maintenance could, on the basis of the evidence put forward by the appellant, be found to extend to the prevention of injury from falling rock.

Even with the duty of care established, it is necessary to explore two aspects in order to determine whether liability may be imposed upon the respondent. First, the applicable legislation must be reviewed to see if it imposes any obligation upon the respondent to maintain its highways or alternatively if it provides an exemption from liability for failure to so maintain them. Secondly, it must be determined whether the province is exempted from liability on the grounds that the system of inspections, including their quantity and quality, constituted a "policy" decision of a government agency and was thus exempt from liability.

[After considering the relevant legislation and concluding that it did not provide an exemption from liability but rather imposed a duty of maintenance on the department, he continued.]

> ### *Was the Decision of the Rock Section as to the Quantity and Quality of Inspections a "Policy" Decision Exempting the Respondent from Liability?*

The respondent placed great reliance on the decision of this Court in *Barratt v. District of North Vancouver* [1980] 2 SCR 418 (BC). ...

[Cory J here considered *Barratt*, including *dicta* of Martland J to the effect that, in the policy domain, no duty of care rested on statutory authorities.]

With the greatest respect, I am of the view that the portion of the reasons relied on by the respondent went farther than was necessary to the decision or appropriate as a statement of principle. For example, the Court would not have approved as "policy" a system that called for the inspection of the roads in a large urban municipality once every five years. Once a policy to inspect is established then it must be open to a litigant to attack the system as not having been adopted in a *bona fide* exercise of discretion and to demonstrate that in all the circumstances, including budgetary restraints, it is appropriate for a court to make a finding on the issue.

The functions of government and government agencies have multiplied enormously in this century. Often government agencies were and continue to be the best suited entities and indeed the only organizations which could protect the public in the diverse and difficult situations arising in so many fields. They may encompass such matters as the manufacture and distribution of food and drug products, energy production, environmental protection, transportation and tourism, fire prevention and building developments. The increasing complexities of life involve agencies of government in almost every aspect of daily living. Over the passage of time the increased government activities gave rise to incidents that would have led to tortious liability if they had occurred between private citizens. The early governmental immunity from tortious liability became intolerable. This led to the enactment of legislation which in general imposed liability on the Crown for its acts as though it were a person. However, the Crown is not a person and must be free to govern and make true policy decisions without becoming subject to tort liability as a result of those decisions. On the other hand, complete Crown immunity should not be restored by having every government decision designated as one of policy. Thus the dilemma giving rise to the continuing judicial struggle to differentiate between policy and operation. Particularly difficult decisions will arise in situations where governmental inspections may be expected.

The dividing line between "policy" and "operation" is difficult to fix, yet it is essential that it be done. The need for drawing the line was expressed with great clarity by Becker J of the United States District Court in *Blessing v. United States*, 447 FS 1160 (1978).

[Cory J here quoted from that judgment, part of which reads:

Read as a whole and with an eye to discerning a policy behind this provision, [the section] seems to us only to articulate a policy of preventing tort actions from becoming a vehicle for judicial interference with decisionmaking that is properly exercised by other branches of the government and of protecting "the Government from liability that would seriously handicap efficient government operations," ... Statutes, regulations, and discretionary functions

... are, as a rule, manifestations of policy judgments made by the political branches. In our tripartite governmental structure, the courts generally have no substantive part to play in such decisions. Rather, the judiciary confines itself—or, under laws such as the [*Federal Tort Claims Act*] discretionary function exception, is confined—to adjudication of facts based on discernible objective standards of law. In the context of tort actions, with which we are here concerned, these objective standards are notably lacking when the question is not negligence but social wisdom, not due care but political practicability, not reasonableness but economic expediency. Tort law simply furnishes an inadequate crucible for testing the merits of social, political or economic decisions.]

The need for distinguishing between a governmental policy decision and its operational implementation is thus clear. True policy decisions should be exempt from tortious claims so that governments are not restricted in making decisions based upon social, political or economic factors. However, the implementation of those decisions may well be subject to claims in tort. What guidelines are there to assist courts in differentiating between policy and operation?

Mason J, speaking for himself and one other member of the Australian High Court in *Sutherland Shire Council v. Heyman* (1985) 60 ALR 1 (HCA NSW), set out what I find to be most helpful guidelines. He wrote:

[Only part of the quotation is included.]

The distinction between policy and operational factors is not easy to formulate, but the dividing line between them will be observed if we recognize that *a public authority is under no duty of care in relation to decisions which involve or are dictated by financial, economic, social or political factors or constraints.* Thus budgetary allocations and the constraints which they entail in terms of allocation of resources cannot be made the subject of a duty of care. *But it may be otherwise when the courts are called upon to apply a standard of care to action or inaction that is merely the product of administrative direction, expert or professional opinion, technical standards or general standards of reasonableness.* [Emphasis added.]

The duty of care should apply to a public authority unless there is a valid basis for its exclusion. A true policy decision undertaken by a government agency constitutes such a valid basis for exclusion. What constitutes a policy decision may vary infinitely and may be made at different levels although usually at a high level.

The decisions in *Anns v. Merton London Borough Council* and *City of Kamloops v. Nielsen* indicate that a government agency in reaching a decision pertaining to inspection must act in a reasonable manner which constitutes a *bona fide* exercise of discretion. To do so they must specifically consider whether to inspect and if so, the system of inspection must be a reasonable one in all the circumstances.

For example, at a high level there may be a policy decision made concerning the inspection of lighthouses. If the policy decision is made that there is such a pressing need to maintain air safety by the construction of additional airport facilities with the result that no funds can be made available for lighthouse inspection, then this would constitute a *bona fide* exercise of discretion that would be unassailable. Should then a lighthouse beacon be extinguished as a result of the lack of inspection and a shipwreck ensue, no liability can be placed upon the government agency. The result would be the same if a policy decision were made to increase the funds for job retraining and reduce the funds for lighthouse inspection so that a beacon could only be inspected every second year and as a result the light was extinguished. Once again this would constitute the *bona fide* exercise of discretion. Thus a decision either not to inspect at all or to reduce the number of inspections may be an unassailable policy decision. This is so provided it constitutes a reasonable exercise of *bona fide* discretion based, for example, upon the availability of funds.

On the other hand, if a decision is made to inspect lighthouse facilities, the system of inspections must be reasonable and they must be made properly ... . Thus once the policy decision to inspect has been made, the Court may review the scheme of inspection to ensure it is reasonable and has been reasonably carried out in light of all the circumstances, including the availability of funds, to determine whether the government agency has met the requisite standard of care.

At a lower level, government aircraft inspectors checking on the quality of manufactured aircraft parts at a factory may make a policy decision to make a spot check of manufactured items throughout the day as opposed to checking every item manufactured in the course of one hour of the day. Such a check as to how the inspection was to be undertaken could well be necessitated by the lack of both trained personnel and funds to provide such inspection personnel. In those circumstances the policy decision that a spot check inspection would be made could not be attacked. ...

Thus a true policy decision may be made at a lower level provided that the government agency establishes that it was reasonable decision in light of the surrounding circumstances.

The consideration of the duty of care that may be owed must be kept separate and distinct from the consideration of the standard of care that should be maintained by the government agency involved.

Let us assume a case where a duty of care is clearly owed by a governmental agency to an individual that is not exempted either by a statutory provision or because it was a true policy decision. In those circumstances the duty of care owed by the government agency would be the same as that owed by one person to another. Nevertheless the standard of care imposed upon the Crown may not be the same as that owed by an individual. An individual is expected to maintain his or her sidewalk or driveway reasonably, while a government agency such as the respondent may be responsible for the maintenance of hundreds of miles of highway. The frequency and the nature of inspection required of the individual may well be different from that required of the Crown. In each case the frequency and method must be reasonable in light of all the surrounding circumstances. The governmental agency should be entitled to demonstrate that balanced against the nature and quantity of the risk involved, its system of inspection was reasonable in light of all the circumstances including budgetary limits, the personnel and equipment available to it and that it had met the standard duty of care imposed upon it.

It may be convenient at this stage to summarize what I consider to be the principles applicable and the manner of proceeding in cases of this kind. As a general rule, the traditional tort law duty of care will apply to a government agency in the same way that it will apply to an individual. In determining whether a duty of care exists the first question to be resolved is whether the parties are in a relationship of sufficient proximity to warrant the imposition of such a duty. In the case of a government agency, exemption from this imposition of duty may occur as a result of an explicit statutory exemption. Alternatively, the exemption may arise as a result of the nature of the decision made by the government agency. That is, a government agency will be exempt from the imposition of a duty of care in situations which arise from its pure policy decisions.

In determining what constitutes such a policy decision, it should be borne in mind that such decisions are generally made by persons of a high level of authority in the agency, but may also properly be made by persons of a lower level of authority. The characterization of such a decision rests on the nature of the decision and not on the identity of the actors. As a general rule, decisions concerning budgetary allotments for departments or government agencies will be classified as policy decisions. Further, it must be recalled that a policy decision is open to challenge on the basis that it is not made in the *bona fide* exercise of discretion. If after due consideration it is found that a duty of care is owed by the government agency and no exemption by way of statute or policy decision-making is found to exist, a traditional torts analysis ensues and the issue of standard of care required of the government agency must next be considered.

The manner and quality of an inspection system is clearly part of the operational aspect of a governmental activity and falls to be assessed in the consideration of the standard of care issue. At this stage, the requisite standard of care to be applied to the particular operation must be assessed in light of all the surrounding circumstances including, for example, budgetary restraints and the availability of qualified personnel and equipment.

Turning to the case at bar it is now appropriate to apply the principles set forth by Mason J in *Sutherland Shire Council v. Heyman, supra*, to determine whether the decision or decisions of the government agency were policy decisions exempting the province from liability. Here what was challenged was the manner in which the inspections were carried out, their frequency or infrequency and how and when trees above the rock cut should have been inspected, and the manner in which the cutting and scaling operations should have been carried out. In short, the public authority had settled on a plan which called upon it to inspect all slopes visually and then conduct further inspections of those slopes where the taking of additional safety measures was warranted. Those matters are all part and parcel of what Mason J described as "the product of administrative direction, expert or professional opinion, technical standards or general standards of care." They were not decisions that could be designated as policy decisions. Rather they were manifestations of the implementation of the policy decision to inspect and were operational in nature. As such, they were subject to review by the Court to determine whether the respondent had been negligent or had satisfied the appropriate standard of care.

At trial the conclusion was reached that the number and frequency of inspections, of scaling and other remedial measures were matters of policy; as a result no findings of fact were made on the issues bearing on the standard of care. Since the matter was one of operation the respondent was not immune from suit and the negligence issue had to be canvassed in its entirety. The appellant was therefore entitled to a finding of fact on these questions and a new trial should be directed to accomplish this.

It may well be that the respondent at the new trial will satisfy the Court that it has met the requisite standard of care. It is apparent that although the *Crown Proceeding Act* imposes the liability of a person upon the Crown, it is not in the same position as an individual. To repeat, the respondent is responsible not for the maintenance of a single private road or driveway but for the maintenance of many hundreds of miles of highway running through difficult mountainous terrain, all of it to be undertaken within budgetary restraints. As noted earlier, decisions reached as to budgetary allotment for departments or government agencies will in the usual course of events be policy decisions that cannot be the basis for imposing liability in tort even though these political policy decisions will have an effect upon the frequency of inspections and the manner in which they may be carried out. All of these factors should be taken into account in determining whether the system was adopted in *bona fide* exercise of discretion and whether within that system the frequency, quality and manner of inspection were reasonable.

To proceed in this way is fair to both the government agency and the litigant. Once a duty of care that is not exempted has been established the trial will determine whether the government agency has met the requisite standard of care. At that stage the system and manner of inspection may be reviewed. However, the review will be undertaken bearing in mind the budgetary restraints imposed and the availability of personnel and equipment to carry out such an inspection.

Appeal allowed and new trial ordered.

NOTES

1. On the retrial, the BC Supreme Court found that the requisite standard of care had not been met and Just recovered damages of approximately $1 million: (1991), 60 BCLR 209 (SC).

2. Sopinka J's dissent was founded to an extent on a sense that there is a crisis in the domain of fault-based liability stemming at least in part from the expansion of the liability of public authorities in negligence. In his view, the impact of the majority judgment was in reality a movement in the direction of court assessment of policy decisions to the extent that the exercise of judgment as to the "extent and manner of inspection of the inspection program" would be subject to a negligence standard.

3. In an era in which municipalities and government departments frequently contract out their statutory responsibilities, it is also important that the court continues to recognize the concept of non-delegable duty that prevents a public defendant pleading that the damage was caused by an independent contractor: *Lewis (Guardian ad litem of) v. British Columbia*, [1997] 3 SCR 1145 (BC) and *Mochinski v. Trendline Industries Ltd.*, [1997] 3 SCR 1176 (BC). However, to the extent that this depends on an interpretation of the statute, there always exists the possibility that, by suitably worded language or by reference to the overall structure and purposes of the Act, liability has been excluded entirely or has been passed on to the independent contractor: see, for example, *KLB v. British Columbia*, [2003] 2 SCR 403 (BC); *EDG v. Hammer*, [2003] 2 SCR 459 (BC); *Blackwater v. Plint*, [2005] 3 SCR 3 (BC); and *Reference re Broome v. Prince Edward Island*, 2010 SCC 11 (PEI).

4. For a favourable analysis of *Just* from a theoretical perspective, see Galloway, "The Liability of Government: Just, or Just and Reasonable?" (1990), 41 *Admin. LR* 133. Galloway prefers *Just* to the approach of the Judicial Committee of the Privy Council in *Rowling v. Takaro Properties*, [1988] AC 473 (PC NZ) in which serious concerns are raised as to the viability of the policy–operations distinction. Moreover, insofar as he had concerns with the

judgment, Galloway was of the view that it did not go quite far enough in terms of its delineation of when a duty of care might arise as between government and a private citizen. MacLauchlan, however, expressed concerns about the judgment in terms of its impact on the day-to-day operations of government ("Developments in Administrative Law: The 1989-90 Term" (1991), 2 *Sup. Ct. L Rev.* (2d), at 36-39.) In so doing, at 38-39, he echoed and elaborated on some of the criticisms articulated by Sopinka J:

> Are the users of highways not the beneficiaries of a public service? Is it realistic to proceed into the fiscally impoverished 1990s with an expanded potential for negligence in relation to public service activities, at a time when our capacity to maintain those services is being eroded? Unless we elaborate on the idea of the *user* as an integral element of the *public*, what are we to do with highways and swimming pools and libraries? We will either have to close them altogether or elaborate on a concept of user as a risk-taker. The second element that remains to be developed is how we apply the "reasonable person" standard to modern administration. The motivations of and constraints upon public officials/institutions will have to be better understood before a finder of fact can reliably apply standards of reasonableness to government action or inaction. The third issue is what interests ought to be protected and compensated. There is no necessary reason to believe that the interests of private property and physical integrity ought to be protected against negligence in the operation of public policy, or that other interests ought to be denied protection.

5. Indeed, while the Supreme Court of Canada continues to adhere to the principles laid down in *Anns*, the House of Lords some time ago repudiated Lord Wilberforce's approach in that case: *Murphy v. Brentwood District Council*, [1991] AC 398 (Eng. HL). Specifically, the House of Lords rejected the proposition established in *Anns* that municipalities and other statutory authorities had a duty to use reasonable care to prevent economic loss in the form of the diminished value of a defectively constructed house, a condition that was alleged in *Murphy* to have been in part the responsibility of the municipality by reason of its statutory duty of inspection. More generally, the Law Lords renounced the overall approach of *Anns* in favour of one that was predicated at least partially on concerns expressed by members of the House of Lords that the *Anns* approach to liability placed potentially too great a burden on the community (through the agency of government) for losses that were more appropriately left to the realm of private insurance. More specifically, the House of Lords rejected the collapsing of proximity and harm into one stage of the test for liability and the leaving of issues whether there were any reasons for reducing or eliminating the scope of liability to the second stage of the inquiry. Rather, proximity was a matter that should be dealt with separately and provided a vehicle for inquiring at an early stage whether there were any policy reasons for not finding a duty of care in the circumstances, an inquiry that previously was lost or obscured at that point because of the emphasis on foreseeability. (Among the numerous accounts and discussions, see Fleming, "Requiem for *Anns*" (1990), 106 *LQR* 525 (terse); Howarth, "Negligence After *Murphy*: Time To Rethink" (1991), 50 *Camb. LJ* 58 (in-depth and critical); Reynolds and Hicks, "New Directions for the Civil Liability of Public Authorities in Canada" (1992), 71 *Can. Bar Rev.* 1, at 19-20 (commenting on some of the possible implications of the Canadian courts following this approach)).

In any event, the Supreme Court of Canada in *CNR v. Norsk Pacific Steamship Co.*, [1992] 1 SCR 1021 (Can.) (in extending recovery for economic loss in tort) declared that *Murphy* did not represent Canadian law (at least with respect to its pronouncements on liability for economic loss). As well, the court continues to maintain the policy–operations distinction as a vital component in the determination of liability, notwithstanding the arguments of academic critics and an increasing scepticism as its value or centrality on the part of the English courts (as reflected in the reservations expressed by the Judicial Committee of the Privy Council in *Rowling v. Takaro Properties*, [1988] AC 473 (PCNZ)).

In the two cases that follow, the court (again through Cory J) attempted to further refine the difference between policy and operational decisions, with Sopinka J continuing to be a lone voice for a radically different approach. In reading them, evaluate whether the attempts at clearer delineation succeeded in the sense of making it readily predictable in most such situations whether the relevant decisions are ones of a policy or an operational variety. Also consider the extent to which they represent a step back from the precipice that loomed for Sopinka J in *Just*.

Brown v. British Columbia (Minister of Transportation and Highways)
[1994] 1 SCR 420 (BC)

[Brown suffered injuries when his car skidded on an icy patch of highway. Before this, the RCMP had requested that a sand truck be sent to the area because of the icy conditions. However, at the time, the Highways Department was still operating its sanding services on summer schedule. It was contended that this consideration and the fact that the on-duty employee at the department's control tower did not have the telephone number of the duty employee assigned to handle emergencies were factors in the problem not having been dealt with at the time of Brown's accident.]

CORY J (concurred in by Gonthier, Iacobucci and Major JJ):

[After holding that the department was under a statutory duty to maintain the highway, Cory J continued:]

That duty to maintain would extend to the prevention of injury to users of the road by icy conditions. However the Department is only responsible for taking reasonable steps to prevent injury. Ice is a natural hazard of Canadian winters. It can form quickly and unexpectedly. Although it is an expected hazard it is one that can never be completely prevented. Any attempt to do so would be prohibitively expensive. It can be expected that a Department of Highways will develop policies to cope with the hazards of ice. Before applying the principles set out in *Just* to determine what may be the policy pertaining to ice and what may be the operational aspects of that policy it should be determined whether, as the respondent contends, there are any statutory provisions that would exempt the Department from the imposition of a duty of care in the repair and maintenance of highways.

[Cory J concluded that there were no such statutory exemptions.]

D. Policy or Operations: Was the Decision of the Department to Maintain the Summer Schedule in Effect at the Time of the Accident a Policy Decision or an Operational Decision?

In distinguishing what is policy and what operations, it may be helpful to review some of the relevant factors that should be considered in making that determination. These factors can be derived from the following decisions of this Court: *Laurentide Motels Ltd. v. Beauport (City)* [1989] 1 SCR 705 (Que.); *Barratt v. District of North Vancouver* [1980] 2 SCR 418 (BC); and *Just, supra*; and can be summarized as follows:

> True policy decisions involve social, political and economic factors. In such decisions, the authority attempts to strike a balance between efficiency and thrift, in the context of planning and predetermining the boundaries of its undertakings and of their actual performance. True policy decisions will usually be dictated by financial, economic, social and political factors or constraints.

> The operational area is concerned with the practical implementation of the formulated policies, it mainly covers the performance or carrying out of a policy. Operational decisions will usually be made on the basis of administrative direction, expert or professional opinion, technical standards or general standards of reasonableness.

In my view, the decision of the Department to maintain a summer schedule, with all that it entailed, was a policy decision. Whether the winter or summer schedule was to be followed involved a consideration of matters of finance and personnel. Clearly the decision required the Department to discuss and negotiate the dates for the commencement of the summer and winter schedules with its unions. This was a policy decision involving classic policy considerations of financial resources, personnel and, as well, significant negotiations with government unions. It was truly a governmental decision involving social, political and economic factors.

Nor can I accept the suggestion that the Gold River area should be operated in the same manner as Campbell River. Campbell River is a larger region which requires a larger work force and a different approach to its operations. If this is not an attempt to compare apples and oranges, it is at least seeking to compare grapefruits to tangerines. Any difference in the manner of operating between the Campbell River area and the Gold River area is based upon their size. Surely what is appropriate for a larger centre need not be routinely applied to a smaller unit.

I should not leave this issue without addressing the two bases put forward by the appellant for the interpretation and application of *Just*. First, the appellant contended that policy decisions must be limited to so-called threshold decisions, that is to say, broad initial decisions as to whether something will or will not be done. This would be contrary to the principles set out in *Just* referred to earlier. Therefore, this submission cannot be accepted. Policy decisions can be made by persons at all levels of authority. In determining whether an impugned decision is one of policy, it is the nature of the decision itself that must be scrutinized, rather than the position of the person who makes it. The appellant next alleges that the system itself was unreasonable. As I have already said, this decision was clearly one of policy. Such a policy decision cannot be reviewed on a private law standard of reasonableness. Since no allegation was made that the decision was not *bona fide* or was so irrational that it could not constitute a proper exercise of discretion, it cannot be attacked.

[On the issue whether there was actual negligence in the working of the system that was in place, the court relied in part on the finding at trial that even if the Tower had had the duty employee's number, the accident would not have been prevented; negligence was therefore not a cause of the accident.]

SOPINKA J: I have read the reasons of my colleague Cory J and agree with the conclusion that he reaches. I would, however, adopt a somewhat different approach in arriving at this conclusion. The respondent does not have a statutory duty to maintain its highways. It has the power to do so, the manner and extent to which the power is exercised is a matter of statutory discretion. See *Barratt v. District of North Vancouver* [1980] 2 SCR 418 (BC). Indeed, if a statutory duty to maintain existed as it does in some provinces, it would be unnecessary to find a private law duty on the basis of the neighbourhood principle in *Anns v. Merton London Borough Council* [1978] AC 728 (Eng. HL). Moreover, it is only necessary to consider the policy/operational dichotomy in connection with the search for a private law duty of care.

The conduct complained of in this case, with the exception of the matters referred to by Cory J as operational, were within the exercise of the respondent's statutory discretion. Provided that a public authority exercises its discretion in accordance with the power conferred on it, its actions are not reviewable by the courts under the aegis of a private law duty of care. I agree with Cory J that with respect to the matters discussed by him under the heading The Operational Aspect that no liability for negligence arises for the reasons that he gives. I would prefer not to use the "policy/operational" test as the touchstone of liability. This principle, which was formally adopted in *Anns*, was imported from the United States. It has since been rejected by the Supreme Court of the United States and by the House of Lords as an exclusive test of liability. (See *United States v. Gaubert*, 111 SCt 1267 (1991), and *Rowling v. Takaro Properties Ltd.* [1988] AC 473 (PC NZ).) There is some doubt as to its status in Australia. (See *Sutherland Shire Council v. Heyman* (1985) 157 CLR 424 (NSW).) It has been criticized as ineffective and unreliable by academic writers Cohen and Smith, Woodall, Smillie, Bailey and Bowman, and Klar. (See Cohen and Smith, "Entitlement and the Body Politic: Rethinking Negligence in Public Law" (1986) 64 *Can. Bar Rev.* 1; Woodall, "Private Law Liability of Public Authorities for Negligent Inspection and Regulation" (1992) 37 *McGill LJ* 83; Smillie, "Liability of Public Authorities for Negligence" (1985) 23 *UWOLR* 213; Bailey and Bowman, "The Policy/Operational Dichotomy—A Cuckoo in the Nest" [1986] *Cambridge LJ* 430; and Klar, "The Supreme Court of Canada: Extending the Tort Liability of Public Authorities" (1990) 28 *Alta. LR* 648 at 655.) In "Negligence Claims Against Public Authorities" (1994) 16 *Advocates' Q* 48 at 57, Perell states:

> Whatever the criteria used, the cases show that characterizing the public authority's activity as a policy decision or operational activity is problematic and often unpredictable. In the *Just* case, of the 11 judges that gave judgments, six concluded that the province's actions were operational and five that the actions were a policy decision.

In view of the above, the Court may wish to reconsider at some future time the continued usefulness of this test as an exclusive touchstone of liability.

[In both this case and the one that follows, the other two judges, La Forest and McLachlin JJ (while generally agreeing with Cory J) adopted an intermediate position between that taken by Cory J and that taken by Sopinka J. They held that a private law duty only arose in cases such as this—where there was a statutory power but not a duty to do anything—when a policy decision was taken to do something. At that point, a duty of care arose in the operation or carrying out of that policy decision.]

Appeal dismissed.

Swinamer v. Nova Scotia (Attorney General)
[1994] 1 SCR 445 (NS)

[Swinamer was injured when a tree fell from private property onto a highway under the control of the provincial Department of Transportation. Not only did the department have authority to enter on private land for the purposes of removing trees that were likely to fall on the highway but it in fact did so when its personnel or the public drew attention to such a tree. A foreman had also conducted a survey of trees abutting highways in the region of the accident and had identified 234 trees in need of removal (though not the tree which had caused the accident) and had requested funding for their removal. That request was met only partially and spread out over a three-year period. At trial, the department was found liable in negligence for not having the inspection carried out by a person with proper training and for not taking appropriate steps to remove the tree ((1991), 101 NSR (2d) 333 (TD)). This finding was reversed by the Nova Scotia Court of Appeal ((1992), 108 NSR (2d) 254 (AD)) and Swinamer obtained leave to appeal to the Supreme Court of Canada.]

CORY J (Gonthier, Iacobucci, and Major JJ concurring): ... The trial judge, in his reasons, reviewed the Department's decision to conduct a survey with the object of ascertaining whether it constituted a policy decision which would exempt the respondent from the duty to remove the tree which caused the accident. This is not the correct approach. The enquiry should not be aimed at determining whether a policy decision has been made which specifically exempts a governmental authority from tort liability. Rather, it should be directed at determining what decisions constituted policy and were thus exempt from tort liability and what decisions or actions were operational and thus could, if negligent, attract liability.

In this case, the survey was undertaken in order to identify dead trees and those trees which represented obvious dangers to travellers on the highway. There was no general policy in effect to inspect trees. This is what distinguishes this case from *Just*, where there was a general policy to inspect potentially dangerous rocks and to take steps to eliminate them. Here the policy was limited. Its purpose was to identify obviously dead and dangerous trees in order to apply for funds to remove them. This flows from the uncontradicted evidence of the divisional engineer, the superintendent and the surveyor. The removal of trees involved the expenditure of funds which would have to be derived from funds allocated for other highway maintenance projects. The survey is an example of a preliminary step in what will eventually become a policy decision involving the expenditure and allocation of funds.

That this was in fact a policy decision can be seen from the trial judge's reasons. He considered factors such as past practice, budget, cost, the possibility of closing the road, the nature of the inspection team and concluded that there was "the will, the plan and the money to remove trees which were an immediate hazard." ... The trial judge expressed the view that money could be found or that the needed inspection could be made at little cost. These are all questions of expenditure and allocation of funds and they provide clear indications that this was a policy decision. Moreover, the fact that budgetary considerations are questions of policy is not changed by the fact that the cost of the measures sought may be small. The trial judge was in effect substituting his policy decision for that of the Department of Transportation. This was inappropriate and constitutes an error in law.

It is significant that Mr. Colburn, the divisional engineer, testified that if he had decided to use the money from his general budget to cut the identified trees, he would have had to make cuts in other maintenance activities which could equally adversely affect the security of users of the highway. He was, in fact, setting priorities for the allocation of the available funds. It is also significant that the requested funding for the removal of the 234 identified trees was only partially allowed, and that over a three-year span. The evidence demonstrates this to be a classic example of a policy decision.

The decision to inspect and identify dead trees was taken as a preliminary step in the policy making process. There is no suggestion that this was not a *bona fide* decision or that it was so irrational as to constitute an improper exercise of governmental discretion. Policy decisions of government must be immune from the application of private law standards of tort liability. ...

Appeal dismissed.

NOTES

1. Assuming that the policy–operations distinction has value, should it be maintained as a bright-line criterion for differentiating liability based on bad faith and patent unreasonableness from that based on negligence? Accepting that policy decisions may occur at any level of a statutory authority's hierarchy, and given that a discretionary decision about the allocation of funds seems now to always amount to a policy decision, should the courts always abstain from considering the merits of all such allocative decisions on a negligence basis? After all, assuming that all employees are working to their full capacity and that there is no slack in an organization, is not any decision about where to deploy resources at base a decision about the allocation of funds, as embodied in the personnel available for the performance of tasks?

2. In the context of the previous questions, consider the following statement made by Cory J in considering whether the Department had failed at an operational level to keep the highway safe.

In passing, I would again observe that the common law duty of maintaining the highways would require the Department to remove trees which constituted an apparent danger to travellers of the road. A dead tree or a tree leaning over the road at an acute and threatening angle would constitute a danger. That danger would be just as demanding of attention from the Department as would a hole which was deteriorating to the extent that it could lead a driver to lose control. Failure to fill the hole or remove the obviously dangerous tree could equally, in the circumstances of a particular case, constitute negligence attributable to the Department. This is not the situation presented in this case. Here, it was a tree in apparent good health that collapsed due to the ravages of a disease that could not be perceived in the course of a careful layman's inspection.

In the case of an obviously dead tree, should it make any difference that the tree had not been removed because of negligence in the carrying out of inspections or a failure to have a system of inspection in place? Should the answer to that question further depend on whether the failure to have a system of inspection in place resulted from an explicit budget allocation decision or a failure to deploy workers for that purpose?

This statement by Cory J also begs questions in terms of the judgment of Beetz J for the majority in *Laurentide Motels Ltd. v. Beauport (City)*, [1989] 1 SCR 705 (Que.), a case dealing with the liability under Québec *extra-contractuelle* and *Civil Code* principles of a municipality for damage caused by a fire. Once the municipality decided to exercise its discretion and create a fire brigade, it assumed certain operational responsibilities including the inspection and repair of fire hydrants. It did not matter that the municipality had no policy in place about such matters. But, what if it had? Would that have exempted the municipality from liability provided the policy had been observed? What is to be made of Beetz J's statement to the effect that "in the absence of a policy decision to which the omission alleged to have caused the damage can be attributed, the inspection and repair of the fire hydrants must be taken to be in the operational sphere." Do this and Cory J's analysis suggest that, once there is a policy in place at this level, the dimensions of the case are changed utterly and there can be liability only where the policy is made in bad faith or is patently unreasonable? Of course, such a rule may have the advantage of providing a massive incentive for municipalities and other government agencies to make sure that they have written policies in place governing every facet of their operations. The reward in terms of immunity from suit are potentially significant, as the award of $2.5 million in *Beauport* demonstrates.

3. As opposed to *Nielsen*, the decisions in *Just*, *Brown*, and *Swinamer* are all cases in which the courts were dealing with a government-run enterprise, in each case a highway, as opposed to government in its role of regulator of the private sector. The next two cases return to that sphere.

Swanson Estate v. Canada
(1991), 80 DLR (4th) 741 (FCA)

[This was an action in which the estate was suing the pilot, the airline, and Transport Canada as a result of the death of two family members in a plane crash. In the case of Transport Canada, the estate was alleging negligence based on lax enforcement against the airline of safety regulations and rules.]

LINDEN JA (Heald and MacGuigan JJA concurring): ... In this case, the trial judge correctly decided that the Crown's response to the complaints and reports was an operational decision, not a policy matter. His statement to the effect that it "constituted a conscious decision not to act on policy grounds" was meant in a more general, non-technical sense, or else it was a slip, inconsistent with his other statements and the entire tenor of his reasons. He later concluded that it was "more than a matter of policy but one of operation." The official making the enforcement decisions was not a high elected official like a Minister or even a Deputy Minister; he was only a regional director. His work involved not policy, planning or governing, but only administering, operations or servicing. The decision had no "polycentric" aspects, nor was there evidence of any lack of resources to permit more rigorous enforcement of the regulations. There were available numerous specific guidelines upon which the court could rely in evaluating the conduct of the decision-maker. This was not a budgetary, macro-exercise.

These people were essentially inspectors of airlines, aircraft and pilots, who did not make policy, but rather implemented it, although they certainly had to exercise some discretion and judgment during the course of their work, much like other professional people. I agree with Walsh J ([1990] 2 FC 619 (TD)) when he stated:

> The *Aeronautics Act* and Regulations made thereunder if not explicitly imposing a duty of care to the general public, at least do so by implication in that this is the very reason for their existence. The flying public has no protection against avaricious airlines, irresponsible or inadequately trained pilots, and defective aircraft if not the Department of Transport and must rely on it for enforcement of the law and regulations in the interest of public safety. Its expressed policy is, as it must be, to enforce these Regulations, but when the extent and manner of the enforcement is insufficient and inadequate to provide the necessary protection, then it becomes more than a matter of policy but one of operation and must not be carried out negligently or inadequately. While there may be no contractual duty of care owed to the public, as plaintiff suggests, this does not of itself protect defendant from liability in tort.

These officials were not involved in any decisions involving "social, political or economic factors." Indeed, it was another emanation of the Department of Transport altogether, the Canadian Transport Commission, a *quasi*-judicial body whose function it was to take into account such grounds, which granted the initial licence to Wapiti and other airlines, whereas this branch concerned itself with operating certificates that focused mainly on the matter of safety. These officials were not concerned with the health of the airline industry, with supplying service to remote areas or with employment for young pilots and, if such matters were considered by them in making their decisions, they probably should not have been. Nor was it their job to worry about airlines "going political." Their task was to enforce the regulations and the ANOs as far as safety was concerned to the best of their ability with the resources at their disposal. This function was clearly operational. Hence, a civil duty of care was owed to the plaintiffs to exercise reasonable care in the circumstances.

· · ·

While governments must certainly be free to govern, it is not acceptable for all bureaucrats who must exercise professional judgment to clothe themselves in the vestments of policy-making functions and thereby seek to avoid any responsibility for their negligence. This is especially so for officials charged with the duty of maintaining safety. They cannot be protected by an immunity, but must be encouraged, just like other professionals, to perform their duties carefully. They must learn that negligence, like crime, does not pay.

2. The Negligence Issue

Having decided that Transport Canada owed a civil duty to the passengers of Wapiti and was not immune from negligence liability, it is now necessary to decide whether the servants of the Crown were negligent in their supervision of Wapiti and its pilots.

The government is not an insurer; it is not strictly liable for all air crashes, only for those caused by the negligence of its servants. The standard of care required of these inspectors, like every other individual engaged in activity, is that of a reasonable person in their position. What is required of them is that they perform their duties in a reasonably competent way, to behave as would reasonably competent inspectors in similar circumstances, no more and no less. In evaluating their conduct, courts will consider custom and practice, any legislative provisions and any other guidelines that are relevant. The risk of harm and its severity will be balanced against the object and the cost of the remedial measures. In the end, the court must determine whether the employees of the defendant lived up to or departed from the standard of care demanded of them, in the same way as in other negligence cases: see, generally, Fleming, *The Law of Torts* (7th ed. 1987) at 96.

In accordance with the directions of the Supreme Court of Canada in *Just*, it is necessary to consider, in assessing the conduct of the defendant, matters such as resources available. Surgeons who stop at the side of the road to help injured motorists, cannot, of course, be expected to perform at the same level as they could in an operating theatre of a major hospital. Similarly, an inspection staff of a few cannot be expected to deliver the same quality of service that a larger team could. What is expected of both is reasonable care in the circumstances, including the resources available to them. An underfunded government inspection staff is no different than a surgeon operating on an accident victim at the side of a road. Neither is responsible for circumstances beyond their control, but each must use his resources as would fellow professionals of reasonable competence in the same circumstances.

The trial judge clearly understood that the plaintiff had to "establish that Transport Canada was negligent with respect to the steps it did not take before the crash." He held that there was negligence by the defendant's employees in "allowing Wapiti to continue single pilot IFR operation despite previous infractions," there being "plenty of time to remedy this by withdrawing permission." He found that the "pressure put on pilots to undertake flights in contravention of regulations despite some defects in equipment was known to the defendant some time before the crash." He also held that the plane "had only one … direction finder or if it had two the other was not working" as it was required to be. He decided also that there "was plenty of time to take stronger action in May and again in August before the crash took place in October." I am of the view that these findings of negligence are amply supported by the evidence presented at the trial.

The regulations and the Air Navigation Orders prescribe the procedures to be followed, the purpose for which those procedures existed and the duties of those who performed them. A general description of an inspector's job is found in ANO Series 7, from which Inspector Lidstone of Transport Canada quoted in evidence:

> It is the civil aviation inspector's duty to be familiar with all statutory requirements and to check during the course of his inspections that they are complied with in full. *No deviation from essential safety standards can be permitted.* (Emphasis mine.)

The need for strict compliance with safety standards underscores the obvious importance of passenger safety. The defendant is responsible for the certification of each carrier and their inspection, airworthiness of the equipment and its maintenance. Not only is the granting of the licence the job of this department, but also the need to monitor the airlines to ensure that they remain qualified. One of the warning signs which may alert an inspector that an air carrier is not operating safely, as set out in the Air Carrier Certification Manual, is high pilot turnover. Another is inadequate maintenance. Both of these danger signals were abundantly apparent to Transport Canada as they observed Wapiti.

There were also standards set out for enforcement. Four official enforcement techniques were available to Transport Canada: warning, suspension, prosecution and cancellation of a licence. Warnings were used in the case of most first offences. These enforcement techniques could be carried out through four different types of action: referral, administrative, judicial, and joint administrative and judicial. While administrative action was to be used in most cases, the Transport Canada Enforcement Manual stated that it was not to be employed in cases "where it would be clearly ineffective in promoting flight safety and compliance." The regional director had the power to suspend operating certificates, permits, licences and other flight authorization documents.

. . .

Appeal dismissed.

NOTE

How far should the holding in this case extend? Should it cover economic losses arising as a consequence of regulatory failure? The judgment that follows suggests not, at least as a general rule. Consider also the extent to which the judgment calls into question the authority of *Swanson Estate.*

Cooper v. Hobart
[2001] 3 SCR 537

[As a consequence of the unauthorized use of funds advanced to a mortgage broker, over 3,000 investors lost much of their investment. In October 1997, the statutory regulator suspended the mortgage broker's licence and issued a freeze order on the broker's assets. However, the disappointed investors asserted that the registrar knew at least 14 months earlier that the broker had committed serious violations of the relevant legislation. As a consequence, they claimed that the registrar should have acted earlier to suspend his licence and notify the investors. They claimed that these actions would have at least reduced the losses that the investors had suffered. As a consequence, one of the investors commenced an action in negligence against the registrar, claiming that the registrar's failure to act breached the duty of care that was owed to investors, and applied to have the action certified as a class proceeding. The first instance judge ruled that the pleadings disclosed a cause of action and that the action should be certified as a class proceeding. However, the BC Court of Appeal reversed, holding that the pleadings did not disclose a cause of action: (2000), 184 DLR (4th) 287. The plaintiff secured leave to appeal to the Supreme Court of Canada.]

McLACHLIN CJ and MAJOR J (delivering the judgment of the Court): ...

III. Issue

Does a statutory regulator owe a private law duty of care to members of the investing public for (alleged) negligence in failing to properly oversee the conduct of an investment company licensed by the regulator?

IV. Analysis

Canadian courts have not thus far recognized the duty of care that the appellants allege in this case. The question is therefore whether the law of negligence should be extended to reach this situation.

· · ·

In brief compass, we suggest that at this stage in the evolution of the law, both in Canada and abroad, the *Anns* analysis is best understood as follows. At the first stage of the *Anns* test, two questions arise: (1) was the harm that occurred the reasonably foreseeable consequence of the defendant's act? and (2) are there reasons, notwithstanding the proximity between the parties established in the first part of this test, that tort liability should not be recognized here? The proximity analysis involved at the first stage of the *Anns* test focuses on factors arising from the relationship between the plaintiff and the defendant. These factors include questions of policy, in the broad sense of that word. If foreseeability and proximity are established at the first stage, a *prima facie* duty of care arises. At the second stage of the *Anns* test, the question still remains whether there are residual policy considerations outside the relationship of the parties that may negative the imposition of a duty of care. It may be, as the Privy Council suggests in *Yuen Kun Yeu* [*v. Hong Kong (Attorney General)*, [1988] 1 AC 175 (HK PC)], that such considerations will not often prevail. However, we think it useful expressly to ask, before imposing a new duty of care, whether despite foreseeability and proximity of relationship, there are other policy reasons why the duty should not be imposed.

On the first branch of the *Anns* test, reasonable foreseeability of the harm must be supplemented by proximity. The question is what is meant by proximity. Two things may be said. The first is that "proximity" is generally used in the authorities to characterize the type of relationship in which a duty of care may arise. The second is that sufficiently proximate relationships are identified through the use of categories. The categories are not closed and new categories of negligence may be introduced. But generally, proximity is established by reference to these categories. This provides certainty to the law of negligence, while still permitting it to evolve to meet the needs of new circumstances.

. . .

Defining the relationship may involve looking at expectations, representations, reliance, and the property or other interests involved. Essentially, these are factors that allow us to evaluate the closeness of the relationship between the plaintiff and the defendant and to determine whether it is just and fair having regard to that relationship to impose a duty of care in law upon the defendant.

The factors which may satisfy the requirement of proximity are diverse and depend on the circumstances of the case. One searches in vain for a single unifying characteristic. ...

What then are the categories in which proximity has been recognized? First, of course, is the situation where the defendant's act foreseeably causes physical harm to the plaintiff or the plaintiff's property. This has been extended to nervous shock (see, for example, *Alcock v. Chief Constable of the South Yorkshire Police* [1991] 4 All ER 907 (Eng. HL)). Yet other categories are liability for negligent misstatement: *Hedley Byrne & Co. v. Heller & Partners Ltd.* [1963] 2 All ER 575 (Eng. HL), and misfeasance in public office. A duty to warn of the risk of danger has been recognized: *Rivtow Marine Ltd. v. Washington Iron Works* [1974] SCR 1189 (BC). Again, a municipality has been held to owe a duty to prospective purchasers of real estate to inspect housing developments without negligence: *Anns, supra; Kamloops, supra*. Similarly, governmental authorities who have undertaken a policy of road maintenance have been held to owe a duty of care to execute the maintenance in a non-negligent manner: *Just v. British Columbia* [1989] 2 SCR 1228 (BC), *Swinamer v. Nova Scotia (Attorney General)* [1994] 1 SCR 445 (NS). Relational economic loss (related to a contract's performance) may give rise to a tort duty of care in certain situations, as where the claimant has a possessory or proprietary interest in the property, the general average cases, and cases where the relationship between the claimant and the property owner constitutes a joint venture: *Canadian National Railway Co. v. Norsk Pacific Steamship Co.*, [1992] 1 SCR 1021; *Bow Valley Husky (Bermuda) Ltd. v. Saint John Shipbuilding Ltd.*, [1997] 3 SCR 1210. When a case falls within one of these situations or an analogous one and reasonable foreseeability is established, a *prima facie* duty of care may be posited.

This brings us to the second stage of the *Anns* test. As the majority of this Court held in *Norsk* at 1155, residual policy considerations fall to be considered here. These are not concerned with the relationship between the parties, but with the effect of recognizing a duty of care on other legal obligations, the legal system and society more generally. Does the law already provide a remedy? Would recognition of the duty of care create the spectre of unlimited liability to an unlimited class? Are there other reasons of broad policy that suggest that the duty of care should not be recognized? Following this approach, this Court declined to find liability in *Hercules Managements* [Ltd. v. Ernst & Young, [1997] 2 SCR 165] on the ground that to recognize a duty of care would raise the spectre of liability to an indeterminate class of people.

It is at this second stage of the analysis that the distinction between government policy and execution of policy falls to be considered. It is established that government actors are not liable in negligence for policy decisions, but only operational decisions. The basis of this immunity is that policy is the prerogative of the elected Legislature. It is inappropriate for courts to impose liability for the consequences of a particular policy decision. On the other hand, a government actor may be liable in negligence for the manner in which it executes or carries out the policy. In our view, the exclusion of liability for policy decisions is properly regarded as an application of the second stage of the *Anns* test. The exclusion does not relate to the relationship between the parties. Apart from the legal characterization of the government duty as a matter of policy, plaintiffs can and do recover. The exclusion of liability is better viewed as an immunity imposed because of considerations outside the relationship for policy reasons—more precisely, because it is inappropriate for courts to second-guess elected legislators on policy matters. Similar considerations may arise where the decision in question is quasi-judicial (see *Edwards v. Law Society of Upper Canada*, [2001] 3 SCR 562, 2001 SCC 80 (Ont.)).

The second step of *Anns* generally arises only in cases where the duty of care asserted does not fall within a recognized category of recovery. Where it does, we may be satisfied that there are no overriding policy considerations that would negative the duty of care. In this sense, I agree with the Privy Council in *Yuen Kun Yeu* that the second stage of *Anns* will seldom arise and that questions of liability will be determined primarily by reference to established and analogous categories of recovery. However, where a duty of care in a novel situation is alleged, as here, we believe it necessary to consider both steps of the *Anns* test as discussed above. This ensures that before a duty of care is imposed in a new situation, not only are foreseeability and relational proximity present, but there are no broader considerations that would make imposition of a duty of care unwise.

VI. Application of the Test

The appellants submit that the Registrar of Mortgage Brokers owed them, as investors with a firm falling under the Registrar's administrative mandate, a duty of care giving rise to liability for negligence and damages for losses that they sustained. The investors allege that the Registrar should have acted earlier to suspend Eron or warn them of Eron's breaches of the Act's requirements, and that their losses are traceable to the Registrar's failure to act more promptly.

The first question is whether the circumstances disclose reasonably foreseeable harm and proximity sufficient to establish a *prima facie* duty of care. The first inquiry at this stage is whether the case falls within or is analogous to a category of cases in which a duty of care has previously been recognized. The answer to this question is no.

The next question is whether this is a situation in which a new duty of care should be recognized. It may be that the investors can show that it was reasonably foreseeable that the alleged negligence in failing to suspend Eron or issue warnings might result in financial loss to the plaintiffs. However, as discussed, mere foreseeability is not enough to establish a *prima facie* duty of care. The plaintiffs must also show proximity—that the Registrar was in a close and direct relationship to them making it just to impose a duty of care upon him toward the plaintiffs. In addition to showing foreseeability, the plaintiffs must point to factors arising from the circumstances of the relationship that impose a duty.

In this case, the factors giving rise to proximity, if they exist, must arise from the statute under which the Registrar is appointed. That statute is the only source of his duties, private or public. Apart from that statute, he is in no different position than the ordinary man or woman on the street. If a duty to investors with regulated mortgage brokers is to be found, it must be in the statute.

In this case, the statute does not impose a duty of care on the Registrar to investors with mortgage brokers regulated by the Act. The Registrar's duty is rather to the public as a whole. Indeed, a duty to individual investors would potentially conflict with the Registrar's overarching duty to the public.

A brief review of the relevant powers and duties of the Registrar under the Act confirms this conclusion. Part I sets out the Registrar's regulatory powers with respect to the operation of mortgage brokers and submortgage brokers in British Columbia. Specifically, s. 4 provides that the Registrar must grant registration or renewal of registration to an applicant if, in his opinion, the applicant is "suitable" for registration and the proposed registration is "not objectionable." He may also attach such conditions and restrictions to the registration as he considers necessary. Once registered, a mortgage broker must comply with s. 6 of the Regulations which mandates that registrants maintain proper books and records and file annual financial statements with the Registrar.

Sections 5 and 6 of the Act cover the investigatory powers of the Registrar. Pursuant to s. 5, the Registrar may, and on receipt of a sworn complaint must, investigate any matter arising out of the Act or Regulations. In pursuit of this purpose, the Registrar may examine any records and documents of the person being investigated. He may summon witnesses and compel them to give evidence on oath or otherwise and to produce records, property, assets or things in the same manner as the court does for the trial of civil actions. Section 7 allows the Registrar to "freeze" funds or securities where he has made or is about to make a direction, decision, order or ruling suspending or cancelling the registration of a person under the Act. He may also apply to the court for an appointment of a receiver, or a receiver and manager, or trustee of the property of the person.

Under s. 8, the Registrar may, after giving a person registered under the Act an opportunity to be heard, suspend or cancel any registration if, in his opinion, any of the following or other conditions apply: the person would be disentitled to registration if the person were an applicant under s. 4; the person is in breach of a condition of registration; the person is a party to a mortgage transaction which is harsh and unconscionable or otherwise inequitable; or the person has conducted or is conducting business in a manner that is otherwise prejudicial to the public interest. Section 14 prohibits a broker from making any false, misleading or deceptive statements in any advertisement, circular or similar material. Part II of the Act is directed towards the protection of borrowers, investors and lenders, mandating in part specific disclosure requirements by mortgage lenders and their agents. Section 8 of the Regulations provides that every direction, decision, order or ruling of the Registrar refusing registration, refusing to renew registration, suspending registration or cancelling registration shall be made in writing and shall be open to public inspection.

Finally, s. 20 exempts the Registrar or any person acting under his authority from any action brought for anything done in the performance of duties under the Act or Regulations, or in pursuance or intended or supposed pursuance of the Act or Regulations, unless it was done in bad faith.

The regulatory scheme governing mortgage brokers provides a general framework to ensure the efficient operation of the mortgage marketplace. The Registrar must balance a myriad of competing interests, ensuring that the public has access to capital through mortgage financing while at the same time instilling public confidence in the system by determining who is "suitable" and whose proposed registration as a broker is "not objectionable." All of the powers or tools conferred by the Act on the Registrar are necessary to undertake this delicate balancing. Even though to some degree the provisions of the Act serve to protect the interests of investors, the overall scheme of the Act mandates that the Registrar's duty of care is not owed to investors exclusively but to the public as a whole.

Accordingly, we agree with the Court of Appeal *per* Newbury JA: even though the Registrar might reasonably have foreseen that losses to investors in Eron would result if he was careless in carrying out his duties under the Act, there was insufficient proximity between the Registrar and the investors to ground a *prima facie* duty of care. The statute cannot be construed to impose a duty of care on the Registrar specific to investments with mortgage brokers. Such a duty would no doubt come at the expense of other important interests, of efficiency and finally at the expense of public confidence in the system as a whole.

Having found no proximity sufficient to found a duty of care owed by the Registrar to the investors, we need not proceed to the second branch of the *Anns* test and the question of whether there exist policy considerations apart from those considered in determining a relationship of proximity, which would negative a *prima facie* duty of care, had one been found. However, the matter having been fully argued, it may be useful to comment on those submissions.

In our view, even if a *prima facie* duty of care had been established under the first branch of the *Anns* test, it would have been negated at the second stage for overriding policy reasons. The decision of whether to suspend a broker involves both policy and *quasi*-judicial elements. The decision requires the Registrar to balance the public and private interests. The Registrar is not simply carrying out a pre-determined government policy, but deciding, as an agent of the executive branch of government, what that policy should be. Moreover, the decision is *quasi*-judicial. The Registrar must act fairly or judicially in removing a broker's licence. These requirements are inconsistent with a duty of care to investors. Such a duty would undermine these obligations, imposed by the Legislature on the Registrar. Thus even if a *prima facie* duty of care could be posited, it would be negated by other overriding policy considerations.

The *prima facie* duty of care is also negated on the basis of the distinction between government policy and the execution of policy. As stated, the Registrar must make difficult discretionary decisions in the area of public policy, decisions which command deference. As Huddart JA (concurring in the result) found, the decisions made by the Registrar were made within the limits of the powers conferred upon him in the public interest.

Further, the spectre of indeterminate liability would loom large if a duty of care was recognized as between the Registrar and investors in this case. The Act itself imposes no limit and the Registrar has no means of controlling the number of investors or the amount of money invested in the mortgage brokerage system.

Finally, we must consider the impact of a duty of care on the taxpayers, who did not agree to assume the risk of private loss to persons in the situation of the investors. To impose a duty of care in these circumstances would be to effectively create an insurance scheme for investors at great cost to the taxpaying public. There is no indication that the Legislature intended that result.

In the result the judgment of the British Columbia Court of Appeal is affirmed and the appeal is dismissed with costs.

Appeal dismissed.

NOTES

1. In another judgment handed down the same day as *Cooper*, the court also rejected a similar claim made against the Law Society of Upper Canada for failing to intervene once it had knowledge of the unorthodox use by a lawyer of his trust account: *Edwards v. Law Society of Upper Canada*, [2001] 3 SCR 562, 2001 SCC 80 (Ont.). For commentary, see Brown, "Still Crazy After All These Years: *Anns, Cooper v. Hobart* and Pure Economic Loss" (2003), 36 *UBC Law Rev.* 159. See also *Hill v. Hamilton-Wentworth Regional Police Services Board*, [2007] 3 SCR 129, 2007 SCC 41 (Ont.), where a sharply divided court held by a majority of 6:3 that the court should recognize a tort of negligent investigation, fixing the police with potential liability toward those subject to investigation. In so holding, the majority and minority divided on whether there was sufficient proximity between suspects and the investigating police force, and on whether there were compelling policy reasons under *Anns* and *Cooper v. Hobart* to negate the duty of care arising out of the finding of reasonable foreseeability and sufficient proximity. See also *Syl Apps Secure Treatment Centre v. BD*, [2007] 3 SCR 83, 2007 SCC 38 (Ont.); *River Valley Poultry Farm Ltd. v. Canada (Attorney General)*, (2009) 95 OR (3d) 1, 2009 ONCA 326; and *Williams v. Ontario*, (2009), 95 OR (3d) 401, 2009 ONCA 378, all rejecting regulatory liability on the basis of a lack of sufficient proximity.

2. In what circumstances are members of the public in a sufficiently proximate relationship with regulators of commercial activities to justify the test laid down in this case?

3. The difficult issues raised in this section are not confined to situations where the plaintiff is attempting to hold a governmental authority liable in negligence. Questions of the appropriate scope of governmental liability for the tort of nuisance or under the principles of *Rylands v. Fletcher* raise many of the same risk-allocation issues albeit within a somewhat different legal framework, traditionally the defence of statutory authority. For a re-evaluation of the nature and scope of the statutory authority defence, see *Tock v. St. John's Metropolitan Area Board*, [1989] 2 SCR 1181 (Nfld.) and, in particular, the judgment of La Forest J in which he rejected the analysis of such cases in terms of whether the activity in question is statutorily authorized and proposed a form of enterprise liability. For contrasting evaluations of this judgment, see Hogg, "Torts—Nuisance—Defence of Statutory Authority" (1990), 69 *Can. Bar Rev.* 590, and MacLauchlan, "Developments in Administrative Law: The 1989-90 Term" (1991), 2 *Sup. Ct. L Rev.* (2d) 1, at 40-42. Subsequently, the court explicitly rejected the La Forest J position and reaffirmed the traditional approach in *Ryan v. Victoria (City)*, [1999] 1 SCR 201 (BC). Under that approach, the defendant succeeds if it can establish that the activity is authorized by statute and that the harm suffered was an inevitable consequence of performing the activity.

4. In the light of the various cases considered in this section, study the following fact situations and explain whether they would produce liability on the part of the relevant statutory authorities and/or officials.

a. K died of carbon monoxide poisoning in a house he was renting because the door covering the fan compartment at the rear of the furnace was left off. The furnace, which had been oil-burning, was converted to gas in 1965 and approved by a gas inspector as required under relevant regulations. In 1962, the Canadian Standards Association had adopted a provision requiring all new furnaces to carry a warning of the necessity to keep the fan compartment closed at all times. The gas standards branch of the relevant government department was a member of the CSA but had not done anything to draw this to the attention of the owners of furnaces manufactured before 1962. The relevant legislation was clearly aimed, *inter alia*, at safety to the public in the use of gas and, under it, the lieutenant governor had broad regulation-making powers in relation to all aspects of gas regulations. The deceased's estate brought a cause of action alleging negligence against the Crown in the following ways:

i. Failure of the minister and the lieutenant governor to pass a regulation requiring the attachment of the CSA warning to old furnaces.

ii. Failure of the Gas Protection Branch in breach of its statutory duty to provide gas inspectors with tags containing the warning to attach to old furnaces during conversion and other inspections.

iii. Negligence of the branch's inspector in not providing a warning to the owner at the time of the conversion.

iv. Failure of the relevant officials in the branch in breach of a statutory duty to recommend to the minister a regulation mandating warnings to be placed on old furnaces.

(See *Kwong v. The Queen in right of Alberta* (1978), 96 DLR (3d) 214 (Alta. SCAD); aff'd. [1979] 2 SCR 1010 (Alta.).)

b. As a result of a drunken frolic in a car by W, an inmate of a federal penal institution, T, was severely injured. W had been released on a temporary absence pass by the warden of the institution, acting under a statutory provision entitling him to do so if he was of the opinion that it was necessary or desirable, *inter alia*, to assist in the rehabilitation of the inmate. W had been released on temporary leaves many times previously and had on many occasions breached the conditions of his leave permit, although, aside from his frequent late returns, none of this was actually known to the warden. Nothing had been done about his late returns nor had any check been made of his whereabouts during his temporary absences. The warden is sued for negligence in authorizing W's release.

(See *Toews v. MacKenzie* (1977), 81 DLR (3d) 302 (BC SC).)

c. P is an Ontario Provincial Police officer. He is stationed at a small holiday resort town on Lake Huron and is the only police officer on duty at the station on a mid-summer Sunday. In the past he has complained to his superiors about the difficult conditions under which he has to work during the summer. This concern is also reflected in an internal report prepared for the OPP commissioner the previous year, which stated that it was totally inadequate to have only one officer on duty at the station at a time during the summer. However, nothing has been done in response to P's complaints or the report. This Sunday is particularly busy with troublemakers and, as a result of processing a number of people who have been arrested, P misses a phone call to the station. It turns out that, if the phone had been answered, a serious beating would have been prevented. The victim sues the OPP commissioner in negligence for failing to have a sufficient complement on duty at the station. The *Police Act*, RSO 1980, c. 381 contains the following provision:

> 43(2) Subject to the direction of the Ontario Police Commission as approved by the Solicitor General, the Commissioner has the general control and administration of the Ontario Provincial Police Force and the employees connected therewith.

Also, s. 47 specifies in greater detail the responsibilities of constables, but makes them all subject to the orders of the commissioner.

d. A board has extensive powers to regulate a natural resource. This includes a wide discretion to set and vary quotas for production. The board made an order reducing the quotas of "foreign-owned" producers. This order caused great loss to the plaintiff, a corporation owned in the United States, and it claimed damages. The nationality of the ownership of the producers is an "improper consideration." Is the board liable?

e. A hospital has the power to discharge a patient who has been treated for emotional problems "if it is satisfied that discharge of the patient will not create an unreasonable risk of harm to himself or herself, or to others." The hospital confused the files of two patients, and released one who, if the mistake had not been made, would not have been released. The patient caused predictable harm to the plaintiff. Is the hospital liable? Would the result be any different if a parole board made the same kind of mistake?

f. The *Historical Preservation and Restoration Act* gives a board the power to make regulations for preserving and restoring our history, including buildings. (1) The board made a regulation giving itself the power to declare buildings to be "historical" sites. Once a declaration is made, the uses of the buildings are sharply limited. The board made a declaration about the plaintiff's cabin. As a result, the value of the cabin declined drastically. The plaintiff claimed damages. The regulation is *ultra vires*. Is the board liable? (2) The regulation included a power to restore the buildings to their original condition, and workers employed by the board removed all the plaintiff's improvements and "restored" the cabin. Again, the regulation is *ultra vires*. Is the board liable for trespass?

g. An official has power to destroy an orchard if it is diseased. The official destroyed the plaintiff's orchard and the plaintiff claimed damages. (1) The official should have given a hearing and did not. (2) The orchard was not diseased. (3) The statute gives power to destroy the orchard, if, "in the opinion" of the official, it is diseased. The official concluded that it was diseased, but made only a superficial examination. (4) The statute also contains this provision: "The official is not liable for anything done or purporting to be done under or in pursuance of this Act."

h. A university has statutory power to grant tenure. The decision about tenure for individual candidates is made by a committee. The plaintiff in a cause of action claiming damages was considered for tenure last year and was denied tenure. (1) One member of the committee was biased. (2) The committee accepted the recommendation of a departmental committee without adequately considering the merits. (3) The committee refused to give adequate disclosure of assessments of scholarship and, in particular, refused to give the names of the assessors.

    i. D, a former prisoner with continuing pyromaniac tendencies according to his pre-release report, set fire to a rooming house in which he was living. His accommodation was arranged by B, a probation officer exercising a statutory discretion with respect to arranging for the post-release life of prisoners. H, the owner of the house, knew that D had been in prison, but B did not alert her to the fears expressed in the pre-release report. H sues D, B, and the Crown for damages, alleging negligence against B and the Crown.

(See *Hendrick v. De Marsh* (1986), 26 DLR (4th) 130 (Ont. CA).)

Constitutional Torts

It is clear that s. 24(1), the remedies or enforcement provision of the Charter, provides a sufficient basis for the availability of a damages remedy for Charter violations:

> 24(1) Anyone whose rights or freedoms, as guaranteed by this Charter, have been infringed or denied may apply to a court of competent jurisdiction to obtain such remedy as the court considers appropriate and just in the circumstances.

Yet, s. 24(1) is not as explicit as the comparable provision in the Québec *Charter of Human Rights and Freedoms* on the availability of damages:

> 49. Any unlawful interference with any right or freedom recognized by this Charter entitles the victim to obtain the cessation of such interference and compensation for the moral and material prejudice resulting therefrom.
>
> In case of unlawful and intentional interference, the tribunal may, in addition, condemn the person guilty of it to exemplary damages.

In its early Charter jurisprudence, the Supreme Court limited the seemingly open invitation to the courts to develop s. 24(1) remedies on a broadly discretionary basis, requiring that the court from which a particular remedy is sought be a court that has competence to otherwise entertain a proceeding for that kind of relief: *Mills v. The Queen*, [1986] 1 SCR 863 (Ont.). In the context of claims for damages, this was interpreted as meaning not only that the court must be one that has jurisdiction to award damages but also that the particular form of proceeding must be one in which damages may be sought: *Collin v. Lussier*, [1985] 1 FC 124 (CA); rev'g. [1983] 1 FC 218 (TD) (no jurisdiction to award damages in the context of an application for relief in the nature of *certiorari* under the *Federal Court Act*).

    Despite the fact that the Charter has now been in force for almost 30 years, the jurisprudence in this domain remains relatively sparse and underdeveloped. This is so notwithstanding substantial academic advocacy of the availability of damages in vindication of violations of Charter rights, as well as significant United States jurisprudence in this area.

    There have been cases in which damages have been recovered for Charter violations. One of the earliest examples was *Crossman v. The Queen*, [1984] 1 FC 681 (TD). Here, Walsh J awarded punitive damages of $500 against the Crown for police denial of the right to counsel as guaranteed in s. 10(b) of the Charter. Walsh J allowed the claim by reference to s. 24(1) of the Charter and was prepared to find the Crown liable, notwithstanding the fact that Crossman had pleaded guilty to the charges on which he had been arrested.

The holding of the court in this case involved at least two crucial assumptions as to the availability of damages for breach of the Charter. First, while the Supreme Court of Canada has repudiated the existence of a tort of breach of statutory duty in Canada (*The Queen in right of Canada v. Saskatchewan Wheat Pool*, [1983] 1 SCR 205 (Sask.)), the finding of liability in *Crossman* sprang directly from the violation of the Charter. There was no suggestion of the need to link such a cause of action with a recognized tort, nor did the court seem to require that the plaintiff show malice or knowing breach of the Charter to succeed. Second, the court was prepared to hold the Crown liable and award punitive damages notwithstanding that the plaintiff had not established harm or damage. In other words, the constitutional tort was actionable *per se*; it did not involve proof of actual damage.

These aspects of this case continue to encapsulate many of the matters of ongoing controversy as to the availability and scope of damages as a Charter remedy. Does every violation of the Charter constitute a tort (for example, the denial of the benefit of the principles of fundamental justice as guaranteed by s. 7), and, if so, does it automatically give rise to a claim under s. 24(1)? If not, what are the additional elements that have to be established in order to ground such a claim? Is the answer the same for all Charter violations? Or, are there some where links with an existing tort (trespass, false arrest, malicious prosecution) or proof of deliberate or malicious breach are essential? On this point, see, for example, *Vespoli v. The Queen* (1984), 55 NR 269 (FCA) (mere illegality of search under s. 8 of the Charter not sufficient of itself to give rise to claim for damages), although contrast the majority judgment in *Ward v. Vancouver* (2009), 89 BCLR (4th) 217, 2009 BCCA 23, now under reserve in the Supreme Court of Canada: [2009] SCCA No. 125 (QL).

Further, should the context of the violation make a difference—statute, regulation, adjudication, executive action, enforcement? Should it matter whether the suit is being brought against the Crown or against an individual officer or servant of the state? If so, in what respects? Should there be a good faith defence to some or all actions founded on a Charter breach? Are there other possibilities and nuances that have claim to recognition? Should Charter breaches be actionable *per se* or only on proof of damage? If the former, should there be no more than an entitlement to nominal damages or should substantial damages be available in such cases? If the latter, what should constitute damage for these purposes? What are or should be the principles governing the award of punitive or exemplary damages for breach of a person's Charter rights? It may be that *Ward* will provide clearer answers to some of these questions.

To the extent that much of administrative law is untouched by the Charter, at least as it is currently interpreted and applied, these questions are in some sense of marginal consequence. Nevertheless, despite the fact that much of the jurisprudence in this domain has so far been concentrated in the criminal and correctional law domains, these issues do have a potentially much broader reach—for example, immigration or administrative search, seizure, and enforcement.

One of the central themes of this chapter, governmental immunity from suits in tort, arose in *Prete v. Ontario (Attorney General)* (1993), 110 DLR (4th) 110 (Ont. CA). In this case, the Ontario Court of Appeal responded to one of the possibilities suggested in the judgment of Lamer CJ in *Nelles*, above. In the context of a Charter claim against the Crown in right of Ontario for an alleged preferral of an indictment in violation of the plaintiff's Charter rights, the court held that s. 5(6) of the Ontario *Proceedings Against the Crown Act*, RSO 1990, c. P.27 was inapplicable to claims of Charter violations. This provision immunizes the Crown in right of Ontario from liability for

> anything done or omitted to be done by a person while discharging or purporting to discharge responsibilities of a judicial nature vested in him or responsibilities that he has in connection with the execution of the judicial process.

Similarly, the court held that a statutory six-month limitation period was not applicable to actions against the Crown, assistant Crown attorneys, and police officers founded on breaches of the Charter. As a consequence, claims against all defendants were allowed to proceed. However, see *Alexis v. Toronto Police Service Board* (2009), 259 OAC 148, 2009 ONCA 847, rejecting *Prete* to the extent that it held the limitation period inoperative in the case of Charter claims, and expressing a preference for dealing with issues of delay by reference to general principle of *lâches*.

Also relevant in this context is the judgment of the Judicial Committee of the Privy Council in *Maharaj v. Attorney General of Trinidad and Tobago (No. 2)*, [1979] AC 385 (PC T&T). There, the court held that the Crown was clearly subject to the provisions of the constitution of Trinidad and Tobago, even to the extent of being liable for constitutional breaches committed by superior court judges. However, the court emphasized that this was not an instance of vicarious liability but of separate state liability. This raised the possibility that, under the Canadian Charter, such actions should be directed at the state itself, at least to the extent that some of the traditional and statutory immunities of judges and public officials themselves may still be upheld. After all, as far as adjudicators to whom s. 11(d) applies are concerned, the guarantee of "an independent and impartial tribunal" may imply at least some continuing degree of personal immunity from suit, and similar considerations may intrude in terms of decision-makers to which s. 7 and the principles of fundamental justice apply or within the framework of a s. 1 justification of an immunity provision: see *Royer v. Mignault* (1988), 50 DLR (4th) 343 (Que. CA) and the *dicta* of McDonald J in *Germain v. The Queen* (1985), 10 CRR 232 (Alta. QB). Consider, however, the extent to which the following analysis of damages claims under s. 24(1) of the Charter precludes the development of *Maharaj*-type relief and, more generally, imposes a proof of fault requirement for liability for any manner of Charter infringement.

Mackin v. New Brunswick (Minister of Finance)
[2002] 1 SCR 405, 2002 SCC 13 (NB)

[Were the province and responsible ministers liable in damages when they passed legislation that infringed on the Charter right to independence of a category of superior court judge—those who were supernumerary?]

GONTHIER J (L'Heureux-Dubé, Iacobucci, Major and Arbour JJ concurring):

(1) Damages

According to a general rule of public law, absent conduct that is clearly wrong, in bad faith or an abuse of power, the courts will not award damages for the harm suffered as a result of the mere enactment or application of a law that is subsequently declared to be unconstitutional (*Welbridge Holdings Ltd. v. Greater Winnipeg* [1971] SCR 957 (Man.); *Central Canada Potash Co. v. Government of Saskatchewan* [1979] 1 SCR 42 (Sask.)). In other words "[i]nvalidity of governmental action, without more, clearly should not be a basis for liability for harm caused by the action" (K.C. Davis, 3 *Administrative Law Treatise* (1958) at p. 487). In the legal sense, therefore, both public officials and legislative bodies enjoy limited immunity against actions in civil liability based on the fact that a legislative instrument is invalid. With respect to the possibility that a legislative assembly will be held liable for enacting a statute that is subsequently declared unconstitutional, R. Dussault and L. Borgeat confirmed in their 5 *Administrative Law: A Treatise* (2nd ed. 1990) at p. 177, that:

> In our parliamentary system of government, Parliament or a legislature of a province cannot be held liable for anything it does in exercising its legislative powers. The law is the source of duty, as much as for citizens as for the Administration, and while a wrong and damaging failure to respect the law may for anyone raise a liability, it is hard to imagine that either Parliament or a legislature can as the lawmaker be held accountable for harm caused to an individual following the enactment of legislation.

However, as I stated in *Guimond* [*v. Quebec (Attorney General)*, [1996] 3 SCR 347 (Que.)], since the adoption of the Charter, a plaintiff is no longer restricted to an action in damages based on the general law of civil liability. In theory, a plaintiff could seek compensatory and punitive damages by way of "appropriate and just" remedy under s. 24(1) of the Charter. The limited immunity given to government is specifically a means of creating a balance between the protection of constitutional rights and the need for effective government. In other words, this doctrine makes it possible to determine whether a remedy is appropriate and just in the circumstances. Consequently, the reasons that inform the general principle of public law are also relevant in a Charter context. Thus, the government and its representatives are required to exercise their powers in good faith and to respect the "established and indisputable" laws that define the constitutional rights of individuals. However, if they act in good faith and without abusing their power under prevailing law and only subsequently are their acts found to be unconstitutional, they will not be liable. Otherwise, the effectiveness and efficiency of government action would be excessively constrained. Laws must be given their full force and effect as long as they are not declared invalid. Thus it is only in the event of conduct that is clearly wrong, in bad faith or an abuse of power that damages may be awarded (*Crown Trust Co. v. The Queen in Right of Ontario* (1986), 26 DLR (4th) 41 (Ont. Div. Ct.)).

Thus, it is against this backdrop that we must read the following comments made by Lamer CJ in *Schachter* [*v. Canada*, [1992] 2 SCR 679 (Can.),] at p. 720:

> An individual remedy under s. 24(1) of the Charter will rarely be available in conjunction with action under s. 52 of the *Constitution Act, 1982*. Ordinarily, where a provision is de-

clared unconstitutional and immediately struck down pursuant to s. 52, that will be *the end of the matter*. No retroactive s. 24 remedy will be available. [Emphasis added.]

In short, although it cannot be asserted that damages may never be obtained following a declaration of unconstitutionality, it is true that, as a rule, an action for damages brought under s. 24(1) of the Charter cannot be combined with an action for a declaration of invalidity based on s. 52 of the *Constitution Act, 1982*.

Applying these principles to the situation before us, it is clear that the respondents are not entitled to damages merely because the enactment of Bill 7 was unconstitutional. On the other hand, I do not find any evidence that might suggest that the government of New Brunswick acted negligently, in bad faith or by abusing its powers. Its knowledge of the unconstitutionality of eliminating the office of supernumerary judge has never been established. On the contrary, Bill 7 came into force on April 1, 1995, more than two years before this Court expressed its opinion in the *Provincial Court Judges Reference* [[1997] 3 SCR 3 (PEI)] which, it must be recognized, substantially altered the situation in terms of the institutional independence of the judiciary. Consequently, it may not reasonably be suggested that the government of New Brunswick displayed negligence, bad faith or wilful blindness with respect to its constitutional obligations at that time.

Furthermore, I cannot accept the statement of Ryan JA of the Court of Appeal that the failure of the Minister of Justice to keep his promise to refer Bill 7 to the Law Amendments Committee was an instance of bad faith that justified the awards of damages. Even if admitted to be true, such evidence is far from establishing a negligent or unreasonable attitude on the part of government. In fact, it has no probative value as to whether, in the circumstances, the legislation was enacted wrongly, for ulterior motives or with knowledge of its unconstitutionality.

The claim of the respondent judges for damages is accordingly dismissed.

NOTES

1. This case involved issues of liability for passing and giving effect to unconstitutional legislation. Is it in that narrow context or more generally that Gonthier J required proof of fault in order to establish liability for damages under s. 24(1)? In other words, is this also a governing authority on unconstitutional action taken under a valid statute? Should it be?

2. The following represent some of the extensive academic literature on this potentially very significant subject: Roach, *Constitutional Remedies in Canada* (Aurora, ON: Canada Law Book, 1994), Chapter 11; Dussault and Borgeat, 5 *Traité de droit administratif*, 2d ed. (Québec: University of Laval Press, 1989), Part 4, Chapter 2, Section 4; Cooper-Stevenson, *Charter Damages Claims* (Scarborough, ON: Carswell, 1990); Hogg and Monahan, *Liability of the Crown*, 3d ed. (Toronto: Carswell, 2000); Pilkington, "Monetary Redress for Charter Infringement," in Sharpe, ed., *Charter Litigation* (Toronto: Butterworths, 1987); and Otis, "Constitutional Liability for the Infringement of Rights *Per Se*: A Misguided Theory" (1992), *UBC L Rev*. 21.

Immunities from Suit

We have not attempted in this section to provide a comprehensive account of the various immunities that apply in this domain. However, in the course of our consideration of remedies generally and the various ways of securing financial relief against governments and their servants and agents, we have identified a number of the situations where claims of immunity are likely to arise.

At common law, the Crown possessed an immunity from suit that extended to, or came to apply for the benefit of, at least some officials holding office under the Crown. This included judges of the superior courts and, in a modified form, those exercising other forms of judicial (including prosecutorial) and legislative powers. Gradually, the various immunities of the Crown have been diminished as reflected in legislation on Crown liability and Crown proceedings, both federally and in the various provinces. As well, the courts have been involved in this process of refining and confining, by, for example, narrowing the reach of what constitutes the Crown for various purposes and by diminishing the extent of the immunities of those exercising judicial and prosecutorial functions.

However, the potential sources of immunities from suit are by no means confined to this narrow band of common law or the domain of Crown proceedings and Crown liability legislation. There are still a large number of special statutory immunities possessed by agencies, tribunals, and public officers and servants of all kinds. It is also necessary to factor in to any examination of this topic the perpetuation of the rule that the Crown is not bound by any statute, absent express legislative provision as well as all the adjectival aspects of the law that confer special litigation advantages on those same agencies, tribunals, and public officers and servants. These include short limitation periods, various testimonial immunities and privileges, limitations on liability, and restrictions on the enforcement of judgments and orders.

Moreover, in relation to certain statutory bodies, there is the problem posed by jurisprudence to the effect that these bodies are immune from actions brought against them on the basis that they are not suable entities (see, for example, *MacLean v. Liquor Licence Board of Ontario* (1975), 61 DLR (3d) 237 (Ont. Div. Ct.)). In such cases, this eliminates the possibility of actions for damages and declaratory and injunctive relief against such bodies, and often leaves those affected by their decisions to whatever claim they may have in damages against the individual members of that agency. This is an unsatisfactory state of affairs if the officials themselves also possess some form of qualified or absolute immunity.

Details of this technical aspect of the law are elaborated in Hogg and Monahan, *Liability of the Crown*, 3d ed. (Toronto: Carswell, 2000). Suffice it to say for present purposes that this area of the law is rife with inconsistencies and, in many respects, lacking in any comprehensible policy basis. As a consequence, there has been consensus among law reform agencies that have studied this problem that there is a demonstrated case for comprehensive reform. (See, for example, Ontario Law Reform Commission, *Report on the Liability of the Crown* (Toronto: OLRC, 1989).)

In the absence of legislative action, there is some room for arguing that, in the age of the Charter, there are grounds for attacking the constitutionality of some Crown immunities and litigation advantages. Indeed, recollect the suggestion in *Nelles* that, insofar as there was an absolute immunity from suit on the part of those involved in prosecutorial decisions, it might not stand up constitutionally, at least where the suit was one involving a violation of Charter rights.

Nonetheless, attempts to undermine Crown immunities by reference to Charter values have so far, with the notable exception of *Prete*, been unsuccessful: *Canada (Attorney General) v. Central Cartage Co. (No. 1)*, [1990] 2 FC 641 (CA) and *Canadian Association of Regulated Importers v. Canada (Attorney General)* (1991), 87 DLR (4th) 730 (FCA) (Crown or executive privilege provisions of the *Canada Evidence Act*, RSC 1985, c. C-5 are not contrary to s. 7 or 15 of the Charter (see also *Babcock v. Canada (Attorney General)*, 2002 SCC 57) nor do they violate the guaranteed core of superior court power emanating from ss. 96-100 of the *Constitution Act, 1867*); *Rudolph Wolff & Co. v. Canada*, [1990] 1 SCR 695 (NS) (requiring suits against the Crown to proceed in Federal Court, while giving the Crown ability to take action against a citizen in provincial superior courts, was not an inequality in terms of s. 15(1) of the Charter on the basis that litigants in general were not a discrete and insular minority or an historically disadvantaged group coming within the anti-discrimination objectives of that provision); *Energy Probe v. Canada (Attorney General)* (1994), 17 OR (3d) 717 (Gen. Div.) (restrictions on amounts recoverable against nuclear facilities for losses suffered in event of nuclear accident were not a violation of s. 7 of the Charter). For the moment, therefore, any hopes for reform must rest with the legislature, save to the extent that the immunity or privilege in question depends solely on common law principles (as exemplified by the restatement of the Ontario law of executive or Crown privilege in *Carey v. Ontario*, [1986] 2 SCR 637 (Ont.)).

Appendixes

Constitution Act, 1982

PART I
CANADIAN CHARTER OF RIGHTS AND FREEDOMS

Whereas Canada is founded upon principles that recognize the supremacy of God and the rule of law:

Guarantee of Rights and Freedoms

Rights and freedoms in Canada

1. The *Canadian Charter of Rights and Freedoms* guarantees the rights and freedoms set out in it subject only to such reasonable limits prescribed by law as can be demonstrably justified in a free and democratic society.

Fundamental Freedoms

Fundamental freedoms

2. Everyone has the following fundamental freedoms:

    (a) freedom of conscience and religion;

    (b) freedom of thought, belief, opinion and expression, including freedom of the press and other media of communication;

    (c) freedom of peaceful assembly; and

    (d) freedom of association.

Democratic Rights

Democratic rights of citizens

3. Every citizen of Canada has the right to vote in an election of members of the House of Commons or of a legislative assembly and to be qualified for membership therein.

Maximum duration of legislative bodies

4(1) No House of Commons and no legislative assembly shall continue for longer than five years from the date fixed for the return of the writs of a general election of its members.

Continuation in special circumstances

(2) In time of real or apprehended war, invasion or insurrection, a House of Commons may be continued by Parliament and a legislative assembly may be continued by the legislature beyond five years if such continuation is not opposed by the votes of more than one-third of the members of the House of Commons or the legislative assembly, as the case may be.

Annual sitting of legislative bodies

5. There shall be a sitting of Parliament and of each legislature at least once every twelve months.

Mobility Rights

Mobility of citizens

6(1) Every citizen of Canada has the right to enter, remain in and leave Canada.

Rights to move and gain livelihood

(2) Every citizen of Canada and every person who has the status of a permanent resident of Canada has the right

(a) to move to and take up residence in any province; and

(b) to pursue the gaining of a livelihood in any province.

Limitation

(3) The rights specified in subsection (2) are subject to

(a) any laws or practices of general application in force in a province other than those that discriminate among persons primarily on the basis of province of present or previous residence; and

(b) any laws providing for reasonable residency requirements as a qualification for the receipt of publicly provided social services.

Affirmative action programs

(4) Subsections (2) and (3) do not preclude any law, program or activity that has as its object the amelioration in a province of conditions of individuals in that province who are socially or economically disadvantaged if the rate of employment in that province is below the rate of employment in Canada.

Legal Rights

Life, liberty and security of person

7. Everyone has the right to life, liberty and security of the person and the right not to be deprived thereof except in accordance with the principles of fundamental justice.

Search or seizure

8. Everyone has the right to be secure against unreasonable search or seizure.

Detention or imprisonment

9. Everyone has the right not to be arbitrarily detained or imprisoned.

Arrest or detention

10. Everyone has the right on arrest or detention

(a) to be informed promptly of the reasons therefor;

(b) to retain and instruct counsel without delay and to be informed of that right; and

(c) to have the validity of the detention determined by way of *habeas corpus* and to be released if the detention is not lawful.

Proceedings in criminal and penal matters

11. Any person charged with an offence has the right

(a) to be informed without unreasonable delay of the specific offence;

(b) to be tried within a reasonable time;

(c) not to be compelled to be a witness in proceedings against that person in respect of the offence;

(d) to be presumed innocent until proven guilty according to law in a fair and public hearing by an independent and impartial tribunal;

(e) not to be denied reasonable bail without just cause;

(f) except in the case of an offence under military law tried before a military tribunal, to the benefit of trial by jury where the maximum punishment for the offence is imprisonment for five years or a more severe punishment;

(g) not to be found guilty on account of any act or omission unless, at the time of the act or omission, it constituted an offence under Canadian or international law or was criminal according to the general principles of law recognized by the community of nations;

(h) if finally acquitted of the offence, not to be tried for it again and, if finally found guilty and punished for the offence, not to be tried or punished for it again; and

(i) if found guilty of the offence and if the punishment for the offence has been varied between the time of commission and the time of sentencing, to the benefit of the lesser punishment.

Treatment or punishment

12. Everyone has the right not to be subjected to any cruel and unusual treatment or punishment.

Self-crimination

13. A witness who testifies in any proceedings has the right not to have any incriminating evidence so given used to incriminate that witness in any other proceedings, except in a prosecution for perjury or for the giving of contradictory evidence.

Interpreter

14. A party or witness in any proceedings who does not understand or speak the language in which the proceedings are conducted or who is deaf has the right to the assistance of an interpreter.

Equality Rights

Equality before and under law and equal protection and benefit of law

15(1) Every individual is equal before and under the law and has the right to the equal protection and equal benefit of the law without discrimination and, in particular, without discrimination based on race, national or ethnic origin, colour, religion, sex, age or mental or physical disability.

Affirmative action programs

(2) Subsection (1) does not preclude any law, program or activity that has as its object the amelioration of conditions of disadvantaged individuals or groups including those that are disadvantaged because of race, national or ethnic origin, colour, religion, sex, age or mental or physical disability.

Official Languages of Canada

Official languages of Canada

16(1) English and French are the official languages of Canada and have equality of status and equal rights and privileges as to their use in all institutions of the Parliament and government of Canada.

Official languages of New Brunswick

(2) English and French are the official languages of New Brunswick and have equality of status and equal rights and privileges as to their use in all institutions of the legislature and government of New Brunswick.

Advancement of status and use

(3) Nothing in this Charter limits the authority of Parliament or a legislature to advance the equality of status or use of English and French.

English and French linguistic communities in New Brunswick
16.1(1) The English linguistic community and the French linguistic community in New Brunswick have equality of status and equal rights and privileges, including the right to distinct educational institutions and such distinct cultural institutions as are necessary for the preservation and promotion of those communities.

Role of the legislature and government of New Brunswick
(2) The role of the legislature and government of New Brunswick to preserve and promote the status, rights and privileges referred to in subsection (1) is affirmed.

Proceedings of Parliament
17(1) Everyone has the right to use English or French in any debates and other proceedings of Parliament.

Proceedings of New Brunswick legislature
(2) Everyone has the right to use English or French in any debates and other proceedings of the legislature of New Brunswick.

Parliamentary statutes and records
18(1) The statutes, records and journals of Parliament shall be printed and published in English and French and both language versions are equally authoritative.

New Brunswick statutes and records
(2) The statutes, records and journals of the legislature of New Brunswick shall be printed and published in English and French and both language versions are equally authoritative.

Proceedings in courts established by Parliament
19(1) Either English or French may be used by any person in, or in any pleading in or process issuing from, any court established by Parliament.

Proceedings in New Brunswick courts
(2) Either English or French may be used by any person in, or in any pleading in or process issuing from, any court of New Brunswick.

Communications by public with federal institutions
20(1) Any member of the public in Canada has the right to communicate with, and to receive available services from, any head or central office of an institution of the Parliament or government of Canada in English or French, and has the same right with respect to any other office of any such institution where
(a) there is a significant demand for communications with and services from that office in such language; or
(b) due to the nature of the office, it is reasonable that communications with and services from that office be available in both English and French.

Communications by public with New Brunswick institutions
(2) Any member of the public in New Brunswick has the right to communicate with, and to receive available services from, any office of an institution of the legislature or government of New Brunswick in English or French.

Continuation of existing constitutional provisions

21. Nothing in sections 16 to 20 abrogates or derogates from any right, privilege or obligation with respect to the English and French languages, or either of them, that exists or is continued by virtue of any other provision of the Constitution of Canada.

Rights and privileges preserved

22. Nothing in sections 16 to 20 abrogates or derogates from any legal or customary right or privilege acquired or enjoyed either before or after the coming into force of this Charter with respect to any language that is not English or French.

Minority Language Educational Rights

Language of instruction

23(1) Citizens of Canada

(a) whose first language learned and still understood is that of the English or French linguistic minority population of the province in which they reside, or

(b) who have received their primary school instruction in Canada in English or French and reside in a province where the language in which they received that instruction is the language of the English or French linguistic minority population of the province,

have the right to have their children receive primary and secondary school instruction in that language in that province.

Continuity of language instruction

(2) Citizens of Canada of whom any child has received or is receiving primary or secondary school instruction in English or French in Canada, have the right to have all their children receive primary and secondary school instruction in the same language.

Application where numbers warrant

(3) The right of citizens of Canada under subsections (1) and (2) to have their children receive primary and secondary school instruction in the language of the English or French linguistic minority population of a province

(a) applies wherever in the province the number of children of citizens who have such a right is sufficient to warrant the provision to them out of public funds of minority language instruction; and

(b) includes, where the number of those children so warrants, the right to have them receive that instruction in minority language educational facilities provided out of public funds.

Enforcement

Enforcement of guaranteed rights and freedoms

24(1) Anyone whose rights or freedoms, as guaranteed by this Charter, have been infringed or denied may apply to a court of competent jurisdiction to obtain such remedy as the court considers appropriate and just in the circumstances.

Exclusion of evidence bringing administration of justice into disrepute

(2) Where, in proceedings under subsection (1), a court concludes that evidence was obtained in a manner that infringed or denied any rights or freedoms guaranteed by this Charter, the evidence shall be excluded if it is established that, having regard to all the circumstances, the admission of it in the proceedings would bring the administration of justice into disrepute.

General

Aboriginal rights and freedoms not affected by Charter

25. The guarantee in this Charter of certain rights and freedoms shall not be construed so as to abrogate or derogate from any aboriginal, treaty or other rights or freedoms that pertain to the aboriginal peoples of Canada including

(a) any rights or freedoms that have been recognized by the Royal Proclamation of October 7, 1763; and

(b) any rights or freedoms that now exist by way of land claims agreements or may be so acquired.

Other rights and freedoms not affected by Charter

26. The guarantee in this Charter of certain rights and freedoms shall not be construed as denying the existence of any other rights or freedoms that exist in Canada.

Multicultural heritage

27. This Charter shall be interpreted in a manner consistent with the preservation and enhancement of the multicultural heritage of Canadians.

Rights guaranteed equally to both sexes

28. Notwithstanding anything in this Charter, the rights and freedoms referred to in it are guaranteed equally to male and female persons.

Rights respecting certain schools preserved

29. Nothing in this Charter abrogates or derogates from any rights or privileges guaranteed by or under the Constitution of Canada in respect of denominational, separate or dissentient schools.

Application to territories and territorial authorities

30. A reference in this Charter to a Province or to the legislative assembly or legislature of a province shall be deemed to include a reference to the Yukon Territory and the Northwest Territories, or to the appropriate legislative authority thereof, as the case may be.

Legislative powers not extended

31. Nothing in this Charter extends the legislative powers of any body or authority.

Application of Charter

Application of Charter

32(1) This Charter applies

(a) to the Parliament and government of Canada in respect of all matters within the authority of Parliament including all matters relating to the Yukon Territory and Northwest Territories; and

(b) to the legislature and government of each province in respect of all matters within the authority of the legislature of each province.

Exception

(2) Notwithstanding subsection (1), section 15 shall not have effect until three years after this section comes into force.

Exception where express declaration

33(1) Parliament or the legislature of a province may expressly declare in an Act of Parliament or of the legislature, as the case may be, that the Act or a provision thereof shall operate notwithstanding a provision included in section 2 or sections 7 to 15 of this Charter.

Operation of exception

(2) An Act or a provision of an Act in respect of which a declaration made under this section is in effect shall have such operation as it would have but for the provision of this Charter referred to in the declaration.

Five year limitation

(3) A declaration made under subsection (1) shall cease to have effect five years after it comes into force or on such earlier date as may be specified in the declaration.

Re-enactment

(4) Parliament or the legislature of a province may re-enact a declaration made under subsection (1).

Five year limitation

(5) Subsection (3) applies in respect of a re-enactment made under subsection (4).

Citation

Citation

34. This Part may be cited as the *Canadian Charter of Rights and Freedoms*.

Québec: Charter of Human Rights and Freedoms

CHARTER OF HUMAN RIGHTS AND FREEDOMS
RSQ, c. C-12

Preamble

WHEREAS every human being possesses intrinsic rights and freedoms designed to ensure his protection and development;

Whereas all human beings are equal in worth and dignity, and are entitled to equal protection of the law;

Whereas respect for the dignity of human beings, equality of women and men, and recognition of their rights and freedoms constitute the foundation of justice, liberty and peace;

Whereas the rights and freedoms of the human person are inseparable from the rights and freedoms of others and from the common well-being;

Whereas it is expedient to solemnly declare the fundamental human rights and freedoms in a Charter, so that they may be guaranteed by the collective will and better protected against any violation;

Therefore, Her Majesty, with the advice and consent of the National Assembly of Québec, enacts as follows:

PART I
HUMAN RIGHTS AND FREEDOMS

CHAPTER I
FUNDAMENTAL FREEDOMS AND RIGHTS

Right to life

1. Every human being has a right to life, and to personal security, inviolability and freedom.

Juridical personality

He also possesses juridical personality.

Right to assistance

2. Every human being whose life is in peril has a right to assistance.

Aiding person whose life is in peril

Every person must come to the aid of anyone whose life is in peril, either personally or calling for aid, by giving him the necessary and immediate physical assistance, unless it involves danger to himself or a third person, or he has another valid reason.

Fundamental freedoms

3. Every person is the possessor of the fundamental freedoms, including freedom of conscience, freedom of religion, freedom of opinion, freedom of expression, freedom of peaceful assembly and freedom of association.

Safeguard of dignity

4. Every person has a right to the safeguard of his dignity, honour and reputation.

Respect for private life

5. Every person has a right to respect for his private life.

Peaceful enjoyment of property

6. Every person has a right to the peaceful enjoyment and free disposition of his property, except to the extent provided by law.

Home inviolable

7. A person's home is inviolable.

Respect for private property

8. No one may enter upon the property of another or take anything therefrom without his express or implied consent.

Right to secrecy

9. Every person has a right to non-disclosure of confidential information.

Disclosure of confidential information

No person bound to professional secrecy by law and no priest or other minister of religion may, even in judicial proceedings, disclose confidential information revealed to him by reason of his position or profession, unless he is authorized to do so by the person who confided such information to him or by an express provision of law.

Duty of tribunal

The tribunal must, *ex officio*, ensure that professional secrecy is respected.

Exercise of rights and freedoms

9.1. In exercising his fundamental freedoms and rights, a person shall maintain a proper regard for democratic values, public order and the general well-being of the citizens of Québec.

Scope fixed by law

In this respect, the scope of the freedoms and rights, and limits to their exercise, may be fixed by law.

CHAPTER I.1
RIGHT TO EQUAL RECOGNITION AND EXERCISE OF RIGHTS AND FREEDOMS

Discrimination forbidden

10. Every person has a right to full and equal recognition and exercise of his human rights and freedoms, without distinction, exclusion or preference based on race, colour, sex, pregnancy, sexual orientation, civil status, age except as provided by law, religion, political convictions, language, ethnic or national origin, social condition, a handicap or the use of any means to palliate a handicap.

Discrimination defined

Discrimination exists where such a distinction, exclusion or preference has the effect of nullifying or impairing such right.

Harassment

10.1. No one may harass a person on the basis of any ground mentioned in section 10.

Discriminatory notice forbidden

11. No one may distribute, publish or publicly exhibit a notice, symbol or sign involving discrimination, or authorize anyone to do so.

Discrimination in juridical acts

12. No one may, through discrimination, refuse to make a juridical act concerning goods or services ordinarily offered to the public.

Clause forbidden

13. No one may in a juridical act stipulate a clause involving discrimination.

Nullity

Such a clause is without effect.

Lease of a room in a dwelling

14. The prohibitions contemplated in sections 12 and 13 do not apply to the person who leases a room situated in a dwelling if the lessor or his family resides in such dwelling, leases only one room and does not advertise the room for lease by a notice or any other public means of solicitation.

Public places available to everyone

15. No one may, through discrimination, inhibit the access of another to public transportation or a public place, such as a commercial establishment, hotel, restaurant, theatre, cinema, park, camping ground or trailer park, or his obtaining the goods and services available there.

Non-discrimination in employment

16. No one may practise discrimination in respect of the hiring, apprenticeship, duration of the probationary period, vocational training, promotion, transfer, displacement, laying-off, suspension, dismissal or conditions of employment of a person or in the establishment of categories or classes of employment.

Discrimination by association or professional order forbidden

17. No one may practise discrimination in respect of the admission, enjoyment of benefits, suspension or expulsion of a person to, of or from an association of employers or employees or any professional order or association of persons carrying on the same occupation.

Discrimination by employment bureau

18. No employment bureau may practise discrimination in respect of the reception, classification or processing of a job application or in any document intended for submitting an application to a prospective employer.

Information on job application

18.1. No one may, in an employment application form or employment interview, require a person to give information regarding any ground mentioned in section 10 unless the information is useful for the application of section 20 or the implementation of an affirmative action program in existence at the time of the application.

Penal or criminal offence

18.2. No one may dismiss, refuse to hire or otherwise penalize a person in his employment owing to the mere fact that he was convicted of a penal or criminal offence, if the offence was in no way connected with the employment or if the person has obtained a pardon for the offence.

Equal salary for equivalent work

19. Every employer must, without discrimination, grant equal salary or wages to the members of his personnel who perform equivalent work at the same place.

Difference based on experience, non-discriminatory

A difference in salary or wages based on experience, seniority, years of service, merit, productivity or overtime is not considered discriminatory if such criteria are common to all members of the personnel.

Non-discrimination

Adjustments in compensation and a pay equity plan are deemed not to discriminate on the basis of gender if they are established in accordance with the Pay Equity Act (chapter E-12.001).

Distinction based on aptitudes, non-discriminatory

20. A distinction, exclusion or preference based on the aptitudes or qualifications required for an employment, or justified by the charitable, philanthropic, religious, political or educational nature of a non-profit institution or of an institution devoted exclusively to the well-being of an ethnic group, is deemed non-discriminatory.

Presumption

20.1. In an insurance or pension contract, a social benefits plan, a retirement, pension or insurance plan, or a public pension or public insurance plan, a distinction, exclusion or preference based on age, sex or civil status is deemed non-discriminatory where the use thereof is warranted and the basis therefor is a risk determination factor based on actuarial data.

Discrimination

In such contracts or plans, the use of health as a risk determination factor does not constitute discrimination within the meaning of section 10.

CHAPTER II
POLITICAL RIGHTS

Petition to Assembly

21. Every person has a right of petition to the National Assembly for the redress of grievances.

Right to be candidate and to vote

22. Every person legally capable and qualified has the right to be a candidate and to vote at an election.

CHAPTER III
JUDICIAL RIGHTS

Impartial hearing before independent tribunal

23. Every person has a right to a full and equal, public and fair hearing by an independent and impartial tribunal, for the determination of his rights and obligations or of the merits of any charge brought against him.

Sittings *in camera*

The tribunal may decide to sit *in camera*, however, in the interests of morality or public order.

Grounds for deprivation of liberty

24. No one may be deprived of his liberty or of his rights except on grounds provided by law and in accordance with prescribed procedure.

Search and seizure

24.1. No one may be subjected to unreasonable search or seizure.

Treatment of person arrested

25. Every person arrested or detained must be treated with humanity and with the respect due to the human person.

Right to separate treatment

26. Every person confined to a correctional facility has the right to separate treatment appropriate to his sex, his age and his physical or mental condition.

Person awaiting outcome of his trial to be kept apart

27. Every person confined to a correctional facility while awaiting the outcome of his trial has the right to be kept apart, until final judgment, from prisoners serving sentence.

Information on grounds of arrest

28. Every person arrested or detained has a right to be promptly informed, in a language he understands, of the grounds of his arrest or detention.

Rights of accused person

28.1. Every accused person has a right to be promptly informed of the specific offence with which he is charged.

Right to advise next of kin

29. Every person arrested or detained has a right to immediately advise his next of kin thereof and to have recourse to the assistance of an advocate. He has a right to be informed promptly of those rights.

Right to be brought before tribunal

30. Every person arrested or detained must be brought promptly before the competent tribunal or released.

Right to be released on undertaking

31. No person arrested or detained may be deprived without just cause of the right to be released on undertaking, with or without deposit or surety, to appear before the tribunal at the appointed time.

Habeas corpus

32. Every person deprived of his liberty has a right of recourse to *habeas corpus*.

Right to trial

32.1. Every accused person has a right to be tried within a reasonable time.

Presumption of innocence

33. Every accused person is presumed innocent until proven guilty according to law.

Self-incrimination

33.1. No accused person may be compelled to testify against himself at his trial.

Right to advocate

34. Every person has a right to be represented by an advocate or to be assisted by one before any tribunal.

Full and complete defence

35. Every accused person has a right to a full and complete defense and has the right to examine and cross-examine witnesses.

Interpreter

36. Every accused person has a right to be assisted free of charge by an interpreter if he does not understand the language used at the hearing or if he is deaf.

Non-retroactivity of law

37. No accused person may be held guilty on account of any act or omission which, at the time when it was committed, did not constitute a violation of the law.

Res judicata

37.1. No person may be tried again for an offence of which he has been acquitted or of which he has been found guilty by a judgment that has acquired status as *res judicata*.

Lesser punishment

37.2. Where the punishment for an offence has been varied between the time of commission and the time of sentencing, the accused person has a right to the lesser punishment.

Self-incrimination

38. No testimony before a tribunal may be used to incriminate the person who gives it, except in a prosecution for perjury or for the giving of contradictory evidence.

CHAPTER IV
ECONOMIC AND SOCIAL RIGHTS

Protection

39. Every child has a right to the protection, security and attention that his parents or the persons acting in their stead are capable of providing.

Free public education

40. Every person has a right, to the extent and according to the standards provided for by law, to free public education.

Religious and moral education

41. Parents or the persons acting in their stead have a right to give their children a religious and moral education in keeping with their convictions and with proper regard for their children's rights and interests.

Private educational establishments

42. Parents or the persons acting in their stead have a right to choose private educational establishments for their children, provided such establishments comply with the standards prescribed or approved by virtue of the law.

Cultural interests of minorities

43. Persons belonging to ethnic minorities have a right to maintain and develop their own cultural interests with the other members of their group.

Right to information

44. Every person has a right to information to the extent provided by law.

Financial assistance

45. Every person in need has a right, for himself and his family, to measures of financial assistance and to social measures provided for by law, susceptible of ensuring such person an acceptable standard of living.

Conditions of employment

46. Every person who works has a right, in accordance with the law, to fair and reasonable conditions of employment which have proper regard for his health, safety and physical well-being.

Right to healthful environment

46.1. Every person has a right to live in a healthful environment in which biodiversity is preserved, to the extent and according to the standards provided by law.

Equal rights of spouses

47. Married or civil union spouses have, in the marriage or civil union, the same rights, obligations and responsibilities.

Moral guidance of family

Together they provide the moral guidance and material support of the family and the education of their common offspring.

Protection of aged and handicapped persons

48. Every aged person and every handicapped person has a right to protection against any form of exploitation.

Family protection

Such a person also has a right to the protection and security that must be provided to him by his family or the persons acting in their stead.

CHAPTER V
SPECIAL AND INTERPRETATIVE PROVISIONS

Recourse of victim for unlawful interference

49. Any unlawful interference with any right or freedom recognized by this Charter entitles the victim to obtain the cessation of such interference and compensation for the moral or material prejudice resulting therefrom.

Punitive damages

In case of unlawful and intentional interference, the tribunal may, in addition, condemn the person guilty of it to punitive damages.

Complaint or dispute

49.1. Any complaint, dispute or remedy the subject-matter of which is covered by the Pay Equity Act (chapter E-12.001) shall be dealt with exclusively in accordance with the provisions of that Act.

Enterprise with fewer than 10 employees

Moreover, any question concerning pay equity between a predominantly female job class and a predominantly male job class in an enterprise employing fewer than 10 employees shall be settled by the Commission de l'équité salariale in accordance with section 19 of this Charter.

No suppression of right

50. The Charter shall not be so interpreted as to suppress or limit the enjoyment or exercise of any human right or freedom not enumerated herein.

Rights guaranteed

50.1. The rights and freedoms set forth in this Charter are guaranteed equally to women and men.

No extension of provision of law

51. The Charter shall not be so interpreted as to extend, limit or amend the scope of a provision of law except to the extent provided in section 52.

Sections to prevail over subsequent Act

52. No provision of any Act, even subsequent to the Charter, may derogate from sections 1 to 38, except so far as provided by those sections, unless such Act expressly states that it applies despite the Charter.

Doubt in interpretation

53. If any doubt arises in the interpretation of a provision of the Act, it shall be resolved in keeping with the intent of the Charter.

State bound

54. The Charter binds the State.

Jurisdiction of Charter

55. The Charter affects those matters that come under the legislative authority of Québec.

"*tribunal*"

56(1) In sections 9, 23, 30, 31, 34 and 38, in Chapter III of Part II and in Part IV, the word "tribunal" includes a coroner, a fire investigation commissioner, an inquiry commission, and any person or agency exercising quasi judicial functions.

"*salary*" and "*wages*"

(2) In section 19, the words "salary" and "wages" include the compensations or benefits of pecuniary value connected with the employment.

"*law*" or "*Act*"

(3) In the Charter, the word "law" or "Act" includes a regulation, a decree, an ordinance or an order in council made under the authority of any Act.

Provincial Procedural Statutory Codes

ADMINISTRATIVE PROCEDURES AND JURISDICTION ACT
RSA 2000, c. A-3

HER MAJESTY, by and with the advice and consent of the Legislative Assembly of Alberta, enacts as follows:

PART 1
ADMINISTRATIVE PROCEDURES

Definitions

1 In this Act,

(a) "authority" means a person authorized to exercise a statutory power;

(b) "party" means a person whose rights will be varied or affected by the exercise of a statutory power or by an act or thing done pursuant to that power;

(c) "statutory power" means an administrative, quasi-judicial or judicial power conferred by statute, other than a power conferred on a court of record of civil or criminal jurisdiction or a power to make regulations, and for greater certainty, but without restricting the generality of the foregoing, includes a power

(i) to grant, suspend or revoke a charter or letters patent,

(ii) to grant, renew, refuse, suspend or revoke a permission to do an act or thing that, but for the permission, would be unlawful, whether the permission is called a licence or permit or certificate or is in any other form,

(iii) to declare or establish a status provided for under a statute for a person and to suspend or revoke that status,

(iv) to approve or authorize the doing or omission by a person of an act or thing that, but for the approval or authorization, would be unlawful or unauthorized,

(v) to declare or establish a right or duty of a person under a statute, whether in a dispute with another person or otherwise, or

(vi) to make an order, decision, direction or finding prohibiting a person from doing an act or thing that, but for the order, decision, direction or finding, it would be lawful for the person to do, or any combination of those powers.

Application of Part

2(1) This Part applies to an authority only to the extent provided under this section.

(2) The Lieutenant Governor in Council may, by regulation,

(a) designate any authority as an authority to which this Part applies in whole or in part;

(b) designate the statutory power of the authority in respect of which this Part applies in whole or in part;

(c) designate the provisions of this Part that are applicable to the authority in the exercise of that statutory power, and the extent to which they apply;

(d) prescribe the form of notices for the purposes of this Part;

(e) prescribe the length of time that is adequate for the giving of a notice under this Part.

Notice to parties

3 When

(a) an application is made to an authority, or

(b) an authority on its own initiative proposes

to exercise a statutory power, the authority shall give to all parties adequate notice of the application that it has before it or of the power that it intends to exercise.

Evidence and representations

4 Before an authority, in the exercise of a statutory power, refuses the application of or makes a decision or order adversely affecting the rights of a party, the authority

(a) shall give the party a reasonable opportunity of furnishing relevant evidence to the authority,

(b) shall inform the party of the facts in its possession or the allegations made to it contrary to the interests of the party in sufficient detail

(i) to permit the party to understand the facts or allegations, and

(ii) to afford the party a reasonable opportunity to furnish relevant evidence to contradict or explain the facts or allegations,

and

(c) shall give the party an adequate opportunity of making representations by way of argument to the authority.

Cross-examination

5 When an authority has informed a party of facts or allegations and that party

(a) is entitled under section 4 to contradict or explain them, but

(b) will not have a fair opportunity of doing so without cross-examination of the person making the statements that constitute the facts or allegations,

the authority shall afford the party an opportunity of cross-examination in the presence of the authority or of a person authorized to hear or take evidence for the authority.

When certain representations not permitted

6 Where by this Part a party is entitled to make representations to an authority with respect to the exercise of a statutory power, the authority is not by this Part required to afford an opportunity to the party

(a) to make oral representations, or

(b) to be represented by counsel,

if the authority affords the party an opportunity to make representations adequately in writing, but nothing in this Part deprives a party of a right conferred by any other Act to make oral representations or to be represented by counsel.

Written decision with reasons

7 When an authority exercises a statutory power so as to adversely affect the rights of a party, the authority shall furnish to each party a written statement of its decision setting out

(a) the findings of fact on which it based its decision, and

(b) the reasons for the decision.

Requirements of other Acts

8 Nothing in this Part relieves an authority from complying with any procedure to be followed by it under any other Act relating to the exercise of its statutory power.

Rules of evidence

9 Nothing in this Part

(a) requires that any evidence or allegations of fact made to an authority be made under oath, or

(b) requires any authority to adhere to the rules of evidence applicable to courts of civil or criminal jurisdiction.

PART 2
JURISDICTION TO DETERMINE QUESTIONS OF CONSTITUTIONAL LAW

Definitions

10 In this Part,

(a) "court" means the Court of Queen's Bench of Alberta;

(b) "decision maker" means an individual appointed or a body established by or under an Act of Alberta to decide matters in accordance with the authority given under that Act, but does not include

(i) The Provincial Court of Alberta or a judge of that Court,

(ii) a sitting justice of the peace conferred with the authority to determine a question of constitutional law under the *Provincial Court Act*,

(iii) the Court of Queen's Bench of Alberta or a judge or master in chambers of that Court, or

(iv) the Court of Appeal of Alberta or a judge of that Court;

(c) "designated decision maker" means a decision maker designated under section 16(a) as a decision maker that has jurisdiction to determine one or more questions of constitutional law under section 16(b);

(d) "question of constitutional law" means

(i) any challenge, by virtue of the Constitution of Canada or the *Alberta Bill of Rights*, to the applicability or validity of an enactment of the Parliament of Canada or an enactment of the Legislature of Alberta, or

(ii) a determination of any right under the Constitution of Canada or the *Alberta Bill of Rights*.

Lack of jurisdiction

11 Notwithstanding any other enactment, a decision maker has no jurisdiction to determine a question of constitutional law unless a regulation made under section 16 has conferred jurisdiction on that decision maker to do so.

Notice of question of constitutional law

12(1) Except in circumstances where only the exclusion of evidence is sought under the *Canadian Charter of Rights and Freedoms*, a person who intends to raise a question of constitutional law at a proceeding before a designated decision maker that has jurisdiction to determine such a question

(a) must provide written notice of the person's intention to do so at least 14 days before the date of the proceeding

(i) to the Attorney General of Canada,

(ii) to the Minister of Justice and Attorney General of Alberta, and

(iii) to the parties to the proceeding,

and

(b) must provide written notice of the person's intention to do so to the designated decision maker.

(2) Until subsection (1) is complied with, the decision maker must not begin the determination of the question of constitutional law.

(3) Nothing in this section affects the power of a decision maker to make any interim order, decision, directive or declaration it considers necessary pending the final determination of any matter before it.

(4) The notice under subsection (1) must be in the form and contain the information provided for in the regulations.

Referral of question of constitutional law

13(1) With respect to a question of constitutional law over which a designated decision maker has jurisdiction and in respect of which a notice has been given under section 12, if the designated decision maker is of the opinion that the court is a more appropriate forum to decide the question, the designated decision maker may, instead of deciding the question,

(a) direct the person who provided the notice under section 12 to apply to the court to have the question determined by that court, or

(b) state the question of constitutional law in the form of a special case to the court for the opinion of the court.

(2) Before acting under subsection (1)(a) or (b), the designated decision maker may conduct any inquiries the designated decision maker considers necessary.

(3) Where the designated decision maker acts under subsection (1)(a) or (b), the designated decision maker must, unless otherwise directed by the court, suspend the proceeding, or any part of the proceeding, as it relates to the question to be heard by the court under subsection (1) until the decision of the court has been given.

(4) A question of constitutional law in respect of which an application has been directed to be made to the court under subsection (1)(a) must be brought on for hearing as soon as practicable.

(5) The court must hear and determine the question of constitutional law submitted to it under this section and give its decision as soon as practicable.

(6) The designated decision maker may and, at the request of the court, shall provide the court with any record and documentation that may assist the court in determining the question of constitutional law submitted to it under this section.

Attorney General of Canada and Minister of Justice and Attorney General of Alberta

14 In any proceeding relating to the determination of a question of constitutional law before a decision maker or before the court under this Part, or in any subsequent proceeding on appeal or judicial review,

(a) the Attorney General of Canada and the Minister of Justice and Attorney General of Alberta are entitled as of right to be heard, in person or by counsel,

(b) no person other than the Minister of Justice and Attorney General of Alberta or counsel designated by the Minister of Justice and Attorney General of Alberta shall, on behalf of Her Majesty in right of Alberta, or on behalf of an agent of Her Majesty in right of Alberta, appear and participate, and

(c) if the Minister of Justice and Attorney General of Alberta or counsel designated by the Minister of Justice and Attorney General of Alberta appears, the Minister of Justice and Attorney General of Alberta is deemed to be a party and has the same rights as any other party.

Transitional

15 Where proceedings to determine a question of constitutional law have commenced but have not been concluded before the coming into force of this Part, the decision maker hearing the question may continue the proceedings as if this Part had not come into force.

Regulations

16 The Lieutenant Governor in Council may make regulations

(a) designating decision makers as having jurisdiction to determine questions of constitutional law;

(b) respecting the questions of constitutional law that decision makers designated under a regulation made under clause (a) have jurisdiction to determine;

(c) respecting the referral of questions of constitutional law to the court;

(d) respecting the form and contents of the notice under section 12(1).

STATUTORY POWERS PROCEDURE ACT
RSO 1990, c. S.22

Interpretation

1(1) In this Act,

"electronic hearing" means a hearing held by conference telephone or some other form of electronic technology allowing persons to hear one another; ("audience électronique")

"hearing" means a hearing in any proceeding; ("audience")

"licence" includes any permit, certificate, approval, registration or similar form of permission required by law; ("autorisation")

"municipality" has the same meaning as in the *Municipal Affairs Act*; ("municipalité")

"oral hearing" means a hearing at which the parties or their representatives attend before the tribunal in person; ("audience orale")

"proceeding" means a proceeding to which this Act applies; ("instance") "representative" means, in respect of a proceeding to which this Act applies, a person authorized under the *Law Society Act* to represent a person in that proceeding; ("représentant")

"statutory power of decision" means a power or right, conferred by or under a statute, to make a decision deciding or prescribing,

(a) the legal rights, powers, privileges, immunities, duties or liabilities of any person or party, or

(b) the eligibility of any person or party to receive, or to the continuation of, a benefit or licence, whether the person is legally entitled thereto or not; ("compétence légale de décision")

"tribunal" means one or more persons, whether or not incorporated and however described, upon which a statutory power of decision is conferred by or under a statute; ("tribunal")

"written hearing" means a hearing held by means of the exchange of documents, whether in written form or by electronic means. ("audience écrite")

Meaning of "person" extended

(2) A municipality, an unincorporated association of employers, a trade union or council of trade unions who may be a party to a proceeding in the exercise of a statutory power of decision under the statute conferring the power shall be deemed to be a person for the purpose of any provision of this Act or of any rule made under this Act that applies to parties.

Liberal construction of Act and rules

2. This Act, and any rule made by a tribunal under subsection 17.1 (4) or section 25.1, shall be liberally construed to secure the just, most expeditious and cost-effective determination of every proceeding on its merits.

Application of Act

3(1) Subject to subsection (2), this Act applies to a proceeding by a tribunal in the exercise of a statutory power of decision conferred by or under an Act of the Legislature, where the tribunal is required by or under such Act or otherwise by law to hold or to afford to the parties to the proceeding an opportunity for a hearing before making a decision.

Where Act does not apply

(2) This Act does not apply to a proceeding,

(a) before the Assembly or any committee of the Assembly;
(b) in or before,
    (i) the Court of Appeal,
    (ii) the Superior Court of Justice,
    (iii) the Ontario Court of Justice,
    (iv) the Family Court of the Superior Court of Justice,
    (v) the Small Claims Court, or
    (vi) a justice of the peace;
(c) to which the Rules of Civil Procedure apply;
(d) before an arbitrator to which the *Arbitrations Act* or the *Labour Relations Act* applies;
(e) at a coroner's inquest;
(f) of a commission appointed under the *Public Inquiries Act*;

Note: On a day to be named by proclamation of the Lieutenant Governor, clause (f) is amended by striking out "*Public Inquiries Act*" and substituting "*Public Inquiries Act, 2009*."

   (g) of one or more persons required to make an investigation and to make a report, with or without recommendations, where the report is for the information or advice of the person to whom it is made and does not in any way legally bind or limit that person in any decision he or she may have power to make; or

   (h) of a tribunal empowered to make regulations, rules or by-laws in so far as its power to make regulations, rules or by-laws is concerned.

Waiver
Waiver of procedural requirement

   4(1) Any procedural requirement of this Act, or of another Act or a regulation that applies to a proceeding, may be waived with the consent of the parties and the tribunal.

Same, rules

   (2) Any provision of a tribunal's rules made under section 25.1 may be waived in accordance with the rules.

Disposition without hearing

   4.1 If the parties consent, a proceeding may be disposed of by a decision of the tribunal given without a hearing, unless another Act or a regulation that applies to the proceeding provides otherwise.

Panels, certain matters

   4.2(1) A procedural or interlocutory matter in a proceeding may be heard and determined by a panel consisting of one or more members of the tribunal, as assigned by the chair of the tribunal.

Assignments

   (2) In assigning members of the tribunal to a panel, the chair shall take into consideration any requirement imposed by another Act or a regulation that applies to the proceeding that the tribunal be representative of specific interests.

Decision of panel

   (3) The decision of a majority of the members of a panel, or their unanimous decision in the case of a two-member panel, is the tribunal's decision.

Panel of one, reduced panel
Panel of one

   4.2.1(1) The chair of a tribunal may decide that a proceeding be heard by a panel of one person and assign the person to hear the proceeding unless there is a statutory requirement in another Act that the proceeding be heard by a panel of more than one person.

Reduction in number of panel members

   (2) Where there is a statutory requirement in another Act that a proceeding be heard by a panel of a specified number of persons, the chair of the tribunal may assign to the panel one person or any lesser number of persons than the number specified in the other Act if all parties to the proceeding consent.

Expiry of term

4.3 If the term of office of a member of a tribunal who has participated in a hearing expires before a decision is given, the term shall be deemed to continue, but only for the purpose of participating in the decision and for no other purpose.

Incapacity of member

4.4(1) If a member of a tribunal who has participated in a hearing becomes unable, for any reason, to complete the hearing or to participate in the decision, the remaining member or members may complete the hearing and give a decision.

Other Acts and regulations

(2) Subsection (1) does not apply if another Act or a regulation specifically deals with the issue of what takes place in the circumstances described in subsection (1).

Decision not to process commencement of proceeding

4.5(1) Subject to subsection (3), upon receiving documents relating to the commencement of a proceeding, a tribunal or its administrative staff may decide not to process the documents relating to the commencement of the proceeding if,

(a) the documents are incomplete;

(b) the documents are received after the time required for commencing the proceeding has elapsed;

(c) the fee required for commencing the proceeding is not paid; or

(d) there is some other technical defect in the commencement of the proceeding.

Notice

(2) A tribunal or its administrative staff shall give the party who commences a proceeding notice of its decision under subsection (1) and shall set out in the notice the reasons for the decision and the requirements for resuming the processing of the documents.

Rules under s. 25.1

(3) A tribunal or its administrative staff shall not make a decision under subsection (1) unless the tribunal has made rules under section 25.1 respecting the making of such decisions and those rules shall set out,

(a) any of the grounds referred to in subsection (1) upon which the tribunal or its administrative staff may decide not to process the documents relating to the commencement of a proceeding; and

(b) the requirements for the processing of the documents to be resumed.

Continuance of provisions in other statutes

(4) Despite section 32, nothing in this section shall prevent a tribunal or its administrative staff from deciding not to process documents relating to the commencement of a proceeding on grounds that differ from those referred to in subsection (1) or without complying with subsection (2) or (3) if the tribunal or its staff does so in accordance with the provisions of an Act that are in force on the day this section comes into force.

Dismissal of proceeding without hearing

4.6(1) Subject to subsections (5) and (6), a tribunal may dismiss a proceeding without a hearing if,

(a) the proceeding is frivolous, vexatious or is commenced in bad faith;

(b) the proceeding relates to matters that are outside the jurisdiction of the tribunal; or

(c) some aspect of the statutory requirements for bringing the proceeding has not been met.

Notice

(2) Before dismissing a proceeding under this section, a tribunal shall give notice of its intention to dismiss the proceeding to,

(a) all parties to the proceeding if the proceeding is being dismissed for reasons referred to in clause (1)(b); or

(b) the party who commences the proceeding if the proceeding is being dismissed for any other reason.

Same

(3) The notice of intention to dismiss a proceeding shall set out the reasons for the dismissal and inform the parties of their right to make written submissions to the tribunal with respect to the dismissal within the time specified in the notice.

Right to make submissions

(4) A party who receives a notice under subsection (2) may make written submissions to the tribunal with respect to the dismissal within the time specified in the notice.

Dismissal

(5) A tribunal shall not dismiss a proceeding under this section until it has given notice under subsection (2) and considered any submissions made under subsection (4).

Rules

(6) A tribunal shall not dismiss a proceeding under this section unless it has made rules under section 25.1 respecting the early dismissal of proceedings and those rules shall include,

(a) any of the grounds referred to in subsection (1) upon which a proceeding may be dismissed;

(b) the right of the parties who are entitled to receive notice under subsection (2) to make submissions with respect to the dismissal; and

(c) the time within which the submissions must be made.

Continuance of provisions in other statutes

(7) Despite section 32, nothing in this section shall prevent a tribunal from dismissing a proceeding on grounds other than those referred to in subsection (1) or without complying with subsections (2) to (6) if the tribunal dismisses the proceeding in accordance with the provisions of an Act that are in force on the day this section comes into force.

Classifying proceedings

4.7 A tribunal may make rules under section 25.1 classifying the types of proceedings that come before it and setting guidelines as to the procedural steps or processes (such as preliminary motions, pre-hearing conferences, alternative dispute resolution mechanisms, expedited hearings) that apply to each type of proceeding and the circumstances in which other procedures may apply.

Alternative dispute resolution

4.8(1) A tribunal may direct the parties to a proceeding to participate in an alternative dispute resolution mechanism for the purposes of resolving the proceeding or an issue arising in the proceeding if,

(a) it has made rules under section 25.1 respecting the use of alternative dispute resolution mechanisms; and

(b) all parties consent to participating in the alternative dispute resolution mechanism.

Definition

(2) In this section,

"alternative dispute resolution mechanism" includes mediation, conciliation, negotiation or any other means of facilitating the resolution of issues in dispute.

Rules

(3) A rule under section 25.1 respecting the use of alternative dispute resolution mechanisms shall include procedural guidelines to deal with the following:

1. The circumstances in which a settlement achieved by means of an alternative dispute resolution mechanism must be reviewed and approved by the tribunal.

2. Any requirement, statutory or otherwise, that there be an order by the tribunal.

Mandatory alternative dispute resolution

(4) A rule under subsection (3) may provide that participation in an alternative dispute resolution mechanism is mandatory or that it is mandatory in certain specified circumstances.

Person appointed to mediate, etc.

(5) A rule under subsection (3) may provide that a person appointed to mediate, conciliate, negotiate or help resolve a matter by means of an alternative dispute resolution mechanism be a member of the tribunal or a person independent of the tribunal. However, a member of the tribunal who is so appointed with respect to a matter in a proceeding shall not subsequently hear the matter if it comes before the tribunal unless the parties consent.

Continuance of provisions in other statutes

(6) Despite section 32, nothing in this section shall prevent a tribunal from directing parties to a proceeding to participate in an alternative dispute resolution mechanism even though the requirements of subsections (1) to (5) have not been met if the tribunal does so in accordance with the provisions of an Act that are in force on the day this section comes into force.

Mediators, etc.: not compellable, notes not evidence

Mediators, etc., not compellable

4.9(1) No person employed as a mediator, conciliator or negotiator or otherwise appointed to facilitate the resolution of a matter before a tribunal by means of an alternative dispute resolution mechanism shall be compelled to give testimony or produce documents in a proceeding before the tribunal or in a civil proceeding with respect to matters that come to his or her knowledge in the course of exercising his or her duties under this or any other Act.

Evidence in civil proceedings

(2) No notes or records kept by a mediator, conciliator or negotiator or by any other person appointed to facilitate the resolution of a matter before a tribunal by means of an alternative dispute resolution mechanism under this or any other Act are admissible in a civil proceeding.

Parties

5. The parties to a proceeding shall be the persons specified as parties by or under the statute under which the proceeding arises or, if not so specified, persons entitled by law to be parties to the proceeding.

Written hearings

5.1(1) A tribunal whose rules made under section 25.1 deal with written hearings may hold a written hearing in a proceeding.

Exception

(2) The tribunal shall not hold a written hearing if a party satisfies the tribunal that there is good reason for not doing so.

Same

(2.1) Subsection (2) does not apply if the only purpose of the hearing is to deal with procedural matters.

Documents

(3) In a written hearing, all the parties are entitled to receive every document that the tribunal receives in the proceeding.

Electronic hearings

5.2(1) A tribunal whose rules made under section 25.1 deal with electronic hearings may hold an electronic hearing in a proceeding.

Exception

(2) The tribunal shall not hold an electronic hearing if a party satisfies the tribunal that holding an electronic rather than an oral hearing is likely to cause the party significant prejudice.

Same

(3) Subsection (2) does not apply if the only purpose of the hearing is to deal with procedural matters.

Participants to be able to hear one another

(4) In an electronic hearing, all the parties and the members of the tribunal participating in the hearing must be able to hear one another and any witnesses throughout the hearing.

Different kinds of hearings in one proceeding

5.2.1 A tribunal may, in a proceeding, hold any combination of written, electronic and oral hearings.

Pre-hearing conferences

5.3(1) If the tribunal's rules made under section 25.1 deal with pre-hearing conferences, the tribunal may direct the parties to participate in a pre-hearing conference to consider,

    (a) the settlement of any or all of the issues;

    (b) the simplification of the issues;

    (c) facts or evidence that may be agreed upon;

    (d) the dates by which any steps in the proceeding are to be taken or begun;

    (e) the estimated duration of the hearing; and

    (f) any other matter that may assist in the just and most expeditious disposition of the proceeding.

Other Acts and regulations

(1.1) The tribunal's power to direct the parties to participate in a pre-hearing conference is subject to any other Act or regulation that applies to the proceeding.

Who presides

(2) The chair of the tribunal may designate a member of the tribunal or any other person to preside at the pre-hearing conference.

Orders

(3) A member who presides at a pre-hearing conference may make such orders as he or she considers necessary or advisable with respect to the conduct of the proceeding, including adding parties.

Disqualification

(4) A member who presides at a pre-hearing conference at which the parties attempt to settle issues shall not preside at the hearing of the proceeding unless the parties consent.

Application of s. 5.2

(5) Section 5.2 applies to a pre-hearing conference, with necessary modifications.

Disclosure

5.4(1) If the tribunal's rules made under section 25.1 deal with disclosure, the tribunal may, at any stage of the proceeding before all hearings are complete, make orders for,

(a) the exchange of documents;

(b) the oral or written examination of a party;

(c) the exchange of witness statements and reports of expert witnesses;

(d) the provision of particulars;

(e) any other form of disclosure.

Other Acts and regulations

(1.1) The tribunal's power to make orders for disclosure is subject to any other Act or regulation that applies to the proceeding.

Exception, privileged information

(2) Subsection (1) does not authorize the making of an order requiring disclosure of privileged information.

Notice of hearing

6(1) The parties to a proceeding shall be given reasonable notice of the hearing by the tribunal.

Statutory authority

(2) A notice of a hearing shall include a reference to the statutory authority under which the hearing will be held.

Oral hearing

(3) A notice of an oral hearing shall include,

(a) a statement of the time, place and purpose of the hearing; and

(b) a statement that if the party notified does not attend at the hearing, the tribunal may proceed in the party's absence and the party will not be entitled to any further notice in the proceeding.

Written hearing

(4) A notice of a written hearing shall include,

(a) a statement of the date and purpose of the hearing, and details about the manner in which the hearing will be held;

(b) a statement that the hearing shall not be held as a written hearing if the party satisfies the tribunal that there is good reason for not holding a written hearing (in which case the tribunal is required to hold it as an electronic or oral hearing) and an indication of the procedure to be followed for that purpose;

(c) a statement that if the party notified neither acts under clause (b) nor participates in the hearing in accordance with the notice, the tribunal may proceed without the party's participation and the party will not be entitled to any further notice in the proceeding.

Electronic hearing

(5) A notice of an electronic hearing shall include,

(a) a statement of the time and purpose of the hearing, and details about the manner in which the hearing will be held;

(b) a statement that the only purpose of the hearing is to deal with procedural matters, if that is the case;

(c) if clause (b) does not apply, a statement that the party notified may, by satisfying the tribunal that holding the hearing as an electronic hearing is likely to cause the party significant prejudice, require the tribunal to hold the hearing as an oral hearing, and an indication of the procedure to be followed for that purpose; and

(d) a statement that if the party notified neither acts under clause (c), if applicable, nor participates in the hearing in accordance with the notice, the tribunal may proceed without the party's participation and the party will not be entitled to any further notice in the proceeding.

Effect of non-attendance at hearing after due notice

7(1) Where notice of an oral hearing has been given to a party to a proceeding in accordance with this Act and the party does not attend at the hearing, the tribunal may proceed in the absence of the party and the party is not entitled to any further notice in the proceeding.

Same, written hearings

(2) Where notice of a written hearing has been given to a party to a proceeding in accordance with this Act and the party neither acts under clause 6(4)(b) nor participates in the hearing in accordance with the notice, the tribunal may proceed without the party's participation and the party is not entitled to any further notice in the proceeding.

Same, electronic hearings

(3) Where notice of an electronic hearing has been given to a party to a proceeding in accordance with this Act and the party neither acts under clause 6(5)(c), if applicable, nor participates in the hearing in accordance with the notice, the tribunal may proceed without the party's participation and the party is not entitled to any further notice in the proceeding.

Where character, etc., of a party is in issue

8. Where the good character, propriety of conduct or competence of a party is an issue in a proceeding, the party is entitled to be furnished prior to the hearing with reasonable information of any allegations with respect thereto.

Hearings to be public; maintenance of order

Hearings to be public, exceptions

9(1) An oral hearing shall be open to the public except where the tribunal is of the opinion that,

(a) matters involving public security may be disclosed; or

(b) intimate financial or personal matters or other matters may be disclosed at the hearing of such a nature, having regard to the circumstances, that the desirability of avoiding disclosure thereof in the interests of any person affected or in the public interest outweighs the desirability of adhering to the principle that hearings be open to the public,

in which case the tribunal may hold the hearing in the absence of the public.

Written hearings

(1.1) In a written hearing, members of the public are entitled to reasonable access to the documents submitted, unless the tribunal is of the opinion that clause (1)(a) or (b) applies.

Electronic hearings

(1.2) An electronic hearing shall be open to the public unless the tribunal is of the opinion that,

(a) it is not practical to hold the hearing in a manner that is open to the public; or

(b) clause (1)(a) or (b) applies.

Maintenance of order at hearings

(2) A tribunal may make such orders or give such directions at an oral or electronic hearing as it considers necessary for the maintenance of order at the hearing, and, if any person disobeys or fails to comply with any such order or direction, the tribunal or a member thereof may call for the assistance of any peace officer to enforce the order or direction, and every peace officer so called upon shall take such action as is necessary to enforce the order or direction and may use such force as is reasonably required for that purpose.

Proceedings involving similar questions

9.1(1) If two or more proceedings before a tribunal involve the same or similar questions of fact, law or policy, the tribunal may,

(a) combine the proceedings or any part of them, with the consent of the parties;

(b) hear the proceedings at the same time, with the consent of the parties;

(c) hear the proceedings one immediately after the other; or

(d) stay one or more of the proceedings until after the determination of another one of them.

Exception

(2) Subsection (1) does not apply to proceedings to which the *Consolidated Hearings Act* applies.

Same

(3) Clauses (1)(a) and (b) do not apply to a proceeding if,

(a) any other Act or regulation that applies to the proceeding requires that it be heard in private;

(b) the tribunal is of the opinion that clause 9(1)(a) or (b) applies to the proceeding.

Conflict, consent requirements

(4) The consent requirements of clauses (1)(a) and (b) do not apply if another Act or a regulation that applies to the proceedings allows the tribunal to combine them or hear them at the same time without the consent of the parties.

Use of same evidence

(5) If the parties to the second-named proceeding consent, the tribunal may treat evidence that is admitted in a proceeding as if it were also admitted in another proceeding that is heard at the same time under clause (1)(b).

Right to representation

10. A party to a proceeding may be represented by a representative.

Examination of witnesses

10.1 A party to a proceeding may, at an oral or electronic hearing,

(a) call and examine witnesses and present evidence and submissions; and

(b) conduct cross-examinations of witnesses at the hearing reasonably required for a full and fair disclosure of all matters relevant to the issues in the proceeding.

Rights of witnesses to representation

11(1) A witness at an oral or electronic hearing is entitled to be advised by a representative as to his or her rights, but such representative may take no other part in the hearing without leave of the tribunal.

Idem

(2) Where an oral hearing is closed to the public, the witness's representative is not entitled to be present except when that witness is giving evidence.

Summonses

12(1) A tribunal may require any person, including a party, by summons,

(a) to give evidence on oath or affirmation at an oral or electronic hearing; and

(b) to produce in evidence at an oral or electronic hearing documents and things specified by the tribunal,

relevant to the subject-matter of the proceeding and admissible at a hearing.

Form and service of summons

(2) A summons issued under subsection (1) shall be in the prescribed form (in English or French) and,

(a) where the tribunal consists of one person, shall be signed by him or her;

(b) where the tribunal consists of more than one person, shall be signed by the chair of the tribunal or in such other manner as documents on behalf of the tribunal may be signed under the statute constituting the tribunal.

Same

(3) The summons shall be served personally on the person summoned.

Fees and allowances

(3.1) The person summoned is entitled to receive the same fees or allowances for attending at or otherwise participating in the hearing as are paid to a person summoned to attend before the Superior Court of Justice.

Bench warrant

(4) A judge of the Superior Court of Justice may issue a warrant against a person if the judge is satisfied that,

(a) a summons was served on the person under this section;

(b) the person has failed to attend or to remain in attendance at the hearing (in the case of an oral hearing) or has failed otherwise to participate in the hearing (in the case of an electronic hearing) in accordance with the summons; and

(c) the person's attendance or participation is material to the ends of justice.

Same

(4.1) The warrant shall be in the prescribed form (in English or French), directed to any police officer, and shall require the person to be apprehended anywhere within Ontario, brought before the tribunal forthwith and,

(a) detained in custody as the judge may order until the person's presence as a witness is no longer required; or

(b) in the judge's discretion, released on a recognizance, with or without sureties, conditioned for attendance or participation to give evidence.

Proof of service

(5) Service of a summons may be proved by affidavit in an application to have a warrant issued under subsection (4).

Certificate of facts

(6) Where an application to have a warrant issued is made on behalf of a tribunal, the person constituting the tribunal or, if the tribunal consists of more than one person, the chair of the tribunal may certify to the judge the facts relied on to establish that the attendance or other participation of the person summoned is material to the ends of justice, and the judge may accept the certificate as proof of the facts.

Same

(7) Where the application is made by a party to the proceeding, the facts relied on to establish that the attendance or other participation of the person is material to the ends of justice may be proved by the party's affidavit.

Contempt proceedings

13(1) Where any person without lawful excuse,

(a) on being duly summoned under section 12 as a witness at a hearing makes default in attending at the hearing; or

(b) being in attendance as a witness at an oral hearing or otherwise participating as a witness at an electronic hearing, refuses to take an oath or to make an affirmation legally required by the tribunal to be taken or made, or to produce any document or thing in his or her power or control legally required by the tribunal to be produced by him or her or to answer any question to which the tribunal may legally require an answer; or

(c) does any other thing that would, if the tribunal had been a court of law having power to commit for contempt, have been contempt of that court,

the tribunal may, of its own motion or on the motion of a party to the proceeding, state a case to the Divisional Court setting out the facts and that court may inquire into the matter and, after hearing any witnesses who may be produced against or on behalf of that person and after hearing any statement that may be offered in defence, punish or take steps for the punishment of that person in like manner as if he or she had been guilty of contempt of the court.

Same

(2) Subsection (1) also applies to a person who,

(a) having objected under clause 6(4)(b) to a hearing being held as a written hearing, fails without lawful excuse to participate in the oral or electronic hearing of the matter; or

(b) being a party, fails without lawful excuse to attend a pre-hearing conference when so directed by the tribunal.

Protection for witnesses

14(1) A witness at an oral or electronic hearing shall be deemed to have objected to answer any question asked him or her upon the ground that the answer may tend to criminate him or her or may tend to establish his or her liability to civil proceedings at the instance of the Crown, or of any person, and no answer given by a witness at a hearing shall be used or be receivable in evidence against the witness in any trial or other proceeding against him or her thereafter taking place, other than a prosecution for perjury in giving such evidence.

(2) Repealed.

Evidence

What is admissible in evidence at a hearing

15(1) Subject to subsections (2) and (3), a tribunal may admit as evidence at a hearing, whether or not given or proven under oath or affirmation or admissible as evidence in a court,

(a) any oral testimony; and

(b) any document or other thing,

relevant to the subject-matter of the proceeding and may act on such evidence, but the tribunal may exclude anything unduly repetitious.

What is inadmissible in evidence at a hearing

(2) Nothing is admissible in evidence at a hearing,

(a) that would be inadmissible in a court by reason of any privilege under the law of evidence; or

(b) that is inadmissible by the statute under which the proceeding arises or any other statute.

Conflicts

(3) Nothing in subsection (1) overrides the provisions of any Act expressly limiting the extent to or purposes for which any oral testimony, documents or things may be admitted or used in evidence in any proceeding.

Copies

(4) Where a tribunal is satisfied as to its authenticity, a copy of a document or other thing may be admitted as evidence at a hearing.

Photocopies

(5) Where a document has been filed in evidence at a hearing, the tribunal may, or the person producing it or entitled to it may with the leave of the tribunal, cause the document to be photocopied and the tribunal may authorize the photocopy to be filed in evidence in the place of the document filed and release the document filed, or may furnish to the person producing it or the person entitled to it a photocopy of the document filed certified by a member of the tribunal.

Certified copy admissible in evidence

(6) A document purporting to be a copy of a document filed in evidence at a hearing, certified to be a copy thereof by a member of the tribunal, is admissible in evidence in proceedings in which the document is admissible as evidence of the document.

Use of previously admitted evidence

15.1(1) The tribunal may treat previously admitted evidence as if it had been admitted in a proceeding before the tribunal, if the parties to the proceeding consent.

Definition

(2) In subsection (1),

"previously admitted evidence" means evidence that was admitted, before the hearing of the proceeding referred to in that subsection, in any other proceeding before a court or tribunal, whether in or outside Ontario.

Additional power

(3) This power conferred by this section is in addition to the tribunal's power to admit evidence under section 15.

Witness panels

15.2 A tribunal may receive evidence from panels of witnesses composed of two or more persons, if the parties have first had an opportunity to make submissions in that regard.

Notice of facts and opinions

16. A tribunal may, in making its decision in any proceeding,

(a) take notice of facts that may be judicially noticed; and

(b) take notice of any generally recognized scientific or technical facts, information or opinions within its scientific or specialized knowledge.

Interim decisions and orders

16.1(1) A tribunal may make interim decisions and orders.

Conditions

(2) A tribunal may impose conditions on an interim decision or order.

Reasons

(3) An interim decision or order need not be accompanied by reasons.

Time frames

16.2 A tribunal shall establish guidelines setting out the usual time frame for completing proceedings that come before the tribunal and for completing the procedural steps within those proceedings.

Decision; interest

Decision

17(1) A tribunal shall give its final decision and order, if any, in any proceeding in writing and shall give reasons in writing therefor if requested by a party.

Interest

(2) A tribunal that makes an order for the payment of money shall set out in the order the principal sum, and if interest is payable, the rate of interest and the date from which it is to be calculated.

Costs

17.1(1) Subject to subsection (2), a tribunal may, in the circumstances set out in rules made under subsection (4), order a party to pay all or part of another party's costs in a proceeding.

Exception

(2) A tribunal shall not make an order to pay costs under this section unless,

(a) the conduct or course of conduct of a party has been unreasonable, frivolous or vexatious or a party has acted in bad faith; and

(b) the tribunal has made rules under subsection (4).

Amount of costs

(3) The amount of the costs ordered under this section shall be determined in accordance with the rules made under subsection (4).

Rules

(4) A tribunal may make rules with respect to,

(a) the ordering of costs;

(b) the circumstances in which costs may be ordered; and

(c) the amount of costs or the manner in which the amount of costs is to be determined.

Same

(5) Subsections 25.1(3), (4), (5) and (6) apply with respect to rules made under subsection (4).

Continuance of provisions in other statutes

(6) Despite section 32, nothing in this section shall prevent a tribunal from ordering a party to pay all or part of another party's costs in a proceeding in circumstances other than those set out in, and without complying with, subsections (1) to (3) if the tribunal makes the order in accordance with the provisions of an Act that are in force on February 14, 2000.

Transition

(7) This section, as it read on the day before the effective date, continues to apply to proceedings commenced before the effective date.

Same

(8) Rules that are made under section 25.1 before the effective date and comply with subsection (4) are deemed to be rules made under subsection (4) until the earlier of the following days:

1. The first anniversary of the effective date.

2. The day on which the tribunal makes rules under subsection (4).

Definition

(9) In subsections (7) and (8),

"effective date" means the day on which section 21 of Schedule B to the *Good Government Act, 2006* comes into force.

Notice of decision

18(1) The tribunal shall send each party who participated in the proceeding, or the party's representative, a copy of its final decision or order, including the reasons if any have been given,

(a) by regular lettermail;

(b) by electronic transmission;

(c) by telephone transmission of a facsimile; or

(d) by some other method that allows proof of receipt, if the tribunal's rules made under section 25.1 deal with the matter.

Use of mail

(2) If the copy is sent by regular lettermail, it shall be sent to the most recent addresses known to the tribunal and shall be deemed to be received by the party on the fifth day after the day it is mailed.

Use of electronic or telephone transmission

(3) If the copy is sent by electronic transmission or by telephone transmission of a facsimile, it shall be deemed to be received on the day after it was sent, unless that day is a holiday, in which case the copy shall be deemed to be received on the next day that is not a holiday.

Use of other method

(4) If the copy is sent by a method referred to in clause (1)(d), the tribunal's rules made under section 25.1 govern its deemed day of receipt.

Failure to receive copy

(5) If a party that acts in good faith does not, through absence, accident, illness or other cause beyond the party's control, receive the copy until a later date than the deemed day of receipt, subsection (2), (3) or (4), as the case may be, does not apply.

Enforcement of orders

19(1) A certified copy of a tribunal's decision or order in a proceeding may be filed in the Superior Court of Justice by the tribunal or by a party and on filing shall be deemed to be an order of that court and is enforceable as such.

Notice of filing

(2) A party who files an order under subsection (1) shall notify the tribunal within 10 days after the filing.

Order for payment of money

(3) On receiving a certified copy of a tribunal's order for the payment of money, the sheriff shall enforce the order as if it were an execution issued by the Superior Court of Justice.

Record of proceeding

20. A tribunal shall compile a record of any proceeding in which a hearing has been held which shall include,

(a) any application, complaint, reference or other document, if any, by which the proceeding was commenced;

(b) the notice of any hearing;

(c) any interlocutory orders made by the tribunal;

(d) all documentary evidence filed with the tribunal, subject to any limitation expressly imposed by any other Act on the extent to or the purposes for which any such documents may be used in evidence in any proceeding;

(e) the transcript, if any, of the oral evidence given at the hearing; and

(f) the decision of the tribunal and the reasons therefor, where reasons have been given.

Adjournments

21. A hearing may be adjourned from time to time by a tribunal of its own motion or where it is shown to the satisfaction of the tribunal that the adjournment is required to permit an adequate hearing to be held.

Correction of errors

21.1 A tribunal may at any time correct a typographical error, error of calculation or similar error made in its decision or order.

Power to review

21.2(1) A tribunal may, if it considers it advisable and if its rules made under section 25.1 deal with the matter, review all or part of its own decision or order, and may confirm, vary, suspend or cancel the decision or order.

Time for review

(2) The review shall take place within a reasonable time after the decision or order is made.

Conflict

(3) In the event of a conflict between this section and any other Act, the other Act prevails.

Administration of oaths

22. A member of a tribunal has power to administer oaths and affirmations for the purpose of any of its proceedings and the tribunal may require evidence before it to be given under oath or affirmation.

Powers re control of proceedings

Abuse of processes

23(1) A tribunal may make such orders or give such directions in proceedings before it as it considers proper to prevent abuse of its processes.

Limitation on examination

(2) A tribunal may reasonably limit further examination or cross-examination of a witness where it is satisfied that the examination or cross-examination has been sufficient to disclose fully and fairly all matters relevant to the issues in the proceeding.

Exclusion of representatives

(3) A tribunal may exclude from a hearing anyone, other than a person licensed under the *Law Society Act*, appearing on behalf of a party or as an adviser to a witness if it finds that such person is not competent properly to represent or to advise the party or witness, or does not understand and comply at the hearing with the duties and responsibilities of an advocate or adviser.

Notice, etc.

24(1) Where a tribunal is of the opinion that because the parties to any proceeding before it are so numerous or for any other reason, it is impracticable,

    (a) to give notice of the hearing; or

    (b) to send its decision and the material mentioned in section 18,

to all or any of the parties individually, the tribunal may, instead of doing so, cause reasonable notice of the hearing or of its decision to be given to such parties by public advertisement or otherwise as the tribunal may direct.

Contents of notice

(2) A notice of a decision given by a tribunal under clause (1)(b) shall inform the parties of the place where copies of the decision and the reasons therefor, if reasons were given, may be obtained.

Appeal operates as stay, exception

25(1) An appeal from a decision of a tribunal to a court or other appellate body operates as a stay in the matter unless,

(a) another Act or a regulation that applies to the proceeding expressly provides to the contrary; or

(b) the tribunal or the court or other appellate body orders otherwise.

Idem

(2) An application for judicial review under the *Judicial Review Procedure Act*, or the bringing of proceedings specified in subsection 2(1) of that Act is not an appeal within the meaning of subsection (1).

Control of process

25.0.1 A tribunal has the power to determine its own procedures and practices and may for that purpose,

(a) make orders with respect to the procedures and practices that apply in any particular proceeding; and

(b) establish rules under section 25.1.

Rules

25.1(1) A tribunal may make rules governing the practice and procedure before it.

Application

(2) The rules may be of general or particular application.

Consistency with Acts

(3) The rules shall be consistent with this Act and with the other Acts to which they relate.

Public access

(4) The tribunal shall make the rules available to the public in English and in French.

***Legislation Act, 2006*, Part III**

(5) Rules adopted under this section are not regulations as defined in Part III (Regulations) of the *Legislation Act, 2006*.

Additional power

(6) The power conferred by this section is in addition to any power to adopt rules that the tribunal may have under another Act.

Regulations

26. The Lieutenant Governor in Council may make regulations prescribing forms for the purpose of section 12.

Rules, etc., available to public

27. A tribunal shall make any rules or guidelines established under this or any other Act available for examination by the public.

Substantial compliance

28. Substantial compliance with requirements respecting the content of forms, notices or documents under this Act or any rule made under this or any other Act is sufficient.

Conflict

32. Unless it is expressly provided in any other Act that its provisions and regulations, rules or by-laws made under it apply despite anything in this Act, the provisions of this Act prevail over the provisions of such other Act and over regulations, rules or by-laws made under such other Act which conflict therewith.

AN ACT RESPECTING ADMINISTRATIVE JUSTICE
RSQ, c. J-3

Purpose

1. The purpose of this Act is to affirm the specific character of administrative justice, to ensure its quality, promptness and accessibility and to safeguard the fundamental rights of citizens.

Rules of procedure

This Act establishes the general rules of procedure applicable to individual decisions made in respect of a citizen. Such rules of procedure differ according to whether a decision is made in the exercise of an administrative or adjudicative function, and are, if necessary, supplemented by special rules established by law or under its authority.

Administrative Tribunal

This Act also institutes the Administrative Tribunal of Québec and the Conseil de la justice administrative.

TITLE I
GENERAL RULES GOVERNING INDIVIDUAL DECISIONS MADE IN RESPECT OF A CITIZEN

CHAPTER I
RULES SPECIFIC TO DECISIONS MADE IN THE EXERCISE OF AN ADMINISTRATIVE FUNCTION

Procedures

2. The procedures leading to an individual decision to be made by the Administration, pursuant to norms or standards prescribed by law, in respect of a citizen shall be conducted in keeping with the duty to act fairly.

Administration

3. The Administration consists of the government departments and bodies whose members are in the majority appointed by the Government or by a minister and whose personnel is appointed in accordance with the Public Service Act (chapter F-3.1.1).

Duties

4. The Administration shall take appropriate measures to ensure

(1) that procedures are conducted in accordance with legislative and administrative norms or standards and with other applicable rules of law, according to simple and flexible rules devoid of formalism, with respect, prudence and promptness, in accordance with the norms and standards of ethics and discipline governing its agents and with the requirements of good faith;

(2) that the citizen is given the opportunity to provide any information useful for the making of the decision and, where necessary, to complete his file;

(3) that decisions are made with diligence, are communicated to the person concerned in clear and concise terms and contain the information required to enable the person to communicate with the Administration;

(4) that the directives governing agents charged with making a decision are in keeping with the principles and obligations under this chapter and are available for consultation by the citizen.

Order or unfavourable decision

5. An administrative authority may not issue an order to do or not do something or make an unfavourable decision concerning a permit or licence or other authorization of like nature without first having

(1) informed the citizen of its intention and the reasons therefor;

(2) informed the citizen of the substance of any complaints or objections that concern him;

(3) given the citizen the opportunity to present observations and, where necessary, to produce documents to complete his file.

Exception

An exception shall be made to such prior obligations if the order or the decision is issued or made in urgent circumstances or to prevent irreparable harm to persons, their property or the environment and the authority is authorized by law to reexamine the situation or review the decision.

Decision

6. An administrative authority that is about to make a decision in relation to an indemnity or a benefit which is unfavourable to a citizen must ensure that the citizen has received the information enabling him to communicate with the authority and that the citizen's file contains all information useful for the making of the decision. If the authority ascertains that such is not the case or that the file is incomplete, it shall postpone its decision for as long as is required to communicate with the citizen and to give the citizen the opportunity to provide the pertinent information or documents to complete his file.

Application for review

In communicating the decision, the administrative authority must inform the citizen that he has the right to apply, within the time indicated, to have the decision reviewed by the administrative authority.

Observations

7. Where, upon the request of a citizen, a situation is reexamined or a decision is reviewed, the administrative authority shall give the citizen the opportunity to present observations and, where necessary, to produce documents to complete his file.

Reasons

8. An administrative authority shall give reasons for all unfavourable decisions it makes, and shall indicate any non-judicial proceeding available under the law and the time limits applicable.

CHAPTER II
RULES SPECIFIC TO DECISIONS IN THE EXERCISE OF AN
ADJUDICATIVE FUNCTION

Procedures

9. The procedures leading to a decision to be made by the Administrative Tribunal of Québec or by another body of the administrative branch charged with settling disputes between a citizen and an administrative authority or a decentralized authority must, so as to ensure a fair process, be conducted in keeping with the duty to act impartially.

Hearing

10. The body is required to give the parties the opportunity to be heard.

Hearings

The hearings shall be held in public. The body may, however, even of its own initiative, order hearings to be held *in camera* where necessary to maintain public order.

Hearing

11. The body has, within the scope of the law, full authority over the conduct of the hearing. It shall, in conducting the proceedings, be flexible and ensure that the substantive law is rendered effective and is carried out.

Evidence

It shall rule on the admissibility of evidence and means of proof and may, for that purpose, follow the ordinary rules of evidence applicable in civil matters. It shall, however, even of its own initiative, reject any evidence which was obtained under such circumstances that fundamental rights and freedoms are breached and the use of which could bring the administration of justice into disrepute. The use of evidence obtained in violation of the right to professional secrecy is deemed to bring the administration of justice into disrepute.

Requirements

12. The body is required to

(1) take measures to circumscribe the issue and, where expedient, to promote reconciliation between the parties;

(2) give the parties the opportunity to prove the facts in support of their allegations and to present arguments;

(3) provide, if necessary, fair and impartial assistance to each party during the hearing;

(4) allow each party to be assisted or represented by persons empowered by law to do so.

Decisions

13. Every decision rendered by the body must be communicated in clear and concise terms to the parties and to every other person that the law indicates.

Decisions

Every decision terminating a matter, even a decision communicated orally to the parties, must be in writing together with the reasons on which it is based.

TITLE II
ADMINISTRATIVE TRIBUNAL OF QUÉBEC

CHAPTER I
INSTITUTION

Administrative Tribunal

14. The Administrative Tribunal of Québec is hereby instituted.

Function

The function of the Tribunal, in the cases provided for by law, is to make determinations in respect of proceedings brought against an administrative authority or a decentralized authority.

Jurisdiction

Except where otherwise provided by law, the Tribunal shall exercise its jurisdiction to the exclusion of any other tribunal or adjucative body.

Power

15. The Tribunal has the power to decide any question of law or fact necessary for the exercise of its jurisdiction.

Decision

In the case of the contestation of a decision, the Tribunal may confirm, vary or quash the contested decision and, if appropriate, make the decision which, in its opinion, should have been made initially.

Seat

16. The seat of the Tribunal shall be situated in the territory of Ville de Québec, at the place determined by the Government; a notice of the address of the seat of the Tribunal shall be published in the *Gazette officielle du Québec*.

Divisions

17. The Tribunal shall consist of four divisions:
- the social affairs division;
- the immovable property division;
- the territory and environment division; and
- the economic affairs division.

CHAPTER II
COMPETENCE OF DIVISIONS AS TO SUBJECT-MATTER

DIVISION I
SOCIAL AFFAIRS DIVISION

Jurisdiction

18. The social affairs division is charged with making determinations in respect of the proceedings pertaining to matters of income security or support and social aid and allowances, of protection of persons whose mental state presents a danger to themselves or to others, of health services and social services, of pension plans, of compensation and of immigration, which proceedings are listed in Schedule I.

Review Board

19. Moreover, the social affairs division is designated as a Review Board within the meaning of sections 672.38 and following of the Criminal Code (Revised Statutes of Canada, 1985, chapter C-46) to make or review dispositions concerning any accused in respect of whom a verdict of not criminally responsible by reason of mental disorder has been rendered or who has been found unfit to stand trial.

Criminal Code

In exercising this function, the social affairs division shall act in accordance with the provisions of the Criminal Code.

Chairperson

The powers and duties conferred on the chairperson of a Review Board shall be exercised by the vice-president responsible for the division or by another member of the division designated by the Government.

Jurisdiction

20. In matters of income security or support and social aid and allowances, the social affairs division is charged with making determinations in respect of the proceedings referred to in section 1 of Schedule I which pertain in particular to decisions concerning financial aid.

Panel

21. Proceedings shall be heard and determined by a panel of two members, only one of whom shall be an advocate or notary.

Physician

The other member must be a physician in the case of proceedings

(1) under section 28 of the Act respecting family benefits (chapter P-19.1), to contest a decision determining, pursuant to section 11 of that Act, whether a child has a handicap within the meaning assigned by government regulation;

(2) under section 118 of the Individual and Family Assistance Act (chapter A-13.1.1), to contest a decision concerning the assessment of a temporarily limited capacity for the reason set out in subparagraph 1 of the first paragraph of section 53 of that Act or the assessment of a severely limited capacity for employment referred to in section 70 of that Act;

(3) under section 16.4 of the Act respecting the Société de l'assurance automobile du Québec (chapter S-11.011), to contest a decision concerning a road vehicle to be adapted so that it may be driven by or be accessible to a handicapped person.

(4) under section 1029.8.61.41 of the Taxation Act (chapter I-3), to contest a decision determining, pursuant to section 1029.8.61.19 of that Act, whether a child has, according to the rules set out in the regulation made under that section, an impairment or a developmental disability that substantially limits the child in the activities of daily living during a foreseeable period of at least one year.

Persons under confinement

22. In matters of protection of persons whose mental state presents a danger to themselves or to others, the social affairs division is charged with making determinations in respect of proceedings referred to in section 2 of Schedule I pertaining to the continued confinement of, or decisions made concerning, a person under confinement under the Act respecting the protection of persons whose mental state presents a danger to themselves or to others (chapter P-38.001).

Three-member panel

22.1. Such proceedings shall be heard and determined by a panel of three members composed of an advocate or a notary, a psychiatrist and a social worker or a psychologist.

23. In matters of measures concerning an accused in respect of whom a verdict of not criminally responsible by reason of mental disorder has been rendered or who has been found unfit to stand trial, the social affairs division is charged with making determinations in respect of the cases referred to in section 2.1 of Schedule I.

Jurisdiction

24. In matters of health services and social services, education and road safety, the social affairs division is charged with making determinations in respect of the proceedings referred to in section 3 of Schedule I pertaining in particular, as regards health services and social services matters, to decisions relating to access to documents or information concerning a beneficiary, a person's eligibility for a health insurance program, the evacuation and relocation of certain persons, a permit issued to a health services or social services institution, to an organ and tissue bank, to a laboratory or to other services or an adapted enterprise certificate, or decisions concerning a health professional or the members of the board of directors of an institution.

Panel

25. Proceedings referred to in paragraphs 2, 2.2, 7, 10 and 12 of section 3 of Schedule I shall be heard and determined by a panel of two members, one of whom shall be an advocate or notary and the other, a physician.

Advocate or notary

Proceedings referred to in paragraphs 1, 2.1.1, 2.3, 3, 5, 6, 8, 9, 11, 12.0.1, 12.1, 13 and 14 of section 3 of Schedule I shall be heard and determined by a single member who shall be an advocate or notary.

Proceedings

Proceedings referred to in paragraphs 2.1 and 5.1 of section 3 of Schedule I shall be heard and determined by a panel of two members, one of whom shall be an advocate or notary and the other, a person well-acquainted with the field of education.

Advocate or notary

Proceedings referred to in paragraph 8.1 of section 3 of Schedule I shall be heard and determined by a single member who shall be an advocate or notary. However, where the proceeding concerns a decision based on any of the grounds set out in paragraph 1 of section 67 of the Act respecting pre-hospital emergency services (chapter S-6.2), the proceeding must be heard and determined by a panel of two members, one of whom shall be an advocate or notary and the other, a physician.

Jurisdiction

26. In pension plan matters, the social affairs division is charged with making determinations in respect of proceedings referred to in section 4 of Schedule I pertaining to decisions made by the Régie des rentes du Québec in particular concerning an application for a benefit or the partition of earnings or decisions made by the Commission administrative des régimes de retraite et d'assurances in particular concerning eligibility for the Pension Plan of Elected Municipal Officers, the number of years of service, pensionable salary or the amount of contributions or of a pension.

Panel

27. Proceedings shall be heard and determined by a single member who shall be an advocate or notary.

Panel

However, proceedings under section 188 of the Act respecting the Québec Pension Plan (chapter R-9) brought against a decision based on a person's disability shall be heard and determined by a panel of two members one of whom shall be an advocate or notary and the other, a physician.

Jurisdiction

28. In compensation matters, the social affairs division is charged with making determinations in respect of proceedings referred to in section 5 of Schedule I pertaining in particular to decisions concerning the right to or amount of compensation.

Panel

29. Proceedings shall be heard and determined by a panel of two members, one of whom shall be an advocate or notary and the other, a physician.

Jurisdiction

30. In immigration matters, the social affairs division is charged with making determinations in respect of proceedings referred to in section 6 of Schedule I pertaining to decisions made by the minister responsible for the administration of the Act respecting immigration to Québec (chapter I-0.2) concerning an undertaking, a selection certificate or a certificate of acceptance.

Advocate or notary

31. Proceedings shall be heard and determined by a single member who shall be an advocate or notary.

DIVISION II

IMMOVABLE PROPERTY DIVISION

Jurisdiction

32. The immovable property division is charged with making determinations in respect of proceedings pertaining in particular to the accuracy, presence or absence of an entry on the property assessment roll or on the roll of rental values, exemptions from or refunds of property taxes or the business tax, the fixing of the indemnities arising from the establishment of reserves for public purposes or from the expropriation of immovables or immovable real rights or from damage caused by

public works or the value or acquisition price of certain property, which proceedings are listed in Schedule II.

Panel

33. Proceedings shall be heard and determined by a panel of two members, one of whom shall be an advocate or notary and the other a chartered appraiser.

Advocate, notary or chartered appraiser

However, proceedings under the Act respecting municipal taxation (chapter F-2.1) relating to a unit of assessment or a business establishment whose property value or rental value entered on the roll is lower than the value fixed by regulation of the Government shall be heard and determined by a single member who shall be an advocate, a notary or a chartered appraiser.

DIVISION III

TERRITORY AND ENVIRONMENT DIVISION

Jurisdiction

34. The territory and environment division is charged with making determinations in respect of proceedings pertaining in particular to decisions made or orders issued concerning the use, subdivision or alienation of a lot, the inclusion or exclusion of a lot in or from an agricultural zone, the removal of topsoil, the emission, deposit, issuance or discharge of contaminants in the environment or the carrying on of an activity likely to affect the quality of the environment, or the erection of certain roadside advertising signs, which are listed in Schedule III.

Panel

35. Proceedings shall be heard and determined by a panel of two members, only one of whom shall be an advocate or notary.

DIVISION IV

ECONOMIC AFFAIRS DIVISION

Jurisdiction

36. The economic affairs division is charged with making determinations in respect of proceedings pertaining in particular to decisions concerning permits, licences, certificates or authorizations to carry on a trade or a professional, economic, industrial or commercial activity, which are listed in Schedule IV.

Panel

37. Proceedings shall be heard and determined by a panel of two members, only one of whom shall be an advocate or notary.

CHAPTER III
COMPOSITION

DIVISION I
APPOINTMENT OF MEMBERS

Members

38. The Tribunal shall be composed of independent and impartial members appointed by the Government, in a number determined according to the needs of the Tribunal, to hold office during good behaviour.

Division

39. The division to which a member is assigned shall be determined in the instrument of appointment.

Place of residence.

39.1. The Government may determine the place of residence of a member.

Social affairs division.

40. In the social affairs division, at least 10 members shall be physicians, including at least four psychiatrists, at least two members shall be social workers and at least two other members shall be psychologists.

DIVISION II
RECRUITING AND SELECTION OF MEMBERS

Qualifications

41. Only a person who has the qualifications required by law and at least ten years' experience pertinent to the exercise of the functions of the Tribunal may be a member of the Tribunal.

Selection

42. Members shall be selected among persons declared apt according to the recruiting and selection procedure established by government regulation. The regulation may, in particular,

(1) determine the publicity that must be given to the recruiting procedure and the content of such publicity;

(2) determine the procedure by which a person may become a candidate;

(3) authorize the establishment of selection committees to assess the aptitude of candidates and formulate an opinion concerning them;

(4) fix the composition of the committees and mode of appointment of committee members, ensuring, where appropriate, adequate representation of the sectors concerned;

(5) determine the selection criteria to be taken into account by the committees;

(6) determine the information a committee may require from a candidate and the consultations it may hold.

Register

43. The names of the persons declared apt shall be recorded in a register kept at the Ministère du Conseil exécutif.

Declaration of aptitude

44. A declaration of aptitude shall be valid for a period of 18 months or for any other period fixed by regulation of the Government.

Selection committee

45. Members of a selection committee shall receive no remuneration except in such cases, subject to such conditions and to such extent as may be determined by the Government.

Expenses

They are, however, entitled to the reimbursement of expenses incurred in the performance of their duties, subject to the conditions and to the extent determined by the Government.

DIVISION III

Repealed

[Sections 46 to 50 repealed.]

DIVISION IV

TERMINATION OF APPOINTMENT AND SUSPENSION

Termination

51. The appointment of a member may terminate only on the member's retirement or resignation, or on his being dismissed or otherwise removed from office in the circumstances referred to in this division.

Resignation

52. To resign, a member must give the Minister reasonable notice in writing, sending a copy to the president of the Tribunal.

Dismissal

53. The Government may dismiss a member if the Conseil de la justice administrative so recommends, after an inquiry conducted following the lodging of a complaint pursuant to section 182.

Suspension

The Government may also suspend the member with or without remuneration for the period recommended by the Conseil de la justice administrative.

Removal of member

54. The Government may also remove a member from office for either of the following reasons:

(1) loss of a qualification required by law for holding the office of member;

(2) permanent disability which, in the opinion of the Government, prevents the member from performing the duties of his office satisfactorily; permanent disability is ascertained by the Conseil de la justice administrative, after an inquiry conducted at the request of the Minister or of the president of the Tribunal.

DIVISION V
OTHER PROVISIONS REGARDING TERMINATION OF DUTIES

Expiry of term

55. Any member who has retired or resigned may, with the authorization of and for the time determined by the president of the Tribunal, continue to perform his duties in order to conclude the cases he has begun to hear but has yet to determine; he shall be a supernumerary member for the time required.

DIVISION VI
REMUNERATION AND OTHER CONDITIONS OF OFFICE

Regulations

56. The Government shall make regulations determining

(1) the mode of remuneration of the members and the applicable standards and scales, and the method for determining the annual percentage of salary advancement up to the maximum salary rate and of the adjustment of the remuneration of members whose salary has reached the maximum rate;

(2) the conditions subject to which and the extent to which a member may be reimbursed the expenses incurred in the performance of his duties.

Conditions of office

The Government may make regulations determining other conditions of office applicable to all or certain members, including social benefits other than the pension plan.

Regulatory provisions

The regulatory provisions may vary according to whether they apply to full-time or part-time members or to a member charged with an administrative office within the Tribunal.

Coming into force

The regulations come into force on the fifteenth day following the date of their publication in the *Gazette officielle du Québec* or on any later date indicated therein.

Remuneration

57. The Government shall fix, in accordance with the regulations, the remuneration, social benefits and other conditions of office of the members.

Reduction

58. Once fixed, a member's remuneration may not be reduced, except to take into account a retirement pension from the Québec public sector that is paid to the member.

Termination

However, additional remuneration attaching to an administrative office within the Tribunal shall cease upon termination of such office.

Pension plan

59. The pension plan of full-time members shall be determined pursuant to the Act respecting the Pension Plan of Management Personnel (chapter R-12.1) or the Act respecting the Civil Service Superannuation Plan (chapter R-12), as the case may be.

Public servants

60. A public servant appointed as a member of the Tribunal ceases to be a public servant.

DIVISION VII

ADMINISTRATIVE OFFICE

President, vice-presidents

61. The Government shall designate, among the members of the Tribunal who are advocates or notaries, a president and vice-presidents in the number it determines.

Vice-presidents

The instrument of appointment of a vice-president shall determine the divisions under his responsibility.

Duties

62. The president and the vice-presidents shall exercise their duties on a full-time basis.

Replacement

63. The Minister shall designate a vice-president to replace the president or another vice-president temporarily when required.

Replacement

If the vice-president so designated is himself absent or unable to act, the Minister shall designate another vice-president as a replacement.

Administrative office

64. The administrative office of the president or a vice-president is of a fixed duration determined in the instrument of appointment or renewal.

Termination

65. The administrative office of the president or a vice-president may terminate prematurely only on his relinquishing such office, on the termination of his appointment or on his removal or dismissal from his administrative office in the circumstances referred to in this division.

Removal

66. The Government may remove the president or a vice-president from his administrative office if the Conseil de la justice administrative so recommends, after an inquiry conducted at the Minister's request concerning a lapse pertaining only to his administrative duties.

Dismissal

67. The Government may also dismiss the president or a vice-president from his administrative office for loss of a qualification required by law for holding such office.

CHAPTER IV
DUTIES AND POWERS OF MEMBERS

Oath

68. Before taking office, every member shall take an oath, solemnly affirming the following: "I ... swear that I will exercise the powers and fulfill the duties of my office impartially and honestly and to the best of my knowledge and abilities.".

President

The oath shall be taken before the president of the Tribunal. The president of the Tribunal shall take the oath before a judge of the Court of Québec.

Minister

The writing evidencing the oath shall be sent to the Minister.

Conflict of interest

69. A member may not, on pain of forfeiture of office, have a direct or indirect interest in any enterprise that could cause a conflict between his personal interest and his duties of office, unless the interest devolves to him by succession or gift and he renounces it or disposes of it with dispatch.

Code of ethics

70. In addition to observing conflict of interest requirements and the rules of conduct and duties imposed by the code of ethics adopted under this Act, a member may not pursue an activity or place himself in a situation incompatible, within the meaning of the code of ethics, with the exercise of his office.

Exclusivity

71. Full-time members shall devote themselves exclusively to their office, save the exceptions that follow.

Mandates

72. A member may carry out any mandate entrusted to him by order of the Government after consultation with the president of the Tribunal.

Teaching activities

73. A member may, with the written consent of the president of the Tribunal, engage in teaching activities and receive remuneration therefor.

Powers and immunity

74. The Tribunal and its members are vested with the powers and immunity of commissioners appointed under the Act respecting public inquiry commissions (chapter C-37), except the power to order imprisonment.

Powers

They are also vested with all the powers necessary for the performance of their duties; they may, in particular, make any order they consider appropriate to safeguard the rights of the parties.

Immunity

No judicial proceedings may be brought against them by reason of an act done in good faith in the performance of their duties.

CHAPTER V
OPERATION

DIVISION I
MANAGEMENT AND ADMINISTRATION OF THE TRIBUNAL

Administration

75. In addition to the powers and duties that may otherwise be assigned to him, the president is charged with the administration and general management of the Tribunal.

Duties

The duties of the president include

(1) fostering the participation of members in the formulation of guiding principles for the Tribunal so as to maintain a high level of quality and coherence of decisions;

(2) coordinating the activities of and assigning work to the members of the Tribunal who shall comply with his orders and directives in that regard; and

(3) seeing to the observance of standards of ethical conduct;

(4) promoting professional development of the members as regards the exercise of their functions;

(5) periodically evaluating the knowledge and skills of the members in the performance of their duties and their contribution to the processing of the cases before the Tribunal and to the achievement of the objectives of this Act;

(6) designating a member to coordinate the activities of the Tribunal in one or more regions and, if the volume of proceedings so requires, determining that the place of residence of that member is to be in one of those regions.

Code of ethics

76. The president shall establish a code of ethics applicable to the conciliators and see that it is observed.

Coming into force

The code of ethics comes into force on the fifteenth day following the date of its publication in the *Gazette officielle du Québec* or on any later date indicated therein.

Assignment of member

77. To expedite the business of the Tribunal, the president may, after consultation with the vice-presidents responsible for the divisions concerned, assign a member temporarily to another division.

Management objectives

78. Each year, the president shall present a plan to the Minister in which he shall state his management objectives aimed at ensuring the accessibility of the Tribunal and the quality and promptness of its decision-making process and give an account of the results achieved in the preceding year.

Information

The president shall include in the plan, in addition to the information requested by the Minister, the following information, compiled by the Tribunal on a monthly basis in respect of each division:

(1) the number of days on which hearings were held and the average number of hours devoted to them;

(2) the number of postponements granted;

(3) the nature and number of cases in which conciliation was held, and the number of such cases where the parties reached an agreement;

(4) the number of cases heard, the nature thereof and the places and dates of the hearings;

(5) the number of cases taken under advisement, the nature thereof and the time devoted to advisement;

(6) the number of decisions made;

(7) the time devoted to the proceedings, from the date of the introductory motion until the beginning of the hearing or the making of the decision.

Delegation

79. The president may delegate all or part of his powers and duties to the vice-presidents.

Vice-presidents

80. The vice-presidents shall assist and advise the president in the performance of his duties and perform their administrative duties under the president's authority.

Vice-presidents

81. In addition to the powers and duties that may otherwise be assigned to him or delegated to him by the president, the duties of a vice-president include

(1) assigning cases and scheduling sittings in the division under his responsibility; the members shall comply with his orders and directives in that regard;

(2) participating in the temporary assignment of a member to another division.

DIVISION II

SITTINGS

Sittings

82. The president, the vice-president responsible for the division or any member designated by either shall determine which members are to take part in each sitting.

Panels

The president may, where he considers it expedient in view of the complexity of a case or importance of a matter, form a panel comprising a greater number of members than that provided for in Chapter II, but not exceeding five.

Panel

He may also, where he considers it expedient, form a panel of only one member to hear and determine the proceedings he determines and which, by reason of their nature and the facts, do not raise particular difficulties and do not require a second expert opinion.

Single member

In all cases, one member only is called to sit where measures relating to the management of proceedings or matters incidental thereto are to be determined.

Sittings

83. The sittings shall be presided by the president, the vice-president responsible for the division or a member designated by either of them among the members.

Location

84. The Tribunal may sit at any place in Québec. If the Tribunal holds a hearing in a locality where a court sits, the clerk of the court shall allow the Tribunal to use premises used by the court unless they are being used for sittings of the court.

Property assessment

85. In property assessment matters, the Tribunal may sit in the territory of the local municipality whose roll is involved if the dispute concerns a unit of assessment or a business establishment whose property value or rental value entered on the roll is equal to or lower than the value fixed by regulation of the Government.

Grouping of territories

However, the president of the Tribunal, in cooperation with the vice-president responsible for the immovable property division, may group the territories of several local municipalities within a radius of 100 kilometres, and designate the municipal territory in which the Tribunal shall sit.

Territory

With the consent of the applicant, the Tribunal may sit outside the territory of the local municipality or the limits determined.

DIVISION III

PERSONNEL AND PHYSICAL AND FINANCIAL RESOURCES

Personnel

86. The secretary of the Tribunal and the other members of the personnel of the Tribunal shall be appointed in accordance with the Public Service Act (chapter F-3.1.1).

Immunity

No judicial proceedings may be brought against them for any act done in good faith in the performance of their duties.

Records

87. The secretary shall have custody of the records of the Tribunal.

Authenticity

88. The documents emanating from the Tribunal are authentic if they are signed, as are copies of such documents if they are certified true, by a member of the Tribunal or by the secretary.

Access to records

89. Notwithstanding section 9 of the Act respecting Access to documents held by public bodies and the Protection of personal information (chapter A-2.1), only a person authorized by the Tribunal may have access, for good reason, to any record of the social affairs division that contains information on the physical or mental health of a person or information the Tribunal considers to be confidential which, if disclosed, would be prejudicial to a person.

Confidentiality

Any person authorized to examine such a record is required to maintain its confidentiality. If a copy or extract is given to him, he must destroy it as soon as it is no longer of use to him.

Bank of jurisprudence

90. The Tribunal shall establish a bank of jurisprudence and shall, in cooperation with the Société québécoise d'information juridique, ensure public access to all or part of the decisions made by the Tribunal.

Names

The Tribunal shall omit the names of the persons concerned by decisions of the social affairs division.

Exhibits

91. Once proceedings have been completed, the parties shall take back the exhibits they produced and the documents they filed.

Destruction

Failing that, such exhibits and documents may be destroyed after the expiry of one year from the date of the final decision of the Tribunal or of the proceeding terminating the proceedings, unless the president decides otherwise.

Tariff

92. The Government may, by regulation, determine a tariff of the administrative fees, professional fees and other charges attached to proceedings before the Tribunal as well as the classes of persons which may be exempted therefrom.

Financial year

93. The financial year of the Tribunal shall end on 31 March.

Budgetary estimates

94. Each year, the president of the Tribunal shall submit the budgetary estimates of the Tribunal for the following financial year to the Minister according to the form, tenor and schedule determined by the Minister. The estimates shall be submitted to the Government for approval.

Audit

95. The books and accounts of the Tribunal shall be audited by the Auditor General once a year and whenever ordered by the Government.

Report

96. Not later than 30 June each year, the Tribunal shall present a report to the Minister on its operations for the preceding financial year.

Tabling

The Minister shall lay the report before the National Assembly within 30 days of receiving it if the Assembly is in session or, if it is not, within 30 days of the opening of the next session.

Report

The report shall not designate by name any person concerned by the matters brought before the Tribunal.

Fund

97. The sums required for the purposes of this Title shall be taken out of the fund of the Administrative Tribunal of Québec.

Fund

The fund shall be made up of the following sums:

(1) the sums paid into it by the Minister out of the appropriations granted each year for that purpose by the National Assembly;

(2) the sums paid into it by the Commission de la santé et de la sécurité du travail, the Minister responsible for the application of the Individual and Family Assistance Act (chapter A-13.1.1), the Régie des rentes du Québec and the Société de l'assurance automobile du Québec, the amount and manner of payment of which shall be determined, for each, by the Government;

(3) the sums collected in accordance with the tariff of administrative fees, professional fees and other charges for proceedings before the Tribunal.

Consolidated revenue fund

98. The Government may, on the conditions it determines, authorize the Minister of Finance to advance to the fund of the Tribunal sums taken out of the consolidated revenue fund. Any advance paid shall be repayable out of the fund of the Tribunal.

CHAPTER VI
RULES OF EVIDENCE AND OF PROCEDURE

DIVISION I
PURPOSE

Rules

99. This chapter prescribes basic rules to supplement the general rules of Chapter II of Title I which pertain to decisions made in the exercise of an adjudicative function.

DIVISION II
GENERAL PROVISIONS

Hearing

100. The Tribunal may not decide a matter if the parties have not been heard or summoned.

Exemption

It is exempted from that requirement in regard to a party to grant an uncontested application. The Tribunal is also exempted therefrom if all of the parties consent to its proceeding on the basis of the record, subject to the power of the Tribunal to summon the parties in order to hear them.

Failure to appear

In addition, if a party who has been summoned does not appear at the time fixed for the hearing without having provided a valid excuse for his absence, or appears at the hearing but refuses to be heard, the Tribunal may nonetheless proceed and make a decision.

Parties

101. The parties to a proceeding are, in addition to the person and administrative authority or decentralized authority directly interested therein, any person so designated by law.

Representation

102. The parties may be represented by the person of their choice before the social affairs division, in the case of a proceeding pertaining to compensation for rescuers and victims of crime, a proceeding under section 65 of the Workmen's Compensation Act (chapter A-3) or a proceeding under section 12 of the Act respecting indemnities for victims of asbestosis and silicosis in mines and quarries (chapter I-7); however, a professional who has been removed from the roll or declared disqualified to practise, or whose right to engage in professional activities has been restricted or suspended in accordance with the Professional Code (chapter C-26) or any legislation governing a profession may not act as a representative.

Representation

The Minister of Employment and Social Solidarity or a body which is the Minister's delegatee for the purposes of the Individual and Family Assistance Act (chapter A-13.1.1) may be represented by the person of his or its choice before the social affairs division in the case of a proceeding brought under that Act or this Act in a matter of income security or support or social aid and allowances.

Representation

The applicant may, before the social affairs division in the case of a proceeding in a matter of immigration, be represented by a relative or by a non-profit organization devoted to the defense or interests of immigrants, if he is unable to be present himself by reason of absence from Québec. In the latter case, the mandatary must provide the Tribunal with a mandate in writing, signed by the person represented, indicating the gratuitous nature of the mandate.

Advocate

103. Where the Tribunal is seized of a proceeding under section 21 of the Act respecting the protection of persons whose mental state presents a danger to themselves or to others (chapter P-38.001), it shall ascertain that the applicant has been given an opportunity to retain the services of an advocate.

Assistance

104. The members of the personnel of the Tribunal shall assist any person who so requests in drafting a motion, an intervention or any other written proceeding directed to the Tribunal.

Defects of form

105. The Tribunal may accept a written proceeding despite a defect of form or an irregularity.

Failure to act

106. The Tribunal may relieve a party from failure to act within the time prescribed by law if the party establishes that he was unable, for valid reasons, to act sooner and if the Tribunal considers that no other party suffers serious harm therefrom.

Execution of decision

107. A proceeding before the Tribunal does not suspend the execution of the contested decision, unless a provision of law provides otherwise or, upon a motion heard and judged by preference, a member of the Tribunal orders otherwise by reason of urgency or of the risk of serious and irreparable harm.

Proceeding

If the law provides that the proceeding suspends the execution of the decision, or if the Tribunal issues such an order, the proceeding shall be heard and judged by preference.

Absence of provisions

108. In the absence of provisions applicable to a particular case, the Tribunal may remedy the inadequacy by any procedure consistent with law or with its rules of procedure.

Rules of procedure

109. The Tribunal may, by a regulation adopted by a majority vote of its members, make rules of procedure specifying the manner in which the rules established in this chapter or in the special Acts under which proceedings are brought are to be applied.

Divisions

Such rules of procedure may differ according to the divisions or, in the case of the social affairs division, according to the matters to which they apply.

Approval

The regulation is subject to the approval of the Government.

DIVISION III

INTRODUCTORY AND PRELIMINARY PROCEDURE

Motion

110. A proceeding is brought before the Tribunal by a motion filed at the secretariat of the Tribunal within 30 days after notification to the applicant of the contested decision or after the occurrence of the facts giving rise to the proceeding; a proceeding must, however, be brought within 60 days if it pertains to a matter within the purview of the social affairs division. There is no time limit for bringing a proceeding arising out of the failure by the administrative authority to dispose of an application for an administrative review within the time prescribed by law.

Court of Québec

The motion may also be filed in any office of the Court of Québec, in which case the clerk shall transmit the motion forthwith to the secretary of the Tribunal.

Content of motion

111. The motion shall state the decision in respect of which the proceeding is brought or the facts giving rise thereto, and shall contain a short statement of the grounds invoked in support of the proceeding and set out the conclusions sought.

Information

It shall contain any other information required by the rules of procedure of the Tribunal, and shall, where applicable, state the name, address, phone number and fax number of the representative of the applicant.

Rules

112. The rules pertaining to the notices provided for in article 95 of the Code of Civil Procedure (chapter C-25) apply, with the necessary modifications, to motions presented before the Tribunal.

Copy of motion

113. Upon receipt of the motion, the secretary of the Tribunal shall send a copy of it to the party against whom the proceeding is brought and to the persons indicated by law.

Record

114. The administrative authority whose decision is contested must, within 30 days of receipt of a copy of the motion, send a copy of the record relating to the matter and the name, address, phone number and fax number of its representative to the secretary of the Tribunal and to the applicant.

Documents

Within the same time, the municipal body responsible for the assessment must send the application for review and the assessor's proposal or decision, the documents received by the assessor for the purposes of the review and the documents to which the assessor's proposal or decision refers, as well as any certificate issued by the assessor since the filing of the motion instituting the proceedings.

Access to records

Access to any record sent pursuant to this section shall continue to be governed by the Act applicable to the administrative authority having sent it.

Indemnity

114.1. If an administrative authority fails to send a copy of the case record within the time prescribed in section 114, the applicant may request that the Tribunal fix an indemnity it considers fair and reasonable considering the circumstances of the case and the extent of the delay.

Dismissal of proceedings

115. The Tribunal may, upon a motion, dismiss a proceeding it deems improper or dilatory or subject it to certain conditions.

Suspension of case

116. Where, on examining the motion and the contested decision, the Tribunal ascertains that the authority concerned failed to rule upon certain questions although it was required to do so by law, the Tribunal may, if the date of the hearing has not been fixed, suspend the case for the time it fixes so that the administrative authority or decentralized authority may act.

Expiry of time

If, at the expiry of the allotted time, the proceeding before the Tribunal is maintained, the Tribunal shall hear the proceeding as though it were a proceeding in respect of the original decision.

Referral

117. Where, during a proceeding before the social affairs division, a question is raised respecting Title III of the Act respecting the Québec Pension Plan (chapter R-9), the Tribunal must, subject to the exceptions contemplated in section 76 of the said Act, order the referral of the matter to the Court of Québec for a ruling on the question raised. In such case, the secretary of the Tribunal shall give notice thereof to the Minister of Revenue without delay.

Ruling

Where the ruling of the court does not put an end to the dispute, the matter is referred back to the Tribunal.

Joinder

118. Cases in which the questions in dispute are substantially the same or whose subject-matters could suitably be combined, whether or not the same parties are involved, may be joined by order of

the president of the Tribunal or of the vice-president responsible for the division concerned, on the conditions he fixes.

Revocation
An order made under the first paragraph may be revoked by the Tribunal upon hearing the matter if it is of the opinion that the interests of justice will be better served by doing so.

Hearing by preference
119. The following proceedings shall be heard and decided by preference:

(1) a proceeding under section 68 of the Act respecting prescription drug insurance (chapter A-29.01) which pertains to the withdrawal of recognition by the Minister from a manufacturer or from a wholesaler of medications;

(2) a proceeding under section 53.13 of the Expropriation Act (chapter E-24) which pertains to a provisional indemnity;

(3) (paragraph repealed);

(4) a proceeding under section 21 of the Act respecting the protection of persons whose mental state presents a danger to themselves or to others (chapter P-38.001) which pertains to a person under confinement in a health or social services institution;

(5) a proceeding under section 21.1 of the Act respecting the preservation of agricultural land and agricultural activities (chapter P-41.1) which pertains to an order of the Commission de protection du territoire agricole du Québec;

(5.1) a proceeding under section 57 of the Act respecting pre-hospital emergency services (chapter S-6.2) which pertains to the suspension, revocation or non-renewal of, or a denial of authorization in respect of the transfer or assignment of, an ambulance service permit or to a denial of authorization in respect of the transfer or assignment of share ownership;

(5.2) a proceeding under section 346.0.16 of the Act respecting health services and social services (chapter S-4.2) which pertains to the refusal of an application for or the suspension, revocation or non-renewal of a certificate of compliance;

(6) a proceeding under section 453 of the Act respecting health services and social services (chapter S-4.2) or under section 182.1 of the Act respecting health services and social services for Cree Native persons (chapter S-5) which pertains to the decision to evacuate and relocate any persons lodged in a facility where activities are carried on without a permit;

(7) a proceeding under section 202.6.11 of the Highway Safety Code (chapter C-24.2) following a decision to suspend a licence or the right to obtain a licence for 30 or 60 days for speeding or 90 days for the presence of alcohol in the driver's body.

DIVISION III.1
CASE MANAGEMENT CONFERENCE

Case management conference
119.1. Where warranted by the circumstances of a case, in particular where one of the parties fails to act within the time prescribed by law, the president of the Tribunal, the vice-president responsible for the division concerned or the member designated by either may, on his or her own initiative or at the request of one of the parties, convene the parties to a case management conference in order to

(1) come to an agreement with the parties as to the conduct of the proceeding, specifying the undertakings of the parties and determining the timetable to be complied with within the prescribed time;

(2) if the parties fail to agree, determine a timetable for the proceeding, which is binding on the parties;

(3) determine how the conduct of the proceeding may be simplified or accelerated and the hearing shortened, among other things by better defining the questions at issue or admitting any fact or document;

(4) invite the parties to a conciliation session.

Agreement

An agreement under subparagraph 1 must cover, among other subjects, the procedure and time limit for the communication of exhibits, written statements in lieu of testimony and detailed affidavits, and experts' appraisals.

Minutes

119.2. The minutes of the conference shall be drawn up and signed by the member having conducted the conference.

Failure to attend conference

119.3. If one of the parties fails to attend the conference, the Tribunal shall record the failure and make the decisions it considers appropriate.

[Section 119.4 not in force.]

Failure to comply with timetable

119.5. If the parties fail to comply with the timetable, the member may make the appropriate determinations, including foreclosure. The member may, on request, relieve a defaulting party from default if required in the interest of justice.

DIVISION IV

CONCILIATION

Conciliation session

119.6. Upon receipt by the Tribunal of a copy of a case record pertaining to indemnification or benefits, and if the matter and circumstances so permit, the president of the Tribunal, the vice-president in charge of the division concerned or the member designated by either of them must offer the parties a conciliation session conducted by a member or a personnel member chosen by the president of the Tribunal or a person designated by the president.

Suspension of proceedings

120. If he considers it expedient and if the subject-matter and circumstances of the case permit it, the president of the Tribunal, the vice-president responsible for the division concerned, the member designated by either of them or any member called on to hear the case may, with the consent of the parties, at any time before the case is taken under advisement, preside a conciliation session or allow such a session to be conducted by a personnel member chosen by the president of the Tribunal or by the person chosen by the president of the Tribunal.

Conciliation session

In the case of a proceeding pertaining to a decision claiming the repayment of social security benefits wrongly received, a proceeding pertaining to a decision based on a person's disability in a pension plan matter or a proceeding regarding compensation under the Automobile Insurance Act (chapter A-25), the president of the Tribunal or the vice-president responsible for the division concerned may convene the parties to an initial conciliation session and designate the conciliator. The parties are bound to attend.

Purpose

121. The purpose of conciliation is to facilitate dialogue between the parties and help them to identify their interests, assess their positions, negotiate and explore mutually satisfactory solutions.

Suspension of proceedings

Conciliation does not suspend the proceedings.

Rules

121.1. After consulting with the parties, the conciliator shall define the rules applicable to the conciliation and any measure to facilitate its conduct, and determine the schedule of sessions.

Private sessions

Conciliation sessions are held in private, at no cost to the parties and without formality, and require no prior written documents.

Attending parties

Conciliation sessions are held in the presence of the parties and their representatives. With the consent of the parties, the conciliator may meet with the parties separately. Other persons may also take part in the sessions if the conciliator or the parties consider that their presence would be helpful in resolving the dispute.

Modification

121.2. A member of the Tribunal presiding a conciliation session may, if necessary, modify the proceeding timetable.

Settlement

However, if no settlement is reached, a member of the Tribunal having presided a conciliation session may not hear any application regarding the dispute.

Admissibility as evidence

122. Unless the parties consent thereto, nothing that is said or written in the course of conciliation may be admitted as evidence before a court of justice or before a person or body of the administrative branch exercising adjudicative functions. The parties must be so informed by the conciliator.

Disclosure

123. A conciliator may not be compelled to disclose anything made revealed to or learned by him in the exercise of his functions or produce a document prepared or obtained in the course of such exercise before a court of justice or before a person or body of the administrative branch exercising adjudicative functions.

Access to documents

Notwithstanding section 9 of the Act respecting Access to documents held by public bodies and the Protection of personal information (chapter A-2.1), no person may have access to a document contained in the conciliation record.

Agreement

124. Any agreement reached shall be recorded in writing and signed by the conciliator, the parties and their representatives, if any. It is binding on the parties.

Agreement

If the agreement is reached following a conciliation session presided by a member of the Tribunal, it terminates the proceedings and is enforceable as a decision of the Tribunal; if the agreement is reached following a conciliation session conducted by a personnel member, it has the same effects provided it is homologated by the Tribunal.

DIVISION V

PRE-HEARING CONFERENCE

Pre-hearing conference

125. The president of the Tribunal, the vice-president responsible for the division concerned or the member designated by either of them may call the parties to a pre-hearing conference if he considers it useful and the circumstances of the case allow it.

Purpose

126. The purpose of the pre-hearing conference is

(1) to define the questions to be dealt with at the hearing;

(2) to assess the advisability of clarifying and specifying the pretensions of the parties and the conclusions sought;

(3) to ensure that all documentary evidence is exchanged by the parties;

(4) to plan the conduct of the proceedings and proof at the hearing;

(5) to examine the possibility for the parties of admitting certain facts or of proving them by means of sworn statements;

(6) to examine any other question likely to simplify or accelerate the conduct of the hearing.

Minutes

127. Minutes of the pre-hearing conference shall be drawn up and signed by the parties and by the member who called the parties to the conference.

Agreements and decisions

Agreements and decisions recorded in the minutes shall, as far as they may apply, govern the conduct of the proceeding, unless the Tribunal, when hearing the matter, permits a derogation therefrom to prevent an injustice.

DIVISION VI
HEARING

Hearing

128. The Tribunal shall, so far as is possible, facilitate the holding of a hearing at a date and time when the parties and their witnesses, if any, are able to attend without unduly disrupting their usual occupations.

Notice

129. Notice shall be sent to the parties within reasonable time before the hearing or within the time fixed by law, stating

(1) the purpose, date, time and place of the hearing;

(2) that the parties have the right to be assisted or represented, and listing the classes of persons authorized by law to assist or represent a party before the Tribunal;

(3) that the Tribunal has the authority to proceed, without further delay or notice, despite the failure of a party to appear at the time and place fixed if no valid excuse is provided.

Journalists

130. A journalist who proves his status shall be admitted, without further formality, to any hearing held *in camera*, unless the Tribunal considers that the presence of the journalist can be prejudicial to a person whose interests may be affected by the proceeding.

Publication of information

No such journalist shall publish or broadcast information that would allow the identification of a person concerned, unless the journalist is authorized to do so by the law or by the Tribunal.

Publication ban

131. The Tribunal may, of its own initiative or on an application by a party, ban or restrict the disclosure, publication or dissemination of any information or documents it indicates, where necessary to maintain public order or where the confidential nature of the information or documents requires the prohibition or restriction to ensure the proper administration of justice.

Subpoena

132. Any party wishing to summon a witness shall do so by means of a subpoena issued by a member or by the advocate representing the party and served in accordance with the rules of procedure of the Tribunal.

Examination

Any party may examine and cross-examine witnesses to the extent necessary to ensure a fair process.

Witnesses

133. A witness may not refuse, without valid reason, to answer a question legally put to him by the Tribunal or by the parties.

Exception

However, no witness may be compelled to answer in the cases and conditions described in articles 307 and 308 of the Code of Civil Procedure (chapter C-25).

Adjournment

134. The Tribunal may adjourn the hearing, on the conditions it determines, if it is of the opinion that the adjournment will not cause unreasonable delay in the proceeding or a denial of justice, in particular, for the purpose of fostering an amicable settlement.

Depositions

135. In matters of expropriation, and in matters of municipal taxation where a proceeding pertains to a unit of assessment or business establishment whose property value or rental value entered on the roll is equal to or greater than the value fixed by the Government, all depositions shall be conserved by stenography or by a recording, according to the method authorized by the Tribunal, unless the parties waive their right to appeal from the decision. Any such waiver shall be in writing or be recorded in the minutes of the proceedings.

Depositions

In the case of other proceedings heard by the immovable property division and of proceedings heard in matters concerning the preservation of agricultural land, depositions shall be conserved only if the applicant so requests in writing.

Continuance of hearing

136. Where a member is unable to continue a hearing, another member designated by the president of the Tribunal or by the vice-president responsible for the division concerned may, with the consent of the parties, continue the hearing and, in the case of oral evidence already produced, rely on the notes and minutes of the hearing or on the stenographer's notes or the recording of the hearing, if any.

Continuance of hearing

The same rule also applies in the case of a hearing continued after a member who began to hear the matter ceases to hold office.

DIVISION VII

EVIDENCE

Grounds of law or fact

137. Each party may plead any ground of law or fact relevant to the determination of his rights and obligations.

Prior communication

138. The Tribunal may make the admission of evidence subject to rules on prior communication.

Refusal of evidence

139. The Tribunal may refuse to admit any evidence that is not relevant or that is not of a nature likely to further the interests of justice.

Judicial notice

140. In addition to facts so well-known as to not reasonably be questionable, the Tribunal must take judicial notice of the law in force in Québec in the fields within its jurisdiction. Unless the law provides otherwise, statutory instruments not published in the *Gazette officielle du Québec* or in any other manner provided for by law must be pleaded.

Judicial notice

141. A member shall take judicial notice of facts that are generally recognized and of opinions and information which fall within his area of specialization or that of the division to which he is assigned.

Evidence

142. No evidence may be relied on by the Tribunal in making its decision unless the parties have been given an opportunity to comment on the substance of the evidence or to refute it.

Observations

Other than in the case of facts of which judicial notice must be taken pursuant to section 140, the Tribunal may not base its decision on grounds of law or fact judicially noticed by a member if it has not first given the parties, other than parties who have waived their right to state their allegations, an opportunity to present their observations.

DIVISION VIII

RECUSATION OF A MEMBER

Cause

143. A member who has knowledge of a valid cause for his recusation must declare that cause in a writing filed in the record and must advise the parties of it.

Recusation

144. A party may, at any time before the decision and provided he acts with dispatch, apply for the recusation of a member seized of the case if he has good reason to believe that a cause for recusation exists.

Application

The application for recusation shall be addressed to the president of the Tribunal. Unless the member removes himself from the case, the application shall be decided by the president, by the vice-president responsible for the division concerned or by a member designated by either of them.

DIVISION IX

DECISIONS

Decision

145. Where a matter is heard by more than one member, it shall be decided by the majority of the members having heard it. If any member dissents, the grounds for his dissent must be recorded in the decision.

Referral

When opinions are equally divided on a question, it shall be referred to the president, the vice-president responsible for the division concerned or a member designated by either of them among the members who shall decide according to law.

Advisement

146. In any matter of whatever nature, the decision must be given within three months after being taken under advisement, unless, for a valid reason, the president of the Tribunal has granted an extension.

Withdrawal

Where a member seized of a matter fails to give a decision within three months or, as the case may be, within such additional time as has been granted, the president may, of his own initiative or on an application by a party, withdraw the matter from the member.

Extension or withdrawal

Before granting an extension or withdrawing a matter from a member who has failed to give his decision within the required time, the president shall take account of the circumstances and of the interests of the parties.

Decision

147. A matter that has been withdrawn from a member shall be decided by the other members having heard the matter if their number is sufficient to constitute a quorum. Failing a quorum, the matter shall be heard again.

Rules

148. A matter heard by a member and which has not been decided at the time the member ceases to hold office is governed by the rules set forth in section 147.

Oral testimony

149. The president, a vice-president or any member called upon to hear a matter pursuant to the second paragraph of section 145 or to section 147 or 148 may, as regards oral testimony, and with the consent of the parties, rely on the notes and minutes of the hearing or on the stenographer's notes or the recording of the hearing, if any. If the vice-president or member finds them insufficient, he may recall a witness or require any other evidence.

Signature

150. Where a member is unable to act or has ceased to hold office and cannot sign the minute of a decision given at the hearing, another member designated by the president of the Tribunal or by the vice-president responsible for the division concerned may sign the minute of the decision.

Order

151. Any order made by the Tribunal in the course of a proceeding for a hearing to be held *in camera* or banning disclosure, publication or dissemination of documents or information shall be stated expressly in the decision.

Copy

152. A copy of the decision shall be sent to each of the parties and to any other person specified by law.

Clerical errors

153. A decision containing an error in writing or in calculation or any other clerical error may be corrected, in the record and without further formality, by the member who made the decision.

Correction

Where the member is unable to act or has ceased to hold office, another member designated by the president of the Tribunal or by the vice-president responsible for the division concerned may, on an application by a party, correct the decision.

Review or revocation

154. The Tribunal, on an application, may review or revoke any decision it has made

(1) where a new fact is discovered which, had it been known in time, could have warranted a different decision;

(2) where a party, owing to reasons considered sufficient, could not be heard;

(3) where a substantive or procedural defect is of a nature likely to invalidate the decision.

Restriction

In the case described in subparagraph 3, the decision may not be reviewed or revoked by the members having made the decision.

Motion

155. Proceedings for review or revocation are brought before the Tribunal by a motion filed at the secretariat of the Tribunal within reasonable time following the decision concerned or following the discovery of a new fact susceptible of warranting a different decision. The motion shall refer to the decision concerned and state the grounds invoked in support of the motion. It shall contain any other information required by the rules of procedure of the Tribunal, and shall indicate, where applicable, the name, address, telephone number and fax number of the representative of the applicant.

Copy

The secretary of the Tribunal shall send a copy of the motion to the other parties, who may respond to it in writing within 30 days after receiving it.

Record

The Tribunal shall proceed on the basis of the record; it may, however, if it considers it appropriate or if a party requests it, hear the parties.

Decisions

156. Decisions of the Tribunal are executory according to the terms and conditions stated therein provided the parties have received a copy of the decision or have otherwise been advised of it.

Compulsory execution

Compulsory execution of decisions is effected, by deposit at the office of the competent court, in accordance with the prescriptions of the Code of Civil Procedure (chapter C-25).

Rules

However, execution of a decision that contains a determination in respect of a proceeding under the provisions of the Expropriation Act (chapter E-24) is effected according to the rules prescribed in the said Act.

Contempt

157. Any person who contravenes a decision or an order which is executory is guilty of contempt.

Recourses

158. Except on a question of jurisdiction, none of the recourses provided in articles 33 and 834 to 846 of the Code of Civil Procedure (chapter C-25) may be exercised and no injunction may be granted against the Tribunal or against any of its members acting in their official capacity.

Judgment

A judge of the Court of Appeal may, upon a motion, annul by a summary proceeding any judgment rendered or order or injunction pronounced contrary to this section.

DIVISION X

APPEALS

Appeal

159. An appeal lies to the Court of Québec, irrespective of the amount involved, from decisions rendered by the Tribunal in matters heard by the immovable property division, and from decisions rendered in matters concerning the preservation of agricultural land, with leave of a judge, where the matter at issue is one which ought to be submitted to the Court of Québec.

Application for leave to appeal

160. An application for leave to appeal shall be made in the office of the Court of Québec of the place where the property is situated, and shall be presented by motion accompanied by a copy of the decision and of the documents of the contestation, if they are not reproduced in the decision.

Time limit

The application shall be made within 30 days of the decision. The time limit is peremptory; it may be extended only if a party establishes that he was unable to act.

Service

161. An application for leave to appeal, accompanied by a notice of presentation, shall be served on the adverse party and filed in the office of the Court of Québec. The application shall state the conclusions sought, and shall summarize the grounds the applicant intends to set up.

Execution of decision

162. An application for leave to appeal does not suspend execution of the decision. However, a judge of the Court of Québec may, on a motion, suspend such execution if the application establishes that such execution would cause serious harm and that he has filed an application for leave to appeal.

Judgment

163. If an application for leave to appeal is granted, the judgment authorizing the appeal shall stand for the inscription in appeal. The clerk of the Court of Québec shall transmit a copy of the decision without delay to the Tribunal and to the parties and their attorneys.

Respondent

In the same manner and within the same time limits, the respondent may bring an appeal or an incidental appeal.

Execution of decision

Except where provisional execution is ordered, an appeal suspends the execution of the decision.

Hearing

164. The Court of Québec hears the appeal according to the evidence presented before the Tribunal, without further proof. No appeal lies from the decision of the Court of Québec.

TITLE III
CONSEIL DE LA JUSTICE ADMINISTRATIVE AND ETHICS

CHAPTER I
INSTITUTION AND ORGANIZATION

Institution

165. A council bearing the name "Conseil de la justice administrative" is hereby instituted.

Seat

166. The council shall have its seat in the territory of Ville de Québec. Notice of the address of the seat shall be published in the *Gazette officielle du Québec*.

Members

167. The council shall be composed of the following members:

(1) the president of the Administrative Tribunal of Québec;

(2) a member of the Administrative Tribunal of Québec other than the vice-president, chosen after consultation with all the members of the Tribunal;

(3) the president of the Commission des lésions professionnelles;

(4) a member of the Commission des lésions professionnelles other than the vice-president, chosen after consultation with all the commissioners of that Commission;

(5) the president of the Commission des relations du travail;

(6) a member of the Commission des relations du travail other than the vice-president, chosen after consultation with all the commissioners of that Commission;

(7) the chairman of the Régie du logement;

(8) a member of the Régie du logement other than the vice-chairman, after consultation with all the commissioners of the Régie; and

(9) nine other persons who are not members of any of those bodies, two of whom only shall be advocates or notaries chosen after consultation with their professional order.

Appointment

168. The members referred to in paragraphs 2, 4, 6, 8 and 9 of section 167 shall be appointed by the Government, which shall designate the chairman of the council from among the members who are not members of any of the bodies referred to in paragraphs 1 to 8 of that section.

Term of office

The term of office of the members is three years and may be renewed only once.

Expiry of term of office

At the expiry of their term, the members shall remain in office until they are replaced or reappointed.

Duties

At the end of his term, each member may continue to perform his duties to conclude the cases he has begun to hear but has yet to determine.

Vacancy

169. Any vacancy which occurs during a term of office shall be filled according to the rules of composition and for the term set out in sections 167 and 168.

Oath

170. Before they may sit on the council, each member shall have taken an oath, solemnly affirming the following: "I … swear that I will neither reveal nor disclose, without being authorized to do so by law, anything of which I may gain knowledge in the performance of the duties of my office and that I will perform those duties impartially and honestly to the best of my knowledge and abilities.".

Chairman

The oath shall be taken before the chairman of the council. The chairman shall take the oath before a judge of the Court of Québec.

Remuneration

171. The members of the council receive no remuneration, except in the cases, on the conditions and to the extent that may be determined by the Government.

Expenses

The members are, however, entitled to the reimbursement of expenses incurred in the performance of their duties, on the conditions and to the extent determined by the Government.

Chairman

171.1. The chairman is in charge of the administration of the council. If absent or unable to act, the chairman shall be replaced by the member designated by the Minister.

Secretary

172. The secretary of the Tribunal shall act as secretary of the council.

Meetings

173. The council shall meet as often as necessary, at the request of the chairman, of a majority of the members or of the Minister.

Location

The council may hold its sittings at any place in Québec. The sittings shall be held in public, unless the council orders them to be held *in camera* where necessary to preserve public order.

Authenticity

174. The minutes of the sittings of the council or of any of its committees are authentic if they are approved by the members and are signed by the chairman of the sitting or by the secretary.

Authenticity

Similarly, documents emanating from the council or forming part of its records are authentic if they are signed, as are copies of such documents if they are certified true, by the chairman of the council or by the secretary.

Council

175. The council may make rules for its internal management, form committees and determine their powers and duties.

Reports

176. The council shall provide the Minister with any report or information he requires on its activities.

CHAPTER II
FUNCTIONS AND POWERS

Functions

177. In addition to the functions assigned to it by law, the functions of the council in respect of the Administrative Tribunal of Québec and its members are

(1) (subparagraph repealed);

(2) to establish a code of ethics applicable to the members of the Tribunal;

(3) to receive and examine any complaint lodged against a member pursuant to Chapter IV;

(4) to inquire, at the request of the Minister or of the president of the Tribunal, into whether a member is suffering from a permanent disability;

(5) to inquire, at the request of the Minister, into any lapse raised as grounds for removal of the president or a vice-president of the Tribunal from his administrative office in the case provided for in section 66;

(6) (subparagraph repealed).

Report

The council may also report to the Minister on any matter the Minister may submit to the council and make recommendations to the Minister concerning the administration of administrative justice by the bodies of the Administration whose president or chairman is a member of the council.

List

178. The council shall publish annually in the *Gazette officielle du Québec* a list of the departments and bodies that make up the Administration within the meaning of section 3 and of the bodies and decentralized authorities referred to in section 9.

Rules of evidence

179. The council may, by by-law, make rules of evidence and procedure applicable to the conduct of its inquiries. The by-law shall be submitted to the Government for approval.

CHAPTER III
ETHICS

Responsibilities

179.1. The members of the Tribunal must perform their duties purposefully, maintain their competence and act diligently. They must avoid placing themselves in a position that undermines such performance of their duties and must conduct themselves in a manner fully compatible with the honour, dignity and integrity required by adjudicative functions.

Code of ethics

180. The council, after consultation with the president, vice-presidents and members of the Tribunal, shall, by regulation, establish a code of ethics which shall be applicable to them.

Approval

The code of ethics shall be submitted to the Government for approval.

Content

181. The code of ethics shall set out the rules of conduct and the duties of the members of the Tribunal towards the public, the parties, their witnesses and the persons who represent them. It shall indicate, in particular, conduct that is derogatory to the honour, dignity or integrity of the members. In addition, the code of ethics may determine activities or situations that are incompatible with their office, their obligations concerning disclosure of interest, and the duties they may perform gratuitously.

Maintenance of competence

The code of ethics shall also set out rules concerning the maintenance of competence of members in the exercise of their functions.

Special rules

The code of ethics may provide special rules applicable to part-time members.

CHAPTER IV
COMPLAINTS

Complaints

182. Any person may lodge a complaint with the council against a member of the Tribunal for breach of the code of ethics, of a duty under this Act or of the prescriptions governing conflicts of interest and incompatible functions.

Complaints

183. A complaint must be in writing and must briefly state the reasons on which it is based.

Seat of council

It shall be transmitted to the seat of the council.

Member

184. If the complaint is lodged by a member of the council, that member cannot take part in the examination of the complaint.

Copy

184.1. The council shall send of copy of the complaint to the Tribunal member concerned and may ask the member for an explanation.

Committee

184.2. Unless the complaint is lodged by the Minister, the council shall form a committee, composed of seven council members, to determine whether a complaint is admissible.

Members

Three committee members shall be chosen from among the council members referred to in paragraph 9 of section 167; the other committee members shall be chosen from among the council members representing a body of the Administration whose president or chair is a council member.

Information

184.3. The committee may require of any person the information it considers necessary and examine the relevant record even if it is confidential under section 89.

Unfounded complaint

185. The committee may dismiss any clearly unfounded complaint.

Decision

The committee shall forward a copy of its decision, with reasons, to the complainant and to the council.

Copy

186. Where the complaint has been determined admissible, or where the complaint is lodged by the Minister, the council shall transmit a copy of it to the member and, where necessary, to the Minister.

Inquiry committee

The council shall form an inquiry committee composed of three members, which shall be entrusted with conducting an inquiry into the complaint and disposing of it on behalf of the council.

Members

Two members of the inquiry committee shall be chosen from among the members of the council referred to in paragraphs 3 to 9 of section 167, at least one of whom shall neither practise a legal profession nor be a member of a body of the Administration whose president or chairman is a member of the council. The third member of the inquiry committee shall be the member of the council referred to in paragraph 2 of that section or shall be chosen from a list drawn up by the president of the Tribunal, after consulting all the members of the Tribunal. In the latter case and if the inquiry committee finds the complaint to be justified, the third member shall take part in the deliberations of the council for the purpose of determining a penalty.

Chairman

187. The council shall designate a chairman from among the members of the committee who are advocates or notaries; the chairman shall call committee sittings.

Powers and immunity

188. For the purposes of an inquiry, the inquiry committee and its members are vested with the powers and immunity of commissioners appointed under the Act respecting public inquiry commissions (chapter C-37), except the power to order imprisonment.

Suspension

189. The council may, for a compelling reason and after consultation with the inquiry committee, suspend the member for the duration of the inquiry.

Decision

190. After giving the member who is the subject of the complaint, the Minister and the complainant an opportunity to be heard, the committee shall decide the complaint.

Recommendation

If the committee finds the complaint to be justified, it may recommend that the member be reprimanded, suspended with or without remuneration for the period it determines or dismissed.

Inquiry report

The committee shall send its inquiry report and conclusions, with reasons therefor, to the council together with its recommendations, if any, concerning the penalty.

Copy

191. The council shall then send a copy of the inquiry report and of the committee's conclusions to the member who is the subject of the complaint, to the complainant and to the Minister.

Reprimand

192. If the committee finds the complaint to be justified, the council, depending on the committee's recommendation, shall administer a reprimand to the member and advise the Minister and the complainant thereof, or shall send the recommendation for a suspension or for dismissal to the Minister and advise the member and the complainant.

Suspension

Where the recommended penalty is the member's dismissal, the council may immediately suspend the member for a period of 30 days.

CHAPTER V
PERMANENT DISABILITY OF A MEMBER AND LAPSE IN THE EXERCISE OF AN ADMINISTRATIVE OFFICE

Inquiry committee

193. At the request of the Minister, who shall send a copy of his request to the member of the Tribunal concerned, the council shall form an inquiry committee entrusted with

(1) determining on its behalf whether the member is suffering from a permanent disability which prevents him from discharging the duties of his office; or

(2) examining a lapse raised as grounds for removal of the president or a vice-president from his administrative office.

Member's disability

In cases pertaining to a member's disability, the council shall act also on a request made by the president of the Tribunal.

Committee

194. The committee shall be formed and chaired according to the rules provided for in the second and third paragraphs of section 186 and in section 187. The committee and its members are vested with the powers and immunity referred to in section 188.

Suspension

195. The council may, for a compelling reason and after consultation with the inquiry committee, suspend the member, the president or the vice-president concerned for the duration of the inquiry.

Conclusions

196. After giving the member, the president or the vice-president concerned and the person having requested an inquiry an opportunity to be heard, the committee shall send its conclusions, with the reasons therefor, to the council.

Recommendation

Where the committee finds there was a lapse in the exercise of an administrative office, the committee may recommend removal from that office. In such case, the committee shall transmit its recommendation and inquiry report to the council.

Copy

197. The council shall transmit a copy of the committee's conclusions to the member, the president or the vice-president concerned and to the person having requested the inquiry.

Recommendation

Where applicable, it shall also transmit to them the committee's recommendation and inquiry report.

Sums

198. The sums required for the purposes of this Title shall be taken out of the sums voted annually by the National Assembly.

FINAL PROVISIONS

Minister responsible

199. The Minister of Justice is responsible for the carrying out of this Act.

Report

200. The Minister shall, not later than 1 April 2003, make a report to the Government on the implementation of this Act and on the advisability of amending it.

Tabling

The report shall be tabled in the National Assembly, within 15 days of that date if the Assembly is sitting or, if it is not sitting, within 15 days of resumption.

Examination and hearing

Within one year of the tabling of the report, the competent committee of the National Assembly shall examine the report and hear submissions by interested persons and bodies.

201. (Omitted).

SCHEDULE I
SOCIAL AFFAIRS DIVISION

1. In matters of income security or support and social aid and allowances, the social affairs division hears and determines

(1) proceedings against decisions pertaining to entitlement to a benefit, brought under section 20 of the Act respecting family assistance allowances (chapter A-17);

(1.1) proceedings under section 40 of the Act respecting parental insurance (chapter A-29.011);

(2) proceedings under section 48 of the Act to secure handicapped persons in the exercise of their rights with a view to achieving social, school and workplace integration (chapter E-20.1);

(2.1) proceedings against decisions pertaining to entitlement to benefits under section 28 of the Act respecting family benefits (chapter P-19.1);

(3) proceedings under section 112 or 118 of the Individual and Family Assistance Act (chapter A-13.1.1) or under section 18 of the Act respecting the Cree Hunters and Trappers Income Security Board (chapter O-2.1);

(4) (paragraph repealed);

(5) proceedings against decisions pertaining to exemptions from payment, brought under section 517 of the Act respecting health services and social services (chapter S-4.2) and against deci-

sions pertaining to exemptions from payment or payment of an expense allowance, brought under section 162 of the Act respecting health services and social services for Cree Native persons (chapter S-5);

(6) proceedings under section 16.4 of the Act respecting the Société de l'assurance automobile du Québec (chapter S-11.011);

(7) proceedings against decisions pertaining to the entitlement to receive an amount in respect of a child assistance payment under Division II.11.2 of Chapter III.1 of Title III of Book IX of Part I of the Taxation Act (chapter I-3), brought under section 1029.8.61.41 of that Act.

2. In matters of protection of persons whose mental state presents a danger to themselves or to others, the social affairs division hears and determines proceedings under section 21 of the Act respecting the protection of persons whose mental state presents a danger to themselves or to others (chapter P-38.001).

2.1. In matters of measures concerning an accused in respect of whom a verdict of not criminally responsible by reason of mental disorder has been rendered or who has been found unfit to stand trial, the social affairs division hears and determines cases submitted to a Review Board under sections 672.38 and following of the Criminal Code (Revised Statutes of Canada, 1985, chapter C-46).

3. In matters of health services and social services, education and road safety, the social affairs division hears and determines

(1) proceedings by manufacturers or wholesalers of medications under section 68 of the Act respecting prescription drug insurance (chapter A-29.01);

(2) proceedings against decisions of the Régie de l'assurance maladie du Québec under section 18.4 or 50 of the Health Insurance Act (chapter A-29);

(2.1) proceedings under section 83.4 of the Charter of the French language (chapter C-11);

(2.1.1) proceedings under section 202.6.11 of the Highway Safety Code (chapter C-24.2);

(2.2) proceedings under paragraph 1 of section 560 of the Highway Safety Code;

(2.3) proceedings under section 121.1 of the Act respecting private education (chapter E-9.1);

(3) proceedings under section 20 of the Act to secure handicapped persons in the exercise of their rights with a view to achieving social, school and workplace integration (chapter E-20.1);

(4) (paragraph repealed);

(5) proceedings under section 44 of the Act to secure handicapped persons in the exercise of their rights with a view to achieving social, school and workplace integration;

(5.1) proceedings under section 34.7 of the Education Act (chapter I-13.3);

(6) proceedings against decisions relating to permits under section 41 of the Act respecting medical laboratories, organ, tissue, gamete and embryo conservation, and the disposal of human bodies (chapter L-0.2);

(7) proceedings under section 120 of the Act respecting occupational health and safety (chapter S-2.1);

(8) proceedings under section 104 of the Educational Childcare Act (chapter S-4.1.1);

(8.1) proceedings under section 57 or 73 of the Act respecting pre-hospital emergency services (chapter S-6.2);

(9) proceedings under section 27 of the Act respecting health services and social services (chapter S-4.2) or under the seventh paragraph of section 7 of the Act respecting health services and social services for Cree Native persons (chapter S-5);

(10) proceedings by physicians, dentists or pharmacists under section 132 of the Act respecting health services and social services for Cree Native persons;

(11) proceedings to contest or annul an election or appointment brought under section 148, 530.16, 530.67 or 530.97 of the Act respecting health services and social services or under section 48 or 59 of the Act respecting health services and social services for Cree Native persons;

(12) proceedings by physicians or dentists under section 205 or 252 of the Act respecting health services and social services, by pharmacists under section 253 of that Act or by midwives under section 259.8 of that Act;

(12.0.1) proceedings under section 305.1 of the Act respecting health services and social services;

(12.1) proceedings by applicants for or holders of a certificate of compliance under section 346.0.16 of the Act respecting health services and social services;

(13) proceedings against decisions pertaining to permits, brought under section 450 of the Act respecting health services and social services or under section 148 of the Act respecting health services and social services for Cree Native persons;

(14) proceedings under section 453 of the Act respecting health services and social services or under section 182.1 of the Act respecting health services and social services for Cree Native persons.

4. In pension plan matters, the social affairs division hears and determines

(1) proceedings against decisions made by the Régie des rentes, brought under section 188 of the Act respecting the Québec Pension Plan (chapter R-9);

(2) (paragraph repealed).

5. In compensation matters, the social affairs division hears and determines

(1) proceedings against decisions pertaining to the degree of impairment of earning capacity, brought under section 65 of the Workmen's Compensation Act (chapter A-3) for the purposes of the Act to promote good citizenship (chapter C-20) and the Crime Victims Compensation Act (chapter I-6);

(2) proceedings against decisions pertaining to the right to an indemnity and the quantum of an indemnity, brought under section 65 of the Workmen's Compensation Act for the purposes of the Act to promote good citizenship and the Crime Victims Compensation Act;

(2.1) proceedings against decisions pertaining to the admissibility of an application by a close relation of a crime victim referred to in section 5.1 of the Crime Victims Compensation Act for psychotherapeutic rehabilitation services, brought under section 65 of the Workers' Compensation Act for the purposes of the Crime Victims Compensation Act;

(3) proceedings under section 65 of the Workmen's Compensation Act or section 12 of the Act respecting indemnities for victims of asbestosis and silicosis in mines and quarries (chapter I-7) pursuant to section 579 of the Act respecting industrial accidents and occupational diseases (chapter A-3.001);

(4) proceedings under section 83.49 of the Automobile Insurance Act (chapter A-25);

(5) proceedings against decisions pertaining to indemnities for victims of immunization, brought under section 76 of the Public Health Act (chapter S-2.2);

(6) proceedings against decisions pertaining to a claimant's entitlement to a benefit or the amount of that benefit, brought under section 138 of the Act respecting assistance and compensation for victims of crime (chapter A-13.2.1) for the purposes of that Act and the Act to promote good citizenship, in respect of a review application brought on or after *(insert here the date of the coming into force of chapter 54 of the statutes of 1993)*.

6. In immigration matters, the social affairs division hears and determines proceedings against decisions of the Minister responsible for the administration of the Act respecting immigration to Québec (chapter I-0.2), brought under section 17 of the said Act.

SCHEDULE II
IMMOVABLE PROPERTY DIVISION

The immovable property division hears and determines

(1) proceedings under section 117.7 of the Act respecting land use planning and development (chapter A-19.1);

(2) proceedings under section 68 of the Act respecting the National Assembly (chapter A-23.1) to determine the price or indemnity arising from the acquisition of an immovable belonging to a Member;

(3) proceedings under section 43 of the Cultural Property Act (chapter B-4) to determine the indemnity arising from damages suffered;

[Sections 6(3.0.1), (3.1), and (3.2) repealed.]

(3.3) proceedings under section 104 of the Act respecting the Communauté métropolitaine de Montréal (chapter C-37.01);

(3.4) proceedings under section 97 of the Act respecting the Communauté métropolitaine de Québec (chapter C-37.02);

(3.5) proceedings under section 74 of the Municipal Powers Act (chapter C-47.1);

(3.6) proceedings under section 107 of the Municipal Powers Act to fix the indemnity for damage caused by a regional county municipality in the exercise of its jurisdiction with respect to watercourses;

(4) proceedings under the Expropriation Act (chapter E-24) to determine the amount of indemnities arising from the establishment of reserves for public purposes and from the expropriation of immovables or immovable real rights;

(5) proceedings under Chapter X of the Act respecting municipal taxation (chapter F-2.1);

[Sections 6(6), (7), and (8) repealed.]

(9) proceedings under section 13 of the Watercourses Act (chapter R-13) to assess and fix damages sustained;

(10) proceedings under section 45, 137 or 191.29 of the Act respecting the land regime in the James Bay and New Québec territories (chapter R-13.1) to determine the compensation arising from an expropriation;

(11) (paragraph repealed);

(12) proceedings under sections 184 and 192 of Schedule C to the Charter of Ville de Montréal (chapter C-11.4);

(13) proceedings under sections 56 and 86 of Schedule C to the Charter of Ville de Québec (chapter C-11.5);

(14) proceedings under section 13 of the Act respecting the reconstruction and redevelopment of areas affected by the torrential rains of 19 and 20 July 1996 in the Saguenay—Lac-Saint-Jean region (1997, chapter 60);

(15) proceedings under section 9 of the Act respecting Ville de Varennes (1997, chapter 106);

(16) proceedings under section 9 of the Act respecting Ville de Saint-Basile-le-Grand (1999, chapter 97);

(17) proceedings under section 9 of the Act respecting Ville de Contrecoeur (2002, chapter 95);

(18) proceedings under section 10 of the Act respecting Ville de Brownsburg-Chatham, Ville de Lachute and Municipalité de Wentworth-Nord (2004, chapter 46).

SCHEDULE III
TERRITORY AND ENVIRONMENT DIVISION

The territory and environment division hears and determines

(0.1) proceedings against decisions of the Commission de protection du territoire agricole, brought under section 34 of the Act respecting the acquisition of farm land by non-residents (chapter A-4.1);

(1) (paragraph repealed);

(1.1) (paragraph repealed);

(1.2) proceedings against decisions or orders of the Communauté métropolitaine de Montréal or, in the case of delegation, the head of a department or an officer brought under section 159.2 or 159.14 of the Act respecting the Communauté métropolitaine de Montréal (chapter C-37.01);

(1.3) proceedings against decisions or orders of Ville de Québec or, in the case of delegation, the executive committee or a department head brought under section 104 of the Charter of Ville de Québec (chapter C-11.5);

(1.4) proceedings against decisions or orders of Ville de Gatineau or, in the case of a delegation, decisions or orders of the executive committee or of a department head, brought under section 66 of the Charter of Ville de Gatineau (chapter C-11.1);

(2) proceedings against decisions or orders of the Commission de protection du territoire agricole du Québec, brought under section 21.1 of the Act respecting the preservation of agricultural land and agricultural activities (chapter P-41.1);

(2.1) proceedings against decisions made by the Minister of Transport, brought under section 10.1 of the Roadside Advertising Act (chapter P-44);

(3) proceedings against decisions or orders made by the Minister of Sustainable Development, Environment and Parks, brought under section 9 of the Act respecting the boundaries of the waters in the domain of the State and the protection of wetlands along part of the Richelieu River (2009, chapter 31), sections 24 and 64 of the Natural Heritage Conservation Act (chapter C-61.01), section 96 of the Environment Quality Act (chapter Q-2) or section 68 of the Pesticides Act (chapter P-9.3);

(4) proceedings against decisions of the Minister under sections 12, 14, 17, 23 and 25 of the Dam Safety Act (chapter S-3.1.01);

(5) (paragraph repealed);

(6) proceedings under section 27 of the Act respecting roads (chapter V-9).

SCHEDULE IV
ECONOMIC AFFAIRS DIVISION

The economic affairs division hears and determines proceedings under

(1) section 13.2 of the Travel Agents Act (chapter A-10);

(1.1) section 48 of the Act respecting commercial aquaculture (chapter A-20.2);

(2) section 45 of the Act respecting prearranged funeral services and sepultures (chapter A-23.001);

(3) (paragraph repealed);

(4) section 366 of the Act respecting insurance (chapter A-32);

(4.0.1) section 17 of the Act respecting the Bureau d'accréditation des pêcheurs et des aides-pêcheurs du Québec (chapter B-7.1);

(4.1) (paragraph repealed);

(5) section 154 of the Cinema Act (chapter C-18.1);

(6) paragraph 2 of section 560 of the Highway Safety Code (chapter C-24.2);

(7) section 123.145 of the Companies Act (chapter C-38);

(7.1) section 25.1 of the Act respecting financial services cooperatives (chapter C-67.3);

(8) section 26 of the Act respecting the development of Québec firms in the book industry (chapter D-8.1);

(9) section 15 of the Act respecting tourist accommodation establishments (chapter E-14.2);

(9.1) (paragraph repealed);

(10) (paragraph repealed);

(11) section 26 of the Act respecting stuffing and upholstered and stuffed articles (chapter M-5);

(12) section 22 of the Cullers Act (chapter M-12.1);

(13) sections 36.14 and 36.16 of the Act respecting the Ministère de l'Agriculture, des Pêcheries et de l'Alimentation (chapter M-14);

(13.1) section 191.1 of the Act respecting the marketing of agricultural, food and fish products (chapter M-35.1);

(14) section 21 of the Act respecting commercial fishing and commercial harvesting of aquatic plants (chapter P-9.01);

(14.1) section 51.1 of the Farm Producers Act (chapter P-28);

(15) section 17 of the Food Products Act (chapter P-29);

(15.1) (paragraph repealed);

(15.2) (paragraph repealed);

(16) section 339 of the Consumer Protection Act (chapter P-40.1);

(17) section 55.35 of the Animal Health Protection Act (chapter P-42);

(18) section 35 of the Act respecting the class action (chapter R-2.1);

(19) section 36 of the Act respecting the collection of certain debts (chapter R-2.2);

(19.1) section 40.1 of the Act respecting the Régie des alcools, des courses et des jeux (chapter R-6.1);

(20) (paragraph repealed);

(20.1) section 243 of the Supplemental Pension Plans Act (chapter R-15.1);

(20.2) section 22.3 of the Act respecting supplemental pension plans (chapter R-17);

(21) section 53.1 of the Act respecting safety in sports (chapter S-3.1);

(22) section 36 of the Act respecting the Société des alcools du Québec (chapter S-13);

(22.1) section 5.7 of the Act respecting farmers' and dairymen's associations (chapter S-23);

(22.2) section 18 of the Horticultural Societies Act (chapter S-27);

(23) section 251 of the Act respecting trust companies and savings companies (chapter S-29.01);

(24) section 22 of the Marine Products Processing Act (chapter T-11.01);

(24.1) section 85 of the Act respecting transportation services by taxi (chapter S-6.01);

(25) section 51 of the Transport Act (chapter T-12);

(26) (paragraph repealed);

(27) (paragraph repealed);

(28) section 23.1 of the Act to promote workforce skills development and recognition (chapter D-8.3);

(29) section 38 of the Act respecting owners, operators and drivers of heavy vehicles (chapter P-30.3);

(30) (paragraph repealed);

(31) section 37 of the Private Security Act (chapter S-3.5).

REPEAL SCHEDULE

In accordance with section 9 of the Act respecting the consolidation of the statutes and regulations (chapter R-3), chapter 54 of the statutes of 1996, in force on 1 April 1998, is repealed, except section 201, effective from the coming into force of chapter J-3 of the Revised Statutes.

PROPERTY OF
SENECA COLLEGE
LIBRARIES
@ YORK CAMPUS